musicHound Jazz

musicHound Jazz

The Essential Album Guide

edited by Steve Holtje
and Nancy Ann Lee

foreword by T.S. Monk

SCHIRMER TRADE BOOKS
NEW YORK/LONDON/PARIS/SYDNEY/COPENHAGEN/MADRID

Copyright © 1998 by Schirmer Trade Books,
A Division of Music Sales Corporation, New York
This book was originally published in 1998 by Visible Ink Press®

A Cunning Canine Production®

Cover photo of Roy Hargrove © Jack Vartoogian

Order No. MH 10004
International Standard Book Number: 0.8256.7253.8

Exclusive Distributors:
Music Sales Corporation
257 Park Avenue South, New York, NY 10010 USA
Music Sales Limited
8/9 Frith Street, London W1D 3JB England
Music Sales Pty. Limited
120 Rothschild Street, Rosebery, Sydney, NSW 2018, Australia

Library of Congress Cataloging-in-Publication Data
MusicHound jazz: the essential album guide/edited by Steve Holtje and
    Nancy Ann Lee
        p. cm.
    Includes bibliographical references (p.   ) and index.
    ISBN 1-57859-031-0 (alk. paper)
    1. Jazz—Discography. I. Holtje, Steve, 1961– . II. Lee,
Nancy Ann,   1939– .
ML156.4.J3M87 1998
781.65'0266—dc21   97-9713
                                                         CIP
                                                         MN

Printed in the United States of America

musicHound *contents*

Jazz is an inner voice expressed through music that mirrors the bottom-line emotions of the human psyche. The term comes from the word *jas,* a Creole word for whorehouse, where the first musicians played this kind of music. It wasn't until the music came up North that the name was altered to jazz. Max Roach told me this.

Jazz is the only art form America can claim as its own; everything else has been imported. Jazz represents a very unique social, economic, political, and ethnic convergence. It's a reflection of the democratic ideal, a reflection of free thought—all Western, truly American. It couldn't have happened anywhere else.

I grew up in a house of music. My father was the most unique of a group of guys that were all really geniuses. The list is very short, but it includes names like Charlie Parker, John Coltrane, Max Roach, Art Blakey, Miles Davis, and Dizzy Gillespie. Growing up so close to the source, I really didn't become acutely aware of the influence my father had on other musicians until a couple of days after his death. He was somewhat inaccessible for the final eight years of his life, so afterwards a tremendous number of musicians appeared who just wanted to vent and to share the experiences they'd had with Thelonious.

My father listened to the likes of Art Tatum, Willie "The Lion" Smith, Jelly Roll Morton, Duke Ellington, and Coleman Hawkins. Despite his accomplishments, despite his *Time* magazine cover in 1964, my dad died feeling somewhat disillusioned by the entire industry. It wasn't really until the last decade that his music has become widely recognized.

For too long now jazz has been treated like a stepchild. Record companies don't seem to try to sell the music—there is no marketing. What does it take to sell the late great grand masters?

The albums are placed on the shelf, and they are sold; there is no conscious effort to push the product. The labels tend to accept the fact that jazz represents only three percent of the marketplace. They fail to see that the percentage could grow, with perhaps just a little help.

I am very supportive of the art form and of the artists, and it's important that we lead through example. I like going into record stores and browsing. If someone has a record that I'm interested in, I want to buy it. I don't want them to give it to me—it's a personal thing. I also like to keep abreast of what's in the marketplace. It's just like pop or classical or country—the characteristics of quality are the same. In other words, the good stuff swings; it's clear, not confusing, and easy to understand.

A definitive guide to the genre like *MusicHound Jazz* is very important because the biggest impediment to the popularity of jazz in the latter part of the twentieth century has been the lack of information, both historical and popular; neither has gotten out to the public, in truth or in fiction.

I think the future of jazz is very healthy and secure. Young kids, particularly teens, are getting into the music: there is an absolute explosion of high schoolers interested in jazz, in part because it's so accessible. The issue here is not so much that these kids party to the music, like generations before them did, but that they are studying the music and understanding the value.

My first drum set was given to me by Art Blakey when I was 15, and Max Roach gave me my first drum lesson. I've played in just about all musical genres, only coming back to playing jazz in the last eight years. It's been an almost magical experience, playing this music. It has always felt so easy and so right.

The great Kenny Dorham once said, "Break out your horn, play two choruses of your best shit, pack up and go home!"

T.S. Monk, a drummer and jazz educator, has recorded albums as a leader for Blue Note and N2K Encoded Music. He was taught by Max Roach and Stanley Spector and toured with, among other jazz greats, his father, the legendary pianist/composer Thelonious Monk. In the late 1980s he formed his own sextet, which has become one of the premier hard-bop repertory groups in jazz. Monk also serves as chairman of the Thelonious Monk Institute of Jazz, sponsoring jazz education programs and an annual contest that has helped advance the careers of such players as Bill Cunliffe, Joshua Redman, Ryan Kisor, and Jacky Terrasson. Visit his website at http://www.jazz corner.com/monk.html.

musicHound *introduction*

by steve holtje **xi**

On the one hand, jazz has been called America's greatest artistic contribution to the world; on the other hand, its death has been announced with numbing regularity over the past six decades, often with specific culprits fingered. Nobody knows how to define jazz, but everybody's sure they know it when they hear it—though "they" often disagree even when listening to the same performance. The musicians themselves can't even decide what the music should be called. Some famous players dislike the term "jazz" or its various subcategories, whether for sociological or economic reasons, and have used phrases such as "Ecstatic Music," "Autophysiopsychic Music," "Great Black Music," or just plain "improvised music."

So jazz is a big subject, filled with contradictions. In fact, some observers have suggested that jazz has packed into its century-long life the phases that took classical music a millenium to rack up. There are a few players active today whose lives encompass almost all of that century, 96-year-old alto saxophonist Benny Waters being the most prominent—and most extreme—example. Jazz isn't dead; it just keeps accumulating more treasures, all available for us to hear. Consider that plenty of players are around who learned the earliest styles of jazz directly from the original creators and plenty more from the subsequent periods. We have a huge musical smorgasbord to choose from.

And practically the entire history of jazz has been recorded. While the first recording of jazz is considered to have been made in 1917 by the Original Dixieland Jazz Band, which would seem to indicate that the first two decades got left out, in fact, many of the earlier players were recorded subsequently. That such legendary icons as New Orleans trumpeter Buddy Bolden

weren't recorded is so exceptional that it's part of their legend. Classical musicians have no idea, really, what the music of Hildegard von Bingen sounded like when it was performed over a thousand years ago. They make educated guesses and debate the authenticity of the results. Jazz fans can hear their music's beginnings by putting on albums by King Oliver, Eubie Blake, and Jelly Roll Morton. Think of it: practically the entire history of a musical style, all theoretically available for anyone who wants to hear it.

Of course, that's a whole lotta albums. And they're not all good. It can seem daunting to beginners. In fact, the editors of this book each own over three thousand jazz albums but realize that's a mere drop in the bucket. And that's where *MusicHound Jazz* comes in. Within these pages you'll find every facet of jazz covered, from the early New Orleans style of Bunk Johnson to the fusion of Weather Report; from swing kings Benny Goodman and Count Basie to avant-gardists Cecil Taylor and Anthony Braxton; from bebop innovators Charlie Parker and Thelonious Monk to acid jazz experimenters Digable Planets and Gang Starr; from smooth jazz superstars Jeff Lorber and Kenny G to screaming free jazz wildmen Sonny Sharrock and Frank Wright.

Maybe you've heard that Yusef Lateef is fantastic and you should check him out. But you go to your local music emporium and there are 25 Lateef albums in the bin. Which ones are great, which are merely good, and which ones seem in retrospect to have been ill advised? We'll tell you. And if you're really fanatical and buy all of his CDs, yet find your Lateef craving knows no bounds, we'll tell you which out-of-print LPs you'll find rewarding. Or maybe you're not a beginner. You have some old Lateef LPs and you want to replace your scratched-up vinyl with shiny new CDs. We'll tell you which ones are available and which of the good ones you're lucky to still have on LP. And after you've taken care of that, you decide you want to catch up with what he's been up to in the last 20 years. Not only will we tell you the changes his music went through, we'll even cover the multitude of CDs he's issued on his own label in the past six years.

No other album guide combines a consumer-friendly and easy-to-follow format, depth and breadth of coverage, and priority attention to what's available now the way *MusicHound Jazz* does—plus an abundance of great photos and 100 sidebars highlighting memorable solos of various artists. That's why we're suitable to all sorts of buyers, from neophytes to those of you who have had to take all the books off your bookshelves and stick them in boxes because there's just no more space for more shelves and, darn it, you've gotta put those albums on a shelf somewhere be-

cause you keep tripping over the CD-filled shoeboxes strewn around your floor (we know what this is like).

Which brings me to another point. Some of you may be thinking, why single out Yusef Lateef? Why not John Coltrane, Louis Armstrong, Miles Davis, and other jazz immortals? Well, we've got them covered too, in equally considerable detail. But we're fanatics, and we go beyond the obvious choices. Of course, telling you that we've got Matthew Shipp, Assif Tsahar, Junko Onishi, D.D. Jackson, Babkas, Whit Dickey, 8 Bold Souls, Joe Maneri, and a whole bunch of other up-and-coming players will look a lot more impressive in five years or so (when they'll be stars) than it does right now (when most of you haven't heard of them). You'll just have to take our word for it. Or better yet, buy their albums according to our recommendations and be ahead of the curve. You won't be sorry.

So how do you use *MusicHound Jazz*? Here's what you'll find in the entries, and what we intend to accomplish with each point:

• An introductory paragraph, which will give you not only biographical information but also a sense of the artist's or group's sound and its stature in the jazz—and overall music—pantheon.

• **what to buy:** The album or albums that we feel are essential purchases for consuming this act. It may be a greatest hits set, or it may be a particular album that captures the essence of the artist in question. In any event, this is where you should start—and don't think it wasn't hard to make these choices when eyeballing the catalogs of Coleman Hawkins, Harry James, Gerry Mulligan, and some of the other jazz titans. Note that for acts with a limited catalog, **what's available** may take the place of **what to buy** and the other sections.

• **what to buy next:** In other words, once you're hooked, these will be the most rewarding next purchases.

• **what to avoid:** This category could include albums the world would be better off without, or it may designate work that newcomers to the particular artist are better off saving for later. Checking the bone ratings—and of course the writer's comments—usually makes it clear whether we're saying "avoid this forever, and cover your ears if anybody plays it in your vicinity," or merely indicating it's "for specialists."

• **the rest:** Everything else that's available for this act, rated with the Hound's trusty bone scale (see below for more on this). Note that for some artists with sizable catalogs, we've condensed this section down to **best of the rest.**

• **worth searching for:** An out-of-print gem. A bootleg. A guest appearance on another artist's album or a film soundtrack. Something that may require some looking but will reward you for the effort.

• ◄◄: The crucial influences on this act's music.

• ►►: The acts that have been influenced by this artist or group. Used only where applicable; it's a little early for Teodross Avery, Mark Elf, or Mat Maneri to have influenced anybody.

We should also remind you that *MusicHound Jazz* is a *buyer's* guide. Therefore, for the most part we only discuss CDs that are currently in print and available in the United States.

Now, you ask, what's with those bones? (Down, boy! Sheesh. . . .) It's not hard to figure out— ♫♫♫♫♫ is nirvana (not Nirvana), a **woof!** is dog food. Keep in mind that the bone ratings don't pertain just to the act's own catalog, but to its worth in the whole music realm. Therefore a lesser act's **what to buy** choice might rate no more than ♫♫♫; some even rate ♫♫𝒱, a not-so-subtle sign that you might want to think twice about that act.

As with any opinions, all of what you're about to read is subjective and personal. MusicHound has a bit of junkyard dog in it, too; it likes to start fights. We hope it does, too. Ultimately, we think the Hound will point you in the right direction, and if you buy the ♫♫♫♫♫ and ♫♫♫♫ choices, you'll have an album collection to howl about. But if you've got a bone to pick, the Hound wants to hear about it—and promises not to bite (but maybe bark a little bit). If you think we're wagging our tails in the wrong direction or lifting our leg at something that doesn't deserve it, let us know. If you think an act has been capriciously excluded—or charitably included—tell us. Your comments and suggestions will serve the greater MusicHound audience and future projects, so don't be shy.

Editor

Steve Holtje has contributed to *MusicHound Rock, Country, Blues, R&B,* and *Classical.* Currently jazz and classical editor at CDnow, he was previously senior editor at *Creem* and *New Review of Records* and managing editor of *NPG* and the book *The Ballplayers* (Arbor House, 1990), a biographical encyclopedia of baseball that has since gone online as part of Sportsline.com's Baseball Online Library. He is a regular contributor to the *Wire, Jazziz,* and *RhythmMusic,* and has also written for *Newsday,* Allstarmag.com, and many other magazines, newspapers, and online publications. He spent several years on the other side of the music biz as mail order manager and press bio author for Sphere Marketing, the American office of the Black Saint and Soul Note labels, and he has also written liner notes for albums on Black Saint, Soul Note, Evidence, and hatOLOGY. When not working, he's a poet (with NYC readings and international publications), classical music composer, party mix taper who thinks nothing of segueing from Count Basie to the Ramones, and feared softball player.

Nancy Ann Lee is a Cleveland-based freelance journalist-photographer. She began a lifelong love of jazz in the 1940s after hearing big band recordings from the family collection. Her tastes were reinforced during the 1950s when Dave Brubeck, Peggy Lee, the Modern Jazz Quartet, Ahmad Jamal, and other artists turned on the college generation with their Cool Jazz movement. After a hiatus to raise three children, Lee actively returned to jazz in 1969. Experiencing a mid-life crisis two decades later, she began a second career as a jazz journalist-photographer, and in 1989 was invited into Dizzy Gillespie's inner circle with her camera. She has since photographed countless musicians and conducted memorable interviews with artists such as Ray Brown, Al Di Meola, Kenny Garrett, Benny Green, Jim Hall, Joe Lovano, Ken Peplowski, Claudio Roditi, Arturo Sandoval, Son Seals, Junior Wells, and others. She is a regular *JazzTimes* contributor, and her articles and photographs have appeared in *Down Beat, The Plain Dealer, Cleveland Free-Times,* and other newspapers, books, and magazines. This was her first book-editing project and, after listening to hundreds of CDs, she loves and respects jazz even more today.

Supervising Editor

Gary Graff is an award-winning music journalist and supervising editor of the MusicHound album guide series. A native of Pittsburgh, Pennsylvania, his work is published regularly by Reuters, *Guitar World, ICE,* the *San Francisco Chronicle, The Plain Dealer,* Michigan's *Oakland Press,* SW Radio Networks, *Country Song Roundup,* and other publications. A regular contributor to the Web sites Mr. Showbiz/Wall of Sound, Jam TV, and Electric Village, his weekly "Rock 'n' Roll Insider" report airs on Detroit rock station WRIF-FM (101.1). He also appears on public TV station WTVS' *Backstage Pass* program and is a board member of the North American Music Critics Association and co-producer of the annual Detroit Music Awards. He lives in the Detroit suburbs with his wife, daughter, and two stepsons.

Managing Editor

Judy Galens is a senior editor at Visible Ink Press and the managing editor of *MusicHound Folk.* She has edited books on a variety of subjects, including hockey, tennis, inventing, food festivals, and, of course, music. Galens lives in a Detroit suburb with her husband and some pets.

Associate Managing Editor

Dean Dauphinais is a senior editor at Visible Ink Press and a contributor to *MusicHound Rock* and *MusicHound R&B*. A huge fan of Frank Sinatra, Antonio Carlos Jobim, and Diana Krall, he's convinced that the only thing better than listening to Ms. Krall sing "Peel Me a Grape" would be if she were in the same room singing it just to him. The co-author of two books, *Astounding Averages!* and *Car Crazy,* Dauphinais lives in suburban Detroit with his jazzy (and jealous) wife, Kathy, and two sons, Sam and Josh.

Copy Editors

Pam Shelton is a freelance writer and copy editor living in Connecticut. She used to write a bluegrass column for *Country in the City News.*

Brigham Narins, who frequently dogs the Hound's grammar, is a freelance copy editor who lives in suburban Detroit with his lovely wife and assorted pets. Working on this book he came to realize the ways in which "jazz is different."

Publisher

Martin Connors

MusicHound Staff

Michelle Banks, Christa Brelin, Jim Craddock, Beth Fhaner, Jeff Hermann, Heather Mack, Brad Morgan, Matt Nowinski, Carol Schwartz, Devra Sladics, Christine Tomassini

Proofreading

Ellen Cothran, Kathy Dauphinais, Diane L. Dupuis, Sean Mc-Cready

Art Direction

Tracey Rowens, Michelle DiMercurio, Cindy Baldwin

Contributing Photographers

Jack and Linda Vartoogian grew up in late 1950s Detroit and heard, but did not get to see, some of the best performers in music. To compensate, they have devoted themselves to photographing musicians (and dancers) from across the country and around the world. While their New York City home virtually guarantees that, eventually, most acts come to them, they continue to seek opportunities to discover new talent and new venues—the farther from home the better. Their images appear regularly in *The New York Times, Time, Newsweek, Living Blues,* and *JazzTimes,* among many others, as well as in innumerable books, including their own *Afropop!* (Chartwell Books, 1995) and *The Living World of Dance* (Smithmark, 1997), and

MusicHound Blues, MusicHound R&B, MusicHound Lounge, and *MusicHound Folk.*

Ken Settle is a Detroit-area photographer who has specialized in music photography for over 16 years. His photos have been published worldwide in magazines such as *Rolling Stone, People, Guitar Player, Playboy, Audio,* Japan's *Player,* France's *Guitarist,* and Australia's *Who Weekly.* His work also appears in *MusicHound Country, MusicHound Blues, MusicHound R&B, MusicHound Lounge,* and *MusicHound Folk.*

Graphic Services

Randy Bassett, Pam Reed, Barbara Yarrow

Permissions

Maria L. Franklin, Michele M. Lonoconus

Production

Mary Beth Trimper, Dorothy Maki, Evi Seoud, Wendy Blurton, Debbie Milliken

Technology Wizard

Jeffrey Muhr

Typesetting Virtuoso

Marco Di Vita of the Graphix Group

Marketing & Promotion

Marilou Carlin, Nancy Hammond, Kim Marich, Betsy Rovegno, Susan Stefani, Lauri Taylor

MusicHound Development

Julia Furtaw

Contributors

Giacomo Aula writes for the Italian magazine *Fedeltà del Suono.* He is also a pianist who has worked with James Newton, Larry Schneider, Gianni Basso, Enrico Rava, Peter Erskine, John Taylor, and many other jazz musicians. In 1997 he recorded *Jazz Inside,* his first CD, for the Musikat label in Stuttgart, Germany.

Greg Baise is a freelance writer and concert promoter who can be found browsing in the slinky, funky, slow-and-low analog proto-hip-hop-dub no wave Scandinavian death metal section. He writes frequently about music and the arts for the *Metro Times* (Detroit).

Andrew Bartlett lives in Seattle, Washington, with his family. A longtime Ph.D. student focusing on cultural aesthetics and jazz, Bartlett now works in the nexus between the music and software industries. As a freelance writer, he contributes to numerous print and online periodicals.

Susan K. Berlowitz is originally from the Midwest. She has worked for the past several years as a photojournalist for a monthly jazz publication and as a DJ and producer on the radio. Currently, Berlowitz operates a freelance publicity business in New York City and is a member of the jazz faculty at Merkin Hall.

Will Bickart is a clinical psychologist living in San Francisco. He has been listening to jazz for over 20 years and his knowledge of the idiom is extensive. Although he uses his writing skills in his profession, the entries written for *MusicHound Jazz* are his first attempts at jazz writing.

Dan Bindert is music editor and jazz columnist at *City Newspaper* in Rochester, New York, and a regular contributor to the Canadian magazine *The Jazz Report*. His work has also appeared in *Blues Connection, Urban Network,* and *Frederick Douglass Voice.* Bindert is also a radio announcer at Rochester NPR-affiliate WXXI, where he has been hosting *Blues Spectrum* and various jazz programs since 1989.

John Bitter is a retired procedures analyst whose hobby since his early teens has been jazz record collecting, sparked by working six years as a full-time jazz buyer in a Lakewood, Ohio, record shop. His interests are wide and varied and for the last 20 years he has been a photojournalist on the jazz party/festival scene. He is currently a contributing editor for *Mississippi Rag,* a traditional jazz publication for which he began writing in the early 1980s.

James Bradley is a freelance writer and reporter based in Brooklyn.

Steve Braun is a Chicago-based national correspondent for the *Los Angeles Times.* He covered the second Woodstock and the Rock and Roll Hall of Fame concert and has written about Jerry Lee Lewis's brushes with the law.

Keith Brickhouse is a jazz journalist/independent radio producer who lives and works in New York City. He has produced the nationally syndicated public radio programs *Highlights of Montreux Live* (a thirteen-part series) and *A Postcard from Bern,* a two-hour special as part of *The Jazz Traveler* series. Each program features live music and interviews with artists from these world-renowned jazz festivals. His radio programs may be heard on public radio stations WBGO-FM in New York and WGBH-FM in Boston. His programs have also been broadcast on WUTC in Chattanooga, Tennessee, WCLK in Atlanta,

Georgia, WDNA in Miami, Florida, KCLM in San Mateo, California, and WSHA in Raleigh, North Carolina.

Stuart Broomer is a resident of Toronto who writes regularly for *Cadence* and *Coda.* His writings on jazz have also appeared in *The Globe and Mail* and *Sub Rosa.* He has written liner notes for artists as diverse and significant as Evan Parker, Marilyn Crispell, Satoko Fujii, and Jimmy Amadie. He appears regularly as a guest on CKLN-FM's *Dat Dere* and has published a baseball biography, *Paul Molitor: Good Timing.* He is also the author of the "Monster Solo" sidebars in *MusicHound Jazz.*

Ken Burke is a singer-songwriter whose column, "The Continuing Saga of Dr. Iguana (The Story So Far)," has been running in small press publications since 1985. He lives in Arizona with the two best people he knows: his wife Lorraine and daughter Emily.

Salvatore Caputo is a freelance writer living in Phoenix with his wife and three kids. The pop music columnist for *The Arizona Republic* from 1990 to 1997, he was a finalist in the 1996 Music Journalism Awards for his retrospective column on Dean Martin.

Norene Cashen writes for *Alternative Press,* Detroit's *Metro Times,* and *Etch.*

Jeff "DJ Zen" Chang is a writer, a record company hack, and, most shockingly, a father living in the Bay Area on little more than rice and water. He has written for more magazines than you've ever heard of.

Spence D. is a Bay Area journalist who first began writing about hip-hop culture in 1990 for the underground rap 'zine *The Bomb.* The Writer Also Known As Spence Dookey regularly contributes to *The Source, Urb, Raygun, Option, Gavin, Bikini,* and *Slap,* and even writes about film for Roughcut.com.

Dean Dauphinais is co–managing editor of Visible Ink Press' *MusicHound* series.

Eric Deggans is the television and pop culture critic for the *St. Petersburg Times* newspaper in Florida, where he's inspired by three children, a wife, and two cats. In that order.

Steve Dollar is chief pop music critic for the *Atlanta Journal-Constitution.* His articles have appeared in *GQ, Jazziz, Down Beat, Contents, Red Bass, Request,* and the *Independent Film & Video Monthly.* He was jazz editor for the now-defunct *CD Review.*

Josh Freedom du Lac is the co-editor of *MusicHound R&B* and has been the pop music critic for *The Sacramento Bee* since 1994.

Daniel Durchholz is co-editor of the forthcoming second edition of *MusicHound Rock* and a contributor to *MusicHound Country, MusicHound R&B, MusicHound Blues, MusicHound Folk,* and *MusicHound Lounge.* He was founding editor of the now-defunct *Replay* magazine, and is a former associate editor of *Request* magazine and St. Louis, Missouri's *Riverfront Times.* He writes for various magazines, newspapers, and Web sites from his home outside St. Louis.

James Eason has covered music, news, and sports for ABC Radio and ABC Online (abc.com, abcnews.com, and abcmnf.com) since 1991. He is also a stereotypically struggling saxophonist in NYC.

Yvonne Ervin is the executive director of the Tucson Jazz Society and jazz projects coordinator for the Western States Arts Federation. She has worked as a jazz radio announcer for 20 years and has written liner notes for RCA and Capri records. She has written for *Down Beat* and for many local newspapers and magazines.

Walter Faber is a freelance reviewer who has contributed to *NPG* and CDnow. He lives a quiet existence in Brooklyn, New York, with his three cats and way too many CDs and LPs.

Jason Ferguson is a freelance music writer based in Columbia, South Carolina. His work has appeared in *Entertainment Weekly, Audio, Request, Raygun, Urb, Alternative Press,* and many other magazines, as well as on MTV Online and SonicNet and in the 1997 edition of the *Trouser Press Record Guide.* Additionally, he is the manager/buyer at Papa Jazz Record Shoppe, the Southeast's best and most comprehensive record store (shameless plug: come visit at www.papajazz.com). The first John Coltrane record he ever bought was *Om,* and his life hasn't been the same since.

David Finkel is a freelance writer who lives in Michigan.

George Foley is a nationally known ragtime pianist who cut his first album while still in his teens. He performs regularly in the Cleveland area and elsewhere in North America.

Lawrence Gabriel is a Detroit-based writer, poet, and musician who is also editor of Detroit's *Metro Times.*

Andrew Gilbert is a Bay Area–based writer who contributes regularly to *The San Diego Union-Tribune, Contra Costa Times, East Bay Express,* and the on-line magazine Salon. His writing on jazz has also appeared in the Los Angeles *Reader,* the Los Angeles *View,* the San Jose *Metro,* the Santa Cruz *County Sen-*

tinel, Musician, and *Jazziz.* Born and raised in Los Angeles, Gilbert was first exposed to jazz at the Kuumbwa Jazz Center in Santa Cruz, California. For two years in the mid-'90s he was manager of the Jazz Bakery Performance Space in Los Angeles. He is currently working on a documentary on the singer Weslia Whitfield. He can be reached at jazzscribe@aol.com.

Alex Gordon is an associate editor of *Inside Sports* magazine and the co-author of the book *College: The Best Five Years of Your Life,* published by Hysteria Press and available in finer bookstores.

Gary Graff is supervising editor of Visible Ink Press' Music-Hound series.

David Greenberger has been publishing *The Duplex Planet* since 1979. His commentaries and music reviews are heard regularly on National Public Radio's *All Things Considered.*

Larry Grogan has been writing about music, both above- and underground, for 15 years. In his 'zines *Incognito, Evil Eye,* and *Gone,* as well as in several New Jersey newspapers, he has annotated his love for everything from Monk to Piazzolla to Mose Allison and Hamza El Din. He is 35 and lives in South River, New Jersey.

David C. Gross writes about jazz, bass, Judaism, and other subjects. He lives in New York City.

Stacey Hale is an 18-year veteran Master Mixer/DJ with numerous awards to her credit. She is president of the Detroit Regional Music Conference, an annual event she founded in 1993.

Joe S. Harrington is a freelance writer living in Massachusetts.

Ed Hazell is a freelance jazz writer who contributes regularly to the *Boston Phoenix.* He is the author of *Berklee: The First 50 Years,* an authorized history of the Berklee College of Music, and a contributor to *Jazz: From Its Origins to the Present,* by Lewis Porter and Michael Ullman (Prentice Hall). His articles, interviews, and reviews have also appeared in *The Boston Globe,* and in *Coda, Cadence,* and *Planet Jazz* magazines.

Alex Henderson is a Philadelphia-based journalist, public relations writer, and technology enthusiast whose work has appeared in *Billboard, Spin, Pulse!, Jazziz,* and many other national publications. He has a broad range of experience that includes everything from writing and coordinating news-features for the Los Angeles *News Globe* in 1987–88 to writing promotional material for Priority Records and serving as a columnist for *Jazz-Times.* Henderson (who has written liner notes for Rhino, Concord Jazz, Del-Fi, and many other labels) turned to more high-tech subjects in the 1990s, often examining technology and the Internet as they relate to everything from business, law, and medicine to media, fashion, the arts, and politics. He currently also writes high-tech press releases for the Internet-based company Vision X Software and its popular DigiDay Web site.

W. Kim Heron has been involved with jazz since the early '70s as a journalist, poet, photographer, broadcaster, and occasional percussionist. For the past 10 years, he has hosted a jazz program on Detroit's public radio station, WDET-FM, and he currently is the managing editor of the *Metro Times,* an alternative news weekly. Heron is the co-creator of an online display "Swinging through Time: The Graystone Museum and and the History of Detroit Jazz," an exhibit within the Internet Public Library at www.ipl.org.

Christopher Hovan is a record collector and historian who specializes in jazz of the 1950s and 1960s. He has worked in public radio as both a disc jockey and producer/writer of jazz-related educational programs. Hovan has also served as jazz buyer for a Cleveland-area record store. In addition to his full-time endeavors as a teacher, Hovan is active as a freelance musician and writes about music for several publications.

B.J. Huchtemann is a freelance music journalist who writes for *Blues Access* magazine and Chicago's *Screamin'* magazine. She is a staff music reviewer and interviewer for the *Reader* in Omaha, Nebraska. When not out supporting live music, she also writes advertising and promotional copy for radio and television.

Robert Iannapollo has been listening to jazz since he impulsively bought Gary Burton's *Genuine Tong Funeral* with his 1968 Christmas money. He is a regular writer for *Cadence* and has also written for *Opprobrium* (New Zealand), *Jazz Nytt* (Norway), and *Option* (USA). He is also a contributor to *The New Grove Dictionary of Jazz.*

Jazzbo is Joseph Monish Patel, a San Francisco–based music journalist and writer who contributes to several print and Internet publications, including *Rap Pages, The Source, Urb, Raygun,* and Mr. Showbiz.

Gregg Juke is a producer, musician, songwriter, music journalist, educator, and music entrepreneur. He has contributed to CDnow, *Western New York Musician,* and the upcoming three-volume encyclopedia *20th Century Music.* A former jazz and pop radio program host and producer, Juke is proprietor of Nocturnal Productions, a full-service music agency and publishing company.

Dan Keener is a 23-year-old young man from Denver, Colorado. He has a real-life job that is about as removed from writing about jazz as you can get—he teaches lawyers how to use computers. Dan became connected with this project because he loves music and because he likes the idea of seeing his name all over a book.

Chris Kelsey is a saxophonist who has studied saxophone with Lee Konitz and jazz history with Max Roach. He has written about music for *Jazz Now, Jazziz,* and *Cadence.* For more information on Kelsey, check out his entry in *MusicHound Jazz.*

Gregory Kiewiet is pursuing his MA in English at Wayne State University in Detroit. A published poet, he received his bachelor's degree in English and art history at Oakland University. Kiewiet lives in Royal Oak, Michigan.

Steve Knopper is a Chicago-based freelance writer who has contributed to *Rolling Stone, George, Newsday,* the *Chicago Tribune, Request, Billboard, Yahoo! Internet Life,* the Knight-Ridder Newspapers wire service, and SW Radio Networks. The former music critic for Boulder, Colorado's *Daily Camera,* he's editor of *MusicHound Lounge: The Essential Album Guide to Martini Music and Easy Listening.*

John Koetzner is a freelance music critic who has written for *Down Beat, Bass Player, Mix, Relix, BAM,* the *Reno News & Review,* California's *Press Democrat* and *Healdsburg Tribune,* and numerous other publications. He attended his first blues concert, performed by John Lee Hooker and Johnny Shines, at age 16 and has followed the blues for the past 27 years.

Mark Ladenson has written for *Coda, JazzTimes,* and the *IAJRC* (International Association of Jazz Record Collectors) *Journal.* His reviews appear regularly in *Marge Hofacre's Jazz News* and his photographs appear regularly in *Cadence.*

Eric J. Lawrence is a music journalist and DJ in Los Angeles. His show *Dragnet* airs on radio station KCRW. Like many of us, he is a frustrated musician.

Jim Lester is a retired psychologist, moonlighting musician, and author of *Too Marvelous for Words: The Life and Genius of Art Tatum* (Oxford University Press, 1994).

Jim Linduff is a collector of jazz and blues recordings, a moderator of jazz and blues history classes at the University of Cincinnati, and a contributor to *Jazz Sounds,* a publication of the Jazz Club of Sarasota, Florida.

Paul MacArthur is a native of Syracuse, New York, and has been a jazz radio personality for over a decade. He is a contributing writer for *Jazziz, The Jazz Report,* and *Lounge* magazines, and a former compilations editor of *Leak CD Music Magazine.* Along with David Skolnick, he has published *Wrestling Perspective,* a newsletter that analyzes the professional wrestling industry, since 1990. MacArthur has taught at Cazenovia College and Onondaga Community College (both located in central New York) and recently completed a three-year appointment as an Assistant Professor of Communication Arts & Sciences at Lyndon State College in Vermont, where he oversaw the Radio Performance and Writing program. MacArthur is currently teaching in the Radio-Television-Film Department at Sam Houston State University in Huntsville, Texas, and is the director of jazz programming for KSHU-FM.

Garaud MacTaggart is a Buffalo, New York–based freelance writer with twenty years experience in music retailing (management/buyer). He believes in the holy jazz trinity of Duke, Monk, and Mingus. Most of his work has appeared in newspapers such as the Buffalo *News,* the *Daily Tribune* (Royal Oak, MI), the *Metro Times* (Detroit, MI), the *Orlando Weekly,* the *Columbus Guardian,* and *In These Times* (Chicago). His interests include all genres of music, cooking, basketball, and camping/travel.

Tali Madden is a contributing writer to *Blues Access* magazine and a freelance music journalist. A former NPR-affiliate jazz and blues broadcaster/programmer, he is currently based in Portland, Oregon.

Chris Meloche is a composer, broadcaster, and music writer. Born in 1957 in Windsor, Ontario, Canada, he has been based in London, Ontario, since 1979. His music has been featured around the world from the UK to Russia. His radio program *Wired for Sound* can be heard locally on CHRW-FM as well as internationally via RealAudio on the Internet.

Bill Moody is the author of *The Jazz Exiles: American Musicians Abroad* and three jazz mysteries: *Solo Hand, Death of a Tenor Man,* and *Sound of the Trumpet.* As a drummer, Moody toured and recorded with Jon Hendricks, Earl "Fatha" Hines, Lou Rawls, and Maynard Ferguson.

D. Thomas Moon is a Chicago-based educator, guitarist, and music journalist. His writings have appeared in CD liner notes and in *Blues Access, Living Blues, Blues Revue,* and *Latin Beat* magazines. He is currently working on a children's picture book, *Wang Dang Doodle Day.*

Patricia Myers has been a jazz columnist and critic since 1972. She has written profiles and reviewed major festivals, concerts, and albums in the U.S. and Europe. A contributing writer since 1985 to *JazzTimes* magazine and other music publications, she lives in Scottsdale, Arizona.

David Okamoto is the music editor at *The Dallas Morning News* and a contributing editor to *ICE* magazine. His work has also appeared in *CD Review, Rolling Stone, Jazziz,* and multiple volumes in the MusicHound series.

Jim O'Rourke is a musician/producer who has worked in areas as diverse as improvisation (Derek Bailey, Gunter Muller, etc.), production (Faust, Stereolab), electronic music, remixing, and film music. He has run the reissue labels Dexter's Cigar and Moikai, been an organizer of improvised and new music in Chicago, and continues to make records under his own name and with diverse assemblages.

Ted Panken has broadcast jazz and "new music" on WKCR-FM, in New York City, since 1985. He's written numerous liner notes and articles and interviewed hundreds of musicians. He's deeply involved in documenting the music through oral history.

Damon Percy, a freelance writer, is a former associate editor for Gale Research's *Dictionary of Literary Biography* online series. His work has appeared in the *Detroit Free Press, Vibe,* and the hip-hop magazine *Beat Down.*

Dan Polletta is the longtime evening jazz host at WCPN-FM, Cleveland Public Radio. He has produced and hosted live-recorded concert programs featuring Abbey Lincoln and the Mingus Big Band, which have been distributed to National Public Radio stations around the country. For ten years he served as jazz buyer for the now-defunct Wax Stacks, Cleveland's premier jazz record store, and guided many customers toward discovering more about jazz.

Debra Pontac is a longtime Los Angeles jazz fan familiar with many of the great players of that city. Before Donte's closed, she used to joke that she was there so often, she should have been paying rent.

Sam Prestianni is an unrepentant music junkie, writer, teacher, musician, and music journalist/critic. He has published widely for the past 12 years in dozens of magazines and newspapers, including *Option, Raygun,* and *Alternative Press.* He currently pens features and reviews for the San Francisco *Weekly,* San Francisco *Sidewalk, Speak, Soma,* and other freelance outlets.

He is also the "Outside/In" columnist for *Jazziz*. Contact him at: johnnycritic@earthlink.net.

Bret Primack has been writing about jazz musicians since 1977. A former East Coast editor of *Down Beat* and director of Jazz Central Station, his articles and interviews have appeared in publications such as *Down Beat, JazzTimes, Swing Journal,* and *People* magazine. Co-founder of the Jazz Theater Workshop and author of the *Ben Hecht Show,* Primack has also written liner notes for artists such as McCoy Tyner, Ella Fitzgerald, Clark Terry, and Arturo Sandoval.

David Prince's words on music have appeared as album liner notes and in a number of publications including the Boston *Phoenix,* Santa Fe *Reporter, Cadence, Raygun, Stereophile, Schwann/Spectrum,* the Albuquerque *Tribune,* and the *Village Voice.* He has produced and hosted jazz and freeform radio programs at both commercial and community stations in Santa Fe, New Mexico, as well as for Albuquerque's NPR affiliate, KUNM-FM. He can be reached via e-mail at Flight505@aol.com.

Jim Prohaska, a resident of Lakewood, Ohio, is an avid collector and enthusiast of vintage jazz and blues of the 1920s and 1930s, owning well over 20,000 jazz and blues 78 rpm records and 10,000 LPs. His specialized interests include early New Orleans bands and recordings, regional recordings made throughout the U.S. from 1921 through 1940 that help trace the growth of jazz, and discographical research. Prohaska has donated and/or loaned material from his collection to the Rock and Roll Hall of Fame and Museum, the Western Reserve Historical Society, and the Cuyahoga Community College (Tri-C) JazzFest, and he buys and sells vintage recordings worldwide. He has written liner notes and supplied recordings from his collection for the Document recording label's complete pre-war blues reissue series and other CD projects. He is a member of the International Association of Jazz Record Collectors (IAJRC), and his well-researched articles on jazz have been published in the *IAJRC Journal* and other publications.

Carl Quintanilla is a Chicago-based staff reporter for *The Wall Street Journal.*

Dennis Rea is a guitarist/composer/writer who plays with the ambient-improv group LAND and in numerous collaborative projects in Seattle. He is co-director of the Seattle Improvised Music Festival, co-editor of the *Tentacle,* and author of the forthcoming "Live at the Forbidden City," an account of his experiences performing music in China and Taiwan. His company,

Nunatak Press and Music, can be found on the Web at http://www.wolfenet.com/~nunatak/.

Bryan Reesman is a graduate of NYU's Tisch School of the Arts with a B.F.A. in film, a former story analyst for Miramax Films, New Line Cinema, and Imagine Entertainment, and an aspiring drummer. He currently freelances for music publications nationwide. He writes regularly for *Allstar, Gig, Goldmine, Keyboard, Magnet, Mix, Mixmag,* and MTV Online, and has also been published in *Bikini,* the Boston *Phoenix, Detour, Guitar Player,* the *Improper Bostonian, Requestline,* and numerous other publications.

John K. Richmond has pursued his love of jazz since high school. He was a clarinetist and saxophonist in the U.S. Navy, and later earned a degree in jazz history and communications from Capitol University in Ohio. He has produced jazz history programs for radio, has written about jazz for two major daily newspapers, the *Cleveland Press* and *The Plain Dealer,* and frequently gives lectures and film programs on jazz. Richmond serves as executive director of the jazz support organization the Northeast Ohio Jazz Society, is a jazz history instructor at Cleveland State University, and is a working jazz musician.

Leland Rucker has been writing about popular music since 1975 and is the managing editor of *Blues Access,* a quarterly journal of blues music. He is the co-author of *The Toy Book* (Knopf, 1992) and editor of *MusicHound Blues.*

Jeff Samoray is an editorial assistant and reporter for *The Detroit News.* His interests include writing, baseball history, absurdist theater, and the music of John Coltrane.

Wally Shoup is a free-improvising saxophonist (Project W) who has been involved in improvisation for over 20 years: as a writer for the *Improvisor,* as an organizer of the Seattle Improvised Music Festivals, and as a dedicated player.

D. Strauss is a writer and DJ who, like many rodents, resides in New York City. His work appears regularly in the *New York Observer, Spin, Icon,* the *Village Voice, Minneapolis City Pages,* and the on-line magazine Salon.

Corey Takahashi is a freelance journalist based (for now) in banana-slug-infested Santa Cruz, California. His work has appeared in *The Oregonian, SF Weekly, A.Magazine,* and *Asian Week.*

Lucy Tauss is a music journalist, radio producer, and entertainment news reporter who writes for a variety of publications, including *Jazziz.* She lives in New York.

Chris Tower is a freelance writer and college radio broadcaster who lives in Richland, Michigan, with his ghost cat, Bumba-Head. His work has appeared in *CyberHound's Web Guide,* Michigan's *Kalamazoo Gazette,* and a variety of national and international magazines.

Bob Townsend is a freelance critic who lives in Atlanta and writes for the Atlanta *Journal-Constitution, No Depression,* and *Stomp and Stammer.*

Bill Wahl is the founder and editor of *Jazz & Blues Report* magazine. He first published the free-of-charge monthly in Buffalo, New York, in 1974, where he also worked as a drummer, hosted a jazz radio program on WBFO-FM, and produced numerous jazz shows at the original Tralfamadore Café. Wahl introduced the *Jazz & Blues Report* to Cleveland, Ohio, in 1978, perma-nently relocated to the city in 1980, and continues to publish the magazine. He has also produced over 200 jazz and blues shows at Peabody's DownUnder, a Cleveland Flats nightspot.

Ron Weinstock, a resident of Falls Church, Virginia, is a federal government attorney who has been listening to and writing about blues and jazz since he was an undergraduate student at Case Western Reserve University in Cleveland, Ohio. He believes he has fairly catholic tastes in both blues and jazz and listens to a wide range of artists from the earliest to the avant-garde. Over the years he has contributed to a variety of publications including *Blues Unlimited, Blues World, Living Blues, Cadence,* and *Jazz & Blues Report.* He is currently music editor of the *D.C. Blues Calendar,* the newsletter of the D.C. Blues Society.

David Yonke writes about popular music for the Toledo *Blade.*

musicHound *acknowledgments*

I would like to thank all the generous CD providers without whose cooperation this book couldn't have happened: Flavio Bonandrini (Black Saint/Soul Note), Ann Braithwaite, Brian Coleman, and Doug Quintal (Braithwaite & Katz), Kevin Calabro (32 Jazz), Phil Cassese (Arabesque), Bob Cummins (India Navigation), Dr. Jazz, Michael Ehlers (Eremite), Donald Elfman and Naomi Yoshi (Koch Jazz), Doug Engel (Delmark), Carl Ericson (Cadence/CIMP), Leo Feigin (Leo), David Ginochio (Concord), Bernardo Goldowski (Sphere), Jerry Gordon (Evidence), Kevin Gore and Margaret Mair (Sony), Debra Harner (Debra Harner J. Media Relations), Terri Hinte (Fantasy), Glenn Ito (EuroJazz), Steve Joerg (AUM Fidelity), Jim Keuther (DA), Marilyn Laverty and Mark Satlof (Shore Fire Media), Jean-Pierre Leduc (Justin Time), Michel Levasseur (Victo), Rozanne Levine (Acoustics), Don Lucoff (DL Media), Heather Mount (Knitting Factory Works), Tina Pelikan (ECM), John Priestley (Sirocco), Tony Reif (Songlines), J.R. Rich (Blue Note), Andrew Seidenfeld (No Problem Productions), Steve Smith (Screwgun), Kazunori Sugiyama (Avant/DIW), Frank Tafuri (Arkadia), Werner X. Uehlinger (hat ART), Chris Wheat (Impulse!), and Mike Wilpizeski (Verve).

I'd also like to thank the following musicians, some of whom provided CDs and information and sometimes much more, and all of whom continue to create beauty despite all the barriers the music business poses: John Altenburgh, Babkas (Aaron Alexander, Brad Sheppik, and Briggan Krauss), Borah Bergman, Jean-Paul Bourelly, Marc Edwards, Bruce Eisenbeil, Mark Elf, Zusaan Kali Fasteau, Charles Gayle, Susie Ibarra, Darrell Katz, Chris Kelsey, Franklin Kiermyer, Dan Krimm, Yusef Lateef, John Lockwood, Mat Maneri, Joe Morris, Joe Mulholland, William Parker, Eric Person, Mark Reboul, Marc Ribot, Adam Rudolph, Matthew Shipp, Rolf Sturm, Assif Tsahar, James Blood Ulmer, and Tom Varner.

Thanks for the experience and tolerance to my editors past and present, some of whom put up with my topsy-turvy schedule during the creation of this massive project and/or helped me find writers: Brad Balfour, Larry Blumenfeld, Tony Herrington, John Leper, Rich Masio, Chris Nadler, Mark Petracca, Jack Rabid, Kami Sanders, Dante Sawyer, Mark Schwartz, Paul Semel, and Mike Shatzkin.

Thanks to the MusicHound crew: Dean Dauphinais, Martin Connors, Josh Freedom du Lac, Jim McFarlin, Dan Durchholz, Leland Rucker, Brian Mansfield, Neal Walters, Steve Knopper, Dave Wagner, and especially Gary Graff, Judy Galens, and Nancy Ann Lee. We did it!

And I'd especially like to thank the people whose contributions to this book fall into none of the above categories. Some of them may even be surprised to be listed, but without these people I might not have made it all the way: Michael B. Ackerman, Esq., Grant Alden, Frank Capalbo, Steve Dalachinsky, Bruce Gallanter, Mary Greenfield, Steve Greenfield, Karen Knobel, Margo Myles, Norman Oder, Allan Orski, Yuko Otomo, Emily Schaab, Fred Schwarz, Julie Taraska, Tom Terrell, Rob Thacher, and most of all, Debra Pontac.

Finally, I'd like to thank my father, David Louis Holtje, for his constant encouragement and help throughout my life, and I wish to dedicate my share of this tome to my late mother, Marjorie Oliver Holtje, and to her mother, Josephine Oliver. They implanted in me the love of music that has brightened my life every day and the values that kept me from wasting what small talents I have.

Steve Holtje

When I returned to college in the mid-1970s, attending nights to complete the degree I'd started twenty years earlier, I had to write a paper for a Principles of Management business course about where I expected to be in my career in the year 2001. One of the goals I imagined was completing a best-selling book in 1998. Life is certainly full of ironies. Toward this goal, I had quit my full-time secretarial job in 1989 to freelance as a jazz journalist and photographer and, by June 1997, when the fledgling *MusicHound Jazz* was presented to me, I was looking for a book project.

Thanks to co-editor Steve Holtje, not only for his all-around knowledge and experience that he lent to the project, but for injecting humor into the process when we were both stressed to the max. That we've managed to complete this project amiably without ever meeting in person is still amazing to me. With tips from Steve, I was able to hit the ground running with my new computer and modem, mastering the art of e-mail and online research, and weathering a change of Internet service providers in mid-stream. Without the guidance of Visible Ink project manager Judy Galens, whose cool-headed perspective helped me through some very distressing times, I couldn't have accomplished writing or co-writing numerous entries and editing half of the book.

A big thank you to John Leper, former publisher of the CD-ROM magazine, *Listen to the Music,* first, for challenging me with the opportunity to write for him in the mid-1990s, but especially for contacting me with the tip that Steve was looking for a co-editor.

My sincerest appreciation goes to the writers I assigned to this project when I officially came aboard. Whether they took one entry or fifty, they came through with flying colors, enduring my nit-picking editing queries by e-mail. It was an honor and a pleasure to work with them, including those couple of writers who generated some hair-raising moments with missed deadlines.

I am always amazed at the creativity of the thousands of musicians who make this wonderful music. Because of them, it was easy to become immersed in and even more enamored of this art form. Listening to hundreds of CDs expanded my ears and boosted my wonder and appreciation that jazz has the capacity to absorb so many diverse artists and styles. There were times when the music was so breathtaking and powerful, I was at a loss for words. I couldn't absorb all of an artist's rich, diverse, and inventive works in one marathon listening session and needed tranquil interludes to digest such powerful music.

The record label publicists who provided me with review copies of CDs deserve my undying gratitude. Those who were most understanding and courteous will have nearly their entire jazz catalogs reviewed within these pages. I also wish to thank Helene Stern, the music librarian of the Cleveland Heights/University Heights Public Library System. Her intelligent buying provided me with many of the CDs I was unable to get from labels.

Thanks, too, for the encouragement from numerous editors of newspapers, magazines, and other publications that have published my jazz articles and photographs over the years, especially Mike Joyce at *JazzTimes,* for keeping me on as a regular reviewer since 1992. Special thanks to editors who cut me some deadline slack while *MusicHound Jazz* was in progress.

Deserving heartfelt thanks is my 86-year-old mother, Mary R. DeLong, a long-retired school administrator who listened to my grousing and provided encouragement, wisdom, and occasional tips on the phone (and never nagged me about not visiting more often during this all-consuming, year-long project). I'm grateful, too, for the legacy of excellence in journalism set by my late stepfather, George J. DeLong, and my uncle, Severino P. Severino, both staff writers for major daily newspapers, and to my father, Joseph C. Valenti, for his self-employment work ethic. Thanks for the understanding of my adult children and five grandchildren; I missed you a lot during this project.

The Northeast Ohio Jazz Society (a Cleveland-based jazz support organization incorporated in 1978) has my gratitude for its role in promoting jazz in the region and for allowing me to serve as a Board Trustee in the late 1980s. Those were mind-expanding years.

Someone once told me that the best job is the one you create for yourself. My career as a jazz journalist would not have been possible without the inspiration of the late Chris Colombi, an ardent jazz fan, jazz radio host, and instructor who taught the History of Jazz class I took at Cleveland State University in 1981. I dedicate this book to his memory. His enthusiastic support (and 'A' grades for my many papers) definitely led to my decision to become a jazz journalist. Raised on sounds of the big bands, I was already listening to jazz, but Colombi opened my ears to a vast smorgasbord of sounds and styles, forever influencing my broad approach as a jazz reviewer.

Finally, I'd like to thank you, the reader, for purchasing this book. Jazz needs as many fans as possible, and every jazz CD you purchase helps keep this American art form alive. So keep on listening and thanks for your support.

Nancy Ann Lee

A

Greg Abate

Born May 31, 1947, in Fall Rivers, MA.

A fine bop-based saxophonist, Greg Abate is a well-traveled veteran who started recording relatively late in his career. Though he plays almost all the saxes, his slashing alto attack makes it his most identifiable horn. He is a prolific writer who has penned many attractive tunes, sometimes leaning in the modal direction. Abate joined the Ray Charles band in 1973, replacing David "Fathead" Newman, and spent two years touring with the orchestra. He joined the revived Artie Shaw Band under the direction of Dick Johnson in 1985 and stepped out on his own in 1987. Since the early 1990s, he's recorded a series of exciting albums for Candid featuring top-flight bands.

what to buy: Greg Abate's sophomore recording, *Straight Ahead* 🎵🎵🎵 (Candid, 1993, prod. Mark Morganelli), features an exciting Latin-tinged band with pianist Hilton Ruiz, bassist George Mraz, drummer Kenny Washington, and trumpeter Claudio Roditi. He switches between alto and tenor, achieving a warm, singing tone on the larger horn and a hot, searing alto sound, especially attractive on his ballad "Denise Marie." Roditi's flugelhorn blends beautifully with the alto on Abate's "Bossa for Gregory," while the two horns play pure bop on Abate's title track, an appropriately named adaptation of "Groovin' High." In addition to his six originals, Abate covers Horace Silver's "Nica's Dream," Gillespie's "Con Alma," and Cole Porter's "It's All Right with Me." Abate keeps only the best

company on *Bop Lives!* 🎵🎵🎵 (Blue Chip Jazz, 1996, prod. Mark Morganelli), with Kenny Barron (piano), Rufus Reid (bass), Ben Riley (drums), and Claudio Roditi playing trumpet and flugelhorn on five of the nine tracks. Dedicating himself exclusively to alto, this is Abate's best album yet, with particularly strong outings on Hank Mobley's "This I Dig of You," his attractive original "Children's Waltz," and a romping 11-minute version of "Speak Low," which includes some serious trumpet/alto jousting. The rhythm section plays with both sensitivity and hard-driving authority, and Barron is featured on a lovely version of his tune "Voyage."

what to buy next: Abate's debut as a leader after many years buried in big bands, *Bop City* 🎵🎵🎵 (Candid, 1991, prod. Mark Morganelli) is a live session recorded at Birdland with a top-flight New York rhythm section featuring pianist James Williams, bassist Rufus Reid, and drummer Kenny Washington. Playing soprano, alto, tenor, and flute, Abate doesn't give himself a chance to establish an identity on any one horn, though his alto work stands out on Hal Crook's bop anthem "Basting the Bird." He plays some attractive, if unspectacular soprano on his Coltranish "Andromeda" and the Latin-tinged "Minorism." The rhythm session offers exemplary support throughout, with Williams featured to advantage on "These Foolish Things" and Washington particularly effective on Abate's "Peaks Beaks."

what to avoid: A disappointing outing between two bop-minded saxophonists, *Dr. Jekyll & Mr. Hyde* 🎵🎵 (Candid, 1995, prod. Greg Abate, Alan Bates) pairs Abate with alto saxophonist Richie Cole. Abate contributes 11 of the album's 12 tunes, covering only Johnny Mandel's "Tommyhawk," and displays his full instrumental arsenal, playing soprano, alto, tenor, baritone sax, and flute. Though "Tommyhawk" is a fun filled romp, the album doesn't really heat up until toward the end. A little variety in the material would have helped keep things interesting. Occasional intonation glitches, as on the ensemble of the modal title track, were left in the mix. The rhythm section features pianist Chris Neville, bassist Paul Del Nero, and drummer Artie Cabral.

best of the rest:
Bird Lives ♪♪♪♪ (Candid, 1992)

worth searching for: Abate contributes two tunes to trumpeter Claudio Roditi's excellent *Samba Manhattan Style* ♪♪♪♪♪ (Reservoir, 1996, prod. Claudio Roditi, Mark Feldman), playing alto on his Brazilian–flavored "My Friend from Rio" and "Vera's Song," and tenor on Wayne Shorter's "Footprints." The session also features trombonist Jay Ashby, pianist Helio Alves, and drummer Duduka Da Fonseca.

influences:
◀◀ Phil Woods, Wayne Shorter, Sonny Stitt

Andrew Gilbert

Ahmed Abdullah

Born May 10, 1947, in New York, NY.

This underappreciated trumpeter made his mark as a part of New York's loose-knit "loft" improviser-scene, which also included such players as Marion Brown, Byard Lancaster, Sam Rivers, and Sunny Murray. Although his name may not be well-known, that shouldn't diminish appreciation for Abdullah's strong horn work, which, in addition to his solo records, can also be found on some of Sun Ra's late 1960s and late 1980s work.

what to buy: Of the two records he cut for Silkheart in 1987, the quartet outing *Liquid Magic* ♪♪♪♪ (Silkheart, 1987, prod. Ahmed Abdullah), with tenor player Charles Brackeen, bassist/AACM-er Malachi Favors, and drummer Alvin Fielder is the stronger, and certainly a great place to get introduced to Abdullah's Sun Ra–influenced compositional style. Although only one Sun Ra cut actually gets played ("Mystery of Two"), the remainder of the LP is infused with the same sort of focused-but-free-wheeling style. Though Abdullah's trumpet playing sometimes gets pushed to the wayside both by his group and by his propensity for sitting at the piano, this is nonetheless a great example of his style.

the rest:
Life's Force ♪♪♪ (About Time, 1979, LP only)
And the Solomonic Quintet ♪♪♪♪ (Silkheart, 1987)

worth searching for: *Live at Ali's Alley* ♪♪♪♪ (Cadence, 1978, prod. Bob Rusch, LP only) can be had through Cadence/North Country's mail order service and is worth the effort, a loft-jazz classic with an unusual instrumentation including French horn and cello plus tenor saxophonist Chico Freeman in an inspired, fiery mood.

influences:
◀◀ Louis Armstrong, Sun Ra

Jason Ferguson

Ahmed Abdul-Malik

Born January 3, 1927, in New York, NY. Died October 2, 1993, in New York, NY.

As one of the better—if underrated—bassists during the 1950s, Ahmed Abdul-Malik's reputation would have been sealed had he never gone beyond his work in the 1950s and 1960s with Thelonious Monk, Randy Weston, and Nina Simone. However, in addition to being a strong bass player, the Brooklyn native of Sudanese descent was also one of the first jazz musicians to introduce an oud into the instrumentation, resulting in a legitimate, and swinging, permutation of jazz and Arabic/Middle Eastern music that is never coy or "exotic" in its flavor. (Abdul-Malik can be heard playing oud on several of the versions of "India" that John Coltrane recorded during the epic 1961 live recordings at the Village Vanguard.) Of the six solo records he made, only one (luckily his best) is currently in print, with the others fetching collectors' prices.

what to buy: Abdul-Malik delicately treads the line between "jazzing up" traditional Eastern melodies and simply adding an oud to some bop tunes on *Jazz Sahara* ♪♪♪♪ (Riverside, 1958, prod. Bill Grauer). Fellow Monk sideman Johnny Griffin provides some high-flying tenor work, and the drummer is Al Harewood. The group also included violin, *kanoon, darabeka,* and *duf.* Essential for aficionados of either music.

what to buy next: Thelonious Monk's *Thelonious in Action* ♪♪♪♪ (Riverside, 1958, prod. Orrin Keepnews) and *Misterioso* ♪♪♪♪ (Riverside, 1958, prod. Orrin Keepnews) both come from live performances by the Monk quartet with Abdul-Malik, Griffin, and Roy Haynes, and the bassist is occasionally featured to good advantage.

worth searching for: The out-of-print albums are worth hearing. The best of them is *East Meets West* ♪♪♪♪ (RCA, 1959, prod. Lee Schapiro) with Lee Morgan, Benny Golson, and Johnny Griffin among the players. One side of *Sounds of Africa*

𝄢𝄢𝄢 (New Jazz, 1962, prod. Esmond Edwards) is more jazz-oriented than the other, with Tommy Turrentine, Andrew Cyrille, and Richard Williams making appearances. A similar lineup graces the marginally better *The Music of Ahmed Abdul-Malik* 𝄢𝄢𝄢 (New Jazz, 1961, prod. Esmond Edwards).

influences:

◄◄ Wilbur Ware

►► Yusef Lateef

Jason Ferguson

John Abercrombie

Born December 16, 1944, in Port Chester, NY.

Abercrombie started playing rock riffs in high school prior to enrolling at the Berklee School of Music in Boston. One of his first gigs as a jazz musician came with organist Johnny Hammond Smith, and Abercrombie has often returned to the organ-guitar-drums format in following decades. Abercrombie also worked with the Brecker Brothers in a jazz/rock hybrid called Dreams, recording an album with them before graduating from Berklee in 1969. Since that time he has played with Chico Hamilton, Billy Cobham, and Gil Evans, among others.

Abercrombie's first solo album, *Timeless*, featured keyboard wiz Jan Hammer (in his post-Mahavishnu Orchestra incarnation) along with drummer Jack DeJohnette. The collaboration with DeJohnette was to prove particularly fruitful when Abercrombie later recorded with the drummer and bassist Dave Holland in a trio called Gateway in addition to playing in De-Johnette's group, Special Edition.

The guitarist's angular yet dense style can fit as easily into the post-Larry Young organ trio dates he plays with Dan Walls and Adam Nussbaum as it does into the Jimi Hendrix tribute albums built around Dr. Lonnie Smith's organ playing. He has recorded duet albums with guitarists Ralph Towner and John Scofield plus a host of quintets and quartets with Andy LaVerne, Dave Liebman, Don Thompson, and others. A gifted session musician, Abercrombie has also appeared on albums by Jan Garbarek, Colin Walcott, Richie Beirach, and Kenny Wheeler.

what to buy: Since Abercrombie is generally the "melody" player in most Gateway tunes, the argument can be posited that all Gateway releases should be filed under Abercrombie even though the ad hoc group is, to a large extent, a cooperative venture. In 1994, after not playing together as Gateway for years, the musicians got into a studio and recorded *Homecoming* 𝄢𝄢𝄢𝄢 (ECM, 1995, prod. Manfred Eicher), certainly their best album since their 1975 debut, and perhaps their best album period. There are tunes to hum and tunes to explore with as Abercrombie's guitar playing glides and wails at the music's beck and call. Bassist Dave Holland and Abercrombie wrote most of the material, but DeJohnette's two songs "7th D" and "Oneness," provide the real yin and yang example of what Gateway can do. The former provides the most opportunities for adventuresome playing, while the latter, sans drums and with DeJohnette on piano, is a melodic, reflective piece for acoustic instruments. *Timeless* 𝄢𝄢𝄢𝄢 (ECM, 1975, prod. Manfred Eicher) was an organ trio for the 1970s, with Jan Hammer on keyboards, DeJohnette on drums, and Abercrombie on guitars. While not as adventurous as Larry Young, Hammer's organ playing still had enough power and drive to stand up to Abercrombie's flashes of energy and DeJohnette's percussive palette. The Abercrombie-penned "Ralph's Piano Waltz" features a standard organ trio groove at its core, but the guitar playing is just enough outside to make conservative ears itch. ECM has put together a handy little sampler of Abercrombie's work for them covering 1975–1984. *Works* 𝄢𝄢𝄢 (ECM, 1994, prod. Manfred Eicher) is a good introduction to the guitarist, for it gives the listener a snapshot from albums Abercrombie recorded under his own name and sessions on which he was a sideman. Out of the eight cuts on this release, five feature the ongoing partnership between Abercrombie's pungent guitar lines and DeJohnette's superbly played polyrhythms.

what to buy next: *While We're Young* 𝄢𝄢𝄢 (ECM, 1993, prod. Manfred Eicher) was the first album with Abercrombie, organist Dan Wall, and drummer Adam Nussbaum playing together as a trio. Wall feeds rich chord mixtures to Abercrombie for the guitarist to pull and fragment into different textures while Nussbaum's drumming provides a constant wash of accents rather than a strict pulse. The first recording by this trio, *Gateway* 𝄢𝄢𝄢𝄢 (ECM, 1975, prod. Manfred Eicher) (Abercrombie, Holland and DeJohnette) is filled with great vehicles for the band to strut their stuff, but the musicality of the group is such that nobody overplays. Holland writes most of the songs but Abercrombie shares credit with DeJohnette on "Unshielded Desire." The group playing is particularly effective on the catchy "Back-Woods Song" and the borderline free-form "Jamala," on which Abercrombie sounds like a less frantic John McLaughlin with better tone.

best of the rest:

Gateway 2 𝄢𝄢𝄢 (ECM, 1977)

Current Events 𝄢𝄢𝄢 (ECM, 1985)

Getting There 𝄢𝄢𝄢 (ECM, 1988)

November 🎵🎵🎵 (ECM, 1993)
Speak of the Devil 🎵🎵🎵 (ECM, 1994)
Tactics 🎵🎵🎵🎵 (ECM, 1997)

worth searching for: For a real Abercrombie rarity, try to find the self-titled LP of the cooperative group *Friends* 🎵🎵🎵🎵 (Caroline/Virgin, 1975, prod. Marc Cohen, Fred Seibert) with Abercrombie joining saxophonist Marc Cohen, bassist Clint Houston, and drummer Jeff Williams in a 1972 recording made at Columbia University's radio station and sounding very *Bitches Brew/Jack Johnson*-influenced. ECM has let a number of Abercrombie-led albums go out of print, but the LPs are often found in used bins. The most beautiful are by Abercrombie's quartet with Richie Beirach (piano), George Mraz (bass), and Peter Donald (drums), with Abercrombie and Beirach splitting compositional duties: *Arcade* 🎵🎵🎵 (ECM, 1979, prod. Manfred Eicher), *Abercrombie Quartet* 🎵🎵🎵🎵 (ECM, 1979, prod. Manfred Eicher), and *M* 🎵🎵🎵🎵 (ECM, 1981, prod. Manfred Eicher).

influences:

◀◀ Jim Hall, Jimi Hendrix

▶▶ Nguyen Le

Garaud MacTaggart

Muhal Richard Abrams

Born September 19, 1930, in Chicago, IL.

Abrams started studying piano at 17 and attended Chicago Music College. He started his professional career in 1948 and began writing arrangements for King Fleming in 1950. In the late 1950s and early 1960s he performed with a number of top musicians as they came through Chicago, including Miles Davis, Sonny Rollins, and Johnny Griffin. In 1961 he formed the Experimental Band with Roscoe Mitchell, Eddie Harris, and Donald Garrett, which led to the formation of the AACM (Association for the Advancement of Creative Musicians) with Henry Threadgill, Joseph Jarman, Fred Anderson, and Steve McCall.

In 1977 he moved to New York, performing and recording solo as well as with Amina Claudine Myers, Anthony Braxton, Leroy Jenkins and others. He formed an important relationship with the Italian label Black Saint and over the next two decades released 16 albums on that label as leader or co-leader. He is still recording and touring, creating some of the more vibrant music of the Jazz language while drawing on jazz's roots in the blues. His music truly looks forward and backward at the same time.

what to buy: *Levels and Degrees of Light* 🎵🎵🎵🎵🎵 (Delmark, 1967, prod. Robert G. Koester) is a landmark recording featuring poetry, vocals, free improvisation, and blues. Featured are Anthony Braxton on alto sax, Leroy Jenkins on violin, and Thurman Barker on drums. *The Hearinga Suite* 🎵🎵🎵🎵 (Black Saint, 1989, prod. Muhal Richard Abrams) is a classic avant-big band recording. *Blu Blu Blu* 🎵🎵🎵🎵🎵 (Black Saint, 1991, prod. Muhal Richard Abrams), another big band album, is both aggressive and uplifting. Check out Joel Brandon whistling his solo on "One for the Whistler." *Think All, Focus One* 🎵🎵🎵🎵🎵 (Black Saint, 1995, prod. Muhal Richard Abrams) is a more recent release that is both challenging to the musicians involved and compelling to the listener. The very solid band features Eddie Allen (trumpet), Eugene Ghee (tenor sax, bass clarinet), Alfred Peterson (trombone), David Gilmore (guitar), Brad Jones (bass), and Reggie Nicholson (drums).

what to buy next: The band on *Familytalk* 🎵🎵🎵🎵🎵 (Black Saint, 1993, prod. Flavio Bonandrini) utilizes Jack Walrath (trumpet), Patience Higgins (reeds), Warren Smith (vibes, marimba, timpani, gongs), Jones, and Nicholson on an adventurous program, which finds Abrams using the synthesizer imaginatively.

what to avoid: Though not without its interesting moments, *Duet* 🎵🎵 (Black Saint, 1981) with Amina Claudine Myers seems rather listless compared with Abrams's usual standard, as though the two-piano format was not colorful enough to inspire him.

the rest:
Young at Heart, Wise in Time 🎵🎵🎵🎵 (Delmark 1969)
Afrisong 🎵🎵🎵 (India Navigation, 1975)
(With Malachi Favors) *Sightsong* 🎵🎵🎵 (Black Saint, 1976)
(With Leroy Jenkins) *Lifelong Ambitions* 🎵🎵🎵 (Black Saint, 1977)
1-OQA+19 🎵🎵🎵 (Black Saint, 1978)
Lifea Blinec 🎵🎵🎵 (Novus, 1978)
Spiral Live in Montreux 🎵🎵🎵🎵 (Arista, 1978)
Spihumonesty 🎵🎵🎵🎵 (Black Saint, 1980)
Mama and Daddy 🎵🎵🎵🎵 (Black Saint, 1980)
Blues Forever 🎵🎵🎵🎵 (Black Saint, 1981)
Rejoicing with the Light 🎵🎵🎵🎵 (Black Saint, 1983)
View from Within 🎵🎵🎵🎵 (Black Saint, 1985)
Colors in Thirty-Third 🎵🎵🎵🎵 (Black Saint, 1987)
(With Roscoe Mitchell) *Duets and Solos* 🎵🎵🎵🎵 (Black Saint, 1990)
One Line, Two Views 🎵🎵🎵🎵 (New World, 1995)
Song for All 🎵🎵🎵🎵 (Black Saint, 1997)

worth searching for: *Things to Come from Those Now Gone* 🎵🎵🎵🎵 (Delmark, 1972, prod. Robert G. Koester) has great compositions and concise and sparkling solos. The multi-artist, four-CD set *Interpretations of Monk* 🎵🎵🎵🎵 (DIW, 1994, prod. Verna Gillis) documents a 1981 Monk tribute concert. Abrams is the pianist for the first CD, playing a lovely unaccompanied "Crepuscule with Nellie" and joined for the rest of the program by Don Cherry, Steve Lacy, Charlie Rouse, Roswell Rudd, Richard Davis, and longtime Monk drummer Ben Riley.

influences:

◀◀ James P. Johnson, Thelonious Monk, Howlin' Wolf, Muddy Waters, Roscoe Mitchell, Eddie Harris, Donald Garrett, Henry Threadgill, Joseph Jarman, Fred Anderson, Steve Mc-Call

▶▶ All of the students at the AACM school for young musicians

David C. Gross

Acoustic Alchemy

Formed 1979, in London, England.

Nick Webb, steel-string guitar (1979–present); Simon James, nylon-string guitar (1979–1985); Greg Carmichael, nylon-string guitar (1985–present).

Every once in a great while a group comes along and, quite by accident, becomes a defining force behind an entire musical genre. Such is the case with Acoustic Alchemy's signature latticework of steel- and nylon-string guitars. When the "Wave" (New Adult Contemporary) radio format was launched in 1987, nearly every track on Acoustic Alchemy's American debut *Red Dust and Spanish Lace* charted. America immediately embraced their music with great enthusiasm. This seemed a pleasant reward after the duo literally "worked their way to America" as the in-flight entertainment for Virgin Airlines' Trans-Atlantic route.

Founder Nick Webb learned about jazz guitar and harmony at Leeds College of Music in England, where he met Simon James, who was studying classical guitar. Although they played a few duets together, it wasn't until a few years later when Webb moved to London that the two, quite by accident, met again and started playing together. The duo found the purist attitude around London that "Charlie Parker was great and all pop-oriented sounds were rubbish" did not encourage their musical direction. After several years of scraping gigs and using the profits to record, it slowly fell apart. Simon drifted off to pursue a solo career and Webb determined to find a replacement. Through their double bass player Jeff Clyne, Nick heard about nylon jazz/classical player Greg Carmichael, who had studied at the London College of Music. A few months after Nick went to see Greg's band the Holloways, they began practicing and writing together. With nine successful albums to their credit,

many receiving Grammy nominations, Acoustic Alchemy continues to record and tour. Although their music is classified as light instrumental, Acoustic Alchemy has never lost its ability to churn out infectious melodies that are occasionally punchy and always fresh and energetic.

what to buy: *Red Dust and Spanish Lace* ♪♪♪♪♫ (MCA Master Series, 1987, prod. John Parsons) is the album that broke the group through to a wide audience.

what to buy next: *Arcanum* ♪♪♪♪ (GRP, 1996, prod. Steven Jones) has fresh arrangements of previously released material with the addition of electric guitar and a string section.

the rest:

Natural Elements ♪♪♪ (MCA Master Series, 1988)
Blue Chip ♪♪♪ (MCA Master Series, 1989)
Back on the Case ♪♪♪ (GRP, 1991)
Reference Point ♪♪♪♪ (GRP, 1991)
Early Alchemy ♪♪♪♪ (GRP, 1992)
The New Edge ♪♪♪ (GRP, 1993)
Against the Grain ♪♪ (GRP, 1994)

worth searching for: Search out *Acoustic Alchemy* ♪♪♪ (Moonstone Records, 1982) just to say you own it. Most of this material was remastered for *Early Alchemy*.

influences:

◀◀ The Beatles, James Taylor, John Martyn, Steeleye Span

▶▶ Strunz and Farrah, Fowler and Barancha

Ralph Burnett

George Adams

Born April 29, 1940, in Covington, GA. Died November 14, 1992, in New York, NY.

George Adams was one of the most powerful and consistently creative tenor saxophonists of the 1970s and '80s. Whether playing with Roy Haynes, Charles Mingus, or McCoy Tyner, leading his own sessions, or most notably with his and pianist Don Pullen's quartet, Adams played with an intensity and exhilaration that knew no stylistic bounds. His thick, brawny sound, reminiscent of Ben Webster and Coleman Hawkins, was equally effective on ballads or at scorching tempos, where he moved easily between complex post-bop lines and late Coltrane harmonic freedom. But Adams's deep blues and gospel roots were always immediately evident in his solos.

After early piano lessons, Adams started playing R&B tenor sax in high school. In the summer of 1961 he toured with Sam Cooke and spent much of the 1960s in Ohio working in organ combos. He moved to New York in 1968 and made a name for himself with Haynes, Art Blakey, and Gil Evans, but it was his three-year stint with Mingus (1973–76) that established his reputation and solidified his emotional, extroverted style. The Adams-Pullen Quartet grew out of the Mingus band and featured bassist Cameron Brown and longtime Mingus drummer Dannie Richmond. The quartet recorded until Adams's death and was one of the most formidable groups of the '80s. Any of their recordings are highly recommended. Towards the end of his life, Adams also played with Phalanx, a powerful group with guitarist James "Blood" Ulmer, bassist Sirone, and drummer Rashied Ali, and worked occasionally with various incarnations of Mingus Dynasty, most notably on the *Epitaph* album, where he was a featured soloist.

what to buy: A great blowing session co-led by Adams and Dannie Richmond, the hard-charging *Hand to Hand* ♫♫♫♫ (Soul Note, 1980, prod. Giovanni Bonandrini) features Adams having a blast with three other jazz originals: Richmond, trombonist Jimmy Knepper and the late, under-appreciated pianist Hugh Lawson, with bass duty handled ably by Mike Richmond (no relation to Dannie). Though recorded during a Mingus Dynasty tour, the band plays its own music, tearing through two fine pieces by Lawson and Adams's gorgeous melody "Yamani's Passion." More than a typically hot album by the George Adams/Don Pullen Quartet, *Live at Montmarte* ♫♫♫♫ (Timeless, 1986, prod. Wim Wigt) is a torrid session recorded live in Denmark's Jazzhus Montmarte club. The presence of guitarist John Scofield makes for spontaneous combustion, as Adams is clearly inspired by Scofield's tricky, fluid lines and digs deep into his blues bag to respond in kind. *Song Everlasting* ♫♫♫♫ (Blue Note, 1987, prod. Michael Cuscuna) is a powerful session by an always rewarding band, designed to display the group's vast range. From Adams's funky "1529 Gunn Street" to their perennial hymn "Sing Me a Song Everlasting," which features Adams at his most lyrical, the Pullen/Adams Quartet draws on 70 years of jazz history and sounds as fresh as tomorrow.

what to buy next: Jazz just doesn't get much more exciting than the two live discs *Live at Village Vanguard, Vol. 1 & Vol. 2* ♫♫♫♫♫ (Soul Note, 1985, prod. Giovanni Bonandrini), which capture the quartet at the peak of its powers. Adams's explosive solos are matched in intensity by Pullen's punishing piano work. A live session billed as George Adams, Hannibal & Friends, *More Sightings* ♫♫♫♫ (Enja, 1984, prod. Stefan Winter) was recorded in Zurich. The pairing of Adams's towering tenor with the stylistically flexible trumpet work of Marvin "Hannibal" Peterson and the greasy guitar of John Scofield pro-

duces terrifically exciting music, with each player spurring the others on to deeper, more emotionally heated solos. *Old Feeling* ♫♫♫♫ (Blue Note, 1991, prod. Kazunori Sugiyama) is a delightfully strange but potent session that opens with the classic Mingus romp "Better Git Hit in Yo' Soul" and closes with Billy Joel's "Just the Way You Are." The album features trumpeter Hannibal, guitarist Jean-Paul Bourelly, bassist Santi DeBriano, drummer Lewis Nash, and pianist Ray Gallon. Adams sounds more restrained than usual and treats each tune with respect.

best of the rest:
(With Pullen Quartet) *Don't Lose Control* ♫♫♫♫ (Soul Note, 1979)
Paradise Space Shuttle ♫♫♫♫ (Timeless Muse, 1981)
(With Pullen Quartet) *Earth Beams* ♫♫♫♫ (Timeless, 1982)
(With Pullen Quartet) *Life Line* ♫♫♫♫♫ (Timeless, 1982)
Gentleman's Agreement ♫♫♫♫♫ (Soul Note, 1983)
(With Pullen Quartet) *Decisions* ♫♫♫♫♫ (Timeless, 1985)
(With Pullen Quartet) *City Lights* ♫♫♫♫♫ (Timeless, 1987)
(With Pullen Quartet) *Melodic Excursions* ♫♫♫♫♫ (Timeless, 1987)
(With Pullen Quartet) *Breakthrough* ♫♫♫♫♫ (Blue Note, 1987)
Nightingale ♫♫♫ (Blue Note, 1988)
America ♫♫♫♫ (Blue Note, 1989)

worth searching for: One of Charles Mingus's last great albums, *Changes One* ♫♫♫♫ (Atlantic/Rhino, 1975, prod. Ilhan Mimaroglu) is a tour de force that features Adams in consistently excellent form throughout, from the surprisingly melodic "Remember Rockefeller at Attica" to the 12-minute masterpiece "Duke Ellington's Sounds of Love," which Adams turns into a personal tribute to Ben Webster and Paul Gonsalves. Adams even sings an effective, gravelly blues on "Devil Blues," something he was known to do in his own performances. Adams's *Sound Suggestions* ♫♫♫♫ (ECM, 1980, prod. Manfred Eicher) is one of his tamer sessions, but his gorgeous, throaty sound has rarely been recorded so well. Fans of the great tenor saxophonist don't want to miss this one.

influences:
◀◀ Coleman Hawkins, Chu Berry, Paul Gonsalves, John Coltrane, Sonny Rollins, Albert Ayler

Andrew Gilbert

Johnny Adams
Born January 5, 1932, in New Orleans, LA.

With his gritty baritone curling around lyrics like honeyed sandpaper, Adams is one of the most versatile and effective balladeers around. The roots of his approach to song come from his early training in the church where Adams used to sing with gospel great Bessie Griffin. Known as the Tan Canary, Adams has long been thought of as a soulful blues artist capable of singing R&B tunes and Nashville's best corn with equal aplomb. He had a series of regional hits for New Orleans companies like Ric, Watch, and Hep Me back in the 1960s, but has appeared on a variety of other labels over the years.

In the 1980s Adams signed a pact with Rounder Records that paired him with a sympathetic producer (Scott Billington) and allowed him to explore other musical avenues than the straight soul blues riffs and country weepers that other companies were having him do.

what to buy: *Walking on a Tightrope: The Songs of Percy Mayfield* ♪♪♪♪ (Rounder, 1989, prod. Scott Billington) is dedicated to the memory of one of the finest crossover composers ever. Mayfield was on Ray Charles's payroll for a few years and gave his boss a series of hits that were popular with both the mainstream pop audience and jazz aficionados. Adams wraps his voice around these gorgeous tunes and their well-crafted lyrics in a way that pays homage to a master without being derivative of someone else's style. Ably supported by guitar wizard Duke Robillard and a kickin' batch of New Orleans-based musicians including Walter "Wolfman" Washington (guitar), Johnny Vidacovich (drums), and reedman Bill Samuels, Adams crafts near-definitive versions of the title tune, "Danger Zone," "You're in for a Big Surprise," and seven other solid senders.

what to buy next: *Good Morning Heartache* ♪♪♪♪ (Rounder, 1993, prod. Scott Billington) is billed as Adams's first jazz album, but he sounds like he's been doing it for ages. He sings songs from the jazz sainthood of Gershwin, Mercer, and Arlen and does solid work on tunes associated with such vocal angels as Dinah Washington and Billie Holiday. All of this is framed in big band settings from Wardell Quezergue and in small group arrangements by pianist David Torkanowsky. Adams even plays his "mouth trombone," imitating the swells and blares of the real thing. The title tune and "Back to Normal" are standouts. *The Verdict* ♪♪♪♪ (Rounder, 1995, prod. Scott Billington) finds Adams fronting a variety of forces from quartets to sextets and nonets, with the occasional nightclub-style piano/vocal duo. There are a few stars on these sessions; Harry Connick Jr. is the pianist dueting with Adams on a beautiful version of "Blue Gardenia," and tenor saxophonist Houston Person brings the art of rib joint balladeering to New Orleans for the title tune, "I Cover the Waterfront," and "Willow Weep for Me." Seven-string guitarist Steve Masakowski also plays on a couple songs, but the rest of the players are from the pool of

talented New Orleans musicians that Billington and Adams usually work with.

the rest:
After Dark ♪♪♪ (Rounder, 1986)
Room With a View of the Blues ♪♪♪♪ (Rounder, 1988)
Johnny Adams Sings Doc Pomus—The Real Me ♪♪♪♪ (Rounder, 1991)
I Won't Cry ♪♪♪ (Rounder, 1992)

influences:
◀◀ Percy Mayfield, Joe Williams, Lou Rawls

▶▶ Dalton Reed

Garaud MacTaggart

Pepper (Park) Adams

Born October 8, 1930, in Highland Park, MI. Died September 10, 1986, in New York, NY.

Although Pepper Adams had a well-documented career as a leader, it's as a sideman that he is perhaps best remembered—his steely yet supple baritone saxophone added depth and appeal to any number of postbop sessions, with Monk's celebrated *Orchestra at Town Hall* and the Mingus Workshop heard on *Blues & Roots* among the essential ones. Indeed, his "Moanin'" riff off the latter has taken on nearly mythic proportions. But it is the solo work that offers the clearest picture of Adams's gem-hard attack and nimble, predominantly vertical improvisatory conception, attributes that set him apart from (and according to many, above) the far more popular Gerry Mulligan.

what to buy: *10 to 4 at the 5 Spot* ♪♪♪♪♪ (Riverside, 1958, prod. Orrin Keepnews) is a lively, live document of the Bobby Timmons–Doug Watkins–Elvin Jones edition of the cooperative quintet co-led by Adams and trumpeter Donald Byrd between 1958 and 1962. This is the set by which the rest must be judged. The original tunes by Byrd and Thad Jones are attractive and filled with forward momentum, and all concerned play with bite and conviction, Byrd's occasionally tenuous articulation notwithstanding.

what to buy next: Adams was never less than polished. His playing didn't necessarily grow exponentially as he matured, nor did it dissipate—he came on the scene fully formed, and he stayed that way, so individual recordings are many times a matter of sidemen and material. . . . *Plays Charlie Mingus* ♪♪♪♪ (Fresh Sounds, 1964, prod. Pepper Adams, Teddy Charles) boasts Hank and Thad Jones, Dannie Richmond, Charles McPherson, Benny Powell, Zoot Sims, and Bob Cranshaw doing

a smart selection of Mingus's marvelous structures. The 1985 meeting between Adams and Frank Foster with a rhythm section of Tommy Flanagan, Ron Carter, and Billy Hart, *The Adams Effect* ♫♫♫♪ (Uptown, 1985, prod. Robert E. Sunenblick, Mabel Fraser) is fiery. *Encounter!* ♫♫♫♪ (Prestige, 1969, prod. F. Norsworthy, O. Gust) is a spirited blowing session with Sims, Flanagan, Carter, and Elvin Jones.

what to avoid: If there's anything in the Adams family to avoid, it's *California Cookin'* ♫♫ (Interplay, 1983), a "festival" recording wherein the late Victor Feldman is sloppy on piano and Adams himself doesn't even appear on a couple of tracks.

best of the rest:
Pepper Adams Quintet ♫♫♫ (Mode/VSOP, 1957)
The Cool Sounds of Pepper Adams ♫♫♫ (Savoy, 1957)
Motor City Scene ♫♫♫ (Bethlehem, 1959)
Mean What You Say ♫♫♫ (Milestone, 1966)
Conjuration ♫♫♫ (Reservoir, 1983)

worth searching for: Flanagan (again), George Mraz, and Leroy Williams lend sedate support to *The Master* ♫♫♫♪ (Muse, 1980, prod. Mitch Farber), on which the concluding "My Shining Hour" saves the day.

influences:
◀◀ Coleman Hawkins, Harry Carney, Charlie Parker

▶▶ Patience Higgins, Jon Raskin

David Prince

Julian "Cannonball" Adderley

Born September 15, 1928, in Tampa, FL. Died August 8, 1975, in Gary, IN.

Adderley started performing in the Tampa area in the 1940s and played in Army bands from 1950 to 1953. Having directed the high school band in Fort Lauderdale, Cannonball (a corruption of "Cannibal," a nickname earned by his healthy appetite) continued to teach until 1955, when he moved to New York, joined Oscar Pettiford's band, and recorded his first LP as a leader. He started a band with his brother Nat in 1956 and joined the Miles Davis quintet in 1957. After his stint with Miles, which included the seminal recordings *Kind of Blue* and *Milestones*, he re-formed his band with brother Nat and it stayed together until his death in 1975, including over its life

Cannonball Adderley **(Archive Photos)**

such major players as Joe Zawinul, Yusef Lateef, George Duke, Walter Booker, Sam Jones, Louis Hayes, and Roy McCurdy. The group gained pop recognition with the Zawinul composition "Mercy, Mercy, Mercy," which reached #11 on the *Billboard* chart. Adderley suffered a stroke in 1975 a few days after appearing in the Clint Eastwood film *Play Misty for Me*.

what to buy: His first recording as a leader, *Spontaneous Combustion* ♫♫♫♪ (Savoy, 1955, prod. Ozzie Cadena) showcases his fiery alto with an obvious nod to Charlie Parker. Whether you believe *Somethin' Else* ♫♫♫♫♪ (Blue Note, 1958, prod. Alfred Lion) is a Cannonball album or a Miles recording under Cannonball's name is immaterial. This is an extraordinary date. "Autumn Leaves" and "Dancing in the Dark" are favorites. This was a period of intense growth for Cannonball. *Mercy, Mercy, Mercy!* ♫♫♫♫♪ (Capitol, 1966, prod. David Axelrod) features Cannonball and brother Nat on cornet along with Joe Zawinul (piano), Victor Gaskin (bass), and Roy McCurdy (drums). This recording foreshadowed the funky rhythm changes and hollering gospel testimonies that distinguish contemporary jazz and new jack fusion, but with a greasy vitality and cerebral harmonic elegance often lacking in today's imitations.

what to buy next: Back in the 1970s a group of British jazz critics selected *Alabama Concerto* ♫♫♫♪ (Riverside, 1958, prod. Orrin Keepnews) as one of the 200 essential recordings of the last 25 years. Based on folk materials created by the pianist on the date, composer John Benson Brooks, and executed flawlessly by the quintet, this recording is an important addition to the Cannonball legacy.

what to avoid: *Julian Cannonball Adderley and Strings* ♫♫ (Verve, 1995, prod. Bob Shad) features good solos but sloppy arrangements.

best of the rest:
Discoveries ♫♫♪ (Savoy, 1955)
Presenting Cannonball ♫♫♪ (Savoy, 1955)
In the Land of HiFi ♫♫♪ (EmArcy, 1956)
Sophisticated Swing: The EmArcy Small Group Sessions ♫♫♫ (EmArcy, 1957)
Portrait of Cannonball ♫♫♫♪ (Riverside, 1958)
Things Are Getting Better ♫♫♫♪ (Riverside, 1958)
Cannonball Adderley Quintet in San Francisco ♫♫♫♫♪ (Riverside, 1959)
What Is This Thing Called Soul ♫♫♫ (Pablo, 1960)
Jazz at the Philharmonic ♫♫♫ (Pablo, 1960)
Know What I Mean? ♫♫♫ (Riverside, 1961)
African Waltz ♫♫♫ (Riverside, 1961)
In New York ♫♫♫♪ (Riverside, 1962)
Nippon Soul ♫♫♫♫♪ (Riverside, 1963)

Cannonball Live in Japan ♫♫ (Capitol, 1966)
Country Preacher ♫♫♫ (Capitol, 1969)
The Price You Got to Pay to Be Free ♫♫♫ (Capitol, 1970)
Inside Straight ♫♫♫ (Fantasy, 1973)

worth searching for: You will have to search the LP bins and cut out cassettes to find *Black Messiah* ♫♫♫♫ (Capitol, 1970, prod. Cannonball Adderley), an important document of 1970s fusion. The standout tracks are "Dr. Honoris Causa" (a dedication by Zawinul to Herbie Hancock after receiving his honorary doctorate) and "The Chocolate Nuisance," which lays the groove down.

influences:

◀◀ Charlie Parker

▶▶ Steve Coleman, Eric Alexander

David C. Gross

Nat Adderley

Born November 25, 1931, in Tampa, FL.

Though Nat Adderley recorded numerous albums of his own, and early in his career worked with Lionel Hampton, J.J. Johnson, and Woody Herman, it's his association with his brother Cannonball Adderley that shaped his career. Strongly influenced by Miles Davis and Clark Terry, Nat usually plays cornet, except for big band sessions when he plays trumpet. Though often overshadowed by his brother in their enormously popular quintets and sextets, in his prime Nat was a potent hard bop improvisor whose sound blended well with Cannonball's alto. Nat also penned a number of jazz standards, including "Work Song," "Sermonette," "Jive Samba," and "The Old Country."

Nat began playing trumpet in 1946 and switched to cornet in 1950. He spent the early 1950s in the service, playing in an Army band and made his first recording in 1955. An early version of Cannonball's quintet (1956–57) didn't catch on and Nat spent time with J.J. Johnson and Woody Herman. When Cannonball re-formed the quintet in 1959 the group caught on quickly with music fans and remained one of jazz's most popular combos until Cannonball's death in 1975. In the proceeding years Nat continued to work in Cannonball's format, employing a steady stream of high-energy alto saxophonists (most notably Sonny Fortune, Antonio Hart, and Vincent Herring) while recording for a number of independent labels. Though his chops have declined, and he lost his right leg to diabetes in 1997, Adderley continues to work with strong bands and make worthwhile albums.

what to buy: *Branching Out* ♫♫♫♫ (Riverside, 1958, prod. Orrin Keepnews) was Nat's first session without Cannonball, and he responded to the spotlight by playing some of the finest solos of his career. The session features the rampaging tenor of Johnny Griffin and the blues-drenched Three Sounds rhythm section with Gene Harris (piano), Andy Simpkins (bass), and Bill Dowdy (drums). Nat's cornet sizzles throughout, and his solos are particularly powerful on the title track and Thelonious Monk's "Well, You Needn't." One of Adderley's best sessions as a leader, *That's Right!* ♫♫♫♫ (Riverside, 1960, prod. Orrin Keepnews) is a hard-swinging all-star session with Cannonball, Yusef Lateef, Jimmy Heath, Charlie Rouse, and Tate Houston. Nat has rarely sounded as impassioned and his energy is matched by his bandmates on this thoroughly enjoyable recording. Heath supplies most of the smart arrangements, which leave plenty of room for solos. *Work Songs* ♫♫♫♫ (Riverside, 1960, prod. Orrin Keepnews) is a fascinating session with guitarist Wes Montgomery and the ultimate hard-bop rhythm section in Bobby Timmons (piano), Louis Hayes (drums), and bassists Percy Heath or Ketter Betts. Betts and Sam Jones also alternate playing pizzicato cello. The shifting personnel and multiple plucked strings make this an unusual but always engaging album. Nat's slightly sour cornet cuts through the ensemble on his original "Work Song" and Cannonball's "Sack O' Woe." *Blue Autumn* ♫♫♫ (Evidence, 1992, prod. Nat Adderley) captures one of Nat's best working bands live at San Francisco's Keystone Korner in 1983. Adderley is in fine form, but alto saxophonist Sonny Fortune is the more aggressive player, taking a number of thrilling solos, especially on his original "For Duke and Cannon." The top-notch rhythm section (pianist Larry Willis, bassist Walter Booker, and drummer Jimmy Cobb) keeps the music charging forward, though overall the album has a disjointed quality, as if something was lost in the editing.

what to buy next: *Mercy, Mercy, Mercy* ♫♫♫♫ (Evidence, 1997, prod. Satoshi Hirano) is a smoking, funky session with Antonio Hart stepping into the Cannonball role and taking the lion's share of solos. Adderley conserves his energy, making his pungent notes count, and even sings two tunes. As if the presence of Booker and Cobb wasn't enough to evoke Cannonball, the band plays a classic arrangement of "What Is This Thing Called Love?" from the old quintet days and the late altoist's "Spontaneous Combustion." *In the Bag* ♫♫♫♫ (Riverside, 1962, prod. Orrin Keepnews) was recorded in New Orleans and features a fascinating sextet with Cannonball, Sam Jones, and three New Orleans modernists: Nat Perrilliat (tenor sax), Ellis Marsalis (piano), and James Black (drums). The Crescent City musicians provide much of the deeply soulful material and Nat is generous with solo space, but he digs as deeply into the material as his bandmates.

what to avoid: Adderley was having problems with his chops on *Talkin' About You* ♫♫ (Landmark, 1991, prod. Orrin Keepnews), though Vincent Herring's alto work soars and Rob Bargad, Walter Booker, and Jimmy Cobb are a top-flight rhythm section. There are many much better Adderley discs available.

best of the rest:
That's Nat Adderley ♫♫♫ (Savoy, 1955)
Introducing Nat Adderley ♫♫♫ (EmArcy, 1955)
To the Ivy League from Nat ♫♫♫ (EmArcy, 1956)
Much Brass ♫♫♫♫ (Riverside, 1959)
Autumn Leaves ♫♫♫ (Evidence, 1990)
The Old Country ♫♫♫ (Enja, 1991)
Workin' ♫♫♫ (Timeless, 1992)

worth searching for: Just about any Adderley brothers album from the '50s and '60s is worth a listen, but *Dizzy's Business* ♫♫♫♫ (Milestone, 1993, prod. Orrin Keepnews) is hard to top. Featuring one of Cannonball's best sextets recorded live in 1962 and '63—with Yusef Lateef (reeds) Joe Zawinul (piano), Sam Jones, and Louis Hayes—jazz just doesn't get much hotter. Nat is an essential element in the mix and he holds his own on stage with his charismatic brother.

influences:
◀◀ Miles Davis, Dizzy Gillespie, Kenny Dorham

Andrew Gilbert

Ron Affif

Born December 30, 1965, in Pittsburgh, PA.

Affif is heading for a land beyond that inhabited by the merely talented. His guitar playing is already a source of wonderment for such musicians as Jimmy Bruno and George Benson, but his harmonic conception and willingness to experiment are already taking him into new territory. Originally a bop-oriented guitarist, Affif has a healthy respect for tradition even as he seeks to move on. Affif's uncle Ron Anthony gave the budding guitarist his first lessons and he continued to learn from local teachers including Jerry Conderato and Joe Negri. Even though Affif won a scholarship to attend Duquesne University, he ended up moving (in 1984) to Los Angeles where his uncle was working with Frank Sinatra and George Shearing. While there he played with Pete Christlieb, Dave Pike, and Andy Simpkins,

JULIAN "CANNONBALL" ADDERLEY

song "Somethin' Else"
album Somethin' Else
(Blue Note, 1958/1986)
instrument Alto saxophone

Monster Solo

among others. He went to live in Brooklyn in 1989 and has worked with Sheila Jordan, Leon Parker, Bill Mays, Steve Kuhn, and Ralph LaLama.

what to buy: Affif brings his blazing plectrum and often quirky sense of time to the trio date *52nd Street* ♫♫♫♫ (1996, Pablo, prod. Eric Miller). Ostensibly an album celebrating the cradle of bebop sensibilities, the tunes feature a lineup of period pieces ("Yardbird Suite", "Stompin' at the Savoy," etc.). Drummer Jeff "Tain" Watts and the doubly named bassist Essiet Essiet match Affif riff for riff, plucking his ideas from midair and acting on them in nanoseconds. Arrangements hang pretty close to the melody for the most part and the excitement of creative minds melding with muscular technique is heady throughout, but when the group decides to throw the listener a changeup, things get exciting. The Oscar Pettiford classic "Bohemia After Dark" opens the album with a perfect example of this kind of group interplay. The bass and drum kit mix powerful speed with Affif's unique timing. Essiet is a revelation. He might end up revolutionizing bass concepts in the same way Scott LaFaro did decades ago with Ornette Coleman.

what to buy next: His producer convinced Affif to devote an album to material associated with Miles Davis and the wonderful result is *Vierd Blues* ✍✍✍ (1994, Pablo, prod. Eric Miller). Affif performs with the basic quartet he used on his self-titled debut album for Pablo. Augmenting them on "Solar" and the title song are Affif's uncle, guitarist Ron Anthony, and percussionist Brian Kilgore. Brian O'Rourke's piano playing sparkles throughout and bassist Andy Simpkins has a nice walking solo on "Blue in Green." Affif proves that he has more than speed at his command with some thoughtful solos, especially on the band's take of "All Blues."

the rest:
Ron Affif ✍✍✍ (1993, Pablo)
Ringside ✍✍✍ (Pablo, 1997)

worth searching for: Affif's very first album (recorded for Van Belt and currently out of print) will probably approach mythic status soon. Affif can also be heard playing alongside former Joe Pass associate John Pisano on *Among Friends* (Pablo, 1995, prod. Eric Miller) on "D'Joe" and "If I Should Lose You."

influences:
◄◄ Pat Martino, Joe Pass, Ron Anthony, George Benson, Wes Montgomery

Garaud MacTaggart

The Afro Blue Band

Rather than a regular working band, the Afro Blue Band represents a one-time, all-star gathering of players from New York City, Miami, and San Francisco, with one common tie. Most of them worked for many years at the San Francisco jazz club, Keystone Corner, owned from 1972–1983 by Todd Barkan, the producer of this album. At their session recorded in 1994, the 15-musician band highlighted talents of top Afro-Cuban jazz leaders, many who have recorded with their own groups or with foremost Afro-Cuban jazz bands.

what's available: *Impressions* ✍✍✍ (Milestone, 1995, prod. Todd Barkan) runs the gamut from edgy, hot-blowing to melodic, straight-ahead jazz built on the modern arrangements of saxophonist Arthur Barron and others. Guest soloists include reedists Dave Liebman, Mario Rivera, Mel Martin, trumpeter Melton Mustafa, pianist Hilton Ruiz (all who have albums as leaders) and, part of the extended Keystone family, percussionists Steve Berrios (leader, Son Bachéche) and trumpeter-conguero Jerry Gonzalez (leader, Fort Apache Band). Mel Martin's arrangement of "For Pearl," brings one of the calmer, sweeter interludes, giving vent to his own lush, alto flute and bass clarinet solos in a trio setting that includes Ruiz.

influences:
◄◄ Fort Apache Band

Nancy Ann Lee

Air
/New Air
Formed 1975, in New York, NY.

Henry Threadgill, alto, tenor, baritone saxophones, flute, hubkaphone, eastern banjo; Fred Hopkins, bass; Steve McCall, drums (1975–82); Pheeroan AkLaff, drums (1982–85); Andrew Cyrille, drums (1985–86).

Threadgill, Hopkins, and McCall joined together under the rubric Reflections in 1971 when Threadgill was asked to do some arrangements of Scott Joplin material for a Columbia College theatrical production. In 1972 McCall went to Europe, but the three reunited in 1975 in New York. They became part of the burgeoning New York loft jazz scene and were performing continuously. Equally at home in completely unscripted free improvisation, Threadgill's intricate compositions, or explorations of blues and early jazz, the trio was never predictable and always thought-provoking. In 1982 when McCall moved back to Chicago they added Pheeroan AkLaff on drums and renamed themselves New Air. In 1985 AkLaff was replaced by Andrew Cyrille, but the group split a year later, with Threadgill going on to a successful and idiosyncratic solo career.

what to buy: Threadgill and company perform with an intuitiveness that is uncanny on *Live Air* ✍✍✍✍ (Black Saint, 1977, prod. Giovanni Bonandrini), their first release with widespread U.S. distribution. Threadgill's flute work is in evidence on this CD. Hopkins walks with aplomb and his arco work is tender yet forceful. Pheeroan AkLaff gave the group a more aggressive stance on *New Air Live at Montreux International Jazz Festival* ✍✍✍✍ (Black Saint, 1983, prod. New Air). The interplay between Hopkins and AkLaff is rough in spots, but that added tension is what makes this CD cook. As always Threadgill is inventive and exploratory.

what to buy next: New Air's *Air Show No. 1* ✍✍✍✍ (Black Saint, 1986, prod. Giovanni Bonandrini) features three tracks with vocalist Cassandra Wilson (Threadgill's wife at the time). "Don't

Drink That Corner, My Life Is in the Bush" is a tribute to winos and street drinkers featuring superb arco work by Hopkins. Threadgill increases his arsenal by including the eastern banjo on this track. *Air Mail* 𝄢𝄢𝄢𝄢 (Black Saint, 1980, prod. Air) at 35 minutes is relatively short by today's standards, but the music more than compensates. Hopkins adds ostinatos and plaintive arco work to the proceedings. McCall is a master at understatement, and Threadgill's three compositions explore territory akin to the Art Ensemble and Muhal Richard Abrams.

best of the rest:
Air Time 𝄢𝄢𝄢 (Nessa, 1977)
Open Air Suit 𝄢𝄢𝄢 (Novus, 1978)
Montreux Suisse 𝄢𝄢𝄢𝄢 (Novus, 1978)
80 Degrees Below 82 𝄢𝄢𝄢 (Antilles, 1982)

worth searching for: *Air Song* 𝄢𝄢𝄢𝄢 (India Navigation, 1975, prod. Air) was originally released in Japan and although it is not available on CD is still one of the most important recordings to find. Steve McCall is at his creative best on this LP. The band is in fine form with dynamics and textures at the fore. The out-of-print *Air Lore* 𝄢𝄢𝄢𝄢 (Novus, 1979, prod. Michael Cuscuna) documented the group's interest in early jazz, consisting mostly of Scott Joplin and Jelly Roll Morton tunes.

influences:
◀◀ Art Ensemble of Chicago, Muhal Richard Abrams, Howlin' Wolf

▶▶ Dave Douglas, Tiny Bell Trio

David C. Gross

Kei Akagi

Born March 16, 1953, in Japan.

An extremely versatile player with a highly individual style and lengthy resume, Akagi maintains his own sound no matter what the context. In the last two decades his credits include significant stints with Miles Davis, Stanley Turrentine, Art Pepper, Slide Hampton, Joe Farrell, Airto Moreira, James Newton, Sadao Watanabe, and fusion stalwarts Al DiMeola, Jean-Luc Ponty, and Allan Holdsworth. First influenced by Bud Powell, Akagi came of age listening to everyone from Oscar Peterson, Bill Evans, and Sonny Rollins to late Coltrane and Miles's seminal fusion. His family moved to the U.S. when he was four and he spent his late teens back in Japan, playing guitar and studying composition at the International Christian University in Tokyo. Returning to the States, he became a philosophy grad student at the University of California, Santa Barbara, but after

two years decided to play music full-time. After early gigs with Blue Mitchell, Art Pepper, and Eddie Harris, Akagi hooked up with Airto and Flora Purim in 1979 and stayed with them until 1985. He spent two years with Miles (1990–91) and much of the rest of the decade with Turrentine. Based in Los Angeles, Akagi is a fine composer who writes angular, dramatic tunes. Akagi's first album was *Symphonic Fusion—The Earth*, a five-part funk-jazz concerto recorded in the early 1980s for a Japanese label.

what to buy: *Mirror Puzzle* 𝄢𝄢𝄢𝄢 (Audioquest, 1994, prod. Joe Harley) is a challenging quartet session with Rick Margitza on tenor and soprano sax, Charles Fambrough on bass, and Willie Jones III on drums, featuring mostly Akagi originals. "Splinter Unity" flirts with dissonance and doesn't so much end as stop, while "Too Much Remembered" features Margitza's excellent tenor work. This consistently involving session is the work of a major talent whose music should be further documented.

what to buy next: *Sound Circle* 𝄢𝄢𝄢 (Evidence, 1995, prod. Akira Tana) features the Asian American Jazz Trio playing a diverse body of music. Akagi and longtime rhythm section mates Rufus Reid (bass) and Akira Tana (drums) recorded this session in late 1992 after working at the Asian American Jazz Festival. Akagi contributes one tune, "Cotati," and fits in easily with two of jazz's premier accompanists, demonstrating his quick and fertile harmonic imagination.

influences:
◀◀ McCoy Tyner, Bud Powell, Bill Evans

Andrew Gilbert

Toshiko Akiyoshi

Born December 12, 1929, in Darien, Manchuria, China.

Toshiko Akiyoshi is living proof that jazz is a world-wide phenomenon. Born in China and raised in Japan, Akiyoshi was introduced to jazz when she was still in her teens through recordings of Teddy Wilson. While in her twenties and performing around Tokyo, she was heard by Oscar Peterson, who then told impresario Norman Granz that Akiyoshi was "the greatest female jazz pianist." This in turn led to her receiving a scholarship for the Berklee School of Music.

She later formed a quartet with her husband at the time, alto saxophonist Charlie Mariano, recording for the Candid label prior to hooking up briefly with Charles Mingus in 1962. Shortly after the Mingus stint, Akiyoshi went back to Japan before returning to America where, in 1965, she was a piano teacher at jazz clinics in Reno, Nevada and Salt Lake City, Utah.

Since that time she has founded her big band, now known as the Toshiko Akiyoshi Jazz Orchestra (featuring saxophonist Lew Tabackin, her current husband), and recorded with it for RCA, Jam, and Ascent. The orchestra is now considered her main musical voice and her writing and arranging for them are widely considered to be among the best in the world. Akiyoshi's music is a skilled blend of East and West, often melding lessons learned from Charles Mingus, Duke Ellington, and Gil Evans with Oriental themes and instruments. Her albums have garnered numerous Grammy nominations and she was voted the best arranger in a 1978 *Down Beat* readers poll.

what to buy: The wonderfully recorded live set *Carnegie Hall Concert* ♫♫♫♫ (Columbia, 1992, prod. Dr. George Butler) documents Akiyoshi's orchestra at the peak of perfection, playing material arranged by her and, with the exception of Frank Wess's "Your Beauty Is a Song of Love," written by her. The voicings used by Akiyoshi can roar or offer soloists a lush sonic backdrop, and the slate of guest notables for this date is impressive, with trumpeter Freddie Hubbard and vocalist Nnenna Freelon heading the list. The section lineup is pretty strong as well, with ex-Basie stalwart Wess (on alto saxophone and flute) lining up in the reeds with the orchestra's main tenor soloist, Lew Tabackin. Standout moments include the duet between Hubbard and Tabackin on "Chasing After Love" where the band lays out and the two soloists do battle. Akiyoshi's orchestration of Japanese vocals and Tabackin's oriental–flavored flute playing into the texture of a gently swinging yet powerful "Children of the Universe" is another highlight.

In the mid-1970s, Akiyoshi was just starting to hit her stride as a composer/arranger for an innovative series of albums released by RCA. *Toshiko Akiyoshi–Lew Tabackin Big Band* ♫♫♫♫ (Novus, compilation issued 1991, prod. Hiroshi Isaka/compilation prod. John Snyder) is only a taste of what was an important band, and until RCA or Novus chooses to reissue the full recordings from this period, this is the only way to go. Works from the acclaimed *Long Yellow Road* and the underrated *Kogun* are particularly welcome.

what to buy next: In the exposed environment of the solo recital *Maybeck Recital Hall Series, Vol. 36* ♫♫♫♫ (Concord Jazz, 1995, prod. Carl E. Jefferson), Akiyoshi has to provide both melody and rhythm. This is where her strong left-hand playing comes into play, especially on the set's opening number, "The Village." As written for her big band, this song needs a rapid-fire pulse, and in the absence of a rhythm section, Akiyoshi proves equal to her task. The Maybeck series, while it often brings out the best in the featured artists, also seems to contain a large number of cover versions, even when the performer is as distinguished a composer as Akiyoshi is. This volume is no exception since it includes songs by two of her major influences, Duke Ellington and Bud Powell, plus a host of older pop standards to go with her own "Quadrille, Anyone?" and the previously mentioned "The Village." Despite those admittedly minor caveats, this is still a marvelous performance. Bud Powell was an influence and a mentor to Akiyoshi, both as a performer and as a composer, so *Remembering Bud: Cleopatra's Dream* ♫♫♫♫ (Evidence, 1992, prod. Toshiko Akiyoshi) makes sense. This set list includes nine Powell-penned tunes and an instrumental tribute by Akiyoshi called "Remembering Bud." Here's a chance to hear Akiyoshi in a trio setting where her keyboard skills are more exposed than in the big band, but with the rhythm support that allows her a modicum of melodic freedom. There's some good playing here, with well-chosen material including Powell favorites like "Tempus Fugit" and "Un Poco Loco." The mix and match trio shifts lineups between the two bassists (George Mraz and Ray Drummond) and a pair of drummers (Lewis Nash and Al Harewood).

the rest:
Toshiko Mariano Quartet ♫♫♫ (Candid, 1961)
Finesse ♫♫ (Concord Jazz, 1978)
Interlude ♫♫♫ (Concord Jazz, 1987)
Desert Lady–Fantasy ♫♫♫♫ (Columbia, 1995)

worth searching for: They may be out of print in the U.S., but there are Japanese reissues of the RCA-period big band albums, and they are worth the effort to find if you don't already have the vinyl versions. Especially notable are *Tales of a Courtesan* ♫♫♫♫ (RCA, 1976, prod. Hiroshi Isaka), *Road Time* ♫♫♫♫ (RCA, 1976, prod. Hiroshi Isaka), *Long Yellow Road* ♫♫♫♫ (RCA, 1975, prod. Hiroshi Isaka) and *Insights* ♫♫♫♫ (RCA, 1977, prod. Hiroshi Isaka). Another wonderful album (and also out of print), *Tanuki's Night Out* ♫♫♫♫ (JAM, 1981, prod. Toshiko Akiyoshi, Lew Tabackin), featured Toshiko Akiyoshi arrangements of six compositions by Lew Tabackin.

influences:
◀◀ Bud Powell, Charles Mingus, Duke Ellington, Gil Evans
▶▶ Maria Schneider

Joe Albany

Born Joseph Albani, January 24, 1924, in Atlantic City, NJ. Died January 11, 1988, in New York, NY.

Though Joe Albany was an important figure early in the bebop movement, the pianist's extremely unsettled life kept him from participating in the jazz scene for decades. Drug and alcohol addiction derailed his career from the mid-1940s until the early 1970s, when he made a tentative comeback. His first instrument was the accordion, but he switched to piano in high school and joined scat singer Leo Watson's band in 1942. In the mid-1940s he worked with such top bandleaders as Benny Carter, Georgie Auld, and Boyd Raeburn. However, it was his gigs with Charlie Parker, some of which were released on live albums, and his 1946 Aladdin recordings with Lester Young, that established his reputation as a significant modernist. But Albany only recorded once between 1947 and 1971, a desolate period he described in the harrowing 1980 documentary *Joe Albany . . . A Jazz Life*. He did play briefly with Charles Mingus in the mid-1960s, but otherwise Albany was a completely obscure figure until 1972. Over the next decade he recorded sessions for Revelation, Horo, Inner City, Sea Breeze, and Interplay, though few have appeared on CD.

what to buy: Though it's the tape of an informal rehearsal session from 1957, *The Right Combination* ♫♫♫ (Riverside/OJC, 1990) is a worthwhile recording as virtually the only documentation of bebop pianist Joe Albany's lost years. Though the sound isn't great and the material is mostly well-worn standards, Albany shows flashes of brilliance with his jagged right-hand lines while accompanying the great tenor saxophonist Warne Marsh (along with bassist Bobby Whitlock).

best of the rest:
Birdtown Blues ♫♫♫ (SteepleChase, 1973/1995)

worth searching for: *Bird Lives!* ♫♫♫ (Storyville, 1979, prod. Toshiya Taenaka) finds Albany in his element, tearing his way through a set of Charlie Parker tunes, mostly consisting of 12-bar blues. Fans of bebop piano will be rewarded if they uncover this trio session, which features exemplary support by bassist Art Davis and drummer Roy Haynes.

influences:

◀◀ Al Haig, Bud Powell, Thelonious Monk

Andrew Gilbert

Gerald Albright

Born 1957.

An expressive saxman whose influences range from John Coltrane to soul-jazz heroes, Gerald Albright is more than capable of delivering first-class jazz. But on the whole, he has chosen to embrace lightweight "muzak" along the lines of Najee and George Howard. Albright set the tone for his career with 1988's *Just Between Us*, an overproduced date that made him a hit on so-called "smooth jazz" radio stations. Subsequent albums *Bermuda Nights* and *Dream Come True* were equally contrived, but Albright (who has done session work for the Temptations, Anita Baker, and other R&B artists) had an impressive straight-ahead jazz album in 1991's *Live at Birdland West*.

what to buy: Albright's crowning achievement, *Live at Birdland West* ♫♫♫ (Atlantic, 1991) showed just how commanding an improviser he can be. Albright truly burns on John Coltrane's "Impressions," and "Georgia on My Mind" exemplifies his ballad playing at its most heartfelt and moving. Guests range from Eddie Harris to saxman Kirk Whalum, and Albright plays postbop, hard bop, and soul-jazz with splendid results. For once, he celebrates his improvisatory skills instead of so shamelessly wasting them.

what to avoid: Typical of Albright's commercial output, the homogenized recordings *Dream Come True* ♫ (Atlantic, 1990, prod. Gerald Albright) and *Smooth* ♫ (Atlantic, 1994, prod. Gerald Albright) are formulaic "smooth jazz" discs that throw artistic considerations to the wind and concern themselves only with radio airplay. Except for *Live at Birdland West*, none of Albright's albums are worth owning.

influences:

◀◀ Grover Washington Jr., John Coltrane, Eddie Harris, David "Fathead" Newman, Hank Crawford

▶▶ Art Porter Jr., Paul Taylor

Alex Henderson

Howard Alden

Born October 17, 1958, in Newport Beach, CA.

Alden is to the Concord Jazz label what Grant Green was to Blue Note: the house guitarist of choice. He has played on albums by Ruby Braff, Monty Alexander, and Ken Peplowski in addition to recording with a pioneer of the seven-string guitar, George Van Eps. As part of the burgeoning new generation of swing practitioners, Alden has gone straight to the source, learning by playing with some of the best-known masters of the form: Woody Herman, Dizzy Gillespie, Clark Terry, Benny Carter, Kenny Davern, Flip Phillips and Red Norvo to name just a few. Not bad for a kid who started off playing banjo in California pizza restaurants before he was 18 years old.

The guitarist lists piano players Duke Ellington, Bill Evans, and Thelonious Monk as his favorite composers, so when he was introduced to the seven-string guitar through Van Eps, Alden was delighted to find that the extra low string aided him in playing tunes by those giants. Most of his current work features the hybrid guitar.

what to buy: Alden's use of the seven-string guitar for *Your Story—The Music of Bill Evans* 𝄫𝄫𝄫𝄫 (Concord Jazz, 1994, prod. Carl E. Jefferson) allows him a wider sonic range, all the better to play music defined by the piano of the great Bill Evans. Many of Evans's compositions are of a refined, introspective nature, but to put him in that bag decries the possibilities of other material he had written. Alden's retrospective shows us the way. For this exercise in swing Alden is joined by Frank Wess on tenor saxophone and flute in addition to former Evans sideman Michael Moore on bass and drummer Al Harewood. Ken Peplowski, the superb clarinet player, gets co-billing on *Live at Centre Concord: Encore!* 𝄫𝄫𝄫𝄫 (Concord Jazz, 1995, prod. Carl E. Jefferson). For five out of the nine cuts, Alden and Peplowski play as a duo and are nothing short of marvelous. The remaining tracks feature Jeff Chambers on bass and Colin Bailey on drums and things still stay marvelous, especially when Peplowski pulls out his tenor saxophone for two tunes within the quartet format.

what to buy next: On *Misterioso* 𝄫𝄫𝄫𝄫 (Concord Jazz, 1991, prod. Carl E. Jefferson) Alden does the jazz world a service by bringing Bud Freeman's "Song of the Dove" back into the light of day. This is one of those songs with a melody so beautiful that it cries out to be performed more. Other than that gem, Alden does an exemplary job with a couple Monk pieces (the title track and "We See"), a pair of Ellingtonian numbers, some Broadway show chestnuts, a Jelly Roll Morton classic (the delightful "The Pearls"), and one of Alden's own compositions. The trio for this date gets its pulse from drummer Keith Copeland (whose father, Ray, played on the original version of "We See") and bassist Frank Tate. The variety of settings found on *Take Your Pick* 𝄫𝄫𝄫𝄫 (Concord Jazz, 1997, prod. Allen Farnham, John Burk) include a welcome reminder of how well Alden plays when paired with a really good horn player in a quintet. The duet with pianist Renee Rosnes is nicely done, but the six tracks with Lew

Tabackin on tenor saxophone or flute lift the session into something more than just another tasteful album. Take note of the nice opening on the lead-off tune, "I Concentrate on You," where Alden riffs over the rhythm section before Tabackin starts trading lines with Alden, Rosnes, and the rest of the band. Longtime Alden associate Michael Moore (bass) and drummer Bill Goodwin provide the pulse for most of the session.

the rest:
(With the Howard Alden/Dan Barrett Quartet) *Swing Street* 𝄫𝄫𝄫 (Concord Jazz, 1988)
The Howard Alden Trio 𝄫𝄫𝄫 (Concord Jazz, 1989)
(With the Howard Alden/Dan Barrett Quartet) *ABQ Salutes Buck Clayton* 𝄫𝄫𝄫 (Concord Jazz, 1989)
(With Jack Lesberg) *No Amps Allowed* 𝄫𝄫𝄫 (Chiaroscuro, 1989)
Snowy Morning Blues 𝄫𝄫 (Concord Jazz, 1990)
(With George Van Eps) *13 Strings* 𝄫𝄫𝄫 (Concord Jazz, 1991)
(With George Van Eps) *Hand Crafted Swing* 𝄫𝄫 (Concord Jazz, 1992)
A Good Likeness 𝄫𝄫𝄫 (Concord Jazz, 1993)
(With George Van Eps) *Seven & Seven* 𝄫𝄫 (Concord Jazz, 1993)
(With Ken Peplowski) *Concord Duo Series, Vol. 3* 𝄫𝄫𝄫 (Concord Jazz, 1993)
(With Frank Vignola and Jimmy Bruno) *Concord Jazz Guitar Collective* 𝄫𝄫𝄫 (Concord Jazz, 1995)
(With George Van Eps) *Keepin' Time* 𝄫𝄫𝄫 (Concord Jazz, 1996)

worth searching for: The two-CD set *Fujitsu-Concord 25th Jazz Festival Silver Anniversary Set* 𝄫𝄫𝄫𝄫 (Concord Jazz, 1996, prod. Carl E. Jefferson) includes six tunes from the Howard Alden Trio along with seven from Gene Harris and another seven from Marian McPartland. The overall quality of the playing is good, but the Alden trio sides are reason enough to clamor for a live album from this talented guitarist.

influences:
◀◀ Charlie Christian, Barney Kessel, Bucky Pizzarelli
▶▶ Ron Affif

Garaud MacTaggart

Brian Ales

Born July 25, 1960.

Brian Ales is the modern equivalent of the jazz arranger; while he does play some guitar and electronics (keyboards, samplers, and the like), his main role is that of audio constructor, with the recording studio as his instrument. Likening his methods to a film director, Ales digitally manipulates the recording of his collaborators. Framing and reorganizing the sounds to fit his own unique sonic vision, he often juxtaposes elements from various genres to create a type of ethno-ambient music. While this type of assemblage may seem sterile, his recordings are remarkably warm, intimate, and musically diverse, demonstrating that Ales is a young talent with whom to be reckoned.

It should come as no surprise that Ales began his musical career as an engineer, eventually reaching a level of renown where his services were requested by jazz innovators Bob Moses, Lyle Mays, Joe Lovano, and Oliver Lake. Ales relocated from Boston to Canada in the late 1980s, accepting a position as artist/technologist in residence at the Banff Centre for the Arts, where he produced his debut CD, *Naivete* (eventually released in 1995). After a brief stay in Los Angeles, working mainly in film composition, Ales moved to New York, where he continues to create his own music, as well as work with members of the cutting-edge New York City jazz scene (i.e., the Knitting Factory stable of artists) in the role of producer and engineer.

what to buy: On his second solo release, *Creature of Habit* 𝄢𝄢𝄢𝄢 (Intuition, 1997, prod. Brian Ales), Ales demonstrates his knack for using a wide range of ethnic instrumentation to create totally unique music that suggests no individual region and avoids the cliches of much World music. Bulgarian bagpipes join African drums, Indian tablas, and Japanese flutes in a coherent communion of sound that comes off as neither forced nor free form. Preferring to create in the studio instead of with a prepared written score, Ales generates tunes that retain the vitality of jazz despite the rather eclectic orchestrations. Ales's own guitar playing, highlighted by short solo passages interspersed between tracks, recalls the textured, spacious work of his frequent collaborator Bill Frisell.

what to buy next: *Naivete* 𝄢𝄢𝄢 (Intuition, 1995, prod. Brian Ales) is the domestic issue of Ales's debut, recorded over the span of several years. Like any artist's first steps, this record seems protean, but the ideas and technique are clearly there. Frisell's presence helps.

worth searching for: *American Blood/Safety in Numbers* 𝄢𝄢𝄢 (Intuition, 1995, prod. Brian Ales, Bill Frisell) contains two highly conceptual pieces, one collaboration between Ales, Frisell, and vocalist Victor Bruce Godsey, the other Ales's manipulation of an extended Frisell guitar solo.

influences:
◄◄ Bill Frisell

Eric J. Lawrence

Eric Alexander

Born August 4, 1968, in Galesburg, IL.

One of the few "young lions" who is more influenced by Dexter Gordon and George Coleman than by John Coltrane and Sonny Rollins, tenor saxophonist Eric Alexander has come very far with his music in a short period of time. Following his first year of studying classical music at Indiana University as an alto player, Alexander picked up the tenor, made the switch to jazz, and the next year transferred to William Patterson College in New Jersey. In 1991, Alexander finished second to Joshua Redman in the Thelonious Monk Institute's tenor saxophone competition. He worked frequently in the Chicago area with Charles Earland, Jack McDuff, and Cecil Payne, and others before heading to New York. Since his arrival in the summer of 1992, he has continued to develop his approach and his melodic, middle-register sound (the one element he takes most seriously), and to record for the Criss Cross Jazz label as both a leader and frequent sideman.

what to buy: *Straight Up* 𝄢𝄢𝄢 (Delmark, 1992, prod. Robert G. Koester) is the debut Chicago set that clearly shows a budding talent in the making and includes some wonderful piano work from Harold Mabern. On *New York Calling* 𝄢𝄢𝄢 (Criss Cross Jazz, 1992, prod. Gerry Teekens), Alexander holds his own in the talented company of trumpeter John Swana, pianist Richard Wyands, and rhythm mates Peter and Kenny Washington. This is very solid stuff! Alexander's *Eric Alexander in Europe* 𝄢𝄢𝄢𝄢 (Criss Cross Jazz, 1996, prod. Gerry Teekens) finds him working in an organ combo with Melvin Rhyne and guitarist Bobby Broom. Alexander simply shines and presents the most cogent recorded example of his ability to be technically adept while also really telling a story and communicating with the listener.

the rest:
Up, Over, and Out 𝄢𝄢𝄢 (Delmark, 1995)
Full Range 𝄢𝄢𝄢 (Criss Cross Jazz, 1995)
(With Lin Halliday) *Stablemates* 𝄢𝄢𝄢𝄢 (Delmark, 1996)
One for All 𝄢𝄢𝄢 (Sharp Nine, 1997)

worth searching for: Alexander performs as part of The Tenor Triangle with the Melvin Rhyne Trio on *Tell It Like It Is* 𝄢𝄢𝄢 (Criss Cross Jazz, 1994, prod. Gerry Teekens), another fine example of Alexander's work in an organ combo where he blows up a storm alongside other tenor heavies Tad Shull and Ralph Lalama.

influences:

◄◄ Coleman Hawkins, Dexter Gordon, George Coleman, Sonny Stitt

Chris Hovan

Monty Alexander

Born Montgomery Bernard, June 6, 1944, in Kingston, Jamaica.

A dazzling pianist who effectively combines Caribbean and jazz rhythms, Alexander tends to be overlooked despite fellow musicians' respect for his playing. Alexander has incorporated the influences of Oscar Peterson, Ahmad Jamal, and Nat "King" Cole into a highly personal sound that relies as much on his joyful, emotionally charged sensibility as his virtuosity. A frequent sideman with Ray Brown and Milt Jackson in the 1970s, Alexander has recorded a few dozen albums of his own and formed a Jamaican band in the 1980s, Ivory and Steel, featuring steel drums.

Alexander began playing professionally in Jamaican clubs while still a teenager, and his band Monty and the Cyclones developed a strong following in the late 1950s. His first U.S. gig was in Las Vegas with Art Mooney's orchestra, but he soon found work as a singers' accompanist and became friends with Milt Jackson. Alexander made a strong reputation with albums he recorded for Pacific Jazz, RCA, and Verve in the 1960s. In the 1970s, he recorded for MPS, Pablo, and Concord, the label with which he is still associated. His albums are consistently rewarding, marked by his hard, swinging attack and attention to dynamics.

what to buy: Alexander shines in the rare solo session *Monty Alexander at Maybeck, Maybeck Recital Hall Series, Vol. 40* ♪♪♪♪ (Concord, 1995, prod. Carl E. Jefferson), displaying his affinity for pre-bop piano styles. From a two-fisted "When the Saints Go Marching In" to his smoking, gospel-tinged "The Serpent," Alexander shows that his powerful left hand is all the accompaniment he needs to swing like a monster. His emotional range comes through with a delicate, thoughtful reading of "Close Enough for Love" and a ravishing version of his spiritual "Renewal." *Triple Treat* ♪♪♪♪ (Concord Jazz, 1982, prod. Carl E. Jefferson) is the first in a series of playfully virtuoso sessions featuring Alexander, Ray Brown, and Herb Ellis. The material is mostly well-worn (except for a swinging version of *The Flintstones* theme) but when the three veterans bring their ample wit and even more ample chops to "But Not for Me," it's hard to resist. Alexander turns Blue Mitchell's "Funji Mama" into a calypso excursion, while "Triple Treat Blues" sounds suspiciously

like "After Hours." Alexander thrives in the trio format, and *Steamin'* ♪♪♪♪ (Concord, 1995, prod. Carl E. Jefferson) is a typically swinging affair featuring bassist Ira Coleman and drummer Dion Parson. There's nothing usual about the material, though, as Alexander explores a baker's dozen of rarely played tunes, from Bob Marley's "Lively Up Yourself" and a playful version of Jerome Kern's "Make Believe" to a graceful, perfectly crafted "Pure Imagination" from the movie *Willy Wonka and the Chocolate Factory.* He closes the album striding through a bravura solo version of "Young at Heart." A Frank Sinatra tribute, *Echoes of Jilly's* ♪♪♪♪ (Concord Jazz, 1997, prod. Allen Farnham) isn't what one might expect from Alexander, but turning him loose on 13 standards with equally confident triomates is a pretty surefire formula, with John Patitucci (bass) and Troy Davis (drums) providing strong support. Alexander plays with our knowledge of Sinatra's recordings, referencing Nelson Riddle's arrangement on the opener, "I've Got You Under My Skin," but he imposes his own identity on the tunes. The trio sails through "Come Fly With Me" and "Fly Me to the Moon," while Alexander plays gorgeous solo versions of "I'm a Fool to Want You" and "Here's That Rainy Day." Jilly's, by the way, was a 1960s New York nightspot that Frank frequented.

what to buy next: *Reunion in Europe* ♪♪♪♪ (Concord Jazz, 1984, prod. Jeff Hamilton) was recorded live in Stuttgart, Germany, re-uniting one of the most exciting mainstream piano trios of the 1970s. The rapport between Alexander, the ostensible leader, and John Clayton (bass) and Jeff Hamilton (drums) infuses each track, and there's really no frontline instrument. Alexander tips his hat to Art Tatum on "Yesterdays" and shows off his earthy side on his "Blues for Stephanie," while Clayton takes a beautiful arco bass solo on "Smile." *The River* ♪♪♪♪ (Concord Jazz, 1985, prod. Monty Alexander) is a fascinating album of diverse spiritual music, from gospel and Negro spirituals to hymns and jazz compositions. With John Clayton (bass) and Ed Thigpen (drums), this session also features two of Alexander's most beautiful tunes, the title track and "Renewal." "David Danced" by Duke Ellington and the traditional spiritual "Ain't Gonna Study War No More" also make for powerful material.

best of the rest:

Facets ♪♪♪♪ (Concord, 1980)
Duke Ellington Songbook ♪♪♪♪ (Verve, 1983)
Full Steam Ahead ♪♪♪♪ (Concord, 1985)
Jamboree: Monty Alexander's Ivory and Steel ♪♪♪♪ (Concord Picante, 1988)
Triple Treat II ♪♪♪♪ (Concord, 1989)
Triple Treat III ♪♪♪♪ (Concord, 1989)
Caribbean Circle ♪♪♪♪ (Chesky, 1992)

Monty Alexander's Ivory and Steel: To the Ends of the Earth 𝄞𝄞𝄞 (Concord Picante, 1996)

worth searching for: Alexander's first of many recordings for the label, *Soul Fusion* 𝄞𝄞𝄞 (Pablo, 1977, prod. Norman Granz) is an exercise in funky virtuosity, well worth searching the used record bins for.

influences:

◀◀ Oscar Peterson, Gene Harris, Nat "King" Cole

Andrew Gilbert

Carl Allen

Born April, 1961, in Milwaukee, WI.

One of the leading drummers of his generation, Carl Allen has quickly become a favorite among the greats of hard bop and beyond. He landed his first major gig at the age of 16 with Sonny Stitt and in his early twenties began a long association with Freddie Hubbard, recording frequently with the trumpeter throughout the 1980s. Over the past decade and a half Allen has worked and/or recorded with veterans George Coleman, Johnny Griffin, Don Pullen, Randy Weston, Jackie McLean, Art Farmer, Benny Golson, Phil Woods, and Dewey Redman and recorded with contemporaries and young lions such as Vincent Herring, Don Braden, Cyrus Chestnut, Benny Green, Donald Harrison, Javon Jackson, and Anthony Wonsey. Like one of his main influences, Art Blakey, Allen has made a concerted effort to find and nurture young players.

what to buy: A hard-swinging if not particularly inventive album, *The Pursuer* 𝄞𝄞𝄞 (Atlantic, 1994, prod. Carl Allen) features a host of up-and-coming young players (Vincent Herring, Teodross Avery, Marcus Printup, Ed Simon, and Ben Wolfe) and two special guests (George Coleman and Steve Turre). Allen's powerful drum work pushes the young soloists, though the best track, "Hidden Agenda," features just Coleman with the rhythm section. Allen wrote all of the arrangements and tunes except for Wayne Shorter's "Each One, Teach One" and "Amazing Grace." Another album in the hard bop mode, *Testimonial* 𝄞𝄞𝄞 (Atlantic Jazz, 1995, prod. Carl Allen) features some of the leading young musicians in mainstream jazz playing hard bop with a heavy dose of gospel. Allen's frequent collaborator Vincent Herring (alto sax) and Nicholas Payton (trumpet) make a potent front line, while pianists Cyrus Chestnut and Anthony Wonsey and bassists Reuben Rogers and Christian McBride split rhythm section duties. Allen supplied most of the tunes,

but not surprisingly, Ellington's "Come Sunday" and Cedar Walton's "Holy Land" are the most memorable tracks.

what to buy next: Allen is the ostensible leader on a thematic addition to Evidence's Manhattan Projects series, *The Dark Side of Dewey* 𝄞𝄞𝄞 (Evidence, 1992, prod. Tetsuo Hara, Carl Allen). Originally released on the Japanese Alfa label, this quintet session was conceived as a tribute to Miles Dewey Davis. Featuring Herring, Payton, Mulgrew Miller (piano), and Dwayne Burno (bass), *The Dark Side* kicks off with the tasty, modal-feeling Allen original "Opening Statement" and includes a number of tunes written by or associated with Davis ("All Blues," "My Funny Valentine," and "Just Squeeze Me"). Payton sounds nothing like Davis, and blends well with Herring, which helps makes this a rewarding session. Allen makes his presence felt throughout with his lively trap work, but he doesn't dominate the session.

influences:

◀◀ Art Blakey, Billy Higgins, Max Roach, Philly Joe Jones

Andrew Gilbert

Geri Allen

Born June 12, 1957, in Pontiac, MI.

While many folks have yet to discover Geri Allen, she is a talented artist who ranks high among the most creative pianists of her generation, and her excellent musicianship was internationally recognized in 1996 when she was the first woman to win the coveted JAZZPAR Prize in Copenhagen. A post-bop stylist raised in the fertile Detroit music scene, Allen began piano lessons at age 10, continuing studies as she attended Cass Technical High School where she was mentored by Motor City trumpeter Marcus Belgrave, who set her on a career path of frequent study and collaboration. She earned her undergraduate degree in jazz studies in 1979 from Howard University in Washington, D.C., then headed for New York were she studied with pianist Kenny Barron on an NEA grant. Urged by jazz educator Nathan Davis, Allen enrolled in studies at the University of Pittsburgh where she earned an M.A. in Ethnomusicology. She returned to New York in 1982 and launched her recording career. Allen's kaleidoscopic musical experiences include her early Western European (classical) training, albums as side player in with saxophonist Oliver Lake's reggae-funk Jump Up

Geri Allen (© Jack Vartoogian)

band, stints with the funk-metal band Living Colour and with M-Base (a Brooklyn-based funk, hip-hop, and jazz cooperative). Allen has accrued an extensive discography as leader and has worked and recorded with many cutting-edge jazz players such as Coleman, Lake, Lester Bowie, Joseph Jarman, James Newton, Paul Motian, Dewey Redman, Andrew Cyrille, and Betty Carter.

As leader, Allen has not veered significantly from the path she set on her first recording. Though confined occasionally by conventional mainstream stylings, her albums to date could generally be characterized as quests for new territories in jazz. Allen is a skilled improviser who invents with fresh vitality, drawing from myriad musical sources and incorporating a wide range of ideas that unpredictably weave in and out of her compositions. Her works, from bop to free-jazz, derive from well-grounded melodies, rich colors, harmonies, and textures, and make use of the full percussive capabilities of the piano. She is dedicated to rhythmically fascinating improvisations, rife with unexpected twists and turns, and has used many of the most creative drummers and percussionists on her recordings. In both live performances and on her recordings, Allen paints with the broadest pallette, carefully blending and slowly developing traditional approaches to jazz with infusions of avant garde, and Afro-folk and pop themes.

what to buy: Though her music on *Eyes . . . In the Back of Your Head* ♫♫♫♫ (Blue Note, 1997, prod. Teo Macero, Geri Allen, Herb Jordan) seldom swings, this is one of Geri Allen's most stirring sessions, tastefully melodic and beautiful. Offering an array of 10 tunes penned mostly by Allen, this is her fourth Blue Note album and features percussionist Cyro Baptista in a central role, with alto saxophonist Ornette Coleman punching up some of the 10 tunes with his freestyled solos, and her husband, trumpeter Wallace Roney, adding artfully to the session. Allen takes opportunities for pensive solo space (especially lovely on "New Eyes Opening," obviously inspired by the arrival of their new baby boy) and interacts with Roney and Baptista in fresh ways. The best moments occur when the improvisations teeter on the inside edge. *Some Aspects of Water* ♫♫♫♫ (Storyville, 1997, prod. Ib Skovgaard) is from the live-recorded performance that documents her commissioned JAZZPAR work with members of the Danish Radio Jazz Orchestra. Performing six tunes (including three originals) with her core trio of Palle Danielsson (bass) and drummer Lenny White, Allen launches the album with a nearly 11-minute version of improvisations based on the catchy melody of her trademark tune, "Feed the Fire" (which she has recorded on at least two previous albums

as leader and which was the title tune of a Betty Carter album on which Allen played). By this point in her career, Allen's playing in the post-bop and free jazz realms had matured considerably. A strong, two-handed player, her keyboard technique is intricate and densely chordal, and she is able to stretch out on a melody line to create luxuriously fresh inventions that still yield her side players plenty of room. A veteran of the Ellington, Basie, Mingus, and other major orchestras, Johnny Coles, joins the trio with a warm flugelhorn solo on the ballad "Old Folks," and generates equally fine muted work with the JAZZPAR nonet on "Smooth Attitudes." But the piece de resistance is Allen's 19-minute commissioned title tune, a venturesome, tempo- and mood-switching arrangement performed with a nonet of Danish musicians, especially highlighting the talents of reeds player Uffe Markussen. This album admirably points up Allen's broad-based musical talents. *Maroons* ♫♫♫♫ (Blue Note, 1992, prod. Geri Allen, Kazunori Sugiyama), Allen's second Blue Note album and one of her most popular recordings, maintains a bracing modern edge, unyielding individual and collective creativity, and pleasing equilibrium throughout. All but two of the 15 selections are originals featuring African roots music, blues, and straight-ahead swing that bond with Allen's musical and politically based interests. Allen's husband, trumpeter Wallace Roney, darts in and out of various settings with sidemen Anthony Cox or Dwayne Dolphin on bass, and Pheeroan AkLaff or Tani Tabbal, drums. Trumpeter Marcus Belgrave guests triumphantly. It's an unhurried mainstream jazz session, yet crafted with Allen's changing time signatures and odd meters. *Twenty One* ♫♫♫♫ (Blue Note, 1994, prod. Teo Macero, Herb Jordan, Geri Allen) ranks indeed as one of Allen's most ebullient and interactive trio sessions. With masterful accomplices bassist Ron Carter and drummer Tony Williams, Allen stretches out to perform a mixture of 12 standards and originals which showcase her consistently fresh ideas, facile technique, and spellbinding themes.

what to buy next: Primarily a straight-ahead, sextet outing, *The Nurturer* ♫♫♫ (Blue Note, 1991, prod. Geri Allen) features compositions from the then "young lions," bassist Robert Hurst, drummer Jeff "Tain" Watts, and saxophonist Kenny Garrett, with brief contributions from Allen's mentor, trumpeter Marcus Belgrave. Percussionist Eli Fountain adds special flair to the session. Allen has recorded several highly praised albums with Ornette Coleman of which her 1997 session is the best.

what to avoid: *Open on All Sides in the Middle* ♫♫♫ (Minor Music, 1987, prod. Geri Allen, Steve Coleman) offers commercial jazz-rock fusion fare that includes a vocalist and a tap dancer on some tracks. With Allen playing keyboards in a lesser role, there's not much to attract the devoted listener to the nine jazzy pop tunes. Though this disc may hold appeal for contemporary jazz fans, Allen's performance here is certainly not up to the level of her later work.

best of the rest:

Segments ♪♪♪♪ (DIW, 1989)

Twylight ♪♪♪♪ (Verve, 1989)

In the Year of the Dragon ♪♪♪♪ (Verve, 1990)

worth searching for: Allen collaborates best with mature players known for their unrivaled impressionistic creations. Her synergistic collaborations with bassist Charlie Haden and drummer Paul Motian rank superior among such sessions and *Etudes* ♪♪♪♪ (Soul Note, 1988, prod. Giovanni Bonandrini) finds Allen artfully free-improvising on an array of boppers to ballads and beyond, written by Haden, Motian, and Ornette Coleman. Among Allen's first-rate collaborations with avant-garde jazz saxophonist Ornette Coleman (one of the prime innovators of the past three decades), *Sound Museum: Hidden Man* ♪♪♪♪ (Harmolodic/Verve, 1996, prod. Denardo Coleman) and *Sound Museum: Three Women* ♪♪♪♪ (Harmolodic/Verve, 1996, prod. Denardo Coleman) present ultimate challenges for Allen to hold her own (mostly spontaneously comping) with Coleman (who plays sax, trumpet, and violin on both albums), bassist Charnett Moffett, and drummer Denardo Coleman. The 14 restless tunes of each album are intruded only occasionally by pensive, melodic themes, but keep an open mind when you listen to their crashing, cascading cacophony and try to capture how well each musician plays off the other. Allen has recorded mostly straight-ahead sessions with her husband, trumpeter Wallace Roney. She is spotlighted on *Crunchin'* ♪♪♪♪ (Muse, 1993, prod. Don Sickler), a warm, accessible session of eight standards led by Roney with bassist Ron Carter, drummer Kenny Washington, and saxophonist Antonio Hart. Augmented with a studio orchestra, Roney's *Misterios* ♪♪♪♪ (Warner, 1994, prod. Ted Macero, Matt Pierson) is a contemplative (some would say, sleepy) session, featuring 10 romantic ballads by composers ranging from Pat Metheny and John Lennon, to Egberto Gismonti, to Dolly Parton (!), with guest soloists, tenor saxophonists Antoine Roney and Ravi Coltrane, and keyboardist Gil Goldstein. Clarence Seay (bass) and Eric Allen (drums) complete the rhythm section. One of the more upbeat numbers, Gismonti's "Café," is an intriguing odd-metered piece that almost swings, but mostly, dark-harmonied, mysterious themes prevail. Maybe you can still find LP versions of *The Printmakers* ♪♪♪♪ (Minor Music, 1984, prod. Stephan Meyner),

GERI ALLEN (WITH CHARLIE HADEN AND PAUL MOTIAN)

song "Oblivion"

album *In the Year of the Dragon* (Verve, 1989/1990)

instrument Piano

Allen's exciting debut as leader of a trio with drummer Andrew Cyrille and bassist Anthony Cox on which Allen demonstrates impeccable, chord-crunching technique, an explorative nature that was to become her trademark, and an ability to create alluring melodies and harmonies. As she has continued to demonstrate on subsequent recordings, Allen masters her spontaneous creations, confidently playing both inside and outside of the chord changes, interacting tightly with her cohorts, and allowing them plenty of space for solos.

influences:

◀◀ Anthony Davis, Don Pullen, Keith Jarrett, Randy Weston

Nancy Ann Lee

Harry Allen

Born October 12, 1966, in Maryland.

Almost ten years after his recording debut at age 22, tenor saxophonist Harry Allen still bears a youthful countenance that makes his mature, warm, full-bodied, assertive sound all the more remarkable. Allen is very much a torch-bearer for the diminishing Swing-era tenor sax style. Raised in Rhode Island, the state that also produced tenor sax notables and major Allen influences Scott Hamilton and Paul Gonsalves, Allen was introduced to jazz through his drummer father's record collection. He started on clarinet at age ten and switched to tenor sax at age 12, making unbelievable progress which resulted in a debut at the Newport Jazz Festival at age 14. By age 17, Allen had subbed for Zoot Sims and was gigging around New York. While attending Rutgers University where he graduated with a Bachelor of Music degree in 1988, Allen concentrated on tenor sax players such as Ben Webster, Zoot Sims, Stan Getz, Lester Young, and Coleman Hawkins.

Introduced to drummer Oliver Jackson by a mutual friend, bassist Major Holley, Allen toured extensively through Europe with Jackson, gaining experience and finding a large appreciative audience for his dynamic, ever-swinging tenor sax. Allen has worked extensively with pianist Keith Ingham, guitarist John Pizzarelli, and other mainstream musicians, including Scott Hamilton, Warren Vaché, Dave McKenna, Ruby Braff, Dan Barrett, Howard Alden, Randy Sandke, and John Bunch. Allen can be heard at various U.S. jazz festivals, parties, and concerts, but he now tours Europe regularly, spending a good portion of the year overseas.

what to buy: *Jazz Im Amerika Haus, Vol. 1* ♫♫♫♪ (Nagel-Heyer, 1994, prod. Sabine Nagel-Heyer, Hans Nagel-Heyer) recorded for the German label at a May 1994 concert in Hamburg, Germany, finds the now hard-driving, now languid, tenor man in the company of a first-class rhythm section—pianist John Bunch, bassist Dennis Irwin, and drummer Duffy Jackson. The Harry Allen Quartet coaxes fresh life into an even mix of standard fare such as "Limehouse Blues," "My Heart Stood Still," "Honeysuckle Rose," "But Beautiful," and shifts into high gear for "'Deed I Do." *A Night at Birdland, Volume 2* ♫♫♫♫ (Nagel-Heyer, 1995, prod. Sabine Nagel-Heyer, Hans Nagel-Heyer) features the Harry Allen Quintet recorded at a Hamburg jazz club in November 1993. Allen's tenor sax is confident yet lyrical, and works well with the slightly boppish trumpet of Randy Sandke. With two Brits, Brian Dee on piano and Len Skeat on bass, the quintet is nicely propelled by drummer Oliver Jackson, in what was probably his final recorded performance. From the opening, "Isn't This a Lovely Day," to the ultra-relaxed "My Foolish Heart," through a quirky "Blues My Naughty Sweetie Gives to Me," to the closing "Lover Come Back to Me," this is a well-balanced set of tunes and performances. *A Night at Birdland, Vol-*

ume 1 ♫♫♫♫ (Nagel-Heyer, 1994, prod. Sabine Nagel-Heyer, Hans Nagel-Heyer), from the same dates and setting as Volume 2, above, features Allen and Sandie on a well-recorded romp through extended versions of "On a Slow Boat to China," "How Deep Is the Ocean?," "The Man I Love," and other standards.

what to buy next: *The Harry Allen–Keith Ingham Quintet: Are You Having Any Fun?* ♫♫♫♫ (Audiophile, 1991, prod. Harry Allen, Keith Ingham) is a celebration of composer Sammy Fain and a good excuse to showcase the ballad stylings of Harry Allen and his frequent collaborator, pianist Keith Ingham, on some rarely heard tunes done up in fine lyrical fashion. The rhythm section is fleshed out nicely by guitarist John Pizzarelli, bassist Dennis Irwin, and Allen's mentor, drummer Oliver Jackson. Not a misplaced note anywhere. *Blue Skies* ♫♫♫♫ (John Marks Records, 1994), a session recorded in May, 1994, offers more superior and intimate quartet work from Allen, Bunch, Irwin and Jackson. The Jerome Kern gem, "Nobody Else But Me," gets a gorgeous reading.

best of the rest:
Someone to Light up My Life ♫♫♫♪ (Mastermix, 1991)
I Know That You Know ♫♫♫♫ (Mastermix, 1992)
I'll Never Be the Same ♫♫♫♫ (Mastermix, 1993)
How Long Has This Been Going On? ♫♫♫ (Progressive, 1993)
My Little Brown Book: A Celebration of Billy Strayhorn's Music, Volume 1 ♫♫♫♪ (Progressive, 1994)
The Intimacy of the Blues: A Celebration of Billy Strayhorn's Music, Volume 2 ♫♫♫♪ (Progressive, 1994)
Live at Renouft's ♫♫♫♫ (Mastermix, 1996)
A Little Touch of Harry ♫♫♫♫ (Mastermix, 1997)

influences:
◀◀ Paul Gonsalves, Ben Webster, Stan Getz, Lester Young, Coleman Hawkins, Scott Hamilton

John T. Bitter

Henry "Red" Allen

Born Henry James Allen Jr., January 7, 1908, in Algiers, LA. Died on April 17, 1967, in New York, NY.

Henry "Red" Allen was one of the last great New Orleans trumpeters to emerge during the post Louis Armstrong era. He learned trumpet in the New Orleans brass band led by his father, Henry Allen Sr. The young Allen worked with various Crescent City bands, including the George Lewis band, and joined King Oliver's band in St. Louis in 1927, traveling with Oliver to New York City, where Allen recorded with Clarence Williams. Allen played in the Mississippi riverboat bands of Fate Marable from 1928–1929 and was discovered by Victor reps who were searching for a trumpeter to rival the popularity of Louis Armstrong on OKeh, a competing label. Allen recorded four sides with members of Luis Russell's band in July 1929, and on the merits of his playing, began a lengthy stint as lead trumpeter with the Russell band from 1929–32. He later performed in the big bands of Fletcher Henderson (1933–34), and the Mills Blue Rhythm Band (1934–37) before embarking on a solo career as a leading trumpet soloist, setting the standards for the early swing era. Allen returned to Russell's band in 1937, which by then was accompanying Louis Armstrong. He left this band in 1940 to become a player in the growing traditional-jazz movement, and recorded New Orleans–style music with Jelly Roll Morton, Sidney Bechet, and with his own groups. Allen gained visibility during the 1940s and 1950s as a prominent figure in mainstream jazz, adapting his style to perform with Coleman Hawkins, Buster Bailey, Pee Wee Russell, J. C. Higginbotham, and others. During the 1950s–1960s, he held lengthy club engagements and toured Europe several times. Allen remained active until his death.

Allen's early playing, similar to Louis Armstrong's, developed into a fluid, light, articulate style, that took full advantage of the full range of timbral effects of his instrument. In earlier years he used trills, smears, growls, glissandos, and splattered notes with expertise that inspired the free-jazz players. In later years he moved away from swing-influenced playing to focus on New Orleans combo-style jazz and the blues. His career is sequentially documented on import recordings from Jazz Chronological Classics (covering the years from 1929–1941), and on a series of volumes from Collectors Classics (Storyville).

what's available: Representing Allen's only domestic recording in print, *World on a String* 🎵🎵🎵🎵 (RCA/Bluebird, 1957/1991, prod. Fred Reynolds) is an exuberant romp which features the trumpeter backed by a pert rhythm crew—Marty Napoleon (piano), Everett Barksdale (guitar), Lloyd Trotman (bass), and Cozy Cole (drums). Tenor saxophonist Coleman Hawkins is aptly spotlighted. Trombonist J. C. Higginbotham and clarinetist Buster Bailey add to the session. Includes classic tunes such as "St James Infirmary," "Sweet Lorraine," "Ain't She Sweet," the title tune, and seven more. Orrin Keepnews produced the digitally remastered reissue of the original session recorded during March and April, 1957.

influences:

◀◀ Louis Armstrong

▶▶ Clark Terry, Rex Stewart, Harry "Sweets" Edison, Freddie Hubbard, Woody Shaw

Nancy Ann Lee

HENRY "RED" ALLEN (WITH COLEMAN HAWKINS)

song "Sweet Lorraine"

album *A Retrospective* (RCA Bluebird, 1957/1995)

instrument Trumpet

Monster Solo

Steve Allen

Born December 21, 1921, in New York, NY.

If anyone fits the rather broad (and often overused) category of "quintessential renaissance man," it is certainly Steve Allen. His varied career in entertainment and the arts draws from many areas. As a youngster, he played piano from an early age and traveled with his parents who were vaudeville performers. In the 1940s, he was a radio deejay and successfully switched his career to television in the 1950s. Although most widely known as a TV talk show host (the original *Tonight Show*) and comedian, Allen is both a prolific songwriter and author (nearly 5,000 songs and over 40 books) and has had an almost 50-year career that includes stints as a musician, movie actor (title role in the 1955 film *The Benny Goodman Story*), and TV and film writer-producer.

Jazz has always been an important if not high-profile part of Allen's career. His TV shows featured him often at the piano, creating jazz improvisations, and singing his own music, frequently ad-libbing with his musical director, the jazz vibraphonist Terry Gibbs. In the 1950s and 1960s, Allen recorded a number of successful (but now unavailable) albums for labels such as Coral, which showcased his writing abilities and piano performances. He also co-wrote and performed on the projects of others (as with the classic, but now extremely hard to find recordings with Al "Jazzbo" Collins). Allen continues to compose and perform, and a few of his tunes have actually established themselves to some degree as jazz and popular standards ("Gravy Waltz," "This Could Be the Start of Something Big," "Impossible").

what to buy: Definitely not bop, but bop-inflected, *Steve Allen Plays Jazz Tonight* ♫♫♫♫ (Concord Jazz, 1993, prod. Carl E. Jefferson) features Allen in a sextet setting, performing originals and standards in a Swing/Trad-Jazz/New Orleans mode. There are some nice tunes and performances by Allen. Other Concord stalwarts on this album include guitarist Howard Alden, swinging drummer Frank Capp (who also leads his Juggernaut band which has recorded for Concord), growling tenorist and clarinetist Ken Peplowski, and others displaying Dixieland-flavored ensemble soloing and tailgating. Highlights include enjoyable and convincing ballad performances on classics such as "Body and Soul" and "I Can't Get Started," Allen's original "Don't Cry, Little Girl," and an absolute swinger in "Steve's Blues."

the rest:
Steve Allen Plays Cool, Quiet Bossa Nova ♫♫♫ (Laserlight, 1993)
Steve Allen Plays Hi-Fi Music for Influentials ♫♫♫ (Varese Vintage, 1996)

Gregg Juke and Nancy Ann Lee

Ben Allison

Born November 17, 1966, in New Haven CT.

As of this date in mid-1997, composer and bassist Ben Allison is relatively new to the scene, but his CD debut as a leader and work spearheading the New York-based, nonprofit Jazz Composers' Collective bode well for the future. For Allison, the writing is as important as the freedom and chops his players bring to the individual pieces, and in this way his music echoes that of innovators such as (fellow bassists) Oscar Pettiford and Charles Mingus, pianist Andrew Hill, trombonist Grachan Moncur III and drummer Joe Chambers. Allison can also be heard to good advantage on albums by fellow-JCCers Frank Kimbrough and Ted Nash (see separate listings), as well as with Lee Konitz, Peggy Stern, and Eddie Gale. Mapleshade Records is planning

to put out a second Ben Allison Quintet record, titled *Random Sex and Violins*, early in 1998.

what's available: *Seven Arrows* ♫♫♫♫ (Koch Jazz, 1996, prod. Ben Allison) is comprised of material first presented during a 1995 concert, and it paints a striking picture, from the opening "Dragzilla," with its rhythmic urgency, Colemansesque flavor (trumpeter Ron Horton smears notes like a Don Cherry in full flight) and clever, ever-shifting sectional outline to "Delirioso," with its shades-of-Dave-Holland opening and *Conference of the Birds* theme, and the serpentine "King of a One Man Planet" that closes the proceedings in high style. "Little Boy" is especially noteworthy, a piece that draws thematic parallels to Mingus's "Oh Lord, Don't Let Them Drop That Atomic Bomb on Me," although Allison's vision is horrific and literal, an aural evocation of the second A-bomb dropped on Japan in August, 1945.

influences:
◀◀ Either/Orchestra, Phillip Johnston's Big Trouble

David Prince

Mose Allison

Born November 11, 1927, in Tippo, MS.

A glance at Mose Allison's past would reveal sideman stints with Stan Getz, Gerry Mulligan, and Al Cohn, but Allison has led his own combos and sung his own unique tunes for so long that some folks might have a hard time envisioning him doing anything else.

As a piano player, Allison has some of the same disdain for conventional structure that Thelonious Monk had, but the way he constructs his music, while quite different from the norm, is eminently logical. He has created music that's deeply rooted in the blues while devising some of the most interesting and, at times, sardonic lyrics of any jazz musician on the planet. As a lyricist, Allison creates titles and wordplay for his songs that reveal a sonic satirist with the power to ridicule the pretentious and make them like it. The secret to Allison's art seems to be his reliance on the sketch instead of the grand tapestry, the essay instead of the tome. That may be why you won't find many epic-length performances in his repertoire (although you could probably make a case for "Back Country Suite," the title tune from his debut album).

Mose Allison (Archive Photos)

what to buy: The two-CD set *Allison Wonderland: The Mose Allison Anthology* 𝄞𝄞𝄞𝄞 (Atlantic, 1994, prod. various) is the place to start if you have no Mose Allison in your collection. It's a comprehensive distillation of Allison's recorded history, covering all the crucial tunes in his oeuvre that you need to know before moving on to his more contemporary work. *Greatest Hits* 𝄞𝄞𝄞𝄞 (OJC, 1988, prod. Bob Weinstock, Esmond Edwards) focuses on Allison's earliest vocals and classic performances of songs he was to repeat for other labels, making this collection even more to the point than the Atlantic anthology. It's the difference between single malt whiskey and a blended Scotch. Included are such hits as "Parchman Farm" (no relation to the Bukka White tune), "Young Man's Blues," and Allison's wondrous version of Willie Dixon's "Seventh Son."

what to buy next: *Gimcracks and Gewgaws* 𝄞𝄞𝄞𝄞 (Blue Note, 1998, prod. Ben Sidran) is a fine quintet date featuring Paul Motian, arguably the most sensitive drummer for Allison's needs. His uptempo brush work behind the pianist on the title tune works with Ratzo Harris's bass to provide a soft-focus hard drive (not a contradiction) to a typically constructed Allison composition. Russell Malone displays some strong blues-inflected guitar playing on "St. Louis Blues" and "The More You Get," while tenorman Mark Shim is strong and idiomatic throughout. Allison sticks to his typical lyric and melody tricks for much of the album, but such wonderful reflective songs as "Texana" and "Fires of Spring" act as well-weighted counterbalances. *High Jinks! The Mose Allison Trilogy* 𝄞𝄞𝄞𝄞 (Columbia, 1994, prod. various) binds Allison's post-Prestige releases (before he split to Atlantic records) into an entertaining three-CD set. The material covered comes from a period in his recording career that is often overlooked in comparison to his work before and after these albums. The previously unreleased tracks make this a worthy buy. Ben Sidran has taken huge chunks from the Allison legacy to create his own vision, and it's about time he paid the man back. *Ever Since the World Ended* 𝄞𝄞𝄞𝄞 (Blue Note, 1987, prod. Ben Sidran) is as good a start as any. Allison is aided by a comfortable rhythm section and a select group of upper echelon "sidemen." Guitarist Kenny Burrell contributes his fluid, bop-oriented lines to three tunes including the witty "Top Forty," wherein Allison describes, in the most cutting way possible, what it might take for him to get a hit song on the radio. The saxophone ensemble heard on some cuts includes Arthur Blythe, Bennie Wallace, and Bob Malach.

the rest:
Back Country Suite 𝄞𝄞𝄞𝄞 (OJC, 1957)
Local Color 𝄞𝄞𝄞 (OJC, 1957)
Autumn Song 𝄞𝄞𝄞𝄞 (OJC, 1959)
I Don't Worry about a Thing 𝄞𝄞𝄞𝄞𝄞 (Atlantic, 1962)
Lessons in Living 𝄞𝄞𝄞 (Discovery, 1982)
Middle Class White Boy 𝄞𝄞𝄞 (Discovery, 1982)
My Backyard 𝄞𝄞𝄞 (Blue Note, 1990)
Earth Wants You Too 𝄞𝄞𝄞 (Blue Note, 1994)
Pure Mose 𝄞𝄞𝄞 (32 Records, 1994)

influences:
◀◀ Thelonious Monk, Percy Mayfield, Sonny Boy Williamson II
▶▶ Ben Sidran

Garaud MacTaggart

Alloy Orchestra

Ken Winokur, percussion; Caleb Sampson, keyboards; Terry Donahue, percussion, accordion.

The Alloy Orchestra is a three-man ensemble writing and performing live accompaniment to classic silent films using an unusual combination of homemade percussion, junk metal objects, modified electronics, drums, brass, piano and synthesizer, and state of the art electronics to give the Orchestra the ability to create any sound imaginable. The Orchestra has scored music for nine silent films and has appeared on CDs with Morphine, Hal Willner, and Roger Miller. Sampson has written scores for *Sesame Street, NOVA,* MTV, and Showtime, and commercials for Chase Manhattan Bank and McDonalds.

what's available: On *New Music for Silent Films* 𝄞𝄞𝄞𝄞 (Accurate Records, 1994, prod. Alloy Orchestra) the melodies, crashes, and electronic swoops are augmented by saxophonist Neil Leonard for scores to *Metropolis, Aelita, Queen of Mars, Sylvester, The Wind,* and *First Night.* The music definitely speaks for itself and watching along with the films demonstrates how powerful silent films are. *Lonesome* 𝄞𝄞𝄞 (Bib Records, 1994, prod. Bill Pence) is the complete score to the 1928 film *Lonesome,* Hungarian director Paul Fejos's first Hollywood production. The Telluride and Pordenone Film Festivals commissioned the soundtrack.

influences:
◀◀ Ennio Morricone, Karlheinz Stockhausen

David C. Gross

Karrin Allyson

Born c. 1963, in Great Bend, KS.

Karrin Allyson (pronounced KAR-in) is one of the strongest jazz singers to emerge in the 1990s, a musician who can scat with authority, handle slow tempos with ease, and swing with abandon. She is as comfortable transforming contemporary pop tunes by the likes of Janis Ian and Bonnie Raitt as singing American Songbook standards and jazz tunes. Raised in Omaha, Nebraska, Allyson studied classical piano and moved to the San Francisco Bay Area in high school. She attended the University of Nebraska, where she graduated with a classical piano major in 1987. She was first exposed to jazz in college, and began working regularly at nightspots around Minneapolis, where she moved in 1987. She settled in Kansas City, Missouri, where she still lives, after a successful run at her uncle's club Phoenix in the early 1990s. Her four albums for Concord Jazz and appearances at numerous jazz festivals have gained her a well-deserved national reputation.

what to buy: There's no sophomore jinx on Allyson's second release *Sweet Home Cookin'* 𝄢𝄢𝄢𝄢 (Concord Jazz, 1994, prod. Carl E. Jefferson), an excellent album featuring a top-flight rhythm section and well-paced program. Alan Broadbent handles piano and arranging duties, surrounding Allyson's sprightly, devil-may-care vocals with lean but lush support from (the late) tenor saxophonist Bob Cooper and trumpeter Randy Sandke. With Putter Smith on bass, Danny Embry on guitar, and Sherman Ferguson on drums, Allyson has all the support she needs to sail through Jobim's "One Note Samba" and "Dindi" and tear into "No Moon at All" and Gigi Gryce's "Social Call." Allyson's third album, *Azure-Te* 𝄢𝄢𝄢𝄢 (Concord Jazz, 1995, prod. Carl E. Jefferson) isn't as consistently riveting as her previous one, but she does expand her emotional range with an achingly sensual reading of "Blame It on My Youth" and a thrilling vocal/alto sax duet with Kim Park on Charlie Parker's "Yardbird Suite." Equally at home with Swing Era tunes as bebop, Allyson interacts wonderfully with Claude "Fiddler" Williams on the old Don Redman/Andy Razaf standard "Gee Baby (Ain't I Good to You)" and races pianist Paul Smith to the finish on "Stompin' at the Savoy."

what to buy next: As the title of her fourth album suggests, on *Collage* 𝄢𝄢𝄢𝄢 (Concord Jazz, 1996, prod. Nick Phillips) Allyson offers up a varied program, handling herself well on most of the material. The opening medley of "It Could Happen to You" with Dexter Gordon's "Fried Bananas" gets things off to an exciting start, and she follows it up with a soulful version of "Autumn Leaves" in both French and English. Quite the polyglot, Allyson handles the Portuguese lyric (not to mention the Brazilian rhythm) of Djavan's "Faltando Um Pedaco" with style. However, her blues inflection on Bonnie Raitt's "Give It Up or Let Me Go"

isn't entirely convincing. Allyson's debut *I Didn't Know about You* 𝄢𝄢𝄢𝄢 (Concord Jazz, 1993, prod. Karrin Allyson, Danny Embry) is a hit-or-miss affair, but she shows great potential on a program that includes everything from Randy Newman's "Guilty" and Janis Ian's "Jesse" to Gerry Mulligan's "Line for Lyons" and a samba version of "It Might as Well Be Spring." Allyson accompanies herself on piano on a number of tracks, and while her classical background serves her well on a Chopin introduction to Jobim's "Insensatez," she swings much harder with Paul Smith on the ivories.

worth searching for: Allyson fans might want to check out *Fujitsu–Concord 27th Jazz Festival* 𝄢𝄢𝄢𝄢 (Concord Jazz, 1996, prod. John Burk) a two-disc set recorded live at the Concord Pavilion. Featured on the first disc where she sings five tunes with Allen Farnham (piano), Bob Bowman (bass), Danny Embrey (guitar), and Colin Baily (drums), Allyson is in excellent form, especially on Jerome Kern's "In Love in Vain" and Jobim's "No More Blues." Scott Hamilton, Howard Alden, Louie Bellson, Ray Brown, Benny Green, Chris Potter, and Rickey Woodard are featured on the bulk of the album.

influences:

◄◄ Betty Carter, Nancy Wilson, Sarah Vaughan, Ella Fitzgerald

Andrew Gilbert

Laurindo Almeida

Born September 2, 1917, in Sao Paulo, Brazil. Died July 26, 1995, in Los Angeles, CA.

Though Laurindo Almeida was never a great jazz guitarist, he played a significant role in introducing Brazilian music to the American jazz world. A virtuoso concert guitarist who recorded a dozen classical albums for Capitol in the 1950s and 1960s, Almeida was nominated for 15 Grammys and won six (including one he shared with Igor Stravinsky for the best contemporary composition in 1961). Almeida was a popular musician in Brazil who had extensive radio and studio experience when he came to the United States in the late 1940s to work in the Hollywood studios. In 1947, Stan Kenton heard him and invited him to join his orchestra, where Almeida became a featured soloist on "Peanut Vendor" (Kenton's most popular tune) and Pete Rugulo's "Lament," a tune written specially for Almeida. By 1950, he was working steadily as a studio musician, and in 1953 recorded a landmark session with Bud Shank, which essentially anticipated Stan Getz's discovery of bossa nova by a decade. In the early 1960s, Almeida recorded some best-selling bossa nova sessions for Capitol and toured and recorded with the MJQ. In the 1970s, he made some rewarding albums on Concord with Charlie Byrd and co-founded the L.A.4, a chamber jazz group with Bud Shank, Ray Brown, and Shelly Manne (later replaced by Jeff Hamilton).

what to buy: Perhaps the first fusion of jazz and Brazilian music, *Brazilliance, Vol. 1* 🎵🎵🎵🎵 (World Pacific, 1953, prod. Richard Bock) is a groundbreaking session that perfectly mates the pastel West Coast sound with the sensual rhythms and melodies of Brazil. A quartet session with Bud Shank (alto sax), Harry Babasin (bass), and Roy Harte (drums), the album features mostly jazz interpretations of traditional Brazilian tunes, though there are also beautiful versions of "Stairway to the Stars" and "Speak Low." Almeida brings together his three great musical loves on the introspective session *Chamber Jazz* 🎵🎵🎵🎵 (Concord Jazz, 1979, prod. Carl E. Jefferson), blending jazz with Brazilian and classical music. Almeida's arrangements don't leave much room for improvising, but he gets strong, sensitive support from bassist Bob Magnusson and drummer Jeff Hamilton. Whether transporting Debussy to Bahia in "Claire de Lune Samba" or interpreting Bach or the great Brazilian composer Ernesto Nazareth, Almeida renders each tune with captivating virtuosity. A typically diverse program by a consistently inventive group, *Executive Suite* 🎵🎵🎵 (Concord Jazz, 1983, prod. Carl E. Jefferson) features the L.A.4's second incarnation with drummer Jeff Hamilton, Almeida, Bud Shank on alto sax and flute, and Ray Brown on bass. All of the elements of the band's attractive chamber jazz approach are in full bloom here, as the group moves gracefully between blues, Bach, Brazil, and standards. Almeida's beautifully exotic composition "Amazonia" is one of the album's highlights. A pure delight for fans of Brazilian guitar, *Music of the Brazilian Masters* 🎵🎵🎵🎵 (Concord Picante, 1989, prod. Carl E. Jefferson) features Almeida with fellow countryman Carlos Barbosa-Lima and Charlie Byrd on guitars with Larry Grenadier (bass) and Michael Shapiro (drums). Strong material covering a wide spectrum of Brazilian music, from the early 20th century giant Ernesto Nazareth to Heitor Villa-Lobos and Jobim, makes this a consistently engaging recording. As the senior fretman on board, Almeida sets the tone with his perfectly placed notes. The three guitarists work well together throughout, for the most part keeping the music clean and uncluttered.

what to buy next: *Brazilliance, Vol. 2* 🎵🎵🎵 (World Pacific, 1958, prod. Richard Bock) isn't as interesting a session as the first volume, but is still a fascinating fusion of jazz and Brazilian music. Accompanied by Shank on alto sax and flute, Gary Peacock on bass, and Chuck Flores on drums, Almeida plays with

his usual grace and style. What he lacks in swing he makes up for with feeling. *Artistry in Rhythm* 🎵🎵🎵🎵 (Concord Jazz, 1984, prod. Carl E. Jefferson) is a winning session by the Almeida trio with Bob Magnusson (bass) and Milt Holland (drums). The highlights are many: start with Almeida's tour de force version of Stan Kenton's "Artistry in Rhythm," then check out his gorgeous ballad work on Richard Rodgers's rarely played "Slaughter on Tenth Avenue," and finish with the delicately textured bossa nova "Astronauto." This is good music that goes down easy.

best of the rest:

Concierto De Aranjuez 🎵🎵🎵🎵 (Inner City, 1978)
(With the L.A.4) *Zaca* 🎵🎵🎵 (Concord Jazz, 1980)
(With the L.A.4) *Montage* 🎵🎵🎵 (Concord Jazz, 1981)
Brazilian Soul 🎵🎵🎵 (Concord Jazz, 1981)
Tango: Laurindo Almeida and Charlie Byrd 🎵🎵🎵🎵 (Concord Jazz, 1985)
Outra Vez 🎵🎵🎵 (Concord Jazz, 1992)

influences:

◀◀ Heitor Villa-Lobos, Stan Kenton

▶▶ Charlie Byrd, Stan Getz

Andrew Gilbert

Herb Alpert

Born March 31, 1937, in Los Angeles, CA.

Herb Alpert began playing trumpet at the age of eight, although he started in the music business as a songwriter, co-writing "Wonderful World" with Lou Adler, which was made into a hit by Sam Cooke. Inspired by an actual bullfight in 1962, he released "The Lonely Bull" on his own A&M imprint (he'd founded the label that year with Jerry Moss). As the proprietor of A&M, he released not only a string of albums by his own highly successful Tijuana Brass, but masterminded some of the more saccharin pop sensations of the day, from the We Five to, ultimately, the Carpenters. During the years 1962–68, only the Beatles sold more LPs than the Tijuana Brass. Unfortunately, most of their recordings were watered-down samba and light jazz. Thirty years later, a *Suddenly Susan* episode made fun of the insistently chirpy hit "Tijuana Taxi." Meanwhile, Alpert and Moss had a new label, Almo, and Alpert made a strongly Latin-flavored comeback. Not much of an improvisor, Alpert has retained his recognizable tone on trumpet.

what to buy: Give credit to *Whipped Cream (& Other Delights)* 🎵🎵🎵 (A&M, 1965, prod. Herb Alpert, Jerry Moss) for having the ultimate cocktease/come-hither album cover. It was hard to find a household in the 1960s that didn't own it—and a junk store that doesn't now.

what to buy next: *The Lonely Bull* 🎵🎵🎵 (A&M, 1962, prod. Herb Alpert, Jerry Moss) is the same as *Whipped Cream*, without the excellent album cover—this time you get to look at Herb instead of the whipped cream–covered babe. *A Taste of Honey* 🎵🎵🎵 (A&M, 1965, prod. Herb Alpert, Jerry Moss) is not utterly terrible 1960s psuedo-bossanova muzak (made hipper by the subsequent post-modern appreciation of such things).

what to avoid: Two times in his career, Alpert has strayed from his proven formula for a strike at the hit parade, and both times he has met with #1 success—first in 1968 with a rare (and strained) Alpert vocal on "This Guy's in Love with You" (the Bacharach-David song, complete with a bloated Bacharach MOR orchestral arrangement), and again, in 1979, with the pseudo-funk/disco "Rise," his biggest hit. But the real question is: if the original stuff was tepid to begin with, what does that make these compromises? Certainly they should only be owned in a "best-of" context rather than on the original albums *The Beat of the Brass* 🎵🎵 (A&M, 1968, prod. Herb Alpert, Jerry Moss) and *Rise* 🎵 (A&M, 1979, prod. Herb Alpert, Jerry Moss) where they're surrounded by filler.

best of the rest:
A&M Classics, Vol. 1 🎵🎵🎵 (A&M, 1987)
A&M Classics, Vol. 2 🎵🎵🎵 (A&M, 1987)
Passion Dance 🎵🎵🎵 (Almo, 1997)

influences:
◄◄ Astrud Gilberto, Chet Baker

►► Chuck Mangione, Baja Marimba Band, Rick Braun

Joe S. Harrington

John Altenburgh

Born April 20, 1960, in Wausau, WI.

Keyboardist John Altenburgh has documented the Wisconsin jazz scene since 1990 on his label, Altenburgh Records, which has featured not only his own music but also that of Mark Ladley, Mike Metheny, Rebecca Parris, John Greiner, the Kenny Hadley Big Band, Gary Sivils, and more.

Altenburgh played in rock bands in high school. He got into jazz and blues while studying Recording Engineering at the University of Wisconsin–Oshkosh. In 1988 he opened RiverSide Productions Recording Studio. At first he concentrated on writing and arranging advertising jingles (winning two Addy Awards for

his work), but in 1990 he put out his first album, *Old City*, and within five years the label had 25 releases. His three most recent albums as a leader have made national jazz radio charts.

what to buy: The aptly titled *Heartland '95* 🎵🎵🎵 (Altenburgh, 1995, prod. John Altenburgh) is accessible instrumental jazz that never panders, offering hummable melodies without the saccharine production that ruins major labels' lowest common denominator–oriented pop-jazz. Altenburgh's warm arrangements and tuneful playing are augmented by tenor saxophonist John Greiner's rich tone and soulful style.

what to buy next: *Legends of Keelerville* 🎵🎵🎵 (Altenburgh, 1997, prod. John Altenburgh) has some more elaborate arrangements, with the swinging "Simmer Down," a nice greasy chunk of organ-driven soul jazz adorned with exciting horn charts, and "Dining with Mrs. Blair" cushioning Bob Kase's lovely flugelhorn playing with lush synth-string lines.

the rest:
Old City 🎵🎵 (Altenburgh, 1990)
Vol. II 🎵🎵🎵 (Altenburgh, 1992)
Generations 🎵🎵🎵 (Altenburgh, 1993)

influences:
◄◄ Pat Metheny Group, Groove Holmes

►► John Greiner, Mark Ladley

Steve Holtje

Barry Altschul

Born January 6, 1943, in the Bronx, NY.

Self-taught on drums as a teenager, supplemented by later studies with Charlie Persip, Altschul came to public attention through a long 1960s stint with pianist Paul Bley. His excellent work with Bley, especially in trio with bassist Gary Peacock, gave him a reputation as a sterling free improvisor, and while in Europe in the early 1970s he co-founded the short-lived but much celebrated collective Circle (with Anthony Braxton, Chick Corea, and Dave Holland). Two related bands of similarly short duration also made noteworthy albums, as did Circle, for the fledgling ECM label: a trio with Corea and Holland (*A.R.C.*) and a quartet led by Holland with Altschul, Braxton, and Sam Rivers (*Conference of the Birds*).

But Altschul was never just a free player, working with some frequency in bebop contexts and integrating the breadth of jazz history reaching all the way back to New Orleans into both his rhythmic concepts and his writing. This has allowed him a flourishing sideman career with the likes of Kenny Drew Sr., Andrew Hill, Sonny Criss, Hampton Hawes, Tony Scott, Art Pepper, Babs Gonzales, Gato Barbieri, and even blues guitarist Buddy Guy. Meanwhile he continued to play in the bands of prime avant-gardists, including Braxton, Steve Lacy, Alan Silva, and others.

what to buy: *Irina* 𝄞𝄞𝄞𝄞 (Soul Note, 1983, prod. Giovanni Bonandrini) is Altschul's masterpiece as a leader, running the gamut from outside excursions to Fats Waller's "Jitterbug Waltz." The rest of the quartet—Enrico Rava (trumpet, flugelhorn), John Surman (baritone and soprano saxes), and Mark Helias (bass)—walk the fine line between adding their own considerable inspiration yet not overwhelming the leader's concepts.

what to buy next: *Virtuosi* 𝄞𝄞𝄞𝄞 (Improvising Artists, Inc., 1967, prod. Paul Bley) with Paul Bley and Gary Peacock is somewhat short measure time-wise, consisting of two Annette Peacock-penned tracks of 16 and 17 minutes, but to hear this trio's kaleidoscopic deployment of its considerable yet restrained resources is to witness improvisational interaction at the highest level. Bley was the leader, but his propensity for giving his sidemen co-billing combined with alphabetical order to put this in Altschul's bin. A reunion of these forces, recorded at a 1976 Japanese festival, produced *Japan Suite* 𝄞𝄞𝄞𝄞 (Improvising Artists, Inc., 1977/1992, prod. Paul Bley), but Bley's name comes first on that one, another shorty at 32 minutes.

Partially presaging Circle five weeks before *Paris-Concert* was recorded, *A.R.C.* 𝄞𝄞𝄞𝄞 (ECM, 1971, prod. Manfred Eicher) with Chick Corea and David Holland ranges from a cover of Wayne Shorter's "Nefertitti" (also played by the quartet) to free improvisation. The general mood is abstract and exploratory, less prone to ecstatic flights and more controlled than Circle (perhaps the difference between studio and live recording), but still probing and stimulating. Altschul's ear for subtle percussion timbres is clearly on display, freed from normal time-keeping duties and functioning instead as an equal musical partner.

what to avoid: The problem with *That's Nice* 𝄞𝄞 (Soul Note, 1986, prod. Giovanni Bonandrini) is summed up by its bland title, which matches the bland music. Perhaps it was important to Altschul to demonstrate his mainstream abilities with a group of non-stars (pianist Mike Melillo is the best-known player here), but the enervated results sound shallow.

the rest:
Another Time, Another Place 𝄞𝄞𝄞𝄞 (Muse, 1978)
For Stu 𝄞𝄞𝄞 (Soul Note, 1981)

worth searching for: *You Can't Name Your Own Tune* 𝄞𝄞𝄞𝄞 (Muse, 1977, prod. Michael Cuscuna, Barry Altschul) was technically the first album by Altschul as sole leader, but once again he's in an all-star setting, with Sam Rivers (saxes, flute), Muhal Richard Abrams (piano), George Lewis (trombone), and Holland. More than his Soul Note albums, this record shows how Altschul's best music combines characteristics from across jazz history while sounding thoroughly modern, and his writing and the players' solos are both at a very high level here. Abrams plays some of the best piano of his distinguished career, in fact. Hopefully as the Muse catalog is transferred to its new owner, this and Altschul's other Muse LP will find their way onto CD again.

influences:
◀◀ Charlie Persip, Billy Higgins
▶▶ Michael Sarin, Jim Black

Steve Holtje

Franco Ambrosetti

Born December 10, 1941, in Lugano, Switzerland.

While jazz can certainly be found in your soul, it can also show up in your genes. Franco Ambrosetti was born just as his father, bebop alto saxophonist/vibraphonist Flavio (born October 8, 1919, in Lugano, Switzerland), was beginning his career as a working jazzman. Having the opportunity to hang out with his father's local jazz buddies, as well as the occasional touring superstar, Franco caught the bug, and at age 17 switched from studying classical piano to teaching himself trumpet. A few years later, he was winning awards for his snappy solos. Along with his father, Franco played extensively with local pianist and impresario George Grunz in a series of progressive big bands throughout the 1960s. Their relationship proved to be quite fruitful, eventually leading to his cofounding of Gruntz's Concert Jazz Band in 1972 and a continued relationship for the next decade. Since the late 1970s, Ambrosetti has recorded for the Enja label, while simultaneously working as an executive in the family's industrial plant, as his father did before him. Ambrosetti plays with a tart sound and favors large ensembles with often complicated arrangements, sometimes approaching fusion-like jams. However, his solos are superb, full of dynamic playing and creative energy.

what to buy: Ambrosetti's second collection of radical reworkings of "classic" movie themes, *Movies, Too* 𝄞𝄞𝄞𝄞 (Enja, 1989, prod. Matthias Winckelmann), features a tight band including pianist Geri Allen and guitarist John Scofield; a bit more exciting than the first CD, despite odd song selections ("Theme from Superman," "What's New Pussycat"). *Wings* ♪♪♪♪ (Enja, 1984, prod. Horst Weber, Matthias Winckelmann) is a good example of Ambrosetti's soloing in a relatively uncluttered setting, a sextet featuring Michael Brecker, Kenny Kirkland, and Buster Williams.

what to buy next: *Movies* ♪♪♪ (Enja, 1987, prod. Matthias Winckelmann) was Ambrosetti's first attempt to reinterpret movie themes. Though ambitious, it just misses the mark. *Music for Symphony and Jazz Band* ♪♪♪ (Enja, 1991, prod. Wolfgang Kunert) is another ambitious project, this time with the NDR-Radio Orchestra Hannover. Alto saxophonist Greg Osby helps keep things together.

the rest:
Close Encounter ♪♪♪ (Enja, 1978)
Heart Bop ♪♪♪ (Enja, 1982)
Tentets ♪♪♪ (Enja, 1985)
Gin and Pentatonic ♪♪♪ (Enja, 1992)
Live at the Blue Note ♪♪♪ (Enja, 1993)

worth searching for: *Flavio Ambrosetti: Anniversary* ♪♪♪♪ (Enja, 1996, prod. various) is a two-CD collection of work by Franco's father ranging from 1949 to 1976, with many tracks featuring early work from the younger Ambrosetti. *A Jazz Portrait of Franco Ambrosetti* ♪♪♪ (Right Tempo Classic, 1996, reissue prod. Stefano Gidari) reissues seven 1965 tracks supplemented by nine previously unreleased alternate takes from the same session. Hearing Ambrosetti this early in his career, with just a trio behind him (Franco D'Andrea, piano; Giorgio Azzolini, bass; Franco Mondini, drums) on such classics as "Blue in Green," "My Old Flame," "Bye Bye Blackbird," and the like helps put his artistry in context.

influences:
◄◄ Chet Baker
►► Jon Faddis, Enrico Rava

Eric J. Lawrence

Albert Ammons

Born September 23, 1907, in Chicago, IL. Died December 2, 1949, in Chicago, IL.

Most of Albert Ammon's life was spent in Chicago, where he learned the art of the rolling bass line so essential to boogie woogie piano stylings. Ammons and his contemporaries, Meade "Lux" Lewis and Pete Johnson, were the keyboard triumvirate

for 1938's historically important Spirituals to Swing concert (organized by John Hammond at Carnegie Hall), and their collective digital prowess created a sensation. Alan Lomax recorded the trio for the Library of Congress soon after the concert.

Technically the most gifted of the three, Ammons was also the one whose inclinations were closer to jazz than blues, although he was heavily influenced by the young blues prodigy Hersal Wallace and the house rent stylings of the neglected Jimmy Yancey.

In addition to duets and trios with Lewis and Johnson, Ammons recorded a wonderful batch of piano solos and in groups with his Rhythm Kings, Harry James, J.C. Higginbotham, and the Port of Harlem Jazzmen. He also accompanied Big Bill Broonzy and Joe Turner, among others. In the 1940s he cut sides with Louis Jordan, Lonnie Johnson, and Sippie Wallace. His son, Gene Ammons, was one of the most important post-war tenor sax players and actually recorded for Mercury with the senior Ammons in 1947. Albert joined the Lionel Hampton band in 1949, mere months before he died.

what to buy: *1936–1939* ♪♪♪♪ (Jazz Chronological Classics, 1993, prod. various) is a good overall introduction to Ammons since it features the pianist in a variety of settings. The first four cuts come from 1936 and feature Albert Ammons and His Rhythm Kings, which included the great Israel Crosby on bass. The playing on "Nagasaki" and "Boogie Woogie Stomp" shows Ammons to be a sympathetic accompanist when he wasn't playing leads. Everything else comes from 1939. The two pieces with Harry James and the Boogie Woogie Trio have the trumpeter playing quite well, and the Port of Harlem Jazzmen cuts are wonderful. The heart of the album is in the solo spots with 10 tunes that distill the left-hand boogie and right-hand filigree, including a romping solo version of "Boogie Woogie Stomp" and a finely nuanced "Backwater Blues." The first recording sessions for Alfred Lion's new Blue Note label, *The First Day* ♪♪♪♪ (Blue Note, 1939, prod. Alfred Lion/1992, reissue prod. Michael Cuscuna) yielded a treasure trove of marvelous piano playing. The CD is split between solo Ammons material, duets with Meade "Lux" Lewis, and some fine Lewis solo tunes. Nine of the 10 Ammons cuts on this disc appear on the Classics recording, but the two duets with Lewis do not. The choice is between the more complete survey on the Classics album and the better sound quality of the Blue Note release.

what to buy next: *Master of Boogie* ♪♪♪ (Milan, 1992) contains live recordings from Le Hot Club de France and have Ammons playing in different situations. He has solo spots, a few duos with Meade "Lux" Lewis, some small group material, one cut accompanying blues singer Big Bill Broonzy, and a hot three-piano date with Lewis and Pete Johnson. All of it comes from sessions in 1938 and 1939, mastered by S.E.I. Gilbert Prenneron in surprisingly good sound.

worth searching for: Mosaic, the mail order audiophiles, put out a limited edition box set on vinyl, *The Complete Blue Note Albert Ammons and Meade Lux Lewis* 𝄢𝄢𝄢𝄢 (Blue Note, 1939–44, prod. Alfred Lion/Mosaic, prod. Michael Cuscuna, Charlie Lourie), including eight otherwise unavailable songs. This set was a limited edition of 5,000 and is currently out of print.

influences:

◄◄ Hersal Wallace, Jimmy Yancey, Pine Top Smith

►► Judy Carmichael

Garaud MacTaggart

Gene "Jug" Ammons

Born Eugene Ammons, April, 14, 1925, in Chicago, IL. Died August 6, 1974, in Chicago, IL

Gene Ammons was the son of the great boogie woogie piano player Albert Ammons and even made some of his first recordings (for Mercury in 1947) with his father on piano. The younger Ammons first made a name for himself in Billy Eckstine's band during the mid-1940s where his tenor "battles" with section mate Dexter Gordon led to a hit for the band called "Blowing the Blues Away." After leaving the band, Ammons formed his own group and recorded a song called "Red Top" in 1947 (mere months before the session with his father) which became an instrumental hit first, until King Pleasure put words to it and had another hit with his vocal version. In 1949 Ammons replaced Stan Getz in Woody Herman's band for a while before leaving to form a septet with his former Eckstine bandmate, Sonny Stitt. The Herman job was to be Ammons's last gig as a sideman.

The Stitt-Ammons band only lasted a few years but the two good friends would periodically get together for blowing sessions, live and on record. Ammons's popularity encouraged his record company to book studio time for a raft of blowing sessions which only consolidated his hold on his fans. In 1958 he was sentenced to do time in prison on a narcotics possession charge. When he was finally released, and after recording a string of hits, he got nailed on possession charges once again (in 1962) and ended up spending seven years in prison. After doing his last stretch of time, Ammons dug back into the music scene, recording some of

his best material, before he finally died five years later from bone cancer complicated by pneumonia.

what to buy: The first four cuts on *Red Top* 𝄢𝄢𝄢𝄢 (1947–1953, Savoy, prod. Teddy Reig, Lew Simpkins) are actually from a date under the nominal leadership of baritone sax player Leo Parker. The session participants were more star-studded (with Junior Mance on piano, Howard McGhee on trumpet, Gene Wright on bass, and Chuck Williams on drums) than on the balance of the album, but the spark is missing. Ammons does better when he's the leader of an octet whose only other real "star" is trumpeter Johnny Coles. Beginning with "Just Chips," a hard-charging tune that's right up Ammons's alley (as you can tell from his initial solo), things really cook. Even the ballads he played had the trademark big sound and sustained tension, as heard on "Stairway to the Stars." The version of "Red Top" heard on this album is a 1953 remake of his first big hit. Ammons seems at peace on the first cut of *Jug* 𝄢𝄢𝄢𝄢 (Prestige, 1961, prod. Esmond Edwards), his version of "Ol' Man River," and his big, softly booting sound nails it by palpably holding back from the powerful swinging attack Ammons was capable of. He definitely knew that sometimes less is more. By the end of the album however, there is a romping version of "Tangerine" where Ammons starts riffing like he could go on for hours. The rhythm section includes drummer J.C. Heard and conga player Ray Barretto, who can be heard trading fours in mid-tune. Bassist Doug Watkins is the walking rock of time, while Richard Wyands on piano feeds the big man all the right chords. In between these two songs are a couple Ammons originals and some tasty arrangements on classic pop tunes.

what to buy next: Prestige recorded a lot of Gene Ammons's playing in situations just like *The Happy Blues* 𝄢𝄢𝄢 (Prestige, 1956, prod. Bob Weinstock). Call up some musicians for the date, get a sketchy arrangement or two ready for the recording and then drive to Hackensack, New Jersey where Rudy Van Gelder would engineer the jams played. Sometimes they worked and other times (including the gigs where John Coltrane played alto) they cruised on name recognition, not musical worth. This was one of those special moments where things worked out just the way they were supposed to. The septet for this album featured trumpeter Art Farmer (who gets credit for "writing" the title tune) and pianist Duke Jordan with Jackie McLean as the alto foil for Gene's broad tenor. Rhythm chores were handled by Art's brother Addison, on bass, Candido on congas, and the other Art (Taylor) on drums. The group runs through some mid and up-tempo songs before closing with "Madhouse," a real barn burner that has the frontline players trading licks in rapid succession while the pulsing rhythm section goes into overdrive. Sonny Stitt gets co-leader billing with Ammons on *Boss Tenors* 🎵🎵🎵✧ (1961, Verve, prod. Creed Taylor) and the two tenors do the aural duking just like they used to in the Eckstine band. This is not a subtle session. Even an ostensible ballad ("Autumn Leaves") gets a little boot with a vaguely Latin rhythm starting the tune off. Stitt plays alto on "There Is No Greater Love" and the swing generated by Ammons and Stitt is contagious. The rhythm section is solid and supportive throughout, but the date belongs to the leaders.

best of the rest:

Jammin' with Gene 🎵🎵🎵✧ (Prestige, 1956)
Jammin' in Hi Fi 🎵🎵🎵✧ (Prestige, 1957)
Blue Gene 🎵🎵🎵✧ (Prestige, 1958)
Boss Tenor 🎵🎵🎵✧ (Prestige, 1960)
(With Sonny Stitt) *We'll Be Together Again* 🎵🎵🎵✧ (Prestige, 1961)
(With Dexter Gordon) *The Chase* 🎵🎵🎵 (Prestige, 1971)
(With Dodo Marmarosa) *Jug & Dodo* 🎵🎵🎵✧ (Prestige, 1972)
The Gene Ammons Story: Gentle Jug 🎵🎵🎵✧ (Prestige, 1992)

influences:

◀◀ Coleman Hawkins, Chu Berry

▶▶ A.C. Reed, Eddie Shaw, David S. Ware

Garaud MacTaggart

Chris Anderson

Born February 26, 1926, in Chicago, IL.

Chris Anderson is a self-taught pianist with remarkable improvisatory skills that use harmony as a base more often than melody. His first influences didn't come from jazz artists of the day as much as from the movie scores he heard during the 1930s and 1940s. His eyesight was already fading at this time (he's blind, and also afflicted by a congenital condition colloquially known as "soft bones") and he used to tell what the action on the screen was going to be by the musical cues. Anderson later got a job in a record store, where he was exposed to the music of Nat "King" Cole, Art Tatum, and Duke Ellington. By the time he was in his early twenties, Anderson had picked up the skills he needed to play with Chicago musicians such as Von Freeman. He left Chicago as an accompanist to singer Dinah Washington, who fired Anderson six weeks later while on the New York City leg of a tour. The pianist took this opportunity to make New York City his home, playing in small clubs as an accompanist or with his own small groups. His homegrown, harmonic sense was strong enough and impressive enough that Herbie Hancock, already an accomplished player, started

studying ("through osmosis," according to Anderson) with the pianist.

what to buy: *Solo Ballads* 🎵🎵🎵🎵 (Alsut, 1997, prod. Al Sutton) finds Anderson dipping into Ellingtonia and the showtune bag for six wonderful tunes which he stretches into advanced harmonic experiments. Spacing and pacing are the elements which Anderson uses to frame his musical thoughts, as the shortest rendition on the album is an eight-minute version of "I Got It Bad" with the rest hovering between 10 and 16 minutes. The melodies appear, hide, and show themselves again in seemingly endless variations of stately beauty. Barry Harris wrote the liner notes.

what to buy next: Recorded in 1987 but not released until 1993, the solo piano album *Love Locked Out* 🎵🎵🎵🎵 (Mapleshade, 1993, prod. Clifford Jordan, Pierre M. Sprey) was an afterthought to a still unreleased session Mapleshade was doing with Clifford Jordan and Anderson. It includes three originals and six show tune standards with an amazing version of Stephen Sondheim's often overworked "Send in the Clowns." The piano playing is stunning throughout and there are two charming, if idiosyncratic, vocals. If heaven has a piano bar for jazzers, this is probably what it sounds like.

worth searching for: Anderson's earliest recorded appearance is on the Charlie Parker album *An Evening at Home with the Bird* 🎵🎵🎵 (Savoy, 1993), which he remembers (contrary to the album liner notes) as two disparate club gigs with saxophonist Von Freeman that Parker sat in on. Anderson also recorded an album for a Riverside subsidiary, *Inverted Image* 🎵🎵🎵 (Jazzland, 1962, prod. Orrin Keepnews) and a trio date with bassist Ray Drummond and drummer Billy Higgins called *Blues One* 🎵🎵🎵🎵 (DIW, 1993, prod. Mickey Bass). Perhaps the oddest project the pianist was involved with is *The Sun Ra Sextet at the Village Vanguard* 🎵🎵🎵 (Rounder, 1993, prod. John Snyder), a 1991 live date with Sun Ra playing synthesizer over Anderson's piano.

influences:

◀◀ Duke Ellington, Nat "King" Cole, Art Tatum

▶▶ Herbie Hancock, Jason Linder, Mfergu

Garaud MacTaggart

Clifton Anderson

Born October 5, 1957, in New York, NY.

The nephew of Sonny Rollins may have come to public attention in his uncle's band, but his only album shows a musician who can stand on his own. Anderson boasts a refulgent tone with plenty of body to it and a clean, dexterous technique. He's obviously listened to J.J. Johnson, but his sound is mellower and more burnished. Another connection with his uncle is calypso, a style in which Anderson played extensively at one time while living in New York and which shows up on his only album. Perhaps in the future Anderson will add to his already impressive talents elements of his time spent with Lester Bowie and James Jabbo Ware and his expressed admiration for the writing of Muhal Richard Abrams, taking his music into newer territory.

what's available: Anderson's rhythm section on *Landmarks* 𝄞𝄞𝄞𝄞 (Milestone, 1996, prod. Clifton Anderson, Victor See Yuen) has Rollins's bassist and drummer, Bob Cranshaw and Al Foster, plus Jamaican pianist Monty Alexander and percussionist Victor See Yuen, while Anderson shares the frontline on one tune each with trumpeter Wallace Roney and alto saxophonist Kenny Garrett. The style is basically soulful bebop, which these guys could play in their sleep, but there's no snoring on this gig. Between Alexander and Foster, the groove is so deep it's practically gospel on "Mommy." There are excursions into Latin rhythms elsewhere, two standards, and a calypso tune by Clifton's mother. Anderson's five originals are well-written and arranged, and this is quite a high-caliber debut.

worth searching for: Among the Sonny Rollins albums on which Anderson can be heard are *Sunny Days, Starry Nights* 𝄞𝄞𝄞𝄞 (Milestone, 1984, prod. Sonny Rollins, Lucille Rollins), *G-Man* 𝄞𝄞𝄞𝄞 (Milestone, 1986, prod. Sonny Rollins, Lucille Rollins), *Dancing in the Dark* 𝄞𝄞𝄞𝄞 (Milestone, 1987, prod. Sonny Rollins, Lucille Rollins), and *Here's to the People* 𝄞𝄞𝄞𝄞 (Milestone, 1991, prod. Sonny Rollins, Lucille Rollins).

influences:
◀◀ J.J. Johnson

Steve Holtje

Ernestine Anderson

Born November 11, 1928, in Houston, TX.

A versatile singer who helped create R&B in the 1940s, Ernestine Anderson is a soulful jazz vocalist who is equally at home singing blues and pop. Influenced strongly by Dinah Washington early in her career, Anderson developed her own sound based deeply in the big band swing and jump blues tradition, though she occasionally draws on bebop, too. Since her re-emergence in the mid-1970s, she's been one of the most consistently swinging vocalists in jazz.

Anderson was raised in Seattle and sang in her church's choir as a teenager. She toured widely in the 1940s, working with the bands of Russell Jacquet (with whom she made her first recording in 1947), Shifty Henry, Eddie Heywood, and R&B pioneer Johnny Otis. In the 1950s, Anderson began carving out a niche as a straight-ahead jazz singer, working with Lionel Hampton in 1952–53 and performing around New York. Through Hampton's band, Anderson connected with Quincy Jones and Gigi Gryce, recording with Jones in 1953 and Gryce in 1955. During a tour of Sweden with trumpeter Rolf Ericson in 1956, she recorded an album with the Harry Arnold Orchestra, *Hot Cargo*, that helped establish her reputation when it was released in the U.S. by Mercury. She won *Down Beat*'s "New Star" critics award in 1959, appeared at the Monterey Jazz festival, and made a number of well-received albums for Mercury in the early 1960s. But the ascendancy of rock 'n' roll led to difficult times and Anderson moved to England in 1965. Her sensational appearance at the 1976 Concord Jazz Festival, engineered by bassist Ray Brown, marked her return to prominence and the beginning of a long, fruitful association with the Concord label, including albums with pianists Hank Jones and Monty Alexander, the Clayton-Hamilton Jazz Orchestra, and the Capp/Pierce Juggernaut. With her theme song "Never Make Your Move Too Soon," Anderson developed a repertoire of raucous blues, beautifully rendered swing-era standards, and jazzy contemporary pop tunes.

what to buy: An excellent introduction to this highly enjoyable singer, *Great Moments with Ernestine Anderson* 𝄞𝄞𝄞𝄞 (Concord Jazz, 1993, prod. various) covers her almost two-decade association with the Concord label. A flexible vocalist, Anderson makes herself at home with a variety of accompanists, including pianists Dave McKenna, Monty Alexander, Gene Harris, and Hank Jones. She is equally comfortable singing gorgeous standards ("Skylark" and "Time after Time") as she is belting definitive versions of the blues ("Someone Else Is Steppin' In") and delivering her theme song ("Never Make Your Move Too Soon"), heard here in a 10-minute live version with the Frank Capp/Nat Pierce Juggernaut. Another fine quartet session with a first-rate rhythm section, *Never Make Your Move Too Soon* 𝄞𝄞𝄞𝄞 (Concord Jazz, 1981, prod. Carl E. Jefferson) is possibly Anderson's definitive Concord session. Singing with effortless swing, she sails through a program of blues and standards. Opening with the title track, a tune that became her theme song, she offers a tribute to Dinah Washington (one of her main influences) with "What a Diff'rence a Day Made," and breathes new life into "Old Folks," which somehow works with Monty Alexander's Fender Rhodes accompaniment. With bassist Ray

Brown and drummer Frank Gant rounding out the rhythm section, Anderson breezes through mid-tempo versions of "As Long As I Live" and a bop-tinged "My Shining Hour." Like Oscar Peterson, the prodigious pianist George Shearing has done some of his best work as an accompanist for confident singers. *A Perfect Match* 𝄢𝄢𝄢 (Concord Jazz, 1988, prod. Carl E. Jefferson) pairs Anderson, a singer who holds her own with anybody, with Shearing's trio, featuring bassist Neil Swainson and drummer Jeff Hamilton. The program consists of 13 mostly well-worn standards and the Benny Golson classic "I Remember Clifford," but the trio plays with such energy and Anderson projects so much joyful feeling into the music, it's no strain hearing these tunes again (and again). Highlights include "Falling in Love with Love" and a lilting version of the seldom-played Rodgers and Hammerstein song "That's for Me."

what to buy next: Anderson's Concord debut and first recording in years, *Hello Like Before* 𝄢𝄢𝄢 (Concord Jazz, 1977, prod. Carl E. Jefferson) finds her in the inimitable hands of Hank Jones (piano), Ray Brown (bass), and Jimmie Smith (drums). This is the album that re-established her reputation as one of the most forthrightly soulful singers in jazz. Though there are only two blues tunes on the album, she infuses everything she sings with down-home feeling, moving easily between 1930s classics "It Don't Mean a Thing . . . " and "Tain't Nobody's Bizness If I Do," and contemporary tunes such as Stevie Wonder's "Bird of Beauty" and a down-to-earth version of "Send in the Clowns."

Anderson gets deep into the blues on *When the Sun Goes Down* 𝄢𝄢𝄢𝄢 (Concord Jazz, 1985, prod. Carl E. Jefferson), a smokin' session featuring Gene Harris (piano), Ray Brown (bass), Gerryck King (drums), and Red Holloway (tenor sax). From the books of Count Basie and Duke Ellington ("Goin' to Chicago Blues" and "I'm Just a Lucky So and So") to a rare vocal version of Joe Zawinul's hit "Mercy, Mercy, Mercy," Anderson is completely at home wailing the blues. Holloway and Anderson blow up a storm together on "Someone Else Is Steppin' In," a tune that became a permanent part of her repertoire. Though *Ernestine Anderson* 𝄢𝄢𝄢 (PolyGram, 1958/Verve, 1992) contains barely over a half-hour of music, the CD captures the singer at the height of her Dinah Washington phase. Her first full-length U.S. session, the album features orchestrations by Pete Rugolo. Anderson swings but doesn't do much improvising. She is particularly effective on "Stardust" and "My Ship."

best of the rest:

Live from Concord to London 𝄢𝄢𝄢 (Concord Jazz, 1978/1990)
Sunshine 𝄢𝄢𝄢 (Concord Jazz, 1979/1991)
Big City 𝄢𝄢𝄢 (Concord Jazz, 1983/1989)

Live at the Alley Cat 𝄢𝄢𝄢 (Concord Jazz, 1987)
Be Mine Tonight 𝄢𝄢𝄢 (Concord Jazz, 1987)
Boogie Down 𝄢𝄢𝄢 (Concord Jazz, 1990)
Live at the 1990 Concord Festival—Third Set 𝄢𝄢𝄢 (Concord Jazz, 1991)
Now & Then 𝄢𝄢 (Qwest, 1993)
Blues, Dues & Love News 𝄢𝄢 (Qwest, 1996)

influences:

◀◀ Dinah Washington

▶▶ Barbara Morrison

Andrew Gilbert

Fred Anderson

Born March 22, 1929, in Monroe, LA.

Although a co-founder of the AACM (he played at the first concert) and sporadically recorded over the last 30 years (he can be heard on Joseph Jarman's landmark *Song For*, finally issued on CD by Delmark), Anderson has only been justly documented over the last few years, and this by the small labels dedicated to covering Chicago's vibrant and underrecorded scene, which his bar, the Velvet Lounge, has done much to incubate. Late in life, he is finally coming into his own as a hero of both his instrument and a guiding light for younger musicians. With the exception of some Ornette Coleman acolytes such as Dewey Redman and (the also underappreciated) James Clay, he is probably the tenor player who has best absorbed Coleman's lessons of the early 1960s, and he often sounds as if he could fit right in on one of Coleman's Atlantic LPs. But Anderson is from Coleman's generation, and although Coleman was a large inspiration, they absorbed many of the same influences, such as Don Byas and Lester Young (let us not forget that Ornette started as a tenor player, and that has much to do with his most vocal of approaches). Anderson possesses a distinctive sound, gliding without being facile, with a Rollins-esque honk and agility at glancing moments similar to David S. Ware's. Like Ware, he can worry a phrase until it burrows a hole to China. He seems to take the same scalar inspiration from Coltrane that Rollins did. For the last couple of decades, Anderson's bands and informal students have included Chico Freeman, George Lewis, and Douglas Ewart. He has continued a fruitful mentorship of the drummer Hamid Drake, although Drake doesn't appear on his latest.

what to buy: Anderson's latest is also his finest, the sprawling two-CD release *Chicago Chamber Music* 𝄢𝄢𝄢𝄢 (Southport, 1997, prod. Bradley Parker-Sparrow) that's half a trio with bassist Tatsu Aoki and drummer Afifi Phillard, the other half a duo with Aoki. Also producer Parker-Sparrow's piano joins in for a couple of cuts. *Birdhouse* ♫♫♫♪ (Okkadisk, 1996, prod. Fred Anderson, Bruno Johnson) is named after Anderson's old club, which was often harassed by cops who couldn't understand why a jazz club wouldn't sell alcohol. It's a quartet date with youthful Chicago veterans Drake, Harrison Bankhead on bass, and Jim Baker on piano. Tender interplay features on some ferociously free tracks, while "Like Sonny" sounds more like Ornette as played by David S. Ware, with Bankhead approaching his instrument with confluence to Ware bandmate Matt Shipp.

what to buy next: It's hard to see why the 1979 session *The Missing Link* (Nessa, 1984, prod. Fred Anderson, Chuck Nessa) ♫♫♫♫ didn't broaden Anderson's career prospects. Anderson's tone has deepened since this recording, which is somewhat more traditional than his recent releases and relatively funkier (that's relatively), with two percussionists (Drake and Adam Rudolph) and occasional ostinato bass (Larry Hayrod). Once again, though, Anderson's imagination is hard to predict, and that's the fun of it. On CD there's an extra 15-minute track by Drake. *Destiny* ♫♫♫ (Okkadisk, 1994, prod. Fred Anderson, Bruno Johnson) can't go wrong with Marilyn Crispell on piano and Drake, again.

the rest:
Accents ♫♫♫ (EMI, 1977)
Another Place ♫♫♫ (Moers, 1978),
Vintage Duets: Chicago 1/11/80 ♫♫♫ (Okkadisk, 1994)
Fred Anderson/DKV Trio ♫♫♫ (Okkadisk, 1997)

worth searching for: Anderson rarely (if ever) gets out of Chicago, but his music must have, as *Dark Day* ♫♫♫ (Messenger, 1979) is an Austrian release of a concert at the Chicago Museum of Contemporary Art.

influences:
◀◀ Ornette Coleman, Sonny Rollins, Joseph Jarman
▶▶ David S. Ware, Tim Berne

D. Strauss

Ray Anderson

Born October 16, 1952, in Chicago, IL.

Though he's been criticized for his exaggerated trombone techniques that defy any classical training on his instrument, jazz fans admire Ray Anderson's exuberant spirit, innovative ideas, and the colorful musical statements he has been making since the 1970s. He's viewed by many insiders as one of the most re-

freshing instrumentalists on the jazz scene. His music is filled with intelligence, wit, and multi-phonics produced by simultaneously singing and blowing into his instrument. Anderson evokes growls, slides and distortions from his trombone, and occasionally plays other brass instruments including alto trombone, slide trumpet, cornet, tuba, and even some percussion. A rare and revered artist, his jovial, extroverted personality comes through in his innovative recordings and in live performances. Anderson sings on many of his albums, especially with his Alligatory Band and the cooperative funk group, Slickaphonics. In the 1980s, Anderson developed a split-tone vocals style (simultaneously singing two notes a minor third apart) when he had Bell's Palsy (a condition that causes partial paralysis of the facial nerves) and temporarily couldn't play trombone. Whether leading freestyled jazz, blues, bop-oriented sessions, or performing arrangements with an all 'bone group, or employing a traditional New Orleans approach, Anderson is a trombonist of great range and flexibility.

Born and raised in Chicago, Anderson learned trombone from an early age and absorbed classical, blues, funk, and New Orleans jazz, as well as being influenced by the Chicago-based AACM (Association for the Advancement of Creative Musicians). After brief stays in Minnesota and California, Anderson moved to New York in 1972, where he worked in the new music scene and freelanced in New York's Latin bands. On many endeavors, his partners included fellow Chicagoans George Lewis (whom he's been friends with since third grade) and Anthony Davis, as well as Mark Helias and Gerry Hemingway, two players who would ultimately become part of Anderson's Bass-DrumBone trio. Anderson gained wider notice in 1977 after replacing George Lewis in Anthony Braxton's ensemble, and began to record in 1980 under his own name for various European labels. Since the 1970s, he has appeared as sideman on numerous albums with a wide range of jazz stylists. He has also worked and recorded with Barry Altschul, the George Gruntz Concert Band, Charlie Haden's Liberation Music Orchestra, and Bennie Wallace, as well as with the Slickaphonics, and a collective trio with Han Bennink and Christy Doran.

what to buy: You can start about anywhere in Anderson's sizable discography, depending on your tastes. Anderson has recorded inventive avant-garde and free-jazz sessions, boisterous rock-influenced funk, classy orchestral oeuvres, a tasty trombone quartet, and more. For a rockin' good time, select *Don't Mow Your Lawn* ♫♫♫♫ (Enja, 1996, prod. Mark Helias), a set launched with Anderson's raspy singing of the anti-suburbia title tune lyrics. A fun-filled, eight-tune romp with Anderson's rousing Alligatory Band, this March, 1994 Brooklyn studio session finds the trombonist collaborating with Jerome Harris (guitar, background vocals), trumpeter Lew Soloff (who sometimes takes a front-line spot with Anderson or creates in-tandem tension), and a rousing rhythm section (percussionist Frank Colon, drummer Tommy Campbell, bassist Gregory Jones). Anderson revs up some raw, wrangling lines and everyone has a great time on upbeat tempos and spirited call-and-response elements of this animated romp. Anderson's Alligatory Band delivers a mostly mainstream-jazz session on *Heads and Tales* ♫♫♫♫ (Enja, 1996, prod. Mark Helias, Ray Anderson). Nine tunes include his cleverly devised, slice-of-life suite, titled *The Four Reasons,* and its diverse movements, "Hunting and Gathering," "Heads and Tales," "Matters of the Heart," and "Unsung Songs." Anderson draws from sundry musical sources including Latin and New Orleans jazz, and funk. He sings on a couple of tunes and, on the first movement of the funky suite injects a humorous trombone "quote" mimicking a childhood taunt. Forming a band around one instrument has been successful for the World Saxophone Quartet, Rova, the 29th Street Saxophone Quartet, and others groups. But it's rare that an all-trombone group like Slideride arises to perform with the verve and freedom of this foursome formed by Ray Anderson and Craig Harris with George Lewis, and Gary Valente documented on *Slideride* ♫♫♫♫♫ (hat ART, 1994). On the 11 tunes performed, the group traces the history of trombone, packing a wallop with freestyled jazz originals, plush ballads (Billy Strayhorn's "Lotus Blossom"), jive cookers (the Ellington/Hodges tune, "The Jeep Is Jumping"), and more. At times, Anderson's 'bonisms sound like wounded elephants or a nest of buzzing hornets. With his cohorts, their blended performance sings like an a capella choir. But it's all serious good fun, a provocative, abstract session that stretches the instrument's range and challenges the listener's ears. At the 1991 Chicago Jazz Festival, Anderson performed the *Chicago Cantata* with the George Gruntz Concert Jazz Band. Their exploratory styles are well-matched and it's evident on the boisterous, swinging nine tunes of Anderson's *Big Band Record* ♫♫♫♫ (Gramavision, 1994, prod. Ray Anderson, George Gruntz). The trombonist exhibits his characteristic playfulness, especially on "Raven-A-Ning" (a romping tune written for one of his children) and on the last track, an orchestrated version of "Don't Mow Your Lawn," from his like-titled Enja album. For Anderson's original compositions, Gruntz has written complex, adventurous, swinging jazz charts. Powerful and unpredictable, these awesome arrangements leave space for solos from Anderson, who delivers fanciful honks, sputters, and gravelly grumblings, and from other top soloists including Lew Soloff, Tim Berne,

Herb Robertson, Tom Rainey, and Marty Ehrlich. With 75 minutes of music, this is a wonderful, roguish, big band album. *Blues Bred in the Bone* ♫♫♫♫ (Enja, 1989, prod. Ray Anderson) features instrumentation similar to Anderson's out-of-print Gramavision dates and is different from any small group dates reviewed above because it includes piano. Performing seven modern arrangements (four originals) with Anthony Davis (piano), Mark Dresser (bass), Johnny Vidocovich (drums), Anderson strives to show the full range of his instrument and give his sidemen plenty of room. Guesting soloist, guitarist John Scofield, lends a couple of tracks a fusiony feel which Anderson keeps in check with his grounded 'bonisms. Some critics have panned this album for Anderson's upper register wranglings even though Anderson balances them with low register grumblings and some serious straight-ahead swing and bop. The fun grooves and the collaborative effort of these musicians, especially on the Latin-Americanized pulsations of the pop tune, "Mona Lisa," Anderson's bop speedball, "Datune," and their chatty creeper, "I Don't Want to Set the World on Fire," makes this album very much worthy of attention.

what to buy next: On *Cheer Up* ♫♫♫♫ (hat ART, 1995, prod. Peter Pfister), Anderson plays trombone and tuba, collaborating creatively (often, humorously) on nine tunes with like-minded drummer Han Bennink and guitarist Christy Doran. As always, his sounds range from freestyled bursts, sputters, and gusts, to sensibly melodic mood generators. All but one tune on the Zurich session are originals by Anderson and/or his cohorts. Their music is serious but it's all good fun with curious titles such as "My Children Are the Reason Why I Need to Own My Publishing" (an Anderson-penned original on which he delivers an accessibly palatable trombone solo with smooth underpinning from his teammates), "Tabasco Cart" (a scrambling, spicy caper that turns darkly ominous), "Buckethead" (a brief, freerolling, drum-laden piece), and the ethereal title tune (with Anderson playing muted trombone). Painted with the broadest pallette, and often teetering on the outside edge, their imaginative creations continue to appeal to fans. A hat ART release recorded a year earlier, *Azurety* ♫♫♫♫ (hat ART, 1995, prod. Peter Pfister) introduces this synergistic team to fans and features similar material and provocative Anderson titles, plus Anderson's wonderful interpretation of Ellington's "Just Squeeze Me." The fare on this April 21–22, 1994 Zurich studio session is more abstract, less playful, and prominently features the churning guitar work of Christy Doran. Although Anderson plays innovatively, equitable interaction between Doran, drummer Han Bennink, and Anderson has not quite evolved to the level on their upbeat *Cheer Up* album, and this session comes across as overly serious, except for Anderson's whisper-like sauciness on the all-too-brief nod to Ellington. Anderson works with a larger ensemble on *It Just So Happens* 🎵🎵🎵 (Enja, 1987/1992, prod. Matthias Winckelmann), one of his more rhythmically accentuated, straight-ahead albums. On the nine catchy tunes (including two takes on the standard, "Once in a While"), his crew gets a workout, especially drummer Ronnie Burrage who cleverly spurs soloists Anderson, Stanton Davis (trumpet), Perry Robinson (clarinet), and Bob Stewart (tuba), powerfully from underneath in conjunction with bassist Mark Dress on this outstanding session recorded in New York on January 31 and February 1, 1987. Anderson contributes six originals, ranging from serious explorations such as "Fatelet" (which features Dresser), to a rambunctious visit to the Caribbean on "Raven's Jolly Jump-Up," to a peppy New Orleans–styled "Fishin' with Gramps."

best of the rest:
(With Mark Helias, Gerry Hemingway) *Right Down Your Alley* 🎵🎵🎵 (Soul Note, 1984)
(With Mark Helias, Gerry Hemingway) *You Be* 🎵🎵🎵 (Minor Music, 1985/1996)
(With Slickaphonics) *Wow Bag* 🎵🎵🎵 (Enja, 1986)

worth searching for: Recorded with Slickaphonics, *Modern Life* 🎵🎵🎵 (Enja, 1983, prod. Slickaphonics) is a bawdy, brassy, boisterous outing featuring funky, deep-groove dance beats. As well as Anderson's raw and rowdy vocals and 'bonisms, the 11-tune session spotlights Daniel Wilensky (saxophonist), Allan Jaffe (guitar), Mark Helias (bass), and Jim Payne (drums). Also search-worthy is Anderson's imaginative trio recording with BassDrumBone (with bassist Mark Helias and drummer Gerry Hemmingway). On the diverse tempos of eight originals, the musicians percolate with breezy familiarity on *Wooferloo* 🎵🎵🎵 (Soul Note, 1989, prod. Giovanni Bonandrini). Jazz chameleon Anderson stretches out with exotic trombone moans, groans, splats, and sputters. With the exception of Anderson's big band recording, most of his excellent Gramavision dates are out-of-print. Check used or cut-out bins for *Every One of Us* 🎵🎵🎵 (Gramavision, 1992), featuring Anderson with Simon Nabatov (piano), Charlie Haden (acoustic bass), and Ed Blackwell (drums). It's a classic that features fine music, and Anderson's woeful vocals on the 1932 Jay Gorney tune, "Brother, Can You Spare a Dime?" *Wishbone* 🎵🎵🎵 (Gramavision, 1991, prod. Ray Anderson, Mark Helias) is special for introducing Anderson's playful junket, "The Gahtooze," and his popular original, "Cheek to Cheek." An Anderson-led quintet session which includes John Hicks (piano),

Allan Jaffe (guitar), Mark Dresser (bass), Pheeroan akLaff (drums), *What Because* 🎵🎵🎵 (Gramavision, 1990, prod. Mark Helias, Ray Anderson) contains the stylistic seeds of Anderson's Alligatory Band, with the jousting kick-off tune, "Alligatory Crocodile."

influences:
◀◀ Albert Mangelsdorff, Sam Nanton, J.C. Higginbotham, Vic Dickenson

▶▶ Craig Harris, George Lewis, Gary Valente, Robin Eubanks, Wycliffe Gordon

see also: *Mark Helias, George Lewis*

Nancy Ann Lee

Wessell Anderson

Born November 27, 1964, in Brooklyn, NY.

Wessell Anderson is one of the many important new players to come through the Wynton Marsalis finishing school. One of the imprints Marsalis leaves on his sidemen is the need to understand where jazz comes from, the roots of the form. Anderson might not have needed too much of a boost in that direction since his father was a professional drummer who used to tour with Cecil Payne. Attending the Jazzmobile workshops enabled the budding young reed player to learn from such experienced musicians as Frank Wess and Frank Foster, who taught Anderson the rudiments of theory and performance. His next important teacher, clarinetist Alvin Batiste, was referred to him by Branford Marsalis, who met Anderson after a Jazzmobile concert featuring Art Blakey & his Jazz Messengers. The next steps came in 1988 when Anderson worked for a few months with vocalist Betty Carter before hiring on with the Wynton Marsalis septet. Anderson has played on some of Marsalis's most heralded albums, including *In This House on This Morning* and *Levee Low Moan* in addition to carving out a solo career.

what to buy: *Warmdaddy in the Garden of Swing* 🎵🎵🎵 (Atlantic, 1994, prod. David M. Robinson) is an enjoyable first date for Anderson and finds him in the company of a fellow Marsalis bandmate, pianist Eric Reed. The playing is fluid throughout and if there are caveats to be voiced, they might focus on the rhythm section of Ben Wolfe (bass) and Donald Edwards (drums), which tends to disappear at times while Reed is prone to overplaying in the excitement of the moment. The overall impression of the album is that the players had a good time making it and this is communicated even in the slower pieces. Most of the material is written by Anderson, and he proves himself a capable tunesmith if not yet a major craftsman. The title song, featuring the composer playing alto over a slow blues motif voiced by Reed, is a winner, as is the vaguely Latin-esque "Go Slow for Mo'." The New Orleans-inflected bop groove of "Finger Painted Swing" is ingratiating as well.

what to buy next: There's a shift in personnel between the first album and *The Ways of Warmdaddy* ♪♪♪♬ (Atlantic, 1996, prod. Billy Banks). Only Anderson and drummer Edwards remain from the debut effort. Ellis Marsalis sits on the piano bench, Taurus Mateen provides bottom on bass, and Antoine Drye has been added on trumpet to give the album some frontline options. Marsalis is more relaxed in his solos and comping than Reed was on the first release, which translates into a comfort factor missing from the sometimes overeager playing heard on the debut. However, Drye is merely adequate, not quite pushing Anderson as expected given the chances offered. The leader is solid throughout and the material is well-chosen, with the band's take on Ellington's "Rockin' in Rhythm" particularly effective. Anderson is experimenting with his writing here and offers up some performance alternatives to the basic quintet, in particular the pianoless trio heard on "Desimonae."

influences:

◄◄ Charlie Parker, Alvin Batiste, Frank Wess, Frank Foster

Garaud MacTaggart

Ernie Andrews

Born December 25, 1927, in Philadelphia, PA.

Although a bluesy shouter at heart, Ernie Andrews is versatile singer who has never experienced the success his talents merit. His recording career began in the late 1940s while he was still attending high school in Los Angeles. He was discovered after winning a local amateur contest by songwriter Joe Greene who started his own record label to record the young singer Andrews's early Billy Eckstine-influenced recordings. He gained national recognition and was one of the mainstays of the L.A. Central Avenue scene in the late 1940s and early 1950s. Since the early 1950s, Andrews has been associated with top-level jazz talent including Andy Kirk, Benny Carter, Cannonball Adderly, The Frank Capp-Nat Pierce Juggernaut band, Gene Harris, Harry James (whom he sang for from 1959–1969), Don Redman, Jimmy Rogers, and Kenny Burrell, but the singer has fallen through the cracks in terms of long-term stardom. He's been overshadowed by Billy Eckstine, Arthur Prysock, and Al Hibbler. Andrews has recorded for 30 different labels (including Decca,

Dot, Columbia, and Capitol) since the late 1940s, but none of his albums are in-print (including two albums issued on Muse in the 1990s). The newly formed label, 32 Jazz, has been reissuing some albums from the Muse catalog, and the former Muse producer, now head of HighNote Records, is also releasing albums by some former Muse artists. Someone should make an effort to revive the Andrews catalog. There is too much good Andrews music sitting in the vaults.

the rest:

No Regrets ♪♪♪ (Muse, 1993)

worth searching for: Check used bins for *The Great City* ♪♪♪♬ (Muse, 1995, prod. Houston Person) where Andrews is supported by Frank Wess, Peter Washington , Lewis Nash and longtime associate, Richard Wyands. Andrews is in good form on this 1995 recording. The song selections feature a standard mix of traditional ballads and blues, with the exception of James Taylor's "Fire and Rain" which Andrews converts to a shouting vehicle. A good recording that shows Andrews still has his fire.

influences:

◄◄ Billy Eckstine, King Pleasure, Eddie Jefferson, Jimmy Rushing, Joe Turner

►► Lou Rawls

Paul MacArthur and Nancy Ann Lee

Fela Anikulapo-Kuti

Born October 15, 1938, in Abeokuta, Nigeria.

In Africa, Fela Anikulapo-Kuti is best known as a musician, political irritant, and supporter of Pan-Africanism. Afrobeat, the musical hybrid created by Anikupalo-Kuti, combines elements of highlife (via Ghana), soul (a la James Brown), and jazz for a potent rhythmic force to which he adds lyrics decrying government corruption sung in either Yoruba or pidgin English. He got his performance baptism as a vocalist with trumpeter and highlife superstar Victor Olaiya. In 1958 Anikupalo-Kuti went to London and studied at Trinity College of Music. While in England he formed a highlife band known as Koola Lobitos. After studying trumpet and musical theory for four years, he returned to Nigeria, where he re-formed Koola Lobitos. Between 1963 and 1968 Anikupalo-Kuti unveiled the first version of "Afrobeat," but it was his trip to the United States in 1969 that helped to crystallize his musical ideas. Anikupalo-Kuti lived and recorded in Los Angeles for most of the year, absorbing lessons in black history and Black Power through an impressive reading regimen that helped develop his political consciousness. He also rethought his approach to music, as he said in an interview that he had been "using Jazz to play African music, when really I should be using African music to play Jazz." The horn-section work from James Brown's funk band also made an impression on Fela at this time. 1970 found him back in Nigeria with a newly minted evolution of Afrobeat, a band (Africa 70), and a vision of social justice that endeared him to much of the African populace while marking him as a gadfly for the ruling establishment. Since then Anikupalo-Kuti has released more than 40 albums, been harassed, beaten up, and imprisoned by Nigerian governments, renamed his band Egypt 80, and remained as popular with the African masses as ever.

what to buy: After his release from prison in 1986 (he had been charged with money laundering by the ruling Nigerian military junta) Anikupalo-Kuti reclaimed his band, enlarged it to 40 pieces, and jumped back into the musical fray. *O.D.O.O. (Overtake Don Overtake Overtake)* 𝄞𝄞𝄞𝄞 (Shanachie, 1990, prod. Fela Anikulapo-Kuti, Sodi) shows a strengthening of Anikulapo-Kuti's composing, arranging, and playing skills. There are only two pieces on the album, each hovering around the half hour mark, and both contain fiery solos within the context of Anikupalo-Kuti's rhythm and polemic. *Black Man's Cry* 𝄞𝄞𝄞𝄞 (Shanachie, 1992, comp. prod. Fela Anikulapo-Kuti) is probably the best single-volume Fela sampler now available, binding together six of his most popular performances from the mid- to late '70s. The version of "Black Man's Cry" comes from a 1975 recording that Anikulapo-Kuti made with rock drummer Ginger Baker, while "Zombie," with its constantly moving rhythm accents, post-Masekela trumpet, and Maceo Parker-inspired sax playing, is a true Afrobeat classic.

what to buy next: In the early days of Afrobeat, drummer Tony Allen defined the jazz-oriented rhythm that would drive Anikupalo-Kuti's music. The songs on *Open & Close* 𝄞𝄞𝄞𝄞 (Stern's African Classics, 1971, prod. Fela Ransome Kuti) were breaking the five-minute barrier that many of Anikupalo-Kuti's pre-Africa 70 songs had hovered near, and Allen's flexible stick work and sophisticated cymbal splashing provided the constant push needed to enhance the leader's horn charts. "Gbagada Gbagada Gbogodo Gbogodo" provides ample evidence of Allen's importance to this edition of the band, while the title tune, purporting to provide instruction for a brand new dance, is one of the last apolitical works Anikupalo-Kuti recorded.

best of the rest:
Original Sufferhead 𝄞𝄞𝄞𝄞 (Shanachie, 1981)
Beasts of No Nation 𝄞𝄞𝄞𝄞 (Shanachie, 1989)
Volumes 1 & 2 𝄞𝄞𝄞𝄞 (M.I.L. Multimedia, 1996)

worth searching for: A biography of Anikulapo-Kuti written by Carlos Moore, *Fela: This Bitch of a Life* (Allison & Busby) maintains a similar contact with reality as Charles Mingus's autobiography, *Beneath the Underdog*. In other words, there are fantasy sequences woven through the text that may or may not illuminate episodes in Anikupalo-Kuti's life. Included are interviews with the musician and some of his 27 (and counting) wives.

influences:
◀◀ Victor Olaiya, Guy Warren, Miles Davis, John Coltrane, Thad Jones, James Brown

▶▶ Femi Kuti, Sonny Okosun

Garaud MacTaggart

Peter Apfelbaum

Born August, 21, 1960, in Berkeley, CA.

Saxophonist/keyboardist/percussionist Apfelbaum was one of the first of the Berkeley/Bay Area multi-cultural jazz crowd to achieve national exposure in the 1990s with his 15-member Hieroglyphics Ensemble, whose shifting personnel on record included such soon-familiar names as guitarist/keyboardist Jai Uttal, guitarist Will Bernard, trombonist Jeff Cressman, and drummer Josh Jones V. Earlier incarnations (Apfelbaum first put the group together in 1977, mostly drawing on fellow Berkeley High School students) included pianist Benny Green and saxophonists Craig Handy and Joshua Redman. A four-year-plus stint in New York City, where he moved at age 19, led to work with Karl Berger, Carla Bley, and Eddie Jefferson. Apfelbaum moved back home and revived the group, and starting in 1988 famed trumpeter Don Cherry began appearing with it. Apfelbaum and two other band members joined with Cherry to tour as the MultiKulti quartet. After the Hieroglyphics Ensemble was dropped by Antilles, Apfelbaum began working with smaller groups, including the Hieroglyphics Ensemble members on the sextet album released by Gramavision, but fortunately the Hieroglyphics Ensemble continues to exist, for that is his most interesting musical context. Apfelbaum's multi-instrumental skills are significant, but what sets him apart are his eclectic arrangements, which draw on a variety of jazz and world music genres (especially African rhythms and structures) while managing to maintain stylistic coherence.

what to buy: *Jodoji Brightness* 𝄞𝄞𝄞𝄞 (Antilles, 1992, prod. Hans Wendl, Wayne Horvitz) has the deepest grooves and the most tightly knit arrangements the Hieroglyphics Ensemble has put on record, plus an intriguing setting of Dylan Thomas's "The Hand That Signed the Paper."

what to buy next: *Signs of Life* ♫♫♫ (Antilles, 1991, prod. Hans Wendl, Wayne Horvitz) was the Hieroglyphics Ensemble's major label debut, but its assured stylistic mixture reflects the group's long history.

the rest:
Luminous Charms ♫♫♫ (Gramavision, 1996)

worth searching for: Don Cherry's *MultiKulti* ♫♫♫ (A&M, 1990) finds the group supporting the late legendary trumpeter in his omnivorous musical pursuits.

influences:
◄◄ Art Ensemble of Chicago, King Sunny Ade, Mario Bauzá
►► Graham Haynes, T.J. Kirk

Steve Holtje

Peter Appleyard
Born August 26, 1928, in Cleethorpes, England.

Appleyard is an accomplished vibraphone player seldom heard in the U.S. He played drums in British dance bands and briefly with the Royal Canadian Air Force band before moving for three years to Bermuda, then to Toronto (1951). He took up vibes on the Toronto club circuit and made radio and TV appearances with pianist Calvin Jackson. Working with Canadian and U.S. musicians, Appleyard has performed and recorded as leader since 1957, even touring with the Benny Goodman band occasionally and hosting his own TV show in the 1970s. He continued to tour as leader and sideman during the 1980s and 1990s, particularly with Peanuts Hucko (a fellow member of the Pied Piper Quintet). His only two albums currently available are Appleyard's 1990s CDs for Concord.

what's available: Recorded live February 17–18, 1990 at a jazz party in Barbados, *Barbados Heat* ♫♫♫ (Concord, 1990, prod. Robert E. Neal) features the seldom-heard Canadian vibraphonist Peter Appleyard. This collection of eight standards performed with veterans Major Holly (bass), Butch Miles (drums), Bucky Pizzarelli (guitar) and Rick Wilkins (tenor saxophone), contains some provocative straight-ahead stylings. When Appleyard steps to the bars, he shows considerable expertise and vitality, especially on the bracing up-tempo version of Ellington's "Caravan" and the gorgeous romantic ballad, "Here's That Rainy Day." Other highlights include Boss Brass star Wilkins's impassioned solos on the supple interpretation of "Body and

Soul" and a swinging rendition of "Take the 'A' Train," and Pizzarelli's luxuriant (melody) head and solo on a trio version (with Miles and Holley) of Django Reinhardt's "Nuages." Their foot-tapping finale, "Sing, Sing, Sing," largely dependent on former Basie band drummer Miles's throbbing jungle beats, gives vent to pleasureful solos from everyone, especially Holley's rough-hewn, scat-harmonizing with his bass solo in Slam Stewart style. A fun party. From the same event and same team, *Barbados Cool* ♫♫♫ (Concord, 1991, prod. Robert E. Heal) features Appleyard contributing some tricky mallet-work on vibraphone. He spends more time in the spotlight on the 1991 release and proves to be adept at both up-tempo tunes and ballads. Selections include superb interpretations of "Prelude to a Kiss," "Passion Flower," "Django," "Cherokee," and six more standards. The two albums are meant to be companions. Buy both.

influences:
◄◄ Lionel Hampton

Nancy Ann Lee

Louis Armstrong
Born August 4, 1901, in New Orleans, LA. Died July 6, 1971, in New York, NY.

As if it were not enough that Louis Armstrong was the most influential instrumentalist in the first half of the history of jazz (some would say in the entire history of the music), he was also the most influential vocalist, not only in jazz, but in pop as well. It is no wonder that he became the first jazz superstar and America's jazz ambassador to the world.

A generation of New Orleans jazz musicians came before Louis Armstrong, but technology and the music industry dealt them a cruel blow. Until Armstrong's first recordings with King Oliver in 1923, no significant recordings were made of New Orleans artists. In fact, even these 1923 efforts featured precious little of Armstrong as a soloist, and it is as a soloist that he made his mark. By the time he reached New York in 1924, Armstrong had mastered the art of compressing some notes and lengthening others to make the music swing. In addition, he was a melodically daring improvisor, had great range, and possessed a beautiful tone. His Hot Five and Hot Seven recordings from 1925 through 1928 and his slightly later collaborations with pianist Earl Hines were the avant-garde jazz of their day, and still inspire musicians of all generations. Armstrong fronted big bands for most of the 1930s and early 1940s, a period in his career during which he developed an on-stage persona which for the remain-

der of his career often detracted from his continued artistry. In 1947, he returned to leading a small band, his six-piece All Stars, and kept that format for the remainder of his career.

what to buy: There are hundreds of Louis Armstrong recordings in print. To be selective, consider the Armstrong sides that first turned heads, the 1925 through 1928 recordings: *Hot Fives, Vol. 1* ⚫⚫⚫⚫ (Columbia, 1988), *Hot Fives and Hot Sevens, Vol. 2* ⚫⚫⚫⚫ (Columbia, 1988) and *Hot Fives and Hot Sevens, Vol. 3* ⚫⚫⚫⚫ (Columbia, 1989). Also consider buying *Louis Armstrong and Earl Hines, Vol. 4* ⚫⚫⚫⚫, (Columbia, 1989), featuring Armstrong's 1928 collaborations with Hines from early 78 rpm recordings. First issued by Columbia on LP in the 1950s, the collection includes a very free "Weather Bird." *Louis Armstrong Plays W.C. Handy* ⚫⚫⚫⚫⚫ (Columbia, 1954/1997, prod. George Avakian) is a masterpiece with sensitive, swinging playing and singing by Armstrong, including one chorus on which his trumpet perfectly complements his vocalizing through thoughtful overdubbing. Be careful to get the CD version with the 11 original tracks and five bonus tracks. An earlier CD used a number of inferior alternate takes. One way to acquire all of the Armstrong-led sessions in chronological order from the mid-1920s through the mid-1940s, with discography information but without alternate takes, is to buy the 14 separate CDs released by the Classics label in the 1990s. The discs, which include earlier 78 rpm recordings from various labels, are not designated by volume number or name, but by recording years (e.g., 1926–1927, etc.). There are some weak tracks from the 1930s big band sessions, but the incredible quality and well-established historical value of the best garners the series the highest ranking.

what to buy next: If you're not interested in the entire Classics series, at least consider the following individual volumes, *Louis Armstrong: 1934–1936* ⚫⚫⚫⚫ (Classics, 1990, prod. Gilles Petard) and *Louis Armstrong: 1936–1937* ⚫⚫⚫⚫ (Classics, 1991, prod. Gilles Petard), which include the best of Armstrong's 1930s big band output, including a perfectly paced "Thanks a Million" and a delightfully exhibitionistic "Swing That Music." *Louis Armstrong: 1940–1942* ⚫⚫⚫⚫ (Classics, 1991) includes a reunion between Armstrong and soprano saxophonist Sidney Bechet, one of the few musicians to challenge Armstrong's solo powers in recording sessions. By November 1947, which is after the period currently covered by the Classics series, Armstrong's All Stars, with clarinetist Barney Bigard and trombonist

Jack Teagarden, had coalesced into a tightly knit, swinging unit, evidenced in *Satchmo at Symphony Hall* ⚫⚫⚫⚫ (Decca, 1950s/1996, reissue prod. Orrin Keepnews). Armstrong's mid-1950s remakes of some Hot Five and Hot Seven tunes are included in the limited edition 6-CD set, *The Complete Decca Studio Recordings of Louis Armstrong and the All-Stars* ⚫⚫⚫⚫ (Mosaic, prod. Michael Cuscuna) and are superior to the originals, but are offset by the inclusion of more commercial fare.

what to avoid: Most performances from Armstrong's twilight years were recorded and many of them have been issued (usually on small labels), with too often poor sound and/or less than spirited performances of a predictable repertoire. Avoid them, unless you can check them out first. Two examples are *Louis Armstrong: What a Wonderful World* ⚫⚫ (Milan, 1994) and *Louis Armstrong: Blueberry Hill* ⚫⚫ (Milan, 1992). Although Armstrong's indomitable spirit is evident, stay clear of the LP *Louis "Country & Western" Armstrong* ⚫ (Avco Embassy, prod. Ivan Mogull, Jack Clement).

best of the rest:

Louis Armstrong: Hello Dolly ⚫⚫⚫ (Kapp/MCA, 1964)
Armstrong/Ellington: Together for the First Time ⚫⚫⚫⚫ (Roulette, 1990)
Louis in New York, Vol. 5 ⚫⚫⚫⚫ (Columbia, 1990)
St. Louis Blues ⚫⚫⚫⚫ (Columbia, 1991)
Louis Armstrong: The Complete RCA Victor Recordings ⚫⚫⚫⚫ (4 CDs) (RCA, 1997)
Now You Has Jazz ⚫⚫⚫ (Rhino, 1997)
The Complete Ella Fitzgerald and Louis Armstrong ⚫⚫⚫⚫ (Verve, 1997)

worth searching for: *Satch Plays Fats* ⚫⚫⚫⚫ (Columbia, 1955, prod. George Avakian), featured the Armstrong All Stars in fine versions of Fats Waller compositions, some of which Armstrong had recorded when they were new. In what must have been an attempt to sell additional copies to collectors already owning the album, it was reissued on LP and CD using inferior alternate takes. Find the original, and hope for an honest CD reissue. *Louis Armstrong Plays W.C. Handy* (mentioned above) went through a history parallel to *Satch Plays Fats*, but was eventually reissued with the original takes, plus some rehearsal sequences. If you're interested in hearing about Louis Armstrong or are a jazz history buff, search for the following LPs: *Satchmo and Me* ⚫⚫⚫ (Riverside), on which the second Mrs. Armstrong, pianist Lil, tells of their days with King Oliver and the Hot Five and Seven sessions, and *Satchmo* ⚫⚫⚫ (Varese, 1976, prod. Dub Taylor), which features Satch in a 1954 interview.

influences:

◀◀ King Oliver, Freddie Keppard

Louis Armstrong **(Archive Photos)**

▶▶ Louis Prima, Red Allen, Roy Eldridge, Wingy Mannone, Harry James, Hot Lips Page

John K. Richmond

Lynn Arriale

Born in Milwaukee, WI.

Pianist Lynne Arriale embraces a full range of expressions in her recordings. From strongly blues-tinged offerings to elegant ballads, Arriale achieves a pleasing balance with an approach that is neither too dreamlike nor too reformist. Bolstered with a masters degree in classical training from the Wisconsin Conservatory of Music, Arriale triumphs in the jazz idiom, creating and conveying her fresh ideas with sensibly lean phrasing, pleasing harmonies, and unexpected rhythmic twists. She studied jazz with David Hazeltine in Milwaukee, and after playing the local scene as side player and leader, moved to NYC. Her first big break came in the summer of 1991 when she was invited to tour Japan with other American jazz piano greats as part of "100 Golden Fingers." Shortly after, she guested on Marian McPartland's National Public Radio show, *Piano Jazz*. Arriale gained broader exposure after winning the 1993 International Great American Jazz Piano competition, and signed with DMP. Arriale has earned widespread media acclaim for her rich lyricism, harmonic sophistication, abundant passion, and fine art of improvisation.

what to buy: Arriale's third DMP album, *The Lynne Arriale Trio: With Words Unspoken* ♫♫♫♫ (DMP, 1996, prod. Lynne Arriale, Tom Jung) features her trio with bassist Drew Gress and drummer Steve Davis. Delivering six romantic standards and three originals, mainstream jazz fare similar to earlier outings, Arriale engages in interactive "conversation" with her sidemen. Davis creatively sculpts each tune with grandeur, and Gress is compatibly warm and lissome. Whether mining standards or mapping originals, this exceptional trio maintains an observant edge, reinventing classics such as Gillespie's "Woody n' You," Monk's "Think of One," Jimmy Rowles's "The Peacocks," and Gershwin's "I Loves You Porgy." A magnificent album! Arriale's second album for the label, *When You Listen* ♫♫♫♫ (DMP, 1995, prod. Lynne Arriale, Tom Jung) demonstrates her penchant for picking and writing material accessible to the listener, and then leading her creative cohorts, bassist Drew Gress and drummer Steve Davis, to stimulating heights on fresh interpretations of lush romantic standards such as "How Deep Is the Ocean," "In the Wee Small Hours of the Morning," "My Shining Hour," and more of her appealing originals.

what to buy next: *The Lynne Arriale Trio: The Eyes Have It* ♫♫♫♫ (DMP, 1994, prod. Lynne Arriale, Tom Jung), Arriale's debut DMP album with drummer Steve Davis and bassist Jay Anderson, introduces her virtuosity, sublime technique, and thoughtful elegance on a mix of 10 classics and originals. Destined to become the earmark of all her recordings, Arriale aims at creating amazingly fresh arrangements of familiar favorites. The shifting time signatures on "Witchcraft," an up-tempo version of "Yesterdays," a totally fresh reading of "Alone Together," are prime examples of her artistry in a trio setting.

the rest:
A Long Road Home ♫♫♫♫ (TCB, 1997)

solo outings:
Steve Davis:
Songs We Know ♫♫♫ (DMP, 1996)

influences:
◀◀ Keith Jarrett, Tommy Flanagan, Hank Jones, Kenny Barron

Nancy Ann Lee

Art Ensemble of Chicago

Formed 1969, in Chicago, IL.

Roscoe Mitchell, saxophones and various reed, wind, and percussion instruments; Joseph Jarman, saxophones and various reed, wind, and percussion instruments (1969–93); Lester Bowie, trumpet; Malachi Favors, bass; Famoudou Don Moye, percussion (1970–present).

The Art Ensemble of Chicago's formation was fostered by the boisterous 1960s laboratory of the windy city's Association for the Advancement of Creative Musicians (AACM), within which the members who would become the Art Ensemble ran some of the most important musical experiments with one another and various others. Both Lester Bowie and Malachi Favors were in on Roscoe Mitchell's debut 1966 recording *Sound*, for example, which was a signal recording for the entire movement with its embrace of silence, textural concerns, improvisational nerve and compositional savvy. It was an early expression of the breadth of the AACM credo of "Great Black Music," Bowie's coinage for an all-encompassing umbrella covering everything from gut-bucket to the freedom styles of Ornette Coleman, John Coltrane, and Albert Ayler. Bowie and Favors were among Mitchell's most important collaborators over the next few years. Joseph Jarman joined that trio on Bowie's now out-of-print *Nos. 1 & 2* sessions in 1967, and permanently in 1969 following the collapse of his own group after the deaths of promising pianist Chris Gaddy and bassist Charles Clark. Then known as the Art Ensemble, this drummerless quartet appended "Chicago" to their moniker on arriving in Paris for a two-year stay. Playing a plethora of instruments—including everything from kazoos to parade drums—they took their music in an almost mind-blowing number of directions, from extensions of the New York avant garde to proto-punk rock to wacked-out marches to subtle pastel landscapes to twisted bop. The addition of the appropriately resourceful percussionist Don Moye in 1970 brought the group new power and propulsion, although it also made them a more conventional outfit that *could* call a standard rhythm section into play. They continued to make strong records into the 1980s as their individual careers came to loom larger than the AEC, but by the 1990s there was a question (on record at least) of what was left to say as a group. In 1993 founding member Jarman left, announcing his retirement from music to pursue his long-standing interest in Buddhism (he is an ordained Shinshu priest). He has since returned to music, and has performed sessions with Myra Melford, Marilyn Crispell, and Leroy Jenkins. Bowie was quoted in 1993, saying Jarman "can come back to the band anytime he feels like it." In the meantime, the group was making plans to record for the first time since Jarman's departure.

what to buy: Out-there-but-darn-friendly was the subtext of *Nice Guys* ⚜⚜⚜⚜ (ECM, 1979/1994, prod. Manfred Eicher), which remains the most accessible introduction to the AEC's range and power. The record comprises a mid-length cut, including an almost giddy, reggae-influenced ditty about Bowie's affection for Jamaica, slowly transmuting sonic textures both pleasant and mysterious, and a full-blown rave, "Dreaming of the Master," that moves with cocky cool on the edge of an explosion that takes the quintet into unbridled overdrive. Having been thus introduced to the AEC in so many cuts, try their non-stop live "manifestation" (part medley, part cue-system improv, part on-the-fly, whatever) at full gale force in the double-CD set *Urban Bushmen* ⚜⚜⚜⚜ (ECM, 1982/1994, prod. Manfred Eicher). Arguably the best live document of a band that is best live, *Bushmen* ranges from a percussion processional to the poignancy of Bowie's ballad "New York is Full of Lonely People," to the kaleidoscopic abstractions of Mitchell's "Uncle," to the flag-waving closer, "Odwalla," built on the ballast of twin bass saxophones dancing a funkafied second line while Bowie slings fleet trumpet riffs overhead. It all flows seamlessly for an hour and a half.

what to buy next: *Full Force* ⚜⚜⚜ (ECM, 1980/1994, prod. Manfred Eicher) and *Third Decade* ⚜⚜⚜ (ECM, 1985/1994, prod. Manfred Eicher) follow the *Nice Guys* outre variety-show approach. The former gives a full side over to a rare Favors com-

LOUIS ARMSTRONG

song "West End Blues"
album Louis Armstrong, Volume IV: Louis Armstrong and Earl Hines
(Columbia, 1928/1989)
instrument Trumpet

Monster Solo

position that builds from silence (an AEC staple), only to wail over a Favors ostinato and reach resolution in a intricate, sunshiny 45-second Mitchell composition. The latter includes one of the more unusual AEC pieces, "Prayer for Jimbo Kwesi," evoking the sound of military music of centuries gone by. *The Spiritual* ⚜⚜⚜⚜ (Black Lion, 1997, prod. Chris Whent, Alan Bates) and *Tutankhamun* ⚜⚜⚜⚜ (Black Lion, 1997, prod. Chris Whent, Alan Bates) catch the AEC's quartet era when surreal, avant jug-band theatrics filled a good deal of the musical space left by the absence of a drummer. *Tutankhamun* fades from a sort of spoken pseudo-language into a sort of musical drama. *The Spiritual* evokes a tale of plantation rebellion and violence, tells us "that song ain't got no name, it's just a spiritual," and gives way to a surreal hoe-down and mysterious cacophony.

best of the rest:
Dreaming of the Masters, Volume I: Ancient to the Future ⚜⚜⚜ (DIW, 1987)
The Alternate Express ⚜⚜⚜⚜ (DIW, 1989/1994)
(With Lester Bowie's Brass Fantasy) *The Art Ensemble of Chicago and Lester Bowie's Brass Fantasy* ⚜⚜⚜ (DIW, 1990)

Live ♪♪♪♪ (Delmark, 1991)
Dreaming of the Masters, Volume II: Thelonious Sphere Monk ♪♪♪♪ (DIW, 1991)
America-South Africa ♪♪♪ (DIW, 1991)

worth searching for: The limited edition five-CD *The Art Ensemble 1967/68* ♪♪♪♪ (Nessa, 1993) anthologizes early LPs and previously unavailable sessions led by Bowie and Mitchell. It includes the first session with the Bowie-Mitchell-Favors-Jarman line-up, which would be dubbed the Art Ensemble of Chicago after arriving in Paris in 1969. The many out-of-print vinyl gems include *Bap-Tizum* ♪♪♪♪ (Atlantic, 1973); *Fanfare for the Warriors* ♪♪♪♪♪ (Atlantic, 1974) with pianist Muhal Richard Abrams; *Kabalaba* ♪♪♪♪♪ (AECO, 1978), also with Abrams; *People in Sorrow* ♪♪♪♪♪ (Nessa, 1969), a masterpiece of slowly unfolding dynamics; and a soundtrack album, *Les Stance à Sophie* ♪♪♪♪ (Nessa, 1970), featuring Fontella Bass on an AEC jam just made for a dance-hall discovery.

solo outings:
Lester Bowie:
All the Magic! /The One and Only ♪♪♪♪ (ECM, 1994)
The Great Pretender ♪♪♪♪ (ECM, 1994)
Works ♪♪♪♪♪ (ECM, 1994)
(With Lester Bowie's Brass Fantasy) *Avant Pop* ♪♪♪ (ECM, 1994)
(With Lester Bowie's Brass Fantasy) *I Only Have Eyes for You* ♪♪♪ (ECM, 1994)
The Fifth Power ♪♪♪♪ (Black Saint, 1994)
Funky T Cool T ♪♪♪♪ (DIW, 1994)
(With Lester Bowie's Brass Fantasy Band) *The Fire This Time* ♪♪♪♪♪ (In & Out, 1995)

Roscoe Mitchell:
(With the Sound Ensemble) *Nonaah* ♪♪♪♪ (Nessa, 1976)
(With the Sound Ensemble) *Snurdy McGurdy and Her Dancing Shoes* (Nessa, 1980)
(With the Sound Ensemble) *3 X 4 Eye* ♪♪♪♪ (Black Saint, 1981/1994)
(With the Sound Ensemble) *Sound and Space Ensembles* ♪♪♪♪ (Black Saint, 1983/1994)
(With the Sound Ensemble) *Live at the Knitting Factory* ♪♪♪ (Black Saint, 1990)
Songs in the Wind ♪♪♪♪ (Victo, 1991)
(With the Scandinavian Brus Trio) *After Fallen Leaves* ♪♪♪♪ (Silkheart, 1992)
(With the Note Factory) *This Dance Is for Steve McCall* ♪♪♪♪♪ (Black Saint, 1993)
The Flow of Things ♪♪♪♪ (Black Saint, 1994)
Hey, Donald ♪♪♪♪ (Delmark, 1995)
(With Borah Bergman and Tom Buckner) *First Meeting* ♪♪♪♪ (Knitting Factory Works, 1995)
Sound ♪♪♪♪ (Delmark, 1996)
Sound Songs ♪♪♪♪ (Delmark, 1997)

Joseph Jarman:
Sunbound Volume I ♪♪♪♪♪ (AECO, 1978)
Song For ♪♪♪♪♪ (Delmark, 1991)
As If It Were Seasons ♪♪♪♪ (Delmark, 1996)
(With Famoudou Don Moye) *Egwu-Anwu* ♪♪♪♪ (India Navigation, 1997)
(With Marilyn Crispell) *Connecting Spirits* ♪♪♪♪♪ (Music & Arts, 1997)

Famoudou Don Moye:
Sun Percussion Volume I ♪♪♪♪♪ (AECO, 1975)
Jam for Your Life ♪♪♪♪ (AECO, 1991)
(With Enoch Williamson) *Afrikan Song* ♪♪♪♪ (AECO/Southport, 1996)

influences:

◀◀ Thelonious Monk, Ornette Coleman, John Coltrane, Albert Ayler, George Russell, Eric Dolphy, Sun Ra, Duke Ellington

▶▶ Oliver Lake, Julius Hemphill, Revolutionary Ensemble, John Zorn

see also: *Lester Bowie, Joseph Jarman, Famoudou Don Moye, Roscoe Mitchell*

W. Kim Heron

Dorothy Ashby

Born August 6, 1932, in Detroit, MI. Died April 13, 1986, in Santa Monica, CA.

It's a notoriously temperamental instrument, going out of tune with the slightest change in temperature or humidity, but jazz harp swings and all because Dorothy Ashby made it do so. While not the first jazz harpist recorded (Casper Reardon gets the nod for that one, recording with Jack Teagarden in 1934), she is arguably the most important, Alice Coltrane and Deborah Henson-Conant not withstanding. Originally a pianist at Wayne State University, Ashby switched to harp in 1952 and with a great deal of perseverance (insisting on leading groups herself in an effort to be taken seriously as a jazz player) she made her first recording in 1956. She made albums for (among others) Savoy, Prestige, Cadet, and Atlantic, including a harp transcription of Rodrigo's "Concierto de Aranjuez," the same work that Miles Davis and Gil Evans arranged on *Sketches of Spain*.

what to buy: The delightful *In a Minor Groove* ♪♪♪♪ (Prestige, 1958, prod. Bob Weinstock) deserves to be heard by more people. It's actually a combination of two albums, *Hip Harp* and *In a Minor Groove*, with co-leaders Ashby and flutist Frank Wess. Herman Wright is the bassist on both sessions, with the drum chair switching from Art Taylor (the first seven tracks) to Roy Haynes. The album opens up with an Ashby composition, "Pawky," where she plays the harp as if it were an especially gifted guitar while Wess has his extended solo. Then she jumps in with a set of runs that include the occasional glissando along with some single-note riffing that sounds Wes Montgomery-esque. Wright's solo follows before Ashby jumps in again to vamp the way out with Wess following behind. In other words, it's another typical jazz album, with good tunes played by top-notch soloists and sympathetic rhythm support. Ashby probably wanted it that way.

what to buy next: Ashby's first solo album, *The Jazz Harpist* ♪♪♪ (Savoy, 1956, prod. Ozzie Cadena), also has Wess on flute, plus Ed Thigpen on drums, and Eddie Jones and Wendell Marshall splitting bass chores. It's interesting to hear the harpist developing a style that made her more than just a novelty, but you also get to check out how difficult it is breaking the stereotypical mold of the instrument, even for Ashby. The beginnings of her mature style can be heard in "Aeolian Groove" when she trades fours with Wess.

influences:
▶▶ Deborah Henson-Conant

Garaud MacTaggart

Eden Atwood

Born January 11, 1969, in Memphis, TN.

Skirting the line between cabaret and jazz, Eden Atwood is a singer who interprets lyrics with dramatic flair, though her emotional readings don't involve much improvisation. She has a small, attractive voice that can be effective on ballads, but so far she's interesting more for her potential than for anything she's recorded. Raised in a musical family (her father, Hub Atwood, was a composer/arranger who worked with Frank Sinatra and Harry James), Eden grew up in Montana with her mother, where she studied drama and musical theatre at the University of Montana. At age 19, she moved to Chicago where she performed at the Gold Star Sardine Bar. After stints in acting and modeling, she decided to devote herself to singing full time. She has performed at many of New York's leading rooms, including Michael's Pub and Tavern on the Green, and major jazz events such as the North Sea and Fujitsu-Concord festivals. She has recorded four albums for Concord.

what to buy: Eden Atwood's second album, *Cat on a Hot Tin Roof* ♪♪♪ (Concord Jazz, 1994, prod. Carl E. Jefferson) is an enjoyable session featuring first-rate accompanists such as pianist Allen Farnham, drummer Alan Dawson, alto saxophonist Jesse Davis, and clarinetist/tenor saxophonist Ken Peplowski (who gets to stretch out on a number of tunes). Though at

times she comes across as trying too hard to project emotion into a tune, she swings convincingly on Johnny Mercer's and Marian McPartland's "Twilight World," and makes fine use of her attractive voice on Yip Harburg's and Harold Arlen's "Right As Rain." Most impressive, however, are the title track and "Silent Movie," which showcase her considerable talent as a lyricist. Both tunes deserve to be recorded by other singers.

what to buy next: Atwood knows her way around a ballad, though on *A Night in the Life* ♪♪♪ (Concord Jazz, 1996, prod. Allen Farnham) her choice of material tends toward the well trod. Accompanied by pianist Jeremy Kahn, bassist Larry Kohut, and drummer Joel Spencer, Atwood is especially effective on "Spring Can Really Hang You up the Most," where she's joined by Chris Potter on tenor sax (he sits in on four tunes). Her readings of standards can come across as a little overwrought, such as her duet with Kahn on "The Folks Who Live on the Hill," but her desire to wring every ounce of emotion out of a tune might appeal to some.

the rest:
No One Ever Tells You ♪♪♪ (Concord Jazz, 1992)
There Again ♪♪♪ (Concord Jazz, 1995)

influences:
◀◀ Abbey Lincoln, Shirley Horn, Sarah Vaughan

Andrew Gilbert

Brian Auger

Born 1939, in London, England.

Auger was an award-winning, hard bop-oriented jazz pianist when he opted for an R&B-oriented rhythm section in 1964, much to the dismay of London's jazz aficionados. His first band, Trinity, started up in that year and featured bassist Rick Laird and guitarist John McLaughlin (who later went on to play with Miles Davis and form the Mahavishnu Orchestra with Laird). A few months later the lineup changed again, with Auger switching to organ and picking up a new rhythm section. During this time he was also doing a lot of studio work, including playing harpsichord on the Yardbirds hit "For Your Love."

Subsequent editions of Trinity often featured a young singer named Julie Driscoll, whose vocals owed a lot to her admiration of Nina Simone. By this time the band's hybrid approach to rock and jazz was established, and they had several British hits, including their take on Bob Dylan's "This Wheel's on Fire," later used as the theme for the British television comedy series *Absolutely Fabulous.* They were also the first fusion band to play the Montreux and Berlin Jazz Festivals. In the early 1970s, after hearing *In a Silent Way* by Miles Davis, Auger formed the Oblivion Express with a revolving lineup of musicians that concentrated on jazz fusion styles. By 1973 Auger had moved to the States and released the album *Closer to It*, which landed on *Billboard*'s rock, jazz, and R&B charts. At first Auger performed all the vocals in an earnest manner, but later editions of the band with singer Alex Ligertwood, while weaker in terms of material, were stronger vocally and as a concert headliner.

These days Auger is once again releasing albums under his own name and has achieved a certain notoriety in the acid jazz community when his versions of "Indian Rope Man" and "Light My Fire" were used in samples by young British chart toppers. One Way Records, a company specializing in reissues, has most of Auger's back catalog.

what to buy: *Closer to It* 𝄢𝄢𝄢 (1973, One Way Records reissue, prod. Brian Auger) by Brian Auger and the Oblivion Express is a good sample of Auger's jazz-rock fusion. It features Auger's Jimmy Smith–derived keyboard playing on Eugene McDaniels's "Compared to What" and Marvin Gaye's "Inner City Blues," along with four originals in a programming formula that was to last as long as the band was performing.

what to buy next: On *Encore* 𝄢𝄢𝄢 (1978, One Way Records reissue, prod. Brian Auger), Auger reunited with Julie Tippetts (née Driscoll). It features cover tunes from Milton Nascimento, Al Jarreau, and Pops Staples plus two Auger originals. Tippetts had, by this time, already done a lot of work in Britain's free jazz community with her husband Keith Tippetts in addition to performing with some avant-garde vocal ensembles, so she was far closer to the cutting edge of what was happening in European jazz at the time than was Auger. While Auger had done all of the production and arranging for this album, it was Tippetts who provided the artistic focus. The Nina Simone influence in her singing was still noticeable but Tippetts had taken those elements and fashioned a mature style with its own power, something which would transform pop tunes such as "Don't Let Me Be Misunderstood" into emotional gutwrenchers.

best of the rest:
(With the Trinity) *Jools and Brian* 𝄢𝄢 (1969, One Way Records)
(With the Trinity) *Befour* 𝄢𝄢 (1970, One Way Records)
(With the Oblivion Express) *Straight Ahead* 𝄢𝄢𝄢 (1973, One Way Records)
(With the Oblivion Express) *The Best of Brian Auger's Oblivion Express* 𝄢𝄢𝄢 (1996, One Way Records)
The Best of Brian Auger 𝄢𝄢𝄢𝄢 (1997, One Way Records)

worth searching for: The high point, artistically speaking, of Julie Driscoll's stay with Brian Auger came on a two-LP set *Street Noise* 𝄢𝄢𝄢𝄢 (Atco, 1969, prod. Giorgio Gomelsky) which featured cover art by Ralph Steadman, an interesting version of the Miles Davis tune "All Blues," and a chilling rendition of an old folk song, "When I Was a Young Girl." Auger's organ playing was solidly in the Jimmy Smith tradition on many of the more up-tempo numbers.

influences:
◀◀ Jimmy Smith

▶▶ Jimmy Z, Barbara Dennerlein

Garaud MacTaggart

Avenue Blue /Jeff Golub

Formed early 1990s, in Los Angeles.

Jeff Golub (born April 15, 1955, in Akron, OH), guitarist; Jim Biggins, saxophone; Lincoln Goines, bass; Steve Gaboury, keyboards; Jeff Levine, organ; Steve Barbuto, drums; Roger Squitero, percussion.

Led by accomplished guitarist Jeff Golub, Avenue Blue is one of contemporary jazz's most versatile ensembles; its repertoire includes blues, jazz, pop, rock, R&B, and funk. Golub began playing guitar at age eight and was drawn to the blues in general and to jazz guitar icon Wes Montgomery in specific. Educated at Boston's Berklee College of Music, Golub performed throughout the Boston area, but upon relocating to New York in 1980, he decided to concentrate more on rock and pop. Golub then spent several years as a sideman, performing with rock artists like Billy Squier and Peter Wolf, as well as with jazz saxophonist Bill Evans. In 1988 he began a seven-year association with Rod Stewart, and met his longtime producer and collaborator, trumpeter Rick Braun. Golub formed Avenue Blue to incorporate a variety of styles, especially blues, but always improvisational. The group has become a chart-topping staple on smooth-jazz radio, and Golub continues to perform as a session musician for commercials, soundtracks, and artists such as Vanessa Williams, Bob James, and Ashford and Simpson.

what to buy: *Avenue Blue* 𝄢𝄢𝄢 (Bluemoon, 1994, prod. Rick Braun) is a well-crafted first effort that amply demonstrates the band's musical aptitude and versatility, from the bluesy "West Side Serenade" to the Jeff Beck-esque "Stockholm" to the lovely acoustic ballad "Atlanta Nights." The group's jazzy side is showcased on the spirited ensemble piece "Lucy, I'm Home," which suddenly turns Brazilian before returning to its main theme, and a swinging trio version of Henry Mancini's classic "Moon River."

what to buy next: *Naked City* ♫♫♫ (Mesa/Bluemoon, 1996, prod. Rick Braun, Jeff Golub) is a bit jazzier than its predecessor, *Avenue Blue*, especially on "The Conversation," in which Golub and guest Bob James trade licks comfortably. Other standout tracks include the spirited retro jazz-blues-funk hybrid "Mama Didn't Raise No Fool" and the lively jam "Yohimbe," featuring a nice flute turn by Jim Biggins.

the rest:
Nightlife ♫♫♫♪ (Mesa/Bluemoon, 1997)

worth searching for: The core band on Jeff Golub's out-of-print *Unspoken Words* ♫♫♫ (Gaia, 1988, prod. Jeff Golub) includes familiar names: Jim Biggins and Steve Gaboury are in Avenue Blue, and the other two members of the quintet, Chris Bishop (bass) and Michael Dawe (drums), were heard with the rest on two tracks on *Avenue Blue*. But this album sounds a bit different from Avenue Blue the band, with more 1980s production, more scorching guitar solos, and more variety of mood.

influences:
◀◀ B.B. King, Albert King, Jeff Beck, Wes Montgomery
▶▶ Chieli Minucci

Lucy Tauss and Steve Holtje

Teodross Avery
Born July 2, 1973, in Fairfield, CA.

Born in a suburb of Oakland, Avery was encouraged by his father to study classical guitar at age 10. He switched to alto sax at 13, then to tenor, and was influenced to play jazz by his dad's record collections, which featured John Coltrane, Jimi Hendrix, Rahsaan Roland Kirk, Eddie Harris, and Dexter Gordon. He spent his high school years sitting in with Art Blakey, Donald Byrd, Branford and Wynton Marsalis, and other artists when they visited the Bay Area, and studied with Joe Henderson, and then attended Berklee College of Music. Avery made his first album appearance on drummer Carl Allen's *Pursuer* in 1993. The next year he released his debut as a leader. He shows considerable promise as a player and writer and seems to have strong major-label support, but it's too early to tell, on the strength of just two uneven albums, whether his promise can be fulfilled.

what to buy: Avery's debut, *In Other Words* ♫♫♫♪ (GRP, 1994, prod. Michael Cuscuna) was made with his regular quartet, in-cluding pianist Charles Craig, bassist Reuben Rogers, and drummer Mark Simmons. Trumpeter Roy Hargrove sits in on three tunes. The practiced interaction of the quartet, and Avery's solid post-bop writing, are the setting for his amalgamation of the Dex and Trane strains in his playing, making for a pleasant if not quite distinctive set.

what to buy next: Avery's compositions are still a strong point on most of *My Generation* ♫♫♫ (Impulse!, 1996, prod. Carl Griffin), but the switch to a different rhythm section and a procession of guest guitarists (John Scofield, Mark Whitfield, Peter Bernstein), with Craig playing piano on only four tracks, diffuses the album's focus. The half-hearted attempts to fulfill the album's title include covers of Nick Cave and Janet Jackson songs and an uncompelling rap number with a hip-hop flavor.

worth searching for: The Los Angeles group Black/Note's *Nothin' But the Swing* ♫♫♫ (Impulse!, 1996, prod. Mark Anthony Shelby, Willie Jones III) has two guest shots by Avery, including "Gettin' Your Trane On," which caters to his strengths as an improvisor.

influences:
◀◀ John Coltrane

Steve Holtje

Roy Ayers
Born September 19, 1940, in Los Angeles, CA.

The legend of Roy Ayers begins when he was five years old and was presented with a pair of mallets by jazz vibraphonist Lionel Hampton. Maybe that had something to do with his choice to switch from piano to vibes when he was in high school. In his early 20s, an accomplished Ayers played with jazz luminaries such as Teddy Edwards, Chico Hamilton, Wayne Henderson, and Gerald Wilson's big band on the Los Angeles scene. During the mid-1960s he signed with Atlantic. Ayers played with the renowned jazz flutist Herbie Mann from 1966 to 1970, recording on Mann's huge hit, *Memphis Underground* and recording his first three records on the label under Mann's production expertise. Ayers left Mann in 1970 and formed his group, Ubiquity, featuring drummer Billy Cobham, guitarist George Benson, trombonist Wayne Henderson, and vocalist Dee Dee Bridgewater. Ayers signed with Polydor and released several critically acclaimed jazz records featuring soulful performers such as Sonny Fortune, Billy Cobham, Omar Hakim, and Alphonse Mouzon. In 1976 Ayers bravely stepped away from the warm embrace of jazz circles by experimenting with the sounds of R&B on *Mystic Voyage* and

Everybody Loves Sunshine. His undaunted innovations paid off when both records charted, and fans of electrified funk-soul jazz followed him reluctantly through a series of ever-changing styles. After 1977's *Vibrations*, Ayers entered a mellow period that yielded softer, smoother grooves. In 1980 he toured Africa with Fela Anikulapo-Kuti and made *Africa, Center of the World*. As much as he has been inspired by his collaborations and tours with artists from around the world, Ayers has been an inspiration to many. On April 6, 1986, the city of Los Angeles celebrated an official "Roy Ayers Day." After some experimentation with hip-hop/jazz blends in the early 1990s with various artists, Ayers has returned to jazz, recording as leader a series of soul-influenced records for Ronnie Scott's Jazz House label. The recent Verve reissue of the live-recorded Ayers performance at the 1972 Montreux Festival, containing straight-ahead, fusion, and soul-influenced jazz styles should bring his playing to the forefront for new fans.

what to buy: The two discs of *Evolution: The Polydor Anthology* 𝄢𝄢𝄢𝄢 (Polydor, 1995. prod. various) offer a thorough overview featuring guest artists such as Fortune, Cobham, Ron Carter, and Gloria Jones. The tracks were originally produced by Roy Ayers, Myrnaleah Williams, and Jerry Schoenbaum.

what to buy next: Check out Ayer's *Mystic Voyage* 𝄢𝄢𝄢 (Polydor, 1976/1993, prod. Roy Ayers), his first full-fledged foray into the R&B world, which benefitted from his tasty fusion sensibility.

best of the rest:
Roy Ayers: Live at the Montreux Jazz Festival 𝄢𝄢𝄢𝄢 (Verve, 1972/1996)
Wake Up 𝄢𝄢𝄢 (Ichiban, 1990)
Everybody Loves the Sunshine 𝄢𝄢𝄢 (Polydor, 1993)
Naste' 𝄢𝄢𝄢 (RCA, 1995)
Searchin' 𝄢𝄢𝄢 (Ronnie Scott's Jazz House, 1996)
Best of Roy Ayers 𝄢𝄢𝄢𝄢 (Polydor, 1997)

worth searching for: Search the used bins for the vinyl edition of flutist Herbie Mann's *Impressions of the Middle East* 𝄢𝄢𝄢𝄢 (Atlantic, 1966, prod. Nesuhi Ertegun, Arif Mardin), an album on which Ayers contributes his impressions of Turkish music melded to jazz. Ayers is also featured on the more popular Mann album, *Memphis Underground* 𝄢𝄢𝄢𝄢 (Atlantic, 1969) with guitarists Larry Coryell and Sonny Sharrock. The danceable R&B beats, tinged with Memphis-inspired sound, offer an appealing (though perhaps dated) listen.

influences:
◄◄ Lionel Hampton, Herbie Mann
►► A Tribe Called Quest, Guru (of Gang Starr), Brand Nubian, Galliano, Groove Collective

Norene Cashen and Nancy Ann Lee

Albert Ayler
Born July 13, 1936, in Cleveland, OH. Died November 25, 1973, in New York, NY.

Albert Ayler's first "professional" gigs were as a ten-year-old alto player in a Cleveland group—led by his tenor-playing father—that played at funerals. Other than historical curiosity, this fact is relevant because the two things that punctuated all of his playing were honest, gut-level emotion and an overwhelming sense of mournful searching. That the combination of these two elements has made Ayler one of the most reviled and revered players in the genre is testament only to how seamlessly he melded them. From his first major impact on the burgeoning "New Thing" scene—a performance with Cecil Taylor's trio at New York's Philharmonic Hall on New Year's Eve, 1963—through his groundbreaking oeuvre of solo work to the day his body was found floating in the Hudson River, every time Ayler played, someone was amazed and someone was disgusted.

Initially joining Taylor's group in late 1962 for a tour of Scandinavia, Ayler's return to U.S. soil was brief, and he soon found himself back in Denmark, performing live and recording his first dates for far more money than he could have possibly made in the States. On these early sessions, Ayler's squonky, New Orleans-style bellow was in its nascency. It wasn't until his return to New York that Ayler would fully hit his stride. By connecting with Don Cherry and Sunny Murray, he found compatible souls and—most notably on the stirring *Witches and Devils* sessions (with Murray, Henry Grimes, and Norman Howard—began making the kind of soulfully free music for which he would be known. By the time Ayler recorded his landmark *Spiritual Unity* in 1964, he was shattering senses on every level. Longtime aficionados of free music, barely able to get their ears around a decade of Ornette Coleman, John Coltrane, and Taylor, were faced with an entirely different mode of attack. Ayler pared the blues to its most basic emotional elements, playing furiously and without restraint. Most people truly didn't know what to make of it. A series of groundbreaking concerts and albums followed, but Ayler was distraught over the negative criticism hurled his way. Unable to understand why equally emotional players such as Coltrane were not only respected but well paid, Ayler assumed it was because he wasn't playing the right kind of music and turned out an alarming chain of polished "free R&B" records in pursuit of a hit. Of course, they weren't hits and, seeing no hope for his future, Ayler took his own life.

what to buy: The frenzied emotional interplay between the trio on the live *Spiritual Unity* 𝄢𝄢𝄢𝄢 (ESP-Disk, 1964) is a landmark of the genre and Ayler's heartachingly honest playing is at a peak. The anthemic "Ghosts," a final, ten-minute climax, is devastating: No matter what anybody tells you, this is not untrained, it's just unharnessed. Recorded at two performances, *In Greenwich Village* 🎵🎵🎵🎵 (Impulse!, 1967, prod. Bob Thiele) captures the essence of Ayler's latter, pre-polish period. It captures Ayler at a focused, clear, and powerfully creative point.

what to buy next: For *Vibrations* 🎵🎵🎵🎵 (Freedom, 1964, prod. Alan Bates), Don Cherry's fiercely poetic cornet is added to the trio and, again with "Ghosts" as a centerpiece, this studio set demonstrates how integral interaction was to Ayler's improvisations. The studio sessions from 1967 and 1968 on *Love Cry* 🎵🎵🎵🎵 (Impulse!, 1968, prod. Bob Thiele) suffer only in comparison to the live fire of the Greenwich Village shows. The album is essential both for the mind-bendingly powerful "Universal Indians" and the fact that this is perhaps the only album where Ayler cleanly delivered his pro-black freedom message without resorting to the oddities on his soon-to-come vocal records.

the rest:
The First Recording, Volume II 🎵🎵 (1962/DIW, 1990)
My Name Is Albert Ayler 🎵🎵🎵 (Black Lion, 1963)
Goin' Home 🎵🎵🎵 (Black Lion, 1964)
Witches and Devils 🎵🎵🎵🎵 (Freedom, 1964)
The Hilversum Session 🎵🎵🎵🎵 (Coppens, 1964)
Bells/Prophecy 🎵🎵🎵 (ESP-Disk, 1964)
Spirits Rejoice 🎵🎵🎵🎵 (ESP-Disk, 1965)
New York Eye & Ear Control 🎵🎵🎵 (ESP-Disk, 1965)
At Slugs Saloon, Volumes I and II 🎵🎵🎵🎵 (ESP-Disk, 1966)
Lorrach/Paris 🎵🎵🎵 (hat ART, 1966)

worth searching for: In all likelihood, *Music Is the Healing Force of the Universe* 🎵🎵🎵🎵 (Impulse!, 1969, prod. Ed Michel) will never be reissued on CD, since it—in some people's minds—is part of the rash of "sell-out" records Ayler recorded before his death. But in actuality, none of them are that bad; they're just not jazz. However, all of them are brimming with black-power messages, odd instrumentation, uplifting sentiments, and Ayler's unmistakable tone. His playing is simultaneously ferocious and restrained.

influences:
◀◀ Charlie Parker, Illinois Jacquet

▶▶ John Coltrane, Pharoah Sanders, Frank Wright, Roscoe Mitchell, David Murray, Charles Gayle, Assif Tsahar

Jason Ferguson

Albert Ayler

song "Change Has Come"

album *Albert Ayler in Greenwich Village* (Impulse!, 1967)

instrument Tenor saxophone

Monster Solo

B

Mr. B

Born Mark Lincoln Braun, February 19, 1957, in Flint, MI.

Mark Braun started playing piano at the relatively late age of 16, soon after his father gave him a Jimmy Yancey album. The subtle boogie of this relatively unsung master of the blues piano became a gateway for Braun's budding musical interest. The moment he met journeyman pianist Boogie Woogie Red (who used to record with John Lee Hooker), Braun realized he had found the talented and well-traveled instructor who was willing to induct him into the ways of a bluesman. Under the tutelage of his new-found teacher, Braun practiced until he was strong enough to go out on his own. A few years later, while playing in various bars around southeastern Michigan, Braun acquired his nickname from the Ann Arbor-based blues guitarist Steve Nardella. Now dubbed Mr. B, Braun was not content playing only the standard boogie-woogie blues riffs, and became an avid listener to many of the funkier jazz keyboard players, such as Ray Bryant, Bobby Timmons, and Gene Harris. While he doesn't consider himself to be a jazz pianist ("I don't know 200 standards to play off"), Mr. B believes that he is more than a blues musician, a belief borne out by his performances since the early 1990s.

what to buy: *Hallelujah Train* ✻✻✻✻ (Schoolkids, 1995, prod. Mr. B, Paul Keller) is an exciting example of big band jump and boogie. B's driving piano and occasional vocals front a ten-piece horn section in a well-recorded live session that kicks, screams, and moans with the best of them. Particularly notable is the horn arrangement (by trumpeter Paul Finkbeiner) on "My Sunday Best" that starts in church before heading uptown for some fiery honking and wailing.

what to buy next: The best parts of the live *My Sunday Best* ✻✻✻✻ (Schoolkids, 1991, prod. Jean-Michel Creviere) are solo performances, such as the title tune, but the duo and trio recordings are still pretty good. B's playing hovers between his boogie-woogie roots and the funk of 1960s-era Horace Silver or Bobby Timmons.

the rest:
Shining the Pearls ✻✻✻ (Blind Pig, 1995)

influences:
◄◄ Boogie Woogie Red, Little Brother Montgomery, Ray Bryant, Horace Silver, Gene Harris, Bobby Timmons, Jimmy Yancey

Garaud MacTaggart

B Sharp Jazz Quartet

Formed 1990s.

Randall Willis, alto, tenor, soprano saxophones (1993–present); Herb Graham Jr., drums (1993–present); Reggie Carson, bass (1993–95); Eliot Douglass, piano (1993–94); Rodney Lee, piano, Hammond B3 organ (1994–present); Osama Afifi, bass (1995–present).

One of the best young groups to emerge from the Los Angeles jazz scene in the 1990s, B Sharp uses hard bop as a jumping-off point for more adventurous explorations. Co-led by drummer Herb Graham Jr. and saxophonist Randall Willis (who are responsible for most of the band's tunes and arrangements), B Sharp evolved out of Billy Higgins's World Stage performance space and Fifth Street Dick's coffee house in the Los Angeles Crenshaw District in the early 1990s. The band has undergone a number of personnel

changes, but powered by Graham's driving drum work, B Sharp continues to incorporate new influences, from funk and hip hop to avant garde, while never forgetting to swing like hell. The band has released three strong albums on the MAMA Foundation label.

what to buy: *B Sharp Jazz Quartet* ✻✻✻✻ (MAMA Foundation, 1994, prod. Herb Graham Jr., Randall Willis) is an impressive debut by four hard swinging young musicians—Graham (drums), Willis (tenor, alto saxophones), Reggie Carson (bass), and Eliot Douglass (piano). Graham, the heart and soul of the band, knows how to turn a beat around and handles Latin, funk, and straight-ahead rhythms with equal facility. Willis is a powerful player, especially on tenor, and he takes charge on the pianoless burner "How's That?" Other highlights are the excellent ensemble work on Willis's "Almost Next" and Graham's funky crowd-pleaser "Father Knows Best." If B Sharp's second release *Mirage* ✻✻✻ (MAMA Foundation, 1995, prod. Herb Graham Jr.) is a bit disappointing, it's only because their debut raised high expectations. This album hews closer to the hard bop tradition, though there are a number of adventurous touches, such as guest singer Carmen Bradford's wordless vocals on Graham's "Velvet Touch" and the Latin-tinged version of Joe Henderson's "Inner Urge." The title track and an 11-minute version of Freddie Hubbard's "The Intrepid Fox" are potent if somewhat conventional hard bop vehicles, with Willis blowing passionately and pianist Rodney Lee (replacing Douglass) taking some tasty choruses. *Searching for the One* ✻✻✻✻ (MAMA Foundation, 1996, prod. Herb Graham Jr.) finds the band stretching out, exploring some difficult musical territory (and with a new bassist, as Osama Afifi replaces founding member Carson). The album opens and closes with effective spoken word passages by Crenshaw District bard Kamau Daaood, linking the band to the pre-rap poetry tradition of Watts. The melancholy, pensive mood Willis achieves on Graham's abstract ballad "After" shows his tenor playing continues to mature. The band cuts loose on Rodney Lee's "12 Tone Blue" which sounds like a meeting between Roland Kirk and James Brown. Overall, the album is marked by a cohesive, group approach to playing that sets B Sharp apart from many bands.

the rest:
Tha Go 'Round ✻✻✻ (MAMA Foundation, 1997)

influences:
◄◄ Horace Silver, Jazz Messengers

Andrew Gilbert

Babkas

Formed 1992, in Seattle, WA.

Briggan Krauss, alto saxophone; Brad Schoeppach, guitar; Aaron Alexander, drums.

Teetering on the line between composition and free improvisation, this New York City trio of Brad Schoeppach (shimmering, biting electric guitar), Briggan Krauss (probing alto sax with a keening tone), and Aaron Alexander (versatile, pointillistic drumming) recalls the instrumentation–if only occasionally the style–of the Paul Motian Trio with Joe Lovano and Bill Frisell. The members of Babkas are all from Seattle, but the group's formation was circuitous and didn't take place until after Schoeppach moved to New York in 1990. During separate 1992 visits to Schoeppach's home in Brooklyn, Krauss and Alexander talked about uniting to rehearse, perform, and record some music, but it didn't happen until Schoeppach went home for the holidays at the end of the year. The trio sold the resulting masters to the Vancouver-based Canadian label Songlines, which has released all their albums so far. Eventually they changed their base of operations to Brooklyn; Alexander moved to New York in November 1993, and Krauss followed in May 1994.

All three have thrived in other contexts as well. Alexander plays with the band Hasidic New Wave, which has released two albums (including an Alexander number), subs with the Klezmatics, and appears with several other klezmer groups. He recently formed a quartet with Stomu Takeishi, Cuong Vu, and Jamie Saft. Previously Alexander led his Raggedy Time Band (get it?). Krauss is a member of Wayne Horvitz's Pigpen and Steve Bernstein's Sex Mob and has recorded as a leader. Schoeppach plays in Dave Douglas's Tiny Bell Trio and, as Brad Shepik, plays in Pachora and leads the Commuters, the latter especially leaning towards world music sounds. In addition, Alexander, Krauss, and Shoeppach have all backed vocalist Jay Clayton. Babkas remains a going concern, with tours of the United States, Canada, and Europe, and has performed at the Knitting Factory's annual What is Jazz? Festival.

what to buy: *Fratelli* ♪♪♪♪ (Songlines, 1996, prod. Tim Berne, Babkas) is the most assured and unself-conscious-sounding of this trio's efforts so far. The stylistic shifts sound organic and unforced and the music has a fine sense of proportion among its parts. There are a few free-improv squalls of appealing energy and jagged intervals, but most of the album is marked by a fluid, low-key virtuosity, and the individual members (Krauss in particular) and the group as a whole have clearly found their own voices, sounding like a well-honed unit.

what to buy next: Compositionally speaking, Schoeppach dominates *Ants to the Moon* ♪♪♪ (Songlines, 1994, prod. Babkas), so there are lots of off-kilter rhythms and themes redolent of Ornette Coleman and Middle Eastern/Eastern European music. "Rocky and Rachel" (the only Alexander-penned track) has a lopsidedly reeling circus feel. There are lots of stimulating stylistic juxtapositions, with everything from cabaret to free jazz touched on. The overall feeling is abstract, but with a sense of humor. *Babkas* ♪♪♪ (Songlines, 1993, prod. Tony Reif, Babkas) is where Babkas comes closest, on a few tracks, to the Paul Motian Trio's sound (Schoeppach's tonal palette still recalls Frisell's here), but with more outside excursions, suggestions of Ornette Coleman's Prime Time band, and post-modern cuts between a variety of styles and moods. Seamlessly mixing composition and improvisation, this debut is tight and refreshingly uncliched, occasionally even movingly lyrical. An effective cover of Brahms's Hungarian Dance #20 has the woozy, semi-martial feel of Kurt Weill in his subdued moments, broken up by a short and speedy mosh bit in the middle.

worth searching for: *The Songlines Anthology* ♪♪♪♪ (Songlines, 1996, comp. prod. Tony Reif) includes an alternate take of *Ants to the Moon*'s "This" that is sufficiently different (yet equally good) to be worth acquiring. The rest of the album consists of similarly previously unreleased material from other artists on this fine Canadian label, including Dave Douglas, Tiny Bell Trio, and Ellery Eskelin.

solo outings:
Briggan Krauss:
Good Kitty ♪♪♪ (Knitting Factory, 1996)

Brad Shepik and the Commuters:
The Loan ♪♪♪ (Songlines, 1997)

influences:
◄◄ Bill Frisell, Paul Motian, Ornette Coleman, John Zorn

Steve Holtje

Erykah Badu

Born Erica Wright, February 26, 1961, in Dallas, TX.

Emerging as a pop diva in 1997, Badu deftly mixes hip-hop and jazz into a strong soul music base. She honed these singing and songwriting crafts in Erykah Free, a relatively successful duo she formed with her cousin. Badu has a distinctive soul style that sounds radical in the 1990s but draws on African American pop traditions dating as far back as the 1940s. Her song "Afro" is a for-real blues song. "Certainly" bounces along with jazz piano chording, slinky trumpet sneaking in and out, walking bass on the chorus, and background vocal harmonies any big band would love. She even has the nerve to open the disc with "Rimshot," electric fusion piano riding on the oldest bass riff in the book. Often compared to Billie Holiday, Badu does share a sultry delivery, odd and ironic lyrics, and bohemian persona with Lady Day. Ultimately her destiny lies on the R&B/pop side of the continuum—*Baduizm* topped the R&B chart and hit #2 on the pop side—but she's infused enough roots into her sound to be more authentic than most of what is considered contemporary jazz.

what's available: *Baduizm* 🎵🎵🎵🎵 (Universal, 1997, prod. various) shows real talent and more roots than most of what is considered contemporary jazz. Stripped of much of the studio pop veneer, *Live* 🎵🎵🎵🎵 (Universal, 1997, prod. Erykah Badu, Norman Hurt) covers most of the same material as her debut album to mostly better effect. Backed by a trio of bass, drums, and keyboards, Badu's voice comes to the fore as a lead instrument totally capable of carrying the show. The stretched out (12-minute) version of "Next Lifetime" shows true improvisational ability and the new tune "Tyrone" is catchy enough to attract even jaded ears.

influences:

⏪ Arrested Development, Billie Holiday, Minnie Riperton, Marvin Gaye

Larry Gabriel

Derek Bailey

Born January 29, 1932, in Sheffield, Yorkshire, England.

Derek Bailey is one of those rare examples of someone who changed an instrument so radically that everyone who has come afterward owes a debt to his expansion of the language. Unlike many other improvisers, Bailey has continued to redefine himself throughout the years, and even a cursory listen to a disc will reveal what era, or mode, Bailey is in. Bailey cofounded the Incus label which was the primary publishing house for improvisation from England. All of the classics of the early English improvised scene were on there, from *Topography of the Lungs*, a searing trio of Bailey, Evan Parker, and Han Bennink, to solo records of Bailey, Parker, and Tony Oxley.

what to buy: *Aida* 🎵🎵🎵🎵 (Dexter's Cigar, 1976/1997) stands out as a favorite. It has Bailey both at his most abstract and most lyrical, revealing an incredible ability for guitaristic klangfarbenmelodie, where a line is made of regular plucked notes,

harmonics, scrapes on the body, picking behind the bridge, sustained feedback, and light finger-sweeping against the strings.

what to buy next: *One Time* 🎵🎵🎵🎵 (Incus, 1995) is a perfect example of what makes Bailey a great improviser: his ability to make any situation, here a trio with percussionist John Stevens and bassist Kent Carter, more than it would be in the hands of another. His skills both in interplay and comment reveal his multi-tiered aesthetics of what improvising is.

what to avoid: *The Sign of 4* 🎵 (Knitting Factory, 1997, prod. Gregg Bendian) is the atrocious three-CD set with Pat Metheny, Gregg Bendian, and Paul Wertico. While Bailey still shines, when you can hear him, the rest of the ensemble are not in his league.

best of the rest:

(With Cecil Taylor) *Pleistozaen Mit Waasser* 🎵🎵🎵🎵 (FMP, 1989)
(With the Ruins) *Saisoro* 🎵🎵🎵🎵 (Tzadik, 1995)
Incus Taps 🎵🎵🎵🎵 (Organ of Corti, 1995)
(With Han Bennink) *Verity's Place* 🎵🎵🎵 (Organ of Corti, 1995)
(With John Zorn and William Parker) *Harras* 🎵🎵🎵 (Avant, 1995)
(With Min Tanaka) *Song and Dance* 🎵🎵🎵 (Revenant, 1996)
(With Tony Williams and Bill Laswell) *Arcana* 🎵🎵🎵🎵 (Avant, 1996)
Lace 🎵🎵🎵🎵 (Emanem, 1996)
(With DJ Ninj) *Guitar, Drum 'n' Bass* 🎵🎵🎵 (Avant, 1996)
(With Keiji Haino) *Drawing Close, Attuning the Respective Signs of Order and Chaos* 🎵🎵🎵 (PSF, 1997)

influences:

⏪ Anton Webern

⏩ Henry Kaiser, Eugene Chadbourne, Fred Frith

Jim O'Rourke

Ernest Harold "Benny" Bailey

Born August 13, 1925, in Cleveland, OH.

Primarily a hard-bop stylist, Benny Bailey cuts a distinctive figure among trumpeters of his generation for his bright tone and distinctive intervallic approach to improvisation. In Cleveland, Bailey formed his first band, the Counts of Rhythm, while a high school student at East Tech, eventually playing in well-known Cleveland nitespots such as the Cedar Gardens and Club Rendevous. Bailey was influenced by Cleveland trumpet legend Freddie Webster, who was eight years older, as well as by a local player Hubert Kidd. Hearing Dizzy Gillespie play bebop in a 1940s jam session one night at Cleveland's Majestic Hotel, Bailey was inspired. In the early 1940s, Bailey worked with Bullmoose Jackson and Scatman Crothers, and followed the latter to the West Coast where he remained for a few years. During this time, he also toured with Jay McShann and performed with Teddy Edwards. In the late 1940s, Bailey stinted with Dizzy Gillespie and was a prime soloist with Lionel Hampton from 1948 until the mid-1950s, and did a lot of writing for the band. After a late 1950s tour to Europe with Hampton, Bailey remained awhile to work with Harry Arnold's band on Swedish radio from 1955–1959. He returned briefly to the U.S. to work with Quincy Jones before moving permanently to Europe in 1961. During the 1960s, Bailey worked as first trumpet with the Kenny Clarke–Francy Boland Orchestra, and he's continued to supplement solo gigs with employment in countless studio orchestras.

what to buy: Bailey was 35-years-old when he made his first recording as a leader *Big Brass* &&&& (Candid, 1960/1992, prod. Nat Hentoff), a session that displays his confident power and technique. Intelligent programming by producer Hentoff, a hard-swinging rhythm section (pianist Tommy Flanagan, bassist Buddy Catlett, drummer Arthur Taylor), and great arrangements by Quincy Jones, Hale Smith, and Tom McIntosh comprise an album's worth of Bailey's passionate, witty improvising. On *For Heaven's Sake* &&&& (Hot House, 1989, prod. Edward Dipple, Mike Hennessey), Bailey and English reed master Tony Coe are an assured front line on this relaxed bebop date. Horace Parlan, Jimmy Woode, and Idris Muhammad are a top-shelf rhythm section. The studio date *No Refill* &&&& (TCB, 1992, prod. Carlo Schöb, Peter Eigenmann, Peter Schindlin) is a good representation of the sound of Bailey's typical working groups. Challenging tunes and masterful presentation make for an enjoyable set.

what to avoid: Form and function don't mesh on *Islands* && (Enja, 1976, prod. Mladen Gutesha), a rock-inflected session. Bailey's playing is superb, but bassist Eberhard Weber and guitarist-sitarist Siggi Schwab aren't in synch. If you want to hear Bailey in this context, get the record, but it's not the most felicitous setting for him.

worth searching for: During his voluminous recordings with big bands, Bailey's had ample opportunity to shine. *Quincy Jones Round Midnight* &&&& (Verve, 1997, prod. Michael Lang) features Quincy Jones's concerto, "Meet Benny Bailey," a virtuoso turn, and a thrilling interpretation of "Moonglow," both recorded with the Harry Arnold Orchestra in 1958. Bailey appears on many Clarke-Boland big band recordings, and a few highlights include *Fire, Heat and Guts* &&&& (MPS, 1967, prod.

Gigi Campi) which features an archetypal hot, bop-inflected Bailey solo, and *Latin Kaleidoscope* (MPS, 1968, prod. Gigi Campi) which spotlights Bailey's dark, lyrical solos on "Crepuscule y Aurora."

influences:
◀◀ Roy Eldridge, Hubert Kidd, Freddie Webster, Dizzy Gillespie

Ted Panken

Mildred Bailey

Born Mildred Rinker on February 27, 1907, in Tekoa, WA. Died December 12, 1951, in Poughkeepsie, WA.

Great artists don't necessarily have great tools, they just know how to use what they have. Or as Mildred Bailey, many years later honored with her own U.S. postage stamp, once said, "Hell honey, I just sing." Critics loved to cite her "little girl" voice and her portly physique, pointing out the incongruous pairing. Stories of Bailey's tremendous rages or her prodigious capacity for food show the singer in an unfavorable light, but other tales tell us that she was a pro. Once she hit the stage Bailey focused on the job at hand, no matter what else might be going on in her personal life.

Bailey got her break with Paul Whiteman's orchestra after she sent the leader a demo of her singing and got the call to join his band. While with Whiteman she started singing "Rockin' Chair," a song that was to be closely associated with Bailey for the balance of her career. When she married Red Norvo in 1933, Bailey was about to enter a decade of success. During this time she made recordings with the Dorsey Brothers, Benny Goodman, the Red Norvo Orchestra, and her own group, Mildred Bailey and Her Alley Cats. The latter ensemble featured big-name players such as Bunny Berigan, Johnny Hodges, and Teddy Wilson. After divorcing Norvo in 1943, Bailey's career began a gradual decline made worse by her increasingly bad health until, in 1951, she died a pauper.

what to buy: The only way *The Rockin' Chair Lady: 1931–1950* &&&& (Decca Jazz, 1994, reissue prod. Orrin Keepnews) could be supplanted as the top recommendation for Bailey's oeuvre would be if there was a CD out containing the sides with Dorsey, Goodman, and the others mentioned above. As it is this highly enjoyable set places Bailey in a variety of musical surroundings, all guaranteed to show her flexible, youngish voice to best advantage. She covers such songs as "Honeysuckle Rose," "Georgia on My Mind," and the obligatory "Rockin' Chair." Her accompanists include the neglected Herman Chittison on piano and the aforementioned Alley Cats. Most of the material dates from the early 1930s until the early 1940s, with the notable exception of two songs recorded in 1950 with Vic Schoen and His Orchestra. The Schoen tunes include a prophetic "Blue Prelude" with the couplet, "Won't be long 'til my song will be through/ 'Cause I know I'm on my last go 'round."

what to buy next: The fact that *Me and the Blues* ♫♫♫ (Savoy, 1946–1947, prod. Ozzie Cadena) is only a hair over 30 minutes long is what keeps the rating lower than what it could be, for some of these performances far outclass what is heard on the Decca release. This version of "Lover Come Back to Me" with the Ellis Larkins Orchestra is informed by the vicissitudes of a career in decline, and her vocals, in this regard only, might be compared to later recordings by Billie Holiday for poignancy. The earlier version swings, but in a relatively carefree manner by contrast. Pianist Larkins and his trio back Bailey up on the album's last three songs, and his sensitive solo slot on "Born to Be Blue" compares well with anything he recorded as Ella Fitzgerald's accompanist.

the rest:
Rockin' Chair: The Legendary V-Disc Sessions ♫♫♫ (VJC, 1990)
Harlem Lullaby ♫♫♫ (ASV Living Era, 1992)
That Rockin' Chair Lady ♫♫♫ (Topaz, 1994)

worth searching for: There was a three-LP set *Her Greatest Performances* ♫♫♫ (Columbia Special Products, 1981, prod. various) that covered the essential Mildred Bailey recordings in one fell swoop; all the cool stuff with Benny Goodman, Red Norvo, Teddy Wilson, and Eddie Sauter. In a better world these performances would be back on the market in a CD box set, complete with the original liner notes from John Hammond, Bing Crosby, Irving Townsend, and Bucklin Moon.

influences:
◀◀ Annette Hanshaw, Bessie Smith
▶▶ Diane Schuur

Garaud MacTaggart

Chet Baker

Born December 23, 1929, in Yale, OK. Died May 13, 1988, in Amsterdam, Netherlands.

Underneath the messiness of his life and fog of myth surrounding Chet Baker is the undeniable fact he was one of jazz's great lyric trumpeters, a natural musician with a gift for melodic invention. Strongly influenced by Miles Davis, Baker developed a singular ballad style and was fully capable of playing effective bop-derived lines. The vulnerability and fragility he communicated with his voice made him a compelling, charismatic singer, though late in his career it became impossible to separate the pathos of his life from his art.

After leaving the Army, Baker played with Charlie Parker on the West Coast in 1952. He joined Gerry Mulligan's groundbreaking pianoless quartet at the Haig in Los Angeles and it soon became one of the hottest groups in jazz. Baker struck out on his own in the mid-1950s, but drug addiction and his undisciplined lifestyle soon began taking a toll on his career. A 1960 drug bust in Italy marked the start of a precipitous decline, and Baker lost much of the 1960s to addiction, though he did manage to make a few recordings worthy of his talent. At his nadir in 1968, Baker had his teeth knocked out in a drug-related incident, though a few years later he began an amazing comeback. He spent much of the latter part of his life in Europe, returning occasionally to the United States and recording much too frequently for a myriad of labels. Though his voice was little but a whisper in his last decade, he remained a fine trumpeter right up until his death, when he either fell or was pushed out of a hotel window. A beautiful man who could have been a model or a movie star, Baker by the end of his life looked like Dorian Grey's portrait, with a lifetime of hard living etched in his face. Since his death, Baker's great 1950s Pacific Jazz recordings have been reissued in many different forms, from "best of" anthologies to completist multi-disc collections.

what to buy: *The Best of the Gerry Mulligan Quartet with Chet Baker* ♫♫♫♫ (Pacific Jazz, 1991, prod. Dick Bock) is an anthology of the classic 1952–53 sessions by one of the great small groups in modern jazz. With either Bobby Whitlock or Carson Smith on bass and Chico Hamilton or Larry Bunker on drums, these 15 tracks are consistently rewarding due to Mulligan's ingenious charts and the scintillating baritone sax/trumpet interplay. An essential part of any jazz collection. Baker was at the peak of his popularity when *Quartet: Russ Freeman and Chet Baker* ♫♫♫♫ (Pacific Jazz, 1956, prod. Richard Bock) was released, featuring Los Angeles stalwarts Leroy Vinnegar (bass) and Shelly Manne (drums). Freeman, a brilliant writer and improvisor, composed all the material except for the opening "Love Nest" and a gorgeous, early version of Billy Strayhorn's "Lush Life." The rapport between Freeman and Baker makes this one of the trumpeter's strongest sessions, a long hard-to-

Chet Baker **(Archive Photos)**

find gem that bears repeated listening. *The Route* ♫♫♫♫ (Pacific Jazz, 1956, prod. Richard Bock) unites Baker and alto saxophonist Art Pepper, two of jazz's most chaotic figures. This session gives the lie to the lightweight rap on West Coast jazz, as Baker and Pepper play tough, hard-swinging music. Baker's breathy trumpet sound blends well with Pepper's hot and lustrous alto. Pianist Pete Jolly is also in fine form, contributing a number of sparkling solos. Baker's finest vocal album, *It Could Happen to You* ♫♫♫♫ (Riverside, 1958, prod. Bill Grauer) was recorded when his voice was still fresh and sweet but already marked by the terrible knowledge of self-destruction. Baker croons a dozen standards, including his classic version of "Everything Happens to Me," accompanied by pianist Kenny Drew, and either Sam Jones or George Morrow on bass and Philly Joe Jones or Dannie Richmond on drums. Other standout tracks include "Old Devil Moon" and the irony-tinged "I'm Old Fashioned."

what to buy next: Though the sound quality isn't great, *Witch Doctor* ♫♫♫♫ (Contemporary, 1985, prod. Lester Koenig) is a fascinating slice of history, recorded live at the Lighthouse in the summer of 1953 during one of the legendary Sunday jam sessions. Baker, who had recently left Gerry Mulligan's popular quartet, is in top form battling with trumpeter Rolf Ericson. Also on hand are saxophonists Bud Shank, Jimmy Giuffre, and Bob Cooper, pianists Russ Freeman and Claude Williamson, bassist Howard Rumsey, and drummers Max Roach and Shelly Manne. This session was released for the first time in 1985. *Songs for Lovers* ♫♫♫♫ (Pacific Jazz, 1997, prod. Richard Bock) is a compilation of a dozen standards Baker recorded in the mid-1950s for Pacific Jazz. Baker's voice is an acquired taste, but he was at his best singing world-weary romantic ballads. Accompanied mostly by rhythm sections lead by pianist Russ Freeman, Baker sings affecting versions of "My Old Flame," "Darn that Dream" and especially "Lush Life." *Chet Baker in New York* ♫♫♫♫ (Riverside, 1958, prod. Orrin Keepnews) is a strong session matching West Coast-typecast Baker with a tough East Coast rhythm section of Al Haig (piano), Paul Chambers (bass), and Philly Joe Jones (drums), with tenor saxophonist Johnny Griffin on three tracks. Baker easily holds his own, and shows he wasn't afraid of being compared to Miles Davis by playing a number of tunes associated with him ("Solar" and "When Lights Are Low"). One of Baker's last quality sessions, *The Legacy, Vol. 1* ♫♫♫♫ (Enja, 1995, prod. Matthias Winckelmann) was recorded live in 1987 in Hamburg, Germany with the NDR Big Band directed by Dieter Glawischnig. The band includes Baker's old West Coast compatriots Herb Geller (alto sax) and Walter Norris (piano), but

Baker is the featured soloist and he was still a capable improvisor. The program is mostly mid-tempo standards and ballads, but his playing on Herbie Hancock's "Dolphin Dance" and Hal Galper's "Mister B" show that Baker kept his ears open until the end.

what to avoid: Chet Baker lovers might want this one, but with the plodding orchestra charts and unchanging tempos, *Chet Baker with 50 Italian Strings* ♫♫ (Riverside, 1960, prod. Orrin Keepnews) is a snooze.

best of the rest:
Pacific Jazz Years ♫♫♫♫ (Pacific Jazz, 1952–57)
Complete Pacific Jazz Studio Recordings of the Chet Baker Quartet with Russ Freeman ♫♫♫♫ (Mosaic, 1953–56)
Complete Pacific Jazz Live Recordings ♫♫♫♫ (Mosaic, 1954)
Chet in Paris, Vol 1–4 ♫♫♫♫ (EmArcy, 1955–56)
Playboys ♫♫♫♫ (Pacific Jazz, 1957)
Embraceable You ♫♫♫♫ (Pacific Jazz, 1958)
Plays the Best of Lerner and Lowe ♫♫♫♫ (Riverside, 1959)
Chet ♫♫♫♫ (Riverside, 1960)
Lonely Star ♫♫♫♫ (Prestige, 1965)
On a Misty Night ♫♫♫♫ (Prestige, 1965)
Blues for a Reason ♫♫♫♫ (Criss Cross, 1985)
My Favorite Songs ♫♫♫♫ (Enja, 1988)
Chet Baker in Tokyo ♫♫♫♫ (Evidence, 1993)

worth searching for: Chet was often at his best with spare accompaniment, and *Chet's Choice* ♫♫♫♫ (Criss Cross, 1985, prod. Gerry Teekens) finds him in a trio context with guitarist Philip Catherine and bassist Jean-Louis Rassinfosse. His gift for melodiousness is very intact and this is one of his best later sessions.

influences:
◄◄ Bix Beiderbecke, Miles Davis, Kenny Dorham
►► Rick Braun

Andrew Gilbert

Ginger Baker
Born Peter Baker, August 19, 1939, in London, England.

Ginger Baker is best known as a rock drummer who made his mark in the 1960s with the power trio Cream (with Eric Clapton and Jack Bruce) and the rock supergroup, Blind Faith. He later led his own 10-piece band with three drummers, Ginger Baker's Air Force. But, before his stardom in the rock genre, Baker worked in a number of jazz groups in London as well as Alexis Korner's Blues Incorporated.

After some journeys into the World Music arena, Ginger Baker teamed up with guitarist Bill Frisell and bassist Charlie Haden in 1994 for a trio venture which produced two recordings for Atlantic Records. Released under Baker's name, these discs show him to be a much better jazz drummer than most would expect.

what to buy: *Going Back Home* ♪♪♪♪ (Atlantic, 1994, prod. Chip Stern) an excellent group effort from Baker with Bill Frisell (guitar) and Charlie Haden (bass). The trio's unique sound is both quirky and loads of fun. Songs include originals, plus Monk's "Straight, No Chaser" and Arnaud Coleman's "Ramblin'."

what to buy next: *Falling off the Roof* ♪♪♪ (Atlantic, 1996, prod. Ginger Baker, Malcolm Cecil) features the same trio of Baker, Frisell, and Haden from the 1994 disc, plus guests Bela Fleck and Jerry Hahn—more good, fun music, but not quite up to the level of its predecessor.

Bill Wahl

Billy Bang

Born William Walker Vincent, September 20, 1947, in Mobile, AL.

One of the few great jazz violinists, Bang is largely self-taught and immediately identifiable. After growing up in the Bronx and Harlem areas of New York City, he served a tour in Vietnam and on his return to the United States took up violin, which he had played in his youth. His love for the style of swing violinist Stuff Smith and Leroy Jenkins's mentorship combined in Bang to produce a sweet, bluesy, occasionally gritty style which never lacks verve and which he has built up over the years into a superb technique. In 1977 he co-founded the String Trio of New York, remaining in the group for a decade, with a brief time-out for a stint in the Sun Ra Arkestra. Many early recordings are long out-of-print, but fortunately all his Soul Note material is available on CD, and a few guest spots with other artists are easily found, with Marilyn Crispell's *Live in Berlin* and Kalil El'Zabar's Ritual Trio album *Big Cliff* two examples. The most notable guest appearance on one of Bang's albums, on the other hand, is easily Ra's membership in the one-time-only quartet which pays tribute to Smith, whom Ra had played with in Chicago in the 1950s. It's believed to be Ra's final studio recording.

what to buy: *Rainbow Gladiator* ♪♪♪♪ (Soul Note, 1981, prod. Giovanni Bonandrini) is an exuberant, swinging quintet session with Charles Tyler (alto and baritone saxes), Michele Rosewoman (piano), Wilbur Morris (bass), and Dennis Charles (drums). Bang plays the material with raw excitement and generous humor, while Tyler and Rosewoman display a gusto per-

haps unmatched on their own records. Unlike some of Bang's albums, which can get looser than more traditional listeners would like, this group is tightly coordinated yet comfortably relaxed—witness the tempo changes on the rollicking title track.

what to buy next: *Spirits Gathering* ♪♪♪♪ (CIMP, 1996, prod. Robert D. Rusch) is a quartet with Brett Allen (guitar), Akira Ando (bass), and Denis Charles (he changed the spelling himself). Allen's cool chording allows a feeling of space without ever sounding thin, and the players are equally comfortable exuding a quiet, confident intensity or rocking out joyously. Highlights include the Japanese folk song "Tanko Bushi" and a bluesy swing through Sonny Rollins's "Pent Up House." *Commandment* ♪♪♪♪ (No More, 1997, prod. Alan Schneider) is the only solo Bang currently available. Recorded at a concert inspired by Alain Kirili sculptures, it ranges from what sound like free improvisations to "Swing Low Sweet Chariot," and the violinist's between-tunes comments and the slight flaws and hesitations here and there are all of a charming piece.

the rest:
Changing Seasons ♪♪♪ (Bellows, 1980)
Invitation ♪♪♪♪ (Soul Note, 1982)
Outline No. 12 ♪♪♪ (Celluloid, 1983)
The Fire from Within ♪♪♪ (Soul Note, 1985)
Live at Carlos 1 ♪♪♪♪ (Soul Note, 1987)
Valve No. 10 ♪♪♪♪ (Soul Note, 1991)
(With Sun Ra) *A Tribute to Stuff Smith* ♪♪♪ (Soul Note, 1993)
Bang On! ♪♪♪♪ (Justin Time, 1997)

worth searching for: At least two of Bang's out-of-print LPs are worth tracking down in the used bins—both concert recordings. *Sweet Space* ♪♪♪♪ (Anima, 1979, prod. John Mingione, Billy Bang) adds tenor saxophonist Frank Lowe to Bang's sextet with Butch Morris (cornet), Luther Thomas (alto sax), Curtis Clark (piano), Wilbur Morris (bass), and Steve McCall (drums). Permutations of elemental riffs ground exciting improvisations. *Live at Green Space* ♪♪♪♪ (Anima, 1982, prod. John Mingione) is a duo between Bang, who also plays mbira (African thumb piano) here, and Charles Tyler, who plays alto and baritone saxes, harmonica, and bells. It's a bit diffuse at times, but at its peak this is swinging, penetrating improvisation. Easier to find will be the multiple-artists compilation *A Confederacy of Dances, Vol. 1* ♪♪♪♪ (Einstein, 1992, prod. Jim Staley, David Weinstein), which has a live solo performance of "One for Albert" recorded at Roulette in February 1988. As one would expect from a tribute to free jazz icon Albert Ayler, it's full of wailing intensity, but also reflects the R&B roots of that sound.

influences:

◀◀ Stuff Smith, Leroy Jenkins, Sun Ra, Albert Ayler

▶▶ Jason Hwang

see also: *String Trio of New York*

Steve Holtje

Nancie Banks Orchestra

Formed 1989, in New York, NY.

Nancie Banks, conductor-vocalist; Oliver Von Essen, piano; Kerry Politzer, piano; Joe Knight, piano; Edwin Swanson, piano; Michael Max Fleming, bass; Brian Grice, drums; Vinnie Johnson, drums; Dave Gibson, drums; Tony Barrero, trumpet; Kenny Rampton, trumpet; Winston Byrd, trumpet; Frank Gordon, trumpet; James Zollar, trumpet; Eddie Allen, trumpet; Valery Ponomarev, trumpet; John Gordon, trombone; Alfred Patterson, trombone; Aaron Johnson, trombone; Jack Jeffers, trombone; Enrique Fernandez, alto saxophone; Alexander McCabe, alto saxophone; Patience Higgins, tenor saxophone (1989–95); Neal Sugarman, tenor saxophone; Marshall McDonald, tenor saxophone; Mitch Frohman, tenor saxophone; Richard Johnson, baritone saxophone.

Bandleader-vocalist Nancie Banks, a multi-faceted musician who also composes and arranges, has led her own 17-player big band since 1989. Banks (née Manzuk) was born in Morgantown, West Virginia, on July 12, 1951, and grew up in Pittsburgh. At an early age, Banks learned piano from her mother, a classically trained church pianist, and drew inspiration as a singer from her father, a vocalist with a wide range. Banks came to New York as a teenager and eventually studied with Barry Harris, Alberto Socarras (pioneer in Afro-Cuban jazz), and Edward Boatner (whose spiritual arrangements influenced Banks's orchestral voicings). She attended New York City's Jazzmobile Workshops for 15 years, experience that reinforced her writing and arranging skills. As a singer, Banks performed with Jon Hendricks's Vocalstra, the female vocal group Joyspring, the Lionel Hampton Orchestra, Dexter Gordon with Strings and Voices, the Barry Harris Jazz Ensemble, Walter Bishop Jr., and others. Banks, also a music copyist, worked for Buck Clayton and George Benson, and for major motion pictures, including Spike Lee's *Mo Better Blues*. Banks continues to perform regionally as a singer, with her own quintet, and with her orchestra at festivals, clubs, concerts, and private parties. She is married to trombonist Clarence Banks, who has guested on her albums and performs with the band when he's not touring with the Count Basie Orchestra. While everyone is making a big fuss over bandleader Maria Schneider, multi-talented Nancie Banks goes about her work largely unheralded. She certainly deserves wider recognition.

what's available: The debut recording by the Nancie Banks Orchestra, *Waves of Peace* ♫♫♫✧ (Consolidated Artists, 1992, prod. Nancie Banks) offers the studio session of 11 straight-ahead and Afro-Cuban jazz tunes, as well as fresh arrangements of featured tunes by composers Billy Strayhorn ("Chelsea Bridge"), Walter Bishop Jr. ("Coral Keys"), Charlie Parker ("Little Lou"), Dizzy Gillespie ("Tin Tin Deo"), and others, including two Banks originals. Highlights focus on Banks's superb composing-arranging skills and some fine solos from baritone saxophonist Charles Davis, tenor saxman Patience Higgins, alto saxist Bobby Porcelli, pianist Lynne Arriale, and others. The versatile rhythm section keeps the uncluttered music flowing smoothly forward, especially on the Afro-Cuban numbers "Coral Keys" and "Tin Tin Deo," and the thickly arranged, briskly paced Bud Powell tune, "Tempus Fugit." Arrangements are nicely balanced and tightly blended, yielding to the talents of the soloists, and allow each section to shine. Banks is not overbearing in her arrangements—she makes all the instrumental voices fit. And, as singer, she doesn't try to hog the limelight; her brief sweet-voiced singing graces only a couple of tunes. Only one or two rough spots generated by soloists mar this otherwise fine debut. The second Nancie Banks Orchestra recording, *Bert's Blues* ♫♫♫♫ (Consolidated Artists, 1995, prod. Grover Mitchell), is a flawless outing. The sound quality is so greatly improved (engineered by Rudy Van Gelder) compared to her first album, I'd suggest buying this one first. But you'll want to own both, eventually. Bossier, bluesier, and brassier, *Bert's Blues* is propelled throughout by great charts from Banks and others, and by excellent section work and solos. The satisfying mix of tunes includes a beefy version of "Night and Day," a lush version of "You Go to My Head" (featuring Banks's sensuous vocals and a mellow trumpet solo from Frank Gordon), a light-swinging treatment of Charlie Parker's "Quasimodo/Quasimoto," Banks's original "Bert's Blues" (which resonates with orchestral colors), and more great music. Grice and Fleming return, with Joe Knight, Edwin Swanson, and Oliver Von Essen sharing piano duties. Some of the same section players return, and Nancie's husband, Clarence Banks (trombone), and Charles Davis (tenor saxophone) are again brilliantly featured. There's not a dull moment among the 10 tunes and, though featured on only three tunes, Banks's honeyed singing is simply sumptuous. (If you can't find these albums in your local stores, both albums are available by mail by calling 800-BEBOP-YO.)

influences:

◀◀ Duke Ellington

Nancy Ann Lee

Chris Barber

Born April 17, 1930, in Welwyn Garden City, Hertfordshire, England.

Trombonist Chris Barber led one of the first, and most popular, "trad jazz" bands in postwar England, and his all-star groups were a big influence on the next generation of Brit musicians, whether they were blues revivalists like Alexis Korner, or skiffle bands like the early Beatles. Barber's whole approach was a formalized take on Dixieland, a fairly tame rendition, actually. However, New Orleans and Dixieland jazz had been extensively analyzed in the British music journals and, during the mid-1950s, the time was right for a genuine revival in the clubs. Barber led the way until rock took over a decade later, actually achieving hit parade status. He commanded a large following and earned large sums of money in pre-Beatle Britain. Though basically steeped in Dixieland, Barber was open-minded about music, playing various jazz styles, as well as directly helping foster the Brits' appreciation of the blues by bringing American artists such as Muddy Waters, and Sonny Terry and Brownie McGhee to England.

what to buy: *Copulatin' Jazz* ♫♫♫ (Great Southern, 1994, prod. Chris Barber) features spirited arrangements of American standards and the hottest Dixieland performances (compared with Barber's other recordings) from lively Pat Halcox on trumpet, reedmen John Crocker and Ian Wheeler, and trombonist-leader Barber on the front line. Their collective energy propels classics such as "Down by the Riverside," "Swanee River," and "When the Saints Go Marching In" to new levels. Other down-South favorites include "Sweet Sue," "My Old Kentucky Home," "Dipper Mouth Blues (Sugar Foot Stomp)," and the ditty that still occasionally ends ballroom dances, "Goodnight Sweetheart." The album is a pleaser, especially for Dixieland fans.

best of the rest:

The Original Copenhagen Concert ♫♫♫ (Storyville, 1954)
In Budapest ♫♫♫ (Storyville, 1962)

influences:

◀◀ Louis Armstrong, Ken Colyer

▶▶ Alexis Korner, Graham Bond, Cyril Davies, Rolling Stones

Joe S. Harrington

Gato Barbieri

Born Leandro J. Barbieri, November 28, 1934, in Rosario, Argentina.

Barbieri's career has to frustrate the hell out of any jazz fan, which might be a surprise to the millions of "jazz" fans who have wholeheartedly embraced the light Latin and easy-listening pabulum that has made "El Gato" rather wealthy over the last 20 years. His current situation seems highly unlikely in light of his early career. Starting with Lalo Schifrin's band in the early 1950s, Barbieri moved to Rome in the early 1960s. He was discovered by Don Cherry during Cherry's mid-'60s troubadour period, recording with his landmark *Symphony for Improvisers* large band, as well as *Complete Communion* and a quartet LP. Barbieri was one of the first to reconnect free playing to the folk music that inspired it, and often explored South American rhythms and modal local melodies. But the money shot was his screaming, passionate tenor—often verging on the cusp of parody, but rarely tipping over.

Pharoah Sanders was no doubt an influence and a model, although Barbieri attempted to put distance between himself and the comparison. "I do not scream for the reasons Pharoah Sanders screams," he says in the liner notes of *Confluence*. Like Sanders, he was inspired in completely free contexts, but managed to reach out to a mass audience in an honest manner, at least until the mid-1970s. His experience with folk music made him one of the highlights of Charlie Haden's first *Liberation Music Orchestra* LP, and he also appeared on a few of LMO arranger/composer Carla Bley's LPs (he is listed as "Unidentified Cat" on her *Tropic Appetites*, but his tone is unmistakable), as well as her flagship, the JCOA. There were gigs with many musicians passing through Europe in the late 1960s, including Steve Lacy and Alan Shorter (good luck tracking down Shorter's Verve LP *Orgasm* with Barbieri, Muhammad, and Rashied Ali).

Barbieri's recordings for Flying Dutchman and his first few for Impulse! (that exclamation point surely suited Gato's style) remain high points in accessible free-ish playing, often highlighting Latin musicians and melodies. They were increasingly popular—never had cacophony seemed so catchy. Many popular players such as Stanley Clarke and John Abercrombie make early appearances. Barbieri no doubt paid attention to Sanders's chart success with *Karma* and *Thembi* and managed to top him when his soundtrack to Bernardo Bertolucci's *Last Tango in Paris* became a monster seller. It is not a bad album, but, artistically, it did more harm than good. While many of the artists recording for Bob Thiele's Flying Dutchman label, playing out of a *musical* compulsion, managed to straddle the line between commercial compromise and searching music rather adroitly (Lonnie Liston Smith comes to mind), as the 1970s progressed and popular music became less polyrhythmical, the balance shifted and Barbieri seems to have fallen right on the noggin.

When he recovered . . . let's just say that *Caliente* remains immensely popular, still selling upwards of 225,000 copies a year worldwide. It is produced by Herb Alpert and features a cast of L.A. session ringers. The exotic became successfully exoticized and Latin America transformed into Los Angeles. After the success of that LP, Barbieri continued to drip melodrama into the deepest bowels of Fusion and has been cited as a pioneering figure by "Quiet Storm" station programmers. He even placed a song in a "Miami Vice" episode. Still, there is no denying the power in Barbieri's first decade of recording. He remains one of jazz's few consistent draws, despite a heart attack a couple of years ago, and recently released his first album in 15 years.

what to buy: *Confluence* 🎵🎵🎵🎵 (Freedom, 1968, prod. Mario Nicalaio) is a luminous series of duets with pianist Abdullah Ibrahim (then still known as Dollar Brand), often venturing into uncharted territory. An atypical LP for both of them, but informative of the free spirit that informs their more "accessible" works. Which is to say, lots of dark drama, but also contemplative in the Ibrahim manner. *The Third World* 🎵🎵🎵🎵 (Flying Dutchman, 1969, prod. Bob Thiele) boasts an insanely excellent lineup, (trombonist Roswell Rudd, pianist Lonnie Liston Smith, bassist Charlie Haden, and drummer Beaver Harris) and mixes African, African American, and South American motifs, as was the fashion back then (and it's a shame it has passed). Unlike most of Barbieri's Thiele-produced releases, the sessions and personnel remain constant. *Gato Chapter One: Latin America* 🎵🎵🎵🎵 (Impulse!, 1973, prod. Ed Michel) was recorded in Argentina; Barbieri started playing with more South American musicians around this time and his music became folksier and, for lack of a better word, earthier. The engineering of the Impulse! LPs is also much better than the Flying Dutchman ones, which are often tinny. *Last Tango in Paris* 🎵🎵🎵🎵 (United Artists, 1972) is the ultimate Barbieri release, if not the best one. Arrangements are by the erratic Oliver Nelson. Plenty of strings over which Barbieri solos aplenty, often among the hissing of accordion, and the tone gets a little, well, ripe, which certainly served the spirit of the film. The butter, please.

what to buy next: With Latin musicians and melodies, *Gato Chapter Two: Hasta Siempre* 🎵🎵🎵🎵 (Impulse!, 1973, prod. Ed Michel) is passionate, political and rhythmic, the way jazz should be, baby! What differentiates the Impulse! from the Dutchman releases is that the Impulse! ones tend to be more self-consciously "ethnic," while the Dutchman ones tend to favor Bob Thiele standbys such as Oliver Nelson, Pretty Purdie, and Lonnie Liston Smith, although there's plenty of overlap on the former. Compare and contrast, folks! Percussionist Nana

Vasconcelos kicks ass and Barbieri rises to the challenge on *Fenix* 🎵🎵🎵🎵 (Flying Dutchman, 1971, prod. Bob Thiele). This is the LP that really broke him to a larger public. Also features bassist Ron Carter, keyboardist Lonnie Liston Smith, guitarist Joe Beck, and drummer Lenny White. *In Search of Mystery* 🎵🎵🎵🎵 (ESP-disc, 1967, prod. Gato Barbieri) is European Barbieri at his most frenetic (and least rhythmically Latin) on two sidelong pieces, including the oft-essayed "Michelle." With Sirone on bass, Carlo Scott on very spacey cello, and Robert "Bobby" Kapp on drums.

what to avoid: Although his concurrent work was actually lamer, *Caliente* 🎵 (A&M, 1976, prod. Herb Alpert) is the great divide between the listenable and unlistenable in the Barbieri oeuvre (there are earlier moments of worry, though, so caveat emptor). A large band lays down MOR so that Barbieri can set lovers' tongues aflame.

the rest:
El Gato 🎵🎵🎵 (Flying Dutchman, 1971)
El Pampero 🎵🎵🎵 (Flying Dutchman, 1971)
Under Fire 🎵🎵🎵🎵 (Flying Dutchman, 1971)
Bolivia 🎵🎵🎵 (Flying Dutchman, 1973)
The Legend of Gato Barbieri 🎵🎵🎵🎵 (Flying Dutchman, 1973)
Yesterday 🎵🎵🎵🎵 (Flying Dutchman, 1974)
Gato Chapter Three: Viva Emiliano Zapata 🎵🎵 (Impulse!, 1974)
The Third World Revisited 🎵🎵🎵🎵 (Bluebird, 1974)
Gato Chapter Four: Alive in New York 🎵🎵🎵🎵 (Impulse!, 1975)
Ruby, Ruby 🎵 (A&M, 1978)
Tropico **woof!** (A&M, 1978)
Euphoria **woof!** (A&M, 1979)
Para Los Amigos!! 🎵🎵🎵 (Doctor Jazz, 1981)
Apasionado 🎵🎵🎵 (Doctor Jazz, 1983)
Bahia 🎵🎵 (Fania, 1983)
Fire and Passion **woof!** (A&M, 1988)
Que Pasa **woof!** (Sony, 1997)
Priceless Jazz Collection 🎵 (GRP, 1997)

worth searching for: Don Cherry was the Ed Sullivan of the European avant-garde—talent scout #1—and although *Gato Barbieri and Don Cherry* 🎵🎵🎵🎵 (Durium Records, 1965) is essentially his LP (with a lineup derived from the *Complete Communion* group), Barbieri gets plenty of solo space, though little of his trademark sound is in evidence. On a suite entitled "Togetherness," the tune heads are rather Ornette-y (later re-released by Inner City). Not really a Barbieri LP per se, *Two Pictures, Years 1965–1968* 🎵🎵🎵🎵 (Luito, 1968, prod. Piero Umilani) contains two soundtracks by pianist Piero Umilani that feature the cream of Italian jazz players, including Enrico Rava and Giovanni Tommaso. But most important, the LP includes "Mana-

Mana" from the film *Sweden: Heaven and Hell,* later popularized by the Muppets.

influences:

◀◀ John Coltrane, Pharoah Sanders, John Klemmer

▶▶ Ivo Perelman, Steve Turre

D. Strauss

Carlos Barbosa-Lima

Born December 17, 1944, in São Paulo, Brazil.

One of the foremost classical guitar players in the world, Carlos Barbosa-Lima is also a pretty good jazz guitarist. His understanding of, and versatility in, both genres has made him one of the most formidable technical players around. It should come as no surprise that Barbosa-Lima has authored at least eight books on classical, jazz, and Brazilian technique in addition to serving as a faculty member at the Manhattan School of Music. Much of Barbosa-Lima's jazz performing and recording has been in the company of Charlie Byrd and Laurindo Almeida, two marvelous guitarists and influential aficionados of Brazilian jazz. He has also recorded with Byrd as part of the Washington Guitar Quintet. Barbosa-Lima's playing is characterized by precision but, within the context of Brazilian repertoire, also possessed of a remarkable sense of swing which easily translates into his performances of music by Joplin and Gershwin.

what to buy: Barbosa-Lima's performances of Joplin or Gershwin and Jobim, while recommendable in their own way, don't have the swing and sheer joie de vivre of the solo recital *Plays the Music of Luiz Bonfá & Cole Porter* 𝄞𝄞𝄞𝄞 (Concord Concerto, 1984, prod. Carl E. Jefferson, Charles E. Brown). Bonfá composed such wonderful songs as "Manha de Carnaval" and "Samba de Orfeu" and toured the States with Stan Getz during the height of the bossa nova craze. Cole Porter was the composer of witty songs like "Night and Day," "Love for Sale," and "In the Still of the Night" that hundreds of jazz musicians have used as a road map for improvisation. Barbosa-Lima does a great job with this.

what to buy next: *Plays the Music of Antonio Carlos Jobim & George Gershwin* 𝄞𝄞𝄞 (Concord Concerto, 1982, prod. Carl E. Jefferson) in some ways is more of a classical recording than a jazz one, but the material is so close to the hearts of jazz musicians and fans that it deserves some recognition. The playing is lovely and these are some of the most wonderful tunes of the century.

best of the rest:

(With Sharon Isbin) *Brazil, With Love* 𝄞𝄞𝄞 (Concord Picante, 1987)

(With Sharon Isbin) *Rhapsody in Blue/West Side Story* 𝄞𝄞𝄞 (Concord Concerto, 1988)

(With Laurindo Almeida and Charlie Byrd) *Music of the Brazilian Masters* 𝄞𝄞𝄞𝄞 (Concord Picante, 1989)

(With the Washington Guitar Quintet) *Charlie Byrd & the Washington Guitar Quintet* 𝄞𝄞𝄞𝄞 (Concord Concerto, 1992)

(With the Washington Guitar Quintet) *Aquarelle* 𝄞𝄞𝄞 (Concord Jazz, 1994)

worth searching for: *Chants for the Chief* 𝄞𝄞𝄞𝄞 (Concord Picante, 1991) is more of a Brazilian-flavored classical recording than a jazz one, but the rhythms and percussive effects give the works a flexibility and third world swing that most classical music just doesn't have. Barbosa-Lima and composer/percussionist Thiago DeMello perform a 10-movement work titled "Chants for the Chief" and then the guitarist plays six solo guitar works by various Brazilian composers who use folk melodies as a starting point for their compositions.

influences:

◀◀ Andres Segovia, Atahualpa Yupanqui

▶▶ Sharon Isbin, Manuel Barrueco

Garaud MacTaggart

A. Spencer Barefield

Born May 27, 1953, in Detroit, MI.

A guitarist with both classical and jazz training, Barefield combines the free-blowing and structured compositional elements of the "free jazz" tradition. Barefield has extended, in both musical and geographic terms, the impetus toward self-determination launched in Chicago by Muhal Richard Abrams's Association for the Advancement of Creative Musicians (AACM) While developing a growing national and international reputation, he remains rooted in Detroit, committed to artistic survival amidst a crisis of public funding and airplay for creative jazz. ("It's like someone dropped a bomb on the vanguard of music," he told *Coda* magazine).

After studying under AACM stalwart Roscoe Mitchell in the early '70s at Michigan State University, where the idea of the Creative Arts Collective was born, Barefield in 1978 founded the CAC as a tax-exempt organization and has served ever since as its Artistic and Executive Director. In this capacity he has organized numerous concert series featuring his own compositions and those of guest artists including Abrams, Lester Bowie, Anthony Braxton, Roy Brooks, Leroy Jenkins, Oliver

Lake, and Mitchell. He is the musical organizer and a performer at the "Day of Discovery" at the annual Montreux-Detroit International Jazz Festival.

what to buy: Barefield's range of expression is on full display on *Xenogenesis 2000* 🎵🎵🎵 (CAC) featuring trio, quartet, and Chamber Jazz Ensemble with Richard Davis (bass), James Carter (reeds), and a string section including Regina Carter (violin) and Tani Tabbal (percussion). Tunes include Roland Kirk's "A Handful of Fives," Richard Davis's "Jumonji," and Thelonious Monk's little-heard "Ugly Beauty" as well as Barefield's extended compositions.

what to buy next: *Live at Leverkusener Jazztage* 🎵🎵🎵 (Sound Aspects), with Oliver Lake and Andrew Cyrille, and *After the End* 🎵🎵🎵 (Sound Aspects) with Lake, Cyrille, Davis, and trumpeter Hugh Ragin, illustrate Barefield's wide-ranging musical collaborations in the 1990s.

the rest:
(With the Barefield-Holland-Tabbal Trio) *Transdimensional Space Window* 🎵🎵🎵 (CAC, 1980) (LP only)
(With the Barefield-Holland-Tabbal Trio) *Live at Nickelsdorf Konfrontationen* 🎵🎵🎵 (Sound Aspects, 1985)

worth searching for: You'll have to find old LP outlets to lay hands on some of Barefield's 1980s recordings with the Roscoe Mitchell Sound Ensemble, *Live in Detroit* 🎵🎵🎵 (CECMA) or *Snurdy McGurdy and Her Dancing Shoes* 🎵🎵🎵 (Nessa, 1980), but the 1981 session *3 X 4 Eye* 🎵🎵🎵 (Black Saint, 1981/1994) and the highly experimental and rather weird *Sound and Space Ensembles* 🎵🎵🎵 (Black Saint, 1983/1994) are available on CD. The insertion of Barefield's guitar sound—slightly metallic and difficult to record to best advantage, but not distorted or rock-like—into the AACM mix indicates things to come.

influences:
◀◀ Roscoe Mitchell, Muhal Richard Abrams, Thelonious Monk, Kenny Burrell, Manuel de Falla, Joaquin Rodrigo

▶▶ James Carter, Regina Carter, Gerald Cleaver, Cassius Richmond, Rodney Whitaker

David Finkel

Danny Barker

Born January 13, 1909, in New Orleans, LA. Died March 14, 1994, New Orleans, LA.

Danny Barker played guitar, banjo, composed music, and sang. In his childhood, he learned clarinet, ukulele, and finally banjo from his grandfather, Isadore Barbarin, who played alto horn in the Onward Brass Band. Barker played with the Boozan Kings, and in the early 1920s toured with Little Brother Montgomery and trumpeter Willie Pajeaud. He joined trumpeter Lee Collins and saxophonist David Jones for a 1928 tour of Florida. In 1930 Barker and his wife, singer Louise "Blue Lu" Barker, moved to New York and Danny found work the following year with trumpeter Dave Nelson, trombonist Harry White, and others, including Fats Waller. In the rewarding, personal freedom of New York, Barker absorbed everything around him during the Harlem Renaissance, and flourished as a musician. He soon switched from banjo to rhythm guitar, and during the 1930s mainly performed with Sidney Bechet, Fess Williams, Albert Nicholas, and James P. Johnson. In the late 1930s he recorded with his wife and with Henry "Red" Allen, worked in the big bands of Lucky Millinder (1937–38), Benny Carter (1938), and Cab Calloway (1939–46), and began to work with small groups. Barker participated in a Dixieland revival through a series of "This Is Jazz" radio broadcasts and recorded with Mutt Carey and Bunk Johnson. About the same time, he began to play six-string banjo. In 1948 the Barkers spent a long stretch in California, where Lu recorded an album for Capitol. Danny recorded various sides in Los Angeles and New Orleans before returning to New York where he performed throughout the 1950s at Ryan's, often with trombonists Conrad Janis and Wilbur DeParis, and with his own band. In 1965 Barker and his wife returned to New Orleans and re-established their careers there. Until 1975 Danny served as assistant curator of the New Orleans Jazz Museum. He continued to work as a bandleader, guitarist, and from 1965 to 1972 led the Onward Brass Band. In later years he also recorded with Wynton Marsalis and the Dirty Dozen Brass Band. His notable compositions are "Don't You Feel My Leg," written for his wife, and "Save the Bones (for Henry Jones)," which was recorded by Nat King Cole. He wrote and lectured about jazz and taught young musicians. He wrote about his life in music in the now out-of-print 1986 book, *A Life in Jazz,* and worked to keep New Orleans jazz alive until his death. When Barker died in 1994 he left a trail of compositions and a discography of considerable range. A distinguished rhythm guitarist, he was also an accomplished six-string guitar player who made over 1,000 recordings as sideman, but only a couple of recordings as leader exist.

what to buy: A fun-filled, somewhat autobiographical, solo studio session, *Save the Bones* 🎵🎵🎵 (Orleans, 1991, prod. Carlo Ditta) features Barker's crisp vocals with self-accompanying rhythm guitar on an array of 11 originals and chestnuts such as "Nevertheless (I'm in Love with You)," "Nobody Knows You

When You're Down and Out," "St. James Infirmary," and "When You're Smiling." But most enjoyable are his originals, written often with self-revealing lyrics about saloons, and humorous, down-home themes. "Ham & Eggs" kicks off the set with the ringing bell of a wind-up alarm clock and continues with Barker weaving a tale about a Depression-era worker yearning for a buck and a square meal. His title tune is a classic, a chuckler about saving the bones for Henry, a vegetarian, who "doesn't eat no meat" but "loves the gristle." The 1988 session, recorded when Barker was in his mid-80s, preserves the tradition of the early troubadours, and Barker's simple, hard-times tunes sometimes bring to mind Woody Guthrie's "Dust Bowl Ballads." Other Barker originals with their humorous lyrics (and Barker's asides) and his unique treatment of classics make this a delightfully intimate session. *Live at the New Orleans Jazz Festival* ♪♪♪♪ (Orleans, 1998, prod. Carlo Ditta) features Blue Lu and Danny Barker in their last performance at the 1989 New Orleans Jazz and Heritage Festival. Danny was 80, Blue Lu, 75. Accompanied mostly by Danny's guitar, the ailing Lu sings fives songs in a hoarse voice (after throat surgery had affected her vocal cords). However, the spirit of the jazz/blues singer remains, especially when she sings Danny's original, "Don't You Feel My Legs," a risque tune she first recorded in 1938. Accompanied by his Jazz Hounds (a traditional New Orleans band), Danny sings and plays guitar on "Save the Bones," "St. James Infirmary," "You Got the Right Key, But the Wrong Keyhole," "Bourbon Street Parade," and a wonderful New Orleans rouser, "The Second Line." This CD preserves a special slice of jazz history.

influences:

◀◀ Johnny St. Cyr, Little Brother Montgomery, Jimmie Noone, Sidney Bechet, George Lewis

▶▶ Burt Bales, Lawrence Marrero, Eddie Smith, Stu Morrison, Johnny McCallum

Nancy Ann Lee

Charlie Barnet

Born October 26, 1913, in New York, NY. Died September 4, 1991.

Charlie Barnet could afford to be a liberal dilettante (he was born into a wealthy family), but it is a tribute to his basic instincts that he became a solid musician and a deceptively casual social do-gooder. Even though Barnet was a big fan of the Fletcher Henderson and Duke Ellington big bands, his outfits of the early 1930s were more like the white society bands of Paul Whiteman with a jazzier edge. By the mid-1930s Barnet's band

had more of a swinging jazz flavor and he cut some records with Red Norvo that included Artie Shaw and Teddy Wilson backing up Barnet's Coleman Hawkins–inspired tenor playing. 1939 was the year of "Cherokee," the Ray Noble barnburner that became Barnet's theme and one of the most frequently played of all jazz standards. From that point and on into the mid-1940s, Barnet was at his peak. He was also playing a lot of Ellington charts during this period and Duke remarked (in his autobiography *Music Is My Mistress*) that ". . . he constantly bolstered my ego by playing a book almost full of our compositions." Barnet was so enamored of Ellington that he would sometimes hire Duke's band for his own private parties.

Barnet also led the first white band to play the Apollo Theater and his colorblind hiring practices prevented him from playing a lot of venues during this period. The role call of major musicians that spent time in his band is remarkable. A very short list would include singers Lena Horne and Kay Starr and trumpeters Clark Terry and Doc Severinsen, along with arrangers Benny Carter and Eddie Sauter, but it would leave out even more big-time players. When Barnet gave up his big band he would still go out with an occasional sextet/septet or, in the case of his 1958 studio dates, work with an amazing big band (featuring Phil Woods, Charlie Shavers, Milt Hinton, and Nat Pierce), but most of his time was spent in comfortable retirement.

what to buy: *An Introduction to Charlie Barnet: His Best Recordings, 1935–1944* ♪♪♪♪ (Best of Jazz, 1996) is a well-conceived overview of Barnet's most popular and important recordings for Bluebird and Decca. If there is a weakness to the set, it is the underrepresentation of Barnet's hottest band of the mid-1940s, with only three of the Decca sides included. For that, get *Drop Me Off in Harlem* ♪♪♪♪ (Decca Jazz, 1992). Barnet's band of the early to mid-1940s included a fair number of proto-boppers and swing practitioners playing together in harmony, and artistically they may be more rewarding than earlier bands, although this shouldn't be taken as a knock on some of their predecessors. Members of the band during this time included pianist Dodo Mamarosa, guitarist Barney Kessel, and trumpet king Roy Eldridge. This album contains Barnet's biggest hit from the post-Bluebird years, "Skyliner."

the rest:

Clap Hands, Here Comes Charlie ♪♪♪ (Bluebird, 1987)
Cherokee ♪♪♪♪ (Bluebird, 1992)
Charlie Barnet and his Orchestra: 1941 ♪♪♪ (Circle, 1992)
Charlie Barnet and his Orchestra: 1942 ♪♪♪ (Circle, 1992)
Cherokee ♪♪♪▽ (Evidence, 1993)
More ♪♪♪ (Evidence, 1995)

worth searching for: Back in the days of vinyl, Bluebird had an awesome six-volume set of "twofers," *Complete Charlie Barnet, Vols. 1–6* 𝄞𝄞𝄞𝄞 (Bluebird, 1935–42, prod. various) which, if it were in print today, would go right to the top of the list.

influences:

◀◀ Coleman Hawkins, Johnny Hodges, Duke Ellington

▶▶ Pete Christlieb

Garaud MacTaggart

Joey Baron /Baron Down

Born June 26, 1955, in Richmond, VA. Baron Down formed c. 1990, in New York, NY.

Joey Baron, drums; Steve Swell, trombone; Ellery Eskelin, tenor sax.

Probably the most versatile and accomplished drummer in the Downtown NYC avant scene, Joey Baron can be counted on to keep the meter, no matter how crazy the circumstances. Besides being called on to blend Carl Stalling, grindcore, Ornette Coleman, and klezmer for John Zorn, Baron has also been found on recordings by artists as diverse as Arto Lindsay and Toots Thielemans. Heck, he even played on one of the more listenable David Sanborn efforts out there, *Another Hand*. Playing with Zorn must have helped keep Baron on his toes, for he's always ready to shift genres impeccably, based on who he's playing with as well as what he's playing. Although his discographical appearances are mostly as a sideman, some of those side dates are the most substantial in contemporary jazz (e.g. Naked City, Masada), and Baron consistently creates brilliant improv with Zorn, Frisell, and Miniature, the trio he has with Tim Berne and cellist Hank Roberts. Plus, through his trio Baron Down, he makes his own imprint on the face of contemporary avant garde jazz.

what to buy: If you're a fan of the downtown sound, then any Baron Down release should be scarfed up on sight. Start at the beginning and you'll find that *Tongue in Groove* 𝄞𝄞𝄞𝄞 (JMT, 1991, prod. David Breskin) offers a varied blur of jazz, from the crazed "Yow" to the humor injections of "Scottie Pippen" and the closing studio skit goofiness of "Mr. Pretension." By the way, the booklet informs that *Tongue* is an "all-acoustic all-live no mix edit gutbucket digital recording"—quite the punk-jazz credo. On the next Baron Down release, *Raised Pleasure Dot* 𝄞𝄞𝄞𝄞 (New World Records/CounterCurrents, 1993), some of the bossa nova beats that inform Baron's playing get deconstructed through "The Girl from Ipanema Blues," while Baron

also offers such rip-it-out scorchers as "Unleashing the Dobermans."

what to avoid: Although the lineup of Baron leading Arthur Blythe, Ron Carter, and Bill Frisell might seem enticing, *Down Home* 𝄞𝄞 (Intuition, 1997, prod. Lee Townsend) rests in a placid Virginian tobacco field compared to the urban clangor of his Baron Down releases. Seemingly marketed in a similar manner to Frisell's *Nashville*, *Down Home* also has a similar ready-for-NPR gloss to it—not too offensive or bad, just strictly Yuppieville middle-of-the-road music that's not as exciting as, say, *Another Hand*. So if you're looking for that crazy, cutting-edge downtown racket, stay away from *Down Home*.

worth searching for: A Japanese import, the Baron Down disc *Crackshot* 𝄞𝄞𝄞𝄞 (Avant, 1995, prod. David Breskin) features all-Baron penned tunes recorded in the same all-or-nothing style as *Tongue in Groove*.

influences:

◀◀ Bobby Previte, John Zorn

▶▶ Jim Black

see also: *Tim Berne, John Zorn*

Greg Baise

Dan Barrett

Born December 14, 1955, in Pasadena, CA.

Although he doubles on cornet and trumpet, Dan Barrett is best known for his gorgeous trombone sound. Barrett learned trombone and trumpet in junior high school, heard his first live jazz played by the South Frisco Jazz Band and, by age 15, was subbing in the band. Shortly after, he played with New Orleans veterans Ed Garland, Barney Bigard, Joe Darensbourg, and Nappy Lamare. Barrett was influenced by recordings of Al Jenkins, Lou McGarity, Jack Teagarden, and many other favorites including Dickie Wells, Vic Dickenson, and Tommy Dorsey. While continually distilling and reworking those trombone sounds into a style all his own, Barrett spent most of the late 1970s and early 1980s on the West Coast working with Dick Shooshan's Golden Eagles, and with professionals Eddie Miller, Jake Hanna, Dick Cary, and Gene Estes. In that period, Barrett also played the Breda, Holland Jazz Festival, recorded with Ray Skjelbred and his Port Costa Yeti Chasers, and with Dick Sudhalter, before moving to join Howard Alden in New York City in 1983.

In New York, Barrett played and arranged for the Widespread Depression Orchestra, worked with Bob Wilber, and with Terry

Waldo's Gotham City Jazz Band. He played at the last Eddie Condon's, performed with the Woody Herman Orchestra at Carnegie Hall, and made additional recordings as sideman. Barrett played lead trombone and soloed in Benny Goodman's last big band in 1985 and 1986. After Goodman's death, Barrett concentrated on the Alden-Barrett Quintet, organized in 1984. This fleet little band approaches swing in much the same manner as the John Kirby Sextet and the highly acclaimed Red Norvo groups, a style that found favor with trumpeter-arranger Buck Clayton who re-entered the jazz scene to write original tunes for the Alden-Barrett quintet. By the mid-1990s, Barrett was one of the busiest jazz musicians in the U.S. and international festival scene. He appears on numerous recordings, and on movie soundtracks for *The Cotton Club, Brighton Beach Memoirs,* and Woody Allen's *Bullets Over Broadway,* where he is seen briefly on camera. Barrett consults to the Arbors label and has appeared on many of their recordings.

what to buy: A laid-back duo album, *Two Sleepy People* 🎜🎜🎜 (Arbors, 1996, prod. Rachel Domber, Mat Domber) teams two world-class players, Barrett and pianist John Sheridan, both tune-sleuths who have found some fairly obscure melodies to explore. Barrett employs a variety of trombone mutes and switches to cornet occasionally to provide diversity of sound and Sheridan, sounding at times like John Bunch or Dick Hyman, is a one-man rhythm section at the piano. For folks who appreciate classy forays into the American popular songbook, they play 10 gems such as "Remember Me," "Oh, You Crazy Moon," "Why Do I Lie to Myself About You?," "Who Loves You?," "Moanin' Low," and other tunes. A trombone buff's delight, *Jubilesta!* 🎜🎜🎜 (Arbors, 1992, prod. Rachel Domber, Mat Domber) features Barrett in trio and quartet settings on a well-recorded display of the leader's mastery of the difficult instrument. He's aided by pianist Ray Sherman, bassist David Stone, and drummer Jake Hanna. The musicians pay tribute to Chu Berry ("Blue Chu"), Roy Eldridge ("Little Jazz"), Duke Ellington ("Jubilesta") and a wide range of trombone stylists. On the warmly rendered studio session, *The A-B-Q Salutes Buck Clayton* 🎜🎜🎜 (Concord Jazz, 1989, prod. Howard Alden, Dan Barrett), Barrett and Alden send their solid little band through a relaxed set of Buck Clayton originals. Swing is the watchword as reedman Chuck Wilson, bassist Frank Tate and drummer Jackie Williams join the co-leaders in 13 polished performances of Clayton favorites.

what to buy next: *Swing Street* 🎜🎜🎜 (Concord, 1987, prod. Howard Alden, Dan Barrett) finds the Alden-Barrett Quintet making easy work out of some swing classics with their com-

fortable but solid approach to tunes such as "Cottontail," "Stompin' at the Savoy," and "Lullaby in Rhythm." Guitarist Alden has effortless technique, a marvelous sense of rhythmic concept somewhere between swing and modern. Barrett is a licensed swinger with an endless bag of dynamic trombone sounds. *Strictly Instrumental* 🎜🎜🎜 (Concord, 1987, prod. Carl Jefferson) features the Dan Barrett Octet, especially the leader's trombone and Howard Alden's guitar, but probably underutilizes front-line players Ken Peplowski and Warren Vaché Jr. This album is special because it is Dick Wellstood's last record date and his piano shines on "Sleep" and the title tune.

the rest:
Reunion with Al 🎜🎜🎜 (Arbors, 1992)
(With George Masso) *Let's Be Buddies* 🎜🎜🎜 (Arbors, 1994)
Dan Barrett and Tom Baker in Austrialia 🎜🎜🎜 (Arbors, 1997)

worth searching for: Excellent examples of Barrett's arranging skills can be found on *Bobby Short with the Alden-Barrett Quintet: Swing That Music* 🎜🎜🎜 (Telarc, 1993, prod. John Snyder) which was nominated for a Grammy award.

influences:
◄◄ Al Jenkins, Lou McGarity, Jack Teagarden

John T. Bitter

Sweet Emma Barrett

Born March 25, 1897, in New Orleans, LA. Died January 28, 1983, in New Orleans LA.

With a career that began in the early 1920s as the pianist in Papa Celestin's Original Tuxedo Orchestra, "Sweet Emma" Barrett became best known for playing her hard-driving, authentic, New Orleans piano, and her vocal style reminiscent of the old-time blues singers. A distinctively colorful character, Barrett was commonly known to her audiences as "The Bell Gal," because she always sported a red beanie cap with "Sweet Emma the Bell Gal" inscribed on it, wore a red dress, and beneath the dress, wore red garters with dozens of tiny bells sewn into them. After her stint with Papa Celestin, she played and sang with Sidney Desvigne, John Robichaux, and Armand Piron, and during the 1940s and 1950s, performed with various local small groups. After 1961 Barrett became the regular pianist at Preservation Hall, and in addition, appeared on *The Ed Sullivan Show,* performed at the Stork Club in New York, and made numerous trips to Disneyland. Although she suffered from a stroke in 1968 that left her paralyzed on her left side, Barrett continued to perform up until her death, playing with only her right hand.

what to buy: There is very little available in print for Barrett. But check out the inspiring and authentic New Orleans jazz on *Sweet Emma—New Orleans: The Living Legends* 🎵🎵🎵🎵 (Riverside, 1961, prod. Chris Albertson/OJC, 1994, reissue prod. Phil De Lancie). The band, with trumpeter Percy Humphrey, trombonist Jim Robinson, and clarinetist Willie Humphrey, demonstrates why they became a favorite at Preservation Hall. With Barrett belting out four vocals, including "Bill Bailey (Won't You Please Come Home?)" and "St. Louis Blues," the energy level during the session keeps climbing. A must have-CD, particularly if you are a fan of New Orleans jazz.

influences:
◀◀ George C. McCullum, Papa Celestin

Susan K. Berlowitz

Ray Barretto

Born April 29, 1929, in Brooklyn, NY.

During the late 1940s Ray Barretto, fresh from his tour of duty with the Army, was hanging out in Harlem and partaking in the famous jam sessions that went on at Minton's and the Apollo Bar. Playing alongside such members of the bop elite as Sonny Stitt and Charlie Parker was inspirational for the career path Barretto was to take. From there he went on to play in Latin bands led by José Curbelo and Tito Puente (where he replaced Mongo Santamaria). After Barretto recorded with Red Garland on *Manteca*, receiving special guest artist billing on the cover of the album, he became the first choice for jazz musicians looking for a bit of Latin percussion. Some of the jazz artists he has worked with include Lou Donaldson, Gene Ammons, Dizzy Gillespie (an early influence along with Chano Pozo), and Sonny Stitt, but as a crack sessionman he has also played on the pop side of the ledger with the Rolling Stones and Bette Midler, to name just a few.

While working the jazz scene has always been special to Barretto, a lot of his recordings and commercial success came out of the Latin arena. In 1961 he recorded a novelty tune, "El Watusi," for Tico Records that became a big hit for him in 1963, lasting seven weeks on *Billboard* magazine's Top 40 charts. Fania Records was the next major recording home for Barretto. While with Fania he recorded several groundbreaking Latin albums including *Acid*, which included elements of jazz, Latin, and soul that capitalized on the bugalú craze of the moment. Barreto has also been a key member of the Fania All-Stars since their founding in 1968. In 1990 his collaboration with Celia Cruz, *Ritmo En El Corazón*, won a Grammy Award. His more re-cent albums have swung back towards Latin-influenced jazz with 1994's *Taboo* and 1996's *My Summertime* receiving Grammy nominations for Best Latin Jazz Performance.

what to buy: With his group New World Spirit, Barretto is in the running for most interesting Latin jazz group of the 1990s. The personnel has stayed fairly consistent over the years, but the lineup on *Taboo* 🎵🎵🎵🎵 (Concord Picante, 1994, prod. Allen Farnham) featured Latin trumpet legend Ray Vega soaring over the keyboard fantasies of Colombian-born pianist Hector Martignon, with Barretto's always-interesting percussion playing binding the whole together. Martignon is also an interesting composer with the sensuous midtempo "Guaji-rita" sustaining rhythmic tension where a lesser band and composer would probably want to sprint for the finish instead of enjoying the ride. Barretto's songs, including "Bomba-riquen" and "Montuno Blue," are also worth a mention as is his choice of covers with McCoy Tyner's "Effendi" and Nat Adderly's always welcome "Work Song." *My Summertime* 🎵🎵🎵🎵 (Blue Note, 1996, prod. Jean-Jacques Pussiau) is another fine mix of covers and originals from Barretto and his New World Spirit band. Trumpeter Michael Philip Mossman, though relatively young, is already a veteran of the Latin jazz world, having appeared on the last two Mario Bauzá albums in addition to playing with such jazz stars as Gene Harris, Horace Silver, and Toshiko Akiyoshi. Pianist Martignon and bassist Jairo Moreno have been part of Barretto's band for years and help form the rhythm core along with drummer Vince Cherico. Barretto is his usual superb self on congas.

what to buy next: *Handprints* 🎵🎵🎵 (Concord Picante, 1991, prod. Ray Barretto, Eric Kressmann) is definitely a percussion album. Barretto and drummer Ed Uribe wrote 40 percent of the album and provide a percolating rhythm bed for the band to float improvisations over. This early edition of New World Spirit was already a pretty happening band and a lot of that is owed to Barretto's guidance and playing along with his ability to attract young, high-caliber talent and (in the case of Hector Martignon and Jairo Moreno) to keep them. Saxophonist Steve Slagle is the other major player on the album and contributes three fine songs, with the album's leadoff tune, "Tercer Ojo," taking high honors.

best of the rest:
Carnaval 🎵🎵🎵 (Fantasy, 1962)
La Cuna 🎵🎵🎵 (Epic, 1979)
Rican/Struction 🎵🎵🎵 (Fania/Charly, 1979)
(With Celia Cruz) *Ritmo En El Corazón* 🎵🎵🎵 (Fania/Charly, 1988)
Latin Gold Collection 🎵🎵🎵 (PolyGram Latino, 1995)

worth searching for: Red Garland's album *Manteca* ♫♫♫ (Prestige, 1958, prod. Bob Weinstock) was the first real jazz album to feature Barretto as a sideman. The same year Garland's trio once again gave Barretto featured billing on *Rojo* ♫♫♫ (Prestige, 1958, prod. Bob Weinstock).

influences:

◀◀ Chano Pozo, Mongo Santamaria, Tito Puente

▶▶ Giovanni Hidalgo

Garaud MacTaggart

Kenny Barron

Born June 9, 1943, in Philadelphia, PA.

The younger brother of Bill Barron, the late and neglected saxophonist, Kenny Barron has been acclaimed as one of the finest piano players of recent vintage. Like Hank Jones and Tommy Flanagan, Barron has that elusive sense for playing just what is called for at any moment and making it sound so easy and natural that his work can initially be taken for granted. In 1961, Barron moved to New York where he worked with Roy Haynes, Lee Morgan, James Moody, and Lou Donaldson. He spent a particularly fruitful association with Dizzy Gillespie's band between 1962 and 1966. Later work included stints with Freddie Hubbard, Yusef Lateef, Ron Carter, and the Thelonious Monk tribute band, Sphere. His work with Stan Getz just prior to the saxophonist's death is also of major importance. With a sizeable lot of good albums under his own name and scores of others as a sideman now available, Barron finds himself in the enviable position of being known as one of the true masters of the art.

what to buy: *New York Attitude* ♫♫♫♫ (Uptown, 1984, prod. Robert Sunenblick, David Sunenblick) is one of Barron's finest trio efforts with Rufus Reid and the late Freddie Waits on hand. *Quickstep* ♫♫♫♫ (Enja, 1991, prod. Joanne Klein) is one of the few recordings available with Barron's stellar quintet of Eddie Henderson, John Stubblefield, David Williams, and Victor Lewis. A lengthy version of Victor Lewis's sublime "Big Girls" is a highlight of this truly inspired set.

what to buy next: Working with bassist Dave Holland and drummer Daniel Humair on *Scratch* ♫♫♫♫ (Enja, 1985, prod. Matthias Winckelmann), Barron contributes some originals to the session and is roused to some of his most imaginative playing. *The Only One* ♫♫♫♫ (Reservoir, 1990, prod. Mark Feldman, Joanne Klein) is my favorite disc of standards played by Barron's trio with Ray Drummond and Ben Riley. Simply gorgeous

stuff! *Wanton Spirit* ♫♫♫♫ (Verve, 1994, prod. Joanne Klein) reveals Barron inspired to some truly creative heights in this genuine meeting of giants with Charlie Haden and Roy Haynes.

best of the rest:

Sunset at Dawn ♫♫♫ (Muse, 1973)
Peruvian Blue ♫♫♫ (Muse, 1974)
Golden Lotus ♫♫♫ (Muse, 1980)
At the Piano ♫♫♫ (Xanadu, 1981)
Green Chimneys ♫♫♫♫ (Criss Cross Jazz, 1983)
What If? ♫♫♫♫ (Enja, 1986)
Two as One ♫♫♫ (Red, 1986)
Live at Fat Tuesdays ♫♫♫ (Enja, 1988)
Rhythm-A-Ning ♫♫♫♫ (Candid, 1989)
Live at Maybeck Recital Hall ♫♫♫♫ (Concord, 1990)
Invitation ♫♫♫♫ (Criss Cross Jazz, 1991)
Lemuria-Seascape ♫♫♫♫ (Candid, 1991)
The Moment ♫♫♫♫ (Reservoir, 1992)
Sambao ♫♫♫ (Verve, 1992)
Other Places ♫♫♫ (Verve, 1993)
Swamp Sally ♫♫♫♫ (Verve, 1996)

influences:

◀◀ Art Tatum, Elmo Hope, Wynton Kelly

Chris Hovan

Bruce Barth

Born September 7, 1968, in Pasadena, CA.

An exciting young pianist with a strong compositional sensibility, Bruce Barth is a graceful improvisor with a lithe but harmonically rich sound. His solos have an edited feel, as if shorn of extraneous notes, and he adds percussive accents to a style rooted in Herbie Hancock's and Chick Corea's mid-1960s sounds. Barth moved to New York in the late 1980s, where he's freelanced extensively, including tours with Stanley Turrentine and Nat Adderley. He joined Terence Blanchard's quintet in 1990, and made a number of albums with the trumpeter. He has also recorded with saxophonist Vincent Herring, vibraphonist Monte Croft, singer Dominque Eade, trumpeter Ingrid Jensen, composer George Russell, guitarist Dave Stryker, alto saxophonist Steve Wilson, and the ensemble Orange Then Blue. Since leaving Blanchard in 1994, Barth has worked with the Mingus Big Band and bassist John Patitucci, and led his own groups, appearing at Bradley's and Sweet Basil in New York with bands featuring leading young players such as Wilson, Larry Grenadier, Ed Howard, Leon Parker, Billy Drummond, Adam Cruz, and Scott Wendholt. Considering his work as a sideman and his two albums for Enja, Barth has emerged as a talent to watch.

what to buy: A quintet session with some of the most inventive young mainstream players in jazz, *Morning Call* 🎵🎵🎵🎵 (Enja, 1995, prod. Bruce Barth) features the same front line as his debut recording—Steve Wilson on soprano and alto sax and Scott Wendholt on trumpet and flugelhorn—with bassist Larry Grenadier and drummer Leon Parker. Though Barth opens with two standards, a re-harmonized version of "April in Paris" featuring a thrilling Wilson alto solo, and a trio version of "In the Still of the Night," the bulk of the album consists of his original tunes. Most notable is his two-part tune "Where Eagles Fly," with its movement between turbulence and serenity. His title track is another multifaceted piece that flows through a variety of moods, highlighted by Wilson's piquant soprano solo. Parker's traps work is a revelation throughout, with his inventive textural sense and skin-tight connection to Grenadier's excellent bass playing.

what to buy next: An extremely impressive debut session by the 25-year old pianist, *In Focus* 🎵🎵🎵🎵 (Enja, 1993, prod. Horst Weber) features Steve Wilson on soprano and alto sax, Scott Wendholt on trumpet, Robert Hurst on bass, and Lewis Nash on drums. Barth wrote six of the 10 tunes, including the freewheeling, Latin-tinged "In Search Of . . . ," and the gorgeous ballad "Louise," but tips his hat to one of his main compositional influences with lyrical versions of two Wayne Shorter tunes, "Pinocchio" and "Wildflower," the latter featuring a particularly sensitive piano solo. Another highlight is his reworking of Ellington's perennial "I Got It Bad and That Ain't Good," a keyboard tour de force where Barth alternates single-note lines, lush block chords, and sneaky register jumps.

worth searching for: Though he's listed in the album credits as Bruce Bath, it's Barth who holds down the piano chair on *The Malcolm X Jazz Suite* 🎵🎵🎵🎵 (Columbia, 1993, prod. Terence Blanchard), one of trumpeter Blanchard's most impressive outings. A quintet session featuring tenor saxophonist Sam Newsome, bassist Tarus Mateen, and drummer Troy Davis, the album holds together as a suite through Blanchard's use of reoccurring motifs. The trumpeter uses Barth's sinuous lines and beautiful, bell-like tone, and Davis's cymbal work as the suite's foundation. This is an album that gets better with each listen.

influences:

◀◀ Herbie Hancock, Kenny Barron

Andrew Gilbert

Gary Bartz

Born June 26, 1940, in Baltimore, MD.

Bartz has added fervent alto in the bands of some of jazz's biggest names, including Miles Davis, McCoy Tyner, Max Roach, and Art Blakey but he will always be unjustly thought of as a sellout by the jazz bourgeois for a series of increasingly R&B-oriented LPs that he put out through the mid-1970s into the early 1980s. This is too bad—Bartz's so-called commercial LPs reveal an active conceptual mind and remain fresh two decades later, even if anything that smacks of fusion is held in suspicion by the status quo nowadays. It's a shame that the recent recordings of Bartz's "comeback" have reduced him to little more than pretty and/or fiery blowing—and, no question, it is pretty and/or fiery—but this is not uncommon for many of the 1960s innovators who have managed to scramble back into the public eye.

A Juilliard graduate, Bartz's first break was with the Max Roach/Abbey Lincoln band in 1964 when both were at the height of their powers. Bebop drummers seemed more willing to embrace the New Music than their contemporaries (see Roy Haynes, Art Taylor, and Philly Joe Jones), particularly those with a political orientation, and Roach and Lincoln could get pretty far out—Lincoln turning Billie Holiday's moan into the screams of an ex-slave. When Bartz went solo with his NTU Troop ("NTU" means "unity" in Bantu), he extended the concept, and it is true that his early LPs as a leader are his high point. Uncompromising free blowing with African-ish percussion, they are finally getting reissued in the United Kingdom (and on vinyl, no less). During the late 1960s and early 1970s, he appeared on several classic recordings, including Pharoah Sanders's *Sumnen, Bukmen, Umyun*, Lee Konitz's *Altissimo*, and several McCoy Tyner LPs, including *Extensions*, the pianist's finest album as a leader in a very fine career. But most importantly, he was drafted into the Miles Davis band as Wayne Shorter's replacement, and as jazz history has shown, this tends to be a life-changing event. Davis was under heavy attack during that period for so-called commercial concessions but any cursory listen to the recordings of that period—*Dark Magus, Get Up With It, On the Corner* and the like—will show some of the most oddball artwork in American history: un-funk rhythms with anti-jazz playing razor-bladed apart and together again by producer Teo Macero into an unrepeatable conjecture of the darkest cocaine feel. Miles did manage to insure his status as a public figure, but by his "retirement" in 1975, his LPs were selling as poorly as they ever had. Commercial concessions, indeed. Because of the nature of the recordings, Bartz can only be heard for certain on live recordings such as the *Isle of Wight* track and *Live-Evil* and his playing may be the finest on that double disc.

This digression on Miles is to show the turn of jazz at the start of the 1970s. Much of the avant-garde developed from the sonic attack of R&B and it should not be surprising that as other forms of black pop music took over the airwaves, some experimental musicians might be honestly interested. Bartz's first several albums in this new vein weren't R&B proper, although he would cover songs such as "Betcha by Golly Wow." He was often accompanied by underground legend Andy Bey on vocals and keyboards. The African influence was still there, and he would play in a more mainstream fashion on occasion, such as on *Ju Ju Man*. These LPs are generally reviewed diffidently, but Bartz's disco records are a real bugbear in the jazz community, if a boon to the more historically minded (i.e. better) Hip-Hop groups such as A Tribe Called Quest, who have been faithfully sampling them over the last decade. No doubt his work with Davis and drummer Norman Connors was an influence (they recorded several LPs together). Like Connors, Pharoah Sanders, and many others during that period, they did not separate their interest in Stevie Wonder-esque pop and avant-jazz; in fact, both had similar social roots. Although it was a shame to lose such a vibrant member of the avant-garde, hindsight fails to show what the fuss was about, and it is time to reevaluate them. It did not help that he finally fully converted to the cause as disco was grunting its death rattle, nor that he was disappearing into anonymous pop session work, but these records hold up a lot better than the Neo-con stylings and faux-Rap (no doubt the imperative is "always connect") of his recent Atlantic releases. Still, let's not begrudge a great improviser a half-hearted comeback (Atlantic has since dumped him). His roots, and I expect his heart, are not in either of these musics, but in the avant-garde and 1970s funk-soul.

what to buy: Bartz's group Harlem Bush Music made *Taifa* ♫♫♫♫ (Milestone, 1970, prod. Orrin Keepnews) and *Uhuru* ♫♫♫♫ (Milestone, 1971), combined on a single import CD on BGP and it's the best Bartz out there, with Bey, bassist Ron Carter, and percussionist Nat Bettis among others. Uncompromising and political ("Viet Cong," anyone?), but, like the best Bartz, always humanistic. *Another Earth* ♫♫♫♫ (Milestone, 1968) turned a lot of heads in its time. Pharoah Sanders guests and the vibe is actually a bit wilder than the hippy-dippy stuff he was making his name in.

what to buy next: *Ju Ju Street Songs* ♫♫♫♫ (Prestige, 1973, prod. Gary Bartz) and *Follow the Medicine Man* ♫♫♫♫ (Prestige,

1973, prod. Gary Bartz) feature the same personnel, were recorded around the same time, and were reissued on a single CD (minus one song from *Medicine Man*) by Fantasy in 1997. This is where you really start to notice a change. Bartz's lines become snakier, the tunes Wonder-esque, and there's a fair amount of singing. The soul stuff is in a Gil Scott-Heron vibe (not quite as adroitly wordy, as you might imagine). Still harder-edged than, say, Lonnie Liston Smith and really quite ahead of its time by being altogether of it. Song quality does vary, though. *Singerella: A Ghetto Fairy Tale* ♫♫♫ (Prestige, 1974) . . . they don't write ghetto fairy tales the way they used to. Silliness is abated by fine soloing.

what to avoid: *Blues Chronicles: Tales of Life* ♫♫ (Atlantic, 1996, prod. Gary Bartz, Eulis Cathey) might seem a curious choice for those used to flogging the disco stuff, but Bartz's recent Atlantic releases have been ponderous, turgid affairs. The playing is okay and sometimes inspired, but the ideas—either the placid muting of Young Lions, or (on a few tracks on this disc) a decade-old take on "currency"—don't support them. On one hand, like many great jazz artists searching for relevancy, the kids they think are kids have kids. And likewise, when an old lion tries to sound like a young one sounding like an old one, he becomes redundant.

best of the rest:
Home ♫♫♫♫ (Milestone, 1969)
I've Known Rivers and Other Bodies ♫♫♫♫ (Prestige, 1974)
Jujuman ♫♫♫ (Catalyst, 1976)
Ode to Super ♫♫♫ (SteepleChase)
(With Leon Thomas) *Precious Energy* ♫♫♫♫ (Mapleshade, 1987)
Monsoon ♫♫♫ (SteepleChase, 1988)
Reflections of Monk: The Final Frontier ♫♫♫ (SteepleChase, 1988)
There Goes the Neighborhood ♫♫♫ (Candid, 1990)
West 42nd Street ♫♫♫ (Candid, 1990)
Shadows ♫♫♫ (Timeless, 1993)
Episode One Children of Harlem Jazz ♫♫♫♫ (Challenge, 1994)
Red & Orange Poems ♫♫♫ (Atlantic, 1994)

worth searching for: Bartz's finest straight-ahead disc as a leader is also his earliest, *Libra* ♫♫♫♫ (Milestone, 1969, prod. Orrin Keepnews), which would make sense after being on the road with Art Blakey for two years. With the underrated duo of trumpeter Jimmy Owens and pianist Kenny Barron. Bartz's first unabashedly pop album, *Music Is My Sanctuary* ♫♫♫♫ (Capitol, 1975), is his best, as funk rhythms tend to be more productive than disco. It didn't hurt to have some crack jazzmen in with the session guys, such as pianist George Cables and trumpeter Eddie Henderson. Fonce Mizell does his thing here, creating a rich backdrop with lots of keyboards and a touch of the sort of cheese that gives these things a shelf life as fascinating documents. Maybe this will some day come out again on Blue Note! There's a mother lode of samples on *The Shadow Do* ♪♪♪♪ (Prestige, 1975, prod. Larry Mizell, Fonce Mizell, Gary Bartz). As producers, the Mizells are best known for their work with Donald Byrd in the 1970s. The music here is too active to remain in the background for long, however, and with improv always creeping around the edges of the vamps, it never really gets down, which is the archetypal problem for jazz-funk. That is, it's always jazz's fault. Don't let this dissuade you, however (not that you could find the disc anyway).

influences:

◀◀ Charlie Parker, Jackie McLean

▶▶ Greg Osby, Joshua Redman

D. Strauss

Count Basie

Born William Basie, August 21, 1904, in Red Bank, NJ. Died April 26, 1984, in Hollywood, CA.

If music alone were the criteria for crowning jazz royalty, William Basie would have been the King of Swing, not merely a Count. Basie's riff-based big band was the epitome of swing. The band's streamlined "All American Rhythm Section" had its rhythm firmly locked in, providing a perfect springboard on which the band's jazz giants could launch their developing solo skills.

Count Basie's career provides an excellent example of how the movements of individual musicians influenced the spread of jazz styles. In the early 1920s, Basie became a professional New York pianist, learning at the feet of stride masters such as James P. Johnson and Fats Waller. Strong, though simplified, stride elements permeated Basie's piano work throughout his career. In 1927, Basie made a western tour with the Gonzel White vaudeville company. When the company became stranded in Kansas City, Basie joined Walter Page's Blue Devils, then Bennie Moten's Kansas City Orchestra, introducing his already modified New York stride to the hard-riffing Kansas City jazz. This electrifying combination was the foundation on which Count Basie built his new band of 1935, which he formed from remnants of the Moten orchestra. In 1936 Basie and his band gave New York its first extended taste of hard-swinging Kansas City jazz. The band's influence was unquestionable. So too was the influence of Basie drummer Jo Jones, tenor saxophonist Lester Young, and trumpeters Buck Clayton and Harry Edison.

Jones and Young, in particular, laid the groundwork for the boppers waiting just over the horizon.

The rising cost of touring a big band, coupled with diminishing revenue, led Basie to disband at the end of 1949. For the next couple of years he led a small group, usually a septet, that at best boasted boppers Clark Terry (trumpet), Wardell Grey (tenor saxophone), and Buddy DeFranco (clarinet) in the front line, and a Basie rhythm section that swung harder than ever. This often overlooked small band should be considered one of several musical high points in Basie's career. Then, bucking economic trends, Basie organized another big band in 1952. With personnel changes, this is the band he led for the remainder of his life, and which exists in the late 1990s under the direction of Grover Mitchell. While Basie's 1930s-40s band, now referred to as the "Old Testament" band, based much of its repertoire on head arrangements developed in rehearsal and on gigs, this "New Testament" band relied heavily on its arrangers, notably Ernie Wilkins, Neal Hefti, and Frank Foster, to set its style. But the band still boasted great soloists, including at various times trumpeters Thad Jones and Joe Newman, trombonists Al Grey and Benny Powell, and saxophonists Frank Foster, Frank Wess, and Eddie "Lockjaw" Davis. Two 1955 hit recordings, the instrumental "April in Paris" and "Everyday I Have the Blues," featuring band vocalist Joe Williams, assured success for this new Basie band.

The exciting formative years of Basie's "New Testament" band were recorded on Norman Granz's Clef and Verve labels until 1958, when Basie jumped to Roulette, the label which captured the band's greatest work. After leaving Roulette in 1962, Basie appeared on many different labels, with often indifferent results. In 1972, he was reunited with Granz, this time on Pablo. Many fine Basie Band albums resulted, though none up to the level of the best on Roulette. But Granz, perhaps the greatest matchmaker in the history of jazz, also recorded Basie in many jam sessions and combos, utilizing Basie sidemen, visiting veterans, and interesting guests. Basie's last gig, however, was in Burlington, Vermont, with his regular band, during a tour of one night stands.

Basie's band influenced most big bands after the late 1930s, especially the Harry James Band. Basie's rhythm section opened up the music for modern jazz by keeping the rhythm solid yet uncluttered. Basie's spare piano style laid the groundwork for the coming of modern jazz pianists. The light, airy, and very swinging work of Basie saxophonist Lester Young influenced most modern players—saxophonists, trumpeters, guitarists, and others, especially Zoot Sims, Al Cohn, Bill Perkins, Bob Cooper, Art Pepper, Phil Woods, Shorty Rogers, Miles Davis, Bill deArango, and Chuck Wayne. Virtually every musician of the so-called West Coast Cool Jazz school of the 1950s cited Young's influence.

what to buy: *The Complete Decca Recordings* 🎵🎵🎵🎵 (GRP–Decca Jazz, 1992, prod. Orrin Keepnews) magnificently documents the Basie band's first New York recordings, those of 1937 through 1939. The transfers are first class, and the annotation thorough, but most importantly, the band's tremendous sense of swing and the soloists' bristling creativity is constantly in evidence. These band sides include about 25 sax solos by Lester Young (and one on clarinet), and dozens by saxophonist Hershel Evans, trumpeter Buck Clayton, trombonists Benny Morton and Dickie Wells, vocalist Jimmy Rushing and others, but it is the locked-in rhythm section of Basie, guitarist Freddie Green, bassist Walter Page, and drummer Jo Jones that keeps things solid and swinging. *The Essential Count Basie, Vol. 1* 🎵🎵🎵🎵 (Columbia/OKeh, 1987–88, prod. Bob Altshuler, Mike Berniker), *The Essential Count Basie, Vol. 2* 🎵🎵🎵🎵 (Columbia/OKeh, 1987–88, prod. Bob Altshuler, Mike Berniker), and *The Essential Count Basie, Vol. 3* 🎵🎵🎵🎵 (Columbia/OKeh, 1987–88, prod. Bob Altshuler, Mike Berniker) contain many moments equal to those on the Decca reissue, but are a little less consistent, and not as well produced than the first-mentioned album. These three CDs still include a lot of Lester Young and the other stars of the Decca sides, although by 1941, which hits mid-way through Volume 3, there were quite a few defections, including Young, who is replaced by Coleman Hawkins on two tunes. Basie's "New Testament" band's best period is thoroughly documented on two limited edition sets available by mail order only from Mosaic (phone: 203-327-7111 or FAX: 201-323-3526). The ten-CD set *The Complete Roulette Studio Recordings of Count Basie and His Orchestra* 🎵🎵🎵🎵 (Roulette, late 1950s–early 1960s, prod. Teddy Reig/Mosaic, 1993, reissue prod. Michael Cuscuna) and the eight-CD set *The Complete Roulette Live Recordings of Count Basie and His Orchestra* 🎵🎵🎵🎵 (Roulette, 1959–62, prod. Teddy Reig/Mosaic, 1991, reissue prod. Michael Cuscuna) include few alternate takes on the studio sessions, keeping these CDs listenable. All of the great Neal Hefti charts from *Basie* (see below) are included, and saxophonists "Lockjaw" Davis, Frank Foster, and Frank Wess, trumpeters Thad Jones, Joe Newman, and Snooky Young, trombonists Al Grey and Benny Powell, and of course pianist Basie are among those who keep the music inspired. Many tunes are repeated on different nights on the live set, but hard-core collectors will be pleased to note that only 28 of the 133 selections have been issued before.

what to buy next: Basie's 1950s output for Norman Granz's Clef and Verve labels has not been systematically reissued, but there are still a couple of must-have CDs. *April in Paris* 🎵🎵🎵🎵 (Verve, 1956, prod. Norman Granz) includes 1955–56 Basie classics such as the hit title tune (a Wild Bill Davis arrangement), Freddie Green's fine "Corner Pocket," and Frank Foster's "Shiny Stockings." Also from 1955, *Count Basie Swings, Joe Williams Sings* 🎵🎵🎵🎵 (Verve, 1955/1993, prod. Norman Granz) is arguably the finest vocalist with big band album ever. Everything clicks. Williams is at his peak; the band cooks, playing fine charts mostly by Frank Foster, and the soloists shine, especially Foster and section-mate Frank Wess on tenor sax. The album includes the classic "Everyday I Have the Blues," the equally fine "The Comeback," and the nearly as good "Roll 'Em, Pete." If you do not want to spend big bucks on the limited-edition Mosaic sets (or if you wait too long and they're gone), you may wish to pick up *Basie* 🎵🎵🎵🎵 (Roulette, 1957/1994, prod. Teddy Reig). This CD, which retains the famous atomic bomb album cover, includes arranger Neal Hefti's best charts: "The Kid from Red Bank" (with kicking Basie stride-piano), "Whirly-Bird" (with drummer Sonny Payne's rim shots adding punch to the work of the trumpet section), and the slow and sexy "Lil' Darlin'," (which quickly attained "jazz standard" status). *Sing Along with Basie* 🎵🎵🎵🎵 (Roulette, 1959/1991, prod. Teddy Reig) was a change of pace from Basie's usual big band fare, featuring the star vocalese group, Lambert Hendricks & Ross, singing many of the band parts and vocally recreating previously improvised instrumental solos. Unlike many later vocalese groups, whose strident singing too often reflects Broadway roots, LH&R had cut their teeth in jazz clubs of the era, and their work swung like mad. Have no fear if you're buying the "complete" Roulette studio set on Mosaic. It doesn't include sessions with guest vocalists, such as this.

what to avoid: If shopping for LPs (some of which are bound to show up on CD), be careful of Basie albums recorded from the time he left Roulette in 1962 to before he joined Pablo in 1972. Certainly some are fine, but there are too many others pairing Basie with inappropriate material or guest artists. Basie albums with Sammy Davis Jr. (Verve, 1964), the Alan Copeland Singers (ABC, 1966), Jackie Wilson (Brunswick, 1968), and Bing Crosby (Daybreak, 1972), just don't work. Other flops include bland attempts at the music from *Half a Sixpence* 🎵 (Dot, 1967) and Walt Disney's *The Happiest Millionaire* 🎵 (Coliseum, 1967),

Count Basie **(AP/Wide World Photos)**

lame musicals to begin with, and *Basie Meets Bond* ♂ (United Artists, 1966) and *Basie on the Beatles* ♂ (Happy Tiger, 1970). Professional musicianship is up to par and good solo moments do occur but they are few and far between on these recordings. They deserve a woof or two additional for content.

best of the rest:

Basie in London ♫♫♫♫ (Verve, 1957/1988)
Count Basie at Newport ♫♫♫♫ (Verve, 1957/1989)
Count Basie and the Kansas City Seven ♫♫♫♫♫ (Impulse!, 1962/1996)
First Time ♫♫♫♫ (Columbia, 1987)
88 Basie Street ♫♫♫♫ (Pablo, 1987)
The Golden Years, Vol. 1–3 and 5 ♫♫♫♫ (EPM, 1988–93) (Air checks and broadcast transcriptions)
Beaver Junction ♫♫♫♫ (VJC, 1991) (Air checks and broadcast transcriptions)
Corner Pocket ♫♫♫♫ (Laserlight, 1992)
Shoutin' Blues ♫♫♫♫ (RCA Victor, Various 78s/Bluebird, 1993)
Count Basie and the Stars of Birdland ♫♫♫♫ (Jazz, 1996)
The Bosses, with Joe Turner ♫♫♫♫ (Pablo)

worth searching for: As exciting as the Basie Band's first Decca studio recordings were, broadcast recordings from the same period kick even more. The earliest, from a February 1937, Pittsburgh date, are on *The Count at the Chatterbox* ♫♫♫♫ (Jazz Archive, 1974). Lester Young, Buck Clayton, and many of the others are all over the place, darting in and out of the ensemble, and soaring through their solos. The next air checks, as well as some transcription recordings, are on *The Golden Years* already mentioned, but Volume 4 went out of print in the blink of an eye. This CD is worth a hard search, for it documented work by the band during the musician's union recording ban of the war years, a period during which Lester Young returned, playing his tail off. A sub-rosa LP (which may see daylight on CD eventually), *Featuring Wardell Gray* ♫♫♫♫ (Ozone, 1948–51) spotlights tenorist Gray in live sessions by Basie's big band of 1948, and the kickin' small group of 1951. Although the music is top-notch, it's a poorly produced LP. A fantastic, full-fidelity LP performance by Basie's Band, including trumpeter Roy

Eldridge and tenor saxophonist "Lockjaw" Davis, was recorded at the 1966 Newport Jazz Festival and issued on one side of *Basie, Lambert, Hendricks, Ross* &&&& (Europa/Giganti Jazz). As one might guess, Lambert, Hendricks, and Ross dominate the other side, which is from Newport, 1959. The liner notes lie about the dates and personnel, but the music doesn't lie. It's top notch, with "Lockjaw's" sax work and the trumpet section tearing up "St. Louis Blues." The LH&R side isn't bad, but you'll never go back to it after you hear the Basie.

influences:

⏪ Fats Waller, James P. Johnson, Bennie Moten

⏩ The Henry James Band, most big bands

John K. Richmond

Django Bates

Born October 2, 1960, in Beckenham, England.

Playing piano, keyboards, E-flat peck horn, guitar, tenor horn, trumpet, and various percussion instruments, Django Bates is arguably the most daring bandleader among the younger crop of British jazzmen. While a prominent figure on the English scene, his intriguing and colorful music has not received the attention it deserves on the other side of the Atlantic. He has recorded with a few prominent artists—Tim Berne (*Nice View*), Hank Roberts (*Little Motor People*), and Bill Bruford (*Earthworks*, *Dig?*, and *Earthworks Live: Stamping Ground*) being the best-known in the United States—but has decided to focus on working as a leader. If none of his albums have the focus that sets apart masterpieces, they are all full of good ideas and engaging playing.

what to buy: There's a circusy atmosphere on *Summer Fruits (and Unrest)* &&&& (JMT, 1993, prod. Stefan F. Winter) which mixes seven tracks by the large and versatile English group Delightful Precipice with four by the occasionally augmented quartet Human Chain, both led by Bates, who here plays piano, keyboards, E-flat peck horn, and guitar. The large-group pieces are dense and mercurial, sometimes more flashy and postmodernly ironic than necessary, but winningly hyperactive. The greater space in the small group allows for some exciting improvisations.

what to buy next: *Autumn Fires (and Green Shoots)* &&&& (JMT, 1994, prod. Stefan F. Winter) is a nicely quirky solo piano album. Bates's pianistic influences come from jazz (Mal Waldron, Keith Jarrett, Richie Beirach) and beyond, with natural incorporations of harmonies redolent of Debussy and Scriabin.

There's always the off-kilter sense that anything could happen, but nothing sounds contrived or disproportionate as Bates straddles the border between inside and outside.

the rest:
Winter Truce (and Homes Ablaze) &&&& (JMT, 1995)

worth searching for: *Music for the Third Policeman* &&& (Ah Um, 1990) is inspired by a book by Flann O'Brien and ends up functioning like a soundtrack. There are a lot of sudden stylistic shifts, and the music sounds mostly composed; this is arguably more of a classical release than jazz, but offers Bates fans, who don't have a lot of his music to pick up, a look at another side of his music.

influences:

⏪ Mal Waldron, Keith Jarrett, Richie Beirach, John Zorn

Steve Holtje

Alvin Batiste

Born 1937, in New Orleans, LA.

One of jazz's great modern clarinetists, Batiste has inexplicably spent most of his career completely overlooked by record labels large and small. An original stylist whose playing can't be categorized, Batiste possesses a beautiful tone and a fertile, avant-garde-leaning harmonic vocabulary. He has spent most of his career as an educator in Louisiana, which partially explains his relative obscurity. A childhood friend of drummer Ed Blackwell, Batiste spent some time in Los Angeles in the mid-1950s, where he played with Ornette Coleman. He also played with Cannonball Adderley and toured with Ray Charles in 1958 but remained a hometown legend until recording three albums with the group Clarinet Summit (with David Murray, John Carter, and Jimmy Hamilton) in the 1980s. He recorded a few hard-to-find albums for India Navigation and finally made his major label debut in 1993 on Columbia's bizarrely titled "Legendary Pioneers of Jazz" series. Despite this, Batiste continues to be one of jazz's great but under-recorded players, a daring improvisor with an entirely original sound.

what to buy: *Late* &&&& (Columbia, 1993, prod. Alvin Batiste) pairs Batiste with a bebop rhythm section and the results are entirely pleasing. Kenny Barron (piano), Rufus Reid (bass), and Herman Jackson provide effective straight-ahead accompaniment while Batiste keeps slipping out of their harmonic grasp. Things start off strong with the New Orleans blues "Late," pick up with the complex Coltrane-inspired "Imp and Perry," and remain interesting until the unfortunate modal version of "When the Saints." The album otherwise features all Batiste material except for "Body and Soul" (which also features alto saxophonist Wes Anderson) and the tasty Ray Charles lick "Ray's Segue." *Southern Bells* 𝄢𝄢𝄢𝄢 (Black Saint, 1987, prod. David Murray) is a brilliant album by the collective Clarinet Summit, a quartet of reed masters spanning three generations from the longtime Ellingtonian Jimmy Hamilton to avant-garde pioneers Batiste, John Carter, and David Murray, whose always rewarding bass clarinet work anchors the ensemble. Batiste contributes two tunes to the session, the whimsical, interval-leaping "Fluffy's Blues" and the hip-hop-tinged "Beat Box."

the rest:

(With Clarinet Summit) *You Better Fly Away* 𝄢𝄢𝄢𝄢 (MPS, 1980)
(With Clarinet Summit) *In Concert at the Public Theater* 𝄢𝄢𝄢𝄢 (India Navigation, 1983)
Musique d'Afrique Nouvelle Orleans 𝄢𝄢𝄢𝄢 (India Navigation, 1984)
(With Clarinet Summit) *Clarinet Summit, Vol. 2* 𝄢𝄢𝄢𝄢 (India Navigation, 1985)
Bayou Magic 𝄢𝄢𝄢𝄢 (India Navigation, 1989)

influences:

◀◀ Ornette Coleman
▶▶ Don Byron

Andrew Gilbert

Mario Bauzá

Born April 28, 1911, in Havana, Cuba. Died July 11, 1993, in New York, NY.

Mario Bauzá was involved in two of the major jazz and Latin trends of the 1930s and 1940s. He was responsible for introducing Dizzy Gillespie to conga legend Chano Pozo and for bringing the standard Cuban rhythm section into line with the big band sound of Cab Calloway and Chick Webb. The meeting of Gillespie and Pozo was influential in the development of a hybrid known as Cubop which included among its proponents Stan Getz and Charlie Parker. The blending of big band arrangements with Cuban rhythms made Bauzá's brother-in-law, Machito (Frank Grillo), the leader of what was arguably the most influential Latin-flavored band in the first half of this century.

Bauzá's first instruments were the clarinet and the bass clarinet, which he played in the Havana Philharmonic. In 1930, shortly after arriving in the United States, Bauzá got a job with Cuarteto Machin playing trumpet, an instrument he learned to play in the two weeks preceding his first job with the band. His first major jazz gig was with Chick Webb in 1933 and from there

Bauzá worked briefly with bands led by Don Redman and Fletcher Henderson before joining Cab Calloway's outfit in 1939. In 1940 Bauzá made the move to Machito's newly formed band as the musical director, and there he stayed until 1976.

During the late 1970s and early 1980s Bauzá and Graciela (his sister-in-law and former vocalist with Machito) recorded a couple albums for small labels which have since turned into prized collector's items. It was in 1992 that he made a recording featuring Chico O'Farrill's arrangement of "Tanga," a tune originally written by Bauzá back in 1943, and this led to a resurgence in his career.

what to buy: *Tanga* 𝄢𝄢𝄢𝄢 (Messidor, 1992, prod. Mario Bauzá, Götz A. Wörner) is by a truly big band, something like 24 pieces not counting vocalists and special guest Paquito D'Rivera. Things could get messy when arrangers work with an ensemble this big, but everyone involved in this project is top-notch. Special honors go to Chico O'Farrill, whose transformation of Bauzá's "Tanga" into the subtitled "Afro-Cuban Jazz Suite in Five Movements" is a masterpiece. There is not a weak moment in the whole album. The end result is not only a paean to the spirit of Latin jazz but a celebration of one of its cardinal figures, Mario Bauzá. *My Time Is Now* 𝄢𝄢𝄢𝄢 (Messidor, 1993, prod. Mario Bauzá, Götz A. Wörner) is another splendid album from one of the most important musicians in Latin jazz history. The band romps through Cuban classics by Arsenio Rodríguez ("La Vida Es Un Sueño") and Moíses Simons ("El Manisero," otherwise known as "The Peanut Vendor") in addition to rearranging Kurt Weill's "Moritat" into a Latin version of "Jack the Knife" (no, that's not a typo). Many of the players from *Tanga* show up on this album, including major participants vocalist Rudy Calzado, drummer Bobby Sanabria, and conga legend Carlos "Patato" Valdéz.

what to buy next: Two months before he died, Bauzá was actively involved in recording what would be his swan song. On *944 Columbus* 𝄢𝄢𝄢𝄢 (Messidor, 1994, prod. Mario Bauzá, Götz A. Wörner), the writing, arranging, and playing are still at a remarkably high level from all the participants, but that spark of genius that informed the other two efforts on Messidor was starting to fade along with the leader. There are still crucial performances on this disc, however, and it is almost too easy to read some sort of subliminal clue into the titles chosen for inclusion on this album. One of the Bauzá-composed works is entitled "Lourdes' Lullaby" and there is a version of Dizzy Gillespie's "Night in Tunisia" to go with "Chano" by Cascaser and Joe Santiago.

worth searching for: One of the albums Bauzá recorded with Graciela after Machito's death in 1984 was *Afro-Cuban Jazz* 🎵🎵🎵 (Caiman, 1984). It has a dream team lineup of personnel including Paquito D'Rivera, Claudio Roditi, Daniel Ponce, and Jorge Dalto.

influences:

◄◄ Antonio Machin, Don Apiazo, Cab Calloway

►► Dizzy Gillespie, Tito Puente

Garaud MacTaggart

Sidney Bechet

Born May 14, 1897, in New Orleans, LA. Died May 14, 1959, in Paris, France.

While Sidney Bechet never really received the public acclaim he deserved during his lifetime, or even since in the United States, his status among musicians and jazz connoisseurs as a true jazz giant has never been in question. Bechet learned to play clarinet as a child growing up in New Orleans, falling under the influence of early jazz notables such as Lorenzo Tio and Big Eye Nelson. In 1917 he made his way to that cauldron of early jazz, Chicago, and played in the bands of such pioneers as Freddie Keppard, King Oliver, and Lawrence Duhe. Bechet's genius was already apparent, and became even more so when he went to Europe as a member of Will Marion Cook's Orchestra and took up his primary instrument, the soprano saxophone. The soprano was always a signature of Bechet's, and its power-ful tone allowed Bechet to dominate early jazz ensembles as only trumpets had before.

Bechet made his recording debut in 1923 with the Clarence Williams Blue Five, and joined an early incarnation of the Duke Ellington Orchestra in 1924, where he had a profound influence on a young Johnny Hodges. In 1925, Bechet recorded again with Williams in a group called the Red Onion Jazz Babies, and for the first time matched wits with a young Louis Armstrong. As early jazz progressed in the 1920s, so did Bechet's promi-nence, and he became the first jazz soloist on record in 1925. His virtuosity and presence as a soloist was unmatched by any other reed player at the time, and really only Armstrong on trumpet can be considered his equal.

During the late 1920s, Bechet was back in Europe, wandering and playing and even spending some time in jail. After returning to the States in the 1930s, Bechet was veiled in obscurity, as more popularly pleasing ensembles led by the likes of Ellington and Armstrong were garnering all the attention. But in the late

SIDNEY BECHET

song "Summertime"
album *The Best of Sidney Bechet*
(Blue Note, 1939/1994)
instrument Soprano saxophone

1930s, due to a Dixieland revival, Bechet was again being hailed by critics as a luminary, and he began making some classic recordings (for Hughes Panassie) on Bluebird, and also on the fledgling Blue Note label. During the late 1930s and early 1940s, Bechet met once again with Armstrong on record, and also with Jelly Roll Morton, Earl Hines, and Eddie Condon. When Bechet returned to France, this time for good, he was surrounded by an adoring French audience. His celebrity status there would last until his death in 1959 of cancer.

The Sidney Bechet discography is a mess of overlapping reis-sues of varying availability and quality. Completists and partic-ular fans of Bechet will want to head for either the Masters of Jazz or Classics reissue series. The recommendation here is the Masters of Jazz set, which includes notable sessions Bechet recorded as a sideman (for instance, those with Morton and Armstrong).

what to buy: The single CD compilation *Really the Blues* 🎵🎵🎵 (Living Era, 1993, prod. Vic Bellerby) is an excellent place to start for fans just beginning to enjoy Bechet. It includes high-lights from all of the classic sessions of one of his most prolific and important periods. Of particular interest are "2.19 Blues" with Armstrong and "Blues in Thirds" with Hines. *Volume 2: 1923–1932* 🎶🎶🎶🎶 (Masters of Jazz, 1992, prod. Alain Thomas, Fabrice Zammarchi) is classic early Bechet, including his first recordings with Clarence Williams and the Red Onion Jazz Babies sides from 1925. Many of these recordings are landmarks of early jazz. *Best of Sidney Bechet on Blue Note* 🎶🎶🎶🎶 (Blue Note, 1939–53/1994, prod. Alfred Lion, reissue prod. Michael Cuscuna) includes his now famous readings of "Blue Horizon" and "Summertime."

what to buy next: The live recording *Jazz at Storyville* 🎶🎶🎶🎶 (Black Lion, 1953/1992, prod. Alan Bates) was made during one of Bechet's visits to the U.S. later in his life. Bechet sounds as exciting as ever, teamed with trombonist Vic Dickenson and pianist and club owner George Wein. Most of *In Paris, Vol. 1* 🎶🎶🎶🎶 (Vogue, 1952–53/1995) features Bechet as a soloist for two ballet scores, "La Colline du Delta" and "La Nuit est une Sorciere." The settings are not typical for the Dixieland master, and he almost sounds out of place at times, but the combination works for the most part.

what to avoid: The title of *Sidney Bechet and Art Tatum* 🎶🎶 (Bechet, 1940/Collectables, 1995) is quite misleading, for the two giants Bechet and Tatum never appear together on this CD of questionable sound quality. The Bechet sides are from a rather unsuccessful endeavor at early Latin jazz titled *Haitian Moods*.

the rest:

The Complete Blue Note Recordings 🎶🎶🎶🎶 (Blue Note, 1939–53/Mosaic)
Summertime 🎶🎶🎶 (Musical Memories, 1940/1992)
(With Muggsy Spanier) *Double Dixie* 🎶🎶 (Drive Archive, 1940–57/1994)
New Orleans Jazz 🎶🎶🎶 (Columbia, 1949/1989)
Spirits of New Orleans 🎶🎶🎶 (Vogue, 1949/1993)
And Friends 🎶🎶 (Verve, 1950s/1990)
Le Legende de Sidney Bechet 🎶🎶🎶 (Vogue, 1953)
Salle Pleyel: 31 January 52 🎶🎶🎶 (Vogue, 1953)
Parisian Encounter 🎶🎶 (Vogue, 1959)
Live in New York, 1950–1951 🎶🎶 (Storyville, 1989)
Master Takes: The Victor Sessions (1932–1943) 🎶🎶🎶🎶 (Bluebird, 1990)
Olympia Concert, October 19, 1955 🎶🎶🎶 (Vogue, 1990)
1923–1936 🎶🎶🎶 (Classics, 1991)
1937–1938 🎶🎶🎶 (Classics, 1991)
1938–1940 🎶🎶🎶🎶 (Classics, 1991)
1940 🎶🎶🎶🎶 (Classics, 1991)
1940–41 🎶🎶🎶 (Classics, 1991)

Volume 1: 1923 🎶🎶🎶 (Masters of Jazz, 1992)
Sidney Bechet in New York, 1937–1940 🎶🎶🎶 (JSP, 1992)
Volume 3: 1931–1937 🎶🎶🎶 (Masters of Jazz, 1994)
Volume 6: 1939 🎶🎶🎶 (Masters of Jazz, 1995)
Volume 7: 1940 🎶🎶🎶 (Masters of Jazz, 1995)
En Concert Avec Europe 1: 1957–1958 🎶🎶🎶 (RTE, 1995)
Volume 8: 1940 🎶🎶🎶 (Masters of Jazz, 1996)

worth searching for: RCA thoughtfully reissued all the Bechet sides they had in 1994 on three groups of 2 CDs: *The Complete, Vol. 1 & 2* 🎶🎶🎶🎶 (RCA, 1932–41/1994, prod. Jean-Paul Guiter), *The Complete, Vol. 3 & 4* 🎶🎶🎶🎶 (RCA, 1941/1994, prod. Jean-Paul Guiter), and *The Complete, Vol. 5 & 6* 🎶🎶🎶🎶 (RCA, 1938–43/1994, prod. Jean-Paul Guiter). However, they are already out of print, making these reissues well worth picking up if seen.

influences:

◀◀ Lorenzo Tio Jr., Big Eye Nelson, Lawrence Duhe

▶▶ Johnny Hodges, Bob Wilber, Steve Lacy

Dan Keener

Joe Beck

Born July 29, 1945, in Philadelphia, PA.

The jazz highway is busy with the comings and goings of innumerable guitarists. Joe Beck has managed to carve out an almost 30-year niche of recording, producing, and performing in a notable yet relatively low-profile manner. Beck is skilled at both a traditional straight-ahead style and able to transition into a harder mode when the music requires. He has managed both a solo recording career and the demands of a lengthy and full studio/accompanist career. He came to New York right after college and immediately was in demand as a session player, at a time in the mid-1960s when studio work first began to include guitarists conversant with rock styles. Within four years, Beck became the first electric guitarist to record with Miles Davis, although Columbia didn't release his tracks from those December 1967 sessions until 1979 (on *Circle in the Round*) and 1981 (on *Directions*). Beck's widely heard 1975 solo effort *Beck* coupled him with a young David Sanborn at the beginning of his solo career with some dynamic results. Followed by a couple of less successful recordings, Beck turned to studio work, becoming a sought-after player for his soaring fat tone and brilliant rhythm playing. His CTI collaborations with vocalist Esther Phillips produced a series of good selling recordings. He appeared on Steely Dan studio sessions as well as numerous other dates with a wide range of artists in pop and jazz. Beck

did a series of quality accessible jazz CDs for the small audio-phile DMP label throughout the 1980s and continues to release under that label, in addition to other solo projects such as the excellent 1995 Wavetone release *Fingerpainting*. It gives the listener solid, accessible jazz guitar from a veteran player who has several decades of experience to cull from.

what to buy: The most recent recording, *Alto* 𝄞𝄞𝄞𝄞 (DMP, 1997) is primarily a duet effort with Beck on specially tuned alto gui-tar accompanying Ali Ryerson on alto flute, with light occa-sional percussion from Steve Davis. The charming and subdued affair covers standards such as "Summertime," "Billie's Bounce," "'Round Midnight," and others. Ryerson's rich alto flute tones blend beautifully with Beck's guitar for one of the more delightful and laid-back duet offerings in recent memory. One of Beck's strongest outings, *Fingerpainting* 𝄞𝄞𝄞𝄞 (Wave-tone, 1995, prod. Mark Egan) is primarily a trio effort with pro-ducer Mark Egan on fretless electric bass and Egan's fellow for-mer Pat Metheny Group member Danny Gottlieb on drums. Saxophonist Bill Evans joins in on some selections on tenor or soprano. Beck's electric playing here is commanding and a pleasure to hear as he and the rhythm section groove through ten tunes with barely a dull moment. Alternately picking tasty solos and pouring on deliciously lush chordings, this recording is one of the best examples of Beck's "power" playing since his 1975 Kudu release. Indeed, two tunes from that outing are re-visited here with fine results, "Red Eye" and "Texas Ann." Also outstanding is the dramatic version of "Summertime" and a fun piece with nice Evans sax work, "The Kramer."

what to buy next: Beck comes more alive on *The Journey* 𝄞𝄞𝄞 (DMP, 1991, prod. Joe Beck, Tom Jung) than on previous DMP sessions, with a nice visit to "Killer Joe" and his own strong title piece, where he cuts loose with some intense and soaring solo-ing. The seminal pop/jazz *Beck* 𝄞𝄞𝄞𝄞 (Kudu, 1975/Columbia Legacy 1997, prod. Creed Taylor) with its up-front mix of Dave Sanborn's fiery alto sax work and Beck's hard rock–inflected soloing still remains fresh listening today. Also accompanying are the late Don Grolnick on keyboards, Will Lee on bass, and Chris Parker on drums, with barely audible rhythm guitar work from session and solo artist Steve Khan. The band grooves through brooding ballads like "Cactus" and smoking blues romps such as Gene Dinwiddie's "Cafe Black Rose." While pre-sent on some selections, the ubiquitous CTI signature Don Sebesky string arrangements are unobtrusive.

what to avoid: The remainder of the DMP catalog falls into an almost easy listening, soft-commercial jazz vein. While well

performed and recorded, *Relaxin'* 𝄞𝄞 (DMP, 1983 prod. Joe Beck, Tom Jung) and *Friends* 𝄞𝄞 (DMP, 1984, prod. Joe Beck, Tom Jung) are rather bland, making for good background music. *Back to Beck* (DMP, 1988, prod. Joe Beck, Tom Jung) 𝄞𝄞𝄞 fares slightly better, but still falls victim to formulaic blandness to an extent.

worth searching for: The more interesting of the two released items from Beck's 1967 session with Miles Davis is the 26-minute title track of the odds-and-ends collection *Circle in the Round* 𝄞𝄞𝄞 (Columbia, 1979, prod. Jim Fishel, Joe McEwen). Beck's thrumming, drone-like guitar line may sound unde-manding, but it's an integral part of a piece that was something of a missing link between the music Davis made with his mid-1960s quintet and the sprawling fusion jams to come.

influences:

◀◀ Grant Green, Wes Montgomery

▶▶ Emily Remler, Buzz Feiten, Steve Khan, Mike Stern

Tali Madden

BeebleBrox

Formed in Germany in 1983; re-formed in the United States in 1988.

Peter Kienle, guitar; Monika Herzig, keyboards, acoustic piano; Greg Riley, saxophone (1988–89); Robert Dickson, bass (1988–91); Woody Williams, drums (1988–89), Greg Chambers, saxophone (1988–91); Don Davis, drums (1988–91); Tom Clark, saxophone/EWI (1995–pre-sent); Jonathan Paul, bass (1991–92); Jack Helsley, bass (1994–96); Danny Kiely, bass (1996–97); Dan Immel, bass (1997); Dan Vonnegut, drums (1991–95); Jamey Reid, drums (1995–96).

Guitarist Peter Kienle founded BeebleBrox in Albstadt, Ger-many, in 1983 and teamed up with keyboardist Monika Herzig when he moved to the States in 1988. Together, the husband-wife team reincarnated the jazz-fusion band in 1991 in Tuscaloosa, Alabama, then moved to the Bloomington-Indi-anapolis, Indiana, area where they perform regularly as a quar-tet at clubs, festivals, and for name-act openers. The group de-rives its name from Zaphod Beeblebrox, one of the main char-acters in the sci-fi novel *The Hitchhiker's Guide to the Galaxy*. And, while their music often contains galactic dreaminess, it also features palpable elements influenced by 1970s jazz groups Return to Forever, Weather Report, and Mahavishnu Or-chestra. Make no mistake; this is no cover band. All their mate-rial is original, with Kienle writing the more fusion-laden pieces, and Herzig contributing acoustic and swing pieces. Herzig earned her Ph. D. in Music Education and jazz studies at

Indiana University in 1997. Since their first album in 1991 (first CD in 1994), this versatile, modern band has toured and performed at festivals around the U.S. and in Germany.

what to buy: BeebleBrox has improved with each recording, so buy in reverse order. Their third CD, *Indianapolis Intergalactic Spaceport* ✍✍✍✍ (Acme, 1997, prod. Dave Weber), finds them better entrenched in their trademark jazz—bright, attractively layered tunes influenced by 1970s fusion. Yet, the fare is more balanced on this album, as they also deliver some acoustic straight-ahead swing and some blues-groove numbers. The talented saxophonist Tom Clark returns from their second recording, and except for electric bassist Jack Helsley who plays on three tracks, most of the six players are new to the group and the best acclimated team for switching styles. This is a pleasing album for fans of jazz past and present. The second BeebleBrox CD, *Quantumn Tweezers* ✍✍✍ (Acme Records, 1996, prod. Peter Kienle, Monika Herzig), follows along the multi-colored, jazz-fusion path (the leaders prefer you call their music "original jazz") coursed by Kienle and Herzig on their debut album (see below). Drawing from various musical influences and performing all original work by band members, this cohesive session is more listener friendly and aware, compared with their more self-indulgent debut. BeebleBrox's expressions retain the ethereal feel of their first album, yet are substantially augmented by newcomers, bassist Jack Helsley, and especially tenor saxophonist/flutist Tom Clark. Returning for this outing are electric violinist Cathy Morris and drummer Dan Vonnegut. Percussionist Russ May augments some tunes. Herzig's original song, "The Saga of C. and C.," featuring the pianist in fresh, beautiful collaboration with Morris, is one of the album's high points. Their albums are available through North Country Distributors or by mail from ACME Records, 3374 Old Meyers Road, Bloomington, IN 47408.

what to buy next: On their debut album *Raw Material* ✍✍✍ (B'Brox Productions, 1994, prod. Peter Kienle, Monika Herzig), BeebleBrox musicians don't rush to fill all the spaces. Hence, there's a spacey quality to their original work. Settings and personnel change, yet their sound is consistent—1970s (heavily electric) jazz fusion, laced with world music percussion, an occasional acoustic break, and even a playful calliope-like riff that segues into fusion. Regular and guest musicians include electric violinist Cathy Morris, Larry Calland and Russ May (percussion), John Huber (upright bass), Jonathan Paul (electric bass), and drummers Dan Vonnegut and Pete Wilhoit. Kienle's modal, rock-oriented compositions give vent to his Scofield-like sound that is sometimes overly intrusive. Classically

trained Herzig is the star of this session, exhibiting warmth and maturity at the keyboards and contributing fine original melodies.

worth searching for: Before BeebleBrox recorded their three CDs, they made four jazz-fusion recordings on cassette. *Entropy* (1990), *The Thing* (1991), and *Bloomington* (1992). These, and cassette copies of *Raw Material*, are available through ACME Records.

influences:

◀◀ Chick Corea's Return to Forever, Weather Report, Mahavishnu Orchestra

Nancy Ann Lee

Bix Beiderbecke

Born March 10, 1903, in Davenport, IA. Died August 6, 1931, in New York, NY.

One of the true legends of jazz, Leon Bix Beiderbecke's stunning trumpet tone, unique phrasing, and impeccable rhythmic sense made him the idol of other early jazz musicians as well as the collegiate crowd of the "Roaring Twenties." Beiderbecke's velvet sound and his refreshing approach to the music of the era remains as attractive today as it was when first recorded during the "Golden Age" of jazz in the 1920s and 1930s.

Beiderbecke showed an early precociousness for music. By age seven he was a prodigy on piano, yet had never taken a lesson. When his older brother returned from World War I with some Original Dixieland Jazz Band records, Beiderbecke became infatuated with the music and borrowed a neighbor's cornet so that he could try to emulate ODJB cornetist Nick LaRocca. Thus, he learned how to play jazz entirely on his own, developing a style and approach absolutely unique. He started playing professionally while still in high school. Beiderbecke's parents, in trying to dissuade his musical career, sent him away to school at Lake Forest Academy (just north of downtown Chicago) where he promptly spent most of his time absorbing the exploding Chicago jazz scene. Music ultimately won out over schooling, and Beiderbecke joined a band called the Wolverines, with whom he made his first recordings in February of 1924. The Wolverines, quite often unjustly maligned by some critics, were an enthusiastic and inspired young group whose music seems perfect for Beiderbecke's inspired horn. The acoustic recordings

Bix Beiderbecke **(Archive Photos)**

the Wolverines made for Gennett records showcase a self-assured and remarkably creative young cornetist.

Beiderbecke then joined Frankie Trumbauer's band in St. Louis in September of 1925. When Trumbauer disbanded in mid-1926, he and Beiderbecke joined the Jean Goldkette Orchestra. The Goldkette Orchestra's recordings and radio broadcasts brought national recognition to Beiderbecke. During the summer of 1927, Beiderbecke started to record both under his own name and with Frankie Trumbauer for OKeh records. These sessions yielded some of his finest solo work, and are high-level marks of jazz improvisation. Beiderbecke then joined Paul Whiteman and His Orchestra in October 1927. Although often buried in the section work of Whiteman's orchestra, the arrangements by Bill Challis gave Beiderbecke room to showcase his talents. Many fine examples of Beiderbecke's solo and ensemble mastery exist on his Whiteman recordings for Victor and Columbia. Sadly, complications derived from Beiderbecke's acute alcoholism quickly brought about a decline in his career, and ultimately killed him, leaving behind an early jazz legend from a now-legendary time.

what to buy: The definitive Beiderbecke (i.e., a current CD release of all titles and takes) has yet to be done with high-quality reproduction. For those seeking an introduction to Beiderbecke's music, there are some fine reissues to choose from. For a cross-section of some (but not all) of Beiderbecke's finest recordings done in stellar sound, the CD *Bix Beiderbecke 1924–1930* (Jazz Classics in Digital Stereo, 1995, prod. Robert Parker) is a good introduction to Beiderbecke. The Wolverines titles can be found on *Bix Beiderbecke and the Wolverines* ♫♫♫♫ (Timeless, 1993, prod. Chris Barber, Wim Wigt) and *The Complete New Orleans Rhythm Kings, Vol. 2 (1923) /The Complete Wolverines (1924)* ♫♫♫♫ (King Jazz, 1923–24/1992, prod. Alessandro Protti, Roberto Capasso, Gianni Tollara). Both CDs feature wonderful transfers from the acoustic Gennett recordings. The Timeless compilation includes the two Sioux City Six titles, the two Bix and His Rhythm Jugglers titles, and the two Wolverines titles (featuring Jimmy McPartland) made after Beiderbecke left. The King Jazz CD only contains the Wolverines titles, but also has the last six titles (plus alternates) recorded for Gennett by the New Orleans Rhythm Kings (who were so very influential not only to Beiderbecke, but a whole generation of young, white Chicago musicians). Any doubts about the prowess of the Wolverines as a jazz unit can be quickly laid to rest by listening to "Fidgety Feet." As for Beiderbecke, he shines on all titles. Solos on two tunes, "Oh Baby" and "I Need Some Pettin'," quickly prove Beiderbecke's young genius. *Bix*

Beiderbecke, Vol. 1: Singin' the Blues (1927) ♫♫♫♫ (Columbia, 1990, prod. Michael Brooks) and *Bix Beiderbecke, Vol. 2: At the Jazz Band Ball (1927–28)* ♫♫♫♫ (Columbia, 1991, prod. Michael Brooks) provide recordings from Beiderbecke's zenith. The rightly touted "Singin' the Blues" (some say one of the finest early jazz records made), "Riverboat Shuffle," and "I'm Coming Virginia" (dig the breathtaking "blue" note Beiderbecke takes in the 32nd bar of his solo) are a few examples of the best that Beiderbecke can offer.

what to buy next: *Bix Lives* ♫♫♫ (Bluebird, 1991, prod. Steve Backer) and the two-CD set *The Indispensable Bix Beiderbecke 1924–1930* ♫♫♫ (RCA, 1924–1930/1995, prod. various) feature Beiderbecke in the Goldkette and Whiteman bands. All of Beiderbecke's critical recordings with these RCA Victor bands are covered here. Full, well-arranged scores present Beiderbecke and other fine soloists in wonderful period tune settings.

best of the rest:
Bix Beiderbecke 1924–27 ♫♫♫ (Classics, 1994)
Bix Beiderbecke 1927–30 ♫♫♫ (Classics, 1994)
Masters of Jazz Series: The Complete Bix Beiderbecke ♫♫♫♫♫ (Media 7, 1997)

influences:

◀◀ Louis Armstrong, Dominick "Nick" LaRocca, Emmet Hardy, New Orleans Rhythm Kings

▶▶ Louis Armstrong, Rex Stewart, Lester Young, Jimmy McPartland, Red Nichols, Andy Secrest, Roland "Bunny" Berrigan

Jim Prohaska

Richie Beirach

Born May 23, 1947, in New York, NY.

Richie Beirach is a prolific yet underrated pianist whose catalog has been ill-served (by ECM in particular), leaving most of it, including some of his best work, to be searched out in the used-CD/LP bins. He has forged a unique style equal parts classical—especially the amorphous harmonies of Scriabin and Takemitsu—and jazz, drawing on the lyricism of Bill Evans (with whom he studied), McCoy Tyner's modality, and a number of other sources. Beirach expanded from his early classical piano lessons into jazz, studying at Berklee and the Manhattan School of Music (with a degree in music theory and composition). He paid his sideman dues with Stan Getz, Chet Baker, Lee Konitz, and others, and worked in a more collaborative vein with soprano saxophonist David Liebman, both as a duo and in the groups Lookout Farm and Quest, and with guitarist John Abercrombie's quartet (*Arcade*, *Abercrombie Quartet*, and *M*, all now deleted).

what to buy: Fortunately Beirach's most remarkable album is easily acquired. *Antarctica* (Pathfinder, 1985/Evidence, 1994, prod. Richie Beirach, Lee Ann Ledgerwood, Douglas Lichterman) is a suite for solo piano (with overdubs) that perfectly embodies the icy vastness of its subject with dissonant grandeur. Impressionism and the fourths-based harmonies of Scriabin are at the core of the otherwordly sound; rather than the pastels of Beirach's playing elsewhere, here we get the startlingly delineated chiaroscuro effects of light glinting off dark waters. Though not widely known, this is one of the greatest and most distinctive solo piano albums in jazz history. On *Trust* (Unicom, 1993/Evidence, 1996, prod. Ken Inaoka, Richie Beirach) Beirach filters the pastel lyricism of Bill Evans through the fractured geometries of Paul Bley, fusing breathtaking beauty to restless energy and lush harmonies to off-kilter accents. Joined by bassist Dave Holland and drummer Jack DeJohnette (the latter ensuring the tension never slackens), Beirach plays six originals plus tunes by Holland, Gary Peacock, and Wayne Shorter ("Nefertiti"). The free and spontaneous trio interplay is masterfully tight-knit and responsive.

what to buy next: The covers album *Double Edge* w/David Liebman (Storyville, 1985, prod. Arnvid Meyer) is a fine duo record with Beirach's most frequent collaborator. The soprano saxophonist's playing is occasionally a bit sappy, but it's interesting to hear Beirach dig into "Naima," "'Round Midnight," "India," "On Green Dolphin Street," "Lover Man," "Some Other Time," and "Oleo." Similarly, *Maybeck Recital Hall Series, Volume 19* (Concord, 1992, prod. Nick Phillips) doesn't rank with Beirach's best solo work but is valuable for revealing his takes on 11 standards (plus his own classic "Elm"), spotlighting the Bill Evans influence in his playing.

the rest:

(With John Abercrombie) *Emerald City* (1987/Evidence, 1994)
Common Heart (Owl, 1987)
(With George Coleman) *Convergence* (Triloka, 1991)
The Snow Leopard (Evidence, 1997)

worth searching for: The solo *Sunday Songs* (Blue Note, 1992, prod. Richie Beirach) is one of the few albums to successfully use largely familiar classical music (by Chopin, Debussy, Schumann, and Mompou) in an improvisatory context which compromises the integrity of neither world but rather sounds natural and unforced, the improvisational parts and altered harmonies seeming to flow organically from the original pieces. There is also an affecting take on Bill Evans's "Peace Piece" (which certainly fits in this context) as well as Beirach originals and bassist George Mraz's "Wisteria." It's a shame that Blue Note has let this lapse from their catalog. Other excellent but out-of-print solo piano albums include *Hubris* (ECM, 1977, prod. Manfred Eicher); *Breathing of Statues* (CMP, 1982/Magenta/Windham Hill, 1985, prod. Kurt Renker); *Continuum* (Eastwind/IMC, 1987, prod. Hiroaki Itoh/Lighthouse, Richie Beirach, David Parker); and *Self-Portraits* (CMP, 1992, prod. Kurt Renker, Walter Quintus, Richie Beirach). Excellent duos include *Rendezvous* (IPI, 1981, prod. Dean Roumanis, Jonathan Horwich), with George Mraz; *The Duo Live* (Advance, 1986, prod. Hans Gruber), with David Liebman; and the short but remarkable *Kahuna, Keeper of Secrets* (Trio, 1978, prod. Ken Inaoka), a direct-to-masterdisk LP from Japan with one side of solo free improvisation and the other an improvised duet with legendary Japanese free jazz drummer Masahiko Togashi, revealing an especially adventurous side of Beirach not heard as often as it should be. Easy to find if you look under bassist/leader George Mraz's name is *My Foolish Heart* (Alfa, 1995/Milestone, 1996, prod. Todd Barkan, Satoshi Hirano), a trio album with Beirach and drummer Billy Hart that mixes Thelonious Monk's "Ask Me Now," Miles Davis's "Blue in Green," Beirach's "Sunday Song," three Mraz originals, and standards. For Beirach's most muscular playing on record, find the leaderless *Tribute to John Coltrane: Live under the Sky* (King, 1987/Columbia, 1989), with Wayne Shorter and David Liebman on soprano saxes and Beirach joined in the rhythm section by Eddie Gomez (bass) and Jack DeJohnette (drums). On "Mr. P.C." and the medleys "After the Rain/Naima" (a Liebman/Beirach duo) and "India/Impressions," Beirach plays in the language of McCoy Tyner while speaking it with his own accent.

influences:

◀◀ Bill Evans, McCoy Tyner, Herbie Hancock, Paul Bley, Chick Corea, Alexander Scriabin, Toru Takemitsu

▶▶ Ketil Bjørnstad

see also: *Quest*

Steve Holtje

Bob Belden

Born October 31, 1956, in Charleston, SC.

Bob Belden has a dual career as a jazz reissue producer for labels such as Blue Note and Columbia (he's an expert in Miles

Davis's electric period) and as an arranger with a penchant for nudging pop into a jazzier direction. Sometimes overlooked is that he can also hold his own as a tenor saxophonist, but he tends not to feature himself the way some arrangers would. Belden grew up in the South, listening to pop music. His family had a piano, and he played in his school's concert band and jazz ensembles, his curiosity leading him to try playing his bandmates' instruments too. He then attended North Texas State, a well-known jazz college (he calls it "a jazz prison") and also played in an R&B cover band that did material such as the Commodores' "Brick House."

After college, Belden played with the Woody Herman Band from January 1979 to May 1980. "It's the same sentence you would get if you were caught for burglary for the first time," he says. On a more serious level, he points out, "It was with him that I first started seeing the effects of jazz on pop on a jazz level. In the '70s, most jazz attempts at pop were pop itself—original material aping pop music. Very few people were arranging contemporary material for jazz style. They were making it pop and just having instrumental versions of jazz hits. The Woody Herman Band recorded half an album of Steely Dan tunes, and we used to play it when we were on the road." Later Belden worked with Donald Byrd, another jazzman who worked well with pop material.

Belden recorded an album of his own compositions and then moved into the role he's best known for, recording albums of arrangements built around a songwriter or style. One won't be possible to track down: his Puccini project, released in Japan, has been blocked for export by the Puccini estate. The rest have been luckier, although his best effort remains another Japanese release.

what to buy: *Shades of Blue* 𝄞𝄞𝄞𝄞 (Blue Note, 1996, prod. Bob Belden) is a tribute not to a specific writer but to the music of the Blue Note label. Herbie Hancock's "Maiden Voyage," Bud Powell's "Un Poco Loco," Horace Silver's "Song for My Father," and Thelonious Monk's "Evidence" are the most famous tunes, with others by Wayne Shorter, Andrew Hill, Herbie Nichols, McCoy Tyner, Kenny Dorham, etc. The all-star cast of current Blue Note artists Belden features includes singers Dianne Reeves, Cassandra Wilson, Holly Cole, and Kurt Elling, guitarist John Scofield, trumpeters Tim Hagans and Marcus Printup, pianists Jacky Terrasson, Geri Allen, Geoff Keezer, Eliane Elias, and Renee Rosnes, bassist Ron Carter, and drummer T.S. Monk, with a wealth of other stars assisting the leaders of the various tracks. Belden's arrangements walk the fine line of respecting

the originals yet making them different enough to be interesting rather than a pale rehash.

what to buy next: *The Music of Sting: Straight to My Heart* 𝄞𝄞𝄞𝄞 (Blue Note, 1991, prod. Matt Pierson) reworks the songs of the former bassist for the pop/rock band the Police, using material from that group and his solo work. There's enough latent jazz content in the originals that this project never sounds forced. Reeves, Scofield, Hagans, guitarist Fareed Haque, tenor saxophonist Rick Margitza, pianists Joey Calderazzo and Marc Copland, and alto saxophonist Bobby Watson are among those featured. There are some tracks that stumble (Phil Perry's overwrought vocal on "Sister Moon," the way-too-slick stylings on "Every Breath You Take" by vocalist Mark Ledford and tenor saxman Kirk Whalum—ruining an interestingly percussive chart), but by and large it's a very swinging album that twists familiar material into clever and stimulating new shapes. Many tracks feature a large band, and show Belden to be a moderately original band arranger with an upfront sound that mixes the brassy energy of Bob Holman with an appreciation for the timbres of Gil Evans's craft.

what to avoid: *When Doves Cry: The Music of Prince* 𝄞𝄞 (Somethin' Else/Toshiba-EMI, 1994/Blue Note, 1995, prod. Bob Belden) was known in Japan as *Purple Rain*. Though it has a few good moments, sub-par vocalists (Phil Perry, Jimi Tunnell) and cheesy players (especially saxophonist Everette Harp) drag the project down, and even when the more talented singers (Cassandra Wilson, Holly Cole) are spotlighted, they can't shake the memories of the original versions of the songs, perhaps partly because Belden's arrangements seem to hold back from doing anything too uncommercial.

the rest:
Treasure Island 𝄞𝄞𝄞 (Sunnyside, 1990)

worth searching for: *PrinceJazz* 𝄞𝄞𝄞𝄞 (Somethin' Else/Toshiba-EMI, 1994, prod. Bob Belden) is much less commercial—and much more interesting to jazz fans—than the more widely available album of Prince arrangements listed above. Well worth tracking down as a Japanese import, it would be a great stumper in blindfold tests, because it draws strongly on Miles Davis's spacey electric music of the 1970s (while using, on "Electric Chair," members of Davis's 1980s band). Trumpeters Tim Hagans and Wallace Roney do a good job in a demanding role, Belden gets to play more than usual, and the shifting ensembles of young New York jazzmen dig into the material with relish and help Belden completely reinvent it. It's a

Marcus Belgrave **(© Jack Vartoogian)**

tribute to Prince, actually, that they find so much to do with these songs, which aren't even his best-known tunes.

influences:

◀◀ Miles Davis, Gil Evans, Duke Ellington, Gil Evans, Woody Herman

Steve Holtje

Marcus Belgrave

Born June 30, 1936, in Chester, PA.

Woody Shaw once called him the greatest living trumpet player in jazz; Charles Mingus said if he could get Marcus Belgrave to New York, "I'd have the best band in the world." Belgrave proves that you can be the contemporary and musical equal of Lee Morgan and Freddie Hubbard without becoming famous, let alone rich. You hear him as a teenager on some classic Ray Charles late 1950s sides. After an early '60s stint in the Motown studios, he settled for good in Detroit in 1967, establishing a

career as both educator and nightclub performer, while periodically touring with Mercer Ellington, Charles, and more recently, the Lincoln Center Jazz Orchestra. Belgrave's fluid sound and attack are deeply rooted in the style of classic bebop trumpeters Fats Navarro and Clifford Brown, yet his performances cover a wide variety of idioms, from duets with Sammy Price and Art Hodes to appearances with the avant-garde Creative Arts Collective. Seriously under-recorded throughout most of the 1970s and the Reagan-era jazz depression, Belgrave's profile has become higher in recent years, both as leader and as featured sideman on the recordings of some of his proteges, notably Geri Allen and Robert Hurst, alumni of his Jazz Development Workshop.

what to buy: A long-time partnership with percussionist Lawrence Williams bore fruit with *Working Together* 🎵🎵🎵🎵 (Detroit Jazz Musicians Co-op Productions, 1992). Especially with Williams's intricate compositions, here's a recording that does not rely on standard hard-bop lines or try to recreate your classic Blue Note sessions. It rates full marks for its performance excellence plus that rarest of qualities—originality—and it also features pianists Geri Allen and Kirk Lightsey, saxophonist Ikeda Atsushi, and several prominent Detroit rhythm section players.

what to buy next: *Marcus Belgrave with Detroit's Jazz Piano Legacy Volume 1* 𝄞𝄞𝄞 (DJM) features Belgrave in the company of three pianists: bebop master Tommy Flanagan, young star Geri Allen, and Gary Schunk. Allen and Belgrave in particular set the sparks flying on her composition, "Dolphy's Dance." You also get a taste of Belgrave's vocal style on "Sweet Geri" (a.k.a. "Sweet Lorraine")—a loving tribute to Satchmo that admittedly goes down better in the club with a few beers. In a traditional vein, Belgrave appears on the Canadian Parkwood label as co-leader with veteran pianist Art Hodes *Hot 'n' Cool Blues* (Parkwood, 1989) and saxophonist Franz Jackson *Franz Jackson & Marcus Belgrave* (Parkwood, 1994) and in a sideman role on Parkwood sets by pianists Earl Van Riper and Sammy Price.

worth searching for: A session co-led with alto saxophonist Phil Lasley, *Live in Amsterdam* 𝄞𝄞𝄞𝄞 (Phil Lasley, 1993) has been released on cassette only. Extended treatments of familiar favorites "Ray's Idea," "Alone Together," "Poinciana," and "Quasimodo" conjure the atmosphere of a Detroit club, ironic since the session happened at Bimhuis, in Amsterdam, with a Dutch rhythm section. And several cuts from the long-unavailable *Gemini II* (Belgrave, 1974) have been re-released by the Japanese Blues Interaction label as part of an anthology of the defunct Tribe label, an early self-determination project of Detroit musicians.

influences:

◀◀ Fats Navarro, Clifford Brown, Louis Armstrong

▶▶ Geri Allen, Kenny Garrett, Robert Hurst, Cassius Richmond, James Carter

David Finkel

Louie Bellson

Born Luigi Paolino Balassoni, July 26, 1924, in Rock Fall, IL.

One of jazz's greatest drummers, Bellson is equally effective powering a big band or accompanying a small group. He gained fame in the 1950s with his solos using two bass drums, but Bellson has never emphasized flash over musical substance. He played with many of the leading Swing Era orchestras, including stints with Benny Goodman (1943 and 1946), Tommy Dorsey (1947–49), and Harry James (1950–51). Part of the Great James Robbery, when Duke Ellington hired Bellson, Willie

Smith, and Juan Tizol away from James in 1951, Bellson became the first white musician to play a significant role in the Ellington band. He left Ellington in 1953 to act as musical director for his wife, singer Pearl Bailey, and made a number of tours with Jazz at the Philharmonic (1954–55, 1967, and 1972). Along with Benny Carter, Bellson played on the classic *Art Tatum Group Masterpieces, Vol. 1*. He rejoined Ellington in 1965–66 and made a number of recordings with him on Pablo. Bellson is a noted composer whose works include "Skin Deep" and "The Hawk Talks." Active in music education since the 1960s, Bellson gives frequent clinics. He has recorded extensively for Verve, Pablo, Concord, MusicMasters, Telarc, and other labels and maintains East Coast and West Coast versions of his big band, for which he writes many of the tunes and arrangements.

what to buy: *Duke Ellington: Black, Brown & Beige* 𝄞𝄞𝄞𝄞 (MusicMasters, 1992, prod. Teo Macero) is a brilliant recreation of Ellington's landmark jazz symphony. Featuring his own orchestra conducted by Maurice Peress with Clark Terry playing Johnny Hodges's role on "Come Sunday" and Joe Williams singing "The Blues" passage, Bellson takes liberties with BB&B but stays true to Ellington's vision. The album also includes fine versions of Bellson's "Hawk Talks" and "Skin Deep" and his "Ellington-Strayhorn Suite." A smokin' session paying tribute to a dozen of his fellow drum masters, from Big Sid Catlett and Chick Webb to Dennis Chambers and Steve Gadd, *Their Time Was the Greatest!* 𝄞𝄞𝄞𝄞 (Concord Jazz, 1996, prod. John Burk, Nick Phillips) features Bellson's West Coast big band playing ten of his original compositions and two standards. Bellson's consistently inventive trap work, tight arrangements, and strong solos by pianist Frank Strazzeri, tenor saxophonist Pete Christlieb, and trumpeter Conte Candoli make this an all-around winner. *Live at the Concord Summer Festival* 𝄞𝄞𝄞𝄞 (Concord Jazz, 1976, prod. Carl E. Jefferson) is a typical Bellson small group session, featuring world-class but underappreciated players. With trumpeter Blue Mitchell and Christlieb on board, Bellson wisely cuts back on his solos and lets his sidemen shine, though his presence is constantly felt as he pushes the band hard on Christlieb's "Now and Then" and Mitchell's "Tru Blue." Dick Nash (trombone), Ross Tompkins (piano), John Williams (bass), and Grant Geissman (guitar) round out the septet. With only two of eight tracks longer than five minutes, *Prime Time* 𝄞𝄞𝄞𝄞 (Concord Jazz, 1978, prod. Carl E. Jefferson) features tight arrangements on a program that mixes straight-ahead numbers with Latin, calypso and funk. The first four tracks feature Bellson's working quintet of Christlieb, Blue Mitchell, Tompkins, and John Williams, with guitarist Bob Bain and percussionist Emil Richards spicing up the last four numbers. Highlights include Christlieb's powerhouse tenor work on Marian McPartland's "With You in Mind" and Ellington's "Cottontail" and Tompkins's commanding version of "What's New."

what to buy next: *Louis in London* 🎵🎵🎵 (DRG, 1970, prod. Derek Boulton) features a British big band playing Bellson's compositions inspired by his experiences in London. Bellson is in top form, driving the band with precision. The band handles Bellson's music with skill, though few of the featured musicians make a strong impression. Recorded a little more than a year before the Maestro's death, *Duke's Big Four* 🎵🎵🎵🎵 (Pablo, 1974, prod. Norman Granz) features four giants—Duke, Joe Pass, Ray Brown, and Bellson—playing six Ellington classics. Duke pays the drummer the ultimate compliment by covering Bellson's best-known tune, "The Hawk Talks." *Raincheck* 🎵🎵🎵🎵 (Concord Jazz, 1978, prod. Carl E. Jefferson) is another strong session by a Bellson small group, featuring Mitchell, Tompkins, Joel DiBartolo (bass), and the brilliant but now obscure Ted Nash (alto and tenor sax). The varied program ranges from "Alone Together," which features Nash's beautiful ballad work, to Sonny Rollins's "Oleo," where Bellson puts down his brushes and plays a blistering solo. Bellson always hires top flight musicians and *Live at Joe Segal's Jazz Showcase* 🎵🎵🎵 (Concord Jazz, 1988, prod. Louie Bellson) continues that tradition. The quartet session features the fiery Don Menza (flute and tenor sax), Larry Novak (piano), and former Basie-ite John Heard (bass). Highlights include Bellson's tribute to Buddy Rich, "Walkin' with Buddy," and a no holds barred "Cherokee" taken at a breakneck tempo.

what to avoid: Even drum fanatics might want to give *Ecue Ritmos Cubanos* 🎵🎵 (Pablo/OJC, 1977, prod. Norman Granz) a pass. Bellson is part of the supporting cast for Cuban percussionist Walfredo De Los Reyes in a band with eight percussionists, two bassists, keyboards, and three horns. There's a lot of energy expended in this dense percussion session, but little variety in the music.

best of the rest:
The Louie Bellson Explosion 🎵🎵🎵🎵 (Pablo, 1975)
Dynamite 🎵🎵🎵🎵 (Concord Jazz, 1979)
Louie Bellson Jam with Blue Mitchell 🎵🎵🎵🎵 (Pablo, 1979)
Cool, Cool, Blue 🎵🎵🎵🎵🎵 (Pablo, 1983)
Hot 🎵🎵🎵🎵 (MusicMasters, 1989)
Jazz Giants 🎵🎵🎵🎵🎵 (MusicMasters, 1989)
Peaceful Thunder 🎵🎵🎵🎵 (MusicMasters, 1992)
Live from New York 🎵🎵🎵🎵 (MusicMasters, 1994)
Air Bellson 🎵🎵🎵🎵🎵 (Concord Jazz, 1997)

worth searching for: The excellent *Side Track* 🎵🎵🎵🎵 (Concord Jazz, 1979, prod. Carl E. Jefferson) features Bellson in a particularly forceful session, driving his working band with energy and precision.

influences:
◀◀ Gene Krupa, Chick Webb, Jo Jones
▶▶ Frank Capp, Jeff Hamilton, Mel Lewis

Andrew Gilbert

Gregg Bendian
Born July 13, 1963, in Englewood, NJ.

Gregg Bendian was raised in Teaneck, New Jersey, began percussion studies at age seven, and piano at age ten. While still in high school, he was first exposed to avant-garde classical music through studies with composer Jeff Kreske at William Paterson College. He furthered his studies at Rutgers University with Third Stream composer Noel DaCosta. Studies with drummers Andrew Cyrille and Steve McCall, both former members of Cecil Taylor's groups, also fortified his surrealistic work. Since 1980 Bendian has composed and performed his own work and collaborated with members of the New York City's "downtown" scene, including John Zorn, Ned Rothenberg, Tom Cora, Bill Frisell, Mark Dresser, and others.

what to buy: Consisting of spontaneously composed percussion duets *Bang!* 🎵🎵🎵🎵 (Truemedia Jazzworks, 1994, prod. Gregg Bendian, Paul Wertico) is an extraordinary recording featuring drummer Paul Wertico. Four selections were recorded live at the Hot House in Chicago and another four were recorded in the studio. It is hard to believe that there are no electronic instruments and no overdubbing! *Gregg Bendian's Interzone* 🎵🎵🎵🎵 (Eremite, 1996, prod. Gregg Bendian, Michael Ehlers) finds the versatile percussionist exclusively playing vibraphone and glockenspiel, his best instruments. West Coast improvisor Alex Cline handles the drum chores, with his brother Nels on guitar, and Mark Dresser on bass. Bendian's intricate compositions are highly structured but leave room for all concerned to deploy imaginative solos. Bendian can sometimes seem a bit dry, but not here! If this disc proves hard to find, it's worth contacting the label directly at eremite@javanet.com. Bendian interacts with bassist Dresser, reed man Vinny Golia, and trumpeter Paul Smoker on *Counterparts* 🎵🎵🎵🎵 (CIMP, 1996, prod. Gregg Bendian), a session that highlights these innovators as they soar with freedom and polyrhythmic action through six challenging compositions.

what to buy next: Derek Bailey and Bendian's free-improvisation duo *Banter* 🎵🎵🎵 (OO Discs, 1995, prod. Derek Bailey, Gregg Bendian) is heavy sledding for novices: Bailey long ago pioneered a totally atonal guitar style, abandoning melody and harmony in favor of extending the instrument's timbral range. Percussionist Bendian also plays freely, and more from a jazz perspective than Bailey. As the album title hints, these improvised duets are musical conversations between the two. As spontaneous as this all is, it has a musical logic and intuitive structure that repay intensive, open-minded listening.

the rest:
Definite Pitch 🎵🎵🎵 (Aggregate, 1989/1994)

worth searching for: Jointly credited to Derek Bailey, Pat Metheny, Bendian, and Paul Wertico, the three-CD (but bargain-priced) *The Sign of 4* 🎵🎵🎵🎵 (Knitting Factory Works, 1997, prod. Gregg Bendian) is mostly scorching free improvisation too "out" for Metheny fans and too loud for Bailey's followers, but just right for listeners seeking an uncategorizable roller-coaster ride on the profusely flowing inspirations of this adventurous, one-time-only quartet. The two discs recorded live at the Knitting Factory offer burly, unbridled intensity, while the middle disc has cooler but no less scintillating studio improvisations. Bendian plays a vast and colorful array of drums and percussion.

influences:
◀◀ Ornette Coleman, Anthony Braxton, Cecil Taylor, Anton Webern, Edgar Varese

David C. Gross and Steve Holtje

Don Bennett

Born August, 14, 1941, in Chicago, IL.

A talented pianist who had not gained widespread notice before his two CDs for Candid, Don Bennett twice came close to appearing as sideman on albums which were never released. Bennett's early roots included listening to Bud Powell and Ahmad Jamal, and you hear those influences in his playing, along with bits of Wynton Kelly and Red Garland. Once established as a pianist in Chicago, Bennett worked with Von Freeman, Betty Carter, Gene Ammons, and Sonny Stitt. Bennett left Chicago in the early 1960s for Los Angeles where he studied with Phineas Newborn for a year. Fortified by his West Coast experiences and playing with Harold Land, Cal Tjader, and others, Bennett returned to Chicago and spent three and a half years with Mari Jo Johnson. He quit playing for a decade to raise his family. Drawn back into the music in the late 1980s, Bennett eased back into the scene, ultimately moving to New York City, where he taught at the New School for a couple of years before leaving for Europe, returning to Chicago in 1988, and moving to Holland in 1993.

what to buy: Recorded in Chicago in May, 1990 and originally released in limited edition by Southport, the bold and brassy *Chicago Calling!* 🎵🎵🎵 (Southport, 1990/Candid, 1995, prod. Ed Crilly) was rereleased by Candid in 1995. Featuring a slew of Chicago-based players—Arthur Hoyle or Steve Smyth (trumpet), Art Porter (alto/soprano saxes), Eddie Peterson (tenor saxophone), with Eric Hochbert (bass), Paul Wertico or Darryl Ervin (drums)—the recording reveals Bennett's many talents as much as it is a showcase for the vibrant Chicago scene and its fine players. Bennett includes highly energized moments where he comps under the tight-and-tidy frontline horns (for which he wrote the arrangements) and his spotlighted moments on ballads such as his lyrical "Love Found Me," featuring Porter's soprano sax and Ervin's tasty brushwork. Bennett is broadly conversant, unfurling single-note runs, smooth blues-tinged phrasing, and relaxed yet polished technique. In various settings, he gives his splendid hometown soloists plenty of space to conquer assorted themes. Fortified by Ed Crilly's studio production skills, the musicians created 75 minutes of spectacular recorded music. *Solar: The Don Bennett Trio* 🎵🎵🎵 (Candid, 1995, prod. Don Bennett, Alan Bates) features Bennett at the piano, James Long on bass, and Douglas Sides on drums covering a sparkling 11-tune set ranging from blues, to romantic ballads, to bubbling bop. Bennett's knack for swinging, bluesy stylings was undoubtedly influenced by the Chicago-born musician's early roots and career collaborations. Highlights include a hard-swinging interpretation of Miles Davis's title tune, a dramatic version of the classic, "You Don't Know What Love Is," and a lovely waltzing interpretation of John Lewis's "Afternoon in Paris." This outing is a pleasantly accessible session that reveals the breadth of Bennett's worldly talents and inspirations—his flowing lyricism, his eloquent phrasing, and his joyfulness. A delightful album.

influences:
◀◀ Ahmad Jamal, Bud Powell, Wynton Kelly, Red Garland

Nancy Ann Lee

Tony Bennett

Born Anthony Dominick Benedetto, August 3, 1926, Astoria, Queens, NY.

Singer Tony Bennett is one of the essential interpreters of the American songbook, matching (perhaps surpassing) the individual worldwide contributions of Ella Fitzgerald, Frank Sinatra, and Bing Crosby. His warm style has made him as popular today with all ages of fans as he was during the 1950s and 1960s. His affinity for jazz musicians and his often swinging style, as well as his precise phrasing and impeccable tone, which has grown deeper and stronger over the years, are archetypal traits to which singers have aspired for the past five decades.

Bennett grew up singing but things didn't start to happen for him until after serving in the Army for three years. Discharged in 1946, he used the G. I. Bill to study voice, then began singing in New York City saloons. His years of scuffling began to diminish in 1949 when he auditioned for a revue Pearl Bailey was in at the Greenwich Village Inn. Bob Hope heard the young singer (then working as Joe Bari) and invited him to sing with his show at the Paramount Theater and go on a subsequent ten-day tour. It was Hope who named him "Tony Bennett."

In 1951 Bennett auditioned at Columbia Records, singing a demo of "Boulevard of Broken Dreams." Mitch Miller signed him to the label and the tune became a moderate hit, launching Bennett's career in the United States. In 1962 he became an international star with his signature recording, "I Left My Heart in San Francisco," and through 1964 Bennett made two dozen Top 40 hits, including "Because of You," "Cold, Cold Heart," "Rags to Riches," and "Stranger in Paradise." As the record industry changed with emphasis shifted from singles to albums in the 1950s, Bennett continued to draw on material from the great American songbook, classic songs by composers George and Ira Gershwin, Irving Berlin, Cole Porter, Harold Arlen, Johnny Mercer, and others. A jazz stylist at heart, Bennett continued to nurture his ties to the idiom, working with orchestras led by Count Basie, Dizzy Gillespie, Duke Ellington, and numerous others.

Bennett recorded infrequently during the 1970s and 1980s, partly because he resisted pressure from Columbia to record more mainstream pop. Instead, he concentrated on touring and his other talent, painting. He revived his career in the 1990s, finding new popularity with the Generation Xers by making appearances on MTV, the late-night TV talk circuit, and even *The Simpsons.* He released an album from his *MTV Unplugged* appearance, toured regularly, and recorded several well-executed concept albums paying tribute to Sinatra, Fred Astaire, Billie Holiday, and others. Bennett's voice today has a huskier edge than the smooth tone of his younger days, but he retains the same sense of swing, passion for lyrical expression and drama, and sincere, warmhearted delivery. Bennett has basically re-

mained with the same label since 1961 (with a hiatus from recording during the 1970s and 1980s), and has had the same pianist/musical director, Ralph Sharon, for over five decades. Bennett continues to tour internationally and has received numerous awards and honors for his achievements.

what to buy: If you want to dig into Bennett's jazz roots, check out *Tony Bennett: Jazz* ♫♫♫♫ (Columbia, 1987, reissue prod. James Isaacs, Joe McEwen), a compilation of 22 previously recorded songs made between 1954–67 with various jazz musicians, including the Count Basie Orchestra, and groups of various size led by Ralph Sharon, Marion Evans, Ralph Burns, Chuck Wayne, and others. An array of jazz notables perform, including Herbie Hancock, Stan Getz, Art Blakey, Nat Adderley, Chico Hamilton, Ed Shaughnessy, and more. With heartfelt warmth, Bennett delivers classics such as "On Green Dolphin Street;" Ellington's "Solitude" and an uptempo "Lullaby of Broadway" (both backed by a swinging Basie Orchestra); a quirky, kicking version of "Just One of Those Things" featuring Art Blakey; and the shuffle-beat swinger "Crazy Rhythm" featuring the artistry of drummer Chico Hamilton. Among the most enjoyable songs are those performed with backing from tenor saxophonist Stan Getz, pianist Herbie Hancock, bassist Ron Carter, and drummer Elvin Jones—"Clear out of This World," "Just Friends," "Have You Met Miss Jones?," and a gorgeous, previously unissued track, "Danny Boy," where Getz weaves his embellishments around Bennett's vocals. One of Bennett's best performances on this album of ballads and swingers is his caressing, intimate performance on the bluesy ballad "When Lights Are Low," performed with Ralph Sharon (piano), Hal Gaylor (bass), and William Exiner (drums). These may not be his biggest hits, but the way he handles them, with ultimate jazz sensibility, demonstrates the finesse he has cultivated throughout his career. A highly recommended album. Another charming album recommended for the jazz fan, is Bennett's intimate duet album with pianist Bill Evans, *The Tony Bennett/Bill Evans Album* ♫♫♫♫ (Fantasy/OJC, 1975, prod. Helen Keane). Bennett has a wonderful way with tenderhearted laments such as "Young and Foolish," "Some Other Time," "We'll Be Together Again," "My Foolish Heart," the Evans original, "Waltz for Debby" (with lyrics by Gene Lees), and four more tunes that prominently feature the empathetic and lyrical Evans five years before his death. A relaxed listen, suited for healing the wounds of a broken romance. Recorded when he was edging toward age 40, *I Left My Heart in San Francisco* ♫♫♫♫ (Columbia, 1962/1988 prod. Ernest Altschuler) is Bennett's first great studio album. Backed by an unnamed studio orchestra (with added strings on some tracks), the 12-tune session contains jazz standards such as "Love for Sale," swing-infected versions of "Taking a Chance on Love" and "The Best Is Yet to Come," and the unforgettable title track, which won him two 1962 Grammys, for Record of the Year and Best Solo Vocal Performance, Male. That single, a gold-selling Top 10 hit, remained on the charts for nearly three years. Bennett's voice is deepening from tenor toward baritone by the time of this recording, and his warmth and intimacy come through strongly, in spite of the less-than-perfect sound quality. In 1997 Columbia released a three-CD set that combines *I Left My Heart in San Francisco* and *I Wanna Be Around* and other material, but the album reviewed above is Bennett's single disc release. The CD reissue of *I Wanna Be Around* 𝄢𝄢𝄢𝄢 (Columbia, 1963/1995, prod. Ernie Altschuler) draws from the original LP released the year after Bennett's breakthrough hit, "I Left My Heart in San Francisco," and includes additional material, mostly from the album, *This Is All I Ask*. Of the 18 tunes Included here, both the title tune and "The Good Life" became top 20 hits. Bennett also sings lovely arrangements of Antonio Carlos Jobim's "Quiet Nights of Quiet Stars (Corcovado)," "Once upon a Summertime," "Young and Foolish," and the delicately swinging Freddie Green composition, "Until I Met You" (which is really Green's melody, "Corner Pocket," a trademark tune of the Basie Orchestra). Exceptional reproduction quality captures Bennett's voice in peerless clear, crisp form on this mixture of jazz and pop tunes performed with two separate orchestras led by conductor-arrangers Marty Manning and Ralph Burns. Songs recorded with the latter orchestra, highlight the Ralph Sharon Trio. If you're ready to lay down greenbacks for Bennett, *Forty Years: The Artistry of Tony Bennett* 𝄢𝄢𝄢𝄢 (Columbia, 1991/1997, prod. Didier Deutsch), is recommended. This four-CD box set offers an overview of Bennett's career at that point, with 87 song arranged chronologically. The original four-CD box set came with a booklet. The collection was re-reissued in 1997 in an unabridged, more affordable, slip-case package.

what to buy next: Bennett's fans welcomed him back after a recording hiatus of several years (and his return to Columbia after 14 years) with the release of a series of top-notch albums featuring fresh material and concepts, including *The Art of Excellence* 𝄢𝄢𝄢𝄢 (Columbia, 1986/1997), *Astoria: Portrait of the Artist* 𝄢𝄢𝄢𝄢 (Columbia, 1989/1997, prod. Ettore Stratta, Danny Bennett), and *Perfectly Frank* 𝄢𝄢𝄢𝄢 (Columbia, 1992, prod. Andre Fischer). *The Art of Excellence* offers a collection of old and new songs performed with the Ralph Sharon Trio (Sharon, piano; Paul Langosch, bass; Joe LaBarbera, drums) and the

U.K. Orchestra Limited, conducted by Jorge Calandrelli. Bennett is in excellent form throughout this strings-enriched session, and delivers with awesome power fresh material such as the Bergman-Legrand song, "How Do You Keep the Music Playing?" Ray Charles makes a cameo appearance singing and pattering with Bennett on "Everybody Has the Blues." *Astoria: Portrait of the Artist* honors Bennett's birthplace with liner photos from his childhood and he sings a collection of admired classics such as "Speak Low," "Body and Soul," "The Folks That Live on the Hill," as well as appealing songs from a newly discovered songwriter, Charles DeForest. At this point, the Ralph Sharon Trio included pianist Sharon, bassist Paul Langosch, and drummer Joe LaBarbera. Bennett is also backed by the U.K. Orchestra Limited on some songs recorded in Wembley, England in May 1989, and other tunes were recorded in Astoria, New York the following month. On *Perfectly Frank* Bennett honors one of his best admirers—"Old Blue Eyes," a.k.a. "The Chairman of the Board." Singing torch and saloon songs Frank Sinatra made famous, Bennett (with the Ralph Sharon Trio) puts his indelible mark on a 24-tune collection of popular favorites, including some swing-tinged jazz standards such as "I Thought about You," "Night and Day," "The Lady Is a Tramp," "One for My Baby," and classic ballads such as "I've Got the World on a String," "Here's That Rainy Day," "A Foggy Day," and "Angel Eyes." While some of these tunes are better done by Sinatra, Bennett and his trio lend classy elegance to them, making the session a refreshing and agreeable listen. *Steppin' Out* 𝄢𝄢𝄢𝄢 (Columbia, 1993, prod. David Kahne) features Bennett with his regular group, the Ralph Sharon Trio (Sharon on piano, Doug Richeson, bass; Clayton Cameron, drums) on a tantalizing mix of 18 American songbook swingers and ballads dedicated to dance master Fred Astaire. The session reflects Bennett's successfully reignited career (engineered by his son and manager, Danny Bennett). Lively and engaging, the tunes hold appeal for an active generation that laughs, loves, and laments, as well as for Bennett's gray-haired fans who will find memories among the Irving Berlin, Cole Porter, George and Ira Gershwin tunes, and classics such as "Dancing in the Dark" (ladies, you'll swear he's humming in your ear as, eyes closed, you glide together across the dance floor). Performed lovingly by Bennett and the trio, "He Loves and She Loves" is a delicate, waltzing masterpiece, alone worth the album price. Now in the midst of a full-fledged comeback, Bennett won a Grammy for *MTV Unplugged* 𝄢𝄢𝄢𝄢 (Columbia, 1994, prod. David Kahne), a collection of 20

Tony Bennett (© Ken Settle)

live-recorded tunes delivered for the television special on MTV and aimed at Generation Xers. Bennett sings in his joyful, confident, commanding manner with the Ralph Sharon Trio (Sharon, piano; Doug Richeson, bass; Clayton Cameron, drums), swinging through jazz classics such as "Fly Me to the Moon," "When Joanna Loved Me," "A Foggy Day," "Body and Soul," "It Don't Mean a Thing If It Ain't Got That Swing," and his trademark tunes such as "I Left My Heart in San Francisco," "Rags to Riches," and more. Elvis Costello and k.d. lang stumble through cameo appearances.

best of the rest:

The Beat of My Heart ✍✍✍ (Columbia, 1957/1997)
In Person! With the Count Basie Orchestra ✍✍✍ (Columbia, 1959/1994)
Tony Sings for Two ✍✍✍ (Columbia, 1960/1996)
At Carnegie Hall: The Complete Concert ✍✍✍✍ (Columbia, 1962/1997)
Who Can I Turn To? ✍✍✍ (Columbia, 1964/1995)
If I Ruled the World: Songs for the Jet Set ✍✍✍ (Columbia, 1965/1997)
The Movie Song Album ✍✍✍ (Columbia, 1966/1988)
Something ✍✍✍ (Columbia, 1970/1995)
All-Time Hall of Fame Hits ✍✍✍ (Columbia, 1970/1987)
The Very Thought of You ✍✍✍ (Columbia, 1971/1995)
All-Time Greatest Hits ✍✍✍ (Columbia, 1972/1987)
Rodgers and Hart Songbook ✍✍✍ (DRG, 1973/WMO, 1997)
Bennett/Berlin ✍✍✍ (Columbia, 1987)
Here's to the Ladies ✍✍✍ (Columbia, 1995)
On Holiday ✍✍✍ (Columbia, 1997)

worth searching for: Imagine hearing Bennett, Bing Crosby, Rosemary Clooney, and Woody Herman on one CD. *A Tribute to Duke* ✍✍✍ (Concord, 1977, prod. Carl E. Jefferson) combines the contributions of these major talents with a West Coast swing combo that includes pianist Nat Pierce, tenor saxophonist Scott Hamilton, trumpeter Bill Berry, bassist Monty Budwig, and drummer Jake Hanna. Although Bennett is featured on only two songs ("Prelude to a Kiss" and "I'm Just a Lucky So and So"), this Ellington homage is an enjoyable listen for the singers and fine instrumentals. It's especially rewarding if you're a fan of Scott Hamilton's warm tenor saxophone style. Not easily found the rest of the year, *Snowfall: The Tony Bennett Christmas Album* ✍✍✍ (Columbia, 1968/1994, prod. Jack Gold) is a gem featuring Bennett backed by a fabulous strings-sweetened orchestra (and, on some selections, a vocal choir) conducted by the esteemed Robert Farnon, whose arrangements of favorite holiday songs are the classiest best. Bennett is in superb form on this recording, singing 12 holiday favorites and spreading cheer with non-seasonal classics such as "My Favorite Things," "Where Is Love," and "I've Got My Love to

Keep Me Warm." This disc is a must for inclusion in your Christmas music collection.

influences:

◀◀ Art Tatum, Mildred Bailey, Louis Armstrong, Bing Crosby, Charlie Parker, John Coltrane, Fred Astaire, Frank Sinatra, Ella Fitzgerald

▶▶ Chet Baker, Harry Connick Jr., Holly Cole, Kurt Elling, Shirley Horn, Susannah McCorkle

Nancy Ann Lee

Han Bennink

Born April 17, 1942, in Zaandam, Netherlands.

Arguably the premier European percussionist, Han Bennink is a drummer for all seasons. Initially influenced by his father, a classical percussionist, by the early 1960s he gravitated towards jazz and improvised music. He became the drummer of choice for visiting American jazzmen, including Eric Dolphy, Dexter Gordon, and Sonny Rollins.

In 1967, along with Misha Mengelberg and Willem Breuker, Bennink formed the Instant Composer's Pool (I.C.P.), a nonprofit organization that released recordings and sponsored performances by members of the Dutch avant-garde. In 1968 he participated in the session that resulted in the seminal European free-jazz album *Machine Gun* by the Peter Brötzmann Octet. In 1969 he joined a cooperative trio with German saxophonist Brötzmann and Belgian pianist Fred van Hove. From 1969–76, this group forged a unique and powerful brand of improvisation that drew from not only American sources (primarily Albert Ayler's groups and post-*Ascension* John Coltrane), but also from European folk melodies and the performance aesthetic of the Fluxus group. Bennink's apocalyptic drumming drove Brötzmann's frenzied saxophonics to ever-further heights as van Hove etched a wry commentary underneath. After van Hove left in 1976, Brotzmann and Bennink continued as a duo, occasionally augmented by pianist Mengelberg until 1980.

Since the '80s Bennink has shown a willingness to explore virtually any musical situation. In addition to performing solo and in an endless array of duos (with guitarist Derek Bailey, trombonist Conrad Bauer, and pianist Cecil Taylor), he has also worked with Dutch anarcho-punks experimentalists the Ex. A steady and highly fruitful alliance was formed with reedman Michael Moore and cellist Ernst Reijseger as Clusone 3, who have released four albums since 1990. Another trio with trombonist Ray Anderson and guitarist Christy Doran has released two recordings. Bennink's most steady partnership has been with pianist Mengelberg, which has been documented on record since 1964. They have a number of duo albums that are now out of print. But they continue to be the engine of the I.C.P. Orchestra.

If Sunny Murray's drumming has been described as the continuous sound of shattering glass, Bennink's could be described as the continuous sound of collapsing buildings. But that would not take into account a drummer of enormous subtlety and wit. He incorporates elements of African drumming, gamelan music, tap dance, and big band swing. He's also a very theatrical performer whose penchant for absurdity (his flaming hi-hat trick is quite impressive) shows his fondness for Dada and his sense of humor. Above all, Bennink is one of jazz/improvised music's most swinging drummers.

what to buy: *Han* 𝄞𝄞𝄞𝄞 (Incus, 1986) is a recording with guitarist Derek Bailey and thus stars improvised music's very own Felix and Oscar. Bennink and Bailey seem to have diametrically opposed aesthetics, though this collaboration has been going since 1972. Each brings unexpected responses out of the other's playing. *Serpentine* 𝄞𝄞𝄞 (Songlines, 1996) finds Bennink paired with a more recent collaborator, trumpeter Dave Douglas, who is an excellent foil for Bennink. He knows Bennink's tricks and throws in a few of his own.

what to buy next: *Brotzmann-Van Hove-Bennink with Albert Manglesdorff Live in Berlin '71* 𝄞𝄞𝄞𝄞 (F.M.P., 1971, prod. Jost Gebers) is a 2-CD set reissue of a legendary three-album set recorded at two separate concerts during the Berlin Free Music Market of 1971. This is the classic trio augmented by trombonist Manglesdorff. What impressed on its initial release was the sheer unadulterated power of this trio and its Gotterdamerung sensibility. (The last installment wasn't called "The End" for nothing.) Over time, this music has retained its impact, thought its subtleties, especially those of Van Hove and Bennink, are much more apparent.

best of the rest:
Azurety 𝄞𝄞𝄞𝄞 (hat ART, 1994)

worth searching for: *Change of Season* 𝄞𝄞𝄞𝄞 (Soul Note, 1984) is a Mengelberg release. It is a companion to *Regeneration*, with George Lewis in place of trombonist Roswell Rudd. All compositions are by pianist Herbie Nichols. Lewis gives the music a smoother texture and Bennink's adjusts his playing accordingly. *Last Date* 𝄞𝄞𝄞 (PolyGram, 1964) is an Eric Dolphy release featuring Bennink and Mengelberg. They are two-thirds of the rhythm section backing Dolphy on his last studio session. Even

though Bennink is a bit too klompen, he plays with enthusiasm throughout. Dolphy sounds quite inspired. This record was reissued on CD but may be difficult to locate. *Regeneration* 𝄞𝄞𝄞𝄞 (Soul Note, 1982, prod. Giovanni Bonandrini), released under trombonist Roswell Rudd's name, consists of three Thelonious Monk and three Herbie Nichols compositions. Bennink expertly propels a quintet of Rudd, Bennink, soprano saxophonist Steve Lacy, pianist Mengelberg, and bassist Kent Carter. The demanding rhythmic contours of these compositions are expertly maneuvered by Bennink. *Peter Brotzman Octet Machine Gun* 𝄞𝄞𝄞𝄞 (F.M.P, 1968, prod. Jost Gebers) is the defining document of European free jazz, an all-out rapid-fire assault by an octet of musicians from Britain, the Netherlands, and Germany. Even after 30 years it still comes across as the feral European cousin to Coltrane's *Ascencion*. Bennink propels a 12-piece band and an octet on *I.C.P. Orchestra Performs Nichols and Monk* 𝄞𝄞𝄞𝄞 (I.C.P., 1984–86, prod. I.C.P.) The two ensembles perform the music of Nichols and Monk respectively. The entire record is very much in the tradition. Bennink adheres to the standard without sacrificing his individuality. One of saxist Steve Lacy's most brilliant recordings, *Lumps* 𝄞𝄞𝄞𝄞 (I.C.P., 1974) features Bennink and two of Holland's finest: Michel Waiswisz on electronics and Maarten Altena on bass. Bennink punctuates Lacy's themes with shattering explosions, chattering commentary and (on "Snips") some dangerous sounding work on scissors. This is Bennink at his most manic.

influences:
◄◄ Baby Dodds, Sunny Murray
►► Bill Stewart, Jim Black, Michael Sarin

Robert Iannapollo

David Benoit
Born August 18, 1953, in Bakersfield, CA.

David Benoit's brand of pop-jazz can be described with the same adjectives used to describe a lake at sunset: cool, breezy, romantic, and sometimes a little damp. His determination to pursue challenging extensions rather than carbon copy sequels to his past successes certainly elevates Benoit above most of his peers on the contemporary jazz charts, but if record sales and concert attendance measure success, Benoit has been entirely successful. One thing that separates Benoit from the swarm of contemporary jazz artists is his intrinsic ability to compose melodies that stick. On the piano, he certainly owns his own "sound." His style echoes the delicate touch of Bill Evans with the melodic grace of Vince Guaraldi, an underappreciated talent that shines best when he strips back his often busy arrangements and plays acoustic piano.

The son of a jazz guitarist father and a piano-playing mother, he began playing piano at age 14. He continued with various bands after his family moved to Hermosa Beach, near Los Angeles. His first big break came when film composer Richard Baskin invited Benoit to play on the soundtrack to the legendary Robert Altman film of 1975, *Nashville*. It is fitting that Benoit's first studio session was Alphonse Mouzon's 1975 *The Man Incognito*, featuring future GRP labelmates Dave Grusin and Lee Ritenour. Benoit's solo career began with several albums on the AVI label: *Heavier Than Yesterday*, *Can You Imagine*, *Stages* (a smash hit in the Philippines), *Digits*, and *Waves of Raves*. During this time, he was sharpening his composing/bandleading skills, which led to his 1985 album for Spindletop, *This Side Up*, a turning point for the pianist.

It was that album that attracted the ear of Larry Rosen and Dave Grusin, then starting a new label called GRP (Grusin Rosen Productions). Benoit became one of the label's initial signings, providing a strong foundation for GRP's extraordinary success. The cache of albums that Benoit has recorded as a leader for GRP over the past decade, 10 in all, has made him one of the highest-selling jazz artists of the period. And although most people associate the Benoit sound with glossy melodies that could easily be mistaken for (and sometimes are) TV and film themes, his more "serious" albums such as *Waiting for Spring* and *Letter to Evan* leave the mainstream critics cold. Now that Mesa/Bluemoon Records has reissued his AVI catalog, it is evident to a wider audience that Benoit's jazz roots run deep.

Aside from his own albums, Benoit has served as producer on over 10 albums and added his keyboard talents to scores of others, including those of such artists as Emily Remler, Diane Schuur, Kenny Loggins, Patti Austin, and the Rippingtons. He has also appeared as guest conductor and pianist with The New World Symphony, The Dresden Philharmonic, The Royal Winnipeg Ballet, The New Jazz Philharmonic, The Los Angeles Philharmonic, and the Los Angeles Composer's Guild. Each new release provides further proof that Benoit's sturdy musical stamp of well-stated and highly accessible melodies is indelible.

what to buy: *Waiting for Spring* ♫♫♫♫ (GRP, 1989, prod. Jeffrey Weber, David Benoit) topped the *Billboard* jazz album listings for eight weeks, unseating the immensely popular *When Harry Met Sally* soundtrack as the #1 album. It isn't as shocking as hearing Kenny G play Coltrane, but given his previous pop-ori-

ented output, it was a pleasant surprise. Backed by a trio including Peter Erskine and Emily Remler, Benoit pays homage to such heroes as Evans and Guaraldi and delivers a gorgeous instrumental version of Doris Day's "Secret Love," flexing the straight-ahead muscles that were in danger of atrophying. Of his early pop-jazz excursions, the glistening *Freedom at Midnight* ♫♫♫ (GRP, 1987, prod. Jeffrey Weber) holds up the best. The melodic bliss of "Kei's Song," "Along the Milky Way," and the title track evoke an unabashed beauty that later would occasionally lapse into saccharine.

what to buy next: *Christmastime* ♫♫♫♫ (AVI/Bluemoon, 1983, prod. David Benoit) was actually recorded at Christmas time, initially as a personal gift to friends. (Most Christmas albums are recorded in the dead of summer to make the retail stores by the holidays.) AVI heard it and wisely released it the next year. Embracing the grand scope of Aaron Copland, the orchestral *American Landscape* ♫♫♫ (GRP, 1997, prod. David Benoit, Al Schmitt) captures the purple mountain's majesty but stays grounded with Benoit's engaging piano playing.

what to avoid: *Urban Daydreams* ♫ (GRP, 1989, prod. David Benoit, Don Grusin) is a cold, overblown synthesizer-driven effort that makes Mannheim Steamroller sound like the Modern Jazz Quartet.

the rest:
Heavier than Yesterday ♫♫♫ (AVI/Bluemoon, 1977)
Life is Like a Samba ♫♫ (AVI, 1979)
Can You Imagine ♫♫♫ (AVI/Bluemoon, 1980)
Stages ♫♫♫ (AVI/Bluemoon, 1982)
Digits ♫♫♫♫ (AVI/Bluemoon, 1983)
Every Step of the Way ♫♫♫♫ (GRP, 1987)
Urban Daydreams ♫♫♫ (GRP, 1988)
Inner Motion ♫♫♫ (GRP, 1990)
Shadows ♫♫ (GRP, 1991)
Waves of Raves ♫♫♫ (Bluemoon, 1991)
Letter to Evan ♫♫♫♫ (GRP, 1992)
Shaken Not Stirred ♫♫ (GRP, 1994)
Benoit Freeman Project ♫♫♫♫ (GRP, 1994)
Lost and Found ♫♫♫ (Rhino, 1994)
Best of David Benoit 1987–1995 ♫♫♫ (GRP, 1995)
Remembering Christmas ♫♫♫ (GRP, 1996)
To: '87 ♫♫♫ (Marquee Music, 1996)

worth searching for: *This Side Up* ♫♫♫♫ (Spindletop, 1991) reached the #4 position on *Billboard*'s jazz chart. It offers bright and upbeat instrumentals ranging from the enticing "Beach Trails" to Evans's "Waltz for Debbie" to Benoit's first attempt at Guaraldi's "Linus and Lucy."

influences:

⏪ Ramsey Lewis, Henry Mancini

⏩ Kym Pencyl, Rob Mullins, Pat Coil

Ralph Burnett and David Okamoto

George Benson

Born March 22, 1943, in Pittsburgh, PA.

Like legendary predecessors such as Nat "King" Cole and Louis Armstrong, singer/guitarist George Benson has become one of the few jazz artists to notch nearly equal acclaim as both an instrumental improvisor and pop vocal star. While recent fans may only know his scat-singing solo style and R&B-flavored jazz-pop records, Benson's recording career actually began at age 10, when he cut several R&B singles for a small label after sporadic gigs as an amateur singer and street musician in Pittsburgh. Inspired to learn jazz after hearing groundbreaking saxophonist Charlie Parker, Benson eventually traveled to New York in 1963, where he joined groups led by organists "Brother" Jack McDuff and Jimmy Smith. Befriending his soon-to-be mentor and most obvious influence, jazz guitar great Wes Montgomery, the talented young guitarist scored his first record deal in the mid-1960s—courtesy of producer John Hammond, who has discovered everyone from Charlie Christian to Bob Dylan. Supposedly, Benson was required to sing as part of the deal, but that talent didn't emerge during his three records with Hammond. In the years that followed, Benson would move from Columbia to Verve, A&M, and then CTI, also appearing on albums by Herbie Hancock, Freddie Hubbard, and Miles Davis. Following the lead of Montgomery—who recorded successful records in the mid-1960s featuring covers of Beatles tunes—Benson even presented an album, "The Other Side of Abbey Road," that featured his take on the Fab Four's entire opus. Fans of his instrumental work, featuring a fluid tone and thick chordal work that recalled Montgomery, say that the albums Benson crafted for CTI stand as some of his best-ever recording as a player.

By the mid-1970s, producer Tommy LiPuma convinced Benson to go the pop route, assembling the landmark LP *Breezin'*. Benson, who reportedly received the biggest advance ever given a jazz artist, repaid Warner Bros. with the first jazz album ever to sell over one million copies. Showcasing the guitarist's amazing ability to scat sing and play guitar lines in unison, the album became an instant classic, shaping Benson's approach to R&B-flavored jazz-pop forevermore. After nearly 20 years as an R&B star, during which period his guitar playing receded into the background of his music, Benson turned back to jazz in 1990, recording with the Count Basie Orchestra and, later, his own quartet, leapfrogging between more commercially successful and artistically demanding styles.

what to buy: For all his commercial success, Benson also offers jazz fans a chance to hear one of the best instrumental improvisers around. *George Benson Verve Jazz Masters #21* 🎷🎷🎷🎷 (Verve, 1994, compilation prod. Michael Lang) features liberal amounts of the guitarist's best instrumental work, including selections from *The Shape of Things to Come* and *The Other Side of Abbey Road*, along with an appearance by his former boss, Jimmy Smith. *White Rabbit* 🎷🎷🎷🎷 (CTI, 1971, prod. Creed Taylor) stands as one of Benson's best CTI gigs, offering a wonderful reworking of the Jefferson Airplane hit on the title cut and one of the first recorded appearances by Earl Klugh.

what to buy next: *Breezin'* 🎷🎷🎷🎷 (Warner Bros., 1976, prod. Tommy LiPuma) helped define the best and worst of what has become today's "smooth jazz" phenomenon—fleshing out classic cuts such as the title track and Leon Russell's "This Masquerade" with seamless production value and an unerring instinct for pop appeal. The follow-up record, the live *Weekend in L.A.* 🎷🎷🎷🎷 (Warner Bros., 1977, prod. Tommy LiPuma) gave Benson his other enduring hit, "On Broadway," while cementing his reputation as consummate singer and entertainer. Benson's album with R&B production master Quincy Jones, *Give Me the Night* 🎷🎷🎷🎷, (Warner Bros., 1980, prod. Quincy Jones) succeeded nearly as well, fueled by the percolating hit title track and a tribute to saxophonist James Moody, "Moody's Mood."

what to avoid: Benson's efforts to win pop acclaim weren't always so successful, as shown by the empty pop confection *20/20* **woof!** (Warner Bros., 1984, prod. Russ Titelman). Weighed down by empty commercial arrangements, this lightweight record shows off the dangers of placing sales concerns above artistic effort. Almost as bad for different reasons is *Big Boss Band* 🎷 (Warner Bros., 1990, prod. George Benson), a directionless bit of confusion that smells suspiciously like Benson trying to cash in on his jazz credentials when the crossover hits had stopped coming. Not even the fact that he was recording with the Count Basie Band could save this one.

the rest:

The New Boss Guitar of George Benson with the Brother Jack McDuff Quartet 🎷🎷🎷 (OJC, 1964)

Benson Burner 🎷🎷🎷 (Columbia, 1965)

$\frac{9}{8}$ | *george benson*

George Benson (© Jack Vartoogian)

The Most Exciting New Guitarist on the Jazz Scene Today—It's Uptown with the George Benson Quartet 𝄞𝄞𝄞𝄇 (Columbia, 1966)

The George Benson Cookbook 𝄞𝄞𝄞𝄇 (Columbia, 1966)

The Shape of Things to Come 𝄞𝄞𝄇 (A&M, 1967)

Blue Benson 𝄞𝄞𝄇 (Polydor, 1968)

Body Talk 𝄞𝄇 (CTI, 1973)

Beyond the Blue Horizon 𝄞𝄞𝄇 (CTI, 1973)

Bad Benson 𝄞𝄞𝄞𝄇 (CTI, 1974)

Good King Bad 𝄞𝄞𝄇 (CTI, 1975)

In Concert at Carnegie Hall 𝄞𝄇 (CTI, 1975)

George Benson and Joe Farrell 𝄞𝄞𝄇 (CTI, 1976)

In Flight 𝄞𝄞𝄞𝄇 (Warner Bros., 1976)

Livin' Inside Your Love 𝄞𝄞𝄞𝄞𝄇 (Warner Bros., 1979)

The George Benson Collection 𝄞𝄞𝄇 (Warner Bros., 1981)

The Best 𝄇𝄇 (Rebound, 1981)

In Your Eyes 𝄞𝄇𝄇 (Warner Bros., 1983)

While the City Sleeps 𝄞𝄇𝄇 (Warner Bros., 1986)

Silver Collection 𝄞𝄞𝄞𝄇 (Verve, 1987)

Compact Jazz 𝄞𝄇𝄇 (Verve, 1987)

Tenderly 𝄞𝄇 (Warner Bros., 1989)

Love Remembers, 𝄇 (Warner Bros., 1993)

Witchcraft 𝄇𝄇 (Jazz Hour, 1995)

The Best of George Benson 𝄞𝄞𝄞𝄇 (Warner Bros., 1995)

That's Right 𝄞𝄞𝄇 (GRP, 1996)

Revue Collection 𝄞𝄇 (One Way, 1996)

This Is Jazz #9 𝄞𝄞𝄞𝄇 (Columbia Legacy, 1996)

Talkin' Verve 𝄞𝄞𝄇 (Verve, 1997)

worth searching for: It's fascinating to hear a master instrumentalist tackle masterful songs intended for another genre. *The Other Side of Abbey Road* 𝄞𝄞𝄞𝄇 (A&M, 1995) is a wonderful work, available only as a Japanese import.

influences:

◀◀ Wes Montgomery, Charlie Christian, Grant Green

▶▶ Ronnie Jordan, Mark Whitfield, Stanley Jordan

Eric Deggans

Steve Beresford

Born 1950, in Wellington, Shropshire, England.

Some fans may perceive Steve Beresford as a true musical schizophrenic. He has recorded albums with many of Europe's top free-jazz improvisers, but he has concurrently recorded albums of middle-of-the-road lounge music. In between, he has produced and performed on albums of dub, classic South African jazz, and rock. In 1974, after he left York University, where he produced British avant-garde jazz concerts, Beresford moved to London and dove into the free improvisation scene. His most important early alliance was with the group Alterations, with whom he recorded three albums. During the early '80s, he was also involved in dub experiments, most notably on Prince Far I's *Cry Tough Dub Encounter, Chapter 3*. Beresford's first solo album, *The Bath of Surprise*, consisted of home and studio recordings from 1977–80 and reflected his varied interests.

By the mid-'80s he had formed the duo General Strike with David Toop, and they released the cassette-only *Danger in Paradise*. With the Melody Four (a trio with Beresford and saxophonists Lol Coxhill and Tony Coe), he put out a series of love songs, TV themes, and Spanish music, on a French record label. Under his own name, he released the music of French songwriter Charles Trenet and songs associated with crooner Doris Day. More recently, he has worked on film scores and TV projects, but also continued with free improvisation and surreal middle-of-the-road music.

what to buy: The unpredictable and winning *Signals for Tea* ✍✍✍✍ (Avant, 1994, prod. Steve Beresford, John Zorn), a middle-of-the-road album, includes Andrew Bremmer's absurdist lyrics, music ranging from hipster jazz to cheesy bossa nova, saxophonist John Zorn, and trumpeter Dave Douglas. *Avril Brise* ✍✍✍✍ (Cinenato, 1987, prod. Jean Rochard) is a haunting score Beresford wrote for an obscure 1933 film. The remarkable music incorporates some electronics and slight ethnic touches, and shows Beresford's more sober side.

what to buy next: The Melody Four's *Melody Four-TV? Mais Oui!* ✍✍✍✍ (Nato, 1986, prod. Jean Rochard) focuses on television themes, played like you have never heard them before. Beresford's Cecil Taylor-style take on the *Dallas* theme is not to be missed. It also comes with a hip reading of Laurie Johnson's theme to *The Avengers*. *Short in the U.K.* ✍✍✍✍ (Incus, 1994) includes two free improvisors from Britain and two from the United States, and all manner of mayhem ensues. Like most of

Beresford's forays into free improvisation, it's not about solos, it's about group interaction.

best of the rest:
(With General Strike) *Danger in Paradise* ✍✍✍ (Piano/Echo Beach, 1985)
(With David Toop, John Zorn, and Tonie Marshall) *Deadly Weapons* ✍✍✍✍ (NATO, 1986)
(With Melody Four) *Shopping for Melodies* ✍✍✍ (Nato, 1989)
Fish of the Week ✍✍✍ (Scatter, 1993)

worth searching for: Beresford's *L'Extraordinaire Jardin de Charles Trenet* ✍✍✍✍ (Chabada, 1987), another offbeat but brilliant work, focuses on Trenet, a venerated French songwriter whose best-known composition is "La Mer" ("Somewhere beyond the Sea"). The album of four singers and a small ensemble was originally released as part of Chabada's 10" series.

influences:
◀◀ David Toop, Bob Dorough
▶▶ Lee Feldman

Robert Iannapollo

Bob Berg

Born April 7, 1951, in New York, NY.

Bob Berg's reputation as a world class tenor player has been carefully constructed through stints with Miles Davis and Chick Corea, as well as his own groups, including a fusion band he co-leads with long time collaborator, guitarist Mike Stern. While at Juilliard, Berg was offered a tour with organist Jack McDuff, which launched his career as a jazz musician. In 1973 he joined Horace Silver's band and remained there for three years. Pianist Cedar Walton's quartet, Eastern Rebellion was Berg's next stop, where he replaced George Coleman for nearly five years. In 1984 Berg joined Miles Davis for three years, touring the world with the Davis group. After leaving Davis, he embarked on a solo recording career, as well as an ongoing collaboration with guitarist Mike Stern. Concurrently, from 1992–96, Berg was part of Chick Corea's Acoustic Quartet, also recording for Corea's Stretch Records. A free-jazz player with energy and style in the 1960s, Berg assimilated the Coltrane influence and became a respected orthodox hard-bop soloist in the 1970s. When he joined Davis in the mid-1980s, he began playing fusion music as well. His later releases successfully balance traditional and contemporary elements.

what to buy: Although many know Berg from his fusion work with Davis and in the group he co-leads with Stern, the tenor and soprano saxophonist is very much at home with standards in the straight-ahead tradition. On *Another Standard* ♫♫♫♫ (Stretch, 1997, prod. Bob Berg, David Kikoski, John Burk), he's at the height of his post-bop creativity. He burns on a blazing "You And the Night and the Music," creates memorable lines on "All the Way," chills out on "Summer Wind," and offers a Coltrane-esque soprano on the unlikely "It Was a Very Good Year." Thoughtfulness and depth throughout mark Berg as an experienced master. Berg's second Stretch recording, *Enter the Spirit* ♫♫♫♫ (Stretch, 1997, prod. Bob Berg, Ron Moss), focuses on his straight-ahead roots with a supporting cast that includes Corea and solid support from bassist James Genus and drummer Dennis Chambers. Berg's emotional tenor really shines on his compositions "Nature of the Beat," and "Snapshot," as well as Corea's "Some Other Time" and Sonny Rollins "No Moe," with Berg's moving rendition of "I Loves You Porgy" recalling the Miles Davis/Gil Evans collaboration. Berg's third Denon release, *In the Shadows* ♫♫♫♫ (Denon, 1990, prod. Bob Berg, Mike Stern), is a pleasant mix of old and new, with re-worked standards "I Thought about You" and "Autumn Leaves" alongside the fusion title track (featuring Randy Brecker on muted trumpet), which echoes Berg's days with Davis. Dennis Chambers's fiery drumming, Lincoln Goines's solid bass and Jim Beard's imaginative keyboards help to elevate the proceedings and allow Berg to offer a refreshing take on contemporary sounds. Berg's Stretch debut, *Riddles* ♫♫♫♫ (Stretch, 1994, prod. Jim Beard), is a fusion-based offering that shows an imaginative use of the genre, thanks to the accordion of Gil Goldstein and Jim Beard's keyboards. Propelled by Steve Gadd's precision percussion, Berg's soprano sax is almost up to his tenor here in intensity and originality. In addition to his originals, Berg's imaginative renditions of Wayne Shorter's "Children of the Night," George Harrison's "Something," and Stevie Wonder's "Ebony Eyes" make this a good introduction for new listeners.

what to buy next: A change of pace finds Berg focusing on fusion and country with his regular band mates on *Backroads* ♫♫♫ (Denon, 1991, prod. Bob Berg). He shows that country/jazz doesn't have to be corny on the title track and "Traveling Man," while staying in touch with jazz roots on "When I Fall in Love." A tip of the hat to fusion as it should be played on *Cycles* ♫♫♫ (Denon, 1989, prod. Bob Berg), featuring strong blowing, strong compositions, including "Someone to Watch over Me," and a strong band with pianists Don Grolnick and David Kikoski, guitarist Stern, and drummer Chambers. This session was recorded just after Berg left Davis. *Short Sto-*

ries ♫♫♫♫ (Denon, 1988, prod. Don Grolnick) finds Berg anxious to stretch the limits of everything he touches, from the bluesy "Friday Night at the Cadillac Club," which recalls the tear-ass tenor players who used to walk the bar, to the African influenced "Kalimba," climaxing in some remarkable Berg/David Sanborn interplay.

what to avoid: Berg's solos are always good but the setting on *Virtual Reality* ♫ (Denon, 1993, prod. Jim Beard) is pedestrian funk, disappointing and unimaginative, not worthy of his talent.

worth searching for: *Games* ♫♫♫♫ (Jazz Door, 1992), a European import, is a live date for the Bob Berg/Mike Stern Group and three extended tracks offer Berg and Stern the opportunity to really stretch out. Berg's tenor seems to grow in intensity with his solos. Backed by an Italian rhythm section, Berg is fiery and sensitive on a 1982 live date, *Steppin'—Live in Europe* ♫♫♫♫ (Red, 1994). Now out of print, *New Birth* ♫♫♫♫ (Xanadu, 1978), Berg's auspicious debut, features trumpeter Tom Harrell and pianist Cedar Walton.

influences:

◀◀ John Coltrane, Sonny Rollins, Wayne Shorter

▶▶ Bob Malach, Bob Mintzer, Jerry Bergonzi, Michael Brecker

Bret Primack

Karl Berger

Born March 30, 1935, in Heidelberg, Germany.

Karl Berger favors melodic and improvisational concepts pioneered by his mentor Ornette Coleman. Like Coleman's early work, Berger's music is generally a type of tuneful freebop—modally based, swinging, with little or no chordal accompaniment. Berger's choice of instruments mitigates a degree of expressiveness; neither the vibes or piano are capable of the same tonal malleability as the saxophone. Consequently, Berger's style is dependent more upon the quality and clarity of his ideas.

As a youngster in Heidelberg, Berger learned to play modern jazz while accompanying visiting American mainstream jazz players. In the 1960s, he played and recorded with Don Cherry's Paris-based ensemble. After moving to New York in 1966, he worked with the pianist Horacee Arnold and led his own bands. In 1972 Berger and Coleman founded the Creative Music Studio in Woodstock, New York. Berger headed the school until its closing in the mid-1980s. He became progressively more interested in the melding of world music traditions with jazz improvisation, performing with such non-jazz musicians as the African percussionist Baba Olatunji and the Japanese shakuhachi player Hozan Yamahoto.

what to buy: *Transit* ♫♫♫♫ (Black Saint, 1986, prod. Giovanni Bonandrini), a trio date with drummer Ed Blackwell and bassist Dave Holland, presents Berger at his percussively resonant best. The tracks with Berger on piano are not as strong as those on which he plays vibes; on the latter instrument, the thoroughness of his technique and distinctiveness of his approach shine through.

what to buy next: *Karl Berger Quartet* ♫♫♫ (ESP, 1966) is a solid effort that gives valuable insight into the artist's early development, as well as the time and place in which it was recorded.

the rest:
We Are You ♫♫♫ (Enja, 1971)
Around ♫♫♫♫ (Black Saint, 1990)
Crystal Fire ♫♫♫♫ (Enja, 1991)
Conversations ♫♫♫♫ (In + Out, 1995)

influences:
◄◄ Ornette Coleman

Chris Kelsey

Borah Bergman

Born December 13, 1933, in Brooklyn, NY.

When Borah Bergman asked a drummer he played with what he felt Bergman did best, the answer was, "Borah, the thing you do best is make tumult" (a story Bergman told on himself when interviewed by Francis Davis). As much as it is possible to not have influences, Bergman's piano style is unique. He has spent his career developing his left-hand dexterity to the point where he can do anything with his left hand that he can with his right hand, perhaps even more, and he does this not in a style such as stride, where the left hand's function is clearly defined and relegated to specific duties, but in an utterly unfettered free jazz style.

Born in Brooklyn, Bergman played clarinet as a child but began playing piano seriously only in his twenties, conceptually inspired both by John Coltrane's "Chasin' the Trane" for the example of combined intensity and endurance it set and by the Abstract Expressionist painters such as Jackson Pollack. He has supported himself as a teacher for many years, going his solitary way at first in jazz with solo piano recordings in the 1970s (two out-of-print albums on Chiaroscuro) and 1980s (another two, on Soul Note). In the 1990s he began playing duos on a

semi-regular basis, and all his 1990s recordings so far have been collaborations.

what to buy: *Reflections on Ornette Coleman and the Stone House* ♫♫♫♫ (Soul Note, 1995, prod. Borah Bergman) is the best of the pianist's several fine duo albums, matching him with Chicago-based drummer Hamid Drake. The title of this concert album derives from five of its six tracks taking Ornette tunes as their starting points ("Lonely Woman," "Peace," "Congeniality," and long and short takes of "Focus on Sanity"), plus Bergman's favorite original, "The Stone House." The Ornette themes appear as heads, harmonically reconfigured, and then give way to excursive if not unrelated improvisations in a bold reimagining of a seminal jazz legacy.

what to buy next: At the moment, Bergman has only two solo piano albums available on CD, including *A New Frontier* ♫♫♫♫ (Soul Note, 1983, prod. Giovanni Bonandrini). Though he since has moved on from this sound, it remains a stunning monument of pianistic imagination and energy, though with enough variety of mood to not be exhausting. The title track of *Upside Down Visions* ♫♫♫♫ (Soul Note, 1985, prod. Giovanni Bonandrini)) is an excellent example of Bergman's style, with the left hand playing cross-handed above the right hand.

what to avoid: *First Meeting* ♫♫ (Knitting Factory, 1995, prod. Thomas Buckner) is largely improvised duos between Bergman and saxophonist Roscoe Mitchell, with vocalist Thomas Buckner joining on the 14-minute suite which ends the record. Mitchell and Bergman are, in a sense, too well-matched, their approaches so similarly monolithic that the listener feels buffeted about by their dense blocks of sound when both are playing at peak energy. Individually each of their four duets is successful, but they all follow roughly the same structure of opening quietly and gradually building, lending a predictability to the proceedings. Buckner's avant vocals could provide a contrast, but are perhaps too much of an acquired taste. This is not an album to write off permanently, but with Bergman's recent spurt of productivity in the realm of collaborations, there are plenty more rewarding discs of similar vintage.

the rest:
(With Thomas Chapin) *Inversions* ♫♫♫♫ (MuWorks, 1992)
(With Andrew Cyrille) *The Human Factor* ♫♫♫♫ (Soul Note, 1993)
(With Evan Parker) *The Fire Tale* ♫♫♫♫ (Soul Note, 1994)
(With Thomas Borgmann and Peter Brötzmann) *Ride into the Blue* ♫♫♫♫ (Konnex, 1995)
(With Peter Brötzmann and Andrew Cyrille) *Exhilaration* ♫♫♫♫ (Soul Note, 1997)

(With Peter Brötzmann and Anthony Braxton) *Eight by Three* 𝄞𝄞𝄞𝄞 (Mixtery, 1997)

worth searching for: *Discover* 𝄞𝄞 (Chiarascuro, 1975, prod. Hank O'Neal) was Bergman's debut album, and finds his ideas taken to dual extremes: side one, "Perpetual Springs," is an 18-minute free improvisation for piano four hands, with Bergman overdubbing himself. The ceaseless onslaught of notes is frightening, but an interesting suggestion of the sound he aims for even while using just two hands. One of the two tracks on side two is "normal," but the other is for left hand alone, though a casual listen wouldn't suggest one-handedness; it's designed to show off the amazing technique he's built up in the "weak" hand. The only document of Bergman in a quartet setting is *The October Revolution* 𝄞𝄞𝄞𝄞 (Evidence, 1996, prod. John F. Szwed, Matthews Szwed), a 1994 concert (the CD is not credited to a particular artist, so who knows where it'll be filed in record stores) commemorating the Bill Dixon-organized concert series of the same title 30 years before. Bergman joins saxophonist/flugelhornist Joe McPhee, drummer Rashied Ali, and bassist Wilber Morris for two long freeform dedications to Dixon. The sound is a bit below ideal balance—sometimes Ali overpowers, and woe betide McPhee whenever he moves slightly off-mike while playing tenor sax—but this is great music-making in the heat of the moment, full of energy, unfettered, and uninhibited. McPhee in particular is heard too infrequently and shows how deep his talents are. On the second improvisation, a much more contemplative piece than the first track, duo passages between McPhee and Bergman are stunning in their quiet intensity.

influences:

⏪ John Coltrane, Cecil Taylor, Bud Powell, Lennie Tristano, Ornette Coleman

Steve Holtje

Jerry Bergonzi

Born 1947, in Boston, MA.

Compared to John Coltrane for his knife-like tone and questing improvisations, Bergonzi adds elements of Sonny Rollins, Joe Henderson, and Wayne Shorter for a style of his own. He made a strong impression on the New York scene in the 1970s, playing with Tom Harrell and Harvie Swartz and in a couple of Dave Brubeck's bands for almost a decade. He continued to refine his sound, becoming noted for his rhythmic incisiveness. He's had his flings with American labels, but "The Gonz" remains best represented by his albums for the Italian label Red Record,

which fortunately (and somewhat ironically) are also his most widely distributed even in the United States.

Bergonzi has written three respected books about improvisation (*Melodic Structures, Pentatonics,* and *Bebop Scales,* all published by Advance Music), with a fourth volume forthcoming; the series is called Inside Improvisation and the instructional books come with play-along CDs and videos. He received his B.A. in music education from the University of Lowell and teaches at the New England Conservatory in addition to being an in-demand jazz clinician throughout the United States and Europe.

what to buy: *Tilt* 𝄞𝄞𝄞𝄞 (Red, 1991, prod. Jerry Bergonzi, Sergio Veschi) offers seven Bergonzi originals (two played twice) in the program which best shows his writing talents. The cleverly titled "On the Brink," which opens with a bravura display of unaccompanied sax fireworks, encapsulates Bergonzi's style: always near the edge, but never falling off, playing "inside" with "outside" fire and passion and daring. The responsive rhythm section is Andy Laverne on piano (replaced by Salvatore Bonafede on the title track), Bruce Gertz on bass, and Salvatore Tranchini on drums. *On Again* 𝄞𝄞𝄞𝄞 (Ram, 1996, prod. Raimondo Meli Lupi) is a Boston all-star session, with the leader (on tenor and soprano saxes) joined by guitarist Mick Goodrick, Gertz, and drummer Adam Nussbaum. The Gonz displays his less-heard tender lyricism on tracks where Goodrick lays out shimmering harmonies underneath, and as usual Bergonzi blows through the changes authoritatively on the up-tempo numbers, with the contrasting styles making for an appealing program.

what to buy next: *Just Within* 𝄞𝄞𝄞𝄞 (Double-Time, 1997, prod. Jamey D. Aebersold) stands out for its context: an organ trio with Dan Wall on B-3 and Nussbaum. The most audacious track is "Giant Steps," recast in 5/4 time and played in a relaxed fashion (at first; it heats up a bit as it goes on) which suggests nothing so much as a waltz with half its measures lopped off early. Bergonzi's formidable technique (the altissimo passage in his solo on "The Ray" is gorgeous) and fine composing are once again showcased on one of his most soulful outings. *Lineage* 𝄞𝄞𝄞𝄞 (Red, 1991, prod. Jerry Bergonzi) captures an exciting 1989 concert in quartet with Mulgrew Miller (piano), Dave Santoro (bass), and Nussbaum. It kicks off with a driving version of Joe Henderson's "Inner Urge"—always a superb blowing vehicle—and follows with a tender "Everything Happens to Me." Bergonzi's three originals are also compelling, and with every cut topping the 10-minute mark, Bergonzi (and Miller) have plenty of time to stretch out.

the rest:

Jerry on Red 🎵🎵🎵 (Red, 1989)

Inside Out 🎵🎵🎵 (Red, 1992)

Peek a Boo 🎵🎵🎵 (Label Bleu, 1993/Evidence, 1995)

(With ETC Plus One) *ETC & Jerry Bergonzi* 🎵🎵🎵 (Red, 1993)

(With Trio Idea) *Napoli Connection* 🎵🎵🎵 (Red, 1994)

Vertical Reality 🎵🎵🎵🎵 (Musidisc, 1995)

(With Red Records All Stars: Bobby Watson, Victor Lewis, Kenny Barron) *Together Again for the First Time* 🎵🎵🎵🎵 (Red, 1997)

worth searching for: It's a shame that *Standard Gonz* 🎵🎵🎵🎵 (Blue Note, 1990, prod. Jerry Bergonzi) has been allowed to lapse out-of-print. Backed by pianist Joey Calderazzo, Santoro, and Nussbaum, Bergonzi plays with enthusiasm on a mix of standards (thus the title) and originals (including "McCoy," a highly idiomatic tribute to Coltrane pianist McCoy Tyner). Among the surprises are the way Bergonzi treats "If I Were a Bell" with much more intensity than it usually receives and his clever adaptation of Cole Porter's "Night and Day" to the chord changes of "Giant Steps." Though drummer Alex Riel is credited as the leader, the 1993 concert on *Emergence!* 🎵🎵🎵🎵 (Red, 1994, prod. Lars Goran Ulander, Neils Lan Doky) consists entirely of the saxophonist's compositions. Energetic, inventive lines spill from his horn in abundance as Bergonzi takes advantage of the improvisational space and freedom allowed by the tenor/bass/drums format. Riel's flexibility, brush work, and gentle swing are assets, while bassist Jesper Lundgaard's rich-toned solos offer plenty of melodic content and structural integrity.

influences:

◄◄ John Coltrane, Sonny Rollins, Joe Henderson, Wayne Shorter

►► Joshua Redman, Ken Field

Steve Holtje

Bunny Berigan

Born Roland Bernard Berigan, November 2, 1908, in Hilbert, WI. Died June 2, 1942, in New York, NY.

Bunny Berigan's fiery trumpet tone and unmistakable growl provides excitement for even the casual jazz listener. No ordinary big band sideman or leader, Berigan's sheer force and inventive attack could spark any variety of musical settings. Berigan's musical career began at age eight on violin. By age 13, he had started to play trumpet, and by the next year, he played

**BUNNY BERIGAN
(WITH BENNY GOODMAN)**

song "King Porter Stomp"

album *The Birth of Swing*
(Bluebird, 1935/1991)

instrument Trumpet

Monster Solo

well enough to join some local bands. Soon, he quit school and became a professional musician. His travels ultimately took him to New York City, where he joined Hal Kemp's Orchestra and made his first recordings in 1930.

After quitting Kemp, Berigan freelanced around New York extensively, spending brief periods with the bands of Paul Whiteman, Fred Rich, Ben Selvin, Bennie Krueger, and others. He was continually in recording studios because of his quick reading skills and improvisational expertise. Thus, from 1931 to 1936, hundreds of exciting examples exist of Berigan playing with various large and small groups. Berigan was a regular fixture on 52nd Street, and his presence on many small group swing records of this period are gems of 1930s jazz. After a short stint with Benny Goodman's Orchestra in 1935 and Tommy Dorsey's Orchestra in 1937, Berigan formed his own big band and recorded for RCA Victor from mid-1937 until the band went bankrupt in 1940. Bunny Berigan was a stellar trumpet player and a workaholic. Unfortunately, he was not a good businessman, and was also a heavy drinker. Collectively,

these factors ultimately brought on his untimely death at age 33 in 1942.

what to buy: Some of Berigan's best recordings from the early to mid-1930s can be found on *Portrait of Bunny Berigan* ♫♫♫♫ (ASV Living Era, 1992) and *Swingin' High* ♫♫♫♫ (Topaz, 1993). On these, Berigan is featured with the Dorsey Brothers, Frankie Trumbauer, Glenn Miller ("Solo Hop" is a Berigan tour de force), Gene Gifford, Bud Freeman, and others. Berigan recordings under his own name on the Classics label present a fine way to obtain his recordings as leader. *Bunny Berigan and His Boys: 1935–36* ♫♫♫♫ (Classics, 1993, prod. Gilles Petard), *Bunny Berigan: 1936–37* ♫♫♫♫ (Classics, 1993, prod. Gilles Petard), *Bunny Berigan: 1937* ♫♫♫♫ (Classics, 1994, prod. Gilles Petard), *Bunny Berigan: 1937–38* ♫♫♫♫ (Classics, 1994, prod. Gilles Petard), and *Bunny Berigan: 1938* ♫♫♫♫ (Classics, 1995, prod. Gilles Petard) cover possibly the best period of Berigan's career. The Bunny Berigan and His Boys period was Berigan's 52nd Street group before forming his Big Band. Unfortunately, the 1936–37 Classic reissue copies the old Epic LP, which chopped out Chick Bullock's vocals, also axing some beautiful solo work by Berigan taking place behind Chick's vocals. To make up for it, four Frank Froeba and His Swing Band titles from Columbia (1936) are included, which showcase some tasty Berigan. The other volumes take the listener into the beginning years of Berigan's big band, which feature not only Berigan, but solos by Georgie Auld, Joe Dixon, George Wettling (and Buddy Rich, a little later), plus the arrangements of Ray Conniff. Berigan's classic "I Can't Get Started," "Black Bottom," "Prisoner's Song," and others, including those labeled by Victor as "Swing Classics," are primary examples of what made Berigan popular with record buyers and musicians alike.

what to buy next: To just get a taste of Berigan's prowess, the *Bunny Berigan: Pied Piper* ♫♫♫♫ (Bluebird, 1995, prod. Steve Backer) offers a nice cross-section of Berigan's Victor recordings. Berigan's entire output on radio transcription recordings have been released on the two-CD set *Bunny Berigan and the Rhythm Makers* ♫♫♫ (Jazz Classics, 1996). These have good fidelity, plus a lot of titles that were never commercially recorded. Although many titles are pop tunes, Berigan's solos add quite a bit of spark to these performances. "Shanghai

Shuffle," "Sing You Sinners," and other titles make this acquisition most worthwhile.

best of the rest:
The Complete Bunny Berigan, Volume III ♫♫ (Bluebird, 1993) (two-CD set)
Bunny Berigan: 1938–1942 ♫♫ (Classics, 1996)

worth searching for: Berigan was always at his best in a small group setting. The 1935 and 1936 recordings with Red McKenzie's group, the *Mound City Blues Blowers* ♫♫♫♫ (Timeless, 1994, prod. Chris Barber, Wim Wigt) feature Berigan extensively. Titles such as "What's the Reason," "Indiana," and "I'm Gonna Sit Right Down and Write Myself a Letter," should leave the listener in awe as Berigan rips through his solos, teases with muted accompaniment, then pounces once again, exuding a fire to which few other trumpet players could come even close. For listeners interested in recordings before Berigan's Victor recording period, the trumpeter can be appreciated to great advantage on *Harlem Lullaby* ♫♫♫♫ (Hep, 1992, prod. Alastair Robertson, John R.T. Davies) or *Best of the Big Bands: Dorsey Brothers* ♫♫♫♫ (Columbia, 1992, prod. Michael Brooks). His awe-inspiring solos on "She's Funny That Way," "Shim Sham Shimmy," and "She Reminds Me of You" (which might well be one of Berigan's best-ever offerings), are added bonuses to overall fine recordings by the Dorsey Brothers' band.

influences:

◄◄ Louis Armstrong, Bix Beiderbecke, Bob Mayhew

►► Manny Klein, Pee Wee Irwin, Roy Eldridge, Johnny Best, Billy Butterfield, Charlie Spivak

Jim Prohaska

Dick Berk

Born May 22, 1939, in San Francisco, CA.

Dick Berk is a highly musical drummer who has consistently sought out and nurtured gifted young musicians for his band The Jazz Adoption Agency. A professional by age 14, Berk had already gigged with Billie Holiday, Anita O'Day, and Art Pepper before attending the Berklee School of Music and studying with Alan Dawson. He spent much of the 1960s in New York, working with such creative musicians as Charles Mingus, Monty Alexander, Nick Brignola, Freddie Hubbard, and the Ted Curson/Bill Barron group. He moved to Los Angeles in 1968 and worked regularly with Cal Tjader from 1969 to 1975, performed with George Duke and Gabor Szabo, and gigged and recorded with Milt Jackson. As an actor, he had roles in the films *New York, New York*

Bunny Berigan (standing) with Georgie Auld and Joe Dixon **(Archive Photos)**

(he also played on the soundtrack), *Raging Bull,* and *Scarface* and has made numerous stage and TV appearances.

what to buy: Berk made the trip east with two of his young proteges for *East Coast Stroll* 𝄞𝄞𝄞 (Reservoir, 1993, prod. Mark Feldman), a session featuring veterans John Hicks (piano) and Ray Drummond (bass) and newcomers Jay Collins (tenor sax) and Dan Faehnle (guitar). The emphasis is more on blowing than on ensemble work, but this is a fine straight-ahead album with a good selection of tunes, including Johnny Griffin's corker "That Party Upstairs" and Charlie Parker's "Klactoveedsetene." Berk presents four excellent young West Coast musicians on *Let's Cool One* 𝄞𝄞𝄞𝄞 (Reservoir, 1992, prod. Mark Feldman), an album by his New Jazz Adoption Agency. Featuring exciting young tenor player Jay Collins, longtime Adoption member Andy Martin on trombone, highly skilled and well-traveled pianist Tad Weed, and rock solid bassist Jeff Littleton, the session includes strong original material by Weed and a fine version of Duke Pearson's ballad "You Know I Care." *One by One* 𝄞𝄞𝄞𝄞 (Reservoir, 1996, prod. Mark Feldman) is a very successful session with the unusual instrumentation of two trombones (Andy Martin on slide and Mike Fahn on valve), piano (Tad Weed), guitar (Dan Faehnle), and bass (Phil Baker). Three tunes from the Blakey book show that this session is about hard swinging, but Weed's arrangements are thoughtful and original, making the most out of the contrast between Fahn's outside approach and Martin's hard-charging, straight-ahead sound. Berk's nimble drumming keeps the music moving briskly without drawing needless attention to itself. The two-trombone quintet session *Bouncin' with Berk* 𝄞𝄞𝄞 (9 Winds, 1991, prod. Vinny Golia, Richard Lubovitch) again pits Andy Martin's slide against Mike Fahn's valve. The rhythm section features bassist Ken Filiano and Weed, whose arrangements provide a sturdy framework for the horn players to joust. J.J. Johnson's "Lament" is particularly memorable, though Weed's "In Remembrance of Bud" is a worthy tribute to Mr. Powell.

the rest:
The Rare One 𝄞𝄞𝄞 (Discovery, 1983)

worth searching for: A fine session with a host of up-and-coming young players, *More Birds, Less Feathers* 𝄞𝄞𝄞𝄞 (Discovery, 1986, prod. Albert L. Marx) also features veteran baritone master Nick Brignola, who steals the show, though Weed is again very impressive.

influences:
◀◀ Art Blakey, Max Roach, Philly Joe Jones

Andrew Gilbert

Tim Berne

Born October 16, 1954 in Syracuse, NY.

Saxophonist Tim Berne, a Julius Hemphill acolyte who spoke at Hemphill's memorial service, was a latecomer to jazz but has made up for lost time with his prolific output, in styles ranging from complex compositions to sprawling free improvisation. Berne bought his first alto saxophone on a whim while in college in Oregon. Then came the event that changed his life. "I hadn't listened to much jazz," Berne once said, "but then I heard Julius Hemphill's album *Dogon A.D.*, and that completely turned me around. It captured everything I liked in music. It had this Stax/R&B sensibility and it had this other wildness. It was incredible. That's when I started playing." He moved to New York in 1974 and tracked down Hemphill, beginning a long period of private study with the co-founder of—and main composer in—the World Saxophone Quartet. After Hemphill's health prevented him from playing, Berne stood in for his mentor as a player in the Julius Hemphill Sextet (he can be heard on the group's album *Five Chord Stud*).

Berne put out his first five albums on his own Empire label (long since defunct, although his current label plans to reissue the four currently unavailable ones in a limited edition box set) and made two albums for the Italian Soul Note label. Berne was then given a deal by Columbia—something of a surprise in a decade when avant-garde jazz was given as little respect by major labels as has perhaps ever been the case. He made no compromises in his music and Columbia put out only two of his albums, both of which have fortunately been reissued by Koch. German producer Stefan Winter then signed Berne to his JMT label (the acronym is for "Jazz Music Today"), for which Berne was prolific until the label was brought by PolyGram, its U.S. distributor (through its Verve office), which cherry-picked the best-selling titles and eventually shut the label down. (Berne fans will want to buy the JMT material while it's still "selling through" as it may be unavailable after that.) In that period, Berne formed the cooperative trio Miniature with Hank Roberts and Joey Baron and recorded with two bands of his own, Caos Totale and Bloodcount, with a group of Paris concerts by the latter yielding a series of albums.

Though Berne recorded an album for Winter's new label with his trio Big Satan (with Marc Ducret and Tom Rainey), his focus shifted back to self-issued albums, and he formed the label Screwgun. Its first four releases continued Berne's prolific spate of live albums in true *samizdat* fashion.

what to buy: *Diminutive Mysteries (Mostly Hemphill)* 𝄞𝄞𝄞𝄞 (JMT, 1993, prod. Stefan F. Winter) consists of Hemphill compositions apparently written specifically for this album, the exception being a Berne-penned track. Berne is joined by David Sanborn (alto and sopranino saxophones), Marc Ducret (electric guitar), Hank Roberts (cello), and Joey Baron (drums), with Herb Robertson (trumpet, cornet, flugelhorn) and Mark Dresser (bass) added for the lengthy, multi-faceted Berne composition, aptly titled "The Maze" (which is a superb example of the style of writing found on *Nice View*). The Hemphill compositions tend toward an autumnal mood, especially the beautiful and touching "Writhing Love Lines" and the elegaic "Mystery to Me." The quartet album *Fulton Street Maul* ♫♫♫♪ (Columbia, 1987/Koch Jazz, 1996, prod. Gary Lucas) mixes the tight structures of the Soul Note albums with more complex arrangements, a move away from typical jazz textures, and an occasionally more aggressive edge. On "Unknown Disaster," Bill Frisell's electric guitar parts are like icy shards protruding from the roiling textures, with Hank Roberts sawing away ferociously on cello and drummer Alex Cline pounding out polyrhythms that wouldn't be out of place in Mahavishnu Orchestra's or Return to Forever's less twee moments. "Icicles Revisted" features a darkly lyrical cello melody. "Miniature" has a martial drive. "Federico" offers a warped version of cool jazz. The hypnotic "Betsy" is a sonic sculpture of metallic timbres.

what to buy next: The only one of Berne's Empire albums in print at this writing, . . . *theoretically* ♫♫♫♪ (Empire, 1986/Minor Music, 1996, prod. Bill Frisell, Tim Berne, Jon Rosenberg) is an anomaly in Berne's career, but a fascinating one. A duo album (dually credited) with guitarist Frisell, it's not only a studio creation, it's carefully arranged using multiple overdubs of Berne's sax lines, which, combined with Frisell's shimmering soundscapes, result in a low-key tension and subtle beauty.

the rest:
The Ancestors ♫♫♫♪ (Soul Note, 1983)
Mutant Variation ♫♫♫ (Soul Note, 1984)
Sanctified Dreams ♫♫♫ (Columbia, 1987/Koch Jazz, 1996)
Fractured Fairy Tales ♫♫♫♫ (JMT, 1989)
(With Caos Totale) *Pace Yourself* ♫♫♫♫ (JMT, 1991)
(With Michael Formanek and Jeff Hirshfield) *Loose Cannon* ♫♫♫♪ (Soul Note, 1993)
(With Bloodcount) *Lowlife* ♫♫♫♪ (JMT, 1993)
(With Bloodcount) *Poisoned Minds* ♫♫♫ (JMT, 1993)
(With Caos Totale) *Nice View* ♫♫♫♫ (JMT, 1994)
(With Marilyn Crispell) *Inference* ♫♫♫♫ (Music & Arts, 1995)
(With Bloodcount) *Memory Select: The Paris Concert* ♫♫♫ (JMT, 1996)
(With Big Satan) *I Think They Liked It, Honey* ♫♫♫♫ (Winter & Winter, 1997)

worth searching for: In the wake of JMT's demise, Berne has formed his own label and issued limited-edition CDs. Three are by Bloodcount, his quartet (it was a quintet in the JMT years, with Ducret) with Chris Speed (tenor sax, clarinet), Michael Formanek (bass), and Jim Black (drums). *Unwound* ♫♫♫♫ (Screwgun, 1996.) is a somewhat forbidding three-CD collection drawn from two concerts and shows Berne's style becoming rawer and more discursive. *Discretion* ♫♫♫♫ (Screwgun, 1997) continues this trend, as does the mail-order-only *Saturation Point* ♫♫♫♫ (Screwgun, 1997). Berne has also formed the trio Paraphrase with bassist Drew Gress and drummer Tom Rainey. *Visitation Rites* ♫♫♫♫ (Screwgun, 1997) sounds like its three tracks are all free-form improvisations, though each member gets a sole composer credit for one track. There are moments where inspiration flags and is substituted for by energy alone, but most of the time the three interact with invigorating freshness and dynamic variety. The Rova Saxophone Quartet's *The Works (Volume 2)* ♫♫♫♫ (Black Saint, 1996, prod. Rova Saxophone Quartet) contains Berne's "The Visible Man," which the group commissioned as part of its series dedicated to important new jazz composers. At first, its taut mixture of composition and improvisation is propelled by the baritone saxophone's semi-ostinato figures as he honks and slap-tongues a bassline. Above that, one sax (sometimes more) solos while the other two play lush sustained lines, riff together, or intertwine abstractly. The moods and textures begin to vary even more after a while, but the piece develops organically and suggests a direction Berne will hopefully explore further.

influences:
◀◀ Julius Hemphill, Ornette Coleman
▶▶ Chris Speed

Steve Holtje

Peter Bernstein
Born September 3, 1967, in New York, NY.

Guitarist Peter Bernstein possesses great talent that may be elusive to most listeners at first. His style is not one of bombast and fireworks but, like his main influence Grant Green, Bernstein possesses a melodic sensibility and feeling for the blues which cuts to the heart of any situation and makes him truly one of the most important guitarists of his generation. Largely self-taught, Bernstein came to jazz through such early blues and rock heroes as Jimi Hendrix and B.B. King and then eventually gravitated toward the works of John Abercrombie, Pat Metheny, Charlie Christian, Wes Montgomery, Jim Hall, and

Kenny Burrell. Since 1990, Bernstein has worked steadily in the New York area with Lou Donaldson, Melvin Rhyne, Eric Alexander, Walt Weiskopf, and Jesse Davis. One of the best ways to hear Bernstein is in the organ combos of Larry Goldings and the legendary Melvin Rhyne. Bernstein also recently joined Joshua Redman's group, where he truly adds a great deal to the originality and balance of that ensemble. In addition, he has recorded on an impressive number of jazz dates plus he has led three sets of his own for Criss Cross Jazz.

what's available: The guitarist's debut set as a leader, *Something's Burning* 𝄢𝄢𝄢𝄢 (Criss Cross Jazz, 1993, prod. Gerry Teekens), is a strong start, but bigger and better things were on the way. On *Signs of Life* 𝄢𝄢𝄢𝄢 (Criss Cross Jazz, 1995, prod. Gerry Teekens), Bernstein truly impresses with some of his best playing on record, with a strong set of originals and some well-selected standards. Brad Mehldau, Christian McBride, and Gregory Hutchinson are equally inspired. A glance at the line-up (Eric Alexander, Steve Davis, Larry Goldings, and Billy Drummond) hints at the excellent musicianship on *Brain Dance* 𝄢𝄢𝄢𝄢 (Criss Cross Jazz, 1997, prod. Gerry Teekens). Bernstein's melodic, single-note lines speak volumes and mesh perfectly with Goldings's contemporary-sounding organ work.

worth searching for: Melvin Rhyne's *Mel's Spell* 𝄢𝄢𝄢𝄢 (Criss Cross Jazz, 1996, prod. Gerry Teekens) is a perfect opportunity to hear Bernstein in the company of the legendary organist Mel Rhyne and drummer Kenny Washington. This is bluesy stuff that brings out the best in the guitarist. On Joshua Redman's *Freedom in the Groove* 𝄢𝄢𝄢𝄢 (Warner Bros., 1996, prod. Matt Pierson), Bernstein was just what Redman's group needed. The guitarist adds another color and dimension to the saxophonist's signature sound. Grant Stewart's *More Urban Tones* 𝄢𝄢𝄢𝄢 (Criss Cross Jazz, 1996, prod. Gerry Teekens) is probably the most impressive appearance Bernstein has made as a sideman. In this quartet session, Bernstein provides main support to tenor saxophonist Stewart and contributes choice solos.

influences:

◀◀ Grant Green, Jim Hall, Wes Montgomery

Chris Hovan

Steve Berrios

Born Stephen Ramon Berrios, February 24, 1945, in New York, NY.

Drummer/percussionist/arranger Steve Berrios grew up in a musical home, influenced by his father (Steve Berrios Sr.), a professional drummer from the mid-1940s through 1970s in the

bands of Marcelino Guerra, Noro Morales, and Migelito Valdez, and house drummer for leading Latin music clubs such as the Stork Club, El Morocco, Copacabana, and Habana Madrid. Growing up, young Berrios was surrounded by his father's musician friends and listened to recorded music by everyone from Machito to Duke Ellington. His father often took the family to Harlem's Apollo Theater where Berrios heard bands led by Dizzy Gillespie, Count Basie, Stan Kenton, and others. Berrios began to surreptitiously experiment with his father's instruments, playing along with recordings. He began his formal studies on a bugle at age 11, continuing with trumpet studies through high school. At age 16, with a jazz combo he'd organized with high school friend and subsequent Fort Apache Band collaborator Larry Willis, Berrios won his first of five Apollo Theater amateur contests as a trumpeter.

Berrios's first major career break on drums occurred when he was age 19 and subbed for his father at the Alameda Room in the midtown Manhattan Great Northern Hotel. He spent four years there as house drummer, working with New York City's finest Latin musicians, including Pucho and the Latin Soul Brothers and Joe Panama, and was able to move easily among various musical idioms. Berrios's playing caught the attention of bandleader Mongo Santamaria, whose first performance in the United States was with Berrios's father. Berrios joined Santamaria's band, spending the next 20 years working intermittently with the legendary conguero. During this time, Berrios developed his skills, adapting Afro-Cuban rhythms to the drum set, introducing timbales and other percussion instruments into his playing, and enhancing his performances with complicated and sophisticated rhythmic patterns. His vast experience and extensive knowledge of both Afro-Cuban music and modern bebop allows him to create adroitly in both worlds, and in addition to his tenure with Mongo Santamaria, Berrios has toured and performed with Kenny Kirkland, Randy Weston, Michael Brecker, Hilton Ruiz, Paquito D'Rivera, Leon Thomas, Art Blakey and the Jazz Messengers, and other mainstream jazz artists. Since 1980 Berrios has been drummer-percussionist with Jerry Gonzalez and the Fort Apache Band, and has performed and regularly recorded since 1991 with M'Boom, led by Max Roach. In 1995 Berrios made his recording debut as leader with his Milestone album, *First World*.

what to buy: Steve Berrios and Son Bachéche (translated roughly, "the sound is happening") prove their equally balanced stances in straight-ahead jazz and traditional Latin music on *First World* 𝄢𝄢𝄢𝄢 (Milestone, 1995, prod. Todd Barkan, Steve Berrios), a collection of 15 tunes. Berrios is an accomplished arranger/drummer and, with an array of fine guest soloists and solid sidemen, proves it on this debut as leader. Berrios mixes it up with the instrumentalists, including his long-time associates Larry Willis (piano) and Joe Ford (alto sax) (who also perform with the Fort Apache band), and George Mraz (bass), George Washington Jr. (soprano saxophone), Eddie Henderson (trumpet), Freddie Cole (vocals), and a crew of talented Latin-jazz instrumentalists and choral singers. In various instrumental and vocals-enhanced ensembles, the musicians create a variety of moods, with Berrios's expertise on traps and hand drums underpinning each tune. Berrios's dramatic polyrhythmic solo (performed on tympani, bass drum, gongs, traps set, guataca, conga) on "Talkin' to Myself," proves he knows his stuff. His arrangements are equally enticing, especially on Latin tunes such as "Iremowire," with Julito Collazo trading call-and-response vocals with a chorus shored up with Berrios's gentle percussions. With generous amounts of straight-ahead jazz and Latin-jazz totaling over 64 minutes, there's plenty here to satisfy both camps. If you favor both styles, there isn't a dull track on the album. On *And Then Some!* ♫♫♫♫ (Milestone, 1996, prod. Todd Barkan, Steve Berrios) vocalist Julito Collazo, saxophonist Joe Ford, bassist George Mraz, and others return to perform 11-tunes with professionalism and vitality. It's infrequent that a follow-up album matches a great debut, but this one with Berrios and Son Bachéche does. The brassy horns, well-blended vocals, and prevailing Afro-Cuban rhythms are authentic, exciting, and bewitching. As with his 1995 album, Berrios successfully straddles both camps, playing straight-ahead and Latin jazz styles with equally matched expertise. Highlights include a refreshing modern version of Monk's "Bemsha Swing," performed as a duo by Berrios and soprano saxist Joe Ford, a Latin percussion/vocals spree fired by singer Pedro Morejon on "Chamalongo," and a lush interpretation of George Mraz' jazz ballad, "Blues for Šarka," which features Mraz, Ford (on soprano sax), and Berrios's fine traps brushwork. Berrios is a versatile leader, arranger, and performer and both of his recorded dates are gems that leave the listener yearning for more.

worth searching for: If you can't get enough of Berrios, check out his playing with Jerry Gonzalez and The Fort Apache Band on *Pensativo* ♫♫♫♫ (Milestone, 1995, prod. Todd Barkan). Gonzalez plays trumpet, flugelhorn, and congas, and his band features tenor saxman John Stubblefield, Berrios on drums, marimba, and percussion, Joe Ford on saxophones, and Larry Willis on piano. Berrios adds significant percussive flair to the easy-swaying nine-tune Latin-jazz session, and contributes his

original, "Jungle Plum," a duo with bassist Andy Gonzalez that highlights Berrios playing marimba and a combination of drums. Berrios also augments the 1994 Fort Apache release, *Crossroads* ♫♫♫ (Milestone, 1994, prod. Todd Barkan), contributing four originals co-written with Gonzalez, and plays drums, bells, guagua, claves, guataca, shakere, and other percussion instruments. From a slow start, the set builds dramatically with same band (as above) performing 12 modern Latin-laced bebop tunes and traditional material. Berrios is prominently featured throughout. Berrios can also be heard playing percussion and timbales with Mongo Santamaria on the four Afro-Cuban jazz tunes of *Summertime* ♫♫♫♫ (OJC, 1981/1991), which also features live-recorded dates with guests Dizzy Gillespie, Toots Thielemans, and others. Berrios is also featured on *Mongo Returns* ♫♫♫♫ (Milestone, 1995, prod. Todd Barkan) an excellent nine-tune collection of modern Latin-jazz arrangements featuring a steamy horn section and throbbing rhythms from Santa Maria, Berrios, and four other percussionists.

influences:

◄◄ Mongo Santamaria, Machito, Chano Pozo, Art Blakey, Willie Bobo, Philly Joe Jones, Eddie Palmieri, Tito Puente

►► Bobby Sanabria, Poncho Sanchez

see also: *Jerry Gonzalez, Larry Willis, John Stubblefield, M'Boom, Mongo Santamaria*

Nancy Ann Lee

Chu Berry

Born Leon Brown, September 13, 1910, in Wheeling, WV. Died October 30, 1941, in Conneaut, OH.

One of the finest tenor saxophonists of the 1930s, almost on the same level as Coleman Hawkins and Lester Young, Chu Berry recorded prolifically but remains under-celebrated today. A powerful riff-based player with a huge, blowzy sound, Berry was an extroverted improvisor who often waxed sentimental on ballads and played with a keening, upper register wail on flag wavers.

Berry played alto in college and switched to tenor when he joined Sammy Stewart's band in 1929. He came to New York in 1930 and worked with Benny Carter at the Savoy. He made a number of classic recordings with Spike Hughes in 1933, was featured in the orchestras of Teddy Hill (1933–35) and Fletcher Henderson (1936) and in 1937 joined Cab Calloway's hugely popular band, where he spent the rest of his life. Berry recorded often with his cutting-contest partner Roy Eldridge and Lionel Hampton. He died after a car crash (which also killed Calloway saxophonist Andy Brown) at the age of 33. Many anthologies of Cab Calloway hits feature Berry solos.

what's available: *Chu Berry Story 1936–39* 🎵🎵🎵🎵 (Jazz Archives, prod. various) features a number of classic Berry sessions with Lionel Hampton, Wingy Malone, and Gene Krupa, among others. He clearly reveled in the opportunity to stretch out in small group settings. *Giants of the Tenor Sax* 🎵🎵🎵🎵 (Commodore, 1938–1941, prod. Milt Gabler) is small group swing at its very best, as Berry battles with worthy adversaries in Roy Eldridge and Hot Lips Page. The 1941 session, with classic versions of "Body and Soul" and "On the Sunny Side of the Street," was recorded just before Berry's death, underlining the huge loss suffered by jazz with his passing.

worth searching for: Recorded at the height of the swing era, *Cab Calloway 1939–40* 🎵🎵🎵🎵 (Classics, prod. various) documents one of Calloway's greatest bands, with top flight soloists such as Berry, Ben Webster, and a young Dizzy Gillespie (still in thrall to Roy Eldridge). Berry is one of the featured soloists and he gets plenty of support from the rhythm section, which features Danny Barker (guitar), Milt Hinton (bass) and Cozy Cole (drums). The tracks on the European release *Cab Calloway 1940* 🎵🎵🎵🎵 (Classics, prod. various) include Berry's classic version of "Ghost of a Chance." Though most of the 22 pieces are vocal features, there are many fine solos, including Dizzy Gillespie's on "Bye Bye Blues." Calloway didn't have the best band of the swing era, but he did know a great improvisor when he heard one, and he made sure Berry was prominently featured. Berry also appears extensively on *The Calloway Years: 1937–41* 🎵🎵🎵🎵 (Merrit, prod. various), a collection of classic and not-so-classic Cab Calloway recordings. His highly distinctive tenor is immediately identifiable, and always powerfully emotive.

influences:
◀◀ Coleman Hawkins
▶▶ Don Byas, Yusef Lateef

Andrew Gilbert

Gene Bertoncini

Born April 6, 1937, in New York, NY.

One of the most tasteful, elegant, and harmonically sophisticated guitarists in the business, Gene Bertoncini is a rhythmically supple improvisor who plays with a light, fluid tone. Valued as an accompanist for his deft touch, Bertoncini is a soft, unimposing improvisor who plays beautifully constructed melodic phrases. He started playing guitar at age 9 and by 16 was working professionally. He studied architecture at Notre Dame, but decided to pursue a career in music. He has performed with Buddy Rich, Nancy Wilson, Tony Bennett, Clark Terry, and Paul Winter and in the 1960s played in the studio orchestras of Merv Griffin and Skitch Henderson. In the 1970s Bertoncini collaborated with Charles McPherson and Wayne Shorter and formed an inspired, long-lived duo with bassist Michael Moore.

what to buy: A beautiful, deceptively easy-listening album, *Two in Time* 🎵🎵🎵🎵 (Chiaroscuro, 1989, prod. Hank O'Neal, Andrew Sordoni) captures the inspired pairing of Bertoncini and bassist Michael Moore after almost two decades of partnership. Their blend of soft jazz, classical, and popular music is hard to resist and they come up with ingenious medleys, combining David Raksin's "The Bad and the Beautiful" with his best known tune, "Laura," and making a seasonal connection between "It Might as Well Be Spring" and the gorgeous lament "Spring Can Really Hang You up the Most."

what to buy next: *Roger Kellaway Meets Gene Bertoncini and Michael Moore* 🎵🎵🎵🎵 (Chiaroscuro, 1992, prod. Hank O'Neal, Andrew Sordoni) throws the musically volatile pianist Roger Kellaway in with two masters of understatement. The results are wonderful, as Kellaway plays dense clusters of chords on Bertoncini's "Soflee" and spare, delicate notes on Moore's "Old New Waltz." Jobim's rarely played "If You Come to Me" brings to the fore the latent Brazilian vibe present in much of this music.

best of the rest:
O Grande Amor 🎵🎵🎵🎵 (Stash, 1986)
Strollin' 🎵🎵🎵🎵 (Stash, 1987)
Art of the Duo 🎵🎵🎵🎵 (Stash, 1987)

influences:
◀◀ Jim Hall

Andrew Gilbert

Andy Bey

Born October 28, 1939, in Newark, NJ.

Because he finds the business of music so abhorrent, Bey has been content to make only sporadic live appearances and occasional forays into the studio. As a child, he was a prodigy, playing the Apollo Theater with Louis Jordan's jump band by the time he was 14. Throughout the 1950s, he performed with his siblings, Salome and Geraldine, as Andy and the Bey Sisters.

Several albums, all out-of-print, date from this period. Later, he guested with Horace Silver during the pianist's "Acid, Pills or Pot" psychedelic phase, and with Gary Bartz's NTU ensemble. Early Bey can be viewed in Bruce Weber's cinematic portrait of Chet Baker, "Let's Get Lost."

what's available: At the end of 1996, Bey openly declared his longstanding homosexuality (he is, in addition, HIV-positive, though presumably in "good health"), and began another comeback with his only in-print album, *Ballads, Blues & Bey* ♫♫♫♪ (Evidence Music, 1996, prod. Herb Jordan), an intimate recording that eschews sidemen in favor of the sound of Bey's four-octave voice accompanied by his own spare piano stylings. At the lowest, bass/baritone end of his range, he is not unlike Johnny Hartman with a pronounced vibrato. But it is at the top that he really shines. His falsetto is creamy, evocative, and chill-inducing. The program is made up of Tin Pan Alley standards and Ellingtonia, with nods to gay composers Cole Porter ("You'd Be So Nice to Come Home To") and Billy Strayhorn ("Day Dream") thrown in for good measure. There are no finger-snapping up-tempo outings from Andy Bey this time around, but if you're in the mood for some unhurried and unabashedly romantic, late-night musings, Andy's your man.

David Prince

Ed Bickert

Born November 29, 1932, in Hochfeld, Manitoba, Canada.

Until he toured the States with Paul Desmond in the mid-1970s, Ed Bickert wasn't getting the international acclaim a guitarist of his caliber deserved. Based in Toronto, Bickert was doing commercial work in addition to appearing with such Canadian jazz stars as Phil Nimmons, Moe Koffman, and Rob McConnell when it was recommended to Desmond that he hire Bickert for a gig the alto player had in Toronto. Desmond was so enamored of the guitarist's playing that he would later rave (in the liner notes to *The Paul Desmond Quartet Live*), " . . . how does he get to play chorus after chorus of chord sequences which could not possibly sound better on a keyboard?"

Bickert's skills are acknowledged in more countries now but he still resides in Toronto where he likes the pace of life better than if he were in a high-powered market like New York City. He still plays with some of his old cohorts, especially with Rob McConnell's Boss Brass, and his recording career is doing fine as well. Since 1983 when he recorded a session with Rosemary

Clooney for the Concord Jazz label, most of his album work has come through that company.

what to buy: *Third Floor Richard* ♫♫♫♪ (Concord Jazz, 1989, prod. Carl E. Jefferson) is a trio date, with bassist Neil Swainson and drummer Terry Clarke, that has the added attraction of pianist Dave McKenna guesting on four cuts. The title tune is an interesting Charles Lloyd work with Monkish lines that lets the members of the trio all have their say, with Bickert's smooth, bop-influenced lines swinging the theme. In "Louisiana" it's interesting to hear McKenna comp and then echo Bickert's lead for a second before diving back into the rhythm. The pianist has a nice solo slot on this tune which is followed by another one of those subtly impossible runs from Bickert that Paul Desmond used to marvel at before McKenna and the guitarist start trading licks back and forth.

what to buy next: Bickert shares top of the bill on *This Is New* ♫♫♫♪ (Concord Jazz, 1990, prod. Phil Sheridan) with fellow guitarist Lorne Lofsky. The expected plectra fireworks occur. The younger Lofsky pushes Bickert to some of his best playing and vice versa. Throughout the set there are chances for rapid riff exchange and the rhythm section of Swainson and drummer Jerry Fuller (who used to play with Bickert in the Paul Desmond Quartet) are right on the case. When the tempos slow down for swinging ballads such as "Elsa," the creative tension never lets up either. All in all, this is a fine album with much to commend it if not quite enough to dislodge *Third Floor Richard* as the top dog in the Bickert discography.

the rest:
I Wished on the Moon ♫♫♫ (Concord Jazz, 1985)
(With Rob McConnell) *Mutual Street* ♫♫♫ (The Jazz Alliance, 1991)
(With Rob McConnell and Neil Swainson) *Trio Sketches* ♫♫♫ (Concord Jazz, 1994)
(With Bill Mays) *Concord Duo Series, Vol. 7* ♫♫♫♪ (Concord Jazz, 1994)
(With Rob McConnell and Don Thompson) *Three For the Road* ♫♫♫♪ (Concord Jazz, 1997)

worth searching for: To get an idea of Bickert's playing with Desmond, the curious should pick up *Like Someone in Love* ♫♫♫♪ (Telarc, 1992, prod. John Snyder) by the Paul Desmond Quartet, recorded live in Toronto. Bickert gets so much solo space that the album should probably be credited to the Desmond/Bickert Quartet.

influences:
◄◄ Jim Hall, Kenny Burrell
►► Lorne Lofsky

Garaud MacTaggart

Barney Bigard

Born Albany Leon Bigard, March 3, 1906, in New Orleans, LA. Died June 27, 1980, in Culver City, CA.

Barney Bigard was one of jazz's greatest clarinetists, a brilliant and distinctive exemplar of the New Orleans tradition. As the title of his brief but valuable autobiography *With Louis and the Duke* suggests, his two longest and by far most significant musical relationships were with Armstrong and the Ellington orchestra, where his gorgeous, woody tone and thrilling, serpentine mobility made him a major voice in the band for decades. Though as a youth he studied with Lorenz Tio Jr., the greatest clarinet teacher in New Orleans, Bigard first made a name for himself in the early 1920s as a tenor saxophonist, then considered a novelty instrument. He used a tongue-slapping technique while playing with bandleader Albert Nichols (another great New Orleans clarinetist). Considering the few recordings he made on tenor, including a session with Luis Russell, Bigard could have been a great saxophonist, but when summoned to Chicago in late 1924 to join King Oliver, he went back to the clarinet. He stayed with Oliver until 1927—also freelancing with Jelly Roll Morton, Johnny Dodds, and Louis Armstrong—but when work slowed down in Chicago he joined Ellington in New York for the first season at the Cotton Club. He stayed with Ellington until 1942, contributing countless solos and a number of melodic lines that Ellington used as the basis for such classics as "Mood Indigo," "C-Jam Blues," and "Clarinet Lament." Sick of life on the road, Bigard left Ellington in 1942 and settled in Los Angeles, which he used as a base for freelancing around the West Coast through the mid-1940s, including long stints with Freddie Slack's big band and Kid Ory's New Orleans group. He appeared in the 1947 movie *New Orleans* and the same year joined Armstrong's All-Stars, touring widely with the hugely popular band from 1947–55. Once again burned out with road life, he left Armstrong and freelanced around Los Angeles, working with Ben Pollack and Cozy Cole (and rejoining Armstrong briefly in 1960–61). Though semi-retired after the early 1960s, he continued to work and record intermittently (including sessions with Art Hodes and Earl Hines) until his death in 1980.

what's available: A co-led session with fellow giants Benny Carter and Ben Webster, *BBB & Co.* 𝄞𝄞𝄞𝄞 (Prestige/Swingville/ OJC, 1962, prod. Leonard Feather) is a delightful recording that ends far too quickly after 35 minutes. Featuring the superlative accompaniment of Jimmy Rowles (piano), Dave Barbour (guitar), Leroy Vinnegar (bass), and Mel Lewis (drums), the swing titans stretch out on two extended blues and Carter's tunes "Lula" and "When Lights Are Low." Though then on the verge of

going into semi-retirement, Bigard was in top form, his translucent sound and spectacular dexterity undiminished.

worth searching for: Bigard is featured throughout the classic recordings *Duke Ellington: Small Groups, Vol. 1* 𝄞𝄞𝄞𝄞 (Columbia, 1934–38, prod. Helen Oakley Dance, Harry Grey) including three sessions (from 1936–38) under his nominal leadership, billed as Barney Bigard and His Jazzopators. His highly distinctive clarinet sound helped make Juan Tizol's "Caravan" a hit, and check out Bigard's and Cootie Williams's solos on "Clouds in My Heart." One of the best recordings by Louis Armstrong and His All-Stars, *Louis Armstrong Plays W.C. Handy* 𝄞𝄞𝄞𝄞 (Columbia, 1954/1986, prod. George Avakian) features Satchmo with Bigard, Trummy Young (trombone) Billy Kyle (piano), Arvell Shaw (bass), Barrett Deems (drums), and Velma Middleton (vocals). Bigard's style is more modern and swing-oriented than the rest of the band, but his New Orleans roots give him plenty of common ground and he is a powerful and persuasive blues player.

influences:

◀◀ Lorenzo Tio Jr.

▶▶ Edmond Hall, Joe Marsala

Andrew Gilbert

Biota

Formed c. 1991, in Fort Collins, CO.

James Gardner, fluegelhorn, ney; Tom Katsimpalis, guitars, keyboards; Mark Piersel, guitars, trumpet, processing; Steve Scholbe, guitars, reeds; William Sharp, processing, tapes, voice; Gordon Whitlow, keyboards, accordion, bass guitar; Larry Wilson, drums; Randy Yeates, keyboards, concertina, percussion; additional guests.

Hailing from the unlikely backwater of Fort Collins, Colorado, experimental music collective Biota concocts a truly unclassifiable sonic brew that is equal parts real-time performance and radical studio production. The group's music shares a tenuous link with jazz in its reliance on improvisation to generate musical material, but the music is subsequently fragmented and recombined using sophisticated processing and collage techniques to produce a warped, carnival-mirror refraction of the original. In addition to traditional instrumentation such as guitars, reeds, drums, and various keyboards, Biota's sonic arsenal includes curiosities like the hurdy-gurdy, psaltery, penny whistle and "marxophone." Heavy processing and layering render many of these instruments virtually unidentifiable, but that is evidently the group's intention—the effect is something like hearing an orchestra turned inside-out. For all its murkiness, there is a great deal of variety in Biota's music; *Almost Never* is dreamlike, almost ambient, while *Bellowing Room*, by contrast, contains passages of almost terrifying intensity. Despite the absence of recognizable musical signposts, there is much to savor in Biota's dense, epic sound masses.

what to buy: *Almost Never* ♫♫♫ (Recommended, 1992) is a sort of surrealist ambient music, with vaguely familiar musical motifs occasionally rising to the surface of a mix reminiscent of a prehistoric lagoon.

what to buy next: Sections of *Bellowing Room/Tinct* ♫♫♫ (Recommended, 1992) suggests the sound of a jazz-rock big band being sucked through a breach in a spacecraft's hull. An exceedingly strange CD.

the rest:
Tumble ♫♫ (Recommended, 1992)
Object Holder ♫♫ (Recommended, 1995)

influences:

◀◀ Pierre Henry, Pierre Schaefer, Karlheinz Stockhausen, Faust

▶▶ Zygmunt Krause, David Shea

Dennis Rea

Walter Bishop Jr.

Born October 4, 1927, in New York, NY. Died January 24, 1998.

The son of a noted songwriter, by age 25 Walter Bishop had been present on noted early recordings of Art Blakey, Miles Davis, Stan Getz, and Milt Jackson. He worked frequently (possibly more than any other pianist) with Charlie Parker during the last four years of Bird's life, both in small groups and in the Bird-with-strings ensemble.

In the 40-plus years since Parker left us, Bishop's musical activity has waxed and waned with the general ups and downs of the fortunes of jazz, weathering periods in which he recorded fairly actively as leader and sideman with the cream of jazzdom's horn players, and alternating with long bouts of relative inactivity. In the early 1970s, he spent five years in Los Angeles running a small music school and studying with Lyle Murphy. One product of these studies was his 1976 book, *A Theory of Fourths.*

what to buy: *Midnight Blue* ♫♫♫♫ (Red, 1991, prod. Sergio Veschi) is an extremely tasteful piano-trio album drawn mostly from the great pop standards. While, clearly, Bishop has been highly valued for his abilities as an accompanist by the greatest

of his contemporaries, he doesn't have his own instantly identifiable solo sound. Nevertheless, in contrast to some of his earlier work, the style on these pieces is consistent throughout the disc and does not put one immediately in mind of one or more other prominent pianists. *What's New* ♫♫♫♫ (DIW, 1990, prod. Mickey Bass), recorded 13½ months before *Midnight Blue*, is quite similar in material, quality, and Bishop's sound. Perhaps on this disc he interjects more quotes from other pieces in his solos. Worthy of special note is his minor-key "Waltz Zweetie."

the rest:
The Walter Bishop Jr. Trio ♫♫♫♫ (Opus, 1962/Cotillion, 1963/OJC, 1997)

worth searching for: Bishop appears as sideman on numerous albums, but there are several vital with other leaders. *Swedish Schnapps* ♫♫♫♫ (Verve, 1951/1991, prod. Norman Granz) represents Bishop's first recording session with Charlie Parker. Although Bishop's solo space is limited, it far exceeds that on his earlier recordings with Blakey, Getz, and Jackson. Bishop has said that one of his major influences was Nat King Cole and one hears it in these solos. What is most notable about the session, however, is the recording of "Star Eyes." Bishop did not know the Raye-DePaul song, yet came up with an intro that, at least for the purposes of jazz players, has become part of the piece. Caution: Parker recorded "Star Eyes" eight months earlier with Hank Jones on piano; to hear the recording with the famous intro be sure to obtain the version with Bishop. Bishop appears with leader Kenny Dorham on *West 42nd Street* ♫♫♫♫ (Jazztime, 1961/Black Lion, 1989, prod. Fred Norsworthy), an album of great interest for the presence of obscure tenorist, Rocky Boyd (under whose name this date was originally issued on the Jazztime label), and for the track, "Why Not?," written by the date's drummer, Pete La Roca, a tune which would be recorded later in 1961 by John Coltrane as the immortal "Impressions." Bishop's comping behind Boyd's modal blowing on this track is outstanding, showing that he had fully mastered the innovation of Miles Davis's recording of "So What" two years earlier. He also has a fine solo here as he does on several other tracks, including the minor-key blues, "Avars," on which he also comps beautifully on bassist Ron Carter's solo. With Ken McIntyre as leader on *Looking Ahead* ♫♫♫♫ (New Jazz, 1960/OJC, c. 1986, prod. Esmond Edwards), Bishop's Bud Powell influence is greatly perceptible. (A phrase at the beginning and end of his solo on "Curtsy" is reminiscent of Bud's introduction to "Dance of the Infidels.") The seeming incongruity of matching trailblazing reedists McIntyre and Eric Dolphy with the straightahead rhythm section of Bishop, Sam Jones, and Art Taylor vanishes on hearing this disc. As bizarre as Dolphy's playing may have sounded when it was new, with some later exceptions he by-and-large stayed inside standard chord patterns and rhythms. Bishop's familiar bebop comping thus augments Dolphy's (and McIntyre's) solos quite nicely. Bishop also appears on *Matador/Inta Somethin'* ✍✍✍✍ (Pacific Jazz, 1961/Blue Note, 1991, prod. Richard Bock), with leader Kenny Dorham, which reissues two LPs in one disc. Bishop is present only on *Inta Somthin'*, a live-recorded date at San Francisco's Jazz Workshop. With Dorham and Jackie McLean in the front line, Bishop's solos evolve to contain a hard-boppish character. He comps nicely behind Jackie on his beautiful rendition of "Lover Man." *Milestones* ✍✍✍✍ (Jazztime, 1961/Black Lion, 1989, prod. Fred Norsworthy) was Bishop's first date as a leader. Influences of both Red Garland and Wynton Kelly are present in his sound here and in some of his other work. Also worth searching for are the following albums on vinyl: *Bish Bash* ✍✍✍✍ (Xanadu, 1977, prod. Walter Bishop Jr., Don Schlitten) includes three long tracks by a Bishop-led quartet, recorded (badly) at a 1964 club date, yet valuable for the presence of the late obscure George Coleman–soundalike tenorist, Frank Haynes. The remaining tracks are a self-produced Bishop-led trio set from 1968, which didn't make it to vinyl until this LP was issued nine years later. *They All Played Bebop* ✍✍✍✍ (CBS, 1977, prod. Henri Renaud) is a double LP, featuring eight different pianists in a trio setting, each doing three tracks. Bishop reprises "Star Eyes" and "Au Privave" from his first recording date with Parker, and for his third track does bop warhorse "Ornithology." Very Powell-ish here. (The other pianists on the issue are Al Haig, Duke Jordan, John Lewis, Sadik Hakim, Barry Harris, Tommy Flanagan, and Jimmie Rowles).

influences:

◀◀ Nat King Cole, Bud Powell

Mark Ladenson

The Blackbyrds

Formed 1972, in Washington, DC.

Allan Barnes, tenor and soprano saxophones, vocals; Joe Hall, bass, vocals; Perk Jacobs, percussion, vocals; Keith Killgo, drums, vocals; Barney Perry, guitar, vocals; Kevin Toney, keyboards, vocals.

While Donald Byrd was heading up the music school at Washington, D.C.'s Howard University, he corralled six of his students and formed the Blackbyrds. As a sort of logical extension of Byrd's dabbling in R&B and pop, the Blackbyrds actually made the infectious, funk-laden gems that Byrd was attempt-

ing. With no pretense of "jazz," their early albums nonetheless maintained the polyrhythms and loose-limbed stylings of the era's better fusion. However, as time progressed and their fame grew, the quality of their work diminished considerably, yet remains of interest to intense acid-jazzers.

what to buy: Funky and fun, *The Blackbyrds/Flying Start* ✍✍✍✍ (Fantasy, 1974/1996, prod. Larry Mizell, Donald Byrd) (two albums combined on one CD) show the group at its best. Unlike the more radical stylings of then-contemporaries Earth, Wind & Fire, the Blackbyrds play it pretty straight, dishing up tasty, poppy melodies. The few vocal tracks are far better than some of the lightweight instrumental numbers (which seem interminable at times), yet on balance, it's a good time.

what to buy next: Retaining some of the freewheeling fire of the first two albums, the two mid-period albums *City Life/Unfinished Business* ✍✍✍ (Fantasy, 1975–76/Beat Goes Public, 1994, prod. Donald Byrd), find the band focusing a little much on the slick end of things (due mostly to Byrd's direction), but numbers such as "Hash and Eggs" are sure to keep the party going.

what to avoid: Too thoroughly influenced by disco and bad pop-fusion, the combined albums *Action/Better Days* ✍✍ (Fantasy, 1977–80/Beat Goes Public, 1994, prod. Donald Byrd, George Duke) are pure easy listening.

the rest:
Greatest Hits ✍✍✍ (Fantasy, 1989)

influences:

◀◀ Kool & the Gang

Jason Ferguson

Cindy Blackman

Born November 18, 1959, in Yellow Springs, OH.

Cindy Blackman can be a flashy drummer at times but her basic training and technique is solid, befitting an artist who learned her skills at the University of Hartford (classical percussion) and the Berklee College of Music (with Alan Dawson and Lennie Nelson). After moving to New York City in 1982, Blackman achieved the respect of her jazz compatriots through work with Jackie McLean, Sam Rivers, Ted Curson, and Joe Henderson. She has also garnered some notoriety through her recording and touring with rock musician Lenny Kravitz. As a leader Blackman has recorded four albums for Muse, featuring a variety of new and established talent including Kenny Barron, Ron

Carter, Jacky Terrasson, and the Roney brothers, Wallace and Antoine.

what to buy: Ignore the cover photo on *Telepathy* 🎵🎵🎵 (1994, Muse, prod. Cindy Blackman, Don Sickler) because the ragamuffin sex symbol image Blackman conveys on the outside of the album has no musical relationship to the Tony Williams-inspired drumming heard on the inside. This, her third album as a leader, was recorded shortly before Blackman went out on tour with Kravitz in 1994, and it seems as if she were trying to compress all the jazz she wouldn't be playing over the next few months into one intense session. All but two of the songs on the album were written by Blackman, and they reveal a composer at least partially influenced by Steve Coleman and the people in the M-Base school of thought. Her theme song for the album, "Reves Electriques" (written as a mini-suite for morning, noon, and evening) is a case in point. Blackman and the members of her quartet do an adequate version of Monk's "Well You Needn't" but they seem more at home with her material and the one song ("Club House") written by Jacky Terrasson. Her cohorts in the quartet include Terrasson on piano, Antoine Roney on reeds, and bassist Clarence Seay.

what to buy next: Blackman is actually a coleader on *Trio + Two* 🎵🎵🎵🎵 (1990, Free Lance, prod. Santi Debriano, Jean-Paul Rodrique) with bassist Santi Debriano (who writes most of the material) and electric guitarist Dave Fiuczynski (best known for his work with keyboard player John Medeski, drummer Billy Hart, and the rock group Screaming Headless Torsos). Guest artists include alto player Greg Osby on three cuts and conga wiz Jerry Gonzalez on another, but the trio performances actually have more meat to them than the augmented ones. The compositions, combined with the avant-garde proclivities of Debriano and Fiuczynski, require more of an "outside" approach than what Blackman uses on her own releases as a leader, but she is up to the task. The one song she contributes to the date ("Next Time Forever") is a number for the trio featuring an impressive, albeit short, drum solo which leads into Fiuczynski's moderately skewed guitar playing. In fact, if truth be known, Blackman's drumming on this album is actually more impressive than on her own projects.

the rest:
Arcane 🎵🎵🎵 (1988, Muse)
Code Red 🎵🎵🎵 (1992, Muse)
The Oracle 🎵🎵🎵 (1996, Muse)

worth searching for: Blackman and reed player Ravi Coltrane are the mainstays of Grand Central, a blowing group with two albums. Their first project *Sax Storm* 🎵🎵🎵 (Evidence, 1993, prod. Satoshi Hirano, Todd Barkan) has the same players heard on Blackman's *Telepathy* (with the addition of Coltrane) while their second title *Tenor Conclave* 🎵🎵🎵 (Evidence, 1995, prod. Todd Barkan) is a tribute to Hank Mobley with Craig Handy, Billy Childs, and Dwayne Burno on hand.

influences:
◀◀ Tony Williams, Art Blakey, Alan Dawson
▶▶ Carola Grey

Garaud MacTaggart

Black/Note
Formed in Los Angeles, CA.

Mark Anthony Shelby, bass; Willie Jones III, drums; James Mahone, alto saxophone; Ark Sano, piano; Gilbert Castellanos, trumpet.

An ambitious, hard swinging group out of L.A.'s Crenshaw District, the Black/Note quintet came together at Billy Higgins's World Stage performance space in the early 1990s. Led by bassist/composer Mark Shelby, the band includes some extremely talented young players, most notably drummer Willie Jones III, who has gigged with Eric Reed, Kei Akagi, Cedar Walton, Billy Childs, and Milt Jackson. Pianist Ark Sano draws widely for inspiration, calling to mind Herbie Hancock on his solos. On alto sax, James Mahone develops long, flowing lines out of a tune's melody, building momentum until his smooth, full-bodied sound takes on a thicker tone. Gilbert Castellanos is a hard bop trumpeter who has listened closely to Kenny Dorham. Each of Black/Note's three albums is on a different label and has featured new musicians, though Shelby's writing and arranging and Jones's expressive trap work have helped the group maintain a core identity. The group has appeared at the Monterey and JVC jazz festivals and mostly plays material composed by band members.

what to buy: Opening with the voice of Malcolm X, *Jungle Music* 🎵🎵🎵 (Columbia, 1994, prod. Al Pryor) features all original tunes by the band, here a sextet with the addition of the versatile tenor and soprano saxophonist Phil Vieux. The band hews pretty closely to the Jazz Messenger sound, but adds its own twist to the hard bop tradition with well-crafted arrangements. Standout tracks include Shelby's Mingus-minded blues "Elizabeth Brown" and Sano's modal excursion "Evil Dancer." *Nothin' But the Swing* 🎵🎵🎵🎵 (Impulse!, 1996, prod. Mark Shelby, Willie Jones III) kicks off with a forceful version of Freddie Hubbard's "The Core," which lets you know you're heading straight into Jazz Messenger-land. But this is a disciplined album, full of concise, focused solos (8 of the 13 tracks are under five minutes). The first four quintet tracks feature up-and-coming pianist Greg Kurstin (who works regularly with Charles MacPherson) in place of Ark Sano and trumpeter Nicholas Payton sitting in for Gilbert Castellanos. Though the band is self-consciously trying to link its music to the Southern California experience, it stands up quite well as 1990s hard bop.

the rest:

L.A. Underground (Red, 1995) 🎵🎵🎵

worth searching for: *43rd & Degnan* 🎵🎵🎵 (World Stage, 1991, prod. Dennis Sullivan, Uthman Ray III) is a strong debut by a band that was figuring out its sound. Sano's piano and Jones's tasty drum work make a strong impression, promising better things to come.

influences:

◀◀ Jazz Messengers

Andrew Gilbert

Alfonzo Blackwell

Born in 1973.

Contemporary jazz has been an issue of great debate since the passing of many of the pioneers of the traditional and be-bop movements. Although, more pop and R&B has been combined with that sound, and ushered in a new crop of artists, it still remains jazz nonetheless. A multi-instrumentalist who plays alto saxophone, piano, keyboards, and other instruments on his albums, Alfonzo Blackwell is one of the most talented new artists to emerge in the last few years. Since his debut in 1995, he has shown the promise to remain longer.

what to buy: Blackwell has released two top-selling solid collections to good reviews. *Let's Imagine* 🎵🎵🎵 (Scotti Bros., 1995, prod. Yasha Barjone) and *Alfonzo Blackwell* 🎵🎵🎵 (Street Life, 1996) both exhibit the artist's flexibility between the traditional and urban-contemporary jazz formats. His influences are very much heard here and hopefully in the next few releases Blackwell will have crafted his own sound and feel.

influences:

◀◀ Najee, Grover Washington Jr., James Carter, George Howard, Kirk Whalum, David Sanborn

Damon Percy

Ed Blackwell

Born October 10, 1927, in New Orleans, LA; died October 8, 1992, in Hartford, CT.

Ed Blackwell drummed with everyone from Ray Charles and Earl King to Thelonious Monk, John Coltrane, Randy Weston, Archie Shepp, and Anthony Braxton. But his work with Ornette Coleman—and the other musicians, most notably Don Cherry, who also played with the revolutionary altoist—remains his best-known contribution to jazz history.

Blackwell studied snare drum in high school in New Orleans and was heavily influenced by Baby Dodds and Zutty Singleton; he played his first full drum set, though, in Plas Johnson's R&B band in 1949. He hooked up with Ornette Coleman in Los Angeles in 1951, and he encouraged the saxophonist's experiments and the two performed as a duo for some time. Later, he teamed with Coleman in New York; his flexible, responsive style made him a perfect running mate. He was one of the drummers (along with former student Billy Higgins, who had replaced him in Coleman's group) on Ornette's ground-breaking *Free Jazz*. His playing remained vital throughout the 1970s and 1980s, showing its qualities most prominently with Don Cherry's group NU, where his insatiable appetite for rhythmic melodicism naturally led him to incorporate aspects of "world music" into his New Orleans–based style. Blackwell also worked with the Coleman alumni group Old and New Dreams, along with Cherry, Dewey Redman, and Charlie Haden. In 1992 Blackwell finally succumbed to the kidney failure that plagued him for 20 years, and jazz lost one of its most melodic drummers.

what to buy: The two-CD set *Walls-Bridges* 🎵🎵🎵🎵 (Black Saint, 1996, prod. Glenn Siegel, WMUA-FM) was originally released as one CD. It is now newly remastered, with an additional track, still at the cost of one CD. Blackwell, then in the last year of his life, works with frequent collaborator and fellow Coleman alumnus Dewey Redman (tenor saxophone), as well as Cameron Brown (bass), in a scorching, near-telepathic concert performance. Redman in particular excels with a tour-de-force performance characterized by highly inventive improvisations of corruscating brilliance. But this music is quite democratic, and Blackwell's aggressive accents and intricate, interlocking polyrhythms are not consigned to the background.

what to buy next: Jointly credited to Redman and Blackwell, *Red and Black in Willisau* 🎵🎵🎵🎵 (Black Saint, 1985, prod. Giovanni Bonandrini) is a 1980 festival recording of their duo. Their styles are laid bare in the spare format, though they certainly fill up the space most of the time. This naked music communicates with a touching emotional directness. Dewey Redman is one of the great (if underrated) saxophonists of our time, and the ceaseless flow of imagination he displays here on a program consisting entirely of his compositions is wondrous, with Blackwell shadowing his every move with peppy polyrhythms that show his trademark melodic sense.

what to avoid: Bypass the one-CD version of *Walls-Bridges* **woof!** (Black Saint, 1996, prod. Glenn Siegel, WMUA-FM) no matter how cheaply it's selling for. It was mastered at too high a speed.

the rest:
What It Is? ♫♫♫ (Enja, 1993)
What It Be Like? ♫♫♫ (Enja, 1994)

influences:
◀◀ Baby Dodds, Zutty Singleton, Max Roach
▶▶ Billy Higgins, Andrew Cyrille, Whit Dickey

see also: *Old and New Dreams*

Wally Shoup and Steve Holtje

Terry Blaine
Born in New York, NY.

Terry Blaine is a singer with a gentle, natural swing whose choice of material helps link her with the jazz tradition of singers such as Connee Boswell, Ethel Waters, Lee Wiley, Mildred Bailey, and Billie Holiday. Although Blaine studied classical music at the University of Buffalo, graduating as a *summa cum laude* flute player, she has been singing most of her life. Her association with jazz pianist Mark Shane began in the mid-1980s and strengthened her jazz credentials. Together, they held a lengthy engagement at Café Society in Greenwich Village, toured the U.S. and internationally, and recorded a highly acclaimed CD cited by critics as one among the *Jazz Journal* International recordings of the year picks. Blaine continues to perform with Shane, and also with Ed Polcer and his Midtown Jazz band.

what's available: The acclaimed top-selling recording, *Whose Honey Are You?* ♫♫♫♫ (Jukebox Jazz, 1994, prod. Tom Desisto), was a break-through session in the careers of vocalist Terry Blaine and her pianist-arranger and mentor, Mark Shane. The two swinging principals are in good company with cornetist Ed Polcer, trombonist Tom Artin, and reed players Ken Peplowski or Dick Meldonian on this array of 14 good tunes with infectious beats. Blaine's easygoing approach and pleasing, low,

throaty voice are completely in sync with her swing-era roots on her debut recording as leader. Blaine is in top form as are her sidemen, especially Shane, whose excellent piano solos shine on "What a Little Moonlight Can Do", "A Little Bit Independent," and "I Can't Give You Anything But Love, Baby." Frank Vignola (guitar), Russell George (bass) and Danny D'Imperio (drums) round out the rhythm team. A small amount of vocal overdubbing is intelligently employed and unobtrusive. Lots of fans have bought this CD to have the copy of "Louisiana Fairy Tale," still a runaway hit. Even folks who don't enjoy vocals have praised this highly recommended album. Captured at a live-recorded concert in Cleveland, *Terry Blaine in Concert with the Mark Shane Quintet* ♫♫♫♫ (Jukebox Jazz, 1995, prod. Tom Desisto) finds the ebullient Blaine and her companions, cornetist Ed Polcer and pianist Shane, in top form as they swing through 18 tunes. Blaine's warm, no-nonsense singing style swings like mad through some standards and a few obscure tunes from the 1920s and 1930s. Included in the well-planned mix are songs associated with Ethel Waters ("Guess Who's in Town"), Billie Holiday ("Them There Eyes" and "Eeny, Meeny, Miney, Mo"), Mildred Bailey, ("I'd Love to Take Orders from You"), and Fats Waller ("A Little Bit Independent," "Keepin' Out of Mischief Now," "Baby Brown," and "Louisiana Fairy Tale"). The other members of the group, Allan Vache, Ed Polcer, Dale Cornutt, and David Lopez, contribute some fine moments. A good-time, good listening performance.

John T. Bitter

Eubie Blake
Born February 7, 1883, in Baltimore, MD. Died February 12, 1983, in New York, NY.

Classifiable more as a ragtimer than as a jazz musician, pianist Eubie Blake exerted an influence on early jazz players with his energetic and bluesy pianistics. By 1915, he had teamed up with Noble Sissle in vaudeville and songwriting. Their 1921 hit show *Shuffle Along* introduced jazz dancing to New York and included the perennial favorite "I'm Just Wild about Harry," which Harry Truman used as his campaign song years later. Benny Goodman used Blake's 1930 gem, "Memories of You," throughout his career to great effect.

From the 1940s through 1960s, Blake was in semi-retirement, though he practiced every day. The 1969 double-LP, *The 86 Years of Eubie Blake*, now out of print, jump-started a second career which lasted almost until Blake's death at age 100, plus five days.

Eubie Blake (© Jack Vartoogian)

what to buy: *Tricky Fingers* ♪♪♪ (Quicksilver,1994, prod.) and *Piano Jazz with Eubie Blake* ♪♪♪ (from Marian McPartland's NPR radio show) (The Jazz Alliance, 1993) captures Blake in good form. The latter gives a good idea of his warmth and humor.

what to buy next: Blake's piano rolls of blues, spirituals, and rags are among the most exciting of the 1920s. His combination of syncopation, the blues, and a kind of earthy sophistication highlight the few Blake rolls on *The Greatest Ragtime of the Century* ♪♪♪♪ (Biograph, 1987, prod. Arnold S. Caplin) and *Memories of You* ♪♪♪ (Biograph, 1990, prod. Arnold S. Caplin).

worth searching for: There have been several LPs released that feature Blake, even a few from the 1950s. But, without a doubt, the one most ripe for CD reissue is *The 86 Years of Eubie Blake* (Columbia, 1969, prod. John Hammond). Blake's close friends Bolcom and Morris showcase an overview of his beautiful compositions on *Wild about Eubie* ♪♪♪♪ (Columbia, 1977, prod. Sam Parkins) including Blake on three solos and a duo.

influences:

◀◀ Jesse Pickett, Will Turk, Kitchen Tom

▶▶ Luckey Roberts, James P. Johnson, Willie "The Lion" Smith, Terry Waldo, Mike Lipskin

George Foley

Kenny Blake

Born May 31, 1950, in Pittsburgh, PA.

Pittsburgh saxophonist Kenny Blake draws from many musical sources, including 1950–60s influences of Cannonball Adderly and Stanley Turrentine, to create a distinctive voice and a style that straddles both mainstream and contemporary jazz. On both tenor and alto, his stylings are blues-balanced, full of spunk, and funk-filled. Although he began playing reeds as a youngster, Blake's musical career really began taking shape in the 1980s. Blake left Pittsburgh for boarding school in Andover, Massachusetts, and attended Columbia University as a pre-med student. After his intrinsic musical aspirations won out over academia, he headed to New York for a brief foray into the jazz scene. Returning to Pittsburgh in the late 1970s, Blake entrenched himself in the local scene. He formed the Steel City's first definitive fusion band, King Solomon, and toured the Northeast with Billy Prince and the Keystone Rhythm Band, Kid Smoker, and G.H. Flyer. Blake formed a jazz trio in the 1980s which opened for touring artists, but gained widest exposure touring with the pop-jazz band Cabo Frio between 1987–89. Blake signed with Heads Up after Michael Hurzon, a Pittsburgh concert promoter and radio consultant, brought his talents to the attention of president Dave Love. Blake has made four Heads Up recordings and has toured the U.S. and abroad.

what to buy: You can't go wrong starting with saxophonist Kenny Blake's 1991 international recording debut album, *Interior Design* ♪♪♪♪ (Heads Up, 1991, prod. Dave Love, Kenny Blake). On the collection of 10 tunes, half are Blake's compositions. Beats are punchy, reminiscing on Blake's two years with Cabo Frio, and instrumental layering is colorful and uncluttered. Both standards and Blake's original music receive royal treatment in various ensembles from his band mates–Keith Stebler (piano and synthesizer), Joe McBride (piano, synthesizer, vocals), Max Leake (synthesizer), Tony Janflone (guitars), Ron Fudoli (bass), George Jones (percussion), Steve Trettle (drums), and Peter Morley (vocals). The pleasing mix of funk, rock, and bluesy jazz is nicely balanced, and the musicians navigate tunes without treading on each others' toes. Not a bad song in the bunch. Blake selects another batch of attractive tunes with swinging grooves on his second album. With some personnel changes, *Rumor Has It* ♪♪♪♪ (Heads Up, 1992, prod. Dave Love) continues along paths similar to his debut disc, with Blake deferring more to his team mates, yet still executing innovative alto and tenor saxisms. Trettle's beats keep things together tightly, Janflone's guitar augments, Bob Thompson tickles the keys of both piano and B-3 organ. Highlights are many among the well-planned, 11-tune mix of bubblers and ballads. This album receives the high rating for a hot-blowing, toe-tappin' kickoff with "Night Train," SteelyDan–like vocalized versions of "Black Hat" and "Bennie and the Jets," and my all-time favorite Blake tune, the upbeat, South-of-the-Border swinger, "Coffee Bean," on which Blake's generous, straight-ahead blowing packs particular wallop. Start with his previous album if you prefer instrumentals over vocals. If not, both albums are pleasers.

what to buy next: You hear Blake moving in a smoother direction on *Since You Asked* ♪♪♪♪ (Heads Up, 1993, prod. Dave

Love), a 12-tune, mixed collection with an all-new crew. This disc successfully straddles two camps, a contemporary jazz audience and fans who prefer melodic straight-ahead jazz, proving that Blake has chops to excel in both camps. Highlights feature Peter Morley's return to sing his hip, bluesy original, "The Windfall," and Blake's best testifyin' solos on his original ballad, "Next With Me," and the warhorse, "What's New." An appealing album for its diversity. Blake took a three-year hiatus before recording his fourth album, *An Intimate Affair* ♪♪♪ (Heads Up, 1996, prod. Erik Huber). A multi-media, enhanced CD containing 30 minutes of video and artist profiles, this outing has appeal for smooth jazz fans or those who dig grooves. Even though Blake plays passionately, the production (played on my audio component system) sounds muddy and over-synthesized. Sadly, gone are Blake's distinctive, blues-funk Steel City licks, leaving him sounding like every other contemporary jazz sax player.

Nancy Ann Lee

Ran Blake

Born April 20, 1935, in Springfield, MA.

There's an obvious and freely acknowledged debt to Thelonious Monk in Blake's pianism, but nobody else has ever taken Monk's ideas and distilled out of them such an equally personal and inimitable style. Blake can have the lightest touch one moment, then switch into a highly rhythmic, stride-influenced groove the next. There are plenty of pianists with better technique, but few who can make such strong statements in a solo context. In a way this is because, despite all his remarkable harmonies and his elusively dreamlike musical logic, his biggest influence after Monk is singers, especially the Pentecostal black gospel singing that made a vivid early impression on him while he was growing up. So no matter how far-out his playing gets, it retains an inherent soulfulness that always communicates. And since his technique focuses on timbre and his rhythm is so personal, he works most often, and best, in solo or duo formats.

The first jazz major at Bard College, he also studied summers at the innovative Lenox School of Jazz, founded by John Lewis (of the Modern Jazz Quartet) and Gunther Schuller. Blake also studied privately with Lewis, Oscar Peterson, Bill Evans, Mal Waldron, and to a degree with Monk. Schuller got Blake his long-time teaching position at the New England Conservatory of Music, and Schuller and Blake are both associated with so-called Third Stream Music, a term coined to describe the flowing together of the classical and jazz streams. Blake played a major role in broadening the boundaries of Third Stream by adding pop and ethnic music to the mix.

what to buy: *Epistrophy* 🎵🎵🎵🎵 (Soul Note, 1992, prod. Giovanni Bonandrini) is the most intimate, personal, and effective tribute to Thelonious Monk any pianist has made, a mature tip of the hat from one master to another. Blake's Monk influence by this time was so thoroughly absorbed into his own unique style that these solo piano renditions of Monk tunes and standards associated with Monk have not the slightest whiff of imitation about them, just a somewhat shared vocabulary. It's like hearing Monk if he had chosen to concentrate on the most subtle timbral aspects of his technique and develop them into defining characteristics—a fascinating sound. On the mostly solo *Unmarked Van (A Tribute to Sarah Vaughan)* 🎵🎵🎵🎵 (Soul Note, 1997, prod. Giovanni Bonandrini) Blake's experience of Sarah Vaughan is so imbued with his personal reactions to her music that he is paying tribute not to her singing style, not to her era, but to her emotional presentation and the effect it has on him as a listener. The songs themselves are often utterly transformed in a hallucinatory manner: has "Old Devil Moon" ever sounded so truly devilish as it does here, with tightly voiced dissonances contrasted with throbbing bass? The four quite different versions of "Tenderly" are particularly astonishing in their imagination and fluidity, and "Whatever Lola Wants" has never been more questioning. Blake mixes in a few originals that are even more elusive yet indescribably apt.

what to buy next: Blake rarely works in the common quartet setting, so the darkly beautiful *The Short Life of Barbara Monk* 🎵🎵🎵🎵 (Soul Note, 1986, prod. Greg Silberman) is a valuable document, not only for format reasons but because Blake surprises (shocks might even be the word) with two considerably stripped-down covers of Stan Kenton Band material. Saxophonist Ricky Ford pensively probes the pieces' tender spots, and Blake is his usual cinematic self. With Houston Person, *Suffield Gothic* 🎵🎵🎵 (Soul Note, 1984, prod. Giovanni Bonandrini) is a look back at his early life in Suffield, Connecticut, and Blake's tribute to the music he absorbed in black churches (though there's also a surprising version of "Stars and Stripes Forever"). Though that quality of soul may not be what listeners first associate with Blake's chiaroscuro piano style, here those gospel (and blues) roots well up from deep within him, without partaking of any obvious clichés. Saxophonist Person, of course, has soul to burn, and on the three tracks on which they collaborate, their styles meet midway; on Person's solo

number, Blake's "Vanguard," he moves deeper into the composer's highly personal sound world.

best of the rest:
Ran Blake Plays Solo Piano 🎵🎵🎵 (ESP, 1966)
Breakthru 🎵🎵🎵 (Improvising Artists, Inc., 1976)
(With Jaki Byard) *Improvisations* 🎵🎵🎵 (Soul Note, 1981)
Duke Dreams: The Legacy of Strayhorn-Ellington 🎵🎵🎵 (Soul Note, 1981)
(With Jeanne Lee) *You Stepped Out of a Cloud* 🎵🎵🎵 (Owl, 1989)
Painted Rhythms 🎵🎵🎵 (GM, 1994)
Painted Rhythms V. II 🎵🎵🎵 (GM, 1994)
(With Clifford Jordan) *Masters from Different Worlds* 🎵🎵🎵 (Mapleshade, 1994)
(With Christine Correa) *Round About* 🎵🎵🎵 (Music & Arts, 1994)
A Memory of Vienna 🎵🎵🎵 (hatOLOGY, 1997)

worth searching for: The out-of-print solo album *The Blue Potato and Other Outrages* 🎵🎵🎵🎵 (Milestone, 1969, prod. Mait Edey) is the political Blake. Even standards are used to comment on events of the day: "Chicago" refers to the violence at the 1968 Democratic Convention, "Never on Sunday" reflects Greece's 1967 coup, "All or Nothing at All" and "Stars Fell on Alabama" obliquely refer to America's racial divide. Blake also covers Mingus's "Fables of Faubus" and Max Roach's "Garvey's Ghost," both politically intended from the beginning, and Blake's originals mince no words either. Musically the most important development here is his incorporation of Greek music, not only Manos Hadjidakis's "Never on Sunday" but also Mikis Theodorakis's "Vradiazi." Another solo masterpiece, *The Realization of a Dream* 🎵🎵🎵🎵 (Owl, 1978, prod. Jean-Jacques Pussiau) is the best of Blake's albums on the French Owl label (unlike his Owl album with Jeanne Lee, it still awaits CD issue in the U.S.) and makes most explicit the importance of the dream state in his music's structural and textural conception. Only recently out of print, *That Certain Feeling* 🎵🎵🎵 (hat ART, 1991, prod. Pia Uehlinger, Werner X. Uehlinger) is Blake's George Gershwin tribute, and includes Steve Lacy (soprano saxophone) and Ricky Ford (tenor saxophone). "It Ain't Necessarily So," "The Man I Love," "Oh Where's My Bess," "I Got Rhythm," and other favorites are reexamined, with surprising facets revealed as always in Blake's deeply reinterpretive art.

influences:
⏪ Thelonious Monk, Bill Evans, Erik Satie, Anton Webern, Henry Cowell, Billie Holiday

⏩ Richie Beirach, Matthew Shipp

Steve Holtje

Seamus Blake

Born 1969, in England.

Along with Joshua Redman and Eric Alexander, tenor saxophonist Seamus Blake is one of the finest players of his generation. Raised in Vancouver, British Columbia, he began studies on the violin at the age of 10 and later played alto saxophone in his high school stage band. After graduation, Blake headed to Boston's Berklee College of Music where he would make important connections with peers such as Geoff Keezer, Roy Hargrove, Mark Turner, and Joshua Redman. In the Fall of 1992, the saxophonist moved to New York and soon was a regular member of Victor Lewis's combo, and found work with pianist Kevin Hays and trumpeter Franco Ambrosetti. Currently, Blake holds his chair with Lewis's group, tours with the Mingus Big Band, and continues to record as leader for the Criss Cross label.

what to buy: *The Call* ♫♫♫♫ (Criss Cross Jazz, 1994, prod. Gerry Teekens) is an impressive disc by any standard, and even more so considering it was Blake's debut as a leader. Blake's tone is especially distinctive, full-bodied at the lower end and razor-sharp in the upper register. The Joe Lovano influence is noticeable. Blake's soprano work is equally impressive and his own originals are meaty and challenging. *Four Track Mind* ♫♫♫♫ (Criss Cross Jazz, 1997, prod. Gerry Teekens) was actually recorded at the end of 1994. This set finds Blake making a very comfortable mix of his two personalities, the straight-ahead and the more adventurous. Kevin Hays uses both electric and acoustic piano, and front-line partners Mark Turner and Tim Hagans mesh well with Blake. Aside from one number, all the tunes are originals, which also contributes to the success of this recording.

what to avoid: A real departure from his debut set, *The Bloomdaddies* ♫♫♫ (Criss Cross Jazz, 1996, prod. Gerry Teekens) primarily features Blake's electric band. Blake too is plugged in with an electronic device that he hooks up to his horns. Though you can't blame him for trying to stretch the music, this one's a bit uneven.

worth searching for: Victor Lewis's *Eeeyyess!* ♫♫♫♫ (Enja, 1997, prod. Matthias Winckelmann) is Blake's best showing on record with Lewis's group, and a good place to hear the electronics that he often attaches to his horns. Unlike others before him, Blake uses the devices in a highly musical manner.

Chris Hovan

Art Blakey

Born October 11, 1919, in Pittsburgh, PA; died October 16, 1990, in New York City.

Art Blakey never held back, not one little bit, when he hit the bandstand. One of the great ensemble drummers in the history of jazz, he did as much as anyone to spread the music's message. Blakey exemplified the timeless role of the drum. He cited Chick Webb and Sid Catlett, the master drummer-orchestrator of the 1930s, as primary early influences, the primal sophisticate Webb for bringing the drums to the forefront as an instrument of equal value in the ensemble, Catlett for his seamless dynamics, polished finesse, and spectacular technique.

A working musician since his early teens, Blakey stinted between 1939 and 1943, at one time or another in the hard-swinging dance bands of Fletcher Henderson, Lucky Millinder, Andy Kirk, Jimmie Lunceford, and Fletcher Henderson (he toured the South with Henderson in 1943–44). Known as a shuffle drummer when he joined the Billy Eckstine Orchestra in 1944, Blakey was forced to adapt his style (under Dizzy Gillespie's tutelage) to the complex velocities of bebop. He began to superimpose triplet figures over four-four time, setting up overt dialogue with the front line. When Eckstine broke up the band in 1947, Blakey settled in New York City and began forming ensembles under the Jazz Messengers sobriquet. In 1948–49, while traveling in Africa to observe Islamic culture, he absorbed musical devices that he incorporated into his swing concept of drumming.

Over the next decade he developed drum tunings on the traps kit to produce the deep, speech-like tones of Afro-Cuban percussion styles introduced to jazz by Gillespie and Chano Pozo. His primal sound—an unmistakable amalgam of earthy tom-tom tones, roaring press rolls, perfectly placed rimshots, and a forcefully closed hi-hat on two and four—shaped the solos of his musicians, defined and linked the bands with which he played. He needed to hear an arrangement once to memorize it; his interpretation would sound inevitable, preordained. Blakey's contribution transcended notes and beats. He perceived his band as a showcase for young talent, a training ground for future leaders, believed his musicians must have room for expression and a chance to grow. During his 35 years as a bandleader, Blakey groomed a staggering array of talented improvisers: Hank Mobley, Jackie McLean, Wayne Shorter, Bobby Watson, Bill Pierce, Donald Harrison, Kenny Garrett, Donald Byrd, Lee Morgan, Freddie Hubbard, Woody Shaw, Wynton Marsalis, Terence Blanchard, Wallace Roney, Brian Lynch, Curtis Fuller, Steve Turre, Horace Silver, Cedar Walton, Bobby

Timmons, James Williams, Mulgrew Miller, Donald Brown, Benny Green, and Geoff Keezer, to name a few. And these musicians put to admirable use not only Blakey's lessons on presentation, but his philosophy of life, after they dove into the treacherous waters of the jazz business.

what to buy: The recorded output of the Jazz Messengers was tremendously consistent. The selections in this section can be considered as landmarks in Blakey's career. The sound Blakey eventually settled on was deeply influenced by the drummer's association with pianist Horace Silver and tenor saxophonist-composer Benny Golson. The astonishing primal drive Silver and Blakey could conjure was never more convincingly documented than on the astonishing live date on the two CDs, *A Night at Birdland, Volume One* 𝄞𝄞𝄞𝄞 (Blue Note, 1954/1988, prod. Alfred Lion) and *A Night at Birdland, Volume Two* 𝄞𝄞𝄞𝄞 (Blue Note, 1954/1988, prod. Alfred Lion), featuring a front line of Clifford Brown on trumpet and Lou Donaldson on alto saxophone. Blakey's style is fully evolved by now, and he pushes Brown and Donaldson to improvisatorial heights on Silver compositions "Mayreh" and "Weedot," a spectacular "Night in Tunisia," and many others. After Silver departed to begin his own career as a bandleader, Blakey became sole leader of the Messengers. The band lacked stylistic direction until Benny Golson, a veteran of the R&B wars and two years of heavy apprenticeship with Gillespie, joined him in 1958. Golson's signature stamps every note of *Moanin'* 𝄞𝄞𝄞𝄞 (Blue Note, 1958/1988, prod. Alfred Lion), an iconic document of what jazz musicians were thinking about in the late 1950s. Golson's classic compositions "Blues March," "Along Came Betty," and "Are You Real" receive their definitive interpretations, and the title track is the first of a long string of soul jazz hits for pianist Bobby Timmons. Golson knew how to showcase Blakey's shuffle-based style with a mix of sanctified blues, marches, and bop lines that matched catchy melodies with progressive harmonies, and Blakey adhered to that conception for the next 30 years. Not of least interest, it's Lee Morgan's spectacular Messenger debut. Perhaps the most adventurous edition of the Jazz Messengers featured fearless trumpeter Freddie Hubbard in youthful, exploratory bloom, a rapidly maturing Wayne Shorter on tenor saxophone, trombone virtuoso Curtis Fuller, and pianist-composer Cedar Walton. *Mosaic* 𝄞𝄞𝄞𝄞 (Blue Note, 1961/1988, prod. Alfred Lion) is a good introduction to this extraordinary group, featuring the complex Walton title track,

Hubbard's anthemic "Crisis," Shorter's driving "Children of the Night," and Fuller's classic modal vamp "Arabia." After three years, the band was ready to stretch to the heavens, per its penultimate statement, *Free for All* 𝄞𝄞𝄞𝄞 (Blue Note, 1964/1987, prod. Alfred Lion), propelled by Blakey's urgent, primal polyrhythms.

what to buy next: In the mid-1950s, Blakey and Silver co-led a classy unit that retained the Jazz Messengers' name with sinuous tenor saxophonist Hank Mobley and incisive trumpeter Kenny Dorham on the front line. They were in great form on the two-night session *At the Cafe Bohemia, Volume One* 𝄞𝄞𝄞𝄞 (Blue Note, 1955/1988, prod. Alfred Lion) and *At the Cafe Bohemia, Volume Two* 𝄞𝄞𝄞 (Blue Note 1955/1988, prod. Alfred Lion) were recorded. The proceedings include Kenny Dorham gems "Prince Albert" and "Minor's Holiday," and Mobley's Latinate "Avila and Tequila." Donald Byrd took the trumpet chair in 1956 and participated in the eponymous *Art Blakey and the Jazz Messengers* 𝄞𝄞𝄞𝄞 (Columbia, 1956/1997, prod. George Avakian, Michael Cuscuna), featuring everyone at the top of their game on a beautifully balanced set. Compositions include Silver's evocative "Nica's Dream" and the roaring "Ecaroh," and Mobley's "Infra-Rae." Blakey's superimposition of triplet figures over a driving shuffle was deeply rooted in his assimilation of African and Afro-Cuban rhythms, codified in jazz by Gillespie. On *Orgy in Rhythm* 𝄞𝄞𝄞 (Blue Note, 1958/1997, prod. Alfred Lion, Michael Cuscuna) he brought together jazz trap drummers Arthur Taylor, Jo Jones, and Specs Wright with five of New York top Latin percussionists: Sabu Martinez, Carlos "Patato" Valdez, Jose Valiente, Ubaldo Nieto, and Evilio Quintero. They course through eight performances evoking a wide array of rhythmic narrative and drum texture on this two-LPs-on-one-CD reissue. Blakey made eight recordings with the tenor-trumpet front line of Lee Morgan and Wayne Shorter, pianist Bobby Timmons and bassist Jymie Merritt, including *A Night in Tunisia* 𝄞𝄞𝄞𝄞 (Capitol, 1960/1989, prod. Alfred Lion), a personal favorite. This features Blakey's breathtaking arrangement of Gillespie's famed title track, two superb Morgan compositions (the trumpeter never played so beautifully as on "Yama"), a fine signature Shorter tune which twists progressive harmonies into lyrical melodies, and a fundamental offering by Bobby Timmons. The listener intrigued by the Morgan-Shorter chemistry can hear a year's worth of studio recordings on limited-edition, six CD set, *The 1960 Jazz Messengers* 𝄞𝄞𝄞𝄞 (Mosaic, 1960/1997, prod. Alfred Lion, Michael Cuscuna). If *Mosaic* is the most unified document of the Shorter-Hubbard-Fuller-Walton unit, *Ugetsu* 𝄞𝄞𝄞𝄞 (Riverside/OJC, 1963/1989,

Art Blakey (Archive Photos)

prod. Orrin Keepnews), another Birdland recording, is perhaps the most diverse, featuring Walton's evocative title track, Shorter classics "Ping Pong" and "On the Ginza". It's a beautifully paced, streamlined recording by a band that had been working steadily for two years on their home turf. One of the stronger later Messengers recordings is *Album of the Year* ♫♫♫♫ (Timeless, 1981/1994, prod. Wim Wigt), featuring an all-star Messengers unit of Bobby Watson on alto sax, Bill Pierce on tenor sax, Wynton Marsalis on trumpet, James Williams on piano, and Charles Fambrough on bass. Recorded at the end of nine months of steady work on one-nighters and week-long stands, there isn't a wasted note on this energetic steamer. Branford Marsalis replaces Watson to join his brother on the front line, and Donald Brown is the piano on *Keystone 3* ♫♫♫♫ (Concord, 1982/1990, prod. Carl E. Jefferson).

best of the rest:

Art Blakey's Jazz Messengers with Thelonious Monk ♫♫♫♫♪ (Atlantic, 1957/1987)
The Big Beat ♫♫♫♫ (Blue Note, 1960/1995)
Buhaina's Delight ♫♫♫♫ (Blue Note, 1960/1992)
Art Blakey and the Jazz Messengers ♫♫♫♫ (Impulse!, 1961/1996)
Indestructible ♫♫♫♫ (Blue Note, 1964/1995)
New York Scene ♫♫♫♫ (Concord, 1984/1987)
Chippin' In ♫♫♫♪ (Timeless, 1990)

influences:

◄◄ Chick Webb, Sid Catlett, Ray Bauduc, Max Roach, Kenny Clarke

►► Tony Williams, Jack DeJohnette, Jeff Watts, Carl Allen, Marvin "Smitty" Smith, Tony Reedus

Ted Panken

Terence Blanchard

Born March 13, 1962, in New Orleans, LA.

Along with the Marsalis brothers and saxophonist Donald Harrison, trumpeter Blanchard was one of the "young lions" who helped fuel the resurgence of bebop and traditional jazz forms in the mid-1980s. Coached by a strong father who ran an insurance company by day and sang opera part-time by night, Blanchard eventually studied with patriarch Ellis Marsalis, who introduced him to legendary jazz horn men such as Clifford Brown and Miles Davis. Schooled at New Jersey's Rutgers University on a scholarship, Blanchard eventually joined Lionel Hampton's touring band through a connection with a professor there. The Marsalis connection paid off two years later, when Wynton called Blanchard and Harrison to join Art Blakey's Jazz

Messengers, a group that served as a launching pad for many of jazz's biggest stars. Indeed, Harrison and Blanchard split with Blakey four years later to start their own quintet, recording five albums before Blanchard struck out on his own as a leader in 1990. His public profile had grown, thanks to work scoring Spike Lee films such as *School Daze, Do the Right Thing,* and the homage to new traditionalist jazz, *Mo' Better Blues.* His first two records were merely competent, but Blanchard's reworking of the score to Lee's film *Malcolm X* into a jazz suite helped cement his reputation with critics as a talented composer. Balancing work scoring films such as *The Inkwell, Sugar Hill,* and *Crooklyn* with an ambitious take on songs made famous by legendary jazz singer Billie Holiday, Blanchard continues to ambitiously straddle the roles of performer and composer.

what to buy: As a work that echoes Duke Ellington's famous jazz suites, Blanchard's *The Malcolm X Jazz Suite* ♫♫♫♫ (Sony, 1993, prod. Terence Blanchard) serves as a wondrous, impressive example of how young musicians could add to the traditional jazz canon and not merely copy it. It should not be confused with the soundtrack collection of period recordings and new R&B items. Blanchard's second solo outing, *Simply Stated* ♫♫♫♫ (Sony, 1992, prod. Terence Blanchard) presents a confident, blazing talent. Though Blanchard was fighting embouchure problems that would eventually sideline him for a year, this record still offers some compelling playing.

what to buy next: Ambitious and headstrong, the soundtrack to Spike Lee's *Mo' Better Blues* ♫♫♫♫ (Columbia, 1990, prod. various) is much like the character in the film—brash, adventurous and convinced that its sound is the best thing around. Featuring members of Wynton Marsalis's blazing 1980s-era band, including drummer Jeff "Tain" Watts, and an inspired jazz-backed rap from actor Denzel Washington, this record proved one of the more surprising jazz albums of the year.

what to avoid: Tentative and a little too correct, Blanchard's first album as a leader, *Terence Blanchard* ♫♪ (Sony, 1991, prod. Dr. George Butler) is too busy touching all the right bases to be adventurous or passionate—two things that always characterize the best jazz music.

the rest:

(With Donald Harrison) *New York Second Line* ♫♫ (Concord Jazz, 1983)
(With Art Blakey) *New York Scene* ♫♫♫ (Concord Jazz, 1984)
(With Donald Harrison) *Discernment* ♫♫♫ (Concord Jazz, 1986)
(With Donald Harrison) *Nascence* ♫♫♪ (Columbia, 1986)
(With Donald Harrison) *Crystal Stair* ♫♫ (Columbia, 1987)

Terence Blanchard (© Jack Vartoogian)

(With Art Blakey) *Live at Kimball's* ♫♫♫ (Concord Jazz, 1987)
(With Donald Harrison) *Black Pearl* ♫♫♫ (Columbia, 1988)
(With Art Blakey) *Blue Night* ♫♫ (Timeless, 1991)
(With Art Blakey) *Dr. Jekyll* ♫♫ (Evidence, 1992)
(With Art Blakey) *New Year's Eve at Sweet Basil* ♫♫♫ (Evidence, 1992)
(With Art Blakey) *Hard Champion* ♫♫ (Evidence, 1992)
In My Solitude: The Billie Holiday Songbook ♫♫♫ (Sony, 1994)
Romantic Defiance ♫♫♫ (Sony, 1995)
The Heart Speaks ♫♫♫ (Sony, 1996)

worth searching for: Recorded in 1986 with the identical rhythm section that backed Dolphy and Little on the classic Five Spot gig a quarter-century earlier, *Eric Dolphy and Booker Little Remembered Live at Sweet Basil* and *Fire Waltz* ♫♫♫ (Evidence, 1993, prod. Horst Liepolt, Shigeyuki Kawashima) crackles with the intensity of two young lions paying homage to important influences as Blanchard and Harrison join forces with Mal Waldron, Richard Davis, and Ed Blackwell. One of the two soundtracks to *Back Beat* ♫♫♫ (Virgin, 1994, prod. Don Was) essays mid-'60s jazz styles on compositions penned by Don Was,

with the band including not only the young trumpeter but also David McMurray (sax) and Eric Reed (piano), among others. Blanchard's mute work makes a clear connection with Miles Davis's sound.

influences:

◀◀ Clifford Brown, Miles Davis, Booker Little

▶▶ Marcus Printup, Wallace Roney

Eric Deggans

Carla Bley

Born Carla Borg, May 11, 1938, in Oakland, CA.

Carla Bley was a church musician's daughter whose early musical grounding included endless variations on "Onward Christian Soldiers." Leaving the straight and narrow for New York's Bohemia as a teen, she was eventually pressed into service as a composer by her first husband, Paul Bley, to keep royalties in the family. (Well, that's a version that Carla Bley has relayed at times.) Marked by charm and wit, her pieces were also recorded by George Russell (with whom she studied, and with whose work her early efforts display a particular affinity), Jimmy Giuffre, and others, and her 1967 suite for Gary Burton, *A Genuine Tong Funeral*, hinted at the extended works to come. With next hubby, Michael Mantler, she was in on the ground floor of what became the Jazz Composers Orchestra Association as pianist on their first record, and the ringleader/composer for the JCOA's sprawling 1971 release, the three-LP set *Escalator over the Hill*, a category-defying surreal opera blending jazz, rock, Kurt Weill, country & Western, and Eastern elements, with a cast including Jack Bruce, Linda Ronstadt, John McLaughlin, and Don Cherry. She may have been coming out of the free-jazz scene, but the emphasis was on coming *out* of it to more ordered music. In subsequent releases, it became all the clearer that her affinities were more with Kurt Weill and the Beatles than the screaming scene around her, and which the New Music Distribution Service (a JCOA spinoff in which Mantler and Bley were heavily involved) was instrumental in promoting. A key step for her came with the 1977 formation and subsequent institutionalization of the Carla Bley Band as her main musical platform. On a good night, she said, she felt like "Countess Basie" as she presided over madcap assemblages of first-rate improvisers, though over the years the group has displayed less of its initial mania as it reaches for a more controlled, if off-kilter, majesty. Small group projects outside of the big band have sometimes overexposed her modest keyboard work, though band recordings tend to be good to excellent, with the exception of generally lackluster mellow jazz forays. Bley's later work includes frequent musical collaborations with Steve Swallow, her significant other of many years now.

what to buy: Check out *Big Band Theory* ♪♪♪♪ (ECM, 1994, prod. Carla Bley, Steve Swallow) for an introduction to the mature Bley Band at a peak. Highlights include violinist Alex Balanescu's work on "Birds of Paradise" and a rare arrangement of another composer's work, Charles Mingus's "Goodbye Pork Pie Hat," with trombone solo honors going to Gary Valente. An early recording with the JCOA, *Escalator over the Hill* ♪♪♪♪♪ (ECM, 1971/1994, prod. Michael Mantler), with its revolving cast of musicians and wild stylistic swings, stands somewhat apart from the Bley oeuvre, but its brilliance endures. Highlights include Don Cherry's lead and solo work on "A.I.R.," the power trio of guitarist John McLaughlin, bassist Jack Bruce, and drummer Paul Motian, and "The Hotel Overture" with powerful solos from Roswell Rudd on trombone and pre-crossover Gato Barbieri on tenor sax.

what to buy next: *Live!* ♪♪♪♪♪ (ECM, 1994, prod. Carla Bley), recorded in 1982, explains how this band caught on, with lots of hard rocking, roof-raising horn lines and a contagious sense of having a good time. Bley's "Song Sung Long" gets a serious workout here. *European Tour 1997* ♪♪♪♪♪ (ECM, 1978/1994, prod. Carla Bley) was the band's grand debut, calling on more old hands than the later bands. The voluble Roswell Rudd is here on trombone, Andrew Cyrille on drums, and the wild-card piano playing of Terry Adams in addition to Bley. Not that many have tried, but few bands have evoked a loutish drunken swagger so well as this crew on "Drinking Music," or satirized nationalism so well as "Spangled Banner Minor and Other Patriotic Songs."

best of the rest:
Dinner Music ♪♪♪♪ (ECM, 1976/1994)
Musique Mechanique ♪♪♪♪♪ (ECM, 1979/1994)
The Very Big Carla Bley Band ♪♪♪♪ (ECM, 1991)
Sextet ♪♪♪ (ECM, 1994)
Go Together (ECM, 1994) ♪♪♪♪
Duets: Carla Bley and Steve Swallow ♪♪♪♪ (ECM, 1994)
Social Studies ♪♪♪♪ (ECM, 1994)
Night-Glo ♪♪♪ (ECM, 1994)
Heavy Heart ♪♪♪ (ECM, 1994)
Fleur Carnivore ♪♪♪♪♪ (ECM, 1994)
Songs with Legs ♪♪♪♪ (ECM, 1994)
The Carla Bley Big Band Goes to Church ♪♪♪♪ (ECM, 1996)
I Hate to Sing ♪♪♪♪ (ECM, 1997)

worth searching for: Recorded in 1966, *Jazz Realities* ♪♪♪ (Fontana) finds Bley and Mantler in a small, free-leaning combo with saxophonist Steve Lacy. Interesting takes on Bley compositions, although her playing is not particularly forceful.

influences:

◀◀ Miles Davis, Thelonious Monk, Ornette Coleman, Don Cherry

▶▶ George Russell, Jimmy Giuffre, Art Farmer

W. Kim Heron

Paul Bley

Born November 10, 1932, in Montreal, Quebec, Canada.

By creating music of terse lyricism, rhythmic individuality, and great formal freedom, Bley occupies a unique place in avant-garde jazz. He has also displayed a remarkable ability to keep his music fresh and evolving. In Montreal, Bley played with Charlie Parker at the Jazz Workshop (1953). Moving to the U.S., he played at the Hillcrest Club in Los Angeles with a quintet that included Ornette Coleman, Don Cherry, Charlie Haden, and Billy Higgins (1958). Moving to New York in 1959, Bley recorded with George Russell (1960), Charles Mingus (1960), Sonny Rollins (1963), and was a member of the Jimmy Guiffre 3 with Steve Swallow (1961–62). He also participated in the October Revolution and Jazz Composers Guild (1964) and performed with Albert Ayler. Beginning in 1962, he began to record more on his own, usually in trios that included as various times bassists Swallow (1962–65), Kent Carter (1965), Mark Levinson (1966), Gary Peacock (1967), and Mario Pavone (1968); and drummers Pete LaRoca (1962), Barry Altschul (1965–69), and Billy Elgart (1968). These trios explored the structural freedoms of new jazz with fine-tuned equilateral interplay. Their performances were notable for Bley's lyrical abstraction and performances of compositions by Carla Bley or Annette Peacock.

Bley was among the first jazz musicians to recognize the potential of synthesizers, although his foray into electronics was more interesting for his provocative theorizing than for actual realization. From 1969 to 1974, he used synthesizer and electronic keyboards to extend his timbral palette and range. Starting with his 1972 ECM album *Open, to Love,* Bley began to play unaccompanied solos more often and developed into one of the music's most engaging solo improvisors. In 1974, he founded Improvising Artists, Inc. along with artist Carol Goss, and released records by himself and others, including Lester Bowie, Steve Lacy, Sun Ra, and Sam Rivers. His groups in the 1980s often featured guitarists, including John Abercrombie (1986, 1988–89), John Scofield (1985), and Bill Frisell (1986). Late in the 1980s, Bley frequently returned to the standard and bebop repertoire, interpreting old tunes with a fresh ear in a style that owed little to the bebop vocabulary. Recorded reunions with Guiffre and Swallow (1989, 1992–93) are also notable for their refusal to give in to nostalgia. He has recently recorded more often with saxophone players, including Jane Bunnett (1993), Evan Parker (1994), and John Surman (1986, 1991).

Bley's poetically concise improvisations are frequently propelled by idiosyncratic left-hand figures that avoid the familiar approaches of stride, swing, and bebop in favor of wholly original patterns. As a soloist he gets lots of mileage out of just a few notes or motifs, although his development of them is often oblique and full of surprising leaps in logic. He is also an especially empathetic group player.

what to buy: *Closer* 🎵🎵🎵 (ESP, 1965, prod. Bernard Stollman) features a trio with Swallow and Altschul notable for its exceptional melodiousness and group interplay. Bley embarks in an

PAUL BLEY

song "Ida Lupino"
album *Open, to Love*
(ECM, 1972/1991)
instrument Piano

entirely personal direction in free jazz, different in every way from Cecil Taylor's, but no less compelling. Bley's freely evolving lines are dark and poetic on *Touching* 🎵🎵🎵 (Black Lion, 1965–66), airy, oblique, and tightly empathetic recordings by two of his 1960s trios working at their peak. *Open, to Love* 🎵🎵🎵🎵 (ECM, 1972, prod. Manfred Eicher) was Bley's first, and still one of his best, solo albums. Piano haiku written in stillness, sudden eruptions of romantic longing, and quirky twists in logic played on a great piano and captured in pristine fidelity. *Bebop* 🎵🎵🎵 (SteepleChase, 1989, prod. Nils Winther) blows away neo-bop conservatives with imaginative interpretations of the repertoire, a lesson in how to be innovative within the tradition.

what to buy next: *Japan Suite* 🎵🎵🎵 (IAI, 1976, prod. Paul Bley, Carol Goss) is a telepathic trio with Gary Peacock and Barry Altschul which stretches the piano trio format as far as it will go. This group was prone to highly elliptical counterpoint and jump cuts in tempo and direction, but absolutely welded together as a unit. Bley and Steve Swallow were members of

Guiffre's innovative trio 30 years prior to making *The Life of a Trio: Saturday* and *The Life of a Trio: Sunday* ♫♫♫ (Owl, 1989, prod. Jean-Jacques Pussiau, Francois Lemaire) and the intervening years have only made them all cagier improvisors. A bracing, uncompromising set of solo, duo, and trio groupings that find freedom in discipline. On *Memoirs* ♫♫♫ (Soul Note, 1990, prod. Giovanni Bonandrini) Bley and two old friends, bassist Charlie Haden and drummer Paul Motian, use their years of experience to craft a subdued gem. They let the music unfold slowly, follow each stray thought and indirection, and create an album of unforced subtly and beauty.

best of the rest:

Introducing Paul Bley ♫♫♫♪ (Debut, 1953)
Footloose ♫♫♫♪ (Savoy, 1962–63)
Ramblin' ♫♫♫♪ (Red, 1966)
Jaco ♫♫♫♪ (IAI, 1974)
Alone, Again ♫♫♫ (IAI, 1975)
Tango Palace ♫♫♫♪ (Soul Note, 1983)
Blues for Red ♫♫♫♪ (Red, 1989)
Annette ♫♫♫♪ (hat ART, 1992)
Time Will Tell ♫♫♫♪ (ECM, 1994)
(With Gary Peacock) *Mindset* ♫♫♫♪ (Soul Note, 1997)

worth searching for: *Mr. Joy* ♫♫♫ (Limelight, 1968) is a superb performance by a trio featuring Gary Peacock and the vastly underrated drummer Billy Elgart. The version of the title track is definitive and Elgart's rich sonority adds another melodic dimension to the always fascinating Peacock-Bley interplay.

influences:

◀◀ Bud Powell, Thelonious Monk, Lennie Tristano

▶▶ Keith Jarrett, Martial Solal

Ed Hazell

Blood, Sweat & Tears

Formed 1967, in New York, NY.

Al Kooper, keyboards, vocals (1967–68); Steve Katz, guitar, vocals (1967–72); Fred Lipsius, saxophone, piano (1967–72); Jim Fielder, bass (1967–73); Bobby Colomby, drums (1967–76); Dick Halligan, keyboards, trombone, flute (1967–72); Randy Brecker, trumpet, flugelhorn (1967–68); Jerry Weiss, trumpet, flugelhorn (1967–68); David Clayton-Thomas, vocals (1968–72, 1974–present); Chuck Winfield, trumpet, flugelhorn (1968–72); Lew Soloff, trumpet, flugelhorn (1968–73); Jerry Hyman, trombone (1968–70); Dave Bargero, trumpet, trombone, tuba (1970–76); Bobby Dole, vocals (1972); Lou Marini Jr., reeds (1972-73); George Wadenius, guitar (1972–75); Jerry Fisher, vocals (1972–74); Tom Malone, trumpet,
flugelhorn, trombone, saxophone (1972–73); Ron McClure, bass (1973–75); Jerry LaCroix, vocals, reeds, harmonica (1973–74); Joe Giorgianni, trumpet, flugelhorn (1974–75); and many others over the years.

When the band Blood, Sweat & Tears was formed, rock and roll had taken over the United States and plenty of jazz musicians were looking for work. With a style influenced by the big bands of Maynard Ferguson and Stan Kenton, the jazz-rock group employed many of these musicians, making use of their mastery of brass instruments. Drawing from some elements of jazz, they created the appealing crossover meld of jazz, rock, and blues. Formed by Blues Project refugees Al Kooper and Steve Katz, BS&T made one landmark album—*Child Is Father to the Man*—and assembled an array of musicians (including jazz players Randy Brecker, Lew Soloff, Ron McClure and others) that would change from album to album. Kooper was one of the first out, bristling over group demands that he step aside from or at least share the vocal spot. The difficulties of keeping a large band together prevailed, and over the years BS&T would shift personnel with almost every album. Like the Maynard Ferguson band and many other jazz bands, Blood, Sweat & Tears became a musical lab for hot young players. That is, in fact, how frontman David Clayton-Thomas—the voice behind hits such as "Spinning Wheel," "You've Made Me So Very Happy," and "Hi-De-Ho"—runs the band these days. Ironically, BS&T has in fact become what it set out not to be—a family-oriented show band playing big, brassy hits in casinos, nightclubs, and parks.

what to buy: *Child Is Father to the Man* ♫♫♫♪ (Columbia, 1968/1987, prod. John Simon) is indeed a landmark synthesis of styles and musical sensibilities, winding jazzy horn charts, lush string sections, and a soulful rhythm section into the same song. It still sounds fresh today though, to be honest, Kooper's thin vocals do keep the album just a wee bit earthbound. *The Best of Blood, Sweat & Tears: What Goes Up!* ♫♫♫ (Columbia/Legacy, 1995, prod. various) is a strong two-CD compiling the group's recordings up to 1976, when drummer Colomby was the final original member to leave the band.

what to buy next: The bands that recorded *Live & Improvised* ♫♫♫ (Columbia/Legacy, 1991, prod. Bobby Colomby) in 1975 may not resemble the first two or three BS&T lineups at all, but they're still hot ensembles (including Clayton-Thomas and guitarists Mike Stern and Steve Kahn) that wail away on long, jamming versions of some of BS&T's best-known songs.

what to avoid: Things get a little bit out there on *Blood, Sweat & Tears 3*, 🎵🎵 (Columbia, 1970/1987, prod. Bobby Colomby, Roy Halee) especially on the ill-advised "Symphony for the Devil/Sympathy for the Devil" suite.

best of the rest:
Blood, Sweat & Tears 🎵🎵🎵 (Columbia, 1969/1988)
BS&T 4 🎵🎵🎵 (Columbia/Legacy, 1971/1996)
Greatest Hits 🎵🎵🎵 (Columbia, 1972/1987)
Found Treasures 🎵🎵🎵 (Columbia Special Products, 1972/1995)
Live 🎵🎵🎵 (Avenue, 1980/1994)
Nuclear Blues 🎵🎵 (Avenue, 1980/1995)

worth searching for: The out-of-print *Mirror Image* 🎵🎵🎵 (Columbia, 1974), is worth a listen; it features an interesting version of the band fronted by full-throated singer Jerry LaCroix, a musician who brings more of a player's sensibility to the group.

influences:

◀◀ Blues Project, Maynard Ferguson, Stan Kenton, Duke Ellington, Count Basie, Beatles, Ike Turner's Kings of Rhythm

▶▶ Chicago, Michael Bolton, Brecker Brothers, Stevie Wonder

Gary Graff and Nancy Ann Lee

Jane Ira Bloom

Born 1955, in Newton, MA.

Soprano saxophonist and composer Jane Ira Bloom is one of the most ardent and accomplished improvisers on her instrument and has carved out a completely distinctive sound. She began playing at the age of 12, studied at Boston's Berklee College of Music, and went to Yale in 1972 where she earned a master's degree in music. She settled in New York City in the late 1970s where she studied saxophone with George Coleman. Bloom recorded her first album in 1978 and numerous albums followed, many with Fred Hersch with whom she first recorded in duo and quartet settings. She has performed with Ed Blackwell, Charlie Haden, Bobby McFerrin, David Friedman, Jay Clayton, and other artists. An artist of international stature, she is noted for using live electronic effects on stage to shape her improvisations. She is the first musician to receive a commission from the NASA Art Program (documented on her *Art and Aviation* album), for which she visited the Kennedy Space Center, and spent a year developing the music to document the sights and sounds of the space shuttle *Discovery*'s return to flight. As well as clubs and concert halls, Bloom has performed at major festivals in Paris, Berlin, Montreal, and New York. She has also composed works for dance companies such as Philobus, and has written for television movie features. Bloom has recorded albums between 1986–89 for Columbia (recently reissued on CD by Koch) and more recent sessions for Arabesque. If you've never seen Bloom perform, she's a treat to watch as well. She bobs and twists with the music as she changes tempos in midstream, creates spontaneous harmonics, and impassionedly waves her horn as she adds subtle live electronics. Check Bloom's website (http://www.tuna.net/janeirabloom) for information on current recording activities and concerts.

what to buy: Following a recording hiatus from her 1988 album, *Modern Drama*, Bloom returned with her well-conceived *Art and Aviation* 🎵🎵🎵🎵 (Arabesque, 1992, prod. Jane Ira Bloom), a collection of nine tunes, including "Most Distant Galaxy," from her commissioned four-part suite for the NASA Art Program. As she crafts her soprano sax inventions enhanced by live electronics, she is accompanied by Kenny Wheeler (flugelhorn, trumpet), Rufus Reid (bass), Kenny Werner (piano), Jerry Granelli (drums, elektro-acoustic percussion), Michael Formanek (bass), and Ron Horton (trumpet). The array of talented musicians (especially the percussionists and an added frontline horn) give this album extra-special flair. Bloom's music defies category, but it's best described as solidly palatable "inside-out" music; it soars, bubbles, streams, and flows. Close your eyes, listen, and zoom through another dimension as Bloom draws inspiration from jazz pianist Thelonious Monk, Oshumare (the African Goddess of the rainbow), artist Joan Miro, Coleman Hawkins, and other sources. The musicians are of one mind and, in addition to Bloom's stellar playing throughout, solos from Werner, Reid, and Wheeler provide many peak moments. There's abundant substance for experienced ears in Bloom's music that invites repeated listening. Newcomers, as well as devoted fans of Bloom's music, may want to purchase the next recommendation to get acquainted with her artistry. *The Nearness* 🎵🎵🎵🎵 (Arabesque, 1995, prod. Jane Ira Bloom) finds her in an innovative session, delivering harmonically pleasing, mostly "inside" (with some free-jazz blowing) improvisations, featuring an expanded front-line embellished warmly by trombonist Julian Priester. Trumpeter Kenny Wheeler returns and rhythm masters Fred Hersch (piano), bassist Rufus Reid, and drummer Bobby Previte provide wide-open support. Among her 13 original tunes, Bloom puts new twists on time-honored favorites such as "Nearly Summertime," "Midnight Round/'Round Midnight," "Midnight's Measure/In the Wee Small Hours of the Morning," "Monk's Tale/The Nearness of You," and others performed in settings from duo to sextet.

Bloom's work is always full of surprises, witty asides, episodic swing, and edgy unexpected harmonics, and this attractive album is no exception. It belongs in any collection.

what to buy next: *Modern Drama* 🎵🎵🎵🎵 (Columbia, 1987/Koch, 1996, prod. Jane Ira Bloom) sounds as fresh today as it did more than a decade ago. With Fred Hersch on piano and Hammond B3 organ, Ratzo Harris on acoustic and electric bass, Bloom delivers a very innovative nine-tune session of originals. Three selections are colored by the artistry of David Friedman playing vibes, marimba, or percussion. And percussionist Isidro Bobadilla adds interest to two tunes. Bloom's soprano sax improvisations are palatable and engaging, ranging from swinging sprees to free-jazz glissandos embellished with live electronics. She has said that the titles of her tunes come from the way they sound. So when you listen to her originals such as "Overstars," "Cagney," "More Than Sinatra," and (especially) her witty "NFL," you'll revel in her imaginative renderings. On this session, her side players are experienced Bloom travelers, and can shift on a dime to the inside or outside, no matter what path Bloom takes. The propulsion of her virtuosic, high-energy music makes this one of the most exciting albums in jazz.

best of the rest:

Mighty Lights 🎵🎵🎵🎵 (Enja, 1983)
(With Fred Hersch) *As One* 🎵🎵🎵🎵 (JMT, 1985)
Slalom 🎵🎵🎵🎵 (Columbia, 1987/Koch Jazz, 1996)

influences:

◄◄ Steve Lacy

Nancy Ann Lee

Hamiet Bluiett

Born September 16, 1940, in Lovejoy, IL.

Hamiet Bluiett is the most significant baritone sax specialist since Gerry Mulligan and Pepper Adams. His ability to provide a stabilizing rhythm (as he frequently does in the World Saxophone Quartet) or to just flat out wail in free-form abandon has been apparent since his involvement with St. Louis' legendary BAG (Black Artists Group) collective in the mid-1960s. By the time he moved to New York City in 1969 he had already worked with his future WSQ partners, Oliver Lake and Julius Hemphill. By 1972, after playing with Sam Rivers, the Thad Jones–Mel Louis Orchestra, and others, Bluiett became an on-again, off-again member of Charles Mingus's quintet, subject to the whims of the bassist and Bluiett's own admitted personal problems at the time. In 1977 Bluiett became (along with Lake,

Hemphill, and David Murray) a founding member of the World Saxophone Quartet. His career since that time still includes the WSQ as well as a host of other side projects including the Clarinet Family and Bluiett's Barbeque Band. In 1991 and 1992, Bluiett was voted the top baritone player in *Downbeat*'s annual International Critics Poll. He can also be heard on recordings by Babatunde Olatunji, Stevie Wonder, Marvin Gaye, Eddie Jefferson, and Randy Weston.

what to buy: The sextet album *Young Warrior, Old Warrior* 🎵🎵🎵🎵 (Mapleshade, 1995, prod. Hamiet Bluiett) displays the kind of music which transcends jazz denominations. There are some beautiful ballads here and there is also a drummer/baritone duet which verges on commercially viable free jazz. Bluiett has taken the core of Dinah Washington's old rhythm section (bassist Keter Betts and drummer Jimmy Cobb), blended in a 20-something tenor player with chops beyond his years, an innovative trumpeter/arranger, a monster pianist, and his own powerful brand of baritone playing.

what to buy next: People are used to solo recitals from piano players and guitarists where chords can be formed easily, often providing comfort to the listener searching for something to hang on to. A solo horn outing such as *Birthright: A Solo Blues Record* 🎵🎵🎵🎵 (1977, India Navigation, prod. Bob Cummins) is even more exposed, with the potential to be more boring or excruciating than many people are willing to endure. That's what makes this album by Bluiett such an exceptional release. Dip into it and hear the history of jazz up to 1977. There's a tune dedicated to Ellington's great baritone player, Harry Carney, and the gospel-tinged "Doll Baby" to give the recital the feel of aural history. Then Bluiett's baritone saxophone hops through such avant-garde performance staples as overblowing, squawks, and squeals, but within the context of the album's blues-tinged material. All these noises refer the listener back to eras where these sounds were an accepted part of bandstand showmanship. Not for everyone, but a wonderful album nonetheless. Recorded in 1994, the quartet date *Ballads & Blues: Live at the Village Vanguard* 🎵🎵🎵🎵 (Soul Note, 1997, prod. Hamiet Bluiett) features Bluiett with the kind of sidemen leaders dream about—a sensitive yet unconventional guitarist (Ted Dunbar), a bassist with solid compositional chops to go along with his performance abilities (Clint Houston), and a drummer who can fully explore a wide range of percussive sounds without being bombastic (Ben Riley). While Bluiett wrote the majority of music played on this date, Houston's "Darian" and Dunbar's "Rare Moments" are fine works too. Just for good measure the group tosses in a few standards, making this album one of the most consistently accessible releases in Bluiett's catalog. With the exception of "Route 66," every cut on *Makin' Whoopee: Tribute to the King Cole Trio* ♪♪♪ (Maple-shade, 1997, prod. Hamiet Bluiett) features a trio of Bluiett on either baritone sax or contrabass clarinet, bassist Keter Betts, and guitars by either Rodney Jones or Ed Cherry. Even though no ivories are tickled on this disc, it is still an effective (albeit quirky) tribute to the music Nat "King" Cole played. The ballads, for instance "When I Fall In Love" and "These Foolish Things," work best but the quirky energy invested in up-tempo tunes such as "Straighten Up and Fly Right" and "Paper Moon" has its charms as well.

the rest:

Resolution ♪♪♪♪ (Black Saint, 1977)
Dangerously Suite ♪♪♪ (Soul Note, 1981)
The Clarinet Family ♪♪♪♪ (Black Saint, 1984)
EBU ♪♪♪ (Soul Note, 1984)
Nali Kola ♪♪♪ (Soul Note, 1987)
If You Have to Ask. . . . ♪♪♪ (Tutu, 1992)
Sankofa/Rear Garde ♪♪♪ (Soul Note, 1993)
Bearer of the Holy Flame ♪♪♪ (Black Fire, 1994)
Bluiett's Barbeque Band ♪♪♪ (Mapleshade, 1996)
Bluiett Baritone Saxophone Group: Live at the Knitting Factory ♪♪♪ (Knitting Factory, 1998)

influences:

◀◀ Harry Carney, Pepper Adams
▶▶ James Carter

Garaud MacTaggart

Arthur Blythe

Born July 5, 1940, in Los Angeles, CA.

A powerful sax player with a unique sound (partially due to a broad vibrato) that fits in with the avant-garde and the new traditionalists, Arthur Blythe came out of the same Los Angeles scene (where he called himself Black Arthur) that spawned James Newton. Another alumni of Horace Tapscott's West Coast ensembles, Blythe made quite an impression when he finally reached New York City in the mid-1970s, playing with Chico Hamilton, Gil Evans, Lester Bowie, and Jack DeJohnette in addition to leading his own groups. After recording albums for Adelphi and India Navigation, Blythe was signed to Columbia and released a series of albums with innovative lineups and programming that were artistically successful but didn't generate the number of units sold that the big company was looking for. Since that time Blythe has continued to lead his own groups

and maintain membership in several others (the World Saxophone Quartet, Roots, and the Leaders.)

what to buy: Combine *Calling Card* ♪♪♪♪ (Enja, 1995, prod. Matthias Winckelmann) with *Retroflection* and you have an audio snapshot of the concerts Blythe and company did at the Village Vanguard in June 1993. The group features longtime Blythe associate Bobby Battle on drums, bassist Cecil McBee, and pianist John Hicks. Some of Blythe's original material has been recorded on other Blythe albums (notably "Hip Dripper" and "Break Tune"), but the playing makes everything fresh again. Hicks contributes his beautiful "Naima's Love Song" to the date and there is also a strong version of Fats Waller's "Jitterbug Waltz." *Night Song* ♪♪♪♪ (Clarity, 1997, prod. Chico Freeman) is the best thing Blythe has done in years. His accompanists are Bob Stewart on tuba, Gust Tsillis on marimbas and vibes, producer Freeman on bass clarinet, and a quartet of percussionists (including Freeman). The music bobs and floats over a sea of rhythm even as it echoes the more adventurous recordings (by virtue of its instrumental lineup) Blythe made for Columbia eons ago. Check out his version of Billy Strayhorn's "Blood Count" and Monk's "We See" as well as a healthy, interesting batch of originals by Blythe and Tsillis. Clarity produces audiophile recordings with a reasonable price tag and this is one of their best releases.

what to buy next: The seven songs heard on *Retroflection* ♪♪♪♪ (Enja, 1994, prod. Matthias Winckelmann) come from two days of recording at New York's Village Vanguard. This album actually appeared on the market a year before *Calling Card*. The material is still strong although performances used on *Calling Card* flow together better. (*Retroflection*'s playing comes from June 25 & 26, 1993 while the *Calling Card* album is taken only from the June 26 concert.) The band's cover of "Light Blue" by Thelonious Monk is marvelous and the Blythe-penned "Lenox Avenue Breakdown" is interesting but lacks the punch of the original version Blythe recorded on a classic, now out-of-print Columbia release.

the rest:

Hipmotism ♪♪♪ (Enja, 1991)
Metamorphosis/The Grip ♪♪♪ (India Navigation, reissue 1991)

worth searching for: Almost all of the out-of-print Columbia releases, including *Lenox Avenue Breakdown* ♪♪♪♪ (Columbia, 1979), *In the Tradition* ♪♪♪♪ (Columbia, 1979), and *Basic Blythe* ♪♪♪♪ (Columbia, 1988), deserve to be reissued on CD. If you can track down the vinyl versions, these are worth picking up for the uniformly high level of playing and the unique instrumental lineups (tuba and cello included) which give a special, and at times, definitive slant to Blythe's compositions.

influences:

⏪ Johnny Hodges, Earl Bostic, Tab Smith, Julian "Cannonball" Adderley, Thelonious Monk, Kirt Bradford, John Coltrane

⏩ Chico Freeman

Garaud MacTaggart

Angela Bofill

Born 1954, in New York, NY.

Migrating between contemporary jazz and slick pop, Bofill's biggest successes came within the realm of the latter, though at both the beginning of her professional career (with Dizzy Gillespie, Cannonball Adderley, and others) and then after its commercial success waned, she performed in genuine jazz contexts. The Hispanic multi-instrumental prodigy grew up in the Bronx and performed on the Latin music scene, most notably with the salsa band led by Ricardo Morrero known simply as The Group. Flutist Dave Valentin of that band introduced her to the owners of GRP, who launched her career with an album that made the jazz charts. After her second album for GRP, she disputed her royalties and subsequently her contract was moved to Arista, which promoted her solely as an R&B artist and similarly focused the production on her albums. Though she never broke through to the mainstream, she had a number of R&B hits and her mid-1980s albums charted consistently. She had the greatest success with Narada Michael Walden, who like Bofill directed jazz chops in a commercial direction. By the latter part of the decade, however, her sound was no longer current, and later efforts to update it came off awkwardly. Finally on her Shanachie album she returned to her old style, at least sounding comfortable again.

what to buy: *Best of Angela Bofill (1978–1985)* ⅉⅉⅉ (Arista, 1986, prod. various) in trying to represent her entire GRP/Arista career ends up with too much of her mediocre work, but it's all that's available at the moment, and does have some of the good Michael Narada Walden material.

what to buy next: *Love in Slow Motion* ⅉⅉⅉ (Shanachie Cachet, 1996) is Bofill's most recent album and marks a return to her old virtues, if in somewhat muted form, with a mellow jazziness whose time has come back around at some radio formats if not on the singles charts.

what to avoid: *Intuition* ⅉ (Capitol, 1988, prod. Norman Connors) flitted desperately from cliché to cliché both lyrically and sonically as Bofill's producers weighed her down with inferior songs, except for the old Gino Vannelli hit "I Just Wanna Stop," which is the high point if you can conceive of such dire straits.

the rest:
Something About You ⅉⅉⅉ (Arista, 1981)
Let Me Be the One ⅉⅉⅉ (Arista, 1984)
Tell Me Tomorrow ⅉⅉⅉ (Arista, 1985)
Love Is in Your Eyes ⅉⅉ (Capitol, 1991)
I Wanna Love Somebody ⅉⅉ (Jive, 1993)

worth searching for: Of Bofill's out-of-print material, a pair of 1983 pop albums stand out as worthy of reissue. *Too Tough* ⅉⅉⅉⅉ (Arista, 1983, prod. Narada Michael Walden, Angela Bofill) flaunts her four-octave vocal range on a mix of pretty ballads and slightly up-tempo tracks mildly inflected with dance production effects on Walden's half of the album (originally side one of the LP). Bofill wrote or cowrote all the tunes on her side, which is gentler and falters on the sappy closing track "Rainbow Inside My Heart," complete with kiddie chorus. *Teaser* ⅉⅉⅉ (Arista, 1983, prod. Narada Michael Walden, Denny Diante) is energetic enough that the dated production doesn't dampen the fun. It helps that Walden and various collaborators (including Bofill) came up with plenty of massive hooks for Bofill to belt out. *Angie* ⅉⅉ (GRP/Arista, 1978, prod. Dave Grusin, Larry Rosen) and *Angel of the Night* ⅉⅉ (GRP/Arista, 1979, prod. Dave Grusin, Larry Rosen) catch her before the jazz content of her music was crowded out by pop.

influences:

⏪ Dionne Warwick, Minnie Riperton

⏩ Whitney Houston, Mariah Carey

Steve Holtje

Claude Bolling

Born April 10, 1930, in Cannes, France.

French pianist, composer, and bandleader Claude Bolling was a piano prodigy as a child. After winning an amateur jazz contest in Paris In 1944, Bolling formed a small jazz ensemble that was influenced by New Orleans jazz and by Duke Ellington's small groups. In the 1940s Bolling played swing jazz with American musicians such as Roy Eldridge, Lionel Hampton, Rex Stewart, Cat Anderson, and Paul Gonsalves, and from 1955 has led his own orchestras. He has written for films, and became notable for his semi-classical compositions, for which he gained acclaim in the United States beginning in 1975 with a series of jazz collaborations with classical musicians such as Jean-Pierre Rampal. Their *Suite for Flute and Jazz Piano Trio* remained on classical charts for 530 weeks, including two years in the top 40. Albums with guitarist Alexandre Lagoya, trumpeter Maurice André, violinist Pinchas Zukerman, and others followed. Bolling has also recorded ragtime piano albums, tributes to Duke Ellington, and original music for orchestra and small groups. Bolling's productivity includes over 30 albums, 38 film scores and more than 40 TV shows and theatrical productions.

what to buy: If you're not familiar with Bolling's 1970s albums, you may wish to start with the compilation, *Vintage Bolling* ♪♪♪♪ (Milan, 1995, prod. Claude Bolling), which contains buoyant jazz selections from three semi-classical/jazz albums with flutist Jean Pierre Rampal and others: Bolling's Grammy-winning *Suite for Flute and Jazz Piano Trio* with Rampal (which sold nearly two million copies internationally), *Suite for Violin and Jazz Piano Trio* (with Pinchas Zukerman), and *Concerto for Guitar and Jazz Piano Trio* (with Alexandre Lagoya). The fourth album sampled is Bolling's 1993 *Cross over U.S.A.*, featuring swing classics such as "Way Down Yonder in New Orleans," "Do You Know What It Means to Miss New Orleans," and "Back Home in Indiana," performed with Rampal and guitarist Eric Franceries. *Vintage Bolling* is a pleasant introduction to Bolling's small group works, but if you find this album to your liking, you'll want to own the original albums. Exemplary of Bolling's splendid original film scores, *California Suite* ♪♪♪♪ (CBS, 1978/1989, prod. Claude Bolling), offers the original soundtrack recording from Neil Simon's film and features the pianist leading a small combo with bassist Chuck Damonico, drummer Shelly Manne, and Herbert Laws on flute. This album has much of the flavor of Bolling's pairings with Rampal (on *Suite for Flue and Jazz Piano Trio*), but with a more solid jazz slant. Bud Shank (flute and soprano saxophone), Tommy Tedesco (guitar), and Ralph Grierson (piano) augment some selections. Notable tracks include, "Black Folks," a lively chase that features the two flutists trading solos with excellent backing from the rhythm section, "Hannah's Theme" featuring a romantic theme performed with Tedesco, and the sprightly dancer, "California," performed with soloist Laws to launch and close this delightful album. One of his many tributes to his alter-ego, *Bolling Plays Ellington, Volume I* ♪♪♪♪ (CBS, 1987) features Bolling's big band performing 11 Elllington classics, such as "Cotton Tail," "Sophisticated Lady," "It Don't Mean a Thing If It Ain't Got That Swing," "In a Mellow Tone," and "Rockin' in Rhythm." The band's fine soloists and the superb arrangements

keep Ellington's music alive, and make this an enjoyable listen, but for the real thing, seek out Duke's original versions.

what to buy next: Bolling's talents with a big band are artfully highlighted on *Cinemadreams* ♪♪♪♪ (Milan, 1996), a nostalgic tribute to cinema music. The Paris studio session features his big band performing arrangements of 12 movie themes. Bolling's original theme from *Borsalino* gives him vent for his polished honky-tonk piano chops. He takes a back seat as performer on other tunes, deferring to the sophisticated vocalists Jeffery Smith and Laika, and to the fine instrumental soloists. Bolling's provocative, swinging arrangements revive the catchy "Theme from Pink Panther," and the swinger, "Everybody Wants to Be a Cat," from the full-length Disney cartoon, *The Aristocats*. A superb big band album that highlights fine solos from the French musicians who, collectively, execute fine section work and hit tight, swinging grooves. *Jazz Brunch* ♪♪♪ (CBS, 1988, prod. Claude Bolling) features performances by the Claude Bolling Big Band, interspersed with glimmering moments when Bolling shows off his fine piano skills with the rhythm section. The full band sweeps through 11 charts by Ernie Wilkins, George and Ira Gershwin, Duke Ellington, Neal Hefti, and others. Bolling contributes his original, a three-part Basie-tribute, which features 20 minutes of smartly swinging, blues-inflected mainstream jazz. The 16-musician European band swings hard but, on this CD, lacks the vitality of American-bred bands like Frank Capp's Juggernaut, the Count Basie Orchestra, and other units that perform densely textured, dynamic, and colorful arrangements with intensive punch. Somewhat distracting, vocalist Annette Lowman warbles with too much vibrato on her five selections, and strives for effect rather than remaining true to lyrics. The most engaging moments occur with the band-within-a-band, when Bolling tastefully performs (and improvises) with bass, guitar, and drums, and horn soloists.

best of the rest:

Suite for Flute and Jazz Piano Trio ♪♪♪♪♪ (CBS, 1975/Milan, 1993)
Concerto for Classic Guitar and Jazz Piano ♪♪♪♪ (CBS, 1975/1993)
Original Ragtime ♪♪♪♪ (CBS, 1976/1987)
Suite for Violin and Jazz Piano ♪♪♪♪ (CBS, 1978/Milan, 1993)
Bolling Plays Ellington, Volume II ♪♪♪ (CBS, 1985)
Toot Suite ♪♪♪♪ (Sony, 1987)
Bolling's Greatest Hits ♪♪♪♪ (CBS, 1988)
Claude Bolling Plays Duke Ellington: Black Brown & Beige ♪♪♪♪ (Milan, 1993)
(With Claude Bolling Big Band) *The Victory Concert: Echos of 1944–45* ♪♪♪♪ (Milan, 1994)
(With the Claude Bolling Big Band) *The Drum Is a Woman* ♪♪♪ (Milan, 1996)

influences:

◄◄ Duke Ellington

►► John Williams, Peter Nero, Dudley Moore

Nancy Ann Lee

Joe Bonner

Born April 20, 1948, in Rocky Mountain, NC.

Joe Bonner played with some of the hipper members of the avant-garde (Pharoah Sanders, Roy Haynes) during the music's true heyday (late 1960s/early 1970s). He began playing piano at an early age, studying formally at Virginia State. Moving to New York at the age of 21, in 1969, he played with Roy Haynes's ensemble and with Freddie Hubbard (1971–72). He reached his bounty on a pair of way, way out albums recorded with Pharoah Sanders in 1972 and 1973 respectively: *Black Unity* and *Elevation*. In the late 1970s, as many members of the avant-garde were wont to do, he toured Europe (with Billy Harper) while being based in Copenhagen. Returning to the United States in 1980, he worked in and out of New York, including a stint in Denver. He also led a trio featuring renowned Ornette Coleman drummer/collaborator Billy Higgins.

what to buy: *Parade* ♫♫♫♫ (SteepleChase, 1979, prod. Nils Winther) finds Bonner leading a trio featuring Johnny Dyani (bass) and Billy Higgins (drums).

what to buy next: *Suburban Fantasies* ♫♫♫ (SteepleChase, 1983, prod. Nils Winther) is a great duet record with Dyani (Bonner also recorded a solo piano record for the same label, the same year, which is also recommended).

best of the rest:

Suite for Chocolate ♫♫♫ (SteepleChase, 1985)
New Life ♫♫♫ (SteepleChase, 1986)
The Lost Melody ♫♫♫♫ (SteepleChase, 1987)
Impressions of Copenhagen ♫♫♫ (Evidence, 1992)

worth searching for: *Angel Eyes* ♫♫♫ (Muse, 1976, prod. Joe Bonner, Michael Cuscuna) has Leroy Jenkins (violin), Linda Sharrock (vocals), Billy Harper (tenor sax), etc. Only question is, which is more shrill—Jenkins's violin or Sharrock's vocals? Muse is defunct, but its owner may reissue its albums through a new company.

influences:

◄◄ Thelonious Monk, McCoy Tyner

►► Bill Henderson

Joe S. Harrington

James Booker

Born December 17, 1939, in New Orleans, LA. Died 1983, in New Orleans, LA.

The troubled, flamboyant master of New Orleans piano, James Carroll Booker had so much technique and energy that other keyboard players were in awe. On a good night Booker could take those 88s and drive tunes into an ever-widening spiral of improvisation that left performers such as Mac Rebennack (a.k.a. Dr. John) and Allen Toussaint with their jaws hanging to the floor. Trained in the classics and picking up R&B licks on the side, Booker had the kind of technical grounding which let him segue from Chopin to bop-influenced riffs and traditional New Orleans habanera-tinged barrelhouse with ease. Rebennack has called Booker a genius, and few who have heard him on a good night would deny the possibility.

In 1960 Booker had a Top 40 hit with "Gonzo," a raucous organ instrumental released on Don Robey's Peacock label. He also did a lot of session work for Imperial, King, and Reprise in addition to working with Fats Domino, Sam Cooke, Aretha Franklin, B.B. King, Little Richard, Wilson Pickett, Joe Tex, and Lloyd Price, among others. Still, idiosyncrasies and drug dependency had derailed other major talents, keeping them from a life their abilities deserved, and Booker was no exception to the rule. A convicted felon and drug addict, having spent time at Louisiana's Angola State Prison and the Anchora Mental Institution, Booker's offstage behavior often interfered with his onstage responsibilities. The last year of his life found him working a day job in the New Orleans city hall.

what to buy: There is no better way to introduce someone to the genius of James Booker than *Junco Partner* ♫♫♫♫ (Hannibal, 1976, reissued 1993, prod. Joe Boyd), a well-recorded document of pianistic power combined with a catchy back-of-the-throat tenor warble on the vocal cuts. Starting out with Booker's instrumental take on Chopin ("Black Minute Waltz") and rolling through Leadbelly's "Good Night Irene" sets the listener up for the best of Booker. His original tunes are filled with the essence of New Orleans piano and the standards are filled with life. The title song, in Booker's rendition, is a lyrically disturbing work touching on the grip of heroin and cocaine on this talented man's life, surrounded by rolling left-hand bass lines and right-hand filigree.

what to buy next: *Resurrection of the Bayou Maharajah* ♫♫♫♫ (Rounder, 1993, prod. Scott Billington, John Parsons) and *Spiders on the Keys* ♫♫♫ (Rounder, 1993, prod. Scott Billington, John Parsons) should be paired for consideration, stemming as they do from more than 60 hours of tape recorded at James Booker's last consistent New Orleans venue, the Maple Leaf Bar. They capture him in full improvisatory flight with a sympathetic if at times boisterous audience. It's the small crowd's vocal appreciation for Booker's playing and singing that drag the rating down half a point. *Maharajah* contains a slew of medleys wherein keys modulate all over the place, snatches of classical pieces bump up against blues ribaldry, and rhythms change in surprisingly logical nanoseconds. *Spiders* is more of a straightforward tune fest containing Booker's take on such chestnuts as "Besame Mucho" and "Sunny Side of the Street." Some of Booker's standard repertoire appears on both albums, but the different takes give you a glimpse of the pianist's ever-evolving creative vision. "Papa Was a Rascal" is paired with "Tico Tico" on *Maharajah* and is a suitably entertaining vocal performance, but the instrumental version on *Spiders* is an almost eight-minute long improvisational tour-de-force with Booker playing like a gumbo-fied Art Tatum.

the rest:
New Orleans Piano Wizard: Live! ♪♪♪ (Rounder, 1981)
Classified ♪♪♪ (Rounder, 1982)
The Lost Paramount Tapes ♪♪♫ (DJM, 1995)
Gonzo: More Than All the 45's ♪♪♫ (Night Train, 1996)

influences:
◀◀ Professor Longhair, Art Tatum, Lloyd Glenn, Huey "Piano" Smith, Tuts Washington, Jelly Roll Morton, Frederic Chopin, Louis Moreau Gottschalk, Meade Lux Lewis

▶▶ Little Richard, Henry Butler, George Winston, Mac Rebennack (Dr. John), Allen Toussaint, Harry Connick Jr.

Garaud MacTaggart

Earl Bostic

Born April 25, 1913, in Tulsa, OK. Died October 25, 1965, in Rochester, NY.

Alto saxophonist Earl Bostic started in jazz, playing in several Midwest bands in the early 1930s before he studied at Xavier University. He left school to tour and worked with various bands, including one co-led by Fate Marable and Charlie Creath. In the late 1930s Bostic moved to New York where he performed as a soloist in jazz bands led by Lionel Hampton, Don Redman, and Edgar Hayes, as well as leading his own small groups which included jazz players such as Jimmy Cobb, Blue Mitchell, Stanley Turrentine, Benny Golson, and John Coltrane. Throughout the 1950s Bostic toured extensively while recording more than 400 singles for King records. Bostic's sparse style and subtle phrasing differed from other players out of the Swing era, and eventually he opted for the better suited R&B scene, to which Bostic turned during the 1950s as a bandleader and performer. Hits among his King Records included the 1951 smash "Flamingo" and other well-known songs such as "Temptation" and "You Go to My Head." A heart attack slowed him during the early 1960s, and the jazz influence crept back into his music, though he never lost the honking R&B edge that helped establish his reputation.

what to buy: *The Best of Earl Bostic* ♪♪♪♪ (Deluxe, 1956/King, 1989, prod. various) and *All His Hits* ♪♪♪♪ (King, 1996, prod. various) are pretty much what the titles describe and are both good introductions to this under-celebrated talent.

what to buy next: *Dance Music from the Bostic Workshop* ♪♪♪♪ (King, 1988) focuses on the funkier selections in Bostic's catalog.

the rest:
For You ♪♪♪ (King, 1956)
Let's Dance with Earl Bostic ♪♪♪♫ (King, 1957)
Alto Magic in Hi-Fi ♪♪♪♫ (King, 1958)
Blow a Fuse ♪♪♫ (Charly)

influences:
◀◀ Lionel Hampton, Charlie Creath, Edgar Hayes
▶▶ John Coltrane, Stanley Turrentine, King Curtis

Gary Graff and Nancy Ann Lee

Jean-Paul Bourelly

Born November 23, 1960, in Chicago, IL.

Jazz fans know this guitarist for his work on Miles Davis, McCoy Tyner/Elvin Jones, Muhal Richard Abrams, and Cassandra Wilson albums (he co-produced Wilson's *Dance to the Drums Again*), while R&B/hip-hop fans have heard him on Jody Watley, DJ Jazzy Jeff & Fresh Prince, Bel Biv Devoe, and Charles & Eddie records. Unbelievably, he's only been able to make albums on German and Japanese labels of often-tenuous U.S. distribution, though fortunately some records have been licensed by U.S. companies. He combines the influences of a number of greats in his own distinctive, uniquely rich guitar sound. Mixing jazz/blues/rock playing and his gruffly soulful vocals with funk and hip-hop rhythms, often with his group Blue Wave (sometimes Bluwave) Bandits, he builds dense, complex music he calls "New Breed Funk Jazz." Bassists Melvin Gibbs (Rollins Band), Darryl Jones (Rolling Stones), and Me'shell NdegoCello all passed through his groups prior to their more famous gigs, and "Kundalini" Mark Batson of the hip-hop group Get Set VOP plays keyboards (very Sly Stone) and sometimes raps for Bourelly's Blue Wave Bandits.

what to buy: For a few years, *Fade to Cacophony* ♫♫♫ (DIW, 1995/Evidence, 1996, prod. Jean-Paul Bourelly, Kazunori Sugiyama) was the most easily found Bourelly album. With its seven live tracks (plus one previously unreleased studio track) providing a cross section of his first three albums with added concert vigor, it's also a good introduction.

what to buy next: *Trippin'* ♫♫♫ (Enemy, 1991, prod. Jean-Paul Bourelly) features some of Bourelly's best guitar playing, focusing on his integration of lead and rhythm, and some of his tighter material. The lush, intensely lovely instrumental rave-up "Love Crime" is especially memorable.

the rest:
Blackadelic-Blu ♫♫♫ (DIW, 1994)
Tribute to Jimi ♫♫♫ (DIW, 1994/Koch Jazz, 1998)
Rock the Cathartic Spirits: Vibe Music and the Blues! ♫♫♫ (DIW, 1997/ Koch Jazz, 1998)

worth searching for: Bourelly's debut as a leader, *Jungle Cowboy* ♫♫♫♫ (JMT, 1987, prod. Stefan Winter, Jean-Paul Bourelly), is his best album, but JMT's U.S. distributor, Verve, doesn't carry it. It predates Bourelly's incorporation of hip-hop beats, and late sax great Julius Hemphill guested. *Saints & Sinners* ♫♫♫♫ (DIW, 1993, prod. Jean-Paul Bourelly, Kazunori Sugiyama) distills the core of Bourelly's stylistic fusion on "Got to Be Able to Know" and "Rumble in the Jungle," while "Muddy Waters (Blues for Muddy)" is a slow, simmering update of the blues. Many tracks, especially "Skin I'm In," show his matter-of-fact socio-political/racial consciousness without being preachy. Additionally, a couple albums that Bourelly produced, played on extensively, and largely composed are worth mentioning even though they're not in his name. He's actually a member of Ayibobo, whose *Freestyle* ♫♫♫ (DIW, 1993, prod. Jean-Paul Bourelly, Kazunori Sugiyama) combines Haitian singers and drummers with jazz horns, Bourelly's style, and EU drummer Ju Ju House. Jazz violinist Sonya Robinson's *Sonya* ♫♫♫♫ (Columbia, 1987, prod. Jean-Paul Bourelly) lets Bourelly stretch out more than usual (even playing keyboards) on a mostly instrumental album that contains his prettiest writing.

influences:
◀◀ Muddy Waters, Jimi Hendrix, Wes Montgomery, Jimmy Page, John McLaughlin, Sly & the Family Stone, Frank Zappa, Miles Davis

▶▶ Sonya Robinson

Steve Holtje

Lester Bowie

Born October 11, 1941, in Frederick, MD.

Lester Bowie's sputtering, squawking, mewling, moaning trumpet style has caused dispute among some jazz fans who would probably prefer he stuck to bebop. Yet, avant-garde jazz afficionados enjoy his trumpet and flugelhorn performances (which can sometimes be quite humorous), and admire him as a major jazz innovator and composer who draws from rock, gospel, R&B, soul, and other influences. Raised in a musical home in Little Rock, Arkansas, and St. Louis, Missouri, Bowie was influenced by his father who was a musician-educator, and by his grandfather, a trombonist. Bowie began playing trumpet in 1946, and from age 10 participated in musical activities at school and religious gatherings. By age 16 he was leading his own group. After military service, he spent several years working with R&B groups around the South and Midwest, played jazz gigs, recorded some R&B sessions for Chess Records, and performed with singer Fontella Bass, and with Frank Foster. In the late 1960s Bowie helped form the St. Louis musicians cooperative, Black Artists Group (BAG), and the Great Black Music Orchestra. In 1969 Bowie recorded with Archie Shepp, Sunny Murray, Jimmy Lyons, Cecil Taylor, and others, and also wrote, conducted, and recorded *Gettin' to Know Y' All* with the 50-piece Baden-Baden Free Jazz Orchestra, and performed the work again at the 1970 Frankfurt jazz festival.

Bowie moved to Chicago where by 1965 he began to gain recognition with members of the Chicago musicians cooperative, the AACM (Association for the Advancement of Creative Musicians), serving as its second president (after the founder, pianist/composer Muhal Richard Abrams). In 1969 a group of AACM members—Bowie, Roscoe Mitchell, Joseph Jarman, Malachi Favors, and Don Moye—formed the cooperative group the Art Ensemble of Chicago. Bowie continues to compose and play trumpet, flugelhorn, and percussion on recordings with the AEC, as well as perform and record with his New York Organ Ensemble and his Brass Fantasy band.

A live performance by Bowie's Brass Fantasy commonly finds the leader in perpetual motion at center stage, alternately leading the ten-piece ensemble and playing his trumpet or flugelhorn, as his trademark silvery lab coat shimmers under the spotlights. Tagged "avant pop," the music played by Brass Fantasy blends leading-edge jazz, pop, funk, and R&B, packed into stunningly modern pop-jazz arrangements. Brass Fantasy puts its own twist on tunes by Michael Jackson, James Brown, and other pop icons, creating engaging original works that skillfully combine musical genres. Drawing from a pool of 20 musicians, Brass Fantasy often includes AACM members and players from the Art Ensemble of Chicago, including Moye, who also adds percussive flair to Bowie's New York Organ Ensemble, a group styled after 1950s organ-combos.

Bowie also performs with the Leaders, a venturesome sextet of individual bandleaders that gathers on rare occasions when schedules permit. The Leaders first performed together at European jazz festivals during 1984–85. Formed in 1984 by saxophonist Chico Freeman and drummer/percussionist Moye, the Leaders includes pianist Kirk Lightsey, alto saxist Arthur Blythe, and bassist Cecil McBee. Bowie replaced Don Cherry in the Leaders' front line in 1986. Since 1986, when they released *Mudfoot*, they have released a few albums featuring original works by group members. Their ensemble sound ranges from smooth and tight straight-ahead journeys, to a mix of gritty blues, to New Orleans boisterousness and raw lyricism, to tunes laced with angular rhythms and free-style playing.

While Bowie is central to the serious musical efforts of the bands with which he performs, and is able to coax beautiful, pure, round tones from his trumpet, he is often responsible for comedic aspects and flamboyant visual and dramatic expressions during live performances with his groups. For example, at the 1992 Chicago Jazz Festival during a Brass Fantasy performance, the band was playing Bowie's compelling arrangement of Billie Holiday's "Strange Fruit" and, for dramatic effect, Bowie unexpectedly fired a gunshot over the heads of the audience. In a lighter vein, Bowie has been known during performances to pour water into his trumpet to create hilarious gurgling effects at the microphone, or to make his trumpet humorously "speak" with tonal inflections of animated human conversation. He makes his music fun, and is a one-of-a-kind musician who has no known imitators.

what to buy: A good overview of Bowie's ideas, solos, and collaborations, *Works* 𝄞𝄞𝄞𝄞 (ECM, 1980, 1981, 1983, 1985, 1986/1994, prod. Manfred Eicher) offers nine tunes compiled from Bowie's ECM recordings with the Art Ensemble of Chicago (*Full Force*), with Brass Fantasy (*Avant Pop*), and other sessions as leader (*I Only Have Eyes for You*, *All the Magic!*, and *The Great Pretender*). While this compilation contains neither Bowie's most popular tunes nor his more adventurous "trumpetisms," it is a good introduction to his consummate musicianship and influential leadership. Prominently featuring Bowie as performer and composer, the two-CD set, *All the Magic/The One and Only* 𝄞𝄞𝄞𝄞 (ECM, 1983, prod. Manfred Eicher), combining two earlier

LESTER BOWIE
(WITH ART ENSEMBLE OF CHICAGO)

song "The Bell Piece"
album *The Third Decade*
(ECM, 1984)
instrument Trumpet

Monster Solo

albums, could be considered the definitive Bowie showcase featuring Bowie with a group, Bowie soloing, and Bowie as the composer with a special knack for drawing from the entire spectrum of "Great Black Music." While some listeners may find Bowie's trumpet splats, splatters, growls, smears, gargles, and other sounds quite unorthodox, his devotees laud him for his creativity, his wide range of musical expressions, and his sociopolitical musical commentary. Disc one, *All the Magic*, features trumpeter Bowie in rousing collaborations with Ari Brown (tenor/soprano saxes), Art Matthews (piano), Fred Williams (Bass), Phillip Wilson (drums), and vocalists Fontella Bass and David Peaston. The team performs stimulating versions of Bowie's arrangements, ranging from the tender, gospel-inspired Armstrong tribute, "For Louie," to the free-jazz spree "Spacehead," to an Afro-Caribbean influenced version of Albert Ayler's "Ghosts", to Bowie's all-inclusive original "Trans Traditional Suite" which takes the listener on a free-jazz to R&B journey from Africa to America (with Fontella Bass's powerful vocal version of "Everything Must Change" in the middle). The closer offers a rockin' reminder of "Let the Good Times Roll." Disc two, *The One and Only,* features Bowie in solo performance of his 12 originals, playing trumpet and creating other sounds, with an array of percussive instruments, to stretch beyond the traditional. He is sometimes dramatically serious, other times quite humorous. Overall, this two-CD set is a scintillating, ear-expanding Bowie feast. One of Bowie's most fun-filled sessions, *The Great Pretender* ♫♫♫♪ (ECM, 1982, prod. Manfred Eicher) stretches the form on six pop classics and Bowie originals, including his 16:50-minute spoof on the title tune. The quartet stretches Bowie's avant-garde arrangement of "When the Doom (Moon) Comes over the Mountain" to new dimensions. Disappointingly brief, the calliope-like version of "Howdy Doody Time" (theme from the 1950s children's TV puppet show) warrants further development. Bowie contributes three serious and rhythmically diverse original tunes, and is more often spotlighted on this 1982 set with Donald Smith (piano, organ), Fred Williams (bass, electric bass), and guest soloist Hamiet Bluiett (baritone sax on the title tune). This album still ranks among Bowie's best sessions. You can't go wrong with any recording by Lester Bowie's Brass Fantasy, a listener-friendly and pop-oriented brass ensemble. Bowie's fine-tuned, modern arrangements for four trumpets, two trombones, French horn, tuba, percussion and traps drums draw from all eras and genres of "Great Black Music," including New Orleans-styled jazz, early rock, gospel-blues, carnival themes, plus other rousing, fun-filled fare. Arrangements seem to improve with each recording. And while Bowie may defer to other soloists and the dazzling horn-section maneuvers, his spirit and energy permeate each outing. *My Way* ♫♫♫♪ (DIW, 1990, prod. Art Ensemble of Chicago) finds the ten-piece ensemble performing six extended arrangements of originals and pop standards. The orchestrated ballad version of Paul Anka's "My Way" features a warm trombone solo from Steve Turre. Rousing versions of Bill Doggett's "Honky Tonk," and James Brown's "I Got You" put talented trombonist Frank Lacy in the spotlight, who also sings on the latter.

what to buy next: A rambunctious Brass Fantasy set, *The Fire This Time* ♫♫♫♪ (In & Out, 1992, prod. Lester Bowie, Famoudou Don Moye) is built on complex arrangements, tight harmonies, expert section work, brilliant dynamics, and finely executed solos from the talented musicians. Bowie leads (and joins) trumpeters E. J. Allen, Gerald Brazel and Tony Barrero; Vincent Chancey (French horn); Frank Lacy and Louis Bonilla (trombones); Bob Stewart (tuba); Vinnie Johnson (drums); and percussionist Famoudou Don Moye. For freewheeling arrangements of Michael Jackson's "Black or White" and "Remember

the Time," (arranged by E.J. Allen), and refreshing versions of the earlier recorded, "The Great Pretender," and "Strange Fruit," this album packs a knockout punch. Frank Lacy laudably launches *Serious Fun* ♫♫♫♫ (DIW, 1989, prod. Art Ensemble of Chicago) with his vocalizing on Brass Fantasy's version of the James Brown pop classic, "Papa's Got a Brand New Bag." This seven-tune session includes a deft arrangement of "Smooth Operator," providing foundation for a French horn solo from Vincent Chancy. Fine solos from trumpeter Stanton Davis and trombonist Steve Turre are the core of the 15-minute ballad-cum-bossa "God Bless the Child." Bowie has trumpet fun on the funky "Da Butt," which also highlights Bob Stewart's tuba artistry. The mirthful arrangement of Bobby McFerrin's "Don't Worry Be Happy" provides momentary levity before the finale, a powerful, soul-stirring requiem on Billie Holiday's "Strange Fruit," inspired after the legendary singer witnessed a Southern lynching. One of the earliest Brass Fantasy sessions, *Avant Pop* ♫♫♫♪ (ECM, 1986, prod. Manfred Eicher) contains rousing versions of the pop tunes, "Saving All My Love for You," "Blueberry Hill," and "Oh, What a Night," as well as originals by Bowie and trombonist Steve Turre. Their brass-possessed version of Willie Nelson's ballad, "Crazy," is alone worth the album price. Beefed up by Bob Stewart's big tuba tempos and drumming by Phillip Wilson, arrangements are colorfully pleasing, and allow soloists plenty of room. The trumpets played by Bowie, Stanton Davis, Malachi Thompson, and Rasul Sidduk blend tightly with trombones of Turre and Frank Lacy, and Vincent Chancey's French horn to make this an absorbing listen. For a modern twist on the nostalgic 1950s organ combos, check out Bowie's New York Organ Ensemble on *The Organizer* ♫♫♫♪ (DIW, 1991, prod Lester Bowie). While this is a sedate set compared to the usual raw, bluesy, organ-ensemble sound, the six-tunes set a straight-ahead and swinging path, and are enhanced by Bowie's characteristic trumpet coaxings and imprinted with African themes and free-jazz expeditions. Organist Amina Claudine Myers provides good foundations for solos from Bowie, trombonist Steve Turre, and tenor saxist James Carter, with drummer-percussionist Famoudou Don Moye (Phillip Wilson subs on three tracks) performing with his customary flair. While this album is not as exciting as Bowie's other recorded groups, it fittingly represents yet another aspect of his all-embracing musical persona.

best of the rest:
(With the Art Ensemble of Chicago) *Nice Guys* ♫♫♫♪ (ECM, 1979/1994)
(With the Art Ensemble of Chicago) *Full Force* ♫♫♫♪ (ECM, 1980/1994)
(With the Art Ensemble of Chicago) *Urban Bushmen* ♫♫♫♪ (ECM, 1982/1994, 2-CD set)

(With the Art Ensemble of Chicago) *The Third Decade* 𝄞𝄞𝄞 (ECM, 1984/1994)

(With the Leaders) *Unforeseen Blessings* 𝄞𝄞𝄞 (Black Saint, 1989)

(With Art Ensemble of Chicago & Lester Bowie's Brass Fantasy) *Live at the 6th Tokyo Music Joy '90* 𝄞𝄞𝄞 (DIW, 1990)

(With the Art Ensemble of Chicago) *Dreaming of the Masters, Volume II: Thelonious Sphere Monk* 𝄞𝄞𝄞 (DIW, 1991)

(With the Art Ensemble of Chicago) *Art Ensemble of Soweto: America-South Africa* 𝄞𝄞𝄞 (DIW, 1991)

influences:

◄◄ Louis Armstrong, Kenny Dorham

►► Malachi Thompson, Orbert Davis

see also: *Art Ensemble of Chicago*

Nancy Ann Lee

Ronnie Boykins

Born c. 1935, in Chicago, IL. Died April 20, 1980, in New York, NY.

As bassist with Sun Ra's Arkestra between 1958 and 1966 (and off and on in later years), contributing to the, um, stellar *Heliocentric Worlds* records and many others (most notably *Jazz in Silhouette* and *The Magic City*), Boykins could have left well enough alone and been relegated to history as a solid, if inconsequential, sideman. However, he challenged fate and, a decade later, with Marzette Watts behind the boards, let loose one solid, if uneventful, piece of Ra-inspired freedom, his only album as a leader.

Less well-known is Boykins's early background in Chicago, where he studied with local legends Walter Dyett and Ernie Shepard, and his work with other musicians. Boykins recorded with a surprisingly broad range of jazzmen, from Bill Barron and Elmo Hope to Rahsaan Roland Kirk, Charles Tyler, Steve Lacy, and Archie Shepp and the New York Contemporary Five. He even played with Mary Lou Williams and Sarah Vaughan.

what's available: Although sometimes Boykins's quest for Arkestral improvisation turns into uncomfortable clunkiness, *Ronnie Boykins* 𝄞𝄞𝄞 (ESP, 1975) is actually quite enjoyable. However, his bass playing, appropriate within the framework of Ra's large-scale ensemble madness, is actually diminished by the context of this comparatively smaller septet, and too often Boykins sounds as if he's trying too hard to be a leader, rather than let the members work things out on their own.

influences:

◄◄ Walter Dyett, Ernie Shepard, Wilbur Ware, Henry Grimes

►► Alejandro Blake, Richard Williams, Rollo Redford, Tyler Mitchell

Jason Ferguson

Charles Brackeen

Born March 13, 1940, in Eufaula, OK.

Charles Brackeen lived on a cattle and hog farm in Eufaula until he was 11, then moved to Paris, Texas, internalizing the capacious Southwest tenor sound and incantational Amerindian rhythms in his mind's ear. He played piano and violin from the age of six, on which he'd accompany his aunt at church services, and began playing saxophone at age 10. At 14 he moved to New York, where various "hip" relatives gradually introduced him to the music of Charlie Parker, Stan Getz, Sonny Rollins, and John Coltrane. During a late-teens sojourn to Los Angeles he met Ornette Coleman, Don Cherry, Billy Higgins, Paul Bley, and other pioneers of New Jazz. During the 1960s and early 1970s in New York, tenor/soprano saxophonist Brackeen established himself as a thoroughly individual and personal voice in the avant-garde realm. During the 1980s, he was sought out by the manager of the Silkheart label and invited to record three dates between 1986–1987. Although Brackeen has had long hiatuses from recording, his documented work is highly energetic and invigorating.

what's available: *Rhythm X* 𝄞𝄞𝄞𝄞 (Strata East, 1968, prod. Clifford Jordan), Brackeen's previously long-out-of-print stunning debut recording with Don Cherry, Charlie Haden, and Ed Blackwell was put back in the catalog a few years ago. Three Silkheart recordings are magnificent documents that display the mercurial and concise playing of a singular artist whose music is instilled with a gentle spirituality during even the most intense passages. *Bannar* 𝄞𝄞𝄞𝄞 (Silkheart, 1987, prod. Keith Knox) features Brackeen freely improvising in the style of Ornette Coleman or Albert Ayler, joined by AACM veterans Malachi Favors (bass) and Alvin Fielder (drums), and trumpeter Dennis Gonzalez. The musicians are in peak form on both *Attainment* 𝄞𝄞𝄞𝄞 (Silkheart, 1987, prod. Manfred Eicher) and *Worshippers Come Nigh* 𝄞𝄞𝄞𝄞 (Silkheart, 1987, prod. Manfred Eicher), sessions where Brackeen is abetted by Mississippi-born trumpeter Olu Dara (who plays cornet on both dates), and the incendiary pair of Fred Hopkins (bass) and Andrew Cyrille (drums).

worth searching for: You can hear Brackeen's dry sound in utter clarity on two Paul Motian recordings, *Dance* 𝄞𝄞𝄞𝄞 (ECM, 1977, prod. Manfred Eicher) and *Le Voyage* 𝄞𝄞𝄞 (ECM, 1979, prod. Manfred Eicher). And Brackeen appears to great effect with Ahmed Abdullah's *Liquid Magic* &&&&& (Silkheart, 1987, prod. Keith Knox).

influences:

Sonny Rollins, John Coltrane, Ornette Coleman, Albert Ayler

Ted Panken

JoAnne Brackeen

Born JoAnne Grogan, July 26, 1938, in Ventura, CA.

"I *never* think in terms of women," pianist JoAnne Brackeen, has said. "I think of music, period. It wasn't until 1978 that I even heard (the phrase) 'women in jazz.' By then I'd been playing all over the world. I just thought jazz was jazz and whoever played it, that was that." Noted for her free, atonal improvisations as well as her romanticism, the California-born, self-taught, post-bop pianist spontaneously infuses "warhorse" standards, as well as her own highly original compositions, with fresh energy, keeping everything together technically, melodically, and harmonically.

Born in Ventura in 1938, Brackeen taught herself to play by copying Frankie Carle records note-for-note. When she was 16, her family moved to Los Angeles, where, in her late teens, she joined the jazz scene, favoring experimental jazz musicians. She worked with Teddy Edwards, Dexter Gordon, Harold Land, and Charles Lloyd in the late 1950s in L.A., married tenor saxist Charles Brackeen in 1960 (divorced in the 1980s), and they moved to New York in 1965. One night, at a Lower East Side jazz club where Art Blakey and the Jazz Messengers were playing, Brackeen saw that his young pianist had become lost in the challenging music—she politely sat in and was invited to join the band, becoming the first woman player to remain with the Messengers for any significant period (1969–72). Brackeen worked with Joe Henderson (1972–75) and, one of her most notable associations, with Stan Getz (1975–77) before leading her own groups. An internationally recognized artist and composer, Brackeen continues to explore and record the gamut of jazz styles from straight-ahead, to avant garde and Brazilian jazz, using her forceful percussive approach, novel ideas, and polished phrasing. An exuberant, adventurous, and confident player, Brackeen was the first modern female jazz pianist who went the route the guys went, with no mentors, and her travails have inspired countless keyboard sisters such as Carla Bley, Geri Allen, Renee Rosnes, and others. Brackeen is a true virtuoso on today's jazz scene.

what to buy: One of her more adventurous sessions, *Fi-Fi Goes to Heaven* &&&&& (Concord, 1987, prod. Carl E. Jefferson) features Brackeen leading an exciting, all-star quintet that includes trumpeter Terence Blanchard, alto/soprano saxophonist Branford Marsalis, bassist Cecil McBee, and drummer Al Foster. With tantamount verve, these musicians stretch and explore extraordinary Brackeen originals such as the grandiose, carnival-like "Estilo Magnifico," the playfully hip modal piece "Fi-Fi Goes to Heaven," the cacophonous churner "Cosmonaut," and the hard-edged "Dr. Chang." This most exciting album finds Brackeen in top form and, for the adventurous spirit displayed by the pianist and her cohorts in solos and ensembles, should be part of any jazz collection. While Brackeen sticks mostly to standards on her live-recorded 11-tune solo piano performance on *Live at Maybeck Recital Hall, Volume I* &&&&& (Concord, 1990, prod. Carl E. Jefferson), she also includes four originals which, as always, are among her best tunes. She draws inspiration from many sources for compositions and her brawny piece "Dr. Chu Chow" (dedicated to a master of Chi Kung) strongly features her left hand underpinnings, Asian themes, and Pullen-like key-crunching runs. Equally enjoyable are her tricky time signature shifting on "Curved Space," her composition "African Aztec," which alternates with chugging left-hand riffs suggestive of boogie-woogie while her right hand plays counter-melody, and "Calling Carl," a spontaneously invented piece devoted to a Concord producer who Brackeen urged to record her solo performance, thus launching the entire solo piano recital series. Sensitive to her audience, Brackeen also includes popular favorites such as "Thou Swell," "The Most Beautiful Girl in the World," "My Foolish Heart," "I'm Old Fashioned," and, the closer, a lightly cavorting, straight-ahead spree on George and Ira Gershwin's "Strike up the Band." From start to finish, this Maybeck solo piano recording still ranks as one of the best of the 40 sessions recorded by various artists. *Six Ate* &&&&& (Candid/Choice, 1975/1996, prod. Gerry MacDonald) compiles selections from her first album in 1975 (*Snooze*) and others performed with bassist Cecil McBee and drummer Billy Hart, two artful players who sensitively inspire and cavort with the pianist on the eight tunes (including a CD-reissue bonus track, "I Didn't Know What Time It Was"). As with all of her recordings, Brackeen performs imaginative, stirring originals, and this March 16, 1975 New York studio session sounds as fresh today as when it was recorded.

what to buy next: A more recent trio session with next-generation players, *Power Talk* &&&& (Turnipseed Music, 1994, prod. Don Turnipseed) documents a well-produced, live-recorded trio performance at the Contemporary Arts Center, in New Orleans, Louisiana, on April 16, 1994. Brackeen delivers an eight-tune mixture of originals and standards in a trio session with bassist Ira Coleman and drummer Tony Reedus. Their collective energy and rapport (as well as some fine solos) on "(There Is) No Greater Love," "My Funny Valentine," "Just One of Those Things," "Darn That Dream," "Caravan," and Brackeen's three originals, make this a very special trio outing from this small independent New Orleans label. *Turnaround* 🎵🎵🎵🎵 (Evidence, 1992/1995, prod. JoAnne Brackeen) finds pianist Brackeen leading her quartet through a progressive, live-recorded performance at New York's Sweet Basil. Three originals and three standards equitably spotlight Brackeen, Blakey alumnus Donald Harrison on alto sax, the sought-after *Tonight Show* drummer Marvin "Smitty" Smith, and bassist Cecil McBee, with whom Brackeen has worked for two decades. Brackeen, prodded underneath by Smith, uses the keyboard's full range sometimes creating rolling crescendos, churning sheets of sound. Yet she doesn't upstage singularly outstanding contributions from her sidemen who ably weave their way through her demanding compositions such as "Rubies and Diamonds," "Picasso," and others. At midpoint, she delivers a lush, lyrical solo interpretation of the Rodgers-Hart classic, "Bewitched, Bothered and Bewildered." Titled after the Ornette Coleman tune on the album, *Turnaround* is an agreeable listen. *Breath of Brazil* 🎵🎵🎵🎵 (Concord Picante, 1991, prod. Carl E. Jefferson) displays Brackeen's interest in Brazilian jazz as she romps through nine compositions by Brazilian masters and three originals. With graceful vigor, Brackeen, Eddie Gómez (bass), Duduka Fonseca (drums), and Waltinho Anastácio (percussion) breeze through the engaging, lightly swaying mixture of three originals and nine Brazilian-jazz standards from composers Ivan Lins, Antonio Carlos Jobim, Egberto Gismonti, and others. Listen to her soft and gentle interpretation of Jobim's "Aguas De Marco," and her original title tune (a Brazilian-bopper that cries out for lyrics), and you'll understand how well-versed she is in the Brazilian-jazz domain. Gomez, whose roots are in San Juan, is an expert bassist (best known for his decade with Bill Evans) who adds splendor with his support and lyrical pizzicato solos. Brackeen's playing is exhilarating throughout as she nicely blends rhythms and styles, develops intriguing harmonies, builds dynamics, and displays superb technique. She is spurred to greater heights by her chosen team who make this a successful session. Fans of this genre should find this CD authentic and enjoyable. Recorded two years later in 1993, *Take A Chance* 🎵🎵🎵 (Concord, 1994, prod. Carl E. Jefferson) finds Brackeen with the same Brazilian-jazz experts—Eddie Gómez (bass), Duduka Da Fonseca (drums), and

JoAnne Brackeen

song "Bewitched, Bothered and Bewildered"

album Turnaround
(Evidence, 1992/1995)

instrument Piano

Waltinho Anástacio (percussion). Highlights among the eight Brazilian tunes and three originals include an elegant reading of the Brazilian classic, "Estaté," and Bracken's Brazilian-bop meld on her original title tune. This album teeters more on a straight-ahead edge, and lacks some of the energy of her earlier Brazilian-jazz album, but is equally enjoyable as Brackeen lends her expansive style to the 11 selections with effective support from her side team.

best of the rest:

(With Clint Houston and Billy Hart) *Invitation* 🎵🎵🎵🎵 (Black Lion, 1976/1995)

Aft 🎵🎵🎵🎵 (Timeless, 1977/1993)

worth searching for: Currently out-of-print, *Havin' Fun* 🎵🎵🎵🎵 (Concord, 1985, prod. Carl E. Jefferson) features Brackeen in an eight-tune studio session recorded in June 1985 with bassist Cecil McBee and drummer Al Foster. The artistry of this trio as they skirt through the American songbook warrants a CD re-release, especially for their kicking versions of classics such as

"I've Got the World on a String" and "Just One of Those Things," Bracken's flowery waltz version of the Mercer-Mandel treasure, "Emily," her grandly sweeping "This Is Always," and a benchmark version (over seven minutes) of Bonfa's bossa-nova classic, "Manha De Carnaval." Visit the Concord website and register your vote for re-releasing this exceptional CD.

influences:

◀◀ Bud Powell, McCoy Tyner, Chick Corea, Herbie Hancock, Joe Henderson, Art Blakey

▶▶ Carla Bley, Geri Allen, Renee Rosnes, Junko Onishi, Aki Takase

Nancy Ann Lee

Don Braden

Born November 20, 1963, in Cincinnati, OH.

Don Braden started playing contemporary jazz professionally at age 15 after two years learning to play tenor sax in Louisville, Kentucky. After time at Harvard (during which he studied with Jerry Bergonzi and Bill Pierce), he moved to New York in 1984 and began gigging with a variety of mainstream artists, starting with the Harper Brothers Quintet and Lonnie Smith, with many more (most notably Tony Williams, Betty Carter (*Look What I Got*), Wynton Marsalis, Out of the Blue, J.J. Johnson, Tom Harrell, Art Farmer, Freddie Hubbard, and Roy Haynes) after he had established himself as a talent to watch, which led to recordings as a leader with small labels. After one album for a Sony subsidiary, Braden was dropped, but caught a break when he was picked to provide the music for jazz-lover Bill Cosby's TV show *Cosby.*

what to buy: *Organic* ♪♪♪ (Epicure/550 Sony, 1995, prod. Joel Dorn) is a throwback to the glory days of organ-based soul-jazz, with Larry Goldings and Jack McDuff alternating at the Hammonds. Like those old albums, it's not afraid to draw on contemporary pop, so we get a swinging cover of "Saving All My Love for You" (complete with hand claps). Braden writes idiomatically, and when McDuff and guest David "Fathead" Newman chip in tunes, you know they're good 'n' greasy. Cecil Brooks III and Winard Harper both lay down deep grooves during their turns in the drum chair.

what to buy next: *The Voice of the Saxophone* ♪♪♪ (RCA Victor, 1997, prod. Don Braden), as its title hints, is a tribute to Braden's predecessors. Tunes by or associated with Hank Mobley, Wayne Shorter, Grover Washington Jr., John Coltrane, Sam Rivers, and Jimmy Heath bracket the album. In a way this is a

better record than *Organic* just because the material's so classic, but it's a lot tougher to match the standards set by those greats. On the other hand, Braden's no slouch, and he's put together a superb octet to play much of this album, with Hamiet Bluiett and Vincent Herring the other saxes and Randy Brecker (trumpet, flugelhorn) and Frank Lacy (trombone) the brass. The theme from *Cosby,* the Cosby/Benny Golson-penned "Monk's Hat," also appears in a driving Latinized arrangement.

the rest:

Time Is Now ♪♪♡ (Criss Cross, 1991)
Wish List ♪♪♡ (Criss Cross, 1991)
Landing Zone ♪♪♪ (Landmark, 1994)

influences:

◀◀ Joe Henderson, Bill Pierce, Jerry Bergonzi, Wilton Felder

Steve Holtje

Bobby Bradford

Born July 19, 1934, in Cleveland, MS.

A leading though largely overlooked figure in the avant-garde since the late 1950s, cornetist Bobby Bradford is a passionate, incisive player whose small discography contains a number of gems. Though best known as the first trumpeter in Ornette Coleman's quartet and for his work with clarinetist/composer John Carter, Bradford is a fine composer in his own right and a visionary improvisor who brings a deep feeling for the blues to everything he plays. Raised in Dallas, Bradford was fully versed in the bop tradition, playing with such local contemporaries as Cedar Walton and David Newman and working with the legendary alto saxophonist Buster Smith. He moved to Los Angeles in 1953 and began associating with Eric Dolphy and Coleman, who was still developing his radical harmolodic approach. Bradford also worked with Gerald Wilson and Wardell Grey before serving in the military in the late 1950s. He returned to L.A. after the service to study for his masters, then moved to New York to replace Don Cherry in Coleman's quartet in 1961–62, a period when Coleman played infrequently and didn't record. Over the years, Bradford has been hired by Coleman for various performances but has only appeared on record with him twice, on Coleman's early 1970s Columbia albums *Science Fiction* and *Broken Shadows.*

Bradford eventually settled back in Los Angeles in the mid-1960s and began teaching, though he didn't play much publicly until 1968 after forming the New Art Jazz Ensemble (1965–71) with reed master John Carter. The group only made two recordings, both of which have been reissued on CD, though Bradford played on many of Carter's later albums, including his five-volume Roots and Folklore series on Gramavision and Black Saint. After the breakup of his marriage to singer Melba Joyce (their daughter is jazz singer Carmen Bradford), he moved to England for a year in 1973, where he formed strong musical relationships with such British avant-gardists as drummer John Stevens, with whom he recorded a number of albums. Upon returning to Los Angeles, Bradford started teaching music history at a number of Southland colleges and continued to work with Carter and occasionally lead his own groups. He has recorded a number of times with David Murray and performed with Charlie Haden's Liberation Music Orchestra. Since the early 1980s, Bradford has called his band the Mo'tet, a quintet that often features multi-reed player Vinny Golia.

what to buy: The best example of Bobby Bradford's compositional sensibility, *One Night Stand* ♫♫♫♫ (Soul Note, 1989, prod. William Kennally) also captures the inventive trumpeter in top form, burning through his organically developing themes with his crackling, warm, middle-register lines. Recorded live in Gainesville, Florida, in 1986 with pianist Frank Sullivan, bassist Scott Walton, and drummer Billy Bowker, the quartet starts things off with a incendiary version of "Comin' On," a free tune Bradford recorded again two years later with John Carter. Bradford displays his deep feeling for the blues on the 12-bar "Sho' Nuff Blues," and his bop roots on "All the Things Your Mother Didn't Tell You," based on the chord changes of "All the Things You Are." Another highlight is Bradford's tribute to Ornette Coleman, the 11-minute "Ornate," a free piece that moves in a number of directions, but maintains a unified feel throughout. Originally released on the tiny Revelation label, *Seeking* ♫♫♫♫ (hat ART, 1969, prod. J.W. Hardy, Pete Welding) is the debut recording by Bradford and John Carter's New Art Jazz Ensemble, a pioneering avant-garde group that expanded on some of the directions first explored by Ornette Coleman. Bradford contributes one tune, his sorrowful "Song of the Unsung," while his warm trumpet sound contrasts effectively with Carter's keening reed work. Later on, Carter played clarinet exclusively, but in the late 1960s he was still playing flute, alto, and tenor sax. His alto playing here is particularly luminous. The transition between bop and the avant-garde is captured concisely in Bradford's solo on "The Village Dancers." Tom Williamson's understated bass work anchors the session, while drummer Bruz Freeman (the brother of Chicago tenorman Von Freeman) plays with admirable attention to texture and dramatic development.

what to buy next: An exciting, hard-blowing quintet session, *Lost in L.A.* ♫♫♫♫ (Soul Note, 1984, prod. Giovanni Bonandrini) fea-

tures James Kousakis on alto sax, Sherman Ferguson on drums, and bassists Mark Dresser and Roberto Miranda. Bradford revisits a number of tunes he's recorded before, including a down-and-dirty version of "Sho' Nuff Blues," an epic, almost 12-minute version of "Ornate," and "Ashes," a concise, sunny, funky piece reminiscent of an early Ornette Coleman line. The two bassists, on separate stereo channels, trade walking and solo duties, creating constant textural shifts, and Ferguson's active drumming keeps the soloists on their toes. Bradford's cornet work is consistently inventive, but Kousakis's alto isn't as rigorous as other Bradford reed partners (such as David Murray or Marty Ehrlich), putting this session firmly in the good-but-not-great camp.

best of the rest:

Comin' On ♫♫♫ (hat ART, 1989)
Detail: In Time Was ♫♫♫♫ (Circulatione Totale, 1990)

worth searching for: A real treasure, *West Coast Hot* ♫♫♫♫♫ (Novus, 1969, prod. J.W. Hardy, Bob Thiele) collects two landmark L.A. sessions, Bradford's and John Carter's second New Art Jazz Ensemble recording for the Revelation label and pianist/composer Horace Tapscott's debut on the Flying Dutchman label, *The Giant Is Awakened*, featuring a young Arthur Blythe. Bradford's playing is particularly powerful on the opening "Call to the Festival." The NAJE also features drummer Bruz Freeman and bassists Tom Williamson and Henry Franklin (though Franklin is uncredited on the album). This is brave, uncompromising music largely ignored at the time of its release. The first suite in John Carter's series of five octet sessions in his Roots and Folklore series, *Dauwhe* ♫♫♫♫ (Black Saint, 1982, prod. John Carter) is also the best, a brilliant album that draws on a huge swath of African American music. Bradford's glorious cornet work shines through on the ensemble passages, while his solos on the title track and "Mating Ritual" add a good deal of flesh and blood to Carter's music. With James Newton on flute, Red Callender on tuba, Charles Owens on reeds, and Roberto Miranda on bass, the album features a who's who of advanced West Coast improvisors.

influences:

◄◄ Fats Navarro, Kenny Dorham

►► Don Cherry, Baikida Carroll

Andrew Gilbert

Ruby Braff

Born Reuben Braff, March 16, 1927, in Boston, MA.

A remarkable swing cornet player in the classic New Orleans style, Ruby Braff has developed a distinctive sound of his own.

After working in Boston and building a reputation, Braff moved to New York City in 1953. He recorded and performed with Pee Wee Russell, Vic Dickenson, Urbie Green, and Buck Clayton. Although his work was greatly respected and critically acclaimed, Braff had a difficult time finding work throughout the 1960s because the classic style was not in demand. In 1971 he began working as soloist with Tony Bennett, and subsequently, in 1973, formed a successful quartet with guitarist George Barnes. Since that time he has kept busy performing and recording with such jazz greats as Dick Hyman, Ellis Larkins, Scott Hamilton, and Howard Alden.

The cornet is a brass instrument which may have first appeared in an orchestra in 1829. It has a tone somewhere between the bright-sounding trumpet and deeper-toned horn. Braff is one of few jazz players who performs solely on cornet. He has mastered the instrument, playing fluidly and with a sound that is warm-toned and engaging, especially on ballads.

what to buy: Braff has recorded frequently with tenor saxophonist Scott Hamilton since these two February 1985 sessions made at Penny Lane Studios, *A First* 𝄞𝄞𝄞𝄞 (Concord, 1985, prod. Carl E. Jefferson) and *Sailboat in the Moonlight* 𝄞𝄞𝄞𝄞 (Concord, 1986, prod. Carl E. Jefferson). Both sessions feature Braff interpreting time-honored swing classics with Hamilton, pianist John Bunch, bassist Phil Flanigan, guitarist Chris Flory, and drummer Chuck Riggs. On *Sailboat in the Moonlight* the like-minded leaders revisit "Lover Come Back to Me," "Jeepers Creepers," "'Deed I Do," the title tune, and four more gems. Braff is in top, friendly toned form throughout, with a particularly enticing cornet solo on the seductive ballad, "When the Lights Are Low" (written by Benny Carter). On *A First*, there are also peak moments, with Braff equally at his best on slow swingers such as "Rockin' Chair" and uptempo numbers such as "Dinah" (which also yields the limelight to Flory and Riggs) and the finale, a toe-tapping jam on Basie's "Bugle Blues." While Hamilton lays down some warm tenorisms, he tends to lay back and not interfere with Braff's cornet improvisations, yet he's able to pick up lines where Braff leaves off and create his own fine solos. On both albums, the group follows an arranged sounding, head-solos-head format and swings intently, with Braff and Hamilton interacting comfortably and generating attractive solos. Both albums are recommended for swing-minded jazz fans. You can't buy just one without the other! Having first recorded an album of duets together in 1955, pianist Ellis Larkins and cornetist Ruby Braff reunite for the first time since 1972 on the critically acclaimed *Calling Berlin, Volume 1* 𝄞𝄞𝄞𝄞 (Arbors, 1995, prod. Rachel and Matthew

Domber). As they explore tunes from the Irving Berlin songbook, the rapport between the two is refreshing, swinging, and conversational, with the lyrics clearly and sensitively interpreted. Guitarist Bucky Pizzarelli joins the duo for "It's a Lovely Day Today," and "Russian Lullaby." Other classic Berlin tunes include "Blue Skies," "How Deep Is the Ocean?," and "Let's Face the Music and Dance." *Calling Berlin, Volume 2* 𝄞𝄞𝄞𝄞 (Arbors, 1997, prod. Rachel and Matthew Domber) provides more of the same satisfying music as Ellis Larkins and Braff continue their explorations of Berlin's music. And this disc proves to be another tasty treat from the duo. With emotion, the duo delivers "Cheek to Cheek," "What'll I Do?," "Isn't It a Lovely Day?," and "Always," among others.

what to buy next: *Salutes Rodgers and Hart* 𝄞𝄞𝄞𝄞 (Concord, 1975, prod. Carl E. Jefferson) features Braff and guitarist George Barnes leading a quartet with rhythm guitarist Wayne Wright and bassist Michael Moore. Together, this foursome demonstrates a high level of musicianship on the 10 tunes, swinging through the opener, "Mountain Greenery," then slowing to a breathtaking, intimate rendition of "Isn't It Romantic," guaranteed to pull at your heart strings. Other tunes include romantic Rodgers and Hart classics such as "Lover," "Thou Swell," "Spring Is Here," and "There's a Small Hotel." *Plays Gershwin* 𝄞𝄞𝄞𝄞 (Concord, 1975, prod. Carl E. Jefferson) also features the Braff/Barnes Quartet with guitarist Wright and bassist Moore on a session recorded at Concord Boulevard Park. The musicians swing and improvise through such tunes as "'S Wonderful," "I Got Rhythm," "Somebody Loves Me," and eight other swing gems. A tribute to Louis Armstrong, *Being with You* 𝄞𝄞𝄞𝄞 (Arbors, 1996, prod. Rachel and Matthew Domber) features Braff with a nine-piece New Orleans-style band. Joined by soloist Joe Wilder on flugelhorn, they play tunes such as "Royal Garden Blues."

best of the rest:

Hustlin' and Bustlin' 𝄞𝄞𝄞𝄞 (Black Lion, 1955/1992)
(With the Ruby Braff Trio) *Bravura Eloquence* 𝄞𝄞𝄞 (Concord, 1988)
(With the Ruby Braff Trio) *Me, Myself and I* 𝄞𝄞𝄞 (Concord, 1988)
Cornet Chop Suey 𝄞𝄞𝄞 (Concord, 1991)
(With Ruby Braff & His Buddies) *Controlled Nonchalance, Volume 1* 𝄞𝄞𝄞𝄞 (Arbors, 1993)
(With the Ruby Braff Quartet) *Live at the Regattabar* 𝄞𝄞𝄞𝄞 (Arbors, 1993)
(With Roger Kellaway) *Inside & Out* 𝄞𝄞𝄞𝄞 (Concord, 1995)

influences:

◀◀ Bunny Berigan, Bix Biederbecke, Jimmy McPartland, Bobby Hackett, Buck Clayton

▶▶ Warren Vache

Susan K. Berlowitz and Nancy Ann Lee

Brand X
Formed in 1975.

John Goodsall, guitar; Percy Jones, bass; Robin Lumley, keyboards; Phil Collins, drums.

While some tremendous and lasting music came out of the fusion/jazz-rock era of the 1970s and 1980s, an equal amount of banal, inaccessible, and pseudo-important recordings were produced in an effort to hop on the fusion bandwagon. Brand X, a British jazz-rock group that never crossed the line into unacceptable musical excess, was one band that always took the high ground where matters of composition, melodiousness, accessibility, and pure chops were concerned. Brand X's genesis was in recording sessions that included the best of England's then young, progressive, electric-oriented musicians. Originally formed in 1975 while the group was recording as sidemen on another artist's project, the core members were John Goodsall (formerly of Atomic Rooster), Percy Jones (England's answer to Jaco Pastorius), Trident Studio's producer/keyboardist Robin Lumley, and Genesis drummer Phil Collins. Later, the inventive percussionist Morris Pert was added. After recording seven albums on Charisma and fielding a revolving roster of some of the finest jazz and instrumental progressive rock musicians, the group disbanded subsequent to their 1981 CBS debut. Former "deputies"/associate members include drummers Bill Bruford (Yes, Genesis, King Crimson, National Health), Chuck Burghi (Al Di Meola), Mike Clarke (Herbie Hancock), and Kenwood Dennard (PDB), as well as keyboardist Peter Robinson (Stanley Clarke).

A re-formed version of the band appeared in 1992 (featuring Goodsall, Jones, drummer Frank Katz, and vibist Mark Wagnon), and has remained active, releasing new material via two studio albums and a live recording to date. Reforming to pursue new musical directions, the band has continued to produce quality electric improvisational music, whatever ill-suited tag ("fusion," "jazz-rock," "progressive rock," etc.) is foisted upon them. Drummer Pierre Moerlen (Gong) has also been retained as a Brand X associate musician. Most of the early Charisma/Passport Brand X catalog has been reissued on the Caroline label.

what to buy: Tunes that were originally recorded for the "Product" sessions ended up on *Do They Hurt?* 𝄢𝄢𝄢𝄢 (Caroline,

1980/1989, prod. Brand X, Neil Kernon), a much better album as a whole. New Orleans via Oakland drummer Mike Clarke puts in a superb performance, as does Phil Collins (who by this time held only part-time member/"special guest" status with the band). The album contains great tunes by Jones and Goodsall. Standout tracks include "Noddy Goes to Sweden" (with the intentionally "backwards-masked" story of Noddy read by Michael Palin), "Voidarama," "D.M.Z," and the tour-de-force "Cambodia." Percy Jones rivals Jaco Pastorius as the archetypal modern electric bassist on this release. *Masques* 𝄢𝄢𝄢𝄢 (Caroline, 1978/1989, prod. Robin Lumley) offers a little something for all types of electric jazz fans, featuring a mix of funk-oriented material and a generous helping of straight-ahead jazz-rock/fusion (lots of 32nd-note speed solos, ensemble riffing, and odd time signatures), and even an extremely beautiful ballad in Morris Pert's composition "Black Moon." Peter Robinson is the designated keyboardist, but Robin Lumley puts in admirable oversight as producer of these sessions. *Manifest Destiny* 𝄢𝄢𝄢𝄢 (Outer Music/Pangea, 1997, prod. David Hentschel) amazingly achieves two seemingly contradictory things—the album is both a natural extension of the band's musical legacy, and a fresh, ground-breaking effort. With a pared-down lineup and a more contemporary focus, Brand X uses modern technology such as sampling and MIDI instrumentation combined with a stripped down monster groove to create some great music; all under the watchful eye of producer/engineer David Hentschel. The group's interest in Middle Eastern/exotic musical material remains extant, while the whole project sounds the way Steps Ahead may have if they had hired Adrian Belew, Allan Holdsworth, or Frank Zappa to play guitar and veered off in a harder, more "metallic-funk" direction. Pick hits include the title cut, "True to the Clik," "Virus," "Drum Ddu," and "Operation Hearts and Minds." The CD also includes two "hidden bonus tracks" that were recorded live and feature Gong's Pierre Moerlen on drums. *A History: 1976–1980* 𝄢𝄢𝄢𝄢 (Caroline, 1997, prod. various) features a sampling of material from various studio (and live) albums including the 1977 concert recording "Livestock." Phil Collins is represented here as a drummer and vocalist in a way that those only familiar with his top-40 successes could never dream of. Many rock and fusion all-stars put in stellar performances as well, and the in-depth liner notes by Chris Welch provide plenty of historical perspective and at least a few useable questions and answers for a late night game of music trivia.

what to buy next: The very "unorthodox" debut recording from Brand X, *Unorthodox Behaviour* 𝄢𝄢𝄢𝄢 (Caroline, 1976/1989, prod. Brand X, Dennis MacKay), is heavy fusion at its finest ("Nuclear Burn"). Instrumental pyrotechnics abound, but not at the expense of composition or musical form. Features the original four-piece band lineup of John Goodsall, Percy Jones, Robin Lumley, and Phil Collins.

best of the rest:
Moroccan Roll 𝄞𝄞𝄞𝄞 (Caroline, 1977/1989)
Livestock 𝄞𝄞𝄞 (Caroline, 1977/1989)
Product 𝄞𝄞𝄞 (Caroline, 1979/1989)

worth searching for: The "final" Brand X album (before the 1990s re-formation), *Is There Anything About?* 𝄞𝄞𝄞 (Passport/ CBS, 1982) is out of print and pretty scarce.

influences:
◀◀ Tony Williams Lifetime, Gong, Weather Report
▶▶ Uzeb, Jeff Lorber Fusion, Gamalon

Gregg Juke

Rick Braun

Born July 6, 1955, in Allentown, PA.

Los Angeles–based trumpeter Rick Braun's music lives on the fringes of jazz. His playing, which is superbly nuanced, has definite jazz roots, but his music as a whole has a mellow pop feel. This has made him quite successful (and influential) in the smooth-jazz field, however. Braun began playing trumpet in third grade and has credited Herb Alpert's records as an early influence—he played along with them while growing up. His musical interests have been diverse. He attended the Eastman School of Music in Rochester, a prestigious college with a classical leaning, and while there formed a fusion group, Auracle, which recorded two albums before lack of success led to the group's breakup. Braun has attributed that commercial failure to the music being "more adventurous and complicated than the other fusion groups that were working at the time," and it may be that this lesson has had the biggest influence on his subsequent music. His first solo recording was actually a pop vocal album done for a Japanese label.

Braun's first success came as a songwriter: in 1988 the soft-rock band REO Speedwagon had a Top 20 hit with his tune "Here with Me." He subsequently carved out a career as a background player (and singer) and has toured with many of the biggest names in pop music: Rickie Lee Jones, Sade, Rod Stewart, Tina Turner, Glenn Frey, Natalie Cole, Tom Petty, Crowded House, Phoebe Snow, and War. He also was heard playing the trumpet lead on the theme to the TV series *Mid-*

night Caller. His solo success has led him to shift his outside-work focus to production for Mesa/Bluemoon, most prominently acoustic guitarist Peppino D'Agostino, guitar and violin duo Willie and Lobo, and contemporary jazzers Avenue Blue.

what to buy: A big hit on contemporary jazz radio, Braun's breakthrough album *Night Walk* 𝄞𝄞𝄞 (Mesa/Bluemoon, 1994, prod. Rick Braun) was strongly influenced by the music Braun had played while he was the touring trumpeter for Sade on the *Love Deluxe* tour. Braun took that band's jazzy, lightly funky, and darkly ruminative sound, subtracted the vocals, substituted his mellow, rounded trumpet tone, and added some synthesizer and slightly richer harmonies for an appealing if unambitious sound which proclaims him the Herb Alpert of the '90s.

what to buy next: *Beat Street* 𝄞𝄞𝄞 (Mesa/Bluemoon, 1995, prod. Rick Braun) was influenced by another touring situation, Braun's time with the veteran funk band War, a lively and spontaneous group diametrically opposed in approach to the slickly polished and somber Sade. Though still slick in sound, it's more overtly funky and more of a loose blowing album, with not only Braun but tenor saxophonist Boney James and guitarist Jeff Golub distinguishing themselves soloistically.

what to avoid: *Christmas Present* 𝄞𝄞 (Mesa/Bluemoon, 1994/1997, prod. Rick Braun) mixes familiar Christmas material ("The Little Drummer Boy," Mel Tormé's "The Christmas Song," "Jingle Bells," "Do You Hear What I Hear," "O Tannenbaum") with Braun-penned songs. The selection of old stuff leans much too heavily on clichéd choices (mostly musically insignificant) and dresses them in overly smooth arrangements. A few of the new compositions are nice, but have more of a new-age feeling than anything jazz-like about them. It all adds up to nothing more than background music you'll only play one month a year, if then.

the rest:
Intimate Secrets 𝄞𝄞 (Mesa/Bluemoon, 1993)
Body and Soul 𝄞𝄞𝄞 (Mesa/Bluemoon, 1997)

influences:
◀◀ Herb Alpert, Miles Davis, Clifford Brown
▶▶ Chris Botti, Greg Adams, Mark Ledford

Steve Holtje

Anthony Braxton

Born June 4, 1945, in Chicago, IL.

It is no overstatement to say that Anthony Braxton is one of the most important composers of our time ... and, luckily, also one of the best-documented, with well over 100 albums issued in nearly 30 years (including those as a sideman and conductor). The scope of his compositions range from solo saxophone pieces to large ensemble works, which would more comfortably be classified in the genre of contemporary classical music.

Braxton studied at Chicago Musical College, then spent 1964–66 in the Army. Returning to Chicago, he joined the Association for the Advancement of Creative Musicians (AACM) and in 1968 made his first recordings as a solo artist, the double LP *For Alto*, and as a band leader, *Three Compositions of New Jazz* (with Leo Smith, Leroy Jenkins, and Muhal Richard Abrams). Both of these albums eventually made their appearance on Chicago's Delmark label. He moved to New York, where he lived with Ornette Coleman for a while. After giving up music for a year and supporting himself as a chess player, he began working with Chick Corea, which led to his joining the cooperative free jazz quartet Circle (with Corea, Dave Holland, and Barry Altschul). The group's two-year existence, and Delmark's release in 1971 of *For Alto* at a time when horn players rarely recorded solo recitals, served to finally bring attention to Braxton's distinctive music.

Since then, the sky has been the limit. Braxton has produced albums of standards with musicians including Mal Waldron, Cecil McBee, and Andrew Cyrille. He has also released recordings of very large ensembles such as *Composition No. 96*, *Two Compositions (Ensemble) 1989/91*, and *Composition No. 165*. Perhaps the performance format for which he is best-known and most praised is his quartet, which worked extensively in the 1980s and which included Marilyn Crispell (piano), Gerry Hemingway (percussion), and Mark Dresser (bass). Early charges that Braxton couldn't swing have long since been refuted; it's now clear that he can, when he wants to, but much of his music is not based on traditional jazz rhythms and structures.

In recent years, Braxton has set his sights on the piano and has made many recordings both solo and as a member of an ensemble. Hildegard Kleeb has also recorded a four-CD set on hat ART of the composer's notated piano works dating back to 1968. Possibly one of the most important developments in Braxton's career has been the formation of his own imprint called Braxton House. This new recording label was formed by Braxton and longtime associate Velibor Pedevski and has now become the main outlet for his musical voice. The initial string of releases includes a number of recordings of what Braxton has termed Ghost Trance Music. This music has its origins in culturally sacred, ritualistic music based on repeating phrases.

ANTHONY BRAXTON

song "Dewey Square"
album *Charlie Parker Project 1993*
(hat ART, 1993/1995)
instrument Alto saxophone

The tribes who would play such music could go on for hours, even days. Braxton has taken the spirit of this type of music and placed it in a secular context. Depending upon the intent of each piece, the recorded performances range from quartets to ensembles of eight to 11 players and last from 10 minutes to an hour. In each case, the effect is hypnotic, as one would expect in "trance" music. Short repeating phrases are unfolded in layers over a long period of time with an alternating focus on a group context or solo players. In the end, it is difficult to divorce this style of music from the American minimalist movement of the 1960s—i.e. Terry Riley, Steve Reich, etc. The effect is probably closer to Riley's *In C* than anything else of this type, but it could also make the listener think of Steve Reich's *Drumming* as well.

what to buy: *Willisau (Quartet) 1991* ♫♫♫♫ (hat ART, 1992, prod. Pia Uehlinger, Werner X. Uehlinger) is a four-CD set featuring some of the most polished playing by the classical quartet. Half of the set is studio recordings, the rest is a concert document. *Creative Orchestra 1976* ♫♫♫♫ (Arista, 1976, prod.

Steve Backer) and *Creative Orchestra (Köln) 1978* 🎵🎵🎵🎵 (hat ART, 1996, prod. Manfred Niehaus, WDR Köln) both document Braxton as composer and arranger. The first album is a studio recording and the second album represents a live concert performance taken from the archives of German radio many years later. On the double disc set *Charlie Parker Project 1993* 🎵🎵🎵🎵 (hat ART, 1993/1995, prod. Ulrich Kurth, Pia Uehlinger, Werner X. Uehlinger), Braxton leads an all-star cast including Paul Smoker (trumpet), Ari Brown (sax), Misha Mengelberg (piano), Joe Fonda (bass), and drummers Han Bennink and Pheeroan AkLaff on a full-tilt tribute to Bird's music. The first disc is recorded in concert (with Bennink) and the other disc is a studio recording (with AkLaff).

what to buy next: *Quartet (Birmingham) 1985* 🎵🎵🎵🎵 (Leo, 1991, prod. Leo Feigin), *Quartet (London) 1985* 🎵🎵🎵🎵 (Leo, 1990, prod. Leo Feigin), and *Quartet (Coventry) 1985* 🎵🎵🎵🎵 (Leo, 1993, prod. Leo Feigin) make up a trio of documents from the classic quartet's British tour. This tour was the subject of the book *Forces in Motion* by Graham Lock (see below). *Birth and Rebirth* 🎵🎵🎵🎵 (1978, Black Saint, prod. Giacomo Pelliccciotti) is a fine set of interactions between Braxton and drummer Max Roach. Recorded at the Victoriaville Festival in Quebec, Canada, *Victoriaville 1988* 🎵🎵🎵🎵 (Victo, 1992, prod. SRC) features a cooking seven-piece band with Evan Parker (sax), Bobby Naughton (vibes), Joelle Leandre (bass), Gerry Hemingway (drums), Paul Smoker (trumpet), and George Lewis (trombone). *Victoriaville 1992* 🎵🎵🎵 (Victo, 1993, prod. SRC) has the classic quartet, with bonus material on the CD version. *Four Compositions (Quartet) 1995* 🎵🎵🎵🎵 (Braxton House, 1997, prod. Anthony Braxton, Velibor Pedevski) contains four pieces of Ghost Trance Music stripped down to a quartet format. The works range from 10 to 20 minutes in length and give a good overview of Braxton's GTM. The quartet features Braxton along with Ted Reichman (accordion), Joe Fonda (bass), and Kevin Norton (percussion). *Tentet (New York) 1996* 🎵🎵🎵🎵 (Braxton House, 1996, prod. Anthony Braxton, Velibor Pedevski) features a larger ensemble performing Ghost Trance Music. The bigger group of musicians gives a lot of room for changing density and texture in the music.

what to avoid: Braxton's recent leanings towards performing on the piano have brought some mixed results. These should be approached well after the listener has gained an appreciation for his other work. For example, the set *Knitting Factory (Piano/Quartet) 1994, Vol. 1* 🎵🎵🎵 (Leo, 1995, prod. Leo Feigin) may be somewhat off-putting at first. Although the group of standards are rather lengthy, the recordings tend to fade out

before the pieces have a chance to resolve. Braxton's double disc *Solo Piano (Standards) 1995* 🎵🎵🎵 (No More, 1995, prod. Alan Schneider) is a slightly more accessible place to start with Braxton's piano musings.

best of the rest:

Three Compositions of New Jazz 🎵🎵🎵 (Delmark, 1968)
For Alto 🎵🎵🎵 (Delmark, 1968)
Composition No. 96 🎵🎵🎵 (Leo Records, 1981)
(With Richard Teitelbaum) *Open Aspects '82* 🎵🎵🎵 (hat ART, 1982/1995)
Four Compositions (Quartet) 1983 🎵🎵🎵 (Black Saint, 1983)
(With Gino Robair) *Duets 1987* 🎵🎵🎵🎵 (Rastascan, 1987)
19 (Solo) Improvisations 1988 🎵🎵🎵 (New Albion, 1988)
Seven Compositions (Trio) 1989 🎵🎵🎵🎵 (hat ART, 1989)
Eight (+3) Tristano Compositions 1989 🎵🎵🎵🎵 (hat ART, 1989)
(With Marilyn Crispell) *Duets Vancouver 1989* 🎵🎵🎵 (Music & Arts, 1989)
Eugene 1989 🎵🎵🎵🎵 (Black Saint, 1989)
Two Compositions (Ensemble) 1989/1991 🎵🎵🎵🎵 (hat ART, 1989/1991)
Dortmund (Quartet) 1976 🎵🎵🎵🎵 (hat ART, 1991)
Town Hall (Trio & Quintet) 1972 🎵🎵🎵🎵 (hat ART, 1992)
Composition No. 165 🎵🎵🎵 (New Albion, 1992)
Wesleyan 12 (Altosolos) 1992 🎵🎵🎵 (hat ART, 1993)
(With Evan Parker) *Duo (London) 1993* 🎵🎵🎵🎵 (Leo Records, 1995)
Composition No. 173 🎵🎵🎵 (Black Saint, 1996)
(With Fred Simmons) *9 Standards (Quartet) 1993* 🎵🎵🎵 (Leo Records, 1996)
Composition No. 102 for Orchestra & Puppet Theatre 🎵🎵🎵 (Braxton House, 1996)
Sextet (Instanbul) 1996 🎵🎵🎵🎵 (Braxton House, 1996)
(With Brett Larner) *11 Compositions (Duo) 1995* 🎵🎵🎵 (Leo Records, 1997)
Ensemble (New York) 1995 🎵🎵🎵🎵 (Braxton House, 1997)

worth searching for: The LP *New York, Fall 1974* 🎵🎵🎵🎵 (Arista, 1975, prod. Michael Cuscuna) contains six compositions which feature Kenny Wheeler, Dave Holland, Richard Teitelbaum, Julius Hemphill, Oliver Lake, Hamiet Bluiett, and Leroy Jenkins. The sequel LP *Five Piece Pieces 1975* 🎵🎵🎵🎵 (Arista, 1975, prod. Michael Cuscuna) offers five more works recorded in New York with Wheeler, Holland, and Barry Altschul. Braxton has been the subject of a number of books on his work. Two worth starting with are the biography *New Musical Figurations* by Ronald M. Radano (University of Chicago Press, 1993) and the document of his 1985 British tour *Forces in Motion* (Quartet Books, 1988) by Graham Lock. These are essential reads for any fan wanting to learn more about the composer. Braxton has also compiled his own books dealing with his works. This has taken the form of a pair of multiple volumes. Firstly, there are the *Tri-Axium Writings* (Synthesis Music, 1985), a three-volume set of the composer's theories. Secondly, there are five volumes of

Composition Notes (Synthesis Music, 1988) which detail the structure and theory behind the individual compositions. These are both very dense sets of books which are recommended to the most serious fans or students of the composer.

influences:

◀◀ Association for the Advancement of Creative Musicians, Art Ensemble of Chicago, John Coltrane, Charlie Parker, Paul Desmond, Lee Konitz, Eric Dolphy, Karlheinz Stockhausen

▶▶ Steve Norton, Marilyn Crispell

Chris Meloche

Joshua Breakstone

Born 1955, in Elizabeth, NJ.

Berklee graduate Breakstone is a well-grounded, bop-influenced guitarist, educator, and clinician. He has taught at the Rhode Island Conservatory of Music and given clinics at the University of South Florida, the University of Miami, the University of North Florida, and the University of Alberta (Canada). Breakstone has recorded albums with Tommy Flanagan, Barry Harris, Jack McDuff, and Joanne Brackeen in addition to working with kindred guitarists Emily Remler and Vic Juris.

what to buy: The quartet session *Self Portrait in Swing* ♫♫♫♫ (Contemporary, 1989, prod. Joshua Breakstone) with Kenny Barron on piano, Dennis Irwin on bass, and drummer Kenny Washington sounds like it was fun. The up-tempo title tune whizzes by the ear with everything in perfect control before settling in to land on Irving Berlin's luscious ballad "Count Your Blessings." Breakstone the composer has two songs on this album, the title piece and a mildly Caribbean-flavored "Salisway," scoring with the prior and whiffing on the second. The cover tunes make the album work, especially the bossa nova-style arrangement of Lerner and Lowe's "If Ever I Would Leave You."

what to buy next: *Remembering Grant Green* ♫♫♫ (Evidence, 1993, prod. Joshua Breakstone) is meant as a tribute to the great guitarist Grant Green, dwelling mostly on material plucked from the classic Blue Note releases. It helps that Breakstone enlisted organist Jack McDuff and drummer Al Harewood to play on most of these tunes, since McDuff is one of the many B-3 players who worked with Green, while Harewood had a hand in two of Green's finest albums, *Idle Moments* and *Grandstand*. That stab at authenticity aside, Breakstone has produced pleasant readings of Grant's classic performances on "Grandstand," "Green's Greenery," and Duke Pearson's "Idle Moments," but nothing that will supplant the origi-

nals. Still, it's a well-crafted album and deserves a hearing from guitar aficionados.

the rest:

Evening Star ♫♫♫ (Contemporary, 1987)
9 By 3 ♫♫♫ (Contemporary, 1991)
Walk, Don't Run ♫♫♫ (Evidence, 1993)

influences:

◀◀ Barney Kessel, Johnny Smith, Grant Green, Lee Morgan, Charlie Parker

Garaud MacTaggart

Lenny Breau

Born August 5, 1941, in Auburn, ME. Died August 12, 1984, in Los Angeles, CA.

As a guitarist, Maine native Lenny Breau strung together elements of jazz, rock, and classical. Growing up, his musical influences included his own parents, who were the country and western performing duo Hal "Lone Pine" Breau and Betty Cody. Although he began playing country in the style of his parents, mostly in Canada, in the late 1960s he recorded two LPs with his own trio that established him as primarily a jazz guitarist in the vein of George Benson (whom he later played with). Other musicians he worked with included Don Thompson (Canadian double-bass player and pianist) and Claude Ranger (Canadian drummer) and, in a return to his country roots, Chet Atkins. Breau was compared to pianist Bill Evans for the way he changed the inner workings of chords in a creative way. Meanwhile, he sang in a style reminiscent of Chet Baker. He also wrote a monthly instructional column for *Guitar Player* from 1981 until his untimely death just days after his 43rd birthday.

what to buy: *The Velvet Touch of Lenny Breau* ♫♫♫♫ (RCA/One Way, 1969, prod. Danny Davis, Ronny Light) is fantastic. This live album, recorded at Shelley's Manne-hole, is probably his all-time best.

the rest:

Five O'Clock Bells/Mo' Breau ♫♫♫ (Genes, 1989)
Last Sessions ♫♫♫ (Genes, 1988)

worth searching for: *Chance Meeting* ♫♫♫♫ (Guitarchives) pairs Breau with fellow six-stringer Tal Farlow. This Canadian release feature all standards, including "My Foolish Heart," "Cherokee," and "My Funny Valentine."

influences:

◀◀ Bill Evans, George Benson, Chet Baker

Joe S. Harrington

Zachary Breaux

Born June 26, 1960, in Port Arthur, TX. Died February 20, 1997, in Miami, FL.

Breaux took jazz and his native Texas blues and combined them with hip-hop and funk rhythms to create a distinctive and very contemporary sound. As a youngster growing up in Port Arthur, Texas (the birthplace of Janis Joplin), Breaux began playing the guitar at age nine and performed in bands throughout high school. He attended North Texas State University, where he studied composition. On the advice of veteran trumpeter Donald Byrd, Breaux relocated to New York City during the mid-1980s and performed with many well-known artists, including Byrd, saxophonist Stanley Turrentine, violinist Noel Pointer, and vibraphonist Roy Ayers, in whose band he played for six years. Breaux's first solo album *Groovin'* was recorded live at Ronnie Scott's legendary London jazz club during an Ayers performance and features a guest appearance by Ayers.

Groovin' was critically well-received and launched Breaux on a promising solo career. His last recording, *Uptown Groove*, reached #1 on the smooth-jazz radio charts even before its release in late January 1997. Breaux seemed to be poised for major stardom, but his life was cut short by a tragic accident. While vacationing in Miami with his family, he dove into the ocean to rescue a swimmer caught in a riptide. Breaux, who was in excellent physical shape, had saved a swimmer from drowning a few years earlier while on tour in Italy, but this time he too was caught in the powerful current and suffered a fatal heart attack when he was pulled ashore.

what to buy: *Uptown Groove* ♫♫♫♫ (Zebra Records, 1997, prod. Zachary Breaux) offered more elaborate production than on Breaux's earlier efforts. This album features a collection of well-crafted, highly accessible tunes, including a catchy cover of Isaac Hayes's "Cafe Reggio," a respectful yet completely updated take on Miles Davis's classic "All Blues," and the retro-jazzy-bluesy-funky title track.

what to buy next: *Groovin'* ♫♫♫♫ (NYC, 1992, prod. Chris Lewis, Zachary Breaux) was an auspicious debut that amply showcases Breaux's astounding versatility, as he moves effortlessly from the Latin-spiced Tito Puente tune "Piccadillo" to the stately self-penned blues "Alice (Down in Parks Louisiana—August 1906–August 1991)." The production isn't the greatest—pianist Rex Rideout is a bit buried—but it demonstrates Breaux's easy give-and-take with his band, his marvelous technique, and his improvisational talent.

the rest:
Laidback ♫♫♫ (NYC Records, 1994, prod. Zachary Breaux)

influences:
◄◄ George Benson, Wes Montgomery, B.B. King

Lucy Tauss

Michael Brecker

Born March 29, 1949, in Philadelphia, PA.

Michael Brecker is among that generation of jazz musicians that saw rock music not as the enemy, but as a viable musical option. After only a year at Indiana University, he moved to New York City in 1970 and quickly carved out a niche for himself as a dynamic and exciting soloist. He picked up the gauntlet laid down by King Curtis and Maceo Parker to become the preeminent pop/R&B/funk saxophone soloist of the 1970s and early 1980s. He first made his mark at age 21 as a member of the jazz/rock band Dreams—a band that included brother Randy, Billy Cobham, Jeff Kent, and Doug Lubahn. Dreams was short-lived, lasting only a year, but influential (Miles Davis was seen at some gigs prior to his recording *Jack Johnson*).

Despite the limited success of Dreams, it was apparent that Brecker was a soloist to be reckoned with. Most of his early work is marked by an approach informed as much by rock guitar as by R&B saxophone. After Dreams, he worked with Horace Silver and then Billy Cobham before he and brother Randy teamed up once again. The newly formed Brecker Brothers Band played fusion that was equal parts bar band, Thelonious Monk, and Sly Stone. The band followed the trail blazed by Miles Davis's 1970s bands and Weather Report, but with more attention to structured arrangements, a heavier backbeat, and stronger rock influence. The band stayed together from 1975 to 1982 with consistent success and musicality.

At the same time, Brecker put his stamp on numerous pop and rock recordings with brief but energizing solos. His most notable collaborations were with James Taylor, Steely Dan, Donald Fagen, and Joni Mitchell. His solos on Fagen's "Maxine" and Joni Mitchell's version of "Dry Cleaner from Des Moines" are particularly noteworthy. During the early 1980s he was also a member of NBC's *Saturday Night Live* band. Brecker can be seen in the background sporting shades during Eddie Murphy's parody of James Brown, "Get in the Hot Tub."

Michael Brecker **(AP/Wide World Photos)**

After a brief stint co-leading all-star group Steps Ahead with Mike Mainieri, Brecker finally went solo. His eponymously titled debut album marked his return to a more traditional jazz setting, highlighted his compositional talents, and featured the EWI (Electronic Wind Instrument), a saxophone-triggered synthesizer. Given a chance to stretch out on his solo projects, Brecker takes full advantage and shows off his considerable tenor chops. His following solo releases, as well as Brecker Brothers reunion albums, maintain the high standard of musicianship established on his first solo album. His bright incisive tone, jaw-dropping technique, and harmonic daring are instantly recognizable. All of this, combined with his unmatched versatility, has made him one of the most recorded saxophonists since 1975. His mainstream credentials have by now been firmly established by his work with McCoy Tyner.

what to buy: His solo debut album *Michael Brecker* 𝄞𝄞𝄞𝄞 (Impulse!, 1987, prod. Don Grolnick, Michael Brecker) features Brecker in top form with the added bonus of outstanding supporting players (Jack DeJohnette, Charlie Haden, Pat Metheny, and Kenny Kirkland). The return to a jazzier setting is liberating. Brecker's playing is more rhythmically adventurous and he seems eager to explore small melodic motifs and new sonorities. "Original Rays" and "Syzygy" highlight his knack for sophisticated jazz fusion composition. Overall, the album is harmonically and rhythmically complex but at the same time very accessible. Nearly 20 years after it was recorded, the Brecker Brothers' funk/rock live recording *Heavy Metal Be-Bop* 𝄞𝄞𝄞𝄞 (Arista, 1978/One Way, 1996, prod. Randy Brecker, Michael Brecker) still gets the "chicken neck" going. You can't help yourself, it's just that funky. Randy plays the be-bop to Michael's heavy metal. Both add a variety of electronic effects and pedals to their instruments. Whipping the crowd into a frenzy on "Inside Out," "Sponge," and their signature tune "Some Skunk Funk," they show off their unique brand of jazz funk to its fullest. Michael's cadenza on "Funky Sea, Funky Dew" is a brilliant display of his trademark pyrotechnical saxophone playing.

what to buy next: Cut from the same mold as his solo debut, *Tales from the Hudson* (Impulse!, 1996, prod. George Whity, Michael Brecker) shows Brecker's continuing growth and development as a composer and performer. The album is more relaxed and confident than his three previous outings. Gigging and recording with McCoy Tyner seems to have sparked his debt to Coltrane. The title of *Now You See It . . . (Now You Don't)* 𝄞𝄞𝄞𝄞 (GRP Records, 1990, prod. Don Grolnick) is a sly reference to a pop tune Michael was unceremoniously mixed out of. The album shows Brecker leaning more on his fusion

roots than on his solo debut, with increased EWI contributions. His compositions show a rhythmic and harmonic sophistication not found in most typical fusion recordings. "Ode to the Doo Da Day" and "Peep" point to a humorous and carefree side of Brecker's playing. "Escher Sketch" demonstrates a particular flair for time changes without sacrificing the heavy groove.

what to avoid: Despite the group's reputed influence, *Dreams* 𝄞 (Columbia/Legacy, 1992, prod. Fred Weinberg, Dreams) doesn't show off its strengths. Limited solos and a late 1960s/early 1970s style of jazz/rock that hasn't aged well drag the album down. Reportedly, they were amazing in concert. They'd have to have been.

the rest:

(With the Brecker Brothers) *The Brecker Brothers* 𝄞𝄞𝄞 (Arista, 1975/One Way)

(With the Brecker Brothers) *Back to Back* 𝄞𝄞𝄞 (Arista, 1976/One Way)

(With the Brecker Brothers) *Don't Stop the Music* 𝄞𝄞𝄞 (Arista, 1977/One Way)

(With the Brecker Brothers) *Detente* 𝄞𝄞 (Arista, 1980/One Way, 1996)

(With the Brecker Brothers) *Straphangin'* 𝄞𝄞𝄞 (Arista, 1981/One Way, 1995)

Don't Try This at Home 𝄞𝄞𝄞 (Impulse!, 1988)

(With the Brecker Brothers) *The Brecker Brothers Collection, Vol. 1* 𝄞𝄞𝄞 (Novus, 1990)

(With the Brecker Brothers) *The Brecker Brothers Collection, Vol. 2* 𝄞𝄞𝄞 (Novus, 1991)

(With the Brecker Brothers) *Return of the Brecker Brothers* 𝄞𝄞𝄞 (GRP, 1992)

(With the Brecker Brothers) *Out of the Loop* 𝄞𝄞𝄞 (GRP, 1994)

worth searching for: Guitarist Jack Wilkins's *You Can't Live Without It* 𝄞𝄞𝄞𝄞 (Chiaroscuro, 1977, prod. Hank O'Neal) features Michael flexing his jazz chops early in his career on standards such as "What's New," "What Is This Thing Called Love," and "Invitation." (It may currently be more easily found as part of the double album *Merge*.) McCoy Tyner's *Infinity* 𝄞𝄞𝄞𝄞 (Impulse!, 1995, prod. Michael Cuscuna) finds Brecker exercising his Coltrane muscles, most notably on the sax legend's own "Impressions."

influences:

◄◄ John Coltrane, Joe Henderson, Wayne Shorter

►► Bob Berg, Warren Hill, Donny McCaslin

James Eason

Randy Brecker

Born November 27, 1945, in Philadelphia, PA.

Randy Brecker made a name for himself as one of the first true jazz/rock crossover artists, appearing on records by Blood, Sweat and Tears and Steely Dan. With his brother, Michael, he formed the Brecker Brothers, who specialized in staccato funk rhythms (as the semi-hit "Some Skunk Funk" demonstrates). Over the years, he has acted as a sideman for many notable jazz and rock musicians. A partial list includes Clark Terry, Duke Pearson, Thad Jones, Mel Lewis, Joe Henderson, Frank Foster, Dreams, Larry Coryell, Billy Cobham, Steely Dan, Lou Reed, and Aerosmith. The Brecker Brothers reunited in the 1980s and 1990s, but by then it was an idea that had gone stale.

what to buy: Randy's *Score* 🎵🎵🎵 (Blue Note, 1969, prod. Duke Pearson) features Larry Coryell. *The Brecker Brothers* 🎵🎵🎵 (Arista 1975, prod. Randy Brecker, Michael Brecker) contains "Some Skunk Funk," a minor funk/disco/fusion hit. Randy's *In the Idiom* 🎵🎵🎵 (Denon, 1988, prod. Randy Brecker) has Joe Henderson, Dave Kikoski, Ron Carter, and Al Foster. It's a step above fusion, but a step below respectable jazz.

what to buy next: The Brecker Brothers' live album *Heavy Metal Be-Bop* 🎵🎵🎵 (Arista, 1978/One Way, 1996, prod. Randy Brecker, Michael Brecker) shows why these two musicians/showmen captured the fancy of the studio/sidemen set in the 1970s—and ultimately why they should've remained in the studio. Randy's *Live at Sweet Basil* 🎵🎵🎵 (GNP/Crescendo, 1988) showcases occasional moments of brilliance and features a sterling cast including Bob Berg, Dave Kikoski, Dieter Ilg, and Joey Baron.

what to avoid: *Detente* **woof!** (Arista, 1980/One Way, 1996, prod. George Duke) is total disco dreck, with a cast of no-names (Ginch Howard?) replacing the usual stalwarts.

the rest:
(With the Brecker Brothers) *Back to Back* 🎵🎵 (Arista, 1976/One Way)
(With the Brecker Brothers) *Don't Stop the Music* 🎵🎵 (Arista, 1977/One Way)
(With the Brecker Brothers) *Straphangin'* 🎵🎵🎵 (Arista, 1981/One Way, 1995)
(With the Brecker Brothers) *The Brecker Brothers Collection, Vol. 1* 🎵🎵🎵 (Novus, 1990)
(With the Brecker Brothers) *The Brecker Brothers Collection, Vol. 2* 🎵🎵🎵 (Novus, 1991)
(With the Brecker Brothers) *Return of the Brecker Brothers* 🎵🎵🎵 (GRP, 1992)
(With the Brecker Brothers) *Out of the Loop* 🎵🎵 (GRP, 1994)
Into the Sun 🎵🎵🎵 (Concord Vista, 1997)

worth searching for: Some of Randy Brecker's many sideman gigs shed light on his abilities. Larry Coryell's *Introducing Larry Coryell & the 11th House* 🎵🎵🎵 (Vanguard, 1972) is a sterling fusion super session with Brecker, Alphonse Mouzon, Mike Man-

dell (keyboards), and Danny Trifan (bass). Billy Cobham's *Cross-winds* 🎵🎵🎵 (Atlantic, 1974, prod. Billy Cobham) at the time was considered one of the five great fusion records, but actually it's fusion for easy listening. *Me, Myself an Eye* 🎵🎵🎵 (Atlantic, 1978, prod. Ilhan Mimaroglu) was the last album by famed bassist Charles Mingus, with an assortment of glad-hands on deck, including both Breckers.

influences:
◀◀ Miles Davis, Blood, Sweat & Tears

Joe S. Harrington

Willem Breuker

Born November 4, 1944, in Amsterdam, Netherlands.

Reedman, composer, and arranger Willem Breuker is one of the most important musicians to emerge from the Netherlands. In 1967, along with Misha Mengelberg and Han Bennink, he co-founded the Instant Composers Pool, a nonprofit organization that sponsored concerts and issued recordings by the Dutch avant-garde. While he was involved with the organization, from 1967–72, he issued four albums, including a legendary duo session with drummer Bennink full of fire and anarchy. But at the same time he was issuing albums of composed barrel organ, opera, film, and small-group music. A major participant in the free-jazz ferment brewing throughout Europe in the late '60s, he played with the Peter Brotzmann Octet, the initial Globe Unity Orchestra, and Gunter Hampel's quartet.

In the early '70s, Breuker eschewed the anarchy associated with the Instant Composers Pool and formed his own ensemble (Kollektief) and record label (Bvhaast), both of which have lasted for 25 years. Initially, Kollektief performed his compositions, but its repertoire grew to include compositions by Kurt Weill and Bertolt Brecht, Duke Ellington, Erik Satie, George Gershwin, and Ennio Morricone. In live performance, the Kollektief developed an antic style, sometimes surreal and sometimes bordering on vaudeville. Although the Kollektief has been his main focus, Breuker has also composed orchestral and chamber works.

what to buy: *De Onderste Steen* 🎵🎵🎵🎵 (Entr'acte, 1972/1991, prod. Channel Classics Studio, Willem Breuker), a sampler of Breuker's Instant Composers Pool work dating to 1972, includes a tango, an orchestral work from 1978, and a piece written for jazz accordionist Johnny Meyer. There's also a healthy dose of Kollektief material, including Breuker's haunting elegy to Duke Ellington, "Duke Edward/Miserere" with a beautiful wah-wah solo by trumpeter Boy Raaymakers. With so much more work out of print, a more appropriate title might be "The Incomplete Breuker." But, as it stands, it's an excellent introduction to his music. The Kollektief's *Bob's Gallery* 𝄞𝄞𝄞𝄞 (Bvhaast, 1987, prod. Willem Breuker, Kollektief), a rousing selection of mostly Breuker compositions played by a strong edition of the Kollektief, includes a 24-minute title track that ends wildly, a mock-Philip Glass piece played with verve, and a wonderful tribute to obscure Boston pianist Dick Twardzik. *A Paris Summer Music* 𝄞𝄞𝄞𝄞 (Marge, 1978, prod. Gerard Terrones) is the only disc available with the looser, solo-heavy '70s edition of the Kollektief. Also, the group had three of its best voices in the burly tenor saxophone of Maarten van Norden, the expressive trombone of William van Manan, and a true original, pianist Leo Cuypers (who sings a devastating "Let's Fall in Love").

what to buy next: Breuker's *Baal Brecht Breuker Handke* 𝄞𝄞𝄞𝄞 (Bvhaast, 1973–74, prod. Willem Breuker) inclues music for two theatre pieces from the days just before he formed the Kollektief. Although this music for Brecht's "Baal" is mostly composed, the tart, distinctive voicings could only come from Breuker. The CD, like its LP predecessor, comes in a burlap sack. The Kollektief's *Vera Beths—Mondriaan Strings* (Bvhaast, 1987–88, prod. Willem Breuker, Kollektief) includes four Gershwin pieces, such as an arrangement of "An American in Paris" by the Kollektief's pianist Henk de Jonge. It also includes the Kollektief in a North African mode on the leader's "Sahara Sack" and a version of Alexander von Schlippenbach's "Minor Double Blues" with strings.

what to avoid: The Kollektief's *Sensemaya* 𝄞𝄞𝄞 (Bvhaast, 1995) is a program of odds and ends, mostly light classics including Antheil's "Jazz Symphony" and Leroy Anderson's "The Typewriter." But there are two Breuker pieces worth hearing: "Four City Views" and the oboe concerto "Han De Vries." Best of all is a 12-minute kaleidoscopic arrangement of Gershwin's "Night and Day."

best of the rest:
Overtime/Uberstunden 𝄞𝄞𝄞𝄞 (NM Classics, 1993)
(With Kollektief) *Metropolis* 𝄞𝄞𝄞𝄞 (Bvhaast, 1987–89)
(With Kollektief) *Parade* 𝄞𝄞𝄞𝄞 (Bvhaast, 1990–91)
(With Kollektief) *Heibel* 𝄞𝄞𝄞𝄞 (Bvhaast, 1991)

worth searching for: Breuker's *Instant Composers Pool 007/008* 𝄞𝄞𝄞𝄞 (I.C.P., 1968–70), like the entire Instant Composers Pool back catalog, should be reissued. Originally packaged in a circular box, this two-LP set collected various Breuker recordings for theatre, live excerpts, and a piece for a mandolin orchestra.

influences:
◀◀ Kurt Weill, Duke Ellington, Nino Rota, Rahsaan Roland Kirk
▶▶ Gunter Hampel, John Zorn

Robert Iannapollo

Dee Dee Bridgewater
Born May 27, 1950, in Memphis, TN.

One of best and most charismatic jazz singers of her generation, Dee Dee Bridgewater has emerged in the 1990s as a worthy heir to Ella, Sarah, and Dinah. Whether singing standards or improvising ferociously as she scats, Bridgewater maintains a commanding stage presence, honed by her years of experience on and off Broadway. As a jazz singer, she long ago surpassed her early influences—Nina Simone, Nancy Wilson, Lena Horne, and Gloria Lynne—though in recent years her voice has taken on shades of Sarah Vaughan and Carmen McRae. Bridgewater was raised in a musical family (her father was a trumpeter) and began singing as a teenager. She met her first husband, trumpeter Cecil Bridgewater, while he was working with Horace Silver. She sang with the Thad Jones/Mel Lewis Orchestra in 1972–74, but recorded with the band only once, a wordless vocal on "Suite for Pops." She began a parallel stage career in the mid-1970s, appearing in *The Wiz, Sophisticated Ladies, Lady Day,* and other shows. She moved to France in the early 1980s and began reestablishing herself as a jazz singer, but legal disputes with a label kept her from recording. Her albums for Verve in the 1990s paved the way for an extremely successful U.S. tour in 1997.

what to buy: It had been years since she had released an album, so the appearance of *In Montreux* 𝄞𝄞𝄞𝄞 (Verve, 1991, prod. Dee Dee Bridgewater) created quite a stir. Accompanied by her top-notch European rhythm section, Bridgewater keeps thing loose by letting the band stretch out. She handles a range of material with style, from a gentle version of Jobim's "How Insensitive" to a thrilling three-tune Horace Silver medley. This is the work of a great musician coming into her own. Though not quite as exciting as her first Verve release, *Keeping Tradition* 𝄞𝄞𝄞𝄞 (Verve, 1993, prod. Dee Dee Bridgewater) finds Bridgewater exploring 13 standards. Completely at ease with her excellent accompanists (pianist Theirry Eliez, drummer Andre Ceccarelli, and bassist Hein Van de Geyn, who also wrote all the arrangements), Bridgewater shows off her chops on

"Fascinating Rhythm" and once again finds treasures in the Horace Silver songbook with "Love Vibrations" and "Sister Sadie." One of the best vocal albums of the decade, *Love and Peace: A Tribute to Horace Silver* ♫♫♫♫ (Verve, 1995, prod. Dee Dee Bridgewater) is a delight from start to finish. Silver's lyrics aren't always as inspired as his music, but Bridgewater, accompanied by her working European quintet, brings so much vitality and energy to this session she carries the music along with the force of her personality. The Maestro himself plays piano on his two best-known tunes, "Nica's Dream" and "Song for My Father," and Jimmy Smith's organ pushes the soul quotient on "Filthy McNasty" and "The Jody Grind."

what to buy next: A well-crafted though somewhat subdued album, *Prelude to a Kiss* ♫♫♫♫ (Philips, 1996, prod. Robert Sadin) features an ad hoc all-star jazz band billed as the Hollywood Bowl Orchestra playing a dozen Ellington classics. Bridgewater sings on six tracks, including a sultry "I'm Beginning to See the Light" and a movingly plaintive "Come Sunday." With Wynton Marsalis, Charles McPherson, Bobby Watson, Cyrus Chestnut, Ira Coleman, and Jeff Hamilton all featured soloists, Bridgewater could have been given more room to stretch out and more creatively integrated into the ensemble.

the rest:
Just Family ♫♫♫ (Elektra, 1977)
Live in Paris ♫♫♫♫ (MCA, 1987)
Dear Ella ♫♫♫♫ (Verve, 1997)

influences:
◀◀ Lena Horne, Nancy Wilson, Sarah Vaughan, Ella Fitzgerald

Andrew Gilbert

Nick Brignola

Born July 17, 1936, in Troy, NY.

One of the premier baritone saxophonists in jazz, Nick Brignola is a hard-charging player capable of generating tremendous momentum on up-tempo pieces and playing with great lyricism on ballads. Using the large horn's entire range, Brignola is a nimble improvisor firmly rooted in the bop tradition. He is also an accomplished soprano and tenor saxophonist, but his baritone playing marks him as one of the instrument's very best practitioners. Brignola started on alto and began playing baritone when he was 19. He attended Berklee and played with Herb Pomeroy, Cal Tjader, and the Mastersounds early in his career. He toured with Woody Herman in 1963 and in 1967 worked widely in Europe with Ted Curson. His credits also include dates with such diverse musicians as Jay McShann, Doc

Cheatham, Clark Terry, Chet Baker, Ralph Towner, Dewey Redman, Pat Metheny, and Lee Konitz. An extremely versatile musician, Brignola has played both Dixieland and free jazz and led fusion bands for much of the 1970s and early 1980s, including one with bassist Dave Holland, though since the mid-'80s he's mostly led small acoustic combos. Brignola has recorded for Beehive, Interplay, and Discovery, though besides one session on Night Life, his excellent series of albums for Reservoir are his only sessions available on CD.

what to buy: From the title track's opening note, Brignola's powerful baritone is hurdling down the track like a runaway locomotive on *Like Old Times* ♫♫♫♫ (Reservoir, 1994, prod. Mark Feldman), an excellent quintet session featuring Claudio Roditi (trumpet, flugelhorn), John Hicks (piano), George Mraz (bass), and Dick Berk (drums). He switches to soprano on Roditi's attractive Brazilian-calypso "Lambari" and plays some impressively fluid clarinet on "More Than You Know." He plays bari, though, on the album's highlight, the jam session–like version of "The Night Has a Thousand Eyes," featuring strong solos all around and some highly kinetic trap work by Berk. With the redoubtable rhythm section of Kenny Barron (piano), Rufus Reid (bass), and Victor Lewis (drums), *The Flight of the Eagle* ♫♫♫♫ (Reservoir, 1996, prod. Mark Feldman) is simply great straight-ahead jazz played by four masters. Brignola sticks entirely to bari, which is just fine because no one plays the large horn with as much energy and dexterity. Brignola offers a classy tip of the hat to fellow bari master with "Gerrylike," based on the opening phrase of Mulligan's "Youngblood," and evokes the spirit of Wayne Shorter with the title track (which features some striking piano work). Lewis plays with great power and sensitivity throughout, though he's sitting out on two of the album's most memorable tunes, a mid-tempo version of "Body and Soul" and an achingly tender reading of "My Foolish Heart."

what to buy next: Brignola shows off his eclectic taste on *Raincheck* ♫♫♫♫ (Reservoir, 1988, prod. Mark Feldman), a strong quartet session with an all-star rhythm section featuring Kenny Barron (piano), George Mraz (bass), and Billy Hart (drums). Highlights include the marvelously inventive piano/baritone duet on "Darn That Dream," Brignola's intensely lyrical version of "My Ship," and his swinging take on Cannonball Adderley's "Hurricane Connie." He also shows off his piquant, woody soprano sound on Ralph Towner's "North Star" and his liquid clarinet work on "Tenderly." Brignola sticks mostly to the bari throughout *On a Different Level* ♫♫♫♫ (Reservoir, 1989, prod. Mark Feldman), a tough session featuring longtime collaborator Holland, frequent recording partner Barron, and powerhouse drummer Jack DeJohnette. The material ranges from a sinuous samba version of Benny Carter's "Key Largo" and a torrid run through Tadd Dameron's bebop anthem "Hot House" to a deeply expressive take on Ornette Coleman's "Tears Inside" and a gorgeous, singing version of Mingus's "Duke Ellington's Sounds of Love."

best of the rest:
L.A. Bound ����� (Night Life, 1990)
What It Takes ����� (Reservoir, 1991)
It's Time ����� (Reservoir, 1992)
Live at Sweet Basil, First Set ����� (Reservoir, 1993)

worth searching for: Brignola's huge bari sound gives Phil Woods's octet the heft of a big band on *Evolution* ����� (Concord Jazz, 1988, prod. Bill Goodwin), a strong session with three horns augmenting the alto saxophonist's regular quintet with trumpeter Tom Harrell. Featured on Woods's tune "Song for Sisyphus," Brignola solos with high flying passion.

influences:
◀◀ Pepper Adams, Serge Chaloff, Cecil Payne

Andrew Gilbert

Alan Broadbent

Born April 23, 1947, in Auckland, New Zealand.

Alan Broadbent is a Berklee College of Music alumnus, having won a *Downbeat* scholarship in the mid-1960s which led him to leave his native New Zealand and attend the school. While at Berklee, Broadbent also spent some time studying with pianist and composer Lennie Tristano. Best known as an arranger, Broadbent has done charts for Woody Herman (with whom he was nominated for two Grammy Awards), Sheila Jordan, Natalie Cole, and a wide variety of other artists. He is a talented pianist and an in-demand accompanist for singers and other instrumentalists. His performing credits include having played with Bud Shank, Irene Kral, Sue Raney, and Charlie Haden in addition to leading his own groups. While his bread-and-butter focus as a composer lies with his jazz work, Broadbent has also written original works for orchestra that blend jazz and traditional European classical elements.

what to buy: Once again, the Concord Jazz Maybeck Recital series has come up with a winner; *Live at Maybeck Recital Hall, Vol. 14* ����� (Concord Jazz, 1991, prod. Carl E. Jefferson, Nick Phillips) is the kind of album you play for people needing an introduction to the artist as piano player. Broadbent is a solid, focused pianist and his arranging skills help him present an inter-

esting selection of music in the best possible light. Titles by Lennie Tristano ("Lennie's Pennies") and Bud Powell ("Parisian Thoroughfare") pay tribute to two of Broadbent's influences, while his own remembrance of Woody Herman ("Woody 'n' I") is a stunningly beautiful melody.

what to buy next: *Better Days* ����� (Discovery, 1992, prod. Albert Marx) is a selection of Broadbent performances from three 1980s-era trio dates produced for Discovery. They feature the pianist in the company of Patrick "Putter" Smith on bass and fellow New Zealander Frank Gibson Jr. behind the drum kit. It's a comfortable-sounding collection (despite some virtuoso flourishes from the pianist) with a nice selection of Broadbent-penned tunes combined with Lennie Tristano's classy "317 East 32nd Street" (the address of Tristano's studio during the 1950s) and material from John Coltrane and Clifford Brown tossed in for good measure. *Pacific Standard Time* ����� (Concord Jazz, 1995, prod. Nick Phillips) reunites the trio of Broadbent, Putter, and Gibson in a slightly more relaxed set of sessions. Concord Jazz sessions usually don't feature a lot of original material, preferring instead to have their performers cover a variety of standards. In this case, they should have allowed Broadbent a little more flexibility given his compositional skills. Only one original surfaces here, the marvelously idiomatic "This One's for Bud," but given the prior caveat, the rest of this recording offers up some nice interpretations of such chestnuts as "Someday My Prince Will Come," Cole Porter's "Easy to Love," and a really moving rendition of John Lewis's classic "Django."

the rest:
(With Gary Foster) *Concord Duo Series, Vol. 4* ����� (Concord Jazz, 1993)
Personal Standards ����� (Concord Jazz, 1996/1997)

influences:
◀◀ Lennie Tristano, Bud Powell, Bill Evans, Charlie Parker

Garaud MacTaggart

Bob Brookmeyer

Born December 19, 1929, in Kansas City, MO.

Having originally studied piano, Bob Brookmeyer took up valve trombone when he was 23 years old. As a pianist, Brookmeyer worked with the Tex Beneke band in 1951, with Claude Thornhill as trombonist and second piano in 1952, and with Teddy Charles in 1954. Emerging on the scene as a major jazz figure in 1953, he worked with Stan Getz, then replaced Chet Baker in the Gerry Mulligan Quartet, and also gained notoriety as a member of the Jimmy Guiffre Three, an unprecedented trio, with Guiffre on reeds and guitarist Jim Hall. When Mulligan formed his Concert Jazz Band, Brookmeyer joined the group as an arranger, often playing trombone and occasionally switching to piano. Few people are aware of his extraordinary skills as a pianist, however, and that he and Bill Evans once played a two-piano engagement, with Brookmeyer's talents equal to the task. From 1961–68, Brookmeyer co-led a prominent quintet with Clark Terry, and in 1965 was one of the founding members of the Mel Lewis—Thad Jones Orchestra, an ensemble that would become an important finishing ground for many young, up-and-coming musicians. After moving to California in 1968 Brookmeyer was fairly inactive on the jazz scene throughout the 1970s, although he was associated with several television series, including *The Della Reese Show* in 1969–70. After Jones's death in 1986, Brookmeyer took over as musical director of the band and became known for the complex charts he created for the group. He is a polished arranger who draws from modern classical music and other sources in his works.

what to buy: Brookmeyer composed all the music and performs as soloist on valve trombone on the 1991 studio session, *Electricity* 𝄞𝄞𝄞𝄞 (ACT Music, 1994, prod. Wolfgang Hirschmann), an intriguing recording that finds him directing the WDR Big Band and guesting soloists, John Abercrombie (guitar), Rainer Brüninghaus, and Frank Chastenier (keyboards), Dieter Ilg (bass), and Danny Gottlieb (drums). From the opener "Farewell, New York," a nearly 17-minute powerful, electrifying dirge-like movement that sucker-punches you right in the gut, Brookmeyer's formidable talents are on display throughout the six modern pieces arranged in a suite titled, "Electricity." This was the composer's last piece written in New York, and there is a melancholy feel to the entire album, but there are passionate, highly charged sections, such as "Say Ah," which brilliantly features Abercrombie. When this composition was completed, Brookmeyer moved to Rotterdam to start a new school, which he subsequently put aside, and in 1996 he became Chief Conductor of the Danish Radio Big Band. Brookmeyer's music explores dissonant contrapuntal themes, melodic blues and hard-edge rock derivations, shifting time signatures, humming sonorous textures, and spontaneous improvisations to create the ultimate ear-expanding listen. This is serious stuff, so if you believe all jazz must swing, move to the next listen. Featuring Brookmeyer playing both valve trombone and piano, *The Dual Role of Bob Brookmeyer* 𝄞𝄞𝄞𝄞 (Prestige/OJC, 1954, 1955/1989, prod. Ira Gitler, Bob Weinstock), combines eight selections from two previous recordings made in 1954 and 1955. The 1954 date features Brookmeyer with the

ALAN BROADBENT

song "Ballad Impromptu"
album *Personal Standards*
(Concord, 1996/1997)

instrument Piano

Monster Solo

Teddy Charles Quartet, and the 1955 session highlights the leader with his own quartet. This CD offers the opportunity to hear Brookmeyer as pianist in fine form, particularly on the Teddy Charles tune, "Loup-Garou."

best of the rest:
And Friends 𝄞𝄞𝄞 (Columbia, 1964/Sony-Tristar, 1995)
Paris Suite 𝄞𝄞𝄞 (Challenge, 1993)
Back Again 𝄞𝄞𝄞 (Sonet, 1978–79/Gazell, 1992)
Oslo 𝄞𝄞𝄞 (Concord, 1992)

Susan K. Berlowitz and Nancy Ann Lee

Roy Brooks
Born March 9, 1938, in Detroit, MI.

Percussionist Roy Brooks says he was born "the same year as Superman," but in solo performance is more likely to assume the persona of the "Mystical Afronaut." After a musical schooling at Cass Tech High School, Brooks emerged in the late 1950s with Horace Silver and toured with a variety of acts for the next couple of decades. In the process he became an elder states-man of the Detroit bebop generation. Brooks's percussion inter-ests range as far as you can get beyond the traditional drum kit: vibes, marimba, steel drums, musical saw, gongs and a "Breathatone" of his own creation, a device that the drummer employs to vary the pitch of the snare drum. He's been known to stage solo percussion concerts with a stage full of all the above and more: One of his compositions, "Basketball," features Brooks not only rhythmically dribbling the ball but sinking a 15-foot jumper with a higher percentage than, say, Dennis Rodman. Brooks is a veteran member of M'Boom, the percussion ensem-ble headed up by colleague and friend Max Roach. His own small groups perform under the name of Artistic Truth, and he heads his own Aboriginal Percussion Choir. The latter performs a variety of compositions of Brooks and others, including his no-table expansion of Eddie Harris's "Freedom Jazz Dance," which Brooks styles "Kujichagalea" (self-determination). This would be impossible to capture on CD; somebody needs to do a video.

what to buy: There's not a lot of choice, but *Duet in Detroit* ♫♫♫♫ (Enja, 1994) documents part of a series of duet concerts that Brooks staged at the Detroit Institute of Arts in 1983 and 1984. These featured collaborators Geri Allen, Don Pullen, pi-anist Randy Weston, and trumpeter Woody Shaw. Brooks re-tained the tapes and was able to put this together after a decade's delay. Conditional on its success, there's certainly enough in the can for a second volume. It's certainly not coinci-dental that Brooks found kindred spirits in pianists with power-ful percussive instincts of their own.

worth searching for: Brooks can be heard as a featured side-man on Enja recordings of 1970s with Abdullah Ibrahim (when he was known as Dollar Brand), African Space Program and the Children of Africa, and Coleman Hawkins's Supreme, where Brooks joins Barry Harris and Gene Taylor in backing Hawk from a 1966 session that was finally unearthed and released in 1995.

influences:

◀◀ Max Roach, Kenny Clarke, Sid Catlett, J.C. Heard

▶▶ Geri Allen, James Carter, Tani Tabbal

David Finkel

Tina Brooks

Born Harold Floyd Brooks, June 7, 1932, in Fayetteville, NC. Died Au-gust 13, 1974, in New York, NY.

Blue Note was the only label to pay any attention whatsoever to the tragically short-lived hard bop tenorist Tina Brooks. And even

they were slow to put his intelligent, fluid, passionate music in front of the public, and have not done a good job of keeping it there. He appeared as a sideman on such Blue Note sessions as Jimmy Smith's *House Party*, *The Sermon*, *Confirmation*, and *Cool Blues*; Kenny Burrell's *Blue Lights*, *Swingin'*, and *At the Five Spot Cafe*; Jackie McLean's *Jackie's Bag* and *Street Singer*; Freddie Hubbard's *Open Sesame*; and Freddie Redd's *Shades of Redd*. After drug problems loomed, Brooks made no recordings in the last 12 years of his life. He died of kidney failure at age 42.

worth searching for: Of the four albums' worth of prime hard-bop quintet sides he and his uniformly excellent cohorts laid down for Alfred Lion and Francis Wolff's trendsetting label between March 1958 and March 1961, only one session, *True Blue* ♫♫♫♫ (Blue Note, 1960/1994, prod. Alfred Lion), with Freddie Hubbard, Duke Jordan, Sam Jones, and Art Taylor, was released during Brooks's lifetime, and that's also the only one available recently (in 1994 Blue Note issued it in their limited edition Connoisseur series, and it is still available from Mosaic on LP). The earlier *Minor Move* ♫♫♫♫ (Blue Note, 1958/1980, prod. Alfred Lion), with Lee Mor-gan, Sonny Clark, Doug Watkins, and Art Blakey, was finally is-sued in 1980, while the legendary—it had been erroneously listed as available for years before it actually was—*Back to the Tracks* ♫♫♫♫ (Blue Note, 1960, prod. Alfred Lion), with Blue Mitchell, Kenny Drew, Paul Chambers, and Taylor, languished until Mosaic Records made it available, along with all the above and an unti-tled 1961 date with Johnny Coles, Drew, Wilbur Ware, and Philly Joe Jones, in a limited-edition boxed set, *The Complete Blue Note Recordings of the Tina Brooks Quintet* ♫♫♫♫ (Mosaic, 1985, reis-sue prod. Michael Cuscuna), which is also now out of print. There are plans for Mosaic to issue *Back to the Tracks* on LP while Blue Note puts it out on CD, though these have not appeared as this is written. Additionally, Japanese facsimiles of Tina Brooks's records appear from time to time. Given the short shelf-life of this mater-ial when it does appear, grab it when you see it. Despite his com-parative obscurity, Tina Brooks's legacy is as rich as any in Blue Note history.

influences:

◀◀ Dexter Gordon, Wardell Gray

▶▶ Wayne Shorter

David Prince

Peter Brotzmann

Born March, 6, 1941, in Remschied, Germany.

Peter Brotzmann cut his teeth by playing in various Dixieland bands. Subsequently, he played improvised jazz beginning in the early 1960s and had achieved a sound similar in ferocity to that of American saxophonist Albert Ayler by the time of his initial recordings. *Machine Gun* shook the foundation of European jazz at its core with its octet centering on three saxophonists—Brotzmann, Evan Parker, and Willem Breuker.

Over the years, Brotzmann has recorded with some of the greats of improvised jazz including Barre Philips (bass), Albert Mangelsdorf (trombone), Han Bennink (percussion), and William Parker (bass). He was an active member of the Globe Unity orchestra for a number of years and has also collaborated with his son, guitarist Caspar Brotzmann. In 1986, Brotzmann was a co-founder of the free jazz supergroup Last Exit with Sonny Sharrock (guitar), Bill Laswell (bass), and Ronald Shannon Jackson (drums). In this context, the group seemed to be approaching the searing intensity of Brotzmann's *Machine Gun* project of nearly 20 years before.

what to buy: *Machine Gun* ♪♪♪♪ (self-released/FMP, 1968, prod. Peter Brotzmann, Jost Gebers) is an album of some of the most intense sonic assaults to emerge from Europe in the late 1960s. The lineup is Brotzmann (tenor, baritone sax), Willem Breuker (tenor sax, bass clarinet), Evan Parker (tenor sax), Fred van Hove (piano), Peter Kowald (bass), Buschi Niebergall (bass), Han Bennink (drums) and Sven-Ake Johansson (drums). *Die Like a Dog* ♪♪♪♪ (FMP, 1994, prod. Peter Brotzmann) is subtitled *Fragments of Music, Life and Death of Albert Ayler*. Brotzmann pays his respects to the late American saxophonist. The quartet has Toshinori Kondo (trumpet, effects), William Parker (bass), and Hamid Drake (percussion). While the works on this disc are mainly credited to Brotzmann, he admits to using "very short quotations out of Albert Ayler's music in different variations."

what to buy next: *Songlines* ♪♪♪ (FMP, 1994, prod. Jost Gebers) is a trio recording with Fred Hopkins (double bass) and Rashied Ali (drums). The liner notes say "music is a memory for finding one's way out of the world." That seems quite appropriate as the trio seems to create their own small universe in the language of music. It is a fine balance of dynamics and musical density. As the cover credits imply, the Brotzmann/Drake Duo's *Dried Rat Dog* ♪♪♪ (Okka Disk, 1995, prod. Peter Brotzmann, Hamid Drake, John Corbett) is a duet performance with percussionist Hamid Drake. It is in the tradition of other such recent pairings as those by Urs Leimgruber and Fritz Hauser as well as the famed John Coltrane/Rashied Ali *Interstellar Space*. While the absence of a bassist to flesh out the recording may, at first,

seem a bit disconcerting, repeated listenings reveal that this is not a drawback.

what to avoid: *Last Home* ♪♪ (Pathological, 1990) is a collaborative effort between Brotzmann and his son Caspar (guitar). Overall, the picture is not focused with no real sense of cohesion or reason.

best of the rest:

The Berlin Concert ♪♪♪ (FMP, 1971)
Reserve ♪♪♪ (FMP, 1988)
Wie Das Leben So Spielt ♪♪♪ (FMP, 1989)
No Nothing ♪♪♪ (FMP, 1990) solo recording
Dare Devil ♪♪♪♪ (DIW, 1991)
The Martz Combo ♪♪♪ (FMP, 1992)

influences:

◀◀ Albert Ayler, John Coltrane, Pharoah Sanders, Frank Wright

▶▶ Mats Gustafsson, Werner Ludi

Chris Meloche

Ari Brown

Born 1944, in Chicago, IL.

Ari Brown was fascinated by his mother's fingers as she played the piano, but he did not play piano seriously until 1961 at Wilson Junior College, where he met Joseph Jarman, Roscoe Mitchell, and Henry Threadgill. Mitchell urged Ari to start on saxophone in 1965 when he was playing with soul and blues bands. In 1971 he began focusing exclusively on jazz and joined the Association for the Advancement of Creative Musicians (AACM). He recorded with a group featuring Rufus Reid on bass called the Awakening. He stopped playing piano in the early 1970s, but took it up again after he lost a few teeth in a car accident in 1974 and couldn't play sax for a while. He has worked with McCoy Tyner, Elvin Jones, Anthony Braxton, Big John Patton, Sonny Stitt, Von Freeman, Frank Gordon, Bobby Watson, and Lester Bowie. In 1989 he joined Kahil El'Zabar's Ritual Trio. He also led a group with bassist Fred Hopkins called Ultimate Frontier.

what's available: The quartet session *Ultimate Frontier* ♪♪♪♪ (Delmark, 1995, prod. Steve Wagner) is Brown's first recording as a leader (at age 52!) and was worth waiting for. His tenor is strong and vibrant and he goes outside with his alto, particularly on "Lester Bowie's Gumbo Stew." "One for Luba" is a beautiful ballad creating an air of sadness.

worth searching for: Brown's sax work with Kahil El'Zabar's Ritual Trio can be sampled on *The Renaissance of the Resistance*

𝄞𝄞𝄞𝄞 (Delmark, 1994, prod. Robert G. Koester), with El'Zabar on drums and Malachi Favors on bass, and *Big Cliff* 𝄞𝄞𝄞 (Delmark, 1995, prod. Robert G. Koester) on which Brown adds piano to his duties and the group is joined by violinist Billy Bang in an explosive live recording. For sax work of earlier vintage, hear Brown on the 1978 sessions led by Frank Walton on *Reality* 𝄞𝄞𝄞 (Delmark, 1993, prod. Robert G. Koester), which includes two Brown compositions. His bebop roots can be glimpsed on Anthony Braxton's *Charlie Parker Project 1993* 𝄞𝄞𝄞𝄞 (hat ART, 1995, prod. WDR Köln/hat HUT Records), though of course, the players perform Parker's compositions with an exciting awareness of the passage of time.

influences:

◄◄ Charlie Parker, Roscoe Mitchell

David C. Gross and Steve Holtje

Charles Brown

Born September 13, 1922, in Texas City, TX.

Charles Brown, like Johnny Adams, is a performer whose abilities spread across genres, but with a recorded history leaning towards the blues. Brown first came to the public's attention as the voice of "Driftin' Blues," a hit in 1946 for the West Coast–based Johnny Moore's Three Blazers. That song, with its vocal similarities to the popular Nat "King" Cole, sparked a whole school of "cool" blues performers who took Cole's croon and swung it with a soft blues beat.

Brown's subtle piano playing and smoky voice helped him have an impressive number of hits after leaving the Three Blazers in 1948. That was also the year he recorded "Merry Christmas Baby," a perennial holiday classic. Brown's vocal style was to make a big impression on the young Ray Charles, but hits stopped coming after 1952 as the music-buying public started swinging towards a harder-edged approach, keeping Brown's cocktail voice off the charts.

When Alligator Records reissued an import recording in 1989 called *One More for the Road*, Brown's career reentered the limelight. Since then, he has made a series of well-received albums for the Bullseye Blues label that showcase Brown's still solid piano playing and smoky voice within a blues context, plus two other releases on Verve and Muse that are more jazz-oriented.

what to buy: Even though his music has always had a jazzy flavor to it, Charles Brown wears the blues label a little easier. *Blues and Other Love Songs* 𝄞𝄞𝄞𝄞 (Muse, 1992, prod. Houston Person) is one of only two releases by the pianist that could fit the jazz tag with ease, although it's probably not the title that will move him out of the blues section in music stores. Brown's piano playing is deceptively laid back and this has never been more apparent then on his rendition of Thelonious Monk's "'Round Midnight." His playing is a bit more square than what folks might be used to on this tune, but the blues content behind the writing is brought to the fore. The phrasing verges on delicate, but the tone (thanks to a well-recorded piano) is full-bodied in that smoky bar room sort of way. Throughout the album, Brown's in fine voice expressing cool heartbreak on standouts "Fool That I Am" and "Who's Beating My Time." The latter tune and "I've Got a Right to Cry" are decidedly intimate, with Brown being the sole performer, crooning sad lyrics and playing his piano like it's three in the morning. Saxophonist Houston Person produced these sessions and plays his forceful, soulful tenor on four cuts, but guitarist Danny Caron is the real deal foil for Brown, comping when needed and never overplaying, delivering solos with just enough power to fill the spaces and times. The rhythm section of bassist Ruth Davies and drummer Gaylord Birch never gets in the way and that's a compliment.

what to buy next: *These Blues* 𝄞𝄞𝄞𝄞 (Verve, 1994, prod. John Snyder) features the same rhythm gang as *Blues and Other Love Songs*, but Clifford Solomon has stepped into the tenor saxophone role and there is more variety in the lineups being used. The songs range from duets and drummerless trios to the Ellington standard "I Got It Bad (And That Ain't Good)" and "Amazing Grace," where Brown's piano and vocals play sans accompaniment. Danny Caron has graduated to the role of musical director and his guitar playing is still tasteful and swinging, especially during his solo on the Louis Jordan–penned "Is You Is, Or Is You Ain't (Ma Baby)."

the rest:

Boss of the Blues 𝄞𝄞𝄞 (Mainstream, 1983)
One More for the Road 𝄞𝄞𝄞𝄞 (Blue Side, 1986/Alligator, 1989)
All My Life 𝄞𝄞𝄞𝄞 (Bullseye Blues, 1990)
Someone to Love 𝄞𝄞𝄞 (Bullseye Blues, 1992)
Just a Lucky So and So 𝄞𝄞𝄞𝄞 (Bullseye Blues, 1994)
Charles Brown's Cool Christmas Blues 𝄞𝄞𝄞 (Bullseye Blues, 1994)
Honey Dripper 𝄞𝄞𝄞𝄞 (Verve, 1996)
1946 𝄞𝄞𝄞𝄞 (Classics, 1997)

worth searching for: If you can find it, the limited edition box set *The Complete Aladdin Recordings of Charles Brown* 𝄞𝄞𝄞𝄞 (Mosaic, 1994, prod. Michael Cuscuna) gives you all the early

Charles Brown recordings you will ever need. Strictly speaking, it's not jazz but, at times, it's good enough and close enough.

influences:

 Nat "King" Cole

 Ray Charles, Willie Littlefield, Percy Mayfield

Garaud MacTaggart

Clifford Brown

Born October 30, 1930, in Wilmington, DE. Died June 25, 1956, in PA.

That Clifford Brown's extremely short career in jazz is so well documented is a testament to his immense impact on post-bebop in general and the trumpet in specific. He was an unmistakably brilliant musical thinker, constructing intricate, jubilantly bouncing solos that rivaled Dizzy Gillespie's complexity. He was also a likable fellow, kind and lacking the baggage of drug addictions or the temperamental problems that have afflicted other musicians of his era. At the time of his death, in a car accident on the Pennsylvania Turnpike, Brown had ascended from the hard-driving soulfulness of Art Blakey and Horace Silver's Jazz Messengers (before Silver's departure) to wow audiences and musicians alike. So impressed were his peers and audiences that drummer Max Roach, by the early 1950s a veritable institution in jazz, would agree to not only form a co-op band with Brown, but also to allow the trumpeter's name to share top billing in the group's title. Quickly, the Roach-Brown group cut a spree of driven, edgy LPs with tenor saxophonist Harold Land and pianist Richie Powell, younger brother of bebop scion Bud Powell. When Land decided to curtail the lengthy road trips and remain in California, where the band was nominally based, Roach and Brown hired Sonny Rollins to play tenor. Thus was born one of the two most significant hard bop units of the 1950s. Brown came to jazz almost accidentally, after getting a trumpet as a teenager when he reportedly had no interest in jazz. He headed from his native Wilmington, Delaware, to Delaware State College, where he studied mathematics on a music scholarship for a year before moving to Maryland State College in 1950. In this period, Brown met Fats Navarro, one of his idols, and was seriously injured in a car accident. By mid-1951, Brown was touring with Chris Powell and His Blue Flames, playing R&B. Brown cut his first Blue Note session in August 1953, before heading to Europe; he opened 1954 with Art Blakey and then won *Down Beat* magazine's "New Star of the Year" award.

Brown's recording career comes in three overlapping phases: first with Vogue, then Blue Note, and finally EmArcy. Even the

CLIFFORD BROWN

song "I'll Remember April"

album *Clifford Brown and Max Roach at Basin Street* (EmArcy, 1956/1990)

instrument Trumpet

Monster Solo

moments when he was still developing a personal sound and style sound as top-notch as anything else happening in the mid-1950s. And they were merely foreshadowing for the 1954–55 era, during which he produced some flawlessly beautiful ballads, riveting solos, and a host of precious tunes with the music's foremost leaders. Cut down at a creative zenith, Brown was a prime mover in the history of jazz trumpet.

what to buy: The anthology *Clifford Brown-Max Roach Alone Together: The Best of the Mercury Years* ♫♫♫ (Mercury/Verve, 1995, prod. various) opens the door to one of the most economical, driving hard bop ensembles in jazz history.

what to buy next: *Brownie: The Complete EmArcy Recordings of Clifford Brown* ♫♫♫♫ (Mercury/Verve, 1989, prod. various), a ten-CD set, encompasses all the Roach-Brown quintet recordings, including many outtakes, false starts, and unreleased pieces, as well as "All-Star" sessions led by Brown, a vaunted date with a string section, and two vocalist-led sessions. It's ripe for completists but also valuable to any fan of Brown's—as it includes some of his most mature, riveting work. The book-like four-CD package *The Complete Blue Note and Pacific Jazz Recordings* 𝄫𝄫𝄫𝄫 (Blue Note/Capitol, 1995, prod. Michael Cuscuna) features an extensive essay, discography, and series of photographs by Blue Note Records official Francis Wolff. Two of the discs feature Brown as the star of Art Blakey's early Jazz Messengers group, and while Brown is an unfettered, bouncy post-bop enthusiast, he's also incomparably articulate in phrasing and beautiful on the slow numbers.

the rest:

The Clifford Brown Sextet in Paris 𝄫𝄫 (Fantasy, 1989)
The Clifford Brown Quartet in Paris 𝄫𝄫 (Fantasy, 1989)
The Clifford Brown Big Band in Paris 𝄫𝄫 (Fantasy, 1989)
The Complete Paris Sessions, Volume 1 𝄫𝄫 (BMG, 1997)

influences:

◄◄ Roy Eldridge, Dizzy Gillespie

►► Lee Morgan, Randy Brecker, Wynton Marsalis, Rick Braun

Andrew Bartlett

Donald Brown

Born March 28, 1954, in Hernando, MS.

An adept high school drummer and trumpeter, Brown began to study piano during his freshman year at Memphis State University. He moved to Boston after graduation, and followed college friend James Williams to the piano chair in Art Blakey's Jazz Messengers in 1981. His expertise as soloist and accompanist also enhanced groups led by Donald Byrd, Art Farmer, Freddie Hubbard, and Milt Jackson. Donald Brown began to compose and arrange during junior high school, and has evolved to become a premier composer of the 1980s and 1990s, one of an elite group that includes Billy Strayhorn, Duke Ellington, Tadd Dameron, Thelonious Monk, Horace Silver, Thad Jones, and Wayne Shorter. His composing has taken front seat to his playing during the past 15 years and his compositions have been recorded by his Messenger mates, Wynton Marsalis and Billy Pierce, as well as by Elvin Jones, Jon Faddis, Ralph Moore, Renee Rosnes, and other top artists. In a small group setting, Brown's arrangements set him apart from his contemporaries. Brown is also a resourceful and imaginative pianist, and his recorded solos display his natural gift of melody and an inquisitory, spirited, rhythmic feel that draws on the percussive characteristics of the piano. However, in recent years, Brown's playing has been circumscribed by severe rheumatoid arthritis, and in the 1990s he's been teaching at the University of Tennessee.

what to buy: Brown recorded an astonishingly resourceful series of recordings for minimal budgets between 1987–1993, cutting a broad swath through contemporary improvisation. Each is a self-contained unit, telling a story; each shines for the originality of Brown's compositions and the quality of top shelf improvisers rising to the challenge. *Sources of Inspiration* 𝄫𝄫𝄫𝄫 (Muse, 1989, prod. Don Sickler) is a fabulous date with inspired improvising on Brown's superb compositions and arrangements by Gary Bartz (alto and soprano saxophone), Eddie Henderson (trumpet), Buster Williams (bass), and Carl Allen (drums). *Cause and Effect* 𝄫𝄫𝄫𝄫 (Muse, 1991, prod. Don Sickler) is a strong programmatic recording with veterans Joe Henderson on tenor and James Spaulding on flute. Brown explores the permutations of the voice and the drum on this richly layered date. *Send One Your Love* 𝄫𝄫𝄫𝄫 (Muse, 1992, prod. Don Sickler) offers lots of trio on this session of mixed configurations. The constant is drum master Louis Hayes. "Crazeology" showcases Brown's talents as a top shelf bebopper. Brown varies the tempos and displays his innate sense of dynamics throughout the presentation. *Car Tunes* 𝄫𝄫𝄫𝄫 (Muse, 1993, prod. Don Sickler) features Brown's great ensemble writing on ten originals. Brown prevails, getting way inside the blues on this fifth and final Muse date featuring altoist Steve Wilson and tenor saxist Don Braden, who are superb on their spotlighted moments.

what to buy next: Brown's debut as leader, *Early Bird Gets the Short End of the Stick* 𝄫𝄫𝄫𝄫 (Sunnyside, 1987, prod. James Williams, Francois Zalacain), is an energetic, Jazz Messenger-inflected session with many strong moments. Highlights are the harmonically challenging "Early Bird," and Brown's solo feature on Tadd Dameron's "If You Could See Me Now." His collaborators are Donald Harrison (saxes and flute), Bill Mobley (trumpet/flugelhorn), Steve Nelson, (vibraphone), Bob Hurst (bass), and Jeff Watts (drums). *People Music* 𝄫𝄫𝄫𝄫 (Muse, 1990, prod. Don Sickler) is an ambitious program exploring many vernacular dance rhythms of Afro-America. There's something a bit formulaic on this recording that doesn't crop up on the others, but it's a strong session nonetheless.

worth searching for: An intimate classic with Steve Nelson (vibraphone), Charnett Moffett (bass), and Alan Dawson (drums), *The Sweetest Sounds* 𝄫𝄫𝄫𝄫 (Jazz City, 1988) is unavailable in the States unless you're lucky enough to find an import copy. Art Blakey & the Jazz Messengers recorded *Keystone 3* 𝄫𝄫𝄫𝄫 (Concord, 1982), a smoking Jazz Messengers date to which Brown imparts cohesion. It also features Charles Fambrough (bass), Wynton Marsalis (trumpet), and Bill Pierce (tenor sax). Compositions include "Smile of the Snake" and "New York."

With former Messengers Christian McBride and Billy Drummond, Brown sparkles throughout Bill Easley's *Easley Said* 𝄞𝄞𝄞𝄞 (Evidence, 1997, prod. James Williams), an inspired homage to Thelonious Monk and Sonny Rollins. Brown contributes the humorously dissonant "In Walked Toot."

influences:

◀◀ Oscar Peterson, Phineas Newborn, Harold Mabern, Thelonious Monk, Bud Powell, Tadd Dameron, Cedar Walton, James Williams

▶▶ Geoff Keezer, James Hurt

Ted Panken

Jeri Brown

Born March 20, 1952, in St. Louis, MO.

Jazz vocalist Jeri Brown is an uncommon stylist who favors the era of classic jazz singers between the 1920–1940s. Yet, she is one of the most versatile singers on the modern scene with her outstanding four-octave vocal range which she flexes and uses well. She has recorded five albums for Justin Time, each one focusing on a fresh theme and featuring different musicians. Brown's U.S. appearances are rare, but her adventurous spirit, expert use of dynamics, and her trademark scat singing have won her critical acclaim throughout Canada and in Europe.

Brown grew up in St. Louis amidst a musical family. Her uncle was trumpeter Virgil Carter whom she often heard rehearsing with Dizzy Gillespie, Miles Davis and Clark Terry in her grandparents' basement. Her fascination with music led to opera lessons at age 12 and her early talents won her a scholarship to Westmar College in Iowa where she graduated in 1975 with dual teaching degrees in music and English. During college, she toured Europe as lead soloist with a light opera chorale. Brown moved to the Cleveland, Ohio area in 1976, attended Kent State University to complete her Masters studies in education, and taught at Oberlin Conservatory of Music, Cleveland State University, The University of Akron, and Cuyahoga Community College. She performed with the Cleveland Jazz Orchestra and the Cleveland Chamber Symphony. Cleveland drummer Bob McKee (who performed on the then locally produced Mike Douglas TV show) invited Brown to sing with his small groups throughout Ohio, exposure and training which led to performances with Ellis Marsalis, Billy Taylor and Dizzy Gillespie. Brown moved to Montreal in 1989 to teach at Concordia University, made her recording debut on Justin Time Records in 1991, and has since relocated to Nova Scotia, where she teaches at St. Francis Xavier University.

what to buy: Brown's best collaboration to date, *A Timeless Place* 𝄞𝄞𝄞𝄞 (Justin Time, 1995, prod. Jim West), features her singing mostly ballads with pianist-composer-lyricist Jimmy Rowles (who died in May 1996, two years after this studio session) and bassist Eric Von Essen. Rowles never received the recognition he deserved and Brown's attention to his nine originals, a mix of ballads and easy-swingers, not only represents the perfect choice of material for a singer who loves standards, but brings attention to Rowles's craftsmanship. Brown exhibits assurance, unpredictable phrasing, and breathy, sensuous lyricism. With saucy verve, Brown delivers the bittersweet, yet humorous, tune, "Fraser," alone worth the album price. Adding icing to the cake, Rowles superbly accompanies and briefly sings on his tune, "Baby Don't Quit Now." A banner album. With *Fresh Start* 𝄞𝄞𝄞𝄞 (Justin Time, 1996, prod. Jeri Brown, Jim West), Brown sings mostly in mid-to-low vocal range, a lá Betty Carter style. Accompanied by pianist Cyrus Chestnut, bassist Avery Sharpe, drummer Wali Muhammad, whose spotlighted moments cap this ebullient outing, Brown bends and shapes 12 intriguing original tunes with her smoldering, sultry delivery and tasteful scatting.

what to buy next: Brown's fifth session *April in Paris* 𝄞𝄞𝄞𝄞 (Justin Time, 1996, prod. Jim West), a classy collection of 11 romantic ballads recorded in France with a trio from the Paris scene, finds the singer artfully gliding up and down her four-octave range. Her devotion to lyrics and whisper-to-gleeful dynamics draw the listener into the heart of standards such as "Once Upon a Summertime," "The Twelfth of Never," "Who Can I Turn To," "When April Comes Again," "Summertime," and others. Accordion player Roberto De Brashov augments two tracks, a special touch that gives European flavor to the album. Perhaps Brown's idea to record her Rowles's tribute originated from her second recording, *The Peacocks* 𝄞𝄞𝄞 (Justin Time, 1993, prod. Jim West, Jeri Brown), titled after Rowles's beloved song. A pleasing straight-ahead session of eight ballads and light swingers, the album features tunes penned by Tony Lavorgna (a saxophonist Brown recorded with in Cleveland), Abdullah Ibrahim, Tadd Dameron, Dizzy Gillespie, and Fred Hersch. Brown's top-notch musician team includes Kirk Lightsey (piano), Peter Leitch (guitar), Wali Muhammad (drums), and Rufus Reid (bass). Guest Michel Dubeau adds eerie touches with his Shakuhachi flute on the title tune and "Jean," an ethereal piece which hints at Brown's early opera training. A wonderful album. Her major label debut, *Mirage* 𝄞𝄞𝄞 (Justin Time,

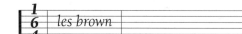

1991, prod. Jim West) features Brown backed by pianist Fred Hersch and bassist Daniel Lessard. While her singing lacks the maturity and control of her later recordings, for a debut she shows remarkable promise.

influences:

Sarah Vaughan, Betty Carter

Nancy Ann Lee

Les Brown /Les Brown & His Band of Renown

Born Lester Raymond Brown, March 14, 1912, in Reinerton, PA.

Best known as the house band on *The Dean Martin Show* and countless Bob Hope TV specials, Les Brown and His Band of Renown was arguably the most versatile orchestra of the big-band era. Brown's outfit could blow sweet and reedy like Isham Jones or Sammy Kaye, update the classics Freddy Martin and Frankie Carle-style, and wail hot and brassy a la Glenn Miller or Stan Kenton. And you could always dance to it. A clarinetist, Brown led his first band at Duke University (the Duke Blue Devils), and worked as a professional arranger for orchestras led by Ruby Newman, Isham Jones, Jimmy Dorsey, Larry Clinton, and Red Nichols before going out on his own. Immediately, his sense of organization and professionalism won him the respect of bookers and top vocalists alike, and he scored some fair-sized hits with "'Tis Autumn," "Bizet Has His Day," and "Mexican Hat Dance." The turning point in Brown's career came when he hired Doris Day away from Bob Crosby's band. Their collaboration on such hits as "Sentimental Journey," "You Won't Be Satisfied until You Break My Heart," and "My Dream's Keep Getting Better All the Time" made them both household names. After Day's departure, Brown's orchestra continued to thrive with records like "I've Got My Love to Keep Me Warm" and their jumpin' theme "Leap Year." Never lacking for fine warblers, at one time or another Brown's orchestra employed Miriam Shaw, Betty Bonney, Ray Kellogg, Lucy Polk, and novelty singer-saxophonist Butch Stone. During the 1950s, while competing bands were retiring or being forced out of the business by rock 'n' roll, Brown's orchestra was busier than ever and won *Down Beat* magazine's Best Dance Band Poll five years in a row. By 1962 Brown had tired of the road and settled his orchestra into a staff job at NBC, recording occasionally. His band's work behind Dean Martin, the Gold Diggers, and Bob Hope was the best of any prime-time orchestra, and led in no

small part to a big-band resurgence in the late 1970s. These days, the retired Brown has handed the baton to his son, Les Brown Jr.

what to buy: The best-known numbers by Brown and his Band of Renown are on *Les Brown: Best of the Big Bands* ♫♫♫♫ (Legacy, 1990, comp. prod. Michael Brooks), including "Leap Frog," "Sentimental Journey," "My Dreams Are Getting Better All the Time," "Bizet Has His Day," and "Mexican Hat Dance." It's an excellent sampler and starting point for this versatile band.

what to buy next: The best numbers sung with Brown's best singers (including Doris Day) are on *Best of the Big Bands: His Great Vocalists* ♫♫♫♫ (Legacy, 1995, prod. Didier C. Deutsch). There's romance a-plenty in "I Guess I'll Have to Dream the Rest," "I Got It Bad and That Ain't Good," and the flirty "Rock Me to Sleep." Equally fine is *The Essence of Les Brown* ♫♫♫♫ (Legacy, 1994, comp. prod. Michael Brooks), which contains some similar tracks, plus the good-humored jive of "Joltin' Joe DiMaggio" and many others.

what to avoid: The song selection is good, but the sound quality awfully thin on *Giants of the Big Band Era* ♫♫ (Pilz, 1994).

the rest:
The Uncollected Les Brown & His Orchestra 1944–46 ♫♫♫ (Hindsight, 1977/1994)
The Uncollected Les Brown & His Orchestra, Volume II ♫♫♫ (Hindsight, 1978/1994)
Digital Swing ♫♫♫ (Fantasy, 1986)
Twenty-Two Original Big Band Recordings ♫♫♫ (Hindsight, 1987/1992)
Jazz Collector Edition ♫♫ (LaserLight, 1992)
1944–1946 ♫♫♫ (Circle, 1992)
Greatest Hits ♫♫♫ (Curb, 1993)
Live at Elitch Gardens 1959 ♫♫♫ (Status, 1994)
Part II, Live at Elitch Gardens 1959 ♫♫♫ (Status, 1994)
Sentimental Journey ♫♫♫ (Columbia Special Products, 1994)
Anything Goes ♫♫ (USA, 1994)
America Swings—The Great Les Brown ♫♫ (Hindsight, 1995)
Lullaby in Rhythm ♫♫ (Drive Archive, 1995)
At the Hollywood Palladium ♫♫♫ (Starline, 1995)
Sentimental Journey ♫♫♫ (MCA Special Products, 1995)

worth searching for: Featured vocalists Margaret Whiting, Johnny Mercer, and Jimmy Wakely bring extra zest to the swinging *The Les Brown Show from Hollywood 1953* ♫♫♫ (Magic, 1994, prod. various), which you might find in the import racks. Also, during the big prom scene of *The Nutty Professor* (Paramount, 1963, director Jerry Lewis), Professor Julius Kelp can't keep still while Les Brown and His Band of Renown play their hit theme "Leap Frog." Neither will you.

influences:

◀◀ Isham Jones, Jimmy Dorsey, Red Nichols, Glenn Miller

▶▶ Si Zentner, Randy Brooks, Les Brown Jr.

Ken Burke

Marion Brown

Born September 8, 1935, in Atlanta, GA.

A subtle and inveterate trickster, Brown has never been an easy musician to pin down. A passionate free jazz altoist, he possesses an ethnomusicologist's knowledge of African American culture and a love of game-playing that is almost classical in its conception, although certainly many AACM musicians share his interest in this, as well as genre-straddlers such as John Zorn. Those who think of free music as mere macho aggression would do well to consider Brown's counter-example; he is rather lyrical and diverse, and a perusal of his oeuvre suggests an obsession with silence similar to the trumpeter Leo Smith, with whom Brown has recorded some of his finest performances. But Brown can howl with the best of them, as his many European blowing sessions testify. Arriving in New York City in 1962, Brown certainly hooked up with the right names, practicing with Ornette Coleman (Brown would play Coleman's plastic alto, while Coleman worked on his trumpet), playing with Sun Ra, and gigging on John Coltrane's chest-beating landmark *Ascension* and Archie Shepp's rococo *Fire Music*. Shepp took Brown under his wing and produced *Three for Shepp* for him, at a time when Shepp's name was in ascendance. There was a spell in Europe in the late 1960s, where Brown struck up fruitful alliances with Gunter Hampel and Jeanne Lee, among others. Back in America, he recorded a string of remarkable LPs in a variety of settings, and even played the 1972 Ann Arbor Jazz and Blues Festival in duet with Smith.

It is impossible to separate Brown's beliefs in collective improv from his political concerns, and this goes far to explain the diversity of his music. He often made a point of including non-musicians in his works, and of exploring themes of concern to the African American community, particularly of the South. Having spent much of the 1970s and 1980s in the academy (as both student and teacher, and not only of jazz), Brown's profile abated somewhat, and many of his later LPs suffer from contrived standards and commercial compromise, which is odd as his music anticipated much of what was going on in the Studio

Rivbea scene during the same period. Serious illness (brain cancer) has kept him out of view for most of this decade. A 1994 benefit concert at the Cooler in New York City brought out many of jazz's leading lights in a show of great affection.

what to buy: *Porto Nova* ♫♫♫♫ (Freedom, 1967/Black Lion, 1996, prod. Foppe Damste) is free and freaky, although Brown often works off of heads in a Rollins-esque mode. Accompanying him are the new Euro-improvisors, Maarten Altena on bass and Han Bennink on all sorts of percussion. The CD possesses a couple of bonus tracks from 1970, scored duets with Leo Smith. *Reeds 'n' Vibes* ♫♫♫ (IAI, 1978, prod. Paul Bley) offers empathetic duets with vibist Gunter Hampel.

what to buy next: *Why Not?* ♫♫♫♫ (ESP-disc, 1966) is the later and better of Brown's two ESP albums, featuring Stanley Cowell (piano), Sirone (bass), and Rashied Ali (drums). Amina Claudine Myers's *Poems for Piano: The Music of Marion Brown* ♫♫♫ (Sweet Earth Records, 1979, prod. Rick Jeffery), with the exception of one Myers piece, consists of piano works by Brown. It's a bit treacly at times, but gives insight into Brown's compositional method.

what to avoid: *La Placita—Live in Willisau* ♫♫ (Timeless, 1979, prod. Wim Wigt) is evidence that, as with many free players in the 1970s (such as Brown mentor Archie Shepp), finances dictated that edges got blunted and dissonance were blocked, particularly when it came to the festival crowd. Hence a live quartet date with "Sonnymoon for Two," "Soft Winds," and some unsearching if not unevocative originals. One can apply as much glop about "appreciation of past masters" as one wants: this is a compromise, plain and simple, and it became increasingly and unfortunately evident in Brown's later work.

the rest:

Marion Brown Quartet ♫♫♫♫ (ESP-disc, 1965)
Juba-Lee ♫♫♫♫ (Fontana, 1966)
Vista ♫♫ (Impulse!, 1975)
Solo Saxophone ♫♫♫♫ (Sweet Earth, 1977)
November Cotton Flower ♫♫♫♫ (Baystate, 1979)
Back to Paris ♫♫♫ (Freelance, 1980)
Back to Basics ♫♫♫ (Freelance, 1980)
Gemini w/Gunter Hampel ♫♫♫ (Birth, 1983)
Recollections: Ballads and Blues for Saxophone ♫♫♫ (Creative Works, 1985)
(With Mal Waldron) *Songs of Love and Regret* ♫♫♫♫ (Free Lance, 1985)
Native Land ♫♫ (ITM, 1990)
Offering I ♫♫♫ (Venus Records, 1992)
Mirambe de Vale: Offering II ♫♫♫ (Venus Records, 1993)

worth searching for: Ironically, Brown's success at getting major jazz labels to issue his records ended up hurting the availability of his best albums, since those companies are less likely to keep items in print. *Geechee Recollections* 𝄞𝄞𝄞𝄞 (Impulse!, 1973, prod. Ed Michel) is a masterful connection of the African and the African American which features several amateur percussionists (as well as the very professional Steve McCall), a Jean Toomer recitation, and trumpeter Leo Smith, Robin to Brown's Batman. Intense yet recessive, Jimmy Jefferson's bass intro to "Once Upon a Time" will stick in the crawl, but good. Consistently understated and off-kilter, this is one of the transcendent LPs of the 1970s. Featuring many homemade instruments, *Afternoon of a Georgia Faun* 𝄞𝄞𝄞𝄞 (ECM, 1970, prod. Manfred Eicher) is Brown's most famous "game" piece, and one of the LPs that launched ECM. Brown took writer's credits, but claimed the results of "six players, two vocalists and three assistants," including Chick Corea, Anthony Braxton, Jeanne Lee, Bernie Maupin, and Andrew Cyrille. The title side is rather sparse, about as far from the roar of *Porto Nova* as could be imagined. *Three for Shepp* 𝄞𝄞𝄞 (Impulse!, 1966, prod. Archie Shepp) was considerably acclaimed on its release, but it has not been available for some time. Shepp and Brown divide the compositions and this is thoughtful free jazz at its finest. Shepp's arrangements during this period (many done by the trumpeter Bill Dixon) are some of the finest in jazz history. *Sweet Earth Flying* 𝄞𝄞𝄞𝄞 (Impulse!, 1974, prod. Ed Michel) consists of two sidelong suites featuring some of Brown's finest soloing, but both Paul Bley and Muhal Richard Abrams set the mood on a variety of acoustic, electric, and electronic keyboards. *Duets* 𝄞𝄞𝄞𝄞 (Arista, 1975, prod. Marion Brown, Elliott Schwartz, Leo Smith, Bowdin Music Press) is a compilation of two separate LPs recorded with trumpeter Leo Smith and classical pianist Elliot Schwartz.

influences:

◀◀ Archie Shepp, Anthony Braxton

▶▶ John Zorn, Marty Ehrlich

D. Strauss

Ray Brown

Born October 13, 1926, in Pittsburgh, PA.

Ray Brown, noted for his precise pitch, emerged in the mid-1940s as one of the foremost bassists of the bebop era, and has remained vital as a sideman and a leader ever since. Bursting upon the New York bop scene in 1945, he played with Charlie Parker, Dizzy Gillespie, and Bud Powell and was hired by Gillespie to help propel his innovative big band. In the late 1940s, Brown played and toured with Jazz at the Philharmonic during some of that outfit's most exciting gigs featuring, among others, Parker, Lester Young, and Buddy Rich. Brown married singer Ella Fitzgerald in 1948; although the marriage only lasted a few years, Brown led a trio to back Fitzgerald for a time. In 1951, Brown recorded with Milt Jackson and John Lewis in a quartet that was a forerunner the Modern Jazz Quartet. Later that year, Brown joined the Oscar Peterson trio, where he would remain for 15 years. During this period with the popular pianist, Brown also recorded with JATP and other big acts, making him widely recorded and relatively famous.

When Brown left Peterson (though there have been subsequent reunions), he settled in California and concentrated more on producing and managing such acts as the MJQ and Quincy Jones. In 1974 he co-founded the L.A. Four with guitarist Laurindo Almeida, saxophonist Bud Shank, and drummer Shelly Manne. Brown also began recording extensively as a leader on the Concord Jazz label in the mid-1970s, and continued to do so all through the 1980s. In the 1990s Brown continues to be a formidable bassist and a prodigious recorder, leading a solid trio for Telarc that includes pianist Benny Green and drummer Greg Hutchison.

what to buy: *Black Orpheus* 𝄞𝄞𝄞𝄞 (Evidence, 1989, prod. Takao Ishizuka) was made by a trio that was arguably Brown's strongest, with pianist Gene Harris and drummer Jeff Hamilton. Tempos are slow and soulful for the most part, but excitement and creativity are certainly not lacking. *Much in Common* 𝄞𝄞𝄞𝄞 (Verve, 1963–65/1996, prod. Michael Lang) with Milt Jackson is a recent two-CD reissue of what had previously been three LPs recorded between 1962 and 1965. In addition to Brown and vibist Jackson, this set also features altoist Cannonball Adderley, trumpeter Clark Terry, gospel singer Marion Williams, and pianist Tommy Flanagan in enjoyable settings.

what to buy next: One of Brown's first major recordings as a leader, *Something for Lester* 𝄞𝄞𝄞𝄞 (Contemporary, 1977/OJC, 1995, prod. John Koenig, Lester Koenig) features a strong trio with pianist Cedar Walton and drummer Elvin Jones. *Summer Wind* 𝄞𝄞𝄞𝄞 (Concord Jazz, 1990, prod. Carl Jefferson) is another compelling recording from Brown's 1980s trio with Harris and Hamilton. Tunes include Johnny Mercer's title track, Gerry Mulli-

Ray Brown (AP/Wide World Photos)

gan's "Mona Lisa," Milt Jackson's "Bluesology," and the Ellingtonian standard "It Don't Mean a Thing."

what to avoid: *Bye Bye Blackbird* ♫♫ (Paddle Wheel, 1984) suffers in comparison to recordings on Concord from the same period that are much more stimulating and inspired.

the rest:
Brown's Bag ♫♫♫ (Concord Jazz, 1975)
As Good as It Gets ♫♫♫ (Concord Jazz, 1977)
Live at the Concord Jazz Festival ♫♫♫♫ (Concord Jazz, 1980)
Ray Brown Three ♫♫♫♫ (Concord Jazz, 1982)
Milt Jackson/Ray Brown Jam ♫♫♫♫ (Pablo, 1982/OJC, 1989)
Soular Energy ♫♫♫♫ (Concord Jazz, 1984)
Don't Forget the Blues ♫♫♫ (Concord Jazz, 1985)
The Red Hot Ray Brown Trio ♫♫♫ (Concord Jazz, 1986)
Bam Bam Bam ♫♫♫ (Concord Jazz, 1988)
Super Bass ♫♫♫ (Capri, 1989)
Moore Makes 4 ♫♫♫♫ (Concord Jazz, 1990)
New Two Bass Hits ♫♫♫ (Capri, 1991)
Three Dimensional ♫♫♫♫ (Concord Jazz, 1991)
Ray Brown/Jimmy Rowles ♫♫♫ (Concord Jazz, 1992)
Bass Face: Live at Kuumbwa ♫♫♫ (Concord Jazz, 1993)
Don't Get Sassy ♫♫♫♫ (Telarc, 1994)
Some of My Best Friends are . . . The Piano Players ♫♫♫♫ (Telarc, 1994)
Seven Steps to Heaven ♫♫♫♫ (Telarc, 1995)
Some of My Best Friends are . . . The Sax Players ♫♫♫♫ (Telarc, 1996)
Live at Sculler's ♫♫♫♫ (Telarc, 1997)

worth searching for: *This One's for Blanton* ♫♫♫♫ (OJC, 1972) is a tribute to great Ellington bassist Jimmy Blanton which swings consistently and recognizes one of Brown's main influences. You won't have to search too hard for this collection of duets co-led by Brown and pianist Duke Ellington—just look under Ellington's name at the record store.

influences:
◀◀ Jimmy Blanton, Oscar Pettiford
▶▶ Percy Heath, Ron Carter

Dan Keener

Rob Brown

Born February 27, 1962, in Hampton, VA.

Rob Brown started on piano in second grade and later switched to saxophones and other reeds, working with a swing/blues group while in high school and becoming fascinated with Charlie Parker. He began his college years at James Madison University, then switched to Berklee College, where he was a student of Joe Viola (saxophone) and John LaPorta (ensemble perfor-

mance). While in Boston he hooked up with pianist Matt Shipp. Moving to New York University, he studied with Lee Konitz and Joe Lovano while earning his B.S. in music, later taking private lessons from John Coltrane's teacher, Dennis Sandole. His debut recording was a duo album with Shipp, and they have worked together frequently. Brown has also played with a who's who of the jazz avant-garde, including Cecil Taylor, Rashied Ali, Fred Hopkins, Grachan Moncur III, Tim Berne, Mark Dresser, Dennis Charles, Billy Bang, and Borah Bergman. He's a member of William Parker's groups In Order to Survive and Little Huey Creative Music Orchestra and has recorded with both as well as with drummer Mark Edwards and Shipp. He has often worked with modern dance companies and is the music director of two.

what to buy: Long-time collaborators Brown and Shipp are marvelously responsive on the live duo album *Blink of an Eye* ♫♫♫♫ (No More Records, 1997, prod. Alan Schneider). Two of its three free improvisations are each in the half-hour range but masterfully sustained. Brown's flute playing is a revelation, and his tone on alto sax is sometimes big enough to be mistaken for a tenor—also, he doesn't spend a lot of time screaming in the upper register, using the whole range of the horn and exploring the full range of sonic effects available. He varies his sound, and his split tones and hoarse, nearly vocalized cries have strong musical logic (as on the long unaccompanied passage near the beginning of the second track) and emotional impact. Brown and Shipp alternate contrasting styles and matching figures, with the congruity of their wild flurries remarkably aligned. Even when Shipp crescendos to loud, fierce climaxes, Brown matches his fervor and excitement. The volume and density of their intertwining figures may vary (and the density is remarkable for two musicians, even if one is a pianist), but their intensity is remarkably sustained. This indie label's e-mail address, in case the CD is hard to find in stores, is nomore@bway.net.

what to buy next: On *High Wire* ♫♫♫♫ (Soul Note, 1996, prod. Flavio Bonandrini), one of his more structured efforts, Brown's rhythmically limber and harmonically daring post-bop melodic configurations are supported by the sympathetic accompaniment of bassist William Parker and drummer Jackson Krall, who provide a multi-layered foundation without ever being merely busy. Brown shows a mature voice of his own on a compelling album of intricate original compositions.

the rest:
(With Matthew Shipp) *Sonic Explorations* ♫♫♫ (Cadence, 1988)
Breath Rhyme ♫♫♫ (Silkheart, 1990)
(As Joe Morris–Rob Brown Quartet) *Illuminate* ♫♫♫♫ (Leo, 1994)

worth searching for: Brown, drummer Whit Dickey, and guitarist Joe Morris are jointly credited on *Youniverse* 𝄞𝄞𝄞 (Riti, 1993), which Morris issued on his own label (contact ritirec@ici.net). Six of the eight tracks are by Brown (the other two are spontaneous group improvisations), and the space and the shape of the instrumental lines often suggest (without copying) Ornette Coleman. The lack of a bass player and a chordal instrument (Morris usually plays lines rather than chords) really opens up the music and gives it a stark clarity which Brown's sonically denser projects don't have, allowing some of his more subtle timbral effects full exposure.

influences:

◀◀ Albert Ayler, Ornette Coleman, Jimmy Lyons, Roscoe Mitchell, Charlie Parker, Cecil Taylor

Steve Holtje

Ruth Brown

Born Ruth Alston Weston, January 30, 1928, in Portsmouth, VA.

Ruth Brown's earliest inspiration came from jazz singers such as Billie Holiday, Sarah Vaughan, and Dinah Washington, and stints with jazz orchestras led by Lucky Millinder (1947), Blanche Calloway, and others. Although she's appeared in Hollywood films, music fans probably know Brown best as the host of the National Public Radio broadcast series, "Blues Stage." However, Brown's more resonant legacy is her string of hits for Atlantic Records during the 1950s, which not only helped establish that label but also boosted her crossover appeal among jazz, blues, and rock fans. Brown's first hits ("So Long," "Teardrops from My Eyes," "I'll Wait for You") were torchy jazz renderings. But as the age of rock 'n' roll dawned, she developed her own rough and ready style. Tunes such as "(Mama) He Treats Your Daughter Mean," "Wild Wild Young Men," "Mambo Baby," and "As Long as I'm Moving" were squealing, rocking paeans to youthful expectations, sexuality, and groove. Brown mixed her bawdy rockin' with sensual, romantic songs such as "Oh What a Dream" (written for her by Chuck Willis), "Love Has Joined Us Together" (with Clyde McPhatter), and "It's Love Baby." Her biggest hits were 1957's "Lucky Lips," a mainstream pop record that seems beneath her today, and the 1958 teen romper "This Little Girl's Gone Rockin'" (written by Bobby Darin), which eventually inspired a popular video on the Disney Channel. By the end of the 1950s, hits for Brown were not coming as easily, and she was lost in the shuffle on Atlantic's crowded roster of stars. Signing with Phillips/Mercury, Brown recorded two solid LPs and had a minor hit single with her ver-

sion of Faye Adams's "Shake a Hand" in 1962. Brown's career tailspinned badly after that. Though she cut well-regarded LPs for the DCC and Capitol Jazz labels, sales were slow and live gigs were not plentiful. To keep her family fed and clothed, Brown joined the Head Start program and trained to be a beautician while working as a maid, nurse's aide, cashier, and babysitter. During the mid-1970s, comedian Redd Foxx helped revive Brown's career by bringing her to Los Angeles and casting her in bit parts on his hit sitcom *Sanford & Son*. Brown also had recurring roles on the ill-fated sitcoms *Hello Larry* and *Checking In,* but her experiences in live theater would ultimately prove more rewarding. Roles in *Amen Corner* and *Staggerlee* won her critical praise and led to her Tony Award-winning role in 1989's *Black & Blue*. Brown signed with Fantasy Records in 1988 and has recorded four well-regarded discs featuring fresh interpretations of jazz and blues standards. Other successes just as important followed. Her decade-old legal battle with Atlantic over unpaid royalties was finally resolved in her favor, and her old label helped set up the Rhythm & Blues Foundation as part of the settlement. Brown was elected to the Rock 'n' Roll Hall of Fame in 1991. As for her acting career, which began decades ago when she hosted her groundbreaking TV program, *Showtime at the Apollo* in 1955, she would portray Motormouth Mabel in the 1988 Hollywood film *Hairspray,* and win a Tony Award for her 1989 role in the Broadway revue *Black and Blue*. These days, Brown still records and plays live dates whenever time and health permits. 1996 saw the release of her autobiography, *Miss Rhythm*.

what to buy: The great string of records that resulted in Atlantic Records being nicknamed "The House That Ruth Built" are on the excellent *Rockin' in Rhythm—The Best of Ruth Brown* 𝄞𝄞𝄞𝄞 (Rhino, 1996, prod. Ahmet Ertegun, Jerry Wexler, Herb Abramson, Jerry Leiber, Mike Stoller; reissue prod. James Austin, Peter Grendysa), a 23-track compilation featuring her biggest hits as well as previously unreleased live versions of "(Mama) He Treats Your Daughter Mean" and "Oh What a Dream" from 1959. For a smart introduction to Brown's resurrection as a purveyor of soulful jazz, check out *Blues on Broadway* 𝄞𝄞𝄞 (Fantasy, 1989, prod. Ralph Jungheim), which earned her a Grammy Award for Best Jazz Female Vocal Performance with its mix of torch songs with such ribald sass as "If I Can't Sell It, I'll Keep Sittin' on It," and "Tain't Nobody's Biz-ness If I Do."

what to buy next: Many additional facets of Brown's salad days are revealed through *Miss Rhythm: Greatest Hits and More* 𝄞𝄞𝄞𝄞 (Atlantic, 1989, prod. Ahmet Ertegun; reissue prod. Bob Porter), a 40-song, two-CD set that not only includes all her Atlantic hits but also several pleasing LP tracks and four fine pre-viously unreleased songs. And Brown proves she's lost none of her vocal chops or dramatic verve on *R+B = Ruth Brown* ♫♫♫ (Bullseye Blues, 1997, prod. Scott Billington), a potent grab-bag of blues, R&B, and jazz featuring highly entertaining guest spots by Johnny Adams, Clarence "Gatemouth" Brown, and Bonnie Raitt.

what to avoid: For completists only, *Fine Brown Frame* ♫♫ (EMI/Capitol, 1993, prod. Sonny Lester; reissue prod. Michael Cuscuna) is not so much a bad LP as it is a disappointing one. Brown is in fine voice, but the Thad Jones/Mel Lewis Orchestra distracts from her performance with its brassy, jazz effrontery.

best of the rest:
Black Is Brown and Brown Is Beautiful ♫♫♫ (DCC Records, 1981/1995)
Have a Good Time ♫♫♫ (Fantasy, 1988)
Blues on Broadway ♫♫♫♫ (Fantasy, 1989)
Fine and Mellow ♫♫♫ (Fantasy 1991)
Sweet Baby of Mine ♫♫♫ (Route 66, 1992)
The Songs of My Life ♫♫♫ (Fantasy, 1993)

worth searching for: Hit the import racks for *Late Date with Ruth Brown* ♫♫♫♫ (Atlantic, 1956, prod. Ahmet Ertegun, Jerry Wexler), a reissue of Brown's best early LP, with romantic stan-dards gorgeously framed by arranger/conductor Richard Wess.

influences:
◀◀ Billie Holiday, Dinah Washington, Sarah Vaughan
▶▶ Irma Thomas, Little Richard, Koko Taylor, Bonnie Raitt

Ken Burke and Nancy Ann Lee

Tom Browne

Born October 13, 1954, in Queens, NY.

Influenced by Clifford Brown, Tom Browne can play a fat, brassy hard bop trumpet when he puts his mind to it. But for the most part, he's chosen not to, and has emphasized funk and R&B in-stead. Browne's big sellers, including 1981's *Magic*, may have contained one or two jazz instrumentals, but soul was domi-nant. Browne first attracted the attention of the R&B world in 1980 with his infectious hit "Funkin' for Jamaica" and returned to the R&B charts in 1981 with the equally addictive funk smoker "Thighs High (Grip Your Hips and Move)" and in 1983 with the synth-funk tune "Rockin' Radio." Browne wasn't very visible in the mid-to-late 1980s or early 1990s, although the mid-1990s found him recording everything from R&B to hard bop for the Hip Bop Essence label.

what to buy: Arguably Browne's best album, *Magic* ♫♫♫♫ (Arista, 1981, prod. Tom Browne) had much more to offer from an R&B standpoint than from a jazz standpoint. Though he does put his jazz trumpeting skills to good use on Billie Holiday's "God Bless the Child," it was the danceable funk and soul jew-els "Thighs High (Grip Your Hips and Move)" and the title song which made the album a hit. *Rockin' Radio* ♫♫♫ (Arista, 1983, prod. Tom Browne) was best known for the high-tech title track, but the best songs on this R&B-oriented date include the sassy "Mr. Business" and the emotional "Brighter Tomorrow." Browne did the unexpected when he recorded the enjoyable hard bop album *Another Shade of Browne* ♫♫♫♫ (Hip Bop Essence, 1996, prod. Tom Browne), which employed bassist Ron Carter, tenor saxman Javon Jackson, and drummer Idris Muhammad.

best of the rest:
Mo' Jamaica Funk ♫♫♫ (Hip Bop Essence, 1994, prod. Tom Browne)

influences:
◀◀ Clifford Brown, Lee Morgan

Alex Henderson

Dave Brubeck

Born December 6, 1920, in Concord, CA.

Dave Brubeck is the single artist most usually blamed by purists for corrupting jazz and making it "square" and "respectable" in the 1950s and early 1960s—the flip side being that he expanded the jazz audience in ways no other jazz artist had before, in the process becoming one of the largest-selling and most popular mainstream jazz artists of all time. Studying with Darius Mil-haud in the late 1940s, Brubeck was a pioneer in the synthesis of jazz and classical music. His piano work featured dense har-monies, a studied sense of rhythm, and the use of elements pre-viously alien to jazz such as the 12-tone row and odd time signa-tures. Brubeck was lucky in that he had an excellent alto sax player in his band in Paul Desmond (who once told an inter-viewer he wanted his alto to sound like a very dry martini).

Brubeck was featured on the cover of *Time* in 1954, a contro-versial move that outraged the black jazz community (though Miles Davis covered his tunes "The Duke" and "In Your Own Sweet Way"). This period also signaled the apex of cool jazz, stereotyped as a laidback West Coast form of improvising based more on theory than soul. With Brubeck's tidy song structures, unusual time signatures, and horn-rimmed glasses, and Desmond's laidback, light sound, the Brubeck Quartet was sometimes seen as a prime exponent of the style, with which

Dave Brubeck (© Jack Vartoogian)

they shared some characteristics without really being part of the movement. More importantly, they were the first band to tap the commercial potential of the college touring circuit, as documented on a string of college-titled albums.

But Brubeck really broke through with his 1960 album *Time Out*, thanks to the famous 5/4-meter tune "Take Five," which even reached #25 on the pop charts when released as a single in 1961. By that point the personnel in his quartet with Desmond (who actually wrote "Take Five") had stabilized, with the superb Joe Morello on drums (able to swing even in 5/4) and Eugene Wright on bass. Eventually, Brubeck tried his hand at more improvisational modern-rock textures in collaborations with his three sons, Chris, Darius, and Danny. In more recent years he has turned more towards large-scale compositions, often of works with a sacred leaning.

what to buy: If there's one Brubeck album to buy, it's *Time Out* ♫♫♫♫ (Columbia, 1960, prod. Teo Macero) with the classics

"Take Five" and "Blue Rondo a la Turk." *1975: The Duets* ♫♫♫♫ (A&M, 1975, prod. John Snyder) finds Brubeck in absolutely his finest form on duets with Desmond.

what to buy next: *Time Signatures: A Career Retrospective* ♫♫♫♫ (Columbia Legacy, 1992, compilation prod. Russell Gloyd, Amy Herot) covers his career from 1946 through 1991, although obviously focusing on his Columbia years, with an 80-page booklet offering helpful documentation. Featuring "Brother Can You Spare a Dime" and "Pennies from Heaven," *Brubeck Time* ♫♫♫♫ (Columbia, 1955, prod. George Avakian) has an earlier version of the quartet with Desmond, Joe Dodge (drums), and Bob Bates (bass). That LP makes up the bulk of the CD *Interchanges '54: Featuring Paul Desmond*, along with half of *Red Hot and Cool*.

what to avoid: On *Adventures in Time* ♫♫ (Columbia, 1972) Brubeck goes progressive, but doesn't quite pull it off.

best of the rest:
Jazz at Oberlin 𝄢𝄢𝄢 (Fantasy, 1953)
Jazz at the College of the Pacific 𝄢𝄢𝄢𝄢 (Fantasy, 1953)
Jazz Goes to College 𝄢𝄢𝄢𝄢 (Columbia, 1954)
In Europe 𝄢𝄢𝄢𝄢 (Columbia, 1958)
Newport 1958 𝄢𝄢𝄢𝄢 (Columbia, 1959)
Time Further Out 𝄢𝄢𝄢𝄢 (Columbia, 1961)
Countdown Time in Outer Space 𝄢𝄢𝄢𝄢 (Columbia, 1962)
Two Generations of Brubeck—Brother the Great Spirit Made Us All 𝄢𝄢𝄢 (Atlantic, 1973)

influences:

◀◀ Darius Milhaud

▶▶ Paul Desmond

Joe S. Harrington and Steve Holtje

Bill Bruford

Born William Scott Bruford, May 17, 1949, in Sevenoaks, England.

Bill Bruford's name is more associated with 1970s British progressive or art-rock music than jazz. But as a percussionist for Yes (he played on the hit single "Roundabout" and the albums *Fragile* and *Close to the Edge*), King Crimson, and other influential groups, he made his mark with a style that brought a jazz aesthetic to what would otherwise be called "rock" music. After departing Yes, Bruford replaced Ian Wallace in King Crimson, where he showed a more complex side of his work on studio albums such as *Larks' Tongue in Aspic* and the live *U.S.A.*. In the more straightforward jazz context, Bruford recorded two albums with guitarist David Torn—*Cloud about Mercury* and *Door X*—and several solo albums that cover rock, jazz, and various ethnic influences. He continues to show up periodically for Yes reunions (including the short-lived Anderson, Bruford, Wakeman and Howe).

what to buy: Bruford's collaboration with David Torn on *Cloud about Mercury* 𝄢𝄢𝄢 (ECM, 1986, prod. Manfred Eicher) is eclectic, electric jazz with the main focus on Torn's guitar and electronics. The line-up also includes Tony Levin (bass), and Mark Isham (trumpet). The main drawback is the work sometimes gets bogged down with the heavy electronic effects and synthesized drums. Bruford also shines on the title track of King Crimson's *Larks' Tongue in Aspic* 𝄢𝄢𝄢𝄢 (Atlantic, 1973, prod. King Crimson) and he is also featured heavily on "The Talking Drum."

what to buy next: Bruford's solo album *Feels Good to Me* 𝄢𝄢𝄢 (Polydor, 1978, prod. Robin Lumley, Bill Bruford) is filled with

well-crafted works that cross over between pop and jazz. Annette Peacock's vocals are a highlight.

what to avoid: Absolute Elsewhere's post–King Crimson session *In Search of Ancient Gods* 𝄢 (Warner Bros., 1976, prod. Jack Fishman, Paul Fishman) is a bland concept album based around the UFO writings of Erich von Daniken.

best of the rest:
One of a Kind 𝄢𝄢𝄢 (Polydor, 1979)
Bruford Tapes 𝄢𝄢𝄢 (Polydor, 1980)
Gradually Growing Tornado 𝄢𝄢𝄢 (Polydor, 1980)

worth searching for: Recorded with Ralph Towner and Eddie Gomez, *If Summer Had Its Ghosts* 𝄢𝄢𝄢 (Discipline Global Mobile, 1997, prod. Bill Bruford), is as close as Bruford has gotten to mainstream acoustic jazz, with Towner (acoustic guitarist of Oregon fame) and Gomez (ex–Bill Evans Trio bassist) defining the sound. Bruford swings more than his background might lead many listeners to expect. This album is on King Crimson leader Robert Fripp's label; if it's not stocked in your local CD emporium, contact the American distributor at PossProd@aol.com or call 310-435-5901.

influences:

◀◀ Buddy Rich, Gene Krupa, Keith Moon, Ringo Starr

▶▶ Carl Palmer, Alan White, Neil Peart, Ian Wallace, Jamie Muir

Chris Meloche

Jimmy Bruno

Born July 22, 1953, in Philadelphia, PA.

Jimmy Bruno learned guitar from his father, Jimmy Bruno Sr., a one-time guitarist for Nat "King" Cole. When the junior Bruno was 19, he started his professional career with Buddy Rich by going on the road with the demanding drummer/bandleader. Since that time Bruno has worked with singers Lena Horne and Frank Sinatra in addition to a surprising number of fellow guitarists—Joe Pass, Tal Farlow, Bucky Pizzarelli, and session wizard Tommy Tedesco. Currently working as a professor of jazz guitar performance and jazz improvisation at Philadelphia's University of the Arts (he has also released an instruction video), Bruno is a technically astute player partial to blazing single-note runs. The Wes Montgomery–style octave leap is also in his bag of tricks.

what to buy: Organ master Joey DeFrancesco gets special guest billing on Bruno's *Like That* 𝄢𝄢𝄢𝄢 (Concord Jazz, 1996, prod. Allen Farnham) as two of Philadelphia's finest jazz speed merchants hook up for an album that might be the best thing that either of them has done. Their interplay is so tight, clear, and impressive, particularly at the high speeds each of them seems to favor, that they might as well be twins. Both of these guys are mighty good at slow tempos too, as their playing on Bruno's moody "Night Dreamer" should prove. Steve Holloway on drums and Craig Thomas on bass are good, but they fade into the background when Bruno and DeFrancesco are working up a sweat. In addition to DeFrancesco's normal organ chores, he can be heard playing trumpet on "There Is No Greater Love" and "Stars Fell on Alabama."

what to buy next: *Burnin'* 𝄞𝄞𝄞 (Concord Jazz, 1994, prod. Jimmy Bruno) is a trio outing with the same rhythm section that appears on *Like That*. He makes some pretty astute program choices here, including a lot of material (other than the occasional obligatory original) you don't normally hear a guitarist do. He takes off on a torrid pace with Sonny Stitt's barn burner "Eternal Triangle" and then goes to another great sax player for Gene Ammons's "One for Amos," not to mention John Coltrane's "Giant Steps." Bruno breaks out the acoustic guitar for a fairly sensitive rendition of Gershwin's "Love Is Here to Stay," but then he ups the amperage again with the self-penned title tune. The guitarist doesn't quite erase memories of Johnny Smith on the gentle ballad "Moonlight in Vermont," but you have to give him points for a decent job.

the rest:
Sleight Of Hand 𝄞𝄞𝄞 (Concord Jazz, 1992)
(With Howard Alden and Frank Vignola) *Concord Jazz Guitar Collective* 𝄞𝄞𝄞 (Concord Jazz, 1995)

influences:
◀◀ John Bruno, Sr., Tommy Tedesco, Tony Mottola, Bucky Pizzarelli, Tal Farlow

Garaud MacTaggart

Ray (Raphael) Bryant

Born December 24, 1931, in Philadelphia, PA.

Ray Bryant absorbed the lessons of bebop, but his powerfully swinging and deeply soulful keyboard style also incorporates a strong dose of gospel, blues, boogie woogie, and even stride. An effective accompanist, he can also hold his own in solo recitals, as some of his most memorable sessions attest. Bryant hails from a highly musical family—his older brother is bassist Tommy Bryant and his nephews are Kevin and Robin Eubanks. His first important gig was with Tiny Grimes in the late 1940s, but he really established himself in 1953 while working as the house pianist at the Blue Note in Philly, where he accompanied such jazz stars as Miles Davis, Lester Young, and Charlie Parker. Bryant made his first significant recording on the 1955 session with Miles Davis that produced the classic *Quintet/Sextet* album with Jackie McLean and Milt Jackson. He worked as Carmen McRae's accompanist in 1956–57 and backed Coleman Hawkins and Roy Eldridge on their live recording at the 1957 Newport Jazz Festival as part of Jo Jones's trio. In 1959, the pianist made the move to New York and recorded extensively as a sideman on Prestige and Blue Note, including sessions by Sonny Rollins, Coleman Hawkins, Art Blakey, Budd Johnson, and Charlie Shavers, as well as leading his own trio. He got a taste of commercial success with a number of funky hits in the early 1960s, including "Cubano Chant," "Pawn Ticket," "Madison Time," and "Little Susie." Bryant has recorded prolifically since the late 1950s for such labels as Columbia, Cadet, Pablo, EmArcy, and Atlantic, and a number of his recordings have been reissued on CD.

what to buy: *Ray Bryant Trio* 𝄞𝄞𝄞𝄞 (Prestige, 1957/OJC, 1993, prod. Bob Weinstock) is the pianist's impressive debut as a leader. Bryant, bassist Ike Isaacs, and drummer Specs Wright were working together as Carmen McRae's rhythm section when this session was recorded, and their cohesion is evident from the first note. From Bryant's gospel-tinged originals "Blues Changes" and "Splittin'" through the modern jazz standards "Django," "Daahoud" and the Gerald Wiggins/Kenny Clarke tune "Solar," Bryant plays with the funkiness, rhythmic conviction, and harmonic insight of a major new voice. A very popular album, *Con Alma* 𝄞𝄞𝄞 (Columbia, 1961/1988, prod. John Hammond) distills the essence of Bryant's keyboard style. There's the Latin funk of "Con Alma" and "Cubano Chant," the tricky bop lines of "Milestones," the down-and-dirty "C-Jam Blues," and the lithe lyricism of "Autumn Leaves" and "Django." The album's loose and easy swinging feel can partly be attributed to bassist Bill Lee and drummer Mickey Roker, who were in Bryant's working trio at the time. Covering ballads, blues, and standards, *Solo Flight* 𝄞𝄞𝄞𝄞 (Pablo/OJC, 1977, prod. Norman Granz) is a smokin' solo set by a pianist with enough chops, personality, and swing to make a rhythm section superfluous. Whether revitalizing the archaic "Blues in Da Big Brass Bed" or reworking "Take the 'A' Train" and "St. Louis Blues," Bryant renders each tune in his inimitable and deeply soulful style.

what to buy next: The title isn't exactly accurate, as *All Blues* 𝄞𝄞𝄞𝄞 (Pablo, 1978/OJC, 1995, prod. Norman Granz) also contains "Please Send Me Someone to Love," but Bryant plays the

Percy Mayfield lament with such feeling it may as well be a blues. Accompanied by the superlative bassist Sam Jones and drummer Grady Tate, Bryant shows there's more than one way to skin a blues as he employs various grooves and styles on "C-Jam Blues," "Billie's Bounce," and his original "Blues Changes." Always known for his extensive repertoire, Bryant really stretches out on *Ray's Tribute to His Jazz Piano Friends* ♫♫♫♫ (JMI, 1998, prod. Larry Hathaway), a session ranging from Dave Brubeck ("The Duke") and Horace Silver ("Doodlin'") to Kenny Barron ("Sunshower") and Randy Weston ("Hi-Fly"). Backed by bassist Ray Drummond and drummer Winard Harper, Bryant plays with all the soul, intelligence, and unpredictability that have been the hallmark of his style for more than four decades. Bryant was already an excellent accompanist when he made his recording debut backing singer Betty Carter on *Meet Betty Carter and Ray Bryant* ♫♫♫♫ (Columbia/Legacy, 1955–56, prod. Marv Holzman). This reissue contains a big band session featuring four Gigi Gryce arrangements (reissued previously on the Betty Carter album *Social Call*), a trio session augmented on three tracks by Jerome Richardson's flute, and eight tracks of Bryant's trio, featuring Wendell Marshall (bass) and Philly Joe Jones (drums), without Carter. Bryant provides Carter, who sounds so fresh and original it's hard to understand how she was overlooked for so long, with deft and sensitive support throughout. On his trio tracks he plays three strong originals and joyously romps through the standards "Old Devil Moon" and "Get Happy."

best of the rest:

Alone With the Blues ♫♫♫♫ (New Jazz/OJC, 1959)
Here's Ray Bryant ♫♫♫♫ (Pablo/OJC, 1976)
Montreux '77 ♫♫♫♫ (Pablo/OJC, 1977)
Solo Flight ♫♫♫♫ (Pablo/OJC, 1977)
Potpourri ♫♫♫♫ (Pablo, 1980/OJC, 1997)

worth searching for: One of Bryant's better solo outings of the past decade, *Plays Blues and Ballads* ♫♫♫♫ (Jazz Connaisseur, 1991, prod. Jorg Koran) captures the pianist in peak form, exploring a host of tunes, mostly dating from the 1920s and 1930s. Most memorable is his medley linking "She's Funny That Way," "Memories of You," and "I Surrender Dear" and his gospel finale "Blues in the Pulpit."

influences:

◀◀ Teddy Wilson, Art Tatum, Red Garland
▶▶ Eric Reed, Cyrus Chestnut

Andrew Gilbert

Jeanie Bryson
Born c. 1958.

A talented pop-jazz singer with a small, husky, sensual voice, Jeanie Bryson is more an interpreter of songs than an improvisor. She can swing hard when she wants to, but is at her best phrasing gracefully on ballads or finger-snapping, mid-tempo arrangements. Raised in a musical household, she cites her main influences as Billie Holiday, Carmen McRae, and Dinah Washington. Bryson began singing professionally in college and in 1987 quit her day job to sing full time. In the early 1990s, Bryson revealed that her father was Dizzy Gillespie. Though they had little contact while she was growing up, he encouraged her once she decided on a career in music. Bryson has made guest appearances on albums by Larry Coryell and Grover Washington Jr. and released three fine albums on Telarc.

what to buy: An impressive debut, *I Love Being Here with You* ♫♫♫♫ (Telarc, 1993, prod. John Snyder) pays tribute to her favorite singers. She evokes Billie Holiday with "You've Changed" and honors Ernestine Anderson with the title track. Bryson holds her own with the world class rhythm section—Kenny Barron (piano), Ray Drummond (bass), Vic Juris (guitar), and Ron Davis (drums)—and vibraphonist Steve Nelson, tenor saxophonist Don Braden, and trumpeter Wallace Roney add to the album's jazz content. Her wonderfully exotic version of Barron's "Sunshower" is the album's standout track. Recording an album of tunes by or associated with Peggy Lee, *Some Cats Know* ♫♫♫♫ (Telarc, 1996, prod. John Snyder), was a stroke of genius. Though Bryson has a very different sound than the Peg, like Lee she has learned to make the most of her small voice. Pianist Terry Trotter, bassist Jim Hughart, and drummer Harold Jones make a cohesive rhythm section and tenor saxophonist Red Holloway handles the blues duties. Bryson rounds up the usual suspects—"Some Cats Know," "Why Don't You Do Right?," "Fever," and Lee's own "I Didn't Know Enough About You"—and with Lee collaborator/guitarist John Chiodini on hand, Bryson manages the difficult feat of honoring Lee without imitating her.

what to buy next: *Tonight I Need You So* ♫♫♫♫ (Telarc, 1994, prod. John Snyder) is a worthy sophomore effort that features both pop and jazz tunes. Bryson's direct, unadorned singing style is perfectly suited to her material, turning the well-worn standards "Honeysuckle Rose" and "Willow Weep for Me" into rewarding listening. Highlights include a delicate duet with guitarist Vic Juris on "The Face I Love" and an intimate interpretation of the bossa nova "Solamente Tu." And Bryson once again features top-flight players such as Don Braden, Paquito D'Rivera, Claudio Roditi, Danilo Perez, Jay Ashby, and Steve Nelson. Pianist Ted Brancato supplies most of the arrangements.

worth searching for: One of trumpeter Terence Blanchard's weaker sessions, *The Billie Holiday Songbook* 𝄞𝄞𝄞 (Columbia, 1994, prod. Terence Blanchard, Miles Goodman) features Jeanie Bryson singing on five of the 12 tracks. The arrangements are attractive, but don't leave much room for Bryson to maneuver. She avoids sounding like Holiday, but doesn't really put her own stamp on the music either.

influences:
◀◀ Billie Holiday, Carmen McRae, Dinah Washington

▶▶ Nnenna Freelon

Andrew Gilbert

Milt Buckner

Born July 10, 1915, in St. Louis, MO. Died July 27, 1977, in Chicago, IL.

Milt Buckner, a pioneer of the use of organ in jazz, began as a pianist and arranger in the swing era. He arranged for McKinneys Cotton Pickers in 1934, but it was during a long and fruitful run with Lionel Hampton's orchestra in the 1940s (he reunited with Hamp a few times in later years) that Buckner really started to attract attention. His unique "locked hands" piano technique was utilized by many, including George Shearing. While associated with Hampton, Buckner penned the classic "Hamps Boogie Woogie," among others. By the early 1950s Buckner was playing organ and fronting a small group of his own. The jumping R&B and blues of this era, including Buckner's minor hit "Trapped," has survived much better than the ballads. He continued to occasionally perform and record on piano (and vibes), but it was on the organ, both as a sideman with frequent partner Illinois Jacquet and on his own, that his exuberant personality was expressed most fully. His ability to create a swelling, pulsating flow of sound was perhaps put to its best use on the European recordings he made in the early 1970s with Clarence "Gatemouth" Brown and others. Often, Buckner could be heard on recordings grunting, singing, and shouting encouragement to himself as he played. Buckner, younger brother of the Jimmie Lunceford band's swing/hot sax star Teddy Buckner, played happy, good-time music that had more to do with lifting the spirits of the listeners than it had to do with technical virtuosity, though his skills were considerable.

what to buy: There's nothing in print under Buckner's name. A good sampling of his work with Lionel Hampton in the 1940s

can be found on the excellent two-CD set *Hamp* 𝄞𝄞𝄞𝄞 (MCA, 1996). Buckner's 1970s work on both organ and piano, in a sideman role, can be heard to great advantage on a pair of fine Clarence "Gatemouth" Brown reissues, *Pressure Cooker* 𝄞𝄞𝄞𝄞 (Alligator, 1986) and *Just Got Lucky* 𝄞𝄞𝄞 (Evidence, 1993).

what to avoid: You'd have to search pretty hard to find *Mighty High* 𝄞𝄞 (Argo, 1959), *Please Mr. Organ Player* 𝄞 (Argo, 1960), and *Midnight Mood* 𝄞 (Argo, 1961), but you needn't bother unless you're a completist or a big fan of mellow organ mood music.

worth searching for: Any of the French Black and Blue label 1970s releases featuring Buckner's organ are recommended, but they are hard to find. Best is *Green Onions* 𝄞𝄞𝄞 (Black and Blue, 1975, prod. Jacques Morgantini), which includes a wild, romping version of the title track in which Buckner sings of culinary delights and drives the point with swirling bursts of the mighty Hammond organ. Also, Illinois Jacquet's *Genius at Work* 𝄞𝄞𝄞 (Black Lion, 1971) is a fun, if not especially sophisticated, live set recorded at Ronnie Scott's London jazz club in 1971—a good display of the raw excitement generated by Jacquet and Buckner when they were loose. The LP *Rockin Hammond* 𝄞𝄞𝄞 (Capitol, 1956) collects some of Buckners three-minute jukebox singles.

influences:
◀◀ Count Basie, Fats Waller, "Wild" Bill Davis

▶▶ Bill Doggett, Doc Bagby, Jimmy McGriff, George Shearing, Dave Brubeck

Dan Bindert

Alex Bugnon

Born October 10, 1958, in Montreux, Switzerland.

Although his music may spark debates on classification, contemporary jazz pianist Alex Bugnon, a talented European jazz pianist working in the United States, has captured the attention of music audiences world-wide with his unique style of playing. As a young musician in Montreux, Switzerland, growing up under the shadow of Europe's most famous jazz festival, Bugnon witnessed many diverse musical styles. After studying piano in Switzerland, he moved to France for formal piano training at a Paris conservatory, and then to Boston, Massachusetts to continue his education at the Berklee College of Music. Bugnon gained experience performing and touring with local gospel groups and left Boston for New York, where he spent four years working as sideman for musicians such as Najee, Freddie Jackson, Keith Sweat, Patti Austin, and James Ingram before landing his first record contract. Not wanting to be boxed into one particular style, Bugnon's music spans multiple genres from 1970s funk to traditional jazz, and includes gospel, R&B, and classical. His earlier recordings reflect the influences of his long-time friend, pianist Herbie Hancock, as well as the electrified funk of George Duke that has made a partial impact on his style.

what to buy: Bugnon's *Tales from the Bright Side* ⚹⚹⚹⚹, (RCA, 1995, prod. Alex Bugnon, Charles Bell, Bernard Wright) is by far the most far-reaching of his work. With all but one arrangement written by Bugnon, this CD reveals a direction toward more mainstream music than past releases. Numbers such as "Okra," although using programmed effects, display an original sound and his piano playing is more expansive. The number "Yaslyn," is a straight-ahead piece in trio setting without synthesizers and is overall quite impressive. Bugnon's accomplished piano work, thoughtful yet provoking, is helped by a warm, spirited solo by Vincent Henry on tenor saxophone. Anthony Jackson on bass guitar and Poogie Bell on drums add nice rhythm, rounding out what is an impressive tune. "Waltz in G Minor" is a reflective number with Bugnon performing solo piano, a classical arrangement portraying another dimension of his talent on piano.

what to buy next: Bugnon's second release on Epic, *This Time Around* ⚹⚹⚹ (Sony, 1993), gives a good indication of the diverse styles influencing his play. His original, "The Way We Used to Be," is a soft yet enlightening ballad exhibiting his piano capabilities backed by a solid horn arrangement. "Sweet Sticky Thing," "This Time Around," and "Klook Mop," are bright contemporary tunes with interesting rhythm sections containing strong funk and R&B influences. Bugnon's first solo Epic release, *107 Degrees in the Shade* ⚹⚹⚹, (Sony, 1991, prod. Alex Bugnon) is a collection of 10 mostly contemporary tunes with five of the numbers written and arraigned exclusively by Bugnon. With a feel that captures his profound talent and love of music, most of the numbers on this release are synthesized studio creations with their roots in the R&B vein that seems to have shaped a major part of Bugnon's musical life. If you shy away from the preordained selections touted by the record company (although strong sellers on the contemporary music charts), tunes such as "When I Think about Home"—a beautiful creation written by Bugnon—and "The Lone Crusader" are exceptionally well crafted and convey the vibrancy, skills, and originality that he brings with him to the piano.

the rest:
Love Season ⚹⚹⚹ (Capitol, 1989)
Head over Heels ⚹⚹⚹ (Capitol, 1990)

influences:
◄◄ Carlos Santana, Aretha Franklin, Les McCann, Billy Cobham, George Duke, Herbie Hancock

Keith Brickhouse

John Bunch

Born December 1, 1921, in Tipton, IN.

John Bunch began playing piano in a small Indiana town in the early 1930s and, by age 12, was appearing in clubs all over the state that officially honored him at the 1996 Elkhart Jazz Festival. An Army Air Force enlistee in 1942, Bunch was shot down and captured during his 17th mission over Germany. He passed time as a prisoner playing with the camp band and wrote his first arrangement there. Upon his return to the U.S., Bunch entered Indiana University, graduating in 1950. He mostly put music aside until age 34, when he headed for California and a spot in Woody Herman's band, followed by band work with Benny Goodman and Maynard Ferguson, and subsequent dates around New York City with Urbie Green. In December, 1966, Bunch joined Tony Bennett as accompanist and musical director for six years, and was appropriately referred to by the singer as "Gentleman John Bunch."

In 1972, Bunch returned to jazz full-time. As well as working solo over the years, he worked with the Scott Hamilton Quintet, frequently returned to the Benny Goodman fold, and played mostly in small groups. He currently works with guitarist Bucky Pizzarelli and bassist Jay Leonhart in a powerhouse combine dubbed New York Swing. Bunch has been around long enough to come under the spell of Fats Waller and Teddy Wilson, but was young enough to adopt some Bud Powell mannerisms and sophisticated harmonies. Bunch remains very much a melody player with a delicate keyboard touch and yet can swing with the best.

what to buy: *John Bunch Solo* ⚹⚹⚹⚹ (Arbors, 1997, prod. Rachel Domber, Mat Domber) is a superb solo outing that finds Bunch revisiting tunes by Fats Waller ("Ain't Misbehavin'," "Honeysuckle Rose," "Keepin' Out of Mischief Now"), Ellington/Strayhorn ("Something to Live For," "Isfahan"), Rowles ("We Take the Cake"), and Brubeck ("The Duke") along with a batch of standards containing some subtle surprises. Bunch always keeps in touch with the melodies. Bunch teams with longtime rhythm cohort Phil Flanigan on *Struttin'* ⚹⚹⚹⚹ (Arbors, 1996, prod. Rachel Domber, Mat Domber). Together they work their way through a collection of enduring standards, including "On a Slow Boat to China" and "Struttin' with Some Barbeque." Other interesting stops along the way include a warmly rendered version of "Smoke Gets in Your Eyes," an apt-named "Sultry Serenade," and a romping "As Long as I Live."

what to buy next: *John Bunch Plays Kurt Weill* ♪♪♪♪ (Chiaroscuro, 1991, prod. Hank O'Neal) is a solo piano album that is remarkable on several counts. Weill's tunes are seldom heard in a jazz context, original 1975 tracks are seamlessly reproduced with additional cuts, and Bunch's provocative tempos and rhythmic approach make for a very stimulating listen. *The Best Thing for You* ♪♪♪ (Concord Jazz, 1987, prod. Ed Trabanco) is a trio session featuring Bunch, bassist Phil Flanigan, and drummer Chuck Riggs, all members of the Scott Hamilton Quintet at the time. It's no wonder they have the sound of a working unit on the agreeable mix of tunes, including "Au Privave," "I Can't Get Started," and "Jitterbug Waltz."

the rest:
(With Bucky Pizzarelli) *NY Swing* ♪♪♪ (LRC Ltd., 1992)
Cole Porter Collective by NY Swing ♪♪♪ (LRC Ltd., 1992)
New York Swing Plays Rodgers and Hart ♪♪♪ (LRC Ltd., 1993)
New York Swing Plays Jerome Kern ♪♪♪ (LRC Ltd., 1994)

influences:
◀◀ Fats Waller, Teddy Wilson, Bud Powell

John T. Bitter

Jane Bunnett

Born 1955, in Toronto, Ontario, Canada.

Bunnett was originally trained as a classical pianist but had to give up that career option when tendinitis made it too difficult for her to play. Traveling to San Francisco to recoup her energies, Bunnett heard a series of concerts by Charles Mingus at Keystone Corners which inspired her to change her instrumental focus to the flute. She is also a gifted soprano saxophone player, having studied with Steve Lacy and won a couple of *Down Beat* polls for the instrument. Another crucial element in her musical history revolves around her discovery of Cuban rhythms and musicians. Before this time, she was a fairly straight-ahead post-bop player with interesting, if conventional, ideas. Bunnett's exposure to Cuban music has opened up new vistas in her playing and widened her compositional palette.

what to buy: Although Bunnett became a fan of Latin rhythms prior to her first trip to Cuba, it was that physical journey that introduced her to some of the most talented musicians in the genre and helped make possible the wonderful *Spirits of Ha-*

vana ♪♪♪♪ (Messidor, 1991, prod. Guillermo Barreto, Danny Greenspoon). Bunnett's flute solo over the percussion ensemble Grupo Yoruba Andabo ("Hymn") is squarely in the tradition of such Cuban masters as Fajardo and Filiberto Rico, while the group's take on Thelonious Monk's "Epistrophy," with Bunnett on soprano saxophone, has interesting rhythms percolating beneath the surface courtesy of pianist Gonzalo Rubalcaba and a slew of percussion. The focus of the album is on the sound of the group although there are spaces for soloists. Other participants in the sessions include pianist Hilario Durán, vocalist Merceditas Valdes, bassist Kieran Overs, trumpeter Larry Cramer, and timbales player Guillermo Barreto, to whom the album is dedicated.

what to buy next: On *New York Duets* ♪♪♪ (Denon/Music & Arts, 1989, prod. Larry Cramer), Bunnett and Mingus alumnus Don Pullen engage in some playing that rides the razor's edge between intellect and heart. Pianist Pullen writes nice tunes and it's good to see two of them, "Double Arc Jake" and "Gratitude," here. Also welcome are the two Monk pieces that open and close the album, "Bye-ya" and "Little Rootie Tootie." Bunnett writes the bulk of the material on this project and shifts between post-bop extremism (Pullen keeps up with her in this regard) and simple melodies played with beguiling prowess. Her flute and sax playing is always commendable and she makes an interesting instrumental choice during "For Merceditas" when she plays the pan pipes. Vocalists Jeanne Lee and Sheila Jordan are part of the Bunnett sound picture on *The Water Is Wide* ♪♪♪ (Evidence, 1994, prod. Larry Cramer). Although they don't sing on every song, when they do sing, Lee and Jordan prove why they are tops in their field. Their work on the title tune (an old spiritual) is packed with emotion, trading stanzas with each other before melding their vocals on the last verse. Pullen and Overs spring the rhythm with master drummer Billy Hart, and trumpeter/producer Cramer proves to be an interesting composer as well with "Burning Tear" and "Influence Peddling." Bunnett does her usual sterling job on soprano sax along with some particularly noteworthy flute playing on Monk's "Pannonica."

the rest:
Live at Sweet Basil ♪♪♪ (Denon/Music & Arts, 1991)
Rendez-Vous Brazil/Cuba ♪♪♪ (Justin Time, 1995)
Jane Bunnett & the Cuban Piano Masters ♪♪♪ (World Pacific, 1996)
Chamalongo ♪♪♪ (Blue Note, 1998)

influences:
◀◀ Steve Lacy

Garaud MacTaggart

Dave Burrell

Born September 10, 1940, in Middletown, OH.

Firmly entrenched in the history of jazz piano, Burrell invokes everything from ragtime to hard bop in his playing. However, as a product of the mid to late 1960s free scene and student of Third Stream ideas, he always takes these elements and pushes them forward and outward. The results are outstanding, if sometimes confounding.

Burrell's first musical influences were his mother, a pianist/organist and singer, and his father, also a singer. He remembers that when his family moved to Hawaii when he was still young, the only records which made the trip with them were by Louis Armstrong and Jimmie Lunceford. A visit by Ellington vocalist Herb Jeffries to his family steered Burrell's musical ambitions towards jazz and he eventually enrolled at the Berklee School of Music in Boston. Burrell's early work with Tony Williams, Marion Brown, and Grachan Moncur III led to the late 1960s formation of the Untraditional Jazz Improvisational Team with Byard Lancaster and the 360 Degree Music Experience with Beaver Harris and Moncur. This gave way to work with Archie Shepp, Sunny Murray and others, as well as to a career as a leader and solo performer.

what to buy: *High One High Two* ♫♫♫ (Freedom/Black Lion, 1968, prod. Alan Douglas) has guest star Pharoah Sanders . . . on tambourine. Regardless, this fine album (which also includes drummer Bobby Kapp and bassist Sirone from the Untraditional group, as well as Sunny Murray) finds Burrell slicing and dicing *West Side Story* into a mind-bending medley. Additionally, all the songs found on side two get reworked into a "Theme Stream Medley" of their own and all in their own ways are successful. Burrell's piano work is as wide-ranging as it will ever be, with passages ranging from baroque flourishes to bop stride and, of course, free banging. Although conceived as an opera, *Windward Passages* ♫♫♫ (hat HUT, 1980, prod. Pia Uehlinger, Werner X. Uehlinger)—on this record, at least—takes the form of a cathartic, autobiographical solo piano piece. Showcasing Burrell's stylistic panoply, this album shows that Third Stream can have soul too.

what to buy next: Four collaborations with David Murray, *Daybreak* ♫♫♫ (Gazell, 1989, prod. Sam Charters), *In Concert* ♫♫♫♫ (Victo, 1991), *Brother to Brother* ♫♫♫ (Gazell, 1993, prod. Sam Charters), and *Windward Passages* ♫♫♫♫ (Black Saint, 1997, prod. Giovanni Bonandrini) don't really exhibit much of Burrell's pianistic grace, but they do show how easily he can shift from swingin' stride playing to out-and-out percussive pounding. These two artists have influenced each other through the past and it's illustrative to hear their relationship manifest itself in these performances.

the rest:
Plays Ellington and Monk ♫♫ (Denon, 1978)
Jelly Roll Joys ♫♫ (Gazell, 1991)

worth searching for: Loosely based on Puccini's opera, *La Vie de Bohême* ♫♫♫♫ (BYG, 1970, prod. Georgakarakos Young, Jean-Luc Young) is among Burrell's finest moments. Burrell (who also plays harp on this set) is accompanied in fine style by Grachan Moncur III, trumpeter Ric Colbeck, and phenomenal tenor player Kenneth Terroade. Although it may sound like a conceptually heavy load, Burrell's glistening arrangements and fluid playing style combine with an enthusiastic band and, rather than come off dull and analytical, *Bohême* swings and squeals in a quite nonclassical manner.

influences:
⏪ Fats Waller, Cecil Taylor
⏩ Anthony Davis

Jason Ferguson

Kenny Burrell

Born July 31, 1931, in Detroit, MI.

An amazing, consistent musician who has recorded countless albums, guitarist Kenny Burrell has retained essentially the same style throughout his career. Why change perfection? With his light, cool tone, Burrell developed his own approach to bebop guitar, expanding on Charlie Christian's innovations with his finely honed harmonic sensibility. Burrell rarely dazzles with his technique. Rather, he voices and places his notes with precision, preferring subtlety and understatement to flash. Wes Montgomery cited Burrell as one of his early influences.

Surrounded by music as a child, Burrell bought his first guitar at age 13 and soon began participating in the vibrant Detroit jazz scene. He made his first recordings six years later with Dizzy Gillespie and earned a B.A. in music composition and theory from Wayne State University. After graduating, Burrell impressed Oscar Peterson enough during a nightclub session that the pianist recruited him to fill in for Herb Ellis, and Burrell spent six months touring with Peterson's trio. Burrell settled in New York in 1956 and quickly became a mainstay on both the jazz and studio scene. As both a sideman and a leader, he has recorded with a who's who of jazz, including John Coltrane, Coleman Hawkins, Billie Holiday, Kenny Dorham, Jimmy Smith,

Kenny Burrell **(Archive Photos)**

Sonny Rollins, Stan Getz, and Milt Jackson. One of the great interpreters of Ellingtonia (he was Ellington's favorite guitarist), Burrell always includes an Ellington section in his performances and has recorded Duke's music extensively. Long involved in jazz education, Burrell took over UCLA's jazz program in the mid-1990s.

what to buy: Burrell played on many Prestige blowing sessions, and *Kenny Burrell and John Coltrane* 🎵🎵🎵🎵 (Prestige, 1958/1987, prod. Bob Weinstock) stands out as one of his best dates from the late 1950s. The contrast between 'Trane's "sheets of sound" approach and Burrell's more restrained playing makes for a felicitous pairing, especially their duet on "Why Was I Born." The rhythm section features Tommy Flanagan (piano), Paul Chambers (bass), and Jimmy Cobb (drums). *Guitar Forms* 🎵🎵🎵🎵 (Verve, 1965/1997, prod. Creed Taylor) is a classic session featuring Gil Evans's arrangements for Burrell's guitar, expanded on the CD reissue with 11 additional tracks covering multiple takes of the small group material. Designed to demon-

strate Burrell's versatility, the five tracks with the Evans orchestra include a ballad, a bossa nova, and a classical piece. Three tunes feature a quintet with pianist Roger Kellaway, and Burrell, who is the album's only soloist, plays Gershwin's "Prelude No. 2" unaccompanied. With a dozen tunes from the Ellington/Strayhorn songbook *Ellington Is Forever, Volume I* 🎵🎵🎵🎵 (Fantasy, 1975/1993, prod. Kenny Burrell) is an inventive, well-conceived tribute by one of Ellington's foremost interpreters. Burrell recruited a top-flight band with organist Jimmy Smith, trumpeters Thad Jones, Snooky Young, and Jon Faddis and tenors Joe Henderson and Jerome Richardson, giving them all ample room to solo. Ernie Andrews sings on two tracks and pianist Jimmy Jones leads the formidable rhythm section. *Then Along Came Kenny* 🎵🎵🎵🎵 (Evidence, 1996, prod. Kenny Burrell, Yoichi Nakao) is one of Burrell's most satisfying albums of the '90s, recorded live at the Village Vanguard in 1993. Featuring the brilliant, bluesy pianist James Williams, bassist Peter Washington, and longtime Burrell sideman drummer Sherman Ferguson, the quartet plays Monk ("I Mean You"), bop ("Yardbird

Suite"), Latin ("Manteca"), funky calypso ("Funji Mama"), ballads, and blues. The band swings hard and Burrell is clearly enjoying the proceedings.

what to buy next: With only 37-minutes of music *Kenny Burrell* 𝄽𝄽𝄽𝄽 (Prestige, 1957/OJC, 1993, prod. Bob Weinstock) could be a better value. But the mix of Cecil Payne's gruff but flexible baritone sax with Burrell's light and mellow guitar is irresistible. Powered by a tough all-Detroit rhythm section featuring Tommy Flanagan (piano), Doug Watkins (bass), and Elvin Jones (drums), this music still sounds fresh today, especially the opening "Don't Cry Baby." A two-disc reissue that includes two albums *Blue Lights, Volumes I & II* 𝄽𝄽𝄽𝄽 (Blue Note, 1958/1997, prod. Alfred Lion) is a better-than-average bop-based blowing session that's especially notable for the presence of two fine but forgotten horn players in trumpeter Louis Smith and tenor Tina Brooks (Junior Cook is also featured on tenor). The horn men take advantage of the ample solo space, propelled by Burrell, Sam Jones (bass), Art Blakey (drums) and either Duke Jordan or Bobby Timmons (piano). Burrell penned four of the nine tunes, including the funky blues "Yes Baby." By recruiting excellent but diverse musicians and varying personnel from track to track, Burrell created another masterpiece *Ellington Is Forever, Volume II* 𝄽𝄽𝄽𝄽 (Fantasy, 1975/1994, prod. Kenny Burrell) a fitting tribute to one of jazz's Olympian figures. In addition to Jimmy Smith, Thad Jones, Snooky Young, Joe Henderson, and Jerome Richardson, the second session features Nat Adderley, Gary Bartz and former Ellingtonian Quentin Jackson. The highlights are many, including Thad and Snooky's unison work on "Come Sunday" and Ernie Andrews singing "Satin Doll." One of Burrell's more lyrical, introspective sessions *Lotus Blossom* 𝄽𝄽𝄽𝄽 (Concord, 1995, prod. John Burk) features him on electric and acoustic guitars. Of the 13 tracks, he plays six solo (including ravishing versions of Ellington's "Warm Valley" and Strayhorn's title track), four in duo with bassist Ray Drummond, and three with a trio adding drummer Yoron Israel. Though Burrell sounds less comfortable on the acoustic than the electric guitar, he gets a beautiful tone on the "unplugged" instrument.

what to avoid: *God Bless the Child* 𝄽𝄽 (CTI, 1971/Sony, 1987, prod. Creed Taylor) is a lugubrious, overproduced session with far too many cellos, though the presence of Freddie Hubbard and Burrell's always tasteful musicianship prevent it from being a total dog.

best of the rest:
All Day Long 𝄽𝄽𝄽𝄽 (Prestige, 1957/1990)
All Night Long 𝄽𝄽𝄽𝄽 (Prestige, 1957/1990)
Two Guitars 𝄽𝄽𝄽𝄽 (Prestige, 1957/1992)

Tin Tin Deo 𝄽𝄽𝄽𝄽 (Concord, 1977/1994)
Guiding Spirit 𝄽𝄽𝄽𝄽 (Contemporary, 1990)
Sunup to Sundown 𝄽𝄽𝄽𝄽 (Contemporary, 1991)
Midnight at the Village Vanguard 𝄽𝄽𝄽𝄽 (Evidence, 1993)

worth searching for: *Midnight Blue* 𝄽𝄽𝄽𝄽 (Blue Note, 1963 prod. Alfred Lion) is an excellent turn-the-lights-down-low blues session with tenor saxophonist Stanley Turrentine.

influences:
◀◀ Charlie Christian

▶▶ Wes Montgomery, Grant Green, Rodney Jones, Bobby Broom

Andrew Gilbert

Gary Burton

Born January 23, 1943, in Anderson, IN.

A major innovator on the vibraphone, Gary Burton first studied piano and composition during high school, receiving lessons that were to form the heart of his subsequent approach to melody and harmony. By using four mallets instead of the traditional two, Burton created a new sound platform from which future vibes players (using techniques pioneered by Burton) could launch their exploratory solos. Burton worked in Nashville, Tennessee when he was 17, recording with guitarists Hank Garland and Chet Atkins among others. After studying at Berklee College of Music, he joined George Shearing's quintet (1963) prior to working with Stan Getz in 1964. By 1967 Burton was heading a quartet—with guitarist Larry Coryell, bassist Steve Swallow, and drummer Bob Moses—introduced rock elements into the language of jazz and created one of the legendary hybrid albums of the 1960s, *A Genuine Tong Funeral*, featuring material composed by Carla Bley. Since that time Burton has recorded in a wide variety of formats and with a corresponding number of master musicians, including violinist Stephane Grappelli, bandoneon player Astor Piazzolla, and pianists Keith Jarrett, Chick Corea, and Fred Hersch. Burton's sessions as a leader for RCA, Atlantic, and GRP have all been pretty solid but his recorded legacy is strongest with the series of releases he created with ECM under the guidance of producer Manfred Eicher. Burton has gotten heavily involved with the academic side of jazz through clinics and his work with Berklee College of Music. A mainstay at Berklee, where he has worked for over 25 years, Burton has attained the position of executive vice president after having risen through the ranks as a professor and dean of curriculum. He has also won three Grammy awards and been voted to the Percussive Arts Society's Hall of Fame.

what to buy: The (now out-of-print) album that Burton made with Piazzolla back in the '70s was a subtle marvel, but *Astor Piazzolla Reunion* 𝄞𝄞𝄞𝄞 (Concord Jazz, 1998, prod. Gary Burton, Marcelo Morano), a memorial to the deceased tango master and bandoneon wizard, is a more than adequate replacement. All the material here was written by Piazzolla, combining tango's passion with the spirit of jazz improvisation. Burton's vibes provide an open, airy touch that works well within Piazzolla's prescribed limits and Fernando Suarez-Paz (violin) and Horacio Malvicino (guitar), who worked with Piazzolla, add the imprint of authenticity to the sessions. Other than some studio trickery that meshes Burton with Piazzolla on "Mi Refugio," one of the composer's signature tunes, all of the bandoneon parts are played by either Daniel Binelli or Marcelo Nisinman. By the time *Dreams So Real: Music of Carla Bley* 𝄞𝄞𝄞𝄞 (ECM, 1976/1994, prod. Manfred Eicher) had been recorded, both Burton and Bley had grown in performance and compositional stature since the halcyon days of *A Genuine Tong Funeral.* The music is wonderful, skewed as it is toward the unconventional, with a plethora of basically hummable melodies. "Vox Humana" and the medley of "Ictus/Syndrome/Wrong Key Donkey," receive recordings that come close to definitive. The quintet features the twin guitars of Pat Metheny and Mick Goodrick along with bassist Steve Swallow and drummer Bob Moses, surely one of Burton's great groups. *Passengers* 𝄞𝄞𝄞𝄞 (ECM, 1977/1994, prod. Manfred Eicher) is probably the most accessible of Burton's ECM quartet/quintet albums. Pat Metheny's playing has the liquid lyricism that has made him such a popular jazz guitarist but he isn't challenged in quite the same way he was when Mick Goodrick was in the band. Songs by Corea and Metheny make up the bulk of the set with bassists Eberhard Weber and Steve Swallow also contributing material. Corea's "Sea Journey" is the standout while Weber's "Yellow Fields" is an oft-recorded ECM standard from that decade.

what to buy next: *The New Quartet* 𝄞𝄞𝄞𝄞 (ECM, 1973/1994, prod. Manfred Eicher) showcases a pre-Metheny quartet that is a bit tougher sounding than on some of Burton's other ECM releases. Abraham Laboriel's bass playing adds the closest thing to funk that the label had experienced to that time. Mick Goodrick's guitar lines are harder edged than would be the rule in later Burton groups but not quite as in-your-face as Larry Coryell's playing was in Burton's earlier ensembles. The vibraphonist has consistently championed some fine writers and this album features good stuff from Corea, Keith Jarrett, Bley, Mike Gibbs, and Gordon Beck plus one song from Burton himself ("Brownout"). *Departure* 𝄞𝄞𝄞𝄞 (Concord Jazz, 1997, prod.

KENNY BURRELL

song "It Don't Mean a Thing (If It Ain't Got That Swing)"
album *Ellington Is Forever: Volume 1* (Fantasy, 1975/1993)
instrument Guitar

Gary Burton, Tommy Kamp) shows us no new tricks but ends up as a satisfying listen anyway with fine versions of "Poinciana" and "If I Were a Bell." "Tossed Salads and Scrambled Eggs" (the theme from the television series *Frasier*) is the closest thing to a blemish on the release but even that has a rather kitschy charm. Burton's sidemen include pianist Fred Hersch, guitarist John Scofield, bassist John Pattitucci, and drummer Peter Erskine. *Face to Face* 𝄞𝄞𝄞𝄞 (GRP, 1995, prod. Gary Burton) is a duet album with Burton's long time associate, pianist Makoto Ozone. While not perhaps in the same rarefied air as the Burton/Corea collaborations have been there is something more satisfying about this release. The release of intellect and swing in equal amounts which evades the more cerebral Burton/Corea projects is not a problem here. Check out their tributes to Thelonious Monk ("Monk's Dream" and "Blue Monk") or the delightful "My Romance."

best of the rest:
New Vibe Man in Town 𝄞𝄞𝄞 (RCA, 1961/1995)
A Genuine Tong Funeral 𝄞𝄞𝄞𝄞 (RCA, 1967/One Way, 1997)

Lofty Fake Anagram 𝄞𝄞𝄞✔ (RCA, 1967/One Way, 1996)
Gary Burton and Keith Jarrett/Throb 𝄞𝄞𝄞 (Atlantic, 1971/1969)
Ring 𝄞𝄞𝄞 (ECM, 1974/1994)
(With Chick Corea) *Duet* 𝄞𝄞𝄞 (ECM, 1979)
Real Life Hits 𝄞𝄞𝄞✔ (ECM, 1985/1994)
Whiz Kids 𝄞𝄞𝄞✔ (ECM, 1987/1994)
Works 𝄞𝄞𝄞✔ (ECM, 1988/1994)
Reunion 𝄞𝄞𝄞✔ (GRP, 1990)
Gary Burton and the Berklee All-Stars 𝄞𝄞𝄞 (JVC, 1995)
Collection 𝄞𝄞𝄞✔ (GRP, 1996)
Duster 𝄞𝄞𝄞✔ (Koch Jazz, 1997)
(With Chick Corea) *Native Sense* 𝄞𝄞𝄞𝄞 (Stretch/Concord Jazz, 1997)

worth searching for: While there are some live performances available of Burton with Getz, the earliest pairing of the two can be found on *Nobody Else But Me* 𝄞𝄞𝄞𝄞 (Verve, 1994, prod. Creed Taylor), a Stan Getz studio album. Recorded in 1964, just as the Getz album with João Gilberto was setting off the bossa nova wave, this was a fine sampling of early Burton and mid-period Getz. It includes plenty of show-tune standards but also features two Burton compositions ("6-Nix-Quix-Flix" and "Out of Focus") and a tune by Mike Gibbs ("Sweet Sorrow"), an important writer of material for Burton's later catalog. *Alone at Last* 𝄞𝄞𝄞𝄞 (Atlantic, 1971, prod. Joel Dorn) an out-of-print album that displays Burton's awesome mallet technique on four solo performances and, through the miracle of overdubbing, his keyboard skills on three others. The solo renditions are what make this album worthwhile, especially a knockout version of the Antonio Carlos Jobim tune "Chega De Saudade (No More Blues)."

influences:

◀◀ Harry Partch, Bill Evans, Stan Getz, Thelonious Monk

▶▶ Dave Samuels

see also: *Chick Corea, Larry Coryell, Makoto Ozone*

Garaud MacTaggart

Jonathan Butler

Born 1961, in Capetown, South Africa.

A native of South Africa, Jonathan Butler has parlayed his angst and frustration about apartheid and his homeland into a successful musical career. Primarily a jazz guitarist and vocalist, the expatriate has extended himself into the realms of pop, funk, rhythm and blues, gospel, reggae, and his innate African rhythms. Growing up in England, he added fusion to his style and has made major progressions in his music without disregarding his roots or audience. His 1977 debut, *Introducing Jonathan Butler* on the Jive/Novus label, presented him solely

as an instrumentalist. After a ten-year recording hiatus, Butler was reintroduced by the label on *Jonathan Butler*, presenting himself more confident and polished.

what to buy: *More than Friends* 𝄞𝄞𝄞𝄞 (Jive/Novus, 1988, prod. Barry J. Eastmond, Loris Holland, Timmy Allen, Teddy Riley) is a very solid collection and exhibits Butler's talents fully without his songs of protest and antagonism which have dominated much of his recorded work. *The Best of Jonathan Butler* 𝄞𝄞𝄞𝄞 (Jive/Novus, 1993, prod. Barry Eastmond) presents the best of the best. For a good feel of the progression and development of Butler as an artist, this is a disc to have.

what to buy next: *Deliverance* 𝄞𝄞𝄞 (Jive/Novus, 1990, prod. Wayne Brathwaite) is an album of originals which are almost a testament to his roots and the problems in South Africa. In addition to featuring jazz artists such as saxophonist Michael Brecker, pianist Bobby Lyle, percussionist Don Alias, and many other musicians, the album is peppered with just the right amount of variance to make it enjoyable.

what to avoid: *Head to Head* 𝄞𝄞 (Mercury, 1994, prod. Gerry E. Brown, Jonathan Butler) is not one of his best albums; to knock some sense into him, somebody should have hit Butler on the head. Experimentation is fine, but trying to compete with the young R&B set is silly. A few of the songs stand out, but the rest will make you cringe. If you see it, leave it.

best of the rest:
Heal Our Land 𝄞𝄞𝄞✔ (Jive/Novus, 1990)
Do You Love Me? 𝄞𝄞𝄞𝄞 (N2K Encoded Music, 1997)

influences:

◀◀ Earl Klugh, Grover Washington Jr., George Benson, David Sanborn

▶▶ Waymon Tisdale, Wyclef Jean, Eric Benet

Damon Percy

Jaki Byard

Born June 6, 1922, in Worcester, MA.

Jaki Byard is one of the most versatile jazz musicians around and one of the more talented, if under appreciated, composers in the idiom. As befitting a true renaissance man, Byard's piano playing embraces the stride elements of James P. Johnson and the tonal clusters of Henry Cowell with equal fervor. His ability to play in just about any style a band leader could want made him the perfect choice to fill the piano chair for some of Charles Mingus's greatest groups. Byard's compositions embrace eclecticism ranging from early New Orleans stylings to bebop, including operas and a trumpet concerto. Much of Byard's life has been spent in the halls of academia, teaching at Bennington College, the New England Conservatory of Music, and Mannes College of Music at the New School for Social Research.

Byard got his first formal piano lessons when he was eight years old. From there he went on to learn the trumpet, the trombone (picked up in the Army band during World War II), and the saxophone. Somewhere along the line he also educated himself on the guitar. His first gigs as pianist were with Earl Bostic and Herb Pomeroy before hooking up with one of Maynard Ferguson's better outfits in 1959. Then Byard made the big leap in 1962 to Charles Mingus and working alongside Eric Dolphy, Booker Ervin, Sam Rivers, and Roland Kirk. He has also played in piano bars where he learned to please audiences by performing show tunes and popular favorites of the day.

what to buy: More than just another solo piano album *Empirical* 𝄞𝄞𝄞𝄞 (Muse, 1972/1992, prod. Don Schlitten) has been a benchmark performance for Byard over the course of a couple decades. Most of the album is devoted to Byard's compositions and they reveal his ability to play stride with the best of them ("To Bob Vatel of Paris") just before blowing self-righteous old fogies away by twisting a standard inside out with something so out yet so logical that their preconceptions are challenged (Leonard Bernstein's "Lonely Town"). This is a musician who was picking up on his roots long before the young Marsalis clan was even a glint in Ellis's eyes, yet Byard always checks out what's happening on the edge, too. Over the years Byard's solo piano outings have been the best way to sample his ideas and *At Maybeck: Live at Maybeck Recital Hall Series, Volume 17* 𝄞𝄞𝄞𝄞 (Concord Jazz, 1992, prod. Carl Jefferson) part of the highly touted Maybeck series is certainly among his most accessible. He covers Rodgers & Hammerstein and a delightful rendition of "My One and Only Love," but it is his medley of Thelonious Monk tunes and a couple Byard originals that take the album beyond the ordinary. After making a veiled reference to Ravel's "Piano Concerto for the Left Hand," Byard proceeds to play Monk's "'Round Midnight" with only his left hand, then segueing into "Friday The Thirteenth" showing some delicate, right-hand filigree work. "Tribute to the Ticklers" has shown up on other Byard albums but this might be the definitive version of his paean to stride piano giants. And his "Family Suite" is a successful blend of jazz sensibilities wedded to classical technique. *Blues for Smoke* 𝄞𝄞𝄞𝄞 (Candid, 1960/1989, prod. Alan Bates, Nat Hentoff) is another solo piano album, but this time Byard is also the only com-

poser represented. His "Excerpts from European Episode" switches between European-based rhythms and jazz accents with all due logic and speed. The pensive "Aluminum Baby" dates from Byard's employment with Herb Pomeroy in the 1950s, but the harmonies and voicings are timeless. Everything he plays works. What else could a listener want?

what to buy next: *Here's Jaki* 𝄞𝄞𝄞𝄞 (OJC, 1961/1995, prod. Esmond Edwards) is a solid, well-played set that finds Byard working with a dream rhythm section (Ron Carter, bass, and Roy Haynes, drums) and romping through a fine selection of Byard compositions, John Coltrane's "Giant Steps," and a Gershwin medley of "Bess You Is My Woman" and "It Ain't Necessarily So." The tune "Mellow Septet" shows up later in his oeuvre as the first part of Byard's "Concerto Grosso." Featuring Jaki Byard and the Apollo Stompers, *Phantasies II* 𝄞𝄞𝄞𝄞 (Soul Note, 1991/1994, prod. Giovanni Bonandrini) is a big band outing containing a mix of pop tunes, jazz classics, and Byard originals that makes for interesting listening. Despite the lack of marquee names (other than trumpeter Graham Haynes and guitarist Peter Leitch) this album is a solid effort from beginning to end. Leitch's soloing on Byard's tribute to B.B. King, "BJC Blues" is well thought out, and the band's version of Roland Kirk's "Bright Moments" has a pretty high fun quotient which is appropriate for this bouncy, mid-tempo classic.

best of the rest:
Hi-Fly 𝄞𝄞𝄞 (OJC, 1962/1996)
Out Front! 𝄞𝄞𝄞𝄞 (OJC, 1964/1994)
Live! 𝄞𝄞𝄞𝄞 (Prestige, 1965/1992)
(With Ran Blake) *Improvisations* 𝄞𝄞𝄞 (Soul Note, 1981)
To Them, to Us 𝄞𝄞𝄞 (Soul Note, 1981/1993)
(With the Apollo Stompers) *Phantasies* 𝄞𝄞 (Soul Note, 1984/1988)
Foolin' Myself 𝄞𝄞𝄞 (Soul Note, 1988/1994)
Freedom Together 𝄞𝄞𝄞𝄞 (OJC, 1997)
(With David Eyges) *Night Leaves* 𝄞𝄞𝄞 (Brownstone, 1997)

worth searching for: Someday Original Jazz Classics may reissue the other great showpiece for Byard's digital prowess, *Solo Piano* 𝄞𝄞𝄞𝄞 (OJC, 1969, prod. Don Schlitten) or the exquisite trio date from 1968 that set Byard with bassist David Izenzon and drummer Elvin Jones, *Sunshine of My Soul* 𝄞𝄞𝄞𝄞 (prod. Don Schlitten). Izenzon was playing with Ornette Coleman at the time and his bass playing was pushing Byard to do some of his most interesting performances, especially on *Sunshine of My Soul* where Byard explodes in a flurry of note spinning that still manages to swing around Jones's swirling pulse. There are also two interesting solo piano cuts by Byard on an album dedicated to the music of Fellini's favorite film composer, *Amarcord Nino Rota: Interpretations of Nino Rota's Music* ����� (Hannibal, 1981, prod. Hal Willner).

influences:

◀◀ James P. Johnson, Erroll Garner, Art Tatum, Bud Powell

▶▶ D.D. Jackson, Ted Rosenthal, Jeff Gardner, Greg Kurstow

Garaud MacTaggart

Don Byas

Born October 21, 1912, in Muskogee, OK. Died August 24, 1972, in Amsterdam, Holland.

Tenor saxophonist Don Byas is among the handful of jazz musicians whose popularity in Europe always far exceeded their acclaim at home, and who have tended to become underrated figures in jazz history as a result. Yet despite the expatriate status he held for most of his career, Byas is considered one of the greats on his instrument by those in the know. Byas came up in the 1930s through the bands of Lionel Hampton, Buck Clayton, Don Redman, Andy Kirk, and Count Basie. Early on, he sounded a great deal like his primary influence, Coleman Hawkins. But in the 1940s, Byas began bridging the stylistic gap between swing and bop, playing at Minton's Playhouse with Dizzy Gillespie and cutting some memorable early-bop duets with bassist Slam Stewart. In 1946 Byas went to Europe and, except for sporadic visits back home, stayed there for the rest of his life. Byas played and recorded regularly with other Americans living in Europe, with touring groups, and with local musicians. Because of his distant locale, Byas did not have the direct influence on younger tenors that he might have otherwise had; but he always commanded the utmost respect for his virtuosity and individuality on his instrument.

what to buy: One of his last recordings, *A Night in Tunisia* ����� (Black Lion, 1963/1989, prod. Alan Bates), is also one of Byas's best. Backed by a strong trio of European musicians, he stretches out in exciting form on the title track, "I'll Remember April," Tad Dameron's "Ladybird," and other standards. *Savoy Jam Party* ����� (Savoy, 1944-46/1995) compiles sides Byas cut for Savoy in the mid-'40s and combines the raucous, happy energy of the best swing bands with the sophistication of early bebop. When one listens to these recordings—made shortly before Byas went to Europe for good—it is easy to wonder about the kind of jazz superstardom Byas would have encountered had he stayed in the States.

what to buy next: *A Tribute to Cannonball* ���� (Columbia, 1962/1997, prod. Julian Adderley, reissue prod. Orrin Keepnews) is a tribute only in the very loosest sense; Cannonball Adderley's only relation to this album is that he was its producer. Nevertheless, this session, co-led by pianist Bud Powell and featuring a strong lineup also consisting of bassist Pierre Michelot, drummer Kenny Clarke, and trumpeter Idrees Sulieman, is particularly enjoyable. Furthermore, it has finally been marvelously reissued on CD as part of Columbia's new campaign. Well worth picking up.

the rest:
Tenor Giant ���� (Drive Archive, 1945/1996)
Walkin' ���� (Black Lion, 1963/1992)
Don Byas 1944-1945 ��� (Classics, 1996)
Don Byas 1945 ��� (Classics, 1997)

worth searching for: *On Blue Star* ��� (Verve, 1954/1991) is a 23-tune collection of mostly ballads recorded during Byas's early years (1947–52) in Europe. It was reissued on CD, but is already out of print and rather hard to find.

influences:

◀◀ Coleman Hawkins

▶▶ John Coltrane

Dan Keener

Charlie Byrd

Born September 16, 1925, in Chuckatuck, VA.

Guitarist Charlie Byrd is a perfect example of an artist in the right place at the right time. In 1961, when Dave Brubeck was forced to cancel a U.S. State Department-sponsored tour of South America, Byrd agreed to take his place. What he found there forever changed the sound of jazz. He had already made a name for himself as a notable acoustic player, having jammed with Django Reinhardt during World War II, studied with legendary classical guitarists Sophocles Papas and Andres Segovia in the early 1950s, and returned to jazz for some sessions with Woody Herman, as well as a leader of his own Washington D.C.-based trio. But his breakthrough came after introducing Stan Getz to the Brazilian tunes he encountered while touring South America. This fortuitous exchange led to the seminal 1962 recording *Jazz Samba*, featuring historic interpretations of songs by the likes of Antonio Carlos Jobim, among others. The record was a smash and ignited a U.S. bossa nova craze of near-monstrous proportions. While Getz proved to be the most successful practitioner of the genre, Byrd himself was no slouch, and he recorded a series of fine Afro-Latin albums, in addition to some straight-ahead jazz recordings as well. After a series of syrupy releases on the Columbia label, Byrd reemerged in the mid-1970s as a member of the Great Guitars group, along with Barney Kessel and Herb Ellis, and has continued to records (mainly for the Concord label) in trio, quartet, and sextet configurations.

By combining the precision of classical guitar with the improvisational style of jazz, Byrd has established himself as among the best of a small group of acoustic, nylon-string players (Byrd's excursions into electric guitar are few and far between). His bright, bouncy sound is well-suited for the bossa nova, but he is equally adept at other styles, from blues to flamenco. His unamplified guitar is best heard in trio settings, as other instruments can drown him out, but Byrd occasionally adds sax players to the mix, including Bud Shank, Scott Hamilton, and Ken Peplowski, usually to lesser effect. His brother Joe (Gene) Byrd frequently accompanies him on bass.

what to buy: *Latin Byrd* 🎵🎵🎵 (Milestone, 1961–63/1996, prod. Orrin Keepnews, Ed Michel) reissues on CD two early 1960s Riverside sessions, *Latin Impressions* and *Charlie Byrd's Bossa Nova*, which had been previously available as a two-LP set in the 1970s. The 23 Brazilian jazz selections are lovely renderings and include Byrd in unaccompanied solos, with his quartet, and with additional instrumentation. Five Byrd originals are highlighted. *Jazz 'n' Samba* 🎵🎵🎵 (Hindsight, 1995, prod. Pete Kline) offers previously unreleased recordings from 1965 incorporating both Latin and straight-ahead jazz performances, featuring soon-to-be fellow Great Guitars member Herb Ellis on electric guitar.

what to buy next: *Byrd at the Gate* 🎵🎵🎵 (Riverside/OJC, 1963/1992, prod. Orrin Keepnews) is a fine live date, emphasizing the non-Latin side of Byrd's talents. The straight-ahead set documents Byrd in a live performance at the Village Gate in New York City, with bassist Keter Betts, drummer Bill Reichenbach, veteran tenor saxophonist Seldon Powell, and guest trumpeter Clark Terry. Included among the 11 tunes are swing classics such as Louis Armstrong's "Butter and Egg Man" and Frank Foster's "Shiny Stockings," as well as the Byrd originals "Blues for Night People" and "Ela Me Deixou." Although *Latin Odyssey* 🎵🎵🎵 (Concord, 1983, prod. Carl E. Jefferson) is listed under guitarist Laurindo Almeida as leader, it's really an equal billing of two compatriots who often work together. On this elegant later-day pairing of the two guitarists on several Brazilian jazz tunes, backing is by

bassists Joe Byrd or Bob Magnusson, drummers Jeff Hamilton or Chuck Redd.

what to avoid: If you come across *The Touch of Gold* 🎵 (Columbia, 1966, prod. Teo Macero), even in the used bins, it's no bargain. The album includes three Beatles songs, a Sinatra favorite, and the theme from *Bonanza*! This album is like virtually all of Byrd's Columbia releases, which are for kitsch value only. *Brazilian Bird* is the exception.

best of the rest:

Jazz Recital 🎵🎵🎵 (Savoy, 1957/1993)
At the Village Vanguard 🎵🎵🎵 (Riverside/OJC, 1961/1991)
Bossa Nova Pelos Passaros 🎵🎵🎵 (Riverside/OJC, 1963/1992)
Brazilian Byrd 🎵🎵🎵 (Columbia, 1965/1994)
(With Great Guitars: Barney Kessel, Herb Ellis) *Great Guitars* 🎵🎵🎵 (Concord, 1976)
Bluebyrd 🎵🎵🎵 (Concord, 1979/1991)
(With Great Guitars: Barney Kessel, Herb Ellis) *Straight Tracks* 🎵🎵🎵 (Concord, 1979)
Sugarloaf Suite 🎵🎵🎵 (Concord, 1980)
(With Great Guitars: Barney Kessel, Herb Ellis) *At the Winery* 🎵🎵🎵 (Concord, 1980)
(With Bud Shank) *Brazilville* 🎵🎵🎵 (Concord, 1982)
(With Great Guitars: Barney Kessel, Herb Ellis) *At Charlie's Georgetown* 🎵🎵🎵 (Concord, 1983)
Isn't It Romantic 🎵🎵🎵 (Concord, 1984)
(With the Annapolis Brass Quintet) *Byrd & Brass* 🎵🎵 (Concord, 1986)
(With Scott Hamilton) *It's a Wonderful World* 🎵🎵🎵 (Concord, 1989)
(With Ken Peplowski) *The Bossa Nova Years* 🎵🎵🎵 (Concord, 1991)
Charlie Byrd/Washington Guitar Quintet 🎵🎵🎵 (Concord, 1992)
(With the Washington Guitar Quintet & Ken Peplowski) *Aquarelle* 🎵🎵🎵 (Concord, 1994)
(With Ken Peplowski) *Moments like This* 🎵🎵🎵 (Concord, 1994)
(With Great Guitars: Barney Kessel, Herb Ellis) *Great Guitars II* 🎵🎵🎵 (Concord, 1995)
Du Hot Club De Concord 🎵🎵🎵 (Concord, 1995)

worth searching for: *Midnight Guitar* 🎵🎵🎵 (Savoy, 1957/1994, prod. Ozzie Cadena) was Byrd's second album as leader and features his trio with bassist Keter Betts, and drummer Gus Johnson. Recorded around 1957, prior to Byrd's bossa nova recordings, this is a good example of Byrd's talents beyond the Latin realm. Featured are swing-era tunes, including the catchy three-part "Blues for Night People."

influences:

⏪ Django Reinhardt, Andres Segovia, Antonio Carlos Jobim

⏩ Howard Alden

Eric J. Lawrence

Donald Byrd

Born December 9, 1932, in Detroit, MI.

Nobody could ever accuse Donald Byrd of being afraid to try new things. By the same token, nobody could ever credit the man with staying true to his creative vision. As the trumpeter moved from bop and hard bop through soul-jazz and fusion and right on to some of the most execrable examples of crossover pop schmaltz, he's displayed an ironic dichotomy that ranks right up there with Herbie Hancock's: a strong player with a highly individual voice that, aside from commercial success, never really made any significant inroads of his own. In other words, he's one of jazz's most popular and better players, yet rather than pursue innovation, he's been more content to "please the people." Needless to say, this mindset has had mixed results. However, although he has made some of the worst "jazz" records ever, he's also made some of the best and, to his credit, has consistently stood by his belief in the higher, more noble powers of music itself . . . no matter what it sounds like.

Coming up in Detroit along with Yusef Lateef and Pepper Adams, Byrd's career began in earnest after Air Force duty and the earning of a master's degree in music education at Manhattan School of Music. His first, full-time band was one he co-led with Pepper Adams (documented on the excellent *Motor City Scene* LP). However by this time, Byrd had racked up hours of studio time under his own name, as well as made a trip to Europe. It wasn't until his 1958 arrival at Blue Note that Byrd found his groove, cutting more than a dozen high-quality hard bop albums between 1958 and 1967 that, along with Lee Morgan's concurrent work, would define the genre. Yet, in 1969—two months before session work got underway on *Bitches Brew*—Byrd cut *Fancy Free*, which found the trumpeter accompanied by electric keyboards, funky polyrhythms, and (horrors!) overdriven guitar. However, as is well known, *Fancy Free* didn't have quite the impact that *Bitches Brew* did, nor did Byrd use it as a jumping off point to better things.

Rather, in between making straight-up R&B records with the Blackbyrds and dishing up tasty (but ultimately insubstantial) soul-jazz treats in the next couple years, Byrd began charting his steady, but swift, decline by making a series of fusion records that started out enticing (*Electric Byrd*), yet wound up artless, vapid, and achingly commercial (*Places and Spaces* and the uniformly horrible *Caricatures*). In 1978 he left Blue Note in pursuit of commercial fame, and though the two albums that followed (1978's *Thank You for F.U.M.L.* and 1981's *And 125th St. N.Y.C.*) met with marginal success, they were, to be generous, terrible. In the mid-1980s, Byrd returned, like so many of his pop/fusion counterparts, to mainstream bop, and he cut a couple of albums that are enjoyable, if not great. Unfortunately, those records have been deleted, while his recent work with rapper Guru as well as his catholic deification by acid jazzers and his jazz music written for ballet, has brought the lesser Byrd back into the spotlight once again.

what to buy: *Byrd in Paris, Volume I ♪♪♪♪* (Polydor/Verve, 1958/1989) , a strong, underappreciated set by a fresh-faced Byrd, finds him and his thumping quintet near the end of a four-month European voyage and, accordingly, they're tight. Each player (especially the usually reserved piano of Walter Davis Jr.) attacks each piece enthusiastically, yet leaves plenty of open spaces. An outstanding document. Doubtlessly, *Byrd in Flight ♪♪♪♪♪* (Blue Note, 1960/1996, prod. Alfred Lion) is Byrd's best record. This amazing set (augmented by three bonus cuts on CD) puts Byrd in the august (and fiery) company of Jackie McLean (alto saxophone), Hank Mobley (tenor saxophone), Duke Pearson (piano), Reggie Workman and Doug Watkins (bass), and Lex Humphries (drums). The result of this teaming is one of the quintessential hard bop records: one that flexes its technical muscles while allowing plenty of room for melodicism and improvisational interplay. Pearson's groove-centric piano lines on this date foreshadow his arrangements with Byrd nearly a decade later. *Early Byrd: The Best of the Jazz Soul Years ♪♪♪♪* (Blue Note, 1960–72/1993, comp. prod. Dean Rudland) is the Byrd for funkateers. Although the cuts here span an insanely large amount of time (1960–72) for an artist as prone to change as Byrd, the *modus operandi* is nonetheless consistent: groove-heavy, R&B-influenced, and funky, funky, funky. These cuts show that Byrd was more than capable of making accessible, enjoyable records that didn't sacrifice artistic integrity for dollar signs. Strong, fun and, most importantly, it's still jazz. Not an LP proper, *Kofi ♪♪♪♪* (Blue Note, 1969–70/1995, prod. Duke Pearson) was compiled onto CD from two sessions a year apart and features two almost completely different bands. However, the slow-burning, Afro-electric groove Byrd manifests on these two sessions is consistent and makes for one heck of a good record. Although it could be dismissed as another step on his stairway

Donald Byrd **(AP/Wide World Photos)**

to pop hell, this album actually demonstrates considerable thought and conveys an intense musicality that rivals most of its contemporaries.

what to buy next: *Motor City Scene* ♫♫♫ (Bethlehem, 1960) As co-leader with Pepper Adams, Byrd takes a hot band—Kenny Burrell (guitar), Tommy Flanagan (piano), Louis Hayes (drums), Paul Chambers (bass)—through some stunning bebop workouts. A run through Erroll Garner's "Trio" gives each player some solo room and is the highlight of this fine record. *Fuego* ♫♫♫ (Blue Note, 1960/1988, prod. Alfred Lion) is a rather typical Blue Note blowing session. Of course, "typical" means outstanding. Jackie McLean and Duke Pearson duke it out on a few melody lines, leaving Byrd to keep things anchored. An excellent example of hard bop done right. *A New Perspective* ♫♫♫ (Blue Note, 1963/1988, prod. Alfred Lion) is unabashedly high-concept, although the actual concept is never quite clear. Nonetheless, Byrd and arranger Pearson created one of the trumpeter's most organically intellectual records and, with the eight-member Coleridge Perkinson Choir on hand, run through a stirringly emotional record. However, the ideas too often get scattered and the actual band (Mobley, Burrell, Hancock, Humphries and others) tend to get lost in the shuffle. A noble effort, yet, with the exception of the mind-blowing "Christo Redentor," a bit of a muddle. Byrd's first full-fledged attempt to make an R&B record actually managed to work out pretty well. *Street Lady* ♫♫♫ (Blue Note, 1973/1997, prod. Larry Mizell) a disgraceful record by "jazz" standards, however, as a meaty piece of early '70s funk, it's an undeniable success. The guttural synths on "Sister Love" must be heard to be believed, however I don't actually recall hearing any trumpet-playing. Oh well. If you can't dance to this, you just can't dance.

what to avoid: *Places and Spaces* **woof!** (Blue Note, 1975/1997, prod. Larry and Fonce Mizell) is as empty as the blue skies portrayed on its cover, with noodling electric instrumentation providing more atmosphere than musical substance. An attempt at validation is made by tagging it as part of Blue Note's "Rare Groove" reissue series, but it actually sounds more like the soundtrack to a low-budget porn flick. *And 125th Street, N.Y.C.* **woof!** (Elektra/Musicraft, 1979/1994, prod. Donald Byrd) is just a miserably contrived stab at pop acceptance. It worked. But then again, disco was still pretty popular in 1979, too. These are bad records and no amount of sampling will change that fact.

the rest:
Byrd's Word ♫♫♫ (Savoy, 1952/1992)
First Flight ♫♫ (Delmark, 1955/1990)

Free Form ♫♫♫ (Blue Note, 1961/1989)
Groovin' for Nat ♫♫♫ (Black Lion, 1962/1992)
Byrd in Hand ♫♫♫ (Blue Note, 1969/1995)
Fancy Free ♫♫ (Blue Note, 1969/1993)
Electric Byrd ♫♫♫ (Blue Note, 1970/1996)
Black Byrd ♫♫ (Blue Note, 1973/1992)
Best of Donald Byrd ♫♫♫ (Blue Note, 1992)

influences:
◄◄ Clifford Brown

Jason Ferguson

Don Byron

Born November 8, 1958, in New York, NY.

One of the most versatile jazz musicians on the scene today, clarinetist Don Byron is a classically trained musician who was born in Manhattan and raised in the Bronx amidst a musically appreciative family. He attended the High School of Music and Art, then went on to the New England Conservatory of Music in Boston, where he also embraced jazz, and in 1980, while still an undergrad student, found work in the revival of Eastern European, clarinet-led klezmer music. Byron fronted the Klezmer Conservatory Band from 1980–87, and gained visibility as this music was advancing its crossover appeal. An open-minded musician who has gained international recognition as the foremost innovator on clarinet, Byron embraces jazz into his eclectic musical style. His inspiration comes from his rich musical upbringing and broad exposure to everything from classical to Motown, and from the Latin-jazz of Eddie Palmieri to the avant-garde creations of Henry Threadgill. Based in New York where he leads a jazz quintet, a classical chamber group (Semaphore), and other groups, Byron joyously extends the boundaries of his music, immersing himself in the most adventurous circles of New York's music scene, and performing often at the Knitting Factory where he feels at home. He has led an Afro-Cuban ensemble, written commissioned classical works for Kronos Quartet (*There Goes the Neighborhood*, 1994 London premiere), and has appeared at major international festivals. As sideman, Byron has performed and recorded since 1984 with an array of cutting-edge innovators, including Hamiet Bluiett, Bill Frisell, Craig Harris, Marilyn Crispell, Gerry Hemingway, Leroy Jenkins, Steve Coleman, Bobby Previte, and others. Byron was also featured in the Hollywood film, *Kansas City*, and can be heard on the 1997 soundtrack album.

what to buy: Byron's first album, the critically hailed *Tuskegee Experiments* ♫♫♫♫ (Elektra/Nonesuch, 1992, prod. Arthur

Moorehead), established him as a clarinet virtuoso, earned him 1993 citations from *Down Beat* critics and readers as favorite clarinet player, and helped further a revival of the instrument in jazz. On the album's nine originals, Byron interacts freely and masterfully with a group of veteran improvisers: Bill Frisell (guitar), Joe Berkovitz and Edsel Gomez (piano), Kenny Davis, Lonnie Plaxico, and Reggie Workman (bass), Richie Schwartz (marimba), Pheeroan AkLaff and Ralph Peterson (drums). A combination of social commentary (on the African American trigger-word "Tuskegee," as Byron explains in liner notes) and haunting and scorching improvisations, *Tuskegee Experiments* features many exceptional moments. From Byron's buoyant clarinet solo on the opener ("Waltz for Ellen"), to dazzling full group settings highlighting Frisell's incendiary improvs, from the near-traditional to free-form inventions, the music takes the listener on a constantly changing, radically different trip where no two tunes are alike. Highlights include "In Memoriam: Uncle Dan," a haunting duo piece performed on bass clarinet with bassist Workman; the "Tuskegee Strutter's Ball," which contrasts Frisell's fusiony licks and Byron's light, spontaneous clarinet improvs against swing tempos, and the *piece de resistance,* the churning title piece interspersed with poetry (read by Sadiq) that weaves the tragic tale of the 40-year medical experiment on African Americans by the U.S. Public Health Service. So well-programmed, this disturbing piece is then followed by "Auf einer Burg," a brief, classically tinged dirge Byron performs with pianist Gomez. *Tuskegee Experiments* offers some of Byron's most compelling work and is a must-own album for anyone seeking to know the breadth of Byron's musical talents. On the lighter side, Bryon and his cohorts exuberantly explore and celebrate 16 early jazz classics on *Bug Music* ♪♪♪♪♪ (Elektra/Nonesuch, 1996, prod. Don Byron), a lively tribute to the music of Duke Ellington, Billy Strayhorn, the John Kirby sextet, and the Raymond Scott Quintette. Supported by his ensemble, Byron is prominently featured, gliding and weaving this clarinet solos throughout. Alto saxophonist Steve Wilson, trombonist Craig Harris, and pianist Uri Caine are also spotlighted in fine solos. Four other horn players and different sets of rhythm players add to the appeal of this album. Bryon also contributes skillful arrangements of overlooked Ellington tunes such as "Dicty Glide," "Cotton Club Stomp," and "Blue Bubbles," as well as other lesser-known gems honoring swing-stylists Kirby and Scott. Light and lively throughout, this venture into the jazz vaults holds greatest appeal for the swing-minded set.

what to buy next: Byron gained widespread notice with *Don Byron Plays the Music of Mickey Katz* ♪♪♪♪ (Elektra/None-

DON BYRON (WITH VERNON REID)

song "You Say He's Just a Psychic Friend"

album Mistaken Identity
(Sony, 1996)

instrument Clarinet

such, 1993, prod. Hans Wendl), an album that pays homage to Mickey Katz who, along the lines of his former affiliation with the zany, spoofing Spike Jones band, made a name for himself with recordings of his 1950s Yiddish parodies of American pop tunes. Byron offers high-spirited, accountable covers of Katz classics with some of New York's hottest talent including trumpeter Dave Douglas, violinist Mark Feldman, trombonist Josh Roseman, and reedman J.D. Parran. Several guest artists add to the fun-filled Katz revival. As one of the best sites for explorative music, New York's Knitting Factory has hosted groundbreaking groups over the years. Byron leads a live-recorded, January 7, 1996 session at the club on *No Vibe Zone* ♪♪♪♪ (Knitting Factory Works, 1996, prod. Don Byron, Hope Carr). A snow emergency kept most fans away except for a select few, hence your listening won't be distracted by audience patter. The clarinetist coaxes nearly 68 minutes (five tunes) of fine, wide-ranging jazz styles from his crew, guitarist David Gilmore, bassist Kenny Davis, and drummer Marvin "Smitty" Smith. They infuse the opener, Ornette Coleman's "WRU," with fiery avant-energy led by Gilmore's grinding guitar-led sketches. You'll want to hit replay for Byron's "Sex/Work," a seductive, lightly pulsating, Latin-influenced spree highlighting Smith and Caine. Byron's mellifluously soaring clarinet solos on the 17-minute "Next Love/The Allure of Entanglement" finds him digging into the jazz archives to build solos from familiar themes. Johnny Mercer's "Tangerine" allows the musicians to brandish their straight-ahead chops. The finale, another version of Byron's "Tuskegee Strutter's Ball" builds stark, thrashing rhythms and contrapuntal themes laced with Byron's inventive solos and Gilmore's incendiary electric guitar before it ends in a happy, swing-style romp. *No-Vibe Zone* contains enough diversity and plenty of individual artistry to satisfy all jazz fans.

the rest:
Music for Six Musicians ♫♫♫ (Elektra/Nonesuch, 1995)

worth searching for: Playing bass clarinet, Bryon appears (briefly) as guest soloist and with the ensemble on pianist Uri Caine's *Toys* ♫♫♫♫ (Verve/JMT, 1995, prod. Stefan F. Winter), an exhilarating 1995 Verve outing containing a mixture of rhythms from bossa, to bop, to Afro-Cuban beats, to the bold and free, with innovators Gary Thomas (flute, tenor sax), Dave Douglas (trumpet), Joshua Roseman (trombone), David Holland (bass), and Ralph Peterson (drums). Byron is highlighted only on an African-motif track (Joni Mitchell's "Black Crow") of jazz singer Cassandra Wilson's *Blue Light 'til Dawn* ♫♫♫♫ (Blue Note, 1993, prod. Craig Street), but his unbridled solo against Cyro Baptista's percussion, and his interwoven lines with Wilson's eerie vocals, add to the enjoyment of this uncommon album and further demonstrate his versatility. For those seeking more ear-expanding music, check out drummer Bobby Previte's adventuresome *Weather Clear and Track Fast* ♫♫♫♫ (Enja, 1994, prod. Matthias Winckelmann) on which Byron adds his virtuosity on clarinet and baritone saxophone to the well-layered ensemble encounters.

influences:

◀◀ Jimmie Noone, George Lewis, Sidney Bechet, Albert Nicholas, Buddy DeFranco, Harry Carney, John Carter, Anthony Braxton, Eric Dolphy, Eddie Palmieri, Henry Threadgill, Dizzy Gillespie

▶▶ Ben Goldberg

Nancy Ann Lee

George Cables
Born November 14, 1944, in New York, NY.

Pianist George Cables attended Brooklyn's famed High School of Performing Arts, and his first significant gigs after graduating from Mannes College were with drummers Art Blakey and Max Roach. Cables then went from accompanying masters of rhythm to working with wizards of the reed and horn: Sonny Rollins, Joe Henderson, Freddie Hubbard, Dexter Gordon and, most significantly, Art Pepper. Cables has also done some notable recording with vibist Bobby Hutcherson among others. From the mid-1980s onward, he has increasingly donned the role of main man for a series of albums that showcase both his talents as a soloist and, all too infrequently, as a composer. Cables moved to the West Coast in 1971 where, at last word, he was an active educator working at San Jose State University.

what to buy: The Maybeck Recital Hall solo piano series is turning into a litmus test for pianistic greatness. Always well recorded, the stream of albums flowing into the market with this imprint consistently delivers the artistic goods and in many cases redefines the first choice for exploring a keyboard artist's work. Certainly it's hard to go wrong with *At Maybeck, Volume 35* ♫♫♫♫ (Concord Jazz, 1994, prod. Carl E. Jefferson). Cables's choice of material encompasses three Gershwin standards (including a great version of "My Man's Gone Now" that nearly makes the ivories weep), Bobby Hutcherson's classy "Little B's Poem," and a couple of Cables originals (the pensive and beautiful "Lullaby" takes the honors here). Cables performs the rest of the songs well, and brings forth his best playing with attention to the inner voicings of the works. Comparing the solo recital *Person to Person* ♫♫♫♫ (SteepleChase, 1995, prod. Nils Winther) with the Maybeck release, it's the selection of material, not necessarily Cables's uniformly marvelous playing, that makes this album work. Cables contributes four of his own compositions to the recording and they stand up well against standards from Gershwin, Ellington, Monk, and Golson. "Blue Nights," with its moody, minor-flavored rhythmic pulse hovering behind Cables's ornamental right-hand work, is a particular joy. *By George: George Cables Plays the Music of George Gershwin* ♫♫♫♫ (Contemporary, 1987, prod. George Cables) features another rendition of the previously recorded (on the Maybeck recital) classic, "Someone to Watch over Me." Cables's playing is uncluttered on this tune and less concerned with ripples, flourishes, and frills at the beginning of this version than he is in the Maybeck accounting. This is not meant to imply that he won't add some filigree to the melody later on, it just means that listeners have more time to prepare themselves as the technical artistry unveils. The trio portion of this album has Cables backed by the capable bassist John Heard and drummer Ralph Penland. Heard's bass playing adds some nice bottom color to the band's arrangement of "Bess, You Is My Woman Now," and he takes a nice solo on the rendering of "My Man's Gone Now." Penland is solid throughout. Essentially another album of standards (and one original composition), *Skylark* ♪♪♪♪ (SteepleChase, 1996, prod. Nils Winther) is presented with Cables's usual skill and grace. He never overplays and the choice of material ranges from Brazilian chestnuts like "Manha Da Carnival" and "Samba De Orfeu" to American jazz classics from Monk ("Pannonica") and Hoagy Carmichael (the title tune). Rhythm is the key to the success or failure of this session since many of the songs covered don't just sit in 4/4 or 3/4 waiting for the beat. For this trio date, Cables has chosen his support well. Bassist Jay Anderson is much better here than he was on Cables's earlier release, *I Mean You*, and drummer Albert "Tootie" Heath, of the fabulous Heath brothers, adjusts to the varying time conundrums and keeps the rhythms driving the melodies.

what to buy next: *I Mean You* ♪♪♪ (SteepleChase, 1994) is a well-played set from Cables, but the rhythm section of drummer Adam Nussbaum and bassist Jay Anderson doesn't jell with Cables as well as past collaborators. Still, there are gems here from Cables as composer. "Blackfoot" with its Tyner-esque sound blocks implies the music of Native Americans, while the rocking-chair melody of "But He Knows" deserves to be heard more. The best of the cover tunes is probably the Billy Strayhorn standard, "Lush Life."

the rest:

Cables's Vision ♪♪♪♪ (OJC, 1979)
Cables's Fables ♪♪♪ (SteepleChase, 1991)
Night and Day ♪♪♪ (DIW, 1991)
Quiet Fire ♪♪♪ (SteepleChase, 1994)

influences:

◀◀ Thelonious Monk, McCoy Tyner, Bud Powell, Herbie Hancock

▶▶ Craig Taborn

Garaud MacTaggart

Cachao

Born Israel Lopez, September 14, 1918, in Havana, Cuba.

Israel Lopez, a bassist and composer-arranger (who also plays trumpet, piano, celesta, and bongos) is better known as Cachao, a central figure in the development of Cuban music for a substantial portion of the twentieth century. He, along with his brother Orestes, presided over the mutation of *danzón* (a Cuban ballroom dance in rather staid rondo form) into the mambo, with arrangements written for bandleader/flautist Antonio Arcaño Betancourt and his group, Arcaño y Sus Maravillas. The Latin jam session known as a *descarga* might not have evolved into the vital training ground for young Latin jazz players that it later became if Cachao hadn't encouraged his compatriots to be more daring in their improvisations. Pianist Bebo Valdes has been quoted as saying, "if Cachao and Arsenio Rodriguez had never been born, the Cuban music of the fifties and perhaps the last thirty years, would have sounded like the music of the thirties."

After a series of ground-breaking *descarga* albums for Panart, Maype, and Bonita, Cachao moved to New York City where he worked with Charlie Palmieri, Tito Rodriguez, and Eddie Palmieri before finally settling in Miami. Throughout the 1960s, 1970s, and 1980s he appeared on albums with musicians/fans such as Hubert Laws, Mongo Santamaria, Eddie Palmieri, and Grupo Niche, while concertizing with Tito Puente, José Fajardo, and Chocolate Armenteros. He has even played with the Miami Symphony Orchestra.

what to buy: There is a whole story included behind the 12-tune album, *Master Sessions, Volume 1* ♪♪♪♪ (Crescent Moon/Epic, 1994, prod. Andy Garcia), that deals with the years of neglect and poor-paying gigs endured by one of the major figures in Latin music history and it has been made into an award-winning video by the actor Andy Garcia that is making new fans for Cachao's music. The albums around which the video revolves have also won awards and the music is an awesome tribute to the man and his music. From the opening notes of "Al Fin Te Vi," a duet between Cachao's bowed bass and Paquito D'Rivera's clarinet, the album rolls through a sublime primer in the art of Afro-Cuban music. There can be no stand-out performances when everything is this good.

what to buy next: On *Master Sessions, Volume 2* ♪♪♪♪ (Crescent Moon/Epic, 1995, prod. Andy Garcia), 24 of the 30 songs cut during one historic week with Cachao have been released. Both of the Master Sessions albums are so good that the next question a listener should ask after hearing both CD's is,

"When are the other six tunes coming out?" The sidemen include many greats from the Latin music community including trumpeter Alfredo "Chocolate" Armenteros, reed man extraordinaire Paquito D'Rivera, and flautist Nestor Torres. The percussion section has so many time signatures going on that it's a good thing the melody players are used to floating with a polyrhythmic pulse.

best of the rest:

Latin Jazz Descarga, Part I ♫♫♫ (Tania, 1985/1994)

Maestro De Maestros ♫♫♫♪ (Tania, 1986)

Cuban Jam Session, Volume II, Descargas Cubanas ♫♫♫♪ (Rodven, 1987)

worth searching for: Check out the companion documentary video to the Master Session albums, *Cachao . . . Como Su Ritmo No Hay Dos (Like His Rhythm There Is No Other),* available from Epic Music Video, for an intriguing, well-constructed view of Latin music from the inside.

influences:

◀◀ Sexteto Habanero, Arsenio Rodriguez

▶▶ Machito, Mario Bauzá, Chico O'Farrill, Tito Puente

Garaud MacTaggart

Uri Caine

Born in Philadelphia, PA.

One of the more gifted and intuitive sidemen working in the so-called "downtown" jazz scene of New York, pianist Uri Caine is as comfortable working the standards—as he often did as a regular at Ortlieb's Jazz Haus in his hometown of Philadelphia—as comping behind "old school" rap star Biz Markie in an ensemble led by steady employer Don Byron. His own solo career has been slowly gathering momentum, balanced between slightly off-mainstream jazz sessions that delightfully display the influence of Herbie Hancock and no lack of "Hasidic tinge," and investigations of classical repertoire—Mahler, Wagner—by way of the Knitting Factory all-star team of which he is an MVP.

what's available: *Wagner e Venezia* ♫♫♫ (Winter & Winter, 1997, prod. Stefan Winter) is an homage to Richard Wagner's "greatest hits"—adaptations of excerpts from *Tristan und Isolde* and *Lohengrin* and the like—recorded live in Venice. The classy packaging suits the performances (top string players Erik Friedlander and Mark Feldman are featured), which taper the tragic grandiosity of the music to a chamber-style intimacy without losing punch. You'll have to find this and its immediate predecessor, *Primal Light* ♫♫♫ (Winter & Winter, 1996, prod.

Stefan Winter), which offers a similar approach to Mahler, as imports.

worth searching for: Caine has two jazzier discs that are easily recommended if potentially difficult to find since JMT was bought by PolyGram and shut down; though some JMT releases are being kept in print, others are "selling through" and will be gone when stock is exhausted. This has already happened with *Sphere Music* ♫♫♫ (JMT, 1993, prod. Uri Caine), which features Ralph Peterson on drums, Anthony Cox or Kenny Davis on bass, and guests Gary Thomas (tenor sax), Graham Haynes (cornet), and Don Byron (clarinet). A couple Thelonious Monk tunes and the standard "Just in Time" are mixed with an attractive original program that shows Caine to be a distinctive performer in a post-bop idiom. The more recent *Toys* ♫♫♫ (JMT, 1995, prod. Stefan Winter) can still be found in stores at the time this is written. At first glance it's practically a Herbie Hancock tribute album, with covers of his "Canteloupe Island," "The Prisoner," "Dolphin Dance," and "Toys," but there are also a number of Latin-influenced uptempo numbers on the album, on which Caine's piano style gets much more full-blooded and aggressive, quite a contrast to the more lyrical Hancock items. Peterson, Byron (on bass clarinet this time), and Thomas (adding flute to his arsenal) return from the earlier album, joined by bassist Dave Holland, percussionist Don Alias, trumpeter Dave Douglas, and trombonist Joshua Roseman. The arrangements are quite colorful and may be Caine's greatest talent.

influences:

◀◀ Herbie Hancock, Horace Silver

▶▶ Mel Waldron

Steve Dollar

Joey Calderazzo

Born 1966, in New Rochelle, NY.

Pianist Joey Calderazzo burst onto the scene in 1987 as sideman with Michael Brecker's band. He made a few recordings with Brecker and was still touring with the band in 1997. Calderazzo has also recorded as sideman with Bob Belden, Rick Margitza, John Blake, Bruce Gertz, Branford Marsalis (Buckshot LeFonque), and other groups. In 1991 Calderazzo was signed to Blue Note and recorded three albums (*In the Door, To Know One,* and *Traveler*) which are now out of print. The albums failed to generate lasting excitement, and Calderazzo was dropped by the label. He has since recorded excellent sessions as leader for Audioquest and the Canadian label, Lost

Chart Records. With each new recording, Calderazzo displays growing musicianship and remains a talent to watch.

what to buy: One of Calderazzo's best sessions to date, *Simply Music* 𝕚𝕚𝕚𝕚 (Lost Chart, 1997, prod. Alain de Grosbois) features the pianist in a trio setting with bassist Sylvain Gagnon, and drummer Jeff "Tain" Watts. Recorded in Montreal on dates in September 1995 and May 1996, the trio performs superbly on the diverse, eight-tune session, delivering mostly originals by the principals, a hard-swinging version of Wayne Shorter's "Speak No Evil," and adroit interpretations of two other standards. Each tune is a capsulated, ear-pleasing melodic excursion. Most notable is Watts's "Blu Tain," a hard-driving, harmonious bop spree. Watts was twice-named Best Acoustic Jazz Drummer by readers of *Modern Drummer* and demonstrates his polyrhythmic skills on this CD, artfully prodding the others from underneath and keeping tidy tempos throughout. Gagnon works well with Watts, creating responsive pulses and helping to build drama into each tune. Calderazzo lends significant lyricism to this tasteful session, and contributes two originals, "Catania," a lovely pensive ballad, and "Mikell's," a subtle swinger. Calderazzo shows mastery of keyboard technique and an original style. His playing is rife with unpredictable ideas, and while his phrasing and lines are melodically sensible, sincere, fleet-fingered, and often elegant, he can swing mightily. No matter if this trio recording was a chance meeting of the three musicians or the result of ongoing collaboration, the chemistry seems right, and the result is some outstanding jazz. Another knockout album, *Secrets* 𝕚𝕚𝕚𝕚 (Audioquest, 1995, prod. Joe Harley) finds pianist Joey Calderazzo and his trio—bassist James Genus and drummer Clarence Penn—mixing it up in various group settings with Tim Hagans (trumpet, flugelhorn), John Clark (French horn), Earl McIntyre (bass trombone/tuba), Tim Ries (soprano sax/flute) Charlie Pillow (tenor sax/bass clarinet/English horn), Fareed Haque (guitar) and Tomas Ulrich (cello). Calderazzo wrote six of the eight compositions and Bob Belden contributes superb arrangements for the horn ensembles. Calderazzo's playing shows maturity and improvement from earlier recordings, particularly his right-hand playing on uptempo numbers with the trio. Maintaining dynamic control, Calderazzo keeps things intriguing and exciting without cranking up the volume. Everything is tastefully delivered and everyone shines. Ballads are elegant and sweetly romantic, and bebop tunes burn, building dramatically on atypical melodies and harmonies. On this album, Calderazzo's focus is his music. Throughout this sparkling session, all the elements are in place to make this a true delight for the listener.

worth searching for: Although Calderazzo's Blue Note recordings are out of print and he is no longer with the label, search for *The Traveler* 𝕚𝕚𝕚𝕚 (Capitol/Blue Note, 1993, prod. Joey Calderazzo, Michael Cuscuna) on which Calderazzo employs two different rhythm teams, performing five tunes with drummer Peter Erskine and bassist John Patitucci, and four with drummer Jeff Hirshfield and acoustic bassist Jay Anderson. Calderazzo and cohorts create a seamless, straight-ahead session, generating kicking bop tunes and warm-toned ballads on this 10-tune album that includes three of his warmly accessible originals. Calderazzo doesn't cut new paths, yet he displays passionate mastery of the ivories. Check out an earlier session that brought Watts and Calderazzo together with leader Rick Margitza on *This Is New* 𝕚𝕚𝕚 (Blue Note, 1991, prod. Matt Pierson). Calderazzo demonstrates his artistry, performing at a variety of tempos on all but two tracks with the quartet. Margitza's supple saxisms predominate, but Calderazzo has his share of the spotlight and thrives in uptempo versions of "Just In Time" and "Invitation." Since 1988 when they met at one of Jerry Bergonzi's Vermont Jazz gigs, Calderazzo has collaborated with the Bruce Gertz Quintet. Their most recent U.S. release is *Blueprint* 𝕚𝕚𝕚 (Evidence, 1997, prod. Bruce Gertz), a harmonically modern session that features 11 enticing originals from the bassist-leader, performed with John Abercrombie (guitar), Jerry Bergonzi (tenor sax), and Adam Nussbaum (drums). Calderazzo adapts readily to the spirit of the 1991-recorded session, enhancing the sturdy rhythm section, and shining in his spotlighted moments.

influences:

◀◀ Red Garland, Herbie Hancock, McCoy Tyner, Benny Green

see also: *Michael Brecker, Bruce Gertz*

Nancy Ann Lee

Red Callender

Born George Sylvester Callender, March 6, 1916, in Hainesville, VA. Died March 8, 1992, in Saugus, CA.

Callender began his musical career with a brief stint in New York in the 1930s, but settled in Los Angeles in 1936. He made his recording debut that year with Louis Armstrong and spent the next several years playing with various small groups in Los Angeles. In the 1940s, Callender made several important recordings with Errol Garner, Charlie Parker, Dexter Gordon, and Wardell Gray, among others. From the 1950s on, Callender would be mostly involved in commercial recording and work for television. However, he continued participating in stimulating jazz sessions on the side, most notably with Art Tatum on Pablo.

what to buy: On Art Tatum's *The Tatum Group Masterpieces: Vol. 6* 𝄞𝄞𝄞𝄞 (Pablo, 1956, prod. Norman Granz) the pianist, of course, is the main star, but the trio with Callender and drummer "Papa" Jo Jones really cooks on such standards as "Just One of Those Things" and "Love for Sale."

the rest:
Swingin' Suite 𝄞𝄞𝄞 (Modern, 1956)
The Lowest 𝄞𝄞𝄞 (Metrojazz, 1960)
Night Mist Blues 𝄞𝄞𝄞 (Hemisphere, 1984)

worth searching for: Unfortunately, all of Callender's discography as a leader fits in this category, as none of it is currently available on CD. *Red Callender Speaks Low* 𝄞𝄞𝄞 (Crown, 1954) stands out as especially worth searching for because, though Callender is mainly known to jazz enthusiasts as a bassist, he becomes one of the first jazz tuba soloists on this record.

influences:
◀◀ Walter Page
▶▶ Don Butterfield

Dan Keener

Cab Calloway

Born Cabell Calloway, December 25, 1907, in Rochester, NY. Died November 18, 1994, in Delaware, RI.

Known to most as the "hi-de-ho" man, Cab Calloway was one of the greatest entertainers of all time, a consummate showman. Growing up in Baltimore, at an early age he sometimes sang with the Baltimore Melody Boys. His brother, Elmer, and sister Blanche both became bandleaders. After moving to Chicago with his family, Calloway briefly studied law at Crane College, and with Blanche, appeared in the notable black revue, *Plantation Days* at the Loop Theater. He also worked as master of ceremonies and as a relief drummer at the Sunset Cafe. In 1928–29, he took over leadership of the 11-piece Chicago band, the Alabamians, but their appearance in New York met with tough competition and, parted from the band, Calloway found work in *Connie's Hot Chocolate* revues at Connie's Inn. In the spring of 1930 he signed on to lead the Missourians at the Savoy. With his demonstrative all-encompassing energy, Calloway breathed a new life into the band, engaging the audience with a fire, and soon, they were employed and working at the Cotton Club.

With the hit theme song "Minnie the Moocher," Calloway gained a national reputation, and was one of the most recog-

nized black performers in America, with a salary that belied the depression and enabled him to pay his band members very well. He reigned at the Cotton Club into May 1940. Among his most famous recordings are "Reefer Man," "Kicking the Gong Around," "Minnie the Moocher's Wedding Day," and "You Gotta Hi-De-Ho," with many of his hits featuring his innovative scat vocals. His sidemen included Milt Hinton, "Doc" Cheatham, Eddie Barefield, Cozy Cole, Jonah Jones, "Panama" Francis, Mario Bauzá, Chu Berry, Dizzy Gillespie, and Tyree Glenn, among others. Calloway appeared in numerous films, including "Stormy Weather" with Lena Horne, in 1943. Due to the changing times, Calloway disbanded his orchestra in 1948, and fronted various small groups on into 1952, when he accepted the role of Sportin' Life in Gershwin's *Porgy and Bess,* which included a run in London. Returning to nightclub solo work, he sometimes reassembled the band for short stints. During the mid-1960s, Calloway was featured with the touring Harlem Globetrotters Show, and in the late 1960s, he appeared on stage with Pearl Bailey in *Hello Dolly.* His autobiography, *Of Minnie the Moocher and Me,* published in 1976, unfortunately, is out of print. Throughout the rest of his life, Calloway continued to appear before fans and, always the ultimate entertainer, gave them what they wanted, "Minnie the Moocher." Continuing to perform well into the 1980s, Calloway also made some film appearances, including the 1980 film, *The Blues Brothers.* Calloway also remains notable for boosting the careers of legendary musicians such as Doc Cheatham, Ben Webster, Milt Hinton, Cozy Cole, Jonah Jones, Dizzy Gillespie, Ike Quebec, and others who achieved great success.

what to buy: Many of Calloway's recordings are on import labels. One of his best and most accessible domestic albums, *Are You Hep to the Jive?* 𝄞𝄞𝄞𝄞 (OKeh/Vocalion/Columbia, 1940–47/Sony Legacy Series, 1994, prod. various) is a 22-tune compilation produced by Bob Irwin that showcases Cab Calloway vocalizing at his best and leading his band through his 11 originals and the remaining novelty numbers, and other version (1942) of his classic, "Minnie the Moocher." Including three previously unreleased tracks, the 1940s-era sides were lovingly restored to exceptional sound quality, and current young jump-swing fans should find the danceable beats appealing, especially tunes like "The Calloway Boogie," which features the quavering sax section playing in unison and the full band kicking big-time. Older fans should find reminiscences in the jive

Cab Calloway **(AP/Wide World Photos)**

jargon of the lyrics, such as on "Are You All Reet?" While some may quibble about Calloway's contributions to jazz and think of his music as corny by today's standards, he was a true entertainer, a powerful, popular singer and bandleader who managed to keep his band working during the Depression and beyond, and with considerable flawlessness! If he were directing his band today, he'd probably be leading the jump-swing revival. This disc displays Calloway's copious talents and high-energy performances, as well as fine instrumental solos and tight, buoyant ensemble work from his band. A great introduction to Calloway. The only drawback to this compilation is that the liner booklet gives no information about the fine soloists or band members, but in the earliest years this CD covers, soloists with the band included trumpeters Dizzy Gillespie and Jonah Jones, tenor saxman Chu Berry, drummer Cozy Cole, and other then and soon-to-be notables. For that information, you'll have to investigate the series of CDs from Jazz Chronological Classics. Backtrack a bit to the beginning of Calloway's career and check out *Cab Calloway (1930–1931)* (Various, 1930–31/Classics, 1994, prod. various) ♪♪♪♪. One of the best in the series of 11 CDs compiled on Jazz Chronological Classics, it contains his first 24 sides (including his original version of "Minnie the Moocher"), and highlights tunes associated with other band leaders, as well as popular favorites such as "Some of These Days," "St. James Infirmary," "St. Louis Blues," and other gems. This is a good introduction to the series which ends with the years 1941–42. These albums are usually found in Borders bookstores and can be special ordered online at amazon.com.

best of the rest:

Cab Calloway & Company ♪♪♪♪ (RCA, 1931–49/1994)
Radio Years 1940–1945 ♪♪♪♪ (1940–45/Storyville, 1997)
Cab Calloway (1931–1932) ♪♪♪♪ (Classics, 1994)
Cab Calloway (1939–1940) ♪♪♪♪♪ (Classics, 1994)
Cab Calloway (1940) ♪♪♪♪♪ (Classics, 1994)
Minnie the Moocher ♪♪♪♪♪ (MCA, 1995)

influences:

◀◀ Blanche Calloway, Duke Ellington, Louis Armstrong

▶▶ George Gershwin, Louis Jordan

Susan K. Berlowitz and Nancy Ann Lee

John Campbell

Born July 7, 1955, in Bloomington, IL.

John Campbell is a strong technical pianist whose playing harkens back to the elegant Pittsburgh school of Erroll Garner and Ahmad Jamal, with a little Art Tatum or Oscar Peterson

tossed in for good effect. While in college he played bass in the Illinois State University big band but it's as a piano player that Campbell first started receiving notice. After moving to Chicago from southern Illinois where he had grown up and gone to school, Campbell became the local guy many touring artists hired when they passed through the Windy City. He moved to the highly competitive environment of New York City in 1984 and quickly managed to achieve a status similar to the one he enjoyed in Chicago. The pianist has worked as an accompanist for Mel Tormé and Eddie Jefferson in addition to recording with Clark Terry and the Gibbs-DeFranco group. Campbell has also played alongside Eddie Harris, James Moody, and Stan Getz.

what to buy: When many pianists play Maybeck Recital Hall they feel that they need to turn the recital into a technical tour de force or it won't be a success. There is a bit of that on *At Maybeck, Volume 29* ♪♪♪♪ (Concord Jazz, 1993, prod. Carl E. Jefferson) where Campbell's formidable skills are on display all the time. A recurring trick used in this recording finds him shifting from one key to another in every song. As Campbell performs, he often reveals stimulating turns of phrase but sometimes it's tempting to listen more to how he plays than what he plays. Luckily, there is enough music in this album to forgive the sometimes heavy-handed focus on technique versus feel. When Campbell takes his time with works like "Darn That Dream" and "Easy to Love," the rewards come because the music is served so well by his formidable abilities.

what to buy next: *Turning Point* ♪♪♪ (Contemporary, 1990, prod. Terry Gibbs), an exemplary second album from pianist Campbell, finds him in the company of a solid rhythm section (Jay Anderson on bass and drummer Joel Spencer) and, on four cuts, with his old employer, master trumpeter Clark Terry. The title tune, written by Campbell, is a bit of a surprise since you might reasonably expect blazing keyboard antics from this master technician but, it's a pleasant mid-tempo romp threatening to be a ballad. His version of "Tin Tin Deo" weds technique and flash with good results and Terry's call-and-response work with Campbell on "This Time the Dream's on Me" is an awful lot of fun.

the rest:

After Hours ♪♪♪ (Contemporary, 1989)

influences:

◀◀ Bill Evans, Erroll Garner, Ahmad Jamal, Oscar Peterson, Ramsey Lewis

Garaud MacTaggart

Roy Campbell

Born September 29, 1952, in Los Angeles, CA.

A performer, composer, arranger, music director, and teacher, Roy Campbell has been a fixture on the underground music scene for over two decades. Playing trumpet, flugelhorn, and flute, Campbell has accrued credits in the David Murray Octet and Billy Bang's group, as well as recording albums as leader for the Delmark label and for the Swedish label, Silkheart. Campbell's family moved to New York when he was a child and he began playing piano at age six and switched to trumpet in high school. As a member of the Jazzmobile Workshop from 1971 to 1973, Campbell pursued advanced trumpet studies with Lee Morgan and Kenny Dorham. An eclectic musician, Campbell has dabbled in an array of musical genres, including R&B, funk, bebop, standards, and has found his home in the avant garde, to which he brings all of these influences in collaborations with Cecil Taylor, Sunny Murray, Henry Threadgill, Jemeel Moondoc, Craig Harris, Woody Shaw, and others. Campbell's expertise in orchestration (he's written for 15- to 20-piece orchestras), past collaborations with leading jazz innovators, and ability to draw inspiration from a variety of sources, set him apart from the trumpet herd. In the late 1980s and early 1990s Campbell split his time between New York and Rotterdam, where he toured with bass saxophonist Klaas Hekman and took over the helm of the Thelonious New World Orchestra there. He now leads a New York–based trio with fluctuating personnel, plays in William Parker's Little Huey Creative Music Orchestra, and co-leads the group Other Dimensions In Music with Daniel Carter (alto/tenor saxophones, flute, trumpet), William Parker (bass), and Rashid Bakr.

what to buy: Campbell has forged a solid second outing as leader with *La Tierra del Fuego (The Land of Fire)* &&&& (Delmark, 1994, prod. Steve Wagner), composing all but one of the seven tunes. This album features tenor saxman Zane Massey, Ricardo Strobert (alto sax, flute), Rahn Burton (piano), Hideiji Taninaka (bass), Reggie Nicholson (drums), Talik Abdullah (percussion), with Klaus Hekman (bass sax) and Alex Lodico (trombone) guesting on two tracks each. Campbell composes on Spanish motifs, at times inflecting haunting or fiery rhythms laden with percussion. The centerpiece of the album is the 17-minute title tune, a three-movement suite that builds on Spanish folk melodies and third world sounds. The leader creates festive colors and pleasing textures that make this session eminently more interesting than those of most young trumpet players recording today. It's a tough choice between Campbell's two Delmark albums and *New Kingdom* &&&& (Delmark, 1992,

prod. Steve Wagner), Campbell's debut album for the label could just as easily be a first pick since it was so highly praised by fans and critics when it came out. Delmark is a fitting choice for Campbell's innovative music that seems to draw, in part, from AACM (Association for the Advancement of Creative Musicians) influences as well as from the New York City avant-garde scene. The leader mostly adheres to melody frameworks as he generates open and muted trumpet/flugelhorn smears, sputters, splashes, splats, and straight-up renderings, leading innovative trio settings with William Parker (bass) and Zen Matsuura (drums), and expanding the group to a quintet featuring Ricardo Strobert (alto sax, flute) and Bryan Carrott (vibes), and a sextet with guesting tenor saxophonist Zane Massey (on two tracks). In addition to Campbell's accomplished trumpet skills, his talents as composer are impressive; he wrote five of the album's eight tunes. (Parker contributes two originals, Massey one.) Both albums are enjoyable; if you like one, you'll want the other.

the rest:
(With Pyramid) *Communion* &&&& (Silkheart, 1995)

see also: *Other Dimensions in Music*

Nancy Ann Lee

Valerie Capers

Born May 24, 1935, in New York, NY.

While pianist/vocalist Valerie Capers has not recorded much, she's certainly made her mark on the scene. And when she does record, it's with a sturdy two-handed, dramatic approach and the ultimate sensitivity to her material. Before Capers lost her sight at the age of six, she was playing piano and picking up songs by ear. Encouraged by a supportive family, she graduated from the New York Institute for the Education of the Blind where she began classical piano studies. She received her B.S. and M.S. degrees, in 1959 and 1960, respectively, from Juilliard School of Music, the first blind graduate. Although she was playing classical repertoire, she ventured into jazz with encouragement from her brother, Bobby Capers, then a saxophonist/flutist with Mongo Santamaria. Capers began her career in jazz as composer-arranger for Mongo Santamaria's Afro-Cuban-jazz band, contributing his hits, "El Toro" (recorded on his *Live at the Village Gate* album), "Uh-Huh," and the bossa nova, "Sarai." She formed her own trio and made her 1967 recording debut on Atlantic with *Portrait in Soul*, and recorded a 1982 album, *Affirmation*. In between, she worked with Ray Brown, Slide Hampton, James Moody, Max Roach, Dizzy Gillespie, and others. She has appeared at Newport, Kool, JVC, North Sea, and other festivals, and performs regularly in New York clubs. Capers has conducted various performances, including the 1978 Christmas jazz cantata *Sing About Love* at Carnegie Hall and her own "opertorio" *Sojourner* which premiered at New York's St. Peter's Church (1981). Her teaching credentials include stints at the Manhattan School of Music and her current position as Professor Emeritus and Artist-in-Residence at Bronx Community College of the City University of New York (CUNY), where she was Chairman of the Department of Music and Art (1987–1995). She has received numerous awards, honors, and music grants and, in 1996, was awarded an honorary Doctor of Fine Arts degree from Susquehanna University for her achievements as a scholar, educator, and musician. Fifteen years after her 1982 recording, she made her only album currently in print.

what's available: A robust nine-tune session by pianist Valerie Capers and her trio with Terry Clarke (drums), John Robinson III or Bob Cranshaw (bass), *Come on Home* ♪♪♪♪ (Columbia, 1995, prod. Frank Zuback) is part of Columbia's Legendary Pioneers of Jazz series. Special guests Wynton Marsalis (trumpet), Paquito D'Rivera (alto sax), and Mongo Santamaria (conga drums) add vitality to the session, appearing on a couple of tracks each. Capers shows off her accomplished Afro-Cuban rhythms, kicking off with a bubbling version of Dizzy Gillespie's "A Night in Tunisia," and frolicking on "One Note Samba." While she can hit-and-run with hard-bop, she is equally adept with her delicate pianoisms, especially on the romantic Loesser classic, "I've Never Been in Love Before." She adds special verve with her mid-range vocals on her soul-stirring torch song, "Out of All (He's Chosen Me)," the bluesy title tune, and one more. Capers is a tasteful performer with diverse influences at her fingertips. No imitator, she owns her turf.

Nancy Ann Lee

Frank Capp

Born August 20, 1931, in Worcester, MA.

A solid big band and swinging small-ensemble drummer, Frank Capp was 19 when he replaced Shelly Manne in the Stan Kenton band in 1951. Capp then joined the bands of Neal Hefti, Billy May, Benny Goodman, and Bob Florence. He also worked and/or recorded with major jazz stars, including Ella Fitzgerald, Benny Goodman, Andre Previn, Art Pepper, and Turk Murphy, and played in bands of the *Merv Griffin, Red Skelton,* and *Steve Allen* TV shows.

Always in demand as a studio musician, Capp is known for lay-

ing down a solid beat while accenting the melody of each song. He worked for Warner Bros. Studio and fueled combos for vocalists Peggy Lee and Shirley Horn, pianist Roger Kellaway, trumpeter Ruby Braff, and trombonists Al Grey and Rob McConnell. Capp performs in small combos at jazz parties and festivals around the nation, as well as leading the Frank Capp Juggernaut big band.

Juggernaut effectively emulates the tight section work and exciting solos of the Basie bands, and has earned fans and record-chart recognition via tours to England and Japan. Juggernaut originated as a one-nighter in 1975 when Capp was contracting for the Neal Hefti band and the leader decided to break up the orchestra. Capp and pianist Nat Pierce agreed to stage a concert tribute to Count Basie using top Los Angeles session musicians. The band proved to be such an irresistible musical force that it turned into a twice-monthly nightclub gig. Two decades later, Juggernaut is still alive and swinging, albeit with varying personnel and existing mostly for recording dates and special gigs that include corporate shows. Capp has continued to lead the band after Pierce's death in 1992, with Gerald Wiggins at the piano. Vocalists Joe Williams, Ernie Andrews, and Ernestine Anderson have performed with Juggernaut, but the main focus is on instrumental power and polish. The band's changing cast of musicians has included trumpeters Blue Mitchell, Snooky Young, Conte Candoli, Bobby Shew, Bill Berry, Carl Saunders and Frank Szabo; saxophonists Marshal Royal, Red Holloway, Bob Cooper, Lanny Morgan, Plas Johnson, Richie Kamuca, Pete Christlieb, Jack Nimitz, Jackie Kelso and Rickey Woodard; trombonists Buster Cooper, Thurman Green and George Bohanon; and bassists Chuck Berghofer and Bob Maize.

what to buy: The band's first album, *Juggernaut* ♪♪♪♪ (Concord, 1977/1991, prod. Carl Jefferson), was recorded live at the band's debut nightclub in Hollywood, King Arthur's. The sound on eight Basie charts is solidly propelled by Capp. "Roll 'em Pete" is sparked by the fiery solos of trumpeter Blue Mitchell and tenorman Plas Johnson. The medium-tempo "Moten Swing" showcases co-leader and pianist Nat Pierce, altoist Marshal Royal shines on "Wee Baby Blues," and vocalist Ernie Andrews takes "Take the 'A' Train" on a new route via witty excerpts from other standards. The band works 16 Neal Hefti charts on *The Frank Capp Juggernaut: In a Hefti Bag* ♪♪♪♪ (Concord, 1995, prod. Frank Capp). "Li'l Darlin'" lets trumpeter Snooky Young handle the solo on Hefti's most famous chart, while "Cute" provides Capp exposure for clever brush work. But it's "Whirly Bird" that brings out the best in the band, tenormen Pete Christlieb and Rickey Woodard soloing with dynamic energy. "Duet" features solos by trumpeters Conte Candoli and Young. The album was alto saxophonist Marshal Royal's farewell recording shortly before his death. *Frank Capp Juggernaut: Play It Again, Sam* 𝄞𝄞𝄞𝄞 (Concord, 1997, prod. Frank Capp) showcases the band's solid section and solo work on a dozen tracks from Basie arranger Sammy Nestico. Trumpeter Conte Candoli is featured on several tracks, including "Warm Breeze" and "The Heat's On." Gerald Wiggins delivers Basie's signature one-note piano skirmishes but also explores longer melodic riffs on an unusual ballad-style working of "Ja-Da." A burning duet by tenormen Pete Christlieb and Rickey Woodard, plus a satisfying Capp segment, give "Wind Machine" its power. *Frank Capp Quartet Featuring Rickey Woodard: Quality Time* 𝄞𝄞𝄞 (Concord, 1995, prod. Frank Capp) finds Capp leading a quartet behind guest Rickey Woodard, one of Juggernaut's tenor saxophonists. It's a well-balanced issue of three original charts and several evergreens, including Duke Ellington's "Sophisticated Lady" and "Things Ain't What They Used to Be." Woodard plays alto on Frank Loesser's "I've Never Been in Love Before" and Tadd Dameron's "Tadd's Delight." Clifford Brown's "Daahoud" is a vehicle to prove trumpeter Nolan Smith's fiery flair, while Woodard's original blues, "Dip Stick," stars both the saxophonist and pianist Tom Ranier. Capp propels cleanly and without intrusion throughout.

what to buy next: *The Capp-Pierce Juggernaut: Live at the Century Plaza* 𝄞𝄞𝄞 (Concord, 1978/1987, prod. Carl Jefferson) is a high-energy live outing that includes two Nat Pierce originals, "Basie's Deep Fry" and "Capp This!" The sax section is especially strong on Buck Clayton's "Swing Shift" and Al Cohn's "Tarragon." The album features brandy-smooth Joe Williams on the final two tracks, "Joe's Blues" and "What the World Needs Now." Unfortunately, the liner notes list only the co-leaders and not the band members of this early aggregation. *Juggernaut Strikes Again!* 𝄞𝄞𝄞 (Concord, 1982/1990, prod. Frank Capp, Nat Pierce) is another powerhouse outing that adds Ernie Andrews on ballads and blues. A medley paying tribute to Charlie Parker offers two of Bird's best, "Parker's Mood" and "Word from Bird." Ellington gets a swinging salute from trombonist Buster Cooper on "Things Ain't What They Used to Be." *Live at the Alley Cat* 𝄞𝄞𝄞 (Concord, 1987, prod. Chris Long) is the last Capp-Pierce co-led issue, full of energy and expertise on evergreens such as "Street of Dreams," "It Might As Well Be Spring" and "Spring Is Here." Top solos are delivered by trumpeters Conte Candoli and Snooky Young, saxophonists Bob Cooper and Red Holloway, and guitarist Ken Pohlman.

the rest:
Frank Capp Trio Presents Rickey Woodard 𝄞𝄞𝄞 (Concord, 1991)

influences:
◀◀ Ornette Coleman
▶▶ David Murray, Don Byron

Patricia Myers

Ana Caram

Born October 1, 1958, in Sao Paulo, Brazil.

Brazilian guitarist/vocalist Ana Caram has roots in a musical family and is undoubtedly influenced by songwriter Antonio Carlos Jobim and his contributions to the international *bossa nova* boom. Like Jobim, Caram delivers haunting, subtle melodies melded to jazz improvisations, although she rarely composes tunes. Caram's career as a singer-guitarist began in Brazil, but a trip to perform at a festival in Finland and a subsequent invitation from Paquito D'Rivera to sing with his band at the JVC Festival at Carnegie Hall eventually led her to New York City. The night of that performance she was introduced to David Chesky of Chesky Records and in 1989 Caram released her debut album, *Rio after Dark*. She has since recorded four more albums for the label.

what to buy: With illustrious guests Paquito D'Rivera (saxophone/clarinet) and the Brazilian jazz god himself, Antonio Carlos Jobim (piano/vocals), Caram makes her debut on *Rio after Dark* 𝄞𝄞𝄞 (Chesky, 1989, prod. David Chesky). The 15 selections include two originals, tunes by Brazilian composers (including Jobim), and other composers. The familiar theme of Jobim's "Meditation" features Caram singing English and Portuguese lyrics, and a brief duet with Jobim, who plays piano on this track. Along with Caram's guitar finesse and vocals, D'Rivera's beautifully improvised saxophone solo on David Chesky's subtle swayer, "Summer Days," makes this song a delightful listen. The fare, which has crossover appeal for World music fans, is evenly balanced with ballads, uptempo percussive-laden Brazilian pieces, and even the familiar Carol King song, "You've Got a Friend." Though Caram plays guitar admirably, her sweet, soft vocals, often interwoven with the improvised solos of the instrumentalists, are the real treasure. After releasing a mixed bag of selections under the dubious musical direction of Leandro Braga on her second album, *Amazonia*, Caram returned to more familiar turf, the Jobim-styled Brazilian jazz found on *The Other Side of Jobim* 𝄞𝄞𝄞𝄞 (Chesky, 1992, prod. David Chesky). On this album of 11 lesser-known

Jobim compositions, her team is significantly enhanced by guitarist/musical director/arranger, Sergio Assad, and the creative flair of percussionist Jamey Haddad. Other fine musicians include Steve Sacks (soprano sax/flute), Erik Friedlander (cello), Matthew Dine (oboe), and David Finck (bass). Assad's arrangements are unmatchably rich and beautiful and perfectly suited to Caram's singing style. She caresses the lyrics, especially on tunes like "Sem Voce," and "Falando De Amor." This is a well-programmed, well-produced project, containing a mixture of Brazilian-jazz classics, romantic ballads sung in Portuguese, and modern uptempo numbers such as "Demais." The colorful music holds broad appeal for Brazilian-jazz lovers, World music fans, classical crossover fans, and anyone who appreciates expertly arranged, softly melodic music.

what to buy next: A veteran of Caram's groups since her first Chesky album, Steve Sacks serves as musical director, arranging the 12 modern tunes of *Maracanã* ♫♫♫ (Chesky, 1993, prod. David Chesky, Nelson Motta, Steve Sacks). Often with backing from excellent horn arrangements, Caram sings in her native language and in English. As on previous albums, her guitar playing receives less emphasis, but the efforts of regular cohorts, instrumentalists such as David Finck (bass), Steve Sacks (saxophones and flutes), David Sacks (trombone), Erik Friedlander (cello), and special guest Raul Jaurena on bandoneon, make this a pleasurable venture.

the rest:
Amazonia ♫♫♫ (Chesky, 1990)
Bossa Nova ♫♫♫♫ (Chesky, 1995)

influences:
◀◀ Astrud Gilberto, Antonio Carlos Jobim, Dori Caymmi

Nancy Ann Lee

Larry Carlton

Born March 2, 1949, in Torrance, CA.

Larry Carlton is a guitar legend. He has rightly and long been called "the guitarist's guitarist" and "the musician's musician." His signature guitar sound has been added to over 5,000 sessions, including over 100 gold and platinum albums, and he has received seven Grammy nominations, winning two. The problem with most studio musicians is that over time they loose their ability to play something that is all their own. This has never been a problem for Carlton, a sure-handed technician who plays with a plethora of honesty and emotion.

From the age of six, receiving encouragement from his mother,

Carlton learned note reading, time signatures and chords, performing at local talent shows in Los Angeles until he was 14. It was in junior-high school that Carlton was introduced to jazz through the Gerald Wilson Big Band album *Moment of Truth*, which featured guitarist Joe Pass. Carlton's first paid studio session was at age 16 (because that's when he could drive), for a California surf-band called the Challengers. Prior to that, at age 13, he did a session for Tommy Reddick, (the original "Jeff" on the *Lassie* TV series), who formed a group called the Tokens and recorded a tune called "Oh, What a Night." Three months later, Carlton heard the track on KRLA, L.A.'s big pop station, and realized he had cut his first "hit" record.

Carlton spent three years (1967–69) at Harbor College and Long Beach State University, majoring in music. A brief association with the Fifth Dimension augmented his first year of academic study. In 1968 he recorded his first LP, *With a Little Help from My Friends*, which led to his joining the Going Thing, a group of jingle singers that did Ford commercials. Carlton's exposure through on-camera and radio commercials for Ford led to his call on the *Lohman and Barkley Show* for NBC-TV. During the program's second season, he became musical director on a different NBC-TV project, *Ms. Alphabet,* a children's show that was nominated for an Emmy award. The program also featured his acting talents as the co-star "Larry Guitar." The calls began to increase significantly as Carlton gained studio notoriety. Carlton broke new ground with his volume pedal technique when he was asked to play with the Crusaders on their *Crusader One* album in 1971. Joni Mitchell's *Court and Spark* album is another fine example of this technique. During his tenure (through late 1976), Carlton was featured on 13 Crusader albums, often contributing material.

In 1973 Carlton released his first solo recording, *Singing/Playing* on Blue Thumb Records. His demand as a session player was now at a zenith (averaging 15 calls a week) juxtaposed against 50 live dates a year with the Crusaders. He was featured with stars from every imaginable genre—Sammy Davis, Herb Alpert, Quincy Jones, Paul Anka, Michael Jackson, Christopher Cross, John Lennon, Jerry Garcia, Neil Diamond, Bobby Bland, Dolly Parton, Linda Ronstadt, Ray Charles, and others. He also produced and co-wrote the television theme for *Who's the Boss* and the movie soundtrack for *Against All Odds.* Carlton also arranged two albums (*Superman* and *Songbird*) for Barbra Streisand, and arranged Joan Baez's *Diamonds and Rust* LP.

As his association with the Crusaders drew to a close, Carlton began to focus more intensively on his solo career, signing with Warner Bros. in 1977. An anxious audience responded to his

Larry Carlton, hot on the heels of his debut session with Steely Dan. *Rolling Stone* magazine lists Carlton's guitar solo on "Kid Charlemagne" as "one of the three best licks in rock music." His four-album association with Steely Dan would later segue into a close working relationship with Donald Fagen on the widely acclaimed *Nightfly* release. By the early 1980s, with over 3,000 studio sessions completed, Carlton had received four Grammy nominations, and in 1981, he and Mike Post won the "Best Pop Instrumental Performance" Grammy for the *Hill Street Blues* theme. He was also voted N.A.R.A.S.'s "Most Valuable Player" for three consecutive years. From 1973 to 1978 he released four albums for Warner Bros. and two in Japan that attained gold and silver status. Three months after the release of *Friends*, Carlton, along with other jazz artists, was abruptly dropped from the label, having been told that there was no longer any interest in their type of music. After a two-year sabbatical, Carlton signed with MCA Nashville, deciding to switch to acoustic guitar to express himself in a more personal way. His two initial releases, *Alone/But Never Alone* and *Discovery*, were both chart-topping efforts, the latter winning a Grammy for "Best Pop Instrumental" for his arrangement of the Doobie Brothers' "Minute by Minute."

It was announced in 1986 that Carlton would record a combined 13 albums for MCA proper and MCA Master Series. After the success of his live album *Last Nite* in 1987 and while working on his next album, he became the victim of random gun violence, being shot once in the throat by juveniles outside his private studio in North Hollywood, California. The bullet shattered his vocal cord and caused significant nerve trauma, but through intensive therapy and a relentless desire to heal, Carlton completed work on *On Solid Ground* in 1989. In keeping with Carlton's desire to put a positive spin on everything, he formed Helping Innocent People (HIP), the first emergency response program in Los Angeles that aids the critical needs of victims of random gun violence. Meanwhile, with their acquisition in 1989 by MCA, the remainder of Carlton's contract was transferred to GRP, where he continues to extend his notoriety.

what to buy: *Discovery* 𝄪𝄪𝄪𝄪 (MCA Master Series, 1987, prod. Larry Carlton) garnered a Grammy for "Best Pop Instrumental Performance" with "Minute by Minute," performed by the original composer and pianist, Michael McDonald. Also, this was probably the first song on a jazz record label to be released as a CD single.

what to buy next: *Last Night* 𝄪𝄪𝄪𝄪 (MCA, 1987, prod. Larry Carlton) was recorded live at the Baked Potato in North Holly-

wood and is an excellent example of Carlton's focused energy and ability to make the electric guitar "talk" instead of just generating notes. This record was also nominated for a Grammy in the "Best Jazz Instrumental Performance" category.

the rest:
With a Little Help from My Friends 𝄪𝄪𝄪 (Uni, 1968/Edsel, 1996)
Larry Carlton 𝄪𝄪𝄪𝄪 (Warner Bros., 1978/MCA, 1988)
Strikes Twice 𝄪𝄪𝄪𝄪 (Warner Bros., 1980/MCA, 1988)
Sleepwalk 𝄪𝄪𝄪 (Warner Bros., 1982/MCA, 1988)
Friends 𝄪𝄪𝄪 (Warner Bros., 1983/MCA, 1988)
Alone/But Never Alone 𝄪𝄪𝄪 (MCA Master Series, 1986)
On Solid Ground 𝄪𝄪𝄪𝄪 (MCA, 1989)
Christmas at My House 𝄪𝄪𝄪𝄪 (MCA Master Series, 1989)
Collection 𝄪𝄪𝄪 (GRP, 1990)
Kid Gloves 𝄪𝄪𝄪 (GRP, 1992)
Renegade Gentleman 𝄪𝄪𝄪 (GRP, 1993)
Playing/Singing 𝄪𝄪𝄪 (Edsel, 1995)
Larry & Lee 𝄪𝄪𝄪𝄪 (GRP, 1995)
The Gift 𝄪𝄪𝄪 (GRP, 1996)

influences:
◀◀ Joe Pass, John Coltrane, Wes Montgomery, Barney Kessel, B.B. King

Ralph Burnett

Judy Carmichael

Born November 27, 1952, Pico Rivera, CA.

Born into a musical family, Judy Carmichael began to study piano at an early age. When her grandfather offered $50 to the first grandchild who could play "Maple Leaf Rag," she taught herself the piece and collected the reward. While attending college at Cal State Fullerton, Carmichael took a part-time job playing ragtime piano on the Balboa Pavilion Queen Riverboat. Since she drew larger crowds than the regular pianist, Carmichael soon took over on a full-time basis. Because she was so consistently booked as a pianist, after two years of college, she dropped out, and at the age of 21, first heard Fats Waller's recordings, and began to move from the ragtime style into stride. In 1977 Carmichael was hired to play stride piano at Disneyland. She made her first recording for the Progressive label in 1980 and moved on to New York the following year. Bringing a freshness to the stride music that is so deeply ingrained in her soul, Carmichael plays beyond interpretation, with both authority and authenticity, almost as if she invented the musical style herself. Carmichael plays clubs, concert halls and festivals around the world. In addition to recording for Progressive/Statiras and other labels, she has recorded for her own label, C&D Productions.

what to buy: On *Judy Carmichael . . . and Basie Called Her Stride* 𝄞𝄞𝄞𝄞 (C & D Productions, 1983/1993, prod. Judy Carmichael), Carmichael sounds as if she were born in an earlier era, and then transported here in some magical way. Her sound and stride style are authentic. This CD includes her work from her first two albums, and she is accompanied by top-notch musicians, including Marshal Royal, Freddie Green, Red Callender, and Harold Jones. Interpreting the music of Fats Waller and James P. Johnson, among others, Judy swings, and once you hear her work, you'll understand why pianist-bandleader Count Basie referred to her as "Stride."

best of the rest:

Pearls 𝄞𝄞𝄞𝄞 (Jazzology, 1993)
Chops 𝄞𝄞𝄞𝄞 (C & D Productions, 1996)

influences:

◀◀ Scott Joplin, James P. Johnson, Fats Waller

Susan K. Berlowitz

Bakida Carroll

Born 1947, in St. Louis, MO.

Bakida Carroll spent his teen years immersed in R&B, blues, and jazz. He joined the U.S. Army band in 1968, then returned to St. Louis and joined the Black Artists Group (BAG). This began a lifelong association with Julius Hemphill and Oliver Lake. In 1972 he moved to Paris and formed a band with Brazilian percussionist Nana Vasconcelos. Carroll moved to New York in 1975 and has performed with artists as diverse as Albert King, John Carter, Oliver Nelson, Dr. John, David Murray, Muhal Richard Abrams, and Sam and Dave. A composer of great talent and style, he has written music for poet/playwright Ntozake Shange, playwright Richard Wesley, and Kermit Frazier. Carroll has also collaborated with choreographer Diane McIntyre, written for TV and film, and been awarded numerous grants and commissions.

what to buy: *Door of the Cage* 𝄞𝄞𝄞𝄞 (Soul Note, 1994, prod. Bakida Carroll, Flavio Bonandrini) features beautiful compositions with a groove. A flair for the outside complements this release featuring Erica Lindsay on tenor, Santi Debriano on bass, Pheeroan Aklaff on drums, and Steve Adegoke Colson on piano.

the rest:

Shadows and Reflections 𝄞𝄞𝄞𝄞 (Soul Note, 1982)

David C. Gross

Benny Carter

Born Bennett Lester Carter August 8, 1907, in New York, NY.

Deeply entrenched in the Swing tradition, Benny Carter has had one of the most successful, all-encompassing jazz careers, spanning over 70 years as a multi-instrumentalist, arranger, composer, educator, and bandleader. Carter has played trumpet and alto saxophone since the start of his career in the 1920s. In 1925 Carter enrolled at Wilberforce College in Ohio to study theology, but soon left to join Horace Henderson's band. Late in 1928, he formed and toured with his first band, playing the Arcadia Ballroom in New York City. In addition to short stints with Fletcher Henderson and Chick Webb, as well as a year with Charlie Johnson, with whom he first recorded in 1927, Carter took the position of musical director for McKinney's Cotton Pickers during the summer of 1931. During the 1930s, he also wrote for Benny Goodman. In 1936 Carter moved to England, where he worked for the BBC, leading a staff band of American and British musicians. Returning to the States in 1938, he led his own small and large ensembles, with sidemen including Vic Dickenson, Jonah Jones, Eddie Heywood, Dizzy Gillespie, and Tyree Glenn, among others, and completed a residency at the Apollo Theater in 1944. In 1943 Carter formed a West Coast band that included sidemen such as Max Roach, Buddy Rich and J.J. Johnson. In addition, he was one of the first black musicians to work in the Hollywood studios as a writer/arranger, moving permanently to Los Angeles in early 1945.

In Hollywood, Carter worked on numerous film scores, including *The Snows of Kilimanjaro* and the television series, *Mod Squad*. During the 1950s and 1960s, he also arranged for some of the finest jazz singers, including Sarah Vaughan and Abbey Lincoln. Because he was so busy writing, Carter's schedule left little time for playing, but by the mid-1970s, he returned to a busy performance schedule, and still continues to perform, write, and arrange successfully. His rich recorded legacy documents his incredible talents as composer-arranger. Along with Johnny Hodges, Carter, with his rich tone and flawless technique, is considered one of the most important influences of the 1930s, and his influence continues today, reaching around the world.

what to buy: You really can't go astray with any domestic-label recordings with Carter as leader. You'll be well rewarded if you're a swing fan, as most Carter-led sessions swing ferociously. If you're just becoming acquainted with Carter, check out the compilation on *The Best of Benny Carter* 𝄞𝄞𝄞𝄞 (Pablo, 1980/1987, prod. Norman Granz, Benny Carter), which features him with stalwart swing masters performing some of his best tunes from the Pablo vaults ("In A Mellow Tone," "Wave," "Squatty Roo," and others). It's not the definitive Carter, but as you become enamored of his playing you'll want to check out other CDs. From his early career, *Benny Carter: The Complete Recordings, 1930–1940, Volume I* ♪♪♪♪ (Various, 1930–40/ Charly/Affinity, 1991, prod. Francis Hood, Joop Visser) is a three-CD set important for its documentation of Carter's beginning years. The set includes 1928 recordings for Columbia with the Chocolate Dandies as well as 1931 recordings with McKinney's Cottonpickers for Victor. The Chocolate Dandies was a recording group made up of men from Fletcher Henderson's band, and included notable players such as trumpeter Rex Stewart, saxophonist Coleman Hawkins, pianist Horace Henderson, trombonist Jimmy Harrison, either Clarence Holiday (Billie Holiday's father) or Benny Jackson on guitar, and bassist John Kirby. The 1928 session includes the songs "Goodbye Blues" (with vocals by Carter and his sixteen-bar alto solo), "Cloudy Skies," "Got Another Sweetie," and "Bugle Call Rag," on which he solos on both alto saxophone and clarinet. In August 1931, Carter joined McKinney's Cotton Pickers as their music director. In addition to acting as music director, Carter also played clarinet on both "Do You Believe in Love at First Sight" and "Wrap Your Troubles in Dreams," which were recorded in September 1931. This version of McKinney's Cotton Pickers included noted musicians such as Rex Stewart and Doc Cheatham (trumpet); Ed Cuffee and Quentin Jackson (trombone); Joe Moxley and Hilton Jefferson (clarinet and alto saxophone); Prince Robinson (clarinet and tenor saxophone); pianist Todd Rhodes; Dave Wilborn (guitar and banjo); string bassist Richard Fullbright; and drummer Cuba Austin. "Synthetic Love," recorded with his own orchestra on March 14, 1933 for Columbia, contains his first recorded trumpet solo, in addition to his vocals. Also included on the first disc is another session recorded under the name Chocolate Dandies. The musicians include trumpeter Max Kaminsky, trombonist Floyd O'Brien, tenor saxophonist Chu Berry, pianist Teddy Wilson, guitarist Lawrence Lucie, string bassist Ernest Hill, and drummer Sid Catlett. Carter performs on both trumpet and alto saxophones, demonstrating his agility on both instruments on the tune, "I Never Knew." For this session, Carter wrote and arranged all but one of the tunes, and includes the first recording of "Blue Interlude," one of Carter's many standards. The second disc represents Carter's work under his own name, with recording sessions in New York City, London, and Copenhagen. Carter wrote most of the compositions and arrangements. This disc includes "These Foolish Things," recorded April 15, 1936,

BENNY CARTER

song "Frenesi"

album Cosmopolite:
The Oscar Peterson Verve Sessions
(Verve, 1954/1994)

instrument Alto saxophone

Monster Solo

with Carter soloing on trumpet, clarinet, and alto saxophone, as well as the original recording of "When Lights Are Low," recorded June 20, 1936, with Elizabeth Welsh on vocals. In addition, this disc includes "You Understand," Carter's first recorded piano solo. The third disc from this set includes sessions recorded in London, Copenhagen, and Stockholm, and is the least interesting of the set. *Benny Carter: The Oscar Peterson Verve Sessions* ♪♪♪♪ (Verve, 1952–55, prod. Norman Granz) offers previously unissued alternative tracks of the first session, which took place on September 18, 1952 in New York City, and is interesting because we have a chance to hear how the tunes evolved. All four sessions feature Carter playing alto saxophone with pianist Peterson, guitarist Barney Kessel, bassist Ray Brown, and drummer Buddy Rich. This quintet recorded "Gone with the Wind," "I Got It Bad (and That Ain't Good)," "Long Ago (and Far Away)," and "I've Got the World on a String." This CD also contains three other separate sessions. The second session, recorded on December 4, 1952 in Los Angeles, included pianist Peterson, guitarist Kessel, bassist

Brown, and drummer J.C. Heard. Tunes recorded by this group include Alfred Newman's "Street Scene" and Cole Porter's "I Get a Kick out of You." The third session features Peterson, trombonist Bill Harris, guitarist Herb Ellis, bassist Brown, and drummer Rich. This session was recorded on September 14, 1954 in New York City, and was originally issued under two titles, *Benny Carter Plays Pretty* and *New Jazz Sounds*. The fourth session features Peterson, guitarist Ellis, bassist Brown, and drummer Bobby White. Tunes included from this session are "A Foggy Day," "You Took Advantage of Me," "Prisoner of Love," and "Frenesi." A high level of musicianship prevails throughout all four sessions, and the musicians generate hard-swinging, inspired sets as they play off of each other and improvise with mastery to create spontaneous, energetic teamwork that's listener friendly. Swinging from the start, *Benny Carter Meets Oscar Peterson* ♫♫♫♫ (Pablo, 1987/OJC, 1995, prod. Norman Granz) offers stately jazz created by pairing Carter with Peterson, guitarist Joe Pass, bassist Dave Young, and drummer Martin Drew. Recorded in Hollywood on November 14, 1986, the set launches with an uptempo version of the classic, "Just Friends," which establishes everyone's chops—Peterson's ivories artistry, Carter's gracefully flowing altoisms, and Pass's warmly precise picking. The seven-tune set includes hard-swinging, inventive remakes of classics such as "Baubles, Bangles, and Beads" and "Whispering," a bluesy closer, "Some Kind of Blues," and a warm rendering of the ballad, "If I Had You." Carter, 79 years old at the time of this session with Peterson (their first since the 1950s), plays with facility and warmheartedness, appearing to have lost little of his earlier verve. The session conveys the extraordinary, effortlessly swinging rapport among these musicians and is highly recommended as documentation of Carter's later career efforts. Carter is ensconced in various small combos *Benny Carter: The Verve Small Group Sessions* ♫♫♫♫ (Verve, 1955/1991, prod. Norman Granz). The first setting featured ingeniously matches Carter with Teddy Wilson and Jo Jones. The energy is exciting, as they execute on such tunes as "Little Girl Blue," "Rosetta," "When the Moon Is Low," and "Birth of the Blues," among others. Prior to the release of this CD, a recording of this session had been released only in Japan. The second session finds Carter performing with pianist Don Abney, bassist George Duvivier, and drummer Louis Bellson reinventing tunes such as "Moonglow," "Tenderly," "Unforgettable," and "Ruby" with a superior level of musicianship. The third session features Carter with the Oscar Peterson Trio and drummer White; this CD includes three previously unissued tracks from that recording date, "Don't You Think," "Will You Still Be Mine?," and "We'll Be To-

gether Again." *Benny Carter: The King* ♫♫♫♫ (Pablo, 1976/OJC, 1996, prod. Norman Granz) is a sextet date recorded on February 11, 1976, as Carter is joined by vibist Milt Jackson, guitarist Joe Pass, pianist Tommy Flanagan, bassist John B. Williams, and drummer Jake Hanna in performing an entire session of Carter compositions. Tunes included are "A Walkin' Thing," "My Kind of Trouble Is You," "Easy Money," "Blue Star," "I Still Love Him So," and "Green Wine", and others. With original liner notes from Leonard Feather, as well as an explanation from Norman Granz regarding the title of the session and the nickname given to Carter by tenor saxophonist Ben Webster, this CD offers a cohesively swinging session, Carter's first small-group session since 1966. Solidly crafted and sensitively improvised lines from each musician on this date add to the energy and emotion. There's nothing like a live performance to energize jazz musicians and *Live and Well in Japan* ♫♫♫♫ (Pablo, 1978/OJC, 1992, prod. Benny Carter) is proof. Performing before a highly receptive Japanese audience at Kosei Nenkin Hall in Tokyo on April 29, 1977, Carter, playing both alto saxophone and trumpet, leads a fine group of swing stalwarts, including Budd Johnson (tenor, soprano saxophones), Cecil Payne (baritone saxophone, flute), Britt Woodman (trombone), Cat Anderson and Joe Newman (trumpets), Nat Pierce (piano), Mundell Lowe (guitar), George Duvivier (bass), and Harold Jones (drums). Old-time swing is the focus and your foot will be tapping throughout the nearly 42 minutes of exceptional jazz, executed upon Carter's arrangements written specially for the performance. From the opener, a romping version of Johnny Hodges's "Squatty Roo," to the grandly hip (almost 11-minute) finale, "It Don't Mean a Thing (If It Ain't Got That Swing)," these swing masters are in prime form. Cat Anderson's trumpet solo on three-tune Satchmo dedication, "Tribute to Louis Armstrong" and Joe Newman's fine vocal impersonation of Satchmo on "When You're Smiling," are alone worth the album price. Even though Carter doesn't take the limelight often, this session is testament to his entrenchment in the Swing era and his exceptional abilities as arranger and leader. It's also hard evidence of the Japanese yen for jazz; this is one of the most enthusiastic audiences in the history of recorded music.

what to buy next: *Montreux 1977* ♫♫♫♫ (Pablo, 1977/OJC, 1989) finds Carter leading a sterling quartet at the 1977 Montreux (Switzerland) Jazz Festival. And considering the year and

Betty Carter (© Jack Vartoogian)

recordings by other labels that came out of that year's festival, the music documented on this disc represents some of the most straight-ahead and swinging jazz presented. Carter mixes it up playing alto saxophone and trumpet on seven standards with backing from pianist Ray Bryant, bassist Niels Pedersen, and drummer Jimmie Smith. Highlights include a toe-tapping version of Ellington's "In a Mellow Tone" which features Carter's inventive alto sax improvs, and a lovely rendering of the ballad, "Body and Soul," which features his superbly phrased trumpet and alto interpretations balanced against Bryant's lovely piano expressions. Equally enticing is "On Green Dolphin Street," a warhorse that is given fresh treatment by everyone, but sparked especially by Carter's joyful altoisms. Prominently featuring Carter's inventiveness on both alto sax and trumpet, this is a gorgeous quartet session. *Swingin' the '20s* 𝄞𝄞𝄞 (Contemporary, 1958/OJC, 1988, prod. Lester Koenig) was recorded in Los Angeles on November 2, 1958, and features Carter on both trumpet and alto saxophone, with pianist Earl Hines, bassist Leroy Vinnegar, and drummer Shelly Manne. This session, totally improvised, is the first pairing of Carter with Hines, and features hit tunes from the 1920s such as "Thou Swell," "My Blue Heaven," "Sweet Lorraine," "Who's Sorry Now," and "Someone to Watch over Me," among others. Moments to note are the melodic and emotional solo work from both Carter and Hines on "Sweet Lorraine," and the call-and-response between the trio and Carter on Irving Berlin's "All Alone." Three alternate takes not on the LP version are added to the CD reissue. This is a spontaneous, swinging first-time documentation of Carter and Hines together. *Benny Carter, Dizzy Gillespie, Inc.* 𝄞𝄞𝄞 (Pablo, 1976/OJC, 1992, prod. Norman Granz) opens with two bars from bassist Al McKibbon on the Latinate "Sweet and Lovely," followed by two bars from drummer Mickey Roker, after which they are joined by trumpeter Gillespie, alto saxophonist Carter, pianist Tommy Flanagan, and guitarist Joe Pass. The entire session is full of inspiration and hard-swinging energy. At the time of this recording, Carter was 70 years old, and Gillespie sixty. Two fairly obscure and masterful compositions included on this recording are Carter's "The Courtship" and Gillespie's "Constantinople." Other tunes interpreted by this ensemble are "Broadway," "Nobody Knows the Trouble I've Seen," featuring effective and stirring vocals from drummer Mickey Roker, and the Gillespie trademark tune, "A Night in Tunisia." *Jazz Giant* 𝄞𝄞𝄞 (Contemporary, 1957–58/OJC, 1987, prod. Lester Koenig) features Carter playing alto sax and trumpet with on this compilation of sessions recorded in the late 1950s with Ben Webster (tenor sax), Frank Rosolino (trombone), Barney Kessel (guitar), Leroy

Vinnegar (bass), Shelly Manne (drums), and Andre Previn and Jimmy Rowles (piano). Don't shun this seven-tune session of mostly lesser-known tunes, because you'll be missing some fine playing by Carter (especially his trumpet renderings on "I'm Coming Virginia") and his original tunes—the deep-grooved Carter classic "A Walkin' Thing," and his bop-based swinger, "Blues My Naughty Sweety Gives to Me." Both tunes give his soloists solid, melodic launch-pads. Considering the recording year and plethora of talent on this small-group outing, it's a must-own gem. A more recent two-CD set, *Harlem Renaissance* 𝄞𝄞𝄞𝄞 (Music Masters, 1992, prod. Ed Berger), is an 85th birthday celebration of sorts that showcases Carter's broad talents. Highlighted are his performances, his majestic compositions, and his leadership abilities. Disc one contains Carter originals "Evening Star" and "Vine Street Rumble," and arrangements of classics such as "How High the Moon" and "I Can't Get Started," performed by the Benny Carter Big Band featuring fine players such as trumpeter Michael Mossman, trombonist Curtis Hasselbring, reedman Frank Wess, drummer Kenny Washington, and others of considerable talent. Disc two documents the February 1992 premiere of two of Carter's five-movement suites commissioned by the Institute of Jazz Studies of Rutgers University with a grant from the National Endowment for the Arts. Performed by the Rutgers University Orchestra and the Benny Carter Big Band, "Tales of the Rising Sun" reflects Carter's love of Japan, where he has had warm reception for his live performances. The other work, "Harlem Renaissance" chronicles the story of Harlem during the 1920s. Both works are filled with great emotion and beauty.

best of the rest:

BBB & Co. 𝄞𝄞𝄞 (Prestige/OJC, 1962)
In the Mood for Swing 𝄞𝄞𝄞 (MusicMasters, 1987)
My Kind of Trouble 𝄞𝄞𝄞 (Pablo, 1988/OJC, 1989)
(With Phil Woods) *My Man Benny, My Man Phil* 𝄞𝄞𝄞𝄞 (MusicMasters, 1990)
Legends 𝄞𝄞𝄞𝄞 (Music Masters, 1992)
Songbook 𝄞𝄞𝄞𝄞 (MusicMasters, 1995)

influences:

◄◄ Bubber Miley, Bill Challis, Frank Trumbauer

Susan K. Berlowitz and Nancy Ann Lee

Betty Carter

Born May 16, 1929, in Flint, MI.

Whitney Balliett once observed that if she'd been blowing a horn rather than her pipes Betty Carter would be considered one of the finest improvisers of them all. Ditto for her small combo arranging, and certainly her record as a talent scout compares favorably to Art Blakey's. She's nurtured Cyrus Chestnut, Benny Green, Mulgrew Miller, and Stephen Scott to mention a few of her "young lion" pianists alone. A teen on the Detroit-area jazz scene of the late 1940s, Carter jammed with Charlie Parker and other boppers on the traveling circuit. She garnered early experience, spending two and a half years on the road with Lionel Hampton's before settling in New York in 1951. There she enjoyed a modest career that included regular Apollo Theatre gigs and road work with Ray Charles. With the withering of the mainstream jazz scene in the 1960s, Carter found demand for her craft roughly on par with calls for, say, a typewriter repair person at Microsoft headquarters. Nonetheless, she built an underground rep playing anywhere she could, releasing music on her own Bet-Car label, and, most important, pushing the boundaries of her art and building a following. In the 1980s her alliance with Verve, which included the re-release of Bet-Car material, finally connected her with an audience of the proportions she deserved. She is the reigning queen of scat, which doesn't mean that she can't deliver a lyric like a countess.

what to buy: *The Audience with Betty Carter* 𝄢𝄢𝄢𝄢 (Verve, 1979/1992, prod. Betty Carter) is a well-recorded, live, two-CD set, heavy on the audience-tested material, and celebrating Carter's long climb from obscurity to star status with a glorious take on her largely improvised "Sounds Movin' On." The album also highlights one of her best trios, with John Hicks, piano, Curtis Lundy, bass, and Kenneth Washington, drums. *The Betty Carter Album* 𝄢𝄢𝄢𝄢 (Verve, 1972/1992, prod. Betty Carter) overcomes its mediocre recording quality with spunk, wit, and imagination.

what to buy next: *Droppin' Things* 𝄢𝄢𝄢 (Verve, 1990, prod. Betty Carter) serves up superior Carter originals (the title tune and "30 Years"), and guest-spots Freddie Hubbard and Geri Allen. *Look What I Got* 𝄢𝄢𝄢𝄢 (Verve, 1988, prod. Betty Carter) contains "The Man I Love" with high drama, and features pianists Benny Green and Stephen Scott as belt-notches for Carter the talent scout.

what to avoid: *'Round Midnight* 𝄢 (Atlantic, 1963/1992, prod. Nesuhi Ertegun, Jerry Wexler, Arif Mardin), with that choir, those tunes, those overblown orchestrations, is one Carter disc to pass up in the bins!

best of the rest:
I Can't Help It 𝄢𝄢𝄢 (GRP, 1958/1992)

BETTY CARTER

song "All or Nothing at All"
album Feed the Fire
(Verve, 1993/1995)
instrument Vocals

Inside Betty Carter 𝄢𝄢𝄢 (Capitol, 1965/1993)
It's Not about the Melody 𝄢𝄢𝄢𝄢 (Verve, 1992)
Feed the Fire 𝄢𝄢𝄢 (Verve, 1993/1995)
I'm Yours, You're Mine 𝄢𝄢𝄢 (Jazz Ahead, 1996)

influences:

⏪ Billie Holiday, Leo Watson, Sarah Vaughan, Ella Fitzgerald

⏩ Dee Dee Bridgewater

W. Kim Heron

James Carter
Born January 3, 1969, in Detroit, MI.

The recent young lion movement came to the fore with an undercurrent (sometimes not even so "under") of disdain for the 1960s and 1970s avant garde. So there was nothing so refreshing as the arrival of a young cat who could meet the Wynton Marsalis litmus tests *without* renouncing his affection for Sun Ra. Saxophonist James Carter's breadth isn't surprising given his middle-school experience in the unique Detroit band Bird-Trane-Sco-Now, a reference to Parker, Coltrane, and Roscoe Mitchell. But equally important, Carter has the mustered depth of instrumental prowess to unite those disparate realms. Even as a teen he became a sought-after player for local and national groups (including Marsalis), and barely out of his teens he was at work with former Art Ensemble trumpeter Lester Bowie, with gigs in Julius Hemphill's Sextet, and others to follow. When it came time to form his own group, Carter tapped back to the drum-bass team of Tani Tabbal and Jaribu Shahid, which for years had propelled Griot Galaxy. By then defunct, in its prime the Galaxy featured hometown heroes renowned for their ability to make the avant accessible. The piano chair was filled by Ann Arbor–based Craig Taborn, one of the Detroit area's brightest up-and-coming pianists and another player comfortable traversing the inside-to-outside continuum. Carter swings like mad, spins ideas at prodigious rates, and draws freely on the saxophonic vocabularies of recent past masters like David Murray as much as from those of Ben Webster and honking Gene Ammons. Moreover, he is proving to be adept at saxophones from soprano to baritone, not to mention the bass and contrabass clarinets and bass flute. A prodigious talent and still shy of age 30, the chief question is how he'll find compositional challenges commensurate with his instrumental prowess.

what to buy: *JC on the Set* 𝄞𝄞𝄞𝄞 (DIW/Columbia, 1993, prod. Kazunori Sugiyama) is easily the most startling debut recording of the last decade. And the follow-up, the all-standards *Jurassic Classics* 𝄞𝄞𝄞𝄞 (DIW/Columbia, 1994, prod. Kazunori Sugiyama) is a more worthy successor. Carter tackles compositions from Sun Ra to Ellington and the obscure John Hardee. In fact, on *JC on the Set* Carter gives "Caravan" one of its best workouts in recent memory.

what to buy next: *The Real Quiet Storm* 𝄞𝄞𝄞𝄞 (Atlantic, 1995, prod. Yves Beauvais) steps back from the fury of the DIW's and puts more emphasis on balladry. Not that there aren't surprises, such as following the umpteenth version of "'Round Midnight" with Sun Ra and Hobart Dodson's "You Never Told Me That You Care," and giving us unusual choices from the repertoires of Ellington ("The Stevedore's Serenade") and Don Byas ("1944 Stomp"). *Conversin' with the Elders* 𝄞𝄞𝄞𝄞 (Atlantic, 1996, prod. Yves Beauvais) puts Carter in the company (one per cut) of the Art Ensemble of Chicago's Lester Bowie, the World Saxophone Quartet's Hamiet Bluiett, swing era survivors Buddy Tate and Harry "Sweets" Edison and Detroit-based bopper extraordinaire Larry Smith, but without the focus one would hope for.

influences:

⏮ Ben Webster, Sun Ra, Art Ensemble of Chicago, Julius Hemphill, Sonny Rollins, Don Byas, Gene Ammons, John Coltrane, John Gilmore, Lester Bowie, Hamiet Bluiett, Buddy Tate, Harry "Sweets" Edison, Larry Smith

W. Kim Heron

John Carter

Born September 24, 1929, in Fort Worth TX., Died March 31, 1991, in Los Angeles, CA.

An important jazz composer of the 1980s, John Carter was also a clarinet virtuoso who did more than any other modern figure to bring the instrument into contemporary jazz. As a teenager, he played with Ornette Coleman and Charles Moffett, but the most significant early milestones in his career were meeting trumpeter Bobby Bradford, with whom he performed regularly until his death, and the founding of the New Art Jazz Ensemble in Los Angeles in 1964. Among the first West Coast free jazz groups, the band was at times reminiscent of Coleman's classic quartet in sound and conception.

The other important step came in 1974, when Carter gave up his other horns (alto and tenor saxophones) to play clarinet exclusively. He grew into the most important clarinetist in new music of his day, incorporating blues and vocal inflections into a contemporary vocabulary of wide intervalic leaps, angular lines, dramatic dynamic contracts, and a formidably extended range. Beginning in the early '80s, he was a member of Clarinet Summit with David Murray, Alvin Batiste, and Jimmy Hamilton. He also recorded as a sideman in small and large ensembles with saxophonist Vinny Golia, and with pianist Horace Tapscott. But Carter's greatest legacy is a series of five suites titled "Roots and Folklore: Episodes in the Development of American Folk Music," which he began composing and recording in 1982 with *Dauwhe*. A monumental programmatic work for octet, "Roots and Folklore" traces the history of African American music from its origins in Africa, *Dauwhe*, through the departure of slaves to America, *Castles of Ghana*, and the horrors of the Middle Passage, *Dance of the Love Ghosts*, to the foundations of African American culture in the rural South, *Fields*, and the migrations to the cities of the North and the establishment of black urban culture, *Shadows on a Wall*. This profound meditation on national, racial, and personal history incorporates elements of African music, country blues, gospel, big band swing, and bebop into a contemporary vocabulary in an entirely organic and convincing way. Each suite is satisfying on its own, but together they make up one of the most impressive and enduring artistic successes of the 1980s.

what to buy: *Castles of Ghana* 🎵🎵🎵 (Gramavision, 1986, prod. Jonathan F.P. Rose) is the only one of the four segments of the suite recorded by Gramavision currently in print. This is a harrowing depiction of the departure of Africans slaves to America that manages to be both sorrowful and ennobling at the same time. It features beautiful writing by Carter and crack ensemble work and solos from a band that includes Marty Ehrlich, Bobby Bradford, and Andrew Cyrille. *Seeking* 🎵🎵🎵 (1969/hat ART, prod. Pia and Werner X. Uehlinger) is a reissue of an album by the early Carter-Bradford New Art Jazz Ensemble. It's not fully mature, but still a scorching album, full of the spirit of adventure. *Tandem 1 & 2* 🎵🎵🎵 (Emanem, 1996, prod. Martin Davidson) is a somewhat low-fi recording (volume one was recorded on a rare East Coast tour in 1982, volume two in Los Angeles in 1979). Still, the record is an excellent example of the rapport shared by Carter and Bradford, and the startling forcefulness of Carter's playing throughout the remarkably extended range of his instrument.

worth searching for: *Dauwhe* 🎵🎵🎵 (Black Saint, 1982, prod. John Carter) features some marvelously celebratory playing despite some shaky moments in the opening. *Night Fire* 🎵🎵🎵 (Black Saint, 1980, prod. Giovanni Bonandrini)is an uneven album by a Los Angeles ensemble. But it's notable for Carter's first recorded compositions using folk elements. *Fields* 🎵🎵🎵🎵 (Gramavision, 1988) is the most personal of the five "Roots and Folklore" suites. Childhood reminiscences by Carter's 90-year-old uncle threads through some tracks. The record features the best of the octets involved in the project, varied and focused composing with devastating Carter solos.

Ed Hazell

Regina Carter

Born 1959, in Detroit, MI.

Regina Carter is one of the leading voices of a new generation of jazz violinists. Firmly rooted in the jazz tradition of Stuff Smith, Stephane Grappelli, and Joe Venuti, her style also reflects the musical peregrinations of Jean-Luc Ponty and Noel Pointer, as well as sophisticated funk. Born in Detroit, Carter gigged with local musicians before joining the all-female jazz quintet Straight Ahead, and the acclaim she received from her performances served as the catalyst for her move to New York in 1991. Carter quickly became active in the New Music scene, premiering composer/saxophonist Oliver Lake's composition

JAMES CARTER

song "Equinox"
album *Jurassic Classics*
(DIW-Columbia, 1994)
instrument Tenor saxophone

for violin and piano at the Library of Congress. With a wide array of influences, Carter was soon comfortable doing sessions with Dolly Parton, Mary J. Blige, and the String Trio of New York. Carter's self-titled 1995 debut propelled her to the attention of the national media. In the 44th Annual Critics Poll published by *Down Beat,* she was voted Number One in the category of Violin Talent Deserving of Wider Recognition. After the release of her second CD, "Something for Grace," she began touring regularly with her own group.

what to buy: In Carter's hands, the violin reveals both its melodic side and its potential for percussive expression. Her debut, *Regina Carter* 🎵🎵🎵🎵 (Atlantic, 1995, prod. Victor Bailey), demonstrates an eagerness to explore musical combinations and contexts both familiar and unexpected. On "Beau Regard," Carter's sinuous playing joins forces with Steve Turre's trombone and Abdoulaye Epizo Bangoura's African djembe drum to create an exotically mesmerizing atmosphere. Another highlight is her quietly powerful version of Billie Holiday's "Don't Explain," performed as a stark, plaintive duet with bassist Lonnie Plaxico. Yet for all its complex musical references, the recording is not esoteric or difficult, but a joyful creative expression, her technical proficiency and profound compositional and improvisational gifts offering a fresh, aggressive approach to the instrument. Following the path set by her debut, on her second release, *Something for Grace* ⅃⅃⅃ (Atlantic, 1997, prod. Arif Mardin, Regina Carter, Yves Beauvais, Werner Gierig, Oriente Lopez, Michael Bearden), Carter again successfully creates an upbeat mix of funk, soul, and jazz. The mix includes five originals, most notably the title track, a sensitive ballad written for her mother, and five covers including "Listen Here," the Eddie Harris/Les McCann rouser. Carter seems at home in any genre, be it the solid Latin groove she strikes on "Centro Habana," to Mal Waldron's "Soul Eyes," the ballad popularized by John Coltrane. Happily, Carter doesn't dilute her style for the sake of production and accessibility. Always aggressive and interesting, she's amazingly versatile.

influences:

◀◀ Stuff Smith, Joe Venuti, Jean-Luc Ponty, Noel Pointer

▶▶ Stephane Grappelli, Didier Lockwood, John Blake, Michael Urbaniak

Bret Primack

Ron Carter

Born May 4, 1937, in Ferndale, MI.

Ron Carter's acoustic bass work with Miles Davis Quartet in the mid- to late 1960s made him an instant luminary on the instrument and, but for a fleeting flirtation with electric bass in the 1960s and 1970s, he has remained an acoustic bassist throughout his career. Growing up in Detroit, where his parents moved when he was four, Carter began classical studies on cello at age ten, and by his graduation from high school was playing bass and violin, as well as clarinet, trombone, and tuba. An early career choice as a symphonic cellist was forestalled by the race barrier that existed in the field of classical music at that time, yet today Carter has performed as a bassist with major symphony orchestras around the world. In 1955 Carter won a scholarship to pursue classical studies at the Eastman School of Music in Rochester, New York, and after graduating in 1959, headed for New York City where he entered the Manhattan School of Music (graduating with a master's in bass in 1961). While at MSM, he hooked up briefly with Chico Hamilton in a band that also included Eric Dolphy. Carter freelanced extensively, working with Jaki Byard, Randy Weston, Wes Montgomery, and Bobby Timmons, and toured Europe with Cannon-

ball Adderley. After Hamilton returned to the West Coast in 1960, Carter remained in New York, working with Dolphy and Mal Waldron, recording a series of notable albums for Prestige with them in 1961. From 1963–68 he toured and recorded with the Miles Davis band. During this time, he also wrote a series of bass instruction books, played numerous clubs, and recorded sessions with a variety of leaders including Joe Henderson, Stan Getz, Sonny Rollins, and a stint with Herbie Hancock and Tony Williams that laid the groundwork for a looser rhythm-section sound.

With about 400 albums behind him, Carter recorded his first solo album, *Uptown Conversation*, for Atlantic in 1971, and shortly after, signed with CTI Records, where he made a series of recordings until he left the label in 1976. When Carter first considered forming his own group, the bass was not viewed as a lead instrument. Carter met this challenge by using a piccolo bass—an instrument one-half the size of a full-size bass—and tuned the instrument to evoke an unusual sound quality that stands out in an ensemble backed by piano, drums, percussion, and an additional bass. He has played the piccolo bass in many settings, included the Ron Carter Nonet, an innovative nine-piece, chamber-jazz ensemble that includes four cellos, a rhythm section, and a percussionist. One of the most prolific and influential bassists, Carter can be heard on over 2,000 recordings made as sideman and leader since the late 1940s. He's appeared as sideman with a veritable array of stylists, the who's who in jazz, from Stan Getz, Eric Dolphy, Coleman Hawkins, Jaki Byard, Randy Weston, Miles Davis, George Benson, Herbie Hancock, and countless others. According to some accounts, Carter appeared on 49 CD reissues and new releases in 1997 alone! Throughout his career, he has won honors around the world for his performances and been cited in numerous critics and readers polls. His solo bass recording of the Bach Cello Suites on compact disc was certified gold in 1988. He earned a Grammy award in 1988 for his composition "Call Sheet Blues" in the film, *'Round Midnight,* and received another Grammy in 1993 for Best Jazz Instrumental Group, with the Miles Davis Tribute Band. He has scored and arranged music for other films, including *Beatrice, Haruka,* and for the television movies *Exit Ten* and *A Gathering of Old Men.* In January 1998, at the International Association of Jazz Educators Conference, Carter was awarded the prestigious American Jazz Master fellowship by the National Endowment for the Arts. Carter is an active music educator, and is currently a Distinguished Professor of Music at the City College of New York. He continues to record and perform and tour worldwide.

what to buy: Carter's career covers so many decades, it's advisable to find recordings from each to understand the full scope of his talents and accomplishments. If you're new to Ron Carter, you might want to check out the Milestone compilation *Standard Bearers* 𝄞𝄞𝄞𝄞 (Milestone/OJC, 1972–79/1988, prod. various), which gathers small-group dates recorded between August 4, 1972 and March 1979, with Kenny Barron, Jack De-Johnette, Red Garland, Jim Hall, Herbie Hancock, Philly Joe Jones, Ben Riley, McCoy Tyner, Buster Williams, Tony Williams, and other musicians. The compilation features eight standards (with the CD bonus track, "All Blues" from Carter's *Pick 'Em* album). While this isn't the "definitive" compilation, the performances drawn from several Milestone albums should give you an idea of Carter's skillful abilities as soloist and supporter during this period. Essential to any collection, Carter's first date as leader, *Where?* 𝄞𝄞𝄞𝄞 (New Jazz Records, 1961/OJC, 1990, prod. Esmond Edwards), is a 1961 session that features him playing bass and cello on six tunes (two originals) with an inventive team that includes Eric Dolphy (bass clarinet, alto saxophone, flute), Mal Waldron (piano), and Charles Persip (drums). Bassist George Duvivier takes over bass duties when Carter plays cello on a couple of tunes, plus they lightly go at it on "Bass Duet." Carter's performances, both bowed and pizzicato, are calm, compelling and classic throughout the session and, combined with Dolphy's impassioned playing, make this album a delightfully attractive listen that offers many peak moments, including a soulful ballad version of the title tune composed by Randy Weston. *Patrão* 𝄞𝄞𝄞𝄞 (Milestone/OJC, 1980/1993) is a five-tune studio session that features Carter with trumpeter Chet Baker, pianist Kenny Barron, and drummer Jack De-Johnette on three solid, straight-ahead jazz musings. The two Latin numbers which begin and end the session feature additional musicians, mostly providing percussion. But it is Baker's cool, muted, and open playing throughout all five tunes and Carter's walking basslines that steal the limelight on this session, especially on the bluesy Carter original, "Nearly," and his tasty swinger, "Tail Feathers." This is one of the leader's best sessions from the Milestone years. There's nothing wrong with the bassist stealing the melody, considering that there are plenty of albums out there where you can hardly hear the acoustic bass! *Jazz, My Romance* 𝄞𝄞𝄞𝄞 (Blue Note, 1994, prod. Ron Carter) is an exquisite exercise in understated elegance, with Carter leading a lyrical Kenny Barron on piano, and a relaxed Herb Ellis on guitar. The unique trio remakes classics such as "My Romance" (alternating swing and waltz tempos), "Airgin" (a racing reading with Carter adding percussive touches and a fine solo), and "Summertime" (a lilting, bluesy

REGINA CARTER
(WITH STRING TRIO OF NEW YORK)

song "Speedball"
album Blues . . . ?
(Soul Note, 1995)
instrument Violin

interpretation), and delivers equally engaging renditions of "I Fall in Love Too Easily" and "Sweet Lorraine," along with three diverse Carter originals, the hip "Blues for D.P.," a gentle "Quiet Times," and the playfully pattering "For Toddlers Only." This album is a refreshing, laid-back listen recommended for the over-50 crowd or younger folks who want to slow down their pace. Carter again romances the acoustic bass on *The Bass and I* 𝄞𝄞𝄞𝄞 (Blue Note, 1997, prod. Ron Carter), a charming session that features the bassist leading a crew of young lions—Stephen Scott on piano, Lewis Nash on drums, and Steve Kroon on percussion. With this good supportive team, Carter revisits his compositions, "Blues for D.P." and "Mr. Bow-Tie," and adds heartfelt artistry to "You and the Night and the Music," "Someday My Prince Will Come," "I Remember Clifford," and two more tunes. Though Carter garners much of the limelight, Scott and Lewis, two of today's most adaptable innovators, have plenty of opportunities to show off their chops, and they enhance this session with their understated gracefulness and blues-based sensibilities. If Carter is passing along a

legacy to these young players, it's his penchant for warm-toned wooing of each tune. Recorded in a 1984 live performance at the Concord Jazz Festival, Carter and guitarist Jim Hall deliver a stately seven-tune duo session, *Telephone* ✍✍✍✍ (Concord, 1992, prod. Carl E. Jefferson), which features two originals from each player, plus three standards. "Alone Together" is a revisit from their first album together in 1970. The album a tasteful performance between compatriots whose paths have crossed and intertwined for decades before and after their first duo album together in 1970. This is their third recording together and it's carried out in most comfortable fashion. Another of the famous live-recorded duet sessions with guitarist Jim Hall, *Live at Village West* ✍✍✍✍ (Concord, 1984, prod. Carl E. Jefferson) captures the interaction between these two top improvisers in a stunning 10-tune performance that, besides one original each, includes jazz standards such as Milt Jackson's blues-tinged "Bags Groove," Thelonious Monk's "Blue Monk," Sonny Rollin's Latinate "St. Thomas," and popular favorites such as "Embraceable You," "All the Things You Are," and "Baubles, Bangles and Beads." By the time of this recording, the two classically trained veterans had developed a spiritual affinity for performing together after numerous concerts and recordings. Recorded in a New York City jazz club, this is one of their best duets together.

what to buy next: A mid-1970s date that remains unique amidst Carter's vast discography, *Pastels* ✍✍✍ (Milestone, 1976/OJC, 1991) prominently features Carter playing bass and piccolo bass on his five original tunes performed with Kenny Barron (piano), Hugh McCracken (electric and acoustic guitars), Harvey Mason (drums), and a 15-musician string section conducted by Don Sebesky. Arrangements of Carter's originals by Sebesky and Carter draw upon the bassist's classical training, especially no-ticeable on Carter's lush "Ballad" (the longest piece at 8:45 minutes), which gives vent to an edgy piccolo bass solo that is sweetened with the strings. The catchy "One Bass Rag" is a light-swinging spree again colored with strings. There's some-thing here for everyone, and steadfast Carter (and bass) fans should find this album best showcases his creativity on both in-struments. The strings are an added bonus. *Spanish Blue* ✍✍✍ (Columbia, 1975/1991, prod. Creed Taylor) shows off Carter's comprehension of Spanish themes and catchy rhythms. With his simpatico sidemen, drummer Billy Cobham, pianist Roland

Hanna (subbed by electric pianist Leon Pendarvis on one track), guitarist Jay Berliner, percussionist Ralph MacDonald, and flutist Hubert Laws, Carter performs his originals, "El Noche Sol," "Sabado Sombrero," and the ten-minute, infectious blues-funk piece, "Arkansas," featuring Carter's overdubbed piccolo bass work and "another" bass line underneath. The one stan-dard is a kickin', 11-minute, tempo-shifting version of Miles Davis's "So What?" featuring scintillating solos from Laws, Hanna (on electric piano), and the flashy Cobham. Because of the electric piano, the 34-minute session sounds a tad dated today, but Carter was there on (mostly) acoustic bass when the rest of the jazz world was jacking up the amps. *Third Plane* ✍✍✍ (Milestone, 1977/OJC, 1992) is a harmonious, straight-ahead, six-tune set that reunites the bassist with his companions from the 1960s Miles Davis rhythm section, Herbie Hancock (piano), and Tony Williams (drums). While there are few fireworks, this date demonstrates their flexible ease and equality when work-ing together. While not one of Carter's essential albums, it does offers some pleasing interpretations of Hancock's "Dolphin Dance," Carter's "Quiet Times" (as well as his title tune and "United Blues"), Williams's "Lawra," and a warmly romantic ver-sion of "Stella by Starlight." Bill Evans (tenor/soprano saxo-phones), Art Farmer (trumpet/flugelhorn), and drummer Tony Williams join bassist Ron Carter on *Etudes* ✍✍✍ (Elektra, 1983/Discovery, 1994, prod. Ron Carter). The elegant pianoless quartet gives Carter more license for launching melodic inter-ventions. While it's not one of his critically acclaimed sessions, it's an attractive listen for its subtleties. The best interactions come to the fore on the airy and spacious, "Bottoms Up," a tidy time-switching study that seems to float to the finish on Carter's lyricism. Carter sometimes carries the melodies, with the usu-ally aggressive Williams totally harnessed to shading with cym-bals, except for the drummer's two originals, "Arboretum" and "Doctor's Row," where he breaks out with some polyrhythmic pizzazz. Evans gets his moment to shine on "Rufus," a boppish number that finds everyone working tight and in top form. Farmer is best featured in a long flugelhorn solo on the final (sixth) tune, "Doctor's Row." At 36 minutes, the album cheats Carter fans, but his focused energy and fine solos achieve a bal-ance that makes this a satisfying listen.

best of the rest:

Peg Leg ✍✍✍ (Milestone, 1977/OJC, 1991)
New York Slick ✍✍✍ (Milestone, 1977/OJC, 1988)
Meets Bach ✍✍✍ (Blue Note, 1992)
Friends ✍✍✍ (Blue Note, 1993)
Mr. Bow Tie ✍✍✍ (Blue Note, 1996)
Brandenburg Concerto ✍✍✍ (Blue Note, 1997)

Ron Carter (© Jack Vartoogian)

worth searching for: One of Carter's more intriguing albums as leader during the 1970s, *Piccolo* ♫♫♫♫ (Milestone, 1977, prod. Orrin Keepnews) has not been released on CD. The two-record LP documents his live-recorded, two-bass, quartet performance on March 25–26, 1977 at Sweet Basil in New York City. Carter plays his unique-sounding piccolo bass. Side one contains an 18:25 version of his original, "Saguaro," giving Carter, pianist Kenny Barron, bassist Buster Williams, and drummer Ben Riley, plenty of stretching room. On the other sides, the tight-knit team performs Carter's "Sun Shower," "Laverne Walk," "Little Waltz," and "Tambien Conocido Como," and the time-honored gems "Blue Monk" and "Three Little Words." Aside from the talented side players, the attractive sound of the piccolo bass against the Williams's double-bass, makes this an enjoyable listen, one of Carter's more lively and engaging small-group performances. If you find this vinyl set in the secondhand market, snatch it up. If not, hope for a CD reissue.

influences:

◀◀ Jimmy Blanton, Ray Brown, Oscar Pettiford

▶▶ Scott LaFaro, Chuck Israels, Charlie Haden

Nancy Ann Lee

Michael Carvin

Born December 12, 1944 in Houston, TX.

Michael Carvin, whose father was also a drummer, began playing professionally with Earl Grant's Big Band in the early 1960s. After a stint in Vietnam (1966–68), he worked with blues guitarist B.B. King, and in the early to mid-1970s worked with jazz musicians Freddie Hubbard, Pharoah Sanders, Lonnie Liston Smith, McCoy Tyner, Jackie McLean, and others. He also stinted with the group Atmospheres (led by saxophonist Clive Stevens). In the 1980s Carvin spent much of his time teaching and made occasional albums for Muse that gave him some visibility. Carvin's style of drumming, similar to Billy Cobham's, helped pioneer a polyrhythmic style that came to characterize much jazz-rock fusion in the modern era.

what to buy: *Between You and Me* ♫♫♫♫ (Muse, 1989, prod. Cecil Bridgewater) is a good, fairly up-to-date session featuring soloists Cecil Bridgewater (trumpet), Claudio Roditi (trumpet), Ron Bridgewater (tenor), John Stubblefield (tenor), and rhythm players Cyrus Chestnut (piano) and Calvin Hill (bass). Seven tunes are written mostly by group members, including one original from Carvin, who fires up his team with his drumming.

what to buy next: *The Camel* ♫♫♫ (Inner City, 1975/Steeple-Chase, 1994), Carvin's debut as leader, is a solid session that features Bridgewater, Ron Burton, Sonny Fortune, and Hill playing seven tunes, with three composed by Carvin. This is a good mainstream outing, with tinges of fusion and some avant-garde twists.

the rest:

Revelation ♫♫♫♫ (Muse, 1989)
Each One Teach One ♫♫♫ (Muse, 1992)
(With Hamiet Bluiett) *Explorations 4: Drum Concerto at Dawn* ♫♫♫♫ (Mapleshade, 1996)

influences:

◀◀ Tony Williams

▶▶ Billy Cobham

Joe S. Harrington and Nancy Ann Lee

Laura Caviani

Born October 11, 1962, in Duluth, MN.

Laura Caviani is a melodious, inventive pianist whose substantive style reflects her European classical music training as well as her penchant for creating fresh mainstream-jazz improvisations. A Midwesterner, Caviani obtained her Master of Music degree at the University of Michigan at Ann Arbor. In addition to performing at festivals with Stan Getz, Bob Mintzer, and Dave Liebman, she has written a number of works for the Kansas City Symphony Orchestra, the Central Wisconsin Symphony Orchestra, and pieces for jazz combos and full jazz bands. A versatile pianist/composer/jazz educator, Caviani made her recording debut in 1995 on the independent label Igmod. She tours as a solo artist, with her trio, or her horns-augmented quintet, as well as performing and recording with Concord recording artist vocalist Karrin Allyson and other jazz musicians. Caviani has held several teaching posts in the Midwest, and currently resides in St. Paul, Minnesota, where she teaches privately through two universities.

what to buy: Caviani's debut recording as leader, *Dreamlife* ♫♫♫♫ (Igmod Records, 1995, prod. Laura Caviani, Terry Burns, Jay Epstein), offers 11 sparkling tunes which readily demonstrate her varicolored style. Her technique is flawless, yet not self-conscious. She works the keyboard in a sturdy, precise manner, creating gleefully swinging bop sprees and romantic renderings. Her passionate jazz phrasing and open, unpredictable lines make this collection of standards and originals a pleasurable listen. Caviani stretches, pushing to the outer edge, as well as playing inside chordal structures. Acoustic bassist Terry Burns and drummer Jay Epstein generate inspired teamwork as the threesome shifts rhythms, and explores harmonies and dynamics to add colorful splashes to each unique tune. This trio album triumphs with magnificent musicianship, imagination, and sophistication.

what to buy next: Caviani's second album, *As One* ✔✔✔✔ (Igmod, 1998, prod. Laura Caviani), is equally appealing. This 11-tune session of standards and originals fortifies Caviani's talents as composer and interpreter of stimulating jazz tunes. Her core trio, with bassist Bob Bowman and drummer Todd Strait, is augmented by guitarists Danny Embrey and Rod Fleeman, who split rhythm/solo flourishes on six tunes. Returning the favor, Concord recording artist Karrin Allyson joins the leader, sweetly singing two Caviani originals. Overall, Caviani's second outing trades hard-driving New-Yorkish forays of her debut album for soft-edged, warmer, even bluesier, expressions. Highlights include kickin' numbers such as the opener, "Fast Track" (a crew-introduction reminiscent of 1970s Ramsey Lewis), a bracing quartet version of "If I Should Lose You" (featuring Embrey's talents), the groovin' foot-tapper "Moanin'" (displaying Fleeman's Wes-like guitar plus some of Caviani's most inspired playing), and a lesser-known Monk tune, "Bye Ya." Two stunningly fresh solo piano sittings feature Caviani's improvisations on the Monk warhorse "Well You Needn't," and her smooth, churchy version of "Swing Low, Sweet Chariot."

worth searching for: If you dig Caviani's chops, you'll also want to hear her prominent playing on singer Karrin Allyson's album, *Collage* ✔✔✔✔ (Concord, 1996, prod. Nick Phillips). Both versatile expressionists, they make a highly compatible team deserving of wider recognition.

see also: *Karrin Allyson*

Nancy Ann Lee

Serge Chaloff

Born November 24, 1923, in Boston, MA. Died July 16, 1957, in Boston, MA.

Serge Chaloff was among the first baritone saxophonists to master the bebop vocabulary and one of the instrument's greatest players. His father was a pianist with the Boston Symphony Orchestra, and his mother, Madame Margaret Chaloff, was a legendary piano teacher. Chaloff's first influences were Ellington baritone saxophonist Harry Carney and Count Basie's Jack Washington. After short stints with Boyd Raeburn's progressive big band (1944–45), Georgie Auld's band (1945–46),

and Jimmy Dorsey (1946–47), Chaloff joined the Woody Herman Orchestra of 1947–49 and rose to his greatest fame as one of the Four Brothers saxophone section. Although this was a fertile period musically for Chaloff, personal problems associated with heroin addiction made his tenure with the band a rocky one. When the band broke up, he spent a short time with Count Basie (1950), then went back to Boston. Although he recorded and performed less frequently for the rest of his short life, it was during these last years in Boston that Chaloff grew to full maturity and made his greatest artistic statements. Paralyzed by a malignant tumor in 1956, he continued to play (a jam session with Max Roach and Clifford Brown is legendary), and recorded a reunion album with the Four Brothers shortly before he died. Chaloff maintained full control of a lush tone throughout the baritone's entire range. His use of abrupt and extreme contrasts in dynamics—distinctively varied and irregular phrasing and deliberate pacing—lent his solos drama and volatility that few saxophonists have ever matched.

what to buy: *Blue Serge* ✔✔✔✔ (Capitol, 1956, prod. Bill Miller) is Chaloff's masterpiece. It was recorded on a short tour of the West Coast with a crack pick-up rhythm section of Sonny Clark, Leroy Vinnegar, and Philly Joe Jones. *Boston Blow Up* (Capitol, 1955, prod. Stan Kenton) ✔✔✔✔ finds Chaloff in the company of his working Boston band, playing with special depth and grace. His "Body and Soul" on this session ranks with the greatest versions of that standard ever recorded. *Fable of Mabel* ✔✔✔ (Black Lion, 1954, prod. George Wein) is marred only by some rough ensemble playing. This session with some of Boston's flourishing bebop community, including the rarely recorded pianist Dick Twardzik, sounds astonishingly fresh and progressive even today.

the rest:
The Four Brothers Together Again! ✔✔✔ (RCA, 1957)
Boston 1950 ✔✔✔ (Uptown, 1994)

worth searching for: *The Complete Serge Chaloff Sessions* ✔✔✔✔ (Mosaic, 1993, prod. Michael Cuscuna) is available through the mail order-only label Mosaic. It is a collection of all of Chaloff's sessions as a leader, including those with Capitol and Fable of Mable, as well as some very obscure small-label sessions, in a superbly remastered three-CD set.

influences:

◄◄ Harry Carney, Jack Washington

Ed Hazell

Joe Chambers

Born June 25, 1942, in Stoneacre, VA.

Most of Joe Chambers's early career was spent in Washington, D.C., and Philadelphia, where his first professional job (at the age of 12 years) involved drumming for strip routines. For a while Chambers also worked in various rhythm and blues bands with James Brown, the Shirelles, and Bobby Charles. He studied at the Philadelphia Conservatory and took composition classes with Hall Overton. In 1963 Chambers moved to New York City where he played with Eric Dolphy, Lou Donaldson, Jimmy Giuffre, and Andrew Hill. He made his recording and compositional debut in 1964 with Freddie Hubbard, who performed Chamber's "Mirrors." Working with vibist Bobby Hutcherson provided Chambers with his first long-term gig and an important creative partnership as well, since the drummer wrote material for the albums *Dialogue*, *Components*, *Spiral*, *Patterns*, and *Medina*, all classics in Hutcherson's catalog. Since that time Chambers has also worked with Joe Henderson, Sam Rivers, Sonny Rollins, the percussion ensemble M'Boom, Tommy Flanagan, and Larry Young. As a drummer, he is talented and versatile, able to play with tradition-oriented bands or with more modern free-jazz and post-bop players.

what to buy: *Phantom of the City* 🎵🎵🎵 (Candid, 1991, prod. Mark Morganelli) was recorded live at Birdland in 1991. This release features bassist Santi Debriano and pianist George Cables who wrote the title track. Cables, like Chambers, has worked with and written material for vibist Hutcherson. Despite Chambers's prowess as a composer, there are only two of his tunes played on this album. They are the valedictory "For Miles," with a sensitive tenor solo from Bob Berg, and "Nuevo Mundo," featuring Berg with trumpeter Philip Harper. The other songs on the album include one made famous by Billie Holiday, "You've Changed," and material from Miles Davis, Wayne Shorter, and Joe Henderson.

worth searching for: Chambers's best material is out of print currently, so it might be hard to find the albums he recorded for Muse, but the hunt could be worth it. Try to find *The Almoravid* 🎵🎵🎵 (Muse, 1974), which combines material from three separate sessions stretching from 1971–73. The result is a splendid rhythm journey with instrumental flavors from North Africa and Moorish Spain within a seventies-era, post-bop framework. The melodic aspects of percussion are highlighted by Cedar Walton's piano and marimba playing from David Friedman, while Omar Clay, Doug Hawthorne, and Ray Mantilla take care of various shaking and banging things. Hutcherson has been the beneficiary of some of Chambers's best playing and writing. Listening to the Hutcherson version of Chambers's *Medina* (from the album of the same name), one gets this double dose of good writing and a master class in how to use a cymbal subtly while forcefully pushing the music.

influences:

◄◄ Max Roach, Elvin Jones, Kenny Clarke, Roy Haynes, Miles Davis, Jimmy Giuffre

►► Tani Tabaal

Garaud MacTaggart

Paul Chambers

Born Paul Laurence Dunbar Chambers, April 22, 1935, in Pittsburgh, PA. Died January 4, 1969 in New York, NY.

Paul Chambers was raised in Detroit where he initially played baritone horn and tuba before learning the rudiments of bass playing. In 1952 he solidified his skills by taking lessons with one of the bassists in the Detroit Symphony Orchestra. During this time he was playing bass in the Cass Tech High orchestra in addition to occasionally working with fellow Michiganders Thad Jones and Barry Harris. Chambers's first important job was with Paul Quinichette followed by gigs with Bennie Green, George Wallington, and the trombone duo of J.J. Johnson and Kai Winding. In 1955, after moving to New York, he began working with Miles Davis and finding himself at the rhythm core of such outstanding albums as *Kind of Blue*, *Milestones*, and *'Round about Midnight*. When Chambers finally left Davis in 1963 he performed in a trio with Wynton Kelly and Jimmy Cobb. He also did a lot of session work, showing up on albums by Sonny Rollins, Bud Powell, Kenny Clarke, Johnny Griffin, Donald Byrd, Hank Mobley, and Lee Morgan. Chambers's skill with arco or bowed bass playing added a new dimension to the music he played.

what to buy: If you love bass playing, then *Bass on Top* 🎵🎵🎵🎵 (Blue Note, 1957/1995, prod. Alfred Lion) is probably the album to buy first. Chambers was a virtuoso and this album let him show off his skills in a more exposed way than any other album on which he had worked. We are talking bass solos, bass leads, arco bass, and plucked bass, and ensemble work, all designed to showcase Chambers. Don't assume that the high quality sidemen get stiffed in the solos department; it just means that they are accompanists and the leader gets to strut his stuff. After Chambers has his first tour de force on "Yesterdays," the overwhelming (but excellent) bass playing subsides to a level where you can hear how marvelous the rest of the band is. Guitarist Kenny Burrell gets the first non-Chambers solo (on "You'd Be So Nice to Come Home To"), closely followed by pianist

Hank Jones on the same piece. Drummer Art Taylor has to wait a little longer for his propers on "Chasin' the Bird." Burrell's lead on "Dear Old Stockholm" is another highlight. *Paul Chambers Quintet* 𝄞𝄞𝄞𝄞 (Blue Note, 1957/1996, prod. Alfred Lion) is a fine recording by important jazz musicians at what amounts to the beginnings of their careers. Chambers himself had most of a decade left to work with Miles Davis, and drummer Elvin Jones was three years away from joining the groundbreaking John Coltrane Quartet. Pianist Tommy Flanagan was developing a major reputation as an accompanist about this time, long before his work with Ella Fitzgerald, and the horn section of trumpeter Donald Byrd and tenor man Clifford Jordan were just embarking on fulfilling journeys of their own. Benny Golson had written a couple of tunes especially for this date ("Minor Run-Down" and "Four Strings", a showpiece for Chambers), and the leader had composed some lovely songs as well ("The Hand of Love" and "Beauteous"). Everything came together for this album, making it one of the gems in the Blue Note catalog.

what to buy next: The sextet for Chambers's first album has some pretty heavy dudes in it. There's Byrd, Burrell, Coltrane, Horace Silver, "Philly" Joe Jones, and the leader himself. It's a surprise in some ways that Silver who was such a strong song writer didn't contribute any compositions to *Whims of Chambers* 𝄞𝄞𝄞 (Blue Note, 1956/1996, prod. Alfred Lion). Despite that, the material heard here is pretty solid. Chambers wrote three, Coltrane contributed two, and Byrd tossed in another two. Byrd's piece "Omicron" is the lead-off tune and features some interesting time signature experiments bracketing a rather straightahead blowing session. Coltrane has already started to develop his big tenor sound by this time and his playing is only two years away from some of his best Prestige dates. While "OMICRON" may be the most overtly radical work on the album, Coltrane's "Just for Love" hints at the stuff he was to record on *Soultrane*.

the rest:
Chambers Music 𝄞𝄞𝄞 (Blue Note, 1956/1995)

influences:
◀◀ Jimmy Blanton, Ray Brown, Charles Mingus

▶▶ Christian McBride

Garaud MacTaggart

Thomas Chapin

Born March 9, 1957, in Manchester, CT. Died February 13, 1998, in Providence, RI.

Though leukemia tragically ended saxophonist Thomas Chapin's life when he was only 40 years old, he spent nearly a decade working as a leader and left behind a legacy of many excellent albums and performances and a reputation as a versatile musician's musician who was unfailingly gentlemanly. He moved freely between the dual (and sometimes dueling) New York City factions of the avant-garde downtown scene and the mainstream scene and was respected in both. Though in his trio work he would sometimes play outside time, unlike some avant-gardists he often played metered music even in nonmainstream settings. His natural exuberance made him an expressive showman, yet there was never the slightest sense that he compromised his musicality in any context; he was able to communicate directly and unassumingly in even the most challenging sonic contexts.

Chapin attended the Hartt School of Music at the University of Hartford and later went to Rutgers University, studying with Jackie McLean, Paul Jeffrey, Ted Dunbar, and Kenny Barron. Starting in 1981 he spent six years as the musical director for Lionel Hampton's big band; he also worked in Chico Hamilton's group for a while. In the late 1980s Chapin formed his own groups and soon made a name for himself. When the downtown NYC club the Knitting Factory started a record label, Chapin was the first artist it signed. Bassist Mario Pavone was a frequent collaborator, and they worked closely in Chapin's trio and in Pavone's own bands. Chapin's versatility made him a popular addition to many groups, from obscure avant-garde big bands in which he was sometimes the most famous player (Walter Thompson Big Band, Joe Gallant's Illuminati) and improvisors on the fringes of jazz (John McCracken, Machine Gun) to such notables as John Zorn, Ned Rothenberg, and Anthony Braxton.

Chapin's final album was recorded in 1996 but delayed until he could work on its production during a period of remission from his illness. It came out the same week he died. The Chapin-penned poem in the CD booklet, called "Sky Piece," captures its mood perfectly: "So much sky/in the space of desert/my soul/rises/from a mournful Earth/into a clarity/above Time./ While Time is/it is best to be/in both worlds/Music/as the bridge."

what to buy: Chapin's final release, the trio album *Sky Piece* 𝄞𝄞𝄞𝄞 (Knitting Factory, 1998, prod. Thomas Chapin) sounds like a benediction, with a feeling of quiet peace on many tracks. His flute playing is especially striking. The centerpiece of the album, however, is the 11-minute "Night Bird Song," anchored by Pavone's vamp-like basslines and including a Rahsaanesque section where Chapin plays two saxes in an ecstatic climax. For Chapin's mainstream side only, go straight to *You*

Don't Know Me ♫♫♫♫ (Arabesque, 1995, prod. Thomas Chapin, Daniel Chriss), an absolutely burning bebop session. Chapin flies through the changes with assured ease, with the flute ballad "Namibian Sunset" for variety. Chapin surrounds himself with an excellent cast of Tom Harrell (trumpet, flugelhorn), Peter Madsen (piano), Kiyoto Fujiwara (bass), and Reggie Nicholson (drums) on a program of six fine originals and two standards.

what to buy next: *Insomnia* ♫♫♫♫ (Knitting Factory, 1992, prod. Thomas Chapin), by the Thomas Chapin Trio Plus Brass, is the best album for listeners who want to hear a cross between Chapin's mainstream and more outside efforts. Adding two trumpets, two trombones, and tuba fills out the trio's textures nicely and in quieter moments recalls the sound of Gil Evans, especially when Chapin is playing flute. On this live recording, the arrangements are precise yet relaxed on the all-original program. *Radius* ♫♫♫♫ (MuWorks, 1990, prod. Robert Musso) is Chapin's second-best mainstream album, with a fine rhythm section of Ronnie Mathews, Ray Drummond, and John Betsch and an attractive cover of Fats Waller's "Jitterbug Waltz" on which Chapin plays mezzo-soprano (F) sax. The other five tracks are by Chapin, all excellent, with the exotic "Forgotten Game" standing out for the use of oud (played by Ara Dinkjian), which works well with Chapin's cool flute playing. Chapin's most outside playing on record by far is heard on his duo free-improv album with pianist Borah Bergman, *Inversions* ♫♫♫♫ (MuWorks, 1992, prod. Robert Musso). The unstinting flow of imagination both players exhibit, and the lyricism of Chapin's playing, even in this intensely dense context (Bergman is an extremely active pianist), sets it apart from the free-jazz norm.

the rest:
Third Force ♫♫♫♫ (Knitting Factory, 1991)
Anima ♫♫♫♫ (Knitting Factory, 1992)
I've Got Your Number ♫♫♫♫ (Arabesque, 1993)
Menagerie Dreams ♫♫♫♫ (Knitting Factory, 1994)
(With the Thomas Chapin Trio Plus Strings) *Haywire* ♫♫♫ (Knitting Factory, 1996)

worth searching for: An old promo CD put out in advance of a package tour, *Knitting Factory Tours Europe* ♫♫♫♫ (Knitting Factory/Enemy, 1991, prod. Bob Appel) contains a noiresque outtake from *Third Force*, "Walking Mystery Man," which sounds like a cross between early Ornette Coleman and a spy movie theme, complete with a cool-walking quarter-note bassline by Mario Pavone (its composer). There's also an alternate take of "Ahab's Leg." The multiple-artists compilation *What Is Jazz? 1996* ♫♫♫♫ (Knitting Factory, 1996, prod. Brett

Heinz, Mark Perlson), recorded live at the eponymous annual festival of the album title, includes the rollicking, rhythmically charged, nine-minute Chapin trio track "A Drunken Monkey," with Pavone and Sarin. Chapin's lengthy, ecstatic solo is a must-own. He's also heard on the same album's Mario Pavone Sextet track. The saxophonist's work on Pavone's albums is interesting for its more arranged context, and Pavone's *Song for (Septet)* ♫♫♫♫ (New World Countercurrents, 1994, prod. Marty Ehrlich) and the sextet album *Dancers Tales* ♫♫♫♫ (Knitting Factory, 1997, prod. Marty Ehrlich) are important parts of Chapin's legacy. Sure, he shares the frontline (and thus solo space) with fellow saxophonist Marty Ehrlich and trombonist Peter McEachern—but it's the overall music that counts, a fact Chapin always made his top priority. For a completely different context, there's the Anthony Braxton-Mario Pavone Quintet's *Seven Standards 1996* ♫♫♫♫ (Knitting Factory, 1997, prod. Anthony Braxton, Mario Pavone), with Braxton on piano rather than reeds, plus Dave Douglas (trumpet) and Pheeroan AkLaff (drums). It's a classic bebop format, and they explore tunes by Charlie Parker, Thelonious Monk, and John Coltrane as well as four standards. As a pianist, Braxton's not up to the high level of the others, but he comps adequately behind their superb solos—Chapin sounds invigorated by the challenges of "Dewey Square" and "Straight Life."

influences:

◀◀ Rahsaan Roland Kirk, Earl Bostic, Jackie McLean

▶▶ Chris Kelsey

Steve Holtje

Bill Charlap

Born October 15, 1966, in New York City, NY.

Able to paint with a rich and melodic pallet, while possessing a pure and bell-like tone, pianist Bill Charlap is a player who is actively looking for new ways to express himself and compliment any musical situation. His sophisticated harmonic knowledge and sense of drama make him one of the most stimulating pianists around. It should come as no surprise that Charlap would pursue a career in music; his parents are Broadway composer Moose Charlap and vocalist Sandy Stewart. At the age of three, Charlap began his piano studies, and his formal musical education included graduation from New York's High School of the Performing Arts.

Over the past several years, Charlap has gained valuable experience through work with Gerry Mulligan, Benny Carter, Louis

Bellson, Sheila Jordan, Bobby Short, Barry Manilow, and Tony Bennett, among many others. He has been a key member of the Phil Woods Quintet since 1995, a position that has found him appearing at many of the world's major jazz festivals, and even guesting on Marian McPartland's *Piano Jazz* radio show. He also leads his own piano trio and has recorded for the Chiaroscuro and Criss Cross labels. A major voice, Bill Charlap's talent is worthy of wider critical attention and public awareness.

what to buy: *Souvenir* ✍✍✍✍ (Criss Cross Jazz, 1995, prod. Gerry Teekens) was Charlap's first date for Criss Cross and his second as a leader. Charlap's trio with Scott Colley and Dennis Mackrel is very attuned to each other's sensibilities and whims. For adventure, there's a wonderfully inventive version of Ornette Coleman's "Turnaround," while the lush title track and "Goodbye Mr. Evans" show how maturely Charlap can handle a ballad. *Distant Star* ✍✍✍✍ (Criss Cross, 1997, prod. Gerry Teekens) features bassist Sean Smith and drummer Bill Stewart on the best effort yet from this intriguing pianist. There are a few originals here, but mainly the program consists of little-known standards. The trio gives each number a definitive treatment and proves that it's still possible to say something new while working in the tradition.

the rest:
Along with Me ✍✍✍ (Chiaroscuro, 1994)

influences:
◀◀ Bill Evans, Herbie Hancock

Chris Hovan

Ray Charles
Born Ray Charles Robinson, September 23, 1930, in Albany, GA.

Not for nothing was Charles known as "the Genius." In his extraordinary recording career, he's done more than almost any other artist to obliterate the lines between genres of nearly every stripe, from R&B and gospel to country and pop to blues and rock. Beginning as an imitator of the smooth stylings of Nat "King" Cole and Charles Brown, Charles eventually forged his own style, combining gospel music and harmonies with decidedly earthier lyrics reflecting love, lust, heartbreak and hard times. He was passionate about jazz, recording Count Basie–style big band arrangements on the one hand, and stripped-down bluesy bop with Milt Jackson on the other. A bigger leap still were his two albums of country & western music that Charles infused with righteous soul. A man of Herculean determination, few opponents have faced him down. Not all of

his decisions have been right ones, but he stands behind them all. And why not? His voice is one of the most recognizable in all of music, thanks to such timeless hits as "I Got a Woman," "What'd I Say," "The Night Time Is the Right Time," "Hit the Road Jack," "Georgia on My Mind," "Unchain My Heart," "You Don't Know Me," "Busted," and countless others, to say nothing of his famous Diet Pepsi commercials. Over the years, many of his albums have gone out of print, but plenty of quality box sets, anthologies, and samplers exist. Meanwhile, Rhino records is currently on an ambitious reissue campaign, offering a number of the original works configured as two-fers. Most of these are worth seeking out, though the place to start with Charles is one of the best-of sets.

what to buy: It's big and expensive, but you won't find many box sets that are the equal of the five-CD set *Genius & Soul: The 50th Anniversary Collection* ✍✍✍✍ (Rhino, 1997, prod. various), the first collection that successfully represents every phase of Charles's career, with material from every label. The music is unparalleled, the sound is terrific, the notes are scholarly, and the back of the booklet is even in Braille. This set belongs in every serious collection of twentieth-century American music. The merely curious or the more budget minded, on the other hand, might want to sample the two main periods of Charles's early career with *Anthology* ✍✍✍✍ (Rhino, 1988, prod. various) and *The Best of Ray Charles: The Atlantic Years* ✍✍✍✍ (Rhino, 1994, prod. Jerry Wexler, Zenas Sears, Nesuhi Ertegun, Ahmet Ertegun). The 20-track *Anthology* contains some of the ABC material, including "Georgia on My Mind," "Let's Go Get Stoned," "Eleanor Rigby," "Hit the Road Jack," and "Unchain My Heart." *The Atlantic Years*, which also contains 20 tracks, features "I Got a Woman," "What'd I Say," "The Night Time Is the Right Time," and "Drown in My Own Tears."

what to buy next: For those wanting to delve a little deeper into the Atlantic material, you can't go wrong with *The Birth of Soul: The Complete Atlantic Rhythm & Blues Recordings, 1952–1959* ✍✍✍✍ (Rhino, 1991, prod. various), a three-CD chronicle tracking Charles's development from his years as a Cole imitator to his breakout as a talent of almost unparalleled intuition and ability. The focus is on his blues and jazz sides on the two-CD anthology appropriately titled *Blues + Jazz* ✍✍✍✍ (Rhino, 1994). Charles is an explosive live performer, and two of his best in-concert albums, 1958's *Ray Charles at Newport* and 1969's *Ray Charles in Person* are now configured as *Ray Charles Live* ✍✍✍✍ (Atlantic, 1973/1987, prod. Nesuhi Ertegun, Zenas Sears). The experiments Charles was carrying out in the studio are extended to the stage, and his feverish versions of "The

Right Time," "What'd I Say," and "Drown in My Own Tears," among others, shout, plead, testify, and rock.

what to avoid: Some of Charles's albums are ill-conceived or poorly executed, but none are truly wretched. Beware of numerous cheap repackagings of his hits; if it's not on Atlantic, ABC, Columbia, Warner Bros., or Rhino, proceed with caution.

the rest:

The Great Ray Charles/The Genius after Hours 🎵🎵🎵 (Atlantic, 1957/ 1961/Rhino, 1987)

(With Milt Jackson) *Soul Brothers/Soul Meeting* 🎵🎵🎵 (Atlantic, 1958/1961/Rhino, 1989)

The Genius of Ray Charles 🎵🎵🎵🎵 (Atlantic, 1959/Rhino, 1990)

The Genius Hits the Road 🎵🎵🎵 (ABC/Paramount, 1960/Rhino, 1997)

Genius + Soul = Jazz/My Kind of Jazz 🎵🎵🎵🎵 (Impulse!, 1961/Tangerine, 1970/Rhino, 1997)

Modern Sounds in Country and Western Music 🎵🎵🎵🎵🎵 (ABC/Paramount, 1962/Rhino, 1988)

Ingredients in a Recipe for Soul/Have a Smile with Me 🎵🎵🎵🎵 (ABC/ Paramount, 1963/1964/Rhino, 1997)

Sweet & Sour Tears 🎵🎵🎵 (ABC/Paramount, 1964/Rhino, 1997)

Super Hits (a.k.a. Friendship) 🎵🎵🎵 (Columbia, 1984/1998)

The Spirit of Christmas 🎵🎵🎵 (Columbia, 1985)

Greatest Hits, Vol. 1 🎵🎵🎵🎵 (Rhino, 1988)

Greatest Hits, Vol. 2 🎵🎵🎵🎵 (Rhino, 1988)

Would You Believe? 🎵🎵 (Warner Bros., 1990)

My World 🎵🎵🎵 (Warner Bros., 1993)

Ain't That Fine 🎵🎵🎵 (Drive Archive, 1994)

The Early Years 🎵🎵🎵 (Tomato, 1994)

Classics 🎵🎵🎵🎵 (Rhino, 1995)

Strong Love Affair 🎵🎵🎵 (Qwest, 1996)

Berlin, 1962 🎵🎵🎵🎵 (Pablo, 1996)

Standards 🎵🎵🎵🎵 (Rhino, 1998)

worth searching for: *Ray Charles and Betty Carter* 🎵🎵🎵🎵 (ABC/Paramount, 1961) was reissued a few years ago by DCC, though it's now out of print. It brings together two classic voices for some terrific duets, including the definitive version of "Baby, It's Cold Outside."

influences:

◀◀ Nat "King" Cole, Charles Brown, Count Basie, the Grand Ole Opry, Louis Jordan, Claude Jeter

▶▶ Van Morrison, Billy Joel, Joe Cocker

Daniel Durchholz

Teddy Charles

Born Theodore Charles Cohen, April 13, 1928, in Chicopee Falls, MA.

After an initial period of study at Juilliard, Charles rode out the

end of the Big Band era with Benny Goodman (1948) and Artie Shaw (1949). His own early 1950s combos worked extensively with modes and polytonality, the direct result of Charles's study with pianist/arranger Hall Overton. In the early to mid-1950s he led a number of small group sessions, many with West Coast cool stars such as Jimmy Giuffre and Shorty Rogers and bop tenor legend Wardell Gray. Charles combined advanced ideas in composing and arranging (such as playing around key centers rather than over chord changes) with a formidable talent on the vibes. While continually on the cutting edge, Charles never sacrificed listenability, achieving an ultra-cool take on bop. The latter part of the decade saw him participating in Charles Mingus's Jazz Composers Workshop. He assembled a series of tentets in 1956, recording his own progressive arrangements as well as several from Gil Evans, Giuffre, and George Russell, all of whom, like Charles, presaged the 1960s avant-garde. Charles was also connected (mainly by association) with the Third Stream movement. In the 1960s he continued to tour and perform with his New Directions combos and founded pop label Polaris Records.

what to buy: Charles's 1950s small-group sessions are gathered on a number of reissues. *Collaboration West* 🎵🎵🎵🎵 (Prestige/OJC, 1992, prod. Teddy Charles, Ira Gitler) collects three separate sessions from 1952–53. It's essential (and above all listenable) early avant-bop for anyone who thinks *Kind of Blue*-era Miles Davis and early Ornette Coleman popped up out of nowhere. "Variations on a Motive by Bud" is stunning. *The Teddy Charles Tentet* 🎵🎵🎵🎵 (Atlantic, 1956/1988, prod. Nesuhi Ertegun) collects the entire *Tentet* LP as well as selections from *The Word from Bird* and a quartet session featuring Mingus. It has some great large group sounds reaching a satisfying middle-ground sensibility between Gil Evans and Mingus.

what to buy next: *Evolution* 🎵🎵🎵 (Prestige/OJC, 1992, prod. Bob Weinstock) has more small group recordings from the August 31, 1953 sessions on *Collaboration West* and a 1955 session featuring J.R. Monterose on tenor. More standards here, but the avant flavor is still present. The CD reissue of *Wardell Gray Memorial, Vol. 2* 🎵🎵🎵🎵 (Prestige/OJC, 1992, prod. Teddy Charles) contains a 1953 session by Teddy Charles's West Coasters, valuable for the presence of the mighty Gray as well as the recording debuts of Sonny Clark and Frank Morgan.

the rest:

The Vibraphone Players of Bethlehem, vol. 1 🎵🎵🎵 (Bethlehem, 1959/ 1994)

Live at the Verona Jazz Festival, 1988 🎵🎵🎵 (Soul Note, 1989)

worth searching for: *The Dual Role of Bob Brookmeyer* 🎵🎵🎵 (Prestige/OJC, 1989, prod. Ira Gitler) includes a 1954 session of a Charles-led quartet featuring Brookmeyer on valve trombone and piano as well as beatnik vocal by Hall Overton's wife Nancy on "Nobody's Heart." *The Birth of the Third Stream* 🎵🎵 (Columbia Legacy, 1996, prod. George Avakian) incorporates all of the *Music for Brass* (1957) and two-thirds of the *Modern Jazz Concert* (1958) LPs. It includes Charles playing in the large group arrangements by Mingus, Giuffre, Russell, and Gunther Schuller taken from the latter album.

influences:

◀◀ Lionel Hampton, Milt Jackson, Lennie Tristano

▶▶ Bobby Hutcherson, Ornette Coleman

Larry Grogan

Allan Chase

Born June 22, 1956, in Willimantic, CT.

Completely at home in any number of modern jazz styles from bop and swing to free and third stream, altoist/sopranist Allan Chase is a thoughtful soloist with a keen sense of architectural space and proportion, as well as compelling rhythmic drive. His previous associations include Boston's esteemed Your Neighborhood Saxophone Quartet (which also launched the career of current ROVA member Steve Adams), Rashied Ali, Gunther Schuller, and vocalist Dominique Eade, to whom he is married.

what's available: His only date as a leader, thus far, *Dark Clouds with Silver Linings* 🎵🎵🎵🎵 (Accurate, 1995, prod. Allan Chase) is a handsome "concept" album, of sorts. The leader's pianoless quartet—himself, trumpeter Ron Horton, bassist Tony Scherr, and drummer Matt Wilson—plays a program of tunes almost exclusively associated with pianists, among them compositions by Sun Ra (the quirky, ebullient title cut), Horace Silver's joyous, melodically infectious "Yeah," and a pair of lines by Bud Powell, "Borderick" and the infrequently heard "Comin' Up." In the liner notes, Chase writes: "The instrumentation brings Ornette Coleman to mind, but the way we play these tunes owes more to the two-horn quartets of Sonny Rollins and Gerry Mulligan." He's absolutely right. This is a beautifully warm, accessible album.

influences:

◀◀ Lee Konitz

David Prince

Doc Cheatham

Born Adolphus Anthony Cheatham, June 13, 1905, in Nashville, TN. Died June 2, 1997, in Washington, D.C.

Doc Cheatham is a unique figure in jazz, a trumpeter whose career spanned almost the entire history of the music and who came into his own as an improvisor at an age when most of his contemporaries were either dead, retired, or long past their peak as musicians. An elegant and supremely sensitive player, Cheatham just seemed to get better as he got older, his pure tone and spare, gracefully constructed improvisations honed to diamond brilliance. He liked to play in the middle register, but could hit and sustain high notes without a quaver until the end of his life. He only began singing in public in his seventies, choosing songs that perfectly reflected his fey, self-deprecating wit. Like Louis Armstrong, who first influenced him to pick up the trumpet, Cheatham's singing seemed to extend directly from his playing.

Cheatham started making music when he was 15, first playing drums, then moving to saxophone and cornet. By the early 1920s he was working in the pit band at the Bijou Theater in Nashville, where he played behind many of the great blues singers, including the three Smiths (Bessie, Mamie, and Clara, no relation) and Ethel Waters. He picked up his nickname while working in a small group at Meharry Medical College. He moved to Chicago in the mid-1920s, played soprano saxophone on a record session with Ma Rainey, worked with Albert Wynn, and first heard his lifelong idol, Louis Armstrong. It was at this time that he substituted for Armstrong in the Erskine Tate Orchestra at the Vendome Theater, a much-remarked upon aspect of the Cheatham legend. Doc left Chicago in 1927 and worked with Wilbur DeParis in Philadelphia, then in 1928 moved to New York City, where he was hired by Chick Webb. He spent three years playing lead trumpet with Sam Wooding's band in Europe and when he returned to the U.S. became a member of McKinney's Cotton Pickers' formidable trumpet section (with Rex Stewart and Joe Smith). Cheatham spent most of the 1930s with Cab Calloway's hugely popular band, though due to his beautiful tone and wide range he played lead almost exclusively and rarely soloed. Struck by disabling fatigue in the late 1930s, Cheatham was on and off the jazz scene through the mid-1940s, playing in the big bands of Benny Carter and Teddy Wilson and later in Eddie Heywood's small group. He spent most of the 1950s and 1960s playing in Dixieland and Latin bands (Machito, Ricardo Rey, Perez Prado, and Herbie Mann). In 1957 he appeared on the CBS television show *Sound of Jazz* with such legendary trumpeters as Rex Allen, Rex Stewart, Joe

Wilder, and Roy Eldridge. He wouldn't solo, but agreed to play behind Billie Holiday on "Fine and Mellow." It was with Benny Goodman (1966–67) that Cheatham started to emerge as an improvisor. Always a highly lyrical player, he methodically set about developing his ear, listening closely to later trumpet stars such as Clifford Brown. Cheatham started recording prolifically in the mid-1970s for independent labels such as Sackville, New York Jazz, Stash, GHB, and Parkwood as well as a number of European labels. By the 1980s he had become a jazz star for the first time in his career, playing jazz festivals and clubs, while his long-running weekly Sunday brunch performances at Sweet Basil became a New York institution. Cheatham performed right up until the last week of his life.

what to buy: Trumpeters usually start to fade in their sixties, but as *The Eighty-Seven Years of Doc Cheatham* ♪♪♪♪ (Columbia, 1993, prod. Phil Schaap) makes clear, Cheatham became virtually the first octogenarian to achieve greatness on the horn. Playing with poise, power and profundity, his solos are perfectly crafted gems. Accompanied by his working rhythm section led by pianist Chuck Folds, Cheatham also sings a number of tunes. His wry, sweet vocals on the tunes "My Buddy" and "I Guess I'll Get the Papers and Go Home," among others, are priceless. This album is highly recommended. *Doc Cheatham & Nicholas Payton* ♪♪♪♪ (Verve, 1997, prod. Andrea du Plessis, Jerry Block, George Hocutt) pairs an excellent 23-year-old trumpeter who worships Louis Armstrong with the 91-year-old Cheatham who subbed for Armstrong in 1926. The session was recorded in New Orleans and both trumpeters invoke the spirit of Satchmo as they stroll through 14 timeless standards with insouciance. They are accompanied by a fine, alternating cast of Crescent City musicians and pianist Butch Thompson. There are many transcendent moments on this quiet, intimate album, such as the interplay between the trumpeters on "Out of Nowhere," accompanied only by guitar and bass. Cheatham also sings on 10 of the tracks.

what to buy next: Doc Cheatham was a completely obscure figure when *Shorty and Doc* ♪♪♪♪ (Swingville/OJC, 1961, prod. Esmond Edwards) was recorded, while trumpeter Shorty Baker was better known through his tenure with Duke Ellington. Baker often takes the lead on solos, but this is a friendly session and the two lyric-minded trumpeters don't take each other on as much as play with each other. Cheatham's Dixieland ap-

proach sounds a little out of place with the more modern rhythm section (Walter Bishop Jr. on piano, Wendall Marshall on bass, and J.C. Heard on drums), but the makings of a great improvisor are apparent.

best of the rest:
Black Beauty ♪♪♪♪ (Sackville, 1980)
Too Marvelous for Words ♪♪♪♪ (New York Jazz, 1982)
I've Got a Crush on You ♪♪♪♪ (New York Jazz, 1982)
It's a Good Life ♪♪♪♪ (Parkwood, 1983)
The Fabulous Doc Cheatham ♪♪♪♪♪ (Parkwood, 1984)
Tribute to Billie Holiday ♪♪♪♪ (Kenneth, 1987)
Tribute to Louis Armstrong ♪♪♪♪ (Kenneth, 1988)

worth searching for: *Live!* ♪♪♪♪ (Natasha Imports, 1993, prod. Bernard Brightman, Will Friedwald) documents two 1985 concerts in Jack Kleinsinger's long-running Highlights in Jazz series, one with a sextet including swing tenorist George Kelly and pianist Richard Wyands, the second a septet with tenor revivalist Loren Schoenberg and pianist Marty Napoleon. Cheatham takes vocals on "Sweet Lorraine" and "You're Lucky to Me."

influences:
◄◄ Louis Armstrong, Bix Beiderbecke, Joe Smith
►► Nicholas Payton

Andrew Gilbert

Jeannie & Jimmy Cheatham & the Sweet Baby Blues Band
Formed mid-1980s.

Jeannie Cheatham, piano/vocals; Jimmy Cheatham, bass trombone; Clora Bryant, trumpet, (1990); Red Callender, bass (1984–92); John Harris, drums, (1984–present); Dinky Morris, tenor, soprano, baritone saxophones, (1985–present); Jimmie Noone Jr., clarinet, soprano and tenor saxophones, (1984–91); Charles Owens, alto and baritone saxophones, (1993–present); Curtis Peagler, alto and tenor saxophones, (1984–92); Richard Reid, bass, (1992–present); Herman Riley, tenor and soprano saxophones, (1988); Nolan Smith, trumpet, flugelhorn, (1990–present); Louis Taylor, alto and soprano saxophones, (1996–present); Rickey Woodard, tenor and alto saxophones, clarinet, (1991–present); Snooky Young, trumpet and flugelhorn, (1984–present).

The Sweet Baby Blues Band is an earthy jump-blues combo that plays funky, hard-swinging, booty-busting music. A throwback to the pre-R&B 1940s when big bands were scaling down and playing blues-oriented dance music, the SBB Band adds a

Doc Cheatham (© Jack Vartoogian)

dash of bop to the mix, but never strays far from the funk. The Cheathams founded the band in the mid-1980s, but they've been working together for 45 years and married since the late 1950s. Both have long, varied careers in the music business.

Jeannie Cheatham, an Akron, Ohio native, is a vibrant, joyful vocalist and pianist who had been working in clubs when she met Jimmy on stage in his hometown of Buffalo. She studied piano from a young age and has accompanied Dinah Washington, Al Hibbler, and Jimmy Witherspoon. Jimmy Cheatham is a bass trombonist who had worked in Broadway and television bands, and has performed with Duke Ellington, Bill Dixon, Thad Jones, Lionel Hampton, Ornette Coleman, and Chico Hamilton. Together, they attended the University of Wisconsin in the 1970s, then settled in San Diego, which is still their home base. Since the mid-1980s, they've recorded a number of irresistible albums for Concord, featuring guest stars such as Hank Crawford, Eddie "Lockjaw" Davis, Eddie "Cleanhead" Vinson, and Plas Johnson. But the now-ten-piece band has plenty of its own fire power, as its regular members have been a who's who of underrecognized players, such as clarinetist/tenor saxophonist Jimmie Noone, bassist Red Callender, and alto saxophonist Curtis Peagler (all deceased), trumpeter Snooky Young, and saxophonists Rickey Woodard and Charles Owens.

what to buy: The album that started it all, *Sweet Baby Blues* 𝄞𝄞𝄞𝄞 (Concord Jazz, 1984,/1989 prod. Carl E. Jefferson), features bassist/tuba specialist Callender, and he had such a good time he later became a member of the band. The Cheathams established their successful formula early: inventive arrangements that make the SBB Band sound like a big band, lots of solo space, top-shelf improvisors, and Jeannie's spirited vocals. A superior session by the dependable Cheathams, *Homeward Bound* 𝄞𝄞𝄞𝄞 (Concord Jazz, 1987/1995, prod. Carl E. Jefferson) features special guest alto saxophonist Cleanhead Vinson on three tracks. But solo honors go to trumpeter Snooky Young, whose spectacular plunger work steals the show. With Jeannie's joyful vocals and Jimmy's excellent arrangements, this session transcends the feel-good party music genre, though it fits comfortably there too. Over the years death has taken its toll on the Cheatham's band, but *Blues and the Boogie Masters* 𝄞𝄞𝄞𝄞 (Concord Jazz, 1993, prod. Nick Phillips) finds the SBB Band in fine shape with a first-class horn section. In fact, Charles Owens and Rickey Woodard outplay special guest Hank Crawford, who sits in on four tracks. Just another fine session by a great working band. The good news is that *Gud Nuz Blues* 𝄞𝄞𝄞𝄞 (Concord Jazz, 1996, prod. Nick Phillips) continues the Cheathams' tradition of playing stompin' blues-drenched music

with a generous helping of jazz improvisation. The great, underappreciated tenor saxophonist Plas Johnson is special guest and he fits right in. Jimmy's smart arrangements, lots of solo space, and players with plenty to say make this session another winner.

what to buy next: The Cheathams' second album with the SBB Band, *Midnight Mama* 𝄞𝄞𝄞 (Concord Jazz, 1986, prod. Carl E. Jefferson) is a bit of a letdown, even with the presence of the great Eddie "Lockjaw" Davis, who does a fine job leading a vocal chorus on "Reel Ya' Deel Ya'," and also engages Jimmie Noone and Curtis Peagler in some worthy jousting. While it's not the band's smoothest outing, there are many fine moments. One of the Cheatham's most bluesy albums *Luv in the Afternoon* 𝄞𝄞𝄞𝄞 (Concord Jazz, 1991, prod. Carl E. Jefferson) features special guest Clarence "Gatemouth" Brown. Tunes includes Muddy Waters's "Baby Please Don't Go" and Danny Barker's classic "Don't You Feel My Leg," which is a delightful instrumental feature for Snooky Young. The fine horn section has plenty of room to stretch out, and trumpeter Nolan Smith and alto saxophonist Curtis Peagler make the most of their solo space. *Basket Full of Blues* 𝄞𝄞𝄞𝄞 (Concord Jazz, 1992, prod. Carl E. Jefferson) features tenor saxophonist Frank Wess as special guest, and the old Basie-ite fits right into the swinging proceedings. Changes in personnel haven't detracted from the band's cohesiveness or the talent level of the horn section. One of the Cheathams' more interesting albums, *Back to the Neighborhood* 𝄞𝄞𝄞𝄞 (Concord Jazz, 1989, prod. Carl E. Jefferson) adds violinist Papa John Creach into the mix with variable results. Otherwise, this is a typically well-played, foot-stomping session by the Cheathams.

influences:

◀◀ Louis Jordan

Andrew Gilbert

Chelsea Bridge

Formed 1992, in Ottawa, Canada.

Rob Frayner, saxophone; John Geggie, bass; Jean Martin, drummer; Tena Palmer, vocals.

The Ottawa-based Chelsea Bridge had been together only one year when the quartet won the grand prize at the 1993 Montreal Jazz Festival. The group, led by saxophonist Rob Frayne, includes bassist John Geggie, drummer Jean Martin, and singer Tena Palmer. They came together after individually racking up substantial musical credits. Frayne studied with Joe Lovano, has recorded as leader on Unity, and has performed with Shuffle Demons, Timewarp, Gil Evans, Kenny Wheeler, Fred Stone, and others. Palmer, a Montreal resident, studied voice in New York City with Janet Lawson and has performed with a variety of bands at Canadian jazz festivals. Geggie has performed and recorded with jazz musicians Bill Watrous, Jamey Abersold, David Baker's 21st Century Bebop Band, Troika, and others, and also performed orchestral music with the National Arts Centre Orchestra, a baroque ensemble, a New Music group, and with a Celtic-folk group. Martin also performs with a wide array of contemporary groups in Ottawa.

what to buy: The critically acclaimed Chelsea Bridge debut album, *Blues in Sharp Sea* 🎵🎵🎵 (Unity Records, 1992, prod. Glenn Trilley, Ross Murray), gives you an idea of why they are an award-winning group, and why, after this album, they made the 1993 playlists of jazz radio hosts like Oscar Treadwell. In their eclectic approach to jazz, Chelsea Bridge does what its name implies, melds Celtic folk melodies with jazz improvisations and also performs bopping originals. Frayne excels on tenor and soprano saxes, and flute. Palmer's chameleon-like, clear soprano voice approaches the uninhibited ease of Sheila Jordan. She is extremely adept at using her voice like an instrument, most apparent when she trades off with Frayne on "The Eyes Are Worth 1,000 Words." Her broad compositional talents are equally notable, and most evident when she switches from her award-winning composition, "The Hills of Loch Katerine" to a country-western original, "Kiss and a Bedtime Story." The 11 tunes are augmented by guest soloists Don Rooke (kona, lap steel guitar), James Stephens (violin), Sara Louise Seck (alto flute), and Peter Kiesewalter (clarinet). If you're looking for a fresh listen and musical adventure, this is a compelling album.

what to buy next: Their sophomore album, *Double Feature* 🎵🎵🎵 (Unity Records, 1995, prod. Ross Murray), shows how far they've come. Recorded live at a 1995 concert performance at the National Library of Canada, it's a hip, sophisticated affair of nine tunes that combines lush orchestrations, seductive improvised jazz instrumental solos, some free-bop stylings, and Palmer's wide-ranging vocals, scatting, and recitations. Virtuosic guest players contribute significantly to this date. Guitarist Roddy Ellias is fluent and versatile. David Mott lays down bursting baritone saxisms that sound like an aircraft carrier. Kevin Turcotte is warmly precise in his trumpet and flugelhorn renderings. Sara Louis Seck (flutes, piccolo) and Joey Skrapek (clarinets) add special color to the richly layered orchestrations. With these players, the extended Chelsea Bridge is even more versatile than on their debut recording, sounding at vari-

Don Cherry
(with Carla Bley/Paul Haines)

song "A.I.R. (All India Radio)"
album Escalator over the Hill
(ECM, 1969/1990)
instrument Trumpet

Monster Solo

ous times like a pastoral Metheny-Haden meeting, or an orchestrated, rowdy Brass Fantasy bash, or a jazz-rock fusion fracas, and more. Chelsea Bridge is one of the most varicolored, provocative groups to come along in years, and they cut a wide berth to provide an out-of-the-ordinary listening experience.

the rest:
Tatamgouche . . . Next Left 🎵🎵🎵 (Unity Jazz, 1994)

Nancy Ann Lee

Don Cherry

Born November 18, 1936, in Oklahoma City, OK. Died October 19, 1995, in Malaga, Spain.

"All the jazz musicians I've liked have had a special quality of making me feel the wind in my face," trumpeter Don Cherry once said. But he moved far and wide through the world of jazz as if the wind was at his back. An acolyte and co-conspirator in Ornette Coleman's late 1950s jazz revolution, Cherry spread the gospel on the New York and European scenes (check out his collaborations with John Coltrane, Sonny Rollins, Steve Lacy, Archie Shepp, and the New York Contemporary 5). And, in his first recordings as a leader, Cherry documented a sort of outre medley-making that was as influential as it was innovative. His musical orbit widened in the late 1960s as he traveled the world. More than any other individual, it was Cherry who self-consciously positioned jazz as a nexus for something called World Music. To talk of only his influence on the form of jazz, though misses much of his importance. There was the joy and heartbreak of his melodies, with his trumpet lines exploring the territory that Coleman had opened up and often including a clarion motif that owed little or nothing to Coleman. A player for all sessions, Cherry's collaborators were widely diverse. He sporadically reunited with Coleman, and he played Coleman's music without Coleman in the band Old and New Dreams. He collaborated with percussionists Colin Walcott and Nana Vasconcelos in Codona. His presence is pivotal on dates by Johnny Dyani (*Song for Biko*), and the Jazz Composers Orchestra (both *Escalator over the Hill* and *The Jazz Composers Orchestra*), to name just a few, and his rock-session employers included Lou Reed, Steve Hillage, and Bong Water. Cherry died at age 58 in 1995.

what to buy: Tragically little of the music Cherry recorded as a leader music is currently available. Start with *Symphony for Improvisers* 🎵🎵🎵 (Blue Note, 1966/1994, prod. Alfred Lion), the second of three 1965–66 sessions for the label that introduced his medley approach with a melodic charm and improv wit that have rarely been matched. *Symphony for Improvisors* features Cherry playing cornet, with Gato Barbieri (tenor saxophone), Pharoah Sanders (tenor sax, piccolo), Karl Berger (vibraphone, piano), Henry Grimes and Jenny Clark (bass), and Edward Blackwell (drums) in two far-ranging, roller-coaster suites that are by turns confrontational and conversational, serious and light-hearted, turbulent and serene. Fans of latter-day Barbieri may be amazed by his Coltranesque early days; fans of drummer Blackwell will be hard-pressed to find their man sounding more at home than in these Cherry sessions. The shortcomings here are Sanders's ineffectual piccolo on the title suite and the missed opportunity on "Manhattan Cry" for Sanders and Barbieri to play simultaneously. *El Corazon* 🎵🎵🎵 (ECM, 1982/1994, prod. Manfred Eicher) captures stately, varied duets by Cherry and frequent collaborator Blackwell on drums. The material ranges from Monk, to the evocation of a street dance, to textural forays, to a haunting, delicate melodica-drum tribute to the memory of Egyptian songstress Oum Kaltsom. *Mu* 🎵🎵🎵 (Le Jazz, 1996, prod. Jean Georgakarakos, Jean-Luc Young) finds the same duo in an altogether wilder live exchange recorded almost 25 years earlier. *Dona Nostra* 🎵🎵 (ECM, 1994, prod. Manfred Eicher) is a sympathetic if merely pleasant session.

worth searching for: Items well-worth looking for include the other two out-of-print Blue Note sessions, *Complete Communion* 🎵🎵🎵🎵 (Blue Note, 1965, prod. Alfred Lion) and *Where Is Brooklyn* 🎵🎵🎵🎵 (Blue Note, 1961, prod. Alfred Lion). Both dates are lovingly packaged along with *Symphony for Improvisers* in the now-unavailable, limited-edition Mosaic recordings, *The Complete Blue Note Recordings of Don Cherry* 🎵🎵🎵🎵 (Mosaic, 1993, prod. Alfred Lion, Michael Cuscuna). Also worth searching for is a vinyl or CD issue of *Brown Rice* 🎵🎵🎵 (A&M, 1975/1988, prod. Corrado Baccheli), Cherry's successful navigation of the line between fusion accessibility and the breadth of his musical interests. *Relativity Suite* 🎵🎵🎵🎵 (JCOA, 1973, prod. Don Cherry, Jazz Composers Orchestra Association) expands the Blue Note ideas into a manifesto on jazz globalism. *The Third World-Underground* 🎵🎵🎵 (Trio, 1973, prod. Dollar Brand, As-Sham), under the leadership of pianist Abdullah Ibrahim (then known as Dollar Brand) and saxophonist Carlos Ward, is a loose but exciting outing. *MultiKulti* 🎵🎵🎵 (A&M, 1990, prod. John Snyder, Don Cherry, John L. Price) was the last superior Cherry record, and while the recording is hard to find, a video of the same title is available through View Video.

influences:

◀◀ Fats Navarro, Ornette Coleman, Miles Davis, Clifford Brown, Thelonious Monk

▶▶ Lester Bowie, Wynton Marsalis, Butch Morris, Graham Haynes, Oregon

W. Kim Heron

Cyrus Chestnut

Born January 17, 1963, in Baltimore, MD.

A lot of great jazz piano players first performed live in the church and so it is no surprise that Cyrus Chestnut has come from those beginnings. The first time he played for the multitudes, he was seven years old and the place was the Mt. Calvary Baptist Church in Baltimore. From there he went on to study piano and music theory at a prep school before attending the Berklee College of Music. Since graduation, Chestnut has worked with Jon Hendricks, the Blanchard-Harrison Quintet, Wynton Marsalis, Betty Carter, and others. It was during the two years and counting that he spent with Carter when Chestnut started developing the need to go off on his own. When his boss told him he was ready get his own group together, the piano player took her advice and ended up cutting his very first album for a major label when he was 30 years old. Chestnut served as pianist in the Lincoln Center Jazz Orchestra during the 1995–96 season and maintains a busy touring schedule.

what to buy: *Earth Stories* &&&& (Atlantic, 1996, prod. Yves Beauvais, Cyrus Chestnut) is Chestnut's first album with horns but, he eases into the brass and reed work by playing with his trio prior to inviting the three horn players in. When the saxophones of Antonio Hart and Steven Carrington combine with Eddie Allen's trumpet and the trio for "Cooldaddy's Perspective," they brew up a swinging groove. Just as he does in concert, Chestnut leaves a little something for the listener to think about. In this case, he closes out his performance with a lovely version of the spiritual "In the Garden," a work arranged for solo piano that points the way toward the gospel album he would release later that year. With *Blessed Quietness: A Collection of Hymns, Spirituals, and Carols* &&&&& (Atlantic, 1996, prod. Yves Beauvais, Cyrus Chestnut), Chestnut takes another step towards greatness. The playing and phrasing is wonderful, which one would hope for when the practitioner has spent a near lifetime in the church. His choice of material is strong but there is also the seasonal factor to consider when you factor in titles like "We Three Kings," "The First Noel," and "Silent Night." But the timelessness of "Amazing Grace" and "Sometimes I Feel like a Motherless Child" should dissolve any problems a potential listener might have.

what to buy next: On *The Dark before the Dawn* &&&& (Atlantic, 1995, prod. Yves Beauvais) Chestnut demonstrates the kind of technique and power that can shake you out from your seat at twenty paces. Within the confines of this trio date he proves that he also has the sense and taste to use it sparingly, only when the music commands it. Chestnut also has a winning delicacy of touch that really comes through when he grafts part of a Bach invention onto "Baroque Impressions." His rendition of the old gospel tune, "It Is Well (With My Soul)" contains power as well, but it's the restrained power of quiet faith. To follow that song with the boisterous exuberance of "Kattin'" is to follow Chestnut back into the real world, rejuvenated and refreshed.

the rest:
Nut &&& (Evidence, 1992)
Another Direction &&& (Evidence, 1993)
Revelation &&&& (Atlantic, 1994)

influences:
⏪ James P. Johnson, Fats Waller, Art Tatum, Bud Powell

Garaud MacTaggart

Billy Childs

Born March 8, 1957, in Los Angeles, CA.

Pianist-composer Billy Childs has not yet made it into most jazz encyclopedias or into the publicity mainstream, yet he's been leaving his indelible mark on the scene, particularly with his composing skills. At the keyboards, he shows imagination and accomplished technique, creating fresh improvisations and interacting comprehensively with this side players. Childs began piano studies at age six. But it wasn't until he was age 14 and a student at Midland, a boy's boarding school in California, that he started serious piano studies. His exposure to jazz had occurred earlier and he was especially taken with trumpeter Freddie Hubbard's 1970 classic album, *Red Clay*. While attending a pre-college program, Childs met a fellow student, Larry Klein, who was to later gain recognition as a bassist and producer and who would eventually introduce Childs to Hubbard. During his undergraduate studies at the University of Southern California, Childs joined Hubbard's band in 1978. A simple twist of fate occurred when Childs was discouraged from majoring in piano studies and was steered by his teacher to study composition instead. Childs absorbed his lessons well as he continued to do after graduation, when he rejoined Hubbard's band for a six-year period and performed on Hubbard's 1981 releases, *Born to Be Blue* and *Keystone Bop: Sunday Night*. Childs recorded his first album as leader, *Take for Example This . . .*, for Windham Hill in 1988. After four more Windham Hill albums, Childs released albums for Stretch/GRP in 1995 and Shanachie in 1996, for which he began to receive the wider recognition he deserves. Childs began writing commissioned works for symphonies in 1992. In addition to leading his own groups, Childs collaborated with vocalist Diane Reeves, appearing on her two Blue Note recording sessions (*The Palo Alto Sessions* and *I Remember*), and worked with an array of other artists including Joe Locke, Bruce Forman, Allan Holdsworth, Eddie Daniels. Childs's dynamic two-handed keyboard approach makes him a stalwart player and combined with his talents as composer, he shows potential for becoming one of the idiom's celebrated musicians.

what's available: *The Child Within* &&&&& (Shanachie, 1996, prod. Billy Childs) finds the pianist leading a versatile session of ten tunes, a pleasing assortment of originals and classics.

With Dave Holland on bass and Jeff Watts on drums, two experts who are given room to expand, the energy is electric! Switching time signatures, swinging beats, brilliant spontaneous inventions, and Childs's unending melodic creativity contribute to one of his accessible best sessions. Add soloists such as trumpeter Terence Blanchard, saxophonists Steve Wilson and Ravi Coltrane, and trombonist Luis Bonilla, and you have a crackling session. Kicking off with an unhackneyed take on "Lover Man," the crew plows through three originals, then on to the blistering pace of "Alone Together" (enhanced by Blanchard in a top-flight solo), Childs's solo piano sitting on the reinvented Monk classic, "Pannonica," and three more gems. One of the best piano albums out there! On Chick Corea's Stretch Records, Billy Childs tests a new path after his Windham Hill dates. *I've Known Rivers* ♪♪♪♪ (Stretch/GRP, 1995, prod. Billy Childs) finds Childs exploring more contemporary-sounding turf. Inspired by the poetry of Langston Hughes, Rainer Maria Rilke, Walt Whitman, and others, he collaborates with featured soloists Bob Sheppard (reeds), Scott Henderson (electric guitar), and rhythm-makers Jimmy Johnson (electric bass), and Michael Baker (drums). Vocalist Diane Reeves guests on one track and Wren Brown recites Langston Hughes poetry preceding the title tune. Nine compositions/arrangements by Childs serve as a showcase for another side of his musical personality. Briefly exposing his mainstream musings, Childs keeps the session in balance for those fans, but the beats and musical flow are definitely on the contemporary side.

worth searching for: Two top-notch sessions, both out of print, were originally recorded on what can be considered as a stylistically unsuitable label for a straight-ahead jazz musician. Check used bins for Childs's album *Take for Example This . . .* ♪♪♪♪ (Windham Hill, 1988, prod. Billy Childs, Andy Narell). A collection of eight originals, performed in settings from trio to quartet, the album focus is on the leader's idea-rich, lyrical, oft-swinging, straight-ahead stylings and his bop to ballad compositions which lay the groundwork for fine soloing by saxophonist Bob Sheppard, and assorted rhythm players. Also out of print, *Portrait of a Player* ♪♪♪♪ (Windham Hill, 1993, prod. Billy Childs, Andy Narell) features Childs in an A-one mainstream jazz trio setting with bassist Tony Dumas and drummer Billy Kilson. Childs draws from the vast piano tradition, featuring compositions by Bill Evans, Cedar Walton, Ivan Lins, and others. Highlights from the mixture of 10 standards and Childs's originals, include a sweet reading of Walton's "Bolivia," a sentimental version of popular gem, "Darn That Dream," and two Childs's originals, the darkly romantic "The End of Innocence"

and the cleverly paced bopper, "Flanagan." The album is another splendid showcase for this fluent pianist and it's a shame that it's unavailable.

Nancy Ann Lee

Ellen Christi
Born 1950.

Ellen Christi is one of the great undiscovered vocalists in jazz and improvised music. Her art incorporates a wide range of vocal effects (shrieks, whispers, growls, melismatic warbles) as well as more standard jazz singing. But she's less rooted in the jazz tradition than her contemporaries, and she has a tendency to work in unusual group formats. Christi's first recordings were with the New York City Arts Collective, a loose grouping of musicians, film, and visual artists. She recording several albums with the collective, put out a few solo albums and worked with other artists, such as singer Lisa Sokolov and the Italian quartet Art Studio. As a lyricist, she's unafraid to tackle sensitive subjects (drug abuse, homelessness) in an unsentimental manner.

what to buy: Christi's collaboration with Fiorenzo Sordini and other members of Art Studio, *A Piece of the Rock* ♪♪♪♪ (Splasc(h), 1990, prod. Peppo Spagnoli) is a rhythmically solid set, and the three-horn front line (Christi frequently plays horn) gives it a full texture. *Instant Reality* ♪♪♪♪ (Network, 1992, prod. Ellen Christi), a quintet recording with her New York group, includes tight interplay between Christi and cellist Thomas Ulrich. The set contains a wonderful cover of Charlie Haden's "Silence" and versions of her previously recorded "Senza Parole" and "Captain Gregor."

what to buy next: With Claudio Lodati, another member of Art Studio and frequent Christi collaborator, *Dreamers* ♪♪♪♪ (Splasc(h), 1990, prod. Peppo Spagnoli) is an intimate work with two players remarkably well attuned to each other. At its best, on the languid "Malibu" and the apocalyptic "Captain Gregor," the album contains some of Christi's best singing.

best of the rest:
(With Claudio Lodati) *Vocal Desires* ♪♪♪ (CMC, 1994)

Robert Iannapollo

Charlie Christian
Born July 29, 1916, in Dallas, TX. Died March 2, 1942, in New York, NY.

Though he was not quite the first electric guitarist in jazz (Eddie Durham beat him to it), Charlie Christian raised the electric guitar from novelty to prominence in the genre. For the first time, guitar could be properly heard over the other players in large ensembles (before the days of P.A. systems and mixing consoles) and thus could move from being strictly a rhythm section instrument to playing an important solo role.

In 1939, John Hammond learned of Christian's talent and managed to hook him up with Benny Goodman. Most of the material we have from Christian was recorded from that time up until his death. Christian was also among the players of the time, like Charlie Parker and Dizzy Gillespie, who rode the crest of the wave that carried them from swing to bebop. In 1941, he came down with tuberculosis and died the next year at a mere 25 years of age.

what to buy: *The Genius of the Electric Guitar* 𝄫𝄫𝄫𝄫 (Columbia, 1987, prod. John Hammond) concentrates on Christian's recordings with Benny Goodman from 1939 to 1941. They include "Solo Flight," "Good Enough to Keep" (a.k.a. "Air Mail Special"), and "Honeysuckle Rose." The template for jazz guitar for the next 30 years (at least) is laid out here, though much of the music when Christian isn't playing is dated.

what to buy next: Christian is featured on the 1941 jam session recording *Swing to Bop* 𝄫𝄫𝄫 (Natasha, 1993) from the legendary New York nightclub Minton's with Thelonious Monk (piano), Kenny Clarke (drums), Joe Guy (trumpet), and Nick Fenton (bass). It includes five tracks including "Swing to Bop" and "Stompin' at the Savoy." While the recording quality is primitive, the spirit of the session is definitely captured and of incredible historical significance.

influences:

◄◄ Charlie Parker, Dizzy Gillespie, Benny Goodman

►► Wes Montgomery, Barney Kessel, George Benson, Herb Ellis, Pat Martino

Chris Meloche

Jodie Christian

Born February 2, 1932, in Chicago, IL.

With a nearly five-decade career behind him, pianist Jodie Christian still isn't an often-heard name. Yet, the veteran Chicago jazz pianist, a self-described "professional sideman," has performed with major jazz musicians and recorded with Stan Getz, Eddie Harris, Chet Baker, Sonny Stitt, Buddy Montgomery, Roscoe Mitchell, and others since his career began in 1948. Christian's accolades, as with many other jazz artists who choose to remain in their home towns away from New York City, have come only recently as he gained wider exposure. In 1994 he was honored for his lengthy, fruitful career and his commitment to community by being named an Arts Midwest Jazz Master. Christian's early influences came from his parents, self-taught pianists who played for church and house parties. Christian went to Chicago School of Music to study piano in the 1940s. As did many African American jazz musicians, Christian fortified his playing in church. Yet, he was also influenced by artists of the day, singer-pianist Nat King Cole, for one. Christian still sings adeptly, although his focus remains on his piano skills. The lifelong Southsider was a charter member of Chicago's Association for the Advancement of Creative Musicians (AACM) in 1965, and although those avant-garde influences can often be heard in his playing, he considers himself a bebop-influenced player who can play outside the music. During the 1970s Christian toured for several years with saxophonist Eddie Harris, and has toured overseas with E. Parker McDougal and Roscoe Mitchell, as well as accompanying many visiting jazz greats at Chicago venues such as the Jazz Showcase and the Green Mill. Although recording many albums as a sideman on Verve, Cadet/Argo, Prestige, and other labels, Christian didn't make his debut as leader until his 1992 Delmark album. Since then he has recorded as leader and sideman with Chicagoans Lin Halliday, Ira Sullivan, Frank Walton, Brad Goode, Mike Smith, Roscoe Mitchell, Malachi Favors, and others, and has toured Europe with other Delmark artists such as avant-garde saxophonist Fred Anderson and drummer/percussionist Kahil El'Zabar. Christian's devotion as a Jehovah's Witness for over 25 years certainly seems to influence his playing. He talks about trying to keep his life in balance, and you'll hear a sense of equilibrium in his work with musicians in a variety of settings from avant garde to traditional.

what to buy: *Front Line* 𝄫𝄫𝄫𝄫 (Delmark, 1996, prod. Robert G. Koester) finds Christian leading an energized ten-tune session featuring fellow Arts Midwest Jazz Master Norris Turney on alto sax. They're joined by Sonny Cohn (a Basie band trumpeter from 1960–84), and tenor saxist Eddie Johnson (who stinted with Coleman Hawkins, Louis Jordan, and Cootie Williams). John Whitfield plays bass, while Gerryck King and Ernie Adams split drum duties. Christian plays brilliantly throughout the mixture of standards and originals, taking these illustrious veterans on a delightfully pleasing journey. These cats swing elegantly, especially on the Ellington classics, "In a Mellow Tone" and "Don't Get around Much Any More." But they're not so entrenched in the Swing era that they can't play harmonically advanced pieces such as the superbly arranged, horns-heavy version of Wayne Shorter's "Lester Left Town." A lot of accrued experience and compatibility among these players equates to an excellent listen and a top recommendation. Recorded in August, 1994, *Soul Fountain* ♫♫♫♫ (Delmark, 1997, prod. Robert. G. Koester) is Christian's fourth Delmark CD. The intimate nine-tune session showcases his warmly personal style as well as his skills as composer, especially on his solo piano renderings of "Abstract Impressions" and "Blessings." He's joined by bassist John Whitfield, drummer Ernie Adams, with alto saxophonist Art Porter and trumpeter Odies Williams expanding the trio to a quartet and quintet on some numbers. It's notable that the late young alto saxophonist Art Porter, who once told this writer that despite his bent on commercially viable contemporary jazz, he *could* comfortably play straight-ahead as he proves on a warm, elegant solo during his beautiful duo with Christian on the classic ballad, "My One and Only Love." Fans of the AACM (and Roscoe Mitchell) will enjoy Christian's avant-garde original, "Consequences," an engrossing quartet explosion with Mitchell at the helm playing soprano sax. These musicians work compatibly throughout, whether playing inside the chord changes or improvising beyond the boundaries.

what to buy next: *Rain or Shine* ♫♫♫♫ (Delmark, 1994, prod. Robert G. Koester), Christian's second album as leader, finds him mixing it up with Chicago's top players as sidemen in three dates in May and June, 1993. Christian is indeed challenged to perfection, showing off his vast musical experience with his talented Chicago-based cohorts—reedman Roscoe Mitchell, alto saxophonist Art Porter, trumpeter Paul McKee, bassist Larry Gray, and drummers Ernie Adams or Vincent Davis. Christian has an marvelous ability to draft uncommon original melodies, and his original "Coltrane's View" conveys masterful spirituality and free-wheeling AACM-influenced characteristics, greatly enhanced with Roscoe Mitchell blowing soprano sax on an extended solo. The nine selections offer a pleasant mix of styles and prove that Christian is as adept at comping as he is at creating exciting, contemporary solos. He may be in his senior years, but his nimble fingers can still fly over the keys as evidenced on the lightening-paced version of the standard, "Cherokee." Christian is a true craftsman at the keys! *Experience* ♫♫♫♫ (Delmark, 1992, prod. Robert G. Koester) is Christian's first album under his own direction. Featuring mostly standards, Christian executes a strong right-handed style on solo piano, performing a mixture of soothing, melodious selections (he even whistles accompaniment on "Blues Holiday") and joins with two other competent Chicagoans, bassist Larry Gray and drummer Vincent Davis. While his solo piano is tender and lyrical, Christian is equally expressive and comfortable in the interactive trio setting.

the rest:
Blues Holiday ♫♫♫ (SteepleChase, 1994)

influences:
◀◀ Nat King Cole, Art Tatum, Bud Powell, Pee Wee Wheaton

Nancy Ann Lee

Pete Christlieb

Born February 16, 1945, in Los Angeles, CA.

Living on the West Coast has rarely been the path to jazz stardom, which partially explains why Pete Christlieb, one of the most powerful tenor saxophonists of the past 30 years, remains a "musician's musician" rather than a festival headliner. A monster on up-tempo tunes, where his articulate, high-velocity lines spill out of his horn, he can also play blues and ballads with complete authority. Christlieb, whose father was a noted master of double reed instruments, started playing sax at 13. He worked with Chet Baker and Woody Herman in the '60s, then began his long association with Louie Bellson. He has played on sessions with Count Basie, Mel Lewis, Quincy Jones, Shelly Manne, and Gene Ammons among others and worked in bands accompanying Sarah Vaughan and Della Reese. A 25-year member of the old *Tonight Show* band, Christlieb has worked extensively in the studios on television and movie projects. He founded his own record label, Bosco, in the '80s, and released albums by Bellson, Bob Florence, and himself. In recent years he's been featured in Bill Holman's big band and Frank Capp's Juggernaut. His recordings for Bosco, Rahmp, Warner Bros., and Criss Cross are hard to find but well worth the effort. The best way to experience Christlieb is to look for him on Bellson's recordings since the late '60s, many of which feature him extensively.

what to buy: *Apogee* ♫♫♫♫ (Warner Bros., 1978, prod. Walter Becker, Donald Fagen) made quite a splash when it was released, since the pop press was trying to figure out why the cats behind Steely Dan produced an album by two little-known saxophonists, Christlieb and Warne Marsh. The answer was Becker and Fagan had big ears, and the pairing of two highly distinctive tenor players make *Apogee* one of the best blowing sessions of the late '70s. The rhythm section features pianist Lou Levy, bassist Jim Hughart, and drummer Nick Ceroli.

what to buy next: Louie Bellson's *Live at the Concord Summer Festival* ♫♫♫♫ (Concord Jazz, 1976, prod. Carl E. Jefferson) opens with Christlieb surging through his original "Now and Then." His ballad playing on "These Foolish Things" brings to mind Ben Webster, while Christlieb and trumpeter Blue Mitchell mix it up on "Tru Blue." The session also features Dick Nash (trombone), Ross Tompkins (piano), John Williams (bass), and Grant Geissman (guitar). A number of Christlieb's different sides come out on Louie Bellson's *Prime Time* ♫♫♫♫ (Concord Jazz, 1978, prod. Carl E. Jefferson), which mixes straight-ahead numbers with Latin, calypso, and funk. Christlieb takes a forceful solo on the opener, "Step Lightly," but really starts cooking on Ellington's "Cottontail." Christlieb shows off his gorgeous ballad style on Marian McPartland's "With You in Mind" and "What's New," while his own "Thrash-In" is an opportunity for some funky wailing. The session also features Ross Tompkins (piano) and John Williams (bass), with guitarist Bob Bain and percussionist Emil Richards added on the last four numbers.

best of the rest:

Jazz City ♫♫♫♫ (Rahmp, 1977)
Conversations with Warne Volume 1 ♫♫♫♫♫ (Criss Cross, 1979)
Going My Way ♫♫♫♫ (Bosco, 1982)
Mosaic ♫♫♫♫♫ (Capri, 1990)

influences:

⏮ Johnny Griffin

⏭ Rickey Woodard

Andrew Gilbert

June Christy

Born Shirley Luster, November 20, 1925, in Springfield, IL. Died June 21, 1990, in Los Angeles, CA.

After a typically rough, Depression-era childhood, June Christy started her professional singing career at the tender age of 13, fronting a button-down, society dance band. After a short string of similar gigs, she made her way in 1945 to the front of Stan Kenton's orchestra, replacing Anita O'Day. And, though many of her critics would say that she sounded too much like O'Day (just like Chris Connor, Christy's replacement in the orchestra, would be accused of sounding too much like Christy), it was during her three-year stint with the Kenton orchestra that she met her life-long husband (tenor saxophonist Bob Cooper) and, just as importantly, developed her huskily gentle and entirely individual singing style.

However, it wasn't until she left Kenton (entirely amicably, it must be noted, for he is the one who helped her sign with his label, Capitol) that Christy truly left her mark on music. Her 1955 *piece de resistance, Something Cool,* is a milestone and the flurry of recording activity that immediately followed it (seven albums' worth in four years) resulted, to varying degrees, in the high caliber work on which her legend is based.

Unfortunately, after that, little was heard from Christy, who died of kidney failure.

what to buy: The line between pop and jazz singers is a blurry one at best, and Christy is a typical example of a singer with feet planted firmly on both sides of the line. Certainly not prone to improvisational flights of fancy, she nonetheless evinces a singular style and, on *Something Cool* ♫♫♫♫ (Capitol, 1955/ 1991, prod. Bill Miller), more than any of her other recordings, it is matched with material that is off-beat enough to make the singer *and* the song shine beautifully. A sort of looney-tune song suite that benefitted equally from Christy's voice and conductor/arranger Pete Rugolo (a longtime Kenton collaborator), LP pressings from the early 1960s on were actually a re-recording of the suite made simply so it could be reprocessed into stereo. Thankfully, for the CD reissue, Capitol restored it to the original mono version and added 10 other 1950s-era tracks to round it out. This is an essential introduction to Christy, as well as a strong case for a reassessment of 1950s jazz/pop singers. Ironically, the 18-track *Great Ladies of Song: Spotlight on June Christy* ♫♫♫♫ (Alliance, 1994, prod. various) includes only two songs from the LP (and not even the gently mind-blowing title track), yet nonetheless provides a broad overview of Christy's Capitol catalog.

what to buy next: *The Misty Miss Christy* ♫♫♫♫ (Capitol, 1956/1992, reissue prod. Michael Cuscuna) is certainly her second best LP set, finding her settling back into more "acceptable" pop/torch setting (with a glorious reading of "'Round Midnight"), featuring Maynard Ferguson, Bud Shank, and hubby Cooper, and again conducted by Rugolo.

what to avoid: A flimsy compilation of Christy's late 1950s work with Shelly Manne's group and the Jerry Grey Orchestra, *A Lovely Way to Spend an Evening* ♫♫♫ (Jasmine, 1994) suffers both from poor sound and bad arrangements. Although the songs are swinging and Christy's voice is in good form, these were not her better days.

the rest:

Day Dreams ♫♫♫ (Capitol, 1955)
The Song Is June ♫♫♫ (Capitol, 1958)

worth searching for: Though not that shocking on paper, *Duet* ♫♫♫♫ (Capitol, 1955, reissue prod. Michael Cuscuna), a re-teaming of Christy with Stan Kenton, actually turns out to be a very strange-sounding record. Kenton's piano accompaniment varies between dissonant and subversively inappropriate, while Christy's vocal lines are pointed and darkly melancholic, resulting in tunes that may sound relatively straight-ahead but are, in essence, truly idiosyncratic.

influences:

◀◀ Anita O'Day

▶▶ Holly Cole, Diana Krall

Jason Ferguson

The Jim Cifelli New York Nonet

Formed 1996, in New York, NY.

Jim Cifelli, trumpet; Tim Horner, drums; Joel Frahm, tenor saxophone; Barbara Cifelli, baritone saxophone, bass clarinet, flute; Andy Gravish, trumpet; Cliff Lyons, alto and soprano saxophones, flute; Mary Ann McSweeney, bass; Pete McCann, guitar; Pete McGuiness, trombone.

After spending nearly ten years as a freelance trumpeter and composer, Jim Cifelli formed this nonet so he could hear his charts played. Based in Manhattan, the band utilized the Musician's Union Local 802 rehearsal hall. Their various credits describe a veritable history of jazz performance ensembles over the past several decades (Hank Jones, Clifford Jordan, Maynard Ferguson, Betty Carter, Toshiko Akiyoshi, Woody Herman, Buddy Rich, Phil Woods, Randy Brecker, etc.) Cifelli made the calls and set up the ensemble, and as he said, "If you make the calls, people call it your band." Starting out with just one of his own compositions and a handful of charts he bought from publishers (there's not an abundance of readily available material for the nonet), Cifelli eventually came to do more and more of the writing; thus, what had started as a sort of collective of active New York City players came to be called The Jim Cifelli New York Nonet. *Bullet Train* was released at the start of 1998 on Cifelli's own label, and it marked their active emergence as a performing ensemble. In addition to his work with the Nonet, Cifelli has been commissioned to write music for others, including his trumpet and piano sonata for the Canadian Brass.

what's available: *Bullet Train* 𝄞𝄞𝄞 (Short Notice Music, 1998, prod. Jim Cifelli, John Guth) is a smart mingling of tonal playfulness, strong themes, and inventive soloists. As a writer Cifelli is clearly in the tradition of other writer/arrangers who created works that exploit the strengths and character of the ensemble's players, while also fitting them into a nicely unified small bigband.

influences:

◀◀ Duke Ellington, Oliver Nelson, George Russell, Gil Evans

David Greenberger

Circle

Formed 1971.

Anthony Braxton, reeds, percussion; Chick Corea, piano; David Holland, bass, cello; Barry Altschul, drums.

This brief-lived avant-garde supergroup existed for a little more than a year and recorded one classic album. Corea and Holland had been playing in Miles Davis's quintet; they recorded with Altschul, and when Braxton was added, magic was bound to happen. After touring the United States and Europe, in the process of which their double live album was recorded at a Paris concert, the group officially ceased to exist in early 1972 when Corea left to pursue considerably more populist paths. The remaining members added multi-instrumentalist Sam Rivers and recorded another classic, *Conference of the Birds*, under Holland's leadership. Other reconfigurations, under Braxton's leadership, added trumpeter Kenny Wheeler or trombonist George Lewis to the fourth slot.

what's available: *Paris-Concert* 𝄞𝄞𝄞𝄞 (ECM, 1972, prod. Manfred Eicher) is a two-CD set which belongs in the collections of all who have even the slightest inclination towards the avant-garde. It blasts off with a cover of the Wayne Shorter–penned Miles Davis Quintet classic "Nefertiti" (which ECM consistently spells "Nefertitti" for unknown reasons), wends through tunes by the quartet members, and closes with an amazing interpretation of the standard "No Greater Love." Any jazz latecomers who doubt Corea's credentials as a serious musician are especially advised to check out "Duet," his track with Braxton. The ease with which all concerned move between "inside" and "outside" playing and between composition and improvisation, often recombining in different configurations (solos, duos, trios, quartet), makes this a *tour de force* of all the things that produce exciting jazz.

influences:

◀◀ Miles Davis Quintet

▶▶ Anthony Braxton Quartet, Dave Holland

Steve Holtje

Sonny Clark

Born July 21, 1931, in Herminie, PA. Died January 13, 1963, in New York, NY.

One of the best pianists within the bop/hard bop category (only eclipsed by Bud Powell and, to a different extent, Monk), it's unfortunate that Sonny Clark will probably be more remembered for the all-too common heroin/alcohol addictions that he struggled with than he will be for his genre-defining piano playing. It is fortunate, however, that the scant remaining evidence of his playing is some of his strongest. Born in a small (pop. 800) coal-mining town outside Pittsburgh, Clark moved out to the West Coast when he was 20 and began making the rounds with players like Wardell Gray and Oscar Pettiford. Replacing Kenny Drew in Buddy DeFranco's quartet in 1953, Clark served a two-year stint with the group that took him to Europe, Hawaii, and back to the West coast. In 1956 he worked with Harold Rumsey's All-Stars, as well as in the studio with Serge Chaloff (recording the seminal *Blue Serge*). In 1957 Clark went on the road as Dinah Washington's accompanist, winding up in New York, which is where he made his mark. His five Blue Note dates (recorded between July 1957 and November 1961) were his only as a leader and, though a few spotty live records round out his discography, those are the ones that find him at the height of his powers. Oddly enough, the effects of his addictions never showed in the ebullient, yet relaxed grooves of his playing. However, they certainly took their toll and before he turned 32, Clark was another of jazz's unfulfilled promises.

what to buy: By far his strongest date, *Cool Struttin'* ♫♫♫♫ (Blue Note, 1958, prod. Alfred Lion) is a hard-bop masterpiece that finds Clark in esteemed company. Jackie McLean, Art Farmer, Paul Chambers, and Philly Joe Jones all shine brightly on this inspired album. With selections that mirror Clark's easygoing demeanor, the four songs here (with two more from the same session appended on the CD) illustrate perfectly the appeal of hard bop without falling into any cornbread skillets along the way. The effortless interplay between the five players is a joy (especially on their nearly giddy take on "Sippin' at Bells") and, though Clark is certainly the star here, he's unafraid to let the group dazzle as well.

what to buy next: Clark's debut as a leader, *Dial "S" for Sonny* ♫♫♫♫ (Blue Note, 1957, prod. Alfred Lion), demonstrates two things. One, he knows the right people, as Art Farmer, Curtis Fuller, Hank Mobley, Wilbur Ware, and Louis Hayes all make marvelous contributions here. Two, to have been one of the strongest hard bop pianists around, he sure does seem to have a good time playing. Light hearted and groove-heavy, *Dial "S"* still retains a strict adherence to form, never failing to deliver on any of its many melodic promises. By 1961 Clark's ideas had shifted somewhat and *Leapin' and Lopin'* ♫♫♫♫ (Blue Note, 1961, prod. Alfred Lion), which would also be his last, finds him moving into slightly funkier territories with Tommy Turrentine (trumpet), Charlie Rouse (tenor sax), Butch Warren (bass), and Billy Higgins (drums). Yet his playing is at its strongest and,

---

SONNY CLARK (WITH GRANT GREEN)

song "It Ain't Necessarily So"

album *The Complete Quartets with Sonny Clark*
(Blue Note, 1961/1997)

instrument Piano

Monster Solo

---

sadly enough, gives only slight indication as to the direction he would have taken had he lived. Clark's seminal "Voodoo" is included here.

the rest:
Oakland 1955 ♫♫♫ (Uptown, 1955/1995)
Sonny Clark Trio ♫♫♫ (Blue Note, 1957/1988)
Trio 1960 ♫♫♫ (Jazz View, 1960)

worth searching for: The gem *Sonny's Crib* ♫♫♫♫ (Blue Note, 1957, prod. Alfred Lion) is currently out of print; it was reissued once in 1987 and then disappeared. However, it is well worth seeking out, given the top-notch performance by Clark as he is accompanied in fine style by John Coltrane, Donald Byrd, and Curtis Fuller. Not a masterpiece, but a cut above your average blowing session.

influences:
◀◀ Bud Powell, Horace Silver
▶▶ Herbie Hancock

Jason Ferguson

Kenny Clarke

Born January 9, 1914, in Pittsburgh, PA. Died January 26, 1985, in Paris, France.

Clarke was probably the most important figure in the transition from swing to early bebop drumming. His most notable innovation was shifting the basic time-keeping role from the bass drum to the ride cymbal, and then using the bass and snare drums to interject accents against the beat.

Clarke got his musical start in his home town of Pittsburgh, where he came up in bands led by Roy Eldridge, Claude Hopkins and Teddy Hill. In the early 1940s, he was in the house band at that cauldron of early bebop, Minton's Playhouse, where he came into musical contact with bebop founders Thelonious Monk, Dizzy Gillespie, Charlie Christian, and Bud Powell. There Clarke began developing his own influential ideas about timekeeping, earning the name "Klook" or "Klook-mop" for his distinctive style. After a short stint in the military, Clarke returned to New York and recorded prolifically with virtually all the top bop players. Clarke was a founding member of the Modern Jazz Quartet in 1951 and played with that group until 1955, when he moved to Paris, where he worked regularly with other expatriate or visiting American musicians, most notably with Bud Powell from 1959 to 1962. He also co-led the stimulating Clarke-Bolland Big Band in the 1960s. In addition to his influence on jazz drumming, Clarke is also well known for cowriting the bop classics "Salt Peanuts" (with Gillespie) and "Epistrophy" (with Monk).

what to buy: *Bohemia after Dark* ♫♫♫♫♫ (Savoy, 1956/1996, prod. Ozzie Cadena) is a classic hard bop session most notable for being the recording debut of the Adderley brothers, "Cannonball" and Nat. However, it is also a sterling example of how a strong drummer can effectively lead a diverse group of soloists. In addition to the Adderleys, this session features trumpeter Donald Byrd, tenor Jerome Richardson, pianists Horace Silver and Hank Jones, and bassist Paul Chambers.

what to buy next: *Pieces of Time* ♫♫♫♫ (Soul Note, 1983, prod. Giovanni Bonandrini) presents a rather novel idea in recorded jazz—several drummers playing together with no other instruments. Clarke is the eldest of the group, which also consists of Andrew Cyrille, Milford Graves, and Famoudou Don Moye, and he is probably the most conservative. However, he is also the most firmly in control. This distinctive record is well worth picking up.

what to avoid: Clarke recorded *The Paris Bebop Sessions* ♫♫ (Prestige, 1950/Disques Swing, 1990) with mostly French musi-

cians—and it shows why musicians in Europe usually sought out fellow Americans when possible.

the rest:
Special Kenny Clarke ♫♫♫♫ (1938–59/Jazz Time, 1991)
Telefunken Blues ♫♫♫ (Savoy, 1955/1993)
Kenny Clarke and Ernie Wilkins ♫♫♫ (Savoy, 1955)
Transatlantic Meetings ♫♫♫ (Vogue, 1955/1989)
Discoveries ♫♫♫♫ (Savoy, 1955/1990)
Klook's Clique ♫♫♫♫ (Savoy, 1957/1988)
Meets the Detroit Jazzmen ♫♫♫ (Savoy, 1957/1992)
Plays Andre Hodeir ♫♫♫♫ (Philips, 1957/1993)

worth searching for: Because the Clarke-Bolland big band worked only in Europe, they were never very popular in the States, so it's still hard to find any of their music in American stores. But their import CD *Three Adventures* ♫♫♫ (MPS, 1968/1992) can in fact be found and is worthwhile for documenting an important aspect of Clarke's European career.

influences:
◀◀ "Papa" Jo Jones
▶▶ Max Roach, Art Blakey, Connie Kay

see also: *Modern Jazz Quartet*

Dan Keener

Stanley Clarke

Born June 30, 1951, in Philadelphia, PA.

Few players can claim they've revolutionized their instrument. Stanley Clarke can. In the early 1970s, as a member of Return to Forever and as a solo artist, Clarke changed the bass vocabulary by incorporating and expanding upon the funk slap-'n'-pop style first popularized by Larry Graham. His solos were filled with rock lines derivative of Jimi Hendrix and John McLaughlin, while his backing and melodic style owed much to Scott LaFaro. It was Clarke's desire to be a melody player and soloist that led him to develop the electric version of the piccolo bass (a smaller bass tuned one octave higher than a normal bass). Clarke also uses a tenor bass (a regular bass, tuned one fourth higher, with lighter gauge strings) and the Flyde acoustic bass guitar (looks like a guitar, but is tuned lower and has four strings).

Boasting both impressive technical prowess and a broad musical palette, Clarke's career has been all over the map. The classically trained musician played with a number of R&B groups as a teenager, yet upon moving to New York after high school, he became a jazz purist. During the early 1970s Clarke established himself as solid straight-ahead bassist by playing with

Stanley Clarke **(Archive Photos)**

Joe Henderson, Dexter Gordon, Art Blakey, Gil Evans, Mel Lewis, Pharoah Sanders, Horace Silver, and Stan Getz. In 1972, Clarke joined Chick Corea on the groundbreaking *Return to Forever* album with Joe Farrell, Airto Moreira, and Flora Purim. Within a year, Clarke's solo career started to take off. At the same time he and Corea formed the second, more rock-oriented incarnation of Return to Forever, which attained tremendous commercial success. After the breakup of RTF in 1976, though he still toured with other musicians, including stints with Jeff Beck and the New Barbarians (featuring Keith Richards and Ron Wood), Clarke focused on his solo career, as he had already attained almost legendary status as a player.

Clarke's solo efforts, which include some classic albums, were generally in the jazz/rock vein in the mid-1970s, though they had some traditional influences. By the late 1970s, Clarke moved towards a more funk-oriented style and completely consummated his funk direction with the 1981 dance record he co-led with George Duke. The Clarke/Duke pairing was an instant

success, generating a top 20 hit, and the two toured together for four years. While there was no denying it was good funk, critics and jazz fans were hoping Clarke would return to a more jazz-based style, which he did when he toured with the excellent straight-ahead Echoes of an Era band. Since the mid-1980s, Clarke's output has drifted between hot contemporary jazz, innocuous smooth jazz, and R&B. His straight-ahead playing, however, has been rare. He's also taken some artistic chances, including a solo electric bass tour in 1986. An underrated composer, Clarke has scored a number of movie soundtracks, and from an arranging standpoint, his albums of late have been strong. He's also been an in-demand producer, overseeing recordings for Ramsey Lewis, Nancy Wilson, Roy Buchanan, Dee Dee Bridgewater, Flora Purim, and Maynard Ferguson.

Like many of the first generation of fusion players, Clarke constantly shifts directions, but there is no question that when he wants to be, he is still one of the baddest bass players on the scene.

what to buy: Easily one of the best albums from the mid-1970s, *Journey to Love* 𝄢𝄢𝄢 (Epic, 1975, prod. Stanley Clarke, Ken Scott) is all over the road with songs such as "Silly Putty" (which sounds like a soundtrack to a blaxploitation film) to the R&B-styled psychedelic title track to a full-scale jam with Jeff Beck and the overblown "Concerto for Jazz/Rock Orchestra." But the best performance is the two-part "Song for John" featuring John McLaughlin, Chick Corea, and Clarke performing an acoustic tribute to John Coltrane, which ranks as one of the top moments in the lauded careers of all three men. *School Days* 𝄢𝄢𝄢 (Epic, 1976, prod. Stanley Clarke) is a classic fusion album noted for the title track. The other five songs mix Clarke's rock, jazz, and R&B influences quite nicely. But it's the all-acoustic "Desert Song" with John McLaughlin that blows away everything else. How hot was Clarke's band in the mid-1970s? Very hot. Taken mostly from live concerts (there is a studio outtake with McLaughlin), *Live 1976–1977* 𝄢𝄢𝄢 (Epic, 1991, prod. Stanley Clarke) features Clarke playing great hits such as "School Days." A standout duet with David Sancious on "Bass Folk Song No. 3" proves to be the album's majestic high point, with great colors and nuances. *If This Bass Could Only Talk* 𝄢𝄢𝄢 (Portrait, 1988, prod. Stanley Clarke) is a good mix of fusion and contemporary jazz, almost a welcome-back-from-funk album for jazzers. "Goodbye Pork Pie Hat" is killer and two duets with Gregory Hines, who provides percussion via tapping (reminiscent of a machine gun at one point), are the epitome of cool. It was easily Clarke's best album in years.

what to buy next: Clarke's friends on *Stanley Clarke & Friends: Live at the Greek* 𝄢𝄢𝄢 (Epic, 1994, prod. Stanley Clarke) are Larry Carlton, Billy Cobham, Najee, and Deron Johnson. It's really a great set as they plow through material like "All Blues," "Goodbye Pork Pie Hat," "Stratus," and full scale 21-minute "School Days" jam with a Clarke/Cobham duet intro. A classic live set, complete with long solos, makes it lots of fun. Stanley plays well and Najee shows he can be something other than a smooth jazz blower. With fusion heavyweights Tony Williams, Jan Hammer, and Bill Connors, *Stanley Clarke* 𝄢𝄢𝄢 (Epic, 1974, prod. Stanley Clarke) is very typical of the pre-R&B fusion movement. It's filled with hot rock–influenced playing by the better musicans of the period, but it really does sound somewhat dated. *At the Movies* 𝄢𝄢𝄢 (Epic, 1995, prod. Stanley Clarke) is a great place to hear how Clarke has taken new directions in his composition. Not a spectacular bass record, and some spots sound too much like "movie" music, but it's still filled with some good material. Smooth jazz is rarely done so well as *East River Drive* 𝄢𝄢𝄢 (Epic, 1993, prod. Stanley Clarke). Scoring soundtracks has improved Clarke's compositional abili-

ties, and while there is not a lot of fire or showmanship in his playing, the songs are good and the solos have a more melodic structure on this underrated album.

what to avoid: *Rock, Pebbles and Sand* 𝄢𝄢 (Epic, 1980, prod. Stanley Clarke) has some cool spots on it that are fun, but most of it is just plain bad hard rock or bad soul.

the rest:
I Wanna Play For You 𝄢𝄢𝄢 (Epic, 1979)
Clarke/Duke Project 𝄢𝄢𝄢 (Epic, 1981)
Clarke/Duke Project II 𝄢𝄢 (Epic, 1983)
Time Exposure 𝄢𝄢𝄢 (Epic, 1984)
Find Out! 𝄢𝄢𝄢 (Epic, 1985)
Hideaway 𝄢𝄢𝄢 (Epic, 1986)
Clarke/Duke Project III 𝄢𝄢𝄢 (Epic, 1990)
Passenger 57 Soundtrack 𝄢𝄢 (Slamm Dunk/Epic, 1992)

worth searching for: *Echoes of an Era* 𝄢𝄢𝄢 (Elektra Musician, 1982, prod. Lenny White) is a great straight-ahead date you probably will find in used record stores under Chick Corea or Freddie Hubbard. Chaka Khan, Joe Henderson, and Lenny White join in the festivities. This answers in the affirmative the question of whether Clarke could still swing.

influences:
◄◄ Charles Mingus, Paul Chambers, Ron Carter, Ray Brown, Larry Graham, Bootsy Collins, Scott LaFaro

►► Charles Fambrough, Victor Wooten, Kim Clarke, Abe Laboriel, John Patitucci, Alphonso Johnson

Paul MacArthur

James Clay

Born September 8, 1935, in Dallas, TX.

A reclusive performer, James Clay is among several Texas tenor players to have made a mark on the jazz scene (others include Illinois Jacquet and David "Fathead" Newman). Clay began playing the alto while in high school, then tenor and flute professionally in 1954. He moved to Los Angeles in 1956, where he made his first recordings as a sideman with Lawrence Marable and Red Mitchell. At that time he gained the attention of Cannonball Adderley, who subsequently produced his first album as a leader. Clay continued to record as a leader and sideman through the early 1960s before joining Ray Charles for a ten-year period. Clay then retired from the music scene, but re-emerged as a sideman with Billy Higgins and Paul Geurrero in the early 1980s. He began leading his own sessions again in the early 1990s. Though never known as a composer, and with no traces of the "free-jazz" movement in his music, Clay is said to have influenced Ornette Coleman, with whom Clay rehearsed in Los Angeles in the mid 1950s.

what to buy: Clay's flute playing on *A Double Dose of Soul* ♫♫♫ (Riverside, 1960/OJC, 1991, prod. Orrin Keepnews) makes the disc worthwhile, despite his shortcomings on tenor. The most noteworthy selections are "Pavanne" and the two takes of "New Delhi," in which Clay is teamed with composer/vibist Victor Feldman. The lone sax standout is the ballad "Lost Tears," where Clay plays with more lyricism than in the compositions of a faster tempo. Clay likely returns a favor to Cannonball Adderley who helped him get started on Riverside in 1960. Cornetist Nat Adderley, bassist Sam Jones, drummer Louis Hayes, were Cannonball's sideman. Gene Harris on piano rounds out the team. Unlike their initial collaboration on *The Sound of the Wide Open Spaces*, Clay is every bit David Newman's equal on *Cookin' at the Continental* ♫♫♫ (Antilles, 1992, prod. John Snyder). Clay keeps pace with Newman on the title track and the updated, more compact "Wide Open Spaces," though their marchy rendition of Bobby Timmons's "Moanin'" is less appealing. Contributions by trumpeter Roy Hargrove add to the brassy texture of "Sister Sadie," and bassist Christian McBride is paired with Clay for a unique duet version of "Crazeology."

what to avoid: Clay is upstaged on *The Sound of the Wide Open Spaces* ♫♫ (OJC, 1960, prod. Julian "Cannonball" Adderley) by the driving, authoritative play of fellow Texan (and co-leader) David "Fathead" Newman on tenor and pianist Wynton Kelly. Otherwise, the result of Adderley's first effort as a producer, available only on album, is a rather ordinary blowing session.

worth searching for: In one of his earliest recording dates, Clay displays inventiveness and dexterity on tenor and flute as a sideman on *Presenting Red Mitchell* ♫♫♫ (OJC, 1957, prod. Lester Koenig). Hearing Clay's mellow, smooth flute makes one wonder what he would offer today on that instrument. Now out of print, Clay's first offering as a leader after emerging from retirement, *I Let a Song Go out of My Heart* ♫♫♫ (Antilles, 1991, prod. John Snyder), displays his rhythm-and-blues approach to jazz, perhaps forged by his years with Ray Charles. Accompanied by the Cedar Walton trio, Clay presents fine readings of "Body and Soul" and "My Foolish Heart." Exceptionally fine is the Clay/Walton duet on "I Can't Get Started."

influences:

◄◄ Buster Smith, Sonny Rollins

►► Ornette Coleman

Jeff Samoray

Buck Clayton

Born Wilbur Dorsey Clayton, November 11, 1907, in Parsons, KS. Died December 8, 1991, in New York, NY.

After learning piano from his father, Buck Clayton switched to trumpet in his teens, and is known for his solo work and arrangements created for Count Basie during the late 1930s and early 1940s. Clayton began his professional career in Los Angeles, where he led a 14-piece band, which he took to Shanghai from 1934–36. When he returned to the United States, Clayton led his own groups. However, when he stopped in Kansas City on his way to New York to join Willie Bryant's band, Count Basie convinced him to take the trumpet spot recently vacated by Hot Lips Page. In 1943 Clayton was drafted by the Army, and spent most of his time in Kilmer, New Jersey, playing in various service bands. He was honorably discharged in 1946 and began writing arrangements for various bands, including Count Basie, Benny Goodman, and Harry James. In October 1946 Clayton took part in the first national Jazz at the Philharmonic tour organized by Norman Granz, and subsequently played on several other Granz tours. During the late 1940s and 1950s, Clayton worked with notable jazz musicians such as Joe Bushkin, Tony Parenti, and Jimmy Rushing. He led a sextet at Barney Josephson's Café Society in 1947, and toured Europe several times. In the mid-50s Clayton organized a series of remarkable recordings for Columbia, under the title of *Jam Session*, and in 1956 he led a combo at the Newport Jazz Festival that included Coleman Hawkins. During 1954 Clayton appeared in the film, *The Benny Goodman Story*. In late 1959 he joined Eddie Condon, touring Japan, and he toured Australia in 1964. Clayton can be seen in *Jazz on A Summer's Day*, a documentary film of the 1959 Newport Jazz Festival. Throughout the 1960s he continued to tour and record, but after 1969 was absent from music for a time due to lip and hernia surgery. Recommencing practice again in 1971, Clayton again began to tour and perform, and started teaching at Hunter College in New York City in the early 1980s. In 1983 he led a group of Basie sidemen to Europe, followed by his own big band in 1987. His autobiography, *Buck Clayton's Jazz World,* written with author/photographer Nancy Miller-Elliot, was published that same year.

what to buy: Just as the title states, *The Classic Swing of Buck Clayton* ♫♫♫♫ (Riverside, 1946/OJC, 1990), a compilation of three separate sessions, swings cohesively throughout. The first session, recorded in New York on July 24, 1946, includes trombonists Trummy Young and Dicky Wells, alto saxophonist George Johnson, a young Billy Taylor on piano, guitarist Brick

Fleagle, bassist Al McKibbon, and drummer Jimmy Crawford, playing songs such as Dick Vance's "Harlem Cradle Song" and "Sentimental Summer." Buck Clayton's Big Four, an unusual configuration of musicians recorded on June 26, 1946, features trumpeter Clayton, clarinetist Scoville Brown, guitarist Tiny Grimes, and bassist Sid Weiss performing Dick Wells's "Dawn Dance" and "Well-a-Poppin'," and Brick Fleagle's "It's Dizzy" and "Basie's Morning Bluesicale." Trummy Young's Big Seven headlines the third session during the fall of 1946, and features trumpeter Buck Clayton, trombonist Trummy Young, clarinetist Buster Bailey, alto saxophonist George Johnson, pianist Jimmy Jones, bassist John Levy, and drummer Cozy Cole. These sessions demonstrate the authentic sound of the swing era, nearly at its end in 1946, as well as documenting the biting clarity of Clayton's sound. *Goin' to Kansas City* ♫♫♫ (Riverside, 1960/OJC, 1990, prod. Tommy Gwaltney) was recorded in New York City on October 5–6, 1960, and features swinging arrangements from both Tommy Newsom and Tommy Gwaltney. Clayton/Gwaltney's Kansas City Nine features co-leaders Clayton (trumpet) and Gwaltney (alto sax, clarinet, vibes) with musicians Bobby Zottola (trumpet), Dickie Wells (trombone), Tommy Newsom (tenor saxophone, clarinet), Charlie Byrd (guitar), John Bunch (piano), Whitey Mitchell (bass), and drummer Buddy Schutz. Gwaltney's theme during this session, and purpose, was to pay tribute to the many influences that contributed to the Kansas City swing sound. To accomplish this, he and Tommy Newsom created new and modern arrangements to several tunes, without destroying the authenticity of the pieces. This CD includes several obscurities, such as Andy Razaf and Don Redman's "An Old Manuscript," Jay McShann and Charlie Parker's "The Jumping Blues," Jelly Roll Morton's "Midnight Mama," Count Basie's "John's Idea," Mary Lou Williams's "Steppin' Pretty," and Bennie Moten's "The New Tulsa Blues," among others. A fine tribute to an era that continues to give birth to fresh and vibrant ideas, even today.

what to buy next: *Buck & Buddy* ♫♫♫ (Prestige/Swingville, 1960/OJC, 1992, prod. Esmond Edwards) features Clayton leading a quintet featuring tenor saxophonist Buddy Tate, pianist Sir Charles Thompson, bassist Gene Ramey, and drummer Mousey Alexander. Clayton's muted and open horn work stand out remarkably throughout the session. The recording includes three original Clayton compositions: "High Life," "Birdland Betty," and "Kansas City Nights," as well as three standards, "When a Woman Loves a Man," "Thou Swell," and "Can't We Be Friends." These players definitely understand the blues, evoking emotion and instilling a solid swinging groove

throughout their work on all six tunes. Clayton and Buddy Tate *can* blow the blues, and prove it on *Buck & Buddy Blow the Blues* ♫♫♫ (Prestige/Swingville, 1961/OJC, 1995, prod. Esmond Edwards). This recording exemplifies classic swing era grooves inspired by Count Basie. The quintet for this session includes pianist Sir Charles Thompson, bassist Gene Ramey, and drummer Gus Johnson, in addition to Clayton and Tate. Three compositions, "Rompin' at Red Bank," "Blue Creek," and "Don't Mind if I Do," were composed by Tate, while the other four compositions, "A Swingin' Doll," "Dallas Delight," "Blue Breeze," and "Blue Ebony," were composed by Clayton. All six tunes are drawn from the blues, and whether the group is playing beautifully constructed lines of a sensitive slow blues, such as "Blue Creek," or an uptempo foot-tapping blues, such as "A Swingin' Doll," these musicians hit solid swinging grooves at all times. Pianist Thompson is the only non-Basie-ite, however, he clearly understands the task at hand. Clayton's brilliant sound and subtle muted work, in addition to Tate's warmth, pervade the session. The music is infectious, making this CD worthy of adding to any collection.

influences:
◀◀ Louis Armstrong

Susan K. Berlowitz

Clayton-Hamilton Orchestra
See: Jeff Hamilton

Clever Jeff
Born Jeff Jones.

Jazzier than D.J. Jeff and fresher than the Prince of Bel Air, Jeff Jones is one of the better examples of what happens when a hip-hop artist just can't shake his jazz jones. The son of a female jazz singer, Jeff grew up playing drums and keyboards and formed a funk band in high school. In 1993, he hooked up with producer Dave G, signed a deal with Qwest, and released an underrated debut, *Jazz Hop Soul.* The hip-hop world wasn't hip to the album, though, and Jeff was released by Qwest. The Bay Area–based artist recently resurfaced on the progressive San Francisco hip-hop/dance label, OM, to release his second album, *God Quality.*

what's available: Hip-bop hooray for *Jazz Hop Soul* ♫♫♫ (Qwest/Warner, 1994, prod. Dave G), a swinging, verve-filled album that isn't far removed in sound or spirit from Guru's Jazzmatazz. With a guest list that includes singer Mike Marshall (ex–Timex Social Club/Club Nouveau) and heralded young saxophonist Dave Ellis (ex–Charlie Hunter Trio), *God Quality* ♫♫♫

(OM, 1997, prod. various) has many of the same qualities that made *Jazz Hop Soul* such a winner. Of particular note is "The Ghetto Anthem," which makes a socially conscious effort to keep it real *positive*.

influences:

◀◀ Jazzmatazz, Dream Warriors

Josh Freedom du Lac

Alex Cline

Born 1956.

Alex Cline belongs to that rare breed of percussionists who value space, silence, and understatement as much as pulse and activity. Employing a panoply of Western and non-Western percussion instruments, Cline displays an acute sensitivity to finer nuances of sonority usually overlooked by mere "drummers." Not that he can't summon energy when the situation demands it—check out his dates with reed omnivore Vinny Golia and guitarist G.E. Stinson for a taste of his more swinging, propulsive work. Like his brother, guitarist Nels Cline (with Alex a key member of Los Angeles' furtive musical avant-garde), Alex is a musician's musician who is equally comfortable playing inside or outside conventional musical structures.

The recordings released under Cline's own name tend to favor sparse settings for voice, strings, bells, and delicate percussion. These outings sometimes veer perilously close to New Age bathos, but with rather more intelligence, depth, and musicality.

what to buy: *The Lamp and the Star* ♪♪♪♪ (ECM, 1987, prod. Manfred Eicher) is understated, folk-inflected chamber jazz featuring the ethereal vocals of Aina Kemanis.

the rest:

Montsalvat ♪♪♪ (Nine Winds, 1995)

worth searching for: *Gregg Bendian's Interzone* ♪♪♪♪ (Eremite, 1996, prod. Gregg Bendian, Michael Ehlers) finds Cline in the drum chair while his fellow percussionist sticks with vibes and glockenspiel, and the tightly structured Bendian compositions offer Cline quite a showcase for his kaleidoscopic playing.

influences:

◀◀ Famoudou Don Moye, Milford Graves, Andrew Cyrille

▶▶ Gregg Bendian, Lena Willemark, Ale Moller

Dennis Rea

Nels Cline

Born 1956.

Nels Cline is one of the most versatile, imaginative, and criminally unheralded guitarists active today, a dubious distinction he shares with Christy Doran, James Emery, and a handful of others. Combining jaw-dropping chops with a keen musical intelligence, Cline displays an encyclopedic mastery of guitar styles that encompasses delicate lyricism, sonic abstractions, and skull-crunching metallic flights. In the late 1970s, Cline played in the chamber-jazz group Quartet Music with his brother, percussionist Alex Cline, and other rising talents on the Los Angeles new music scene. He emerged from several years in relative obscurity with his 1987 release, *Angelica*, which added acid-toned New York City altoist Tim Berne to a roster of longtime Cline collaborators. In the early 1990s, the guitarist formed the amped-up Nels Cline Trio, perhaps the best vehicle to date for Cline's guitar excursions, which range from probing, reflective balladry to knotty riffing to bracing freeform assaults. In addition to his trio, Cline regularly performs with his brother and the constellation of creative musicians associated with reedsman Vinny Golia's adventurous Nine Winds record label. He is also active in the rock domain, collaborating with ex-Minuteman Mike Watt, avant country-rockers Geraldine Fibbers, and Sonic Youth guitar terrorist Thurston Moore, among others.

what to buy: The trio date *Silencer* ♪♪♪♪ (Enja, 1992, prod. Alex Cline, Jeff Gauthier), a well-balanced mix of energetic throwdowns and winsome ballads, serves as an excellent overview of Cline's multifarious playing talents.

what to buy next: On *Chest* ♪♪♪♪ (Little Brother, 1996, prod. Nels Cline, Brian Rosser), Cline probes the interface of music and noise in his most extreme recording as a leader.

the rest:

Angelica ♪♪♪ (Enja, 1987)
Ground ♪♪♪ (Krown Pocket, 1995)

influences:

◀◀ John Abercrombie, Pat Metheny, Bill Frisell

▶▶ Christy Doran, Brad Shoeppach

Dennis Rea

Rosemary Clooney

Born May 23, 1928, in Maysville, KY.

Among the finest jazz-influenced popular singers of the post-

World War II era, Rosemary Clooney is a masterful interpreter of the American songbook. Though she rose to popularity singing novelty tunes, she has always possessed a warm, husky voice and the gift, like all great singers, to emotionally inhabit her material. Though she isn't an improvisor herself, with her inimitable phrasing and excellent sense of time she is always at home working with jazz musicians. Clooney broke into show business singing on the radio in Cincinnati with her sister Betty. Local gigs brought them to the attention of band leader Tony Pastor, and in 1947 the Clooney Sisters made their debut in Atlantic City. After two years on the road, Betty returned to Cincinnati and Rosemary went to New York, where she was quickly signed by Columbia Records. Beginning in the early 1950s, Clooney scored a series of hits produced by Mitch Miller, starting with "Come on-a My House." Her fame increased when she moved to Hollywood, married actor Jose Ferrer, and began appearing in movies, including *Here Come the Girls, The Stars and Singing,* and *White Christmas,* which began her long association with Bing Crosby. She maintained her jazz credentials through her recordings with the Benny Goodman Sextet, Woody Herman and the Hi-Lo's, and her classic album with Duke Ellington and Billy Strayhorn, *Blue Rose.* Prescription drug abuse and emotional problems sidelined Clooney in the late 1960s, but she began performing again in the mid-1970s and by the end of the decade had begun her remarkable series of albums for the Concord label. Working with tenor saxophonist Scott Hamilton, cornetist Warren Vache Jr., and other musicians from the Concord roster, Clooney has recorded nearly two dozen albums, often focusing on the work of one composer, or lyricist, or song-writing team.

what to buy: *Love* ♫♫♫♫ (Reprise, 1963/1995, prod. Dick Peirce) is the perfect pop/jazz vocal album, a masterpiece with Clooney in top form singing a dozen tunes arranged by Nelson Riddle (with whom she was involved at the time). The soft, dreamy Riddle arrangements bring out Clooney's sensual side and she sings with an intimacy and emotional knowledge that are rarely heard in pop music. Random highlights include the opening "Invitation," and the deeply felt "More Than You Know." The CD also includes two bonus tracks arranged by Bob Thompson. *Sings the Music of Harold Arlen* ♫♫♫♫ (Concord Jazz, 1983, prod. Carl E. Jefferson) lets Clooney sample from the vast book of the great composer, and she selects tunes like someone shopping at Tiffany's. "My Shining Hour," "Stormy Weather," and "Hurray for Love" are all interpreted masterfully by Clooney, who also has fun with "Ding Dong the Witch Is Dead." Clooney revisits her formative years in the big band era

with *Girl Singer* ♫♫♫♫ (Concord Jazz, 1992, prod. Carl E. Jefferson), a lush session with well-conceived arrangements by John Oddo and Peter Matz. No nostalgia here though, as she covers contemporary gems by Jobim, Dave Frishberg, and Johnny Mandel as well as Ellington, Porter, and Vernon Duke. The introduction to "Straighten up and Fly Right" is from the Clooney Sisters' 1945 audition tape! There's no overarching theme on *Do You Miss New York?* ♫♫♫♫ (Concord Jazz, 1993, prod. Carl E. Jefferson) except good songs and great singing. She seems to have a special relationship with every song. "I Ain't Got Nothin' but the Blues" was dropped in from her Ellington/Strayhorn album *Blue Rose.* "As Long as I Live" and "It's Only a Paper Moon," performed as duets with John Pizzarelli, were written by her close friend Harold Arlen. She is joined once again by Hamilton, Vache, guitarist Bucky Pizzarelli, and her musical director John Oddo.

what to buy next: It had been more than a decade since Clooney had made a good record when *Everything's Coming up Rosie* ♫♫♫♫ (Concord Jazz, 1977, prod. Carl E. Jefferson) came out, marking the beginning of her remarkable comeback. It also began her relationship with tenor saxophonist Scott Hamilton and the Concord studio players, a rare example of complete trust between a singer and jazz musicians. *Sings the Lyrics of Ira Gershwin* ♫♫♫♫ (Concord Jazz, 1987, prod. Carl E. Jefferson) brings Clooney together with the music of her old friend and next-door neighbor. She gives the grade-A material first-class treatment and the Concord regulars are on hand to make this another exemplary small group session. *Sings the Lyrics of Johnny Mercer* ♫♫♫♫ (Concord Jazz, 1987, prod. Carl E. Jefferson) pairs a great lyric interpreter with America's greatest lyricist. Joined by the usual suspects—tenor saxophonist Hamilton, cornetist Warren Vache, trombonist Dan Barrett, guitarist Ed Bickert, and pianist/musical director Oddo—Clooney sings both Mercer standards ("Laura" and "Skylark") and his lesser-known tunes ("When October Comes" and "P.S. I Love You"). Most singers of her generation long ago embraced nostalgia as a career move, but with *For the Duration* ♫♫♫♫ (Concord Jazz, 1991, prod. Carl E. Jefferson) Clooney sings 14 tunes associated with World War II and never makes a false emotional step. Oddo wrote tasteful string charts for six tunes, including a beautiful version of "September Song."

best of the rest:
Rosie Sings Bing ♫♫♫♫ (Concord Jazz, 1978)
Sings the Music of Cole Porter ♫♫♫♫ (Concord Jazz, 1982)
Sings the Music of Irving Berlin ♫♫♫♫ (Concord Jazz, 1984)
Sings the Music of Jimmy Van Heusen ♫♫♫♫ (Concord Jazz, 1986)

Sings Rodgers, Hart, and Hammerstein 🎵🎵🎵🎵 (Concord Jazz, 1990)
Still on the Road 🎵🎵🎵 (Concord Jazz, 1994)
Dedicated to Nelson 🎵🎵🎵 (Concord Jazz, 1996)

worth searching for: A masterpiece with gorgeous, haunting Billy Strayhorn arrangements, *Blue Rose* 🎵🎵🎵🎵 (Columbia, 1956, prod. Irving Townsend) captures Clooney at her sultry best. She covers Ellington standards "Sophisticated Lady" and "It Don't Mean a Thing," and obscure numbers such as "Grievin'" and "I'm Checkin' out, Goom Bye." *Marian McPartland's Piano Jazz with Guest Rosemary Clooney* 🎵🎵🎵🎵 (Jazz Alliance, 1992, prod. Dick Phipps) presents just two grand old dames having a wonderful time with each other, sharing their love of great songs and jazz.

influences:

◀◀ Jo Stafford, Patti Page

▶▶ Doris Day, Teresa Brewer

Andrew Gilbert

Clusone 3

Formed 1988, in Italy.

Han Bennink, drums; Michael Moore, reeds; Ernst Reijseger, cello.

The members of this trio had played together since 1980 when they joined with a pianist for a gig at Italy's Clusone Festival; since then they've kept the name. They're all-stars of the European avant-jazz circuit and leaven their musical adventures with a healthy dollop of humor, as expected from most Bennink projects.

what to buy: *Soft Lights & Sweet Music* (hat ART, 1995, prod. Westdeutscher Rudfunk, hat HUT Records, Ltd.) delivers a mostly Irving Berlin program with tongue firmly in cheek, but there is an obvious affection for this material as well. By turns tender ("What'll I Do") and raucous (a rowdy "Cheek to Cheek" married to a South African stomp by Sean Bergin), this recording finds Bennink in peak, playful form.

what to buy next: *Love Henry* 🎵🎵🎵🎵 (Gramavision, 1996, prod. Hans Wendl) has the advantage of presenting a complete concert by the trio which splendidly demonstrates the group dynamic as the members shift seamlessly from song to improvisation to song. One of the most arresting moments in their entire output is when they segue from a wild free improvisation into a gorgeous rendition of Kurt Weill's "Bilbao Song." The trio's second album, *I Am an Indian* 🎵🎵🎵🎵 (Gramavision, 1992, prod. Michael Moore, Ernst Reijseger, Han Bennink) is a collec-

tion of tracks from their North American and European tours. The enjoyable selection includes the rousing Berlin tune "I'm an Indian, Too" (twice) and delightful interpretations of two Herbie Nichols compositions.

the rest:

Clusone 3 🎵🎵🎵 (Ramboy, 1990)

influences:

◀◀ Irving Berlin

▶▶ Tiny Bell Trio, Babkas, Spanish Fly

Robert Iannapollo and Steve Holtje

Arnett Cobb

Born August 10, 1918, Houston, TX. Died March 24, 1989, Houston, TX.

Often known as "The Wild Man of the Tenor" and "The World's Wildest Tenorman," Arnett Cobb gained his first notoriety as a soloist in Lionel Hampton's band from 1942 to 1947. Even more noteworthy in documenting the spirit of this very soulful player is that, while illness and accidents plagued his career beginning shortly after he left Hampton's band, he never did give up performing. His big, fat, vivid tone is a jazz classic. His notes are filled with emotion whether he's blowing a muscular, up-tempo solo or slowly romancing a ballad. Along with Illinois Jacquet, Cobb's colorful, stomping style defined the early Houston, Texas tenor sound, a swingin' sound equally at home in jazz, soul/blues, or early R&B.

Cobb's father died of tuberculosis when he was six, and he was raised by his mother and maternal grandfather. He took up music at an early age, playing piano under the instruction of his grandmother. He tried the violin, trumpet, and C melody sax before taking up the tenor horn. Mostly self-taught on saxophone, Cobb performed in the marching band and stage band at Phyllis Wheatley High School until he graduated in 1935. A summer job between his junior and senior years touring with Frank Davis introduced Cobb to trumpet player Chester Boone. Back in Houston, Boone started a band to play the Harlem Grill, and Cobb held down the tenor chair six nights a week while he finished high school and into 1936. Cobb left Boone's band to play with Milton Larkin's band from 1936–42. Newly married in 1939, Cobb turned down Count Basie's offer to join his horn section as the replacement for Herschel Evans that year.

In 1942, Lionel Hampton invited Cobb to replace another well-known Houston tenor man, Illinois Jacquet. This time, Cobb said yes. Cobb took over not only Jacquet's slot in the band, but his famous solo on "Flyin' Home," since the tune was considered the property of the Hampton band. This famous piece was ultimately associated as much with Cobb as with Jacquet, thanks to Cobb's reworking, his many live performances and the recording of "Flyin' Home No. 2" by Cobb with Hampton. It was with Hampton's band that the "wild man" nickname stuck, as Cobb fit in easily with the frantic, feverish approach which characterized the old Hampton band. Often Hampton would march his band around the old Strand Theatre on Broadway, many times leading them strutting and leaping into the street.

Cobb stayed with Hampton until 1947, leaving to start his own combo. They recorded for Columbia and OKeh, and even backed Ruth Brown on some of her Atlantic records. He was a popular figure on the New York jazz scene when a spinal operation and a period of illness sidelined him from 1948–51. On the comeback trail, a near-fatal auto accident broke both legs, variously documented as in 1956 or 1957. Doctors told him he would not play again. Despite being handicapped to the extent of being forced to walk with crutches, Cobb would not give up music. Amazingly, the following year Cobb was not only playing again, but recording, with his first in a series of excellent sessions for the Prestige label, *Blow, Arnett, Blow*. Cobb lived in New Jersey and gigged with his small band, Cobb's Mobb, during the period when most of the Prestige recordings were made.

Eventually he returned to live primarily in Houston, playing nightly in a small cafe, in his words, playing "a little jazz, commercial music and what have you." Cobb made a number of recordings even into his later years and continued to record until near his death, even touring Europe in a tenor sax blowout with Jimmy Heath and Joe Henderson documented by Soul Note. The availability of various sessions ebbs and flows a bit, with import versions popping up and then falling out of print.

what to buy: *Arnett Blows for 1300* 𝄞𝄞𝄞𝄞 (Apollo Records, 1947/Delmark Records, 1994, reissue prod. Robert G. Koester, Steve Wagner) contains Cobb's first two recording sessions as a bandleader. He signed to Apollo Records while filling in for Billie Holiday at the Baby Grand nightclub in Harlem. Cobb's chops are solid and his playing swings. It's stomping, sizzling, textbook Texas tenor sax from the get-go. The first sessions were recorded while Cobb's band was playing nightly to SRO crowds at the Baby Grand. Listening, you feel a real resonance of time and place, an electric energy and sassy sophistication which reflects the times. "Cobb's Idea" was written by Cobb during his tenure with Hampton. Because most bandleaders retained co-composer credits for tunes written or improvised by members, "Top Flight" and "Still Flyin'" may sound familiar; they're slight revisions of Hampton-era tunes "Air Mail Special" and the clas-

sic "Flyin' Home." Cobb's former boss Milt Larkin is the vocalist. A sax player friend calls *Blow Arnett, Blow* a.k.a. *Go Power!!!* 𝄞𝄞𝄞𝄞 (Prestige, 1959) "the musical equivalent of a monster truck battle." The pairing of sax greats Cobb and Eddie "Lockjaw" Davis is a natural and the music is, well, monstrous. Included are later interpretations of three Cobb standards, "When I Grow Too Old to Dream," "Go, Red, Go," and "Dutch Kitchen Bounce." Exceptionally strong supporting musicians make for a vibrant ensemble sound. The more melancholy pieces on *Blue and Sentimental* 𝄞𝄞𝄞𝄞 (Prestige, 1960) with the Red Garland Trio make the title apt, but there is invention where you might expect clichés, and some up-tempo tunes that are equally surprising. Cobb had a way with ballads that was as provocative as the swingin' approach which got him his "wild man" nickname.

what to buy next: *Party Time* 𝄞𝄞𝄞 (Prestige, 1959) shines throughout, and includes a jaunty, swing-infused "Flying Home." The warm, fluid, vibrant solos Cobb puts down on his mellow composition "Slow Poke" are exceptionally beautiful, and the liner notes reveal this striking version was a "run-down" rehearsal take, accidentally recorded, which on playback proved to be a sparkling keeper. The title track of *Smooth Sailing* 𝄞𝄞𝄞 (Prestige, 1959) was written by Cobb and recorded by him on Columbia in 1950, a now out-of-print recording which was so popular in its day that Ella Fitzgerald later recorded a scat vocal of Cobb's solo on Decca. "I Don't Stand a Ghost of a Chance with You" was a Cobb staple in live performance; recorded here for the first time, it's an interesting showcase for Cobb's style, moving from moody and evocative to upbeat and wailing all in a single arrangement.

the rest:
(With Jimmy Heath and Joe Henderson) *Tenor Tribute* 𝄞𝄞𝄞𝄞 (Soul Note, 1990)
(With Jimmy Heath and Joe Henderson) *Tenor Tribute vol.2* 𝄞𝄞𝄞𝄞 (Soul Note, 1993)

worth searching for: The box set *Hamp: The Legendary Decca Recordings of Lionel Hampton* 𝄞𝄞𝄞𝄞 (Decca Jazz, 1996, reissue prod. Orrin Keepnews) archives the Hampton band's recordings on Decca from 1942 to 1963 and contains work by Jacquet and Cobb, as well as later tenor players. "Foot Pattin'" from *Blues Wail: Coleman Hawkins Plays the Blues* 𝄞𝄞𝄞𝄞 (Prestige, 1996, compilation prod. Ed Michel) features Cobb, Hawkins, Eddie "Lockjaw" Davis, and another Texan, Buddy Tate, and is taken from the currently out of print *Very Saxy* 𝄞𝄞𝄞𝄞 (Prestige, 1959) truly an all-star tenor sax album. Cobb recorded extensively throughout his career. If you're hooked, it's worth checking the used record shops for the original vinyl from his recording sessions on Columbia/OKeh, Progressive, Muse, and Bee Hive, as well as other Prestige efforts. From France, the rockin', bluesy 1970s Black & White label sessions include Milt Buckner and Gatemouth Brown. Also be on the lookout for *Show Time* ♪♪♪ (Fantasy, 1988, prod. David Thompson, Steve Williams) recorded live in Houston with personnel including Dizzy Gillespie and Jewel Brown.

influences:

◀◀ Coleman Hawkins, Illinois Jacquet, Ben Webster, Lester Young

▶▶ King Curtis, David "Fathead" Newman, Sonny Rollins

B.J. Huchtemann

Billy Cobham

Born May 16, 1944, in Gatun, Panama.

Billy Cobham's earliest influences were the carnival and parade music of his native land. As a young child in 1948, he moved with his family from Panama to Harlem, and later to Brooklyn, New York. He got his first set of drums at age four, and later got his foundation from playing in the drum corps (Marching and Maneuvering Corps), a statewide organization of bands promoted by Catholic churches. Cobham attended the Music & Arts high school, along with Al Foster, Larry Willis, Jimmy Owens, George Cables, and other budding jazz musicians. He enlisted in the Army in 1965 and after his release in 1968, Cobham joined Manhattan's jazz scene, performing with Jimmy Owens and Ron Carter in the New York Jazz Sextet. He toured with Horace Silver's group and met future jazz-rock fusion trendsetters Joe Zawinul, Wayne Shorter, Miroslav Vitous, John McLaughlin, Larry Coryell, and Chick Corea at Bank Street Recording studio. Cobham broke into studio work, playing with George Benson and James Brown, and played timbales at uptown Latin dances where he met trombonist Barry Rogers who was forming the horn-fronted rock band, Dreams. Cobham received broader exposure as a member of this band, an embryonic group that included the Brecker brothers and John Abercrombie. They recorded two albums together before disbanding in 1970.

Cobham also toured with Miles Davis and recorded several albums with the trumpeter during the 1970s. But the gig that brought him greatest prominence, securing his reputation for life, was as drummer for John McLaughlin's Mahavishnu Orchestra. Assembled a year after Weather Report, the band made three albums for Columbia from 1971–1973. A powerful drummer, Cobham revolutionized that decade's drum set tech-

nique, integrating easily into the high-decibel music which formed the core of their supergroup sets. Cobham certainly started off on the right foot as far as his solo career was concerned. His 1973 release *Spectrum* was a highlight of the jazz fusion era. It also contained some of the late rock guitarist Tommy Bolin's most shining moments (in duet with Jan Hammer) captured on tape. His album *Crosswinds* continued along similar lines but, the absence of Bolin's force was certainly felt. By the early 1980s, Cobham's career was becoming flat, and he took studio work making commercials and performed in the *Saturday Night Live Band*. He moved to Zurich, and though he kept busy globetrotting, he hardly played in the United States for five years. In the early 1990s, he traveled all over the world for clinics and performances, and by the mid-1990s was back on track, touring in the U. S. with his band. Since that time, he has continued to work as a session player with Stanley Clarke, Ron Carter, and others. Most of his solo outings have been less than spectacular compared to his earliest releases, and with the exception of two recordings with McLaughlin's Mahavishnu Orchestra, little of his work from the 1970s is available on CD.

what to buy: *Spectrum* ♪♪♪ (Atlantic, 1973/Rhino, 1992, prod. Billy Cobham) was one of the highlights of the 1970s jazz-rock fusion genre. The standout track on the album is "Stratus" which features the guitar proto-technics of Tommy Bolin along with Jan Hammer's Moog-synthesizer work. This is all held together by Cobham's drumming which is synched to the groove basslines of Lee Sklar. Recorded on May 14–16, 1973 in New York City, the album features 11 tunes, and includes soloists Joe Farrell (soprano/alto saxophones) and Jimmy Owens (flugelhorn/trumpet).

best of the rest:

Best of Billy Cobham ♪♪♪ (Atlantic/Rhino, 1987)
Billy's Best Hits ♪♪ (GRP, 1987)
The Traveler ♪♪♪ (Evidence, 1994)

worth searching for: Check out the CD reissues of the first two recordings featuring Cobham with John McLaughlin's Mahavishnu Orchestra, the classic *The Inner Mounting Flame* ♪♪♪♪ (Columbia, 1972/1989), and its follow up *Birds of Fire* ♪♪♪ (Columbia, 1973/1987).

influences:

◀◀ Elvin Jones, Tony Williams

▶▶ Lenny White, Peter Erskine

see also: *John McLaughlin*

Chris Meloche and Nancy Ann Lee

Al Cohn

Born November 24, 1925, in Brooklyn, NY. Died February 15, 1988, in Stroudsburg, PA.

Alvin Gilbert Cohn was a gifted arranger, prolific composer, and a master at finding the right notes to fit into his well-constructed, inventive, tenor saxophone solos, although his often dark, broad, brooding sound and driving rhythmic thrusts probably received more accolades from his musical peers than from the casual listening public. Cohn's studies included piano at age six and clarinet at 12, but he received no formal tenor sax training. He played in the Erasmus High School Band in his native Brooklyn and dabbled in arranging but took no courses in orchestration. He had a tremendous grasp of music theory and a harmonic sense beyond impressive, which, coupled with his ability to absorb the best from his musical experiences, led him to writing for radio and big bands. Cohn's personal tenor sax favorites included Zoot Sims, Sonny Stitt, and Lester Young.

During World War II years, he joined the bands of Joe Marsala and George Auld. In the late 1940s, Cohn played and arranged for Boyd Raeburn, Alvino Rey, Buddy Rich, and, later, the Woody Herman Second Herd, and the Artie Shaw Orchestra, where his section-mate was Zoot Sims. Following a brief hiatus from the music world, Cohn joined Elliot Lawrence as sideman-arranger in 1952, and subsequently free-lanced as writer-arranger for CBS radio and for television shows—*Hit Parade, Andy Williams,* and *Steve Allen.* From 1954–1956, Cohn was affiliated with RCA Victor and producer Jack Lewis, arranging and playing as leader and sideman on numerous jazz albums, with Joe Newman, Dick Collins, Ernie Wilkins, Freddie Green, and his old section-mate, Sims, with whom he formed the Al Cohn-Zoot Sims Quintet in 1957. By 1959, these two modernists had played many gigs together, spending much of their time at the Half-Note, a comfortable spot near New York City's Greenwich Village. The pair continued their friendly association, off and on, until Sims's untimely death in 1985. Cohn played, recorded and wrote throughout the 1960s, 1970s, and into the 1980s, receiving Broadway credits along the way as principal arranger for musicals *Raisin, Music, Music, Music,* and *Sophisticated Ladies.* During the 1980s, Cohn did more club dates and festivals, playing his horn almost up to the time of his death from liver cancer in 1988. He left a legacy of charts and hundreds of recordings, not many of which have been reissued on CD.

Billy Cobham **(AP/Wide World Photos)**

what to buy: The Al Cohn duets with pianist Jimmy Rowles, *Heavy Love* ♫♫♫♫ (Xanadu, 1978/1995, prod. Don Schlitten) features the compatible proponents of hard-swinging jazz as they swagger, strut, and joyfully celebrate. This session catches the pair at the top of their game, hooking listeners from the first tune, "Them There Eyes," which is full of crazy breaks, chases, stop-time variations, and broken chords. Cohen's earthy, confident lines blend perfectly with Rowles's off-beat chords and dazzling, single-line excursions. *Rifftide* ♫♫♫♫ (Timeless, 1987, prod. Wim Wigt), recorded in Holland in June, 1987 with a solid Dutch rhythm section, finds Cohn exploring an array of engaging standards by top jazz composers. *Al and Zoot* ♫♫♫♫ (Coral, 1957/Decca-MCA, 1990) documents an earlier collaboration between Cohn and Sims (originally titled *The Al Cohn Quintet featuring Zoot Sims, 1957*) aided and abetted by drummer Nick Stabulas, bassist Teddy Kotick, and long-time Cohn associate, pianist Mose Allison. Highlights include a delightful boppish interweaving of the two horns on "Halley's Comet" and "Two Funky People," where they both switch to clarinet to yield an earthy blues performance. *Standards of Excellence* ♫♫♫♫ (Concord, 1984, prod. Frank Dorritie) offers Cohn playing a tasteful batch of standards and sharing the solo spot with guitarist Herb Ellis, supported by bassist Monty Budwig and drummer Jimmie Smith. Johnny Mercer's "I Remember You" and the Gershwin's "Embraceable You" are among tunes receiving tender, loving care.

what to buy next: *Body and Soul* ♫♫♫♫ (Muse, 1988/32 Jazz, 1997, prod. Don Schlitten) is one of the best of the two tenor offerings of Cohn and Sims, because of strong rhythmic support from pianist Jaki Byard, bassist George Duvivier, and drummer Mel Lewis. On *Nonpareil* ♫♫♫♫ (Concord, 1981, prod. Carl Jefferson), Cohn returns to the quartet format with former Woody Herman teammate, Lou Levy. Concord regulars Jake Hanna (drums) and Marty Budwig (bass) join in to give special treatment to Billy Strayhorn's "Raincheck" and Kurt Weill's "This Is New." For those who want to check out Cohn's early work from the 1950s, search for the 1994 Savoy CD reissue of *The Progressive Al Cohn* ♫♫♫♫ (Progressive, 1953, prod. Gus Statiras). Be advised that Savoy also reissued the same material on CD under the name of *Cohn's Tones.* Hints of Don Byas and Ben Webster are evident along with more obvious Lesterisms. *Overtones* ♫♫♫♫ (Concord, 1982, prod. Carl Jefferson) is a strong, small group date featuring four Cohn originals and another Cohn, son Joe, who makes eloquent guitar contributions. Old pros pianist Hank Jones and bassist George Duvivier provide the right chemistry behind the leader's hard-swinging tenor sax.

best of the rest:
(With Zoot Sims) *Either Way* 𝄢𝄢𝄢𝄢 (Evidence, 1961)
(With Scott Hamilton and Buddy Tate) *Tour De Force* 𝄢𝄢𝄢 (Concord Jazz, 1982)
Al Cohn Meets the Jazz 7: Keeper of the Flame 𝄢𝄢𝄢 (Ronnie Scott's Jazz House, 1995)
Skylark 𝄢𝄢𝄢 (E.J.'s Records, 1996, 2-CD set)

worth searching for: *Al Cohn: The Final Performance* 𝄢𝄢𝄢𝄢 (Raz-M-Taz, 1988, prod. Al Porcino, Roger Rhodes) is a misnomer because Cohn would play another six months and record at least two more sessions before his death. As fine as his performance is on this classic big band material, the album (also released by Red Baron as *Al Cohn Meets Al Porcino*), is out of print. Also out of print is Cohn's album, *From A to Z and Beyond* 𝄢𝄢𝄢 (RCA/Bluebird 1987, prod. Ed Michel), mid-1950s material featuring material by Sims and Cohn, Ralph Burns, Ernie Wilkins, and others, and a dynamite rhythm section that includes Dave McKenna or Hank Jones on piano, bassist Milt Hinton, and drummer Osi Johnson. One more sterling session, *Be Loose* 𝄢𝄢𝄢𝄢 (Biograph, 1979), was reissued on a now out-of-print CD from the original 1956 Dawn recordings. The session won five stars in *Down Beat* magazine when originally issued and it is one of Al Cohn's best efforts ever.

John T. Bitter

Pat Coil
Born September 21, 1954, in Jefferson City, MO.

For those who follow television and film music, Pat Coil is a familiar name. He has added his keyboard magic to shows such as *Star Trek: The Next Generation, Voyager, Matlock, Murphy Brown, Knot's Landing, Dallas,* and *Falcon Crest,* among many others, and films such as *Star Trek: The Undiscovered Country,* and *Throw Momma from the Train.* Since moving to Tennessee from Los Angeles, Coil has served as music director for gospel singer Cee Cee Winans's show, *Cee Cee's Place,* and played on various TV specials. Besides three albums he recorded as a leader, Coil has played on dozens of projects, including Natalie Cole's 1992 Grammy winner, *Unforgetable,* as well as albums by Peter Cetera, Trisha Yearwood, Nancy Wilson, and Barry Manilow. He spent four years at North Texas State University, renowned for its jazz program, through which Coil, a tuba scholarship winner, quickly worked his way into the top group,

the One O'Clock Band. Upon leaving school, Woody Herman invited him to join one of his Thundering Heard installments, and Coil recorded several albums with Herman. He spent five years in Dallas, where he became an active session musician, mostly performing on radio and television commercials, and formed his own band, Recoil, before joining the Pat Metheny Group. Soon after his move to Los Angeles, Coil became a "first call" studio musician, working on albums by Tom Scott, Lyle Mays, Gerald Albright, Paulihno Da Costa, and the list goes on.

what to buy: *Schemes and Dreams* 𝄢𝄢𝄢𝄢 (Sheffield Lab, 1994, prod. Lyle Mays, Steve Rodby) shows Coil and his college roommate, Lyle Mays, know each other well. Although the recording contains a couple of burning tracks, it mostly explores the quieter nuances of jazz.

what to buy next: *Just Ahead* 𝄢𝄢𝄢𝄢 (Sheffield Lab, 1992, prod. Clair Marlo), a punchy contemporary jazz album, is full of clean-sounding, heartfelt performances.

the rest:
Steps 𝄢𝄢𝄢𝄢 (Sheffield Lab, 1990)
Gold 𝄢𝄢𝄢𝄢 (Sheffield Lab, 1996)

influences:
◀◀ Ramsey Lewis, Stan Kenton, The Beatles, Oscar Peterson, Ahmad Jamal

▶▶ Rob Mullins, Kym Pensyl, Alex Bugnon, Jim Beard

Ralph Burnett

Freddy Cole
Born October 15, 1931, in Chicago, IL.

Although singer-pianist Freddy Cole sounds a lot like his famous brother, Nat "King" Cole (d. 1965), he has a style all his own. The youngest of the five children of Edward and Paulina Nancy Cole, Freddy was influenced by three older brothers, Eddie, Ike, and Nat. The family moved from Alabama to the South side of Chicago where Freddy was born. He had started playing by age six; by his early he teens was playing professionally. Brother Eddie (d. 1970) was a bassist who led his own bands, Nat played piano, and brother Ike resides and works as a singer-pianist in Arizona. Cole has been recording since he was 21 years old, starting his career in 1952 with the single, "The Joke's on Me," for the obscure, Chicago-based Topper Records. Some moderate hit singles for various small labels followed and, in the 1980s, Cole formed his own label, First Shot.

In spite of his early talents, Cole was set to pursue a career in football until he injured his hand at age 16, and subsequent infection, operations, and intensive physical therapy kept him from realizing his gridiron dream. He began playing piano and singing in hometown clubs, pursued formal musical education at the Roosevelt Institute in Chicago, and in 1951 was accepted into the Juilliard School of Music. In 1953 he spent several months on the road with Earl Bostic's band with Johnny Coles and Benny Golson. He studied further at Boston's New England Conservatory of Music, earning a master's degree in 1956. In New York City Cole established his career, developing a vast repertoire of songs in Manhattan's posh bistros, performing commercial studio work as a pianist, and later, as vocalist. His recordings during the 1970s helped establish his international career and, able to sing a few songs in French, Portuguese, and Spanish, he continues to enjoy a big following in Brazil. Living in the shadow of older brother Nat, fame eluded Cole for years until his pivotal 1991 Sunnyside album, *I'm Not My Brother, I'm Me* (now out of print), and albums as leader for Sunnyside, Laserlight, and Muse. After signing with the Fantasy label in 1994 and making four albums, Cole has achieved the broader recognition he deserves. He tours widely with his trio throughout Europe, the Far East, and Brazil, in addition to performing at major U.S. jazz festivals and in nightclubs.

what to buy: A stickler for presentation, Cole has established himself best at shaping love ballads, selecting material listeners will find familiar and palatable, and choosing the right musicians to bring it all home. His performances are so perfected and his accompaniment so superb on each album that you could start with any of the recommended albums and base your purchase purely on which of your favorite tunes are featured. On *Always* 𝄞𝄞𝄞𝄞 (Fantasy, 1995, prod. Todd Barkan), Cole concentrates on delivering his laid-back vocals and leaves piano duties to the young, talented Cyrus Chestnut, who plays outstanding accompaniment on the eleven romantic ballads. Cole is a veteran whose confident treatment of lyrics yields a heart-warming listen. This album works because of tight, fluid interactions between the velvet-toned crooner and his superb instrumentalists. Bassist Tom Hubbard and drummer Yoron Israel complete the rhythm team, and an assortment of musicians assist, including saxophonists Antonio Hart, Grover Washington Jr, and Javon Jackson; trumpeters Byron Stripling, and Robin Eubanks; and string players Eileen Folson, Lesa Terry, Sanford Allen, and Al Brown. Cole's vocals are beautifully delivered and interwoven with memorable instrumental solos tucked into the splendid arrangements of classics such as

"Isn't She Lovely," "You Must Believe in Spring," "If," and surprise selections like Buffy Sainte-Marie's "Until It's Time for You to Go," and Robin Eubanks's "Interlude." Each track contains special moments, like Joe Locke's tender vibraphone solo on "Remember," Grover Washington's lyrical solo on "You Must Believe in Spring," Roger Rosenberg's lovesome baritone sax and clarinet solos on "I'm a Fool to Want You," and Eubanks's trombone solo on "Maybe You'll Be There." Cole and his cohorts put romance on the front burner with ultimate elegance and finesse. A romantic 14-tune album, *It's Crazy, but I'm in Love* 𝄞𝄞𝄞𝄞 (After 9, 1996, prod. Tony Smythe) features the singer in various settings, including a jazz orchestra augmented by strings. The versatile session is undated, but Cole claims he recorded the previously unreleased material "several years ago" and Touchwood Records (the parent company of After 9) bought the masters. Featured soloists include saxophonists George Young and Dave Tofani, trumpeter Marvin Stamm, pianist James Williams, vibraphonist Joe Locke, and a slew of other accomplished musicians, including the vocal team, Group Five. Cole has definitely found a formula for romancing classics such as "An Affair to Remember," "Where Can I Go without You," "My Heart Stood Still," and "You're Sensational." He renders upbeat swingers such as "Send for Me," "As Long as I'm Singing," and bluesy heart-warmers like "An Old Piano Plays the Blues" (featuring Williams at the keys) with equal panache. Instrumental soloists are given plenty of space and the elegant session flows along in smooth and easy fashion. Kick off your shoes, settle into your easy chair, and listen to a master crooner.

what to buy next: On *To the Ends of the Earth* 𝄞𝄞𝄞𝄞 (Fantasy, 1997, prod. Todd Barkan), Cole delivers 13 tunes in various ensembles featuring his guests. He ups the tempo a tad from previous Fantasy albums, yet retains the same romantic flavor with tunes such as "In the Still of the Night," "Candy," "Love Walked In," "I'll Be Seeing You," and other popular favorites given jazzy flair. The core rhythm section features Cyrus Chestnut on piano, George Mraz or Tom Hubbard on bass, and Steve Berrios or Yoron Israel on drums. Vibraphonist Joe Locke and saxophonist Joe Ford augment nicely. Numerous other instrumentalists endow this session with their talents, including, on a two-tune medley, Eubanks (trombone), Stripling (trumpet), Javon Jackson (tenor sax), and Antonio Hart (alto sax). Throughout, Cole maintains meticulous control, holding true to the lyrics and phrasing in a natural, easy manner. Vibraphonist Joe Locke adds significantly to this set, helping to create the desired mood for each song. This is a comfortable session in the style of bona fide balladeers. Cole proves he knows how to turn a phrase on *A Circle of Love* 𝄪𝄪𝄪 (Fantasy, 1993, prod. Todd Barkan, Makoto Kimata). He's picked 12 of the prettiest sentimental songs and delivers them so earnestly, with prime sidemen to achieve maximum passion and impact. Chestnut, Larry Willis, and Cole take turns at the acoustic piano, and the leader mixes it up in different settings, subtracting from or adding to two fabulous core trios—Chestnut, Mraz (bass), Steve Berrios (drums) or Willis, Hubbard (bass), Berrios. Cole performs at the keys (replacing Willis) for a couple of tunes with Hubbard and Berrios. Various guest soloists add color and texture. Cole delivers straightforward versions of beautiful ballads such as Paul Williams's "You're Nice to Be Around," and Kern's "They Didn't Believe Me," Abbey Lincoln's "A Circle of Love," and then switches to Latin beats with Bonfa's "Manha de Carnaval." Cole artfully swings on "All Too Soon" and "Angel Eyes," both songs featuring Danny Moore's crisp Harmon-muted trumpet solos. Cole accompanies his vocals on the poignant Gladys Shelley tune "I Wonder Who My Daddy Is" (the lyrics will bring tears to your eyes) and is a wonderful stylist who creates an intimate, romantic album that invites repeated listening.

the rest:
I Want a Smile for Christmas 𝄪𝄪𝄪 (Fantasy, 1995)
Love Makes the Changes 𝄪𝄪𝄪𝄪 (Fantasy, 1998)

influences:
◀◀ Billie Holiday, Dinah Washington, Billy Eckstine

Nancy Ann Lee

Holly Cole

Born 1963, in Halifax, Nova Scotia, Canada.

Canadian jazz chanteuse Holly Cole specializes in creating brooding cabaret classics out of material drawn from such left-field sources as Lyle Lovett, Johnny Nash, Everything but the Girl, Tom Waits, and Sly Stone. Making her debut in Canada in 1990 with an independent direct-to-two-track recording called *Girl Talk*, she was signed to Blue Note/Capitol's contemporary-jazz subsidiary Manhattan in 1991 and made her stateside bow with *Blame It on My Youth*, which instantly established her as an interpretive force to be reckoned with. Backed by long-time pianist Aaron Davis and former Chet Baker bassist David Piltch, Cole sings in a husky, haunting voice that fills in the purposeful spaces of her minimalist arrangements with sensual nuances that never deteriorate into camp.

what to buy: Cole's *Temptation* 𝄪𝄪𝄪𝄪 (Metro Blue/Blue Note, 1995, prod. Craig Street) is a gorgeous homage to Tom Waits

that avoids his overly familiar favorites in favor of his darker, more obscure story-oriented gems. While her cool, seductive phrasing is certainly more commercially palatable than Waits's whiskey-coated, cigarette-ravaged howl, the acoustic arrangements and starkly intimate production are as jarringly iconoclastic as some of his recent work. Highlights include a lullaby-like reworking of "I Don't Wanna Grow Up" and the achingly beautiful "I Want You."

the rest:
Blame It on My Youth 𝄪𝄪𝄪 (Manhattan, 1991)
Don't Smoke in Bed 𝄪𝄪𝄪𝄪 (Manhattan, 1993)
It Happened One Night 𝄪𝄪𝄪 (Metro Blue/Blue Note, 1996)

worth searching for: Her yearning version of "Christmas Blues" can be found on *Jazz to the World* 𝄪𝄪𝄪 (Blue Note, 1995, prod. Christine Martin).

influences:
◀◀ Sarah Vaughan, Tom Waits, Nina Simone
▶▶ Diana Krall, k.d. lang, Madeleine Peyroux

David Okamoto

Khani Cole

Born May 7, in Milwaukee, WI.

The product of a musical family, Khani Cole sang practically right out of the cradle. She cites Minnie Riperton, Gladys Knight, Billie Holiday, Barbra Streisand, and Nat King Cole as early influences. She studied operatic technique at the Milwaukee Conservatory of Music and developed a lounge-singing career in the Midwest before moving from Milwaukee to Phoenix in the early 1990s. Her chief assets are crystal-clear articulation, dramatic phrasing, and a vocal range said to encompass four-and-a-half octaves.

what's available: *Piece of My Heart* 𝄪𝄪𝄪 (Fahrenheit, 1996, prod. Kevin Stoller) shows Cole to be a singer who comes in on the jazzy end of rhythm and blues—the same general area inhabited by Anita Baker. There's not much straight-ahead swing here, but Cole uses strong jazz players such as organist-trumpeter Joey DeFrancesco (who spends a good deal of time in Phoenix) and bassist Brian Bromberg to keep her pop tunes from sounding canned. Her slides into the high end of her range on such tunes as "Everytime He Comes Around" are almost shocking in their starkness. Her version of Knight's "If I Were Your Woman" is a show-stopping nod to one of her chief influences.

Nat "King" Cole

Born Nathaniel Adams Cole, March 17, 1917, in Montgomery, AL. Died February 15, 1965, in Santa Monica, CA.

He was known as the "King," and during his incredible, too-brief reign he actually ruled over two domains. Nathaniel Adams Cole was one of the finest jazz swing pianists in history, drawing deeply from the inspiration of Earl "Fatha" Hines. And he became one of the single most successful pop ballad singers of the twentieth century, with a voice so warm, rich, and unmistakable that it seems nearly impossible to believe he spent the early years of his career trying to make it as a piano player! After his family moved to Chicago from the Deep South, Cole began taking keyboard lessons while playing the organ and singing in church. He made his professional debut in 1936 on *Eddie Cole's Solid Swingers*, a record fronted by his brother, Eddie, with brothers Fred and Isaac accompanying. He left the group to conduct the band for *Shuffle Along*, a touring music revue; when the show closed in Los Angeles, he settled there. Struggling to find his place in the music world, Cole finally managed to organize the King Cole Trio with guitarist Oscar Moore and bassist Wesley Prince and began performing on radio. The combo became popular when they recorded Cole's "Sweet Lorraine" in 1940, and other musicians (notably Art Tatum and Oscar Peterson) formed their own trios, inspired by his sound. Johnny Miller replaced Prince and the trio rose to prominence during that decade, recording exciting jazz music, mostly for Capitol, and performing in the movies *Here Comes Elmer* and *Pistol Packin' Mama* and the first-ever Jazz at the Philharmonic concert. Along the way, Cole grew more confident in his vocal ability and became increasingly more popular as a singer. When a string of now-classic recordings, including "The Christmas Song," "I Love You for Sentimental Reasons," and "Nature Boy" culminated in a #1 hit with "Mona Lisa" in 1950, Cole became a pop singer full-time. Though he continued to dabble in jazz, playing keyboards on the 1956 release *After Midnight*, Cole's vocals catapulted him to such superstardom that many of his newer fans weren't aware he could play piano. He landed his own NBC-TV series from 1956 to 1957, an almost unheard-of accomplishment for a black man of the era. Despite being accompanied by the Nelson Riddle Orchestra and hosting many of the biggest stars of the day (Tony Bennett, Sammy Davis Jr., Peggy Lee), the show ultimately died due to lack of sponsorship and the refusal of some stations to carry it. Cole continued to be a major attraction, appearing in many movies (including *Cat Ballou* and *The Nat King Cole Story*) and becoming a musical holiday tradition at Christmas. One of the regal trademarks of the "King" was a lit cigarette in a cigarette holder, but when he died of lung cancer at the age of 47, the world mourned the loss of one of the most beloved voices of all time.

what to buy: Why it took the success of Natalie Cole's *Unforgettable* tribute to her father to prompt the release of a hit singles collection for Cole is inconceivable, but *The Greatest Hits* ⅋⅋⅋⅋ (Capitol/EMI, 1994, prod. various) is such a package. Covering the King's work from 1944 through 1963 in 62 minutes and 22 tracks, the collection skips some of his famous Christmas songs but does focus on his best pop productions such as "Mona Lisa" and "Sentimental Reasons." The cuts are arranged by style and quality rather than chronology, which gives an imperfect sense of history but a better sense of the music. *Jazz Encounters* ⅋⅋⅋⅋ (Blue Note, 1992, prod. Michael Cuscuna) combines the great work of jazz masters like Coleman Hawkins, Benny Carter, and Dizzy Gillespie with Cole's piano and vocal stylings. Here you'll find Cole's non-trio performances and some of his best collaborations with Woody Herman and Johnny Mercer.

what to buy next: If you're looking for big box sets, start with *Nat King Cole* ⅋⅋⅋⅋ (Capitol/EMI, 1992, prod. Lee Gillette), which boasts 4 discs and a 60-page booklet covering 20 years in 100 different tracks. As a side dish, you'll find the previously unreleased novelty "Mr. Cole Won't Rock & Roll" as well as Leonard Feather liner notes, complete track annotations, rare photographs, and some of the King's most inspiring jazz sets. Starting with records like *Lush Life* ⅋⅋⅋⅋ (EMI/Capitol, 1993), with the Pete Rugolo Orchestra, Cole was phasing out of trio work and trying to establish a vocal career over his keyboard fare. There's still jazz here, but lots of great vocals on tunes that are memorable and representative of Cole's best musical work.

what to avoid: Some musicians just could do no wrong—you didn't think they called him "King" simply because his last name was Cole, did you? His only albums worth avoiding are ones with weak or offbeat selections, such as *Greatest Country Hits* ⅋⅋ (Curb, 1990).

the rest:

Big Band Cole ⅋⅋⅋⅋⅋ (EMI/Capitol, 1950)
The Billy May Sessions ⅋⅋⅋⅋⅋ (EMI/Capitol, 1951)
Nat King Cole Live ⅋⅋⅋ (A Touch of Magic)
Early American ⅋⅋ (A Touch of Magic)

(With the Nat King Cole Trio) *Hit That Jive, Jack: The Earliest Recordings (1940–41)* 🎵🎵🎵 (Decca/MCA Jazz, 1990)

The Very Thought of You 🎵🎵🎵🎵 (Capitol/EMI, 1991)

The Jazz Collector Edition 🎵🎵🎵 (Laserlight, 1991)

(With the Nat King Cole Trio) *The Trio Recordings* 🎵🎵🎵 (Laserlight, 1991)

(With the Nat King Cole Trio) *The Complete Capitol Recordings of the Nat King Cole Trio* 🎵🎵🎵🎵 (Capitol/EMI, 1991)

(With the Nat King Cole Trio) *The Trio Recordings, Vol.2* 🎵🎵🎵 (Laserlight, 1991)

(With the Nat King Cole Trio) *The Trio Recordings, Vol. 3* 🎵🎵🎵 (Laserlight, 1991)

(With the Nat King Cole Trio) *The Trio Recordings, Vol. 4* 🎵🎵🎵 (Laserlight, 1991)

The Unforgettable Nat King Cole 🎵🎵🎵🎵 (Capitol/EMI, 1992)

(With the Nat King Cole Trio) *The Best of the Nat King Cole Trio: Instrumental Classics* 🎵🎵🎵 (Capitol/EMI, 1992)

The Piano Style of Nat "King" Cole 🎵🎵🎵 (Capitol/EMI, 1993)

(With the Nat King Cole Trio) *Early Years of Nat King Cole Trio* 🎵🎵🎵 (Sound Hills, 1993)

(With the Nat King Cole Trio) *Nat King Cole & the King Cole Trio: Straighten Up & Fly Right (Radio Broadcasts 1942–1948)* 🎵🎵🎵 (VJC, 1993)

(With the Nat King Cole Trio) *The Nat King Cole Trio: World War II Transcriptions* 🎵🎵🎵🎵 (Music & Arts Programs of America, 1994)

Spotlight on Nat King Cole 🎵🎵🎵 (Capitol/EMI, 1995)

The Jazzman 🎵🎵🎵🎵 (Topaz Jazz, 1995)

To Whom It May Concern 🎵🎵🎵 (Capitol/EMI, 1995)

Swinging Easy Down Memory Lane 🎵🎵🎵 (Skylark Jazz, 1995)

The Complete After Midnight Sessions 🎵🎵🎵🎵 (Capitol/EMI, 1996)

Sweet Lorraine (1938–1941 Transcriptions) 🎵🎵🎵 (Jazz Classics, 1996)

The Vocal Classics 🎵🎵🎵 (Capitol/EMI, 1996)

The Nat King Cole TV Show 🎵🎵🎵 (Sandy Hook, 1996)

The McGregor Years (1941–1945) 🎵🎵🎵🎵 (Music & Arts Programs of America, 1996)

Love Is the Thing (Gold Disc) 🎵🎵🎵🎵 (DCC, 1997)

worth searching for: For a fascinating insight into the performing medium and the painstaking polishing of brilliance, Cole's *Anatomy of a Jam Session* 🎵🎵🎵🎵 (Black Lion, 1945) with drummer Buddy Rich is especially choice. Cole attacks the keys only, no vocals, and his dynamic jams with Charlie Shavers, Herbie Hayner, John Simmons, and Rich are superb. The solos that emanate from the 12 songs, five as a quintet, make this a very memorable disc and worth hunting down. Famous for his rendering of "The Christmas Song" and "Frosty the Snowman," Cole became the unofficial herald angel of Christmas. If you take the time to hunt down the reissues of *The Christmas Song* 🎵🎵🎵 (Capitol,

Nat "King" Cole **(AP/Wide World Photos)**

1990, prod. Lee Gillette) and *Cole, Christmas and Kids* 🎵🎵🎵🎵 (Capitol, 1990, prod. Lee Gillette), you won't be sorry.

influences:

◀◀ Billy Kyle, Louis Armstrong, Louis Jordan, Duke Ellington, Teddy Wilson, Earl "Fatha" Hines

▶▶ Johnny Mathis, Frank Sinatra, Johnny Hartman, Oscar Peterson, Al Jarreau, Bing Crosby, Mel Tormé, Billy Eckstine

Chris Tower

Richie Cole

Born February 29, 1948, in Trenton, NJ.

Richie Cole is a dedicated bebopper whose infectious, high-spirited solos won him considerable attention during the commercial nadir of acoustic jazz in the mid-1970s. Though known for his exuberant playing, he can often put his passion to better use on ballads, where he is capable of deeply moving and finely crafted statements. Exposed to jazz at an early age at his father's New Jersey jazz club, Cole began playing alto at age 10 and later attended Berklee for two years. Strongly influenced by Charlie Parker and Phil Woods (the latter a mentor to him), he joined Buddy Rich's big band in 1969 and later worked with Lionel Hampton. He toured and recorded frequently with singer Eddie Jefferson through the late 1970s, making some of the best albums of his career for Muse. At the same time, Cole founded the band Alto Madness, which used the gimmick of transforming novelty tunes such as the *I Love Lucy* theme, the *Star Trek* theme, and "Holiday for Strings" into effective bop vehicles. Though his career has been interrupted a number of times due to personal problems, Cole's recent recordings for Heads Up indicate he is still a powerful improvisor.

what to buy: An almost inevitable pairing, *Side by Side* 🎵🎵🎵 (Muse, 1980, prod. Mitch Farber) features Richie Cole with one of his main inspirations, Phil Woods. Recorded live in Denver, the two like-minded alto players clearly relish each other's company, battling through such bop standards as "Donna Lee" and "Scrapple from the Apple." Tenor giant Eddie "Lockjaw" Davis contributes some brawny playing on "Save Your Love for Me," while the top-flight rhythm section of John Hicks (piano), Walter Booker (bass), and Jimmy Cobb (drums) keeps the music lithe and energized. Any doubts about Cole's chops after a number of years off the scene were erased with *Kush: The Music of Dizzy Gillespie* 🎵🎵🎵 (Heads Up, 1995, prod. Bob Belden), a fine album featuring interesting brass arrangements by Bob Belden. Covering nine tunes by Dizzy Gillespie (as well as, strangely, "You Go to My Head" by J. Fred Coots and Haven Gillespie), Cole is at his best jousting with Paquito D'Rivera on the title track and matching wits with trumpeter Jack Walrath on "Birk's Works" and "A Night in Tunisia."

what to buy next: One of the best albums recorded by "Alto Madness," the band co-led by Richie Cole and Eddie Jefferson, *New York Afternoon* ♫♫♫ (Muse, 1977, prod. Eddie Jefferson) is a fun and often exciting session featuring two Jefferson vocals and numerous spirited Cole solos. The album's highlights include "Stormy Weather" and an exuberant version of "Alto Madness." *Profile* ♫♫♫ (Heads Up, 1993, prod. Carroll Coates) marked Cole's returned to the jazz scene after a number of years of inactivity, but his style had changed little. Backed by an able rhythm section featuring pianist Dick Hindman, guitarist Henry Johnson, bassist Seward McCain, and drummer Scott Morris, Cole takes on such interesting material as Tom Waits's "A Foreign Affair," the pop song "Volare," and a number of excellent tunes by songwriter (and album producer) Carroll Coates.

best of the rest:

Yakety Madness ♫♫ (Laserlight, 1983)
Popbob ♫♫ (Milestone, 1987)
Pure Imagination ♫♫♫ (Concord, 1987)
Signature ♫♫♫ (Milestone, 1989)
Bossa Nova International ♫♫♫ (Milestone, 1990)
Plays Westside Story ♫♫♫ (MusicMasters, 1997)

influences:

◄◄ Charlie Parker, Sonny Stitt, Phil Woods

Andrew Gilbert

Cecilia Coleman

Born September 8, 1962, in Long Beach, CA.

Pianist Cecilia Coleman shows depth, passion, and understanding in her performances, and has been making a name for herself on the Los Angeles jazz scene since she was 19 years old. Coleman began Classical and popular piano studies at age five. Ten years later, after being inspired by the Count Basie-Oscar Peterson album, *Satch and Josh*, Coleman began studies with pianist Eloise Ferguson, who introduced her to the music of famed jazz pianists Red Garland and Wynton Kelly. Coleman studied with vibist Charlie Shoemake at California State University-Long Beach, graduating in 1986. She became partners for five years with tenor saxophonist Benn Clatworthy, and gained wider notice in 1990 when she won the Los Angeles Jazz Society's Shelly Manne Memorial New Talent Award. She soon formed her own trio (later expanded it to a quintet) and, as

leader, recorded three albums of bop-oriented, harder-edged jazz, which she compares to the music of Art Blakey.

what to buy: Together more than two years by the time of this recording, pianist Cecilia Coleman's cohesive, swinging quintet generates energy aplenty on *Cecilia Coleman: Home* ♫♫♫ (Resurgent Music, 1995, prod. Cecilia Coleman, Robert Bennett), her third CD as leader. Eleven sparkling straight-ahead originals display her brilliant craftsmanship as performer-composer. Her melodious creations inspire resplendent solos from veteran trumpeter Steve Huffsteter and saxophonist Andy Suzuki, and top-notch backing from Dean Taba (bass), Kendall Kay (drums), and Dee Huffsteter (percussion). The sophisticated team radiates sprightly propulsion, engaging harmonies, and imaginative colors and textures. Coleman's previous session (her second CD), *Young and Foolish* ♫♫♫ (Resurgent Music, 1994, prod. Cecilia Coleman, Dean Taba), featured the same personnel (minus Dee Huffsteter), and she varies ensemble settings on her seven originals and the two standards. Navigating tight, front-line horn arrangements, the full quintet is reminiscent of Blakey's Jazz Messengers, with drummer Kendall Kay's imaginative rhythms frequently punching, knockout style, from underneath. And Coleman's modern-edged trio forges ahead on her sturdy improvisations, yielding invigorating coactions. Considering the all-around competent performances on both sessions, you can't go wrong with either disc.

what to buy next: Hinting at better things to come, Coleman's debut CD as leader, *Words of Wisdom* ♫♫♫ (L.A.P. Records, 1992, prod. Cecilia Coleman, John Wood), with bassists Eric Von Essen or Jimmy Hoff, and drummer Kendall Kay, enriches the listener's experience with refreshing standards by Wayne Shorter, Bud Powell, and Thelonious Monk, and three attractive Coleman originals. Tenor saxophonist Benn Clatworthy and trumpeter Oscar Brashear nicely augment some of the nine selections. Highlights include Coleman's pulsating title tune, a warm rendition of the warhorse, "I'll Get By" (prominently featuring Brashear's crisp trumpet renderings), and the gracefully floating trio version of "Nature Boy."

influences:

◄◄ Red Garland, Bill Evans, Mulgrew Miller, Benny Green

Nancy Ann Lee

George Coleman

Born March 8, 1935, in Memphis, TN.

Wear your life jacket when you listen to George Coleman, or

you're liable to be swept away by the onrushing torrent of swinging sound pouring from his tenor saxophone. Coleman chews up chord changes at a rapid clip, creating long solo lines which build in intensity or swoop and swirl through a ballad. His clear tone projects beauty and power, and his style is often tinged with a Memphis-bred feel for the blues. Coleman grew up amidst a Memphis filled with budding jazz musicians, including school chums pianist Harold Mabern, trumpeter Booker Little, and altoist Frank Strozier. His first horn was the alto which he started playing at 15. Not surprising, Charlie Parker was Coleman's major inspiration and Bird's influence can still be heard in the tenorman's flowing lines. During a two-year stint with B.B. King in the early 1950s, Coleman began playing tenor. In 1957, Coleman headed to Chicago with Booker Little and together they joined the Max Roach band the following year. On John Coltrane's recommendation, Miles Davis hired Coleman in 1963. After a year with the trumpeter, Coleman left and began playing dates as sideman with Herbie Hancock, Lee Morgan and Chet Baker. Since the late 1960s, Coleman has been leading and recording his own ensembles, sometimes playing horns in addition to his tenor.

what to buy: Coleman has chosen to record infrequently rather than bend to the whims of producers who have their own ideas of what he should do. Most often, he records for small labels that give him final say about the sessions. This can make it hard to find his albums as they fall in and out of print. The best of the lot is *Amsterdam After Dark* (Timeless, 1979), a quartet set with no weak tunes. Check out the heartfelt cadenza on "Autumn in New York." Two live quartet dates from the 1980s with frequent collaborator Harold Mabern at the piano were originally done for Theresa. Featuring no-holds-barred performances, they have been reissued by Evidence. *Manhattan Panorama* (Evidence, 1985, prod. George Coleman) and *At Yoshi's* (Evidence, 1989, prod. George Coleman) showcase Coleman's hard-charging tenor exploding with melodic intensity. Both albums contain fine medium tempo and ballad performances allowing Coleman's rhapsodic approach to shine, especially on *At Yoshi's*. Although he includes what seems to be an obligatory double-time section during ballads, something that tends to spoil the beautiful moods he has created, it's a minor quibble. Don't let it stop you from grabbing these sessions.

what to buy next: In his autobiography *Miles*, Miles Davis wrote that he had never heard Coleman play better than the 1964 Davis quintet concert at New York's Philharmonic Hall. No argument here. Run, don't walk, to get the two-CD set of this performance captured on *The Complete Concert: 1964* (Columbia) under Miles's name. You won't go wrong with Herbie Hancock's *Maiden Voyage* (Blue Note) or the 1975 album *Eastern Rebellion* (Timeless) by the band of the same name–though sometimes it's filed under Cedar Walton.

what to avoid: *Meditation* (Timeless, 1977) is disappointing. With all due respect to Coleman and his duo partner, pianist Tete Montoliu, were these guys in the same room for this session?

the rest:
Playing Changes (Ronnie Scott's Jazz House, 1989),
My Horns of Plenty (Verve, 1991),
Blues Inside Out (Ronnie Scott's Jazz House, 1996),

worth searching for: Wham! Coleman's tenor exudes power in this punching, near-rocking octet on *Big George* (Charly, 1977), especially on racing versions of "On Green Dolphin Street" and "Joggin'." Underrated soloists abound in the ensemble including Mabern, saxophonists Strozier, Junior Cook, and trumpeter Danny Moore.

influences:
◀◀ Charlie Parker, John Coltrane

Dan Polletta

Ornette Coleman

Born March 9, 1930, in Fort Worth, TX.

No figure has ever begun so far from the mainstream of jazz and proceeded to shake the music so thoroughly to its core as has Ornette Coleman. Saxophonist Charlie Parker, for instance, worked though the ranks with the acknowledged Jay McShann in fomenting the bebop revolution; the idiosyncratically self-taught saxophonist Ornette Coleman paid his dues on the road with Silas Green's later-day minstrel show, and with Pee Wee Crayton's obscure R&B band. Relocating to Los Angeles in the early 1950s, Coleman found his originality unwelcome in bands and jams. He made his living as an elevator operator and at other nonmusical jobs while studying music theory on his own and generally upending traditional notions of harmony with a mix of intuition, insight, and (according to many commentators) outright error. Most important, though, he found a small circle of generally younger acolytes, including trumpeter Don Cherry and bassist Charlie Haden, sympathetic to his cause.

An audition to sell his compositions to Lester Koenig at Contemporary Records led to a chance to make two recordings for that label, although Coleman compromised by using more "name" sidemen than musicians familiar with his concepts. The

next Coleman recordings were totally his, recorded in the wake of his 1959 debut at New York's Five Spot in one of the most talked about gigs in the history of jazz—and rightly so. Chord changes were gone, solos overlapped, beat gave way to pulse and flow, melodies were achingly and unexpectedly beautiful—or just a pain to the detractors. But a mere three years later, having set in motion a new jazz era, Coleman withdrew from the scene as he would a number of times subsequently.

A 1965 comeback saw him adding violin and trumpet to his instrumental arsenal. The mid-1970s heard Coleman's radical take on jazz-rock with his group Prime Time (which spun off a virtual harmolodic fusion genre of former Coleman associates James "Blood" Ulmer, Ronald Shannon Jackson, and Jamaaladeen Tacuma). Sporadic acoustic outings for the next 20 years would almost invariably be in the company of longtime collaborators like Haden and Cherry (who also played the acoustic Coleman book in the Coleman alum group Old and New Dreams). A recent deal for his own Harmolodic label through Verve is seeing Coleman record in a wider variety of settings and re-releasing long unavailable material on CD. Pianist Paul Bley once said that Coleman threw a monkey wrench into the course of jazz by showing up 10 years early, showing musicians how to leap "outside" of chord changes at a time when musicians were still progressively and productively loosening the shackles of changes from "inside." And Coleman's compositions are increasingly played by others. "Lonely Woman," in particular, has virtually become a standard.

Harmolodic was not the first label Coleman started. In the mid-1970s he released some well-designed LPs by himself and other musicians on the label, Artist's House; at least two of those albums, *Soapsuds, Soapsuds* and *Body Meta*, have been released on the Harmolodic/Verve label.

what to buy: *Beauty Is a Rare Thing: The Complete Atlantic Recordings* 𝄞𝄞𝄞𝄞 (Atlantic, 1959–61/Rhino, 1993, prod. Yves Beauvais/Nesuhi Ertegun, John Lewis) collects all 57 surviving recordings of Coleman's 1959–61 Atlantic sessions in a six-CD box set featuring the original core of collaborators: trumpeter Don Cherry, bassists Charlie Haden and Scott LaFaro, drummers Ed Blackwell and Billy Higgins in quartets, and all of them plus bass clarinetist Eric Dolphy and trumpeter Freddie Hubbard in the double-quartet session that named a movement, *Free Jazz.* Also included are an augmented Coleman quartet

Ornette Coleman **(Archive Photos)**

ORNETTE COLEMAN

song "R.P.D.D. (The Relation of the Poet to Day-Dreaming)"

album *Beauty Is a Rare Thing: The Complete Atlantic Recordings* (Atlantic, 1959–61/Rhino, 1993)

instrument Alto saxophone

Monster Solo

playing Third Stream pieces composed by Gunther Schuller and based on the work of Coleman and Thelonious Monk, respectively. *The Art of the Improvisers* 𝄞𝄞𝄞𝄞 (Atlantic, 1988, prod. Nesuhi Ertegun) offers a smaller sampling (of the quartet dates only) from the same period. Throughout, the uptempo tunes create a sort of zippy tumult with shifting directions and solos that seem to burst; the ballads float without moorings.

what to buy next: *At the Golden Circle in Stockholm, Volume 1* 𝄞𝄞𝄞𝄞 (Blue Note, 1965/1987, prod. Francis Wolff) and *At the Golden Circle in Stockholm, Volume 2* 𝄞𝄞𝄞𝄞 (Blue Note, 1987, prod. Francis Wolff) capture Coleman live in a trio format with drummer Charles Moffett and bassist David Izenzon during Coleman's 1965 comeback. Hear Coleman in his controversial trumpet and violin styles as well as his alto sax. Even if Moffett and Izenzon aren't quite as distinctive musical personalities as Haden and Blackwell, this trio has a feisty energy of its own (not to mention a sense of humor) that is entirely in sync with Coleman's. The Coleman-Cherry give-and-take gives way to an even more assertive Coleman in *In All Languages* 🎝🎝🎝🎝 (Harmolodic/Verve, 1997, prod. Denardo Coleman). The recording captures Coleman with acoustic associates from 1957 and his then-current (1987) Prime Time lineup for compare-and-contrast takes on the same set of tunes. It's a good introduction to Prime Time, in this edition essentially two guitar-bass-drum trios plus Coleman, which can sound like at least three bands at once, none of them conventionally in sync. Yet it all works, from stuttering funk to evocations of loopy hoedowns. Coleman's recent collaborations with pianist Geri Allen reintroduces the piano to his group after 35 years on the simultaneously released, *Sound Museum: Three Women* 🎝🎝🎝🎝 (Harmolodic/Verve, 1996) and *Sound Museum: Hidden Man* 🎝🎝🎝🎝 (Harmologic/Verve, 1996). The inflexible tuning of piano and its harmonic orientation have long been considered antithetical to Coleman's polytonal free jazz and its variable tuning inflections, yet it all works well on the 14 tracks on each album due to the intelligent creations of pianist Allen, with Coleman on sax, trumpet, and violin, bassist Charnett Moffett, and drummer Denardo Coleman (Ornette's son). Without repeating itself, the music furnishes a clear example of Ornette's self-proclaimed harmolodic system (where HARmony, MOtion, and meLODIC elements are equal rather than hierarchical), beating his attempts to explain it with words. Coleman's imaginative playing combines melodic flights of Parker-like bebop with blues-derived intonational nuances that early in his career led some critics to claim Coleman couldn't play in tune. Allen plays fluid yet angular lines and sounds as comfortable and exciting stylistically as on her 1980s recordings with Charlie Haden (an original Coleman Quartet member) and drummer Paul Motian, as well as on most recent adventurous outings as leader.

what to avoid: *Broken Shadows* **woof!** (Moon, 1972/1990) contains sloppy track listings to complement execrable recording quality.

best of the rest:
The Shape of Jazz to Come 🎝🎝🎝🎝 (Contemporary, 1959/OJC, 1988)
Tomorrow Is the Question! 🎝🎝🎝🎝 (Contemporary, 1959/OJC, 1988)
Ornette on Tenor 🎝🎝🎝🎝 (Atlantic, 1961/Rhino, 1993)
The Empty Foxhole 🎝🎝🎝 (Blue Note, 1966/1994)
Love Call 🎝🎝🎝🎝 (Blue Note, 1968/1990)
New York Is Now 🎝🎝🎝🎝 (Blue Note, 1968/1990)
Body Meta 🎝🎝🎝🎝 (Artists House, 1977/Verve, 1996)
(With Charlie Haden) *Soapsuds, Soapsuds* 🎝🎝🎝🎝 (Artists House, 1977/Verve, 1996)
Virgin Beauty 🎝🎝🎝🎝 (Portrait, 1988)
Live at the Tivoli 1965 🎝🎝🎝🎝 (Magnetic, 1993)
Tone Dialing 🎝🎝🎝 (Harmolodic/Verve, 1996)

(With Joachim Kuhn) *Colors: Live from Leipzig* 🎝🎝🎝🎝 (Harmolodic/Verve, 1997)

worth searching for: *Crisis* 🎝🎝🎝🎝 (Impulse!, 1972, prod. Ornette Coleman) is a live concert recording with a stunning rendition of Haden's "Song for Che" and two of the free-est Coleman ensemble pieces ever—"Trouble in the East" and "Space Jungle." Its only weakness is a mix that hides the full extent of the action. *Skies of America* 🎝🎝🎝🎝🎝 (Columbia, 1972, prod. James Jordan) is the most successful of several Coleman recordings with strings, a sweeping work that brings in a traps drum and Coleman's alto sax at key points over the London Symphony Orchestra. *Science Fiction* 🎝🎝🎝🎝🎝 (Columbia, 1971, prod. James Jordan) includes Coleman's only recorded return to something akin to his *Free Jazz* format, not to mention two ballads lovingly sung by vocalist Asha Puthli and smaller groups. *Dancing in Your Head* 🎝🎝🎝🎝 (Horizon/A&M, 1977, prod. Ornette Coleman) dishes up a movement from the symphonic "Skies of America" for Coleman's electric band, Prime Time, and kicks off the harmolodic fusion school in 26 minutes of hectic jamming.

influences:

◀◀ Charlie Parker, Thelonious Monk

▶▶ Charlie Haden, Don Cherry, John Carter, Bobby Bradford, Billy Higgins, Ed Blackwell, Dewey Redman, Old & New Dreams, Ronald Shannon Jackson & His Decoding Society, Jamaaladeen Tacuma, James (Blood) Ulmer, Charles Brackeen, Leroy Jenkins, Anthony Braxton, Roscoe Mitchell, Pat Metheny, John Coltrane, Miles Davis, Bern Nix, Geri Allen

W. Kim Heron

Steve Coleman

Born September 20, 1956, in Chicago, IL.

One of the most interesting new conceptualizers on the scene, Steve Coleman walks both sides of the funk/jazz line and has done so from an early age. He was playing alto saxophone in high school and patterning his playing after that of James Brown's horn man, Maceo Parker. While Coleman was working the funk side of the equation in various R&B bands he came to appreciate Charlie Parker and jazz playing through his father's urging and by watching Chicago legend Von Freeman gigging in area clubs. When Coleman finally left Chicago for New York City in 1978 he ended up playing on the streets before catching work with the Thad Jones-Mel Lewis Big Band, Sam Rivers, and Cecil Taylor. Record dates with David Murray, Stanley Cowell, Abbey

Lincoln, and Doug Hammond followed. His stint with bassist Dave Holland in 1984 brought Coleman the greatest amount of notoriety, especially in Europe where he has toured often. Coleman is also the main proponent of the Macro-Basic Array of Structured Extemporizations (M-Base) concept. Known chiefly by its acronym, M-Base appears to be more of a philosophical set of guidelines than a hard and fast definition of style. Elements of non-European rhythm, funk, and rap/poetry seem to blend with post-bop sensibilities in music associated with the concept. Coleman has worked with an impressive array of relatively new talent to spread the M-Base word: saxophonists Greg Osby, Steve Williamson, and Craig Handy, trumpeter/cornetist Graham Haynes, guitarists Kelvyn Bell, Jean-Paul Bourelly, David Gilmore, and Vernon Reid, keyboard players Geri Allen and Andy Milne, and vocalist Cassandra Wilson have each used M-Base techniques in some, if not all, of their music. Over the years Coleman has also been on the faculty of the Banff (Canada) School of Fine Arts and founded his own music publishing firms and record companies in addition to producing videos and leading at least five different musical ensembles.

what to buy: In 1995 Coleman recorded a trio of live albums at the Hot Brass Club in Paris, France, using three different groups to expose the various facets of his music. *Curves of Live* 𝄢𝄢𝄢𝄢 (BMG, 1995, prod. Steve Coleman), featuring Coleman and Five Elements, is closer to traditional post-bop modes than much of his other music, even though the thumb-popping bass lines of Reggie Washington and the snapping snare and slick cymbal work of drummer Gene Lake owe a great deal to the funk revolution of James Brown and George Clinton. Tenor saxophonist David Murray guests on "Country Bama" and "I'm Burning Up," offering an interesting audio alternative to Coleman's dryer alto, hovering around the beat more often than playing on or with it. Three rappers (Black Indian, Sub-Zero and Kokayi) knock out syllables on "I'm Burning Up" like latter-day Last Poets. The band's take on "'Round Midnight" is an interesting arrangement that occasionally touches the melody line while building M-Base derived improvisational structures on the song's basic framework.

what to buy next: One of Coleman's many projects has been to investigate rhythms of the African Diaspora, especially the Yoruban sound artifacts at the heart of such Caribbean sects as Santeria, Candomble, and Vodun. When he got in touch with the Cuban folklore ensemble AfroCuba de Matanzas, he hit the motherlode of African rhythms in the Western Hemisphere. *The Sign and the Seal* 𝄢𝄢𝄢𝄢 (BMG, 1996, prod. Steve Coleman) explores traditional African rhythms preserved by AfroCuba de

Matanzas while weaving Coleman's formulaic yet intriguing jazz visions through an ageless, percussive tapestry. The result, on the surface, could be compared to the music Charlie Parker and Dizzy Gillespie were playing with Machito's band spurring them on, but Coleman's blending of styles with the Cuban group approaches current world-music standards with greater ease than it does the hallowed halls of bebop or Latin jazz. The ensemble is the Mystic Rhythm Society, featuring such Coleman associates as keyboard player Andy Milne, trumpeter Ralph Alessi, and drummer Gene Lake, with tenor saxophonist Ravi Coltrane providing an aural counterweight for the leader's astringent alto. *Anatomy of a Groove* 𝄢𝄢𝄢𝄢 (DIW/Columbia, 1992, prod. Steve Coleman) is listed as by the M-Base Collective, but for all intents and purposes it's a Coleman album: He produced it, wrote or co-wrote four of the songs, provided the basic methodology, and played on every cut. The musicians include drummer Marvin "Smitty" Smith, bassists Reggie Washington and Kevin Harris, keyboard players Andy Milne and James Weidman, guitarist David Gilmore, saxophonists Coleman, Greg Osby, and Jimmy Cozier, and trumpeters Mark Ledford and Graham Haynes, with vocalist Cassandra Wilson tossed in for good measure. The basic Coleman concepts are laid out in an aural showcase which makes this album a perfect starting point if you want an example of the M-Base idea in one of its more coherent midlife incarnations.

the rest:
(With Dave Holland) *Phase Space* 𝄢𝄢𝄢 (DIW, 1991)
(With Five Elements) *Drop Kick* 𝄢𝄢𝄢 (Novus, 1992)
(With Five Elements) *The Tao of Mad Phat-Fringe Zones* 𝄢𝄢𝄢 (Novus, 1993)
(With Five Elements) *Def Trance Beat* 𝄢𝄢𝄢 (Novus, 1995)
(With Metrics) *The Way of the Cipher* 𝄢𝄢𝄢 (BMG, 1995)
(With Metrics) *A Tale of Three Cities* 𝄢𝄢𝄢 (Novus, 1995)

influences:
◀◀ Maceo Parker, Von Freeman, Doug Hammond
▶▶ M-Base Collective

Garaud MacTaggart

William "Bill" Coleman

Born William Johnson Coleman, August 4, 1904, in Paris, KY. Died August 24, 1981, in Toulouse, France.

Trumpet player Bill Coleman reached his zenith in the mid- and late 1930s as one of the many Black American jazz artists to travel to Europe. As a child, he moved with his family to the Cincinnati area in 1909. Southern Ohio, an area rich in jazz and blues by the early 1920s, was an inspiring region for Coleman to learn music. By the mid-1920s, he was playing professionally with Cecil Scott's band from Springfield, Ohio. The band traveled to New York in 1927, where Coleman left for a period to join Luis Russell's Orchestra (for whom he made his first records). By the early 1930s, he had traveled briefly to Europe with Lucky Millinder, and played trumpet with a number of other Harlem bands, including Fats Waller's.

Coleman's second trip to Europe was far more extensive and far-reaching. His talents were showcased in many fine small group recordings made while abroad. Coleman initially went to Europe with Freddy Taylor's Band. He toured all of Europe plus parts of Egypt and India from 1935 until 1940, when the threat of war forced him back to the United States. Coleman stayed extremely active while back in the U.S. He led his own trio, as well as playing for various big bands (Andy Kirk, Fats Waller, Noble Sissle) and small groups (Mary Lou Williams, Teddy Wilson, John Kirby) before going back to Europe permanently in 1948. Bill maintained an exquisite tone and wonderful, almost romantic improvisational sense throughout his career. He continued to perform and travel extensively right up to his death.

what to buy: Bill Coleman's best period stylistically and with regard to creativity were his earliest years, especially those recordings done in Europe. *Bill Coleman: 1929–1940* 𝄞𝄞𝄞𝄞 (Jazz Archive, 1994) and *Hangin' Around* 𝄞𝄞𝄞𝄞 (Topaz, 1993) provide some of Coleman's earliest recordings. There is duplication of titles here, but availability might be the qualifier. Either one serves as a great introduction to Coleman's playing. *Bill Coleman 1936–1938* 𝄞𝄞𝄞𝄞 (Classics, 1994, prod. Gilles Petard) starts with Coleman's first sessions overseas. "What's the Reason" and "After You've Gone" are two wonderful tunes, examples of his lyrical playing and unique robust sound. Later sessions find Django Reinhardt in accompaniment, a talented guitarist always a joy to have on a date and, coupled with Coleman's forceful lead, Reinhardt's unmatched rhythm gives these recordings a wonderful buoyancy and swing. In his later years, Coleman still maintained rich ideas and could swing, but without the youthful bravura found in the pre-War recordings. *Bill Coleman Meets Guy Lafitte* 𝄞𝄞𝄞 (Black Lion, 1992, prod. Alan Bates), recorded in 1973, features Coleman to good advantage in a quintet setting.

the rest:
Bill Coleman + 4 𝄞𝄞𝄞 (Jazzology, 1997)

influences:
◀◀ Louis Armstrong, Red Allen

Jim Prohaska

Johnny Coles

Born July 3, 1926, in Trenton, NJ. Died December 21, 1997, in Philadelphia, PA.

The distinctive trumpet sound of Johnny Coles is marked by a cry of yearning. Despite being a major talent who has been on the jazz scene for decades, popularity and acclaim have largely eluded him. He started his career with work in the R&B bands of Eddie "Cleanhead" Vinson, Bull Moose Jackson, and Earl Bostic. During the late 1950s he became part of James Moody's group, followed by a lengthy and fruitful association with Gil Evans and his orchestra. Other notable gigs have included stays with Charles Mingus, Herbie Hancock, Ray Charles, Duke Ellington, and Dameronia. Sadly, he has recorded very few times under his own name, making the few sessions he has done highly prized among fans and collectors.

what to buy: A very aptly titled album, *The Warm Sound* 𝄞𝄞𝄞𝄞 (Koch Jazz, 1961, prod. Mike Berniker) was originally issued on Epic and quickly became a rarity, making this a highly rewarding reissue. Fronting a quartet with Kenny Drew at the piano, Coles explores a nice set of tunes, including four Randy Weston classics. *Little Johnny C* 𝄞𝄞𝄞𝄞 (Blue Note, 1963, prod. Alfred Lion) is a Blue Note classic and Coles's finest moment. This wonderful set finds the trumpeter paired with tenor saxophonist Joe Henderson for some textbook hard bop. Although Coles has always had a dark lyricism to his playing, he can bop with the best of them!

what to buy next: Since so little is available under his own name, it's only logical to go to these fine sideman appearances with the Gil Evans Orchestra. Coles is featured prominently throughout and the music as a whole is simply excellent: *New Bottle, Old Wine* 𝄞𝄞𝄞𝄞 (Pacific Jazz, 1958, prod. Dick Bock), *Great Jazz Standards* 𝄞𝄞𝄞𝄞 (Pacific Jazz, 1959, prod. Dick Bock), *Out of the Cool* 𝄞𝄞𝄞𝄞 (Impulse!, 1961, prod. Creed Taylor).

the rest:
New Morning 𝄞𝄞𝄞𝄞 (Criss Cross Jazz, 1982)

worth searching for: If you still own a turntable and can find Frank Wess/Johnny Coles: *Two at the Top* 𝄞𝄞𝄞𝄞 (Uptown, 1983, prod. Mark Feldman, Robert Sunenblick), don't hesitate to pick it up. Wess and Coles make a superb front line and you can't lose with Kenny Barron at the keyboard and Kenny Washington on drums. As an added treat, the program includes a few choice tunes by Gigi Gryce, Kenny Dorham, and Benny Golson.

influences:
◀◀ Freddie Webster, Miles Davis

▶▶ Tim Hagans, John Swana

Chris Hovan

Buddy Collette

Born William Marcel Collette, August 6, 1921, in Los Angeles, CA.

A pillar of the Los Angeles jazz scene since the early 1940s, Buddy Collette is a fine improvisor on alto and tenor sax, clarinet and especially flute, an instrument on which he was an early innovator. Though best known for his long-time friendship and musical association with Charles Mingus, Collette also played an important role breaking down the color barrier in L.A. studios in the early 1950s. Collette took piano lessons as a youth before moving on to various wind instruments. He played with a number of bands, including Les Hite, in the early 1940s, and then led a dance band in the Navy. He founded the short-lived Stars of Swing with Lucky Thompson, Britt Woodman, and Mingus in 1946, then became a busy freelancer, working for such leading West Coast bandleaders as Benny Carter, Gerald Wilson, Johnny Otis, Louis Jordan, and Edgar Hayes. He became the first black musician to hold a staff position in a Los Angeles studio band, playing on Groucho Marx's TV and radio shows (1951–55), among others. He gained widespread exposure with the original edition of drummer Chico Hamilton's popular "cello" quintet (the group was featured in the 1958 film, *Jazz on a Summer's Day,* about the Newport Jazz Festival) and made a number of strong recordings of his own for Contemporary in the late 1950s. In 1964 Collette gained attention for organizing the band Mingus triumphed with at Monterey, and two years later he assembled a big band for Dizzy Gillespie's Monterey appearance. He continues to work and teach around L.A., and though he has never achieved national attention commensurate with his talents, a number of his students—including flutist James Newton, who can be heard with Collette on *Flute Talk*—have gone on to become major figures. In 1994 Issues Records released a two-CD "audio biography," a fascinating, episodic oral history covering Collette's career and his relationships with Mingus, Eric Dolphy, Groucho, and the racial and Cold War politics of the 1950s.

what to buy: Collette's debut as a leader, *Man of Many Parts* ♫♫♫♫ (Contemporary/OJC, 1956/1992, prod. Lester Koenig) displays his skills as a multi-instrumentalist and a composer. The album features three bands: an octet featuring bassist Red Callendar and trumpeter Gerald Wilson, a quintet with guitarist Barney Kessel, and a quartet with pianist Gerald Wiggins. Collette wrote nine of the 12 tunes, and some of his work is quite

daring for the time. As good as his fluid, Lester Young-influenced tenor and alto playing sounds, it's his flute and clarinet work that impress the most.

what to buy next: A pleasing session that never really breaks a sweat, *Nice Day with Buddy Collette* ♫♫♫♪ (Contemporary/OJC, 1957/1992, prod. Lester Koenig) showcases his talents on tenor, alto, and especially clarinet and flute. Covering five standards and five originals, Collette leads three different quartets. Highlights include a potent version of "Moten Swing" on clarinet with Calvin Jackson (piano), Leroy Vinnegar (bass), and Shelly Manne (drums), and his lovely flute work on "Over the Rainbow" with a trio led by pianist Don Friedman.

best of the rest:

Tanganyika ♫♫♫♫ (VSOP, 1954)
Jazz Loves Paris ♫♫♫ (Specialty/OJC, 1958/1991)
Flute Talk ♫♫♫♪ (Soul Note, 1988)

influences:

◀◀ Lester Young, Charlie Parker

▶▶ James Newton, Eric Dolphy

Andrew Gilbert

Jay Collins

Born July 22, 1968, in New York, NY.

An exciting young tenor player who has made a big impression with a few recordings, Jay Collins can play serious blues, reference 60 years of tenor sax tradition, and render ballads with a knife-edge lyricism. His highly charged solos develop organically, and are full of low honks and high squeals, pushing the range of the tenor but never slipping out of tune. Raised in Portland, Oregon, Collins was a professional break dancer at age 15 and began playing tenor at 16. Sitting in at jam sessions around Portland, he developed formative relationships with bassist Leroy Vinnegar, pianist/composer Andrew Hill, and drummer Dick Berk. His only formal training took place at the Banff Centre for the Arts in Alberta, where he studied with Steve Coleman and Dave Holland. Collins debuted on Berk's Reservoir album *Let's Cool One* in 1991, and made strong contributions to 1993's *East Coast Stroll*. He settled in New York in 1992 and has worked with Frank Lacy's big band Vibe Tribe and the acid jazz group, Groove Collective. Influenced by the group Old and New Dreams, he has begun incorporating his interest in folk music into his compositions. Collins has released two excellent albums on Reservoir. He also leads an acid jazz band called Tuba.

what to buy: Collins imposes his identity on a wide range of material on *Uncommon Threads* ♫♫♫♫ (Reservoir, 1995, prod. Mark Feldman), an extremely impressive debut. He makes himself right at home with the distinguished rhythm section featuring Kenny Barron (piano), Rufus Reid (bass), and Ben Riley (drums). He turns the folk song "When Irish Eyes Are Smiling" into an effective jazz vehicle, and gamely tackles the rarely heard Monk tune "Played Twice." He contributes three of his own tunes, most notably the "The Great Spirit," a kinetic waltz he composed for the late Jim Pepper, whom he subbed for occasionally in Oregon.

what to buy next: A strong second album by Collins, *Reality Tonic* ♫♫♫♫ (Reservoir, 1996, prod. Mark Feldman) finds the tenor player developing a compositional approach based on folk melodies. The session features James Hurt (piano) Santi Debriano (bass), Michael Mazor (drums), and Frank Lacy (trombone and flugelhorn). Collins composed five of the album's nine tunes, including "Unsung Hero," based on a melody from Cameroon, and "Folk Study," which superimposes an Irish real over a swing groove. Also ambitious in his choice of straightahead material, Collins covers Monk's often neglected "Ugly Beauty" and Mingus's "Self Portrait in Three Colors."

influences:

◄◄ Dewey Redman, John Coltrane, Wayne Shorter, Jackie McLean

Andrew Gilbert

John Coltrane

Born September 23, 1926, in Hamlet, NC. Died July 17, 1967, in New York, NY.

John Coltrane, a deeply spiritual man who devoted much of his career to reaching new musical heights, ranks with Charlie Parker and Louis Armstrong in terms of the breadth and pervasiveness of his influence on jazz history and players.

Coltrane's father played violin and clarinet and taught his son, who learned clarinet and later alto sax, the rudiments of music. The family moved to Philadelphia in 1944, and Coltrane served in the Navy from 1945–46, playing in a Navy band in Hawaii. After returning to Philadelphia, he worked in the bands of King Kolax and Joe Webb before joining Eddie "Cleanhead" Vinson's band starting in 1947, picking up tenor sax to do so. Subsequently he played with Jimmy Heath, Howard McGhee, Earl Bostic, Gay Crosse, Dizzy Gillespie (with whom Coltrane made his debut on record), Johnny Hodges, Jimmy Smith, and R&B

groups. His main influences on tenor at this time were Sonny Stitt and Dexter Gordon.

Coltrane first reached a broad audience after joining Miles Davis's quintet in 1955. Criticism of the unknown's tone, considered harsh (on faster material) compared to Gordon and other established tenor sax role models, was gradually leavened by growing admiration for his harmonic resources. The group's string of impressive albums for Prestige and then Columbia made Davis a star and went a ways towards doing the same for the tenor saxophonist, who began recording as a leader for Prestige in 1956.

Davis dismissed Coltrane in 1957 after his drug addiction made him unreliable, but going home to Philadelphia, Coltrane (who had by then picked up the nickname "Trane") kicked his habits, underwent a spiritual awakening, and returned to New York that summer to join pianist Thelonious Monk's quartet. That group had a famous residency at the Five Spot Cafe, which returned Coltrane to the public eye with solo spots where the pianist "strolled" (dropped out) and Trane soloed over just bass and drums, fueling his quickly growing legend. Many years later a tape made by Coltrane's wife Naima at the club appeared on Blue Note as *Discovery!* and offers valuable evidence of this historic collaboration, although it was apparently recorded not in 1957 but rather the next year, when Coltrane filled in for Johnny Griffin. Monk also recorded a few 1957 studio sessions with Coltrane in various lineups; *Thelonious Monk with John Coltrane* and *Monk's Music* contain the results.

Monk was a valuable mentor for Coltrane during their brief time together, and Trane's music took a great leap forward, as shown on his Prestige albums *Settin' the Pace* and especially *Black Pearls*. This was where Coltrane started being admired not just as a fine player but as an innovator. His music became harmonically dense. The phrase "Coltrane changes" came into use among musicians to describe chord changes which move by at the fast pace of every two beats rather than every bar or two. Even on material which didn't have such fast changes, Coltrane would insert them—"substitutions" were a common enough bebop practice, where a common chord was replaced by a more complex chord containing higher intervals, but Coltrane took this practice to an extreme which led to his playing being described as "sheets of sound" as he crammed sub-

John Coltrane **(Wide World Photos)**

stitutions together and played flurries of 16th notes in the process.

Miles Davis invited Coltrane to rejoin his group in 1958 and Coltrane stayed into 1960, with the lineup being a sextet including alto saxophonist Cannonball Adderley much of that time. The music the sextet made is all classic (*Milestones* especially), but of special note is the groundbreaking 1959 album *Kind of Blue*, which explored the use of modality (playing on scales rather than chord progressions). Instead of being structured by rapidly moving chord changes, Coltrane's solos spun out over long sections where the harmonic content was dictated by a single mode/scale. His playing became even freer and sometimes flowed even faster as a result.

Coltrane's contract with Prestige ran out in December 1958 and he switched to Atlantic. It took a year for his Atlantic recordings to start appearing, but when they did, Trane leapt from star to superstar. The album that did it was *Giant Steps*, which marked the first time he'd made a record consisting entirely of his own compositions. "Giant Steps" itself amazed his peers through the ease with which he negotiated its tricky chord changes; the blistering "Countdown" found him playing faster than ever in a bravura display of technique and harmonic knowledge. Conversely, the ballad "Naima" became a jazz standard, as did "Mr. P.C.", Trane's tribute to his bassist, Paul Chambers. The success of *Giant Steps* allowed Coltrane to leave Davis's group after a Spring 1960 European tour with the quintet (which has been documented on some fabulous bootleg concert recordings) and strike out on his solo career in earnest, exploring new ideas. The mid-1960 sessions that produced *The Avant-Garde* (not released until 1966) found Trane recording on soprano saxophone for the first time and working with trumpeter Don Cherry, bassists Charlie Haden and Percy Heath (one at a time), and Ed Blackwell, tenuously exploring Ornette Coleman's groundbreaking free jazz style with Ornette's musicians.

The success of *Giant Steps* also induced Atlantic to start issuing his albums at a pace more in line with Coltrane's wishes—1961 brought *Coltrane Jazz* in February and *My Favorite Things* in March. "My Favorite Things" was an unlikely success, a minor-key show tune which he deconstructed, rendering it modally while playing soprano saxophone, until then an instrument whose last days of popularity had come in the early days of jazz and which mostly survived in 1961 in Dixieland bands. Coltrane's recording of the ditty was a genuine pop hit. It also opened the ears of many jazz musicians, sparking interest in both modality and the soprano sax. "My Favorite Things" was also nearly 14 minutes long, emphasizing both its exploratory

aspect and a trance-like quality accented even more by the Middle Eastern sound Coltrane drew from his soprano sax. He, Eric Dolphy, and Yusef Lateef were exposing themselves and each other to music from Africa and Asia in an attempt to expand their musical resources and vocabularies. The other three songs chosen for the LP were also standards, making his innovations more accessible with familiar tunes. Additionally, the album introduced his new rhythm trio of pianist McCoy Tyner, bassist Steve Davis, and drummer Elvin Jones. Within a year he would switch to Art Davis and then Reggie Workman on bass, but Tyner and Jones would stay with him for years as the foundation of the classic Coltrane Quartet. Trane's Atlantic recordings put him atop the jazz world. There are still players whose entire goal in life is to master the styles epitomized by "Giant Steps" and "My Favorite Things."

Still eager to venture into even newer and more challenging territory, Coltrane switched to the Impulse! label in 1961, where his highly sympathetic producer, Bob Thiele, allowed him to record prolifically and where his records were issued faster and more frequently. The first fruits of the new relationship (though actually produced by Creed Taylor) came on *Africa/Brass*, which featured complex arrangements (mostly by Eric Dolphy) and unusual instrumentation, including bassoon and the Arabic oud. Coltrane then took yet another major leap forward with a concert album, *Live at the Village Vanguard*, which extended some of the *Africa/Brass* material but most notably featured "Chasin' the Trane," which consisted entirely of Trane improvising over bass and drums (no piano) with a white-hot intensity few had ever heard before. "Chasin' the Trane," though based on the familiar blues progression, had no pre-determined theme and found Coltrane venturing far beyond the chord changes, making sounds not then accepted as good saxophone technique (braying, squawking, splitting his tones)—and still not accepted in some quarters—to convey deep emotion. At the Vanguard, Coltrane took his interests in modality to new levels of inspiration with his daring improvisations on "Impressions" (derived from Miles Davis's "So What" being sped up considerably) and "Spiritual." His incorporation of ideas associated with Indian ragas also blossomed here with "India." This was music which cast aside the comfortable parameters of melody, steady rhythm, and chord progressions in favor of more primal yet more sophisticated methods of organization. The music had moved towards drones and vamps defining its motion and its gravity, and this required bassists to change their entire way of thinking. Reggie Workman worked alongside new bassist Jimmy Garrison, and then Garrison became the regular bassist of the quartet, staying in Coltrane's group for the rest of Trane's life.

On Impulse! Coltrane took major risks in exploring new and challenging realms, proving that a jazz musician could be popular (he was one of the biggest attractions in jazz) without being "pop." He did a few tracks which could be seen as concessions to his audience. Examples included "Greensleeves," easily pegged as another 3/4 modal recasting of a familiar tune a la "My Favorite Things," and the standard "Softly as in a Morning Sunrise," a pretty ballad. (There were even two ballads albums, *Ballads* and a collaboration with the singer Johnny Hartman.) In effect, they ease the audience into the heavier forays, but they are equally masterful in their own way and hardly compromise—just more facets of Coltrane's all-encompassing style. It must be noted that many jazz fans were befuddled by the revolutionary changes in the music.

More unsettling developments lay in store. But first, after a string of masterful albums in 1962–64, came *A Love Supreme*, another incredibly popular album. Coltrane's spirituality came to the fore, not only in the playing and composing but in his liner note and poem. The first section of the four-part suite which made up the album even found him chanting "a love supreme, a love supreme" on the piece's simple, haunting theme. Though his music retained its questing quality, it temporarily acquired an inner peacefulness which was reflected in the relative lack of complexity of the music's basic materials.

In mid-1965, however, Coltrane moved towards the most controversial period of his career by diving into the most radical stream of the avant-garde, a movement in which free improvisation, foreshadowed by his own "Chasin' the Trane," and extreme intensity of playing were wedded in dense music which many observers saw (contrary to Coltrane's opinion, if not those of some of his collaborators) as angry, even hostile. He made the album *Ascension* with his quartet augmented by three other saxophonists, two trumpeters, and bassist Art Davis. Its structure and construction had been anticipated by Ornette Coleman's revolutionary 1960 recording *Free Jazz*, with minimal thematic material interspersed at widely spaced intervals among vast swatches of collective improvisation which used neither chords nor modes nor any pre-set arrangements, and thus tended towards atonality. The ferocious improvisations of fellow tenor saxists Archie Shepp and Pharoah Sanders took the language of Coltrane's "Chasin' the Trane" and Albert Ayler's textural approach to saxophone tone to its logical extreme in a music in which the point was not the notes, but the sounds with which they were voiced. It was music which alienated most of the mainstream even as it fascinated a core of listeners who reveled in its emotional and sonic intensity.

Sanders became a regular member of Coltrane's band, and before the end of the year, another drummer was added, Rashied Ali. Both Jones and Ali played in the group for a while, eventually prompting Tyner to decide to leave the group, frustrated that his playing couldn't be heard about theirs. Jones also left, and Alice Coltrane, John's second wife, took over on piano. If she was hardly the virtuoso that Tyner had become, she and Garrison were adept at filling musical space and thus providing Coltrane's music with the sonic heft he sought—virtuosity was not a goal. This quintet was the group Coltrane used for most of 1966 and until his death in 1967, and it has been consistently underrated by jazz historians unsympathetic to the territory where Trane's continuing quest for new sounds had taken him. His final recording, *Expression*, has something of the quality of ambition unrealized, but his premature passing, at age 40 due to liver cancer, left unanswered the question of where his music's final destination might have been. Certainly his intensely documented career left enough greatness to be thankful for in every stage.

what to buy: *Blue Train* ♫♫♫♫ (Blue Note, 1957, prod. Alfred Lion/1997, reissue prod. Michael Cuscuna) was a one-off recording made while Coltrane was contracted to Prestige. Working with a stellar lineup of Lee Morgan (trumpet), Curtis Fuller (trombone), Kenny Drew (piano), Paul Chambers (bass), and Philly Joe Jones (drums), Coltrane served notice that he was not only an inventive improvisor but also a masterful composer and arranger, with four of the five pieces—"Blue Train," "Moment's Notice," "Locomotion," and "Lazy Bird"—his own, most now classics. Spring for the 20-bit Super Bit Mapping remaster on the enhanced CD that proclaims itself "The Ultimate Blue Train." Not only does it have nifty CD-ROM material, it also boasts superb sound and alternate takes of the title track and "Lazy Bird." Recommending a seven-CD box set as a first purchase is not to be taken lightly, but *The Heavyweight Champion: The Complete Atlantic Recordings* ♫♫♫♫ (Atlantic Jazz/Rhino, 1995, prod. Nesuhi Ertegun, reissue prod. Joel Dorn) is not only consistently inspired across every one of the nine-plus albums' worth of material it contains (with the additional bonus of many originally unissued takes), it also covers Coltrane's most accessible period. His tone had shed some of its previous harshness, and whereas the "sheets of sound" approach of his later Prestige period had sometimes sounded slightly forced, he had since then grown so confident that the lightning-fast 16th notes flowed from him with ease. Coltrane recorded for Atlantic from January 1959 through May 1961, making seven absolutely essential albums whose contents are rearranged here in chronological order (including alternate takes) over the first six discs, starting with the blues-and-standards jam session *Bags Meets Trane* issued under vibist Milt Jackson's leadership. Two of the Atlantic albums, *Giant Steps* and *My Favorite Things*, changed the face of jazz, first in 1960 with the unusual and challenging chord progression of "Giant Steps," destined to be a proving ground for many tenor players to follow, and then in 1961 with "My Favorite Things," which put modal jazz (and the supposedly obsolete soprano saxophone) on the pop charts. Along with his various innovations and explorations, he was always comfortable on blues progressions, which allowed his earthier side to be expressed, and for that reason *Coltrane Plays the Blues* is one of his best LPs for its concentrated feeling. The final gem from his Atlantic output was *Olé Coltrane*, issued in February 1962 and drawn entirely from a May 1961 session that included guests Eric Dolphy (flute, alto sax) and Freddie Hubbard (trumpet), with Art Davis and Reggie Workman taking over the bass chores, sometimes together. This is where Tyner's piano style achieved its trademark weight and breadth, developing the modal style in an even more hypnotic, groove-like way. The title track is an 18-minute exploration of a simple flamenco riff Tyner embroiders constantly while the soloists wax lyrical. Things build to a feverish pitch of intensity, especially during Coltrane's second solo. Coltrane was already a star when he brought his quintet, with Dolphy (alto sax, bass clarinet), Tyner, Workman, and Jones, supplemented by Jimmy Garrison (bass) and including guests Ahmed Abdul-Malik (oud), Garvin Bushell (oboe, contrabassoon), and Roy Haynes (drums), to the November 1–5, 1961 gig documented on *The Complete 1961 Village Vanguard Recordings* ♫♫♫♫ (Impulse!, 1997, prod. Bob Thiele, reissue prod. Michael Cuscuna). The appearance of the original LP *Live at the Village Vanguard* in 1962 (his second album on Impulse!) vaulted Coltrane's already great reputation to an even higher level as musicians and fans alike marveled at the spontaneous invention of "Chasin' the Trane," the epic tenor/bass/drums blues improvisation which finally revealed to record buyers the overwhelming fervor Coltrane brought to live performances, where he could solo for 15 minutes at a stretch. Tapes from four nights of recording exist, and eventually three more fine albums were issued by Impulse!—*Impressions*, the logically titled *More Live at the Village Vanguard*, and *Trane's Modes*, all apparently withdrawn now that the box has appeared and rendered them redundant. Eric Dolphy is nearly the leader's match in imaginative soloing and Jones is a drumming marvel. Tyner

sounds slightly tentative, but not enough to complain about. *A Love Supreme* ♫♫♫♫ (Impulse!, 1964, prod. Bob Thiele) is a strong contender for the title of "greatest jazz album ever." The trancelike intensity of the solos' repetitive development of thematic figures is totally natural-sounding yet completely fresh. Jones swings polyrhythms as if he has four hands, Garrison lays down a solid bottom, and Tyner revolutionizes "comping" with a fully realized style that's heavily modal but harmonically rich. This instant classic remains as moving and musically rich as when it first appeared. *Interstellar Space* ♫♫♫♫ (Impulse!, 1974/1991, prod. John Coltrane, reissue prod. Michael Cuscuna) was recorded in February 1967, but not released until after Coltrane's death. It's a remarkable duo album by Coltrane and drummer Rashied Ali. Propelled by Ali's free polyrhythms, Coltrane reaches the stratosphere in unfettered improvisations which stand as the greatest work of his "late" period.

what to buy next: *The Prestige Recordings* ♫♫♫♫ (Prestige, 1991, prod. Bob Weinstock, Esmond Edwards; reissue prod. Orrin Keepnews) is, amazingly, a 16-CD box set documenting just three years, 1956–58, and isn't even everything he recorded for Prestige in that time since all the Miles Davis–led sessions with Trane are on the also crucial Miles Davis 8-CD box set *The Complete Prestige Recordings, 1951–1956* ♫♫♫♫ (Prestige, 1980/1987, prod. Bob Weinstock, Ira Gitler; reissue prod. Orrin Keepnews). The quality of the 25 sessions (as both leader and sideman) on the Coltrane box varies, with some dates sounding unprepared, but Coltrane himself is always interesting, and the microscopic view this box offers of his development is invaluable. It's true that a 16-CD set is a hefty investment, and jazz newcomers may initially prefer to sample the Prestige period via the Coltrane-led individual albums listed below, but this box offers excellent value and is better-organized thanks to its chronological presentation. The vast majority of the Coltrane-led sessions feature two rhythm section cohorts from Davis's band, Red Garland (piano) and Paul Chambers (bass), but with Art Taylor on drums rather than Philly Joe Jones. If there is any complaint besides the occasional lapses caused by inadequate rehearsal, it's that the lack of preparation also led to a reliance on standards and head arrangements of common chord progressions rather than original compositions (though "Straight Street" and a few other Trane-penned classics appear), but of course Coltrane was capable of making any musical material fascinating. Coltrane's Impulse! years were not devoted exclusively to pushing the boundaries of jazz, and even projects of a commercial nature produced artistically satisfying results. The all-ballads session *John Coltrane and Johnny Hartman* ♫♫♫♫♫ (Impulse!, 1963, prod. Bob

Thiele) matched Coltrane, whose superlative ballad playing was overshadowed by his other attributes, with the unsurpassed honey-smooth voice and phrasing of Johnny Hartman. Hartman had a versatile baritone, light and creamy on top, with an expressive but not overdone terminal vibrato; in lower ranges he sounds heftier yet consummately mellow. Pairing Hartman with the Coltrane Quartet was producer Bob Thiele's idea, and the result is a small gem of expression and emotion, an even better place to luxuriate in Coltrane's ballad-playing than the *Ballads* album itself. On the opposite end of the musical spectrum, *The Major Works of John Coltrane* 🎵🎵🎵🎵 (Impulse!, 1965/1992, prod. Bob Thiele, John Coltrane) is a two-CD set which most notably contains the two mind-blowing 40-minute free improvisations each known as *Ascension*, which in either version ranks among the densest, most intense music in the "energy" vein of free improv and still stand as monolithic landmarks. Modeled to an extent on Ornette Coleman's *Free Jazz*, it uses an expanded group with Coltrane, Tyner, Garrison, and Jones joined by saxophonists Archie Shepp, Pharoah Sanders, John Tchicai, and Marion Brown, trumpeters Freddie Hubbard and Dewey Johnson, and bassist Art Davis. Dissenting critics consider the playing to be mere screaming, but rarely have screams been so eloquent. The three other tracks, of similar vintage and including Sanders, multi-instrumentalist Donald Garrett, and others, are hardly "major works" by Coltrane's standards but have their moments. The four-CD *Live in Japan* 🎵🎵🎵🎵 (Impulse!, 1973/1991, prod. Michael Cuscuna) offers an extraordinary July 1966 concert document of the quintet with Sanders, only one disc's worth of which was released on LP. "My Favorite Things" is over 57 minutes and finds Coltrane playing the theme and soloing on alto sax rather than soprano sax (though well into the performance he also solos on soprano). "Crescent" gets a 54-and-a-half minute reading, while "Afro Blue" and "Leo" receive only slightly less epic performances and "Peace on Earth" is heard twice in 25- and 26-minute versions, demonstrating the storied live excursions this group was famous for. Inevitably there are slack moments; certainly few listeners will take much away from Garrison's 13-minute bass solo on "Crescent." But ironically it's not that, but rather the truly overwhelming intensity of the horns which presents the biggest challenge to listeners—but a challenge well worth accepting, without which no one's understanding of Coltrane's body of work is complete.

what to avoid: There is absolutely no John Coltrane recording which should be truly avoided. However, the two-CD *The Bethlehem Years* 🎵🎵 (Bethlehem, 1957), as enjoyable as it is at times, is one of the least crucial to his legacy, involving no sessions on

J OHN COLTRANE

song "Out of This World"

album *Coltrane*
(Impulse!, 1962/1997)

instrument Tenor saxophone

Monster Solo

which he was a leader and only one Trane tune, "Pristine." It combines two 1957 recording dates—an Art Blakey big band album (plus two quintet tracks) and an all-star big band jam session. Two other albums feature only one or two appearances by Trane's group. Of these, the somewhat deceptively packaged *New Thing at Newport* 🎵🎵🎵 (Impulse!, 1965/1991, prod. Bob Thiele, reissue prod. Michael Cuscuna) contains two tracks by the Coltrane Quartet and five by Archie Shepp's group, with no collaborations between the two saxophonists. All the material has value, and for that matter this might serve as a good introduction to Shepp's playing; nonetheless this album isn't a priority, Coltrane-wise. Similarly, *The New Wave in Jazz* 🎵🎵🎵 (Impulse!, 1968/1994, prod. Bob Thiele, reissue prod. Michael Cuscuna) documents a 1965 benefit concert where the only Coltrane track is a classic-quartet reading of "Nature Boy." The other groups included are variously led by Archie Shepp, Charles Tolliver, and Grachan Moncur III.

the rest:
Dakar 🎵🎵🎵 (Prestige, 1957)

Cattin' with Coltrane and Quinichette 𝄞𝄞𝄞𝄞 (Prestige, 1957)
Coltrane 𝄞𝄞𝄞𝄞𝄞 (Prestige, 1957)
Lush Life 𝄞𝄞𝄞𝄞 (Prestige, 1957)
Traneing In 𝄞𝄞𝄞𝄞 (Prestige, 1957)
The Last Trane 𝄞𝄞𝄞𝄞 (Prestige, 1957–58)
Soultrane 𝄞𝄞𝄞𝄞 (Prestige, 1958)
The Believer 𝄞𝄞𝄞𝄞𝄞 (Prestige, 1958)
Kenny Burrell & John Coltrane 𝄞𝄞𝄞𝄞𝄞 (New Jazz, 1958)
Settin' the Pace 𝄞𝄞𝄞𝄞 (Prestige, 1958)
Black Pearls 𝄞𝄞𝄞𝄞𝄞 (Prestige, 1958)
Standard Coltrane 𝄞𝄞𝄞𝄞 (Prestige, 1958)
Stardust 𝄞𝄞𝄞𝄞 (Prestige, 1958)
Bahia 𝄞𝄞𝄞𝄞𝄞 (Prestige, 1958)
Giant Steps 𝄞𝄞𝄞𝄞𝄞 (Atlantic, 1960)
Coltrane Jazz 𝄞𝄞𝄞𝄞𝄞 (Atlantic, 1961)
My Favorite Things 𝄞𝄞𝄞𝄞𝄞 (Atlantic, 1961)
(With Milt Jackson) *Bags & Trane* 𝄞𝄞𝄞𝄞 (Atlantic, 1961)
The Complete Africa/Brass Sessions 𝄞𝄞𝄞𝄞𝄞 (Impulse!, 1961)
The Paris Concert 𝄞𝄞𝄞𝄞 (Pablo, 1961 or 1962/1979)
Olé 𝄞𝄞𝄞𝄞 (Atlantic, 1962)
Coltrane Plays the Blues 𝄞𝄞𝄞𝄞𝄞 (Atlantic, 1962)
Bye Bye Blackbird 𝄞𝄞𝄞𝄞 (Pablo, 1962/1981)
The European Tour 𝄞𝄞𝄞𝄞 (Pablo, 1962/1980)
Ballads 𝄞𝄞𝄞𝄞𝄞 (Impulse!, 1962)
Duke Ellington and John Coltrane 𝄞𝄞𝄞𝄞 (Impulse!, 1962)
Coltrane 𝄞𝄞𝄞𝄞 (Impulse!, 1962/1997)
Dear Old Stockholm 𝄞𝄞𝄞𝄞 (Impulse!, 1963 & 1965)
Afro-Blue Impressions 𝄞𝄞𝄞𝄞𝄞 (Pablo, 1963/1977)
Coltrane Live at Birdland 𝄞𝄞𝄞𝄞𝄞 (Impulse!, 1963)
Coltrane's Sound 𝄞𝄞𝄞𝄞𝄞 (Atlantic, 1964)
Crescent 𝄞𝄞𝄞𝄞𝄞 (Impulse!, 1964)
Sun Ship 𝄞𝄞𝄞𝄞 (Impulse!, 1965)
John Coltrane Quartet Plays . . . 𝄞𝄞𝄞 (Impulse!, 1965)
First Meditations 𝄞𝄞𝄞𝄞 (Impulse!, 1965/1977)
Transition 𝄞𝄞𝄞𝄞 (Impulse!, 1965/1970)
Live at the Village Vanguard Again! 𝄞𝄞𝄞𝄞𝄞 (Impulse!, 1966)
Live in Seattle 𝄞𝄞𝄞𝄞 (Impulse!, 1966)
Meditations 𝄞𝄞𝄞𝄞𝄞 (Impulse!, 1966)
The Avant-Garde 𝄞𝄞𝄞𝄞 (Atlantic, 1966)
Expression 𝄞𝄞𝄞𝄞 (Impulse!, 1967)
The Coltrane Legacy 𝄞𝄞𝄞 (Atlantic, 1970)
The Gentle Side of John Coltrane 𝄞𝄞𝄞𝄞 (Impulse!, 1974–75)
Newport '63 𝄞𝄞𝄞𝄞 (Impulse!, 1993)
Stellar Regions 𝄞𝄞𝄞𝄞 (Impulse!, 1995)

worth searching for: *Coltrane Time* 𝄞𝄞𝄞𝄞 (Douglas/United Artists, 1972, prod. Tom Wilson) is a slightly unnerving 1958 recording, somewhat daring for its time, with Cecil Taylor (piano), Kenny Dorham (trumpet), Chuck Israels (bass), and Louis Hayes (drums). The clash of different worlds, with Trane the sonic intermediary between the revolutionary Taylor and the boppers, produces an odd tension. This record is mostly interesting for the interactions between Taylor and Coltrane. Thanks to Italy's exceptional view of publishing matters up until a few years ago, companies based in that country were able to issue a wealth of concert recordings which were technically not bootlegs. One such Coltrane item is *The Promise* 𝄞𝄞𝄞𝄞 (Moon, 1994), which contains six live tracks with the classic Tyner/Garrison/Jones quartet, half from Stuttgart, Germany on November 4, 1963, and half from Belgium in 1965, the latter including a nearly 21-minute "My Favorite Things."

influences:

◄◄ Johnny Hodges, Charlie Parker, Sonny Stitt, Dexter Gordon, Thelonious Monk, John Gilmore, Albert Ayler, Ornette Coleman, Ravi Shankar

►► Pharoah Sanders, Archie Shepp, Branford Marsalis, Myron Walden, David Liebman, Steve Grossman, Charles Gayle, Zusaan Kali Fasteau, David Murray, Gato Barbieri, Billy Harper, Jerry Bergonzi, Peter Brotzmann, Sonny Sharrock, Jerry Garcia, Carlos Santana, John McLaughlin, Charles Lloyd, Javon Jackson, Joe Lovano, Borah Bergman, Michael Marcus, Ivo Perelman, Courtney Pine, Joshua Redman, James Carter, John Stubblefield, Michael Brecker, Frank Wright, Charles Tyler, Glenn Spearman

Steve Holtje

Turiya Alice Coltrane

Born Turiya McLeod, August 27, 1937, in Detroit, MI.

If music is a vibration engendering meditative introspection and cosmic awareness, Turiya Alice Coltrane has been a prime U.S.-born practitioner. She learned keyboard through her membership at Detroit's Mount Olive Baptist Church, study of European classical forms, and training from Bud Powell. Her mastery of the harp as an improvisatory device has enamored her to aficionados and new listeners alike. Coltrane is one of the three women (along with Dorothy Ashby and Patrice Nasoma Williams—also from Detroit) who have most thoroughly extended the language of jazz through use of the decidedly difficult-to-manipulate instrument.

Turiya Alice Coltrane was a member of groups led by Kenny Burrell, Johnny Griffin, Lucky Thompson, Yusef Lateef, and Terry Gibbs. She met seminal saxophonist-composer John Coltrane and married him in 1965, replacing McCoy Tyner as pianist in John's group the following year; she can be heard on such albums as *Live at the Village Vanguard Again!*, *Expression*, *Live in*

Japan, and *Stellar Regions*. Their three children are also musicians (Miki, Oran, Ravi). Alice Coltrane's investigation of composition, arrangement, and spiritual themes through music continued after her husband's passing in 1967. Hinduism became her religious practice, and as her oeuvre expanded, jazz and European classical underpinnings supported her work with classic Indian instrumentation, string arrangements, and collaboration with veterans such as Pharoah Sanders, Joe Henderson, Ben Riley, Rashied Ali, Ornette Coleman, and Carlos Santana. Her fusing of jazz with Indian and Hindi musical forms has yielded heavenly chants, compositions named for her guru ("Journey into Satchidananda") and other works in which her "out" style on organ and harmonium resonate. Her reading of Igor Stravinsky's "The Rite of Spring" goes deep as a bottomless well.

Aside from appearances at a New York tribute to John Coltrane with her sons, and another in Los Angeles with Ravi, Oran, and Miki, Alice Coltrane's career as performer and recording artist seems to have concluded in the late 1970s. Few of her albums as a leader remain in print in this country, though some are on CD in Europe.

what to buy: *Ptah the el Daoud* ✗✗✗✗ (Impulse!, 1970) is jazz exemplifying all its profound elements. It's satisfyingly grounded and it's available, too! Alice plays piano on some tunes, harp on the others. With both Pharoah Sanders and Joe Henderson blowing and the double percussion of Ben Riley and Rashied Ali, this entire album is a gem.

what to buy next: The title track of *Journey into Satchidananda* ✗✗✗✗ (Impulse!, 1971) and "Something about John Coltrane" are fascinating glimpses into the results of Alice Coltrane's creative processing. Working as usual with the cream of musicians, she made an album which, like *Ptah the el Daoud*, will draw in new listeners and alert veteran listeners to why they're alive.

the rest:
A Monastic Trio ✗✗✗ (Impulse!, 1968)
(With John Coltrane) *Cosmic Music* ✗✗✗ (Impulse!, 1968)
Universal Consciousness ✗✗✗✗ (Impulse!, 1972)
(With Joe Henderson) *The Elements* ✗✗✗✗ (Fantasy, 1973/1996)
(With Carlos Santana) *Illuminations* ✗✗✗✗ (CBS, 1974; Columbia/Sony, 1996)
Eternity ✗✗✗✗ (Warner Bros., 1976)
Radha-Krsna Nama Sankirtana ✗✗✗ (Warner Bros., 1977)
Transcendence ✗✗✗ (Warner Bros., 1977)
Transfiguration ✗✗✗ (Warner Bros., 1978)

worth searching for: The collaboration between Marian McPartland and Alice Coltrane, *Piano Jazz* ✗✗✗✗ (Jazz Alliance,

1985), was recorded for broadcast on McPartland's syndicated National Public Radio program. It includes conversation, solo piano, and duets by both. Now, who can resist the conversation of two women geniuses? *Infinity* ✗✗✗✗ (Impulse!, 1972) takes 1960s recordings of the John Coltrane quartet as its basis. Years later, Alice went in the studio with more musicians and in effect created a new work using the original recordings as the foundation. With Trane working out amid swirls of atonal strings, this is a statement of transformative energy. Listen especially to "Living Space."

influences:
◀◀ Dorothy Ashby, Bud Powell
▶▶ Zusaan Kali Fasteau

Nkenge Zola

Eddie Condon

Born Albert Edwin Condon, November 16, 1905, in Goodland, IN. Died August 4, 1973, in New York, NY.

Eddie Condon was a well-known entrepreneur, raconteur, a possessor of a quick and acerbic wit, who had an affinity for bow ties, slicked-down hair, double-breasted suits, and, as befitted his Gallic heritage, a taste for Irish whiskey. He was also a sometime rhythm guitarist, a splendid organizer, and a spokesman for and a champion of Chicago-styled music. The term "Chicago style" originally embraced unarranged small group improvisation performed in a direct, straight-ahead fashion, using sparsely placed notes and hot intonation and intensity, rather than slick virtuosity. Coincident with World War II and the traditional jazz revival, Chicago jazz came to be associated with solo-dominated Dixieland (a term that has since fallen out of favor) and hell-bent-for-leather ensembles. Condon took part in the first jazz album ever made, producer George Avakian's 1939–1940 Decca recording, *Chicago Jazz*, which included four sides each by Eddie Condon and his Chicagoans, Jimmy McPartland and his Orchestra, and George Wettling's Chicago Rhythm Kings.

Albert Edwin Condon grew up in a musical family in which his father played violin, all four sisters were pianists, brother Cliff sang in a barbershop quartet and played alto horn, and brother Jim handed down first his ukelele and then his short-necked tenor banjo to young Eddie. By age 16, in the spring of 1922, Condon was on the road with Hollis Peavey's Jazz Bandits. Working out of the jazz mecca that was Chicago in 1924, Condon heard King Oliver and Louis Armstrong at the Lincoln Gardens, fell under the spell of cornetist Bix Beiderbecke, and hung out with young Chicago apprentice musicians like Benny Goodman, Bud Freeman, Jimmy McPartland, and Dave Tough. In 1927, he co-led the "McKenzie-Condon Chicagoans" on a groundbreaking record date for OKeh which gave definition to the term "Chicago Jazz." Fellow groundbreakers included clarinetist Frank Teschmacher, cornetist Jimmy McPartland, tenor saxophonist Bud Freeman, bassist Jim Lanigan, pianist Joe Sullivan, and young drummer Gene Krupa. In 1928, Eddie Condon moved to New York, found that work was scarce, and managed to ride out the Depression playing banjo with the Mound City Blue Blowers and making a few record dates.

As the changing sound of jazz made for subtle rhythm section alterations (tubas and banjos out, string basses and guitars in), Condon chose a full-size Gibson L-5 guitar with four strings and banjo tuning, dubbed his "porkchop" because of its shape. He played along 52nnd Street in the mid-1930s, co-led a band with clarinetist Joe Marsala during 1936–1937, and recorded as a sideman with Tempo King, Putney Dandridge, Sharkey Bonano, Bunny Berigan, Red McKenzie, and Marsala. Condon moved to Greenwich Village in 1937 to be close to the bandstand at the famed nitespot, Nick's ("home of breaks and sizzling steaks"), where he was either leader or sideman for seven years. Condon also acted as house leader for the newly formed Commodore Records in 1938, and he organized and/or led many exciting sessions for that label, working with Commodore prexy, Milt Gabler, who would later supervise Condon's Decca record dates.

In 1944, Condon began a scheduled half-hour radio show on the Blue Network, which brought what announcer Fred Robbins called freewheeling "Americondon" music into New York concert halls. The Armed Forces Radio Service transcribed 48 of the concerts and sent them around the world to U.S. troops. These broadcasts have been reissued on CD and are still thrilling to hear some 50-odd years later, with outstanding performances by many jazz giants such as Jack Teagarden, Bobby Hackett, Wild Bill Davison, The Dorsey Brothers, Pee Wee Russell, Yank Lawson, Jess Stacy, Lee Wiley, and Sidney Bechet, all at their peak during those War years. Amazing as it might seem now, Condon, who never soloed, won the *Down Beat* poll for jazz guitar playing in 1943 and 1944. He had well-connected publicist friends and he appeared regularly in the pages of *Time, Life, New Yorker,* and the *New York Times.* His weekly wartime concert broadcasts in the early 1940s were far-reaching at home and abroad. Condon was, however, when he wanted to play, a dynamic rhythm man with a keen sense of chordal voicing. One could sense or feel his four-string guitar at times when you couldn't really hear it.

In 1945, Condon opened his own club at 47 West Third Street and played host to visiting celebrities, fellow musicians, and jazz fans galore until the lease expired in 1958 and forced a relocation to the elite East side. He renewed his association with producer George Avakian by shifting from Commodore and Decca to Columbia Records in the 1950s. Condon authored or collaborated on three books, *We Called It Music, Eddie Condon's Treasure of Jazz,* and *Eddie Condon's Scrapbook of Jazz,* which provided jazz fans with witty insights and some valuable photographic memories of Eddie Condon's life, his work, and some of his notable musical friends. Condon's last dozen years or so were spent making occasional overseas tours and a few record dates. Serious traditional or mainstream record collectors cannot get by without a healthy dose of Eddie Condon in their record or CD libraries.

what to buy: A generous offering of Condon-style jazz is contained in the 20-track CD *Eddie Condon, 1938–1940* ♪♪♪♪ (Commodore and Decca, 1938–1940, prod. various/Classics, 1994, prod. Gilles Petard), which highlights six sessions made originally for Commodore or Decca over a 31-month span. Clarinetist Pee Wee Russell and the leader are common to all the sides, with frontline horn men Bobby Hackett, Max Kaminsky, Muggsy Spanier, and Marty Marsala appearing here and there with some nifty contributions. Trombonists Jack Teagarden, Brad Gowans, Miff Mole, and George Brunis get in their licks, and tenor saxophonist Bud Freeman brings his looping, loping, elliptical style to a dozen tunes. The August 3, 1939 Decca session *Chicago Jazz* actually features Freeman's own Summa Cum Laude Orchestra with a couple of ringers. Pianists Jess Stacy, Joe Bushkin, and Joe Sullivan take their turns, and the last session of November 11, 1940 has Fats Waller on board with some scintillating piano work. It's hard to be glum when listening to the veteran jazzmen "swing out" on these classic jazz sides. Twenty later cuts by many of these hardy swingsters are collected in *Eddie Condon: Dixieland All-Stars* ♪♪♪♪ (Decca, 1939, 1944–1946, prod. George Avakian, Milt Gabler/GRP, 1994, reissue prod. Orrin Keepnews). The four "Chicago Jazz" sides repeated here (produced by Avakian) contain two unissued alternate takes ("There'll Be Some Changes Made" and "Someday, Sweetheart"). There are eight Gershwin tunes (among 16 tunes produced by Gabler) with sparkling contributions from trumpeters Yank Lawson, Bobby Hackett, Billy Butterfield, and Max Kaminsky; trombonists Jack Teagarden or Lou McGarity; and clarinetists Joe Dixon, Pee Wee Russell or Edmond Hall. A truly classic ballad performance of "When Your Lover Has Gone," features Hackett, Teagarden, and Butterfield. Lee Wiley lends her warm vocalizing to "Someone to Watch Over Me" and "The Man I Love." Pianists Gene Schroeder, Joe Bushkin, Joe Sullivan, and Jess Stacy alternate, while Dave Tough, Johnny Blowers, and George Wettling take turns behind the drum kit. This set has a nice mix of the relaxed and hot sides from Condon's Decca period and is recommended for the swing-minded traditionalist. The Condon Town Hall concert broadcasts were an absolute listening must for jazz fans who owned radios back in the 1944–1945 war years. The 48 broadcasts that survived via Armed Forces Radio Service Transcriptions have been made available on a series of CDs by Jazzology Records. Chances are that if you buy one, you'll want more. *The Town Hall Concerts, Vol. 7* 🎵🎵🎵 (Jazzology, 1991, prod. George H. Buck Jr.) is a good place to start because it contains some fine trombone by Jack Teagarden and rare appearances by his sister, pianist Norma Teagarden, and trumpeter Wingy Manone. Also featured at length are Condon stalwarts clarinetist Pee Wee Russell, trumpeter Max Kaminsky, baritone saxist Ernie Caceres, cornetist Bobby Hackett, pianist Jess Stacy, and frequent guest, soprano saxophonist Sidney Bechet. Condon and host Fred Robbins chat a bit between numbers, which reminds the listener that this was, after all, a radio broadcast. The series gives a glimpse of many seldom-heard musicians such as James P. Johnson, Willie "The Lion" Smith, Oran "Hot Lips" Page, Joe Marsala, Bill Harris, Benny Morton, Bob Haggart, Edmond Hall, Jonah Jones, and Muggsy Spanier, along with the familiar names of Gene Krupa, Jimmy and Tommy Dorsey, and Woody Herman, who all gave generously of their time for this musical corner of the war effort.

what to buy next: The Associated Transcription Services is the source of a 21-tune, 33-track (including alternate takes and breakdowns) collection served up in *The Definitive Eddie Condon and His Jazz Concert All-Stars, Vol. 1* 🎵🎵🎵 (Stash, 1990, prod. Jerry Valburn, Will Friedwald). Members of the Condon mob visited the Musak Studios twice in 1944 and came up with some straight-ahead, Condon-style performances containing some very attractive solos scattered throughout. The June 8th session has some lyrical Bobby Hackett cornet, some rolling and rollicking Gene Schroeder piano, generous doses of Ernie Caceres's booming baritone sax, and Pee Wee Russell's spiky eccentric clarinet work. Hot Lips Page is on hand for his "Uncle Sam's Blues" ("Uncle Sam ain't no woman, but he sure can take your man"), a minor classic. Billy Butterfield reprises his famous solo on Bob Haggart's "What's New?," with the composer himself in the rhythm section. All in all, it's a relaxed, easygoing slice of "Americondon." Vintage Condon is visited in *Eddie Condon, 1927–1938* 🎵🎵🎵 (Classics, 1994, prod. Anatol Schenker) which

reissues the classic McKenzie and Condon's Chicagoans efforts for the OKeh label, Eddie Condon's 1928 quartet with Frank Teschmacher, the 1928 Victor recordings by Eddie Condon and his Footwarmers & his Hot Shots, the 1933 Brunswick recordings, and the start of the 1938 Commodore sessions. These are all classics of their genre and sound as good now as they did decades ago. If you haven't discovered these or if your old 78s are as worn as most, this CD is a sound investment. *The Complete CBS Recordings of Eddie Condon and His All-Stars* 🎵🎵🎵🎵 (CBS, 1953–1957, prod. various/Mosaic, 1994, reissue prod. Michael Cuscuna) is a limited edition set that seemingly transports the earth shaking activities from Condon's Club to the recording studios. In the era of the longplaying record, the time limits imposed by 78rpm recordings are removed here and the improvements in recording techniques are obvious in this five-CD collection of sessions produced by George Avakian (1953–1957), Bob Morgan (January 1962), Teo Macero (September 1962), bringing all the Columbia dates together in one package. There are 72 tracks, and the 57 produced by George Avakian are pure gems. The remaining 15 certainly have their moments, but the rapport between Condon and producer Avakian makes for the finer musical happenings in this monster collection. Condonites Bobby Hackett, Billy Butterfield, Lou McGarity, Cutty Cutshall, Vic Dickenson, Peanuts Hucko, Bud Freeman, and Pee Wee Russell are all in top form. Edmond Hall and Bob Wilber are also on hand to provide outstanding examples of jazz clarinet on the 42 tracks split between them. Gene Schroeder, at the piano, offers some of his best recorded efforts. George Wettling and Cliff Leeman split the drum chores on all but eight tunes which are handled by Bostonian Buzzy Drootin. The versatile Dick Cary appears on eight cuts doubling on trumpet and his mellow alto horn, then switches to piano for 10 additional tunes in 1962. Wild Bill Davison, who shows here that he came by his name with good reason, has some of his most exciting solos on these swinging Columbia sides. Eddie Condon can be heard directing traffic on some numbers, shouting encouragement or wisecracking on others, and his guitar can be felt throughout these sessions. This set is available by mail-order from Mosaic Records, 35 Melrose Place, Stamford, CT 06902-7533 (Phone: 203-327-7111).

best of the rest:

Eddie Condon & His All-Stars Dixieland Jam 🎵🎵🎵 (Columbia, 1989)
Eddie Condon Live in Japan 🎵🎵🎵 (Chiaroscuro, 1991)
Live at the New School 🎵🎵🎵 (Chiaroscuro, 1991)
We Dig Dixieland 🎵🎵🎵 (Savoy, 1992)
Dr. Jazz Vol. 1: Eddie Condon with Johnny Windhurst, No. 1 🎵🎵🎵 (radio air checks) (Storyville, 1993)
Eddie Condon, 1942–1943 🎵🎵🎵 (Classics, 1994)

Ringside at Condon's 🎵🎵🎵 (Savoy, 1994)

Eddie Condon, 1933–1940 🎵🎵🎵 (Jazz Portraits, 1994)

Windy City Jazz 🎵🎵🎵 (Topaz, 1995)

Dr. Jazz Vol. 8: Eddie Condon with Johnny Windhurst, No. 2 🎵🎵🎵 (radio air checks) (Storyville, 1995)

Dr. Jazz Vol. 5: Eddie Condon with Wild Bill Davison, No. 1 🎵🎵🎵 (radio air checks) (Storyville, 1995)

Dr. Jazz Vol. 11: Eddie Condon with Wild Bill Davison, No. 2 🎵🎵🎵 (radio air checks) (Storyville, 1995)

Eddie Condon: Chicago Style 🎵🎵🎵 (ASV/Living Era, 1996)

Eddie Condon, 1928–1931 🎵🎵🎵 (Timeless, 1996)

influences:

▶▶ Marty Grosz, Ed Polcer, James Dapogny, The Original Salty Dogs

John T. Bitter

Graham Connah

Born August 14, 1961, in Charlotte, NC.

Graham Connah has been playing piano around the San Francisco Bay Area for about a decade. A skilled composer and improviser, he's performed in numerous professional contexts, from an appearance at the Monterey Jazz Festival in 1995 to a lengthy stint as house pianist at Harris's, a premier beef eatery in the city by the bay. Other festival gigs include the prestigious San Francisco Jazz Fest (1997) and the 8th Annual Eddie Moore Jazz Fest (1997). Connah has successfully worked in a wide range of ensemble configurations, from small improvising combos to his 13-piece big band, NoPorkestra & Chorus. But it's with his regular sextet, Sour Note Six, that the pianist truly stands out as a composer with a solid vision. Although his tunes allow for dynamic blowing, Connah's sophisticated melodic/harmonic concepts steer the thematic development throughout. The artist likes to write a lot of notes and play around with time and tempo shifts, all of which contribute to an exciting (and accessible) listen that will appeal to fans from all over the jazz map.

what to buy: *My God Has Fleas* 🎵🎵🎵 (Rastascan, 1996) showcases Connah's Sour Note Six (with clarinetist Ben Goldberg, saxophonist Rob Sudduth, trombonist Marty Wehner, bassist Trevor Dunn, and drummer Elliot Kavee). There are spectacular performances from the entire group, with plenty of harmonic movement built in multiple layers of crisscrossing melody. Focused compositions, tight ensemble execution, and inspired solos give the music an immediacy and flow.

what to buy next: Connah's self-produced debut, *Snaps Erupt at Pure Spans* 🎵🎵🎵 (Sour Note, 1994, prod. Graham Connah),

marks the genesis of the leader's Graham Connah Group with Goldberg, Sudduth, Dunn, and drummer Kenny Wollesen (just before he moved to New York to work with John Zorn, among others). The album features six extended compositions along the lines of *My God*, including a masterful collective improv on the self-effacing "Another Gratuitous Narcissistic Pseudo-Musical Experiment Utilizing Live Human Subjects."

influences:

◀◀ Charles Mingus, Andrew Hill, Steve Lacy

Sam Prestianni

Harry Connick Jr.

Born September 11, 1967, in New Orleans, LA.

Harry Connick Jr. could be largely responsible for the renaissance of big band swing and 1940s crooners among the MTV generation. The versatile entertainer began his musical career playing in Bourbon Street saloons at the age of six. Still in his youth, he collaborated with legends such as Eubie Blake, and studied with pianist James Booker. Connick made his first recording (*11*), at age 11, playing piano with a New Orleans-styled trad ensemble. Fortified with his earlier classical training, Connick received his most comprehensive jazz education from his studies with jazz pianist/educator Ellis Marsalis (father of Wynton and Branford), at the New Orleans Center for the Creative Arts. Connick moved to New York City at age 18 and studied less than two months at the Manhattan School of Music, abandoning academia to perform in churches, small jazz clubs, and on street corners in order to pursue his goal of landing a record contract with Columbia. In 1986 Connick was signed to Columbia and, after two albums, recorded his first platinum album, *When Harry Met Sally*, featuring his Sinatra-style vocals, solo piano, and performances with his big band. Along with his musical talents, Connick's matinee idol looks have helped him establish himself as a gifted actor. His acting debut was in *Memphis Belle* (1990), and he has since held supporting roles in *Little Man Tate* (1991), *Copycat* (1995), *Independence Day* (1996), and *Excess Baggage* (1997). Connick also has a starring role opposite Sandra Bullock in *Hope Floats* (1998).

what to buy: Connick's popularity exploded with the release of the soundtrack of *When Harry Met Sally* 🎵🎵🎵🎵 (Columbia, 1989, prod. Marc Shaiman, Harry Connick Jr.), a collection of classic love songs such as "Love Is Here to Stay" and "It Had to

Harry Connick Jr. **(Archive Photos)**

Be You," enhanced by Connick's sultry voice and smooth jazz style. On his album *25* ♫♫♫♫ (Columbia, 1992, prod. Tracey Freeman), Connick alternates his vocals with instrumental solos for a unique and fun mix. This recording features several jazz staples, everything from "Lazybones" to "Muskrat Ramble" to "I'm an Old Cowhand (from the Rio Grande)," and the last is truly a delight. Connick's Sinatra-like sounds are well represented in *Blue Light, Red Light* ♫♫♫♫ (Columbia, 1991, prod. Tracey Freeman), which finds Connick conducting a full-blown big band featuring, among other talents, the trumpets of Leroy Jones and Jeremy Davenport (the latter made his 1996 recording debut on Telarc with his Connick-influenced vocals). The songs, all written or co-written by Connick, run the gamut of emotions, from the stunning love ballad "Jill" to the big band electrified "Just Kiss Me."

what to buy next: *She* ♫♫♫ (Columbia, 1994, prod. Tracey Freeman) marks Connick's move from the big band style to the funky sounds reflecting his New Orleans roots. Here he explores a variety of styles, from funky instrumentals to minimalist vocal recitations, and uses only local musicians. He continues this hometown tribute in *Star Turtle* ♫♫♫ (Columbia, 1996, prod. Tracey Freeman), a concept album in which Connick meets up with a turtle from outer space and shows the visitor around the city. While most of the songs superbly meld his funky/jazzy/bluesy sounds, you'll enjoy the disc more if you skip the four "Star Turtle" tracks altogether. Connick's *To See You* ♫♫♫♫ (Columbia, 1997, prod. Tracey Freeman) offers a return to the mellow croonings that popularized him originally, combining the jazz quartet with the orchestra to produce a collection of love ballads ideal for romance. As well as playing piano and singing, Connick conducts a 65-piece orchestra, and he wrote and arranged all of the tunes.

the rest:
11 ♫♫♫ (Columbia, 1978/1992)
Harry Connick Jr. ♫♫♫ (CBS, 1987)
20 ♫♫♫ (CBS, 1988)
We Are in Love ♫♫♫♫ (Sony, 1990)
Lofty's Roach Souffle ♫♫♫ (CBS, 1990)
When My Heart Finds Christmas ♫♫♫♫ (Columbia, 1993)

influences:

◀◀ Fats Waller, Earl Hines, Erroll Garner, Hoagy Carmichael, Duke Ellington, Ellis Marsalis, James Booker, Nat "King" Cole, Frank Sinatra, Tony Bennett, Mel Tormé

Dana Barnes and Nancy Ann Lee

Chris Connor

Born November 8, 1927, in Kansas City, MO.

Evolving out of the cool-school of jazz, Chris Connor was recommended to Stan Kenton in the early 1950s by June Christy, who left the band. Connor is known for her relaxed yet controlled interpretations, sung with warmth and an understated, sparing use of dynamics, all of which helped to lend an individual style and sound to her work. Studying clarinet at the age of eight, Connor began singing in her teens, and was later vocalist with a big band at the University of Missouri. Moving back to Kansas City for a short time, she worked with Bob Brookmeyer as vocalist in a small group. In 1949 she moved to New York City and sang with Claude Thornhill as a member of his vocal group, Snowflakes, as well as with Herbie Fields. Joining Stan Kenton's band in 1952, she recorded her famed version of "All about Ronnie." After going out on her own in 1953, Connor was picked up by Bethlehem Records, who hired Sy Oliver to put together a band to back her. Record sales, for that time, were phenomenal. When she performed at Basin Street East and the Village Vanguard, people lined up around the block to see and hear her. Recording for Atlantic in 1956, Connor's records continued to sell at an unprecedented rate. In the 1960s pop music changed considerably, and with the advent of rock and roll, the sound of the Cool disappeared. Connor's comeback in the mid-70s, brought her back into the public eye, with sessions that included a recording with the Maynard Ferguson Band. She has continued to record and perform on into the 1990s, including a recording for Enja in 1992.

what to buy: *Chris Connor Sings Lullabys of Birdland* ♫♫♫♫ (Bethlehem/Charly, 1954/1997) finds Connor accompanied by the Ellis Larkin Trio and Vinnie Burke's quartet with Art Mardigan on drums. Connor is in great form on this recording as she interprets the material, which includes "Lullaby of Birdland," as well as "What Is There to Say", "Chiquita from Chi-Wah-Wah," and "A Cottage for Sale." *Sings the George Gershwin Almanac of Song* ♫♫♫♫ (Atlantic, 1961/1989, prod. various) finds Connor flawlessly interpreting Gershwin classics with such depth of feeling that she leaves the listener breathless. Included are gems such as "I've Got a Crush on You," a medley from "Porgy and Bess," "They Can't Take That Away from Me," "Fascinatin' Rhythm," "Our Love Is Here to Stay," "Embraceable You," and others. Connor is accompanied by 10 different bands, including those led by Doc Severinsen and Herbie Mann.

best of the rest:
A Jazz Date with Chris Connor/Chris Craft ♫♫♫♫ (Atlantic/Rhino, 1958/1994)
As Time Goes By ♫♫♫ (Enja, 1992)

Lover Come Back to Me 🎵🎵🎵🎵 (Evidence, 1995)

influences:
◀◀ Anita O'Day
▶▶ Irene Kral, Morgana King

Susan K. Berlowitz

Bill Connors

Born September 24, 1949, in Los Angeles, CA.

Bill Connors started playing guitar at age 14 during the "English Invasion." In the early 1970s he moved to San Francisco and played with Mike Nock and Steve Swallow. Connors gained greater visibility with Chick Corea from 1973–74 as the first guitarist for Return to Forever, featuring Stanley Clarke and Lenny White. But Connors was inspired to head in another direction and focused his attention on the acoustic nylon-string guitar. A stint with Jan Garbarek in the late 1970s rekindled Connors's interest in the electric guitar and he began a practice regimen that incorporated classical right hand technique with the legato sound of John Coltrane's horn. In the early 1980s Connors formed and recorded with the first of his electric trios. He has recorded albums for ECM, some of which have not been released in the United States, but check out the ECM website for ordering information.

what to buy: *Step It!* 🎵🎵🎵🎵 (Evidence, 1984/1994, prod. Steve Khan, Doug Epstein) is a landmark in guitar fusion session featuring interesting compositions and creative playing with drummer Dave Weckl (just before Weckl joined Chick Corea's Elektric Band) and the unsung Tom Kennedy on bass. More creative tunes plus the addition of Kim Plainfield on drums makes *Double Up* 🎵🎵🎵🎵 (Evidence, 1986/1994, prod. Bill Connors, Doug Epstein) a most satisfying listening experience. Odd time signatures and flowing technique are the modus operandi.

the rest:
Theme to a Guardian 🎵🎵🎵🎵 (ECM 1974/1994)
Assembler 🎵🎵🎵🎵 (Evidence, 1987/1994)

worth searching for: A 1974 studio date that may be hard to find, *Quiet Song* 🎵🎵🎵🎵 (Improvising Artists, 1978/1994 prod. Paul Bley, Carol Goss) features Paul Bley (acoustic piano, Fender Rhodes electric piano), Jimmy Guiffre (alto flute, clarinet), and Connors (acoustic guitar) performing in various configurations. Included are 10 introspective and freely improvised originals (mostly written by Bley) that tend to plod along at the same tempos. Still, there are moments among the contemplative art songs when the music is attractively melodic and textu-

rally well-blended, especially when Connors adds his sparse guitar improvs to "Goodbye," with Bley playing both acoustic piano and the Fender Rhodes, and Guiffre lending bittersweet clarinet cries to this blue and melancholy version of the Gordon Jenkins song. That head-turning tune makes this session a worthwhile. Look for it under Bley or Guiffre.

influences:
◀◀ The Beatles, the Rolling Stones, Cream, John Coltrane, Eric Clapton, Julian Bream

David C. Gross and Nancy Ann Lee

Norman Connors

Born March 1, 1948, in Philadelphia, PA.

With success as an instrumentalist, composer, singer, producer, and astute talent scout, Norman Connors has built a career to confound those who would limit drummers to work behind the trap set. Early on, he became one of jazz fusion's first artists, moving from work recording with John Coltrane, Pharoah Sanders, and Archie Shepp to leading a crack band featuring Stanley Clarke, Ron Carter, and Hubert Laws. A drummer since age five, Connors began recording as a teen with stars such as Coltrane and "Brother" Jack McDuff. Joining Sanders's band shortly after a move to New York in 1971, he eventually found himself offered contracts with two record labels. Choosing musical freedom over a company that wanted to mold him into yet another soul/jazz artist, Connors embarked on a series of records for Buddah subsidiary Cobblestone Records that helped define the fusion jazz movement. Aided by bandmates Clarke, Herbie Hancock, and Airto, he stirred funk, jazz, and soul rhythms into a heady stew of albums. But his biggest success would come with a more conventional tune, "You Are My Starship," a ballad smash he recorded in 1976 that would be his biggest hit. As the advent of disco made his type of soul more obsolete, Connors turned to producing and discovering other artists, including Dee Dee Bridgewater (who wrote "Starship"), Angela Bofill, Phyllis Hyman, Glenn Jones, Norman Brown, and Marion Meadows. Even now, Connors continues to tour with his Starship Orchestra, producing records for several artists on Motown's jazz label, MoJazz.

what to buy: Filled with classic cuts from his Buddah Records period, *The Best of Norman Connors and Friends* 🎵🎵🎵🎵 (The Right Stuff, 1997, prod. various) lines up all of his most famous cuts, from the dreamy "You Are My Starship" to his thrilling duet with Phyllis Hyman on the Stylistics's "Betcha by Golly Wow."

what to buy next: As the best of his expansive, 1970s-era jazz records, *Dark of Light/Dance of Magic* 🎵🎵🎵 (Sequel, 1996, prod. various) stands as a quality combo pack of albums—assembled by Sequel into one unit for fans. Featuring powerhouse bass work from Clarke and Airto's nimble percussion efforts, these early '70s albums stand as a funkified precursor to the musical gymnastics bands such as Return to Forever would bring to modern jazz.

what to avoid: When it comes to artists with careers as long and varied as Connors', bad greatest-hits collections are often a fan's worst pitfall. That's why all but the most serious completists should stay clear of *The Best of Norman Connors* **woof!** (Sequel, 1995, prod. various), which only features a few quality cuts along with a bunch of filler.

the rest:
Slewfoot 🎵🎵🎵 (Buddah, 1974)
Love from the Sun 🎵🎵🎵 (Buddah, 1974)
Saturday Night Special 🎵🎵 (Buddah, 1975)
Aquarian Dream 🎵🎵🎵 (Buddah, 1976)
This Is Your Life 🎵🎵 (Arista, 1977)
You Are My Starship 🎵🎵🎵 (Capitol, 1977)
Remember Who You Are 🎵🎵🎵 (MoJazz, 1993)
Romantic Journey 🎵🎵 (Capitol, 1994)
Easy Living 🎵🎵 (MoJazz, 1997)

worth searching for: To hear Connors's abilities as a producer and talent coach, check out Norman Brown's *Just between Us* 🎵🎵🎵 (MoJazz, 1992, prod. Norman Connors) and Phyllis Hyman's *Under Her Spell: Greatest Hits* 🎵🎵🎵 (Arista, 1995, prod. various), both sturdy albums that showcase their stars' talent well.

influences:
◀◀ Art Blakey, Quincy Jones, Max Roach, Pharoah Sanders

▶▶ Lenny White, Artist Formerly Known as Prince

Eric Deggans

Junior Cook
Born Herman Cook, July 22, 1934, in Pensacola, FL. Died February 4, 1992, in New York, NY.

Tenor saxophonist Junior Cook was a prominent figure in New York jazz ensembles from the mid-1950s until his untimely passing in 1992. A hard-toned and astute instrumentalist, he was noted for intelligent, lucid improvisations. Cook came to New York in the mid-1950s and joined Dizzy Gillespie's group briefly in 1958. But that same year, he became a member of Horace Silver's Quintet, replacing Clifford Jordan. His association with Silver, who led one of the most popular ensembles of the hard-bop

period, continued until 1964 and established his reputation as a soloist. After Silver, Cook worked and recorded with Barry Harris, Blue Mitchell, and Don Patterson, as well with trumpeter Freddie Hubbard. Cook also spent a year teaching at the Berklee College of Music. In the mid-1970s, he co-led the Bill Hardman/Junior Cook Quintet; before his death he also performed regularly with Clifford Jordan's orchestra and McCoy Tyner's Big Band.

what to buy: *The Place to Be* 🎵🎵🎵🎵 (SteepleChase, 1989/1994, prod. Nils Winther) highlights Cook's no-nonsense tenor at front and center on this classic blowing session that features longtime collaborators pianist Mickey Tucker, bassist Walter Booker, and drummer Leroy Williams. What could have been another pedestrian bebop session is enhanced by Cook's energetic, intriguing improvisations, humorous asides, and unexpected twists and turns, most notably his solos on "Cedar's Blues," and "She Rote." Tadd Dameron's "On a Misty Night" shows off Cook's sensitive side. Backed by what could be one of the best rhythm sections around—pianist Cedar Walter, bassist Buster Williams, and drummer Billy Higgins—Cook pulls out all the stops on *Something's Cookin'* 🎵🎵🎵🎵 (Muse, 1981, prod. Joe Fields), a 1981 session that finds his tenor solid and earthy after years of consistence and unswerving swing. What pushes this beyond the typical Muse blowing date is the choice of material and flexibility of moods, from Walton's tasty "Fiesta Espanol" to "Detour Ahead." There's some serious cookin' and sensitive moments as well on the quartet date *On Misty Night* 🎵🎵🎵🎵 (SteepleChase, 1989/1995, prod. Nils Winther), recorded during the same sessions that produced *The Place to Be*. The title track is an absolute beauty, as if Cook is reaching out to the tune's composer, Tadd Dameron. Also tasty is Cannonball Adderley's "Wabash," a toe-tapping medium swinger.

the rest:
You Leave Me Breathless 🎵🎵🎵🎵 (SteepleChase, 1997)

influences:
◀◀ Horace Silver, Clifford Jordan, Eddie "Lockjaw" Davis, Hank Mobley, Sonny Stitt

▶▶ Javon Jackson, Billy Pierce, Benny Golson, Wayne Shorter

Bret Primack

Bob Cooper
Born December 6, 1925, in Pittsburgh, PA. Died August 6, 1993, in Los Angeles, CA.

Multi-reedist Bob Cooper's father was a professional hockey player who moved from Canada to the United States to play in

Pittsburgh. Cooper started playing clarinet in 1940, switching to tenor sax within a year. He played in local bands, subbed in the Stan Kenton Orchestra and, starting in 1945, formed a six-year association with Kenton which led to a Capitol Recording contract. On January 14, 1947, he married band singer, June Christy. Cooper moved to California, settling in Sherman Oaks at the same address for the next 35 years. Cooper performed with Jerry Gray in 1953, with Shorty Rogers and Pete Rugulo in 1954. About this time, Cooper turned to serious study of the oboe and orchestration, all the while strengthening his West Coast jazz affiliations. When he joined the Lighthouse All-Stars at Hermosa Beach in 1954, Cooper had a lighter tenor sound, not unlike his contemporaries Stan Getz and Zoot Sims.

Over the next 30 years, Cooper's saxophone sound grew broader and heavier, and his attack harder and more assertive, yet it remained as swinging as ever. During these years, he made lasting associations with Bud Shank, Bill Holman, and Conte Candoli. Always open, friendly, and helpful, Cooper was mentor to younger players, including tenor saxophonist Pete Christlieb and left-handed bass wizard John Leitham. Although his playing and writing skills were first-class, Cooper seemed to shun the limelight, making decisions throughout his life that kept him more in the background than many of his cohorts.

what to buy: If one wanted to remember Bob Cooper, *Bob Cooper–Conte Candoli Quintet* ♫♫♫♫ (V.S.O.P./Mode, 1994, prod. Dick Bank), recorded six weeks before Cooper's death, would be his most memorable session of his later years when his playing was strongest. Among nine tunes is a definitive version of Billy Strayhorn's "Come Sunday," with Cooper playing a well-conceived tenor sax solo. The rhythm team of pianist Ross Tompkins, drummer Paul Kreibich, and bassist John Leitham is up to the high standard set by Cooper and trumpeter Candoli. Their version of "We'll Be Together Again" could well be used as a model on how to play a jazz ballad. *Coop!* ♫♫♫♫ (OJC/Contemporary, 1957, prod. Lester Koenig) is a gathering of archetypical West Coast swingsters. Backing Cooper's light, feathery tenor sax stylings are the Candoli brothers and the brilliant Don Fagerquist (trumpets), Frank Rosolino and Johnny Halliburton (trombones), Lou Levy (piano), Vic Feldman (vibraharp), Max Bennett (bass), and Mel Lewis (drums). Cooper delivers an extended version of his original "Jazz Themes and Variations," as well as five well-chosen standards, and heats up "Frankie and Johnny," a rendering that hints at his burgeoning intensity to come in later years.

what to buy next: *Pete Christlieb–Bob Cooper: Live* ♫♫♫♫ (Capri, 1991, prod. Tom Burns, Pete Christlieb) was recorded at a free-flowing 1990 club date in Portland, Oregon. The album features the tenor sax interplay of old pro Cooper and the younger Christlieb. High points include eloquent interpretations of "Passion Flower," "Rain," and another lovely reading by Cooper of Strayhorn's "Come Sunday." Rhythm support is provided by pianist Mike Wofford, bassist Chuck Berghofer, and, an alumnus of the Lighthouse All-Stars, drummer Donald Bailey. *Rumsey's Lighthouse All-Stars: Jazz Invention* documents a 1989 reunion of Howard Rumsey's Lighthouse All-Stars, with Cooper serving as music director and arranger for the Hermosa Beach, California, concert session. Monty Budwig fills in on bass for the retired Rumsey and Lighthouse veterans Bud Shank, Conte Candoli, Bob Enevoldsen, Claude Williamson, and John Guerin give that light, swinging West Coast touch to 10 intricate and textured arrangements.

the rest:
Milano Blues ♫♫♫ (Fresh Sound, 1957)
For All We Know ♫♫♫ (Fresh Sound, 1990)

John T. Bitter

Marc Copland

Born May 27, 1948 in Philadelphia, PA.

Pianist Marc Copland actually began his career in New York as a saxophonist from 1970 to 1973 and worked with jazz artists such as Chico Hamilton, John Abercrombie, Ralph Towner, and others. His pioneering work on the electric alto saxophone yielded the album *Friends*, which received a five-star rating in *Down Beat*. His penchant for playing intense blow outs began to yield to the more lyrical side of his musical personality and Copland left New York to take a hiatus to develop his piano chops. He re-emerged in 1986 as a mature player, receiving critical acclaim after his decade of musical exploration. Today, Copland tours and records with his trio (Gary Peacock, bass; Billy Hart or Bill Stewart, drums), and also leads various versions of his all-star quartet.

what to buy: It seems fitting that, after his hard work at reinventing himself as a pianist, Copland should be rewarded by working with the most creative players in jazz. With bassist Gary Peacock and drummer Billy Hart on *Paradiso* ♫♫♫♫ (Soul Note, 1997, prod. Marc Copland), Copland's harmonically rich style shines on this nine-tune session of mostly originals. He outdoes himself on his third Savoy release, *Softly* ♫♫♫♫ (Savoy Jazz, 1998, prod. Marc Copland). With bassist Peacock and drummer Bill Stewart generating brawny energy, Copland brilliantly stretches out on nine exciting tunes. His fertile ideas

and keyboard mastery shine throughout, and he attains a new plateau of excellence with this recording.

what to buy next: Copland swapped saxophone for piano, polished his chops a-plenty for a decade, and it paid off as evidenced on his album, *Stompin' with Savoy* ♪♪♪ (Savoy, 1995, prod. Takao Ogawa), a spectacular session that also brings out the best in his team: Bob Berg (saxophone/arranger), Randy Brecker (trumpet), James Genus (bass), and Dennis Chambers (drums). Their camaraderie and previous collaborations result in a cohesive, interactive session of 10 standards. Copland chooses treatment that is contemporaneous and leading-edge, neither too far out nor too ordinary. Selections span several decades, with American compositions from jazzmen Dizzy Gillespie, John Coltrane, Wayne Shorter, and popular Broadway composers George and Ira Coleman and Cole Porter. It's a well-rounded, straight-ahead session that gives everyone spectacular moments in the spotlight.

the rest:
At Night ♪♪♪ (Sunnyside, 1996)
Second Look ♪♪♪ (Savoy Jazz, 1996)

influences:
⏮ Bill Evans, Keith Jarrett

Nancy Ann Lee

Chick Corea

Born Armando Anthony Corea, June 12, 1941, in Chelsea, MA.

If he had quit recording and performing two decades ago, Chick Corea would still be a piano legend. But it's impossible to find a common cord that tethers his career: Corea's musical curiosity has led him to try many avenues, changing directions many times along the way. Corea began playing piano when he was four. By the time he made his recording debut as a leader in 1966, he had already gained valuable experience working with Mongo Santamatia and Willie Bobo (1962–63), Blue Mitchell (1964–66), Herbie Mann, and Stan Getz. He then joined Miles Davis's band, replacing Herbie Hancock during Davis's important transitional period (1968–70). Persuaded by Davis to play electric piano, Corea contributed to such fusion classics as *In a Silent Way* and *Bitches Brew*. After that, he formed an avant-garde quartet with Anthony Braxton, Dave Holland, and Barry Altschul called Circle, before switching styles yet again in 1971.

Chick Corea **(AP/Wide World Photos)**

CHICK COREA

song "Drone"
album *The Song of Singing*
(Blue Note, 1970/1989)
instrument Piano

Monster Solo

After a short stint with Getz, Corea formed Return to Forever, which started as a South American group with Stanley Clarke, Joe Farrell, Airto, and Flora Purim but morphed into a high-power fusion band. After that, he matured, branching out in a variety of contexts but generally emphasizing his acoustic roots and playing duet tours with Gary Burton and Herbie Hancock, a quartet with Michael Brecker, trios with Miroslav Vitous and Roy Haynes, a tribute to Thelonious Monk, and even some classical music. In 1995 Corea formed a new fusion group, the Elektric Band, then pruned it to a trio known as the Akoustic Band. Corea's jazz standards include "Spain," "La Fiesta" and "Windows," a small portion of his legacy as one of the most significant jazzmen of the past 30 years.

what to buy: *Now He Sings, Now He Sobs* ♪♪♪♪ (Blue Note, 1968/1988, prod. Sonny Lester, reissue prod. Michael Cuscuna) features Corea's best original writing and a superb trio with Miroslav Vitous and Roy Haynes. The reissue adds eight tracks, including revealing covers of the standard "My One and Only Love" and Thelonious Monk's "Pannonica." *Piano Improvisa-*

tions, Vol. 1 𝄞𝄞𝄞𝄞 (ECM, 1970, prod. Manfred Eicher) and *Piano Improvisations, Vol. 2* 𝄞𝄞𝄞𝄞 (ECM, 1971, prod. Manfred Eicher) are Chick by himself. Any company would be too much on these classic recordings. This soul-felt collection of solo piano pieces is the cornerstone of what defines masterful improvisation.

what to buy next: *A.R.C.* 𝄞𝄞𝄞𝄞 (ECM, 1971, prod. Manfred Eicher) is a trio with bassist Dave Holland and drummer Barry Altschul, and not surprisingly some Circle material appears. The mood is just as free and probing as that quartet, but less shocking minus Braxton. This is an essential side of Corea that has been overshadowed by his mainstream successes. Corea pays tribute to an important influence on *Remembering Bud Powell* 𝄞𝄞𝄞𝄞 (Stretch, 1997, prod. Chick Corea, Ron Moss, Bernie Kirsh) and in the process of returning to his roots reminds straight-ahead jazz fans that when challenged by solid material (in this case, all but one track by the bebop piano archetype), the pianist's shallower style falls away and an imaginative improvisor with an elegant touch emerges. The core band is Corea, trumpeter Wallace Roney, bassist Christian McBride, and drummer Roy Haynes, with saxophonists Kenny Garrett and/or Joshua Redman joining on some tracks.

what to avoid: *Children's Songs* 𝄞𝄞 (ECM, 1983, prod. Manfred Eicher) confuses simplicity with simple-mindedness.

best of the rest:

Inner Space 𝄞𝄞𝄞𝄞 (Atlantic, 1966)
Early Circle 𝄞𝄞𝄞𝄞 (Blue Note, 1970)
Song of Singing 𝄞𝄞𝄞 (Blue Note, 1970)
The Beginning 𝄞𝄞𝄞 (LRC/Delta Music, 1970)
ECM Works 𝄞𝄞𝄞 (ECM, 1971)
Children of Forever 𝄞𝄞𝄞 (Polydor, 1972)
Crystal Silence 𝄞𝄞𝄞 (ECM, 1972)
Where Have I Known You Before 𝄞𝄞𝄞𝄞 (Polydor, 1974)
Leprechaun 𝄞𝄞𝄞 (Polydor, 1975)
My Spanish Heart 𝄞𝄞𝄞𝄞 (Polydor, 1976)
Chick Corea and Gary Burton in Concert 𝄞𝄞𝄞 (ECM, 1978)
Evening with Herbie Hancock 𝄞𝄞𝄞 (Polydor, 1978)
Friends 𝄞𝄞𝄞𝄞 (Polydor, 1978)
Mad Hatter 𝄞𝄞𝄞𝄞 (Polydor, 1978)
Tap Step 𝄞𝄞𝄞 (Warner Bros., 1978)
Chick Corea, Herbie Hancock, Keith Jarrett 𝄞𝄞𝄞 (Atlantic, 1981)
Three Quartets 𝄞𝄞𝄞𝄞 (Warner Bros., 1981/Stretch, 1997)
Trio Music 𝄞𝄞𝄞𝄞 (ECM, 1981)
Touchstone 𝄞𝄞𝄞 (Stretch, 1982)
Again and Again 𝄞𝄞𝄞 (Elektra, 1982)
Trio Music: Live in Europe 𝄞𝄞𝄞 (ECM, 1984)
Chick Corea 𝄞𝄞𝄞 (ECM, 1985)
Elektric Band 𝄞𝄞𝄞 (GRP, 1986)
Light Years 𝄞𝄞𝄞𝄞 (GRP, 1987)

Eye of the Beholder 𝄞𝄞𝄞𝄞 (GRP, 1988)
Akoustic Band 𝄞𝄞𝄞 (GRP, 1989)
Music Forever and Beyond: The Selected Works 𝄞𝄞𝄞𝄞𝄞 (GRP, 1989)
Inside Out 𝄞𝄞𝄞𝄞 (GRP, 1990)
Alive 𝄞𝄞𝄞 (GRP, 1991)
Beneath the Mask 𝄞𝄞𝄞 (GRP, 1991)
Piano Greats 𝄞𝄞𝄞 (Laserlight, 1991)
Live in Tokyo 𝄞𝄞𝄞 (Pacific Arts, 1992)
Compact Jazz: the Seventies 𝄞𝄞𝄞 (Verve, 1993)
Paint the World 𝄞𝄞𝄞𝄞 (GRP, 1993)
Best of Chick Corea 𝄞𝄞𝄞 (Capitol, 1993)
Expressions 𝄞𝄞𝄞𝄞 (GRP, 1994)
Verve Jazz Masters 3: Chick Corea 𝄞𝄞𝄞 (Verve, 1994)
Time Warp 𝄞𝄞𝄞 (GRP, 1995)
Live in Montreux 𝄞𝄞𝄞 (Stretch, 1996)

worth searching for: The Pete LaRoca (later known as Pete Sims) album *Turkish Women at the Bath* 𝄞𝄞𝄞𝄞 (32 Jazz, 1997, prod. Alan Douglas) has an unusual history to go with its unusual personnel (drummer LaRoca/Sims, Corea, Sun Ra tenor saxophonist John Gilmore, and bassist Walter Booker). It was recorded in 1967 as a LaRoca session (he wrote all seven tracks), but when it was sold to Muse, it was released as a Corea album. LaRoca sued, it was withdrawn, and finally it has reappeared. It teeters on the edge of the avant-garde and makes for uneasy but fascinating listening.

influences:

◀◀ Horace Silver, Bud Powell, Bill Evans, Miles Davis, Art Tatum, McCoy Tyner

▶▶ Marc Copland, David Benoit

see also: *Circle, Return to Forever*

Ralph Burnett

Rich Corpolongo

In one of his rare, hometown performances, Chicago reedman/composer Rich Corpolongo played the 1997 Chicago Jazz Festival with his quartet, which includes the same musicians heard on his only CD as leader. Corpolongo is a gifted musician, adept at styles from bebop to modal and free jazz, with tinges of European classical tossed into his mix. He regularly sits in with Barrett Deems's Big Band, and has also performed with all of the major orchestras in Chicago, including the Chicago Symphony Orchestra. Corpolongo studied with saxophonist Joe Daley, and at Roosevelt University, where as a student he co-led a bop group which featured pianist Herbie Hancock. After graduation, Corpolongo did commercial jingle work, played a variety of jobbing dates, and taught privately. During the 1970s, he explored avant garde jazz with Joe Daley's Quorum and has co-led free-improvisation groups (the Spontaneous Composition trio and the mid-1970s quartet, Enigma). Corpolongo has a Masters degree in classical composition from Roosevelt University, and his training is evident in his jazz compositions which reflect his passion for composers such as Mozart, Stravinsky, Hindemith, and Penderecki.

what's available: A versatile, long-standing Chicago musician, multi-reed player Rich Corpolongo inexplicably waited decades to showcase his amazing talents as leader, performer and composer on *Just Found Joy* ♫♫♫♫ (Delmark, 1996, prod. Robert G. Koester). Whether performing with warm romanticism or blowing hard and free, Corpolongo's soprano and alto musings, as well as his plump-toned clarinet, are fluent and polished, easily matching world class jazz luminaries. Corpolongo's clarity, finesse, ingenuity, and spontaneous inventions provide peak moments throughout to make this a rapturous outing for musicians and listeners alike. His next album, *Smiles* ♫♫♫♫ (Delmark, 1998, prod. Steve Krasinsky), is of equal caliber, exploring cooler hues and drawing inspiration from Chicago's avant-garde scene as well as European classical themes. A sterling reedman, Corpolongo excels with burnished, crisp precision throughout, aided by his regular crew—pianist Larry Luchowski, bassist Eric Hochberg, and drummer/percussionist Mike Raynor.

Nancy Ann Lee

Larry Coryell

Born April 2, 1943, in Galveston, TX.

A founding father of the fusion movement, an amazing live musician, and one of the most important jazz musicians to emerge in the 1960s, Larry Coryell is an influential though often underrated and sometimes inconsistent guitarist. His playing contains more blues influence than most jazz/rock players and he is probably the most lyrical jazz/rock guitarist spawned from that era (few guitarists have ever written anything as catchy as "Bicentennial Headfest"). Like fellow fusion pioneer John McLaughlin, Coryell has stunning technique and grows restless playing any one style.

Shortly after his recording debut with Chico Hamilton in 1966, Coryell co-founded the Free Spirits, a Byrds-influenced rock band with jazz undertones. He joined Gary Burton in 1967, and while his reputation as a versatile rock-influenced jazz player grew with Burton, it was in 1969, when he recorded his first two groundbreaking solo albums—*Lady Coryell* and the out-of-print

Coryell—that he became recognized as a world-beater. Both albums combine rock, jazz, folk, classical, and country influences, have a sense of experimentation that was typical of that era, and are filled with some wild guitar playing. During the 1970s Coryell was all over the road stylistically. He kicked off the decade by recording the legendary *Spaces* album with John McLaughlin, which pretty much guaranteed both guitarists a place in jazz history. From there, the 1970s saw Coryell form his own fusion band, the Eleventh House (with Alphonze Mouzon and Mike Mandel); record a classic album, *The Restful Mind* with Ralph Towner (currently out of print); make several solo albums that ranged from jazz-rock to challenging acoustic adventures; and record two excellent duets with guitarist Philip Catherine, *Twin House* and *Splendid* (both are out of print). Coryell also recorded with Joe Beck and John Scofield and in 1979 formed the first version of the Acoustic Guitar Super Trio with McLaughlin and Paco de Lucia. He showed he was also an adept flamenco player (is there a style he isn't adept at?) as the trio barnstormed Europe and made an excellent live-video from Royal Albert Hall (if you can find it send me a copy). However, by the time the trio hit he United States, Coryell was replaced by Al Di Meola, though accounts vary as to why. In the early 1980s, Coryell, who has a strong classical background, embarked on the ambitious project of scoring and recording famous orchestral works by Stravinsky and Rimsky-Korsakov for solo acoustic guitar (*The Rite of Spring* and *Scherazade*—both out of print); he has scored and recorded works by Ravel and Gershwin. The 1980s also saw Coryell form a partnership with Brian Keane, record an indispensable duet album with Emily Remler, and embark on a number of straight-ahead albums. The 1990s have been typically all over the road for Coryell. He has recorded albums in the smooth jazz and world genres, made acoustic dates with heavy folk influences, and most recently has revisited the fusion landscape he mapped out over 27 years ago.

Coryell has been active in education, had a regular guitar column in the magazine *Guitar Player* for several years, and has two sons who are also musicians (music has long been a family affair, as his former wife Julie wrote songs for him). Despite Coryell's status as one of the most important jazz guitarists of the past 30 years, the current state of his catalog is a disgrace. Despite making over 50 recordings as leader, only a small percentage are in print and the record companies are not making a concerted effort to reissue his material on CD. This is problematic, as while his catalog has its share of inconsistent dates, there are a number of historic recordings sitting on the shelves. Coryell deserves better.

what to buy: On *Spaces* ♫♫♫♫ (Vanguard, 1970, prod. Danny Weiss) guitar pioneers Coryell and John McLaughlin are joined by Billy Cobham, Chick Corea, and Miroslav Vitous for one of the very best fusion recordings ever made. In 1970, Coryell and McLaughlin were two hot guns developing a new musical vocabulary. The playing is tremendous, though less rock-oriented in tone and style than their individual efforts. A guitar hero recording? Yes, but it's also a musical landmark. Those who've bastardized fusion since the late 1970s should listen to this to understand from whence they came. The Eleventh House probably doesn't get the recognition it should because it was overshadowed by more popular bands, the Mahavishu Orchestra and Return to Forever, and was not a precedent-setter like the Tony Williams Lifetime. But the fact is they could play, as heard clearly on *Larry Coryell & the Eleventh House at Montreux* ♫♫♫♫ (Vanguard, 1978, prod. Vince Cirrincione, Tom Paine). Recorded at the Montreux Jazz and Pop Festival in 1974, an inspired Coryell wails throughout the half-hour set, has a great time, and even quotes Jimi Hendrix. The band lends Coryell excellent support, but it was clearly the guitarist's night. A good way to sample the variety of Coryell's acoustic styles, *Bolero* ♫♫♫♫ (Evidence, 1993, prod. Larry Coryell) is a compilation of mostly solo music Coryell recorded from 1981 to 1983. The title track is a standout, as Ravel's "Bolero" has never had this much bite to it. Coryell's arrangement for acoustic guitar is filled with wild bends and cool fills (though it's even better to hear him play it live). The rest of the date finds Coryell moving from classically influenced pieces (including another Ravel composition) to flamenco, country fingerpicking, and jazz styles. Several tracks from *Just Like Being Born*, a duet album with former student Brian Keane, fill out the rest of the album. Coryell's playing is strong throughout and the arrangements are varied. *Together* ♫♫♫♫ (Concord, 1985, prod. Larry Coryell) is a duet date with the late Emily Remler, matching the seasoned pro with the up-and-comer. The two support each other marvelously and their lead playing is strong on one of Coryell's more memorable recordings.

what to buy next: The folk influences are stronger on the all-acoustic set *Dragon Gate* ♫♫♫♫ (Shanachie, 1989, prod. Larry Coryell) than on most of his albums, and the playing is brilliant. A true master of acoustic guitar subtleties, Coryell's 10 performances, some with overdubs and two duets with Stefan Grossman, paint several contrasting pictures, both big and little, with beauty and flair. No one makes notes ring quite like Coryell on the ballads and few jazz players can bend the blues so well. "Bottleneck Blackout" is one of the hottest acoustic folk blues jams ever made. *The Essential Larry Coryell* ♫♫♫♫ (Vanguard, 1975/1991, prod. various) samples Coryell's early years on Vanguard and has some of the obvious choices from his first few albums. Because Vanguard has been slow in releasing Coryell's catalog on CD, this is the only place to get "Jam with Albert," "Scotland I," and the very pop-ish "Are You Too Clever" on CD. Curiously, the original artwork has names of several musicians who do not appear on the CD version—tracks from the LP version were omitted for space reasons (which denies us any of the Coryell/Towner recordings, as *The Restful Mind* is still out of print). Ten years after *Lady Coryell* ♫♫♫♫ (Vanguard, 1969, prod. Danny Weiss) came out, most fusion was dull and programmed, with little fire and few mistakes. *Lady Coryell* isn't the greatest technical record you'll ever hear, but Coryell and drummer Bob Moses create excitement throughout and it is filled with raw, unadulterated fire. Coryell teams up with Billy Cobham, Richard Bona, and Bireli Lagrene on *Spaces Revisited* ♫♫♫♫ (Shanachie, 1997, prod. Larry Coryell, Danny Weiss) 27 years after *Spaces* and does a great job of recapturing much of the magic from the original session. While Lagrene is no McLaughlin, he is a great foil with outstanding chops. Coryell hasn't sounded this inspired from start to finish for some time—no doubt Cobham gets credit for some of that.

the rest:
Introducing the Eleventh House ♫♫♫♪ (Vanguard, 1974)
Planet End ♫♫♪ (Vanguard, 1975)
Twelve Frets to One Octave ♫♫♫♫ (Shanachie, 1991)
Live from Bahia ♫♫♫♪ (CTI, 1992)
Sketches of Coryell ♫♫♫♪ (Shanachie, 1996)

worth searching for: One of the ultimate late-1960s rock records was made by a jazz player. On *Coryell* ♫♫♫♫ (Vanguard, 1969, prod. Danny Weiss) the songs range from a hardcore psychedelic opener called "Sex" to a folk-influenced tune with an electric edge, "Beautiful Woman," a glorious hard-rocking blowing session, "The Jam with Albert," to the wonderful ballad "Ah Wuv Oo." More rock-oriented than most of Coryell's albums, it is nonetheless filled with passion and fire. Sure his vocals leave a lot to be desired, but they don't detract from the power of the album. More so than any other record, this got me through my sophomore year of college (16 years after it was released no less). Note to Vanguard: PLEASE reissue this. My vinyl copy is almost worn out.

influences:
◄◄ Wes Montgomery, Jimi Hendrix, Django Reinhardt
►► Steve Khan

Paul MacArthur

Stanley Cowell

Born May 5, 1941, in Toledo, OH.

Stanley Cowell grew up in the same Toledo neighborhood that was home to Jon Hendricks and the great Art Tatum. In a story that has all the hallmarks of potential legend, it is said that Tatum sat down at the Cowell family piano one afternoon and played a few tunes. While Tatum is a definite influence in Cowell's playing, young Stanley didn't really pick up on what the piano god was putting down until a couple decades later. Cowell, who had studied piano since he was four, collected degrees from Oberlin College Conservatory and the University of Michigan before moving to New York in 1966. His prodigious skills soon attracted attention, garnering an impressive resumé that includes work with Stan Getz, Max Roach, Archie Shepp, Oliver Nelson, Bobby Hutcherson, and Marion Brown among others. He also was co-founder, along with Charles Tolliver, of Strata-East, a record company with releases by Gil Scott-Heron, Sonny Fortune, Music Inc. (a project of Tolliver's), and Cowell himself. From the mid-1970s through the early '80s Cowell worked with the Heath Brothers and started his teaching career at the Herbert Lehman College, part of the City of New York collegiate system.

what to buy: Cowell has lots of technique, especially in the left hand, and he got to let it all hang out in what is now one of the most prestigious solo piano venues in the jazz world on *Live at Maybeck Recital Hall Volume 5* ♪♪♪♪ (Concord Jazz, 1990, prod. Nick Phillips). He starts the show off by playing "Softly, as in a Morning Sunrise" by modulating through 12 keys in two minutes plus and still makes it sound good. Later in the program, Cowell shows off his left-hand prowess by playing J.J. Johnson's ballad, "Lament," with only one hand. Guess which one? (Jaki Byard was to pull off the same trick on Monk's "'Round Midnight" in volume 17 of the Maybeck series.) The rest is well chosen, including three originals by Cowell with "Cal Massey" taking pride of place.

what to buy next: There are other worthy Cowell albums that could go in this slot, including some the trio dates on Steeple-Chase, but *Setup* ♪♪♪♪ (SteepleChase, 1994, prod. Nils Winther) stands out by showcasing a different facet of the pianist, playing with some pretty high-powered talent in a sextet where everybody can solo and comp with taste, which means they know when to lay back and when to power forward. This presents pianist/composer/leader Cowell with a different set of tasks than what he would have to deal with in a solo or trio situation, and it is to his credit that the man has not forgotten his skills as an accompanist. All of the material was written by Cowell, and there are some real treats, especially the title tune with a densely textured, bottom-heavy beginning blending into Henderson's Miles Davis-flavored mute playing. Another standout is "Sendai Sendoff," with a tasteful solo from Washington, Hart's percolating cymbal work, and Cowell's slick keyboard trills and flourishes setting up nice solo work from the horn section.

the rest:
Brilliant Circles ♪♪♪♪ (Black Lion, 1969)
We Three ♪♪♪ (DIW, 1988)
Sienna ♪♪♪♪ (SteepleChase, 1989)
Back to the Beautiful ♪♪♪ (Concord Jazz, 1989)
Close to You Alone ♪♪♪♪ (DIW, 1991)
Angel Eyes ♪♪♪♪ (SteepleChase, 1994)

worth searching for: ECM should reissue Cowell's 1972 trio setting of *Illusion Suite*, which contains some drop-dead gorgeous music, including "Cal Massey," which shows up on many of Cowell's later albums. Another one to look for would be *Musa: Ancestral Streams*, the solo album that the pianist did for Strata-East, which includes two sections from *Illusion Suite*.

influences:
◀◀ Art Tatum, Erroll Garner, Bud Powell, Ray Bryant
▶▶ Mitch Hampton

Garaud MacTaggart

Ida Cox

Born February 25, 1896, in Toccoa, GA. Died November 10, 1967, in Knoxville, TN.

Vocalist Ida Cox (often billed as "The Uncrowned Queen of the Blues") started her show business career very young. She ran away from home around 1910 to join the theater but ended up with the famous Rabbit Foot Minstrels, as well as other African American troupes. As she got experience, she started working with traveling shows such as Silas Green's Minstrels (from New Orleans), which crisscrossed the South with their talent. Ida was a member of these shows into the early 1920s. By 1923, she had made her home base in Chicago and had signed with the Paramount record label. Ida recorded exclusively for Paramount, and made almost 90 titles for the company during the 1920s. Her fame was widespread, and her recordings show a rich, distinctive voice with crisp diction. Although most of her recordings are blues tunes (most of which she composed herself), her live shows contained a wide variety of songs and music. In her heyday, Ida Cox's troupe (containing 16 chorus girls and a band) traveled extensively in the eastern and southern U.S. until the early 1930s. Her recordings all feature fine jazz accompaniment, some of which have become jazz classics. During the Depression and after, she toured with smaller groups, spending a lot of time in New York City in the late 1930s. After World War II, she retired from music, although she occasionally performed in theaters. She made her last recording date in 1961, accompanied by an all-star group led by Coleman Hawkins for the Riverside label. Miss Cox died from cancer in 1967.

what to buy: Fortunately, as of this writing, Ida Cox's entire recording output is available on CD. The high point of her recordings were certainly the Paramount titles from the 1920s. These can be found in their entirety on the Document label: *Ida Cox—Vol. 1 (1923)* 🎵🎵🎵🎵 (Document, 1995, prod. Johnny Parth), *Ida Cox—Vol. 2 (1924–25)* 🎵🎵🎵🎵 (Document, 1995, prod. Johnny Parth) , *Ida Cox—Vol. 3 (1925–27)* 🎵🎵🎵🎵 (Document, 1995, prod. Johnny Parth), and *Ida Cox—Vol. 4 (1927–38)* 🎵🎵🎵🎵 (Document, 1995, prod. Johnny Parth). Titles such as "I've Got the Blues for Rampart Street" and "Ida Cox's Lawdy Lawdy Blues" (both found on Vol. 1) are high water marks of early blues. On "Rampart Street," the listener takes an evening walk down Rampart Street in New Orleans with Ida as she names each night club on the way, encouraged along by the exquisite trumpet of Tommy Ladnier. The beauty of Ida Cox's recordings are enhanced by the musicians who accompanied her, including her husband, pianist Jesse Crump. Their duet on "Alphonia Blues" (Vol. 3) is absolutely marvelous. King Oliver's nephew, Dave Nelson, joins with Crump on a later session, which produced such titles as "Fogyism" (having to do with superstitious activities), "Papa Tree Top Tall," and others (all on Vol. 4). Here, Ida's low, rich voice is captured to good quality and understated grandeur.

what to buy next: After 1938, Ida did not record again until 1961. *Ida Cox: Blues for Rampart Street* 🎵🎵🎵🎵 (OJC, 1991, prod. Bill Grauer) was originally recorded for the Riverside label and finds Ida in the company of Coleman Hawkins, Roy Eldridge, Sammy Lewis (piano), Milt Hinton (bass), and Jo Jones on drums. Although beyond her prime, Ida had not lost her quality. The tunes are a little slower, and not necessarily perfect, but the session is a poignant reminder of the classic 1920s, and of a singer who was one of the best of her genre.

the rest:
Ida Cox: Uncrowned Queen of the Blues 🎵🎵🎵🎵 (Black Swan, 1996)

Jim Prohaska

Hank Crawford

Born Bennie Ross Crawford Jr., December 21, 1934, in Memphis, TN.

It's hard to grow up as a wannabe-musician in Memphis and not have a lot of soul, as alto saxophonist Hank Crawford ably demonstrates. Through the years his distinctive, full-bodied tone has come to exemplify soul-jazz, and his trademark approach to bluesy ballads continues to influence each new generation of players. Crawford started out on piano, but soon switched to saxophone with immediate success, playing in the band at Manassas High School, a noted source of fine jazz players. His R&B leanings led him to work with B.B. King, Bobby "Blue" Bland, and Ike Turner before heading off to college to study music theory in 1952. He attended Tennessee State in Nashville, which afforded him the opportunity to learn the finer points of composition during the day while at night jamming with the big-time musicians who came to town, from Nat King Cole to Charlie Parker. Shortly after graduating, Crawford came to the attention of Ray Charles, who in 1958 hired him on as a member of his small combo. It proved to be a perfect match, and by 1960 Crawford was promoted to music director, arranging and composing for Charles until 1963, when he began his own career as a leader. The years with Charles were invaluable to him, not only in terms of public exposure, but also in terms of experience, as Crawford has rarely strayed from the ground-breaking mix of R&B, jazz, and blues that he helped to perfect with Charles. Crawford continues to record regularly, and has provided arrangements for numerous other performers. Crawford's recording career neatly divides into three parts: his '60s work with Atlantic, following in the tradition of Brother Ray; a series of slick, commercial recordings for Creed Taylor's Kudu label during the '70s, which would be best forgotten; and a return to form during the '80s and '90s with albums recorded for Milestone, including several with organist Jimmy McGriff. All of his recordings (even the abhorrent Kudu ones) feature his highly emotional, bluesy solos, and he tends to favor melodic ballads, where his evocative playing takes on the role of the singer, belting out every soulful line of the song. As might be expected from such a savvy arranger, Crawford is also a multi-instrumentalist, occasionally playing baritone sax and piano. Regular contributors to his records include Bernard Purdie, Dr. John, and fellow Ray Charles protege David "Fathead" Newman.

what to buy: Hands down, the definitive collection from one of the giants in soul-jazz, *Heart and Soul: The Hank Crawford Anthology* 🎵🎵🎵🎵 (Rhino, 1994, prod. various) covers all bases, from the early days with Charles to recent work with McGriff.

Every track drips with soul, demonstrating Crawford's mastery of the fertile middle-ground between bebop and R&B.

what to buy next: One of the best of the Atlantic (and the only one available on CD) is *After Hours* 𝄢𝄢𝄢𝄢 (Atlantic, 1966, prod. Nesuhi Ertegun, Phil Iehle). *On the Blue Side* 𝄢𝄢𝄢𝄢 (Milestone, 1990, prod. Bob Porter) is arguably the finest of the Crawford/McGriff collaborations. Their soulful work on tracks like "Any Day Now" and "Hank's Groove" is a treat for music fans of all types.

what to avoid: Crawford is completely out of his element on the bland, glassy *We Got a Good Thing Going* 𝄢𝄢 (Kudu, 1972, prod. Creed Taylor), complete with syrupy string section. None of the Kudu records should be trusted, but tracks from this one can be safely sampled on the Rhino collection.

the rest:
More Soul 𝄢𝄢𝄢𝄢 (Atlantic, 1961)
The Soul Clinic 𝄢𝄢𝄢𝄢 (Atlantic, 1961)
From the Heart 𝄢𝄢𝄢𝄢 (Atlantic, 1962)
Soul of the Ballad 𝄢𝄢𝄢𝄢 (Atlantic, 1963)
True Blue 𝄢𝄢𝄢𝄢 (Atlantic, 1964)
Dig These Blues 𝄢𝄢𝄢𝄢 (Atlantic, 1965)
Mr. Blues 𝄢𝄢𝄢𝄢 (Atlantic, 1966)
Double Cross 𝄢𝄢𝄢𝄢 (Atlantic, 1968)
It's a Funky Thing to Do 𝄢𝄢𝄢𝄢 (Cotillion, 1971)
Wildflower 𝄢𝄢 (Kudu, 1973)
I Hear a Symphony 𝄢𝄢 (Kudu, 1975)
Hank Crawford's Back 𝄢𝄢 (Kudu, 1976)
Tico Rico 𝄢𝄢 (Kudu, 1977)
Cajun Sunrise 𝄢𝄢 (Kudu, 1978)
Centerpiece 𝄢𝄢 (Buddah, 1979)
Indigo Blue 𝄢𝄢𝄢 (Milestone, 1983)
Midnight Ramble 𝄢𝄢𝄢 (Milestone, 1983)
Down on the Deuce 𝄢𝄢𝄢 (Milestone, 1984)
Roadhouse Symphony 𝄢𝄢𝄢 (Milestone, 1985)
(With Jimmy McGriff) *Soul Survivors* 𝄢𝄢𝄢𝄢 (Milestone, 1986)
(With Jimmy McGriff) *Soul Brothers* 𝄢𝄢𝄢𝄢 (Milestone, 1986)
Mr. Chips 𝄢𝄢 (Milestone, 1987)
(With Jimmy McGriff) *Steppin' Up* 𝄢𝄢𝄢𝄢 (Milestone, 1987)
Night Beat 𝄢𝄢𝄢𝄢 (Milestone, 1989)
Groove Master 𝄢𝄢𝄢 (Milestone, 1990)
Portrait 𝄢𝄢𝄢𝄢 (Milestone, 1991)
South-Central 𝄢𝄢𝄢𝄢 (Milestone, 1993)
Tight 𝄢𝄢𝄢𝄢 (Milestone, 1996)
Road Tested 𝄢𝄢𝄢𝄢 (Milestone, 1997)

worth searching for: *Mr. Blues Plays Lady Soul* 𝄢𝄢𝄢𝄢 (Atlantic, 1969, prod. Joel Dorn) is a terrific set of songs popularized by

MARILYN CRISPELL

song "Cascades"
album Cascades
(Music and Arts, 1993/1995)
instrument Piano

Monster Solo

Aretha Franklin, where Crawford's voice-like voicings really come through.

influences:
◀◀ Louis Jordan, Johnny Hodges
▶▶ David Sanborn

Eric J. Lawrence

Marilyn Crispell
Born March 30, 1947, in Philadelphia, PA.

Crispell played classical piano from age seven and graduated from the New England Conservatory in 1968, having focused on piano and composition. Yet, she was much more attracted to improvisation, although in a non-jazz context. She gave up music in favor of medicine for six years, but after the breakup of her marriage began singing blues in a folk-rock group for the catharsis it offered. After a pianist turned her on to some jazz albums, she experienced a personal revelation upon listening to John Coltrane's *A Love Supreme* and decided to learn to play jazz. Eventually this led her to move to Woodstock, where she studied and then taught at Karl Berger's Creative Music Studio until it shut down in the early 1980s. During this time she worked in the groups of Anthony Braxton, Roscoe Mitchell, and Leo Smith, with the Braxton association proving particularly lasting. Cecil Taylor was both an inspiration and an influence, and it is to his playing that hers is most often compared, though she has developed a style of her own over the years.

what to buy: *For Coltrane* 𝄢𝄢𝄢𝄢 (Leo, 1993, prod. Leo Feigin) is an intense 1987 solo concert where Crispell links John Coltrane's legacy to the piano with four covers of Coltrane-penned tunes and three improvised "collages." She covers several periods of his quickly developing career, and her startling, virtuosic technique and highly personal free jazz language make her one of the few active pianists capable of dealing with the density of the great saxophonist's later style and the delicacy of some of his themes.

what to buy next: *Marilyn Crispell & Gerry Hemingway Duo* 𝄢𝄢𝄢𝄢 (Knitting Factory, 1992, prod. Marilyn Crispell, Gerry Hemingway) alternates writing credits from track to track but seems to be pure free improvisation. It shows Crispell often exploring quieter textures (sometimes inside the piano), with the pieces where Hemingway plays vibes offering an attractively cool sound.

the rest:
Spirit Music 𝄢𝄢𝄢 (Cadence, 1982)
Live in Berlin 𝄢𝄢𝄢 (Black Saint, 1983)
Live in San Francisco 𝄢𝄢𝄢 (Music & Arts, 1990)
Marilyn Crispell Trio 𝄢𝄢𝄢 (Music & Arts, 1993)
Labyrinths 𝄢𝄢𝄢 (Victo, 1995)
Live at Mills College 1995 𝄢𝄢𝄢𝄢 (Music & Arts, 1996)
Contrasts: Live at Yoshi's 𝄢𝄢𝄢𝄢 (Music & Arts, 1996)
Woodstock Concert 𝄢𝄢𝄢 (Music & Arts, 1996)
Nothing Ever Was, Anyway: The Music of Annette Peacock 𝄢𝄢𝄢 (ECM, 1997)

worth searching for: Crispell's work with Anthony Braxton is heard at its best on the two-CD live set *Quartet (Santa Cruz) 1993* 𝄢𝄢𝄢𝄢 (Hat Jazz, 1997, prod. Larry Blood), with the leader on reeds, Crispell, bassist Mark Dresser, and Hemingway. She takes some energetic, unfettered solos that display her Cecil Taylor influence and interacts tightly with the group.

influences:
◀◀ Cecil Taylor, John Coltrane, Paul Hindemith
▶▶ Myra Melford

Walter Faber

Sonny Criss

Born William Criss, October 25, 1927, in Memphis, TN. Died November 19, 1977, in Los Angeles, CA.

Saxophonist Sonny Criss had the misfortune to spend most of his career on the West Coast away from what was then the heartbeat of jazz central, New York City. Still, his reputation as a top-flight soloist in the Charlie Parker tradition would secure him occasional jobs showcasing light, fluid alto playing characterized by an amazing sense of swing and lift. His earliest on-the-job training occurred in Los Angeles with Howard McGhee, Billy Eckstine, Stan Kenton, and Gerald Wilson before going on tour with drummer Buddy Rich in the 1950s. He also recorded albums for Imperial and Peacock during this time that were poorly promoted but whose current rarity has blessed them with "collector's item" status among jazz cognoscenti. Criss lived in Europe from 1962 to 1965 and returned there after returning to the States for periodic tours. During the 1960s and 1970s, he recorded sessions for Xanadu, Muse, Prestige, and Impulse!, many of which have provided a firm foundation for his reputation as one of the finest saxophone players in jazz. He was later diagnosed with cancer and found dead of a self-inflicted gunshot wound in 1977.

what to buy: From the opening tune, Horace Tapscott's "The Isle of Celia," and on into the rest of *Crisscraft* 𝄢𝄢𝄢𝄢 (Muse, 1975/32 Jazz, 1998, prod. Bob Porter), Criss is at his best. Solos glide from his horn with the seeming ease that is the true hallmark of a virtuoso but the ideas behind the notes tell of genius if only the listener will hear. It's hard to believe now but this was Criss's first recording in six years. The rhythm section was working for Harry "Sweets" Edison at the time of this recording and their working relationship blended beautifully with what the saxophonist was playing. Pianist Dolo Coker, drummer Jimmy Smith, and bassist Larry Gales are in top form while guitarist Ray Crawford is solid, if unspectacular. *Portrait of Sonny Criss* 𝄢𝄢𝄢𝄢 (OJC, 1967/1991, prod. Don Schlitten) shows that pairing Criss with a stellar rhythm section was the "no brainer" way of getting a good album for the saxophonist. The support for this date was indeed top caliber, with Paul Chambers and Alan Dawson providing the pulse from bass and drums, respectively, while pianist Walter Davis feeds Criss chords to embroider. Top tunes for the session are "God Bless the Child" and "On a Clear Day." *Saturday Morning* 𝄢𝄢𝄢𝄢 (Xanadu, 1965/1975, prod. Don Schlitten) is a combination of two sessions. The five cuts from 1965 originate with an acetate Criss gave to producer Don Schlitten and feature the saxophonist in company with pianist Hampton Hawes, bassist Clarence

Johnson, and drummer Frank Butler. The remaining six performances were recorded in 1975 with Barry Harris on piano, Leroy Vinnegar on bass, and Lennie McBrowne working the drum kit. The title tune is common to both dates, but the versions could not be more different. The 1965 version is a nice blowing ballad with plenty of pretty notes in all the right spots but by 1975 the song had mutated into something less facile and more heartfelt. Harris plays a chord, Criss answers, the bass thrums, and then another chord from the piano and a corresponding reply from the sax; pretty soon everyone is in on the action with some of the best blue edged playing Criss has ever done. The album is almost a document of Criss's increasing dissatisfaction with life.

what to buy next: *This Is Criss!* 𝄞𝄞𝄞𝄞 (OJC, 1966/1990, prod. Don Schlitten) has the same quartet heard on *Portrait of Sonny Criss* and, while they miss the very last scintilla of greatness squeezed out on that album, they're pretty damn close. "Greasy" is an instrumental version of the vocal blues romps Wynonie Harris and Roy Brown used to be famous for. "Days of Wine and Roses" punches the tempo for a version quite unlike any other as Dawson plays with the beat and Criss is a volcano of riffs. An all-around solid album.

the rest:
Sonny's Dream (Birth of the New Cool) 𝄞𝄞𝄞𝄞 (OJC, 1968/1992)
I'll Catch the Sun 𝄞𝄞𝄞𝄞 (OJC, 1969/1994)
Out of Nowhere 𝄞𝄞𝄞 (Muse, 1975/32 Jazz, 1997)
Intermission Riff 𝄞𝄞𝄞 (Pablo, 1987/OJC, 1998)

influences:
◀◀ Charlie Parker, Johnny Hodges

Garaud MacTaggart

Bing Crosby

Born Harry Lillis Crosby, May 3, 1903, in Tacoma, WA. Died October 14, 1977, in Madrid, Spain.

Bing Crosby is to jazz what Elvis Presley is to rock. Neither the first nor necessarily the best, his unprecedented popularity would pave the way to the commercial mainstream for countless jazz vocalists. Whereas Presley brought elements of the blues to his recordings, Crosby brought shades of jazz to his interpretations of swing, cowboy, Hawaiian, boogie-woogie, polkas, and religious material. His distinctive style and versatility allowed him a now-unheard-of longevity in the face of changing musical trends. Crosby's 50-year recording career spawned more than 200 hit records, and was the launching

pad for equally successful forays into radio, motion pictures, and television.

Crosby began his career in 1925 singing and playing drums for Al Rinker's Musicaladers orchestra. The following year, Rinker and Crosby recorded their first Columbia single, "I've Got the Girl," as a duet, just before joining bandleader Paul Whiteman's orchestra. Whiteman teamed them with Harry Barris and dubbed his new trio the Rhythm Boys, recording dozens of hits (including "Side by Side," "I'm Coming Virginia," "Three Little Words," and "My Blue Heaven") with them. The Rhythm Boys left Whiteman in 1930 to establish themselves as a solo act and constant chart presence. Crosby's increasingly popular solo spots, combined with union problems (concerning missed bookings), broke up the act, and he signed with Brunswick in 1931. Under the direction of Jack Kapp, his recording career exploded. His jazz-influenced phrasing and casual, erudite manner led to major hits, such as "Just One More Chance," "I Surrender Dear," and "Where the Blue of the Night" (where he whistles and scats the immortal phrase "boo-boo-boo-boo"), and established him as a household name. Crosby's concurrent rise as a radio and motion picture star dovetailed into a publicity bonanza, and he became King of the Crooners, the biggest star of the Depression Era. However, his enormously busy schedule was not without consequence: After severely straining his vocal chords with his forced tenor warbling, he had to lower his pitch and be coached on proper breathing technique. The result was the warmer, more intimate style most people associate with Bing Crosby.

When Kapp left Brunswick for Decca Records in 1934, Crosby went with him and continued his dominance of the charts with such classics as "Pennies from Heaven," "Sweet Leilani," "I'm an Old Cowhand," and dozens of others. Kapp was instrumental in expanding Crosby's style to other genres, and paired him with such stars as the Mills Brothers, Connee Boswell, Louis Armstrong, Judy Garland, Johnny Mercer, Louis Jordan, Les Paul, and the Andrews Sisters for a series of amazingly popular discs. And if Crosby was hot in the 1930s, he supernovaed in the 1940s. He became Hollywood's leading box office draw (with and without his *Road* picture partner, Bob Hope), had one of the highest rated radio shows in the country, and recorded the biggest-selling single of all-time, "White Christmas" (from the 1942 movie *Holiday Inn*). A seasonal Top 10 record for the next several years, Decca pressed so many copies of "White Christmas," that the company damaged the master recording and had to re-record the tune in 1947. Perhaps Crosby's absolute peak as a multi-media star was in 1944, when he won a best-actor Oscar for *Going My Way,* as well as scoring seven #1 hit records ("Swinging on a Star," "Don't Fence Me In," and "I'll Be Seeing You" among them). Crosby also weathered the rise of a new crooner who threatened his popularity: Frank Sinatra, of whom he said, "A voice like that comes along once in a generation. Why did it have to be mine?" Despite Sinatra's sudden fame, Crosby sold more records.

Crosby's enormous popularity extended well past the war years into television's golden age, but his amazing string of hit records dried up after 1951. His final Top 10 hit, "True Love," (a duet with Grace Kelly from the film *High Society),* came in 1956. Though generally considered one of the greatest mainstream pop singers, Crosby allied himself with jazz artists throughout his career, especially after leaving Decca Records to freelance with other labels. During the 1950s Crosby returned to his jazz roots at Verve, cut some swing and standards at RCA, and released movie soundtracks and remakes through MGM and Capitol. Throughout the 1960s he generally attempted to update his pop style for Sinatra's Reprise Records and other labels. By the 1970s a "semi-retired" Crosby hosted occasional TV specials and golf tournaments, made commercials, took feature parts in movies, recorded two LPs for United Artists (one with Count Basie), and profited handsomely from his many entertainment business interests. Throughout, Crosby never lost the aura of the "educated hipster" who delighted in finding the jazz in everything he did.

what to buy: Some of Crosby's best moments as a jazz singer are included on *That's Jazz* 𝄢𝄢𝄢 (Pearl, 1991, compilation prod. Tony Watts), a 22-song collection culled from the early to-mid-1930s and featuring hot takes on such classics as "Dinah," "Sweet Georgia Brown," "St. Louis Blues," and "Pennies from Heaven." Equally good, and maybe a little easier to find is *Sixteen Most Requested Songs* 𝄢𝄢𝄢𝄢 (Columbia/Legacy, 1992, compilation prod. Didier C. Deutsch), a mid-price compilation with many similar tracks that features backing from the Dorsey Brothers, Woody Herman, Eddie Lang, and Bunny Berigan. A nice starting point for Crosby's great run of popular hits can be found on *Bing's Gold Records* 𝄢𝄢𝄢𝄢 (Decca, 1997, compilation prod. Andy McKaie), which has 21 songs and encompasses the best of the MCA releases from 1987 (*Best of Bing*) and 1995 (*Greatest Hits*), both which are currently unavailable. The CD contains 21 Bing classics such as "Swinging on a Star," "Don't Fence Me In," "Sam's Song," "Now Is the Hour," and other popular favorites, including his Irish and Christmas hits. Also featured are the Andrew Sisters, Al Jolson, Fred Waring's orchestra, and Carmen Cavellero.

what to buy next: Crosby swings hot and croons cool on *The Jazzin' Bing Crosby 1927–40* 𝄢𝄢𝄢 (Affinity, 1992, prod. various), a two-disc, 50-song set featuring recordings with such notables as Paul Whiteman, Bix Beiderbecke, Duke Ellington, Joe Venuti, and Tommy Dorsey. However, the epiphany of true Bing-ness can be achieved by purchasing *Bing Crosby: His Legendary Years 1931–1957* 𝄢𝄢𝄢𝄢 (MCA, 1993, compilation prod. Steve Lasker, Andy McKaie), a four-CD, 101-track box set culled from his great years with Decca that includes hit collaborations with the Andrews Sisters, Judy Garland, Louis Armstrong, Louis Jordan, and Crosby's son, Gary, as well as a comprehensive 68-page booklet.

what to avoid: They're OK for completists, but don't be misled. *Christmas through the Years* 𝄢𝄢 (Laserlight, 1995) and *White Christmas* 𝄢𝄢 (Laserlight, 1993) do not feature Crosby's original Decca renditions of his famous seasonal offerings. Also, Crosby himself considered *Hey Jude/Hey Bing!* 𝄢 (Amos, 1969, prod. Jimmy Bowen) the worst LP of his career.

best of the rest:
Blue Skies 𝄢𝄢𝄢 (Sandy Hook, 1946/1996)
Bing's Buddies 𝄢𝄢𝄢 (Magic, 1951/1994)
Best of Bing Crosby & Fred Astaire: A Couple of Song & Dance Men 𝄢𝄢𝄢 (Curb 1975/1993)
Bing Crosby's Christmas Classic 𝄢𝄢𝄢 (Capitol/EMI, 1977/1997)
Bing Crosby Sings Again 𝄢𝄢𝄢𝄢 (MCA, 1986)
Radio Years–20 Songs 𝄢𝄢𝄢𝄢 (GNP/Crescendo, 1987)
Radio Years–25 Songs 𝄢𝄢𝄢 (GNP/Crescendo, 1988)
Remembering 1927–34 𝄢𝄢𝄢𝄢 (Happy Days, 1989)
The All-Time Best of Bing Crosby 𝄢𝄢𝄢 (Curb, 1990)
Bing Crosby & Some Jazz Friends 𝄢𝄢𝄢𝄢 (Decca Jazz, 1991)
On the Sentimental Side 𝄢𝄢𝄢 (ASV, 1992)
Here Lies Love 𝄢𝄢𝄢𝄢 (ASV, 1992)
Merry Christmas 𝄢𝄢𝄢𝄢 (MCA, 1993)
The Great Years 𝄢𝄢𝄢𝄢 (Pearl, 1993)
Classic Bing Crosby 1931–1938 𝄢𝄢𝄢 (DRG/ABC, 1994)
World War II Radio, Volume 3 𝄢𝄢𝄢 (Laserlight, 1994)
Bing Crosby 1927–1934 𝄢𝄢𝄢𝄢 (Mobile Fidelity, 1995)
Swingin' on a Star 𝄢𝄢𝄢 (Flapper, 1996)
I'm an Old Cow Hand 𝄢𝄢𝄢 (Living Era, 1995)
Duets 1947–1949 𝄢𝄢𝄢 (Viper's Nest, 1996)
Bing Crosby/Andrews Sisters: Their Complete Recordings 𝄢𝄢𝄢𝄢 (MCA, 1996)
Bing Sings whilst Bregman Swings 𝄢𝄢𝄢𝄢 (Mobile Fidelity, 1996)
My Favorite Cowboy Songs 𝄢𝄢𝄢𝄢 (MCA, 1996)
A Little Bit of Irish 𝄢𝄢𝄢 (Atlantic, 1996)

Bing Crosby **(Archive Photos)**

worth searching for: Crosby's early years as a young sensation with a high, hard vocal technique are on *The Crooner: The Columbia Years 1928–1934* ♫♫♫ (Columbia, 1988, prod. various), which has 67 tracks, including his work as part of the Rhythm Boys, with Paul Whiteman, and his first solo efforts. Also, *Two Fantastic Stories* ♫♫♫ (MCA, 1957/1962/1993, prod. various) features Crosby's eloquent readings of *The Small One* and *The Happy Prince* (with Orson Welles). For a first-rate example of how Der Bingle got better as he aged, dig through the $1.99 vinyl racks for *Bing Crosby: A Legendary Performer* ♫♫♫ (RCA, 1977, compilation prod. Ethel Gabriel). Side one features early hits "Just One More Chance," "Just a Gigolo," and others recorded with the Paul Whiteman, Duke Ellington, and Gus Arnheim orchestras in the late 1920s and early 1930s. Side two has six cool and jazzy tracks recorded in 1957 with Bob Scobey's Frisco Jazz Band.

influences:

◀◀ Rudy Vallee, Mildred Bailey, Al Jolson, Louis Armstrong, Ethel Waters, Paul Whiteman

▶▶ Russ Columbo, Dick Haymes, Frank Sinatra, Dean Martin, Frankie Laine, Perry Como, Boswell Sisters, Tony Bennett

Ken Burke

Connie Crothers

Born May 2, 1941, in Palo Alto, CA.

In 1955, upon hearing of the death of Charlie "Bird" Parker, Lennie Tristano composed "Requiem." A few years later, when the Atlantic recording of that tribute reached the ears of a student pianist and music major at the University of California in Berkeley who "could not personally identify with contemporary approaches to composition," Connie Crothers knew where she needed to be. Moving to New York in 1962, Crothers missed the Berkeley student revolt but found her musical voice during a ten-year course of study with Tristano (while working as a typist and on typesetting jobs). By 1972 Tristano was presenting her in performances at his home and then at Carnegie Recital Hall. In 1979, the year after his death, she co-founded the Lennie Tristano Foundation.

It's regrettable that historiographic conventional wisdom consigns Tristano to an isolated corner as the founder of a school of cerebrally brilliant but "emotionless," rhythmically neutral playing. The recorded output of Crothers (with several close collaborators) could help to dispel that. True, this isn't hard-bop and doesn't grab for the nearest blue note in the clinches.

It often sounds like (and sometimes is) an intimate, privately recorded musical conversation or soliloquy, with not-completely obvious harmonic rules of discourse. The audience, perhaps, is invited to listen in more than to be the object of entertainment. In addition to other treats, you get to play the jazz lover's favorite game of decoding the derivation of various compositions from standards ("Soul Sayer" from "Body and Soul," "Angel in Disguise" from "Angel Eyes," "Leave Me" from "Love Me or Leave Me," etc.). But "emotionless"? Hardly. There's a wide range of expression, considerable rhythmic power, and especially a lot of love conveyed in her work. In addition to her working and recording quartet co-led with tenor saxophonist Lenny Popkin, Crothers also leads an as-yet-unrecorded quartet with alto saxophonist Richard Tabnik, drummer Roger Mancuso, and bassists Ed Broderick, Calvin Hill, and Sean Smith.

what to buy: Solowise, *Music from Everyday Life* ♫♫♫♫ (New Artists, 1997, prod. Connie Crothers) compiles Crothers's favorite recordings in her own studio between 1993 and mid-1996, including standards, originals and an improvisation on Bela Bartok's "Buciumeana." *Swish* ♫♫♫♫ (New Artists, 1982) is a highly distinctive 1982 duet recording with Max Roach that launched the New Artists label. Some of the same interplay that characterizes the phenomenal Roach–Cecil Taylor collaboration is on display, but with a much lighter touch and compact format. Among the four recordings of the Connie Crothers–Lenny Popkin Quartet, with bassist Cameron Brown and drummer Carol Tristano, the most extroverted and accessible is *New York Night* ♫♫♫♫ (New Artists, 1989), a live 1989 club date.

what to buy next: The solo 1984 *Concert at Cooper Union* ♫♫♫♫ (New Artists, 1984) culminates in a fine "Trilogy (Prediction/In the Blues Mode/Love as a Force in History)." Two duet recordings, 1987's *Duo Dimension* ♫♫♫ (New Artists, 1987) with Richard Tabnik and 1994's *Deep into the Center* ♫♫♫ (New Artists, 1994) with Roger Mancuso, are collaborations with fellow disciples of Lennie Tristano. Mancuso's drumming in particular drives a high-energy partnership, particularly on the title cut, appropriately programmed "deep into the center" of the CD. The Crothers–Popkin Quartet has recorded both *New York Night* and *Love Energy* ♫♫♫ (New Artists, 1988), *Jazz Spring* ♫♫♫ (New Artists, 1992), and *In Motion* ♫♫♫ (New Artists, 1989). The slightly lower rating of *In Motion* (a recording session for Belgian radio and television) reflects not the quality of the playing, but the rather short 35-minute playing time. Here is one of the jazz rarities, a combination that not only plays but thinks and breathes together. Cameron Brown, a Detroit native who played with everyone from Art Blakey to Massimo Urbani, comes from outside the Tristano circle strictly speaking, while Popkin's tenor shows a lot of Warne Marsh in the middle and lower ranges and plenty of Lee Konitz in the upper. Carol Tristano is a drummer who propels the music without abusing it. Here's hoping they last a long time.

influences:

⏮ Louis Armstrong, Kenny Clarke, Billie Holiday, Lee Konitz, Warne Marsh, Sal Mosca, Fats Navarro, Charlie Parker, Oscar Pettiford, Bud Powell, Lennie Tristano, Lester Young

⏭ Liz Gorrill

David Finkel

Crusaders /Jazz Crusaders

Formed as the Jazz Crusaders in 1961 in Los Angeles, CA. Disbanded as the Crusaders in 1991.

Joe Sample, piano; Wilton Felder, tenor saxophone; Nesbert "Stix" Hooper, drums (1961–83); Wayne Henderson, trombone (1961–75); Larry Carlton, guitar (1971–91).

From their origins as a group of teenaged soul-jazz aficionados to their last days as a contemporary R&B/funk outfit, the Crusaders were successful throughout all stages of their career. Houston natives Joe Sample, Wilton Felder, Stix Hooper, and Wayne Henderson first started playing together in high school in the early '50s as the Swingsters. After a series of name changes—from the Modern Jazz Sextet to the Nighthawks—and an eventual relocation to California, the foursome finally arrived as the Jazz Crusaders and began their recording career in Los Angeles in 1961, releasing a series of well-received albums on the Pacific Jazz label that feature a soulful (and popular) brand of hard bop. Guest appearances included Jimmy Vaughan, Monk Montgomery, Joe Pass, and an old friend from their Houston days, Hubert Laws. As the 1970s approached, the group began concentrating their efforts exclusively on the studio, enabling them to experiment by adding elements of funk and rock into their sound. In 1971 they dropped the "Jazz" from their name and moved even further into a contemporary vibe with the inclusion of electric piano, electric bass, and, most importantly, electric guitar, supplied by virtual fifth member, Larry Carlton. Initially, this change in direction gave the band new energy, inspiring them to create some of the best non-fusion fusion of the time. The group's popularity soared even higher, with a gig opening for the Rolling Stones in 1975

and a number of hit records, especially *Street Life* in 1979. But after Henderson left in 1975 to focus on his career as a producer, the group's sound became increasingly watered-down and less "jazzy." Hooper's departure in 1983 essentially sounded the death-knell for the band, although Sample has maintained an active solo career. The Jazz Crusaders' material captured a vigorous bop style within an ensemble setting, giving each player the opportunity to display his own improvisational flair. Yet, with years of playing together, their various parts fit perfectly with each other. All four players contributed compositions, keeping the mix varied with slow-burning ballads, up-tempo romps, and everything in between, and their unique trombone-tenor combination suited both the "jazz" and "non-jazz" configurations. Although they eventually forsook pure jazz, the Crusaders left their mark with a number of recordings that show what can be done with its finest elements.

what to buy: Their first and best record from the "jazz" period, *Freedom Sound* ♫♫♫♫ (Pacific Jazz, 1961, prod. Richard Bock) is a clutch of snappy originals and the "Theme from Exodus," a great soul-jazz set. The two-LP set, *The Young Rabbits* ♫♫♫♫ (Blue Note, 1975, prod. Richard Bock), is the most comprehensive compilation of their first decade, although still unavailable on CD. Digital junkies will have to settle for the pared-down collection *The Best of the Jazz Crusaders* ♫♫♫♫ (Pacific Jazz, 1993, prod. Richard Bock).

what to buy next: Jazzy R&B from the height of their popularity, *Southern Comfort* ♫♫♫ (Blue Thumb, 1974, prod. Crusaders) prominently features Carlton and was Henderson's last hurrah. The three-CD set, *The Golden Years* ♫♫♫ (GRP, 1992, prod. various) focuses mainly on material from the hit days of the 1970s, with a couple of oldies thrown in.

what to avoid: There is no excuse for the slick, synthesized monstrosity *Life in the Modern World* **woof!** (MCA, 1988, prod. Stewart Levine). The ghost had been given up years before, and the album is typical of the Crusaders' tired '80s work.

the rest:
Jazz Crusaders:
Lookin' Ahead ♫♫♫♫ (Pacific Jazz, 1962)
At the Lighthouse ♫♫♫♫ (Pacific Jazz, 1962)
Tough Talk ♫♫♫ (Pacific Jazz, 1963)
Heat Wave ♫♫♫ (Pacific Jazz, 1964)
Stretchin' Out ♫♫♫♫ (Pacific Jazz, 1964)
The Thing ♫♫♫ (Pacific Jazz, 1965)
Chile Con Soul ♫♫♫♫ (Pacific Jazz, 1965)
Live at the Lighthouse 1966 ♫♫♫♫ (Pacific Jazz, 1966)

Talk that Talk 🎵🎵🎵 (Pacific Jazz, 1966)
Festival Album 🎵🎵🎵 (Pacific Jazz, 1967)
Uh Huh 🎵🎵🎵🎵 (Pacific Jazz, 1967)
Lighthouse 68 🎵🎵🎵🎵 (Pacific Jazz, 1968)
Powerhouse 🎵🎵🎵🎵 (Pacific Jazz, 1969)
Lighthouse 1969 🎵🎵🎵🎵 (Pacific Jazz, 1969)

Crusaders:

Old Socks, New Shoes 🎵🎵🎵🎵 (Chisa, 1970)
Crusaders I 🎵🎵🎵🎵 (Chisa, 1972)
The Second Crusade 🎵🎵🎵 (Blue Thumb, 1973)
Unsung Heroes 🎵🎵🎵 (Blue Thumb, 1973)
Chain Reaction 🎵🎵🎵 (Blue Thumb, 1975)
Scratch 🎵🎵🎵 (Blue Thumb, 1975)
Those Southern Knights 🎵🎵🎵 (Blue Thumb, 1976)
Free as the Wind 🎵🎵🎵 (Blue Thumb, 1977)
Images 🎵🎵 (Blue Thumb, 1978)
Street Life 🎵🎵 (Blue Thumb, 1979)

worth searching for: Having dropped the "Jazz" from their name, *Pass the Plate* 🎵🎵🎵🎵 (Chisa/MoJazz, 1971, prod. Crusaders) clearly sets them on the road of contemporary funk while still showing their roots; the update on their classic "Young Rabbits" alone speaks volumes.

influences:

◀◀ Ramsey Lewis Trio, JBs

▶▶ B-Sharp Jazz Quartet, Blackbyrds

Eric J. Lawrence

Celia Cruz

Born in Havana, Cuba.

Celia Cruz is the salsa singer non pareil, considered by many to be the "Queen of Salsa," a feminine icon in a notoriously macho field. She has been performing for well over four decades, but just how many years past those two score years is a matter of conjecture since Cruz is rather closed-mouthed when it comes to her age. Her voice transcends matters of age, however, and while not quite as flexible in the 1990s as it was during her artistic heyday in the early 1950s, Cruz has proven that she still carries surprising power in her singing.

In 1950 Cruz became the lead singer for Sonora Matancera, one of the leading Cuban orchestras of the time. This was the start of her "classic" period, when she was cementing her reputation as the most popular female singer in Cuba. Her recordings from the period she spent with Sonora Matancera (until 1965) were originally released through Seeco Records and some have been reissued through Palladium and Poly-

Gram Latino. It was also during this time that Cruz and the band left Cuba for a tour that never made it back to their homeland, applying for residency in the United States when they were able to secure a long-term gig at the Hollywood Palladium. Cruz had a commercial downturn from the mid-1960s through the early 1970s as the Latin audience turned to newer Latin styles like bugálu. By the mid-1970s she was making the climb back into popularity with a performance at Carnegie Hall in 1973, and a series of releases with Johnny Pacheco that were big sellers within the Hispanic community. By the late 1980s, her role as "Queen of Salsa" was the real deal. She received an honorary doctorate degree in music from Yale in 1989 and her album with Ray Barretto (*Ritmo en el Corazón*) won a Grammy Award in 1990, the same year her star appeared on the Hollywood Walk of Fame. She has also made cinematic appearances in the movies the *Mambo Kings Play Songs of Love* and *The Perez Family*. Cruz's later albums on RMM still carry some Latin-jazz punch but, in general, they target salsa fans.

what to buy: *Canciones Premiadas* 🎵🎵🎵🎵 (Palladium, 1994) is a collection of Cruz's classic performances with the Sonora Matancera, originally released on Seeco. She is in marvelous voice and the Sonora Matancera is an amazingly flexible instrumental ensemble. Certain aspects of the music may sound dated but, to keep things in perspective, so do the early Ella Fitzgerald sides with Chick Webb that don't have nearly as much raw power and assurance as heard from this top Latin act at the height of its popularity. Cruz has managed to remain the ruling diva of salsa by changing her style just enough to accommodate the latest recording techniques and keep pace with the younger singers in today's market. *Irrepetible* 🎵🎵🎵 (RMM, 1994, prod. Willy Chirino) was a 1996 Grammy nominee for Best Tropical Latin Performance and is a pretty good sample of Cruz's more recent recordings. The material is more pop oriented in some ways but the musicians and arrangers working with her are more than capable of making Cruz sound contemporary without gutting the vocal fire that makes her "The Queen." The rhythm riffs on "La Guagua" and "Cuando Cuba Se Ababe de Liberar" still have the deep Afro-Cuban roots that no amount of production work can weaken.

what to buy next: *La Dinamica Celia Cruz* 🎵🎵🎵 (Palladium, 1991) is yet another album from the Seeco vaults with the Sonora Matancera accompanying Cruz. From the first song ("Tamborilero"), this album is a primer of Afro-Cuban rhythms with mambos, rumbas, merengues, sones, and even a cha-cha-cha generating heat. The sound is a bit cheesy but the music is loads of fun. Cruz swears she's a devout Roman Catholic but she somehow recorded *Homenaje a los Santos* 𝄞𝄞𝄞𝄾 (PolyGram Latino, 1994), an album for Seeco that uses Santeria texts in praise of the various Orishas. It's an aural curiosity that works because understanding the basic Yoruba rhythms behind the music is the ticket to a fuller understanding of Latin Jazz and salsa.

best of the rest:

(With Ray Barretto) *Ritmon en el Corazón* 𝄞𝄞𝄞𝄾 (Fania/Charly, 1988)
The Best of Celia Cruz 𝄞𝄞𝄞𝄾 (Sony Discos, 1994)
Las Guaracheras de la Guaracha 𝄞𝄞𝄞 (PolyGram Latino, 1994)
Mi Llaman la Reina (They Call Me the Queen) 𝄞𝄞𝄞 (Laserlight, 1996)

influences:

◀◀ Graciela

▶▶ Gloria Estefan, India

Garaud MacTaggart

Ronnie Cuber

Born December 25, 1941, in New York, NY.

One of jazz's greatest living baritone saxophonists, Ronnie Cuber is a powerful player with complete control of his horn in both the upper and lower registers. His improvisational approach is rooted in bebop, though he has also recorded R&B sessions and injects a deep blues feeling into many of his solos. Raised in a musically inclined family, he began playing tenor sax in high school and picked up the baritone only after he had made a strong impression auditioning for the Newport Youth Band in 1959. The band already had enough tenor players, so Cuber agreed to switch to bari. Cuber has worked steadily over the years, including stints with Slide Hampton (1962), Maynard Ferguson (1963–65), George Benson (1966–67), Lionel Hampton (1968), and Woody Herman (1969). He has also worked extensively with Latin-jazz pianist/composer Eddie Palmieri. His first recordings as a leader were two excellent albums for Xanadu in 1976 and 1978, and he has also made fine recordings for Dire, King, SteepleChase, and ProJazz. Over the year's, however, he's gained far more exposure through his many tours and recordings with pop, soul, and R&B artists such as King Curtis, Steve Gadd, Aretha Franklin, Paul Simon, and the Saturday Night Live Band. Since the mid-1990s, he's been featured in the Mingus Big Band.

what to buy: A fine quartet session with Cuber exclusively playing his huge, swaggering baritone sax, *In a New York Minute*

𝄞𝄞𝄞𝄞 (SteepleChase, 1995, prod. Nils Winther) features the brilliant young pianist Kenny Drew Jr., bassist Andy McKee, and versatile drummer Adam Cruz. Cuber shows off his bop shops on Miles Davis's "Dig," waxes extremely lyrical on Johnny Mandel's "Emily," and makes fast tracks through the desert sand of Juan Tizol's classic Ellingtonia, "Caravan," while providing five of his own tunes. Most impressive is his hot-blooded emotionalism on "Con Pasion" and an incredibly nimble workout on the duet "For Bari & Bass." Drew, a bandmate of Cuber's in the Mingus Big Band, develops a beautiful melodic line on the title track, while McKee and Cruz lock into a irresistible groove on "Bu's Beat."

what to buy next: With his eclectic career, bari master Cuber decided to display a few of his many sides on *The Scene Is Clean* 𝄞𝄞𝄞 (Milestone, 1994, prod. Roberta Arnold), an enjoyable session covering everything from Latin jazz with Palmieri's "Adoracion," to hard bop with Tadd Dameron's title track, to an impassioned modal outing on his "Song for Pharoah," and a soulful tribute to the keyboardist Richard Tee with "Tee's Bag," featuring organist Joey DeFrancesco. The album is suffused with a Latin feel, and Cuber makes extensive use of overdubbing to create his own horn section. The results are effective if not especially memorable.

best of the rest:

Cuber Libre 𝄞𝄞𝄞𝄞 (Xanadu, 1976)
Live at the Blue Note 𝄞𝄞𝄾 (ProJazz, 1987)
Passion Fruit 𝄞𝄞 (ProJazz, 1988)
Two Brothers 𝄞𝄞𝄾 (Projazz, 1988)
Cubism 𝄞𝄞𝄞 (Freshsound, 1992)
Airplay 𝄞𝄞𝄞𝄞 (SteepleChase, 1996)

worth searching for: Cuber opens his arrangement of "Nostalgia in Times Square" with a story about sitting in with Mingus at Birdland, *Mingus Big Band 93* 𝄞𝄞𝄞𝄞 (Dreyfus, 1993, prod. Sue Mingus), kicking off one of the best post-Mingus albums with just the right note of jazz-musician solidarity. He is also featured on a stomping nine-minute version of "Moanin'," one of Mingus's great roots tunes. With its passion and bluesy swagger, Cuber's solo would have pleased Mingus himself. His huge sound supplies this excellent orchestra with much of its sonic punch.

influences:

◀◀ Pepper Adams, Cecil Payne, Sonny Rollins, Eddie "Lockjaw" Davis

Andrew Gilbert

Brian Culbertson

Born January 12, 1973, in Decatur, IL.

With encouragement from his father (a high-school jazz band director), contemporary jazz multi-instrumentalist Brian Culbertson began piano studies at age eight, and tried drums, trombone, and bass by age twelve. As a high school student, he began experimenting with MIDI keyboard programming. While in high school, he received six individual citations from *Down Beat* magazine. By then, influenced by contemporary players such as David Sanborn, Marcus Miller, and horn-led bands such as Earth, Wind & Fire and Chicago, he was still trying to find his niche but was composing his own material. Culbertson attended DePaul University, and signed with Bluemoon while a 20-year-old junior, releasing his debut recording, *Long Night Out,* in 1994. He has since released three more albums for the label. In addition to performing, touring, and recording, Culbertson has written radio and TV jingles for national clients. What sets Culbertson apart from the contemporary jazz herd is his penchant for creating catchy, unique melodies that blend pop, jazz, and cityscape sounds with funky, riveting beats.

what to buy: Brian Culbertson's 1997 album, *Secret* 𝄞𝄞𝄞𝄞 (Bluemoon, 1997, prod. Brian Culbertson, prod. various) shows how far this versatile musician has come since his 1994 debut CD. His piano and keyboard performances on this nine-tune set show greater confidence, maturity, and more melodic and harmonic flexibility. Mastering an urban-beat edge, Culbertson engages various musicians, including his old friend Steve Finckle on saxophones, Atlantic group label–mate Gerald Albright, whose alto sax punctuates "One More Day," and Bluemoon companion, Jeff Golub, whose guitar work combines with Ricky Peterson's B-3 to make "At the Backroom" a down-to-business funk-beat track. Culbertson's eight originals range from stealth-like, tip-toeing numbers to upbeat, peppy messages, and he nods to one of his influences with Marcus Miller's romantic ballad "Straight to the Heart," to which Lenny Castro adds piquant percussion. Rhythm and diversity are the focus on Culbertson's catchy third album, *After Hours* 𝄞𝄞𝄞𝄞 (Bluemoon, 1996, prod. Brian Culbertson). The leader mixes it up with an array of musicians, including his guests, percussionist Steve Reid, tenor saxman Steve Finckle, and even a real string orchestra conducted by Cliff Colnot. As on his previous recordings, on the 13 originals of this CD, Culbertson plays piano, keyboards, organ, trombone, and designs drum programming. Guitarist Harry Mura, a regular, appearing on all of Culbertson's sessions thus far, adds pleasing textures to some tracks. Although there are many highlights, extra points go to the lyrical

"Shadow's Dance" to which Reid's percussion complements Culbertson's acoustic piano, the strings, Mura's guitar, and Tom Hipskind's drums, and to the danceable, funky-pop lines of "Inside Pocket."

what to buy next: Culbertson hit the top of the adult alternative radio charts with *Modern Life* 𝄞𝄞𝄞𝄞 (Bluemoon, 1995, prod. Brian Culbertson, Harry Mura), playing with an assortment of musicians on the 11 tracks, including Chicago guitarist Fareed Haque on a sugary ballad ("Without the Rain") and Gerald Albright on a funky A-2 tune ("Take Me Home to You"). Saxophonist Steve Finckle creates the contemporary-styled trademark soaring saxisms. Culbertson shows a knack for creating likeable smooth melodies and intricately blending harmonies. A promising debut for a 21 year old, Culbertson recorded *Long Night Out* 𝄞𝄞𝄞𝄞 (Bluemoon, 1994, prod. Brian Culbertson) in the bedroom of his Chicago apartment he was sharing with three other DePaul University students at the time. But don't let the locale lead you to believe it isn't a top-notch album. Culbertson has created a solid, intelligent approach to his keyboards with emotionally charged lead lines, snappy sequences, and superb production quality. The young marvel also plays bass and trombone, programs drum sequences, and sings, with accompaniment on his 11 originals from Mark Colby (saxophones), Harry Mura (guitars), and guests. With such abundant talent, Culbertson should be around a long while.

Nancy Ann Lee

Jim Cullum
/Jim Cullum Jazz Band

Born September 20, 1941, in San Antonio, TX.

Jim Cullum, a cornetist influenced primarily by Louis Armstrong, has led his San Antonio-based Jim Cullum Jazz Band since the death (in 1973) of his father, a clarinetist and former leader of the Cullum band forerunner, the Happy Jazz Band. If you listen to National Public Radio, you've probably heard his informative and entertaining *Riverwalk: Live from the Landing* series, which began around 1988 and now broadcasts to more than 200 NPR-affiliate stations nationwide. Cullum owns the club where his band of full-time, professional musicians hold fort, and he's had the good fortune to perform along with illustrious guests such as Lionel Hampton, Doc Cheatham, Benny Carter, Banu Gibson, and a host of other traditional-jazz stylists. When Cullum was 12, his family moved to San Antonio, where he spent his lonely hours listening to and committing to memory (by whistling) his father's 78 rpm recordings of Bix Bei- derbecke and other inspiring classic jazz players. Cullum wanted to play the music he loved and tried trombone first be- fore he found a beat-up cornet in a hock shop. He taught him- self to play with help from his father, a wholesale grocer and part-time clarinetist whose friends Bobby Hackett, Adrian Rollini, and Jack Teagarden would gather at the Cullum home to jam when they were in town. Cullum eventually formed a band with his father, getting his first professional gigs playing in the 1960s with the Happy Jazz Band at a local beer joint. His knowl- edge is vast, and his playing, steeped in the classic jazz/Dix- ieland, pre-bop style, is featured on numerous albums pro- duced with his band. If you can't find their albums in your local stores, check out the Jim Cullum Jazz Band Website at http://www.riverwalk.org for more information.

what to buy: You'll be transported back to the turn of the cen- tury with the classic jazz (Dixieland) on one of the earliest recordings of the Jim Cullum Jazz Band. The 1986-recorded ses- sion, *Super Satch* 𝄞𝄞𝄞𝄞 (Stomp Off, 1986, prod. Mike Cogan), finds the seven-musician team romping through 12 (mostly) Louis Armstrong compositions, with some tunes reminiscing on Satchmo's Hot Five and Hot Seven (small ensemble) repertoire. Cullum leads with his fine cornet solos dedicated to his idol, accompanied by equally innovative solos and tight ensemble playing from Allan Vaché (clarinet), Ed Hubble or Randy Rein- hart (trombone), John Sheridan (piano), Howard Elkins (banjo, guitar, vocals), Jack Wyatt (string bass), and Ed Torres (drums). Everyone is enlivened—especially pianist Sheridan—on the collection of pianist Jelly Roll Morton's ragtime classics ren- dered by the Jim Cullum band on *Shootin' the Agate* 𝄞𝄞𝄞𝄞 (Stomp Off, 1993, prod. Mike Cogan). On "Kansas City Stomp," the seven-musician crew pulls out the stops for a bustling and brassy rendition of this warhorse. Cullum's warm-toned solo on the appropriately titled "Sweet Substitute" shows his soul-felt command of his instrument. Other highlights include Sheri- dan's awesome solo piano performance on "Fingerbuster," one of the most difficult ragtime piano pieces to perform, as you might guess from the title. If you aren't already enamored of Sheridan's playing, after hearing this number, you'll want to go out and buy his recordings as leader. He also helps put the focus on the rhythm team on "Tank Town Bump," which fea- tures tidy solos and comping from Don Mopsik (bass) and Ed Torres (drums). The full ensemble leads off before Cullum takes over with a gorgeous cornet solo on "Buddy Bolden's Blues." Remaining personnel include Allan Vaché (clarinet), Mike Pitts- ley (trombone), and Howard Elkins (banjo, guitar). These are all

very talented players and, combined with the wonderfully exe- cuted old-time charts, this album is highly recommended. Pi- anist Sheridan is prominently featured on *Hooray for Hoagy!* 𝄞𝄞𝄞𝄞 (Audiophile, 1990, prod. Jim Cullum), a 14-tune celebra- tion of 1920s–1940s music by composer-pianist Hoagy Car- michael. The Jim Cullum Jazz Band authentically performs Carmichael's most popular ballads, "Star Dust" and "Skylark," spotlighting lovely, fluent solos from Cullum, Allan Vaché (clar- inet), and Mike Pittsley (trombone). The rhythm team of Sheri- dan (piano), Elkins (guitar/banjo), Jack Wyatt (bass), and Torres (drums) keep "Washboard Blues," "I Walk with the Music," "Boneyard Shuffle," and other seldom-heard delights swinging with hot fervor. A nostalgic listen for the solos and the melodic ensemble arrangements.

what to buy next: One way to get a healthy dose of jazz history with Jim Cullum Jazz Band music is to pick up any of the albums from the NPR broadcast series, *Riverwalk: Live at the Landing.* The several live-recorded performances will inform you with brief narratives from host David Holt, sound clips from historic jazz artists, and delightful, reminiscent music performed by the Band, with an array of stellar guests. *New Year's All-Star Jam, Volume 1* 𝄞𝄞𝄞𝄞 (Riverwalk Live, 1993, prod. Margaret Pick, Lynne Cruise, Jim Cullum) launches the series. Containing 12 tunes, this album features guest soloists Dick Hyman (piano), Doc Cheatham (trumpet/vocals), Dan Barrett (trombone), Carol Woods (vocalist), Marty Grosz (guitar/vocals), and Bob Hag- gart (bass). Bette Midler's version of "Big Noise from Win- netka" may be the boldest, but you'll want this album for the fun-filled version of the tune by its composer, bassist Bob Hag- gart, performed as a duo with drummer Torres. If you pick up this album, you'll undoubtedly want the rest. Capturing all the energy of the live performances, they're very well produced and contain plenty of swing-minded fun. Another of the best of the series is *American Love Songs, Volume 7* 𝄞𝄞𝄞𝄞 (Riverwalk Live, 199, prod. Margaret Pick, Lynne Cruise, Jim Cullum), which features guests Benny Carter (alto sax), Dick Hyman (piano), and Carol Woods, Nina Ferro, and Joe Williams (vocals). Vocalist Woods has a powerful, big voice yet handles the ballad medley "Lover Man/Body and Soul" with controlled, soulful ease and is nicely accompanied by alto saxophonist Fred Salas. The band's other regular soloists also make significant contribu- tions to the 15 tunes, yet cameo appearances by so many illus- trious guests give the album added oomph, including Joe Williams singing and swingin' through "Singin' in the Rain," with all of the fine ensemble backing and instrumental solos. Benny Carter renders a toasty alto sax solo on "When the

Lights Are Low," and, without band backing, Hyman and Sheridan offer a pleasing two-piano duet on "My Fate Is in Your Hands." The romantic theme slows the band down from their usual swinging, brassy-sound, and they master the 15 sentimental ballads and light swingers with seasoned flair.

the rest:
(With Dick Hyman) *The Boogie Woogie Craze: Volume 2* ♫♫♫ Riverwalk Live, 1994)

(With Topsy Chapman) *The Bessie Smith Story: Bessie & The Blues, Volume 3* ♫♫♫ (Riverwalk Live, 1994)

(With Banu Gibson & the New Orleans Hot Jazz and others) *Battle of the Bands: San Antonio vs. New Orleans, Volume 4* ♫♫♫♫ (Riverwalk Live, 1994)

(With others) *Hot Jazz for a Cool Yule, Volume 5* ♫♫♫ (Riverwalk Live, 1995)

(With Lionel Hampton and others) *Fireworks! Red Hot & Blues, Volume 6* ♫♫♫ (Riverwalk Live, 1996)

influences:

◀◀ Bix Beiderbecke, King Oliver, Louis Armstrong, Yank Lawson, Bobby Hackett, Garner Clark

▶▶ Randy Sandke, Ken Peplowski

see also: *John Sheridan, Dick Hyman, Ken Peplowski, Bix Beiderbecke, King Oliver, Dan Barrett*

Nancy Ann Lee

Bill Cunliffe

Born June 26, 1956, in Lawrence, MA.

While at Duke University, Cunliffe studied with piano great Mary Lou Williams. He later studied with pianist Bill Dobbins at the Eastman School of Music, where he got his Master's degree. After three years of teaching, Cunliffe toured with the Buddy Rich Big Band. Other notables he's worked with include Woody Shaw, Joe Henderson, Freddie Hubbard, Art Farmer, James Moody, Joshua Redman, Art Blakey, the Clayton Hamilton Jazz Orchestra, and Natalie Cole.

Many jazz fans first noticed Cunliffe in 1989 when he won the Thelonious Monk International Jazz Piano Award. Currently based in Los Angeles, he often works as a studio musician (but don't be tempted by his presence in the Jazz at the Movies Band, which has done a series of Muzaky arrangements of film soundtrack themes). A lyrical player and composer, his work sometimes skirts "contemporary jazz" but maintains straight-ahead credibility.

what to buy: *A Rare Connection* ♫♫♫ (Discovery, 1994, prod. Bob Sheppard, Bill Cunliffe) offers the biggest dose of Cunliffe's tuneful writing, with seven originals out of 10 tracks. It starts like jazzy easy listening music with a cover of "Stella by Starlight" replete with cheesy synth backgrounds, but the fleet Corea tribute "Chick It Out" soon sets things straight. His style-hopping tendency is strongest on "Jamaican Lounge Lizards," which mixes reggae and stride. On most of the album he's joined by horns (Cunliffe's arrangements are nicely voiced), and Bob Sheppard provides some hot solos. The drummer throughout is former Weather Reporter Peter Erskine.

what to buy next: Throughout much of *Bill in Brazil* ♫♫♫ (Discovery, 1995, prod. Bill Cunliffe, Bones Howe), Cunliffe, of course, plays with Brazilian musicians, and there are classics by Caetano Veloso, Luis Bonfa, and Baden Powell as well as Vince Guaraldi's "Cast Your Fate to the Wind" and Paul Simon's "She Moves On." The prevailing mood is mellow, but the percolating rhythms keep even the most laid-back sambas from stagnating.

the rest:
A Paul Simon Songbook ♫♫♫ (Discovery, 1993)

worth searching for: *Just Duet* ♫♫♫ (Azica, 1998, prod. Gary Wright) is a duo album with flutist Holly Hofmann that contains some of Cunliffe's most mainstream material, including "Bag's Groove" (Milt Jackson), "Powell's Prances" (Bud Powell), "I Mean You" (Thelonious Monk), and the standards "But Not for Me," "Old Folks," and "Willow Weep for Me." There's even an arrangement of classical composer Robert Schumann's "Three Romances," as well as three Cunliffe originals and a collaboration with Hofmann. Unlike the highly produced Discovery albums, which tend to highlight the piano in the mix and surround it with a gauzy halo, this album has a very pure sound and shows his sensitive pianistic touch, with a gorgeous legato beyond even many classical players. The spontaneity and give-and-take here make it in some ways Cunliffe's best recording—and Hofmann's a fine flute player who avoids the cheap sentimentality of many jazz flutists.

influences:

◀◀ Bill Evans, Chick Corea, Oscar Peterson, Tommy Flanagan, Wynton Kelly, Herbie Hancock, Lyle Mays

Steve Holtje

Ted Curson

Born June 3, 1935, in Philadelphia, PA.

While growing up, trumpeter Ted Curson lived close to the

Heath family, and the first band he played in (before he was even deep into his teens) featured Albert Heath on drums and Sam Reed on alto. He studied music with Albert's older brother, Jimmy, and went to a high school where other juveniles like Jimmy Bond, Lex Humphries and Henry Grimes were in the same music program. Curson worked with Lee Morgan, Bobby Timmons, and Odean Pope before moving to New York, where the trumpeter found himself working with pianists like Red Garland and Mal Waldron. While heady stuff, this hardly prepared him for the tumult of brief associations with pianist Cecil Taylor and bassist Charles Mingus. Curson only worked briefly with both bandleaders, but the Mingus association was the famous piano-less outfit featuring Dannie Richmond on drums and Eric Dolphy on reeds and flutes that took part in some of the most interesting jazz performances on the cusp of the 1960s. Since then Curson has played with Bill Barron and Max Roach. Most of his live shows the past few decades have been confined to Europe, especially Finland. He has even recorded an album with a Siberian sextet called the Siberian Jazz Project and has also led his own groups on recordings for Old Town, Prestige, Atlantic, and King.

what to buy: After all these years, *Fire down Below* ♪♪♪♪ (OJC, 1963, prod. Ozzie Cadena) is still the Curson solo album to start your collection. There are none of the avant-garde fireworks of the Taylor/Mingus period; instead, you get a well-played, bop-pish set of covers, heavy on show-tune classics. Of the six cuts, four feature conga playing from Montego Joe, and the Latin percussion riffs work well with what master drummer Roy Haynes has popping in the background. Gildo Mahones was a solid pianist but he, like Dodo Marmarosa, never really got a whole lot of press. Bassist George Tucker is best known for his work with Jaki Byard, Kenny Burrell, and Earl Hines. Curson's balladeering is wonderful on "The Very Young," and "Show Me" features some nice mute work.

what to buy next: *Traveling On* ♪♪♪ (Evidence, 1996, prod. Yoichi Nakao) shows what Curson has been up to lately. The old-line players are Curson and bassist Ray Drummond; new blood comes from solid young tenor player Mark Gross, drummer Sylvia Cuenca, and pianist Misako Kano. Four cuts feature a percussion ensemble which gives an interesting lift to Herbie Hancock's "Watermelon Man" and one of Curson's classic compositions, "Flatted Fifth." Curson shows that he hasn't really lost a step. His playing still has fire, and when he revisits earlier compositions he does an interesting job of rearranging them. Curson uses some of Mingus's compositional strategies on "Reava's Walty (More Mingus)," including a marvelous opening bass line from Drummond.

the rest:
Tears for Dolphy ♪♪♪ (Black Lion, 1964)
Plenty of Horn ♪♪♪ (Boplicity, 1994)
Cattin' Curson ♪♪♪ (EPM, 1996)

worth searching for: Discs by Curson are not going to be that hard to find. The almost telepathic compatibility of Eric Dolphy and Curson in the Charles Mingus Quartet is at another level than that reserved for mere mortals. The best example of this can be heard on "Folk Forms, No. 1," from *Charles Mingus Presents Charles Mingus* ♪♪♪♪ (Candid, 1961, prod. Nat Hentoff). Curson has never played so intensely or so well since.

influences:

◀◀ Dizzy Gillespie, Miles Davis, Clifford Brown

▶▶ Charles Tolliver

Garaud MacTaggart

Andrew Cyrille

Born November 20, 1939, in New York, NY.

Andrew Cyrille began playing at age 11 in a drum-and-bugle corps, and at age 15 performed in a trio that included Eric Gale. From the early 1950s, Cyrille performed with a variety of musicians including Illinois Jacquet, Babatunde Olatunji, Walt Dickerson, Coleman Hawkins, Bill Barron, and Rahsaan Roland Kirk. In 1958, Cyrille began percussion studies at the Juilliard School. Cyrille replaced Sunny Murray in pianist Cecil Taylor's group in 1964, and became notable for his long-term association with the avant-garde visionary until 1975. Cyrille showed amazing ability to interact with Taylor and to influence the direction of Taylor's music, certainly a testament to Cyrille's strong rhythmic and melodic sense. Since the 1960s, Cyrille has collaborated with Marion Brown, the Jazz Composers Orchestra, Grachan Moncur III, and Peter Brötzmann. As a member of the collective called the Group, Cyrille joined free-boppers such as Billy Bang, Marion Brown, Ahmed Abdullah, Fred Hopkins, and Sirone. He's also performed with drum ensembles that included Milford Graves and Rashid Ali, and duos with Famadou Don Moye or Joseph Jarman, which should give an idea of the scope of his credits as a performer. In recent years, Cyrille has focused on his role as a clinician-educator, serving as artist-in-residence at Antioch College, and as clinician at other educational institutions. He is now on the jazz division faculty of the New School for Social Research.

what to buy: *Metamusicians' Stomp* ♪♪♪♪ (Black Saint, 1978, prod. Giacomo Pellicciotti) is the best recording Cyrille did with his 1970s band Maono. Featuring Ted Daniel (trumpet, flugelhorn, flute), David S. Ware (tenor saxophone/flute), and Nick DiGeronimo (bass), the session offers some of the more intense "outside" playing in the drummer's catalog, with an interesting read on the popular Kurt Weill tune "My Ship." The other compositions are by Cyrille, a much better composer than is the norm among drummers. The motivic shapes and the instrumentation combine to recall the classic Ornette Coleman–Don Cherry Quartet, especially on "5-4-3-2." Most impressive is the extended suite "Spiegelgasse 14." *Ode to the Living Tree* ♫♫♫♫ (Venus, 1995, prod. Tetsuo Hara/Evidence, 1997) is the first jazz album to be recorded in Senegal, West Africa. The first and last tracks are drum duets with Mor Thiam on African drums and between these are standards such as "Mr. P.C." and "A Love Supreme," and originals from Cyrille, bandmate David Murray, and pianist Adegoke Steve Colson. Bassist Fred Hopkins adds his usual best and Oliver Lake joins in on alto.

what to buy next: On *Special People* ♫♫♫♫ (Soul Note, 1981, prod. Giovanni Bonardrini) Ware is heard again, starring on the opening Ornette Coleman tune and on "High Priest," which Cyrille penned with Ware in mind. The leader's fluid, subtly startling rhythms hold together a deeply involving inside/outside date. *Good to Go* ♫♫♫♫ (Soul Note, 1997, prod. Flavio Bonandrini) contains a stunning tribute, heard in two versions, to fellow drum great Art Blakey (Abdullah Buhainia). The album is a trio with Lisle Atkinson on bass and James Newton on flute and mostly consists of band originals, stretching stylistically from the depths of African drumming to the cool of a Blue Note session (complete with Andrew Hill's "Nicodemus").

best of the rest:
Nuba ♫♫♫♪ (Black Saint, 1979)
The Navigator ♫♫♫♪ (Soul Note, 1983)
My Friend Louis ♫♫♫♪ (Columbia, 1992)
X Man ♫♫♫♪ (Soul Note, 1994)
Double Clutch ♫♫♫♫ (Silkheart, 1997)

worth searching for: Cyrille's long association with Cecil Taylor bandmate/alto saxophonist Jimmy Lyons continues on the duo albums *Something in Return* ♫♫♫♫ (Black Saint, 1988) and *Burnt Offering* ♫♫♫♫ (Black Saint, 1991), recorded respectively at 1981 and 1982 concerts and dually credited but with Lyons's name listed first. Lyons's level of improvisatory imagination is positively spellbinding in its unceasing flow and ability to startle, his light tone and insinuating style never hectoring or wearing thin. And Cyrille's mastery of rhythm is at its peak in this context: never rote, always probing, yet rock-solid.

influences:

◀◀ Cecil Taylor, Ornette Coleman, Duke Ellington, Milford Graves, Sunny Murray, Max Roach

▶▶ Susie Ibarra, Whit Dickey, Michael Sarin

David C. Gross, Nancy Ann Lee, and Steve Holtje

Tadd Dameron

Born Tadley Ewing Dameron, February 21, 1917, in Cleveland, OH. Died March 8, 1965, in New York, NY.

To the public, composer-arranger Tadd Dameron's flame never shone as brightly as it should have. A number of his tunes have become standards—including "Hot House," "Our Delight," and "If You Could See Me Now"—and there are indeed occasional efforts to promote the oeuvre of the man Stanley Crouch has hailed as "the most influential arranger of the bebop era." Dameron sang with the band of Freddie Webster in his hometown of Cleveland before switching to piano. Subsequent gigs included the band of Cab Calloway's sister, Blanche Calloway; the band of Zack Whyte (where he inherited and absorbed charts left behind by the redoubtable Sy Oliver); and eventually, after moving to Kansas City, the band of Harlan Leonard. While in Kansas City Dameron had his first exposure to Charlie Parker. Moving to New York, he wrote for Jimmie Lunceford and a number of others. He got with the bop though, and penned for the Dizzy Gillespie big band and led his own fine combo with the equally doomed trumpeter Fats Navarro. He spent two years living in England and returned to the United States in 1951 after Navarro had died. In 1957 or '58 (sources vary), Dameron began serving a drug sentence. In 1961, still confined at a Federal penitentiary for drug rehab, he wrote charts (and tunes) for trumpeter Blue Mitchell's Riverside album with string and brass arrangements and mailed them in. His career never fully revived despite one more good session, *The Magic Touch*, with a 14-piece big band in 1962. It was his last album. Dameron died of cancer three years later.

what to buy: The first CD of the two-disc set *Fats Navarro and Tadd Dameron: The Complete Blue Note and Capitol Recordings* ♫♫♫♫ (Blue Note, 1995, prod. Michael Cuscuna) is all Dameron material. First comes the Dameron/Navarro sextet (with Ernie Henry on alto sax, Charlie Rouse on tenor, Nelson Boyd on bass, and Shadow Wilson on drums), records recorded for Blue Note in 1947: "The Chase," "The Squirrel," "Our Delight," and "Dameronia," all favorites and heard in two versions each. The 1948 sextet (tenor saxes Allen Eager and Wardell Gray, bassist Curly Russell, and drummer Kenny Clarke, with Chino Pozo on bongos on two cuts and vocalist Kenny Hagood on one), again on Blue Note, has "Jahbero," "Lady Bird," "Symphonette" (all with alternate takes), and "I Think I'll Go Away." This is bebop of the highest order, with some pieces anticipating cool jazz. The two 1949 Dameron/Navarro ten-piece recordings for Capitol (trombonist Kai Winding, alto saxist Sahib Shihab, tenor Dexter Gordon, baritones Cecil Payne, Russell, and Clarke, percussionists Diego Ibarra and Vidal Bolado, plus Rae Pearl contributing one vocal) are "Sid's Delight" and "Casbah." Especially interesting from the cool jazz perspective are Dameron's 1949 sides for Capitol with Miles Davis (trumpet), J.J. Johnson (trombone), Shihab, tenor Ben Lundy, Payne, guitarist John Collins, Russell, Clarke, and vocalist Kay Penton on the double-entendre song "Heaven's Doors Are Wide Open." All this material constitutes the core of the Dameron legacy, and some of the finest music of its time.

what to buy next: *Fountainbleau* 🎵🎵🎵🎵 (Prestige, 1956, prod. Bob Weinstock) features the lovely and entirely composed three-movement title track (conveying Dameron's impressions of the French palace of that name), though there are fine solos elsewhere from Kenny Dorham and others in the medium-sized combo. The quartet album recorded with John Coltrane, *Mating Call* 🎵🎵🎵🎵 (Prestige, 1956, prod. Bob Weinstock), recorded earlier in 1956 than *Fountainbleau*, proves an excellent setting for the tenor saxophonist, with "Soultrane" (like all the tunes, a Dameron composition) a highlight.

the rest:
The Magic Touch 🎵🎵🎵 (Riverside, 1962)

worth searching for: *Fats Navarro Featured with the Tadd Dameron Band* 🎵🎵🎵🎵 (Milestone, 1989, prod. Orrin Keepnews), though credited to the trumpeter, is essentially a Dameron recording. The material comes from 1948, and if not as superb as the Blue Notes, is nonetheless valuable documentation of two under-recorded greats.

influences:

◀◀ Duke Ellington, Sy Oliver

▶▶ Horace Silver, Benny Golson, Gigi Gryce, Dameronia

W. Kim Heron and Steve Holtje

Eddie Daniels

Born October 19, 1941, New York, NY.

Eddie Daniels is one of the great clarinetists, matching the talents of Buddy DeFranco and Benny Goodman. Daniels can play jazz and European classical music with equal facility, and has performed with small jazz ensembles as well as with symphony orchestras. In recent years, he has also returned to his earliest reed instrument, tenor saxophone. Daniels attended the High School of Performing Arts in New York and played alto saxophone in Marshall Brown's Youth Band at the 1957 Newport Jazz Festival. He graduated from Brooklyn College in 1963, studied clarinet at the Juilliard School (earning his master's degree in 1966), and, the same year, joined the Thad Jones–Mel Lewis Orchestra, remaining with the band for six years. Daniels has moved back and forth between the jazz and classical worlds throughout his career. In the 1970s he recorded with jazz musicians Freddie Hubbard, Richard Davis, Don Patterson, Bucky Pizzarelli, Airto Moreira, and as leader of his own group. Daniels's series of albums for GRP, beginning with *Breakthrough* in 1986, gave him wider visibility. In the early 1990s he began doubling on tenor saxophone again, once he had accrued much success playing clarinet, on which Daniels is a technically gifted player with a beautiful tone.

what to buy: *Real Time* 🎵🎵🎵🎵 (Chesky, 1994, prod. David Chesky) is a wonderful album that finds Daniels splitting his playing almost evenly between clarinet and tenor sax. Leading a sprightly session of 11 tunes with guitarist Chuck Loeb, bassist Ned Mann, and drummer Adam Nussbaum, Daniels displays dexterously distinct personas; he forges muscular, fiery and passionate saxisms, and light, airy clarinet lines with classical perfection. Deftly delivering standards such as a seductive clarinet solo on "The Man I Love," a soaring "My Foolish Heart," and a bopped-up version of "You Stepped out of a Dream," the reedman shines as player. Plus, he contributes his gorgeous, head-turning originals: "Blue Bolero," "Thad's Lament," and "Farrell," the latter two pay tributes to Thad Jones and Joe Farrell, honoring Daniels's Monday nights with New York's Village Vanguard band beginning in the mid-1960s. A wonderful player with great technique and understanding, Daniels is always a joy to hear, especially on straight-ahead sessions like this gem. Daniels extends his virtuosity playing clarinet, bass clarinet, flute, and alto flute on *Blue Bossa* 🎵🎵🎵🎵 (Candid, 1972/1996, prod. Gerry MacDonald), an exquisite album (recorded on four New York studio dates in 1972 and 1973) that includes an array of 14 tunes recorded in duets with (surprise!) guitarist Bucky Pizzarelli. Because of Daniels's diversity, there are numerous highlights on this album, such as his flute solo on the Johnny Mandel ballad, "Emily," his bass clarinet improvisations on the opening title tune, his clarinet reading of the lightly swinging Harold Arlen tune, "As Long as I Live," his solo bass clarinet track overdubbed with his flute improvs on Roland Hanna's "A Flower for All Seasons," and more. Pizzarelli has many laudable moments in the spotlight and his supportive role fits Daniels's intentions perfectly. A very different venture considering Daniels's later work. *Under the Influence* 𝄢𝄢𝄢𝄢 (GRP, 1990, prod. Eddie Daniels, Michael Abene) marks Daniels's recorded return to doubling on alto saxophone. In a quartet setting with Alan Pasqua on piano, Mike Formanek on bass, and Peter Erskine on drums and percussion, he plays tenor sax or clarinet on the mixture of 11 originals and jazz standards that include favorites such as "I Hear a Rhapsody," "I Fall in Love Too Easily," and Daniels's originals, "Mr. Cool (for Stan)," "Waltz for Bill (Evans)," and other treasures. One of his best sessions.

what to buy next: Featuring Daniels with vibraphonist Gary Burton, *Benny Rides Again* 𝄢𝄢𝄢𝄢 (GRP, 1992, prod. Eddie Daniels, Gary Burton) is an uplifting, joyful tribute to Benny Goodman and Lionel Hampton. Reinterpreting music that is well known and giving it fresh perspective, vibraphonist Burton and clarinetist Daniels offer a swinging mainstream jazz sound backed by a modern rhythm section—Mulgrew Miller (piano), Marc Johnson (bass), and Peter Erskine (drums). (Somebody was reminiscing!) These 13 selections will take fans back to the 1930s and 1940s with Goodman tunes such as "Sing, Sing, Sing," "Stompin' at the Savoy," "Moonglow," "Airmail Special," "Let's Dance," "Avalon," and "After You've Gone." "Memories of You" and "Goodbye" conjure up images of crowded dance floors and the big band sounds, while pianist Miller plays a boogie-woogie motif on a 12-bar blues "Grand Slam." Daniels, a master on both saxophone and clarinet, has been concentrating on the latter since 1986 and is exceptionally fluid. He makes incredibly warm, articulate statements and is able to bend melody lines. Burton is a lyrical player able to play straight-ahead as well as modern jazz styles. He appropriately plays wooden bars (marimba) on the punfully fun "Knockin' on Wood." Interaction by the two musicians is superb. There are a few tinges of trad jazz, but mostly, *Benny Rides Again* offers Goodman's straight-ahead stuff without Daniels sounding like Goodman, nor Burton like Hampton. This is a most enjoyable collaboration for the non-purist listener. Included in the package is a 19-page booklet of informative liner notes with brief histories of these Goodman tunes. *Beautiful Love* 𝄢𝄢𝄢𝄢

(Shanachie, 1997, prod. Eddie Daniels, Chuck Loeb) contains a pleasing array of improvised romantic tunes from jazz and classical realms, as well as originals from clarinetist Daniels and guitarist Chuck Loeb. Bob James (piano), Wolfgang Haffner (drums), and bassist David Finck or Tim LeFebvre join the principals. Guests include percussionist David Charles and Lawrence Feldman on alto flute. It's a pretty album with no ground being broken, just a joyfully upbeat listen that demonstrates Daniels's woody tone and facile, lyrical technique. *Collection* 𝄢𝄢𝄢𝄢 (GRP, 1986/1994, prod. various), compiled from previous recordings by clarinetist Daniels, offers a mixture of mainstream and contemporary jazz-styled tunes recorded from 1986 to 1994. The clarinet is not an easy instrument with which to forge a reputation as a straight-ahead jazz player, but Daniels has done so with panache for many years. He weaves his lines through those of his guesting sidemen: pianist Mulgrew Miller, guitarist Chuck Loeb, and pianist Billy Childs. Fans should find his voicings varied and interesting especially tunes such as Benny Goodman's "Stompin' at the Savoy," and the funky, "P.I." (which includes the astounding drumwork of Dave Weckl), the slippery "East of the Sun," and the slow-grinding throbber, "Equinox" (a banner track with Weckl and John Patitucci because the melody line follows the first few measures of Ellington's "Black and Tan Fantasy"). A good sampler featuring the versatility of leader Daniels.

the rest:
First Prize 𝄢𝄢𝄢𝄢 (Prestige/OJC, 1966/1993)
Nepenthe 𝄢𝄢𝄢𝄢 (GRP, 1990)
This Is Now 𝄢𝄢𝄢𝄢 (GRP, 1991)
The Five Seasons 𝄢𝄢𝄢𝄢 (Shanachie, 1996)

worth searching for: Check the cut-out bins or the second-hard markets for *Breakthrough* 𝄢𝄢𝄢𝄢𝄢 (GRP, 1986, prod. Jorge Calandrelli, Eddie Daniels, Ettore Stratta), which is Daniels's debut on the GRP label. The recording that established his formidable clarinet chops, it remains one of his best showcases, blending European classical and jazz styles. Performing with the Philharmonic Orchestra and a jazz trio that includes Fred Hersh (piano), Allan Walley (bass) and Martin Drew (drums), Daniels shows his fluent technique and his ability to shift on a dime between the two musical genres. Bassist Marc Johnson and drummer Joey Baron are replacements on the joyful, melodious waltzing Daniels original, "Circle Dance." The three-movement "Concerto for Jazz Clarinet," composed by conductor-arranger Jorge Calandrelli, is most exciting, and Daniels navigates through the 22-minute piece with grace, beauty, and improvising ease.

influences:

◀◀ Benny Goodman, Artie Shaw, Buddy DeFranco

Nancy Ann Lee

Harold Danko

Born June 13, 1947, in Youngstown, OH.

An often overlooked pianist, Harold Danko is best known for his long-term associations with Chet Baker, the Thad Jones–Mel Lewis Jazz Orchestra, Gerry Mulligan, Woody Herman, and Lee Konitz. Danko received his undergraduate degree in music education at the Youngstown State University Dana School of Music and pursued graduate studies there and at Juilliard School of Music. He also studied privately with Chick Corea, Jaki Byard, and others. As well as performing duo piano performances with Kirk Lightsey and leading his own trio, Danko has composed music for television and off-Broadway productions. He is also a jazz educator who taught at the Manhattan School of Music (1984–85), Jersey City State College (1980–85), and Concordia College in New Jersey (1981–83), and conducted numerous clinics and workshops and authored piano instruction books and videos. Danko is a modern pianist who can play a range of styles, but seems most comfortable in small group sessions that give vent to the romantic side of his musical personality. He has recorded as leader for Sunnyside and other import labels, as well as recording numerous sessions as sideman for domestic and import labels.

what to buy: A critically acclaimed session of duets with bassist Rufus Reid, *Mirth Song* ♫♫♫♫ (Sunnyside, 1991, prod. Francois Zalacain) documents two 1982 studio dates featuring the pair performing an array of nine standards and Danko originals. With two of the most lyrical players in jazz, you can only expect the best poetry in motion, and that's exactly what you'll hear on this matchless album.

what to buy next: Harold Danko's romantic album, *Alone but Not Forgotten* ♫♫♫ (Sunnyside, 1989, prod. George Galip), contains a collection of eight romantic tunes (five originals) recorded with his trio in various studio sessions in 1985 and 1986. His side team includes Woody Herman alumni and former Bill Evans trio members, drummer Joe LaBarbera, and bassists Marc Johnson (tracks 2, 6, 8) and Michael Moore. Some tunes include strings (arranged by LaBarbera) and Bob Dorough sings on the finale, Bill Evans's classic, "Laurie." Danko's romanticism comes through best on his own compositions, the tempo-shifting, strings-enhanced ballad "Martina," his peaceful and pretty ballad, "When Everything Gets Quiet," an elegant

trio piece, "Candlelight Shadows," and the strings-sweetened title tune. This is a lovely trio date that originally began as a demo.

best of the rest:
(With Kirk Lightsey) *Shorter by Two* ♫♫♫♫ (Sunnyside, 1989)
(With Harold Danko Quartet) *New Autumn* ♫♫♫ (SteepleChase, 1995)
(With Harold Danko Quartet) *Tidal Breeze* ♫♫♫ (SteepleChase, 1997)

influences:

◀◀ Bill Evans, Chick Corea, Jaki Byard, John Lewis, Kirk Lightsey

▶▶ Mulgrew Miller, Bill Dobbins

Nancy Ann Lee

James Dapogny

Born September 3, 1940, in Berwyn, IL.

James Dapogny is a scholar/musician whose efforts to keep traditional jazz alive and viable have been amazingly successful, both in academia and on the bandstand. With his Chicago Jazz Band, Dapogny has documented early performance practice through concerts and on recordings, and he is one of the foremost authorities on the music of Ferdinand "Jelly Roll" Morton. Dapogny is the editor of *Jelly Roll Morton: The Collected Piano Music* and has taught jazz history and theory at the University of Michigan for more than 20 years. Despite all the ivory-tower credentials, the bottom line is that Dapogny appears to be concert oriented. (One of his earliest recorded projects was in bringing the great classic blues singer Sippie Wallace back into the fold of performing artists.) Whether on disc or live, the Chicago Jazz Band, under Dapogny, treats traditional jazz like a living, breathing art form capable of great subtlety and joy, not the mummified remains promulgated by many traditional outfits. His playing and arranging honor the forerunners of today's jazz with performances that don't trivialize their tunes.

what to buy: Just the title *Laughing at Life* ♫♫♫♫ (Discovery, 1992, prod. James Dapogny) does a great job of encapsulating this band's mission in life; the sense of joy is palpable on this fine set that includes old war-horses like the title tune, "St. James Infirmary" and "Lulu's Back in Town" with arrangements that make every one sparkle like new. Jelly Roll Morton is represented with "Blue Blood Blues" and "Grandpa's Spells" while Ellington shows up in a deftly swinging "Caravan" and the relatively unknown "Dooft Wooft." In addition to Dapogny's crisp piano playing, trumpeter Jon-Erik Kellso and clarinetist Kim Cusack deserve special mention. *Hot Club Stomp* ♫♫♫ (Discovery, 1994, prod. James Dapogny) is a change of pace from what the Chicago Jazz Band has been know to do, since it moves ever so slightly into the swing era of the early and mid-1930s. Charts are being played, but the overall feel leans towards flexibility over stiffness. Once again, trumpeter Kellso merits kudos. Other than the Library of Congress sessions released by Rounder, *Original Jelly Roll Blues* 𝄞𝄞𝄞𝄞 (Discovery, 1993, prod. James Dapogny) may be the best way to get your fill of Jelly Roll. Dapogny is a formidable Morton scholar, and these performances have the stamp of all that knowledge blended with the usual strong performances from the Chicago Jazz Band. "Sidewalk Blues" is a nice showpiece for Kellso, and the tuba playing of guest musician Mike Walbridge brings an authentic bass line to songs like "Little Lawrence" and "Pontchartrain."

what to buy next: Meant as a celebration of the James Dapogny's Chicago Jazz Band and their 20 years as a performing entity, *On the Road* 𝄞𝄞𝄞 (Schoolkids', 1996, prod. James Dapogny) has a lot going for it. There's the longevity factor involved in playing this sort of music for so many years that it's second nature. Toss in the fact that even after a couple decades these guys still sound excited, primed, and ready to go. That's good because this is the sort of music which, if not delivered with skill and love, can become real old, real quick. Standouts include Wingy Manone's "San Antonio Strut," Hoagy Carmichael's "Old Man Harlem," Benny Goodman's flag-waver "Flying Home," and a unique take on John Philip Sousa's 1899 showpiece, "The Washington Post March."

worth searching for: Dapogny did a nice little album with fellow archival pianist Butch Thompson titled *How Could We Be Blue* on the Stomp Off label that would be good to see on CD one day.

influences:

◀◀ Ferdinand "Jelly Roll" Morton

Garaud MacTaggart

Jeremy Davenport

Born in St. Louis, MO.

Jeremy Davenport grew up in a musical family; his father has been a longtime trombonist with the St. Louis Symphony and his mother is a vocal music teacher. Davenport received classical trumpet training from members of the St. Louis Symphony, and was hooked on jazz after hearing a Miles Davis recording. By junior high school, Davenport had formed the Todd Williams Quintet, whose members would go on to perform with Joshua

Redman and Wynton Marsalis. Davenport received further training as a merit scholar at the Manhattan School of Music, and studied with Wynton Marsalis who introduced him to Harry Connick Jr. Davenport joined Connick's band, making four international tours, before settling in Connick's hometown in 1989 to study under Ellis Marsalis at the University of New Orleans. By 1990 Davenport had perfected his round, warm tones and splendid technique, and won second place in the International Trumpet Guild Jazz Competition. Davenport invites comparison with Connick on many counts, but especially his romantic vocal style. The trumpeter has performed with Wynton Marsalis, Branford Marsalis, Eric Reed, Marcus Roberts, and Nicholas Payton, and has recorded two albums for the Telarc label.

what to buy: *Jeremy Davenport* (Telarc, 1996, prod. Robert Woods, Elaine Martone) is a promising self-titled debut that features the trumpeter/vocalist mixing it up with Peter Martin on piano, Christopher Thomas on bass, and Channon Powell on drums. Davenport's rhythm team on two tracks are Glenn Patscha, piano; Neal Caine, bass; and Martin Butler, drums. Recorded in New York City, September 26–28, 1995, the session is reminiscent of early efforts by vocalists Frank Sinatra and Tony Bennett and trumpeter/vocalist Chet Baker, or more recent endeavors by technically proficient, introspective trumpeter Tom Harrell. Davenport makes the song his focus and the intimate, melodic warmth of his boy-next-door vocals equals the moods of his pensive, lyrical horn playing on the album's 10 tunes, especially sentimental favorites such as "They Can't Take That away from Me," "I See Your Face," "I'm Old-Fashioned," and "I'm in the Mood for Love." Davenport phrases naturally, even comfortably, adding the slightest hint of swing influenced by 1940s crooners, and displays an intimate charm destined to capture the hearts of his fans. Plus, he's versatile enough to effortlessly improvise some trumpet bebop licks on "Lora with an O." Expect a second Telarc release in 1998 featuring Davenport's quartet and guest vocalist Diana Krall.

influences:

◀◀ Miles Davis, Chet Baker, Clark Terry, Harry Connick Jr., Wynton Marsalis

Nancy Ann Lee

Kenny Davern

Born January 7, 1935, in Huntington, NY.

Kenny Davern is a swinging mainstream clarinetist with strong traditional roots. A consummate, uncompromising artist on an unwieldy instrument, Davern has the tone, passion, humor, lyricism, convictions, and sense of adventure that sets him apart. John Kenneth Davern began his professional career while still in high school in Queens, New York, and made his recording debut at age 19 with Jack Teagarden's Band. He played and recorded with trumpeters Pee Wee Erwin and Phil Napoleon in the mid-1950s and fronted his own group at Nick's in Greenwich Village in 1961. While playing around New York City with Red Allen, Buck Clayton, Ruby Braff, and Eddie Condon, Davern became good friends with one of his early influences, clarinetist Pee Wee Russell. Another significant association began in 1963 when Davern met pianist Dick Wellstood with whom he would periodically play and record for the next 20 years. Davern helped organize and, with Bob Wilber, co-lead the well-known Soprano Summit during the 1970s when Davern was playing soprano sax and other reeds in addition to clarinet. Always open-minded and willing to take risks, Davern recorded with modernists Steve Lacy and Paul Motian in 1978, the same year he was touring extensively with Wild Bill Davison, who, like Davern, was something of an iconoclast.

Ever since Soprano Summit disbanded, Davern has concentrated solely on clarinet. His travels expanded in the 1980s with the advent of more jazz parties and festivals at home and ever-expanding club dates and festivals in the U.K. and the rest of Europe. Recordings made in Sweden, Norway, and England during this period are still sought after by collectors. When Soprano Summit was revived in the 1990s, the name had to be changed to Summit Reunion because Davern would only play his preferred instrument, the clarinet. Davern has long enjoyed playing in a small group format, often favoring the guitar over piano, which seems to give him more freedom. He prefers to play with a natural, acoustic sound, turning off sound systems when and where he can. Davern has listened carefully to the jazz clarinetists who preceded him and has distilled the best from the past into a truly distinguished and unique, recognizable style.

what to buy: Produced by Davern who knew exactly what he wanted, *Breezin' Along* 𝄞𝄞𝄞𝄞 (Arbors, 1997, prod. Kenny Davern) is a 10-tune collection as good as it gets. Davern's clarinet has never sounded better with Howard Alden's solo guitar in the front line, and Bucky Pizzarelli's guitar, Greg Cohen's bass, and Tony DeNicola's drums all in perfect rhythmic support. No matter how old the tune (e.g., "Jazz Me Blues," "Dark Eyes," and "Rose Room"), these performances are all brand new. Highly recommended. *I'll See You in My Dreams* 𝄞𝄞𝄞𝄞 (MusicMasters, 1989, prod. Leroy Parkins) features Davern in one of his favorite formats, the quartet, with Howard Alden (guitar), Phil Flanagan (bass), and Giampaolo Biagi (drums), swinging lightly and not-

so-politely through 10 newborn evergreens such as "Sweet and Lovely," "Solitude," and the title tune. Good therapy and good listening. *Never in a Million Years* 𝄞𝄞𝄞𝄞 (Challenge, 1995, prod. Dick Sudhalter) is taken from the PBS radio series *Jazz at the Vineyard*. This hour is an excellent introduction to the interactive team of pianist Dick Wellstood and reedman Kenny Davern. For fans who saw them in this live-recorded performance, the interviews and the commentary by the two protagonists should bring smiles. For others, the music speaks for itself. *Kenny Davern's Big Three: Playing for Kicks* 𝄞𝄞𝄞𝄞 (Jazzology, 1989, prod. James Asumn), catches Davern at the Pizza Express in Soho, London in 1985, with England's versatile Martin Litton on piano and fellow Brit John Petters on drums. There is lots of room for Davern's clarinet to roam through an agreeable range of 10 diverse tunes from "Willie the Weeper," to "Drop Me Off in Harlem," to "Lullaby of the Leaves," and more, including the pleasant closer, "Dinah." This one is for clarinet hounds, small band lovers, and folks who like good old tunes that swing with a touch of traditional jazz on the side.

what to buy next: *Stretchin' Out* 𝄞𝄞𝄞𝄞 (Jazzology, 1989, prod. Gus P. Statiras, Kenny Davern) is an adventuresome trio session that finds Davern's clarinet in tandem with Dick Wellstood's piano and Chuck Rigg's drums, probing a set of six classy standards. "The Man I Love, " "Love Me or Leave Me," and the old Jimmy Noone rouser, "Chicago Rhythm," receive extended treatments. Some of the choruses are filled with quirks and little surprises. This one is not for the faint of heart. A collection of eight extended performances, *Kenny Davern and the Rhythm Men* 𝄞𝄞𝄞𝄞 (Arbors, 1996, prod. Kenny Davern), is another must for Davern fans. A heated 1995 quintet session, very well recorded, finds Davern in front of the swinging John Bunch (piano), veteran bassist Bob Haggart, and Davern's favorite, the tasteful drummer Tony DeNicola, with Bucky Pizzarelli in the dual role of soloist and rhythm guitarist. "Out of Nowhere" features Pizzarelli and attractive, melodious and wistful solos from Davern, supported by Bunch and Haggart. It's over before you realize that almost 10 minutes have gone by. "Three Little Words," "Say It Isn't So," and "Cherry" are also especially attractive, and on "That Rhythm Man," everyone on the date is off and running.

best of the rest:

Bob Wilber–Kenny Davern: Soprano Summit in Concert 𝄞𝄞𝄞𝄞 (Concord, 1976)

Kenny Davern Quartet: One Hour Tonight 𝄞𝄞𝄞𝄞 (MusicMasters, 1988)

Bob Wilber and Kenny Davern: Summit Reunion 𝄞𝄞𝄞𝄞 (Chiaroscuro, 1990)

Soprano Summit: Live at Concord '77 𝄞𝄞𝄞𝄞 (Concord, 1991)

Kenny Davern: My Inspiration ♫♫♫ (MusicMasters, 1992)

Jazz Im Amerika House, Vol. 5: Summit Reunion ♫♫♫ (Nagel-Heyer, 1994)

Summit Reunion, 1992 ♫♫♫ (Chiaroscuro, 1994)

Kenny Davern and His Jazz Band: East Side, West Side ♫♫♫ (Arbors, 1994)

Bob Wilber and Kenny Davern: Soprano Summit ♫♫♫♫ (Chiaroscuro, 1994)

Summit Reunion: Yellow Dog Blues ♫♫♫♫ (Chiaroscuro, 1996)

John T. Bitter

Lowell Davidson

Born November 20, 1941, in Boston, MA. Died July 31, 1990.

Growing up in Boston, Lowell Davidson played organ and led the choir in Emanuel Episcopal Church and played tuba in his high school's band. He attended the prestigious Boston Latin School and went on to study biochemistry at Harvard. In the mid-1960s he moved to New York for a while, playing with Ornette Coleman and recording his only album in 1965 for the renegade ESP label, which specialized in documenting New York's free-jazz scene. Later he played drums in an early lineup of the New York Art Quartet. Returning to Massachusetts, he continued to play off and on with local musicians including guitarist Joe Morris (with whom Davidson dueted on an aluminum-bodied double bass), though no documents of Davidson's later work have emerged as of yet. His musical career was aborted after a lab accident afflicted him both mentally and physically, leading to a premature death at age 49.

what's available: *Lowell Davidson Trio* ♫♫♫ (ESP Disk, 1965) would rate even higher if not for sound that's tinny, muffled, and constricted even by ESP's standards (bassist Gary Peacock can barely be heard except in moments when the piano drops out). The music itself deserves only the highest praise. In tandem with drummer Milford Graves, whose colorful, non-metered pulses are incredibly variegated and polyrhythmic, Davidson (sticking solely to piano) unleashes wispy, serpentine flurries of right-hand runs and latches onto improvised motivic cells and prods them from all angles. He uses much more space than free piano icon Cecil Taylor and avoids (if this can be judged by this sonically flawed document) his loud and dense aspects.

influences:

◀◀ Herbie Nichols, Thelonious Monk, Paul Bley, Ornette Coleman

▶▶ Joe Morris

Steve Holtje

Anthony Davis

Born February 20, 1951, in Paterson, NJ.

Imagine walking through a museum of Anthony Davis's musical influences: there's a diorama showing Duke Ellington at the piano, another showing a young Davis in Leo Smith's Band, kiosks explaining the relative powers of notation and improvisation, and a map of Davis's musical world with prominent pins in the capitals of Europe and the island of Bali. Think of Davis as a one-man Third Stream. The son of Charles T. Davis, a noted professor and authority on African American literature, Davis studied music at Yale and became part of an improv scene that included his contemporary George Lewis and the older AACM veteran, Leo Smith. After moving to New York in his mid-20s, Davis began important collaborations with violinist Leroy Jenkins, saxophonist Oliver Lake, and, for a time, co-led a group with like-minded flutist James Newton. Early releases strive to synthesize the AACM stream with Ellington and elements of the conservatory. Over the years, his palette broadened to include more conservatory elements and, in a number of cases, cycling rhythmic motifs out of Balinese music. He has composed extensively for dance performances and in recent years has been almost entirely focused on operatic projects, most notably *X: The Life of Malcolm X.*

what to buy: *X: The Life of Malcolm X* ♫♫♫♫ (Gramavision, 1992, prod. Max Wilcox) is an ambitious melding of nearly every technique in Davis's bag, a two-disc set telling an epic saga. The opera in three acts covers three eras in Malcolm X's life: Act One (1931–45) includes his Lansing, Michigan, roots to prison; Act Two (1946–63) picks up in prison and continues to the Muslim Mosque/Velvet Drive; and Act Three (1963–65) continues from Velvet Drive, Phoenix to the finale in the Audubon Ballroom in Harlem. The opera features many cutting-edge jazz musicians among the instrumental ensemble, including Marty Ehrlich, J.D. Parran, Mark Dresser, Gerry Hemingway, Pheeroan AkLaff, Marilyn Crispell, and others, and Davis himself plays celesta. An extensive libretto, written by Thulani Davis, is included in the package. *Hidden Voices* ♫♫♫♫ by the Anthony Davis–James Newton Quartet (India Navigation, 1996, prod. Bob Cummins), recorded in the late 1970s, is one of Davis's rare, straightforward, swinging combo dates in the excellent company of flutist Newton and trombonist George Lewis.

what to buy next: *Episteme* ♫♫♫♫ (Gramavision, 1995, prod. Jonathan F.P. Rose) offers superb ten-piece ensemble (including trombonist George Lewis) that works through Davis's infatuation with Bali through tightly controlled settings for improvisation, thus foreshadowing *X. Lady of the Mirrors* 𝄞𝄞𝄞𝄞 (India Navigation, 1991, prod. India Navigation Co.) contains solo piano from thoughtful to bursts of speed and Pullenesque clusters.

best of the rest:

The Ghost Factory 𝄞𝄞𝄞𝄞 (Gramavision, 1982/1991)
Trio, Volume II 𝄞𝄞𝄞𝄞 (Gramavision, 1991)
I've Known Rivers 𝄞𝄞𝄞𝄞 (Gramavision, 1994)

influences:

⏪ Duke Ellington, Thelonious Monk, Cecil Taylor, Don Pullen

⏩ Matthew Shipp, Marilyn Crispell, Myra Melford

W. Kim Heron

Eddie "Lockjaw" Davis

Born March 2, 1922, in New York, NY. Died November 3, 1986, in Culver City, CA.

Taking his cue from Ben Webster and Coleman Hawkins, tenor saxophonist Eddie "Lockjaw" Davis was a rough-and-tumble player with a sound and attack that were immediately recognizable. He first made a name for himself in the 1940s while a member of the big bands of Cootie Williams, Lucky Millinder, Andy Kirk, and others. He also became a star soloist with the Count Basie Orchestra on many occasions, first from 1952–1953, then during 1957, and again from 1964–1973. One of Davis's most memorable associations was with organist Shirley Scott during the late 1950s. Their famous "Cookbook" sessions virtually defined the organ-tenor combo. A true heavyweight in every manner, Davis most benefitted from the quintet he co-led with Johnny Griffin during the 1960s. Virtually every recording this group made brims with excitement. A more incendiary pairing hadn't been heard since the days of Dexter Gordon and Wardell Gray. Up until his untimely death in 1986, Davis maintained his "tough tenor" stance and continued to record music of great interest and virility.

what to buy: Available as three separate discs, *The Eddie "Lockjaw" Davis Cookbook, Volumes 1, 2, 3* 𝄞𝄞𝄞𝄞 (Prestige, 1958, prod. Esmond Edwards), find Lockjaw in top form. In addition, organist Shirley Scott proves you don't have to be all sound and fury to say something special on the organ. These classics belong in any definitive collection!

what to buy next: *Trane Whistle* 𝄞𝄞𝄞𝄞 (Prestige, 1960/OJC, 1992, prod. Esmond Edwards) finds "Jaws" supported by Oliver Nelson's large ensemble and the results are truly explosive. As good as Davis's small combo work is, he's a natural when placed in front of a big band. Fronting a large trumpet and per-

EDDIE "LOCKJAW" DAVIS

song "The Stolen Moment"

album *Trane Whistle*
(Prestige, 1960/OJC, 1992)

instrument Tenor saxophone

cussion section, Davis goes south-of-the-border for spirited versions of "Tin Tin Deo" and "Alma Alegre" and other tunes on *Afro-Jaws* 𝄞𝄞𝄞𝄞 (Riverside, 1961, prod. Orrin Keepnews). Fortunately, several recordings exist which feature Johnny Griffin and the "Lockjaw" Davis Quintet, the group that Davis co-led with Johnny Griffin. *Tough Tenor Favorites* 𝄞𝄞𝄞𝄞 (Riverside, 1962, prod. Orrin Keepnews) is one of their better efforts, also due in no small way to the fine piano work of Horace Parlan.

the rest:

Jaws 𝄞𝄞𝄞 (Prestige/OJC, 1958)
Smokin' 𝄞𝄞𝄞 (Prestige, 1958)
Jaws in Orbit 𝄞𝄞𝄞𝄞 (Prestige/OJC, 1959)
(With Buddy Tate, Coleman Hawkins, Arnett Cobb) *Very Saxy* 𝄞𝄞𝄞𝄞 (Prestige, 1959)
Gentle Jaws 𝄞𝄞𝄞𝄞 (Prestige, 1960)
(With Johnny Griffin) *The Tenor Scene* 𝄞𝄞𝄞𝄞 (Prestige, 1961)
Streetlights 𝄞𝄞𝄞𝄞 (Prestige, 1962)
Swingin' 'til the Girls Come Home 𝄞𝄞𝄞𝄞 (SteepleChase, 1976)
Straight Ahead 𝄞𝄞𝄞 (Pablo, 1976)
Montreux '77 𝄞𝄞𝄞 (Pablo, 1977)

Jaw's Blues ♫♫♫ (Enja, 1981)
All of Me ♫♫♫♫ (SteepleChase, 1983)

worth searching for: Sometimes seen on Japanese import, Johnny Griffin/Eddie "Lockjaw" Davis: *Lookin' at Monk* ♫♫♫♫♫ (Jazzland, 1961, prod. Orrin Keepnews), is well worth the search. With Thelonious Monk's tunes as a base, Griffin and Davis engage in spirited exchanges that rank among the best this group had to offer. Although no longer available on CD, you may find the little-known gem, *Save Your Love for Me* ♫♫♫♫ (Bluebird, 1988, prod. Ed Michel), in the used bins. This is a fine compilation of Davis's mid-1960s RCA dates that includes a big band set and a pairing with Paul Gonsalves.

influences:

◀◀ Coleman Hawkins, Ben Webster

Chris Hovan

Jesse Davis

Born September 11, 1965, in New Orleans, LA.

In the wake of Wynton, it seems that a number of players have emerged from the musically fertile Crescent City, including alto saxophonist Jesse Davis. A member of the house of Bird-Cannonball-Stitt-McLean, Davis has followed examples of his predecessors by absorbing ideas that have come before him, then attempting to add his own voice to the mix. That goal has been met with a good deal of success. At the New Orleans Center for Creative Arts, teacher Ellis Marsalis turned the budding alto player on to Charlie Parker. Davis went to Chicago to study in the early 1980s, then on to New York to further his education. While still a student in 1987, Jesse joined the Illinois Jacquet Big Band for three years and also led his own bands. It was his playing on a TanaReid album for Concord, *Yours and Mine*, that landed Davis a recording contract with the label.

what to buy: Davis has made five albums for Concord. These aren't "groundbreaking" or "innovative" sessions if one accepts the definitions for those terms crafted by the *avant garde* crowd. What you'll get is a mix of well-played originals and standards interpreted in a bop to post-bop style. Each album has its high points. Start with Davis's second album, *As We Speak* ♫♫♫♫ (Concord, 1992, prod. Carl Jefferson), which features an unusual front line of alto, trombone (Robert Trowers), and guitar (Peter Bernstein). The album contains Jesse's most engaging originals, including the burning "Wake Up Call" and "'Tudes," plus two haunting songs, the title composition and

"Hipnotism." Special nod to the empathetic rhythm section of Jackie Terrason, Dwayne Burno and Leon Parker.

what to buy next: On his third session, *Young at Art* ♫♫♫ (Concord, 1993, prod. Carl Jefferson, Allen Farnham), Davis omits the trombone and enlists pianist Brad Mehldau. The rest of the band is the same as the *As We Speak* date. The album is a worthy buy for their treatment of Cole Porter's "I Love Paris" and Davis's two original waltzes, "Broj Roj" and "Waltz for Andre." On album number four, *High Standards* ♫♫♫ (Concord, 1994, prod. Carl Jefferson), Bernstein is replaced by trumpeter Nicholas Payton, and trombonist Trowers returns with the appropriately titled "Rush Hour." "Isms" offers a good representation of Davis's composing style, rich lines with a tinge of melancholy written over a simple but grooving rhythm. Extra tail wags for digging out Wayne Shorter's "Big Push" and a boppish take on "I Hear a Rhapsody." Jesse's fifth date, *From Within* ♫♫♫ (Concord, 1996, prod. Allen Farnham), features his most conventional and distinguished lineup—Payton, Hank Jones and Lewis Nash. Good ballad playing is the order of the day on chestnuts such as "You've Changed," "If I Should Lose You," and Davis's "Portrait of Desiree." The groove picks up on Oliver Nelson's "Six and Four," and Davis's original "Tai's Tune."

the rest:
Horn of Passion ♫♫♫ (Concord, 1991, prod. Carl Jefferson)

influences:

◀◀ Charlie Parker, Cannonball Adderley, Sonny Stitt, Jackie McLean

Dan Polletta

Miles Davis

Born May 26, 1926, in Alton, IL. Died September 28, 1991, in Santa Monica, CA.

Miles Davis changed the style of his music more often than any other jazz musician of his stature. His career had at least eight distinct phases, most of them influencing the course of jazz history and all of them controversial to some degree. Everything from his instrumental abilities to his choice of sidemen was questioned, yet again and again Davis rose to the top of his profession, in the process becoming known as an astute judge of talent who led several of the greatest units in jazz.

Miles Davis (© Jack Vartoogian)

Davis was raised in a land-owning upper-middle-class family (his father was a dentist who also raised pedigreed hogs) in East St. Louis. He received a trumpet for his 13th birthday and soon began taking private lessons from Elwood Buchanan, who had played in the Andy Kirk band. Buchanan suggested trumpeter Harold "Shorty" Baker and cornetist Bobby Hackett, both excellent ballad players, as models. Already Davis was going against the tide, since most trumpeters modeled themselves on Louis Armstrong or his disciples (most prominently Roy Eldridge), who were more aggressive in tone and style. Davis was encouraged to develop the warm, vibrato-free tone that would set him apart for the rest of his career. He also studied with the first trumpeter of the St. Louis Symphony Orchestra. By the time he was 16 years old, Davis was playing professionally on the local scene and got a regular gig with Eddie Randle's Blue Devils, a jump blues/R&B group.

At 18, Davis moved to New York City, ostensibly to study at Julliard but really to track down Charlie Parker (not yet famous except among the cognoscenti) and play with him. Davis finally found him at a jam session and they hung out; within a day, Parker had invited himself to share Davis's apartment. Shortly before Davis turned 19, he made his first recordings, as a sideman with Herbie Fields's band accompanying the singer Rubberlegs Williams, material that is included on the Savoy collection *First Miles*. Of greater importance were the musical ideas Davis was absorbing in day-long discussions at Dizzy Gillespie's house that included Thelonious Monk, Kenny Dorham, Max Roach, and other bebop founders. Soon Davis was playing with Coleman Hawkins and Eddie "Lockjaw" Davis, and when Parker and Gillespie split up over Parker's unreliability, Davis became Parker's trumpet player. Davis was not as technically proficient as Gillespie, whose brilliant, speedy high-note runs were his trademark, and was a complement rather than a match to Parker's own proficiency. On November 26, 1945, Davis recorded with Parker for the first time, for Savoy. Dizzy Gillespie, playing piano on the gig, had to stand in for Davis on "Ko Ko," a "Cherokee" derivative that Davis was unable to master. Nonetheless, the three tracks on which Davis did play during this much-anticipated session spread his name beyond New York.

Parker and Davis went to California in 1946, splitting up while out there (Parker eventually ended up in Camarillo, a sanitarium). Davis played with then-unknown Charles Mingus before joining the Billy Eckstine band and returning to New York, where he played in the trumpet section of Gillespie's big band. When Parker also returned, in 1947, he reunited with Davis and they made a series of classic quintet recordings for Dial and Savoy, the latter including Davis's debut as a leader (with Parker on tenor sax) on August 14, 1947 as heard on *First Miles*. They also did regular radio broadcasts from the Royal Roost nightclub which have been preserved. The legendary status of this group and its records cannot be overstated. Playing regularly with Parker was a baptism by fire for Davis, whose technique improved considerably. Finally at the end of 1948 Davis and Roach left Parker to pursue Miles's considerably different ideas.

A group of adventurous musicians—Davis, Gerry Mulligan, Lee Konitz, Tadd Dameron (in whose group Davis played at times) and others—had gathered around Gil Evans, an arranger for the Claude Thornhill band. Evans was not satisfied with the normal range of instrumental effects and put together groups which included French horn and tuba to play arrangements typified by rich, complex harmonies and a "cooler," less frenetic sound than that pioneered by Parker. Davis put together a nonet to play in this new style. It performed a few times over the next few years, impressing fellow musicians and making a few poor-selling 78-rpm singles for Capitol, but however little commercial success it had, this nonet pioneered the style which became known as "cool jazz." Davis, still something of a controversial figure merely by virtue of not being Dizzy Gillespie, had upset bebop orthodoxy even further by de-emphasizing its aggressiveness and emphasis on soloists. But by the time cool jazz was popular in the mainstream, Davis had moved on.

It was around this time that Davis imperiled his career with a heroin addiction which apparently started in 1949 after years of staying clean despite the temptations of the scene. His playing became temporarily erratic, as did his reliability, and his career momentum was slowed. There was a reunion in the studio with Parker which was recorded for Verve; on the same day, Davis recorded his first session for Prestige—using, among others, a young Sonny Rollins; Miles was the first important player to hire him. Davis's second Prestige session, in 1951, would be memorable not only for being his first not recorded on the 78-rpm discs, which restricted performance length to three or four minutes, but also for the recording debut of Jackie McLean. Davis was beginning to establish a track record for sniffing out new talent which would eventually become legendary. But his unreliability at this time led Prestige to let his contract lapse, and he recorded for Blue Note in 1952. A return to Prestige in 1953 found Davis noticeably suffering the effects of his addiction, with his trumpet technique quite sloppy at times. Finally, after some time in Los Angeles, he went home to St. Louis and his parents' house, locked himself in his room, and went cold turkey for two weeks. He rebuilt his chops outside the limelight by moving to Detroit and playing regularly there. When he returned to New York, he soon changed jazz history again.

Davis's first recording session after his return was for Blue Note on March 6, 1954, with pianist Horace Silver (another Davis discovery), bassist Percy Heath, and drummer Art Blakey, presaging Davis's new style. The same group recorded for Prestige a mere four days later as Davis resumed a regular relationship with that label. But it was on April 29, with Silver, Heath, trombonist J.J. Johnson, tenor saxophonist Lucky Thompson, and drummer Kenny Clarke, that Davis recorded "Walkin'" and "Blue 'n' Boogie." Cool jazz, many had said, omitted a crucial element: the blues. Davis put the blues back in, practically inventing the hard bop genre (of which Silver would soon be perceived as a major icon) and revitalizing the New York scene—and, in fact, all of jazz. Ironically, just before "Walkin'" was issued, Capitol put out an LP (still a new format then) collecting eight of Davis's nonet recordings titled *Birth of the Cool*, reminding the public of Davis's innovations of five years earlier and in fact introducing these recordings to a broader audience than had heard them the first time.

Davis had a short-lived quintet with Rollins, Silver, Heath, and Clarke, but it broke up when the latter two became half of the Modern Jazz Quartet and Silver and Blakey co-founded the Jazz Messengers. In 1955 Davis began recording with a new rhythm section that featured drummer Philly Joe Jones and pianist Red Garland, whom Davis encouraged to copy then-popular pianist Ahmad Jamal's spare style. Later that year Paul Chambers took over the bass slot. When Sonny Rollins quit and moved (temporarily) to Chicago, he was eventually replaced, on the advice of Jones, by a raw young talent who would quickly become legendary: John Coltrane. The personnel would become known, simply, as The Quintet. The new group first recorded in October 1955 for Columbia (the start of an artist-label association which would last three decades), but the results were not immediately released because Davis had not come even close to fulfilling his contract with Prestige. This situation was remedied through some extremely productive sessions. On November 16, 1955 the quintet cut six tracks which were issued as *The New Miles Davis Quintet*, the title reflecting the anticipation which had been building about the group among those in the know. There was a later session with an all-star group. Then came the quintet flood: a May 11, 1956 session that produced 13 tracks, all first takes (two are minute-plus versions of "The Theme"), and an October 26 date of 12 tunes. The first selection of material Prestige issued from these two quintet marathons was

Cookin' with the Miles Davis Quintet, which came out before the end of the year and impressed many with its largely uptempo swingers plus the starkly different "My Funny Valentine," a truly classic ballad reading which led to the song being a fixture in Davis's set for years to come. In the meantime, Columbia had continued to record the quintet (in much less frenzied fashion), and after this Prestige release was apparently finally allowed to put out its first Davis album, *Round about Midnight*, which focused on his ballad playing. Prestige copied that strategy with its next album, *Relaxin' with the Miles Davis Quintet*, in early 1957, followed a few months later by the more haphazardly programmed *Workin' with the Miles Davis Quintet*. It would not be until 1961 that Prestige issued its last LP drawing on these sessions, *Steamin' with the Miles Davis Quintet*. These Prestige albums all quickly became known by the first word in each title. The high quality and considerable ingenuity of these Prestige and Columbia records, not to mention the publicity Davis's new (and major) label generated, made him a bigger star than ever, and labeled Coltrane as a hot young talent too. They also established a highly influential new bebop prototype which continues to be used to this day.

Though Davis remained clean, the rest of the quintet members had serious heroin problems, and by the end of 1956 the group had been disbanded. It re-formed the next year, and then Coltrane's drug problem became so bad that Davis fired him, with Rollins taking his place. Davis switched his attention, at least in recording terms, to a completely different type of music which would prove to be just as groundbreaking and, at least with the record-buying public, even more popular, working with arranger Gil Evans. Their first project found Davis backed by a 19-piece band on the album *Miles Ahead*, with Evans's lush and innovative arrangements setting off the haunting trumpet sound of Davis, who took all the solos. Similar projects in the next two years, *Porgy and Bess* (for years Davis's best-selling album) and *Sketches of Spain*, would also prove successful musically, critically, and commercially, making Davis not just a star but a superstar, quite possibly the most popular jazz musician around during what was a golden age for the genre.

Meanwhile, in 1957 Rollins had been replaced by another star-to-be, alto saxophonist Julian "Cannonball" Adderley, in the quintet, which although inactive in the studio was still Davis's main group for live performances. Then, at the end of the year, with Coltrane having conquered his addiction, Davis invited him back—but kept the soulful Adderley. Thus was born the Miles Davis Sextet, superior to even the Quintet in artistic accomplishment and innovation. Though it had all the members of the

Quintet, it would develop in a different and startling direction, supplanting the previously unquestioned reliance on chord progressions with a new system of improvisation based on scales. Before it was fully developed, there was a magnificent transition album, *Milestones*, recorded in April 1958 and marking the group's studio debut. The title track shows the group's new direction best. Davis was not the first to write using modes; George Russell had started experimenting with them in 1947. But Davis's success with the concept firmly established its viability. After replacing Garland with pianist Bill Evans (another brilliant and unexpected talent move by the leader), and with Jimmy Cobb taking over on drums, the Sextet was nearly ready to give itself over completely to the new style. Columbia recorded the group prolifically in 1958, though not all the results were released immediately. The final step into modality was recorded in March and April of 1959: *Kind of Blue*, which makes every short list of the greatest jazz albums ever. Making the sextet's music even more remarkable was its spontaneity. Evans, who spent eight months playing with the group, said they never had a rehearsal in that time, and that all the performances on *Kind of Blue* were first takes of brand-new material. Also notable was that Coltrane was reaching new peaks of inspiration.

By the end of the year, however, Adderley had left, going on to a highly popular career as a leader. Wynton Kelly had replaced Evans on piano, bringing a bluesier sound back to the group. This lineup of the Quintet made a lengthy European tour in early 1960 which was documented by amateur tapers, and a Stockholm concert, the most readily available, is valuable for documenting the last days of Coltrane's membership in the group. Coltrane's career as a leader had taken off after he signed with Atlantic, and his landmark album *Giant Steps* had been released in January 1960. After the tour, he too quit Davis's group. For the next four years, although Davis would make much fine music, his group was unsettled as he went through many saxophonists, looking for a replacement. Jimmy Heath, Sonny Stitt, Hank Mobley, Rocky Boyd, Wayne Shorter, Frank Stozier, George Coleman, and Sam Rivers all came and went with varying degrees of success. At the same time, new jazz innovators were coming up, stealing some of Davis's thunder. Not only was Coltrane revolutionizing the music, Ornette Coleman's quartet had produced some avant-garde notions which were shaking the jazz world to its foundation and causing considerable controversy. Davis's albums were still best-sellers, however, and Columbia ensured a steady flow of them by recording Davis's groups in concert.

At the end of 1962 his rhythm section departed to become the Wynton Kelly Trio, and though it was a disastrous turn of events

for Davis at the time (he was sued by promotors when he had to cancel concert appearances), it forced him to start accumulating some young musicians who eventually would help him reach the top of the jazz world yet again. First came bassist Ron Carter, followed by teenage drum prodigy Tony Williams, who first played with Miles when Williams was just 17 years old. When pianist Herbie Hancock was hired, the puzzle was almost complete. With tenor saxophonist George Coleman, this lineup was recorded in concert in February 1964, resulting in the classic live albums *'Four' and More* and *My Funny Valentine*; once again, a Davis group sounded adventurous and willing to take risks, though Coleman less so than the rhythm section. A couple months later, Coleman quit, replaced temporarily by Sam Rivers, who proved too avant-garde for Davis's tastes.

Davis determinedly pursued Wayne Shorter, who had played with him briefly a few years earlier, to fill the sax slot, and finally got his man in mid-1964. The lineup of Davis's second classic Quintet was set. Davis was invigorated by the new group, which over the next three years proceeded to make a series of albums which—a familiar circumstance in Davis's fabled career—again changed the face of jazz: *E.S.P.*, *Miles Smiles*, *Sorcerer*, *Nefertiti*, *Miles in the Sky*, and *Filles de Kilimanjaro*. Though the impact on other musicians, critics, and the public was not as immediate as had been the case with Davis's previous phases, undoubtedly due to the combined effects of rock and the avant-garde, this group nonetheless stands as classic, if considerably less settled and more restless. Its earlier albums, *Miles Smiles* in particular, offered a new template for group interaction and a redefinition of the roles of the members of the rhythm section – Hancock's piano parts use chords much less than the norm, bassist Carter is the rhythmic anchor of the group, and Williams's drum parts manipulate the rhythm more like a lead instrument would. The peak of this extraordinary group's development (aside from *Miles Smiles*) was only heard years later, when selections from a December 1965 engagement at the Plugged Nickel, a Chicago jazz club, were issued piecemeal at first and then finally in total on a magnificent box set. Modal jazz was taken to a new level of complexity, especially rhythmically, and many consider this period to be Davis's most challenging. Later albums by the group had guests or substitutions, and it gradually dissolved into different lineups, often expanded into larger groups, as Davis began to pursue yet another musical direction.

By the late 1960s, Davis had accomplished enough to fill the careers of three or four lesser greats, but his restless genius and a thirst for continuing relevance led him beyond acoustic jazz into electric territory barely explored by his peers. Many of his experiments in this new direction remained unissued for years, with only electric guitarist George Benson's guest appearance in a very subordinate role the year before as precedent, so *In a Silent Way*, recorded in February of 1969, seemed like a more radical leap than it was. All of a sudden, Davis, Shorter, and Williams were recording with three electric pianists at once (Hancock, Chick Corea, who had replaced Hancock in the Quintet, and Josef Zawinul, who also played organ), electric guitarist John McLaughlin, and new bassist Dave Holland. On the surface, the music they made, although sonically denser than the Quintet, was simpler and smoother. Jazz purists, many already uncomfortable with the Quintet's knotty creations, reacted with disappointment or outrage.

Just adding electric guitar and electric piano was enough to incite cries of "sellout"; soon, he went further with electric Fender bass, synthesizer, even a wah-wah attachment for his trumpet. But while he incorporated rock and funk rhythms into his music, he never watered down his style; actually, it became denser and eventually more complex. If his bold action caused a schism in the jazz world that still inspires impassioned debate today, it also jumpstarted a new style, fusion (the major players of which were groomed in his bands: Hancock, Zawinul, and Shorter of Weather Report, Billy Cobham, Jack deJohnette, McLaughlin, Corea, etc.), and revived jazz's commercial fortunes after rock had captured the spotlight. Davis and producer Teo Macero also pioneered what for jazz was a new and equally controversial method of recording, laying down hours and hours of improvisation (in the studio or in concert) and then constructing tracks by splicing different segments together.

Starting with *Bitches Brew* in 1969, the double LP was Miles's favorite form for six years, allowing the audience greater access to his prolific expression. The studio doubles often were heavily chopped up by Macero, but the concert doubles sometimes allowed the ebbs and flows of live freeform improvisation to survive in their natural state. Pre-existing tunes/vamps were connected by improvised bridges or by suddenly switching into contrasting moods after musical cues by Davis (sometimes abrupt, dissonant synthesizer clusters) or stop-time silences of a couple beats or a measure. Far from being the commercial concession detractors claimed, these records were if anything more forbidding than ever, although in general the soloistic achievements of the other players ranked considerably lower than those of the earlier groups. However, this was partly because Davis was more concerned than ever with his music's overall texture. Thanks to a recent reissue program by Colum-

bia, some of the more disparaged sets are getting a second hearing, their merits more apparent after 20-odd years. Soon after the epochal 1975 concerts documented on the *Agharta* and *Pangaea* albums, Davis's health forced a six-year retirement. He returned in 1981, and if he was no longer on the edge—even surprising fans with returns to his older styles—neither was he standing still; his last studio album heavily incorporated hip-hop and rap. Still, even though he made much excellent music in the final phase of his career, which continued until his death, much of it also seemed uninspired compared to his many previous innovations, and his post-retirement comeback is mostly an appendix to his earlier career.

what to buy: Newcomers looking for a comprehensive career overview are in more luck with Davis than they would be with most jazz artists, since Davis spent 30 years recording for Columbia. The four-CD set *The Columbia Years 1955–1985* ♪♪♪♪ (CBS, 1988, prod. Jeff Rosen) is arranged by category: Blues, Standards, Originals, Moods, Electric. It will allow total newcomers to jazz to figure out what they like and which albums they might want to explore next. In no way is it adequate by itself in documenting Davis's greatness, but it touches on nearly every aspect thereof, and unlike other, more stylistically coherent Columbia compilations, this set doesn't slight the post-1968 period. *Birth of the Cool* ♪♪♪♪ (Capitol, 1957, prod. Walter Rivers) is the album that confirmed that Davis was destined to be an innovator. Recorded in 1949 (eight tracks) and 1950 (four tracks), these nonet arrangements were issued piecemeal until parts were collected on an album which was given its title to acknowledge the incredible influence this music had on the "cool jazz" genre. The ground-breaking arrangements, which extend the multi-hued style Gil Evans had developed in the Claude Thornhill band, were by not only Evans and Davis but also baritone sax great Gerry Mulligan (heard throughout), pianist John Lewis, and Johnny Carisi (composer of the immortal "Israel"). The gem-like perfection of the music falters only on the twelfth track, the mediocre ballad "Darn That Dream" featuring vocalist Kenny Hagood. *Kind of Blue* ♪♪♪♪ (Columbia, 1959, prod. Teo Macero) is arguably the most perfect album in jazz history and is certainly Davis's greatest creation. This landmark recording by a short-lived sextet brought modal playing to the mainstream. Miles's achingly fragile trumpet tone was never complemented better than by uncredited co-writer Bill Evans's delicately lush piano (Wynton Kelly replaces him on the blues "Freddie Freeloader"), and John Coltrane never played tenor sax more romantically. "All Blues," "Blue in Green," "Flamenco Sketches," and "So What" are all top-shelf classics. This album changed jazz history through its popularization of the use of modes rather than chord changes. *Miles Smiles* 𝄪𝄪𝄪𝄪 (Columbia, 1966, prod. Teo Macero) is the pinnacle of studio achievement by the second of Davis's classic Quintets. Wayne Shorter (tenor sax), Herbie Hancock (piano), Ron Carter (bass), and Tony Williams (drums) nudged the leader, who'd been making anti-avant-garde statements in the early and mid-1960s, into a drastic extension of his modal ideas. The material on this album, unlike some later Quintet releases, is tightly conceived and tautly played. Though not the first fusion album, *In a Silent Way* 𝄪𝄪𝄪𝄪 (Columbia, 1969, prod. Teo Macero) was the first of significant and enduring value. Davis's and Wayne Shorter's plangent tones, the shimmering electric keyboards of Joe Zawinul and Chick Corea, the steady but subtly varied pulses of drummer Tony Williams, John McLaughlin's guitar filigree, and the rock-solid bass lines of Dave Holland weave a meditative spell not of new-agey emptiness but rather of ecstatically infinite interest and tonal beauty. The double album *Bitches Brew* 𝄪𝄪𝄪𝄪 (Columbia, 1969, prod. Teo Macero) supplemented the previous album's players (minus Williams) with more future fusion all-stars, with Bennie Maupin's bass clarinet the most important new tonal color and multiple drummers adding layers of rhythmic complexity on one of the most profound albums ever in any genre. Actually, no future fusion came anywhere near the depth and adventurousness of *Bitches Brew*.

what to buy next: It is no small thing to suggest that an eight-CD box set is an essential purchase while at the same time admitting the flawed nature of many of the recordings it contains; nonetheless, *Chronicle: The Complete Prestige Recordings 1951–1956* 𝄪𝄪𝄪 (Prestige, 1980/1987, prod. Orrin Keepnews) is a must-own. While it's true that Davis was not at his best technically speaking, on the early material it contains, there were still interesting ideas and exciting new players (Jackie McLean, Sonny Rollins) on the dates. More to the point, the straight CD reissues of the separate original albums (at about $12 apiece) have short overall times and often split sessions up over several albums, so the largely chronological structure of the box set (selling for around $125), and the presence of roughly 15 albums on eight CDs makes for better value historically and monetarily. Collectors on a budget can start with the three absolutely essential Prestige albums: *Walkin'* 𝄪𝄪𝄪𝄪 (Prestige, 1955, prod. Bob Weinstock), *Cookin' with the Miles Davis Quintet* 𝄪𝄪𝄪𝄪 (Prestige, 1956, prod. Bob Weinstock), and *Relaxin' with the Miles Davis Quintet* 𝄪𝄪𝄪𝄪 (Prestige, 1957, prod. Bob Weinstock). *Cookin'* and *Relaxin'* are the best of the Prestige albums drawn from the famed Quintet marathon

sessions of 1956, while *Walkin'* signaled Davis's rejuvenation with the groups that included Horace Silver. Davis's three magnificent classics with Gil Evans are *Miles Ahead* 𝄪𝄪𝄪𝄪 (Columbia, 1957, prod. George Avakian), *Porgy and Bess* 𝄪𝄪𝄪𝄪 (Columbia, 1958, prod. Cal Lampley), and *Sketches of Spain* 𝄪𝄪𝄪𝄪 (Columbia, 1959, prod. Teo Macero, John Hammond, Irving Townsend). They not only feature some of Davis's most exquisitely delicate playing, they also show Evans taking large jazz ensemble arranging to levels unmatched in combining complex harmonies with pastel delicacy and shimmering beauty. After years of mistreating some of these classic collaborations, Columbia has provided a scholarly and complete compilation, *Miles Davis & Gil Evans: The Complete Columbia Studio Recordings* 𝄪𝄪𝄪 (Columbia Legacy, 1996, prod. Phil Schaap, Bob Belden), with the fat booklet explaining practically every sound. It contains all three of the above albums, and fans who have none of them (or maybe none on CD yet) should consider getting the whole package. Evans's difficult charts for *Miles Ahead*, which backed Davis with a 19-piece group, were learned in short sections extensively documented on two additional CDs of rehearsal takes (which also contain *Porgy* and *Sketches'* rehearsal material). Though the presence of these scraps increases appreciation of Evans's contributions, to which this set stands as a well-deserved monument, it doesn't make for an aesthetic listening experience; casual fans may prefer to pick up the three most important albums rather than the box. Besides those three famous albums, this six-CD box includes the less recommendable *Quiet Nights* (see below), three songs from a 1962 session with vocalist Bob Dorough, the previously unreleased but excellent incidental music taped in 1963 to accompany the play *The Time of the Barracudas,* and the pair's last recorded large-group collaboration, "Falling Water." The sextet album *Milestones* 𝄪𝄪𝄪𝄪 (Columbia, 1958, prod. Teo Macero) is aptly named. Considering the importance of the title track to his direction at the time, the Sextet with Adderley, Coltrane, Garland, Chambers, and Jones is at its peak. With Davis playing some of his best muted trumpet on "Miles"; a showcase for the rhythm section alone on "Billy Boy"; and excellent renditions of "Straight, No Chaser," "Dr. Jackyl" (consistently misidentified as "Dr. Jekyll"), "Sid's Ahead," and "Two Bass Hit," *Milestones* ranks very high among the Columbia albums of the 1950s. *The Complete Live at the Plugged Nickel 1965* 𝄪𝄪𝄪𝄪 (Columbia Legacy, 1995, prod. Teo Macero, Michael Cuscuna) documents two nights and a total of seven sets by one of the most exciting live bands in jazz history, the Miles Davis Quintet with Wayne Shorter, Herbie Hancock, Ron Carter, and Tony Williams. It's fascinating to hear how this group deconstructs the older Davis repertoire—"If I Were a Bell," "Stella by Starlight," "Walkin'," "My Funny Valentine," etc., many performed several times (but always differently enough that it doesn't feel like duplication). In a way, it makes the group's advanced concept a little easier to grasp than the new material it played on its solo albums. If the eight-CD box is too much for some fans, the single CD *Highlights from the Plugged Nickel* 𝄞𝄞𝄞𝄞 (Columbia Legacy, 1995, prod. Teo Macero, Michael Cuscuna) can provide a sampling. From early in Davis's electric period, *A Tribute to Jack Johnson* 𝄞𝄞𝄞𝄞𝄞 (Columbia, 1970, prod. Teo Macero) is the soundtrack to a film about the titular boxing great. It consists of two long tunes each originally an entire LP side, one of funky aggression (featuring MacLaughlin's great riff) and another of meditative tranquility with references back to Davis's earlier work. The studio disc *On the Corner* 𝄞𝄞𝄞𝄞 (Columbia, 1972, prod. Teo Macero) is Davis's most rhythmically oriented album and, in a way, his most avant-garde, structurally and sonically influenced by the sound sculptures of classical avant-gardist Karlheinz Stockhausen without ever sounding like the German's work, thanks to ultra-funky rhythms. The double live albums *Agharta* 𝄞𝄞𝄞𝄞𝄞 (Sony, 1976, prod. Teo Macero) and *Pangaea* 𝄞𝄞𝄞𝄞𝄞 (Sony, 1975, prod. Teo Macero) were recorded the same day, at, respectively, afternoon and evening concerts in Japan. With Miles almost more active as a sort of conductor than as a player, the heroes on these recordings, where the quiet moods are as intense as the full-force grooves, are electric guitarists Pete Cosey and Reggie Lucas and saxophonist/flutist Sonny Fortune. Cosey in particular unleashes a vast array of unearthly sounds and wild freakouts, and this music is as much about sonic sculpture as it is about rhythm. No matter what the volume or the rhythm, the tension never lets up, with moments of shattering beauty and soul-rending vehemence combined.

what to avoid: No Miles albums are totally lacking in interest, but these are at the bottom of the list, given that so much better work is available from this artist. European critics have wildly overpraised *Ascenseur pour l'echafaud* 𝄞𝄞 (Fontana, 1958/PolyGram, 1988) (translated as Lift to the Scaffold), the soundtrack to a Louis Malle film known in the United States as *Frantic*. As padded here for completists, it includes all the takes of the various cues in order of recording, followed by the 10 cues actually used on the original soundtrack, which had a huge amount of reverb added in some cases. Because of that, the way some tracks end with annoying abruptness, and the almost parodistic sense of "cool" of all but a few tracks, this is a vastly overrated project in terms of a solely aural experience. *The Man with the*

MILES DAVIS

song "So What"
album *Kind of Blue*
(Columbia, 1959/1997)
instrument Trumpet

Monster Solo

Horn 𝄞 (Columbia, 1980, prod. Teo Macero) was Davis's comeback from retirement, and his chops were rusty, sabotaging material which in any case is merely mediocre. The sappy, self-congratulatory title track, complete with an unctuous vocal, is far below even mediocrity. *Doo-Bop* 𝄞 (Warner Bros., 1992, prod. Easy Mo Bee), Davis's final studio album, found him exploring hip-hop. As acid jazz it's okay, and Miles plays as though invigorated by the rhythms, but the rapping (only three tunes, fortunately) suffers from banal lyrics and the backing tracks ultimately offer little depth on repeat listens. A word of warning is in order for Davis fans regarding *Miles & Monk at Newport* 𝄞𝄞𝄞𝄞 (Columbia, 1958/1994, prod. Teo Macero, Nedra Olds-Neal). It's a two-CD set, with the first CD consisting of the Davis sextet's 1958 Newport Jazz Festival performance but the other CD being the Thelonious Monk Quartet's 1963 gig at the same venue. Davis and Monk do not play together, and all the Davis material except the set-closing "The Theme" is on the below-listed *Miles & Coltrane* album, which adds two 1955 non-album tracks. (The Monk CD is superb.)

the rest:

First Miles (Savoy, 1988)

(With Sonny Rollins) *Dig* (Prestige, 1951)

Miles Davis, Volume I (Blue Note, 1952, 1954/1990)

Miles Davis, Volume II (Blue Note, 1953/1990)

And Horns (Prestige, 1953)

Miles Davis & the Lighthouse All-Stars: At Last! (Contemporary, 1953/1985)

Blue Haze (Prestige, 1954)

Bags' Groove (Prestige, 1955)

Miles Davis and the Modern Jazz Giants (Prestige, 1955)

The Musings of Miles (Prestige, 1955)

The New Miles Davis Quintet (Prestige, 1955)

Quintet/Sextet w/Milt Jackson (Prestige, 1955)

Collectors' Items (Prestige, 1956/1987)

Blue Moods (Debut, 1956)

Round about Midnight (Columbia, 1956)

Workin' (Prestige, 1957)

Miles & Coltrane (Columbia, 1958/1988)

'58 Miles (Columbia Legacy, 1958/1991)

Steamin' (Prestige, 1961)

Quiet Nights (Columbia, 1962)

The Legendary Stockholm Concert, March 22, 1960 (1960/Natasha Imports, 1992)

In Person at the Blackhawk, San Francisco: Friday and Saturday Nights (Columbia, 1961)

At Carnegie Hall (Columbia, 1961)

Live Miles: More Music from the Legendary Carnegie Hall Concert (1961/Columbia, 1987)

Someday My Prince Will Come (Columbia, 1962)

Seven Steps to Heaven (Columbia, 1963)

The Complete Concert 1964: My Funny Valentine + Four & More (Columbia, 1964/1965/1992)

E.S.P. (Columbia, 1965)

Sorcerer (Columbia, 1967)

Nefertiti (Columbia, 1967)

Miles in the Sky (Columbia, 1968)

Filles de Kilimanjaro (Columbia, 1968)

At Fillmore (Columbia, 1970)

Black Beauty: At Fillmore West (CBS/Sony, 1970)

Live-Evil (Columbia, 1970)

In Concert (Columbia, 1973)

Big Fun (Columbia, 1974)

Dark Magus (CBS/Sony, 1977)

Circle in the Round (CBS, 1979)

We Want Miles (Columbia, 1981)

Star People (Columbia, 1982)

Decoy (Columbia, 1984)

You're under Arrest (Columbia, 1985)

Miles Davis and the Jazz Giants (Prestige, 1986)

Tutu (Warner Bros., 1986)

Siesta (Warner Bros., 1987)

Amandla (Warner Bros., 1989)

Aura (CBS, 1989)

Miles Davis and Quincy Jones Live at Montreux (Warner Bros., 1993)

Live around the World (Warner Bros., 1996)

This Is Jazz 8: Miles Davis Acoustic (Columbia Legacy, 1996)

This Is Jazz 22: Miles Davis Plays Ballads (Columbia Legacy, 1997)

worth searching for: Given Davis's cachet, it boggles the mind that Sony doesn't keep all his work in print. Though a recent batch of reissues restored five of the 1970s doubles to domestic circulation, still missing in action is *Get up with It* (Columbia, 1974, prod. Teo Macero), last seen here as a pricey limited edition 20-bit two-CD remaster imported from Japan. Dedicated to the then-recently deceased Duke Ellington, this studio double features the fantastically atmospheric tribute "He Loved Him Madly," which gently undulates for a whole LP side without ever having a real theme or melody yet remains interesting throughout for its shifting textures. The rest of the album, recorded over a five-year period, has more variety than most of Davis's 1970s work. From the same series come *Miles in Tokyo* (CBS, 1977, prod. Kiyoshi Itoh) and *Miles in Berlin* (CBS, 1976, prod. Rudy Wolpert), both live albums recorded in 1964. The Tokyo concert is valuable for documenting Sam Rivers's short time in the Quintet, while the later Berlin gig is the first to capture Wayne Shorter after he joined permanently. Lest it seem that the main attraction is the rest of the band, Miles is in superb form on both gigs. Davis concert bootlegs sometimes document otherwise unrecorded configurations of Davis's bands or present the only live evidence of some lineups. *Double Image* (Moon, 1989), with Shorter, Corea, Holland, and DeJohnette in Paris in 1969, presents inspired, extremely freeform improvisations, though Davis manages to insert an extremely abstract version of "'Round Midnight." *In Sweden 1971* has saxist Gary Bartz, Keith Jarrett, electric bassist Mike Henderson, and three drummers; Jarrett's time with Davis was short and such documentation as in this Uppsala University show is valuable and offers some priceless soloing. *What I Say? Volume I* (Jazz Music Yesterday, 1994) contains a large chunk of a Vienna concert (November 5, 1971) with the same group as the Sweden show. The muscular improvisations flow organically. *What I Say? Volume II* (Jazz Music Yesterday, 1994) continues the Vienna gig and tacks on three tracks from a Fillmore West show (October 17, 1970; different drummers), but the muffled sound of the latter doesn't measure up to the radio sound of Vienna. In 1986 Davis recorded a few interesting studio tracks with Prince that have seen some underground circulation on tape, although they have never been officially released, apparently because Prince was not happy with the results. The soundtrack to Dennis Hopper's noir film *Hot Spot* 🎵🎵🎵🎵 (Antilles, 1990, prod. Michael Hoenig, Jack Nitzsche) teams Davis with blues greats John Lee Hooker and Taj Mahal in a series of moody, evocative cues written by veteran Jack Nitzsche. Considering Davis's fluency in the blues, it's surprising that this is the only time he was ever recorded with actual bluesmen; the experiment was a complete success.

influences:

◀◀ Elwood Buchanan, Harold "Shorty" Baker, Bobby Hackett, Fats Navarro, Freddie Webster, Dizzy Gillespie, Charlie Parker, Thelonious Monk, Ahmad Jamal, Ornette Coleman, James Brown, Sly & the Family Stone, Karlheinz Stockhausen

▶▶ Art Farmer, Chet Baker, Shorty Rogers, Don Cherry, Bill Dixon, Weather Report, Mahavishnu, Herbie Hancock, Return to Forever, Bill Laswell/Material, Jon Hassell, Wynton Marsalis, Wallace Roney, Rick Braun, Nicholas Payton, Vernon Reid/Living Colour

Steve Holtje

Richard Davis

Born April 15, 1930, in Chicago, IL.

One of the premier jazz bassists, Richard Davis is also among the most venerable jazz sidemen. Davis studied bass with Walter H. Dyett at DuSable High School in Chicago and spent 10 years studying classical technique with Rudolf Fahsbender (contra bassist with the Chicago Symphony). Davis became interested in jazz and started playing after four years of instruction, working parties with high school chums Clifford Jordan, Harold Ousley, Ira Sullivan, and Andrew Hill. After playing in dance bands in Chicago, Davis performed with Ahmad Jamal in 1953–54 and pianist Don Shirley in 1954–55 and, with the latter group, made it to New York where he remained until 1977. In the late 1950s, Davis worked with the Sauter-Finegan Orchestra and with Charlie Ventura before a five-year stint with Sarah Vaughan that included tours of Europe and South America. In the 1960s and 1970s, he worked on a freelance basis performing with symphony orchestras under Igor Stravinsky and Leonard Bernstein, with the Gunther Schuller Orchestra, and he even backed folk musicians. His gigs as sideman with small jazz groups in the 1960s included performances and several

recording dates with the Eric Dolphy/Booker Little Quintet. Around this time, he picked up an electric bass and began to do some commercial studio work recording jingles as well as a variety of recording dates. From 1966 to 1972, Davis was a regular performer with the Thad Jones–Mel Lewis Orchestra and was cited in a 1966 *Down Beat* critics poll as "Talent Deserving Wider Recognition." Davis performed during the 1970s with the New York Philharmonic and gigged as sideman with jazz artists such as Helen Merrill, Roland Hanna, and others as well as making recordings with Al Cohn/Zoot Sims, Andrew Hill, and James Moody. He was a member of bassist Bill Lee's legendary New York Bass Violin Choir, an orchestra of seven bassists that also included Ron Carter, Lisle Atkinson, Milt Hinton, Sam Jones, and Michael Fleming. For his bass playing, Davis received accolades in *Down Beat* readers polls from 1967 to 1972, yet Davis's expertise extends far beyond jazz as one of the most versatile bassists in the business.

In addition to performing with top jazz innovators and many distinguished classical conductors, Davis has also backed pop artists such as Frank Sinatra, Barbra Streisand, John Lennon, Bruce Springsteen, and Paul Simon in concerts and on recordings. After 23 years in New York City, Davis left in 1977 to become professor of bass and black music studies at the University of Wisconsin. He has received numerous awards and grants, including the prestigious 1993 Arts Midwest Jazz Master Award for his lifelong commitment to many facets of the music. Unfortunately, of his many recordings as leader, few are currently in print.

what's available: *Richard Davis and Friends: Live at Sweet Basil* 🎵🎵🎵🎵 (Evidence, 1994, prod. Horst Liepolt, Shigeyuki Kawashima) features the bassist leading a four-tune session (51 minutes) recorded live on August 8–9, 1990, at the famed New York jazz club. His side team includes pianist Sir Roland Hanna (his musical partner for more than 30 years), drummer Ronnie Burrage, tenor saxophonist Ricky Ford, and trumpeter Cecil Bridgewater. The group shines in collective and individual improvisations on the 16-plus minute version of Grofe's classical piece, "On the Trail," recorded on May 21, 1991, with George Cables subbing on piano. Davis is the star on the jazz interpretation of this number, kicking off the melody head, and taking an extended solo using a number of spark-generating techniques before handing off to Ford. Cables's backing is busier than Hanna's and he lends lyricism to this piece, creating ear-pleasing underpinnings to Ford's raucous solo. Davis, Bridgewater, and Hanna contribute one tune each. Davis's blues-tinged modal tune, "Dealin'" dates from the 1970s when he recorded a like-titled Muse album, which is out of print. The version that kicks off this date features a hot tenor blowout from Ford that squeaks and squeals into the instrument's upper registers, a grandiose solo from Hanna, with Davis playing a supportive role throughout. Bridgewater's "Samba Para Ustedes Dos" follows, changing the mood and rhythmic thrust, and providing launching pads for fine solos, especially from Ford. Davis plays a dominant bassline riff on Hanna's "Manhattan Safari," and everyone struts their solo stuff, including Burrage who's at his best on this number. This album has it all, from the straight-ahead and lyrical, to the near-free and avant-garde, to blues-influenced figures, and more. The individual and collective musicianship of these players makes this CD a highly enjoyable listen from the first note to the last.

worth searching for: You have many choices to hear Davis as a sideman, especially in small group sessions. His association with Eric Dolphy (1960–64) influenced him greatly and one of their highly rated recorded dates includes *Out to Lunch* &&&&&& (Blue Note, 1964, prod. Rudy Van Gelder), a classic Dolphy session featuring young musicians who would become famous: bassist Davis, vibraphonist Bobby Hutcherson, drummer Tony Williams, and trumpeter Freddie Hubbard. Another classic date of this period was Davis's collaboration with pianist Andrew Hill on *Point of Departure* &&&& (Blue Note, 1964, prod. Rudy Van Gelder), an avant-garde session that documents the artistry of saxophonist Joe Henderson, trumpeter Kenny Dorham, reeds player Eric Dolphy, and drummer Tony Williams in their early years.

influences:

◀◀ Duke Ellington, Jimmy Blanton, Oscar Pettiford, Eric Dolphy

▶▶ Charlie Haden, Christian McBride, Charnett Moffett

see also: *Jaki Byard, Eric Dolphy, Andrew Hill*

Nancy Ann Lee and Joe S. Harrington

Steve Davis

Born April 14, 1967, in Worcester, MA.

Taking his cue from his father's jazz records, Steve Davis took up the trumpet before he came under the spell of Curtis Fuller, leading him to switch to the trombone when he was 14 years old. Following high school, Davis entered the Hartt School of Music at the University of Hartford, studying with and eventually taking a spot in Jackie McLean's legendary band. During the same period he also got a chance to sit in with visiting play-

ers such as Pepper Adams and Eddie Henderson. Upon graduation, Davis hooked up with Art Blakey, making several tours and recording two albums with the master drummer. His playing continues to be influenced by his stint with Blakey, and he exhibits a fluid, melody-based, mainstream style. Davis currently teaches at both Hartt and McLean's Artist Collective, leads his own ensembles, and is still a member of McLean's group.

what's available: For his debut as a leader, *The Jaunt* &&&& (Criss Cross Jazz, 1996, prod. Gerry Teekens), Davis pairs up with tenor man Eric Alexander and a talented cast that includes the fine drummer Eric McPherson. The originals are quite good and Davis's unique arrangements of several choice standards makes this more than an average blowing date.

worth searching for: When one's appreciation of this fine player has developed, these dates where he appears as a sideman are the next valuable places to look for sustenance: Jackie McLean: *Rhythm of the Earth* &&&& (Antilles, 1992, prod. Jean-Francois Deiber); John Swana: *In the Moment* &&&& (Criss Cross Jazz, 1996, prod. Gerry Teekens); Peter Bernstein: *Brain Dance* &&&&& (Criss Cross Jazz, 1997, prod. Gerry Teekens).

influences:

◀◀ Curtis Fuller, J.J. Johnson

Chris Hovan

Walter Davis Jr.

Born September 2, 1932, in Richmond, VA. Died July 2, 1990, in New York, NY.

One of the more underrated bebop pianists of his time, Walter Davis Jr. played his first gig with Charlie Parker at the Apollo Theater in 1949. Months later, Davis became a regular on the New York City nightclub scene, mentored by Thelonious Monk and Bud Powell. He played with Parker and Max Roach in the early 1950s and began a long association with Dizzy Gillespie in 1956. Davis played with Art Blakey in the early 1960s and again in the mid-1970s, and also performed with Miles Davis and Sonny Rollins. Davis released many solo albums, most now out-of-print, but was better-known as an excellent bop sideman. He died of untreated diabetes and high blood pressure in 1990.

what to buy: *In Walked Thelonious* &&&& (Mapleshade, 1994, prod. Pierre M. Sprey) finds Davis playing 14 well-known and lesser-known songs from the Monk canon in a solo setting. His approach is economical and effective. This work is a serious interpretation of Monk and thus a must for any fan of Monk's music.

what to buy next: *Davis Cup* ♫♫♫ (Blue Note, 1959/1995, prod. Alfred Lion) was the pianist's first album as a leader, remastered for disc by Michael Cuscuna. His writing and the personnel (Jackie McLean, Donald Byrd, Sam Jones, Art Taylor) make it quite the hard bop outing.

the rest:
Blues Walk ♫♫♫♫ (Red, 1979)
400 Years Ago, Tomorrow ♫♫♫ (Owl, 1979)
Illumination ♫♫♫♫ (Denon, 1988)

worth searching for: Davis made a strong contribution as player and composer to Jackie McLean's *New Soil* ♫♫♫♫ (Blue Note, 1959, prod. Alfred Lion) shortly before making his own *Davis Cup* with the same horns. Here the rhythm section is Paul Chambers and Pete LaRoca, and if anything *New Soil* hits even harder.

influences:

◀◀ Art Tatum, Thelonious Monk, Bud Powell, Horace Silver, Wynton Kelly, John Lewis

▶▶ Herbie Hancock, Stephen Scott

Paul MacArthur

Wild Bill Davison

Born January 5, 1906, in Defiance, OH. Died November 14, 1989, in Santa Barbara, CA.

Cornetist Wild Bill Davison, with his surprising placement of high notes and his gift for direct melodic variation, was one of the most forceful voices of Chicago-style jazz from the 1920s to the 1980s. Davison's style was marked by his early childhood. Deserted by his parents, he was raised by grandparents who ran the Defiance Public Library. Condemned to spend much of his childhood in silence in the library's basement, Davison would later practice his cornet in the middle of a lake. In Chicago in the 1920s, Davison became associated with young Chicagoans Frank Teschemacher and Eddie Condon, who were under the sway of the many New Orleans musicians in the city such as Joe Oliver, Jimmy Noone, brothers Baby and Johnny Dodds, and, especially, Louis Armstrong. Davison was initially inspired by the subtle approach of Bix Beiderbecke, but the impact of Armstrong erased this early influence. Davison had found a style that suited his own brash personality, and he would remain true to it, and the cornet, for the next six decades. Unfortunately, his career was frequently derailed by

bad luck. He was injured in the 1932 car accident that killed Teschemacher and, upon moving to Wisconsin, he suffered a serious lip injury from a flying beer mug in Milwaukee. In the 1940s he was in New York, playing regularly with Condon at the guitarist's club and elsewhere, and making distinguished records with Sidney Bechet and Art Hodes. Whether leading his own band or working as a visiting soloist in Dixieland revival bands, Davison worked steadily in the later decades of his life. His style was particularly popular in Europe, and he spent the 1970s residing in Denmark. *The Wildest One: The Life of Wild Bill Davison,* by Hal Willard (Monkton, MD: Avondale Press, 1996), is an excellent full-length account of the cornetist's colorful life and career.

what to buy: Davison's finest moments in the studio came in the 1943 sessions now heard on *Commodore Master Takes* ♫♫♫♫ (Commodore/GRP, 1997, prod. Milt Gabler) that epitomize Chicago-style jazz with his strident horn perfectly complemented by a band that includes Pee Wee Russell on clarinet, Condon on guitar, and Dave Tough on drums. *Jazz Giants* ♫♫♫♫ (Sackville, 1968/1997, prod. John Norris, Bill Smith) is an excellent performance with Davison in a band of veteran peers, most more oriented to swing than the Dixieland that Davison often played. It includes the underrated Herb Hall on clarinet, Benny Morton on trombone, and Claude Hopkins responsible for musical direction as well as piano. It's vital and swaggering, serene and profound, and filled with wit and high spirits.

what to buy next: *Solo Flight* ♫♫♫ (Jazzology, 1994, prod. George Buck) provides a late and engaging look at Davison in an unusual context, displaying his still strong trumpet in a 1981 quartet with two guitars and bass. The excitement that Davison could bring as a guest with revivalist bands can be heard on *Wild Bill Davison with the Alex Welsh Band* ♫♫♫ (Jazzology, 1997, prod. George Buck). A performance recorded in England in 1966, it features aggressive sparring between Davison's cornet and Welsh's trumpet.

best of the rest:
Showcase ♫♫♫ (Jazzology, 1994)
AfterHours ♫♫♫ (Jazzology, 1994)
Lady of the Evening ♫♫♫ (Jazzology, 1994)
'S Wonderful ♫♫♫ (Jazzology, 1994)

influences:

◀◀ Bix Beiderbecke, Louis Armstrong

▶▶ Tom Saunders, Alex Welsh

Stuart Broomer

Blossom Dearie

Born April 28, 1926, East Durham, NY.

With a small, girlish voice and a devotion to bright, snappy songs, singer/pianist Blossom Dearie has staked her claim as one of the more distinctive performers in the world of vocal jazz. She began her career in various vocal groups, including the Blue Flames (from Woody Herman's orchestra) and the Blue Reys (with Alvino Rey's band). A trip to Paris in the early 1950s proved profitable, where she performed with Annie Ross, as well as scored a hit with her own group, the Blue Stars, singing a French version of "Lullaby in Birdland." Dearie returned to the States in 1956, and recorded a series of albums for Verve, heading small groups that variously included guitarists Herb Ellis and Kenny Burrell, bassist Ray Brown, and drummers Jo Jones and Ed Thigpen. In 1973, she started her own label, Daffodil Records, and has recorded regularly since then.

Dearie sings with great wit, clarity, and style, as her unique delivery aggressively punctuates certain phrases, while still leaving room for her to savor others. While her early recordings are mostly comprised of dynamic interpretations of show tune standards (i.e. "The Surrey with the Fringe on Top"), her later work favors cabaret-style originals and the kitschy, musical wordplay of songwriters like Dave Frishberg and occasional duet partner Bob Dorough (children of the 1970s may recognize Dearie as one of the voices of the animated Saturday morning educational series, *Schoolhouse Rock,* for which Dorough served as musical director). In addition to singing, Dearie backs herself on piano on most tracks, and her elegant, spare playing is underrated.

what to buy: *Blossom Dearie– Jazz Masters 51* ♫♫♫♫ (Verve, 1996, prod. Norman Granz) is part of Verve's budget compilation series and provides a perfect overview of Dearie's talents in her most jazzy settings.

what to buy next: *Give Him the Ooh-La-La* ♫♫♫♫ (Verve, 1958, prod. Norman Granz) and *Once Upon a Summertime* ♫♫♫♫ (Verve, 1959, prod. Norman Granz) are two prime late 1950s sessions.

best of the rest:
Blossom Dearie ♫♫♫ (Verve, 1957)
Blossom Dearie Sings Comden and Green ♫♫♫ (Verve, 1959)
My Gentleman Friend ♫♫♫ (Verve, 1959)
Soubrette Sings Broadway Hit Songs ♫♫♫ (Verve, 1960)
May I Come In? ♫♫♫ (Capitol, 1964)
Blossom Dearie Sings ♫♫ (Daffodil, 1973)

Tweedledum & Tweedledee ♫♫ (Daffodil, 1991)
Our Favorite Songs ♫♫♫ (Daffodil, 1995)

Eric J. Lawrence

Dedication Orchestra

Formed 1992, in London, England.

Louis Moholo, drums; Kenny Wheeler, trumpet; Keith Tippett, piano; Lol Coxhill, saxophone; Evan Parker, saxophone; Harry Beckett, trumpet; Claude Deppa, trumpet; Dave Amis, trombone; Malcolm Griffiths, trombone; Paul Rutherford, trombone; Dave Powell, tuba; Neil Metcalf, flute; Elton Dean, saxophone; Chris Briscoe, saxophone; Ray Warleigh, alto sax; Paul Rogers, bass.

The Dedication Orchestra, led by drummer Louis Moholo, is a eulogy not to a musician or group, but to the entire musical scene that grew around the expatriate South African group, the Blue Notes, after their arrival in England. Leaving apartheid behind, they brought with them a jazz language evolved half a world away, that included rhythmic drive, vibrant folk and ethnic themes and, as pianist-producer Steve Beresford has written, "an utterly uninhibited attitude" toward expressing themselves. Just what the British scene needed. When the Blue Notes splintered in 1968, members fanned out, spreading that ethos in a wave of individual bands, Chris McGregor's Brotherhood of Breath being the most prominent. Then came the deaths. By 1990, drummer Louis Moholo was the sole survivor of the half-dozen South Africans who'd been key to the scene. Saxophonist Dudu Puwana, bassists Johnny Dyani and Harry Miller, trumpeter Mongezi Feza, and pianist McGregor were all gone. Two years later, Moholo formed the Dedication Orchestra as a charity fund-raiser and tribute, bringing in stars such as trumpeter Kenny Wheeler, pianist Keith Tippet, and saxophonists Lol Coxhill and Evan Parker.

what's available: On *Spirits Rejoice* ♫♫♫♫ (Ogun, 1992, prod. Steve Beresford), the writing swells what were generally small combo pieces to big-band strength without losing the original vibes. Dudu Pukwana's ballad "B My Dear" gets a majestic arrangement from Wheeler and a crack solo from alto saxophonist Ray Warleigh. *Ixesha* ♫♫♫♫♫ (Ogun, 1994, prod. Steve Beresford) at double-CD length, also boasts a cleaner recorded sound and more precise ensemble playing with no diminution of feeling. Not to be missed are the soulfully sung "Sondela" (composed by Mongezi Feza, with a vocal quartet including Julie Tippets and Maggie Nichols) and a quick-witted take on Dudu Pukwana's "Bird Lives." (Available from Ogun Records at 36 Dunboyne Road, London NW3 2YY, England.)

influences:

◀◀ Chris McGregor, the Brotherhood of Breath, Mongezi Feza, Dudu Pukwana, Johnny Dyani, Hugh Masekela

▶▶ Abdullah Ibrahim, African Jazz Pioneers

W. Kim Heron

Barrett Deems

Born March 1, 1913, in Springfield, IL.

Drummer Barrett Deems, nicknamed "Deemus," remains active in Chicago, leading his 18-musician big band, a 10-musician ensemble, and smaller groups. Best known for his stint as touring drummer for Louis Armstrong's All-Stars from 1954–58, Deems has enjoyed a lengthy career since his first professional gig with the Paul Ash band at age 15. Deems admirably drove many swing era bands with his skillful swing-style drumming, as well as heading his own groups. He toured with the bands of Joe Venuti (1937–44), Red Norvo (1948), Charlie Barnett (1951), and Muggsy Spanier (1951–54), and enjoyed brief stints in the 1940s with Jimmy Dorsey and Woody Herman. Deems settled in Chicago after a stint with Jack Teagarden (1960–63), toured Eastern Europe with the Benny Goodman sextet in 1976 and traveled with Wild Bill Davison to South America. Deems continues to lead his own modern groups and, in addition to playing on recordings with Louis Armstrong, Art Hodes, Red Norvo, and various Dixieland compilations, has recorded two Delmark albums as leader.

what's available: *Deemus* 🎵🎵🎵🎵 (Delmark, 1997), initially recorded in Lake Geneva, WI in 1978 as an LP and distributed on a limited scale. A delightful reissue of eight happy-time swingers, the disc features fine solos by clarinetist Chuck Hedges, vibraphonist Don DeMichael, and lead guitarist Bob Roberts, with Deems leading a sterling rhythm section featuring Steve Behr at piano, John Defauw on rhythm guitar, and Wilson McKindra on bass. The mixture of toe-tapping standards and sweet ballads allows Deems to show off his fine skills, especially on sprinters like "Get Happy, " where he displays the speed for which he was tagged "the world's fastest drummer." Musicianship is superb, with clarinetist Chuck Hedges adding buoyancy to "Deed I Do," authenticity to "New Orleans," and lushness to "New Orleans." Vibraphonist Don DeMichael and lead guitarist Bobby Roberts are deceased, but, at this writing, Deems, dubbed as "the oldest living teenager" by Chicago saxophonist Rich Corpolongo, was still performing regular Saturday nights with pianist Steve Behr, and working with Defauw, now in his seventies. Deems's recording of his Chicago-based,

18-member big band, *How D'You Like It So Far?* 🎵🎵🎵🎵 (Delmark, 1994, prod. Robert G. Koester, Jane Johnson) showcases his talents for driving a large, modern band, brandishing big-stick technique and subtle, soft brushwork, as well as offering brief, expressive solos. Section work on all 16 tunes is brassy-tight, and soloists are among Chicago's best. A choice album for fans of hard-swinging, modern big bands.

worth searching for: In a July, 1997 interview with this writer, Deems confided that his Louis Armstrong sessions on Columbia are being reissued on CD. Take note of the years Deems was with the band, and watch for these reissues. In addition, Deems recorded some tasty swing-jazz numbers with pianist Art Hodes on *Up in Volley's Room* (Delmark, 1972). Their best session together, it's a laid-back date that features Hodes's understated piano playing, strong support from bassist Truck Parham, and fine solos from Chicago clarinetist Volley DeFaut (former recording partner with Jelly Roll Morton) and trumpeter Nappy Trottier.

influences:

◀◀ Gene Krupa, Dave Tough

Nancy Ann Lee

Joey DeFrancesco

Born April 10, 1971, in Springfield, PA.

Although keyboard prodigy Joey DeFrancesco used to do Elvis Presley imitations on stage and came onto the national scene in the late 1980s Miles Davis band that produced *Amandla*, this young lion's recorded work owes everything to the mainstream and swinging soul jazz of the 1960s. His father, Papa John DeFrancesco, taught Joey to play the Hammond B-3 organ at a young age. Raised in Philadelphia, Joey won the Philadelphia Jazz Society's McCoy Tyner scholarship and was a finalist in the first Thelonious Monk International Jazz Piano Competition in 1987. He's been leading his own groups ever since he left Davis's band and has been a prolific session player as well, showing up on albums by his mentor Jack McDuff, guitarist John McLaughlin, tenor saxophonist Houston Person, and Papa John DeFrancesco. In addition, Joey also plays trumpet well, although not as brilliantly as he plays organ.

what to buy: *All of Me* 🎵🎵🎵🎵 (Columbia, 1989) is an energetic, swinging debut that ranges from the Jimmy Smith tune "Blues for J" to the standard "All of Me" to the Bacharach-David pop hit "Close to You," along with DeFrancesco's tasty originals. Just as good is *Where Were You?* 🎵🎵🎵🎵 (Columbia, 1990), his second album, which features a number of guests including tenor saxophonists Illinois Jacquet and Kirk Whalum and guitarist John Scofield in a set that's heavier on the standards than the originals.

what to buy next: *Reboppin'* 𝄢𝄢𝄢 (Columbia, 1992, Joey DeFrancesco, Cheryl Carte) and *Live at the Five Spot* 𝄢𝄢𝄢 (Columbia, 1993, prod. Joey DeFrancesco) feature slightly less stellar work than DeFrancesco's best, but they're still albums full of that accessible, rollicking organ sound and swinging arrangements. On *Reboppin'*, DeFrancesco augments his regular trio—guitarist Paul Bollenback and drummer Byron "Wookie" Landham—with friends he made hanging out in Phoenix, challenging tenor saxophonist Tony Malaby and trumpeter Jim Henry. There's also a "Family Jam" featuring DeFrancesco's brother Johnny on guitar and their father, John, on organ. On the live album, the "duel" between DeFrancesco and Jack McDuff on "Spectator" is fun.

the rest:
Part III 𝄢𝄢𝄢 (Columbia, 1991)
The Street of Dreams 𝄢𝄢𝄢 (Big Mo, 1995)

worth searching for: Try the second-hand market for *All about My Girl* 𝄢𝄢𝄢 (Muse, 1994), an album that went out of print when the Muse label folded. For DeFrancesco's guest shots with tenor saxman Houston Person check out *Party* 𝄢𝄢𝄢 (Muse, 1989) and *Why Not!* 𝄢𝄢𝄢 (Muse, 1990). These were DeFrancesco's best performances as sideman, although his appearance on McDuff's *It's about Time* 𝄢𝄢𝄢 (Concord Jazz, 1995) has a certain sentimental charm.

influences:
◀◀ Jack McDuff, Jimmy Smith

see also: *Miles Davis*

Salvatore Caputo

Buddy DeFranco

Born December 17, 1923, in Camden, NJ.

Equally at home with bop, swing or cool jazz and any combination of the three styles, Buddy DeFranco is a magnificent clarinetist with a wondrous technique and a tone other reedmen must envy. DeFranco's sound is warm, his facility breath-taking, and his concept modern. Heavily influenced by Charlie Parker, DeFranco emerged from the 1940s and to this date remains the pacesetter for the modern clarinet sound. Christened Boniface Ferdinand Leonardo DeFranco, he grew up in a tough South Philadelphia neighborhood where he was encouraged by his

father, a blind piano tuner. Young DeFranco started clarinet lessons at age nine, developed a solid classical background, and after junior high school received a thorough musical training at the Mastbaum Vocational School where classmates included trumpeters Red Rodney and Joe Wilder. DeFranco won an amateur swing music contest in 1937, sponsored by Tommy Dorsey, a bandleader with whom DeFranco worked off and on in the 1940s. Following stints with Johnny "Scat" Davis, Ted Fiorito, Charlie Barnet, and Gene Krupa, DeFranco twice attempted to lead his own big bands, but the times and economic climate proved to be wrong and he was unsuccessful.

In 1950, DeFranco held a front-line spot with a small Count Basie group, alongside trumpeter Clark Terry. DeFranco organized a quartet in 1952 which toured and recorded at length for three years before he joined the Jazz at the Philharmonic troops. Using California as his base, DeFranco's solo career abated in the late 1950s, and he did studio work, often with Nelson Riddle (his old roommate from his Dorsey days). In the 1960s, DeFranco teamed with accordionist Tommy Gumina in a quartet and became leader of the revived Glenn Miller Orchestra (1966). He remained in front of the Miller band for eight years, and met his wife, Joyce, while on the road. DeFranco and his wife moved to Florida in 1974, where he did some teaching, performed periodic club dates, and during the 1980s, formed new musical collaborations. DeFranco performed, toured, and recorded with vibist Terry Gibbs, Scottish guitarist Martin Taylor, and British clarinet virtuoso, John Deman. In the 1990s, he continues to record and perform internationally.

what to buy: *Like Someone in Love* 𝄢𝄢𝄢𝄢 (Progressive, 1989, prod. Gus P. Statiras) is a DeFranco-led quintet session that hits a relaxed groove and maintains it throughout the eight tunes with successful backing from bassist George Duvivier, guitarist Tal Farlow, pianist Derek Smith and Drummer Ronnie Bedford. Any track on the album sells you on its merits. Previously available on two LPs, *The Buenos Aires Concerts* 𝄢𝄢𝄢𝄢 (Hep, 1980/1995 prod. Alastair Robertson) find DeFranco at the top of his game in a series of eight dazzling and satisfying extended performances (shortest tune is 8:15). Definitive versions of often-played DeFranco favorites, "Street of Dreams," "Billie's Bounce," and "The Song Is You," are among the offerings. *Chip off the Old Bop* 𝄢𝄢𝄢𝄢 (Concord, 1992, prod. Allen Farnham) finds DeFranco and his rhythm cohorts presenting a well-programmed mix of 12 originals and standards. Support here is first rate, coming from bassist Keter Betts, drummer Jimmy Cobb, pianist Larry Novak, and guitarist Joe Cohn. The array of tunes includes such popular favorites as "Makin'

Whoopee," "Moon Song," "You're Blase," "If You Could See Me Now," and a roaring closer, "Hashimoto's Blues," a clever re-working of the venerable "Limehouse Blues."

what to buy next: *You Must Believe in Swing* 𝄞𝄞𝄞𝄞 (Concord, 1997, prod. Allen Farnham) features DeFranco's quicksilver clarinet in duo setting with the one-man rhythm section, pianist Dave McKenna. They produce an outstanding mainstream jazz recording of eight standards, the bluesy title tune, and a swinging "Anthropology." A satisfying compilation of bop and swing tunes, *Holiday for Swing* 𝄞𝄞𝄞𝄞 (Contemporary, 1988, prod. Ralph Kaffel, Terry Gibbs) is typical of the Gibbs/DeFranco collaborations (Gibbs leads four more for the Contemporary label).

what to avoid: *The Essential Glenn Miller Orchestra, Directed by Buddy DeFranco* 𝄞𝄞𝄞 (Sony, 1988, prod. Bob Morgan) is an agreeable 1972 re-creation of the Miller sound, with auditory nuggets of Bobby Hackett, Al Klink, and Ray McKinley, who lend authenticity to the project, but there is little of DeFranco's clarinet featured.

best of the rest:
Free Fall 𝄞𝄞𝄞𝄞 (Choice, 1974/Candid, 1996)
(With the Oscar Peterson Quartet) *Hark* 𝄞𝄞𝄞𝄞 (Pablo, 1985/OJC, 1996)
Born to Swing 𝄞𝄞𝄞 (Hindsight, 1993)
Mr. Lucky 𝄞𝄞𝄞 (Pablo/OJC, 1997)

worth searching for: In print but hard to find, *Whirligig* 𝄞𝄞𝄞𝄞 (Bis-Ludco, 1995, prod. Jim Bastin, Jeff Haskell, Paula Fan) features DeFranco and John Denman on clarinets. The original 1983 Arizona date issued on LP, garnered five stars from *Down Beat* magazine. With six more tracks from a later date added, it is truly a magnificent collection of 15 tunes. *Nobody Else but Me* 𝄞𝄞𝄞𝄞 (Hark Records, 1997, prod. Joyce DeFranco, Buddy DeFranco) is a limited edition pressing of 15 tunes arranged by Rob Pronk, which reflect DeFranco's 1980s Holland appearances with the Metropole Orchestra. This set of standards and originals is a personal favorite of the DeFranco's and is available from them by sending $15 (+$3 S&H) to Buddy DeFranco Enterprises, P. O. Box 252, Sunnyside, FL 32461. *The Complete Verve Recordings of Buddy DeFranco Quartet/Quintet with Sonny Clark* 𝄞𝄞𝄞𝄞𝄞 (Verve, 1954–55, prod. Norman Granz/Mosaic Records, 1991, prod. Michael Cuscuna) are now out-of-print, but you might stumble across a set somewhere out there.

influences:
◀◀ Johnny Mince, Benny Goodman, Artie Shaw, Charlie Parker
▶▶ Eddie Daniels, Ron Odrich, Rolf Kuhn

John T. Bitter

Jack DeJohnette

Born 1942, in Chicago, IL.

Jack DeJohnette has been one of the most inventive and prolific drummers since he first appeared in the mid '60s playing with the Charles Lloyd Quartet. The enormous popularity of that outfit, as well as their inroads into the rock marketplace (they'd share concert bills with the Grateful Dead, Jimi Hendrix, and many others, appearing often at the Fillmore in San Francisco), no doubt shaped many of the decisions DeJohnette subsequently made in terms of the possibilities available to him if he didn't keep himself confined to one domain. A stint with Miles Davis (replacing Tony Williams and first appearing on *Bitches Brew*) brought him in contact with a range of players with whom he has continued to work. Moving on from Davis, he formed Compost, a sort of fusion variant. By the mid-70s he began a long association with the ECM label, recording under his own name as well as appearing in many other settings. As an adolescent, DeJohnette studied classical piano for ten years, graduating from Chicago's American Conservatory of Music. This is an instrument he continues to explore regularly, even recording a solo piano album in the '80s. Inspired by his exposure to Max Roach, he took up drumming in high school. His first album as a leader (1969's *Complex*) also introduced him as the only known recording artist who doubles on drums and Melodica. His ensembles over the years have all drawn their strengths from the inherent chemistry of the chosen players (Gateway, New Directions, and Special Edition each are represented by numerous recordings). DeJohnette's drumming is always sensitive to what needs to be underscored and how to best serve the overall piece. As a composer he shows an equally wide range of interests and skills. Even a casual look into this man's output reveals a rich, highly contrasting but always rewarding approach to music. Besides his own ensembles, he's been the drummer in Keith Jarrett's standards trio for the past fifteen years and his playing has been a key component in albums by everyone from Sonny Rollins to Herbie Hancock.

what to buy: *Complex* 𝄞𝄞𝄞𝄞 (Milestone, 1969, prod. Orrin Keepnews, Dick Katz) exhibits the charms of an eager first album, but also solidly makes a case for DeJohnette as a composer and leader. *Special Edition* 𝄞𝄞𝄞𝄞𝄞 (ECM, 1980, prod. Jack DeJohnette) became the name for one of his ongoing outfits, featuring David Murray (tenor saxophone, bass clarinet), Arthur Blythe (alto saxophone), and Peter Warren (bass, cello). Personnel shifted, and all of them are worthwhile, so why not start with the first one? He also assembled two different trios, both essentially guitar-bass-drums, with DeJohnette also playing

Jack DeJohnette **(Archive Photos)**

piano at times. *Rypdal/Vitous/DeJohnette* 𝄾𝄾𝄾 (ECM, 1979, prod. Manfred Eicher) and *Gateway 2* 𝄾𝄾𝄾𝄾 (ECM, 1978, prod. Manfred Eicher) are a study in contrasts between guitarists and bass players. Europeans Terje Rypdal and Miroslav Vitous comprise the former, and Americans John Abercrombie and Dave Holland the latter. DeJohnette's most recent work includes pianist Michael Cain. With reed player Steve Gorn, *Dancing with Nature Spirits* 𝄾𝄾𝄾𝄾 (ECM, 1996, prod. Manfred Eicher) is a powerfully atmospheric trio, with a rhythmic base drawing from DeJohnette's study of Native American culture. That was followed with *Oneness* 𝄾𝄾𝄾𝄾𝄾 (ECM, 1997, prod. Manfred Eicher), which omits reeds but adds Don Alias on percussion and Jerome Harris on bass and guitar.

what to buy next: *Sorcery* 𝄾𝄾𝄾 (Prestige, 1974, prod. Jack DeJohnette) features a two-guitar lineup (Abercrombie and Mick Goodrick) as well as bass guitar (Bennie Maupin) and trombone (Michael Fellerman). It's from the era of fusion, and although it isn't anywhere near as rock-bound as latter-day Re-

turn to Forever, it does bear some of the marks of misguided hybrids. *New Directions: In Europe* 𝄾𝄾𝄾 (ECM, 1980, prod. Manfred Eicher) is a live date of his quartet with Lester Bowie (trumpet), John Abercrombie (guitar), and Eddie Gomez (bass). Not a lineup anyone would have guessed, they do interact bracingly at times, but also can sound like disparate elements politely gathered. By the time of *Irresistible Forces* 𝄾𝄾𝄾 (MCA, 1987, prod. Jack DeJohnette) DeJohnette's Special Edition was finding and featuring a new generation of players (Gary Thomas and Greg Osby on saxes). This album suffers only from production values that sacrifice some of the sterling clarity found on the ECM releases for contemporary polish; this identifies it with its decade in ways that his earlier recordings don't. *Zebra* 𝄾𝄾𝄾 (MCA, 1986, prod. Kousaku Makita) is a rewarding exploration with DeJohnette on synthesizers and Lester Bowie on trumpet. *Works* 𝄾𝄾𝄾 (ECM, 1985, prod. Manfred Eicher) is a compilation drawing from a some of his ECM work (1975–81). However, most of the albums these tracks are pulled from have their own proper shape and flow and are strong, complete statements at their full length. This set serves only as a very brief overview.

influences:

◄◄ Max Roach, Elvin Jones, Philly Joe Jones

►► Bobby Previte, Pheeroan ak Laff

David Greenberger

Peter Delano

Born September 28, 1976, in New York, NY.

Although the record industry's love of lucre and pablum seems almost certain to turn jazz into background music for the Jacuzzi set, serious players such as Peter Delano continue to emerge. Delano began playing piano at six and by age nine was working on transforming blues progressions. He studied jazz at the New School and by the time he was 16 had released his first album. Showing a taste for the mainstream styles from the '50s and '60s, Delano's solos can be elegant or rough-and-tumble. They are always intelligent. His compositions are driven as much by mood as by intellect.

what to buy: *Bite of the Apple* ✍✍✍✍ (Verve, 1994, prod. Peter Delano, Bob Belden) shows off a 17-year-old pianist-composer with the poise and taste of a master musician. The independence of his left-hand rhythmic-harmonic statements from his spiraling right hand makes him a formidable improviser, especially on such full-speed-ahead solos as his own "Spontaneous id" and Richard Rodgers's "The Sweetest Sounds." Delano's compositions are well crafted and mature and cover a wide range of textures and emotions, from the wistfully romantic "Heartfelt" to the muscularly assertive "Demonic Disorder" and the Latin-flavored straight-ahead groove of "Castellaras." Delano proves most adaptable as well, leading and writing for eight different combinations of fine New York players, including altoist Gary Bartz and bass-player Eddie Gomez, with equal rapport.

what to buy next: *Peter Delano* ✍✍✍ (Verve, 1993, prod. Peter Delano, Guy Eckstine) is an eye-opening debut by this prodigy amidst stellar backup that includes drummer Lewis Nash, tenor man Michael Brecker, and altoist Gary Bartz. Delano mixes interesting original compositions with John Coltrane's "Miles' Mode" and Benny Golson's "I Remember Clifford," and finds something new to say on the often-addressed "Autumn Leaves."

influences:

◄◄ McCoy Tyner

Salvatore Caputo

Barbara Dennerlein

Born September 25, 1964, in Munich, Germany.

Barbara Dennerlein started playing organ when she was 11 years old, was playing clubs at 15, and had her first appearance on record in 1983. Since that time she has become one of the most popular touring jazz artists in Europe, receiving the German Critic's Award twice and scoring high in *Down Beat* magazine critic's polls. In a field of players defined by Jimmy Smith, Dennerlein has managed to carve out her own niche with a highly original style that laces samplers and synthesizers to her Hammond B-3. She has also developed a foot-pedal setup that gives her a string bass sound that helps her stand out from other organ players. Dennerlein's composing skills take advantage of her virtuoso performance capabilities, while her arranging talents find new ways to blend aural colors with the straight-ahead swing/Latin/funk hybrid she is developing.

what to buy: From a performance standpoint Dennerlein may be the most exciting talent to come along on her instrument in decades, perhaps even since the hallowed days of Larry Young (although their styles are totally different). That said, many of the players on *Take Off!* ✍✍✍✍ (Verve, 1995, prod. Barbara Dennerlein) have the kind of major-league talent that she deserves to have on her sessions. The horn section includes Ray Anderson, Mike Sim, and Roy Hargrove, while percussion is in good hands with Dennis Chambers and Don Alias. Bassist Lonnie Plaxico joins in on some songs, and Joe Locke's vibes playing provides an interesting textural contrast to Dennerlein's washes of sound. The organist is maturing as a composer. Standout tunes include the Latinesque "Fly Away," with solos from Locke, Dennerlein, Hargrove, and Watkins pushing the groove along, and the title song, a ten-minute funk extravaganza that owes a debt of gratitude to old James Brown rhythm anthems.

what to buy next: *Hot Stuff* ✍✍✍ (Enja, 1990, prod. Barbara Dennerlein), a quartet date with Dennerlein, guitarist Watkins, drummer Mark Modesir, and tenor sax man Andy Sheppard, is pretty exciting if you ignore the excesses of the title tune, which sounds like the kind of "suite" routinely cranked out by early 1970s fusioneers. Dennerlein covers Benny Golson's "Killer Joe" and the Miles Davis classic "Seven Steps to Heaven," both of which receive credible performances, but her most vibrant playing is reserved for her own material. "Top Secret," which leaves Sheppard out of the mix, features some nice escalating interplay between the remaining threesome, and "Birthday Blues" is the kind of tune one expects to hear in

Paul Desmond (© Jack Vartoogian)

a 21st-century rib joint. But the closer, "Toscanian Sunset," is the kind of timeless ballad that begs other artists to record it.

the rest:

Straight Ahead ♫♫♫ (Enja, 1988)
That's Me ♫♫♫ (Enja, 1992)

influences:

◀◀ Jimmy Smith

Garaud MacTaggart

Paul Desmond

Born Paul Emil Breitenfeld, November 25, 1924, in San Francisco, CA. Died May 30, 1977, in New York, NY.

Paul Desmond's career and royalty checks were shaped by one of the largest hits any jazz composer has ever had, "Take Five." The music licensing organization BMI (Broadcast Music Incorporated), which monitors such things, has tracked over one million performances of the tune. The only Desmond contribu-

tion to the now-classic Dave Brubeck Quartet album *Time Out*, "Take Five" was an infectious experiment in 5/4 that swung its parent release onto the turntables of middle-brow America. Desmond and Brubeck were a team through the mid-1960s, but they had actually been playing together since the late 1940s when the altoist first recorded with Brubeck's Octet prior to actually joining the band. After leaving the band, Desmond formed his own ad hoc groups for recording purposes in addition to playing or recording with the Modern Jazz Quartet, Gerry Mulligan, and occasional reunion tours with Brubeck. His light, intuitive playing style owed a lot to Lester Young as filtered by Lee Konitz. While Desmond was quoted as calling himself "an arch conservative" in matters of performance, Anthony Braxton, one of the foremost avant garde players of this century, was a fan of the older man's approach to the alto.

what to buy: Desmond's always intelligent playing and improvising were often set off best within the Brubeck Quartet. That said, the dates he recorded under his own name are still worth having, especially if guitarist Jim Hall was involved. *Take Ten* 🎵🎵🎵 (RCA/Bluebird, 1963, prod. George Avakian) features Hall and Desmond in the company of bassist Gene Cherico (the title tune features Brubeck's bassist Gene Wright) and drummer Connie Kay from the Modern Jazz Quartet. In addition to three songs written by Desmond (including "Take Ten," a tasteful exercise in self-plagiarism), there are a couple of well-played Luiz Bonfa pieces ("Samba De Orpheu" and "The Theme from 'Black Orpheus'") that cashed in on the bossa nova craze of the time as well as three chestnuts from the standard repertoire. Hall's guitar artistry is a perfect foil for Desmond's cool, precise playing, giving these performances the feel of a pleasant chamber music recital. Any major artist with more than one album out on a label almost automatically provides fodder for the "Best of" monster. There should be a law mandating that music companies must state on the packaging that such and such a compilation is selected only from recordings made for that particular label. With that caveat given, the selections on *The Best of Paul Desmond* 🎵🎵🎵 (CTI/Columbia, 1990, prod. Creed Taylor) come from Desmond's association with Creed Taylor and his label, CTI. The sound is good and the personnel includes guitarists Gabor Szabo and Ed Bickert, drummers Connie Kay and Jack DeJohnette, bassist Ron Carter, and Bob James on keyboards. While not as comfortable sounding as the recordings Desmond made with Jim Hall, there are still some good performances here, including "Skylark", "Nuages," and a slightly harder edged "Take Ten" than what appeared on the Bluebird release.

what to buy next: The only reason *Polka Dots and Moonbeams* 🎵🎵🎵 (Bluebird, 1992, prod. GeorgeAvakian) isn't in the "must get" category lies with the brevity of the album. Four cuts have been trimmed from the original release, which means that this album barely tops the half hour mark. Desmond, Hall, and Kay are back, with the bass chores being split between Eugene Wright, Gene Cherico, and Percy Heath. All the recordings are mid-1960s cover versions of standards, including the title tune, "Easy Living," and "Bewitched." Despite the short shrift in playing time, this is a wonderful collection. *Like Someone in Love* 🎵🎵🎵 (Telarc, 1992, prod. John Snyder) offers a nice aural snapshot of Desmond and his Canadian-based quartet (Ed Bickert on guitar, Don Thompson on bass, and drummer, Jerry Fuller) in a concert setting. The playing is relaxed but not sloppy, with everybody floating comfortably in a simpatico groove. Bickert's comping and soloing is strong and subtle even if it won't erase memories of the Desmond/Hall team. This is the same group and location that (a few months later)

PAUL DESMOND
(WITH GERRY MULLIGAN)

song "The Way You Look Tonight"
album *Two of a Mind*
(RCA, 1962/1996)
instrument Alto saxophone

Monster Solo

figured in a wonderful (now out of print) double album called *The Paul Desmond Quartet Live*.

best of the rest:

The Paul Desmond Quintet/Quartet 🎵🎵 (OJC, 1956/1992)
Late Lament 🎵🎵🎵 (Bluebird, 1962/1987)
Desmond Blue 🎵🎵🎵 (RCA, 1962/1997)
Easy Living 🎵🎵🎵 (Bluebird 1964/1990)
(With the Modern Jazz Quartet) *Paul Desmond & the Modern Jazz Quartet* 🎵🎵🎵 (Columbia, 1971/1993)
Skylark 🎵🎵🎵 (CTI/CBS, 1973/1997)
Pure Desmond 🎵🎵🎵 (CTI/CBS, 1974/1987)

worth searching for: There was a limited-edition box set from Mosaic that contained all the Paul Desmond/Jim Hall recordings from 1959–65 and was mastered better than the snippets released so far by RCA/Bluebird. It would also be nice if the *Paul Desmond Quartet Live* album recorded in Toronto, Canada (and released through Horizon/A&M) showed up on CD someday.

influences:

◄◄ Lester Young, Lee Konitz

►► Julius Hemphill, Anthony Braxton

Garaud MacTaggart

Al Di Meola

Born July 22, 1954, in Jersey City, NJ.

A second-generation fusion trailblazer much like his fusion forefathers, Al Di Meola has refused to be pigeonholed in the jazz/rock genre. He was barely 20 when he became a guitar hero in 1974 by replacing Bill Connors in Chick Corea's high profile group Return to Forever. One of the guitar's most proficient players, Di Meola awed fans with his tremendous technique, so much so he won *Guitar Player*'s best Jazz Guitarist Award five years in a row and is a member of the magazine's "Gallery of Greats." Heavily influenced by Larry Coryell and John McLaughlin, Di Meola followed their lead by using high-speed single-note runs and incorporated flamenco and classical elements in his playing. However, unlike Coryell or McLaughlin, he had little variation in his speed, so while his runs sounded impressive, detractors claimed he was merely running up and down the fretboard with no musical purpose. To that end, some of his early songs are mechanical sounding and do lack the fire of Return to Forever, Mahavishnu Orchestra, or Lifetime. However, part of this could be attributed to the fact that Di Meola never had a great band after Return to Forever broke up in 1976. While his musicians were all solid axemen, they never really pushed him. It's therefore not surprising that the songs that brought out his best musicianship featured guest appearances by Chick Corea and Paco de Lucia.

In 1980 Di Meola teamed up with John McLaughlin and Paco de Lucia to form the legendary Guitar Trio. Noted for pure technical virtuosity and showmanship, their tour and first album were filled with excellent musicianship. McLaughlin and de Lucia proved to be an inspiration as they got more than just notes out of Di Meola. It was after the trio's 1983 tour that Di Meola's recorded work started to show less flame-throwing and more musical ideas. With his 1985 releases *Cielo e Terra* and *Soaring Through a Dream* Di Meola used acoustic and electric guitars in a more melodic and atmospheric style. Since that turning point, Di Meola has continued to expand his musical direction through explorations of world music, Astor Piazzolla's tango repertoire, and the occasional fusion effort. He reunited with the Guitar Trio for an album and tour in 1996 that saw all three men still at the top of their game, though it regrettably will probably be the last time the three play together. Di Meola remains a tremendous technician, but his playing continues to mature beyond the fusion speed racer, though he can still be one on occasion.

what to buy: *Friday Night in San Francisco* ♪♪♪♪ (Columbia, 1981, prod. John McLaughlin, Al Di Meola, Paco de Lucia) shows the fire-breathing acoustic guitar trio of Al Di Meola, John McLaughlin, and Paco de Lucia tearing down the house on December 5, 1980 with their mind-blowing techniques. Yet while this concert is a guitar hero worshiper's dream—complete with awesome duels and clever quotes—it is the musicianship that stands out within the flurries of notes. This may really be the first place on record that Di Meola showed he was more than just an axemaster. Di Meola has dismissed *Passion, Grace & Fire* ♪♪♪♪ (Columbia, 1983, prod. John McLaughlin, Al Di Meola, Paco de Lucia) in recent interviews and that's a shame, because the fact is McLaughlin and de Lucia got more out of him on this record than any of the "hot" studio musicians he worked with during his Columbia days. "Orient Blue Suite" is one of Di Meola's best compositions and the trio's performance is typically top-notch. The third trio album with McLaughlin and de Lucia, *The Guitar Trio* ♪♪♪♪ (Verve, 1996, prod. John McLaughlin, Al Di Meola, Paco de Lucia) has less dueling than their first two, but the technique is still dazzling. What this lacks in high-speed chases, it makes up for in interplay and sophistication. The three always had good musical chemistry, but what's surprising is that after over a decade apart (save for a track on John McLaughlin's *The Promise*, which inspired this release), their chemistry actually sounded better.

what to buy next: With Jan Hammer, Steve Gadd, Mingo Lewis, Anthony Jackson, and Victor Godsey in tow, *Tour de Force "Live"* ♪♪♪ (CBS, prod. Al Di Meola) is probably the best of Di Meola's early fusion efforts. The musicians connect here better than on many of Di Meola's more antiseptic studio recordings. Like most of his recordings from this period, it is inconsistent, but when it is hot, it burns.

what to avoid: On *Scenario* ♪♪ (Columbia, 1983, prod. Dennis MacKay), Al goes commercial with mixed results.

best of the rest:
Land of the Midnight Sun ♪♪♪ (Columbia, 1976)
Elegant Gypsy ♪♪♪ (Columbia, 1977)

Casino 🎵🎵🎵🎵 (Columbia, 1978)
Spendido Hotel 🎵🎵🎵 (Columbia, 1980)
Electric Rendezvous 🎵🎵🎵 (Columbia, 1982)
Di Meola Plays Piazzolla 🎵🎵🎵 (Bluemoon, 1996)

influences:

⏪ John McLaughlin, Larry Coryell, Allan Holdsworth, Jeff Beck, Bill Connors, Astor Piazzolla

⏩ Yngwie Malmsteen, Tony MacAlpine, Bireli Lagrene

Paul MacArthur

Walt Dickerson

Born in 1931, in Philadelphia, PA.

As mysterious as he wants to be, vibist Walt Dickerson, like Wayne Shorter, seems to prefer not recording by choice, although when he does, it's usually in a flurry of activity. What he has ended up with is a body of work with nary a clunker and an influence on the instrument as great as Bobby Hutcherson, whom he anticipated although he's less well known. Dickerson has been called the Coltrane of his instrument, much as Larry Young (who, tellingly, also recorded an LP titled *Unity*) is the Coltrane of the organ. That is, he has come to symbolize the Quest, and his playing often possesses an otherworldly quality. A musician of many contradictions, Dickerson's use of two mallets instead of the normal four has, oddly, only led to a greater harmonic exploration. Likewise, his particularly hard and metallic touch creates great clouds of overtones, and he often sounds as if he's emerging from the mists (into a solid form). A bit of a fuss was raised when he first appeared in the early 1960s, but his inactivity has kept him a cult figure, and perhaps drugs were involved as he seems to have recorded a lot in the Netherlands (or it could merely be that Nils Winther dug him). He has developed close relationships with drummer Andrew Cyrille, bassist Richard Davis, and Sun Ra, with whom he recorded two sublime LPs of duets (and often helped find work in his scuffling early days in New York City). Dickerson still occasionally gigs around Philadelphia, but hasn't recorded in several years. When he does, it will no doubt be in the same modest vein he has pursued in the past, and many can't wait.

what to buy: Lobby Verve to re-release *Impressions of a Patch of Blue* 🎵🎵🎵🎵 (MGM, 1965), a perfect LP that changes hands for a pretty penny nowadays. Sun Ra had a knack for turning pox into gold, and Jerry Goldsmith's manipulative score is barely noticeable under all the art. Dickerson and Ra are perfect compliments (vibe sets are often muddled by piano) and

an enormous sense of search and drama is created from a minimalist approach. Bassist Bob Cunningham keeps the low end admirably in balance. Also, Roger Blank on drums. Whoever came up with the stupid idea for this (probably someone at Audio Fidelity, the Roger Corman of the record industry) set in motion an accidental masterpiece, one of the five greatest vibes albums of all time. Only Milt Jackson's work with John Lewis rivals Dickerson's vibe mesh with piano, and he certainly knows how to pick a band—pianist Andrew Hill, drummer Andrew Cyrille, and bassist George Tucker—for *To My Queen* 🎵🎵🎵🎵 (New Jazz, 1962, prod. Esmond Edwards). The title track is his most famous composition (revisited on the good, but inferior *Revisited*). As Dickerson wanders off while Hill worries a phrase in his manner, one can feel the earth spinning on its axis as it revolves around the sun. Cyrille possess an aggressive patience, and he knows Dickerson's music inside and out. *Peace* 🎵🎵🎵🎵 (SteepleChase, 1976, prod. Nils Winther), a set of duets, is everything that could be hoped for.

what to buy next: *Divine Gemini* 🎵🎵🎵🎵 (SteepleChase, 1977, prod. Nils Winther) and *Tenderness* 🎵🎵🎵🎵 (SteepleChase, 1977, prod. Nils Winther), both recorded with Richard Davis, have been combined into a single CD under the title *Dialogue* (and not quite on the same level of Bobby Hutcherson's LP of the same name). Like most of Dickerson's oeuvre, modest and accurate. *Relativity* 🎵🎵🎵🎵 (New Jazz, 1962, prod. Esmond Edwards) is half standards, and they work with no small measure of sonorous support from former Monk bassist Ahmed Abdul-Malik. The recording features Cyrille again, along with Austin Crowe's competent piano. Though Dickerson's second pairing with Sun Ra doesn't reach as deeply as the first (I sort of wish he'd whipped out his Astro-Infinity Space Organ), *Visions* 🎵🎵🎵🎵 (SteepleChase, 1978, prod. Nils Winther) is easily available and you can really hear their thought processes at work as each responds to the other. An improvisation textbook, really.

the rest:
This Is Walt Dickerson! 🎵🎵🎵🎵 (Prestige, 1961)
A Sense of Direction 🎵🎵🎵🎵 (New Jazz, 1961)
Jazz Impressions of Lawrence of Arabia 🎵🎵🎵🎵 (Audio Fidelity, 1963)
Tell Us Only the Beautiful Things 🎵🎵🎵🎵 (Whynot, 1975)
Serendipity 🎵🎵🎵🎵 (SteepleChase, 1976)
Shades of Love 🎵🎵🎵🎵 (SteepleChase, 1978)
To My Queen Revisited 🎵🎵🎵 (SteepleChase, 1978)
To My Son 🎵🎵🎵🎵 (SteepleChase, 1978)
Landscape with Open Door 🎵🎵🎵🎵 (SteepleChase, 1978)
I Hear You John 🎵🎵🎵🎵 (SteepleChase, 1979)
Life Rays 🎵🎵🎵🎵 (Soul Note, 1982)

worth searching for: Cyrille and Edgar Bateman ratchet around on double drum sets as pianist Walter Davis plays bop on *Unity* ♫♫♫♫ (Audio Fidelity, 1964), which is all the more modern for sounding a bit schizo.

influences:

⏪ Milt Jackson, John Coltrane

⏩ Khan Jamal, Bill Ware, Damon Choice

D. Strauss

Whit Dickey

Born May 28, 1954, in New York, NY.

Drummer Whit Dickey graduated from Bennington College, where he studied under drummer Milford Graves and in ensemble courses taught by Bill Dixon in the Black Music Department. He then attended New England Conservatory, where his main focus was studying composition with Hank Usnetsky. He has worked at length with Matthew Shipp, Rob Brown, David S. Ware, and Joe Morris, all of whom he has recorded with. Graves, something of a mentor to him (as to so many free drummers on the New York scene), is the clearest influence on his playing, which is often stark and abstract and always offers a punctuating counterpoint to the other instruments' lines.

what's available: Dickey's only album as a leader, *Transonic* ♫♫♫♫ (AUM Fidelity, 1998, prod. Whit Dickey, Steven Joerg), is a trio with Rob Brown (alto sax, flute) and Chris Lightcap (bass). It focuses on his composing; only two tracks, "Second Skin" and "Kinesis," out of eight are group improvisations. On either haltingly lyrical or busily uptempo tracks, Dickey favors tricky, asymmetrical lines that are more like motivic cells than full-blown melodies. Of course, it helps that Brown, a fine player and frequent collaborator with Dickey, skillfully develops the leader's material as he expands upon it in his solos. Dickey's skittering pulses sometimes suggest an extension of post-bop, and he swings more now than he did earlier in his career, though stylistically he remains proudly "outside."

influences:

⏪ Milford Graves, Elvin Jones, Billy Higgins, Steve McCall

⏩ Susie Ibarra

Steve Holtje

Digable Planets

Formed 1991, in Washington, DC.

Butterfly, vocals; Doodlebug/Knowledge, vocals; Ladybug/Mecca, vocals.

Revolutionary in song and soul, this gender-mixed trio helped revitalize rap during one of its most daunting stages of stagnation. But it wasn't necessarily that the Digable Planets did something new. In fact, in classic hip-hop tradition, their genius comes in doing something *old*. In the early 1990s, that meant integrating be-bop flavor into an increasingly fragmented music scene. Digging into the crates for jazz samples and adopting '60s communitarianism while articulating it all to hip-cat syncopation, the Digable Planets earned a Grammy and briefly diverted attention away from hip-hop's creative slump. The group, which was conceived while its members were still college students, had found both a modern way to make Miles Davis important, and, to the surprise of some, a receptive audience spanning the rap savant to the average MTV viewer. A year after their debut, they dropped a less experimental follow-up, favoring nationalism and spartan soundscapes. The catchy loops and hooks that made their first effort so accessible were lost in the face of a decidedly message-oriented project. Nevertheless, an aura of progressive '60s coolness—mainly lyrical—emanates from the Brooklyn-based clan so artistically ahead (and behind) the times.

what to buy: *Reachin' (A New Refutation of Time and Space)* ♫♫♫♫ (Pendulum/Elektra, 1993, prod. various) brings the Digable Planets—and thereby jazz-hop—into the national spotlight with a coffee-house anthem built around samples of Art Blakey and the Jazz Messengers. "Rebirth of Slick (Cool Like Dat)" orders a call for change—musically through buoyant horns, and verbally through beatnik rhymes, which accurately boast "the Puba of the styles, like Miles, my man" over a descending bass riff. Most of the album follows stylistic suit, with rhymes either celebrating community pride or drifting into politics. "La Femme Fetal" even offers a hip-hop perspective on the pro-life lobby.

the rest:

Blowout Comb ♫♫♫♫ (Pendulum/EMI, 1994)

influences:

⏪ Miles Davis, Gang Starr, De La Soul, A Tribe Called Quest, Dream Warriors

⏩ Fugees, Camp Lo

Corey Takahashi

Joe Diorio

Born August 6, 1936, in Waterbury, CT.

Although he has a bold spirit and is equally at home in boppish and free-form expressions, guitarist Joe Diorio is an exceptionally talented player who has been mostly overlooked by mainstream jazz enthusiasts. Diorio began his career during the 1960s based in Chicago where he performed with Sonny Stitt, Eddie Harris, and Bennie Green. He moved to Miami from 1968–1977 where he performed with Stan Getz, Ira Sullivan, Stanley Turrentine, Freddie Hubbard, and others, then relocated to Los Angeles where he freelanced and began gaining a reputation as a notable teacher. He was one of the founding instructors at the Guitar Institute of Technology in Hollywood, but left when school management shifted away from jazz. Diorio currently teaches at the University of Southern California. He tours extensively and has conducted jazz guitar seminars throughout the United States, Europe, and Brazil. In addition to a series of albums as leader for the RAM label in the late 1980s and throughout the 1990s, Diorio has released instructional videos and books. He is also an accomplished artist who creates works in watercolors, charcoal, and ink. In 1998, Diorio spent the first three months of the year touring Italy, France, and Switzerland. Diorio has his own website where you'll find information about his current activities.

what to buy: *The Breeze and I* 𝄞𝄞𝄞𝄞 {RAM Records, 1994, prod. Raimondo Meli Lupi) is an airy, melodious session that pairs the guitarist with Ira Sullivan, a multi-faceted musician who plays flute, alto flute, soprano/alto saxophones, and percussion, all with expertise, passion and sweet harmonies. Diorio accompanies with rhythm guitar, sometimes with walking lines, and renders plump-toned, warm solos. It's an uplifting, soothing session geared for listeners to kick back and forget woes and just let the calm moods of the beautiful ballads wash over you. This is an anti-frantic album featuring lush and lovely standards such as "I Wish You Love," "Beautiful Love," "Day by Day," and other tunes. After a few contemplative releases in a row, you begin to wonder if Diorio can swing a phrase, or budge himself out of his pensive mode. Recorded in the same Pennsylvania studio the day before his session with Ira Sullivan, *More Than Friends* 𝄞𝄞𝄞𝄞 (RAM, 1994, prod. Raimondo Meli Lupi) is an impassioned 10-tune session of standards and originals by Diorio, bassist Steve LaSpina, and drummer Steve Bagby made while they were all assembled for the 13th Central Pennsylvania Jazz Festival (in June, 1993). Swinging versions of "Just Friends" and "The Man I Love," along with Diorio's buoyant original "Blues for Jim Hall" and the freely improvised "The

Owl and the Bridge," contribute to the success of this album. Each musician offers a solo performance: LaSpina goes solo on "Eclipse," Bagby on his polyrhythmic "Drums Solo," and Diorio on a four-minute spontaneous improv on "Lovely Afternoon." This is Diorio's best session to date for the RAM label. Diorio does it again, generating excitement as he coleads a quartet with trombonist Hal Crook on *Narayani* 𝄞𝄞𝄞𝄞 (RAM, 1997, prod. Raimondo Meli Lupi), a 10-tune set of mostly originals by the leaders recorded in Italy on February 28 and March 1, 1994. Crook's playing matches Diorio's for its warmth and melodiousness, and with the same rhythm team from his album *More Than Friends*, Diorio is obviously relaxed and comfortable as he and his cohorts weave through the varying tempos of their original works. Diorio and Crook act often as if they were *both* frontline horns, locked in blended unity and breaking out with energetic trades. This is a unique and well-crafted session with the musicians remaking popular favorites such as "Because of You," "Darn That Dream," "I'll Be Seeing You," and Miles Davis's "Solar."

what to buy next: Joe Diorio's first session for the Italian label, RAM records, and perhaps his most pensive, *Double Take* 𝄞𝄞𝄞𝄞 (RAM, 1993, prod. Raimondo Meli Lupi) was recorded live with bassist Riccardo Del Fra during a 1992 tour of several cities in Italy. It's a gorgeous, lyrical and relaxed collection of six standards (including two takes of Gershwin's "Summertime") and the closing piece, Diorio's original, "Chetadananda." Well worth hearing, Diorio's original is a freely improvised piece that gives both players expanding room; Del Fra finally picks up his bow for some arco work as Diorio romps with dazzling artistry through his mellow, deep-toned, well-crafted solos. After hearing Diorio's playing for 74 minutes on this CD, you'll be convinced of his technical expertise, and your stress should be eased away. *We Will Meet Again* 𝄞𝄞𝄞𝄞 (RAM, 1993) is a lovely solo guitar album of 14 tunes (including five originals) that demonstrates how well Diorio devises counter melodies to accompany himself, picking the melody line while creating complex harmonies underneath. With such fine technical expertise and warmth, he delivers graceful renderings of classics such as "Summertime," "Lover Man," "All the Things You Are," and the title tune, a Bill Evans composition. Diorio also engages the listener with his brief, but pleasant, original vignettes.

the rest:

(With Goodrick) *Rare Birds* 𝄞𝄞𝄞𝄞 (RAM, 1993)
To Jobim with Love 𝄞𝄞𝄞𝄞 (RAM, 1996)

influences:

◀◀ Jim Hall

Nancy Ann Lee

Dirty Dozen Brass Band

Formed 1979, in New Orleans, LA.

Gregory Davis, trumpet, vocals, percussion; Efrem Towns, trumpet; Charles Joseph (1979–91), trombone; Revert Andrews (1992–present), trombone, percussion; Kevin Harris, tenor saxophone, vocals, percussion; Roger Lewis, baritone and soprano saxophones, percussion; Kirk Joseph (1979–91), Sousaphone; Keith Anderson (1992–94), Sousaphone, trombone; Julius McKee (1995–present) Sousaphone, acoustic and electric basses; Jenell Marshall, drums; Lionel Paul Batiste Jr., drums; Raymond Weber (1991), drums; Terence Higgins (1995–present) drums, vocals; Richard Knox (keyboards).

The Dirty Dozen Brass Band grew out of young trumpeter Leroy Jones's Hurricane Brass Band, which included his St. Augustine High classmate Gregory Davis. After Jones left the group, it became the Tornado Brass Band. When it merged with a percussion group, the DDBB was born. Struggling for work on the Crescent City's crowded brass band scene, the players' love for everything from Duke Ellington and Charlie Parker to James Brown helped them forge a new style in which the traditional favorites were augmented by such rocking tunes as "Night Train." When the group incorporated such material into its public repertoire, brass band traditionalists were not amused, but audiences (whether in parades or at clubs) appreciated the newer songs, and soon Sousaphone player Kirk Joseph's funky basslines became influential on the next generation of brass bands. The group found a national audience after Columbia signed it and released four albums (plus a compilation). A reliance on album concepts and guest vocalist, whether New Orleans legends such as Danny Barker and Dr. John or rock stars such as Elvis Costello, continued to make the group controversial in its hometown. Finally the group dropped "Brass Band" from its name and expanded its instrumentation to include keyboards, bass, and a trapset drummer at the same time it switched to indie rock label Mammoth; its Mammoth debut includes outright funk cuts.

what to buy: It's hard to go wrong playing Jelly Roll Morton tunes, and *Jelly* ✹✹✹✹ (Columbia, 1993, prod. Scott Billington) gets a slight nod over the band's other energetic albums thanks to the undeniable quality of the material. New Orleans institution Danny Barker, who played guitar with Morton, adds to the historic aura here with between-songs stories. The

rowdy octet doesn't dim their energy just because they're playing practically sacred material, though, romping through such classics as "Milenberg Joys," "Wolverine Blues," and "Kansas City Stomp" with the same unbridled enthusiasm for reworking the music as on their other albums.

what to buy next: *Voodoo* ✹✹✹✹ (Columbia, 1989, prod. Scott Billington) was the DDBB's major-label debut, and they pull out all the stops aiming for national popularity, with guests Dr. John and Dizzy Gillespie singing and playing on, respectively, "It's All over Now" and "Oop Pop a Dah" (on "Moose the Mooche," Branford Marsalis sticks to playing tenor sax). There's even a cover of Stevie Wonder's "Don't Drive Drunk." The mood is fun and the music is funky.

the rest:
My Feet Can't Fail Me Now ✹✹✹ (George Wein Collection/Concord, 1984)
Live: Mardi Gras in Montreux ✹✹✹✹ (Rounder, 1985)
The New Orleans Album ✹✹✹ (Columbia, 1990)
Open Up . . . Whatcha Gonna Do for the Rest of Your Life ✹✹✹ (Columbia, 1991)
Ears to the Wall ✹✹ (Mammoth, 1996)
This Is Jazz #30 ✹✹✹ (Columbia, 1997)

influences:

◀◀ Olympia Brass Band, Eureka Brass Band, Dukes of Dixieland, Parliament

▶▶ Rebirth Brass Band, Treme Brass Band

Walter Faber

Diva

Formed 1993.

Sherrie Maricle, drums; Nicki Parrott, bass; Jill McCarron, piano; Laura Dreyer, alto saxophone; Jenny Hill, alto saxophone; Cynthia Mullis, tenor saxophone; Grazia DiGiorgio, tenor saxophone; Claire Daly, baritone saxophone; Lolly Bienenfeld, trombone; Deborah Weisz, trombone; Leslie Havens, bass trombone; Liesl Whitaker, lead trumpet; Barbara Laronga, trumpet; Pam Fleming, trumpet; Jami Dauber, trumpet.

The 15-musician, all-female band Diva draws from a pool of about 120 players from all over the United States, many of them graduates of college music programs at Berklee College of Music, the University of North Texas, the New England Conservatory of Music, and elsewhere. Based in New York City, the spirited Diva band—a hard-swinging unit in the tradition of the Buddy Rich, Count Basie, and Woody Herman orchestras—plays contemporary, mainstream big band charts arranged by band members and renowned musicians Tommy Newsom, Michael Abene, John LaBarbera, and Jerry Dodgion. Many of the band members, professional musicians with years of experience, have performed with other big bands such as the Thad Jones/Mel Lewis Orchestra, Toshiko Akiyoshi, and Doc Severinsen.

Forming the band was the idea of Stanley Kay, a 50-year music business veteran and former manager/relief drummer for the Buddy Rich Big Band, who conducted a band in 1990 where freelance drummer Maricle was playing. Impressed with her skill, he wondered if there existed other women musicians of similar caliber and began a nationwide audition that resulted in Diva's formation by Kay, Maricle, and John LaBarbera. Diva's premiere concert was in March 1993. The band now tours extensively, playing prestigious U.S. venues such as Carnegie Hall, the Smithsonian Institute, the Kennedy Center, New York's Blue Note, the Playboy Jazz Festival at the Hollywood Bowl, and others, in addition to regular New York club gigs and appearances at festivals abroad.

what's available: Diva's debut album, *Something's Coming* ♫♫♫♫ (Perfect Sound, 1995, prod. Stanley Kay), features 11 deep-grooving tunes, classics such as "You Stepped out of a Dream," "Caravan," and more, including tunes by John LaBarbera, Stanley Kay, and Sherrie Maricle, and a lush rendering of Hoagy Carmichael's "Stardust," which gives soloists Liesl Sagartz Whitaker on trumpet and Virginia Mahew (tenor sax) room to shine. Newsom's arrangement of "Ding Dong the Witch Is Dead" is a ferociously swinging, fun-filled romp that features fine soloing and section work, with a brief spotlight on the rhythm section. Diva delivers this modern, tight session with vitality and precision, offering colorful, textured arrangements, tight teamwork, and masterful solos. Maricle commendably drives the big band. With more than half of the personnel returning, Diva's second album, *Leave It to Diva* ♫♫♫♫ (self-released, 1997, prod. Sherrie Maricle, Tommy Newsom, John LaBarbera), features equally hard-swinging grooves, spectacular solos, more focus on the rhythm section, and brassy, tight horn work on longtime favorites such as "Trolley Song," "Makin' Whoopee," "All of You," "Begin the Beguine," "Them There Eyes" (the latter, arranged by Scott Whitfield, features spectacular baritone sax soloing by Claire Daley), and other classics, some arranged by band members. Newsom's arrangement of "Inka Dinka Doo" is a lighthearted pleaser that tips the hat to the late composer Jimmy Durante who made it his TV theme song. You can't go wrong with either album. Both CDs feature ambitious arrangements by some of the best in the business, and these women players definitely meet the challenges.

influences:

◀◀ Buddy Rich Orchestra, Count Basie Orchestra, Woody Herman Orchestra

Nancy Ann Lee

Bill Dixon

Born October 5, 1925 in Nantucket, MA.

Bill Dixon has long been the supreme groundbreaker of the trumpet avant-garde, conjuring a vast array of nuanced sounds never heard before but much copied since. There are only 19 items on his discography, including his appearances on other people's albums, as his main focuses have been the process of creating music (rather than its preservation) and education. His importance to the free jazz movement results from providing the impetus behind bands or organizations of historical importance. Dixon and Archie Shepp co-founded the seminal group New York Contemporary Five in 1963, though Dixon didn't record with the group. In 1964 Dixon organized the famous four-day concert series billed as the October Revolution in Jazz, which showcased 20 avant-garde jazz groups that had largely been unable to find bookings on the New York City club scene. He followed up by forming (with charter members Cecil Taylor, Sun Ra, Shepp, George Russell, Carla Bley, and Paul Bley) the Jazz Composers' Guild to promote jazz styles not being served by the American Federation of Musicians. In 1968 Dixon began teaching at Bennington College, in Vermont, a position he held until 1996, establishing a respected Black Music department. He has also been a guest professor or lecturer at the University of Wisconsin, Ohio State, George Washington University, Columbia University, and more. In 1984 he was the recipient of a BMI Jazz Pioneer Award.

Dixon was a producer for the Savoy label in the early 1960s, and it was on Savoy that his first two releases appeared. In 1966 he played on the famed Cecil Taylor album *Conquistador*. He can also be heard on one short track on *The Marzette Watts Ensemble*, a 1968 Savoy release. A Dixon-led 1967 album on RCA, *Intents and Purposes: The Jazz Artistry of Bill Dixon*, is long-gone from circulation, as are all his 1970s recordings, which appeared on small (usually European) labels. He made a guest appearance with fellow trumpeter Franz Koglmann in 1976 on one track of an Austrian album. Fortunately, the last two decades find Dixon's catalog in much better shape. Except for one 1980 concert performance on an Italian magazine's compilation of various artists' Verona Jazz Festival appearances, all of his 1980s and 1990s work was recorded for Soul Note, which admirably keeps its entire catalog in print. Dixon, something of a Renaissance man, studied painting at Boston University and is a talented artist whose work, beyond gracing his Soul Note album covers, has also been commissioned for events such as that in Villeurbanne, France, in 1994 at the Union Regionale pour le Developpement de la Lithographie d'Art, where he spent two months in residence.

what to buy: Despite the wide span of time between their release dates, *Vade Mecum* ♫♫♫♫ (Soul Note, 1994, prod. Giovanni Bonandrini) and *Vade Mecum II* ♫♫♫♫ (Soul Note, 1997, prod. Giovanni Bonandrini) were recorded at the same three-day session in August 1993. Dixon's broad sonic palette has plenty of room around it, which, with the contrasting approaches of bassists William Parker and Barry Guy, plus Tony Oxley's sensitive splashes of percussion, produces a masterpiece of implication and understatement. On the classic *Son of Sisyphus* ♫♫♫♫ (Soul Note, 1990, prod. Giovanni Bonandrini) Dixon plays both piano and trumpet with an unusual backing of double bass (rising star Mario Pavone), drums (longtime cohort Laurence Cook), and tuba (John Buckingham), exploring subtle textural contrasts rarely heard in any context. The music's cool beauty and somber gravity convey much with economical means of expression.

what to buy next: *In Italy, Volume I* ♫♫♫♫ (Soul Note, 1980, prod. Giovanni Bonandrini) and *In Italy, Volume II* ♫♫♫♫ (Soul Note, 1981, prod. Giovanni Bonandrini) feature another unusual lineup; the band has not only Dixon on trumpet (he again also plays piano) but also Arthur Brooks and Stephen Haynes, along with Stephen Horenstein (tenor and baritone saxophones), Alan Silva (bass), and Freddie Waits (drums). Dixon's spare sonic sculptures highlight timbre contrasts of fragile beauty. Also of interest are the two fat CD booklets, containing between them a lengthy and fascinating 1980 interview with the highly articulate Dixon.

the rest:
November 1981 ♫♫♫ (Soul Note, 1982)
Thoughts ♫♫♫ (Soul Note, 1987)

worth searching for: Dixon's early, out-of-print LPs are necessary for a complete picture of his style. *Archie Shepp–Bill Dixon Quartet* ♫♫♫♫♫ (Savoy, 1962, prod. Bill Dixon, Archie Shepp), which was reissued many years ago as *Peace* by the French label BYG, finds Dixon (and Shepp) at an early stage playing more "inside," though at the time this was still fairly avant-

garde. There are four tracks. "Trio" is modal jazz, more low-key than, say, the Coltrane Quartet of the same period, though Dixon plays more assertively than his later style. "Peace" is the Ornette Coleman tune, and Dixon's ties to Don Cherry become clear, though his tone is clearer and stronger. "Quartet" is an uptempo swinger that could qualify as bebop, and Dixon sounds superb as he spins out flowing lines in a style reminiscent at first of Miles Davis, though he goes more outside in the middle of his solo. "Somewhere," the Leonard Bernstein tune from *West Side Story,* has its rhythms squared off a bit. Dixon plays a tender solo, while Shepp gets more raucous. *7-tette* ♫♫♫♫ (Savoy, 1962) is Dixon's half of a split LP (the other side is Shepp and the New York Contemporary Five, though not including Dixon). BYG picked up this one too, retitling it *Consequences*. The recorded sound is a bit flat and distant, but the music is fascinating. The two Dixon compositions are tightly arranged in the style of Gil Evans's contemporary work, with the low-pitched instruments defining the sound. Joining the trumpeter are Howard Johnson (tuba, baritone), Ken McIntyre (alto saxophone, oboe), George Barrow (tenor saxophone), bassists Dave Izenson and Hal Dodson, and swinging drummer Howard McRae. Dixon is the featured soloist on the Tony Oxley Celebration Orchestra's *The Enchanted Messenger* ♫♫♫♫ (Soul Note, 1996, prod. George Gruntz), recorded live at the Berlin Jazz Fest. The single lengthy piece consists of 19 "mobiles" that unfold kaleidoscopically, their timbral variety especially enhanced by Phil Minton's imaginative vocalese and probing solos by Dixon and trombonist Johannes Bauer.

influences:

◄◄ Rex Stewart, Don Cherry, Cecil Taylor

►► Herb Robertson, Dave Douglas, Steve Bernstein

Steve Holtje

DJ Krush

While DJ Shadow was making noise stateside with a decidedly progressive brand of abstract hip-hop, his eventual MoWax labelmate DJ Krush was doing likewise in Japan, although Krush's warm soundscapes lean on jazz much harder than Shadow's moody breakbeat collages.

what to buy: Guest appearances by jazz-minded MCs CL Smooth, Guru, and the Roots' Black Thought and Malik B. are a nice touch, but *Meiso* ♫♫♫♫ (MoWax, 1996, prod. DJ Krush) is clearly Krush's show, as he concocts a series of soothing, dynamic ambient soundscapes that rarely meander. Fellow abstract hip-hop heavyweight DJ Shadow emerges from the album's shadows, too, for the stunning "Duality."

what to buy next: Old-school beats and older-school horn lines mark the improvisational *DJ Krush* 𝄢𝄢𝄢 (Shadow, 1995, prod. DJ Krush), on which Krush is joined by capable Japanese jazz musicians.

the rest:
MiLight 𝄢𝄢𝄢 (MoWax/ffrr/London, 1997)

influences:
◀◀ DJ Premier, Ali Shaheed Muhammad
▶▶ DJ Honda

Josh Freedom du Lac

Baby Dodds

Born Warren Dodds, December 24, 1898, in New Orleans, LA. Died February 14, 1959, in Chicago, IL.

The younger brother of clarinetist Johnny Dodds, Baby Dodds enjoyed both the classic period of the 1920s and the revival of the 1940s. He started taking drum lessons at age 14 and was soon playing in parade and dance bands with Bunk Johnson and Papa Celestin. In 1918 he joined Fate Marable's riverboat orchestra, working on the *S.S. Sidney*. After joining King Oliver's band in 1922, his career was intertwined with his brother Johnny's, including regular work with Oliver and Johnny Dodds's own bands and frequent recording sessions. Dodds was often out of music in the 1930s, working for another brother's taxi firm in Chicago. The rise of popularity of traditional jazz in the 1940s gave new life to his career, and he was able to play regularly with the bands of trumpeter Bunk Johnson and clarinetist George Lewis, as well as recording with the fine Chicago pianist Art Hodes. Dodds suffered a stroke in 1949 that restricted his ability to play in the final decade of his life. Baby Dodds is present on many of the key recordings of New Orleans-style jazz, beginning with King Oliver's Creole Jazz Band in 1923. However, the acoustic recording technology available severely restricted the use of drums in the studio, and Dodds was limited to the creative use of woodblocks and cymbals. On several recordings with Johnny in the late 1920s, Baby plays only washboard. Dodds has been generally considered the first drummer "to swing," and his drumming is an essential part of jazz in the twenties and the later revival of New Orleans-style music. His shifting rhythm patterns, inventive accents, tuning, and flamboyant use of percussion effects were to touch later stages in the music from Max Roach to the Art Ensemble

of Chicago. An autobiography *The Baby Dodds Story* by Dodds and Larry Gara (1959/1992, Louisiana State University Press) provides a fascinating look at Dodds's career and the New Orleans musical background.

what's available: Only two CDs under Baby Dodds's name are currently available. One, *Baby Dodds* 𝄢𝄢𝄢 (American Music 1945/1995, prod. Bill Russell), combines material from Bunk Johnson sessions with both a six-piece ensemble and Johnson's brass band, Dodds playing snare drum in the latter. The CD is supplemented by tapes of Dodds's conversation. The other recording is *Talking and Drum Solos, Footnotes to Jazz, Volume I* 𝄢𝄢𝄢 (Folkways, 1951/Smithsonian, 1997, prod. Moe Asch), rich in both oral history and its demonstration of the drumming patterns of traditional jazz.

worth searching for: *Bunk Johnson 1944* 𝄢𝄢𝄢 (American Music, 1995, prod. Bill Russell) shows more of Dodds's drumming on a number of traditional warhorses, including "Tiger Rag" and "Darktown Strutters' Ball." While the musicians are clearly not of the level of those Dodds worked with in the 1920s, his playing is better represented in these later recordings, and certainly easier to hear.

influences:
▶▶ Zutty Singleton, Dave Tough, George Wettling, Gene Krupa, Max Roach, Milford Graves

see also: *King Oliver, Louis Armstrong, Johnny Dodds, Bunk Johnson, Art Hodes*

Stuart Broomer

Johnny Dodds

Born April 12, 1892, in Waverley, LA. Died August 8, 1940, in Chicago, IL.

Johnny Dodds took up the clarinet at 17 and, apart from a few lessons with the New Orleans master Lorenzo Tio Jr., he was virtually self-taught on the instrument. Dodds joined the Kid Ory band in 1912 and played in it intermittently until 1919, leaving to play with Fate Marable's riverboat band in 1917. During the 1920s he enjoyed long engagements in Chicago, playing in King Oliver's Creole Jazz Band with Louis Armstrong and his brother Baby Dodds. After leaving Oliver in 1924, Dodds worked with the legendary New Orleans cornetist Freddie Keppard at Bert Kelly's Stable, eventually taking over leadership of the group and remaining there until 1930. During the 1930s he was relatively inactive musically, recording infrequently, his music passed by with changing fashions. At the time of his death he was managing a Chicago apartment building in which he had invested. Dodds appeared as a sideman on many of the most important recordings of early jazz history—King Oliver's Creole Jazz Band of 1923, the Louis Armstrong Hot Fives and Sevens, and in a trio with Jelly Roll Morton. From 1926 to 1930 he recorded in Chicago with numerous bands, whether as leader or as a sideman to associates like pianists Lil Hardin Armstrong and Jimmy Blythe and percussionist Jimmy Bertand. Dodds's abilities have been subject to wildly varying assessments, with some commentators finding his technique and rhythmic placement lacking. While Armstrong was developing a new place for the soloist in jazz, Dodds's greatest strengths belonged to the classic New Orleans polyphonic style with a balance of parts, a style apparent on his own recordings. He possessed a tremendously expressive tone, especially on blues, a fluent sense of collective improvisation, and great rhythmic drive. His own recordings are some of the finest examples of early jazz, worthy to stand beside the work of Oliver and Morton. They're frequently looser and more spirited.

what to buy: The best introduction to Dodds is *Wild Man Blues* 𝅘𝅥𝅮𝅘𝅥𝅮𝅘𝅥𝅮𝅘𝅥𝅮 (ASV/ Living Era, 1998, prod. various). It includes samples of his work under the leadership of Oliver, Armstrong, and Jelly Roll Morton, and provides a broad cross-section of the clarinetist's activities with the New Orleans Wanderers, the Chicago Footwarmers, etc. The version of "Wild Man Blues" was recorded by Dodds's Black Bottom Stompers with Louis Armstrong two weeks before Armstrong recorded it with the Hot Seven. The earlier recording heard here is more confident and accomplished than the one recorded under Armstrong's own name. Dodds's fluent soloing is especially apparent on trio tracks "Clarinet Wobble" from 1927 and "Indigo Stomp" from 1929.

what to buy next: For a fuller treatment of Dodds's great and various work from the late 1920s, there's *Johnny Dodds 1926* 𝅘𝅥𝅮𝅘𝅥𝅮𝅘𝅥𝅮𝅘𝅥𝅮 (Jazz Chronological Classics, 1991, prod. various), which includes, among much else, the existing output of the Dixieland Jug Blowers and Blythe's Washboard Ragamuffins. Despite some novelty instrumentation, these are fine bands. On the former's "Memphis Shake," Dodds soars over the jug "bass." Among the groups represented on *Johnny Dodds 1927* 𝅘𝅥𝅮𝅘𝅥𝅮𝅘𝅥𝅮𝅘𝅥𝅮 (Jazz Chronological Classics, 1991), there are four tracks each by the Black Bottom Stompers, including "Wild Man Blues," and Jimmy Bertrand's Washboard Wizards, behind whose obscure name lurks a brilliant band with Dodds, pianist Jimmy Blythe, and Louis Armstrong.

best of the rest:
Johnny Dodds 1927–1928 𝅘𝅥𝅮𝅘𝅥𝅮𝅘𝅥𝅮𝅘𝅥𝅮 (Jazz Chronological Classics, 1991)
Johnny Dodds 1928–1940 𝅘𝅥𝅮𝅘𝅥𝅮𝅘𝅥𝅮 (Jazz Chronological Classics, 1992)

Johnny Dodds & Jimmy Blythe 𝅘𝅥𝅮𝅘𝅥𝅮𝅘𝅥𝅮𝅘𝅥𝅮 (Timeless, 1994)
Johnny Dodds 1923–1940 𝅘𝅥𝅮𝅘𝅥𝅮𝅘𝅥𝅮 (Best of Jazz, 1994)
The Johnny Dodds Story 1923–1929 𝅘𝅥𝅮𝅘𝅥𝅮𝅘𝅥𝅮 (Jazz Archives, 1996)

influences:
▶▶ Jimmie Noone, George Lewis

see also: *Louis Armstrong, King Oliver, Jelly Roll Morton*

Stuart Broomer

Bill Doggett

Born February 16, 1916, in Philadelphia, PA. Died November 13, 1996, in New York, NY.

After making his initial mark as a pianist and arranger during the late '30s and '40s, most notably with bands led by Lucky Millinder and Louis Jordan, Bill Doggett followed former Jordan pianist "Wild" Bill Davis's lead by switching over to the Hammond organ. Leading his own small groups after 1952, Doggett became the most popular organist of the '50s. His combos (usually four or five pieces) boiled big-band swing and postwar R&B into a frequently imitated sound that proved ideal for three-minute jukebox records. Recording for the King label throughout the '50s, Doggett had a string of successful singles, including "Ram-Bunk-Shush," "Slow Walk," and "Rainbow Riot," but it was with "Honky Tonk," which hit Number Two on the pop charts in 1956, that Doggett made his most lasting impression. "Honky Tonk," with its loping rhythm, was one of the all-time great R&B grooves, but Doggett's groups also created schmaltzy, mellow mood music, and they remained popular up to Doggett's death. In addition to his solo legacy, he was an important arranger, working with the Ink Spots, Jimmy Rushing, and Ella Fitzgerald, whom he backed on the hit "Smooth Sailing."

what to buy: *Greatest Hits* 𝅘𝅥𝅮𝅘𝅥𝅮𝅘𝅥𝅮𝅘𝅥𝅮 (King, 1994) is a good starting point, a concise but budget-priced collection with eight of the classic '50s recordings, including "Honky Tonk," "Hold It," and "Ram-Bunk-Shush."

what to buy next: *The Right Choice* 𝅘𝅥𝅮𝅘𝅥𝅮𝅘𝅥𝅮 (After Hours, 1991, prod. Marty Duda) is on the same level as the best Jimmy McGriff CDs in the '90s. Recorded with saxophonist Bubba Brooks and drummer Bernard Purdie, Doggett grooves and stretches out on mostly newer material. *All His Hits* 𝅘𝅥𝅮𝅘𝅥𝅮𝅘𝅥𝅮 (King, 1996) is a more thorough collection of Doggett's classic '50s period on King.

what to avoid: *Dame Dreaming* 𝅘𝅥𝅮 (King, 1995) and *As You Desire Me* 𝅘𝅥𝅮 (King, 1995) are for fans of Doggett's mellow side only.

the rest:

Dance Awhile 🎵🎵 (King, 1995)

Doggett Beat for Dancing Feet 🎵🎵🎵 (King, 1995)

worth searching for: *Finger Tips* 🎵🎵 (Columbia, 1963) finds Doggett in an upbeat, soul-flavored groove on tunes like "The Worm." One of the better non-King titles, it's not yet available on CD.

influences:

◀◀ Count Basie, Fats Waller, "Wild" Bill Davis, Milt Buckner

▶▶ Hank Marr, Jimmy McGriff, Booker T. & the MG's

Dan Bindert

Eric Dolphy

Born June 20, 1928, in Los Angeles, CA. Died June 29, 1964, in Berlin, Germany.

Recording as a leader and with John Coltrane, Chico Hamilton, Ornette Coleman, Charles Mingus, Mal Waldron, and others, Eric Dolphy left an impressive legacy of imagination and versatility despite barely making it to age 36. He fortunately produced a sizeable body of work due to a prolific recording schedule, thanks at first to the Prestige label and its subsidiary New Jazz and later to European bootleggers. Dolphy crafted a distinctively angular style that extended bebop into new harmonic realms, acting as a bridge between bebop and free jazz. Besides mastering alto sax, he made bass clarinet and flute respectable jazz instruments. He and his musical cohorts, especially pianist Waldron, were among the numerous innovators in that period who extended jazz composition into new forms and structures, freeing it from the show tune/blues templates and permitting new expression. But most of all, Dolphy was an exciting and inventive improvisor.

The son of emigrants from Panama, Dolphy started out on clarinet at age seven. He first heard jazz while in junior high school, and took up alto saxophone while in high school. After spending 1950–53 in the army, he played as a leader and with Gerald Wilson and Buddy Collette around his native Los Angeles. He then achieved prominence during a year's time in the popular Chico Hamilton Quintet (1958–59), replacing Collette, and was in the band at the 1958 Newport Jazz Festival, as featured in the film *Jazz on a Summer's Day,* which includes Dolphy playing a flute solo. Dolphy then moved to New York and joined Charles Mingus's groups, working with Mingus off and on and cramming a tremendous amount of music-making into the years 1960–61. He features prominently on Ornette Cole-

man's groundbreaking 1960 album *Free Jazz.* In 1961–62 Dolphy was a semi-regular member of John Coltrane's band (he arranged most of *Africa/Brass,* and the 1961 Village Vanguard sessions feature some fine Dolphy solos); Dolphy, Coltrane, and Yusef Lateef worked together privately to expand their concepts, exploring different scales and music from other cultures.

Noted as a "clean" jazzman whose only addiction was to practicing, Dolphy's sudden death of diabetes while touring in Europe shocked the jazz world and cut short a career which, given his rapid development in the space of five years, seemed likely to take him in new and potentially influential directions beyond even the fine work he left. Though usually excellent from the standpoint of his playing, his recorded legacy often suffered on other terms. Some of his finest solos on record came with European bands below his level (though a few bands were exceptions). Dolphy's potentially finest live session found Mal Waldron wrestling with a blatantly out-of-tune piano. Much of Dolphy's better playing must be searched out on other people's record dates. It always rewards the effort.

what to buy: *Out to Lunch!* 🎵🎵🎵🎵 (Blue Note, 1964, prod. Alfred Lion) is Dolphy's most mature studio statement and finds him in the company of musicians more than capable of keeping up with him: Freddie Hubbard, Bobby Hutcherson, Richard Davis, and Tony Williams. The cool textures of Hutcherson's vibes, which opened up the sound in a way piano hadn't on Dolphy's other albums, provide the signature sound of the session. Tunes such as "Hat and Beard" (a tribute to Thelonious Monk), "Something Sweet, Something Tender," and the title track are among Dolphy's greatest creations. *Last Date* 🎵🎵🎵🎵 (Limelight, 1964/Verve, 1986, prod. Michiel de Ruyter) isn't actually the last documentation of Dolphy, but it's close. It was recorded in a Holland studio (with a small audience) while he was on his final European tour, with a fine rhythm section of Misha Mengelberg (piano), Jacques Schols (bass), and Han Bennink (drums). Mengelberg's Monkish comping in particular seems to fit Dolphy's style, and it was perhaps in acknowledgement of this that they open with Monk's "Epistrophy." The players learned three of Dolphy's tunes, including "Miss Ann," and also play a Mengelberg original and "You Don't Know What Love Is."

what to buy next: The nine-CD chronological box set *The Complete Prestige Recordings* 🎵🎵🎵 (Prestige/Fantasy, 1995, prod.

Eric Dolphy **(Archive Photos)**

Esmond Edwards, comp. prod. Eric Miller) constitutes the core of Dolphy's pre-1964 output as a leader and displays an amazing burst of creative energy. From his first album as a leader recorded April 1, 1960, through a pair of live dates in Copenhagen on September 6 and 8, 1961—under a year and a half—he was on 13 sessions yielding 17 Prestige/New Jazz albums as a leader (ten), co-leader with Ken McIntyre (one, with lots of good ideas), or featured sideman on two Oliver Nelson dates (very good) and one each for Mal Waldron (excellent), Ron Carter (interesting), and the Latin Jazz Quintet (a poor fit between guest and band), plus a date in the sax section of Eddie "Lockjaw" Davis's big band (with no Dolphy solos; even that's included to make it a truly complete set). It's possible over that short span to hear him develop in leaps and bounds, going from a good player with interesting compositional ideas that occasionally receive slightly awkward execution to a master of his instruments whose every move is fluid and organic. Though the box set is a great value (it sells for around $140; his 10 albums as a leader alone would total $120 if purchased separately), some listeners will inevitably want to economize by getting only the most crucial elements. The main priority, the monumental 1961 Five Spot club gig with the equally ill-fated Booker Little (trumpet), Waldron (piano), Richard Davis (bass), and Ed Blackwell (drums), was spread out across three LPs when issued and as separate CDs—*Eric Dolphy at the Five Spot, Volume I* ♪♪♪♪ (New Jazz, 1961), *Eric Dolphy at the Five Spot, Volume II* ♪♪♪♪ (Prestige, 1961/1964), and *Memorial Album* ♪♪♪♪ (Prestige, 1961/1964)—remains so, though it would fit comfortably on two. However one acquires it, the music is superb. Dolphy and Little are extremely complementary frontline partners, and the rhythm section is top-notch. With Dolphy and Waldron tunes in the set lists, so is the material, with "The Prophet," "Fire Waltz," and "Status Seeking" highlights. Stretching out in the club context, the players probe each piece at length, seemingly extracting every last ounce of meaning even from Little's relatively inconsequential "Bee Vamp." (All three albums are docked half a bone each because of the excrutiatingly out-of-tune piano.) And the December 1960 studio recording *Far Cry* ♪♪♪♪ (New Jazz, 1962) marked the first pairing of Dolphy and Little, with the rhythm section being Jaki Byard, Ron Carter, and Roy Haynes. The classic tunes are the title track, "Miss Ann," and Waldron's "Left Alone." Dolphy and Little play with an edge, the cry in their tones cutting right through the listener. Of the many concerts from Dolphy's European tours that have been issued posthumously, *Berlin Concerts* ♪♪♪♪ (Enja, 1961/1990, prod. Horst Weber) is the best by a slight margin, thanks to trumpeter Benny Bailey and a

fairly good rhythm section: pianist Pepsi Auer (the weak link), bassist George Joyner (a.k.a. Jamil Nasser), and drummer Buster Smith. Smith is the secret weapon, to the extent that he relentlessly stokes the fires on the uptempo numbers.

what to avoid: *Other Aspects* ♪♪ (Blue Note, 1987, prod. Eric Dolphy, James Newton) is a hodgepodge of Dolphy's private recordings from 1960 and 1962, and is strictly for Dolphy fanatics, though they will find its two unaccompanied flute solos, the alto sax duet with bassist Ron Carter, and two lengthy group improvisations fascinating and full of hints on both Dolphy's influences and his future interests.

best of the rest:
Outward Bound ♪♪♪♪ (New Jazz, 1960)
Out There ♪♪♪♪ (New Jazz, 1960)
Candid Dolphy ♪♪♪♪ (Candid, 1960–61/1989)
Here & There ♪♪♪♪♪ (Prestige, 1960–61/1965)
In Europe, Volume I ♪♪♪♪ (Prestige, 1961/1964)
In Europe, Volume II ♪♪♪♪ (Prestige, 1961/1965)
In Europe, Volume III ♪♪♪ (Prestige, 1961/1965)
Stockholm Sessions ♪♪♪♪ (Enja, 1961/1988)
Vintage Dolphy ♪♪♪ (GM, 1962–63/1995)
Naima ♪♪♪♪ (West Wind, 1964)
Unrealized Tapes ♪♪♪♪ (West Wind, 1964)
The Essential Eric Dolphy ♪♪♪♪ (Prestige, 1991)
Iron Man ♪♪♪♪ (Metrotone/Restless, 1992)
Conversations ♪♪♪♪ (Metrotone/Restless, 1992)

worth searching for: Chico Hamilton's *Gongs East!* ♪♪♪♪ (Discovery, 1958, prod. Albert Marx) is a good source for pre-New York Dolphy and has superb solos on the title track, "Tuesday at Two," and "Nature, by Emerson," among others. Ornette Coleman's *Free Jazz* ♪♪♪♪♪ (Atlantic, 1960, prod. Nesuhi Ertegun) provides the most "outside" context in which to hear Dolphy and ranks high among the most important jazz albums. Arranger George Russell's *Ezz-thetic* ♪♪♪♪ (Riverside, 1961, prod. Orrin Keepnews) finds Dolphy apparently inspired by playing in the context of the leader's "Lydian Chromatic Concept of Tonal Organization," which freed up all 12 tones of the scale for use in improvisation while still referring to blues harmony. Russell's originals and a cover of Monk's "'Round Midnight" are especially good. The John Coltrane November 1–5, 1961 gigs documented on *The Complete 1961 Village Vanguard Recordings* ♪♪♪♪ (Impulse!, 1997, prod. Bob Thiele, reissue prod. Michael Cuscuna) find Dolphy nearly the leader's match in imaginative soloing, though of course not featured so strongly. However, he has major solos on both versions of "Naima," two of the "Impressions" performances, "Brasilia," both takes on "Miles' Mode" (which Dolphy may have written), and even two versions of "Chasin' the Trane." Oliver Nelson's *Blues and the Abstract Truth* ♫♫♫♫ (Impulse!, 1961, prod. Creed Taylor) is the culmination of the path Nelson started on with his Prestige albums. Dolphy solos on all but one track. Most of all, Dolphy fans will enjoy his work on several of Charles Mingus's live albums, where he had room to stretch out in the company of superb musicians playing familiar material. Of these, *Town Hall Concert* ♫♫♫♫ (Jazz Workshop, 1964) is the best-distributed. It's practically dedicated to him, consisting of two long tracks titled "So Long Eric" and "Praying with Eric" ("Meditations for a Pair of Wirecutters" renamed) and featuring brilliant solos. A few odd edits (or bad splices?) are the only problem. (It should not be confused with a 1963 Town Hall concert now on Blue Note.) The band has Johnny Coles (trumpet), Clifford Jordan (tenor sax), Jaki Byard (piano), the leader on bass, and Dannie Richmond (drums), a sterling unit capable of building to tremendous levels of excitement, especially when they riff behind the soloist. *Live in Oslo 1964* ♫♫♫♫ (JazzUp/ New Sound Planet, 1989) is a bootleg recording from the same period. It has clear sound considering the circumstances and the time period; variable volume levels, the cymbals sometimes being higher in the mix than the piano, and the final track, "Take the 'A' Train," cutting off right after Dolphy's bass clarinet solo are flaws. The playing is inspired; personnel and the musical merits are the same as on the Town Hall album but in inferior sound. A 1960 concert at the Antibes Jazz Festival is heard on the 71-minute *Mingus at Antibes* ♫♫♫♫ (Rhino, 1994, prod. Nesuhi Ertegun) with Booker Ervin (tenor sax), Ted Curson (trumpet), and Richmond. Dolphy's alto solo on "Folk Forms No. 2" is particularly fine.

influences:

◀◀ Eureka Jazz Band, Johnny Hodges, Lloyd Reece, Charlie Parker, Thelonious Monk, Severino Gazzeloni

▶▶ John Coltrane, Yusef Lateef, Oliver Lake, Henry Threadgill, David Murray, James Newton, Donald Harrison

Steve Holtje

Lou Donaldson

Born November 1, 1926, in Badin, NC.

The bluesier aspects of Charlie Parker's playing are where Lou Donaldson found his initial inspiration. In the 1950s Donaldson could be found on recordings by Milt Jackson and Thelonious Monk in addition to working briefly with Charles Mingus, Sonny Stitt, Horace Silver, and Art Blakey before stepping out on his own as a leader. By the time the '60s rolled around, Donaldson

ERIC DOLPHY

song "The Prophet"
album *Eric Dolphy: The Complete Prestige Recordings*
(Prestige, 1961/1995)
instrument Alto saxophone

had been gravitating towards what would later be called "soul jazz," employing organists like Baby Face Willette and Big John Patton. As Donaldson entered the '70s he started creating overblown masses of studio funk that layered orchestral sounds over neo-psychedelic electronics. This trend continued through the early '70s in what was probably his most commercially successful period with hits like "Here 'Tis" and "Alligator Boogaloo." By the end of the decade Donaldson had reverted to a neo-bop phase, paying homage to Bird without abandoning some of the soulful playing that characterized his basic style.

what to buy: Unless you're a glutton for funk punishment, *The Best of Lou Donaldson Volume I* ♫♫♫♫ (Blue Note, 1993, prod. various) may be the only Donaldson album you definitely need. It covers the decade 1957–67 and charts the progression of Donaldson from bluesy bopper to rib-joint funk master. The biggest hits from this era, including the two previously mentioned, are included. The list of sidemen is pretty impressive, with such luminaries as Donald Byrd, Sonny Clark, Horace Parlan, George Benson, Wayne Shorter, and Grant Green making appearances.

what to buy next: Donaldson has fashioned a viable career for more than 40 years, which is not easy to do unless you're a shrewd judge of popular taste. *Play the Right Thing* ♪♪♪♪ (1991, Milestone, prod. Bob Porter) comes from phase three of his career. Donaldson's instincts have him heading back towards his bop roots, but he's taking along the organ underpinnings from his soul jazz years. Dr. Lonnie Smith, the organist on some of Donaldson's biggest hits (think "Alligator Boogaloo") is joined by guitarist Peter Bernstein, conga player Ralph Dorsey, and career funk session drummer Bernard Purdie. Toss in standards like "I Had the Craziest Dream" and Charlie Parker's "Marmaduke," and things start getting respectable. The one tune that doesn't quite have the punch it needs is "Harlem Nocturne," which, except for Bernstein's guitar solo, weaves along in slow motion like a blasted wino.

best of the rest:

Blues Walk ♪♪♪♪ (Blue Note, 1958)
Birdseed ♪♪♪ (Milestone, 1992)

influences:

◀◀ Charlie Parker

▶▶ Cannonball Adderley

Garaud MacTaggart

Dorothy Donegan

Born April 6, 1922, in Chicago, IL. Died May 19, 1998 in Los Angeles, CA.

On her recordings, the virtuosic pianist Dorothy Donegan always conveys an enthusiastic exuberance. Donegan capably played swing, bop, stride, and boogie-woogie styles, and often added European classical motifs or switched among various styles during a single tune. A well-schooled musician who studied classical music with various teachers from an early age, she attended the Chicago Conservatory and the Chicago Musical College. When Art Tatum once traveled to Chicago, he was told that there was a young woman in town who could play faster than he could. As the story goes, Tatum climbed six flights of stairs to hear the then-25-year-old Donegan. He then took her under his wing, and taught her his technique, which was continually evident in her playing. Donegan first recorded on the Bluebird label in 1942, and during the mid-1940s recorded several sides for the Continental label. In 1943 Donegan became the first woman, as well as the first black, to play Orchestra Hall, sharing the bill with Vladimir Horowitz. Although she was

honored in 1992 with an American Jazz Masters award from the National Endowment for the Arts, Donegan never received the widespread recognition she deserved. Yet her live performances drew devoted fans who admired her showmanship. She was known to kick up her heels at the piano, engage her audience with witty asides, and entertain with resilient spirit unmatched by many musicians today.

what to buy: On *Live at the 1990 Floating Jazz Festival* ♪♪♪♪♪ (Chiaroscuro, 1992, prod. Hank O'Neal, Shelley M. Shier) Donegan demonstrates why she was such a powerful jazz pianist. Her cohesive trio with bassist Jon Burr and drummer Ray Mosca was recorded live between October 27–November 2, 1990 during Floating Jazz Festival performances aboard the *S.S. Norway* in the Caribbean Sea. The ultimate entertainer, Donegan offers a definitive version of "My Funny Valentine," injects quotes from other tunes into a flowery version of Erroll Garner's "Misty" and segues into an uptempo, swinging, Ellington-inspired, "Caravan Medley." Her technique is awesome: she exhibits amazing facility as her right hand rips through melody lines using single-note, scalar runs, trills, sturdy chords, and unexpected flourishes that command listener attention. Donegan uses her left hand supportively, often adding downscale bassline runs, boogie-woogie and stride riffs, and other powerhouse techniques. For ultimate impact, she varies dynamics from percussive key-pounding to the most soft and delicate phrasing. Plus, as demonstrated on the tune, "Lena, Eartha, Pearl & Billie," it doesn't take much audience coaxing to get her to sing or invoke witty (sometimes politically incorrect) asides that will have you laughing out loud. This album conveys precisely the nature of Donegan's intimate, live performances. An added bonus is a brief recorded monologue with Donegan telling about her musical influences and her lifestyle. *Dorothy Romps: A Piano Retrospective (1953–1979)* ♪♪♪♪ (Various, 1953/Rosetta, 1979, prod. Rosetta Reitz) offers a top-notch compilation of 15 tunes, including several Donegan originals, as well as standards such as "Just in Time," "That Old Black Magic," "Limehouse Blues," and "Lullaby of Birdland." Most of the tunes compiled here are drawn from obscure labels, out-of-print albums, and some previously unreleased material, with lengthy and meticulous liner notes researched and put together by Rosetta Reitz that add to the CD package. Donegan is in peak form on each selection, brandishing her trademark wit, fluency, and uncontrived switching of styles.

best of the rest:

The Explosive Dorothy Donegan ♪♪♪♪ (Audiophile, 1980/1995)

(With Clark Terry) *Live at the 1992 Floating Jazz Festival* ♫♫♫♫ (Chiaroscuro, 1993)
Live at Widder Bar ♫♫♫♫ (Timeless, 1993)
I Just Want to Sing ♫♫♫ (Audiophile, 1995)
Dorothy Donegan Trio ♫♫♫♫ (Storyville, 1996)

influences:

◀◀ Art Tatum, Erroll Garner, George Shearing, Victor Borge, Thelonious Monk, Cecil Taylor, Vladimir Horowitz, Vladimir Ashkenazy, Alicia De La Rocha

Susan K. Berlowitz and Nancy Ann Lee

Kenny Dorham

Born August 30, 1924, near Fairfield, TX. Died December 5, 1972, in New York, NY.

A first-generation bop trumpeter, Kenny Dorham never achieved the same degree of fame as his peers Dizzy Gillespie, Miles Davis, or Fats Navarro. He played in the innovative bop big bands of Gillespie and Billy Eckstine (1945), but his first important gig was as the replacement for Miles Davis in the Charlie Parker Quintet from 1948 to 1950. Always an in-demand sideman, he recorded with Thelonious Monk for Blue Note in 1952, was a founding member of the Jazz Messengers in 1954, and briefly led a similar group called the Jazz Prophets from 1955 to 1956, when Max Roach asked him to join his group after the death of Clifford Brown. Dorham remained with Roach until 1958, appearing on several albums, including *The Max Roach 4 Plays Charlie Parker*. After leaving Roach, Dorham struck out on his own as a leader, recording a string of remarkably consistent hard bop albums with a variety of groups. In the 1960s he was frequently paired with Joe Henderson on several Blue Note albums. Dorham also appeared as a sideman on several unexpected albums including *Coltrane Time* with John Coltrane and Cecil Taylor and on Andrew Hill's *Point of Departure* with Eric Dolphy and Tony Williams. Dorham's solos display an exceptionally pretty sense of melody and graceful linear development. His dark, rounded tone bears a resemblance to Davis (an early influence whom he outgrew) but lacks the smoldering anger and vulnerability that marks Davis's playing. Although he was a virtuoso, Dorham never gave in to mere technical display; he simply made beautiful music of great clarity and swing.

what to buy: *Whistle Stop* ♫♫♫♫ (Blue Note, 1961, prod. Alfred Lion) is a slight concept (all the tunes refer to Dorham's Southwest roots) fleshed out into a major statement by a crack quintet with Hank Mobley, Philly Joe Jones, Paul Chambers, and

Kenny Drew. With saxophonist Jackie McLean sharing the front line, *'Round Midnight at the Cafe Bohemia* ♫♫♫♫ (Blue Note, 1956, prod. Alfred Lion), which captures Dorham's Jazz Prophets live and in superior form, and *Matador/Inta Something* ♫♫♫♫ (Blue Note, 1962/61, prod. Alan Douglas, Richard Bock) feature Dorham playing with special fire and coherence.

what to buy next: *Jazz Contemporary* ♫♫♫♫ (Bainbridge, 1960, prod. Bob Shad) is solidly played and a good example of Dorham's great sense of time. Without a piano, the variety of Dorham's lines and his keen sense of phrasing and time stand out in high relief on *2 Horns/2 Rhythm* ♫♫♫♫ (OJC, 1957, prod. Orrin Keepnews).

best of the rest:
Afro-Cuban ♫♫♫ (Blue Note, 1955)
Quiet Kenny ♫♫♫♫ (OJC, 1959)

worth searching for: None of the albums featuring Henderson under Dorham's name are currently in print, but *Una Mas* ♫♫♫♫ (Blue Note, 1963) is a good one, especially for the grooving title track, a bossa nova that swings with a harder edge than most.

influences:

◀◀ Miles Davis, Dizzy Gillespie

▶▶ Wynton Marsalis

see also: *Dizzy Gillespie, Fats Navarro, Miles Davis, Max Roach, Charlie Parker*

Ed Hazell

Bob Dorough

Born December 12, 1923, in Cherry Hill, AR.

In the world of jazz vocals, Bob Dorough truly is an unsung hero (pun fully intended). Although he has never received as much critical attention as many of his peers, he has made his mark in some unexpected ways. After dabbling with music in high school and during his stint in the Army, Dorough got serious in 1945 and studied composition and piano at North Texas State Teachers' College, the first American school with a jazz curriculum. He moved to New York in 1949, pursuing further studies at Columbia University (1949–52). He eventually immersed himself in the local jazz scene, picking up along the way a love of singing. During the early 1950s, Dorough accompanied boxer Sugar Ray Robinson's musical revue, then performed in Paris with Blossom Dearie and her Blue Stars. He returned to New York in 1955 and recorded his first session as a leader a year later (released on Bethlehem), featuring his vocalese tribute to Charlie Parker, *Yardbird Suite*. It wasn't until several years later, in 1962, that Dorough got his next real break, but what a break! Miles Davis asked him to write some songs for his band, resulting in the decidedly unsentimental Christmas tune "Blue Xmas," as well as "Nothing Like You," which seemed out of place when it finally surfaced on Davis's *Sorcerer* album in 1967. The notoriety gained by this unlikely pairing eventually faded, and the lack of worthy gigs led Dorough to seek work writing ad jingles. However, it was in this realm that Dorough made his most memorable contributions to the world of music, when in 1970 he became musical director and principle songwriter for *Schoolhouse Rock!,* the series of short animated instructional television programs that helped teach math, grammar, science, and history to millions of kids across the U.S. Since then, Dorough has returned to straight jazz performances, with both club dates and the occasional recording. But his *Schoolhouse Rock!* songs have garnered him the most acclaim, culminating in a full-scale revival in 1996 with the Rhino Records release of a four-CD box set of all the tunes from these much-loved cartoons.

Dorough's unique style incorporates clarity, charm, and a slight southern twang, which well suits the wry, jaunty numbers that he favors. While neither trained as a vocalist nor blessed with a particularly beautiful voice, Dorough manages to convey a wide range of emotions from childlike glee to bittersweet remembrance in a genuine, folksy manner. At the same time, he remains perfectly, timelessly hip. He is also a more than competent pianist, to boot.

what to buy: OK, so the jazz content may be a little slight in *Schoolhouse Rock!* ♫♫♫♫ (Rhino, 1996, prod. Bob Dorough), but don't let the word "rock" in the title fool you—there are many other musical styles represented by these songs, from the bluesy "Conjunction Junction" to the fugue-like "Figure Eight," and they are all informed by Dorough's jazzy sense of how to write and sing a song. The album features many of Dorough's jazz buddies, including singer Blossom Dearie, drummer Grady Tate, and trumpeter Jack Sheldon, guaranteeing fun for the whole family (when was the last time a record did that?). *Schoolhouse Rock!* is available as a box set or four individual CDs, of which *Multiplication Rock* is the most essential. *Devil May Care* ♫♫♫♫ (Bethlehem, 1956/1996, prod. Joe Quinn) (reissued on Bethlehem in 1976 as *Yardbird Suite*) was Dorough's debut which caught the ear of Miles. Including some great originals, old classics, and "Yardbird Suite," with a sympathetic band featuring longtime partner bassist Bill Takas, it stills stand up today.

what to buy next: At age 73, Dorough makes his major-label "debut," with *Right on My Way Home* ♫♫♫♫ (Blue Note, 1997, prod. Bill Goodwin), a snappy collection of songs. Several tracks feature guests Billy Hart, Christian McBride, and Joe Lovano.

what to avoid: *Oliver! An Excursion through Songs from the Hit Show* ♫♫ (Music Minus One, 1963) is not so much a bad record, but as Dorough only plays piano throughout, one wishes he would sing. Clark Terry's presence does help.

the rest:
Just About Everything ♫♫♫♪ (Focus, 1966)
Beginning to See the Light ♫♫♫♪ (Laissez-Faire, 1976)
Devil May Care II ♫♫♫ (52 Rue Est, French import, 1982)
(With Phil Woods) *Memorial Charlie Parker* ♫♫♫♫ (Philology, 1985)
Skabadabba ♫♫♫ (Pinnacle, 1987)

worth searching for: *That's the Way I Feel Now: A Tribute to Thelonious Monk* ♫♫♫♫ (A&M, 1984, prod. Hal Willner) contains Dorough's contribution to this stellar compilation, a nifty duet with Bobby McFerrin on "Friday the Thirteenth."

influences:

◄◄ Eddie Jefferson, Johnny Mercer

►► Dave Frischberg, Blossom Dearie

Eric J. Lawrence

Jimmy Dorsey

Born February 29, 1904, in Shenandoah, PA. Died June 12, 1957, in New York, NY.

Fairly or not, Jimmy Dorsey's reputation is often overshadowed by the musical endeavors of his younger brother Tommy, even though Jimmy's alto saxophone skills (he was also adept on clarinet) found admirers in such bop legends as Lester Young and Charlie Parker. The brothers started their careers playing in many of the same bands before creating their own short-lived group in 1934. Both men had terrible tempers, and their disagreements were the stuff of legend and gossip. One night in 1935 Tommy and Jimmy got into an argument which resulted in Tommy walking off the stage and out of Jimmy's life until the mid-1950s, when they reunited.

The brothers grew up the sons of an ex-coal miner who became a music teacher. Jimmy started off playing trumpet and cornet but switched to the reed family around his tenth birthday. He started playing in small groups with his brother in the early 1920s before moving to New York City, where he joined (sometimes with Tommy) a wide variety of popular bands including groups led by Paul Whiteman, Jean Goldkette, Red Nichols, and Ted Lewis. After Tommy left the Dorsey Brothers Band, Jimmy took over the leadership role and led one of the more jazz-oriented of the white swing bands, with sidemen including Ray McKinley, Freddy Slack, Herb Ellis, and vocalist Helen O'Connell. The other singer during the heyday of Jimmy Dorsey's band was Bob Eberly, whose balladeering would often set the audience up for the livelier tunes—"Amapola," "Green Eyes," and the band's biggest hit, "Tangerine," which featured O'Connell. Dorsey's career continued to be strong right up through the early 1950s, at which time he disbanded his group to join the ensemble led by his brother. Prior to that time Dorsey had many hit records, and the band's popularity was such that it was able to survive when many big bands were biting the dust. He also appeared in such films as *Lady Be Good* (1940), *Four Jills and a Jeep* (1944), and the somewhat fictionalized documentary, *The Fabulous Dorseys* (1947).

what to buy: *Contrasts* ♫♫♫♫ (Decca/GRP, reissue prod. Orrin Keepnews, 1993) is the hands-down best album to get if you want a solid sampling of Dorsey as a jazz man as opposed to Dorsey the pop hit-maker. The period represented here ranges from 1936 to 1943 and features such important figures as drummer Ray McKinley (whose solo in "Dusk in Upper Sandusky" proves that Gene Krupa wasn't the era's only percussive firebrand), pianists Freddy Slack and Johnny Guarnieri, and singers Helen O'Connell and Bob Eberly. The remastering is solid throughout and Dorsey's alto playing justifies the high opinion accorded him by notables like Lester Young and Coleman Hawkins.

what to buy next: The previously unreleased radio broadcasts on *1939–1940* ♫♫♫ (Hindsight, 1977, prod. Wally Heider) show what the band's concerts sounded like at the height of its popularity. Included are Dorsey's theme song, "Contrasts," a few pop tunes of the day, and a novelty tune ("Shoot the Meatballs to Me Dominick Boy") that mercifully has not become a standard. This album pays more attention to the dance band angle of Dorsey's career than it does the jazz elements but the groove is infectious and the group falls into it surreptitiously and often. Vocals are by O'Connell and Eberly. The budget release *Perfidia* ♫♫♫ (LaserLight, 1992, prod. Frank Donovan) contains excerpts from radio broadcasts of the early 1950s featuring fine jazz musicians, including guitarist Herb Ellis and saxophonist Bob Lawson. The material includes standards like "Love for Sale" and "Moten Swing" alongside pop classics by Sammy Cahn and Hoagy Carmichael. Bop elements that one would not normally associate with Dorsey start showing up in his solo during Tadd Dameron's "Bula Beige," proving that the man was paying at-

tention to which way the wind was blowing. Guitarist Ellis gets the spotlight on "Hip Hop," a tune he co-wrote with Dorsey.

best of the rest:
Greatest Hits ♫♫♫ (Curb, 1991)
Jazz Collector Edition ♫♫♫ (LaserLight, 1991)

influences:
◄◄ Leon Roppolo, Jimmie Noone, Frankie Trumbauer
►► Lester Young, Charlie Parker

Garaud MacTaggart

Tommy Dorsey

Born November 19, 1905, in Shenandoah, PA. Died November 26, 1956, in Greenwich, CT.

For decades Tommy Dorsey's name stood for supreme excellence of trombone playing. His superbly polished and lyrical style could present a melody as movingly as any singer, and in fact was a model for many singers (most notably Frank Sinatra) as well as for other trombonists. He was more than competent in the jazz style current during the 1920s (he was an admirer of Miff Mole) and recorded with some of the best-known artists of the time but, in the swing era, the ballad was his personal medium. As leader of one of the best-known big-bands of the 1930s and 1940s, Dorsey was known as "the sentimental gentleman of swing."

His father, originally a coal-miner, was a self-taught musician who eventually taught music in Lansford, Pennsylvania and became a band-master. He taught Tommy both trumpet and trombone. In Lansford, Tommy, his brother Jimmy (destined to be another of the big-band era greats), and their father formed several bands in which Tommy apprenticed (starting with the Way Back When band, which evolved into Dorsey's Novelty Six and then Dorsey's Wild Canaries). By 1925 Tommy was in much demand for freelance radio and recording work with Paul Whiteman, Vincent Lopez, Roger Wolfe Kahn, Nathaniel Shilkret, Rudy Vallee, Victor Young, and others. In the late 1920s and early 1930s he also co-led several bands with his brother Jimmy. In 1935 he split with Jimmy and formed his own band, which eventually became one of the groups defining the big-band era. The critic George T. Simon thought that "Dorsey's must be recognized as the greatest all-round dance band of them all." Although he was known for his ballad style, Dorsey and his band also created their share of classic big-band swing arrangements (with those of Sy Oliver being the most outstanding). His recording of Pine Top Smith's "Boogie Woogie"

was a huge success, as were later recordings of "Well, Git It!" and "On the Sunny Side of the Street." Dorsey's band always included at least a few top jazz performers, such as Buddy Rich, Dave Tough, and Louis Bellson (drums); Peanuts Hucko, Johnny Mince, and Buddy DeFranco (clarinet); Ziggy Elman, Bunny Berigan, and Yank Lawson (trumpet); and Joe Bushkin (piano). He nurtured a number of vocalists who went on to outstanding careers on their own: Sinatra, of course, but also Dick Haymes, Bob Eberly, Connie Haines, Jo Stafford, and the Pied Pipers. Because of its prominence among the big bands, the Dorsey band was showcased in at least nine feature films including *A Song Is Born* and *The Fabulous Dorseys*. His accidental death in 1956, at age 51 (he choked in his sleep), took Dorsey off in his prime, and he was much mourned by trombonists of all stripes (Count Basie's jazz trombonist said, "I've never heard enough praise for him. It's really been disgusting since he died.") and by big-band fans. A Dorsey "ghost band"—first led by trombonist Buddy Morrow, later by Warren Covington, and now by Larry O'Brien—has continued to present the Tommy Dorsey sound.

what to buy: There are numerous recordings available featuring the Tommy Dorsey Orchestra, many of them on import labels. *Having a Wonderful Time* 𝄞𝄞𝄞𝄞 (RCA, 1940/1994, prod. Rolf Enoch) features a small group called the Clambake Seven from within the Dorsey band, on recordings made between 1935 and 1940. The 16 tracks comprise mainly jazzy versions of pop tunes, with many fine solos by the likes of Max Kaminsky, Bud Freeman, and Johnny Mince, and showing Dorsey in his best jazz style which was closely tied to Dixieland. "When the Midnight Choo Choo Leaves for Alabam'" and "Chinatown, My Chinatown" rollick nicely, and a gentler mood pervades "Head on My Pillow" (with Bunny Berigan, Buddy Rich, and Joe Bushkin and a smooth vocal by a very young Frank Sinatra) and "Don't Be a Baby, Baby," which offers a very rare vocal by arranger Sy Oliver and a backing that includes Charlie Shavers, Ziggy Elman, and Buddy DeFranco. *The Best of Tommy Dorsey* 𝄞𝄞𝄞𝄞 (Bluebird, 1992, prod. Steve Backer) provides an agreeable sampling of the full band's developing styles between 1936 (Royal Garden Blues) and 1944 (Opus One), with Dorsey featured mainly in his ballad mode. The 15 tracks include some of the numbers that established the band's reputation ("Marie," "Song of India," "Boogie Woogie," "Who?") and also some of his later hits

("Opus One," "Yes Indeed," "Star Dust," and "I'll Never Smile Again").

what to buy next: You can't fully understand the tremendous appeal of the Dorsey band without hearing Sinatra's work, so check out *Tommy Dorsey and Frank Sinatra: Stardust* 𝄞𝄞𝄞𝄞 (Bluebird, 1992, prod. Steve Backer) and *Tommy Dorsey—Frank Sinatra: I'll Be Seeing You* 𝄞𝄞𝄞𝄞 (RCA, 1994, prod. Paul Williams). Both offer a sampling of the many sides this pair recorded in the early 1940s. About half the tunes on each disc are also on the other, and there's little to choose between them. If you're a serious Sinatra fan you should know that *Tommy Dorsey—Frank Sinatra: The Song Is You* 𝄞𝄞𝄞𝄞𝄞 (RCA, 1994, prod. Paul Williams), a five-disc set, includes every studio master recorded, as well as 21 previously unreleased live performances and the four Sinatra/Stordahl recordings.

best of the rest:

The 17 Number Ones 𝄞𝄞𝄞𝄞 (RCA, 1990)
The Great Tommy Dorsey 𝄞𝄞𝄞𝄞 (Pearl, 1991)
Stop, Look, and Listen 𝄞𝄞𝄞 (Living Era, 1993)
Tommy Dorsey: Greatest Hits 𝄞𝄞𝄞𝄞 (RCA, 1996)

worth searching for: There are plenty of titles available that capture the Dorsey sound, but there are two that offer less conventional selections from his work. For the most jazz-oriented collection of TD's big band recordings try to find *Yes, Indeed!* 𝄞𝄞𝄞𝄞𝄞 (Bluebird, 1990, prod. Orrin Keepnews), a compilation that emphasizes jazz charts and plays down Dorsey's sentimental side. And for the most obscure list of titles from the Dorsey book the award goes to *Jazz Collector's Edition, Volume I* 𝄞𝄞𝄞𝄞 (Laserlight, 1991) and *Jazz Collector's Edition, Volume II* 𝄞𝄞𝄞𝄞 (Laserlight, 1991).

influences:

⏮ Jimmy Dorsey, Jean Goldkette Orchestra, Paul Whiteman Orchestra, Jack Teagarden, Miff Mole

⏭ Frank Rosolino, Vic Dickenson, Dan Barrett

see also: *Frank Sinatra*

Jim Lester

Dave Douglas
/Tiny Bell Trio
/New & Used

Born March 24, 1963 in Montclair, NJ.

Tiny Bell Trio: Dave Douglas, trumpet; Brad Schoeppach, guitar; Jim Black, drums. **New and Used:** Dave Douglas, trumpet; Kermit Driscoll,

Tommy Dorsey **(Archive Photos)**

bass; Mark Feldman, violin; Andy Laster, saxophone; Tom Rainey, drums.

After one-year stints at New England Conservatory and Berklee, trumpeter Dave Douglas moved to New York City to attend NYU and gradually became a major force on the freewheeling downtown scene. Among his other high-profile jobs, covering a broad range of styles, have been concerts and/or records with the Nick Didkovsky-led band Dr. Nerve (Douglas's first gig in New York), Horace Silver, saxophonist Vincent Herring, a duo with drummer Han Bennink, Don Byron's Mickey Katz tribute, John Zorn's quartet Masada, Anthony Braxton's Charlie Parker Project, a couple of Myra Melford groups, bassist Mark Dresser, and Ned Rothenberg. He mixes interests in Eastern European music and klezmer with classical concepts and structures (several albums have included arrangements of Robert Schumann's music), 1960s jazz avant-garde, and free improvisation. In the process, Douglas coaxes as many sounds from an unmodified trumpet as is sonically possible, without sacrificing an iota of control—he studied with trumpet chops guru Carmine Caruso, whose students included Freddie Hubbard.

As a player, Douglas considers his stronger influences to be Miles Davis and Woody Shaw, but he's also done a Booker Little tribute and often plays in ultra-flexible post-modern settings. He's said, "In my writing I really try to get away from the habits and clichés and patterns and traps of jazz, improvised music." This perhaps partially explains his penchant for unusual instrumentations. His Tiny Bell Trio (named for the small Bell Café) includes electric guitarist Brad Schoeppach and drummer Jim Black, and his "String Group" (with which he's made two fine albums for Soul Note) is a quintet with violinist Mark Feldman on violin, Erik Friedlander on cello, Mark Dresser or Drew Gress on bass, and Michael Sarin on drums. Douglas's pieces, especially with the Tiny Bell Trio, can slip quickly from style to style in a dizzying and exciting amalgam, but as his Booker Little and Wayne Shorter tributes prove, he can also more than hold his own in complex post-bop.

what to buy: Nowhere is Douglas's seriously playful ethos laid as bare as with the limber Tiny Bell Trio, and *Live in Europe* 𝄞𝄞𝄞𝄞 (Arabesque, 1997, prod. Dave Douglas) shows that live performance is the group's best context. Schoeppach alternates ripping single-note guitar lines, pizzicato backgrounds, Frisell-like shimmering chords, and more sparely constructed, tartly sweet chords. Black lays down limber grooves or plays free with an intuitive pulse. Meanwhile Douglas's trumpet burbles, wheezes, croons, squeals, chuckles, whispers, trills, and blares, sometimes to the fore and other times playing a bassline or sketching out the structure for the other players' solos. As always with this group, the compositions (drawing frequently on Balkan music) and/or arrangements are Douglas's, with the latter including a Robert Schumann cover and the style-hopping showstopper "Czardas," a traditional Hungarian dance. It's practically a summary of Douglas's styles.

what to buy next: How to describe *Sanctuary* 𝄞𝄞𝄞𝄞 (Avant, 1997, prod. Kazunori Sugiyama)? Using two trumpeters, two samplers, two bassists, a saxophonist, and a drummer, it has some of the quiet twilight mood and acoustic/electric timbres of Miles Davis (circa *In a Silent Way* and *Bitches Brew*) and recalls the organizational principles of Ornette Coleman's *Free Jazz*, but it wouldn't be mistaken for either—not least because among the instruments is a sampler. It's a lengthy, sprawling two-CD set, but it never seems distended or verbose. And there's a good chance that when the decade is over, *Sanctuary* will rank as one of its free-jazz milestones. *Five* 𝄞𝄞𝄞𝄞 (Soul Note, 1996, prod. Dave Douglas) was the second CD by Douglas's "string group." It combines original tributes (most notably to Woody Shaw) with two imaginative covers, Thelonious Monk's "Who Knows" and Rahsaan Roland Kirk's "The Inflated Tear." Douglas displays his broad, colorful sonic palette, and drummer Sarin's subtle pointillism keeps the rhythm flowing.

what to avoid: Don't avoid *Serpentine* 𝄞𝄞 (Songlines, 1996, prod. Dave Douglas), just save it for last. Eventually, you'll want to hear Douglas in this trumpet-drums duo with Han Bennink just to be amazed at how many sounds he can get out of his instrument, but the slapstick drumming of Bennink is too much of an acquired taste.

the rest:
Parallel Worlds 𝄞𝄞𝄞 (Soul Note, 1993)
(With the Tiny Bell Trio) *The Tiny Bell Trio* 𝄞𝄞𝄞 (Songlines, 1994)
(With the Tiny Bell Trio) *Constellations* 𝄞𝄞𝄞 (hat ART, 1995)
In Our Lifetime 𝄞𝄞𝄞 (New World, 1995)
Stargazer 𝄞𝄞𝄞 (Arabesque, 1997)

worth searching for: *The Songlines Anthology* 𝄞𝄞𝄞 (Songlines, 1996, comp. prod. Tony Reif) consists entirely of music by this label's artists "released on CD for the first time," including a live, ten-minute version of Tiny Bell Trio's "Head-on Kouvlodsko." Other artists on this sampler included Babkas and Ellery Eskelin. Dating from the late 1970s, the cooperative band Mosaic Sextet grew out of an informal workshop arrangement and consisted of Douglas, Michael Jefry Stevens (piano), Mark Feldman (violin), Michael Rabinowitz (bassoon), Joe Fonda (bass), and Harvey Sorgen (drums). Though all are composers, on the German album *Today, This Moment* ♪♪♪♪ (Konnex, 1993, prod. Mosaic Sextet) Douglas and Stevens split the composing evenly (five tracks each) on sessions recorded in 1988–90. This is Douglas at his most abstract, working in the area where the jazz avant-garde intersects the classical avant-garde (both structurally and texturally), although still with room for improvisation. New and Used is also a cooperative group, but with all members contributing material to its two albums so far. Douglas is joined by Kermit Driscoll (bass), Mark Feldman (violin), Andy Laster (saxophones), and Tom Rainey (drums) on *Souvenir* ♪♪♪ (Knitting Factory, 1992, prod. New & Used) and *Consensus* ♪♪♪♪ (Knitting Factory, 1995, prod. New & Used), which have a loose, sometimes Ornette Coleman-esque feel to them.

influences:

◀◀ Miles Davis, Herb Robertson, Lester Bowie, Henry Threadgill's Very Very Circus, Carla Bley

▶▶ Spanish Fly, Babkas

see also: *Masada*

Steve Holtje

Will Downing

Born in New York, NY.

During the late 1970s Will Downing was a highly sought-after session singer with a resume that included work for acts like Rose Royce and Billy Ocean. When Downing finally went out on his own, he was still considered a soul singer, but his first album revealed some jazz leanings when he included a re-arranged version of John Coltrane's "A Love Supreme" that had lyrics. Downing and other singers like him pose the perpetual question: What is jazz? Downing has a marvelous baritone voice, and the jazz phrasing he picked up while attending Brooklyn's Erasmus Hall High School (distinguished alumni include Barbra Streisand and Mickey Spillane) combined with his penchant for hiring trained jazz musicians for his record dates are all an indisputable part of his artistry. Downing's biggest audience right now is in Europe, where his first album was a Top 20 hit in Great Britain. Despite somewhat weaker sales in his homeland, Downing has still managed to carve out a living in the States with the advent of the Quiet Storm radio format—radio programming that features soulful ballads and light, jazz-inflected instrumentals. On his albums, Downing has done a lot of work with contemporary jazz saxophonists like Art Porter and Gerald Albright in addition to recording with keyboard

DAVE DOUGLAS

song "Forward Flight"
album *In Our Lifetime*
(New World, 1994/1995)
instrument Trumpet

Monster Solo

players Ronnie Foster and Onaje Allan Gumbs. Even jazz stalwarts Stanley Turrentine, Marvin "Smitty" Smith, and Harvey Mason have turned up. If what Downing is doing isn't some kind of jazz, it sure is close.

what to buy: Despite the mini-plethora of producers on this project, the overall sound of *Love's the Place to Be* ♪♪♪♪ (Mercury, 1993, prod. Will Downing, Rex Rideout, Bob Baldwin, Barry Eastmond, Ronnie Foster) provides a lush bed for Downing's flexible, jazz-inflected croon. Foster, who used to play keyboards for Grant Green, appears to be responsible, either as a producer or writer, for the jazzier cuts, and his vibes solo on "Love's the Place to Be" perks through a lavish string arrangement. Then there's the roll-call of jazz players to walk through: Gerald Albright, Kevin Eubanks, Marion Meadows, Harvey Mason. Stevie Wonder plays harmonica on "That's All."

the rest:
Will Downing ♪♪ (Island, 1988)
Come Together As One ♪♪♪ (Island, 1989)

A Dream Fulfilled &&& (Island, 1991)
Moods &&&& (Mercury, 1995)
Invitation Only &&&& (Mercury, 1997)

influences:

◄◄ Donny Hathaway, Nat King Cole, Johnny Hartman, Luther Vandross, Marvin Gaye, Al Jarreau

Garaud MacTaggart

Arthur Doyle

Born June 26, 1944, Birmingham, AL.

First coming to attention in the New York loft scene of the late '70s, Doyle (who holds a Master of Arts in music education from Tennessee State) gigged around with guitarist Rudolph Grey and drummer Beaver Harris, confounding listeners with his extraordinarily free, "skronky" tenor work. He's sporadically appeared on records since 1969 with the likes of Milford Graves, Noah Howard, and Alan Silva and made live appearances with everybody from Sun Ra and Pharoah Sanders to Bill Dixon and Frank Lowe. But it seems that making friends with Sonic Youth guitarist Thurston Moore was the best thing to happen to Doyle's career, since Moore not only brought him some much-deserved attention, but also aided him in releasing records on his Ecstatic Peace label. Apparently relocated out of the Big Apple, Doyle now teaches in Binghamton, New York, yet continues to play around the city.

what to buy: *Plays and Sings from the Songbook, Vol. 1* &&&& (Audible Hiss, 1995) is one of the most disturbingly open jazz albums ever. Doyle clomps around on piano and flute, while co-mingling his "singing" voice with his tenor voice to emerge with a breathy scream that evokes Albert Ayler as a mental patient. The way he vocally drones through "Just Get the Funk Spot" provides a perfect foil to his searching tenor squawk. The work is scary, but gut-wrenchingly great.

what to buy next: *The Songwriter* &&& (Ecstatic Peace, 1994), in a similar, though less shocking, vein as *Songbook*, finds Doyle on the opposite end of Charles Gayle's post-Ayler spectrum. *Live At The Cooler* &&& (Lotus Sound, 1997) finds Doyle re-teaming with guitarist Rudolph Grey in a quartet setting that also features drummer Tom Surgal and bassist Wilbur Morris. It's loose and primitive, though there's not much interaction between the two free-wheelers.

worth searching for: *Plays More Alabama Feeling* &&& (Ecstatic Peace, 1990) is a one-sided record that is unmercifully short

and gives only a slight glimpse into Doyle's breathtaking style. Should be heard, if only to hear Doyle rip into "Nature Boy."

influences:

◄◄ Albert Ayler

►► Charles Gayle

Jason Ferguson

Dream Warriors

Formed in Canada.

Capitol Q; King Lou.

Along with Gang Starr, A Tribe Called Quest, and the Young Disciples, the Dream Warriors (Capitol Q and King Lou) were one of the driving forces behind hip-hop's early '90s jazz infusion. But after a three-year hiatus, which saw the addition of two more members, and thanks to the fickleness of the hip-hop audience, the group fell out of favor with a once-adoring public.

what to buy: *And Now the Legacy Begins* &&& (4th and B'Way, 1991, prod. Dream Warriors) is one of the seminal albums from hip-hop's *Rebirth of Cool* jazz era. "My Definition of a Boombastic Jazz Style" samples the brassy kitsch of an old Canadian game show and makes for a new way of creating music. You'd think the album might sound dated now, but the glowing innocence of songs like "Wash Your Face in My Sink" still resonate with optimism.

what to avoid: Three years is a lifetime in hip-hop, and waiting that long before releasing the follow up, *Subliminal Simulation* & (EMI/Pendulum, 1994, prod. Dream Warriors) ultimately cost the group a shot at longevity. Of course, the group's attempt at publicizing its newfound, quasi-spiritual, cafe-induced intellectualism through promotional comic books and indecipherable liner notes didn't help, either.

worth searching for: In the early '90s, 4th and B'Way's U.K. division began issuing a series of *Rebirth of Cool* compilations focusing on contemporary soul, jazz, and jazz-inspired hip-hop. *Rebirth of Cool: Volume 2* &&&& (4th and B'Way UK, 1992, prod. various) features the spellbinding, UK-only single "I've Lost My Ignorance (and Don't Know Where to Find It)," which matches the Dream Warriors with Gang Starr. While the song also appears on *Subliminal Simulation*, this version is better.

influences:

◄◄ De La Soul, Gang Starr

►► Arrested Development, Digable Planets

Jazzbo

Mark Dresser

Born September 26, 1952, in Los Angeles, CA.

Dresser, a virtuoso bassist, has been composing and working professionally since 1972. He holds both B.A. and M.A. degrees in Music from U.C. San Diego where he studied contrabass with the seminal virtuoso of 20th-century performance practice, Bertam Turetzky. Additionally, Dresser was awarded a 1983 Fulbright Fellowship for advanced contrabass study with Franco Petracchi. Besides solo bass work, his main projects as a leader are his trio and the group Force Green. He also has worked with the quartet Tambastics (with Robert Dick on flute, Denman Maroney on piano, and Gerry Hemingway on drums) and was a founding member of the Arcado String Trio (with violinist Mark Feldman and cellist Hank Roberts, the latter later replaced by Ernst Reijseger)—which, combined with the Trio du Clarinettes, becomes the Double Trio. For ten years he was a member of the Anthony Braxton Quartet, as well as diverse groups led by Ray Anderson, Tim Berne, Anthony Davis, Gerry Hemingway, John Zorn, Dave Douglas, and others; Dresser can be heard on over 60 albums. He also wrote solo bass music for the New York Shakespeare Festival Production of *Henry VI* and has received commissions for composed music.

what to buy: *Force Green* ♫♫♫♫ (Soul Note, 1995, prod. Mark Dresser, Tim Berne) is an extraordinary recording featuring the vocal talent of Theo Bleckmann, Dave Douglas on trumpet, Denman Maroney on piano, and Phil Haynes on drums. Like a post-modern Mingus, Dresser writes flexible music suited to the voices he's working with. Bleckman and Douglas mesh wonderfully; the many styles contrast without clashing. The material constantly takes chances but there is a beautiful lyricism to the proceedings. *The Cabinet of Dr. Caligari* ♫♫♫♫ (Knitting Factory Works, 1994, prod. Mark Dresser) arose from a Sunday afternoon series at the Knitting Factory where downtown musicians provide soundtracks for famous silent films. Working in a trio with Douglas and Maroney, Dresser crafts an atmospheric and occasionally dramatic aural complement to the German Expressionist landmark, reflects the film's uneasy ambiguity.

what to buy next: The solo bass recital *Invocation* ♫♫♫♫ (Knitting Factory Works, 1996, prod. Mark Dresser, Lamont Wolfe) includes four 1983 tracks utilizing overdubbing (most notably on Gerry Hemingway's "Threnody for Charles Mingus") and minimal electronic processing in collaboration with co-composer Lamont Wolfe, while the three more recent tracks find Dresser working alone (but again overdubbing). Though the frequencies are definitely bass, the fullness of the compositions and the attention to sonic detail make the results practically orchestral in effect.

the rest:

Tambastics ♫♫♫ (Music and Arts, 1992)
Banquet ♫♫♫♪ (Tzadik, 1997)
Un Chien Andalou ♫♫♫♫ (Knitting Factory Works, 1998)
The Arcado String Trio:
Arcado ♫♫♫ (JMT, 1989)
Behind the Myth ♫♫♫♪ (JMT, 1990)
(With the Köln Radio Orchestra) *For Three Strings and Orchestra* ♫♫♫♪ (JMT, 1991)
Live in Europe ♫♫♫♫ (Avant, 1994)

influences:

◀◀ Charles Mingus, Wilbur Ware, Bertam Turetzky, Ornette Coleman, Charlie Haden, Ray Brown, Sonny Rollins, Anthony Braxton

David C. Gross and Steve Holtje

Kenny Drew

Born August 28, 1928, in New York, NY. Died August 4, 1993, in Copenhagen, Denmark.

Journeyman pianist Kenny Drew was one of the most widely recorded sidemen of the hard bop era. Drew was perhaps more famous for his adaptability and consistency than for the depth of his musical insights. However, he displayed a polished technique and a peerless sense of swing, and sessions usually were better for his presence at the keyboard. Drew's recording debut was on a Howard McGhee session in 1949, followed by a Sonny Stitt date a few months later. Although he led sessions for Riverside, Norgran, and Blue Note from 1953 until 1960, Drew's most significant work during this period was as a sideman. He recorded with Sonny Rollins and John Coltrane in the late 1950s, during crucial phases in the development of both of those artists. He also had strong outings on Blue Note in support of Kenny Dorham, Tina Brooks, and Jackie McLean. In the early 1960s, Drew left the American jazz scene and moved to Europe, where he was to remain for the rest of his life. Dexter Gordon's early 1960s albums with Drew were a high point in the careers of both artists, and the two of them would reunite several times over the next ten years. Drew led the house band at the Jazzhaus Montmarte in Copenhagen into the 1970s, performing with many prominent expatriate jazzmen. Here he began a productive musical partnership with Scandinavian bassist Niels-Henning Orsted Pederson which would last into the 1970s. Although he made some solid recordings as a leader throughout his career, Drew is heard to best advantage supporting other artists of stronger musical personality. His recordings with Ben Webster, Johnny Griffin, Jackie McLean, Dexter Gordon, Sonny Rollins, and John Coltrane were high points in the careers of those artists. Few pianists of his generation could claim such a distinguished résumé.

what to buy: With an association spanning many years and countless club dates, Drew achieved a special rapport with bassist Niels-Henning Orsted Pederson. Pederson's crisp, assertive style was a good foil to Drew's fluent, almost glossy technique. Of their many recordings together, *Dark and Beautiful* ♫♫♫ (SteepleChase, 1974/1995, prod. Nils Winther) may be their finest. On this two CD set, Drew and Pederson are reunited with former Montmarte drummer Albert "Tootie" Heath.

what to buy next: *Pal Joey* ♫♫♫ (OJC, 1957/1992, prod. Orrin Keepnews) is the best of Drew's late 1950s trio recordings. The up-tempo numbers are the standouts; like Oscar Peterson, Drew was at his best reeling off blues riffs at a swinging tempo. The backing of Wilbur Ware (bass) and Philly Joe Jones (drums) is top-notch. Good sessions like *Undercurrent* ♫♫♫ (Blue Note, 1960/1996, prod. Alfred Lion) were a dime a dozen in the early 1960s, and although this session doesn't necessarily stand out from the pack, it is certainly well worth hearing. Drew's compositions are not particularly memorable, but the front line of Freddie Hubbard and Hank Mobley can always be counted on for fine soloing, and Drew ably holds his own with the talented hornmen.

what to avoid: *Everything I Love* ♫♫ (SteepleChase, 1973/1995, prod. Nils Winther) is a rather bland solo outing for Drew. There are pleasant moments, but the album does not leave a lasting impression.

best of the rest:
The Kenny Drew Trio ♫♫♫ (OJC, 1956/1992)
Lite Flite ♫♫♫ (SteepleChase, 1977/1994)

worth searching for: During Drew's tenure at the Montmarte he had opportunity to record live dates with three of the best tenor saxophonists of his era. Recorded in 1967 but previously unreleased, Dexter Gordon's *The Squirrel* ♫♫♫ (Blue Note, 1997, prod. Ib Skovgaard) is one of several Gordon club dates he would record with Drew at the Montmarte. It stands as one of Gordon's fieriest performances. *Stormy Weather* ♫♫♫♫ (Black Lion, 1965/1988, prod. Alan Bates) is an essential document of Ben Webster's autumnal stage. Drew teamed up with Johnny Griffin on *Blues for Harvey* ♫♫♫ (SteepleChase, 1973/1995,

prod. Nils Winther, Johnny Griffin). Griffin displays his R&B roots in flamboyant form on this loose-sounding session.

influences:
◀◀ Bud Powell, Oscar Peterson, Hampton Hawes

Will Bickart

Kenny Drew Jr.

Born 1958, in New York, NY.

There's little stylistic similarity between Kenny Drew Jr. and his father, the great bebop pianist, which isn't surprising considering that he was raised by his aunt and grandparents. Still, Drew has developed into a formidable player who matures with each new release. Drew began classical piano lessons at an early age, taught by his mother and grandmother (who had also taught Drew Sr.). Drew spent the early '80s working in Florida, playing in rock, R&B, funk, and blues bands and made his first jazz recording on a 1989 album by bassist Charnett Moffett. Tours with guitarist Stanley Jordan and Blue Note's Young Lion showcase OTB followed, as well as recording dates with Eddie Gomez and Sadao Watanabe. He has also worked with Slide Hampton, Stanley Turrentine, and Frank Morgan and toured and recorded with the Mingus Dynasty big band. Drew's handful of U.S. releases indicate he is rapidly becoming a major jazz talent, combining his classical training and rock experiences with the influences of Hancock, Peterson, Corea, Evans, and Monk. He has also recorded a number of albums for small Japanese and European labels.

what to buy: *Kenny Drew Jr.* ♫♫♫♫ (Antilles, 1992, prod. John Snyder, Jerry Wexler) is an impressive debut by a pianist who arrives preceded by high expectations. He occasionally rushes his solos and relies too much on his technique, but his talent is beyond question. Drew's second American release *A Look Inside* ♫♫♫♫♫ (Antilles, 1993, prod. John Snyder, Jerry Wexler) demonstrates considerable growth in a short period. The album features Drew in alternating duo, trio, and quartet settings, with tenor saxophonists David Sanchez and Joshua Redman, bassists George Mraz and Charnett Moffett, and drummers Lewis Nash and Codaryl Moffett. Highlights include the interplay with Redman on a duo version of Monk's "Ugly Beauty" and Drew's use of space in the duet with Sanchez on Wayne Shorter's "Nefertiti." Rising to the challenge of a solo recital, Drew comes of age as a top-shelf improvisor with *Kenny Drew Jr. at Maybeck* ♫♫♫♫♫ (Concord Jazz, 1995, prod. Carl E. Jefferson). The program consists mostly of well-worn standards, which Drew reinvents and personalizes with his commanding technique. He turns Monk's "Well, You Needn't" into a stunning torrent of notes and plays a ravishingly rhapsodic version of Horace Silver's "Peace." Drew never coasts or simply plays notes; he starts each tune with an idea of where he wants to go, though the path often takes surprising turns.

the rest:

The Flame Within 🎷🎷🎷 (Jazz City, 1988)
Third Phase 🎷🎷🎷 (Jazz City, 1990)

influences:

◀◀ Thelonious Monk, McCoy Tyner, Bill Evans

Andrew Gilbert

Paquito D'Rivera

Born June 4, 1948, in Havana, Cuba.

If there is a singular musician carrying on the legacy of Dizzy Gillespie, it is bandleader and reeds player Paquito D'Rivera. Inspired at a young age by the music of John Coltrane, Charlie Parker, and Lee Konitz, D'Rivera added rhythms from his native Cuba and melded them into bopped-up, romantic, salty, and sensuous sounds. In Cuba he was influenced by his father, a classical saxophonist who introduced his son to the recordings of Charlie Parker. Young D'Rivera was a prodigy who was playing professionally by his mid-teens, entered the Havana Conservatory in 1960 to pursue classical studies, joined the Orquesta Cubana de Música Moderna in 1967, and with some of the members of the Orquesta, formed Irakere, an 11-member band that played a sizzling mixture of jazz, rock, classical, and traditional Cuban music from 1973–80. Irakere performed in the United States during 1978 at the Newport Jazz Festival as well as others worldwide, causing a sensation that resulted in an historic March 1979 concert in Cuba featuring an array of American pop artists who performed along with the best musicians of the contemporary Cuban music scene. The event was documented on two albums, *Havana Jam* and *Havana Jam II*. Albums with his group Irakere followed in 1979 and 1980. While on tour in Spain with Irakere in 1980, D'Rivera defected. He eventually settled in New York and within three years was playing in the most prestigious clubs and concert halls, and touring Europe with Dizzy Gillespie. Throughout the 1980s he continued performing, recording, and touring globally with his own groups. After performing regularly in Gillespie's United Nation Orchestra (UNO), which Gillespie founded in 1988, D'Rivera took over leadership of the band following its leader's death in 1993. His first albums as leader, *Paquito Blowin'* in 1981 and *Mariel* in 1982, solidified his reputation in the United States,

and numerous albums as leader and sideman have followed. As well as recording as sideman with McCoy Tyner, Hendrik Meurkens, Claudio Roditi, Arturo Sandoval, Bobby Sanabria, Richie Cole, the Caribbean Jazz Project, and many others, he has chalked up a significant number of richly diverse albums for Columbia, Chesky, Messidor, Candid, and TropiJazz. D'Rivera's broad-based performances and recordings continue to brilliantly straddle the fence between modern American music and his native Cuban rhythms.

what to buy: Not only do you get a broad sampling of Cuban music on *Paquito D'Rivera Presents: Forty Years of Cuban Jam Session* 🎷🎷🎷🎷 (Messidor, 1993, prod. Götz A. Wörner, Paquito D'Rivera, Brenda Feliciano), but the booklet enclosed with this CD presents a brief history explaining the origin and impact of American jazz on Cuban rhythms. The gathering of 23 Cuban players from all over the world originated from a party to honor two veteran Cuban-jazz reed players, Gustavo Mas and José "Chambo" Silva. The 11-selection Cuban "descarga" (jam session), recorded in Miami in February 1993, features leader D'Rivera playing clarinet and alto saxophone on six of the 11 tunes, accompanied by a flexible rhythm that includes Horacio Hernández and Rogelio Rivero (drums, timbales), and Rigo Herrera and Victor Valdés (percussion). Among the many fine soloists is trombonist Leopoldo "Pucho" Escalante who shines on "Despojo (Exorcism)," a powerful Yoruban-inspired percussive number performed with the full ensemble. This is a wonderfully loose and captivating album, less influenced by modern themes than some of D'Rivera's recent albums. Meanwhile, the UNO has continued to perform and tour, although with mostly new (and younger) personnel on their second live-recorded performance under D'Rivera's leadership, *Paquito D'Rivera & the United Nation Orchestra Live at Manchester Craftsmen's Guild* 🎷🎷🎷🎷 (Blue Jackel, 1997, prod. Marty Ashby, Jay Ashby). This performance, recorded on February 14, 1997, features 10 Latin and Afro-Caribbean tunes arranged by D'Rivera and band members. Ranging from full orchestra forays to a gorgeous duet featuring D'Rivera on clarinet and Oscar Stagnaro (bassist from Peru), the music covers classic Caribbean numbers to funk-tinged modern pieces, and draws from D'Rivera's days with Irakere and the Orquesta Cubana de Música Moderna. D'Rivera takes tasteful extended solos (alto/soprano saxes and clarinet) and the arrangements spotlight other top-flight soloists as well, including trombonist Conrad Herwig, who contributes the tune, "Quasi Modal." Guitarist Fareed Haque can be heard to great advantage, Dario Eskenazi (Argentina) commendably holds the former piano chair of Danilo Perez, and bari saxman Marshall McDonald is a talent deserving of wider exposure. Under D'Rivera's leadership, the band—truly an amalgam of musicians from the States and points south—conveys with expertise the rhythms native to Argentina, Brazil, Uruguay, Cuba, and Puerto Rico. The UNO is exceptional and the colorful, lightly textured arrangements warrant repeated listening, especially the closing dedication to Dizzy, a modern interpretation of his "A Night in Tunisia," which has become the UNO theme. An earlier recording featuring D'Rivera at the helm of the UNO, *A Night in Englewood* ✍✍✍✍ (Messidor, 1993, prod. Götz A. Wörner, Paquito D'Rivera, Brenda Feliciano), is an excellent session of nine Afro-Cuban jazz selections that spotlight some of the best soloists in the business and also feature topnotch, tight, and gorgeously textured ensemble playing on arrangements by D'Rivera. Guest artists include Slide Hampton (trombone), Claudio Roditi (trumpet), Dave Samuels (marimba, vibraphone), and Raul Jaurena (bandoneon). Filling Gillespie's shoes is not an easy task, yet this band carries on the Afro-Cuban jazz tradition with matchless vitality and inventiveness under D'Rivera's leadership. This passionate tribute to the memory of Gillespie is a must-own CD. D'Rivera and trumpeter Arturo Sandoval, former members of the groundbreaking Orquesta Cubana de Música Moderna and the innovative Cuban band, Irakere, mix it up with exciting side players on *Reunion* ✍✍✍✍ (Messidor, 1991, prod. Götz A. Wörner, Uwe Feltens). Fluent in Afro-Cuban rhythms, bassist David Finck, guitarist Fareed Haque, percussionist Giovani Hidalgo, pianist Danilo Perez, and drummer Mark Walker add panache to this nine-tune session. D'Rivera soars, Sandoval sings. It's a sizzling session all the way, featuring Gillespie's Cubop number, "Tanga," as well as tunes by Chucho Valdés (leader of Irakere), and members of the group. Haque contributes two parts (and solos elegantly) on the sweet, three-part Latin-American suite that also highlights Paquito's fluid clarinet mastery. A bounteous CD for its south-of-the-border rhythms. *Havana Café* ✍✍✍✍ (Chesky, 1992, prod. David Chesky, Paquito D'Rivera) is a studio session with frequent partners pianist Danilo Perez, bassist David Finck, and guitarist Fareed Haque, as well as drummer Jorge Rossy, percussionist Sammy Figueroa, and guitarist Ed Cherry who guests on two tracks. D'Rivera leads the sextet session infusing energy into authentic Cuban melodies and rhythms and modern Latin-influenced tunes such as Haque's, "The Search,"a powerful ensemble number that must have rattled the studio rafters. Yet D'Rivera capably harnesses his energy to produce brief vignettes in a guitar-clarinet duo on his "Improvalsation,"

and his unaccompanied clarinet solo on "Contradanza." Also included is a nod to James Moody, on the D'Rivera/Roditi original, "Who's Smoking?" (a revisit of the title tune of his 1991 release for Candid). Recorded in August 1991, this remains one of D'Rivera's freshest sounding, vigorous sessions, with 10 excellent tunes composed mostly by D'Rivera and band members. Everyone shines throughout the nearly 60 minutes of this unique and exciting listen.

what to buy next: *A Taste of Paquito D'Rivera* ✍✍✍ (Columbia, 1981–86/Legacy, 1994, prod. various) is a 12-tune compilation from D'Rivera's Columbia albums after he settled in the United States that features tracks that demonstrate his fluent, fiery expressions on both alto saxophone and clarinet. On the mix of standards and originals, he is assisted by a who's who of Afro-Cuban jazz, including bassist Eddie Gomez, drummer Ignacio Berroa, trumpeter Claudio Roditi, pianist Hilton Ruiz, and others who play this music with flawless ardor. The modern orchestral version of Gillespie's "Manteca" features D'Rivera playing both alto sax and clarinet, and also spotlights Claudio Roditi (trumpet) and Michel Camilo (piano). An album of quite different flavor (and more sedate), but also one to suitably acquaint you with D'Rivera's artistry, *Tico! Tico!* ✍✍✍ (Chesky, 1989, prod. David Chesky, Paquito D'Rivera) is most enjoyable for its focus on authentic Cuban rhythms and themes. While this session may lack the consistent, fiery explosiveness of some of his other albums, D'Rivera's clarinet playing is gorgeously romantic and he plays alto and tenor saxophones with equal skill. Plus, he is backed in small group settings by wonderful players such as Danilo Perez (piano), bassists David Finck or Nillson Matta, Portinho (drums), and others. In addition to an excellent reading of the title tune made famous by Carmen Miranda in the 1940s, the 12 assorted tunes include D'Rivera's two originals and compositions by David Chesky, Claudio Roditi, Danilo Perez, and traditional Cuban composers. *Portraits of Cuba* ✍✍✍✍ (Chesky, 1996, prod. David Chesky, Carlos Franzetti) features D'Rivera collaborating with musical arranger Carlos Franzetti who conducts the 14-member orchestra enhanced by guest soloists on this jazz tribute to the Cuban tradition (recorded in February 1996 during New York's "blizzard of the century"). Bolstered by a band that includes top session players—tenor saxman Dick Oatts, trumpeter Lew Soloff, Paquito's regular pianist Dario Eskenazi, to name a

Paquito D' Rivera (© Nancy Ann Lee)

few—D'Rivera shines in the spotlight playing clarinet, and soprano and alto saxophones. Franzetti, who has collaborated and performed with D'Rivera for many years, crafted sophisticated arrangements of Cuban music from the past century by composers from Jose White to D'Rivera. His familiarity with D'Rivera's stylings empowered him to create elaborate, dense charts, full of the dreamy colors and the beauty and passion of Cuba. This is a resplendent album that demands repeated listening, not only for D'Rivera's masterful solos, but for Franzetti's extraordinarily beautiful arrangements. *The Caribbean Jazz Project* 🎵🎵🎵 (Heads Up, 1995, prod. Caribbean Jazz Project) showcases a collaborative unit led by Dave Samuels, D'Rivera, and Andy Narell, all veteran jazz players-composers. An invigorating session of 11 originals by the co-leaders, this album features a range of music from modern contemporary jazz with Caribbean beats to a seductive, traditional bolero. D'Rivera (clarinet, alto saxophone), Samuels (vibraphone/marimba), and Narell (steel pans) add spicy Caribbean flavor to their jazz, energized by a solid rhythm section and creative percussionists.

the rest:

Manhattan Burn 🎵🎵🎵 (Columbia, 1987)
La Habana-Rio Conexion 🎵🎵🎵 (Rounder, 1992)
(With Bebo and Chucho Valdéz) *Cuba Jazz* 🎵🎵🎵🎵 (TropiJazz, 1996)
(With Caribbean Jazz Project) *Island Stories* 🎵🎵🎵🎵 (Heads Up, 1996)

worth searching for: To hear how well D'Rivera works with a singer/pianist in a small setting, seek out *Come on Home* 🎵🎵🎵🎵🎵 (Columbia, 1995, prod. Frank Zuback), a robust nine-tune CD by pianist Valerie Capers and her trio. D'Rivera guests on four tracks of this pleasing album, weaving his alto sax lines around Capers's piano melodies or her vocals, but adding particular passion to her torchy love ballad, "Out of All (He's Chosen Me)." He also joins leader-pianist Bebo Valdés on *Bebo Rides Again* 🎵🎵🎵🎵 (Messidor, 1995, prod. Paquito D'Rivera), a tribute to the many other talented musicians who have fled Cuba. Valdés (b. 1918) was an important figure in Cuban music before fleeing Cuba in 1960 and this November, 1994, German studio session was his first recording in 34 years. The 11 tunes, mostly varied danceable Cuban originals by Valdés, are performed by 10 musicians who deliver a cohesive, bubbling Cuban-jazz session, with stand-out solos from D'Rivera, trumpeter Diego Urcola, conguero Potato Valdés, and guitarist Carlos Emilio Morales. Valdés was 76 when this session was recorded and his piano technique remains vibrant (one can hear where his son, pianist Chucho Valdés, got his chops). An exciting sampler containing (no lie) "the finest contemporary Latin music," *United Rhythms*

of Messidor 🎵🎵🎵 (Messidor, 1994, prod. various) features 13 tracks compiled by Michael Barth from albums by the label's top performers in Latin jazz: D'Rivera, the late band leader Mario Bauzá, flutist/soprano saxist Jane Bunnett, the late bandoneon player Astor Piazzolla, jazz pianists Gonzalo Rubalcaba and Jesus "Chucho" Valdés, percussionist Giovanni Hidalgo, and more. There's no question about the caliber and authenticity of the Latin beats from these musicians. If you're into Latin jazz, you've probably heard some of the tunes before or already own the albums. Paquito performs on "Tanga," "Blues for Astor," and "Despojo." Covering a broad cross-section of Latin styles, this enjoyable CD also serves as entree to the albums from which these tunes have been extracted.

influences:

◀◀ Mario Bauzá, Bebo Valdéz, Chico O'Farrill, Benny Goodman, Charlie Parker, Dizzy Gillespie, John Coltrane, Lee Konitz

see also: *Dizzy Gillespie, Claudio Roditi, Arturo Sandoval*

Nancy Ann Lee

Billy Drummond

Born 1959, in Newport News, VA.

A member of the thirty-something generation, drummer Billy Drummond made a name for himself in the early 1990s and has become one of the most sought-after players on the current jazz scene. Music was a natural for Billy. His dad, Billy Sr., was a drummer with a large record collection. The younger Drummond picked up a pair of sticks at age four and had a pop band with a few school mates when he was only 10. After earning a college degree in music performance, Drummond headed for New York in 1988. During this period he worked with the group Out of the Blue, Joe Henderson, Bobby Hutcherson, Horace Silver, Ralph Moore, and his wife, pianist Renee Rosnes. The main attraction to Drummond is his full, vibrant drum sound and the totally musical approach to what he plays. Much like Elvin Jones, his ideas typically spill over bar lines and his phrasing is as flawless as any horn player's.

what to buy: In addition to having three superb records of his own available on Criss Cross, Drummond can be found on scores of current releases for a variety of labels where his versatility and fire are hot commodities. *Native Colours* 🎵🎵🎵🎵 (Criss Cross Jazz, 1992, prod. Peter Leitch) is the drummer's impressive debut session recorded beautifully by the legendary Rudy Van Gelder. The wonderful blend of Steve Wilson's saxophones and

Steve Nelson's vibes make for a stellar front line, plus pianist Renee Rosnes contributes some of her finest writing and playing on record. *The Gift* ✍✍✍✍ (Criss Cross Jazz, 1994, prod. Gerry Teekens) opts for a quartet with Rosnes, bassist Peter Washington, and up-and-coming saxophonist Seamus Blake. Drummond's penchant for obscure tunes pays off with great versions of Charles Lloyd's "Apex" and Clifford Jordan's "Dear Old Chicago." *Dubai* ✍✍✍✍ (Criss Cross Jazz, 1996, prod. Gerry Teekens) is easily Drummond's finest recorded work to date. This piano-less quartet features the horns of Chris Potter and Walt Weiskopf. The latter, in particular, contributes some exquisite writing and his solo work makes me wonder why he's not better known. This is state-of-the-art stuff!

what to buy next: Although I recommend picking up anything with Drummond on it, I single out this date from very talented pianist-composer Jonny King: *Notes From the Underground* ✍✍✍✍ (Enja, 1996, prod. Matthias Winckelmann). Drummond adapts with ease to the range of styles the music covers. Walt Weiskopf's *Song for My Mother* ✍✍✍✍ (Criss Cross Jazz, 1997, prod. Gerry Teekens), is definitely Drummond's finest hour as a sideman. Weiskopf's program of originals for a nine-piece group brings out the best in the drummer and everyone else involved.

influences:
◀◀ Philly Joe Jones, Elvin Jones, Tony Williams, Eric Gravatt, Max Roach

Chris Hovan

Ray Drummond

Born November 23, 1946, in Brookline, MA.

The son of an Army colonel, bassist Ray Drummond attended 14 schools around the world. He began at age eight on trumpet and, later, french horn before switching to bass at age 15. He later taught himself piano. After his family settled in California, Drummond earned a B.A. in Political Science from Claremont (CA) Men's College in 1968. His first corporate employer sent him to earn his MBA at Stanford. Bored, he left to become a full-time musician in San Francisco in 1971. After another stint in corporate life from 1974 to 1977, he made the break complete and went to New York City where his solid rhythm and harmonic innovations landed him gigs with the Thad Jones/Mel Lewis Jazz Orchestra and Betty Carter. Since then, he has recorded more than 200 albums as a sideman with artists such as Woody Shaw, Art Farmer, Benny Golson, Wynton Marsalis, Pharoah Sanders, and Johnny Griffin. But his greatest contribution to the music has been as a leader and composer. His dates as leader are rare but excellent. Like Charles Mingus before him, while he can play bop backgrounds with the best of them, he has the technical facility and lyricism to make the bass a true solo instrument. He possesses an intimate understanding of jazz and its roots. Many of his original compositions meld African inspirations, modal moods, and a touch of classicism. Yet his imaginative blend remains accessible to the average listener.

what to buy: *Excursion* ✍✍✍✍ (Arabesque, 1993, prod. Ray Drummond), gleaned from music Drummond composed during his musically soul searching years in the early 1970s, features a five-part suite, "Excursion," with some of Marvin "Smitty" Smith's best work, accentuated by Senegalese percussion master Mor Thiam. As a musician and producer, Drummond has a keen ear for great artists. Joe Lovano, Craig Handy, and Danilo Perez are featured on this album recorded before they became big names. *Excursion* was followed by *Continuum* ✍✍✍✍ (Arabesque, 1994, prod. Ray Drummond) where Drummond takes the blues and explores its continuum into modern jazz and world music with quirky arrangements of standards and originals enhanced by the guitar work of John Scofield. *Vignettes* ✍✍✍✍ (Arabesque, 1996, prod. Ray Drummond) is comprised of sketches from Drummond's musical life with neo-bop and "Africanized" originals, with third stream renderings by pianist Renee Rosnes on two "Ballades Poetiques." Drummond's foundation in straight-ahead jazz can be heard in *The Essence* ✍✍✍✍ (DMP, 1991, prod. Ray Drummond, Tom Jung), which captures Drummond as he could often be heard at the now-defunct Bradley's in Greenwich Village. Pianist Hank Jones and drummer Billy Higgins share equal time on standards and a few originals.

the rest:
Camera in a Bag ✍✍✍✍ (Crisscross, 1989/1994)
(With Bill Mays) *One to One* ✍✍✍✍ (DMP, 1989)
One to One II ✍✍✍✍ (DMP 1990)

influences:
◀◀ Charles Mingus
▶▶ Christian McBride

Yvonne Ervin

George Duke

Born January 12, 1946, in San Rafael, CA.

George Duke is one of the most prolific and eclectic musicians of his generation, continually redefining his range as a keyboardist, songwriter, singer, and producer. In addition to making his own trendsetting fusion LPs both as a solo artist and with other jazz musicians such as bassist Stanley Clarke, Duke has pursued numerous, quite diverse musical projects that have jazz purists accusing him of abandoning his roots. He toured with Frank Zappa and the Mothers of Invention, produced three LPs for Jeffrey Osborne, and played on Michael Jackson's *Off the Wall* album. Yet, Duke is a jazz cat at his core: he often tells the story of how his mother took him to see Duke Ellington in concert when he was four, an experience which sent him racing around his house yelling, "Get me a piano!" Heavily influenced by giants such as Miles Davis, Les McCann, and Cal Tjader, Duke graduated from the San Francisco Conservatory of Music and formed his first jazz combo with a young singer named Al Jarreau. He went on to blaze new trails in jazz with violinist Jean-Luc Ponty in his George Duke Trio; tour with sax great Cannonball Adderley and drummer Billy Cobham; and enjoy a series of successful solo funk-fusion LPs beginning in 1976 with *From Me to You.* Turning his interests to producing, Duke made his first vocal album with singer Dee Dee Bridgewater, then earned his breakthrough with the group A Taste of Honey when his production on their album yielded a Number One single on the R&B, pop, and Adult Contemporary charts in "Sukiyaki," selling over two million copies. He has since worked as producer and/or musician for many of popular music's brightest stars, ranging from Sarah Vaughan, Anita Baker, and Gladys Knight to the Winans, Keith Washington, and his cousin, Dianne Reeves, and won a 1989 Grammy for producing the late Miles Davis's album *Tutu.* As the Clarke/Duke Project, the keyboardist recorded a series of lively jazz-funk duo albums with bassist Stanley Clarke.

what to buy: The obvious choice here would be *The Best of George Duke* 🎵🎵🎵🎵 (Epic, 1996, prod. various), and it is a wondrous work, assembling "Dukey Stick," "Reach for It," "Sweet Baby," and other key tracks from his solo albums and work with the Clarke/Duke Project. However, for a sensational example of Duke's dedication to and innovation within the jazz idiom, check out *Muir Woods Suite* 🎵🎵🎵🎵 (Warner Bros., 1996, prod. George Duke), a brilliant composition recorded live at the Montreux Jazz Festival that glides between intimate jazz trio (with Clarke and drummer Chester Thompson) and full orchestra with electrifying interplay between the two.

what to buy next: The first of the three albums from *The Clarke/Duke Project* 🎵🎵🎵🎵 (Epic, 1981, prod. Stanley Clarke, George Duke) is arguably still the best, with the breath of new collaboration and experimentation inspiring such cuts as "Winners" and "Touch and Go" in addition to the duo's best-known hit, "Sweet Baby."

what to avoid: Of Duke's many pop-jazz confections, *Rendezvous* 🎵🎵 (Epic, 1995) is the most lightweight and disposable.

the rest:
Dream On 🎵🎵🎵 (Epic, 1982)
Don't Let Go 🎵🎵🎵🎵 (Legacy, 1990)
Stanley Clarke/George Duke 3 🎵🎵🎵 (Epic, 1990)
Reach for It 🎵🎵🎵 (Legacy, 1991)
Snapshot 🎵🎵🎵🎵 (Warner Bros., 1992)
Three Originals 🎵🎵🎵 (Verve, 1993)
A Brazilian Love Affair 🎵🎵🎵🎵 (Legacy, 1994)
Clarke/Duke Project II 🎵🎵🎵🎵 (Epic, 1995)
Guardian of the Light 🎵🎵🎵 (Epic, 1995)
Illusions 🎵🎵🎵 (Warner Bros., 1995)
Is Love Enough? 🎵🎵🎵 (Warner Bros., 1997)

influences:

⏪ Cannonball Adderley, Miles Davis, Les McCann, Cal Tjader, Frank Zappa, Sonny Rollins, Chick Corea

⏩ Jaco Pastorius, Patrice Rushen, Everette Harp, Dianne Reeves

see also: *Stanley Clarke*

Stacey Hale

Ted Dunbar

Born January 17, 1937, in Port Arthur, TX.

Ted Dunbar's parents were both pharmacists, and that's the field Dunbar was headed for when he graduated from Texas Southern University and got his pharmacy license. He started learning guitar when he was ten, and he had played trumpet in high school, but music was always more of a sideline for him, something to do while preparing for a "real" career. While Dunbar was going to college he would play guitar with local heroes Arnett Cobb and Don Wilkerson, and while in Indianapolis on a school study trip he heard the Wes Montgomery Trio, and his life was changed. The guitarist moved to Indianapolis and started playing gigs and jamming with Freddie Hubbard, Slide Hampton, and Dave Baker. While in Indianapolis Dunbar was introduced to George Russell's Lydian concept, which led, years later, to writing books on guitar techniques, improvisation, arranging, and composing. After a brief return to Texas, where he played with Red Garland and David Newman, in 1966 it was on to New York, where his first record date had him working with Gil Evans. Dunbar was still working the pharmacy angle even as he was gigging with Ron Carter, Sonny Rollins, and McCoy Tyner. Finally, in 1972, he retreated from the druggists' counter to the world of academia and Rutgers University, where he teaches jazz guitar and jazz improvisation. He's still one of the top session guys in the market in addition to being a respected educator.

what's available: *Gentle Time Alone* 🎵🎵🎵 (SteepleChase, 1992, prod. Nils Winther) is the only Dunbar album currently in print. Even though he espouses some interesting theoretical concepts regarding playing and composition, Wes Montgomery's influence is plainer on this album than it is in any of his session work. He even does some of the octave leaping that was a Montgomery trademark. It's quite a pleasant release, featuring nine of Dunbar's compositions played by a strong quartet, but it's only a decent stop gap until someone produces the really good album of which this guitarist is capable. The players include Dunbar, pianist Mickey Tucker, bassist Ray Drummond, and drummer David Jones with flautist Dotti Anita Taylor appearing on one cut.

worth searching for: The Xanadu label is back in business so there may be a possibility that Dunbar's *Opening Remarks* 🎵🎵🎵 (Xanadu, 1978, prod. Don Schlitten) will come back into print on CD. The writing is more focused than on *Gentle Time Alone*, the playing is a little tougher and the sidemen (Tommy Flanagan, Sam Jones and Leroy Williams) are among the best in the biz. Otherwise Dunbar has done a lot of interesting session work, including his brief solo on "Kucheza Blues" from the Randy Weston/Melba Liston album *Volcano Blues* 🎵🎵🎵 (Antilles, 1993, prod. Randy Weston, Brian Bacchus, Jean-Philippe Allard). Dunbar's work on Hamiet Bluiett's *Live at the Village Vanguard: Ballads & Blues* 🎵🎵🎵 (Soul Note, 1997, prod. Hamiet Bluiett) is probably the best thing that Dunbar has done since his days with Xanadu. His playing is responsible for much of what is right with this album and his composition "Rare Moments" is one of the finest moments on the release.

influences:
⏮ Wes Montgomery, George Russell

Garaud MacTaggart

Dominique Eade
Born 1958.

A faculty member at Boston's New England Conservatory of Music since 1984, Dominique Eade is well-versed in the Third Stream airs of pianist/academician Ran Blake as well as the adventurous approaches of collaborators Either/Orchestra and Butch Morris. She's worthy of such free-thinking company, having recorded two discs for Boston's artist-centered independent label, Accurate, using her fluid alto voice to advance the art of scat singing while keeping an eye on jazz tradition.

what to buy: On her second album, *My Resistance Is Low* 🎵🎵🎵 (Accurate 1995, prod. Dominique Eade), Eade and her crack quartet (drummer Lewis Nash, pianist Bruce Barth, and bassist George Mraz) buoy a collection of standards, obscurities, and originals made refreshing by the singer's eagerness to tamper with tempo. She takes "The Tender Trap" at the speed of light and eases down Hoagy Carmichael's title track into blissful pre-pillow talk without succumbing to mere theatrics.

the rest:
The Ruby and the Pearl 🎵🎵🎵 (Accurate, 1990)
When the Wind Was Cool 🎵🎵🎵 (RCA Victor, 1997)

Steve Dollar

Charles Earland
Born May 24, 1941, in Philadelphia, PA.

Charles Earland was the sax player in organist Jimmy McGriff's band at the start of the 1960s, but he learned the rudiments of the Hammond B-3 well enough to go out on his own in 1963. His first major employer after McGriff was saxophonist Lou Donaldson, with whom he recorded *Hot Dog* and *Black and Proud* before forming his own group in 1969. Earland had an immediate hit with *Black Talk!*, still a classic in "acid jazz" circles, and he recorded a slew of albums for Prestige, Mercury, Columbia, and Muse that all feature his punchy keyboard attack. He has also been instrumental in the careers of guitarist Pat Martino, to whom Earland gave his first touring gig, and Jamaaladeen Tacuma, who was a teenage bass wizard before splitting to work with Ornette Coleman. Earland has worked on albums by Boogaloo Joe Jones and Rusty Bryant, while trumpeter Lee Morgan played on two of Earland's better post-*Black Talk!* releases, *Intensity* and *Charles III*.

what to buy: Earland reached the pinnacle of his career with *Black Talk!* 🎵🎵🎵🎵 (OJC, 1969, prod. Bob Porter), and every subsequent release has been an attempt to climb the mountain one more time. Funk is all over this album, even making "Aquarius" (from the Broadway play, *Hair*) a foot pattin' exercise. The horn players, whose solos kick like a bull-rider's nightmare, are tenor man Houston Person (who would produce some of Earland's later sessions for Muse) and trumpeter Virgil Jones. Drummer Idris Muhammad, who had worked with Earland in Donaldson's band, guitarist Melvin Sparks and percussionist Buddy Caldwell fill out the rest of the band.

what to buy next: *Living Black!* ♫♫♫ (Prestige, 1970, prod. Ed Michel), a live date recorded with the same instrumental line-up as on *Black Talk!* in Newark, New Jersey, features tenor saxophonist Grover Washington Jr. before he became a solo artist. The organist almost always includes some current hit tune in his sets, and this time the choices are (remember, this is the early '70s) "Westbound #9" and "More Today Than Yesterday." There's also a kicking version of Benny Golson's "Killer Joe" to boot things along. Earland has taken a long time to hit a groove with any real consistency, but *Ready 'n' Able* ♫♫♫ (Muse, 1995, prod. Charles Earland) is the first one he's done in years with more than a hint of what could have been. The great young tenor sax player Eric Alexander had been working on Earland's sessions since 1992, and ace trumpeter Lou Soloff helps give the front line some punch. The material the band works with is fairly strong, although the organist once again tosses a few recent (at the time) chart toppers into the mix, including "Free" by Denise Williams and "Nick of Time" from Bonnie Raitt, with a golden funk oldie from the George Clinton songbook, "Knee Deep," chucked in for good measure. Earland's "Giving Praise" may be the best thing he's done in awhile.

what to avoid: *The Great Pyramid* **woof!** (Mercury, 1976, prod. Robin McBride, Charles Earland) is a big-time mega woof actually, about as low as Earland could go in his search for commercial relevance. Some of the musicians actually had careers after this piece of near-transcendental garbage; if you ask Gabor Szabo, Jon Faddis, Randy Brecker, or Chris Brubeck for a list of vocational highlights, chances are that this wouldn't be one of them. Synthesizer washes and ballads in search of a click track are not the kind of stuff that will get you enshrined in the Hall of Fame except as a memorial to all that was tacky about the mid-'70s. As an album, this is a sinful waste of polyvinyl chloride; pray that some misguided record company exec doesn't feel the need to market this piece of sonic toxicity on disc.

the rest:
Leaving This Planet ♫♫♫ (Prestige, 1973)
Front Burner ♫♫♫ (Milestone, 1988)
Third Degree Burn ♫♫♫ (Milestone, 1989)
Whip Appeal ♫♫♫ (Muse, 1991)
Unforgettable ♫ (Muse, 1993)
I Ain't Jivin', I'm Jammin' ♫♫♫ (Muse, 1994)

worth searching for: Released in 1972 on Prestige, *Intensity* features two of Earland's larger horn sections. The trumpet

line-up includes Lee Morgan, Virgil Jones, Victor Paz, and Jon Faddis, Hubert Laws plays flute and piccolo while Billy Cobham anchors the rhythm section from behind his kit. Billy Harper has the tenor sax solo on "Morgan," dedicated to Lee Morgan, who died shortly after this session was in the can. Earland even works magic on Chicago's pop hit "Happy 'Cause I'm Goin' Home," and the album is way better than most of the Earland catalog now in print.

influences:
◄◄ Jimmy McGriff, Jimmy Smith, Don Patterson, Jack McDuff

Garaud MacTaggart

Bill Easley

Born 1946, in Olean, NY.

Bill Easley has been a working musician since age 13. The talented multi-instrumentalist first hit the road with George Benson from 1968 to 1970, then moved to Pittsburgh, and subsequently Memphis, where he attended Memphis State University and worked in the Stax-Volt Studios mentoring young musicians like James Williams, Donald Brown, and Mulgrew Miller. Easley joined Mercer Ellington in the late 1970s. Among numerous jobs Easley held after moving to New York in 1981 are the reed chairs with Illinois Jacquet's Big Band, with Panama Francis and the Savoy Sultans, and with the American Jazz Orchestra. Easley has established himself as one of New York's premier session musicians. As Michael Bourne writes in the liner notes to *Easley Said*, "While others of his generation scuffle for work, Bill Easley is working all the time. He might be playing soul tenor with Charles Earland, Jimmy McGriff, or Ruth Brown. Or swing clarinet among the 20-somethings in the Lincoln Center Jazz Orchestra. Or whatever horn in whatever style is needed in Broadway's show pits. And he'll always be soulful, swinging and himself—even more so when fronting his own session."

what to buy: You can begin with *Wind Inventions* ♫♫♫ (Sunnyside, 1986/1996, prod. Francois Zalacain), a showcase for Easley's expressive clarinet, and there aren't too many who play jazz on it with more range and understated virtuosity than he. From the overdubbed rubato intro on clarinet and flutes on the intro, to the title track (variations on "All the Things You Are") which morphs into a bullet-speed clarinet solo on the changes, to the fundamental blues that follows it, to the idiomatic drama of "Come Sunday" and "All Too Soon," it's a challenging session that never lets the listener presume the next step. Mulgrew Miller (piano), Victor Gaskin (bass), and

Tony Reedus (drums) are the first-rate rhythm section. Also check out *Easley Said* ♫♫♫ (Evidence, 1997, prod. James Williams), which offers great post-bop playing on a challenging range of compositions by an outstanding sextet, matching Easley (primarily on alto sax) with veteran Memphis-born tenor saxophonist George Coleman, trumpeter Bill Mobley, pianist Donald Brown, bassist Ron Carter, and drummer Billy Higgins. Listen to Easley's masterful ballad reading of "Nina Never Knew," how he dances through the changes of "Runnin'," Frank Strozier's "Rhythm" variant, and how Easley makes his modal original "Born Out of Darkness" sing. Easley shines in the heavy company.

what to buy next: *First Call* ♫♫ (Milestone, 1991, prod. Bob Porter) finds Easley playing tenor and alto sax on an October, 1990 soul-bop date with a schizophrenic identity. The four performances with Roland Hanna (piano), J.J. Wiggins (bass), Grady Tate (drums), and George Caldwell (synthesizer, two tracks) are well-played as you'd expect, but never really transcend routine genre formulations. The four tracks by the quintet of Bill Mobley (trumpet), James Williams (piano), Dave Jackson (bass), Tate, and Caldwell sparkle with soul, wit, and invention. The latter crew makes a sprightly bossa out of "How Long Has This Been Going On," goes deep into church on the Ruth Brown feature "Oh, What a Dream," and explores the blues in depth on "Soulful Bill" and "Blues for Stitt."

influences:

◀◀ Sonny Stitt, Hank Crawford, George Coleman, Stanley Turrentine, Cannonball Adderley, Barney Bigard, Jimmy Hamilton

Ted Panken

Madeline Eastman

Born in San Francisco, CA.

Madeline Eastman is a consummate professional, a jazz singer with a polished approach who's not afraid to take chances or to take charge. Eastman made her recording debut with the Bay area group, Full Faith & Credit Big Band, co-founded Mad-Kat Records with Bay-area singer Kitty Margolis, and has her own website. She has recorded three albums as leader since 1990 and maintains a busy international touring schedule, performing at festivals, clubs, and at workshops in Finland, Scotland, and Germany. She is founder and head of the jazz vocal department at the Stanford Jazz workshop at Stanford University in California and is on the international staff at both the Pop/Jazz Conservatory and the Sibelius Conservatory in Helsinki, Fin-

land. Over the years, she has served in a variety of other teaching posts, including ongoing summer jazz camps. Eastman was cited by a 1993 *Down Beat* critic's poll as Talent Deserving Wider Recognition. She has been gaining global acclaim for her confident, dynamic style and technique, her velvety warmth and wit, her mastery of vocalese, and her innovative interpretations of jazz standards.

what to buy: If singers are known by the company they keep, then vocalist Eastman is in great company on her 1992 release, *Mad about Madeline!* ♫♫♫ (Mad-Kat, 1992, prod. Paul Potyen). With her illustrious crew—alto saxophonist Phil Woods, pianist Cedar Walton, bassist Tony Dumas, and drummer Vince Lateano—Eastman swoops through the 11-tune collection, including a compatible vocal duet with guest Mark Murphy on the swinging take of Bob Dorough's tune "You're the Dangerous Type." She brilliantly refreshes standards, delivering a romantically sweet and swinging version of "All of You," an upbeat "Cheek to Cheek," and a tender treatment of the Bill Evans ballad, "Turn out the Stars," with Walton creating luxuriant piano accompaniment. With saxman Woods, Eastman generates an angular, modern version of Eddie Harris's classic, "Freedom Jazz Dance," scatting unison lines with the sax genius, and yielding room for his excellent solo. They also work together comfortably on two other tunes. Walton is a remarkable match for this expressive singer, and their closing song together, "Never Never Land," is a beauty. This is an A-plus album. Her most recent CD, *Art Attack* ♫♫♫ (Mad-Kat, 1994, prod. Paul Potyen), features Eastman in a sophisticated and diverse 14-tune set, accompanied mainly by pianist Kenny Barron, bassist Peter Barshay, and drummer Tony Williams, with two tunes enhanced by the Turtle Island String Quartet (TISQ). Eastman's percussion-enhanced group, an alternate assemblage featuring Marcos Silva or Pablo Perez on piano, Jeff Buenz on guitar, David Belove on bass, and Michael Spiro on percussion, backs the singer in various configurations. Their Brazilian/Latin jazz tunes include the soft, guitar accompaniment on the remake of "The Thrill Is Gone," and the collaborative effort from Perez, Belove, and Spiro with the TISQ on a lively Afro-Cuban-tinged version of Monk's "Evidence." Eastman handles these varied tempos with complete ease. The ultimate artist, she can unleash a standard ballad such as "Say It Isn't So," with an engaging suppleness that makes you believe the lyrics. She manipulates her voice in all the best ways, phrasing with unexpected twists and turns at any tempo, and employing warbles and vibrato only for dramatic effect. Plus, she leaves plenty of space for her side players, especially the lyrical Barron. This wonderful album offers hard-swinging tempos and warm ballads with Barron at the keys, and Latin-tinged tunes from the other team. If you own one of her albums, you'll want all three. They can be ordered from her website: www.madelineeastman.com.

the rest:

Point of Departure 𝄞𝄞𝄞𝄞 (Mad-Kat, 1990)

influences:

⏮ Billie Holiday, Miles Davis, Mark Murphy, Carmen McRae

Nancy Ann Lee

Peter Ecklund

Born September 27, 1945, in San Diego, CA.

Trumpeter, cornetist and guitarist Peter Ecklund was raised in Woodbridge, Connecticut. He attended Yale University where he played mostly classical music, but also was exposed to and started playing traditional jazz. After his 1967 graduation, Ecklund taught elementary and high school social studies in the Boston area, and became a founding member of the Galvanized Jazz Band. Ecklund became a full-time musician in 1972, and the following year moved to New York City where he toured, arranged, and recorded with pop and blues artists Maria Muldaur, Greg Allman, David Bromberg, Bonnie Raitt, Paul Butterfield, Paula Lockheart, and others. In the 1980s, Ecklund played an eclectic mix of early pop and jazz with Leon Redbone, and freelanced on jazz gigs with other musicians. Ecklund moved away from pop and rock by 1984. He subbed in Vince Giordano's Nighthawks, arranged for the Widespread Jazz Orchestra and other groups, and played with Terry Waldo's Gotham City Band. Ecklund became lead trumpeter with the Nighthawks in 1986, worked frequently at Manhattan clubs with his own quartet, and often teamed with acoustic guitarist Marty Grosz. At the 1988 Conneaut Lake Jazz Party in Western Pennsylvania, he and Grosz premiered The Orphan Newsboys band, which performs for jazz parties and U.S. festivals. Ecklund enjoys the freedom a small group affords and sometimes travels nearly four hours to Boston to sub with the Black Eagle Jazz Band. As a stylist, he draws influences from Louis Armstrong, Red Allen, Bix Beiderbecke, and Miles Davis, and a joyous mix of these traditional and modern stylists can be detected in his playing.

what's available: *Strings Attached* 𝄞𝄞𝄞𝄞 (Arbors, 1996, prod. Peter Ecklund) features "string" players bassists Greg Cohen and Murray Wall, guitarists Marty Grosz, Frank Vignola, Chris

Flory, Molly Mason, and Ecklund, who sometimes doubles on second guitar. The album draws from six sessions recorded with varying personnel between 1992–1995. Ecklund's warm cornet and some savvy guitar plucking, strumming, and chording are featured throughout. Seven standards are included, along with nine Ecklund originals, some with slightly eccentric titles such as "Get Out of My Way," "Excessively Happy Tune," "Waltz For Another Time," and "12 Country Miles." Not your average fare. *Ecklund At Elkhart* 𝄞𝄞𝄞𝄞 (Jazzology, 1995, prod. George H. Buck Jr.) was captured at the 1994 Elkhart, Indiana Jazz Festival and features him performing with the Classic All-Stars. The album offers a well-balanced set of evergreens and warhorses played by a traditional-style band which appears from its lineup to be an augmented version of The Orphan Newsboys, a band Ecklund co-leads with guitarist Marty Grosz. Joining Ecklund and guitarist Marty Grosz are clarinetist Bobby Gordon, bassist Greg Cohen, trombonist Dan Barrett, drummer Hal Smith and pianist Mark Shane. Worthy of repeat listening, "Where the Blue of the Night" features the leader's puckish whistling and hot, hot cornet renderings.

influences:

⏮ Louis Armstrong, Red Allen, Bix Beiderbecke, Miles Davis

see also: *The Orphan Newsboys, Marty Grosz*

John T. Bitter

Billy "Mr. B" Eckstine

Born July 8, 1914, in Pittsburgh, PA. Died March 8, 1993, in Pittsburgh, PA.

Billy Eckstine is an important, intriguing historical figure for two rather unrelated reasons. The first is that he led one of the first successful working bebop big bands, a proving ground for people like Dizzy Gillespie, Sarah Vaughan, Dexter Gordon, and Art Blakey, to name a few. The second reason is that Eckstine was perhaps the very first black male sex symbol in mainstream American pop culture, creating a role that would later be filled by early rock musicians.

Eckstine got his musical start with the Earl Hines big band in the late 1930s, where he quickly made a name for himself with his silky baritone voice. He was instrumental in bringing brilliant young musicians such as Gillespie, Vaughan, and Charlie Parker into Hines's band, and hired many of them into his own group after 1943. The bop big band Mr. B led in 1944–47 was mostly unsuccessful at the time, but is now highly acclaimed, both for the music it created and the impact it had on the development of modern jazz. When he was forced to break up the band due to financial constraints, Eckstine signed with MGM and became a popular romantic balladeer. However, he never lost his jazz sensibilities, as shown by his recordings for Roulette in 1959–60.

what to buy: *Airmail Special* 𝄞𝄞𝄞𝄞 (Drive Archive, 1996, prod Lynn Franey) is a collection of 1945 recordings featuring the Eckstine big band at its swinging best. A young Sarah Vaughan is heard on a few tunes, and Mr. B himself delivers memorable versions of many of his own compositions, including "I Want to Talk About You" and "Airmail Special." The two-CD set *Everything I Have Is Yours* 𝄞𝄞𝄞𝄞 (Verve, 1994, prod. Bob Porter, Richard Seidel) is an excellent overview of Eckstine's career, covering the years 1947–57. The first disc is mostly a collection of ballads from his MGM years, while the second contains more of the important bop band material.

what to buy next: *Basie and Eckstine, Inc.* 𝄞𝄞𝄞𝄞 (Roulette, 1960/1994, prod. Teddy Reig) finds Eckstine in top form in front of one of the great swing bands. Among other things, this album shows his great versatility as a vocalist.

what to avoid: A 1950s collaboration with Sarah Vaughan, *Irving Berlin Songbook* 𝄞𝄞 (Mercury, 1958/Verve, 1995, prod. Bob Shad) fails to recreate the magic of the sessions from the previous decade.

the rest:
Mister B and the Band 𝄞𝄞𝄞𝄞 (Savoy, 1945–47/1995)
Billy Eckstine's Imagination 𝄞𝄞𝄞𝄞 (EmArcy, 1958/1992)
No Cover, No Minimum 𝄞𝄞𝄞𝄞 (Roulette, 1961/1993)
At Basin Street East 𝄞𝄞𝄞 (EmArcy, 1962/1990)
Sings with Benny Carter 𝄞𝄞𝄞𝄞 (Verve, 1986)
Stormy/Feel the Warm 𝄞𝄞𝄞 (Stax, 1994)

worth searching for: The LP *I Want to Talk about You* 𝄞𝄞𝄞𝄞 (Xanadu, 1940–45) collected Eckstine's earliest recordings, made with Earl Hines in 1940—a collection of ballads well worth looking for.

influences:
◀◀ Cab Calloway, Herb Jeffries
▶▶ Nat "King" Cole, Johnny Hartman

Dan Keener

Harry "Sweets" Edison

Born October 10, 1915, in Columbus, OH.

One of the most distinctive trumpeters in jazz history, Harry "Sweets" Edison can say more with one note than most trum-

peters can say in five choruses. A master of understatement with a wry, backhanded sense of humor and a blues-drenched sensibility, Edison is also one of the few trumpeters from his generation influenced by Dizzy Gillespie. One of the great stylists with a Harmon mute, Edison swings potently while playing softly, repeating seemingly simple phrases while building clever, perfectly constructed solos. Since the '80s his style has grown even more concise as his chops have diminished, but he is still an inimitable improvisor who places notes with surgical precision. First influenced by Louis Armstrong, whom he heard play at a neighborhood dance hall, Edison was raised by his aunt and uncle in Kentucky, and he credits his uncle with giving him a solid musical education. He toured widely with some of the best territory bands, including Jeter-Pillars and Earl Hood, and landed a job with Lucky Millinder when he arrived in New York in 1937. Fired by Millinder in place of Gillespie, Edison was quickly hired in early 1938 by Count Basie, where he was dubbed "Sweets" by Lester Young. Featured on many of Basie's greatest recordings, he stayed with the classic band until Basie broke it up in 1950. In the second phases of his career Edison toured with Jazz at the Philharmonic, served as Josephine Baker's music director, and began a long association with Frank Sinatra, with whom he performed and recorded for years. His contributions to Sinatra's classic Nelson Riddle albums on Capitol—*Songs for Swingin' Lovers!*, *Swing Easy*, and *A Swingin' Affair*—can't be overrated. Edison settled in Los Angeles in the early '50s and became one of the first black musicians to break into the studios, where he worked too much to keep up much of a jazz profile. He reunited with Basie numerous times for concerts and recording dates (many documented on Pablo) and often worked with Benny Carter and tenor saxophonist Eddie "Lockjaw" Davis.

what to buy: A two-CD set that contains three Verve records, including Edison's *Gee Baby, Ain't I Good to You*, *The Soul of Ben Webster* (Verve, 1957–58, prod. Norman Granz) is a treasure trove featuring long-out-of-print sessions by three jazz giants. The Edison album pairs his witty, hide-and-seek trumpet with the robust, breathy tenor of Ben Webster. The rhythm section features Oscar Peterson's propulsive piano work, Barney Kessel or Herb Ellis on guitar, Ray Brown on bass, and Alvin Stoller on drums. (The other albums are *The Soul of Ben Webster*, which pairs the tenor giant with trumpeter Art Farmer, and the great Ellington altoist Johnny Hodges's *Blues-a-Plenty* with Webster, Roy Eldridge, Vic Dickenson, and Billy Strayhorn.) *Jawbreakers* 𝄞𝄞𝄞𝄞 (Riverside, 1962, prod. Orrin Keepnews) is a rambunctious session featuring the two former Basie-ites: Edison and tough tenor Eddie "Lockjaw" Davis. Hugh Lawson (piano), Ike Isaac (bass), and Clarence Johnston (drums) made up Edison's working rhythm section at the time, and they swing with conviction. Check out Lawson's McCoy Tynerish touch on Edison's title track. Steeped in the blues but hardly trapped in the swing era, Edison and Davis make a timeless duo. At first glance *Oscar Peterson & Harry Edison* 𝄢𝄢𝄢𝄢 (Pablo, 1974, prod. Norman Granz) might seem like a highly unlikely pairing, but such are the mysteries of jazz. The combination of one of the most prodigious players with one of the great minimalists produces an album for the ages, a set full of thrilling interplay and fascinating improvisational contrasts. Though *Edison's Lights* 𝄢𝄢𝄢𝄢 (Pablo, 1976, prod. Norman Granz) once again unites Edison with the great "Lockjaw" Davis, it's the presence of Count Basie that makes this an event. Their joy at working together again is reflected directly into the music.

what to buy next: Not one of the greatest sessions with Edison and "Lockjaw" Davis, *Simply Sweets* 𝄢𝄢𝄢 (Pablo, 1978, prod. Norman Granz) features the two swinging veterans on a program of five blues and a few ballads, including the unfortunate "Feelings." Still, Edison and Davis are endlessly inventive blues players, and the rhythm section features the too-little-recorded Dolo Coker (piano), Harvey Newmark (bass), and Jimmie Smith (drums). A solid session with a strong band, *For My Pals* 𝄢𝄢𝄢 (Pablo, 1988, prod. Eric Miller) features the powerful saxophonist Curtis Peagler, trombonist Buster Cooper, pianist Art Hillery, bassist Andy Simpkins, and drummer Tootie Heath. Sweets shows off his lyrical side, especially on "There Is No Great Love," but he really cuts loose on the concluding 11-minute "Blue for the Cats," which was added to the CD reissue. A hard-driving album recorded live in Tokyo by the Frank Wess-Harry Edison Orchestra, *Dear Mr. Basie* 𝄢𝄢𝄢𝄢 (Concord Jazz, 1991, prod. Carl E. Jefferson) isn't really a Basie tribute. Which isn't a complaint, 'cause this all-star session swings like mad and features some strong solos, including Edison's on "I Wish I Knew." Snooky Young and Curtis Peagler are also in top form.

best of the rest:
'S Wonderful 𝄢𝄢𝄢𝄢 (Pablo, 1982)
Just Friends 𝄢𝄢𝄢𝄢 (Pablo, 1983)
Swing Summit 𝄢𝄢𝄢𝄢 (Candid, 1991)

worth searching for: Recorded live at the legendary Lighthouse in Hermosa Beach, *The Inventive Mr. Edison* 𝄢𝄢𝄢𝄢 (Pacific Jazz, 1953, prod. Dick Bock) features a top-flight West Coast band and Edison stretching out in one of his first small group recordings after leaving Basie.

influences:
◀◀ Louis Armstrong, Rex Stewart
▶▶ Bobby Hackett, Miles Davis

Andrew Gilbert

Marc Edwards

Born July 23, 1949 in New York, NY.

Marc Edwards is a free jazz drummer who has recorded with Cecil Taylor (*Dark to Themselves*), David S. Ware (*Passage to Music*, *Great Bliss Volumes 1 and 2*, *Flight of i*), and Charles Gayle (*More Live at the Knitting Factory*). He started leading his own groups in 1990 and has issued two albums on his Alpha Phonics label (distributed by North Country/Cadence). The seemingly tireless Edwards has a formidable technique which he sometimes uses to create stunningly dense polyrhythms, though he is not averse to using a sparer style when appropriate. But it's his powerful, extended rolls—from his rock-solid rudiments it's clear his time in drum-and-bugle corps was well-spent—that are his trademark, providing a massive and stimulating foundation for the frontline instruments. He also studied with a number of respected drum teachers, most notably Tony Williams's teacher, Alan Dawson.

what's available: Most recent and perhaps easiest to find of Edwards's releases is *Red Sprites & Blue Jets* 𝄢𝄢𝄢𝄢 (CIMP, 1997, prod. Robert Rusch). The title refers to lightning, and there's plenty of thunder too. Tenor saxophonist Sabir Mateen matches the leader's boundless energy and free-flowing inventiveness throughout, no small feat. Bassist Hill Greene often gets lost in the mix—which isn't the fault of the recording, as that's the group's natural sound—but his contribution to the low end is felt nonetheless as he strums (and sometimes bows) the drones that prompt Edwards to call him a "flamenco bassist." "Positive Charge-Negative Release" is a wild and exhilarating storm, while "Upper Atmosphere" offers a contrasting quiet opening where the trio effectively explores more subtle timbres before heating up. "African Rain Dance," which opens with a multifaceted drum solo, later shows that, unlike some free jazz drummers, Edwards doesn't always shun a steady groove, though his is certainly complex. Mateen gets the start of the title track to himself and contrasts swirling lines across a wide range against timbral effects until the bass and drums enter with a roiling cloudburst. Greene gets to start the final "Morning Dew" with a pretty arco solo, switches to pizzicato, and is joined by Mateen more than five minutes in as Edwards enters gently behind them, in keeping with the title. The intensity, density, and volume build gradually through this 21-minute piece, but the mood remains reverential and meditative for most of the track. This album is a tour de force of free playing.

worth searching for: Both of Edwards's self-produced-and-issued albums feature alto saxophonist Rob Brown. *Black Queen* ♪♪♪♪ (Alpha Phonics, 1991, prod. Marc Edwards) is slightly better thanks to veteran bassist Fred Hopkins and innovative pianist Matthew Shipp, whose wide-voiced chords sometimes suggest huge tolling bells and set the overall tone of the album. Two cuts are graced by Edwards's poetry (don't worry, it's much better than the usual jazz poetry) as recited by actress Laverne Maxwell. The playing here seems to encompass the world. Going beyond even that is the full-out blowing session *Time & Space, Volume I* ♪♪♪ (Alpha Phonics, 1993, prod. Marc Edwards), which was partially inspired by Edwards's interest in outer space exploration. Hill Greene is energetic and full-toned but lacks Hopkins's finesse, while alto saxophonist Cara Silvernail is the fourth member instead of Shipp.

influences:

◀◀ Max Roach, Tony Williams, Rashied Ali

Steve Holtje

Teddy Edwards

Born Theodore Marcus Edwards, April 26, 1924, in Jackson, MS.

Saxophonist Teddy Edwards would be a much more recognized player if he hadn't the misfortune to make the West Coast his home base. Although he played a pivotal role in the development of bop in the late '40s and early '50s, all of the attention was on the East Coast scene, and he is often overlooked by the general jazz fan. Nevertheless, Edwards has proven to be a versatile musician and has made many fine recordings, both as a leader and a sideman. He began his career as an alto player, bouncing around Detroit and Tampa and touring with Ernie Field's orchestra before finally settling in Los Angeles in 1945 as a member of Roy Milton's big band. He switched to tenor sax after being invited to join Howard McGhee's group, and that remains his primary instrument. It was at this time that Edwards had the chance to help create a new sound by performing and recording with a wide range of artists, including Benny Carter, Red Callender, Max Roach, Clifford Brown, Dexter Gordon, Gerald Wilson, and many others. The early '60s were his most productive time as a leader, resulting in a series of excellent albums on Contemporary. The rest of the '60s and '70s were characterized by touring and occasional recording with a focus

on composing and arranging for television, radio, and film. Edwards kept a lower profile during the '80s, but revitalized his recording career in the '90s, courtesy in part to the efforts of singer Tom Waits, who helped him secure a new record deal and appeared on his Antilles debut. Edwards has a big, warm sound easily adaptable to both bluesy ballads and powerful solo flights, which made him a popular choice to pair with other tenor players. He also matched well with trumpeter Howard McGhee and pianist Phineas Newborn Jr. on his Contemporary records. Probably due to his years in scoring for TV and the like, his most recent releases have tended toward sentimental, orchestrated pieces that dilute some of the power of his playing. Nonetheless, he still has the stuff, as evidenced on his 1995 album of trio sessions, *Tango in Harlem*.

what to buy: *Together Again!!!!* ♪♪♪♪ (Contemporary, 1961, prod. Lester Koenig) is a tremendous pairing with Howard McGhee and a crack band of Phineas Newborn Jr., Ray Brown, and Ed Thigpen. Everything clicks on this set of nifty bop burners, from Charlie Parker's "Perhaps" to Brown's frenetic "Up There" to Edwards's own title track—it's clearly the product of some old friends jamming together once again.

what to buy next: With a quartet setting, Edwards really shows his stuff on *Good Gravy!* ♪♪♪♪ (Contemporary, 1962, prod. Lester Koenig). Most of the piano is reliably played by Danny Horton, but the two tracks on which Newborn contributes especially shine. *Back to Avalon* ♪♪♪ (Contemporary, 1995, prod. Lester Koenig) includes some previously unreleased sessions from 1960, with unusual octet arrangements by Edwards that feature some of his overlooked West Coast chums.

the rest:

Teddy's Ready ♪♪♪ (Contemporary, 1960)
Heart and Soul ♪♪♪ (Contemporary, 1962)
Nothin' but the Truth ♪♪♪ (Prestige, 1967)
It's All Right ♪♪♪ (Prestige, 1968)
Feelin's ♪♪♪ (Muse, 1974)
Out of This World ♪♪♪ (SteepleChase, 1981)
Mississippi Lad ♪♪ (Antilles, 1991)
Blue Saxophone ♪♪♪ (Antilles, 1992)
Tango in Harlem ♪♪♪ (Gitanes/Verve, 1995)
(With Houston Person) *Horn to Horn* ♪♪♪ (Muse, 1996)

influences:

◀◀ Don Byas

▶▶ Ernie Watts

Eric J. Lawrence

Mark Egan

Born January 14, 1951, in Brockton, MA.

Mark Egan has been an influential electric bassist well-known throughout the jazz scene for his use of electronic effects and for having a sound similar to that of Jaco Pastorius. Egan started playing trumpet at the age of 10. Picking up bass as a teenager, he played with R&B groups and his high school's jazz band. Egan went to the University of Miami (Ohio) under the direction of Jerry Coker, studied privately with Jaco Pastorius, and in Florida formed a band with fellow University students Hiram Bullock, Clifford Carter, Phyllis Hyman, and Bill Bowker. Egan also played in the Baker's Dozen band with Pastorius and Ira Sullivan.

In 1976, Egan went to New York, studied with Dave Holland, and worked with him. From 1977–1980, Egan was a member of the Pat Metheny Group, which included drummer Danny Gottlieb. Leaving that group, Egan joined the Gil Evans Orchestra (1983–1985), and performed on Monday nights at the Village Vanguard. An in-demand studio bassist, Egan's credits include work with the Pointer Sisters, David Sanborn, Deodato, Joan Osborne, Michael Franks, Rory Block, Joe Beck, Marianne Faithful, Arcadia, Laurie Anderson, Mike Stern, Richie Havens, Sting, and many more. Egan's greatest visibility since 1982 has been as coleader of Elements, his band with longtime compatriot Danny Gottlieb, which for many years featured old bandmate Clifford Carter.

what to buy: *Beyond Words* &&&& (Mesa/Bluemoon, 1991, prod. Mark Egan) features Egan with an all-star cast of Elements collaborators—Steve Khan, Danny Gottlieb, Bill Evans, and Clifford Carter—plus Manolo Badrena, Toninho Horta, Don Alias, and Gordon Gottlieb. Egan's compositions are quite tuneful and often pretty.

the rest:
Mosaic &&& (Hip Pocket, 1985/Wavetone Records, 1993)

worth searching for: Using an eight-string as well as a four-string fretless electric bass, Egan weaves his way through nine originals on the out-of-print *A Touch of Light* &&&& (GRP, 1988, prod. Mark Egan), showcasing, in myriad ways, how well the bass can be used as a melodic instrument. From funky to pensive passages, this is an enjoyable album.

influences:
◄◄ Miles Davis, Kenny Dorham, John Coltrane, Jack Cassidy, Jack Bruce, Chuck Rainey, James Jamerson, Stanley Clarke, Jaco Pastorius, Eberhard Weber, Steve Swallow, Ron Carter, Paul Chambers, Scott LaFaro

►► Abraham Laboriel, John Patitucci

see also: *Elements*

David C. Gross

Marty Ehrlich

Born May 31, 1955, in St. Paul, MN.

Elements of bop, pop, free, and contemporary classical work their way into the elegant music of composer/arranger/multi-instrumentalist Marty Ehrlich. A graduate of the New England Conservatory of Music, Ehrlich's musical associations are an indication of the depth of his commitment to expanding the boundaries of jazz: he's been a member of bands led by Anthony's Braxton and Davis; Muhal Richard Abrams depends upon him in his larger ensembles; he played in Julius Hemphill's all-reed sextet and later took over as the group's musical director after its founder's death; and he was an integral part of the late John Carter's celebrated octet. Perhaps the Hemphill and Carter references are the most telling, because they point out Ehrlich's affinity for the "Fort Worth" school of soulful improvising and "composer-ly" attributes that characterized the work of both these past masters, as well as that of Ornette Coleman, whose influence on Ehrlich is plainly apparent on any number of tunes (try, for example, "Generosity" on *The Welcome*). The other player who comes to mind is, of course, Eric Dolphy, who pioneered the modern-day, multi-reed approach and whose flute technique is the clear precursor of Ehrlich's own (in this respect, note the covers of Charles Mingus and John Coltrane tunes on *The Traveller's Tale*). In any event, Ehrlich's warm and woody, yet ever-so-slightly astringent tone on saxophone (alto is his main ax) is distinctive and immediately identifiable.

what to buy: Ehrlich's solo output is extremely balanced, quality-wise. There's not a clinker in the bunch, so the places to start and where to go next are mostly a matter of personal preference. If you like your improvising relatively unadulterated and straight-ahead, try the "power-trio" outlines of his debut as leader, *The Welcome* &&&& (Sound Aspects, 1984, prod. P. DeFreitas), where he's teamed with the marvelous bassist Anthony Cox and the splashy drumming of Pheeroan Aklaff. Then again, several of Ehrlich's best outings have been those where he's paired with the fine and under appreciated Boston-based saxophonist, Stan Strickland, which produces an extremely pleasing yin-yang effect in the front line. *Can You Hear a Motion* &&&& (Enja, 1994, prod. Marty Ehrlich) pairs the two hornmen with the striking bassist Michael Formanek and the bright, explosive percussion of Bobby Previte; *The Traveller's Tale* (Enja, 1990, prod. Marty Ehrlich) ✍✍✍ substitutes Lindsey Horner for Formanek; and the cleverly titled *Pliant Plaint* ✍✍✍ (Enja, 1988, prod. Marty Ehrlich) is a muscular set (dig Strickland's barwalking tenor intro to "The All-Told Alto Blues") that features an Ehrlich-Strickland-Cox-Previte line-up. Ehrlich and Strickland join forces with drummer Bill Stewart, bassist Formanek, and pianist Michael Cain for the enormously satisfying *New York Child* ✍✍✍✍ (Enja, 1996, prod. Marty Ehrlich).

what to buy next: The other Ehrlich-led band to feature a keyboardist—in this instance Wayne Horvitz—is heard on *Side by Side* ✍✍✍ (Enja, 1991, prod. Matthias Winckelmann), an attimes cacophonous outing that also includes trombonist Frank Lacy, Anthony Cox, and Andrew Cyrille. Ehrlich's chamber-like Dark Woods Ensemble is more classically informed than his other projects. *Emergency Peace* ✍✍✍ (New World, 1991, prod. Lee Townsend) includes Horner, cellist Abdul Wadud, and Richard Muhal Abrams on two tracks. *Just before the Dawn* ✍✍✍ (New World, 1995, prod. Wayne Horvitz) has Vincent Chancey on French horn, Erik Friedlander on cello, Mark Helias's bass, and Don Alias's percussion. *Dark Woods Ensemble, Live* ✍✍✍ (Music & Arts, 1997, prod. Marty Ehrlich) includes Helias and Friedlander. Ehrlich and Cox teamed up in 1989 for a stunning set of duets, released as *Falling Man* ✍✍✍ (Muse, 1991, prod. Marty Ehrlich, Anthony Cox).

influences:

◀◀ Ornette Coleman, Julius Hemphill, John Carter, Eric Dolphy

▶▶ Tim Berne, Sam Furnace

David Prince

Eight Bold Souls /Ed Wilkerson Jr.

Formed 1985, in Chicago, IL.

Ed Wilkerson Jr., tenor, alto, and bass saxophones, clarinet, alto clarinet; Mwata Bowden, clarinet, baritone and tenor saxophones; Robert Griffin, trumpet and flugelhorn; Isaiah Jackson, trombone; Aaron Dodo, tuba; Naomi Millender, cello; Harrison Bankhead, bass; Dushun Mosley, drums.

Eight Bold Souls is a remarkably consistent Chicago octet led by Ed Wilkerson Jr. that follows the example of fellow AACM member Muhal Richard Abrams in composing music that's highly structured yet loose and daring and hard to categorize— too planned to be called free jazz, more far-out than bebop or

post-bop, but definitely stimulating and satisfying. There are moments in some of the group's music which suggest early Ornette Coleman as an influence. Wilkerson formed the group for a four-concert series to present his octet music, and the musical results and the audience's response led to its perpetuation. 8BS's size and instrumentation help it to stand out from the AACM crowd and provide a musical experience of considerable stylistic and timbral variety. The group's debut album was issued on Wilkerson's own label; for information, contact sessomsmus@aol.com or P.O. Box 6812, Chicago, Illinois 60680. Two releases on Arabesque have led to a higher profile.

what to buy: *Ant Farm* ✍✍✍ (Arabesque, 1994, prod. Eight Bold Souls) mixes bluesy rhythms and the undulating feel and good humor of early jazz from New Orleans and Chicago, yet is recognizably modern. The complexity of some of the charts never inhibits the relaxed improvisations on six tracks ranging in length from 8:27 to 16:07—this is a band which, when it stretches out, never stretches its material too thin.

what to buy next: *Sideshow* ✍✍✍ (Arabesque, 1992, prod. Eight Bold Souls) also finds the octet stretching out on some highly evocative mood pieces. A cover of Coleman's "Lonely Woman" helps define Wilkerson's music's relationship to the composer; for one thing, they share a warmth which is very inviting.

the rest:

Eight Bold Souls ✍✍✍ (Sessoms, 1987)

worth searching for: Wilkerson leads a quartet with trumpeter Rod McGaha, 8BS bassist Harrison Bankhead, and stalwart drummer Reggie Nicholson on *Light on the Path* ✍✍✍ (Sound Aspects, 1994, prod. Pedro de Freitas), released by a small German label (available in the United States through Cadence). Nicholson's more mainstream pulse balances the longer, more freewheeling and spontaneous structures (Wilkerson wrote all songs on both CDs), and McGaha's improvisations and tensile tone (a cross between Miles Davis and Don Cherry) almost steal the show.

influences:

◀◀ Muhal Richard Abrams, Ornette Coleman

Steve Holtje

Either/Orchestra

Formed 1985, in Boston. MA.

Russ Gershon, tenor and soprano saxophones; Tom Halter, trumpet, fluegelhorn; John Carlson, trumpet, fluegelhorn; Bob Seely, trumpet

(1985–86); Dan Drexler, trumpet (1985–86); Dave Ballou, trumpet (1985–86); Russell Jewell, trombone (1985–93); Josh Roseman, trombone (1985–86); Curtis Hasselbring, trombone (1986–93); Dan Fox, trombone (1993–present); Robb Rawlings, alto saxophone, clarinet (1985–89); Douglas Yates, alto saxophone, clarinet (1989–90); Andrew D'Angelo, alto saxophone, clarinet (1993–94); Charlie Kohlhase, alto and baritone saxophone (1987–present); Oscar Noriega, alto saxophone, clarinet (1995–present); Steve Norton, baritone saxophone (1985–86); John Dirac, guitar (1985–89); Kenny Freundlich, keyboards (1985–88); John Medeski, keyboards (1988–92); Chris Taylor, keyboards (1993–present); Michael Shea, keyboards (1992–93); Michael Rivard, bass (1985–89); Bob Nieske, bass (1989–92); John Turner, bass (1992–present); Jerome Deupree, drums (1985–90); Matt Wilson, drums (1990–94); Eric Rosenthal, drums (1994–present).

The musically fertile Boston area has produced a plethora of talented jazz musicians, many of whom find a performance home with the eclectic and exciting Either/Orchestra. It is one of the few large jazz ensembles able to mount wide-ranging tours with any real consistency, having played all over the United States, Canada, and Europe. Founded in 1985 by saxophonist Russ Gershon (who also runs the label, Accurate, for which the group records), the Either/Orchestra keeps mutating, spinning off one world-class player after another and replacing them with other talented artists. Over the years, the Either/Orchestra has also played with high-quality guest musicians like saxophonists John Tchicai and Jay Brandford, guitarist Jerry Hahn, drummer Chris Wood, and vocalist Dominique Eade. While Gershon leads the Either/Orchestra, contributing a substantial portion of their "book" and playing saxophones, there are other members and associates of the band writing and arranging material for the ensemble. In addition to music written especially for them, the band also performs intriguing renditions of standards from talents as diverse as Duke Ellington, Sonny Simmons and Burt Bacharach.

what to buy: The Either/Orchestra is so good that the two-CD album of out-takes *Across the Omniverse* ♫♫♫♫ (Accurate, 1995, prod. Russ Gershon) is one of the outstanding releases in its already strong catalog. It gives a wonderful overview of the band's career through 1994, with killer versions of Juan Tizol's immortal "Caravan" and sounding perfectly natural on Lennon/McCartney's "(I Want You) She's So Heavy." *Brunt* ♫♫♫♫ (Accurate, 1993, prod. Russ Gershon) features absolutely classy playing—with verve, bite, and humor. There is a simply outstanding take on Mal Waldron's "Hard Talk" to go along with inventive charts from trombonist Hasselbring (the

title tune) and the tongue-in-cheek "Notes on a Cliff." A fine mix of live and studio performances, *The Calculus of Pleasure* ♫♫♫♫ (Accurate, 1992, prod. Russ Gershon) is a beguiling blend of fanciful humor and serious professionalism, including the intriguing pastiche of Mingus-isms, "Bennie Moten's Weird Nightmare," and one of the best recordings of Julius Hemphill's "The Hard Blues."

what to buy next: With the introduction of keyboardist (and organ specialist) John Medeski on *The Half-Life of Desire* ♫♫♫♫ (Accurate, 1990, prod. Russ Gershon), the Either/Orchestra gained an element of edgy fun and modern funk. The resulting album moved the band up another notch, from being merely very good to verging on wonderful. The medley of Miles Davis's "Circle in the Round" and the Ellington standard "I Got It Bad" is a major highlight.

the rest:
Dial E ♫♫♫ (Accurate, 1986)
Radium ♫♫♫ (Accurate, 1988)

influences:
◀◀ Duke Ellington, Charles Mingus, Don Ellis
▶▶ Jazz Composers Alliance Orchestra

Garaud MacTaggart

Roy Eldridge

Born January 30, 1911, in Pittsburgh, PA. Died February 26, 1989, in Valley Stream, NY.

Roy Eldridge is often first thought of as a stylistic bridge between Louis Armstrong and Dizzy Gillespie. But Eldridge's innovation and virtuosity on the trumpet indicate that he deserves mention as an equal to those two greats.

Eldridge began playing with territory bands in the mid-east in the early 1930s, but his big musical break came when he hooked up with Teddy Hill's group in 1935. He also backed Billie Holiday, played with Fletcher Henderson, and by the end of the 1930s, Eldridge was probably the most important trumpeter in jazz. The early 1940s saw Eldridge, who had gained the nickname "Little Jazz," presented with lucrative offers to join the popular bands of Gene Krupa and Artie Shaw. But by the end of the 1940s, Eldridge's playing had gone out of style, and he went to Europe for a couple of years. He returned to the United States in 1951 with renewed confidence and was embraced as part of the resurgence in mainstream jazz. Eldridge went on to make many stimulating recordings—mostly for Norman Granz's labels Verve, Clef, and Pablo—in the 1950s, 1960s, and 1970s.

Eldridge's style, like that of any trumpeter of the era, was profoundly influenced by Louis Armstrong. But he also assimilated the longer lines and fluid articulation of prominent reed players, especially Coleman Hawkins and Benny Carter, and in this way had a major influence on bop trumpeters. These influences, combined with Eldridge's own ebullient nature, combined to make him one of the most exciting jazz soloists of his era, or of any other.

what to buy: *Little Jazz* ♫♫♫♫ (Columbia, 1989, prod. Michael Brooks) is an incredible collection of early Eldridge recorded from 1935–40, featuring many exciting cuts made with Teddy Hill, Billie Holiday, and Fletcher Henderson. But the real gems are the records made under Eldridge's own leadership as part of the "Heckler's Hop" session of 1937; these are important documents in the career of a trumpet giant. Producer Norman Granz was famous for bringing together formidable musicians in interesting settings. On *Roy and Diz* ♫♫♫♫ (Verve, 1955/1994, prod. Norman Granz), he teams the combative Eldridge with the jazz giant who looked up to him as a mentor. Rarely did Granz's machinations work this wonderfully. Sometimes this CD sounds like a cutting contest, sometimes like a mutual admiration society—but it always sounds like great jazz. Also worth noting is the wonderful backing provided by the Oscar Peterson trio. Eldridge called all the shots on *The Nifty Cat* ♫♫♫♫ (New World, 1970/1986, prod. Bill Weilbacher), made rather late in his life—he chose the tunes (all his own), hired the musicians, and just about everything else. The result is reminiscent of a self-portrait by an aging painter; it is as personal a statement as Eldridge would ever make.

what to buy next: *After You've Gone* ♫♫♫ (GRP Decca, 1991, prod. Orrin Keepnews) is another excellent CD compilation of early Eldridge recorded 1936–46, featuring quite a few tracks with Gene Krupa and Anita O'Day. *Montreux '77* ♫♫♫♫ (Pablo, 1978/OJC, 1989, prod. Norman Granz) is the last recording Eldridge would make, and it's also one of his best. How a musician in his late 60s with fading chops could still sound so incandescent and exuberant is a marvel. The last two tunes especially, "Perdido" and "Bye Bye Blackbird," provide a fitting testament to a brilliant career.

what to avoid: *Jazz Maturity . . . Where It's Coming From* ♫♫ (Pablo, 1978/OJC, 1994, prod. Norman Granz) is a second meeting between Eldridge and Gillespie that doesn't even come close to creating the fireworks of the first meeting. It's not bad music, but after the 1955 record, it's a bit of a disappointment.

the rest:
Roy Eldridge in Paris ♫♫♫ (Vogue, 1950/1995)
Little Jazz: The Best of the Verve Years ♫♫♫♫ (Verve, 1951–60/1994)
1957 Live ♫♫♫ (Jazz Band, 1959)
Count Basie and Roy Eldridge ♫♫♫ (Pablo, 1972/OJC, 1988)
Happy Time ♫♫♫ (Pablo, 1975/OJC, 1991)
What It's All About ♫♫♫ (Pablo, 1976/OJC, 1995)
Roy Eldridge and Vic Dickenson ♫♫♫ (Storyville, 1978)
Just You, Just Me—Live in '59 ♫♫♫ (Stash, 1990)
(With Gene Krupa, Anita O'Day) Uptown ♫♫♫ (Columbia, 1990)
Heckler's Hop ♫♫♫♫ (Hep CD, 1993)
Eldridge, 1935–1940 ♫♫♫♫ (Classics, 1993)
The Big Sound of Little Jazz ♫♫♫♫ (Topaz, 1995)

worth searching for: The two-LP set *Dale's Wail* ♫♫♫♫ (Clef, 1954, prod. Norman Granz) has yet to be reissued on CD, but the music is certainly deserving. Although he's backed by such stars as Oscar Peterson and Buddy Rich, Eldridge is alone, front and center throughout.

influences:

◄◄ Louis Armstrong, Coleman Hawkins

►► Dizzy Gillespie, Howard McGhee, Fats Navarro

Dan Keener

Elements

Formed 1982, in New York, NY.

Mark Egan, bass; Danny Gottlieb, drums.

Egan and Gottlieb were the rhythm section of the Pat Metheny Group from 1977 to 1980 and reunited in Elements. Though Egan and Gottlieb are the only official members, for a long time the group also regularly featured keyboardist Clifford Carter and saxophonist Bill Evans, with other guests including guitarist Steve Khan. They play thoughtful, uncompromised fusion that's as deep as it is tuneful, with Egan doing the bulk of the writing. Unfortunately, little of the group's work remains in print despite its consistent quality.

what to buy: *Far East, Vol. 1* and *Far East, Vol. 2* ♫♫♫♫ (Wavetone, 1993, prod. Mark Egan) document an exciting Japanese live gig and are the group's most recent recordings, released on Egan's own label. Here the quartet is filled out by saxist David Mann and keyboardist Gil Goldstein, and they stretch out more and play more exciting up-tempo numbers in the live context than they tended to in the studio.

what to avoid: *Blown Away* ♪ (Passport, 1987, prod. Mark Egan, Danny Gottlieb) is the only other Elements album still in print. The soundtrack to a windsurfing movie of the same title, it's much simpler than their other work and frankly sounds slapped together, often leaning towards smooth jazz vapidity. Tracks including guitarist Joe Caro's emptyheaded, clichéd solos are the worst.

the rest:
Forward Motion ♪♪♪ (Antilles/Island, 1984)
Illumination ♪♪♪♪ (Novus, 1988)
Liberal Arts ♪♪♪ (Novus, 1989)
Spirit River ♪♪♪ (Novus, 1990)

worth searching for: All the group's out-of-print material is worth hearing. Especially crucial is the debut, *Elements* ♪♪♪♪ (Antilles/Island, 1983, prod. Mark Egan, Danny Gottlieb, Rich Brownstein), which recalls the sounds and textures of Weather Report. But any 1980s guitarless fusion quartet inevitably would, and though keyboardist Clifford Carter and Bill Evans when he's playing soprano saxophone hardly reduce the comparisons, Egan's compositions and the leaders' strong musical personalities define the quartet beyond the obvious similarities. There's an almost meditative peacefulness to many of the tracks, and the lines flow organically. The exciting exception is Gottlieb's only writing contribution, "Conundrum," with Evans switching to tenor sax (on which he's more assertive) as the group builds up a head of steam, pushed by Gottlieb's joyously bashing beat. Danny Gottlieb's out-of-print *Whirlwind* ♪♪♪ (Atlantic, 1989, prod. Doug Hall) still finds him contributing relatively few compositions, with producer/keyboardist Doug Hall pitching in and several guest tunes and group efforts. The guests, in fact, are the main attraction, with guitarists John Abercrombie and Chuck Loeb especially standing out.

influences:
◀◀ Pat Metheny Group, Weather Report
▶▶ Jan Garbarek

see also: *Mark Egan*

Steve Holtje

Mark Elf

Born December 13, 1949, in Queens, NY.

Elf is a real fret-burner, a hardcore bebop guitarist whose specialty is energetic runs through classic bebop tunes. He tends to play in a detached style, though he can phrase smoothly when he feels like it, and he has the timeless electric hollow body guitar sound of ringing, rounded tones.

Elf attended Berklee (1969–71) and studied privately with Barry Gailbraith and Chuck Wayne. He has recorded or performed in concert with a huge number of jazz luminaries: Lou Donaldson, Freddie Hubbard, Joe Henderson, Jimmy McGriff, Groove Holmes, Junior Cook, Bill Hardman, Wynton Marsalis, Benny Golson, Al Grey, Lonnie Smith, Charles Earland, Clark Terry, Dizzy Gillespie, Lionel Hampton, Walter Bishop, Jr., Kenny Barron, Jimmy Heath (with whose quartet he spent a fair amount of time) and the Heath Brothers, Curtis Fuller, Joe Newman, Barry Harris, Branford Marsalis, Slide Hampton, Jimmy Cobb, Donald Byrd, and Al Foster, as well as backing singers Jon Hendricks, Dakota Staton, Cab Calloway, Joe Williams, Etta Jones, Ruth Brown, and Liza Minelli. His long-gone first recording, on the Half Note label, came in 1986, but a lack of recorded exposure as a leader commensurate with the respect he has in the jazz community led him to start his own label, Jen Bay (www.jenbayjazz.com), on which he has released an album a year starting in 1996. He also works as an educator and private instructor from his home base on Long Island, New York.

what to buy: *Trickynometry* ♪♪♪♪ (Jen Bay, 1998, prod. Mark Elf) finds Elf the composer stepping out more than on his earlier albums, with eight originals out of twelve tracks. As expected, he stays firmly in the bebop tradition, using blues progressions and familiar changes (the title track is based on "Lover Come Back to Me"). The personnel varies from track to track; the core trio is drummer Yuron Israel and Christian McBride or Neal Miner on bass, with trumpeter Nicholas Payton the most famous guest. Vocals by the agile Miles Griffith and the inimitable Grady Tate provide changes of pace. Elf's speed runs are tamed down just enough that he never sounds like he's showing off, which allows more room for nuance and attractive legato playing.

what to buy next: *Minor Scramble* ♪♪♪♪ (Jen Bay, 1997, prod. Mark Elf) is another all-star album, with Payton, tenorman Eric Alexander, pianist Benny Green, and a variety of bassists and drummers (eight of the twelve tracks are trio numbers). Elf rips through "After You've Gone" with great verve, whizzing through until a slow coda, and has fun on the Latin classic "Tico Tico." *Eternal Triangle* ♪♪♪♪ (Jen Bay, 1996, prod. Mark Elf) was recorded in 1988 with pianist Hank Jones, bassist Ray Drummond, and drummer Ben Riley, with Jimmy Heath joining on tenor sax on some numbers. It has Elf's usual fine mix of standards ("Why Do I Love You," "Prelude to a Kiss," and "This Is

All I Ask"), bebop classics (by Sonny Stitt, Tadd Dameron, Benny Golson, Kenny Dorham, and Freddie Redd), and two Elf originals. The mood is a bit more laid-back than on the later albums, making it a nice change of pace after the more recent barn burners—which isn't to say Elf had any less technique back then!

worth searching for: *Mark Elf Trio* ♫♫♫♪ (Alerce, 1994, prod. Alejandro Espinosa) comes from a label based in Chile and, despite its title, is not entirely a trio production. There are horns on "Sweet and Lovely" and a female vocalist of no particular distinction on "Body and Soul," and Elf plays the final track, "Darn That Dream," by himself in a gorgeous arrangement. He also scats in unison with himself on "It's You or No One," which is exciting until his playing gets too far beyond his vocal range. The highlights are his changes-devouring romps through "Giant Steps" and a super fast "Shaw Nuff" and his funky "Tribute to Wes."

influences:

◀◀ Charlie Parker, Bud Powell, Tal Farlow, Joe Pass, Wes Montgomery, Pat Martino, Jimmy Raney, George Benson

Steve Holtje

Eliane Elias

Born March 19, 1960, in Sao Paulo, Brazil.

Eliane Elias is a powerful two-handed linear pianist whose fleeting lines are punctuated with chords and varied by altering dynamics, diverse phrasing ideas, and a wide range of moods and emotions. In Brazil, Elias began classical piano studies at age 10 and two years later was considered an accomplished classical pianist. She pursued further studies at a school run by the jazz-oriented instrumental group, the Zimbo Trio, the Centrol Livre de Apremdizagem Music (or Free Center of Music Apprenticeship). She began as a student and ended up teaching by the age of 15. She was simultaneously performing in local jazz and bossa nova clubs, blending Brazilian rhythms with her newfound influences Herbie Hancock and Chick Corea. Bassist Eddie Gomez heard Elias play in Paris and recommended she move to New York, which she did in 1981. Elias became a member of the group Steps Ahead two years later. After leaving the group in 1984, Elias performed and recorded with her husband, Randy Brecker. She made her debut as leader in 1986, signed with the Blue Note label in 1989, and toured with her trio.

what to buy: Elias not only understands how to make great music, but has wisdom, confidence and perseverance to keep it

happening. *The Three Americas* ♫♫♫♫ (Blue Note, 1997, prod. Eliane Elias) is her 11th album in as many years, but mining her native rhythms makes this her most authentic journey. Taking new chances on 10 originals and two Jobim classics of *The Three Americas*, Brazilian-born pianist Elias melds influences of Central and South America to North American jazz. Elias is a powerful lyrical pianist who has demonstrated on previous recordings that she can imaginatively stretch out. On this disc, Elias displays her keyboard prowess (and occasionally sings in cool bossa style) as she artfully merges and shifts among various Brazilian beats, Cuban rhythms, Argentinean nuevo tango, and straight-ahead jazz—occasionally, in the same tune! Such diversity is served well by Elias's cohesive core companions, bassist Marc Johnson and drummer Satoshi Takeishi, and special guests, flutist Dave Valentin, accordionist Gil Goldstein, violinist Mark Feldman, guitarist Oscar Castro-Neves, and percussionists Manolo Badrena and Cafe, among others. In the company of bassist Eddie Gomez, drummer Jack DeJohnette, and percussionist Nana Vasconselos, Elias leads a stunning tribute to Brazilian composer Antonio Carlos Jobim on *Eliane Elias Plays Jobim* ♫♫♫♫♫ (Blue Note, 1990, prod. Eliane Elias, Randy Brecker), an 11-tune album that remains one of her best. Merging her jazz sensibilities with native Brazilian rhythms, Elias eloquently performs Jobim classics such as "Agua de Beber," "Passarim," "Dindi," "One-Note Samba," and more. Gomez is gorgeously in his element, and DeJohnette is painterly in his expressions. This an engaging and memorable album, alone worth the price for the leader's lush version of "Don't Ever Go Away."

what to buy next: For her eighth Blue Note album, *Solos and Duets* ♫♫♫♫ (Blue Note, 1995, prod. Eliane Elias), Elias records her first entire album of solo piano selections and jazz-based improvisations, featuring guest Herbie Hancock. The duets were recorded in New York, the four solo selections, in Brazil. Expressions range from sweet simplicity, to experimentally free, to almost Bartokian stylings with Hancock—angular, powerful, and very classically contemporary. Hancock and Elias are well matched, inspiring freedom for each other's improvisations on their collaborative pieces, especially the last four of the 11 tracks, titled "Messages" (Parts 1–4). Elias and Hancock produce fresh and provocative improvisations, and alone, Elias shows profound talent. An impressive album!

the rest:
Cross Currents ♫♫♫♪ (Denon, 1988)
So Far So Close ♫♫♫♪ (Blue Note, 1989)
Illusions ♫♫♫ (Denon, 1990)

A Long Story ♪♪♪♪ (Blue Note, 1991)
Fantasia ♪♪♪♪ (Blue Note, 1992)
Paulistana ♪♪♪♪♪ (Blue Note, 1993)
Best of Eliane Elias ♪♪♪ (Denon, 1995)

influences:

◄◄ Bud Powell, Keith Jarrett, Art Tatum, Herbie Hancock, Chick Corea, Ivan Lins, Antonio Carlos Jobim

Nancy Ann Lee

Kurt Elling

Born November 2, 1967, in Chicago, IL.

Kurt Elling is a strong but sensitive hipster-songster who draws particularly on the style of Mark Murphy. He turns a lyric with the right dose of histrionics and musical acumen. He's a fearless scatter, matching lines with post-Coltrane saxophone screams, which puts him in over his head, but what a show. His greatest originality is in bringing semi-improvised poetic "rants" into his work, diving off the board of Murphy's vaunted monologue-poetry-song experiments. A University of Chicago Divinity School drop-out (one degree short of his M.A., he reports), Elling took to the city's jazz scene, where he hooked up with his regular pianist Laurence Hobgood.

what's available: As a debut recording *Close Your Eyes* ♪♪♪♪♪ (Blue Note, 1995, prod. Laurence Hobgood) held so many surprises that its Grammy nomination came as little surprise. Elling mixes up what sounds like off-the-cuff stream of consciousness with poetry by the likes of Kenneth Rexroth and Rilke, and he pulls off even "Never Never Land." On *The Messenger* ♪♪♪ (Blue Note, 1996, prod. Laurence Hobgood, Kurt Elling) the inspired poetics of 1995 sometimes sink to inspirational verse worthy of greeting cards. There's a steamy duet with Cassandra Wilson, though one wishes there had been a weightier vehicle than "Time of the Season," and he doesn't add much new to "Nature Boy." But he's as inspired as ever reworking Donald Byrd's "Tanya Jean," and his scatting is more assured. Hopefully this is just a sophomore slump for a major talent.

influences:

◄◄ Lou Rawls, Mark Murphy, Jon Hendricks, Eddie Jefferson

►► Kevin Mahogany, Dennis Rowland, Harvey Thompson

W. Kim Heron

Duke Ellington

Born Edward Kennedy Ellington, April 29, 1899, in Washington, DC. Died May 24, 1974, in New York, NY.

Truly the essence of the gentleman genius, the impact that Duke Ellington had on music—all music, not just jazz—could hardly be overstated. As probably the most important composer of the 20th century, it was Ellington who, during the crucial formative stages of the genre, pushed jazz beyond being mere "colored entertainment" and transformed it into a genuinely complex and artful musical form. He informed his compositions with thoughtful, grandiose statements and simultaneously kept his band swinging hard. And, rather than simply being content as a crack bandleader from "the early days," Ellington refused to be sentimental and kept growing and changing, always aware of and involved with the mutating beast known as jazz.

Ellington first started playing the piano at age seven and, by the age of 18, had formed his first band, the Duke's Serenaders, and written his first composition, "The Soda Fountain Rag" (were it not for Ellington's job at the Poodle Dog Cafe, a D.C. soda counter, no telling what would have happened, for it was there that he got both his nickname and the inspiration for his first tune). Although the Serenaders were moderately successful and Ellington had just married and had a son, Mercer, it was decided in 1923 to attempt success in New York after being offered a gig with Wilbur Sweatman's band. Although it didn't pan out, Ellington was smitten with Harlem and, after a brief return to D.C., Duke and his "Washingtonians" (as the band was now called) headed back to the city. For good. The next four years (1923–27) laid the foundation for Ellington's future. The band had a steady gig at Club Hollywood (which became Club Kentucky after a fire), as well as weekly radio broadcasts. It was during this time that Ellington hired trumpeter Bubber Miley, who, for his brief period in the orchestra, would be a guiding light until his drinking forced his "early retirement" in 1929. However, it was in 1927, after the group's last season at Club Kentucky, that Ellington's star began to arc irreversibly skyward, since this was the year that the Duke Ellington Orchestra found itself hired at the renowned Cotton Club. Their "jungle nights" shows became the stuff of legend, with Ellington arranging and overseeing the outrageous floor show that brought in the huge crowds—black and white—every night. It was during this Cotton Club period that Ellington began composing in earnest, producing "Mood Indigo," "Tiger Rag," "The Mooche," "Black and Tan Fantasy," and many others. Also while at the Cotton Club, he hired an alto player who would in-

Duke Ellington **(Archive Photos)**

form most of the music he would make over the next 40 years: Johnny Hodges.

In 1931 Ellington left the Cotton Club and headed out on the road, where he would stay for much of the next four decades. This was the era of the swingin' big band and Ellington did not disappoint, not only by making his band one of the top concert attractions, but also by composing dozens of hits, most of which would become standards over the years: "Sophisticated Lady," "Solitude," "Prelude to a Kiss," "It Don't Mean a Thing If It Ain't Got That Swing," and others. When tenor player Ben Webster, bassist Jimmy Blanton, and trumpeter Ray Nance joined in the early 1940s, Ellington had under his wing some of the best soloists in the business and the Orchestra's work blossomed accordingly. More importantly however was the arrival of Billy Strayhorn, who not only aided Duke by creating masterful arrangements and compositions of his own, but also by becoming one of Ellington's closest friends. During this period, the band was at one of its strongest peaks, and Ellington also

debuted (at Carnegie Hall, no less) his first major, extended piece, "Black, Brown, and Beige." With the end of the war and the close of the big-band era, however, Ellington found the Orchestra struggling a bit, but with the royalty money from his compositions, he managed to stay on the road. Nonetheless, the replacement rate in the band was pretty high (even Hodges split for a while) and it wasn't until the early 1950s, with the return of Hodges and the arrival of masterful tenor player Paul Gonsalves (as well as the Duke's subtle assimilation of bebop forms) that the Ellington band was ready for action.

Arriving at the 1956 Newport Jazz Festival fully intent on unveiling a new work—the aptly titled "Newport Jazz Festival Suite"—Ellington was ready for action again. However, what he was *not* ready for was a riot. In one of the few real "historic moments" in jazz, the 7,000-strong crowd at the festival exploded in joyous rapture in the midst of Gonsalves's 27-chorus solo during "Diminuendo and Crescendo in Blue." Headlines were made and Ellington was back on top. The period that immediately followed yielded few new major compositions (except, of course, "Satin Doll"), however the band, featuring Clark Terry, Cat Anderson, Buster Cooper, as well as Hodges, Nance, and Gonsalves, was certainly one to contend with. It wasn't until the 1960s (especially after a State Department-sponsored tour through the Middle and Far East) that Ellington again began unveiling compositional masterworks. All magnificent and of varying complexity (but consistent beauty), pieces like "The Far East Suite" (1966), "Money Jungle" (1962), "La Plus Belle Africaine" (1966), and "The Afro-Eurasian Eclipse" (1971), show that, even near the end, Ellington never lost his genius. After outliving nearly everyone in his earlier bands, Sir Duke died of cancer four weeks after his 75th birthday, leaving a legacy that will be felt for many, many years to come.

what to buy: With nearly 200 Ellington CDs currently in print, and many times issued on record in the past, it would be unreasonable to try to list and grade them all. Rather, what follows is an informative entrée into this legend's prodigious output. Keep in mind, there is no such thing as a *bad* Ellington record, only ones that suffer from substandard sound (as is the case with many of the more historical documents) or less-than-perfect—though still better-than-average—performances. Of all the many documents of Club Kentucky/Cotton Club-era Ellington, the triple-disc set *Early Ellington: The Complete Brunswick and Vocalion Recordings, 1926–31* ♫♫♫♫♫ (Decca, 1926–31/1994) is certainly the best. Due both to its scope (77 cuts, with a good dozen alternate takes) and the surprisingly good sound quality, this compiles all the sides that Ellington cut for Brunswick and Vocalion before 1931. Illustrative of the band's formative stylings, as well as Ellington's early compositional proficiency ("Tiger Rag," "East St. Louis," "Toodle-Oo," and "Black and Tan Fantasy" can all be found here), this is definitely the place to start to get a handle on the genesis of a genius. *The Blanton-Webster Band* ♫♫♫♫♫ (RCA, 1940–42/1987, reissue prod. Bob Porter) covers what is unquestionably one of the Ellington band's finest (if not *the* finest) eras. These three discs cover, logically enough, the strong and swinging combination of Jimmy Blanton's individualistic bass playing, the deadly tenor-alto combination of Hodges and Ben Webster, and the first collaborations with Strayhorn. Between 1940 and 1942 the Orchestra was unstoppable and this necessary set shows why. *Carnegie Hall Concerts, January 1943* ♫♫♫♫♫ (Prestige, 1943/1991) contains Duke's first (of many) appearance at Carnegie Hall and, for the illustrious occasion, he debuted "Black, Brown, and Beige" in its entirety. Unfortunately, this two-disc set isn't entirely his-

torically correct (some parts are spliced in from a Boston concert a few days later, due to the loss/damage of the original acetates). And, furthermore, the premiering suite winds up split between the last part of the first disc and the first part of the second. Regardless, between the mind-melting power of Hodges and Webster and the overall impact of the orchestra, this is valuable as both a document and a portrait of a genius moving from strength to strength. Although Hodges and Webster weren't present on *Uptown* ♫♫♫♫ (Columbia, 1952/1987, prod. George Avakian) (Hodges having temporarily struck out on his own; Webster permanently), new kids on the block Gonsalves, trumpeter Clark Terry, and powerhouse drummer Louie Bellson were on hand for this comeback of sorts. Alternating between pieces old and new ("The Mooche" and "Perdido" rest nicely next to more modern numbers like "Harlem" and "The Controversial Suite"), this studio set doesn't exactly break any ground, but, due to its undeniable strengths, it did help re-invigorate Ellington at a time when the least likely thing in the world was a successful big band. Ah, the show! . . . if you own only one live jazz album, let it be *Ellington at Newport* ♫♫♫♫ (Columbia, 1956/1987, prod. George Avakian). In an era of bebop, post-bop and hard bop, only Ellington's band could make a crowd lose its mind by having a tenor player wrench out a 27-chorus blues solo. "The Newport Jazz Suite" is here too, and it's certainly quite nice, but you've gotta hear that solo to understand why improvisation is the key to this music. Often overlooked, *The Great Paris Concert* ♫♫♫♫♫ (Atlantic, 1963/1989, prod. Ilhan Mimaroglu) is a stunning set (actually culled from four different concerts) which is exuberant and full of power. With Hodges now well back in the fold (with the inimitable Gonsalves as his tenor foil), and mainstays like trumpeters Cootie Williams and Cat Anderson, trombonist Buster Cooper, and baritone saxman Harry Carney, Ellington blazes through mostly newer material (the recorded debut of "Suite Thursday," his odd theme for TV's *The Asphalt Jungle*) with typical enthusiasm. *And His Mother Called Him Bill* ♫♫♫♫♫ (Bluebird, 1967/1988, prod. Brad McCuen) is a touching, but not moribund, tribute to the then-recently deceased Strayhorn (who died just three months previous to the recordings). The session finds Ellington and a 15-member group lovingly moving through 16 wonderful, yet less-known Strayhorn compositions (there's no "Lush Life" here). The playing here is tasteful, yet remarkably unrestrained, with Hodges letting loose some his most blistering solos to date.

what to buy next: *Solos, Duets, and Trios* ♫♫♫♫ (Bluebird, 1932–67/1990, prod. various) presents one of the strongest showcases of the Duke's piano playing. Although it spans an insanely large time frame, it's nonetheless consistent and, given that there are relatively few examples of his pure piano work, this is a necessary addition to any collection. Two separate two-disc sets, *The Duke's Men: Small Groups, Volume I* ♫♫♫♫ (Columbia, 1934–39/1993, prod. Helen Oakley) and *The Duke's Men: Small Groups, Volume II* ♫♫♫♫ (Columbia, 1934–39/1993, prod. Helen Oakley), showcase the strengths of Ellington's players in small group settings, rather than as soloists and section players. Everyone, from Hodges and Williams to Rex Stewart and Juan Tizol, has the opportunity to shine here. Thankfully kept to a rather limited time-frame, the music here is consistent and actually showcases a few hard-to-find Ellington compositions. Although this same show is available as two single discs, the double-disc set *Fargo, North Dakota, 1940* ♫♫♫♫ (Vintage Jazz Classics, 1940/1996) comes recommended because of *slightly* better sound quality and sheer convenience. But that's not what matters. What's important here is this is the Blanton-Webster band at their strongest and this was the very first show with trumpeter Ray Nance. This concert helps explain why Ellington's orchestra was the one to beat during this era. Although some pundits disregard *Piano Duets: Great Times with Billy Strayhorn* ♫♫♫ (Riverside/OJC, 1950) as a mere historical footnote, in truth, it's both highly enjoyable and astonishingly diverse. Although the tunestack is a bit predictable ("Perdido," "C Jam Blues," "Take the 'A' Train"), some surprises do pop up, most notably the uniformly odd "Tonk." More interesting still is the format that Ellington and Strayhorn utilize for their duos. On eight of the cuts, it's simply the two augmented by a bass player, which, on its own, merits a listen. However, the last four tracks find bassist Lloyd Trotman and workhorse drummer Jo Jones abetting Ellington on piano, Strayhorn on celeste(!) and, wait for it, Oscar Pettiford on cello. Now, given that the players are all quite into it and the proceedings are kept decidedly lighthearted, could a record like that be dull? Although *First Time! The Count Meets the Duke* ♫♫♫♫ (Columbia, 1961/1987, prod. Teo Macero) could have been better, it's hard to imagine how, especially when one considers that 1961 was not the best of times for either of these big band powerhouses. With both the Duke and the Count at the piano for most of the cuts and, generally, both bands in full swing at all times, the fact that the song selection is rather mundane is far eclipsed by the sheer joyousness of the proceedings. *Money Jungle* ♫♫♫♫ (United Artists, 1962/Blue Note, 1989, prod. Alan Douglas) is again an underrated Ellington classic. Whether a calculated move or not, this date—with Charles Mingus and Max Roach—more than proved that the

DUKE ELLINGTON

song "Money Jungle"
album Money Jungle
(Blue Note, 1962/1987)
instrument Piano

Monster Solo

Duke was the very essence of hip, unafraid to hold his own against the new wave of jazz. This intimate trio setting works incredibly well, and though Mingus attempts some scenery-chewing pyrotechnics every now and then, this is among each of the participants' finest hours as players. *Far East Suite* ♫♫♫♫ (RCA, 1966/Bluebird, 1995) documents the first of a slew of extended mid-1960s suites that saw Ellington incorporating elements both modern and exotic into his big band mix. Rather than lower himself to making pseudo-ethnic easy listening records, he instead borrowed ideas like tuning and syncopation (and even drone) from the countries he'd visited, emerging with a suite that evoked, without ever directly quoting, the music that had inspired it. Daring and very, very successful. Although not quite as stunning musically as *The Far East Suite*, *The Afro-Eurasian Eclipse* ♫♫♫♫ (Fantasy, 1971/OJC, 1991) , is nonetheless fairly theoretically advanced. Using as a springboard Marshall McLuhan's prophetic theory that national/regional/ethnic differences would soon be superceded by a sort of Orientalized superrace, the works here evoke a sort of vague internationalism (tinged, of course, with an Eastern touch) that Ellington's last band does a marvelous job of interpreting.

best of the rest:

In a Mellotone ♫♫♫ (RCA, 1940–42/1995)
Black, Brown & Beige ♫♫♫♫♫ (RCA/Bluebird, 1944–46/1988)
Carnegie Hall Concerts, January 1946 ♫♫♫ (Prestige, 1946/1991)
The Great Chicago Concerts ♫♫♫♫ (MusicMasters, 1946/1994)
Carnegie Hall Concerts, December 1947 ♫♫♫ (Prestige, 1947/1991)
Piano Reflections ♫♫♫ (Capitol, 1953/1989)
Jazz Party ♫♫♫ (Columbia, 1959/1987)
Ellington Suites ♫♫♫ (OJC, 1959–72/1990)
The Duke Ellington–Louis Armstrong Years ♫♫♫♫♫ (Columbia, 1961)
The Feeling of Jazz ♫♫♫ (Black Lion, 1962/1992)
New Mood Indigo ♫♫♫ (Doctor Jazz, 1962–66/Columbia, 1991)
All Star Road Bands, Volume I ♫♫♫ (Doctor Jazz, 1964/Columbia, 1989)
All Star Road Bands, Volume II ♫♫♫ (Doctor Jazz, 1964/Columbia, 1990)
Second Sacred Concert ♫♫♫♫ (Prestige, 1968/1990)
New Orleans Suite ♫♫♫♫♫ (Atlantic, 1970/1993)
Latin American Suite ♫♫♫♫ (Riverside/OJC, 1972/1990)
Live at the Whitney ♫♫♫ (Impulse!, 1972/1995)
Togo Brava Suite ♫♫♫ (United Artists/Capitol, 1972)

influences:

◀◀ Willie "The Lion" Smith, Eubie Blake

▶▶ Thelonious Monk, Charles Mingus, Miles Davis, Gil Evans, Bill Holman, Maria Schneider, Cecil Taylor

see also: *Ella Fitzgerald, Frank Sinatra*

Jason Ferguson

Mercer Ellington

Born March 11, 1919, in Washington, DC. Died February 8, 1996, in Copenhagen, Denmark.

Mercer Ellington could never escape the overwhelming shadow of his father, Duke Ellington, but he never really tried. Instead, he strove to perpetuate his father's legacy after his death. Mercer learned music in Washington, D.C. while growing up, and after moving to New York, he tried to start up his own bands in the late 1930s and early 1940s. He was ultimately unsuccessful, despite having sidemen such as Billy Strayhorn, Cat Anderson, Clark Terry, and Carmen McRae. During this time he also made notable contributions to the Duke Ellington songbook, writing "Things Ain't What They Used to Be" and "Blue Serge" (among others). Through the next few decades, Ellington would work in many capacities within the music industry, trying his hand at managing, sales, disc jockeying, and trumpet work for his father and Cootie Williams. After Duke's death in 1974, Mercer took over his band, making some enjoyable, but not very

important, music in that capacity. He also wrote a biography of his father titled *Duke Ellington in Person.*

what to buy: For *Digital Duke* ♫♫♫♫ (GRP, 1987, prod. Michael Abene, Mercer Ellington), Mercer's group mixed such Ellington alumni as trumpeter Clark Terry, altoist Norris Turney, and trombonist Britt Woodman with other talented musicians, including saxophonist Branford Marsalis and pianist Sir Roland Hanna. The result is an enjoyable set of classics with a fresh feeling.

what to buy next: *Only God Can Make a Tree* ♫♫♫ (MusicMasters, 1995, prod. Steve Fox) has a worldly, environmental theme and features interesting arrangements of such Ellington standards as "Caravan" and "Sophisticated Lady." It's rather run of the mill, but still a good example of what Mercer did with the band after his father's passing.

what to avoid: *Take the Holiday Train* ♫ (Special Music, 1992, prod. Mercer Ellington) is the kind of lazy, commercial album Mercer's father never would have made, relying more on cliches and a few big names than on originality. The Duke-ish renditions of Christmas tunes are worth skipping.

the rest:

Continuum ♫♫♫ (Fantasy, 1975)
Hot and Bothered ♫♫ (Doctor Jazz, 1984)
Music Is My Mistress ♫♫♫ (MusicMasters, 1988)

worth searching for: With a cast including tenorman Ben Webster, altoist Johnny Hodges, pianist Strayhorn, and trumpeter Terry, one would hardly know the strong *Black and Tan Fantasy* ♫♫♫♫ (Coral, 1958, prod. Mercer Ellington) was an album by Mercer and not his father's orchestra.

influences:

◀◀ Duke Ellington

▶▶ Quincy Jones, T.S. Monk Jr.

Dan Keener

Richard Elliot

Born in Glasgow, Scotland.

Raised in Los Angeles, Richard Elliot has been a professional musician since his teens. At age 16, he traded in his high school band uniform for a slot touring Europe with Natalie Cole and the Pointer Sisters. Moving from pop/R&B to fusion, Elliot joined the West Coast band Kittyhawk. He also became an in-demand studio player for artists including Smokey Robinson, the Four Tops, and the Temptations, and toured with Rickie Lee Jones. Asked to join the high-profile band the Yellowjackets, Elliot played on that band's second album and tour. He was part of Melissa Manchester's backing band while playing occasionally with Tower of Power. From 1982–88, Elliot was a permanent part of the famed Tower of Power horn section, and can be heard on TOP's recording *Power*. Elliot has been creating solo recordings since 1986. His reverb-laden style on tenor and soprano sax is soaring, powerful, and sensuous. He succeeds in combining an earthy, muscular energy with a breezy lyricism. His first five recordings were originally released on the Enigma Records label. Often imitated, his style has helped define the sound associated with the popular "Smooth Jazz" FM radio format, or, as Elliot prefers to call the genre, "Contemporary Instrumental."

what to buy: *Jumpin' Off* 𝄢𝄢𝄢𝄢 (Metro Blue, 1997, prod. Paul Brown) is Elliot's first work with an outside producer since his first two solo recordings. Freed from the producer's chair, he seems to bring more of the intensity, passion, and energy of his live performances to these studio tracks. Like a fine wine, Elliot's style matures with age. His mid-'90s discs *City Speak* 𝄢𝄢𝄢𝄢 (Blue Note Contemporary/Capitol, 1996, prod. Richard Elliot) and *After Dark* 𝄢𝄢𝄢𝄢 (Blue Note Contemporary/Capitol, 1994, prod. Richard Elliot) solidify his unique personal sound. Elliot's wailing, transcendent interpretation of "When a Man Loves a Woman" on *Take It to the Skies* 𝄢𝄢𝄢𝄢 (Manhattan-EMI, 1989, prod. Richard Elliot) sets a standard for instrumental ballads in the 1990s.

what to buy next: *On the Town* 𝄢𝄢𝄢𝄢 (Manhattan-EMI, 1991, prod. Richard Elliot) contains "Over the Rainbow," another signature-defining tune in Elliot's repertoire. The ballad gets a lush, romantic treatment that's spinetingling. The rest of the disc is almost as good as this remarkably sexy presentation. Several tracks on *Soul Embrace* 𝄢𝄢𝄢 (Manhattan-EMI, 1993, prod. Richard Elliot), including "Sweat" and "Deep Blue," continue to get popular airplay within today's Smooth Jazz FM radio format. *The Power of Suggestion* 𝄢𝄢𝄢 (Manhattan-EMI, 1988, prod. Richard Elliot) has the Tower of Power horn section guesting on three tracks: "Oompong," "Neon Nights," and "Spare Time."

the rest:
Trolltown 𝄢𝄢𝄢 (Manhattan-EMI, 1986)
Initial Approach 𝄢𝄢𝄢 (Manhattan-EMI, 1987)

influences:

◀◀ The Yellowjackets, Tower of Power, David Sanborn

▶▶ Boney James, Eric Marienthal

B.J. Huchtemann

Bᴜʙʙᴇʀ Mɪʟᴇʏ
(ᴡɪᴛʜ Dᴜᴋᴇ Eʟʟɪɴɢᴛᴏɴ)

song "Black and Tan Fantasy"
album *The Brunswick Era,*
Volume 1: 1926–29
(Decca, 1927/1990)

instrument Trumpet

Dave Ellis

Born December 1, 1967, in Fontana, CA.

With his big, smooth-toned tenor sound and wide-ranging musical taste, Dave Ellis plays an artful blend of jazz, funk, and pop while avoiding most of the pitfalls of radio-slated jazz-lite. A product of the Berkeley High School jazz program, Ellis has played an important role on the vibrant San Francisco Bay scene in developing funk/jazz hybrids. Ellis has toured and recorded with a number of other Bay Area musicians, including guitarist Charlie Hunter and trumpeter Dmitri Matheny. He has also toured with Ratdog, a blues/rock band led by former Grateful Dead guitarist Bob Weir. His debut release is a stylistically diverse affair that delves into acid jazz but also explores advanced mainstream jazz compositions.

what's available: A fine debut by a gifted player with a foot in both the jazz and acid jazz worlds, *Raven* 𝄢𝄢𝄢𝄢 (Monarch Records, 1996, prod. Bud Spangler) features a who's who of the Bay Area's youthful jazz scene. The album opens with a smokin' trio version of Jackie McLean's "Little Melanie," with Charlie Hunter (eight-string guitar) and Mike Clark (drums), and closes with the same players on the Beatles' "Tomorrow Never Knows." Though there are some light-weight tracks (Ronnie Laws's "Always There"), much of the music is quite rewarding, especially a sextet arrangement of Woody Shaw's "A Rose for Rose," and a quartet version of McCoy Tyner's "Contemplation."

influences:

◀◀ Wayne Shorter, Joe Henderson

Andrew Gilbert

Don Ellis

Born July 25, 1934, in Los Angeles, CA. Died December 17, 1978, in Hollywood, CA.

Trumpeter Don Ellis was hailed as "the Stan Kenton of the younger generation" when he presented his first big band in the late 1960s. Ellis had already paid his dues with big bands led by Woody Herman, Claude Thornhill, Lionel Hampton, Charlie Barnet, and Maynard Ferguson. In search of advanced harmonic and rhythmic ideas, he even spent two years with George Russell, as well as collaborating with Hari Har Rao in the Hindustani Jazz Sextet. When Ellis moved to Los Angeles in the mid-1960s, he turned away from all avant-garde experimentation and formed a 21-piece orchestra, striving to reach a younger audience. The group achieved great success following an appearance at the Monterey Jazz Festival in 1966. Its innovations included extensive use of odd time signatures, the first use of electronics in a big band, the fusion of Indian music and jazz, use of quarter tones for solos and ensemble passages and a vocal quartet used as instrumentalists. Even though the band was riding a wave of commercial acceptance, Ellis kept changing its instrumentation, concept, and direction. As a result, he had no identifiable style, except that he was a proselytizer for new musical developments.

what's available: Ellis was a true innovator and the 1963 session *New Ideas* ♫♫♫♫ (OJC, 1963, prod. Orrin Keepnews), featuring pianist Jaki Byard, bassist Ron Carter, and drummer Charlie Persip, is jazz for intellectuals, the trumpeter's unique musical path resting somewhere between the classically based "Third Stream" and more adventurous avant garde. *New Ideas* is an eclectic musical brew, from the conventional "Natural H" to the atonal "Tragedy" and "Imitation." The trumpeter's extemporized solo trumpet voyage, aptly titled "Solo," shows off an impressive knowledge of the horn, and throughout this adventurous recording Ellis's compelling music warrants com-

plete attention for its freshness, ingenuity, and the striking originality of its conception. The execution is also particularly stunning, not surprising considering the musicians present. If you have a sense of adventure, run, don't walk to your nearest CD outlet and purchase the re-release of *Electric Bath* ♫♫♫♫ (GNP/ Crescendo, 1996, prod. John Hammond Jr.), a classic 1960s musical tapestry that features one of the most innovative musicians of the era. Recorded in 1968, Ellis and his big band broke the mold. Informed by rock, they were among the first groups to utilize electronics constructively, seldom losing touch with jazz. Unique harmonies and time signatures were their calling card, with "Turkish Bath," a case in point. The composition, coming out of the blues, is in five. It showcases Ellis's use of microtones, which are achieved by his use of a specially made, four-valve trumpet. The reed section is also tuned to quarter tones, and on this track their sound is amazingly kaleidoscopic. If Jelly Roll Morton had returned in a time machine and dropped some acid before the gig, this music might have been the result. *Out of Nowhere* ♫♫♫ (Candid, 1961, prod. Nat Hentoff), a date from the beginning of the decade, recorded just after Ellis left Maynard Ferguson's big band, is a nice, simple blowing session unlike his other music. Standards like "My Funny Valentine" and "Sweet and Lovely" are front and center here, played by a tasty quartet that features Paul Bley on piano and a very young Steve Swallow on bass. Ellis plays his version of Ferguson's upper-register trumpet gymnastics throughout, but with taste and verve. Interestingly, this was one of the recordings that writer Nat Hentoff produced for the Candid label, an association that was rather short-lived.

influences:

◀◀ Stan Kenton, Gil Evans, George Russell, Maynard Ferguson

▶▶ George Gruntz, Chuck Mangione, Sun Ra, Toshiko Akiyoshi

Bret Primack

Herb Ellis

Born Mitchell Herbert Ellis, August 4, 1929, in Farmersville, TX.

Guitarist Herb Ellis is a fine bop stylist who has worked with an array of top musicians since his career began in the 1940s. Ellis attended North Texas State University from 1941–43. His early performances included stints with the Casa Loma Orchestra (1944), Jimmy Dorsey (1945–47), and the Soft Winds Trio with pianist Lou Carter and violinist/bassist Johnny Frigo. Ellis gained greatest visibility when he replaced Barney Kessel in the Oscar Peterson trio (1953–58) and he made a life-long friend of bassist Ray Brown, with whom he has performed and recorded for nearly 45 years. Ellis moved to Southern California in the 1960s where he played area nightclubs, but mostly worked in Los Angeles television and recording studios, including on *The Steve Allen Show* with Don Trencher's band from 1964–65, and on shows hosted by Joey Bishop and Merv Griffin. Ellis began an association with Concord Records in 1973 that has yielded nearly 30 albums. He also recorded with the Dukes of Dixieland, Stuff Smith, and joined forces with guitarist Joe Pass in 1973 and they recorded albums together. In 1974 Ellis formed Great Guitars with Charlie Byrd and Barney Kessel, and they toured as a threesome yet were often joined by a bassist and drummer. Ellis has a technically accomplished, warm, woody tone, and a solid, straight-ahead, boppish-to-bluesy, swinging style that can be heard on numerous albums as sideman and leader for a variety of labels including Verve, Concord, Justice, and others.

what to buy: *Together!* ♫♫♫♫ (Epic, 1963/Koch Classics, 1995, prod. John Hammond) documents a delightful session Ellis recorded in Hollywood with violinist Stuff Smith, a prime statesman of swing 12 years older than the guitarist. This was a nostalgic session for Ellis, because Stuff's trio was the first professional jazz group Ellis ever sat in with on New York's 52nd Street in 1944. The swinging nine-tune session, produced by John Hammond, features mostly Smith originals performed by Ellis, Smith, Lou Levy (piano), Shelly Manne (drums), and Al McKibbon (bass), with guest solos from Bob Enevoldsen (tenor sax, valve trombone). Trust Houston-based Justice Records for solid, blues-based releases such as Ellis's *Roll Call* ♫♫♫♫ (Justice, 1991, prod. Randall Hage Jamail), an exciting session of 11 improvised swingers recorded with B-3 organist Melvin Rhyne, drummer Jake Hanna, and guest soloists Johnny Frigo (violin) and Jay Thomas (tenor sax, flugelhorn). Among the standard blues fare such as "Lime House Blues," Wes Montgomery's racing "Naptown Blues," "Blues for Bernie," and others are four Ellis originals that highlight his best-picking session in recent years. Frigo is wonderful in his sharings with Ellis on "Isn't It Wonderful." Rhyne (who worked with guitar god Wes Montgomery) adds extra grit to this heartfelt, helluva swinging session. *Windflower* ♫♫♫♫ (Concord, 1978, prod. Carl E. Jefferson) documents a rare and lovely recording highlighting guitarist Remo Palmier, a leader Ellis met during his 52nd Street days in New York. Thirty-seven years passed until they got together on this studio session with bassist George Duvivier and drummer Ron Traxler. It's worth the wait. They share a special musical relationship that makes for a noticeably different listen from Ellis's recordings

with other guitarists. The nine tunes, a mixture of standards, give the musicians room for amicable guitar-focused explorations. Ellis and Joe Pass first performed together at a Los Angeles jazz club over two decades ago and the 13 duets on *Two for the Road* ♫♫♫♫ (Pablo, 1974/OJC, 1992, prod. Herb Ellis, Joe Pass) capture them as they compatibly intertwine lines and engage in some exciting exchanges. You'll be amazed at their technically proficient picking and the one-mindedness of their improvs, especially their speedy call-and-response on the uptempo "Seven Come Eleven." An engaging album all the way through. Ellis and Pass came together again, this time with bassist Ray Brown and drummer Jake Hanna on *Seven, Come Eleven* ♫♫♫♫ (Concord, 1974, prod. Carl E. Jefferson), a live-recorded concert of seven standards performed at the Concord Summer Festival. A delightful listen, especially the Ellis-Pass exchanges on "Prelude to a Kiss," with Ellis leading off with a beautiful melody head.

what to buy next: Another in the series of albums recorded with Brown and Hanna, *Jazz/Concord* ♫♫♫♫ (Concord, 1972, prod. Carl E. Jefferson) is a tasteful quartet session of standards performed with fellow guitarist Pass (the first album Concord released). While some of their music is laid-back, this foursome can generate fearsome swing, evident on the boppish "Stuffy," with Ellis and Pass co-mingling their lines, and Brown's bass (locked with Hanna's tidy brushwork) pulsing underneath. The slow, drawling "Georgia" is pure blues-tinged pleasure. Play this with your morning coffee and ease into your day. Add the piano flair of George Duke to the Ray Brown-Jake Hanna team, sprinkle some trumpet from Harry "Sweets" Edison, and you have *Soft Shoe* ♫♫♫♫ (Concord, 1974, prod. Carl E. Jefferson), a seven-tune studio set that swings like a Southern gate and surrenders supple ballads such as the title tune featuring a wonderfully warm, muted solo from "Sweets." Ellis generously defers to his illustrious team mates, but contributes a lovely solo on a waltzing blues-tinged version of Irving Berlin's "Easter Parade." This disc also contains a rare recorded take on "The Flintstones Theme" on which everyone excels at the breakneck tempos. The same musicians can be heard, plus wrenching and warm tenor saxisms from Plas Johnson, on *After You've Gone* ♫♫♫♫ (Concord, 1975, prod. Carl E. Jefferson), a pert, seven-tune (two Ellis originals) performance live-recorded at the 1974 Concord Festival. An alluring listen throughout with excellent ensemble work and superb spotlighted moments from Ellis, "Sweets," and Johnson. The best and longest track (9:40) is Brown's "Fatty McShatty," a rousing number that sends the full ensemble on a deep-grooving bluesy spree. Ellis plays a warm and swinging guitar on *Texas Swings* 𝄢𝄢𝄢 (Justice, 1992, prod. Randall Hage Jamail), accompanied by seven musicians (including Willie Nelson on guitar) who pay homage to music from the Lone Star State. The array of 10 standards including "Scrapple from the Apple," "It Had to Be You," "Sweet Georgia Brown," and other toe-tappers featuring fine soloing from Herb Remington (steel guitar), Tommy Alsup (bass), Tommy Perkins (drums), Floyd Domino (piano), and violinists Johnny Gimble and Bobby Bruce. Relaxed and lightly swinging jazz with a Texas twang, it is a slightly different setting for Ellis and fun for fans of this style. From a series of recordings made with Barney Kessel and Charlie Byrd, *Great Guitars at Charlie's Georgetown* 𝄢𝄢𝄢 (Concord, 1983/1994, prod. Carl E. Jefferson) features the musicians delivering perky versions of "When the Saints Go Marching In," "Change Partners," and "Get Happy," enhanced by Chuck Redd's zesty drum work. Their remakes of pleasant standards such as Al Cohn's "Pensive" (bonus track on the CD version), and the lilting classic, "Old Folks," where the three guitars blend comfortably, make this CD a serene listen for frayed nerves. *Hot Tracks* 𝄢𝄢𝄢 (Concord, 1976, prod. Carl E. Jefferson) finds the Ellis/Brown Sextet with trumpeter "Sweets" Edison, drummer Jake Hanna, tenor saxophonist Plas Johnson, and pianist Mike Melvoin in a 1976 studio session of eight tunes, mostly well-arranged, incendiary swingers by band members. The set includes Ellis's hoppin' original, "Onion Roll," two blues-drenched tunes from Ray Brown ("Spherikhal," "Blues for Minnie"), Edison's "Sweetback," and Plas Johnson's "Bones," all top-quality melodies on which the ensemble expands and the soloists strut their stuff. Jazz veterans Ellis and bassist Red Mitchell (both born in the 1920s) got together on a March 1988 live-record duet performance on *Doggin' Around* 𝄢𝄢𝄢 (Concord, 1989, prod. Carl E. Jefferson). Recorded at the Loa, in Santa Monica, California, the album features the pair picking their way through 10 standards and two Mitchell originals. A soothing listen recommended for late-night relaxation.

best of the rest:

(With Freddie Green) *Rhythm Willie* 𝄢𝄢𝄢 (Concord, 1975)
(With Barney Kessel) *Poor Butterfly* 𝄢𝄢𝄢 (Concord, 1977/1995)
Soft and Mellow 𝄢𝄢𝄢 (Concord, 1979)
Great Guitars at the Winery 𝄢𝄢𝄢 (Concord, 1980)
(With the Justice All-Stars) *Down-Home* 𝄢𝄢𝄢 (Justice, 1996)

influences:

◀◀ Charlie Christian, Wes Montgomery

Nancy Ann Lee

Lisle Ellis

Born November 17, 1951, in Campbell River, British Columbia, Canada.

Bassist Lisle Ellis has been active in improvisational music since high school. Early on he was so influenced by the blues that he would drive to Chicago to catch concerts by Albert King, Muddy Waters, Paul Butterfield, and the like; through the blues he found jazz. After being blown away by Rahsaan Roland Kirk's horn-juggling act and experiencing the music of Wes Montgomery and Charles Mingus, there was no looking back. A master improviser with a no-holds-barred attitude, Ellis has since 1978 contributed to more than a dozen albums, including the powerful *Density of Lovestruck Demons* with longtime associate Paul Plimley, and *The Fields* with the Glenn Spearman Double Trio. Over the years he has also worked with such luminaries as Cecil Taylor, Paul Bley, Rashid Bakr, Andrew Cyrille, and Rova Saxophone Quartet. Since moving to the Bay Area in 1992 he has collaborated with the scene's most commanding improvisers and composers, including Spearman, Ben Goldberg, and Rova's Larry Ochs. A thoughtful, serious artist, Ellis makes the distinction between so-called free jazz and more commercial enterprises. "This music is not entertainment in terms of diversion or distraction," he insists. Bemoaning the common misperceptions of the music, he explains, "Free form does not mean that we're throwing form away. Maybe we're free to inspect and investigate other forms. There are all kinds of forms in nature. . . . Music takes many forms and we can trust that." Taking a break from live performance for a spell, Ellis is currently focusing on composition. His latest large-scale work—a two-part/ten-section suite entitled *Children in Peril* with Joe McPhee (sax), Marco Eneidi (sax), Dana Reason (piano), and Peter Apfelbaum (drums)—is scheduled for release on Music & Arts in the near future.

what to buy: *What We Live* 𝄢𝄢𝄢𝄢 (DIW, 1996, prod. Larry Ochs) is the self-titled debut (though it was recorded a year later than the next album) of an improvisational trio with Rova saxophonist Larry Ochs and drummer Donald Robinson which grew out of Ellis's interest in exploring bass-driven structures. Each individual brings a very personal vocabulary to the proceedings and they've developed a remarkably intuitive collective language which rivals that of the U.K.'s infamous Evan Parker–Barry Guy–Paul Lytton group. The title of *What We Live Fo(u)r* 𝄢𝄢𝄢𝄢 (Black Saint, 1996, prod. Don Paul) is a play on words and a play on the *What We Live* concept, as this exceptional disc expands the Ellis-Ochs-Robinson trio to a quartet on six of the seven tracks. Guest artists include Ben Goldberg (bass clarinet), Glenn Spearman (flute, sax), Miya Masaoka (koto), William Winant (vibes), Paul Plimley (piano), and India Cooke (violin). While improvisation is a key to the album's success, unlike the trio disc, all of the music on *What We Live Fo(u)r* was composed beforehand, with five tunes by Ellis and a pair by Ochs.

what to buy next: Ellis has referred to *Elevations* ♫♫♫♫ (Victo, 1994, prod. Don Paul) as a "house cleaning," documenting the development of his structural/compositional ideas, some of which date back 20 years. The reed-heavy septet includes Glenn Spearman, Larry Ochs, and Joe McPhee. The collective effort is electric.

influences:

◀◀ Muddy Waters, Wes Montgomery, Charles Mingus, Charlie Haden

▶▶ Trevor Dunn, George Cremaschi

Sam Prestianni

Kahil El'Zabar

Born November 11, 1953.

Kahil El'Zabar is a versatile Chicago-based percussionist who at the age of 18 joined the Association for the Advancement of Creative Musicians (AACM). Raised on Chicago's South Side, he absorbed the sounds of music around him, including gospel, bebop, and the blues. He furthered his studies at the Chicago Conservatory of Music and at Lake Forest College and received seven months of additional formal training in Ghana, West Africa. He has performed and recorded worldwide with jazz luminaries such as Dizzy Gillespie, David Murray, Henry Threadgill, Lester Bowie, Cannonball Adderley, Billy Bang, Arthur Blythe, World Saxophone Quartet, as well as with many members of the AACM. More than 20 years ago, he formed and currently leads the experimental Ethnic Heritage Ensemble, which currently includes Joseph Bowie, Ernest "Khabeer" Dawkins (who replaced Ed Wilkerson Jr. in 1997), and Atu Harald Murray. He also leads two other groups, the Ritual Trio, an AACM-influenced group that includes saxophonist Ari Brown and bassist Malachi Favors, and Afrocentrix, a "21st-century dance band." The Ritual Trio began around 1985 as a way to bring together two generations of AACM musicians, and the first grouping featured trumpeter Lester Bowie and bassist Favors (both of Art Ensemble of Chicago fame). The group acquired its name with El'Zabar's 1984 recording, *The Ritual* for Sound Aspects Records. One year later, violinist Billy Bang replaced Bowie, and by the 1990s, Ari Brown assumed Bang's spot. A renais-

sance man of sorts, El'Zabar has scored two feature films, Damon Wayan's *Mo' Money* and Darrell Roberts's *How U Like Me Now.* He was also cast in a number of films, including a co-starring role in the 1988 feature film *Savannah,* an award-winning performance in the 1989 independent film short *So Low But Not Alone,* and roles in the DeWayne Johnson Cochran film, *The Last Set,* and a more recent role in *Love Jones.* He had his first book of poetry and prose published in 1993 and in 1995 was honored as *Chicago Tribune* Artist of the Year. He is a full professor of interdisciplinary arts at the University of Illinois at Chicago and also teaches at the University of Nebraska and at the Art Institute of Chicago. He serves on the boards of many national arts organizations. El'Zabar plays a number of percussion instruments—congas, bongos, African drums, balaphon, marimba, barimbau, sanza, shekere, African thumb piano, traps drums, and other miscellaneous instruments. He also plays woodwinds and bass bamboo flute. He has recorded albums for Sound Aspects, Silkheart, and Delmark. For more information about El'Zabar and his Ethnic Heritage Ensemble, check their Web site at http://www.fred.net/jbowie/, and if you want to learn more about these and other Chicago musicians, check the Centerstage site at http://centerstage.net/chicago/music/whoswho/, and other sites.

what to buy: This newer generation of AACM-influenced musicians continues to push and stretch the boundaries of improvised music. The music performed by the Ethnic Heritage Ensemble (EHE) is composed mostly by El'Zabar to draw from African and African American traditions. On *The Continuum* ♫♫♫♫ (Delmark, 1998, prod. Kahil El'Zabar), the focus is on deep-toned, hypnotic rhythms created by percussionist El'Zabar and Murray, with the horn soloists Joseph Bowie and Dawkins adding splashes of colorful melodic riffs and free-jazz improvisations. Among the seven tunes the musicians also marry African-themes to jazz standards such as "Well You Needn't" and "All Blues." The EHE revisits "Ornette," a tune dedicated to Ornette Coleman which was recorded with the trio on their 1993 album, *Dance with the Ancestors.* On this track, El'Zabar adds his scat vocals to the 11:47-minute classic, underpinned with the repetitive happy rhythms that will draw you into the piece. Because of their busy schedules, this group doesn't often tour extensively or come together in the studio all that often. But when they do, it's worth the wait. *Dance with the Ancestors* ♫♫♫♫ (Chameleon, 1993, prod. Kahil El'Zabar) features the EHE as a trio, blending free jazz, African rhythms, voice, and unique instrumental sounds. Evolved from a larger group, the Ensemble evolved into the present cooperative of two horns and percussion. Making their debut on an American label with this album, the EHE freely melds El'Zabar's syncopated African hand drum rhythms and melodies on African thumb piano to jazz standards and some original tunes with an overall feeling of harmony and peace. Of musically similar minds are Ed Wilkerson Jr. (tenor sax, alto clarinet, percussion, vocals) and the funk-oriented younger brother of trumpeter Lester, Joseph Bowie, (trombone, congas, percussion, vocals) who merged with the group in 1976 and 1986, respectively. Ten selections, arranged or written by El'Zabar, transport your visions to Africa yet remain grounded in the black American experience, especially "Ornette," where El'Zabar's repeated acclamations, "Ornette! . . . Coleman!" remind you that jazz *was* born in the United States (despite its more enthusiastic overseas reception). The most recognizable (yet amazingly unique) tune is the reconstructed Ellington theme, Billy Strayhorn's "Take the 'A' Train." The most recent recording by El'Zabar's Ritual Trio, *Jitterbug Junction* ♫♫♫♫ (CIMP, 1997, prod. Robert D. Rusch) finds the leader playing primarily traps drums as he and cohorts Ari Brown (tenor and soprano saxophones) and Malachi Favors (bass) romp inside and out of six originals that range from the bop-influenced ("From Whence It Came") to music inspired by Jelly Roll Morton (the title tune) to musings on Coltrane (Billy Brimfield's composition, "One for John"), to Favors's spiritually fed arrangement of the traditional Negro spiritual, "This Little Light of Mine," and more. There's a unity of spirit evident on this June 10, 1997 recording that gives grounding to their free-jazz improvisations. Perhaps their inspired playing is due to the studio atmosphere of the north country setting in Redwood, New York, or to producer Bob Rusch's enthusiasm. Whatever the reasons, this is another outing where they've put their best musical energies forth.

what to buy next: The illustrious avant-garde violinist Billy Bang joins the Ritual Trio on *Big Cliff* ♫♫♫♫ (Delmark, 1995, prod. Robert G. Koester), an album that documents their live-recorded performance at the Underground Fest, on September 3, 1994. Bang had played in the band in its earlier days, so this is a meeting of old friends, cohesive and adventurous. El'Zabar focuses on conga drums and thumb pianos with this group, creating catchy, danceable African rhythms. The current trio—percussionist El'Zabar, pianist Ari Brown, and bassist Malachi Favors—delivers four tunes that range between the ten-minute "Another Kind of Groove," to the 21-plus-minute "Blue Rwanda." The extended times give these extraordinary avant-garde musicians plenty of stretching

room and, encouraged by the enthusiastic audience, they generate some free-wheeling blow-outs, especially on the title piece. A drastic shift of pace follows that piece with "For the Love of My Father," a powerful, passionate ballad dedicated to the late Clifton Henry Blackburn Sr., El'Zabar's father. All of their music is engaging and Billy Bang's presence is a bonus. Regarding the band's name, El'Zabar has said, "The idea was that the nature of the performance and the band itself would be related to a ritual, such as those that exist in folk cultures around the world. It's musicians relating those folk traditions to the urban contemporary experience." This album, and all others by El'Zabar, are recommended for AACM lovers and other adventurous jazz fans who seek to expand their listening skills. El'Zabar's Ritual Trio shines on *Renaissance of the Resistance* ♫♫♫♫ (Delmark, 1994, prod. Steve Wagner), an album offering divergent flavors of the avant garde served up by AACM-influenced players. The catchy African rhythms, sparse lines, players who don't push the music but rather let it flow, and primitive energies forged to new ideas can all be found on this trio release led by El'Zabar with long-known impressionistic fashioners Favors (bass) and Brown (saxes). Their music is so counter to the raging bebop lines or rap rousings of today's young black musicians, it seems almost to come from a different culture. The music from this trio is laden with emotion that conjures up ancient themes and images that will take you on a musical journey to the African continent. Perhaps it is the repetitive bass lines or throbbing beats of the hand drums. Perhaps it is that the AACM-ers allow space for listeners to absorb their musical ideas. El'Zabar has composed nearly all of the music, and his team capably stretches out their statements on familiar frameworks that identify their roots in the Association which has nurtured so many great innovators.

influences:

◀◀ Art Ensemble of Chicago

Nancy Ann Lee

Bobby Enriquez

Born 1943, on Mindanao Island, Philippines. Died August 6, 1996.

Pianist Bobby Enriquez, the "Madman of Mindanao," was a tremendous talent in the tradition of Erroll Garner, Art Tatum, Oscar Peterson, and Bud Powell. His prodigious technique was ever-present, but it always complemented, never distracted, from the music. Enriquez was largely (and strangely) unknown to all but in-the-know musicians and the most cognizant of jazz fans and piano trio aficionados, but he left a legacy of several fine recordings that feature his technical, lyrical, humorous, and aggressive style. Shelly Manne once remarked that Enriquez was "the only piano player that was trained by Bruce Lee," but Enriquez' taste and versatility allowed him to follow a blistering be-bop number with the most genuinely sensitive ballad without the slightest hint of contrivance. He was influenced by Arthur Rubenstein and Vladimir Horowitz as much as he was by Parker and Tatum, and his ability to absorb and filter these influences in his own inimitable way was truly unique. After performing throughout the Philippines and Japan, Enriquez arrived in the United States in the early 1970s and began a long association with alto saxophonist Richie Cole. He also worked with Dizzy Gillespie in the early '80s. In 1980 Enriquez recorded the first of many solo efforts, mostly released on the GNP/Crescendo label. His untimely death deprived the jazz world of an expressive musician and singular talent.

what to buy: *The Prodigious Piano of Bobby Enriquez* 🎵🎵🎵🎵 (GNP/Crescendo, 1991, prod. Gene Norman) is a "best of" including live recordings featuring Alex Acuna and John Pena performing burning and creative versions of Chick Corea's "Spain," Miles Davis's "Boplicity," and the Gillespie bop standard "Night in Tunisia." Pristine recording and superior performances.

what to buy next: *Live! In Tokyo* 🎵🎵🎵🎵 (GNP/Crescendo, 1983, prod. Gene Norman) offers more standards and jazz tunes performed in the incendiary Enriquez style, this time backed by a Japanese rhythm section consisting of Isso Fukui on bass and Shinji Mori on drums. The group swings hard through 15 tunes. A truly impressive surprise is the trio's version of David Rose's "Holiday for Strings."

the rest:
The Wild Man 🎵🎵🎵 (GNP/Crescendo, 1980)
Live at Concerts by the Sea Volume II 🎵🎵🎵🎵 (GNP/Crescendo, 1982)
Live! In Tokyo Volume II 🎵🎵🎵🎵 (GNP/Crescendo, 1983)
The Wildman Returns 🎵🎵🎵 (Evidence, 1993)

worth searching for: The out-of-print *Live at Concerts by the Sea Volume I* 🎵🎵🎵🎵 (GNP/Crescendo, 1982) offers more burning tunes on vinyl.

influences:
◀◀ Erroll Garner, Oscar Peterson, Red Garland

▶▶ Chick Corea, Makoto Ozone

Gregg Juke

Peter Erskine

Born June 5, 1954, in Somers Point, NJ.

Peter Erskine first came to prominence with the Stan Kenton Orchestra, but it was his tenure with Weather Report and his rhythmic symbiosis with legendary electric bassist Jaco Pastorius that established his place in jazz history. Along the way he has performed and recorded with artists as diverse as Chick Corea, Freddie Hubbard, Joni Mitchell, Steely Dan, Jan Garbarek, Steps Ahead, and many others. In a career that has spanned a quarter century, he has been involved in nearly 300 albums and remains active as a "first-call" touring and studio musician. Erskine has enjoyed a long-standing relationship with ECM Records as both a recording artist and sideman, appearing on many of the label's releases. A world-class, tasteful, and very musical jazz percussionist, Erskine has re-invented himself as the quintessential modern music entrepreneur, having pursued and attained success as a producer, independent record label owner (Fuzzy Music), music educator, author, and composer. He continues to influence the next generation of jazz drummers while simultaneously juggling several aspects of a very successful musical career.

what to buy: A tremendous album, the only shortcoming on *Peter Erskine* 🎵🎵🎵🎵 (Contemporary/OJC, 1982, prod. John Koenig, Peter Erskine) is the dearth of tracks—the seven outstanding tunes leave the listener wanting more. Tracks include a handful of originals, a few jazz covers ("ESP," "Change of Mind") and a standard ("My Ship"). Featuring superb performances by the Brecker brothers, Bob Mintzer, Mike Mainieri, Don Grolnick, Kenny Kirkland, Eddie Gomez, and Don Alias, the disc is a worthy investment for any modern jazz enthusiast.

what to buy next: A date co-led by Erskine and tenor saxophonist Richard Torres, *From Kenton to Now* 🎵🎵🎵🎵 (Fuzzy Music, 1995, prod. Peter Erskine) is one of the CDs available on Erskine's independent imprint that exhibits fine performances from both leaders, as well as from bassist Dave Carpenter and former Tony Williams Lifetime keyboardist Alan Pasqua. Post-bop modern jazz in a straight-ahead acoustic vein provides these musicians with an excellent vehicle through which to shine. Stand-out cuts include "L.A. Stomp," the All-Blues-inspired "Blues for All," Kenton's "Artistry in Rhythm," "Modern Drummer Blues," "Intermission Riff," and "Happy Day"—which, if not for the saxophone lead, could have been taken straight from the Ahmad Jamal *Live at the Pershing* sessions.

the rest:
Transition 🎵🎵🎵 (Denon, 1986)

John Abercrombie, Marc Johnson, Peter Erskine ♫♫♫♪ (ECM, 1988)
Motion Poet ♫♫♫♪ (Denon, 1988)
Sweet Soul ♫♫♫♪ (BMG, 1990)
Miroslav Vitous/Jan Garbarek/Peter Erskine: Star ♫♫♫♪ (ECM, 1991)
Big Theatre ♫♫♫♪ (ah um, 1991)
John Abercrombie, Marc Johnson, Peter Erskine: November ♫♫♫♪ (ECM, 1992)
You Never Know ♫♫♫♪ (ECM, 1992)
Time Being ♫♫♫♪ (ECM, 1993)
The History of the Drum ♫♫♫♪ (Interworld, 1994)
As It Is ♫♫♫♪ (ECM, 1996)
Peter Erskine & the Lounge Art Ensemble: Lava Jazz ♫♫♫♪ (Fuzzy Music, 1997)
Juni ♫♫♫♪ (ECM, 1998)

influences:

◄◄ Elvin Jones, Mel Lewis, Paul Motian, Shelly Manne

►► Ralph Peterson, Lewis Nash, Adam Nusbaum

Gregg Juke

Booker Ervin

Born October 31, 1930 , in Denison, TX. Died July 31, 1970, in New York, NY.

Among the significant accomplishments credited to Booker Ervin is the establishment of an early 1960s saxophone-piano-bass-drums quartet in the mold of neither the Thelonious Monk nor John Coltrane combos. But neither Ervin's group concept nor his brilliantly voluble saxophonics ignited commensurate fire under his relatively short life and career: Born in 1930, he had his big break with Charles Mingus in 1959 and died before his 40th birthday. And this relative obscurity comes despite bracing work with both Mingus and Randy Weston, and a string of good-to-superior recordings. Ervin's earthiness kept him a member in good standing in the bluesy brotherhood of tough Texas tenors. He absorbed lessons, too, from saxophonists, his acknowledged idol Dexter Gordon, and Sonny Stitt among others, then extended what he had learned into a personal style that showed brilliantly in lengthy thematic explorations. And in the era when Coltrane and Sonny Rollins were magnets, Ervin explicitly tried to resist their pull and pursue his own thing.

what to buy: *The Freedom Book* ♫♫♫♫♫ (Prestige, 1964/OJC, 1995, prod. Don Schlitten) and *The Space Book* ♫♫♫♫♫ (Prestige, 1964/OJC, 1996, prod. Don Schlitten), sessions that Ervin recorded with pianist Jaki Byard, bassist Richard Davis, and drummer Allen Dawson (originally for Prestige), are musts that are central to Ervin's output. This is the Ervin group sound at its most grand. Pianist Byard in particular spurs Ervin to impas-sioned solos with his hearty percussive flair. "I Can't Get Started" had been a favorite vehicle for Ervin's former employer Mingus, but on *Space Book* Ervin gives it his own indelible stamp, finding in the tune a heretofore unheard soulfulness, transforming the song over the space of his solo from a witty observation to a histrionic plea. *Space Book* also offers "Mojo," the spirited, angular composition that has become Ervin's best known. On *Freedom Book* the musicians display the same dazzling flexibility; the selections include Ervin's "A Day to Mourn," a heartfelt reaction to the assassination of President John F. Kennedy.

what to buy next: Reggie Workman replaces Richard Davis in the quartet for an exciting 1965 live date as the group meets with one of Ervin's main musical models, Dexter Gordon, on *Setting the Pace* ♫♫♫♫ (OJC, 1993, prod. Don Schlitten). The tenors perform two Gordon compositions, clocking in around 20 ecstatic minutes apiece. In both, Ervin melds Gordon's flurried passages with Ervinesque bluesy wails and screaming punctuations. It's a jam session in the best sense, all about throwing down and rising to challenges. Minus Gordon, the group settles back to a mid-tempo lament for then recently deceased bassist George Tucker, "The Trance," and revs up again for Kurt Weill's "Speak Low." *The Song Book* ♫♫♫♫ (Prestige, 1964/OJC, 1993, prod. Don Schlitten), recorded with Davis, Dawson, and pianist Tommy Flanagan, is relatively relaxed and more conventional than the Byard sessions, but the all-standards format allows Ervin to shine in a different context (and check out Davis's "Just Friends" solo).

the rest:
Cookin' ♫♫♫♪ (Savoy, 1960/1993)
Exultation! ♫♫♫♪ (Prestige, 1963/OJC, 1994)
The Blues Book ♫♫♫♪ (Prestige, 1964/OJC, 1993)
The Trance ♫♫♫♪ (Prestige, 1965/OJC, 1997)

worth searching for: *Back from the Gig* ♫♫♫♪ (Blue Note, 1976, prod. Alfred Lion) is a vinyl two-fer of previously unreleased 1960s material. A 1963 session finds the Texas tenor with pianist Horace Parlan, who, like Byard, was an Ervin associate through the Mingus band, and a splendid partner outside of the bassist's company as well (witness the up-tempo theatrics of Parlan's solo on "Dexi"). A 1968 session features up-and-coming artists Kenny Barron on piano and Woody Shaw on trumpet. The session swings with an elan that makes inexplicable the eight-year delay in its release. On *The Book Cooks* ♫♫♫♪ (Bethlehem, 1977, prod. Teddy Charles) Ervin locks tenors with Zoot Sims on the first Ervin-led session (1960). The uptempo title track posits both tenors as fonts of inspiration as the tune gives most of its nearly 11 minutes over to dozens of sparring four-bar exchanges between the two.

influences:

◀◀ Dexter Gordon, Sonny Stitt, Lester Young, Buster Smith, Charles Mingus, Randy Weston

▶▶ Dewey Redman, Billy Harper

W. Kim Heron

Ron Eschete

Born 1948, in Houma, LA.

Best known for his work in pianist Gene Harris's blues-drenched quartet, Ron Eschete is a nimble, harmonically inventive improvisor who has played mainly seven-string guitar since 1982. He studied classical guitar at Loyola University for three years and played jazz and R&B on New Orleans' Bourbon Street before going out on the road with Buddy Greco. He moved to Southern California in 1974 and worked with vibraphonist Dave Pike. He began teaching at various Southland colleges in the mid-1970s and established a reputation as the consummate sideman, working with fellow guitarists Joe Diorio, Joe Pass, George Van Eps, and Herb Ellis, pianists Alan Broadbent, Hampton Hawes, and Bill Mays, and saxophonists Pete Christlieb, Harold Land, Bob Cooper, Gary Foster, Jeff Clayton, and Warne Marsh, among many others. A long-running gig in San Diego starting in 1988 led Eschete to pursue his own recordings, resulting in a series of fine albums for Concord. At about the same time, he joined Harris's quartet, a group with which he's toured and recorded (for Concord) extensively.

what to buy: An elegantly swinging guitarist firmly in the mainstream jazz tradition, Ron Eschete plays with consistent taste throughout *Rain or Shine* ♫♫♫♫ (Concord Jazz, 1995, prod. Ron Eschete). With Todd Johnson on six-string electric bass and drummer Paul Humphrey (his bandmate from the Gene Harris quartet), he leads a relaxed trio session augmented on four tunes by the deft percussion work of Poncho Sanchez, who adds some wonderful textures to Victor Feldman's "Azul Serape" (originally recorded by Cannonball Adderley), and a mid-tempo version of Coltrane's "Naima." Eschete moves seamlessly between Bobby Timmons's hardbop classic "Moanin'" and a Brazilian-tinged version of Django Reinhardt's impressionistic rhapsody "Nuages," maintaining a constant dialogue with Johnson's rich and supple bass lines.

what to buy next: The release of Joe Pass's *Virtuoso* set a seemingly impossible standard for solo jazz guitar projects, but

Eschete boldly meets the challenge with *A Closer Look* ♫♫♫♫ (Concord Jazz, 1994, prod. Ron Eschete), a finely crafted session featuring a dozen deftly rendered tunes. Playing seven-string guitar, Eschete sticks close to the melodies of such standards as "Stardust," "My Foolish Heart," and "Like Someone in Love," alternating fleet single-note lines and harmonically rich chords while supplying his own bass line. The session's highlight is his four-tune, Deep South medley, a picaresque journey of varying textures, grooves, and keys linking "When It's Sleepy Time Down South," "Do You Know What It Means to Miss New Orleans?," "Stars Fell on Alabama," and "Birth of the Blues."

best of the rest:

Mo' Strings Attached ♫♫♫♫ (Jazz Alliance, 1993)
Soft Winds ♫♫♫♫ (Concord Jazz, 1996)

worth searching for: Variety isn't a hallmark of Gene Harris Quartet albums, but *Brotherhood* ♫♫♫♫ (Concord Jazz, 1995, prod. Carl E. Jefferson) is a particularly rewarding session covering a variety of moods besides his patented blend of gospel, blues, and jazz. Eschete provides both harmonic depth and rhythmic drive to the band, though he doesn't have many chances to solo. Still, this is a particularly good session in the setting Eschete is heard in most often. The quartet also features Luther Hughes on bass and Paul Humphrey on drums.

influences:

◀◀ Jim Hall, Wes Montgomery, Kenny Burrell

Andrew Gilbert

Pete Escovedo

Born July 13, 1935, in Pittsburg, CA.

Percussionist Pete Escovedo has been an active force in Latin jazz since the 1960s as both a session player and a solo recording artist; his credits include work with Carlos Santana, Herbie Hancock, Mongo Santamaria, Angela Bofill, Barry White, Cal Tjader, Tito Puente, Woody Herman, Billy Cobham, Anita Baker, Stephen Stills, Bobby McFerrin, Chris Isaak, Boz Scaggs, and George Duke. Escovedo has released a number of fine contemporary jazz-pop albums as a leader on the Concord label; although the "jazz-pop" categorization might be somewhat deceiving. The trademark Escovedo sound combines equal parts jazz, salsa, funk, Brazilian, pop, and rock influences with traditional Afro-Cuban sounds and odd meters to create a very listenable, cohesive whole. He has also made musical history as co-leader (with brother Coke Escovedo) of the ground-breaking Latin/fusion big-band Azteca. The Escovedo musical dynasty in the San Francisco Bay area is similar to that which the Marsalis family has achieved in New Orleans. Pete is not only the brother of Coke (deceased) and Phil Escovedo—both performing musicians and former members of the Escovedo Brothers Band—but also the father of Sheila "E" Escovedo—L.A. studio percussionist and former pop-singing Prince-protege—and musician/producer/arranger and studio engineer Peter Michael Escovedo. Pete Escovedo continues to perform and record as a leader, with various members of his family, and in support of some of the world's most famous jazz and pop acts.

what to buy: *E Street* 🎵🎵🎵 (Concord, 1997, prod. Pete Escovedo) features Sheila E, Gerald Albright, Ray Obiedo, and more special guests and Escovedo progeny performing tunes by Obiedo, Stevie Wonder, and Sheila E. A mixed-bag of styles with some slick production. George Duke, Andy Narell, and Najee make guest appearances on *Flying South* 🎵🎵🎵 (Concord, 1996, prod. Pete Escovedo, Peter Michael Escovedo). Highlights include "Flying South," "Tiemblas," "Flying Easy," Cal Tjader's "Leyte," and the more folkloric-oriented "Canto Para Chango."

what to buy next: *Yesterday's Memories—Tomorrow's Dreams* 🎵🎵🎵 (Concord/Crossover, 1987) is the Pete Escovedo Orchestra captured live and in concert, including a medley of Azteca-inspired tunes called "The E Medley." The 10 cuts on *Mister E* 🎵🎵🎵 (Concord/Crossover, 1988) include tracks featuring Sheila E and *The Tonight Show*'s Vicki Randle. Of note is a cover of Earl Klugh's "Dr. Macumba."

worth searching for: Both of the out-of-print Azteca albums—the eponymous debut *Azteca* (Columbia, 1972, prod. Azteca) and *Pyramid of the Moon* (CBS, 1973, prod. Azteca)—are available only on vinyl.

influences:

◀◀ Mongo Santamaria, Tito Puente, Carlos Santana

▶▶ Koinania, Alex Acuna & the Unknowns

Gregg Juke

Ellery Eskelin

Born August 16, 1959, in Wichita, KS.

Tenor saxophonist Eskelin, raised in Baltimore, Maryland, from 1961, was influenced by his musical family. His mother, Bobbie Lee, was a Hammond B3 organist leading her own group in the 1960s, and his late father, Rodd Keith, was a pop cult hero. Ellery studied classical woodwinds and jazz at Towson State

University and started his professional career doing one-nighters with swing-era trombonist Buddy Morrow. Moving to New York City in 1983, he played with trumpeter Paul Smoker in the cooperative Joint Venture. He is currently performing with his own group featuring Andrea Parkins on accordion and sampler and Jim Black on drums. He performs with Joey Baron's group Baron Down, the new Gerry Hemingway quartet, and Mark Helias's Attack the Future. Ellery pushes the boundaries of modern jazz, challenging the listener and his musicians alike with unconventional groupings of instruments. His influences include not only the saxophonists listed below but also contemporary classical composers, world music, rock, and DJ culture.

what to buy: Groove, humor, and chops abound in Ellery's compositions and improvisations on *Figure of Speech* 🎵🎵🎵🎵 (Soul Note, 1993, prod. Ellery Eskelin). The trio with Joe Daley on tuba and Arto Tuncboyaciyan on drums and percussion leaves a lot of musical/sonic space between the instruments, letting timbral subtleties cut through unobscured. Eskelin's imaginative structures go beyond the usual head-solos-head organization to provide a sense of organic surprise. Utilizing just Eskelin and Andrea Parkins on sampler, the duo outing *Green Bermudas* 🎵🎵🎵🎵 (Eremite, 1996, prod. Ellery Eskelin) covers the gamut from free jazz to country to rock to you name it in a supple demonstration of improvisational flexibility.

what to buy next: The stimulating *Jazz Trash* 🎵🎵🎵 (Songlines, 1995, prod. Karl Hereim) is by Eskelin's trio with Parkins on accordion and sampler and Jim Black on drums. The structures are loose but not chaotic, blurring the distinction between writing and improvisation, with all parts sounding spontaneous. Those who shy from accordion have nothing to fear, by the way—woozy sentimentality never intrudes. The solo tenor musings of *Premonition* 🎵🎵🎵 (Prime Source, 1993, prod. Ellery Eskelin) show Eskelin to be fully capable of creating a wide range of ideas and emotions on his own in the always-treacherous unaccompanied-horn format.

the rest:
Forms 🎵🎵◐ (Open Minds, 1991)
The Sun Died 🎵🎵🎵 (Soul Note, 1996)
One Great Day 🎵🎵🎵 (hatOLOGY, 1997)

worth searching for: *Setting the Standard* 🎵🎵🎵 (Cadence Jazz 1988 prod. Ellery Eskelin) is only available on vinyl or cassette at present. It features Eskelin, with full-bodied bassist Drew Gress and driving drummer Phil Haynes, deconstructing standards in a more familiar trio format than his usual unusual lineups.

influences:

Gene Ammons, John Coltrane, Stan Getz, Lee Konitz, Sonny Stitt

David C. Gross and Steve Holtje

The Ethnic Heritage Ensemble

See: Kahil El'Zabar

Kevin Eubanks

Born November 15, 1957, in Philadelphia, PA.

Thanks to his inherited position as *The Tonight Show* band leader, guitarist Kevin Eubanks is one of the most-seen musicians in the world. His ability and willingness to play just about anything makes him a perfect foil for host Jay Leno, but sometimes all that talent seems wasted on what he plays. Eubanks began recording as a leader during the mid-1980s on GRP with a popish, fusion sound that allowed some of his deeper jazz roots to show through—he'd previously worked with Art Blakey. His switch to Blue Note in 1991 sparked a more cool jazz-cum-New Age feel to his music. Throughout his career Eubanks has revealed himself to be an enterprising composer and adept on acoustic and electric guitar. He treads a highly melodic line between post-bop and contemporary styles with great chops and judicious restraint. His brother is trombonist Robin Eubanks.

what to buy: Though all songs but one were composed by bassist Dave Holland, *Spirit Talk* 🎵🎵🎵 (Blue Note, 1993, prod. Kevin Eubanks) provides some of Eubanks's best work. The New Age overtones are there, but there is some understated swing and even a rock tune—"Earth Party." *Spirit Talk 2* 🎵🎵🎵 (Blue Note, 1995, prod. Kevin Eubanks) takes the same direction but this time with Eubanks's own compositions. It swings just a bit more and takes a little chance with the jagged-but-comfortable "Being."

what to buy next: *Live at Bradley's* 🎵🎵🎵 (Blue Note, 1996, prod. Kevin Eubanks, Michael Cuscuna) portrays his swingability for jazz purists in a trio with Bob Hurst and James Williams to good advantage.

what to avoid: If the naked torso on the cover doesn't tell you enough, *The Heat of Heat* 🎵🎵 (GRP, 1987) tells you even less.

the rest:
Opening Night 🎵🎵🎵 (GRP, 1985)
Face to Face 🎵🎵🎵 (GRP, 1986)
Shadow Prophets 🎵🎵 (GRP, 1988)

E̲LLERY E̲SKELIN

song "Ca' Purange"
album *The Sun Died*
(Soul Note, 1996)
instrument Tenor saxophone

Monster Solo

The Searcher 🎵🎵🎵 (GRP, 1988)
Promise of Tomorrow 🎵🎵🎵 (GRP, 1990)
Turning Point 🎵🎵🎵🎵 (Blue Note, 1992)

worth searching for: If you're a fan, seek out *Guitarist* 🎵🎵🎵🎵 (Elektra, 1982), which portrays Eubanks solo and with a small group, including trombonist brother Robin.

influences:

George Benson, Kenny Burrell, Grant Green, Oregon

Larry Gabriel

Robin Eubanks

Born October 25, 1955, in Philadelphia, PA.

The brother of guitarist Kevin Eubanks, Robin is a protégé of Slide Hampton. After moving to New York in 1980, he came to prominence as a member of the loosely knit group of young Brooklyn-based musicians gathered around alto saxophonists Steve Coleman and Greg Osby, who called their music M-Base

and incorporated funk into jazz by favoring tricky, angular grooves and intervallic leaps. Eubanks's mellifluous tone and sterling technique made him an in-demand player in many contexts, however, and after paying his dues in the big bands of Hampton and Sun Ra (how's that for stylistic breadth?), he played with everyone from McCoy Tyner's big band and Art Blakey (where he was the Jazz Messengers' musical director) to Don Grolnick and Stevie Wonder, plus work in the orchestra pits of Broadway.

what to buy: Unlike most of his JMT albums, *Wake Up Call* ♫♫♫♫ (Sirroco, 1997, prod. Robin Eubanks, John Priestley) places Eubanks firmly in a straight-ahead context, with three originals augmented by tracks penned by Wayne Shorter (two), Lee Morgan, Charlie Parker ("Scrapple from the Apple") plus Rodgers and Hart's "You Are Too Beautiful." Eubanks's compositions, especially the tricky "Wake Up Call," keep the album from being an exercise in nostalgia, and the fine playing—Antonio Hart shines on alto sax, Duane Eubanks's trumpet playing suggests the family's produced yet another fine musician, and Robin (the only horn to play on every track) is stellar—makes it a solidly worthwhile effort. The flexible rhythm section is Eric Lewis (piano), Lonnie Plaxico (bass), and Gene Jackson (drums).

what to buy next: *Mental Images* ♫♫♫ (JMT, 1994, prod. Robin Eubanks, Stefan F. Winter) is Eubanks's most successful incorporation of M-Base principles as a leader, notable for some wild and intricate horn charts and tricky meters (try 9/4) that groove hard anyway. Varying the personnel from track to track—Eubanks alone, duets with brother Kevin and drummer Marvin "Smitty" Smith, a couple of trios, and pairs of sextet and septet tracks—moves it through a nicely varied array of styles and sounds. Stimulating solos are provided by Robin and Kevin, Hart, trumpeter Randy Brecker, and pianist Michael Cain.

what to avoid: The unfocused *Karma* ♫♫ (JMT, 1991, prod. Stefan F. Winter, Robin Eubanks) isn't all that bad—except for the opening title track, a laughable attempt at rap with lyrics aiming at profundity but achieving only awkward, half-formed clichés. Otherwise, the main problem is just a lack of overall cohesion.

the rest:
Different Perspectives ♫♫♫ (JMT, 1988)
(With Steve Turre) *Dedication* ♫♫♫♫ (JMT, 1989)

Kevin Eubanks (AP/Wide World Photos)

worth searching for: Steve Coleman and Five Elements' *World Expansion (By the M-Base Neophyte)* ♫♫♫♫ (JMT, 1987, prod. Steve Coleman) remains the high point of the M-Basers. With Cassandra Wilson and superdiva D.K. Dyson splitting the vocal chores, a monster rhythm section of Geri Allen (piano), Kelvyn Bell (guitar), Kevin Bruce Harris (bass), and Mark Johnson (drums) laying out those unique M-Base grooves, and a trio of superb horns—the leader, Eubanks, and trumpeter Graham Haynes—the disparate elements of this album come together to prove that it's possible to be adventurous and accessible at the same time.

influences:
◀◀ J.J. Johnson, Slide Hampton

Steve Holtje

Bill Evans

Born August 16, 1929, in Plainfield, NJ. Died September 15, 1980, in New York, NY.

Bill Evans was one of the most widely influential pianists of the 1960s and 1970s, a powerfully original improvisor who seemed to emerge in the late 1950s as a fully formed player. A ravishingly lyrical and harmonically sophisticated musician, Evans attained an immediately recognizable ringing tone from the piano. When playing long, flowing up-tempo lines, his sound revealed elements of Bud Powell, Nat "King" Cole, Horace Silver and especially Lennie Tristano. On meditative ballads with his trio, his introspective approach was entirely distinctive. His most profound innovations came through his groundbreaking trios, which developed a new conception for small group interplay involving simultaneous improvisation. Though many pianists who cite him as a primary influence draw on his more rhythmically attenuated style, Evans could swing with authority when he wanted. His early death at age 51 was partly precipitated by his lifelong struggle with drug addiction. His influence has continued to expand since his death, through his own recordings and as an element in the styles of such major figures as Herbie Hancock and Keith Jarrett. Evans was a prolific composer whose music was long neglected, but in recent years musicians such as guitarists John McLaughlin and Howard Alden have recorded entire albums devoted to his tunes.

Evans began playing piano at age six, and later took lessons on violin and flute. He graduated with a music education major in 1950 from Southeastern Louisiana College and before joining the Army (1951–54) gigged with Mundell Lowe and Red Mitchell and worked in saxophonist Herbie Fields's band. After the ser-

Bill Evans **(Archive Photos)**

vice he freelanced around New York, working with Jerry Wald and Tony Scott. His first album as a leader, *New Jazz Conceptions*, solidified his growing reputation as an innovator. Much in demand as a sideman in the late 1950s, Evans recorded with George Russell, Bob Brookmeyer, Art Farmer, Lee Konitz, Jimmy Giuffre, Cannonball Adderley, Eddie Costa, and on Charles Mingus's *East Coasting* album. Evans spent most of 1958 with John Coltrane and Cannonball Adderley in the Miles Davis Sextet, an association that had enormous musical repercussions for both Evans and Davis and for jazz. Though he didn't record much with the group, Evans helped pave the way for Davis's modal experiments on the seminal 1959 album *Kind of Blue*, on which Evans played "So What" and contributed his best known tune, "Blue in Green." Also in 1959, Evans founded his own trio with bassist Scott LaFaro and drummer Paul Motian, a group that developed a seemingly telepathic rapport. Recorded extensively while playing at the Village Vanguard in 1961, the trio introduced radical new possibilities for musicians in rhythm sec-

tions and small groups by erasing boundaries between accompanist and soloist. Shortly afterward, LaFaro was killed in a car crash and Evans spent months in seclusion before reforming the trio with bassist Chuck Israels and Motian (soon replaced by Larry Bunker). He recorded two classic albums with guitarist Jim Hall and for the rest of his life continued to work with excellent trios featuring such sidemen as bassists Gary Peacock (1963), Eddie Gomez (1966–77), and Marc Johnson (1978–80), and drummers Philly Joe Jones (1967), Jack DeJohnette (1968), Marty Morrell (1969–75), Eliot Zigmund (1975–78), and Joe LaBarbera (1979–80). Evans recorded extensively for Riverside, Fantasy, Verve, and Warner Bros., much of which is in print and available on individual CDs or multi-disc box sets. In recent years, Warner Bros. and Fantasy have released large box sets of previously unissued Bill Evans concert recordings.

what to buy: A studio session by Bill Evans's greatest trio, *Explorations* 𝄃𝄃𝄃𝄃 (Riverside, 1961, prod. Orrin Keepnews) features the majestic bass of Scott LaFaro and intuitive drum work of Paul Motian. With a year of road experience behind them, the trio was coalescing into one of the most remarkable units in jazz. Check out the evolving interplay on "Israel," a tune originally recorded on the *Birth of the Cool* sessions, or on Miles's tune "Nardis." The legendary session *Sunday at the Village Vanguard* ♫♫♫♫ (Riverside, 1961, prod. Orrin Keepnews) is one of the most influential trio albums in jazz. The level of interaction between Evans, LaFaro, and Motian was unprecedented and continues to amaze. This album is an essential part of any jazz collection. A brilliant collaboration with guitarist Jim Hall and trumpeter Freddie Hubbard, *Interplay* ♫♫♫♫ (Riverside, 1963, prod. Orrin Keepnews) shows that Evans could thrive outside his trio. Though at first glance this seems like a hard bop session, with Evans swinging hard, the pianist reworks the material ingeniously and uses Hall's guitar in the ensemble like a horn. *Cross-Currents* ♫♫♫♫ (Fantasy, 1978, prod. Helen Keane) adds the brilliant and too-little-recorded tenor saxophonist Warne Marsh and brilliant much-recorded alto saxophonist Lee Konitz to Evans's working trio with Eddie Gomez (bass) and Eliot Zigmund (drums). The Konitz/Evans duet on "When I Fall in Love" alone justifies the purchase of this CD.

what to buy next: *Everybody Digs Bill Evans* ♫♫♫♫ (Riverside, 1959, prod. Orrin Keepnews) and this album shows why. With the propulsive accompaniment of Sam Jones (bass) and Philly Joe Jones (drums), Evans plays a set of standards, including a driving take of "Night and Day," and jazz tunes such as "Oleo" and "Minority." But it's his stunning and highly influential theme "Peace Piece" that stands out as the essential track. The second album of material from the classic trio's well-documented 1961 engagement at the Village Vanguard, *Waltz for Debby* ♫♫♫♫ (Riverside, 1962, prod. Orrin Keepnews) captures Evans, LaFaro and Motian playing at a level of communication that borders on the preternatural. As fascinating an album as it is beautiful, *Alone (Again)* ♫♫♫♫ (Fantasy, 1977, prod. Helen Keane) is a solo session where Evans explores five tunes. He searches out the nooks and crannies of each piece before settling on one idea and taking it in a surprising direction. A rare quintet date, *Quintessence* ♫♫♫♫ (Fantasy, 1977, prod. Helen Keane) features the great tenor saxophonist Harold Land, guitarist Kenny Burrell, bassist Ray Brown, and drummer Philly Joe Jones. Not surprisingly, there's much sensitive interplay, and Evans's playing on Thad Jones "A Child is Born" is particularly gorgeous. Completists with the spare cash can now pick up *The Complete Bill Evans on Verve* ♫♫♫♫ (Verve, 1997, prod. various). Though docked half a point for not living up to its title—it

BILL EVANS

song "Stella by Starlight"
album *Conversations with Myself*
(Verve, 1963/1997)
instrument Piano

Monster Solo

includes only one of his Verve sessions as a sideman and lacks both 1963's rare (and critically panned) LP *Theme from the VIPs and Other Great Songs* plus Town Hall concert material—the confusingly organized package partially compensates with a wealth of unreleased material from the 1967 Vanguard sessions.

what to avoid: *Symbiosis* ♫♫ (Verve, 1974, prod. Helen Keane) is an utterly forgettable session featuring Evans playing two extended movements composed and arranged by Claus Ogermann. Why the label decided to reissue this when there are so many great Evans albums languishing in the Verve vaults is a mystery.

best of the rest:
New Jazz Conceptions ♫♫♫♫ (Riverside, 1957)
Portrait in Jazz ♫♫♫♫ (Riverside, 1960)
Moonbeams ♫♫♫♫ (Riverside, 1962)
How My Heart Sings! ♫♫♫♫ (Riverside, 1963)
At Shelly's Manne-Hole ♫♫♫♫ (Riverside, 1964)
Re: Person I Knew ♫♫♫♫ (Fantasy, 1974)

$\frac{3}{8}$ $\frac{8}{8}$ *gil evans*

The Tony Bennett/Bill Evans Album ♪♪♪♪ (Fantasy, 1975)
New Conversations ♪♪♪♪ (Warner Bros., 1978)
We Will Meet Again ♪♪♪♪ (Warner Bros., 1980)
Highlights from Turn Out the Stars ♪♪♪♪ (Warner Bros., 1996)

worth searching for: An amazingly sensitive artist right up until his death, Evans is in top form on *Paris Concert, Edition One* ♪♪♪♪ (Elektra, 1980, prod. Helen Keane) a trio session with Marc Johnson (bass) and Joe LaBarbera. His last trio was also one of his best, capable of (and captured here) playing music at the highest level of communication. Marian McPartland coaxes the reserved Evans to talk about himself on *Marian McPartland's Piano Jazz with Guest Bill Evans* ♪♪♪♪ (Jazz Alliance, 1978, prod. Dick Phipps), taken from her always engaging *Piano Jazz* radio show. The two also make very sympathetic partners as they play a series of fascinating piano duets.

influences:

◄◄ Lennie Tristano, Bud Powell, Horace Silver, Nat "King" Cole

►► Herbie Hancock, Keith Jarrett, Chick Corea, Richie Beirach, Fred Hersch, Alan Broadbent

Andrew Gilbert

Gil Evans

Born Ian Ernest Gilmore Green, May 13, 1912, in Toronto, Canada. Died March 20, 1988, in Cuernavaca, Mexico

Completely self-taught and remarkably unprolific, Gil Evans nonetheless ranks among the greatest arrangers in jazz history, arguably surpassed only by Duke Ellington. Though musically he could be a perfectionist, he was distinctly unassertive in terms of self-promotion, and his career follows one of the oddest trajectories ever seen in the competitive world of jazz.

Evans grew up on the Pacific coast and first established himself while leading a Stockton, California-based band starting in 1933. It eventually became the house group at the Rendezvous Ballroom in Balboa Beach. In 1937 he ceded control of the band to its singer, Skinnay Ennis, and continued on as its arranger, joined in that role by Claude Thornhill. Thornhill moved to New York and started his own band, and in 1941 invited Evans to join him and write arrangements. Though nominally a dance band, the Thornhill group had a number of excellent jazz soloists (including Lee Konitz and Red Rodney) and made a name for itself through its expanded instrumentation, which included French horn and tuba, and its repertoire, which featured bebop tunes such as "Anthropology," "Yardbird Suite," and "Donna Lee." The last, by Miles Davis, led to Evans's introduction to the man with whom he would make several of jazz's most sophisticated

and intricately arranged albums. The Thornhill band's sound became defined by the lush, hazy, floating textures Evans favored, and if not a commercial leader, it made a big impression on other jazz musicians.

Evans's open and tolerant personality and willingness to share his knowledge soon made him the vortex of a coterie of younger musicians looking to expand the range of bebop. His Manhattan apartment became the center of ongoing discussions involving Davis, Gerry Mulligan, John Lewis, Tadd Dameron, Johnny Carisi, J.J. Johnson, George Russell, and other innovators. The first public manifestation of these sonic revolutionaries came in the form of a Davis-led nonet that gigged in 1948 and which in 1949–50 recorded 12 tracks (written and/or arranged by Mulligan, Lewis, Evans, Davis, and Carisi) for Capitol. To the typical bebop quintet (trumpet, alto sax, piano, drums, bass) were added trombone, French horn, baritone sax, and tuba, all lower-pitched instruments than trumpet and alto sax, thus providing a broader array of timbres. Once again, the impact on open-minded musicians was greater than the immediate public acceptance. Within a few years, the style that sprang from these experiments retroactively named the new sound; the nonet's music was subsequently collected on an album dubbed *Birth of the Cool*. Mulligan (who dubbed Evans "Svengali," an anagram of his name) had moved to California and spread the gospel of the style, which toned down the emphasis on individual solos, favored intertwining lines, expanded the harmonies, and used less aggressive rhythms than bebop.

Evans added to his reputation by arranging languid singer Helen Merrill's 1956 EmArcy album *Dream of You*, and then achieved lasting fame through a series of classic Miles Davis albums in the late 1950s. *Miles Ahead*, *Porgy and Bess*, and *Sketches of Spain* used larger groups (*Miles Ahead* sports on its cover the legend "Miles Davis + 19") and provided exquisitely detailed settings that display Davis's vulnerable tone in gem-like solos. The importance of Evans's vision on these albums is properly reflected in the dual accreditation on the 1996 box set *Miles Davis & Gil Evans: The Complete Columbia Studio Recordings*. The immediate popularity and importance of *Miles Ahead* brought Evans to the attention of the record industry, and he finally began recording as a leader in 1957 at age 45, adding soprano saxophone and bassoon to his arrangements for the Prestige album *Gil Evans & Ten*, on which he played piano in his spare, self-taught style.

Intermittently, there were other Evans-led albums, for Pacific Jazz, Impulse!, and Verve, and more collaborations with

Davis—the inconsistent, semi-bossa nova album *Quiet Nights*, a concert at Carnegie Hall, and music for a play in California (*The Time of the Barracudas*). A rare six-week engagement in 1960 (at the Jazz Gallery in New York, alternating sets with the John Coltrane Quartet) led to Evans's most notable album, *Out of the Cool* (1961), which included two fine original compositions by Evans himself. Most odd was its follow-up, *Into the Hot*, on which none of the tracks were either Evans-arranged or led and on which he played not a note despite the billing of the Gil Evans Orchestra; half were Johnny Carisi originals (which did use Evans Orchestra regulars) and half were Cecil Taylor compositions played by Taylor's group. Though nothing on the album jacket gave any hint of this, the notes inside correctly stated that it was "entirely in character for *Evans* to decide to devote this album to two strongly individual jazz composers who were invited to function here on their own terms under Gil's aegis." A later four-album deal with Verve resulted in just one album being completed, and subsequent Davis projects produced even less fruit. Evans did arrangements for albums led by Kenny Burrell and Astrud Gilberto and entered the soundtrack world with scores to obscure films by Nogata (*Fragments*, 1967), Gittler (*Parachute to Paradise*, 1969), and Lee (*The Sea in Your Future*, 1970). There were occasional group performances, but little documentation. Various proposed projects with Davis were not followed through on.

Evans began a complete turnaround in 1969, when he began playing regularly, continuing to do so until his death. The turnaround also involved the sound of his music. Always a voracious listener of broad tastes, he had become attracted to the music of Jimi Hendrix; they had booked studio time to work together, but Hendrix's premature death intervened. Finally, in 1974, Evans recorded a legendary album of nine Hendrix tunes for RCA, arranging two songs himself while band members contributed the rest of the charts. Evans moved to a less precisely notated style and incorporated electric instruments. His concern for timbre remained, however; even when the front-line instruments were playing unisons, they had a unique quality.

As always, there were plenty of admiring musicians eager to work with Evans. Most prominent in the early edition of his new band was tenor saxophonist Billy Harper, whose earthy modality as both player and composer (his "Thoroughbred" and "Priestess" became standards in the Evans repertoire) typified the leader's new direction. Among the many other bandleaders in their own right who contributed to the band in the 1970s and 1980s were trumpeters Johnny Coles, Lew Soloff, Jon Faddis, Terumasa Hino, and Hannibal Marvin Peterson, saxophonists

David Sanborn, Arthur Blythe, Hamiet Bluiett, and George Adams, trombonists Jimmy Knepper and George Lewis, French horn players John Clark and Sharon Freeman, multi-instrumentalist Howard Johnson, guitarists Joe Beck, John Abercrombie, Hiram Bullock, and Ryo Kawasaki, and drummers Tony Williams, Billy Cobham, and Lenny White.

Evans's new momentum culminated in the famous Monday Night Orchestra, which from April 1983 until January 1988—a couple of months before Evans's death—played a weekly Monday-night gig at Sweet Basil. (Mondays being the slow night for jazz clubs after the weekend, they've been the traditional night when club owners will take chances and when players are reliably free enough, commitment-wise, to form large groups.) A plenitude of live albums document the final phase of Evans's career. The rock musician Sting, a fan of Evans's music, used the Evans band on his Top 10 1987 album *Nothing like the Sun* for a cover of Hendrix's "Little Wing," and there's even a curious but fairly successful album, *Last Session*, recorded live at an Italian jazz festival that year, on which Sting sings throughout on material ranging from the hits of his former band, the Police, to Hendrix songs and even "Strange Fruit." Also noteworthy, if also peripheral to Evans's legacy, were occasional duo gigs, which showed that the man who with good humor described his instrumental abilities by saying he played "cheerleader's piano" had finally, after many years, become more comfortable as a player. Evans even revisited his past to an extent by once again, over 30 years after their first album, arranging Helen Merrill's *Collaboration*, and by working with French admirer Laurent Cugny's Big Band Lumiere.

what to buy: Among all Evans's recordings as a leader, *Out of the Cool* ♫♫♫♫ (Impulse!, 1961/1996, prod. Creed Taylor, reissue prod. Michael Cuscuna) remains the touchstone of his incredible artistry. The long Evans original "La Nevada" kicks off the album and somewhat foreshadows his later style. The gorgeous, mesmerizing "Where Flamingos Fly" (written by John Benson Brooks) is prototypical Evans, shimmering gently under Jimmy Knepper's solo. Kurt Weill's "Bilbao Song" is the ultimate arranger's showcase. George Russell's blues "Stratusphunk" is also heavily arranged, but allows a little room for improvisation. Evans's "Sunken Treasure" is a successful experiment in melody-less thematic material, with trumpeter Johnny Coles (who throughout the album fills the Miles Davis role exquisitely) providing the element of melody in his solo improvisation. Left off the original LP, and in a completely different and revelatory mood from the rest of the material, is Evans's funky take on Horace Silver's "Sister Sadie," proving that hard bop and cool jazz can intersect magnificently. Evans's final style receives its most extended and extreme workout on *Live at Sweet Basil* 🎵🎵🎵🎵 (King, 1984/Evidence, 1992, prod. Shigeyuki Kawashima, Horst Liepolt) and *Live at Sweet Basil, Volume 2* 🎵🎵🎵🎵 (King, 1984/Evidence, 1992, prod. Shigeyuki Kawashima, Horst Liepolt), which feature his Monday Night Orchestra that had been playing every week for nearly a year and a half when these albums (originally double-LP sets) were recorded. His unique sonic touches show up constantly even in this format; the most striking is giving the electric guitar riff of Hendrix's "Voodoo Chile" not to guitarist Hiram Bullock (who solos with abandon elsewhere) but to tuba player Howard Johnson (who also plays baritone sax and bass clarinet on other tracks). The trumpet stars are Lew Soloff and Hannibal Marvin Peterson, while George Adams on tenor and Chris Hunter on alto get the sax honors. The material includes two other Hendrix tunes, a lengthy Charlie Parker medley, compositions by Charles Mingus, Wayne Shorter, Thelonious Monk, and Herbie Hancock, and a few Evans originals. Everybody really stretches out, with the shambling nature of the arrangements more than compensated for by the ebullient solos and the infectious sense of comfortable camaraderie.

what to buy next: Sometimes overlooked amid the praise for Evans's overall sound is that the best musicians have always wanted to play in his bands, and that even his most heavily scored music frequently left them ample room to exhibit their talents. *The Individualism of Gil Evans* 🎵🎵🎵🎵 (Verve, 1964/1988, prod. Creed Taylor, reissue prod. Michael Cuscuna, Richard Seidel, Seth Rothstein) not only has some of Evans's richest arrangements—"Time of the Barracudas" (a.k.a. "General Assembly"), Kurt Weill's "Barbara Song," "Hotel Me" (a.k.a. "Jelly Rolls")—it also stars Wayne Shorter, Phil Woods, Thad Jones, and Kenny Burrell in prominent solo roles. Recorded live in 1977, *Priestess* 🎵🎵🎵🎵 (Antilles, 1983/1991, prod. John Simon) is a classic late-period album on the strength of the nearly 20-minute "Priestess," a soulful Billy Harper tune featuring stirring alto sax solos by David Sanborn and Arthur Blythe.

what to avoid: Though nobody will be disappointed by the spirited performances on *Tribute to Gil* 🎵🎵 (Soul Note, 1989, prod. Giovanni Bonandrini), this festival concert document is a low-priority acquisition, given the profusion of live recordings from Evans's late period and the poor sound quality here. Evans's absence from the proceedings, recorded four months after his death, seems to spur the musicians on, and the rating here is the result of a two-notch penalty for the dull sonics.

the rest:
Gil Evans and Ten 🎵🎵🎵🎵 (Prestige, 1957/OJC, 1989)
New Bottle, Old Wine 🎵🎵🎵🎵 (Pacific Jazz, 1958/Blue Note, 1997)
Great Jazz Standards 🎵🎵🎵🎵 (Pacific Jazz, 1958/Blue Note, 1997)
Into the Hot 🎵🎵🎵🎵 (Impulse!, 1961/1988)
Blues in Orbit 🎵🎵🎵 (Ampex, 1969/Enja, 1985)
Plays the Music of Jimi Hendrix 🎵🎵🎵🎵 (RCA Bluebird, 1974/1988)
There Comes a Time 🎵🎵🎵🎵 (RCA Bluebird, 1976)
Live at the Public Theater, Volume I 🎵🎵🎵🎵 (King, 1980/Evidence, 1994)
Live at the Public Theater, Volume II 🎵🎵🎵🎵 (King, 1980/Evidence, 1994)
In Memoriam: Bud & Bird 🎵🎵🎵🎵 (King, 1987/Evidence, 1994)
Farewell 🎵🎵🎵🎵 (King, 1988/Evidence, 1992)
(With Steve Lacy) *Paris Blues* 🎵🎵🎵 (Owl, 1988)
(With the Laurent Cugny Big Band Lumiere) *Rhythm-a-ning* 🎵🎵🎵 (EmArcy, 1988)
Little Wing 🎵🎵🎵 (DIW, 1989)
(With Lee Konitz) *Heroes* 🎵🎵🎵🎵 (Verve, 1991)
(With Lee Konitz) *Anti Heroes* 🎵🎵🎵🎵 (Verve, 1991)
(With Sting) *Last Session* 🎵🎵🎵 (Jazz Door, 1992)

worth searching for: *Where Flamingos Fly* 🎵🎵🎵🎵 (Artists House, 1981/A&M, 1989/Musical Heritage Society, 1990, prod. John Simon) first came out on Ornette Coleman's label 10 years after it was recorded and offers a fascinating look at the early years of the style which Evans would expand on for the rest of his life. The band on the two long tracks (Evans's "Zee Zee" and Kenny Dorham's "El Matador") that bookend the disc was smaller than previous or subsequent groups would be, but Evans's incorporation of electric instruments (shocking to some at the time), including Joe Beck on guitar, filled out the sound. Billy Harper (tenor sax) and Johnny Coles (trumpet) are the solo stars, with Airto Moreira and Flora Purim overdubbed later. It's also interesting to hear the way the title track had changed since *Out of the Cool*. That *Svengali* 🎵🎵🎵🎵 (Atlantic, 1973, prod. Kenneth Noland, Gil Evans), Evans's finest 1970s album, has lapsed from Atlantic's catalog is a crime. Two superb Billy Harper compositions and a gorgeous "Summertime" are highlights, and there are fine solos by Harper, Sanborn, and guitarist Ted Dunbar. Listeners who find the less structured live albums of Evans's last decade too meandering will appreciate the greater precision of this studio effort.

influences:

◀◀ Claude Debussy, Duke Ellington, Claude Thornhill, Bud Powell, Jimi Hendrix

▶▶ George Russell, Oliver Nelson, Quincy Jones, Michel Legrand, Maria Schneider, Laurent Cugny, Palle Mikkelborg

Steve Holtje

Douglas Ewart

Born September 13, 1946, in Kingston, Jamaica.

As a child in Jamaica, the story goes, Douglas Ewart was always building things, from go-carts, to kites, to musical instruments, fashioning drums and shakers, and even then seizing on the possibilities of flutes made from bamboo. When his family moved to Chicago in 1963, Ewart attended vocational school where he studied tailoring. Music entered his life forcefully, though, through his association with the Association for the Advancement of Creative Musicians, which as part of its activist outreach, ran a music school where Ewart studied with founding members Muhal Richard Abrams, Roscoe Mitchell, and Joseph Jarman. Ewart has since blossomed both as a maker of music and musical instruments, particularly bamboo instruments. He has performed on flutes, saxophones, and electronics with many of his fellow Chicagoans, including recording sessions with pianist Abrams; saxophonists Chico Freeman, Henry Threadgill, and Anthony Braxton; and trombonist George Lewis, with whom he shared the eponymous duets project, *George Lewis/Douglas Ewart*. Ewart is also a sculptor and educator. He has been chairman of the AACM and participant in panels for the National Endowment for the Arts and other arts organizations. Under an NEA fellowship, he studied the crafting and playing of shakuhachi flutes in Japan for a year.

worth searching for: Until a commercial release matches the power of his best live performances and his private-issue records and tapes on his Arawak label, few of Ewart's potential listeners will know what they've missed. Among the Arawak tapes *The Bamboo Forest* 𝄢𝄢𝄢𝄢 (Arawak, 1990, prod. Douglas Ewart) is particularly worth seeking out, ranging from a sort of rustic minimalism to the superimposition of strident horn lines over percussion that boasts the influence of Rastafarian roots music. The only Arawak CD, *Bamboo Meditations at Banff* 𝄢𝄢𝄢 (Arawak, 1994, prod. Douglas Ewart) is an ever-changing scrim of dreamy flute atmospherics (Available by mail, P.O. Box 7987, Chicago, Illinois 60680). *George Lewis/Douglas Ewart* 𝄢𝄢𝄢 (Black Saint, 1979, prod. Giacomo Pellicciotti) gives a side to the compositions of each of the duet participants in a sort of AACM-style chamber music in which the precision (and delicacy) can give way to more impassioned improvising, and vice versa. Ewart's "Save! Mon," sends the musicians into pointillist sparring and finally an exotic soundscape of percussive and electronic sounds.

influences:

◄◄ Yusef Lateef, Art Ensemble of Chicago

W. Kim Heron

Jon Faddis

Born July 24, 1953, in Oakland, CA.

Faddis got his start with San Francisco R&B bands in the late 1960s. He joined Lionel Hampton in 1971, and then later that same year was playing with the Thad Jones–Mel Lewis big band. Faddis also gained valuable experience in the 1970s playing with Charles Mingus, Gil Evans, Chuck Mangione, and Dizzy Gillespie. Starting in the late 1970s and into the 1990s, Faddis has mostly led his own groups, and in 1993 became the director of the Carnegie Hall Jazz Orchestra. Stylistically, he's always been thought of as a close approximation of his primary influence, Dizzy Gillespie. But since the mid-1980s, he has gained a slightly more individualistic style (characterized especially by lots of high notes!).

what to buy: On *Legacy* 𝄢𝄢𝄢 (Concord, 1985, prod. Bennett Rubin) Faddis pays tribute to all of his trumpet idols—Louis Armstrong ("West End Blues"), Roy Eldridge ("Little Jazz"), and Dizzy Gillespie ("A Night in Tunisia"). Also included are Benny Golson's "Whisper Not" and a Faddis original. Faddis does little that is truly original or startling, but he shows his dazzling technique and a hearty appreciation for the past.

what to buy next: *Into the Faddisphere* 𝄢𝄢𝄢 (Epic, 1989, prod. Jon Faddis) features some dazzling trumpet work on a group of tunes dominated by Faddis originals. This recording also marks, by Faddis's own admission, the first time he really stopped trying to sound like Dizzy Gillespie.

what to avoid: Not only is *Hornucopia* 𝄢𝄢 (Epic, 1991, prod. Jon Faddis) as a whole not that good, this album gains a dubious distinction for one track in particular, the ill-advised "Rapartee." As if this rather pathetic attempt at jazz-rap fusion isn't bad enough on its own, Faddis brings the immortal Dizzy Gillespie into the fray, making this a true abomination. One only wonders what these two men may have thought they were accomplishing here.

the rest:
(With Billy Harper) *Jon and Billy* 𝄢𝄢𝄢 (Evidence, 1975)
Oscar Peterson and Jon Faddis 𝄢𝄢𝄢 (Pablo, 1975)

worth searching for: With *Youngblood* 𝄢𝄢𝄢 (Pablo, 1976, prod. Norman Granz), his debut recording as a leader, Faddis made an emphatic statement with his trumpet virtuosity.

influences:

◄◄ Dizzy Gillespie

►► Roy Hargrove, Carnegie Hall Jazz Orchestra

Dan Keener

Charles Fambrough

Born August 25, 1950, in Philadelphia, PA.

Bassist Charles Fambrough is one of the few musicians who can genuinely lay claim to being a totally "well-rounded" player. Inspired in part by his father who was a singer in the church choir, Fambrough undertook classical studies with a member of the Philadelphia Orchestra while in middle school and he's played world music with percussionist Airto, tiptoed into the fusion bag via a gig with Grover Washington Jr., and gained valuable mainstream jazz knowledge through stints with McCoy Tyner and Art Blakey's Jazz Messengers. His record dates as leader during the past few years—for labels including CTI, Audioquest, and Evidence—reflect the multi-directional outlook that results from Fambrough's musical experiences and personality. He shows great skill as a composer and his sound is distinctive for its deep and resounding sonority. Capable of a full and rich tone in all the registers, his solo lines often hit the upper range, where he obtains a cello-like resonance. As his background would suggest, Fambrough is equally adept at accompanying any size ensemble or providing melodic leads, making him a versatile and valuable jazz artist.

what to buy: *Blues at Bradley's* ♫♫♫♫ (CTI, 1993, prod. Creed Taylor) catches a live set at the now-defunct club where some spirited playing is put forth from the front line of Joe Ford, Donald Harrison, and Steve Turre. Four of the five tunes are Fambrough originals and they show him to be a composer of some merit.

what to buy next: *The Charmer* ♫♫♫♫ (CTI, 1992, prod. Creed Taylor) is not the swinger that *Blues at Bradley's* is and not as successful on the commercial side as Fambrough's first CTI release (which is unfortunately out-of-print on disc), but it has some admirable moments and features some substantial original pieces.

the rest:
Keeper of the Spirit ♫♫♫ (Audioquest, 1995)
City Tribes ♫♫♫ (Evidence Music, 1996)
Upright Citizen ♫♫♫ (Nu Groove, 1997)

worth searching for: *The Proper Angle* ♫♫♫♫ (CTI, 1991, prod. Creed Taylor) was Fambrough's debut set as a leader and re-

mains his strongest recorded work to date. The variety of straight-ahead and Latin-inspired romps can't be beat. Soloists include Kenny Kirkland, Wynton and Branford Marsalis, and Roy Hargrove, and for his strong efforts as an engineer, Rudy Van Gelder won a French award for excellence in recorded sound. Look for this out-of-print disc on tape or in the used record shops.

influences:

◄◄ Paul Chambers, Jimmy Garrison, Jymie Merritt

Chris Hovan

Tal Farlow

Born Talmage Holt Farlow, June 7, 1921, in Greensboro, NC.

A late bloomer who didn't start playing guitar until he was in his 20s, Tal Farlow is a self-taught player who didn't read music. Nevertheless, by the time he was 30, the inventive guitarist had scored gigs with clarinetist Buddy De Franco and vibraphonist Red Norvo. Blessed with blinding speed, an unerring knack for great melodies and a deft touch, he won critical acclaim in the early '50s for his work with Norvo and trumpeter Artie Shaw. He led his own trio until a distaste for the music business led him to return to North Carolina for work as a sign painter. By the late '60s, he was making irregular appearances at festivals, and by the '80s he had resumed his partnership with Norvo, surprising audiences who had never heard his now-out-of-print seminal recordings.

what to buy: Featuring an impressive take on "My Romance," Farlow's comeback record, *The Return of Tal Farlow* ♫♫♫♫ (OJC, 1969, prod. Don Schlitten) sounds as if he never left, with lots of fleet-fingered melodicism and a backing group led by drummer-extraordinaire Alan Dawson.

what to buy next: For an overview of Farlow's talents, *Verve Jazz Masters 41* ♫♫♫♫ (Verve, 1995, prod. Norman Granz) offers 16 different cuts full of fire, including such standards as "Stella by Starlight," "Autumn Leaves," and "Cherokee" with players that include Oscar Pettiford, Ray Brown, Joe Morello, and Chico Hamilton.

what to avoid: With backing from legendary bassist Ray Brown and pianist Hank Jones, this record couldn't be horrible–still, there's something missing from *A Sign of the Times* ♫♫♫ (Concord Jazz, 1977). Despite inspired standards such as "Georgia on My Mind" and "Put on a Happy Face," there's a little too much sizzle missing from this steak.

the rest:

The Tal Farlow Album 🎵🎵🎵 (Verve, 1954)
Fascinating Rhythm 🎵🎵🎵 (Norgran, 1955)
Recital by Tal Farlow 🎵🎵🎵 (Norgran, 1955)
Tal 🎵🎵🎵 (PolyGram, 1956)
Fuerst Set 🎵🎵🎵🎵 (Xanadu, 1956)
Second Set 🎵🎵🎵🎵 (Xanadu, 1956)
This Is Tal Farlow 🎵🎵🎵 (Verve, 1958)
The Guitar Artistry of Tal Farlow 🎵🎵🎵🎵 (Verve, 1968)

worth searching for: Planned as an homage to the man that inspired them all, *A Tribute to Wes Montgomery* 🎵🎵🎵🎵 (Project G-5, 1994) aligned Farlow with Herb Ellis, Jimmy Raney, Cal Collins, and Royce Campbell tipping a hat to the legendary six-stringer with lots of inspired guitar blowing.

influences:

◀◀ Charlie Christian, Wes Montgomery

▶▶ Joe Pass, Kenny Burrell, Pat Martino

Eric Deggans

Art Farmer

Born August 21, 1928, in Council Bluffs, IA.

Art Farmer is one of jazz's most profoundly lyrical improvisors, a flugelhornist whose deceptively placid attack is marked by incisive, highly nuanced emotional insight and undergirded by a singular harmonic sensibility. A second generation bebopper, Farmer early on developed along similar lines as Miles Davis, but from his earliest recordings as a leader displayed his own personality. Though largely overshadowed in his formative years, Farmer is one of jazz's most consistently inspired players, a musician who has continued to refine his approach throughout his career. Along with Miles Davis and Clark Terry, Farmer popularized the flugelhorn, which he's played in small group contexts almost exclusively since the early 1960s.

Raised in Phoenix, Farmer and his twin brother, bassist Addison Farmer (1928–63), moved to Los Angeles in 1945, and Allen quickly found work on Central Avenue with Johnny Otis, Jay McShann, and Benny Carter, and in the bebop-influenced bands of Roy Porter and Gerald Wilson. In the early 1950s he toured and recorded with Wardell Grey and Lionel Hampton, and made a number of records with Hampton sidemen such as Clifford Brown and Gigi Gryce. He played on many of Prestige's jam session recordings in the mid- and late 1950s with players such as Gene Ammons and Donald Byrd, and also recorded with noted composer George Russell. Throughout the first half of his career, Farmer preferred to share the spotlight and formed a se-

ries of rewarding partnerships. Settling in New York, he led a succession of bands with Gryce (1954–56), Horace Silver (1956–58), Gerry Mulligan (1958–59), and the popular Jazztet with Benny Golson (1959–62). Between 1962 and 1965, his own quartet featured Jim Hall and later Steve Kuhn and for a while he co-led a group with Jimmy Heath. He began making regular trips to Europe in the mid-1960s and by 1968 had settled in Vienna, becoming a member of the Austrian Radio Orchestra and appearing as a featured soloist in the Kenny Clarke/Francy Boland Big Band. Since the early 1980s, he has made regular trips back to the United States. Over the years, Farmer has recorded numerous sessions as a leader, including albums for Prestige, Contemporary, Chess, CTI, Concord, United Artists, Mercury, Atlantic, Soul Note, Arabesque, Monarch, and Enja. Many of his albums are still available.

what to buy: Containing a quintet session with Sonny Rollins and a quartet session with pianist Wynton Kelly, *Early Art* 🎵🎵🎵🎵 (Prestige/OJC, 1954, prod. Bob Weinstock) is an excellent album documenting Farmer's early, hard-swinging bop sound. The four quintet tracks feature a rhythm section Farmer recorded with a number of times—pianist Horace Silver, bassist Percy Heath, and drummer Kenny Clarke—playing three strong Farmer originals as well as "I'll Take Romance." The second rhythm section isn't as lively, but provides strong support on the five ballads and Farmer-penned blues, "Pre Amp." After a year in Lionel Hampton's trumpet section sitting next to Clifford Brown, Farmer had clearly come into his own by the time of these recordings, all marked by his light, luminous, but introspective sound. A classic session with strong material, inventive arrangements and an all-star line up, *Farmer's Market* 🎵🎵🎵🎵 (Prestige/OJC, 1956, prod. Bob Weinstock) features tenor saxophonist Hank Mobley, pianist Kenny Drew, bassist Addison Farmer, and drummer Elvin Jones. Highlights include his second-version "Farmer's Market," a tune made famous by Annie Ross's vocalese, taken here at a faster clip than the original recording with Wardell Gray; Farmer's sensitive ballad work on Gigi Gryce's "Reminiscing"; and the standard, "By Myself," the latter two *sans* Mobley. One of the finest Billy Strayhorn tributes ever recorded, *Something to Live For: The Music of Billy Strayhorn* 🎵🎵🎵🎵 (Contemporary, 1987, prod. Helen Keane) is a brilliant quintet session with Clifford Jordan (tenor sax), James Williams (piano), Rufus Reid (bass), and Marvin "Smitty" Smith (drums). Farmer's achingly poignant flugelhorn sound and deep harmonic insight make him particularly well suited to explore Strayhorn's music, while Jordan and Williams both bring their passionate lyricism and hard swinging romanticism to the seven

Strayhorn classics, including "Isfahan," "Johnny Come Lately," and "Raincheck." One of Farmer's best albums of the 1980s, *Blame It on My Youth* ♪♪♪♪ (Contemporary, 1988, prod. Helen Keane) features Clifford Jordan (tenor and soprano sax), James Williams (piano), Rufus Reid (bass), and Victor Lewis (drums). Brilliant soloists and challenging material make this a consistently rewarding session. Opening and closing with classic ballads, the title track and Alec Wilder's "I'll Be Around," respectively, the album features strong pieces by Jordan, Williams, and pianist Donald Brown ("The Smile of the Snake"), though Benny Carter's "Summer Serenade" is the album's highpoint, with sublime contributions by the entire band.

what to buy next: *Portrait of Art Farmer* ♪♪♪♪ (Contemporary/OJC, 1958, prod. Nat Hentoff) is one of Farmer's better albums, a quartet session with his brother Addison Farmer on bass, Hank Jones on piano, and Roy Haynes on drums. Farmer contributed two blues and a blowing tune, and selected a good range of material including George Russell's "Nita," Benny Golson's "Stablemates," and the standard ballads "By Myself," "Too Late Now," and "The Folks Who Live on the Hill," which he renders with his supreme lyricism. Haynes and Jones are the perfect sidemen, listening actively and offering knowing support while stoking the rhythm section with fiery precision. Combining two sessions by the second version of the Jazztet, *Blues on Down* ♪♪♪♪ (Chess/GRP, 1960–61, prod. Kay Norton, Jack Tracy) features Farmer and Benny Golson (tenor sax) with trombonist Tom MacIntosh (replacing Curtis Fuller), pianist Cedar Walton (replacing McCoy Tyner), bassist Tommy Williams, and drummer Tootie Heath. *Warm Valley* ♪♪♪ (Concord Jazz, 1983, prod. Carl E. Jefferson) pairs Farmer with pianist Fred Hersch, whose finely honed lyricism makes him a well-suited accompanist for the flugelhornist. The album develops as if the quartet were playing a set, opening with a brief bop workout on "Moose the Mooche," through a rapid version of "Three Little Words," kicked off by Akira Tana's deft stick work, into Tommy Flanagan's Latin-tinged "Eclypso," and Billy Strayhorn's swinging "UMMG." The set concludes with a gorgeous version of Ellington's "Warm Valley," a perfect vehicle for Farmer's glowing, burnished horn. Recorded live at Kimball's East, across the bay from San Francisco, *Central Avenue Reunion* ♪♪♪♪ (Contemporary, 1990, prod. Helen Keane) brings together Farmer and his former L.A. jam session mate, alto saxophonist Frank Morgan. Accompanied by Lou Levy (piano), Eric Von Essen (bass), and Tootie Heath (drums), the two bop-era veterans apply their lyrical approaches to seven tunes from standard and hard-bop repertoire, including two fine Sonny Clark tunes,

"Blue Minor" and "Cool Struttin,'" and Farmer's best known piece, "Farmer's Market." This album is the first (and to date only) time Farmer and Morgan recorded together.

what to avoid: There's nothing wrong with Farmer's horn work on *Gentle Eyes* ♪♪ (Mainstream, 1972, prod. Bob Shad). In fact, he sounds typically beautiful, but he's often accompanied by treacly, sentimental orchestrations and totally superfluous vocals by the Swedish Radio group. Even dedicated Farmer fans probably want to skip this CD reissue.

best of the rest:

The Art Farmer Septet ♪♪♪♪ (Prestige/OJC, 1953–56)
(With Gigi Gryce) *When Farmer Met Gryce* ♪♪♪♪ (Prestige/OJC, 1955)
(With Donald Bird) *2 Trumpets* ♪♪♪♪ (Prestige/OJC, 1956)
Meet the Jazztet ♪♪♪♪♪ (Chess/MCA, 1960)
On the Road ♪♪♪♪ (Contemporary/OJC, 1976)
A Work of Art ♪♪♪♪ (Concord Jazz, 1982)
Manhattan ♪♪♪♪♪ (Soul Note, 1982)
(With the Jazztet) *Moment to Moment* ♪♪♪♪♪ (Soul Note, 1984)
Ph.D. ♪♪♪♪♪ (Contemporary, 1990)
(With the Art Farmer Quintet featuring Clifford Jordan) *Live at Sweet Basil* ♪♪♪♪♪ (Evidence, 1994)
The Company I Keep ♪♪♪♪ (Arabesque, 1994)
The Meaning of Art ♪♪♪♪ (Arabesque, 1995)
Live at Stanford Jazz Workshop ♪♪♪♪ (Monarch, 1997)

worth searching for: Farmer shines throughout *Art Farmer, Lee Konitz with the Joe Carter Quartet & Trio* ♪♪♪♪♪ (Stash, 1993, prod. Joe Carter), a session led by the under-appreciated guitarist Joe Carter with bassist Harvie Swartz and drummer Akira Tana. Highlights include the timeless ballad "My Foolish Heart," with beautiful solos by both Farmer and Carter, and Chick Corea's "Day Waves." The last two tracks feature Carter and Swartz with Lee Konitz playing two tunes by the alto saxophonist.

influences:

◀◀ Kenny Dorham, Miles Davis, Clark Terry

▶▶ Donald Byrd, Tom Harrell

Andrew Gilbert

Allen Farnham

Born May 19, 1961, in Boston, MA.

A 1983 graduate of the Oberlin Conservatory of Music, Allen Farnham received degrees in classical piano and jazz studies before briefly studying classical Indian music with Tamnad V. Ragavan. He is a versatile pianist who has served as an accompanist for Mel Tormé and Susannah McCorkle in addition to backing up Arthur Blythe, Junior Cook, and Frank Foster, and has also produced albums by Lew Tabackin, Ray Barretto, Jimmy Bruno, and Peter Leitch. His post-bop orientation towards piano shows up on his own albums, which are slightly more adventurous than the ones usually released by Concord Jazz.

what to buy: Joe Lovano, the amazing tenor saxophonist who Farnham used to perform with in Cleveland, joins the pianist in an interesting program, *5th House* 🎵🎵🎵 (Concord Jazz, 1990, prod. Carl E. Jefferson, Allen Farnham), which features material by John Coltrane (the title tune), Duke Pearson ("You Know I Care"), and Chick Corea ("Now He Sings, Now He Sobs"). Farnham the composer is represented with five songs. The rhythm section (Jamey Haddad on drums and percussion and Drew Gress on bass) had also known the pianist from his Ohio days and provides sympathetic support throughout. Haddad in particular, is a find.

what to buy next: *Play-cation* 🎵🎵🎵 (Concord Jazz, 1992, prod. Allen Farnham, John Burk) is pretty solid, with no major caveats. The song selection backs off from the adventurous (for Concord Jazz) line-up on *5th House*: Covers of Gershwin, Kern, Golson, and Ellington join with four Farnham compositions and the classic Dietz/Schwartz tune "Alone Together."

the rest:
The Common Thread 🎵🎵🎵 (Concord Jazz, 1995)
At Maybeck Volume 41 🎵🎵🎵 (Concord Jazz, 1996)

influences:
◀◀ Lennie Tristano, Dodo Marmarosa

Garaud MacTaggart

Joe Farrell

Born Joseph Carl Firrantello, December 16, 1937, in Chicago Heights, IL. Died January 10, 1986, in Los Angeles, CA.

Joe Farrell began studying tenor saxophone at 16 and moved to New York after receiving a degree in music education from the University of Illinois. He began working with Maynard Ferguson and also worked and/or recorded with Charles Mingus, Slide Hampton, Dizzy Reece, Jaki Byard and others in the early 1960s. Farrell quickly rose to prominence in the late 1960s for his creations as a founding member of the Thad Jones-Mel Lewis Orchestra and as a featured soloist with Elvin Jones. In the early 1970s, Farrell's saxophone and flute solos reached wider audiences through his stints with two of the three versions of Chick Corea's Return of Forever. During that same period, he recorded several albums for Creed Taylor's CTI label, which showed him to be one of the finest voices of that period

on tenor and soprano saxophones and flute, playing all with equal finesse. Although he was at home in a variety of contexts, Farrell's modal and hard bop work was most exceptional.

Unfortunately, Joe Farrell was extremely underrated and he did not become the huge name that many had expected. For the latter part of the 1970s he worked with Flora Purim and Airto, among others, and in jazz-rock contexts before he joined the Mingus Dynasty band in 1979. The 1980s found him back in a mainstream jazz direction and he recorded albums for Xanadu, Timeless and Contemporary and toured with Joanne Brackeen before his untimely passing in 1986. Over the years, Joe Farrell recorded with numerous jazz and pop artists. Unfortunately, many of his own albums are currently out-of-print.

what to buy: A modal mainstream gem, the CD reissue of Farrell's 1980 Contemporary Records LP, *Sonic Text* 🎵🎵🎵🎵 (Fantasy/OJC, 1990, prod. John Koenig) rates among Farrell's finest work. The quintet includes Freddie Hubbard and George Cables who, along with Joe, penned the six compositions which offer plenty of room to stretch out. *Joe Farrell Quartet* 🎵🎵🎵🎵 (Columbia, 1987, prod. Creed Taylor), a CD-reissue of Farrell's 1970 CTI album, mixes jazz with doses of rock and a touch of avant-garde and includes John McLaughlin, Chick Corea, Dave Holland and Jack DeJohnette. McLaughlin's spooky "Follow Your Heart" is a real treat.

what to buy next: A reissue of Farrell's 1972 CTI session, *Moon Germs* 🎵🎵🎵 (CTI/CBS, 1987, prod. Creed Taylor), is a must for anyone who enjoys early Return to Forever. Although Herbie Hancock plays the electric piano rather than Corea, Stanley Clarke and Farrell are present (along with Jack DeJohnette) as are two RTF style songs, Clarke's "Bass Folk Song" and Corea's "Times Lie."

the rest:
(With Art Pepper) *Darn That Dream* 🎵🎵🎵 (Drive Archive, 1982)
(With Louis Hayes) *Vim 'N Vigor* 🎵🎵🎵 (Timeless, 1983)

worth searching for: It's inconceivable that Farrell's best CTI LP album, *Outback* 🎵🎵🎵🎵 (CTI, 1971, prod. Creed Taylor), has not yet been reissued by Columbia. It offers four Farrell originals and features Chick Corea, Buster Williams and Airto. Best of all, Farrell is reunited with drummer Elvin Jones, with whom he had worked for the three years prior to this recording. Everyone shines. Try to find the LP version for now.

influences:
◀◀ Sonny Rollins, John Coltrane

Bill Wahl

Zusaan Kali Fasteau

Born March 9, 1947, in Newark, NJ.

Fasteau first made her mark in the Sea Ensemble, a duo with her late husband Donald Raphael Garrett, who recorded with John Coltrane. The Sea Ensemble's eponymous album on ESP is something of a classic of the type, which is purely spontaneous multi-instrumental free improvisation. Fasteau's music is impossible to pigeonhole, full of influences and sound sources from around the globe, but if there is one category (besides the impossibly broad "world music") it fits into, it would be free jazz. She sees music as a healing force, but doesn't let that turn her art into new age pablum. Her ideals reflect and expand on those of the late 1960s and early 1970s the same way her music does, with Coltrane—as he is to so many free improvisors—a special inspiration but far from the only ingredient in her musical stew.

Fasteau has spent considerable time living abroad, often studying the music of the cultures she was living in (France, Turkey, and especially India). She has acquired not only a knowledge of the complex Indian ragas, but also a formidable arsenal of instruments which may strike many jazz listeners as exotic: ney (nasal Middle Eastern flute), shakuhachi (Japanese bamboo flute), kaval (like a ney, but more folk-oriented), mizmar (small reed pipe, also called flagolet), sanza (African thumb piano, also called mbira), sheng (Chinese mouth organ made with bamboo pipes and a metal base, sort of like a harmonica), moursin (the South Indian name for Jew's harp), and berimbau (Brazilian stringed instrument, basically the bow of a bow and arrow) are the ones which require some explanation, but counting Western instruments alone she's already quite versatile. On her Flying Note label, Fasteau released three albums on cassette tape in 1986–88, and three CDs since then, most recently 1997's live collection *Sensual Hearing* (there's another Flying Note CD in the works) as well as a trio album on CIMP.

what to buy: *Worlds beyond Words* ♪♪♪♪ (Flying Note, 1989, prod. Zusaan Kali Fasteau) may attract knowledgeable jazz fans first with its Rashied Ali credit, and those expecting Coltranesque music as a result of his presence will not be disappointed by what they hear, especially when the leader plays soprano sax. This CD largely draws on two of Fasteau's earlier cassette tapes (see below) and features her in a broad variety of contexts. *Prophecy* ♪♪♪♪ (Flying Note, 1993, prod. Zusaan Kali Fasteau, James C. Jamison III) finds Ali replaced by drummers Ronnie Burrage and Newman Taylor Baker, with bassist William Parker and tabla player Badal Roy among the other familiar names. On both albums, a number of tracks are derived from ragas: "From Above," "A Gift," and "Sourceress" on *Worlds Beyond Words* and "Lunar Wisdom" and "Cosmopolis" on the highly focused *Prophecy*. Since Coltrane spent the last part of his life exploring Indian music, there's a further parallel between Fasteau's music and his, although she definitely has her own voice.

what to buy next: *Expatriate Kin* ♪♪♪ (CIMP, 1997, prod. Robert D. Rusch) is a trio album with Noah Howard (alto sax) and Bobby Few (piano), musicians Fasteau played with when she lived in Paris. On this CD she sticks to soprano sax, cello, and vocals, which in this company and with those instruments makes this the most solidly jazz-oriented of her albums. *The Sea Ensemble* ♪♪♪ (ESP, 1974) is less structured than Fasteau's music under her own name. It's somewhat "of its time," but continues to have some historical importance and contains attractive sections amid its ebbs and flows.

the rest:
Sensual Hearing ♪♪♪♪ (Flying Note, 1997)

worth searching for: When Fasteau started her label, her first three releases were cassettes. *Bliss* ♪♪♪♪ (Flying Note, 1986, prod. Zusaan Kali Fasteau) is in some ways the most interesting of them, meditational music she plays entirely herself through overdubbing. The predominant instrument is the shakuhachi, and many of the pieces are built over drones. Three of the tracks on *Beyond Words* ♪♪♪♪ (Flying Note, 1987, prod. Zusaan Kali Fasteau) and most of *Affinity* ♪♪♪♪ (Flying Note, 1988, prod. Zusaan Kali Fasteau) are not on the *Worlds Beyond Words* CD. These are the sessions with Ali on drums, and enthusiasts will find them worth hearing. They can be obtained from Fasteau at zkfasteau@msn.com. The Sea Ensemble LPs *Manzara* ♪♪ (Red, 1978, prod. Sergio Veschi, Alberto Alberti) and *After Nature* ♪♪ (Red, 1978, prod. Sergio Veschi, Alberto Alberti) have not appeared on CD and may be of interest to completists. They ramble a bit (the musicians expected one LP's worth of material to be chosen) but contain moments of inspiration.

influences:
◀◀ John Coltrane, Yusef Lateef, Tony Scott
▶▶ Regina Carter

Steve Holtje

Pierre Favre

Born June 2, 1937, in Le Locle, Switzerland.

Drummer/percussionist Pierre Favre's style, which peaked in

the European free jazz scene of the late '60s, has always been characterized by subtle, shifting textures and tonalities. He began playing professionally in the late 1950s, apprenticing in both bop and Dixieland bands. He moved to Paris in the early '60s and gained a reputation by backing visiting Americans such as pianist Bud Powell and trumpeter Benny Bailey. A move to Cologne, Germany, in 1967 found Favre working for the Paiste Company as a gong and cymbal maker, assisting in the design and testing of the instruments, during which time he began recording albums as a solo artist and with various combos. In concert, his standard drum kit was augmented by a vast array of gongs and cymbals, and he started working internationally, with musicians like the Indian percussionist T.V. Gopalakrishnan and the French singer Tamia. While a rhythmically strong drummer, Favre is also known for melodic contours and shifting textural emphasis.

what to buy: A lovely collaboration with Tamia, *Solitudes* 𝄢𝄢𝄢𝄢 (ECM, 1991, prod. Manfred Eicher) is at times orchestral and times an intimate one-to-one. *Irene Schweitzer/Pierre Favre* 𝄢𝄢𝄢𝄢 (Intakt, 1990, prod. Irene Schweitzer) is a reunion of Favre with pianist Schweitzer, his free-jazz group companion of the '60s. Although they occasionally take too much time to set up their ideas (the pace here is a little more leisurely than it was in their '60s group), this is a solid set with little dead wood.

what to buy next: Although French reed player Michelle Portal is the main focus, *Arrivederci La Choutarse* 𝄢𝄢𝄢𝄢 (hat ART, 1981, prod. Werner Uehlinger, Pia Uehlinger) is perhaps the best way to hear Favre in a typical jazz setting. It's successful due to Favre's open ears and his effortless command of mood, rhythm, and texture.

best of the rest:
Drum Orchestra 𝄢𝄢𝄢 (ECM, 1984)

worth searching for: The vinyl-only *Pierre Favre Quartet* 𝄢𝄢𝄢𝄢 (Wergo, 1969) is an excellent example of European free jazz played with the fire and fervor of the era. Favre's high-energy drumming, coupled with his unique textural emphasis makes this a worthwhile recording, definitely worth reissuing on CD.

Robert Iannapollo

John Fedchock

Born September 18, 1957, in Cleveland, OH.

Trombonist-bandleader John Fedchock is a musician's musician, admired by colleagues as well as fans for his laidback, smooth playing, and for his skillful musical arranging. Fedchock grew up in the Cleveland area, attended Ohio State University, and earned his Master's degree in jazz studies at Eastman School of Music. With the Woody Herman band from 1980 until Herman's death in 1987, Fedchock served as Herman's musical coordinator and chief arranger for four of those years, including two Grammy-nominated albums for Concord. Fedchock has also toured with Gerry Mulligan's Concert Jazz Band, Louie Bellson's Big Band, the Bob Belden Ensemble, The Carnegie Hall Jazz Band, and other groups. He is an active arranger and performer in New York City, and, as a solo artist, travels as clinician to colleges and universities and performs overseas. Fedchock has performed or recorded with artists such as Rosemary Clooney, Tony Bennett, Nancy Wilson, and Joe Williams. His first big band album was released in 1995 and a second is due out in early 1998. Fedchock is definitely a talent to track.

what's available: Fedchock's creamy-toned trombone solos and his meticulously drafted, dense ensemble arrangements keep his 18-piece jazz orchestra (formed in 1989) swinging mightily on this explosive debut album as leader, *New York Big Band* 𝄢𝄢𝄢𝄢 (Reservoir, 1995, prod. John Fedchock). Steering his brawny band through eleven standards and originals, Fedchock brings out the best of their talents and steals some sparkling solo time to feature his own soft-edged, supple, and swift stylings. Fedchock's tasteful, classy playing is always the icing on the cake and his second release with his New York Big Band, *On the Edge* 𝄢𝄢𝄢𝄢 (Reservoir, 1998, prod. John Fedchock), contains his soulfully warm trombone solos, deft and diverse arrangements, and splendid instrumental solos from his colleagues. Drifting to the edge, this is another buoyant big band session that aptly documents Fedchock's burgeoning talents.

worth searching for: Recorded live in in San Francisco's Great American Music Hall in March, 1986, the Woody Herman album, *50th Anniversary Tour* 𝄢𝄢𝄢𝄢 (Concord, 1986, Carl E. Jefferson), prominently features Fedchock's arrangements which pack the wallop for which the Herman band has always been noted. Seven of the eight charts are his and they allow the 16-piece band a cohesive agility usually found only in small combos. Fedchock also contributes a hard-swinging original, "Blues for Red," a tribute to bassist Red Kelly that features a scat-vocal/arco-bass sequence by Lynn Seaton, a clarinet solo from Woody, and other fine spotlighted moments. On another hard-swinging big band affair, *Woody's Gold Star* 𝄢𝄢𝄢𝄢 (Concord, 1987, prod. Carl E. Jefferson), Fedchock arranged all exciting nine charts, including a full-throttle version of Miles Davis's "Dig," a lyrical medley of "Rose Room" and "In a Mellow Tone," a rousing opener on Ellington's "Battle Royal," a funky, beat-laden version of Herbie Hancock's "Watermelon Man," and other pleasers. Included in the live-recorded performance at the Willows Theater in Concord, California, (March, 1987) is Fedchock's original, "The Great Escape," a rollicking album centerpiece. In 1989, Fedchock and Maria Schneider formed a band together in New York City after he left the Woody Herman Orchestra and moved to New York. Schneider's current group, the Maria Schneider Jazz Orchestra, is an offshoot of that original band and can be heard on its debut recording *Evanescence* ♫♫♫♫ (Enja, 1994, prod. Maria Schneider). Fedchock solos artfully on the dramatic, 10-minute opening track, "Wyrgly."

influences:

◀◀ J.J. Johnson, Curtis Fuller, Slide Hampton, Herbie Green

see also: *Woody Herman, Maria Schneider*

Nancy Ann Lee

Maynard Ferguson

Born May 4, 1928, in Montreal, Quebec, Canada.

Probably best known as the trumpeter who screams in the upper register with burning intensity, Maynard Ferguson has enjoyed six-decades of playing. Ferguson's talents were evident at a young age. Growing up in Montreal, he was playing piano and violin before discovering the trumpet at age nine. He won a scholarship to the French Conservatory of Music where he received formal training. At age 13 Ferguson soloed with the Canadian Broadcasting Company Orchestra and two years later began to gain the attention of leaders of the big band era. He played in a 14-musician local band that opened for touring big band acts. While still a teenager, Ferguson moved to the U.S., and he has since established himself far beyond his abilities as a trumpet player and composer.

Ferguson came to the United States to join Stan Kenton's Orchestra. When Kenton took a one-year hiatus, Ferguson pursued stints with bands led by Boyd Rayburn, Charlie Barnet, and Jimmy Dorsey before joining Kenton for three years. Leaving Kenton in 1953, Ferguson worked extensively as a Los Angeles studio musician and performed with Leonard Bernstein and the New York Philharmonic in a performance of William Russo's "Symphony No. 2 in C ('Titans')." In 1956 Ferguson formed an all-star jazz band, featuring pianist Hank Jones, saxophonist Budd Johnson, bassist Milt Hinton, and others, for an

extended run at the famous New York club, Birdland. Over the next decade, Ferguson recorded in big band and sextet settings and toured the college circuit before living and touring in Spain, England, and India in the late 1960s and early 1970s. He returned to the U.S. in 1974 and signed with Columbia, for which he produced some now out-of-print jazz-fusion albums (*M.F. Horn, Vol. One, M.F. Horn, Vol. Two*, and two more volumes in that series, of which *MF Horn, 4 & 5* is considered a best example of his jazz playing during the 1970s). He also released the Columbia albums *Chameleon* (1974) and *Conquistador* (1977), a gold album that cracked the pop charts with its featured theme from the *Rocky* soundtrack ("Gonna Fly Now"). After leaving Columbia, Ferguson recorded two lackluster albums with his funk-fusion combo, High Voltage. In the late 1980s Ferguson returned to the bop-oriented roots of his earlier years and created what has proved to be one of his most successful bands, Big Bop Nouveau, a 10-musician ensemble of shifting young players with whom he has released four CDs to date, two on the Jazz Alliance label and two more after joining the Concord Jazz roster in 1995. Ferguson has recorded on about 200 albums as sideman and leader, not all of which are available or reissued on CD. He has designed instruments, produced recordings, served as an educator/clinician, and been a consistent jazz poll winner. Ferguson now resides in Ojai, California, about 90 miles north of Los Angeles. With his Big Bop Nouveau band, he tours regularly (and intensely), maintaining a somewhat grueling schedule that probably accounts for the personnel turnover. A musician first, educator second, Ferguson also tours internationally, instructing students at universities around the world.

what to buy: One word that best describes Maynard Ferguson's music is "energetic." And nowhere is it more evident than on his top-notch performances live-recorded at Ronnie Scott's Club, *Live from London* ♫♫♫♫ (Avenue Jazz/Rhino, 1994, prod. Maynard Ferguson, Jim Exon, Chip McNeill). Ferguson takes standards such as Dizzy Gillespie's "A Night in Tunisia," Duke Ellington's "In a Mellow Tone," Sonny Rollins's "St. Thomas," and other gems and turns them inside out with blistering solos and tumultuous big band charts from a variety of the best arrangers for this band. Soloists such as the fabulous tenor/soprano saxophonist Chip McNeill (especially on McNeill's own rousing original, "Rhythm Method") and baritone saxophonist Glenn Kostur (on the Ernie Wilkins swinging arrangement of "Glenn's Den") match the supreme, reigning rules of musicianship Ferguson sets, adding significantly to this exciting listening adventure. An equally enjoyable listen, *Footpath Café*

ƧƧƧƧ (Jazz Alliance, 1992/1995, prod. Maynard Ferguson, Frank Kleinschmidt) was recorded live at a jazz club in Belgium. The eight-tune set featuring Maynard Ferguson and his Big Bop Nouveau Band is a combustive session that leans to bluesy edges, with fine contributions from soloists McNeill, Kostur, alto saxophonist Mike Scaglione, and a rhythm section comprising pianist Doug Bickel, bassist Dennis Marks, and drummer Jim White. Ferguson delivers some spectacular trumpet solos throughout, hitting those quavering high notes with screeching fervor. The title tune by Ferguson (arranged by Christian Jacob) is a grooving treat, as is Ferguson's "Poison Ya' Blues" (arranged by McNeill), which contains vocals by Matt Wallace and solos from Ferguson, Roger Ingram (plunger trumpet), and Dante Luciani (trombone), which soar above the dense, full band arrangement. McNeill's charts are always dense, gutsy, and exciting, and his arrangement of his original tune, "Break the Ice," is a crowd pleaser that features Ferguson and the band's best soloists, adding to the satisfaction of this top-notch album. Saxophonist-arranger Chip McNeil is still with the band on *These Cats Can Swing!* ƧƧƧƧ (Concord, 1995, prod. Maynard Ferguson), and he wrote all but two of the seven arrangements. Tunes of various flavors feature Ferguson's squealing trumpet as well as top-notch solos from the others. From Stanley Turrentine's bluesy "Sugar" to Ferguson's Middle Eastern-tinged "Sweet Baba Suite (Bai Rav)," from Ellington's "Caravan" to the straight-ahead Alec Wilder romancer "I'll Be Around," and including Ferguson's "He Can't Swing" and "It's the Gospel Truth," the material here is engaging and unusual, making this a must-own album for any Maynard fan. On the studio session *One More Trip to Birdland* ƧƧƧƧ (Concord, 1996, prod. Maynard Ferguson), Ferguson and Big Bop Nouveau perform a mixture of band originals and bop-oriented standards by Dizzy Gillespie ("Manteca"), Miles Davis ("Milestones"), a Duke Ellington swing classic ("It Don't Mean a Thing If It Ain't Got That Swing"), and the Joe Zawinul gem, "Birdland." Ferguson actually delivers some warm solos that don't screech excessively into the upper register, especially on hard-swinging "The Vibe." Absent from this date is Chip McNeill, whose indelible imprint was felt and heard on earlier Maynard Ferguson recordings. Replacing him in stature is the fine trombonist (and guitarist) Tom Garling, who also arranges some of the nine tunes. It's a hot session all the way through as old-timers and newcomers alike unveil their best musicianship. Ferguson's band is always best in live performance and *Live from San Francisco* (Avenue Jazz/Rhino, 1994, prod. Maynard Ferguson, Jeffrey Weber) ƧƧƧƧ is no exception. The 12-musician band (including Ferguson) is documented in a seven-tune

performance recorded on May 27, 1983, at the Great American Music Hall and features fine solos. While their expressions still retain some funk flavor, there are some splendid straight-ahead jazz numbers (Strayhorn's "Lush Life," Gillespie's "BeBop Buffet," and the standard, "On the Sunny Side of the Street") that make this CD an agreeable listen.

what to buy next: If you're new to Maynard Ferguson, you might want to check out *The Essence of Maynard Ferguson* ƧƧƧƧ (Columbia/Legacy, 1993, reissue prod. Nedra Olds-Neal), part of the *I Like Jazz* album series. The eight tunes are compiled from Ferguson's period with the Columbia label during the 1970s, and they feature him leading the band and blowing trumpet on distinctive jazz classics such as "'Round Midnight," "Birdland," "I Can't Get Started," the bop-oriented "The Fox Hunt," the bluesy "Everybody Loves the Blues," and his more pop-oriented tunes like "MacArthur Park" and "Conquistador." It's a good sampling of his facile, razor-sharp chops and his piercing solos. For long-time Ferguson fans, this compilation features some of his best jazz efforts during that period (mainly from his MF Horn album series). Unfortunately, the other soloists are unlisted, as are the original recording dates. *Storm* ƧƧƧ (Palo Alto, 1982/Avenue Jazz, 1994, prod. Jeffrey Weber) tries to cover too much musical turf and comes off as uneven. Yet this CD contains a rare recorded big band version of "Sesame Street," a delightful hard-swinging straight-ahead jazz number that features Denis DiBlasio's big baritone solo, in addition to some hot blowing from Maynard. Other jazz classics among the eight tunes on the album include an uptempo version of Ellington's "Take the 'A' Train" and the ballad "As Time Goes By," a smoky treat featuring vocals from Ferguson and a closing trumpet solo. A representative album from Ferguson's 1970s period, *Chameleon* ƧƧƧ (Columbia, 1974/1990, prod. Teo Macero) displays both the best and worst aspects of his populist style of that era. Herbie Hancock's funky title tune is more appealing than jazz purists offended by the Fender Rhodes electric piano and rock-style electric guitar will ever admit. Chick Corea's "La Fiesta" is exciting, and Ferguson's fairly subdued (not that there aren't plenty of high notes) take on the warhorse "I Can't Get Started" finds him updating vocal lyrics with witticisms such as "Linda Lovelace thinks I'm obscene." Pop covers such as Paul McCartney's "Jet," Stevie Wonder's "Livin' for the City," and the Barbra Streisand hit "The Way We Were," end up sounding like garish compromises. Yet if one doesn't mind shallowness, these tunes have a certain gaudy attraction for fans of kitsch. From this same period is the slightly better album *Conquistador* ƧƧƧ (Columbia, 1997/

1987, prod. Jay Chattaway), tolerable for the classic "Gonna Fly Now" (the *Rocky* theme) which features Ferguson's familiar squealing trumpet melody. Featured soloists include guests such as guitarist George Benson and pianist Bob James, and, one of the 13 MF Band members, flutist Bobby Militello (a long-time Dave Brubeck sideman) who plays the "Theme from Star Trek." The title tune is a funkified Spanish bull-fighter theme with a distant vocal chorus and plenty of drama . . . a hokey Hollywood production that seems to come right off a 1970s movie set. A slew of prime studio heavies of that time appear in addition to the regular MF Band—among them, the young trumpeter Jon Faddis, who would eventually come to emulate the leader's screeching style.

what to avoid: *High Voltage* ♫♫ (Intima, 1987, prod. Maynard Ferguson, Jim Exon) features Ferguson leading a small two-horn combo with saxophonist Denis DiBlasio (one of Ferguson's big band regulars), keyboardist Todd Carlon, drummer Ray Brinker, bassist Rick Shaw, guitarist Michael Higgins, and percussionist Steve Fisher. Despite Ferguson's fine solo on the 3:40 version of Hoagy Carmichael's "Stardust," there's little that can save this studio venture. Even a second-hand copy is no bargain unless you can tolerate overpowering reverb, rock-jazz fusion with excessively heavy drumming, and uninspired playing by the sidemen.

best of the rest:
The Complete Roulette Recordings of the Maynard Ferguson Orchestra ♫♫♫♫ (Roulette, 1958–62/Mosaic, 1996)
(With Chris Connor) *Two's Company* ♫♫♫ (Roulette, 1960/1996)
Body & Soul ♫♫♫ (Jazz Alliance, 1986/1995)
Verve Jazz Masters, Vol. 52 ♫♫♫♫ (Verve, 1996)

worth searching for: *The Blues Roar* ♫♫♫♫ (Mainstream, 1965/Mobile Fidelity, prod. Bob Shad) features a typically brassy Ferguson big band (complete with tuba) and satisfyingly multi-layered arrangements by Don Sebesky, Mike Abene, and Willie Maiden of blues and R&B chestnuts such as "Every Day I Have the Blues," "Night Train," etc. and lots of Ray Charles numbers ("Mary Ann," "I Believe to My Soul," "What'd I Say," "I've Got a Woman"). The leader is the star, of course, playing a bit of flugelhorn and valve trombone in addition to his trade-mark screaming trumpet, but there are plenty of other fine players, including trombonist Urbie Green, alto saxophonist Lanny Morgan (who doubles on clarinet and flute), and alto

Maynard Ferguson **(Archive Photos)**

saxist Charlie Mariano (listed in the track-by-track rundown of soloists although not in the personnel column). The rhythm section is superb—Mike Abene (piano), Barry Galbraith (guitar), Richard Davis (bass), and Mel Lewis (drums)—making this a swinging, richly-arranged blues affair throughout.

influences:
◀◀ Dizzy Gillespie, Clark Terry, Stan Kenton, Doc Severinsen
▶▶ Marvin Stamm, Chuck Mangione, Jon Faddis, Brian Lynch

Nancy Ann Lee and Steve Holtje

Rachelle Ferrell

Born 1961, in Berwyn, PA.

A professional singer since the age of 13, Rachelle Ferrell has an unusual, two-label recording contract. She records R&B for Capitol and jazz for Blue Note, and no matter what she's singing, her multi-octave vocals are a joy to listen to. Ferrell—who accompanies herself on keyboards and is also a classically trained violinist—attended Boston's Berklee College of Music with Branford Marsalis and later taught music for the New Jersey State Council of the Arts with Dizzy Gillespie. In fact, it was Gillespie who once told Ferrell's parents that she would be a "major force" in the music industry. For such a prolific composer, Ferrell records relatively infrequently (two albums in eight years), something her devoted fans hope changes in the not too distant future.

what to buy: Originally released only in Japan in 1990, *First Instrument* ♫♫♫♫ (Somethin' Else, 1990/Blue Note, 1995, prod. Hitoshi Namekata, Lenny White) showcases Ferrell's incredible range as a jazz vocalist. Backed by Stanley Clarke, Lenny White, Wayne Shorter, and Terrence Blanchard, Ferrell glides effortlessly through standards like "Bye Bye Blackbird" and "What Is This Thing Called Love," with a couple of original compositions thrown in for good measure. One of those, "Don't Waste Your Time," is the disc's finest track.

what to buy next: *Rachelle Ferrell* ♫♫♫♫ (Capitol/Manhattan, 1992, prod. George Duke, Michael J. Powell, Barry J. Eastmond, Rachelle Ferrell, Erik Zobler) is Ferrell's R&B/pop album. Her powerful vocals and songwriting abilities—she wrote or co-wrote 10 of the album's 13 cuts—helped keep this collection on the R&B charts for almost three years. Highlights include "With Open Arms," "Nothing Has Ever Felt Like This" (a vocal duet with Will Downing), and the gospel-tinged "Peace on Earth."

worth searching for: Okay, so it's not a CD; it's a videotape. Nevertheless, *Manhattan Project* is worth checking out. It features the live recording of "Autumn Leaves" from *First Instrument*, allowing one to see, as well as hear, the talented Ferrell in action.

influences:

Billie Holiday, Betty Carter, Shirley Horn, Anita Baker

Dean Dauphinais

Glenn Ferris

Born June 27, 1950, in Los Angeles, CA.

Glenn Ferris discovered the trombone at eight years old, studied classically, and later studied theory and improvisation with Don Ellis (1964–66). He joined Don Ellis's innovative big band when he was 16, touring and performing until 1970. His warm, mellow sound was inspiring and admired, and he worked around Los Angeles in the 1970s with Frank Zappa, Harry James, Billy Cobham, Bobby Bradford, and also played in a number of classical, pop, rock, and R&B groups. He formed a duo with Milcho Leviev and organized his own 10-piece band, Celebration, in the late 1970s. During the 1980s, he recorded with Tony Scott and toured Europe with Jack Walrath's quintet. Since settling in Europe in 1980, he's played and recorded with Steve Lacy, Barry Altschul, Chris McGregor, Louis Sclavis, Franco D'Andrea, Peter Schärli, Enrico Rava, Michel Portal, Joachim Kuhn, Aldo Romano, and Henri Texier.

what's available: Either *Flesh & Stone* ♪♪♪ (Enja, 1994, prod. Werner Aldinger, Glenn Ferris) or *Face Lift* ♪♪♪ (Enja, 1995, prod. Horst Weber, Glenn Ferris) can give an adventurous listener an idea of the bottom-heavy instrumentations to which Paris-based Ferris is attracted for their rich, wooden timbres. Both recordings feature Ferris's resourceful compositions for trombone, cello (Vincent Segal), and bass (Bruno Rousselet). The threesome creates delightfully different music that ranges from free-styled, pulsating rhythms to virtuosic, insightful readings of Duke Ellington's "Azure," and John Lewis's European-flavored "Django."

worth searching for: Hear Ferris on Barry Alschul's *That's Nice* ♪♪♪ (Soul Note, 1985) and with the Peter Schärli Quintet, on *Tomorrow* ♪♪♪ (Enja, 1992). Ferris has chances to stretch out as sideman on these dates and the results are salutary.

influences:

Lawrence Brown, Dicky Wells, Jimmy Knepper, Roswell Rudd

Ted Panken

Garrison Fewell

Born October 14, 1953, in Charlottesville, VA.

Garrison Fewell is a talented guitarist and instructor at Berklee College of Music whose performing and recording resume includes gigs with Herbie Hancock, Tim Hagans, Buster Williams, Larry Coryell, and Cecil McBee. McBee has returned the favor by appearing on the guitarist's first two releases as a solo artist. In addition to playing and teaching, Fewell has written a book on jazz improvisation and appeared at a slew of big-name jazz festivals, including North Sea and Montreux.

what to buy: For his first solo album, *A Blue Deeper than the Blue* ♪♪♪♪ (Accurate, 1993, prod. Garrison Fewell), Fewell has done himself proud. Recorded live at Scullers Jazz Club in Boston, it is blessed with good sound and fine playing from a well-chosen support staff, including the deep, woody bass of McBee, fine piano work from Fred Hersch, and Matt Wilson's steady drumming. Garrison's playing is, for lack of a better word, smooth. It glides and floats above the rhythm with occasional swift darts in and around the melody like a bee looking for just the right flower. McBee is awesome when he needs to be and his introductory solo on Fewell's beautiful "Brazilian Breeze" is marvelous. The band performs two Benny Golson tunes, a Frank Foster cover, and four originals from the guitarist before an appreciative (but not obnoxiously so) audience. Only the setting and the piano player have changed for Fewell's second album, *Are You Afraid of the Dark?* ♪♪♪♪ (Accurate, 1995, prod. Garrison Fewell), a studio date with Laszlo Gardony replacing Hersch but with the top-notch rhythm section of McBee and Wilson still along for the cruise. The playing is at least as good as on Fewell's first release, but the tunes seemed to swing a bit more on the debut. Check out "Alto Blues."

what to buy next: *Reflection of a Clear Moon* ♪♪♪ (Accurate, 1997, prod. Garrison Fewell) is actually a duet pairing Gardony and Fewell for a concert held in Gardony's old home town of Budapest, Hungary. The level of communication is strong, but a whole album of beautiful moments like this one should be dipped into rather than absorbed whole, depending on whether you like your music transcendental or earthy. The music starts to sound like it comes from the tofu and whole-grains crowd.

influences:

Tal Farlow, Jimmy Raney

Garaud MacTaggart

Ella Fitzgerald **(UPI/Corbis-Bettmann)**

Dale Fielder

Born 1956, in East Liverpool, OH.

Equally at home on the tenor and the alto saxophones, Dale Fielder is an important figure on the Crenshaw District jazz scene that emerged in Los Angeles in the early 1990s. Raised near Pittsburgh, Fielder started on clarinet and switched to alto in junior high. By high school, he was playing R&B tenor with bands on the Stax Records circuit, but using alto on jazz gigs. Fielder formed a band with his older brother that included Geri Allen on piano. Years later, when Fielder arrived in New York, he again hooked up with Allen. He studied Ethnomusicology at the University of Pittsburgh, and made it to New York after replacing Steve Coleman and spending almost three years touring with calypso pioneer band, The Mighty Sparrow. Fielder moved to Los Angeles in 1989 and has worked steadily, leading both a quartet and a quintet, and recording two strong CDs for his Clarion Jazz label. He recorded an LP with Allen on Clarion in 1983, *Scene from a Dream*.

what to buy: Dale Fielder pays homage to the great saxophonist/composer both through playing his tunes and arrangements and with his own Shorter-esque pieces on *Dear Sir: Tribute to Wayne Shorter* ♪♪♪♪ (Clarion, 1996, prod. Dale Fielder), an impressive session featuring Mingus Workshop alumnus Jane Getz (piano), Bill Markus (bass), Thomas White (drums), and trumpeter Dan Bagasoul on two tracks. Sticking entirely to tenor, Fielder chooses some lesser-known Shorter pieces, including "Teru" and the lovely, impressionistic "Dear Sir," as well as Shorter's chart for Gil Evans's "Barracudas." Of Fielder's six tunes, most impressive are the waltz "Believer," where his tenor sound evokes Coltrane, and the bright, sunny "Afternoon in L.A."

what to buy next: A strong debut CD by one of Los Angeles' leading hard-bop players, *Know Thyself* ♪♪♪♪ (Clarion Jazz, 1995, prod. Dale Fielder) is a quintet session that features some very promising young players, including the appropriately named trumpeter Dan Bagasoul, bassist Bill Markus, drummer Ocie Davis III, and especially the imaginative, hard-swinging pianist Greg Kurstin. Fielder plays both alto and tenor and contributes six of the nine tunes, including the hard-charging "Strivers Row" and winsome "Dreamlife." He displays his lyrical side with the ballads "But Beautiful" and "Sometime Ago," and his strong hard bop chops (and taste) with Tina Brooks's "Theme for Doris."

the rest:
Free Flow ♫♫♫ (Clarion Jazz, 1993)

influences:
◀◀ John Coltrane, Sonny Stitt, Wayne Shorter

Andrew Gilbert

Ella Fitzgerald

Born April 25, 1918, in Newport News, VA. Died June 15, 1997, in Beverly Hills, CA.

Ella Fitzgerald, often referred to as "the First Lady of Song," built a solid reputation as a jazz musician, and gained notoriety around the world as possibly the best vocalist of the twentieth century. Her clear-ringing sound, far-reaching range, and rhythmically, her innate swing, all helped to set Fitzgerald apart from other vocalists. Throughout her life, she claimed that Connee Boswell was her single most important influence. Although the tales concerning Fitzgerald's debut often vary, most agree that she entered an amateur contest at the Apollo Theater (some sources say it was the Harlem Opera House) in 1934, intending to dance. But, intimidated by the Edwards Sisters who preceded her, Fitzgerald opted to sing instead. Stepping up to the microphone, she sang "Judy." Encores ensued as the world was introduced to Fitzgerald. She soon met Chick Webb through Bardu Ali, who fronted Webb's band and had heard the young vocalist at her stage debut. Other sources say that Benny Carter was responsible for the introduction. Regardless, Fitzgerald auditioned, and although Webb was hesitant at first, he hired her, and took her under his wing, legally taking on the responsibilities as her guardian.

In 1935 she recorded "Love and Kisses" and "I'll Chase the Blues Away," Fitzgerald's first recordings with the band, on which she sang only on the second chorus. In April 1936 she recorded "Rhythm and Romance," and had progressed to coming back in for a sixteen-bar out chorus, in addition to singing the second chorus. Her voice quickly became a main feature of Webb's band, and in October 1936, when she recorded "You'll Have to Swing It (Mr. Paganini)" with the band, Fitzgerald opens the song, and additionally, sings short scat phrases.

During the big band years, orchestras had to swing and satisfy the dancers. Webb's band, performing regularly at the Savoy and showcasing Fitzgerald, accomplished this with ease and style. By 1937 Fitzgerald was, without a doubt, the main feature of the band. In 1938 she had an idea for a song, "A-Tisket, a-Tasket," adapted from the nursery rhyme. With the music and arrangement by staff arranger Van Alexander, the tune was recorded by Decca on May 2, 1938, and almost immediately shot to the top of the charts, giving the band national recognition, and establishing Fitzgerald as a star.

With a sound and a distinctive developing style, Fitzgerald continued to perform and record with the Chick Webb Band. When Webb passed away on June 16, 1939, she took over as leader of the band, until 1941, when she began to pursue a solo career, continuing to record with Decca. During the mid-1940s, she traveled with Dizzy Gillespie, which put her into the midst of the bop movement, and created an experience that was an important influence on her subsequent work. In addition, Fitzgerald's association with Norman Granz began in 1946, when she took part in his newly created Jazz at the Philharmonic. In 1945 she had a hit with "Flying Home," her first solely instrumental recording, and in 1947 her "How High the Moon" became a hit. Both tunes are examples of Fitzgerald's abilities as a bop singer, demonstrating her fine ear, extraordinary musicianship, and flexible voice, as well as her progression as an artist. During this time she also recorded with the Ink Spots, Louis Jordan, the Delta Rhythm Boys, and Louis Armstrong. In 1948 she married bassist Ray Brown, whose ensembles often accompanied her, including on the recording "Airmail Special" in January 1952, with Fitzgerald masterfully scatting the choruses in the true spirit of Benny Goodman and Charlie Christian. A highlight of her Decca years is a duo recording of Gershwin tunes with Ellis Larkins in 1950.

After appearing in the film *Pete Kelly's Blues* in 1955, Fitzgerald left Decca, and signed with Granz, beginning her Verve years. Within the next few years, she recorded the famous *Songbooks* series, dedicated to the various great American songwriters, including Cole Porter, Harold Arlen, Rogers and Hart, Irving Berlin, Gershwin, Jerome Kern, Johnny Mercer, and Duke Ellington. In addition, many live recordings were issued, including the classic 1960 *Ella in Berlin*, with her famed rendition of "Mack the Knife." The Verve years, with Granz as her manager, took her around the world, and offered her the opportunity to record prolifically. When Granz formed the Pablo label, Fitzgerald was again consistently featured in jazz settings. In 1972 she performed her first concert with the Boston Pops, and by 1975,

Fitzgerald had performed with more than 40 American symphony orchestras. During these years, the quality of her voice began to decline, and because of eye trouble that had begun in 1971, she gradually began to cut back on her working schedule until personal appearances became rare events. Throughout her working years, Fitzgerald accumulated 11 Grammy awards, and for 18 consecutive years, she was voted Best Female Singer in the *Down Beat* Reader's Poll. The name Ella Fitzgerald remains synonymous with jazz.

what to buy: Wondering where to begin in Fitzgerald's vast discography? There's so much out there, once you become a fan and start collecting all that's in print for the songstress, you'll find plenty to keep you holed up listening for months. If you're compulsive and have to start at the beginning, check out the Fitzgerald series on the import label Jazz Chronological Classics. The series captures the singer's performances with the Chick Webb Band in one-year spans (e.g., 1937–38) into the 1940s. If you're new to Ella and want to test the waters, start with a collection such as the highly acclaimed two-CD set *75th Birthday Celebration* 𝄪𝄪𝄪𝄪 (Decca, 1938–55/GRP, 1993, prod. Milt Gabler, Orrin Keepnews), which was compiled in recognition of Fitzgerald's 75th birthday. Tracking her work between 1938 and 1955, the compilation begins with her classic, "A-Tisket, a-Tasket," and includes recordings with Louis Jordan ("Stone Cold Dead in the Market"), Louis Armstrong ("You Won't Be Satisfied"), and the Ink Spots ("Cow Cow Boogie"), as well as numerous other memorable Fitzgerald moments. For jazz purists, her first recorded renditions of "Flying Home" (October 4, 1945) and "Airmail Special" (January 4, 1952) are also included. Additionally, "How High the Moon," recorded on December 20, 1947, is important because it demonstrates her first recorded scat solo on this tune, a vocal technique she continued to develop throughout her career. This two-CD set is vital to any jazz collection. To check out Fitzgerald in a more intimate setting, *The Intimate Ella* 𝄪𝄪𝄪𝄪 (Verve, 1960/1990, prod. Norman Granz), originally released as *Ella Fitzgerald sings Songs from the Soundtrack of Let No Man Write My Epitaph*. The film flopped and the Fitzgerald recording was soon forgotten until it was discovered in the vaults and reissued on CD. This recording captures the singer accompanied in lovely duos with pianist Paul Smith, as they tenderly interpret 13 songs such as "Black Coffee," "Angel Eyes," "Misty," "I Cried for You," "I Hadn't Anyone 'till You," "September Song," "Who's Sorry Now?," and other American songbook gems. Ella (aged 42 at the time of this 1960 recording) is in exquisite vocal form, gracefully singing with a tad more vibrato than usual, and

stretching comfortably into the upper register on this relaxed, gorgeously romantic session. You'll swear she is right there in the room with you. Once introduced, you'll likely be craving more Fitzgerald and eventually be ready for the hefty four-CD set, *The Concert Years* 𝄪𝄪𝄪𝄪 (Pablo, 1994, prod. Norman Granz), crammed with over five hours of stunning performances. This set compiles previously released material from performances between 1953–83 concerts around the globe. Twenty songs on disc one are from two 1953 live-recorded performances in Japan (originally released on *Jazz at the Philharmonic in Tokyo*), with Ella accompanied by a quartet on delightful renditions of a swinging "On the Sunny Side of the Street," a step-up speedball scat version of "How High the Moon," and her playful, gravel-voiced imitation of Satchmo (Louis Armstrong) on "Frim Fram Sauce." Also included are five tunes performed with the Duke Ellington Orchestra (1966) in Stockholm and selections from two 1967 performances in New York City. With the backing of the big band behind her, Ella really wails, especially on the bluesy Ellington-Strayhorn arrangement of "Imagine My Frustration." The orchestra's all-star soloists are also spotlighted. Disc two begins with an enchanting 13-tune set recorded in 1971 in Nice, France (originally released on *Ella a Nice*). Backed by pianist Tommy Flanagan, bassist Frank De-LaRosa, and drummer Ed Thigpen, Fitzgerald covers an array of moods and tempos from blues, to bossa, to ballads as she honors songwriters Cole Porter, George and Ira Gershwin, and Antonio Carlos Jobim. Also on disc two are performances from a June 1, 1992 concert in Santa Monica, California, with two different bands. Originally released on *Jazz at the Santa Monica Civic '72*, these dates include classics such as "Spring Can Really Hang You up the Most," "Shiny Stockings," and a jumping scat-vocals version of "C-Jam Blues" with top-notch instrumental solos from trombonist Al Grey, tenor saxophonist Stan Getz, trumpeter Harry "Sweets" Edison, and others. Disc three focuses on an April 1974 performances at the famous London club, Ronnie Scott's, with a quartet featuring pianist Tommy Flanagan, guitarist Joe Pass, bassist Keter Betts, and drummer Bobby Durham, and a trio (same personnel, without Pass) at the 1975 Montreux (Switzerland) Jazz Festival. (Compiled material was originally released on *Ella in London* and *Ella Fitzgerald at the Montreux Jazz Festival 1975*, respectively). These two dates contain 23 standards, including a passionate rendering of "Ev'ry Time We Say Goodbye," which Fitzgerald tells the audience she never sings anywhere else but in London. There's a certain warmth to these performances, a charming quality that's probably due to the presence of the lyrical pianist Flanagan. Disc four finds Fitzgerald in two live-recorded sets at the

July 1977 Montreux Jazz Festival; one with her trio with Flanagan, Betts, and Durham (originally documented on *Montreux '77*) and another with the Count Basie Orchestra. As with her performances on the previous discs, she's in top form, hitting those high notes with crisp accuracy. We come full circle in the final two performances on this well-conceived box set, closing with 1983 concerts in Tokyo. Pianist Paul Smith replaces Flanagan in the trio setting, and the larger ensemble includes Oscar Peterson (piano), Joe Pass (guitar), Niels-Henning Ørsted Pedersen (bass), Louie Belson (drums), and Sweets Edison, Al Grey, J.J. Johnson, Zoot Sims, and Eddie Lockjaw Davis who perform on the nearly nine-minute finale, "Flying Home." There's not a weak disc in this entire set. If you can't afford to lay out the cash for the box set, some of these tunes (and more) are available on the original single discs. *Ella a Nice* ♫♫♫ (Pablo, 1971/OJC, 1990, prod. Norman Granz) contains a total of 22 songs from this date, (compared with 13 songs included in the box set *The Concert Years*). Recorded before a respectful and receptive audience, the session covers ballads, bossas, and bluesy swingers that Fitzgerald delivers in fine vocal form, especially on the graceful ballads with trio backing led by pianist Tommy Flanagan. Also available as a single, *Ella in London* ♫♫♫♫ (Pablo, 1974/1987, prod. Norman Granz) features Fitzgerald with pianist Tommy Flanagan, guitarist Joe Pass, bassist Keter Betts, and drummer Bobby Durham, performing at Ronnie Scott's. Opening with "Sweet Georgia Brown," Ella proves, despite recent health problems and eye surgery, that she is still "the first lady of song." Her voice is flexible and her natural improvisatory ability is unmatchable as she sings "They Can't Take That away from Me," "It Don't Mean a Thing," and "The Man I Love." A three-CD set, *Sings the George and Ira Gershwin Songbook* ♫♫♫♫ (Verve, 1959/ 1987, prod. Norman Granz) features Fitzgerald singing the best of Gershwin, with arrangements by Nelson Riddle. From the opening "Sam and Delilah" to the closing "I Got Rhythm," Fitzgerald performs exquisitely. She puts her own stamp on "Strike up the Band," "Soon," "Fascinatin' Rhythm," "Just Another Rhumba," "They All Laughed," "Oh, Lady Be Good," "I've Got a Crush on You," and other tunes. A classic performance featuring musicians Ellis Larkins, Flanagan, Al Grey, and Eddie "Lockjaw" Davis, *Newport Jazz Festival: Live at Carnegie Hall* ♫♫♫♫ (Columbia, 1973/Legacy, 1995, prod. John Hammond, Teo Macero) includes eight previously unissued tracks. Fitzgerald is in excellent form, backed by an orchestra constructed to recreate the Chick Webb Band. Former Webb bandmembers Eddie Barefield, Taft Jordan, Dick Vance, George Matthews, Pete Clarke, and Arthur Clarke enhance the performances. Songs includes "A-Tisket, a-Tas-

ket," "Smooth Sailing," and "Indian Summer." In addition, Ella performs a duo with Ellis Larkin, and with the Tommy Flanagan Quartet. The Jazz at Carnegie All-Stars perform "Stardust," "Avalon," and "C-Jam Blues." An unusual departure for the singer, Fitzgerald goes Brazilian on *Ella Abraca Jobim* ♫♫♫♫ (Pablo, 1980–81/1991, prod. Norman Granz), singing 17 jazz songs built on compositions by Antonio Carlos Jobim, including popular favorites such as "Wave," "Quiet Nights of Quiet Stars (Corcovado)," "The Girl from Ipanema," "Dindi," "One-Note Samba (Samba de Uma Nota Só)," and others. She is backed by accomplished musicians including solo guitarists Joe Pass and Oscar Castro-Neves, drummer Alex Acuna, percussionist Paulinho da Costa (who served as leader of the all-important rhythm section), and guest soloists Clark Terry (trumpet), Zoot Sims (tenor sax), Toots Thielemans (harmonica), and others. Sounding as fresh as ever, she proves on "The Girl from Ipanema" (which she converts to "The Boy from . . .") that her voice is still in great shape, and she glides through this song offering supple scatting vocals. Backed by explosive Brazilian rhythms, Fitzgerald creates paramount excitement on *Ella Abraca Jobim* and there isn't a bad tune among the bunch. This is a marvelous session from a singer who, by the time of this recording, had nearly five decades of wonderful performances behind her.

what to buy next: *The Early Years, Part I* ♫♫♫ (Decca, 1935–38/GRP, 1992, reissue prod. Orrin Keepnews) documents Fitzgerald's earliest recordings with the Chick Webb Orchestra, beginning with "I'll Chase the Blues Away." Although she is young, Fitzgerald is already singing with distinctive characteristics. She swings and sings with a voice as clear as a bell, scatting short artful phrases on "You'll Have to Swing It (Mr. Paganini)." When Webb died in June 1939, Fitzgerald stepped forward to lead the band, keeping the unit together for another two years. *The Early Years, Part II* ♫♫♫♫ (Decca, 1939–41, GRP, 1993, reissue prod. Orrin Keepnews) reflects an assured, confident Fitzgerald fronting the band. However, she is artistically hampered at times, because everything had to be arranged in dance tempos. Included in the two-CD set are the 1939 version of "Undecided" and the 1936 version of "Moon Ray." The material on the preceding two CDs, is also available as a four-CD box set, *The Early Years: Parts I & II* (Decca, 1995). Fitzgerald joins with Louis Armstrong as they work their way through 11 chestnuts, singing and swinging with vibrance and a tight, natural blend on *Ella and Louis* ♫♫♫♫ (Verve, 1956, prod. Norman Granz). Accompaniment is by pianist Oscar Peterson, guitarist Herb Ellis, bassist Ray Brown, and drummer Buddy Rich. Highlights include "Can't We Be Friends," "Isn't This a Lovely Day," and "Cheek to Cheek." Reunited for their second of three collaborations, Fitzgerald and Armstrong continue to have fun with the music on *Ella and Louis Again* 🎵🎵🎵 (Verve, 1957/1990, prod. Norman Granz). Accompanied by pianist Peterson, guitarist Ellis, bassist Brown, and drummer Louis Bellson, the duo also performs "Autumn in New York," "I Won't Dance," and "I'm Putting All My Eggs in One Basket," among 12 tunes. As with the first recording, Armstrong plays some trumpet, but the emphasis is definitely on vocal performing. The three-CD set *Sings the Duke Ellington Song Book* 🎵🎵🎵 (Verve, 1957/1988, prod. Norman Granz) includes both small group and big band recordings, and features noted musicians such as Ben Webster, Peterson, Barney Kessel, and Billy Strayhorn in addition to the Duke Ellington band. Ellington and Strayhorn composed together, specifically for these sessions, a four-movement suite, titled "Portrait of Ella Fitzgerald." Also included are various Ellington classics, such as "Take the A Train," "I Ain't Got Nothing but the Blues," "Solitude," "Don't Get around Much Anymore," "Cottontail," and "Rocks in my Bed." Among the best intimate and warmly rendered duo sessions Ella recorded with guitarist Joe Pass is *Take Love Easy* 🎵🎵🎵🎵 (Pablo, 1974/1987, prod. Norman Granz), which contains a collection of nine romantic ballads recorded in the studio in 1973. They offer gorgeous renditions of "Once I Loved," "Lush Life," "A Foggy Day," and other songs that Fitzgerald handles with seasoning and great finesse with lyrical contributions from Pass. An earlier duo recording with Pass, *Easy Living* 🎵🎵🎵 (Pablo, 1966/1989, prod. Norman Granz) conveys the same intimacy, but gives Pass a bit more solo space as he accompanies Fitzgerald on a mixture of 15 soft, sweet, swinging gems and lush ballads, including "My Ship," "My Man," "I Don't Stand a Ghost of a Chance," "Love for Sale," "Green Dolphin Street," and other popular favorites. Her voice is more strained on this recording, but it's a pleasant listen nonetheless. *Clap Hands, Here Comes Charlie* 🎵🎵🎵 (Verve, 1961/1989, prod. Norman Granz) features Fitzgerald performing with pianist Lou Levy, guitarist Herb Ellis, bassists Joe Mondragon or Wilfred Middlebrooks, and drummers Gus Johnson or Stan Levey. In addition to the title track, Fitzgerald swings through "Night in Tunisia," "Jersey Bounce," "Music Goes 'round and 'Round," and other classics. Nelson Riddle is the arranger and conductor for the orchestra on *The Best Is Yet to Come* 🎵🎵🎵🎵 (Pablo, 1982/1987, prod. Norman Granz) and Fitzgerald joins with musicians Jimmy Rowles (piano), Shelly Manne (drums), Bill Watrous (trombone), and Joe Pass (guitar), among others. In addition to her finesse with the title track, a very difficult tune to sing, Fitzger-

ELLA FITZGERALD

song "Oh, Lady Be Good!"
album The Best of Ella Fitzgerald
(Decca, 1947/1996)
instrument Vocals

Monster Solo

ald embraces "You're Driving Me Crazy," "Somewhere in the Night," "Autumn in New York," and "Deep Purple." *The Essential Ella Fitzgerald: The Great Songs* 🎵🎵🎵 (Verve, 1957–63/1992, prod. Norman Granz) is a compilation that includes two versions of "Oh, Lady Be Good," "Angel Eyes" (with accompaniment from pianist Paul Smith), "Summertime" (with Louis Armstrong), and "Spring Can Really Hang You up the Most" (with Lou Levy). "A-Tisket, a-Tasket," however, is a live 1961 version, not the original from 1938. Recorded at the Chicago Opera House, *At the Opera House* 🎵🎵🎵 (Verve, 1957/1986, prod. Norman Granz) features Fitzgerald accompanied by pianist Peterson, guitarist Ellis, bassist Brown, and drummer Jo Jones on the first nine tracks. The other nine tracks were recorded at the Shrine Auditorium in Los Angeles, and the last of these features finds the quartet joined by Roy Eldridge, J.J. Johnson, Stan Getz, Lester Young, Coleman Hawkins, Illinois Jacquet, and Sonny Stitt. Although many people think that Fitzgerald shouldn't have recorded this last session, on *All That Jazz* 🎵🎵🎵 (Pablo, 1990, prod. Norman Granz) she swings hard and, with backing from great musicians, has moments of brilliance with good intonation and excellent pitch. In fact, Fitzgerald on her worst day is still better than any of today's singers at their best.

best of the rest:

Dreams Come True 𝄞𝄞𝄞 (Drive Archive, 1935/1995)

The Best of Ella Fitzgerald with Chick Webb and his Orchestra 𝄞𝄞𝄞𝄞 (Decca Jazz, 1939/1996)

The War Years 𝄞𝄞𝄞𝄞 (Decca, 1941–47/GRP, 1994)

First Lady of Song 𝄞𝄞𝄞𝄞𝄞 (Verve, 1949–66/1994)

Pure Ella 𝄞𝄞𝄞𝄞 (Decca, 1950–54//GRP, 1994)

Bluella: Ella Fitzgerald Sings the Blues 𝄞𝄞𝄞 (Pablo, 1953/1996)

Ella & Louis 𝄞𝄞𝄞𝄞 (Verve, 1956/1972)

Sings the Rodgers & Hart Songbook, Volumes I & II 𝄞𝄞𝄞𝄞𝄞 (Verve, 1956/1997)

Like Someone in Love 𝄞𝄞𝄞 (Verve, 1957/1991)

Compact Jazz: Ella & Duke 𝄞𝄞𝄞𝄞𝄞 (Verve, 1957–66/1993)

Ella Swings Lightly 𝄞𝄞𝄞𝄞 (Verve, 1958/1992)

Ella in Rome: The Birthday Concert 𝄞𝄞𝄞𝄞𝄞 (Verve, 1958/1988)

Ella Swings Brightly with Nelson 𝄞𝄞𝄞𝄞𝄞 (Verve, 1959/1993)

The Harold Arlen Songbook Volume I 𝄞𝄞𝄞 (Verve, 1960/1988)

The Harold Arlen Songbook Volume II 𝄞𝄞𝄞 (Verve, 1960/1988)

Returns to Berlin 𝄞𝄞𝄞𝄞 (Verve, 1961/1991)

Ella Swings Gently with Nelson 𝄞𝄞𝄞𝄞 (Verve, 1961/1993)

Ella & Basie 𝄞𝄞𝄞𝄞𝄞 (Verve, 1963)

These Are the Blues 𝄞𝄞𝄞 (Verve, 1963/1987)

The Jerome Kern Songbook 𝄞𝄞𝄞𝄞𝄞 (Verve, 1963/1987)

The Johnny Mercer Songbook 𝄞𝄞𝄞 (Verve, 1964/1997)

The Best of Ella Fitzgerald 𝄞𝄞𝄞𝄞 (Pablo, 1974–82/1988)

Fine and Mellow 𝄞𝄞𝄞 (Pablo, 1974/1987)

At the Montreux Jazz Festival, 1975 𝄞𝄞𝄞𝄞 (Pablo, 1975/OJC, 1993)

Ella and Oscar 𝄞𝄞𝄞 (Pablo, 1975/1987/1991)

Fitzgerald and Pass . . . Again 𝄞𝄞𝄞𝄞 (Pablo, 1976/1988)

Dream Dancing 𝄞𝄞 (Pablo, 1978/1987)

Lady Time 𝄞𝄞𝄞 (Pablo, 1978/1995)

(With Count Basie and Joe Pass) *Live: Digital 3 at Montreux* 𝄞𝄞𝄞 (Pablo, 1979)

Ella Fitzgerald & Count Basie: A Classy Pair 𝄞𝄞𝄞 (Pablo, 1979/1989)

Ella Fitzgerald & Count Basie: A Perfect Match 𝄞𝄞𝄞𝄞 (Pablo, 1979/1989)

Ella Fitzgerald & Joe Pass: Speak Love 𝄞𝄞𝄞 (Pablo, 1983/1987)

The Best Is Yet to Come 𝄞𝄞𝄞 (Pablo, 1983/1996)

The Irving Berlin Songbook Volume I 𝄞𝄞𝄞𝄞 (Verve, 1986)

The Irving Berlin Songbook Volume II 𝄞𝄞𝄞𝄞𝄞 (Verve, 1986)

Silver Collection: The Songbooks 𝄞𝄞𝄞𝄞 (Verve, 1987)

Ella Fitzgerald & Louis Armstrong, Compact Jazz 𝄞𝄞𝄞𝄞 (Verve, 1988)

Ella Fitzgerald/Tommy Flanagan, Montreux 1977 𝄞𝄞𝄞 (OJC, 1989)

The Best of Ella Fitzgerald 𝄞𝄞𝄞𝄞 (Curb, 1993)

The Best of the Songbooks: The Ballads 𝄞𝄞𝄞𝄞 (Verve, 1994)

Verve Jazz Masters 6 𝄞𝄞𝄞 (Verve, 1994)

Ella: The Legendary Decca Recordings 𝄞𝄞𝄞𝄞𝄞 (Decca Jazz, 1995)

Daydream: The Best of the Duke Ellington Songbook 𝄞𝄞𝄞𝄞 (Verve, 1995)

Love Songs: Best of the Verve Songbooks 𝄞𝄞𝄞𝄞𝄞 (Verve, 1996)

Oh, Lady Be Good! Best of the Gershwin Songbook 𝄞𝄞𝄞𝄞 (Verve, 1996)

Ella & Friends 𝄞𝄞 (Decca Jazz, 1996)

The Best of Ella Fitzgerald & Louis Armstrong on Verve 𝄞𝄞𝄞𝄞𝄞 (Verve, 1997)

The Complete Ella Fitzgerald & Louis Armstrong on Verve 𝄞𝄞𝄞𝄞𝄞 (Verve, 1997)

Ella Fitzgerald with the Tommy Flanagan Trio 𝄞𝄞𝄞 (Laserlight, 1997)

Priceless Jazz Collection 𝄞𝄞𝄞𝄞 (GRP, 1997)

influences:

◄◄ Maxine Sullivan, Connee Boswell, Billie Holiday, Bessie Smith

►► Sarah Vaughan, Lena Horne, Betty Carter, Mel Tormé, Carmen McRae, Joe Williams, Shirley Horn, Diana Ross, Whitney Houston, Gladys Knight, Bette Midler, Barbra Streisand

Susan K. Berlowitz and Nancy Ann Lee

David Fiuczynski

Born March 5, 1964, in Newark, NJ.

David Fiuczynski attended the New England Conservatory during the mid-'80s with fellow students John Medeski and Chris Wood before moving to New York City in 1988. There he formed a group called Screaming Headless Torsos that bridged the nervous chasm between experimental rock and edgy loft jazz and released an album on Discovery in 1995. Since arriving in New York, Fiuczynski's jazz-oriented playing has been heard with Muhal Richard Abrams, Billy Hart, Ronald Shannon Jackson, Jack Walrath, and John Zorn.

what's available: *Lunar Crush* 𝄞𝄞𝄞𝄞 (Gramavision, 1994, prod. Jim Payne) is actually an album under the double leadership of Fiuczynski and keyboardist John Medeski of Medeski, Martin, and Wood, but the music is closer to Screaming Headless Torsos, powerful distorted guitar lines weaving around Medeski's fluid keyboard playing with vocals a la Meredith Monk from Michelle Johnson and Gloria Tropp. Gene Lake, best known for his drumming with Steve Coleman, guests on most tracks, but the Torsos rhythm section, bassist Fima Ephron and drummer Jojo Mayer, also appears. "Pineapple" is a hard-charging fusion instrumental much like the kind of thing John Abercrombie was doing with Jan Hammer on Abercrombie's *Timeless* sessions while "Slow Blues for Fuzy's Momma" is a warped yet angular take on blues from the 21st century. Rock fans are more likely to appreciate this album than mainstream jazz aficionados.

worth searching for: Billy Hart's *Amethyst* 𝄞𝄞𝄞𝄞 (Arabesque, 1993, prod. Marc Copland) has Fiuczynski playing guitar in an interesting post-bop ensemble. He even wrote one tune ("Melanos") where his guitar playing pops out of the arrangement with a high-flying flair while still playing within the context of the group's sound. His solo on Hart's "Irah" is even more intriguing. Also worth seeking out is *Trio + Two* 𝄞𝄞𝄞𝄞 (Free Lance, 1990, prod. Santi Debriano, Jean-Paul Rodrique), the album Fiuczynski recorded with drummer Cindy Blackman and bassist Santi Debriano.

influences:

◀◀ Mick Goodrick, John Abercrombie

Garaud MacTaggart

Tommy Flanagan

Born March 16, 1930, in Detroit, MI.

With his subtle touch, pianist Tommy Flanagan has crafted improvisations that catch the ear by making one listen closely for the melodic gems fluidly woven into his understated work. Flanagan seems to be getting better with age, although he was no slouch when he left the active Detroit jazz scene for New York in 1956 with fellow Motor City musician guitarist Kenny Burrell. Flanagan became an in-demand pianist, playing with Charlie Parker, Dizzy Gillespie, and Ben Webster, and recording countless sidemen dates, including highly regarded, classic sessions such as *Saxophone Colossus* with Sonny Rollins and *Giant Steps* with John Coltrane.

Flanagan had two stints as Ella Fitzgerald's accompanist—from 1962–1965 and again from 1968–1978. Since leaving Fitzgerald in 1978, Flanagan has focused attention on his own trio. The pianist's recordings have been met with critical acclaim. In 1993, he received the prestigious international prize, the JAZZPAR award.

what to buy: The legendary modern jazz composer Tadd Dameron said: "When I write something, it's with beauty in mind. It's got to swing, sure, but it has to be beautiful." Flanagan seems to have applied that maxim to his playing. He's a modernist with a love for lyricism that is continually reflected in his improvisations. Don't be mistaken, Flanagan's playing is not effete. He can spin out bluesy, complex, modern jazz lines with the best, but his lines swing and sing, as evidenced on his album *Giant Steps* 𝄞𝄞𝄞𝄞 (Enja, 1982, prod. Horst Weber), a re-

visit to material he recorded with John Coltrane. Flanagan's clean playing on this recording seems to wring more emotion out of the tunes than on the earlier, like-titled Coltrane album. Flanagan brings the melodic beauty of each song to the fore without ever losing the sense of drive associated with songs like "Mr. P.C." The same holds true on *Thelonica* 𝄞𝄞𝄞𝄞 (Enja, 1983, prod. Matthias Winckelmann) on which Flanagan explores the music of Thelonious Monk. Flanagan knows better that to try to play like the idiosyncratic composer of those songs. Instead, his light touch makes Monk's melodies shine on "Pannonica", "Light Blue," and "Ask Me Now." And the trio cooks on the lesser known "North of the Sunset" and "Thelonious." If you like your trio more up-tempo, get *Giant Steps*, more introspective, *Thelonica*. Save yourself the decision, buy both. Then grab *Jazz Poet* 𝄞𝄞𝄞𝄞 (Timeless, 1989, prod. Wim Wigt) which is a well balanced set of cookers and ballads with booming bass from George Mraz and brushwork extraordinaire from Kenny Washington. "Caravan," "St. Louis Blues," and "Willow Weep for Me" receive fresh treatments, the band bops on "Mean Streets," and romantic subtleties of Flanagan's touch emerge on "Lament" and "Glad to Be Unhappy." Flanagan is equally compelling as a solo pianist, which you'll find on *Adelina Too Long* 𝄞𝄞𝄞𝄞 (Demon, 1984, prod. Yoshio Ogawa). The song "Dignified Appearance" is quintessential Flanagan. The pianist slowly builds to an emotional resolution without resorting to theatrics. The same holds true on "Maybe September."

what to buy next: Flanagan teams with old friend Burrell on *Beyond the Bluebird* 𝄞𝄞𝄞𝄞 (Timeless, 1991, prod. Diana Flanagan) as they revisit some tunes from their salad days at the Bluebird Club in Detroit, including "Yesterdays," on which Flanagan plays the rarely heard verse before beginning its familiar theme. *Sea Changes* 𝄞𝄞𝄞𝄞 (Evidence, 1997, prod. Todd Barkan, Satoshi Hirano) finds the pianist and his trio of five years returning to several songs Flanagan recorded on his first album as a leader (see *Worth Searching For* below). The trio's interplay is prominent as bassist Peter Washington and drummer Lewis Nash provide Flanagan with tasteful, yet swinging, support from start to finish. Flanagan's band mates on his late 1970s sessions, bassist George Mraz and drummer Elvin Jones, provide similar backing. All of their dates are solid. Seek out *Eclypso* 𝄞𝄞𝄞𝄞 (Enja, 1977, prod. Horst Weber) for its songs, including boppish takes of "Oleo," "Relaxin at Camarillo," and an obscure Dameron ballad, "A Blue Time."

the rest:
Plays the Music of Rodgers and Hammerstein 𝄞𝄞 (Savoy, 1957)

The Tommy Flanagan Trio 🎵🎵🎵 (OJC, 1960)

The Tokyo Recital 🎵🎵🎵 (OJC, 1975)

Tommy Flanagan Three: Montreux '77, 1977 🎵🎵🎵 (OJC)

The Best of Tommy Flanagan, 1991 🎵🎵🎵 (OJC, combines material from preceding two recordings)

Confirmation 🎵🎵🎵🎵 (Enja, 1977)

Something Borrowed, Something Blue 🎵🎵🎵 (OJC, 1978)

Our Delights 🎵🎵🎵 (OJC, 1979) (duets with Hank Jones)

Ballads and Blues 🎵🎵🎵🎵 (Enja, 1979)

Super Session 🎵🎵🎵 (Enja, 1980)

You're Me 🎵🎵🎵 (Phontastic, 1980)

The Magnificent Tommy Flanagan 🎵🎵🎵 (Progressive, 1981)

Nights at the Vanguard 🎵🎵🎵 (Uptown, 1986)

Let's 🎵🎵🎵🎵 (Enja, 1993)

Lady Be Good 🎵🎵🎵 (Verve, 1994)

Flanagan's Shenanigans 🎵🎵🎵 (Storyville, 1994)

worth searching for: Flanagan made his first recording as a leader while touring Europe with J. J. Johnson in 1957. Entitled *The Complete Overseas* 🎵🎵🎵🎵 (DIW, 1957), it featured the pianist teamed with bassist Wilbur Little and drummer Elvin Jones—worth finding not only for its historical significance in the Flanagan discography, but also because the album showcases a more hard-driving Flanagan and Elvin's brushwork could paint a house.

influences:

◀◀ Art Tatum, Nat "King" Cole, Teddy Wilson, Bud Powell, Tadd Dameron, Duke Ellington

Dan Polletta

Bela Fleck & the Flecktones

Formed 1990, in Nashville, TN.

Bela Fleck, banjo; Victor Wooten, bass; Roy "Future Man" Wooten, Synth-axe Drumitar and percussion; Howard Levy, harmonica and keyboards (1990–93).

Jazz scholars will remind us that the idea of playing jazz with a banjo isn't original or sacrilegious: Vess Ossman and Fred Van Eps were among the five-string specialists who helped usher in ragtime and Dixieland at the turn of the century. But Bela Fleck, a renowned Nashville musician with a bluegrass pedigree and a Charlie Parker fixation, has elevated the banjo to new levels of respectability and flexibility. Apprenticing in such bluegrass ensembles as Tasty Licks and the revered New Grass Revival, Fleck got some flack for turning his back on his country roots in 1990 when he left NGR to form his own band, which initially was considered a nifty novelty act. But he and bassist Victor Wooten and percussionist Roy "Future Man" Wooten (who plays a homemade, guitar-shaped drum machine) have honed a boundary-defying, relentlessly evolving sound that marks the most significant milestone in contemporary jazz since the formation of the Pat Metheny Group. Employing amplification, reverb, and synthesizers that allow him to trigger sounds of other instruments, Fleck and his Flecktones deftly tackle everything from funky fusion romps to blues and bebop-based improvisations without letting their predilection for high-tech experimentation mar their melodic grace.

what to buy: Credited as a "solo" project but featuring the Flecktones on virtually every track, the richly textured *Tales from the Acoustic Planet* 🎵🎵🎵🎵 (Warner Bros., 1995, prod. Bela Fleck) is a sterling back-to-basics consolidation of Fleck's jazz and bluegrass roots. The delicate melodies, classical overtones, and live-in-the-studio workouts with Bruce Hornsby, Tony Rice, and Branford Marsalis recall the bounce and beauty of David Grisman's early "dawg" music projects; it's highlighted by a madcap piano/banjo duet with Chick Corea called "Bicyclops." The Flecktones' second album, *Flight of the Cosmic Hippo* 🎵🎵🎵🎵 (Warner Bros., 1991, prod. Bela Fleck), captures the group as it finds its sound. From the hard-rocking "Turtle Rock" to the loping New Orleans bounce of the title track to barely discernible improvs on "The Star Spangled Banner" and the Beatles' "Michelle," these arrangements—featuring the haunting harmonica of since-departed Howard Levy—suggest just how far "out there" they would eventually venture.

what to buy next: *Live Art* 🎵🎵🎵🎵 (Warner Bros., 1996, prod. Bela Fleck) is a generous, crisply recorded double-CD of live performances spanning 1992–96. In between reworkings of such old favorites as "Flight of the Cosmic Hippo" and "Sinister Minister," the group stretches out on such new tunes as "New South Africa" and "Far East Medley" while Fleck merges country, Bach, and *The Beverly Hillbillies* on his solos and Victor Wooten deconstructs "Amazing Grace" into a funky seven-minute solo bass number.

what to avoid: With its offbeat instrumentation and wobbly merger of bluegrass and fusion, *Bela Fleck and the Flecktones* 🎵🎵🎵 (Warner Bros., 1990, prod. Bela Fleck) offers an unusual sound but an unfocused vision. "The Sinister Minister," however, hints at the greater accomplishments to come.

the rest:

UFO TOFU 🎵🎵🎵🎵 (Warner Bros., 1992)

Three Flew over the Cuckoo's Nest 🎵🎵🎵🎵 (Warner Bros., 1993)

worth searching for: Fleck released eight solo titles on Rounder before forming the Flecktones, most of them straight bluegrass efforts. Recorded with his New Grass Revival pals, *Inroads* ♫♫♫ (Rounder, 1986, prod. Bela Fleck) dabbles in jazz and offers the first sign that he would soon boldly go with the banjo where no one had gone before.

Victor Wooten:
A Show of Hands ♫♫♫ (Compass, 1996)

influences:

◀◀ Mark O'Connor, David Grisman, Return to Forever, Dixie Dregs

▶▶ Rob Wasserman, Modern Mandolin Quartet

David Okamoto

Flim & the BB's

Formed in Minneapolis, MN, in 1973. Disbanded in 1993.

Jimmy Johnson, bass; Billy Barber, keyboards; Bill Berg, drums; Dick Oatts, reeds.

Flim & the BB's began as a lark in 1973 at the Longhorn Bar in Minneapolis, when five-string bassist Jimmy Johnson and drummer Bill Berg—already the Twin Cities' most in-demand rhythm section—got together with keyboardist Billy Barber. Not yet an official member, Dick Oatts regularly sat in on sax. The group's name came from a nickname of founding member Jimmy "Flim" Johnson, and the "BB's" are Barber and Berg. The wealth of experience that each member brought to the quartet added to a canvas of many colors. Barber (composer of most of the group's material) wrote the 1985 hit "Little Things" for the Oak Ridge Boys, as well as the Ray Charles single, "Love Is Worth the Pain." Bassist Johnson has recorded and toured with James Taylor, Alan Holdsworth, Sergio Mendez, Lee Ritenour, Don Grusin, Billy Childs, and Brandon Fields. In addition to recording in the studio with Bob Dylan, Cat Stevens, Leo Kottke, and others, drummer Berg is also a key animator who worked extensively on the Walt Disney hits *The Little Mermaid* and *Beauty and the Beast.* Saxman Dick Oatts includes the Mel Lewis/Thad Jones Orchestra, Eddie Gomez, Roland Valesquez, and Red Rodney in his extensive recording and performing schedule. The quartet's first recording came at the invitation of studio owner Tom Jung, for experimentation with a prototype digital tape machine. The 1977 session was one of the first non-classical digital recordings and, being pre-CD, was pressed direct-to-vinyl. Enough copies were collected by hi-fi buffs and jazz lovers alike to build a faithful following. (Sadly, the 3M prototype has since been dismantled, and the original masters can no longer be played.) In 1982 Jung formed Digital Music Prod-

ucts (DMP) and, naturally, Flim and the BB's became one of its flagship groups.

what to buy: *New Pants* ♫♫♫♫ (Warner Bros., 1989, prod. George Massenberg, Flim & the BB's) displays the maturity of the quartet with an ear more tuned to improvisation. This was the first pairing with George Massenberg (of Little Feet and Linda Ronstadt fame). As with all of its catalog, the sonic quality is clean and punchy.

what to buy next: *Tricycle* ♫♫♫ (DMP, 1983, prod. Flim & the BB's, Tom Jung) is Flim and the BBs' undisputed cornerstone recording. It was named a "Number-One Compact Disc" title for demos, according to a 1985 dealer survey by *AudioVideo International* magazine.

the rest:
Tunnel ♫♫♫ (DMP, 1984)
Big Notes ♫♫♫ (DMP, 1985)
Neon ♫♫♫ (DMP, 1987)
Further Adventures ♫♫ (DMP, 1988)
This Is a Recording ♫♫♫ (Warner Bros., 1992)
Big Notes/Gold ♫♫♫ (DMP, 1995)
Tricycle/Gold ♫♫♫♫ (DMP, 1995)
Vintage BBs ♫♫♫♫ (DMP, 1995)

worth searching for: The vinyl-only *Flim & the BB's* ♫♫♫ (3M prototype/Tom Jung, 1977), with no master recording to convert to compact disc, is the rarest of rarities.

influences:

◀◀ The Crusaders, Joe Sample, Return to Forever

▶▶ Fattburger, Bob's Diner, The Dolphins

Ralph Burnett

Bob Florence

Born May 20, 1932, in Los Angeles, CA.

A challenging and highly imaginative arranger, Bob Florence has sporadically maintained an orchestra to play his charts since 1958, though his Limited Edition band has worked steadily since the late 1970s. Strongly influenced by Bill Holman, Florence studied arranging at Los Angeles City College and played weekend gigs with saxophonists Lanny Morgan and Herb Geller in the mid-'50s. But his career in the music industry really took off when his arrangement of "Up the Lazy River" became a hit in 1960 for Si Zentner's band, with whom he worked as pianist and arranger from 1959–64. A mainstay on the L.A. studio scene, Florence also served as Julie Andrews's music director for years. Though he made a number of obscure albums in the late '50s and '60s, he came into his own as a band leader in 1978, when he began a series of big-band sessions featuring top LA jazz and studio players. Though his writing is solidly in the modern, mainstream, big-band tradition, his idiosyncratic and sometimes brilliant charts demonstrate just how much room there is for individuality within that tradition. Since the late '70s he has recorded for Trend, USA, Discovery, and Bosco, though in the 1990s he's done some of his best work for the MAMA Foundation label.

what to buy: An absolutely fabulous session that fully realizes Florence's dense, idiosyncratic but highly swinging orchestral vision, *With All the Bells and Whistles* &&&&& (MAMA Foundation, 1995, prod. Bob Florence, Don Shelton) ranks with the best big-band recordings of the decade. Powered by bassist Tom Warrington and drummer Steve Houghton, the 18-piece band sounds like a well-rehearsed unit, and though there are few name members, the solos are consistently incisive and in the spirit of Florence's music. Among the many highlights are Dick Mitchell's and Terry Herrington's tenor battle on "Tenors, Anyone?" and Don Shelton's ethereal clarinet work on "Shimmery."

what to buy next: As its title suggests, *Funupmanship* &&&& (MAMA Foundation, 1993, prod. Bob Florence, Don Shelton) is a thrilling, fun-house adventure of a big-band session. Most of the material consists of Florence originals, though even the occasional standard, such as "Come Rain or Come Shine," is completely reworked and sounds as if it was written for the Limited Edition. From the roaring, densely kinetic harmonies of the title track to the playfully feline medley of "The Cats' Waltzes," Florence takes each piece in unexpected directions. Among the best solos are Dick Mitchell's powerful tenor work on Wayne Shorter's "Lester Left Town" and Lanny Morgan's fluid alto on "Leicester (Lester) Leaps In."

best of the rest:
Soaring &&&& (Sea Breeze, 1982)
Treasure Chest &&&& (USA Music Group, 1994)
Earth &&&&& (MAMA Foundation, 1997)

worth searching for: A strong session consisting mostly of reworked standards, *State of the Art* &&&& (USA Music Group, 1988, prod. Bob Florence) features excellent solos by saxophonists Bob Cooper, Kim Richmond, and Lanny Morgan and trumpeter Steve Huffsteter. Florence successfully pushes the envelope with his morose version of "Auld Land Syne," but goes over-the-top with a Brazilian-flavored take on "Moonlight Serenade."

influences:
◀◀ Bill Holman

Andrew Gilbert

Ricky Ford

Born March 4, 1954, in Boston, MA.

Ricky Ford has the distinction of being the last tenor player to be hired by Charles Mingus (replacing George Adams) at the tender age of 22. Despite Ford's relative youth, he already had studied at the New England Conservatory, recorded with Gunther Schuller, Ran Blake, and Jaki Byard and played with Mercer Ellington. Ford's post-Mingus career has included work with Danny Richmond, Lionel Hampton, Mingus Dynasty, and Abdullah Ibrahim. He directs the jazz ensemble and gives private lessons at Brandeis University.

what to buy: Ford has recorded three albums for Candid with a dream rhythm section of elder statesmen: pianist Jaki Byard, drummer Ben Riley, and bassist Milt Hinton. *American-African Blues* &&&& (Candid, 1993, prod. Mark Morganelli), a live one-nighter from Birdland in New York City, is the absolute cream of the crop. Everything—tunes, playing, even the recorded sound—comes together into a marvelous listening experience. Ford wrote every song. The title piece is played in two versions and, at one point, features Hinton slapping his bass solo in a way that actually works within the tune's post-bop context. The bluesy "Of" is filled with a rootsy kind of barbecue soloing ala John Coltrane, Dexter Gordon, or Houston Person and is an inspired conglomeration of 1960s-era jamming saxophone. The spotlight tune for veteran bassist Hinton, "Mostly Arco" is another gem. Fans will recognize the allusion to the Sonny Rollins-John Coltrane classic of burning improv in the title of *Tenor Madness Too!* &&&& (Muse, 1995, prod. Don Sickler). But Ford and Antoine Roney are just following in the hallowed tradition of other two-tenor jams—from Ammons and Stitt to Gordon and Gray. "Summer Summit" is a blowing session all the way, with Ford and Roney continually upping one another. By the Dizzy Gillespie classic, "Con Alma," it becomes apparent that these guys have absorbed the lessons of the past and can apply them in new, interesting ways.

what to buy next: The septet for *Hot Brass* &&&& (Candid, 1992, prod. Mark Morganelli) features trumpeters Lew Soloff and Claudio Roditi, trombonist Steve Turre, pianist Danilo Perez, and the rhythm section of bassist Christian McBride and drummer Carl Allen in addition to Ford on tenor saxophone. A lot of the tunes have a definite retro feel. On Ford's "Banging, Bashing, Bowing, and Blowing," McBride slaps his bass like Milt Hinton, Turre pulls Tricky Sam Nanton's growling mute work out of his bag, and everyone just lays back in the groove while Ford whacks out a Coleman Hawkins-inspired turn. *Ebony Rhapsody* ✎✎✎ (Candid, 1990, prod. Mark Morganelli) is the same setting and ensemble that appeared on Ford's excellent *American-African Blues* with a lesser set of material. That said, there is still plenty of good playing, and an interesting arrangement of a Franz Liszt work which, when renamed, became the album title. Ford's originals are consistently interesting, leaving lots of room for the soloists.

the rest:

Loxodonta Africa ✎✎✎ (New World, 1977)
Saxotic Stomp ✎✎✎ (Muse, 1988)
Manhattan Blues ✎✎✎ (Candid, 1990)
Hard Groovin' ✎✎✎ (Muse, 1991)

worth searching for: Ford recorded a lot of nice material for Muse that hasn't reached CD status. *Flying Colors* ✎✎✎ (Muse, 1980, prod. Don Schlitten), *Tenor for the Times* ✎✎✎ (Muse, 1981, prod. Don Schlitten), and *Shorter Ideas* ✎✎✎ (Muse, 1984, prod. Don Sickler) all deserve to be reissued.

influences:

◀◀ Dexter Gordon, John Coltrane, Sonny Rollins, Rahsaan Roland Kirk

▶▶ Antoine Roney

Garaud MacTaggart

Jimmy Forrest

Born January 24, 1920, in St. Louis, MO. Died August 26, 1980, in Grand Rapids, MI.

A career in music was inevitable for tenor saxophonist Jimmy Forrest, who made his debut at age 12 with his mother's band, Eva Forrest's Stompers. With a big, husky tone and a breathy ballad style, Forrest was at home in just about any situation and even hit the charts with his take on Duke Ellington's "Happy Go Lucky Local," which he turned into "Night Train." His first important gig was with the Jay McShann Orchestra in 1940, which at the time also featured an up-and-coming Charlie Parker. Until his untimely death in 1980, Forrest also worked for a period with Harry "Sweets" Edison, was a member of both the Basie and Ellington bands, and co-led a group with trombonist Al Grey. As part of his small body of recorded performances, Forrest's several dates as a leader for the Prestige label rank among his finest moments.

what to buy: *Night Train* ✎✎✎ (Delmark, 1951–1953, prod. Bob Koester) was originally recorded for the United label. This set includes the hugely successful title track and other fun numbers in Forrest's early R&B style. *All the Gin Is Gone* ✎✎✎ (Delmark, 1959, prod. Bob Koester) is solid hard bop fare that features the first recordings of guitarist Grant Green and includes an early look at drummer Elvin Jones.

what to buy next: *Out of the Forrest* ✎✎✎ (Prestige, 1961, prod. Esmond Edwards) features the opener "Bolo Blues," an all-time classic. Forrest's husky voicings often take on the leaner sensibilities of Lester Young, making the ballad features especially attractive. Fans of pianist Joe Zawinul will find his fine work here surprising. A free-wheeling quartet date with the underappreciated pianist Hugh Lawson, *Most Much* ✎✎✎ (Prestige, 1961, prod. Esmond Edwards) contains some of Forrest's finest work. A must hear!

the rest:

Forrest Fire ✎✎✎ (Prestige, 1960)
(With Oliver Nelson, King Curtis) *Soul Battle* ✎✎✎ (Prestige, 1960)
Sit Down and Relax with Jimmy Forrest ✎✎✎ (Prestige, 1961)
Heart of the Forrest ✎✎✎ (Palo Alto, 1983)

worth searching for: Although long out of print, *Soul Street* ✎✎✎ (Prestige, 1962, prod. Esmond Edwards) is worth searching for because of three cuts that feature Forrest in a large ensemble arranged and conducted by Oliver Nelson.

Chris Hovan

Joel Forrester

Born May 2, 1946, in New Kensington, PA.

Forever the ironist, pianist/composer Joel Forrester is quick to describe himself as the "odd man out" among his family's four siblings, all of whom have careers in music. But while the others are immersed in the world of classical music, Forrester is a self-taught improviser and free-jazz conceptualist. Along with saxophonist Phillip Johnston, he formed the Microscopic Septet, mixing musical metaphors with abandon over the course of a dozen years and four albums, all now extremely rare.

what's available: Forrester's debut as a bona-fide leader, *No . . . Really!* ✎✎✎ (Koch Jazz, 1997, prod. Joel Forrester, Claire Daly, Dave Hofstra, Denis Charles, Donald Elfman) is credited on its label to his working quartet, People like Us, with Claire Daly on baritone (joined for a couple of cuts by former Microscopic Dave Sewelson), Dave Hofstra on bass, and the magnificent

Denis Charles, whose associations include Cecil Taylor and Steve Lacy, on drums. The 10 original tunes are steeped in the rainments of the bop tradition but adorned with enough idiomatic touches to place them far beyond the mundane or predictable. Above all, they echo Forrester's fondness for Thelonious Monk, whom he sought for counsel in the older man's last years. Forrester plays with finesse, toying with time and phrase lengths to keep the listener off balance, while the rest of his stellar cast swings hard, wide, and very happily. Even Peter Keepnews's liner essay and Forrester's brief comments on the individual pieces are a delight.

influences:

◀◀ Meade Lux Lewis, Thelonious Monk, Duke Ellington

David Prince

Fort Apache Band

See: Jerry Gonzalez & the Fort Apache Band

Sonny Fortune

Born Cornelius Fortune, May 19, 1939, in Philadelphia, PA.

Sonny Fortune is a highly underrated alto saxophonist. He is also a fine composer and many of his best recordings are versions of his own material. A hard-bop player who is equally at home on alto and soprano saxes and flute, Fortune has a passionate, unmistakable style which often sounds as though he's either laughing or crying through his instrument.

After moving to New York in 1967, Fortune began working with Elvin Jones, an association that continues sporadically today, and he also performed and recorded with Mongo Santamaria, McCoy Tyner, and Miles Davis. Fortune recorded albums as a leader for Strata-East, A&M Horizon, and Atlantic in the mid- to late 1970s, becoming a bit more commercial with each release. However, his live shows were far from commercial, with Fortune taking solos of 30 minutes or more with the right audience. Fortune recorded for the Konnex label and toured and recorded in the 1980s with Nat Adderley (with whom his style fit perfectly). Working with Elvin Jones in the early 1990s, Fortune, by Jones's request, has played tenor. Fortune signed with Blue Note Records as a leader in 1993.

what to buy: *From Now On* ✍✍✍✍ (Blue Note, 1996, prod. Sonny Fortune, Marty Kahn) is an excellent CD featuring mostly his own compositions and the contributions of Joe Lovano, Eddie Henderson, John Hicks and others. *A Better Understanding* ✍✍✍✍ (Blue Note, 1995, prod. Sonny Fortune, Marty Kahn) provides more top-shelf music, all Fortune originals, with Jerry

Gonzalez, Robin Eubanks, Kenny Barron, Billy Hart, and others. Some of the songs on both of these are new versions of his 1970s recordings.

what to buy next: Fortune's Blue Note debut, entitled *Four in One* ✍✍✍✍ (Blue Note, 1994, prod. Sonny Fortune, Marty Kahn), features strictly Thelonious Monk compositions performed in the company of pianist Kirk Lightsey, bassist Buster Williams and drummer Billy Hart.

worth searching for: His debut LP, *Long Before Our Mothers Cried* ✍✍✍✍ (Strata-East, 1974, prod. Sonny Fortune), is a real gem with five original compositions and an octet that includes Charles Sullivan, Stanley Cowell, Wayne Dockery, Chip Lyle and three percussionists. *Awakening* ✍✍✍ (Horizon, 1975, prod. Ed Michel) and *In Waves of Dreams* ✍✍✍ (Horizon, 1976, prod. Ed Michel) are both favorable LP finds from the defunct A&M Horizon label. Recorded just before Fortune's more commercial Atlantic sides, both feature top players such as Kenny Barron, John Hicks, Billy Hart, Charles Sullivan, Buster Williams, and others performing mainly Fortune originals.

influences:

◀◀ John Coltrane, Cannonball Adderley

Bill Wahl

Frank Foster

Born September 23, 1928, in Cincinnati, OH.

A warm-hearted tenor saxophonist, arranger-composer, and former member and subsequent leader of the Count Basie Orchestra, Frank Foster proved to be musically adept from an early age, and by the time he entered high school, he was writing and arranging for his own 12-piece band. While studying music at Wilberforce University (now Central State University), Foster composed, arranged, and played alto and tenor saxophones with the Wilberforce Collegians, a 20-piece band. Following his college years, he joined the "Snooky" Young band in Detroit as an alto saxophonist, and worked as a freelance artist with Milt Jackson and Wardell Gray. After returning from the Far East in 1953, where he served with the 7th Army Infantry Division Band, Foster joined the Count Basie Band as a tenor saxophonist. In addition to performing, he made significant contributions to the band with his compositions and arrangements, which included "Down for the Count," "Blues Backstage," "Shiny Stockings," and "Four-Five-Six," among others. Foster remained with the Basie Band until 1964. In addition to touring and recording with his own groups, he has worked with Clark

Terry, Elvin Jones, the Johnny Richards Orchestra, Dexter Gordon, the Thad Jones-Mel Lewis Orchestra, and Benny Goodman. In 1980 Foster was commissioned by Jazzmobile to write a suite dedicated to the Winter Olympics. The resulting *Lake Placid Suite* was performed at the Olympics by a 20-piece orchestra, under Foster's direction. On June 18, 1986, Foster took over the leadership of the Count Basie Orchestra, writing and arranging for the band until he resigned on July 3, 1995. During these years, his arrangements helped to earn the band numerous Grammy nominations, two of which resulted in Grammy awards. Foster's Loud Minority Big Band, which he formed during the early 1980s, has reunited and is still performing today.

what's available: The Loud Minority is Frank Foster's big band, and on *The Loud Minority* ♫♫♫ (Mainstream, 1983, prod. Bob Shad), Foster features players such as saxophonist Kenny Rogers; trumpeters Cecil Bridgewater, Charles McGee and Marvin Peterson; trombonist Dick Griffin; guitarist Earl Dunbar; bassists Stanley Clarke and Gene Perla; pianists Harold Mabern and Jan Hammer; drummers Richard Pratt, Omar Clay, and Elvin Jones; percussionist Airto Moreira; and vocalist Dee Dee Bridgewater. All compositions were written and arranged by Foster, including "The Loud Minority," "Requiem for Dusty," "J.P.'s Thing," and "E.W.—Beautiful People." The band has a distinctly different, more dissonant sound and tone than the works Foster created with Basie. *Frankly Speaking* ♫♫♫ (Concord, 1984, prod. Bennett Rubin) exhibits a hard-swinging rhythm section with pianist Kenny Barron, bassist Rufus Reid, and drummer Marvin "Smitty" Smith. "The Two Franks," Frank Wess (tenor saxophone and flute) and Frank Foster (tenor and soprano saxophones), add their remarkable rapport to the energy, executing flawlessly throughout the session. Opening with "An' All Such Stuff as 'Dat," a Foster original, the quintet hits a natural swinging groove throughout the recording. Other tunes include "The Summer Knows," "When Did You Leave Heaven," "One Morning in May," and "This Is All I Ask," in addition to Neal Hefti's classic composition, "Two Franks." Paying their respects to Count Basie on this recording, Foster states, "We're propelling the Basie tradition into this decade." *Two for the Blues* ♫♫♫ (Pablo, 1983/OJC, 1993, prod. Bennett Rubin) is a reissue that brings Foster (tenor and soprano saxophones) and Frank Wess (tenor and alto saxophones and flute) together, recording the energy that had been so important to the Basie band during the late 1950s and into the 1960s. The rhythm section swings with abandon, highlighting the handiwork of Barron, Reid, and drummer Smith. Opening with Neal Hefti's composition, "Two for the Blues," the "Two Franks"

demonstrate why their sound and style captivated audiences. Included on this CD are "Send in the Clowns" and "Spring Can Really Hang You up the Most," both of which are usually performed as ballads but on this session are arranged in up-tempo, swing style, demonstrating the versatility of good tunes. Frank Wess contributes three originals while Foster contributes "Heat of Winter" to the mix.

influences:
◄◄ Sonny Stitt, Don Byas

Susan K. Berlowitz

Gary Foster
Born May 25, 1936 in Leavenworth, KS.

Gary Foster studied clarinet at the University of Kansas but plays flute and soprano, tenor, and alto saxophone. He moved to Los Angeles in 1961, where he began a long association with pianist-composer Clare Fischer in 1965 and was as a busy studio musician. Admired for his cool-tone, straight-ahead approach, Foster continued his jazz work as a sideman in the big bands of Louie Bellson, Mike Barone, and Toshiko Akiyoshi (1970s), as well as with small groups led by Dennis Budmir, Jimmy Rowles, Warne Marsh, and Laurindo Almeida. Foster has recorded with Cal Tjader, Poncho Sanchez, and Mel Tormé. He continues to be active in studio work, primarily because of his flute and clarinet abilities.

what to buy: *Make Your Own Fun* ♫♫♫ (Concord, 1994, prod. Carl E. Jefferson) is a great collection of standards and jazz favorites with a rhythm section of Jimmy Rowles (piano), John Heard (bass), and Joe LaBarbera (drums). Foster is in particularly fine form on "Nica's Dream," as he negotiates the Horace Silver tune with ease with a sound that perhaps can be best described as a muscular Paul Desmond. Rowles compliments Foster perfectly on "The Peacocks," and Foster's nod to his mentor Warne Marsh on "Warne-ing" is one of the highlights of this fine album.

what to buy next: Foster is featured with pianist Alan Broadbent on *Concord Duo Series, Volume Four* ♫♫♫♫ (Concord, 1995, prod. Carl E. Jefferson), a wonderful duo recording that displays the amazing interplay between these two musicians. Foster romps through "Relaxin' at Camarillo," and provides softer readings of two popular ballads, "In Your Own Sweet Way" and "If You Could See Me Now" by Tadd Dameron that show that his alto playing draws inspiration from Lee Konitz. Foster's fluency and warmth on this session demonstrate why he's such an in-demand session player.

influences:

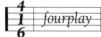 Warne Marsh, Lee Konitz, Lennie Tristano

Bill Moody

Fourplay

Formed 1990, in Los Angeles, CA.

Bob James, keyboards; Lee Ritenour, guitar (1990–98); Larry Carlton, guitar (1998–present); Nathan East, bass; Harvey Mason, drums.

Fourplay is not just a band—it's a quartet, with all the "real" jazz connotations the word suggests. Blending acoustic instruments and the latest MIDI digital technology, the all-star collective lives up to its mission statement—four musicians playing together in the studio rather than simply overdubbing their parts—while avoiding the mindless solo volleying that often results in cold fusion. Radio listeners who know Fourplay only for its playlist-pandering duets with guest vocalists like El DeBarge (Marvin Gaye's "After the Dance") and Chaka Khan (the Isley Brothers' "Between the Sheets") will wonder what all the fuss is about. But at its instrumental best, the group brings a refreshing sense of integrity and improvisation to a genre known more for merry melodies, sleepy rhythms, and Kenny G, not surprising since two of its original members—pianist Bob James and guitarist Lee Ritenour—rank among the most noble guardians of post-fusion contemporary jazz. Ritenour, who recently launched his own record label, withdrew from the band in early 1998 due to conflicting commitments.

what to buy: *Fourplay* ♪♪♪♪ (Warner Bros., 1991, prod. Fourplay) is state-of-the-art pop/jazz. From the swaying blues of the title track to the elegant melodies of "Bali Run," "Moonjogger," and "101 Eastbound," this 11-track debut teases and seduces with gentle but intoxicating rhythms and delicate but distinctive playing.

the rest:
Between the Sheets ♪♪♪ (Warner Bros., 1993)
Elixir ♪♪♪ (Warner Bros., 1995)
The Best of Fourplay ♪♪♪ (Warner Bros., 1997)

influences:

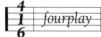 George Benson, Pat Metheny Group

David Okamoto

Pete Fountain

Born July 3, 1930, in New Orleans, LA.

Pete Fountain identifies strongly with New Orleans: He was born there, learned to play there, and continues to perform there in a nightclub in the Hilton hotel, complete with red velvet on the walls, that bears his iconic name. Although he borrowed a great deal from Benny Goodman, Fountain's most enduring influence on clarinet was his teacher and early mentor, Irving Fazola. By 1950, after playing with various New Orleans-based Dixieland combos, Fountain made his recording debut with Phil Zito's International Dixieland band. In the '50s, he led his own combo, and toured Chicago with the Dukes of Dixieland. From 1957 to 1959, Fountain achieved widespread popularity during a stint with *The Lawrence Welk Show,* on which he played Dixieland numbers. After leaving Welk, Fountain returned to New Orleans, purchased his first nightclub, and began a productive association with the Decca subsidiary Coral Records. Little else has changed since then—Fountain is still a New Orleans monument, he still plays with the same warm tone and Dixieland style, and he still wanders into the studio every now and then.

what to buy: *Do You Know What it Means to Miss New Orleans?* ♪♪♪♪ (Decca, 1996, prod. Orrin Keepnews), a two-CD compilation subtitled "Playing Dixieland Classics and Louis Armstrong Favorites," is a well-conceived, enjoyable program, collecting the best of Fountain's Coral recordings from the '60s.

what to avoid: *A Touch of Class* ♪ (Ranwood, 1995, prod. Owen Bradley) has nothing new to offer. The accompanying musicians are sub par, and Fountain sounds bored on a lazy set of ballads.

the rest:
The Blues ♪♪♪ (Coral, 1959)
Pete Fountain Day ♪♪ (Coral, 1960)
Pete Fountain's French Quarter ♪♪♪♪ (Coral, 1961)
Standing Room Only ♪♪♪ (Coral, 1965)
Swingin' Blues ♪♪ (Ranwood, 1990)
Live at the Ryman ♪♪ (Sacramento, 1992)
Cheek to Cheek ♪♪ (Ranwood, 1993)
Country ♪♪ (Ranwood, 1994)
The Best of Pete Fountain ♪♪♪♪ (Decca, 1996)

worth searching for: *Pete Fountain's New Orleans* ♪♪♪ (Coral, 1959/MCA, 1993) is one of the few individual albums Fountain cut for Coral that has actually been reissued on CD, but it is currently out of print. Many New Orleans favorites are included, like "When the Saints Go Marching In" and "When It's Sleepy Time Down South."

influences:

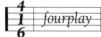 Irving Fazola, Benny Goodman, Johnny Dodds, Louis Armstrong

▶▶ Michael White, Al Hirt

Dan Keener

Michael Franks

Born September 18, 1944, in La Jolla, CA.

Franks has not been given his due as a songwriter in the Bob Dorough tradition of cleverly twisted lyrics. Jazz purists claim his music is pop, not jazz, and there' a certain justification to this, yet Franks has always used jazz musicians on his albums, from Michael Brecker and David Sanborn to Toots Thielemans and Eliane Elias, and Carmen McRae, Mark Murphy, the Manhattan Transfer, and Dee Dee Bridgewater have covered his songs.

Franks started playing in folk and rock bands while in high school, and he partially supported himself with professional gigs while in college. He moved to Canada in the late 1960s and worked with Lighthouse, a popular band of the time. Later he taught undergraduate music courses while earning a Ph.D. He was studying songwriting and saw himself as a songwriter. Three songs Franks wrote for the blues duo of Sonny Terry and Brownie McGhee were recorded by them on an A&M album. While he was touring with them, Brut did a documentary on the pair, and they recommended Franks to the Brut label as a recording artist, leading to his 1973 self-titled debut album. It contains songs written with other performers in mind, including rock star Rod Stewart, as well as things he had written for himself, and "Can't Seem to Shake This Rock 'n' Roll" got some attention as a single.

A music research project for Warner Bros. led to Franks's signing with Reprise, a subsidiary. His Reprise debut, *The Art of Tea*, was recorded with several members of the Crusaders. "Popsicle Toes" proved to be a hit, and Franks has recorded for Warner Bros. ever since. An interest in Brazilian music led to a friendship with Antonio Carlos Jobim, whose music Franks had used to learn to play guitar. "Antonio's Song/The Rainbow" on 1977's *Sleeping Gypsy* was dedicated to Jobim, as was the entire album *The Abandoned Garden* following Jobim's death. Franks incorporated Brazilian music into his own style, which sometimes made his albums fairly low-key compared to his snappier pop-jazz tunes, but the singer's fans haven't objected, and he has been quite commercially successful. A patch of work in the 1980s when Rob Mounsey was his producer moved Franks further from jazz with extremely slick productions keyed to the current styles of the times. Franks was not without ambitions, however, and wrote a musical based on the life of the painter Paul Gauguin after he moved to Tahiti. Some of this music was used for the album *Blue Pacific*.

what to buy: *The Art of Tea* 🎵🎵🎵🎵 (Reprise/Warner Bros., 1976, prod. Tommy LiPuma) is Franks's major label debut, with the hit "Popsicle Toes" and a program balancing similarly witty lyrics with the occasional ballad. The core of the superb supporting cast is keyboardist Joe Sample, guitarist Larry Carlton, bassist Wilton Felder (all three were in the Crusaders at the time), and drummer John Guerin, with Larry Bunker on vibes and Michael Brecker and David Sanborn featured on sax solos. The album was recorded live in the studio in three days, and though hardly unpolished, it avoids the offputting slickness of productions to come. It's funky pop-jazz at its finest.

what to buy next: *Sleeping Gypsy* 🎵🎵🎵 (Warner Bros., 1977, prod. Tommy LiPuma) was the follow-up, with the same core band of Sample, Carlton, Felder, and Guerin. Brecker and Sanborn appear with greater frequency (one at a time), with the final lazy samba track lacking a sax solo. The highlight is "Chain Reaction," cowritten with Sample (and also recorded by the Crusaders). Franks's infatuation with Brazilian music leads to occasional lapses into mellowness greater than the average jazz fan will tolerate, but overall this is still an enjoyable effort.

what to avoid: *Skin Dive* 🎵🎵 (Warner Bros., 1985, prod. Rob Mounsey) and *The Camera Never Lies* 🎵 (Warner Bros., 1987, prod. Rob Mounsey) are the nadir of Mounsey's productions. The 1987 album in particular is horribly dated and inhuman-sounding thanks to some inflexible drum machine tracks.

the rest:

Michael Franks (Brut/Buddah, 1973) a.k.a. *Previously Unavailable* 🎵🎵🎵
(John Hammond, 1983/DRG, 1989)
Burchfield Nines 🎵🎵🎵 (Warner Bros., 1978)
Tiger in the Rain 🎵🎵🎵 (Warner Bros., 1979)
One Bad Habit 🎵🎵🎵🎵 (Warner Bros., 1980)
Objects of Desire 🎵🎵🎵🎵 (Warner Bros., 1982)
Passion Fruit 🎵🎵🎵 (Warner Bros., 1983)
Blue Pacific 🎵🎵🎵 (Reprise/Warner Bros., 1990)
Dragonfly Summer 🎵🎵🎵 (Reprise/Warner Bros., 1993)
Abandoned Garden 🎵🎵🎵 (Warner Bros., 1995)
The Best of Michael Franks: A Backward Glance 🎵🎵🎵🎵 (Warner Bros., 1998)

worth searching for: There has long been talk among Franks fans of "when will he finally make a live album?" Actually, he already did, it just wasn't issued in the U.S. *With Crossfire: Live* 🎵🎵🎵🎵 (WEA, 1980, prod. Michael Franks) was recorded with a band of unknowns on a tour of Australia and New Zealand and released there on LP. Using material from the first three Warner Bros. albums, including "Chain Reaction" (given a funkier arrangement than in the studio) and "Popsicle Toes," it's got four tracks per side and only one ballad each, a percentage Franks would be well-advised to remember. The band plays

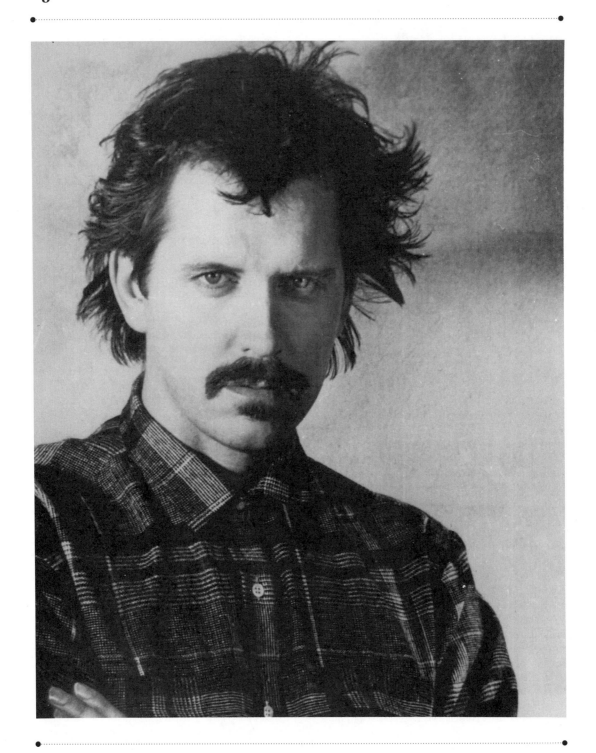

well up to the standards of those early albums but with the relaxed feel of a road-tested group, making for a very satisfying run through this material. The Christmas compilation *Jazz Christmas Party* 🎵🎵 (Warner Bros., 1997, prod. various) contains the wry Franks contribution "I Bought You a Plastic Star for Your Aluminum Tree."

influences:

⏪ Bob Dorough, Antonio Carlos Jobim, Ben Sidran, Dave Frishberg

⏩ Gino Vanelli, Laura Fygi

Steve Holtje

Rebecca Coupe Franks

Born November 27, 1961.

Rebecca Coupe Franks has gained considerable recognition playing trumpet and flugelhorn with great technical skill. From an early age, Franks wanted to play the trumpet; her brother played the instrument and she loved hearing the sound. Beginning in the fifth grade, she began taking private lessons, and in ninth grade, she began playing with the nearby college band. By the time she was in high school, Franks was performing nightly in a local restaurant with much older players. Finishing high school, she then moved to San Francisco, where she joined the band Chevere and met Virginia Mayhew. Moving on to New York, Franks co-led a group with Mayhew, playing Monday nights at the Blue Note. She has performed or recorded with Milt Hinton, Lou Donaldson, and other players.

what's available:: *Suit of Armor* 🎵🎵🎵 (Justice, 1991, prod. Randall Hage Jamail) features mostly original tunes by Franks, played with brilliance and emotion on flugelhorn and trumpet. Among the 10 selections are Ellington's "I'm Beginning to See the Light" and John Lewis's "Afternoon in Paris." Franks is joined on this outing by saxophonist Joe Henderson, pianist Kenny Barron, guitarist Leni Stern, bassist Buster Williams, drummer Ben Riley, and percussionist Carolyn Brandy. This album is highly recommended. With a touch of gospel, funk, and the blues on *All of a Sudden* 🎵🎵🎵 (Justice, 1992, prod. Randall Hage Jamail), Franks proves she is a skillful player, with expressive tone and good technique. She plays down and gritty blues or straight-ahead jazz, with support from pianist Kevin Hays, bassist Scott Colley, drummer Yoron Israel, and guest

soloist Javon Jackson on tenor sax. Franks composed and arranged most of the 11 tunes and, in addition to her originals, the crew performs Ellington's "I Let a Song Go out of My Heart" (listen to the interplay between Franks and bassist Scott Colley), and Thad Jones's "A Child Is Born." The band is both swinging and soulful, with a high level of musicianship.

influences:

⏪ Ruby Braff, Clark Terry

Susan K. Berlowitz

Rob Fraynor

See: Chelsea Bridge

Free Music Quintet

Formed in the 1960s.

Pierre Coubois, percussion; Peter van der Locht, soprano/tenor saxophone, piccolo flute, percussion; Boy Raaymakers, trumpet, bugle, percussion; Erwin Somer, violin, vibes, percussion; Ferdy Rikkers, bass, percussion.

ESP-disk was a record company and label founded in New York by Bernard Strollman in 1963 that was initially devoted to works by free-jazz players such as Albert Ayler, Ornette Coleman, Pharoah Sanders, Sun Ra, and numerous other artists involved in creating avant-garde jazz. Another of the mysterious ESP ensembles, the Free Music Quintet, was unabashedly European in its approach and its presence on the label reflected ESP's frantic grasping for new energy when the quintet was at the height of its power. The label was active into the 1970s with not much activity thereafter, although some ESP albums have since been reissued by ZYX.

what's available: The group's sole release, *Free Music Quintet* 🎵🎵🎵 (ESP, 1968, prod. Onno Scholtze), was recorded in the Dutch farmhouse of violinist Erwin Somer and the two far-reaching improvisations contained on the disc bear up surprisingly well to repeated listenings.

Jason Ferguson

Nnenna Freelon

Born in Cambridge, MA.

After graduating from Simmons College, Nnenna Freelon worked in the health services field in Durham, North Carolina. Making the decision to pursue a career as a jazz vocalist, Freelon worked diligently learning her craft and, as good fortune sometimes prevails, she took part in a key jam session in

Michael Franks **(AP/Wide World Photos)**

Atlanta that became a very important turning point in her career. While there, she made an indelible impression on fellow performer Ellis Marsalis, who brought her to the attention of Dr. George Butler at Columbia Records. Signed by Columbia, Freelon recorded her self-title debut CD in 1992, dedicated to standard repertoire. Through her recordings, she has begun to stretch, proving an individual talent. After releasing three Columbia albums, Freelon recently switched to Concord.

what to buy: Although in high prominence these days within the realm of the jazz vocal tradition, by following divas such as Ella Fitzgerald and Sarah Vaughan, Freelon has her work cut out for her. Her scatting has little depth and diversity of language and she doesn't come across lyrically. Yet, Freelon's career is in its infancy and she has plenty of time for developing her craft. That said, Freelon performs a pleasing variety of standards on her first recording, *Nnenna Freelon* ♫♫♫ (Columbia, 1992, prod. Dr. George Butler), featuring classics such as "Stella by Starlight," "Angel Eyes," "Skylark," "Yesterdays," "I Fall in Love Too Easily," and others. In addition to a string section, she is accompanied by musicians such as trumpeter Marvin Stamm (who has solos on "Yesterdays" and "Changed"); alto and tenor saxophonist Dave Tofani (who takes an alto solo on "Changed" and a tenor solo on "Future News Blues"); and guitarist Gene Bertoncini; bassists Ron Carter, Dave Finck, and Buster Williams; and drummer Grady Tate. Tate joins Freelon on vocals for "I Fall in Love Too Easily." The recording also includes three original compositions by Freelon.

what to buy next: On *Heritage* ♫♫♫ (Columbia, 1994, prod. Bob Freedman) Freelon is accompanied by top-notch musicians, including pianist Kenny Barron, bassist Christian McBride, drummer Lewis Nash, saxophonist Dave Tofani, and trombonist Jim Pugh. She performs a mixture of 13 standards and lesser-heard tunes, opening with Stevie Wonder's "Girl Blue." She also sings "Tis Autumn," "Comes Love," "Infant Eyes," "Never Let Me Go," and "Young and Foolish," in addition to Duke Ellington's "Heritage," the title track, and "Prelude to a Kiss." *Listen* ♫♫♫ (Columbia, 1994, prod. Bill Fischer) finds Freelon with pianist Bill O' Connell; bassists Ron Carter or Walter Booker; drummer Ricky Sebastian; guitarist Scott Sawyer; flugelhornist Cecil Bridgewater; saxophonists Dick Oatts, Alex Foster, and Dave Valentin; flutist Yusef Lateef; and vibist Bill Fischer, among others, plus a string section. Several compositions, including the title track, were written by Freelon. Standards included are "A Hundred Dreams from Now," "Lost in the Stars," and "Will You Still Love Me Tomorrow."

the rest:
Shaking Free ♫♫♫ (Concord, 1997)

influences:
◀◀ Sarah Vaughan

Susan K. Berlowitz

Bud Freeman

Born Lawrence Freeman, April 13, 1906, in Austin, IL. Died March 15, 1991, Chicago, IL.

Bud Freeman was an innovative jazz great who developed a gutty, bouncy, angular style of playing the tenor sax that was all his own. His performance career spanned seven decades and saw him mature from a largely self-taught founding member of the Chicago-style jazz school to an important sideman in the swing bands of Ray Noble, Tommy Dorsey, and Benny Goodman, and then go on to become a leader of his own groups. Freeman worked constantly to expand his harmonic knowledge, even studying with modernist Lennie Tristano. Freeman continued to broaden his musical horizons and developed a heavily melodic approach as he grew older. A natural-born storyteller, Freeman's anecdotes came as freely as his flowing saxophone lines. He was a confirmed Anglophile and, as early as his Chicago days, affected a distinctive speaking style tinged with an English accent. He was attracted to the arts and also kept a trained eye out for women, right up to the end. Freeman's approach to the tenor saxophone was an alternative to that taken by Coleman Hawkins, and Freeman influenced many players during the 1930s through the 1950s, including the famous Lester Young.

While growing up in Chicago, Freeman was a member of the famed "Austin High Gang," which included the McPartland Brothers, cornetist Jimmy and guitarist Dick, reedman Frank Teschmacher, bassist Jim Lanigan, and pianist Dave North. Freeman was befriended by drummer Dave Tough, who had a girlfriend at Austin, and Tough introduced young Freeman to painting, literature, and modern classical composers such as Debussy, Ravel, Stravinsky, and Holst. At age 17, while still struggling to learn the C-melody saxophone, Freeman (and his friends) heard major influences King Oliver and Louis Armstrong at the Lincoln Gardens. By 1945, Freeman had switched to tenor sax and had begun to read music. By 1927 he had recorded the famous McKenzie-Condon Chicagoan sides for the Okeh label with most of his Austin High friends plus banjoist Eddie Condon, pianist Joe Sullivan, and a very young drummer named Gene Krupa. Freeman was influenced by singer Bessie

Smith and cornetist Bix Beiderbecke, with whom he would record in 1930. Freeman joined Ben Pollack late in 1927 and went with him to New York until mid-1928, and later played aboard a ship while on the way to a gig in France. In 1929, playing mostly in the New York City area, he jobbed around with Zez Confrey, Red Nichols, and others. In the early 1930s, Freeman worked with Paul Whiteman, Gene Kardos, and Roger Wolfe Kahn. For a 1933 Eddie Condon recording date, Freeman unleashed his most famous composition, "The Eel," a serpentine line full of convoluted, writhing phrases that made the most of Freeman's quicky bouncing-ball tenoring. He then gravitated toward the big bands, joining Joe Haymes in 1934, Ray Noble's all-star U.S. band in early 1935, then became a featured soloist with the Tommy Dorsey Orchestra from 1936 to March 1938 when Benny Goodman beckoned.

In April 1939, Freeman formed his famed Summa Cum Laude Orchestra, which included old associates Eddie Condon and Dave Tough, the drummer who had also departed the Dorsey band. The front line of the newly formed eight-piece band included trumpeter Max Kaminsky, clarinetist Pee Wee Russell, and valve-trombonist Brad Gowans, along with the leader's powerhouse tenor saxophone. The band broke up in July 1940 and Freeman toured around before joining Joe Marsala; then he moved back to Chicago before being drafted into the Service in 1943. He served as leader of a Service band at Fort George, Maryland, and later disappeared into the wilds of the Aleutian Islands until his discharge in 1945. Returning to civilian life, Freeman figured he had some catching up to do, so he studied with Lennie Tristano who did not want Freeman to change his well-established style. Freeman freelanced in the 1950s and 1960s, often leading his own groups while also sustaining a long-term association with the "Condon mob." He became a charter member of the World's Greatest Jazz Band in 1969, working with co-leaders Bob Haggart and Yank Lawson into the early 1970s. Freeman moved to London in 1974, lecturing and performing at university and clubs throughout Great Britain, and throughout the decade recorded prolifically both at home and abroad. He returned to the U.S. in 1980 and once again took up residence in Chicago, where he began a series of club dates and occasional forays onto the jazz party circuit. Each year from 1986 through 1989, Freeman was a mainstay at the Conneaut Lake Jazz Festival in Western Pennsylvania, where he performed in 1986 with fellow tenorists Scott Hamilton and old friend, Eddie Miller. Freeman acquired and played on one of Miller's old tenors during his later years, and also found time to author or co-author three autobiographical books, *You Don't*

Look Like a Musician (1974), *If You Know of a Better Life, Please Tell Me* (1976), and *Crazeology* (1989). Freeman died of cancer on March 15, 1991, just a month short of his 85th birthday, thus stilling one of our most articulate, enduring, and original jazz voices.

what to buy: *Bud Freeman 1939–1940* 🎵🎵🎵🎵 (Jazz Chronological Classics, 1995, prod. Anatol Schenker) reissues 24 classic Freeman band sides, 16 by the Summa Cum Laude Orchestra originally issued on RCA Victor's Bluebird label or on Decca, and eight from Colombia's *Comes Jazz* album session by Bud Freeman and his Famous Chicagoans. The 1939 Bluebird sessions reprise Freeman's loping, looping feature, "The Eel," full of elliptical phrasing and brash tenorisms. Eight of the Decca sides are from a 1940 *Fashions in Swing* album that saluted Bix Beiderbecke and the Wolverines with tunes that were originally recorded by that earlier band. Brad Gowans (valve trombone) is present on the first 16 tracks while Jack Teagarden handles the slide trombone in masterful fashion for the last eight tunes. Max Kaminsky (trumpet), Pee Wee Russell (clarinet), leader Freeman, and both trombonists have many sparkling solos through the proceedings, as does pianist Dave Bowman with his Jess Stacy–like keyboarding. The horns, along with Eddie Condon's propulsive guitar, get a solid ensemble drive, and Dave Tough's drumming adds much to the Famous Chicagoan sides. Tough's attention-getting work on "47th and State" is downright magnificent. Teagarden takes the honors on "Jack Hits the Road," and delivers one of his effective laid-back solos on the Freeman original "After Awhile." Eddie Condon's presence, if not clearly heard, is surely felt on all of these rewarding Chicago-style sides. Twenty-two earlier Bud Freeman sides from Okeh, Decca-Parlophone, and Commodore are presented on *Bud Freeman 1928–1938* 🎵🎵🎵 (Jazz Chronological Classics, 1994, prod. Anatol Schenker). Four of the tracks are by Bud Freeman and his Windy City Five, a 1936 session which contains exciting solos by trumpeter Bunny Berigan and finds Freeman playing clarinet as well as tenor sax. The tune "Buzzard" has especially attractive solos by the two horns and a solo chorus by pianist Claude Thornhill. Eleven Commodore sides by the Bud Freeman Trio are a showcase for three veteran Chicagoans—pianist Jess Stacy, drummer George Wettling, and leader Freeman. There is plenty of solo work for pianist Stacy who excels on "Blue Room," "Three Little Words," and "Swingin' without Mezz." Freeman is the only horn on these sides and has ample room to display his swinging wares, his booting tenor saxophone approaching a barrelhouse atmosphere on tunes such as "I Got Rhythm," "My Honey's Lovin'

Arms," and Freeman's favorite anthem, "You Took Advantage of Me." The musical portion of this compilation climaxes with four swinging Commodore sides (wonderful examples of late 1930s small band swing) by Bud Freeman and his Gang which feature cornetist Bobby Hackett, clarinetists Pee Wee Russell, alto saxophonist Dave Matthews, and pianist Stacy. A final track, "Private Jives," a spoof on Noel Coward's "Private Lives," on which would-be actor Freeman brandishes his cultivated English accent. *Muggsy Spanier and Bud Freeman 1944–45: The Complete V-Disc Sessions* ♫♫♫♫ (Jazz Unlimited, 1997) is a collection of final takes, alternate takes, and breakdowns from New York V-Disc sessions held October 17, 1944 (Muggsy Spanier & His V-Disc All Stars), October 22, 1945 (Muggsy Spanier and His V-Disc band), and October 4, 1945 (the V-Disc Jumpers/Bud Freeman and his Stars). Nineteen of the 24 tracks feature the booting tenor sax of Bud Freeman. This set contains three very different versions of "You Took Advantage of Me," Freeman's signature tune that he would play and record repeatedly throughout his lengthy career. He never played it better than he does here in the company of cornetist Muggsy Spanier, clarinetist Peanuts Hucko, trombonist Lou McGarity, pianist Dave Bowman, guitarist Hy White, bassist Trigger Alpert, and drummer George Wettling. The October 4, 1945 date has trumpeter Yank Lawson sharing solo honors with tenor man Freeman and clarinetist Hucko. Ray McKinley's solid drumming lends support as they tear into jazzy renditions of "Love Is Just Around the Corner" and "Coquette," and they parody the then current bebop trend with tunes titled "The Latest Thing in Hot Jazz" and "For Musicians Only." This is a very welcome addition to the recorded legacies of Spanier and Freeman.

what to buy next: Enjoyable mainstream fare, *Superbud* ♫♫♫♫ (77, 1974/Jazzology, 1997, prod. Doug Dobell, reissue prod. George Buck) brings to CD a session originally recorded during one of Freeman's tours of England. Ten tracks feature the tenacious, joyful, swinging tenor sax of the dapper Freeman. Highlights include "Keeping Myself for You," which features the Keith Ingham trio, and five cuts of solo piano added to the reissue by Ingham to bring the original LP to suitable CD length. *California Session* ♫♫♫♫ (Jazzology, 1997, prod. George Buck) finds the tenor man in pleasant California-based company performing eight extended tunes, with appealing solos all around. Supporting the tenor antics of the erudite Freeman are trumpeter Dick Cathcart, multi-instrumentalist Betty O'Hara, clarinetist Bob Reitmeier, pianist Ray Sherman, guitarist Howard Alden, bassist Phil Stephens, and drummer Nick Fatool. Recorded live at the Lost Angel in the last decade of his long career, this has some interesting and inspired work by Freeman on some of his favorites, such as "Crazy Rhythm," "Tea for Two," and "S'Wonderful." A 1962 quartet date, *Something to Remember You By* ♫♫♫♫ (Black Lion, 1990, prod. Alan Bates) finds Freeman performing a pleasant 17-tune mix of melodic ballads and easy swingers. Support here is first-rate with pianist Dave Frishberg carving out some solo highlights, and master bassist Bob Haggart and veteran drummer Don Lamond laying down a solid rhythm background. The seldom heard "You're a Sweetheart," "Please," "Last Night When We Were Young," and the title tune all receive very listenable workouts. Uptempo Rodgers & Hart swingers such as "The Girl Friend" and "It's Only a Paper Moon," and a bluesy "Meet You in San Juan" add spice to the mix. Five alternate takes pad the playing time.

what to avoid: *Bud Freeman 1945–1946 #3* ♫♫♫ (Jazz Chronological Classics, 1997, prod. Anatol Schenker), though an enjoyable album, is recommended for avid Freeman completists only since ten of the tracks showcase the Five De Marco Sisters, accompanied by Bud Freeman and his Orchestra.

best of the rest:
Bud Freeman 1946 ♫♫♫♫ (Jazz Chronological Classics, 1997)
Bud Freeman 1928–1939 ♫♫♫♫ (Giants of Jazz, 1997)

influences:
◀◀ Jack Pettis

▶▶ Lester Young, Babe Russin, Roomie Richmond, Peanuts Hucko

John T. Bitter

Chico Freeman

Born Earl Lavon Freeman Jr., July 17, 1949, in Chicago, IL.

Second-generation tenor saxophonist Chico Freeman (son of Von Freeman) has made a name for himself in the post-Coltrane jazz world. Although he began his musical education on trumpet (inspired by Miles Davis's *Kind of Blue*) and did not start playing sax until his third year at Northwestern University, he quickly mastered the instrument and began performing with a variety of local groups during the early 1970s, as well as joining the Association for the Advancement of Creative Musicians (AACM). Completing his education was Freeman's priority during this time, and eventually he received his Masters degree from Governors State University, but in 1977 he moved to New York and began his jazz career in earnest, playing with Elvin Jones, Sun Ra, the Sam Rivers big band, Jack DeJohnette's Special Edition, and Don Pullen, as well as leading his own groups.

Since then he has been quite prolific, recording with a variety of labels (his best work is with India Navigation) and often with excellent bassist Cecil McBee and even his father joining him. Freeman plays numerous woodwinds, but he is best known for his rich, flexible tone that has made him a leader in the recent bop/post-bop revival and caused some critics to proclaim him the rightful heir to John Coltrane's throne.

what to buy: On *Spirit Sensitive* 𝄞𝄞𝄞𝄞 (India Navigation, 1979, prod. Bob Cummins) Freeman successfully recreates the evocative sound of his idol without sounding derivative. Gentle yet intense, this set is aided by outstanding work by McBee, drummer Billy Hart, and pianist John Hicks. *Kings of Mali* 𝄞𝄞𝄞𝄞 (India Navigation, 1978, prod. India Navigation) is an intriguing free jazz record with an African motif. Vibes and various percussion instruments combine with Freeman's soaring tenor and soprano sax styles to create an original record devoid of pretension.

what to buy next: *Morning Prayer* 𝄞𝄞𝄞𝄞 (India Navigation, 1984, prod. Masahiko Yuh) is a reissue of sessions from 1976. Freeman teams up with visionary reedman Henry Threadgill to good effect on adventurous tracks such as "Pepe's Samba" and "Conversations." *Focus* 𝄞𝄞𝄞𝄞 (Contemporary, 1994, prod. Eric Miller) is a relatively recent album which finds Freeman in fairly straightforward waters, with two Monk compositions and wonderful work from alto player Arthur Blythe.

what to avoid: The problem with *Tangents* 𝄞𝄞 (Elektra Musician, 1984, prod. Chico Freeman, John Koenig) with Bobby McFerrin is that calliope-like vocalist McFerrin is an acquired taste, one Freeman would have done better not to have found.

the rest:
Chico 𝄞𝄞𝄞𝄞 (India Navigation, 1977)
Beyond the Rain 𝄞𝄞𝄞 (Contemporary, 1977)
No Time Left 𝄞𝄞𝄞 (Black Saint, 1979)
Peaceful Heart, Gentle Spirit 𝄞𝄞𝄞 (Contemporary, 1980)
Destiny's Dance 𝄞𝄞𝄞 (Contemporary, 1981)
The Search 𝄞𝄞 (India Navigation, 1982)
Tradition in Transition 𝄞𝄞𝄞 (Elektra Musician, 1982)
The Pied Piper 𝄞𝄞𝄞𝄞 (Black Hawk, 1984)
Tales of Ellington 𝄞𝄞𝄞 (Black Hawk, 1984)
Live at Ronnie Scott's 𝄞𝄞 (Hendring/Wadham, 1986)
You'll Know When You Get There 𝄞𝄞𝄞𝄞 (Black Saint, 1988)
Freeman & Freeman 𝄞𝄞𝄞 (India Navigation, 1989)
The Mystical Dreamer 𝄞𝄞𝄞 (In & Out, 1989)
Up and Down 𝄞𝄞𝄞 (In & Out, 1989)
Sweet Explosion 𝄞𝄞𝄞 (In & Out, 1990)
Threshold 𝄞𝄞𝄞 (In & Out, 1992)
Still Sensitive 𝄞𝄞𝄞𝄞 (India Navigation, 1995)
(With Project Terra Nova) *The Emissary* 𝄞𝄞𝄞 (Clarity, 1996)

worth searching for: *The Outside Within* 𝄞𝄞𝄞𝄞 (India Navigation, 1981, prod. Bob Cummins) finds regulars McBee and Hicks joining Freeman and drummer extraordinaire Jack DeJohnette on the epic "Undercurrent," which shimmers and grooves along the A-side. The other tracks on the flip side don't quite compare, but still merit investigation.

influences:

◀◀ John Coltrane, Von Freeman

Eric J. Lawrence

George Freeman

Born April 10, 1927, in Chicago, IL.

Another talented member of the musical Freeman family of Chicago, George Freeman is a soulful but somewhat idiosyncratic player whose recordings have been infrequent. Freeman was inspired to play guitar after witnessing a performance by T-Bone Walker at a Chicago club in the 1940s, and though he was also inspired by guitarists Charlie Christian, Oscar Moore, and Wes Montgomery, his strongest influences came from non-guitarists—Charlie Parker, Art Tatum, and his saxophonist brother, Von. Freeman was first recorded while backing Parker on a live date released on Savoy. From the late 1940s through the 1950s he backed a series of R&B stars, including Joe Morris, Sil Austin, and Jackie Wilson, before hooking up with "Groove" Holmes in the 1960s. He has since been most often heard in soul-jazz settings, working extensively with Gene Ammons in the late 1960s (Freeman appeared on a few of Ammons's late 1960s Prestige LPs) and with Jimmy McGriff in the early 1970s. He recorded his debut as a leader for Delmark in 1969, an LP for Sonny Lester's Groove Merchant label in 1974 called *New Improved Funk*, and finally resurfaced on CD in the 1990s with a session for Chicago's Southport label. A unique player who has kept his ears wide open to post-bop developments, Freeman exhibits a unique penchant for sprawling rapid-fire lines of notes with unexpected turns.

what to buy: *Birth Sign* 𝄞𝄞𝄞𝄞 (Delmark, 1972/1993, prod. Michael Cuscuna, Robert G. Koester), the best representation of Freeman's style, shows his personality a lot stronger than his gigs as a sideman. His unusual style sets this album apart from typical organ group dates.

what to buy next: *Rebellion* 𝄞𝄞𝄞 (Southport, 1995, prod. Joanie Pallatto, Bradley Parker-Sparrow) finds Freeman taking it further out towards the edge in the 1990s though the songs are all standards. Von Freeman is on hand, as with *Birth Sign*, but on piano instead of saxophone.

worth searching for: *The Groover* 🎵🎵🎵 (Prestige, 1968) is a burning organ trio date under "Groove" Holmes's leadership that has yet to be reissued on CD. Also, Jimmy McGriff's early 1970s Groove Merchant releases featuring Freeman, such as *Fly Dude*, have been reissued in part on the CD *Funkiest Little Band in the Land* 🎵🎵🎵 (LRC/Laserlight, 1996, prod. Sonny Lester).

influences:

◀◀ T-Bone Walker, Charlie Christian, Oscar Moore, Charlie Parker, Von Freeman

▶▶ Melvin Sparks, Pat Martino, Mark Elf, James "Blood" Ulmer

Dan Bindert

Russ Freeman

Born Russell Donald Freeman, May 28, 1926, in Chicago, IL.

Not to be confused with Russ Freeman of the Rippingtons, composer, pianist Freeman studied classical music as a child, moved to Los Angeles, and became involved with bop groups by the 1940s, playing with Dexter Gordon, Charlie Parker, Howard McGhee, Wardell Gray, Art Pepper, and Shorty Rogers. Freeman had a long association with Chet Baker, for whom he served as musical director. He joined Shelly Manne's Men by the mid-1950s and recorded numerous albums with the drummer's group. Freeman also toured Europe in 1959 with Benny Goodman. In 1962 Freeman formed his own publishing company and became musical director for a number of vocalists. He worked on numerous movie sound tracks and continued to compose, although by the 1970s his jazz work had become limited to the occasional appearance. Freeman now lives in Las Vegas, Nevada, and continues to pursue his song-writing career. His piano style is essentially bebop, but he has indicated that his playing was often influenced by bassists and drummers—most notably Manne—rather than by other pianists.

worth searching for: Although Freeman performed with many luminaries, he has nothing in print as a leader. However, search the used LP bins for one of the best examples of his playing on the now-out-of-print LP with Chet Baker, *Russ & Chet* 🎵🎵🎵🎵 (Contemporary, 1955, prod. Dick Bock). Freeman is a solid accompanist and good listener. His comping behind Baker is a model of taste and musicality, as are his own solos. Still in print, *Double Play!* 🎵🎵🎵 (Contemporary, 1957/OJC, 1993) features Freeman co-billed with Andre Previn on a duo outing centered on nine baseball-oriented tunes such as "Take Me out to

the Ball Game," "Called on Account of Rain," "Who's on First?," "In the Cellar Blues," and other such titles. Freeman is a worthy match for Previn and one wishes these two could have been recorded in a setting such as Concord's Maybeck Recital Hall duo series. Shelly Manne & His Men recorded *At the Manne-Hole, Volume 1* 🎵🎵🎵🎵 (Contemporary, 1959/OJC, 1992, prod. Lester Koenig), as well as a follow-up album featuring Freeman, *At the Manne-Hole, Volume 2* 🎵🎵🎵🎵 (Contemporary, 1962/OJC, 1992, prod. Lester Koenig). Volume I offers a hard-swinging, live performance by a group that worked together and could read each others' minds. Freeman shines on "Love for Sale" and "The Champ," feeding the right chords in just the right way to Conte Condoli and Richie Kamuca before he steps up to take his own licks. On the ballad, "How Could This Happen to a Dream," Freeman's rich harmonic sense inspires the rest of the band and his sensitivity to melody makes you think he might have been the composer. Volume II includes classics such as "Green Dolphin Street," "What's New?," "Ev'ry Time We Say Goodbye," and other gems. *The Three and the Two* 🎵🎵🎵🎵 (Contemporary, 1954/OJC, 1994) features drummer Manne leading two separate sets featuring trumpeter Shorty Rogers and reedman Jimmy Giuffre. Freeman's work with Manne features his hard-swinging, bebop style and some great section work as well. The highlight is a duo with Shelly on "Sound Effects Manne." Freeman displays uncanny empathy with the drummer, and without benefit of a bassist, Freeman and Manne work in counterpoint to each other, alternating the lead from drums to piano and back to drums. This track alone is worth the price of the CD to hear these two great musical minds on the same page. *Chet Baker: Boston 1954* 🎵🎵🎵🎵 (Pacific Jazz, 1954/1997, prod. Bob Sanenlick) is a live recording with Baker's working, on-the-road group, and the performances reflect the group's interplay. Although Baker and Stan Getz weren't talking much during the recording of *West Coast Live* 🎵🎵🎵🎵 (Pacific Jazz, 1954/Blue Note, 1998, prod. Dick Bock), they did make some good music and Freeman is much in evidence, providing the bridge to hold these two greats together.

influences:

◀◀ Bud Powell

Bill Moody

Von Freeman

Born Earl Lavon Freeman, October 3, 1922, in Chicago, IL.

Von Freeman is a highly underrated Chicago saxophonist who collaborated with his brothers, guitarist George Freeman and drummer Bruz Freeman, and inspired his son, reedman Chico. Like many Chicago musicians, Von Freeman came under the direction of famed DuSable High School music educator, Captain Walter Dyett, and his first professional gig was at age 12. Inspired by Lester Young and Coleman Hawkins, Freeman's career included stints with the Horace Henderson Orchestra, and with a Navy band while in the service during the 1940s. With his brothers, Freeman also served in the house band at the famed Persian Lounge from 1946–50 where he backed touring artists such as Charlie Parker, Roy Eldridge, Lester Young, and others. During the late 1940s Freeman played in a band at the Club DeLisa, where Sun Ra played occasional piano and later led the band. Freeman played with a variety of musicians on the road during the 1950s, but didn't record as leader until 1972 and rarely since then. Yet, he became a local legend who inspired countless Chicago musicians (and others throughout the Midwest) with his bluesy style. The late Art Porter Jr. claimed that while a young player, he jammed with the veteran saxophone master without fully appreciating Freeman's artistry and importance in shaping Chicago's jazz scene. Freeman has worked with many of the Association for the Advancement of Creative Musicians (AACM), innovators, including Muhal Richard Abrams. But he has mostly led his own bands since the 1960s, recording as leader for Atlantic (1972), Nessa, Daybreak, Columbia, SteepleChase, and the independent Chicago label, Southport.

what to buy: *Walkin' Tuff!* 𝄞𝄞𝄞𝄞 (Southport, 1989, prod. Joanie Pallatto, Bradley Parker-Sparrow) features tenor saxophonist Freeman with two separate Chicago rhythm teams. With pianist Jon Logan, bassist Carroll Crouch, and drummer Wilbur Campbell, Freeman kicks off the album with a swinging version of the title tune, then heads for obviously comfortable bop territory with his original, "Bruz, George, & Chico." Freeman's alternate quartet, with pianist Kenny Prince, bassist Dennis Carroll, and Freeman's drummer Michael Raynor, takes tune three, an up-tempo rendering of "Nature Boy," which gives Freeman vent for some loose-flowing, technically skilled improvisations. He works well with both rhythm teams throughout this seamless collection of eight standards and originals. Demonstrating the full range of his sophisticated, exuberant tenor playing, Freeman shows why he is Chicago's treasure. Yet, it's puzzling as to why he has worked in relative obscurity except for his Steeple-Chase albums, but that makes this rare domestic session even more valuable.

what to buy next: *Fire* 𝄞𝄞𝄞 (Southport, 1996, prod. Tatsu Aoki, Bradley Parker-Sparrow, Joanie Pallatto) features Chicago tenor

sax legend Freeman and his regular drummer Michael Raynor in their first meeting with bassist Tatsu Aoki. Southport partners Bradley Parker-Sparrow (an average pianist), and vocalist Joanie Pallatto round out the team. Freeman stretches out articulately on the 10 selections, leaving plenty of spaces in his saxisms as he entrenches himself in the bop court and experiments with some free-jazz stylings. Best is the freely improvised "Tatsu's Groove," which begins with an inspiring bass riff on which everyone expands, shifting from beat-driven grooves to dreamy, floating schemes. Pallatto's vocals are often distracting, and while Freeman interacts intelligently and gets enough licks in, you'll wish for more from him. The whole session has the feel of a spontaneous jam.

worth searching for: A reissue of a March, 1969 date, *Birth Sign* 𝄞𝄞𝄞 (Delmark, 1993, prod. Robert G. Koester) finds guitarist George Freeman and his brother, saxophonist Von Freeman, leading a quartet that summons some swinging grooves in the style of '60s organ groups. This is George Freeman's first album as leader, and Von's cocky, fluent tenor innovations are featured on four of the seven tracks. George was a stalwart in Groove Holmes's organ group from the mid-1950s into the mid-1960s, but rarely appeared on Holmes's recordings before he quit the road to freelance in Chicago. This album was recorded in two separate sessions just before George joined Gene Ammon's new quintet. Other musicians include organist Sonny Burke and drummer Billy Mitchell. Kalaparusha Maurice McIntyre (tenor sax on three tunes), Lester Lashley (trombone), and organist Robert Pierce are part of the quintet that plays on Michael Cusuna's arrangement of "Must Be, Must Be." A soulful, price-worthy album if only for the closer, a beautiful rendition of the standard, "My Ship," which spotlights romantic solos from both Freeman brothers.

influences:

◀◀ Lester Young, Coleman Hawkins, Gene Ammons, Dave Young

Nancy Ann Lee

Freestyle Fellowship

Formed 1991, in South Central, Los Angeles, CA. Disbanded 1994.

J-Sublimi, vocals (1991–93); Mikah Nine/Microphone Mike, vocals; Self-Jupiter, vocals; Aceyalone, vocals; Peace/Mtulazaji, vocals (1993–94).

Discussions of '90s West Coast hip-hop center on so-called gangsta rap, but for those who really know, the experimental edge of the Los Angeles underground has been as influential as it has been overlooked. All roads begin at an ongoing series of open-mic nights organized in the early '90s by cafe owner and community activist Bea Hall at her South Central site called the Good Life. Attracting a wildly talented group interested in pursuing poetic and rhythmic complexity, these artists worked with the same intensity and dogma of late '60s free jazzers. The similarities don't end there. While they blew down all kinds of artistic borders, they would be received by the public in much the same way—derided, especially, by East Coast critics and fans who favored simplicity and directness. Their innovations would be taken into the mainstream by much less committed artists in the most ironic way: although they were post-gangsta in spirit, the artists' tricky cadences would gain credibility and transform street rap through groups like Bone Thugs-N-Harmony and Crucial Conflict. Although the L.A. rappers' commitment to jazz was strictly in line with their deep understanding of African American music, their quest to make hip-hop more complex would be short-circuited by Kerouac-reading, goateed acid jazz hipsters.

what to buy: By 1991, a loosely configured federation of Good Life alumni calling themselves the Freestyle Fellowship was committing itself to wax on its self-released *To Whom It May Concern* 𝄞𝄞𝄞𝄞 (Sun, 1991, prod. various). The record took on mythic status in some quarters, as much for what it represented as for what it did and said musically. Taking seriously the collectivist vibe of the Native Tongues Movement, vibrant local scenes based around college radio, fanzines, and small open-mic cafes were springing up across the nation. Hip-hop that experimented with jazz structures was the emerging sound of choice. Freestyling—the improvisation of lyrics in shifting rhythmic patterns—was the new standard. Nostalgia for long microphone sessions was chic. Anti–major label independence, articulated by A Tribe Called Quest on *The Low End Theory*'s "Check the Rhime," presented the first sustained do-it-yourself move by hip-hop artists. *To Whom It May Concern* manifests all of these trends, along with a respect for diversity of sound. This diversity makes the album exciting. There are J-Sumbi's political attacks on government on "Legal Alien" and on wack East Coast rhymers on "Sunshine Men." There's Mikah Nine's (here as "Microphone Mike") leaps into rap-scatting and horror-flick psychedelia ("Five O'Clock Follies," "Seventh Seal"); the off-center word experiments of Self-Jupiter ("Jupiter's Journey"); and the Langston Hughes B-boy rebel style of Aceyalone ("My Fantasy," "Here I Am"). Down to Mikah Nine, Self-Jupiter, Aceyalone, and new member Peace, the Fel-

lowship refines its attack on *Inner City Griots* 𝄞𝄞𝄞𝄞 (Island, 1993, prod. Earthquake Brothers, Freestyle Fellowship). The group's musical mission is nothing less than to show that Louis Armstrong, Eddie Jefferson, Art Blakey's Jazz Messengers, and John Coltrane all belong in a deconstructed version of hip-hop. Their approach and their lyrics seem to summon entropy, even while proclaiming "Everything's Everything." Undeniably, tracks like "Hot Potato" and "Cornbread" are hip-hop. But the Freestyle Fellowship forces the listener to answer the question *How?* To those in 1993 for whom hip-hop had become wallpaper music, the challenge was too much. Ignored by everyone except a sizable cult following, the artists went their own ways in 1994—and in Self-Jupiter's tragic case, to jail.

what to buy next: Aceyalone's *All Balls Don't Bounce* 𝄞𝄞𝄞 (Capitol, 1995, prod. Aceyalone, others) is somewhat of a disappointment. A whimsical personality of protean poetic strength on the first two Fellowship albums, Acey is less cohesive over a wide-ranging solo record. There are moments of brilliance, however (the exciting microphone session with Abstract Rude and Mikah Nine of "Knownots," the engaging beat politics of "Headaches and Woes," the spraycan rhythms of "Arhythmaticulas," the deadpan delivery of "I Think") that are insistent enough for all but the most jaded to be hopeful about a hip-hop alternative.

the rest:
Project Blowed 𝄞𝄞𝄞 (Afterlife, 1994/1995)

worth searching for: The underground is always churning with live bootlegs, demos, and rumors of Freestyle Fellowship tracks. One of the more rewarding finds is Abstract Rude's 1996 promotional single, *Oooo I'ma Getcha/Left Hand Sided/Shogun* 𝄞𝄞𝄞 on Grand Royal.

influences:

◄◄ Watts Prophets, De La Soul, Ultramagnetic MC's, Organized Konfusion

►► Bay Area hip-hop underground, Abstract Rude, Bone Thugs-N-Harmony, Crucial Conflict, Busta Rhymes, Wu-Tang Clan

Jeff "DJ Zen" Chang

Don Friedman

Born May 4, 1935, in San Francisco, CA.

Don Friedman began piano studies at age five and acquired an extensive classical background. He began playing professionally in the mid-1950s and worked with many of the most prominent musicians then in California. From the outset of his career, Friedman worked in both the modern mainstream and the avant-garde, playing with Dexter Gordon, Chet Baker, and Ornette Coleman in 1956–57. After moving to New York, he worked with Pepper Adams and his own trio, beginning a series of trio records for Riverside in 1961. In 1964 Friedman was part of trio with Jimmy Giuffre alongside Barre Phillips on bass, a group that unfortunately never recorded. In the same period he co-led a quartet with Hungarian guitarist Attila Zoller that often successfully combined the subtle and experimental interaction of its leaders with potent and changing rhythm sections. In the decades since his New York arrival, Friedman has taught at New York University, spent many years as Clark Terry's regular pianist, and performed regularly in America and abroad in solo dates, duets, and trios. An exceptional pianist, Friedman's subtle skills have often been overlooked, but over his career he has played in a surprising range of settings. He has been as impressive in highly improvised sessions as he is exploring the harmonic potential of a ballad, though it's the lyrical side that predominates in currently available issues.

what to buy: Friedman is featured on his live-recorded solo piano album, *Maybeck Recital Hall Series, Volume 33* ₰₰₰₰ (Concord, 1994, prod. Nick Phillips), a gorgeous solo program, fluid and luminous, with layers of musical invention. Its highlights include "Alone Together," one of Friedman's favorite ballads, and "Memory for Scotty," a tribute to the bassist Scott LaFaro. *The Days of Wine and Roses* ₰₰₰₰ (Soul Note, 1997, prod. Flavio Bonandrini) is an excellent recent trio set that alternates chordal approaches with pieces of free improvisation.

what to buy next: Friedman's first record as leader, *A Day in the City* ₰₰₰₰ (Riverside, 1961/OJC, 1991, prod. Orrin Keepnews) is also one of his most ambitious, a six-part suite that mixes techniques and harmonic languages from jazz and modern European music with excellent support from Chuck Israels and Joe Hunt. Another fine performance is *Opus de Amor* ₰₰₰₰ (Sackville, 1992, prod. John Norris), a series of duets with bassist Don Thompson that includes Friedman's durable originals "Circle Waltz" and "Flashback."

best of the rest:
Circle Waltz ₰₰₰ (Riverside, 1962/OJC, 1996)
Flashback ₰₰₰ (Riverside, 1963/OJC, 1997)
I Hear a Rhapsody ₰₰₰ (Stash, 1994)
My Romance ₰₰₰ (SteepleChase, 1997)

worth searching for: Friedman does a fine job of enriching the distinctive harmonies of Booker Little's *Out Front* ₰₰₰₰ (Can-

did, 1961/1987, prod. Nat Hentoff), a masterpiece of jazz composition. His gift for spontaneous interaction is apparent with Lee Konitz and Attila Zoller on the recent *Thingen* ₰₰₰₰ (hat ART, 1996, prod. Pia Uehlinger, Werner X. Uehlinger), a live performance that celebrates improvisation at its most refined.

influences:
◀◀ Bill Evans, Paul Bley

Stuart Broomer

Johnny Frigo

Born John Virgil Frigo, December 27, 1916, in Chicago, IL.

Johnny Frigo began playing violin as a boy in grade school and switched to the tuba and bass in high school. He made his living as a bassist, playing in small groups such as the Four Californians (a lounge act) from 1934–40, and in the Chico Marx band in 1943–45 as a musician-comedian (singer Mel Tormé was in the group). Frigo joined the Jimmy Dorsey band where he played bass and violin from 1945–47, then left and formed an instrumental-vocal group, Soft Winds Trio, in which he played bass with Dorsey bandmate, guitarist Herb Ellis, and pianist Lou Carter from 1947–52. Their compositions for the group, "Detour Ahead," and "I Told Ya I Love Ya, Now Get Out" were popular and have been recorded by many jazz singers (Billie Holiday, Anita O'Day, etc.). In the 1950s Frigo freelanced in Chicago, did TV and commercial studio work (composing and arranging jingles), recorded as sideman with Dick Marx, Dave Remington, and Buddy Greco, and made one LP as leader (playing violin) for Mercury. During the 1960s he led his own trio at various Chicago clubs and collaborated with singer Mara Lynn Brown, arranging music for and directing her touring band, and playing on her Decca album. Most of his career as a professional musician has been devoted to commercial studio work (he won a Chicago Emmy Award as best lyricist for radio and TV commercials), playing bass on everything from the Pepsodent commercial to Dinah Washington's *What a Difference a Day Makes*. In the 1980s he left studio work to concentrate on jazz violin, guested on an album with Monty Alexander, and became an overnight smash. At age 73 his violin playing and comedic wit were highlighted in two appearances on the *Tonight Show* with Johnny Carson. Frigo has recorded more often as sideman, appearing on a 1991 Herb Ellis recording for Justice (*Roll Call*), and on young John Piazzarelli's 1996 hit album *One Night with You*, but his two albums as leader for Chesky best demonstrate his artistry. Frigo is also an artist who has had one-man shows of his paintings and pastels.

what's available: At the time *Debut of a Legend* 🎻🎻🎻🎻 (Chesky, 1994, prod. David Chesky, Steve Kaiser) was released, Frigo only had one other recording as leader, made for Mercury in the 1950s, and long out of print. *Debut of a Legend* is a lush and lively session of 12 standards (two originals) with backing from guitarist Gene Bertoncini, bassist Michael Moore, drummer Bill Goodwin, pianist Joe Vito, and guest Bob Kindred (tenor sax and clarinet). Digging into his 50-year repertoire, Frigo waxes nostalgic with "I'm Old Fashioned," "Jitterbug Waltz," "I Love Paris," "Here's That Rainy Day," "Lush Life," and other tunes that he translates into his friendly language. Jazz violin albums remain a rarity and Frigo, in his distinctive style, has created a most enjoyable session. An equally enjoyable album, *Live from Studio in New York City* 🎻🎻🎻🎻 (Chesky, 1989, prod. David Chesky) features Frigo with Bucky Pizzarelli and a supreme rhythm team with bassist Ron Carter or Michael Moore, and drummer Butch Miles. Guitarist John Pizzarelli Jr. also joins the festivities. Frigo and Pizzarelli first met in 1988 at Dick Gibson's annual jazz party in Denver, two months before this album was made. Their compatibility is immediately evident and they deliver a mix of 14 lively and lovely tunes, commendable for a version of the Frigo-Carter-Ellis classic "Detour Ahead," smartly swinging chestnuts such as "Do Nothing 'till You Hear from Me" and "Stompin' at the Savoy," hot swingers like "Just Friends" and "The Song Is You," and nostalgic ballads such as "Early Autumn" and "In a Sentimental Mood." Buy both albums and you'll have a complete picture of Frigo's violin mastery.

worth searching for: You'll find fine examples of Frigo's playing on Herb Ellis's *Roll Call* 🎻🎻🎻🎻 (Justice, 1991, prod. Randall Hage Jamail), an exciting session of 11 improvised swingers and standards recorded with B-3 organist Melvin Rhyne, drummer Jake Hanna, and Jay Thomas (tenor sax, flugelhorn). Frigo *is* wonderful in his interactions with Ellis on the appropriately titled, "Isn't It Wonderful."

influences:

◄◄ Stephane Grappelli, Joe Venuti, Stuff Smith

►► Vassar Clements, Matt Glaser, Randy Sabien, Tom Morley

Nancy Ann Lee

Bill Frisell

Born March 18, 1951, in Baltimore, MD.

Bill Frisell's imagination transcends the boundaries of jazz to incorporate spacey soundscapes, country music and Ameri-

cana, the avant-garde, pop and rock, and classical music. His best pure jazz playing can be heard on Paul Motian albums (*The Story of Maryam*, *Jack of Clubs*, *Misterioso*, and especially the trio outings *One Time Out* and *Trioism*); his most far-out and hard-edged sonic adventures come in John Zorn's boundary-smashing group Naked City. His own albums cover the broad range of territory in between those poles.

Frisell grew up in Denver, Colorado. His first instruments were clarinet and alto saxophone. After music studies at the University of North Colorado and Berklee College and private lessons with respected mainstream jazz guitarists Dale Bruning, Jim Hall, and Johnny Smith, Frisell launched into a career which has found him in demand with many musicians in and out of jazz for his distinctively shimmering, gossamer electric guitar style, which can shade into tougher tones depending on the context. He frequently makes use of electronic effects and treatments, but can express himself with complete success on an acoustic guitar. His jazz employers have ranged from Mike Gibbs, Charlie Haden, Bob Moses and Julius Hemphill to Lyle Mays, Jan Garbarek, and Carla Bley, but a series of early 1990s albums for Nonesuch made him a star in his own right.

what to buy: *Have a Little Faith* 🎸🎸🎸🎸 (Elektra/Nonesuch, 1993, prod. Wayne Horvitz) is a conceptual *tour de force*: lump completely disparate American music into one album to show the diversity of our culture, yet knit it all together into a coherent whole. The latter is the hard part, of course, and there are a couple slips here. On repeated listenings, Sousa's "Washington Post March" comes off as merely a joke, while "When I Fall in Love" is too sappy a standard to redeem. But these are balanced out by the surprising successes. Pop star Madonna's "Live to Tell" is understatedly gorgeous and country singer–songwriter John Hiatt's "Have a Little Faith in Me" is so catchy yet previously unknown that it became Frisell's in-concert "hit." A condensation of Aaron Copland's "Billy the Kid" works as prime Americana, and the two excerpts from Charles Ives's "The 'Saint-Gaudens' in Boston Common" give the album some avant-garde spine. Bob Dylan's "Just Like a Woman" and Muddy Waters's "I Can't Be Satisfied" and "Billy Boy" get reinvented by Frisell and his oddly but effectively instrumented group—Don Byron (clarinet, bass clarinet), Guy Klucevsek (accordion), Kermit Driscoll (electric bass), and Joey Baron (drums).

what to buy next: The guitarist's trio with Driscoll and Baron is caught in a 1991 concert on *Live* 🎸🎸🎸 (Gramavision, 1995, prod. Hans Wendl). The variety of Frisell's tones amazes, matched by the range of his compositions (even within a single piece)—from quiet beauty to coruscating energy, from avant-garde scree to circus glee, from heartfelt reinterpretation ("Have a Little Faith in Me") to menacing atmosphere ("Strange Meeting"), with Driscoll's melodicism and Baron's pointillism folding around every mood change. Baron could be less cute sometimes to better effect, but Frisell's brilliance overshadows minor faults. *Before We Were Born* 🎵🎵🎵 (Elektra/Musician, 1989) is good for a taste of two quartets. Frisell made several albums with The Bill Frisell Band, which included himself, cellist Hank Roberts, Driscoll, and Baron. Here they play the long and evocative "Hard Plains Drifter" (written by Frisell, arranged by John Zorn in his typical hard-cut style) and are augmented by alto saxophonists Julius Hemphill and Billey Drewes and baritone saxist Doug Wieselman for the eclectic suite "Some Song and Dance," which features piquant solos by Hemphill. On three shorter tracks, Frisell works with skronk guitarist Arto Lindsay, keyboardist Peter Scherer (who with Lindsay co-lead the group Ambitious Lovers), and Baron, with Cyro Baptista added on shaker for one track. Because of Zorn and Lindsay, *Before We Were Born* has more of an edge than most of Frisell's albums, and for this occasion Frisell draws more on that aspect of his own playing.

what to avoid: *American Blood/Safety in Numbers* 🎵🎵 (Intuition, 1994, prod. Brian Ales, Bill Frisell, Victor Bruce Godsey) with Brian Ales and Victor Bruce Godsey has its moments, but overall will not be especially rewarding to jazz fans. On the 10-section "Safety in Numbers," Ales uses sampling and electronics to restructure fragments of a 27-minute Frisell guitar improvisation, over which Frisell plays a new live part switching between guitar, ukulele, and banjo. Frisell's pastel tones and spidery lines (with occasional blues and rock allusions) gaining added impact from the abstract yet evocative settings. On "American Blood," Frisell and Ales are joined by poet Godsey, who understatedly speaks and sings meditations on mortality. Listeners may find they don't get back enough to reward the attention required to hear the project's merits.

the rest:
In Line 🎵🎵🎵 (ECM, 1983)
Rambler 🎵🎵🎵🎵 (ECM, 1985)
(With Tim Berne) . . . theoretically 🎵🎵🎵🎵 (Minor Music, 1986)
Lookout for Hope 🎵🎵🎵🎵 (ECM, 1988)
Is That You? 🎵🎵🎵 (Elektra/Musician, 1990)
Where in the World 🎵🎵🎵🎵 (Elektra/Musician, 1991)
This Land 🎵🎵🎵🎵 (Elektra/Nonesuch, 1994)
Go West 🎵🎵🎵 (Elektra/Nonesuch, 1995)

BILL FRISELL (WITH PAUL MOTIAN)

song "Mumbo Jumbo"
album Bill Frisell and Joe Lovano
with Paul Motian in Tokyo
(JMT, 1991)
instrument Guitar

Monster Solo

Music for the Films of Buster Keaton: The High Sign/One Week 🎵🎵🎵 (Elektra/Nonesuch, 1995)
Quartet 🎵🎵🎵🎵 (Elektra/Nonesuch, 1996)
Nashville 🎵🎵🎵 (Elektra/Nonesuch, 1997)
Gone, Just Like a Train 🎵🎵🎵 (Elektra/Nonesuch, 1998)

worth searching for: Issued by a German label, *Smash & Scatteration* 🎵🎵🎵🎵 (Minor Music, 1985, prod. David Breskin), with Vernon Reid, is one of the most unusual items in Frisell's discography. He plays a spacey-sounding Roland 300 guitar synthesizer on most of the tracks, which are all duets with fellow guitarist Vernon Reid (leader of Living Colour/former member of Ronald Shannon Jackson's Decoding Society) except for one solo Reid track. They split the composing. Jazz purists may be put off by the drum machines, but then, jazz purists are probably already missing out on Frisell's sonic wizardry. The delight both players take in the multiplicity of sounds they can create (Reid pulls out his six-string banjo for the occasion) is infectious, and there are enough tracks typical of Frisell's sound that his fans can ease into the album slowly. The multiple-artist compilation *A Confederacy of Dances Vol. 1* ♫♫♫ (Einstein, 1992, prod. Jim Staley, David Weinstein) offers an even more unusual side of Frisell: a solo live free improvisation on electric guitar which shows his dark side (sonically speaking, of course).

influences:

◀◀ John Abercrombie, Bern Nix, Sonny Sharrock, Jimi Hendrix, Jim Hall, Johnny Smith, Wes Montgomery

▶▶ Ben Monder, Rolf Sturm, John Scofield

see also: *Naked City, Power Tools*

Steve Holtje

David Frishberg

Born March 23, 1933, in St. Paul, MN.

A clever lyricist and pianist, Dave Frishberg has written dozens of humorous, sophisticated tunes that have been recorded by numerous singers. After studying journalism at the University of Minnesota and spending a couple of years in the U.S. Air Force, Frishberg moved to New York in 1957. A fine swing pianist, he manned the rhythm sections of notables such as Al Cohn, Zoot Sims, and Gene Krupa. In addition, he accompanied a very diverse group of singers, including Carmen McRae, Jimmy Rushing, and Anita O'Day. Frishberg began writing songs during the 1960s, and continues today. After moving to Los Angeles in 1971, he began writing for both television and motion pictures. Since starting to perform his own material regularly during the late 1970s, he has performed around the world. His classic, very "hip" tunes, include "The Underdog," "Peel Me a Grape," "Sweet Kentucky Ham," "My Attorney Bernie," "Van Lingo Mungo," "I'm Hip," "Z's," and "Quality Time," among many others. His remarkably quirky lyrics put a stamp on Frishberg as a unique musical voice in the jazz world.

what to buy: One of the most clever lyricists alive today, Frishberg is a delight. As a very accomplished pianist, he swings, and always injects the humor of the lyrics onto the piano keys. *Live at Vine Street* ♫♫♫♫ (OJC, 1984/1994) captures the enjoyment of a live Frishberg performance. The session includes "One Horse Town," "The Dear Departed Past," and "Blizzard of Lies," as well as a "Johnny Hodges Medley." *Can't Take You Nowhere* ♫♫♫♫ (Fantasy, 1986, prod. Dave Frishberg) includes the title cut, as well as one of his all-time classics "My Attorney Bernie" (which is often performed in live performances by singer-pianist Blossom Dearie), "Sweet Kentucky Ham," and Frishberg's ever popular "I'm Hip." *Quality Time* ♫♫♫♫ (Sterling,

1993, prod. Dave Frishberg) finds Frishberg working with a group that includes Phil Baker, Gary Hobbs, Lee Wuthenow, and Rich Cooper. In addition to the humorous title cut, he charms us with "Eloise," "Dear Bix," and "Matty," and other original tunes. *Getting Some Fun out of Life* ♫♫♫♫ (Concord, 1977, prod. Carl E. Jefferson) is a recording dedicated to the rarely performed work of several composers, including Bix Beiderbecke's "In a Mist," Billy Strayhorn's "Violet Blue," and Fats Waller's "Alligator Crawl." Frishberg wrote all the arrangements and fully captures the beauty and spirit of each tune. In addition to Frishberg, the quintet features Bob Findley, Marshal Royal, Larry Gales, and Steve Schaeffer. Recorded with bassist Steve Gilmore and drummer Bill Goodwin, *Classics* ♫♫♫♫ (Concord, 1983/1991, prod. Bill Goodwin, Chris Fichera) contains many of Frishberg's most notable crafted tunes documented in session during the early to mid-1980s. Frishberg plays piano and sings with bassist Steve Gillmore and drummer Bill Goodwin. His infectiously warm and witty performances include tunes such as "Blizzard of Lies," "Slappin' the Cakes on Me," "My Swan Song," and others.

what to buy next: Opening with the tune "Brenda Starr," the mood of *Let's Eat Home* ♫♫♫ (Concord, 1989, prod. Dave Frishberg, Nick Phillips) continues to escalate with humor and originality, offering another remarkable script from Frishberg and an all-star cast featuring Rob McConnell (valve trombone), Snooky Young (trumpet), Jim Hughart (bass), and Jeff Hamilton (drums). "Matty" and "The Mooche" were "Lookin' Good," and emphatically proclaimed, "Let's Eat Home" tonight, and watch "The Underdog" cast off on "A Ship without a Sail," with a salute to both Al Cohn and Billy Strayhorn. Title-puns aside, this CD features Frishberg at his best. He and cornetist Jim Goodwin collaborate on *Double Play* ♫♫♫ (Arbors, 1992, prod. Rachel Domber, Mat Domber), performing some rare gems such as Irving Berlin's "Russian Lullaby," Billy Hill's "There's a Cabin in the Pines," Cole Porter's "Rosalie," and others. However, there are no original Frishberg tunes included. *Not a Care in the World* ♫♫♫ (Arbors, 1995, prod. Rebecca Kilgore, Dave Frishberg) was recorded with vocalist Rebecca Kilgore and guitarist Dan Faehnle. This session is not a "must have" for Frishberg fans; the vocals lack depth and there are no original Frishberg tunes included on the CD.

influences:

◀◀ Jimmy Rowles, Hank Jones

▶▶ Blossom Dearie

Susan K. Berlowitz

Curtis Fuller

Born December 15, 1934, in Detroit, MI.

Along with J.J. Johnson, Curtis Fuller presents the quintessence of modern trombone playing, with a technical command and fluid sound that set him apart from the swing players that came before him. Picking up the horn at the age of 16, he had the choice opportunity to be part of a fertile Detroit jazz scene that found Donald Byrd, Louis Hayes, Kenny Burrell, Pepper Adams, Tommy Flanagan, and many others, among his peers. Fuller's first important gig was with Yusef Lateef's group, which brought him to New York in the Spring of 1957. Very soon, he became a hot commodity on the scene. Within an eight-month span he recorded six albums as a leader (two on Prestige, the rest on Blue Note) and appeared as sideman on 15 others. Following a brief stay with the Jazztet (which also featured Art Farmer and Benny Golson), Fuller would work with Art Blakey's Jazz Messengers from 1961–1965. Since the 1970s, Fuller has toured with the Count Basie Band, the Timeless All-Stars, Benny Golson, and numerous groups of his own. Indeed, Fuller remains one of the music's most valuable and legendary practitioners of the jazz trombone.

what to buy: *The Complete Blue Note/United Artists Curtis Fuller Sessions* 𝄞𝄞𝄞𝄞 (Mosaic Records, 1996, prod. Michael Cuscuna, Charlie Lourie), a three-CD (five-LP) boxed set only available by mail order, presents the original Blue Note albums *The Opener*, *Bone and Bari*, *Curtis Fuller/Art Farmer*, and *Two Bones*. In addition, you get the previously hard-to-find *Sliding Easy* date from 1959. A must-hear, this is really the smartest place to experience Fuller at his best and in the company of stellar sidemen. The great sound and packaging also make this one a real keeper!

what to buy next: *New Trombone* 𝄞𝄞𝄞 (Prestige, 1957, prod. Ozzie Cadena) was Fuller's strong debut set as a leader, with the alto saxophone work of Sonny Red as an added treat. *Blues-Ette* 𝄞𝄞𝄞𝄞 (Savoy, 1959, prod. Ozzie Cadena) is one of Fuller's most successful and best-known dates. Benny Golson and Tommy Flanagan are on hand and the results are simply sublime. *The Curtis Fuller Jazztet with Benny Golson* 𝄞𝄞𝄞𝄞 (Savoy, 1959, prod. Ozzie Cadena) was the first appearance of a now-legendary group before Golson and Art Farmer took over the name. Among those stoking the fires are Lee Morgan and Wynton Kelly.

the rest:
Curtis Fuller with Red Garland 𝄞𝄞𝄞𝄞 (Prestige/New Jazz, 1957)
Imagination 𝄞𝄞𝄞 (Savoy, 1960)

Images of Curtis Fuller 𝄞𝄞𝄞 (Savoy, 1960)
Four on the Outside 𝄞𝄞𝄞 (Timeless, 1978)
Blues-Ette, Part 2 𝄞𝄞𝄞𝄞 (Savoy, 1993)

influences:

◀◀ Jimmy Cleveland, Urbie Green, Bob Brookmeyer

▶▶ Frank Lacy, Steve Davis, Robin Eubanks

Chris Hovan

Kenny G

Born Kenny Gorelick, June 5, 1957, in Seattle, WA.

Thanks to his knack for a catchy melody and willingness to offer material excruciatingly calculated for wide appeal, saxophonist Kenny G has become something of a punch line in the jazz world—the name you invoke whenever discussing a sell-out, contrived musical effort. Yet, beneath his thicket of curly hair and pop ambitions lie the talent and ability of a master musician. Thrust into the world of professional gigs at age 17, after getting the call to substitute on a show by Barry White's Love Unlimited Orchestra, scrawny Kenneth Gorelick was hooked. A few years later, Gorelick graduated magna cum laude from the University of Washington's business school right into a four-year stint with the Jeff Lorber Fusion, from 1979 through 1982. With Lorber, he learned the ins and outs of the 1980s-era fusion scene, recording his own self-titled solo disc in 1982. Two years later, the saxophonist enlisted Kashif as a producer for his second record, which sold 200,000 copies. Still, it wasn't until his fourth effort, 1986's *Duotones*, that Gorelick perfected the blend of jazz polish and funk-tinged backing grooves that would make his fortune. Powered by the #4 hit "Songbird"—with the novelty of an extra-long note held through circular breathing methods—this album would begin a string of pop success that helped create the modern "smooth jazz" phenomenon. Though some called it "fuzak"—think muzak and fusion together—Gorelick's material produced hit albums in 1988 and 1992, proving his greatest asset was in giving people what they wanted with a nice guy image so squeaky clean, even President Bill Clinton could name him as a favorite without fear. Most recently, he entered the Guinness Book of World Records after holding a single note for 45 minutes.

what to buy: Assuming you can stand his elevator-ready pop stuff, *Silhouette* ♪♪♪ (Arista, 1988, prod. Kenny G, Peter Bunetta, Rick Chudacoff, Preston Glass) offers the best songs, including a touching duet with Smokey Robinson called "We've Saved the Best for Last." And no Kenny G collection would be complete without the album containing "Songbird," *Duotones* ♪♪♪ (Arista, 1986, prod. Preston Glass, Kenny G), a break-through that proved that well-calculated, jazz-tinged pop in-strumental music could top the charts in a big way.

what to buy next: Even though the songs themselves are dead on arrival, the instrumental performances by Kenny G's crack band on the concert disc *Live* ♪♪♪ (Arista, 1989, prod. Kenny G) are spot on—including a bombastic drum solo and kinetic bass workout that lend some life to the saxophonist's bland material.

what to avoid: During the recording of *Kenny G* **woof!** (Arista, 1986, prod. Jeff Lorber) the G-man let producer Jeff Lorber stamp his own personal vision on the proceedings, resulting in a formless collection of tunes that makes the saxophonist sound like a sideman on his own record.

the rest:
G Force ♪♪ (Arista, 1983)
Gravity ♪♪ (Arista, 1985)
Breathless ♪♪ (Arista, 1992)
Miracles: The Holiday Album ♪♪ (Arista, 1994)
The Moment ♪♪ (Arista, 1996)
Greatest Hits ♪♪♪ (Arista, 1997)

worth searching for: Look for Kenny G's team-up with Frank Sinatra on the legendary singer's first *Duets* ♪♪♪ record (Capi-tol, 1993, prod. various) on "All the Way/One For My Baby (And One More for the Road)."

influences:
◀◀ David Sanborn, Spyro Gyra, Jeff Lorber
▶▶ Dave Koz, Boney James, Marion Meadows, Everette Harp

Eric Deggans

Charles Gabriel

Born July 11, 1932, in New Orleans, LA.

Born into the fourth generation of a New Orleans jazz family, saxophone and clarinet player Charles Gabriel began playing professionally at age 11 and worked with family bands and such revered elders as T. Boy Rena's Eureka Jazz Band, Kid Howard, George Lewis, and Kid Sheik. A family move to Detroit in the 1940s resulted in work with Lionel Hampton's young be-boppers, Joe Simon and Motown. While in France with Aretha Franklin in the early '70s, a French critic recognized Gabriel's essentially New Orleans solo style and expressed musical knowledge of Gabriel's grandfather and uncles. Gabriel then devoted himself to exploring roots musical traditions, leading his own bands and working with J.C. Heard, Trevor Richards, Jay McShann, and others.

what to buy: The Hot Club of France gave its 1995 Grand Prix for best foreign record to Gabriel and Red Richards' *Live at the Kerrytown Concert House* ♪♪♪♪ (Gabriel Historical Society, 1995, prod. Charles Gabriel), a duet between two performers each with a personal style yet providing a link with the past. *Gabriel Traditional Jazz Band* ♪♪♪♪ (Gabriel Historical Society, 1992, prod. Charles Gabriel) is a New Orleans traditional outing featuring his uncle—bassist Percy Gabriel—yet pursuing inter-pretations informed by modernism with the likes of trumpeter Marcus Belgrave and avant-gardists Tanni Tabbal and Jaribu Shahid.

what to buy next: *Charlie Gabriel & Friends in Asia* ♪♪♪ (Poly-dor, 1987) features a more contemporary approach, with side-men including El Dee Young and Red Holt on standards and Gabriel originals such as "Miranda" and "I'm Free."

influences:
◀◀ Sidney Bechet, Lucky Thompson, Illinois Jacquet

Larry Gabriel

Steve Gadd

Born April 9, 1945, in Rochester, NY.

One of the most recorded session drummers ever, Steve Gadd has had a truly impressive career and has made a major impact on music and drumming over a three-decade period. His per-forming and recording credits span artists as diverse as Steely Dan, Chuck and Gap Mangione, Chick Corea, Spyro Gyra, Paul McCartney, Paul Simon, Eric Clapton, Frank Sinatra, Rickie Lee Jones, Stuff, the Buddy Rich Big Band, and countless others. Al-though in semi-retirement, Gadd continues to tour and record and will remain a major influence on generations of drummers to come.

what to buy: Featuring Gadd's old Stuff bandmates Richard Tee on keyboards and Cornell Dupree on guitar, plus Eddie Gomez

on bass and an all-star horn section led by Ronnie Cuber and Dave Matthews, *The Gadd Gang* ♫♫♫♪ (Columbia, 1987, prod. Steve Gadd, Kiyoshi Itoh) is Gadd's only in-print album as a leader on a major label. It's not for the "straight-ahead only" fans—R&B, gospel, funk, Latin, blues, pop ballads, and soul all combine to make a tasty blend on his debut album as a leader. Gadd even turns in some convincing scat singing ("Strength") and a surprise Billy Vera-esque lead vocal ("Everything You Do"). A great arrangement of "Honky-Tonk"/"I Can't Stop Loving You" is dedicated to Count Basie and Ray Charles.

the rest:
Gaddabout ♫♫♫ (Pro Jazz, 1988)
Best of Steve Gadd ♫♫♫ (Pro Jazz, 1988)

worth searching for: *Stuff* ♫♫♪ (Warner Bros., 1978, prod. Steve Cropper) is somewhat dated but still-interesting funk-fusion-pop-soul with a band of top session players including Cornell Dupree, Gordon Edwards, Richard Tee, and Eric Gale. It features both Chris Parker and Steve Gadd on drums. *Burning for Buddy—Vols. I and II* ♫♫♫♫ (Atlantic, 1996 and 1997, prod. Neil Peart) is a tribute album featuring top jazz and rock drummers sitting in with the Buddy Rich Big Band. Gadd is showcased on both albums.

influences:
◀◀ John Guerin, Harvey Mason, Max Roach, Mel Lewis
▶▶ Jeff Porcaro, Dave Weckl

Gregg Juke

Slim (Bulee) Gaillard
Born January 1, 1916, in Detroit, MI. Died February 26, 1991, in London, England.

The brightest light of a group of hipster musicians that included Babs Gonzalez, Jack McVea, Leo Watson, and Harry "The Hipster" Gibson, Slim Gaillard combined subversive humor and swinging jazz in a unique way.

At age 12, Slim shipped out with his father on the SS Republic, only to be accidentally left ashore in Crete for six months (where he claimed to have become fluent in Greek, Turkish, and Portuguese). He arrived in New York City in 1936 and hooked up with bassist Slam Stewart at Jock's Place in Harlem the next year. Securing a recording contract with the help of influential New York disc jockey Martin Block, Slim and Slam recorded for Vocalion and OKeh between 1938 and 1942. Their tune "Flat Foot Floogee" became a huge hit (for themselves and for Benny Goodman) and made Gaillard a celebrity. Slim and Slam combined swinging vocals and humorous delivery to great effect. An important part of this was Gaillard's invention of his hipster double talk, "vout" ("oreenie, oroonie," etc.). After spending 1943–45 in the Army Air Corps, Gaillard teamed with bassist "Bam" Brown and headed to the West Coast (during which time he encountered Jack Kerouac, who wrote about him in *On the Road*). In late 1945 he recorded with Brown, Zutty Singleton, and Dodo Marmarosa for a number of small labels (Cadet, Atomic, Bel-Tone, etc.) and headed a legendary session with visiting East Coast bop dignitaries Dizzy Gillespie and Charlie Parker. He was signed by Norman Granz in 1946 and for the next six years recorded for Clef, Norgran, and Verve. Between 1954 and his death Gaillard recorded sporadically, spending more time working in films and television, experiencing a resurgence in popularity in England during the 1980s.

what to buy: There are two essential Gaillard compilations out on major labels. *Slim and Slam: The Groove Juice Special* ♫♫♫♫ (Columbia Legacy, 1996, prod. Michael Brooks) features the best of his 1938–1942 recordings including "Flat Foot Floogee," "Matzoh Balls," the title cut, and the rare "African Jive." *Slim Gaillard: Laughing in Rhythm* ♫♫♫♫ (Verve, 1994, prod. Michael Lang) has the best of his Verve recordings, including the "vout" masterworks "Opera in Vout" and "Yip Roc Heresy."

what to buy next: You can find all of the collaborations with Dizzy and Bird as well as some rare sessions on *Slim's Jam* ♫♫♫ (Drive Archive, 1996 , prod. Lynn Francy). *Slim Gaillard: Birdland 1951* ♫♫♫ (Hep, 1995, prod. Alastair Robertson) contains Symphony Sid air checks from 1951 with appearances by Terry Gibbs, Eddie "Lockjaw" Davis, and Art Blakey.

the rest:
Slim Gaillard 1945 Vol. 1 ♫♫♫ (Classics, 1995)
Slim Gaillard 1945 Vol. 2 ♫♫♫♫ (Classics, 1996)
Slim Gaillard 1940–1942 ♫♫♫ (Classics, 1996)

influences:
◀◀ Fats Waller, Mills Brothers
▶▶ Bob Dorough

Larry Grogan

Eric Gale
Born September 20, 1938, in Brooklyn, NY. Died, May 25, 1994, in Baja California, Mexico.

During the 1960s, after teaching himself to play guitar, Eric Gale lent his identifiable style blending elements of R&B and improvised jazz with funk rhythms to stints and/or recordings with R&B artists King Curtis, Maxine Brown, and Little Anthony and the Imperials. From the early 1970s, he was the session guitarist of choice (especially for CTI), recording and playing on hundreds of jazz, R&B, and pop albums during his career. Among the jazz artists he collaborated with were Carla Bley, Mose Allison, Johnny Hodges, and Grover Washington Jr. A very versatile player, his style was bluesy and somewhat laid back, though he could burn when necessary. Gale was part of the group Stuff, formed with Bob James, Steve Gadd, Richard Tee, and others, and was also the guitarist in the Tom Scott Band when they were the orchestra for the short lived *Pat Sajak* TV show. Like most session players, Gale was a bit of a chameleon, and recorded several dates as a leader, most in the R&B-flavored jazz mode. At the peak of his popularity in the 1970s, he was somewhat overshadowed by the younger Grammy-winning studio musician, Earl Klugh, whose fusion-styled jazz drew from some of the same influences, but had more vitality. Gale died of lung cancer at the age of 55.

what to buy: Originally released as two separate LPs, *Ginseng Woman/Multiplication* 𝄢𝄢𝄢 (Columbia 1977/Legacy, 1991, prod. Bob James) offers 12 selections to satisfy the jazz-funk yearnings in your soul. The selections from *Ginseng Woman* feature a slew of artists, vocalists, strings, and highlights the guitarist mixing it up with notables such as keyboardists Bob James and Richard Tee, drummer Steve Gadd, saxophonist Grover Washinton Jr., and other jazz-funk fusion luminaries. With most arrangements by Bob James, it's still a satisfying listen today for contemporary jazz fans. *Multiplication* included Gale versions of "Sometimes I Feel Like a Motherless Child," "Thumper," "Morning Glory," and three more tunes, but *Ginseng Woman* was the more popular album. While Gale improvises pleasingly in relaxed style on the genre's typical smooth arrangements, he's doesn't make any significant contribution to the art form.

the rest:
Blue Horizon 𝄢𝄢𝄢 (Elektra/Discovery, 1988)
In the Shade of a Tree 𝄢𝄢𝄢 (JVC Classics, 1991/1995)

worth searching for: *In a Jazz Tradition* 𝄢𝄢𝄢 (EmArcy, 1989) finds Gale playing straight-ahead on this out-of-print date, one of the few occasions he chose to do so as a leader. There's nothing of earth-shattering value here, but it's nice to hear Gale actually stretch out and the playing is good.

influences:
◀◀ Charlie Christian, Kenny Burrell, Phil Upchurch, Grant Green, Pat Martino, Wes Montgomery

▶▶ Larry Carlton, Robben Ford, Henry Johnson

Paul MacArthur and Nancy Ann Lee

Hal Galper
Born April 18, 1938, in Salem, MA.

An excellent and highly flexible post-bop pianist, Hal Galper has played in a wide variety of contexts with many of the leading figures in jazz. He studied classical music from 1945–48 and, while attending Berklee in 1955–58, broke into the Boston jazz scene. Galper quickly began working with the city's most creative players, including Herb Pomeroy's big band, Sam Rivers' quartet, and Tony Williams' groups. He became a highly desired accompanist in the 1960s, touring with Chet Baker, Bobby Hutcherson, the Brecker Brothers, Joe Henderson, Stan Getz, and the singers Joe Williams, Chris Connor, and Anita O'Day. He replaced George Duke in the Cannonball Adderley Quintet (1972–75) and spent almost a decade with Phil Woods, starting in 1982. He has recorded a number of fine albums for Enja and Concord Jazz.

what to buy: Galper's first recording after leaving his long-time employer, Phil Woods, *Live at Maybeck Recital Hall, Volume Six* 𝄢𝄢𝄢𝄢 (Concord Jazz, 1990, prod. Carl E. Jefferson) finds the pianist in an expansive mood, stretching out and relishing the freedom of the solo recital. He incorporates a variety of styles into each piece, often making unexpected juxtapositions, and has no trouble generating serious heat *sans* rhythm section. Highlights include "Airegin" and a funky version of Thelonious Monk's "Bemsha Swing." A loose but hard-charging live session with Galper's working trio augmented by brawny tenor saxophonist Jerry Bergonzi, *Rebop* 𝄢𝄢𝄢 (Enja, 1995, prod. Hal Galper) features five standards and Galper's opening original "All the Things You Aren't." Galper plays with wit and considerable personality, interacting subtly with his long-time collaborator, the brilliant but often-overlooked drummer Steve Ellington. With half of the six tracks more than 10 minutes long, including a muscular version of "Laura," Bergonzi and Galper both have plenty of room.

what to buy next: A subtle, superb trio session displaying Galper's stylistic range, *Invitation to a Concert* 𝄢𝄢𝄢 (Concord Jazz, 1991, prod. Carl E. Jefferson) features bassist Todd Coolman and the brilliant drummer Steve Ellington. Though the program consists mostly of ballads and medium-tempo standards, Galper's arrangements are consistently well crafted. A stylistic excursion to the light, bouncy sound pioneered by Nat "King" Cole and later Ahmad Jamal, *Tippin'* 𝄢𝄢𝄢 (Concord Jazz, 1993, prod. Allen Farnham) is a highly enjoyable trio session featuring Wayne Dockery on bass and Steve Ellington on drums. The trio calls Jamal to mind directly with the arrangements of "Serenata" and "Flamingo," while the gorgeous version of "Ebb Tide" was inspired by pianist Steve Kuhn. Only at the end do they really burn, on Miles Davis's "Solar" (erroneously credited to Thelonious Monk).

best of the rest:

Live—Redux '78 ♫♫♫♫♫ (Concord Jazz, 1978)
Ivory Forest ♫♫♫♫ (Enja, 1980)
Dreamsville ♫♫♫♫ (Enja, 1986)
Portrait ♫♫♫ (Concord Jazz, 1989)
Children of the Night ♫♫♫♫ (Doubletime, 1991)
Just Us ♫♫♫♫ (Enja, 1994)

worth searching for: One of alto saxophonist Cannonball Adderley's best later recordings, *Inside Straight* ♫♫♫♫ (Fantasy, 1973, prod. Orrin Keepnews) features Nat Adderley (cornet), Galper, Walter Booker (bass), Roy McCurdy (drums), and King Errisson (percussion). After seven years at Capitol, Cannonball reunited with former Riverside producer Keepnews at Fantasy and moved back toward jazz after many R&B-oriented sessions. Galper contributed three of the album's seven tunes and plays the greasy, blues-drenched music with authority.

influences:

◀◀ Nat "King" Cole, Wynton Kelly, Ahmad Jamal

Andrew Gilbert

Frank Gambale

Born 1959, in Canberra, Australia.

Nicknamed "the Thunder from down Under," Frank Gambale has drawn lots of notice for his prodigious guitar technique, which fueled the mile-a-minute bombast that made Chick Corea's Elektric Band such a formidable presence. Unfortunately, his taste for recognizable, enjoyable melodies is far less advanced, as his solo albums would suggest. Drawn to the guitar at age seven by rock heroes Jimi Hendrix and Eric Clapton, he journeyed to America at the age of 23 to study at California's Guitar Institute of Technology. He eventually became a teacher there, leaving to record three albums for the tiny Legato label and then touring with jazz-fusion violinist Jean-Luc Ponty. After that tour, Gamble auditioned for the Elektric Band after Corea decided to expand his trio to a quintet. Fond of spiked hair and loud (both sonically and visually) guitars, he lent a bit of rock 'n' roll flair to the Elektric Band's efforts. Six years later, Gambale returned to his solo efforts, assembling a series of dense,

chops-heavy fusion records for JVC that showcased both his "sweep" technique for picking amazingly fast guitar runs and his singing ability.

what to buy: Recorded with drummer Jonathan Mover and bassist Stuart Hamm from rocker Joe Satriani's outfit, *The Great Explorers* ♫♫♫♫ (JVC, 1993, prod. Frank Gambale) finds Gambale plumbing more melodic ground—aping modern-day guitar heroes like Satriani and Steve Vai with simpler song structures, less mind-blowing jazz chops and more emotion—a welcome combination.

what to buy next: The title of *Thinking out Loud* ♫♫♫ (JVC, 1995, prod. Frank Gambale) is a bit of a misnomer—actually, this may be the quietest album the guitarist has ever made. Filled with light, keyboard-based cuts and nimble guitar work, it proves a wonderful departure from the waves of notes that fill most Gamble albums.

what to avoid: So dense and busy you can barely make out song structures, let along melodies, *Frank Gambale Live* **woof!** (Legato, 1989, prod. Frank Gambale, Mark Varney) features all the excesses that make this Aussie guitar god's albums so hard to take: overplaying, lack of melodies, uninspired songs, and egotistical musicianship. It'll give you a headache by the end of the first track.

the rest:

Brave New Guitar ♫♫ (Legato, 1986)
Present for the Future ♫♫ (Legato, 1987)
(With the Elektric Band) *Light Years* ♫♫♫♫ (GRP, 1987)
(With the Elektric Band) *Eye of the Beholder* ♫♫♫ (GRP, 1988)
(With the Elektric Band) *Inside Out* ♫♫♫ (GRP, 1990)
Thunder from Down Under ♫♫♫ (JVC, 1990)
(With the Elektric Band) *Beneath the Mask* ♫♫♫ (GRP, 1991)
Note Worker ♫♫ (JVC, 1991)
Passages ♫♫ (JVC, 1994)

worth searching for: It's hard to believe that the kings of fusion guitar overplaying could team up and make a listenable record, but Gambale and Englishman Allan Holdsworth make beautiful music together on *Truth in Shredding* ♫♫♫ (Legato, 1991, prod. Frank Gambale), a meeting of giants that allows the two to flex their prodigious talents while fleshing out some impressive grooves.

influences:

◀◀ Jeff Beck, Al Di Meola, Allan Holdsworth, Eddie Van Halen
▶▶ Eric Johnson, John Petrucci

Eric Deggans

Ganelin Trio
/Vyacheslav Ganelin

Formed in 1973, in Vilnius, Lithuania, USSR.

Vyacheslav Ganelin, piano, bassett, synths, percussion, electric guitar; Vladimir Tarasov, drums, percussion (1973–86); Vladimir Chekasin, bassett-horn, alto saxophone, tenor saxophone, clarinet, flute (1973–86); Victor Fonarev, cello, bass; Mika Markovich, drums; Uri Abramovich, voice.

Although cultural imperialism might dictate otherwise, it's rather apparent that, for once, the West caught on to something a little bit too late. By the time the Soviet Union's most outrageous and impressive free jazz group made its way to Europe—via a March 1984 concert in London only a couple years after the release of the talismanic *Catalogue* LP—the end was already near and, in 1986, the trio would splinter. Thankfully, however, *glasnost* not only accommodated a handful of shows in the West but also helped make available—via Sonore's CD reissues of the awful, state-run Melodiya pressings—nearly all of the Trio's work prior to the mid-'80s intervention of Leo Records. Originally a duo of Vyacheslav Ganelin and Vladimir Tarasov, the Trio coalesced during a time of Soviet expansion and, ironically, a more liberal state's attitude towards the arts. Mutually frustrated and inspired by the music they were hearing, the three began performing their peculiar brand of improvisational music: three parts jazz, two parts classical, one part performance/folk art. The result was a stunningly dense, occasionally humorous, and consistently exciting body of work that was, for the most part, solely performed in the Soviet Union or in Warsaw Pact states. By the time *Catalogue* (made from tapes that Leo boss Leo Feigin smuggled home to London) was released in 1981, the group was still at the height of its strengths, tightly wound, and capable of just about anything. The aforementioned London show inaugurated a short, sporadic string of performances throughout the West that helped solidify the trio's undeniable impact. Ganelin's immigration to Israel and mounting intra-personal tensions within the group effectively put an end to the Ganelin Trio in 1986. Although Ganelin would briefly reactivate the group—with two new players replacing Tarasov and Chekasin—the magic was obviously gone and, though the records this new Trio released were enjoyable, they certainly weren't up to the high standard set by masterworks like *Concerto Grosso*. Ganelin's two solo LPs, however, are of impeccable quality.

what to buy: For a bunch of dour, Soviet jazzers, *Poco-a-Poco* 🎵🎵🎵🎵🎵 (Leo, 1978/1988) is one hell of a joyous record. Nearly rapturous in its abandon, this live show alternates between gentle romance, subtle impressionism, and all-out aggression. The trio is not only intense, strong, and incredibly focused, but, most importantly, they're obviously having a good time. Ganelin and Chekasin's harmonic interplay is not to be missed. *Concerto Grosso* 🎵🎵🎵🎵 (Sonore, 1980/1995, prod. Peter Motovilov), an extended piece, was one of the Trio's first major studio outings and, not surprisingly, the results are wonderful. Dense, tasteful, and mind-blowingly complex, the composition is majestic in its scope and unremorsefully intense in its delivery. An essential moment. *Catalogue: Live in East Germany* 🎵🎵🎵🎵 (Leo, 1979/1981, prod. Leo Feigin) is the record that, for jazz purposes, helped bring down the Iron Curtain. For it was here that we capitalist scum realized not only how influential our music was (to hear "jazz" translated through cloistered ears is a truly revealing experience), but also exactly how limited and indoctrinated even our most adventurous musicians are. Although it may not be their best recorded moment—Chekasin's playing occasionally falters, but one can blame it on the fact that he's probably laughing—it's certainly their most important.

the rest:
Con Anima 🎵🎵🎵🎵 (Sonore, 1977/1995)
Encores 🎵🎵🎵 (Leo, 1978–81/1994)
Non Troppo 🎵🎵🎵 (hat ART, 1980–82/1990)
Poi Seque 🎵🎵🎵 (Sonore, 1981/1995)
Opus A Duo (Ganelin/Tarasov) 🎵🎵🎵 (Sonore, 1982/1995)
Old Bottles 🎵🎵🎵🎵 (Leo, 1982–83/1995)
Semplice 🎵🎵🎵 (Sonore, 1983/1995)
(With the Rova Saxophone Quartet) *San Francisco Holidays* 🎵🎵🎵 (Leo, 1986)
Opuses 🎵🎵🎵 (Leo, 1989)

worth searching for: Of the few albums released by Ganelin Trio Mk. II, *Jerusalem February Cantabile* 🎵🎵🎵🎵 (Leo, 1989, prod. Leo Feigin) is not only the best, but it actually ranks quite highly with the rest of Ganelin's ouevre. Although Ganelin himself relies a bit too heavily on electronics, the ecstatic atmospherics and surprisingly agile interplay of the Trio makes this surprisingly rewarding.

solo outings:
Vyacheslav Ganelin:
Con Amore 🎵🎵🎵🎵 (Leo, 1986)
On Stage . . . Backstage 🎵🎵🎵 (Leo, 1992)

Jason Ferguson

Gang Starr

Formed 1988, in Brooklyn, NY.

Guru, vocals; DJ Premier, DJ.

Although the hip-hop one-two punch of Guru and DJ Premier use the moniker Gang Starr, the two aren't gangstas: Guru's consciousness-raising lyrics recall KRS-One more than Spice 1, while the gritty, jazzbo-cool backing music supplied by Premier is miles closer to "Doo Bop"–era Miles than "Fuck Tha Police"–era Dre. Influenced by jazz at least as much as any other hip-hop group, Gang Starr understands better than the rest the correlation between jazz and rap—two black art forms with similar cadences that thrive on spontaneous innovation. The group's songs typically feature jazzy basslines, horn riffs, and obscure jazz samples laid out over loose hip-hop beats; many could probably work as instrumental tracks. Yet Guru's conversational, laconic vocals weave perfectly through Premier's raw, soulful, and simple constructions, with neither music nor lyrics fighting for attention. How refreshing. Outside of the Gang Starr format, one-time computer science major Premier has become one of the most sought-after producers in East Coast rap, working with the likes of KRS-One, Nas, Jeru the Damaja and Group Home. Meanwhile, Guru has coordinated two jazz-meets-rap projects under the moniker Jazzmatazz.

what to buy: The minimalist *Daily Operation* ♪♪♪♪ (Chrysalis, 1992, prod. DJ Premier, Guru), which samples artists from Mingus to Byrd, is Gang Starr's best, most consistent album, with the thoughtful "Soliloquy of Chaos" (which warns against the cycle of violence) and the tender, respectful "Ex Girl to the Next Girl" serving as antidotes to the killing and misogyny of the day's dominant style, gangsta-©rap. On the racially concerned "Conspiracy," Guru also attacks the shady side of the rap business—an appropriate topic, perhaps, given that he graduated from Morehouse College with a degree in business. *Guru's Jazzmatazz: Vol. I* ♪♪♪♪ (Chrysalis, 1993, prod. Guru) falls on the other side of the jazz-hop fence, using live contributions from jazz legends (Roy Ayers, Donald Byrd, Lonnie Liston Smith) and comers (Ronny Jordan, N'Dea Davenport, Carleen Anderson) instead of old, dusty samples. It also swings more than any Gang Starr album.

what to buy next: The upbeat *No More Mr. Nice Guy* ♪♪♪♪ (Wild Pitch/EMI, 1989, prod. DJ Premier, Guru) features the tone-setting history lesson, "Jazz Thing," based on a poem by the longtime jazz publicist Elliot Horne. Also included is the hip-hop classic, "Manifest," which makes excellent use of a Dizzy Gillespie sample. On *Hard to Earn* ♪♪♪ (Chrysalis/ERG, 1994, prod.

DJ Premier, Guru), Premier strips away much of the jazz influence to reveal old-school hip-hop roots. Yet Guru's cautionary tone of "Tonz 'O' Gunz" is decidedly '90s.

the rest:
Step in the Arena ♪♪♪ (Chrysalis, 1990)
Jazzmatazz Vol. II: The New Reality ♪♪ (Chrysalis/EMI, 1995)
Guru Presents Ill Kid Records ♪♪♪ (Payday, 1995)
Moment of Truth ♪♪♪ (Noo Trybe/Virgin, 1997)

influences:
◄◄ Miles Davis, Jungle Brothers, Eric B. & Rakim, Poor Righteous Teachers

►► Buckshot LeFonque, the Roots, Ronny Jordan, Bahamadia, Digable Planets, Us3, A Tribe Called Quest, Jeru the Damaja

Josh Freedom du Lac

Jan Garbarek

Born March 4, 1947, in Mysen, Norway.

Garbarek was ECM's flagship artist—his 1970 album *Afric Pepperbird* was the label's first release—and his sound and Manfred Eicher's trademark production seem inextricably intertwined by now. Self-taught, with John Coltrane an early inspiration and a four-year period of collaboration with theoretician/composer George Russell also influential in his playing, Garbarek can often seem to be outside the boundaries of jazz. Detractors would say he is more of a new age artist, or even a classy Kenny G, and certainly he neither swings nor develops his themes the way a bebopper would, but there is a solid jazz precedent in some of the late 1960s work of the Miles Davis Quintet.

what to buy: *I Took Up the Runes* ♪♪♪♪ (ECM, 1990, prod. Manfred Eicher) frequently achieves an ecstatic elevation thanks to Garbarek's incantatory style being matched to some superb themes—the five-section "Molde Canticle" uses the most immediately communicative melody of his career, with the direct simplicity of a folk tune—and the propulsive world music percussion of Manu Katché and Nana Vasconcelos. There are some slow but inexorable crescendos to intense peaks that lift the entire record above the usual atmospheric soundscapes.

what to buy next: *Witchi-Tai-To* ♪♪♪ (ECM, 1973, prod. Manfred Eicher) is credited to the Jan Garbarek–Bobo Stenson Quartet, which includes Palle Danielsson on bass and Jon Christensen on drums. At this point in his career, Garbarek was more assertive and jazz-based in his playing. The peak is the

20-minute excursion on Don Cherry's "Desireless," but the track that got the most attention was Jim Pepper's title tune. *Esoteric Circle* 𝄢𝄢𝄢 (Freedom, 1969, prod. George Russell) is slightly earlier in vintage than the album usually referred to as Garbarek's debut, *Afric Pepperbird*, and offers important pointers to Coltrane and Miles Davis (Wayne Shorter's "Nefertiti").

what to avoid: *Officium* **woof!** (ECM, 1994, prod. Manfred Eicher) ranks high (or low) among the most horribly misguided musical concepts ever recorded. The Hilliard Ensemble, a classical choir, sings Gregorian chant and medieval/early Renaissance works and, on too many tracks, Garbarek improvises over them. It's a worse combination than chocolate and sardines. Less of an abomination but symptomatic of the doldrums Garbarek's 1980s work often sank into is *It's Okay to Listen to the Gray Voice* 𝄢𝄢 (ECM, 1985). The material is bland, and Garbarek—perhaps the album title should be sufficient warning—does not feel the need to rise above it.

best of the rest:
Afric Pepperbird 𝄢𝄢𝄢 (ECM, 1970)
Triptykon 𝄢𝄢𝄢 (ECM, 1973)
Dansere 𝄢𝄢𝄢 (ECM, 1976)
Places 𝄢𝄢𝄢 (ECM, 1978)
Wayfarer 𝄢𝄢 (ECM, 1983)
Star 𝄢𝄢𝄢 (ECM, 1991)
Twelve Moons 𝄢𝄢𝄢 (ECM, 1993)

worth searching for: The out-of-print *Eventyr* 𝄢𝄢𝄢 (ECM, 1981, prod. Manfred Eicher) is a trio with guitarist John Abercrombie and percussionist Nana Vasconcelos, and either they or the use of folk themes seem to stimulate the leader a bit more than on his other guitar-centered albums. Or is it just that Garbarek repeated himself more and more as the decade progressed? Regardless, fans should know that this stands out from the many run-of-the-mill Garbarek albums of the 1980s.

influences:

◀◀ John Coltrane, Wayne Shorter, Charles Lloyd, Miles Davis, Albert Ayler

▶▶ David Darling, Arild Anderson, Ketil Bjørnstad

Walter Faber

Red Garland

Born William M. Garland, May 13, 1923, in Dallas, TX. Died April 23, 1984, in Dallas, TX.

Going from clarinet to saxophone to boxer and finally, to pianist, is no common route to artistic success, but Red Garland was not an ordinary piano player. Nearing the end of his military career he started learning how to play piano, and within a decade of that momentous decision, Garland found himself on the East Coast working with big-league saxophone players like Charlie Parker, Lester Young, and Coleman Hawkins. Despite his acceptance by jazz luminaries of the time, it wasn't until Garland joined Miles Davis in 1955, becoming part of the famous quintet with Davis, John Coltrane, Paul Chambers, and Philly Joe Jones, that he was considered more than just another good sideman. His right-hand filigree combined with the block chording from his left influenced the next generation of pianists. After leaving Davis, Garland performed with his own groups before retiring briefly to Dallas in 1965 when his mother died. He reappeared in concert during the 1970s before finally retiring for real at the end of the decade.

what to buy: *Garland of Red* 𝄢𝄢𝄢𝄢 (OJC, 1956, prod. Bob Weinstock), Garland's first album as a leader, laid the blueprint for most of his prolific trio recordings. The material was a heady blend of pop show tunes, a bebop standard (Charlie Parker's "Constellation"), and an original or two by Garland. His sidemen were among the top players of the day: bassist Paul Chambers, Garland's rhythm partner in the Davis Quintet, and drummer Art Taylor, who had played with Bud Powell, one of Garland's big influences. Combine all those things with the solid, at times inspired, playing of the trio and you have one of the great trio recordings from the mid-1950s. It would be tempting to call *Red in Bluesville* 𝄢𝄢𝄢𝄢 (OJC, 1959, prod. Esmond Edwards) just another Red Garland Trio date, but that would be like calling a Stradivarius "just another violin." This time around Garland goes for the blues roots of jazz with some of his most subtle playing aided by Sam Taylor on bass and the perennial Art Taylor on drums. Garland's version of the traditional "See See Rider" might be the slowest rendition available, but the swing is still there, while "Your Red Wagon" and "He's a Real Gone Guy" reveal their jump-blues heritage.

what to buy next: *Manteca* 𝄢𝄢𝄢𝄢 (OJC, 1958, prod. Bob Weinstock) is the album that gave conga player Ray Barretto some recording credibility within the jazz community. The conga playing works most effectively in the title tune, where there is a long percussive dialog between Barretto and drummer Taylor but, for the balance of the album Barretto is relegated to an incidental background role with occasional brief, yet mild, outbursts. Garland is never less than really good and on the ballad "Portrait of Jenny" (a bonus CD track) his use of block chords for deliciously sustained tension is particularly potent.

what to avoid: *Keystones!* **woof!** (Xanadu, 1977, prod. Leroy Vinnegar, Don Schlitten) was recorded by Leroy Vinnegar on a small portable tape recorder at a gig that he was doing with Garland and Philly Joe Jones. It documents the pianist prior to retiring for the last time and, while the playing can still be very good, it wasn't consistent enough to overcome the amateur quality of the recording, especially when Garland has a huge discography that is, for the most part, still in print. For completists only.

best of the rest:

Groovy 🎵🎵🎵 (OJC, 1957)
(With John Coltrane) *All Mornin' Long* 🎵🎵🎵🎶 (OJC, 1957)
(With John Coltrane) *Soul Junction* 🎵🎵🎵🎶 (OJC, 1957)
Solar 🎵🎵🎵 (OJC, 1962)
Red Alert 🎵🎵🎵🎶 (OJC, 1977)
The P.C. Blues 🎵🎵🎵 (OJC, 1996)

influences:

◀◀ Nat "King" Cole, Bud Powell, Art Tatum

▶▶ Gene Harris, Bobby Timmons

Garaud MacTaggart

Erroll Garner

Born June 15, 1921, in Pittsburgh, PA. Died January 2, 1977, in Los Angeles, CA.

It's amazing to listen to pianist Erroll Garner playing his original compositions—many of which, like his tune, "Misty," have become standards—knowing that he never learned to read music. Countless pianists have been inspired by his technique: his cascading, orchestral attack marked by steady, left-hand chords and right-handed, behind-the-beat, single-note lines. One of the most prolific jazz pianists ever to record, Garner was a one-of-a-kind player with an instantly recognizable style. He had a broad range of creative expression at the keyboards, from light and bouncy, to richly romantic, to orchestral, but always with clarity and a freshness that holds up after even all these years. Considering the brevity of most of his recorded tunes, he crammed an amazing amount of clever improvisations into them. Garner's music continues to serve dance theater, films, and television. His best known tune, "Misty," has received much recognition, and in 1991 Garner's original Mercury recording of that tune was voted into the NARAS Hall of Fame. Jazz pianist Benny Green hails Garner as one of his major influences. And, a quick listen to Garner will inform you that Keith Jarrett was *not* the first pianist to hum along with his improvisations!

Garner was raised in a musical family and was playing piano at age three by imitating phonograph recordings. He was playing publicly by age seven, and at age 10 worked on radio with the Kan-D-Kids. In high school, he was advised by a teacher to not take lessons for fear it would misdirect his natural abilities. After performing with local bands in 1937, including some riverboat gigs on the Allegheny, Garner headed for New York City in 1944 and worked a series of gigs on 52nd Street. He performed and recorded with the Slam Stewart trio before forming his own tight unit with a bassist and drummer. From 1945–49, Garner freelanced, making a tremendous number of recordings for various labels. His richly embellished version of "Laura," recorded for Savoy in 1945, certified his abilities as a crossover artist. By the time he signed with Columbia in 1950, Garner had recorded numerous sides as an unaccompanied soloist, in trios, and with alto saxophonists Benny Carter and Charlie Parker, as well as with Don Byas, Coleman Hawkins, Wardell Gray, Lucky Thompson, Teddy Edwards, and the orchestras of Georgie Auld and Boyd Raeburn. His appeal with fans (and jazz critics) was boosted by his many top-shelf Columbia recordings (especially his first live-recorded album, *Concert by the Sea*, in 1955), plus television appearances, and tours in the United States and abroad (he was the first jazz artist booked by impresario Sal Hurok). His best-known work, "Misty," was a big hit in 1959. In 1963 he composed four themes for the film, *A New Kind of Love*. Garner continued to travel and record during the 1960s, making appearances with symphony orchestras from 1957 on, incorporating Latin themes into his music and making more television appearances that most jazz artists at the time. During the early to mid-1970s, Garner toured France, South America, and Asia. He re-recorded his best known composition, "Misty," for the film *Play Misty for Me,* and wrote a series of compositions that appear on his albums during these years. He was diagnosed with lung cancer and died at age 55 on January 2, 1977.

what to buy: Garner's historic first live-recorded performance, *Concert by the Sea* 🎵🎵🎵🎵 (Columbia, 1956/1987), recorded when his reputation was well established, still ranks among his best albums. Recorded on September 19, 1955, in Carmel, California, his trio at the time included bassist Eddie Calhoun and drummer Denzil Best. Garner's gray-haired fans will reminisce and new fans will thrill to his dramatically exciting versions of "Teach Me Tonight," "Autumn Leaves," "It's All Right with Me," "April in Paris," "Where or When," and seven other enjoyable tracks that demonstrate Garner's singular approach to playing. He's one of few pianists in jazz history with a strong, two-handed approach and an inherent understanding of how to best use dynamics to enrich his piano style. You'll hear all of this in his performances on this must-own album. You could start here, then collect the rest, even going back to his initial Columbia recordings made in 1951–52. Those new to Garner will find another excellent introduction in *Compact Jazz: Erroll Garner* ♫♫♫♫ (Mercury, 1954–55/PolyGram, 1987/Verve, 1990, prod. Bob Shad), a compilation recorded during the 1950s. The disc contains some of Garner's best performances with a trio, quartet, and in solo settings. Garner recorded a sparkling set with bassist Wyatt Ruther and drummer Eugene "Fats" Heard in Chicago on July 27, 1954, and the popular percussionist, Candido Camera, joins them on some tracks. Tunes include a delicate "Misty," a hard-swinging "Oh, Lady Be Good" (which showcases Garner's penchant for block chords), a rhythmically fetching "Begin the Beguine," and a highly imaginative, jumping version of "You Are My Sunshine." Excerpts from a solo piano date recorded in New York on March 14, 1995 demonstrate how Garner ably accompanies himself, especially on romantic ballads such as his lyrical take on "A Cottage for Sale," his dramatic original "All My Loves Are You," and a flowery interpretation of "I'll Never Smile Again." Every one of the 14 tunes is enjoyable, making this CD a bargain at any price. You may get acquainted with 1960s Garner on any number of stellar recordings, especially those featuring his regular trio with Eddie Calhoun and Kelly Martin. *Erroll Garner Collection 1: Easy to Love* ♫♫♫♫♫ (EmArcy/Verve, 1988, prod. Martha Glaser), which provides 46-plus minutes from the piano master, includes classics Garner recorded between 1961 and 1965 with his longest-lasting trio (Eddie Calhoun, bass, and Kelly Martin, drums). Just listen to neatly swinging gems as "My Blue Heaven," "Easy to Love," "Somebody Loves Me," and "Lover Come Back to Me" and you'll hear the style that influenced countless pianists who followed, including Gene Harris, Ahmad Jamal, and Benny Green. The CD reissue offers two previously unreleased tracks, "Out of Nowhere," and "Taking a Chance on Love." A companion to the previous album, *The Erroll Garner Collection 2: Dancing on the Ceiling* ♫♫♫♫♫ (EmArcy/Verve, 1989, prod. Martha Glaser) again features Garner with bassist Calhoun and drummer Martin, and combines New York studio dates from 1961, 1964, and 1965. Garner's threesome performs tight, tasty, lilting renderings of "Dancing on the Ceiling," "Crazy Rhythm," "Our Love Is Here to Stay," "After You've Gone," "There Will Never Be Another You," "What Is This Thing Called Love," and five more gems, including a powerful gospel-tinged waltz, "Like Home," penned by Garner. The CD bonus track, "Ain't Misbehavin'," resembles the Ray Brown Trio with

pianist Benny Green. A spectacular album that showcases Garner at the top of his game. Also from the 1960s, *Dreamstreet & One World Concert* ♫♫♫♫ (Telarc, 1995, prod. Martha Glaser) is a listening delight as Garner's regular trio, with bassist Calhoun and drummer Martin, zips through a collection of 17 tunes combined from the two sessions, recorded in 1961 and 1963, respectively. The nine (mostly standard) tunes from the earlier studio session are featured first and contain an elegantly embellished reading of "I'm Getting Sentimental over You," among other classics. *One World Concert*, a live-recorded performance by the Garner trio performance at the 1963 Seattle World's Fair, includes another version of his trademark, "Misty," the sweetly rendered ballad "Happiness Is a Thing Called Joe," an exuberant "Sweet and Lovely," and other delightful renderings.

what to buy next: If you want to truly dig into Garner's earliest roots, check out *Moon Glow* ♫♫♫♫ (Tradition, 1945, 1949/1996, prod. Ralph Bass). The CD compiles original 78-rpm recordings Garner made for various small labels (which were originally released as a collection on the Savoy label). Garner performs with his 1945 trio with bassist John Levy Jr. and Georgie Dellart on drums, and his 1949 trio with bassist John Simmons and drummer Alvin Stollar. Ten popular standards are featured, including "Somebody Loves Me," "Stormy Weather," "I'm Confessin'," "Stompin' at the Savoy," and other swinging numbers that demonstrate the pianist's talents not long after he arrived in New York City in 1944. With the exception of one side recorded in New York with Levy and Dellart, all of the sides were recorded in Los Angeles from February to the summer of 1949. Considering the source material, sound reproduction is not bad, and you'll hear all of the stylistic elements that would make him famous in the 1950s. Garner plays solo piano on this historic two-disc set, *Solo Time!—Volumes 4 and 5* ♫♫♫♫ (EmArcy, 1992), which documents previously unreleased material from a July 7, 1954 marathon studio date where Garner recorded 35 songs in three hours, all of them completed in first takes. Tunes run the gamut from Tin Pan Alley to Broadway to Hollywood movie themes. This recording is a must for Garner fans. *Mambo Moves Garner* ♫♫♫♫ (Mercury, 1954/Verve, 1988), recorded in Chicago in 1954 with bassist Wyatt Ruther, drummer Eugene Heard, and (for the first time) conga player Candido, features Garner debuting 11 tunes with Latin themes. Not one of his best sessions when you compare it to his large body of recorded works, yet it gives us a glimpse of Garner's versatility, presents his two originals "Mambo Blues" and "Mambo Nights," and contains a rare mambo version of Ray Noble's usually racing, "Cherokee."

best of the rest:

Long Ago and Far Away ♫♫♫ (Columbia, 1951/1987)

Body and Soul ♫♫♫ (Columbia, 1952/1991)

The Essence of Erroll Garner ♫♫♫ (Columbia, 1950–57/1994)

Close-Up in Swing/A New Kind of Love ♫♫♫ (Telarc, 1961/1963/1997)

Now Playing: A Night at the Movies/Up in Erroll's Room ♫♫♫ (Telarc, 1964/1968/1996)

That's My Kick/Gemini ♫♫♫ (Telarc, 1967–72/1994)

Magician/Gershwin and Kern ♫♫♫ (Telarc, 1974–76/1995)

influences:

◀◀ Fats Waller, Art Tatum, Earl Hines, Thelonious Monk

▶▶ Thelonious Monk, Ahmad Jamal, Gene Harris, Benny Green

Nancy Ann Lee

Kenny Garrett

Born October 9, 1960 in Detroit, MI.

Kenny Garrett is a promising "young lion" most famous for his stint in Miles Davis's band. He came up in Detroit, where he played with local scene patriarch Marcus Belgrave. After paying his dues in the Mercer Ellington orchestra, Garrett moved to New York in 1980 and spent a while in the retro-bop collective Out of the Blue. Besides Davis, Garrett has recorded with Chick Corea, Art Blakey, Woody Shaw, Freddie Hubbard, Lenny White, Marcus Miller, Al Jarreau, and more.

what to buy: *Black Hope* ♫♫♫ (Warner Bros., 1992, prod. Donald Brown) has killer sidemen (Joe Henderson, Kenny Kirkland, Charnett Moffett, Brian Blade) and a program of fine post-bop Garrett originals—plus a fiery "Bye Bye Blackbird." Nothing's groundbreaking, but it's an enjoyable and moderately deep conception spiced with exciting solos. The short final track, for alto sax alone, makes a nicely bluesy coda.

what to buy next: On *African Exchange Student* ♫♫♫ (Atlantic, 1990, prod. Donald Brown), Garrett's writing is somewhat uneven in inspiration, but his hypnotic, "Caravan"-esquely exotic title track (an original) and a soulful cover of Donny Hathaway's "Someday We'll All Be Free" stand out. There are a few different band configurations, with pianist Mulgrew Miller a reliable constant and Charnett Moffett (bass) and Tony Reedus (drums) spelled by Ron Carter and Elvin Jones.

the rest:

Introducing Kenny Garrett ♫♫ (Criss Cross, 1984)

Triology ♫♫♫ (Warner Bros., 1995)

Pursuance: Music of John Coltrane ♫♫♫ (Warner Bros., 1996)

Songbook ♫♫♫ (Warner Bros., 1997)

worth searching for: *Warner Jams, Volume 1* ♫♫♫ (Warner Bros., 1995, prod. Matt Pierson) puts the label's young stars— Garrett, Joshua Redman, Wallace Roney, Larry Goldings, Brad Mehldau, Peter Bernstein, Clarence Seay, Brian Blade—into a nicely informal setting. Garrett is featured on the Roberta Flack hit "Killing Me Softly with His Song" and originals by himself and Redman. Garrett's best showcase while with Miles Davis came in concert, and *Live around the World* ♫♫♫ (Warner Bros., 1996, prod. Miles Davis) is worth hearing for the saxophonist even when the leader is playing below his peak form. Garrett sounds inspired stretching out in this electric, elastic context, and it's too bad he hasn't explored it on his own records.

influences:

◀◀ Sonny Stitt, Cannonball Adderley, Johnny Hodges, John Coltrane

▶▶ Wessell Anderson

Walter Faber

George Garzone

Born in Boston, MA.

Because he's taught saxophone and harmony at the Berklee School of Music for the past 20 years and, since 1972, has performed primarily with the Fringe (a Boston-based collective ensemble devoted to the outer partials of improvising), saxophonist George Garzone is less known to the public than his immense talent would dictate. Born to a musical family, he's been playing club gigs since age 12, and he plays with operatic passion through the full spectrum of contemporary improvisation, from funk to Latin to bop and free jazz styles. With Coltrane and Rollins as his starting points, Garzone blends the natural quality of an ear player with the tremendous sophistication of the Berklee-trained musician that he is.

what's available: *Alone* ♫♫♫ (NYC, 1995, prod. Chuck Loeb, Mike Mainieri) is Garzone's homage to Stan Getz, his first idol. Joined by Chuck Loeb (guitar), Mike Mainieri (vibraphone), David Kikoski (piano), Eddie Gomez (bass), and Lenny White (drums) in a variety of configurations, Garzone performs a varied program of nine tunes recorded by Getz, plus two originals. Among the numerous highlights: a softly caressed "Spring Can Really Hang You up the Most," a fire-eating "Night and Day," the tender ode "Ballad for Lana" (his daughter), interactive duos with Kikoski on "Lush Life" and Loeb on "Nature Boy," a spitfire tear-through-the-changes "What Is This Thing Called Love," and a truly soulful "Con Alma." A mature interpretation of Getz by a wholly personal improviser. *Four's and Two's* 𝄢𝄢𝄢𝄢 (NYC, 1996, prod. Mike Mainieri, George Garzone), a state-of-the-art tenor battle pairing Garzone and Joe Lovano, finds the Berklee School of Music classmates collaborating on five melodic, harmonically challenging Garzone originals, including a way-up-tempo "Have You Met Miss Jones," plus an unaccompanied duo reading of "In a Sentimental Mood." Garzone performs two original ballads with the rhythm section—pianist Joey Calderazzo, John Lockwood (bassist in the Fringe), and drummer Bill Stewart—a worthy foil for the three rugged individualists. An immensely creative endeavor.

worth searching for: Two albums with Fringe are worth the search. An intimate document, *It's Time for the Fringe* 𝄢𝄢𝄢𝄢 (Soul Note, 1992, prod. Giovanni Bonandrini, Fringe) is the group's 20th anniversary concert before friends and musical family in Boston. They stretch out with detailed collective interplay. *Live in Israel* 𝄢𝄢𝄢𝄢 (Soul Note, 1995, prod. Fringe) is a less intimate, authoritative set, with extraordinary improvising by Garzone, comprehensively documenting what the Fringe is about.

influences:

◀◀ Stan Getz, Sonny Rollins, John Coltrane, Joe Lovano

▶▶ Branford Marsalis, Joshua Redman, Donny McCaslin, Teodross Avery

Ted Panken

Giorgio Gaslini

Born October 22, 1929, Milan, Italy.

Pianist, composer, bandleader, and educator Giorgio Gaslini is well known in his home country as a sort of elder jazz statesman. Although most of his commercially available recordings date from the 1980s, Gaslini has been extremely active in all his musical capacities since at least the 1940s. He has generated wide critical acclaim for his wide breadth of musical interests—expressed in tributes to Thelonious Monk, Robert Schumann, and Albert Ayler—and has put his early classical training and conservatory education to use in his phrasing, compositions, and structural sense. Gaslini's tendrils reach far back into Italian jazz history, to at least the early post-war period. His presence as a performer and conductor (of symphonic groups in addition to jazz ensembles) heightened in the 1960s. But it wasn't until the 1980s, when Italian jazz impresario and Black Saint/Soul Note Records founder Giovanni Bonandrini began releasing Gaslini's records internationally, that this undersung

giant's reputation took off. Gaslini, who has composed an opera based on Malcolm X and a lament for Eric Dolphy and has had his music appear in the films of Michaelangelo Antonioni and Vermuccio, also ventured into musical outreach. His ensembles performed in all manner of venues in Italy, from industrial plants to hospitals. And his string of Soul Note CDs might explain his faith in the art: they are at once moving in a stately, classical vein, and then robustly adventurous. His takes on Schumann and Ayler share the same profound understanding of the music as a continuum of intense, committed expression, and neither veers too far into the land of percussive thuds or ornate classicism. Further, Gaslini's tremendous Globo Quartet likewise captures the polished demeanor of the Modern Jazz Quartet and then heads into the land of abstract, avant-garde jazz, only to periodically re-assert the sort of careful precision that marks more chamber music than post-bebop jazz.

what to buy: *Ayler's Wings* 𝄢𝄢𝄢𝄢 (Soul Note, 1991, prod. Giovanni Bonandrini) is likely one of the top 50 jazz recordings every fan should own. Its muted elegance conveys the enormous respect Gaslini has for the late Ayler, by all accounts an uncompromising outcast of the highest order. The tunes are complexly served with intonations of cerebral classical leanings and spare but thunderous free jazz elements. Virtually all over the jazz map, the Globo Quartet's *Lampi (Lightnings)* 𝄢𝄢𝄢𝄢 (Soul Note, 1994, prod. Giovanni Bonandrini) manages to merge Ellington with Herbie Nichols and Burmese harp with the post-bop, post-classical sweep of Gaslini's title suite. Daniele Di Gregorio's vibraphone and marimba help place this vibes-piano-bass-drums recording in league with the first Modern Jazz Quartet LPs. Spirited by the avant-garde but heavily anchored in simply lovely pianism, *Lampi* is a gem.

what to buy next: More on the classical side, the trio session *Schumann Reflections* 𝄢𝄢𝄢 (Soul Note, 1984, prod. Giovanni Bonandrini) maintains enough angularity and post-bop colorations to attract many a piano-jazz fan, including the free-music aficionado. *Gaslini Plays Monk* 𝄢𝄢𝄢 (Soul Note, 1981, prod. Giovanni Bonandrini) is more stately than most Monk tributes, but it's textured like all Gaslini recordings. It's abstract in some spots, visceral in others, and flat-out entrancing as a whole. On Monk's playful, halting tunes, Gaslini shows he is able to interweave high-spirited humor into his awesome range of talents. Probably Gaslini's most "conventional" date available, *Multipli* 𝄢𝄢𝄢 (Soul Note, 1981, prod. Giovanni Bonandrini) is a relatively straight-ahead quintet date featuring the composer's complex sense of texture. It's part Lennie Tristano, but also part post-free oddness. The twin saxes of Claudio Fasoli

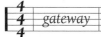

and Roberto Ottaviano have never sounded better placed than in Gaslini's tunes, especially the out-bop of "Ornette or Not."

what to avoid: *Tiziana Ghiglioni Sings Gaslini* ⚖ (Soul Note, 1995, prod. Giovanni Bonandrini) may work in Italy, but it doesn't survive the Atlantic crossing with its charms intact. Ghiglioni's singing is an acquired taste, and though Gaslini's music is as interesting as ever, not many American listeners will care about his original songs—in Italian, no less—gussied up with fancy string arrangements.

the rest:
(With Quintetto Vocale Italiano) *Freedom Jazz Dance: Le Pause Del Silenzio* ⚖⚖ (Soul Note, 1992)

worth searching for: *L'Integrale Antologia Cronologica #1 (1948–63) & #2 (1964)* ⚖⚖⚖ (Soul Note, 1997, prod. Giovanni Bonandrini) and *L'Integrale Antologia Cronologica #3 (1964–65) & #4 (1966–68)* ⚖⚖⚖⚖ (Soul Note, 1997, prod. Giovanni Bonandrini) apparently haven't been released in the United States, but these two-CD collections of Gaslini's formative years are highly attractive. Certainly the 1966 session "Nuovi Sentimenti" (New Feelings) with Don Cherry, Steve Lacy, Gato Barbieri, Enrico Rava, and others in the Gaslini International Ensemble will interest most avant-garde fans!

influences:
◀◀ Thelonious Monk, Bud Powell, John Lewis, Lennie Tristano
▶▶ Franco D'Andrea, Stefano Battaglia

Andrew Bartlett and Steve Holtje

Gateway
Formed in 1975.

John Abercrombie, guitar; Dave Holland, bass; Jack DeJohnette, drums, percussion, keyboards.

The trio of Abercrombie, Holland, and DeJohnette could never be accused of flooding the market with their collaborative efforts. As a group, they have released only four albums in 20 years. Each member of the group brings with them many years of experience as both a leader and sideman, so the result is predictably high quality. Abercrombie made his mark playing with others such as Jan Hammer, Richie Beirach, Jon Christenson, and Peter Erskine. Holland has also been featured in ensembles with the likes of Chick Corea, Anthony Braxton, and Barry Altschul (Circle) as well as with Stan Getz, Paul Bley, and vocalists Abby Lincoln and Betty Carter. DeJohnette's career brought him together with the likes of Miles Davis, Thelonious

Monk, John Coltrane, Keith Jarrett, and Bill Evans. Over the years, each musician could easily be pegged as an example of what has come to be termed the "ECM" sound since the label made its debut nearly 30 years ago.

what to buy: *Gateway* ⚖⚖⚖⚖ (ECM, 1975, prod. Manfred Eicher) is where the trio started. The album contains a wide range of musical dynamics that take the mood from introspective to aggressive.

what to buy next: On *Gateway 2* ⚖⚖⚖ (ECM, 1977, prod. Manfred Eicher), the group moved toward a nearly rock-oriented sound. The dynamic leans toward the louder end of the spectrum and might be the place for rock listeners to begin. After a 17-year break as a trio, the group seems to have not missed a beat with *Homecoming* ⚖⚖⚖⚖ (ECM, 1994, prod. Manfred Eicher). As on their previous recording, the dynamics tend to go toward the rock spectrum. *In the Moment* ⚖⚖⚖⚖ (ECM, 1996, prod. Manfred Eicher) contains a wide slice of sonic elements, from the exotic sounds of Turkish frame drums to DeJohnette's plucking of the strings from inside the piano. With many of these pieces, there is not only an air of improvisation but also sonic experimentation (as with the effects on the guitar).

influences:
◀◀ Pat Metheny Group

Chris Meloche

Charles Gayle
Born February 28, 1939 in Buffalo, NY.

Practically unknown for nearly the first 50 years of his life, in the 1990s Charles Gayle established himself as arguably the greatest purely free-jazz saxophonist of the era. Refusing to compromise his music even while in the most dire of personal circumstances, he has attracted a dedicated following and has made up for lost time with an amazing spurt of productivity, recording 17 albums as a leader in a ten-year period. Gayle grew up listening to and playing bebop. He started on piano, with lessons as a child, but switched to tenor sax because it made it easier to sit in on jam sessions. He moved to New York City in the mid-1960s and participated in the scene that built up around John Coltrane. Gayle says that later, just before the company went under, famed avant-jazz label ESP was going to put out an album of his, which needless to say could have changed his career path. Instead, Gayle moved back upstate, then lived in Germany. In the mid-1980s he returned to New York City, performing with Peter Brötzmann's big band and other groups and as a leader, but became homeless for a considerable period of time and supported himself by playing for money in the city's subway system. Three albums recorded in 1988 for the Swedish label Silkheart helped raise his profile. In the early 1990s Gayle became a regular at the Knitting Factory, where his incendiary live sets became the talk of the scene. Recordings for the club's label were better-distributed than the Silkheart albums and broke him through to a larger audience.

One of the most pure energy improvisors ever, Gayle often opens his first sets with full-bore blasts, sometimes blowing non-stop for a half-hour or more. He has a stunning array of timbres he can coax or rip from his sax, from harmonics, overblowing shrieks, and honking to Ayleresque, vibrato-laden vocalism, all spun out with inexorable intensity. The intuitive structuring of his improvisations contrasts cells in which the motifs may be organized either by linear shape or by sonic character. Occasionally in his second sets he would surprise his listeners with quick forays into bebop or Coltrane tunes, though he has steadfastly refused to document his prowess in such repertoire. His sets have always been purely spontaneous, and he avoids rehearsal. Always searching for music which hasn't been played before, his most withering dismissal is, "It's been done." Powering Gayle's music is a deep religiosity which he sometimes expresses verbally (as on his Victo album) but more often musically and through his song titles.

As Gayle has became better known, he has been able to play more often with top-flight rhythm sections (some of his early trio partners were not especially responsive listeners in performance). When the Knitting Factory had a piano onstage one night, he spent a good portion of his second set at the keyboard, mixing up spartan Monk-isms and powerfully two-fisted free playing, and soon made piano a regular part of his arsenal. It must be said that some commentators have overemphasized Gayle's legendary homelessness, because he progressed to living in a relatively secure squat and then a modest apartment in the East Village long after some writers were still latching onto his homelessness, as though that alone signified some sort of romanticized authenticity. His burgeoning reputation brought him work on the European festival circuit, and he even recorded an album at one of them as a member of a Cecil Taylor group (as documented on Taylor's FMP album *Always a Pleasure*).

Gayle's cathartic intensity has made him popular outside the hardcore jazz audience; a segment of the alternative rock crowd appreciates his energy and uncompromising attitude, which has led to occasional live collaborations with some of the more on-the-edge rock celebrities, including Henry Rollins,

with whom he also recorded (and on whose label a gospel-inflected CD was issued). In Gayle's continuing quest for something new, in 1996 he began using a multi-media presentation in the persona of Streets, performed as a mime clown in full classic costume (ragged suit, bowler hat, red ball nose, big pale gloves—it can be seen in the photo inside the *Delivered* CD booklet) with prerecorded tapes of street sounds, interspersed with lengthy musical interludes where he and his band play appropriately emotional music. Whatever the context, Gayle is a widely admired artist as he closes in on his 60th birthday.

what to buy: The deeply spiritual *Consecration* ♫♫♫♫ (Black Saint, 1993, prod. Flavio Bonandrini) offers transcendent music-making throughout, with better sound than Gayle's many live albums and more focused playing. "Thy Peace" is a subdued yet harrowingly intense showcase for Gayle's formidable bass clarinet skills. Vattel Cherry on bass and William Parker on cello and violin lay out a thick string carpet to support Gayle, while Michael Wimberley on drums proves more responsive than a few predecessors who sometimes plowed ahead overpoweringly.

what to buy next: *Touchin' on Trane* ♫♫♫♫ (FMP, 1993, prod. Jost Gebers) teams Gayle with Parker and Coltrane drummer Rashied Ali and finds Gayle, as the title indicates, looking back towards a major inspiration a bit more than he usually would (as a member of Ali's By Any Means, it's practically a duty to do so). He remains his own man, of course, but the ties to one of his spiritual forefathers make this a special experience—and Ali's superb polyrhythms certainly spur him on. In a mix of concert and studio tracks, *Kingdom Come* ♫♫♫ (Knitting Factory, 1994) matches Gayle with a very different drummer, Sunny Murray, whose relatively spare technique is surprisingly complementary to Gayle and allows him to explore more moods. This was also the first album Gayle played piano on, and his excitement is palpable.

what to avoid: *Always Born* ♫♫ (Silkheart, 1988, prod. Charles Gayle), Gayle's first released album, suffers not from inexperience but rather from the uneasiness between the leader and guest saxophonist John Tchicai, who never really gel.

the rest:
Homeless ♫♫♫ (Silkheart, 1988)
Spirits Before ♫♫♫ (Silkheart, 1988)
Repent ♫♫♫♫ (Knitting Factory, 1992)
Translation ♫♫♫♫ (Silkheart, 1993)
Raining Fire ♫♫♫♫ (Silkheart, 1993)

More Live at the Knitting Factory 𝄢𝄢𝄢𝄢 (Knitting Factory, 1993)
Unto I AM 𝄢𝄢𝄢𝄢 (Victo, 1995)
Testaments 𝄢𝄢𝄢𝄢 (Knitting Factory, 1995)
Delivered 𝄢𝄢𝄢 (2.13.61, 1997)
Solo in Japan 𝄢𝄢𝄢𝄢 (P.S.F., 1997)
Berlin Movement from Future Years 𝄢𝄢𝄢𝄢 (FMP, 1997)
Daily Bread 𝄢𝄢𝄢𝄢 (Black Saint, 1998)

worth searching for: Credited to the Sunny Murray Duo Featuring Charles Gayle and thus probably filed under M, *Illuminators* 𝄢𝄢𝄢𝄢 (Audible Hiss, 1996) again pairs Gayle (on piano and tenor sax) with the ESP legend, with equally fine results. The tour-promoting compilation *Avant Knitting* 𝄢𝄢𝄢𝄢 (Knitting Factory, 1993, prod. Michael Dorf) includes an otherwise unavailable 14-minute improvisation by a Gayle trio. *Live at Disobey* 𝄢𝄢𝄢𝄢 (Blast First/The Wire, 1994) may never have appeared in stores as it was recorded by a British label in conjunction with an anniversary celebration by *The Wire* and made available to subscribers. It captures a fairly intense live set with bassist Hilliard Green and Wimberley, with Gayle on tenor sax and bass clarinet. Gayle completists will want to pick up Henry Rollins's two-CD *Everything* 𝄢𝄢 (2.13.61, 1996, prod. Alyson L. Careaga, Henry Rollins) for the music by Gayle and Ali that appears intermittently and not always in the foreground. (The rating would be higher if this were considered as a spoken word album.)

influences:

◀◀ John Coltrane, Sonny Rollins, Albert Ayler, Thelonious Monk

▶▶ Assif Tsahar, Allan Chase

Steve Holtje

Bruce Gertz

Born December 15, 1952, in Providence, RI.

Bruce Gertz began playing guitar at the age of ten, switched to electric bass four years later, and played primarily rock and blues. He went to the Berklee College of Music as a composition and arranging major, and studied with late John Neves and with William Curtis. Later, Gertz studied more advanced jazz improvisation with the legendary Charlie Banacos. While in Boston, Gertz played with Bill Frisell, Mick Goodrick, Jerry Bergonzi, and Mike Stern He has also performed and recorded with various leaders, including Gil Evans, Dave Brubeck, Joe Lovano, and Lee Konitz. He is on the faculty at Berklee College of Music and has written a bass instruction manual as well as a bass instructional video.

what to buy: *Discovery Zone* 𝄢𝄢𝄢𝄢 (RAM, 1996, prod. Raimondo Meli Lupi) is Bruce Gertz's most warmly accessible, melodious album yet, and certainly the tightest performance from this group since his 1992 debut recording (*Blueprint*) with guitarist John Abercrombie, tenor saxophonist Jerry Bergonzi, pianist Joey Calderazzo, and drummer Adam Nussbaum. Gertz also shows improvement as a composer. The pretty melody of his slow and dreamy original "The Reach" is a pleaser that Bergonzi and Calderazzo develop nicely in their mellifluous solos. Gertz also contributes five more diversities which the crew passionately caresses, and he lays down some funky electric bass lines for Joe Henderson's "The Urge," a collective improvisation similar to their modern-edge creations on earlier albums. The piece de resistance, though, is a beautiful waltzing version of the Rogers/Hart gem, "My Romance," with Abercrombie handling the melody and his fine solo with velvety finesse. *Discovery Zone* is just what the title implies; the musicians seem to be rediscovering themselves and deliver the 11-tune session from their souls.

what to buy next: Gertz's debut as leader, *Blueprint* 𝄢𝄢𝄢𝄢 (Evidence, 1992, prod. Bruce Gertz) finds him heading a solid quintet with John Abercrombie on guitar, Jerry Bergonzi on tenor sax, Joey Calderazzo on piano, and Adam Nussbaum on drums. Gertz penned the 11 modern-edged tunes and gives his buddies plenty of space in the spotlight. These musicians have all worked with Gertz in the past, and their familiarity breeds some good music. On *Third Eye* 𝄢𝄢𝄢𝄢 (RAM, 1994, prod. Bruce Gertz), a 1992 live-recorded date at Somerville Theatre, in Somerville, Massachusetts, Gertz performs with the same illustrious crew as on his Evidence debut. He leads an understated, expansive performance, a suitable homage to the bassists who have gone before. While the group occasionally kicks up some fiery bop tempos and righteous swing on the session of nine Gertz originals, the mostly modern menu balances with uncluttered, airy pieces.

influences:

◀◀ John Coltrane, Wayne Shorter, Herbie Hancock, McCoy Tyner, Scott LaFaro, Ray Brown

▶▶ Stu Hamm, Alain Caron, Victor Bailey, Jeff Andrews, Skuli Sverrisson, Peter Herbert

David C. Gross and Nancy Ann Lee

Stan Getz

Born February 2, 1927, in Philadelphia, PA. Died June 6, 1991, in Malibu, CA.

During his nearly fifty-year career, which began in the 1940s, tenor saxophonist Stan Getz became a revered, world-class jazz player, winning widespread favor with fans and musicians alike for his appealing sense of melody and his robust, luxuriant tone. Getz retains characteristics of his major influence (Lester Young) in his featherweight cool tone, slow rate of vibrato, graceful sense of swing, and melodious improvisation. Yet Getz was one of the few bop tenors who departed from Young's ideas and created his own melodic and rhythmic lexicon. Getz made numerous recordings prior to 1962, but his popularity exploded the year he joined with guitarist Charlie Byrd to record the album *Jazz Samba*. The tune "Desafinado" became a huge hit, popularizing the *bossa nova*, a brilliant meld of jazz with Brazilian rhythms. Riding on this crest, Getz recorded other Brazilian-jazz albums during the next two years and, from his 1964 recording *Getz/Gilberto* (with João Gilberto and Antonio Carlos Jobim), the tune "Girl from Ipanema" sung by Astrud Gilberto, became one of the best-selling records in jazz history. While these recordings gave him greatest visibility, they represent only a small portion of his complete discography.

Getz began playing professionally at age 15 in New York and made his first recording a year later as sideman to Jack Teagarden. He worked in the major big bands led by Stan Kenton (1944–45) and Benny Goodman (1945–46), and in 1947 joined Woody Herman's Second Herd where, with fellow saxophonists Zoot Sims, Serge Chaloff, and Herbie Steward, he became a member of the famous reed section that became known as the Four Brothers. A solo with the Herd on the 1948 version of "Early Autumn" established Getz as a capable swing-style improviser. He left the Herman band in 1949 and began to lead his own small groups which won him popularity and praise in the jazz polls for his instrument.

Getz began the 1950s leading a quartet that included Horace Silver. He toured Sweden in 1951 leading a quintet that co-featured guitarist Jimmy Raney, and from 1953–54 included Bob Brookmeyer in his group. Getz's career was disrupted in 1954 by his drug problems, but he was soon back to his music and toured Europe with Jazz at the Philharmonic during 1957–58. He remained in Europe, working there from 1958–1961 with other American expatriates such as Oscar Pettiford and Kenny Clarke. Returning to the United States around 1961, Getz led his own quartet and between 1962–64 made his popular *bossa nova* albums. Once the Brazilian-jazz craze subsided, Getz continued to lead jazz groups and record with a variety of players, helping to launch the careers of Gary Burton, Chick Corea, and other promising musicians. In 1967 Getz and Corea recorded *Sweet Rain* for Verve. They formed a quintet in 1971 that in-

cluded bassist Stanley Clarke, drummer Tony Williams, and percussionist Airto Moreira and the following year this band made its debut in New York City and recorded the Columbia album *Captain Marvel*.

Getz spent 1969–72 in semi-retirement in Europe (although he recorded an album with French organist Eddy Louiss in 1971). His 1972 album *Captain Marvel* with Chick Corea and his 1975 album, *The Peacocks*, with Jimmy Rowles were highlights of the decade. Getz included pianist JoAnne Brackeen in his group in 1977 and their association is documented on *Live at Montmartre*. Getz subsequently experimented with fusion, but pleased jazz purists when he signed with the Concord label in 1981 and released a series of straight-ahead albums. Throughout the 1980s he worked regularly in the San Francisco Bay area, taught at Stanford University, and though semi-retired by the mid-1980s, made occasional tours even into early 1991. His final recording, *People Time*, made for Concord in 1991, features pianist Kenny Barron. Getz died of cancer in June, 1991.

what to buy: A year and a half before the Beatles' tidal wave hit the American pop music charts, there was a Brazilian invasion and Getz and guitarist Charlie Byrd led the charge with *Jazz Samba* ℐℐℐℐ (Verve, 1963, prod. Creed Taylor), a classic session that introduced many Americans to Brazilian music. The album's two hits were Jobim's "Desafinado" and "One Note Samba," but the entire session perfectly melded the band's lightly swinging take on Brazilian rhythms with Getz's exceptional gift for melody. With Keter Betts (bass), Gene Byrd (guitar and bass), and either Buddy Deppenschmidt or Bill Reichenbach on drums, *Jazz Samba* is a landmark session that opened the door wider for international influences in jazz. Should you want to explore the origins of the bossa nova in grander style, the four-CD set, *The Girl from Ipanema: The Bossa Nova Years* ℐℐℐℐ (Verve, 1964/1989, prod. Richard Seidel, Seth Rothstein, Phil Schaap) compiles the brilliant work that Getz recorded with Charlie Byrd, Antonio Carlos Jobim, João Gilberto, Astrud Gilberto, Luiz Bonfa, and Laurindo Almeida during the early to mid-1960s. The melodic work of these artists generated exquisitely new, graceful standards in the jazz world. Captured throughout the four discs are Brazilian jazz classics such as Jobim's "Desafinado," "Samba de Una Nota So," Bonfa's "Manha De Carnival," "The Girl from Ipanema," "Doralice," "Desafinado," "Corcovado," "O Grande Amor," and many other tunes performed by Getz with an array of sidemen, including bassist Keter Betts, bassist, guitarist Gene Byrd, guitarist Luiz Bonfa, pianist Antonio Carlos Jobim, guitarist João Gilberto, and vocalist Astrud Gilberto. Especially

notable is the October 9, 1964 performance featuring Getz at Carnegie Hall performing with guitarist/vocalist João Gilberto, vibist Gary Burton, bassist Gene Cherico, drummer Joe Hunt, and vocalist Astrud Gilberto. This CD set contains numerous classic bossa nova sessions recorded during their heyday. Brazilian jazz fans should find this a particularly rewarding listen. Some of the more historic jazz ever recorded happened at George Wein's Storyville Club in Boston. This reissue of *Stan Getz at Storyville, Volumes 1 & 2* 🎷🎷🎷 (Blue Note, 1953/1990, prod. Teddy Reig) features Getz in straight-ahead sets (originally recorded for Roost Records) on October 28, 1951, in the middle of a two-week engagement at the club with Charlie Parker's former pianist Al Haig, guitarist Jimmy Raney, 23-year-old bassist Teddy Kotick, and drummer Tiny Kahn. The album includes a racing team blowout built on the chord changes of Ray Noble's classic, "Cherokee" (a speedball tune Charlie Parker made famous), which Getz re-titled "Parker 51." Other notable tracks (from the original Volume 1) include tastily swinging versions of "Thou Swell" and "Pennies from Heaven," a pleasing reading from the saxophonist on the ballad "Everything Happens to Me," and the team effort on Lester Young's swing classics "Jumping with Symphony Sid" and Johnny Mandel's "Hershey Bar." Throughout, Getz (then in his mid-20s) is awesome, as is his young crew (which had not worked together as a team before this engagement). However, within a few weeks after this gig the quintet disbanded. Getz went to work for NBC's studio orchestra, Haig went into semi-retirement for a few years, and Tiny Kahn died of a heart attack at age 29 in 1953. Two decades later, Getz celebrated his 50th birthday in Copenhagen, recording *Live at Montmartre, Volume 2* 🎷🎷🎷 (SteepleChase, 1977/1987, prod. Nils Winther), which was released originally as a double LP but has been reissued as two separate CDs. This volume documents four tunes from his live performance at Montmartre in Copenhagen, Denmark, with a rhythm section that includes pianist JoAnne Brackeen, bassist Niels-Henning Orsted-Pedersen, and drummer Billy Hart. The four tunes included on this CD are Getz's "Blues for Dorte," Steve Swallow's "Eiderdown," and two compositions from Wayne Shorter, "Infant Eyes" and "Lester Left Town." Getz's work on "Infant Eyes" is both tender and melodic, and throughout the CD the quartet demonstrates a cohesive working unit, exploring a range of moods. *Blue Skies* 🎷🎷🎷 (Concord, 1982/1995, prod. Carl E. Jefferson, Steve Getz) is Getz at his late-career best on a lush and dreamy six-tune session with a

Stan Getz (Archive Photos)

S TAN G ETZ (WITH B ILL E VANS T RIO
F EATURING S TAN G ETZ)

song "The Peacocks"
album *But Beautiful*
(Milestone, 1974/1996)
instrument Tenor saxophone

quartet consisting of Jim McNeely (piano), bassist Marc Johnson, and drummer Billy Hart. Getz exhibits pleasantly rich tone and impeccable phrasing, as if he were imparting wonderfully woven stories with his tenor saxophone. McNeely, a lyrical player at heart, is a well-chosen team mate, and Johnson and Hart are equally empathetic throughout. The tunes feature jazz standards such as the Rodgers/Hart classic "Spring in Here," the Gershwin hit ballad "How Long Has This Been Going On?," the title tune by Irving Berlin, originals by Johnson and McNeely, and one obscurity by Ralph Rainger/Leo Robin, "Easy Living." All are given thoughtful, robust readings. For its relaxed romanticism that peaks dramatically on McNeely's time-switching bopper, "There We Go," (track four), and for the well-executed, intricate, straight-ahead solos, this album is highly recommended. Getz left the stage in grand style, recording *People Time* 🎷🎷🎷🎷 (Verve, 1992, prod. Jean-Philippe Allard) just three months before his death. A two-disc set of live duos with the great pianist Kenny Barron, this is a beautiful session with Getz and Barron communicating at a breathtaking level.

The first disc opens with a gorgeous version of "East of the Sun," and though Getz occasionally runs a little short of wind, his playing just gets stronger on the second disc. The almost ten-minute version of Charlie Haden's "First Song" and Mal Waldron's "Soul Eyes" are two highlights, though there's not a weak track among the album's 14 tunes.

what to buy next: *Quartets* 𝄢𝄢𝄢𝄢 (Prestige/OJC, 1949–50/1989, prod. Bob Weinstock) features the tenor saxophone of Stan Getz on three separate recording sessions. The first took place on June 21, 1949, and includes such tunes as "Long Island Sound" and "Indian Summer," performed with pianist Al Haig, bassist Gene Ramey, and drummer Stan Levey. The second date, January 6, 1950, includes pianist Al Haig, bassist Tommy Potter, and drummer Roy Haynes. The third session recorded on April 14, 1950, features pianist Tony Aless, bassist Percy Heath, and drummer Don Lamond. The ballads are gently melodic, and the up-tempo tunes swing with passion. These sessions were recorded directly following Getz's tenure with the Woody Herman band, and helped to establish him as a major jazz soloist and leader. Featuring Getz and Zoot Sims, *The Brothers* 𝄢𝄢𝄢𝄢 (Prestige/OJC, 1949–52/1989, prod. Bob Weinstock) is a compilation that embodies the tenor saxophone sound created when Gene Roland wrote arrangements for Sims, Getz, Jimmy Giuffre, and Herbie Steward when they performed at Pontrelli's Ballroom in Los Angeles. They carried their sound on to fame in Woody Herman's band, with Steward replaced later by Al Cohn and the addition of Serge Chaloff. The first session on this CD, recorded on April 8, 1949, features five tenor saxophonists, including Getz, Sims, Cohn, Allen Eager, and Brew Moore, supported by pianist Walter Bishop, bassist Gene Ramey, and drummer Charlie Perry. The session opens with "Five Brothers," a tune written by Gerry Mulligan, and everyone swings from the first note. Mulligan also composed "Four and One Moore" for this session, which also includes two compositions by Cohn, "Battle of the Saxes" and "Battleground." The second session was recorded on September 8, 1952 and features two tenor saxmen—Sims and Cohn—plus trombonist Kai Winding, pianist George Wallington, bassist Percy Heath, and drummer Art Blakey. Getz seems to have been inspired by using different (and the best) pianists and on *The Peacocks* 𝄢𝄢𝄢𝄢 (Columbia/Legacy, 1977/1994, prod. Stan Getz), one of a series of "Stan Getz presents" albums for Columbia, he anoints the admirable Jimmy Rowles who was not only a sensitively expressive pianist, but a heartfelt, rough-hewn singer, and a superb composer. The 13 tunes feature the tenor saxophonist mixing it up in various configurations with

Rowles, drummer Elvin Jones, bassist Buster Williams, and, on one track only, the vocalese group of Jon, Judy, and Michelle Hendricks and Beverly Getz. The saxophonist is in best form in the duo setting with Rowles on tunes such as "I'll Never Be the Same" (which Rowles sings with his piano accompaniment), and their instrumental duos on "What Am I Here For?," "The Hour of Parting," "Skylark," and the title tune, a Rowles original. Getz and the others step out for two highly pleasing unaccompanied solo sittings by Rowles. Add the sprightly quartet settings, and there's enough diversity here to satisfy everyone. *The Best of Two Worlds* 𝄢𝄢𝄢𝄢 (CBS, 1976/1987, prod. Stan Getz) is a relaxed Brazilian jazz session that features a mixed menu, with sparing amounts of Getz and generous helpings of his inspirator, guitarist/vocalist João Gilberto. Side players also include pianist Albert Dailey, drummers Billy Hart or Grady Tate, bassist Steve Swallow or Clint Houston, and guitarist/arranger Oscar Castro-Nueves, percussionist Airto Moreira (riding the crest of his popularity after arriving in the United States in 1968), and others. While this may not be one of Getz's best Brazilian-jazz sessions, for fans of this beautiful musical genre, it's always wonderful to hear his collaborations with Gilberto. *The Dolphin* 𝄢𝄢𝄢𝄢 (Concord, 1981/1992, prod. Carl E. Jefferson) was Getz's first recording for Concord, and features him leading a six-tune straight-ahead session with Lou Levy (piano), Victor Lewis (drums), and Monty Budwig (bass), in a live-recorded performance at Keystone Korner. Levy is an aggressive innovator whose technique grasps listener attention, and he's spurred by the illustriously colorful drummer Lewis and veteran bassist Budwig. Getz is inspired and so are the other musicians as they cordially wend their way through gems such as the heart-tugging Johnny Mandel ballad "A Time for Love," a buoyant version of Clifford Brown's "Joy Spring," a passionate, unhurried rendering of "My Old Flame," an uptempo bopping reading of "The Night Has a Thousand Eyes" and a fresh take on the Brazilian jazz standard, "The Dolphin." Because of the live audience, perhaps it's the material, but this outing finds Getz (and his team) enthusiastically generating some splendid music. The fifth Concord recording by Getz, *Yours and Mine* 𝄢𝄢𝄢𝄢 (Concord, 1989, prod. Steve Getz) was recorded live (June 29, 1989) by the BBC at the Glasgow International Jazz Festival and features Getz leading a quartet with pianist Kenny Barron, bassist Ray Drummond, and drummer Ben Riley. The leader's easy banter with the crowd pretty much typifies his mood and playing, lyrically fetching and relaxed, except for those times during solos where he energetically jabs at the melody lines. The album contains seven tunes, and Getz is in sublime form, giving a sweetly rendered solo on the title tune by Thad Jones, a lively Latinate version of Dizzy Gillespie's "Con Alma," an exceptionally warm ballad reading of Benny Carter's "People Time," and more broadly appealing tenorisms.

best of the rest:

The Brothers 𝄞𝄞𝄞 (Prestige/OJC, 1949/1989)
Quartets 𝄞𝄞𝄞𝄞 (Prestige/OJC, 1949–1950/1991)
At Storyville, Volume 1 & 2 𝄞𝄞𝄞𝄞 (Roulette/Capitol, 1952/1990)
Stan Getz and the Oscar Peterson Trio 𝄞𝄞𝄞𝄞 (Verve, 1957)
Spring Is Here 𝄞𝄞𝄞 (Concord, 1981)
Billy Highstreet Samba 𝄞𝄞𝄞 (Verve, 1981/1990)
Pure Getz 𝄞𝄞𝄞𝄞 (Concord, 1982/1987)
Serenity 𝄞𝄞𝄞𝄞 (EmArcy, 1987/1991)

worth searching for: Due to the original recordings made between 1958–59, the sound quality is not perfect on *In Denmark 1958–59* 𝄞𝄞𝄞 (Olufsen, 1958–59/1989), yet this hard-to-find import CD does offer a glimpse into Getz's improvisational energies when he was living in Denmark. The live-recorded concert performances throughout mix Getz with various configurations of musicians from America and Denmark (mostly the latter), and feature Getz with Ib Glindemann's big band on three tracks. The best tracks are the three performed with Jan Johansson (piano), expatriate Oscar Pettiford (bass), and Joe Harris (drums). Featuring 11 mostly swinging jazz standards, this is not one of Getz's best recordings, but it documents his years in Europe with some well-conceived solos.

influences:

◀◀ Lester Young, Coleman Hawkins, Ben Webster, Zoot Sims, Benny Carter, Paul Desmond, João Gilberto

▶▶ Scott Hamilton

Nancy Ann Lee, Susan K. Berlowitz, and Andrew Gilbert

Gerry Gibbs

Born January 15, 1964, in New York, NY.

An inventive drummer with a gift for waggish percussion humor, Gerry Gibbs is the son of vibraphonist Terry Gibbs and grew up in Los Angeles surrounded by jazz. As a teenager, he gigged with his father and Buddy DeFranco, and developed a friendship with Alice Coltrane. Through her came a lasting musical relationship with tenor saxophonist Ravi Coltrane. Gibbs moved to New York in 1988 and quickly established a reputation as a creative force through a series of trio gigs at the Village Gate, featuring such up-and-coming players as Danilo Perez and David Sanchez. He has also worked with Patrice Rushen, Phillip Harper, Joe Henderson, Joe Lovano, and Larry

Coryell, and recorded sessions with pianist John Campbell, and with Terry Gibbs/Buddy DeFranco.

what's available: The title may sound like just another hard-bop session, but *The Thrasher* 𝄞𝄞𝄞𝄞 (Qwest, 1996, prod. Stix Hooper) is anything but. With Ravi Coltrane on tenor and soprano sax, Joe Locke on vibes, Mark Feldman on violin, Derek "Oles" Oleszkiewicz on bass, and either Billy Childs or Uri Caine on piano, drummer Gerry Gibbs's extremely impressive debut is the work of an adventurous musician with an unfettered imagination. Besides playing two Ellington classics, "Rockin' in Rhythm" and "In a Sentimental Mood," and Coltrane's "Impressions," Gibbs wrote the remaining eight tunes, including the Caribbean-inflected "F Train to Bermuda," the McCoy Tyner-ish "Miss Nedra Wheeler," and the title track, which combines Eastern harmonics with Feldman's country fiddling and a Charleston shuffle beat. Rather than weighing down the music, Gibbs's highly active traps work, augmented by cowbells, whistles, wood blocks, and various gongs and bells, provides the other players a strong foundation to flow with or push against. Easily one of the best debut albums of that year.

influences:

◀◀ Elvin Jones, Billy Hart, Spike Jones

Andrew Gilbert

Terry Gibbs

Born Julius Gubenko, October 13, 1924, in New York, NY.

Terry Gibbs plays vibes like he talks—loose, wild-fire, run-on lines which he occasionally interrupts with amusing asides. One recent Gibbs collaborator commented that you need footnotes when you talk with the vibist, something you certainly don't need to listen to his straight-ahead swinging music. But it's exactly that characteristic fervid energy that makes Gibbs such a laudable player, a suitable team-mate with Buddy DeFranco, and an excellent bandleader. In December 1996, Gibbs celebrated 60 years of traveling since his playing won a him radio contest on Major Bowes' Amateur Hour at age 12. Gibbs admits he's entrenched in the vibes-clarinet sound and has toured and recorded with clarinetist Buddy DeFranco since 1980. Before settling in Sherman Oaks, California in 1957, Gibbs played in the big bands of Tommy Dorsey, Chubby Jackson, Woody Herman's Second Herd, and Benny Goodman. For 17 years he served as musical director for *The Steve Allen Show* on TV.

Jazz historians consider the Terry Gibbs Dream Band recordings among his best sessions and rank the group as one of the great ensemble bands, along with Woody Herman's Second Herd, Benny Goodman's band with drummer Gene Krupa, and Artie Shaw's band with drummer Buddy Rich. Superb arrangements, combined with Gibbs' infectious personality, infused the band's collective energy, and their dynamic, swinging, and crisp performances, often compared to roller-coaster rides, were exciting to hear with all the yelling, and accelerated dizzying tempos. He formed the much heralded Terry Gibbs Dream Band in the late 1950s and last recorded with the band in 1961. Much of the foot-tapping Dream Band music (documented on five albums) was written by top arrangers before they became famous. The straight-ahead swing-jazz charts by Marty Paich, Bill Holman, Manny Albam, Al Cohn, Bob Brookmeyer, and others helped make Gibbs's band a favorite of fans everywhere.

Gibbs grew up amidst a musical family, inspired by his father, Abe Gubenko, a violinist and bassist who led the Radio Novelty Orchestra which played Jewish music over New York City airwaves, and his older brother who played drums and xylophone, the instrument Gibbs first learned before becoming interested in drums and tympani. During his teen years, Gibbs partnered regularly in bands (playing drums) with his neighbor, pianist Norman "Tiny" Kahn, before doing a stretch in the Army. On furlough in New York City, the two buddies explored the burgeoning jazz scene on 52nd Street, and the music of Charlie Parker and Dizzy Gillespie. Gibbs absorbed their bop styles along with his earlier influences of Benny Goodman, Roy Eldridge, Lester Young, and Art Tatum. After his discharge from the service, Gibbs joined the 52nd Street musicians as a participant with guitarist Bill DeArango's group and in June, 1946 made his first recordings on Xanadu's *Bebop Revisited, Volume 2* with Aaron Sachs, before a six-week stint with Tommy Dorsey's band in California. Returning to New York, Gibbs was taken under the wing of his mentor, Lionel Hampton. In December 1947, Gibbs joined the Chubby Jackson sextet to tour Sweden and record *Bebop Revisited Volume 1*. He worked with Buddy Rich's big band in 1948, then joined Woody Herman's famed Four Brothers band and went on to co-lead a sextet with Charlie Shavers and Louis Belson. Stints with Mel Tormé and Benny Goodman's sextet (1951) followed. Since then, he has led his own groups. He moved to Los Angeles in 1957 and began a lengthy association (which continues today) with Steve Allen, playing clubs, recording, and appearing on TV. Gibbs formed his Dream Band in 1959, and, though long disbanded, it is still considered one of the most exciting big bands. He returned to New York in 1963, remaining until the next year when he went back to California where he did more

TV studio work. Since then, Gibbs has remained active leading small groups, particularly with clarinetist Buddy DeFranco. In recent years, he has become selective about the jobs he accepts, generally taking bookings that will be the most fun for him. He claims his favorite collaborations in recent years are those with clarinetist Buddy DeFranco. Because of his admiration for DeFranco, Gibbs endured a grueling 1995 trans Europe tour of 25 one-nighters (in 29 days) with his long-time cohort. He also goes out alone to star on big band and quartet dates in various parts of the United States.

what to buy: Swing-minded jazz fans and Lounge enthusiasts will dig Gibbs's jousting, danceable beats on his big band albums from the 1950s. First in the series of his boisterous big band albums, *Dream Band* ♪♪♪♪ (Contemporary, 1959/1986, prod. Richard Bock) documents a live-recorded engagement at the Seville in Hollywood, California during March 17–19, 1959. Every successful big band needs a capable leader, talented instrumentalists, a powerhouse drummer (in this case, Mel Lewis), and superb charts. Gibbs's 15-member band had it all. He credits the arrangements by Bill Holman, Bob Brookmeyer, Marty Paich, and Manny Albam (before they hit the big-time) as the impetus that gave this band such distinctive flair. These cats wrote some of the best big band arrangements—colorfully layered musical maps with lots of power, pulsation, and propulsion—many of which continue to be performed today by jazz bands all around the world. Even saxophonist Al Cohn contributes a barreling arrangement of Ellington's "Cottontail." You'll hear Gibbs yell out the count before the band swings into action, pumping through hard-swinging, uptempo numbers such as Marty Paich's arrangement of "Opus One" and "Jumpin' at the Woodside," Holman's rabble-rousing arrangement of "After You've Gone" and his lush charting for "You Go to My Head," and other exhilarating numbers. Gibbs's energy undoubtedly infused his band and his fine solos on the album's 11 tunes. Notable contributions from his lead soloists trumpeter Conte Candoli, tenor saxman Bill Holman, drummer Mel Lewis, valve trombonist Bob Enevoldsen, and others, are simply icing on the cake. A must own album for big band fans. Personnel changes or their larger, new venue (the Sundown, on the Sunset Strip in Hollywood) may account for the slight difference in the joyful spirit and sound of the band on *Dream Band, Volume 2: The Sundown Sessions* ♪♪♪♪ (Contemporary, 1959/1987, prod. Richard Bock), but those differences are minimal and all is copasetic, including the engineer, Wally Heider. So don't let the lower rating deter you from picking up this album, because Gibbs is in usual form in his leadership role and vibraphone solos on the November 1959 set, and charts from Al Cohn ("Moonglow"), Manny Albam ("The Fat Man"), Marty Paich ("Softly, as in a Morning Sunrise"), Bill Holman ("Dancing in the Dark," "No Heat," "My Reverie") and others are well crafted. The band held fort at the Sundown for 18 months, three nights a week, during which the previous album and *Dream Band, Volume 3: Flying Home* 🎵🎵🎵 (Contemporary, 1959/1988) were recorded. Volume three offers some hard-driving charts from the same world-class arrangers. Highlights include Gibbs's solo on "Midnight Sun" (arranged by Med Flory), a kicking Manny Albam arrangement of "Moten Swing," a bluesy Bill Holman original, "Evil Eyes," featuring Pete Jolly at the piano, fine solos from tenor saxophonist Holman, trombonist Joe Cadena, and others, as well as excellent section work, especially from the reeds. Med Flory's arrangement of the title tune is the grand, swinging finale and features Gibbs and a slew of soloists in the seven-plus minutes. For its sheer energy, raucous spirit, and fantastic charts, this was one of the most highly acclaimed big bands in jazz history. Own one of these Dream Band recordings, and you'll want them all. Unfortunately, the CD reissues of Volumes four and five are out of print.

what to buy next: The other important batch of recordings in Gibbs's discography includes the vibraphonist's few albums with clarinetist Buddy DeFranco, one of the most unique-sounding pairings in jazz. The first of these, *Air Mail Special* 🎵🎵🎵🎵 (Contemporary, 1990, prod. Herb Wong), was live-recorded at Carmelo's in Sherman Oaks, California on October 4–5, 1981. Gibbs and DeFranco, like-minded swing-to-bop enthusiasts, go at it, weaving and wending their way through solos, connecting, and comping with a hot rhythm team, pianist Frank Collette, bassist Andy Simpkins, and drummer Jimmy Smith. When the LP was first released under the Palo Alto Jazz label, it garnered the band three TV appearances in an eight-month period on Johnny Carson's *Tonight Show*. However, the label folded before they could make more recordings. Gibbs signed with Contemporary in 1985, acquired the masters from Palo Alto, and after several projects for Contemporary, convinced label president Ralph Kaffel to reissue the album. This delightfully bouncy and unique-sounding album offers 10 tunes, including swing standards ("Air Mail Special," "In a Mellow Tone"), the big bopper ("Now's the Time"), Latin-influenced numbers ("Yesterdays," and Gibbs' "Samba Wazzoo"), romantic ballads ("Body and Soul," "Prelude to a Kiss"), a swing-blues ("Blues for Brody"), and others tunes performed with vitality and warmth by these two masters. Equally fired up on *Chicago Fire* 🎵🎵🎵🎵 (Contemporary, 1987, prod. Richard Bock), the Gibbs-DeFranco quintet delivers a Chicago-style set, live-recorded in 1987 at Joe Segal's Jazz

Showcase at the Blackstone Hotel in Chicago. This set features young Chicagoans John Campbell (piano) and Todd Coolman (bass), and drummer Gerry Gibbs (Terry's son, then 23 years old). There's energy aplenty with many highlights on this intimate set of 10 standards, largely due to Gerry's drumming, solid rhythm support, and A-one soloing from Gibbs and DeFranco. One of the loveliest tracks is the lesser-known ballad, "This Is Always," to which Gibbs and DeFranco lend warm sentimentality. The CD bonus track, "Jitterbug Waltz," provides a nice balance amidst the swing and bop numbers. This is an excellent album. Continuing into the 1990s, the Gibbs-DeFranco team expands to a swing sextet modeled after Goodman's sextet that included vibist Lionel Hampton and guitarist Charlie Christian. Two albums deriving from one engagement at Kimball's East in Emeryville, California from April 13–15, 1991, *Kings of Swing* 🎵🎵🎵🎵 (Contemporary, 1992, prod. Terry Gibbs) and *Memories of You* 🎵🎵🎵🎵 (Contemporary, 1992, prod. Terry Gibbs), feature Gibbs and DeFranco amiably mixing it up with guitarist Herb Ellis, pianist Larry Novak, bassist Milt Hinton, and drummer Butch Miles. *Kings of Swing* delivers their nine-tune set of hard-swinging classics such as the "Seven Come Eleven," "Stompin' at the Savoy," "Undecided," "Just One of Those Things," "Air Mail Special," and pleasing ballads such as "Soft Winds," "The Man I Love," "Body and Soul," and "These Foolish Things (Remind Me of You)," all favorites that allow for these legendary musicians to comfortably romp and reminisce. Dedicated to Benny Goodman, the nine-tune *Memories of You* is alone worth the album price for Milton Hinton's bass-slapping solo and sturdy comping on the opener, "Flying Home." Everyone shares the limelight equally and there's not a dull track on either album. These albums are pure listening delights. Buy both. Recorded in 1974, *Bopstacle Course* 🎵🎵🎵🎵 (Xanadu, 1989/1995, prod. Don Schlitten), features vibist Gibbs with pianist Barry Harris, bassist Sam Jones, and drummer Alan Dawson, as they cut their way as a tight unit through eight tunes, from bop numbers to a jazz waltz, to a Brazilian-jazz track, and more. In addition to standards such as "Body and Soul" and "I'm Getting Sentimental over You," there are Gibbs originals such as the fast-paced title tune (built on the changes of "I Got Rhythm"), "Waltz for My Children," and the beautiful ballad, "Kathleen." Gibbs is as comfortable in the spotlight as he is deferring to his fine side players and this session is a gem, documenting his quartet work and highlighting his fluid, unpredictable phrasing, his penchant for swing and bop, and his wonderful melodicism.

best of the rest:

The Latin Connection 🎵🎵🎵 (Contemporary, 1986/1996)

worth searching for: If you can find either of Gibbs's final two Dream Band sessions which are currently out of print, you're in for a treat. Both albums were recorded in January of 1961 during a three-night stint at the Summit, a Hollywood nightspot. Featuring Gibbs's popular 15-member band, this CD was originally released on LP as *Terry Gibbs and his Exciting Big Band/Explosion* (Mercury, 1962). From the live-recorded stint at Hollywood's Summit, *Terry Gibbs Dream Band, Volume 4: Main Stem* ♫♫♫♫ (Contemporary 1961/1991, prod. Terry Gibbs), contains 10 rousers that showcase the rowdy, musically hip family. Knockout charts from revered big-band arrangers Bill Holman, Manny Albam, and Al Cohn prominently feature unified section work, allowing Gibbs plenty of solo and comping room, and also yielding space for spectacular soloists such as Candoli (trumpet), Rosolino (trombone), and others. Favorites such as "Ja-da," " Day in Day Out," "You Don't Know What Love Is," and "Sweet Georgia Brown," are given the Dream Band treatment. *Terry Gibbs Dream Band, Volume 5: The Big Cat* ♫♫♫♫ (Contemporary, 1961/1991, prod. Terry Gibbs, Jack Tracy) (originally released on LP as *The Exciting Terry Gibbs Big Band*) features the Dream Band driving home 11 tunes from the same live-recorded performance. Collectively and individually, musicianship is supreme and drummer Mel Lewis keeps the band kicking with his big beats, particularly when propelling fast-paced numbers such as the opener "Tico, Tico," Charlie Parker's "Billie's Bounce," and the brassy swinger, "Jump the Blues Away." Gibbs takes some fine solos throughout.

influences:

◀◀ Count Basie, Jo Jones, Benny Goodman, Roy Eldridge, Lester Young, Art Tatum, Lionel Hampton

▶▶ Dave Samuels

see also: *Buddy DeFranco*

Nancy Ann Lee

Banu Gibson

Born October 24, 1947, in Dayton, OH.

Considered to be one of today's best singers and performers of classic jazz from the 1920s and 1930s, Banu (pronounced Bahnew) Gibson has spent most of her life on stage. Gibson's vivacious and ebullient singing style harkens to the golden age of American music where pop and jazz were often one in the same. Gibson is also an accomplished instrumentalist on guitar and banjo, and her strong rhythmic playing blends perfectly on instrumentals featured by her band, the New Orleans Hot Jazz Orchestra.

Growing up in Hollywood, Florida, Banu started dancing by age three, and was taking voice lessons by age nine. She was performing professionally while in her teens, and graduated from college with a degree in music and theater. Performing through a number of venues, she ultimately ended up at Disneyland where she appeared in a Roaring Twenties-style show. This led her to move to New Orleans, where she formed her own band in 1981, and played in a number of clubs in the Crescent City. Various PBS shows and other TV appearances boosted her visibility, and made her known around the world. Along with her Hot New Orleans Jazz Band, Gibson currently tours extensively in the United States and around the world.

what to buy: As the listener will find, especially after hearing Gibson and her band in live performance, not enough of her music is out for consumption. Her *'Zat You, Santa Claus* ♫♫♫♫ (Swing Out, 1995, prod. Banu Gibson) features Banu and the New Orleans Hot Jazz band to great advantage. "Santa Claus Blues" (a classic early 1920s jazz tune) and "Christmas Night in Harlem" (from the early 1930s) showcase the band's many talents across jazz periods and styles, and are indicative of the band's potential. Gibson's voice is always effervescent, and if the listener would like a more intimate setting, her CD *Livin' in a Great Big Way* ♫♫♫♫ (Swing Out CD, 1994, prod. Banu Gibson) features Banu with just piano accompaniment. The keyboard duties are split between her competent pianist/arranger David Boeddinghaus (playing in his Fats Waller cum Teddy Wilson cum Earl Hines style) and John Sheridan, who is the pianist/arranger for the Jim Cullum Jazz Band. Gibson's tune selections are excellent samples from a very large encyclopedia of well-written songs produced from the mid-1920s to the mid-1930s. "It's Been So Long," "About a Quarter to Nine," and "I'll See You in My Dreams" are some of the stand-out tracks.

what to buy next: One of the earlier efforts for Gibson with her New Orleans Hot Jazz Orchestra can be still found on *Jazz Baby* ♫♫♫ (Stomp Off, 1990, prod. Bob Erdos). Banu's singing is fine here. The band is not as coherent as it would become, and some of the performances are uneven. Yet, for Gibson's vocals alone, the CD is certainly worth having on the shelf.

worth searching for: The CD *Battle of the Bands: San Antonio vs. New Orleans* ♫♫♫♫ (Pacific Vista, 1994, prod. Margaret Pick, Lynne Cruise) is volume four in the series Riverwalk Live at the Landing Vintage Jazz Collection (produced for Texas Public Radio), and features The Jim Cullum Jazz Band playing against Banu Gibson & The New Orleans Hot Jazz. The album provides an excellent representation of how Gibson and her band sound in a live setting. Most of the 15 tracks feature Gibson up front, with the band, or with select band members. Well-recorded and well-produced, the CD offers a nice representation of her repertoire. A variety of selections showcase the talents of the group, including wonderful vocals by Gibson on "Down Hearted Blues" and "Wrap Your Cares in Rhythm and Dance" (where she also tap dances along with Savion Glover), and a sizzling instrumental by her band of the Chocolate Dandies' "Krazy Kapers."

Jim Prohaska

João Gilberto

Born June, 1931, in Juazeiro, Brazil.

João Gilberto became interested in samba rhythms and American jazz while still a teenager. After moving to Rio de Janeiro in the early 1950s, he played on sessions for a variety of artists while working with Antonio Carlos Jobim to create the style of music later known as bossa nova. This "new wave" variation on samba reduced the crowded percussion work typical of the style in a manner similar to the development of "cool jazz" as a reaction to harder bop mannerisms. The main innovation contributed by Gilberto to this budding genre was a style of guitar playing called "violão gago," or "stammering guitar." By syncopating his voice with the rhythms generated by his guitar and a small rhythm section, Gilberto was able to build new harmonic patterns akin to chord progressions used in jazz. It was the later development that made bossa nova so seductive to jazz musicians like Stan Getz and Charlie Byrd. After changing the face of Brazilian music forever in 1959 with the hugely influential album that included Jobim masterpieces "Chega De Saudade (No More Blues)" and "Desafinado (Out of Tune)," Gilberto came to the States in 1963 with his wife, Astrud, and Jobim to record with Getz. The version they cut of Jobim's "The Girl from Ipanema" was a massive hit in America, starting a bossa nova craze that lasted for a couple of years. The album they recorded with Getz is still a steady seller.

what to buy: The performances on *The Legendary João Gilberto* ♫♫♫♫♫ (World Pacific, 1990, compilation prod. Ron McMaster, Matt Pierson) are at the core of a music revolution. The combination of Gilberto's gentle, somewhat restricted vocal range and his rhythmically sophisticated guitar playing with Jobim's songs and arrangements are beguiling, to say the least. The CD contains 38 songs in 75 minutes of music in decent sound from Gilberto's first three albums. First performances of masterpieces fill it: "Desafinado," "Samba de Una Nota Sô (One Note

Samba)," and "Insensatez (How Insensitive)" are just a few. Except for a somewhat out of place version of "I'm Looking over a Four-Leaf Clover," which gives a foretaste of crimes committed in the name of bossa nova, this collection is solid. *Getz/Gilberto* ♫♫♫♫♫ (Verve, 1964, prod. Creed Taylor) isn't the first bossa nova influenced jazz album released in the States, but it is the most influential—and quite deservedly so.

what to buy next: The music is marvelous, the performance is good, and (this could be a drawback for some listeners) the audience is enthusiastic for *Live in Montreux* ♫♫♫ (Elektra Musician, 1987, prod. João Gilberto). Luckily, they generally wait until these gently swaying classics have run their course before leaping into the participatory fray with appreciative applause. Gilberto recorded this concert in 1985, nearly three decades after the revolution Jobim and he had popularized. The material holds up well and the intimacy achieved by Gilberto and his guitar are pluses, but the performance is valedictory rather than revelatory. The wonders of modern recording technology paved the way for *João* ♫♫♫ (Verve, 1991, prod. Mayrton Bahia, Carmela Forsin). Gilberto recorded the vocals and guitar parts in Brazil while the orchestration by Clare Fischer was added in Los Angeles. If the folks at Verve had left Gilberto alone to play his guitar backed up by some idiomatic percussion, then this album might score higher. Fischer attempts to duplicate some of Jobim's orchestration on Gilberto's earlier albums, but the result is often a bit over the top. The finest touches place the vocals and rhythm over marvelous arrangements featuring clarinets and alto saxophones ("Little Rose"), where darkly wooded sounds highlight the lightness of Gilberto's singing. When Fischer drops his coverlet of strings over Gilberto's softly swinging vocals (as in "Malaga") the song verges on easy listening instead of art. Still, there is more than enough good stuff here to recommend, albeit with the orchestral caveat.

the rest:
João Gilberto ♫♫♫ (Verve, 1973)
Amoroso/Brasil ♫♫♫ (Warner Bros., 1993)
Personalidade ♫♫♫ (Verve, 1993)
Eu Sei Que Vou Te Amar: Ao Vivo ♫♫♫ (Sony Latin Jazz, 1995)

influences:

◄◄ Gerry Mulligan, Miles Davis, Noel Rosa, Vinícius de Morais, Elizete Cardozo

►► Caetano Veloso, Gilberto Gil, Milton Nascimento, Chico Buarque, Charlie Byrd, Stan Getz

Garaud MacTaggart

Dizzy Gillespie

Born John Birks Gillespie October 21, 1917, in Cheraw, SC. Died January 6, 1993, in Englewood, NJ.

Dizzy Gillespie profoundly influenced jazz on several levels simultaneously. Through his dazzling speed of execution, harmonic ingenuity, rhythmic flair, and painstaking timbral nuance, he totally conquered his instrument, reinventing the way the trumpet is played. Gillespie's ability to dissect and codify rhythmic and harmonic information for arrangers and improvisers made his formulations singularly responsible for the sound of contemporary music. More than any other individual, he morphed the trans-African structures of clave into the swing equation. His compositions ("Anthropology," "Woody 'n' You," "Groovin' High," "Night in Tunisia," "Con Alma," "Bebop," "Birks Works") remain essential vehicles for improvising. And during his half-century of music-making, Gillespie was a global musical ambassador without peer.

Gillespie began playing trumpet when he was 12 years old, and refined his technical and reading abilities at North Carolina's Laurinberg Institute between 1932 and 1935. In Philadelphia by 1935, he joined Frankie Fairfax's Orchestra, where he met trumpeter Charlie Shavers and learned the solos of Roy Eldridge, his primary early influence. He soon moved to New York, where he attracted notice for his proficiency at jam sessions and after-hours situations. He replaced Eldridge in Teddy Hill's prestigious orchestra in 1937, joined them for a European tour, and remained part of Hill's unit and other strong New York big bands until 1939. That's when his friend Mario Bauzá, the great Cuban trumpeter-composer, recommended Gillespie to Cab Calloway, in whose high-paying orchestra he remained until 1941. Hill meanwhile had folded his band to become booking manager for Minton's Playhouse in Harlem, where the after-hours rhythm section included pianist Thelonious Monk and drummer Kenny Clarke who were elaborating a new kind of phrasing and accentuation that demanded virtuosic musicianship, provided by sitters-in like Charlie Christian and, ever more frequently, Gillespie. In 1942 Gillespie recorded a fully developed "bop" solo ("Jersey Bounce" with Les Hite). In 1943 he wound up in the Earl Hines Orchestra with Charlie Parker, and singers Billy Eckstine and Sarah Vaughan who all left the venerable Hines to join Eckstine's breakaway orchestra in 1944, with Gillespie as musical director and Parker as lead alto saxophonist. Gillespie and Parker had established an instant affinity on their first meeting in Kansas City several years earlier. The intense proximity afforded by membership in a traveling orchestra gave ample time to refine their concepts. Gillespie had been bringing the new music "downtown" from Harlem for several years and after he and Parker left Eckstine, they joined forces in small combos on 52nd Street. Their May 1945 Guild recordings of Gillespie's compositions "Shaw Nuff," "Salt Peanuts," and "Hot House" were the first thunderbolt examples of the music known as bebop.

Parker's drug addiction and erratic behavior sundered the magical partnership, and in 1946 Gillespie formed his seminal big band, with arrangements from Tadd Dameron, Gil Fuller, and George Russell. By 1947 he had hired the Cuban drummer Chano Pozo, and integrated Pozo's clave concept into the band's rhythmic framework. By 1948 Gillespie's trademark goatee, horn-rimmed glasses, beret, and hipster patois became bebop's personification in the straight world. Among the musicians who passed through were the rhythm section John Lewis (piano), Ray Brown (bass), Kenny Clarke (drums), and soloists J.J. Johnson, Sonny Stitt, James Moody, John Coltrane, Jimmy Heath, and Paul Gonsalves. After breaking up the big band in 1949, Gillespie assembled satellite ensembles and traveled steadily. In 1956 he formed a second version of the big band, employing arrangers like Quincy Jones (his musical director), Benny Golson, Ernie Wilkins, Melba Liston, and Clare Fischer. In the early 1960s he commissioned concertos from J.J. Johnson and Lalo Schifrin, led a fiery quintet with James Moody, and recorded a variety of theme albums—all the while expanding his luminous reputation. The 1970s and 1980s saw Gillespie consolidating his achievements, settling into puckish elder statesmanship. He continued to perform and record extensively with various small groups, most significantly the All Nation Orchestra, an incubator for talent such as Paquito D'Rivera, Steve Turre, Danilo Perez, David Sanchez, and others.

what to buy: The remarkable two-CD retrospective *Dizzy Gillespie: The Complete RCA-Victor Recordings* ♪♪♪♪ (RCA, 1946–49/1995, prod. Orrin Keepnews) takes the listener through Gillespie's first recorded solos with Teddy Hill in 1937 to his influential 1946 small-band recordings with Don Byas, to his seminal big band dates of 1947. Gillespie recorded four discs for Verve with his superb mid-1950s touring big band, three of which had been long out of print until the release of *Birks Works: The Verve Big Band Sessions* ♪♪♪♪ (Verve, 1956–57/1995, prod. Norman Granz). Never in better form, Gillespie has total control of tone and timbre in his exquisitely structured solos over a band with

Dizzy Gillespie (© Nancy Ann Lee)

the power and smoothness of a Cadillac. His thorough mastery of his instrument was never more stirringly articulated than on the two dates combined on *Gillespiana/Carnegie Hall Concert* 𝄞𝄞𝄞𝄞 (Verve, 1961/1993, prod. Norman Granz). *Gillespiana*, perhaps Gillespie's most successful foray into concert music, is Lalo Schifrin's commissioned suite for brass band, setting up a wide array of rhythms and textures for Gillespie to solo over. *Carnegie Hall Concert* is a live concert featuring Schifrin's strong reconfigured band arrangements of Gillespie classics. For Gillespie's later period, try *Dizzy's Big 4* 𝄞𝄞𝄞𝄞 (Pablo/OJC, 1974/1990, prod. Norman Granz), featuring the maestro simultaneously biting and mellow as fine vintage wine, in a pianoless setting with guitarist Joe Pass, bass maestro Ray Brown, and crackling drummer Mickey Roker. This disc reunites the Jazz at the Philharmonic veterans with producer Granz on a seven-tune session of Gillespie classics.

what to buy next: The serious student of jazz should own all the recordings they can find of Gillespie's collaborations with Charlie Parker. The definitive *Dizzy Gillespie: His Sextets and Orchestra* 𝄞𝄞𝄞𝄞 (Musicraft, 1945–46/1988, prod. Albert Marx) includes the 1945 Guild recordings, the much-listened-to 1946 sextets with Sonny Stitt, and the first, seminal recordings of Gillespie's big band. A classic Parker-Gillespie quintet encounter at Carnegie Hall in September 1947, with fireworks from each to match some pre-concert drama, followed by a rousing performance by Gillespie's big band is contained in its entirety on *Diz 'n' Bird at Carnegie Hall* 𝄞𝄞𝄞𝄞 (Blue Note, 1947/1997, prod. Teddy Reig, Michael Cuscuna). For a comprehensive overview of the Verve years, lovingly broken down into big band recordings, bebop, and rhythms of the African diaspora, with an eye to long unavailable material, you can't do better than the three-CD set, *Dizzy's Diamonds: The Best of the Verve Years* 𝄞𝄞𝄞𝄞 (Verve, 1954–64/1992, prod. Norman Granz). One of the unique items in Gillespie's discography is *Dizzy Gillespie and the Double Six of Paris* 𝄞𝄞𝄞𝄞 (Verve, 1963/1989), with fierce bebop interpretations of 10 1940s Gillespie classics recorded on two separate occasions in 1963 in the company of James Moody, Kenny Barron, Bud Powell, Kenny Clarke, and others, with overdubbed vocalese arrangements (arranged by Lalo Schifrin) and sung in French by the Double-Six of Paris. It sounds odd, but does it ever work!

best of the rest:
(With Charlie Parker, Sonny Stitt, Dexter Gordon, and others) *Groovin' High* 𝄞𝄞𝄞𝄞 (Savoy, 1945–46/1993)
(With Charlie Parker, Sonny Stitt, Dexter Gordon, and others) *Shaw 'Nuff* 𝄞𝄞𝄞𝄞 (Musicraft, 1946/1987)

Verve Jazz Masters Ten 𝄞𝄞𝄞𝄞 (Verve, 1952–64/1994)
Duets 𝄞𝄞𝄞𝄞 (Verve, 1957/1988)
Sonny Side Up 𝄞𝄞𝄞𝄞𝄞 (Verve, 1957/1997)
Perceptions 𝄞𝄞𝄞 (Verve, 1961/1997)
(With Machito) *Afro-Cuban Jazz Moods* 𝄞𝄞𝄞𝄞 (OJC, 1975)
New Faces 𝄞𝄞𝄞 (GRP, 1988)
To Bird with Love 𝄞𝄞𝄞 (Telarc, 1992)
To Diz with Love 𝄞𝄞𝄞 (Telarc, 1992)

worth searching for: If you come across the LP version of *A Portrait of Duke Ellington* 𝄞𝄞𝄞𝄞 (Verve, 1962/1984, prod. Norman Granz), consider it a find. Gillespie's lyrical side bursts forth on fresh, idiomatic performances of 11 Ellington-Strayhorn gems arranged by Clare Fischer. Previously issued on a two-CD set which is apparently now unavailable, *Diz and Roy* 𝄞𝄞𝄞𝄞 (Verve, 1954/1994, prod. Norman Granz) pairs Gillespie with his primary influence, Roy Eldridge. Offering an iconic, inter-generational dialogue between masters, this is a revelatory document that is highly recommended should you come across it in the secondhand market.

influences:

◀◀ Louis Armstrong, Roy Eldridge, Mario Bauzá, Thelonious Monk

▶▶ Miles Davis, James Moody, Lee Morgan, Jon Faddis, Jimmy Heath, Slide Hampton, Steve Turre, David Sanchez, Danilo Perez

Ted Panken

Egberto Gismonti

Born in 1947, in Carmo, Brazil.

Egberto Gismonti is a classically trained pianist, having studied in France with Nadia Boulanger and Jean Baralaque. Moving to Rio de Janeiro in 1968 brought Gismonti into contact with Antonio Carlos Jobim and the guitar music of Baden Powell, which firmed up the young musician's resolve to make a living with his music. He taught himself how to play a standard six-string guitar but soon found it to be inadequate for his musical vision. Gismonti moved on to a seven-string instrument before discovering that an eight-string guitar (for which he had to devise a whole new way of playing) would enable him to cover the wide range of sounds he wanted to employ. His latest recordings find Gismonti using 10- and 12-string guitars with unique tunings. In 1977 Gismonti, while working on a film project in the Amazon basin, was exposed to the music of the Xingu tribes. This was to have a profound effect on his future work. The combination of a classical European background, tribal music, and the urban Brazilian sounds of samba and bossa nova have made him one of the most unique performers in the world. Gismonti has recorded more than 50 different albums in a wide variety of instrumental settings. He is also a well-known producer in Brazil in addition to writing music for film, television, theater, ballet, orchestra, and chamber ensembles.

what to buy: ECM's selection of tracks for *Works* 𝄞𝄞𝄞𝄞 (ECM, 1994, prod. Manfred Eicher) gives you an interesting sample of Gismonti's prolific, wide-ranging catalog. There are cuts featuring his superb piano playing in a group or solo setting as well as performances with Gismonti on guitar, again in group or solo presentations. The musicians appearing on this disc include saxophonist Jan Garbarek, percussionist Nana Vasconcelos, bassist Charlie Haden and Gismonti's long-time associate, bassist Zeca Assumpção. *Sanfona* 𝄞𝄞𝄞𝄞 (ECM, 1981, prod. Manfred Eicher), a superb two-CD set, contains some of Gismonti's most beguiling and accessible music. The first disc features Gismonti and supporting trio Academia de Dança playing five longish tunes and one four-part suite. There is a lot of Gismonti's piano work, certainly more than one hears on his more recent recordings. His keyboard style here hovers between Chick Corea and the sound clusters of Henry Cowell, with a little Villa-Lobos tossed in for good measure. The second CD focuses in on Gismonti as a solo guitarist. With aural colors and lines weaving an impressive tapestry of sound, Gismonti's playing reveals some of his debt to Baden Powell's pioneering performances of the 1960s and early '70s, even as he breaks new ground with his specially built guitars.

what to buy next: *Dança Das Çabecas* 𝄞𝄞𝄞𝄞 (ECM, 1977, prod. Manfred Eicher) is the album that introduced Gismonti to U.S. audiences. Essentially a duet album with percussionist Nana Vasconcelos, *Dança Das Çabecas* was impressive for the sheer number of musical sounds the duo brought to play in what was essentially a Brazilian jazz album. With songs like "Quarto Mundo + 1" and the 12-minute "Tango," it was no wonder the record was nominated for album of the year by *Stereo Review*. Almost 10 years after their initial duet release, Gismonti and Vasconcelos recorded yet another fine album, *Duas Voces* 𝄞𝄞𝄞𝄞 (ECM, 1985, prod. Manfred Eicher). Gismonti's flute playing on "Tomarapeba" shows the influence of his studies of Amazon aboriginal music, an element not heard in the earlier recording.

best of the rest:
Solo 𝄞𝄞𝄞𝄞 (ECM, 1979)
(With Charlie Haden and Jan Garbarek) *Folk Songs* 𝄞𝄞𝄞𝄞 (ECM, 1980)
(With Charlie Haden and Jan Garbarek) *Magico* 𝄞𝄞𝄞 (ECM, 1980)
Dança Dos Escravos 𝄞𝄞𝄞 (ECM, 1989)

Dizzy Gillespie (with various artists)

song "A Night in Tunisia"
album *The Bebop Revolution*
(RCA Bluebird, 1946/1990)
instrument Trumpet

Monster Solo

Infancia 𝄞𝄞𝄞 (ECM, 1991)
Zig Zag 𝄞𝄞𝄞 (ECM, 1996)

influences:
◄◄ Baden Powell, Antonio Carlos Jobim, João Gilberto, Maurice Ravel, Claude Debussy, Heitor Villa-Lobos

Garaud MacTaggart

Jimmy Giuffre
Born April 26, 1921, in Dallas, TX.

Although he could ostensibly have been categorized with the West-Coast cool movement of the 1950s (and in fact played with Howard Rumsey's Lighthouse All-Stars, the veritable finishing school for West Coast players), Jimmy Giuffre wound up spearheading a mellow sort of free jazz that was equal parts improvisation and introspection. Coming up through the ranks via orchestras like Woody Herman's and Jimmy Dorsey's, it was after his 1952–56 stint with Shorty Rogers's All-Stars that Giuffre began staking his own stylistic claim. After moving through several different, no-drummer trio set-ups—the best of which, featuring guitarist Jim Hall and bassist Ralph Peña, can be found on Atlantic's *Jimmy Giuffre 3*—Giuffre debuted what would be his ground-breaking group in 1961. Featuring pianist/composer Paul Bley and bassist Steve Swallow, this trio pulled the rug out from under both bebop and cool jazz with astonishing improvisations that, though they never seemed to heat to more than a slow simmer, were nonetheless enthralling in their complexity and expression. Though the group was short lived, it was thankfully well recorded, and any document is well worth having. Though none of Giuffre's later work would be as quietly revolutionary, it rarely falters in quality, and his reputation as a steadfastly surprising stylist has never been in doubt.

what to buy: Although on *The Jimmy Giuffre 3* 𝄞𝄞𝄞𝄞𝄞 (Atlantic, 1956, prod. Nesuhi Ertegun), Giuffre still seems somewhat indebted to the cool school from which he sprang, his instrumental versatility (he plays clarinet, tenor and even baritone on various tracks) and the consistently high compositional standards here (all but three songs are Giuffre originals) combine with the budding improvisational skills of a strong band to create a stirring and important document. Originally released as two separate Verve LPs recorded only a month apart (*Thesis* and *Fusion*), *1961* 𝄞𝄞𝄞𝄞 (ECM, 1961, prod. Creed Taylor) still neatly functions as a cohesive piece and an important document. Swallow's bass—particularly on tracks like "Trudgin'"—is passionate but restrained, while Bley's complementary piano work is fluid and dynamic. However, Giuffre's beautiful clarinet still dominates these tight-knit improvisations. Mellow without being sleepy, daring without being brash, this is a bold statement of intent that, sadly, was not taken as a call to arms by the rest of the jazz community.

what to buy next: Of the two European concerts released by hat ART, *Emphasis, Stuttgart 1961* 𝄞𝄞𝄞𝄞 (hat ART, 1961/1993, prod. Pia Uehlinger, Werner X. Uehlinger) barely nudges out its companion simply by virtue of strength of the trio's (comparatively) impassioned playing. The set list for the two shows are virtually the same, but on the *Emphasis* version of "Stretching Out," the Bley/Swallow trio was in top form and Giuffre reacts accordingly. Actually not one of Giuffre's best moments, *Dragonfly* 𝄞𝄞𝄞𝄞 (Soul Note, 1983, prod. Giovanni Bonandrini) is nonetheless a sterling example of why, even 20 years later, he was still a strong player. With his trio concept expanded to include a drummer (Randy Kaye) and electric keyboards and synths replacing standard piano accompaniment, this is certainly not cool jazz. Yet, despite all the clunky instrumentation, it still comes off simple and streamlined.

the rest:
Flight, Bremen 1961 𝄞𝄞𝄞𝄞 (hat ART, 1961/1992)
Free Fall 𝄞𝄞𝄞𝄞 (Columbia, 1962)
Giuffre/Konitz/Connors/Bley 𝄞𝄞 (Improvising Artists, 1978)
Quasar 𝄞𝄞𝄞 (Soul Note, 1985)
Eiffel 𝄞𝄞𝄞 (CELP, 1987)
Liquid Dancers 𝄞𝄞𝄞 (Soul Note, 1989)
Diary of A Trio: Saturday 𝄞𝄞𝄞 (Owl, 1989)
Diary of A Trio: Sunday 𝄞𝄞𝄞 (Owl, 1989)
Fly Away Little Bird 𝄞𝄞𝄞 (Owl, 1992)

worth searching for: *River Station* 𝄞𝄞𝄞𝄞 (CELP, 1991) may be tough to find (try Cadence), but it's well worth the search. Featuring multi-instrumentalist Joe McPhee on trombone and André Jaume handling tenor and bass clarinet, this largely improvisatory set is a joy to behold.

influences:
▶▶ Anthony Braxton

Jason Ferguson

Globe Unity Orchestra

Formed in 1966, in Berlin, Germany.

Alexander von Schlippenbach, piano; Peter Kowald, bass, tuba; Evan Parker, soprano/tenor saxophone; Peter Brötzmann, clarinet, tenor saxophone; Anthony Braxton, alto saxophone; Steve Lacy, soprano saxophone; Albert Mangelsdorff, trombone; Paul Lovens, percussion; Derek Bailey, guitar; Alan Silva, bass.

As if the late 1960s Berlin avant-garde scene wasn't free-wheeling enough, along comes pianist Alexander Schlippenbach with the concept of a free-jazz big band that's very big, very free, and that issues forth a beautiful racket that would bring tears to Glenn Miller's eyes. Although Globe Unity is sadly underdocumented, they were (and are) one of the most interesting aberrations in contemporary music. With a sound that pushes the envelope of improvisational organizations, Globe Unity firmly lays to rest the perception that free jazz, structure and humor are mutually exclusive concepts—or that insane Europeans can't swing.

what to buy: *Rumbling* 𝄞𝄞𝄞𝄞 (FMP, 1975, prod. Jost Gebers), a reissue of the *Evidence* twin-LPs, shows off a relatively pared-down line-up (nine members plus an "unidentified dog"). However, though the group does keep it somewhat close to the vest on the more "structured" numbers (they redefine Monk's "Evidence"), there is still plenty of room for fireworks, courtesy mainly of Evan Parker's incessant tenor playing and the twin trombones of Paul Rutherford and Albert Manglesdorff. Still available only on vinyl, *Jahrmarkt/Local Fair* ✍✍✍ (Po Torch, 1977, prod. Peter Kowald, Paul Lovens) is perhaps the only extant jazz recording to feature 26 accordionists on the same track, and along with *Improvisations*, is Globe Unity at their most goofily deranged. Simultaneously evoking European folk songs, heart-rending improvisatory squeals and society-band dance music, this record is as enjoyable as it is confusing. Not for the weak of heart, thanks mainly to the saxophone interplay between Braxton and Brötzmann on side one.

what to buy next: By 1986 Globe Unity had gone from jazz pariahs to German musical ambassadors, touring the world on government grants, and *20th Anniversary* ✍✍✍ (FMP, 1986, prod. Jost Gebers), live from the Berlin Jazzfest, shows a Peter Kowald-less group that sounds more like a small improvisatory ensemble then the lumbering sound-monster of the early days. Strong performances by Parker, Paul Lovens, and the elusive Alan Silva make it worthwhile though.

worth searching for: One of the last Globe Unity records to evince the communal insanity of the group, *Improvisations* ✍✍✍ (Japo, 1978, prod. Thomas Stöwsand) is also one of their best. With Manglesdorff, Brötzmann, Kowald, Parker, and (of course) Schlippenbach providing the majority of the fire here, the four improvisations contained within are bristlingly loose, yet still guarantee a good time.

influences:

◀◀ Stan Kenton, Sun Ra Arkestra

▶▶ Jazz Composers Orchestra, London Jazz Composers Orchestra

Jason Ferguson

Ben Goldberg

Born August 8, 1959, in Sycamore, IL.

Recipient of numerous NEA grants and a 1993 Goldie Award (the *San Francisco Bay Guardian*'s annual creative-music honor), clarinetist Ben Goldberg is one of the leaders of the jazz/improv community in the Bay Area. He has led a variety of combos, including New Klezmer Trio, Junk Genius, Snorkel, and Brainchild (an undocumented but phenomenal large ensemble based on Goldberg's "spontaneous composition" concept of minimally directed, collective improvisation). His efforts have attracted NYC heavyweights like John Zorn and Marty Ehrlich. Tours abroad and appearances on the festival circuit, with a couple of showcases at the distinguished Vancouver Jazz Fest, have begun to spark an international buzz. While Don Byron is

popularly credited as the most adept and adventurous clarinetist in contemporary jazz, a simple comparison of discographies casts Goldberg in a far more progressive light. With New Klezmer Trio, Goldberg was exploring "Radical Jewish Culture" long before Zorn coined the term for his Tzadik imprint (and Byron delved into the *Music of Mickey Katz*). His Junk Genius quartet reworks bebop classics with an up-to-the-minute approach that pushes toward the future. And a handful of new recordings in trio, quartet, and sextet configurations reveals an innovative composer/band leader at the vanguard of creative improvised music. Jumping off from a deceptively simple notion—"Don't improvise, just play the song . . . do what needs to be done"—the clarinetist cuts to the core of what great jazz is all about.

what to buy: *Masks & Faces* ✍✍✍✍ (Nine Winds, 1991/Tzadik, 1996, prod. Ben Goldberg), the debut recording of New Klezmer Trio (with drummer Kenny Wollesen and bassist Dan Seamans) introduced the creative merger of traditional klezmer and forward-pushing jazz. Pre-Masada, pre-Byron-does-Katz, it marks a pivotal moment in the evolution of the art form. From the leader's "Statement of Themes on Contra-alto Clarinet," the sextet on *Twelve Minor* ✍✍✍✍ (Avant, 1997, prod. Ben Goldberg) dives into more than an hour's worth of frighteningly incisive extrapolation. Rob Sudduth is a melodic monster on tenor, and Miya Masaoka and Carla Kihlstedt have to be heard to be believed. On-edge arrangements explode the bebop handbook while respecting the essence of the songs of *Junk Genius* ✍✍✍✍ (Knitting Factory Works, 1996, prod. Ben Goldberg). An almost post-punk energy pumps locomotive tracks like "Tempus Fugit," "Koko," "Shaw Nuff" and the definitive "Bebop." To be sure, this ain't no Wynton Marsalis rehash. *Here by Now* ✍✍✍✍ (Music and Arts, 1997, prod. Ben Goldberg) is a vivid look at how Goldberg's tune-based aesthetic soars in the company of like-minded collaborators. Simple melodies are transformed with ingenuity and intensity without a superfluous note in the lot.

what to buy next: New Klezmer Trio's *Melt Zonk Rewire* ✍✍✍✍ (Tzadik, 1995, prod. Ben Goldberg) expands the equation introduced on *Masks & Faces*. The mondo-"grunge" of Seamans's bass on "Feedback Doina" and Goldberg's clarinet blasted through a Fender amp on "Gas Nine" give klezmer's serpentine melodicism a welcome shock of hard rock electricity. *Light at the Crossroads* ✍✍✍ (Songlines, 1997, prod. Marty Ehrlich, Ben Goldberg) is worth checking out if only for the tone of the woodwinds. Powerful improvising from all members of the quartet. Dunn and Wollesen have never sounded more commanding. Compositions are split between Erlich and Goldberg, with a nod to Wayne Horvitz on "Ask Me Later."

the rest:
What Comes Before ♫♫♫♪ (Tzadik, 1997)

worth searching for: With a deliriously punchy "Salt Peanuts" anticipating Junk Genius, Goldberg and Kenny Wollesen's *The Relative Value of Things* ♫♫♫♫♪ (33 1/4, 1992, prod. Ben Goldberg), a series of inspired duets self-released on Goldberg's literally in-house "label," offers a nascent glimpse of the Goldberg-Wollesen inventions to come.

influences:
◀◀ Charlie Parker, Thelonious Monk, Ornette Coleman, Steve Lacy

▶▶ John Zorn's Masada

Sam Prestianni

Larry Goldings

Born August 28, 1968, in Boston, MA.

Although he is increasingly thought of as one of the most promising young organists in the business, the piano was Larry Goldings's first instrument. After high school, he moved to New York City to attend the New School for Social Research and soon took a job with saxophonist Christopher Hollyday. The young musician's next employer was singer Jon Hendricks, closely followed by guitarist Jim Hall. During his stint with Hall, Goldings started listening to recordings of organists Jimmy Smith, Mel Rhyne and Larry Young before making his first record date as an organist with ex-James Brown horn man Maceo Parker. Since that time Goldings has recorded and toured extensively with guitarist John Scofield, doubling on piano and organ, and recorded on his own.

what to buy: On *Caminhos Cruzados* ♫♫♫♫ (Novus, 1994, prod. Larry Goldings, Ikuyoshi Hirakawa) Goldings's organ style is a lot lighter in tone and less likely to wail in the powerful aural acrobatics usually associated with the instrument. (This makes him the perfect choice of all the young, talented organists now playing to record an album of Brazilian classics.) Composers represented include the cream of the bossa nova/MPB crop (Jobim, Gilberto, and Veloso) in addition to tunes by Kenny Dorham ("UNA MAS") and Rodgers & Hart ("Where or When") adaptable to the Brazilian treatment. Goldings, with his compatriots Peter Bernstein on guitar and Bill Stewart on drums, works with percussionist Guilherme Franco and guest artist

Joshua Redman to make an album packed with the idiomatic grace inherent in the material.

what to buy next: There is more heft in Goldings's organ's playing on his last couple albums, and *Whatever It Takes* ♫♫♫♫ (Warner Bros., 1995, prod. Matt Pierson) is lighter toned than a lot of the funkier players out there, but the added aural weight means that Goldings is coming more to grips with the idea of being an organist, not just a recycled piano player. He is using his stops more and pulling out some licks he never would have played on his previous albums. Maybe the presence of his old employer, Maceo Parker, and another James Brown alum, Fred Wesley, had something to do with it; Goldings cranks it out in true sixties soul/funk style on "If You Want Me to Stay" and the organist's own "Yipes!" Drummer Bill Stewart (Goldings's compatriot in the John Scofield group) kicks up a storm, and all those years playing with Lou Donaldson have given guitarist Peter Bernstein a handle on the funk as well. Bassist Richard Patterson is added on three cuts, freeing Goldings from the bass pedal responsibility on those tunes.

the rest:
The Intimacy of the Blues ♫♫♫ (Verve, 1991)
Big Stuff ♫♫♫ (Warner Bros., 1996)
Light Blue ♫♫♫ (Minor Music, 1996)

worth searching for: Goldings is one of the featured artists on *Warner Jams Volume 1*, an attempt by the label to take some of their young lions and duplicate the era of in studio jams first made popular by the Jazz at the Philharmonic dates. The organist writes the first tune, "Blue Grass," and is featured on the Cole Porter standard "Get out of Town." Fellow players include Kenny Garrett, Joshua Redman, Wallace Roney, Brad Mehldau, Peter Bernstein, Clarence Seay, and Brian Blade.

influences:
◀◀ Jimmy Smith, Mel Rhyne

Garaud MacTaggart

Vinny Golia

Born March 1, 1946, in the Bronx, NY.

Despite a 20-year period of prolific recording and international touring activity, multi-instrumentalist Vinny Golia remains largely an underground figure. This has as much to do with geography (he lives in L.A.) as it does vision. In many ways, Golia is a traditionalist, but he's no slave to any one tradition. So you won't find him keeping ranks with the proselytizers of the Blue Note canon. A virtuosic composer-improviser, he has expanded the lexicon of contemporary jazz to include an unlimited range of inspirational sources, not unlike Anthony Braxton and other leaders of the post-Trane revolution. He writes for everything from chamber trio (winds, piano, bass) to his Large Ensemble (which, involving up to 26 members, has served as a breeding ground for some of L.A.'s most ambitious players). The artist also skillfully wields more than 40 aerophones, including all kinds of saxes (from baritone to sopranino), multiple clarinets, ethnic flutes and other indigenous wind instruments. A former painter, Golia's compositions and improvisations weave stunning visual tales. The moods of his lengthier pieces, particularly for Large Ensemble, unfold in elegant layers of color and texture, no doubt originally styled after Duke Ellington. Though he occasionally records for other independent labels, much of Golia's documented work is available from his DIY imprint, Nine Winds.

what to buy: *haunting the spirits inside them. . . ♪♪♪♪* (Music & Arts, 1995, prod. Nels Cline) is arguably one of the greatest freely improvised summits ever documented. The connection between Golia (on an arsenal of winds from bass clarinet to sheng), world-class bassists and long-time bandmate Ken Filiano, and Joelle Leandre (a French virtuoso) is intuitive and rare. Recorded with the Chamber Trio in 1986, Golia's compositions create an irrepressible forum for pianist Wayne Peet and bassist Filiano to let loose on *Worldwide & Portable* ♪♪♪♪ (Nine Winds, 1990, prod. Vinny Golia). Both the songs and the improvisations pulse with dynamic intensity. The group's *Against the Grain* ♪♪♪♪ (Nine Winds, 1993, prod. Vinny Golia) is the second-generation Vinny Golia Quintet's debut on CD, a reunion of Golia and former bandmate and six-string innovator Nels Cline. All of the Quintet recordings are amazing, but this is the place to start. The tour that became *Portland, 1996* ♪♪♪♪ (Nine Winds, 1996, prod. Vinny Golia) was one of those rarities in modern jazz: a 24-piece creative-music ensemble on the road in the United States. Plus, it's a formidable introduction to Golia's big band. The energy is high and the individual performances (particularly from violinist Jeff Gauthier, tuba player Bill Roper, and of course, Golia) near transcendent. How drummer Alex Cline locks down the colossal grooves is beyond rational.

what to buy next: The Quintet's debut, *The Gift of Fury* ♪♪♪♪ (Nine Winds, 1981, prod. Nels Cline) showcases Golia's trademark compositional elements: fiery propulsion, harmonic sophistication, graceful mood and tempo shifts, lyrical melodies, volcanic swing, slamming backbeats, and structural flexibility. The earliest document of Golia's mature vision. An exemplary showcase for Golia's seemingly inexhaustible flow of ideas is *The Art of Negotiation* ♪♪♪♪ (CIMP, 1996, prod. Robert Rusch). Part-

VINNY GOLIA

song "Big Child on the Loose"
album *Nation of Laws*
(Nine Winds, 1996)
instrument Bass saxophone

ner Filiano creates an improvised framework for Golia to slide in and out of with unwavering lyricism at logic-defying speeds. Note the deconstructed bop, Dolphy-like speech-sound outbursts, and relentless forward momentum. *Triangulation* ♪♪♪♪ (Nine Winds, 1996, prod. Vinny Golia) is Golia at his darkest. The grave, gargantuan, almost apocalyptic tone is absorbing, and not at all what you'd expect from the average threesome. Its a portentous improvised meeting that pushes beyond the boundaries of so-called jazz. A heady two-CD, six-section, 21-part suite titled "One Moment of Truth," on the Large Ensemble's *Commemoration* ♪♪♪♪ (Nine Winds, 1994, prod. Vinny Golia) is dedicated to John Carter. The band's in top form, as usual.

the rest:
Solo ♪♪♪♪ (Nine Winds, 1980)
(With the Golia Trio) *Slice of Life* ♪♪♪♪ (Nine Winds, 1983)
(With the Golia Quintet) *Goin' Ahead* ♪♪♪♪ (Nine Winds, 1985)
(With the Golia Quintet) *Out for Blood* ♪♪♪♪♪ (Nine Winds, 1989)
(With the Golia Large Ensemble) *Pilgrimage to Obscurity* ♪♪♪♪♪ (Nine Winds, 1990)

(With the Golia Large Ensemble) *Decennium Dans Axlan* ♫♫♫♫ (Nine Winds, 1992)

(With the Golia Large Ensemble) *Tutto Contare* ♫♫♫♫ (Nine Winds, 1995)

(With the Golia Quintet) *Razor* ♫♫♫♫♪ (Nine Winds, 1995)

(With the Paul Smoker-Vinny Golia Quartet) *Halloween '96* ♫♫♫♫♪ (CIMP, 1996)

(With Golia-Turetzky) *Eleven Reasons to Begin* ♫♫♫♫♪ (Music & Arts, 1996)

(With the Golia Quintet) *Nation of Laws* ♫♫♫♫ (Nine Winds, 1996)

worth searching for: *spirits in fellowship* ♫♫♫♫♪ (Nine Winds, 1977) is Golia's debut recording, with John Carter on b-flat clarinet.

influences:

◀◀ Jimi Hendrix, Duke Ellington, John Coltrane, Eric Dolphy, Igor Stravinsky

Sam Prestianni

Mac Gollehon

Born in VA.

Mac Gollehon is an oft-recorded studio player with the apparent will and financial resources to attempt to transcend side-man-style anonymity and become a pop jazz star. As a leader, Gollehon plays an undistinguished, synthesized brand of fuzak-funk: "smooth jazz," in the contemporary marketing vernacular. Gollehon has chops galore, and a pleasant sound, but the contexts in which he chooses to work are exceedingly banal. As a teenager, Gollehon played first trumpet with the Roanoke (Virginia) Symphony. After graduation from the Berklee School of Music in Boston, he went on the road with a number of big bands, including those led by Buddy Rich, Buddy Morrow, and Stan Kenton. After moving to New York, Gollehon found his way onto the studio scene. He's played on records by—among others—David Bowie, Mick Jagger, and Duran Duran. He remains a busy session player and leads a band that on occasion features the trumpeter Lester Bowie. Gollehon has also worked in the design and development of brass instruments.

what's available: *Mac's Smoking Section* ♫♫ (McKenzie, 1996, prod. Robert Arron) is a minimally involving record at best (featuring guest stars Bowie, Hilton Ruiz, and Nile Rodgers). Gollehon exhibits a well-developed technique and an affecting lyrical sense that is ill-served by the bland, echo-laden artifice of the electronic backdrops. By the late 1990s, this all-too-obvious try at Kenny G-like stardom was Gollehon's sole release as a leader.

influences:

◀◀ Herb Alpert

Chris Kelsey

Benny Golson

Born January 25, 1929, in Philadelphia, PA.

Though early in his career Benny Golson gained renown for his memorable compositions and well-crafted arrangements, by the late 1950s he had established a strong reputation as a distinctively warm-toned tenor saxophonist. One of the few players of his generation to base his approach largely on Lucky Thompson, Golson at times also called to mind Don Byas. When he returned to jazz in the late 1970s after more than a decade hiatus, his sound had become gruffer and darker, with shades of Archie Shepp.

After Golson attended Howard University in the late 1940s, he moved back home to Philly and hooked up with Bull Moose Jackson's proto-R&B outfit in 1951, while Philly Joe Jones and Tadd Dameron were in the band. Golson played with Dameron's band in 1953, and the seminal bebop composer-arranger became one of his major influences. Before Golson made a name for himself writing for Dizzy Gillespie's big band (1956–58), he played with Lionel Hampton (1953–54), and briefly replaced John Coltrane in Johnny Hodges band (1954) and Stanley Turrentine in Earl Bostic's group (1954–56). His reputation as an improvisor was firmly established during the year (1958–59) he spent with Art Blakey's third edition of the Jazz Messengers, with Lee Morgan and Bobby Timmons. He contributed many tunes and arrangements to Blakey's book, including "Blues March" and "Whisper Not." Golson also wrote a host of other standards around this time, including "I Remember Clifford" in tribute to trumpeter Clifford Brown, "Stablemates," "Out of the Past," and the modal "Killer Joe." He made his first album as a leader for Contemporary in 1957, and recorded a series of strong albums for Riverside and Prestige over the next two years. From 1959–62 he co-led the Jazztet with Art Farmer, then increasingly began working outside of jazz. He spent 1964–66 in Europe and then concentrated on studio work, composing for television. He became active in jazz again in 1977, and has recorded a number of fine albums for Timeless, Dreyfus, Denon, and various Japanese labels. In addition to writing music for famed jazz singers over the years, Golson has crafted commissioned works for symphony orchestras. In 1996, he was honored for his lifetime achievements as a recipient of the National Endowment of the Arts Jazz Master Award.

what to buy: Golson's reputation as a composer-arranger was already firmly established through his work with Dizzy Gillespie when *Benny Golson's New York Scene* ♫♫♫♫ (Contemporary/OJC, 1957, prod. Nat Hentoff) came out, one of his first sessions as a leader. Five tracks feature Art Farmer (trumpet), Wynton Kelly (piano), Paul Chambers (bass), and Charlie Persip (drums). Golson augments the quintet with Julius Watkins (French horn), Jimmy Cleveland (trombone), Sahib Shihab (baritone sax), and Gigi Gryce (alto sax) on three pieces, including beautiful arrangements of his tunes "Whisper Not" and the melancholy "Just by Myself." Farmer and Golson display the intuitive connection and aural affinity they developed further in their Jazztet, creating luminous voicings on the ballad "You're Mine You," and gospel-flavored "Step Lightly." Golson's arrangements show his considerable debt to Tadd Dameron, but also how much he'd developed his own voice as a writer. A true all-star album, *The Modern Touch* ♫♫♫♫ (Riverside/OJC, 1957, prod. Orrin Keepnews) is a relaxed session featuring trumpeter Kenny Dorham, trombonist J. J. Johnson, pianist Wynton Kelly, bassist Paul Chambers, and drummer Max Roach. Golson wrote three of the six tunes, introducing his future standards "Out of the Past" and an 11-minute workout on "Blues on Down." The album includes two tunes by Gigi Gryce, including the Eastern-tinged "Hymn of the Orient" and the pop tune "Namely You." The three horn players all possess supremely burnished, warm tones, and Golson's charts create some deliciously rich textures, making this a highly rewarding recording. Golson stretches out on *Live* ♫♫♫♫ (Dreyfus, 1991), a quartet session recorded in Porto Maggiore, Italy, in 1989. Accompanied by a confident rhythm section with Mulgrew Miller (piano), Peter Washington (bass), and Tony Reedus (drums), Golson blows with conviction, spinning out consistently fresh and inventive lines. The tunes include his standards "I Remember Clifford," "Along Came Betty," and a thrillingly fast "Jam the Avenue," as well as "Sweet and Lovely," and Tom MacIntosh's harmonically challenging "The Cup Bearers." No tune is shorter than 11 minutes. Miller sounds thoroughly energized by the proceedings, taking a number of fluent, discursive solos. Golson plays with a harder, rougher sound than in his Riverside/Prestige days, yet has lost none of the intimacy that marked his early work.

what to buy next: *The Other Side of Benny Golson* ♫♫♫♫ (Riverside/OJC, 1958, prod. Orrin Keepnews) established Golson's reputation as a tenor saxophonist and was the first of many sessions with trombonist Curtis Fuller. Golson doesn't shirk his writing duties, supplying three of the six tunes, including the jaunty "Strut Time" and a soulful "Cry a Blue Tear." Golson shows off his hard-bop chops on Junior Mance's gospel-inflected "Jubilation" and plays with relaxed authority on Richard Evans's "This Night." The rhythm section features Barry Harris (piano), Jymie Merritt (bass), and Philly Joe Jones (drums). Golson and trombonist Curtis Fuller renew their long-running and mutually inspiring collaboration on *Domingo* ♫♫♫♫ (Dreyfus, 1992, prod. Benny Golson, Francis Dreyfus), one of the tenor saxophonist's finest sessions since returning to jazz in 1977. Featuring a youthful rhythm section with pianist Kevin Hays, bassist Tony Reedus, and drummer James Genus, the session includes six Golson tunes, including two Jazztet tunes he reworked for the quintet, "Time Speaks" and "Moment to Moment," Dave Brubeck's "In Your Own Sweet Way," and Fuller's "A La Mode." Trumpeter Jean-Loup Longnom sits in for a rousing version of "Blues March" to close the album.

best of the rest:
Gone with Golson ♫♫♫♫ (Prestige/OJC, 1959/1995)
Groovin' with Golson ♫♫♫♫ (Prestige/OJC, 1959/1993)
Gettin' with It ♫♫♫♫ (Prestige/OJC, 1959/1995)
Meet the Jazztet ♫♫♫♫♫ (Chess/MCA, 1960)
Blues on Down ♫♫♫♫ (Chess/GRP, 1960–61)
I Remember Miles ♫♫♫♫ (Evidence, 1992/1996)

worth searching for: A fascinating session pairing Golson with Pharoah Sanders, *This Is for You, John* ♫♫♫♫ (Timeless, 1983, prod. Benny Golson, Fumimaru Kawashima) is a tribute to Golson's Philly jam session partner, John Coltrane, though the two tenors complement much more than compete with each other. The redoubtable rhythm section features Cedar Walton (piano), Ron Carter (bass), and Jack DeJohnette (drums). Golson wrote five of the seven tunes, which mostly harken back to his and Trane's informal blowing sessions, such as "Jam the Avenue" and the bop chord changes of "Page 12." Golson sounds particularly beautiful on his elegiac ballad for Trane, "A Change of Heart," with Pharoah sitting out. Sanders supplied the unusually structured modal piece "Origin" and the two tenors can't help but evoke Trane on "Greensleeves."

influences:
◀◀ Lucky Thompson, Don Byas, Archie Shepp

Andrew Gilbert

Eddie Gomez

Born October 4, 1944 in Santurce, Puerto Rico.

A soloist of dazzling technique and passionate lyricism, bassist Eddie Gomez first gained renown when he joined pianist Bill Evans Trio in 1965. Since then, his expressive tone, exemplary musicianship, and commitment to jazz have led to partnerships with dozens of equally uncompromising artists, from Hank Jones to McCoy Tyner. Raised in New York, Gomez joined Marshall Brown's Newport Jazz Festival Band at age 14. Turning pro while still in high school, he worked with drummer Rufus Jones, vibist Gary McFarland, and pianist Marian McPartland before joining Paul Bley's influential group. Gomez greatly expanded his bass chops during his 11-year tenure with Evans and gained a reputation for his forays into the bass's upper register and for his melodic adventurousness. He later brought that same technique to the electric bass, though he preferred playing amplified acoustic even in fusion sessions. Since the late 1970s he has been working constantly, helping to found the group Steps, in 1979, backing Chick Corea and Jack DeJohnette, and leading his own groups.

what to buy: *Gomez* 🎵🎵🎵🎵 (Denon, 1987, prod. Siruko Lejuki) is a Japanese import, with Chick Corea, bassist Gomez, and drummer Steve Gadd joined by Yasuaki Shimzu on tenor sax, and Kazumi Watanabe on guitar. Corea, Gomez, and Gadd have worked together repeatedly over the past two decades in a variety of configurations and their individual musical mastery, along with the fact that they've played together, allows a level of communication that elevates these proceedings. Shimizu and Watanabe are promising, but certainly not on the level of their American counterparts. Originals, including Gomez's "Santurce," Corea's "Japanese Waltz," and Bill Evans's "We Will Meet Again," are highlights. *Next Future* 🎵🎵🎵🎵 (Stretch, 1993, prod. Chick Corea, Eddie Gomez), Gomez's first recording for his friend Chick Corea's Stretch Records, is a slick studio session featuring the bassist and two pianists, Corea or James Williams, drummer Lenny White, flautist Jeremy Steig, and saxman Rick Margitza. Steig and Gomez go back to the 1960s, to one of the first true jazz-fusion groups, Jeremy and the Satyrs. Steig plays the flute a la Rahsaan Roland Kirk and Jethro Tull's Ian Anderson, humming the melody while blowing the instrumental simultaneously and his focused intensity is nice addition here. Margitza's smooth tenor also shines, most notably on Corea's "Basic Trane-ing," and "Cheeks," Gomez's humorous dedication to Dizzy Gillespie.

influences:

◀◀ Jimmy Blanton, Scott LaFaro

▶▶ Dave Holland, Miroslav Vitous, Charlie Haden, Marc Johnson

Bret Primack

Paul Gonsalves

Born July 12, 1920, in Boston, MA. Died May 14, 1974, in London, England.

Paul Gonsalves was as important a figure as any in the revival of Duke Ellington's orchestra in the 1950s and '60s, and his sometimes fiery, sometimes gentle playing became a signature of those groups.

After coming up through the big bands of Count Basie and Dizzy Gillespie in the 1940s, Gonsalves joined an Ellingtonian unit in 1950 whose popularity had been faltering. That changed, however, in 1956, after a rousing performance at the Newport Jazz Festival in which a 27-chorus solo by Gonsalves on "Diminuendo and Crescendo in Blue" almost caused a riot—a moment which proved to be as vital for Duke's band's new vitality and fame as it was for Gonsalves's own career. Throughout the rest of the 1950s and up until his death, Gonsalves made his mark on many classic Ellington records, including *The Far East Suite*, . . . *And His Mother Called Him Bill*, and *70th Birthday Concert*. He also made some stimulating records of his own, with various different swing and bop stylists.

what to buy: On *Gettin' Together* 🎵🎵🎵🎵 (Riverside, 1961/ OJC, 1987, prod. Orrin Keepnews), his first date as a leader, Gonsalves is joined by an appealing hard-bop cast of Nat Adderley, Wynton Kelly, Sam Jones, and Jimmy Cobb. The interaction of Gonsalves and Kelly is particularly enjoyable, especially on "Walkin'" and "I Cover the Waterfront." As usual on his many recorded tenor battles, *Salt and Pepper* 🎵🎵🎵🎵 (Impulse!, 1964/1997, prod. Bob Thiele) found the competitive Sonny Stitt bringing out the best in his "opponent." This release has the benefit of having been reissued as part of GRP's superb 20-bit Impulse! remastering series.

what to buy next: *Paul Gonsalves Meets Earl Hines* 🎵🎵🎵🎵 (Black Lion, 1973/1992, prod. Alan Bates) is full of beautiful duets, mostly covering Ellingtonian standards, with the great pianist. Gonsalves sounds very much like his predecessor in the Ellington band, Ben Webster, and this meeting with Hines is reminiscent of the classic encounters between Webster and pianist Art Tatum.

what to avoid: Two great swing veterans are captured at far from their best on *Mexican Bandit Meets Pittsburgh Pirate* 🎵🎵 (Fantasy, 1974/ OJC, 1992, prod. Michael James, Stanley Dance). Roy Eldridge's chops were fading, and Gonsalves was close to his death. This might have been a great record if it were made a few years earlier.

the rest:

Jazz Till Midnight 🎵🎵🎵 (Storyville, 1967)

(With Ray Nance) *Just A-Sittin' and A-Rockin'* 🎵🎵🎵 (Black Lion, 1971/1990)

worth searching for: What? You don't already own *Ellington at Newport* 🎵🎵🎵🎵 (Columbia, 1956, prod. George Avakian)? If ever an album was worth buying for just one performance, it's this classic with Gonsalves's immortal "Diminuendo and Crescendo" solo.

influences:

◀◀ Ben Webster, Coleman Hawkins, Don Byas

▶▶ John Coltrane

Dan Keener

Jerry Gonzalez & the Fort Apache Band

Formed in 1980 in New York, NY.

Jerry Gonzalez (born January 5, 1949), trumpet, flugelhorn, percussion; Andy Gonzalez, bass; John Stubblefield, tenor saxophone; Joe Ford, alto/soprano saxophones; Larry Willis, piano; Andy Gonzalez, bass; Steve Berrios, percussion.

Trumpeter/percussionist Jerry Gonzalez leads one of today's most popular Afro-Cuban-jazz bands, the six-member Fort Apache Band. The multi-talented Gonzalez and his brother, bassist Andy, grew up in the Bronx surrounded by eclectic musical influences. Jerry Gonzalez made his recording debut as leader in 1980 with *Ya Yo Me Cure*. He has also worked as sideman to leaders in both jazz and Latin music, such as Tony Williams, McCoy Tyner, Kenny Dorham, Anthony Braxton, Tito Rodriguez, Ray Barretto, Tito Puente, Paquito D'Rivera, and Machito. Gonzalez began to form his own definition of "Latin" jazz, which was fed by experiences with Dizzy Gillespie (1970), and with the classic Latin-jazz band, El Son, led by pianist Eddie Palmieri (with whom Jerry and Andy both worked). They also worked together with timbalero Manny Oquendo's Conjunto Libre, and other bands before forming their own ensemble which evolved into the Fort Apache Band. While both brothers continued to work as sidemen with various sympathetic jazz players (such as Steve Turre), their 30 years of experience is best brought to fruition within their tight-yet-flexible Fort Apache Band, founded in the early 1980s.

As one of the best-sounding bands arising from New York's Latin scene, the Fort Apache Band generates seamless, sponta-

PAUL GONSALVES
(WITH DUKE ELLINGTON)

song "Diminuendo and Crescendo in Blue"

album *Ellington at Newport* (Columbia, 1956)

instrument Tenor saxophone

Monster Solo

neous shifts between scintillating Afro-Cuban rhythms and straight-ahead, bebop influenced jazz. The Fort Apache Band began as a flexible ensemble of 10–15 pieces in the early 1980s. By 1989 the group had trimmed down to a quintet featuring the Gonzalez brothers with Steve Berrios (drums), Larry Willis (piano), and Carter Jefferson (saxophone). Their first two albums were live-recorded at European jazz festivals. The group gained wider notice in the United States after their 1989 recording *Rumba Para Monk* was cited as Jazz Record of the Year by the French Academie Du Jazz. That recording consolidated their musical concept and led to a citation in the 55th Annual *Down Beat* Readers Poll as the top band in the World Beat category. In 1991 saxophonist Joe Ford joined the group, and following Carter Jefferson's death in 1993, tenor saxman John Stubblefield, who'd previously guested, became a regular member. Gonzalez and his band, often augmented by guest soloists, have continued to build on their successes, releasing a stream of albums for Sunnyside, Milestone, and Enja. Originally launched with more salsa players, Fort Apache now contains musicians equally well versed in jazz, resulting in a nicely balanced sound that smoothly straddles the fence between the two musical genres and contributes to their uniqueness.

what to buy: You could pick any Fort Apache Band album and be satisfied with the creativity of the soloists, the fine Afro-Cuban and jazz arrangements, and the overall tight band sound. Making their Milestone debut on *Crossroads* 🎵🎵🎵🎵 (Milestone, 1994, prod. Todd Barkan), Gonzalez and Fort Apache performs mostly original music from band members. The group successfully melds traditional jazz with Afro-Cuban rhythms and infuses tunes with cutting-edge solos. Tenor saxman Stubblefield, a former Fort Apache member, returns on this outing, replacing Jefferson, who died in 1993. Also on this album with brothers Jerry (trumpet/flugelhorn/ congas) and Andy (bass) Gonzalez, are Joe Ford (alto/soprano saxes), Larry Willis (piano), and Steve Berrios (percussion). These players were with Apache prior to this session and recorded the Sunnyside sessions, *Earthdance* (1991) and *Moliendo Café* (1992). Throughout the diverse array of 12 tunes, *Crossroads* remains a solid, well-produced session that never loses its jazz sensibilities, a fitting dedication to the late Carter Jefferson. On *Pensativo* 🎵🎵🎵🎵 (Milestone 1995 prod. Todd Barkan), the nine compositions, mostly originals by group members, are great vehicles for the superb soloists and equally demonstrate the band's proclivity for unified section work. Rhythms are easy, colors are bright and upbeat, and tunes offer nicely textured blends of Afro-Cuban rhythms with jazz sensibilities. When compared to their debut, this album focuses a bit more on percussion, but always within the framework of jazz. Gentle swayers such as Stubblefield's "Midnight Train" should coax some listeners to dancing. Wayne Shorter's composition, "Dance Cadaverous" and the Monk standard, "Ruby, My Dear," get tender, lush readings from Gonzalez, and Strayhorn's "A Flower Is a Lovesome Thing" provides a gentle, poignant forum for front-line soloists.

what to buy next: Less jazz-influenced, but still one of the best Fort Apache gigs, the live-recorded *Obatalà* 🎵🎵🎵🎵 (Enja, 1989, prod. Matthias Winckelmann) impresses the listener with how much Gonzalez is influenced by Dizzy Gillespie's small-ensemble Afro-Cuban explorations. The session prominently features a tantalizing percussion team (Berrios, Milton Cardona, Hector "Flaco" Hernandez, Nicky Marrero) backing the horns on exhilarating versions of Wayne Shorter's "Nefertiti," the Monk tunes "Evidence" and "Jackie-ing," and Cardona's title tune, plus four more numbers. Recorded at the International Jazz Festival in Zurich on November 6, 1988, this CD is one of Fort Apache's earliest, most Latin-influenced listens. *The River Is Deep* 🎵🎵🎵🎵

(Enja, 1982/1996), another live-recorded date (this time at the Berlin Jazz Days on November 5, 1982), is another more percussion-laden album, with their rousing version of Dizzy's "Bebop," demonstrating Gonazlez's conceptual roots. Blazing horn-section playing, pulsating hand drums, and Gonzalez's bright solos earmark this album which artfully connects musical influences from Africa, the Caribbean, South America, and North America. Melding jazz sensibilities to layers of throbbing percussion, the 13-minute version of Bud Powell's "Parisian Thoroughfare" is pure perfection. Highlighted on that track are the talented pianist Jorge Dalto, alto saxman Wilfredo Velez, trombonist Steve Turre, and various percussionists. In spite of some annoying microphone feedback screeches, the exceptional seven-tune outing is a must-own for fans of Afro-Cuban jazz. Recorded in a New York studio in 1991, *Moliendo Café* 🎵🎵🎵🎵 (Sunnyside, 1992, prod. Todd Barkan, Satoshi Harano) features Fort Apache when tenor saxophonist Carter Jefferson was still with the band. With Latin classics such as "Obsesion" and "Moliendo Café," and jazz standards such as "Stardust" and "Summertime," the musicians stretch the divide between hard-bop and Latin grooves with satiny, cohesive success. Recorded during a live February 2–4, 1996 stint at Blues Alley in Washington, D.C., *Fire Dance* 🎵🎵🎵🎵 (Milestone, 1996) was Fort Apache's first live-in-concert recording with this edition of the band following the death of Jefferson in 1993. Tightly arranged horns and vibrant solos enhance the bop-derived six tunes. Highlights include fine soloing from the fiery John Stubblefield (Jefferson's replacement), especially on the burning 15-minute opener, "Isabel the Liberator," contributed by pianist Larry Willis. Gonzalez offers a pleasing muted solo on "Elegua," a tune augmented with dark, horn-section riffs interspersed between soloists. The remaining tunes include band originals (which begin to sound somewhat alike but for the solos) and fine translations of Monk's "Let's Call This" (given Afro-Cuban seasonings) and "Ugly Beauty" (a vehicle for Gonzalez's most thoughtful solo). For those who prefer Fort Apache's earlier albums, the Latin beats are subdued, but for post-bop and straight-ahead fans, *Fire Dance* is burning perfectionism.

the rest:
Ya Yo Me Cure 🎵🎵🎵🎵 (American Clave, 1979/Sunnyside, 1996)
Rumba Para Monk 🎵🎵🎵🎵 (Sunnyside, 1989/1995)
Earthdance 🎵🎵🎵🎵 (Sunnyside, 1996)

influences:
◀◀ Dizzy Gillespie, Charlie Parker, Mario Bauzá, Machito, Eddie Palmieri, Paquito D'Rivera, John Coltrane, Miles Davis

Nancy Ann Lee

Benny Goodman

Born May 30, 1909, in Chicago, IL. Died June 13, 1986, New York, NY.

Benny Goodman, the first great clarinetist in the history of jazz, perfected a style of playing that is still the dominant influence on the instrument. It is a style based on clearly articulated, hard-swinging melodic lines and related arpeggios, played with a very centered, clear, clarinet tone. Goodman occasionally added a growl to this tone, produced by humming into the clarinet while otherwise playing normally, but only where it added effective emphasis. It was the incredible excitement and clarity of his playing that made it great, rather than any profound harmonic or rhythmic invention. His work was remarkably free of gratuitous musical posturing, and he limited his use of cliches to where they were effective in many of his, and his audiences', favorite tunes. Although Goodman became fantastically popular, and performed a good deal of classical music, he remained first and foremost a jazzman throughout his career.

It is perhaps because of Goodman's enigmatic personality—he tended to be interested in music above all else, even basic social civility—that his role as a jazz explorer has been underappreciated. In the mid-1930s, it was Goodman who first brought the music of the Harlem jazz bands to the general public through his purchase and presentation of the compositions and arrangements of Fletcher Henderson, Edgar Sampson (of the Chick Webb band), and others. He didn't do this to steal anyone's music, and he freely credited his sources, though sometimes adding his own name, as was the questionable custom of the time. He simply wanted the best charts he could get his hands on.

Also in the mid-1930s, Goodman premiered the high-profile presentation of racially mixed ensembles with his inclusion of African American pianist Teddy Wilson and vibraphonist Lionel Hampton in his trio and quartet. (Goodman included these musicians simply because he liked the way they played, rather than to make any social statement.) His sextet of 1939 through 1941, with pioneer amplified-guitarist Charlie Christian, was a breeding ground for bop ideas.

In the early 1940s, Goodman could have been quite successful duplicating his success of the 1930s. Instead, he reached out and featured the difficult, harmonically inventive, and very beautiful arrangements of Eddie Sauter and Mel Powell. They were way ahead of their time.

Historians have referred to Goodman's band of the late 1940s as a brief flirtation with bop. While Goodman himself was never an effective bop soloist, he made sure this edition of his band included, at various times, boppers Fats Navarro, Wardell Grey, Doug Mettome, and others. The band's book was all bop charts, with the older book left in storage. While Goodman never again jumped head first into bop, he often returned to bop principles, especially with the ten-piece band he led in 1959 and 1960.

Goodman's groups were great talent incubators, giving their first prominent exposure, in person or on records, to Billie Holiday, Harry James, Gene Krupa, Teddy Wilson, Lionel Hampton, Charlie Christian, Peggy Lee, Stan Getz, Roland Hanna, Zoot Sims, and many others.

what to buy: There are hundreds of Goodman studio performances and live dates on CD from his peak years, 1937 through 1939. The Victor studio sessions reveal well-rehearsed, precise ensembles, and were well recorded, although they have not always been well remastered for reissue. The best of the live dates are a little muddier, but still sound fine, and reveal a much more exciting band, mistakes and all. The live sessions have the edge. Duplicating the 1950s LPs titled *Jazz Concert No. 2* produced by George Avakian, the two-CD set, *On the Air, 1937–1938* 𝄞𝄞𝄞𝄞 (Columbia, 1993, reissue prod. Michael Brooks), offers a fine set of 14 remastered tracks. The set is a must have, consisting of the most exciting performances drawn from the greatest of Goodman air-checks, many from *Camel Caravan* radio shows. Most are up-tempo, but Fletcher Henderson's sensuous chart of "Sometimes I'm Happy" rivals any of the flag-wavers. Adding interest is Harry James's interpretation of the trumpet solo taken on the Victor recording by the legendary Bunny Berigan. The apogee of Goodman's career was his 1938 Carnegie Hall concert, which was privately recorded, surprisingly quite well. Columbia issued all but two tunes of the concert in 1950, mainly to demonstrate the value of their new LP format. The positive tension felt by the Goodmanites conquering Carnegie in 1938 came through on the LPs, as it does on the two CDs of *Benny Goodman Carnegie Hall Jazz Concert* 𝄞𝄞𝄞𝄞 (Columbia, 1987). "Sing, Sing, Sing" was the concert's high point, with an unexpected Bixian solo by pianist Jess Stacy, and a crowd-pleasing tom-tom solo by Krupa. The Victor sides with their great sound, even in the 1930s, should eventually be issued on CD, complete and in chronological order. The fine three-CD set *Benny Goodman/The Birth of Swing* 𝄞𝄞𝄞𝄞 (Victor-Bluebird 78s/Bluebird, 1991, prod. Orrin Keepnews) appears to be the start of such a project, at least as far as Goodman's big band is concerned. The set documents the start of the Swing era, and includes the sides Bunny Berigan made as a Goodmanite, as well as a session with a very

young Ella Fitzgerald. Delights are found in superior versions of pop songs of the day, as well as in the "killer-dillers." The only reason the set doesn't merit the highest rating is the presence of what sounds like phase distortion on some tracks and an occasional whistling sound, problems which occur with a number of RCA/Bluebird reissues. The Goodman trio and quartet of the 1930s was important for sociological (it was the first high-profile racially integrated jazz ensemble) as well as musical reasons. The entire Victor studio output of these Goodman small groups, including previously unissued alternate takes, was recently released on a three-CD set, *The Complete RCA Victor Small Group Recordings* ♫♫♫♫ (RCA, 1997, reissue prod. Orrin Keepnews), incorporating the following LPs—*The Original Trio & Quartet Sessions, Vol. 1* (Victor/Bluebird 78rpm recordings/Bluebird 1987), and *Avalon: The Small Bands, Vol. 2* (Victor/Bluebird 78rpm recordings/Bluebird 1990).

what to buy next: In 1939, Goodman added Charlie Christian (the first significant electric guitarist in jazz) to his entourage, primarily featuring him in sextet and septet settings. The resulting recordings, many of which are found on *Featuring Charlie Christian* (Columbia 78s, various LP compilations/Columbia, 1989), provided much inspiration for the beboppers coming just around the corner. Columbia has not reissued their wonderful early 1940s Goodman catalog, but until they do, *Featuring Peggy Lee* ♫♫♫♫ (Columbia, OKeh 78s/Columbia, 1993, prod. Michael Brooks) provides great insight into the "let's play beautiful music without getting cutesy or worrying about the jitterbuggers" side of Goodman. Lee, brand new on the scene, sings very well, and the Eddie Sauter and Mel Powell arrangements can be equated to early, very good Gil Evans. On the limited edition, four-CD set *Benny Goodman: Complete Capitol Small Group Recordings* ♫♫♫♫ (Mosaic, 1993, prod. Michael Cuscuna), Goodman displays incredible clarinet technique and seems bound by few stylistic limitations. The eleven years (1944–55) represented here find Goodman employing such sidemen as veteran swing trumpeter Charlie Shavers, vibist Red Norvo, and pianist Teddy Wilson, as well as bop trumpeters Fats Navarro and Doug Mettome, and saxophonist Wardell Grey. Among the many highlights are the angular "Hi 'Ya Sophia"(from 1947), and a slashing "Air Mail Special" (from 1954). Goodman's ten-piece 1959–60 band has been largely forgotten. Too bad—it was one of his loosest, most swinging bands. This fresh group, featuring such inventive sidemen as

Benny Goodman (l) and Gene Krupa
(UPI/Corbis-Bettmann)

saxophonists Jerry Dodgion and Flip Phillips, trumpeter Jack Sheldon, and bop-leaning veteran Red Norvo, didn't rely on any of the old swing charts. Several recent CDs have rectified the band's two commercial recordings (one on MGM and one on Columbia) which didn't capture it at its best. A concert from Basel, Switzerland, is documented on the single CD *Legendary Concert* ♫♫♫♫ (TCB, 1993, prod. Gino Ferlin), as well as on the four-CD set *B.G. World-Wide* ♫♫♫♫ (TCB, 1993, prod. Gino Ferlin). The other three CDs of the TCB issue, recorded in 1956, 1961, and 1980, are equally exciting.

best of the rest:
B.G. in Hi-Fi ♫♫♫ (Capitol, 1954/1989)
Let's Dance ♫♫♫ (Music Masters, 1986)
Benny Goodman's 1934 Bill Dodge All-Star Recordings Complete ♫♫♫♫ (Original broadcast transcriptions/Melodeon LP/ Circle, 1987)
Air Play ♫♫♫♫ (Signature, 1989)
Best of the Big Bands ♫♫♫ (Columbia and OKeh 78s/Columbia, 1990)
Solo Flight ♫♫♫♫ (VJC, 1991)
B.G. & Big Tea in NYC ♫♫♫♫ (Brunswick 78s/Decca, 1992)
Swing, Swing, Swing ♫♫♫♫ (Music Masters, 1993)
The Harry James Years, Vol. 1 ♫♫♫♫ (Victor/Bluebird 78s/Bluebird, 1993)
The Alternative Goodman ♫♫♫♫ (Phontastic, 1993–94)
Swing Sessions ♫♫♫ (Hindsight, 1994)
Undercurrent Blues ♫♫♫♫ (Capitol, various dates/1995)
Wrappin' It Up, The Harry James Years, Part 2 ♫♫♫♫ (Victor and Bluebird 78s/Bluebird, 1995)
Benny Goodman Plays Eddie Sauter ♫♫♫♫ (Columbia and OKeh 78s/Hep, 1996)
Together Again ♫♫♫♫ (RCA Victor, 1964/Bluebird, 1996)
The King of Swing ♫♫♫♫ (Music Masters, 1996)

worth searching for: If you still have a turntable, the three-LP box set (also issued as single LPs) *Treasure Chest Series* ♫♫♫♫ (MGM, c. 1959) is about as good as the previously noted *On the Air, 1937–1938* recordings. These peak-era big band and combo air-checks find Goodman, Harry James, Gene Krupa, and the rest of the Goodman firmament exhibiting the spontaneity that is the essence of jazz. Many of these sides appeared on a hard-to-find Swiss CD, *Hallelujah* (Drive, 1989), while others have appeared on various Verve reissues. The best concert by Goodman's 1959–60 ten-piece band is on the separate LPs *Session* ♫♫♫♫ (Swing House, 1981, prod. Christopher A. Pirie) and *Jam* ♫♫♫♫ (Swing House, 1983, prod. Christopher A. Pirie). Vocalist Anita O'Day was still with the band for this Berlin concert; Goodman fired her shortly thereafter. Until this concert is issued on CD, the band's Swiss concert, previously noted, is a good second choice. A number of out-of-print LPs (which may eventually be released on CD), such as *Hello Benny* ♫♫ (Capitol, 1964, prod. Dave Cavanaugh), *Made in Japan* 𝄢𝄢 (Capitol, 1964, prod. Dave Cavanaugh), and *Let's Dance Again* 𝄢𝄢𝄢 (Mega, 1969, prod. John Franz) should interest completists. Fans should avoid, however, short-lived bootleg CDs that often include Goodman material issued elsewhere with better sound.

influences:

◄◄ Fletcher Henderson, Chick Webb, Casa Loma, Tommy Dorsey, Jimmy Dorsey

►► Peanuts Hucko, Sal Pace, Walt Levinski, Sol Yaged, Henry Cuesta, Bob Wilber, Bobby Gordon, Jack Maheu, Buddy De-Franco, Eddie Daniels, Ken Peplowski

John K. Richmond

Mick Goodrick

Born June 9, 1945, in Sharon, PA.

Mike Goodrick is yet another talented jazz guitarist employed in the halls of academia. A graduate of the Berklee College of Music in Boston, he later returned to teach there and is now ensconced at the New England Conservatory teaching Contemporary Improvisation and Jazz Studies. Early in his career Goodrick played with Woody Herman, but he may be best known for his four-year stint with vibist Gary Burton, where he worked in tandem with one of his students, Pat Metheny on albums like *Dreams So Real* and *The New Quartet*. Goodrick has also worked with the Charlie Haden Liberation Orchestra and Jack DeJohnette's Special Edition. He is a master of guitar technique with a musically adventurous streak that can best be heard on his solo albums.

what to buy: *Biorhythms* 𝄢𝄢𝄢𝄢 (CMP, 1990, prod. Kurt Renker, Walter Quintus) is a guitar tour de force without the flashy moves. The technique is always there but it serves the demands of the music—not the ego. His compatriots for most of the session are bassist Harvie Swartz and drummer Gary Chaffee, a crew with the chops to play any way Goodrick wants them to; funky, spacy, whatever.

what to buy next: *In Passing* 𝄢𝄢𝄢 (ECM, 1979, prod. Manfred Eicher) was Goodrick's first solo album, and why it doesn't have more punch is a mystery until you consider the sort of stuff ECM was putting out about the same time. That doesn't mean that it's bad; there are several interesting moments. Maybe that's the problem. Things are too diffuse. Everybody has space and the groove is on a different plane than the melody.

the rest:

Sunscreams 𝄢𝄢𝄢 (Ram, 1994)
(With Joe Diorio) *Rare Birds* 𝄢𝄢𝄢 (Ram, 1995)

influences:

►► Wolfgang Muthspiel, Pat Metheny, John Scofield, Emily Remler

Garaud MacTaggart

Bobby Gordon

Born 1942, in Hartford, CT.

As a teenager growing up on Long Island, Bobby Gordon received clarinet lessons from a close family friend, well-known Chicago clarinetist Joe Marsala, who was to remain the primary influence on Gordon's easy-going clarinet work. Marsala introduced Gordon to many jazz greats including Jack Teagarden, Eddie Condon and, another important influence, Pee Wee Russell. After high school, Gordon attended Roosevelt University, Berklee School of Music, and the University of California at San Diego. By 1963, he had recorded his Decca LP, *Warm and Sentimental*. Gordon moved to Chicago after college and worked with Wild Bill Davison, Muggsy Spanier, and, briefly, Louis Armstrong. In the mid-1960s, he returned to the East Coast, playing club dates in the New Jersey-New York area, often with leaders Eddy Davis or Max Kaminsky.

Following the death of clarinetist Jim Cullum, Sr. in 1970, Gordon moved to San Antonio, Texas and held down the clarinet chair in the reorganized Jim Cullum Band. He returned to New York City in 1975 to join cornetist Ed Polcer's gang at Condon's. Gordon hooked up with Leon Redbone in 1977 for a series of national tours which ended tragically with a 1981 West Virginia plane crash which killed 12 people. Leaving the hospital after a lengthy convalescence, Gordon rejoined his family in California, eventually settling in San Diego which remains his home base. He gigs around the West Coast, frequently leaving for jazz party appearances throughout the country. At the 1988 Conneaut Lake Jazz Party, Gordon became a charter member of the Marty Grosz-Peter Ecklund Orphan Newsboys, an instrumental quartet that revels in uncovering obscure tunes from the jazz past, performing mostly at jazz festivals. Associations with Grosz and Ecklund, drummer Hal Smith, and pianist Keith Ingham have led to many record dates which provide opportunities to hear and enjoy the fluid, melodic, sometimes whimsical, style of Bobby Gordon.

what to buy: *Jump Presents: Bobby Gordon, Keith Ingham & Hal Smith* ♪♪♪♪ (Jump, c. 1993, prod. Joe Boughton) features the dynamic trio just after a long weekend of performances at the 1990 Conneaut Lake Jazz party, so they were properly warmed up for this well-recorded August session. Gordon lays down some gorgeous low-register clarinet. Delivering tunes that deserve more exposure, clarinetist Gordon, pianist Ingham, and drummer Smith achieve a winning combination of unusual material and tasteful performance. Relaxed swinging samples from this 18-tune collection include "Don't Leave Me Daddy," "Hummin' to Myself," and "Laughing at Life." The same threesome rejoined in April 1993 to record 17 tunes under Ingham's name. (See below, Worth Searching For.) *Bobby Gordon Plays Bing* ♪♪♪♪ (Arbors, 1997, prod. Rachel Domber, Mat Domber) features Gordon leading a solid octet performing 19 delightful tunes associated with singer Bing Crosby, with arrangements and piano by longtime bandmate Ingham. Peter Ecklund and Randy Reinhart alternate on cornet-trumpet, with Dan Barrett on trombone, Scott Robinson on reeds, and Marty Grosz on guitar contributing nifty solos while Greg Cohen (bass) and Hal Smith (drums) anchor the rhythm. Tunes range from Bing's days with the Whiteman band ("There Ain't No Sweet Man" and "From Monday On") to the Hollywood *Road* films with Bob Hope ("Road to Morocco") and nostalgic stops in between with "Sweet and Lovely," "I'm an Old Cowhand," "Just One More Chance," and more. Good tunes, good players, good listening!

what to buy next: A Gordon-led octet session, *The Music of Pee Wee Russell* ♪♪♪♪ (Arbors, 1995, prod. Rachel Domber, Mat Domber), focuses on sensitive readings of 12 Russell compositions with Gordon's playing leaving no doubt about the lasting impression clarinetist Russell made on him. The band's sounds and textures vary from selection to selection, with arrangements and fine solos contributed by Marty Grosz, Dan Barrett, Jon-Erik Kellso, Johnny Varro, and Gordon. Rick Fay is on hand to add some tenor saxisms, and rhythm chores are aptly handled by Varro and Grosz, along with old smoothies Bob Haggart (bass) and Gene Estes (drums). Highlights include the original "The Charles Ellsworth Stomp" (Russell's first and middle names) which grabs the intro from "Hello Lola," and one of Russell's favorites, "I'd Climb the Highest Mountain." *Don't Let It End* ♪♪♪♪ (Arbors, 1992, prod. Rachel Domber, Mat Domber) features an appealing title tune written by Gordon's mentor, Joe Marsala. Marsala's wife, Adele Girard, a swinging harpist, came out of retirement to join the quartet proceedings on some selections, lending an almost ethereal sound which works well with Gordon's middle-register clarinet. With respectable versions of "Exactly Like You," "Do You Ever Think of Me," the lilting Marsala favorite "Singin' the Blues," and a romping "Love Nest," along with a generous helping of other admired Gordon-Marsala tunes, this is a worthwhile addition to a middle-of-the-road jazz collection (no bop or fusion here).

worth searching for: A session recorded with Keith Ingham as leader *Music from the Mauve Decades* ♪♪♪♪ (Sackville, 1993, prod. Keith Ingham, Norris) captures trio spirit similar to *Bobby Gordon, Keith Ingham & Hal Smith*.

see also: *The Orphan Newsboys, Marty Grosz*

John T. Bitter

Dexter Gordon

Born February 27, 1923, in Los Angeles, CA. Died April 26, 1990, in Philadelphia, PA.

One of the prime movers behind the hard bop revolution of the 1960s, Dexter Gordon was one of jazz's most consistently great players and though his personal life was spotty—marked by addiction and jail time and more "comebacks" than any man should have to endure—his playing, a rich, robust tenor sound, never faltered. Unlike many of his contemporaries, he never succumbed to the temptations of fusion or pop-jazz; instead, he became an expatriate, spending much of the 1970s in Europe, spreading the gospel of quality playing to audiences who were actually interested in the real thing.

Born to a "jazz doctor" father (Lionel Hampton and Duke Ellington could be counted among Dr. Frank Gordon's patients), Dexter Keith Gordon began playing the clarinet at age seven. Eventually switching to alto, then tenor, saxophone, Gordon landed his first professional gig with Lionel Hampton's band at age 17. Section work with Fletcher Henderson and Louis Armstrong followed, with Gordon cutting his first side (accompanied by Nat Cole on piano) in 1944. While gigging with Billy Eckstine's band (1944–45), Gordon gained Manhattan notoriety, while L.A. sessions (1945–46) brought him not only West Coast fame, but also a collaborator and foil that would strongly shape Gordon's style—Wardell Gray. It was with Gray that Gordon began developing his highly empathic solo style and, though he played much harder than Gray, the two's recordings from this era are amazingly synergetic. Unfortunately, the only ones currently available suffer from middling sound.

Gordon was sentenced to two years in prison for possession of heroin in 1952. It was the beginning of periodic lapses into addiction that would plague him for much of the next decade and

a half. Accordingly, his work slowed considerably during this time but, thanks to an acceptable "comeback" record in 1960 (*Resurgence*) and his work on the West Coast version of *The Connection*, he soon found himself welcomed into the Blue Note fold, at the genesis of the hard-bop movement. His work during this period (May 1961 to May 1965) was definitely his best, and it found him working with everyone from Herbie Hancock and Bobby Hutcherson to Sonny Stitt and Bud Powell. It was also during this time that Gordon fell in love with Europe, specifically Scandinavia, spending most of his time there. In fact, apart from radio recordings, Gordon wouldn't enter a studio again until 1969, when he cut the first of two records for Prestige. Though those two records were relatively successful in the States, it was not a good time for jazz musicians, especially pure players like Gordon, so it was back to Scandinavia, where he would remain and record until 1976. Relatively quiet during the late 1970s and early 1980s, Gordon surprised most by turning in an astonishingly moving lead role in the 1986 film *Round Midnight,* as well as a remarkable accompanying record (the actual soundtrack was more or less done by Herbie Hancock, with a few tenor injections from Gordon, while *The Other Side of Round Midnight* is all Gordon).

what to buy: The collection *Dexter Gordon: The Complete Dial Sessions* 𝄞𝄞𝄞𝄆 (Spotlite, 1947/1995) only loses points due to its unappealing sound quality. Otherwise, the communicative tenor battles between Gordon and Wardell Gray are astonishing. Blue Note wanted Gordon to follow up his success with *Go!* (1962) so badly that Frank Wolff flew to Paris to record him with Bud Powell, Kenny Clarke and bassist Pierre Michelot, where they created this unqualified masterpiece, *Our Man in Paris* 𝄞𝄞𝄞𝄞 (Blue Note, 1963/1988, prod. Francis Wolff). The results are uniformly stunning with Gordon at the peak of his best period. Riveting hard bop, handled smoothly by the genre's giant. Much better than his other Prestige date, *The Panther!* 𝄞𝄞𝄞 (Prestige/OJC, 1970/1993, prod. Don Schlitten) shows Gordon conveying a wide range of expression and a deeper sense of emotion. Tommy Flanagan is a willing melodic foil here and the rhythm section of Larry Ridley and Alan Dawson is more than up to the task. At a time when most of his contemporaries were content to churn out R&B/pop records, Gordon—who at 50 years old, knew he had no business trying to fit into spandex pants—simply kept making great jazz. The strongest of his mid-1970s dates, *Bouncin' with Dex* 𝄞𝄞𝄞𝄞 (SteepleChase,

DEXTER GORDON

song "Cheese Cake"
album Go
(Blue Note, 1962/1987)
instrument Tenor saxophone

Monster Solo

1975/1995, prod. Nils Winther) features regular European collaborators Tete Montoliu (piano) and bassist Nils-Henning Ørsted-Pedersen, as well as drummer Billy Higgins. The results are outstanding, with Gordon blowing supremely rich lines in a manner that only he could. Expensive, sure. But since you probably *should* own all the Blue Note records anyway, the six-disc box, *The Complete Blue Note Sixties Sessions* 𝄞𝄞𝄞𝄞 (Blue Note, 1996, prod. Alfred Lion, Francis Wolff, Michael Cuscuna, Maxine Gordon) may turn out to be quite cost-effective. With excellent liner notes (featuring correspondence between Gordon and Blue Note's Alfred Lion and Francis Wolff) and a healthy selection of unreleased tracks, this is exemplary of a true giant at the height of his powers (no puns intended).

what to buy next: While it may not be essential Gordon, it is telling to hear how surprisingly strong his playing is after a few years of prison and drug abuse. Adderley's presence on *Resurgence* 𝄞𝄞𝄞 (Jazzland/OJC, 1960/1997, prod. Cannonball Adderley) is minimal, the song selection is pretty weak, but as a warm-up blowing session for the better things to come, this

Dexter Gordon (Archive Photos)

certainly ain't half bad. Featuring Bobby Hutcherson (whose brother went to high school with Gordon) and Billy Higgins, as well as Bob Cranshaw (bass) and Barry Harris (piano), *Gettin' Around* ♫♫♫ (Blue Note, 1965/1987, prod. Alfred Lion) is a strong, challenging set, with Gordon obviously reveling in the odd harmonic changes and forward-moving attitude of the band. *Live at the Montmartre Jazzhaus* ♫♫♫ (Black Lion, 1967/1996) is a box set that collects the same performances found on the individual LPs *Body and Soul*, *Both Sides of Midnight* and *Take the "A" Train*, which were recorded over two nights in Copenhagen. However, there's something besides archival quality that makes it necessary to pick up all three together. It was during this expatriation that Gordon felt most comfortable with his playing and, thankfully, the audiences he played to were appreciative. This set repeats only one tune ("For All We Know") and, even though it's a bit cumbersome to get through, thanks to Gordon's joyous playing and the solid support work of Kenny Drew, Ørsted-Pedersen, and Albert Heath, *Live at the Montmartre Jazzhaus* is both highly informative and highly enjoyable. Although certainly not up to par with Gordon's '60s Blue Note work, *The Other Side of 'Round Midnight* ♫♫♫♫ (Blue Note, 1987) ain't too bad for a 65-year-old movie star. *Blue Dex: Dexter Gordon Plays the Blues* ♫♫♫ (Prestige, 1996, comp. prod. Ed Michel) is a nice compilation of Gordon's best 12-bar blues work for Prestige, culled from the sessions he did for the label between 1969 and 1973. Two alternate takes make it that much more worthwhile.

the rest:
Dexter Rides Again ♫♫♫ (Savoy, 1947/1993)
Dexter Blows Hot and Cool ♫♫ (Fresh Sound, 1955/1991)
Dexter Calling . . . ♫♫♫ (Blue Note, 1961/1988)
Doin' Alright ♫♫♫♫ (Blue Note, 1961/1988)
A Swingin' Affair ♫♫♫ (Blue Note, 1962/1987)
Go! ♫♫♫ (Blue Note, 1962/1988)
Cheese Cake ♫♫♫ (SteepleChase, 1964/1990)
King Neptune ♫♫♫ (SteepleChase, 1964)
One Flight Up ♫♫♫♫ (Blue Note, 1964/1989)
Body and Soul ♫♫♫ (Black Lion, 1967/1992)
Take the "A" Train ♫♫♫ (Black Lion, 1967/1992)
Both Sides of Midnight ♫♫♫ (Black Lion, 1967/1992)
The Tower of Power! ♫♫♫ (Prestige/OJC, 1969/1993)
The Jumpin' Blues ♫♫♫ (Prestige/OJC, 1970/1996)
Generation ♫♫♫ (Prestige/OJC, 1972/1995)
Strings & Things ♫♫ (SteepleChase, 1975–76/1995)
Gotham City ♫♫ (Columbia, 1981/1987)
`Round Midnight: Original Motion Picture Soundtrack ♫♫♫ (Columbia, 1986)
After Hours ♫♫♫ (SteepleChase, 1988/1994)

Best Of ♫♫♫ (Blue Note, 1988)
Ballads ♫♫♫ (Blue Note, 1991)

influences:
◀◀ Lester Young

Jason Ferguson

Danny Gottlieb
See: Elements

Dusko Goykovich
Born Dusan Koykovich, October 14, 1931, in Jajace, Yugoslavia.

A talented bop-based trumpeter who outshines many of his peers, Dusko Goykovich was inspired at age 14 by hearing Dizzy Gillespie and Roy Eldridge on Willis Conover's *Voice of America* radio show. Goykovich studied at the Academy of Music in Belgrade from 1948–53, and started his big band career in 1950, playing in dance orchestras and bands of his native country. He moved in 1953 to Germany where he became active in the jazz scene, playing with the Frankfurt All Stars until 1956, with Max Greger's orchestra, and with Kurt Edelhagen's radio orchestra from 1957–60. He performed at the 1958 Newport Jazz Festival with Marshall Brown's International Youth Band. Three years later, Goykovich returned to the United States with a scholarship to study composition and arranging at Boston's Berklee College of Music, completing four years of study in one and a half years. After graduation, he worked with the Maynard Ferguson and Woody Herman bands before returning to Germany. During the late 60s and early 1970s, Goykovich worked with Sal Nistico and performed as a principal soloist in the Kenny Clark-Francy Boland ensemble and with others, as well as leading and recording with his own groups. He's guested with many world-class jazz bands, written more than 100 big band charts (many for German radio orchestras), and recorded on more than 130 albums. On all of his recordings as leader, Goykovich proves to be a fabulous expressionist, exhibiting utmost passion, drive, and energy, and reaching a high level of excellence as he creates accessible, warm melodies and sensible swing.

what to buy: Whew! Where to begin with Goykovich's recordings? You can't go wrong with any of his high-quality, small-group collaborations with American jazz musicians. If you're a Miles Davis fan, begin with *Soul Connection* ♫♫♫♫♫ (Enja, 1994, prod. Matthias Winckelmann), a beautiful session with nine originals dedicated to Goykovich's musical muse. The 1993 Brooklyn studio session highlights his composing skills on tunes ranging from waltz tempos to bebop and blues. Pianist Tommy Flanagan adds wondrous warmth to the quartet session with bassist Eddie Gomez and drummer Mickey Roker, and tenor saxman Jimmy Heath heartily augments five tunes. Goykovich is a master at creating melodies that get inside your head and this is one of his most listener-friendly sessions. Davis, whom Goykovich met in 1956, would have been proud. On *Bebop City* 𝄞𝄞𝄞𝄞 (Enja, 1995, prod. Matthias Winckelmann), Goykovich salutes New York City with a team of veterans—pianist Kenny Barron, bassist Ray Drummond, drummer Alvin Queen—and guest soloists, Ralph Moore (tenor sax) and Abraham Burton (alto sax). He directs an equitable nine-tune session, shines as a soloist, and contributes seven originals that give his teammates plenty to explore in solos and in the combined horn segments. Goykovich sets the climate for the ballad, "In the Sign of Libra," interweaving his silky lines with Burton's and giving space to a heartfelt romantic solo from Barron. From boppers to ballads, Goykovich is the master of mood-setting, influencing his illustrious team to enkindle some sensational soul-pleasing jazz. *After Hours* 𝄞𝄞𝄞𝄞 (Enja, 1995, prod. Horst Weber) is another romantic date, recorded in Barcelona in 1971, that finds Goykovich leading an interactive mainstream-jazz quartet through three standards and three originals. Always generous with his side mates, Goykovich gives ample space to pianist Tete Montoliui, bassist Rob Langereis, and drummer Joe Nay. Goykovich shows nice tone and sensitivity on their brief version of the Thad Jones gem, "A Child Is Born," and his original, "Old Fisherman's Daughter," a tricky waltz number spotlighting his muted trumpet, at 8:38, gives everyone room for fine solos. (Note: A shorter and equally graceful version of the latter, featuring a flute solo by Nathan Davis, can be found on Goykovich's sextet recording, *Swinging Macedonia*.) Their nine-minute rendering of Cole Porter's "I Love You," swings elegantly. Multi-talented Goykovich writes the stuff of standards and, with this team, delivers the goods with ultimate ear-pleasing artfulness.

what to buy next: A robust big band session, *Balkan Connection* 𝄞𝄞𝄞𝄞 (Enja, 1996, prod. Matthias Winckelmann) features fabulous arrangements from Goykovich, performed by his 16-piece European band, revived in 1986 from its initial formation in 1968. His third Enja CD, this is the first ever album to exclusively feature the leader's big band charts and his own band. Out of the 10 tunes, eight are originals reflecting Goykovich's love for writing and arranging hardy bop and swing tunes. He demonstrates an excellent feel in his expressions drawing upon big band tradition. Tight horns create harmonically fresh,

colorfully upbeat and modern themes. Soloists are superb. The rhythm section dazzles. Overall, this is a highly recommended album, outstanding among overseas big bands.

best of the rest:
Swinging Macedonia 𝄞𝄞𝄞𝄞 (Enja, 1988)
Balkan Blues 𝄞𝄞𝄞 (Enja, 1997)

influences:
◀◀ Miles Davis

Nancy Ann Lee

Jerry Granelli

Born December 30, 1940, in San Francisco, CA.

Jerry Granelli's mentor was Dave Brubeck drummer Joe Morello. Granelli found considerable work as a session drummer in the 1960s and 1970s and played various hits, but jazz fans first noticed him in the 1960s as a member of pianist Vince Guaraldi's group and later with groups led by Ornette Coleman, bassist Charlie Haden, and pianist Denny Zeitlin. More recently, after a long period where his emphasis shifted to music education (at the Cornish Institute in Seattle, the Naropa Institute in Boulder, Colorado, and the Conservatory in Halifax, Nova Scotia), Granelli moved back into regular sideman work in a trio with Ralph Towner and Gary Peacock, also performing with Jane Ira Bloom's group and in a trio with Anthony Cox and David Friedman. He has also accompanied singers from Mose Allison and Jon Hendricks to Rinde Eckert, Jay Clayton, and Annie Wilson. Currently a professor in Berlin, Germany, Granelli works in both straight-ahead and fusion contexts. In 1975 he formed the two-guitar ensemble Visions, and his current fusion effort is his funky UFB quartet with electric guitarists Kai Bruckner and Christian Kogel and bassist Andreas Walter. UFB performs Granelli originals as well as covers ranging from John Coltrane, Charles Mingus, and Ornette Coleman to Prince, Jimi Hendrix, and Peter Gabriel. His current acoustic quintet includes Jane Ira Bloom (soprano sax), Julian Priester (trombone), Anthony Cox (bass), and David Friedman (vibes and marimba).

what to buy: *Another Place* 𝄞𝄞𝄞 (Intuition, 1994, prod. Lee Townsend) has probing post-bop and an adventurous band of Bloom (soprano sax), Priester (trombone), Friedman (vibes/marimba), and Cox (bass), all with solid mainstream jazz chops and imagination. There's a slightly exotic, bittersweet air to the project, akin to Italian art film soundtracks.

what to buy next: UFB is Granelli's fusion quartet with three Germans and is funky and accessible. *News from the Street* ♫♫♫ (Intuition, 1995, prod. Lee Townsend) includes some interesting, well-chosen covers, from Jimi Hendrix's "Little Wing," Little Village's "Big Love," and Bruce Hornsby's "Rainbow's Cadillac" to Thelonious Monk's challenging "Brilliant Corners."

the rest:
One Day at a Time ♫♫♫ (Koch, 1990)
A Song I Thought I Heard Buddy Sing ♫♫♫ (Evidence, 1993)
(With Glen Moore) *Forces of Flight* ♫♫ (ITM, 1995)
Koputai ♫♫♫ (ITM, 1995)
(With UFB) *Broken Circle* ♫♫♫ (Intuition, 1996)

influences:
◀◀ Joe Morello, Jerry Hahn Brotherhood

Walter Faber

Darrell Grant

Born May 30, 1962, in Pittsburgh, PA.

During an interview with drummer Tony Williams, he was asked about the issue of originality. "Originality?" he snorted, "You'd better learn how to play your instrument before you worry about that." Pianist Darrell Grant, who played with Williams, is a good example of Tony's sentiment. While, like many other jazz pianists, Grant hasn't played anything profoundly groundbreaking at the piano, he knows his way around the 88s in a post-bop approach that draws from mid-1960s Herbie Hancock, and also shows promise as a composer.

After gaining music degrees from Eastman and the University of Miami, Grant headed to New York in 1986 where he filled in the Woody Shaw quintet, followed by jobs with Junior Cook, Charlie Persip's Superband and, in 1988, the highly demanding piano chair in the Betty Carter band. Other jobs included stints as musical director for the American Tap Orchestra and singer Leslie Gore, and sideman gigs with saxophonist Frank Morgan and drummer Roy Haynes.

what to buy: Grant has two albums on Criss Cross, both featuring fine drumming by Brian Blade. For its more interesting compositions, the second CD, *The New Bop* ♫♫♫ (Criss Cross, 1995, prod. Gerry Teekens), merits. A quintet session citing Horace Silver as inspiration (check out "The Blues We Ain't No More"), the recording shows Grant's composing and playing contain less of Silver's 1950s–1960s minor key, Latin-tinged sound and more of a 1980s neo-bop approach, especially in the elastic

rhythms. Good tunes include "Struttin' to Tangiers" and "Gettin' Mean with Mateen."

what to buy next: Grant's other recording, *Black Art* ♫♫♫ (Criss Cross, 1994, prod. Gerry Teekens), is a quartet session with trumpeter Wallace Roney. It emphasizes a rhythm section that twists and turns like the mid-1960s Miles ensemble with Hancock, Ron Carter, and Williams.

influences:
◀◀ Herbie Hancock, Thelonious Monk, Horace Silver

Dan Polletta

Stephane Grappelli

Born January 26, 1908, in Paris, France. Died December 1, 1997, in Paris, France.

Stephane Grappelli is considered to be one of the greatest jazz violinists, matching the contributions to jazz by Joe Venuti, Eddie South, and Stuff Smith on his instrument. Mostly self taught from the age of 12, violinist Stephane Grappelli received some formal training at the Paris Conservatory, but dropped out after he heard his first jazz recordings and never returned. He instead played violin in the street and for silent films at a local cinema. In the mid-1920s, Grappelli abandoned violin and learned piano to get work with dance bands. He resumed playing violin again in the late 1920s, years before he teamed up with Belgian gypsy jazz guitarist Django Reinhardt in 1933. Although he is overshadowed by Reinhardt on many recordings with the Quintette Du Hot Club De France (formed in 1934), Grappelli is known best for his performances and recordings with this group which included his violin, three guitars, and a double bass. Annoyed with Grappelli's growing popularity, Reinhardt abruptly left the group in 1939 to return to Paris as World War II broke out. Grappelli remained behind where he established a base and worked with pianist George Shearing throughout the War years. Grappelli returned to Paris in 1946, and worked sporadically with Reinhardt from 1947–49.

During the next two decades, Grappelli performed regularly in clubs and at music festivals throughout Europe, but was less active as a leader and made fewer albums as sideman. Grappelli remained largely unknown to American audiences until his appearance at the 1969 Newport Jazz Festival won him wider appeal in the U.S. Other international festival performances fol-

Stephane Grappelli **(Archive Photos)**

lowed, and a series of successful swing-oriented albums from the 1970s through the 1990s boosted his visibility and popularity. He recorded with an array of musicians including Oscar Peterson, Joe Pass, Quincy Jones, Earl Hines, and McCoy Tyner, as well as classical and rock musicians. He was also well-known for his interpretations of the American Songbook, tunes by composers George Gershwin, Jerome Kern, Cole Porter, and others. As leader, Grappelli recorded for many different labels, with no long-term allegiance to any single one; thus his discography encompasses numerous labels, mostly imports. His last performance before his death on December 1, 1997, was in September at the palace of French President Jacques Chirac where he performed from a wheelchair. Grappelli was 89 years old when he died of complications following a hernia operation.

what to buy: Many of Grappelli's historic best recordings with the Quintette Du Hot Club De France are under Django Reinhardt's name as leader or found on the Jazz Chronological Classics, imports for which promotional copies were unavailable to us for evaluation purposes for this book. Grappelli's playing remained consistent throughout his career, so you may want to consider recordings based on his many different side teams. The variance of ratings, especially in "The Rest" section is a subjective decision, based on the collective musicianship of Grappelli's side teams (whether they could keep up with the energetic violinist), and to what extent Grappelli is showcased on the recordings. The sessions which sound closest to the Quintet of the Hot Club of France can be found on *Shades of Django* &&&& (Verve, 1975/1989, prod. Mike Hennessey), Grappelli's first major studio session recorded in 1975 with Canadian rhythm guitarist Diz Dizley's regular trio (guitarist Ike Isaacs and bassist Isla Eckinger). Add Grappelli and it becomes a pleasing drumless string quartet session of 13 classics that swing tastefully throughout. Grappelli's technique is masterful and his joy unparalleled on classics such as "Sweet Lorraine," "Ain't Misbehavin'," "Lover Come Back to Me," "Hot Lips," "Cherokee," and more light sprees to get your feet a-tappin'. The musicians seem comfortable with each other and their gorgeous, lilting versions of Ellington's ballad, "Solitude" and the chestnut "The Nearness of You," provide heartwarming listening experiences. *Parisian Thoroughfare* &&&& (Laserlight, 1960–1975/1997, prod. various), a compilation of recordings Grappelli made between 1960–75, offers some of the hardest swinging jazz on any of his albums. Best are the nine tunes with backing from pianist Johnny Guarnieri, bassist Slam Stewart, guitarist Jimmy Shirley, and drummer Jackie Williams, all well-matched musicians. Grappelli performs the remaining six

tunes with other musician groupings, yet the tight swingers and warm ballads with rhythm masters (singin' Slam) Stewart and Williams setting the pace are definitely the best. (Note: Don't confuse this CD with the Black Lion album with the same title and different sidemen.) Besides the bargain price, the quality of the music contained on *Parisian Thoroughfare* makes it an attractive buy. Unique for the instrumentation, *Bringing It Together* &&&& (Cymekob, 1984/1995, prod. Andrew Kulberg) captures the relaxed collegial spirit between coleaders Grappelli and Belgian-born Toots Thielemans (harmonica), who are backed warmly by Martin Taylor and Marc Fossett (guitars) and bassist Brian Torff on nine standards. The album is worthwhile if only for Grappelli's performances (and Thielemans wonderful interactions with the violinist) on "Georgia on My Mind," "Jitterbug Waltz," and "You'd Be So Nice to Come Home To." Of Grappelli's late-career recordings, this is one of the best. Grappelli performs 10 duets with pianist McCoy Tyner on *One on One* &&&& (Milestone, 1990, prod. Eric Miller). Their mutual admiration is evident in Grappelli's incredibly spirited duets with Tyner, whose fleet fingering matches Grappelli's lightning-quick lines. The American Songbook standards give both musicians plenty of stretching room and opportunities for intelligent interactions as they survey the jazz tradition on tunes by W. C. Handy ("St. Louis Blues"), to Duke Ellington ("Satin Doll"), to George Gershwin ("Summertime"), and others. Their enthusiastic, charming exchanges provide pleasurable listening.

what to buy next: Recorded when Grappelli was 71 years old, *Tivoli Gardens* &&&& (Pablo Live, 1980/OJC, 1990, prod. Norman Granz) captures the violinist in a live-recorded performance at Tivoli Concert Hall in Copenhagen, Denmark with guitarist Joe Pass and bassist Niels-Henning Orsted Pedersen. While there aren't any surprises, their cheery performances of eight standards make this a worthwhile listen. *Violins No End* &&&& (Pablo, 1957/OJC, 1996, prod. Norman Granz) features violinists Grappelli and Stuff Smith backed on four tunes recorded in a Paris studio session in May 1957, with Oscar Peterson (piano), Herb Ellis (guitar), Ray Brown (bass), and Jo Jones (drums). The remaining three selections feature Smith in a 1957 concert at Salle Pleyel, Paris with the same rhythm team. Musicianship on both dates is superb, tempos upbeat, and spirits joyful. Plus, you'll have a chance to compare the styles of these two violin giants. Another enticing album is the violinist's lyric piano-jazz session with countryman Michel Legrand, bassist George Mraz, and drummer Roy Haynes on *Flamingo* &&&& (Dreyfus Jazz, 1995, prod. Yves Chamberland, Francis Dreyfus). While they perform standards that Grappelli has recorded before, that doesn't matter. These are virtuosic musicians capable of reinventing warhorses and maintaining the mixtures of swingers and rich ballads. *Vintage 1981* ♫♫♫ (Concord, 1981/1992, prod. Carl E. Jefferson) finds Grappelli with guitarists Mike Gari and Martin Taylor, and bassist Jack Sewing in an 11-tune studio session of swinging numbers such as "It's Only a Paper Moon," "I Can't Get Started," "Honeysuckle Rose," and other weathered classics. While there's a lack of spirit between the musicians, there are some surprises, especially when Grappelli (then age 73) plays the Fender Rhodes!

best of the rest:

Stephane Grappelli: Jazz Masters 11 ♫♫♫ (Verve, 1966–1992/1994)
Afternoon in Paris ♫♫♫ (MPS, 1971/Verve, 1994)
Live in London ♫♫♫♫ (Black Lion, 1973/1992)
Just One of Those Things ♫♫♫♫ (EMI Classics, 1973/Angel, 1988)
Satin Doll ♫♫♫ (Vanguard, 1975/1987)
(With Philip Catherine, Larry Coryell, Neils-Henning Ørsted Pedersen) *Young Django* ♫♫♫♫ (PolyGram/MPS, 1979)
At the Winery ♫♫♫ (Concord, 1981/1994)
Stephanova ♫♫♫ (Concord, 1983/1989)
Just One of Those Things ♫♫♫ (EMI, 1984)
(With Yo-Yo Ma) *Anything Goes* ♫♫♫ (CBS, 1989)
Live at the Blue Note ♫♫♫♫ (Telarc, 1996)

worth searching for: The out-of-print disc, *Souvenirs* ♫♫♫♫ (Various, 1938–46/London, 1988, prod. various) compiles original versions of 20 swinging sides (many of their originals) recorded for various labels between 1938–46, capturing Stephane Grappelly (sic) and Django Reinhardt with the Quintet of the Hot Club of France. It's a pleasureful listen. Consider yourself lucky if you come across this disc anywhere. A July 1979 live-recorded, six-tune session at Tivoli Concert Hall in Copenhagen, with Oscar Peterson as leader, *Skol* ♫♫♫♫ (OJC, 1982/1990, prod. Norman Granz) ranks among one of Grappelli's best collaborations. Peterson is cited as leader, but Grappelli gets spotlighted plenty. Guitarist Joe Pass, bassist Niels-Henning Orsted Pedersen, and drummer Mickey Roker also shine in their solos and support. At 41 minutes, it's a short but rich and rewarding concert that includes solid renditions of Django Reinhardt's "Nuages," the Gershwin gem "Someone to Watch over Me," a cohesive, playful "That's All," and, the highly improvised closing jam on Peterson's original, "Skol Blues."

influences:

◀◀ A.J. Piron, Joe Venuti, Eddie South

▶▶ Stuff Smith, Ray Nance, John Frigo, Vassar Clements, Matt Glaser, Randy Sabien, Tom Morley

Nancy Ann Lee

Lou Grassi

Born January 21, 1947, in Summit, NJ.

Like many who toiled in the hardscrabble free-jazz scene of the 1970s, drummer Lou Grassi cut his percussion teeth in the U.S. Army during the 1960s. Upon his return after three years in the military, Grassi began his long career as an accompanist for modern dance troupes as well as an important straight-ahead jazz sideplayer with Sheila Jordan, Johnny Hartman, Charles Byrd, and others. But Grassi blazed many an avant-garde jazz trail, collaborating with other artists and his own PoGressions and Saxtet—in the process embodying Ornette Coleman's suggestions that Dixieland and free jazz are not that far apart. Grassi's work in the "trad jazz" field includes drumming for a half-dozen crack ensembles, and at least one recording with the cracklingly upbeat Dixie Peppers. The powerfully limber drummer balances a variety of teaching gigs around Lodi, New Jersey, and New York City; he has also won Meet the Composer grants four times and a National Endowment of the Arts fellowship in the early 1970s.

what to buy: *Quick Wits* ♫♫♫ (CIMP, 1997, prod. Robert D. Rusch), recorded with his reeds-weighted Saxtet, shows Grassi's swinging power loosely wrapped in smooth but free rhythmic patter.

what to buy next: *PoGressions* ♫♫♫ (Cadence Jazz, 1996, prod. Lou Grassi) is a live date recorded with a dynamic, off-kilter supergroup. Clarinetist Perry Robinson and pianist Burton Greene represent the free jazz polytonalism of the 1960s, and trumpeter Herb Robertson provides blurs of brass amid Grassi's powerhouse percussion.

worth searching for: *Noises from an Open Window* ♫♫♫ (Bridge), the first of two collaborations with Dresden-based keyboardist Andreas Bottcher, is a full-on set of squiggles, dots, and density. Grassi backs up a strong Dixieland ensemble, the Dixie Peppers, on *Hot and Sweet* ♫♫ (Elgee, 1989, prod. Eddy Davis), which includes Arthur Baron on trombone and David Hofstra on bass and tuba. The music is fun and propulsive.

Andrew Bartlett

The Grassy Knoll

Formed early 1990s, in San Francisco, CA.

Bob Green, multi-instrumentalist and sampling guru; Chris Grady, trumpet; David Revelli, drums.

A Dallas–Forth Worth native, Bob Green originally studied photography at the San Francisco Art Institute. Upon returning to

Texas in 1990, he did documentary photo shoots and played in a Beatles-influenced band, which is when he first began to learn about the possibilities of sampling and computers in music. His passion for music took over, and as his aesthetics became more experimental, it became obvious that the brass players Green wanted for his music were more readily available in San Francisco. So he relocated back to the Bay Area, trading in his photo equipment for music gear.

Marrying his affinity for jazz, classic hard rock, and things avant-garde, Bob Green's resultant experimental brainchild is fusion for the modern age. It marries the improvisation and energy of jazz fusion with the seemingly infinite world of electronic sampling and the grooves of funk, hip-hop, and rock. Unlike so much of the so-called "acid jazz" of today (which is merely a half-assed sampling with no soul), The Grassy Knoll's music aptly fits that title. Composer/performer Green himself garners frequent comparisons to Miles Davis circa *Bitches Brew*.

At the heart of his group is a desire to experiment and toss their influences into a musical blender. Theirs is a sonic universe where jazzy trumpet and sax, throbbing bass lines, colorful samples and effects, and hard-hitting grooves collide in aural abandon. Live, the band takes their material to another level; the *Positive* tour was comprised of trumpeter Green leading a rock unit (sans bass) playing to some basic rhythm tracks and samples, and the results were free-flowing and grooving, showcasing a unit capable of creating a mood but also able to rock out.

what to buy: The sophomore GK release *Positive* ♩♩♩ (Antilles, 1996, prod. Bob Green, Jaime Lagueruela) shows Green and his "group" maturing and loosening up. Unlike the noisier feeling of their debut, this time out the group creates a more accessible sound, one which favorably balances melodiousness with dissonance. A recurring motif are the schizoid string samples which squeal during certain numbers. The guitars here are more upfront and the drums less aggressive than on their earlier recording. Overall, *Positive* is more listener-friendly without losing the sense of adventure displayed on their first record.

what to buy next: *The Grassy Knoll* ♩♩♩ (Antilles, 1995, prod. Norm Kerner, Bob Green) is a good debut for the eclectic group. There's a dark undercurrent running beneath many of these discordant tunes, and while occasionally it can be a bit stifling, the record is an interesting listen. Guests artists on this self-titled debut include turn-table pro DJ Quest, Trance Mission clarinetist Beth Custer, and tabla player Baba Duru Demetrius. Be warned that two versions exist. The Antilles version is newer

and has two bonus tracks not on the original disc issued on the Nettwerk label.

influences:

◀◀ Black Sabbath, Deep Purple, Miles Davis, Public Enemy

Bryan Reesman

Milford Graves

Born August 20, 1941 in New York, NY.

Infrequently recorded and seemingly indifferent to the machinery of the music scene, Milford Graves's musical import as one of the first free drummers seems inversely proportional to the length of his discography. He played conga drums as a child and is said to have worked with sticks for the first time at the relatively late age of 17 (studies on tabla came later). In his teens he led a Latin jazz group that had Chick Corea on piano. Graves's concepts emphasize the rumbling, organic, bottom-of-the-drum sound instead of the traditional snap-and-sizzle of combo drumming. Rather than keeping time, Graves suggests simply living in it; his later work is reminiscent of music that would more naturally roll off hillsides than ricochet off the walls of a club or concert hall. Early 1960s associations led to recordings for ESP with Giuseppe Logan, Paul Bley, the New York Art Quartet, and (in a duo) Don Pullen. Graves joined the faculty of Bennington College in Vermont in 1973, where he teaches to the present day, but he continues to live in New York, where he is a mentor to a number of young drummers (Susie Ibarra and Whit Dickey are the most recent to make their marks on the scene) and occasionally puts on much-anticipated small-group concerts at his home. He also teaches martial arts and is a doctor of acupuncture and an herbalist.

what to buy: The roof-rattling *Pieces of Time* ♩♩♩♩ (Soul Note, 1984, prod. Giovanni Bonandrini) is a drum quartet with Don Moye, Kenny Clarke, and Andrew Cyrille. The annotation of instruments and in some cases bar-by-bar sequences allows the listener to compare and contrast these four unique stylists. Finishing off the record, each percussionist takes exactly two minutes for a personal statement.

what to buy next: *Percussion Ensemble* ♩♩♩♩ (ESP, 1965) consists of free-improvisation duos with drummer Sonny Morgan. This is fairly outside stuff, and a useful look at Graves's early style before he mellowed somewhat.

worth searching for: Graves's duo with saxophonist David Murray, *The Real Deal* ♩♩♩♩ (DIW, 1992, prod. Kazunori Sugiyama), has a heavily ritualized vibe. There are moments when the force and power of Graves's 1960s work puts in an appearance, but in general this is a respectful meeting between generations (one is tempted to say, between masters) in which both players listen and respond to each other—which is not to say that many people would find it tame!

influences:

◀◀ Jo Jones, Elvin Jones, Babatunde Olatunji

▶▶ Sonny Murray, Andrew Cyrille, Don Moye, Tony Oxley, Susie Ibarra, Whit Dickey

W. Kim Heron and Steve Holtje

Wardell Gray

Born February 13, 1921, in Oklahoma City, OK. Died May 25, 1955, in Las Vegas, NV.

Raised in the fertile Detroit jazz scene of the late 1930s and early 1940s, Wardell Gray's earliest name-band work was with Earl Hines, at a time when many who would become famous as central figures of the bebop revolution were his band mates. Though he followed them briefly into the Billy Eckstine band, he rejoined the Hines band and with it, relocated to Los Angeles in 1946. Until the end of 1947, he was a major figure in the vibrant Central Avenue scene of club and concert jam sessions. He spent 1948 and 1949 with Benny Goodman's septet, and the big bands of Goodman and Count Basie. When the latter broke up in early 1950, he returned to Detroit, but was soon tapped for a Basie septet. When Basie re-formed his big band in late 1951, Gray chose to remain in Los Angeles, where he was based until his tragic death. During a 1955 sojourn in Las Vegas with a band led by Benny Carter, his body was found in the nearby desert.

One of the most natural swingers and creative improvisors in jazz saxophone history, Gray was called by Basie bio discographer Chris Sheridan, "one of the two or three most articulate tenor players in the band's *50-odd* year history." Despite his associates in the Hines band, and his presence on Charlie Parker's famous "Relaxin' at Camarillo" date for Dial, Gray was not a leading figure of the bebop revolution. Rather, he could play comfortably and swing effortlessly in any setting, in a style that seamlessly melded the characteristics of swing and bebop. The singer Annie Ross paid him tribute by setting to lyrics his solos on three of his recordings.

what to buy: *Wardell Gray Memorial Album, Volume 2* 🎵🎵🎵🎵🎵 (Prestige, 1950/1952/OJC, 1992) consists of three different dates. The first ten tracks (master and alternate takes of four

WARDELL GRAY

song "Twisted" (master take)
album Wardell Gray Memorial: Volume 1
(Prestige-OJC, 1949/1992)
instrument Tenor saxophone

Monster Solo

tunes, two blues, a piece based on the chords of "Blue Moon," and the fairly obscure ballad, "A Sinner Kissed an Angel") find Gray in fine form in Detroit between the demise of Basie's big band and formation of his septet. The next six tracks comprise a date with Gray's proteges, trumpeter Art Farmer (surely among Farmer's first recorded solo work) and pianist Hampton Hawes. Gray's solos on "Farmer's Market" and "Jackie" were vocalized by Annie Ross. But perhaps the standouts of this session are his beautiful ballad treatments of "Sweet and Lovely" and "Lover Man." The disc's final two tracks, recorded at a Los Angeles club, provide a good idea of the sound of Central Avenue jamming by Gray with his fellow saxophonists, Dexter Gordon and Sonny Criss.

what to buy next: *Wardell Gray Memorial Album, Volume 1* 🎵🎵🎵🎵 (Prestige, 1950/1953, prod. Bob Weinstock, Teddy Charles/OJC, 1992) consists of a 1949 Gray-led quartet session with Charlie Parker's rhythm section of that period, and a 1953 session led by vibist Teddy Charles. The first four tracks are the master and three alternates of one of Gray's most famous pieces,

"Twisted." His solo on the master was again vocalized by Annie Ross. One can trace its evolution from a series of standard blues choruses unrelated to the famous head, on the first two takes, to an organic whole on the master. This date's other three pieces were, again, two beautiful ballad performances and a lively pleasant Gray original, "Southside," of which the quartet did seven takes, all included here, which some nonspecialists will probably find tiresome. The group's puzzling difficulty in achieving a strong finish on this piece is revealed in these takes. The four tracks from the 1953 session are notable for perhaps the first appearance on records by altoist Frank Morgan, sounding a great deal like Charlie Parker. With one exception this disc, *How High the Moon* ♪♪♪♪ (Moon, 1950–1952/1997, prod. various), contains television and radio broadcast material by the Basie septet. The last track is a live club jam with Criss and Chet Baker. The rating is for the Basie material. There are fine solos all around. *Wardell Gray: One for Prez* ♪♪♪ (Jazz Selection, 1946, prod. Eddie Laguna/Black Lion, 1988, reissue prod. Alan Bates) is a quartet date, notable for the presence of Dodo Marmarosa, legendary pianist on the California bop scene of the mid-1940s. Five tunes were recorded, "The Man I Love," and four pieces based on the chords of popular songs. The sixteen tracks on this disc are the master and alternate takes of these five tunes. If this were a 10-inch LP consisting only of the master takes of the five tunes, the rating would be considerably higher but the alternate takes do become repetitive. Not the place to start. *Stan Hasselgard with Benny Goodman* ♪♪♪♪ (1948/Phontastic, 1990) is a series of broadcasts by the Goodman septet with its unusual front line of two clarinets (the brilliant young Hasselgard being the second) and Gray's tenor.

worth searching for: The items at a legendary April 29, 1947 concert at the Pasadena Civic Auditorium have been issued many times on "budget label" LPs. As for CD issues, *The Chase!* ♪♪♪♪ (Giants of Jazz, 1992) contains one of Gray's greatest performances, "Blue Lou," with Erroll Garner on piano. Another important track is "Little Pony"—Gray at full speed from start to finish, booted on by a big band put together by Basie only for a recording date during the period of the septet. The title track of this disc is not the classic 1947 recording for Dial, but a 1952 concert performance which reunited Gray and Gordon. The disc also contains their rendition, at that concert, of Charlie Parker's "Steeplechase," which is the same variant on the "I Got Rhythm" changes as Gray's "Easy Swing" on *One for Pres*, recorded more than a year earlier than the Parker date. The remaining tracks duplicate some of the material from the Original Jazz Classics *Memorial Albums*, except for a performance of

"Bebop" by Gray, Criss, Marmarosa, and Howard McGhee from that April 29, 1947 concert. The latter is not as successful as their renditions of "Groovin' High" and "Hot House" to be found on the leaderless disc, *An Unforgettable Session* ♪♪♪♪ (Giants of Jazz, 1992). While all the material on that disc comes from California concert jams of that period, it does not, contrary to the implication of the disc's liner, come from the one concert. Gray recorded with leader Dexter Gordon, *The Chase!* ♪♪♪♪ (Dial, 1947/Stash, 1995, prod. Ross Russell). The rating is for the title track, the only one on which Gray appears, the all-time best-seller in the Dial catalog outselling everything Charlie Parker did for the label. The idea was to capture the kind of music that was made nightly in the Central Avenue clubs, impossible to record on location with the equipment of the time. Gray and Gordon chase each other, trading off solos of progressively shorter length. The remaining Gordon material is worthwhile, and the disc also contains the important "Blues in Teddy's Flat" by tenor Teddy Edwards.

influences:

◀◀ Lester Young, Charlie Parker

▶▶ Frank Foster

Mark Ladenson

Benny Green

Born April 4, 1963, in New York, NY.

Raised in Berkeley, California, pianist Benny Green was inspired by his father's jazz record collection and tenor sax renderings, and began formal classical music studies at age seven. Playing in a series of Bay-area bands of varying sizes as a teenager provided broad-based experience for the young musician, who finally moved back to New York in the spring of 1982. He hooked up with Walter Bishop Jr., who encouraged Green to develop his own sound and to look at the entire jazz piano history to find his niche.

By the time pianist Green hit the scene big-time through stints with vocalist Betty Carter (1983–87), drummer Art Blakey's Jazz Messengers (1987–89), trumpeter Freddie Hubbard, and the Ray Brown Trio, he had been performing for years, had mastered bebop piano, and performed and recorded as leader of his own trio. His recordings during this period include Carter's Grammy-winning *Look What I Got*, three albums with Art Blakey, a date co-led by Blakey and Hubbard, and two albums as leader for the import Criss Cross label (*Prelude* and *In This Direction*). In 1990 Green appeared on Bobby Watson's *The In-*

ventor and made his Blue Note debut with the now out-of-print album *Lineage*. Green admittedly felt greater pressure to focus on career goals after he was awarded Canada's Glenn Gould International Protégé Prize in Music and Communication in 1993, an honor made possible by Canada's foremost jazz pianist, Oscar Peterson, a mentor to Green.

By the time Green's fourth Blue Note album as leader was issued, he had replaced Gene Harris in the Ray Brown Trio. Brown had heard the young pianist play a New York duo gig with Christian McBride, and had Green in mind when a recording date came up. He felt Green knew the history of predecessors on his instrument and had talent, and decided to use him on *Two for the Max*, a Warner album not released in the States. Green made several albums with Brown, remaining with the bassist until 1996, when it was reported he was leaving to pursue his own interests, although, allegedly, he occasionally performs with Brown overseas. With Ray Brown, the pianist's recognizable style was peppered lavishly with rapid-fire runs, interludes of thick ten-finger block chords, lush romanticism, and hard-swinging rhythms that combined elements of gospel, blues and bebop. As leader, Green shows greater maturity, improved technique, and languorous lyricism on his 1997 Blue Note album, *Kaleidscope*.

what to buy: Green's first Blue Note album as leader since 1994 and his sixth for the label, *Kaleidoscope* 𝄞𝄞𝄞𝄞 (Blue Note, 1997, prod. Michael Cuscuna) finds him leading a well-rounded, nine-tune session with bassist Ron Carter (a stalwart in the Cedar Walton trio), fanciful drummer Lewis Nash, and guest soloists Stanley Turrentine (tenor saxophone) and Antonio Hart (alto saxophone). Departing from his characteristic style displayed with the Ray Brown Trio, Green immediately makes his statement of emancipation, stretching his chops in various directions on his original compositions and arrangements. Kicking off (and ending) with separate takes of the title tune, he proves he can compose modern, angular-sounding pieces to give his fleet-fingered solos expressive freedom. Alto saxophonist Hart sweetens "Thursday's Lullaby," a romantic waltz, and three other tunes. Turrentine's rich-toned tenor adds thrust to "Central Park South" and, on the old-style love song, "You're My Melody," blends comfortably with Green. Guitarist Russell Malone renders a fine solo on Green's "The Sexy Mexy," an upbeat, bluesy-riffing piece (that sometimes sounds like "Love Potion No. 9"). The mellow bass-piano duo on Green's ballad "Patience" is the album's lush centerpiece. Hart weaves his harmonies with Malone and solos succinctly with the quintet on "Apricot," a swaying bossa nova. Green shows ultimate versatil-

ity on this outing, leaving the listener wanting more. Drummer Kenny Washington replaces Carl Allen on Green's *The Place to Be* 𝄞𝄞𝄞𝄞 (Blue Note, 1994, prod. Steven Schenfeld) and his loose, flashy style lends exceptional vitality to the set. With bassist Christian McBride rounding out the trio, they creatively carve their way through 12 lesser-known tunes, generating some imaginative solos. Green wrote the orchestrations for top young horn players who guest on a couple tunes and he performs solo on the title tune, the Ray Brown's bluesy "The Gravy Waltz," and Oscar Peterson's "Noreen's Nocturne." His swinging duo with McBride on Green's original, "Which Came First?" is reminiscent of Green's duo performances with Ray Brown, and features the bassist's fine arco solo. Throughout this album, Green varies dynamics, time, ensembles, and he shifts keyboard styles (from straight to stride in one tune) to showcase his rapid-fire romps and rapturous readings of romantic ballads. His skills seem to improve with each recording and, for the listener, this is one of his most engaging recordings.

what to buy next: By the time *That's Right!* 𝄞𝄞𝄞𝄞 (Blue Note, 1993, prod. Michael Cuscuna) was recorded, Green had done considerable "shedding" learning Ray Brown's book. Brown's tutelage is noticeably evident in Green's zestful performance, one of his last with bassist Christian McBride and drummer Carl Allen. Highlights among the 10 tunes include Green's percussive treatment of the nostalgic, straight-ahead swinger "Ain't She Sweet," a sweet solo rendering of "Glad to Be Unhappy," and powerful interpretations of Bud Powell's "Celia," Horace Silver's "Me and My Baby," as well as alluring readings of four originals. Green's second Blue Note album, *Greens* 𝄞𝄞𝄞𝄞 (Blue Note, 1991, prod. Matt Pierson) features Green with McBride on bass, and Allen on drums. With three major label recordings behind him as leader (including two for Criss Cross), Green shows considerable seasoning for such a young player. The album is rife with empathetic camaraderie and individual artistry. Evident on the 12 selections are Green's consistently hard-swinging bluesy tempos, his characteristic light touch and poignant lyricism on ballads, and his overall *joie d'esprit*. Green has admitted he enjoys seeking out old-time gems and, with his able cohorts, he freshly interprets "Time after Time," "Battle Hymn of the Republic," and "I See Your Face before Me," as well as introducing four sparkling originals.

the rest:
Testifyin'! 𝄞𝄞𝄞 (Blue Note, 1992)

worth searching for: Green is showcased in fresh light on the nine tunes of bassist Ray Brown's *Bassface: Live at Kuumbwa*

♫♫♫♫ (Telarc, 1993, prod. Ray Brown) a tight, tasteful, dynamic, and colorful trio set of nine standards. Green masters the bassist's arrangements of "Milestones," "Tin Tin Deo," "Remember," and "Makin' Whoopee," as well as two Brown originals ("CRS-Craft" and "Phineas Can Be"). The integrity their live performance made at Kuumbwa Jazz Center in Santa Cruz, California, April 1–2, 1993, several months after Green joined the trio, stands tall today. He shines throughout, displaying his two-handed unison runs and the swinging style for which he became noted with this trio. Hamilton spurs the others along, and his time-ticking, pill-bottle shaker on "Remember" adds flair to the set.

influences:

🔊 Art Tatum, Erroll Garner, Walter Bishop Jr., Oscar Peterson, Hank Jones, Tommy Flanagan, Thelonious Monk, Horace Silver

Nancy Ann Lee

Grant Green

Born June 6, 1931, in St. Louis, MO. Died January 31, 1979, in New York, NY.

Grant Green was impressed by horn players and adapted some of their ideas for his own playing. When the mid-1960s rolled around he had become one of the most influential guitarists in jazz. Rather than toss a barrage of notes at the listener during a solo, Green would sketch around the spaces, making them hear more by playing less. As the de facto house guitarist for Blue Note Records during that time, his bluesy, single-note runs combined with an uncanny sense of when not to play, made him an in-demand musician on sessions by Lou Donaldson, John Patton, Bobby Hutcherson, Dodo Greene, Sonny Clark, and just about everybody else on the Blue Note roster. The critics noticed and in 1962 Green won his category (New Star) in a *Down Beat* poll. He signed with Verve Records in 1966 and began incorporating soulful versions of the day's hits in his programs, which gave him a modicum of commercial success. He also started to have serious drug problems. When Green finally rejoined Blue Note he was to achieve even greater popularity with the record-buying public by building on the formula that had started to work for him at Verve. He was finally hospitalized in 1978 and died shortly thereafter. His legacy crosses stylistic boundaries. Today's acid-jazz fans are enamored of his later funk-oriented recordings, while the main body of jazz aficionados can lay claim to those first halcyon days at Blue Note.

what to buy: *The Best of Grant Green, Volume I* ♫♫♫♫ (Blue Note, 1993, prod. Alfred Lion) is a good introduction to some of Green's best work under his own name. There are cuts from every major album recorded during his first tour of duty at Blue Note including some (like a version of "Speak Low" with Larry Young on organ, Hank Mobley on tenor, and Elvin Jones on drums) that are not currently available otherwise. The trio format is as good a way as any to tell if a soloist can sustain coherent musical ideas when there is little to fall back upon except a (hopefully) sympathetic rhythm section. How Green came to record within this configuration for *Green Street* ♫♫♫♫ (Blue Note, 1961, prod. Alfred Lion) is far less important than the fact that he did it. On every level, this is a masterful album. Bassist Ben Tucker and drummer Dave Bailey support and push the guitarist depending upon the needs of the song, and Green responds with some of his best playing. The material, including three of the guitarist's originals, is well chosen and the label has included alternate takes of "Green with Envy" and "Alone Together" that weren't on the original album. *Idle Moments* ♫♫♫♫ (Blue Note, 1964, prod. Alfred Lion) demonstrates how Green works well within the context of a larger group even if he is not the consistent focus of attention. Hearing vibist Bobby Hutcherson in the mix is an initial surprise but the interplay between Duke Pearson's piano, Green's guitar and Hutcherson is a continual delight. Joe Henderson's sax playing is pretty heady as well.

what to buy next: Jack McDuff was the organist on *Grantstand* ♫♫♫♫ (Blue Note, 1961, prod. Alfred Lion), and his funky, driving keyboard style meshes well with Green. Yusef Lateef on tenor does a credible job, but he sounds less convinced by what he is doing (especially on the album's putative centerpiece, "Blues in Maude's Flat") than the others do. Lateef's flute playing on "My Funny Valentine" sounds like he's back in the groove. Green, who never leaves it, is, in contrast, almost in the background on *Solid* ♫♫♫♫ (1979, Blue Note, prod. Alfred Lion), a sextet date where everybody gets a turn. And with the caliber players (saxophonists Henderson and James Spaulding, pianist McCoy Tyner, bassist Bob Cranshaw, and polyrhythmic powerhouse Elvin Jones on drums), everybody damn well better get their turn. The groups take of "Ezz-Thetics" by George Russell is a stone gas from beginning to end, with Green riffing note for note with the saxophones.

what to avoid: Green's second stay with Blue Note was commercially successful and some of the albums from this period, like *Green Is Beautiful*, have their adherents among acid jazz fans but *Grant Green Alive!* **woof!** (Blue Note, 1970, prod. Francis Wolff), recorded, appropriately enough, at the Cliché Lounge in Newark, New Jersey, is monochord groove from adequate beginning to the contemptible ending, with a truly wretched version of "Down Here on the Ground" that should wake Wes Montgomery up from his dirt nap to spin a 360.

best of the rest:
Born to be Blue ♪♪♪♪ (Blue Note, 1962)
Feelin' the Spirit ♪♪♪♪ (Blue Note, 1962)
The Matador ♪♪♪♪ (Blue Note, 1964)
Street of Dreams ♪♪♪♪ (Blue Note, 1965)
Iron City ♪♪♪♪ (Cobblestone, 1967/32 Jazz, 1998)
Standards ♪♪♪♪ (compilation) (Blue Note, 1998)

worth searching for: *The Complete Blue Note Recordings of Larry Young* ♪♪♪♪ (Mosaic, 1993, prod. Alfred Lion, Francis Wolff) contains the three albums Green made with organist Young as a sideman (with only *I Want to Hold Your Hand* and *Street of Dreams* currently available) and reveals just how well the guitarist could play when he was with someone who could challenge him to perform at his best.

influences:
◀◀ Charlie Christian

▶▶ Joshua Breakstone, Melvin Sparks

                                  Garaud MacTaggart

Dodo Greene

Born Dorothy Greene, January 1930, in Buffalo, NY.

Dodo Greene was the first vocalist ever signed to an exclusive contract with Blue Note Records and her fans included such reputable students of jazz singing as Sarah Vaughan, Dinah Washington, and Ella Fitzgerald. Greene's first major job came when Cozy Cole's regular singer got sick while on tour in Buffalo and the drummer was hipped to Greene by some local musicians. Declining an offer to join Cole's group, the singer continued to work clubs like the Blue Note in Buffalo until the late 1950s when she moved to Hollis, Queens, New York. Her first album was recorded with Slide Hampton's ten-piece big band for Time Records and released, according to Greene, "in the late '50s or early '60s." Her second album, *My Hour of Need*, was recorded in 1962, and Greene never recorded again, although she sang with Cab Calloway in the '60s and worked the club circuit in New York, Chicago, and Europe. In 1985 Greene moved back to Buffalo after an illness in the family and worked as a nurse's assistant before restarting her singing career.

Nowadays she can be heard singing in venues around Buffalo with drummer Jimmy Gomes and his quartet.

what's available: There aren't many albums that document the kind of gutsy singing heard on *My Hour of Need* ♪♪♪♪ (Blue Note, 1962, prod. Alfred Lion). Greene's vocalizing is a wonderful example of the rib-joint, nightclub songbird. The roots are squarely in the church, but the heart is worn right out on her sleeve for poignant pop standards like "Let There Be Love" and "You Don't Know Me." The musicians were a stellar cast, with Ike Quebec on tenor saxophone, guitarist Grant Green, drummers Billy Higgins and Al Harewood, bassist Milt Hinton, and keyboard players Sir Charles Thompson, Johnny Acea, and Edwin Swantson. The CD has six tracks not found on the original album, including a swinging, gospel-tinged "Jazz in My Soul" accompanied by a booting, big-toned solo from Quebec.

influences:
◀◀ Frank Sinatra, Ella Fitzgerald, Sarah Vaughan, Billie Holiday

                                  Garaud MacTaggart

Phillip Greenlief

Born February 14, 1959, in Los Angeles, CA.

Multi-instrumentalist/composer Phillip Greenlief started on trumpet in the fifth grade. After a few years, he switched to bass (with the occasional piano lesson), and by 10th grade had found his main axe, the tenor saxophone. After a short post-high school stint in Humboldt County, he moved to the San Francisco Bay Area for a period which lasted from 1979–86. Feeling the need to reconcile his literary and musical interests, he returned to Southern California and enrolled in U.S.C. There, he obtained a B.A. in Music Education and an M.A. in English Lit. While in Los Angeles, Greenlief worked regularly in a trio with Ken Filiano and Tootie Heath, and in 1991 performed with Alice Coltrane in the inaugural staging of what has become an annual John Coltrane Memorial Concert. The following year he moved back to the Bay Area where he presently resides.

Love Songs to the Episodes of James Joyce's Ulysses, one of his earliest Bay Area fusions of literature and music, modeled jazz improvisation on the style and structure of Joyce's epic fiction. Other pursuits include a lengthy tenure with the progressive Rough and Tumble Theatre Company, and a recent film score for Finn Taylor's *Dream with the Fishes.* Further, Greenlief has collaborated with Wadada Leo Smith and he co-leads a sextet with Ben Goldberg. He is currently working on a musical interpretation of Rilke's *Duino Elegies* with a new wind trio, including Goldberg and Evelyn Mann.

what to buy: *Phillip Greenlief/Trevor Dunn* ✍✍✍✍ (Evander Music, 1996, prod. Phillip Greenlief) features an exceptional series of improvised duets with bassist Dunn (Ben Goldberg, Graham Connah, Mr. Bungle) and Greenlief on tenor and soprano saxes and various flutes. Tunes like "Itchy and Scratchy" and "Billie" demonstrate the pair's range, from wild up-to-the-minute extrapolations on a cartoon within a cartoon to a sensitive, evocative portrait of Lady Day. The Phillip Greenlief/Scott Amendola Duo is featured on *Collect My Thoughts* ✍✍✍✍ (Nine Winds, 1995, prod. Phillip Greenlief). Greenlief's penetrating freestyle (at times redolent of Ornette Coleman's punchy phrasing and John Coltrane's lyrical steamroll), paired with the supple octopus swing of drummer Amendola (Charlie Hunter, TJ Kirk, Ben Goldberg) yields impressive results, alternately subtle and explosive. These improvised outings are based on conversations between the musicians, and about half the program draws inspiration from the words of courageous writer-thinkers like William S. Burroughs, Zora Neale Hurston, Anne Frank, and Malcolm X. Even our favorite rosy-jowled politico and best-selling author gets a nod on "Gingrich," though Greenlief's whorling free-bop invective seems more like a headbutt than an affirmation.

what to buy next: The disc *Who Ordered the Fish?* ✍✍✍✍ (Evander Music, 1996, prod. Dan Seamans, Phillip Greenlief, Adam Levy), featuring Greenlief, Adam Levy, and Dan Seamans, further demonstrates the saxophonist's range as an improviser. Along with guitarist Levy and bassist Seamans (New Klezmer Trio), Greenlief leads the trio through a traditional program, including tunes like "I Cover the Waterfront" and "Just One of Those Things." Far more convincing than most modern-day standards explorations, the trio even pulls off a beautiful reading of Sam Rivers's "Beatrice."

influences:

◀◀ Lester Young, Dmitry Shostakovich, James Joyce

Sam Prestianni

Al Grey

Born Albert Thornton Grey, June 6, 1925, in Aldie, VA.

The plunger mute used to alter the sound of the trombone and trumpet is most closely identified with players in the Duke Ellington Orchestra of the late 1920s. Trombonist Al Grey carries on this tradition as a master of the plunger, mute, and hat techniques, and his often-humorous improvisations distin-

guish him from trombonists playing today. During his World War II stint with the Navy, Grey played in the famed Great Lakes Naval Training Center band. Following his discharge, he performed with orchestras led by Benny Carter (1945–46), Jimmie Lunceford (1946–47), and Lionel Hampton before hooking up with Count Basie from 1957–61. This was an important career move and with his contributions to Basie band classics, Grey became one of the most impressive soloists of the period. He gained international recognition and recorded albums as leader. From 1961–64, he co-led a sextet with Billy Mitchell, then rejoined Basie, remaining with the Orchestra until late 1976. He worked the studios, toured with Jazz at the Philharmonic, and led his own groups. During the 1970s, he toured and co-led a group with saxophonist Jimmy Forrest. After Forrest died, Gray teamed up with Buddy Tate. Throughout the 1980s, Grey continued to tour internationally and perform with peers such as Lionel Hampton. In the 1990s, Grey performed and recorded as sideman with a number of his colleagues, and recorded on *The Statesmen of Jazz* CD, which also features his son, Mike Grey, on second trombone. Most of his early career recordings since 1958 are out of print, but some Grey gems are currently available on various labels.

what to buy: You've heard plenty of saxophone/B-3 organ groups, but it's rare for a trombone to be included in the instrumental mix. That's what makes *Me 'n' Jack* ✍✍✍✍ (Pullen Music, 1996, prod. Greg Wold) a special listen. Grey's playing does not dominate this cohesive set, but his leadership is felt throughout as Grey and Jack McDuff keep the eight tunes (jazz standards and originals by Grey, McDuff, and Durham) swinging smartly with help from Grey's drummer of over 20 years, Bobby Durham, and bassist Jerome Hunter. Tenor saxophonist Jerry Weldon (Grey's touring partner) boosts the frontline appeal on groovers such as McDuff's "Cap'n Jack" and "Deli's Blues," and guitarist Joe Cohn (a Grey collaborator for over 10 years) has his special spots. Not only is this one of Grey's best albums, but the collegial atmosphere makes this one of the best Hammond B-3 organ dates amidst the recent revival. *Matzoh and Grits* ✍✍✍✍ (Arbors, 1998, prod. Rachel Domber, Mat Domber) features Grey leading a sparkling swing sextet on an 11-tune mixture of standards and two Grey originals. Grey's expressive open and mute trombone playing ranges from rollicking, high-spirited playfulness to lush-toned, warm finesse. One of Grey's most diverse recordings, this CD features material in a variety of tempos, from the swing for which this label is noted, to ballads, bossas, and blues. Grey's backed by a solid rhythm team—Randolph Noel (piano), J.J. Wiggins (bass) and Bobby

Durham (drums), with Cleve Guyton (alto sax/flute) and Joe Cohn (guitar). Grey defers to his sidemen, allowing them plenty of space for solos. But when he steps up to the microphone, Grey makes his plunger-muted trombone sing. The well-shaped sound of his open and muted trombone solos contains the entire history of jazz. He's one of the greatest artists on this instrument and this album finds him in prime form.

what to buy next: Nicknamed "Fab" by Count Basie for his fabulous playing that included his distinctive plunger work, Al Grey used an arsenal of effects as soloist, some of which you'll hear on *Fab* 🎵🎵🎵🎵 (Capri, 1992, prod. Thomas C. Burns, Rosalie Soladar, Al Grey). The New York studio session recorded on July 16 and 17, 1990, features Grey with his son, trombonist Mike, guitarist Joe Cohn (son of Al Cohn), saxophonist Virginia Mayhew, J.J. Wiggins (bassist and son of pianist Gerald Wiggins), pianist-arranger Norman Simmons, drummer Bobby Durham, and veteran Clark Terry (trumpet, flugelhorn). Guesting on one tune each are trombonist Delfeayo Marsalis (of that famed New Orleans family), trumpeter Don Sicker, and vocalist Jon Hendricks. This is a well-organized intergenerational date that captures Grey in some finely honed, plunger mute solos, most notably his collaboration with Terry during the seductive ballad, "Lover Man." Another delight comes with Grey and Terry trading scat vocals on the up-tempo Ellington classic, "Cotton Tail." Tasteful arrangements by Norman Simmons, skillfully crafted to feature the horns and showcase the soloists, add to the enjoyment of the 10 standards and originals by band members. A relaxed and often blues-grooved date that warrants repeat listening.

best of the rest:

Live at the Floating Jazz Festival, (1990) 🎵🎵🎵 (Chiaroscuro, 1992)
The New Al Grey Quintet 🎵🎵🎵 (Chiaroscuro, 1992)
Al Grey Centerpiece: Live at the Blue Note 🎵🎵🎵 (Telarc, 1995)
The Statesmen of Jazz 🎵🎵🎵 (American Federation of Jazz Societies/Arbors, 1995)

Nancy Ann Lee

Johnny Griffin

Born April 24, 1928, in Chicago, IL.

Nicknamed "The Little Giant" because he's a small man with a (very) big sound, Johnny Griffin is one of the more individual tenor stylists around, primarily because he's not afraid to play fast and he's not afraid to play loud. He has consistently surrounded himself with strong players and remained true to his bop/hard bop foundations, resulting in records that are steadfastly exuberant and enjoyable, yet nonetheless substantial

and engaging. After his first gigs with Lionel Hampton's big band and a stint in the service, Griffin left his home town of Chicago for the Big Apple and, once there, made an enormous impact. Although he had recorded a couple of albums under his own name in Chicago, Griffin really hit his stride with a pair of Blue Note albums recorded in 1957. Although his under-regarded 1956 Blue Note debut, *Introducing Johnny Griffin*, was a phenomenal disc, it was with the triple-tenor assault of *A Blowing Session* and the infectious blues-bop of *The Congregation* that Griffin made his mark. In 1957 he began a stint with Art Blakey's Jazz Messengers, appearing on their classic Atlantic date with Thelonious Monk (on which all the tunes were written by Monk, except one Griffin original). This, logically enough, led to a mutually appreciative job with Monk the next year. Griffin would start out the '60s by teaming up with Eddie "Lockjaw" Davis and recording several rock-hard "tenor battles." In '63, like so many of his peers, he lit off to Europe, where he was able to maintain an allegiance to his craft. Accordingly, his albums since have been consistently enjoyable, though sometimes a touch on the sentimental side.

what to buy: On *A Blowing Session* 🎵🎵🎵🎵 (Blue Note, 1957/1988, prod. Alfred Lion), it's almost funny to hear Lee Morgan try to keep up with Griffin's lightning-fast runs on this barn-burner of a jam. However, even though all the players (even pianist Wynton Kelly and the truly gifted rhythm section of Art Blakey and Paul Chambers) were surely out of breath by the end, the way this all-star sextet blows through the four pieces here is truly inspiring. Teaming Griffin with John Coltrane and Hank Mobley was an inspired move on Alfred Lion's part because the three (yes, three!) tenor players interact marvelously, rather than trying to duke it out with solo after solo. Of course, this set is dripping with machismo and there's not a lot of melodic complexity here, but this is definitely a cut (or three) above your average blowing session. A little more restrained, yet no less rewarding, the unequivocal masterpiece, *The Congregation* 🎵🎵🎵🎵 (Blue Note, 1957/1994, prod. Alfred Lion) was recorded just a few months after *A Blowing Session*. With Paul Chambers back for more and Sonny Clark (who was then in the midst of his prime) on the piano, this smaller group gives Griffin all the room he needs to blast his beautifully primal runs. "It's You or No One" is outstanding here: loose and riveting, with a beautiful arco solo by Chambers. This record didn't come about its name by accident, for Griffin summons up a truly religious experience on this one.

what to buy next: A tribute to singer Billie Holiday, *White Gardenia* 🎵🎵🎵 (Riverside, 1961/OJC, 1995, prod. Orrin Keepnews) was recorded exactly two years after her death. This ten-cut tribute to Holiday is warm and reverent, though never overly somber. Griffin (obviously) isn't at his "tough tenor" toughest here, but his passion and intensity are still omnipresent. If *A Blowing Session* wasn't your typical blowing session, then *Tough Tenor Favorites* 𝄞𝄞𝄞 (Jazzland, 1962/OJC, 1994, prod. Orrin Keepnews), a marvelous set with Eddie "Lockjaw" Davis, is certainly a cut above your average tenor battle. With pianist Horace Parlan stuck in the middle, Griffin and Davis get down to business on the seven standards and the proceedings are hot, indeed. A good time, to be sure. Although it wasn't exactly a "return"—more like a visit—the solid date *Return of the Griffin* 𝄞𝄞𝄞 (Galaxy, 1978/OJC, 1996, prod. Orrin Keepnews) celebrates a Griffin tour of the States nearly 15 years after his departure for Europe. It must have been incredibly invigorating for U.S. jazz fans at the time, given the then-climate of the genre. As such, it is still a joy to hear that Griffin had lost none of his style, speed, nor allegiance to hard bop forms.

the rest:
Introducing Johnny Griffin 𝄞𝄞𝄞 (Blue Note, 1956/1995)
Johnny Griffin Sextet 𝄞𝄞𝄞 (Riverside, 1958/OJC, 1994)
Way Out 𝄞𝄞𝄞 (Riverside, 1958/OJC, 1995)
The Little Giant 𝄞𝄞𝄞 (Riverside, 1959/OJC, 1995)
(With the Johnny Griffin Orchestra) *The Big Soul Band* 𝄞𝄞𝄞 (Riverside, 1960/OJC, 1990)
The Man I Love 𝄞𝄞𝄞 (Black Lion, 1967/1992)
Blues for Harvey 𝄞𝄞 (SteepleChase, 1973/1995)
The Cat 𝄞𝄞𝄞 (Antilles, 1991)
Dance of Passion 𝄞𝄞𝄞 (Antilles, 1993)
Chicago, New York, Paris 𝄞𝄞𝄞 (Verve, 1995)

influences:
◀◀ Lester Young
▶▶ Roland Kirk

Jason Ferguson

Henry Grimes

Born November 11, 1935, in Philadelphia, PA. Died 1971.

One of the preeminent free bassists, Grimes first earned his wings as a sideman to such luminaries as Cecil Taylor and Albert Ayler. He studied violin (and later tuba) in junior high. During the 1950s, he attended Julliard and played with Bobby Timmons, Lee Morgan, and Albert Heath. In 1958, he performed at Newport with Benny Goodman's Big Band and Thelonious Monk (he can even be seen in the movie *Jazz on a Summer Day*). However, it is his free playing in the 1960s that he is most known for,

working in tandem with such greats as Taylor, Ayler, and Don Cherry, underlining the ferment that bubbles wildly on top.

what's available: *Henry Grimes Trio* 𝄞𝄞𝄞 (ESP, 1965, prod. Henry Grimes) was Grimes's only album as leader. It's free jazz, but stands apart from the era thanks to Perry Robinson's utterly distinctive clarinet style, which was gutsier than the only other notable clarinetist in the movement, Jimmy Giuffre. Tom Price is the drummer and he and Grimes pursue a less single-minded approach to rhythm than many free players, perhaps reflecting Grimes's varied experience.

worth searching for: Grimes is also heard to good advantage on albums by a number of New York greats from the 1960s. On McCoy Tyner's trio album *Reaching Forth* 𝄞𝄞𝄞 (Impulse!, 1962, prod. Bob Thiele) Grimes takes an exuberant arco solo on the title track. Roy Haynes is the drummer on that session, and on Haynes's own *Out of the Afternoon* 𝄞𝄞𝄞𝄞 (Impulse!, 1962, prod. Bob Thiele) with Rahsaan Roland Kirk, Tommy Flanagan, and Grimes's bowing prominently featured, especially on Haynes's tune "Raoul." Don Cherry's *Where Is Brooklyn?* 𝄞𝄞𝄞𝄞𝄞 (Blue Note, 1966, prod. Rudy Van Gelder) is a kick-ass session from the peak of the free movement, with Grimes, Cherry, Pharoah Sanders, and Ed Blackwell. One of the outstanding features of the album is the contrast in styles among the players. The fiery "Unite" is the album's centerpiece. If the individual album proves hard to locate, get the Cherry box set on Mosaic. Grimes's work with Albert Ayler must be mentioned, of course. Ayler's *Witches and Demons* 𝄞𝄞𝄞𝄞𝄞 (Arista Freedom, 1975) is a posthumous Ayler release of 1964 material featuring Grimes with Sunny Murray (drums), Norman Howard (trumpet) and Ayler. Grimes is most prominent with Earl Henderson in a double-bass duet on the title track. Grimes appears on side two of *Albert Ayler in Greenwich Village* 𝄞𝄞𝄞𝄞𝄞 (Impulse!, 1967, prod. Bob Thiele). His interaction with not only the Ayler brothers but also violinist Michael Sampson on "Truth is Marching In" and "Our Prayer" shows why he was such a valued collaborator, with the two string players bringing a unique sound to jazz at that time. A couple Cecil Taylor classics deserve mention, too. *Unit Structures* 𝄞𝄞𝄞𝄞𝄞 (Blue Note, 1966, prod. Rudy Van Gelder) is a free jazz masterpiece with Grimes, Jimmy Lyons (alto), Ken McIntyre (alto, oboe, etc.), Alan Silva (bass), and Andrew Cyrille (drums). The use of two bassists was becoming a popular approach on the scene, and the contrast between the burly sound of Grimes and the more ephemeral approach of Silva shows the best use of this format. *Conquistador* 𝄞𝄞𝄞𝄞𝄞 (Blue Note, 1967, prod. Rudy Van Gelder) has more peak free playing with Bill Dixon (trumpet), Lyons, Taylor, Grimes, Silva, and Cyrille. Grimes duets with Silva on "With (Exit)," offering an opportunity for direct comparison.

influences:

⏪ Paul Chambers, Charles Mingus

⏩ Malachi Favors

Joe S. Harrington

Lloyd "Tiny" Grimes

Born July 6, 1916, in Newport News, VA. Died March 4, 1989.

One of the rare exponents of the four-string "tenor" guitar, Tiny Grimes is a guitarist important not only to the development of electrically amplified guitar within the realm of blues and jazz but also as developer of rock 'n' roll during its embryonic stages. Although Grimes shouldn't be classified as a virtuoso guitarist, he possessed a beautiful bluesy tone and a tremendous sense of swing, as well as a flair for showmanship. He started out as a dancer and drummer and had been gigging in New York as a pianist in the late 1930s before picking up guitar at the close of the decade. Grimes was heavily influenced by Charlie Christian, though his style never was quite as complex. Grimes used to joke that he started on four-string guitar "because he couldn't afford six." He developed quickly, though, and after less than a year of practice, he had joined the popular pre-war rhythm group the Cats & the Fiddle, with whom he recorded in 1941. Grimes soon joined a trio led by Art Tatum (Slam Stewart was the bassist) that stayed together nearly three years. In 1944 Grimes led a session that included some of the first small group soloing by Charlie Parker, and later in the decade, he formed a group called the Rocking Highlanders who played stomping R&B while wearing kilts. His recordings for Atlantic, beginning in 1947, resulted in at least one hit, "Annie Laurie." Along with his recordings for Gotham in the early '50s, these records were often seen as wild "rock 'n' roll" records, though today they sound fairly tame compared to what came later. Grimes recorded a series of pleasant albums for Prestige in the late '50s and guested on records by Coleman Hawkins (among others). He continued to perform up through the '80s and recorded a few more sessions in later years for both European and American labels.

what to buy: Although the alternate takes may prove to be more than you need and the sound quality is not the greatest, the Spain-based Blue Moon label's five-volume collection, *The Complete Tiny Grimes* ♫♫♫♫ (Blue Moon, 1995), taken as a whole, is the most representative collection of Grimes's work while he was in his occasionally kilted prime (1944–54). It's more R&B than jazz, but that's an accurate reflection of where Grimes was at musically during his peak years. The Blue Moon releases include his work with Parker, his late-'40s Atlantic hits, and his Gotham material, rendering the Collectables sets (which collect the Gotham recordings) obsolete.

what to buy next: For a side of Grimes that was more jazz oriented, *Callin' the Blues* ♫♫♫ (Prestige/OJC, 1958, prod. Bob Weinstock) is a good choice, with four lengthy cuts that find Grimes stretching out alongside trombonist J.C. Higginbotham, pianist Ray Bryant, and "Lockjaw" Davis in swinging, bluesy fashion. Totally relaxed and rarely rising above a mild tepidity, the two remaining releases available in the OJC series *Blues Groove, with Coleman Hawkins* ♫♫♫ (Prestige/OJC, 1958, prod. Bob Weinstock) and *Tiny in Swingville, with Jerome Richardson* ♫♫♫ (Prestige/OJC, 1959, prod. Bob Weinstock) are nonetheless enjoyable examples of Grimes's work in a jazz setting. The sound of his guitar tone alone is worth the price of admission. On the slow, bluesy passages especially, for example "Blues Wail" on *Blues Groove*, Grimes really makes the guitar sing, with each well-placed note just hanging in the air and quivering away.

what to avoid: It's certainly not wretched, but there are better places to hear Grimes's work than on *Tiny Grimes and Friends* ♫♫ (Collectables, 1990), which features a line-up of the Cats and the Fiddle that is about 10 years past its pre-World War II prime.

the rest:

Tiny Grimes & His Rocking Highlanders, Volume One ♫♫♫ (Collectables, 1990)

Tiny Grimes & His Rocking Highlanders, Volume Two ♫♫♫ (Collectables, 1990)

worth searching for: It's no longer in print, but the last of a three-part CD series reissuing Art Tatum's Decca recordings, *I Got Rhythm* ♫♫♫♫ (Decca/GRP, 1993, prod. Orrin Keepnews), includes 10 1994 recordings by the popular trio that included Slam Stewart and Tiny Grimes. Grimes's 1941 recordings with the Cats and the Fiddle were reissued in LP form on *I Miss You So* ♫♫♫♫♫ (RCA Bluebird, 1976, prod. Frank Driggs) but are not currently available on CD. An indispensable document of pre-war, small-group vocal jazz, jive, and blues, the two-LP set contains 11 songs recorded while Grimes was in the group. Also only on vinyl is *Profoundly Blue* ♫♫♫ (Muse, 1973, prod. Don Schlitten), a moderately successful outing proving Grimes's continued vitality in the '70s. The flat-out blues numbers work better than the few somewhat dated attempts at funky jazz—with pianist Harold Mabern and saxophonist Houston Person.

influences:

◀◀ Napoleon "Snags" Allen, Charlie Christian, Teddy Bunn, Oscar Moore

▶▶ Bill Jennings, Barney Kessel, Grant Green, B.B. King

Dan Bindert

Don Grolnick

Born September 23, 1947, in New York, NY. Died June 1, 1996, in New York, NY.

Don Grolnick was a veritable renaissance man of contemporary music. Comfortable in pop, rock, and jazz settings, his prodigious session track record reads like a who's who of popular music. Grolnick grew up in New York City and was bitten by the jazz bug while a youngster. Steeped in bop, blues, Latin, and fusion, he took pleasure in combining all the influences into an articulate musical statement all his own. Early 1970s collaborations with a young Michael Brecker led in a fusion direction, along with an appetite for funk and mainstream pop. His session career flourished, including a 22-year stint as arranger/producer and keyboardist for pop star James Taylor. Grolnick proved to be a brilliant post-bop jazz composer and band leader, as is evidenced by his critically acclaimed Blue Note sessions. Grolnick's solo recording discography is short but virtually without a wasted moment of music. His unfortunate and premature death at 48 brought an end to a remarkable and productive career in music.

what to buy: The Blue Note sessions have been reissued as a double CD package, *The Complete Blue Note Recordings* 𝄞𝄞𝄞𝄞 (Blue Note, 1997, prod. Don Grolnick), a delightful collection of beautifully realized mainstream jazz compositions by Grolnick with a few selections penned by others. On 1988's *Weaver of Dreams* and 1991's *Nighttown* Grolnick leads ensembles that include the Brecker brothers, bassist Dave Holland, sax players Joe Lovano and Marty Ehrlich, and other jazz notables such as Steve Turre, Bob Mintzer, and Peter Erskine. The arrangements recall Charles Mingus, McCoy Tyner, Gil Evans, and Bill Evans, among others, with Grolnick's very own personal compositional language highlighting the entire process. His acoustic piano work here is a treat and a nice departure from the electronics he might be better-known for. Many wonderful touches abound in this near-perfect double-CD set of great jazz.

what to buy next: *Hearts and Numbers* 𝄞𝄞𝄞 (Hip Pocket, 1988, prod. Don Grolnick) is a satisfying set of fusion-oriented grooves with Grolnick's sense of musicality and humor coming through. Hiram Bullock delivers clever guitar work on the driving, high-energy "Human Bites." *Medianoche* 𝄞𝄞𝄞 (Warner Bros., 1996, prod. Don Grolnick, Andy Garcia) was Grolnick's final recording. Combining contemporary and Latin jazz sounds, it includes compositions by Wayne Shorter, Horace Silver, and Chick Corea.

influences:

◀◀ Bill Evans, Chick Corea

▶▶ Pat Coil, John Altenburgh

Tali Madden

Groove Collective

Formed 1990, in New York, NY.

Gordon Clay, percussion; Fabio Morgera, trumpet; Jonathan Maron, guitar, bass; Jay Rodriguez, saxophones; Josh Roseman, trombone, keyboards; Genji Siraisi, drums, programming; Itaal Shur, keyboards, synthesizers; Chris Theberge, percussion; Bill Ware, vibes, keyboards; Richard Worth, flutes.

One of the acid-jazz bands that can actually play jazz, Groove Collective grew from a ongoing Soho dance club jam session aggregation of musicians, rappers, and an MC. Rather than falling into an R&B party, the Collective developed into a fusion unit with a big beat based on Latin percussion. Their first album was recorded as a farewell to their home club after angry neighbors had the place closed down. The instrumentalists have real chops and can stretch out in a number of directions. Mostly an instrumental group, the occasional vocals are doled out to guest artists. All the material on their full CDs is original—no samples, no covers—although the Beatles' "I Want You (She's So Heavy)" shows up on a 1996 EP. Groove Collective captures a sound and energy similar to Miles Davis during his *Bitches Brew-Live Evil* era.

what to buy: The first recording, *Groove Collective* 𝄞𝄞𝄞 (Reprise, 1994, prod. Gary Katz) is fun, and arrangements are surprisingly sparse at times. This is a disciplined outing that establishes serious intent. The band takes a stronger Latin tack on *We the People* 𝄞𝄞𝄞 (Giant Step/GRP, 1996, prod. Genji Siraisi, Groove Collective) and displays even stronger soloing.

the rest:

"I Want You (She's So Heavy)"/"Everybody (We the People)" 𝄞𝄞𝄞 (Giant Step/GRP, 1996)

influences:

⏪ War, Fania All Stars, Miles Davis, Herbie Hancock, Santana

Larry Gabriel

Steve Grossman

Born January 18, 1951, in Brooklyn, NY.

Steve Grossman took up both the tenor and soprano saxophones as a teenager and would become one of the most powerful jazz scene players on these instruments during the 1970s. He developed a brawny, torrid style which was strongly influenced by both Sonny Rollins and John Coltrane. In 1969, Grossman recorded with Miles Davis and joined Davis's band the following year. He worked and recorded with Elvin Jones's band from 1971–73, including the outstanding quartet edition with David Liebman and Gene Perla. Grossman recorded some solo albums for Perla's PM Records in the mid-1970s, and was a founding member of the group Stone Alliance in 1975. His work during the 1970s was totally impassioned and continually on fire. Since the early 1980s, Grossman has been living in Italy. He has recorded several albums for Italy's Red Records and is currently recording for Dreyfus Jazz. His playing style has since mellowed quite a bit, sounding more like his early Rollins-styled approach than his intense Coltrane-derived playing of the 1970s.

what to buy: *Time to Smile* ♫♫♫♫ (Dreyfus Jazz, 1994, prod. Sandro Berti-Ceroni, Keiko Jones) is an outstanding, straight-ahead set which reunites Grossman with Elvin Jones, plus Tom Harrell (trumpet), Willy Pickens (piano), and Cecil McBee (bass). Originally released on PM Records in 1974, Grossman's first album, *Some Shapes to Come* ♫♫♫♫ (One Way, 1994, prod. Gene Perla), is a first-rate, powerful jazz-rock session with Jan Hammer, Gene Perla and Don Alias. Although the synthesizers sound a bit dated today, it's the only example on CD of Grossman's 1970s intensity other than on albums with Miles or Elvin Jones.

what to buy next: An inspired live date with choice material, *In New York* ♫♫♫♫ (Dreyfus Jazz, 1992, prod. Yves Chamberland, Sandro Berti-Ceroni), features McCoy Tyner, Avery Sharp and Art Taylor.

the rest:

Standards ♫♫♫ (DIW, 1985)
Katonah ♫♫♫ (DIW, 1989)
Love Is The Thing ♫♫♫♫ (Red, 1990)
Do It ♫♫♫♫ (Dreyfus Jazz, 1991)
My Second Prime ♫♫♫♫ (Red, 1992)

Way Out East, Vol.1 ♫♫♫♫ (Red, 1993)
Way Out East, Vol.2 ♫♫♫♫ (Red, 1993)
Bouncing with Mr. A. T. ♫♫♫♫ (Dreyfus Jazz, 1996)

worth searching for: *Terra Firma* ♫♫♫ (PM, 1977, prod. Gene Perla), Grossman's second solo LP, with Jan Hammer, Gene Perla, and Don Alias is worth the search, as is *Stone Alliance* ♫♫♫♫ (PM, 1976, prod. Gene Perla), which debuts the power jazz trio of Grossman, Gene Perla and Don Alias. *Marcio Montarroyos* ♫♫♫♫ (PM, 1977, prod. Gene Perla), the second Stone Alliance LP, with Brazilian trumpeter Montarroyos and other guests, was recorded in Brazil. *Con Amigos* ♫♫♫♫ (PM, 1977, prod. Nano Herrera, Gene Perla), the third from Stone Alliance, was recorded in Buenos Aries with several Argentinean guests.

influences:

⏪ Sonny Rollins, John Coltrane

Bill Wahl

Marty Grosz

Born February 28, 1930, in Berlin, Germany.

Marty Grosz is a specialist in uncovering overlooked or forgotten songs of the past and performing them on his acoustic guitar in the company of musicians who are kindred spirits capable of making relics from the 1920s to the 1930s sound fresh and unspoiled. First and foremost a rhythm guitarist, Grosz conjures up exciting chorded solos. His singing, inspired by Fats Waller and Red McKenzie, has strengthened over the years and, like Waller's, is often filled with good humor without disrespect to the material. Grosz is also a skilled arranger whose unique mix of music and on-stage wit were likely inspired by his father, the well-known satirical artist and jazz enthusiast, George Grosz. In 1932, the elder Grosz left Germany to accept a post at the Art Student's League in New York City, and subsequently brought his wife and sons to the U.S. after Hitler seized power in Germany in 1933.

Grosz discovered jazz at age 12 and became fascinated with the unamplified guitar sounds performed by Bernard Addison, Dick McDonough, Carl Kress, and Django Reinhardt. Grosz experimented with a four-string guitar while jamming around New York City. He recorded with pianist Dick Wellstood in 1951 before being drafted into the U. S. Army where he practiced guitar in his spare time. Settling in Chicago in 1954, Grosz played numerous gigs, switching to six-string guitar and part-time banjo in a trio at the Gaslight Club. He co-led an octet on a PBS television show, *The Sounds of Swing*. In 1975, Grosz moved East and joined Soprano Summit as guitarist and vocalist. He later toured 14 countries with Dick Hyman's New York Jazz Repertory Company and formed The Classic Jazz Quartet in 1984 with Joe Muranyi, Dick Sudhalter, and Dick Wellstood, a group which lasted until Wellstood's untimely death in 1987. From the mid-1980s, Grosz began to frequently record as leader and to perform internationally at festivals. He continues to play vintage guitar with integrity and conviction and, now that many jazz party promoters have discovered him, has found a platform for his classic style of non-moldy traditional jazz.

what to buy: *Songs I Learned at My Mother's Knee and Other Low Joints* ✍✍✍✍ (Jazzology, 1993, prod. Gus P. Statiras) features Grosz and Destiny's Tots romping through 17 free-wheeling, swinging chestnuts. Using the same rhythm team but alternating two separate front lines, the band maintains continuity while providing a variety of sounds. The "A" band includes Peter Ecklund (cornet), Dick Meldonian (tenor sax), and Bobby Pring (trombone), with the "B" band sporting Randy Sandke (trumpet), Ken Peplowski (alto sax/clarinet), and Joel Helleny (trombone). Rhythm stalwarts Keith Ingham (piano), Greg Cohen (bass), and Chuck Riggs (drums) with Grosz round out each septet. If you have pleasant memories of the small bands led by Teddy Wilson, Red Allen, or Wingy Manone in the 1930s, you'll probably dig this set which presents the opportunity to hear Ken Peplowski's clarinet and his infrequently heard alto sax, along with talented but seldom recorded Joel Helleny, whose trombone choruses are album highlights. Tunes range from straight-ahead instrumental swingers like "Little by Little" and "Stompy Jones," to many with Grosz's humorous and charming vocals such as "Just a Gigolo," "I Believe in Miracles," and Walter Donaldson's nostalgic, "You." Three trio numbers add spice to the proceedings as Loren Schoenberg, Cohen, and Grosz do their band-within-a-band bit. *Marty Grosz and his Swinging Fools: Ring Dem Bells* ✍✍✍✍ (Nagel-Heyer, 1995, prod. Sabine Nagel-Heyer, Hans Nagel-Heyer), a live recording of a February 1995 concert in Hamburg, Germany, makes for good listening for small band fans who thrive on large doses of infectious rhythm. Grosz sings on only five of the 13 tracks here, which might be a discouragement to his hardcore fans, but his short, creative, almost entirely chorded solos and ever-present rhythmic thrusts are plentiful. England's pianist Martin Litton is a stride monster, blues man, and swinger. Drummer Chuck Riggs employs deft brush work, and bassist Greg Cohen showcases plump tone, melodious solos, and an unerring sense of timing. Jon-Erik Kellso's robust Roy Eldridge-like trumpet gets plenty of solo space as does versatile Scott Robinson whose booting, baritone sax kicks like mad on the

opening "Rose of the Rio Grande." Robinson switches to clarinet and soprano sax with ease as the quintet runs effectively through war horses such as "Baby Won't You Please Come Home?," "She's Crying for Me," and "Nobody's Sweetheart," some Ellington tunes, and ballads. Good choruses by all abound in this well-produced collection and there are plenty of little chases and breaks throughout the 77 minutes to sustain or heighten interest in Grosz's neat arrangements. A typical Grosz small band unit on *Marty Grosz and Destiny's Tots: Swing It!* ✍✍✍✍ (Jazzology, 1988, prod Gus P. Statiras), swings like mad on 16 obscure, mostly pop, tunes from the 1930s. There is a feel of pre-bop 52nd Street in many of the numbers. The title tune, "Let's Swing it," is especially appealing and this version probably marks the first time it has been recorded since Ray Noble and Wingy Manone did it when it appeared in Earl Carroll's Sketchbook of 1935. Grosz band veterans Peter Ecklund (trumpet), Dan Barrett (trombone), Bobby Gordon (clarinet), and Loren Schoenberg (tenor sax) fill out the front line with Grosz's propulsive guitar, Keith Ingham's tasteful piano, Murray Wall's acoustic bass and drummer Hall Smith's full kit providing solid background. If you seek well-crafted solos done in swinging manner, you'll revel in the appealing versions of "Emaline." "What's the Use?," "Love Dropped in for Tea," and more. The leader's vocals lend authenticity and charm to many of the performances but never intrude on the jazz content.

what to buy next: Recommended for vintage tune sleuths and fans who have fond recollection of the good old jazz days, *Unsaturated Fats* ✍✍✍✍ (Stomp Off, 1990, prod. Keith Ingham, Marty Grosz, Doug Pomeroy) is a collection of Waller compositions never recorded by the famous pianist. Recorded under the guise of "Marty Grosz & Keith Ingham and their Paswonky Serenaders," it's marked by Ingham's spirited arrangements and carried off nicely by Grosz, Ingham (piano), brass players Peter Ecklund and Dan Barrett, clarinetist Joe Muranyi, bassist Greg Cohen, and Drummer Arnie Kinsella. These staunch revivalists ensure that tunes such as "Dixie Cinderella," "Strange as It Seems," "Asbestos," and other seldom heard tunes continue to be performed. Marty Grosz and Destiny's Tots recorded eight tunes each in California and New York in 1994 and combine them on *Keep a Song in Your Soul* ✍✍✍✍ (Jazzology, 1995, prod. Marty Grosz) to produce a favorable and often amusing set of 1920s–1930s material for the swing-minded listener. Grosz, Ecklund, and bassist Greg Cohen are constants on both dates. The West Coast team includes reedmen Bobby Gordon and Dan Levinson, pianist Chris Dawson, drummer Hal Smith. The East Coast crew features trombonist Joel Helleny, reedmen Scott

Robinson and Dan Block, pianist Keith Ingham, drummer Arnie Kinsella. Tunes featured include the unusually bright treatment of "I've Got a Crush on You" and "Can't Help Lovin' That Man," which comes across like a Chicago-styled, dirty blues tune.

best of the rest:

Marty Grosz Sings of Love and Other Matters ♪♪♪♪ (Jazzology, 1989)

Keith Ingham + Marty Grosz & Their Hot Cosmopolites: Donaldson Redux ♪♪♪♪ (Stomp Off, 1992)

Just Imagine: The Music of DeSylva, Brown, & Henderson ♪♪♪♪ (Stomp Off, 1994)

Marty Grosz and his Sugar Daddies: On Revival Day ♪♪♪♪ (Jazzology, 1995)

worth searching for: Originally recorded in New York but released in the U.K., *Marty Grosz and the Collectors Items Cats: Thanks* ♪♪♪♪ (J & M Records, 1993, prod. Marty Grosz) is a high-grade collection of 13 obscure tunes and four Grosz originals performed by a small band that features regular Grosz cohorts, Peter Ecklund, Dan Barrett, Scott Robinson, Hal Smith, Greg Cohen, and swing-style pianist Mark Shane in various combinations. This CD has limited distribution in the U.S. Check speciality shops and mail order listings.

see also: *The Orphan Newsboys*

John T. Bitter

Grubbs Brothers

See: The Visitors

Dave Grusin

Born June 26, 1934, in Denver, CO.

Dave Grusin planned a career in academia when he moved to New York in 1959 and enrolled in the Manhattan School of Music but soon found himself playing piano and later serving as musical director for singer Andy Williams. Grusin launched his recording career in the mid-1960s with two piano jazz trio albums, *Subways Are for Sleeping* and *Piano, Strings, and Moonlight*. In 1964 he left *The Andy Williams Show* to work on his first film assignment, the Norman Lear/Bud York production of *Divorce American Style*. This marked the beginning of his career as a film composer. Among his Academy Award-nominated work over the years have been scores for *Heaven Can Wait, On Golden Pond, Tootsie, The Milagro Beanfield War* (which won the 1988 Oscar), *Havana,* and *The Fabulous Baker Boys*. Grusin has also arranged for recording artists, including Sergio Mendes, Quincy Jones, Billy Joel, Peggy Lee, Paul Simon, and Grover Washington Jr. Although he's best known as a prolific composer for television and film who favors studio work,

Grusin still plays piano and his better work is firmly rooted in the jazz tradition, most notably his tributes to Ellington, Gershwin, and Mancini.

what to buy: Unquestionably, the music of Leonard Bernstein's *West Side Story* has become a cherished part of America's artistic canon. On *West Side Story* ♪♪♪♪ (N2K Encoded Music, 1997, prod. Phil Ramone), pianist/composer/arranger Grusin's take on the music is a certified jazz rendition, a risk-taking and grand event produced by Phil Ramone and loaded with pungent soloists such as saxmen Michael Brecker and Bill Evans, flutist Dave Valentin, and guitarist Lee Ritenour. Vocalists Jonathan Butler and Jon Secada present singular renditions of "Maria" and "Somewhere," while Ritenour's solid, rippling, solo leads "Cool." *Two for the Road* ♪♪♪♪ (GRP, 1997, prod. Tommy Lipuma) is a tribute to the late great Henry Mancini and his spirited, harmonically rich compositions. Grusin succeeds in capturing the essence of Mancini while offering his own take the music. "Peter Gunn" is sassy, by way of punchy brass and barrelhouse riffs on the piano. "Baby Elephant Walk" gets a bluesy, pungent, New Orleans rendering while the elegance of Mancini's beaming orchestral arrangements is accented in "Moment to Moment." Sultry and sophisticated, this homage is conceived and executed with a sense of elegance and taste. *The Gershwin Connection* ♪♪♪♪ (GRP, 1991, prod. Larry Rosen, Dave Grusin) features 13 classic American compositions by George Gershwin, yet another lofty creative peak. Joined by such friends as Chick Corea, Lee Ritenour, Gary Burton, Eddie Daniels, and John Patitucci, as well as Grusin's brother, Don, who also plays piano, Grusin succeeds in creating a respectful, well-conceived tribute, breathing fresh life into time honored evergreens like "Summertime" and "Fascinating Rhythm." Grusin's piano duo with Chick Corea on "S'Wonderful," his own solo piano on "Nice Work If You Can Get It," and Eddie Daniels's extraordinary clarinet on "Soon" add up to one of the better recordings of Gershwin in the jazz idiom. In 1987, joined by London Symphony Orchestra and a stellar ensemble on *Cinemagic* ♪♪♪♪ (GRP, 1987, prod. Dave Grusin), Grusin recorded an album of his movie scores. His work from such films as *On Golden Pond, Heaven Can Wait* (with Tom Scott's quirky soprano lead), *An Actor's Life, Tootsie, The Goonies, The Champ, Three Days of the Condor,* and *Little Drummer Girl,* demonstrates why he's one of the most respected film composers and orchestrators of the last quarter century. Grusin's themes are memorable and his voicings rich in texture.

what to buy next: For *One of a Kind* ♪♪♪ (GRP, 1977/1988, prod. Dave Grusin, Larry Rosen), Grusin wrote three of the five tracks and arranged them all, as well as playing keyboards in an all-star group that includes Grover Washington Jr., whose sinewy soprano recalls his seminal CTI sessions; Ron Carter, Steve Gadd, Dave Valentin, Ralph MacDonald, and a luscious string section. For better or worse, *Mountain Dance* ♫♫♫♫ (GRP, 1979/1987, prod. Dave Grusin, Larry Rosen) is the CD that helped define what became contemporary jazz, a commercial version of what started as jazz fusion. If anything, Grusin is diverse, demonstrated in the eclectic mix of sounds and everything from the catchy title track, to the poignant "Thanksong," which features his solo acoustic piano. Grusin's compositions, arrangements, and piano are front and center on *Migration* ♫♫♫♫ (GRP, 1989, prod. Dave Grusin, Larry Rosen), along with the soprano and tenor sax of Branford Marsalis and contributions of South African flugelhornist Hugh Masekela. The album also includes the suite from the score of Grusin's Academy Award–winning soundtrack to *The Milagro Beanfield War*.

influences:

◄◄ Henry Mancini, Stan Kenton, Chet Baker, Gerry Mulligan

►► Bob James, David Sanborn, Don Grusin, Tom Scott

Bret Primack

Gigi Gryce

Born November 28, 1927, in Pensacola, FL. Died March 17, 1983, in Pensacola, FL.

Alto saxophonist Gigi Gryce had the distinction of being one of the few bebop players to absorb the music of Charlie Parker while still maintaining his own quick, razor-sharp sound. Gryce studied at the Boston Conservatory and in Paris, and became a very valuable composer. His "Nica's Tempo" and "Minority" rank among some of the all-time bebop classics. During the 1950s, Gryce worked with a number of jazz luminaries, including Max Roach, Tadd Dameron, Clifford Brown, Lionel Hampton, Thelonious Monk, and Oscar Pettiford. Between 1955 and 1958, Gryce co-led with trumpeter Donald Byrd a superb ensemble known as the Jazz Lab Quintet. The following year, Gryce fronted another group with trumpeter Richard Williams and recorded three excellent sets with the band for the Prestige label. A true loss to the jazz community, Gryce stopped playing altogether by the end of the 1960s, working as a teacher until his death in 1983.

what to buy: *Gigi Gryce and the Jazz Lab Quintet* ♫♫♫♫ (Riverside, 1957, prod. Orrin Keepnews) is a prime example of the work Gryce did with Donald Byrd in a group that would have made a lasting impact on the jazz scene had it stayed around

long enough. *Sayin' Somethin'!* ♫♫♫♫ (Prestige/New Jazz, 1960, prod. Esmond Edwards) was the first record to document Gryce's new ensemble with underrated trumpet whiz Richard Williams, pianist Richard Wyands, and drummer Mickey Roker. The material is soulful and blues-drenched and the soloists are indeed "sayin' somethin'." *The Rat Race Blues* ♫♫♫♫♫ (Prestige/New Jazz, 1960, prod. Esmond Edwards) is Gryce's finest work on record, as both player and composer. Sadly, it was also his last.

the rest:

(With Art Farmer) *When Farmer Met Gryce* ♫♫♫♫ (Prestige, 1955)
Nica's Tempo ♫♫♫ (Savoy, 1955)
The Hap'nin's ♫♫♫♫ (Prestige/New Jazz, 1960)

worth searching for: One side of this long out-of-print album, *The Gigi Gryce/Donald Byrd Jazz Laboratory and the Cecil Taylor Quartet at Newport* ♫♫♫♫ (Verve, 1957, prod. Norman Granz), features the Jazz Lab Quintet live at the Newport Jazz Festival in 1957. As the only known live recording of Gryce, it's a nice piece to have, if you can find it.

influences:

◄◄ Johnny Hodges, Charlie Parker

►► Jon Gordon, Abraham Burton

Chris Hovan

Vince Guaraldi

Born July 17, 1928, in San Francisco, CA. Died February 6, 1976, in Menlo Park, CA.

Vince Guaraldi may not rank as a major pianist in the history of jazz, but his swinging piano jazz albums continue to sell. Though he started his career in a boogie-woogie vein, and polished his chops in Woody Herman's Third Herd for a season and with vibraphonist Cal Tjader for two and a half years in the 1940s, Guaraldi is better known for latching on to the U.S. bossa nova craze to compose and record his single, "Cast Your Fate to the Wind," a unexpected hit tune that remained on the upper part of the charts for nearly six months. However, Guaraldi is most widely recognized for his jazz-influenced scores written for the 1960s *Charlie Brown* television specials beginning with *A Charlie Brown Christmas* in 1965.

Guaraldi was born and raised in San Francisco, graduated from Lincoln High School and San Francisco State College, and was performing at local clubs while in college, occasionally with the Chubby Jackson/Bill Harris band, or with small groups led by Sonny Criss and Bill Harris. His first recorded work was with Cal

Tjader's trio in 1953. Guaraldi didn't record again as leader for a few years but continued to work in San Francisco's beatnik club scene. Beginning in 1955, he formed his own trio with guitarist Eddie Duran and bassist Dean Reilly for a lengthy stay as house pianist at the famous club, hungry i, a popular Bohemian nightspot in the North Beach section of San Francisco. Guaraldi toured early in 1956 with the Woody Herman Third Herd, replacing Nat Pierce. In the 1950s, Guaraldi recorded with Conte Candoli, Frank Rosolino, about 10 albums with Cal Tjader, and with others. The pianist ranked among the best of the predominantly white West Coast musicians influenced by the softer, chamber-like, easy-on-the-ears, cool jazz movement spearheaded by the 1950 Miles Davis album *Birth of the Cool*. Other musicians then working in this style included pianist Dave Brubeck, alto saxophonist Paul Desmond, baritone saxman Gerry Mulligan, bassist Red Mitchell, and drummer Shelly Manne. Guaraldi once described himself as a "reformed boogie woogie pianist," and you can hear those influences occasionally in his playing. He loved to swing and nearly all of his recorded sessions are upbeat toe-tappers. He recorded a series of albums for Fantasy, many of which were remastered in the 1980s and 1990s. As rock began to influence Guaraldi, he switched labels from Fantasy to Warner Bros. and made some spunky quartet albums playing electric harpsichord. His last album as leader, *Alma-Ville*, recorded in 1974, is no longer available. Guaraldi died in 1976 of a heart attack while waiting between sets at a California nightclub. He was 47.

what to buy: Impeccably remastered by Phi De Lancie in 1994, *A Flower Is a Lovesome Thing* ♫♫♫♫ (Fantasy, 1957/1994, prod. Vince Guaraldi) is a fine, eight-tune collection of sentimental, reflective pieces rendered by Guaraldi's drumless trio with guitarist Eddie Duran and drummer Dean Reilly in a 1957 recording. The title track, a Billy Strayhorn composition, is given a sweetly sensitive reading, as if the musicians were coaxing open the flower bud. The trio delivers lightly swinging interpretations of the classic "Softly, as in a Morning Sunrise" and Gershwin's "Looking for a Boy." They also caress the lyrical Guaraldi original, "Like a Mighty Rose" (with Duran's splendid solo) and a classically tinged "Autumn Leaves," and unhinge a soulfully soft and bluesy remake of the ballad, "Willow Weep for Me." For its diversity, the sound quality, and Guaraldi's solidly knit trio, *A Flower Is a Lovesome Thing* is highly recommended as one of his best albums. *Jazz Impressions* ♫♫♫♫ (Fantasy/OJC, 1995) was cut during Guaraldi's days at the hungry i, and is a 37-minute compilation of his warmest cool-jazz hits, with guitarist Duran and bassist Reilly. Featuring the trio's ver-

sions of "Django," "Yesterdays," "A Flower Is a Lovesome Thing," "Willow Weep for Me," and four more, this might be the best album for jazz newcomers to discover Guaraldi's laid-back style. Also recommended as a Guaraldi introduction, *Greatest Hits* ♫♫♫♫ (Fantasy/OJC, 1989) is another compilation of many of his hits. At 58 minutes and 14 tunes it's more extensive, features other musicians besides his regular trio, and includes later hits from Guaraldi's Charlie Brown days. The songs don't repeat on these two compilations so you could safely purchase both to have the best overview of Guaraldi's work. Riding on the crest of the bossa nova/jazz wave, Guaraldi digs into his Brazilian-jazz bag for *Jazz Impressions of Black Orpheus* ♫♫♫♫ (Fantasy, 1965/1990), which features his trio with bassist Monty Budwig and drummer Colin Bailey. This attractive piano trio album features the instantly recognizable original hit, "Cast Your Fate to the Wind," with its alternating time signatures, Budwig's arco bass and happy, pulsating, grooves have all contributed to making this album a winner. Other highlights include a gorgeous version of Antonio Carlos Jobim's "Manha De Carnaval," a waltzing interpretation of "Moon River," and, capping the session, a heartfelt, cool-blues version of "Since I Fell for You." A nostalgic trip for jazz fans who remember the 1960s, and an enticement to buy for those who don't.

what to buy next: For fans who like gentle, swaying Latin jazz or jazz sweetened with strings, check out *The Latin Side of Vince Guaraldi* ♫♫♫ (Fantasy, 1964/1996). Guaraldi performs in various settings with guitarist Duran, bassist Marshall, drummer Jerry Granelli, and Bill Fitch on congas and Benny Velarde on timbales. Best, though, are the strings-enhanced tunes "Corcovado," "Dor Que Faz Doer," "Brasilia," and his trio number, "Treat Street," a peppy tune which quotes from "Hang on, Sloopy," and presages his ultimate success in writing for the *Peanuts* television series. The otherwise fine music loses one bone for uneven sound quality and 32:09 duration. Nearly four generations of kids have been raised on the mellifluous holiday treat, *A Charlie Brown Christmas* ♫♫♫♫ (Fantasy, 1965/1986, prod. Vince Guaraldi). Guaraldi's timeless Christmas gift from his trio is nourishment for future generations of jazz lovers. Together with bassist Monty Budwig and drummer Colin Bailey, Guaraldi generates light, airy renderings on this original soundtrack recording from the animated CBS television special. The album's most recognizable tunes include Guaraldi's originals, the time-shifting, swinging and bouncy "Linus and Lucy," with its left-hand, near-boogie bassline, and his original jazz waltz, "Skating," which gives vent to some tricky right-hand riffs. There are more musical gems which helped make the first telecast of *A Charlie Brown Christmas* on December 9, 1965 a flash hit that has been rebroadcast every holiday season since. At one time or another, every child (and many adults) identified with one of Charles Schultz's Charlie Brown cartoon characters, and Guaraldi's soundtrack tunes from the CBS television special on *A Boy Named Charlie Brown* 𝒜𝒜𝒜𝒶 (Fantasy, 1964/1989) became their theme songs. (What a great way to begin introducing kids to jazz!) The 10 soothing and swinging tunes (an additional track was added to the CD reissue) performed by Guaraldi with Monty Budwig (bass) and Colin Bailey (drums) provide a relaxed and delightful listen.

the rest:

Vince Guaraldi Trio 𝒜𝒜𝒜𝒶 (Fantasy, 1956/OJC, 1987)
Vince Guaraldi in Person 𝒜𝒜𝒜𝒶 (Fantasy, 1962/OJC, 1997)
A Boy Named Charlie Brown 𝒜𝒜𝒶 (Fantasy, 1965/OJC, 1988)
Oh, Good Grief! 𝒜𝒜𝒶 (Warner Bros., 1988)

influences:

⏪ Jimmy Yancey, Art Tatum, Albert Ammons, Pete Johnson, Fats Waller, Bill Harris, Oscar Peterson, Tal Farlow, Cal Tjader, Dave Brubeck, Antonio Carlos Jobim

Nancy Ann Lee

Russell Gunn

Born October 20, 1971, in Chicago, IL.

If Art Blakey were still around driving his Jazz Messengers band with his big beat, it's a good bet that Russell Gunn would have filled the trumpet chair at some point. Gunn's playing exhibits the qualities that drummer Blakey's brass men usually had—a strong technical command of his horn, a feel for the blues, and sound knowledge of the musical language that makes up the bop and post-bop vocabulary of many of today's musicians.

Gunn, who wanted to be a rapper as a kid, became serious about his trumpet in high school at Miles Davis's alma mater in East St. Louis. After a short stint studying music at Jackson State University, Gunn worked some pop jobs, spent two years playing on the Carnival Cruise ships, then headed to New York where he recorded with Oliver Lake *Dedicated to Dolphy*, participated in *Blood on the Fields* by Wynton Marsalis, and played in Branford Marsalis's Buckshot LeFonque group.

what to buy: Football coaches always say that a team shows its greatest improvement from the first to the second game. In Gunn's short recording career the same holds true. His second album, *Gunn Fu* 𝒜𝒜𝒜 (High Note, 1997, prod. Cecil Brooks lll), shows growth from his first. With great success, Gunn displays

ability to reign in the curse of many young musicians to overplay, and the addition of vibes and flute to the traditional trumpet-tenor front line gives the album more texture. The standard, "Invitation," receives refreshing treatment, courtesy of an ingenious arrangement with grooving bass vamp. Fiery contributions from Gunn, pianist James Hurt, and vibist Stefon Harris highlight "The Search" and Booker Little's "Minor Sweet," and showcase the power and beauty of Gunn's tone.

what to buy next: Gunn's *Young Gunn* 𝒜𝒜𝒶 (Muse, 1995, prod. Cecil Brooks III) is a solid debut. Gunn's originals "East St. Louis" and "The Message" employ the 1960s-vintage Blue Note groove and are nicely contrasted by ballad readings of "You Don't Know What Love Is," "There Is No Greater Love," and a duo version of "Pannonica" with pianist John Hicks. Be forewarned: if rap isn't your cup of tea, program your disc player to skip "The Concept."

influences:

⏪ Miles Davis, Lee Morgan

Dan Polletta

Tom Guralnick

Born January 14, 1951, in Boston, MA.

Going back and forth between his self-conceived, experimentally dimensional Mobile Saxophone & Mute Unit and the more conventional confines of his sax-trombone-drums trio, multireedist Tom Guralnick began by studying with theorist/seer/trumpeter Bill Dixon, playing in guitarist Baird Hersey's Year of the Ear, and pairing with percussionist David Moss in a Downtown Improvisers duo. Now that he's made his home in Albuquerque for upwards of 20 years, though, Guralnick is as much of a new jazz legend as the State of New Mexico has produced, a champion of the great outside in the midst of a musical environment better suited to honky tonkin' C&W. Guralnick helped create the presently thriving New Mexico Jazz Workshop, and he currently operates the excellent, not-for-profit Outpost Performance Space, dedicated to a wide spectrum of musical and other artistic statements.

what to buy: *Broken Dances for Muted Pieces* 𝒜𝒜𝒶 (What Next?, 1995, prod. Tom Guralnick, Steve Peters) is a demanding and occasionally acrid cycle of what are in reality modern classical compositions and improvisations for the massive floating opera that is the Mobile Saxophone & Mute Unit. Far more to the point, jazz-wise, is *Pitchin'* 𝒜𝒜𝒶 (PostOut, 1997, prod. Tom Guralnick), the initial CD evidence of the lengthy association between Guralnick, Steven Feld (tenor and bass trombones, bass trumpet, and euphonium), and Jefferson Voorhees (trap drumming and hand percussion). *Pitchin'* walks a stylistic tightrope between Ornette Coleman-styled freebop (the album's concluding "Fornet" is an uncanny evocation of Coleman's sound and phraseology), and the occasional whiff of World Beat. Not for the faint of ear, but then again, that's what makes this stuff enjoyable.

influences:

 Archie Shepp, Igor Stravinsky, Mississippi Fred McDowell

 Dave Douglas, Takemitsu, Beck

David Prince

Charlie Haden

Born August 6, 1937, in Shenandoah, IA.

One of the most imaginative musicians on today's scene, bassist, composer, and bandleader Charlie Haden is an improvising poet, a tune-smith who is creating some of the most compelling recordings in jazz history. The Iowa-born musician began his career singing on radio, and later television, with his family's country and western group. Haden learned to play bass in his teens and after high school graduation moved to Los Angeles where, from 1957 to 1959, he worked with Art Pepper, Hampton Hawes, Dexter Gordon, and Paul Bley. Haden met Ornette Coleman in 1957, and eventually became the bass player for Coleman's adventurous quartet that also included Don Cherry on pocket trumpet and Billy Higgins on drums, a team that would cause a commotion in the jazz world by liberating the soloist from the usual harmonic and rhythmic frameworks. Haden's role in this revolution was his development of a bass style that would sometimes complement the soloist, and other times become an independent inventor with an individual voice. Haden hit New York with Coleman in 1959 and remained with him until 1961, recording some venturesome albums for Atlantic. During the 1960s he worked with pianist Denny Zeitlin, recorded with John Coltrane, rejoined Coleman for some recording dates, began touring and recording with Keith Jarrett (1966–72), and, in 1969, with pianist-composer-arranger-conductor Carla Bley formed the Liberation Music Orchestra, an avant-garde orchestra overt in its recorded musical statements

about freedom against political injustice and repression. From 1976–87, Haden recorded with Cherry, Dewey Redman, and Ed Blackwell (all who had worked closely with Ornette Coleman) as the group, Old and New Dreams, a unit that attempted to keep alive Coleman's music and his compositional and improvisational approaches. In the 1980s and 1990s Haden formed and recorded with his Quartet West (with Ernie Watts, Alan Broadbent, and Larance Marable), occasionally reorganized the Liberation Music Orchestra, and released numerous albums, including the *Montreal Tapes*, made during the 1989 Festival International de Jazz de Montréal in various settings (mostly duet, trio, quartet) with an array of musicians.

what to buy: It's not surprising that *Beyond the Missouri Sky* ♪♪♪♪ (Verve, 1997, prod. Charlie Haden, Pat Metheny) won a Grammy for Best Jazz Instrumental Performance. This writer had picked it as one of five best 1997 albums for the *JazzTimes* Critics' Poll. Recorded in a New York Studio, the album finds both Haden and guitarist Pat Metheny at their contemplative best, celebrating the broad expanse their separate careers have covered since their Midwest origins. Haden asked Metheny to make this dreamy album, a contemporary impressionistic view of America drawing melodies from country-western music, jazz, and American folk themes. In acoustic duets, they perform 13 songs (including original compositions by each player) to create this heart-warming, pastoral, musical landscape. This album is rife with pensive exchanges demonstrating why this pair, since their first meeting in 1973 and their initial collaboration on Metheny's *80/81* album and tour, were heading toward a forum for this imaginative project. Their hearts and minds are certainly one, and each tune rendered by this inspired duo is a richly spiritual, touching, and melodious vignette of Americana. *Beyond the Missouri Sky* is a radiant album from two of the world's best jazz performers. Since Haden began his series of duet dialogues, it was inevitable that he would eventually record a bass-piano album with Kenny Barron, one of the classiest pianists on the scene today, who, like Haden, has contributed to epochal shifts in jazz during the 1960s. On *Night and the City* ♪♪♪♪ (Verve, 1998, prod. Charlie Haden, Ruth Cameron), the pair aurally explores the ever-changing moods that pulsate at the heart of late-night Manhattan. The duo opens with Barron's "Twilight Song," a dreamlike dance nearly 13-minutes long that sets the tone for this album. Throughout the seven tunes of this live-recorded performance at the Iridium in Manhattan, Haden is at his melodically inventive best (especially his solo on the ten-minute, reflective version of "Body and Soul") and Barron is equally inspired, creating peak moments such as his intense solo which builds drama into "For Heaven's Sake." Their empathetic alliance enriches "Spring Is Here," "You Don't Know What Love Is," "The Very Thought of You," and the other standards that you'll swear you're hearing for the first time. Even the clanking dishes add ambience to the sketches of late nights in the Big Apple. A live-recorded trio performance from the 1989 Festival International de Jazz de Montréal, *Charlie Haden, the Montréal Tapes with Gonzalo Rubalcaba and Paul Motian* 🎵🎵🎵🎵 (Verve, 1998, prod. Charlie Haden, Ruth Cameron) is a gorgeous listen featuring Cuban-born pianist Gonzalo Rubalcaba, with whom Haden had previously performed in Cuba in 1986. Because of the United States embargo, a second meeting could not occur on American soil; hence their rare encounter in Montreal, enhanced by drummer Paul Motian. Six lengthy tunes include Haden originals ("La Pasionaria," "Bay City," "Silence"), Gary Peacock's "Vignette," Ornette Coleman's "The Blessing," and Miles Davis's "Solar." Rubalcaba is a powerful pianist capable of a wide range of expressions using the full range and capabilities of the piano and his performance obviously inspires Haden to some of his best improvisations. Motian, a frequent Haden collaborator who impressively plays in tandem with Haden, adds color with responsive shadings and cymbal work and contributes tidy timekeeping. This is one of the best trio sessions on record, certainly one of Haden's all-time best small group collaborations. Hollywood of the 1940s still holds a disarming mystique for film-noir fans and bassist Haden, whose third Quartet West album *Haunted Heart* 🎵🎵🎵🎵 (Gitanes/Verve, 1992, prod. Hans Wendl, Charlie Haden) draws inspiration from films and the aura of that period in Hollywood history. Haden attempts to unfold the 12 tunes "as if it were a film telling a story." While Haden is the leader, tenor saxophonist Ernie Watts is the pivotal player whose playing sets the moods. Pianist Alan Broadbent's original tunes, "Lady in the Lake" and "The Long Goodbye," fit beautifully with Haden's theme. And Larance Marable's drumming (particularly his brushwork) is tasteful throughout. The nostalgic feeling of the album is enhanced by sound clips interwoven with Quartet renderings—Jo Stafford on the title tune (singing with Paul Weston and His Orchestra in 1947), a 1954 interlude with vocalist-pianist Jeri Southern (with the Dave Barbour Trio), and Billie Holiday singing "Deep Song," (backed by Bob Haggart's Orchestra). But these are only part of Haden's "story." Make some microwave popcorn, settle back, and go to the "movies" with this collection of postwar boppers and wistful ballads that evoke nostalgic Hollywood film images of smoke-filled cabarets, torch singers, and the sound of a wailing saxophone. Haden sets you

up perfectly for the aural experience by including a liner quote from Raymond Chandler's novel about 1949 Hollywood and the busy Sunset Strip. Ah, imagination! If you have a thing for strings, check out *Now Is the Hour* 🎵🎵🎵🎵 (Gitanes, 1996, prod. Charlie Haden, Ruth Cameron), featuring Haden's Quartet West backed with strings on seven of the 12 tracks. Based on romantic themes surrounding World War II, Haden features a lovely selection of standards and contributes three originals. Pianist Broadbent wrote the arrangements and conducted the orchestra. Tenor saxophonist Watts performs some of his warmest, lyrically best solos (it's amazing how thoroughly he responds to the strings-sweetened atmosphere). Highlights include Charlie Parker's "Back Home Blues," Haden's beautiful melody on "There in a Dream" enriched by the string orchestra, and "Marable's Parable," a Calypso number by the Quartet (without strings) that yields breakout space to drummer Larance Marable. The sentimental, strings-laden version of the title tune, with Haden's playing, and Watts's lush solo, will leave you breathless (especially if you lived through World War II and recall the meaning behind the lyrics). The liner booklet, with familiar photos from V-Day, is an exceptional piece of art, as is all the gorgeously rendered music on this album.

what to buy next: While Haden's small-group collaborations provide wonderfully intimate and rewarding listening, his recordings with the Liberation Music Orchestra are equally enticing for their focus on his writing. For an understanding of Haden "The Composer," you must hear his Liberation Music Orchestra recordings to understand the scope of this man's awesome musical vision. *Dream Keeper* 🎵🎵🎵🎵 (Blue Note, 1991, prod. Hans Wendl) features Haden's shape-changing Liberation Music Orchestra, this time featuring the contributions of 15 musicians conducted by Carla Bley, with some tunes augmented by the Oakland Youth Chorus (under the direction of Elizabeth Min). Haden's original jazz compositions draw from a variety of sources, including the (again) Spanish traditional music, African beats and themes, mainstream jazz, and Latin-influenced traditions. Among all-star soloists spotlighted are Dewey Redman, Joe Lovano, and Branford Marsalis (saxophones); Tom Harrell (trumpet/flugelhorn); Ray Anderson (trombone); Amina Claudine Myers (piano); Don Alias (percussion); and Paul Motian (drums). Just listen to the quick-paced, post-bop, counterpoint themes stretching into the avant-garde on "Nkosi

Charlie Haden (© **Jack Vartoogian**)

Sikelel'i Afrika (Anthem of the African National Congress)," to readily understand that Haden and his contemporaries are among the best innovators on the scene. That track alone is worth the album price. With these works, Haden ranks among today's most brilliant, highly ranked composers, and the ensemble shines as one of the most vibrant performing in the jazz tradition. This album is highly recommended for the adventurous listener. Haden co-leads (with pianist-composer-arranger Carla Bley) the 11-piece Liberation Music Orchestra on *The Ballad of the Fallen* 🎵🎵🎵🎵 (ECM, 1983/1994, prod. Manfred Eicher), an album containing 10 Spanish-tinged selections arranged by Bley. This is a magnificent session, performed by an all-star team that stretches beyond the jazz framework to meld traditional Spanish Civil War-era themes and modern Liberationist anthems to jazz improvisations. While focusing on extraordinary arrangements by Bley, the session also highlights top-flight instrumental solos by trombonist Gary Valente, trumpeters Don Cherry and Michael Mantler, saxophonists Jim Pepper, Dewey Redman, and Steve Slagle, guitarist Mick Goodrick, and others. Settings vary, and one of Haden's best performances on this album is his melancholy duet ("Too Late") with pianist Bley. The ultimate results of their collaborations are highly enjoyable original works that draw upon many sources to provide a great listen. Good music is good music, no matter how you label it and this CD is one sturdy example of Haden's all-embracing artistry.

best of the rest:

(With Hampton Hawes) *As Long as There's Music* 🎵🎵🎵🎵 (Verve, 1978/1993)
(With Christian Escoudé) *Gitane* 🎵🎵🎵🎵 (Dreyfus, 1979/1991)
Magico 🎵🎵🎵🎵 (ECM, 1979/1994)
Quartet West 🎵🎵🎵🎵 (Verve, 1987)
(With Paul Motian and Geri Allen) *Etudes* 🎵🎵🎵🎵 (Soul Note, 1988)
Always Say Goodbye 🎵🎵🎵🎵 (Gitanes/Verve, 1994)
The Montreal Tapes with Paul Bley and Paul Motian 🎵🎵🎵🎵 (Verve, 1994)
Charlie Haden, the Montreal Tapes with Don Cherry, Ed Blackwell 🎵🎵🎵🎵 (Verve, 1994)
(With Hank Jones) *Steal Away* 🎵🎵🎵🎵 (Verve, 1995)

Nancy Ann Lee

Bob Haggart

Born March 13, 1914, in New York, NY.

Robert Sherwood "Hag" Haggart is an excellent bassist, active at the top of his field for over 60 years. Haggart has achieved legendary status as composer and arranger as well, and is remembered by many for his peculiar style of whistling through his teeth. Haggart has appeared on thousands of records over the years and has the distinction of having recorded with diverse giants such as Louis Armstrong, Billie Holiday, Ella Fitzgerald, Bing Crosby, Frank Sinatra, Duke Ellington, Benny Goodman, and Charlie Parker. He has written familiar songs such as "What's New?," "South Rampart Street Parade," "My Inspiration," and "Big Noise from Winnetka," all composed during his long tenure with the Bob Crosby Orchestra.

Haggart grew up in Douglastown, Long Island, New York, where, as a high school student, he studied guitar with the well-known George Van Eps. Haggart sought musical training on a multitude of instruments including tuba and trumpet, and finally took up the bass at age 17. Starting in 1932, he jobbed around with Bob Sperling's Orchestra, played with Mitch Ayres, and went on to prominence in Bob Crosby's Orchestra, joining in 1935 on string bass. Haggart kept on developing as an arranger and helped put together the ever-expanding Crosby book. He was the only founding member of the Crosby band not originally with Ben Pollack's Orchestra. After the Crosby band's final theater tour in 1942, Haggart didn't move to California, as did most of his band friends, but stayed in New York to arrange for various big bands and to play bass in the busy radio and recording studios for the better part of the decade. Possessing a strong harmonic sense, he did not feel forced to change his style with the advent of bop. In the early 1950s, Haggart reunited with trumpeter Yank Lawson, an ex–Crosby Mate, to record 14 albums of Dixieland jazz as the Lawson-Haggart Jazz Band. This alliance led to many Bob Crosby reunion dates and eventually led to the formation of the World's Greatest Jazz Band in 1968, with Haggart again co-leader with Lawson. The band toured extensively and existed in various forms over the next 10 years but never quite achieved the success it deserved. Haggart has been a fixture at jazz parties and festivals over the past 20 years. Over 80 years old, he is still performing.

what's available: You sense that *Bob Haggart's Swing Three: Hag Leaps In* 🎵🎵🎵🎵 (Arbors, 1996, prod. Rachel Domber, Mat Domber) is something different beginning with the opening strains of "Big Noise from Winnetka." Hag's toothy whistling and solid bass work are evident, and he's in the company of top-flight, veteran swingers—guitarist Bucky Pizzarelli and pianist John Bunch. Employing smartly selected tempos and leaving room for plenty of attractive solos, the trio lays down 14 tracks of classic swing. Included are four Ellington/Strayhorn pieces ("All Too Soon," "I'm Beginning to See the Light," "Passion Flower," and "Chelsea Bridge") and four originals. Using the chords to "I Got Rhythm," the tune "Hag Leaps In" (a nod to

Lester Young) features a walking bassline. "Dot's Cheesecake" is a relaxed excursion into blues territory. Throughout the collection there is dazzling interplay between the musicians, and passages float along as if mounted on ball bearings. Bunch and Pizzarelli achieve some fine moments on tunes that stretch out a bit. Other than the closer, "Air Mail Special," a barn-burner with passages full of diminished chords, this recording—Haggart's first as leader in many years—offers a relaxed and intimate brand of swing in a trio session.

John T. Bitter

Al Haig

Born July 22, 1924, in Newark, NJ. Died November 16, 1982, in New York, NY.

One of the first bebop pianists, Al Haig was a superior accompanist who played in many of the seminal bop bands. His highly uneven career consisted of a glorious early period and a late-blooming renaissance at the end of his life with a long fallow period in between. Haig had already absorbed and personalized Bud Powell's keyboard vocabulary when he joined Dizzy Gillespie's band in 1945, holding his own on the classic quintet session with Charlie Parker that produced "Shaw 'Nuff," "Salt Peanuts," and "Loverman." He worked and recorded with Charlie Parker and Stan Getz in the late '40s and early '50s. While he played brilliantly on other people's sessions, his own recordings (for Spotlite, Dawn, and Prestige) were often disappointing. For reasons known only to himself, Haig increasingly worked in non-jazz settings in the '50s and hardly recorded at all through 1973, when he returned to the jazz scene. During the last decade of his life he gained widespread recognition as a modern jazz master and recorded widely for Inner City, Choice, Sea Breeze, Interplay, and other labels, though few sessions have been reissued on CD.

what's available: *Shaw 'Nuff* ♫♫♫♫ (Musicraft, 1945–46, prod. Albert Marx) contains almost all of Gillespie's classic Musicraft recordings, some of the most influential sessions in jazz history. Haig, a member of Gillespie's band from 1945–46, holds down the piano chair on seven of the 20 tracks, most importantly on the May 11, 1945, quintet session with Charlie Parker that virtually defined bebop. His work on the 1946 sextet sessions with Sonny Stitt, Milt Jackson, Ray Brown, and Kenny Clarke provided the model for future bebop rhythm sections. While the original album contained two Charlie Parker quintet sessions from 1951, *Swedish Schnapps +* ♫♫♫♫ (Verve, 1949–51, prod. Norman Granz) adds four tracks featuring Haig, trumpeter Kenny Dorham, bassist Tommy Potter, and drummer Max Roach. The

group was Bird's working band at the time, and Haig locks into Roach's brilliant and relentlessly swinging trap work. It's also fascinating to compare Haig's playing to John Lewis and Walter Bishop Jr., the pianists on the other two sessions.

influences:

◀◀ Bud Powell

▶▶ Duke Jordan, Hampton Hawes

Andrew Gilbert

Jim Hall

Born April 12, 1930, in Buffalo, NY.

Guitarist Jim Hall is notable for his flawless technique, mellow tone, and imaginative, original compositions. He's been tagged by Pat Metheny as "the greatest living guitarist," and jazz critics have likened him to Django Reinhardt and Charlie Christian in stature and influence. Born in Buffalo, New York, Hall moved with his family to Cleveland, Ohio, when he was eight years old. His introduction to music began at an early age, influenced by a mother who played piano, a grandfather who played violin, and an uncle, guitar. By age 13 Hall was playing professionally, working with small groups around Cleveland. His first Cleveland gigs included stints with clarinetist Angelo Vienna's group, an instrumental lineup that featured accordion, drums, clarinet, and guitar. Hall also worked occasionally with Tony "Big T" Lovano (saxophonist Joe Lovano's father) and Cleveland's popular dance orchestra led by Al Serafini. Hall was greatly inspired by one of his early guitar teachers, the harmonically advanced guitarist Fred Sharp, who had worked with Adrian Rollini and Red Norvo in New York. Sharp introduced 15-year-old Hall to the music of guitarist Django Reinhardt. After graduating from high school, Hall attended the Cleveland Institute of Music (CIM), where he majored in music theory. He performed on weekends but was not all that interested in jazz during this time; instead, he planned to go into classical composing and to teach part time. But in 1955 his yearning to perform interrupted these plans and, after graduating from CIM, he set out for the thriving Los Angeles jazz scene. There he studied with Vincente Gomez, and gained wider exposure with Chico Hamilton's groundbreaking quintet (featuring reeds, guitar, cello, bass, and drums) and with a trio led by Jimmy Giuffre.

Around 1958 Hall moved permanently to New York City. He soon began working with Sonny Rollins, with whom he recorded a series of albums including the 1962 session *The Bridge*, and recording with Paul Desmond (1959–65). During this period Hall also collaborated with John Lewis and Gunther Schuller in third-stream experiments that allowed him to write works for guitar and string quartet, and performed with innovators such as Eric Dolphy, Ornette Coleman, and Scott LaFaro. Hall toured with Ella Fitzgerald and, following her South American tour in the late 1950s, remained in Brazil for six weeks, just as the *bossa nova* was blossoming there. This experience broadened Hall's versatility and influenced some of his later work. During the 1960s he worked as a guitarist on Merv Griffin's television show, made some classic albums both as leader and as sideman with Sonny Rollins and Bill Evans, and co-led a quartet with Art Farmer (1962–64). In the 1970s Hall formed a partnership with bassist Ron Carter. This became an enduring relationship and one of the most empathetic duets in jazz. The duo produced a series of albums together, including their debut, *Alone Together*, which has since become a classic. Hall has continued to experiment since the early 1970s, when he worked with Bob Brookmeyer and recorded a series of vibrant albums with bassist Red Mitchell, drummer Shelly Manne, pianist Michel Petrucciani, saxophonist Wayne Shorter, and other top-flight jazz musicians. In recent years he has been teaching part time and has begun to focus on composing, with the results of his efforts well documented on his 1997 Telarc album, *Textures*. Hall admittedly enjoys working with younger musicians, which keeps his creations fresh, modern, and lively. He has recorded albums for numerous labels including Pacific Jazz, Milestone, Evidence, Concord, MusicMasters, and, most recently, Telarc.

what to buy: Hall's debut recording *Jazz Guitar* ♫♫♫♫ (Pacific, 1957/Capitol, prod. Richard Bock) features the 26-year-old guitarist in a drumless trio with pianist Carl Perkins and bassist Red Mitchell. Kicking off the session with a swinging version of "Stompin' at the Savoy," the trio sets the tone for the remainder of the 11 standards, a mixture of ballads and swingers that includes bluesy favorites such as "Things Ain't What They Used to Be" (two takes), and uptempo numbers such as "Tangerine" and "Look for the Silver Lining," as well as attractive ballads. A pleasing listen and a good starting point. One of Hall's famous live-recorded duet sessions with lyrical bassist Ron Carter, *Live at Village West* ♫♫♫♫ (Concord, 1984, prod. Carl E. Jefferson) captures the interaction between these two top improvisers. Containing 10 tunes (only one original from each musician), the album includes jazz standards such as Milt Jackson's blues-tinged "Bags Groove," Thelonious Monk's "Blue Monk," Sonny Rollins's latinate "St. Thomas," and popular favorites such as "Embraceable You," "All the Things You Are," and "Baubles, Bangles, and Beads," which

are given tasteful treatment by the two master improvisers. At the time of this recording, the classically trained veterans had crossed paths many times in their career. They had developed a spiritual affinity for performing together, and had recorded a previous duet album for Concord, as well as albums together in the 1970s. Each tune is a minuet, a complete and elegant dance, with improvs smoothly shifting back and forth while one player supports the other's solos. Recorded in a New York City jazz club, this is one of their best duet sets. For an idea of what Hall can do when his mind-set is on composing, check out his performances and compositional skills on his third Telarc CD, *Textures* ♫♫♫♫ (Telarc, 1997, prod. John Snyder, Gil Goldstein). One of his best sessions ever, the CD features Hall writing for a modern-sounding brass ensemble, quartets, and a full studio orchestra (with strings). He digs into his roots as a composition student at the Cleveland Institute of Music in the early 1950s to create seven exciting, harmonically advanced tunes that give him and his guest soloists room to expand. Among illustrious soloists building upon Hall's fascinating melodies are Claudio Roditi (flugelhorn), Jim Pugh (trombone), and Joe Lovano (soprano sax). This may be Hall's best recording to date. Certainly, it's one that pleasingly stretches the form and affirms his effectiveness in collaborations with younger musicians.

what to buy next: One in a series of laid-back, tasteful performance by Hall and bassist Ron Carter, compatriots whose paths have crossed and intertwined for decades before and after their first duet recording in 1970, *Telephone* ♫♫♫♫ (Concord, 1985/1992, prod. Carl E. Jefferson) documents a 1984 live performance at the Concord Jazz Festival. One could assume just from the album title how well these musicians communicate with each other. Their interactions on this elegant seven-tune session range from lively time-shifting improvs where one musician throws out a head arrangement for the other to pick up, to pensive, sweet improv collaborations that reflect the quieter sides of both personalities. Included are two originals from each player, plus "Indian Summer," "Stardust," and "Alone Together," a remake of the familiar standard first recorded on their 1972 album, *Alone Together* ♫♫♫♫ (Milestone/OJC, 1972), a session of jazz standards that is also highly recommended. *Telephone* is carried out in most comfortable fashion by these two artful improvisers, who have developed one of the best working relationships in jazz.

best of the rest:

It's Nice to Be with You ♫♫♫ (Verve, 1971)
Where Would I Be? ♫♫♫ (Milestone/OJC, 1971/1991)
Concerto ♫♫♫ (CTI/Columbia, 1975/1997)

Commitment 🎵🎵🎵 (Horizon A&M, 1976)
Circles 🎵🎵🎵 (Concord Jazz, 1981/1992)
Concierto de Aranjuez 🎵🎵🎵 (Evidence, 1981/1992)
Jim Hall's Three 🎵🎵🎵 (Concord Jazz, 1986/1994)
All across the City 🎵🎵🎵 (Concord Jazz, 1989)
Live at Town Hall, Volume 1 🎵🎵🎵🎵 (MusicMasters, 1991)
Live at Town Hall, Volume 2 🎵🎵🎵🎵 (MusicMasters, 1991)
Youkali 🎵🎵 (CTI, 1992)
Subsequently 🎵🎵🎵 (MusicMasters, 1992)
Something Special 🎵🎵🎵🎵 (MusicMasters, 1993)
Dedications & Inspirations 🎵🎵🎵🎵 (Telarc, 1994)
Dialogues 🎵🎵🎵 (Telarc, 1995)
Panorama: Live at the Village Vanguard 🎵🎵🎵 (Telarc, 1997)

worth searching for: Hall appears on Sonny Rollins's *The Bridge* 🎵🎵🎵 (Victor Jazz, 1962/1996, prod. George Avakian), an album that has become a classic. Rollins inspires the lyrical Hall to fine solos and sensitive backing on the six tunes performed with bassist Bob Cranshaw and drummer Ben Riley. Excellent performances from all make this CD is a must for any collection. Hall can also be heard on one of the two albums in the Kronos Quartet compilation, *The Complete Landmark Sessions* 🎵🎵🎵 (32 Jazz, 1997, prod. Orrin Keepnews). He and bassist Eddie Gomez collaborate with Kronos Quartet on the 1986 Landmark album, *Music of Bill Evans*. The musicians maintain a melodically light, romantic flavor as they swing through Evans classics such as "Waltz for Debby," "Time Remembered," "Turn out the Stars," and six more tunes (one by Miles Davis, "Nardis," is thrown in for good measure).

influences:

◄◄ Charlie Christian, Barney Kessel, Django Reinhardt, Ben Webster, Paul Gonsalves, Al Sears, Lucky Thompson, Dexter Gordon, Wardell Gray, Don Byas, Sonny Rollins

►► Bill Frisell, John Abercrombie, Mick Goodrick, Pat Metheny, John Scofield

see also: *Ron Carter, Sonny Rollins, Paul Desmond*

Nancy Ann Lee

Lin Halliday

Born 1936, in DeQueen, AR.

Greatly influenced by Sonny Rollins but more sentimental, Lin Halliday is a veteran hard bopper who didn't record as a leader until he was 55. The big-toned saxman, raised in Little Rock, Arkansas, lived in Los Angeles and New York as a young man and in 1959 replaced Wayne Shorter in Maynard Ferguson's Birdland Band. Stints with Philly Joe Jones and Louie Bellson followed,

JIM HALL (WITH SONNY ROLLINS)

song "Without a Song"
album *The Bridge*
(RCA, 1962/1992)
instrument Guitar

though Halliday remained obscure. He moved to Nashville in 1966 and, in 1980, settled in Chicago, where he became a fixture in jazz clubs. One of Halliday's enthusiastic supporters was Delmark Records founder Bob Koester, who produced his appropriately titled debut album, *Delayed Exposure*, before releasing several more excellent CDs by the hard-blowing tenor.

what to buy: A first-rate hard bop session featuring multi-horn-man Ira Sullivan, Halliday's second album, *East of the Sun* 🎵🎵🎵 (Delmark, 1992, prod. Bob Koester) makes one wish he'd been documented as a leader 20 or 30 years earlier. Whether swinging aggressively on "I Found a New Baby" or decreasing the tempo for "Indian Summer" and "Corcovado," Halliday is consistently soulful and confident.

what to buy next: Halliday spared no passion on either *Delayed Exposure* 🎵🎵🎵 (Delmark, 1991, prod. Bob Koester), or his third album, *Where or When* 🎵🎵🎵 (Delmark, 1993, prod. Kathy Lynch), both of which employ the very flexible Ira Sullivan on various wind instruments. Halliday is invigorating at fast tempos, and interpretations of "Darn That Dream" and "The Man I Love" on *Delayed Exposure* and "Sophisticated Lady" on *Where or When* are fine examples of his moving, heartfelt ballad playing.

the rest:
(With Eric Alexander) *Stablemates* ♫♫♫ (Delmark, 1996)

influences:
◀◀ Sonny Rollins

Alex Henderson

Chico Hamilton

Born September 21, 1921, in Los Angeles, CA.

Drummer Chico Hamilton is probably best known for his skills and abilities as a bandleader and talent scout, very much like the late Art Blakey. Hamilton came up in Los Angeles with such players as Charles Mingus, Illinois Jacquet, and Dexter Gordon, and toured with Lionel Hampton's band in the early 1940s. Following his stint with the military, Hamilton worked with Count Basie, Lester Young, Lena Horne, and Gerry Mulligan before forming his now-legendary chamber jazz group in 1955. Unique in its use of a woodwind player, guitarist, bassist and cello player, this subtle ensemble matched Hamilton's drumming quite well, in that he has always been more concerned with developing melodic and varied textures rather than indulging in overt displays of flashy technique. As a result of the group's appearances in the films *Jazz on a Summer Day* and *The Sweet Smell of Success,* and their numerous recordings for the Pacific jazz label, they became very popular among jazz fans and critics. Eventually, the Hamilton band showed influences of the avant garde and rock scene of the 1960s, with such modern stylists as Gabor Szabo, Charles Lloyd, Larry Coryell, and Arthur Blythe joining the ranks. Weathering the hard times that befell jazz in the 1970s and the focus on "young lions" that dominated the 1980s, Hamilton's refined brand of jazz has continued to prosper. He currently has a number of newer recordings available on the Soul Note label.

what to buy: *Man from Two Worlds* ♫♫♫♫ (Impulse!, 1962/ 1963, prod. Bob Thiele) is a reissue of the original album plus four of the six cuts that appeared on the *Passin' Thru* LP. This is Hamilton's finest group, with multi-reedman Charles Lloyd, guitarist Gabor Szabo, trombonist George Bohanon, and bassist Albert Stinson. The music is adventurous, yet remains melodic and accessible. *The Dealer* ♫♫♫ (Impulse!, 1966, prod. Bob Thiele) is one of the more successful attempts at the fusion of jazz and rock, and features the debut of guitarist Larry Coryell.

what to buy next: *Gongs East* ♫♫♫ (Discovery, 1958, prod. Bob Prince) was originally recorded for Warner Bros. and features Hamilton's chamber jazz group, which included Eric Dolphy at the time. The music is a bit polite but contains some fine Hamilton drumming and some important early work from Dolphy. *Reunion* ♫♫♫♫ (Soul Note, 1989, prod. Giovanni Bonandrini) was cut in 1989 as an anniversary celebration of the founding of the first Hamilton quintet. The original members (with one exception) are on hand and the results are superb.

the rest:
Euphoria ♫♫♫♫ (Soul Note, 1988)
Arroyo ♫♫♫♫ (Soul Note, 1990)
Trio! ♫♫♫ (Soul Note, 1992)
My Panamanian Friend ♫♫♫♫ (Soul Note, 1992)

worth searching for: If you still collect vinyl, *The Chico Hamilton Special* ♫♫♫♫ (Columbia, 1960, prod. Irving Townsend) is worth a search because it marks the first appearance of a then-unknown Charles Lloyd. *Drumfusion* ♫♫♫♫ (Columbia, 1962, prod. Irving Townsend, Teo Macero) is the long out-of-print LP that featured the debut of the new Hamilton group with Charles Lloyd and Gabor Szabo and found the cello replaced with a trombone expertly played by Garnett Brown.

Chris Hovan

Jeff Hamilton

Born August 4, 1953, in Richmond, IN.

Jeff Hamilton is a versatile and musical drummer probably best known for his collaborations with the Ray Brown Trio (1988–1995) and for following Shelly Manne in 1978 as drummer for the L.A.4, a group co-led by Laurindo Almeida and Bud Shank with Ray Brown. Hamilton studied percussion for two years at Indiana University, where his fellow students included Peter Erskine and John Clayton, and he also learned jazz drumming from John Van Ohlen in Indianapolis. Hamilton paid his dues in 1974 drumming with the Tommy Dorsey Orchestra under the leadership of Murray McEachern, and worked briefly with the Lionel Hampton band in 1975, Monty Alexander's trio (1975–77), and Woody Herman's Thundering Herd (1977–78), recording three albums with the latter. After making a series of recordings for the Concord label with the L.A.4, Hamilton became part of the Concord stable, regularly recording as sideman on many albums for the label. From 1983–87 Hamilton performed with Ella Fitzgerald, the Count Basie Orchestra, Rosemary Clooney, and Monty Alexander. During the 1990s Hamilton toured internationally with the Ray Brown Trio and

Oscar Peterson, worked with the Clayton Brothers' Quartet, and, from 1989, co-led the Clayton-Hamilton Orchestra. In addition to recording albums for Capri and Lake Street Records with the Clayton-Hamilton Orchestra, Hamilton has made over 100 recordings with artists such as Natalie Cole, Barbra Streisand, Mel Tormé, George Shearing, Milt Jackson, Herb Ellis, Barney Kessel, Scott Hamilton, Mark Murphy, and Toshiko Akiyoshi. Adept with both sticks and brush work, Hamilton is every bit as comfortable driving a big band or small groups, and has recorded with his own trio, formed in 1994.

what to buy: *Absolutely!* ♫♫♫♫ (Lake Street Records, 1994, prod. Allyn Rosenberg) features the Clayton-Hamilton Orchestra, with drummer Hamilton co-leading the 18-musician band with Jeff Clayton (saxes/woodwinds) and John Clayton Jr. (bass). Completing the hard-driving rhythm team that swings the 10 arrangements by John Clayton Jr. are Bill Cunliffe (piano) and Dave Bjur (bass). On tunes such as "Jazz Party," Hamilton drives the big band with the prowess of one of his early teachers, Midwest drummer John Van Ohlen, known to propel a large unit and soloists with a big sound bubbling from underneath. In addition to his big band beats, Hamilton's brush work is poetry in motion, as his sweet syncopations suggest on the gentle romancer, "For All We Know," where Hamilton, Cunliffe, and Bjur are spotlighted in a trio setting. Hamilton is also showcased on a tasty big band version of his original, "Max." This state-of-the art big band contains some of the finest West Coast session players, many of whom are leaders of their own groups. Expert solos from trumpeters Clay Jenkins and Oscar Brashear, saxmen Rickey Woodard, Jeff Clayton, and Charles Owens, and others, contribute to this must-own album for big band fanciers as well as Hamilton fans. On *Jeff Hamilton Trio: Live!* ♫♫♫♫ (MONS, 1996, prod. Thilo Berg), Hamilton, bassist Lynn Seaton, and pianist Larry Fuller provide a toe-tapping listen on nine drums-based arrangements. Fuller and Seaton are the perfect companions for Hamilton's hard-driving propulsion; both players have accrued credits with the major big bands as well as with smaller groups noted for their swing arrangements. This album was made during a European tour, recorded live in the studio as part of the Saabrücken Radio station's "Jazz Live with Friends" series, and the enthusiasm of the musicians is maintained throughout. This is not your usual piano-bass-drums trio, but a rhythm-driven escapade that features the best of the pyrotechnic Hamilton.

what to buy next: *It's Hamilton Time* ♫♫♫♫ (Lake Street Records, 1994, prod. Allyn Rosenberg) finds the drummer leading a trio with pianist Larry Fuller and bassist Jesse Yusef Murphy that swings with flair throughout the 11 standards. It's obvious that Hamilton and Fuller have worked together in the past. Their compatibility is evident on this recording, especially on "Isn't It Romantic," where bassist Murphy temporarily steps out. There are times when this dramatic trio conjures up the tempo-shifting and stop-time breaks Hamilton helped create with the Ray Brown Trio. Highlights abound, especially on "Max," a hard-swinging Hamilton original that gives the drummer a chance to sport his polyrhythmic polish. The finale, Ellington's "Caravan," features Hamilton playing solo, using the full traps set to create an exciting display of rhythmic activity. The Jeff Hamilton Trio—Hamilton (drums), Lynn Seaton (bass), Larry Fuller (piano)—digs deep grooves and creates delicate backup for the featured guest, vibraphonist Frits Landesbergen on *Dynavibes* ♫♫♫ (MONS, 1997, prod. Thilo Berg). A devotee of Hamilton's, the Holland-based vibist is an inspired player whose talents for swing and subtlety match those of his rhythm cohorts on the eight standards and his two originals. The focus is mostly on the vibes player, yet Hamilton's trio craftily keeps the music lush and lively. Although there are times when this group is reminiscent of Milt Jackson's quartets, Hamilton's artistic leadership is what makes this session distinctive, especially notable on the standard "Cherokee," which is turned into a slow ballad instead of its usual racing tempo, and the bopping version of "Sweet Lorraine," which is highly dependent upon Hamilton's rhythmic expertise. *Dynavibes* is dynamite!

the rest:
(With the Clayton-Hamilton Orchestra) *Groove Shop* ♫♫♫♫ (Capri, 1990)
(With the Clayton-Hamilton Orchestra) *Heart and Soul* ♫♫♫♫ (Capri, 1991)
Jeff Hamilton Trio ♫♫♫♫ (MONS, 1996)
Dynavibes ♫♫♫♫ (MONS, 1997)

worth searching for: For a different taste of Hamilton's percussion art, check out any one of the recordings by the L.A.4. *Zaca* ♫♫♫♫ (Concord, 1980/1993, prod. Carl E. Jefferson) was made in a London studio a couple of years after the quartet performed in Japan. A rhythmically exciting journey of Brazilian-influenced jazz, this outing taps into the individual talents of all the musicians and their ability to perform as a tight unit. Thad Jones's exquisite "A Child Is Born" breathes new life with Shank's flute solos and the added colorful uniqueness of Hamilton's celeste. *Zaca* is a beautiful album. In fact, you really can't go wrong with any of the L.A.4 albums. By their third album, *Watch What Happens* ♫♫♫♫ (Concord, 1978, prod. Carl

E. Jefferson), a simpatico studio session of seven standards, Hamilton's understated art is integral to the success of the group's musical mixture of cool-toned boppers, Brazilian themes, and graceful ballads. Another commendable L.A.4 recording is *Live at Montreux* ✍✍✍ (Concord, 1979, prod. Carl E. Jefferson), which documents a live-recorded, eight-tune performance at the auspicious Montreux Jazz Festival in the summer of 1979. By this recording, Hamilton has integrated his bracing firebolt flair and heartful finesse comfortably into the foursome. Along with an unusual version of Cole Porter's "I Love You," which leads off with Shank and Hamilton performing a sparring duet improv, four of the eight tunes are part of an Ellington medley, "Duke's Mélange," which includes "I Let a Song Go out of My Heart," "Caravan," "Take the 'A' Train," and "Rockin' in Rhythm." *Live at Montreux* must have thrilled the audience, and you'll be captured by the rapture of their inventions as well.

influences:

◀◀ Buddy Rich, Gene Krupa, Philly Joe Jones, John Van Ohlen, Mel Lewis, Ed Thigpen, Shelly Manne, Billy Higgins

see also: *Laurindo Almeida, Ray Brown*

Nancy Ann Lee

Scott Hamilton

Born September 12, 1954, in Providence, RI.

Few young musicians were exploring pre-modern jazz styles when tenor saxophonist Scott Hamilton appeared on the New York jazz scene in the mid-1970s. His warm, inviting tenor sound, equal parts Coleman Hawkins and Lester Young (through Zoot Sims), attracted widespread attention to a whole movement of musicians dedicated to the style developed by the small-group swing bands of the '30s. Hamilton began playing saxophone at 16 and rapidly absorbed the sounds and styles of various swing-era tenor masters. As a teenager he worked in organ trios around Providence and in 1976 moved to New York, where he hooked up with like-minded trombonist Dan Barrett and cornetist Warren Vache Jr. He played with Benny Goodman in the late '70s and began his long-running association with singer Rosemary Clooney, accompanying her in concert and on many of her excellent Concord Jazz releases. Hamilton has recorded extensively and almost exclusively for Concord, often as a leader but also on sessions with Vache, Gerry Mulligan, Gene Harris, Ruby Braff, and the Concord All-Stars. He is a remarkably consistent musician who rarely delivers a sub-par performance.

what to buy: The tenor saxophonist's romantic side is on full view on *Scott Hamilton Plays Ballads* ✍✍✍ (Concord Jazz, 1989, prod. Carl E. Jefferson), a beautiful session featuring John Bunch (piano), Phil Flanigan (bass), Chris Flory (guitar), and Chuck Riggs (drums). The 11 tracks include such classic fare as "Body and Soul," "'Round Midnight," and "Laura." Hamilton is at his best on *Radio City* ✍✍✍ (Concord Jazz, 1990, prod. Carl E. Jefferson), a swinging quartet session. Except for two Hamilton originals, all the material is vintage '30s and '40s, such as Alec Wilder's beautiful ballad "I'll Be Around" and an exquisite, deeply moving version of Ray Noble's "The Touch of Your Lips." With pianist Alan Broadbent's charts for 20-piece string orchestra, *Scott Hamilton with Strings* ✍✍✍ (Concord Jazz, 1993, prod. Carl E. Jefferson) pairs two of the most lyrical talents in jazz. A masterpiece of the soloist-with-strings genre, there are many sublime moments, including Broadbent's arrangement of the verse of "Young and Foolish" and Hamilton's passionate solo on Johnny Mandel's "The Shining Sea."

what to buy next: *Organic Duke* ✍✍✍ (Concord Jazz, 1994, prod. Carl E. Jefferson) features Hamilton playing an Ellingtonian program with organist Mike LeDonne, bassist Dennis Irwin, and drummer Chuck Riggs. Baritone sax master Gerry Mulligan teams up with Hamilton on *Soft Lights and Sweet Music* ✍✍✍ (Concord Jazz, 1986, prod. Carl E. Jefferson), a consistently rewarding program featuring five Mulligan originals. The two saxophonists have a strong rapport, and their sounds blend beautifully. Another felicitous pairing is Hamilton joining the supremely soulful pianist Gene Harris on *At Last* ✍✍✍ (Concord Jazz, 1989, prod. Carl E. Jefferson). With guitarist Herb Ellis, bassist Ray Brown, and drummer Harold Jones, this romping all-star session is suffused in the kind of joyful feeling that never goes out of style. *Groovin' High* ✍✍✍ (Concord Jazz, 1992, prod. Carl E. Jefferson) teams Hamilton up with fellow swing-oriented saxophonists Ken Peplowski and Spike Robinson for a well-organized blowing session.

best of the rest:

Scott Hamilton and Warren Vache ✍✍✍ (Concord Jazz, 1978)
Tenorshoes ✍✍✍ (Concord Jazz, 1980)
Major League ✍✍✍ (Concord Jazz, 1986)
East of the Sun ✍✍✍ (Concord Jazz, 1993)
Live at the Brecon Jazz Festival ✍✍✍ (Concord Jazz, 1995)
My Romance ✍✍✍ (Concord Jazz, 1996)

influences:

◀◀ Coleman Hawkins, Ben Webster, Lester Young, Zoot Sims

Andrew Gilbert

Gunter Hampel

Born August 31, 1937, in Gottingen, Germany.

Although known primarily as a vibes player, Hampel is also proficient on the flute, bass clarinet, and piano. He was among the first of the European avant-gardists to release a record, 1965's *Heartplants*. He worked in a variety of groups in the '60s and, beginning in 1968, began a longtime collaboration with American vocalists. He dabbled in the jazz-rock merger around this time with his group Time Is Now, worked with other European groups, and formed his own record label, Birth Records. Although his activity has slowed down somewhat since 1983 (Birth released 40 records in a 15-year period), Hampel has continued to experiment with group formats. He is primarily a texturalist (a formative influence was Walt Dickerson); his flute playing is piquant but occasionally borders on shrill; his bass clarinet is best when used for group color. Early in his career, his work was prone to free-jazz excess, but his improvisation became more clear in small-group settings in the '70s. (His large-group writing at this time was notably messier and less focused.) But in the '80s, Hampel's writing opened up further and his recent big-band work has shown an assimilation of the arranging ideas of Charles Mingus and Sun Ra.

what to buy: *The 8th of July, 1969* 🎵🎵🎵🎵 (Birth, 1969, prod. Gunter Hampel), a landmark recording, is a fertile cross-section of the European and American avant-garde. "We Move" starts with a clip-clop rhythm and eventually develops into a swirling mass of free improvisation. "Morning Song" is a lengthy, stunning piece, with a Hampel/Anthony Braxton duet and Steve McCall's African-influenced drumming being just two of the highlights. *Celestial Glory* 🎵🎵🎵 (Birth, 1991, prod. Gunter Hampel), a live recording from New York's Knitting Factory, contains the five musicians most closely associated with the Galaxie Dream Band: Hampel, singer Jeanne Lee, clarinetist Perry Robinson, and reed players Mark Whitecage and Thomas Keyserling. With Hampel concentrating on bass clarinet (his vibes work on the first track makes one wish for a lot more) and Lee sounding her most horn-like, the dense horn web sounds like a reed choir. Yet there are also moments of spacious beauty. It's a unique combination.

what to buy next: Hampel's duet with German tenor player Matthias Schubert, *Dialog* 🎵🎵🎵 (Birth, 1992, prod. Gunter Hampel) includes an excellent tenor/vibes collaboration on "Spielplatz," and the record contains some of Hampel's finest bass clarinet playing to date, rich and fully textured. Hampel's composition "After the Fact" and (unusually for Hampel) a

blues song make this one of the finest recent Birth releases. *Fresh Heat, Live at Sweet Basil, New York* 🎵🎵🎵 (Birth, 1985, prod. Gunter Hampel) is a stellar big-band recording, including guitarist Bill Frisell, Bob Stewart on tuba, trombonist Curtis Fowlkes, and Sun Ra space vocalist Art Jenkins, as well as frequent members of Hampel's groups. The charts have a Charles Mingus–like quality, with sections of simultaneous improvisation; nice vocal interplay between Lee and Jenkins is another highlight. This is one of Hampel's most accessible recordings, although there isn't enough of his vibes playing. *Jubilation* 🎵🎵🎵 (Birth, 1983, prod. Gunter Hampel), a special edition of the Galaxie Dream Band, sounds unusually open and unpredictable.

what to avoid: *Time Is Now* 🎵🎵 (Birth, 1992), named for a jazz/rock group Hampel had in the late '60s, never rises above average. The rhythm section functions but makes no interesting detours, guitarist Mark Dietz's standard-issue wigouts are boring, and even Hampel sounds uninspired.

best of the rest:
Music from Europe 🎵🎵🎵 (E.S.P., 1966)

Robert Iannapollo

Lionel Hampton

Born April 20, 1908, in Louisville, KY.

Lionel Hampton, the founding father of jazz vibraphone, has had one of the greatest, most productive careers in jazz. A jazz giant since the early 1930s, Hampton is an exuberant, swing-based improvisor, a tremendously successful bandleader, and one of the keenest talent scouts in jazz history. Through the decades, Hamp has maintained his swing-based approach while hiring and nurturing musicians rooted in subsequent jazz styles. His first instrument was the drums, and he was taught by a Dominican nun while attending Holy Rosary Academy in Kenosha, Wisconsin. When he moved to Chicago he joined the *Chicago Defender* Newspaper Boys Band, where he learned percussion and marimba. His first major inspiration was drummer Jimmy Bertrand, who also occasionally played the xylophone. Hampton moved to Los Angeles around 1927 and worked steadily in bands led by Curtis Mosby, Paul Howard, Vernon Elkins, Detroit Shannon, and Reb Spikes. But his big break came when he joined Les Hite's band, which was backing Louis Armstrong at Sebastian's Cotton Club in Culver City. The gig marked another turning point for Hamp, as he met and soon married Cotton Club dancer Gladys Riddle. Riddle became his business manager and profoundly helped shape his career.

She encouraged him to practice the vibes and to study theory at the University of Southern California. Hampton started his own band in order to feature himself on the vibes, and in 1936 landed a job at the Paradise Cafe in Los Angeles. Benny Goodman came in one night and soon Hamp found himself on stage with the clarinetist, drummer Gene Krupa, and pianist Teddy Wilson. Goodman recorded the group and began featuring Hampton with his quartet on the *Camel Cigarette* program, making the vibraphonist a star. RCA Victor gave Hampton wide latitude to assemble all-star bands in the late 1930s, resulting in 90 sides that mark the high point of the swing era (these 1937–41 recordings were reissued in a six-LP set by Bluebird, but the complete set has yet to be released on CD).

Hampton stayed with Goodman through 1940, including a featured role in the legendary 1938 Carnegie Hall concert, and then left to start his own big band. The group was a tremendous success, and has never strayed far from the formula established with the huge 1942 hit "Flying Home"—potent screaming brass over an insistent, driving rhythm section. Tenor saxophonist Illinois Jacquet's classic "Flying Home" solo was an essential element in the emergence of rhythm and blues, a style Hampton's orchestra incorporated effectively into its hard-charging, extroverted sound. By the mid-'40s, the orchestra had adopted elements of bebop, though Hampton's style remained swing-oriented. Over the decades, the band also became known as one jazz's most fertile proving grounds for young talent. The list of musicians who paid early dues with Hampton is prodigious, starting with Dinah Washington, Betty Carter, Charles Mingus, Dexter Gordon, Clark Terry, Illinois Jacquet, Art Farmer, Fats Navarro, Wes Montgomery, Clifford Brown, and Johnny Griffin. He has recorded prolifically throughout his career for many labels and there are many Hampton CDs available.

Hamp's other ventures have also been very successful, running the gamut from a publishing house and two record labels (Glad Hamp and Who's Who) to the Lionel Hampton Development Corp., which built two apartment complexes in Harlem. By the 1970s Hampton had become an important figure in New York and Republican politics. In 1988 the Lionel Hampton Center for Performing Arts opened in Idaho and there is now also an annual Lionel Hampton Jazz Festival in the state. Despite suffering from a stroke and other health problems in the 1990s, Hampton continues to record for MoJazz and Telarc, and tour

Lionel Hampton (© Jack Vartoogian)

with his big band and his all-star group, the Golden Men of Jazz, featuring such relative youngsters as Clark Terry, Sweets Edison, James Moody, and Al Grey.

what to buy: Until all of Hampton's Decca sessions are reissued on CD, *Midnight Sun* ♫♫♫♫ (Decca, 1946–47/1993, prod. Milt Gabler) is the best place to start. These 20 tracks capture one of the most advanced, bop-influenced big bands of the mid-40s, sessions featuring both up-and-coming jazz stars (Johnny Griffin, Charles Mingus, Arnett Cobb, Joe Wilder, Kenny Dorham, and Milt Buckner) and fine, lesser-known players such as powerhouse trumpeters Jimmy Nottingham and Leo Sheppard and tenor saxophonist John Sparrow. These are consistently excellent, high-spirited recordings and, though Hamp retains his swing style, some tracks (such as "Mingus Fingers") are amazingly bop-oriented. While the music contained here is classic, *Flying Home* ♫♫♫ (MCA, 1942–45/1990, prod. Milt Gabler) loses a bone for its slipshod presentation. Containing 16 Decca tracks alternating between Hampton's septet and orchestra, the album includes the original 1942 hit "Flying Home" with Illinois Jacquet's classic tenor solo (and a 17-year-old Dexter Gordon, on his first major gig). Milt Buckner, Cat Anderson, and Earl Bostic are some of the other young talents featured here, as well as a 19-year-old Dinah Washington, backed by some gritty Arnett Cobb tenor work on "Blow Top Blues." This is a good introduction to Hamp's extroverted style as an improvisor and bandleader. The first disc in RCA's frustrating, incomplete Bluebird reissue series of Hampton's classic all-star sessions, *Hot Mallets, Volume 1* ♫♫♫♫ (Bluebird, 1937–39/1987) contains the four master tracks from the legendary date with Coleman Hawkins, Ben Webster, Chu Berry, Benny Carter, and a young Dizzy Gillespie still under the sway of Roy Eldridge. There's also some glorious work by altoist Johnny Hodges, trumpeter Jonah Jones, and of course the ever-ebullient Hampton. Forget about their ages and allegedly contrasting styles, swing veteran Hampton and cool tenor saxophonist Stan Getz find plenty of common ground on *Hamp and Getz* ♫♫♫♫ (Verve, 1955, prod. Norman Granz), a session featuring some take-no-prisoners jousting. Backed by a top-shelf West Coast rhythm section of Lou Levy (piano), Leroy Vinnegar (bass), and Shelly Manne, Hamp and Getz open with a blistering "Cherokee." They display their lyricism on a ballad medley, then hop back into the fire with a torrid "Jumpin' at the Woodside." The CD also contains an alternate take of Hamp's "Gladys" and a mysterious tune, "Headache," with an unknown trombonist.

what to buy next: An excellent concert album recorded at the Pasadena Civic Auditorium, *Lionel Hampton with the Just Jazz*

All-Stars ✍✍✍ (MCA/GNP, 1947/1993, prod. Gene Norman) features a host of jazz stars, including altoist Willie Smith, trumpeter Charlie Shavers, guitarist Barney Kessel, and bassist Slam Stewart. The material—"Flying Home," "Hamp's Boogie Woogie," and "Perdido"—is from Hamp's standard repertoire, and the solos are consistently strong. *You Better Know It!!!* ✍✍✍✍ (Impulse!, 1965/1994, prod. Bob Thiele) is a wonderful small group session featuring tenor giant Ben Webster, trumpeter Clark Terry, pianist Hank Jones, bassist Milt Hinton, and drummer Osie Johnson. The arrangements are simple and direct, leaving plenty of room for these veterans to stretch out. The third and final installment in RCA's scattered reissue series of Hampton's classic all-star swing sessions, *Tempo and Swing* ✍✍✍ (Bluebird, 1939–40/1992) contains 23 tracks featuring such giants as Ben Webster, Benny Carter, Coleman Hawkins, and the Nat "King" Cole Trio. There's no excuse for RCA dividing up sessions between discs, but Hamp knew how to create excitement and inspire his players and the music here is at an extremely high level. Most of *Reunion at Newport 1967* ✍✍✍ (RCA/Bluebird, 1967/1993, prod. Brad McCuen, Bill Titone) features a big band of Hampton alumni assembled for the Newport Festival, including trombonists Al Grey and Britt Woodman, tenor saxophonists Frank Foster and Jerome Richardson, and trumpeters Snooky Young and Joe Newman. Illinois Jacquet reprises his classic "Flying Home" solo, capping a satisfying, high-energy set. The last part of the album contains part of a mid-1950s session recorded in Spain, highlighted by Hamp's pairing with pianist Tete Montoliu.

what to avoid: Despite the presence of many fine musicians, *For the Love of Music* ✍ (MoJazz, 1995, prod. Gary Haase, Stevie Wonder, Israel Sinfonietta) is an over-produced mess that rarely comes to life. A banal, funkified version of "Flying Home" with keyboardist Patrice Rushen is one low point, while Chaka Kahn is wasted on the piffle of "Gossamer Wings." Hampton clearly has fun sitting in with Tito Puente's band on "Mojazz" and "Don't You Worry 'bout a Thing," two rare high points on this weak effort to package a musician who needs no help from clever producers.

best of the rest:

His Best Records with the Jazz Masters, Volume 1 ✍✍✍ (Black and Blue, 1930–38)

I'm in the Mood for Swing ✍✍✍ (Living Era, 1930–38/1992)

Lionel Hampton and His Orchestra (1937–38) ✍✍✍✍ (Classics, 1937–38)

Lionel Hampton's Jumpin' Jive ✍✍✍ (Bluebird/RCA, 1937–39)

His Best Records with the Jazz Masters, Volume 2 ✍✍✍✍ (Black and Blue, 1938–39)

Lionel Hampton and His Orchestra (1938–39) ✍✍✍✍ (Classics, 1938–39)

In Paris ✍✍✍ (Vogue Disques, 1953/1995)

Flying Home/Hamp's Blues ✍✍✍ (Lester, 1974)

Rare Recordings, Volume 1 ✍✍✍ (Telarchive, 1977/1992)

Mostly Blues ✍✍ (MusicMasters, 1989)

Mostly Ballads ✍✍ (MusicMasters, 1990)

Live at the Blue Note ✍✍✍ (Telarc, 1991)

Just Jazz: Live at the Blue Note ✍✍✍ (Telarc, 1992)

worth searching for: Some of the most thrilling small-group sessions in jazz history, *After You've Gone: The Original Benny Goodman Trio and Quartet Sessions, Volume 1* ✍✍✍✍ (Bluebird, 1935–37/1987) covers 10 tracks by the Benny Goodman Trio, with pianist Teddy Wilson and drummer Gene Krupa, and the first 12 tracks recorded by the Benny Goodman Quartet, which added Hampton's irrepressible vibes to the trio. This is timeless music by what happened to be the first racially mixed bands to work regularly in public.

influences:

◀◀ Jimmy Bertrand, Louis Armstrong

▶▶ Red Norvo, Tyree Glenn, Milt Jackson

Andrew Gilbert

Slide Hampton

Born Locksley Wellington Hampton, April 21, 1932, in Jeannette, PA.

One of the truly underappreciated trombonists in jazz, Slide Hampton demonstrated his prolific skills as composer, arranger, and orchestrator, marking him as indispensable. Raised in Indianapolis, Hampton left his hometown in his 20s to go on the road with a succession of groups, including Lionel Hampton (no relation) and Maynard Ferguson, with whose big band, from 1957–59, Hampton's arranging acumen became legendary. After leaving Ferguson, Hampton formed a New York–based octet that featured his compositions and arrangements, as well as musicians such as George Coleman and Freddie Hubbard. He also performed and recorded with Art Blakey, Dizzy Gillespie, and the Thad Jones–Mel Lewis band. After touring the continent with Woody Herman in the late 1960s, Hampton settled in Berlin, where he became the official arranger of the Berlin Radio Orchestra and undertook other European radio staff orchestra assignments. Hampton returned to New York in 1977 and led his World of Trombones. During the 1980s he toured with and arranged for Dizzy Gillespie's All Nation Orchestra. Active in jazz education, he is now a busy New York session player working with the Carnegie Hall Jazz Band, which features his arrangements, and his own group, Slide Hampton and the JazzMasters.

what's available: *Slide Hampton and the JazzMasters—Dedicated to Diz* ✍✍✍ (Telarc, 1993, prod. Charlie Fishman, John Snyder, Robert Woods) is a potent, energetic, and fitting tribute. This group of accomplished pros—Jimmy Heath, Steve Turre, and Jon Faddis—along with robust up-and-comers Roy Hargrove, Danilo Perez, and David Sanchez, capture the magnificence, virtuosity, and humor of the late trumpeter Gillespie. Hampton's charts are world class, with ensemble sections sounding as if they'd been played for decades and not days. Not surprisingly, Faddis really shines on Dizzy's national anthem for jazz, "A Night in Tunisia," while Hargrove and Claudio Roditi work out with Birks's protégé on Dizzy's "Tour de Force." Another highlight is Hampton's successful amalgam of Gillespie themes on "Overture," a solid feature for Heath's mature tenor. Recorded one month after Dizzy's death, this album obviously inspired everyone involved. Slide Hampton's short-lived World of Trombones is a musical feast on *World of Trombones* ✍✍✍✍ (Black Lion, 1979/1993, prod. Roger Pola), a true arranger's band featuring a front line of nine trombonists, including veterans Curtis Fuller and Steve Turre along with newcomers Robin Eubanks and Papo Vasquez. Everyone gets a chance to stretch out on such gems as Dizzy's "Con Alma" and Thelonious Monk's "'Round Midnight," along with Hampton's own "Chorale." Ambitious without taking advantage of what could have been another gimmick, *World of Trombones* is a delight from start to finish, with contrasting styles and savory arrangements. On *Roots* ✍✍✍ (Criss Cross, 1985/1994, prod. Gerry Teekens), Hampton plays the trombone (an instrument that is almost impossible to master) with a fluency few musicians ever achieve. His musical mastery is judiciously demonstrated in this 1985 session from the Dutch label. Joined by august tenor saxman Clifford Jordan and Cedar Walton's Eastern Rebellion (Walton, piano; David Williams, bass; and Billy Higgins, drums), Hampton takes extended solos on standards "My Old Flame," "Just in Time," jazz classics "Solar" and "Barbados," as well as his own compositions and those of Walton and Jordan. Although this is a blowing session and not a feature for his eminent arrangements, Hampton and his collaborators make it memorable by the caliber of their improvisations.

worth searching for: Hampton led one of the better groups around New York in the early '60s and *Explosion! The Sound of Slide Hampton* ✍✍✍ (Atlantic, 1963, prod. Jerry Wexler) features his extroverted, damn-the-torpedoes arrangements in a ten-piece band that includes tenorman Joe Farrell, bassist Bob Cranshaw, and pianists Horace Parlan and Walter Davis Jr. "Slide's Blues," and "Love Letters," are Gospel-tinged and full of earthy emotion, while "Delilah" and "Begin the Beguine" are given a Latin twist. Lots of variety here as well, including a moving "Maria," and "Your Cheatin' Heart," a country hit given jazz accoutrements. Solo standouts include the leader's trombone and Farrell's energetic tenor.

influences:

◀◀ Dizzy Gillespie, J.J. Johnson

▶▶ Curtis Fuller, Robin Eubanks, Steve Davis

Bret Primack

Herbie Hancock
Born April 12, 1940, in Chicago, IL.

As one of the genre's greatest dichotomies, Herbie Hancock has been (at least for the latter two-thirds of his career) unabashedly in pursuit of commercial success. However, unlike many of his fame-seeking peers, three important factors mitigate his quest for popularity: first, he's one of the best jazz pianists alive, if not ever; second, his records—even the most crassly commercial ones—always retain some kernel (although it's often *very* small) of artistic/creative integrity; and, finally, rather than attempting to please both critics and consumers (an impossible feat), Hancock readily admits that his goal is to make music that people enjoy, leaving the "elitists" to come to terms with it. And, if that's not enough, he wrote "Watermelon Man," for god's sake.

Initially trained as a classical pianist, Hancock first became interested in jazz while in high school. After graduating from college (1960), he began playing jazz in earnest, working Chicago gigs with musicians such as Coleman Hawkins and Donald Byrd. It was with Byrd (a performer whose career arc and musical approach is quite similar) that Hancock made his way to New York and, after a couple studio dates with Byrd (most notably, the impressive *Free Form*), was offered his own Blue Note sessions in 1962. Not too bad for a 22-year-old fresh out of college. A string of consistently excellent albums followed, buoyed equally by Hancock's extraordinary compositional skills (at least a half dozen standards sprang from this period), his boppishly soulful style, and a rash of young, forward-looking sidemen like Grachan Moncur III, Tony Williams, Ron Carter, Freddie Hubbard, Bobby Hutcherson, and Grant Green, each of whom would help, in their own way, define the Blue Note "experimental" school of the mid-1960s. Concurrently, Hancock

Herbie Hancock (© **Jack Vartoogian**)

also became a member of Miles Davis's group from 1963–69. Although he was out of the band by the time *Bitches Brew* was made, it's obvious that the tenure with Davis had a great effect on him, and the groundwork that was laid on albums like *Filles de Kilimanjaro* influenced the work that Hancock did with his newly formed sextet. Active from 1969–72, the group cut three of the fanciest, if oddest, fusion records ever (collected on the *Mwandishi* CD), and illustrated Hancock's new commitment to people-pleasing. When Hancock and Miles reunited for Davis's fantastic *Jack Johnson* LP in 1970, a working relationship was resumed that engendered the making of some of the most influential electric jazz records of all time: Miles's *On the Corner* (on which Hancock played) and, of course, Hancock's *Headhunters*.

Unfortunately, from these successes, it was a quick downhill trip into disco hell, and of all the albums that Hancock has recorded in the more than two decades since, only a few qualify as nearly successful. Although most of his 1970s and 1980s material sold quite well and established him as one of the most popular jazz musicians alive, they were far too pop-oriented to even be considered "jazz" records. Sporadically through the years, though, Hancock has occasionally teamed up with friends and members of Miles's groups—Chick Corea, Tony Williams, Ron Carter—and made exciting (if not groundbreaking) forays into straight-ahead territory.

what to buy: *Takin' Off* 𝄢𝄢𝄢𝄢 (Blue Note, 1962/1987/1996, prod. Alfred Lion) is an incredibly strong solo bow that favorably foretold Hancock's future. It's got Dexter Gordon (then enjoying a strong post-prison/post-addiction comeback) and it's got "Watermelon Man." It cooks and grooves, with Hancock sounding as seasoned and comfortable as a man twice his age. *Maiden Voyage* 𝄢𝄢𝄢𝄢 (Blue Note, 1965/1987, prod. Alfred Lion) is certainly Hancock's finest Blue Note hour and an indisputable masterpiece to boot. With Ron Carter and Tony Williams as an unbeatable rhythm section, Hancock, along with tenor player George Coleman and trumpeter Freddie Hubbard, weaves in and out of dense, melodically rich passages, creating a soulful, forward-looking vibe. One of the first fully formed examples of the Blue Note new school. *Mwandishi: The Complete Warner Bros. Recordings* ♫♫♫♫ (Warner Bros., 1970–72/1994, prod. Herbie Hancock, David Rubinson) collects Hancock's three Warner Bros. outings, *Fat Albert Rotunda*, *Mwandishi* and the excellent *Crossings*. Here, the groups feature luminaries such as Joe Henderson, Buster Williams, Bennie Maupin, Eddie Henderson, and Julian Priester, as well as lesser-known players like Johnny Coles. To understand exactly how funky this record is, you need only know one thing: Bernard Purdie sits in on drums for two tracks. However, the pieces here are far more artful than simply pointless grooves. Pieces like "Water Torture" and "Ostinato" combine rock's electricity, hard bop's soulfulness, funk's power, and Hancock's intrinsic sense of adventure, resulting in tunes that are equally accessible and challenging. *Headhunters* ♫♫♫♫ (Columbia, 1974/1997, prod. David Rubinson, Herbie Hancock) is a damnably great record. Had Hancock not succeeded so completely with *Headhunters* in creating a commercially accessible blend of funk, pop, and jazz that actually held its own artistically, it's doubtful that the pungent morass of fusion would have ever grown to include the horrors that it does today. Not only does he utterly revamp "Watermelon Man" (although the 1962 version is far better than this one) into a slow-burning electric groove, but he also pulls off a piece like the warm, smooth, and aptly titled "Vein Melter." A classic, to be sure. Buy the record or the 1997 remaster, because Columbia's initial "Jazz Masterworks" CDs make these rich, bottom-heavy grooves sound terribly thin.

what to buy next: Rather than enlisting typical Blue Note blowers for the date, on *Inventions & Dimensions* ♫♫♫♫ (Blue Note, 1963/1989, prod. Alfred Lion) Hancock opted to put himself and bassist Paul Chambers in the studio with Latin percussionists Willie Bobo (later of "Spanish Grease" fame) and Osvaldo "Chihuahua" Martinez. The results, though a bit inconsistent, are full of life and, though not overtly "Latin" in tone, all five of Hancock's originals here are certainly bolstered by the new blood. *Empyrean Isles* ♫♫♫♫ (Blue Note, 1964/1987, prod. Alfred Lion) is a classic that's only slightly less perfect than *Maiden Voyage*, mainly due to the absence of George Coleman's tenor. Although it does contain "Cantaloupe Island," the rest of the album—especially the slightly off-putting timbre of "The Egg"—is consistent with the high caliber of work that Hancock was producing at the time. Adventurous but not shocking, this is one of those albums that shows how far out people can go while still staying well inside

the lines. *Future Shock* ♫♫ (Columbia, 1983, prod. Bill Laswell, Herbie Hancock) is not actually all that good, but it does have "Rockit," which is probably the only 1980s Hancock track worth having, for pure kitsch value alone, of course. More synths and beats than any jazz fan could possibly feel comfortable with, this is a success only as an instrumental pop record. *A Jazz Collection* ♫♫♫ (Columbia, 1991) is a nice collection of Hancock's periodic fusion-era explorations into "regular" jazz. Obviously these cuts aren't up to the level of his Blue Note records, but they demonstrate nicely that all that electricity hadn't shocked the chops out of his fingers. Derived from specious origins, *Cantaloupe Island* ♫♫♫♫ (Blue Note, 1994, prod. Alfred Lion) is a compilation of six tracks Blue Note revived to quickly cash in on acid-jazzers Us3's success with "Cantaloop Island," which sampled and was based around . . . well, you know; the selections are quite nice. Packaged to look like an original early 1960s album, these cuts were actually taken from four separate albums, but given the impeccable and consistent quality of those albums (*Maiden Voyage*, *Empyrean Isles*, and others), this compilation stands up as a consonant distillation of Hancock's best work.

what to avoid: *Monster* ♫♫ (Columbia, 1980, prod. David Rubinson, Herbie Hancock) ranks among the worst of Hancock's pop records, and is as close as he ever got to making a completely worthless album. The goofily sappy "Making Love" is just strange enough to get over, yet, even for the few seconds that you may dig on that cut, there are five more that will make you retch with horror. You'd think he would have gotten it out of his system by 1994, but for some reason Hancock felt the need to revivify himself in the eyes of "the kids" and made the wretched, pseudo-African blend of third-rate hip hop and fourth-rate fusion found on *Dis Is da Drum* ♫♫ (Mercury, 1995, prod. Herbie Hancock, Bill Summers). Bad Herbie, bad. *The New Standard* ♫♫ (Verve, 1996, prod. Herbie Hancock, Guy Eckstine) was an excellent idea, but sorry execution. Attempting to inject some new blood into the "standard repertoire," Hancock jazzes up numbers by Nirvana, Sade, Babyface, Peter Gabriel, Prince, the Beatles (hadn't that already been done to death before?), and others. Sadly, although his playing is strong and bluesy, given the lineup (which includes Michael Brecker, John Scofield, Jack DeJohnette, and some atypically intrusive bass playing by Dave Holland), the sound is far too sterile and contemporary. It winds up sounding more like Fuzak than a replacement for Monk and Gershwin.

best of the rest:
My Point of View ♫♫♫♫ (Blue Note, 1963/1996)

Blow Up: Original Motion Picture Soundtrack 𝄞𝄞𝄞𝄞 (Atlantic/Rhino, 1966/1992)

Speak like a Child 𝄞𝄞𝄞𝄞 (Blue Note, 1968/1988)

The Prisoner 𝄞𝄞𝄞𝄞 (Blue Note, 1969/1996)

Man-Child 𝄞𝄞𝄞 (Columbia, 1975/1987)

Secrets 𝄞𝄞 (Columbia, 1976/1988)

Feets Don't Fail Me Now 𝄞𝄞 (Columbia, 1978/1987)

Best of Herbie Hancock 𝄞𝄞 (Columbia, 1979/1988)

Mr. Hands 𝄞𝄞 (Columbia, 1980/1994)

Lite Me Up 𝄞𝄞 (Columbia, 1982)

Quartet 𝄞𝄞𝄞𝄞 (Columbia, 1982/1987)

Sound-System 𝄞𝄞𝄞 (Columbia, 1984)

'Round Midnight: Original Motion Picture Soundtrack 𝄞𝄞𝄞 (Columbia, 1986)

Best of Herbie Hancock: The Blue Note Years 𝄞𝄞𝄞𝄞 (Blue Note, 1962/1988)

Perfect Machine 𝄞𝄞𝄞 (Columbia, 1988)

Jazz Profile 𝄞𝄞𝄞𝄞 (Blue Note, 1997)

(With Wayne Shorter) *1 + 1* 𝄞𝄞𝄞 (Verve, 1997)

influences:

◀◀ Bill Evans, Red Garland, Ahmad Jamal, Ramsey Lewis, Horace Silver, Joe Zawinul

▶▶ Chick Corea, George Duke, Hilton Ruiz

Jason Ferguson

John Handy

Born February 3, 1933, in Dallas, TX.

Alto saxophonist John Handy has worn coats of many cultures throughout his long, prolific career, playing jazz with Charles Mingus, Randy Weston, and his own groups, and collaborating with symphony orchestras, Brazilian guitarist Bola Sete, and Indian traditional master musicians Ravi Shankar, Ali Akbar Khan, and Dr. L. Subramaniam. In addition, he hit the R&B charts in 1976 with "Hard Work." Born in Dallas, Handy began playing the alto at age 11 and moved to Oakland, California in 1948. As a teenager, he played around the Bay Area in blues bands and with jazz artists such as Gerald Wilson, Teddy Edwards, and Frank Morgan. Although his musical approach changed after he heard Charlie Parker at San Francisco's Say When Club, the influence of such earlier saxophone favorites as Johnny Hodges, Louis Jordan, and Earl Bostic remained strong and contributed greatly to the development of his unique, searing style. Handy headed for New York in 1958 and was soon hired by bassist Mingus, who found the saxophonist's highly emotive style ideally suited to his alternately sweet and volatile music. Although Handy was a member of Mingus's band for less than a year, the

association brought him a contract with Roulette Records. Returning to San Francisco in 1962 to finish college, Handy stayed and has led a succession of groups ever since. The most successful was the one that featured violinist Michael White and guitarist Jerry Hahn. They were a sensation at the 1965 Monterey Jazz Festival and recorded several best-selling albums for Columbia. In recent years, Handy has toured and recorded with the Mingus Dynasty and Bebop and Beyond all-star groups, as well as his own group, Class, which features Handy and three classically trained violinists.

what to buy: Handy first made his mark in the jazz world as a member of Charles Mingus's Jazz Workshop. He formed his own group in 1964–65 and at the 1965 Monterey Jazz Festival, recorded the incredible album *Live at the Monterey Jazz Festival* 𝄞𝄞𝄞𝄞 (Koch Jazz, 1996, prod. John Hammond). It features only two tunes, "Spanish Lady," and "If Only We Knew," and earned Grammy nominations for both performance and composition. At the time, this was one of the best and most talked-about jazz groups. In addition to Handy's alto, the quintet features Mike White on violin, Jerry Hahn on guitar, Don Thompson on bass, and Terry Clarke on drums. Extended solos on an LP were a rarity in 1965, but the performances here are so inspired that the label (Columbia) had to release this. There's a sense of excitement that marks this as one of the best live recordings of the era. *New View* 𝄞𝄞𝄞𝄞 (Koch Jazz, 1997, prod. John Hammond) features Handy's second great group of the 1960s, which included vibist Bobby Hutcherson, guitarist Pat Martino (then 23), bassist Albert Stinson, and drummer Doug Side. Once again, there are but three compositions on the recording, done live at New York's Village Gate in 1967, but all three are notable. The group does a haunting version of John Coltrane's "Naima," a splendidly soulful "A Little Quiet," and "Tears of Ole Miss," a heroic, a comprehensive musical work. "Tears" reflects the turbulent times and is infused with the passionate emotions of the civil rights years. Handy pulls out all the stops here, using percussion, whistles, and angry calls and shrieks to set the mood. Accordingly, this is as much a social statement as it is a musical one, yet its contagious blues chorus provides just the right climax. After Handy's triumphant appearance at the Monterey Jazz Festival in 1965, his Quintet recorded *Second John Handy Album* 𝄞𝄞𝄞𝄞 (Koch Jazz, 1997, prod. John Hammond), a 1966 studio outing. Although the sparks weren't flying, this recording benefits from the fact that the group was touring consistently and their cohesiveness can be felt on all tracks. Like the live Monterey date that preceded this, everyone solos tastefully and with great precision, particularly

Handy, violinist Mike White, and guitarist Jerry Hahn. The most jubilant track is "Dancy Dancy," a Handy composition that could easily wake the dead with its buoyant beat.

what to buy next: In the mid-'80s, alto saxophonist Handy, a musician always in search of new musical possibilities, put together this unique quartet, with his alto out front and three violinists, which he called John Handy and Class. Their only recording, *Centerpiece* ♪♪♪♪ (Milestone, 1989, prod. Orrin Keepnews), is a collection of jazz, blues, and popular standards, including Handy's own delightful Louis Jordan-influenced "I Be Itchin' and Scratchin' (To Get You out of My Life)." Accordingly, *Centerpiece* showcases Handy's molten alto saxophone blended with the warm, sinewy violin tones of Class. Handy arranged all the selections and even plays clarinet on a tribute to Barney Bigard, "Mood Indigo."

worth searching for: Recorded in 1975 and 1980, *Karuna Supreme* ♪♪♪♪ (MPS, 1980) is true fusion music performed by Handy's group, Rainbow, with Handy's alto alongside Ali Akbar Khan on sarod, L. Subramaniam on violin, and Zakin Hussain and Shyam Kane on tablas. Handy has repeatedly demonstrated that he can adapt to any setting, and he fits in perfectly with the *karnatak* harmonic language and rhythms of South India. More than just putting jazz on top of traditional Indian music, there's an organic feel to this recording that makes it truly unique. As always, Handy sounds comfortable and serene.

influences:

◄◄ Charlie Parker, Cannonball Adderley, Sonny Stitt, Bunky Green

►► Gary Bartz, Charles McPherson, Phil Woods, Bobby Watson, Greg Osby

Bret Primack

W.C. Handy

Born November 16, 1873, in Florence, AL. Died March 28, 1958.

The "Father of the Blues," W.C. Handy is an important figure in both jazz and blues, but he might be better thought of as a step-parent than the true source for either genre. Handy was a coronet player and band leader who took inspiration from the music of street singers, medicine shows, and other popular sources, often transcribing the tunes and publishing them with his name listed as composer. His primary role in music history first brought him a modicum of fame when he heard an itinerant guitarist singing in a train station in Tutwiler, Mississippi, about "Goin' where the Southern crosses the Yellow Dog." Handy later transcribed and arranged the tune for a Memphis

politician who used it as a campaign song ("Mister Crump"), better known today as "The Memphis Blues." In 1914, buoyed by the success of "The Memphis Blues" and another tune he "wrote" ("The St. Louis Blues"), Handy opened up a publishing firm in Memphis with Harry Pace before moving the company to New York City in 1918. In 1928 he conducted a Carnegie Hall performance of "Yamekraw," a piece written for piano and orchestra by James P. Johnson, with Fats Waller as the soloist. His autobiography, *Father of the Blues,* was published in 1941.

what's available: The rating for *W.C. Handy's Memphis Blues Band* ♪♪♪♪ (Memphis Archives, 1994, prod. Richard James Hite) is more for the historical significance of the release than the audio quality. The songs heard on the album were recorded in New York City circa 1917–23 and, while cleaned up considerably, sound "historic." Handy conducts his ensembles in performances of "St. Louis Blues," "Fuzzy Wuzzy Rag," "That Jazz Dance" and 13 other songs. The style can be compared to the music heard in early sound cartoons and is analogous to concert band music heard in town squares at the turn of the century. That said, these are delightful recordings, full of verve and bounce.

worth searching for: Handy's autobiography, *Father of the Blues,* is required reading for anyone interested in early aspects of jazz or blues. There is also an interesting interview clip with Handy included on the newer reissues of *Louis Armstrong Plays W.C. Handy* ♪♪♪♪ (Columbia, 1954/1997, prod. George Avakian). George Avakian gets Handy to comment on Armstrong and the great trumpeter's performance of Handy's scores.

Garaud MacTaggart

Sir Roland Hanna

Born February 10, 1932, in Detroit, MI.

Technique and a well-developed sense of jazz performance history make Sir Roland Hanna one of the most respected solo and ensemble performers. He has studied at Juilliard and at the Eastman School, receiving a firm grounding in the classics to go along with his ever-developing piano skills. His first gigs of renown came with Benny Goodman and Charles Mingus, but he has led his own trios since 1959, in addition to serving a long stint in the Thad Jones/Mel Lewis Jazz Orchestra (replacing Jones.) Hanna has also served as an accompanist to Sarah Vaughan and done extensive performing with the New York Jazz Quartet, which he helped form in 1974. One of his most recent positions is with the Lincoln Center Jazz Orchestra. During a solo tour of Africa in 1969, Hanna was knighted by President

Tubman of Liberia for his humanitarian work, raising money for the education of African youth.

what to buy: Absolutely one of the best solo piano recitals in the catalog bar none, *Perugia* ⅃⅃⅃⅃ (Freedom, 1975, prod. Alan Bates, Michael Cuscuna) is a truly special album. This live recording from the Montreux Jazz Festival in 1974 packs an artistic wallop. From such Ellingtonia as "Take the 'A' Train" and "I Got It Bad and That Ain't Good" to Hanna originals "Wistful Moment" and the album's eight-minute centerpiece, "Perugia," there are no slack moments. He covers piano literature like a blanket, quoting blues phrases here and Satie or Debussy there. At all times, Hanna's control is at the service of the music.

what to buy next: Despite Hanna's undeniable gifts as an accompanist, solo piano performances are where this gifted pianist really shines. While not the same kind of breathtakingly beautiful performance heard on *Perugia*, *Sir Roland Hanna at Maybeck, Vol. 32* ⅃⅃⅃⅃ (Concord Jazz, 1994, prod. Nick Phillips) is yet another distinguished entry into the Maybeck Hall Recital series. The material dips heavily (three songs and a three-tune medley) into the Gershwin catalog with stopovers for Romberg, Rogers, Strayhorn, and Rollins. About the only disappointment is the lack of Hanna originals.

the rest:
Walkin' ⅃⅃⅃ (Jazz Hour, 1975)
Glove ⅃⅃⅃ (Storyville, 1978)
Bird Tracks: Remembering Charlie Parker ⅃⅃⅃ (Progressive, 1978)
(With the New York Jazz Quartet) *Oasis* ⅃⅃⅃ (Enja, 1981)
Persia My Dear ⅃⅃⅃ (DIW, 1987)
(With Jesper Thilo) *This Time It's Real* ⅃⅃⅃ (Storyville, 1988)
'Round Midnight ⅃⅃⅃ (Town Crier, 1990)
Duke Ellington Piano Solos ⅃⅃⅃⅃ (Music Masters, 1991)
Roland Hanna Plays Gershwin ⅃⅃⅃⅃ (LRC, 1993)
(With the New York Jazz Quartet) *Surge* ⅃⅃⅃⅃ (Enja, 1993)

worth searching for: *Swing Me No Waltzes* ⅃⅃⅃⅃ (Storyville, 1980, prod. Rune Ofwerman) is another wonderful solo album by the pianist, standing out from his other solo releases because it showcases Hanna the composer more than any of his other titles. Seven of the nine tunes on the record (not yet available on CD) are his, with the other songs including a fine rendition of Duke Ellington's "Everything but You" and Hanna's amusing arrangement of "I Hear You Knockin' but You Can't Come In."

influences:
◀◀ Bud Powell, Teddy Wilson, Art Tatum, Erroll Garner
▶▶ Craig Taborn

Garaud MacTaggart

Kip Hanrahan

Born 1937, in the Bronx, NY.

Kip Hanrahan plays percussion, writes poetry replete with sexual and political references, sings (sort of), and composes/arranges music. His biggest contribution to the world of jazz, however, is his ability to attract high-quality musicians of differing styles, toss them together in a recording studio, and emerge with interesting Latino/jazz hybrids. Hanrahan is a compiler who often does not even appear on songs released under his name, credited instead with the concept, conducting, or composing. Hanrahan gained many of the contacts he uses in his work through his early work as a technical assistant for the Jazz Composers Orchestra Association (JCOA), founded in part by Carla Bley and Michael Mantler, among others. He created his own label (American Clave) to release his music and the recordings of other people he admired like Milton Cardona, Astor Piazzola, and Paul Haines. The list of major performers who have contributed to Hanrahan's recording projects includes African guitarists, New Orleans R&B artists, cutting-edge jazz musicians, and a veritable who's who of the Latin percussion community in New York City.

what to buy: Overall, Hanrahan's second album, *Desire Develops an Edge* ⅃⅃⅃⅃ (American Clave, 1983, prod. Kip Hanrahan), is a good indicator of whether listeners will be beguiled by Hanrahan's skills as a compiler of musicians and musics or be outraged by his excesses. It starts out with the title tune, a percussion fest featuring Puntilla Orlando Rios, Milton Cardona, Tico Harry Sylvain, and Jerry Gonzalez. Then he piles on an Afro-Caribbean romp ("What Is This Dance Anyway"), which introduces Jack Bruce on bass and vocals with a horn section. *Conjure: Music for the Texts of Ishmael Reed* ⅃⅃⅃⅃ (American Clave, 1984, prod. Kip Hanrahan) is the first of two Hanrahan projects that pair the poetry of Ishmael Reed with music composed by a variety of musicians. The player/composers heard here include David Murray, Carla Bley, Steve Swallow, Allen Toussaint, Lester Bowie, and Taj Mahal. If not terribly representative, this is probably the most accessible of Hanrahan's albums.

what to buy next: *All Roads Are Made of the Flesh* ⅃⅃⅃ (American Clave, 1995, prod. Kip Hanrahan) is filled with chips left over from other Hanrahan projects. The Jelly Roll Morton tune "Buddy Bolden's Blues" is one of the few cover songs featured on a Hanrahan album, and it is a delight, if only to hear Allen Toussaint's piano playing blend with Don Pullen's electronic keyboard work. Jack Bruce is the vocalist and Charles Neville plays tenor sax.

the rest:
Coup de Tête 𝄠𝄠𝄠𝄠 (American Clave, 1981)
Vertical's Currency 𝄠𝄠𝄠𝄠 (American Clave, 1985)
Days and Nights of Blue Luck Inverted 𝄠𝄠𝄠 (American Clave, 1987)
Conjure: Cab Calloway Stands in for the Moon 𝄠𝄠𝄠 (American Clave, 1988)
Exotica 𝄠𝄠𝄠 (American Clave, 1992)
Tenderness 𝄠𝄠𝄠 (American Clave, 1993)
A Thousand Nights and a Night 𝄠𝄠𝄠 (American Clave, 1997)

worth searching for: Hanrahan released an EP on American Clave in 1986. *A Few Short Notes from the End Run* included two outrageous versions of one of his signature tunes, "The First and Last to Love Me." One was played by three bassists (Jack Bruce, Andy Gonzalez, and Steve Swallow) and two conga players (Giovanni Hidalgo and Milton Cardona) while the other was another percussion outing with Hidalgo, Cardona, and drummer Ignacio Berroa popping along behind Hanrahan's vocals.

influences:
◀◀ Machito, Mario Bauzá, Carla Bley
▶▶ David Byrne

Garaud MacTaggart

Fareed Haque

Born 1963, in Chicago, IL.

A gifted guitarist with a strong classical background, Fareed Haque hasn't recorded an album of his own that, strictly speaking, could be called jazz, though along with Indian music, blues, funk, European classical, and various folk musics, jazz is one of the elements he draws on in his musical amalgam. As a youth, he traveled widely with his parents (who are from Pakistan and Chile), soaking up the sounds in Pakistan and Iran, and listening to Flamenco guitar in Spain. He attended the jazz program at North Texas State University, and now teaches classical and jazz guitar at Northern Illinois University. Haque recorded his first album, *Voices Rising*, in 1989 on Sting's label Pangaea. He has toured with Joe Zawinul, worked with Von Freeman and Tito Puente, and recorded with Paquito D'Rivera, Joey Calderazzo, Renee Rosnes, Richie Cole, Dianne Reeves, and Javon Jackson. From a jazz standpoint, his three albums for Blue Note are a decidedly mixed bag.

what to buy: Fareed Haque plays classical, electric, and sitar guitars on *Opaque* 𝄠𝄠𝄠 (Blue Note, 1995, prod. Rob Eaton, Fareed Haque), an attractive session featuring Mark Walker on drums and percussion, Jonathan Paul on bass, and (on two tunes) Hamid Drake on tabla. Haque plays with considerable

warmth, moving with ease from the impressionistic, Oregon-ish title track to the classically oriented "Duet #2," to the Indian currents of "Tabriz." Despite Haque's considerable technique, the album occasionally lapses into light-weight, atmospheric passages that bog down the music's flow.

what to avoid: An unfortunate, high-concept album features Haque exploring the tunes of Crosby, Stills, and Nash, *Deja Vu* 𝄠𝄠 (Blue Note, 1997, prod. Fareed Haque, Carlos Villalobos). It contains the kind of music that torments you when some business you've called puts you on hold.

the rest:
Voices Rising 𝄠𝄠 (Pangaea, 1989)
Manresa 𝄠𝄠 (Pangaea, 1989)
Sacred Addiction 𝄠𝄠𝄠 (Blue Note, 1993)

worth searching for: Of the various straight-ahead albums he's played on, Haque is particularly effective on tenor saxophonist Javon Jackson's *For One Who Knows* 𝄠𝄠𝄠𝄠 (Blue Note, 1995, prod. Craig Street), a gorgeous session featuring Jacky Terrasson (piano), Peter Washington (bass), Billy Drummond (drums), and Cyro Baptiste (percussion). Haque's acoustic guitar provides perfect atmospheric touches on Brazilian-oriented material including Jobim's "Useless Landscape" and Baden Powell's "Formosa," and on Herbie Hancock's lovely ballad "Jane's Theme," though he also provides deft rhythmic accents on Jackson's "Notes in Three."

influences:
◀◀ John McLaughlin, Earl Klugh

Andrew Gilbert

Paul Hardcastle

Born December 10, 1957, in Chelsea, London, England.

Best known for the controversial single "19," which sold over 3.5 million copies worldwide, Paul Hardcastle is an accomplished keyboardist and producer who occasionally plays in the smooth jazz idiom. Hardcastle's music career began when he served as the keyboardist for the English dance groups Direct Drive and First Light in the early 1980s. In 1983 he formed his own label, Total Control, and scored his first solo hit, the instrumental "Rainforest." Hardcastle struck gold and platinum in 1985 with "19," which reached number one on several European charts and was a Top-15 single in the United States. During the late 1980s he produced for Ian Drury & Blockheads, Barry White, D-Train, and Five Star. Performing under his own name as leader of the Jazzmasters (not to be confused with

Slide Hampton's straight-ahead jazz band), Hardcastle's jazz career has been confined to some smooth jazz albums with lots of programmed rhythms. Although neither of his albums as leader is groundbreaking, nor particularly seductive, the two Jazzmasters' albums dominated the Contemporary Jazz and NAC charts. Hardcastle has sold close to 10 million records and will likely be a smooth jazz staple for some time.

what to buy: A two-CD retrospective of Hardcastle's career, *Cover to Cover* ✍✍✍ (JVC, 1997, prod. Paul Hardcastle) contains dance hits, smooth jazz selections, and a number of obscure songs previously unavailable in the United States. Some of his biggest hits, including "19," "Rainforest," and "King Tut," are here, as are some of the better tracks from his smooth jazz outings. The second CD contains cover tunes. This is the place to start if you are interested in Hardcastle.

what to avoid: *Kiss the Sky: Millennium Skyway* ✍ (JVC, 1994) offers dull smooth jazz with heavy vocal emphasis.

the rest:
Jazzmasters ✍✍ (JVC, 1993)
Hardcastle ✍✍ (JVC, 1994)
Jazzmasters 2 ✍✍ (JVC, 1995)
Hardcastle 2 ✍✍ (JVC, 1996)

Paul MacArthur

Wilbur Harden

Born 1925, in Birmingham, Alabama.

Now an obscure, semi-legendary figure, Wilbur Harden was one of the first to play jazz flugelhorn, and was a once-promising soloist and composer. He began playing professionally in the 1940s with R&B bands led by Roy Brown and Ivory Joe Williams. After playing with the U.S. Navy band, he moved to Detroit, where he replaced trombonist Curtis Fuller in Yusef Lateef's group in the spring of 1957. There, under the influence of Miles Davis's work with Gil Evans, Harden began playing the flugelhorn almost exclusively. He appeared on three albums with Lateef before recording with John Coltrane and leading his own sessions. Harden ceased playing in 1959 due to poor health, and has not recorded since. While his playing was lyrical and inventive, his sessions have remained in print largely due to the presence of players such as Coltrane and Tommy Flanagan.

what to buy: Harden's potential as a composer is revealed on *Mainstream 1958—The East Coast Jazz Scene* ✍✍✍ (Savoy, 1958, prod. Ozzie Cadena), including the standout Latin-esque

"E.F.F.P.H." His smooth flugelhorn is well-complimented by the explosive tenor of John Coltrane and pianist Tommy Flanagan's bop solos.

The title track on *Tanganyika Strut* ✍✍✍ (Savoy, 1958/1993, prod. Ozzie Cadena) chugs along at a bluesy medium tempo (somewhat reminiscent of Coltrane's "Blue Train") with nicely understated solos from Harden, trombonist Curtis Fuller, and Tommy Flanagan. Noteworthy is Harden's beautiful lead on the ballad "Once in a While."

the rest:
Jazz Way Out ✍✍✍ (Savoy, 1958/1992)
The King and I ✍✍✍ (Savoy, 1958/1993)

worth searching for: As a sideman with Coltrane, Harden plays some of his best solos on *The Stardust Sessions* ✍✍✍ (Prestige, 1975, prod. Bob Weinstock, Ralph Kaffel). Of particular interest is his economical phrasing on "I'm a Dreamer Aren't We All" and his bright trumpet solo on the upbeat "Spring Is Here."

influences:
◀◀ Miles Davis, Fats Navarro, Clifford Brown

Jeff Samoray and Nancy Ann Lee

Roy Hargrove

Born October 16, 1969, in Waco, TX.

Revered as one of the most ferocious "young lions," trumpeter Roy Hargrove is the closest thing to a Cinderella story that mainstream jazz has produced. At age 16 Hargrove was studying music at Booker T. Washington High School for the Visual and Performing Arts in Dallas, Texas, when trumpeter Wynton Marsalis visited and caught Hargrove playing with the school band. An impressed Marsalis invited the youngster to join him onstage at Fort Worth's Caravan of Dreams nightclub. The buzz from that performance led to a Berklee College of Music scholarship and an invitation to tour Europe with Frank Morgan. Signed to Novus Records at age 19, the soft-spoken, hard-blowing Texan moved to New York and recorded four solo albums for the now-defunct, RCA-distributed imprint, where he established himself as a riveting, rafter-rattling player on such albums as *Diamond in the Rough* and the live *Of Kindred Souls*. He joined the Verve roster in 1994, where he has created his most impressive work and showcased his versatility on ses-

Roy Hargrove (© Jack Vartoogian)

sions ranging from Cuban jazz (*Habana*) to a Charlie Parker tribute with labelmates Stephen Scott and Christian McBride (*Parker's Mood*). More important, he's matured into a loose, lyrical player who has learned that young lions can be just as effective when they purr as when they roar. And he hasn't even turned 30 yet.

what to buy: Recorded live with his quintet, *Of Kindred Souls* ♫♫♫ (Novus, 1993, prod. Larry Clothier, Roy Hargrove) is Hargrove's Novus swan song but also a stunning showcase of the poise and power he developed during his tenure there. *With the Tenors of Our Time* ♫♫♫ (Verve, 1994, prod. Larry Clothier, Roy Hargrove)—a collaboration with such heroes as Stanley Turrentine and Joe Henderson and peers Branford Marsalis and Joshua Redman—finds Hargrove continuing to explore the keen balance between intensity and intimacy, coolness and warmth. His most impressive statements are made on such quiet numbers as the haunting, Miles-like "When We Were One" and a lovely reading of "Never Let Me Go."

what to buy next: Inspired by Dizzy Gillespie's detours into Afro-Cuban jazz, *Habana* ♫♫♫ (Verve, 1997, prod. Larry Clothier, Roy Hargrove) teams Hargrove with some of Cuba's top players for a feverish, festive session that stands as a testament to his sense of adventure and a sign of true leadership—the willingness to share the spotlight.

what to avoid: *Approaching Standards* ♫♫♫ (Novus, 1994, prod. Larry Clothier, Roy Hargrove) is a predictable contract-fulfilling compilation of standards drawn from his four Novus albums.

the rest:
Diamond in the Rough ♫♫♫ (Novus, 1990)
Public Eye ♫♫♫ (Novus, 1991)
(With Antonio Hart) *Tokyo Sessions* ♫♫♫ (Novus, 1992)
The Vibe ♫♫♫ (Novus, 1992)
Family ♫♫♫♫ (Verve, 1995)
(With Christian McBride and Stephen Scott) *Parker's Mood* ♫♫♫♫ (Verve, 1995)

worth searching for: Recorded live at the JVC Newport Jazz Festival and the Festival de Jazz de Vitoria in Spain in 1991, *Jazz Futures* ♫♫♫ (Novus, 1993, prod. Larry Clothier) collects the then-developing talents of Hargrove, Marlon Jordan, Mark Whitfield, Benny Green, Christian McBride, and others on one stage. Hargrove gets his showcases on his own swinging "Public Eye" and the striking "You Don't Know What Love Is."

influences:
◀◀ Fats Navarro, Dizzy Gillespie, Wynton Marsalis

David Okamoto

Everette Harp
Born August 17, 1961, in Houston, TX.

Born the youngest of eight kids in Houston, Texas, saxophonist Everette Harp started out memorizing solos by bluesy saxophonists such as Stanley Turrentine, Hank Crawford, and Grover Washington Jr. Though he graduated from the well-known North Texas State University and performed in the Houston area between 1981 and 1988, Harp's career didn't take off until 1988, when he moved to Los Angeles. He snared a gig backing Teena Marie, followed by high-profile tours with Anita Baker, Kenny Loggins, and Sheena Easton. He also toured with Rachelle Ferrell in 1992. Harp is definitely a "quiet storm," a contemporary jazz stylist who draws inspiration from gospel and R&B and rarely improvises on his current recordings.

what to buy: Harp's first solo album, *Everette Harp* ♫♫♫ (Capitol, 1992, prod. George Duke), recorded between tours with Duke and Marcus Miller, features R&B-drenched, contemporary jazz that sells records. While Harp plays alto and soprano saxophone on the 13 selections, there's not much that's fresh. With a growing public profile that included a weekly stint with "The Posse" on *The Arsenio Hall Show,* and a duet with President Bill Clinton during his 1993 inauguration celebration, Harp found a little more success with his sophomore album *Common Ground* ♫♫♫ (Blue Note, 1994), a collection of 13 tunes, mostly pop/R&B originals with strong dance beats. Branford Marsalis appears on one track.

what to avoid: Harp's latest and most ambitious effort, a recreation of Marvin Gaye's classic album *What's Going On* woof! (Blue Note, 1997), is a transparent attempt to court listeners by providing an album-length instrumental cover (nine tunes) of one of the best-loved R&B records ever. Not even appearances by Kenny Loggins, Howard Hewitt, and Yolanda Adams could save this one.

influences:
◀◀ Kenny G, David Sanborn

Eric Deggans

Billy Harper
Born January 17, 1943 in Houston, TX.

Billy Harper is a distinctive tenor saxophonist and a masterful composer. Writing vocally or at the piano rather than on saxophone, he strongly roots his hypnotic tunes in gospel. As a soloist, Harper is versatile yet always distinctive, relating to Coltrane (via a parallel path, he points out) but with his own voice. After achieving success in college in Texas, his native state and a heralded wellspring for great tenormen, Harper moved to New York in 1966. He scuffled around for awhile, then found work as a sideman—with his tunes often featured—with Elvin Jones, Lee Morgan, Art Blakey's Jazz Messengers, and Max Roach, among others, plus the big bands of Gil Evans, Randy Weston, McCoy Tyner, and Thad Jones/Mel Lewis. Ironically, his best-known tune, "Priestess," achieved widest dissemination on an Evans album of that title where alto saxophonists David Sanborn and Arthur Blythe, not Harper (who by then had left the group), were the soloists. It's a mystery why Harper is not better known, or for that matter properly appreciated by record companies. Though he has released 16 albums as a leader, only two—*Capra Black* in 1973 and 1995's *Somalia*—have come out on U.S. labels. This is despite a busy recording career in the 1970s, especially on Japanese labels, reflecting his popularity with that country's jazz audience. Harper was just as active in the 1980s, but frequent and far-flung tours kept him out of the studio for most of that decade. A series of live albums on SteepleChase reintroduced him to the record-buying public in the 1990s.

what to buy: Harper's long-standing quintet with near-legendary trumpeter Eddie Henderson, Tyneresque pianist Francesca Tanksley, bassist Louie Spears, and super-tight drummer Newman T. Baker is a thrilling and cohesive unit in concert. A series of albums documenting the group's 1991 tour is a superb introduction to their talents and Harper's repertoire and shows them really stretching out on the material. *Live on Tour in the Far East, Volume 1* 🎵🎵🎵🎵 (SteepleChase, 1992, prod. Nils Winther) has a version of Coltrane's "Countdown." *Live on Tour in the Far East, Volume 2* 🎵🎵🎵🎵 (SteepleChase, 1993, prod. Nils Winther) gives a rare glimpse of Harper playing a standard—"My Funny Valentine," no less—and an elaborate "Priestess." *Live on Tour in the Far East, Volume 3* 🎵🎵🎵🎵 (SteepleChase, 1995, prod. Nils Winther) consists of just three monumental excursions on the Harper classics "Soran Bushi B.H." (his adaptation of a Japanese folk song), "Call of the Wild and Peaceful Heart," and the dramatic "Cry of Hunger."

what to buy next: *In Europe* 🎵🎵🎵🎵 (Soul Note, 1979, prod. Giovanni Bonandrini) contains Harper's most memorable composition, the great "Priestess," on which pianist Fred Hersch's relative understatement offers a highly effective foil to the dual frontline horns of Harper and trumpeter Everett Hollins. Imbued with modal and gospel feeling, "Calvary" and the epic "Illumination" also have a timelessness and equilibrium to them, with fervid solos and nice arranging touches. Harper's only release currently available from a domestic label, *Somalia* 🎵🎵🎵

R OY H ARGROVE
(WITH J ACKIE M C L EAN)

song "Rhythm of the Earth"
album Rhythm of the Earth
(Antilles, 1992)

instrument Trumpet

Monster Solo

(Evidence, 1995, prod. Billy Harper, Mark Rappaport) typifies his best qualities: compelling tunes built around insistent vamps and memorable melodies, with exciting solos by Henderson, Tanksley, and of course the leader. The format stands out from his other work: it's a two-drummer sextet. Typically, the music starts with an introduction—sometimes fanfare-like—reaches the main theme, and then goes into extensive solo development that's more than just a string of choruses. *Black Saint* 🎵🎵🎵 (Black Saint, 1975, prod. Giacomo Pellicciotti) was the Black Saint label's very first album and consists of three classic Harper compositions. The leader's gospel-inflected modal melodies and his Coltrane-esque tenor sax sound are deployed in his favorite format, the quintet with trumpet, with Virgil Jones holding up his share of the frontline with élan. Drummer Malcom Pinson propels the music forward with roiling, Elvin Jones–like fervor, and bassist David Friesen embroiders the bottom. "Dance, Eternal Spirits, Dance" is a modal classic, "Croquet Ballet" is a graceful yet intense waltz, and the 21-plus minute "Call of the Wild and Peaceful Heart" moves through a range of exhilarating moods.

what to avoid: *Capra Black* ♫♫ (Strata East, 1973/Bellaphon, 1993, prod. Billy Harper) is the first and weakest of Harper's albums, not because the material is particularly bad—though he soon became a more assured composer—but because the production is a bit too much of its time to inspire repeat listening outside of the context of Harper's entire body of work. Fans will eventually want to acquire it, however, for some tunes he rarely returned to and for the all-star cast, including George Cables, Reggie Workman, Julian Priester, Billy Cobham, and Elvin Jones.

the rest:
(With Jon Faddis) *Jon & Billy* ♫♫♫ (1974/Evidence, 1993)
The Awakening ♫♫♫ (Marge, 1979)
Trying to Make Heaven My Home ♫♫♫♫ (MPS, 1979)
The Believer ♫♫♫♫ (Baystate, 1980)
Destiny Is Yours ♫♫♫♫ (SteepleChase, 1990)
If Our Hearts Could Only See ♫♫♫♫ (DIW, 1997)

worth searching for: Three classic Japanese releases, all with Hollins on trumpet but long unavailable in the United States, can be obtained on cassette from Harper himself (along with some other albums listed above). *Love on the Sudan* ♫♫♫♫ (Denon, 1977, prod. Yoshio Ozawa) has the first appearance of "Priestess"; *Soran Bushi-B.H.* ♫♫♫♫ (Denon, 1978, prod. Yoshio Ozawa) is a must-own for the title track; *Knowledge of Self* ♫♫♫♫ (Denon, 1979, prod. Yoshio Ozawa) is notable for the presence of Kenny Barron on piano. For information, fax (212) 627-7403.

influences:
◄◄ John Coltrane
►► Mark Masters

Steve Holtje

Tom Harrell

Born June 16, 1946, in Urbana, IL.

In the last two decades, Tom Harrell has emerged as one of the most exciting trumpeters in jazz, a highly lyrical, dazzlingly fluent improviser who is also one of his generation's best composers. Harrell has achieved all this while dealing with schizophrenia. Medication gives him a withdrawn, inwardly focused appearance on stage, but when he solos, he's clearly deeply engaged with his band mates. Raised in the San Francisco area, Harrell started on trumpet at age eight and began working at parties and dances in his early teens. He landed his first important job with Woody Herman (1970–71), then put in a short stint with Jon Hendricks before hooking up for an extended stay with

Horace Silver (1973–77). Harrell began writing seriously in the mid-'70s, and his association with bassist Sam Jones's 12-piece band gave him the opportunity to arrange for a large ensemble. Before joining the Phil Woods Quintet for a long stay (1983–89), Harrell worked with Lionel Hampton, Mel Lewis, Cecil Payne, Bill Evans, George Russell, and Lee Konitz's nonet. Harrell has made albums for Pinnacle, Blackhawk, Criss Cross, and SteepleChase, and since leaving Woods has recorded a series of consistently excellent sessions for Contemporary and Chesky. His tunes have been recorded by Jim Hall, Harold Land, Ronnie Cuber, and Woods, among others.

what to buy: A perfect introduction to the radiant world of Harrell, *Visions* ♫♫♫♫ (Contemporary, 1991, prod. Bill Goodwin) features pieces recorded between 1987–90, played by a series of thrilling small groups with such fellow leading improvisers as Joe Lovano and Bob Berg. But the spotlight here is on Harrell's beautiful trumpet work and finely crafted tunes, which balance melodic inventiveness with harmonic sophistication. *Form* ♫♫♫♫ (Contemporary, 1990, prod. Bill Goodwin) is what great jazz is all about. Harrell, who composed all the music (except "For Heaven's Sake," a CD bonus track), is an artist fully capable expressing his personal vision through his writing and his playing. And his is an expansive vision, best represented here with the 12-minute opus "January Spring," a piece full of stunning vistas and unexpected homages to the giants who inspired him. A smoking sextet session, *Upswing* ♫♫♫♫ (Chesky, 1993, prod. Steve Kaiser, Bill Goodwin) features seven Harrell tunes and Ornette Coleman's classic "Blue Connotation." Highlights include the session's only ballad, "Gratitude," which features a haunting Joe Lovano solo and the densely textured, rhythmically combustible closer, "Tune-a-Tune."

what to buy next: Harrell's first major-label album, *Stories* ♫♫♫♫ (Contemporary, 1988, prod. Bill Goodwin) finds him in a Miles mood. Whether a ballad such as the lovely "Song Flower," or the Spanish-tinged theme "The Water's Edge," Harrell's music is consistently challenging and emotionally engaging. *Sail Away* ♫♫♫♫ (Contemporary, 1989, prod. Bill Goodwin) features an all-Harrell program. There are many stunning moments, from the gorgeous voicings on the "Dancing Trees" to Liebman's scorching outside solo on "Dream in June."

best of the rest:
Play of Light ♫♫♫♫ (Blackhawk, 1982)
Open Air ♫♫♫♫ (SteepleChase, 1986)
Passages ♫♫♫♫ (Chesky, 1993)

worth searching for: With its diverse selection of material, *Moon Alley* 𝄞𝄞𝄞𝄞 (Criss Cross, 1986, prod. Gerry Teekens) captures Harrell in a variety of moods, from the searing "Blues in Six" and the Latin-flavored "Rapture" to "Moon Alley," a delicate, haunting theme destined to become a standard.

influences:

◄◄ Miles Davis, Freddie Hubbard, Kenny Dorham, Clifford Brown, Blue Mitchell

Andrew Gilbert

Allan Harris

Born April 4, 1958, in Brooklyn, NY.

Allan Harris is an emerging jazz vocalist who has made two recordings for the German label MONS. As a youngster in Brooklyn, Harris grew up surrounded by music. His mother was a classically trained pianist and his aunt sang opera. He graduated from the School of the Performing Arts, and after some classical guitar studies with one of New York's top teachers, Harris moved at age 16 to Pittsburgh where he played electric guitar in some rock bands before graduating from California State College in Pittsburgh with a B.S. in biology. Lured by the promise of musical work, he moved to Atlanta in the early 1980s. When his band mate left town, Harris began working as a solo act, singing and playing guitar. The more he sang, the more his audiences liked it, and the more they appreciated him, the further he dug into the "American songbook," harvesting classics by Cole Porter, Jerome Kern, Rodgers and Hart, the Gershwins, and other composers. Harris returned to Brooklyn in 1990, and since then has been performing in New York's best venues as well as recording two albums as leader. He expects to release a tribute album featuring the music of Billy Strayhorn in 1998.

what to buy: Vocalist Harris sings loose and easy on *It's a Wonderful World* 𝄞𝄞𝄞𝄞 (MONS, 1995, prod. Thilo Berg, Alfred Lauer), a collection of 14 ballads and swingers performed with all-star backing from Benny Green (piano), Mark Whitfield (guitar), Ray Brown (bass), and Jeff Hamilton (drums), with Claudio Roditi (trumpet, flugelhorn) and Jeff Varner (French horn) guesting on some tracks. It's a pleasant session as Harris glides and soars through a note-bending, uptempo rendition of "I'll Remember April," gets gritty with the bluesy "Black Coffee Blues," and laments laudably on "Everything Happens to Me," and other sincere readings. This is a singer who knows how to craft a tune and has the range and technique to carry it off. Can

this kid from Brooklyn be the next great male crooner? He's been anointed by Tony Bennett, but time will tell.

what to buy next: On Harris's second recording for the German label, *Here Comes Allan Harris* 𝄞𝄞𝄞𝄞 (MONS, 1997, prod. Thilo Berg), the singer is backed by the Holland-based, 54-piece Metropole Orchestra led by Rob Pronk, as he delivers a lush collection of 15 time-honored jazz classics. Harris is a first-class crooner, warbling straight-up lyrics of classics from the American songbook with heart-warming elegance. Sometimes he sounds like Bennett ("I'm Old Fashioned"), other times he sounds exactly like Nat King Cole ("Smoke Gets in Your Eyes"). The orchestra plays fabulous arrangements with classy verve that brings out the best in Harris, who's at gracious ease fronting this full studio orchestra with strings.

influences:

◄◄ Tony Bennett, Nat "King" Cole, Frank Sinatra, Mel Tormé

Nancy Ann Lee

Barry Harris

Born December 15, 1929, in Detroit, MI.

A bebop-oriented pianist strongly grounded in theory and practice, Barry Harris had a reputation amongst national jazz players even before he left Detroit in 1960. When artists arrived to play clubs like the Blue Bird or the Rouge Lounge, Harris was often the house pianist. He resisted offers to leave town, teaching theory to other local musicians and working with area talents like Thad Jones and Billy Mitchell before finally accepting an opportunity to work with the Cannonball Adderley Quintet (replacing Bobby Timmons). Soon he became an in-demand sessioneer and sideman for Yusef Lateef, Coleman Hawkins, Lee Morgan, Hank Mobley, and Dexter Gordon. Harris is a well-known educator, having started the Jazz Cultural Center in New York City in 1982 as a way for young aspiring musicians to meet active performers, part of the reason he received a Jazz Masters Award from the National Endowment for the Arts in 1989. Currently teaching, writing and playing in New York City, he still goes out on tours, but after his stroke in 1993 he has cut back on what was an extensive performance regime.

what to buy: Although *The Bird of Red and Gold* 𝄞𝄞𝄞𝄞 (Xanadu, 1989, prod. Don Schlitten) is filled with solo piano work, it even features his first recorded vocal on the title tune. Harris's rendition of "Body and Soul" makes this old chestnut live again. "Tea for Two" has a Monkish skew to it, and Monk's "Pannonica" nods to the composer as Harris makes it his own.

A live date, *At the Jazz Workshop* ♫♫♫ (OJC, 1960, prod. Orrin Keepnews) offers a picture of Harris's pianistic prowess from 1960, just months after he joined the Cannonball Adderley Quintet. He continually emphasizes the graceful side of bop for a deceptively easy-sounding aural cruise, even at top speed. *Live at Maybeck Recital Hall, Volume 12* ♫♫♫ (Concord Jazz, 1991, prod. Carl E. Jefferson, Nick Phillips) is a Maybeck recital from back in the days when the venue was just beginning to be the focus of solo piano mania. Harris is able to rise to the occasion with a marvelous show of pianistic artistry, not just note spinning but real music. All of the tunes are standards although Harris's personal muses, Charlie Parker and Bud Powell, are represented by "Parker's Mood" and "I'll Keep Loving You."

what to buy next: Despite the title, *Chasin' the Bird* ♫♫♫ (OJC, 1962, prod. Orrin Keepnews) is not a feast of Charlie Parker songs. Harris plays the title tune plus Monk's "'Round Midnight" and three originals. As one of bop's main practitioners (if not an innovator) Harris has been, and always will be, "Chasin' the Bird." On *Preminado* ♫♫♫ (OJC, 1961, prod. Orrin Keepnews) Elvin Jones gives fellow Michigander Harris a little postbop, modernistic push from behind the drum kit. Bassist Joe Benjamin does a solid job, not getting in the way as Harris and Jones spark each other to some interesting performances.

the rest:
Luminescence ♫♫♫ (OJC, 1967)
(With Charles Davis) *Reflections* ♫♫♫ (Red, 1992)
(With Kenny Barron) *Confirmation* ♫♫ (Candid, 1992)
Live at "DUG" ♫♫♫ (Enja, 1997)

influences:
◄◄ Bud Powell, Charlie Parker, Art Tatum, Thelonious Monk

Garaud MacTaggart

Beaver Harris

Born William Godvin Harris, April 20, 1936, in Pittsburgh, PA. Died December 22, 1991, in New York, NY.

A significant drummer of the 1960s avant-garde, Beaver Harris was among the first musicians of his generation to acknowledge the historical continuities in jazz and make music accordingly. His own band, the 360 Degree Experience, played in a variety of jazz idioms—"from ragtime to no time," as the title of their first album put it—with equal fluency and conviction. Harris played drums from the age of 20 but also spent several years playing baseball in the Negro Leagues. In 1963, after being discharged from the army, he moved to New York, where he worked with Sonny Rollins (1965), Roswell

Rudd (1966), Gato Barbieri (1969–70), Thelonious Monk (1970), and others. In 1966 he began a long association with Archie Shepp, appearing on virtually all of the saxophonist's important albums through the mid-'70s. He also worked with Albert Ayler, appearing on his last Impulse! recordings and touring Europe with him in 1966. In the '70s he played frequently at Rudd's New York club, St. James Infirmary, accompanying Chet Baker, Charlie Rouse, Al Cohn, Lee Konitz, and others, and performed with Cecil Taylor (1977), Steve Lacy (on *Trickles*), and with guitarist Larry Coryell in the mid-'80s. Harris integrated all his wide stylistic skills in the conceptually daring 360 Degree Experience, a collective ensemble he co-founded with trombonist Grachan Moncur III and pianist Dave Burrell in 1968. The band routinely covered a variety of jazz idioms and augmented the standard jazz rhythm section with African and Caribbean percussion and non-Western instruments such as the sitar. Personnel varied over the years, with pianist Don Pullen serving as co-leader in the mid-'80s. Saxophonists Hamiett Bluiett, Ricky Ford, and Ken McIntyre were frequent members, as were steel drummer Francis Haynes and bassists Cameron Brown, Ron Carter, and Buster Williams. Sadly, most of the group's important albums, including their ground-breaking debut *From Ragtime to No Time* with Doc Cheatham on the ragtime tracks, are out of print. Harris was a muscular, propulsive drummer. His great independence of limb enabled him to play polyrhythms and ornate, detailed free pulses in avant-garde settings. He was also a highly interactive bebop percussionist. His splash cymbal work was especially bright and intricate. At home in virtually the entire jazz tradition, he is a surprisingly overlooked figure in jazz drumming of the recent past.

what to buy: The best all-around representation of the 360 Degree Music Experience still in print, *In:Sanity* ♫♫♫ (Black Saint, 1976, prod. Giovanni Bonandrini) also happens to be one of their best albums. Typically wide ranging, it includes one certified classic: "Sahara," in which a steel pan orchestra meets collective jazz improvisation.

what to buy next: *Beautiful Africa* ♫♫♫ (Soul Note, 1979, prod. Giovanni Bonandrini) is a solid session with fine soloing from Moncur and multi-reed player Ken McIntyre.

the rest:
From Ragtime to No Time ♫♫♫ (360, 1975, prod. Timothy Marquand)

worth searching for: *A Well-Kept Secret* ♫♫♫ (Shemp, 1985) was one of the great incarnations of the 360 Degree Experience featuring pianist Pullen and saxophonists Bluiett and Ford, and it makes a strong case for Harris's belief in the continuity of African American musics. The band moves effortlessly from bop to free and back with strong Afro-Caribbean undercurrents provided by steel-pan virtuoso Haynes.

influences:

◀◀ Kenny Clarke, Max Roach, Milford Graves

▶▶ Mike Sarin, Susie Ibarra

Ed Hazell

Bill Harris

Born Willard Palmer Harris, October 28, 1916, in Philadelphia, PA. Died August 21, 1973, in Hallandale, FL.

Harris, the most respected trombonist of the generation immediately preceding the beboppers, is most noted for his several tenures in the Woody Herman big band in the 1940s and 1950s, though he also recorded with Benny Goodman, Charlie Parker, Nat "King" Cole, Lennie Tristano, Chico O'Farrill, Dizzy Gillespie, Benny Carter, and others. J.J. Johnson and other trombonists who followed him often seemed to be obsessed by the quest for agility equal to valve instruments; unlike them, Harris, technically gifted as he was, never abjured the slide-oriented inflections of his instrument.

what's available: *Bill Harris and Friends* ♫♫♫ (Fantasy, 1957/1983/1992) is the only Harris album currently available, but would probably be the top recommendation under any circumstances. It's a quintet session with Ben Webster (tenor sax), Jimmy Rowles (piano), Red Mitchell (bass), and Stan Levey (drums). The interaction between the two horns is warmly affectionate and good-humored, small-group swing at its finest.

influences:

◀◀ Jack Teagarden, J.C. Higginbotham, Vic Dickenson, Lawrence Brown

▶▶ Roswell Rudd

Walter Faber

Craig Harris

Born September 10, 1953, in Hempstead, NY.

Trombonist Craig Harris began his professional career straight out of college, joining the Sun Ra Arkestra in 1976. Harris's later forays into rhythm and blues and funk were perhaps foreshadowed in his early Sun Ra days, when the late bandleader would routinely interweave popular music

and soaring free improvisational solos by bandmembers. Next, Harris played for two years with South African pianist Abdullah Ibrahim. Again, Harris played in a context that strongly emphasized popular melodies with inventive harmonic soloing. Harris's entry in the 1980s into the New York scene was facilitated by stints with numerous veterans of the late-1960s and early-1970s avant-garde: Lester Bowie, Henry Threadgill, and David Murray, among others. With strong musical values that leaned equally towards urban popular music and more rarefied "loft" jazz elements, Harris ventured into a career as a bandleader with two collaborative groups: the jazz-funk ensemble Tailgater's Tales and a James Brown tribute band, Cold Sweat (all the releases of both groups were on JMT and are no longer in print). A more straightforwardly jazz quintet also emerged, with tenor saxist George Adams adding another layer of funky but avant-garde jazz to the band's mix. He also recorded important work in a cooperative group co-led by Art Ensemble of Chicago members Joseph Jarman and Don Moye.

what's available: *Black Bone* ♫♫♫ (Soul Note, 1984, prod. Giovanni Bonandrini) is by an all-star quintet, with Harris joined by George Adams (tenor sax), Donald Smith (piano), Fred Hopkins (bass), and Charli Persip (drums) on a program of five of the trombonist's compositions. *F-Stops* ♫♫♫ (Soul Note, 1994, prod. Craig Harris, Bruce Purse) welds Afro-Cuban–inspired rhythms to structures that build in fervor ("Say Essay") or ebb and flow (the title series). In Harris's compositions, solos rise organically from roiling atmospheres tinged with splashes of synthesizer and electric guitar. Harris shares the frontline with John Stubblefield (tenor sax) and Hamiet Bluiett (baritone sax).

worth searching for: *Tributes* ♫♫♫ (O.T.C., 1985, prod. Jim Silverman) once again shows Harris's ability to assemble superb groups; this one includes Vincent Chauncey (French horn), Olu Dara (cornet, harmonica, African trumpet), Junior Vega (trumpet), Dave Holland (bass), and drummers Billy Higgins and Don Moye. The tributes of the title are to Harris's relatives, and are only a fraction of the album's six compositions, all originals. Harris's compositional abilities were already considerable at this point, and the playing is also fine.

influences:

◀◀ Kid Ory, Jimmy Knepper, Roswell Rudd, Grachan Moncur III, Fred Wesley

▶▶ Ray Anderson

Andrew Bartlett and Steve Holtje

Eddie Harris

Born October 20, 1934, in Chicago, IL. Died November 5, 1996.

Eddie Harris was a jazz iconoclast of the first order. Unafraid to challenge conventions, he was often dismissed by critics as a mere showman. In reality, he was a pioneer, among the first to effectively utilize rock rhythms, incorporate electronic effects, and create new instruments. As a child, Harris studied piano with a cousin and sang with choirs and gospel groups in church. In high school he played vibes, clarinet, and tenor sax. He made his professional debut subbing for Gene Ammons's pianist in his early 20s. He got such a positive response that he was encouraged to pursue music as a career. After touring Europe as a member of the 7th Army Symphony Orchestra, Harris began his music career in earnest and soon experienced unprecedented success by jazz standards; in 1960 his version of "Exodus" became a million-selling Top 40 hit. By 1965 he was recording with Atlantic, where his funky approach to jazz reaped more benefits. In 1966 Miles Davis recorded Harris's "Freedom Jazz Dance" and brought the song into the standard jazz repertoire; in 1968 Harris reached the pop charts once again with "Listen Here." This overwhelming popularity tainted his reputation among jazz purists and critics. Throughout the '60s he continued to experiment with rock rhythms and electronics and easily absorbed the ongoing developments as well. His music even reflects the influence of John Coltrane with his use of freer structures and quartal melodies and harmonies. In 1969 Harris had two more moderate hits, "Cold Duck Time" and "Compared to What," with Les McCann. At the 1970 Newport Jazz Festival he unveiled his unusual innovation: a trumpet played with a reed mouthpiece. He patented the idea, but it never caught on. His work continued to become more commercial and electronic through the rest of the '70s. Unfortunately, it often descended into buffoonery and parody. By the '80s, Harris had begun to move back to more straight-ahead jazz. He put aside the comedy and recorded several excellent jazz albums for a variety of labels. Throughout his career his music retained the funky and soulful sound that was his trademark. Recent reissues have helped to repair Harris's tarnished reputation and reveal his profound impact. He was a masterful player who easily improvised in the upper range of the saxophone, provided bass counterpoint to his own solos, and was a popular composer and an innovator of electronics, utilizing Veritone and echoplex effects.

what to buy: *Electrifying Eddie Harris/Plug Me In* 🎵🎵🎵🎵 (Rhino, 1993, prod. Arif Mardin, Joel Dorn) features the premiere of the veritone and electronic sax. Occasionally, it feels as though Harris is pushing too hard. *The In Sound/Mean Greens* 🎵🎵🎵🎵 (Rhino, 1993, prod. Nesuhi Ertegun, Arif Mardin) is a loping and swinging album. Harris flaunts his altissimo abilities on "It Was a Very Good Year." "Yeah Yeah Yeah" is a terrific Sonny Rollins-style calypso. Also of interest is Harris's shorter, first recording of "Listen Here." *Swiss Movement—Montreux 30th Anniversary Edition* 🎵🎵🎵🎵 (Rhino, 1969) contains plenty of great music plus the hits "Compared to What" and "Cold Duck Time." Groovy, funky jazz at its best. *Artist's Choice: The Eddie Harris Anthology* 🎵🎵🎵🎵🎵 (Rhino, 1994, prod. various) collects the best from his 16 albums, many still out of print, on two discs. Highlights include "1974 Blues" and Harris's version of "Giant Steps."

what to buy next: *All the Way Live* 🎵🎵🎵 (Milestone, 1981, prod. Todd Barkan) is not quite as sublime as the Montreux session, but it is rewarding. "Eight Counts for Rita" is typically groovy Eddie Harris. One has to overlook a few technical liabilities, like a police radio that feeds through the amplification, to get to the music. The first and only collaboration with Jimmy Smith is worth having.

what to avoid: *Bad Luck Is All I Have* **woof!** (Atlantic, 1975) is self-indulgent and clowning. Mostly R&B-based, it covers bland, predictable, familiar territory.

the rest:
Exodus to Jazz 🎵🎵🎵 (Vee-Jay, 1961)
Mighty Like a Rose 🎵🎵🎵 (Vee-Jay, 1961)
Eddie Harris Goes to the Movies 🎵🎵 (Vee-Jay, 1962)
Lost Album Plus the Better Half 🎵🎵🎵 (Vee-Jay, 1962)
Best of Eddie Harris 🎵🎵🎵🎵 (Atlantic, 1965)
Tale of Two Cities 🎵🎵 (Night, 1978)
Steps Up 🎵🎵🎵 (SteepleChase, 1981)
There Was a Time (Echo of Harlem) 🎵🎵 (Enja, 1990)
For You, for Me, for Everyone 🎵🎵 (SteepleChase, 1991)
Funk Project: Listen Here! 🎵🎵🎵 (Enja, 1994)
Vexatious Progressions 🎵🎵🎵 (Flying Heart, 1995)
Dancing by a Rainbow 🎵🎵🎵 (Enja, 1996)
Freedom Jazz Dance 🎵🎵 (Music Master, 1997)
Jazz Dance 🎵🎵🎵 (Jazzfest, 1997)

worth searching for: *Silver Cycles* 🎵🎵🎵🎵 (Atlantic, 1968, prod. Arif Mardin, Joel Dorn) is a brilliantly eclectic album that probably confused fans of "Listen Here." "Free at Last" is familiar Latin/funk, but "1974 Blues" is big band, strings, and choir. "Smoke Signals" is spacey and echoplex-filled, followed by the title cut, "Silver Cycles," an *a cappella* electric-saxophone hymn.

influences:

◀◀ Miles Davis, Milt Jackson, Stan Getz, Charlie Parker, Clifford Brown, Sonny Rollins, John Coltrane

▶▶ George Lewis

James Eason

Gene Harris

Born Eugene Harris, September 1, 1933, in Benton Harbor, MI.

While his simple, soul-driven piano style will never make him a superstar, Gene Harris remains one of the most genial of jazzmen. With his group the Three Sounds and on his own records, he plays an easily digestible, post-bop version of the blues that is always popular and entertaining. Inspired by the classic boogie-woogie players, Harris taught himself piano as a child; while serving in the military he belonged to an Army band through 1954. Two years later, as a civilian, he hooked up with bassist Andy Simpkins and childhood friend drummer Bill Dowdy to form the blues-oriented trio Three Sounds (after a short run as the Four Sounds, with a rotating cast of tenor saxophonists). After playing around the Midwest, they relocated to New York in 1958, incorporated jazz standards and show tunes, and began recording for Blue Note. They became a big hit on the Manhattan supper-club circuit, and worked consistently throughout the early '60s. Though Dowdy and Simpkins left the group later that decade, Harris continued to perform under the Three Sounds name with a variety of other players, most regularly with drummer Carl Burnett, but by the '70s their style had mutated into more contemporary, non-jazz sounds. Harris left the New York high-life for laid-back Boise, Idaho, in 1977, until bassist Ray Brown coaxed him to return to full-time jazz performance in the early '80s. In addition to playing in Brown's trio, Harris participated in a number of festival bands and eventually returned to leading his own groups. He has successfully returned to the straight acoustic style of his early days, with forays into blues and even gospel.

what to buy: *The Best of the Three Sounds* ♫♫♫♪ (Blue Note, 1993, prod. Alfred Lion) is a great sampler from Harris's most fruitful period, with the original Three Sounds, recorded between 1958–62; "Willow Weep for Me" may well be Harris's most lyrical moment. *The Gene Harris Trio Plus One* ♫♫♫♫ (Concord, 1986, prod. Ray Brown, Bennett Rubin), the best of Harris's post-Three Sounds records, is aided by the presence of rock-solid bassist Ray Brown and the "plus one" of the title, tenor great Stanley Turrentine.

what to buy next: *The Three Sounds* ♫♫♫♫ (Blue Note, 1958, prod. Alfred Lion) and *The Three Sounds: Babes Blues* ♫♫♫♫ (Blue Note, 1962, prod. Alfred Lion) are the only other Three Sounds sessions available on CD, both filled with soulful doses of Harris's piano.

best of the rest:

(With the Three Sounds) *Good Deal* ♫♫♫♪ (Blue Note, 1959)
(With the Three Sounds) *Feelin Good* ♫♫♫♪ (Blue Note, 1960)
(With the Three Sounds) *Moods* ♫♫♫♫ (Blue Note, 1960)
(With the Three Sounds) *It Just Has to Be* ♫♫♫♫ (Blue Note, 1961)
(With the Three Sounds) *Here We Come* ♫♫♫♪ (Blue Note, 1961)
(With the Three Sounds) *Hey There* ♫♫♫ (Blue Note, 1961)
(With the Three Sounds) *Black Orchids* ♫♫♫ (Blue Note, 1962)
(With the Three Sounds) *Jazz on Broadway* ♫♫♫♪ (Mercury, 1963)
(With the Three Sounds) *Vibrations* ♫♫♫ (Blue Note, 1966)
(With the Three Sounds) *Coldwater Flat* ♫♫♫ (Blue Note, 1968)
(With the Three Sounds) *Elegant Soul* ♫♫♫ (Blue Note, 1968)
(With the Three Sounds) *Live at the It Club* ♫♫♫ (Blue Note, 1970/1996)
Yesterday, Today, Tomorrow ♫♫♪ (Blue Note, 1973)
Astral Signal ♫♫♫ (Blue Note, 1974)
Hot Lips ♫♫ (JAM, 1982)
Live at Otter Crest ♫♫♪ (Bosco, 1983)
Listen Here ♫♫♫♪ (Concord, 1989)
(With Scott Hamilton) *At Last* ♫♫♫♫ (Concord, 1990)
Black and Blue ♫♫♫ (Concord, 1991)
A Little Piece of Heaven ♫♫♫♪ (Concord, 1993)
(With Jack McDuff) *In His Hands* ♫♫♫♫ (Concord, 1997)

influences:

◀◀ Pete Johnson, Erroll Garner, Oscar Peterson

▶▶ Ramsey Lewis, Les McCann

Eric J. Lawrence

Antonio Hart

Born September 30, 1968, in Baltimore, MD.

Antonio Hart is one of the most exciting young alto saxophonists working in the post-bop tradition. He draws heavily from Gary Bartz and Cannonball Adderley, though he has also listened closely to Johnny Hodges, and he's increasingly coming into his own sound. Hart studied classical saxophone for four years at the Baltimore School of the Arts and didn't start playing jazz until his late teens, just before moving to Boston to study at Berklee. After graduating, he moved to New York in 1990 and hooked up with his Berklee classmate trumpeter Roy Hargrove, with whom he toured extensively and recorded a number of fine albums. Hart has recorded four albums on Novus and appeared as a sideman on sessions with a wide array of musicians, including Phil Woods, Vincent Herring, Freddie Cole, Nat Adderley, Cecil Bridgewater, Monty Alexander, and Robin Eubanks.

what to buy: A particularly strong session by one of the most passionate young alto saxophonists in jazz, Antonio Hart's third album *For Cannonball & Woody* ♫♫♫ (Novus, 1993, prod. Eulis Cathey) features a number of tunes associated with Cannonball Adderley (one of Hart's main inspirations), including a potent quintet version of "Sack O' Woe," with Nat Adderley and Jimmy Cobb. Hart expands three tunes by the late trumpeter Woody Shaw with well-crafted octet and nonet arrangements featuring Steve Turre, Robin Eubanks, Craig Handy, and the redoubtable rhythm section of pianist Mulgrew Miller, bassist Ray Drummond, and drummer Victor Lewis. Hart's solos are both searing and poised and his excellent working group also makes impressive contributions, with the hard-swinging trumpeter Darren Barrett, pianist Carlos McKinney, bassist Omer Avital and the deft drummer Nasheet Waits (son of the late Freddie Waits) holding forth on Hart's "Nine Weeks" and "Cannonball," and Fred Lacey's gorgeous ballad "Theme for Ernie."

what to buy next: Hart's sophomore album shows he's the real deal. *Don't You Know I Care* ♫♫♫ (Novus, 1992, prod. Jimmy Heath) features trumpeter Darren Barrett (making his recording debut), pianist Aaron Graves, bassist Rodney Whitaker, and drummer Greg Hutchinson playing seven Hart originals, Ellington's "Don't You Know I Care," and Quincy Jones's "Jessica's Day," which also features trombonist Jamal Haynes. Hart's material ranges from the Freddie Hubbardish "Zero Grade Reliance," to the lovely ballad, "Black Children," featuring Barrett's effective flugelhorn work. Gary Bartz sits in on the jam session tune "At the Closet Inn," and percussionist Kimitau Dinizulu spices up the restrained but celebratory "Mandela Freed," and gracefully swinging "From Across the Ocean."

the rest:
For the First Time ♫♫♫ (Novus, 1991)
It's All Good ♫♫♫ (Novus, 1995)

worth searching for: Trumpeter Roy Hargrove's best session while sharing frontline duties with Hart, *The Vibe* ♫♫♫ (Novus, 1992, prod. Larry Clothier) features Marc Cary (piano), Rodney Whitaker (bass), Greg Hutchinson (drums), and a number of veteran players as special guests. Hargrove and Hart make a potent combination, playing with both youthful energy and considerable maturity. They're not breaking any new ground, but listen to the precision and drive with which they attack Miles Davis's "Milestone" or Cary's title track. Hart steps into

more adventurous territory than usual for him on Robin Eubanks's exciting *Mental Images* ♫♫♫ (JMT, 1994, prod. Robin Eubanks, Stefan Winter), a session featuring a variety of line-ups, including Dave Holland, Kevin Eubanks, Michael Cain, Gene Jackson, and Marvin "Smitty" Smith, among others. Hart takes a few strong solos, fitting in easily to the session's wide-ranging vistas and expansive post-bop moods.

influences:
◀◀ Gary Bartz, Cannonball Adderley, Johnny Hodges

Andrew Gilbert

Billy Hart

Born November 29, 1940, in Washington, DC.

William W. "Billy" Hart is a drummer who plays comfortably and dynamically through the spectrum of contemporary improvisation. During his long apprenticeship in the 1960s he played deep, in-the-pocket shuffles and beyond with Jimmy Smith, Wes Montgomery, and Eddie Harris. The 1970s found him creating fresh variations on rock-jazz patterns with Herbie Hancock's seminal pre-fusion group Mwandishi, forceful polyrhythms with McCoy Tyner, idiomatic swing with Stan Getz, and texturally nuanced free drumming with a host of speculative improvisers. A loose, flowing, explosive drummer who takes, as Joe Lovano puts it, "big right turns and sharp angles," Hart (nicknamed "Jabali") stimulates the soloist with constantly shifting accents and tempos.

Hart's albums are singular documents, sounding unlike anything recorded contemporaneous to them. He functions primarily as an idea generator, a rhythmic fulcrum. He gathers all-star groups of individualistic, virtuosic musicians who would not otherwise play together, assembles them in various combinations, unifying their distinctive personalities through intense dialogue. Everyone composes, providing an open window of collective narrative concerns. Each performance is an opportunity for Hart to thematically develop a wide array of time signatures, patterns, and timbres.

what's available: You can't go wrong with any of Hart's currently in-print albums. Start with *Amethyst* ♫♫♫ (Arabesque, 1993, prod. Marc Copland) or *Oceans of Time* ♫♫♫ (Arabesque, 1996, prod. David Ballou, Billy Hart). Both recordings employ the strong powerful sextet of saxophonist John Stubblefield, violinist Mark Feldman, pianist David Kikoski, guitarist David Fiuczynski, and bassist Santi Debriano, each of whom composes. Pianist Marc Copland guests on *Amethyst* and saxophonist Chris Potter enhances *Oceans of Time*, the more focused undertaking. Hart outdoes himself on both sessions, conjuring an incessant profusion of ideas. *Oshumare* 𝄞𝄞𝄞𝄞 (Gramavision, 1985/1995, prod. David Baker, Mark Gray) is a propulsive, ebullient session, with a mature Hart empathetically shaping the improvisations of mid-1980s prodigies Steve Coleman, Branford Marsalis, Bill Frisell, Kevin Eubanks, Kenny Kirkland, Mark Gray, and Didier Lockwood; Dave Holland returns. Writing is by Frisell, Eubanks, Kirkland, Coleman, Holland, and Hart.

worth searching for: Much of Hart's recorded work is out of print, but certainly worth a search. Hart is leader on *Enhance* 𝄞𝄞𝄞𝄞 (A&M, 1976, prod. John Snyder), a striking acoustic 1976 session (now out of print) blending, in a variety of combinations, cutting-edge New York musicians Hannibal Marvin Peterson and Eddie Henderson (trumpets), Buster Williams or Dave Holland (bass), Dewey Redman and Oliver Lake (saxophones), Don Pullen (piano), and Michael Carvin (percussion). The compositions by Lake, Pullen, Holland, Redman, Peterson, and Hart explore a broad range of structural and emotional possibilities. *Rah* 𝄞𝄞𝄞𝄞 (Gramavision, 1987, prod. Jonathan F.P. Rose) is preoccupied with impressionism, voicing shapes and colors. Soprano saxophonist Dave Liebman's keening sound permeates the album. A blend of young and experienced improvisers, the session features the return of Frisell, Eubanks, Kirkland, Gray, and Henderson, with Liebman, tenorist Ralph Moore, and bassist Eddie Gomez added to the mix. Frisell, Eubanks, Liebman, Henderson, and Hart contribute pieces, with Hart the emphatic but unobtrusive guiding intelligence. Hart's done hundreds of sideman dates over the years and some samples of his apprenticeships can be heard on the following search-worthy recordings. Herbie Hancock's *Mwandishi: The Complete Warner Bros. Recordings* 𝄞𝄞𝄞𝄞 (Warner, 1969–1972), spotlights Hart's command of the rhythms of what he calls "World Classical Music, a music starting with Jazz," which he believes requires knowledge of African music, Indian music, and the American traditions. Miles Davis turns to the funk, with Hart underneath on *On the Corner* 𝄞𝄞𝄞𝄞 (Columbia, 1970). Hart's playing on the first CD of Joe Lovano's two-CD set, *Quartets: Live at the Village Vanguard* 𝄞𝄞𝄞𝄞 (Blue Note, 1994, prod. Joe Lovano, Michael Cuscuna), could serve as a textbook of how to play open-form drums with exquisite structure, perfect time, and uncanny timbral imagination.

influences:

◀◀ Jimmy Cobb, Philly Joe Jones, Art Blakey, Max Roach, Ben

JOHNNY HARTMAN
(WITH JOHN COLTRANE)

song "My One and Only Love"

album *John Coltrane
and Johnny Hartman*
(Impulse!, 1963/1995)

instrument Vocals

Monster
Solo

Dixon, Grady Tate, Clayton Filliard, Zigaboo Modaliste, Elvin Jones, Tony Williams

▶▶ Bill Stewart

Ted Panken

Johnny Hartman

Born John Maurice Hartman, July 13, 1923, in Chicago, IL. Died September 15, 1983, in New York, NY.

Vocalist Johnny Hartman was virtually forgotten by mass audiences until Hollywood director Clint Eastwood used a few of his tracks in the film *The Bridges of Madison County* in the 1990s. The soundtrack went on to huge sales, and since then jazz labels have been quick to reissue many of his albums. New fans have heard Hartman's deep, resonant baritone voice and discovered his knack for phrasing and reshaping a melody. Although Hartman began playing piano and singing at age eight and received a scholarship in 1939 to study voice at Chicago Musical College, he didn't gain wider notice until he sang with

Earl Hines in 1947. Following stints with Dizzy Gillespie (1948–49) and pianist Erroll Garner (1949), Hartman pursued a solo career in nightclubs and on television. He signed with RCA Victor in 1951, when he was touted as having "Sinatra-type appeal for the gals" and was also compared to Billy Eckstine. Hartman worked with jazz saxophonist John Coltrane during the 1960s and is probably best remembered by his fans for his classic recording made in 1963 with Coltrane. The singer made some recordings in Japan in the 1970s, and in 1981 his album *Once in Every Life* was nominated for a Grammy Award.

what to buy: *All of Me* ✍✍✍✍ (Bethlehem Jazz, 1956/1993) contains 16 swingers, ballads, and blues, and is one of Hartman's best albums. Just listen to his version of "Tenderly," with sublime backing from a strings-laden studio orchestra (probably arranged and conducted by Ernie Wilkins), or how he belts out a note-bending, hard-swinging rendition of "Birth of the Blues." And with candor equal to that of Bennett or Sinatra, Hartman delivers potent American songbook titles such as Cole Porter's "I Concentrate on You," "I Get a Kick out of You," and Berlin's "Blue Skies." Hartman hits those low notes with jolting power, yet can end a phrase on a note nearly two octaves above. Superb instrumental solos boost the appeal of this 51-minute CD, which includes four alternate takes that were not on the LP version. This album is highly recommended. Although Hartman was working with a slew of jazz musicians in the 1950s, it wasn't until *John Coltrane & Johnny Hartman* ✍✍✍✍ (Impulse!, 1963, prod. Bob Thiele) lit the jazz world on fire that the singer won wider visibility. Evocative melodies of romantic ballads such as "Lush Life," "You Are Too Beautiful," "My One and Only Love," and "Autumn Serenade" fit Hartman's style perfectly. And Coltrane, showing miraculous restraint on his tenor saxophone, serves as the ideal accompaniment for Hartman's vocals. Pianist McCoy Tyner, bassist Jim Garrison, and drummer Elvin Jones add utmost flair to the session. This recording is a welcome addition to any music collection. Another gem is the 1959 Roost album, *And I Thought about You* ✍✍✍✍ (Capitol, 1959/Roost, 1997, prod. Rudy Traylor), recorded between Hartman's two Bethlehem albums and his album with Coltrane. Producer/arranger/ orchestra conductor Rudy Traylor devises just the right atmosphere for Hartman's 12 romantic musings. However, ballads such as "Long Ago and Far Away," "I Should Care," "Alone," "After You've Gone," "I Thought about You," and other popular favorites still couldn't keep the original version of this album in print. (Probably, this was due to label problems and the stiff competition among singers during the 1950s and 1960s, with an abundance of suitable contenders competing for the tops spots

held by Frank Sinatra, Tony Bennett, Peggy Lee, Rosemary Clooney, and a few others.) Hartman is at his best on the nearly 34 minutes of music, delivering some of best and most tender renderings of romantic ballads.

what to buy next: The same year Hartman recorded his album with Coltrane, he recorded two more albums, *I Just Dropped By to Say Hello* ✍✍✍ (Impulse!, 1964/1995, prod. Bob Thiele) and *The Voice That Is* ✍✍✍ (Impulse!, 1964/1994, prod. Bob Thiele). *I Just Dropped By to Say Hello* contains 32 minutes (11 tunes) of standards and obscurities, lovely ballads and light swingers. More than a decade after Sinatra recorded, "In the Wee Small Hours of the Morning," Hartman one-ups him with his deep-toned, seductive renderings supported by pianist Hank Jones, bassist Milt Hinton, drummer Elvin Jones, and guest guitarists Jim Hall and Kenny Burrell. The Ellington ballad "Don't You Know I Care (or Don't You Care I Know)" weaves Hartman's phrasing with guest soloist Illinois Jacquet's warm tenorisms. Other highlights include Hartman's straight readings of the title tune, rendered warmly with pianist Jones getting some solo space, and "Stairway to the Stars," again with comping from Jacquet's breathy tenor sax. Once you've heard Hartman for the first time, you'll want to hear more and it probably won't matter whether the tunes are familiar or not as long as you can hear his deep, rich baritone voice. *The Voice That Is*, Hartman's third album for Impulse!, features the singer delivering 11 jazz standards like a crooner should, delicately unfolding the lyrics and phrasing for ultimate effect. He's accompanied by two different groups but the best songs are backed by pianist Hank Jones, guitarist Barry Galbraith, bassist Richard Davis, and drummer Osie Johnson, with whom Hartman sings "My Ship," "The More I See You," "These Foolish Things," "Waltz for Debby," and "It Never Entered My Mind." The remaining tunes lean more toward the pop arena, smacking of the eternal artist's struggle with label magnates over inclusion of pop fare. Fourteen best selections from the 1964 Impulse! sessions are compiled on the single disc *Johnny Hartman* ✍✍✍✍ (GRP, 1964/ 1997), from GRP's Priceless Jazz series. Listeners may also find *Unforgettable* ✍✍✍✍ (Impulse!, 1966/1995, prod. Bob Thiele) a highly enjoyable session. Singing 17 tunes taken from two 1966 LPs (*Unforgettable Songs by Johnny Hartman* and *I Love Everybody*), Hartman is backed by a full orchestra conducted by Gerald Wilson (who also wrote the arrangements). His performances demonstrate his loyalty to lyrics, his ability to build drama into each song, his penchant for swing, and his magnificent voice. These recordings reach into the American songbook and also represent Hartman's only venture into the pop field.

Yet, you'll admire the bluesy edge in his voice and the suppleness with which he shapes a tune in a jazz framework.

best of the rest:

Songs from the Heart 🎵🎵🎵🎵 (Bethlehem, 1955/1992/Charly, 1997)
For Trane 🎵🎵🎵 (Blue Note, 1972/1995)

worth searching for: The soundtrack album for Clint Eastwood's movie *Bridges of Madison County* 🎵🎵🎵🎵 (Malpaso/Warner Bros., 1995, prod. Clint Eastwood) singlehandedly renewed popular interest in Hartman's career. His songs "I See Your Face before Me," "It Was Almost like a Song," and "For All We Know" stand up nicely among tracks by Dinah Washington and Barbara Lewis.

influences:

◀◀ Billy Eckstine, Frank Sinatra, Nat "King" Cole, Joe Williams, Vic Damone, Tony Bennett, Bing Crosby

▶▶ Harry Connick Jr., Allan Harris, Kevin Mahogany

Nancy Ann Lee and Carl Quintanilla

Hampton Hawes

Born November 13, 1928, in Los Angeles, CA. Died May 22, 1977, in Los Angeles, CA.

One of the finest and most influential pianists of the 1950s, Hampton Hawes was a brilliant Bud Powell disciple who injected a bluesy, gospel sensibility into bebop. Based in Los Angeles throughout most of his life, Hawes had a roller-coaster career marked by periods of popular success, imprisonment, and obscurity. Fortunately, he recorded prolifically during the peak of his creativity, and though he self-consciously changed his style in the 1970s, seeking commercial success with the electric piano, his improvisational powers never waned.

Hawes's father was a preacher and his earliest musical experiences were playing in church. Hawes came up on Los Angeles' vibrant Central Avenue scene, where he played with Big Jay McNeely, Charlie Parker, Howard McGhee, Dexter Gordon, Sonny Criss, Teddy Edwards, Billie Holiday, Wardell Grey, and with West Coast jazz progenitors Shorty Rogers and Howard Rumsey's Lighthouse All-Stars. After a stint in the Army (1953–55), mostly in Japan, he returned to Los Angeles and formed a trio, with bassist Red Mitchell and drummer Chuck Thompson, that recorded a series of highly influential sessions for Contemporary. Heroin addiction prevented Hawes from capitalizing on his rising popularity and he spent more than five years in prison (1958–1963) until he was pardoned by President Kennedy. Hawes recorded another series of fine albums for Contempo-

rary in the mid-1960s, and recorded for a host of European labels. Typically playing in trio contexts, Hawes successfully employed keyboards in the early 1970s, but the best playing of his later period was in acoustic settings. His influence is still widespread, though many pianists thought to be under the sway of Horace Silver, who developed a similar, though more spare style, were actually following the lead of Hawes. His bitter, trenchant autobiography, *Raise Up off Me*, is one of the great insider accounts of "the life." Many of Hawes's recordings on Contemporary, Savoy, Xanadu, Black Lion, and Arista/Freedom are still available.

what to buy: The album that put him on the jazz map for good, *Hampton Hawes Trio, Volume One* 🎵🎵🎵🎵 (Contemporary/OJC, 1955, prod. Lester Koenig), is the first of three classic records with the highly distinctive Red Mitchell (bass) and Chuck Thompson (drums). The program consists of standards and Hawes's original blues, where he displays the funky kind of grooves that became widely popular later in the decade. *All Night Session, Vol. 1* 🎵🎵🎵🎵 (Contemporary/OJC, 1958, prod. Lester Koenig) is a quartet album with the emerging giant Jim Hall (guitar), Red Mitchell (bass), and Bruz Freeman (drums). The first of three albums recorded during one late night in November 1956, the interplay between the musicians is consistently inspired. When Hamp starts preaching on "Hampton's Pulpit," it feels like a long drink of water for a thirsty soul. A fascinating session bringing together four unique stylists, *For Real!* 🎵🎵🎵🎵 (Contemporary/OJC, 1958, prod. Lester Koenig) features the great tenor saxophonist Harold Land, the ground-breaking bassist Scott LaFaro, and undeservedly obscure drummer Frank Butler. Highlights include a searing Land solo on "I Love You" and the interplay between Hamp and Butler on Hawes's and Land's "Numbers Game." A trio session recorded at Mitchell's Studio Club (no relation to Red) in 1966, *The Seance* 🎵🎵🎵🎵 (Contemporary/OJC, 1969, prod. Lester Koenig) reunites Hawes and bassist Red Mitchell, one of the great collaborations in modern jazz. Their intuitive interaction on the spontaneous blues of the title track is thrilling, high-wire jazz. Hawes shows off his lyrical side on the ballad "For Heaven's Sake." The capable drummer Donald Bailey fits right in with the session's loose, anything-can-happen feel.

what to buy next: The second volume by Hamp's classic trio with bassist Red Mitchell and drummer Chuck Thompson, *This Is Hampton Hawes, The Trio: Vol. 2* 🎵🎵🎵🎵 (Contemporary/OJC, 1956, prod. Lester Koenig) is a masterpiece. Hawes handles ballads with style, personalizes standards, and plays his own funky tunes with verve. A quartet session with Red Mitchell (bass), Barney Kessel (guitar), and Shelly Manne (drums), *Four!* 🎵🎵🎵🎵 (Contemporary/OJC, 1958, prod. Lester Koenig) catches Hawes in top form, blowing through a set of bop tunes, standards, and, of course, blues, a form in which he was endlessly inventive. Though the producer's liner notes make no reference to it, *The Green Leaves of Summer* 🎵🎵🎵🎵 (Contemporary/OJC, 1964, prod. Lester Koenig) was Hawes's first album after five years in prison. His improvisational powers were clearly unaffected by his incarceration, as his solos are concise and focused. Bassist Monk Montgomery and drummer Steve Ellington (making his recording debut) accompany the master ably.

best of the rest:

Everybody Likes Hampton Hawes, Vol 3: The Trio, 🎵🎵🎵🎵 (Contemporary, 1956/OJC, 1990)
All Night Session, Vol. 2 🎵🎵🎵🎵 (Contemporary, 1958/OJC, 1991)
All Night Session, Vol. 3 🎵🎵🎵🎵 (Contemporary, 1958/OJC, 1991)
Here and Now 🎵🎵🎵🎵 (Contemporary, 1965/OJC, 1991)
I'm All Smiles 🎵🎵🎵🎵 (Contemporary, 1966/OJC, 1993)
Blues for Bud 🎵🎵🎵🎵 (Black Lion, 1968/1992)
Live at the Jazz Showcase in Chicago 🎵🎵🎵🎵 (Enja, 1973/1996)

worth searching for: A reunion of West Coast all-stars, *Live at Memory Lane* 🎵🎵🎵🎵 (Fresh Sound, 1990, prod. Jordi Pujol) was recorded during a 1970 television broadcast, *Jazz on Stage.* Saxophonists Sonny Criss and Teddy Edwards and trumpeter Harry "Sweets" Edison are all in fine form, and the great blues shouter Big Joe Turner dominates "Feelin' Happy" and "Shake, Rattle and Roll." Hawes sounds like he's having a great time, especially on the 13-minute jam session that closes out the album.

influences:

◀◀ Bud Powell, Charlie Parker

▶▶ Andre Previn, Oscar Peterson, Bobby Timmons, Junior Mance

Andrew Gilbert

Coleman Hawkins

Born November 21, 1904, in St. Louis, MO. Died May 19, 1969, in New York, NY.

Historically speaking, Coleman Hawkins (a.k.a. Hawk or Bean) is among the handful of players who developed and pioneered jazz in its formative stages. Widely acknowledged as the music's first major saxophonist, Hawkins came to prominence as a member of vocalist Mamie Smith's Jazz Hounds, but his most famous early association was with the star-studded big band led by Fletcher Henderson, which he joined in 1923 and

left in 1934 when he relocated to Europe. While overseas, he recorded with the great Gypsy guitarist Django Reinhardt, among others. When Hawkins returned to the United States, he made the record that is still considered his most important single achievement, a 1939 version of Johnny Green's "Body and Soul," which remains a riveting and moving emotional performance today. Harmonically, Hawkins was on an advanced level, which, at the time, could only be matched by pianist Art Tatum. By the mid-1940s, Hawkins had moved beyond swing to bebop, and both Max Roach and Thelonious Monk got their initial recording experience as members of his various small combos. But he continued to learn from younger players: in his later recordings, you can hear the harmonic influence of John Coltrane's vertical, scalar approach, as well as the formal, thematic melodicism of Sonny Rollins. Part of Hawkins's recorded legacy includes guest appearances with Monk in 1957 and Charles Mingus in 1960.

what to buy: As you might expect from a player of Hawkins's stature, whose career stretched over five decades, there is a lot of material out there. The problem, therefore, becomes how to choose discs that give a good overview of his art and still manage to touch upon the highlights. This isn't as easy as it seems, simply because the Hawkins catalog is owned by so many different labels. Much of his material has been issued by Columbia under Fletcher Henderson's name, and from this period there are several solos—"The Dicty Blues," "New King Porter Stomp," and "Honeysuckle Rose" among them, all found on the boxed set entitled *The Fletcher Henderson Story: A Study in Frustration* 🎵🎵🎵🎵 (Columbia, 1994, prod. various)—that illustrate Hawk's initial, "slap-tongue" method of instrumental attack and show the influence of Louis Armstrong (the later, arpeggiated Hawkins owed a debt to Art Tatum). Examples of Hawkins's 1929 association with the Mound City Blue Blowers, a group that included Pee Wee Russell, Glenn Miller, and Gene Krupa, can be found on the 2-CD *Coleman Hawkins: A Retrospective 1929–1963* 🎵🎵🎵🎵 (RCA Bluebird, 1995, prod. Orrin Keepnews). There is also a fine single-disc compilation of 1939–56 material called *Coleman Hawkins: Body and Soul* 🎵🎵🎵🎵 (RCA, 1996, prod. various), but this single CD doesn't have any of the Mound City Blue Blowers material; it begins with the sessions that produced "Body and Soul," a piece that demonstrates Hawkins's then-new legato style with heavy vibrato. Perhaps an even better choice (though on a somewhat obscure label) for the early

Coleman Hawkins (r) with George Tucker (Archive Photos)

and middle Hawkins styles would be *Picasso* 𝄢𝄢𝄢𝄢 (Jazz Gi-ants, 1994, prod. various), which features the extremely rare 1948 unaccompanied recording of "Picasso," the piece that foreshadowed the 1960s solo saxophone explosion. Beginning in the 1950s, the individual records are more coherent (which is to say that they were done with LPs in mind, rather than 78 rpm singles). From this later period, the standout is *The Hawk Flies High* 𝄢𝄢𝄢𝄢 (Riverside, 1957/OJC, 1988, prod. Orrin Keepnews). By surrounding Hawkins (who by then veered in and out of the thick vibrato at will) with a dream team of J.J. Johnson, Idrees Sulieman, Hank Jones, Barry Galbraith, Oscar Pettiford, and Jo Jones, Keepnews was able to remain true to the archetypical "Bean" sound and yet give the feeling of being up-to-date and "with it." The record comprises almost entirely minor-feel riffs that leave plenty of room for blowing; the sound is warm, the re-sults outstanding—especially the blues entitled "Juicy Fruit," where Sulieman takes a solo built out of one note, held, Roland Kirk–like, for its entire duration. Not as lofty in its execution, but equally arresting, is Hawkins's last date, from December 1966, entitled *Sirius* 𝄢𝄢𝄢𝄢 (Pablo, 1966/OJC, 1995, prod. Norman Granz), with Barry Harris, Bob Cranshaw, and Eddie Locke. The opening "The Man I Love" is taken at a moderate clip that is ob-viously too strenuous for Hawkins, who was already in a physi-cally debilitated state by this time. But the remainder of the date shows how he compensated, slowing the tempos down to a walk and packing his solos with feeling rather than notes. Here, you can hear both the hard-drinking macho-man that Hawk portrayed to the world, and the softer-hearted sentimen-talist who lurked beneath the gruff surfaces.

what to buy next: The 1945 and 1947 recordings on *Hollywood Stampede* 𝄢𝄢𝄢𝄢 (Capitol, 1989, prod. various) show Hawkins's fascination with bop to good advantage (the title track is a spin on "Ornithology"), with a couple of different groups that include Howard McGhee and Miles Davis, Hank Jones, Oscar Pettiford, Denzil Best, and Max Roach. Another interesting grab-bag is *Rainbow Mist* 𝄢𝄢𝄢𝄢 (Apollo, 1944/Delmark, 1992, prod. Leonard Feather, others, reissue prod. Robert G. Koester, Steve Wagner), which includes a Hawkins Orchestra with Dizzy Gillespie and Leo Parker as well as a sextet with Georgie Auld, Ben Webster, and Charlie Shavers. From his stint with Impulse! in the early 1960s, recorded with the quartet including Tommy Flanagan, Major Hol-ley, and Eddie Locke, came *Then and Now* (Impulse!, 1963/1996, prod. Bob Thiele) 𝄢𝄢𝄢𝄢, an easy-going, solid session.

the rest:
The Complete Coleman Hawkins Keynote Recordings 𝄢𝄢𝄢𝄢 (Keynote, 1944/Mercury, 1994)

Coleman Hawkins Encounters Ben Webster 𝄢𝄢𝄢𝄢 (Verve, 1959)
With the Red Garland Trio 𝄢𝄢𝄢𝄢 (Swingville, 1959/OJC, 1990)
(With Charlie Shavers, Ray Bryant, George Duvivier) *Hawk Eyes* 𝄢𝄢𝄢𝄢 (Prestige, 1959/OJC, 1988)
Soul 𝄢𝄢𝄢𝄢 (Prestige, 1959/OJC, 1990)
(With Eddie "Lockjaw" Davis, Buddy Tate, Arnett Cobb) *Very Saxy* 𝄢𝄢𝄢𝄢 (Prestige, 1959)
At Ease 𝄢𝄢𝄢𝄢 (Moodsville, 1960/OJC, 1992)
(With Eddie "Lockjaw" Davis) *Night Hawk* 𝄢𝄢𝄢𝄢 (Swingville, 1960/OJC, 1990)
(With Pee Wee Russell, Vic Dickenson, J. C. Higginbotham) *Jam Session in Swingville* 𝄢𝄢𝄢𝄢 (Prestige, 1961/OJC, 1992)
(With Kenny Burrell, Ron Carter, Andrew Cyrille) *The Hawk Relaxes* 𝄢𝄢𝄢𝄢 (Moodsville, 1961/OJC, 1992)
Desafinado 𝄢𝄢𝄢𝄢 (Impulse, 1962/1997)
In a Mellow Tone 𝄢𝄢𝄢𝄢 (Pablo, 1962/OJC, 1988)
Wrapped Tight 𝄢𝄢𝄢𝄢 (Impulse!, 1965/1991)
(With Roy Eldridge, Don Byas, Benny Carter, others) *Bean Stalkin'* 𝄢𝄢𝄢𝄢 (Pablo, 1988)
Bean & the Boys 𝄢𝄢𝄢𝄢 (Prestige, 1993)

worth searching for: Hawkins's work with the so-called Choco-late Dandies, a band that also featured Benny Carter and Roy Eldridge, can be found on *Giants of the Tenor Sax* 𝄢𝄢𝄢𝄢 (Com-modore, 1975 prod. Milt Gabler), containing 1940–54 material. A disc of 1944–45 sessions that's shared with Ben Webster, *Bean & Ben* 𝄢𝄢𝄢𝄢 (Harlequin, prod. various) includes the 1944 titles done with Thelonious Monk on piano. You'll be able to pick out a number of Monk's own themes in his intros and brief solos, including the beginnings of "Ruby My Dear" at the outset of "Driftin on a Reed," which is not the Charlie Parker tune of the same name. For those wishing to really, really im-merse themselves in the Hawk's musings, there's a British label's six-CD *Complete Coleman Hawkins Recordings 1929–1941* 𝄢𝄢𝄢𝄢𝄢 (Affinity, 1992, prod. various). This includes, literally, everything from the titular period: the dates with Benny Goodman, Django Reinhardt, Red Allen, the Mound City Blue Blowers, some Count Basie sides, the Chocolate Dandies—all of it. Ultimately, of course, this is for the rabid, hardcore fan only.

influences:

◄◄ Louis Armstrong, the Great God Pan

►► Ben Webster, Charlie Parker, Lester Young, Dexter Gordon, Wardell Gray, Sonny Rollins, John Coltrane, Archie Shepp, Pharoah Sanders, Albert Ayler, Wayne Shorter, Scott Hamil-ton, David Murray

David Prince

Erskine Hawkins

Born July 26, 1914, in Birmingham, AL. Died November, 1993, in Willingbord, NJ.

Erskine Hawkins's first instruments were drums and trombone before he took up the trumpet at 13. As a student at the Alabama State Teachers' College in Montgomery, he became leader of the college band, the 'Bama State Collegians. Initially fronted by J.B. Sims, the band traveled to New York in 1934 to generate money to keep the college afloat during the Depression. The band stayed in New York, with Hawkins gradually emerging as the nominal leader as well. What began as a student band turned into a first-class professional unit, with a talented pianist and arranger in Avery Parrish and good soloists in trumpeter Dud Bascomb and tenorist Paul Bascomb. Hawkins specialized in high-note trumpet effects, billing himself as the "Twentieth-Century Gabriel." The band started recording in 1936 and frequently appeared at the Savoy Ballroom. Hawkins's band was a blues-charged outfit that can be associated with both the Kansas City riffing style of Bennie Moten and Count Basie and the rise of rhythm and blues. It's apparent in the band's two biggest hits, "Tuxedo Junction" in 1939 and Parrish's "After Hours," the quintessential midnight blues vehicle. The success of these recordings allowed Hawkins's band to endure far longer than most big bands of the era, adapting increasingly to rhythm and blues, and stretching into the 1950s before Hawkins downsized to a sextet.

what to buy: *From Alabama to Harlem 1938–40* 🎵🎵🎵🎵 (Black & Blue, 1995, prod. various) is superior to other compilations in its generous playing time and track selection, the best introduction to Hawkins's band in its best period, but it's hard to find. For the original versions of the hits and a good sense of the band's power, the next choice is *Tuxedo Junction* 🎵🎵🎵 (BMG, 1992, prod. various), which is readily available and provides "Tuxedo Junction" and "After Hours." Unfortunately, the CD is very brief, including only 11 tracks. It's not to be confused with *Tuxedo Junction* 🎵🎵 (MCA, 1991, prod. various), which is similarly brief but includes later re-makes of the original tunes with different personnel.

what to buy next: The output of the Hawkins band from 1936 to 1945 is available complete on the French import series Jazz Chronological Classics. The best of these is *Erskine Hawkins 1938–39* 🎵🎵🎵🎵 (Jazz Chronological Classics, 1992, prod. various), which has the original "Tuxedo Junction" and excellent versions of "King Porter Stomp" and Hawkins's own "Gin Mill Special."

COLEMAN **H**AWKINS

song "Body and Soul"

album *A Retrospective*
(RCA Bluebird, 1939/1995)

instrument Tenor saxophone

best of the rest:

Erskine Hawkins & His Orchestra 1936–38 🎵🎵🎵 (Jazz Chronological Classics, 1992)

Erskine Hawkins & His Orchestra 1939–40 🎵🎵🎵🎵 (Jazz Chronological Classics, 1992)

Erskine Hawkins & His Orchestra 1940–41 🎵🎵🎵🎵 (Jazz Chronological Classics, 1993)

Erskine Hawkins & His Orchestra 1941–45 🎵🎵🎵 (Jazz Chronological Classics, 1996)

Original Broadcast Performance, 1945 🎵🎵🎵 (Musidisc, 1992)

influences:

◀◀ Bennie Moten, Count Basie, "Hot Lips" Page

▶▶ Louis Jordan, Joe Morris, Ray Charles

Stuart Broomer

Louis Hayes

Born March 31, 1937, in Detroit, MI.

Long before the term "young lions" became a marketing

concept, Louis Hayes was one of the young musicians who matter-of-factly revitalized jazz in the late 1950s. Before he was 16, he led a group at clubs in Detroit, then moved to New York in 1956 to replace Art Taylor in Horace Silver's working group. After Horace Silver and Art Blakey parted ways in 1956, the 19-year-old Hayes took the drum chair with Silver's quintet until 1959. Though his figures veer from Blakey's base in the shuffle, Hayes's drumming evokes Blakey's primal quality, and the younger man has always followed Blakey's declarative philosophy in the bands he's led, and has, indeed, been the drummer in various Jazz Messenger reunion bands in the 1990s. Leaving Silver, Hayes joined Cannonball Adderley until 1965, then worked with the Oscar Peterson Trio until 1967, after which he formed his own groups with sidemen such as Joe Henderson, James Spaulding, Freddie Hubbard, and Kenny Barron. Hayes rejoined Peterson in 1971 and, beginning in 1972, formed a series of groups with Cedar Walton, Junior Cook, and Woody Shaw. A drum virtuoso with perfect time and impeccable technique to suit every function, Hayes has remained active as leader and esteemed sideman through the '80s and '90s, recording in the past decade for SteepleChase and, most recently, Sharp Nine Records.

what to buy: A recent Hayes release, *Louis at Large* ✍✍✍✍ (Sharp Nine, 1996, prod. Marc Edelman) is a well-organized date with a spontaneous quality, and may be his best. Hayes knows how to drive soloists and how to set them off. And he proves it admirably, enhancing the pealing trumpet lines of Riley Mullins, the lean tenor declamations of Javon Jackson, and the virtuosic inventions of pianist David Hazeltine. The drummer plays on the highest level on nine fiery selections that navigate bop structures without falling into clichés.

what to buy next: *Louis Hayes & Co.: The Super Quartet* ✍✍✍✍ (Timeless, 1994, prod. Wim Wigt) sounds put together for the session, but Javon Jackson, Kirk Lightsey, and Essiet Essiet know how to make Hayes's incendiary exhortations ignite sparks. Jackson and Lightsey are in fine form. *Una Max* ✍✍✍✍ (SteepleChase, 1989, prod. Nils Winther) is a more extemporaneous blowing date, but what blowing! Booted incessantly by Hayes, tenor saxophonist John Stubblefield, trumpeter Charles Tolliver and pianist Kenny Barron have something substantial to say throughout.

influences:

◀◀ Max Roach, Kenny Clarke, Elvin Jones

Ted Panken

Graham Haynes

Born September 16, 1960, in Brooklyn, NY.

As the son of drummer Roy Haynes, Graham Haynes was exposed to jazz musicians at an early age; his neighborhood was home to Jaki Byard and Milt Jackson, and his father would sometimes take him out on gigs, thus introducing him to Thelonious Monk, among others. Haynes played in various local bands with Marcus Miller and Bernard Wright before meeting Steve Coleman in 1979. By 1981 Coleman and Haynes were familiar sights busking in the streets and playing in uptown jam sessions before joining forces with Cassandra Wilson, Jean-Paul Bourelly, Mark Johnson, and Kim Clarke to form the Five Elements (the first group to use M-Base theory in its music.) Haynes's first album as a leader, *What Time It Be*, used M-Base concepts in its writing, but his move to Paris in 1991, where he recorded *Nocturne Parisian*, showed him moving in a different direction. By including music from African, Arabic, and Indian cultures and musicians schooled in those ways of playing, Haynes has taken giant steps away from traditional jazz thinking on his later albums, although some of his experiments point back to *Bitches Brew* and *Crossing* in their use of electronics and exotic rhythms. His latest band, the Ethnotronic Church, features British saxophonist Steve Williamson.

what to buy: There is still a touch of the M-Base phenomenon heard on *Nocturne Parisian* ✍✍✍✍ (Muse, 1992, prod. Graham Haynes), but the influence of other cultures shows up in the number of francophone, Paris-based African musicians Haynes includes in his band. This is the first album recorded with Steve Williamson and his Coltrane/Shorter derived tenor, although he is heard to better advantage on Haynes's later albums.

what to buy next: There are still spots where Haynes's coronet pops out of the mix as a soloist but the overall impression of *Transition* ✍✍✍✍ (Verve, 1995, prod. Graham Haynes) shows the composer more concerned with the aural framework of the piece being played than he is with any single instrument, even his own. Williamson is heard to good effect, but the hard-edged guitar slashing of Vernon Reid and Jean-Paul Bourelly may put parts too close to the rock spectrum for some listeners. The title tune and "Freestylin'" showcase Haynes's newer ideas to best effect, incorporating DJ scratching, guitar wailing, and Latin percussive rhythms to form a jazz hybrid unlike any other.

the rest:

What Time It Be ✍✍✍ (Muse, 1991)
The Griot's Footsteps ✍✍✍ (Antilles, 1994)

influences:

◀◀ Miles Davis, Steve Coleman, Olu Dara, Henry Threadgill, Salif Keita

Garaud MacTaggart

Roy Haynes

Born in March 13, 1926, in Roxbury, MA.

One of the few musicians of his era to have played with nearly every historical jazz great, Roy Haynes has been active as one of jazz drumming's foremost innovators for over 50 years. His breadth of experience ranges from early gigs with Lester Young and Charlie Parker to his time spent backing vocalist Sarah Vaughan, involvement in Gary Burton's early fusion of rock and jazz, exploration of the avant garde with the likes of Andrew Hill and Eric Dolphy, pivotal work with the piano trio of Chick Corea, and recent efforts with guitar master Pat Metheny. Responsible for much of the language which has become part and parcel of contemporary jazz drumming, Haynes developed a style that places more emphasis on the interaction between snare and bass drum and less on the patterned playing of a ride cymbal beat. He regularly breaks up the rhythmic flow by displacing beats and accents among the various drums and cymbals. In addition, his tightly tuned snare drum is used for sharp rim shots and a variety of other colorful effects. Voted by *Down Beat* critics as New Star of 1962 (even though at that point he had been playing professionally for over 15 years!), Haynes led a number of significant record dates during the 1950s and 1960s on top of the scores of sessions he cut as a sideman. Other notable moments for Haynes include time spent with John Coltrane as a sub for Elvin Jones, a 1958 stint with Thelonious Monk, the formation of his own Hip Ensemble, and his receipt in 1994 of the Danish Jazzpar prize. Currently, Haynes maintains an active touring and recording schedule with his own group that recently has included such talented musicians as pianists Darrell Grant and David Kikoski, altoist Donald Harrison, tenorist Don Braden, and bassist Ed Howard.

what to buy: *Out of the Afternoon* ♫♫♫♫ (Impulse!, 1962/1996 prod. Bob Thiele) continues to be one of Haynes's superlative recorded efforts and one of the greatest records of the 1960s. Pianist Tommy Flanagan, multi-instrumentalist Roland Kirk, and bassist Henry Grimes are pushed to new heights by Haynes's explosive drumming. *Cracklin'* ♫♫♫♫ (New Jazz, 1963/OJC, 1994, prod. Ozzie Cadena) features a tightly knit group with pianist Ronnie Mathews and tenor saxophonist Booker Ervin. The

pairing of Haynes with the extroverted styling of Ervin is particularly rewarding.

what to buy next: *Just Us* ♫♫♫♫ (New Jazz, 1960/OJC, 1996, prod. Esmond Edwards) is a piano trio date with Richard Wyands that shows how well Haynes can interact in a small group setting. *Te Vou!* ♫♫♫♫ (Dreyfus, 1994, prod. Roy Haynes) is an all-star jam session that works well on so many levels. Donald Harrison, Pat Metheny, David Kikoski, and Christian McBride contribute powerful work, and the hearty set includes three of Metheny's finest tunes.

best of the rest:

We Three ♫♫♫♫ (New Jazz, 1958/OJC, 1992)
True or False ♫♫♫ (Freelance, 1986/Evidence, 1997)
Homecoming ♫♫♫♫ (Evidence, 1992)
When It's Haynes It Roars ♫♫♫♫ (Dreyfus, 1992)
My Shining Hour ♫♫♫♫ (Storyville, 1994)

influences:

▶▶ Tony Williams, Jack DeJohnette, Billy Drummond, Clarence Penn

Chris Hovan

Jimmy Heath

Born October 15, 1926, in Philadelphia, PA.

A brilliant hard-bop tenor saxophonist and gifted composer/arranger, Jimmy Heath is the middle sibling of the illustrious Heath Brothers (bassist Percy is the elder and drummer Albert "Tootie" the younger). For many years his formidable writing skills overshadowed his considerable powers as an improvisor, and a series of excellent albums for Riverside in the late 1950s and early 1960s did little to remedy his status as one of the greatest underappreciated musicians in jazz. Heath is also an accomplished soprano saxophonist and flutist, but the tenor is his most expressive horn. Raised in Philadelphia during the city's jazz heyday, Heath landed one of his first important gigs out of town with Nat Towels in Omaha, though he returned to Philly to hook up with trumpeter Howard McGhee's seminal bebop sextet in 1947–48. At around the same time, Heath formed his own big band, a group that included Benny Golson and John Coltrane (who cited Heath as an early influence). Known around Philly as "Little Bird," Heath, like many alto saxophonists, switched to tenor in the early 1950s. He played in Dizzy Gillespie's short-lived big band in 1949–50, where his finely crafted charts began establishing his reputation as a composer-arranger. Along with brother Percy, he toured with an all-star group featuring Miles Davis, J. J. Johnson, Milt Jackson, and

Kenny Clarke in the early 1950s; though he recorded infrequently during the first half of the decade, a notable exception is a classic 1953 Miles Davis session for Blue Note featuring J. J. Johnson and Heath on tenor. Chet Baker and Art Blakey used Heath's charts in the mid-1950s, and he made his belated debut as a leader for Riverside in 1959. That year he also worked again with Davis, and with Kenny Dorham and Gil Evans. In the mid-1960s he formed several inspired musical partnerships, recording with Milt Jackson and Art Farmer, and initiated a second career as a music educator. The three siblings formed the Heath Brothers group in 1975, documented by an intermittent series of recordings on the labels Strata East, Columbia, Antilles, and most recently Concord Jazz. Since 1987 Heath has taught at Queens College in New York. His tunes, such as "Gingerbread Boy," "Gemini," "C.T.A.," and "For Minors Only," have been recorded by Miles Davis, Dexter Gordon, Clark Terry, Cannonball Adderley, Ahmad Jamal, Blue Mitchell, and many others. Heath has played on two albums for Milestone with the Riverside Reunion Band and recorded as a leader for Muse, Landmark, Columbia, Soul Note, and SteepleChase. Most of his recordings for Landmark and Columbia haven't been reissued on CD but are relatively easy to find on vinyl.

what to buy: Though Jimmy Heath contributes three excellent tunes to *On the Trail* ♫♫♫♫ (Riverside, 1964/OJC, 1994, prod. Orrin Keepnews), this session highlights his brilliant tenor work. Accompanied by Kenny Burrell (guitar), Wynton Kelly (piano), Paul Chambers (bass), and Tootie Heath (drums), Heath transforms Ferde Grofe's "On the Trail" to the road to soulsville and takes a heated turn on his classic "Gingerbread Boy." The album's highlight is his velvety, tender version of the rarely played pop song "Vanity," backed at first only by Burrell's gentle chords. Despite being one of his best sessions, *On the Trail* was his last recording as a leader for almost a decade. Heath's first album as a leader, *The Thumper* ♫♫♫♫ (Riverside, 1959/OJC, 1994, prod. Orrin Keepnews) was recorded when he was 33 years old. A sextet date with Nat Adderley (cornet), Curtis Fuller (trombone), Wynton Kelly (piano), Paul Chambers (bass), and Tootie Heath (drums), the album features nine highly inventive Heath arrangements, including his standard "For Minors Only" and four other originals. Heath's distinctive, full-bodied tenor is featured with just the rhythm section on the ballads "I Can Make You Love Me" and "Don't You Know I Care," where his playing is particularly lyrical. With a big band drawn from the American Jazz Orchestra, *Little Man Big Band* ♫♫♫♫ (Verve, 1992, prod. Bill Cosby) is a *tour de force* outing showcasing Heath's powerful tenor work and his expert writing

skills. Heath supplied all the tunes and arrangements (besides Bill Cosby's "Two Friends"), using the opportunity to revisit such classics as "C.T.A." and "Gingerbread Boy," and pays tribute to fellow masters with "Trane Connections," "Forever Sonny," and "Ellington's Stray Horn." The ensemble passages are flawless, performed with both passion and precision. Though the band contains no shortage of first-rate improvisors, Heath dominates the proceedings, soloing on every track. Pianist Roland Hanna serves as his musical foil, taking a number of sparking solos. Trumpeters Virgil Jones, John Eckert, Lew Soloff, and Claudio Roditi are all featured during the second half of the session.

what to buy next: An early version of the Heath Brothers band, *The Quota* ♫♫♫♫ (Riverside, 1961/1995, prod. Orrin Keepnews) features bassist Percy and drummer Tootie in a sextet with Freddie Hubbard (trumpet), Julius Watkins (French Horn), and Cedar Walton (piano). Heath wrote four of the tunes and the arrangements for the blowing vehicle "Thinking of You," the pop ballad "When Sonny Gets Blue," and Milt Jackson's "Bells and Horns," which inspires an amazingly expressive solo by Watkins. Highlights include Heath's funky "Down Shift" and the title track, where his charts make the group sound considerably larger than a sextet. After more than a decade hiatus, *As We Were Saying . . .* ♫♫♫♫ (Concord Jazz, 1997, prod. John Burk) revives the Heath Brothers group and finds jazz's first family thriving. With guitarist Mark Elf and either Stanley Cowell or Roland Hanna on piano, the brothers cover four tunes by Jimmy, including "The Newest One," featuring Jon Faddis and Slide Hampton, Tootie's "For Seven's Sake," and Percy's "Dave's Maze." Jimmy displays his gorgeous soprano sound on Billy Strayhorn's "Daydream," and everyone shows off their chops on Fats Navarro's "Nostalgia," which also features Faddis and Hampton. A highly rewarding session by a group of consummate players. The only drawback to this next fine big band session is its length. At 36-minutes, *Really Big!* ♫♫♫♫ (Riverside, 1959, prod. Orrin Keepnews) is really short. Heath wrote the charts for six of the eight tunes, including tightly constructed blues workouts on his originals "Mr. 'P" and "Nails," and the deeply melodic version of "My Ideal." Trombonist Tom McIntosh supplies a marvelously funky arrangement for Bobby Timmons's "Dat Dere," and an appropriately swinging one for "The Picture of Heath." The band features a talent-laden horn section with Clark Terry, McIntosh, the Adderley brothers, Pat Patrick, and Dick Berg (on French horn), and either pianist Cedar Walton or Tommy Flanagan with the other Heath brothers rounding out the rhythm section.

best of the rest:

Nice People 𝄞𝄞𝄞𝄞 (Riverside/OJC, 1959–64)

Passing Thru . . . 𝄞𝄞𝄞 (Columbia, 1978)

New Picture 𝄞𝄞𝄞𝄞 (Landmark, 1985)

Peer Pleasure 𝄞𝄞𝄞𝄞 (Landmark, 1987)

You've Changed 𝄞𝄞𝄞𝄞 (SteepleChase, 1992)

The Time and the Place 𝄞𝄞𝄞𝄞 (Landmark, 1994)

worth searching for: The debut as a leader by one of jazz's greatest trumpeters, *Kenny Dorham Quintet* 𝄞𝄞𝄞𝄞 (Debut/OJC, 1953) features Heath on tenor and baritone sax, Walter Bishop on piano, Percy Heath on bass, and Kenny Clarke on drums. Heath plays written bari lines on Monk's "Ruby, My Dear," "Be My Love," and Cole Porter's "I Love You," but makes the most of his tenor solo spots on KD's "An Oscar for Oscar" and Osie Johnson's "Osmosis." A beautiful Milt Jackson session balancing loose arrangements and Heath's and Kenny Dorham's complex charts, *Invitation* 𝄞𝄞𝄞𝄞 (Riverside/OJC, 1962, prod. Orrin Keepnews) features Heath and Dorham (trumpet) with Tommy Flanagan (piano), Ron Carter (bass), and Connie Kay (drums). Trumpeter Virgil Jones replaces Heath on two tracks. Highlights include the haunting version of the title tune, as well as Monk's "Ruby, My Dear" and Jackson's easy-swinging piece "The Sealer."

influences:

◀◀ Charlie Parker, Dexter Gordon, John Coltrane

▶▶ John Coltrane, Benny Golson

Andrew Gilbert

Percy Heath

Born April 30, 1923, in Wilmington, NC.

The oldest among a trio of musical Heath brothers (the others being saxophonist Jimmy and drummer "Tootie"), Percy Heath has also been one of the more important bassists in modern jazz. After moving to New York with brother Jimmy in 1946, Percy got his musical start with trumpeter Howard McGhee's sextet later that same year. He established a reputation very quickly, playing with all the top bop musicians, including Miles Davis, Fats Navarro, Dizzy Gillespie, Thelonious Monk, and Charlie Parker. During the 1950s, Percy was a mainstay on an almost countless number of important jazz records, especially for the Prestige label. In 1952, Heath became a founding member of the Modern Jazz Quartet with Milt Jackson, John Lewis, and Kenny Clarke, an association that has really defined his career ever since. In addition to recording with the MJQ, Percy has spent much of the last few decades making respectable albums with his brothers.

worth searching for: Percy Heath has never recorded as a leader, but his contributions can be heard on many albums. Among these are Miles Davis's *Bags' Groove* 𝄞𝄞𝄞𝄞 (Prestige, 1955, prod. Bob Weinstock) and *Walkin'* 𝄞𝄞𝄞𝄞 (Prestige, 1954, prod. Bob Weinstock), the MJQ's *Django* 𝄞𝄞𝄞𝄞𝄞 (Prestige, 1953–55, prod. Bob Weinstock), and brother Jimmy's *Really Big!* 𝄞𝄞𝄞𝄞 (Riverside, 1960, prod. Orrin Keepnews) are most heartily recommended.

influences:

◀◀ Ray Brown

▶▶ Ron Carter

see also: *Modern Jazz Quartet*

Dan Keener

Tootie Heath

Born Albert Heath, May 31, 1935, in Philadelphia, PA.

Tootie Heath tends to be overlooked when "great drummer" lists are being assembled, but he is a master who can apply his acute rhythmic sensibility to a wide variety of musical situations. Raised in a musical family (his father was a devoted amateur clarinetist), Tootie is the youngest of the illustrious Heath brothers (his older siblings are bassist Percy, of MJQ fame, and saxophonist Jimmy, another underappreciated giant). He quickly made a reputation for himself on the fertile Philadelphia scene. As a teenager in the house trio at the Showboat, he played with Lester Young, Stan Getz, Oscar Pettiford, Kenny Dorham, and Sonny Stitt. At 19, Heath moved to New York and by 1957 had recorded with John Coltrane. He soon landed gigs with J. J. Johnson (1958–60) and the Art Farmer/Benny Golson Jazztet (1960–61). A prolific sideman, Heath recorded extensively for Riverside, including the classic album *The Incredible Jazz Guitar of Wes Montgomery*. Heath spent most of the 1960s living in Scandinavia, where he worked with touring American musicians and other expatriates such as Dexter Gordon, Don Byas, and Kenny Drew. He was an original member of Herbie Hancock's sextet Mwandishi (1968–69) and spent most of the early 1970s working with Yusef Lateef. A sometimes member of the Heath Brothers band, Tootie settled in Los Angeles in the late 1970s, where he's been one of the city's first-call drummers. He has recorded a number of albums with the Riverside Reunion band and, since the death of Connie Kay in 1995, has held down the drum chair in the Modern Jazz Quartet. He also works around Los Angeles with the cooperatively run quartet the Elders, which features saxophonist Herman Riley, pianist Phil Wright, and bassist James Leary (who replaced John Heard).

worth searching for: *Kwanza* ♫♫♫♫ (Muse, 1973, prod. Don Schlitten) is an excellent album with Tootie Heath's brothers Percy and Jimmy on board, as well as trombonist Curtis Fuller, the underrated guitarist Ted Dunbar, and pianist Kenny Barron. Marked by well-crafted arrangements and Tootie's tasteful traps work, this session has been reissued in Japan but is hard to find in the U.S.

influences:
◄◄ Kenny Clarke, Art Blakey, Specs Wright, Philly Joe Jones, Max Roach

see also: *Modern Jazz Quartet*

Andrew Gilbert

Mark Helias

Born October 1, 1950, in New Brunswick, NY.

Composer/bassist Mark Helias has been making innovative music since finishing a master's degree at the Yale School of Music in 1976. He was a part of the New Haven jazz scene with Anthony Davis, Jay Hoggard, Gerry Hemingway, George Lewis, and Pheeroan Aklaff, and with his impeccable credentials as a virtuoso bassist, composer, and band leader, he has composed for, as well as performed and recorded with, modern masters such as Edward Blackwell, Anthony Davis, Dewey Redman, and Anthony Braxton. Helias's present quintet, Attack the Future, featuring tenor saxophonist Ellery Eskelin, violinist Mark Feldman, drummer Tom Rainey, and West African percussionist Epizo Bangoura, represents the leader's trademark harmonic sensibilities. The music focuses on compositional balance and form, rhythmic interaction, odd metrical subdivisions, and open-form improvisation.

what to buy: On *The Current Set* ♫♫♫♫ (Enja, 1992, prod. Mark Helias), bassist Helias is joined by Herb Robertson (trumpet, cornet, flugelhorn), Robin Eubanks (trombone), Tim Berne (alto sax), Greg Osby (soprano sax), Victor Lewis (drums), and Nana Vasconselos (percussion). Music ranges from contrapuntal exclamations to soulful ballads performed in solos, trios, and other compositional stratagems. On the immensely satisfying recording *Loopin' the Cool* ♫♫♫♫ (Enja, 1996, prod. Mark Helias), Helias leads a team that covers all the bases, including serendipitous compositions, intriguing arrangements, hot blowing, moments of tenderness, earthiness, and constant imagination. Eskelin (tenor sax), Regina Carter (violin), and Rainey (drums, percussion) lend uniqueness to this compelling listen.

the rest:
Split Image ♫♫♫ (Enja 1984)
Desert Blue ♫♫♫ (Enja 1989/1997)
Attack the Future ♫♫♫♫ (Enja 1992)

influences:
◄◄ Hall Overton, Richard Davis, Steve Swallow, Gary Peacock, Dave Holland, Anthony Braxton

David C. Gross

Jonas Hellborg

Born 1958, in Gothenborg, Sweden.

Jonas Hellborg taught himself to play the bass at age 12, and at first played mainly blues and heavy rock, influenced by artists such as Jimi Hendrix, Cream, and Deep Purple. In 1972, he heard the Mahavishnu Orchestra's album *The Inner Mounting Flame*, featuring English guitarist John McLaughlin, a recording that changed his perception of music and altered the direction of his career. Hellborg began formal studies in jazz and classical music at the age of 16, listened to Albert Ayler and John Coltrane, and became involved with a free-form group. He studied Miles Davis's development from the early part of his career through the early fusion albums *In a Silent Way* and *Bitches Brew*, a context where he rediscovered John McLaughlin. McLaughlin served as the main influence for Hellborg, who was exploring a jazz/rock idiom by playing small clubs in the south of Sweden.

Hellborg's command of his instrument flabbergasted musicians when he came out of Sweden in the early 1980s. In 1981, he was invited to play at the Montreux Jazz Festival. Michael Brecker, impressed by Hellborg's playing there, introduced him to many of the jazz greats, including Hellborg's longtime idol, John McLaughlin. In 1982 Hellborg created his own record label, Day Eight Music, in order to allow himself and others to record with full artistic freedom. In 1985 Hellborg and McLaughlin started playing duet concerts where they created an intimate chamber music kind of jazz/funk nearly classical in its texture. The following year saw the release of the album *Adventures in RadioLand* by a reconstituted Mahavishnu that featured Hellborg on bass. In 1990, Hellborg and Bill Laswell created the Greenpoint recording studio in New York. Hellborg has collaborated with Ginger Baker, Michael Shrieve, Buckethead, Peter Brötzmann, Glen Velez, and, most recently, guitarist Shawn Lane.

what to buy: *Temporal Analogues of Paradise* ♫♫♫♫ (Day Eight, 1996, prod. Jonas Hellborg) features Shawn Lane on electric guitar and Apt. Q-258 (a.k.a. Jeff Sipe) on drums. Hellborg returns to his fusion/rock roots as they skip the usual display of virtuosity and resort to a casual, practice-session atmosphere. The solos are moderately brief, making their point before running to the next in an organic flow. *The Word* ♫♫♫ (Axiom Records, 1991, prod. Bill Laswell, Jonas Hellborg) finds Hellborg collaborating with a string quartet and drummer Tony Williams. Hellborg performs on his Wechter acoustic bass guitar, creating a new sound with which he continued to experiment.

what to buy next: Two years after his new label debut, Hellborg recorded *Elegant Punk* ♫♫♫♫ (Day Eight, 1984/1996, prod. Jonas Hellborg), a second solo bass recording that shows his playing has grown and his concept is more firmly in place. *Jonas Hellborg Group* ♫♫♫ (Day Eight, 1988/1990, prod. Jonas Hellborg) displays his more experimental side, featuring Hellborg on double-neck fretted and fretless bass guitar and MIDI bass guitar, Anders Nord on bass guitar, and Jaime Salazar playing electronic drums. *Ars Moriende* ♫♫♫ (Day Eight, 1995, prod. Jonas Hellborg) is an unorthodox recording, a rhythmic session that explores strange, airy textures and contains a duet between Hellborg and frame-drummer Glen Velez.

the rest:
All Our Steps ♫♫♫ (Day Eight, 1983)
Reebop-Melodies in a Jungle Man's Head ♫♫♫ (Day Eight, 1983)
Bass ♫♫♫ (Day Eight 1988/1996)
Adfa ♫♫♫ (Day Eight, 1989/1996)
The Silent Life ♫♫♫♫ (Day Eight, 1991)
E ♫♫♫ (Day Eight, 1993)
(With Buckethead and Michael Shrieve) *Octave of the Holy Innocents* ♫♫♫ (Day Eight, 1993)
Abstract Logic ♫♫♫ (Day Eight, 1995)

worth searching for: Hard to find, Hellborg's debut recording for his own label, *The Bassic Thing* ♫♫♫ (Day Eight, 1982, prod. Jonas Hellborg), is a solo bass tour de force showcasing his monster chops.

influences:
 Jimi Hendrix, John McLaughlin, Cream, Deep Purple, John Coltrane, Albert Ayler, Miles Davis

David C. Gross

Julius Hemphill
Born January 28, 1938, in Fort Worth, TX. Died April 2, 1995, in New York, NY.

Julius Hemphill's first musical instrument was the clarinet, but when he was offered a shot at the saxophone, he took it. As a result, according to critic Bob Blumenthal, "No one has done more in the past two decades to move [jazz] music forward." In

---

JULIUS HEMPHILL

song "For Billie"
album *Julius Hemphill Big Band*
(Elektra, 1988)
instrument Alto saxophone

Monster Solo

---

high school, Hemphill played baritone sax, influenced by Gerry Mulligan's pianoless quartets. Hemphill later studied with John Carter while playing with various R&B outfits before joining the army in 1964. After his tour of duty was over, Hemphill played for a while with Ike Turner's band prior to moving to St. Louis. In 1971 he formed his first working group, then started his own record company, Mbari, and released his first album as a leader, the classic *Dogon A.D.* Appearing occasionally in concert with Anthony Braxton, Hemphill experimented with mixed media, producing 1973's *The Orientation of Sweet Willie Rollbar* and 1974's *Obituary: Cosmos for Three Parts* while appearing on albums by Paul Jeffrey, Lester Bowie, and Braxton. In 1976 Hemphill became a founding member and the principal composer/arranger of the World Saxophone Quartet, then premiered his mixed-media opera *Long Tongues: A Saxophone Opera* at New York's Apollo Theatre. He died after a long battle with heart problems, and the Jazz Composers Alliance posthumously renamed an annual contest the Julius Hemphill Composition Awards.

what to buy: After leaving the World Saxophone Quartet, Hemphill formed his own sextet, which made its debut with *Fat Man and the Hard Blues* 🎵🎵🎵🎵 (Black Saint, 1991, prod. Julius Hemphill, Cynthia B. Herbst), which contains moments of great beauty, including the opening statement by James Carter on "Four Saints" and a flute trio on "Tendrils." The honky-tonk residue of Hemphill's days playing in R&B bands can be heard in "The Hard Blues," a song that first appeared on his 1975 album *Coon Bid'ness. Reflections* 🎵🎵🎵🎵 (Freedom, 1975, prod. Michael Cuscuna, Julius Hemphill) is *Coon Bid'ness* released under a different title. The superb album includes the first appearance of one of Hemphill's signature tunes, "The Hard Blues," which took up a whole LP side. The playing is closer to "free" than on "The Hard Blues," but it's interesting hearing alto saxophonist Arthur Blythe and Hemphill trade cosmic blues licks over structured cacophony.

what to buy next: *Big Band* 🎵🎵🎵 (Elektra Musician, 1988, prod. Robert Hurwitz) may be the only chance to hear how Hemphill wrote for a large ensemble. Ronnie Burrage has a wonderful avant-big-band drum solo in "At Harmony" and Hemphill's alto solo opening for "Leora" plays well off the pensive French horn parts. The 18-minute "Drunk on God" backs up a poem by K. Curtis Lyle. *Five Chord Stud* 🎵🎵🎵 (Black Saint, 1994, prod. Julius Hemphill, Cynthia B. Herbst), featuring an edition of the Julius Hemphill Sextet, plays Hemphill's music without Hemphill playing (he conducts and composes). The pieces and playing are all virtuoso material, with the harmonies heard in "Mirrors" making for the most intriguing recordings Hemphill has been involved with.

the rest:
(With Abdul Wadud) *Live in New York* 🎵🎵 (Red, 1976)
Raw Materials and Residuals 🎵🎵🎵 (Black Saint, 1977)
Flat-out Jump Suite 🎵🎵🎵 (Black Saint, 1992)
Live from the New Music Cafe 🎵🎵🎵 (Music & Arts, 1992)
(With Abdul Wadud) *Oakland Duets* 🎵🎵🎵 (Music & Arts, 1993)

worth searching for: The out-of-print *Dogon A.D.* 🎵🎵🎵🎵 (Mbari, 1972/Freedom, 1977, prod. Julius Hemphill), Hemphill's first release as a leader, is one of the essential Hemphill albums.

influences:
◀◀ Gerry Mulligan, Johnny Hodges, Paul Desmond, Charlie Parker, John Coltrane

▶▶ Tim Berne

Garaud MacTaggart

Bill Henderson

Born March 19, 1930, in Chicago, IL.

With so few great male jazz singers around, there's really no excuse for Bill Henderson's obscurity. A powerful, swinging singer who fits perfectly into the hard-bop style, Henderson can also deliver ballads with élan and shout blues with complete authority. An original stylist, Henderson is a dramatic singer who employs moans and sharp shifts in volume to great effect. Raised in Chicago, he began singing professionally in 1953. After a two-year stint in the Army touring Europe with a Special Services band, he moved to New York in the late 1950s and started leading his own sessions. Henderson waxed the definitive hard-bop vocal on Horace Silver's 1958 jukebox hit, "Senor Blues," one of the few vocal singles recorded by Blue Note during the label's glory years. He also recorded a number of excellent sessions for Vee-Jay with such top flight sidemen as Tommy Flanagan, Eddie Harris, Elvin Jones, Booker Little, and Ramsey Lewis. Henderson toured Japan with the great 1961 edition of Art Blakey and the Jazz Messengers. He recorded a classic album with the Oscar Peterson Trio in 1963, and toured with Count Basie from 1965–66. He settled in Los Angeles in the mid-1960s and his singing was soon supplanted by his acting career. Henderson had roles in such movies as *Trouble Man, Inside Move, Murphy's Law,* and *City Slickers,* and has made numerous television appearances. He continues to sing around the Los Angeles area, often working with pianist Mike Melvoin, and his voice has only grown more expressive with time.

what to buy: Bill Henderson, in his prime, turned standards and pop tunes into pure jazz. *His Complete Vee-Jay Recordings, Vol. 1* 🎵🎵🎵🎵🎵 (Vee-Jay, 1959–60/1993, prod. Sid McCoy) features 18 tracks with Henderson accompanied by a trio led by Ramsey Lewis, a sextet arranged by Benny Golson, a Basie-ite octet with Frank Wess, and the MJT+3. Along with Henderson's *His Complete Vee-Jay Recordings, Vol. 2* 🎵🎵🎵🎵🎵 (Vee-Jay, 1960–61/1993, prod. Sid McCoy), it's a must for fans of jazz vocals. *Vol. 2* features Henderson with an orchestra arranged by pianist Jimmy Jones, the Count Basie band with arrangements by Thad Jones, a quartet led by Tommy Flanagan, a studio big band, and a trio led by pianist Eddie Higgins. With his soulful voice and inimitable phrasing, Henderson is one of jazz's long-overlooked delights.

what to buy next: Originally released on MGM, *Bill Henderson with the Oscar Peterson Trio* 🎵🎵🎵🎵 (Verve, 1963/1989, prod. Jim Davis) was long unavailable until it was reissued in 1989 with four previously unreleased tracks. A precious addition to

Henderson's slim discography, this session features Peterson at his sparkling best, with bassist Ray Brown and drummer Ed Thigpen. This is a tour de force by one of the greatest jazz singers of the past 40 years. Recorded live sometime in the mid-1960s, *Live in Concert with the Count Basie Band* ♫♫♫ (Monad Records, 1995, prod. Alonzo King, Norman Hedman) captures Henderson in top form with a powerfully swinging version (was there any other kind?) of the Basie band. The album deserves five bones for quality, but with only 10 tracks and 26 minutes of music, it loses a bone for brevity.

best of the rest:

Live at the Times ♫♫♫ (Discovery, 1975)
Something's Gotta Give ♫♫♫ (Discovery, 1979/1993)

worth searching for: Never reissued on CD, *A Tribute to Johnny Mercer* ♫♫♫♫ (Discovery, 1982, prod. Albert L. Marx) features Henderson with pianist/vocalist Joyce Collins, his frequent collaborator at the time, and Dave Mackay on keyboards and Joey Baron on drums. A Collins-Henderson vocal duet on the medley of "My Shining Hour" and "I Thought about You" is delightfully inventive, and Henderson's version of "Blues in the Night" is a classic. However, the album only includes nine tracks and fewer than 35 minutes of music.

influences:

⏪ Joe Williams, Ernie Andrews, Johnny Hartman, Ray Charles, Earl Coleman

Andrew Gilbert

Eddie Henderson

Born October 26, 1940, in New York, NY.

After years of mediocre recordings, trumpeter Eddie Henderson came into his own in the late 1980s and has begun to fulfill his potential as one of jazz's leading trumpeters. Strongly influenced by Miles Davis, Henderson has increasingly expanded his warm, highly expressive sound with sharp, muscular phrases. Raised in New York, Henderson had strong show business genes—his mother was a dancer at the Cotton Club and his father sang with Bill Williams and the Charioteers. While Henderson was growing up, his house was frequented by Dizzy Gillespie, Sarah Vaughan, and Duke Ellington. His family moved to San Francisco in 1954, and as a teenager, Henderson studied trumpet and music theory at the San Francisco Conservatory; he was inspired to explore jazz when Miles Davis stayed at his parents' house. He spent the 1960s earning his M.D. at Howard University while working summer gigs with Joe Henderson, John Handy, Big Black, and Philly Joe Jones. From 1968 until the late 1980s, Henderson pursued dual careers in medicine and music.

He gained national exposure as a member of Herbie Hancock's Mwandishi sextet from 1970–73, a band that also included Bennie Maupin, Julian Priester, Buster Williams, and Billy Hart. In the mid-1970s he worked extensively with Pharoah Sanders, spent six months with Art Blakey's Jazz Messengers (1973), a year with the Latin jazz group Azteca (1974), and toured with drummer Norman Connors (1975), with whom he recorded five albums. His own sessions for Capricorn and Blue Note tended to be commercial affairs that didn't reflect his strong talents as an improvisor. Around 1988 he gave up his medical practice to devote himself to jazz full time, replacing Wallace Roney in Kenny Barron's group and recording a very impressive session with Barron for Enja, *Live at Fat Tuesdays*, signaling his belated emergence as an important voice. Since the beginning of the 1990s, he's become a prolific sideman, touring with tenor saxophonist Billy Mitchell and contributing significantly to sessions with Gary Bartz, Sonny Fortune, Benny Golson, Winard Harper, Bill Stewart, and Mal Waldron, among others. After more than a decade's hiatus as a leader, he recorded a series of fine albums for SteepleChase in the late 1980s and early 1990s, and cemented his reputation as a major creative force with two excellent sessions for Milestone.

what to buy: Though Eddie Henderson's approach is still deeply influenced by Miles Davis, on *Dark Shadows* ♫♫♫♫ (Milestone, 1996, prod. Todd Barkan) he plays with such direct and finely nuanced emotionalism, he makes the sound his own. Featuring the same players as his first Milestone CD—vibraphonist Joe Locke, pianist Kevin Hays, bassist Ed Howard, and drummer Lewis Nash—the album covers an impressive array of tunes, including Wayne Shorter's rarely played Latin theme "El Gaucho," Chick Corea's grooving "19th Street," Joe Henderson's surging "Punjab," and Freddie Hubbard's "Lament for Booker." Locke contributes two tunes written for the band's instrumentation, the Mwandishi-flavored "Cerulean Blues," with Hays on Fender Rhodes, and the gorgeous "Dawning Dance," with Steve Berrios sitting in on percussion. Henderson never plays a false or gratuitous note, even transforming the folk tune "The Water Is Wide," with an ethereal, crystalline vocal by his daughter Lee Menzies, into a deeply affecting experience.

what to buy next: A tribute to the many musicians he's worked with over the years, *Inspiration* ♫♫♫♫ (Milestone, 1995, prod. Todd Barkan, Makoto Kimata) is a brilliant session featuring vibraphonist Joe Locke, pianist Kevin Hays, bassist Ed Howard, and drummer Lewis Nash. Grover Washington Jr. sits in on "I Remember Clifford" and Herbie Hancock's "Oliloqui Valley," reminding everyone he can improvise convincingly when he wants. The album's overall tone is set by Henderson's gorgeous ballad work on "When You Wish Upon a Star," Billy Harper's gentle "If One Could Only See," and Kenny Barron's lugubrious "Phantoms." Other highlights include Joe Henderson's angular "Jinriksha," McCoy Tyner's lush "Peresina," and Henderson's tribute to Miles Davis, "On Green Dolphin Street." The combination of vibes and trumpet in the front line is highly effective, creating delicate and swinging melodic vistas.

best of the rest:

Phantoms ♫♫♫ (SteepleChase, 1989)
Think on Me ♫♫♫♫ (SteepleChase, 1990)
Flight of Mind ♫♫♫♫ (SteepleChase, 1991)

worth searching for: *Mwandishi: The Complete Warner Bros. Recordings* ♫♫♫♫ (Warner Archives, 1994, prod. various) is a two-disc set containing three records, *Fat Albert Rotunda*, *Mwandishi*, and *Crossings*, recorded between late 1969 and early 1972. While *Fat Albert Rotunda* features a sextet with Joe Henderson and trumpeter Johnny Coles playing funk themes from the cartoon series, the two later albums feature Hancock's groundbreaking funk/rock/avant-garde jazz sextet with Henderson (heavily influenced by Miles's early fusion sound), Bennie Maupin, Julian Priester, Buster Williams, and the dazzling Billy Hart. Henderson's playing is much richer and more dynamic than his own albums that tried to expand on Hancock's loose, exploratory approach. Henderson plays on six of Mulgrew Miller's eight originals on *Hand to Hand* ♫♫♫♫ (Novus, 1993, prod. Mulgrew Miller, Orrin Keepnews), the best album yet by the gifted pianist. Henderson's tracks feature a world-class septet with Kenny Garrett (alto and soprano sax), Joe Henderson (tenor sax), Steve Nelson (vibes), Christian McBride (bass), and Lewis Nash (drums). Miller writes with a keen ear for melody and Henderson thrives in his airy group concept.

influences:

◀◀ Miles Davis, Clifford Brown, Freddie Hubbard

Andrew Gilbert

Fletcher Henderson

Born December 18, 1897, in Cuthbert, GA. Died December 29, 1952, in New York, NY.

Big bands, featuring brass, sax, and rhythm sections, have been around since at least the teens of this century. But prior to the emergence of the Fletcher Henderson band in the 1920s,

few had more than a passing flirtation with jazz. Henderson, a pianist, led the first great jazz-focused big band, an ensemble through which passed many greats on their way to fame, including trumpeters Louis Armstrong, Cootie Williams, Red Allen, and Roy Eldridge; trombonists Charlie Green, Benny Morton, Jimmy Harrison, and J. C. Higginbotham; saxophonists Coleman Hawkins, Benny Carter, Chu Berry, and Ben Webster; clarinetist Buster Bailey; bassists John Kirby and Israel Crosby; and drummer Sid Catlett.

Serious jazz-band arranging appears to have begun with the charts Don Redman wrote for Henderson in the early 1920s. Shortly thereafter, Benny Carter, Edgar Sampson, and Fletcher's younger brother Horace also contributed to the book. It wasn't until the early 1930s that, on a bet, Fletcher started arranging, but he soon became the dominant style-setter of the era. He arranged not only for his own band, but for many others as well. Reportedly, he sold more than 200 charts to Benny Goodman, who readily acknowledged that Henderson's work was a major factor in Goodman's becoming the "King of Swing."

Though Henderson pioneered the Harlem big band movement, his band was dogged by bad luck, much brought on by Henderson's own lax leadership. Among musicians, especially those who played with Henderson, the story long persisted that the band was great on the job, but froze up in the recording studio. Henderson's recorded legacy does reveal a frequent lack of ensemble precision, but just as often finds the band's soloists turning in performances that set high standards. The bad luck, combined with Henderson's phenomenal success arranging for others, led him to disband on June 8, 1939, just when many other big bands were on the verge of fame. Some of Fletcher's musicians went with his brother Horace's band. Fletcher himself took over the piano chair with Benny Goodman's small groups; then, when Jess Stacy left in a huff, he took over Goodman's big band as well.

Henderson led another band from 1941 through 1947, but it was never very successful, either commercially or artistically. After 1947, Henderson played piano accompaniment for various singers, arranged and played for a review, *The Jazz Train*, and finally led a swing sextet at a New York club, Café Society, where his final performance was recorded as an air check the night of December 21, 1950, mere hours before he suffered a

Fletcher Henderson (Archive Photos)

debilitating stroke. Henderson spent his last two years as an invalid.

Henderson is notable for his band-leading and arranging, not as a pianist. The earliest recorded examples of his piano work reveal the influence of the published light classics and ragtime of the day. In its earliest years, Henderson's band was a commercial dance orchestra sounding somewhat similar to recordings by West Coast leader Art Hickman, with a bit of the spunk of James Reese Europe. The solo work of various jazz giants who passed through the band, notably Louis Armstrong, had a profound impact on its very character. Don Redman's charts for Henderson in the 1920s were the major influence on Henderson's own arrangements of the 1930s.

what to buy: Intended to be a complete set, seventeen separate CDs form the Fletcher Henderson series on the Classics label. Compiled from original 78rpm recordings on many labels, these CD reissues, released in the 1990s, present in chronological order virtually all of Fletcher Henderson's work as a leader from 1921 through 1941. The discs are not designated by volume number or name, but by recording years (e.g., *1921–1923*, etc.). Alternate takes and most of Henderson's work as a blues accompanist are not included, but are hardly missed with the wealth of material present. The completeness of this series, its thorough discography, and good sound (subject to original recording conditions) deserve the highest rating but, as can be expected from a musical pioneer, especially one working within constraints imposed by the entertainment business, the artistic results present a mixed bag to which it is difficult to assign one rating. All in all, completists and serious students of jazz history should find these recordings highly worthy of musical pleasure. Though there are many CDs of Fletcher Henderson's output available, they are all covered by the Classics CDs already noted. But a few are valuable for fans not wanting totality or a lesson in jazz history. Selective buying of the Classics CDs is the first option. The sides including Louis Armstrong, as he showed New Yorkers how to swing, are found on *Fletcher Henderson, 1924, Vol. 3* ♪♪♪♪ (Classics, prod. Gilles Petard), and *Fletcher Henderson: 1924–1925* ♪♪♪♪ (Classics, prod. Gilles Petard). "Everybody Loves My Baby," with Armstrong's first vocal on wax, and the classic "Sugarfoot Stomp," on which Louis plays a solo later copied by innumerable trumpeters, are just a couple of the Armstrong/Henderson gems. *Fletcher Henderson: 1932–1934* ♪♪♪♪ (Classics, prod. various) is a great selection of mature Henderson, including a number of charts later recorded by Benny Goodman, including Fletcher's "King Porter Stomp," "Down South Camp Meetin'," and "Wrappin' It Up," as well as

brother Horace's "Big John's Special." The Henderson/Goodman comparison is interesting. There's more meat to Henderson's readings, and the soloists, especially trumpeter Red Allen, tell more convincing stories. But the Goodman band out-swings Henderson. It's no wonder there was a mutual admiration between Henderson and Goodman.

what to buy next: The last Classics Henderson CD, *Fletcher Henderson: 1940–1941* ♪♪♪ (Classics) is not particularly notable for the 1941 sides by Fletcher, but more for the 1940 output of the Horace Henderson band, which features many of Fletcher's former sidemen and a few of Fletcher's arrangements. This was a great overlooked band. Trumpeter Emmett Berry was its most notable soloist, producing particularly hot work on "Flinging a Whing Ding." But for a broad look at Fletcher Henderson's recorded output, *A Study in Frustration* ♪♪♪♪ (Columbia, 1923–1938/1994, prod. Frank Driggs) is the set to buy. This three-CD reissue of a four-LP set chronicles the band from 1923 through 1938. The selection of tunes is excellent, including many on the individual Classics CDs mentioned above. There is super solo work from a galaxy of jazz legends-to-be, including the aforementioned Armstrong, Hawkins, and Allen, as well as trumpeters Bobby Stark, Tommy Ladnier, Rex Stewart, and Roy Eldridge, trombonists Charlie Green, Jimmy Harrison, and J.C. Higgenbotham, saxophonists Benny Carter, Chu Berry, and Ben Webster, and even a couple of pianists other than Fletcher, notably Fats Waller, and brother Horace Henderson. The notes and discography are excellent, but if you can find the LP set, the booklet contains many fine early photos of the band.

worth searching for: Though not essential, jazz necrophiliacs will undoubtedly search for the LP *Fletcher Henderson's Sextet 1950* ♪♪ (Alamac, 1950). This is pretty low-key stuff, with tenor saxophonist Lucky Thompson providing the most interest. A low-rated effort, this recording is significant because it is Henderson's last LP, recorded the night of his debilitating stroke.

influences:

◀◀ Art Hickman, James Reese Europe

▶▶ Sy Oliver, Edgar Sampson, Jimmy Mundy, Ernie Wilkins, Benny Goodman

John K. Richmond

Joe Henderson

Born April 24, 1937, in Lima, OH.

With the release of 1992's *Lush Life*, Joe Henderson arrived. For 30 years he had been an outstanding and prolific leader and sideman but had remained relatively unknown. Recent acclaim has not made him complacent, however. He continues to play with the same intensity and fire that has been the hallmark of his career. His burnished tone and penchant for melodic ornamentation are instantly identifiable. One of 15 children, Henderson was encouraged by his parents and an older brother to study music. Early musical interests included drums, piano, saxophone, and composition. He was particularly enamored of his brother's record collection and listened to Lester Young, Flip Phillips, Stan Getz, Lee Konitz, Charlie Parker, and the popular Jazz at the Philharmonic recordings. At age 18 Henderson became active on the Detroit jazz scene, playing in jam sessions with visiting New York stars of the mid-1950s. The diverse musical opportunities allowed Henderson to learn flute and bass, as well as further developing his saxophone and compositional skills. By the time he arrived at Detroit's Wayne State University, he had transcribed and memorized so many Lester Young solos that his professors believed he had perfect pitch. Classmates Yusef Lateef, Barry Harris, and Donald Byrd undoubtedly provided additional inspiration. After a two-year hitch in the U.S. Army (1960–62), Henderson arrived in New York, where trumpeter Kenny Dorham provided valuable guidance. Although his earliest recordings were marked by a strong hard-bop influence, his playing encompassed not only the bebop tradition, but R&B, Latin, and avant garde as well. After leaving Silver's band in 1964, Henderson resumed freelancing and also co-led a big band with Kenny Dorham. His arrangements for the band went unrecorded until his Verve album, *Big Band,* in 1996. From 1963 to 1968 Henderson appeared on nearly 30 albums for Blue Note that ranged from relatively conservative hard-bop sessions to more avant-garde explorations. This experience was invaluable to his continuing development. He played a prominent role in many seminal recordings: Horace Silver's swinging and soulful *Song for My Father*, Herbie Hancock's dark and densely orchestrated *Prisoner*, and Eric Dolphy's landmark avant-garde album *Out to Lunch*. This adaptability and eclecticism became even more apparent during his tenure with Milestone during the 1970s.

In 1967 there was a notable, but brief, association with Miles Davis's great quintet featuring Herbie Hancock, Wayne Shorter, Ron Carter, and Tony Williams. Although the band was unrecorded, Henderson is reputed to have occasionally stolen the show. Signing with Orrin Keepnews's fledgling Milestone label in 1967 marked a new phase in Henderson's career. He co-led the Jazz Communicators with Freddie Hubbard from 1967–68, then joined Herbie Hancock's fusion-ish sextet from 1969–70

DICKY WELLS
(WITH FLETCHER HENDERSON)

song "King Porter Stomp"
album *A Study in Frustration*
(Columbia, 1933/1995)
instrument Trombone

Monster Solo

and was featured on *Fat Albert Rotunda*. It was here that Henderson began to experiment with increasingly avant-garde structures, jazz-funk fusion, studio overdubbing, and other electronic effects. Songs and albums titled *Power to the People*, *In Search of Blackness*, and *Black Narcissus* reflected his growing political awareness and social consciousness. After a brief stint with Blood, Sweat and Tears in 1971, Henderson moved to San Francisco and added teaching to his résumé. He continued to record and perform as always, but seemed to be taken for granted. Though he occasionally worked with Echoes of an Era, the Griffith Park Band, and Chick Corea, Henderson remained primarily a leader throughout the 1980s. An accomplished and prolific composer, he began to focus more on reinterpreting standards and his own earlier compositions. Blue Note attempted to position him at the forefront of a resurgent jazz scene in 1986 with *State of the Tenor*. And although the album featured the most notable tenor trio since Sonny Rollins's in 1957, insufficient support from Blue Note prevented wider renown. The recording did, however, establish Hender-

son's basic repertoire for the next seven or eight years, with "Ask Me Now" becoming his signature tune. Verve's recent "songbook" approach to recording Henderson, coupled with a considerable marketing and publicity campaign, has successfully positioned him at the forefront of the current jazz scene. Henderson's sound can float prettily like that of Stan Getz or Lester "Prez" Young, and yet also dig in with the bluesy fervor of T-Bone Walker. The increasing complexity and ornamental nature of his current output suggests Henderson has successfully created his own unique vocabulary of phrases, licks, and saxophone effects.

what to buy: *Mode for Joe* ♪♪♪♪ (Blue Note, 1966, prod. Alfred Lion) is a remarkable example of Henderson's compositional and arranging talents. The three-horn frontline (tenor, trombone, and trumpet) gives the music extra kick. The extended form of Cedar Walton's "Mode for Joe" pushes and prods Henderson into new territory. Although the individual recordings for Milestone are uniformly outstanding, the eight-CD box set *Milestone Years* ♪♪♪♪♪ (Milestone, 1994) clearly portrays a seasoned and mature performer confident enough in his skills to test his own limits. The set ranges from straight-ahead jazz sessions and fantastic live performances to Latin/jazz fusion and effect-laden avant-garde. *An Evening with Joe Henderson* ♪♪♪♪ (Red, 1987, prod. Sergio Veschi, Alberto Alberti) captures Henderson in a trio setting taking on originals and lesser-known standards. In addition to the replacement of Ron Carter with Charlie Haden on bass, this disc captures a looser, more freewheeling performance. "Beatrice" and "Ask Me Now" are twice as long as their Blue Note counterparts, and there is a familiarity with the material that allows the three to coax unexpected twists and turns from the music. In one sense, *Double Rainbow* ♪♪♪♪ (Verve, 1995, prod. Oscar Castro-Neves, Richard Seidel) picks up where Stan Getz left off. By the same token this is an interpretation of Antonio Carlos Jobim that is uniquely Henderson's. From the opening notes of "Felicidade," the supple Brazilian rhythms wash over the listener and at the same time retain the edge and fire that distinguishes Joe Henderson's playing.

what to buy next: *Inner Urge* ♪♪♪♪ (Blue Note, 1964/1989, prod. Alfred Lion) is a particularly strong and focused quartet outing with McCoy Tyner (piano), Bob Cranshaw (bass), and Elvin Jones (drums) recorded at Van Gelder Studio in Engle-

wood, New Jersey, in 1964. All but two of the songs are written by Henderson, and his originals "Inner Urge" and "Isotope" have since become standards. "El Barrio" nicely displays Henderson's flair with Latin tunes. *Straight, No Chaser* ♪♪♪♪ (Verve, 1968/1996 prod. Richard Seidel) catches Henderson on an April 21, 1968, live-recorded performance at Baltimore's Left Bank Jazz Society, sitting in with the Wynton Kelly Trio, featuring pianist Kelly, bassist Paul Chambers, and drummer Jimmy Cobb. Henderson's avant-garde tendencies played over the rock-solid backing of Kelly's trio is a listening delight. Henderson is in top form throughout, but especially on "What Is This Thing Called Love" and "Limehouse Blues," which contain burning, incandescent solos that amaze and astound. *State of the Tenor* ♪♪♪♪ (Blue Note, 1986/1994, prod. Stanley Crouch, Michael Cuscuna) is often overly somber, but is also a remarkable example of Henderson's awesome capacity for melodic development. It is, however, the first recording of the latest chapter of Henderson's career. The delicate interaction of the trio on "Beatrice" and "The Bead Game" approaches telepathic. Combining the exquisite compositions of Billy Strayhorn and a band consisting of trumpeter Wynton Marsalis, pianist Stephen Scott, bassist Christian McBride, and drummer Greg Hutchinson, how could *Lush Life: The Music of Billy Strayhorn* ♪♪♪♪ (Verve, 1992, prod. Richard Seidel, Don Sickler) be anything but a hit? Henderson's reading of "Blood Count" is heartbreaking in its delicacy, and his solo rendition of "Lush Life" is a tour de force on a par with Sonny Rollins's famous solo forays. Also among the 10 tunes are the Strayhorn classics "A Flower Is a Lovesome Thing," "Take the 'A' Train," "Upper Manhattan Medical Group," and "Isfahan."

best of the rest:
Page One ♪♪♪ (Blue Note, 1963/1988)
In 'n' Out ♪♪♪ (Blue Note, 1964/1994)
The Kicker ♪♪♪♪ (Milestone, 1967)
Tetragon ♪♪♪♪ (Milestone, 1968/1995)
Four! ♪♪♪♪ (Verve, 1968/1994)
Multiple ♪♪♪ (Milestone, 1973/OJC, 1993)
The Elements ♪♪♪ (Milestone, 1973/OJC, 1996)
Canyon Lady ♪♪♪ (Milestone, 1973/OJC, 1997)
Barcelona ♪♪♪ (Enja, 1978/1993)
Mirror, Mirror ♪♪♪ (Verve, 1980/1993)
Relaxin' at Camarillo ♪♪♪ (Contemporary, 1981/OJC, 1993)
The Standard Joe ♪♪♪♪ (Red, 1993)
So Near, So Far (Musings for Miles) ♪♪♪♪♪ (Verve, 1993)
Big Band ♪♪♪ (Verve, 1996)

worth searching for: With Chick Corea as leader, *Live in Montreux* ♪♪♪ (Stretch, 1981, prod. Chick Corea) features Hender-

Joe Henderson **(© Nancy Ann Lee)**

son as part of an all-star band with Corea, Roy Haynes, and Gary Peacock playing Corea's brand of post-bop jazz.

influences:

◄◄ Lester Young, Stan Getz, Sonny Stitt

►► Michael Brecker, Joe Lovano, Branford Marsalis, Javon Jackson, Joshua Redman

James Eason

Ernie Henry

Born September 3, 1926, in Brooklyn, NY. Died December 29, 1957, in New York, NY.

Ernie Henry was a gifted bebop alto saxophonist who developed his own emotionally intense and rhythmically nuanced approach to Charlie Parker's sound. During his short career he worked with many of the leading bandleaders and composers in modern jazz. After leaving the Army, Henry broke into the 52nd Street scene with Tadd Dameron in 1947 and then spent two years with Dizzy Gillespie's big band. In the late 1940s he recorded with Dameron, Howard McGhee, and Fats Navarro, among others. Following a two-year stint with Illinois Jacquet (1950–52), Henry dropped out of view for a number of years, concentrating on composing and arranging. He resurfaced in the mid-1950s and quickly landed high-profile gigs with Charles Mingus and Thelonious Monk (appearing on his great *Brilliant Corners* session with Sonny Rollins) and spent a year touring with Dizzy Gillespie's big band until his death in 1957. He recorded three sessions for Riverside, but only one (unfortunately not the best) has been reissued on CD.

what's available: Recorded just months before Ernie Henry's death at the age of 31, *Seven Standards and a Blues* ⅃⅃⅃ (Riverside, 1957/OJC, 1992, prod. Orrin Keepnews) is an occasionally rewarding session that lacks some of the passion of the alto saxophonist's best work. Consisting of seven standards and one Henry original, the album features Wynton Kelly (piano), Wilbur Ware (bass), and Philly Joe Jones (drums). Despite the top-flight personnel, there are a number of glaring miscues, and a couple of the tracks ("My Ideal" and "Love Man") stop before they have a chance to go anywhere.

worth searching for: Henry's last session found him playing for the brilliant but underrated trumpeter Kenny Dorham on *2 Horns/ 2 Rhythm* ⅃⅃⅃⅃ (Riverside, 1957/OJC, 1990, prod. Orrin Keepnews), a pianoless quartet session featuring Eddie Mathias or Wilbur Ware (bass) and G.T. Hogan (drums). Opening with Dorham's gorgeous, eastern-tinged "Lotus Blossom," where

the two horns create a series of unusual voicings, the album provides a number of challenging settings, from the free-for-all of "I'll Be Seeing You" to the counterpoint of Dorham's "Jazz-Classic." *Presenting Ernie Henry* ⅃⅃⅃⅃ (Riverside, 1956, prod. Orrin Keepnews) and *Last Chorus* ⅃⅃⅃⅃⅄ (Riverside, 1957, prod. Orrin Keepnews) are the more assured Riverside albums and hopefully will eventually appear on CD.

influences:

◄◄ Charlie Parker

Andrew Gilbert

Woody Herman

Born Woodrow Charles Thomas Hermann, May 16, 1913, in Milwaukee, WI. Died October 29, 1987, in West Los Angeles, CA.

Woody Herman was the consummate orchestra leader, a "road father" to many of his musicians, and a durable jazzman whose lengthy, difficult career as leader spanned over 50 years. A versatile reedman, he recorded as clarinetist and alto/soprano saxophonist, and was an above-average band vocalist. Like his famous contemporary Duke Ellington, whose first love was his band, Herman often downplayed his instrumental skills, concentrating instead on keeping his top-flight musical aggregations on the road and one step ahead of the competition. The old "Woodchopper" was responsible for unleashing some of the best sidemen and arrangers in the dance-band business. He had a knack for setting the right tempos, discovering fresh, young talent, and keeping abreast of an ever-changing jazz scene. With all the financial and health problems that confronted him near the end of his life, Woody Herman was able to fall back on what he called "the great escape," his love of jazz music.

Woodrow Charles Thomas Hermann (not Woodrow Wilson Herman, as some liner notes state) did some vaudeville song-and-dance routines at an early age and worked the old Orpheum circuit as the "Boy Wonder of the Saxophone." At age 16, still in high school, he played as sideman in Joey Lichter's band at Eagles Million Dollar Ballroom in Milwaukee. In February 1931, Woody Herman entered Brunswick recording studio in Chicago to cut his first records with bandleader Tom Gerun, and in 1932 waxed his first vocals. Leaving Gerun in 1934, Herman returned to Milwaukee, joined Harry Sosnik's band, and later, while touring with Gus Arnheim, met his next employer, famous composer-bandleader Isham Jones. Herman remained with Jones until September 1936 when Jones sought retirement. A hot contingent from the defunct Jones organization formed the nucleus for the band billed as "Woody Herman and the Band That Plays the Blues." Originally a cooperative unit, the band employed a quasi-Dixieland style, struggling at the outset but eventually landing a Decca recording contract. Herman had the support of his new wife, Charlotte, and after scuffling for almost three years, had a big hit single with "Woodchopper's Ball," which really got things moving. The band landed in several movies, started playing major locations, and adopted a new theme song, "Blue Flame."

Tremendous personnel changes occurred in the Herman big band ranks during the early World War II years. The band took on Johnny Bothwell, Cliff Leeman, Vido Musso, and Anita O'Day, and added arrangers Dizzy Gillespie and Dave Matthews to provide a modern touch and an Ellington flavor. Ellington stalwarts such as saxophonists Johnny Hodges and Ben Webster were added for recording dates. By the end of 1944 Herman had assembled the orchestra that eventually became known as the First Herd. It featured wild ensembles, unison brass passages, and arrangements by Ralph Burns and Neal Hefti that were destined to become lasting big band classics. Equally at home with flagwavers or ballads, the First Herd boasted major soloists in trombonist Bill Harris, tenorman Flip Phillips, and a blazing, blasting trumpet section propelled by Pete Condoli and at times featuring Sonny Berman, Shorty Rogers, Neal Hefti, Ray Wetzel, and Conte Candoli. Marjorie Hyams and later, Red Norvo, added vibes to the heady mix, and Woody Herman used his Hodges-style alto with greater frequency. The classy rhythm section consisted of "cheerleader"/bassist Chubby Jackson, masterful drummer Dave Tough (later, Don Lamond), guitarists Billy Bauer or Chuck Wayne, and a succession of pianists including Ralph Burns, Tony Aless, and Jimmy Rowles. The sound of this magnificent band was heard coast to coast via ABC Radio (Saturdays at 8 p.m. EST), and those broadcasts are still fondly remembered by aging swingsters. Due to Herman family problems, the First Herd disbanded at the height of its popularity, after having won the 1946 Best Band awards in *Billboard,* and *Metronome,* and Best Swing Band in *Down Beat.*

In mid-1947, Herman reemerged with the Second Herd, also known as the Four Brothers Band. With baritone saxophonist Serge Chaloff anchoring the sax section, and the three tenors played by Stan Getz, Zoot Sims, and Herb Steward (later, Al Cohn), this band had a sound and a personality all its own when compared to earlier Herman bands. Before its 1949 demise, the Second Herd sound received contributions from Gene Ammons, Jimmy Guiffre, Lou Levy, Oscar Pettiford, Terry Gibbs, and Shelly Manne.

Keeping the Herds straight is difficult, but the leader himself dubbed his early 1950s band of swingers the Third Herd. Featuring a more conservative, danceable style, the new band could not help but swing with top-ranked sidemen such as Conte Candoli, Al Cohn, Dave McKenna, Don Fagerquist, Al Porcino, Urbie Green, Kai Winding, Carl Fontana, Dick Hafer, Bill Perkins, Cy Touff, Nat Pierce, Dick Collins, and Richie Kamuca all passing through its ranks. By the summer of 1955, it was becoming increasingly grueling to maintain a big band, and Woody opted for taking an octet into the Las Vegas gig at the Riviera Hotel. The Herd that formed going into 1956 was a different group in personnel and conception, and by mid-1959 had been identified in an album title as the Fourth Herd. This gang made a U. S. State Department tour of South America, Central America, and the Caribbean in 1958, and upon return went into the recording studios with Tito Puente and a group of his Latin percussionists. The next year jobs were erratic, as Herman was experiencing difficulties booking the big band and was often forced to work with various smaller groups. The early 1960s saw the birth of The Swingin' Herd, and a resurgence of interest in the Woody Herman Band, which now featured the piano and charts of Nat Pierce, Count Basie's alter ego. Trumpeters Bill Chase and Don Rader, trombonist Phil Wilson, tenorman Sal Nistico, and drummer Jake Hanna were at the heart of this edition, which lasted through 1967. In the late 1960s and early 1970s, the Herd of the moment experimented with electric piano and bass, and entered into an era of fusion that lasted for approximately a decade. Pianist/composer/arranger Alan Broadbent joined the band in September 1969, and became a major influence on the band book of the early 1970s. Tenor saxophonist Frank Tiberi joined a month later and remained for years, as acting leader during Herman's illnesses, and after his passing in 1987. The Thundering Herd was home to many youthful talents such as keyboard whiz Andy Laverne; guitarist Joe Beck; trombonist Jim Pugh; tenor saxophonists Gary Anderson, Greg Berbert, and Joe Lovano; baritone saxman Bruce Johnstone; trumpeters Bill Byrne and Allen Vizzutti; drummer Jeff Hamilton; and percussionist Victor Feldman.

Woody Herman and the New Thundering Herd celebrated the leader's 40th anniversary with a noteworthy Carnegie Hall concert on November 20, 1976, which featured some famous alumni along with younger Herdsmen. By the late 1970s, the band was returning to a more swinging, straight-ahead approach and began a fruitful affiliation with Concord Records with the release of their 1979 Monterey Jazz Festival album, *Woody and Friends.* The band retained a high level of performance in the 1980s with an influx of talents like pianist/arranger/composer John Oddo; trombonist/arranger/composer John Fedchock; baritone saxophonist Mike Brignola; trumpeters Mark Lewis, George Rabbai, and Ron Stout; bassists John Leitham and Lynn Seaton; and a most appealing gal vocalist, Polly Bodewell.

Herman's health was in a downward spiral, however, and his personal problems mounted, with pressure from the IRS relating to management problems over the years and the death of his wife of over 46 years, Charlotte. Like his characteristic Herdsmen, he was still full of thunder and enthusiasm, appearing cheerful with his public, and celebrated his 50th anniversary as a bandleader in 1986. Herman was in and out of hospitals until his death in late October 1987, his remarkable longevity taking him through most all of the eras of jazz until the end.

what to buy: The roar and bite of the First Herd is captured in *The Thundering Herds, 1945–1947* 𝄞𝄞𝄞𝄞 (Columbia, 1988, prod. Michael Brooks), which allocates 14 tracks to the explosive 1945–1946 band, and two tracks to the Second Herd (aka, the Four Brothers Band). The precision brass, the propulsive rhythm section, and major soloists Bill Harris (trombone), Flip Phillips (tenor sax), and trumpeters Sonny Berman and Pete Candoli, are all here along with an abundance of Woody Herman's clarinet, alto sax, and vocal stylings. Bassist Chubby Jackson and drummers Don Lamond, Buddy Rich, and the masterful Dave Tough prod the soloists and whip some of the hottest ensembles ever recorded in jazz. Titles include Herman classics "Apple Honey," "Northwest Passage," "Wildroot," and "Your Father's Mustache," which, 50 years later, remain the ultimate in swinging big band fare. The blues-tinged "Goosey Gander" and Neal Hefti's well-constructed "The Good Earth" (originally "Helen of Troy") are welcome additions to the mix. Al Cohn's "The Goof and I" and Jimmy Guiffre's well-known "Flour Brothers" are Second Herd selections featuring Herman luminaries such as Zoot Sims, Stan Getz, Herbie Steward, and Serge Chaloff in a powerhouse sax section. *The First Herd* 𝄞𝄞𝄞𝄞𝄞 (Le Jazz, 1996) is a generous set offering 17 tunes by the full Woody Herman orchestra from 1945–1946 Columbia masters, and adds six exciting Woodchopper-like Keynote sides with Bill Harris, Flip Phillips, and Chubby Jackson at their best. There is some overlap with the Columbia set, but this one includes some obscure minor classics like "Let It Snow" and "Put That Ring on My Finger." For the many Herman fans who can't get enough of the First Herd, seek out *Woody Herman, The V-Disc Years, Vols. 1 & 2, 1944–46* 𝄞𝄞𝄞𝄞 (Hep, 1994, prod. vari-

ous). Restored for reissue by Jack Towers and R.T. Davies, this collection offers extended versions of many of the 1944 to 1946 Herman delights ("Apple Honey," "Wildroot," and "Blowin' Up a Storm"), plus others which were never recorded commercially ("Red Top" and "Jones Beachhead"). The rhythm of Ralph Burns, Billy Bauer, Chubby Jackson, and Dave Tough really cooks on these rare sides and the band exudes excitement. The 19 tunes on *Keeper of the Flame: Complete Capitol Recordings of the Four Brothers Band* 𝄞𝄞𝄞𝄞 (Capitol, 1992, prod. Pete Welding, Michael Cuscuna) contain some of the best tracks by Herman's Second Herd, which had a decided bop flavor and an impressive lineup of soloists such as Al Cohn, Stan Getz, Zoot Sims, Serge Chaloff, Gene Ammons, and Jimmy Guiffre passing through the famed sax section. Other members, from time to time, included Terry Gibbs, Shelly Manne, Red Rodney, Shorty Rogers, Lou Levy, Bill Harris, and Oscar Pettiford. Arrangers Ralph Burns, Johnny Mandel, Jimmy Guiffre, and Shorty Rogers all contributed interesting and influential charts. The lovely "Early Autumn" and "Tenderly" are here amidst the wacky "Lemon Drop," and swingers like "The Great Lie," "More Moon," and "Not Really the Blues." This is a welcomed reissue which provides a good recap of the short-lived Second Herd.

what to buy next: A newly discovered treasure for Herman fans, *Jantzen Beach Oregon 1954* 𝄞𝄞𝄞𝄞 (Status, 1996, prod. Dave Kay) offers previously unissued material recorded live by Wally Heider, and brings the Third Herd to the forefront in a 15-tune collection for a dance date. Considering the source, it is remarkable that the band got away with a virtually all-jazz program. This band, more than preceding Herds, was cast in a Count Basie mold, due in part to the presence of Nat Pierce in both the piano and arranger chairs. There are plenty of inspired solos by trumpeter Dick Collins, bass-trumpeter Cy Touff, and reedmen Bill Perkins, Dick Hafer, Bill Trujillo, and Jerry Coker. Dolly Houston has a couple of pleasant vocals ("Embraceable You" and "That Old Feeling"), and the band works through some attractive arrangements by Pierce, Al Cohn, Manny Albam, Neal Hefti, and Bill Holman. "Moten Swing" is handled neatly under the guise of "Moten Stomp," and charts for "Prez Conference," "Mulligantawny," and "Cohn's Alley" swing in a very relaxed groove as they pay tribute to legendary jazz performers. Lead trumpeter Al Porcino and anchor man baritone saxist Jack Nimitz are two unsung band giants who deserve credit for helping to move this band along on this fine outing. *Verve Jazz Masters 54: Woody Herman* 𝄞𝄞𝄞𝄞 (Verve, 1996, prod. Jack Tracy) is a compilation of 13 driving examples (originally recorded on Phillips between October 1962 and September 1964) by the 1960s band known as the Swingin' Herd. Favored by many Herman fans for its swinging sound, this exhilarating edition of the Herman band includes trumpeter Bill Chase, tenor saxophonist Sal Nistico, trombonist Phil Wilson, bassist Chuck Andrus, and drummer Jake Hanna, along with holdover pianist Nat Pierce. Herman's alto sax generates some exceptional moments on "Body and Soul" and "Deep Purple," and the entire band has a funky approach on "Sister Sadie," "Camel Walk," and "Better Git It in Your Soul." This album is definitely not for the faint-hearted. Another arousing session, recorded live at Basin Street West in San Francisco, *Woody's Winners* ♫♫♫♫ (Columbia, 1965, prod. Teo Macero) highlights a slightly later edition of the band tearing it up, and includes regulars Sal Nistico, Bill Chase, and Nat Pierce, and features trumpeters Don Rader and Dusko Goykovich, and tenor saxist Gary Klein. Chase's "23 Red" is a blistering showcase for the trumpet section. "Greasy Sack Blues" has been in the band book for ages and gets a definitive reading here. Horace Silver's extended "Opus De Funk" is a fitting climax to this eight-tune, big band excursion. Latter-day Herman is represented by several fine Concord Jazz CDs. *The Best of Woody Herman and his Big Band: The Concord Years* ♫♫♫♫ collects 12 selections from nine earlier albums from Herman's Concord recording period between September 1979–March 1987. From the 1979 *Woody and Friends* comes "Woody 'n' You" (spotlighting guests Woody Shaw and Dizzy Gillespie along with arranger-trombonist Slide Hampton), and "What Are You Doing the Rest of Your Life?" (featuring gorgeous tenor saxisms by Herman alumnus Stan Getz). Excerpts from *Live at the Concord Jazz Festival 1981* spotlight tenor saxist Al Cohn on "Things Ain't What They Used to Be" and Stan Getz on Bill Holman's arrangement of "The Dolphin," and offer a reprise of "Lemon Drop," a wacky bop tune from the Second Herd library. However, most arrangements from the Concord period were capably crafted by trombonist John Fedchock and pianist John Oddo. Drawn from *50th Anniversary Tour* are Fedchock arrangements of "It Don't Mean a Thing If It Ain't Got That Swing," "Blues for Red," and Coltrane's tone poem, "Central Park West." *World Class* furnishes "Four Brothers" and "Perdido" (with guest soloist Flip Phillips), and from *Woody's Gold Star* come two more Fedchock gems, "Battle Royal" and Monk's "'Round Midnight."

best of the rest:
Live in Stereo at Marion, June 8, 1957 ♫♫♫♫ (Jazz Hour, 1957/1994)
Live at Peacock Lane, Hollywood 1958 ♫♫♫♫ (Jazz Hour, 1958/1994)
The Fourth Herd/New World of Woody Herman ♫♫♫♫ (Ultradisc, 1959–1962/Mobile Fidelity, 1995)
The Raven Speaks ♫♫♫♫ (OJC, 1972)

Giant Steps ♫♫♫♫ (OJC, 1973/1996)
The Thundering Herd ♫♫♫♫ (OJC, 1974/1995)
Woody Herman Presents, Vol. 1, A Concord Jam ♫♫♫♫ (Concord, 1981/1990)
Woody and Friends ♫♫♫♫ (Concord, 1981/1992)
Woody Herman Big Band Featuring Stan Getz Live at the Concord Jazz Festival ♫♫♫♫ (Concord, 1981/1997)
Woody Herman Presents, Vol. 3, A Great American Evening ♫♫♫♫ (Concord, 1983)
World Class ♫♫♫♫ (Concord, 1984/1987)
50th Anniversary Tour ♫♫♫♫ (Concord, 1986)
Woody's Gold Star ♫♫♫♫ (Concord, 1987/1989)
The Sound of Jazz ♫♫♫♫ (Cleopatra, 1988/1996)
Best of the Big Bands: Woody Herman ♫♫♫♫♫ (Sony/Columbia, 1990)
The Best of Woody Herman and His Orchestra ♫♫♫♫ (Curb/Capitol, 1990)
Blues on Parade ♫♫♫♫ (Decca/GRP, 1991)
Northwest Passage, Vol. 2 ♫♫♫♫♫ (Jass, 1991)
The Herd Rides Again ♫♫♫♫ (Evidence, 1992)
Herman's Heat and Puente's Beat ♫♫♫♫ (Evidence, 1992)
Crown Royal ♫♫♫♫ (Laserlight, 1992)
(With Stan Getz) Early Autumn ♫♫♫♫ (RCA/Bluebird, 1992)
Blowing Up a Storm ♫♫♫♫ (Drive, 1994)
The Essence of Woody Herman ♫♫♫♫ (Columbia/Legacy, 1994)
(With Tito Puente) Blue Gardenia ♫♫♫♫ (Laserlight, 1994)
At the Woodchopper's Ball ♫♫♫♫ (ASA/AJA, 1995)
Woody Herman and the Band That Plays the Blues ♫♫♫♫ (Circle, 1995)
At Lake Compounce 1959/Jantzen Beach '54 ♫♫♫♫♫ (Status, 1995)
Blues and the First Herd, Vol. 1 ♫♫♫♫ (Jazz Archives, 1996)
Amen 1937–1942 ♫♫♫♫ (Aero Space, 1997)
Blues on Parade, 1938–1941 ♫♫♫♫ (Aero Space, 1997)
This Is Jazz 24: Woody Herman ♫♫♫♫♫ (Sony/Columbia, 1997)
The Second Herd ♫♫♫♫ (Storyville, 1997)
Feelin' So Blue ♫♫♫♫ (OJC, 1997)

worth searching for: *The 1940s—The Small Groups: New Directions* ♫♫♫♫ (Columbia, 1988, prod. Michael Brooks) is an anthology, containing selections from the Gene Krupa Trio, a Harry James Octet, and 10 tracks (all jewels) from Woody Herman and the Woodchoppers, a small unit drawn from the First Herd. Trumpeters Sonny Berman and Shorty Rogers have some keen moments and tenor saxophonist Flip Phillips adds some smooth, swinging sounds. Trombonist Bill Harris offers vivid brassy explorations. Woody's alto and clarinet fit well into the small band context. Pianist Jimmy Rowles, bassist Chubby Jackson, guitarist Billy Bauer, and drummer Don Lamond make up the extraordinary rhythm section. Vibraharpist Red Norvo adds spice and color to a multi-textured musical brew. These sides kick and swing, reminiscent of Norvo groups past, and hint at Shorty Rogers units to come. *Woody Herman Presents, Vol. 2—*

Four Others ♫♫♫ (Concord, 1982, prod. Carl E. Jefferson) features four of Woody Herman's stellar tenor sax players from separate, distinctive band periods forming a section and offering individual solos. Al Cohn, Sal Nistico, Bill Perkins, and Flip Phillips sally forth into eight extended pieces from the Herman repertoire. Woody himself was on hand to set the tempos and approve the final takes, adding his sonorous alto to "Tenderly." Johnny Mandel's "Not Really the Blues" and Al Cohn's "The Goof and I" and "Woody's Lament" sail along nicely with solid rhythm from pianist John Bunch, drummer Don Lamond, and bassist George Duvivier. Singer Rosemary Clooney headlines with the Woody Herman big band on *My Buddy* ♫♫♫ (Concord, 1983, prod. Carl E. Jefferson), working well with the band and Woody on an eight-tune set. There is some exceptional arranging by pianist John Oddo, who left the band to join forces with Clooney shortly after this attractive session.

influences:

◄◄ Johnny Hodges, Benny Goodman, Barney Bigard, Duke Ellington, Jimmie Noone, Pee Wee Russell, Frank Teschemacher

see also: *Gene Ammons, Al Cohn, John Fedchock, Stan Getz, Terry Gibbs, Dave McKenna, Zoot Sims*

John T. Bitter

Fred Hersch

Born October 21, 1955, in Cincinnati, OH.

After an illustrious career accompanying many of jazz's leading singers and instrumentalists, pianist Fred Hersch has gradually established himself as an exceptional soloist in his own right. Capable of exquisite lyricism on ballads, he can also swing forcefully while crafting thoughtful, harmonically dazzling improvisations. A graduate of the New England Conservatory, Hersch made the move to New York in 1977. He quickly became a highly regarded sideman, working with Stan Getz and Joe Henderson, and recording with Lee Konitz, Art Farmer, Billy Harper, Gary Burton, Toots Thielemans, Jane Ira Bloom, Chris Connor, and Janis Siegel, while also leading his own groups. He returned to Boston to teach at the New England Conservatory from 1980 to 1986, when he joined the faculty at the New School. In 1994, Hersch produced a gorgeous album, *Last Night When We Were Young* for Classical Action: Performing Arts Against AIDS, featuring, among others, Bobby Watson, Phil Woods, George Shearing, Mark Murphy, and Jane Ira Bloom.

what to buy: A brilliant album featuring Hersch's working band with bassist Drew Gress and drummer Tom Rainey, *The Fred Hersch Trio Plays . . .* ♫♫♫ (Chesky, 1994, prod. David Chesky, Fred Hersch) covers one beautiful Hersch original written for Bill Evans and 11 classic jazz compositions by the likes of Ellington ("Mood Indigo"), Strayhorn ("Daydream"), Monk ("Think of One" and "Played Twice") and Wayne Shorter ("Iris"). A particularly cohesive group where the musicians think and breathe as one, the trio is especially skilled at the use of dynamics. Hersch is at his best exploring ambiguous melodic themes such as Herbie Hancock's "Speak Like a Child" and the passionate reverie of "Daydream." The first song of *Heart Songs* ♫♫♫ (Sunnyside, 1990, prod. Fred Hersch) sets the tone, an extended, subtle exploration of the Gershwins' "The Man I Love." Hersch's trio, with bassist Mike Formanek and drummer Jeff Hirshfield, plays with probing intelligence and openness, always ready to let the music flow someplace unexpected. Hersch penned five of the album's 11 tracks, and his tunes reflect his emotionally vibrant but unsentimental lyricism. Highlights include a masterful version of Wayne Shorter's "Infant Eyes" and Ornette Coleman's "The Sphinx," which closes the album with a burst of melodic quirkiness.

what to buy next: A highly rewarding exploration of the music of one of jazz's greatest composers, *Passion Flower: Fred Hersch Plays Billy Strayhorn* ♫♫♫ (Nonesuch, 1996, prod. Fred Hersch) features Hersch in a variety of settings, from solo piano and a piano duet with Nurit Tilles (on "Tonk") to trio tracks with Drew Gress (bass) and Tom Rainey (drums) and the trio augmented with a string orchestra. Hersch covers both Strayhorn's better-known compositions, including an unspeakably melancholy version of "Lush Life" with strings and a brilliant solo version of "Isfahan," as well as lesser-known works such as the dreamy tunes "Absinthe" and "Ballad for Very Tired and Very Sad Lotus-Eaters." Hersch has an unerring ear for rewarding material, and he found a treasure trove with *I Never Told You* ♫♫♫ (Varese Sarabande, 1995, prod. Bruce Kimmel), a solo session featuring the music of Johnny Mandel. Long a favorite composer among jazz players, Mandel combines graceful melodic lines with interesting harmonic ideas, providing Hersch with a challenging array of material. Highlights include the oft-played "Emily" and "A Time for Love" and the lesser-known "Seascape" and luminous "Moon Song."

best of the rest:

Sarabande ♫♫♫ (Sunnyside, 1987)
Forward Motion ♫♫♫ (Chesky, 1991)
Dancing in the Dark ♫♫♫ (Chesky, 1992)

Red Square Blue ♫♫♫ (Angel, 1993)
Fred Hersch at Maybeck ♫♫♫♫ (Concord Jazz, 1994)
Point in Time ♫♫♫♫ (Enja, 1995)
Fred Hersch Plays Rodgers and Hammerstein ♫♫♫♫ (Nonesuch, 1996)

worth searching for: Art Farmer's *Warm Valley* ♫♫♫♫ (Concord Jazz, 1983, prod. Carl E. Jefferson) pairs the master flugelhornist with Hersch, whose finely honed lyricism make him a well-suited accompanist. The album develops as if the quartet were playing a set, opening with a brief bop workout on "Moose the Mooche," through a rapid version of "Three Little Words," kicked off by Akira Tana's deft stick work. Farmer and Hersch play Benny Golson's "Sad to Say" as an exquisite duet before ending the session with Billy Strayhorn's swinging "UMMG" and Duke Ellington's sensuously charged title track. Found in the classical section of most record stores, the benefit compilation *Memento Bittersweet* ♫♫♫ (Catalyst/BMG, 1994, prod. Andre Gauthier, Cynthia B. Herbst) collects music by HIV-positive composers, including Hersch's lovely "Tango Bittersweet," performed with cellist Erik Friedlander.

influences:
◀◀ Bill Evans, Herbie Hancock, Thelonious Monk

Andrew Gilbert

Monika Herzig
See: Beeblebrox

Al Hibbler
Born August 16, 1915 in Tyro, MS.

Blind from birth, pop-jazz singer Al Hibbler began his professional career in the 1930s, influenced originally by Pha (Elmer) Terrell (a singer with Andy Kirk's band from 1933–41). At age 14, Hibbler entered the Arkansas School for the Blind, where he sang in the choir. Upon leaving school he began singing the blues in roadhouses, but yearned to sing ballads like the great crooners. He sang with local bands in Arkansas and Texas before starting his own band. His first big break occurred with a singing gig at a local radio station, but Hibbler was most interested in singing with big bands, and, after flopping in a first audition for the Ellington Orchestra (he arrived there drunk) in 1942, he joined Jay McShann's band, one of the big-name bands then known for its swinging rhythms and for launching the careers of many musicians. Hibbler stayed with McShann's band for 18 months, then auditioned again for the Ellington Band. With Ellington's band for eight years (1943–51), Hibbler recorded "Do Nothin' Till You Hear from Me," which became a hit. He left Ellington's band over a salary dispute and formed his own group, recording LPs as leader for Decca, Verve, Brunswick, Atlantic, and other labels. Hibbler recorded a hit single in 1955 for Decca, "He," which spent 22 weeks on the charts. But his biggest hit was his single rendition of the Alex North/Hy Zaret song, "Unchained Melody," which Hibbler performed on the soundtrack of an obscure 1955 movie titled *Unchained*. Hibbler also recorded with bands led by Harry Carney (1945), Mercer Ellington (1947), Billy Kyle, and Billy Taylor (both in 1950), as well as with the Ellingtonians, Count Basie, Gerald Wilson, Roland Kirk, and others. Though Hibbler's rich, deep baritone voice and emotive approach suited the 1950s style, when the 1960s ushered in rock 'n' roll, his career began to wane and his recording and performing dates became infrequent.

what's available: At the time of this writing most of Hibbler's catalog is out of print, with a couple of albums available on import labels. The only domestic album available is *After the Lights Go down Low* ♫♫♫ (Atlantic, 1956/1989, prod. Bob Porter), which includes a remake of the Sammy Kahn title tune that was a Hibbler hit in 1956. Hibbler sings an array of 14 tunes, but missing from this collection is his bigger hit, "Unchained Melody."

influences:
◀◀ Pha Terrell, Bing Crosby

Nancy Ann Lee

John Hicks
Born December 21, 1941, in Atlanta, GA.

Along with Tommy Flanagan and Kenny Barron, pianist John Hicks has established himself as a consummate performer and expert accompanist. His ability to play in almost any jazz piano style, from stride to avant garde, makes him valuable in any number of musical situations, whether it's backing singer Betty Carter or fronting his own trio. Following his studies at Lincoln University and the Berklee College of Music in Boston, Hicks headed to New York in 1963 where, over the next several years, he worked with Art Blakey's Jazz Messengers, vocalist Carter, Woody Herman, Oliver Lake, Charles Tolliver, and Chico Freeman. Beginning in the early 1980s, Hicks began to lead his own groups and record for a number of record labels, including Theresa, Strata-East, Timeless, Mapleshade, DIW, Reservoir, and Landmark. He can also be heard frequently with David Murray, Arthur Blythe, and Pharoah Sanders. With an intense and energetic approach that is marked by a good degree of rich harmonic sophistication, Hicks continues to be one of the preeminent pianists of his generation.

what to buy: *East Side Blues* ♫♫♫♫ (DIW/Disc Union, 1988, prod. Shigenobu Mori, John Hicks, Bobby Watson) is currently available via Japan but is well worth the price due to the fine trio that includes bassist Curtis Lundy and Victor Lewis and the choice Hicks's originals. With a wonderful balance of beauty and muscle, Hicks puts down some of his best recorded work. *Beyond Expectations* ♫♫♫♫ (Reservoir, 1993, prod. Mark Feldman) is an aptly titled set that finds Hicks once again saying new and provocative things within the context of the standard piano trio.

what to buy next: *Naima's Love Song* ♫♫♫♫ (DIW/Disc Union, 1988, prod. Shigenobu Mori, John Hicks, Bobby Watson) is the companion piece to the above-mentioned *East Side Blues*, with altoist Bobby Watson added to the group. This is some of the most swinging jazz you're likely to hear, and Hicks's sumptuous title track is not to be missed.

the rest:
Some Other Time ♫♫♫ (Evidence, 1981)
In Concert ♫♫♫♫ (Evidence, 1984)
Luminous ♫♫♫ (Evidence, 1985)
Two of a Kind ♫♫♫ (Evidence, 1987)
Power Trio ♫♫♫♫ (Novus, 1990)
Is That So? ♫♫♫♫ (Timeless, 1990)
Live at Maybeck Recital Hall ♫♫♫♫ (Concord, 1990)
Friends Old and New ♫♫♫♫ (Novus, 1992)
Crazy for You ♫♫♫ (Red Baron, 1992)
Lover Man: Tribute to Billie Holiday ♫♫♫ (Red Baron, 1993)
Single Petal of a Rose ♫♫♫♫ (Mapleshade, 1994)
In the Mix ♫♫♫ (Landmark, 1994)

Chris Hovan

Billy Higgins
Born October 11, 1936, in Los Angeles, CA.

How else to describe Los Angeles–born Billy Higgins but as one of the true undeniable forces of modern jazz drumming? After starting his career in Los Angeles playing in R&B and rock 'n' roll bands and joining with Don Cherry and James Clay to form the Jazz Messiahs (a group that was never recorded), Higgins assured his historical reputation with a series of boundary-obliterating recordings with Ornette Coleman's pianoless quartet in beginning in 1958, and a subsequent stint with Coleman's group in New York City during 1959–60. Over the past four decades, Higgins has been on hand for an inordinately high percentage of seminal recordings with leaders as diverse as Thelonious Monk, John Coltrane, Sonny Rollins, Jackie McLean, David Murray, Donald Byrd, Steve Lacy, Lee Morgan, Frank Mor-

gan, Sonny Clark, Joe Henderson, Milt Jackson, Hank Mobley, Mal Waldron, Joshua Redman, and Dexter Gordon. From 1966 on, Higgins has performed often with Cedar Walton's Trio and has also recorded and performed with the Timeless All-Stars, a sextet formed by label president Wim Wigt around 1981 that includes members Higgins, Harold Land, Curtis Fuller, Bobby Hutcherson, Cedar Walton, and Buster Williams. Whenever Higgins shows up, it's the sweet sensibility—the happy sense of rhythmic interplay that sings and swings, in equal measure—that sets him apart. His community-minded activities also win him accolades. In the late 1980s Higgins and others formed the World Stage, a studio, recording label, cultural center, and performance venue located in Los Angeles' Crenshaw district and dedicated to inspiring and recording fine young musician groups such as the B Sharp Quartet and the Black/Note.

what to buy: With a rhythm team that includes pianist Cedar Walton and bassist David Williams, drummer Higgins subtly spurs soloists Harold Land (tenor sax) and Oscar Brashear (trumpet) on *Billy Higgins Quintet* ♫♫♫♫ (Evidence, 1997, prod. Shigeyuki Kawashima, Horst Liepolt), a seven-tune album recorded in New York City in 1993. The fare is split between originals written by band members and standards such as Tadd Dameron's "Hot House," Thelonious Monk's "Jackie-ing," and Michel Legrand's "You Must Believe in Spring." Land's "Step Right up to the Bottom" is a burning opener that establishes the group's collective and individual artistry, and Brashear's mysterious, angular melody on "Seeker" likewise provides launching pads for excellent solos. Walton's light swinger "The Vision" and the lush ballad "You Must Believe in Spring" highlight Higgins's tidy brush work as well as nicely blended horn arrangements and warmly rendered solos from Walton, Land, and Brashear. Higgins is not prone to taking splashy solos but his tastefully supportive presence is heard and felt throughout this appealing, straight-ahead session with his old friends.

what to buy next: Perhaps because he is such a team player, Higgins in the role of leader seems to defer more solo space to his sidemen. But you need to listen carefully to hear his talent for subtly energizing a session. He's not a flashy drummer like Tony Williams or a bombastic player such as Art Blakey, but when Higgins does take a solo, such as on "Dance of the Clones" on *Mr. Billy Higgins* ♫♫♫♫ (Riza, 1985/Evidence, 1994, prod. Billy Higgins, James Saad), it's usually a relaxed, tasteful improvisation fitting with the tune's mood and melody. Higgins's role as sturdy timekeeper is paramount on this five-tune session recorded in 1984 with reed man Gary Bias, pianist William Henderson, and bassist Tony Dumas. The drummer fluidly shades with cymbals, augments with mallets and brushes, and demonstrates his talent for playing diverse, shifting rhythms with the greatest ease. Most notable among the tunes is the time-shifting, lengthy (12-minute), ethereal "John Coltrane." In addition to his wonderful solos on this relaxed outing unified by Higgins's spirituous refinements, Bias contributes three original tunes.

best of the rest:

Soldier 𝄞𝄞𝄞 (Timeless, 1979/1993)
3/4 for Peace 𝄞𝄞𝄞𝄞 (Red, 1994)
Soweto 𝄞𝄞𝄞 (Red, 1994)
Once More 𝄞𝄞𝄞 (Red, 1995)

worth searching for: As sideman, Higgins has appeared on a list of recordings longer than your arm. A series for Evidence recorded live at Sweet Basil in New York City with pianist Cedar Walton and others are among his most enjoyable straight-ahead sessions. One of the best (most energetic) of these sessions highlights two August, 1993, live-recorded Sweet Basil dates documented on *The Art Blakey Legacy* 𝄞𝄞𝄞𝄞 (Evidence, 1997, prod. Shigeyuki Kawashima, Horst Liepolt). Higgins performs with Walton, bassist David Williams, and soloists Steve Turre (trombone), Philip Harper (trumpet), and Javon Jackson (tenor sax). Featured in numerous solos throughout, Higgins proves that he can generate fiery polyrhythms when the situation warrants. Noteworthy tracks include a stimulating 11-minute version of Duke Ellington's "Caravan," which features a lengthy and stirring Higgins solo, and a 14-minute, energetic rendering of Walton's "Mosaic," with Higgins generating sparks with his wide-ranging artistry.

influences:

◄◄ Kenny Clarke, Ed Blackwell, Roy Haynes, Lawrence Marable, Art Blakey, Philly Joe Jones, Max Roach

►► Carl Allen, Jason Marsalis

see also: *Cedar Walton, Ornette Coleman, Thelonious Monk, B Sharp Quartet*

Nancy Ann Lee and David Prince

Andrew Hill

Born June 30, 1937, in Chicago, IL.

Andrew Hill is certainly one of the strongest individual voices in post-bop piano. His knotty melodies, harmonic ambiguities, use of silence and space, and the frequently oblique development of his solos mark him as an heir to Thelonious Monk and Herbie Nichols with a voice all his own. Hill started playing piano in 1950 and studied composition with classical composer Paul Hindemith. As a teenager, Hill played with Charlie Parker, Miles Davis, and Johnny Griffin in Chicago clubs. In 1961 he moved to New York with Dinah Washington. He played with Roland Kirk in Los Angeles in 1962 and recorded the *Domino* album with him for Mercury. Later that year he returned to New York and made his debut on the Blue Note label on Joe Henderson's *Our Thing*, the beginning of an astonishingly fertile period. Between 1962 and 1970 he recorded many albums as a leader for Blue Note, at least one of which, *Point of Departure*, is one of the essential albums of the decade. He also appeared as a sideman on Bobby Hutcherson's *Dialogue*, Hank Mobley's *No Room for Squares*, and Sam Rivers's *Involution*. After leaving Blue Note, Hill's recorded output declined markedly. In the early 1970s he earned a doctorate from Colgate University, toured occasionally, and made albums for SteepleChase, Freedom, and East Wind. In 1977 he moved to the West Coast and taught in California prisons and public schools. He has made infrequent club and concert appearances in the 1990s, but has not recorded recently.

what to buy: *Point of Departure* 𝄞𝄞𝄞𝄞𝄞 (Blue Note, 1964, prod. Alfred Lion) is a benchmark recording of the 1960s, and surely Hill's masterpiece. In reedman Eric Dolphy, Hill finds a kindred spirit in harmonic and linear exploration and drummer Tony Williams's transformations of tempo inspire some of Hill's most alchemical indirections. Trumpeter Kenny Dorham adds a lyrical dimension and Joe Henderson's dark presence gives the album further depth. There's something unexpected and delightful at every turn. Despite the severe title, *Judgment* 𝄞𝄞𝄞𝄞 (Blue Note, 1964, prod. Alfred Lion) is one of Hill's breeziest sessions. The writing is fiendishly difficult, as usual, but the airy interplay between Hill, vibist Bobby Hutcherson, bassist Richard Davis, and drummer Elvin Jones is joyful and dancing. *Smokestack* 𝄞𝄞𝄞𝄞 (Blue Note, 1963, prod. Alfred Lion) is an excellent showcase for Hill the composer and improviser. Working with a quartet featuring two bassists (Richard Davis and Eddie Kahn) and drummer Roy Haynes, Hill elaborates on the harmonically rich title track, plays cat-and-mouse with the tempo on "Ode to Von," and strikes a lovely balance between percussive chords and sinuous line on "The Day After." *Shades* 𝄞𝄞𝄞𝄞 (Soul Note, 1986, prod. Giovanni Bonandrini) is a return to top form after a period of recordings of erratic quality.

what to buy next: *Verona Rag* 𝄞𝄞𝄞𝄞 (Soul Note, 1986, prod. Giovanni Bonandrini) is a mostly sunny solo album with rollicking vamps, emotionally ambiguous balladry, and characteristically curious turns of phrase.

the rest:
Invitation 🎵🎵🎵 (SteepleChase, 1974)
Strange Serenade 🎵🎵🎵 (Soul Note, 1980)

worth searching for: A dazzling seven-disc anthology of the best of Hill's Blue Note releases, *The Complete Blue Note Andrew Hill Sessions (1963–66)* 🎵🎵🎵🎵 (Mosaic) contains inexhaustibly fascinating listening and is well worth the price. Hill made four albums for Soul Note in the 1980s and two discs featuring saxophonist Greg Osby for Blue Note. The first, *Eternal Spirit*, reunited him with Bobby Hutcherson; *But Not Farewell* also featured trombonist Robin Eubanks. Both are now out of print, and worth searching for.

Ed Hazell

Buck Hill

Born 1928, in Washington, DC.

Buck Hill is a straight-ahead tenor sax player whose career stretches back to 1943 but who has become more familiar to international audiences via his sessions for SteepleChase Records in the late '70s. While Hill's first recording date was with guitarist Charlie Byrd in the '50s, the saxophonist had to take a day job as a postman. He later gained a modicum of notoriety in the Washington, D.C., area as the jazz mailman, a label Hill capitalized on while jump-starting his career in the '70s with a series of albums recorded with trumpeter Allan Houser. Hill has recorded as a leader for SteepleChase, Muse, and Improv in addition to recording and touring with pianist Shirley Horn.

what to buy: While most of his other albums have been recorded with heavyweights like Kenny Barron, Barry Harris, and Billy Hart, *Impulse* 🎵🎵🎵🎵 (Muse, 1995, prod. Houston Person), done with his regular cadre of D.C. players, is perhaps Hill's most relaxed date. He also whips out his clarinet on four cuts, including Ellington's "In a Sentimental Mood" and "Solitude." One of the highlights of this recording is Hill's own "Ottawa Bash," a rib joint workout over Carroll Dashiell's funky, broad-toned bass.

what to buy next: *This Is Buck Hill* 🎵🎵🎵🎵 (SteepleChase, 1978, prod. Nils Winther), Hill's first album for the international market, introduced his Hawkins-influenced tenor playing to a much wider audience. His fellow musicians (Kenny Barron, Buster Williams, and Billy Hart) are heavily credentialed, but that doesn't stop Hill from controlling the sessions with some authoritative performances.

the rest:
Scope 🎵🎵🎵🎵 (SteepleChase, 1979)
Easy to Love 🎵🎵🎵 (SteepleChase, 1981)
Impressions 🎵🎵🎵 (SteepleChase, 1981)
Capital Hill 🎵🎵🎵 (Muse, 1989)
I'm Beginning to See the Light 🎵🎵🎵🎵 (Muse, 1991)

influences:

◀◀ Coleman Hawkins, Lester Young

▶▶ Houston Person

Garaud MacTaggart

Earl "Fatha" Hines

Born December 28, 1903, in Duquesne, PA. Died April 22, 1983, in Oakland, CA.

Modern jazz piano styles had to pass through Earl Hines before they reached their current level of maturity. The ripples he played on the keyboard were to be felt as far away in time as the bebop revolution, when Bud Powell played a mutant version of Fatha's concept.

Hines's first paying gigs were in Pittsburgh with vocalist Lois Deppe, and his move to Chicago in 1923 found him working with some of that city's top bands. It was while working for Carroll Dickerson in 1926 that Hines and Louis Armstrong became associates. After some abortive attempts at a musical and commercial partnership (they ran a nightclub together with Zutty Singleton for less than a year), the two finally hooked up in 1928 for some primal jazz recordings, including their pivotal duet on a King Oliver tune, "Weather Bird."

Few people were playing piano the way Hines did in the 1920s, with his right hand playing single-note improvisations as his left hand picked out counter rhythms, deconstructing the typical pulse of the piece. It also made for the kind of accompaniment that Armstrong was looking for, one that loosened the rhythmic straitjacket he had been playing in with his earlier Hot Five and Hot Seven groups.

In 1928 Hines started up his own band at the Grand Terrace, a gig that was to provide a steady base of income for the leader all through the 1930s. The Grand Terrace group had an enviable security compared to many of the bands playing during that time, freeing them from the constant need to tour. Perhaps that was one reason why Hines was able to attract top-flight arrangers and musicians to his organization, people such as Jimmy Mundy (composer of "Cavernism"), ace trombonist Trummy Young, and Budd Johnson, the reed player and

Earl "Fatha" Hines (Archive Photos)

arranger who was to become Hines's longest musical associate. During the early and mid-'40s, budding beboppers such as Dizzy Gillespie, Charlie Parker, and Billy Eckstine passed through the band on their way into the history books. By the end of the decade however, the Grand Terrace well was starting to dry up and Hines folded up his operation as a bandleader and joined Louis Armstrong's All-Stars for a four-year stint.

The 1950s were a time when Hines's career appeared to be in decline. He still managed to front small groups after leaving Armstrong, but time seemed to be passing him by in pursuit of bop and cool. By the time the 1960s rolled around, Hines was contemplating retirement. What changed all this was a series of concerts in 1964 that were organized by the jazz writer Stanley Dance. The Little Theater Concert of March 7, 1964, is often thought of as the turning point in Hines's later career. Playing solo and within a trio (with guest support from Budd Johnson), Hines whipped through an assortment of medleys, covers, and originals that reminded the critics present that he was still a

force to be contended with. From this point on the pianist was in demand for solo and small group concerts around the world. In 1965, Hines played to enthusiastic audiences at the Newport, Monterey, and Berlin Jazz Festivals in addition to being elected to *Down Beat* magazine's Hall of Fame. Hines continued to amaze and delight jazz fans with consistently impressive recordings and concerts until his death in 1983.

what to buy: *Earl Hines Plays Duke Ellington* ♫♫♫♫ (New World Records, 1988, prod. Bill Weilbacher) and *Earl Hines Plays Duke Ellington, Vol. 2* ♫♫♫♫ (New World Records, 1997, prod. Bill Weilbacher) are both special recordings representing an Olympian nod to the greatest jazz composer from one of the most important pianists in the idiom. These solo recordings were laid down over a five-year period and feature a wide variety of Ellingtonia in brilliant, improvisatory settings by Hines. Familiar classics such as "Sophisticated Lady," "Satin Doll," and "It Don't Mean a Thing" receive fresh treatments while lesser known gems ("Heaven," "All Too Soon," and "Black Butterfly" to name a few) shine like diamonds hidden in the back of the vault. Hines could vamp forever on "Tea for Two" and never repeat the same idea, impressing listeners with his fecund imagination and wide harmonic palette, and *Tour de Force* (Black Lion, 1973, prod. Stanley Dance, Alan Bates) and *Tour de Force Encore* (Black Lion, 1973, prod. Stanley Dance, Alan Bates) are reissues that do honor to the concept, including a healthy dose of previously unreleased gems in addition to performances that should always be in print. Just listening to the alternate takes of "Mack the Knife" (one per album) is enough to make shivers run up and down the spine. The Classics label's chronological approach usually unveils diamonds alongside lumps of coal as they run through a performer's musical timeline. Luckily the periods covered in *1932–1934* (Classics, 1995, prod. various), *1939–1940* (Classics, 1996, prod. various), and *1941* (Classics, 1996, prod. various) document the high points in Hines's career as a big-band leader. He employed vocalists such as Herb Jeffries and Billy Eckstine during this time and backed them up with Trummy Young, Jimmy Mundy, Budd Johnson, and Franz Jackson. This is the era when "Jelly, Jelly" and "Grand Terrace Shuffle" were hits and when Hines's solo piano skills and concepts were proven to be years ahead of his contemporaries in the eerily titled "Child of a Disordered Brain."

what to buy next: *Piano Solos* (LaserLight, 1992, prod. Dave Caughren) is probably the best-bang-for-the-buck Hines CD around. These classy 1974 recordings feature fine performances, good sound and a cheap price tag. Mostly covers of chestnuts ("I Want a Little Girl," "She's Funny That Way," etc.), this album also includes Hines singing like a cross between Charles Brown and Louis Armstrong on his own "So Can I." Hines did a lot of live recording at New York City's Village Vanguard, and *Grand Reunion* (Verve, 1995, prod. David A. Himmelstein, Don Schlitten), documenting a spring night in 1965, is up to his usual high standards, in some cases surpassing them. For this occasion Hines and his battery mates (bassist George Tucker and drummer Oliver Jackson Jr.) were joined by jazz giants Roy Eldridge and Coleman Hawkins. The song selection features a ton of Fats Waller, a few tastefully chosen Ellington classics, and the usual batch of Broadway chestnuts, all revealing new rhythmic and harmonic turns in the hands of Hines and his associates. *Live at the Village Vanguard* (Columbia, 1988, prod. Frank Driggs) offers more well-chosen selections circa 1965. Hines is accompanied by bassist Gene Ramey, drummer Eddie Locke, and (on five tunes) Budd Johnson. "Rosetta" and "Tea For Two" are on the bill but

so is an earlier gem from the Hines folio, "Cavernism" (featuring a fluid soprano solo from Johnson), written by his former arranger, Jimmy Mundy. *Four Jazz Giants* (Solo Art Records, 1997, prod. E.D. Nunn) combines these classic tribute albums from the vinyl era into a two-CD set. Hines's solo recitals were always marvels of economy and thought no matter what high-flying pianistic riffs were bouncing off studio walls. While the W.C. Handy and Louis Armstrong dates got the most press, the Hoagy Carmichael tunes such as "Rockin' Chair," "Stardust," and "Georgia on My Mind" suit Hines's sense of musical adventure even more.

best of the rest:

(With Jimmy Rushing) *Blues and Things* (New World Records, 1967)

Earl Hines at Home (Delmark, 1969)

Blues in Thirds (Black Lion, 1972)

Earl Hines Plays George Gershwin (Musidisc, 1973)

Live at the New School (Chiaroscuro, 1973)

(With Louis Armstrong) *Louis Armstrong and Earl Hines* (Columbia, 1989)

Earl Hines and the Duke's Men (Delmark, 1994)

Earl Hines Plays Cole Porter (New World Records, 1996)

worth searching for: *The Legendary Little Theater Concert of 1964* (Muse, 1983, prod. Gary Giddins) is the concert that generated the buzz that put Hines back into currency after decades of decreasing presence on the jazz scene. All of a sudden people were reminded of just how great a pianist Hines was and how much he still had to offer to contemporary audiences. Recorded with his classic trio of Ahmed Abdul-Malik on bass and Oliver Jackson on drums (with guest Budd Johnson), this album showcases a typical blend of high-powered medleys and intelligent playing. *Here Comes Earl Fatha Hines: Spontaneous Explorations* (Sony/Red Baron, 1982, prod. Bob Thiele) also can be found as part of *The Indispensable Earl Hines, Volumes 5/6: the Bob Thiele Sessions* (RCA/France, 1982, prod. Bob Thiele). Simply incredible solo piano playing is combined with a trio date featuring a rhythm section of (then) young lions, bassist Richard Davis and drummer Elvin Jones. While the solo performances generate major heat, the incandescent versions of "Shoe Shine Boy" and "The Stanley Steamer" by the group are album highlights.

influences:

◀◀ James P. Johnson

▶▶ Mary Lou Williams, Bud Powell, Nat "King" Cole, Jaki Byard

Garaud MacTaggart

Milt Hinton

Born June 23, 1910, in Vicksburg, MS.

With a musical career that has spanned more than 65 years, Milt Hinton continues to have a busy career as both performer and educator. When he was 13 years old, Hinton began playing violin, but soon discovered that he could work more as a bassist, so he made the switch while he was in high school in Chicago. During his early years he worked with Eddie South, Eddie Tate, and Zutty Singleton, and first recorded with Tiny Parham in 1930. In 1936 he joined Cab Calloway, where he remained until 1951. Hinton has appeared on countless records as a sideman, including recordings with Ethel Waters, Billie Holiday (during her early years, and then again on *Lady in Satin*, in 1958), Louis Armstrong, Eubie Blake, Al Cohn, Erroll Garner, and Dick Hyman, among many others. With Jackie Gleason's help, he broke into work as a studio musician in the 1950s, which allowed him to be at home with his family. In 1954, as a staff musician for CBS, Hinton became the bassist in a group that for a couple of years came to be known as the "New York Rhythm Section," and included pianist Hank Jones, guitarist Barry Galbraith, and drummer Osie Johnson, backing many of the popular entertainers of the era. Throughout the 1970s, 1980s, and into the 1990s, Hinton traveled extensively, entertaining audiences around the world with his warmth and vitality, and continuing to exhibit his expertise at "slapping that bass," as well as soloing with a thoroughly modern sound. In 1988 his book *Bass Lines* was published, followed by *Overtime* in 1991. Both books, due to the diversity and longevity of his career, are filled with his priceless photographs, helping to chronicle not only Hinton's life, but also the rich history of jazz music.

what to buy: *Back to Bass-ics* 𝄞𝄞𝄞𝄞 (Progressive, 1984/1989, prod. Jane Jarvis, George H. Buck) features the Milt Hinton Trio, with pianist Jane Jarvis and drummer Louis Bellson, and contains a wide spectrum of tunes, including a swinging original tune "Cut Glass," written in collaboration with the masterful pianist Jarvis. Hinton and Jarvis perform well together, their lines dancing fluidly. Other highlights include "Undecided," "Satin Doll," "My One and Only Love," and "Prelude to a Kiss." "Fascinatin' Rhythm" features Hinton "slapping the bass," an art he works at preserving. Louis Bellson's "Windy City Blues" and Hinton's "Brush String Key" are also included. Jean Bach, who was responsible for the film *A Great Day in Harlem*, wrote the liner notes. If you happen to be in New York City, Hinton and Jarvis sometimes perform together at Zinno, a club in the Village.

what to buy next: Milt "The Judge" Hinton, 85 years old at the time he recorded *Laughing at Life* 𝄞𝄞𝄞𝄞 (Columbia, 1995, prod.

Earl "Fatha" Hines

song "I've Got a Right to Sing the Blues"

album *One for My Baby*
(Black Lion, 1974/1994)

instrument Piano

Monster Solo

Frank Zuback), is teamed with pianists Richard Wyands or Derek Smith, and drummers Dave Ratajczak or Alan Dawson. The CD features Hinton on both bass and vocals, and demonstrates his delightfully personal and intimate style. Trumpeter Jon Faddis is featured on "A Child Is Born," and switches to flugelhorn on Hinton's compositions "Laughing at Life" and "Jon John" (lyrics to the tag of "Laughing at Life" were written by Mona Hinton). Tenor saxophonist Harold Ashby plays warmly, especially on "Prelude to a Kiss," "Old Man Harlem," the title tune, and "Mona's Feeling Lonely," another tune written by Hinton. The session closes with yet another original composition from Hinton titled "The Judge and the Jury" that highlights the solos of bassists Lynn Seaton, Brian Torff, Santi Debriano, and Rufus Reid. Terry Clarke is the drummer. Columbia recorded this CD as part of their Legendary Pioneers of Jazz series. Recorded as part of Marian McPartland's Piano Jazz series on National Public Radio, *Piano Jazz: McPartland/Milt Hinton* 𝄞𝄞𝄞𝄞 (Concord/Jazz Alliance, 1991, prod. Shari Hutchinson) features the bassist guesting with McPartland. The hip Hinton opens with a "rap poem" in which he charmingly describes his musical life. The meeting between the two artists conveys a naturally warm rapport, and provides lessons in jazz history and on the bass. Highlights include duets on "All the Things You Are," "My One and Only Love," "Willow Weep for Me," and "How High the Moon," as well as Hilton's solo performance on "Joshua" on which he demonstrates his art of "slapping the bass."

influences:

◀◀ Jimmy Blanton

▶▶ Niels-Henning Orsted Pedersen, Brian Torff, Bob Haggart

Susan K. Berlowitz

Hiroshima
Formed in the mid-1970s, in Los Angeles, CA.

Dan Kuramoto, saxophones, flute, keyboards, percussion, vocals; June Kuramoto, koto, shamisen, vocals; Johnny Mori, taiko, percussion, vocals; Danny Yamamoto, drums, percussion, vocals; Barbara Long, lead vocals (1987–96); Kimaya Seward, lead vocals (1996–present).

Blending traditional sounds of Japanese music such as the koto (Japanese harp) and taiko drum with R&B-flavored jazz fusion sounds, Hiroshima has been called everything from a new form of urban world music to a bunch of new age, easy-listening "fuzak" pretenders. Formed by producer/leader/saxophonist Kuramoto with his wife and a core of Japanese and American bandmates, the group honed its sound performing in Los Angeles' Crenshaw and South Central neighborhoods as part of the city's CET Professional Musicians Program. Shortly after their major-label debut in 1979, the band earned instant attention for its unique sound, which featured June Kuramoto's agile koto workouts. But it wasn't until nearly 10 years later that the band had a certifiable hit in *Go*, which featured the lightweight title track—presaging the later rise of "smooth jazz" as easy-listening for baby boomers too hip for Muzak. For their next project, the group created a musical drama, *Sansei*, and performed it at the Mark Taper Forum in Los Angeles then turned it into another album, *East*. Despite the disdain its easy-listening sound elicits from critics, the group has formed lasting bonds with several jazz greats, drafting George Duke to co-produce some of their songs, touring with Miles Davis, and joining Quincy Jones's Qwest label in time for an invitation to the Montreux Jazz Festival in 1993.

what to buy: Produced by Crusaders member "Big Daddy" Henderson, their debut record *Hiroshima* 𝄢𝄢𝄢 (Arista, 1979, prod. Big Daddy Henderson) showcases both the best and worst aspects of the group's sound. Spiced with koto and Japanese percussion sounds along with some powerful song ideas, this material sounds like nothing else in contemporary jazz. So what if some of the singing and arrangements sound imported from lounge-land? Even the most successful experiments have a few unanticipated side effects.

what to buy next: As a band prone to inconsistent results on record, it makes sense that its greatest-hits record, *Best of Hiroshima* 𝄢𝄢𝄢 (Epic, 1994, prod. various) would be a prudent purchase. Gathering together classic cuts such as "Go," "One Wish," and "Hawaiian Electric," this record gives you the band's best without the tiresome filler that often muddies their records.

what to avoid: Despite—or maybe, because of—its status as the band's most successful record, *Go* **woof!** (Epic, 1987, prod. Dan Kuramoto, George Duke) stands as a mostly bland piece of jazz-tinged pop confection. It even features "Hawaiian Electric," a commercial jingle the band tried to turn into a full-length song. The surprise is that "Electric" is one of the better cuts.

the rest:
Odori 𝄢𝄢𝄢 (Arista, 1981)
Another Place 𝄢𝄢𝄢 (Epic, 1985)
Third Generation 𝄢𝄢 (Epic, 1985)
East 𝄢𝄢𝄢 (Epic, 1989)
Providence 𝄢𝄢 (Sony, 1992)
L.A. 𝄢𝄢𝄢 (Qwest, 1994)
One Fine Day 𝄢𝄢𝄢 (Qwest, 1995)
Urban World Music 𝄢𝄢𝄢 (Qwest, 1996)

worth searching for: Inspired by fans who wanted to hear the band's earliest origins, *Ongaku* 𝄢𝄢𝄢 (Arista, 1986) combines the best cuts from the band's first two albums, *Hiroshima* and the out-of-print *Odori*.

influences:

◀◀ The Crusaders, Spyro Gyra, Lee Ritenour

▶▶ The Rippingtons

Eric Deggans

Al Hirt
Born Alois Maxwell Hirt, November 7, 1922, in New Orleans, LA.

The rap on trumpeter Al Hirt seems to be that he is an enormously gifted musician who would rather play Dixieland or popular tunes than stretch the boundaries of his talents on more challenging material. Yet, no less an authority than Miles Davis praised Hirt's technique, and to legions of fans, he is the ultimate proponent of Dixieland jazz. He brought sassy modernism to an age-old genre, and his best-selling singles still receive air play on jazz and adult contemporary stations worldwide.

Hirt, a classically trained musician, divided the early part of his career between playing in symphony orchestras and working in the trumpet sections of the Tommy Dorsey, Jimmy Dorsey, Horace Heidt, and Ray McKinley bands. An eight-year stint as the leader of the studio band at a New Orleans radio station led to Hirt's first recordings for Paul Mares's Southland label. Later, Hirt teamed with legendary clarinetist Pete Fountain for a series of recordings on the Verve and Audiophile labels that created quite a stir among Dixieland aficionados. After Fountain left the combo in the late 1950s to become a regular on the *The Lawrence Welk Show,* Hirt signed with RCA. Under the guidance of Steve Sholes (who tamed Elvis Presley's sound for the mass market), Hirt released a series of top-selling singles, such as "Java," "Cotton Candy," "Fancy Pants," "Sugar Lips," and "Up Above My Head," that drew their inspiration from country-pop and gospel as much as Dixieland jazz. Using his own Crescent City club as a base, Hirt made his sound and bearded visage synonymous with New Orleans. Throughout his peak years in the 1960s, Hirt recorded extensively both as a solo act and in pairings with celebrities such as Brenda Lee and Ann-Margret, with over three dozen of his LPs hitting the charts. Hirt's many TV appearances and high-profile concerts with major pops and symphony orchestras showcased his spectacular technique and won him new fans well into the 1970s. In recent times, Hirt's weight-related health problems have kept his name in the news more than his trumpet playing, but his status as an icon of good-time music remains secure.

what to buy: A great introduction to this artist, *Al Hirt: The Collection* 𝄞𝄞𝄞𝄞 (Razor & Tie, 1997, compilation prod. Mike Ragogna), not only features Hirt's instrumental hits "Java," "Cotton Candy," and "Sugar Lips," but a complete reissue of his 1964 duet LP with Ann-Margret as well. Hirt's "gruff 'n' easy" vocals perfectly accent the Hollywood sex kitten's purring on such tracks as "T'Aint What You Do," "Mutual Admiration Society," and "Personality," creating an irresistible chemistry.

what to buy next: A fine testament to Hirt's renovation of the New Orleans style can be found on *That's a Plenty* 𝄞𝄞𝄞𝄞 (Pro Jazz Records, 1988/1996, compilation prod. Steve Vining), performed with Peanuts Hucko, Chris Clarke, Dalton Hagler, Dave Zoller, and Bobby Breaux. *Al Hirt Greatest Hits* 𝄞𝄞𝄞𝄞 (Pro Arte, 1990, compilation prod. Steve Vining) features all his easy listening hits and finest instrumental moments from the early to late 1960s.

what to avoid: Despite its generous 22-track lineup, *The Sound of Christmas* 𝄞 (RCA, 1992, prod. Steve Sholes) is an unusually weak seasonal CD featuring bloated, sugary arrangements and a by-the-numbers approach from Hirt.

the rest:

Al Hirt/Pete Fountain: Super Jazz 𝄞𝄞𝄞𝄞 (Columbia, 1988)
Jazzin' at the Pops 𝄞𝄞 (Pro Arte, 1989)
All-Time Great Hits 𝄞𝄞𝄞𝄞 (RCA, 1989, reissue prod. Chick Crumpacker)
Cotton Candy 𝄞𝄞𝄞 (Pro Jazz Records, 1989/1993)
Al Hirt & the Alliance Hall Band: Dixieland's Greatest Hits 𝄞𝄞𝄞 (Pro Arte,1991)
Raw Sugar, Sweet Sauce, & Banana Pudd'n' 𝄞𝄞 (Monument Records, 1991)
The Golden Trumpet of Al Hirt 𝄞𝄞𝄞 (Spectacular Sound, 1995)
Brassman's Holiday 𝄞𝄞𝄞 (Hindsight, 1996)

worth searching for: A little corny, a little slick, and occasionally brilliant, the out-of-print *Our Man in New Orleans* 𝄞𝄞𝄞𝄞 (RCA, 1962/1992, prod. Steve Sholes) is the quintessential Al Hirt album. With the Anita Kerr Singers providing occasionally lyrical interludes, Hirt's trumpet embraces moods sassy and sensitive, wacky and warm.

influences:

◀◀ Harry James, Roy Eldridge

▶▶ Herb Alpert, Doc Severinsen, Baja Marimba Band

see also: *Pete Fountain*

Ken Burke

Fred Ho

Wind player and composer Fred Ho is one of the leading figures in the Asian American jazz movement, along with pianist Jon Jang, violinist Jason Hwang, and bassist Mark Izu. As leader of the multi-ethnic Asian American Art Ensemble/Afro-Asian Music Ensemble, Ho has made it his mission to unite the disparate legacies of jazz-based improvisation and East Asian traditional music, achieving mixed results. His compositions and arrangements owe a clear debt to Duke Ellington, and they work best when not attempting to force a marriage of Asian and African American musics. The inclusion of traditional Chinese instruments like the erhu (two-stringed fiddle) and the oboelike suona is sometimes inspired, sometimes mere exotica, and frequently deflects attention from his considerable gifts as a jazzman. Ho is also highly politicized, favoring compositions that address issues of Asian American identity. Unfortunately, his agitprop grows wearisome upon repeated listenings, and he should let his music speak for itself—for there is much to appreciate in his intelligent ensemble writing and tasty work on saxophones and flute.

what to buy: *Tomorrow Is Now* 🎵🎵🎵 (Soul Note, 1985) contains precision ensemble work and pithy soloing framed by Ho's finely crafted, wide-ranging charts.

what to avoid: As the title presages, on *We Refuse to Be Used and Abused* 🎵🎵 (Soul Note, 1987, prod. Giovanni Bonandrini), Ho's preachy diatribe on identity politics smothers what is otherwise commendable music.

the rest:
Bamboo That Snaps Back 🎵🎵🎵 (Finnadar, 1985)
The Underground Railway to My Heart 🎵🎵🎵 (Soul Note, 1993)
Fred Ho and the Monkey Orchestra: Monkey: Part One 🎵🎵 (Koch Jazz, 1996)
Turn Pain into Power 🎵🎵🎵 (OO Discs, 1997)

influences:
◀◀ Duke Ellington, Charles Mingus, Charlie Haden's Liberation Music Orchestra

▶▶ Jon Jang, Jason Hwang, Francis Wong, Mark Izu

Dennis Rea

Art Hodes

Born November 14, 1904, in Nikoliev, Russia. Died March 4, 1993, in Park Forest, IL.

Art Hodes was a pianist often associated with traditional jazz and the blues. He was brought to the United States by his parents when he was six months old and grew up in Chicago, where he had the chance to see King Oliver, Louis Armstrong, the Wolverines, and other pioneers. Hodes developed into a wonderful player, rollicking on up-tempo numbers, and always showing a nice sense of pace. His blues playing projected a melancholy flavor, while his up-tempo playing was lively, but not frenzied. He first recorded with Wingy Manone in 1928, then did not record again until he moved to New York, where he worked for labels such as Solo Art, Jazz Record, Signature, and Blue Note. Hodes returned in 1950 to Chicago, which remained his home until his death. He recorded there extensively, always at a consistent level, for many labels including Delmark, Jazzology, and Candid.

what to buy: *The Jazz Record Story* 🎵🎵🎵 (Jazzology 1991) collects solo, trio and small group recordings issued on the Jazz Record label associated with the magazine of the same name that Hodes edited. Sound quality may be rough, but there are many splendid samples of his blues playing, including the

moody "Bed Rock Blues." Other sides are strong traditional jazz-band performances, including "At the Jazz Band Ball" and "That's a Plenty." *Pagin' Mr. Jelly* 🎵🎵🎵🎵 (Candid, 1989, prod. Dave Bennett) is a marvelous solo piano album consisting mostly of tunes written by or associated with Jelly Roll Morton that benefit from Hodes's pacing and wistful playing. *Up in Volly's Room* 🎵🎵🎵 with Volly DeFaut (Delmark, 1992, prod. Robert G. Koester) is comprised mostly of small group performances from the 1970s, along with duets of Hodes and bassist Truck Parham. Among the duets is a pensive "St. Louis Blues." "Ode to Louis Armstrong" is a splendid medley of "Do You Know What It Means to Miss New Orleans," and "Sleepy Time Down South," performed as a duet that segues into a quartet rendition of the latter tune taken at a lazy tempo with exquisite clarinet by Volly DeFaut.

the rest:
Keepin' Out of Mischief Now 🎵🎵🎵🎵 (Candid, 1988)
Hodes's Art 🎵🎵🎵 (Delmark, 1994)
Apex Blues 1944 🎵🎵🎵🎵 (Jazzology, 1996)
Midnight Blue (Jazzology) 🎵🎵🎵

worth searching for: A limited-print reissue now unavailable, *The Complete Art Hodes Blue Note Sessions* 🎵🎵🎵🎵 (Mosaic, 1990, prod. Michael Cuscana) is a wonderful five-record or four-CD boxed set of every recording Hodes made for Blue Note as either leader or sideman with Sidney Bechet, Albert Nicholas, Baby Dodds, Max Kaminsky, and Mezz Mezzrow. The collection is especially valuable to collectors, insofar as there are no albums devoted to Hodes's Blue Note recordings currently available. *The Art Hodes Notebook: Vol. 5, Friar's Inn Revisited* 🎵🎵🎵 (Delmark, 1978, prod. Robert G. Koester) is a wonderful album still available on vinyl, but not yet reissued on compact disc. It is a tribute to the New Orleans Rhythm Kings, an important jazz group of the 1920s, and includes former group members trombonist George Brunis and clarinetist Volly DeFaut.

influences:
◀◀ Louis Armstrong, Bessie Smith, Earl Hines, Jimmy Yancey
▶▶ Erwin Helfer, Ann Rabson

Ron Weinstock

Johnny Hodges

Born July 25, 1907, in Cambridge, MA. Died May 11, 1970, in New York, NY.

It's impossible to overemphasize the importance of Johnny Hodges's supremely lyrical but searingly hot alto saxophone sound to the Duke Ellington Orchestra, where he spent almost his entire career. Hodges was masterful on uptempo flag wavers and could play supremely soulful blues, but his ballad work has never been surpassed. Only Benny Carter comes close to challenging Hodges for the title of greatest alto saxophonist of the '30s, and Hodges's influence is still widespread today. He began playing soprano sax at age 14, modeling himself after his idol, Sidney Bechet, though he soon switched to alto and by 1940 had given up the smaller horn entirely. He developed his style early and never really changed it. Before he joined Ellington in 1928 he had played with Bechet, Chick Webb, Lucky Roberts, and Willie "the Lion" Smith, but it was a fateful day when he replaced Otto Hardwicke in Ellington's saxophone section. Hodges soon became one of the orchestra's most important stars, a dependably brilliant improviser who inspired Ellington (and later Billy Strayhorn) to write countless pieces for him. His sound was a central element in the Ellington orchestra during its greatest decades of the '30s and '40s. Ellington also featured Hodges on many small-group dates featuring Duke's sidemen. The jazz world was shocked when Hodges left the orchestra to lead his own band in 1951, but Hodges had long felt under-appreciated with Ellington. His group, which included a young John Coltrane, met some success, but ultimately Hodges decided to return to the security of the Ellington orchestra in 1955. He continued to record his own sessions, mostly on Verve, and remained with the Ellington band until his death. Though Hodges isn't exactly overlooked, neither is he as celebrated a figure as his music deserves.

what to buy: Recorded between 1938–39, *Hodge Podge* ✗✗✗✗ (Legacy/Epic, 1995, prod. Frank Driggs) brings together some of Hodges's classic small-group sessions. Featuring players from the Ellington orchestra, including Cootie Williams (trumpet), Lawrence Brown (trombone), Harry Carney (baritone sax), Billy Taylor (bass), Sonny Greer (drums), and Ellington himself at the piano, the recordings were conceived as vehicles to highlight the overwhelming beauty of Hodges's alto (and some of his last tunes on soprano). An excellent introduction to this singular artist, *Passion Flower: 1940–46* ✗✗✗✗ (Bluebird, 1995, reissue prod. Orrin Keepnews) brings together two of Hodges's great small-group sessions with Ellington, trumpeters Cootie Williams or Ray Nance, drummer Sonny Greer, and the groundbreaking bassist Jimmy Blanton, performing such classics as Strayhorn's "Day Dream" and "Passion Flower" and Hodges's own "Good Queen Bess" and "Squaty Roo." *Everybody Knows Johnny Hodges* ✗✗✗✗ (Impulse!, 1964, prod. Bob Thiele) combines two records, the title one and *Inspired Abandon* by the Lawrence Brown All-Stars featuring Hodges. These sessions

J OHNN HODGES

song "Warm Valley"
album *Used to Be Duke*
(Verve, 1954/1991)
instrument Alto saxophone

Monster Solo

are basically an expanded version of the old Ellington small-group recordings.

what to buy next: A two-disc set recorded in 1961, *Johnny Hodges at Sportpalast, Berlin* ✗✗✗✗ (Pablo, 1993, prod. Norman Granz) features Hodges with a small Ellingtonian group. The program mostly consists of short arrangements of Ellington's greatest hits, with the occasional standard thrown in, and Hodges sails through the tunes with his glorious tone as perfect as ever. Hodges is actually only present on the first half of *Caravan* ✗✗✗✗ (Prestige, 1992, reissue prod. Ed Michel), but the 12 previously rare tracks from 1947 are classics with gorgeous Billy Strayhorn arrangements (he's also at the piano). The second half of the CD features the Strayhorn and Duke Ellington All-Stars from 1950–51 with the great alto saxophonist Willie Smith, who was hired when Hodges left the orchestra to strike out on his own.

best of the rest:
Triple Play ✗✗✗✗ (Bluebird, 1967)

Complete Johnny Hodges Sessions: 1951–55 🎵🎵🎵🎵 (Mosaic, 1989)
Duke Ellington Small Groups Volume 1 🎵🎵🎵🎵 (Columbia/Legacy, 1991)
The Duke's Men: Small Groups Volume 2 🎵🎵🎵🎵 (Columbia/Legacy, 1993)

worth searching for: *A Smooth One* 🎵🎵🎵🎵 (Verve, 1979, prod. Norman Granz) features two big-band sessions from 1959–60 that went unreleased at the time. Hodges wrote almost all the material, but with a host of past and present Ellington members (Ben Webster, Jimmy Hamilton, Ray Nance, and Lawrence Brown, for starters) the music is familiarly Dukish. This double-LP has yet to be reissued on CD.

influences:

◀◀ Sidney Bechet

▶▶ Charlie Parker, Marshal Royal, Norris Turney, Bobby Watson, Steve Wilson

Andrew Gilbert

Holly Hofmann

Born in Painesville, OH.

One of a number of technically superior mainstream jazz flutists to emerge at the end of the 1980s, Holly Hofmann stands out for the purity of her tone and her gift for cogent phrasing. Hofmann began playing the flute at age five and had extensive classical training before she began to play jazz. Since moving to San Diego in 1984, she has worked with James Moody and Slide Hampton, recorded with Ray Brown, and developed strong musical relationships with a number of top-flight players, including pianists Mike Wofford and Bill Cunliffe and guitarist Mundell Lowe. In 1994 she played the Village Vanguard with an all-star band featuring Hampton, Kenny Barron, Ray Brown, and Victor Lewis. In the mid-'90s she worked briefly with a quartet, Four Women Only, with pianist Cecilia Coleman, bassist Nedra Wheeler, and drummer Jeanette Wrate. She has mostly led her own groups, and recorded a number of fine, straight-ahead albums for Capri, Jazz Alliance, and Azica.

what to buy: A beautiful, swinging session, *Tales of Hofmann* 🎵🎵🎵🎵 (Azica, 1995, prod. Don Better) captures Hofmann's luminous, quicksilver flute work on a wide range of material, from Tom Harrell's "Little Dancer" and Mike Wofford's Coltrane tribute, "Afterthoughts," to Hofmann's own down-home tribute to Art Pepper, "Truer Blues." A highlight is Bill Cunliffe and Hofmann's duet on "Green Dolphin Street," which moves seamlessly between a Brazilian feel, a straight-ahead groove,

and a classical, contrapuntal passage. An eclectic duo session with pianist Bill Cunliffe, *Just Duet* 🎵🎵🎵🎵 (Azica, 1997, prod. Don Better) is a consistently inventive album, covering jazz tunes ("Bag's Groove" and "I Mean You"), standards ("But Not for Me" and "Willow Weep for Me"), Brazilian music (Baden Powell's "Conto de Ossanha"), and classical composition (Schumann's "Three Romances"). Hofmann knows how to caress a melody, but her playing is also full of verve and fire as she and Cunliffe trade ideas on their romping "High Flutin' Blues."

what to buy next: Despite its title, *Duo Personality* 🎵🎵🎵🎵 (Jazz Alliance, 1992, prod. Holly Hofmann, Tony Sidotti) is actually a series of duo and trio tracks with alternating personnel, featuring Mike Wofford (piano), Mundell Lowe (guitar), Bob Magnusson (bass), and Ron Satterfeld (guitar). Hofmann is particularly lyrical on the duo version of Thad Jones's "A Child Is Born" with Lowe, and she sails through Lee Morgan's "Speedball" with Wofford and Magnusson.

the rest:
Further Adventures 🎵🎵🎵🎵 (Capri, 1989)

influences:

◀◀ Frank Wess, Buddy Collette, James Moody

Andrew Gilbert

Robin Holcomb

Born 1954, in GA.

Jazz is just one ingredient in the uncategorizable sound of singer-songwriter Robin Holcomb. Though thought of as a denizen of the New York avant-garde scene, prior to that period of her life she worked as a sharecropper in North Carolina. As ethereal as her music can often sound, it retains that grounded earthiness and deals with common concerns, elements most pronounced in Holcomb's rural imagery (right down to one song having a verse about trading roadkill), quavery vibrato-filled voice redolent of Appalachian folk singing, and general desolation of mood.

what to buy: Holcomb's spare piano style and exploration of more distant strains of Americana—not only gospel and folk but also 19th-century ballads—reach a unique apex in *Little Three* 🎵🎵🎵🎵 (Elektra Nonesuch, 1996, prod. Judith Sherman). A gorgeous solo piano album (Holcomb sings on only two tracks), it combines the feel of Civil War ballads, Indonesian gamelan, minimalism, the polytonality and song quotes of Charles Ives, and many beautiful melodies. The two long tracks seem like suites, with a procession of moods including a strong hoedown rhythm nine minutes into "Wherein Lies the Good." Of all her albums, this is the one most likely to appeal to jazz fans.

what to buy next: The rootsy yet arty songs on *Robin Holcomb* 𝄞𝄞𝄞𝄞 (Elektra Nonesuch, 1990, prod. Wayne Horvitz, Peter Holsapple) are built from the simplest, sparest materials, but with extremely imaginative production. Guitarist Bill Frisell's slippery style relates to slide and pedal steel sounds without being either, while Horvitz (Holcomb's husband) contributes a surprisingly varied palette of gray and beige tones with his keyboard work. A couple of songs are almost straightforward country-rock, though even the fiddle-adorned "Troy" stands somewhat apart from country due to a pronounced New Orleans second-line rhythm on the verses.

the rest:
Rockabye 𝄞𝄞𝄞 (Elektra Nonesuch, 1992)

influences:
◀◀ Stephen Foster, Joni Mitchell, Charles Ives
▶▶ Bill Carrothers

Steve Holtje

BILLIE HOLIDAY

song "Moanin' Low"
album *The Quintessential Billie Holiday, Volume 4*
(Columbia, 1937/1991)
instrument Vocals

Billie Holiday

Born Eleanora Harris, April 7, 1915, in Baltimore, MD. Died July 17, 1959, in New York, NY.

Billie Holiday's voice—sweet, sexy, and pulsing with blues feeling—could chill a soul or warm it up like a fireplace of emotion. Born to teenage parents, Sadie Harris and Clarence Holiday, the singer was raped at the age of 10 and, reflecting the sexual double standard of the day, was sent to a home for wayward girls as a result. Her father, a jazz guitarist with Fletcher Henderson, abandoned her. Today, mental-health professionals believe such abuse will shape and shadow the rest of a victim's life, and Holiday's life did seem to play out with the predestination of a Greek tragedy. Her music rescued her from her teenage careers as a house servant and hooker, but it did not stop her from ravaging herself with drugs, which in her final years took away all but a remnant of her voice. Known affectionately as "Lady Day," a name she was given by Lester Young, she brought the breadth of her worldly experience to the stage and recording studio with a vulnerability that—like all the best blues—didn't just speak of being a victim, but spoke of self-worth betrayed, whether by the world, a lover, or the singer herself. That's not to say that all her songs were sad, but that even her happy tunes had an edge.

She seemed in those happier songs to want to overindulge in every appetite in order to gird herself for the hard times. Offstage, she was dependent on a succession of not-quite-Svengalis, who acted as lovers and father figures. In *God Bless the Child,* she sings what one reviewer called a whiny lyric (her own) about how people court a person who's successful but ignore the same person when "money's gone." Yet she doesn't sound whiny at all. Instead, she's having a gentle laugh at the weakness of human nature.

Talent scout John Hammond found her all but irresistible in live performance, so he advocated her to the top people in jazz. Benny Goodman led her first session in 1933. Teddy Wilson followed. When she hit the peak of her form in the late 1930s, the presence of—and her interplay with—Buck Clayton and Lester Young underscored just how much her singing resembled the playing of an instrumentalist. She sang slowly and "behind the beat" and trailed off her voice for emotional punctuation. (Her influence shows up in the work of many singers who followed, possibly most notably in Frank Sinatra.)

Her fluid phrasing and the rasp in her voice were reminiscent of Louis Armstrong. Although she sang very few actual blues tunes, the blue feeling in her voice descended directly from Bessie Smith. Holiday melded these influences into a completely distinctive sound.

Despite her submissiveness to her lovers, Holiday was strong-willed and moody, which often hindered her career. Yet her landmark 1939 recording "Strange Fruit," a protest against lynchings, was a triumph of determination. Columbia, to which she was signed for the bulk of the 1930s, would not record the tune, so she secured a contract that put her on loan to Milt Gabler's Commodore label for a single session. Gabler later signed her to Decca. In this period of the late '30s and early '40s, she gradually abandoned the jazz settings of her earlier recordings for grander, pop orchestrations. Her voice was at its peak, and her version of "Lover Man" defines her style. By the 1950s, when she signed up with Norman Granz, she had served a late '40s prison term for heroin possession and was on a downward spiral. Although her voice faded in the late stages of her life as a result of her indulgences, Holiday retained her expressive capabilities, so nearly all of her recordings are of interest, although sometimes that interest is of the morbid rubber-necking-at-a-car-wreck variety.

what to buy: Holiday's work is documented on more than 80 CDs and collections, but thanks to the archival genius of the CD age, it's very easy to reduce that number to a core, must-have collection. First of all, the title of Columbia's nine-volume retrospective series, *The Quintessential Billie Holiday* 𝄞𝄞𝄞𝄞 (Columbia, 1987–91, prod. John Hammond, Bernie Hanighen, reissue prod. Michael Brooks) is not far off the mark. In this chronological series of her work for the Columbia, Brunswick, and Vocalion labels, even the most dispensible set, *Volume 1, 1933–35* contains great performances—"Miss Brown to You," "If You Were Mine"—as the new recording artist finds her sea legs. By the last CD, *Volume 9, 1940–42*, Holiday's character and style are completely formed and she sings with absolute certainty on such definitive numbers as "God Bless the Child," "Solitude," and "Gloomy Sunday." For listeners who want to delve deeply into her creative process in the studio, *The Complete Commodore Recordings* 𝄞𝄞𝄞𝄞 (GRP, 1997, prod. Milt Gabler, reissue prod. Orrin Keepnews, Joel Dorn) is a two-CD set full of alternate takes (including a second take of "Strange Fruit") and gives in-

Billie Holiday **(Archive Photos)**

sight into her evolution from the jazz-band–oriented style to full-blown pop. *The Complete Decca Recordings* 𝄞𝄞𝄞𝄞 (GRP, 1991, prod. Milt Gabler, reissue prod. Steven Lasker, Andy McKaie) covers Holiday's best performing period in only two CDs. She recorded only 36 sides for the label, and the definitive "Lover Man" sets the collection's tone. It includes a number of alternate takes but isn't as heavy with them as the Commodore collection. This is the most satisfying and consistent listening experience in Holiday's catalog. After her vacation in the reformatory, producer Norman Granz returned Holiday to jazz-oriented sessions. Her voice was raspier, and sometimes you can hear her struggle for the breath to finish a phrase, but there's a soulfulness that the ravages of abuse bring out in her voice that makes her stint with Granz nearly as memorable as her Decca years. Hence, the ten-CD *The Complete Billie Holiday on Verve 1945–1949* 𝄞𝄞𝄞𝄞 (Verve, 1995, prod. various) is an indispensible collection of the work she did as she collapsed upon herself, including "Lady Sings the Blues," the tune written to capitalize on the title of her autobiography.

what to buy next: *Lady in Satin* 𝄞𝄞𝄞𝄞 (Columbia, 1986, prod. Ray Ellis, reissue prod. Michael Brooks) is based on the template of the original 1958 album that paired Holiday, at her request, with the easy-listening orchestral sounds of Ray Ellis. Technical wizardry creates a stereo take of *The End of a Love Affair,* which previously existed only in a mono master. The juxtaposition of her soulful but nearly shot voice and Ellis's extremely sweet strings gives the project a character it couldn't have had when she was younger. *Billie's Blues* 𝄞𝄞𝄞𝄞 (Blue Note, 1988) features Holiday's top concert recording, from a 1954 date in Europe.

what to avoid: Recorded early in 1959, *Last Recordings* 𝄞 (Verve, 1988, prod. Ray Ellis) is another date with Ellis, absent the triumph of *Lady in Satin*. Besides, you'll get the complete Verve set, right?

best of the rest:
Solitude 𝄞𝄞𝄞𝄞 (Verve, 1952)
All or Nothing at All 𝄞𝄞𝄞𝄞 (Verve, 1955)
The Essential Billie Holiday: Carnegie Hall Concert 𝄞𝄞𝄞𝄞 (Verve, 1956)
Lady Sings the Blues 𝄞𝄞𝄞𝄞 (Verve, 1956)
Songs for Distingue Lovers 𝄞𝄞𝄞𝄞 (Verve, 1957)
Masters of Jazz, Volume 3 𝄞𝄞𝄞𝄞 (Storyville, 1987)
At Storyville 𝄞𝄞𝄞𝄞 (Black Lion, 1988)
Fine and Mellow 𝄞𝄞𝄞𝄞 (Collectables, 1990)
Lady in Autumn: The Best of the Verve Years 𝄞𝄞𝄞𝄞 (Verve, 1991)

worth searching for: Issued by a now-defunct Italian bootleg label, *Live and Private Recordings in Chronological Order* 𝄞𝄞𝄞𝄞

(Jazz Up/New Sound Planet, 1989, prod. various) fills in a number of gaps. This set of 12 CDs (available in four boxes of three CDs each and also issued in a highly limited edition single box in Japan) features Holiday's only recording with Duke Ellington, "Big City Blues (The Saddest Tale)," plus recordings from radio and television and other sources such as private parties. With the first box covering 1935–45, the second 1949–53, the third 1954–56, and the fourth 1956–59, there's an obvious tilt towards the more uneven period of her career, and a few favorite songs recur with great frequency, so this is most suited to fanatical collectors. Some interviews with Holiday are scattered throughout.

influences:

◀◀ Bessie Smith, Louis Armstrong

▶▶ Frank Sinatra, Carmen McRae, Betty Carter, Madeline Peyroux

Salvatore Caputo

Dave Holland

Born October 1, 1946, in Wolverhampton, England.

British musician Dave Holland has rightly earned a reputation as one of the top bassists in the jazz field since he began playing in the early 1960s. He has played as a sideman to a wide variety of musicians, from Kenny Wheeler to Ronnie Scott to John Surman. Perhaps his biggest break as far as increasing his profile came when he was invited to join Miles Davis's group in 1968. He was a featured player on the albums *Bitches Brew*, *In a Silent Way*, and *Filles de Kilimanjaro*. After leaving Miles's band, he joined forces with Anthony Braxton, Chick Corea, and Barry Altschul to form the group Circle. In 1972 Holland also released his first album as group leader, titled *Conference of the Birds*. While releasing a number of solo albums over the years, the bassist can most often still be found playing as a sideman with many of the best in the jazz world.

what to buy: *Conference of the Birds* 🎵🎵🎵🎵 (ECM, 1972, prod. Manfred Eicher) includes Anthony Braxton, Sam Rivers, and Barry Altschul and remains the first title to be mentioned when one is discussing the work of Holland. Although the performance is obviously an ensemble effort, it is always Holland's bass work that draws the attention of the listener.

what to buy next: On *Extensions* 🎵🎵🎵 (ECM, 1989, prod. Manfred Eicher) Holland teams up with some of the younger guard of the jazz scene—Steve Coleman, Kevin Eubanks, and Marvin Smitty Smith—who all prove their worth in the setting. More

recently, Holland's quartet has included Steve Nelson (vibes, marimba), Eric Person (sax), and Gene Jackson (drums). Their recording *Dream of the Elders* 🎵🎵🎵 (ECM, 1996, prod. Manfred Eicher) continues Holland's explorations that put him right in the heart of the distinctive "ECM sound."

best of the rest:

Music for Two Basses 🎵🎵🎵 (ECM, 1971)
Emerald Tears 🎵🎵🎵🎵 (ECM, 1977)
Life Cycle 🎵🎵🎵 (ECM, 1982)
Jumpin' In 🎵🎵🎵🎵 (ECM, 1983)
Seeds of Time 🎵🎵🎵 (ECM, 1984)
The Razor's Edge 🎵🎵🎵 (ECM, 1987)
Triplicate 🎵🎵 (ECM, 1988)
One's All 🎵🎵🎵 (Intuition, 1995)

worth searching for: The collective group Circle's *Paris-Concert* 🎵🎵🎵🎵 (1972, prod. Manfred Eicher) has long been one of the highlights of the early ECM catalog. Holland's touching "Song for the Newborn" and his epic "Toy Room—Q&A" are among the highlights on its two CDs. The ad-hoc duo of Holland and multi-instrumentalist Sam Rivers made two LPs, the confusingly titled *Dave Holland—Sam Rivers* 🎵🎵🎵 (Improvising Artists, 1976, prod. Paul Bley) and *Sam Rivers—Dave Holland* 🎵🎵🎵 (Improvising Artists, 1976, prod. Paul Bley), for pianist Paul Bley's label. They have been reissued through an arrangement with an Italian company and are not too hard to track down.

influences:

◀◀ Gary Peacock, Reggie Workman, Jimmy Garrison

▶▶ Anders Jormin, Barre Philips

Chris Meloche

Major Holley

Born Quincy Holley Jr., July 10, 1924, in Detroit, MI. Died October 25, 1990, in Maplewood, NJ.

Major Holley was a swing and bop double-bass player who started out on violin and tuba. He took up bass while playing in navy bands, and Clark Terry nicknamed him "Mule" for the way he carried his instruments on his back. After his discharge from the navy, Holley played with Dexter Gordon, Charlie Parker, and, in 1950, made some duo recordings with Oscar Peterson that have never been reissued. Holley went to London in the mid-1950s to work as a studio musician for BBC-TV. In 1958 he toured South America with Woody Herman's orchestra and, upon his return to the States, played from 1959 to 1960 with the group led by Al Cohn and Zoot Sims. In addition to performing with an array of artists such as Coleman Hawkins, Kenny Burrell, and Duke Ellington during the 1960s, Holley was in demand for his studio work. From 1967 to 1970 he taught at Berklee College of Music, and throughout the 1970s freelanced in New York, made several tours of Europe with various musicians, and recorded with Roy Eldridge, Lee Konitz, and Roland Hanna. He has also appeared on records by Teddy Wilson, Al Cohn, Sims, Hawkins, Harry "Sweets" Edison, Ray Bryant, and others. Along with bassist Slam Stewart, Holley was instrumental in bringing arco (bowed) bass up to modern times.

what's available: The only album featuring Holley currently in print is a session during which he's basically working with tenor saxophonist Joe van Enkhuizen's trio on *Major Step* 𝄐𝄐𝄐𝄐 (Timeless, 1990). Holley is prominently featured in bass parts on the high-spirited tunes, and brandishes his singalong Slam Stewart–style arco (bowed) playing, which some listeners find intrusive and others find amusing. Pianist Rein De Graaff and drummer Han Bennink round out the European rhythm section.

influences:

◄◄ Slam Stewart, Milt Hinton

►► Lynn Seaton

Joe S. Harrington

Red Holloway

Born James Holloway, May 31, 1927, in Helena, AR.

Red Holloway is a saxophonist whose versatility and deep feeling for the blues have made him a valuable sideman in a number of settings, as well as a fairly engaging leader. He has been in on so many blues-related recordings that his considerable skills as a swing player and a bop soloist have been a bit obscured. In addition to his saxophone work, Holloway takes an occasional blues vocal. While still a teenager, Holloway found his first regular gig with a Chicago-based big band led by Gene Wright during World War II. After a stint in the army, he backed a variety of jazz and blues musicians, including the legendary blues pianist Roosevelt Sykes. During the '50s Holloway led his own group and backed many of the touring blues and R&B stars of the day. The work for which he is best known by jazz listeners is his mid-'60s stint with organist Jack McDuff. McDuff's line-ups changed frequently throughout the decade, but the classic unit was undoubtedly the one he had from roughly 1963–65 that featured drummer Joe Dukes, a very young George Benson on guitar, and saxophonist Holloway. Hol-

loway's robust tenor suited McDuff's no-nonsense organ-group sound, and together they recorded a good portion of the songs by which McDuff's original followers remember him best, including "Rock Candy," "A Real Goodun'," and "Rock-a-Bye." Also beginning in 1963, Holloway recorded a series of his own albums for Prestige, three under his own leadership and one with McDuff as co-leader. He also worked with Lionel Hampton during the 1960s, and after moving to Los Angeles late in the decade became an important presence on the scene there. He was a part of blues-rocker John Mayall's "Jazz/Blues Fusion" band in the early '70s, and during the late '70s and early '80s he worked extensively with Sonny Stitt. While at Concord Records in the late '80s, Holloway also was reunited with McDuff and Benson for McDuff's *Color Me Blue*. Overall, Holloway's work at Concord has proven to be some of his best. Also excellent are the recordings he made as a sideman, backing Etta James and Eddie "Cleanhead" Vinson in 1986 on a pair of live albums recorded in L.A. for Fantasy. When James recorded two discs' worth of jazz ballads for Private Music in the '90s, Holloway was again brought on as a featured soloist. A 1997 release for Chiaroscuro features Harry Edison along with Holloway's Quartet.

what to buy: *Nica's Dream* 𝄐𝄐𝄐𝄐 (SteepleChase, 1995, prod. Nils Winther) is the best recorded example of what Holloway is capable of. This 1984 recording is an especially solid mix of blues, bop, and ballads on which Holloway is backed by pianist Horace Parlan and a pair of European rhythm men. It contains a bit less swing or soul-jazz than his other available titles.

what to buy next: Listeners who favor a milder, but more swing-oriented approach—at times combined with a funky (as in Horace Silver) touch—will want to pick up *Locksmith Blues* 𝄐𝄐𝄐 (Concord, 1989, prod. Carl E. Jefferson), a sextet session that features Clark Terry as co-leader. Those with a taste for a little barbecue will find Holloway's available '60s work *Brother Red* 𝄐𝄐𝄐 (Prestige, 1994, prod. Peter Paul, Lew Futterman), or better yet, Brother Jack McDuff's classic *Live!* 𝄐𝄐𝄐𝄐 (Prestige, 1994, prod. Ozzie Cadena) hitting the soul-jazz spot. Etta James's sublime Billie Holiday tribute *Mystery Lady* 𝄐𝄐𝄐𝄐 (Private, 1994 prod. John Snyder) is also not to be missed, with Holloway playing Lester Young to James's Lady Day.

the rest:

Red Holloway & Company 𝄐𝄐𝄐 (Concord, 1987)
Live at the 1995 Floating Jazz Festival 𝄐𝄐𝄐𝄐 (Chiaroscuro, 1997)

worth searching for: *The Burner* 𝄐𝄐𝄐𝄐 (Prestige, 1963, prod. Ozzie Cadena) finds Holloway backed by a group including organist John Patton and guitarist Eric Gale. Heavy on the gut-bucket blues, it's as steaming a tenor and organ date as any from the era. This one is still yet to be reissued on CD, and the LPs aren't easy to come by either.

influences:

◀◀ Gene Ammons, Eddie "Lockjaw" Davis, Rusty Bryant, Sonny Stitt, Charlie Parker

▶▶ Houston Person, Bill Easley, Scott Hamilton, Terry Myers

Dan Bindert

Ron Holloway

Born 1953, in Washington, DC.

Ron Holloway is a big-toned, hard-bop tenor saxophonist based around Washington, D.C., and has many admirers, including Sonny Rollins. A member of Dizzy Gillespie's last small group, Holloway also has a wide-ranging musical background. He's played and recorded with the late Root Boy Slim and tours frequently with Gil Scott-Heron. Holloway is also a terrific blues player and is often heard in the D.C. area clubs playing with local blues groups. His recordings are fairly consistent, with the two most recent showing his musical openness.

what to buy: Holloway's second album, *Struttin'* 🎵🎵🎵 (Milestone, 1995, prod. Todd Barkan), has him working with pianists Kenny Barron and Larry Willis, and organist Dr. Lonnie Smith. His rendition of Gene Ammons's "Jungle Strut" has Smith effectively showcasing his big tone and vigorous attack.

the rest:

Slanted 🎵🎵🎵 (Milestone, 1994)
Scorcher 🎵🎵🎵 (Milestone, 1996)

influences:

◀◀ Sonny Rollins, Dizzy Gillespie, John Coltrane

Ron Weinstock

Christopher Hollyday

Born January 3, 1970, in New Haven, CT.

Alto saxophonist Christopher Hollyday recorded his first album by the time he was 14. He had already memorized a good chunk of alto legend Charlie Parker's work and was performing regularly in Boston-area clubs. His big break came in 1989, when he signed with Novus/RCA and recorded an impressive, heavily Jackie McLean–influenced major label debut. By 1992 he had cut his fourth release for the label, one that found him

in front of some occasionally stunning Kenny Werner arrangements. Since 1992, though, he hasn't been heard from on CD.

what to buy: His first Novus release, *Christopher Hollyday* 🎵🎵🎵 (Novus, 1989, prod. John Snyder), is still his best. The backing is excellent, with trumpeter Wallace Roney, pianist Cedar Walton, bassist David Williams, and drummer Billy Higgins spurring Hollyday on to a fine performance. His tone on the horn is remarkably close to that of Jackie McLean, and he handles the material, including several McLean pieces, with a fiery confidence.

what to buy next: *On Course* 🎵🎵🎵 (Novus, 1990, prod. John Snyder) was Hollyday's first session with all-original material. The compositions may not be earth-shattering, but they have some nice melodic hooks. Hollyday digs in while Larry Goldings provides a solid underpinning for the music with his sturdy, occasionally funky piano. *And I'll Sing Once More* 🎵🎵🎵 (Novus, 1992, prod. John Snyder) is an adventurous—if not entirely comfortable—journey into large-band territory for Hollyday with some great arrangements by Kenny Werner.

what to avoid: *The Natural Moment* 🎵🎵 (Novus, 1991, prod. John Snyder) sounds almost forced throughout. That McLean-like tone of Hollyday's can become a bit grating when he pushes too hard. It's not without merit, but the other Novus releases are better bets.

worth searching for: Not available on CD, *Reverence* 🎵🎵🎵 (RBI, 1988, prod. Ron Carter, John Snyder) is the best of Hollyday's three pre-Novus releases. Ron Carter, Cedar Walton, and Billy Higgins provide the backup.

influences:

◀◀ Charlie Parker, Jackie McLean, Wayne Shorter

▶▶ Abraham Burton, Vincent Herring

Dan Bindert

Bill Holman

Born May 21, 1927, in Olive, CA.

One of jazz's most gifted arrangers, Bill Holman has quietly accrued a small but highly rewarding collection of albums under his own name, and contributed greatly to the success of such artists as Stan Kenton, Maynard Ferguson, and Natalie Cole. A fine tenor saxophonist strongly under the influence of Lester Young, Holman made a name for himself with his arranging, where he developed a complex but swinging orchestration style that makes effective use of his musicians' abilities both as ensemble players and improvisors. Holman broke into the big-band scene with Charlie Barnett (1950–51), but made his reputation as an advanced arranger with Stan Kenton (1952–56). He recorded a few albums in the late 1950s but by the early 1960s was devoting most of his time to studio work, and didn't record again until the late 1980s, an almost 30-year hiatus. He did find time, however, to write for Gerry Mulligan, Woody Herman, Count Basie, Buddy Rich, Louie Bellson, Terry Gibbs, the Lighthouse All-Stars, Maynard Ferguson, and Doc Severinsen's Tonight Show orchestra. He also produced arrangements for Carmen McRae, Peggy Lee, and for Natalie Cole's hit album *Unforgettable*. He began leading a Los Angeles–based big band in 1975, a group that eventually began recording for JVC in 1988.

what to buy: One of jazz's most rewarding arrangers, Bill Holman creates one of his most fully realized albums with *A View from the Side* 𝄫𝄫𝄫𝄫 (JVC, 1995, prod. Akira Taguchi), a densely scored, convincingly swinging session featuring a host of top Los Angeles players. Though he gives the musicians some solo space, featuring powerhouse tenor saxophonist Pete Christlieb on "But Beautiful" and Bob Efford's bass clarinet on Jimmy Rowles's gorgeous mood piece "The Peacocks," the emphasis here is on his inventive charts, which develop with a compelling narrative flow. Whether transforming "Tennessee Waltz" or building complex, rapidly shifting themes with the *tour de force* opener "No Joy in Mudville," Holman's music bears repeated listening. Other featured players include trombonists Andy Martin and Bob Enevoldsen, saxophonists Lanny Morgan and Bill Perkins, trumpeter Ron Stout, and bassist Dave Carpenter.

A challenging masterpiece by a true jazz original, *Brilliant Corners* 𝄫𝄫𝄫𝄫 (JVC, 1997, prod. Akira Taguchi) is a big-band exploration of the music of Thelonious Monk. Though the music swings, it can take a few listens to hear how he accommodated Monk's deceptively simple and conspicuously difficult tunes to ensemble orchestrations. Particularly rewarding is his forthright version of "Rhythm-a-ning," with a brilliant tenor solo by Pete Christlieb, and his haunting take on "Ruby, My Dear." The opener, "Straight, No Chaser," and the concluding "Brilliant Corners" contain some of the most daring writing of Holman's career. The featured soloists are saxophonists Lanny Morgan and Bill Perkins, trumpeters Bob Summers and Ron Stout, trombonist Andy Martin, and pianist Rich Eames.

what to buy next: A strong session with three Holman originals, *The Bill Holman Big Band* 𝄫𝄫𝄫𝄫 (JVC, 1988, prod. Akira Taguchi) also covers Stevie Wonder's "Isn't She Lovely," Monk's

"I Mean You," and the standard "Just Friends." The session's two highlights are a surprise-filled version of Sonny Rollins's "St. Thomas," and a gorgeously rendered take of Mingus's "Goodbye Porkpie Hat." Tenor saxophonist Bob Cooper takes a number of excellent solos, and alto saxophonist Lanny Morgan and trumpeters Bob Summers and Don Rader are also heard to advantage.

best of the rest:
West Coast Jazz in Hi-Fi 𝄫𝄫𝄫 (Hi-Fi/OJC, 1959)

worth searching for: *Big Band in a Jazz Orbit* 𝄫𝄫𝄫𝄫 (VSOP, 1958, prod. Bill Holman) is an interesting session featuring noted West Coast musicians such as Al Porcino, Jack Sheldon, and Conte Candoli (trumpets); Frank Rosolino and Carl Fontana (trombones); Charlie Mariano, Herb Geller, and Richie Kamuca (reeds); Victor Feldman (piano); and Mel Lewis (drums). Despite the many fine improvisors, this is Holman's session (only the second under his own name), and his charts for the first five tunes, including Billy Strayhorn's "Kissin' Bug" and Gordon Jenkins's "Goodbye," are well crafted, if not particularly adventurous. The second half of the session features his own tunes, which, like the standards, are effective vehicles for his orchestrations.

influences:
◀◀ Gil Evans, Gerry Mulligan
▶▶ Maria Schneider, Don Sebesky, Manny Albam

Andrew Gilbert

Richard "Groove" Holmes

Born May 2, 1931, in Camden, NJ. Died June 29, 1991, in St. Louis, MO.

The year was 1965 and all across the country people were moving to the sounds of organist Richard "Groove" Holmes's hit version of the tune "Misty." Despite the fact that Holmes was a new name to many at the time, he had actually been working and recording on the West Coast for several years prior and had made the first record to pair an organ soloist with a big band (Gerald Wilson's *You Better Believe It*). His own dates at the time for the Pacific Jazz label found him in the company of notables such as Gene Ammons, Ben Webster, Les McCann, and Clifford Scott. Then came "Misty" and the resulting string of popular albums for Prestige Records, followed by some less-memorable experiments with various electronic gear in the 1970s. Holmes hooked up with saxophonist Houston Person in 1977 and launched a recording contract with the Muse label that lasted until his death at age 60. Clearly, what set Holmes apart from other organists was his unwavering sense of swing and his sturdy bass lines (it was surely no coincidence that he was capable of playing acoustic bass). He was one of few players who could express a lot and generate an infectious excitement with even the simplest of phrases.

what to buy: *Groove* 𝄪𝄪𝄪𝄪 (Pacific Jazz, 1961, prod. Richard Bock) finds the organist in the company of tenor star Ben Webster and pianist Les McCann. The music is soulful and robust and the memorable program includes such tunes as "Seven Come Eleven" and "Deep Purple." *Soul Message* 𝄪𝄪𝄪𝄪 (Prestige, 1965, prod. Cal Lampley) contains the hit version of "Misty" and a well-recorded organ sound that reveals Holmes's unique way with a bass line. This is music that is commercially appealing, yet also musically substantial.

what to buy next: The reissue *After Hours* 𝄪𝄪𝄪 (Pacific Jazz, 1961 & 1962, prod. Richard Bock), with its bonus tracks, brings together all of Holmes's trio sides recorded for Pacific Jazz and shows him at his early best. *Blue Groove* 𝄪𝄪𝄪𝄪 (Prestige, 1966/1967, prod. Don Schlitten, Cal Lampley) combines the albums *Get Up and Get It* and *Soul Mist* on one CD. Billy Higgins makes a rare appearance backing an organist, and sidemen such as Teddy Edwards, Harold Vick, Pat Martino, and Blue Mitchell add the sparks to what is already a mighty hot session.

the rest:
Groovin' with Jug 𝄪𝄪𝄪𝄪 (Pacific Jazz, 1961)
Misty 𝄪𝄪𝄪 (Prestige, 1966)
The Groover/That Healin' Feelin' 𝄪𝄪𝄪 (Prestige, 1968)
Blues All Day Long 𝄪𝄪𝄪 (Muse, 1988)

influences:
▶▶ Joey DeFrancesco

Chris Hovan

Adam Holzman

Born February 15, 1958, in New York, NY.

Keyboardist Adam Holzman grew up in California and started classical piano lessons at age 12, but at an early age he was listening to progressive rock and jazz-rock, which led to a growing interest in jazz. His first professional job was playing keyboards on a version of the choral and orchestral work *Carmina Burana* by composer Carl Orff, in a band led by Ray Manzarek (of the Doors) and produced by Philip Glass. He then co-founded a group called Fents, which attracted the attention of singer Randy Hall. At the suggestion of friends, Miles Davis hired Holzman for some keyboard work on *Tutu* and then as second keyboardist for the live tour that followed. While Davis hired and fired musicians

repeatedly during his later years, Holzman was part of the trumpeter's touring group for almost five years, and was promoted to musical director when Robert Irving left the band in 1988. After leaving Davis, Holzman collaborated on a number of projects with Michel Petrucciani. In the 1990s he has also worked with Wayne Shorter, Chaka Khan, Robben Ford, the band Kelvynator, and many others, while also leading his own group, which has achieved a considerable degree of popularity in Europe.

what to buy: Keyboardist Holzman marches to the beat of his own drum and the music he creates with his working group on *Manifesto* 𝄪𝄪𝄪𝄪 (Lipstick, 1995, prod. Adam Holzman) is a clever amalgam of many genres. If categorization is essential, call it early trip-hop, but it's really modern fusion, a pure, dark-cyber-jazz with strong melodies and dark humor ("Airplane Window" was originally titled "If I Ever Had to Get Sucked out of an Airplane Window, Baby It Would Be with You"). Like his mentor Davis (present here via a sample of his voice), Holzman loves to experiment, changing rhythm, dynamics, and mood with great ease, as on "The Grim Reaper" and the aptly titled "Brave New World." *Manifesto* is ear candy for the '90s; big fun for the open minded. *The Big Picture* 𝄪𝄪𝄪𝄪𝄪 (Lipstick, 1996, prod. Adam Holzman), by keyboardist Holzman and his Brave New World, puts forth a fresh vision of the jazz and funk equation. It's darker and more powerful than *Manifesto*, the group's first release. Music of this complexity benefits from the hothouse environment of a working group, and *The Big Picture* was recorded by a band that works consistently. Accordingly, it's an organic amalgam with imagination and solid grooves.

the rest:
Overdrive 𝄪𝄪𝄪 (Lipstick, 1994)

influences:
◀◀ Miles Davis, the Doors, Dr. John
▶▶ Rachel Z., Wayne Shorter, Robben Ford

Bret Primack

St. Elmo Hope

Born Elmo Sylvester Hope, June 27, 1923, in New York, NY. Died May 19, 1967, in NY.

St. Elmo Hope is the guy people write off or forget when talking about great piano players/composers from the 1950s. Hope was influenced by Thelonious Monk but grew up with and played piano alongside Bud Powell. Herbie Nichols is just starting to get his due, decades after his death, and perhaps it's Hope's time, too. Born of Caribbean heritage, Hope's earliest professional jobs were with rhythm and blues bands, but he was giving classical concerts as early as age 13. He was soon working and recording with Clifford Brown, Sonny Rollins, Frank Foster, and Jackie McLean.

what to buy: *Trio and Quintet* 𝄞𝄞𝄞𝄞 (Blue Note, 1991, prod. Alfred Lion, Richard Bock) contains all of the recordings (including alternate takes) Hope did for Blue Note and Pacific Jazz. Hope's "St. Elmo's Fire" is the standout from those sessions. On *Meditations* 𝄞𝄞𝄞𝄞 (OJC, 1955, prod. Bob Weinstock), the devilish, mid-tempo minor chords of "Quit It" stretch time but never to the breaking point, while Hope's trio version of "St. Elmo's Fire" is a softer version of Tatum-meets-Monk than is found on the Blue Note release. His musical sherpas include bassist John Ore (who had played with Lester Young and was to perform in one of Thelonious Monk's famous quartets) and drummer Willie Jones.

what to buy next: Recorded midway in Hope's self-imposed West Coast exile, his piano playing on *The Elmo Hope Trio* 𝄞𝄞𝄞𝄞 (OJC, 1959, prod. David Axelrod) is as strong as ever, but the music, while good, is not as compelling as that found in his earlier recordings. Still, the rhythm section of bassist Jimmy Bond and drummer Frank Butler gives the pianist ample support. *The Final Sessions* 𝄞𝄞𝄞 (Evidence, 1977, prod. Herb Abramson) are the same vintage 1966 recordings that used to be available on Inner City, but this two-disc set now includes the alternate takes and full-length versions of tunes previously heard only in their edited forms. Recorded just a year before he died, these valedictory performances still have a lot of power and beauty, but Hope's gas tank is just about empty, riven by drugs and starting the slow, downward slide.

the rest:
Hope Meets Foster 𝄞𝄞𝄞 (OJC, 1955)
All-Star Sessions 𝄞𝄞𝄞𝄞 (Milestone, 1956)
So Nice 𝄞𝄞𝄞 (OJC, 1959)
Homecoming 𝄞𝄞𝄞 (OJC, 1961)
Hope-Full 𝄞𝄞𝄞𝄞 (OJC, 1962)
Elmo Hope Plays His Original Compositions 𝄞𝄞𝄞𝄞 (Fresh Sounds, 1992)

influences:
◀◀ Bud Powell, Thelonious Monk

Garaud MacTaggart

Glenn Horiuchi

Born February 27, 1955, in Chicago, IL.

Harmonies and hooks alternately drawn from the Occident and the Orient mix and mingle in the music of pianist and composer Glenn Horiuchi, one of the leading lights of the Asian American musical community. Along with fellow pianist Jon Jang, he was instrumental in organizing the AsianImprov record label, and, like Jang, his compositional interests span from boppish works for small combo to large, challenging neo-classical canvases. Along with Thelonious Monk and Cecil Taylor, who both clearly influenced Horiuchi's keyboard technique, the modal concerns of L.A.–based elder statesman Horace Tapscott have guided his pianistic approach.

what to buy: Horiuchi's debut for the Italian Soul Note imprint, *Oxnard Beet* 𝄞𝄞𝄞𝄞 (Soul Note, 1992, prod. Glenn Horiuchi) is a uniformly magnificent record filled with humorous turns and intense musicianship. The title track memorializes a strike by Mexican and Japanese farm workers at the turn of the century, and "Dance for a Nisei Hipster" gives a sly, head-bobbing nod to the sound of juke-joint barwalkers (note the allusion to "Night Train"). But it is the aptly titled, engaging "Striking a Riff" and the thematically connected "Burning Embers" that are the album's focal points.

what to buy next: *Calling Is It and Now* 𝄞𝄞𝄞𝄞 (Soul Note, 1995, prod. Glenn Horiuchi), which the pianist says is part of a continuum with *Oxnard*, is somewhat denser and slightly less accessible. The album's title is an indication of the music's Cecil Taylor-ish intentions, and Horiuchi's playing is accordingly more conceptual and diffuse, especially on the title tune, which meanders from broad section to section over the course of 16 minutes. In addition to Francis Wong's tenor, bassist Anders Swanson and the impressive drummer/percussionist Jeanette Wrate are featured. *Hilltop View* 𝄞𝄞𝄞𝄞 (Music & Arts, 1996, prod. Glenn Horiuchi), a trio date with Wrate and bassist Roberto Miranda, is filled with fiery improvisations, as is 1997's *Mercy* 𝄞𝄞𝄞𝄞 (Music & Arts, 1997, prod. Glenn Horiuchi), on which the Horiuchi-Wrate-Miranda combination is joined by Joseph Jarman.

the rest:
Next Step 𝄞𝄞𝄞 (AsianImprov, 1988)
Manzanar Voices 𝄞𝄞𝄞 (AsianImprov, 1989)
Issei Spirit 𝄞𝄞𝄞 (AsianImprov, 1989)
Poston Sonata 𝄞𝄞𝄞𝄞 (AsianImprov, 1992)
Kenzo's Vision 𝄞𝄞𝄞 (AsianImprov, 1995)

David Prince

Shirley Horn

Born May 1, 1934, in Washington, DC.

One of jazz's most affecting ballad singers, Shirley Horn is also a fine pianist who is among the music's very best self-accompany-

ing vocalists. She can swing powerfully as both a singer and a player, but it's her understated gift for interpreting the emotional implications of a lyric that makes her so effective on slow numbers. Though Horn's languid ballad approach and lithe, harmonically rich piano style remain essentially unchanged since she began recording in the early 1960s, her popular breakthrough didn't take place until the late 1980s, when she signed with Verve, her current label. Horn began playing piano at age four, and quickly proved to be a gifted and single-mindedly devoted student. She studied composition at Howard University at age 12 and later attended the school as an undergraduate, and began working in Washington, D.C., nightspots. Horn made her first album, *Embers and Ashes,* in 1960, a recording that caught the attention of Miles Davis, who recruited Horn to open for him at the Village Vanguard (an event that was captured on the Can-Am LP *Live at the Village Vanguard*). During the early 1960s she worked major jazz clubs, recorded albums with Quincy Jones and Jimmy Jones for Mercury and ABC/Paramount, and sang on the soundtracks of the movies *For the Love of Ivy* and *A Dandy in Aspic.* But by the mid-1960s, Horn dropped out of the national jazz scene and moved back to Washington to raise her daughter, playing enough around the city to sustain her reputation as a local legend. Her comeback started with an appearance at the 1981 North Sea Jazz Festival, which resulted in the best of her four SteepleChase albums. By the late 1980s, Horn was well on her way to her present jazz-star status. Her skill as an accompanist has been utilized by Carmen McRae on her Novus album *Sarah—Dedicated to You* and Toots Thielemans on his EmArcy album *For My Lady.* She also appears in the 1990 movie *Tune in Tomorrow* and sings two songs on Wynton Marsalis's excellent soundtrack.

what to buy: A smoky, atmospheric, unspeakably beautiful album, *You Won't Forget Me* ���� (Verve, 1991, prod. Richard Seidel) features Horn with her impeccable working trio—bassist Charles Ables and drummer Steve Williams—and some very special guests. Each tune seems to flow into the next, as Horn turns the 14 standards into a journey through the various meanings of love. On "Don't Let the Sun Catch You Crying," Wynton Marsalis borrows Clark Terry's sound, adding piquant commentary to the lyrics' warning, while bassist Buster Williams and drummer Billy Hart provide the rhythmic lift that makes Horn's the definitive version of "Come Back to Me." Other highlights include Horn's duet with Toots Thielemans (on harmonica and gui-

tar) on a breathtaking version of "Beautiful Love" and, in one of his very last recordings, Miles Davis accompanying Horn on a hypnotic seven-minute version of the title track. Accompanied by her longtime rhythm section, bassist Charles Abels and drummer Steve Williams, Horn delivers a masterful recital on *Close Enough for Love* ���� (Verve, 1989, prod. Richard Seidel), covering 13 tunes with the utmost style. Highlights include her crystalline solo version of Johnny Mandel's title track and her enthralling stroll through Irving Berlin's "I Got Lost in His Arms." The big-toned tenor saxophonist Buck Hill sits in on five tracks, including Horn's authoritative versions of "Beautiful Friendship," "Come Fly with Me," and "Memories of You." Her piano work is rhythmically supple and full of rich, harmonic nuances throughout the session. Recorded live at the North Sea Jazz Festival, *Violets for Your Furs* ���� (SteepleChase, 1981/1994, prod. Nils Winther) features Horn with bassist Charles Abels and the dynamic drummer Billy Hart on a program of well-worn standards. She stretches out on a 10-minute version of "My Man" and a deeply soulful seven-minute take of "Georgia on My Mind." Her understated sensuality pervades "Lover Man" and her sense of humor shines on Andy Razaf's "Gee Baby, Ain't I Good to You."

what to buy next: Recorded live at the Vine St. Bar & Grill in Hollywood, *I Thought About You* ���� (Verve, 1987, prod. Miriam Cutler, David Kreisberg, Ron Berinstein) was Horn's first album for Verve and catapulted her to national attention. Horn sings eight tunes, including the spirited, rarely heard Harold Arlen/Yip Harburg anthem, "The Eagle and Me," and a sensuous version of "Estaté," and delivers "Isn't It Romantic" as instrumental. "I Thought About You'" and Duke Ellington's "I Got It Bad and That Ain't Good" are also performed with admirable style and swing. This album introduced her longtime working trio with bassist Charles Abels and drummer Steve Williams. Augmenting her excellent working trio with a host of guest stars, *The Main Ingredient* ���� (Verve, 1996, prod. Shirley Horn) is one of Horn's best sessions from the mid-1990s. Tenor saxophonist Buck Hill sits in on "Blues for Sarge," "Keepin' Out of Mischief Now," and spars with Joe Henderson on "All or Nothing at All," which also features Elvin Jones. Henderson and Jones turn Horn's nine-minute version of "You Go to My Head" into the album's centerpiece, though Roy Hargrove's flugelhorn adds considerable bite to "The Meaning of the Blues." And only Blossom Dearie can put as a convincing a spin on Dave Frishberg's ode to caprice, "Peel Me a Grape," featuring Billy Hart's deft drum work. If Shirley Horn seems like an unlikely candidate to produce a tribute to Ray Charles, check out *Light*

Shirley Horn (© Jack Vartoogian)

Out of Darkness 🎵🎵🎵🎵 (Verve, 1993, prod. Shirley Horn), an idiosyncratic but highly rewarding collection of 15 blues, standards, ballads, and soul tunes associated with ol' man Ray. Horn plays six of the pieces with her longtime trio mates Charles Abels (bass and guitar) and Steve Williams (drums), including a devastating version of "The Sun Died," and an erotically charged take of "Just for a Thrill," while alto saxophonist Gary Bartz contributes greatly to six tunes, including "Drown in My Own Tears," "Just a Little Lovin'," and "If You Were Mine." Horn performs "Green (It's Not Easy Being Green)" solo, and adds Hammond B3 to her typically sparkling piano work on "You Don't Know Me," "Hard Hearted Hannah," and a deeply soulful version of "Georgia on My Mind."

what to avoid: *Travelin' Light* 🎵🎵🎵 (Impulse!, 1965/1994, prod. Johnny Pate) gets three bones for the music, but the record company gets sent to the doghouse for reissuing this fine session at full price despite barely 30 minutes of playing time. The 12 tunes feature Horn on vocals and piano with the great guitarist Kenny Burrell heading up a competent rhythm section, and a horn section with Joe Newman (trumpet), Frank Wess (flute and alto sax), and Jerome Richardson (flute). Strike a blow against record company greed and look for it in the used bins.

best of the rest:
Loads of Love/Shirley Horn with Horns 🎵🎵🎵 (Mercury, 1963/Verve, 1990)
Here's to Life 🎵🎵🎵🎵 (Verve, 1992)
I Love You, Paris 🎵🎵🎵🎵 (Verve, 1994)
Loving You 🎵🎵🎵 (Verve, 1997)

worth searching for: Though Horn covers a number of tunes from her regular repertoire on *Softly* 🎵🎵🎵🎵 (Audiophile, 1988/1994, prod. Joel E. Siegel), such as "How Long Has This Been Going On," "Estaté," and "My, How the Time Goes By," she also sings a number of strong but rarely heard pieces, including Richard Rodney Bennett's "I Watch You Sleep," the Latin-tinged "Forget Me" by Valerie Parks Brown, and a solo version of the melancholy ballad "Softly, As I Leave You." Though it's not as consistently rewarding as her first Verve sessions and somewhat difficult to find, this is an all 'round excellent session with Horn's capable trio mates, bassist Charles Abels and drummer Steve Williams.

influences:
◀◀ Billie Holiday, Peggy Lee
▶▶ Diana Krall

Andrew Gilbert

Bill Horvitz

Born May 12, 1947, in New York, NY.

Happenstance placed guitarist Bill Horvitz (brother of Wayne Horvitz) at a point on the musical family tree where rock and roll, as well as jazz, began to influence an improvisational player's choices. His limited recorded output of three albums in a dozen years demonstrates that Horvitz has more than the necessary ability to enable him to leap wide stylistic boundaries in the course of a single, bounding run. Duane Eddy was the first musician he heard in person, and he also listened to early rockabilly and soul artists such as Chuck Berry, Jerry Lee Lewis, Little Richard, and the Everly Brothers, so his choice of the guitar is a natural one. Later listening experience with Jimi Hendrix, Frank Zappa, and John Cippolina (arguably the best of the San Franciscan acid voyagers, from Quicksilver Messanger Service and, later, Copperhead) at once expanded his rock horizons and opened up his jazz ears, which had sprung to life with the Eric Dolphy of the 1960 and '64 Charles Mingus Workshops, Pharoah Sanders, Cecil Taylor, electric Miles Davis, and Weather Report; Elmore James and Jim Hall also offered contrasting views of the selfsame continuum. Horvitz studied at the College of Marin in Kentfield, California, Sonoma State, San Rafael's Ali Akbar College of Music, and in private work with pianist Art Lande and bassist Gary Peacock, among others.

what to buy: The most recent Horvitz on record is not only his first recording in a decade, it's unquestionably his best. The wait was well worth it. *Dust Devil* 🎵🎵🎵🎵🎵 (Music & Arts, 1997, prod. Bill Horvitz) is a beautifully paced selection of interesting, elastic, and aesthetically pleasing themes played to near-perfection by a dream trio of Horvitz on guitar and an assortment of unobtrusive and fascinating effects, multi-woodwinder Steve Adams (who's best known as a current ROVA Quartet member, but started out in Boston's similarly shaped Your Neighborhood Saxophone Quartet), and another, unsung Massachusetts exile, Joseph Sabella, on drums. The group exhibits a finely wrought sense of nuanced interaction throughout, with solo statements wafting in and out of each other rather than entering/exiting through rigid, one- or two-chorus-length doors. Indeed, the individual pieces themselves go through untold changes in their not-immoderate, six- to eight-minute timespans.

what to buy next: Recorded in 1986 and caught somewhere in the middle of his other albums stylistically as well as chronologically, *Solo Electric Guitar/Compositions for Eleven* 🎵🎵🎵 (Ear-Rational, 1989, prod. Bill Horvitz) sets up ethereal and menacing drones that are less successful than his later work. At times, not even the talented large ensemble that includes Vincent Chancey, Herb Robertson, Elliott Sharp, Bobby Previte, Myra Melford, and David Hofstra can save the individual motifs of these sectional pieces from wandering about aimlessly. On the other hand, some of the leader's solo sections within these roiling, Fellini-esque mass-ascensions are very attractive and angular.

worth searching for: The earliest Bill Horvitz album, the harder-to-find *Trios* 𝒜𝒜𝒜 (Dossier, 1986, prod. Bill Horvitz), issued in Germany, boasts the excellent Butch Morris on cornet and piano, plus Morris cohort J.A. Deane on electrically modified trombone and hand percussion. Spacious, vibration-level spaciness is the place where this Horvitz threesome feels most at home. Themes, as such, seem not to exist; mood and intuition are all. This is where Jimi Hendrix was very likely headed, if he abandoned the Big Beat and gave himself up to pure experimental improvisation. In other words, very, very trippy.

influences:

◀◀ John McLaughlin, Robin Trower, Tal Farlow, Sonic Youth

▶▶ David Fiuczynski, Marc Ducret, Marc Ribot

David Prince

Wayne Horvitz

Born 1955, in New York, NY.

Horvitz merges jazz with rock, gospel, country, blues, avant-garde, and more. He had been recording for nearly a decade when, in 1986, he relocated from New York to Seattle with his wife, composer Robin Holcomb, and children. Horvitz and Holcomb cofounded the New York Composers Orchestra, an ensemble formed in 1986 to perform commissioned works by himself and other innovators including Bobby Previte, Lawrence "Butch" Morris, and Anthony Braxton. Since Horvitz's relocation, the NYCO repertoire continues to be performed by the original NYCO ensemble, as well as by a Pacific West group of musicians led by Horvitz, and by other ensembles with Horvitz directing. He also leads the bands Pigpen, Zony Mash, The President, and his trio with Butch Morris and Bobby Previte.

Horvitz has performed and/or recorded as sideman or collaborator with such cutting-edge musicians as Marty Ehrlich, John Zorn, Naked City, Philip Wilson, David Moss, Curlew, Bobby Previte, Robin Holcomb, Bill Frisell, Billy Bang, Kazutoki Umezu, Fred Frith, Carla Bley, Elliott Sharp, and Michael Shrieve. He has composed music for film, television, video, and multimedia educational projects as well as theater and dance productions.

what to buy: A good place to start is with *This New Generation* 𝒜𝒜𝒜𝒜 (Elektra Musician, 1987, prod. Wayne Horvitz), the album that gave Horvitz wider exposure and established his career as a leader. From hard-bop jazz and contemporary classical to tinges of rock, Horvitz blends musical genres on the 15-tune compilation combining original material from his mid-1980s LP releases (initially for Dossier Records, Germany), *Dinner at Eight* and *The President*. Horvitz handles keyboards, drum programming, and harmonica, with better-known collaborators such as Bill Frisell (guitar), Dave Hofstra (bass, tuba), Robin Holcomb (keyboards), Bobby Previte (drums, keys), and others.

what to buy next: *Miss Ann* 𝒜𝒜𝒜𝒜 (Tim/Kerr, 1995, prod. Wayne Horvitz) is by Horvitz's band Pigpen. What would the late Eric Dolphy think of this quartet's mutation of his title-track song? With Horvitz's edgy synthesizer sounds, Fred Chalenor's monolithic electric bass line, and Mike Stone's driving drumming supporting Briggan Krauss's keening alto sax tone, that lead track announces that this will not be generic jazz. The rest of the album, except for a John Zorn piece, is by Horvitz. There's a rock bite to many of his tunes (though they're not fusion), and the greasy organ funk on "Stupid" presages his Zony Mash group, but his themes are extremely strong and the structures are solidly jazz. The Billy Tipton Memorial Saxophone Quartet is added for two of Horvitz's tracks.

best of the rest:

(With Lawrence "Butch" Morris and William Parker) *Some Order, Long Understood* 𝒜𝒜𝒜𝒜 (Black Saint, 1983)

(With the New York Composers Orchestra) *The New York Composers Orchestra* 𝒜𝒜𝒜 (New World/Countercurrents, 1990)

(With the New York Composers Orchestra) *First Program in Standard Time* 𝒜𝒜𝒜𝒜 (New World/Countercurrents, 1992)

(With The President) *Miracle Mile* 𝒜𝒜𝒜 (Nonesuch, 1992)

(With Pigpen) *V as in Victim* 𝒜𝒜𝒜 (Avant, 1994)

(With Pigpen) *Halfrack* 𝒜𝒜𝒜𝒜 (Tim/Kerr, 1994)

(With Pigpen) *Live in Poland* 𝒜𝒜𝒜𝒜 (Cavity Search, 1994)

Monologue: Twenty Compositions for Dance 𝒜𝒜𝒜 (Cavity Search, 1997)

(With Zony Mash) *Cold Spell* 𝒜𝒜𝒜 (Knitting Factory Works, 1997)

influences:

◀◀ John Patton, Miles Davis, Elliott Sharp

▶▶ Babkas, Bobby Previte

David C. Gross, Nancy Ann Lee, and Steve Holtje

George Howard

Born 1957, in Philadelphia, PA. Died March 22, 1998, in Atlanta, GA.

George Howard's sax stylings straddle the fine line between jazz and pop. Born in Philadelphia, he started on clarinet and bassoon before adding the soprano sax to his musical arsenal. Like any developing jazz player, Howard had several influences that deeply affected his music, and he names John Coltrane, Chick Corea, Miles Davis, Sonny Fortune, Herbie Hancock, Eddie Harris, and Wayne Shorter as his principal inspirations. After gigs with local bands, the saxophonist started doing session work for a group of musicians (Kenny Gamble, Leon Huff, and Dexter Wansel) who were known for the "Philly Sound." A major turning point in his career happened when Howard started working with Grover Washington Jr. in 1979. In 1982 he recorded his first album as a leader, *Asphalt Garden*, and after he signed on with GRP he recorded more than 10 others. His album *Midnight Mood* was released in early 1998, shortly before he died of cancer.

what to buy: George Howard plays two roles on *Attitude Adjustment* ♫♫♫♪ (GRP, 1996, prod. George Duke, Speech): his signature lead as romantic balladeer, and a newer pose as a hip street-tough. Over the last decade of his life, he was one of the most consistent "contemporary" jazzmen, offering a smooth, lite-funk suavity that maintains the status quo. On *Attitude Adjustment*, his soprano is as silky as always but there's some breakneck tempos that excite as well. The tune title "A Whole Lotta Drum in Me" sums up the electrified production values—world percussion often meeting industrial punch and ultra-slick hip-hop. Throughout, Howard is aggressive and tenacious. For those in search of enjoyable background music, *A Home Far Away* ♫♫♫♪ (GRP, 1994, prod. George Howard, Rex Rideout) more than fills the bill. It's bouncy and silky and features Howard's characteristic soprano, which seems to float on a cushion that's lighter than air. Howard wrote or co-wrote most of the songs, and his compositions reflect his velvety, melodic approach, notably "Doria" and "Until Tomorrow." The funky, penetrating "Grover's Groove" is a tasteful tribute to his mentor, Grover Washington Jr., while "Renewal, for Our Fathers," shows off Howard's more adventurous side, stretching out far beyond the usual groove. Funk and fusion are foremost on *Do I Ever Cross Your Mind?* ♫♫♫♪ (GRP, 1992, prod. George Howard), with Howard's R&B roots front and center. Aided by vocalists Phil Perry and Carl Anderson, he shows that "jazz lite" need not be "fuzak." This solid, masterful set demonstrates how Howard avoided the pitfalls that pop up all too frequently in this genre. Howard also makes his vocal debut on the title

track, "Do I Ever Cross Your Mind," and like his soprano, his voice is most affable. Howard's first recording for GRP, *Love and Understanding* ♫♫♫ (GRP, 1991, prod. George Howard, George Duke, Victor Bailey), features his originals as well as covers of R&B hits like "Baby Come to Me" and "Everything I Miss at Home." Keyboardist George Duke co-produced and plays on several tracks as well, including "Here for a Minute" and "Interlude." His funky sensibilities add a nice touch to Howard's refined sophistication.

what to buy next: *Steppin' Out* ♫♫♫ (GRP, 1984/1992, prod. George Howard, Dean Gant) is a funky delight, with Howard's patented soprano sax riding the powerful grooves laid down by bassist Nathan East and drummer Ndugu Chancler. "Dream Ride" finds Howard on a magic urban carpet, floating on a journey of delight, while on "Sweet Dreams" he guides listeners to a place resplendent in beauty and happiness. *When Summer Comes* ♫♫♫ (GRP, 1993, prod. George Howard, Carl Griffin), Howard's tenth album as a leader, features "Just for Tonight," with Paul Jackson Jr.'s energizing vocals, along with Howard's hit update of the Hugh Masekela/Friends of Distinction chestnut "Grazin' in the Grass." Other standouts include the jazzy "Three Minute Warning" and the poignant "When a Child Smiles," one of the six songs Howard co-wrote for the album. "Family," a soprano/alto duet with Everett Harp, is a "contemporary jazz" version of the old battle of the saxes, with both emerging as winners.

best of the rest:

Dancing in the Sun ♫♫♫♪ (GRP, 1985/1990)
Love Will Follow ♫♫♫ (GRP, 1991)
Personal ♫♫♫♪ (GRP, 1997)

influences:

◀◀ Wayne Shorter, Herbie Hancock

▶▶ Dave Koz, David Sanborn, Gerald Albright, Grover Washington Jr., Kenny G, Kirk Whalum, Najee

Bret Primack

Noah Howard

Born April 6, 1943, in New Orleans, LA.

Firmly entrenched within the free-jazz movement from the get-go, Noah Howard cut his teeth in the mid-1960s playing his first New York gigs with Marion Brown, Pharoah Sanders, Sun Ra, and Archie Shepp (with whom he played again in 1969). His only two in-print albums were recorded within 10 months of one another and—given that he recorded nearly another dozen before he disappeared in the early '80s—unfairly distort the depth and breadth of Howard's talent on the alto. Further gigs and albums (some of which were released on Howard's own Altosax label) find him in the company of Frank Wright, Arthur Taylor, Burton Greene, Sunny Murray, Muhammad Ali, and others.

what to buy: *At Judson Hall* ♫♫♫♫ (ESP, 1966, prod. Richard Alderson), a live set (with LP art that eerily evokes John Coltrane's *Vanguard Again* cover), is incendiary to the point of beauty, with collapsing improvisatory structures giving way to sheer sonic madness. Catherine Norris's cello is a plus, though it's under-utilized. Dave Burrell is, as usual, fluidly frantic on the piano, and a line-up of unsung players like drummer Robert Kapp and trumpeter Ric Colbeck play as if it's the last gig of their lives. Side two's "Homage to John Coltrane" is simply stunning.

what to buy next: Recorded within a year of Howard's arrival in New York, *Noah Howard Quartet* ♫♫♫ (ESP, 1966, prod. Richard Alderson)—though largely engaging—suffers from an unsettling sense of hesitation, and in each of the four pieces here there are moments of extraordinary perfection set right next to moments that are simply ordinary. However, along with the fabulous bass work of Scott Holt, Howard more than makes it work.

worth searching for: From a Hilversum set with Misha Mengelberg, Han Bennink, and others, Howard released the astonishing *Patterns* ♫♫♫♫ (Altosax, 1971), which somehow reconciles his very American and very free tendencies with the avantgarde improvisations of his European partners. Disconcerting at points, but ultimately rewarding.

influences:

◄◄ Marion Brown

►► Anthony Braxton

Jason Ferguson

Freddie Hubbard

Born April 7, 1938, in Indianapolis, IN.

Running neck-and-neck with Donald Byrd in the good-trumpeters-who-make-terrible-records race, Freddie Hubbard is one confounding musician. From a promising start as part of the Blue Note avant garde, Hubbard inevitably bit of the pop-fusion apple, making some of the most artless "jazz" records of the genre, and later attempts to rekindle some of his former hard-bopping fire were thwarted both by faltering skills as well as a decided loss of momentum. Recognized as neither a free-bop

innovator nor a fusion groove machine (à la Donald Byrd), Hubbard may, unfortunately, wind up being considered an almost pop star who happened to play trumpet. It should be remembered, however, that, at the start, Hubbard was a forward-looking innovator, appearing on groundbreaking albums as diverse as Eric Dolphy's *Out to Lunch* and *Outward Bound*, Oliver Nelson's *Blues and the Abstract Truth*, Ornette Coleman's *Free Jazz*, and John Coltrane's mammoth masterpiece, *Ascension*. That this work came after such formative lessons as stints with Philly Joe Jones and Sonny Rollins should make it clear that Hubbard is not only a strong player (he was, in fact, one of the instrument's best), but also an incredibly diverse one. His first, exploratory Blue Note efforts were recorded during the same period as his work with Art Blakey's Jazz Messengers (1961–64). After Blakey, Hubbard spent some time with Max Roach and in 1966 formed his own group. Hubbard's free-bop period ended in 1970, with an eventual phasing in of fusion elements upon his signing to Creed Taylor's controversial CTI label. Ironically, the beginning of the end (as it were) also saw Hubbard make two rather interesting records, *Red Clay* and *Straight Life*, neither of which, sadly, are currently available. In 1971 Hubbard released *First Light*, his first overtly slick and commercial record, nearly drowning in the shiny polish of overdubs and "atmosphere." People dug it, and Hubbard took the hint, following up with *Sky Dive* which, for better or worse, included his take on the theme to *The Godfather*. A string of four progressively slicker CTI albums followed, and in 1975 Hubbard signed to Columbia for what would be the most artistically barren period of his career. Thankfully, none of the six albums Hubbard recorded for Columbia are currently available on CD—and are also completely unrepresented on any Sony "best of," as they are simply more Vegas than Village Vanguard, with overdubs of overdubs, superfluous string sections and precious little human interaction. Although Hubbard attempted to return to his roots in the '80s, he was foiled by occasional lapses into pop pap and, more significantly, by his own inconsistent playing. A few (comparatively) good records can be found from this period, but, in general, if you've heard the Blue Note and CTI records, you've heard what Hubbard has to offer.

what to buy: One of Hubbard's finest group moments, *The Artistry of Freddie Hubbard* ♫♫♫♫ (Impulse!, 1962, prod. Bob Thiele) finds him teamed up with all-star trombonist Curtis Fuller and tenor man John Gilmore (in one of his rare extra-Arkestral appearances, he's playing surprisingly *in*). Also on the scene are pianist Tommy Flanagan, bassist Art Davis, and drummer Louis Hayes, so needless to say, Hubbard's chops

need to be in order for this date. Thankfully, they are, and the group manages to even make both "Caravan" and "Summertime" sound interesting again. Oddly enough, even with Gilmore on board, Hubbard doesn't go out quite as far here as he does on his Blue Notes of the same period. As with many of Blue Note's 1989 reissue series, *Hub-Tones* &&&&& (Blue Note, 1962, prod. Alfred Lion) has alternate takes and original takes jammed next to one another in the running order, utterly nullifying any effect of musical flow the original LP had in favor of some sort of pseudo-archival feeling. Yet, that's why CD players are programmable and, once the alternates are shuffled to the end (where they should be), this reissue gem shines as it did upon its original release. Herbie Hancock steps up to the keys and he, along with Reggie Workman, James Spaulding, and Clifford Jarvis, invigorate Hubbard. From the fluttering tremolo note that opens *Breaking Point* &&&&& (Blue Note, 1964, prod. Alfred Lion), you know you're in for a treat—and something a little different. Hubbard's flexible, intense playing is in high form at this point in his career. Very nearly free and consistently strong, it's Hubbard at his most ambitious and talented. *This Is Jazz #25* &&&& (CTI/Columbia, 1970–73/1997, prod. Creed Taylor), a 1997 "best of," is all that's available of Hubbard's CTI output. With the chaff removed (did you really want to hear *The Godfather* theme again?), these six remastered tracks demonstrate that while Hubbard's ideals may have been becoming increasingly crass, the music he was making was still maintaining its dignity.

what to buy next: Another fine Blue Note moment, *Here to Stay* &&&& (Blue Note, 1962, prod. Alfred Lion)'s only drawback is its reliance on older material for half the set. Of course, "Body and Soul"—as well as two Cal Massey tunes—don't do too badly by this band which, with Wayne Shorter, Cedar Walton, Reggie Workman, and Philly Joe Jones, was among the most exciting of the Blue Note ensembles. Accordingly, *Here to Stay* bristles with a youthful, pioneering spirit. After a spurt of rather "out" recordings, it must have been a surprise to hear Hubbard take part in the hard-core live blowing session, *The Night of the Cookers: Live at Club La Marchal, Volumes 1 & 2* &&&& (Blue Note, 1965, prod. Alfred Lion). Originally spread out over two albums, this live set from 1965 features Hubbard in the mixed company of Lee Morgan, Harold Mabern, Larry Ridley, James Spaulding, and Pete LaRoca, as well as conga player Big Black.

Freddie Hubbard **(Archive Photos)**

It's nothing but hurricane force from the onset, as the mixture of LaRoca's experimental tendencies blend with the hard bopping Morgan, leaving Hubbard smack in the middle to just blow like it was his last day on Earth. He does. It's a corny concept, granted, but *Ballads* &&&& (Blue Note, 1960–64/1997, prod. Alfred Lion) is actually a pretty decent compilation of Hubbard's more laid-back, early '60s moments. Not groundbreaking—or even exemplary of his Blue Note work—it's nonetheless a nice way to hear the trumpeter being relaxed without being asleep. The first of Hubbard's Atlantic LPs, *Backlash* &&&& (Atlantic, 1966, prod. Arif Mardin) finds him in a natural extension of his Blue Note self. Although this quintet is a little less star-studded, it is nonetheless strong and this album (along with his two other, non-CD Atlantics) was the last cutting-edge, hard bop album Hubbard made before beginning his treacherously commercial (though occasionally rewarding) journey on CTI.

what to avoid: Generally, after Hubbard's peak fusion period (1970–72), it's a quick downhill slope into middling song craft, bad-to-worse playing and, eventually pure pop drivel. Although there are a couple notable exceptions, it's best to approach anything that came after this with extreme caution, if not outright avoidance.

the rest:
Best of &&& (Blue Note, 1960–87/1989)
Minor Mishap &&& (Black Lion, 1961)
Hub Cap &&&& (Blue Note, 1961)
The Body and the Soul &&& (Impulse!, 1963)
Best of &&& (CTI/Epic, 1970–73/1990)
First Light && (CTI, 1971)
Sky Dive && (CTI, 1972)
Best of: Live and in the Studio & (Pablo, 1980–81/1983)
Outpost && (Enja, 1981)
Born to Be Blue && (Prestige/OJC, 1981)
Keystone Bop Volume 1: Sunday && (Prestige, 1981)
Keystone Bop Volume 2: Friday/Saturday && (Prestige, 1981)
(With Oscar Peterson) *Face to Face* && (Pablo, 1982)
Back to Birdland &&& (Real Time/Drive Archive, 1982)
Feel the Wind && (Timeless, 1988)
Topsy: Standard Book && (Evidence, 1991)
Bolivia && (Music Masters, 1991)
Blues for Miles && (Evidence, 1992/1996)
Monk, Miles, Trane, Cannon && (Music Masters, 1994)

worth searching for: *Blue Spirits* &&&& (Blue Note, 1966, prod. Alfred Lion), Hubbard's last studio outing for Blue Note, is among his most challenging avant-bop records and, unfortunately, it's fallen out of print. *Sing Me a Song of Songmy* &&&& (Atlantic, 1971, prod. Ilhan Mimaroglu) is among one of the most outrageous career anomalies around; Hubbard took his quintet into the studio with Mimaroglu, who, in addition to his duties as Atlantic A&R man/producer, was also a not-bad tape manipulator/avant garde classical composer. The resulting album was, to say the least, a shocker, with Hubbard's group being equally bolstered and smothered by the combined effect of tape effects, church organs, recitations and, of course, a full orchestra and chorus. Parts of *Songmy* (including the stunning "Threnody for Sharon Tate") can also be found on the more readily available two-record retrospective, *The Art of Freddie Hubbard* (Atlantic).

influences:

◀◀ Clifford Brown

▶▶ Maynard Ferguson (in substance, not style), Randy Brecker

Jason Ferguson

Helen Humes

Born June 23, 1913, in Louisville, KY. Died September 9, 1981, in Santa Monica, CA.

Helen Humes is often reduced to a footnote as the singer who replaced Billie Holiday in the Count Basie Orchestra, but she was one of the great jazz vocalists, a brilliantly versatile artist who made great recordings from the late 1920s through the 1970s. Her deceptively little-girl voice made her blues vocals especially effective. She also made classic recordings of swing standards, ballads, and early R&B. Though she wasn't always well served by recordings, Humes was a distinctive artist who sang with a high, clear-toned voice and expert, rhythmically compelling jazz phrasing. She played piano and organ in church as a child and made her first recordings in her early teens for OKeh. She worked with Stuff Smith, Jonah Jones, Vernon Andrade, Harry James, and Al Sears in the '30s before hooking up with Count Basie, with whom she spent three years. Unfortunately, her tenure with Basie didn't enhance her reputation, since Jimmy Rushing handled all the blues vocals and she was limited mostly to mediocre pop material. Humes spent the early '40s working around New York with Teddy Wilson, Art Tatum, and others, and then went on the road with Clarence Love. She settled in Los Angeles in the mid-'40s and recorded a number of proto-R&B numbers, including her hit "Million Dollar Secret," a tune that stayed in her repertoire the rest of her life. In the '50s and early '60s, Humes toured with Jazz at the Philharmonic and Red Norvo and recorded three classic albums for Contemporary. She moved to Australia in 1964 but returned to the States to take care of her mother in

1967. Humes dropped out of the music business for a number of years, but her triumph at the Newport festival in 1973 jump-started her career, and she remained busy until the end of her life, performing and recording frequently.

what to buy: The best of the three classic albums Humes recorded for Contemporary, *Songs I Like to Sing!* ♪♪♪♪ (Contemporary/OJC, 1960, prod. Lester Koenig) is a masterpiece, with expert brass and string arrangements by Marty Paich. The band features such jazz giants as Ben Webster, Art Pepper, and Barney Kessel, but it is Humes's vocals, especially on "My Old Flame" and "Mean to Me," that make this such enduring music. A brilliant small-group session, *Swingin' with Humes* ♪♪♪♪ (Contemporary/OJC, 1961, prod. Lester Koenig) captures the irrepressible Humes with an all-star sextet. There's not a weak track, but Humes is at her best on "I'm Confessin'" and "Pennies from Heaven." The first of her Contemporary sessions, *'Tain't Nobody's Biz-ness If I Do* ♪♪♪♪ (Contemporary/OJC, 1959, prod. Lester Koenig), was a quickly organized recording with sketchy arrangements. The band turns the loose atmosphere to its advantage, and Humes sings well-known standards with aplomb. From the ancient "Bill Bailey" to Ellington's "I Got It Bad and That Ain't Good," Humes turns everything she sings into gold. Her version of "Star Dust," with an unspeakably beautiful Benny Carter trumpet solo, is for the ages.

what to buy next: Recorded live at the Back Dancing and Dynamite Society in Half Moon Bay, California, *'Deed I Do* ♪♪♪♪ (Contemporary, 1976, prod. Eric Miller) captures Humes with a solid rhythm section and a program heavy on blues, standards, and novelty numbers, including her perennial ode to gold digging, "Million Dollar Secret." *Helen* ♪♪♪♪ (Muse, 1981, prod. Bob Porter) captures the great singer just a year before her death, and she sounds as lively as ever. Though there are only six songs and about 32 minutes of music, this session is highly recommended for her versions of "Easy Living" and "There'll Be Some Changes Made."

the rest:
E-Baba-Le-Ba: The Rhythm and Blues Years ♪♪♪♪ (Savoy, 1950)
Let the Good Times Roll ♪♪♪♪ (Classic Jazz/Black & Blue, 1973)
Sneakin' Around ♪♪♪♪ (Classic Jazz, 1974)
On the Sunny Side of the Street ♪♪♪♪ (Black Lion, 1974)

worth searching for: The great singer's last classic session, *Helen Humes and the Muse All-Stars* ♪♪♪♪ (Muse, 1980, prod. Bob Porter) pairs her with Eddie "Cleanhead" Vinson on "I'm Going to Move to the Outskirts of Town." Also memorable is her version of "My Old Flame." The presence of tough tenors Arnett

Cobb and Buddy Tate and a rhythm section led by the always-classy Gerald Wiggins make this date a winner.

influences:

◀◀ Ethel Waters, Billie Holiday, Ella Fitzgerald

                                    Andrew Gilbert

Percy Humphrey
See: Preservation Hall Jazz Band

Willie Humphrey
See: Preservation Hall Jazz Band

Alberta Hunter
Born April 1, 1895, in Memphis, TN. Died October 17, 1984, in Roosevelt, NY.

Although she began singing as early as 1912 in Chicago brothels, Alberta Hunter's career as a blues vocalist improved during the 1920s as she worked her way into the prominent cabarets. She signed first with Black Swan, then the more powerful Paramount, writing and recording her own songs, often backed by prominent jazz musicians such as Fletcher Henderson, Sidney Bechet, Fats Waller, and Louis Armstrong. Hunter starred in *Showboat* with Paul Robeson at the London Palladium in the late 1920s and she recorded with orchestras in Paris before returning to the United States to sing for military troops during World War II and the Korean War. Hunter retired from music in 1956 and worked as a nurse for the next 20 years. She made a jazz comeback in the mid-1970s, performing at a club in New York City until she was 89 years old.

what to buy: One of the few documents of Hunter's early material is *Young Alberta Hunter: Songs from the 1920s & 1930s* ♫♫♫♫ (MOJO Music, 1996, prod. various), a compilation of 23 selections performed with the Fletcher Henderson orchestra with guests Louis Armstrong, Eddie Heywood, and others.

best of the rest:

(With Lovie Austin and Her Blues Serenaders) *Chicago: The Living Legends* ♫♫♫♫ (Riverside, 1961/Original Blues Classics, 1991)
(With Lucille Hegamin and Victoria Spivey) *Songs We Taught Your Mother* ♫♫♫♫ (Bluesville, 1961/Original Blues Classics, 1991)
Amtrak Blues ♫♫♫ (CBS, 1978/1988)

influences:

◀◀ Bessie Smith, Ma Rainey, Memphis Minnie, Fletcher Henderson, Sidney Bechet

▶▶ Bonnie Raitt, Saffire—The Uppity Blues Women

                                    Steve Knopper

Charlie Hunter
Born 1968, in RI.

Growing up in Berkeley, California, Charlie Hunter was exposed to a wide variety of music, from jazz and blues to rock and soul. Hunter's mother used to repair guitars, and it was probably only natural that her son migrated towards playing guitar himself. He started learning guitar techniques at 12, and a couple of years later took lessons from Joe Satriani, one of the rock musicians whose instruments his mother would often work on. Hunter's first professional brush with fame came via his friendship with Michael Franti, and evolved into a groundbreaking rap-cum-rock group called the Disposable Heroes of Hiphoprisy. After that troupe split up Hunter took his eight-string guitar and, with a drummer and a saxophonist, formed his own hybrid jazz trio. He blended his by-then formidable technical skills with the potential to play both bass lines and lead on his unique guitar. By piping his playing through either a Leslie speaker (for recording purposes) or a Leslie simulator (on his live gigs) Hunter is able to emulate the sound of an organ, aping the tones of keyboard heroes like John Patton, Larry Young, and Jimmy Smith, while still playing single-note guitar leads. Hunter also plays with an ad hoc group called T.J. Kirk that plays its own idiosyncratic arrangements of music by Thelonious Monk, James Brown, and another of Hunter's idols, Rahsaan Roland Kirk.

what to buy: On *The Return of the Candyman* ♫♫♫♫ (Blue Note, 1998, prod. Lee Townsend), by subtracting saxophones in favor of a vibraphone and miscellaneous percussion, Hunter has delivered a collection of tunes that stretches the already-elastic boundaries of his peculiar take on jazz. The lineup places more of the melodic burden on Hunter's guitar playing as John Santos's percussive fills and Stefon Harris's slick mallet licks (like a young Bobby Hutcherson) blend with Scott Amendola's fierce, in-the-pocket drumming for a more rhythmic sound picture. Other than on a merely adequate rendition of Steve Miller's "Fly Like an Eagle," the band meshes for the finest release of Hunter's career. With his unique guitar and playing style, Hunter approaches the funky organ trio sound of the 1960s on *Bing, Bing, Bing!* ♫♫♫♫ (Blue Note, 1995, prod. Lee Townsend) while giving it a distinctly '90s twist. The playing behind songs like "Fistful of Haggis" and "Scrabbling for

Purchase" belies the superficial, youthful insolence that could be associated with their titles.

what to buy next: The group has evolved from trio to quartet for *Ready . . . Set . . . Shango!* ♫♫♫ (Blue Note, 1996, prod. Lee Townsend), and this is another rib-joint organ-group groove with Hunter's eight-string guitar filtered to sound like the '60s funk keyboard of choice.

the rest:
Charlie Hunter Trio ♫♫♫ (Mammoth, 1993)
(With T.J. Kirk) *T.J. Kirk* ♫♫♫ (Warner Bros., 1995)
(With T.J. Kirk) *If Four Was One* ♫♫♫♫ (Warner Bros., 1996)
Natty Dread ♫♫♫ (Blue Note, 1997)

influences:
◀◀ Rahsaan Roland Kirk, John Patton

Garaud MacTaggart

Robert Hurst III
Born October 4, 1964, in Detroit, MI.

One of the most dependably swinging bassists to emerge in the 1980s, Robert Hurst quickly made a name for himself when Wynton Marsalis hired him to anchor his rhythm section with pianist Marcus Roberts and drummer Jeff "Tain" Watts. Hurst studied guitar with Earl Klugh as a youth, but started playing bass and soon became a presence on the Detroit scene. He played with the band Orange Then Blue in 1985 and then joined Wynton Marsalis's group for a long stint (1986–89), recording a number of albums with the trumpeter. He joined saxophonist Branford Marsalis's group in the late 1980s, and when comedian Jay Leno hired Branford Marsalis to front the new *Tonight Show* band, Hurst landed the high-profile gig, a position he continues to hold under guitarist Kevin Eubanks. A big-toned player strongly influenced by Ron Carter, Hurst has recorded extensively as a sideman, including sessions with pianists Geri Allen, Donald Brown, and Mulgrew Miller, saxophonists Ricky Ford, Vincent Herring, and Rick Margitza, and drummers Tony Williams and Marvin "Smitty" Smith. He works regularly in Los Angeles with saxophonist Ralph Moore, pianist Brad Mehldau, and drummer "Smitty" Smith in the band Escape from New York.

what to buy: Except for Dave Brubeck's perennial "In Your Own Sweet Way," bassist Robert Hurst composed all the music on his second release as a leader, *One for Namesake* ♫♫♫ (DIW/Columbia, 1994, prod. Robert Hurst, Kazunori Sugiyama), a trio session featuring pianist Kenny Kirkland and drummer Elvin Jones. Kirkland and Jones, sounding quite restrained, dig

into Hurst's well-constructed, if not always melodically developed, tunes, resulting in a swinging but not especially memorable session.

what to buy next: A strangely underwhelming album given the surfeit of talent assembled, *Robert Hurst Presents: Robert Hurst* ♫♫♫ (DIW/Columbia, 1993, prod. Robert Hurst, Kazunori Sugiyama) features Branford Marsalis (reeds), Kenny Kirkland (piano), and Jeff "Tain" Watts (drums) from the *Tonight Show* Band, with trumpeter Marcus Belgrave and, on two tunes, reed player Ralph Miles Jones III. Except for an impressive solo bass version of Monk's "Evidence," Hurst composed all the material, which is often complex, but rarely involving. Though the musicians all play with great proficiency, there are few memorable solos. Among the few highlights are Jones's sinuous bass clarinet work on "The Snake Charmer," and Belgrave's warm flugelhorn playing on the ballad "Bert's Flirt."

worth searching for: A smokin' live session by Wynton Marsalis's quartet, *Live at Blues Alley* ♫♫♫♫ (Columbia, 1987, prod. Steve Epstein) features the trumpeter with Marcus Roberts (piano), Hurst (bass), and the powerhouse Jeff "Tain" Watts (drums). Wynton is working through the end of his Miles Davis phase and his exploration of older material, such as "Just Friends" and "Do You Know What It Means to Miss New Orleans," points to his new direction. The rhythm section swings fiercely, powered by Watts's polyrhythmic barrage and anchored harmonically by Hurst's elastic bass lines.

influences:
◀◀ Ron Carter, Paul Chambers

Andrew Gilbert

Bobby Hutcherson
Born January 27, 1941, in Los Angeles, CA.

Bobby Hutcherson's first instrument was the piano, but hearing a record by vibes master Milt Jackson changed his listening and performance habits forever. While still in high school he was taking lessons in music theory from Terry Trotter and honing his vibes chops under the tutelage of Dave Pike. Hutcherson's first professional gigs were with Curtis Amy and Charles Lloyd before joining the Al Grey–Billy Mitchell group. With Grey and Mitchell, Hutcherson finally made it to New York in 1961, where he started playing with other young, cutting-edge musicians like Jackie McLean, Andrew Hill, Tony Williams, Grachan Moncour III, and, perhaps most importantly, Eric Dolphy. The *Out to Lunch* sessions with Dolphy in 1964 gave Hutcherson some serious credentials and made him the first-call vibes player for any of the more adventurous sessions of the day. Also in 1964 Hutcherson won *Down Beat*'s critic's poll as new star. The next year found the vibist working on his debut album as a leader; *Dialogue* also started a long, fruitful creative relationship with drummer/composer Joe Chambers. Upon Hutcherson's return to the West Coast he formed a group with saxophonist Harold Land that had the bad luck to be performing and recording during a time (1967–71) when jazz sales and audiences were in one of their periodic slumps. Still, the quintet managed to record under Hutcherson's name for Blue Note and Land's moniker for Mainstream. There was a noticeable shift in Hutcherson's playing and writing around this time as he started a slow but gradual shift away from free and avant garde playing towards more structured and overtly melodic efforts. The transformation was completed by the late '70s, and Hutcherson has now become a standard-bearer for the mainstream. He has continued to release intelligent, well-crafted albums and remains one of the most influential vibes players (Gary Burton is the other) to come out of the 1960s.

what to buy: *Dialogue* 𝄞𝄞𝄞𝄞 (Blue Note, 1965, prod. Alfred Lion) is not an easy album for listeners only used to the latter-day Hutcherson. It's the roaring young lion, avant-garde version, only his instrument chimes instead of blaring or banging. His debut includes a killer group, every one a leader in those days: Freddie Hubbard on trumpet, Sam Rivers on reeds and flute, Andrew Hill on piano, Richard Davis on bass, and drummer Joe Chambers. Why the people at Blue Note waited more than half a decade to release *Live at Montreux* 𝄞𝄞𝄞𝄞 (Blue Note, 1980, prod. George Butler), a 1973 live concert recording, is unknown, but it's one of the most enjoyable albums in Hutcherson's catalog, and it isn't even with one of the groups most closely associated with him. There is an interesting arrangement of Shaw's "Moontrane," and "Anton's Bail" is one of the finest pieces of music Hutcherson has ever written. Previously available only in Japan, *Oblique* 𝄞𝄞𝄞𝄞 (Blue Note, prod. Alfred Lion, 1990) is a 1967 quartet date featuring Hutcherson with pianist Herbie Hancock, drummer Joe Chambers, and bassist Albert Stinson. Hutcherson contributes three easy-flowing tunes, and Hancock's "Theme from *Blow Up*" (with overt references to "Maiden Voyage") makes the cut as well. Chambers provides the meat for the session, however, with two rhythmically complex and harmonically adventurous compositions, including the title work.

what to buy next: *Components* 𝄞𝄞𝄞𝄞 (Blue Note, 1966, prod. Alfred Lion), Hutcherson's second album as a leader, found him

BOBBY HUTCHERSON

song "Una Muy Bonita"
album *Stick-Up*
(Blue Note, 1966/1997)
instrument Vibraphone

heading yet another band of stars. "Little B's Poem," one of Hutcherson's most enduring songs, makes its debut. *Manhattan Moods* 𝄞𝄞𝄞𝄞 (Blue Note, 1994, prod. Michael Cuscuna) is a duet album with Hutcherson featured on vibes and marimba while McCoy Tyner plays piano. There are no flights of genius here, but the well-planned program and high-class musicianship of the participants make this a fine album. With the exception of producer/drummer Lenny White, everyone on *Acoustic Masters II* 𝄞𝄞𝄞𝄞 (Atlantic, 1994, prod. Lenny White) has had a connection with whatever passes for the edge of art in the time of their youth. Bassist Ron Carter and Hutcherson are the older but wiser heads in the ensemble with pianist Mulgrew Miller following close behind. Trumpeter Jerry Gonzalez combines with Craig Handy on flute and reeds to form the junior end of the partnership.

best of the rest:
Patterns 𝄞𝄞𝄞𝄞 (Blue Note, 1980)
Good Bait 𝄞𝄞𝄞𝄞 (Landmark, 1985)
Vibe Wise 𝄞𝄞𝄞𝄞 (Landmark, 1985–86/32 Jazz, 1998)

In the Vanguard 𝄞𝄞𝄞 (Landmark, 1987)
Mirage 𝄞𝄞𝄞 (Landmark, 1991)
Farewell Keystone 𝄞𝄞𝄞 (Evidence, 1992)

influences:

◄◄ Milt Jackson

►► Jay Hoggard, Steve Nelson

Garaud MacTaggart

Dick Hyman

Born March 8, 1927, in New York, NY.

Produced by a master in many musical fields, Dick Hyman's oeuvre offers a modern recreation of the sounds of yesteryear, specifically the nascent sounds of jazz. Hyman has closely studied the works of all of the early jazz piano greats, and it shows. He seems to know even the most obscure tunes in the Clarence Williams catalog, yet can execute them with all the casualness that he might give to a standard like "I'm Getting Sentimental over You." Hyman fluently interprets styles from Scott Joplin to Fats Waller, but James P. Johnson and Jelly Roll Morton seem to be the twin titans in the Hyman world. You won't be going wrong if you pick up any Hyman records exploring the work of either Johnson or Morton. Beginning with stints playing with Red Norvo and Benny Goodman, Hyman soon found good work in radio, television, and session studios. He played on hundreds of recordings, most notably under the aegis of Enoch Light. Most of these were more pop than jazz, but no matter what the project, Hyman brought a professional, concise approach in his skills not only as a player, but as an arranger. Especially significant was his involvement in the production of prominent jazz historian Leonard Feather's History of Jazz concerts. Such a historical approach was a harbinger for the type of work for which Hyman would become renowned.

In the early 1970s Hyman quickly established himself as one of the most knowledgeable historians, archivists, interpreters, and players of old-time jazz, which is pretty much his creative forte to this day. Even though he can reproduce the idiosyncratic sounds of all the jazz piano greats, when Hyman is just himself he has his own unique voice. Especially recognizable when he steps behind his customized Lowery organ, Hyman has contributed his signature sounds to substantial sessions with artists as diverse as Cozy Cole and Cal Tjader. Also, on the pop side, Hyman arranged "Moritat" for trio plus whistling, sending the Kurt Weill tune into the Top 10 three years before Bobby Darin souped up said song as "Mack the Knife." Besides session work, Hyman has done a lot of work in the motion pic-

ture scoring field, and has been awarded an Emmy. And he's been involved with many soundtracks for Woody Allen movies, beginning with, appropriately enough, *Zelig*.

what to buy: While he usually focuses on one composer, on some live dates Hyman lets loose and jumps around stylistically. *Live from Toronto's Café des Copains* 𝄞𝄞𝄞𝄞 (Music & Arts, 1988, prod. Paul J. Hoeffler) is one such date, wherein standards, tunes from Jelly Roll Morton and James P. Johnson, and even some of Hyman's own music from *The Purple Rose of Cairo* get the treatment of Hyman's learned, agreeable playing. For a good example of the erudition of Hyman's scholarship, find *Face the Music: A Century of Irving Berlin* 𝄞𝄞𝄞𝄞 (MusicMasters, 1988). This solo tribute to Berlin finds Hyman, ever the archivist, digging rarities such as "I'll See You in C.U.B.A." out of the nooks and crannies of the Irving Berlin songbook and placing them alongside standards like "Remember" and "Easter Parade." Another solo disc where Hyman best displays his versatility and knowledge is *Live at Maybeck Recital Hall, Volume Three: Music of 1937* 𝄞𝄞𝄞𝄞 (Concord, 1990, prod. Carl E. Jefferson). Here, Hyman examines tunes like "Caravan," "Someday My Prince Will Come," and "My Funny Valentine," all of which found their creation in the year 1937. Hyman deftly moves among styles, from Benny Goodman to Bob Hope, boogie woogie to balladry, and the disc features shining recording quality as well.

what to buy next: Most of Hyman's discs are either solo or small group. An exception is *From the Age of Swing* 𝄞𝄞𝄞𝄞 (Reference Recordings, 1994), which finds Hyman leading an eight-piece group that includes Bucky Pizzarelli and Milt Hinton. The title clues you in to the tunes selected, but as always there are some surprises, as when Hyman dusts off an arrangement of "Topsy." *Manhattan Jazz* 𝄞𝄞𝄞𝄞 (MusicMasters, 1987) uncovers the tunes of Manhattan's olden days. Material like "Jeepers, Creepers" and "I'm Crazy 'bout My Baby" is performed with an entertaining flair in a Hyman duo with cornetist Ruby Braff, with whom Hyman often worked. An out-of-time anomaly in the Hyman catalog is the greatest Moog record of all time: *Moog: The Electric Eclectics of Dick Hyman* 𝄞𝄞𝄞𝄞 (Varese Sarabande, 1969/1997, prod. Dick Hyman). This proto-electronica record (originally released in 1969), has some of Hyman's most simultaneously commercial and experimental pieces combined on this set of originals, including the hypnotic, minimalist "Minotaur," a bizarre electro-drone-pulse that actually made its way into the Top 40! The compact disc reissue adds some stellar tracks from the follow-up *Age of Electronicus*, including a funky drummer vs. drum machine Moog version of James Brown's "Give It up or Turn It Loose" that must be heard to be believed.

best of the rest:

(With Derek Smith) *Live: They Got Rhythm* 🎵🎵🎵 (Jass, 1983/1992)

Harold Arlen Songs: Blues in the Night 🎵🎵🎵🎵 (MusicMasters, 1990)

Plays Fats Waller 🎵🎵🎵🎵 (Reference Recordings, 1990)

Cole Porter: All through the Night 🎵🎵🎵🎵 (MusicMasters, 1991)

The Gershwin Songbook: Jazz Variations by Dick Hyman 🎵🎵 (Music-Masters, 1992)

Gulf Coast Blues 🎵🎵🎵 (Omega, 1992)

Jelly and James: Music of Jelly Roll Morton and James P. Johnson 🎵🎵🎵🎵 (Sony, 1992)

Plays Duke Ellington 🎵🎵🎵🎵 (Reference Recordings, 1992)

(Dick Hyman/Ralph Sutton) *Concord Duo Series, Volume 6* 🎵🎵🎵 (Concord, 1994)

The Great American Songbook 🎵🎵🎵🎵 (MusicMasters, 1994)

Cheek to Cheek 🎵🎵🎵 (Arbor, 1996)

Swing Is Here 🎵🎵🎵🎵 (Reference Recordings, 1996)

worth searching for: The quintessential document of the nature of Hyman's talent, *Themes and Variations on "A Child Is Born"* 🎵🎵🎵🎵 (Chiaroscuro, 1977) has Hyman interpreting the Thad Jones composition in the style of a dozen pianists, from the roots jazz of James P. Johnson and Jelly Roll Morton through the cool of Bill Evans and the free jazz of Cecil Taylor. The technical and the artistic combine to great effect on this recording, and it's especially revealing when Hyman plays "A Child Is Born" in his own style, that is, in the style of Dick Hyman, a voice that's as distinctive as any of ones he mimics. A prescient piece of space-age bachelor pad music, *Moon Gas* 🎵🎵🎵🎵 (MGM, ca. 1963) teams Hyman with the soprano spaciness of Mary Mayo (where is she now?). Electronic sound effects, organs, including Hyman's signature Lowery, and the Ondioline (a forerunner of modern synthesizers), contribute to a uniquely charming listening experience. It would have been interesting if the popular vocalists of the day had enlisted Hyman to make their own albums from the future. The classic *Music of Jelly Roll Morton* (Smithsonian, 1978) 🎵🎵🎵🎵 impeccably recreates the Morton vibe as Hyman orchestrates a battery of sidemen. This sadly out-of-print record finds its academic achievement matched by the levels of joy and excitement it creates. Finally, most of Hyman's earlier work is tough to come by on CD, and his oeuvre from this period sorely begs to be compiled. A collection with "Moritat," "Topsy," the standards, and his smattering of originals (both solo and with Enoch Light, the Corporation, et al.) would be a worthy addition to any shelf. But until the day when that collection arrives on the market, you'll just have to search the thrift stores for such classic hi-fi records as

Organ-ized, *The Man from O.R.G.A.N.*, *Brazilian Impressions*, and *The Sensuous Organ of "D."*

influences:

⏮ James P. Johnson, Jelly Roll Morton

see also: *Ruby Braff, Ralph Sutton*

Greg Baise

Abdullah Ibrahim /Dollar Brand

Born Adolph Johannes Brand, October 9, 1934, in Cape Town, South Africa.

Rarely has a jazz artist captured such a clear sense of geography in his music as has pianist and composer Abdullah Ibrahim, a.k.a. Dollar Brand. His South African heritage comes through in every song he plays, and yet he works within a traditional jazz context, drawing his greatest musical inspiration from Monk and Ellington. Although he incorporates elements of traditional South African township music into his compositions, it's his strong, spiritual playing that makes his sound so distinctive.

Brand started playing piano at the age of seven, and was soon enraptured by the energy and color of American jazz. He got his nickname, "Dollar," from the American soldiers he would constantly ask to sell him their jazz records, and it was with this name that he first started gigging around town. Brand participated in the pioneering group the Jazz Epistles, featuring trumpeter Hugh Masekela and legendary African saxophonist Kippie Moeketsi, and together they recorded South Africa's first jazz album in 1960. Due to the lack of opportunities in his homeland, Brand and his wife, vocalist Sathima Bea Benjamin, moved to Zurich in 1962. There he and his trio came to the attention of Duke Ellington, who was so impressed by Brand that he took him under his wing, sponsoring a recording session in 1963 and an appearance at the Newport Jazz Festival in 1965 (Brand even substituted for his patron on one of the orchestra's tours). After this endorsed start, he began performing and recording regularly, mostly as the leader of his own group. He converted to Islam in 1968 and began using his Muslim name

Abdullah Ibrahim in the early 1970s. After a series of remarkable ensemble recordings made in South Africa in the mid-1970s (reissued on Kaz in 1988), Ibrahim went into self-imposed exile from his homeland in 1976 to protest the apartheid government, and relocated to New York. He has remained quite prolific, recording mainly for Enja in a variety of configurations, from solo sets and duets with Archie Shepp and Carlos Ward to a series of records with his seven-piece ensemble Ekaya. He has also recorded soundtracks for two films by French director Claire Denis: *Chocolat* (released on CD as *Mindif*) and *No Fear, No Die*. Since the political changes in South Africa, Ibrahim has made a joyous return to the land of his birth.

Ibrahim plays with an especially percussive, left-handed technique that recalls that of his idol Thelonious Monk, whose songs he has frequently performed. He conveys a definite enthusiasm in all of his performances, even on ballads; they may be introspective, but never somber. On solo piano sets, he often clumps several melodies together to create a sort of medley. In addition to piano, Ibrahim occasionally plays flute and soprano saxophone, and every once in a while he will sing (although he should not be encouraged to do this often).

what to buy: Brand's recording debut, *Duke Ellington Presents the Dollar Brand Trio* ✍✍✍✍ (Reprise, 1963, prod. Duke Ellington), catches him at his sharpest and most intense. The pianist boldly stakes his claim on such originals as "Ubu Suku" and "Dollar's Dance" and offers a distinctive take on Monk's "Brilliant Corners." *Tintinyana* ✍✍✍✍ (Kaz, 1988, prod. Rashid Vally) is the best of Kaz's reissues from Ibrahim's 1970s African recordings; exuberant, extended jams like "Soweto Is Where It's At" and "Bra Joe from Kilimanjaro" truly celebrate his homeland, with contributions from Yanks Blue Mitchell and Harold Land and underrated African tenor saxophonist Basil Coetzee. *Live at Montreux* ✍✍✍✍ (Enja, 1980, prod. David Richards) is a particularly snappy live date in front of an appreciative audience; "Whoza Mtwana" and "The Homecoming Song" are standouts. *Ekaya (Home)* ✍✍✍✍ (Ekapa, 1984, prod. Sathima Bea Benjamin, Abdullah Ibrahim) has the debut of Ibrahim's most recent regular band; three reeds and a trombone give him a full sound with which to play around and satisfy the Ellington in him.

what to buy next: A somewhat contemporary sound makes the funky *African Marketplace* ✍✍✍ (Elektra, 1980, prod. Abdullah Ibrahim) sound like an African version of the Crusaders. It features frequent cohort Carlos Ward on alto and soprano saxophones. *Cape Town Flowers* ✍✍✍ (Tiptoe, 1997, prod. Rudy Van

Gelder) is a nice recent trio set. It's mostly new material; a bit on the mellow side, it does prove he still has it in him.

what to avoid: *Knysna Blue* ✍✍ (Enja, 1994, prod. Abdullah Ibrahim) has an interminable autobiographical monologue on top of a synthesized rhythm track and a cheesy calypso number featuring Ibrahim's creaky singing—all of which mar what could have been an otherwise excellent collection of solo ballads.

the rest:
African Sketchbook ✍✍✍✍ (Enja, 1963)
Anatomy of a South African Village ✍✍✍✍ (Enja, 1963)
The Dream ✍✍✍✍ (Black Lion, 1965)
Ancient Africa ✍✍✍✍ (Sackville, 1973)
Fats, Duke & the Monk ✍✍✍✍ (Sackville, 1973)
African Space Program ✍✍✍✍ (Enja, 1973)
Good News from Africa ✍✍✍ (Enja, 1973)
Ode to Duke Ellington ✍✍✍✍ (Inner City, 1974)
Soweto ✍✍✍✍ (Chiaroscuro, 1975)
Cape Town Fringe ✍✍✍✍ (Chiaroscuro, 1975)
Banyana—The Children of Africa ✍✍✍ (Enja, 1976)
The Journey ✍✍✍ (Chiaroscuro, 1977)
Anthem for the New Nations ✍✍✍✍ (Denon Japan, 1978)
Autobiography ✍✍✍ (Plainisphare, 1978/1983)
(With Archie Shepp) *Duet* ✍✍✍ (Denon Japan, 1978/1990)
Africa—Tears and Laughter ✍✍✍ (Enja, 1979)
Echoes from Africa ✍✍✍ (Inner City, 1979)
South African Sunshine ✍✍✍ (Plane German, 1982)
African Dawn ✍✍✍ (Enja, 1982)
Zimbabwe ✍✍✍✍ (Enja, 1983)
Live at Sweet Basil, Vol. 1 ✍✍✍ (Ekapa, 1984)
Water from an Ancient Well ✍✍✍✍ (Black Hawk, 1986)
South Africa ✍✍✍✍ (Enja, 1986)
Mindif ✍✍✍✍ (Enja, 1988)
African Sun ✍✍✍✍ (Kaz, 1988)
Blues for a Hip King ✍✍✍✍ (Kaz, 1988)
Voice of Africa ✍✍✍✍ (Kaz, 1988)
African River ✍✍✍✍ (Enja, 1989)
No Fear, No Die ✍✍✍✍ (Enja, 1990)
Mantra Mode ✍✍✍✍ (Enja, 1991)
Desert Flowers ✍✍✍ (Enja, 1992)
Yarona ✍✍✍✍ (Tiptoe, 1995)

worth searching for: *African Piano* ✍✍✍✍ (ECM, 1969/1973, prod. Dollar Brand) was one of Brand's first solo records and remains one of his best, very rhythmic and stride-influenced.

influences:
◀◀ Thelonious Monk, Duke Ellington

▶▶ Bheki Mseleku

Eric J. Lawrence

I.C.P. Orchestra /Instant Composers Pool

Formed 1967.

Misha Mengelberg, composer, arranger, pianist; other rotating personnel.

The I.C.P. Orchestra is an outgrowth of the Instant Composer's Pool, a non-profit organization founded by Misha Mengelberg, Han Bennink, and Willem Breuker and featuring some of the most prominent musicians of the European and American avant-garde. Although there were large-group concerts given under the I.C.P. banner from the beginning, the first recorded evidence of the group was 1977's *Tetterettet*. Early editions of the orchestra leaned towards free, unstructured passages; in the '80s, the charts became more rigorous, as Mengelberg began arranging more outside material, with a special focus on Thelonious Monk, Herbie Nichols, and Duke Ellington. His original and idiosyncratic arrangements fit the group members' consistently individualistic solo personalities.

what's available: *Bospaadje Konijnenhol I & II* 𝄞𝄞𝄞𝄞 (I.C.P., 1986/1991, prod. Instant Composers Pool) are sold as two individual CDs but are really a set. Volume I starts with the title track and Volume II ends with it; in between is a 40-minute Duke Ellington medley and 23 Mengelberg compositions arranged into four suites. The songs traverse from demented music hall to modern chamber orchestra to full hard-driving modern jazz band. Although the albums were taken from recordings done over a five-year period, the band's membership was surprisingly stable. *I.C.P. Orchestra Performs Nichols–Monk* 𝄞𝄞𝄞𝄞 (I.C.P., 1984–86, prod. Instant Composers Pool) includes several Monk pieces, performed by an octet, ranging from the rarely heard "Hornin' In" to the standard "'Round Midnight."

worth searching for: *Tetterettet* 𝄞𝄞𝄞𝄞 (I.C.P., 1977) is ripe for reissue, mostly because of Mengelberg's composition "Alexander's Marschbefehl," a deranged oompah-band piece also performed by the Globe Unity Orchestra. There's also a version of his composition "Rumboon" and two compositions by Dutch composer (and then-tentet oboist) Gilius van Bergyk.

Robert Iannapollo

Keith Ingham

Born February 5, 1942, in London, England.

Keith Ingham is a fine, swinging pianist with an encyclopedic knowledge of songwriters, overlooked songs, and jazz piano history. An eloquent soloist, Ingham has an excellent reputation as an accomplished vocal accompanist and arranger. His many musical associations and collaborations include singers Susannah McCorkle, Peggy Lee, Barbara Lea, and the late Maxine Sullivan, guitarist Marty Grosz, clarinetists Bobby Gordon and Bob Reitmeier, and tenor saxophonist Harry Allen. Ingham's keyboard approach and sound are often reminiscent of Gene Schroeder or Jess Stacy, but he acknowledges Al Haig and Ellis Larkins as primary influences on his harmonically rich piano style.

Growing up in war-ravaged Britain, Ingham began piano studies at age eight and showed an interest in jazz by his teens. As a prerequisite to an Oxford University scholarship, young Ingham worked for the British Government in Hong Kong. It was there he first played jazz piano, sitting in with a Filipino quartet. Ingham left the Far East in 1962 and majored in classical Chinese language at Oxford, graduating in 1966. He returned to London and started playing in British bands with Humphrey Lyttelton, Sandy Brown, Wally Falkes, Bruce Turner, and others. By 1968, he was accompanying visiting Americans, most notably Red Allen, Pee Wee Russell, Benny Carter, and Ben Webster. In the 1970s, Ingham recorded with Bud Freeman, Bob Wilber, and as leader with vocalist Susannah McCorkle with whom he shared a mutual love of 1920s and 1930s songs. In 1978, McCorkle and visiting musicians Billy Butterfield and Ruby Braff encouraged Ingham to move to the United States. Ingham settled in New York where he freelanced and played occasional dates with Benny Goodman with the World's Greatest Jazz Band, and with McCorkle as her musical director and pianist. He plays the festival scene and selective U.S. club dates, and is a favorite at the annual Allegheny Jazz Society sessions in Western Pennsylvania and environs. He has recorded as sideman and leader, including dates featuring singer Maxine Sullivan, guitarist Marty Grosz, clarinetist Bob Reitmeier, and others. Ingham still finds time, however, to play his special brand of thoughtful, complex jazz piano in various New York venues.

what to buy: Containing tinges of traditional, mainstream, and swing jazz styles, *Music from the Mauve Decades* 𝄞𝄞𝄞𝄞 (Sackville, 1993, prod. Keith Ingham) is a trio outing with Ingham playing some outstanding two-handed piano in the manner of keyboard artists from the old Commodore label. There are unmistakable touches of Joe Bushkin, Gene Schroeder, and Jess Stacy scattered throughout Ingham's fine work on this album. Clarinetist Bobby Gordon and drummer Hal Smith are at their best in this trio setting. The "mauve decades" of the title refer to the period from the turn of the 20th century into the early 1920s, supposedly a time of peace, prosperity, and good living. On this disc, it signifies 17 really old gems given renewed life. If you crave familiar fare, listen to "My Gal Sal," "Oh, You Beautiful Doll," "Some of These Days," and "Poor Butterfly." Less familiar tunes include "Vilia," "I Love a Piano," "Take Me to That Land of Jazz," and "The Love Nest." The collection of 19 tunes on *Bobby Gordon/Keith Ingham/Hal Smith Trio* ✍✍✍ (Jump, 1993, prod. Joe Boughton) offers newer, but perhaps more obscure titles than *The Mauve Decades*, with three tunes reserved for Ingham's solo piano. Teaming up in August, 1990, after a warm-up performance at the Conneaut Lake Jazz Party, the musicians provide a more laid-back session than *Mauve Decades*. If in doubt, buy both. *The Keith Ingham New York 9, Vol. 1* ✍✍✍ (Jump, 1994, prod. Joe Boughton) contains 18 tunes for the swing-minded fan. This set purports to be a salute to those Jump 78 rpm singles, and it succeeds with its attractive, interesting, and instrumentally varied performances on a batch of enjoyable tunes. Ingham contributes fine piano skills and lively arrangements. He leads brassmen Randy Reinhart and Dan Barrett (who play cornet, trumpet, and trombone, and switch at the drop of a note) and saxophonists Phil Bodner and Scott Robinson, with a slick rhythm team of James Chirillo (guitar), Murray Wall or Vince Giordano (bass and bass sax) and Arnie Kinsella. Highlights include the full band blasting through two different melodies titled "I Never Knew," Ingham and Kinsella easing through "Too Good to Be True," Ingham's updated Glenn Miller arrangement for Dorsey's "Mood Hollywood," and two very pretty medleys featuring all nine celebrants in top Condon-style form. There's much good listening in this heady mix of warhorses and neglected songs from the past. Available from your local record store or the Allegheny Jazz Society, 283 Jefferson St., Meadville, PA 16335.

what to buy next: A collection of 18 tunes by composer Victor Young, *The Keith Ingham–Bob Reitmeier Quartet Plays the Music of Victor Young* ✍✍✍ (Jump, 1989, prod. Joe Boughton) is for lovers of melody and relaxed, intimate jazz. Ingham and clarinetist Reitmeier have worked together occasionally since meeting at the 1983 Conneaut Lake Jazz Party, and their solid partnership is suited to performing the popular movie songs of composer Victor Young. Among eight movie-related themes are "Love Letters," "Golden Earrings," "When I Fall in Love," and the haunting, "Stella by Starlight." Of the non-movie tunes, many are familiar to jazz fans—"Street of Dreams," "A Ghost of a Chance," "Can't We Talk It Over?," and the 1928 song "Sweet Sue." Ingham's rich harmonies and Reitmeier's warm, will-o'-the-wisp horn work are given superior rhythm support by Frank Tate's big-toned bass, and veteran Vernel Fournier's sympathetic drumming. Not for the bop or fusion-minded, this one scores big

with the melody crowd. On *Donaldson Redux* ✍✍✍ (Stomp Off, 1991, prod. Keith Ingham, Marty Grosz), the leaders and their Hot Cosmopolites pay homage to prolific songwriter Walter Donaldson with a collection of 20 vintage songs done up in the old hot dance style (with more than a few new licks creeping in). The Hot Cosmopolites are no surprise to Ingham-Grosz fans, who anticipate receiving generous doses of Peter Ecklund's hot cornet, Bobby Gordon's fluid, low-register clarinet, and Dan Barrett's mellow trombone when the co-leaders get together. Loren Schoenberg's booting tenor sax and Vince Giordano's gruff bass sax heighten the fun on several selections. Greg Cohen is on hand on string bass and Hal Smith and Arnie Kinsella split drum chores. Andy Stein (violin), Bill Novick (clarinet), and Frank Vignola (guitar) enter into the cheery spirit of the Donaldson tribute on several tracks. Barrett and the rhythm section do wonders with "Swanee," and Grosz's vocals fit the material. Featured are some well-known tracks ("My Blue Heaven," "Love Me or Leave Me," "At Sundown," "My Baby Just Cares for Me"), but it's the obscurities ("Reaching for Someone," "I've Had My Moments," "An Evening in Caroline," "Riptide") that will satisfy fans looking for something a little different.

the rest:
Keith Ingham: Out of the Past ✍✍✍ (Sackville, 1990)
Marty Grosz & Keith Ingham and Their Paswonky Serenaders: Unsaturated Fats ✍✍✍ (Stomp Off, 1990)
The Harry Allen–Keith Ingham Quintet: Are You Having Any Fun? ✍✍✍ (Audiophile, 1991)
Just Imagine: The Music of DeSylva, Brown & Henderson ✍✍✍ (Stomp Off, 1994)
My Little Brown Book: A Celebration of Billy Strayhorn's Music, Vol. 1 ✍✍✍ (Progressive, 1994)
The Intimacy of the Blues: A Celebration of Billy Strayhorn's Music, Vol. 2 ✍✍✍ (Progressive, 1994)
Keith Ingham–Harry Allen: Back Room Romp ✍✍✍ (Sackville, 1995)

John T. Bitter

Chuck Israels

Born August 10, 1936, in New York, NY.

During the 1960s, bassist Chuck Israels performed in New York and Europe with Bud Powell, Kenny Clarke, Lucky Thompson, George Russell, and Benny Goodman, gaining widest notice with his stint in the Bill Evans Trio from 1961 to 1966. During those years, he also appeared on recordings by J.J. Johnson, Herbie Hancock, Gary Burton, and Stan Getz. Israels quit the road and studied composition and arranging with Hall Overton in 1966, and gained experience on studio and Broadway show gigs. In 1981 he moved to California, where he began writing big-band arrangements and compositions. He founded the National Jazz Ensemble, a repertory orchestra that made a couple of now-out-of-print albums for Chiaroscuro. Since the 1970s Israels has established himself as a notable composer and jazz educator, conducting and writing for various European radio orchestras since the mid-1980s, performing as bassist with the Barry Harris Trio, and serving as director of jazz studies at a school in Bellingham, Washington.

what's available: Although he doesn't play on *Chuck Israels & the Metropole Orchestra: The Eindhoven Concert* ♪♪♪♪ (Azica, 1997, prod. Frits Bayens), the nine selections showcase Israel's wide-ranging talents as composer, arranger, and conductor. He meets a real challenge in composing complex charts for the Metropole, an orchestra the size of the old Hollywood studio orchestras, with an added medium-sized string section, extra woodwinds, one more horn, extra percussion, and a harp. The Metropole musicians exhibit flexibility in handling this varied repertoire and the rhythm section performs excellently in the jazz idiom. The string players are skillful jazz players, as you'll hear in Erno Olah's improvisations on the piece by Israels and Miles Black, "String Fever." Augmenting an album that already packs a punch, Claudio Roditi guests on trumpet and flugelhorn.

worth searching for: Israels appears on two tracks of the Kronos Quartet's: *The Complete Landmark Sessions* ♪♪♪♪ (Landmark, 1985–1986/32 Jazz, 1997, prod. Orrin Keepnews), a two-CD reissue that combines the 1985 *Monk Suite: Kronos Quartet Plays Music of Thelonious Monk* and the 1986 LP *Kronos Quartet: Music of Bill Evans*. Israel performs elegantly with Kronos and drummer Eddie Marshall on the Ellington tracks "It Don't Mean a Thing (If It Ain't Got That Swing)" and "Black and Tan Fantasy." Israels can also be heard on John Coltrane's *Coltrane Time* ♪♪♪♪ (Blue Note, 1958/1991, prod. Tom Wilson) with Cecil Taylor on piano and Louis Hayes on drums, a 1958 session actually led by Cecil Taylor and re-released under Coltrane in 1962. Israels is also prominently featured on the Bill Evans Trio recordings, *Bill Evans Trio at Shelly's Mann-Hole* ♪♪♪ (Riverside/OJC, 1963/1989), *Bill Evans Trio '65* ♪♪♪ (Verve, 1965/1993, prod. Creed Taylor), and *Bill Evans Trio at Town Hall* ♪♪♪♪ (Verve, 1966).

influences:

◄◄ Oscar Pettiford, Charles Mingus, Red Mitchell, Ron Carter, Richard Davis, Malachi Favors

see also: *Bill Evans, John Coltrane*

Nancy Ann Lee

J

D.D. Jackson

Born Robert Cleath Kai-nien Jackson, January 25, 1967, in Ottawa, Ontario, Canada.

D.D. Jackson, born in Canada but now based in New York, has gained attention through the advocacy of saxophonist David Murray and was a protégé of the late Don Pullen, on whose piano style he bases his own. Half African American and half Chinese, Jackson could be seen as a partial fulfillment of the pan-cultural vision Pullen was known for. Of primary interest, of course, is Jackson's flamboyant playing, which is superb and attention-grabbing.

Jackson started as a classical pianist at age six and studied with Menachem Pressler at Indiana University, receiving his degree in classical music in 1989. His late brother had already introduced him to jazz, but his parents' pressure had kept D.D. (which supposedly means "little brother" in Chinese) on the classical path, though he performed in David Baker's bands at Indiana. Jackson finally made the move to jazz by getting his master's degree at Manhattan School of Music, studying with Jaki Byard. It was in 1990 that Jackson met Pullen, whose legacy he helped carry on by stepping into Pullen's shoes in his last project, which combined Pullen's African-Brazilian Connection band, the Native American singing and drumming group the Chief Cliff Singers, and the Garth Fagan Dance Company.

Jackson's other important contact came in 1992 when he was touring with a pair of Kip Hanrahan bands and became acquainted with Murray. He is now a regular member of the David Murray Big Band, Octet, and Quartet, as well as the David Murray/D.D. Jackson Duo, and he appears on Murray's *The Long Goodbye*, a tribute to Pullen. They are also collaborating with blues singer/guitarist Taj Mahal and Grateful Dead singer/guitarist Bob Weir on a Broadway musical about baseball Hall of Fame pitcher Satchel Paige.

what to buy: *Rhythm-Dance* ♪♪♪♪ (Justin Time, 1996, prod. D.D. Jackson) finds Jackson passing the piano-trio test with flying colors. His playing explodes from the speakers in splatters of upper-register color as he deploys the techniques of mentor Don Pullen—clusters, wild glissandi, etc.—and throws in a few of his own. The title track is a veritable cross-section of his styles, starting as a pretty, almost Jarrett-esque tune and then launching into the body of the piece in a fast triple meter as Jackson sets off pianistic firecrackers all over the keyboard. If anything is clear, it's that Jackson loves to dig deep into a groove, which keeps his flights of fancy firmly grounded in accessibility.

what to buy next: Jackson's two duet albums offer a broader stylistic range than his first two records as he adjusts to a variety of partners. *Paired Down, Volume 1* ♫♫♫ (Justin Time, 1997, prod. D.D. Jackson) has saxophonists James Carter, David Murray, and Hamiet Bluiett, trumpeter Hugh Ragin, bassist Santi Debriano, and violinist Billy Bang; *Paired Down, Volume 2* ♫♫♫ (Justin Time, 1997, prod. D.D. Jackson) brings back Murray, Debriano, and Bang and adds clarinetist Don Byron, trombonist Ray Anderson, and flutist Jane Bunnett. The rumbustious Anderson in particular is a good match for Jackson on the rowdy "Catch It." More than his other albums, these two find Jackson's subdued moods lasting not just for a few moments but through entire pieces (for instance, Volume 2's "Flute-Song" and "Love-Song").

the rest:
Peace-Song ♫♫♪ (Justin Time, 1995)

worth searching for: Jackson has made an album as part of a collective trio with baritone saxophonist Hamiet Bluiett and Senegalese drummer/vocalist Mor Thiam that is awaiting release and promises to reveal new facets of his style. His approach to standards (he plays none on his releases as a leader) can be gleaned from his work on Billy Bang's quartet album *Bang On!* ♫♫♫ (Justin Time, 1997, prod. Ronnie Burrage, Billy Bang). The piano is not always in tune, but this gives it a bright, barrelhouse tone that seems apt on "Sweet Georgia Brown" (though Jackson doesn't get to solo on this track). On the uptempo "Yesterdays," Jackson comps in something akin to bebop style but with more percussive accents and solos in more of a single-line fashion than usual. "Willow Weep for Me" gets a bluesy rendition, with Jackson playing small cascading fills in the nooks and crannies of Bang's solo and then a jangling, chordal solo himself.

influences:
◀◀ Don Pullen, Abdullah Ibrahim, Randy Weston, Jaki Byard, Andrew Hill

Steve Holtje

Javon Jackson
Born June 16, 1965, in Carthage, MI.

A facile and gutsy saxophonist with a muscular sound and a penchant for the stylistic nuances of fellow tenor man Joe Hen-

derson, Javon Jackson is clearly entrenched in the classic hard bop approach of the 1950s and 1960s. Raised in Cleveland and Denver, Jackson spent two years at the Berklee College of Music before joining the last edition of Art Blakey's Jazz Messengers in 1987. With his reputation soon established, Jackson promptly became a regular on the New York scene, working with Freddie Hubbard, Elvin Jones, the Harper Brothers, James Williams, Charlie Haden, Benny Green, Mickey Tucker, and Billy Pierce. Aside from his many sideman appearances, Jackson currently records as a leader for the Blue Note label.

what to buy: *Me and Mr. Jones* ♫♫♫♫ (Criss Cross Jazz, 1992, prod. Gerry Teekens) is as impressive a debut release as you're ever likely to hear. With James Williams, Christian McBride, and drum legend Elvin Jones on board, Jackson is pushed to reach for new heights. All the material is excellent and Jones's work is easily his finest of the decade.

what to buy next: *A Look Within* ♫♫♫ (Blue Note, 1996, prod. Craig Street) finds Jackson exploring some new territory, although the Henderson influence in his playing is still marked. Fareed Haque's guitar work and guest shots by Cassandra Wilson and organist Lonnie Smith give the music a different color and texture compared to the rest of Jackson's previous recordings.

the rest:
When the Time Is Right ♫♫♫ (Blue Note, 1993)
For One Who Knows ♫♫♪ (Blue Note, 1995)

influences:
◀◀ Joe Henderson, Billy Pierce, Charlie Parker

Chris Hovan

Milt Jackson
Born January 1, 1923, in Detroit, MI.

Milt "Bags" Jackson is one of jazz's greatest improvisors, a prodigiously gifted blues player who pioneered a saxophone-like style of phrasing on the vibes. An early participant in the bebop movement, Jackson developed an approach marked by his ringing tone, unfailing swing, and deeply felt lyricism. On slow blues and ballads especially, his long flowing lines combine harmonic sophistication with ingenious simplicity. Jackson started out playing guitar at age seven, and at 11 switched to piano. He took up the vibes in his early teens and by high school he was an important figure on the vital Detroit scene, playing with Lucky Thompson and other Motor City innovators. When Dizzy Gillespie heard him playing in Detroit he recruited him for his seminal bebop sextet with Charlie Parker, and Jackson made the move to New York, where he was soon working steadily. Jackson also played in Gillespie's short-lived orchestra in 1946, where he was featured occasionally in a quartet with John Lewis, Ray Brown, and Kenny Clarke. Their quartet was the prototype for the Modern Jazz Quartet, configured to give the orchestra's brass players a rest. In the late 1940s, Jackson worked and recorded with many of the most advanced musicians in jazz, including Thelonious Monk, Charlie Parker, Howard McGhee, and the Woody Herman Orchestra. He began recording as a leader in the late 1940s and rejoined Gillespie's sextet from 1950–52. He recorded a session with Lewis, Percy Heath, and Clarke in a group that soon came to be known as the Modern Jazz Quartet, one of the most popular and celebrated small groups in jazz history. Except for Connie Kay taking over the drum chair from Clarke in 1955, the group maintained the same personnel for almost 40 years. Though he often felt constrained by the MJQ's tightly controlled format, Jackson flourished under the discipline, producing countless deeply affecting performances and recordings with the group. Jackson recorded frequently as a leader throughout his association with the MJQ, and by 1974, feeling stifled by the group's material and frustrated with its financial management, he left to begin a highly productive decade of recording, producing a few dozen albums for Pablo in a wide variety of all-star settings. The MJQ first reunited in 1981 and has continued to perform over the years, with Tootie Heath replacing the late Connie Kay as the band marks its fifth decade of activity. A remarkably consistent player, Jackson has produced few sub-par recordings over the course of his career, which includes albums for Savoy, Blue Note, Atlantic, Prestige, Impulse!, CTI, Riverside, Verve, Limelight, MusicMasters, and his present label, Qwest.

what to buy: Former bandmates in Dizzy Gillespie's early 1950s band, vibes master Milt Jackson and tenor sax giant John Coltrane were reunited on *Bags and Trane* &&&& (Atlantic, 1959/1988, prod. Nesuhi Ertegun), a surprisingly simpatico session that clicks from the first note. Featuring Hank Jones (piano), Paul Chambers (bass), and Connie Kay (drums), the session offers three Jackson originals, three standards, and two jazz classics, the torridly paced "Bebop" and Sweets Edison's "Centerpiece." Trane's first album for Atlantic finds him in a relaxed mood, playing with complete authority without pushing any boundaries. He and Jackson, who is in typically excellent form, open the session with a highly lyrical "Stairway to the Stars" and stretch out on Bags's "The Late Late Blues" and "Blues Legacy," displaying the two masters' endless resourcefulness

MILT JACKSON (WITH MILES DAVIS AND THE MODERN JAZZ GIANTS)

song "Bags' Groove" (take 1)
album Bags' Groove
(Prestige-OJC, 1954/1987)
instrument Vibraphone

Monster Solo

with the blues form. Another great meeting pairs Jackson with the legendary guitarist Wes Montgomery on *Bags Meets Wes!* &&&& (Riverside, 1961/OJC, 1987, prod. Orrin Keepnews), a quintet session with the incomparable rhythm section of Wynton Kelly (piano), Sam Jones (bass) and Philly Joe Jones (drums). Jackson and Montgomery sound like they're having a great time as they toss off one brilliant solo after another, while Kelly also is in superlative form. The material includes the standard "Stairway to the Stars" (which also kicked off Bags's session with Trane), two originals each by Jackson and Montgomery, Benny Golson's "Stablemates," and Victor Feldman's "Delilah." The session is available on the single CD and also as part of *Wes Montgomery: The Complete Riverside Recordings*, which includes an alternate take for every track. Milt Jackson takes just about every solo on *For Someone I Love* &&&& (Riverside, 1963/OJC, 1990, prod. Orrin Keepnews), a wonderfully inventive session marked by Melba Liston's gorgeous and often surprising arrangements for brass orchestra, featuring four or five trumpets, three trombones, three or four French horns, Major

Holley's tuba, and a rhythm section led by Hank Jones. Jackson plays with passion and complete involvement throughout, clearly inspired by the unusual voicings of Liston's finely crafted charts. Highlights include May Lou Williams's "(What's Your Story) Morning Glory," Billy Strayhorn's "Chelsea Bridge," Liston's "Just Waiting," and Henry Mancini's "Days of Wine and Roses." Jackson recorded many times with bassist Ray Brown and guitarist Joe Pass, but *The Big 3* ♫♫♫♫ (Pablo, 1975/OJC, 1994, prod. Norman Granz) is their only trio session, though the results cried out for an encore or two. The three masters make the most of the uncluttered chamber jazz setting, listening closely to each other as they develop rich harmonic lines and swing effectively despite the absence of drums and piano. The material includes two Jackson originals, a couple of standards, and the session's highlights—Jobim's "Wave," an atmospheric version of Django Reinhardt's "Nuages," a brisk take of Kenny Dorham's "Blue Bossa," and a brief, but stunningly beautiful version of Ellington's "Come Sunday."

what to buy next: With strong arrangements by Tadd Dameron and Ernie Wilkins, *Big Bags* ♫♫♫♫ (Riverside, 1962/1989, prod. Orrin Keepnews) is a very successful big-band date. Dameron's ballad charts on his originals "If You Could See Me Now" and "The Dream Is You," and his breathtaking arrangement of Monk's "'Round Midnight," are album highlights. Yet, Wilkins also contributes some excellent orchestrations for Jackson's "Echoes" and the standard "Star Eyes," which also features some beautiful trombone work by Jimmy Cleveland. Jackson takes most of the solos, but James Moody and Jimmy Heath get a chance to play some spirited tenorisms on "Later Than You Think," and Ernie Royal shows off his trumpet chops on Jackson's "Namesake." Jackson and tenor saxophonist Jimmy Heath were frequent collaborators in the 1960s, and *Live at the Village Gate* ♫♫♫♫ (Riverside, 1963/OJC, 1988, prod. Orrin Keepnews) is one of their better dates, an excellent quintet session featuring a top-flight rhythm section with Hank Jones (piano), Bob Cranshaw (bass), and Tootie Heath (drums). The material includes three standards, three tunes by Jackson, and two by Jimmy Heath, most notably his bluesy waltz "Gemini." The album's highlights are a beautiful, flowing version of "Time After Time" and Jackson's two blues, "Ignunt Oil," which he recorded previously with Ray Charles, and the comfortably grooving opener "Bags of Blues." *Soul Fusion* ♫♫♫♫ (Pablo, 1977/OJC, 1992, prod. Norman Granz) pairs Jackson with pianist Monty Alexander's supple, hard-swinging trio, featuring bassist John Clayton and drummer Jeff Hamilton. The meeting results in a consistently rewarding session, as Jackson and Alexander in-

spire each other to dig in rhythmically and play with great sensitivity, especially on Clayton's slow ballad "3000 Miles Ago." Steve Wonder's "Isn't She Lovely" and Jobim's "Once I Loved" are the only standards, and Jackson supplies three tunes, including the tasty title track, but it's Richard Evans's "Bossa Nova Do Marilla" that finds the two principals interacting with the most intuitive connection. One of three albums recorded during a stint at Ronnie Scott's Club in London, *Memories of Thelonious Sphere Monk* ♫♫♫♫ (Pablo, 1982/OJC, 1995, prod. Ray Brown, Milt Jackson) features pianist Monty Alexander, bassist Ray Brown, and drummer Mickey Roker. Though the title implies this is a session of Monk's music, the formidable quartet actually runs through concise versions of four Monk tunes, including brilliant renditions of "Blue Monk," "In Walked Bud" (with some particularly inspired playing by Jackson), and "'Round Midnight," which features Brown's gorgeous arco bass work. The quartet gets a chance to stretch out on a 10-minute version of "Django" and Brown's "Blues for Groundhog."

what to avoid: A rare dud in Jackson's illustrious and consistently inspired discography, *Feelings* ♫♫ (Pablo/OJC, 1976, prod. Norman Granz) suffers from boring string charts and material so undistinguished, even the presence of Tommy Flanagan (piano), Ray Brown (bass), and Jerome Richardson (saxes) can't salvage it. The many strong Jackson sessions available on CD make this one completely expendable.

best of the rest:

Milt Jackson/Sonny Stitt: In The Beginning ♫♫♫ (OJC, 1948/1990)
Milt Jackson Quartet ♫♫♫♫ (Prestige, 1955/OJC, 1987)
Invitation ♫♫♫♫ (Riverside, 1962/OJC, 1988)
Milt Jackson/Ray Brown Jam: Montreux '77 ♫♫♫♫ (Pablo/OJC, 1977)
Ain't But a Few of Us Left ♫♫♫♫ (Pablo, 1977/OJC, 1993)
Night Mist ♫♫♫♫ (Pablo, 1977/OJC, 1994)
Big Mouth ♫♫♫♫ (Pablo, 1977/OJC, 1995)
Bag's Bag ♫♫♫♫ (Pablo, 1977/OJC, 1997)
A London Bridge ♫♫♫♫ (Pablo, 1977/OJC, 1997)
Mostly Duke ♫♫♫♫ (Pablo, 1977/OJC, 1991)
The Duke Ellington Album: All Too Soon ♫♫♫♫ (Pablo/OJC, 1980)
Milt Jackson + Count Basie + The Big Band, Vol. 1 ♫♫♫ (Pablo, 1982/ OJC, 1991)
Milt Jackson + Count Basie + The Big Band, Vol. 2 ♫♫♫ (Pablo, 1982/ OJC, 1991)
It Don't Mean a Thing If You Can't Tap Your Foot to It ♫♫♫♫ (Pablo, 1984/OJC, 1990)
The Harem ♫♫♫♫ (MusicMasters, 1991)
Reverence and Compassion ♫♫♫♫ (Qwest, 1993)
The Prophet Speaks ♫♫♫♫ (Qwest, 1994)
Burnin' in the Woodhouse ♫♫♫♫ (Qwest, 1995)
Sa Va Bella (For Lady Legends) ♫♫♫ (Qwest, 1997)

worth searching for: Some of the most profound and timeless music in the modern jazz canon, *Genius of Modern Music, Vol. 2* 𝄞𝄞𝄞𝄞 (Blue Note, 1951–52, prod. Alfred Lion) includes two of Thelonious Monk's early sessions for Blue Note. The first, from 1951, features a quintet with Jackson, Shihab Sahib on alto, Al McKibbon on bass, and Art Blakey on drums. No musicians ever reached a deeper rapport with Monk than Blakey and Jackson, and this session introduced a number of Monk classics, including "Four in One," "Criss Cross," and "Straight No Chaser." The second session from 1952 features a sextet with Kenny Dorham, Lucky Thompson, Lou Donaldson, and Max Roach.

influences:

◀◀ Charlie Parker, Lucky Thompson

▶▶ Terry Gibbs, Buddy Montgomery, Margie Hyams, Victor Feldman

see also: *Modern Jazz Quartet*

Andrew Gilbert

Paul Jackson Jr.

Born December 30, 1959, in Los Angeles, CA.

Paul Jackson Jr. exhibits an R&B, funk guitar style fused with a definite respect for gospel, and is largely influenced by the electro-contemporary jazz traditionally associated with the West Coast music scene. Born and raised in Los Angeles, he is widely respected as one of the most versatile guitar players to hail from the South Central area. He started playing at age 13, quickly earning a reputation for his sweet soulful phrasing, and through his association with contemporaries such as Patrice Rushen, Gerald Albright, and Bobby Lyle, started doing studio recording work at the age of 16. Recognized for his talents as an arranger, Jackson has recorded with many well-known R&B musicians, pop artists such as Michael Jackson, Anita Baker, Chicago, Luther Vandross, and Whitney Houston, and jazz artists such as guitarists George Benson and Earl Klugh. Both Benson and Klugh influenced Jackson's early style and are credited with being major catalysts in the development of his career. He has also recorded as a sideman with the late vocalist Ella Fitzgerald and Orchestra (for Pablo Today), and with the Sonny Rollins Quartet (for Milestone). As a band leader, Jackson has struggled with his R&B roots in an effort to find his own sound, but with maturity he is becoming more directional with his work.

what to buy: Jackson's Blue Note debut, *Never Alone/Duets* 𝄞𝄞𝄞𝄞 (Blue Note, 1996, prod. Paul Jackson Jr., Ollie E. Brown), is a prime example of Jackson embracing his own musical direction and focus as a band leader. On this effort, he is joined by Harvey Mason, Ray Parker Jr., Ali Ollie Woodson, George Bohanon, Wilton Felder, Howard Hewett, Jasmin, Tim Owens, Sharlotte Gibson, George Duke, Sheila E., Jeff Lorber, Alphonse Mouzon, Kevin Toney, Joe Sample, Najee, Tom Scott, Earl Klugh, Kirk Whalum, and long-time friend and associate Gerald Albright. *Duets, Never Alone*, although more on the contemporary side, is a solid recording with Jackson totally at ease. The duet with Klugh on "Reunited" yields a fluid blend of electric and acoustic guitar accentuating the players' distinct styles, yet offers the listener clear evidence of Jackson's growth as a lead guitarist. His previous release, *A River in the Desert* 𝄞𝄞𝄞 (Atlantic, 1993, prod. Paul Jackson Jr., Ollie E. Brown, Cornelius Mims) clearly defines Jackson's versatility as a jazz guitarist and is a welcome respite from his two earlier releases, in which he seemed to be searching for direction in R&B and electro-contemporary. Jackson's originals, "A Preview of Coming Attractions" and "It's a Start," are delightful presentations of straight-ahead jazz guitar, clearly showing an area of Jackson's repertoire unexplored in earlier releases. Among the slew of players on the album are jazz-fusion stalwarts such as Stanley Clarke, George Duke, Harvey Mason, and others.

what to buy next: To get a full appreciation of Jackson's talent, one must listen to his first two albums, *I Came to Play* 𝄞𝄞 (Atlantic, 1988, prod. Paul Jackson Jr., Cornelius Mims) and *Out of the Shadows* 𝄞𝄞𝄞 (Atlantic, 1990, prod. Paul Jackson Jr., Cornelius Mims, Ollie E. Brown). Both offer nice samples of Jackson's early influences—consisting of R&B, electro-funk, and even rap—but *Out of the Shadows* clearly exhibits his emergence as a blossoming guitar player. "Days Gone By," a vocal piece, unquestionably demonstrates strong guitar changes and hits you like a breath of fresh air in comparison to his earlier work. The number, "I Want Jesus to Walk with Me," stands out as an inspirational message in which Jackson totally shares his depth of emotion and ability through his speed of attack and chord changes. At this point one can appreciate the intensity and talent lying underneath the calm exterior of this young musician.

influences:

◀◀ George Benson, Earl Klugh

Keith Brickhouse

Ronald Shannon Jackson

Born January 12, 1940, in Fort Worth, TX.

The only drummer to record with Albert Ayler, Cecil Taylor, and Ornette Coleman, Ronald Shannon Jackson is a polyrhythmatist of power and imagination who has developed Coleman's harmolodic music in his own highly personal direction with his group the Decoding Society. Jackson came up in Texas playing with such esteemed locals as James Clay. Eventually moving to New York, he became part of the free jazz scene, recording with Albert Ayler (*Live at Slug's*) and Charles Tyler (*Charles Tyler Ensemble*) on ESP. Quite technically adept, he was also working with more mainstream musicians, including Betty Carter and Charles Mingus. In the 1970s he worked extensively in the bands of Ornette Coleman (he can be heard on *Dancing in Your Head*) and Cecil Taylor (*The Cecil Taylor Unit, 3 Phasis, One Too Many Salty Swift and Not Goodbye*). He worked throughout the 1980s as a leader, racking up an impressive discography, while also playing on the first two albums by ex-Coleman bandmate James Blood Ulmer's group Music Revelation Ensemble, the only release by the collective trio Power Tools, and a number of Bill Laswell projects, from Laswell's own albums to the free-jazz supergroup Last Exit and SXL. Since returning to Texas in the 1990s, Jackson has become less prolific, though his Decoding Society still convenes in the studio about once a year and has made some fine albums for the Japanese DIW label. Compositionally, Jackson combines the collective voicing/improvisation principles of harmolodics with his complex polyrhythms, a knowledge of African music gained in travel there, and (though somewhat submerged) a feeling for the blues inherent in his Texas upbringing. He prefers higher-pitched instruments, saying that's where he naturally hears musical lines, which explains his flute playing, his distinctive use of guitars (his *Red Warrior* album has three guitars and no horns), and his preference for alto and soprano saxophonists. His music is full of interlocking lines and rhythms and deserves wider dissemination, though its complexity will undoubtedly work against its casual use by other musicians. Jackson's role as mentor to a generation of young New York musicians should also be noted, with a number of Decoding Society members crediting him musically, philosophically, and in terms of business sense as having shaped their outlooks.

what to buy: *Mandance* ♪♪♪♪♪ (Antilles/Island, 1982, prod. David Breskin, Ronald Shannon Jackson) is the peak combination of players and material, with the most versatile, colorful, and coherent edition of the Decoding Society deployed on Jackson's most evocative and multi-faceted compositions. The lineup is Henry Scott (trumpet, flugelhorn), Zane Massey (saxes), Vernon Reid (electric guitar, steel guitar, guitar synthesizer, banjo), Melvin Gibbs and Reverend Bruce Johnson on electric basses, and, on three tracks, the addition of Lee Rozie

on saxes, with David Gordon replacing Scott. Funk is a strong element but never a cliché, the harmolodic element has been completely absorbed into Jackson's own limber language, and the variety of textures and rhythms is a constant delight.

what to buy next: *What Spirit Say* ♪♪♪♪ (DIW, 1995, prod. Kazunori Sugiyama) offers a smaller and more recent lineup, with James Carter on soprano and tenor sax, Jef Lee Johnson on electric guitar, and Ngolle Pokossi on electric bass. There's a surprising cover of Charlie Parker's "Now's the Time" with Jackson stating the theme on the reedy, metallic shalmei—go find another version of this tune played like that!—before moving to drums. Carter and Johnson combine well on the heads, creating a composite tone it's surprising more groups haven't copied. Moving in and out of free improvisation with ease, Carter shines, and the leader's fine compositions are well served.

what to avoid: *Pulse* ♪♪ (OAO/Celluloid, 1984, prod. David Breskin, Ron Saint-Germain) is admirable in its own way: a mostly solo album of drumming and, on half the tracks, poetry (by Sterling A. Brown, Shakespeare, Poe, Michael S. Harper, and Robert Hayden). Jackson's drum skills are amazing, and his voice is compelling; he comes as close as anyone could to pulling off an impossible task: making an album of drum solos you'd want to listen to more than once. But it's still an album of drum solos with poetry recitations. For die-hards only.

the rest:
Nasty ♪♪♪♭ (Moers, 1981)
Street Priest ♪♪♪ (Moers, 1981)
Barbeque Dog ♪♪♪♪♭ (Antilles/Island, 1983)
Decode Yourself ♪♪♪♪ (Island, 1985)
Live at the Caravan of Dreams ♪♪♭ (Caravan of Dreams, 1986)
When Colors Play ♪♪♪♭ (Caravan of Dreams, 1987)
Texas ♪♪♪♪ (Caravan of Dreams, 1988)
Taboo ♪♪♪♪ (Venture/Virgin, 1990)
Red Warrior ♪♪♪♪ (Axiom/Island, 1990)
Raven Roc ♪♪♪♭ (DIW, 1992)

worth searching for: Recorded early in the existence of a small New York indie label, *Eye on You* ♪♪♪♪♪ (About Time, 1980, prod. Alan Ringel) contains some of Jackson's most Ornette-like music and is an arranging masterpiece. The group, for the only time on record, emphasizes veterans rather than young musicians: Billy Bang (violin), Byard Lancaster and Charles Brackeen (saxes), and fellow Ornette alum Bern Nix (electric guitar) feature strongly, though Reid and Gibbs were already in the band too.

influences:

◀◀ Elvin Jones, Ornette Coleman, Albert Ayler, Cecil Taylor

▶▶ Jamaaladeen Tacuma, David Fiuczynski , Eric Person, Zane Massey, Vernon Reid, Living Colour

see also: *Last Exit, Music Revelation Ensemble, Power Tools*

Steve Holtje

Willis "Gator Tail" Jackson

Born April 25, 1932, in Miami, FL. Died October 25, 1987, in New York, NY.

A genuine crowd-pleaser, tenor saxophonist Willis Jackson was always more at home in local neighborhood bars than in the elite jazz clubs or concert halls. His was an emotionally direct sound that hit the listener instantly and was also likely to induce foot-tapping and finger-popping. A player with a muscular sound, Willis drew from R&B, jazz, soul, and blues, and developed a manner in which effects such as honks and squeals were part of his extroverted approach. Jackson first hit it big when he recorded the boisterous "Gator Tail" (which earned him his nickname) with the Cootie Williams band in 1948. During the 1950s, he recorded under his own name and with his wife at the time, singer Ruth Brown. Starting in 1959, the saxophonist began a very productive association with the Prestige label, which lasted for five years. His organ-combo albums, which often featured the up-and-coming guitarist Pat Martino, became big sellers at the time, and were rediscovered in the mid-1990s by the "acid jazz" crowd who could be found dancing to Jackson's funky records. Largely ignored by the media, Jackson remained active throughout the 1970s and 1980s, playing and recording in a style that seems largely overlooked by today's musicians.

what to buy: *Willis Jackson with Pat Martino* 𝄞𝄞𝄞𝄞 (Prestige, 1964, prod. Ozzie Cadena) pairs the original albums *Jackson's Action!* and *Live Action,* on which the saxophonist's working group was caught before a live crowd in one of the local organ clubs where they often played. Both Martino and Jackson play some funky and choice solos. *Gentle Gator* 𝄞𝄞𝄞𝄞 (Prestige, 1995, prod. Esmond Edwards, Ozzie Cadena) is a compilation of Prestige sides done between 1961 and 1962. While Jackson is best known for his crowd-pleasing histrionics, he could also play a ballad with enough emotion to bring a tear to the eye. This album contains his most gorgeous and lush playing on record, proving that he was indeed a multi-faceted player.

what to buy next: *Bar Wars* 𝄞𝄞𝄞𝄞 (32 Jazz, 1977, prod. Bob Porter) is probably Jackson's most popular album, and for good reason. With Pat Martino and organist Charles Earland, Jackson wails on several up-tempo romps and delivers an extremely soulful message.

the rest:
Call of the Gators 𝄞𝄞𝄞 (Delmark, 1949)
Please Mr. Jackson 𝄞𝄞𝄞 (Prestige, 1959)

influences:

◀◀ Illinois Jacquet

Chris Hovan

Illinois Jacquet

Born Jean Baptiste Jacquet, October 31, 1922, in Broussard, LA.

Tenor saxophonist Illinois Jacquet was raised in Houston, Texas, and that likely influenced his biting, mobile, full-bodied sound, a bluesy style that often stretches into the instrument's upper range and has come to be known as the "Texas tenor style." Jacquet began playing drums as a teenager before learning soprano and alto saxophones. In the late 1930s he performed in various bands before joining Lionel Hampton as a tenor saxophonist and becoming famous in 1942 for his 64-bar honking solo on the original Hampton band single, "Flying Home." After his Hampton stint, Jacquet joined the Cab Calloway band (1943–44), and from 1945–46 worked with the Count Basie Orchestra, while occasionally leading his own groups. From 1950 he toured with Norman Granz's Jazz at the Philharmonic (JATP) as a principal soloist. Jacquet settled in New York and continued to tour Europe with the Texas Tenors, a group that included Arnett Cobb and Buddy Tate. Jacquet worked as sideman to artists such as Milt Buckner (1966–74) and Wild Bill Davis in 1972, and again in 1977. He occasionally participated in all-star reunion bands with Hampton from the late 1960s through 1980. From 1984 into the 1990s, Jacquet led his own Jazz Legends big band. He became a less aggressive player, mellowing over the years, and his later playing took on the warm-toned, silken, mainstream influences of Coleman Hawkins and Lester Young.

what to buy: *Flying Home: The Best of the Verve Years* 𝄞𝄞𝄞𝄞 (Verve, 1951–58/1995, prod. Norman Granz) is a compilation from the Jazz at the Philharmonic (JATP) series and includes recordings Jacquet made between 1951–58 in various settings. Highlights include his version of the title tune as well as 19 others featuring soloists such as Cecil Payne, Joe Newman, and other stalwarts of the JATP scene. Don't confuse this recording with the disc, *Flying Home* ♫♫♫ (Bluebird, 1962/1992, prod. various), which features samples of Jacquet's highly energized, soulful playing mostly from the late 1940s: a version of the title tune, and his originals, "Jet Propulsion," "Try Me One More Time," "Symphony in Sid," "Jacquet for Jack the Bellboy," "Black Velvet," and more. *The Comeback* ♫♫♫ (Black Lion 1971/1992, prod. Alan Bates) features the tenor saxophonist mostly mixing it up with the loud and rumbling organ of Milt Buckner on the title tune, "C-Jam Blues," "Easy Living," "Take the 'A' Train," and two others.

what to buy next: From a musician who was there in the beginning, *Jacquet's Got It!* ♫♫♫ (Atlantic, 1988, prod. Bob Porter) is Jacquet's big-band album, featuring Milt Hinton (bass) and former Basie-band drummer Duffy Jackson driving the rhythm section with Richard Wyands at the piano. Soloists include John Faddis (trumpet), Frank Lacy (trombone), and others, as well as leader–tenor saxman Jacquet on hard-swinging arrangements by Wild Bill Davis, Phil Wilson, and Eddie Barefield. Highlights are many among the eight tracks, but especially notable are their swinging versions of Benny Goodman's "Stompin' at the Savoy" and the classic "Three Buckets of Jive." The band had been together part-time over a decade when this recording was made and they yield one of the most exciting big-band albums of the last 25 years.

best of the rest:
Bottoms Up ♫♫♫ (Prestige, 1968/OJC, 1992)
The Blues: That's Me! ♫♫♫ (Prestige, 1968/OJC, 1991)
The Soul Explosion ♫♫♫ (Prestige, 1969/OJC, 1991)

influences:

◀◀ Coleman Hawkins, Lester Young, Charlie Parker

▶▶ King Curtis, Big Jay McNeely, Joe Houston, James Clay, Willis Jackson, Herschel Evans, Stanley Turrentine

Nancy Ann Lee and Joe S. Harrington

Allan Jaffe

See: Preservation Hall Jazz Band

Ahmad Jamal

Born July 2, 1930, in Pittsburgh, PA.

One of the most influential pianists in modern jazz, Ahmad Jamal has also been one of the most underappreciated. Known for building drama by using space, for being an exciting live player, and for creating a new concept of group sound within a piano trio, Jamal continues making profound and original music to this day. He began playing professionally in his hometown of Pittsburgh when he was 11, but his career really began when he moved to New York and formed his first trio in 1951, at the age of 21. Even at this early stage in his career, Jamal sounded completely original during an era when pianists by the score felt compelled to closely imitate Bud Powell. Jamal's independence and insistence on creating his own sound within a group meant that throughout his career he didn't usually play with what might be considered the top echelon of jazz musicians—a fact that may explain why he has always been so seemingly outside the jazz mainstream despite his accessible sound. Still, musicians have always felt compelled to hear what Jamal has been playing. In the 1950s no less an authority than Miles Davis stated, "I live until (Jamal) makes another record.... All my inspiration today comes from Ahmad Jamal," and he insisted that his own pianist at the time, Red Garland, try to sound like Jamal. In fact, Jamal's influence on the entire Davis quintet of the mid-1950s is apparent. In the 1960s, 1970s, 1980s, and proceeding into the 1990s, he has continued making stimulating records within the same sound, with a few changes in personnel and some moves back and forth between acoustic and electric instruments.

what to buy: Jamal's live recorded performances are generally more spirited and vivacious when compared with his studio sessions. Recorded at the Pershing Club in Chicago, Illinois, *At the Pershing/But Not for Me* ♫♫♫♫ (Chess, 1958/MCA, 1990, prod. Phil Chess) combines material from Jamal's earlier LPs. The way he builds tension with sparse runs of notes at low volume and then releases it with louder, flowing, dense harmonic runs has never ceased to delight his fans, and is shown to full effect on this collection of Jamal standards, including the title tune, Jamal's biggest hit, "Poinciana," and a fresh take on "Woody 'n' You." *Ahmad's Blues* ♫♫♫ (Chess, 1959/GRP, 1994, prod. Phil Chess, reissue prod. Orrin Keepnews) is another incredible live performance of 1958, the CD reissue especially recommended because of its excellent remastering, and because it contains 16 tunes, over an hour of consistently exciting music. The versions of the title tune and "A Gal in Calico" are classic, and the rendition of "Autumn Leaves" returns some of the homage Davis had directed to Jamal when he recorded the tune with Cannonball Adderley earlier that same year. *Chicago Revisited: Live at Joe Segal's Jazz Showcase* ♫♫♫♫ (Telarc, 1993, prod. John Snyder) is a more recent live recording

Ahmad Jamal (© Jack Vartoogian)

by Jamal, just as exciting as the earlier recommendations, but with the added benefit of Telarc's renowned engineering and 20-bit digital recording. It's like having the great pianist in your living room playing tunes such as Clifford Brown's "Daahoud" and George Shearing's "Lullaby of Birdland."

what to buy next: It is interesting to hear how original Jamal's earliest recordings sound. Documenting his trios with guitarist Ray Crawford and bassist Eddie Calhoun or Israel Crosby, *Poinciana* 𝄢𝄢𝄢𝄢 (Chess, 1952–55/Portrait, 1989, prod. John Hammond) is a fine album that features the musicians staking out trio turf Jamal first claimed in between 1951–55. Included are classics such as "Old Devil Moon," "You Don't Know What Love Is," and "Our Delight," as well as three other tunes. Since his recent signing with the Verve subsidiary, Birdology, Jamal has taken something of a new direction, playing more originals and with more electric instruments. On *Big Byrd: The Essence Part 2* 𝄢𝄢𝄢𝄢 (Verve, 1996, prod. Jean-Francois Deiber) he also expands his traditional trio, adding Donald Byrd's trumpet and Joe Kennedy's violin on a tune apiece. The title tune with Byrd is especially exciting and revelatory, and proves that Jamal still has interesting, original things to say.

what to avoid: *Digital Works* 𝄢𝄢 (Atlantic, 1987, prod. John Snyder) is one of Jamal's first experimentations with electric piano and bass, and that aspect of the album works reasonably well, although not as effectively as on his recent Verve records. What this CD really lacks is that electric sense of tension and release that is so prevalent throughout his best records. Also, the selection of some of the tunes leaves something to be desired (the "Theme from *M*A*S*H*," "Misty," and "La Costa" don't really work for Jamal, although Jobim's "Wave" and Shorter's "Footprints" are interesting additions).

the rest:
The Awakening 𝄢𝄢𝄢 (Impulse!, 1970/1997)
Freeflight 𝄢𝄢𝄢𝄢 (Impulse!, 1972/1993)
Live at Bubba's 𝄢𝄢𝄢 (Who's Who in Jazz, 1980/1995)
Live in Concert 𝄢𝄢𝄢 (Chiaroscuro, 1981/1996)
Live at the Montreux Jazz Festival 𝄢𝄢𝄢𝄢 (Atlantic, 1987)
Rossiter Road 𝄢𝄢𝄢 (Atlantic, 1987)
Crystal 𝄢𝄢𝄢 (Atlantic, 1987)
Pittsburgh 𝄢𝄢𝄢 (Atlantic, 1990)
Live in Paris '92 𝄢𝄢𝄢 (Verve, 1993)
The Essence: Part 1 𝄢𝄢𝄢 (Verve, 1995)
I Remember Duke, Hoagy & Strayhorn 𝄢𝄢𝄢 (Telarc, 1995)

worth searching for: Unfortunately, much of Jamal's incredibly important output for Chess records and its subsidiary, Argo, has not been released on CD. *Chamber Music of New Jazz*

𝄢𝄢𝄢𝄢 (Argo, 1955, prod. Phil Chess), with a title that seems to rather accurately describe Jamal's trio concept, is a perfect example. As appreciation for Jamal's work and his importance in jazz history continue to grow, one would hope for some kind of comprehensive reissue of this material on compact disc.

influences:

◀◀ Erroll Garner

▶▶ Red Garland, Bill Evans, McCoy Tyner, Eric Reed

Dan Keener

Bob James

Born December 25, 1939, in Marshall, MO.

In the pantheon of influential jazz keyboardists, no one will ever confuse Bob James with Thelonious Monk. But the bebop-trained pianist/producer/arranger, while not a trailblazing pioneer, has been a pivotal player in the pop-jazz movement that bridges '70s fusion, '80s contemporary jazz, and whatever that stuff is that Kenny G and Boney James are playing these days. Cutting his teeth as in-house producer at CTI Records—where he guided the development of Grover Washington Jr., Eric Gale, Stanley Turrentine, and Ron Carter—James made his commercial breakthrough in 1978, when he was hired to compose the elegant, piano-based scores for the TV series *Taxi,* which resulted in the hit "Angela." Subsequent albums found him floundering from lukewarm funk to classical adaptations, most of them marked by anemic arrangements that relied too heavily on the then-trendy Fender Rhodes. But since leaving Columbia and signing with Warner Bros. in 1985, a reinvigorated James has rediscovered the precarious balance between electronic and acoustic instruments, between melodic grace and improvisatory challenge. In between anchoring Fourplay—the supergroup he formed with Lee Ritenour, Harvey Mason, and Nathan East—and serving as a VP of A&R in Warner Bros.' jazz division, James continues to navigate an assured course through the much-maligned contemporary jazz terrain, eschewing the New Age meandering that marks some of his peers' work and rarely confusing poise with mere polish.

what to buy: Of James's 14 Columbia releases that were reissued in 1995, *Touchdown* 𝄢𝄢𝄢 (Warner Bros./Tappan Zee, 1978, prod. Bob James) retains most of its original Caribbean-spiced, pop-flecked luster, thanks to sidemen David Sanborn, Jon Faddis, Earl Klugh, Ron Carter, and Eric Gale, as well as its endearing "Angela (Theme from *Taxi*)." On *Grand Piano Canyon* 𝄢𝄢𝄢 (Warner Bros., 1990, prod. Bob James), he reclaims the acoustic piano and his jazz roots against fierce, often funky backdrops that leave enough space for him to flaunt his improvisational chops. "Wings for Sarah," a touching tribute to Sarah Vaughan featuring Ritenour, East, and Mason, was the impetus for what became Fourplay. The luscious, self-explanatory *Straight Up* ♪♪♪ (Warner Bros., 1997), with Christian McBride and Brian Blade, boasts a stripped-back revision of his 1977 favorite, "Nightcrawler," and gently swinging versions of Pat Metheny's "James" and Horace Silver's "The Jody Grind."

what to buy next: *All around the Town* ♪♪♪ (Warner Bros./Tappan Zee, 1981, prod. Bob James, Joe Jorgensen, Peter Paul), recorded over a week in such New York landmarks as Town Hall, Carnegie Hall, and the Bottom Line, boasts muscular, stretched-out reworkings of such concert favorites as "Westchester Lady" and "Touchdown," and a 12-minute fusion romp through Boz Scaggs's "We're All Alone." Tom Scott, Joanne Brackeen, Hiram Bullock, Gary King, and Eddie Gomez enliven the surprisingly lively proceedings.

what to avoid: From its *Flashdance*-inspired cover art to an ill-conceived synthesizer medley of Beethoven snippets called "Ludwig," *Foxie* **woof!** (Warner Bros./Tappan Zee, 1983, prod. Bob James) is everything—blasé, not to mention bloodless—James normally avoids.

the rest:
Explosions ♪♪♪ (ESP, 1965)
One ♪♪ (Warner Bros./Tappan Zee, 1974)
Two ♪♪ (Warner Bros./Tappan Zee, 1975)
Three ♪♪ (Warner Bros./Tappan Zee, 1976)
Bob James 4 ♪♪ (Warner Bros./Tappan Zee, 1977)
Heads ♪♪♪ (Warner Bros./Tappan Zee, 1977)
Lucky Seven ♪♪♪ (Warner Bros./Tappan Zee, 1979),
(With Earl Klugh) *One on One* ♪♪♪ (Warner Bros., 1979)
H ♪♪ (Warner Bros./Tappan Zee, 1980)
Sign of the Times ♪♪ (Warner Bros./Tappan Zee, 1981)
Hands Down ♪♪ (Warner Bros./Tappan Zee, 1982)
(With Earl Klugh) *Two of a Kind* ♪♪♪ (Capitol, 1982)
The Genie ♪♪♪ (Warner Bros./Tappan Zee, 1983)
12 ♪♪ (Warner Bros./Tappan Zee, 1984)
(With David Sanborn) *Double Vision* ♪♪♪ (Warner Bros., 1986)
Obsession ♪♪ (Warner Bros., 1987)
Ivory Coast ♪♪♪ (Warner Bros., 1988)
(With Earl Klugh) *Cool* ♪♪ (Warner Bros., 1992)
Restless ♪♪♪ (Warner Bros., 1994)
The Swan ♪♪ (Warner Bros./Tappan Zee, 1995)
(With Hilary James) *Flesh and Blood* ♪♪♪ (Warner Bros., 1995)
(With Kirk Whalum) *Joined at the Hip* ♪♪♪ (Warner Bros., 1996)

worth searching for: James composed and performed the soundtrack for *Hapgood* (Jazz Stuff, 1997), a 1994 Lincoln Center production of a Tom Stoppard play starring Stockard Channing. Only 1,000 CDs were pressed and sold through the keepers of James's Web site, http://www.jazzstuff.com/.

influences:

◀◀ Cecil Taylor, Bill Evans, McCoy Tyner

▶▶ David Benoit, the Rippingtons, Grover Washington Jr.

David Okamoto

Harry James

Born March 15, 1916, in Albany, GA. Died July 5, 1983, in Las Vegas, NV.

The son of a trumpeter, James got his start in his father's circus band. When he arrived in New York, he was a strong player with a loud but impeccably controlled tone. After joining the Ben Pollack band as a teenager, James left for the Benny Goodman band and shot to fame during his two years with the clarinetist. He then became a bandleader in his own right and moved from the "hot" sound to playing "sweet," achieving pop star status in 1941 with "You Made Me Love You." As a result, his career has suffered in retrospect in terms of critical respect, and his catalog is in a somewhat shabby state, but being the most popular bandleader of the 1940s and marrying Betty Grable were rewards enough for James. He continued his career into the 1970s, criticized by purists for copying the Basie band and for his frequent use of non-jazz repertoire. He made no bones about aiming for pop success, and worked with many popular vocalists, including Frank Sinatra, Helen Forrest, Dick Haymes, Rosemary Clooney, Helen Humes, and more (even Grable). But he also hired superb jazz musicians and paid them well enough that he could keep them for a while. Willie Smith (alto sax) and Corky Corcoran (tenor sax) were star soloists, and drummers Buddy Rich and Louis Bellson were among the other stars to pass through the Harry James Orchestra.

what to buy: *The Chronological Harry James Orchestra, 1937–1939* ♪♪♪♪ (Jazz Classics, 1996), *The Chronological Harry James Orchestra, 1939* ♪♪♪♪ (Jazz Classics, 1997), and *The Chronological Harry James Orchestra, 1939–1940* ♪♪♪♪ (Jazz Classics, 1998) systematically collect James's commercial discs, with additional treasures to come as the label continues. So far, it stops short of his biggest hits, which won't particularly bother hardcore swing fans, as what's available so far includes some of his strongest playing.

what to buy next: *Bandstand Memories 1938–48* 𝄞𝄞𝄞𝄞 (Hindsight, 1994) is a three-CD set collecting radio broadcast sessions. Its earlier material overlaps some of the songs on the CDs above, but in different performances. More interesting are the many tracks he didn't release commercially. Vocalists include Sinatra and Forrest.

best of the rest:
Golden Trumpet of Harry James 𝄞𝄞𝄞𝄞 (Verve, 1987)
Silver Collection 𝄞𝄞𝄞𝄞 (Verve, 1987)
King James Version 𝄞𝄞𝄞𝄞 (Sheffield Lab, 1991)
Still Harry after All These Years 𝄞𝄞𝄞𝄞 (Sheffield Lab, 1991)
1943–44 Jump Sauce 𝄞𝄞𝄞𝄞 (Viper's Nest, 1994)
Always: 1943–46 𝄞𝄞𝄞𝄞 (Viper's Nest, 1994)
1964 Live! In the Holiday Ball 𝄞𝄞𝄞 (Jazz Hour, 1994)
Best of Harry James 𝄞𝄞𝄞𝄞 (Sheffield Lab, 1995)
All or Nothing at All 𝄞𝄞𝄞𝄞 (Hindsight, 1995)
Beat of the Big Bands 𝄞𝄞𝄞 (Sony, 1996)
Music Maker 𝄞𝄞𝄞 (Sony, 1996)
Verve Jazz Masters 55 𝄞𝄞𝄞𝄞 (Verve, 1996)
Harry James 1954–1966 𝄞𝄞𝄞𝄞 (Giants of Jazz, 1997)
Comin' from a Good Place 𝄞𝄞𝄞𝄞 (Sheffield Lab, 1997)

worth searching for: The Benny Goodman compilations *The Harry James Years, Vol. 1* 𝄞𝄞𝄞𝄞𝄞 (Bluebird/RCA, 1993, prod. Orrin Keepnews) and *Wrappin' It Up: The Harry James Years, Vol. 2* 𝄞𝄞𝄞𝄞𝄞 (Bluebird/RCA, 1995, prod. Orrin Keepnews) proclaim their obvious interest to James's fans in their title. Many jazz purists consider this James's best work, preferring his early "hot" style for its aggressiveness. The biggest classic among many here is "Sing, Sing, Sing," in two parts on vol. 1; vol. 2 has "The Blue Room."

influences:
◀◀ Louis Armstrong
▶▶ Ray Nance, Kenny Baker

Walter Faber

Jon Jang

Born March 11, 1954, in Los Angeles, CA.

Jon Jang didn't begin playing piano until he was 19, but he must've known where he was headed right from the start. By the time of his initial Soul Note release in 1992, he'd done five independently produced albums *and* the ideas and/or material for the next two projects were already in place.

what to buy: Of the readily available offerings (meaning, the Soul Notes) it's the thematic *Tiananmen!* 𝄞𝄞𝄞𝄞𝄞 (Soul Note, 1993, prod. Jon Jang) that's Jang's towering achievement as of this moment. Featuring his medium-sized Pan-Asian Arkestra

(named after Horace Tapscott's Pan-Afrikan People's Ark, but spiritually connected to Sun Ra as well), this concert-length piece is a moving tone poem-cum-meditation on the 1989 Chinese student uprising. Instruments drawn from China's folk and classical heritage blend with the more usual western assortment in creating a rich, earthy, and truly international musical language, with fabulous playing all around.

what to buy next: *Self Defense!* 𝄞𝄞𝄞𝄞𝄞 (Soul Note, 1992, prod. Jon Jang), recorded during a 1991 Arkestra recital, is nearly as good as the above recording, with a heaven-storming "Night in Tunisia" and Jang's lengthy, layered "Concerto for Jazz Ensemble and Taiko" as bookended high points. *Two Flowers on a Stem* 𝄞𝄞𝄞𝄞𝄞 (Soul Note, 1996, prod. Jon Jang) is a sextet with James Newton, David Murray, Chen Jiebing (erhu), Santi Debriano, and Jabali Billy Hart that's as dense and beautiful as its pedecessors; it's centered around "Meditations on Integration" (Mingus) with Newton's flute and Murray's bass clarinet taking the parts of Roland Kirk and Eric Dolphy, respectively. As always, a version of the popular Chinese ballad "Butterfly Lovers Song"—Jang's "Epistrophy"—is also included.

the rest:
Jang 𝄞𝄞𝄞𝄞 (RPM, 1982)
Are You Chinese or Charlie Chan? 𝄞𝄞𝄞𝄞 (RPM, 1984)
Island: The Immigrant Suite Number 1 𝄞𝄞𝄞𝄞 (Soul Note, 1997)

worth searching for: Jang's albums on the AsianImprov label, which he helped start, have to be searched out. Adding the most to the overall picture are *The Ballad or the Bullet* 𝄞𝄞𝄞𝄞 (AsianImprov, 1987, prod. Jon Jang, Francis Wong), which is credited to Jon Jang and the 4 in One Quartet; *Jangle Bells* 𝄞𝄞𝄞𝄞 (AsianImprov, 1988, prod. Jon Jang), and *Never Give Up!* 𝄞𝄞𝄞𝄞 (AsianImprov, 1989, prod. Jon Jang). It may not be an unfair characterization to say these albums are looser and more fun than the increasingly more serious Soul Note releases.

influences:
◀◀ Duke Ellington, Charles Mingus, Horace Tapscott's Pan-Afrikan People's Arkestra
▶▶ Fred Ho's Afro-Asian Music Ensemble

David Prince

Denise Jannah

Born 1957, in Surinam.

Blessed with a deep, rich voice, a keen insight into lyrics and a fine sense of swing, Denise Jannah has the makings of a major jazz talent. Born in Surinam, she spent her youth in Zeist, Holland. When her family returned to Surinam, she was surrounded by music, as her father (a minister, politician and soccer ref) was an organist and composer. Jannah returned to Holland to finish high school and decided to become a professional singer after a stint in law school. Since 1991, she's recorded a couple of albums for European labels, performed in Japan and at the North Sea Jazz Festival, and appeared in at least eight theatrical productions when she's not teaching at the Conservatory of Rotterdam. Her Blue Note debut is a lavish affair with well-crafted arrangements.

what's available: Jannah gets the royal treatment on her Blue Note debut *I Was Born in Love with You* ♫♫♫♫ (Blue Note, 1995, prod. Gary Giddins), a no-expenses spared session with Bob Beldon's arrangements for an all-star jazz orchestra on about half of the tracks. Jannah is brilliant on "You'd Be So Nice to Come Home to," for which she dug up a rarely sung verse, and Billy Strayhorn's "Something to Live for," with Beldon's Nelson Riddlish charts. Pianist Cyrus Chestnut accompanies Jannah on most of the other tracks, either by himself or with his trio, most memorably on "Them There Eyes," played with a rollicking Afro-Surinamese rhythmic pattern.

influences:

◀◀ Sarah Vaughan, Carmen McRae, Ernestine Anderson, Billie Holiday

Andrew Gilbert

Joseph Jarman

Born September 14, 1937, in Pine Bluff, AR.

Raised in Chicago from 1938, Jarman attended the famed DuSable High School music program under Captain Walter Dyett, playing drums. He joined the Army as a paratrooper between 1955–1958, and played with Army bands, learning saxophones and clarinet. Jarman met Roscoe Mitchell at Chicago's Wilson Junior College (other students were Malachi Favors, Jack De-Johnette, and Henry Threadgill), and at Mitchell's urging began attending sessions of Muhal Richard Abrams's Experimental Band (formed in 1961), and emerged in 1965, when he became a member of Chicago's AACM (Association for the Advancement of Creative Musicians). During the 1960s, Jarman led two small groups simultaneously, one a quintet featuring trumpeter Bill Brimfield and tenor saxophonist Fred Anderson, the other a quartet featuring young virtuosos Christopher Gaddy (piano) and Charles Clark (bass). He made his first album as leader in 1966 (*Song For* on Delmark), which ranks among the early classics of the AACM.

When Gaddy and Clark both died in 1968, Jarman, devastated, joined forces with Roscoe Mitchell, Lester Bowie, and Malachi Favors, and the Roscoe Mitchell Quartet became the Art Ensemble of Chicago. Jarman is best known for his 26-year association with the AEC. His textural/textual concerns and penchant for drama and ritual helped make the AEC a powerful force in contemporary speculative music. His abiding interest in martial arts (ki-aikido) has become his dominant focus over the years, and he's cut back on musical activities (he's now on temporary hiatus from the AEC). Jarman is a singular figure in creative music; the clarity of his musical statements is his consistent stamp.

what to buy: Jarman's spectacular debut as leader, *Song For* ♫♫♫♫ (Delmark, 1966/1991, prod. Robert G. Koester) features legendary tenorist Fred Anderson, trumpeter Bill Brimfield, pianist Christopher Gaddy, bassist Charles Clark, and drummers Thurman Barker and Steve McCall, a document of Jarman's working band of 1965–1967. From the brawny shout of "Little Fox Run" (the CD has an alternate take), to the poem-song of "Non-Cognitive Aspects of the City," to the solemn incantations of "Adam's Rib," to the impressionistic colors of "Song For," this sounds unlike anything recorded contemporaneous to it. Absorb Jarman the incantational ritualist on *As If It Were the Seasons* ♫♫♫♫ (Delmark, 1968/1996, prod. Robert G. Koester). The pristine voice of Sherri Scott blends with the ensemble on "As If It Were the Seasons/Song to Make the Sun Come Up" and "Song for Christopher," the latter a dedication to pianist Christopher Gaddy, who died shortly before the session. A singular document. Drummer Don Moye and Jarman have had a particular affinity since Moye joined the Art Ensemble in 1970. They share an interest in ritual, animist musical forms and the ability to stamp them with their sound in performances, making all Art Ensemble of Chicago performances special. That's the case on their enticing duo session on *Egwu-Anwu* ♫♫♫♫ (India Navigation, 1977/1997, prod. Robert Cummins), a two-CD set. Everything clicked during this December 1977 duo concert at Woodstock, the epiphany of which is Jarman's otherworldly solo on "Ohnedaruth," an evocation to John Coltrane. Moye performs like three drummers. (It would rate ♫♫♫♫ if there was a video.) Recorded with Don Moye and Johnny Dyani, *Black Paladins* ♫♫♫♫ (Black Saint, 1979/CD reissue date uncited, prod. Giovanni Bonandrini) showcases Dyani's deep wood sound and pulsing rhythm. He is the ideal triangulator for Jarman and Moye. The title track is set to a poem by Henry Dumas and there's a stunning version of Kalaparusha Ahra Difda's "Humility in Light of the Creator." The energetic interplay never flags. After several years of semi-retirement (Jarman's a ki-aikido master and runs a Brooklyn dojo), Jarman reemerged to perform with Marilyn Crispell on *Connecting Spirits* ✍✍✍ (Music & Arts, 1996, prod. Scott Fields). Crispell, that most flexible of pianists, is the ideal speculative-music accompanist; her solos elaborate and up the ante on Jarman's centered locutions in this duo concert recorded live in Madison, Wisconsin.

what to buy next: *Earth Passage/Density* ✍✍✍ (Black Saint, 1981, prod. Giovanni Bonandrini), a potentially interesting session matching Chicago creative music veteran Donald Raphael Garrett and trombonist Craig Harris with Moye and Jarman, has a thrown-together quality. The group never really connects, yet Jarman and Moye are in fine form and this is worth owning for Jarman's strong improvising throughout. Jarman contributes "Zulu Village," a suite, "Happiness Is," and "Sun Spots." Featuring Don Pullen and Don Moye, *The Magic Triangle* ✍✍✍✍ (Black Saint, 1979/CD reissue date uncited, prod. Giovanni Bonandrini) offers an interesting study of improvisers with contrasting approaches feeling each other out. Pullen and Jarman have almost too much respect for each other, and neither stretches form as we expect to hear them do. Jarman's poem-song "Lonely Child," and Pullen's blues, "What Was, Ain't," are the date's highlights.

best of the rest:
(With the Art Ensemble of Chicago) *Nice Guys* ✍✍✍ (ECM, 1979/CD reissue date uncited)
(With the Art Ensemble of Chicago) *Full Force* ✍✍✍✍ (ECM, 1980/1994)
(With Famoudou Don Moye's Magic Triangle) *Calypso's Smile* ✍✍✍✍ (AECO, 1984/1992)
(With the Art Ensemble of Chicago) *The Complete Live in Japan—1984* ✍✍✍✍ (DIW, 1984/1994)
(With the Art Ensemble of Chicago) *The Third Decade* ✍✍✍✍ (ECM, 1984/1994)
(With the Art Ensemble of Chicago) *Naked* ✍✍✍✍✍ (DIW, 1986)
(With the Art Ensemble of Chicago) *Soweto* ✍✍✍✍✍ (DIW, 1989–90/1994)
(With Famadou Don Moye) *Egwu-Anwu* ✍✍✍✍ (India Navigation, 1997)

worth searching for: Jarman's compositions appear on numerous Art Ensemble recordings, including the currently in print *Tutankhamun* ✍✍✍✍ (Freedom, 1969/Black Lion, 1996, prod. Chris Whent, Alan Bates) and *The Spiritual* ✍✍✍✍ (Freedom, 1969/Black Lion, 1997, prod. Chris Whent, Alan Bates). Both are wonderful documents of the amazing web of shifting colors, timbres, and events the early AEC could spin. The former features Jarman with Bowie on "That the Evening the Sky Fell Through the Glass Wall and We Stood Alone Somewhere." The latter features Jarman's "Lori Song." A hard to find recording, *Sunbound*

✍✍✍✍ (AECO, 1976) is a superb aural document of the magic Jarman can produce in solo performance, in this case a concert at the New Theater, University of Chicago. Jarman evokes his narrative on alto sax, bass clarinet, soprano sax, flute, and an immense array of percussion instruments. Snap it up if you're lucky enough to find it. Also hard to find, *Inheritance* ✍✍✍✍ (Baybridge, 1983/Four Star, 1991, prod. Jeffrey Kaufman) is a panoramic recording that is a highlight of Jarman's oeuvre. Geri Allen, the most sensitive and nuanced of accompanists, and Fred Hopkins, the strongest New Music bassist of the 1980s, are ideal partners for Moye and Jarman. On the traditional side, there's a lyrical soprano interpretation of Sidney Bechet's "Petite Fleur." Jarman unleashes his Pentecostal spirit-catching inclinations on "Inheritance." His formalist stillness-space explorations of shakuhachi music conclude the proceedings, on the originals "Unicorn in Space," " "Love Song for a Rainy Monday," and "Oh Sensei Ni Sasageru." Another hard-to-find gem, *Poem Song: Joy in the Universe* ✍✍✍✍ (Baybridge, 1990, prod. Yumi Mochizuki) serves up exquisitely beautiful, profoundly peaceful music by Jarman, played with intelligence and rigor with Japanese spirit musicians. Grab this album if you find it. An AEC masterpiece that is also out of print, *Fanfare for the Warriors* ✍✍✍✍✍ (Atlantic, 1973, prod. Michael Cuscuna) finds the group augmented by Muhal Richard Abrams. The title track and "What's to Say" are by Jarman. A hard-to-find CD, *Art Ensemble of Soweto: America–South Africa* ✍✍✍✍ (DIW, 1989–90, prod. Art Ensemble of Chicago) contains collaborations with the Amabutho Male Chorus of Johannesburg, featuring some of the AEC's most stimulating recent work.

influences:
◀◀ Gene Ammons, Eric Dolphy, John Coltrane, Roscoe Mitchell
▶▶ Henry Threadgill, Anthony Braxton, Matt Darriau, Myra Melford

see also: *Art Ensemble of Chicago*

Ted Panken

Al Jarreau

Born Alwyn Lopez Jarreau, March 12, 1940, in Milwaukee, WI.

At a time when jazz vocals were all but ignored, Al Jarreau's multi-dimensional, scat-inspired vocal performances earned him a worldwide following. Throughout the 1980s, Jarreau

Al Jarreau (© Jack Vartoogian)

helped revive the public interest in jazz vocals while becoming one of the genre's most distinctive practitioners. Inspired by a musically inclined family, Jarreau was singing from age four and had his first public concert at age seven. Early musical influences were rooted in big-band and bebop records belonging to his older brother and sisters. Gospel and church music were also a dominant influence. His father, a Seventh-Day Adventist minister, was an accomplished singer, and his mother was a church pianist. Jarreau especially admired the harmonizing ability of the Four Freshman. As a high school student, he sang songs from Broadway shows and deepened his love for jazz. Graduating with a master's degree in psychology from the University of Iowa, he worked as a rehabilitation counselor for the handicapped in San Francisco until he was 28.

In 1968, not satisfied with his casual musical flirtations, Jarreau decided to devote his full attention to his singing career. With acid rock and heavy metal in vogue, performing at even the most visible venues in Los Angeles and New York did not secure Jarreau a recording contract. Persevering, he continued developing his vocal techniques and began creating his own lyrics. Although he had accrued a devoted local following, it wasn't until 1975 that his efforts paid off. After being noticed by Warner Bros. president Mo Austin at the Troubadour in Hollywood, Jarreau was offered and accepted a contract. His debut, *We Got By*, was released to unanimous acclaim that same year, and the ensuing European tour earned him a German Grammy for Best New International Soloist. The enormous popularity of his subsequent recordings and live performances is well represented by the avalanche of awards that has marked his career. After the 1977 release of his second LP, *Glow* (which was named Record of the Year by *Stereo Review*), Jarreau embarked on his first world tour, from which selections for his live double album, *Look to the Rainbow*, were culled. During this time, a second German Grammy for Best International Artist was awarded for *Glow*, as well as Vocalist of the Year honors from the French Music Academy and an Italian Music Critics award for best foreign vocalist. *Performance* voted him both Male Vocalist and Best New Jazz Act, while *Cashbox* placed him as Top New Artist in its jazz awards. *Down Beat* named Jarreau Male Vocalist of the Year consecutively from 1977 to 1981 in its People's Choice awards, and in 1985 he was nominated for an Emmy award for the musical theme to the TV series *Moonlighting*. In all, Jarreau has won five Grammy awards: for Best Jazz Vocal Performance in 1977 (*Look to the Rainbow*, 1978 (*All Fly Home*), and 1981 (*Breakin' Away*); for Best Pop Vocal Performance in 1981; and in 1992 for Best R&B

Male Vocal Performance for *Heaven and Earth*. This makes Jarreau the only artist to have won Grammy awards in three separate vocal categories. Affectionately dubbed the "acrobat of scat," he has secured a permanent place in music history and stands virtually unrivaled by other singers of his generation.

what to buy: *We Got By* ♫♫♫♫ (Reprise, 1975, prod. Al Schmitt) is the result of a vivacious and hungry young singer with a lot of fire in his belly. Although this is Jarreau's major-label debut, the confidence gained through years of live performances is evident from the first track to the last. Musically undated, this record sounds as fresh as it did when it was recorded over two decades ago. The vocal performances are saturated with honesty and passion.

what to buy next: *Breakin' Away* ♫♫♫♫ (Warner Bros., 1981, prod. Jay Graydon) is one of the most polished productions in his catalog. Although some critics think this album is a self-serving attempt by Jarreau to win pop icon status, a 100-percent performance is still a 100-percent performance. Here Jarreau is at 101 percent, with scarcely a scat in sight.

the rest:
1965 ♫♫♫♫ (Bainbridge, 1965)
Glow ♫♫♫ (Reprise, 1976)
Look to the Rainbow ♫♫♫♫ (Warner Bros., 1977)
All Fly Home ♫♫♫ (Warner Bros., 1978)
This Time ♫♫♫♫ (Warner Bros., 1980)
Jarreau ♫♫♫ (Warner Bros., 1983)
Ain't No Sunshine ♫♫♫ (Blue Moon, 1983)
Live in London ♫♫♫♫ (Warner Bros., 1985)
L Is for Lover ♫♫ (Warner Bros., 1986)
Heart's Horizon ♫♫♫ (Reprise, 1988)
High Crime ♫♫ (Warner Bros., 1989)
Heaven and Earth ♫♫♫ (Reprise, 1992)
Tenderness ♫♫♫♫ (Warner Bros., 1994)
Lean on Me ♫♫ (Peter Pan, 1996)
Best of Al Jarreau ♫♫♫♫ (Warner Bros., 1996)

influences:
◀◀ Johnny Mathis, Mel Tormé

▶▶ Bobby McFerrin, Gino Vannelli, Randy Crawford

Ralph Burnett

Keith Jarrett
Born May 8, 1945, Allentown, PA.

You'll have a field day picking recordings by pianist Keith Jarrett, one of the major jazz artists to emerge during the 1960s. For example, *everything* in his ECM catalog is in print. Although Jarrett has gone through several musical incarnations, he is perhaps best known internationally for his spontaneously improvised solo piano concerts recorded in venues around the world. Yet his small group settings are equally attractive, especially his dates recorded in the 1970s with his avant garde "American Quartet," featuring saxophonist Dewey Redman, bassist Charlie Haden, and drummer Paul Motian, or his straight-ahead 1990s trio with bassist Gary Peacock and drummer Jack DeJohnette.

Jarrett grew up in a musical family, encouraged by his parents and surrounded by younger siblings. After his father bought a used piano, the precocious Jarrett began playing by ear and was taking lessons by the time he was three years old. He began to excel and give public performances at a very early age. He appeared on Paul Whiteman's television show at age five, and two years later performed a two-hour piano concert. He began composing and improvising early, creating melodies and rhythmic patterns and writing them down. Although immersed in the piano, sometime during this period he also learned to play drums. In his teens, he began to play popular music, dance music, and jazz with his own group and those led by others. He attended summer jazz camps and Stan Kenton clinics. Jarrett left school at age 16, got a factory office job, and worked occasional gigs with older players in Allentown before he was recommended as a replacement for the house pianist at the Dear Head Inn. After working with other small bands, Jarrett went on tour with Fred Waring's Pennsylvanians. In 1962 he recorded as sideman on a Decca big band album. He received a scholarship to Berklee College of Music, where he briefly bolstered his talents before getting kicked out for playing the inside of one of their grand pianos. He spent 1964 scrappling in Boston with other Berklee dropouts, but there was little jazz work. Jarrett moved to New York and gigged around until he was discovered one night by Art Blakey, who was reforming his Messengers band after trumpeter Lee Morgan had left. At age 20, Jarrett joined Blakey for four months, recording his first full jazz album, *Buttercorn Lady,* with the band. He then joined the adventurous Charles Lloyd Quartet (with Jack DeJohnette and Cecil McBee), touring widely and establishing his reputation. Using his rich imagination and flair for creating percussive and melodic sounds, he treated the piano like a living creature, crouching or standing in front of it and coaxing strange sounds from it by stroking the strings, kicking the pedals, and attacking the keyboard. He remained with Lloyd's group until it disbanded in 1969, making a series of enormously successful albums that became classics, beginning with the March 1966 session documented on *Dream Weavers.*

During his days with Lloyd, Jarrett had formed a trio with bassist Charlie Haden and drummer Paul Motian, and the three continued performing and recording together for 10 years. In June 1970 Jarrett replaced Chick Corea in the Miles Davis fusion band, which also included Jack DeJohnette (who had replaced Tony Williams). Jarrett played piano and organ for Davis for 18 months, recording *Live at the Fillmore* and *Live/Evil.* DeJohnette left the band and Jarrett followed in 1971. During his stint with Davis, Jarrett recorded a 1970 album with vibist Gary Burton, a 1971 album with DeJohnette, and some sessions as leader for Impulse!. He joined the ECM label, recording his acoustic piano album *Facing You* on November 10, 1971. He has been with the label ever since. Between 1974 and 1979, Jarrett recorded a few albums as leader of his "European quartet" with Norwegian saxophonist Jan Garbarek, bassist Palle Danielsson, and drummer Jon Christensen. The 1970s were productive years for Jarrett, and he recorded numerous albums for ECM, including the 1975 album *The Köln Concert,* the first in a series documenting his solo piano concerts. By the 1980s Jarrett was also performing classical music for ECM's New Series, and in the 1990s his performing and recording activities continued at a high level. To learn more about Jarrett, check the many Web sites devoted to his life and works, or read the book *Keith Jarrett: The Man and His Music,* by Ian Carr (De Capo Press, New York, 1991).

what to buy: The remarkable thing about Jarrett's solo piano work is that it holds appeal both for jazz fans who admire his brilliant, on-the-spot improvisations, and for 20th-century classical music lovers for his accomplished technique and tradition-steeped performances that draw upon influences of the great composers. While Jarrett's many spontaneously improvised solo piano recordings are exciting, his trio and quartet recordings have won widest appeal with the general jazz audience, especially his trio with bassist Gary Peacock and drummer Jack DeJohnette, his earliest (avant garde) sets with Charlie Haden, Dewey Redman, and Paul Motian recorded for Atlantic in the early to mid-1970s, or his chamber-like, European quartet with Jan Garbarek. If you wish to start chronologically, a compilation of Jarrett's earliest available recordings for the Atlantic label can be found on the nicely packaged two-disc set *Foundations: The Keith Jarrett Anthology* ♪♪♪♪ (Atlantic, 1971–75/Rhino, 1994, prod. various). Containing an assortment of exciting live and studio sessions recorded as leader between 1966–75 with top luminaries and in solo piano settings, the two discs feature Jarrett playing assorted standards and originals that capture his lyrical side as well as his versatile avant garde expressions. Included are quartet tracks with Charles Lloyd, Cecil McBee, and Jack DeJohnette and with Haden, Motian, and Redman; duo and quintet tracks with Gary Burton; trio tracks with Haden and Motian; and more. Highlights among Jarrett's earliest recorded works abound and this set, with its informative booklet, is highly recommended. Jarrett's first recording for ECM, *Facing You* ♫♫♫♫ (ECM, 1972/1994, prod. Manfred Eicher) still ranks high among his best spontaneously composed solo piano recordings. His improvs on this studio session recorded in Oslo show more melodicism and jazz influence than on many of his more recent, live-recorded solo piano concerts around the world. On his eight originals, he draws influences from popular music of the era (even some gospel-tinged motifs) as well as creating engaging new pieces that hold up today. For a sample of his earliest live-recorded European concerts of spontaneously composed music, check out *Solo Concerts: Bremen/Lausanne* ♫♫♫♫ (ECM, 1973), a two-disc set (originally released as a three-LP set) that documents his two-part concert in Bremen, Germany, and his concert in Lausanne, Switzerland. Jarrett is in rare form in both of these concerts as he generates the works that first made him famous. His improvisations are full of colorful, imaginative ideas as he creates intriguing motifs and then expands upon them. This set provides two hours of his inventive developments. Another of his most popular and highly recommended recordings is *The Köln Concert* ♫♫♫♫ (ECM, 1975/1994, prod. Manfred Eicher), recorded in Germany on January 24, 1975. Again, Jarrett unfolds an amazing range of ideas in a solo piano setting, sometimes augmenting with percussive thumps on the piano pedals, or building tension with thundering left-hand chords and then releasing with a stop-time break, or frequently shifting moods to develop melodious new motifs or themes. Brilliant and gorgeous stuff! Jarrett's trio with Gary Peacock and Jack DeJohnette is also exceptionally stimulating. Even though this trio has recorded two hands' full of albums, once you're thoroughly entrenched in Jarrett's music, you'll want to spring for his transcendent six-disc set, *Keith Jarrett at the Blue Note: The Complete Recordings* ♫♫♫♫ (ECM, 1995, prod. Manfred Eicher), recorded in June 1994 at the famous New York jazz venue with Peacock (double-bass) and DeJohnette (drums). The recordings in this box set find Jarrett in peak form as he reinvents an array of 40 jazz standards and his originals with this spectacular trio, capturing first and second sets recorded from June 3–5, 1994. With its many highlights, including a nearly half-hour version of "Autumn Leaves," a 21-minute interpretation of "Green Dolphin Street," and a lengthy version of the Jarrett original, "Desert Sun" at 28:22 minutes, this set was universally hailed by critics

when it was released in 1995 and it should provide you with many hours of listening pleasure. If you're not into shelling out big bucks, you could settle for one of their single disc recordings. *At the Blue Note* ♫♫♫♫ (ECM, 1995, prod. Manfred Eicher) documents the Keith Jarrett Trio's illustrious Saturday, June 4, 1994, performance at the Blue Note, with standards such as "Autumn Leaves," "Days of Wine and Roses," "You Don't Know What Love Is," "When I Fall in Love," and the Jarrett original, "Bop-Be." On *Bye Bye Blackbird: A Musical Tribute to Miles Davis* ♫♫♫♫ (ECM, 1993, prod. Manfred Eicher), a lively studio session with Peacock and DeJohnette recorded in 1991, the trio interprets two versions of the classic, Ray Henderson–penned title tune—a straight version (the opener) and a totally invented rewrite by the band (the set closer). In between, they reinvent tunes by Oliver Nelson ("Butch and Butch"), Thelonious Monk ("Straight No Chaser"), Jimmy Van Huesen ("I Thought about You"), and some obscurities and originals. This is a great set that finds 50-year-old Jarrett moaning with ecstacy as his ingenious improvisations furiously unfold on uptempo numbers. Again, the Jarrett-Peacock-DeJohnette team serves up some boundlessly swinging, straight-ahead fare on *Standards in Norway* ♫♫♫♫ (ECM, 1995, prod. Manfred Eicher). Collaboration between these musicians is always impressive, yielding jazz that is tight, buoyant, and accessible and charming for the listener. Each musician is at his best without making over-exerted statements in solos or comping. Trio interpretations are cheerful and syncopated on standards such as "All of You," "Just in Time," and "I Hear a Rhapsody," touching and sentimental on "Old Folks," and just as expressive on five other tunes on which Jarrett leads off with melody heads to set resplendent moods. If you're a fan of the avant-garde jazz style, you'll want to check out Jarrett's recordings with his "American Quartet," featuring saxophonist Redman, bassist Haden, and Paul Motian. Two multiple-disc sets from Impulse! document Jarrett's early recordings for the label. *The Impulse! Years, 1973–1974* ♫♫♫♫ (Impulse!, 1977/1997, prod. Ed Michel) is an attractive, four-disc box set that compiles Jarrett's LP-albums *Fort Yawuh*, *Treasure Island*, *Death and the Flower* and *Backhand*, which he recorded with his "American Quartet" and percussionist Guilherme Franco, who appears often. The second four-disc set documenting Jarrett's recordings with his American Quartet was actually reissued first. *Mysteries: The Impulse! Years, 1975–76* ♫♫♫♫ (Impulse!, 1975–76/1996, prod. Esmond Edwards) compiles Jarrett's LP-albums *Shades*, *Mysteries*, *Byablue*, and *Bop-Be*. When originally released, all of the albums contained in these box sets received mixed reviews. They didn't quite mesh with the solo piano concert portion of Jarrett's career, and many critics claimed that Jarrett was just mimicking Ornette Coleman with this group. Nonetheless, these digitally enhanced reissued sets each provide over five hours of music, and when compared to what is being created by many artists today, these recordings remain vital and provocative. You'll have many hours of enjoyable listening with these sets. Plus, each set comes with a booklet full of valuable information.

what to buy next: The single disc *Personal Mountains* ♫♫♫♪ (ECM, 1979/1994, prod. Manfred Eicher) and the two-disc live-recorded Village Vanguard performance on *Nude Ants* ♫♫♫♪ (ECM, 1979/1980/1994, prod. Manfred Eicher) rank among the best recordings featuring Jarrett's "European Quartet" (tenor/soprano saxophonist Jan Garbarek, bassist Palle Danielsson, drummer Jon Christensen). Featuring Jarrett's original music, both albums are exciting, leaning often toward sounding like chamber-jazz, but yielding engaging improvisations that are sometimes full of fire and energy, and other times peaceful and serene. Regardless of the controversy among critics over this band, these sets represent some of Jarrett's most exciting work. You should hear at least one of these albums to learn how they compare with the sound of his American Quartet. *At the Deer Head Inn* ♫♫♫♪ (ECM, 1994, prod. Bill Goodwin) features Jarrett playing piano for the first time in 30 years at the Allentown spot where he performed (playing a variety of instruments) from the time of his high school graduation. The set reunites with Jarrett drummer Paul Motian (after 16 years) and bassist Gary Peacock. A relaxed, refreshing, live-recorded September 16, 1992, jam containing seven standards, including the molasses-sweet, "Basin Street," the lyrical swinger "Bye Bye Blackbird," and the beautifully delicate ballad, "It's Easy to Remember." A wonderful album. One of his recent works, *La Scala* ♫♫♫♪ (ECM, 1997) features Jarrett's three-part solo piano concert recorded live on February 13, 1995, at Teatro alla Scala in Milano, Italy. The first two parts feature him doing what he does best, spontaneously improvising using his vast idea-rich method. You'll be wrung out before you get to part three, an all-too-brief but gorgeously intimate rendition of "Somewhere over the Rainbow." It would have made composer Harold Arlen proud. *Concerts* ♫♫♫♪ (ECM, 1982/1994, prod. Manfred Eicher), live-recorded during a May 21, 1981, concert in Munich, ranks among Jarrett's best solo sittings. His spontaneous melodies are beautiful, his self-accompaniment is clever as he creates wide-ranging moods, and he deeply engages the listener in this four-tune solo sitting. Jarrett expansively landscapes "Part I" and "Part II," the shorter percussive-riffed piece "Untitled," and the sweeping bit of Americana, "Heartland." Drawbacks of this CD reissue are its brevity at 49:35 and the omission of the June 2, 1981, portion that appeared on the three-LP set of the same title. *Vienna Concert* ♫♫♫♪ (ECM, 1992, prod. Manfred Eicher, Keith Jarrett), a live-recorded July 13, 1991, solo concert at the Vienna State Opera, draws inspiration from a stark poem by Robert Bly. Constructed in two parts (Vienna, Part I, at 41:53 minutes, and Vienna, Part II, 26:03 minutes), this is one of Jarrett's better solo sittings. His musical language shifts dynamically and he delves deeply into the inner flames of his inspiration. An attention-holding performance, Jarrett is often intense and original, creating serene pastoral scenes, thunderous low-register rumblings, percussive passages, and melodic meanderings.

best of the rest:
(With Jack DeJohnette) *Ruta and Daitya* ♫♫♫♪ (ECM, 1973/1994)
(With Jan Garbarek, Charlie Haden & String Orchestra) *Arbor Zena* ♫♫♫♪ (ECM, 1976/1994)
(With Dewey Redman, Charlie Haden, and Paul Motian) *Survivor's Suite* ♫♫♫♪ (ECM, 1976/1994)
Sun Bear Concerts ♫♫♫♪ (ECM, 1976/1994), six-CD box set
(With Dewey Redman, Charlie Haden, Paul Motian) *Silence* ♫♫♫♪ (Impulse!, 1977/1992)
(With Jan Garbarek, Palle Danielsson, and Jon Christensen) *My Song* ♫♫♫♪ (1978/1994)
(With Gary Peacock and Jack DeJohnette) *Changes* ♫♫♫♪ (ECM, 1984)
Spirits, Volume 1 & 2 ♫♫♫♪ (ECM, 1986/1994)
(With Gary Peacock and Jack DeJohnette) *Standards Live* ♫♫♫♪ (ECM, 1986/1995)
(With Gary Peacock and Jack DeJohnette) *Standards in Norway* ♫♫♫♪ (ECM, 1989/1995)

influences:
◀◀ Dave Brubeck, Bill Evans, Art Tatum, Thelonious Monk, Bud Powell, McCoy Tyner, Ahmad Jamal, Paul Bley

Nancy Ann Lee

The Jazz Composers Alliance Orchestra

Formed 1985, in Boston, MA.

The JCAO is the resident ensemble of the Jazz Composers Alliance, formed by arrangers Darrell Katz (the group's director) and Ken Schaphorst, with Duane Johnson and Andrew Hurlbut in at the collective's inception and Susan Calkins joining later. The membership has varied over the years, with Katz the only constant. At the moment, the resident composers are Katz, Izhar Schejter, and Laura Andel. Bob Pilkington, David Harris, and Laura Allan are involved as well. Many musicians known from other groups have played in the JCAO, including John Medeski, Andrew D'Angelo, Rob Scheps, and John Dirac. An offshoot is the JCA Sax Quartet, which has recorded an album unreleased at press time.

what's available: *Dreamland* ☝☝☝ (Cadence Jazz, 1993, prod. Darrell Katz, Bob Rusch) spotlights Katz's composing and arranging. Consisting mostly of originals, with the exception of the Ellington/Strayhorn tune "Tonk" and blues-guitar great Albert Collins's "Left Overs," it displays rich, vibrant textures that build on the legacies of Duke Ellington and Charles Mingus but with an expanded harmonic language, occasional polytonality, and touches of outside wildness in some solos. Guest Julius Hemphill (alto sax) solos extensively on "Monk," which has the largest complement of instruments as it incorporates members of Either/Orchestra and Orange then Blue in a concert performance.

worth searching for: *Flux* ☝☝☝ (Northeastern, 1992, prod. George Schuller) was the JCAO's first album. Although the Northeastern label has since decided to confine its work to the classical field, the CD can still be acquired from the JCA, which can be contacted at JCAComp@aol.com. Unlike the Cadence album, *Flux* contains one arrangement by each JCA member. Hemphill's "The Hard Blues" and Sam Rivers's "Flux" are also played, with the composers playing on their respective tracks.

solo outings:
Ken Schaphorst:
Over the Rainbow: The Music of Harold Arlen ☝☝☝ (Accurate, 1996)

influences:
◀◀ Association for the Advancement of Creative Musicians, Jazz Composers' Orchestra, Composers in Red Sneakers

Steve Holtje

The Jazz Passengers
Formed 1987.

Roy Nathanson, reeds; Curtis Fowlkes, trombone; Jim Nolet, violin (1987); Marc Ribot, guitar (1987–early 1990s); Bill Ware, vibes; Brad Jones, bass; E. J. Rodriguez, drums; Rob Thomas, violin.

The Jazz Passengers, formed in 1987, originally consisted of co-leaders Roy Nathanson and Curtis Fowlkes, plus Jim Nolet, Marc Ribot, Bill Ware, Brad Jones, and E. J. Rodriguez. Since then, Ribot has left and Rob Thomas has replaced Nolet. The band ranks among today's major avant-garde groups. Their work contains top-notch collective as well as solo improvisation, provocative compositions and arrangements, and it is always earthy and humor-filled. In recent years, the Passengers

have increasingly featured vocals, some by well-known artists, including Debbie Harry and Elvis Costello.

what to buy: All of the Jazz Passengers' albums are worth owning, but when aesthetic merit and availability are considered, these CDs are recommended: *Implement Yourself* ☝☝☝☝ (New World, 1990, prod. Arthur Moorehead, Hugo Dwyer), *Live at the Knitting Factory* ☝☝☝☝ (Knitting Factory, 1991, prod. Bob Appel, Hugo Dwyer), *Plain Old Joe* ☝☝☝☝ (Knitting Factory, 1993, prod. Hugo Dwyer), and *Jazz Passengers in Love* ☝☝☝☝ (High Street, 1994, prod. Hal Willner, Hugo Dwyer). The New World and Knitting Factory CDs feature the Passengers' instrumental work along with a few vocals and comedy skits. These are loaded with stimulating original compositions. Nathanson, a brilliant soprano, alto, and tenor saxophonist, has been influenced by Ornette Coleman and Eric Dolphy. Fowlkes plays powerfully, exhibiting a fine range. Ware's rich imagination and excellent technique help account for his being one of the finest vibists to emerge in decades. Ribot is among the most innovative guitarists of any kind on the scene. Jones, a consummate bassist, and the subtle, creative Rodriguez make a superb rhythm section team. *Jazz Passengers in Love* contains 15 splendid art songs written or co-written by Passenger members and performed by 11 vocalists, including Debbie Harry, Jimmy Scott, Jeff Buckley, Freedy Johnston, and Mavis Staples. It's a landmark work that transcends genres.

what to buy next: *Individually Twisted* ☝☝☝☝ (32 Records, 1996, prod. Joel Dorn, Adam Dorn) features the singing of Debbie Harry and, on a couple of tracks, Elvis Costello. There are more excellent original compositions, and Harry demonstrates considerable ability and intelligence as a jazz singer, but this is a slightly more commercial album, including jazz standards such as "Li'l Darlin'" and "Jive Samba."

worth searching for: *Broken Night Red Light* ☝☝☝☝ (Crespuscle, 1987, prod. Hugo Dwyer, Curtis Fowlkes, Roy Nathanson) and *Deranged and Decomposed* ☝☝☝☝ (Crespuscle, 1988, prod. Hugo Dwyer) are products of a Belgian label and difficult to find. But the excellent writing and playing make a search well worth the effort.

influences:
◀◀ Ornette Coleman, Eric Dolphy, Charlie Mingus, Grachan Moncur, Bobby Hutcherson, James Brown, Sun Ra

Harvey Pekar

Eddie Jefferson

Born August 3, 1918, in Pittsburgh, PA. Died May 9, 1979, in Detroit, MI.

Singer-lyricist (and tap dancer) Eddie Jefferson created in the late 1940s the style that came to be called jazz vocalese, inspiring countless singers who came after him with his lyrics written to horn lines. Jefferson started his vocal explorations of jazz improvisations around 1938, when he used to sing along with recordings for his own amusement. The Pittsburgh native studied tuba in school, and later learned guitar and drums. His father, also an entertainer, encouraged young Jefferson's venture into show business, and with his brother Charlie, Jefferson formed a song-and-dance act, the Candy Kids, and appeared for four years on a local radio show with Erroll Garner. At age 15, Jefferson appeared with the original Zephyrs in the Chicago World's Fair, and in 1939 worked with Coleman Hawkins's band in Chicago. After World War II, Jefferson resumed his dancing. But he wasn't ignoring his singing; he had learned by heart most of the solos by Lester Young and Hawkins and began to develop words to fit the notes. He did the same thing with the modernists, Charlie Parker, Dizzy Gillespie, Dexter Gordon, James Moody, Wardell Gray, and others. Recordings as early as 1949 find Jefferson pioneering his vocalese by singing lyrics to "Parker's Mood" and Young's solo on "I Cover the Waterfront." But it was his classic lyrics to "Moody's Mood for Love" (first recorded in 1952 by King Pleasure) that brought him wider notice and a studio recording as leader on which he included his version of Hawkins's solo on "Body and Soul." Jefferson made a few more recordings during the 1950s under his own name before working for nearly a decade (until 1962) with James Moody. Forced to take a day job, Jefferson fell into obscurity for several years before recording his 1969 Prestige album, *Body and Soul*, which became a sizeable hit, and his appearance at the 1969 Newport Jazz Festival revived his flagging singing career. Jefferson worked again with Moody from 1968–73. Formed in 1976, Jefferson's partnership with saxman Richie Cole ended with the singer's murder in Detroit in May 1979. Jefferson was a master lyricist who created profound, humorous, and joyful lyrics. He combined elements of jive talk, slang, musical diction, storytelling, and rhythm into musical poetry. With his gravelly voice, he precisely delivered brisk bop lines with passionate power, breaking boundaries of American song. Jefferson inspired many later vocalese groups such as Lambert, Hendricks, and Ross.

what to buy: *The Jazz Singer* ✍✍✍✍ (Evidence, 1959–65/1993, prod. Herb Abramson) is the top pick purely for Jefferson's 1960 version of "Moody's Mood for Love," with falsetto vocals (the female part of the dialogue) that will have you laughing out loud. This disc draws from six sessions recorded in New York City between 1959–65. Included are such vocalese treats as his original 1959 version of "Body and Soul," "Sister Sadie," "Workshop," "Now's the Time," "Night Train," and a hilarious take on Pinetop Smith's "T.D. Boogie Woogie," a third-generation treatment of this tune adapted to big-band use in a 1938 Tommy Dorsey recording. His racing scat version of "Honeysuckle Rose" is another treasure. Six CD-reissue bonus tracks are included, one of which is "I Got the Blues (Lester Leaps In)." Backed by ensembles ranging from six to nine musicians (most of which include James Moody), and a few tracks enhanced by background singers, Jefferson displays witty spirit and versatility throughout the 53 minutes of music on this disc. *Letter from Home* ✍✍✍✍ (Riverside, 1962/OJC, 1987, prod. Orrin Keepnews) finds Jefferson singing 12 classics (includes two CD-reissue bonus tracks) with backing by a either a tentet (with alto saxophonist James Moody) featuring arrangements by Ernie Wilkins, or a quintet that includes soloist Johnny Griffin (tenor sax) with a rhythm section of Junior Mance (piano), Barry Galbraith (guitar), Sam Jones (bass), and Louis Hayes (drums). Tunes include wonderfully hip vocal versions of "Take the 'A' Train," "Night in Tunisia," "Body and Soul (I Feel So Good)," and "Parker's Mood (Bless My Soul)." Among the best tunes are the quintet versions of "Soft and Furry," a tune Jefferson performs with tenor saxophonist Johnny Griffin, and "Keep Walkin'" (take one), which features a perky piano chorus from Mance. This album is highly recommended because it finds Jefferson in peak form and demonstrates his ability to work well with both groups.

what to buy next: If you ignore the intent to "update" Jefferson's style with tunes such as Zawinul's "Mercy, Mercy, Mercy" and other mistakes, you'll find some delightful Jefferson classics on *Body and Soul* ✍✍✍✍ (Prestige, 1968/OJC, 1989, prod. Don Schlitten). Jefferson performs his best interpretations on the tracks "Body and Soul," Miles Davis's "So What," Moody's "There I Go, There I Go Again," and Charlie Parker's "Now's the Time." He is obviously more comfortable with small groups, and this one features Moody (tenor sax), Dave Burns (trumpet), Barry Harris (piano), Steve Davis (bass), and Bill English (drums). Jefferson tells brief stories with his lyrics and that, plus his note-bending slight yodel, his quick wit, and his sparing use of scatting, is what makes his style so endearing. *Come along with Me* ✍✍✍✍ (Prestige, 1969/OJC, 1991, prod. Don Schlitten) features singer Jefferson prominently as he skips through eight popular tunes (including a couple of originals) with backing from Bill Hardman (trumpet), Charles McPherson (alto sax), Barry Harris (piano), Gene Taylor (bass), and English (drums). His humor shines through frequently on tunes such as on his originals "Please Leave Me Alone" and "Baby Girl," and he adeptly navigates "Yardbird Suite," weaving his lines with the horn soloists. The brevity of this recording (36 minutes) will undoubtedly leave you wanting more.

influences:

◀◀ Leo Watson, Coleman Hawkins, Lester Young, Charlie Parker, James Moody, Erroll Garner

▶▶ Lambert, Hendricks & Ross, the Manhattan Transfer, Mark Murphy

Nancy Ann Lee

Herb Jeffries

Born September 24, 1916, in Detroit, MI.

Herb Jeffries wasn't really a jazz vocalist, but he sang with a number of big bands in the 1930s, culminating in a two-year stint with Duke Ellington (1940–42). He struck on his singing style while doing an imitation of Bing Crosby for some members of the Ellington band, and they encouraged him to keep that sound. A deep, rich baritone, Jeffries is a fine singer of swing tunes and ballads, though he's not an improvisor and doesn't really swing on up-tempo numbers. Jeffries worked with Erskine Tate in the early 1930s, spent a number of years in Chicago with Earl Hines (1931–34), and toured with Blanche Calloway (Cab's sister) before finding a niche in Hollywood starring as the Bronze Buckaroo in a series of black westerns. He is the last surviving member of Ellington's most innovative orchestra, known as the Webster/Blanton band, with whom Jeffries scored the huge hit "Flamingo." Since leaving Ellington in 1942, he's worked as a solo act, and has continued to perform through the 1990s.

what to buy: An anthology spanning 1934 to 1995, *A Brief History of Herb Jeffries: The Bronze Buckaroo* ♪♪♪♪♪ (Warner Western, 1995, prod. various) is an eclectic set covering everything from cowboy tunes from his 1930s Westerns, to songs recorded with Earl Hines and Sidney Bechet, to four numbers with the great early 1940s Ellington orchestra, including "Jump for Joy" and "Flamingo." Hardly essential music for a jazz collection, but Jeffries makes effective use of his warm and engaging baritone, right up through the tracks recorded in 1995.

what to buy next: With unobtrusive arrangements by Russ Garcia, *Say It Isn't So* ♪♪♪♪ (Bethlehem, 1957, prod. Red Clyde) is an enjoyable Jeffries set featuring a dozen romantic standards and ballads. Not really a jazz date, Jeffries croons tunes such as "Ghost of a Chance" and "Angel Eyes," sounding like Bing Crosby in a mellow mood. A fascinating album that explores the intersection of jazz with country and western music, *The Bronze Buckaroo Rides Again* ♪♪♪♪ (Warner Western, 1995, prod. Jim Ed Norman) features Jeffries singing 10 swing cowboy tunes, including four he wrote himself. From Benny Carter's classic "Cow Cow Boogie" to Gene Autry's "Back in the Saddle Again," this music is full of surprising connections between genres long thought to be polar opposites.

influences:

◀◀ Bing Crosby, Billy Eckstine

Andrew Gilbert

Leroy Jenkins

Born March 11, 1932, in Chicago, IL.

That hazy, categorical Never-Never Land between free jazz and avant-garde classical music counts violinist Leroy Jenkins as one of its model citizens. A major force for adventurous music since the mid-1960s, when he was teaching in Chicago's public school system by day and playing with members of the burgeoning Association for the Advancement of Creative Musicians by night, Jenkins has performed with a veritable who's-who of modern jazz players while steadily moving into venerated (yet viable) elder-statesman status. By the late '60s Jenkins had moved to Europe, where his brand of eclecticism was better received. While living in Paris he became a founding member of the Creative Construction Company (along with Anthony Braxton, Leo Smith, and Steve McCall) and spent time playing with Ornette Coleman. Returning to the States in 1970 he performed with a wide variety of cutting-edge musicians like Cecil Taylor, Archie Shepp, and Rahsaan Roland Kirk before forming the Revolutionary Ensemble. This trio (composed of Jenkins, bassist Sirone, and percussionist Jerome Cooper) became an artistic force within the new music community—an aesthetic success and a commercial disaster. Since the breakup of the Revolutionary Ensemble, Jenkins has continued making strong, impassioned music with his own small groups and with other like-minded souls. He has also dipped more into the classical end of his performance spectrum with operas and works for chamber ensembles, string quartets and string quintets.

what to buy: Computer Minds is the moniker of Jenkins's group for *Leroy Jenkins Live!* 🎵🎵🎵🎵 (Black Saint, 1993, prod. Leroy Jenkins), and the ensemble features the violinist along with an electrified quartet of guitar, drums, synthesizer, and bass. The energy level throughout is taut yet explosive, with special kudos to "Static in the Attic" and "Computer Minds." Technically speaking, the live *Themes & Improvisations on the Blues* 🎵🎵🎵🎵 (CRI, 1994, prod. Leroy Jenkins) fits more into the avant-garde classical realm, but Jenkins allows his players space to improvise a substantial amount of the time, and these flights of fancy are close enough to jazz to pass muster.

what to buy next: *Urban Blues* 🎵🎵🎵 (Black Saint, 1984, prod. Leroy Jenkins) may still be the place for many beginning listeners to break into the Jenkins experience. With two violins, two guitars, bass, and drums, Jenkins got as commercial with this ensemble as he would ever get. The funk veers off into esoterica at times, but this live recording captures some of the excitement this band could generate on a good night. An earlier version of "Static in the Attic" is the nominal hit here. *Lifelong Ambitions* 🎵🎵🎵 (Black Saint, 1981, prod. Marty Khan), an album of duets with pianist Muhal Richard Abrams, is filled with virtuoso squeaks, squawks, bangs, and strums in the service of art, albeit a tad difficult for the general public to grasp. Still, anyone interested in the acoustic avant garde could do far worse than to start with this performance by two talented and committed artists. "The Blues" and "The Father, the Son, the Holy Ghost" would be the "hits" if such a term could be used properly when considering music of this type.

the rest:
Solo Concert 🎵🎵🎵🎵 (India Navigation, 1977)
The Legend of Ai Gatson 🎵🎵🎵 (Black Saint, 1978)
Mixed Quintet 🎵🎵🎵🎵 (Black Saint, 1983)

influences:
◀◀ Eddie South, Jascha Heifetz, Cecil Taylor
▶▶ Billy Bang, the Soldier String Quartet

Garaud MacTaggart

Ingrid Jensen

Born 1966, in North Vancouver, British Columbia, Canada.

Ingrid Jensen is a top-flight trumpeter with impressive credentials—and her fluegelhorn work may be even better. After graduating from Malaspina College in Canada and Berklee in Boston, Jensen toured with the Vienna Art Orchestra, taught at Austria's Bruckner Conservatory, worked with the Maria Schneider Orchestra, and played trumpet with New York's all-female big band, DIVA. She has also won a Juno award in Canada for "Best Mainstream Album of 1995" in addition to winning the Carmen Caruso International Jazz Solo Trumpet Competition. Jensen's playing has taken pointers from some of the post-bop masters and combines fluid grace with intelligent use of space, winning plaudits from Clark Terry and Art Farmer, among others.

what's available: *Vernal Fields* 🎵🎵🎵 (Enja, 1995, prod. Matthias Winckelmann, Alexander Zivkovic) is a good first effort. Jensen wrote "Skookum Spook," a work for muted trumpet that owes much to early Columbia-era Miles Davis and mid-'60s Blue Note grooves.

influences:
◀◀ Miles Davis, Woody Shaw, Art Farmer

Garaud MacTaggart

Jeru the Damaja

Born Kendrick Jeru Davis, in Brooklyn, NY.

Jeru's deep, dexterous flow over a Charles Mingus bassline on Gang Starr's "I'm the Man" made an indelible imprint on the minds of underground hip-hop heads. So when his cutting, dungeon-esque DJ Premier–produced "Come Clean" was released on the first *Ill Kids* collection released by Gang Starr's Guru, it became more than just a hit record; it (eventually) blew up into one of hip-hop's last true classics. Since he came clean, Jeru has commandeered a nouveau consciousness in music, championing the causes of intelligence, spirituality, and dignity in hip-hop. Jeru, however, hasn't been absent from controversy, scuffling with journalists and engaging in lyrical battles with the Fugees. Still, the self-styled guardian of hip-hop remains one of the few MCs who, once on the microphone, actually has something to say.

what to buy: Released a year after "Come Clean" hit the underground, Jeru's debut album, *The Sun Rises in the East* 🎵🎵🎵🎵 (Payday/ffrr, 1994, prod. DJ Premier) rose above the hip-hop heap not only on the strength of its ideas and rhymes, but also with the help of DJ Premier's beat creation. (Considered to be at his creative pinnacle, Premier actually outdid himself on the closing track "Static" by rocking a loop out of the revolving static found at the end of a record.) Lyrically, Jeru created such hip-hop mainstays as "Mind Spray" and "Can't Stop the Prophet," a superhero battle between Jeru and personified villains like Jealousy and Ignorance.

Antonio Carlos Jobim (r) with Frank Sinatra (**Archive Photos**)

what to buy next: *The Wrath of the Math* 🎵🎵🎵 (Payday/ffrr, 1996, prod. DJ Premier) is a creative letdown, as the majority of the songs are either "sequels" or tracks that were previously on compilations ("Frustrated Nigga," "Invasion"). Many of the songs aren't too compelling, but those that do work do so tremendously: in "Black Cowboy," Jeru engages in some verbal sparring with a few other rappers, and in "One Day," he rescues hip-hop from those who have kidnapped it. Jeru also denounces rappers he thinks are superficial and materialistic on "Ya Playin' Ya Self" as Premier cleverly flips the bassline and cowbell used in Junior M.A.F.I.A.'s "Player's Anthem," leaving no room to guess exactly who is being indicted.

worth searching for: Originally assembled for the soundtrack to Spike Lee's *Crooklyn*, the all-star Crooklyn Dodgers trio returned with an all-new lineup for Lee's *Clockers*. The resultant song, "Return of the Crooklyn Dodgers" (MCA, 1995), features one of Jeru's most poignant verses, along with the resurrection of Chubb Rock and a contribution from the always rock-steady OC.

influences:

⏮ Gang Starr, KRS-One

Jazzbo

Antonio Carlos Jobim

Born January 25, 1927, in Rio de Janeiro, Brazil. Died December 8, 1994, in New York, NY.

Antonio Carlos Jobim has had a tremendous influence on the development of Brazilian jazz in the United States and around the globe. Jobim studied piano as a child and was a classically trained musician who started his career in music in 1954 with a 78-rpm release on the Continental label in his native Brazil. Gifted as a composer, guitarist, pianist, and vocalist, Jobim—originally an architect—gained a high profile in his home country when he wrote "Desafinado," which was recorded in Brazil by João Gilberto in 1957. Collaborating with Gilberto and others, Jobim mounted a serious challenge to the rhythms of the samba, earning an international reputation when he and Luiz Bonfa wrote the score for the 1959 film *Orfeo Negro* (*Black Orpheus*).

In the early 1960s, Jobim became the leading force of a new trend in music. Not content to simply reiterate the sounds of the samba, Jobim slowed down the tempo and added some twists and turns to the music. One of his main influences at the time came from America's West Coast cool-jazz sounds being created by musicians such as Chet Baker and Gerry Mulligan. Jobim's music was also augmented by the harmonic sensibilities of the French classical composer Claude Debussy, and from this hybrid of influences came what was called the *bossa nova* or "new stream." As the growing Brazilian record industry began to export to the United States, Jobim's music began to attract the attention of jazz musicians such as Charlie Byrd, who first heard the bossa nova while on tour in Brazil in 1961 and upon his return recorded an album with Stan Getz that included Jobim's "Desafinado." Although Jobim included "The Girl from Ipanema" on his own 1963 Verve album, *The Composer of Desafinado Plays*, it is the vocal version featuring Astrud Gilberto on the 1963 Stan Getz record, *Getz and Gilberto*, that remains the most popular rendition.

Jobim's invitation to be included in a showcase of Brazilian musicians in New York City in 1962 gained him an international recognition and helped to catapult him to stardom as the leader of the new musical movement. Byrd and Getz became big fans of the musical style and recorded many of Jobim's compositions on albums in the early 1960s. Countless other jazz artists continue to perform and record Jobim compositions, and his ineradicable contributions continue even after his death.

what to buy: *The Man from Ipanema* 𝄞𝄞𝄞𝄞 (Verve, 1995, prod. Creed Taylor) is a deluxe three-CD set that covers the best of Jobim's career, especially classics such as "Desafinado," "Corcovado," "The Girl from Ipanema," "Dindi," and others. The first disc is made up of vocal works, the second features instrumentals, and the third contains numerous alternate takes on many of his most popular works. This is an essential collection that includes a 60-page booklet with biographical information as well as an interview with the artist. Lovingly assembled, this is a treat for both the ears and eyes. *Volume 13: Verve Jazz Masters* 𝄞𝄞𝄞𝄞 (Verve, 1993, prod. various) is a briefer introduction to Jobim's work distilled onto one CD, yet provides another excellent introduction to his music.

what to buy next: *The Composer of Desafinado Plays* 𝄞𝄞𝄞 (Verve, 1963, prod. Creed Taylor) is Jobim's original album featuring "The Girl from Ipanema" (sans Astrud Gilberto's vocals).

Smooth, slick, and brimming with the hallmarks of Jobim's ideas, *Wave* 𝄞𝄞𝄞𝄞 (A&M, 1967/1989, prod. Creed Taylor) and *Tide* 𝄞𝄞𝄞𝄞 (A&M, 1970/1996, prod. Creed Taylor) are two albums almost always considered as a pair. *Urubu* 𝄞𝄞𝄞 (Warner Bros., 1976/1996, prod. Claus Ogerman) is an often-overlooked album, yet it's a showcase for Jobim's more serious music, featuring arrangements by Ogerman.

best of the rest:
Stone Flower 𝄞𝄞𝄞 (CTI, 1971/Sony, 1990)
Terra Brasilis 𝄞𝄞𝄞 (Warner Bros., 1980/1996)
Passarim 𝄞𝄞𝄞 (Verve, 1987)
Personalidade 𝄞𝄞𝄞 (Verve, 1987/1993)
Antonio Carlos Jobim: Composer 𝄞𝄞𝄞 (Warner Bros., 1996)

worth searching for: *Francis Albert Sinatra & Antonio Carlos Jobim* 𝄞𝄞𝄞𝄞 (Reprise, 1967/1988, prod. Sonny Burke) pairs Jobim with the Chairman of the Board. It's a divine album, falling short of perfection only because it clocks in at a measly 28:33.

influences:

◀◀ Gerry Mulligan, Chet Baker

▶▶ Stan Getz, Charlie Byrd, Cal Tjader, Sergio Mendes, Herbie Mann, Flora Purim, Airto

Chris Meloche and Nancy Ann Lee

Budd Johnson

Born Albert J. Johnson, December 14, 1910, in Dallas, TX. Died October 20, 1984, in Kansas City, MO.

Although initially influenced by swing era giant Lester Young, tenor saxophonist Budd Johnson would combine Young's light and swinging approach with a huskier sound and swagger that was uniquely his own. While still in his early 20s, Johnson made his recording debut with Louis Armstrong and during the 1930s and 1940s gigged with such stalwarts as Earl Hines and Fletcher Henderson. What would set Johnson aside from other players of his time was his interest in the developing bebop movement of the late 1940s. While he could be found recording and working with Coleman Hawkins and Dizzy Gillespie, he also was at home in the more mainstream settings of Benny Goodman and Snub Mosley. His gifts as an arranger and composer also placed many of his charts in the books of Woody Herman, Buddy Rich, and Billy Eckstine. Beginning in 1960, Johnson became active in the big bands of Quincy Jones and Count Basie. In addition, he would be part of Jones's group that toured Europe with the production of *Free and Easy*. Johnson led many valuable recording dates over the years for a variety of small labels such as Felsted, Argo/Cadet, Riverside, Prestige, and Uptown. Unfortunately, the majority of these works remain long out-of-print. Prior to his death in 1984, Johnson was working as a teacher and had recorded an excellent album with alto saxophonist Phil Woods that proved he still had much more to say as a musician and composer.

what's available: *Let's Swing* ♫♫♫ (Swingville, 1960/OJC, 1993, prod. Esmond Edwards) finds Johnson working with his trombonist brother Keg on an excellent set of pieces. The crystalline piano work of Tommy Flanagan adds much to this recording, which in addition to being one of Johnson's finest moments is also one of the best albums from Prestige's Swingville series. Regrettably, this is Johnson's only in-print compact disc.

worth searching for: *Budd Johnson & the Four Brass Giants* ♫♫♫ (Riverside, 1960, prod. Cannonball Adderley) is the best all-around set for appreciating not only Johnson's tenor work but also his immense composing and arranging talents. Although previously reissued on vinyl, it is currently out of print. *The Ole Dude and the Fundance Kid* ♫♫♫ (Uptown, 1984, prod. Bob Sunenblick) was Johnson's last recording before his death, yet you'd hardly know the end was near with the spirit and camaraderie that pervades this bristling session.

influences:

◀◀ Lester Young, Coleman Hawkins, Ben Webster

Chris Hovan

Buddy Johnson
Born Woodrow Wilson Johnson, January 10, 1915, in Darlington, SC. Died February 9, 1977, in New York, NY.

Pianist, songwriter, vocalist, and band leader Buddy Johnson led a very popular and influential swing big band that after World War II played a major role in the rise of rhythm and blues music. His band was characterized by a walking rhythm that made them a favorite for dancers. Characterized by clean ensemble work, the band featured interesting arrangements and first-rate solos, usually by saxophonist Purvis Henson. Sister Ella Johnson was main vocalist of the band and was popular for her naive-sounding vocals. Arthur Prysock was also discovered by Johnson.

Johnson recorded for Decca from 1939 to 1952, when he signed with Mercury. Johnson was able to adapt to changing musical tastes and continued to have hit recordings in the early rock-and-roll days. In the 1960s he recorded a session for Roulette, and his 1964 session for Old Town was his last. His big band, which served as the house band for Allen Freed's rock-and-roll dance parties, survived well into the 1950s, playing countless one-nighters. A number of Johnson's songs have become pop standards and have been recorded by such diverse artists as Annie Laurie (with Paul Gayten), Lou Rawls, Ruth Brown, and Muddy Waters. Johnson retired from music in the early 1960s and devoted his remaining years to church activities. He became a minister before dying from cancer in 1977.

what to buy: *Walk 'Em: The Decca Sessions* ♫♫♫♫ (Decca, 1941–1952, prod. various/Ace/UK, 1996, compilation prod. Richard Tapp, John Broven) is a wonderful collection of 24 performances that includes the original recordings of "Since I Fell for You," "Baby You're Always on My Mind," "Satisfy My Soul," and "That's the Stuff You Got to Watch" (wonderfully sung by Sister Ella), Arthur Prysock's "They Say I'm Your Biggest Fool," and Buddy's vocal on "Fine Brown Frame." "Boogie Woogie's Mother-in-Law" features Leonard Ware's slashing guitar.

the rest:

The Chronological Buddy Johnson 1939–1941 ♫♫♫ (Classics, 1996)

worth searching for: *Buddy and Ella Johnson 1953–1964* ♫♫♫♫ (Bear Family, 1992, reissue prod. Richard Wieze) is a four-disc boxed set by a German company, with all the recordings Johnson made after leaving Decca, and including plenty of terrific instrumentals and ballads from Ella.

Ron Weinstock

Bunk Johnson
Born Willie Geary Johnson, December 27, 1879 or 1889, in New Orleans, LA. Died July 27, 1949, in New Iberia, LA.

One of the few contemporaries of the legendary-yet-never-recorded Buddy Bolden, trumpeter and cornetist Bunk Johnson is a link to the music that immediately predated New Orleans jazz in style and repertoire. He was active in New Orleans shortly after the turn of the century when jazz was gelling, and he played on tours throughout the South. Blues, rags, marches, and folk music all found a place in Johnson's interpretations. When waves of musicians left the Crescent City for California or Chicago, Johnson was among the core who stayed home. He disappeared from music in the early 1930s but was "rediscovered" around 1940. He made his first recordings ever in 1942 and rode a wave of popularity during a Dixieland revival that rose up in reaction to bebop. The quality of his playing is uneven on recorded material—some days he was on and others he wasn't. When he was hitting it, Johnson was a master interpreter of the blues.

what to buy: *Bunk Johnson and His Superior Jazz Band* 🎵🎵🎵🎵 (Good Time Jazz, 1942) is his first recording and contains his memorable lineup that included George Lewis and Jim Robinson. It broke with what most people had identified as "Dixieland" music and includes some spoken history from Johnson. *The King of the Blues* 🎵🎵🎵🎵 (American Music, 1989) keeps the same horns and adds stars Baby Dodds and Alcide Pavageau to the rhythm section for some of Johnson's most engaging play.

what to buy next: *Bunk Johnson in San Francisco* 🎵🎵🎵🎵 (American Music, 1991) is a treasure because it includes six duets with pianist Bertha Gonsoulin that clearly display Johnson's significant brass skills without the usual ensemble distractions.

best of the rest:
Bunk and Lou 🎵🎵🎵🎵 (Good Time Jazz, 1944)
Second Masters 🎵🎵🎵🎵 (American Music, 1944)
Bunk Johnson 1944 🎵🎵🎵🎵🎵 (American Music, 1944)
Bunk's Brass Band and Dance Band 🎵🎵🎵🎵 (American Music, 1945)
Bunk Johnson and Mutt Carey in New York 🎵🎵🎵 (American Music, 1947)
The Last Testament of a Great Jazzman 🎵🎵🎵🎵 (CBS, 1974)
Bechet, Bunk and Boston 1945 🎵🎵🎵🎵 (Jazz Archives, 1981)

worth searching for: Johnson's recordings are hard to find, so if you come across Sidney Bechet's *Jazz Nocturne* 🎵🎵🎵 (Fat Cats Jazz, 1982) check it out. Even though Johnson isn't in top form, he's not bad, and you get to hear Bechet's excellent clarinet and soprano work.

influences:
⏩ Freddie Keppard, Kid Rena, Louis Armstrong

Larry Gabriel

Henry Johnson

Born January 1, 1954, in Chicago, IL.

If there is a second coming of George Benson, Henry Johnson is probably it. Both are outstanding guitarists influenced by Wes Montgomery and Kenny Burrell; both played with Jack McDuff; both are excellent jazz players; both love to play R&B; both travel back and forth between mainstream and R&B, depending on the occasion. They both even sing (though Benson wins that category hands down). Raised in Chicago, Johnson was playing guitar for Isaac Hayes by the time he was 14. In 1979 he started long-standing associations with Ramsey Lewis and Joe Williams. A versatile sideman, Johnson has also played with Angela Bofill, the Boston Pops, Count Basie Orchestra, Dizzy

Gillespie, Freddie Hubbard, Jimmy Smith, the Spinners, Stanley Turrentine, and Nancy Wilson. His solo releases are a bit erratic, mixing straight-ahead and R&B-based jazz, usually favoring the later, but he is very strong in the former.

what to buy: *New Beginnings* 🎵🎵🎵 (Heads Up, 1993, prod. Henry Johnson) is a nicely arranged record with a lot of Wes Montgomery influence, even on the pop material. Johnson's playing is very strong, and the take of "Tell Me a Bedtime Story" is straight from the George Benson handbook.

the rest:
Missing You 🎵🎵🎵 (Heads Up, 1994)

influences:
⏪ Kenny Burrell, Grant Green, George Benson, Wes Montgomery

Paul MacArthur

Howard Johnson

Born August 7, 1941, in Montgomery, AL.

A sideman's sideman, Howard Johnson boasts credits that include just about everyone from Carla Bley, Gil Evans, Charles Mingus, and Archie Shepp to John Lennon and the Band, but he didn't get to record as a leader until the '90s. Johnson is a pungently soulful baritone saxophonist, which makes him a mainstay with the likes of Hank Crawford and David (Fathead) Newman. But on the tuba he's been trailblazer, both as an individual performer and as leader of his long-standing tubas-plus-rhythm section group, Gravity, which even showed up in blues singer Taj Mahal's band, for which Johnson wrote brass arrangements.

what's available: *Gravity!!!* 🎵🎵🎵 (Verve, 1996, prod. Suzi Reynolds, Howard Johnson) is direct, soulful, and swinging, despite the big brass ballast.

worth searching for: The Gil Evans Monday Night Orchestra's *Live at Sweet Basil, Volume 1* 🎵🎵🎵🎵 (Gramavision, 1975/Evidence, 1992, prod. Shigeyuki Kawashima, Horst Liepolt) displays Johnson's most striking role as a sideman: playing the guitar riff of Jimi Hendrix's "Voodoo Chile" on tuba. Taj Mahal's two-LP live set *The Real Thing* 🎵🎵🎵🎵 (Columbia, prod. David Rubinson) features Gravity prominently and funkily.

influences:
⏪ Harry Carney, Clifford Brown, Gil Evans
⏩ Bob Stewart, Marcus Rojas

W. Kim Heron

J.J. Johnson

Born James Louis Johnson, January 22, 1924, in Indianapolis, IN.

In the history of jazz there have been dozens of innovators on instruments like piano, saxophone, and the drums. But when you think of jazz trombone, only a handful of names are likely to come to mind, and probably the one that tops most peoples' lists is J.J. Johnson. He made his first appearance during a time of great musical change, and the innovations of players like Charlie Parker and Dizzy Gillespie inspired him to develop his own playing in a way that changed perceptions about the place of trombone in jazz. No longer was it merely a joke instrument, good only for funny effects in swing bands; Johnson legitimized the trombone as a worthy sound for bop and beyond. He first started playing in 1938, after a brief study of piano, but quickly established himself. Within three years Johnson began touring with bands led by Clarence Love and Isaac "Snookum" Russell, where he met Fats Navarro, whose trumpet style would have a direct influence on his own playing. He graduated to Benny Carter's orchestra in 1942, contributing arrangements in addition to his increasingly distinctive soloing. He was invited to perform at the debut Jazz at the Philharmonic concert in 1944 and joined the Count Basie Orchestra a year later. Relocating to New York, Johnson found himself in constant demand, performing with Bud Powell, Miles Davis, Parker, Gillespie, and many others. He even toured Korea in a USO band with Oscar Petiford in 1951. His financial situation was tight, however, and in 1952 he was forced to quit performing in order to work full-time as a blueprint inspector. Johnson soon returned to the music world, teaming up with fellow trombonist Kai Winding in 1954 for what would be a quite successful pairing. The duo, recording under the name of Jay and Kai, recorded a series of popular albums that further established Johnson as the premiere trombonist of his day. In 1956 Johnson formed his own quintet and toured extensively, all the while starting to focus on composing as well as playing, offering epic works like "Perceptions" to Gillespie. For the next decade, he would continue to perform and record, but his compositional ambitions began to dominate his time, and by the late '60s, he had quit performing altogether and eventually moved to Los Angeles to write for film and TV, contributing music for shows like *The Mod Squad*. Absence has made the heart grow fonder, and despite his inactivity as a player, Johnson's stature has only risen, with the result that he is now generally regarded as the best jazz trombonist of all time. He has become more visible lately, recording every now and again with a live appearance or two thrown in for good measure. But his position among the greats is already firmly established. Johnson began his career playing with such speed and clarity that people often assumed he was using a valve trombone, as opposed to a slide. Sometimes this reliance on technique came at the expense of inventiveness, and his soloing had a tendency to sound repetitious. When he began to seriously study composition and arranging in the late '50s, Johnson further developed his sound, adding a cooler, more pensive timbre to his playing that took him beyond mere bebop stylings, a move that can be heard clearly in his big-band recordings from the mid-'60s.

what to buy: Ironically, *The Great Kai and Jay* ♫♫♫♫ (Impulse!, 1961, prod. Creed Taylor), Johnson's best collection of tracks with fellow trombonist Kai Winding, came after their glory days as Jay and Kai. What distinguishes this set is a more mature playing style, a better selection of songs, and elegant soloing; the presence of Bill Evans and Paul Chambers helps too. *Proof Positive* ♫♫♫♫ (Impulse!, 1964, prod. Bob Thiele) shows the trombonist at the height of his powers, particularly on "Minor Blues" and "Lullaby of Jazzland," featuring great backing from McCoy Tyner, Elvin Jones, and Toots Thielemans on guitar. *The Eminent Jay Jay Johnson, Volume 1* ♫♫♫♫ (Blue Note, 1953, prod. Alfred Lion) is good early work from Johnson and gets the nod over *Volume 2*, mainly for the presence of Clifford Brown's peerless trumpet. *Pinnacles* ♫♫♫♫ (Milestone, 1980, prod. Ed Michel), Johnson's first studio album in over a decade, makes clear that he still has the chops and demonstrates that he can play in a more contemporary setting as well.

what to buy next: *The Trombone Master* ♫♫♫♫ (Columbia, 1957–60/1989, prod. George Avakian, Teo Macero) is a worthy sampler of the best of Johnson's post–Jay and Kai Columbia records. Another great compilation, *Say When* ♫♫♫♫ (Bluebird, 1964–66/1987, prod. Jack Somer, Brad McCuen) covers Johnson's mid-'60s big bands.

what to avoid: If you are a *really* big fan of jazz trombone, then *Four Trombones: The Debut Recordings* ♫♫ (Debut, 1953/Prestige, 1981) may suit your fancy; otherwise your attention is likely to flag after a couple of selections from this workshop jam session, despite the presence of Charles Mingus and John Lewis.

the rest:
Mad Bebop ♫♫♫ (Savoy, 1946)
J.J. Johnson's Jazz Quintets ♫♫♫ (Savoy, 1946/1996)
Early Bones ♫♫♫♫ (Prestige, 1949)
Jay & Kai ♫♫♫ (Savoy, 1954/1996)
The Eminent Jay Jay Johnson Volume 2 ♫♫♫♫ (Blue Note, 1954–55)
Trombone for Two ♫♫♫ (Columbia, 1955)
Jay & Kai ♫♫♫ (Columbia, 1956)
Jay & Kai Plus 6 ♫♫♫ (Columbia, 1956)

Jay & Kai at Newport 𝄞𝄞𝄞 (Columbia, 1956)

J Is for Jazz 𝄞𝄞𝄞 (Columbia, 1956)

Dial J.J. 𝄞𝄞𝄞𝄞 (Columbia, 1957)

First Place 𝄞𝄞𝄞𝄞 (Columbia, 1957)

Blue Trombone 𝄞𝄞𝄞𝄞 (Columbia, 1957)

J.J. in Person 𝄞𝄞𝄞𝄞 (Columbia, 1958)

Really Livin' 𝄞𝄞𝄞 (Columbia, 1959)

Trombone & Voices 𝄞𝄞𝄞 (Columbia, 1960)

A Touch of Satin 𝄞𝄞𝄞 (Columbia, 1960)

J.J.'s Broadway 𝄞𝄞𝄞 (Verve, 1963)

Israel 𝄞𝄞𝄞 (A&M, 1968)

Betwixt and Between 𝄞𝄞𝄞 (A&M, 1969)

Stonebone 𝄞𝄞𝄞𝄞 (A&M Japan, 1969)

The Yokohama Concert 𝄞𝄞𝄞 (Pablo, 1977)

Concepts in Blue 𝄞𝄞𝄞𝄞 (Pablo, 1980)

We'll Be Together Again 𝄞𝄞𝄞𝄞 (Pablo, 1983)

Things Are Getting Better All the Time 𝄞𝄞𝄞𝄞 (Pablo, 1984)

Quintergy: Live at the Village Vanguard 𝄞𝄞𝄞𝄞 (Antilles, 1991)

Standards: Live at the Village Vanguard 𝄞𝄞𝄞𝄞 (Antilles, 1991)

Vivian 𝄞𝄞𝄞 (Concord, 1992)

Let's Hang Out 𝄞𝄞𝄞𝄞 (Verve, 1993)

Tangence 𝄞𝄞𝄞 (Verve, 1995)

The Brass Orchestra 𝄞𝄞𝄞𝄞 (Verve, 1997)

worth searching for: A well-rehearsed band, including a hot Freddie Hubbard, supports Johnson through *J.J. Inc.* 𝄞𝄞𝄞𝄞 (Columbia, 1960, prod. Teo Macero), a dynamic set of his own compositions, most notably "Mohawk" and the moody "Aquarius."

influences:

◀◀ Fats Navarro, Fred Beckett

▶▶ Kai Winding, Steve Turre, Howard Johnson

Eric J. Lawrence

James P. (Price) Johnson

Born February 1, 1894 (or 1891), in New Brunswick, NJ. Died November 17, 1955.

James P. Johnson is known as the father of stride piano, a demanding style in which the right hand plays the melody while the left hand pumps away like a piston between bass notes and chords. A sophisticated musician with a broad range of influences, from ragtime and blues to classical music, he established himself early on as one of the best pianists (and arguably the best pianist) in New York.

Johnson made piano rolls in 1916 and his first record in 1917. He was the music director for Bessie Smith's film *St. Louis Blues,* wrote Broadway shows and revues, and was a popular attraction at rent parties, making the rounds with Willie "The Lion"

J.J. JOHNSON
(WITH SONNY ROLLINS)

song "Wail March"

album *Sonny Rollins: Volume 2*
(Blue Note, 1957/1987)

instrument Trombone

Monster
Solo

Smith and Fats Waller. His more ambitious works, such as *Yamacraw* and a symphony, were neglected due to the lack of respect accorded black composers by the classical music world. He was slowed by health problems, but continued working until a 1951 stroke disabled him.

what to buy: *Snowy Morning Blues* 𝄞𝄞𝄞𝄞 (Decca Jazz, 1991) is a sublime collection of Johnson's best tunes. The CD's first four songs are 1930 solo recordings. They are Johnson at his Harlem Stride best, featuring "What Is this Thing Called Love?," "Crying for the Carolines," "You've Got to be Modernistic," and "Jingles." The CD's other 16 tracks are from 1944, with drummer Eddie Dougherty. These are light, airy, and immensely enjoyable Johnson originals and a selection of protégé Fats Waller's tunes, including "Honeysuckle Rose" and "Ain't Misbehavin'," played in a style anticipating Erroll Garner.

what to buy next: *Runnin' Wild (1921–1926)* 𝄞𝄞𝄞 (Tradition, 1997) captures the early stages of Johnson's career, and has some wonderful Harlem Stride classics, particularly "Carolina

Shout," "Arkansas Blues," and his joyous "Runnin' Wild Medley." *Harlem Stride Piano, 1921–1929* ♫♫♫ (Hot 'N Sweet, 1992) suffers from poor sound quality, but does feature a memorable version of "Charleston" and some nice tracks with Cootie Williams, Fats Waller, and King Oliver.

the rest:

The Chronological James P. Johnson 1921–1928 ♫♫♫ (Classics, 1992)
The Chronological James P. Johnson 1928–1938 ♫♫♫ (Classics, 1992)
The Chronological James P. Johnson 1938–1942 ♫♫♫ (Classics, 1993)

influences:

◄◄ Eubie Blake, Scott Joplin

►► Willie "The Lion" Smith, Fats Waller, Thelonious Monk, Erroll Garner, Dick Hyman

James Bradley

Marc Johnson

Born October 21, 1953, in Omaha, NE.

Johnson, one of the most tasteful bassists around, has impeccable jazz credentials. Most notably, he was in pianist Bill Evans's final trio (heard on *We Will Meet Again* and *Turn Out the Stars*) in 1978–80. Johnson first played piano and cello, taking up bass at age 16. By the time he was 19, he was playing professionally with the Fort Worth Symphony. Johnson attended the prestigious jazz college North Texas State University and then paid his dues with Woody Herman, Evans, Stan Getz, and John Abercrombie, among others. His own bands use electric guitars, but Johnson has stuck with the acoustic upright and has a big, rich tone and considerable dexterity without making a fetish of either. His mid-1980s band Bass Desires, with guitarists Bill Frisell and John Scofield and drummer Peter Erskine, did much for the reputations of all concerned, though it put out only two albums. His next documented group, Right Brain Patrol, with guitarist Ben Monder (later replaced by Wolfgang Muthspiel) and percussionist/vocalist Arto Tunçboyaciyan, didn't really contract the size of the group, as Monder sometimes overdubs guitars, but it did expand Johnson's musical concepts thanks to Tunçboyaciyan, whose vocal contributions and frequent use of non-trapset percussion (though he's also a fine traps drummer) recall Nana Vasconcelos's role on some Pat Metheny albums. And a recent Johnson quartet with Frisell, Metheny, and drummer Joey Baron recalls the Bass Desires format. The gaps in between Johnson's albums reflect his busy session schedule; he can be heard on over 100 albums.

what to buy: *Second Sight* ♫♫♫♫ (ECM, 1987, prod. Manfred Eicher) is the second Bass Desires album and far livelier than its predecessor, with some superb writing (shared fairly equally) by all members. Highlights are Erskine's "Sweet Soul" and Scofield's catchy "Twister," which set off the more atmospheric mood pieces by providing contrast. *Right Brain Patrol* ♫♫♫♫ (JMT, 1992, prod. Lee Townsend) debuted the subtle and versatile trio with Monder and Tunçboyaciyan. Johnson's singing tone on his acoustic bass makes him the star without resort to flash, and Monder recalls the spaciness of Metheny and Frisell, but bluesier. The compositions and arrangements (mostly by Johnson and Tunçboyaciyan) move easily from mellow soundscapes to gently grooving world music.

what to buy next: *The Sound of Summer Running* ♫♫♫♫ (Verve, 1998, prod. Lee Townsend) features a quartet with guitarists Bill Frisell and Pat Metheny and drummer Joey Baron, but unlike Bass Desires, this group focuses on Johnson's compositions (though the guitarists contribute a few numbers). This is a major document in the "heartland" movement of songful, simple writing that communicates directly. At times the mood stays mellow for too long, meandering a bit, but overall this is a beautiful record.

the rest:

Bass Desires ♫♫♫♪ (ECM, 1986)
Two by Four ♫♫♪ (EmArcy, 1991)

worth searching for: *Magic Labyrinth* ♫♫♫♪ (JMT, 1995, prod. Stefan Winter) with Right Brain Patrol is currently a casualty of Verve's takeover of JMT. Wolfgang Muthspiel replaces Monder on guitar, and the sound is more often stripped down, with Tunçboyaciyan's hand drumming propelling the music in undulating beats. Covers of Miles Davis's "Solar" and Hermeto Pascual's "Nem Um Talvez" (famous from Davis's recording) fit well in the quietly lyrical mood.

influences:

◄◄ Scott LaFaro, Charlie Haden, Pat Metheny

►► Mark Helias

Steve Holtje

Pete Johnson

Born March 24, 1904, in Kansas City, MO. Died March 23, 1967, in Buffalo, NY.

Along with Albert Ammons and Meade Lux Lewis, Pete Johnson was considered the greatest of the boogie woogie pianists and a great blues player. He was initially a drummer who learned piano from his uncle. After playing in Clarence Love's band,

Johnson, with his firm left hand, became one of Kansas City's busiest solo pianists. He met blues-shouter Joe Turner in the early 1930s, and the pair began their long residence at Sunset Crystal Palace. Producer John Hammond heard them and invited them to New York. Johnson participated in the famous "From Spirituals to Swing" concerts produced by Hammond at Carnegie Hall, backing Turner, and playing with Ammons and Lewis as the Boogie Woogie Trio. The Boogie Woogie Trio and Joe Turner were also a sensation at New York's Cafe Society, and made the first of many recordings. Johnson moved to the West Coast from 1945 to 1950, then to Buffalo, New York, working often outside the music business.

what to buy: Two compilation albums contain some of Pete Johnson's finest playing and historic performances from his Kansas City musical associates. *The Chronological Pete Johnson 1938–1939* 🎵🎵🎵 (Classics, 1992), the first in the series of reissued recordings, combines his early Vocalion and Decca recordings, and *The Chronological Pete Johnson 1939–1941* 🎵🎵🎵 (Classics, 1992, prod. various), the second in the series, contains sides from his Blue Note, Decca, and Victor recordings. As added bonuses, the 1938–1939 sides contain Johnson piano solos from Don Whaley's Solo Art label, the Vocalion recordings of Joe Turner's "Roll 'Em Pete," and a jump-band session featuring Joe Turner's classic first recording of "Cherry Red" backed by trumpeter Hot Lips Page and saxophonist Buster Smith. The 1939–1941 set contains Joe Turner's Decca recording of "Piney Brown Blues" with a small group including Hot Lips Page and Don Byas, and Victor sides that feature eight breathtaking, two-piano romps with fellow Boogie-master Albert Ammons, backed by a drummer. Their playing off each other and interweaving of leads is thrilling on "Boogie Woogie Man."

the rest:
Pete's Blues 🎵🎵🎵 (Savoy, 1946)
Central Avenue Boogie (Delmark, 1994) 🎵🎵🎵
The Chronological Pete Johnson 1944–1946 🎵🎵🎵 (Classics, 1997, prod. various)

worth searching for: Most Pete Johnson albums are compilations he made, with the exception of *Pete's Blues* on Savoy. Some of his greatest piano playing is as an accompanist to Joe Turner. *The Boss of the Blues* 🎵🎵🎵🎵 (Atlantic, 1956, prod. Nesuhi Ertegun, Jerry Wexler) reunited Johnson and Turner with a terrific group of swing-band veterans. Johnson is superb, particularly on "Roll 'Em Pete" and "Cherry Red." Joe Turner with Pete Johnson's Orchestra appears on *Tell Me Pretty Baby* 🎵🎵🎵 (Swingtime, 1948–49, prod. Jack Lauderdale/Arhoolie, 1992,

prod. Chris Strachwitz), which gathers classic recordings, including four Johnson instrumentals from the Swingtime label, a seminal Black-owned label. *Boogie Woogie Boys 1938–1944* 🎵🎵🎵 (Magpie (UK), 1994, reissue) is an invaluable reissue that includes seven previously unissued Johnson (Ammons and Lewis) tracks taken from acetate recordings of the Carnegie Hall "From Spirituals to Swing" concerts, the eight Victor duets by Johnson and Ammons, and ten duets by Ammons and Johnson recorded originally for McGregor transcriptions. *The Boogie Woogie Trio, Vol. 1* 🎵🎵🎵 (Storyville 1994, reissue) is another valuable reissue with 10 recordings by the Boogie Woogie Trio originally on McGregor transcriptions, four 1947 concert tracks by Johnson with a rhythm section, and eight tracks by Meade Lux Lewis from radio air checks.

influences:
▶▶ Jay McShann, Big Joe Duskin, Sammy Price, Leon T. Gross (Archibald)

Ron Weinstock

Phillip Johnston /Big Trouble
Born January 22, 1955, in Chicago, IL.

Joe Ruddick, piano; Bob DeBellis, reeds; Kevin Norton, vibes, marimba, traps; David Hofstra, bass; Jeff Leff, trombone; Steve Swell, trombone; Bob Henke, trumpet; Ron Horton, trumpet.

Because he refuses to deliver the commonplace and/or expected, soprano saxophonist Phillip Johnston, who currently leads a stunning little-big-band dubbed Big Trouble, makes the kind of music many casual listeners will perceive as "difficult." But other than a penchant for outlandish pastiche and an admittedly sophisticated harmonic ear that delights in pitting his own reedy soprano against the bowels-of-the-baritone grumble of Bob DeBellis during ensemble passages, there isn't much that's negative you can say about this inspiring, adventurous band. Prior to this, Johnston fronted the ornery Microscopic Septet with Joel Forrester.

what to buy: Big Trouble's three albums are pretty much uniformly excellent. *Phillip Johnston's Big Trouble* 🎵🎵🎵 (Soul Note, 1993, prod. Phillip Johnston, Richard Dworkin) is filled with clever stylistic and generational juxtapositions. Note how Johnston's "The Invisible World" turns its nervously rockish, spinning theme into a veritable "Stompin' at the Savoy"/JATP revival replete with a Kevin Norton imitation of Gene Krupa and Bob DeBellis grandstanding on an Illinois Jacquet–intense bari solo. *Flood at the Ant Farm* ♪♪♪♪ (Soul Note, 1996, prod. Phillip Johnston, Andrew Caploe) foreshadows "Powerhouse," the tribute to the legendary Raymond Scott that awaits us at the record's end, yet remains innately Steve Lacy-like throughout. Their version of "12 Bars" retains composer Herbie Nichols's characteristic Dixieland dimensions at the same time that it sounds as if it were being played by a bunch of Venusian outcasts.

what to buy next: *The Unknown* ♪♪♪♪ (Avant, 1994, prod. Andrew Caploe, John Zorn) is a hybrid of sorts, written to accompany (and, in turn, comment upon) the action of Todd Browning's florid, silent 1927 psychological thriller set in a seedy Spanish side show and starring Lon Chaney Sr. in his final screen appearance, with an 18-year-old Joan Crawford. Johnston's score is accordingly paced—now prancing, now menacing, now mocking—and highly formalistic.

influences:

◄◄ Carla Bley, Steve Lacy, Misha Mengleberg

David Prince

Randy Johnston

Born 1956, in Detroit, MI.

Hard-bop guitarist Randy Johnston is a veteran sideman whose credentials include associations with Ira Sullivan, Della Griffin, Lou Donaldson, Etta Jones, Houston Person, Sonny Fortune, Wayne Marsh, Lionel Hampton, and Jack McDuff. Johnston began playing guitar around 1970, studied jazz at the University of Miami, and headed for New York in 1981, where he played with a variety of musicians, even backing singers Irene Reid and Della Griffin and others at various venues in uptown Harlem, where he dazzled with his blues-inflected playing. Etta Jones spotted him and recruited him for her Muse album, *Sugar*, a session in which Johnston impressed producer Houston Person to the extent that he hired Johnston to play on his albums *Why Not!* and *The Party*, which also featured organist Joey DeFrancesco. Johnston appeared on a series of Muse albums (mostly produced by Person), including Jack McDuff's *Another Real Good 'Un*, and albums by Lionel Hampton, Della Griffin, and Larry O'Neill, as well as his own albums. As a leader, Johnston owes much to Grant Green, Kenny Burrell, and Wes Montgomery. Johnston made a series of albums for Muse that are currently out of print. A good, though not exceptional player, Johnston has taught at the University of Hartford's Hart School of Music since 1987. He also taught jazz and theory at the Brooklyn Conservatory from 1982–1987.

what's available: *Somewhere in the Night* ♪♪♪♪ (HighNote, 1997, prod. Houston Person) is a pleasant straight-ahead quartet recording with some classic jazz tunes getting a good workout. Johnston is at his best playing hard bop, particularly Cannonball Adderley's "Sack of Woe." His interpretation of "I Wish I Knew How It Would Feel to Be Free" is also a winner. The ballads are fine, but Johnston is better on the up-tempo material, generating excitement with his lightning-quick picking and clean, crisp phrasing.

worth searching for: Johnston's debut album as leader, *Walk On* ♪♪♪♪ (Muse, 1992, prod. Houston Person) is worthy of a search, but it's not the best of his albums for the Muse label. Featuring an all-star assemblage with pianist Benny Green, drummer Kenny Washington, bassist Ray Drummond, and saxophonist Bill Easley, Johnston delivers classic jazz-blues tunes such as "Moanin'," "Jumpin the Blues," and the soul-jazz classic, "Please Send Me Someone to Love." On his 1997 HighNote recording he has a whole new sound, moving away from the groove-oriented, blues-inflected jazz found on this album. If you come across *Jubilation* (Muse, 1992) or *In A-Chord* (Muse, 1994) in used or sale bins, pick them up. Best is the latest date, an organ-combo session featuring guest soloist Eric Alexander (tenor sax) on three tracks, with organist Joey DeFrancesco, and drummer Mickey Roker.

influences:

◄◄ Jimi Hendrix, Charlie Parker, B.B. King, Albert King, Grant Green, George Benson, Wes Montgomery, Kenny Burrell

Paul MacArthur and Nancy Ann Lee

Elvin Jones

Born September 9, 1927, in Pontiac, MI.

Drummer Elvin Jones is one of the four or five most innovative and influential drummers in the history of jazz. A product of Detroit's healthy jazz scene during the early 1950s and a sibling of the late trumpeter Thad Jones and pianist Hank Jones, Jones started to make a name for himself upon moving to New York in 1955. His many appearances with jazz legends such as Donald Byrd, Bud Powell, Mal Waldron, Sonny Rollins, and J. J. Johnson, to name a few, would help develop his style and prepare him for his historic place as a member of the groundbreaking John Coltrane quartet. Joining Coltrane in 1960, Jones stayed with the saxophonist for five years, during which time he put on tape with Coltrane some of the most powerfully rhythmic drumming ever heard. Consult any one of these recordings (particularly the drummer's solo *tour de force*, "The Drum Thing," from Coltrane's

Elvin Jones (© Nancy Ann Lee)

Crescent) to gain insight into Jones's innovative approach, which always finds swing and energy at a maximum. Jones can be forceful, but never uncomplimentary. He favors phrases that carry across bar lines and resolve in an atypical fashion. Whether backing singer Johnny Hartman or tackling the complex music of Andrew Hill, Jones always knows how to best inspire the front-line performers.

Following his stint with Coltrane, the drummer began leading his own groups and released a number of superb albums for the Blue Note label (all currently out of print) featuring worthy saxophonists such as Joe Farrell, Frank Foster, and George Coleman. A partial list of the many talented musicians who've passed through the Elvin Jones Jazz Machine through the years includes Pepper Adams, Dave Liebman, Gene Perla, Pat LaBarbera, Steve Grossman, Sonny Fortune, Ravi Coltrane, Joshua Redman, Jan Hammer, and Nicholas Payton. While Jones has appeared on literally thousands of albums as a sideman, he also lays claim to a distinguished set of recordings under his

own name for Blue Note, Atlantic, Riverside, Impulse!, Enja, Storyville, and several other labels.

what to buy: Any of Jones's recordings with the John Coltrane Quartet are worth picking up for abundant examples of his innovative drumming. *Heavy Sounds* ♪♪♪♪ (Impulse!, 1968, prod. Bob Thiele) is a meeting of giants, with Jones and bassist Richard Davis leading a small group and engaging in some pyrotechnic duets. Frank Foster's "Raunchy Rita" finds everyone in peak form. *Youngblood* ♪♪♪♪ (Enja, 1992, prod. Matthias Winckelmann) features Jones leading a pianoless group with up-and-comers Joshua Redman, Javon Jackson, and Nicholas Payton. With the players arranged in different combinations and a choice, seven-minute drum solo, this is Jones's best recording of recent vintage.

what to buy next: *Elvin!* ♪♪♪♪ (Riverside, 1962, prod. Orrin Keepnews) was the drummer's first date as a leader. Although less dramatic than one might expect, this is an above-average

date well worth checking out. *Dear John C.* ♫♫♫ (Impulse!, 1965, prod. Bob Thiele) shows how well Jones could communicate in a more relaxed and mainstream environment. Bassist Richard Davis and alto saxophonist Charlie Mariano contribute some excellent solos.

the rest:

Very R.A.R.E. ♫♫♫ (Evidence, 1978)
Reunited ♫♫♫ (Evidence, 1982)
The Elvin Jones Jazz Machine in Europe ♫♫♫ (Enja, 1991)
It Don't Mean a Thing ♫♫♫ (Enja, 1993)

worth searching for: *Illumination!* ♫♫♫ (Impulse!, 1963, prod. Bob Thiele) is a fiery sextet date with McCoy Tyner and Jimmy Garrison and a front line that includes avant garde stalwarts Charles Davis, Sonny Simmons, and Prince Lasha. This is Jones's greatest record as a leader and its reissue on CD is long overdue. *Live at the Lighthouse, Vols. 1 & 2* ♫♫♫ (Blue Note, 1972, prod. George Butler) was previously available on CD but is currently and inexplicably out of print. Fronting a strong quartet, this recording provides the best example of how much power Jones can generate in a live setting.

influences:

⏪ Max Roach, Art Blakey, Kenny Clarke, Philly Joe Jones

⏩ Lewis Nash, Brian Blade, Billy Drummond, Kenny Washington

Chris Hovan

Etta Jones

Born November 25, 1928, in Aiken, SC.

Combining measured doses of jazz and blues, vocalist Etta Jones has developed a highly inviting approach that has given her popular appeal since she first appeared with the Buddy Johnson band at the age of 16. She gained further experience in front of the groups of J.C. Heard and Earl Hines in the 1950s, before launching on her solo career. With her 1960 hit recording, *Don't Go to Strangers*, Jones began a productive association with Prestige Records that lasted five years and produced seven albums. For much of the 1970s Jones was relatively inactive until she entered her next great phase of recording activity. Since 1976, she has made albums for the Muse label (many of which are currently unavailable on CD), often in the company of husband Houston Person. Any one of Jones's classic dates re-

Etta Jones (© Jack Vartoogian)

ELVIN JONES (WITH JOHN COLTRANE)

song "The Drum Thing"

album Crescent
(Impulse!, 1965/1997)

instrument Drums

Monster Solo

---

veal her singular way with a song. Much like her inspirations, Billie Holiday and Dinah Washington, Jones clearly enunciates each syllable of a word, milking it for all its potential, and often ends a phrase with a melodic upturn. Although not a technically flashy vocalist, she inflects each performance with an emotional attachment that is always quite direct and inviting.

what to buy: *Don't Go to Strangers* ♫♫♫ (Prestige, 1960, prod. Esmond Edwards) was Jones's hit album and contains more than its share of inspired performances. Add some choice standards and an all-star cast that includes Frank Wess, Richard Wyands, George Duvivier, and Roy Haynes, and you have a classic that is a must-listen. *Something Nice* ♫♫♫ (Prestige, 1961, prod. Esmond Edwards) is the follow-up to the above set and it too features some superb Jones, a well-selected program, and a fine supporting crew that includes Roy Haynes, Lem Winchester, and Oliver Nelson.

what to buy next: *So Warm* ♫♫♫ (Prestige, 1961, prod. Esmond Edwards) finds Jones wrapped around a full orchestra arranged and conducted by Oliver Nelson, who created a rich and inviting showcase for Jones's deeply heartfelt singing, with string charts that are always tasteful and never sappy.

the rest:

Lonely and Blue 🎵🎵🎵 (Prestige, 1962)
Love Shout 🎵🎵🎵 (Prestige, 1963)
My Mother's Eyes 🎵🎵🎵 (Muse/32 Jazz, 1977)

worth searching for: *Etta Jones's Greatest Hits* 🎵🎵🎵 (Prestige, 1966, prod. Don Schlitten) is worth looking for if you still own a turntable. Although "best of" packages are usually cause for wariness, this set is really a well-chosen selection of cuts from her many Prestige albums.

influences:

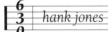 Billie Holiday, Dinah Washington

Chris Hovan

Hank Jones

Born July 31, 1918, in Vicksburg, MS.

Older brother of fellow jazzmen Thad and Elvin, Hank Jones has enjoyed a long and productive career as a session leader and a sideman. Jones began his professional career in the swing era playing piano in territorial bands. He moved to New York in 1944 and began accompanying artists such as Coleman Hawkins, Billy Eckstine, and Andy Kirk. Jones ended that decade as Ella Fitzgerald's accompanist (1948–53) and a some-time member of the Jazz at the Philharmonic ensembles. The flamboyant displays of technique heard on Jones's first solo recordings in the late 1940s reflect the obvious influence of his early idol Art Tatum. But Jones lacked Tatum's expansive per-sonality, and by the 1950s he developed the warmly under-stated, bebop-oriented style that has become his trademark. Over the next two decades, Jones was one of the most exten-sively recorded sidemen on the jazz scene, contributing to fine sessions with John Coltrane, Milt Jackson, Sonny Stitt, Wes Montgomery, Ben Webster, Lucky Thompson, and many others.

Although he was a CBS studio musician from 1959–1976, Jones continued to perform mainstream jazz throughout the 1970s. Many of his recordings from this period were appealing but in-consequential romps with old colleagues, yet his stronger works demonstrate a broadening of his style beyond the con-straints of bebop and the refinement of his craft as a solo recitalist. His late 1970s performances in the Broadway show *Ain't Misbehavin'* provided an opportunity to revisit his roots in stride piano, a style that has increasingly figured in his solo

recital work. In recent years, Jones has continued to find greater depth and authority as a session leader and soloist. His sophisticated sense of harmony, his elegant touch, and his penchant for understatement are still the hallmarks of his style. Other recent recordings include worthwhile pairings with vocalist Abbey Lincoln, bassist Charlie Haden (on a collection of spirituals), and pianist George Shearing.

what to buy: His releases from the last decade rank with his best work. Three stand as minor classics. *Upon Reflection: The Music of Thad Jones* 🎵🎵🎵 (PolyGram, 1994, prod. Jean-Phillipe Allard) is a deeply felt and eloquent tribute to his brother. The somewhat assertive presence of baby brother Elvin Jones (on brushes for most of the session) is one of the quirks that makes this release so endearing. *The Oracle* 🎵🎵🎵 (EmArcy, 1989, prod. Lee Townsend/Verve, 1991), a joint venture with bassist Dave Holland and drummer Billy Higgins, shows Jones at his most quietly compelling. A strength of this set is the well-chosen program of originals and rarely heard jazz standards. On *Live at Maybeck Recital Hall, Vol. 16* 🎵🎵🎵 (Concord, 1992, prod. Carl Jefferson), Jones glides through a program of stan-dards with matchless poise and elegance, his legendary touch always in evidence.

what to buy next: *Lazy Afternoon* 🎵🎵🎵 (Concord, 1989, prod. Carl Jefferson) is an excellent session that features Ken Pe-plowski (clarinet, alto sax) on several tracks. *Hank: Solo Piano* 🎵🎵🎵 (All Art, 1976, prod. Takao Ishizuka) is a collection of 14 miniatures (half are Ellington numbers). The session provides a wonderful example of Jones's craftsmanship, and ranks just be-hind the Maybeck issue as the best example of his solo artistry. Another solo set, *Handful of Keys* 🎵🎵🎵 (Verve, 1993, prod. Jean-Phillipe Allard), features gently swinging renditions of songs associated with Fats Waller. Jones lacks Waller's ebul-lience but the performances are aglow with Jones's affection for the music and the style. *Urbanity* 🎵🎵🎵 (Verve, 1997, prod. Nor-man Granz) is an attractive reissue of 1947 and 1953 sessions, Jones's first recordings as a leader. The stride influence and vir-tuosic embellishments of Art Tatum are amply evident. After these recordings, Jones would rarely put his technique on such conspicuous display. The *Quartet/Quintet* 🎵🎵🎵 (Savoy, 1955/1993, prod. Ozzie Cadena) reissue is the best of his 1950s Savoy sessions as a leader. The band (which includes Kenny Clarke and the young Donald Byrd) sounds as smooth and mel-low as its leader, and the remastering is excellent. It is also easy to recommend *Master Class* 🎵🎵🎵 (32Jazz, 1997, prod. Fred Siebert), a reissue of two excellent 1970s albums of clas-sic bebop compositions, *'bop Redux* and *Groovin' High*.

what to avoid: All of Jones's recordings are safe bets, although some of his 1970s sessions can seem a trifle predictable. It is hard to recommend *Sarala* 🎵🎵🎵 (Verve, 1996, prod. Cheick-Tidi-ane Seck) to mainstream jazz fans. Essentially a worldbeat album, this African project is enjoyable but not quite as engaging as the best of this genre, and Jones is not much of a presence.

best of the rest:

Bluebird 🎵🎵🎵 (Savoy, 1955/1992)

Trio 🎵🎵🎵 (Savoy, 1955/1994)

(With Ray Brown and Jimmie Smith) *Rockin' in Rhythm* 🎵🎵🎵 (Concord, 1977/1992)

Favors 🎵🎵🎵 (Verve, 1977/1997)

Tiptoe Tapdance 🎵🎵🎵 (OJC, 1977/1992)

In Japan 🎵🎵🎵 (All Art, 1979/1991)

worth searching for: Jones's appearances as a sideman in the 1950s and 1960s are well worth exploring. The famous Cannon-ball Adderley session *Somethin' Else* 🎵🎵🎵🎵 (Blue Note, 1958/1986, prod. Alfred Lion) is self-recommending. Among his more recent collaborations, *Steal Away* 🎵🎵🎵🎵 (Verve, 1995, prod. Charlie Haden), a collection of spirituals with bassist Charlie Haden, is the standout. The arrangements are simple and uncluttered (with minimal improvisation), and the performers display a serene dignity throughout. The collaboration with George Shearing, *Spirit of 176* 🎵🎵🎵 (Concord, 1989, prod. Carl Jefferson), is lighter fare, but features some good swinging and shows both pianists to good effect.

influences:

◀◀ Art Tatum, Fats Waller, Bud Powell

▶▶ Ahmad Jamal, Red Garland, Wynton Kelly

Will Bickart

Jo Jones

Born October 7, 1911, in Chicago, IL. Died September 3, 1985, in New York, NY.

With a career spanning 50 years, Jo Jones leads the short list of the most influential jazz drummers. His most significant innovation—marking rhythm on the cymbals while using the bass drum for occasional accents to drive the beat—was the inspiration for the early bebop drummers. Jones's long career began with a brief but formative experience as a tap dancer. His first appearances as a drummer were in the 1920s with territorial bands like Bennie Moten's. Beginning in 1934, Jones keyed the great Basie rhythm session of Jones, bassist Walter Page, guitarist Freddie Green, and Basie himself on piano. This group produced a rhythmic

Hᴀɴᴋ Jᴏɴᴇꜱ

song "Lady Luck"

album *Upon Reflection: The Music of Thad Jones*
(Verve, 1993)

instrument Piano

pulse unlike any heard before, propulsive but never over-driven. Throughout the 1930s and 1940s, Jones's fame and influence were at a peak, and he found the opportunity to record with virtually every significant jazz artist of the era. Despite these side ventures, Jones remained on staff with the Basie band for 14 years, until leaving for good in 1948. By the 1950s, he was a dinosaur of the swing era, revered for both his drumming and his famous and ever-present grin. Producers Norman Granz and John Hammond matched Jones with other swing veterans for some memorable sessions, but only a few with Jones as the front man. Unsurpassed as a timekeeper, he was at his best playing rhythm behind the band. But Jones also came to be known for his distinctive drum solos, which never fail to bring the rhythms of tap dance to mind. Despite failing health in his last years, "Papa" Jones remained on the jazz scene as a performer and storyteller up until the time of his death in 1985.

what to buy: Jones recorded two LP albums for Vanguard in the 1950s, now reissued together as *The Essential Jo Jones* 🎵🎵🎵🎵 (Vanguard, 1977/1995, prod. John Hammond). The first album,

The Jo Jones Special, a longtime favorite of Basie fans, reunites Jones with Walter Page, Freddie Green, and (on one track) Basie himself. Soloists include the under-recorded trumpeter Emmett Berry and tenor saxophonist Lucky Thompson, both in good form. The sleeper, however, is the second album, *The Jo Jones Trio*. There are no fireworks here, just a well-drilled trio (which features the young Ray Bryant on piano) and some of the finest small-ensemble drumming to be heard anywhere. Listeners unfamiliar with Jones's brushwork will be introduced to one of the glories of modern jazz.

what to buy next: *The Main Man* 𝄞𝄞𝄞 (OJC, 1976/1995, prod. Norman Granz) finds Jones in the friendly company of swing-era veterans such as Roy Eldridge, Harry Edison, Eddie "Lock-jaw" Davis, and his old Basie partner, Freddie Green. The aging bandmates may have lost some of their fire, but fans of these artists will appreciate this good-natured session.

worth searching for: Jones's association with Verve in the 1950s resulted in many fine sessions with such greats as Ben Webster, Johnny Hodges, Coleman Hawkins, Roy Eldridge and Benny Carter. A sentimental favorite would have to be the Lester Young/Teddy Wilson album *Pres and Teddy* 𝄞𝄞𝄞𝄞 (Verve, 1956/1986, prod. Norman Granz). The ravaged beauty of Lester Young's late work is not to all tastes, but true "Pres" fans will want to have this great quartet session.

influences:
▶▶ Max Roach, Shadow Wilson, Kenny Clarke

Will Bickart

Oliver Jones

Born September 11, 1934, in Montreal, Quebec, Canada.

Though internationally respected, Oliver Jones has been overlooked in the United States. The outstanding pianist performed his first public concert at the age of five, his first club date at nine. Though he studied with Oscar Peterson's sister, Daisy Peterson Sweeny, for 12 years—and the Peterson style is very evident in his playing and choice of sidemen Ray Brown and Ed Thigpen—he did not gain notoriety on the jazz circuit until the 1980s. From 1962–80 he was the musical director and pianist for pop singer Ken Hamilton and worked in Puerto Rico as a music director for club shows. In 1980 he started his jazz career and has released some very good albums on the Canadian Justin Time label. Though currently in semi-retirement, Jones still tours every year and is a fixture at the International Montreal Jazz Festival.

what to buy: Too often pianists with tremendous technique create unlistenable solo efforts, often too afraid to allow for some space. While Jones is a virtuoso and gives some awesome technical displays on *Just 88* 𝄞𝄞𝄞𝄞 (Justin Time, 1993, prod. Jim West), the disc is filled with nice interpretations and exceptional technique, but most of all, taste. *Have Fingers, Will Travel* 𝄞𝄞𝄞𝄞 (Justin Time, 1997, prod. Jim West, Oliver Jones) includes more great trio playing, this time with Ray Brown and Jeff Hamilton. The only guys playing like this anymore are Jones and Oscar Peterson, but Jones has enough character that he doesn't sound like a clone of the Big O. Terry and Jones play the standards on *Oliver Jones Trio Featuring Clark Terry* 𝄞𝄞𝄞𝄞 (Justin Time, 1989, Jim West, Oliver Jones) with the class and style expected from them. Jones is more restrained as an accompanist, but no less powerful.

what to buy next: *A Class Act* 𝄞𝄞𝄞𝄞 (Justin Time, 1991, prod. Jim West, Oliver Jones) has a classic jazz trio sound with Ed Thigpen and Steve Wallace. Jones's chops are hot, particularly on "Mark My Time," and his renditions of "Very Early" and "Hymn to Freedom" are memorable. *From Lush to Lively* 𝄞𝄞𝄞𝄞 (Justin Time, 1995, prod. Jim West, Oliver Jones, Rick Wilkins) contains ballads and swingers with a big-band sound. Jones's playing is smooth, and while the more uptempo arrangements sometimes fall short, the overall result is still quite good.

the rest:
Yuletide Swing 𝄞𝄞𝄞𝄞 (Justin Time, 1994)

influences:
◀◀ Art Tatum, Oscar Peterson, Erroll Garner, Earl Hines, Bud Powell

Paul MacArthur

"Philly" Joe Jones

Born July 15, 1923, in Philadelphia, PA. Died August 30, 1985, in Philadelphia, PA.

A hard-swinger and superb accompanist, "Philly" Joe Jones was one of the most in-demand drummers of the 1950s, and his prominence helped expand the role of jazz drumming while making him highly influential on future generations. Jones's musical career really began in 1947 when he moved to New York and served as the house drummer at Cafe Society, accompanying top bop musicians Charlie Parker, Fats Navarro, and Dexter Gordon. Jones also worked regularly with Lionel Hampton, Ben Webster, and Tiny Grimes. In the '50s he got important gigs with Tad Dameron and Miles Davis, and from 1955–58, with bassist Paul Chambers and pianist Red Garland, he anchored one of the great rhythm sections in jazz history as part of Davis's classic quintet with John Coltrane. During this period Jones also made significant contributions beyond Davis's working group to many classic sessions of the day, cementing his reputation and place in jazz history. In the '60s Jones was not quite the drummer du jour he was in the late '50s, but he still made some great recordings with Bill Evans, Dameron, his own groups, and even avant-gardeists like Archie Shepp. Upon returning home to Philadelphia after a three-year stint in Europe, Jones formed a short-lived fusion group called Le Grand Prix and toured with Evans and Garland. In the 1980s he formed the group Dameronia to pay tribute to his long-time friend and under-appreciated associate. Although he was considered unreliable and was always plagued by drug problems, Jones is remembered fondly for his sense of humor, and of course, for his uncanny ability to swing a band.

what to buy: *Blues for Dracula* 𝄢𝄢𝄢 (Riverside, 1958/OJC, 1991, prod. Orrin Keepnews) is perhaps best known for its introduction—a humorous but drawn-out impression by the leader of Bela Lugosi's Dracula character. But it settles down into a very strong, hard-bop blowing session with cornetist Nat Adderley, tenor Johnny Griffin, trombonist Julian Priester, and pianist Tommy Flanagan. Jones really seems to be enjoying himself on his first date as a leader.

what to buy next: The concept of *Drums around the World* 𝄢𝄢𝄢 (Riverside, 1959/OJC, 1992, prod. Orrin Keepnews) was, as the name suggests, to bring multicultural influences to a jazz setting. It really just ends up sounding like a typical bop session from the late '50s. Still, the soloists (including trumpeters Lee Morgan and Blue Mitchell, altoist Cannonball Adderley, flautist Herbie Mann, and tenor Benny Golson) shine in front of Jones, with some interesting arrangements by Golson.

what to avoid: *Mo' Joe* 𝄢 (Black Lion, 1969/1991, prod. Alan Bates), from the end of Jones's stay in Europe, came during the height of his personal problems, and it demonstrates that he is really only at his best when accompanying first-rate musicians—here it's just journeymen.

the rest:
Mean What You Say 𝄢𝄢𝄢 (Sonet, 1977)
Philly Mignon 𝄢𝄢𝄢 (Galaxy, 1978)
Advance! 𝄢𝄢𝄢 (Galaxy, 1980)
Look, Stop, and Listen 𝄢𝄢𝄢 (Uptown, 1983)
Showcase 𝄢𝄢𝄢 (Riverside, 1960/OJC, 1990)

worth searching for: *Drum Song* 𝄢𝄢𝄢 (Galaxy, 1979) is another excellent hard-bop session with a strong array of soloists. Blue

Mitchell is featured in one of his last recordings, and Harold Land, Slide Hampton, and Cedar Walton also shine.

influences:
◀◀ Max Roach
▶▶ Elvin Jones

Dan Keener

Quincy Jones

Born Quincy Delight Jones Jr., March 14, 1933, in Chicago, IL.

For as little as he has actually played on record, Quincy Jones has staked out quite a reputation for himself. Of course, a lot of his claim to fame rests on his work as a superstar pop producer for the likes of Michael Jackson, as well as his numerous TV & film scores. But his background is firmly set in the world of jazz. Jones grew up in Seattle, a childhood friend of Ray Charles and equally musically minded. He quickly learned to play the trumpet (at one point under the tutelage of Clark Terry), studied at what would become the Berklee School of Music, and got his first major gig touring with the Lionel Hampton band in the early 1950s. While traveling through Europe, Jones picked up the art of arranging, a skill he has used throughout his career with tremendous success. For the next few years, he kept extremely busy as a freelance arranger, working with artists like Oscar Pettiford, Art Farmer, Count Basie, Cannonball Adderley, and Dinah Washington, to name a few. With arranging taking up most of his time, Jones nearly dropped playing altogether, but he still found time to play trumpet as the music director for Dizzy Gillespie's big band in 1956. Later that year, he called in an all-star collection of friends to record his first major record, *This Is How I Feel about Jazz*. For the rest of the '50s, Jones worked in Paris and New York, producing, arranging, and conducting various groups. After a failed European gig as music director for the blues musical *Free and Easy* (at least Jones got some worthy live dates out of the trip, as documented on *Live in Paris*), he returned to New York and was rewarded with the position of head of A&R for Mercury Records. After further recording and producing, all of his hard work paid off, and in 1964 Jones was named vice president of Mercury, the first African American to reach that level at a major record label. For the rest of his career, straight jazz has played only a part in the projects with which he has been involved: band leader for Frank Sinatra; scoring the soundtracks to *In Cold Blood* and the TV mini-series *Roots*; music director for the Oscars; starting his own label, Qwest; and producing "We Are the World"; not to mention associations with dozens of other R&B

and pop artists. Even his own records, like the Grammy-winning *Walking in Space*, rely so heavily on precise charts and arrangements that the improvisational jazz content is slight, despite the participation of top-notch jazz players. Nevertheless, Jones's contributions to modern music have been significant, helping to develop recent genres like new jack swing and to expand the scope of pop, R&B, and jazz. While a capable musician on trumpet and piano, Jones displays his main art as arranger. His methods involve bringing the feel of small groups to large-band settings and providing vigorous, melodic backdrops into which the soloists can interject their voices. His tight, dramatic style perfectly suits the crime-genre films and TV shows he scores. The ease with which he has been able to move between projects—one minute producing Michael Jackson's latest pop blockbuster, the next coaxing Miles Davis to revisit his Gil Evans–arranged work for a final concert at the 1991 Montreux Jazz Festival—clearly establishes Jones as a major figure in the world of jazz and music in general.

what to buy: It's hard to go wrong on *This Is How I Feel about Jazz* 🎵🎵🎵🎵 (ABC/Impulse!, 1957, prod. Creed Taylor), with a band featuring Art Farmer, Phil Woods, Hank Jones, Zoot Sims, Herbie Mann, Milt Jackson, and Charlie Mingus, not to mention Jones's own swinging tunes and arrangements. Despite the premature closure of the musical *Free and Easy*, Jones kept the assembled band around for a few gigs, including *Q Live in Paris circa 1960* 🎵🎵🎵🎵 (Qwest, 1996). Originally floating around as a much-sought-after bootleg, Jones's own label recently gave it an official release.

what to buy next: Recorded at the height of his powers, *The Quintessence* 🎵🎵🎵🎵 (Impulse!, 1962, prod. Bob Thiele) showcases Jones's affinity for sweet melodies (although some might say too sweet). *Walking in Space* 🎵🎵🎵🎵 (A&M, 1969, prod. Creed Taylor) is a groundbreaking record that reveals the many things to come.

what to avoid: *Back on the Block* **woof!** (Qwest, 1989) is a re-entry to recording and a serious faux pas. Jones attempts to catch up with the times with hip-hop rhythms and special guest rappers (including a brief rap by Quincy himself!). This hodge-podge, guest-laden affair is a precursor to the superior but similarly structured *Q's Juke Joint*.

the rest:
Go West, Man 🎵🎵🎵🎵 (ABC, 1957)
The Great Wide World of Quincy Jones 🎵🎵🎵🎵 (EmArcry, 1960)
Big Band Bossa Nova 🎵🎵🎵🎵 (Mercury, 1963)
Plays Hip Hits 🎵🎵🎵🎵 (Mercury, 1963)

Gula Matari 🎵🎵🎵🎵 (A&M, 1970)
You've Got It Bad Girl 🎵🎵 (A&M, 1973)
Body Heat 🎵🎵 (A&M, 1974)
Mellow Madness 🎵🎵 (A&M, 1975)
I Heard That! 🎵🎵 (A&M, 1976)
Sounds . . . and Stuff Like That! 🎵🎵 (A&M, 1978)
The Dude 🎵 (A&M, 1981)
The Birth of a Band 🎵🎵🎵🎵 (EmArcy, 1984)
The Birth of a Band Volume 2 🎵🎵🎵🎵 (Mercury Japan, 1984)
The Great Wide World of Quincy Jones Live! 🎵🎵🎵🎵 (Mercury Japan, 1984)
Miles Davis & Quincy Jones—Live at Montreux 🎵🎵🎵🎵 (Warner Bros., 1993)
Q's Juke Joint 🎵🎵 (Qwest, 1995)

worth searching for: *Smackwater Jack* 🎵🎵🎵 (A&M, 1971, prod. Quincy Jones, Ray Brown, Phil Ramone) isn't exactly jazz, but a weird, wonderful album that even won a Grammy. It features some great funk workouts with the themes to *Ironside* and *The Bill Cosby Show,* a bizarre medley of guitar styles throughout history, and some rare vocals by Quincy himself on Marvin Gaye's "What's Going On?" and the Carole King–penned title track.

influences:
◀◀ Al Cohn
▶▶ Oliver Nelson

Eric J. Lawrence

Sam Jones

Born November 12, 1924, in Jacksonville, FL. Died December 15, 1981, in New York, NY.

One of the unsung heroes of jazz, Sam Jones, a bassist, cellist, and composer, gained greatest visibility in the late 1950s after moving to New York City, where he began performing and recording with notables such as Kenny Dorham, Illinois Jacquet, Cannonball Adderley, and Dizzy Gillespie. Jones spent eight months with Thelonious Monk, then rejoined Adderley for six years beginning in late 1959, during which time he was also featured on many other recordings, including his sessions as leader (playing both bass and cello) for Riverside and other labels. In February 1966, Jones joined the Oscar Peterson Trio as Ray Brown's first replacement (1966–70), after which he worked with an array of musicians, often with drummer Louis Hayes and instrumentalists from his Riverside dates. A few years before his death, Jones led a big band with Tom Harrell. A cellist of equal virtuosity, Jones has been compared most often to Oscar Pettiford and Ray Brown, two of his influences, and his remarkable double-bass style is quite musical and blues-oriented. Out of his recordings as leader for various labels, the Riverside and SteepleChase albums are still available, but you'll have to search the vinyl used bins for his sessions for Muse, Xanadu, and Discovery. You can also find the versatile Jones as bassist of choice on hundreds of albums recorded since the late 1940s (peaking during the 1960s–70s) with the artists previously mentioned, as well as big-band dates and small-group sessions led by many others. Many of these recordings with Jones as sideman have been reissued on CD and remain in print.

what to buy: On *The Chant* ♪♪♪♪♪ (Riverside, 1961/OJC, 1994, prod. Orrin Keepnews), Jones leads a relaxed and swinging straight-ahead ensemble session configured around the Cannonball Adderley quintet at the time. A stellar rhythm section featuring Wynton Kelly on piano or Victor Feldman on piano/vibes, Jones himself or Keter Betts on bass, and drummer Louis Hayes kicks throughout. Soloists include Nat Adderley (cornet), Blue Mitchell (trumpet), Melba Liston (trombone), Cannonball Adderly (alto sax), Jimmy Heath (tenor sax), and Les Spann (guitar) playing on eight tunes arranged by Feldman and Heath. The fine solos from Jones (on cello and bass) and Betts celebrate the bass, and roomy solos and excellent section work from Mitchell, Nat, and Cannonball add to the album's success. This was Jones's second session for Riverside (released the year after he was cited in the 1960 *Down Beat* critics poll as a "New Star" bassist). You can't go wrong with this enduring, listener-friendly session. *Down Home* ♪♪♪♪ (Riverside, 1962/1995, prod. Orrin Keepnews, Julian Adderley), an eight-tune session recorded on two dates during the summer of 1962, features four configurations of musicians with bassists Jones, Ron Carter, and Israel Crosby (the last session for Crosby, former bassist with the Ahmad Jamal Trio and George Shearing). Jones performs on his original, "Unit 7," leading an octet that includes Joe Zawinul on piano, and trumpet soloists Blue Mitchell and Snooky Young. The session includes more Jones material than some of his earlier recordings for Riverside, and features his tribute to Oscar Pettiford, "O.P.," on which he plays cello, leaving the bass duties to Crosby. Ernie Wilkins arranges and conducts for the largest ensemble, which is the focal point of this recording on four tunes. Woven with Jones's cello intro, Les Spann's flute nicely augments "'Round Midnight," then he generates some mellifluous lines of his own on this classic and the closer, "Falling in Love with Love." An overall pleasant outing for the material as much as the execution.

what to buy next: Enjoyable, but not quite as exciting and exceptional as *The Chant*, this March 10, 1960, studio date, *The*

Soul Society ♪♪♪♪ (Riverside, 1960/OJC, prod. Orrin Keepnews), features Jones leading a swinging sextet on which he plays cello and bass with Nat Adderley (cornet), Jimmy Heath (tenor sax), and a rhythm team with pianist Bobby Timmons, bassist Ketor Betts, and drummer Louis Hayes. Charles Davis (baritone sax) jumps in on four of the eight selections, making it a septet with Jones on bass. Throughout both settings, Jones takes bass or cello melody heads, then puts his improvisational spin the deep-grooved tunes (mostly originals contributed by group members). *Right Down Front* ♪♪♪♪ (Riverside, 1960–62/OJC, prod. various) is a compilation from Jones's Riverside sessions mentioned above, and might be a good place for a jazz newcomer to start if it weren't that the original albums were so fully engaging and enjoyable.

the rest:
Cello Again ♪♪♪♪♪ (Xanadu 1976)
Something in Common ♪♪♪♪ (Muse, 1977)
Something New ♪♪♪♪♪ (Sea Breeze, 1979)
Changes and Things ♪♪♪ (Xanadu, 1979)
The Bassist ♪♪♪♪ (Discovery, 1979)

influences:
◀◀ Oscar Pettiford, Milt Hinton, Al Hall, Ray Brown, Jimmy Blanton, Cannonball Adderley

see also: *Thelonious Monk, Cannonball Adderly, Kenny Dorham, Blue Mitchell, Oscar Peterson*

Nancy Ann Lee

Spike Jones

Born Lindley Armstrong Jones, December 14, 1911, in Long Beach, CA. Died May 1, 1965, in Bel Air, CA.

Among Spike Jones's many musical accomplishments over his 30-plus-year career, perhaps his biggest was introducing such instruments as the latriophone (a toilet seat strung with wire) and the burpaphone (self-explanatory) to the lexicon of American popular music. Much more than a novelty act, Jones was a musical visionary. "I'm the dandruff in longhair music," Jones has said about his comical presence in the world of more serious bandleaders in the 1950s and 1960s. In his high school years, Jones had a hot jazz band that laid the groundwork for the later endeavors of his brilliant ensemble performances, which featured antiquated licks and growls, semi-vulgarities in the lower brass, and sound effects from Jones's expanded traps set. Jones began his career as a studio musician drummer, performing for radio programs such as *Fibber McGee and Molly* and *Kraft Music Hall (The Bing Crosby Show),* and most notably playing on Bing Crosby's monster hit "White Christmas." Bored by conventional music, he began to add unusual instruments to his traps set and in 1940 formed a band, the City Slickers, to fulfill his zany vision that turned the world of pop music on its ear with crazy parodies and bizarre musical collages. Jones's preferred structure was to begin a tune with the melody statement before descending into puckishness rife with sound effects, crude remarks, and hot jazz. The band's unlikely first hit was 1942's Hitler spoof "Der Fuehrer's Face," and on the basis of that hit the band quickly earned a following and had several hit novelty cuts during its first decade. From 1946–53 Jones toured widely with his Musical Depreciation Revue, maintaining their weekly CBS radio show while on the road for nearly two years (1947–49). They undoubtedly won fans when they hit a major city and held their publicity-driven "underwear parade," with Jones and bandmates wearing long underwear. By the late 1940s Jones had expanded the band's live shows to include midgets, jugglers, and loony stage acts, while scoring on the charts with song interpretations like "Cocktails for Two," replete with a hiccuping chorus. Jones and the band appeared in several films, and brought their brand of musical folly to NBC-TV in the 1950s and early 1960s with four versions of *The Spike Jones Show*. Jones and his City Slickers sold more than 30 million recordings for RCA Victor. Later recordings were made for the Starlite, Decca, Kapp, Verve, Warner Bros., and Liberty labels. Jones died of emphysema in 1965, but not before establishing himself as one of the true musical pioneers of the 20th century for his use of sound effects in his performances. There's no disputing that he was easily the most hilarious innovator, responsible for some of most politically incorrect music ever.

what to buy: Probably the most accessible among Jones's numerous greatest-hits packages is an inspired sampling of his lunacy on *The Spike Jones Anthology: Musical Depreciation Revue* ♫♫♫♫ (Rhino, 1994, prod. various), which features 40 classics performed with his touring group. Included are the 1942-recorded spoof about Hitler, "Der Fuehrer's Face," the whistling giddiness on "All I Want for Christmas (Is My Two Front Teeth)," which was Jones's second-biggest record ever, and his famous gargling rendition of "The William Tell Overture." Anyone who doubts Jones's musicianship should check out his sound-effects artistry on "Holiday for Strings" (1945), and other tunes. With their nonsensical antics, the band skewered popular musical acts of the day, including The Ink Spots ("You Always Hurt the One You Love"), Liberace ("I'm in the Mood for Love,"), Desi Arnaz ("Secret Love"), and numerous other irreverences. The set

is rife with goofy sounds and mimicry (band members simulating crying babies, hiccups, belches, hog snorts, and other rude and annoying but hilarious sounds). Band turnover by 1946 left Jones searching for replacements. One of them, clarinetist Mickey Katz, replaced Carl Grayson as the resident "glugger." Inspired by his experience with the Spike Jones bands, clarinetist Katz (the father of entertainer Joel Gray) went on to record some novelty albums of his own during the 1950s. If you're trying to teach your kids to refrain from burping loudly at the dinner table, or you're sick of "knock-knock" jokes, keep the Spike Jones single album *Spiked!* ♫♫♫♫ (Catalyst, 1994, prod. various) away from their innocent ears. Jones performs 23 zany numbers with his City Slickers and his Other Orchestra, including his six-part spoof on Tchaikovsky's "Nutcracker Suite." Anyone who was a kid when these tune were popular during the 1940s and 1950s remembers what listening fun they were compared to the stiff, serious studio music of the day. Although critics bestowed the title "King of Corn" on Jones and his bands, his musicians were accomplished players who could play swing jazz, boogie-woogie, and Dixieland with comfortable ease, as you'll hear on the interludes when they're not poking fun at everything under the sun. Nothing was sacred. The more highbrow, the more deliberate the Spike band spoofs. A prime example is "Pal-Ya-Chee," with vocalists Homer and Jethro (assisted by Sir Frederick Gas) making fun of the famed opera *Pagliacci* (ironically, the translated meaning is "clowns"). Jones and his musicians also mocked white-society band music, and their spoof on big-band singers of the day, "Deep Purple," still evokes a chuckle. A fabulous muted trumpet solo from George Rock on a 1949 recording of "Minka" demonstrates the instrumental prowess of Jones's players and the hard-swinging, versatile arrangements they could produce when they wanted to be serious. This album repeats only a few of the tunes contained in *The Spike Jones Anthology: Musical Depreciation Revue*. If you're sick of Washington politics or other everyday nuisances, just listen to this album. Nothing will ever seem serious again.

what to buy next: The title says it all on *Dinner Music for People Who Aren't Very Hungry* ♫♫♫♫ (Rhino, 1957). The "interpretations" of polite music make it the perfect CD for an intimate date with someone with a sense of humor. You'll have trouble listening to straight renditions of classic carols after hearing *Let's Sing a Song for Christmas* ♫♫♫♫ (MGM, 1978/1997, prod. various).

the rest:
Riot Squad ♫♫♫ (Harlequin, 1989)
Louder & Funnier ♫♫♫ (Harlequin, 1994)

Corn's a-Poppin' ♫♫ (Harlequin, 1995)
Cocktails for Two ♫♫♫ (Pro Arte, 1997)

influences:

◀◀ Al Jolson, Harmonica Frank, Emmett Miller

▶▶ Mickey Katz, "Weird Al" Yankovic, Allan Sherman

Alex Gordon and Nancy Ann Lee

Thad Jones

Born March 28, 1923, in Pontiac, MI. Died August 20, 1986, in Copenhagen, Denmark.

With enviable abilities as both a trumpeter and an extremely talented composer-arranger, Thad Jones is one of the few jazz talents who can accurately be called a "complete" musician. Along with his brothers, drummer Elvin and pianist Hank, Thad was part of a vital jazz scene in Detroit that found him working with Sonny Stitt and Billy Mitchell during the 1940s and 1950s. Following a short stint with Charles Mingus, Jones became a star soloist with Count Basie's Orchestra, where he remained in the trumpet section for several years (1954–1963). During this very productive period, Jones wrote a sizeable number of arrangements and originals for the band, as well as contributing his famous solo on "April in Paris."

His mid-1950s Blue Note recordings as leader reveal a trumpet player of great agility and melodic invention, with a tart and razor-sharp sound. His rare sideman appearances over the next few years with such players as McCoy Tyner and Oliver Nelson further defined his position as a distinctive trumpeter. Then in 1965 Jones embarked on one of his most significant endeavors, teaming up with drummer Mel Lewis to form a big band comprised mainly of top-shelf, New York studio musicians. With several exceptional recordings cut for the Solid State label and a regular Monday night gig at New York's Village Vanguard (which continues to this day, albeit under different leadership and with a rotating cast of players), the Thad Jones–Mel Lewis Jazz Orchestra became one of the most influential and popular big bands of its time. Jones contributed many of his finest pieces to the band's book, including "A Child Is Born," "Kids Are Pretty People," "Fingers," and "Little Pixie." Jones inexplicably left the band in 1978 and headed for Denmark, where he found work as an arranger. A comeback as leader of the Count Basie band in 1984 was short-lived. His ill health ultimately led to his death two years later. Perhaps having not yet earned the full recognition that he rightly deserves, Thad Jones will nonetheless be remembered as a multi-talented musician of great individuality and foresight.

what to buy: Available by mail-order only, *The Complete Solid State Recordings of the Thad Jones/Mel Lewis Orchestra* ♫♫♫♫ (Mosaic, 1966–1970, prod. Michael Cuscuna, Charlie Lourie) is a 5-CD or 7-LP boxed set containing the historic original recordings of this big band, complete with improved fidelity and bonus tracks. The stars of the show here are Jones's distinctive charts and creative soloists such as Eddie Daniels, Joe Farrell, Bob Brookmeyer, Richard Williams, Hank Jones, and Pepper Adams. This is a limited edition, so act quickly!

what to buy next: *The Complete Blue Note/UA/Roulette Recordings of Thad Jones* ♫♫♫♫ (Mosaic, 1956–1959, prod. Michael Cuscuna, Charlie Lourie) contains small-group settings that reveal Jones's great talents as a trumpeter. His three Blue Note sides, *Detroit–New York Junction*, *The Magnificent Thad Jones* and *The Magnificent, Vol.3*, are price-worthy and have been sought out by collectors for years. Taken in tandem with the Solid State set, this 3-CD or 5-LP boxed edition presents the most complete look at Jones to date. Remember, this is available only by mail order and quantities are limited.

the rest:

Fabulous Thad Jones ♫♫♫♫ (Debut, 1955)
After Hours ♫♫♫♫ (Prestige, 1957)
Mean What You Say ♫♫♫♫ (Milestone, 1966)

see also: *Mel Lewis*

Chris Hovan

Betty Joplin

Born May 17, 1942, in Jackson, MI.

Michigan-based singer-pianist Betty Joplin claims her "God-given, natural talent" began at age four as she tapped out finger-beats on the kitchen table. She began tickling the ivories on a used piano her mother bought even before her feet could reach the pedals, and was soon playing in church. Although she deferred her professional career until after raising a family, her first professional nightclub gig in Lake James, Indiana, when she was 32 years old, led to Grammy-nominated recordings for her 1986 duet with Arthur Prysock on the single, "Teach Me Tonight," and for her collaborations on his album *This Guy's in Love with You*. Joplin is a powerful performer who demonstrates a potent, bluesy truth in her singing style and her sturdy piano accompaniment. She has performed and toured with the Duke Ellington Orchestra since 1993, and regularly performs at clubs and festivals in the U.S. and Europe. Joplin's recording career is a real success story. Lake Street Records president and producer Allyn Rosenberg discovered

Joplin's smoky vocals at the end of a demo tape sent by another band. He investigated and learned that Joplin's career had been assisted by Aretha Franklin's brother, Cecil, and by Mercer Ellington. Joplin signed a five-record deal with Lake Street Records in 1995.

what's available: Joplin seduces the listener with her passionate singing style reminiscent of Etta Jones. On her debut as leader, *Blinded by Love* 🎵🎵🎵 (Lake Street Records, 1996, prod. Allyn Rosenberg), Joplin offers a gospel-tinged cache of 10 intimate, torchy classics such as Percy Mayfield's "Please Send Me Someone to Love," Harold Arlen's "Stormy Weather" (a self-accompanied solo), "The Masquerade Is Over," the smoldering title ballad, and other pleasers. Guests include Hammond B-3 organist Jack McDuff, saxophonist Norbert Stachel, and guitarist Phil Upchurch, with backing from bassist Jesse Murphy, and drummer Donald "Duck" Bailey. Richard Hindeman, Peter Horvath, and Joplin split piano duties. It's a promising debut that garnered favorable reviews. Look for a second release in 1998.

worth searching for: Joplin's first album with the late Arthur Prysock, *A Rockin' Good Way* 🎵🎵🎵 (Milestone, 1986, prod. Bob Porter), includes her singing on four tracks, including the Grammy-nominated "Teach Me Tonight," and their second album, *This Guy's in Love with You* 🎵🎵🎵🎵 (Milestone, 1987, prod. Bob Porter), which was nominated for a Grammy award, features Joplin on three tracks.

influences:

◀◀ Etta Jones, Della Reese, Gloria Lynne, Dakota Staton, Dinah Washington

Nancy Ann Lee

Scott Joplin

Born November 24, 1868, in Texarkana, TX. Died April 1, 1917, in New York, NY.

Scott Joplin didn't invent ragtime music, but he was the first to write the music down. After he succeeded in getting his "Maple Leaf Rag" published by John Stark in 1899, everything should have been rosy. The piece sold 75,000 copies of sheet music in its first year, making the song a major turn-of-the-century hit. Stark wanted more of Joplin's tunes and Joplin obliged, but Joplin also had larger aspirations. He believed that ragtime music had potential beyond the sporting houses where it was played. To that end, he kept refining his music, with the result that his rags became increasingly complex. He even conceived a ragtime ballet, *Rag Time Dance,* and two ragtime operas, *A Guest of Honor* and *Treemonisha,* the failure of which helped kill him.

Joplin was born into a musical family. He began taking formal piano lessons from an old German teacher when he was 11. Nonetheless, Joplin's father didn't want him to be a professional musician. As a teenager, he had to leave home to seek his musical fortune. After an itinerant period, he settled in St. Louis, playing in the night spots around the city. His Texas Medley Quartet performed as far afield as New York and introduced some of his early compositions. In 1896 he enrolled at George Smith College in Sedalia, Missouri, and learned to formally write music. After Stark published "Maple Leaf Rag," named after a Sedalia club of the same name, Joplin, recently married, was able to retire from the performing life and focus on composing. *Rag Time Dance* was completed in 1902. A performance was well received, but when Stark published the music, there was little response—an event that began to sour the previously good relationship between composer and publisher. That's probably why *A Guest of Honor,* completed shortly thereafter, was never published. (The score was eventually lost.)

Joplin's marriage deteriorated after a daughter died in her infancy. In 1907 he followed Stark to New York and began performing again. He remarried in 1909—a much happier marriage to a woman who supported his music—and settled in Harlem. The remainder of his life was devoted to *Treemonisha,* which he completed in 1911. He was unable to find backing for it, and finally staged a run-through of the work on his own—without scenery or costumes—at a Harlem theater. The audience didn't respond. Joplin, suffering from the late stages of syphilis, was destroyed by the project's failure. In 1916 he was committed to a state hospital, where he died a year later.

Although only "Maple Leaf Rag" hung on in popularity for many years, Joplin's efforts to write ragtime down helped the music become an underpinning of American pop and jazz. Because of the deep rift between "serious" and "popular" music and the racist dismissal of black culture in the early part of the century, few scholars took Joplin's music as seriously as he took it. Ragtime, played much faster than Joplin wanted, became unfortunately associated with happy-faced effervescence and vacuity. As the nation became more open racially, and later generations of musicians—fluent in both pop and classical idioms—arose, interest in Joplin's compositions grew. In 1973 Marvin Hamlisch orchestrated Joplin's music as the score for the movie *The Sting,* and the soundtrack recording of Joplin's "The Entertainer" became a hit 70 years after it was published.

what to buy: *The Complete Works of Scott Joplin* 🎵🎵🎵🎵 (Laserlight, 1993) is a loving five-CD collection in which pianist Richard Zimmerman plays all of Joplin's song compositions and highlights of *Treemonisha*. The set is sequenced in as-close-to-chronological order as the publication dates will allow, so the listener can hear how Joplin's composing on rags, waltzes, marches, and ballads became increasingly sophisticated. Although Zimmerman holds to Joplin's dictum that "it is never right to play Ragtime fast," he plays it with zest. *Piano Rags by Scott Joplin* 𝄢𝄢𝄢𝄢 (Nonesuch, 1987) combines 17 tracks—including "The Entertainer" and "Maple Leaf Rag"—originally recorded for three vinyl LPs from 1970 to 1974. Joshua Rifkin's versions differ in ambiance from Zimmerman's, sounding as if they were coming from a far-off place.

what to buy next: *The Entertainer, Classic Ragtime from Rare Piano Rolls* 𝄢𝄢𝄢 (Biograph, 1992, prod. Arnold S. Caplin) digitally records the playback of piano rolls on a vintage 19th-century Steinway. Three of the piano rolls were hand-played by Joplin himself, which makes them about as close as we can get to hearing the pieces as Joplin wrote them. However, you can't get away from the fact that a piano roll is a piano roll and not a living pianist. *Elite Syncopations, Classic Ragtime from Rare Piano Rolls* 𝄢𝄢𝄢 (Biograph, 1992, prod. Arnold S. Caplin) includes another three Joplin rolls; *King of the Ragtime Writers* 𝄢𝄢𝄢 (Biograph, 1992, prod. Arnold S. Caplin) does not.

influences:

◀◀ Frederic Chopin, Louis Moreau Gottschalk

▶▶ Eubie Blake, Willie "the Lion" Smith, Reginald Robinson

Salvatore Caputo

Clifford Jordan

Born September 2, 1932, in Chicago, IL. Died May 27, 1993, in New York, NY.

Coming up in Chicago with similarly minded players like John Gilmore, Johnny Griffin, and the ever-underrated John Jenkins (all four actually attended the same high school at the same time), Clifford Jordan was quickly tagged as yet another of the string of brilliant tenor players who seemed to just keep coming out of Chicago in the 1950s. And, though his sound and approach may have been similar to his counterparts', Jordan's music definitely merits individual attention. Although he originally intended to be a horse trainer, his first professional gig at the age of 16 changed all that. After initial gigs with Max Roach, Sonny Stitt, and Horace Silver, Jordan made the pilgrimage to the Big Apple in 1957 and was soon in the Van Gelder studio cutting his Blue Note debut with fellow Chicagoan (and Sun Ra Arkestra member) John Gilmore. Tours with Kenny Dorham and Roach followed, culminating with Jordan taking over Booker

Ervin's spot aboard the wild ride known as Charles Mingus's 1964 Sextet (which also featured Eric Dolphy and Jaki Byard). In the early '70s Jordan teamed up with Stanley Cowell and Charles Tolliver to start their own label, the consistently visionary Strata East. European dates as a leader followed throughout the '70s and, before his death in 1993, Jordan was heading up a big band.

what to buy: *Blowing in from Chicago* 𝄢𝄢𝄢𝄢 (Blue Note, 1957, prod. Alfred Lion), Jordan's recorded debut, is a stunner, pitting him in a thoughtful tenor battle with John Gilmore, who, contrary to perception, was a marvelously gifted, straight-ahead player; here he locks horns brilliantly with Jordan's beefy style, without turning it into an out-and-out blowing session brawl. With more-than-able assistance from Art Blakey, Silver, and bassist Curly Russell, this is a fine hard-bop date for all involved. To leave Blue Note for Riverside may not have seemed the smartest thing for a player to do, but regardless, tempted by Adderley, Jordan made his way to the label and managed to cut *Spellbound* 𝄢𝄢𝄢 (Riverside, 1960/OJC, prod. Cannonball Adderley). Complemented by the water-tight rhythm section of Albert Heath and bassist Spaky DeBrest, as well as the sympathetic piano work of Cedar Walton, Jordan & Co. make right on a set of four solid originals and three covers, including a rather odd, waltzy version of "Lush Life." Not groundbreaking, but a solid example of Jordan's exemplary playing.

what to buy next: The second of Jordan's two Blue Notes, *Cliff Craft* 𝄢𝄢𝄢𝄢 (Blue Note, 1957, prod. Alfred Lion) boasts a strong line-up, and the spirited run-throughs of "Confirmation," "Sophisticated Lady," and "Anthropology" that make up side two are worth the price of admission. Throughout Jordan's European tour of 1975 he made a number of live and studio recordings that were eventually released on the SteepleChase label. *Magic in Munich* 𝄢𝄢𝄢 (SteepleChase, 1975/1995, prod. Nils Winther) would be the place to start, not only since it's inexpensive, but also because this studio date leaves a strong impression of the fire felt between Jordan and his all-star band of Billy Higgins, Sam Jones, and Walton. As with many of his contemporaries, Jordan found in the '70s a Europe that was dying for post-bop done right and, accordingly, he delivered.

the rest:
Bearcat 𝄢𝄢𝄢 (Jazzland, 1962/OJC)
On Stage, Volume 1 𝄢𝄢𝄢𝄢 (SteepleChase, 1975/1994)
On Stage, Volume 2 𝄢𝄢𝄢 (SteepleChase, 1975/1994)
On Stage, Volume 3 𝄢𝄢𝄢𝄢 (SteepleChase, 1975/1994)
Firm Roots 𝄢𝄢𝄢 (SteepleChase, 1975/1987)
The Highest Mountain 𝄢𝄢𝄢𝄢 (SteepleChase, 1975/1989)

Repetition 🎵🎵🎵 (Soul Note, 1984)
Live at Ethell's 🎵🎵🎵 (Mapleshade, 1987)
Masters from Different Worlds 🎵🎵🎵 (Mapleshade, 1989)
Four Play 🎵🎵🎵 (DIW, 1990)
Down through the Years: Live at Condon's 🎵🎵🎵 (Milestone, 1991)

influences:

◀◀ Lester Young

▶▶ Joshua Redman

Jason Ferguson

Duke Jordan

Born April 1, 1922, in New York, NY.

Duke Jordan will be long remembered for the classic sides he recorded with Charlie Parker in 1947. His presence on these seminal recordings place him on the scene during the early days of bebop, and he, along with more famous and technically accomplished pianists like Bud Powell, should be numbered among the founders of the bebop style for the piano. After leaving Parker's group, he performed as a sideman with artists like Stan Getz, Gene Ammons, and Sonny Stitt. Although never blessed with the commanding technique of his early bebop contemporaries, Jordan could be relied upon to provide unintrusive accompaniment and nicely crafted solos. During the early part of his career, Jordan was less active as a session leader than as a sideman. However, he fronted a few good sessions for Savoy and Blue Note in the late 1950s, and he enjoyed a fruitful partnership with baritone saxophonist Cecil Payne that continued until the 1970s. Jordan was also known as a composer of a handful of minor jazz classics (the most widely recorded is "Jordu"). In 1962, he contributed to the score of the French film *Les Liaisons Dangereuses*. In 1973, Jordan ended a decade of obscurity and began recording again for the Danish label SteepleChase. The next 12 years were the most prolific of his career, recording the bulk of his currently available catalog and producing recorded versions of his many compositions. These recordings earned Jordan a small but loyal following that appears to have dwindled somewhat since he stopped recording regularly. The merits of Jordan's legacy on SteepleChase are difficult to assess. Some of Jordan's less significant compositions are of no particular merit, yet they resurface in similar versions on different releases. Other albums feature him matched unfavorably with drummers and bassists who are too assertive for his essentially laid-back style. All the same, Jordan fans will find many pleasures among these recordings. To his fans, Jordan's better compositions become as familiar as

old friends, and they are welcomed each time they reappear in a new version. The performances are usually warm and engaging, and his interpretations of jazz standards (often the strongest tracks on these releases) are full of character and appealing.

what to buy: *Duke Jordan: New York/Bud Powell: Paris* 🎵🎵🎵🎵 (Vogue Disques, 1954/BMG, 1997, prod. Daniel Baumgarten), a collection of trio sides recorded for Vogue in 1954, includes some of Jordan's strongest statements as an improvisor. Jordan was one of the best single-note soloists of his day, and this session affords a rare opportunity to hear him stretch out and allow a solo to develop over several choruses. His trademark left hand style (he usually played chords on the beat, in a steady, gentle manner) offers an interesting contrast to the style of his contemporaries. Some worthwhile Bud Powell recordings (from 1960, with Kenny Clarke) are included as filler.

what to buy next: *Flight to Jordan* 🎵🎵🎵 (Blue Note, 1960/1987/1995, prod. Alfred Lion) is a solid quintet date that features top-flight performances by trumpeter Dizzy Reece and tenor saxophonist Stanley Turrentine. Although some of the compositions (all were written by Jordan) are less than memorable, the strong soloing and top-notch rhythm section carry the day. His first SteepleChase releases *Flight to Denmark* 🎵🎵🎵🎵 (SteepleChase, 1973/1994, prod. Nils Winther) and *Two Loves* 🎵🎵🎵🎵 (SteepleChase, 1973/1995, prod. Nils Winther) are two of Jordan's most successful trio dates for that label. Many of Jordan's best compositions are to be found here, in performances that compare favorably to any of his subsequently recorded versions of these works. However, Jordan's gentle and patient treatments of standards such as "My Old Flame" and "How Deep Is the Ocean" are the highlights of these releases.

what to avoid: *Wait and See* 🎵 (SteepleChase, 1978/1989/1996, prod. Nils Winther) finds Jordan's laid-back style overmatched by the assertive bassist and drummer. Jordan's solo statements are engaging enough, but he all too readily gives way to lengthy and intrusive solos by the rhythm section.

best of the rest:

Osaka Concert: Volume 1 🎵🎵🎵 (SteepleChase, 1976/1990)
When You're Smiling 🎵🎵🎵 (SteepleChase, 1985/1996)
Solo Masterpieces: Volume 2 🎵🎵🎵 (SteepleChase, 1996)

worth searching for: Hardcore Jordan fans will probably want to seek out the two volumes of Jordan's solo performances of his own compositions. The marginally better volume is *Solo Masterpieces: Volume 1* 🎵🎵🎵🎵 (SteepleChase, 1992, prod. Nils Winther). Many of Jordan's significant works are here, including

"Jordu" (called "Mellow Mood") and "Misty Thursday," as well as some compositions of considerably less merit. Jordan creates an atmosphere of intimacy, investing even the thinnest compositions with great patience and warmth.

influences:

◄◄ Bud Powell, Duke Ellington, Teddy Wilson

Will Bickart

Louis Jordan

Born July 8, 1908, in Brinkley, AR. Died February 4, 1975, in Los Angeles, CA.

Listen to a tune by the late jazzman Louis Jordan today and, though the lyrics might seem corny, the 1940s jump-blues and swing tempos will grab you as they did Bo Diddley, B.B. King, Chuck Berry, Albert Collins, Ray Charles, and others who have preserved Jordan's music through the years. A singer, saxophonist, and bandleader, Jordan played a brand of 1940s shuffling rhythms that helped set the standard for an era, and straddled the line between jazz and pop. He offered an alternative to 1940s bebop, and his "race records" (later called R&B) influenced early rock pioneers and today continue to influence contemporary jump-swing bands such as Royal Crown Revue and other such groups.

Jordan learned clarinet and saxophone from his father, a music teacher who led the Rabbit Foot Minstrels. He toured the Theater Owners Booking Association circuit part-time with his dad when he was in high school. He moved to Philadelphia where he worked with Jimmy Winters and Charlie Gaines around 1930, and worked with other musicians in New York City. In 1935 he joined the Chick Webb Orchestra, where he played alto sax and sang occasional vocals before he left the band in 1938. He performed briefly with Fats Waller, leaving to form his own group, the Tympani Five, one of the most successful small groups in jazz history, which recorded over 200 sides for Decca between 1938 and late 1953. Jordan used swing arrangements with comic lyrics depicting everyday activities, the war between the sexes, the down-and-out, and topics shared at Saturday night fish-fry parties. From the mid-1940s to mid-1950s the entertainer was a major influence in revolutionizing post-war jump and boogie-woogie music, with 55 singles reaching the Top 10 on the R&B charts (a feat no musician has since achieved).

He formed a short-lived big band in 1951, but tired of the rigors of the road and went into temporary retirement. Leaving Decca in 1954, Jordan recorded for Aladdin, RCA's short-lived "X" Records, Mercury, and other labels, but by the late 1950s his heyday had come and gone. Although he could play saxophone, Jordan was known more as a songwriter and singer. The late organist Bill Doggett, Jordan's pianist/arranger from 1947–51, once said, "[Jordan] was a tremendous musician. People didn't know about his ability as a saxophonist. . . . Jordan got his fame when he opened his mouth."

what to buy: The best domestic album that captures the spirit of Jordan's fun-filled music is *Best of Louis Jordan* 𝄞𝄞𝄞𝄞 (MCA, 1942–45/1989, prod. various). Jordan performs classics such as "Caledonia," "Choo Choo Ch'Boogie," "Five Guys Named Moe," and "Saturday Night Fish Fry," with that special verve that made him so popular. The CD includes his classics that influenced subsequent rock covers ("Don't Let the Sun Catch You Cryin'" and "Let the Good Times Roll") among the 20 tunes. This is the perfect introductory album, and once you're infected with a big dose of Jordan jive, you can check out the next recommendation. The German import, *Let the Good Times Roll: The Complete Decca Recordings, 1938–54* 𝄞𝄞𝄞𝄞 (Bear Family, 1994, prod. various) is a pricey (and priceless!) nine-CD set that holds great appeal for completists and collectors, as it contains every Decca single (over 200 songs) Jordan recorded for the label, reproduced with quality sound. The set features Jordan's earliest work as well as his later hits like "Choo Choo Ch' Boogie," "Caledonia," "Knock Me a Kiss," and "Is You Is or Is You Ain't My Baby," plus vocal duets with Bing Crosby and Ella Fitzgerald. The booklet that comes with the box set is full of interesting history and photographs. Some of the same Jordan material is repeated on another import label, the Jazz Chronological Classics CD series (from France), but those albums can be purchased as singles.

what to buy next: Harlem-born Clark Peters created the Broadway show *Five Guys Named Moe* (named after one of Jordan's popular tunes). The show (originally produced at the Theatre Royal, Stratford East, London) opened on Broadway in 1992 and is documented on the 23-tune revival version *Five Guys Named Moe* 𝄞𝄞𝄞𝄞 (Columbia, 1992) and the recommended 18-tune compilation performed by Jordan and his musicians, *Five Guys Named Moe: Original Decca Recordings, Volume 2* 𝄞𝄞𝄞𝄞𝄞 (Decca, 1949–1952/1992, prod. various). The Broadway show (primarily a vehicle for Jordan's music) has a thin story line evolving around the love relationship of Nomax, who has been dumped by his girlfriend. Drinking and moping in his room, he is surprised by five "guardian angels" who jump out of his radio garbed in flashy 1940s zoot suits. Singing the often-humorous lyrics of Jordan tunes, the Five Moes—Big Moe, Little Moe, Four-Eyed Moe, No Moe, and Eat Moe—attempt to console Nomax

and advise him on the caprices of women. The Broadway cast captures the essence of Jordan's major hits such as his million-seller "Choo Choo Ch' Boogie" (1946), "Caledonia," "Saturday Night Fish Fry," "Is You Is or Is You Ain't Ma Baby," and "Ain't Nobody Here but Us Chickens," and the title tune, "Five Guys Named Moe." But there's no substitute for the real thing, and the better of the two, hands down, is the Decca recording featuring Jordan himself. A compilation of 1956 tracks, with Quincy Jones as arranger-conductor (seven of the 16 tracks), *The Greatest Hits: No Moe!* ✍✍✍✍ (Mercury, 1992, prod. various) was designed to lure pop, blues, jazz, and early rock fans to Jordan's music. While the tunes lack the raw energy of his recordings of the previous decades, the music is upbeat, and bluesy numbers such as "Early In the Mornin,'" "Let the Good Times Roll," "Knock Me a Kiss," and "Sweet Lorraine" should satisfy blues and jazz fans. Jordan's sincere vocals are augmented with fine instrumental solos from tenor saxmen Budd Johnson and Sam Taylor, trombonist Jimmy Cleveland, and guitarist Mickey Baker. Charlie Persip is the drummer on all but four tracks, and B-3 organist Jackie Davis gets the joint jumpin' on four tracks. There are even a couple of calypso-influenced numbers, a big craze started by Harry Belafonte in the 1950s. Missing from this album is much of the 1940s jive talk material of earlier Jordan albums, but this disc is enjoyable when you frame it in reference to the moderation of the mid-1950s.

best of the rest:
At the Swing Cat's Ball ✍✍✍✍ (JSP, 1937–39)
One Guy Named Louis ✍✍✍✍ (Blue Note, 1954)
Louis Jordan 1941–1943 ✍✍✍✍ (Classics, 1994)

influences:

◀◀ Louis Armstrong, Chick Webb, Bill Doggett, T-Bone Walker

▶▶ Bill Haley & the Comets, Nat "King" Cole, Ray Charles, B.B. King, Chuck Berry, Jeannie & Jimmy Cheatham & the Sweet Baby Blues Band, Royal Crown Revue

Nancy Ann Lee

Marlon Jordan

Born August 21, 1970, in New Orleans, LA.

One of the young rising jazz stars from New Orleans, trumpeter Marlon Jordan, the youngest of seven children of Edward "Kidd" and Edvidge Jordan, grew up in a musical house-

Louis Jordan (Archive Photos)

hold. His father, saxophonist Kidd Jordan, is noted for his journeys into free-jazz, and three of Marlon's older siblings are music performers. Brother Kent plays flute, and introduced Marlon on his 1988 CBS album, *Essence*. Rachael plays violin with the New Orleans Symphony, and Stephanie is a vocalist. As a boy, Marlon was accompanying his dad on the bandstand even before he really knew how to play. After experimenting with saxophone, violin, and drums, Marlon finally settled on trumpet when he was in elementary school. Like the nearly decade-older Wynton Marsalis, Jordan has performed classical concerts with orchestras from a young age. He spent two summers at Tanglewood performing in the Young Artists orchestra with Leonard Bernstein and Seiji Ozawa, and studied with Roger Voisin, principal trumpeter of the Boston Symphony, and with Ralph Smedzig, leader of the Empire Brass Quintet. He also studied with Marsalis in New Orleans, with George Jansen (who also taught Marsalis) at Loyola School of Music in New Orleans, and with New Yorker trumpeter John Longo. Jordan plays a Monette trumpet, the same horn Marsalis used to recorded *J-Mood*. Marsalis gave it to Jordan as a Christmas gift and the younger trumpeter has used it to record all of his albums. Like many other New Orleans musicians of his generation, Jordan has a mature, confident, easygoing interpersonal style that comes across in his music. Although he recorded three albums for Columbia, only one is currently in print. Since his 1993 CBS album, *Undaunted*, was released, Jordan switched recording labels from CBS to Arabesque, took six months to recover from a serious 1995 auto accident in New Orleans, had a second daughter, and moved his family from southern Ohio to hometown New Orleans, where he's now teaching at a private school and performing festival and club dates.

what's available: Jordan is in top form as he adds drama to the seven-tune, mostly Coltrane hard-bop session *Marlon's Mode* ✍✍✍✍ (Arabesque, 1997, prod. Marlon Jordan). With his crisp technique and ear-pleasing phrasing, he makes a personal statement, often drawing from the swinging, Deep South sound of his earlier albums. Jordan's plump-toned Monette trumpet triumphs above swinging grooves from his regular drummer, Troy Davis (three tunes), and sub Jason Marsalis. Clarinetist Alvin Batiste (Jordan's uncle) and saxophonist Victor Goines enhance the album with fine, sophisticated solos, and pianist Victor Atkins from Birmingham and bassist David Pulphus from St. Louis support with expertise. The album centerpiece is a melodic, blended, dirge-like version of Coltrane's "Equinox," the lengthiest track at 13:30.

worth searching for: *For You Only* ♫♫ (Columbia, 1990) and *Learson's Return* ♫♫♫ (Columbia, 1991) were so-so albums and are no longer in print, but you may be able to still find used copies of his third Columbia album, *The Undaunted* ♫♫♫♫ (Columbia, 1993, prod. Marlon Jordan), which features the trumpeter with a tight-knit band of emerging young stars: Tim Warfield Jr. (tenor sax), Troy Davis (drums), Taurus Mateen (bass), and pianist Eric Reed. Jordan gives each musician generous space to develop solos, making this album one of the more exciting from his generation of New Orleans musicians. With the exception of the opener, Coltrane's "Village Blues," all of the compositions are Jordan's. Of particular note, the bluesy "Laurie's Mood" (written for his then two-year-old daughter), features his fine solo with his trumpet mocking the gurgling cries of a child. A churning "In or Out" takes you to the edge. "New Orleans Street Beat" investigates the roots of jazz, transporting you to the Crescent City. There's a distinctive sound inherent in native New Orleans jazz musicians, a bluesy, strolling beat influenced by the Dixieland funeral procession bands in New Orleans, by the sounds of Mardi Gras, and the flavor of 24-hours-a-day music, and it's all present in Jordan's playing.

influences:
◄◄ Wynton Marsalis

Nancy Ann Lee

Ronny Jordan

Born November 29, 1962, in London, England.

The "King of Acid Jazz guitar," Ronny Jordan is a self-taught guitarist who made waves with his debut, *The Antidote*, considered an influence on the acid-jazz movement that included some traditional influences. Jordan's playing has some solid jazz roots, and though more often than not he traverses into R&B and hip-hop territory, he shows signs of having a great pure jazz album in him.

what to buy: *The Antidote* ♫♫♫ (4th & Broadway, 1992, prod. Ronny Jordan) shows acid-jazz's promise as well as its drawbacks. His version of "So What" is daring and swings.

what to buy next: With less emphasis on hip-hop and more attention to smoother sounds, Jordan's sophomore effort, *The Quiet Revolution* ♫♫♫♫ (4th & Broadway, 1993, prod. Ronny Jordan) is more consistent and accessible, but not as biting or daring.

the rest:
Light to Dark ♫♫♫ (4th & Broadway, 1996)

influences:
◄◄ George Benson, Grant Green, Kevin Eubanks

Paul MacArthur

Sheila Jordan

Born November 18, 1928, in Detroit, MI.

Sheila Jordan is one of the most daring and distinctive vocalists in jazz. Though she has a small voice and a limited range, she is a highly creative improviser who brilliantly employs subtle tonal and textural shadings. Her performances can feel like a high-wire act as she improvises lyrics and takes huge musical chances, usually managing to land safely. Raised in Pennsylvania, Jordan took piano lessons and sang in school and on amateur radio shows as a youth. While attending high school she began associating with such leading young Detroit beboppers as Kenny Burrell, Tommy Flanagan, and Barry Harris. At the urging of Charlie Parker, she moved to New York in 1950 and ended up studying with Lennie Tristano. In 1952 she married pianist Duke Jordan (they were later divorced) and by the end of the decade was working regularly in New York clubs. She recorded an innovative version of "You Are My Sunshine" with George Russell in 1962 and the same year led a session for Blue Note, one of label's rare vocal releases. She didn't record again for a decade, however, until her collaborations with Carla Bley and Roswell Rudd appeared in 1973–74. She began touring with the Steve Kuhn Quartet in the late '70s, leading to a number of excellent collaborative sessions on ECM. In 1981 Jordan recorded an album of Steve Swallow's music and she has also collaborated extensively with bassist Harvie Swartz. Along with Mark Murphy, with whom she recorded a magnificent album, she leads a highly regarded vocal clinic every summer in Austria.

what to buy: An album that seemed to come out of nowhere, *Portrait of Sheila* ♫♫♫♫ (Blue Note, 1962/1989, prod. Alfred Lion) is the debut session of a dazzlingly original singer. Accompanied by guitarist Barry Galbraith, bassist Steve Swallow, and drummer Denzil Best, Jordan sings a dozen tunes, from the self-assured funk of Bobby Timmons's "Dat Dere" to the minute-long romp through "Let's Face the Music and Dance" to the resigned ache of "I'm a Fool to Want You." She consistently takes the music in unexpected directions and her sense of rhythm is impeccable throughout. A pairing of two of the most original singers in jazz history, *One for Junior* ♫♫♫♫ (Muse, 1993, prod. Sheila Jordan, Mark Murphy) is a brilliant collaboration with vocalist Mark Murphy. Highlights include "Bird," Jordan's tribute to Charlie Parker, and two ballad medleys that allow both singers to strut their stuff.

what to buy next: *Heart Strings* 𝄢𝄢𝄢𝄢 (Muse, 1994, prod. Sheila Jordan) is a beautiful recording featuring gorgeous arrangements by pianist Alan Broadbent for jazz trio and the Hiraga String Quartet. Covering standards such as "Haunted Heart" and "Comes Love," and jazz pieces such as Tom Harrell's "Out to Sea" and Broadbent and Dave Frishberg's "Heart's Desire," Jordan turns each tune into a highly personal statement.

best of the rest:
Lost and Found 𝄢𝄢𝄢𝄢 (Muse, 1990)
Songs from Within 𝄢𝄢𝄢 (M-A Music, 1993)

influences:
◀◀ Charlie Parker

Andrew Gilbert

Stanley Jordan

Born July 31, 1959, in Chicago, IL.

Just when music fans thought nothing else could be done with a guitar, along came Stanley Jordan. Employing a two-handed "tap and touch" technique, Jordan's hammer-ons, pull-offs, and bends allow him to play walking bass and lead parts simultaneously. The result is a rich, self-contained sound filled with percussive accents, which Jordan uses to great effect on a wide variety of jazz and pop standards as well as his own compositions. A graduate of Princeton University, Jordan recorded his first LP for his own Tangent label in 1982. The following year he attracted attention playing guitar on the streets of New York City, which led to high-profile gigs at the Montreux Jazz Festival and the Village Vanguard. Jordan's first LPs on Blue Note made him a star virtually overnight, and did much to revive jazz in the '80s. At his early peak, Jordan appeared in the Blake Edwards film *Blind Date* (he also played on the soundtrack), but soon shied away from the limelight and deliberately slowed the pace of his burgeoning career. While label-hopping from Capitol to Rounder to Arista, he continued to advance his sense of musical expressionism into the '90s. Not content to be a jazz-based guitar virtuoso, Jordan has widened his stylistic range to include classical, reggae, and funk, and has augmented his sound with layers of electronic instruments, a controversial move with purists. Whether playing solo, with a trio, or banks of studio equipment, Jordan remains the most masterful, distinctive guitarist of our time.

SHEILA JORDAN
(WITH GEORGE RUSSELL)

song "You Are My Sunshine"
album *The Outer View*
(Riverside-OJC, 1962/1992)
instrument Vocals

Monster Solo

what to buy: A very strong introduction to Jordan's revolutionary style and technique can be found on *The Best of Stanley Jordan* 𝄢𝄢𝄢𝄢 (Blue Note, 1995, prod. various), an 11-track sampler culled from his best early LPs. His transformation of Led Zeppelin's "Stairway to Heaven" into a piece of jazz expressionism is worth the price of the LP alone.

what to buy next: Jordan mixes original compositions with daring remakes on *Magic Touch* 𝄢𝄢𝄢 (Blue Note, 1985, prod. Al Di Meola), which features wonderfully inventive versions of Jimi Hendrix's "Angel," the Beatles' "Eleanor Rigby," Thelonious Monk's "'Round Midnight," and Miles Davis's "Freddie the Freeloader."

what to avoid: Stylistically, Jordan is all over the map on *Bolero* 𝄢𝄢 (Blue Note, 1994, prod. Stanley Jordan, Onaje Alan Gumbs), a bloated, overproduced masterpiece of self-indulgence.

the rest:
Standards, Volume 1 𝄢𝄢𝄢𝄢 (Blue Note, 1986)
Cornucopia 𝄢𝄢𝄢 (Blue Note, 1986)

Flying Home ♫♫ (Capitol/EMI, 1988/Alliance, 1997)
El Huracan ♫♫♫ (Rounder, 1989)
Stolen Moments ♫♫♫♫ (Blue Note, 1991)

worth searching for: If you just have to see Jordan and his two-handed piano-style guitar technique, track down the video *Stanley Jordan: The Blue Note Concert* ♫♫♫♫ (Pioneer, 1990), a laser-disc boasting great sound and strong performances.

influences:

◀◀ George Benson, Jimi Hendrix, Roy Buchanan, Carlos Santana

▶▶ Kevin Eubanks, Jeff Healey

Ken Burke

Vic Juris

Born 1953, in Parsippany, NJ.

Initially influenced by rock guitarist Chuck Berry, Vic Juris first came to the notice of jazz fans by playing with saxophonist Eric Kloss. From there he went on to a stint with jazz-rock fusioneer Barry Miles before settling into an important role with saxophonist Richie Cole's fine late-1970s group. It was while playing for Cole that Juris got the chance to record under his own name, an opportunity that resulted in three albums for Muse Records (now out of print). Since his days with Cole, the guitarist has played a supporting role in organ groups led by Don Patterson, Wild Bill Davison, and Jimmy Smith in addition to working in Mel Tormé's backup band. Juris's most recent long-term employer has been saxophonist Dave Liebman. Juris has also worked in tandem with some of the finest jazz guitarists of the 1980s and 1990s, including Larry Coryell and Birelli Lagrene. In the same vein, Juris took part in a 1997 concert with Coryell, David Fiuczynski, Russell Malone, and Jack Wilkins, called Five Guitars Play Mingus. In addition to his regular musicianly duties, Juris has worked the academic angle, teaching jazz improvisation and guitar at the New School (Mannes College), Lehigh University, and William Patterson University.

what to buy: *Moonscape* ♫♫♫♫ (Steeple Chase, 1997, prod. Nils Winther) features wonderful playing from Juris and his associates. Multi-instrumentalist Dick Oatts, best known for his stint with Red Rodney, works well with Juris, adding musical muscle throughout the project. The highlights of their partnership include a flute/guitar duo (the title tune) and an absolutely top-notch rendition of Billy Strayhorn's masterpiece "Blood Count." That last piece, with its deceptively languid pacing, may very well display the most inspired performances by either of these

master technicians and may be reason enough to buy the album.

what to buy next: Juris wrote most of the material on *Night Tripper* ♫♫♫♫ (Steeple Chase, 1995, prod. Nils Winther), although kudos also go to pianist Phil Markowitz for his contribution ("Dekooning"). The guitarist's acoustic playing is best heard on Kurt Weill's superb "Liebeslied" and Bruno Martina's "Estate," but the meat of the project is in the quicksilver plectrum maneuvers and interesting tonal distortions Juris creates on the electric numbers.

the rest:
(With Bireli Lagrene) *Bireli Lagrene Ensemble Live featuring Vic Juris* ♫♫♫ (Jazz Point, 1986)
Music of Alec Wilder ♫♫♫ (Double-Time, 1996)
Pastels ♫♫♫ (Steeple Chase, 1996)

influences:

◀◀ Larry Coryell, John Scofield, Steve Khan, Pat Martino, Charlie Banoros, Ted Dunbar

▶▶ Phil Hopp, B.D. Lenz, Dave Warren

Garaud MacTaggart

Henry Kaiser

Born 1952, in Oakland, CA.

Henry Kaiser is a whole world unto himself. He started as a filmmaker, traveled to Japan to be a director's assistant, and went to Harvard for a business degree. All that changed when he heard the music of Derek Bailey, and the 20-something Kaiser ran out and bought himself a guitar. He became entrenched in Bailey's guitar language, adding his love of Korean and Vietnamese music, Captain Beefheart, and Delta blues. With Larry Ochs of the Rova Saxophone Quartet, Kaiser started his own label, Metalanguage, responsible for documenting the exciting early Bay area scene that included Kaiser, Rova, Greg Goodman, Diamanda Galas, and others. What really sets Kaiser apart from the others is his solo playing, which incorporates many outboard effects and electronics that have altered the sounds of his guitar, making him a pioneer of electric-guitar improvisation. Kaiser also has been a tireless champion of music from unheralded countries and a producer for important recordings from countries like Madagascar and Burma.

what to buy: *Lemon Fish Tweezer* 🎵🎵🎵 (Cunieform, 1992) is a career retrospective of solos. Using a fairly simple setup of delays and filters, Kaiser does something that is so much more intellectually challenging and more beautiful than anything that was being done at the time with the same equipment.

what to buy next: A good sampler of Kaiser's diverse interests, *The Five Heavenly Truths* 🎵🎵🎵 (Fot, 1993) contains more solos and Beefheart-inspired band and group improvisations.

what to avoid: While not a bad record, *Heart's Desire* 🎵🎵🎵 (Reckless, 1994) is the most steeped in Kaiser's love of Dead-inspired jamming. If that's your bag, it's good to hear Kaiser and Bruce Anderson stretch out, but if you want something a bit more elastic, try some other titles in his vast catalog.

the rest:
With Enemies like These, Who Needs Friends? (SST, 1987)
Re-Marrying for Money (SST, 1988)
(With Sergey Kuriyokhin) *Popular Science* (Ryko, 1989)
Tomorrow Knows Where You Live (Victo, 1991)
Hope You Like Our New Direction (Reckless, 1991)
(With Fred Frith) *Crazy Backwards Alphabet* (SST, 1992)
Eternity Blue (Shanachie, 1995)
(With Derek Bailey) *Wireforks* (Shanachie, 1995)
(With David Lindley) *A World Out of Time* (Schanachie, 1995)
Outside Aloha Pleasure (Dexter's Cigar, 1996)
(With John Oswald) *Improvised* (Incus, 1996)

influences:

◀◀ Derek Bailey, Terry Riley

▶▶ Thurston Moore, Reeves Gabrels

Jim O'Rourke

Bruce Katz

Born 1952, in Brooklyn, NY.

Bruce Katz is a Boston-based keyboard ace who has made his presence felt on the music scene as much through his work as a sideman as he has during his turns as a leader. That's not to discount his work under his own name, it's just that Katz has proven to be an especially deft accompanist in a variety of recording situations ranging from blues to rock to soul. It's no coincidence, then, that Katz's work as a leader is flavored by elements of all three aforementioned genres as well as a free-minded, post-bop–based jazz sensibility. His piano work is imbued with touches of a rollicking New Orleans spirit and also

with a sense of creative adventure à la Geri Allen (whom Katz studied with). On the organ, Katz has good taste, an instinctive feel for the blues, and great use of dynamics. Born in Brooklyn, Katz was something of a child prodigy. He had a handle on Mozart by the time he was seven years old. Following graduation from Berklee in 1974, Katz toured as a keyboardist with Johnny Adams and Big Mama Thornton, among others, before beginning a four-year association with Boston rock 'n' roll wildman Barrence Whitfield in the late '80s. In 1992 he released the first of a series of CDs on the Audioquest label. His significant sideman roles also include studio recordings with soul singer Mighty Sam McClain and blues guitarist Ronnie Earl.

what to buy: *Transformation* 🎵🎵🎵 (Audioquest, 1994, prod. Joe Harley) has the most to offer serious jazz fans, with *Crescent Crawl* 🎵🎵🎵 (Audioquest, 1992, prod. Joe Harley) not far behind. Both offer a mix of mostly original compositions by Katz that spotlight both his organ and piano work. Both find bluesy groovers alternating with somewhat angular jazz explorations. *Transformation* is the more exploratory of the two, though *Crescent Crawl* is perhaps more fun. Take your pick.

what to buy next: *Mississippi Moan* 🎵🎵🎵 (Audioquest, 1997, prod. Joe Harley) has a slightly heavier emphasis on the blues, featuring a pair of vocals from Mighty Sam McClain, an excellent soul singer whose Audioquest releases (all of which include Katz as a sideman) are also worth searching out if you are a fan of deep, gospel-inflected soul.

worth searching for: Blues guitarist Ronnie Earl's *Grateful Heart: Blues and Ballads* 🎵🎵🎵🎵 (Bullseye, 1996, prod. Noel Ward) is a high point for both Katz and Earl. An after-hours themed blues-jazz disc not done simply by the numbers, this session has some breathtakingly beautiful moments, and is a must-have for fans of blues-based jazz. Katz is featured on both organ and piano. Also includes David "Fathead" Newman on tenor saxophone.

influences:

◀◀ Don Pullen, Jimmy Smith, Professor Longhair, Geri Allen, Larry Young

▶▶ Larry Goldings, John Medeski, Davell Crawford

Dan Bindert

Connie Kay
See: Modern Jazz Quartet

Sammy Kaye

Born March 13, 1910, in Rocky River, OH. Died June 2, 1987, in Ridgeway, NJ.

"Swing and sway with Sammy Kaye" was this bandleader's famous tag-line, and while he didn't swing particularly hard, his popular "sweet" band racked up nearly 100 chart records between 1937–53. In addition to writing and arranging tunes for his own band, Kaye was a respected songwriter who penned hits for Perry Como ("A—You're Adorable") and Nat "King" Cole ("My Sugar Is so Refined," "Too Young"), among others. Unique among bandleaders, Kaye didn't serve an apprenticeship with any other band—he made a name for himself leading an orchestra at Ohio University, and simply turned pro after graduation. After successful stints on Cincinnati and Pittsburgh radio, Kay and his orchestra hit the big time with a series of such network radio programs as *The Old Gold Cigarette Program* and *The Chesterfield Supper Club.* And on *So You Want to Lead a Band,* Kaye offered fans the opportunity to come on stage, lead his band, and win a band baton, an immensely successful gimmick. This potent exposure resulted in such major hit records as "Until Tomorrow," "Remember Pearl Harbor," "Wanderin'," "Rosalie," and many others. Among Kaye's many vocalists, Tommy Ryan and Don Cornell were able to establish an especially large fan base, and their mellow crooning was responsible for a large portion of Kaye's success. Most of the big bands died out in the 1950s, yet Kaye was able to keep his orchestra's sweet, reed-heavy style popular throughout the decade via his TV version of *So You Want to Lead a Band* and his later show, *The Manhattan Shirt Program.* The 1964 instrumental "Charade" was Kaye's final Top 40 hit. Afterwards, he cut an LP of brassy Dixieland that drew positive reviews, but few sales, and he began slowly phasing himself out of the business. In 1986 he handed the baton over to Roger Thorpe, who toured with a new lineup of the Sammy Kaye Orchestra, though Kaye maintained creative and quality control until his death.

what's available: Kaye's run of hits at Columbia is compiled on *Sammy Kaye: Best of the Big Bands* 🎵🎵🎵 (Columbia, 1990, comp. prod. Nedra Neal) and features the Number One hits "Daddy," "Tennessee Waltz," and "Harbor Lights." Taken from live radio transcriptions, *Sammy Kaye & His Orchestra: 22 Original Big Band Recordings 1941–44* 🎵🎵 (Hindsight, 1987/1993, prod. Wally Heider) has thin sound but is a nice piece of history.

worth searching for: The out-of-print *Sammy Kaye* 🎵🎵🎵 (RCA Special Products, 1993) and *Best of Sammy Kaye* 🎵🎵🎵🎵 (MCA

Jazz, 1974) cover Kaye's big hits and finest moments from his eras with those respective labels.

influences:

◀◀ Isham Jones, Guy Lombardo, Kay Kyser

▶▶ Eddy Howard, Roger Thorpe, Ralph Flanagan

Ken Burke

Geoff Keezer

Born November 21, 1970, in Eau Claire, WI.

Coming from a small farming town in Wisconsin, an unlikely place to find a developing jazz artist one would think, pianist Geoff Keezer was barely of legal age when he joined up as the last pianist in drummer Art Blakey's Jazz Messengers. Rare for his age, Keezer had already developed a maturing style based on the hard-bop tradition. His playing is distinctive in its driving intensity. Both he and his teacher and producer, James Williams, share an affinity for the technical brilliance of the late Phineas Newborn. Thus, Keezer's full sound is marked by thick block chords and two-handed unison lines which are dazzling and incendiary. Unfortunately, most of Keezer's recorded work is done for small independent companies, and a few of the major label dates he led in the early 1990s are already unavailable, making it hard to find the most representative examples of his talent.

what to buy: *Waiting in the Wings* 🎵🎵🎵 (Sunnyside, 1988, prod. James Williams) was recorded just before Keezer turned 18 and it is indeed a very impressive debut. One is struck by his distinguished originals and his technical fluidity at the piano, and you can't beat the strong band, which includes vibist Steve Nelson, saxophonist Billy Pierce, bassist Rufus Reid and drummer Tony Reedus. *Curveball* 🎵🎵🎵 (Sunnyside, 1989, prod. James Williams) was the follow-up to his first Sunnyside date and it too features Keezer's skilled composing and emotionally direct piano work.

the rest:

Live at Maybeck Recital Hall 🎵🎵🎵🎵 (Concord, 1991)

(With Harold Mabern) *For Phineas: Two Piano Jazz* 🎵🎵🎵 (Sackville, 1995)

worth searching for: *Here and Now* 🎵🎵🎵🎵 (Blue Note, 1990, prod. James Williams) is no longer available on CD, but worth looking for in the used bins. Keezer continues his fruitful association with vibist Steve Nelson, and the rhythm section of Peter Washington and Billy Higgins can't be beat. *World Music* 🎵🎵🎵🎵 (DIW/Disc Union, 1992, prod. Geoff Keezer, James

Williams) is currently only obtainable as a Japanese import but is well worth the search and cost. This is Keezer's best effort as a leader to date and the fireworks abound.

influences:

Phineas Newborn, Harold Mabern, James Williams, McCoy Tyner

Chris Hovan

Roger Kellaway

Born November 1, 1939, in Newton, MA.

Even though Roger Kellaway had begun classical piano lessons at an early age, he was playing bass and percussion in high school before finally settling back into his piano studies. He studied composition and piano performance at the New England Conservatory for a couple of years but left to play bass for Jimmy McPartland. When Kellaway moved to New York City in the early 1960s he found steady work as a studio musician in addition to playing with Kai Winding, the Al Cohn/Zoot Sims Quintet, and the Clark Terry/Bob Brookmeyer Quintet and recording with Ben Webster, Oliver Nelson, Wes Montgomery, and Sonny Rollins. When he moved out to the West Coast in the late '60s Kellaway continued his studio work, but added arranging, composing, and producing credits to his resume while continuing to record with top-notch talent like Carmen McRae, Joni Mitchell, and Jimmy Knepper. Kellaway has won Grammy awards (for his work with clarinetist Eddie Daniels) and received Academy Award nominations (for the score to Barbra Streisand's remake of *A Star Is Born)*. His larger classical compositions have been performed by the Los Angeles Philharmonic, the National Symphony, and the New York Philharmonic, while chamber music works like the Cello Quartet have also received a fair number of performances. Kellaway moved back to New York City in 1984 and continues his record of versatility. The list of albums he has recorded on or been involved with tops the 200 mark, including a CD he cut for Piano Disc, meant for use with the new breed of electronic player pianos that company sells.

what to buy: Lest the buyer think that doing all that session work and Hollywood arranging has weakened Kellaway's skills as a highly talented jazz musician, proof to the contrary is available on *Live at Maybeck Recital Hall Volume 11* (Concord Jazz, 1991, prod. Carl E. Jefferson), one of the finest albums in a heralded series of solo piano recitals. He not only has reams of technique at his disposal, Kellaway possesses a sure instinct of what swings and when to swing it. As is the case with most Maybeck releases, the program is heavy with standards, including "How Deep Is the Ocean," "New Orleans," and Ellington's "Creole Love Call." Kellaway's two originals, to his credit, do not sound overwhelmed in those surroundings.

what to buy next: *Life's a Take* (Concord Jazz, 1993, prod. Carl E. Jefferson, Nick Phillips), a duet with bassist Red Mitchell (his last), was recorded at Maybeck Recital Hall as the initial release in Concord Jazz's Duo series. Kellaway and the bassist had a mutual admiration society going that covered most of three decades, and their interplay throughout this set verges on telepathic.

the rest:

Portrait of Roger Kellaway (Fresh Sound, 1963)
(With Red Mitchell) *Fifty-Fifty* (Natasha, 1987)
(With Red Mitchell) *Alone Together* (Dragon, 1988)
Nostalgia Suite (Voss, 1988)
(With Red Mitchell and Putte Wickman) *Some o' This and Some o' That* (Dragon, 1989)
In Japan (All Art Jazz, 1991)
(With Red Mitchell and Jan Allan) *That Was That* (Dragon, 1991)
Roger Kellaway Meets the Duo (Chiaroscuro, 1992)
Windows (Angel, 1994)

influences:

Oscar Peterson, Billy Taylor

Garaud MacTaggart

Wynton Kelly

Born December 2, 1931, in Jamaica. Died April 12, 1971, in Toronto, Ontario, Canada.

Wynton Kelly was a great pianist, but he never seemed to make the turnstiles click, relegating his talents to his role as a sideman for artists like Dinah Washington, Dizzy Gillespie, Charles Mingus, and Miles Davis, with only an occasional session as a leader. His first professional gigs were with R&B bands of the late '40s led by people like Eddie "Cleanhead" Vinson and Eddie "Lockjaw" Davis. Kelly's stint with Miles Davis lasted from 1959–63, during which he worked with rhythm mates Paul Chambers on bass and Jimmy Cobb on drums. When Davis decided to run with a different line-up, his rhythm section continued as a unit, playing under Kelly's leadership. With this trio Kelly recorded dates with Wes Montgomery that later turned up as *Smokin' at the Half Note*. He has also recorded with Cannonball Adderley, Art Pepper, Sonny Rollins, John Coltrane, Abbey Lincoln, and Hank Mobley. While playing in Toronto, Kelly suffered an epileptic seizure and died for lack of assistance.

what to buy: The highly enjoyable *Smokin' at the Half Note* ♫♫♫♫ (Verve, 1965, prod. Creed Taylor) finds Kelly, Chambers, and Cobb in the company of guitarist Wes Montgomery. Kelly, as a former Davis sideman, has a nice, long, funky solo in Davis's "No Blues" that shows why some people compare him to Horace Silver. Chambers and Cobb are impeccable in their roles and Montgomery, the nominal co-leader on this recording, works a little harder than normal to make this one of the better recordings he took part in. *Piano* ♫♫♫♫ (OJC, 1958, prod. Orrin Keepnews), Kelly's second recording as a leader, came a mere seven years after his debut for Blue Note. The quartet sides with Kelly, Chambers, drummer "Philly" Joe Jones, and guitarist Kenny Burrell are filled with solid playing, but the trio versions where Jones drops out are ultimately more rewarding. "Strong Man," an Oscar Brown Jr. tune, is a bright, catchy confection for the trio, while Kelly's "You Can't Get Away" is an uptempo blues piece for the trio done with the sort of chamber music flair you would expect from the Modern Jazz Quartet.

what to buy next: The recordings on *Blues on Purpose* ♫♫♫ (Xanadu, 1983, prod. Don Schlitten) were done at the Half Note during the same time frame as *Smokin' at the Half Note*, but the monaural sound quality is not as strong as the Verve date. Going in its favor though, is some great playing from the trio sans Montgomery.

the rest:
Piano Interpretations ♫♫♫ (Blue Note, 1951)
Kelly Blue ♫♫♫♫ (OJC, 1959)
Kelly at Midnight ♫♫♫ (Vee-Jay, 1960)
Last Trio Session ♫♫♫ (Delmark, 1989)

influences:
◀◀ Art Tatum, Bud Powell
▶▶ Benny Green

Garaud MacTaggart

Chris Kelsey
Born June 5, 1961, in Bangor, ME.

Free jazz player/composer Chris Kelsey grew up in Oklahoma and was taught by his father, a jazz saxophonist and flutist. After getting his bachelor's degree in music education from the University of Central Oklahoma in 1984, he played with jazz and R&B bands in and around Oklahoma City until moving to New York in 1986. A student of Lee Konitz (saxophone) and Max Roach (jazz history), he has worked in the bands of drummer Lou Grassi, composer/bassist Joe Gallant, and saxophonist/composer Marco Eneidi and has also played with William Parker, Matthew Shipp, Phillip Johnston, and Borah Bergman. Kelsey curated the Bunker Annex Series for Free Improvisation from 1995–97, and his music writing has been published in *Jazz Now, Jazziz,* and *Cadence.*

what to buy: *The Ingenious Gentleman of the Lower East Side* ♫♫♫♫ (CIMP, 1997, prod. Robert D. Rusch) compares the stubborn idealism of free-jazz musicians with that of Cervantes's *The Ingenious Gentleman Don Quixote of La Mancha,* with the song title "The Adventure in Which Our Hero Banged His Head against the Wall Repeatedly" summing it up best. Funny titles are not enough, of course, and along with bassist Dominic Duval and drummer Ed Ware, Kelsey goes the rest of the way with enterprising free improvisations that demonstrate an innate structural sense, along with a willingness, less than common in free jazz, to swing unabashedly when the occasion demands it.

the rest:
Observations ♫♫♫ (CIMP, 1996)

worth searching for: *Stomp Own It* (Saxofonis, 1993) is a cassette Kelsey put out himself (he can be contacted at chkelsey@sprintmail.com). He calls the group, with electric bassist Dom Richards and drummer Ed Ware, the Almost Jazz Trio, and it recalls the insouciance of the Lounge Lizards' "fake jazz," although with considerably more instrumental virtuosity and less hip irony from Kelsey than from lead Lizard John Lurie. Kelsey is one of three saxophonists on the Lou Grassi Saxtet's *Quick Wits* ♫♫♫♫ (CIMP, 1996, prod. Robert D. Rusch) but his soprano playing stands out clearly among the sounds of Phillip Johnston's alto and Joe Ruddick's baritone. The saxophonists provide the compositions (with the exception of a clever arrangement of a Bela Bartok piano exercise), and Kelsey's "There's No Business like Jazz Business" (ironic cool jazz) and "I Got Rid of Them" (an affectionate take on early Ellington) are of interest as his only pieces for multiple horns (so far) on record.

influences:
◀◀ Steve Lacy, Sidney Bechet, Lee Konitz

Steve Holtje

Rodney Kendrick
Born April 30, 1960, in Philadelphia, PA.

Known among his fellow-musicians as Monkman, pianist/composer Rodney Kendrick doesn't let his infatuation with his nick-namesake run away with his own individuality. Instead, he uses Thelonious Monk's playful angularity and iconoclastic approach as conceptual models, not etched-in-stone gospel. The result is that Kendrick is among the brightest new lights to emerge in the past several years.

what to buy: Two of the four albums issued under Kendrick's own name (he was previously part of Abbey Lincoln's backup band) are richly textured large-group statements that place the leader's keyboard at the center of a swirling lineup of outstanding sidemen, while his most recent outing is his first in the piano-bass-drums trio setting. *Dance World Dance* ♪♪♪♪ (Verve/Gitanes, 1994, prod. Jean-Philippe Allard) boasts altoist Arthur Blythe, cornetist Graham Haynes, baritonist Patience Higgins, and South African tenorist Bheki Mseleku among its guests, with forces ranging from quintet to tentette on the separate tracks. The trio date, *We Don't Die, We Multiply* ♪♪♪♪ (Verve/Gitanes, 1997, prod. Jean-Philippe Allard) is equally fine, with covers of Randy Weston, Monk, and Lincoln tunes along with some standards and the evocative compositions of the relatively unknown Rhonda Ross.

what to buy next: *Last Chance for Common Sense* ♪♪♪♪ (Verve/Gitanes, 1996, prod. Jean-Philippe Allard) also uses variably sized ensembles (quartet to nonet, with Dewey Redman on several cuts), but is less focused, and the series of brief instrumental interludes that link the tracks are hokey—they detract from, rather than add to, the overall effect. The solo debut, *The Secrets of Rodney Kendrick* ♪♪♪ (Verve/Gitanes, 1993, prod. Jean-Philippe Allard), brings Kenny Garrett, Roy Hargrove, and Houston Person into the mix and has its ups and downs. But regardless, Kendrick's star is definitely on the ascent, a composer/instrumentalist with an extremely bright future.

influences:

◀◀ Thelonious Monk, Abbey Lincoln

David Prince

Stan Kenton

Born February 19, 1912, in Wichita, KS. Died August 25, 1979, in Los Angeles, CA.

Stan Kenton courted controversy through much of his career as a bandleader, arranger, and composer, gaining tremendous popularity then often alienating his fans. He is still something of a cult figure, and though his musical legacy is checkered, his bands often boasted top-flight improvisors. Despite his insistence on giving his bands and albums pretentious names such as "neophonic orchestra" and "innovations," he was a dedicated experimenter who played some advanced, though not always swinging music. An adequate Earl Hines-influenced pianist, Kenton often inspired great loyalty in his sidemen, even when they were frustrated with the band's musical direction.

Raised in Los Angeles, Kenton broke into the West Coast music scene playing piano with Vido Musso and Gus Arnheim's dance bands. He formed his first band in 1941, and by working regularly at the Rendezvous Ballroom in the Southern California town of Balboa Beach, he gradually built up a large popular following. The band's recordings for Decca didn't sell well, however, and a stint as Bob Hope's back-up band ended badly, with Les Brown called in to take Kenton's place. By the mid-1940s, Kenton had recruited a number of top-flight musicians, including Art Pepper, Boots Mussulli, Stan Getz, Bob Cooper, Vido Musso, and especially singer Anita O'Day, resulting in a series of hits. When singer June Christy replaced O'Day and continued to score hits (such as "Tampico"), Kenton was in a position to finance his ambitious project of turning a dance band into a concert orchestra. He called his music "Progressive Jazz," and with Pete Rugolo's charts, Kenton transformed his Lunceford-influenced sound into a radical though sometimes plodding ensemble.

After taking a year off in 1949, Kenton assembled his most ambitious band, the 39-piece Innovations in Modern Music orchestra, with 16 strings, French horns, and a woodwind section. Kenton took the orchestra out on the road twice, but it was economically unsustainable, despite the presence of such talented musicians as Pepper, Maynard Ferguson, Bud Shank, Laurindo Almeida, and Shelly Manne. Playing difficult and advanced music that often looked to the European modernist tradition for inspiration, the unwieldy group did manage to swing on occasion, too. At his most adventurous, Kenton recorded a number of pieces by Bob Graettinger, a brilliantly idiosyncratic arranger/composer who anticipated the Third Stream movement. Reverting to a 19-piece line-up in the early 1950s, the Kenton orchestra became a proving group for arrangers, with such important writers as Bill Holman, Marty Paich, Bill Russo, Gerry Mulligan, Shorty Rogers, and Lennie Niehaus producing highly creative charts for the band. Despite the tendency toward bombast, the early and mid-1950s marked the musical high point of the Kenton organization, which continued to boast a steady stream of top-flight improvisors, including Lee Konitz, Frank Rosolino, Zoot Sims, Bill Perkins, Lucky Thompson, Mel Lewis, and Pepper Adams. Kenton employed four mellophones from 1960–63 and sometimes used them to startling effect, but in the mid-1960s he began focusing more on jazz education, and the level of musicianship in his band dropped considerably.

After 1965 the Kenton band featured a few musicians who went on to significant careers (Peter Erskine, Tim Hagans, and Chuck Findley among them). Kenton recorded prolifically throughout his career, maintaining a relationship with Capitol for 25 years (1943–68), then forming his own label, Creative World, to reissue his past recordings and document his new bands. Many of his albums have been reissued, including two excellent limited-edition box sets by the mail-order label Mosaic. There are numerous import recordings on various labels available, and most of the CDs recommended below are from domestic labels readily available in the United States. Though Kenton's music still retains a hard-core coterie of fans, his artistic reputation has suffered since the 1970s. Still, by making his charts available widely to schools and through his tireless work as an educator, the Kenton sound became prevalent in high school and college jazz programs.

what to buy: Get past the over-long and painfully pretentious "Prologue" in which Kenton introduces the band, and *New Concepts of Artistry in Rhythm* ♫♫♫♫ (Capitol, 1952/1989) offers some fascinating music. The band was still playing some of the challenging music of the unwieldy Innovations Orchestra, but was focusing more on swinging. There are many highlights, from Bill Russo's charts that feature trombonist Frank Rosolino ("Frank Speaking") and Lee Konitz ("My Lady") to Bill Holman's experimental "Invention for Guitar and Trumpet," featuring Sal Salvador and Maynard Ferguson, respectively. A strong two-disc anthology of Kenton's most ambitious band, *The Innovations Orchestra* ♫♫♫ (Capitol, 1950–51/1997, prod. Jim Conkling) gives a good sense of the ensemble's range. With the brilliant arrangements of Bill Russo and Shorty Rogers, and Maynard Ferguson's stratospheric trumpet, Bud Shank's mellifluous flute, Art Pepper's hot and fluid alto, and Conte Candoli's tremendous bebop chops, Kenton had no shortage of talent. Still, the music occasionally sinks under the weight of the 39 players, including a 16-piece string section. The strong solos and often fascinating charts make for highly interesting listening, even when Kenton's ambition oversteps good taste. One of Kenton's best albums from the mid-1950s, *Cuban Fire!* ♫♫♫♫ (Capitol, 1956, 1960/1991) features a six-part suite that made arranger/composer Johnny Richards's reputation. The 27-piece band, with two French horns, a tuba, and seven-piece Latin percussion section, maintains the Afro-Cuban feel quite effectively, though it's the solos by tenor saxophonists Lucky Thompson and Bill

Perkins, trombonist Carl Fontana, and alto saxophonist Lennie Niehaus that carry the day. The CD reissue also contains a previously unreleased suite by Richards, "Tres Corazones," and five pieces by Kenton's 1960 band featuring five mellophones that make for interesting if not repeated listening. There are virtually no precedents in jazz (or European classical music) for *City of Glass* ♫♫♫♫ (Capitol, 1947–53/1995), an amazing CD containing Bob Graettinger's compositions and arrangements for the Kenton orchestra. Still radical-sounding after five decades, Graettinger's music anticipated many of the avant garde experiments of later years. From the astoundingly dense opening track "Thermopylae" to the three movements of the "City of Glass" suite, to the "This Modern World" pieces, Graettinger creates kinetic, sometimes stark, and sometimes brittle soundscapes. Not for the faint of heart, *City of Glass* still retains the power to shock, and it's to Kenton's credit that he championed Graettinger's visionary music.

what to buy next: An excellent session featuring 10 Johnny Richards arrangements of tunes from the musical, *Stan Kenton's West Side Story* ♫♫♫ (Capitol, 1961/1994, prod. Lee Gillette, Kent Larson) offers greater emotional range than many Kenton albums. There are Kenton's trademark roaring brass and fine solos by trumpeter Conte Candoli and alto saxophonist Gabe Baltazar, but there are also some tender and almost sentimental passages. Gene Rolands provides most of the charts for the strong nightclub session *Live from the Las Vegas Tropicana* ♫♫♫ (Capitol, 1959/1996, prod. Lee Gillette, Kent Larson), featuring solos by such fine players as trumpeter Jack Sheldon, tenor saxophonist Richie Kamuca, and alto saxophonist Lennie Niehaus (who also wrote one of the arrangements). The band sounds crisp and focused throughout, and makes a surprising foray into the swing past with interesting versions of "Tuxedo Junction" and "Street Scene." Kenton revisits his past on *Kenton in Hi-Fi* ♫♫♫♫ (Capitol, 1956/1992, prod. Lee Gillette), playing updated, stereo versions of such hits as "The Peanut Vendor," "Intermission Riff," and "Eager Beaver." Tough tenor saxophonist Vido Musso takes most of the solos, but there is also fine work by trumpeters Pete Candoli and Maynard Ferguson, trombonist Milt Berhart, and alto saxophonist Lennie Niehaus. Time hasn't been kind to Stan Kenton's artistic reputation, but the lasting value of his music is evident throughout *Stan Kenton 50th Anniversary Celebration: The Best of Back to Balboa* ♫♫♫♫ (MAMA Foundation, 1992, prod. Gene Czerwinski), a selection of

Stan Kenton **(Archive Photos)**

tracks from an excellent five-disc set documenting a four-day celebration of Kenton in the summer of 1991. The 12 tracks include eight pieces by the Alumni Band, conducted by the original arrangers (including Pete Rugolo, Buddy Childers, Bill Holman, and Lennie Niehaus) and featuring such players as trumpeters Chuck Findley, Steve Huffsteter, and the Candoli brothers, and saxophonists Bob Cooper, Bill Perkins, and Bud Shank. There are also performances by Maynard Ferguson and the Big Bop Nouveau Band, the Bob Florence Limited Edition, the Buddy Childers Big Band, and the Bill Holman Big Band.

influences:

◀◀ Earl Hines, Jimmie Lunceford

Andrew Gilbert

Freddie Keppard

Born February 15, 1889, in New Orleans, LA. Died July 15, 1933, in Chicago, IL.

Along with King Oliver, Freddie Keppard remains one of the most powerful and influential early cornetists of early jazz to have been preserved on record. Keppard, along with his brother Louis (born l888), started playing music at an early age, and had joined various bands in and around New Orleans by the turn of the century. Freddie organized his own Olympia Orchestra by about 1906. A popular player, he continued to play occasional jobs with other groups, especially in Storyville, the red light district of New Orleans. By 1912, Keppard started touring the United States, finally settling in Chicago about 1917. He initiated his brief recording career in 1923 on two numbers for OKeh records with the Erskine Tate Orchestra (with whom he worked on several different occasions). As in New Orleans, he was a player of demand throughout Chicago's South Side before joining "Doc" Cook's popular band. By the late 1920s, Keppard's declining health curtailed his musical activities, and he died in obscurity after a bout with tuberculosis.

In private transcripts, Louis Armstrong had said of Freddie Keppard: "He had the prettiest lips I've ever seen on a man." Those lips gave Keppard a distinctive full and very forceful sound. While still in New Orleans, Keppard and King Joe Oliver would often engage in cutting contests, which sometimes spilled out into the street in front of the club where the battle started. This drew throngs of people and made legends out of both men. Armstrong also claimed that Keppard "did not take the music business seriously." Perhaps that is why so precious few recordings exist of Keppard.

what to buy: Keppard's entire bona fide recorded output (bona fide because critics will continue to argue forever about Keppard's presence on a number of recordings) can be found on *The Complete Freddie Keppard, 1923–27* 𝄞𝄞𝄞𝄞 (King Jazz, 1996, prod. Alessandro Protti, Roberto Capasso, Gianni Tollara). In a small group setting, the titles released under Keppard's name ("It Must Be the Blues" and "Salty Dog," with two takes each) show Keppard's prowess to good advantage, even though recorded acoustically. The best recordings for that "peek behind the curtain" earful of what King Keppard must have sounded like in his prime comes from the electric Columbia recordings by Doc Cook's Orchestra. Cook's recording of Jelly Roll Morton's "Sidewalk Blues" features Keppard on open horn performing a straight lead near the finale. The reeds flutter a riff behind one of the sweetest yet strongest tones to be heard in early jazz. Then Keppard punches the ride out in a jaunty hat-cocked-to-the-side-of-the-head solo that will leave the listener shaking one's head. Keppard is no Armstrong, yet he offers another facet of the rich New Orleans trumpet tradition. There is no one else in recorded jazz quite like Freddie Keppard. For the few recordings left us, we should be thankful at the glimpse of this master of early jazz.

the rest:

The Legendary Freddie Keppard 𝄞𝄞𝄞 (Topaz, 1996)
New Orleans Giants: Keppard/Ory/Dodds/Carey, Vols. 1 & 2, 1922–1928 𝄞𝄞𝄞 (Hot 'N' Sweet, 1996)

Jim Prohaska

Barney Kessel

Born October 17, 1923, Muskogee, OK.

One of the finest guitarists in jazz history, Barney Kessel was largely self-taught after just three months of lessons at the age of 12. By the early 1940s he was working in big bands, playing in 1943 with the Chico Marx orchestra directed by Ben Pollack, and then in a succession of prominent swing bands including those of Charlie Barnet, Hal McIntyre, and Artie Shaw. Kessel also appeared in Shaw's small group, the Gramercy Five. By the late 1940s, he was doing substantial radio work in New York City, and his long career was divided between commercial studio work and more straight-ahead jazz playing. In 1952 he joined the Oscar Peterson trio with bassist Ray Brown. He remained with the group for a year, touring extensively with Norman Granz's Jazz at the Philharmonic, including a European tour backing Lester Young and Ella Fitzgerald. Kessel's flexibility made him a natural for studio work, and he appeared anonymously on countless pop records and TV and film soundtracks, recording with a Who's Who of American pop music that included Elvis Presley, the Coasters, the Beach Boys, Cher, Judy Garland, and Frank Sinatra. His jazz credits stretched from Kid Ory to Sonny Rollins, touching on almost every major figure in between, and he recorded with a variety of fellow guitarists, including T-Bone Walker and Duane Eddy. Though Kessel was a consummate swing and bop musician, his instrument lent itself to the cooler textures of the West Coast style. He became one of the most popular jazz artists of the 1950s, often working with Andre Previn and Shelly Manne on jazz versions of musicals. In the 1960s he took sabbaticals from studio work to play clubs and concerts, and increasingly incorporated Brazilian rhythms into his work. In the 1970s he appeared with Herb Ellis and Charlie Byrd in a group called the Great Guitars. A stroke in 1992 ended his playing career.

The most celebrated jazz guitarist of the late 1950s, Kessel consistently won readers' polls in *Down Beat, Metronome,* and *Playboy.* Among the most talented of Charlie Christian's disciples, he combined great swing, rhythmic inventiveness, a steady flow of melodic ideas, and a technical flare that was evident whether soloing in single notes or chords. His immersion in studio music occasionally colored his own projects, which are sometimes diminished by abysmal pop fare, even including a jazz version of the musical *Hair.* However, despite decades of work in commercial music, as an arranger and producer as well as a guitarist, Kessel remained a great bop soloist, and there are excellent examples of his work from every decade of his career.

what to buy: Much of his finest work is to be found on the dates he recorded in the 1950s for the Contemporary label. *Volume 3: To Swing or Not to Swing* ♪♪♪♪ (Contemporary, 1955/1991, prod. Lester Koenig) presents Kessel in two small group sessions with the emphasis definitely on swing. There's high spirited play on "Begin the Blues," "Moten Swing," and "Twelfth Street Rag," with Kessel clearly fired by the presence of trumpeter Harry Edison, tenor saxophonist Georgie Auld, and pianist Jimmy Rowles. The Poll Winners trio with Shelly Manne and Ray Brown produced lightly swinging, virtuosic music with a brilliant rhythm section highlighting Kessel's invention. *Poll Winners Three!* (Contemporary, 1959/OJC, 1992, prod. Lester Koenig) has great group chemistry throughout with "Soft Winds" and "Mack the Knife" standing out. The piano-less format gives the guitarist tremendous freedom of movement. Kessel's playing had clearly kept developing by the time of the trio's 1975 reunion, *Straight Ahead* ♪♪♪♪ (Contemporary, 1975/OJC, 1992, prod. Lester Koenig), and there's more room to stretch out. Bassist

Brown's springy lines are the perfect foil for Kessel's horn-like attack and subtle placement of notes.

what to buy next: *Solo* ♪♪♪♪ (Concord, 1983/1996, prod. Frank Dorritie) is the only CD available that's devoted to Kessel playing without accompaniment, and it's a showcase for superb playing. Kessel creates masterful chorded solos in a set that mixes strong pieces like "Brazil" and "Manha de Carnaval" with weaker pop tunes like "You Are the Sunshine of My Life" and "People." *Yesterday* ♪♪♪♪ (Black Lion, 1973/1993, prod. Alan Bates) presents Kessel live at the Montreux Jazz Festival. It's lively and relaxed play, ranging from a solo version of the title tune to a sparkling outing with violinist Stephane Grappelli on "Tea for Two."

best of the rest:
Plays Standards ♪♪♪♪ (Contemporary, 1955/OJC, 1987)
PollWinners Ride Again ♪♪♪♪ (Contemporary, 1958/OJC, 1991)
Carmen ♪♪♪♫ (Contemporary, 1958/OJC, 1986)
Workin Out ♪♪♪♫ (Contemporary, 1961/OJC, 1998)
Barney Kessel and Friends ♪♪♪ (Concord, 1975/1992)
Red Hot and Blues ♪♪♪♪ (Contemporary 1988)

influences:
◀◀ Django Reinhardt, Charlie Christian
▶▶ Larry Coryell, John McLaughlin

Stuart Broomer

Steve Khan

Born April 28, 1947, in Los Angeles, CA.

Khan went from being a New York studio musician to a fusioneer to a respected acoustic jazz player. The son of Tin Pan Alley veteran Sammy Cahn, who wrote the lyrics to many a jazz standard, Khan played piano and drums before picking up the guitar. He moved to New York City in 1970 and established himself as a session player on dates with everyone from James Brown, Blood Sweat & Tears, and Joni Mitchell to the Brecker Brothers (*Back to Back, Don't Stop the Music*), Maynard Ferguson, Hubert Laws, and Billy Cobham. He began making fusion albums as a leader in the second half of the decade (on Columbia) and dropped the first notice that he was also adept in straight-ahead jazz with a 1980 album of tunes by Thelonious Monk—several years in advance of the Monk revival, it should be noted—and other jazz greats. In 1981 he put together a steady fusion group, Eyewitness, with Manolo Badrena (percussion, vocals), Anthony Jackson (bass), and Steve Jordan (drums), and temporarily gave up studio work to pursue his career as a leader. With changes in the drum chair, this group has been an ongoing project.

what to buy: *Got My Mental* 🎵🎵🎵 (Evidence, 1997, prod. Steve Khan) has a great program of lesser-known tunes by jazz greats: Ornette Coleman's "R.P.D.D.," Wayne Shorter's "Paraphernalia," Keith Jarrett's "Common Mama," Eddie Harris's "Sham Time," and Lee Morgan's "Cunning Lee." There are also a couple standards, "The Last Dance" (by Sammy Cahn and James van Heusen) and "I Have Dreamed" (Rodgers & Hammerstein) and Khan's own title track. To say that this is straight-ahead jazz, mainstream jazz, is accurate in a way yet not reflective of the imagination with which Khan arranges the material. The core trio of himself, bassist John Patitucci, and drummer Jack DeJohnette is augmented by additional percussionists (sometimes as many as three) on half the tracks, and Patitucci (playing acoustic bass in this format) is often in the foreground. The most exciting parts are when Khan solos, alternating rhythmic displacement of interestingly voiced chords and soul-drenched lead lines. He most often recalls the keyboardless contexts of early Pat Metheny.

what to buy next: *Crossings* 🎵🎵🎵 (Verve Forecast, 1994, prod. Steve Khan) is the most recent manifestation of Khan's group Eyewitness, with the great Dennis Chambers on drums and Michael Brecker adding tenor sax to three of the ten tracks. The major fusion qualities here are some guitar overdubs, electric bass, and Chambers's deep grooves, as the group at this point has moved much closer to Khan's straight-ahead interests. Hence there are tunes by Monk, Tony Williams, Shorter, Morgan, and Joe Henderson (a burning "Inner Urge") and Cole Porter, Bronislau Kaper, and Cahn-Styne standards along with two Khan originals. This has some of Khan's most exciting guitar playing in years.

the rest:
Casa Loco 🎵🎵🎵 (Antilles, 1983)
(With Rob Mounsey) *Local Color* 🎵🎵🎵 (Passport, 1987/Denon, 1990)
Let's Call This 🎵🎵🎵🎵 (Bluemoon, 1991)
Headline 🎵🎵🎵 (Bluemoon, 1992)

worth searching for: First Columbia let their three Kahn-helmed fusion albums go out of print, then they let even the compilation *The Collection* 🎵🎵🎵 (Columbia Legacy, 1994, prod. Bob James, Steve Khan, compilation prod. John Snyder) lapse into unavailability. With everyone from Don Grolnick and Bob James to the Brecker Brothers, David Sanborn, and Steve Gadd, they boasted an all-star crew of the New York session men of the time, with plenty of tasty playing and funky grooves

if not exactly profound composing. And it's really a shame that his first solo acoustic album *Evidence* 🎵🎵🎵 (Novus, 1980, prod. Steve Khan), with its long and loving Monk medley and the layers and layers of guitar overdubs on "In a Silent Way," also seems not to be available at the moment.

influences:
◀◀ Pat Martino, Eric Gale
▶▶ John Abercrombie

Walter Faber

Talib Kibwe

Born in New York, NY.

Talib Kibwe's first instrument was the trumpet, but he traded in the horn for reeds and flute by the time he entered high school. In the mid-1970s Kibwe was studying with the Jazzmobile crew of instructors, including Jimmy Heath, Frank Foster, Thad Jones, and Billy Taylor. By 1977, after he had graduated from NYU and gotten his master's degree in music education from Columbia, Kibwe went on tour with pianist Abdullah Ibrahim. He moved to Paris, France, in 1981 and started working with pianist Randy Weston, eventually becoming Weston's musical director. Kibwe has also played and/or recorded with poet Jayne Cortez, Taja (a group Kibwe co-led with pianist James Weidman), and his own band, T.K. Odyssey.

what's available: *Introducing Talib Kibwe* 🎵🎵🎵 (Evidence, 1996, prod. Cecil Brooks III) is the first mass-distributed release under his own name. There is a strong Randy Weston flavor; the great man plays on his own "Hi Fly," and Kibwe's cohort in the Weston ensemble, trombonist Benny Powell, is included on two cuts.

worth searching for: Kibwe's stay with Weston has been well documented and some of Kibwe's best work can be found on Weston's albums, *The Spirits of Our Ancestors* 🎵🎵🎵🎵 (Antilles, 1992, prod. Randy Weston, Brian Bacchus, Jean-Philippe Allard) and *Volcano Blues* 🎵🎵🎵🎵 (Antilles, 1993, prod. Randy Weston, Brian Bacchus, Jean-Philippe Allard).

influences:
◀◀ Jimmy Heath, Frank Foster, Randy Weston, Abdullah Ibrahim

Garaud MacTaggart

Peter Kienle

See: BeebleBrox

Franklin Kiermyer

Born July 21, 1956, in Montreal, Quebec, Canada.

Franklin Kiermyer is a powerhouse drummer in the Elvin Jones line. Pursuing his musical vision with a single-mindedness rare in the jazz world, he extends the John Coltrane Quartet's aesthetic (what liner notes writer Kevin Whitehead has aptly called "modal expressionism" and Kiermyer himself refers to as Ecstatic American music) by pouring its spirituality into the mold of his personal Jewish faith, and in truth the modality sometimes recalls traditional Jewish music as much as it does Coltrane.

Kiermyer grew up in ethnically diverse Montreal and was first affected by the power of music during Sabbath morning services in the synagogue. He started playing at age 12, and credits his tympani studies and listening to Baby Dodds and Gene Krupa with influencing his style. After starting his professional career, he frequently found himself playing alongside traditional Eastern European musicians and saw the parallels between Middle Eastern, Asian, and Balkan music. During a dues-paying period with touring R&B and dance groups, Kiermyer delved into the contrasting music of the classic Coltrane Quartet.

On his 21st birthday, Kiermyer's loft burned, and all his compositions and his drums were destroyed. He apparently took this as a sign that a clean break with his past was in order and moved to the United States, at first living in Amherst, Massachusetts. Settling into an intense practicing regimen by day and free improvisation by night, with forays to New York City to listen and sit in, he eventually made the move to New York. But he then decided that the sideman's life was not for him, and moved among Toronto, Montreal, and New York while developing his own music before settling again in New York.

Two albums for a German label garnered praise from aficionados, but not much broad-based attention. Signing with a U.S. label, Kiermyer broke through to a larger audience in 1994 with the stunning *Solomon's Daughter*, with guest saxophonist Pharoah Sanders emphasizing the Coltrane connection. He continued to expand his music's base on *Kairos*, incorporating world music. His most recent project, only partially completed, is an album of guitar trios; the first third features Vernon Reid and Reggie Workman.

what to buy: *Solomon's Daughter* ♫♫♫♫♪ (Evidence, 1994, prod. Franklin Kiermyer) is the album that first brought major attention to Kiermyer. Many focused on the high-intensity blowing of Pharoah Sanders throughout the album after his years of more low-key playing, and Sanders truly is marvelous, playing with unrestrained passion and energy. But Kiermyer is the leader, and his powerhouse polyrhythmic drumming and heartfelt compositions deserve to be the focus of the album. Pianist John Esposito fills the Tyner role without sounding slavishly imitative about it, and Drew Gress is stalwart on bass.

what to buy next: On *Kairos* ♫♫♫♫ (Evidence, 1996, prod. Franklin Kiermyer) Coltrane references abound from the opening title track on, but Kiermyer is looking for something even more all-encompassing. Five short tracks offer African, Greek, and Native American music in pure form (the band's not on them), and the cyclic, organic nature of these musics implicitly inspires the band tracks' development beyond Trane. Tenor saxophonist Michael Stuart, pianist John Esposito, and bassist Dom Richards all excel, joined by guest saxists Eric Person and Sam Rivers.

worth searching for: Kiermyer's first two albums, both issued by a German label, offer facets of his music not exposed on his Evidence releases. *Break down the Walls* ♫♫♫ (Konnex, 1993, prod. Franklin Kiermyer) matches the trio of Kiermyer, pianist Peter Madsen, and bassist Tony Scherr with a brass quartet (trumpet, horn, trombone, tuba). In a strategy recalling Herbie Hancock's *Speak Like a Child*, the horn parts are all written out, though of course Kiermyer's focus and harmonic language are different. But the sonorities of the brass, which range from bold to wistful, make it a very special project, and Madsen and the leader improvise stirringly amidst these settings. *In the House of My Fathers* ♫♫♫♫ (Konnex, 1993, prod. Franklin Kiermyer) is notable for variety of both instrumentation and style. Frequent collaborator Esposito makes his first appearance with Kiermyer here, playing on every track except one featuring two electric guitarists, bassist Anthony Cox, and the leader. Other formats range from the trio title track, to quintets with saxophonist John Stubblefield (who's also on the one quartet track) and trumpeter Dave Douglas, to septets with four-horn arrangements like the previous album's.

influences:

◀◀ Elvin Jones, Rashied Ali, Gene Krupa

Steve Holtje

Dave Kikoski

Born 1961, in Milltown, NJ.

Dave Kikoski is one of the most fluent young pianists working in mainstream jazz, a musician who can swing forcefully as an accompanist and apply his adventurous harmonic ideas to various improvisational contexts. Kikoski's father, a part-time musician, started teaching him piano at age seven, beginning with tunes by Count Basie and Duke Ellington. In 1984, Kikoski graduated from the Berklee School of Music (where he met his wife, Argentine reed player Cecilia Tenconi), and about a year later moved to New York. Kikoski has recorded with a host of top-notch musicians, including drummer Billy Hart, trumpeters Randy Brecker and Red Rodney, and saxophonists Craig Handy and Ralph Moore. He started working with the legendary drummer Roy Haynes in the mid-1980s, recording with him frequently, most memorably on the 1992 Dreyfus album *When It's Haynes It Roars*. Comfortable in Latin jazz contexts, he has worked with percussionist Guilhermo Franco. Kikoski has also performed frequently and recorded with tenor saxophonist David Sanchez.

what to buy: Ranging from the edgy, unusual harmonic development of the opening track, "E," to the warped samba of his "B Flat Tune," *Dave Kikoski* 𝄞𝄞𝄞𝄞 (Epicure, 1994, prod. Dave Kikoski, Michael Caplin) is a surprise-filled session. With Essiet Essiet on bass and Al Foster on drums, this trio can move in three different directions at once, or lock into a powerful groove, as on Coltrane's "Giant Steps."

the rest:
Presage 𝄞𝄞𝄞 (Free Lance, 1990)

worth searching for: An excellent showcase for the young pianist, *Persistent Dreams* 𝄞𝄞𝄞𝄞 (Triloka, 1992, prod. Walter Becker) features Kikoski playing a few jazz standards and his own idiosyncratic tunes.

influences:
◀◀ Herbie Hancock, McCoy Tyner

Andrew Gilbert

Rebecca Kilgore
Born September 24, 1949, in Waltham, MA.

Rebecca Kilgore is a vocalist with a gentle, lilting natural swing who also plays rhythm guitar (and plays it very well). Her sound is soothing, often soft and willowy, and easy on the ears. Although she has her own style, at times she sounds as if she had listened at length to Anita O'Day, June Christy, and Ella Fitzgerald. Then again, there is a suggestion of Doris Day in the timbre or tonal quality of her warm delivery. Her material is somewhat eclectic because she is so comfortable with jazz, Country, and Western swing, and with her favorite composers Irving Berlin and Jerome Kern, and other writers of the American popular song.

Kilgore grew up with lots of music and art in her Waltham, Massachusetts, home, her mother being a graphic artist, and her father having a music degree from Harvard, as well as experience as a jazz pianist, a choir director, and writer of choral music. Kilgore began playing guitar while still in high school, attended the University of Massachusetts, became a computer programmer, and studied for a time with a music teacher who had taught at Berklee College of Music. In 1979, she moved to Portland, Oregon, and landed a secretarial job at Reed College. She befriended a girl singer and guitar player, Cyd Smith, who was then with a small swing band, Wholly Cats. Kilgore replaced Smith in the group in 1981, and began easing into a musician's career, learning lyrics, chord changes, and stage presence. She met versatile drummer Hal Smith and trumpeter Chris Tyle while in Wholly Cats, sang with guest artists such as tenor saxman Scott Hamilton, and appeared on the radio with the band in 1983. After Wholly Cats disbanded in 1985, Kilgore freelanced with a number of groups, including a Western swing band, Ranch Dressing; a small Django Reinhart-styled combo, Everything's Jake; and her own country-styled band, Beck-a-Roo. In 1992, Kilgore began singing with noted pianist Dave Frishberg at Portland's Heathman Hotel, giving up her day job and turning full-time to music. Two 1994 record dates prompted national attention and subsequent invitations to jazz parties and festivals, with tours at home and abroad as guitarist-vocalist with Hal Smith's Roadrunners, and as member of another Smith-led group, The California Swing Cats. More record dates followed. In 1997, she appeared at the prestigious Jazz At Chautauqua, accompanied in various sets by pianists Dave McKenna and Keith Ingham, and bands fronted by Dan Barrett and Hal Smith. She continues to dazzle her audiences, making new fans wherever she appears.

what to buy: The first widely distributed and critically acclaimed album for the jazz singer, *I Saw Stars* 𝄞𝄞𝄞𝄞 (Arbors, 1994, prod. Rachel Domber, Mat Domber) finds Kilgore performing with Dan Barrett's Celestial Six. Songs dating from the 1930s and 1940s are enhanced by the free-and-easy delivery of singer Kilgore and her talented accompanists, Barrett (cornet, trombone), Chuck Wilson and Scott Robinson (reeds), Michael Moore (bass), Bucky Pizzarelli (guitar), and longtime Kilgore associate, Dave Frishberg (piano). The 17-tune collection offers abundant solos by all and fresh vocal performances from Kilgore, who even takes up her guitar for a delightful duet with Pizzarelli on "Exactly Like You." A winner album. On Rebecca Kilgore and Dave Frishberg's *Not a Care in the World* 𝄞𝄞𝄞 (Arbors, 1996, prod. Rebecca Kilgore, Dave Frishberg), Frishberg and Kilgore give listeners a sample of what they might hear at the pair's weekly gig at Portland's Heathman Hotel. The collection of 17 tracks, 22 songs from the 1940s and 1950s heyday of jazz, features guitarist Dan Faehnie on 10 tracks, and includes winning performances of "A Kiss to Build a Dream On," "All My Life," and "I've Got a Feelin' You're Foolin'." This set should appeal to fans with leanings toward smart vocals, sensitive piano work, and attractive songs that hold up well 40 or 50 years after being written.

what to buy next: *Looking at You* ♫♫♫ (PHD Music, 1994, prod. Dave Frishberg, Rebecca Kilgore) is another superior vocal-piano album from the Kilgore-Frishberg duo. An eclectic mix of tunes is offered, including "It Might as Well Be Spring," sung in French, a bouncy version of "Robin Hood," a lovely "My Ideal," and an unexpected revival of "There Ain't No Sweet Man That's Worth the Salt of My Tears." They don't write 'em like that any more, and there aren't many collections out there of this quality.

worth searching for: Each of these 20-tune, swinging quintet sessions, *Rhythm, Romance and Roadrunners!* ♫♫♫♫ (Triangle Jazz, 1996, prod. Tom Rippey, Dick Rippey) and *Hal Smith's Roadrunners, Vol. 2* ♫♫♫ (Triangle Jazz, 1996, prod. Tom Rippey, Dick Rippey), features Kilgore's vocals on eight tunes, with fine solos from clarinetist Bobby Gordon, pianist Ray Skjelbred, and relaxed rhythm support from Kilgore (on guitar), bassist Mike Duffy, and leader-drummer Smith. Kilgore also appears on two albums with Smith's California Swing Cats band, *Swing, Brother, Swing* ♫♫♫♫ (Jazzology, 1997, prod. Hal Smith), and *Stealin' Apples* ♫♫♫ (Jazzology, 1997, prod. Hal Smith). Each features nine delightful vocal gems by Kilgore and lots of tasteful swing from Tim Laughlin's fluid clarinet and more of the leader's versatile drumming.

John T. Bitter

Frank Kimbrough

Born November 2, 1956, in Roxboro, NC.

Keeping an eye and ear on pianist Frank Kimbrough becomes easier and more pleasurable as the years and discs go by. The versatile pianist started out his career as a protege of Shirley Horn and in 1985 won the Great American Jazz Piano Competition, sealing his credits as a soulful player with great technique. Since then he has covered a lot of stylistic territory, working with bluesman B.B. King, World fusionist Paul Horn, and avant garde musician Anthony Braxton, as well as appearing on albums by Ted Nash and with the tonally adventurous

Maria Schneider Jazz Orchestra. Although the first couple of recordings under his name (the solo *Star-Crossed Lovers* and piano/drums duet *Double Vision*, both on Mapleshade) were cassette-only affairs that have been discontinued, he has recorded some projects in the 1990s that should be around awhile. A founding member of the Jazz Composers Collective, Kimbrough is a composer-in-residence with the collective and has received grants and fellowships from the National Endowment for the Arts and Meet the Composer. He also serves on the faculties of the Cannon Music Camp at Appalachia State University and at New York University.

what to buy: The late Herbie Nichols is one of those legendary pianists (along with Elmo Hope) who deserve to be placed up there in the ivory pantheon with Bud Powell and Thelonious Monk. All wrote material that challenged the accepted precepts of the time and all, in their own ways and times, were awesome players. Nichols recorded works feature him in a solo or trio format when he would have, according to Roswell Rudd, loved to hear horns playing his tunes. This is where Kimbrough comes in. He started transcribing Nichols music and arranging it for a quintet with piano, bass, drums, saxophone/clarinet, and trumpet/flugelhorn. *The Herbie Nichols Project: Love Is Proximity* ♫♫♫♫ (Soul Note, 1997, prod. Jazz Composers Collective), the result, with the aid of a grant from the National Endowment for the Arts, is spectacular. The album is an at times brilliant, but never less than excellent, sampler of what Nichols's music can sound like in the hands of talented musicians. Kimbrough, reedman Ted Nash, trumpeter Ron Horton, and the rhythm section of Ben Allison on bass and Jeff Ballard on drums have done a wonderful job of playing the music and revealing fresh insights into the audio world of Herbie Nichols. The title tune is a Nichols composition that has never been recorded before, adding a special fillip to this collection of his works. Under Kimbrough's guidance, *Love Is Proximity* proudly takes its place among the finest efforts of its kind, a glowing and important addition to Nichols's posthumous legacy.

what to buy next: *Lonely Woman* ♫♫♫ (Mapleshade, 1990, prod. Pierre M. Sprey) finds Kimbrough in the company of bassist Ben Wolfe and drummer Jeff Williams. This is a well-recorded recital that features some sensitive yet adroit playing from Kimbrough and his partners. As you might expect, the album works best when the group swings hardest, which they seem to do most efficiently on the covers. Nichols's delicious "House Party Starting" prompts leader Kimbrough to dig in deeply and claw his way around the tune's changes. The Nichols piece is particularly interesting from an interpretation standpoint because it pre-dates the NEA grant that Kimbrough received to prepare performance of Nichols's music (although he had been working on the project since 1985). The trio also takes on Ornette Coleman's "Lonely Woman" (from 1959), which for a while was the one Coleman title that other musicians would play. The challenges and rewards it offered on the cusp of the 1960s are well met here, showing the softer, more sensitive (if you will) side of Coleman, and coming equipped with an ever-so-faint Spanish tinge. The other covers include Jimmy Rowles's magnificent "The Peacocks." The rest of the album features tunes contributed by members of the trio who are all fairly talented composers, although Kimbrough's "20 Bars," with its slow, bluesy pace and slightly off-kilter chords, has pride of place. While Williams's and Kimbrough's contributions can be a bit too rhapsodic, Wolfe's "Pete & Repeat" and "Lonely in London" (despite its nearly pulseless, exhausted pacing) rise to the occasion.

influences:

⏮ Shirley Horn, Bud Powell, Herbie Nichols

Garaud MacTaggart and David Prince

King Curtis

Born Curtis Ousley, February 7, 1934, in Fort Worth, TX. Died August 14, 1971, in New York, NY.

With his big, fat tone and guttural growl, King Curtis was at home among the heady rock 'n' roll and R&B scenes of the 1950s and 1960s. His rousing tenor saxophone solo on the Coasters' big hit, "Yakety Yak," set the standard for his trademark style. That's not to say that Curtis wasn't also comfortable working in the jazz and blues fields. Among his early endeavors was a 1951 stint with Lionel Hampton that ultimately placed him in New York, where he soon became an in-demand studio musician. Curtis's most rewarding work, from a jazz perspective, was in the form of several fine dates he led for the Prestige label and in his sideman roles backing such blues legends as Sunnyland Slim, Al Smith, and Roosevelt Sykes. Just prior to his brutal slaying at the age of 37, Curtis had taken on the role of Aretha Franklin's musical director and had appeared at the 1971 Montreux Jazz Festival along with blues great Champion Jack Dupree.

what to buy: *Soul Meeting* 🎵🎵🎵🎵 (Prestige, 1960, prod. Esmond Edwards) pairs the original albums *The New Scene of King Curtis* and *Soul Meeting*, both of which feature Curtis with trumpeter Nat Adderley and pianist Wynton Kelly. This is in-

deed soulful and rewarding music that proved how well Curtis could perform in the jazz idiom. Curtis, the player least associated with a purely jazz style, actually is the one to steal the show on the incendiary and exciting match-up of tough tenors, with Oliver Nelson and Jimmy Forrest, on *Soul Battle* 🎵🎵🎵🎵 (Prestige, 1960, prod. Esmond Edwards).

what to buy next: *Trouble in Mind* 🎵🎵🎵 (Prestige/Tru-Sound, 1961, prod. Esmond Edwards), which finds Curtis blowing and singing the blues, gives us another example of his versatility.

the rest:

Night Train 🎵🎵🎵 (Prestige, 1961, prod. Esmond Edwards)

worth searching for: *Old Gold/Doing the Dixie Twist* 🎵🎵🎵🎵 (Prestige/Tru-Sound, 1961/1962, prod. Esmond Edwards) is a two-on-one CD available from Ace Records out of England. It includes a funky session with organist Jack McDuff and a truly hip date that found Curtis making twist novelties out of such tunes as "St. Louis Blues" and "When the Saints Go Marching In."

Chris Hovan

King Pleasure

Born Clarence Beeks, March 24, 1922, in Oakdale, TN. Died March 21, 1981, in Los Angeles, CA.

A master of vocalese, putting lyrics to jazz solos, King Pleasure came up about the same time as singer Eddie Jefferson (born 1918), who is credited as the "Father of Vocalese." Certainly, their paths must have crossed. Pleasure gained prominence after winning a talent show at Apollo Theatre in New York's Harlem area. He sang Eddie Jefferson's lyrics to James Moody's "I'm in the Mood for Love," which ultimately won him a recording contract with Prestige. His singles "Red Top" and "Parker's Mood" also brought him further notice, but even as he continued recording for Prestige, Jubilee, and Aladdin, Pleasure was unable to sustain his success in the face of the popularity of Al Jarreau, the Manhattan Transfer, and Lambert, Hendricks & Ross.

what to buy: In his day, King Pleasure was considered one of the most innovative singers in jazz, and his album *Moody's Mood for Love* 🎵🎵🎵🎵 (Blue Note, 1955/1992, prod. Alan Douglas) is probably the best of what's out there. Pleasure reinvents classics such as "Old Black Magic," "Sometimes I'm Happy," "It Might As Well Be Spring," "I'm in the Mood for Love" (a.k.a. "Moody's Mood for Love"), and other lesser-known titles.

what to buy next: Compiling material from the classic period of the 1950s, *King Pleasure Sings/Annie Ross Sings* ♫♫♫ (Prestige/OJC, 1952–54, prod. various) features King Pleasure and Annie Ross on a disc that also includes appearances from Betty Carter, John Lewis, Percy Heath, J.J. Johnson, Paul Chambers, Jon Hendricks, Art Blakey, and others. Pleasure sings his hits, "Moody's Mood for Love" (based on the changes of "I'm in the Mood for Love"), "Red Top," "Parker's Mood," and other classics of the day, with four bonus tracks sung by Pleasure on the CD reissue. Ross sings "Farmer's Market," "Twisted," "Annie's Lament," and "The Time Was Right." If you're into vocalese, this is a good album by two of the masters of the form.

the rest:

Golden Days ♫♫♫ (OJC, 1991)

influences:

◀◀ Eddie Jefferson, James Moody, Lester Young

▶▶ Lambert, Hendricks & Ross, Al Jarreau, Manhattan Transfer

Joe S. Harrington

Andy Kirk

Born May 28, 1898, in Newport, KY. Died December 11, 1992, in New York, NY.

Andy Kirk and His Clouds of Joy were one of the finest bands to come out of the Southwest during the late 1920s. His well-dressed and well-rehearsed band represented some of the best in Kansas City Big Band jazz. The fine arrangements coupled with the hot piano of Mary Lou Williams made this band a favorite with dancers and listeners alike. The band recorded frequently and had many juke box hits that boosted their popularity immensely. The Clouds of Joy toured extensively and were a top ballroom attraction.

As a child growing up in Denver, Andrew "Andy" Dewey Kirk received music lessons from Wilberforce Whiteman, Paul Whiteman's father. By 1918, Andy Kirk was playing bass sax, baritone sax, and tuba, and touring professionally. In 1925, he joined Terence Holder's Band, which he eventually took over as leader in 1929. The band's first recordings occurred that year for Brunswick. When Brunswick's A&R man, Jack Kapp, left to form his own record company (Decca), he took many Brunswick artists with him, including Kirk. Decca was priced well (35 cents per disc, or 3 for $1.00). At that price, Decca became a favorite with jukebox vendors, and the danceable Kirk band sold many, many records. The success of Kirk's Decca recordings was bolstered by the sophisticated and silken voice of singer Pha (pro-

nounced "Fay") Terrell. He made hits of "What's Your Story Morning Glory," "Until the Real Thing Comes Along," and others. Kirk kept the band together until 1948, when he semi-retired from the music business then ran a hotel in Harlem for many years. He was also responsible for organizing a local for the Musician's Union in New York City.

what to buy: By far, the "jazziest" or hottest recordings by Andy Kirk and His Clouds of Joy were their earliest recordings for Brunswick (1929–30). These can be found on *Andy Kirk, 1929–31* ♫♫♫♫ (Classics, 1994, prod. Gilles Petard). Titles such as the jaunty "Mess-A-Stomp" and "Sumpin' Low and Slow" showcase the swinging Kansas City style for which the band was so popular. "Mess-A-Stomp" features some tasty Mary Lou Williams on her first date as the Clouds of Joy pianist. She had subbed earlier for the regular band pianist, Marion Jackson, as he was out sick when Jack Kapp set up the recording audition. When the band showed up to cut the actual record (with the recovered Jackson), Kapp insisted that Williams do the recording, and the rest is jazz history. For a cross-section of the band's better instrumental pre-war titles, and showcases for Williams, check out Andy Kirk and Mary Lou Williams on *Twelve Clouds of Joy* ♫♫♫♫ (ASV, 1929–49/1993), and *Mary's Idea* ♫♫♫♫ (Decca, 1936–41/1993 prod. Jack Kapp).

what to buy next: The later they get in to the 1930s, the more ballad-oriented the band becomes; however, there are still musical gems interspersed. The whole Classics series of CDs provides the complete pre-war output of the band, starting with the first Decca recordings *Andy Kirk, 1936–37* ♫♫♫♫ (Classics, 1994, prod. Gilles Petard). Especially good performances of "Christopher Columbus" and "Froggy Bottom" (a reworked, "modern" arrangement of the band's original 1929 recording) are fine examples of the Kirk band of this period. Also included is the Pha Terrell "Until the Real Thing Comes Along" performance that sucked up so many jukebox nickels in 1936. As the band approached the war era, the tunes became more pop oriented (notwithstanding some brief solo passages on the non-instrumentals), with just a few titles here and there remaining out-and-out jazz vehicles.

the rest:

Kansas City Bounce ♫♫♫ (Black & Blue 1992)
A Mellow Bit of Rhythm ♫♫ (RCA, 1993)
Andy Kirk, 1937 ♫♫♫ (Classics, 1994)
Andy Kirk, 1937–38 ♫♫♫ (Classics, 1994)
Andy Kirk, 1939–40 ♫♫♫ (Classics, 1994)
Andy Kirk, 1940–42 ♫♫ (Classics, 1995).

Jim Prohaska

Rahsaan Roland Kirk

Born Ronald Theodore Kirk, August 7, 1936, in Columbus, OH. Died December 5, 1977, in Bloomington, IN.

Gifted with a musical humor midway between that of Charles Mingus and the Art Ensemble of Chicago, and musical inclinations as deep as ragtime and as popish as Burt Bacharach, Rahsaan Roland Kirk stands out as an icon and visionary of post-bop jazz. Blinded as an infant, he was a one-man horn section with the unmatchable skill of playing three saxophones at once. These were usually the tenor, and the rarely played manzello and stritch, on which he harmonized and played contrapuntal lines. Due to his humor and street performer demeanor, his music was at times discounted, but the years have revealed Kirk to be an all-time great. Steeped in every idiom of African-American music, he emerged in the early 1950s as a singular talent without having spent long sojourns as sideman to the stars, though a relationship with Charles Mingus beginning in 1961 helped legitimize Kirk to a mainstream jazz audience. He employed whistles and gongs as compositional and improvisational tools and added his untrained, yet incisive, vocalisms to a number of recordings. His greatest popularity came during the early 1970s, but a 1975 stroke left most of his left side paralyzed. Kirk then fell back on his tenor sax, playing with one hand, to maintain an active touring and concert schedule while playing a vibrant music that still stretched and searched for the unknown.

what to buy: The two-CD set *Does Your House Have Lions: The Rahsaan Roland Kirk Anthology* ♫♫♫♫ (Rhino, 1993, prod. Joel Dorn, Rahsaan Roland Kirk, Nesuhi Ertegun) cuts a swath through Kirk's works (30 selections) during his Atlantic period (1965–76) with such favorites as "Volunteered Slavery" and "Ain't No Sunshine," the masterful composition "The Inflated Tear," and the impressionistic "Seasons." In addition to tenor, manzello, and stritch, he displays his facility on baritone and bass saxophones, clarinet, flute, piccolo, trumpet, and an array of miscellaneous wind and percussion instruments. This is a good album for starters. A single-disc compilation of two of Kirk's 1960s albums, *Rip, Rig, and Panic/Now Please Don't You Cry, Beautiful Edith* ♫♫♫♫ (EmArCy, 1965–67/1990, prod. Richard Seidel, Paul Ramey), divines the music of his early maturity. These sessions feature name sidemen. Pianist Jaki Byard, bassist Richard Davis and drummer Elvin Jones shine on the electric fare of *Rip, Rig, and Panic*, originally a Verve session that was included in a 10-CD Mercury box set. And pianist Lonnie Liston Smith, bassist Ronald Boykins, and drummer Grady Tate join Kirk on *Don't You Cry, Beautiful Edith*, one of Kirk's lesser-known recordings.

what to buy next: *The Inflated Tear* ♫♫♫♫ (Atlantic, 1968/1998, prod. Joel Dorn) addresses Kirk's blindness and exhibits an ability to spur other musicians to his level of vision.

what to avoid: Although Kirk usually managed to eye commercialism while maintaining integrity, his headlong dive with *The Case of the 3-Sided Dream in Audio Color* ♫♫♫ (Atlantic, 1975/1987, prod. Joel Dorn) didn't quite measure up.

best of the rest:

Soulful Saxes ♫♫♫ (Affinity, 1956)
Introducing Roland Kirk ♫♫♫♫ (Chess/MCA, 1960/1990)
(With Jack McDuff) *Kirk's Work* ♫♫♫♫ (OJC, 1961/1990)
We Free Kings ♫♫♫ (PolyGram, 1961/1991)
Reeds and Deeds ♫♫♫ (Mercury, 1963)
I Talk to the Spirits ♫♫♫ (Limelight, 1964)
Left and Right ♫♫♫ (Atlantic, 1968)
The Vibration Continues ♫♫♫♫ (Atlantic, 1968–74)
Volunteered Slavery ♫♫♫♫ (Atlantic/Rhino, 1969/1993)
Rahsaan, Rahsaan ♫♫♫♫ (Atlantic, 1970)
National Black Inventions ♫♫♫ (Atlantic, 1971)
Blacknuss ♫♫♫♫ (Rhino, 1971/1993)
Prepare Thyself to Deal with a Miracle ♫♫♫ (Atlantic, 1972)
(With Al Hibbler) *A Meeting of the Times* ♫♫♫ (Atlantic/Rhino, 1972)
Bright Moments ♫♫♫♫ (Atlantic, 1973/1993)
Kirkatron ♫♫♫ (Warner, 1976)
Man Who Cried Fire ♫♫♫ (Atlantic, 1977)
Boogie Woogie String Along ♫♫♫♫ (Atlantic, 1977)

worth searching for: Most shops don't have 11-CD sets sitting on the shelves, but if you've got the bucks, *Rahsaan—The Complete Mercury Recordings* ♫♫♫♫ (Mercury, 1961–65/PolyGram, 1990) repackages several Kirk albums during a fervent and mature part of his career.

influences:

◀◀ Jelly Roll Morton, Fats Waller, Charles Mingus, Yusef Lateef, Eric Dolphy

▶▶ Art Ensemble of Chicago, David Sanborn, Anthony Braxton, Branford Marsalis

Larry Gabriel

Kenny Kirkland

Born September 28, 1955, in Newport, NY.

One of the most consistently swinging pianists in jazz, Kenny Kirkland has recorded extensively as a sideman since the early

Rahsaan Roland Kirk (AP/**Wide World Photos**)

1980s. Influenced strongly by Herbie Hancock and McCoy Tyner, Kirkland is a highly effective accompanist who can provide a lift to any rhythm section. He began playing piano at age six, and later studied for a while at the Manhattan School of Music. Though he's best known for his work with trumpeter Wynton Marsalis and saxophonist Branford Marsalis, he had worked and recorded with trumpeter Miroslav Vitus, Terumasa Hino, Elvin Jones, and Dizzy Gillespie before joining up with Wynton Marsalis from 1981–85. Kirkland and Branford left Wynton's band in 1985 to tour and record with Sting, but by 1986 Kirkland was back in New York, freelancing steadily. When Branford was hired to front the new *Tonight Show* band in 1991, Kirkland moved to Los Angeles and was reunited with former rhythm section–mates, bassist Robert Hurst and drummer Jeff "Tain" Watts. Kirkland left the *Tonight Show* band after Marsalis's departure and has returned to freelancing. Among some of his credits are albums with Joe Ford, Kenny Garrett, Mark Whitfield, Lew Soloff, Ray Obiedo, and Arturno Sandoval. Strangely for such a prolific musician, he has recorded only one session under his own name.

what to buy: Pianist Kenny Kirkland covers a variety of bases on his only session as a leader, *Kenny Kirkland* ♪♪♪♪ (GRP, 1991, prod. Delfeayo Marsalis, Kenny Kirkland), a fine outing ranging from a piano/percussion duet with Don Alias on Bud Powell's "Celia," to Latinized versions of Monk's "Criss Cross" and Wayne Shorter's "Ana Maria," with Jerry Gonzalez and Steve Berrios on percussion. Three of Kirkland's six original tunes feature a quartet with Branford Marsalis on tenor sax, Charnett Moffett on bass, and Jeff "Tain" Watts on drums, including the smokin' opener "Mr. J.C." The other highlight is a gritty version of Ornette Coleman's "When Will the Blues Leave," with the suspiciously named Roderick Ward on alto.

the rest:
Jazz from Keystone: Thunder and Rainbows ♪♪♪♫ (Sunnyside, 1991)

worth searching for: Kenny Garrett is the most prodigious alto saxophonist of his generation, and *Kenny Garrett Songbook* ♪♪♪♪ (Warner Bros., 1997, prod. Kenny Garrett) backs that statement up with a strong set of original material played by a relentlessly swinging quartet with Kirkland, Nat Reeves (bass) and the consummate drummer Jeff "Tain" Watts. Kirkland shines whenever he's featured, but it's his quicksilver interactions with Tain that will leave listeners shaking their heads.

influences:
◄◄ Herbie Hancock, Keith Jarrett, McCoy Tyner

Andrew Gilbert

John Klemmer

Born July 3, 1946, in Chicago, IL.

A lot of artists start off strong and then lose what first made them special after a while, but saxophonist John Klemmer's descent is particularly disappointing in that he was once a barrier-melting innovator; his work was dominated by blandness after the mid-1970s, blacking out a talent that could have consistently explored new territory in the common ground between jazz, rock, and R&B. Growing up in the Chicago area, Klemmer studied with the charismatic jazz teacher and saxophonist Joe Daley and cut his teeth by playing professionally while still in his mid-teens. Playing with Don Ellis in the late 1960s certainly must have opened the young Klemmer's mind to electric directions in jazz, just as Klemmer's work in Ellis's group must have opened a lot of rock fans' minds to the excitement of the jazz world. (Ellis, with Klemmer as featured soloist, opened for many rock acts in his day, among them Big Brother and the Holding Company). After an all-acoustic first date as a leader, Klemmer began to head into an exciting area where the rock of Hendrix met post-Coltrane soulful saxophone, sometimes beautifully mellow, sometimes incendiary, almost always amazingly agile. After moving to Los Angeles in the early 1970s, Klemmer produced work that became more commercially popular but artistically vapid. Sporadic dates in the 1980s gave way to silence in the 1990s. Adventurous jazz lovers looking for some of the best psychedelic jazz around ought to prepare to do some discographical digging in order to find some of the old, good John Klemmer.

what to buy: Unfortunately, Klemmer's exciting early work, which creatively explored the nexus between electric jazz and rock music, remains out of print. Only *Waterfalls* ♪♪♪♪ (MCA/Impulse!, 1972/1990, prod. Ed Michel) shows the promise that Klemmer had in making commercial yet progressive music. A blend of the mellow and the ferocious, the consistently engaging *Waterfalls* mixes electric jazz and soul without getting too light, even though his heavier years were behind Klemmer at this point.

what to avoid: Unless you have a voracious appetite for light, radio-ready fuzak and saccharine displays of musical emotion, you'll want to avoid the rest of Klemmer's extant catalog. Of course, if you're the kind of music lover who wants to check out the roots of Kenny G or find some authentic-sounding, late-night, romantic-interlude sleaze soundtracks, maybe add a couple of bones to the ratings here. *Touch* ♪♫ (MCA/GRP, 1975/1989/1997) remains popular to this day among fans of urban contemporary-style jazz (it's a classic of the genre), but its light, mellow tones (augmented by such usual suspects as Dave Grusin and Larry Carlton) set such an instantly dated mood that you'll swear you're wearing polyester. And it's pretty much downhill from there, landing at the bottom with *Music woof!* (MCA, 1989, prod. John Klemmer, Stephen Zipper), where Klemmer's smoothness combines with post-Jan Hammer synth and post-Art of Noise, sample-stuttered pronouncements to create a record that's ridiculously b-b-b-b-bad.

the rest:

Barefoot Ballet 🎵🎵 (MCA, 1976)
Cry 🎵🎵 (MCA, 1978/1997)
Arabesque 🎵 (MCA, 1978/1994)
Brazilia 🎵 (MCA, 1979/1997)
Mosaic: The Best of John Klemmer 🎵 (MCA, 1979/1996)
(With Oscar Castro-Neves) *Simpatico* 🎵🎵 (JVC Classics, 1997)

worth searching for: An out-of-print album, *Fresh Feathers* 🎵🎵 (ABC, 1974, prod. John Haeny) at least contained some disco-funk that was mildly captivating. Even better, though, would be to search for the double-LP collection *Blowin' Gold* 🎵🎵🎵🎵 (Chess, 1982, prod. Marshall Chess, Gene Barge, John Klemmer, Bill Wagner), which collects the best tracks from three records released on the highly underrated Cadet/Concept label circa 1969. Had fusion followed the path of such electric blazers as "Excursion #2" and "Children of the Earth Flames," then it probably wouldn't be the much-maligned genre that it is today. Fans of Miles Davis's electric work will definitely want to seek *Blowin' Gold* out, for not only was Klemmer conducting his forays into fusion concurrent with (if not before!) Miles, but he was also utilizing the electric guitar mastery of Pete Cosey, whose searing six-string stylings blew many a mind through his work with Davis, and do so here as well. Klemmer's electric jazz was way more pop-soul-soaked than some other early jazz-rock, but still a lot of his early playing and tunes must be heard to be believed. He gets a bad rap for his later lovers' jazz, but it would be the listener's loss to ignore this colossal collection (barring a cover of "Hey Jude"). And the gorgeous "Rose Petals" provides the best showcase for Klemmer's use of electric modification of his sax sounds: it's haunting and romantic, and it never dips into the maudlin exercises of his indulgent records of echo-plexed sax solos. Finally, the challenging, acoustic, and anomalistically good *Nexus for Duo and Trio* 🎵🎵🎵🎵 (Novus, 1978) serves as the last truly great honk out of a once-promising sax talent.

influences:

⏪ John Coltrane, Don Ellis, Rahsaan Roland Kirk

⏩ Kenny G

Greg Baise

RAHSAAN ROLAND KIRK

song "No Tonic Press"
album *Rip, Rig and Panic*
(EmArcy, 1965/1990)
instrument Tenor saxophone

Monster Solo

Earl Klugh

Born September 16, 1954, in Detroit, MI.

A very talented guitarist, Earl Klugh had studied piano and guitar as a child, opting for the guitar as his main instrument before hitting his teens. Influenced heavily by Chet Atkins and Lenny Breau, Klugh also has a lifelong affection for show tunes and soundtrack music, all of which have shown up in his light, jazz-inflected playing and in many of the songs he chooses to cover on his albums. Klugh was discovered while teaching guitar lessons in a Detroit music store by Yusef Lateef, who used the young guitarist on his 1970 *Suite 16*. Before Klugh was out of his teens he was playing electric guitar with George Benson and with Chick Corea's Return to Forever. Upon returning to Detroit in the mid-'70s, he shifted his allegiance from electric to acoustic guitar and recorded his first album for Blue Note. Since that time he has led his own groups and recorded three albums with Bob James, including *One on One*, which won a Grammy for Klugh. He has also received co-billing on an album he did with one of his old mentors, George Benson (*Collabora-*

tion), and written music for the soundtracks *How to Beat the High Cost of Living* and *Marvin & Tige*. His later albums have found Klugh experimenting more with Latino and Brazilian rhythms.

what to buy: Klugh the movie fan reveals himself on *The Earl Klugh Trio, Volume 1* &&&& (Warner Bros., 1991, prod. Earl Klugh) with "Days of Wine and Roses" and "Love Theme from Spartacus." Klugh the television buff offers up an enjoyable, swinging version of the theme song to "Bewitched." He covers pop tunes from Burt Bacharach–Hal David to Antonio Carlos Jobim and does a really pleasant job of it. It is no sin to prepare a well-crafted dessert, to relax the ears after all that heavy lifting (Ornette Coleman, Sonny Sharrock, etc.).

what to buy next: Collecting the hits that established Klugh as a commercial force made good sense, and *The Best of Earl Klugh* &&&& (Blue Note, 1991, prod. various) is a good deal for someone who wants some of his stuff in a collection, but not too much. "Livin' inside Your Love," "Magic in Your Eyes," and "Dr. Macumba" are all pleasantly swinging acoustic riffs with a touch of soul or perky rhythms, and make up the cream of the pop crop. Klugh never plays less than well. *Solo Guitar* &&&& (Warner Bros., 1989, prod. Earl Klugh) and *Trio Volume 1* would be the top recommendations for Klugh's jazz playing. Both have a definite pop sensibility, but they also show off his very real skills with a guitar.

best of the rest:

Late Night Guitar &&&& (One Way, 1980)
(With George Benson) *Collaboration* &&&& (Warner Bros., 1987)
The Best of Earl Klugh Volume 2 &&& (Blue Note, 1992)
Ballads &&& (Manhattan, 1993)
(With Bob James) *One on One* &&& (Warner Bros., 1993)

influences:

◀◀ Chet Atkins, Lenny Breau, Antonio Carlos Jobim, João Gilberto

Garaud MacTaggart

Jimmy Knepper

Born November 22, 1927, in Los Angeles, CA.

Jimmy Knepper is mostly known for his association with Charles Mingus and the tribute group Mingus Dynasty, and also for being one of the few trombonists of the late bop era not to be especially influenced by J.J. Johnson. Knepper's most valuable early experiences came with the big bands of Woody Herman and Claude Thornhill in the early 1950s. From 1957 to 1962 he added his distinctive sound to many classic jazz records with Mingus, including *Tijuana Moods*, *Mingus Ah Um*, and *Blues and Roots*. Knepper also worked with the big bands of Gil Evans, Stan Kenton, and Thad Jones–Mel Lewis, and toured the world with Benny Goodman and Herbie Mann. In the 1970s he played with Lee Konitz and was a founding member of the Mingus Dynasty in 1979. Knepper has spent the last two decades continuing the Mingus legacy with fellow bandmates, including Dannie Richmond, Sir Roland Hanna, and George Adams, and has cut a few valuable records under his own leadership.

what to buy: *I Dream Too Much* &&&& (Soul Note, 1984, prod. Giovanni Bonandrini) has a distinctive sound because of the all-brass front line Knepper utilizes, including John Eckert's trumpet and John Clark's French horn. In addition to the Jerome Kern title track, three Knepper originals and one by remarkable pianist Roland Hanna are featured.

what to buy next: Although backed by a strong rhythm section of Hanna, Dannie Richmond, and George Mraz, it is the soloing of Knepper and tenor Al Cohn that makes *Cunningbird* &&&& (SteepleChase, 1976/1990, prod. Nils Winther) particularly enjoyable.

what to avoid: *T-Bop* && (Soul Note, 1993, prod. Eric Felten) is a nice effort by Felten, a young admirer of Knepper, to get the veteran some recording exposure, but the album doesn't really work. Knepper sounds a bit lethargic, and the young accompanying group of Harvard and Berklee musicians sounds restrained and unsure in his presence.

the rest:

Jimmy Knepper in L.A. &&& (Inner City, 1978)
Special Relationship &&&& (Hep, 1981)
First Place &&& (Blackhawk, 1982)
Dream Dancing &&&& (Criss Cross, 1986)

worth searching for: *Idol of the Flies* &&&& (Bethlehem, 1958), made during the beginning of his association with Mingus, was Knepper's first album as a leader, and his last for almost 20 years. The cool-sounding work with pianist Bill Evans and altoist Gene Quill is somewhat reminiscent of the Mingus recording from the same year, *East Coasting*.

influences:

◀◀ Frank Rosolino

▶▶ Eric Felten

Dan Keener

Charlie Kohlhase

Born November 28, 1956, in Portsmouth, NH.

Charlie Kohlhase began playing alto saxophone in 1975 and added baritone a year later. He joined the Either/Orchestra in 1987 and has appeared on all their albums except for the first. He also became a member of John Leahman's Mandala Octet in 1987 and has appeared on all their releases. In 1989 he formed a quintet with trombonist Curtis Hasselbring, saxophonist Matt Langley, bassist John Turner, and drummer Matt Wilson. In 1992 trumpeter John Carlson replaced Hasselbring. Besides three CDs of their own, the Charlie Kohlhase Quintet contributed a track to *Wavelength/Infinity (Rastascan)*, an anthology of Sun Ra compositions. In 1993 saxophonist John Tchicai appeared as a special guest with the quintet; trombonist John Rapson joined the band for a short New England tour in 1997. Kohlhase has also appeared in a quartet with saxophonist Michael Marcus. Kohlhase is uncommonly skillful at using elements of the jazz tradition in witty compositions and arrangements that maintain a keen sense of swing as they blend structure and freedom. As a soloist, he is especially good at developing motives and longer linear elements into coherent statements that offer accompanists lots of room for interaction.

what to buy: It took nearly four years of playing and touring before this edition of the Charlie Kohlhase Quintet (with trumpeter Carlson replacing trombonist Curtis Hasselbring) documented their new sound on disc, and *Dart Night* 𝒜𝒜𝒜𝒜 (Accurate, 1996, prod. Charlie Kohlhase) is worth the wait. A fiery session featuring 12 bop-to-avant-garde tunes performed by Kohlhase (alto/baritone saxophonist), Carlson, Matt Langley (tenor/soprano saxophones), John Turner (bass), and Matt Wilson (drums, percussion), it's their best album to date. Kohlhase contributes most of the tunes, and there are many high points as the band members lend color to his impressionistic arrangements with often angular, harmonically adventurous solos and tight, textured horn segments that frequently make the group sound larger than it is. Highlights include their modernized (inside-out) version of "Deep Purple," modeled after the Nino Tempo/April Stevens version of the smoky ballad and augmented with Paul Lichter's brief recitation of the lyrics against Carlson's muted trumpet melody line. Kohlhase's compositions draw inspiration from many sources, making this session his broad-based best.

what to buy next: On *Good Deeds* 𝒜𝒜𝒜𝒾 (Accurate, 1993, prod. Charlie Kohlhase), the Charlie Kohlhase Quintet adds trumpeter Waldron Ricks on two tracks, along with regulars Kohlhase (alto/baritone saxophonist), Hasselbring (trombone),

LEE KONITZ (WITH DON FRIEDMAN AND ATTILA ZOLLER)

song "Alone Together"

album *Thingin*
(hat ART, 1995)

instrument Alto saxophone

Langley (tenor/soprano saxophones), Turner (bass), and Wilson (drums, percussion). Maintaining the high standard set by their debut, the band performs mostly Kohlhase compositions among the 10 selections. *Research and Development* 𝒜𝒜𝒜𝒾 (Accurate, 1991, prod. Charlie Kohlhase) was the impressive and mature debut of the Charlie Kohlhase Quintet, instituting the three-horn frontline and rhythm section. A diverse nine-tune session of Kohlhase originals, Monk's "Off Minor," and Hasselbring's "Got Hooked on Ohio," make this 1990-recorded debut an enjoyable listen throughout.

influences:
◀◀ Roswell Rudd

Ed Hazell and Nancy Ann Lee

Lee Konitz

Born October 13, 1927, in Chicago.

A smooth, pure-toned alto saxophonist of the first order (he also sometimes plays soprano and tenor), Konitz was among the first post-war saxists to develop a style not beholden to the pervasive influence of Charlie Parker. In tone and temperament, Konitz remained closer to Benny Carter, Johnny Hodges, and Lester Young than to Bird, though he was hardly untouched by Parker's innovations. He cut his teeth in diverse contexts, ranging from the big bands of Claude Thornhill and Stan Kenton to the "Birth of the Cool" nonet and septet collaborations of Miles Davis. But he long remained best known for his affiliation with pianist Lennie Tristano and, along with tenorist Warne Marsh, put many of Tristano's ideas into play, although Konitz seems to have long since gotten over Tristano's avoidance of emotion. An inventive strain permeates Konitz's work, which is equal parts fire and ice, dazzling variations and terse phrases, cerebral architectures and a simmering emotionality. He was among the first saxophonists to issue an unaccompanied solo album, an unheard-of idea outside the avant-garde, and was even invited to play on Derek Bailey's *Company Week*. Konitz is most self-assured while improvising within the confines of chord changes or playing free, and uses his full, pristine tone to cover a lot of stylistic ground. He rarely sounds at a loss for ideas, and his sound is remarkably consistent through numerous contexts. He sets a high standard for other mainstream saxophone players to match, most notably by his avoidance of the conventional and his acceptance of the challenging. Among his generation of players, only Miles Davis so consistently avoided the obvious throughout his career—and Konitz, at this writing, is still going strong.

what to buy: *Zounds* 🎵🎵🎵🎵 (Soul Note, 1991, prod. Giovanni Bonandrini) is remarkable. After having prepared charts and rehearsed for this quartet session, Konitz impulsively started over from scratch and produced a rarified mix of free improvisation and standards that finds all the players, especially keyboardist Kenny Werner, playing at the peak of their considerable abilities (the quartet is filled out by bassist Ron McClure and drummer Bill Stewart). Breathtakingly beautiful yet always on the edge, this unique album is a tribute to Konitz's refusal to rest on his laurels. *Live at the Half Note* 🎵🎵🎵🎵 (Verve, 1994, prod. Lee Konitz)— recorded in 1959 but initially released only in edited form on Lenny Tristano's label, with Konitz completely cut out—this two-CD set finds the altoist leading a retrospectively superstar quintet with fellow Tristano disciple Warne Marsh (tenor sax), Bill Evans (piano), Jimmy Garrison (bass), and Paul Motian (drums). The focus is very much on the horns, who evince contrasting styles, Marsh warm and flowing, Konitz probing and asymmetrical. Though low-key, their playing is full of subtle delights. The reper-

toire is a mix of Tristano and Konitz originals, standards such as "It's You or No One," and Charlie Parker's "Scrapple from the Apple." A duo with veteran Italian pianist Franco D'Andrea, *12 Gershwin in 12 Keys* 🎵🎵🎵🎵 (Philology, 1992, prod. Paolo Piangiarelli) is another example of Konitz's habitual spontaneity, a 1988 concert where he decided over dinner with his collaborator just before the show that they would play a dozen Gershwin classics, each in a different key (a Gershwin medley from an earlier concert the same month is tacked on). Actually, some of the tracks can't be pinned down to just one key, and the way many of them unfold nicely varies the usual head-solos-head, with the themes sometimes emerging from nearly free intros and then going through organic permutations; "I Got Rhythm" is a prime example, demonstrating a rare use of this tune as something more than a set of changes for flashy blowing.

what to buy next: When the saxophonist made *The Lee Konitz Duets* 🎵🎵🎵🎵 (Milestone, 1967/1991, prod. Dick Katz), the idea of changing duet partners from track to track was a fresh idea, and this album has subsequently inspired many imitations. There are many stylistic juxtapositions, of course, as Konitz moves from the opening "Struttin' with Some Barbecue" with trombonist Marshall Brown (on the final chorus, Konitz overdubs baritone sax and Brown overdubs euphonium) to "You Don't Know What Love Is" with Joe Henderson. The most interesting track is "Erb," with guitarist Jim Hall, which gets pretty wild by these guys' standards. Other collaborators include pianist Dick Katz, saxman Richie Kamuca, violinist Ray Nance, and, on "Variations on Alone Together," drummer Elvin Jones, vibraphonist Karl Berger, and bassist Eddie Gomez (at first it's just Konitz, then separate duos, and finally they play as a quartet). The final track is with everybody except Nance, sort of a summing up of a landmark recording session. Also a landmark, *Lone-Lee* 🎵🎵🎵🎵 (SteepleChase, 1974, prod. Nils Winther) is, as its title indicates, a solo sax album. It contains very lengthy examinations (one side each on the LP) of the standards "The Song Is You" and "Cherokee," at a time when only Anthony Braxton had done significant work in the solo-sax album format. Konitz's treatments of these tunes are like developing variations, seizing on thematic kernals and seeing how far they can be taken. There is a purity to his essays that transcends abstraction. Another unusual solo album, *Self Portrait* 🎵🎵🎵🎵 (Philology, 1997, prod. Paolo Piangiarelli) goes Bill Evans's groundbreaking *Conversations with Myself* a few steps further, as Konitz constructs several tracks with up to four lines intertwining via overdubbing. Each step in the process follows gradually, so the original tune is heard first and the subsequent elaborations accrete sequentially, baring the creative process. There are surprises even on the truly solo tracks, such as a 16-minute–plus blues tune from a player not normally associated with the rootsier elements of jazz. By contrast, *Live at Laren* ♫♫♫♫ (Soul Note, 1984, prod. Giovanni Bonandrini) is by a star-studded nonet—Red Rodney, Jimmy Knepper, Ronnie Cuber, Ray Drummond, and Billy Hart are among the personnel—caught on tape in 1979 on a set of interesting arrangements (with plenty of room for solo fireworks) of a quirky setlist: Tristano, Knepper, and Chick Corea tunes (two of the latter arranged by the great Sy Johnson) rub up against the standards "Moon Dreams" (arranged by Gil Evans) and "Without a Song." There's an infectiously freewheeling quality to this session, with everybody but Knepper and the rhythm tandem doubling instruments. In a more intimate setting, *Inside Cole Porter* ♫♫♫♫ (Philology, 1997, prod. Paolo Piangiarelli), another collaboration with D'Andrea, is—like this pair's previous duet album of Gershwin tunes—much more than a collection of standards by a famous songwriter. The familiar music, which includes "The Song Is You," "What Is This Thing Called Love," "Everytime We Say Goodbye," "Love for Sale," "Night and Day," and more, is reinvented on the fly through Konitz's melodic imagination and pianist D'Andrea's harmonic wizardry. Konitz croons the themes with caressing tenderness and then slowly flips them into new shapes. The music on much of the album flows from track to track, connected by free improvisations that alter the listening context. Konitz marks a change of his usual boppish pace with *Tenorlee* ♫♫♫♫♫ (Choice 1977–78/Candid, 1997, prod. Gerry MacDonald), an album of 10 romantic ballads and light swingers that captures him solely playing tenor saxophone as a tribute to Richie Kamuca, who died two days before the second session of this intimate album was recorded on July 24, 1977, in Macdonald's Studio in Sea Cliff, New Jersey. With empathetic accompaniment from pianist Jimmy Rowles and bassist Michael Moore, Konitz delivers warmhearted versions of chestnuts such as "Skylark," "Autumn Nocturne," "Tangerine," and other classics. The leader's one original, the title tune, a two-minute unaccompanied spontaneous improv, exemplifies the relaxed nature of this album and segues into a lightly swinging take on "Lady Be Good." In addition to Konitz's flowing raspy-toned tenorisms, Rowles's gentle keyboard touch and Moore's anchoring basslines make this drumless trio recording a soothing and pleasurable listen from start to finish. Two previously unreleased tracks, "The Gypsy" and "'Tis Autumn," enhance the CD version.

what to avoid: With all the recent Konitz material, it's safe to give a wide berth to *So Many Stars* ♫♫ (Philology, 1993, prod.

Paolo Piangiarelli). Konitz plays well enough, as does pianist Stefano Battaglia on the tracks on which he is present, but this album is a collaboration with Italian singer Tiziana Ghiglioni, whose eccentric talents are an acquired taste at best and whose thin, quavery voice is an irritant to most listeners.

best of the rest:

Satori ♫♫♫♫ (Milestone, 1974/1997)
(With Paul Bley, Bill Connors) *Pyramid* ♫♫♫ (Improvising Artists, Inc., 1977)
Dovetail ♫♫♫♫ (Sunnyside, 1983)
Ideal Scene ♫♫♫ (Soul Note, 1986)
Jazz à Juan ♫♫♫ (SteepleChase, 1986)
The New York Album ♫♫♫ (Soul Note, 1988)
(With Space Jazz Trio) *Blew* ♫♫♫ (Philology, 1989)
(With Enrico Pieranunzi) *Solitudes* ♫♫♫♫ (Philology, 1991)
From Newport to Nice ♫♫♫♫ (Philology, 1992)
(With Peggy Stern) *LunaSea* ♫♫♫♫ (Soul Note, 1992)
(With Peggy Stern) *The Jobim Collection* ♫♫♫ (Philology, 1993)
Free with Lee ♫♫♫ (Philology, 1993)
Rhapsody ♫♫♫♫ (King, 1993/Evidence, 1995)
Rhapsody 2 ♫♫♫♫ (King, 1994/Evidence, 1996)
Jazz Nocturne ♫♫♫♫ (Evidence, 1994)
Lullaby of Birdland ♫♫♫ (Candid, 1995)
(With Umberto Petrin) *Breaths and Whispers: Homage to Alexandr Skrjabin* ♫♫♫♫ (Philology, 1995)
(With Franz Koglmann) *We Thought about Duke* ♫♫♫♫ (hat ART, 1995)
(With Attila Zoller and Don Friedman) *Thingin'* ♫♫♫ (hat ART, 1996)
(With Enrico Rava) *L'Age Mür* ♫♫♫♫ (Philology, 1997)
(With Brad Mehldau, Charlie Haden) *Alone Together* ♫♫♫♫ (Blue Note, 1997)

worth searching for: Some Konitz items on Verve should be looked for, one because it will soon disappear and a pair because they've been gone a while. *Motion* ♫♫♫♫ (Verve, 1961/1998, prod. Creed Taylor) is a three-CD limited edition expanded reissue of a classic Konitz trio album with bassist Sonny Dallas and drummer Elvin Jones. The original album is on CD #1, a standards program with "I Remember You," "All of Me," "Foolin' Myself," "You'd Be So Nice to Come Home To," "I'll Remember April," "You Don't Know What Love Is," "These Foolish Things (Remind Me of You)," "Out of Nowhere," and "It's You or No One." The other two CDs in this set are full of rehearsal and alternate takes that are sufficiently different to fully justify their release. The interplay of Konitz and Jones, an unlikely pairing at first sight, works wonderfully, stimulating Konitz more than perhaps any other drummer he's worked with. Of more recent vintage, *Heroes* ♫♫♫♫ (Verve, 1991, prod. John Snyder) and *Anti-Heroes* ♫♫♫♫ (Verve, 1991, prod. John Snyder) are casual duo albums with famed arranger Gil Evans, a colleague from their days with the Claude Thornhill band and then with the Miles Davis "Birth of the Cool" groups. Evans's piano skills are minimal, but that seems only to inspire Konitz to special heights on these recordings from a 1980 restaurant gig. The repertoire is also special in the Konitz discography, including Wayne Shorter's "Prince of Darkness"; Charles Mingus's "Reincarnation of a Lovebird" and "Orange Was the Color of Her Dress, Then Silk Blue"; Chopin's Prelude #20, opus 28; Evans's "Zee Zee" and "Copenhagen Sight"; and some more familiar standards not normally on Konitz's setlists. It's too bad these albums seem to have lapsed out of print.

influences:

◀◀ Lennie Tristano, Benny Carter, Charlie Parker, Lester Young

▶▶ Jimmy Giuffre, Anthony Braxton, Yuko Fujiyama

Wally Shoup, Steve Holtje, and Nancy Ann Lee

Peter Kowald

Born 1944, in Wuppertal, Germany.

Peter Kowald started to play the bass at 17, often visiting the studio of avant-garde saxophonist Peter Brotzmann, and they began collaborating early in both of their careers. By 1962 Kowald had been playing for two years and the pair and was performing the music of Charles Mingus, Miles Davis, Ornette Coleman, and other jazz artists. Kowald participated in the 1966 European tour of the Carla Bley/Michael Manter band, along with Brotzmann, and afterward worked with other German musicians, including the Globe Unity Orchestra from 1966–78. He has continued to work with Brotzmann, including in their Cooperative Trio with drummer Andrew Cyrille, a duo project, and more recent melds of free-jazz, hip-hop, and rap. Because of his versatility, Kowald has worked with a wide variety of improvising musicians worldwide. From 1980–85 he was a member of the London Jazz Composers' Orchestra. He spent time in the United States and Japan and recorded albums with American, European, and Japanese musicians. He also has lived in Greece, working with musicians there. In the 1990s he returned to Germany to pursue various solo projects and group performances. For his trailblazing innovations, Kowald won the 1996 Albert-Mangelsdorff-Preis awarded by the GEMA Foundation and the Union of German Jazz Musicians. The bassist records mostly for the Free Music Production label, formed in Germany around 1969. While you'll have to search the secondhand market for many Free Music Production vinyl releases, Kowald's several CD releases as leader are among about 80 FMP recordings that have been reissued on CD, but they are hard to find.

what to buy: *Die Jungen: Random Generators* ♫♫♫♫ (Free Music Production, 1979, prod. Peter Kowald) contains incredibly inventive bass duos with Barre Phillips. This is where improvised music greets the listener with beauty and a challenge. *Paintings* ♫♫♫♫ (Free Music Production, 1981, prod. Peter Kowald) offers another saga featuring bass duos with master bassist-composer Barry Guy. You can hear these men thinking throughout their soulful, intelligent improvisations. *Open Secrets* ♫♫♫♫ (Free Music Production, 1988, prod. Peter Kowald) is a solo recording that takes the string bass to new levels. Utilizing both his bow and his fingers, Kowald creates dark and brooding music that is at the same time uplifting.

best of the rest:

Two Making a Triangle ♫♫♫♪ (Free Music Production, 1982)
Was da ist? ♫♫♫♫ (Free Music Production, 1994)

influences:

◀◀ Charles Mingus, Ornette Coleman, Miles Davis, John Coltrane, Karlheinz Stockhausen, John Cage

David C. Gross

Dave Koz

Born in San Fernando Valley, CA.

As a testament to fusion keyboardist Jeff Lorber's nose for talent, not only has Lorber's former sideman Kenny G risen to become one of contemporary music's best-selling artists, but his replacement, Dave Koz, is pulling up fast behind. Born and raised in Los Angeles, Koz first got into the saxophone at age 13, inspired by the Tower of Power horn section. After graduating from college, he snagged gigs with Bobby Caldwell and then with Lorber. Both urged him to go solo, so in 1990 he did, releasing a record that spent 25 weeks on *Billboard* magazine's contemporary jazz chart and spawned two Top 10 hits. Koz also found time to sit in with the band on Arsenio Hall's talk show, write a song that became the new theme for the TV show *General Hospital,* and in 1995 start his own syndicated radio interview show about "smooth jazz" artists called *Personal Notes.* Add in appearances on the TV shows *Family Matters* and *Beverly Hills 90210*—along with session work for U2, Curtis Stigers, and Celine Dion, among others—and you have an artist with nearly as much talent for marketing himself as he has for any playing.

what to buy: As a focused example of his commercial style, *Lucky Man* ♫♫♫ (Capitol, 1993, prod. Dave Koz, Jeff Koz, Carl Sturken, Denis Lambert, Evan Rogers, Jeff Lorber) puts it all together—with loads of synthesizers, backing vocalists, sequenced percussion, and hummable melodies.

what to buy next: As a grand experiment, *Off the Beaten Path* ♫♫♫ (Capitol, 1996, prod. Dave Koz, Jeff Koz, Thom Panunzio) works—at least for anyone who likes Koz. Featuring the saxophonist playing live with a real, breathing rhythm section, it manages to shoehorn a little more emotion and guts into his often saccharine arrangements.

what to avoid: A little too derivative and safe, Koz's debut, *Dave Koz* woof! (EMI, 1990, prod. Dave Koz, Jeff Lorber, Jeff Koz, Carl Sturken, Evan Rogers, Elliot Wolff, Claude Gaudette, Randy Nicklaus, Steve Barri, Tony Peluso) only hints at the commercial heights he later scaled with ease.

worth searching for: Recorded before he got too spoiled by success, *Live at the Strand* ♫♫♫ (Capitol, 1991), a team-up with scintillating studio singing legend Phil Perry, shows what the hornman is capable of when he's not trying so hard to sell records.

influences:

◀◀ David Sanborn, Kenny G, Grover Washington Jr.

▶▶ Boney James, Marion Meadows

Eric Deggans

Diana Krall

Born November 16, 1964, in Nanaimo, British Columbia, Canada.

Perhaps it was as simple as trading parent company GRP's logo for the expectation-raising Impulse! imprint. Maybe it was a backhanded bonus of the lounge-music craze. Or maybe it was that there just aren't that many blonde, female singer-pianists working in traditional jazz. Whatever the reason, Diana Krall's third album, *All for You*, a loving tribute to the Nat King Cole Trio, jettisoned the young Canadian toward the top of the jazz charts in 1996 after almost a decade of club-hopping obscurity. Schooled at Berklee and mentored by pianist Jimmy Rowles and bassist Ray Brown, Krall is certainly a dexterous, economical player. But her smoky contralto—a bluesy testament to the emotional wallop of nuance—has developed into one of the decade's most inviting, invigorating vehicles for standards, a reputation solidified with the romantic repertoire of 1997's gorgeous *Love Scenes*, which ranges from the sultry "Peel Me a Grape" to a delightfully intimate reading of "They Can't Take That Away from Me."

what to buy: A tribute to the lighthearted swing of the Nat King Cole Trio, *All for You* ♫♫♫♫ (Impulse!, 1996, prod. Tommy LiPuma) remains faithful to the piano-bass-guitar arrangements of such Cole classics as "I'm an Errand *Girl* for Rhythm," "Gee Baby, Ain't I Good to You," and "Frim Fram Sauce." Krall's singing adds a sense of seductive mischief to what could easily have been a cabaret cakewalk.

the rest:
Stepping Out ♫♫♫ (Justin Time, 1993/Impulse!, 1998)
Only Trust Your Heart ♫♫♫♫ (GRP, 1995)
Love Scenes ♫♫♫♫ (Impulse!, 1997)

worth searching for: The Canadian version of *All for You* ♫♫♫♫ (Justin Time, 1996, prod. Tommy LiPuma) boasts an extra track: the lilting "When I Grow Too Old to Dream."

influences:

◀◀ Carmen McRae, Nat "King" Cole, Shirley Horn

David Okamoto

Ernie Krivda

Born February 6, 1945, in Cleveland, OH.

Tenor saxophonist Ernie Krivda has been a respected pivotal force on the Cleveland, Ohio, jazz scene for many years and his distinctive, staccato-like and hyper-melodic bebop-based playing style is instantly recognizable and attributable to him. Krivda was influenced by his father, a pre-bop style reed player, who ensured that Krivda was exposed to a variety of music and opportunities to develop his musicianship. Krivda was also influenced by listening to trumpet and violin players early in his career and by his involvement with Hungarian folk music as a youngster. He began lessons at the age of seven, and his first professional gigs were on clarinet with polka bands at age 13. He switched to jazz and alto sax in high school, and chose tenor over 30 years ago to fulfill a road gig with the Jimmy Dorsey band. During the late 1960s when jazz jobs were scarce, Krivda earned his way as a studio musician and worked with organist Eddie Baccus, playing for touring R&B bands in Cleveland venues. Before he left Cleveland for a stay in New York City from 1976–80, Krivda spent a year in Los Angeles working with the Quincy Jones band, and for four years led the house band at Cleveland's popular jazz and blues venue, the Smiling Dog Saloon, where he backed touring jazz luminaries such as Keith Jarrett, Herbie Hancock, Elvin Jones, Freddie Hubbard, Art Blakey, McCoy Tyner, and others. Since he returned from New York, Krivda has used his hometown as a launching pad for his myriad projects. He has over 20 albums to his credit (many of which are out-of-print LPs that have not been issued on CD), and he continues to perform, tour, and record. Since the late

1970s Krivda has recorded as leader for Inner City, North Coast Jazz, Cadence, CIMP, and Koch. He also leads Swing City, a band comprised of faculty members from the jazz studies program at Cuyahoga Community College in Cleveland, a septet with a vocalist that released an album in 1998.

what to buy: It's tough to pick a best recommendation from tenor saxophonist Krivda's diverse discography. If you prefer small group recordings, you might enjoy *Ernie Krivda Jazz* ♫♫♫♫ (Cadence, 1992, prod. Ernie Krivda), one of his widely acclaimed sessions. Krivda draws from a pool of 13 Ohio musicians to perform in settings from duo to septet, and contributes six appealing originals to the 10-tune mixture. Musicians in various settings feature Bob Fraser, guitar; Pat Halloran, trombone; drummers Paul Samuels and Scott Davis; pianist Joe Hunter; and bassists Jeff Halsey, Gary Aprile, Roger Hines, and Chris Berger. Trumpeters Dennis Reynolds and Mike Hazlett perform on "The Bozo," a killer modern tune that features Fraser in an electric guitar solo. Duo settings with expressive bassist Jeff Halsey (on "Autumn Leaves," "Blues for Two," and "Over the Rainbow") reflect Krivda's seasoned lyricism. Pete Selvaggio's accordion augments Krivda's ethnic "Old Vienna" (à la Dino Saluzzi) and "Irv's at Midnight," a jaunty version of Krivda's 1981 original (about an after-hours, greasy-food, musician hang). Krivda's continuing open-minded experimentation, and his perfectionism, as well as persistence, reward him well. This is a wonderful listen. One of his recent releases, *Perdido* ♫♫♫♫ (Koch, 1998, prod. Ernie Krivda, Lee Bush) features Krivda and the Fat Tuesday Big Band, an 18-musician big band he has been leading since 1992. The band is not a repertory or nostalgia band, but a true jazz band with talented Ohio players who can attack the most complicated arrangements by Thad Jones, Quincy Jones, Oliver Nelson, Al Cohn, Ernie Wilkins, and other arranger-composers. Krivda's flair as leader-performer, plus a kick-ass rhythm team and competent lead and section players give the 12 "neo–Kansas City swing" selections plenty of punch. (Lounge fans, take heed!) Thad Jones's "Back Bone," the band's 7:39-minute theme song, kicks off the session and features Krivda as well other fine soloists before some socking choruses close the number. The band follows that with a rousing eight-minute interpretation of the title tune by composer Juan Tizol; of particular note is baritone saxophonist Bernie Pelsmajer's big tone and bouncy solo. Right from the start, highlights become too numerous to mention, but an exceptionally hot bopper in the tradition is Ed Finkel's "Leave Us Leap." It's no surprise that this band has gained a following at

every Cleveland venue they've dug into. Krivda's playing throughout is his finest on record. This is a must-own album for jazz big-band fans, lounge fans who dig danceable swingers, and anyone who enjoys good music. If your heart can't handle a rumbling band like Krivda's Fat Tuesday Big Band, then you might prefer *Golden Moments* ♫♫♫♫ (Koch Jazz, 1997, prod. Ernie Krivda, Lee Bush), an album of duets that finds tenor saxophonist Krivda creating unpredictable, shared drama and excitement with the broadly talented pianist Dan Wall. Wall, who has performed for a few years as organ player with John Abercrombie's band, accompanies singers much of the time in Cleveland venues (his wife is a jazz vocalist). Thus, Wall—an adventurous, confident player—is supremely sensitive to Krivda's sax voicings and creates full-bodied accompaniment and artful fills to match Krivda's soaring lyricism. This is teamwork at its best, with neither musician stepping on the other's phrasing. The pair plays five standards and two Krivda originals from live-recorded 1995 performances at Lakeland Community College and the Cleveland Museum of Art. Best among many highlights are their interpretations of the Matt Dennis ballad "Angel Eyes," Irving Berlin's classic "How Deep Is the Ocean," and Cole Porter's "Get out of Town." A highly recommended album.

what to buy next: Unique as a saxophone-piano duo is, it's even more unique for tenor saxophonist Krivda and pianist Bill Dobbins, who come together for the first time in 10 years for nearly an hour to play the six standards on *The Art of the Ballad* ♫♫♫♫ (Koch Jazz, 1995, prod. Ernie Krivda, Lee Bush). On some tracks, Krivda poignantly matches Dobbins's lean and lovely lyricism and his music truly approaches art. The best track is a soulful, live-recorded rendition of a rarely heard Ellington gem, "Volupte." Otherwise, it's fairly standard—"How about You," " My Foolish Heart," "Darn That Dream," and others. Dobbins, from Akron, Ohio, lived and performed in Cleveland in the early 1970s. He's an inventive, mature player with a melodious, exultant style. This album marked Krivda's debut for the Koch label.

the rest:
(With Paula Owen) *So Nice to Meet You* ♫♫♫ (Cadence, 1994)
(With Jeff Halsey and Bob Fraser) *Sarah's Theme* ♫♫♫♫ (CIMP, 1995)

worth searching for: Check secondhand LP markets for the Krivda LP-album, *Tough Tenor—Red Hot* ♫♫♫♫ (Cadence, 1986, prod. Ernie Krivda), a five-tune session featuring his quartet with pianist Chip Stephens, bassist Jeff Halsey, and drummer Joe Brigandi. The same quartet is featured on the sequel, *Well You Needn't* ♫♫♫♫ (Cadence, 1988, prod. Ernie Krivda), a four-tune live-recorded performance at Joe Ricco's Milestones in Buffalo, New York, on May 16, 1987 (about five months before the club closed for good). Another live-recorded session with a different quartet, *Live at Rusty's* ♫♫♫ (North Coast Jazz, 1982, prod. Ernie Krivda) documents a 1981 Krivda-led gig at the Toledo, Ohio, jazz club with pianist Neal Creque (a veteran of groups led by Pharoah Sanders, Leon Thomas, Grant Green, and Carmen McRae), bassist Juny Booth (gigged with McCoy Tyner, Art Blakey, and Elvin Jones), and drummer Paul Samuels (20 years old at the time of this recording). Krivda's playing, like good wine, has mellowed as he's aged, but these sessions document rare quartet sessions with some very fine players.

Nancy Ann Lee

Kronos Quartet

Formed 1973, in San Francisco, CA.

David Harrington, first violin; John Sherba, second violin; Hank Dutt, viola; Joan Jeanrenaud, cello.

Formed over two decades ago, the Kronos Quartet was the first string group to revolutionize contemporary chamber music, emerging on the international scene with a blend of conventional string quartet music and their exuberant explorations into 20th century musical forms such as rock, jazz, blues, country, folk, and more. Kronos paved the way for equally adventurous string groups such as the Uptown String Quartet, Quartette Indigo, Turtle Island String Quartet, and others. Kronos successfully straddles the gulf between the scholarly and the popular. They find insightful approaches to classical masterpieces and at the same time are committed to creating and performing vital new works. Since the unconventional string ensemble first emerged in 1978, they have recorded numerous albums of 20th century music, including works by composers from Bartok, Shostakovich, and Berg, to Philip Glass, John Cage, Terry Riley, Jimi Hendrix, Astor Piazzolla, and others. Kronos performs and tours extensively in North America, Europe, and Japan, and often serve as artists-in-residence on various college campuses and at arts institutions. They are constantly commissioning new works, learning new music, and collaborating with leading 20th century composers.

what to buy: Their jazz-influenced recordings, two albums originally released on LP in the mid-1980s, are good places to start, but eventually inquisitive jazz fans and those who favor modern string quartets will want to explore other Kronos Quartet recordings, some of which are listed below. *The Complete Landmark Sessions* ♫♫♫♫ (Landmark, 1985–1986/32 Jazz, 1997, prod. Orrin Keepnews) combines two earlier LPs, *Monk Suite: Kronos Quartet Plays Music of Thelonious Monk* (with guest bassist Ron Carter, Chuck Israels, bass, and Eddie Marshall, drums) released by Landmark in 1985, and *Kronos Quartet: The Music of Bill Evans* (with Eddie Gomez and Jim Hall) released on Landmark LP in 1986. Performed by David Harrington (first violin), John Sherba (second violin), Hank Dutt (viola), Joan Jeanrenaud (cello) with guest artists, the two-CD set contains the Kronos Quartet recordings that turned on many jazz fans to their music. The group's stately elegance and understanding of composer themes, as well as appearances from guest artists, marks these two discs as the most favored among jazz lovers. The *Monk Suite* includes a sweet version of Ellington's "Black and Tan Fantasy" (with Israels and Marshall) along with other standard Monk gems such as "Misterioso," "'Round Midnight," "Well You Needn't," and three Ellington tunes performed in Monk style. Produced the following year (1986), *Music of Bill Evans* on disc two, features compositions mostly written by the renowned jazz pianist. The fare on disc two maintains a melodically light, romantic flavor as Kronos and guests swing through Evans classics such as "Waltz for Debby," "Time Remembered," "Turn Out the Stars," and six more tunes (one by Miles Davis, "Nardis," is thrown in for good measure). Original album producer Orrin Keepnews was head of Riverside during the late 1950s and early 1960s and produced sessions by both Monk and Evans. He launched the Landmark label in 1985 and produced these Kronos Quartet sessions. His original notes have been revised and are included. With arrangements by Tom Darter, the Kronos Quartet sounds as beautiful and fresh today as they did 20 years ago. New generations of fans should find this attractive, long-awaited, two-disc package a delightful listen.

best of the rest:

Cadenza On the Night Plain ♫♫♫ (Gramavision, 1988)
Pieces of Africa ♫♫♫♫ (Elektra/Nonesuch, 1992)
Short Stores ♫♫♫♫ (Elektra/Nonesuch, 1993)
Kronos Quartet Performs Philip Glass ♫♫♫ (Nonesuch, 1995)

influences:

◀◀ Joe Venuti, Stephane Grappelli, Stuff Smith, Claude Williams, John Frigo, Duke Ellington, Thelonious Monk, John Zorn, Terry Riley, Phillip Glass, Astor Piazzolla

▶▶ Uptown String Quartet, Turtle Island String Quartet, Quartette Indigo

Nancy Ann Lee

Gene Krupa

Born January 15, 1909, in Chicago, IL. Died October 16, 1973, in Yonkers, NY.

Gene Krupa transformed the drums from a mere timekeeping device into a full-fledged solo instrument. Capable of generating a tremendous amount of tension and release, Krupa's explosive solos had kids of the 1930s and 1940s badgering their parents for drums the way later generations would guitars. Whether he played jive and fast with wire brushes or pounded the toms with heavy hands and sticks, Krupa was the most exciting and energetic drummer of his day.

At the tender age of 16, Krupa helped establish the Chicago style of jazz with the Frivolians and Eddie Condon's Austin High School Gang. With the McKenzie/Condon Chicagoans in 1927, Krupa became the first musician to use a full drum kit in a recording studio. A popular session man, Krupa also played in bands fronted by Russ Columbo, Buddy Rogers, and Red Nichols, before joining Benny Goodman's orchestra in 1934. The King of Swing made the most of Krupa's extroverted, highly visual style, and before long Goodman's orchestra was not only perceived as the best, but the most popular as well. Krupa's pneumatic drum solo on the classic "Sing Sing Sing" created a sensation, and his spotlight-stealing performance at Goodman's 1938 Carnegie Hall concert made him a household name. Krupa split with Goodman and formed his own band in 1938. Hits like "Wire Brush Stomp," "Drummin' Man," and "Drum Boogie" propelled the handsome drummer's individual popularity to even greater heights, and led to appearances in over a dozen Hollywood movies. Krupa's band (featuring Roy Eldridge and Anita O'Day, among others) peaked in the early 1940s with hits such as "Bolero at the Savoy," "Let Me Off Uptown," "After You've Gone," "Rockin' Chair," and "Thanks for the Boogie Ride," but it all came crashing down in 1943.

After a drug bust and the resultant waves of bad publicity, Krupa disbanded his orchestra. Once cleared of the charges, he publicly rehabilitated himself in stints with Benny Goodman and Tommy Dorsey. Krupa started another band in 1944, one that allowed the bebop arrangements of Gerry Mulligan to permeate swing-band aesthetics (an artistic and commercial risk at the time). Krupa backed a few more hit records and kept various lineups of his orchestra going until 1951. By then, the big bands were dying, and drummer Buddy Rich's superior technical skill eclipsed Krupa's in the minds of fans. Always a workhorse, Krupa continued recording LPs with trios and quartets throughout the 1950s, and was a featured star of Norman Granz's Jazz at the Philharmonic tours. Interest in his career was revived by the 1959 film *The Gene Krupa Story*. A largely inaccurate Sal Mineo vehicle, the movie's saving grace was Krupa's work on the soundtrack. Krupa recorded with small jazz groups and in big-band reunion settings throughout the 1960s and early 1970s until his death. There are few drummers in either rock music or jazz who don't owe a massive stylistic debt to Gene Krupa.

what to buy: Krupa's best orchestra lineup and their biggest hits can be found on *Drum Boogie* 🎵🎵🎵🎵 (Legacy, 1993, compilation prod. Michael Brooks), an essential introductory collection.

what to buy next: There's more prime Krupa on *Drummer* 🎵🎵🎵🎵 (Pearl 1993, compilation prod. Colin Brown, Tony Watts), a smart selection culled from his 1935 to 1941 output. A good mix of hits and percussion pyrotechnics galore can also be found on *Drummin' Man* 🎵🎵🎵🎵 (Charly, 1989, prod. various).

what to avoid: The sound quality is poor on the budget rack perennial *Giants of the Big Band Era* 🎵 (Pilz, 1992). For a few extra bucks you can get the same tracks with better fidelity elsewhere.

the rest:
Gene Krupa & Buddy Rich 🎵🎵🎵 (Verve, 1955/1994)
Drummer Man 🎵🎵🎵 (Verve, 1956/1996)
Compact Jazz 🎵🎵🎵🎵 (Verve, 1987/1993)
Gene Krupa/Buddy Rich: Compact Jazz 🎵🎵🎵 (Verve 1988/1992)
Gene Krupa—1935–38 🎵🎵🎵🎵 (Classics, 1994)
Gene Krupa—1938 🎵🎵🎵🎵 (Classics, 1994)
1946 Live! 🎵🎵🎵 (Jazz Hour, 1994)
Gene Krupa—1939 🎵🎵🎵🎵 (Classics, 1995)
What's This? 1946, Vol. 1 (Hep, 1995)
Radio Years (1940) 🎵🎵🎵🎵 (Jazz Unlimited, 1995)
Gene Krupa & His Orchestra 🎵🎵🎵🎵 (Jazz Hour, 1995)
The Radio Years 🎵🎵🎵🎵 (Jazz Hour, 1995)
It's Up to You; 1946, Vol. 2 🎵🎵🎵 (Hep, 1995)
The Legendary Big Bands 🎵🎵🎵 (Sony Music Special Products, 1995)
Gene Krupa 1939–40 🎵🎵🎵 (Classics, 1995)
Hollywood Palladium 1/18/45 🎵🎵🎵 (Canby Records, 1995)
Vol. 13—Masterpieces 🎵🎵 (EPM Musique, 1996)
1940, Vol. 2 🎵🎵🎵 (Classics, 1996)
Volume 3: Hop, Skip, & Jump 🎵🎵🎵 (Hep, 1996)
Leave Us Leap 🎵🎵🎵 (Vintage Jazz Classics, 1996)
Swings with Strings 🎵🎵 (Vintage Jazz Classics, 1996)
1940 🎵🎵🎵 (Classics, 1997)

worth searching for: Krupa's sextet delivers some effective hard bop on *Let Me Off Uptown* 🎵🎵🎵 (Drive Archive, 1996), recorded at three live performances circa 1949. Also, for an example of Krupa Hollywood-style check out the Gary Cooper–Barbara

Gene Krupa **(AP/Wide World Photos)**

Stanwyck comedy *Ball of Fire* (Goldwyn Productions, 1941, director Howard Hawks). Krupa's version of "Drum Boogie" on a matchbox is still a killer-diller.

influences:

⏪ Roy C. Knapp, Edward B. Straight, Chick Webb

⏩ Big Sid Catlett, Buddy Rich, Louis Belson, Keith Moon

see also: *Eddie Condon, Tommy Dorsey, Benny Goodman, Red Nichols*

Ken Burke

Joachim Kuhn

Born March 13, 1944, in Leipzig, Germany.

The younger brother of clarinetist Rolf Kuhn, Joachim Kuhn began piano and composition lessons at age five and was already performing classical repertoire when his interests turned fully to jazz when he was 17. During the 1960s he performed regularly with his own trio and often worked in bands led by his brother. He played regularly with violinist Jean-Luc Ponty in 1971 and was often occupied with fusion projects in the 1970s, concentrating on electric keyboards. Since the 1980s Kuhn has worked regularly in a trio setting with drummer Daniel Humair and bassist Jean Francois Jenny-Clark, musicians who are his equals in adventurous creativity and who take the same pleasure in mixing traditional structures and free exploration. Together they've developed a remarkable cohesiveness in their interplay, comparable to the better versions of the Bill Evans Trio but with a broader palette of musical materials. Kuhn has enjoyed a tremendously varied career, from working with vocalists Eartha Kitt and Helen Merrill to mainstream jazz with Joe Henderson and Jerry Bergonzi to his own avant-garde and fusion work. More remarkable still is that he has distinguished himself in every form in which he has played. Whether writing or improvising, Kuhn has strong compositional skills that have led him to explore structures of considerable complexity in his own work.

what to buy: A brilliant series of recent CDs on the French Label Bleu are highlights in Kuhn's career. *Abstracts* ♫♫♫♫ (Label Bleu, 1994, prod. Joachim Kuhn, Walter Quintus) is the most expansive and exploratory of Kuhn's solo recordings, with his brilliant technique always in the service of his demanding imagination. *Usual Confusion* ♫♫♫ (Label Bleu, 1996, prod. Michel Orier) demonstrates the close communication of the Kuhn–Humair–Jenny-Clark trio in a set of originals that range from pensive to frequently explosive.

what to buy next: *Famous Melodies* ♫♫♫ (Label Bleu, 1996, prod. Joachim Kuhn, Walter Quintus) is an entertaining solo session with tunes by Kurt Weill and Cole Porter, and even Bobby McFerrin's "Don't Worry, Be Happy" presented in a rendition that reveals Kuhn's sense of humor. Rather than just another set of solo piano standards, he uses his keen sense of piano sonority to reach through the material to find his own voice.

best of the rest:
From Time to Time Free ♫♫♫ (CMP, 1989)
Easy to Read ♫♫♫ (Mesa/Bluemoon, 1991)
Carambolage ♫♫♫ (CMP, 1992)
Solos ♫♫♫ (Futura, 1996)

worth searching for: Kuhn is outstanding on a recent duet recording with Ornette Coleman, *Colors: Live in Leipzig* ♫♫♫ (Verve, 1997, prod. Denardo Coleman). His rhythmically aggressive, self-directed playing creates one of the most stimulating partnerships that Coleman has found in recent decades.

influences:
◄◄ Bill Evans, Martial Solal, Cecil Taylor

Stuart Broomer

Steve Kuhn

Born March 24, 1938, in Brooklyn, NY.

Pianist/composer Steve Kuhn studied classical piano as a youngster, and began working professionally around age 14. Among his many teachers, he credits Margaret Chaloff as being the most influential. Kuhn freelanced as a teenager in the Boston area, and after his 1959 graduation from Harvard moved to New York, where he played and recorded with Kenny Dorham during 1959–60. Kuhn could've made history by playing in the John Coltrane quartet, but quit after two months to join Stan Getz's quartet (1961–63) and help fashion a style of gently bopping bossa nova. He worked with Art Farmer in the mid-1960s, lived in Europe from 1967 to 1970, and returned to the United States in 1971, where he became an effective part of

the lightweight underground. In the '70s and '80s he gained critical acceptance as a leader on several fine ECM recordings (especially with a quartet that included vocalist Sheila Jordan), and formed the acoustic trio that has since been his main format. In the late 1980s, his trio included bassist Ron Carter and drummer Al Foster; however, he's recorded recent trio sets with bassist David Finck and drummers Joey Baron or Lewis Nash. With a personalized depth and energy, Kuhn's wide-ranging style encompasses everything from straight-ahead jazz to the bossa nova, light blues, and impressionistic and dissonant modal jazz.

what to buy: *Looking Back* ♫♫♫♫ (Concord, 1991, prod. Allen Farnham) features pianist Kuhn performing 10 mostly straight-ahead favorites with bassist David Finck and drummer Lewis Nash, tight-playing partners and tasteful rhythm-mates who can swing with ease and lend lushness to ballads. Kuhn shows imagination and virtuosic, facile fingering and phrasing as he lashes through a stunning, uptempo version of "Alone Together," with Nash punching hard from underneath. Lasting 8:40, this album centerpiece also may be the all-time best version of this standard. The trio also performs the Antonio Carlos Jobim gems "How Insensitive" and "Zingaro" with gentle finesse. Kuhn's touch is exquisite. He often starts a tune with simple lines, then imaginatively increases dynamics, building drama into each tune with sparing use of percussive chording, a technique most noticeable on his buoyant version of "Baubles, Bangles, and Beads." The collective artistry on the trio's interpretation of "Will You Still Be Mine" includes Finck's arco (bowed) playing and Nash's use of mallets. The awesome combined talent here makes *Looking Back* one of the most gorgeous piano trio recordings. Recorded two years later, *Years Later* ♫♫♫♫ (Concord, 1993, prod. Allen Farnham) features the Steve Kuhn Trio (with the same personnel) performing tunes that the pianist listened to growing up. Among the 10 tunes, Kuhn includes classics composed by Duke Ellington ("In a Sentimental Mood"), Billy Strayhorn ("Upper Manhattan Medical Group"), Count Basie ("Good Bait"), Steve Swallow ("Ladies in Mercedes"), Horace Silver ("Silver's Serenade"), and others, including Kuhn's original title song. Kuhn rides to the finish of his version of Mel Tormé's "Born to Be Blue" with a few familiar bluesy quotes. The trio is even more eloquent and unified than on their earlier Concord date, making this CD an extremely satisfying listen for mainstream jazz fans.

what to buy next: *Mostly Ballads* ♫♫♫ (New World Records, 1987, prod. Robert Hurwitz), recorded in 1984, ranks among Kuhn's best recordings. With half the numbers performed solo, half with bassist Harvie Swartz, the album includes lyrical renditions of mostly standards such as "Airegin," "Body and Soul," "How High the Moon," and other favorites. *Live at Maybeck Recital Hall, Volume 13* 𝄞𝄞𝄞𝄞 (Concord, 1991, prod. Carl E. Jefferson), an album in Concord's live-recorded solo piano series, was recorded one month after Kuhn's Concord trio session *Looking Back*. It's on this album that you get to hear how Kuhn develops a tune with his busy right hand, working his melody lines well into the upper octaves, and supporting minimally (sometimes, modally) with his left hand. Highlights include the unusually structured and harmonically adventurous rendition of the Miles Davis tune "Solar," a daringly innovative (nearly 11 minutes) version of "Autumn in New York," and more equally impressive music on his first solo album since his long-out-of-print 1976 studio recording *Ecstacy* for the ECM label. *Remembering Tomorrow* 𝄞𝄞𝄞 (ECM, 1996, prod. Manfred Eicher), his first ECM release in 14 years, features Kuhn's trio with bassist David Finck and drummer Joey Baron, as the leader revisits and updates 11 of his classic tunes, including "The Rain Forest," "Oceans in the Sky," "Life's Backward Glance," and "Silver."

influences:

◀◀ Bill Evans, Horace Silver

Nancy Ann Lee and Joe S. Harrington

STEVE KUHN (WITH BOB MOSES)

song "Autumn Liebs"
album Devotion
(Soul Note, 1979/1996)
instrument Piano

Abraham Laboriel

Born July 17, 1947, in Mexico City, Mexico.

Since following the encouragement of the late Henry Mancini to move to Los Angeles in the late 1970s, bass player Abe Laboriel has played on over 3,000 sessions. He has recorded extensively with such artists as Larry Carlton, Lee Ritenour, George Benson, Joe Sample, Randy Crawford, Dave and Don Grusin, John Klemmer, Kenny Loggins, the Manhattan Transfer, Barbra Streisand, Tim Weisberg, Olivia Newton-John, Melissa Manchester, Justo Almario, Nancy Wilson, Teena Maria, and Al Jarreau. His most noted sessions include Donald Fagen's *Nightfly*, Herb Alpert's *Rise*, Ruben Blades's *Nothing but the Truth*, Joe Cocker's *Best of Joe Cocker*, Robbie Robertson's self-titled release, Maria Muldaur's *Sweet and Slow*, Gilberto Gil's *Nightingale*, and Jennifer Warnes's *Shot through the Heart*. His film credits include *48*

Hours, Against All Odds, Beaches, The Color Purple, Dick Tracy, Last of the Mohicans, Nine to Five, Pretty in Pink, and *Saturday Night Fever*. Originally trained as a classical guitarist, Laboriel incorporated his five-finger flamenco style on the bass guitar when he made the transition to four strings at the Berklee College of Music in Boston. In retrospect, it was also a very wise move for him to study composition as well as guitar, developing a gift solidly evident in his recordings as a leader. Laboriel was also co-founder of the internationally acclaimed jazz-rock group Koinonia with Justo Almario, Alex Acuna, and Bill Maxwell, and a founding member of the highly regarded fusion group Friendship. To witness the energy and joyous passion Laboriel exudes in a live performance (spiced by that infectious smile) is to understand why his recorded performances tend to breathe deep and jump off the track. Bass has always been described as a foundation instrument, and when the player is Laboriel, the foundation is immovable. He has been named the Most Valuable Player as a bassist four years running by the National Association of Recording Arts and Sciences. He is a master at making everybody else sound good.

what to buy: *Dear Friends* ♫♫♫ (Mesa/Bluemoon, 1993) debuts the studio bass giant as a leader. Laboriel's dear friends on this record include Jarreau, Carlton, Grusin, Joe Sample, Philip Bailey, Jim Keltner, Ernie Watts, and Steve Gadd—not bad company even if there is no party dip. From the vocals to the instrumentals, each track stands on its own and brings its own distinct qualities.

what to buy next: *Guidum* ♫♫♫ (101 South, 1994) is a quartet with long-time musical partner and woodwind virtuoso Justo Almario, producer/arranger/composer Greg Mathieson on keyboards, and Laboriel's eldest son Abe Jr. on drums. This record not only documents Laboriel as a great bass player, but proves him to be an outstanding composer as well.

the rest:
Justo & Abe ♫♫♫ (Integrity, 1996)

influences:
◄◄ Carol Kaye, Stanley Clarke
►► Victor Bailey, Nathan East

Ralph Burnett

Steve Lacy

Born July 23, 1934, in New York, NY.

Inspired by Sidney Bechet, soprano saxophonist Steve Lacy first played traditional jazz with Cecil Scott, Rex Stewart, and Dick Sutton, but in 1955 he made a quantum leap to the quartet of Cecil Taylor. In 1957 he recorded with Gil Evans for the first time; he continued to record and perform with Evans up until Evans's death. Lacy played briefly with pianist Thelonious Monk—who probably exerted the single largest influence on Lacy's own music—in 1960 and 1963. He then embarked on a period in Europe during which he played free jazz with Carla Bley and Don Cherry, among others, and recorded his first album of free improvisation. In 1970 he moved to Paris, his home for most of the next 25 years. In the '70s Lacy assembled a quintet consisting of saxophonist Steve Potts, bassist Kent Carter, and drummer Oliver Johnson, with his wife Irene Aebi on cello and vocals. Aebi's voice, another enormous influence on Lacy's music, inspired Lacy's interest in the song form, of which he is a modern master. In 1981 Lacy expanded his band to include pianist Bobby Few, while Jean-Jacques Avenel replaced Kent Carter. Drummer John Betch replaced Johnson in the early 1990s before Lacy finally disbanded the group in 1996. Lacy's music displays a graceful asymmetry, clarity of development, and the influence of literature and the visual arts. His soloing is precise and pared of extra-

neous notes, with a strong, song-like sense of melody. He also has a wry and rather dark sense of humor akin to Samuel Beckett's. His tone is remarkably supple—wire-thin and razor sharp at times, fat and dark at others, and he makes careful, nuanced use of pure sound and a vocabulary of animal-like quacks and growls. Monk is a touchstone for his use of space and emphasis on melodic development, while Gil Evans is an inspiration for his sense of tone color and ensemble coherence.

what to buy: *Reflections* ♫♫♫♫ (OJC, 1958, prod. Rudy Van Gelder) was the first meeting between Mal Waldron and Lacy in a quartet that plays the music of Monk with great insight and swing. The first complete recorded performance of Lacy's "Tao Suite," based on texts by Lau Tzu, played by the fully mature working quintet, is *The Way* ♫♫♫♫ (hat ART, 1979, prod. Pia Uehlinger, Werner X. Uehlinger), a brilliantly attuned ensemble, with Potts serving as a hot counterpart to Lacy's more coolly considered style and Carter and Jackson nailing the tempos. Aebi's alto voice is sonorous and full, and declaims the melodies with a fine ear for the meaning of the texts. *Futurities* ♫♫♫♫ (hat ART, 1984, prod. Pia Uehlinger, Werner X. Uehlinger) is the sextet plus guests in one of Lacy's masterpieces, a suite of settings of Robert Creely love poems. Each intimate song is a gem, and the ensemble plays with great warmth. But while each tune feels modestly scaled, the suite takes on great power and complexity over two CDs. The poems resonate against one another; the seemingly simple melodies conjure up a wide spectrum of emotions; and a quite profound, tough-minded meditation on love and marriage emerges. *Remains* ♫♫♫♫ (hat ART, prod. Pia Uehlinger, Werner X. Uehlinger) is a typically rigorous solo set with a complete rendition of the Tao Suite, a mostly composed suite for dance, and a tune by his beloved and inexhaustable Monk.

what to buy next: The quartet with Rudd playing Monk tunes captured live in all its vitality, daring, and wit is on *School Days* ♫♫♫♫ (hat ART, 1963, prod. Pia Uehlinger, Werner X. Uehlinger). The fidelity (and occasionally the band) is ragged, but little matter—this was a seminal band for all concerned. The Lacy-Waldron duo expound on the compositions of Billy Strayhorn on *Sempre Amor* ♫♫♫♫ (Soul Note, 1986, prod. Giovanni Bonandrini), not a typical program for them, but an exceptionally well-realized album. *Vespers* ♫♫♫♫♫ (Soul Note, 1993, prod. Giovanni Bonandrini, Ann Rebentisch) is another thematic suite played by Lacy's core group plus guests. This one consists of pieces dedicated to the memories of departed friends and colleagues. Once again, complex and tender feelings are evoked with poetic economy.

best of the rest:

Evidence 🎵🎵🎵 (OJC, 1961)

The Forest and the Zoo 🎵🎵🎵 (ESP, 1966)

Weal & Woe 🎵🎵🎵 (Emanem, 1972–73)

Songs 🎵🎵🎵 (hat ART, 1981)

Chirps 🎵🎵🎵 (FMP, 1985)

Morning Joy 🎵🎵🎵 (hat ART, 1986)

More Monk 🎵🎵🎵 (Soul Note, 1989)

Flim-Flam 🎵🎵🎵 (hat ART 1991)

We See 🎵🎵🎵 (hat ART, 1992)

Bye-ya 🎵🎵🎵 (Freelance, 1996)

Five Facings 🎵🎵🎵 (FMP, 1996)

worth searching for: The hat ART label has been Lacy's most sensitive patron; why hasn't it reissued *Prospectus* 🎵🎵🎵 (hat ART, 1983), a stunning session with trombonist George Lewis joining Lacy's working band?

influences:

◀◀ Sidney Bechet

▶▶ Evan Parker, Jane Ira Bloom

Ed Hazell

STEVE LACY
(WITH MAL WALDRON)

song "Snake Out"

album *Live at Dreher, Paris, 1981: Round Midnight, Vol. 1*
(hat ART, 1981/1996)

instrument Soprano saxophone

Monster Solo

Scott LaFaro

Born April 3, 1936, in Newark, NJ. Died July 6, 1961, in Geneva, NY.

Scott LaFaro developed an expanded ensemble role for the bass, with a freer sense of time and greater harmonic and melodic complexity, that exerted an important liberating influence on contemporary bass playing. He took up the bass in 1953, when he began gigging in R&B bands. He traveled with the Buddy Morrow Orchestra to Los Angeles in 1955 and remained in California, where he played or recorded with Chet Baker, Harold Land, Barney Kessel, Paul Bley, Stan Getz, and Cal Tjader. He moved to New York in 1959 and played briefly with Benny Goodman. LaFaro's name is most often linked with the Bill Evans trio that also featured drummer Paul Motian from 1959 to 1961. By alternating counter melodies in free time, walking bass lines, and vamps, LaFaro placed his instrument on a more equal footing with the lead voice of the piano and freed the bass from its traditional role as harmonic/rhythmic foundation. The flexibility and intimate interplay among the members of this Evans trio established a benchmark for piano trios that persists to today. He brought a similarly radical approach to albums by Booker Little and Ornette Coleman, and when playing with Stan Getz at the Newport Jazz Festival days before his death in an automobile accident.

worth searching for: *Bill Evans Trio: Sunday at the Village Vanguard* 🎵🎵🎵 (OJC, 1961/1987, prod. Orrin Keepnews) is an essential jazz album that captures the Evans trio in peak form, a mere 10 days before LaFaro's death. It includes his marvelous composition "Gloria's Step." LaFaro is also highlighted with the Bill Evans Trio on *Waltz for Debbie* 🎵🎵🎵 (OJC, 1961/1994, prod. Orrin Keepnews), the companion volume to *Sunday at the Village Vanguard*. If you want to get confused, highlights from these two albums (the same dates) have been collected on *At the Village Vanguard* (Riverside, 1992, prod. Orrin Keepnews). Another Bill Evans Trio recording that features LaFaro is *Portrait in Jazz* 🎵🎵🎵 (OJC, 1959/1987), a studio session not quite up to their later Vanguard performances, but still very good, especially for the track "Blue in Green." Examples of LaFaro's playing can also be heard on Ornette Coleman's *Beauty Is a Rare Thing: The Complete Atlantic Recordings of Ornette Coleman* 🎵🎵🎵 (Atlantic/Rhino, 1993, prod. Nesuhi Ertegun). Just in case you need another reason to pick up this magnificent six-CD set, it contains every note LaFaro recorded with

Coleman, including the sessions that produced the *Ornette!* and *Free Jazz* albums. LaFaro is also included on the recording with Coleman's Double Quartet, *Free Jazz* 🎵🎵🎵🎵 (Atlantic, 1961/1987). If you can't afford the boxed set (in which this album is included), this is a good single album on which to hear LaFaro's freely wandering, hornlike lines working well with Charlie Haden's rhythmic foundation.

Ed Hazell

Cleo Laine

Born Clementina Dinah Campbell, October 28, 1927, in Southall, Middlesex, England.

An excellent singer who takes cues from Ella Fitzgerald, Peggy Lee, Rosemary Clooney, Helen Merrill, and other pop singers who smooth out the bluesy edges of their styles, Laine has garnered hordes of fans with her smoky, flexible, four-octave voice and her incredible scatting ability. Singing an array of jazz, pop, and classics, Laine has racked up several huge-selling albums, and has appeared in major Broadway concerts and musicals, as well as performing with classical artists James Galway and John Williams. She and her husband, longtime producer and collaborator John Dankworth, create music mostly in the style defined by singers Frank Sinatra and Tony Bennett, and drawing on American Songbook works by Cole Porter, George and Ira Gershwin, Harold Arlen, Lorenz Hart, Duke Ellington, and other composers. Laine frequently performs with philharmonic orchestras, appears at jazz festivals, and, early in her career, even set Shakespeare sonnets to music. In the early 1950s she sang at small British clubs; when she auditioned for then-bandleader Dankworth, he fell for both her music and its maker. Laine joined his band in 1952, married him six years later, and they have been a team ever since. In the late 1950s her acting career took off, with roles in *Valmouth,* the Kurt Weill–Bertold Brecht musical *Seven Deadly Sins,* and a London production of the popular *Show Boat.* After several solo singing tours, in 1973 she began a long-term series of concerts (and subsequent hit live recordings) at New York City's Carnegie Hall. She won a 1983 Grammy Award for her album *The 10th Anniversary Concert,* earned an honorary doctoral degree from Boston's prestigious Berklee College of Music, and, with her husband, continues to perform and teach.

what to buy: *A Beautiful Thing* 🎵🎵🎵🎵 (RCA Victor, 1994, prod. Mike Berniker, Kurt Gebauer, John Dankworth), recorded in 1974 (and partially in 1993) features flutist James Galway and focuses almost exclusively on standards, such as "Send in the Clowns" and "All in Love Is Fair"; the jazzier *Blue & Sentimen-*

tal 🎵🎵🎵🎵 (RCA Victor, 1994, prod. Kurt Gebauer, John Dankworth) features saxophonist Gerry Mulligan (a longtime Laine friend and collaborator) and pianist George Shearing, and snappier numbers such as "Afterglow" and "I've Got a Crush on You."

what to buy next: *The Very Best of Cleo Laine* 🎵🎵🎵 (RCA Victor, 1997, prod. various) collects her biggest hits, including old showtunes like "I Loves You Porgy," big-band classics like Duke Ellington's "Solitude," and interesting but slightly bizarre up-tempo numbers like "Creole Love Call." It's an interesting representation of her long career, but not as valuable as her better solo albums.

what to avoid: "Solitude," with a snippet of Ellington's actual piano playing from 1941 spliced into the new recording, is the centerpiece of Laine's uneven Ellington tribute, *Solitude* 🎵🎵 (RCA Victor, 1995, prod. Steve Vining), in which she fronts the Duke Ellington Band on his old standards, including "I'm Beginning to See the Light," "Sophisticated Lady," and a Laine bastardization titled "Cleo's 'A' Train."

best of the rest:
I Am a Song 🎵🎵🎵 (RCA Victor, 1973/1994)
Cleo at Carnegie Hall: 10th Anniversary 🎵🎵🎵 (RCA Victor, 1983/1993)
That Old Feeling 🎵🎵🎵 (Sony, 1984)
Cleo Laine Sings Sondheim 🎵🎵🎵 (RCA, 1988)
Woman to Woman 🎵🎵🎵 (RCA, 1989)
Jazz 🎵🎵🎵 (RCA Victor, 1991)
Cleo's Choice 🎵🎵🎵 (GNP/Crescendo, 1993)
Live at Carnegie Hall 🎵🎵🎵 (RCA Victor, 1993)

worth searching for: Some of Laine's original LPs have been reissued on CD, but her earliest material, on which you can hear her hunger and freshness, are sadly long gone from the market. Among the best is *All About Me* 🎵🎵🎵 (Fontana, 1962).

influences:
◀◀ Sarah Vaughan, Ella Fitzgerald, Rosemary Clooney, Peggy Lee, Patti Page, Betty Carter

▶▶ Diane Schuur, Helen Merrill, Kitty Margolis, Karin Allyson, Dee Dee Bridgewater

Steve Knopper and Nancy Ann Lee

Oliver Lake

Born September 14, 1942, in Marianna, AR.

Versatility is a good word to use in describing Oliver Lake. Whether playing avant-garde–tinged riffs, reggae stylings, or hard bop licks, composing classically oriented works for string quartet or working on straight-ahead jazz charts, he does it well. Lake's first instrument was drums, closely followed by alto saxophone and flute. After graduating from college, he taught school in St. Louis in addition to playing with members of the Black Artists Group (including Julius Hemphill and Hamiet Bluiett). In 1974 he moved to New York City, where he gigged with various ensembles until 1976, when he joined Hemphill, Bluiett, and David Murray to form the World Saxophone Quartet. Not content with only one outlet for his creativity, Lake formed other bands during this same time, including Jump Up, which used reggae for the base of its improvisations, and a trio with Michael Gregory Jackson and Pheeroan Ak Laff. In addition to his jazz works, Lake has also composed string quartets, large-scale multi-media compositions, and miscellaneous chamber music pieces.

what to buy: *Compilation* ✍✍✍✍ (Gramavision, 1990, prod. Jonathan F.P. Rose, Oliver Lake) is a fairly good introduction to Lake's playing in the late '80s. There is one song from his pseudo-reggae group Jump Up, but the rest of the material hovers between post-modern wailing and adventurous mainstream playing. When Lake takes his heralded versatility outside the norm, the results can be fairly intriguing, as is the case with *Boston Duets* ✍✍✍✍ (Music & Arts, 1992, prod. Donal Leonellis Fox), a 1989 duo concert with classical pianist/composer Donal Leonellis Fox. It's not for everyone, but deserves a listen from the adventurous.

what to buy next: Lake has absorbed many of Eric Dolphy's technical elements into his own unique style and has covered Dolphy tunes before, but *Dedicated to Dolphy* ✍✍✍✍ (Black Saint, 1996, prod. Flavio Bonandrini) is the album that may make Dolphy accessible to mainstream listeners. The result lacks some of the aggressive power and risk-taking Lake has displayed in the past, but the overall performance can't be faulted.

the rest:
Holding Together ✍✍✍ (Black Saint, 1976)
Prophet ✍✍✍✍ (Black Saint, 1981)
Clevont Fitzhubert (A Good Friend of Mine) ✍✍✍ (Black Saint, 1981)
Expandable Language ✍✍✍✍ (Black Saint, 1985)
Again and Again ✍✍✍✍ (Gramavision, 1991)
Zaki ✍✍✍✍ (hat ART, 1992)
Virtual Reality ✍✍✍ (Gazell, 1993)
Edge-ing ✍✍✍ (Black Saint, 1994)

influences:
◄◄ Eric Dolphy

Garaud MacTaggart

Scott LaFaro (with Bill Evans)

song "Solar"
album *Sunday at the Village Vanguard*
(Riverside-OJC, 1961/1992)
instrument Bass

Monster Solo

Lambert, Hendricks & Ross /Lambert, Hendricks & Bavan

Formed 1957. Disbanded 1964.

Dave Lambert (born 1917; died 1966), vocals; Jon Hendricks (born 1921), vocals; Annie Ross (born 1930), vocals (1957–62); Yolande Bavan, vocals, (1962–64).

One of the greatest vocal groups in jazz history, Lambert, Hendricks, and Ross brought together three superior bop-influenced singers who perfected and popularized vocalese, the art of putting lyrics to a previously recorded jazz solo. Dave Lambert and Jon Hendricks were collaborators who were seeking to record an album of Count Basie tunes with a jazz chorus when they met Annie Ross, who was already a respected singer, and decided to make it a trio. The resulting session, *Sing a Song of Basie*, which used over-dubbing to create a chorus effect, catapulted the group into national prominence in 1957. One of the biggest-drawing jazz acts through the late 1950s and early 1960s, the trio recorded a series of classic albums, including collaborations with Basie and Duke Ellington. Health problems led Ross to leave the group in 1962 and she was replaced by Yolande Bavan (transforming the group into Lambert, Hendricks, and Bavan). In 1964 the group disbanded when both Bavan and Lambert decided to move on. LH&R recorded for Columbia, Roulette, World Pacific, and Impulse!, and LH&B recorded for RCA. Their influence is still pervasive among jazz vocal groups, and their vocalese accomplishments have never been surpassed.

what to buy: Perhaps the definitive Lambert, Hendricks, and Ross album, *Everybody's Boppin'* 🎵🎵🎵🎵 (Columbia, 1959–61/ 1989, prod. Irving Townsend, Teo Macero) features the group's astoundingly nimble vocalese arrangements of Bobby Timmons's "Moanin'," Ross's classic chart of Wardell Gray's tenor solo "Twisted," "Sweets" Edison's enduring "Centerpiece" and Hendricks's hilarious original "Gimme That Wine," among other classics. Their stunning lyrical dexterity and vocal chops make this essential listening for any fan of jazz singing. They are accompanied on all tracks by a trio led by the tasteful and swinging pianist Gildo Mahones. The album that made stars of Lambert, Hendricks, and Ross, *Sing a Song of Basie* 🎵🎵🎵🎵 (Impulse!, 1957/GRP, 1992, prod. Bob Thiele) is a landmark in jazz vocal history. Using overdubbing, the trio recreated 10 classic Basie charts, including "One O'Clock Jump," "Little Pony," "Two for the Blues" and "It's Sand, Man." Backed by a nimble rhythm section with pianist Nat Pierce and Basie-ites Freddie Green (guitar), Eddie Jones (bass), and Sonny Payne (drums), the group brought vocalese to an unprecedented level of musicality and lyrical brilliance. Hendricks's lyrics take up 14 pages in the CD booklet!

best of the rest:
The Swingers! 🎵🎵🎵🎵 (Pacific Jazz, 1959/Blue Note, 1995)
The Hottest New Group in Jazz 🎵🎵🎵🎵 (Columbia, 1960/1996)
Twisted: The Best of Lambert, Hendricks, and Ross 🎵🎵🎵🎵 (Rhino, 1992)

solo outings:
Jon Hendricks:
(With Friends) *Freddie Freeloader* 🎵🎵🎵🎵 (Denon, 1990)
Evolution of the Blues Song 🎵🎵🎵🎵 (Collectors, 1994)
Cloudburst 🎵🎵🎵🎵 (Enja, 1994)
Boppin' at the Blue Note 🎵🎵🎵 (Telarc, 1995)

influences:
◀◀ Eddie Jefferson
▶▶ Manhattan Transfer

see also: *Annie Ross*

Andrew Gilbert

Harold Land
Born February 18, 1928, in Houston, TX.

Like so many jazz musicians who have settled on the West Coast, tenor saxophonist Harold Land has never received the attention his accomplishments deserve. A brilliant, original stylist who has continued to assimilate new ideas and sounds throughout his career, Land has incorporated the influences of Coleman Hawkins, Charlie Parker, and John Coltrane while maintaining his own identity. Land's family moved from Houston to San Diego when he was five and he started playing saxophone at 16 after hearing Coleman Hawkins's groundbreaking recording of "Body and Soul." Under the tutelage of trumpeter Froebel Brigham, Land became a mainstay on the active San Diego jazz scene.

On his first recordings, made for Savoy in 1949 (tracks that were reissued years later on the double LP *Black California*), Land is still under Hawkins's sway, but there are hints of bebop and an R&B undercurrent to his solos. Land moved to Los Angeles in the early 1950s, and was discovered by Clifford Brown during a jam session in Eric Dolphy's garage. Land is still best known for the two years he spent in the legendary quintet with Brown and Max Roach (1954–55), a period that produced a number of classic recordings for EmArcy. Leaving Brown and Roach, he returned to Southern California to be with his family and settled in Los Angeles, joining an excellent but often overlooked hard-bop quintet led by bassist Curtis Counce that recorded a number of fine albums for Contemporary. Land made two of his own albums for Contemporary in the late 1950s, and also recorded with Thelonious Monk, Hampton Hawes, Shorty Rogers, and Gerald Wilson, with whom Land was associated for years. In the late 1960s, Land co-led a group with Bobby Hutcherson that recorded a series of challenging albums for Blue Note. The two musicians have continued to work together up to the present. In the 1970s, he co-led a band with Blue Mitchell, and in the 1980s toured with the Timeless All-Stars and Cedar Walton. Land continues to work around Southern California, often with his son, Harold Land Jr., a formidable pianist. Land has recorded for Concord, Muse, Mainstream, Blue Note, Imperial, Atlantic, Cadet, and Postcards, though his discography is sadly limited, and relatively few of his albums are available.

what to buy: One of the great hard-bop albums of the 1950s, *The Fox* 🎵🎵🎵🎵 (Contemporary, 1959/OJC, 1988, prod. David Axelrod) was originally released on the Hifijazz label and is a unique recording for several reasons. Land decided to feature tunes by the brilliant but obscure pianist/composer Elmo Hope, and assembled a quintet including Hope, the 18-year-old bassist Herbie Lewis, powerhouse drummer Frank Butler, and a fiery, gripping trumpeter, Dupree Bolton, who disappeared from the jazz scene immediately after this session, his only recording. A highly rewarding blowing session, *West Coast Blues!* ♪♪♪♪ (Jazzland, 1960/OJC, 1996, prod. Orrin Keepnews) brought together Cannonball Adderley's rhythm section — Barry Harris (piano), Sam Jones (bass) and Louis Hayes (drums) — with guitarist Wes Montgomery, trumpeter Joe Gordon and Land, who was beginning to incorporate the influence of John Coltrane. A companion piece to *The Fox*, *Harold in the Land of Jazz* ♪♪♪♪ (Contemporary, 1958 /1988, prod. Lester Koenig) was originally released as *Grooveyard*, named after the funky piece contributed by pianist Carl Perkins, whose playing is one reason this is such a memorable session. Brilliant arrangements by Land and Elmo Hope are another, with Land also contributing four fine original tunes, as well as many emotionally bracing solos. Swedish trumpeter Rolf Ericson, bassist Leroy Vinnegar and drummer Frank Butler round out the quintet. The only album made by a strong, hard-swinging band co-led by Land and bassist Red Mitchell, *Hear Ye!* ♪♪♪♪ (Atlantic, 1961/1989, prod. Nesuhi Ertegun, Bones Howe) features excellent but overlooked players such as trumpeter Carmell Jones, pianist Frank Strazzeri, and drummer Leon Petties. Land and Mitchell both contribute two tunes to this consistently engaging session.

what to buy next: *Eastward Ho!* ♪♪♪♪ (Jazzland, 1960/OJC, 1990, prod. Orrin Keepnews) is a fine session pairing Land's virile tenor with another brilliant but underappreciated player, trumpeter Kenny Dorham. The unspectacular rhythm section, from the Shorty Rogers group that brought Land to New York where the album was recorded (hence the title), doesn't do much to push the hornmen. Highlights include David Raskin's rarely played ballad "Slowly," and Land's "Okay Blues," a stimulating 12-minute workout. Put this next one under the "it's about time" file. *A Lazy Afternoon* ♪♪♪♪ (Postcards, 1995, prod. Ralph Simon) features Land's gorgeous, fertile tenor work accompanied by a string orchestra conducted by Ray Ellis. Land digs into a dozen standards, turning the melodies into highly personal statements without completely altering them. His version of "You've Changed" is for the ages. The fine Los Angeles pianist Bill Henderson leads the rhythm section. The only recording by the great Harold Land/Blue Mitchell quintet, *Mapenzi* ♪♪♪♪ (Concord Jazz, 1977/1990, prod. Carl E. Jefferson), is a consistently inspired session with pianist Kirk Lightsey. Land and Mitchell blend their distinctive sounds beautifully and both are in top form throughout.

best of the rest:

(With Bobby Hutcherson) *Total Eclipse* ♪♪♪♪ (Blue Note, 1967/Capitol, 1996)

Xocia's Dance ♪♪♪♪ (Muse, 1981)

worth searching for: Though released under vibraphonist Bobby Hutcherson's name, *San Francisco* ♪♪♪♪ (Blue Note, 1970/Capitol, 1995, prod. Alfred Lion) was a session by the band Land co-led with the vibraphonist. An advanced session blending modal melodies, abstract jazz and rock rhythms and intuitive interplay between the long-time collaborators, this album features two masters exploring uncharted territory. Pianist Joe Sample, bassist John Williams, and drummer Mickey Roker make up the effective rhythm section.

influences:

⏪ Coleman Hawkins, Lucky Thompson, John Coltrane, Sonny Rollins

Andrew Gilbert

Art Lande

Born 1947, in New York, NY.

Art Lande is a talented pianist who has performed and/or recorded with Steve Swallow, Gary Peacock, Ted Curson, Jan Garbarek, and various members of Oregon, and as a leader with his own small groups, including Rubisa Patrol and the Russian Dragon Band. He has also been an active clinician and teacher with academic stints at the Cornish College of the Arts, the Jazz School Lucerne, and at the Naropa Institute, in addition to founding his own (short lived) jazz school in the mid-'70s. Lande's personal style is basically reflective (which may be one of the reasons why he was part of the ECM stable) and he has taken a great interest in Eastern thought and ambient music over the last few decades. George Winston has performed material penned by Lande, and the duo of King and Moore has benefited from his arranging talents.

what to buy: His debut, *Red Lanta* ♪♪♪♪ (ECM, 1974, prod. Manfred Eicher), features Lande and flautist/saxophonist Jan Garbarek performing nine Lande compositions. Garbarek has a dry, biting soprano saxophone style that is totally unique albeit sometimes a bit too pinched-sounding to convey much warmth. This actually works to the music's advantage as *Red Lanta* reflects the austere chamber jazz that ECM was becoming known for in the mid-'70s. Lande's tunes are well constructed, even if only one of them ("Verduc") can be said to "swing" in a vaguely traditional way.

what to buy next: Lande and his former Rubisa Patrol associate, Mark Isham, created *We Begin* 🎵🎵🎵 (ECM, 1987), an album that skirts that tricky territory where three genres collide; jazz, new age/ambient, and soundtrack music. Lande plays the acoustic piano lines and Isham and Lande tinker with the electronic gizmos while Isham's trumpet floats above beatbox percussion and hazy, synthesized, washes of sound.

influences:

◀◀ Bill Evans, Paul Horn, Paul McCandless

▶▶ Myra Melford, Michael Powers

Garaud MacTaggart

Ellis Larkins

Born May 15, 1923, in Baltimore, MD.

One would expect a child prodigy who graduated from the Peabody Conservatory and the Juilliard School to have a glorious career as a soloist and/or bandleader. The understated perfection of Ellis Larkins is proof that things aren't always that way. In 1940, just after Larkins had left Juilliard, he started playing in New York clubs, working his way into demand as a studio musician for Coleman Hawkins, Sonny Stitt, and Edmund Hall. Where Larkins has really left his mark in jazz history is as an accompanist to some of jazz's greatest singers: Mildred Bailey, Sarah Vaughan, and Ella Fitzgerald, to name a few. Critics talk about his subtle swing, and vocalists love the way he outlines the melody while gently pulsing the rhythm behind the lyrics.

what's available: The music flows like a waterfall blessed with a rainbow on *Live at Maybeck, Volume 22* 🎵🎵🎵🎵 (Concord Jazz, 1992, prod. Carl E. Jefferson, Nick Phillips). Everything Larkins plays here sounds so deceptively simple and graceful that there are no more superlatives left to communicate the style and understated brilliance he brings to chestnuts like "Lady Be Good," "Blue Skies," and "I Let a Song Go out of My Heart."

worth searching for: Arbors Records released a duet album, *Calling Berlin, Volume 1* (Arbors, 1995, prod. Arbors), with cornet player Ruby Braff getting top billing over Larkins. It features the two on a variety of Irving Berlin standards with occasional assistance from guitarist Bucky Pizzarelli. For an excellent sample of why Larkins was one of Ella Fitzgerald's favorite accompanists, check out *Pure Ella* 🎵🎵🎵 (Decca, 1950–54/GRP, 1994). It is pure voice and piano with no other distractions.

influences:

▶▶ Tommy Flanagan

Garaud MacTaggart

Nick LaRocca

See: Original Dixieland Jazz Band

Mary LaRose

Brooklyn-based Mary LaRose is one of the more purposeful jazz vocalists of her generation. Teamed with her husband, alto saxophonist/composer Jeff Lederer, LaRose makes a grand and reasonably successful attempt to translate the complex instrumental demands of post-bop/free jazz into the vocal realm. Lederer writes imaginative arrangements of off-beat standards like Oliver Nelson's "Teenie's Blues" and Thelonious Monk's "Just You, Just Me"; LaRose pens original lyrics to the tunes, sings the heads, and often transcribes the original instrumental solos for voice. Her version of Eric Dolphy's alto sax improvisation on "Teenie's Blues" is at the very least a noble effort; it's nearly impossible for a vocalist to mimic Dolphy's interval gymnastics accurately, yet LaRose does a commendable job. The two regularly hire such top-notch Downtown NYC sideman as trombonist Steve Swell, violinist Mark Feldman, and bassist Mike Formanek to accompany the singer. LaRose doesn't have the greatest intonation in the world, and she occasionally falls back on some rather hackneyed vocalese mannerisms, but she has a creative nature that more often than not carries her through.

what's available: The couple's only release so far, *Cutting the Chord* 🎵🎵🎵 (Ledhead Productions, 1995, prod. Jeff Lederer) showcases LaRose's vocal ability. The most intriguing aspects, however, are the contexts provided by Lederer; he's an arranger with the soul of a composer and an insightful saxophonist, as well. A promising debut for both.

influences:

◀◀ Jon Hendricks

Chris Kelsey

Last Exit

Formed February 7, 1986, in Germany and New York.

Sonny Sharrock, guitar; Peter Brötzmann, tenor, alto, and bass saxophones, taragato; Bill Laswell, bass; Ronald Shannon Jackson, drums, vocals.

The free improvisation supergroup Last Exit brings together veteran leaders in their own rights: a legendary jazz noise guitarist who played with Miles Davis, Pharoah Sanders, and Herbie Mann; a hard-blowing German avant-garde saxophonist; a versatile master conceptualist who happens to be a monster bassist;

and a technically and imaginatively awesome jazz drummer who has contributed significantly to records by Ornette Coleman, Albert Ayler, and Cecil Taylor. Reviving the spontaneous spirit of 1960s free jazz when it was at a low ebb, they eschewed rehearsals but played with a level of intensity rarely matched.

what to buy: *The Noise of Trouble: Live in Tokyo* 🎵🎵🎵🎵 (Enemy, 1987) ranks among the greatest concerts ever documented on tape. Drawing on two nights in October 1986 (with Japanese saxist Akira Sakata joining throughout and Herbie Hancock contributing effectively on acoustic piano on the final track), it balances the free-for-all improvisation with actual songs and a healthy dose of blues from Sharrock and Jackson.

what to buy next: Drawn from two 1989 concerts, the totally improvised *Headfirst into the Flames* 🎵🎵🎵🎵 (MuWorks, 1993, prod. Robert Musso) is Last Exit's best purely free statement, a masterful display of creative empathy nearly as thrilling as *The Noise of Trouble,* and a sonic improvement.

what to avoid: The unremitting barrage of *Last Exit* 🎵🎵 (Enemy, 1986), the quartet's first actual release, was awe-inspiring at the time, but its muddy sound makes it no match for subsequent releases.

the rest:
From the Board a.k.a. *Cassette Recordings '87* 🎵🎵🎵 (Celluloid, 1988/ Enemy, 1995)
Köln 🎵🎵🎵🎵 (ITM, 1990)

worth searching for: The out-of-print *Iron Path* 🎵🎵🎵🎵 (Venture/Virgin, 1988, prod. Last Exit, Bill Laswell) is Last Exit's only studio album. Laswell scripts some nearly ambient moments and, conversely, a few heavy-metal–like riffs. Pulsating and throbbing, it never explodes but exudes calm majesty.

influences:
◀◀ Albert Ayler, John Coltrane, Blind Willie Johnson
▶▶ Thurston Moore & Lee Ranaldo (of Sonic Youth), William Hooker, Naked City

Steve Holtje

Last Poets
Formed 1967, in Harlem, NY.

Jalal Nuriddin/Alfia Pudim/Lightnin' Rod, vocals (1967–75, 1985–present); Abiodun Oyewole, vocals (1967–71); Umar Bin Hassan, vocals (1967–72, 1992); Nilija, percussion (1967–73); Sulieman El-Hadi, vocals (1972–75, 1985–present).

Backed only by sparse percussion, the Last Poets rode the beat and lived for the music and the power of the word. Black nationalist to the bone, the seminal urban griots were, by the mid-'70s, the first and last word in political raptivism. Their spoken-word aggression has been manifested in the form of more than 12 albums spanning more than two decades. Despite the seemingly spare output, the group's influence has been astounding, as their music and words have inspired and influenced generations of rappers, including Afrika Bambaataa, Chuck D., Ice Cube, the X-Clan, Paris, Michael Franti, and even Too $hort. If nothing else is said about Poets, know that they are unquestionably the Godfathers of modern-day rap. Abiodun Oyewole, Jalal Nuriddin, Umar Bin Hassan, and Nilaja formed the nucleus of the group, which dropped a bomb of a self-titled debut (in the most explosive sense, of course) in 1970. Nuriddin has been the main fixture since, with the group continually splintering around him (the departure of Oyewole, Bin Hassan's comings and goings). Two versions of the Poets exist today: The Nuriddin/Sulieman El-Hadi lineup and the pairing of Oyewole and Bin Hassan. Even without the confusion, though, getting an accurate bead on the Poets' body of work might be rather tricky, since many of the group's records are out of print. And much of their later work is available only as Japanese imports and in various re-release adaptations on the French label On the One. Still, the group's seminal early recordings—originally released by the long-defunct Douglas label—have been reissued several times on CD. Just about any album in the catalog is worth purchasing, but the ones featuring Oyewole and Bin Hassan are your best bet.

what to buy: Originally released in 1970, *Last Poets* 🎵🎵🎵🎵🎵 (Celluloid, 1984) is a poetical, political *tour de force* that blasts away at racism and oppression (while, nevertheless, also attacking Jews and homosexuals) and contains the seminal "Niggers Are Scared of Revolution," a song sampled 20 years later at the end of Too $hort's hit "The Ghetto." Originally released in 1973, *Hustler's Convention* 🎵🎵🎵🎵 (Celluloid, 1984) is credited to one "Lightnin' Rod," who in reality is just Nuriddin. With the help of greasy chops served up by Kool & the Gang, the album is a funky ode to pimps, playas, and macks everywhere. While the sleeve lists 12 tracks, it's really just one long game-related rhyme that became a classic blueprint for the likes of Too $hort, Dru Down, Ice-T, and all the other modern-day hustlers. After almost 20 years of silence, original poet Bin Hassan returned to the studio and unleashed *Be Bop or Be Dead* 🎵🎵🎵🎵🎵 (Axiom, 1993, prod. Bill Laswell). Laswell adds the music of Bootsy Collins, Bernie Worrell, Buddy Miles, Foday Musa Suso, and a host of other prominent musicians from around the globe, placing Bin Hassan's urban street poetry into a global jazz–funk–hard-bop context. Tunes like "Pop" revolve around Middle Eastern raga-tinged rhythms, and "Love" is beefed up by thick Hammond organ vamps and some deep jazz drum work. In addition to new material, the album reworks a couple of Last Poets classics: 1972's "This Is Madness" is given a metallic facelift and is transformed into a hectic aural melee, and 1970's "Niggers Are Scared of Revolution" is given a '90s makeover, thanks to a fast-paced drum track, a thrombobulating bass, and some subdued noize.

what to buy next: Originally issued in 1971, *This Is Madness* ♫♫♫♫ (Celluloid, 1984) is the first Last Poets release without Oyewole. Despite his absence, though, the album still contains plenty of sparks, including the scathing "White Man's Got a God Complex." Bin Hassan left before the 1972 follow-up *Chastisement* ♫♫♫♫ (Celluloid, 1992), and the mediocre Sulieman El-Hadi was brought to fill shoes that were simply too big. The album also features more instrumental accompaniment than the first two. But Nuriddin (here as Pudim) is still a commanding oratorial force. Oyewole retrofitted the 1970 anthem "When the Revolution Comes" for his 25th anniversary celebration *25 Years* ♫♫♫♫ (Black Arc/Rykodisc, 1995, prod. Bill Laswell, others). A tight mixture of intercoastal funk, smoother grit blues, and dusted dubphonics, the album shows that Oyewole hasn't lost any of his verbal tenacity or grace. Yet another Laswell-enhanced update, *Time Has Come* ♫♫♫♫ (Mouth Almighty/Mercury, 1997, prod. Bill Laswell, others) once again shows Oyewole and Bin Hassan working their verbal magic, this time interacting with some of hip-hop's frontiersmen (Chuck D., Keith Shocklee, DXT, etc.). New rappers Jamal Whatley and Khalil Muhammad Hassan flex righteously alongside the elder statesmen on "Kings of Pain," demonstrating how the words (and mic) are passed from generation to generation. And the now-venerable Poets disciple, Chuck D., matches his baritone with the legends on "Down to Now." Quite possibly a minor modern classic.

what to avoid: *Oh My People* ♫♫♫ (Celluloid, 1985, prod. Bill Laswell) shows the Poets (Nuriddin and El-Hadi, anyway) in decline, with lackluster lyrics and musical accompaniment. And the frequent excursions into electro-rhythm just don't work. The disjointed *Freedom Express* ♫♫♫ (Celluloid, 1991) isn't much better—a musical mixture of mediocre jazz, Caribbean shuffles, and just plain cheese with Nuriddin and El-Hadi sounding more like leftovers from the '60s as opposed to inspired poets.

the rest:
Delights of the Garden ♫♫♫ (Celluloid, 1985)
Retrofit ♫♫♫ (Celluloid, 1992)

Holy Terror ♫♫♫ (Black Arc/Rykodisc, 1993/1995)

worth searching for: Gylan Kain's *The Blue Guerrilla* ♫♫♫♫♫ (Collectables, 1990) is a bit of pre-Last Poets wordology. Check the track "Constipated Monkey." Billed as an "exploration into inner-self for the listener," *Right On!* ♫♫♫♫ (Collectables, 1990) is a raw, unfiltered soundtrack to the film of the same name.

influences:

◄◄ Iceberg Slim, Stokely Carmichael, H. Rapp Brown, Malcolm X, Martin Luther King Jr.

►► All of hip-hop

Spence D.

Yusef Lateef

Born William Evans, February 11, 1920, in Chattanooga, TN.

First of all, Yusef Lateef does not like his music to be called jazz because of the origins and connotations of the word. He prefers the self-coined phrase "autophysiopsychic music." Whatever you call the products of his five-decades-and-counting career, his music covers an impressively broad range of styles. Even more astounding is his multi-instrumental virtuosity. Though he is a respected figure, he has received only a fraction of the acclaim his achievements deserve. It's as though his refusal to be pigeonholed, either by genre (consider the oddity of an artist identified with "jazz" winning a Grammy Award in the New Age category for a symphony) or instrumental specialization, has left critics so baffled that they avoid the topics altogether and have no idea how to discuss him.

Growing up in Detroit, a highly fertile musical environment in the 1930s and beyond, Lateef got his first instrument, an $80 Martin alto sax, at age 18. Within a year he was on the road with the 13 Spirits of Swing (arrangements by Milt Buckner). Detroit friend tenorist Lucky Thompson helped Lateef get work with Lucky Millinder in 1946, and though the musician he was brought in to replace ended up not leaving the band, it brought Lateef to New York, where he heard Coleman Hawkins, Charlie Parker, Dizzy Gillespie, etc., and played with Hot Lips Page and Roy Eldridge. He then joined the Ernie Fields Orchestra for about a year. His next stop was Chicago in 1947–48, where he and Sonny Stitt practiced together. It was at the end of 1948 that he made his first released recordings, with bassist Eugene Wright & His Kings of Swing, a group that included Sonny Blount, later known as Sun Ra. And it was in Chicago that he was introduced to Islam, specifically the Ahmadiyya movement, and changed his name from Bill Evans to Yusef Lateef.

Lateef then played tenor in the Gillespie big band for more than a year, recording for RCA and Spotlite, until the economics of post-war jazz broke up that band and he returned to Detroit. He continued playing, with Kenny Burrell and as a leader, worked on an automobile assembly line, and studied at area music schools. He took up flute at the suggestion of Burrell around 1951. Oboe followed, with lessons from the first-chair oboist in the Detroit Symphony, Ronald Odmark. Even working at Chrysler contributed to his musical development when a Syrian coworker made him a rabat (a one-string fiddle made out of horse hair and goat skin) that he later used in a number of pieces instead of bass. Lateef quit Chrysler when his band got a six-nights-a-week job playing at Klein's Show Bar, and in April 1957, 37 years old and a professional musician for more than 17 years, he played his first two sessions as a leader, for Savoy, using his Klein's group of Curtis Fuller (trombone), Hugh Lawson (piano), Ernie Farrow (bass), and Louis Hayes (drums), with percussionist Doug Watkins added for recording. The musical style was basically hard bop, sometimes mixed with R&B/jump blues styles and some early forays into world music–inspired sounds on which he played argol, a Middle Eastern twin-piped reed, and used the aforementioned rabat, exploring a heavily modal sound on some tracks.

Additional sessions for Savoy, Verve, and Prestige over the next two-and-a-half years began to establish his reputation, and he was able to move to New York City, where he joined the Charles Mingus band, which already contained Eric Dolphy and Rahsaan Roland Kirk. He soon expanded the Cannonball Adderley group to a sextet, and his work with that very popular band exposed Lateef's talents on sax, oboe, and flute to a broad audience, with his oboe feature on the blues standard "Trouble in Mind" much noted. In 1963, his profile increasingly more visible and his musical styles becoming more diverse and adventurous, he signed to Impulse!, the same label that was recording his friend John Coltrane, and made *Jazz 'Round the World*, the first of six excellent albums for Impulse!. His discussions with Dolphy and Coltrane were mutually influential, with his interests in world music especially stimulating to them. He later compiled the impressive book *Repository of Scales and Melodic Patterns* (FANA Publishing, Amherst, 1981), which draws on a vast range of material: expansions on scales derived from Scriabin, Berg, and Bartok; Hungarian, Egyptian, Pygmy, Chinese, Mongolian, Japanese, Indian, Persian, Arabic, and archaic Greek scales; Lateef's triple-diminished tone rows; and much more, including "synthetic formations" given to Lateef by Dolphy in 1961. (Lateef has also written *Flute Book of*

the Blues vols. 1 & 2, Method on How to Improvise [Soul Music]*, and *Music for Two Flutes [20 Modern Duets]*, as well as various scholarly papers.)

After Impulse!, Lateef recorded for Atlantic (where he also did session work, often under the pseudonym "Joe Gentle," on records by Little Jimmie Scott, Esther Phillips, Ray Bryant, Roberta Flack, and others) and then CTI, his work on both labels often strongly flavored with pop and R&B sounds. At the same time he was accumulating a considerable number of degrees in music and education, and at the end of the 1970s Lateef interrupted his stateside recording career to move to Nigeria to accept a teaching position. When he returned in the mid-1980s, his musical style changed and he worked in a more composed vein. This frequently misunderstood second Atlantic period includes much beautiful work. His first new recording, *Yusef Lateef's Little Symphony*, released in 1987, won the New Age Grammy Award, though it's more classical in nature. He followed up with *Concerto for Yusef Lateef*, the gorgeous *Nocturnes*, on which he abandoned the use of a rhythm section, and a number of other works also unfairly maligned by critics who dismissed it for not being jazz. When his contract with Atlantic was not renewed, Lateef formed his own label in 1992, YAL, and entered his most prolific period. He is currently ensconced at the University of Massachusetts and at Hampshire College in Amherst, Massachusetts, and continues to explore new systems of musical expression, making some of the best music of his long and fruitful career.

what to buy: *The Centaur and the Phoenix* 🎵🎵🎵🎵 (Riverside, 1960, prod. Orrin Keepnews) contains Lateef's most complex session and largest group of this period, with two trumpets (Clark Terry and Richard Williams), trombonist Fuller, baritone sax (Tate Houston), bassoon (Josea Taylor), Lateef on tenor, oboe, flute, and argol, and a rhythm section of Zawinul, Ben Tucker (bass), and Lex Humphries (drums). The music includes arrangements of material by symphonic composer Charles Mills, plus a pair of considerably less ambitious bonus tracks, probably an aborted single, from 1961. In contrast, the quintet date *Live at Pep's* 🎵🎵🎵🎵 (Impulse!, 1964, prod. Bob Thiele) captures a smoking club gig with trumpeter Williams, pianist Mike Nock, bassist Ernie Farrow, and drummer James Black, a tight working unit. "Sister Mamie" is a classic. With no other Impulse! albums available, this is an especially crucial album. *The World at Peace: Music for 12 Musicians* 🎵🎵🎵🎵 (YAL & Meta, 1996) with Adam Rudolph, a dual release on Lateef's and world percussionist Rudolph's labels, is a major work full of innovative writing that may well be the crowning achievement of Lateef's 1990s work, its high ambition matched by its unfailing execution. His use of unusual compositional processes peaks here. Since Lateef's second affiliation with Atlantic lapsed in 1991, only one album by him has appeared on a label other than YAL: *The African-American Epic Suite* 🎷🎷🎷 (ACT/Blue Jackel, 1994, prod. Ulrich Kurth). It's a four-movement depiction of the African American experience for quintet and orchestra, commissioned for the Köln Radio Orchestra. Given a luxurious eight days to record, the quintet (with Lateef and Ralph Jones III on winds, Federico Ramos on acoustic and electric guitars, Charles Moore on flugelhorn, shofar, dumbek, and conch shell, and Adam Rudolph on percussion) is well integrated within the larger group, and the orchestration is quite effective.

what to buy next: The bands on Lateef's 1950s albums are mostly composed of fellow Detroit residents. *The Sounds of Yusef Lateef* 🎷🎷🎷 (Prestige, 1957, prod. Bob Weinstock) includes a nifty version of "Take the 'A' Train," but caused some controversy with its use of a 7-Up bottle and balloons, making some observers wonder if Lateef, then a newcomer, was serious. He was, and always has been, but he has his humorous side, too, and doesn't see the two moods as exclusive of each other. He also was incorporating instruments from around the world into his music, and plays argol here. *Other Sounds* 🎷🎷🎷 (New Jazz, 1957, prod. Bob Weinstock) is from the same session, with Wilbur Harden (flugelhorn), Hugh Lawson (piano), Ernie Farrow (bass), and Oliver Jackson (drums). A quartet with pianist Barry Harris, Farrow, and Humphries, *Eastern Sounds* 🎷🎷🎷 (Prestige, 1961, prod. Esmond Edwards) is notable for "The Plum Blossom," on which Lateef plays the Chinese globular flute, a pentatonic instrument with only a five-note range. Its restricted range matters little compared to how well he exploits the instrument's unique tone. *Into Something* 🎷🎷🎷 (New Jazz, 1961, prod. Esmond Edwards) offers the most straight-ahead compositions, including a few standards and the oboe blues "Rasheed," with drummer Elvin Jones swinging fiercely throughout. Harris and bassist Herman Wright complete the quartet. Lateef's two stretches on Atlantic don't have a good reputation among jazz purists. Too bad, because they're missing some very interesting music. While it's true that a number of the albums from his earlier Atlantic period have dated, the four reissued on the three-CD set *The Man with the Big Front Yard* 🎷🎷🎷 (32 Jazz, 1998, prod. Joel Dorn) are all winners. *The Complete Yusef Lateef* 🎷🎷🎷🎷 (Atlantic, 1967, prod. Joel Dorn) was his first Atlantic album and is the most straight-ahead session here, a quartet with Hugh Lawson, Cecil McBee, and Roy Brooks (plus a tambourine player) that recalls his Prestige material. *Yusef Lateef's Detroit* 🎷🎷🎷 (Atlantic, 1969, prod. Joel Dorn) starts to get fusiony on some tracks, with Eric Gale on electric guitar and Chuck Rainey on electric bass, but other tracks have the same band as *The Complete Yusef Lateef,* and there are some imaginative arrangements that include strings. *Hush 'n' Thunder* 🎷🎷🎷 (Atlantic, 1973, prod. Joel Dorn) has a heavy gospel feeling on many tracks (the J.C. White Singers are featured), and the keyboardists include Barron, Ray Bryant, and organist Bob Cunningham. Anyone with a tolerance for—or love of—funky fusion will dig *The Doctor Is in . . . and Out* 🎷🎷🎷 (Atlantic, 1976, prod. Joel Dorn), which has Kenny Barron on electric keyboards, Al Foster on drums, Billy Butler on guitar, Cissy Houston on vocals, etc. It's got some experimental tracks to balance the funky stuff, and unlike Yusef's CTI fusion stuff, where he sounds more like a sideman, this is really *him,* so the compositions (half by Barron) are strong and solidly rooted. The unheralded *Nocturnes* 🎷🎷🎷 (Atlantic, 1989, prod. Yusef Lateef) is the best album from Lateef's second Atlantic period, meditative chamber music on which Lateef adds keyboards to his résumé. Lateef also plays flutes, joined by three horns. With no rhythm section, the music floats, creating beautiful soundscapes closer to impressionism than anything else, but utterly original. *Tenors of Yusef Lateef & Archie Shepp* 🎷🎷🎷 (YAL, 1992, prod. Yusef Lateef) is the prize in Lateef's series of two-tenor records, with full-bodied playing by the stars and dedicatory tracks for Thelonious Monk and Gene Ammons. *Fantasia for Flute* 🎷🎷🎷 (YAL, 1996, prod. Yusef Lateef) is stylistically similar to the best of the later Atlantic material, and has Lateef sounding better than ever on flute. *Earth and Sky, Tenors and Flutes* 🎷🎷🎷 (YAL, 1997, prod. Yusef Lateef) finds Lateef sounding vital and imaginative on an album that comes as quite a surprise. Over angular rhythms suggestive of the funk/hip-hop incorporations of Steve Coleman and other M-BASE types, Lateef raps (okay, recites short poetic phrases, does that make purists feel more comfortable?) in hypnotic fashion, which somehow relates back to blues. His speaking voice is a beautiful instrument, and his lyrics reflect his gentle philosophy.

what to avoid: Avoid Lateef's CTI period like the plague (it's all out of print right now, but CTI has started a new reissue program). Creed Taylor's attempts to turn Lateef into a fusion funkateer find the veteran sounding out of place on his own records, sometimes playing sub-mediocre tunes written by studio hacks. *Autophysiopsychic* **woof!** (CTI, 1977, prod. Creed Taylor) might look especially tempting because flugelhornist Art Farmer is on it, but the remake of "Sister Mamie" with Noel Pointer on electric violin was a bad idea. *In a Temple Garden* 🎷 (CTI, 1979, prod. Creed Taylor) is just plain bland. There's a reason these LPs are so cheap and plentiful in the used bins.

best of the rest:

Jazz Moods ♫♫♫ (Savoy, 1957)

Before Dawn ♫♫♫ (Verve, 1957)

Cry-Tender! ♫♫♫ (Prestige, 1959)

The Three Faces of Yusef Lateef ♫♫♫♫ (Riverside, 1960)

Jazz 'Round the World ♫♫♫ (Impulse!, 1963)

A Flat, G Flat and C ♫♫♫ (Impulse!, 1966)

Golden Flute ♫♫♫ (Impulse!, 1966)

In Nigeria ♫♫♫ (Landmark, 1985/YAL, 1995, prod. Yusef Lateef)

Yusef Lateef's Little Symphony ♫♫♫ (Atlantic, 1987)

Concerto for Yusef Lateef ♫♫♫ (Atlantic, 1988)

Yusef Lateef's Encounters ♫♫♫ (Atlantic, 1991)

Tenors of Yusef Lateef & Von Freeman ♫♫♫ (YAL, 1992)

Every Village Has a Song: The Yusef Lateef Anthology ♫♫♫ (Atlantic, 1993)

(With Ralph M. Jones III) Woodwinds ♫♫♫ (YAL, 1993)

Tenors Featuring Rene McLean ♫♫♫ (YAL, 1993)

Tenors of Yusef Lateef & Ricky Ford ♫♫♫ (YAL, 1994)

Full Circle ♫♫♫ (YAL, 1996)

CHNOPS, Gold and Soul ♫♫♫ (YAL, 1997)

worth searching for: All of Lateef's Impulse! albums are worth owning, and it's to be fervently hoped that more than just *Live at Pep's* get reissued. *1984* ♫♫♫ (Impulse!, 1965, prod. Bob Thiele) is a superb quartet with Mike Nock (piano), Reggie Workman (bass), and James Black (drums) and includes Ellington's "Warm Fire" and Lateef's "Sister Soul." *Psychicemotus* ♫♫♫ (Impulse!, 1965, prod. Bob Thiele) is erratic—the cover of Satie's "First Gymnopedie" sounds stilted—but the high points are remarkable: the title track, "Bamboo Flute Blues," "Semi-octo," and Fats Waller's "Ain't Misbehavin'." George Arvenitas replaces Nock. And the LP *Club Date* ♫♫♫ (Impulse!, 1976, prod. Bob Thiele) contains more material from the 1964 gig that yielded *Live at Pep's*. Though three of its six tracks were added to the CD version of *Live at Pep's*, the other three numbers are also worthwhile.

influences:

◄◄ Dexter Gordon, Budd Johnson, Lester Young, Don Byas, Chu Berry

►► John Coltrane, Eric Dolphy, Ralph M. Jones III, Adam Rudolph

Steve Holtje

Andy LaVerne

Born December 4, 1947, in New York, NY.

After attending Ithaca College and Berklee College of Music, pianist Andy LaVerne commenced recording and performing with a wide list of significant jazz artists. Since the early 1970s his résumé includes stints with Woody Herman, John Abercrombie, and Stan Getz, and recording credits with Lee Konitz, Eddie Daniels, Bill Evans (saxophone), and Stan Getz. LaVerne's own albums as leader have appeared on a variety of labels, including SteepleChase, Concord Jazz, Double Time, DMP, and Triloka. He also has an academic bent, writing theory books for Ekay Music (*Handbook of Chord Substitutions* and *Tons of Runs*), serving as a columnist for *Keyboard* magazine, and performing in instructional videotapes for Video Learning Library (*Jazz Piano Standards*) and The Learning Lane (*Andy LaVerne's Guide to Modern Jazz Piano*).

what to buy: LaVerne has a tendency to get caught up in the technical aspects of playing at the expense of inventive improvisation, and his recordings as a leader are rarely as interesting as *Glass Ceiling* ♫♫♫♫ (SteepleChase, 1995, prod. Nils Winther). Ably supported by drummer Anton Fig and bassist Steve LaSpina, LaVerne plays three originals in addition to standards by Clifford Brown, Cole Porter, and Duke Jordan. The Chick Corea tunes "Litha" and "Tones for Joan's Bones" give the truest representation of the bag LaVerne operates out of. Once again, the Maybeck Recital Series draws the best out of a pianist. On *Andy LaVerne at Maybeck Recital Hall, Vol. 28* ♫♫♫♫ (Concord Jazz, 1993, prod. Nick Phillips), LaVerne's prodigious technique gets a surprisingly subtle workout on this program. He still indulges in his love of contra-faction ("Stan Getz in Chappaqua") but the rest of the album is less gimmicky. "I Loves You Porgy" and "Moonlight in Vermont" are beautiful, and his take on Bill Evans's "Turn Out the Stars" does right by the composer.

what to buy next: *Nosmo King* ♫♫♫ (SteepleChase, 1996, prod. Nils Winther) is one in a series of duets LaVerne has done over the years with guitarist John Abercrombie. They are well suited to each other, but may work best if Abercrombie were to provide the guidance instead of LaVerne. Both players are technically able (with Abercrombie getting the nod for emotional communication skills), even though the interpretations sometimes overstay their welcome.

best of the rest:

Another World ♫♫ (SteepleChase, 1978/1995)

Liquid Silver ♫♫♫ (DMP, 1984)

Jazz Piano Lineage ♫♫♫♫ (DMP, 1988)

Plays the Music of Chick Corea ♫♫♫ (Jazzline, 1989)

(With John Abercrombie) Natural Living ♫♫ (Musidisc, 1990)

Frozen Music ♫♫♫ (SteepleChase, 1990)

Pleasure Seekers ♫♫♫ (Triloka, 1992)

Double Standard 🎵🎵🎵 (Triloka, 1993)

Plays Bud Powell 🎵🎵 (SteepleChase, 1993)

Fountainhead 🎵🎵🎵 (SteepleChase, 1994)

Time Well Spent 🎵🎵🎵 (Concord Jazz, 1995)

(With John Abercrombie) *Now It Can Be Played* 🎵🎵🎵 (SteepleChase, 1995)

Buy One, Get One Free 🎵🎵🎵 (SteepleChase, 1995)

First Tango in New York 🎵🎵🎵 (Musidisc, 1996)

Serenade to Silver 🎵🎵🎵 (SteepleChase, 1996)

Standard Eyes 🎵🎵🎵 (SteepleChase, 1996)

Tadd's Delight 🎵🎵🎵 (SteepleChase, 1996)

(With John Abercrombie) *Where We Were* 🎵🎵🎵 (Double Time, 1996)

(With Bill Evans, saxophone) *Modern Days and Nights* 🎵🎵🎵 (Double Time, 1996)

Bud's Beautiful 🎵🎵🎵 (SteepleChase, 1997)

Four Miles 🎵🎵🎵 (Triloka, 1997)

influences:

◀◀ Chick Corea, Bill Evans

▶▶ Jacky Terrasson

Garaud MacTaggart

Azar Lawrence

Born November 3, 1953, in Los Angeles, CA.

A musical prodigy, Lawrence was early on an enormously promising post-Coltrane reedist, playing in a variety of modal and progressive bands in the 1970s, including those of Miles Davis and McCoy Tyner. Like so many, he went the Gary Bartz route (spiritually simple and harmonically complex R&B) without ever grasping the inner beauty of the medium. After that, he sort of petered out and is, as far as I know, bashing around as a session musician. Coming out of Los Angeles' Horace Tapscott cult, he bonded with altoist Arthur Blythe, and did the soul circuit (both Tyner and Lawrence spent time in the Ike and Tina Turner Review in the early 1970s) while still in his teens, then hooked up with Clark Terry and Elvin Jones. This led to Tyner's band, with whom Lawrence became a rising star. Yes, he sounded a lot like Coltrane, but he was more creative than most and who didn't back then? Tyner's live double-LP *Atlantis* shows Lawrence to best effect. Miles took notice and used him on several sessions, including much of *Dark Magus*, on which he intertwines persuasively with Dave Liebman. Lawrence also worked with Woody Shaw (check out Shaw's solid *The Moontrane*, available on 32 Records) and Beaver Harris on *In:Sanity* on Soul Note, and although his most consistent work is as a sideman, his debut LP is an unrecognized classic, effortlessly balancing modal, Latin, and meditative Free interests along with the singing of Jean Carn. Of his own albums as leader, *Summer Solstice* is more straightahead, while *People Moving* is failed pop fusion. Lawrence recorded a rather terrible pop-funk LP for a small label in the 1980s and has not really been heard from since.

what to buy: *Bridge into the New Age* 🎵🎵🎵🎵 (Prestige, 1974, prod. Orrin Keepnews, Jim Stern) is almost a whatever-happened-to project with pianist Joe Bonner, reedman Hadley Caliman, percussionists Guillerme Franco, Kenneth Nash and Mtume, along with the better known altoist Arthur Blythe, trumpeter Woody Shaw, trombonist Julian Preister, and drummer Billy Hart, among others on two different searching and beautiful sessions. The standout track is "The Beautiful and Omnipresent Love," and it slowly unfolds like a glacial force of nature. The track "Forces of Nature," on the other hand, is very much out of McCoy Tyner's work in the 1970s.

the rest:

Summer Solstice 🎵🎵🎵 (Prestige, 1975)

People Moving 🎵🎵 (Prestige, 1976)

influences:

◀◀ John Coltrane

▶▶ Courtney Pine

D. Strauss

Hubert Laws

Born November 10, 1939, in Houston, TX.

Interested in music at a young age, Hubert Laws studied piano, mellophone, and alto sax while in junior high school, developing a talent for jazz, particularly the "Cool" style. In high school, Laws also became interested in classical music and has focused on both forms ever since. He mastered the flute for a high school band performance, yet had not given up the saxophone when, in 1954, he began playing alto in a local band led by Stix Hooper that went under several names (The Nite Hawks, The Swingsters, the Modern Jazz Sextet) and became known in 1960 as the Jazz Crusaders (later shortened to Crusaders). During the six years he spent with the group, Laws attended Texas Southern University, studying classical flute for two years with Clement Barone of the Houston Symphony, who helped the 17-year-old get a performance as soloist with the Houston Youth Symphony. Late in the 1950s, Laws went to Los Angeles with the Nite Hawks, and through a California-based Juilliard Alumni Association won a one-year scholarship to study flute at the Juilliard School of Music. He was so successful there that he won scholarships for two additional years.

Laws began attracting attention with the Berkshire Festival Orchestra and the Third Stream ensemble directed by John Lewis, Orchestra USA. In 1963, Laws worked with Mongo Santamaria (playing tenor sax) and subsequently recorded with Lena Horne, James Moody, J.J. Johnson, Clark Terry, Richard Davis, Arthur Prysock, and Sergio Mendes, among others.

After graduating from Juilliard, Laws remained in New York, where he studied with flutist Julius Baker. His artistry gained the attention of Atlantic Records executives and in 1964 the label released the first in his series of albums. Laws also freelanced doing commercials, Broadway shows, sideman gigs, and subbing with the New York Philharmonic and the Metropolitan Opera Orchestra. Laws got a call from Creed Taylor and left New York to record an album with Stanley Turrentine in Memphis. While there he recorded his first album as leader, *Crying Song*, for Taylor's new record company, CTI. That album caused little stir, but after the release of his second album, *Afro-Classic*, his career took off. In the mid-1970s, Laws switched labels to CBS, released a series of albums, and began winning *Down Beat* readers' and critics' polls. The brother of reeds player Ronnie Laws, Hubert Laws is a virtuoso player, comfortable in both jazz and classical music realms. He has composed and recorded jazz adaptations of works by Mozart, Bach, Stravinsky, Debussy, Ravel, Satie, and others, as well as recording jazz-rock fusion, and, more recently, contemporary jazz.

what to buy: Recorded in 1974, *In the Beginning* ♫♫♫♫ (CTI, 1974/Sony Legacy, 1997, prod. Creed Taylor) still holds up extremely well. The album features Hubert Laws with an all-star cast of improvisers, and is a rare recording featuring composer-arranger Clare Fischer at piano on two tunes (one, on electric piano). The rest of the team forging the classically-tinged jazz blend on eight tunes (originally issued as a double LP) includes pianist Bob James, bassist Ron Carter, drummer Steve Gadd, guitarist Gene Bertoncini, and vibist Dave Friedman, with cameo appearances from organist Richard Tee, brother Ronnie Laws on tenor sax, percussionist Airto, and others. The music is solid all the way through, especially Laws's precise playing on the gorgeous Satie piece "Gymnopedie #1," which he and Bob James adapted for this group. They also give the traditional hymn "Come Ye Disconsolate" a gospel-jazz lilt. Laws performs Sonny Rollins's "Airegin," crafting his improvs with only drums and percussion backing, a novel twist for the old warhorse, and he gives Coltrane's "Moment's Notice" appropriate boppish treatment with cohorts James, Carter, Gadd, and brother Ronnie. *In the Beginning* ranks among the best recordings of Laws's career, an exciting listen that richly showcases the leader's flute virtuosity and broad-based musicianship. *Storm Then the Calm* ♫♫♫♫ (MusicMasters, 1994, prod. Hubert Laws) is a more recent straight-ahead session of nine standards and originals featuring Laws (piccolo, flutes) with pianist John Beasley, drummer Peter Erskine, bassist David Carpenter, and others. Laws plays various flutes with crisp precision on the beautiful jazz ballad "My Ship." The version of his original fusion tune, "Land of Passion" (heard first on his like-titled 1979 Columbia album) is a classic. "Dat Over Dere" is a perky number featuring Laws on piccolo, with backing from pianist David Budway, drummer Harvey Mason, and bassist John Patitucci (the same team performs "Mean Lean"). Overall, this is a pleasant straight-up album with Laws in prime form playing some of his best original works.

what to buy next: *The Laws of Jazz/Flute By-Laws* ♫♫♫♫ (Atlantic, 1965, 1966/Rhino, 1994, prod. Joel Dorn) combines two Atlantic albums from the mid-1960s. *The Laws of Jazz* is a seven-tune straight-ahead session featuring the flutist with a young Armando (Chick) Corea at the piano, with Richard Davis (bass), and drummers Bobby Thomas or Jimmy Cobb. While it's not his most scintillating session, the tunes (mostly by Laws and Thomas) give the team some stretching room, with Laws improvising on his arsenal of flutes. *Flute By-Laws* finds Laws with a studio orchestra performing a mixture of Afro-Cuban jazz and orchestrated ballads that feature his quartet with Corea, Thomas, and Davis. Laws excels on both of these early albums. If you love jazz with Latin beats, this two-fer is a treat. Although his *Afro-Classic* album really boosted his career, the better listen of Laws's earliest two albums for CTI is *Crying Song* ♫♫♫♫ (CTI, 1970/CBS, 1988, prod. Creed Taylor) performed with an array of musicians, including bassist Ron Carter, drummer Billy Cobham, guitarist George Benson, keyboardist Bob James, and a slew of others recorded in Memphis and New York studios during July and September, 1969. The nine tunes swing lightly with a slight jazz-funk feel, and Laws is in rare form throughout this historic date.

the rest:
Afro-Classic ♫♫♫♫ (CTI, 1970/CBS, 1988)
The Best of Hubert Laws ♫♫♫ (CTI, 1970–75/Epic-Legacy, 1990)
Romeo & Juliet ♫♫ (Columbia, 1976/1987)
The San Francisco Concert ♫♫♫♫ (CTI, 1977/CBS, 1987)
My Time Will Come ♫♫♫ (MusicMasters, 1990)

worth searching for: Laws has played as sideman on countless albums with artists as diverse as The Crusaders, Mongo Santamaria (*Skins*), Bob James (a series of albums in the 1970s), Jaco Pastorius (*Jaco Pastorius*), Weather Report (*I Sing* the Body Electric), Claude Bolling (*California Suite*), and others. His performances are always polished and lyrical. (For ratings on these albums, check the entries for each of these leaders.)

influences:

◀◀ Miles Davis, Gil Evans, Herbie Hancock, John Coltrane, Wes Montgomery

Nancy Ann Lee

Ronnie Laws

Born October 3, 1950, in Houston, TX.

A former Earth, Wind, & Fire (EWF) member and the sibling of flutist Hubert Laws and singers Eloise and Debra Laws, Ronnie Laws is a gritty, distinctive "rhythm & jazz" saxman as enamored of soul and funk as he is of jazz. Laws was never one to emphasize complexity for its own sake; influenced by Eddie Harris, the Crusaders, and Grover Washington Jr., Laws at his best is adventurous as well as accessible. After working as a sideman for Quincy Jones, Ramsey Lewis, and Hubert Laws in the early to mid-1970s and playing with EWF in 1972 and 1973, Laws debuted as a leader in 1975 with the promising *Pressure Sensitive*, which boasted his insistently funky hit, "Always There." Balancing commercial and artistic considerations, he enjoyed some attention in the R&B world with *Friends and Strangers* in 1978 and *Every Generation* in 1980, but, unfortunately, too many of his albums were overproduced, forgettable throwaways motivated strictly by a desire for radio airplay that wasted his improvisation skills.

what to buy: Laws's career as a leader was off to an impressive start with *Pressure Sensitive* ♫♫♫ (Blue Note, 1975, prod. Wayne Henderson) and his sophomore effort, *Fever* ♫♫♫ (Blue Note, 1989, prod. Wayne Henderson), both of which show the Crusaders' influence, thanks to Henderson, and illustrate how compatible jazz and R&B can be. After recording his share of disappointing "smooth jazz" albums in the 1980s and 1990s, Laws made a triumphant return to his soul-jazz roots with *A Tribute to the Legendary Eddie Harris* ♫♫♫ (Blue Note, 1997), which celebrated Harris's influence and boasted gutsy interpretations of such classics as "Listen Here" and "Freedom Jazz Dance."

what to buy next: Although not as strong as his first two albums, *Friends and Strangers* ♫♫♫ (United Artists, 1977, prod. Wayne Henderson) and *Flame* ♫♫♫ (United Artists, 1977, prod. Ronnie Laws) are welcome additions to his catalog. "Saturday Evening," from *Friends and Strangers*, shows Laws to be a pleasant and likable R&B singer, while *Flame* marks the first time he did his own producing.

what to avoid: Typical of Laws's radio-oriented recordings of the '80s and '90s, *Identity* ♫ (ATA, 1990) is an overproduced, contrived throwaway that finds him offering an abundance of saccharine "smooth jazz." A few of the songs are worthwhile—namely "Palisades" (an abstract number influenced by Miles Davis's 1980s fusion) and the hip-hop–minded "Street Knowledge." Most of the album, however, is lightweight, vapid elevator music.

the rest:

Every Generation ♫♫♫ (United Artists, 1980)
Solid Ground ♫♫ (Capitol, 1980)

influences:

◀◀ Eddie Harris, Grover Washington Jr., the Crusaders

Alex Henderson

Hugh Lawson

Born Richard Hugh Jerome Lawson, March 12, 1935, in Detroit, MI. Died March 17, 1997, in White Plains, NY.

If Detroit ever wanted to drop its nickname of "Motor City" for something new, one alternative would be the "City of Jazz Pianists." Tommy Flanagan, Barry Harris, Hank Jones, Sir Roland Hanna, and Hugh Lawson learned the tricks of their trade during roughly the same period in Detroit. Lawson is the least known of the bunch, but not for lack of talent. Lawson's early work came with Yusef Lateef in the mid-1950s in Detroit, and then they headed to New York City at the end of the decade. Lawson recorded on Lateef's early Prestige sessions in the late 1950s, spent some time playing and recording with trumpeter Sweets Edison in the early 1960s and then freelanced. In 1972, he helped found the seven-man group of pianists known as the Piano Choir that recorded for Strata East. In the mid- to late 1970s, Lawson toured with Charles Mingus. He recorded as a sideman with Charlie Rouse in the late 1970s and with Mingus alumni George Adams and Dannie Richmond in the early 1980s. He also played in the band Mingus Dynasty.

what's available: Lawson's *Colour* ♫♫♫ (Soul Note, 1983, prod. Giovanni Bonandrini) is a tempered trio affair yet a varied program with many highlights. "The Beast from Bali-Bali" from the Piano Choir days features the album's most engaging theme. "The Tinkler" is a light swinger with Louis Hayes providing brush treatment. "Creepy Chicken" serves up a healthy portion of the blues. Lawson repaints Mussorgsky's "Pictures at an Exhibition" with McCoy Tyner-ish flourishes, then switches to single-note strokes.

worth searching for: Lawson's Bud Powell–influenced approach contains a blues tinge and is heard best on two Soul Note sessions—the George Adams/Dannie Richmond albums *Hand to Hand* 𝄢𝄢𝄢𝄢 (Soul Note, 1980, prod. Giovanni Bonandrini), and *Gentlemen's Agreement* 𝄢𝄢𝄢 (Soul Note, 1983, prod. Giovanni Bonandrini)—sessions to which Lawson contributed two and three original tunes, respectively. Both dates, performed in the company of other Mingus alumni, are free-wheeling, post-bop blowing sessions that crackle with energy. Lawson was also the pianist for a live album made by drummer Roy Brooks, *The Free Slave* 𝄢𝄢𝄢𝄢 (Muse, 1970), a wailing, blowing date with tenor player George Coleman, trumpeter Woody Shaw, and bassist Cecil McBee.

influences:
◀◀ Bud Powell

Dan Polletta

The Leaders

Formed 1984.

Arthur Blythe, alto saxophone; Chico Freeman, tenor/soprano saxophones; Lester Bowie, trumpet; Kirk Lightsey, piano; Cecil McBee, bass; Famoudou Don Moye, drums, percussionist.

Labeling the lovely and strong sextet comprising altoist Arthur Blythe, tenor/soprano master Chico Freeman, trumpeter Lester Bowie, pianist Kirk Lightsey, bassist Cecil McBee, and drummer/percussionist Famoudou Don Moye a "Supergroup" may be technically correct, but it probably does them an ultimate disservice. Named the Leaders because each of the principals is a bandleader, this group has steadfastly eschewed self-congratulatory preening and breast-beating over the course of their more than a decade-long, on-again-off-again career, relying instead on mature and selfless interaction (not to mention healthy doses of humor, courtesy of the saucy Bowie) to deliver their point. The group tours overseas regularly, and Lester Bowie once said about this group that they are "better known in Yugoslavia, than in the U.S." although when they do tour the States, they play to packed halls.

what to buy: Of the relatively few recorded examples of the Leaders' art, *Unforeseen Blessings* 𝄢𝄢𝄢𝄢 (Black Saint, 1990, prod. Giovanni Bonandrini) is the best, mainly because its contours are widely varied (the pieces range from solo statements to full-frontal attacks) and the playing is breathtaking through-

out the 13 originals from pianist Kirk Lightsey, bassist Cecil McBee, drummer/percussionist Famoudou Don Moye, and saxophonist Chico Freeman. The session was recorded in New York in December, 1988.

what to buy next: The band's earliest effort, *Mudfoot* 𝄢𝄢𝄢𝄢 (Blackhawk, 1986, prod. Chico Freeman, Herb Wong), is looser and less focused, but it contains the attractively funky, episodic title track and Freeman's lighthearted yet moving vocal reading of Sam Cooke's "Cupid." Finally, an offshoot/oddity with hilarious liner notes by Richard Santoro, *Heaven Dance* 𝄢𝄢𝄢𝄢 (Sunnyside, 1989, prod. Francois Zalacain) is an eight-tune, May 1988 date comprising originals by pianist Lightsey, bassist McBee, and drummer Moye, performing as the Leaders Trio.

the rest:
Out Here Like This 𝄢𝄢𝄢 (Black Saint, 1988)

David Prince

Peggy Lee

Born Norma Dolores Egstrom, May 26, 1920, in Jamestown, ND.

Peggy Lee, once dubbed "the Queen" of popular song by Duke Ellington, has been considered more of a jazz-influenced pop singer than an outright jazz singer. But no matter how one classifies her, Lee in her prime was one of America's most charismatic and popular female vocalists, a trailblazer with a distinctive, bluesy style that set her apart from all of her peers, especially during the 1940s and 1950s. In her teenage years Lee left North Dakota to seek fame and fortune in Hollywood. She first gained national attention from 1941–43 when she was featured in Benny Goodman's big band, recording in 1942 the first version (for Columbia) of one of her most gorgeously intimate singles, the ballad "The Way You Look Tonight," a laid-back, honey-eyed rendering with celesta backing from Mel Powell. Lee convinced Goodman to let her record the cover of the Lil Green song "Why Don't You Do Right," and her July 27, 1942, recording became her biggest hit with the Goodman band.

Going solo in the mid-1940s, Lee signed with Capitol and enjoyed a string of hits that included another version of "Why Don't You Do Right," and tunes such as "I Don't Know Enough about You" and "Golden Earrings." She married Goodman band guitarist Dave Barbour in 1943 (they divorced in 1951), won a *Down Beat* poll in 1946, and in the 1950s appeared on television and in the film *The Jazz Singer*. In 1956 she received an Academy Award nomination for her singing and acting in the film *Pete Kelly's Blues*. Lee continued to work in clubs, mostly in Las Vegas, and her popularity continued throughout the 1950s, when her hits included "Black Coffee" and her sultry, seductive first version (for which she wrote the lyrics) of the Little Willie John classic, "Fever." During the 1960s she continued her activities as a songwriter and lyricist, and collaborated with composer-arrangers such as Duke Ellington, Quincy Jones, Milton Raskin, Harold Arlen, and Lalo Schifrin. In 1961 Lee traveled to Europe for the first time. During this decade she recorded with the orchestras of Quincy Jones, Lou Levy, and Benny Carter. She recorded more than 60 albums during her career and, as one of the very first female songwriter-performers, she paved the way for countless others to follow. She was sounding good in the 1970s and was still recording in the late 1980s and early 1990s. While her voice on her later recordings may not be up to the quality of her peak years, she retains the same sparse, understated phrasing style for which she became famous. Many of her recordings are on import labels and, while a few of her domestic recordings are available, Capitol has yet to reissue the definitive box set. Today, Lee still occasionally does a special evening performance in a posh Los Angeles hotel-room setting.

what to buy: Containing all of her essential post-war hits of the mid- to late 1940s, *Capitol Collector's Series, Volume 1, The Early Years* 🎵🎵🎵🎵 (Capitol, 1945–50/1997, prod. various) leaves no doubt that when she was in her prime, Lee epitomized jazz-influenced pop perfection. Thanks to digital remastering, gems like "Why Don't You Do Right," "It's a Good Day," and "Don't Smoke in Bed" are heard with a minimum of noise on the 1989 CD. She performs with mostly Capitol studio musicians led by Dave Barbour. Equally superb is *Black Coffee & Other Delights: The Decca Anthology* 🎵🎵🎵🎵 (Decca/MCA, 1952–56/1994, prod. various), a two-CD set focusing on her marvelous Decca output of the early to mid-1950s. Included among the 46 tunes are many of her popular hits, including the more jazzy title tune, and songs that have become jazz standards, such as "It Never Entered My Mind," "My Old Flame," "Street of Dreams," "They Can't Take That away from Me," "Lover," and others.

what to buy next: *The Uncollected Peggy Lee—1948* 🎵🎵🎵🎵 (Hindsight, 1948/1998, prod. various), offers live radio broadcasts that, when recorded, were not intended for commercial release. But thanks to the small Hindsight label, the excellent versions of "Just One of Those Things," "I've Got the World on a String," and other standards featuring Lee with the Dave Barbour and Billy May Bands can be enjoyed by the general public. Of her two late-career recordings still in print, the better is *Love Held Lightly* 🎵🎵🎵🎵 (Angel, 1993, prod. Bill Rudman, Ken Bloom, Keith Ingham). On this 14-tune Harold Arlen tribute, Lee shows

she still has what it takes as she caresses each song in her unique way. Highlights include gorgeous renderings of the Arlen title ballad with lyrics by Johnny Mercer (featuring warm bass flute augmentations from Phil Bodner), the bluesy torcher "Come on Midnight," and probably the best-ever recorded vocal version of the beautiful ballad "My Shining Hour." Sidemen include Keith Ingham (piano), Glenn Zottola (trumpet, flugelhorn), Ken Peplowski (tenor sax), Bodner (alto sax, bass flute), George Mass (trombone), John Chiodini (guitar), Jay Leonhart (bass), Grady Tate (drums), and Mark Sherman (vibes, percussion). Musicianship is superb throughout as the instrumentalists mesh perfectly with Lee, setting easy, light-swinging tempos that add to the high elegance of this recording. Though Lee packed the Hollywood Bowl in a performance with Mel Tormé the same year she recorded *Moments Like This* 🎵🎵 (Chesky, 1992, prod. David Chesky), she must have had a bad day in the studio because her voice sounds tired and lacks the luster of her earlier recordings. Yet she still knows how to turn a phrase artfully as she revisits early hits like "I Don't Know Enough about You," "Why Don't You Do Right," and "Mañana." Pianist Mike Renzi contributes lush, delicate arrangements and side players Jay Leonhart or Steve LaSpina (bass), and drummer Peter Grant provide tasteful support. Soloists Gerry Niewood (tenor sax, flute, bass flute, soprano sax), Tony Monte (keyboards), and Jay Berliner (acoustic and electric guitars) augment some tracks.

best of the rest:

(With George Shearing) *Beauty and the Beat!* 🎵🎵🎵🎵 (Capitol Jazz, 1959)
Basin Street East Proudly Presents 🎵🎵🎵🎵 (Capitol Jazz, 1961/1995)

influences:

◄◄ Maxine Sullivan, Count Basie, Billie Holiday, Ethel Waters, Mildred Bailey

►► Julie London, Chris Connor, Jeanie Bryson, Holly Cole

Nancy Ann Lee and Alex Henderson

Michel Legrand

Born February 24, 1932, in Paris, France.

Michel Legrand is most widely known as a popular composer/conductor out of the classical idiom and for his work on film scores. But he also has a hearty appreciation of jazz, is a decent jazz pianist, and has made his mark on the jazz discography by calling some stellar all-star sessions. Additionally, several of Legrand's tunes, including "What Are You Doing the Rest of Your Life," "The Summer Knows," and "Watch What Happens" have become minor jazz standards.

what to buy: The classic album *Legrand Jazz* 🎵🎵🎵🎵 (Columbia, 1960/Philips, 1989, prod. Michel Legrand) assembles a vast array of top jazz talent and a variety of settings. Miles Davis, Bill Evans, John Coltrane, Ben Webster, Herbie Mann, Phil Woods, and Art Farmer are all featured prominently, performing pieces by Duke Ellington, Django Reinhardt, Earl Hines, Jelly Roll Morton, Thelonious Monk, and Dizzy Gillespie, among others. But despite all of the top names present, Legrand himself doesn't become lost, contributing some strong playing and superlative arrangements.

what to buy next: *After the Rain* 🎵🎵🎵 (Pablo, 1982/OJC, 1994, prod. Michel Legrand, Nat Shapiro) is a collection of six Legrand ballads most enjoyable for the sensitive playing of saxophonists Phil Woods and Zoot Sims. Legrand, bassist Ron Carter, guitarist Gene Bertoncini, and drummer Grady Tate provide equally sensitive support.

what to avoid: For *Michel Plays Legrand* 🎵🎵 (Laserlight, 1994, prod. Michel Legrand), Legrand amassed a typically strong array of jazz talent (including Arturo Sandoval, Bud Shank, Hubert Laws and Bill Watrous), but the affair sounds altogether too relaxed and unexciting. This set of Legrand ballads falls fall short of the music on "After the Rain."

the rest:
I Love Paris 🎵🎵🎵 (1954/Legacy 1994)
At Shelly's Manne Hole 🎵🎵🎵 (Verve, 1968/1989)
Live at Fat Tuesday's 🎵🎵🎵 (Verve, 1985)
(With Miles Davis) *Dingo* 🎵🎵🎵 (Warner Bros., 1991)
Legrand/Grappelli 🎵🎵🎵 (Verve, 1992)
A Warm Shade of Memory 🎵🎵🎵 (Evidence, 1996)

worth searching for: On the import CD *Jazz Grand* 🎵🎵🎵🎵 (Gryphon, 1978/Castle 1990, prod. Norman Schwartz), Legrand combines his work for films with his interest in jazz, performing a jazz suite for big band based on his score for "Les Routes de la Sud." Soloists include Woods, Gerry Mulligan, and trumpeter Jon Faddis.

influences:
◀◀ Leonard Bernstein
▶▶ Dave Grusin

Dan Keener

Peter Leitch

Born 1944, in Ottawa, Ontario, Canada.

An excellent hard-bop based guitarist, Peter Leitch plays linear saxophone-like lines with a gorgeous soft tone and firm attack.

On up-tempo tunes, he tosses off long flowing lines that generate intense momentum, and on ballads his tone seems to expand as his notes float on the melody. Raised in Montreal, Leitch started playing guitar at age 16. His first influences were the Belgian guitarist Rene Thomas (who was living in Toronto at the time), Kenny Burrell, and Wes Montgomery, though he listened to saxophonists (such as Coltrane and Rollins) as much as guitarists. Active on the Toronto scene in the late 1970s and early 1980s, Leitch recorded with Sadik Hakim, Oscar Peterson, and the Al Grey/Jimmy Forrest band before moving to New York in 1983, where he quickly hooked up with organist Jack McDuff. Leitch has worked widely around New York with players such as Bobby Watson and John Hicks, and in the mid-1990s directed a fascinating group, Guitars Play Mingus, but he's best represented by his one dozen albums as a leader, for Jazz House, Criss Cross, Concord, and especially Reservoir.

what to buy: With the release of *Exhilaration* 🎵🎵🎵🎵 (Reservoir, 1993, prod. Mark Feldman), a smoking, mostly Monk session, Peter Leitch moved into the realm of the elite jazz guitarists. Originally released in 1985 on the Uptown label, the album was reissued on CD by Reservoir with two new duo tracks. Featuring the great baritone saxophonist Pepper Adams, the redoubtable pianist John Hicks, rock solid bassist Ray Drummond and dependably brilliant drummer Billy Hart, *Exhilaration* lives up to its title. Highlights include an ingenious arrangement of Monk's "Played Twice," and the guitar/bass duo on "But Not for Me." A strong quartet session, *A Special Rapport* 🎵🎵🎵🎵 (Reservoir, 1994, prod. Mark Feldman) features John Hicks (piano), Ray Drummond (bass), and Marvin "Smitty" Smith (drums). Opening with a blazing version of Charlie Parker's "Relaxin' at Camarillo," the album includes an excellent arrangement of Ahmad Jamal's "New Rhumba," a gorgeous Billy Strayhorn medley and a decidedly Coltranish version of Fats Waller's "Jitterbug Waltz." Leitch and pianist John Hicks had been working together for about a decade when they recorded *Duality* 🎵🎵🎵🎵 (Reservoir, 1995, prod. Mark Feldman). Both are musician's musicians, confident, profound improvisors who bring out the best in each other on this duo session. From Monk's "Epistrophy" and Billy Strayhorn's "Chelsea Bridge," to Jobim's "O Grand Amour" and Hicks's "After the Morning," they listen and play closely together without ever getting in each other's way, producing intimate, but hard-swinging music.

what to buy next: *Mean What You Say* 🎵🎵🎵🎵 (Concord Jazz, 1990, prod. Carl E. Jefferson) is just another brilliant quartet album pairing Leitch with John Hicks (piano), Ray Drummond (bass), and Marvin "Smitty" Smith (drums), a relaxed session full of subtly inspired interplay. Highlights include Leitch's solo version of "In a Sentimental Mood," the scorching "Hick's Time" and Leitch's "Blues on the East Side." Leitch adds a variety of horns on *Colours and Dimensions* ♫♫♫♫ (Reservoir, 1996, prod. Mark Feldman), a superb session featuring Claudio Roditi (trumpet and flugelhorn), Gary Bartz (alto and soprano sax), and Jed Levy (tenor and soprano sax and alto flute). Leitch's lush horn arrangement on his "Song for Jobim" highlights his sensitive acoustic guitar work, while he brings out Mingus's sensual side on "Duke Ellington's Sound of Love." The all-star rhythm section features John Hicks (piano), Rufus Reid (bass), and Marvin "Smitty" Smith (drums). Only Leitch's second trio session as a leader, *Up Front* ♫♫♫♫ (Reservoir, 1997, prod. Mark Feldman) features bassist Sean Smith and the powerhouse drummer Marvin "Smitty" Smith. There's a strong guitar/drum axis on this session, with Smitty really pushing Leitch on the almost frantic "Sea Change." His brush work on "I Didn't Know about You" perfectly supports Leitch's ravishing treatment of the melody, while the drummer plays churning polyrhythms on the quicksilver changes of "Millennium, Part 1."

best of the rest:

On a Misty Night ♫♫♫♫ (Criss Cross, 1987/1994)
Red Zone ♫♫♫♫ (Reservoir, 1987/1993)
Portraits and Dedications ♫♫♫♫ (Criss Cross, 1989/1994)
Trio/Quartet '91 ♫♫♫♫ (Concord Jazz, 1991)
From Another Perspective ♫♫♫♫ (Concord Jazz, 1993)

influences:

◀◀ Kenny Burrell, Jim Hall, Wes Montgomery

Andrew Gilbert

John Leitham

Born August 10, 1953, at Scott Air Force Base, IL.

John Leitham (pronounced LIGHT-um) is a savvy, left-handed bassist whose swinging high-energy performances and remarkable technique have placed him in the jazz forefront through appearances and recordings with luminaries such as Mel Tormé, George Shearing, Herb Geller, Spike Robinson, Bill Perkins, and the late Bob Cooper, his good friend and mentor. Leitham grew up in Reading, Pennsylvania, attended high school in the Philadelphia area and, upon graduation, sang and played electric bass in local groups. As his musical studies became increasingly serious, Leitham switched to acoustic bass under the tutelage of Al Stauffer, who heavily influenced him after Leitham saw Stauffer perform with French jazz pianist Bernard Peiffer. Within a few years, Leitham was playing in big bands and jazz groups, and accompanying well-known traveling performers throughout Eastern Pennsylvania. While working in a South Philadelphia house band, he was recruited for the Woody Herman Young Thundering Herd in 1981, which resulted in extensive touring and exposure to the jazz festival scene.

In 1983, Leitham left Philadelphia for California, where he quickly formed long-term musical associations with Ed Shaughnessy, Bob Cooper, Tommy Tedesco, Bill Watrous, Tom Ranier, and others. While freelancing in the Los Angeles area, Leitham came to the attention of pianist George Shearing, who contacted him in 1987 to play a live-recorded gig at the Paul Masson Winery with singer Mel Tormé. Leitham subsequently recorded nine Tormé CDs, is seen on two of the singer's videos, and was scheduled to tour and record as part of Tormé's rhythm section right up to the time of the singer's August 1996 stroke. Leitham currently works club dates on the West Coast, often with his own trio, and appears throughout the U.S. at festivals, where he has become a crowd favorite for his considerable instrumental skills and his friendly presence.

what to buy: A heady mix of 11 well-arranged standards, lively performances, and fresh material, Leitham's third album, *Lefty Leaps In* ♫♫♫♫ (USA Music Group, 1996, prod. John Leitham), was recorded in three separate sessions during April and May, 1996. Two exciting West Coast tenor saxophonists, Ricky Woodard and Pete Christlieb, join Leitham's trio with Tom Ranier (piano) and Roy McCurdy (drums). Woodard and Christlieb explore the two-tenor format on "Long Ago and Far Away," a blistering "Oleo," a cooking "Lefty Leaps In," and the Bob Cooper original, "Fagin." Guests include trombonist Bill Watrous and guitarist Barry Zweig, who join with Leitham and Ranier as drummer Jeff Hamilton sits in on the playful "Studio City Romp." With the shifting instrumentals on this album, there is little chance of boring the well-trained listener. On *The Southpaw* ♫♫♫♫ (USA Music Group, 1993, prod. John Leitham) Leitham joins with drummer McCurdy and pianist Ranier to form the trio at the heart of these performances. Trumpeter Buddy Childers and the late Bob Cooper's tenor sax add spice to four numbers. Pianist Milco Leviev replaces Ranier on Wayne Shorter's "Fee Fie Fo Fum" and the 7/4-time Leitham original, "Turkish Bizarre." Leitham dazzles with technique while retaining high musical values on this CD.

what to buy next: Leitham's first album as leader, *Leitham Up* ♫♫♫♫ (USA Music Group, 1992, prod. John Leitham), features the bassist leading a trio with drummer Jake Hanna and pianist Tom Ranier. Highlights of the straight-ahead session recorded in Hollywood in May, 1989, include Leitham's blistering arco (bowed) solos on Charlie Parker's "Au Privave," with versatile Ranier soloing on tenor sax, and solid performances of standard tunes composed by Thelonious Monk, Gerry Mulligan, Duke Ellington, and others. Parker's "Moose the Mooche" is deftly handled by Ranier playing bass clarinet in unison with the leader's bass. It's a joyful listen.

worth searching for: A fine example of Leitham's playing exists on the Mel Tormé–George Shearing album *A Vintage Year* 𝄞𝄞𝄞𝄞 (Concord, 1988, prod. Carl E. Jefferson). Leitham's lilting bass-piano duo track with Shearing (while Tormé sat out) on the tune "Bittersweet" is a bonus on this beautiful album.

influences:
◀◀ Oscar Pettiford, Ray Brown

John T. Bitter

Peter Lemer
Born 1942.

As with many ESP-Disk artists of the day, keyboardist Peter Lemer's background is a little sketchy: all that's certain is that he was—from his appropriately mod dress to his tightly wound improvisations—very, very British. Although one album made a moderate impact, Lemer wound up making most of his money by later work with such disparate collaborators as Annette Peacock, prog-rockers Gong, and even the drone-drenched North African Gnawa musicians.

what's available: *Local Colour* 𝄞𝄞𝄞𝄞 (ESP, 1966, prod. Eddie Kramer) is a radiant record. Lemer does fine improvisatory battle with John Surman's booming baritone sax, and the remainder of the quintet—tenor player Nisar Ahmad Khan, drummer John Hiseman, and bassist Tony Reeves—manage to embrace and transcend all the sticky signposts of the late '60s British free scene. Eddie Kramer's rock-oriented production gives Lemer's cluster-bashing the appropriate percussive thrust as well.

influences:
◀◀ Cecil Taylor
▶▶ Myra Melford

Jason Ferguson

Lou Levy
Born March 5, 1928, in Chicago, IL.

Lou Levy is one of jazz's elite accompanists, a fine bop-influ-

enced pianist who has provided excellent support while playing and recording with many of the music's greatest figures, especially vocalists. He broke in with Georgie Auld in 1947 and by the end of the decade had been employed by Sarah Vaughan, Chubby Jackson, and Boyd Raeburn. He worked with Woody Herman's Second Herd, Tommy Dorsey, and Flip Phillips, and later accompanied Peggy Lee, Ella Fitzgerald, Anita O'Day, June Christy, Pinky Winters, Stan Getz, Shorty Rogers, Terry Gibbs, and many others.

what to buy: An excellent quartet session, *Lunarcy* 𝄞𝄞𝄞𝄞 (Verve, 1992, prod. Lou Levy, Daniel Richard) features the deft bop pianist with the great tenor saxophonist Pete Christlieb, the late bassist Eric Von Essen, and powerhouse drummer Ralph Penland. The album opens with two Levy originals, the Monkish title track and the arrestingly difficult "Pathetique," with some fine cello work by Von Essen and superb drumming by Penland. High points include two Johnny Mandel tunes ("The Shadow of Your Smile" and "Zoot"), Al Cohn's "Ah Moore," and a medley of "The Dolphin" and "Carnival" that features a particularly potent Christlieb solo.

best of the rest:
Ya Know 𝄞𝄞𝄞𝄞 (Verve, 1993)

worth searching for: A classic Ella Fitzgerald album from her greatest period, *Clap Hands, Here Comes Charlie!* 𝄞𝄞𝄞𝄞 (Verve, 1961/1989, prod. Norman Granz) features the sparkling accompaniment of Levy, Herb Ellis (guitar), Joe Mondragon (bass), and Stan Levey (drums). Levy easily keeps up with Ella when she's wailing, but he's especially effective on the ballads, building drama into "You're My Thrill" and establishing just the right feeling of world-weary melancholy on a gorgeous version of "Spring Can Really Hang You Up the Most."

influences:
◀◀ Bud Powell, George Wallington

Andrew Gilbert

George Lewis (clarinet)
Born George Zenon, July 13, 1900, in New Orleans, LA. Died December 31, 1968, in New Orleans, LA.

George Lewis took up the clarinet when he was 18, in the same period that many of the finest New Orleans musicians were leaving the city for Chicago and California. In the 1920s he played in various groups, including the Black Eagle Band. Until the 1940s, Lewis played regularly in various bands for dances and other social functions, while usually supporting himself with other work. However, forces in the jazz world conspired to pull him out of this almost anonymous activity. When trumpeter Bunk Johnson was first discovered in the 1940s and touted as a representative of an authentic voice of early jazz, Lewis was in the group assembled to support him. Touring and recording followed, but Lewis found Johnson difficult, and he returned to New Orleans in 1946, having attracted opportunities to record (often for Bill Russell's American Music label). With the passing of Johnson, Lewis gradually assumed the trumpeter's place as the central figure in the New Orleans revivalist movement. Recordings became more frequent, as did tours as far afield as Europe and Japan. Throughout, Lewis remained an essential part of New Orleans traditional musical life, playing in the Eureka Brass Band and with the Preservation Hall Jazz Band. Whether his style is a precursor to the jazz played in Chicago in the 1920s or itself a distinct local evolution is a matter of debate. He possessed a beautifully grainy and expressive sound, a gift for unadorned melodic improvisation, whether as lead or in ensemble, and, at his best, an untrammeled energy.

what to buy: The best of Lewis's work is in the company of a tight band of regular associates, including trumpeter Kid Howard, trombonist Jim Robinson, and the bassist Alcide "Slow Drag" Pavageau. *The Beverly Caverns Sessions* 𝄞𝄞𝄞𝄞 (Good Time Jazz, 1995, prod. Lester Koenig) stands out among their many recordings of a narrow repertoire. These 1953 Hollywood performances are well recorded, Lewis is in excellent form, and the long live selections provide a better sense of the group's developed ensemble improvisation. Lewis's frequently recorded solo feature, "Burgundy Street Blues," is particularly fine here, as is the extended "Tin Roof Blues."

what to buy next: *Jazz at Vespers* 𝄞𝄞𝄞 (Riverside, 1954/OJC, 1993, prod. Bill Grauer) is a recording of hymns and gospel tunes, with the same personnel joining Lewis in evocative renditions that range from "Just a Little While to Stay Here" to "Down by the Riverside."

best of the rest:

Jazz in the Classic New Orleans Tradition 𝄞𝄞𝄞 (Riverside, 1956/OJC, 1991)
George Lewis of New Orleans 𝄞𝄞𝄞 (Riverside, 1958/OJC, 1989)
Plays Hymns 𝄞𝄞𝄞 (Milneburg, 1995)
The Oxford Series Volume 12 𝄞𝄞𝄞 (American Music, 1995)
The Beverly Caverns Sessions, Volume 2 𝄞𝄞𝄞 (Good Time Jazz, 1996)

worth searching for: Lewis's participation in the social rituals of New Orleans is documented with the 11-piece Eureka Brass Band on *New Orleans Funeral and Parade* 𝄞𝄞𝄞 (American

Music, 1951/1994, prod. George Buck). Stirring renditions of "West Lawn Dirge" and "Just a Closer Walk with Thee," with their intense wailing pitch, may give a sense of the New Orleans music that gave rise to jazz in the early years of the century.

influences:

◀◀ Johnny Dodds, Jimmie Noone, Albert Nicholas

see also: *Bunk Johnson*

Stuart Broomer

George Lewis (trombone)

Born July 14, 1952, in Chicago, IL.

An instrumental virtuoso, innovative composer, and pioneer in using electronic instruments and computers as a tool for improvisation, George Lewis is at home in many settings. He began studying trombone in 1961; by the age of 12 he was transcribing solos by tenor saxophonist Lester Young for trombone. He studied with pianist Muhal Richard Abrams and joined the Association for the Advancement of Creative Musicians in 1971. While at Yale he met pianist Anthony Davis, in whose ensemble, Episteme, he later performed, and studied with Fred Anderson back in Chicago. After graduating, he toured with Count Basie for two months in 1976. But a more important association began in May that same year when he joined Anthony Braxton's group. Lewis made an excellent foil for Braxton; he has a quick analytical mind, fast reflexes, and the technical mastery to play Braxton's music. Lewis was artistic director of the Kitchen, an avant-garde cultural center in New York from 1980 to 1982, and today he is on the music faculty of the University of California, San Diego, where he devotes much of his time to interactive computer programs for improvisers. Lewis commands an impressive array of extended techniques, and his improvising can be explosively fragmentary and irreverently humorous, but he also uses a legato delivery that hearkens back to jazz greats like Lester Young. Although he has made frustratingly few albums as a leader, Lewis has recorded extensively as a sideman with significant avant-garde figures on both sides of the Atlantic. He is a member of Slide Ride, a trombone quartet with Ray Anderson, Craig Harris, and Gary Valente, as well as a trio with John Zorn and Bill Frisell called News for Lulu.

what to buy: The title track of *Homage to Charles Parker* 𝄞𝄞𝄞𝄞 (Black Saint, 1979, prod. Giacomo Pellicciotti)—scored for electronics, synthesizer, trombone, piano, and saxophone—is one of the decade's most ravishingly beautiful achievements and a touching tribute to Bird. The other side-long track rips blues sonorities out of their traditional context to gambol in fields of structured free improvisation. *Jile-Save! Mon—The Imaginary Suite ♫♫♫* (Black Saint, 1979, prod. Giacomo Pellicciotti) finds Lewis in an exploratory mood—by turns jovial, impishly flatulent, and soberly lyrical—with his long-time collaborator, saxophonist Douglas Ewart. Lewis has devoted much of his energies recently to developing interactive computer software that can generate music in real time (improvise) or accept music from a human in-strumentalist as input and modify its music in response.

what to buy next: Lewis brings a buoyant spirit of inquiry that lifts *Voyager ♫♫♫* (Avant, 1993, prod. David Wessell) above mere beta testing of the technology. Roscoe Mitchell, at his con-frontational best, guests on half the tracks and puts the ma-chine through its paces. *Shadowgraph No. 5 ♫♫♫* (Black Saint, 1977, prod. Giovanni Bonandrini) is an uncompromising set of avant garde compositions for an all-star ensemble of improvi-sors, including Roscoe Mitchell, Leroy Jenkins, Muhal Richard Abrams, Anthony Davis, and Abdul Wadud. After a long absence from the studio, Lewis returned with *Changing with the Times ♫♫♫* (New World, 1993, prod. George Lewis), an idiosyncratic disc of settings for the spoken word. Full of the usual Lewis wit and technical finesse, but not the first purchase to make.

worth searching for: On *The George Lewis Solo Trombone Album ♫♫♫* (Sackville, 1976, prod. Bill Smith, John Norris) Lewis overdubs three tracks in a long piece that is alternately humorous, lush and sensual, disjointed, and abstract. A lovely version of Ellington's "Lush Life" shows off Lewis's consider-able jazz chops.

influences:

◀◀ Roswell Rudd

▶▶ Robin Eubanks

Ed Hazell

John Lewis

Born May 3, 1920 in La Grange, IL.

Best known for his work in the Modern Jazz Quartet, pianist John Lewis has also led an active life beyond that venerable group. However, his style has remained constant throughout, with a definitively spare, cool sound and an appreciation of classical modes. Lewis's work has made him a pioneer in the "Third Stream" movement, successfully combining the improvi-sational element of jazz with the elegant structures of classical music. Lewis first hooked up with his future MJQ mates while playing in Dizzy Gillespie's big band in 1946–48, after studying

GEORGE LEWIS (WITH INDIA COOKE)

song "Logan's Reel"
album RedHanded
(Music & Arts, 1996)
instrument Trombone

Monster Solo

music at the University of New Mexico and serving in the army. He played with a variety of groups over the next few years, in-cluding for Charlie Parker, Illinois Jacquet, Lester Young, and most notably Miles Davis, participating in Davis's *Birth of the Cool* sessions. In 1951 Lewis joined fellow Gillespie-alum drum-mer Kenny Clarke and vibraphonist Milt Jackson, along with bassist Percy Heath, to form the Milt Jackson Quartet, which al-tered its name to the more familiar moniker—Modern Jazz Quartet—a year later (serendipitously with no change to the initials). When Connie Kay replaced Clarke in 1956, the group had a stable lineup that lasted until 1974, with occasional re-unions thereafter. In this context, Lewis developed his trade-mark sound, and he contributed many memorable composi-tions to the jazz library of songs, including the perennial fa-vorite "Django." He also began composing film scores, collabo-rating with French-horn player and jazz critic Gunther Schuller, and other rewarding side projects. After the MJQ disbanded, Lewis taught at City College and co-founded the American Jazz Orchestra. He continues to contribute to the celebration of jazz as an art form with his crossover recordings and performances. Lewis's economical piano style recalls Count Basie in its perfection of note selection, where every one counts. He works well with earthy artists such as Milt Jackson and Danish violinist Svend Asmussen, who satisfy the blues streak in him. But he is equally at home performing a Bach prelude, of which he has several collections available, capturing his well-tempered piano in all of its eloquent glory.

what to buy: On *Grand Encounter: 2 Degrees East—3 Degrees West* 𝄢𝄢𝄢𝄢 (Pacific Jazz, 1956, prod. Richard Bock) Lewis is joined by MJQ bassist Percy Heath, frequent collaborator Jim Hall on guitar, underrated tenor saxophonist Bill Perkins, and drummer Chico Hamilton for a straight-ahead set of perspicuous standards and one Lewis original. All the parts mesh perfectly for a textbook "cool" album. *The Wonderful World of Jazz* 𝄢𝄢𝄢𝄢 (Atlantic, 1961, prod. Nesuhi Ertegun, Tom Dowd) is a perfect example of Lewis's affection for the blues. "Afternoon in Paris" and an extended take on "Body and Soul" feature larger ensembles than usual, to good effect.

what to buy next: Lewis's first recording with a jazz violinist, *European Encounter* 𝄢𝄢𝄢𝄢 (Atlantic, 1962, prod. John Lewis) worked so well, he'd go back to it later in his career. Svend Asmussen's unorthodox style is a surprisingly good match for Lewis's elegant piano lines, as heard in "If I Were Eve" and a startling arrangement of Ornette Coleman's "Lonely Woman." The relatively recent trio set *The Garden of Delight: Delaunay's Dilemma* 𝄢𝄢𝄢𝄢 (EmArcy, 1988, prod. John Lewis, Kiyoshi Koyama), recorded in Japan, demonstrates that Lewis has not lost a step. Lewis originals such as "Concorde" and "Delaunay's Dilemma" truly sparkle.

what to avoid: *European Windows* 𝄢𝄢 (RCA, 1958, prod. Gene Norman) was an early attempt by Lewis to mix jazz and classical musical elements but unfortunately sounds too jarring to satisfy. It's not a horrible record, but since Lewis refined his methods later, this one may safely be ignored.

the rest:
The John Lewis Piano 𝄢𝄢𝄢𝄢 (Atlantic, 1957)
Afternoon in Paris 𝄢𝄢𝄢𝄢 (Atlantic, 1957)
Improvised Meditations and Excursions 𝄢𝄢𝄢𝄢 (Atlantic, 1959)
Odds against Tomorrow (Soundtrack) 𝄢𝄢𝄢 (United Artists, 1959)
The Golden Striker 𝄢𝄢𝄢 (Atlantic, 1960)
Jazz Abstractions 𝄢𝄢𝄢𝄢 (Atlantic, 1961)
Original Sin 𝄢𝄢 (Atlantic, 1961)
A Milanese Story (Soundtrack) 𝄢𝄢𝄢𝄢 (Atlantic, 1962)
Essence 𝄢𝄢𝄢𝄢 (Atlantic, 1962)
Animal Dance 𝄢𝄢𝄢𝄢 (Atlantic, 1962)

P.O.V. 𝄢𝄢𝄢𝄢 (Columbia, 1975)
An Evening with Two Grand Pianos 𝄢𝄢𝄢 (Little David, 1979)
Kansas City Breaks 𝄢𝄢𝄢𝄢 (Finesse, 1982/Red Baron, 1994)
Bach Preludes and Fugues, Volume 1 𝄢𝄢𝄢𝄢 (Philips, 1984)
Bach Preludes and Fugues, Volume 2 𝄢𝄢𝄢𝄢 (Philips, 1984)
The Bridge Game 𝄢𝄢𝄢𝄢 (Philips, 1986)
(With Ray Brown) *Genes of Jazz* 𝄢𝄢𝄢𝄢 (Sounds of Soul, 1987)
Bach Preludes and Fugues, Volume 3 𝄢𝄢𝄢𝄢 (Philips, 1988)
The Chess Game 𝄢𝄢𝄢𝄢 (Philips, 1988)
(With Ray Brown) *Midnight in Paris* 𝄢𝄢𝄢𝄢 (EmArcy, 1989)
(With Ray Brown) *Private Concert* 𝄢𝄢𝄢𝄢 (EmArcy, 1991)

worth searching for: "Three Little Feelings," Lewis's contribution to the Jazz and Classical Music Society's 1957 album *Music for Brass*, is thankfully included on both the somewhat scattershot compilation *The Jazz Arranger, Volume 2* 𝄢𝄢𝄢𝄢 (Columbia, 1990, prod. various) and the more integrally collected *The Birth of the Third Stream* 𝄢𝄢𝄢𝄢 (Columbia Legacy, 1996, prod. George Avakian), which has all of *Music for Brass* plus two-thirds of *Modern Jazz Concert* with similar efforts by Mingus, Giuffre, Schuller, etc. Lewis's "Three Little Feelings" suite is enough by itself to make either album worth owning, as it is one of his best, brilliantly capturing a melancholy mood in an almost cinematic fashion.

influences:
◀◀ Count Basie, Johann Sebastian Bach
▶▶ Billy Taylor, George Russell

see also: *Modern Jazz Quartet*

Eric J. Lawrence

Meade "Lux" Lewis

Born Meade Anderson Lewis, September 4, 1905, in Chicago, IL, or Louisville, KY. Died June 7, 1964, near Minneapolis, MN.

Figuring out where Meade "Lux" Lewis was born is problematic. All available sources agree that he was born in 1905, but some say he was born in Chicago, moved to Louisville as a young child, and then moved with his family back to Chicago in the early 1920s. The rest place his birth in Louisville while acknowledging Lewis's move to Chicago later. Either way, Lewis became enamored of piano blues in Chicago when he heard his neighbor Jimmy Yancey playing in 1921. In 1927 he went into the studio to record "Honky Tonk Train Blues," one of the first great boogie-woogie tunes. Paramount, his record company, didn't even release the disc until 1929. In 1935 record collector/producer John Hammond discovered Lewis and his housemate Albert Ammons washing cars and driving a taxi for a living. Hammond got Lewis into the studio in November of that year to re-record "Honky Tonk Train Blues." The great boogie-woogie craze that started with the 1938 Spirituals to Swing concert in Carnegie Hall jump-started Lewis's career again, and he began recording and performing in concerts, sometimes with fellow pianists Ammons and Pete Johnson as the Boogie Woogie Trio. A powerful pianist, Lewis didn't have the abundance of technique Ammons had, but his playing was less by rote and, as a result, more interesting. After the dust from the craze settled down in the mid-'40s, Lewis still continued performing and recording. He later moved to Los Angeles, where he engaged in night club and television work. He was driving back from a concert in Minneapolis when he was killed in an auto accident in 1964.

what to buy: The choice between the Blue Note album and the chronological series put out by Classics depends on whether you want an overview of classic boogie woogie (the Blue Note sessions) or whether you are strictly interested in Lewis (Classics). In amongst the 18 songs that make up *The Chronological Meade Lux Lewis: 1927–1939* 𝄢𝄢𝄢𝄢 (Classics, 1993) are three versions of "Honky Tonk Train": the original 1927 version, the John Hammond recorded version from 1935, and one cut in 1937. The last seven performances can also be found on the Blue Note release, but the recording of "Boogie Woogie Prayer Parts 1 & 2" by the piano trio of Lewis, Ammons, and Johnson is only on this set. In addition there are two songs featuring Lewis on celeste ("Celeste Blues" and "I'm in the Mood for Love"). The first recording sessions for Alfred Lion's new Blue Note label yielded a treasure trove of marvelous piano playing. *The First Day* 𝄢𝄢𝄢𝄢 (Blue Note, 1992, prod. Alfred Lion) is split between some fine Lewis solo tunes, two duets with Ammons, and solo material from Ammons. Seven of the Lewis solos appear on the Classics release, but the duets do not. The Blue Note album has better overall sound quality.

what to buy next: *The Blues Piano Artistry of Meade Lux Lewis* 𝄢𝄢𝄢𝄢 (OJC, 1962, prod. Chris Albertson) is unadulterated piano playing by Meade "Lux" Lewis, without vocals or other instruments clamoring for attention. The whole session was recorded in under three hours because Lewis had made an appointment to be somewhere else at the end of the date. Everything was done quickly, just like they used to do in the old days, only with better sound. Results bear out Lewis's calm assurance at the beginning of the session, "Don't worry, we'll make it." In addition to some wonderfully inventive boogie woogie piano playing on his own originals, it's interesting to hear him take off on Duke Ellington's "C-Jam Blues." Lewis also improvises with the celeste's bell-like tones on three songs, making the most of this novelty.

the rest:
Tidal Boogie 𝄢𝄢𝄢 (Tradition, 1954)
Meade Lux Lewis: 1939–1954 𝄢𝄢𝄢 (Story of the Blues, 1991)
Meade Lux Lewis: 1939–1941 𝄢𝄢𝄢𝄢 (Classics, 1994)
Meade Lux Lewis: 1941–1944 𝄢𝄢𝄢𝄢 (Classics, 1994)

influences:
◀◀ Jimmy Yancey, Charles "Cow Cow" Davenport, Cripple Clarence Lofton

▶▶ Lafayette Leake

Garaud MacTaggart

Mel Lewis

Born Melvin Sokoloff, May 10, 1929, in Buffalo, NY. Died February 2, 1990, in New York, NY.

A legendary big-band drummer, Mel Lewis also led one of the most respected big bands as well, the Thad Jones/Mel Lewis Big Band, which played Monday nights at the Village Vanguard for 23 years, until Lewis's death, and continues to this day as the Vanguard Jazz Orchestra. The son of a professional drummer, Lewis began his career working with dance bands in his hometown of Buffalo when he was 14. By 1948 he had played with some of the better dance bands in jazz, including the Boyd Raeburn Orchestra and the bands of Alvino Ray, Tex Beneke, and Ray Anthony. In 1954 he joined the Stan Kenton Orchestra and immediately gained a reputation as a drummer who understood the nuances of working with a big band, swinging the cumbersome Kenton orchestra as never before. After several years on the road with Kenton, he moved to Los Angeles in 1957 and worked with big bands led by Gerald Wilson and Terry Gibbs, as well as in the combos of Hampton Hawes and Frank Rosolino. By the 1960s he was back on the road with Dizzy Gillespie and Benny Goodman. Relocating to New York in the mid-'60s, he was active in the studio scene and in 1965 formed his group with trumpeter Thad Jones. When Jones fled to Europe in the late 1970s, much to the surprise of everyone, including Lewis, the drummer became the orchestra's sole leader. In the 1980s he maintained a busy recording schedule, performing with his own groups, as well as the American Jazz Orchestra.

what to buy: After the departure of Jones in 1978, Lewis kept his band book fresh by commissioning new arrangements. *Live at the Village Vanguard* 𝄢𝄢𝄢𝄢 (DCC, 1980/1991, prod. Norman Schwartz) features the compositions and charts of valve trombonist/arranger Bob Brookmeyer, a charter member of the Jones/Lewis Band at its inception in 1965. In the early 1980s, Brookmeyer also served as musical director for the band. Where

Jones's writing had its roots in Basie, Brookmeyer's concept is informed by modern classical music. Nevertheless, this is one swinging session, thanks to Lewis's driving percussion. Special guest here is Clark Terry, who co-led a quintet with Brookmeyer in the 1960s and whose warm flugelhorn and vocals are featured on the delightful "Ding Dong Ding." A decade after Jones's departure, Lewis pulled out some of Jones's first charts once again and recorded them on *Definitive Thad Jones, Volume 1* ♫♫♫♫ (MusicMasters 1989, prod. John Snyder) with an edition of his famed big band that was among his best, featuring Joe Lovano on tenor and Dick Oatts on alto. Although this was done in the studio, it has the feel of a live date because the solos really stretch out. Gems like "Three in One," which runs 13 minutes, and "Little Pixie" at 15 minutes showcase the soloists and also Jones's intelligent, challenging writing, as well as the finesse of the band's section work. With so much of the band's early work now out of print, this look back to Jones is essential. Lewis's fiery drums ignite the proceedings throughout. When drummer Lewis did his eponymous session, *Mel Lewis* ♫♫♫♫ (VSOP, 1957/1995, prod. Red Clyde), in Los Angeles, he was a busy studio player who was best known for his work with Stan Kenton. Interestingly, it features the work of three choice arrangers, Bill Holman, who plays tenor and baritone here, Marty Paich, who plays piano, and Bob Brookmeyer, who later arranged for Lewis's big band. Also present are alto saxophonist Charlie Mariano, bassist Buddy Clark, and trumpeter Jack Sheldon. This is hard bop with a West Coast feel, more laid back and not as intense as its New York counterpart. Rather than just a blowing session, Lewis and his group work hard to create something original, with "Brookside," "Charlie's Cavern," and "Grey Flannel" as examples of peerless musicianship and first distinctive improvisations. *Lost Art* ♫♫♫♫ (MusicMasters, 1990, prod. John Snyder), a sextet session, was one of Lewis's last recordings and it includes a group of musicians from his big band, notably pianist Kenny Werner, whose compositions and arrangements are featured. Werner is one of the great undiscovered talents in jazz and he gives this hard bop session some really imaginative twists and turns. Lewis never lost his touch, as shown on "4/4." On this date, his sticks and brush work are nothing short of superlative (the title track refers to his brush work). Strong solos from alto saxman Dick Oatts, Werner, and the amazing Gary Smulyan are everywhere.

the rest:

Definitive Thad Jones, Volume 2 ♫♫♫♫ (MusicMasters, 1990)

influences:

◀◀ Chick Webb, Gene Krupa, Jo Jones, Buddy Rich, Louis Bellson, Shelly Manne, Tiny Kahn, Max Roach

▶▶ Duffy Jackson, Butch Miles, Frank Capp, Dennis Mackrell, Jeff Hamilton, Peter Erskine

see also: *Thad Jones*

Bret Primack

Ramsey Lewis

Born Ramsey Emmanuel Lewis Jr., May 27, 1935, in Chicago, IL.

A classically trained musician, Ramsey Lewis is one of the most popular, albeit underrated, jazz pianists in history. He's recorded over 70 albums, 30 of which have made *Billboard* pop charts, and he has over a dozen hit singles to his credit. Lewis started studying piano at the age of four, became interested in jazz at 11, and later attended Chicago Musical College. While playing with the Clefs dance band, he met bassist Eldee Young and drummer Isaac "Red" Holt. After the Clefs disbanded in 1955, Lewis, Young, and Holt formed the original Ramsey Lewis Trio while Lewis was attending De Paul University. A straight-ahead jazz group with a bit of classical influence, the original Ramsey Lewis Trio recorded 17 albums between 1956 and 1965, including the gold *Sound of Christmas*, and were a very popular jazz trio, but their 18th release, *The In Crowd*, recorded in 1965, catapulted them into celebrity.

When they decided to record *The In Crowd* at the Bohemian Caverns, the trio wasn't sure the serious jazz audience would appreciate them covering a Top 40 hit, but they certainly didn't think it would change their lives. It did. *The In Crowd* hit number two and stayed on the pop album charts for 47 weeks. The title track, a Dobbie Gray hit, went to number five, earned gold status, and won a Grammy for best jazz instrumental recording by a small group. The trio's next album, *Hang On Ramsey*, generated two Top 30 hits, and reached number 11. While success gave the trio fame and a major pay increase, it also created internal conflicts and they soon disbanded. Young and Holt formed Young/Holt Unlimited, scored a Top 10 hit with "Soulful Strut," and recorded a few albums before disbanding in 1974.

The second incarnation of the Ramsey Lewis Trio included bassist Cleveland Eaton and drummer Maurice White. Their first effort produced the hit "Wade in the Water," and they usually recorded in larger settings, augmented by woodwinds, brass, and sometimes strings, and continued to have chart success, though their style became simpler. In 1970, White left to form Earth, Wind & Fire (EWF), and was replaced by Morris Jennings. During the early 1970s, Lewis was playing electric piano in scaled-down settings with a more rock-flavored approach than

Ramsey Lewis (© Jack Vartoogian)

his previous work. In 1974, he struck gold again with the million-seller *Sun Goddess*, a jazz-funk classic that featured members of Earth, Wind & Fire. His relationship with EWF continued for the next decade as members of the group made guest appearances on several of his subsequent albums. The R&B-influenced recordings featured Lewis on piano and electric keyboards and varied in quality. Of particular note during this period is his association with guitarist Henry Johnson, who in live performance has tremendous rapport with the pianist.

In the mid- to late 1980s, Lewis was harder to pin down. He released *Classic Encounter* with a symphony orchestra, and *We Meet Again* with Billy Taylor, an excellent traditional duet date. Lately, however, the majority of his releases have been aimed at smooth-jazz radio stations, often including material he recorded years before, with new arrangements that aren't all that insightful. Like his friend Dr. Taylor, Lewis is an ambassador of jazz, hosting the weekly *Ramsey Lewis's Sound & Style* on Black Entertainment Television, and the weekly syndicated

radio series *The Ramsey Lewis Show*. As a musician, Lewis can be brilliant. He is a talented arranger and a smooth player, but often just scratches the surface of his vast talent. Still, he's made some classic recordings and probably has a few left.

what to buy: *The In Crowd* &&&& (Argo, 1965/Chess, 1990) is the first Ramsey Lewis Trio recording to feature the group at their peak. And what a peak it was! The title track is, of course, a classic, but so is rest of the album. There are magic moments like "Love Theme from Spartacus," which moves from a classical to a hard bop interpretation and back without missing a beat, and a superb version of "Come Sunday." There's also great balance in the set with a mix of blues, ballads, and bop selections. Plus there's Eldee Young's "flamenco" bass solo. An indispensable part of any jazz library. The moment Johnny Graham's hot guitar riff opens up the title track it's obvious *Sun Goddess* &&&& (Columbia, 1974/1987, prod. Teo Macero, Ramsey Lewis) is something special. Using Maurice White, Charles Stepney, and members of Earth, Wind & Fire for support, Ramsey Lewis unleashed a tremendous jazz/funk effort with this recording. The grooves are hot, the melodies catchy, the soloing funky, and Lewis's jazz and blues roots shine throughout. Although it's a bit dated now, *Sun Goddess* epitomizes the best of the 1970s jazz/funk genre. Combining his jazz and pop sensibilities with James Mack's tasteful orchestration of the Philharmonia Orchestra, Ramsey Lewis hit one out of the park with *A Classic Encounter* 𝄞𝄞𝄞 (CBS Masterworks, 1988, prod. Ettore Stratta). The songs and orchestrations are mostly on the romantic side and could be relegated to background music because of their lush timbre, but to do so would ignore Lewis's great pop-jazz explorations, which rise far above the typical jazz soloist with symphony fare. For those who want to hear Lewis in a different setting, this album is a must. If anyone ever doubted Ramsey Lewis could still hold his own with top jazz players, his album *We Meet Again* 𝄞𝄞𝄞𝄞 (CBS Masterworks, 1989, prod. Ramsey Lewis, Gary Schultz) erased that doubt. Paired with Billy Taylor in a piano duet setting, the album features two old pros having a good time while providing each other necessary give-and-take to make this setting work. The performances are inspired and the pianists aren't afraid to take risks. This silences those who want to dismiss Lewis as nothing but a pop/jazz player. Or at least it should.

what to buy next: A compilation from three albums released during the late 1950s, *Consider the Source* 𝄞𝄞𝄞 (Argo 1956–1959/Chess 1995, prod. various) is not only an interesting documentation of the early Ramsey Lewis Trio, but it also contains excellent performances and creative arrangements. With the tremendous success of *The In Crowd* and *Sun Goddess*, it's easy to forget the first Ramsey Lewis Trio originally played straight-ahead jazz with some classical influence. Part of the collection on this compilation features the trio playing adventurous arrangements of jazz standards, popular favorites from show tunes to blues and R&B, and even Bizet's "Carmen" and Rimsky-Korsakov's "Song of India." *The Greatest Hits of Ramsey Lewis* 𝄞𝄞𝄞 (Argo/Cadet, 1961–1967/Chess, 1987, prod. various) is a compilation of mostly more pop-oriented material Lewis cut with his first two trios. There are some tasty morsels here, including the hits "Hang On Sloopy," "Wade in the Water," and "A Hard Day's Night," though it has a couple misfires as well. Along with *Consider the Source* and *The In Crowd*, this album shows Lewis's transition from a straight jazz player to a more pop-oriented one. Lewis's first collaboration with arranger/conductor/composer Charles Stepney, *Maiden Voyage (And More)* 𝄞𝄞𝄞 (Argo, 1968/GRP, 1994), is a love it or hate it release with tracks from the original album and four tracks from

Mother Nature's Son. Augmented by strings and voices, Lewis is the featured soloist, and his jams are solid. Stepney's arrangements might be labeled as "elevator music" by some because they are nice-sounding if not overly challenging works. But some of them swing, others are romantic, and this makes for some fun ear-candy. Call it a guilty pleasure. *Tequila Mockingbird* 𝄞𝄞𝄞 (Columbia, 1977/1987, prod. Larry Dunn) is very representative of Lewis's larger scale late 1970s to early 1980s material. It's also pretty funky.

what to avoid: Lewis recorded *Urban Knights* with a group billed as the Urban Knights that featured Grover Washington Jr., Victor Bailey, and Omar Hakim. It was a disappointing R&B/jazz effort that sounded like the artists were coasting, but it contained a couple of decent solos. On *Urban Knights II* 𝄞 (GRP, 1997), Lewis is accompanied by Gerald Albright, Jonathan Butler, Najee, and Sonny Emory, and it's a complete disappointment. There aren't even any decent solos to point out. If Lewis wants to play funk he can do better than this.

the rest:
Ramsey Lewis' Golden Hits (Newly Recorded, All-Time, Non-Stop) 𝄞𝄞𝄞
    (Columbia, 1973/1991)
Electric Collection (1973–80) 𝄞𝄞𝄞 (Columbia 1973–1980/ Legacy 1991)
(With Nancy Wilson) *The Two of Us* 𝄞𝄞𝄞 (Columbia, 1984)
Keys to the City 𝄞𝄞 (Columbia, 1987/1991)
Urban Renewal 𝄞𝄞 (Columbia, 1989)
Ivory Pyramid 𝄞𝄞𝄞 (GRP, 1992)
Sky Islands 𝄞𝄞𝄞 (GRP, 1993)
(With Urban Knights) *Urban Knights* 𝄞𝄞 (GRP, 1995)
Between the Keys 𝄞𝄞𝄞 (GRP, 1996)

worth searching for: By the time they recorded *Barefoot Sunday Blues* 𝄞𝄞𝄞 (Argo, 1962) the original trio had matured into an excellent ensemble. Their song selection was strong, mixing standards with more popular material. Like their sets from the same period, this covers a lot of territory in under 40 minutes. Who can forget the sensual woman moaning "Come on Baby" between nasty piano licks on the closer? In retrospect *Barefoot Sunday Blues* foreshadowed much of what the trio did on *The In Crowd*. The fourth collaboration between Ramsey Lewis and Charles Stepney, *The Piano Player* 𝄞𝄞𝄞 (Cadet, 1969), with some arrangements by Richard Evans, has yet to be reissued in the CD format, but it was their best. Only a couple of pieces push the envelope, with the rest being pretty safe, but everything works so well it's wrong to fault it and Lewis, the master of the grace note here, is interesting. It's also only one of two places where you can find Lewis playing Stepney's wonderful "Close Your Eyes and Remember." In the early 1980s Ramsey

Lewis concerts were all over the road, with pop/jazz selections, solid blues numbers, orchestrated pieces, the hits medley and guest vocalists all a part of the festivities. The live-recorded concert on *Live at the Savoy* 𝄞𝄞𝄞𝄞 (Columbia, 1982) has guest shots by Grover Washington Jr. and Phil Upchurch to add to its star power and it is an accurate snapshot of a Lewis concert from the period. This is the other place to get "Close Your Eyes and Remember."

influences:

⏮ John Lewis, Oscar Peterson, Bud Powell, Art Tatum, Erroll Garner, Ahmad Jamal

⏭ Les McCann, George Duke, Joe Sample

Paul MacArthur

Ottmar Liebert /Luna Negra

Born February 1, 1959, in Cologne, Germany.

Not a technical wizard on guitar, Ottmar Liebert has gained notoriety with his ability to create memorable melodies more sensual than flashy. In fact, most nylon-string purists scorn his hybrid, which he calls nouveau flamenco Spanish gypsy guitar with a contemporary groove. Throughout the '90s, Liebert's prowess as an instrumentalist has steadily improved. The vibrantly raw nature of his early recordings has given way to projects that are more polished and produced. Spending much of his childhood traveling throughout Europe with his family, Liebert was given his first guitar as a Christmas present when he was 11 and began classical training at age 12. At 18 he embarked on a series of musical excursions through Russia and Asia. During the late 1970s and early '80s his attempts at trying to make it big in various jazz-funk bands in Germany, and later in Boston, fell flat. Disillusioned by the East Coast music scene, Liebert headed for California in 1986 but never arrived. A stayover in Santa Fe to visit a friend left him charmed by the city's laid-back and richly artistic ambiance. Encouraged to play music for his own pleasure, Ottmar began performing in local restaurants and found great satisfaction communicating his music *mono y mono*. By 1988 the first incarnation of Luna Negra, a band with bassist Jon Gagan and percussionist Jeff Sussmann, had been born and Liebert's true musical journey began.

what to buy: *Nouveau Flamenco* 𝄞𝄞𝄞𝄞 (Higher Octave, 1990, prod. Ottmar Liebert, Randy Rand) was originally released as the limited-edition CD *Marita: Shadows and Storms*, which

Santa Fe artist Frank Howell planned to distribute along with his drawings. After making its way to West Coast radio stations, indie label Higher Octave Music remastered the tape and released it nationally under its current title. It became one of the first New Age releases to be certified gold in the United States and remained a best seller on *Billboard*'s New Age charts for over 260 weeks.

what to buy next: *Solo para Ti* 𝄞𝄞𝄞𝄞 (Epic, 1992, prod. Ottmar Liebert, Dominic Camardella) is Liebert's major-label debut. Mixed in with the normal fare are two stand-out collaborations with longtime hero Carlos Santana on "Reaching Out to You" and a faithful cover of "Samba Pa Ti" (found on Santana's 1970 classic, *Abraxas*).

the rest:
Poets and Angels 𝄞𝄞𝄞 (Higher Octave, 1990)
Borrasca 𝄞𝄞𝄞 (Higher Octave, 1991)
Hours between Night and Day 𝄞𝄞𝄞 (Epic, 1993)
Euphoria 𝄞𝄞𝄞 (Epic, 1995) (EP)
Viva! 𝄞𝄞𝄞 (Epic, 1995)
Opium 𝄞𝄞𝄞𝄞 (Epic, 1996)
Leaning into the Night 𝄞𝄞𝄞𝄞 (Sony Classical, 1997)

worth searching for: As explained above, *Marita: Shadows and Storms* 𝄞𝄞𝄞𝄞 (Frank Howell Gallery, 1989) is a rarity and hard to find, especially outside Santa Fe.

influences:

⏮ Paco De Lucia, Carlos Santana, Andres Segovia

⏭ Esteban, Strunz & Farah, Peter White

Ralph Burnett

Dave Liebman

Born September 4, 1946, in New York, NY.

A virtuoso on the soprano sax and an innovative composer, Dave Liebman exhibits an attachment to jazz that has always been something more than musical. The spirit behind music and the community of musicians and listeners all figure into his life in jazz. Born in Brooklyn, Liebman grew up playing a variety of instruments and studied with legendary saxophone teacher Joe Allard, as well as with Lennie Tristano and Charles Lloyd. Just after graduating from NYU with a degree in American history, he helped to found Free Life Communication, one of the first jazz musicians' co-operatives. In 1970 he joined Ten Wheel Drive, one of the early jazz/rock fusion groups, and in 1972 joined Elvin Jones. A year later his apprenticeship period reached its zenith when Miles Davis invited him to join his group. Liebman stayed with Davis for almost two years, recording "Dark Magus" and "On the Corner." On his own, Liebman has led groups of varying styles. His first group, which he formed with Bob Moses in 1970, was called Open Sky Trio. In 1973, together with pianist Richard Beirach, he formed Lookout Farm, which toured the world and garnered first place in *Down Beat* magazine's 1976 International Critic's Poll in the category Group Most Deserving of Wider Recognition. In 1981, together with Beirach, George Mraz, and Al Foster, he formed Quest, which reached its peak between 1984 and 1991 after the addition of bassist Ron McClure and drummer Billy Hart. In 1991 Liebman put together his current ensemble, the David Liebman Group. Though he began his career playing tenor at the end of the 1970s, he decided to dedicate himself exclusively to the soprano sax. His other major commitment has been in jazz education. In 1989 he created the International Association of Schools of Jazz, an organization with members in 40 different countries dedicated to connecting jazz teachers to students. But Liebman's first love remains the music itself. He has recorded nearly 75 CDs and albums under his own leadership and co-leadership, and has been a featured sideman on nearly 150 more. After recording CDs on many different labels, mostly European, in 1996 he signed an exclusive recording agreement with New York's Arkadia Jazz, signaling his intention to focus his music-making energies. His first release, *New Vista*, was followed by his recording *John Coltrane's Meditation Suite*, and, in early 1998, *The Elements: Water— Giver of Life*, a collaboration with Pat Metheny. Like his artistic mentor, John Coltrane, Liebman is constantly searching, and his music reflects his never-ending quest. He has recorded for many import labels, including Red, Evidence, Owl, and Soul Note.

what to buy: Ever since "Desafinado," jazz musicians have loved playing Brazilian music. In the hands of a player whose genuine virtuosity and command of his instrument are extraordinary, the music has still has a powerful pull, as is evident on *New Vista* 🎵🎵🎵🎵 (Arkadia Jazz, 1997, prod. Dave Liebman, Bob Karcy). Recorded with his working band, Liebman sounds unusually comfortable and relaxed, as his fluid soprano lines ripple, pulsate, and wiggle through the shifting grooves. With *New Vista*, he successfully fuses Latin modalities with his unique expressionism and the results should appeal to a wide audience. With his working group, including pianist Phil Markowitz, Liebman journeys productively through six originals and two standards on *Voyage* 🎵🎵🎵🎵 (Evidence, 1996, prod. Dave Liebman). A glance at the standards confirms their collective sense of ad-

venture: Herbie Hancock's "Maiden Voyage" is daringly re-harmonized, keeping the listener charmed but off-balance. "Dancing in the Dark," sensuously lyrical on Liebman's soprano, has a corrective undercurrent of thoughtfulness in Markowitz's piano solo. Among the originals, the highlights include "Yildiz," with some exotic percussion, the funky, loose "Cut," and a freejazz, Dachau-visit memoir, "The Gravel and the Bird." After 15 years of focusing on the soprano sax, Liebman has come back to the tenor, the horn that made his reputation with Elvin Jones in the early 1970s. On *Return of the Tenor* 🎵🎵🎵🎵 (Doubletime, 1996, prod. Dave Liebman), he shows he's no longer a Coltrane clone but an individual now, and his expansive, breathy tenor sound, particularly in the low register, is appealing. Although this is essentially a blowing session, Liebman and his five-year-old quintet break things down into quartets and trios and approach standards from anything but a "standard" viewpoint. Melodies are stated intermittently ("All the Things"), or played in two or more keys ("Secret Love"), but always with care and precision, as with "Yesterdays," and "Lover Man." Unbound by convention, Liebman has no qualms about sidestepping harmonic structures and playing beautiful melodies along with those that bristle with dissonance. Davis would have dug the homage *Miles Away* 🎵🎵🎵🎵 (Owl/Blue Note, 1995, prod. Dave Liebman) from his early 1970s sideman. Liebman took 11 tunes associated with the trumpeter and playfully sequenced them in reverse chronological order, managing to inspect all of the stylistic phases that Davis explored in his long career—from the late 1940s' "Birth of the Cool" through the 1980s fusion link. Liebman's unusually flexible working group successfully straddles both acoustic and electric music. Highlights include "In a Silent Way," which floats on Phil Markowitz's keyboards; Wayne Shorter's "Fall," which is slow and sultry; an extra-funky "All Blues"; and "Milestones," which flails furiously. A fitting close is Liebman's spoken tribute: "Thanks, Miles, for all the great music for all those years. We all miss you."

what to buy next: From the tumultuous group interplay of "Little Peanut" and the magical gentleness of "Innocence," to the cacophonous chaos of "Tomato Face," it's obvious from the selections on *Songs for My Daughter* 🎵🎵🎵🎵 (Soul Note, 1995, prod. Dave Liebman) that Liebman knows the joy and pain of parenthood. *Homage to Coltrane* 🎵🎵🎵🎵 (Owl/Blue Note, 1987, prod. Dave Liebman), a collection of rarely played Coltrane compositions, reveals both how highly Liebman values spontaneity and risk and the extent of his continued passion for the music of saxophonist Coltrane. Acoustic and electric groups split the music, which reflects the wide variety of textures and moods Coltrane was capable of creating, from the primal screams of "Untitled Original," to the serenely beautiful "Dear Lord." *Classic Ballads* ♫♫♫♫ (Candid, 1991, prod. Dave Liebman, Alan Bates) finds Liebman's soprano at front and center on eight standards in a cozy sax, guitar (Vic Juris), and bass (Steve Gillmore) setting. Although he has a justified reputation for his sense of adventure, this CD offers the straight-ahead, sensitive side of Liebman on such touchstones as "On Green Dolphin Street," "Stella by Starlight," and "My Funny Valentine." *In the Same Breath* ♫♫♫ (CMP, 1995, prod. Kurt Renker, Walter Quintus), a trio date recorded in Germany, features Liebman's soprano, wooden flute, and occasional piano alongside the work of guitarists Mick Goodrick and Wolfgang Muthspiel. Goodrick takes most of the solo guitar space, but under Liebman's lead both guitarists offer lively comping, counter melodies, ostinatos, and tasty walking lines.

worth searching for: *West Side Story Today* ♫♫♫♫ (Owl/Blue Note, 1990, prod. Dave Liebman) is a collaboration with keyboardist Gil Goldstein that stretches the music of Leonard Bernstein in strange and adventurous ways. *A Tribute to John Coltrane* ♫♫♫♫ (Columbia/Blue Note, 1987, prod. Hiroshi Tanamaki), an energetic soprano sax jam with Liebman and Shorter, was recorded live at Japan's Under the Sky Festival, and serves as an awesome homage to the man who popularized the soprano. There's enough energy here to warm a cold apartment on a frigid winter's day.

influences:

◀◀ John Coltrane, Miles Davis, Elvin Jones, Charles Lloyd, Lennie Tristano

▶▶ Michael Brecker, Bob Mintzer, Steve Grossman, Steve Lacy, Wayne Shorter

Bret Primack

Kirk Lightsey

Born February 15, 1937, in Detroit, MI.

Kirk Lightsey was born in one of the American hotbeds of bop pianism (Detroit), and it is no surprise that the style forms a substantial portion of his musical persona. It was there that he learned piano at an early age before spending some time in his high school band as a clarinet player. After a stint in the Army, Lightsey made a career of accompanying singers such as Ernestine Anderson, Damita Jo, and O.C. Smith before finally getting the chance to record with Sonny Stitt in 1965. Shortly after that, the pianist joined Chet Baker's band, recording a se-

ries of well-received albums with the trumpeter/singer. Lightsey's next marquee setting was with saxophonist Dexter Gordon, and he has also worked and recorded with a wide variety of other players, including Don Cherry, Jimmy Raney, Clifford Jordan, and James Moody. Living in Europe since the 1980s, Lightsey, in addition to leading his own groups and performing solo recitals, is also an important cog in jazz supergroups the Leaders and Roots.

what to buy: Solo piano recitals have always been a test of a musician's abilities, showing whether a pianist's ideas and technique can sustain interest. Lightsey is more than equal to the task on *Lightsey Live* ♫♫♫♫ (SunnySide, 1986, prod. Sam Zappas), on which he runs through a program that includes finger-burners like Monk's "Trinkle Tinkle" alongside elegant standards like "Spring Is Here" and "Just One of Those Things." What impresses most is the way Lightsey goes for substance instead of flash in his playing, digging deep into the heart of the music instead of skittling around the keyboard and trying to impress listeners with his facility. The trio date *Goodbye Mr. Evans* ♫♫♫♫ (Evidence, 1996, prod. T.E.M.P. Musicproduction) sets Lightsey in the company of drummer Famoudou Don Moye and bassist Tibor Elekes, both of whom he has worked with before. Despite the title of the album, this is not a Bill Evans tribute; rather, it reflects the inclusion of the Phil Woods tune by that name that closes out the release. Bassist Elekes contributes an interesting jazz arrangement of Chopin melodies to go along with Lightsey's own classic "Habiba" and a handful of other fine jazz standards, including a medley that meshes Eddie Harris with Wayne Shorter, John Coltrane, and the old pop chestnut "Temptation" by Arthur Freed and Herb Brown.

what to buy next: The solo piano album *Lightsey 1* ♫♫♫♫ (SunnySide, 1983, prod. Francois Zalacain) contains material that has informed Lightsey's concerts for well over a decade. "Habiba" is a perpetual Lightsey vehicle (just like "Nascimento" is for Barry Harris) and "Fee Fi Fo Fum" and "Trinkle Tinkle" showed up on his live disc when released a few years later. Not quite as scintillating as the live album, this disc still serves as an impressive achievement by a pianist who deserves to be heard by more people. Lightsey in a group setting is almost too democratic, especially when there is another potential lead instrument in the ensemble. Luckily, on *Everything Is Changed* ♫♫♫ (SunnySide, 1987, prod. Francois Zalacain) trumpeter Jerry Gonzalez is worth the extra space, especially in "Blues on the Corner." Bassist Santi Debriano's "Nandi" is another highlight, specifically for the rare use of a French horn (ably played by Jerry Routch) within a jazz context.

the rest:
Everything Happens to Me 🎵🎵🎵 (Timeless, 1983)
Isotope 🎵🎵🎵🎵 (Criss Cross, 1983)
Lightsey 2 🎵🎵🎵🎵 (SunnySide, 1985)
(With Harold Danko) *Shorter by Two* 🎵🎵🎵🎵 (SunnySide, 1985)
Everything Is Changed 🎵🎵🎵 (SunnySide, 1986)
Kirk 'n Marcus 🎵🎵🎵🎵 (Criss Cross, 1987)
(With the Leaders Trio) *Heaven Dance* 🎵🎵🎵🎵 (SunnySide, 1988)
Temptation 🎵🎵🎵 (Timeless, 1991)
From Kirk to Nat 🎵🎵🎵🎵 (Criss Cross, 1991)
First Affairs 🎵🎵🎵 (Lime Tree, 1993)

worth searching for: The collaborative group Roots is based around the four horns of Arthur Blythe, Nathan Davis, Chico Freeman, and Benny Golson, but on the live album *Saying Something* 🎵🎵🎵🎵 (In + Out, 1995, prod. Mike Hennessey) pianist Lightsey acquits himself well. "Heaven Dance," which he wrote, is one of the release's highlights, and his sensitive accompaniment throughout is a delight.

influences:

◀◀ Tommy Flanagan, Barry Harris

▶▶ Kenny Kirkland, Laurent de Wilde

see also: *The Leaders*

Garaud MacTaggart

Abbey Lincoln
Born Anna Marie Wooldridge, August 6, 1930, in Chicago, IL.

Abbey Lincoln's career breaks rather neatly into four phases: early releases that hint at what this supper-club singer with sass aplenty would become; experimentation prodded by and often in collaboration with her then-husband Max Roach and others (don't miss her work on Roach's *We Insist! Freedom Now Suite*); a couple of European releases, following a long hiatus, that presaged Lincoln's return as a mature singer-songwriter; and finally, her late flowering on the Verve label with a half-dozen (so far) recordings, often organized around a concept of instrumentation or theme. Lincoln has a modest vocal range but more than compensates with a keen appreciation of how to sculpt nuance with shifting accents and rhythmic delivery as with choice of notes. All the while she seems deceptively conversational, which is to say that she's absorbed much from Billie Holiday and Carmen McRae. And in selecting songs and writing her own, Lin-

Abbey Lincoln (© Nancy Ann Lee)

ABBEY LINCOLN

song "Up Jumped Spring"
album *You Gotta Pay the Band*
(Verve, 1991)

instrument Vocals

Monster Solo

coln delights in delving into less typical topics, sometimes using the stage as a sort of swinging bully pulpit from which to preach perseverance, equality, and pride while decrying a world that seems to be going to hell. During a 1975 trip to Africa, the names Aminata and Moseka were conferred upon her, leading her to also call herself Aminata Moseka. Between the second and third phases of her career, Lincoln worked as an actress.

what to buy: *You Gotta Pay the Band* 🎵🎵🎵🎵 (Verve, 1991, prod. Jean-Philippe Allard) puts Lincoln in all-star company, including pianist Hank Jones and a late-great performance by saxophonist Stan Getz, who's particularly effective on "I'm in Love," giving the opening riff a few obligatos that play off Lincoln's vocals and rendering a rousing solo. *Straight Ahead* 🎵🎵🎵🎵 (Candid, 1961/1988, prod. Nat Hentoff) is Lincoln hitting her somewhat strident 1960's stride with bandmates including Roach, Coleman Hawkins, and Eric Dolphy. She gives "Blue Monk" a set of her own lyrics, performs Billie Holiday's rarely heard "Left Alone," and sings lyrics by poets Langston Hughes and Paul Lawrence Dunbar.

what to buy next: *Devil's Got Your Tongue* ♫♫♫♫ (Verve, 1993, prod. Jean-Philippe Allard) is Lincoln's big-production recording, featuring guests from the Staple Singers to percussionist Babatunde Olatunji without losing bearings. *When There Is Love* ♫♫♫♫ (Verve, 1994, prod. Jean-Philippe Allard), with just Lincoln and sublime pianist Hank Jones, finds Lincoln at her most intimate.

best of the rest:

Affair ♫♫♫ (Capitol, 1956/Blue Note, 1993)
That's Him ♫♫♫♫ (Riverside, 1958/OJC, 1991)
Abbey Is Blue ♫♫♫♫ (Riverside, 1959/OJC, 1991)
Talking to the Sun ♫♫♫♫ (Enja, 1983/1993)
Abbey Sings Billie, Volume 1 ♫♫♫ (Enja, 1992)
Abbey Sings Billie, Volume 2 ♫♫♫ (Enja, 1992)
A Turtle's Dream ♫♫♫♫♫ (Verve, 1995)
Who Used to Dance ♫♫♫♫ (Verve, 1997)

influences:

◀◀ Carmen McRae, Billie Holiday, Thelonious Monk, Max Roach

▶▶ Jeanne Lee

W. Kim Heron

Lincoln Center Jazz Orchestra
Formed 1987.

David Berger, conductor; Wynton Marsalis, trumpet, artistic director; Umar Sharif, trumpet; Lew Soloff, trumpet; Marcus Belgrave, trumpet/flugelhorn; Art Baron, trombone; Wycliffe Gordon, trombone; Britt Woodman, trombone; Bill Easley, clarinet, tenor saxophone; Norris Turney, alto saxophone; Joe Temperley, baritone saxophone; Frank Wess, alto saxophone; Todd Williams, tenor saxophone; Sir Roland Hanna, piano; Reginald Veal, bass; Kenny Washington, drums, timpani; Milt Grayson, vocals.

Formed in 1987 for *Classical Jazz,* the summer concert series of New York City's Lincoln Center for the Performing Arts, the Lincoln Center Jazz Orchestra (LCJO) continues to include several generations of the world's foremost musicians who are dedicated to developing a performance repertory of historic compositions and newly commissioned works for big band. Band personnel and conductors vary on their live and recorded performances. The LCJO repertoire includes music of historic jazz composers such as Duke Ellington, Jelly Roll Morton, Thelonious Monk, Benny Carter, Count Basie, Bennie Moten, Mary Lou Williams, Dizzy Gillespie, Charles Mingus, Jay McShann, and numerous others. In 1991, the Lincoln Center formed the Jazz at Lincoln Center department, which now features concerts

and an array of educational programs to teach adults and children about jazz and its relationship to other art forms. The LCJO first toured in 1992, traveling to 30 cities throughout the United States with a comprehensive Ellington program that showcased the composer's works from the mid-1920s through the early 1970s. During the tour, artistic director Wynton Marsalis led workshops at schools and universities and post-concert programs in many cities. That same year, the LCJO released its debut recording, *Portraits of Ellington*, which reached #4 on *Billboard* charts and was also hailed in Europe and Japan. Overseas tours followed in 1993 and the LCJO again toured 30 U.S. cities during the winter of 1994, then toured during that summer in addition to appearing on "Live from Lincoln Center" with a special nationwide telecast. The LCJO released its second and third recordings in 1994. The LCJO continues to tour into the late 1990s, but has not released any albums since their third CD. For current touring schedule and other information, Jazz at Lincoln Center has its own website at http://www.jazzatlincoln center.org.

what to buy: Best among the LCJO recordings, their third album, *They Came to Swing* ♫♫♫♫ (Columbia, 1994, prod. Jazz at Lincoln Center), features works by Ellington ("Black and Tan Fantasy," "Boy Meets Horn," "Tattooed Bride"), Strayhorn ("Take the 'A' Train"), Thelonious Monk ("Light Blue,"), Wynton Marsalis ("Express Crossing," "Back to Basics"), and others crafted from actual transcriptions or freshly charted. Various personnel are featured on this compilation from different touring performances recorded at halls in New York, New Jersey, Ohio, Michigan, and Iowa between 1992 and 1994. The soloists excel, and the band swings on zestful arrangements conducted by David Berger, Jon Faddis, Wynton Marsalis, and Robert Sadin.

what to buy next: The second recording for the Lincoln Center Jazz Orchestra, *The Fire of the Fundamentals* ♫♫♫♫ (Columbia, 1994, prod. Jazz at Lincoln Center) features the music of Jelly Roll Morton, Thelonious Monk, John Coltrane, Billy Strayhorn, and Miles Davis. The LCJO takes a trip into jazz history (for which they have been both criticized and commended). The live recording, made during 1992–93 at various Jazz at Lincoln Center performances, carries the spark-ignited energy that the debut LCJO album lacked. Among the soloists featured are trumpeter Wynton Marsalis, saxophonists Charles McPherson and Frank Wess, pianists Marcus Roberts and Kenny Barron, vocalists Milt Grayson and Betty Carter, and others. Classic tunes include Morton's "Jungle Blues," Charlie Parker's "Hootie Blues," Miles Davis's "Flamenco Sketches," and more.

the rest:

Portraits by Ellington ♫♫♫ (Columbia, 1992)

influences:

◄◄ Duke Ellington, Jelly Roll Morton, Thelonious Monk, John Coltrane, Billy Strayhorn, Miles Davis, Benny Carter, Count Basie, Bennie Moten, Mary Lou Williams, Dizzy Gillespie, Charles Mingus, Jay McShann

Nancy Ann Lee

Liquid Soul

See: Mars Williams

Melba Liston

Born January 13, 1926, in Kansas City, MO.

Trombonist Melba Liston was virtually the only female brass player to work in the leading big bands of the 1940s and 1950s, but she is best known as an arranger whose longtime relationship with pianist/composer Randy Weston is one of the most profound composer/arranger collaborations in modern jazz. An excellent section musician with a beautiful, burnished tone, Liston was a capable improvisor, but rarely soloed on albums or performances except for ballads.

Born in Kansas City, Liston moved in 1937 with her family to Los Angeles, where she hooked up with music teacher Alma Hightower, who led a neighborhood youth band, and later studied with the legendary Jefferson High music teacher Sam Browne. A professional musician before she graduated, Liston began playing for the Lincoln Theater pit band led by Bardu Ali. Trumpeter Gerald Wilson recruited Liston for his first big band and she toured with him from 1944–1947 and later, with Wilson, joined the Basie band (1948–49), then went on an ill-fated tour with Billie Holiday. Dizzy Gillespie hired Liston for his short-lived 1950 bebop band, and called her again for his great "State Department" band, and she toured the world with him from 1956–57. She later toured with the Quincy Jones band (1959–61) until it broke up in Paris.

A busy session musician in the 1950s and 1960s, Liston recorded with Clark Terry, Freddie Hubbard, Cannonball Adderley, Eddie "Lockjaw" Davis, Dinah Washington, Sarah Vaughan, Betty Carter, Milt Jackson, Art Blakey, J. J. Johnson, Billie Holiday, and Budd Johnson, among others. As a freelance writer she arranged albums for Elvin Jones, Johnny Griffin, Dakota Staton, Milt Jackson, Billy Eckstine, Gloria Lynne, and Junior Mance. But it's her 40-year collaboration with Randy Weston that produced a series of classic albums such as *Little Niles*

and *Open House at the Five Spot with Coleman Hawkins and Kenny Dorham*, which have yet to be reissued on CD. In the late 1960s and 1970s, Liston worked as a staff arranger at Motown, writing and conducting for Marvin Gaye, Diana Ross, and her old friend Billy Eckstine. She spent much of the 1970s teaching music in Jamaica, founding the Popular Music Studies program at the University of the West Indies. Liston triumphantly returned to the States in 1979, when she appeared at the Kansas City Women's Jazz Festival, and soon began touring with her own band. A stroke in 1985 forced Liston give up the trombone, but after years of convalescence she began writing again with the aid of a computer. Since the early 1990s, Liston and Weston have reunited for a series of excellent albums. In recent years she has also written for Abbey Lincoln, Ronnie Mathews, and T.S. Monk.

worth searching for: The only album Liston ever made under her own name, *Melba and Her Bones* ♫♫♫ (Metrojazz, 1959, prod. Leonard Feather) is a collector's item that has never been reissued. The four-trombones-with-rhythm-section arrangements (by Liston and Slide Hampton) work surprisingly well. To hear Liston's work as arranger, check out the album that reunited Liston and Weston after an almost two-decade hiatus, *The Spirits of Our Ancestors* ♫♫♫♫ (Antilles, 1992, prod. Randy Weston, Brian Bacchus, Jean-Philippe Allard). A two-disc set, it features a powerful big band and special guests Pharoah Sanders and Dizzy Gillespie. The instrumentation and compositions reflect Weston's long interest in African music and Liston's potent arrangements are full of fascinating voicings and intricate detail. *Volcano Blues* ♫♫♫♫ (Antilles, 1993, prod. Randy Weston, Brian Bacchus, Jean-Philippe Allard) is a thrilling session with a generation-bridging large band featuring Wallace Roney (trumpet), Benny Powell (trombone), Teddy Edwards (tenor sax), and Hamiet Bluiett (baritone sax). The tunes and arrangements are often tight and focused, with finely textured ensemble passages, though one of the highlights is Edwards's wailing solo on "Mystery of Love" accompanied by just Weston and bassist Jamil Nasser. Tenor saxophonist Johnny Griffin's tribute to Billie Holiday, *White Gardenia* ♫♫♫♫ (Riverside,1961/OJC, 1995, prod. Orrin Keepnews) features six gorgeous arrangements by Liston and four by Norman Simmons. None of the tracks are more than five minutes, and Liston's arrangements are lush and sensitive without being sentimental. Liston's charts are especially effective on "Left Alone" and "God Bless the Child." Griffin is in top form, but Nat Adderley, Clark Terry, and Barry Harris also take fine solos. A reissue combining two amazing Randy Weston albums from the early

1960s, *Uhuru Africa/Highlife* 🎵🎵🎵🎵 (Roulette, 1960, prod. Teddy Reig/Roulette, 1963, prod. Jack Lewis/Combined CD reissue, 1997) was inspired by the decolonization of African countries. *Uhuru Africa* features a huge band, and Liston's arrangements keep things powerfully swinging. *Highlife* is a more traditional 12-piece session, though Julius Watkins's French horn and Aaron Bell's tuba gives Liston a number of unusual orchestral colors. Weston composed almost all the material on both sessions. A classic session with an all-star band and ingenious Liston arrangements, *Tanjah* 🎵🎵🎵🎵 (Verve, 1973/Polydor, 1995, prod. Randy Weston) was the last Liston/Weston project for almost 20 years. Liston's arrangements draw heavily on Weston's interest in African music, but keeps the music effectively organized and swinging. Like Thelonious Monk, Weston revisits his compositions, reinterpreting them again and again, and on *Earth Birth* 🎵🎵🎵🎵 (Verve, 1997, prod. Jean-Philippe Allard) Liston discovers new worlds in his music with her string arrangements. With bassist Christian McBride and drummer extraordinaire Billy Higgins accompanying Weston, Liston wraps Weston's huge piano sound with lithe string charts, remaking such classic tunes as "Little Niles," "Hi-Fly" and "Babe's Blues."

influences:

◀◀ Tadd Dameron, Billy Strayhorn, Duke Ellington, Dizzy Gillespie

Andrew Gilbert

Booker Little

Born April 2, 1938, in Memphis, TN. Died October 5, 1961, New York, NY.

Just as Booker Little's own voice on trumpet was beginning to emerge, his life was over. Dead from uremia at age 23, Little never had the chance to continue what appeared to be a career of great promise. Little's modest recorded legacy documents a trumpeter who was beginning to move out from under the shadow of Clifford Brown into a more individualized conception of self-expression. Little's talent began to emerge during his stint with Max Roach, which began in 1958. The trumpeter spent a year with the drummer, freelanced in New York in 1959, then returned to Roach in 1960. In 1961, Little co-led a quintet with another musician whose career ended too soon, saxophonist Eric Dolphy; they garnered attention during a celebrated stay at the Five Spot in New York City.

what to buy: The must-have Little record is *Out Front* 🎵🎵🎵🎵 (Candid, 1961, prod. Nat Hentoff), which features Dolphy, Roach and trombonist Julian Priester. Little, a warm, melodic player, shared with his major influence, Clifford Brown, a tone

of bell-like clarity and a highly developed melodic sense. Yet, while Brown's playing had a certain sunny optimism, Little, who made judicious use of dissonance, emitted a sound that reflected a melancholy quality, particularly felt on *Out Front* in the work by soloists and in Little's well-structured compositions. There is a sense of symmetry to this date, a sense of controlled experimentation. The musicians were striving for something new but didn't dispense with form for a collection of aimless free blowing that too frequently passed as "cutting edge."

what to buy next: Although it loses some points for incorrect song information and somewhat shaky fidelity, *Booker Little and Friend* 🎵🎵🎵 (Bethlehem, 1961, prod. Teddy Charles) still allows Little's bittersweet lyricism to shine through. (This date has also been issued in the past as *Victory and Sorrow*.) With George Coleman on tenor, the album is more boppish than *Out Front*, and Little's attack is more direct on brisk originals such as "Forward Flight" and "Victory and Sorrow." A straightforward reading of "If I Should Lose You" is especially pretty. Little and Coleman, who grew up together in Memphis, both joined the Max Roach band in 1958. They are featured on *Booker Little 4 and Max Roach* 🎵🎵🎵 (Blue Note, 1958, prod. Tom Wilson). Brownie's influence on Little's playing is more pronounced on this session, especially on swingers like "Milestones" and on a gorgeous rendition of "Moonlight Becomes You." Rounding out the CD are two jam session–type tracks, featuring a number of the Memphis crowd, including Coleman, alto player Frank Strozier, and the Newborn brothers—pianist Phineas and guitarist Calvin.

worth searching for: Although it has been issued by a few different labels under a few different titles, if you see *Booker Little in New York* 🎵🎵🎵🎵 (Jazzview, 1961), buy it. Little's second session as leader is a quartet date with yet another musician who died young, bass virtuoso Scott LaFaro. "Bee Tee's Minor Plea" demonstrates why LaFaro's reputation is well deserved, not only due to his solo but also his supporting lines. The clear resonance of Little's trumpet is evident on "Minor Sweet." With Roy Haynes behind the kit, only favorable comparisons to the Brown-Roach quintet can be drawn on a burning take of Little's "The Grand Valse." To get a complete picture of Little's playing, also seek out the sessions with Max Roach as leader and the more essential albums made under Eric Dolphy's name, including *Far Cry* 🎵🎵🎵🎵 (OJC, 1960, prod Esmond Edwards), and three recordings made at the Five Spot: *At the Five Spot, Volume 1* 🎵🎵🎵🎵 (OJC, 1961, prod. Esmond Edwards), *At the Five Spot, Volume 2* 🎵🎵🎵 (OJC, 1961, prod. Esmond Edwards), and *At the Five Spot, Volume 3* (OJC, 1961, prod. Esmond Edwards). In terms of historical significance, it overstates the case to draw too close a comparison between the Dolphy-Little collaborations and the seminal mid-1940s recordings of Parker and Gillespie, but there are some similarities. Those groundbreaking Bird and Dizzy sessions featured two young musicians with a telepathic sense of interplay searching for new ways to extend the language of jazz. So, too, do the Dolphy-Little recordings, especially the *Five Spot* sessions, which generate an air of excitement and the unexpected.

influences:

◀◀ Clifford Brown

Dan Polletta

Charles Lloyd

Born March 15, 1938, in Memphis, TN.

During a period when John Coltrane and other proponents of the avant garde were alienating some listeners, saxophonist and composer Charles Lloyd was leading a band of soon-to-be stars (i.e., Keith Jarrett and Jack DeJohnette), and performing in rock venues such as the Fillmore. During the last half of the 1960s, Lloyd's group and their music, a wonderfully melodic mix of rock and jazz elements, became eminently popular with not only the jazz cognoscenti, but also the crowd that supported such acts as Jefferson Airplane and Bob Dylan. Following local work in his native Memphis and a subsequent move to Los Angeles that found him working with Gerald Wilson, Lloyd first made a name for himself as a member of Chico Hamilton's distinctive group. Listening to any of the group's Columbia or Impulse! albums of the time reveals that Lloyd was deeply influenced by John Coltrane, yet his searing "cry" was already decidedly his own. Then in 1965 he formed his own ensemble and embarked on a very rigorous four-year journey that included six tours of Europe, a string of hit albums for Atlantic, and an historic appearance at the 1967 Tallinn Jazz Festival in Russia (a first for any American jazz group!). Quiet by comparison, the 1970s had Lloyd engaged in non-musical pursuits. It wasn't until the mid-1980s that he returned to music on a full-time basis. In 1989 he formed a new quartet and signed with ECM Records, launching one of the most highly-touted comebacks in recent memory. In fact, the "chamber jazz" sensibilities of the label perfectly suit Lloyd's musical talents. His deeply emotional tenor saxophone playing is marked by a distinct softness, with a hint of melancholia and yearning, while his flute work is full-bodied and rich. As he continues to strive for new avenues to explore, Lloyd remains one of jazz music's true originals.

what to buy: *Forest Flower* ✍✍✍✍ (Atlantic, 1967/Rhino, 1995, prod. George Avakian) documents Lloyd's historic 1966 performance at the Monterey Jazz Festival. Keith Jarrett and Jack DeJohnette are on board, and this CD reissue also includes the enchanting 1996 *Soundtrack* album.

what to buy next: *A Night in Copenhagen* ✍✍✍ (Blue Note, 1983, prod. Charles Lloyd, Michael Cuscuna) is one of Lloyd's comeback discs from the early 1980s and proves that he lost little of his creative powers and technique while he was off pursuing transcendental meditation in the 1970s. *All My Relations* ✍✍✍✍ (ECM, 1995, prod. Manfred Eicher) still ranks as Lloyd's finest of his recent ECM projects. Working with pianist Bobo Stenson, bassist Anders Jormin, and drummer Billy Hart, he provides some majestic tenor work on several spirited romps and pulls out his flute and Chinese oboe for a few exotic pieces.

the rest:

Fish Out of Water ✍✍✍ (ECM, 1989)
Notes from Big Sur ✍✍✍✍ (ECM, 1991)
The Call ✍✍✍✍ (ECM, 1993)
Acoustic Masters 1 ✍✍✍✍ (Atlantic, 1993)
Canto ✍✍✍ (ECM, 1997)

worth searching for: *Of Course, of Course* ✍✍✍✍ (Columbia, 1965, prod. George Avakian, John Simon) was one of three dates that Lloyd did for Columbia, all of which have yet to be reissued on CD. With Gabor Szabo on guitar and Miles Davis rhythm-mates Ron Carter and Tony Williams, Lloyd demonstrates some of his best early work. *Charles Lloyd in the Soviet Union* ✍✍✍✍ (Atlantic, 1967, prod. George Avakian) documents the Lloyd quartet's Russian concert in 1967. Highlights include a lengthy version of "Sweet Georgia Bright," and Keith Jarrett's positively rhapsodic "Days and Nights Waiting." This one is long overdue for CD reissue.

influences:

◀◀ John Coltrane

Chris Hovan

Joe Locke

Born March 18, 1959, in Palo Alto, CA.

One of the most exciting vibraphonists of his generation, Joe Locke is also a fine arranger who has developed a stimulating group concept for his instrument. Having worked in a wide variety of contexts, from mainstream jazz settings to more edgy situations, Locke has incorporated far-flung influences in his explorations of film-related themes. Strongly influenced by saxophone lines, he often plays long, flowing, harmonically open passages, while his rich, bell-like tone is highly effective on ballads. Raised in Rochester, New York, Locke started playing piano and drums at age eight and vibraphone at 13. As a teenager, he participated in the Eastman School of Music's preparatory department and studied privately with bassist Steve Davis and pianists Phil Markowitz and Bill Dobbins. Right out of high school, he went on the road with Davis and Spider Martin, and was soon recording with saxophonist Pepper Adams and drummer Billy Hart and working alongside saxophonists Sal Nistico and Joe Romano. He made the move to New York in 1981 and has worked and recorded with a wide variety of musicians, from Kenny Barron, Walter Davis Jr., and Eddie Henderson to Marvin "Smitty" Smith, Bob Moses, and Byard Lancaster. He has also worked with Jerry Gonzalez's Fort Apache Band and the Mingus Big Band, participating in the recording and tour of *Epitaph*. Locke has recorded a number of excellent albums for SteepleChase, including a brilliant duo session with Kenny Barron, *Longing*, and contributed four strong arrangements to the Milestone all-star Miles Davis tribute album *Dream Session*.

what's available: A Henry Mancini tribute like you've never heard, Joe Locke's *Moment to Moment* 🎵🎵🎵🎵 (Milestone, 1996, prod. Todd Barkan, Mikoto Kamata) is a gorgeous album featuring the lush but streamlined sound of his quartet, with Billy Childs (piano), Eddie Gomez (bass), and Gene Jackson (drums). Covering both standards ("Moon River" and "The Days of Wine and Roses") and lesser-known tunes ("Loss of Love" and "Whistling Away the Dark," featuring a beautiful arco solo by Gomez), Locke hews closely to Mancini's melodies while making them sound fresh and new. *Sound Tracks* 🎵🎵🎵🎵 (Milestone, 1997, prod. Todd Barkan, Mikoto Kamata) continues Locke's exploration of film music, as he turns nine movie themes into jazz vehicles. A couple, David Raskin's "Laura" and Johnny Mandel's "The Shadow of Your Smile," are longtime favorites of jazz musicians, but most are unusual, yet highly effective themes, such as "The English Patient," "Maturity" from *Cinema Paradiso*, and the album's most haunting track, "Tara's Theme" from *Gone with the Wind*. Bassist Rufus Reid replaces Eddie Gomez in Locke's latest quartet, but drummer Gene Jackson and pianist Billy Childs, who shares Locke's reverence for beautiful melodies, are still in the fold.

influences:

◀◀ Milt Jackson, Bobby Hutcherson

Andrew Gilbert

Giuseppi Logan
Born in 1935.

On a label celebrated for its "outness," Giuseppi Logan still stands out as one of the most out-there characters in modern jazz. Possibly one of the few individuals who gives credence to the typical argument that "anybody can play that crap," Logan, though he was certainly dedicated to the *cause* of free jazz (bringing several artists into the ESP fold), wasn't exactly the most praiseworthy practitioner of it. If, for some reason, these two albums aren't enough, his playing can also be found on Patty Waters's studio album.

what to buy: Bolstered by an astonishing band—drummer Milford Graves, pianist Don Pullen, and bassist Eddie Gomez—Logan actually doesn't come across too terribly on *Giuseppi Logan Quartet* 🎵🎵🎵 (ESP, 1965, prod. Art Crist). His fractured playing (of clarinet and saxophones, among other instruments) seems more of an afterthought, with the other three seldom paying his leads any attention. Smart men.

what to avoid: Although Graves, Pullen, and Gomez return (bassist Reggie Johnson also steps in) only a few months later for *More Giuseppi Logan* 🎵🎵 (ESP, 1965), Logan strains to be heard, breaking notes and tripping all over himself. It's almost depressing to hear the others cope. "Curve Eleven," which purports to be an "impromptu studio recording" of Logan on the piano, must be heard to be believed.

influences:

◀◀ Albert Ayler

Jason Ferguson

Mike Longo
Born March 19, 1940, in Cincinnati, OH.

A versatile pianist best known for his stint with Dizzy Gillespie from 1966 to 1973, Longo now heads his own production company, Consolidated Artists Productions (CAP), as well as performing, composing (over 65 compositions to date), lecturing globally, and creating home study educational materials for musicians. Longo began piano studies at age four, and was playing professionally by age 15, often with his father, a working bassist. Longo worked with Cannonball Adderley (1953–55), then attended college, receiving his Bachelor of Music degree from Western Kentucky University. He moved to New York, where he became house pianist at the Metropole Café (1960–62), working with bands led by Henry Red Allen, Gene Krupa, Coleman Hawkins, Zutty Singleton, Cozy Cole, and others. Performing at a number of NYC clubs, Longo's talents gained notice, and he became an in-demand pianist with singers and jazz musicians alike. Recording contracts followed, and he made some albums as leader for Mainstream, Groove Merchant, Pablo Records, and Laserlight (most of which are out of print). He also recorded with Dizzy Gillespie, James Moody, Richard Groove Holmes, Lee Konitz, and others. In addition to recording for his own label, Longo continues to perform, most notably at the Carlyle Hotel in New York City, where he has been solo pianist in Bemelmann's Bar for the past decade. For more information about Longo, check out the CAP website at http://www.jazzbeat.com.

what to buy: On *Dawn of a New Day* ♪♪♪♪ (CAP, 1997, prod. Mike Longo) Mike Longo performs 11 standards captured in three trio sessions with drummer Ray Mosca (Ignacio Berroa subs on two tracks), and bassists Ben Brown, Paul West, and John Lee. (By the way, Berroa and Lee, former Gillespie-ites, are part of a unit with Longo that presents "Dizzy Gillespie, The Man and His Music" at concerts and festivals worldwide.) Longo has a melody-focused style, with a strong two-handed keyboard approach that uses plenty of chords. He sometimes injects playful quotes, alters dynamics between soft and loud, and adds unexpected time shifts to build drama into each piece. Longo's ballads are rich and passionate (his jazz reading of the ballad "The Shadow of Your Smile" is among the best on record) and he injects blues, funk, bossa beats, and more into the tunes on this disc. Longo's playing on the nearly 12-minute Gershwin medley (with Brown and Mosca) is pure artistry. Listen to the way he constructs a tune and you'll hear the talents that garnered him a gig as Dizzy Gillespie's musical director, especially on Gillespie's "Woody 'n You" and "Tin Tin Deo." Longo aims to please his audience, and this successful, well-produced album is one of the best jazz piano trio sessions out there.

the rest:
The Earth Is but One Country ♪♪♪♪ (CAP, 1990)
I Miss You John ♪♪♪♪ (CAP, 1995)
New York '78 ♪♪♪♪ (CAP, 1996)

influences:
◄◄ Oscar Peterson, Bud Powell

Nancy Ann Lee

Jeff Lorber

Born November 4, 1952, in Philadelphia, PA.

Known in recent years as a record producer, keyboardist Jeff Lorber can write a groove a mile wide. From the late '70s his danceable blend of funk, Latin, and jazz has helped forge the popularity of modern fusion. A studio maven since the late '80s, Lorber's credits read like a Who's Who of Grammy contenders. His producing credits include Kenny G, Dave Koz, Herb Alpert, Michael Franks, Tower of Power, Sheena Easton, Karyn White, Jody Watley, Jon Lucien, Eric Marienthal, Art Porter, and the soundtrack to the movie *Another 48 Hours*. He has added his keyboard mastery to albums by such luminaries as Paula Abdul, the Pointer Sisters, Johnny Mathis, Gladys Knight, Manhattan Transfer, the Isley Brothers, Joe Cocker, and Paul Jackson, Jr. Lorber has also remixed tracks for U2, Chaka Khan, Bruce Hornsby, Luther Vandross, and Duran Duran. On his own releases, however, his abilities as a technician and a soloist leave the critics cold, and it's been suggested that Lorber's primary inspiration is drawn from machines, resulting in pre-packaged tracks that lack any emotionally convincing performances. His more recent work, on the other hand, displays a newly realized freedom and marked maturity as a jazz player.

Lorber is a classically trained pianist who also studied bass, violin, and guitar. He played in R&B and blues bands when he was in high school and later attended Berklee College of Music in Boston. After relocating to Oregon, Lorber began his recording career in 1977 with his group the Jeff Lorber Fusion, which featured the young Kenny Gorelick, a.k.a. Kenny G. Lorber's two Inner City releases, *Jeff Lorber Fusion* and *Soft Space*, became blueprints for the radio formats known today as NAC and Contemporary Jazz. Between 1980 and 1985 Lorber released seven albums on Arista and garnered a Best R&B Instrumental Grammy nomination for the smooth-jazz staple "Pacific Coast Highway." Never manufactured on CD, these titles have become a rare find. Although the demand is great, it is still unclear whether Lorber's Arista catalog will be reissued on CD. (Since unavailable material makes up such a high percentage of this artist's catalog, we list it all below.) Lorber's greatest commercial success came in 1986 when the vocal single "Facts of Love" (from his only Warner Bros. release, *Private Passion*) introduced then-unknown singer Karyn White. The Top-10 pop hit brought Lorber huge crossover success as a vocally oriented singles artist—a blessing and a curse to his established instrumental fusion fan base. In 1991 and 1992 Lorber was voted Best Session Player in *Keyboard* magazine's Annual Reader's Poll, and Best Dance Keyboard Player in 1993. That year also saw the release of his PolyGram debut, *Worth Waiting For* on its forward-looking Verve Forecast label, marking Lorber's first studio project under his own name in seven years. Enthusiastically received, the record made it to the #1 spot on *Billboard*'s Contemporary Jazz chart. The following year, *West Side Stories* was re-leased. For his final Verve Forecast project, *State of Grace*, Lor-ber ties some vintage keyboards to a more simplistic structure, reminiscent of his early compositions. In fact, two of the selec-tions, "Pacific Coast Highway" and "Katherine," were mined from earlier recordings (*Step by Step* and *Soft Space* respec-tively) and given a highly evolved retrofit. Lorber even makes a cameo performance on guitar for three of the tracks. His latest release, *Midnight*, was scheduled to make it to the stores sometime in 1998.

what to buy: The title of *Worth Waiting For* ♫♫♫ (Verve Fore-cast, 1993, prod. Jeff Lorber) is truly stated. Coming after Lorber spent seven years recording other people's records, this project shows the value of Lorber's sabbatical as a leader (although much of the material was written during that time). The tracks on this album heed the production caveat "less is more," and they tend to breathe better than Lorber's previous projects.

what to buy next: On *West Side Stories* ♫♫♫ (Verve Forecast, 1994, prod. Jeff Lorber) Lorber musically chronicles the flavor and ambiance of the West Side of Los Angeles, where he lives. Stylistically it's a seamless continuation of *Worth Wait-ing For*.

the rest:
Soft Space ♫♫♫ (Inner City, 1978)
Water Sign ♫♫♫♫ (Arista, 1979)
Galaxian ♫♫♫ (Arista, 1980)
Wizard Island ♫♫♫ (Arista, 1980)
It's a Fact ♫♫♫ (Arista, 1981)
In the Heat of the Night ♫♫♫ (Arista, 1983)
Lift Off ♫♫ (Arista, 1984)
Step by Step ♫♫♫ (Arista, 1984)
Private Passion ♫♫ (Warner Bros., 1990)
State of Grace ♫♫♫ (Polygram, 1996)

worth searching for: *Jeff Lorber Fusion* ♫♫♫♫ (Inner City, 1977) is one of the few quintessential NAC records that helped define that genre. Released only on vinyl, this recording has become a crown jewel for fusion collectors and one of the luckier finds. This record is a set of tightly knit performances of some very memorable compositions.

influences:
◀◀ The Jazz Crusaders, the Mahavishnu Orchestra, Return to Forever, Tony Williams Lifetime

▶▶ Rob Mullins, Pete Bardens, Brian Culbertson, Kym Pensyl, Bill Myers, Kenny G

Ralph Burnett

Lounge Lizards

Formed 1979, in New York, NY.

John Lurie, soprano and alto saxophones, vocals; Evan Lurie, key-boards (1979–90); Arto Lindsay, guitar (1979–80); Dana Vicek, guitar (1980); Danny Rosen, guitar (1981); Steve Piccolo, bass (1979–81); Anton Fier, drums (1979–81); Peter Zummo, trombone (1983); Tony Garnier, bass (1983); Dougie Bowne, drums (1983–90); Roy Nathanson, soprano, alto, and tenor saxophones (1984–90); Curtis Fowlkes, trombone (1984–90); Marc Ribot, guitar, trumpet, banjo (1984–90); Eric Sanko, drums (1984–90, 1993–present); E.J. Ro-driguez, percussion (1987–90); Michael Blake, soprano and tenor saxophones (1991–present); Steven Bernstein, trumpet, cornet (1991–present); Bryan Carrott, vibraphone, marimba, timpani (1991–92); Michele Navazio, guitar (1991–present); Dave Tronzo, slide guitar (1993–present); Danny Blume, guitar (1993–present); John Medeski, organ (1993); Oren Bloedow, bass (1991–92); Grant Calvin Weston, drums (1991–present); Billy Martin, percussion (1991–93); Jane Scarpantoni, cello (1991–present).

Once upon a time, John Lurie's self-bestowed description "fake jazz" made ironic sense, but his Lounge Lizards long ago grad-uated to a warped version of the real thing, though it goes be-yond jazz boundaries and always has. The key to the band has always been not Lurie, but who's playing with him. Thus the first edition with atonal guitarist Arto Lindsay was stellar; it de-constructed familiar tunes by changing their sonic context, while the Lurie brothers' own compositions posited an alter-nate jazz reality in which cool tunes with jagged edges bespoke a casual yet aware stance. The second lineup with Zummo lost the frenetic, barely contained anarchy and had little to substi-tute, but starting with the third main Lizards lineup African in-fluences could be heard, both in the less square rhythms and in Lurie's keening tone and phrasing. The fourth lineup, with mu-sical director Steve Bernstein (who also leads the post-mod-ernist jazz trio Spanish Fly with Dave Tronzo and tuba player Marcus Rojas), emphasized the worldbeat aspect even more, while throwing in a funky 1960s soul-jazz aspect heard most clearly on the tracks credited to Lurie and arranged by Bern-stein on the *Get Shorty* soundtrack (which includes other artists in related veins). A Lounge Lizards album titled *Queen of All Ears* was supposed to come out on Warner Bros. subsidiary Luaka Bop in 1996, even getting listed in the Schwann catalog, but it never actually appeared, resulting in legal tangles. There are efforts underway to have another label pick it up and possi-bly reissue an album Lurie put out and sold himself that has since gone out of print, so fans should keep their eyes open. Lurie had earlier hooked up with director Jim Jarmusch, who not only had him score three films, but also cast him in *Stranger than Paradise* and *Down by Law,* where his detached presence and iconic good looks work to good *noir* effect (he has appeared in other films as well). Except for *Mystery Train,* which includes period R&B songs of other artists, the albums of John Lurie's film scores include similar work done for other projects.

Evan Lurie has a strong interest in tango; his only solo record released in the United States features respected bandoneon (an elongated accordion) virtuoso Alfredo Pedernera as well as the versatile Ribot. Evan's angular, off-kilter piano style, rife with pregnant dissonances, makes his work stand out and constituted a great deal of the Lounge Lizards' unique sound.

what to buy: *The Lounge Lizards* 🎵🎵🎵🎵 (EG, 1981, prod. Teo Macero) is a brilliant refraction of familiar jazz elements recontextualized. Lindsay's skronk guitar effusions and the covers of two Thelonious Monk tunes and "Harlem Nocturne" stand out.

what to buy next: *Live in Berlin 1991, Volume 1* 🎵🎵🎵🎵 (Intuition, 1993, prod. John Lurie), with the Bernstein-directed lineup, covers all the po-mo bases, and things get stirringly hot or cool according to the circumstance. The overall feeling is looser and more organic than in the earlier versions of the band, and more democratic.

what to avoid: Some of the compositions on *Live from the Drunken Boat* 🎵🎵 (Europa, 1983, prod. Teo Macero, John Lurie) are good, but this studio recording finds Lurie between great band lineups and not yet a strong enough player to carry the album himself.

the rest:
Live 79/81 🎵🎵🎵🎵 (ROIR, 1985)
Live in Tokyo—Big Heart 🎵🎵🎵🎵 (Island, 1986)
No Pain for Cakes 🎵🎵🎵 (Island, 1987)
Live in Berlin 1991 Volume 2 🎵🎵🎵🎵 (Intuition, 1995)

worth searching for: The loose, fun *Voice of CHUNK* 🎵🎵🎵 (Lagarto, 1989) was self-issued by John Lurie and sold via a 1-800 number (which no longer works). It was issued in other countries (including Japan) through more normal distribution routes and can sometimes be found in used bins.

solo outings:
Evan Lurie:
Selling Water by the Side of the River 🎵🎵🎵 (Island, 1990)

John Lurie:
Mystery Train 🎵🎵🎵 (RCA, 1989)
Stranger Than Paradise 🎵🎵🎵 (Enigma, 1986)
Down by Law/Variety 🎵🎵🎵 (Intuition/Capitol, 1987)

Get Shorty 🎵🎵🎵🎵 (Island, 1995)

Michael Blake:
Kingdom of Champa 🎵🎵🎵 (Intuition, 1997)

influences:

◀◀ Thelonious Monk, Charles Mingus, Dollar Brand, Peter Apfelbaum's Heiroglyphics Ensemble

▶▶ Ambitious Lovers, Jazz Passengers, Medeski, Martin & Wood, Squirrel Nut Zippers, Golden Palominos, Spanish Fly

Steve Holtje

Joe Lovano

Born December 29, 1952, in Cleveland, OH.

One of the top saxophonists of the 1990s, Joe Lovano continues to grow and explore as a musician while playing tenor, alto, and soprano saxophones, alto clarinet, and, occasionally, drums. Lovano has a husky tenor tone based in the tradition, but an approach to improvisation that is modern and daring. His father, Tony "Big T" Lovano, a fine Cleveland tenorman, was his first inspiration. He taught Joe all the standards, how to lead a gig, how to pace a set, and how to be versatile enough to always find work. Joe started on alto at age six and switched to tenor five years later. He attended Berklee College of Music before working with Jack McDuff and Lonnie Smith. After three years with Woody Herman's Orchestra, Lovano moved to New York and began playing regularly with Mel Lewis's Big Band. This influence is still present in his solos. He often plays lines that convey the rhythmic drive and punch of an entire horn section. In the early 1980s Lovano worked with Paul Motian's bassless trio and John Scofield's Quartet. Steeped in the tradition of Ornette Coleman, Motian's recordings show off Lovano's avantgarde abilities. John Scofield's Quartet straddled the line between "inside" and "outside." These recordings feature some of Lovano's best work. While with Motian and Scofield, he recorded for smaller, independent labels before signing with Blue Note in the early 1990s. As a leader, Lovano draws from all of his experiences and ends up with diverse, creative, energetic CDs.

what to buy: *From the Soul* 🎵🎵🎵🎵 (Blue Note, 1992, prod. Joe Lovano) improves on the excellent Blue Note debut *Landmarks.* Lovano's playing, in collaboration with pianist Michell Petrucciani, bassist Dave Holland, and drummer Ed Blackwell, is more expansive and free flowing. "Evolution" reflects his debt to Dewey Redman and "Body and Soul" is his terrific contribution

Joe Lovano (© Jack Vartoogian)

to the tenor canon. Recorded live at the Village Vanguard, *Quartets* &&&&ᵛ (Blue Note, 1995, prod. Joe Lovano, Michael Cuscuna) represents Lovano's ongoing exploration of freedom and tradition, performed with two separate quartets. The pianoless quartet (with Tom Harrell, Anthony Cox, and Billy Hart) on disc one exhibits an Ornette Coleman influence, particularly on Lovano's "Fort Worth" and "Uprising." Disc two finds him in a slightly more conservative role, successfully tackling modern standards such as Mingus's "Duke Ellington Sound of Love" and Monk's "Reflections," with pianist Mulgrew Miller, bassist Christian McBride, and drummer Lewis Nash.

what to buy next: *Sounds of Joy* &&&& (Enja, 1991, prod. Horst Weber) is a trio recording that is a bit looser than his subsequent Blue Note recordings. But that is a definite asset. "This One's for Lacy" and "Ettenro" exhibit excellent interplay among Anthony Cox, Ed Blackwell, and Lovano. *Landmarks* &&&& (Blue Note, 1990, prod. John Scofield, Joe Lovano), Lovano's debut on Blue Note, resembles the best of his recordings with John

Scofield. The album consists almost entirely of Lovano compositions, with "Emperor Jones" one of the many highlights.

what to avoid: *Rush Hour* &ᵛ (Blue Note, 1995, prod. Gunther Schuller, Joe Lovano) is an ambitious project that fails to fully capture Lovano's best qualities.

best of the rest:
Tones, Shapes, and Colors &&&ᵛ (Soul Note, 1985)
Village Rhythm &&&ᵛ (Soul Note, 1988)
(With the Joe Lovano Wind Ensemble) *Worlds* &&ᵛ (Evidence, 1989/1995)
Universal Language &&&ᵛ (Blue Note, 1993)
Tenor Legacy &&&ᵛ (Blue Note, 1994)
Ten Tales &&ᵛ (Owl, 1989/Capitol, 1994)
Celebrating Sinatra &&ᵛ (Capitol, 1997)
(With Gonzalo Rubalcaba) *Flying Colors* &&&ᵛ (Blue Note, 1998)

worth searching for: *One Time Out* (Soul Note, 1987, prod. Giovanni Bonandrini) is often listed under Lovano's name, but it's actually a Paul Motian Trio recording. Either way it is an excellent CD. The approach is on a par with Coleman's trio or Old and New Dreams. "Monk's Mood" is stretched to the limit and "One Time Out" crackles with intensity.

influences:

◀◀ Tony "Big T" Lovano, John Coltrane, Dewey Redman, Ornette Coleman

▶▶ George Garzone, Joshua Redman

James Eason

Frank Lowe

Born June 24, 1943, in Memphis, TN.

Frank Lowe is a free-jazz player—he has been quoted as saying he'd rather have his oeuvre called "spontaneous improvisational music"—whose playing has an extremely strong vocal quality he attributes to the early influence of blues and gospel. Like many free players, his stylistic range has proven much broader in the years since he first appeared. Lowe worked for the soul label Stax in its early days. His studio tasks brought him into contact with R&B musicians, and the label was connected to a record store. This is where he began learning about jazz, finding himself particularly attracted to the playing of Ornette Coleman, Eric Dolphy, John Coltrane, and Cecil Taylor. He studied at the University of Kansas, then moved to San Francisco and studied privately with Coltrane sideman Donald Garrett as well as with Bert Wilson and Sonny Simmons. When Lowe arrived in New York, he played with Sun Ra (1966–67), but had trouble finding other musicians who were willing to work with him. He returned to California and studied classical music at the San Francisco Conservatory. His second move to New York found him more accepted on the scene, and he played with Alice Coltrane, Rashied Ali, Don Cherry, Archie Shepp, Milford Graves, Leroy Jenkins, and other free-jazz luminaries as he became more disciplined in his improvising. Like many free players at that time, his recording debut as a leader came with ESP, in 1973, and he was soon recording regularly. He remains active and based in New York.

what to buy: *Black Beings* ♫♫♫♫ (ESP, 1973) is probably Lowe's most famous album and displays prototypical energy playing—as the first and longest (25-minute) track puts it, "In Trane's Name." The sound gets clotted in loud passages on this concert recording, so the solo Lowe track "Brother Joseph" is valuable for showing how much variety of timbre he commanded. Joseph Jarman is on soprano and alto saxes, a violinist credited as the Wizard adds color, bassist William Parker (then 21 years old) makes an early appearance, and the drummer is Rashid Sinan. On *Decision in Paradise* ♫♫♫ (Soul Note, 1985, prod. Giovanni Bonandrini), Lowe's robust tenor tone is complemented by the delicate touch of Don Cherry on pocket trumpet, the strong personality of Grachan Moncur III on trombone, the agile piano of Geri Allen (early in her career, just a year after debuting on record), and the probing, swinging rhythm team of Charnette Moffett (bass) and his father Charles Moffett (drums). The musical style is basically adventurous post-bop of an exploratory bent, more accessible to mainstream listeners if not nearly as crucial to Lowe's legacy as the ESP disc.

what to buy next: *The Flam* ♫♫♫ (Black Saint, 1976, prod. Giacomo Pellicciotti) is a quintet with Joe Bowie (trombone), Leo Smith (trumptet, flugelhorn, wood flute), Alex Blake (acoustic and electric bass), and Charles "Bobo" Shaw (drums). The music is definitely "outside," but the playing has a wider dynamic range than on the ESP album and the recorded sound is far superior. *Bodies & Soul* ♫♫♫ (CIMP, 1996, prod. Robert D. Rusch) documents Lowe's recent playing in a trio with the late Charles Moffett on drums and bassist Tim Flood. Besides four Lowe-penned tracks, there are covers (Coltrane's "Impressions," Pharoah Sanders's "Bethera," Ornette Coleman's "Happy House," Don Cherry's "Art Deco") that nicely delineate Lowe's relation to some of his influences, and there's a lovely, moving solo-tenor version of "Body and Soul."

what to avoid: Recorded in 1982 and released over a decade later in an archival series on a Japanese label, *Live at Soundscape* ♫♫ (DIW, 1994, prod. Verna Gillis) features a solid group (Lowe's regular quintet of the time with Butch Morris, Amina Claudine Myers, Wilber Morris, and Tim Pleasant) saddled with cavernous acoustics and a distant recording. The same lineup is heard to much better effect on *Exotic Heartbreak*.

the rest:

Fresh ♫♫♫ (Freedom, 1975)
Exotic Heartbreak ♫♫♫♫ (Soul Note, 1982)
Vision Blue ♫♫♫ (CIMP, 1997)

worth searching for: Lowe and Michael Marcus (bass sax, manzello) were the motivating forces behind SaxEmble, a sax-quartet-plus-drums whose *SaxEmble* ♫♫♫ (Qwest, 1996, prod. Craig Morton) covers a broad range of jazz, from "Freedom Jazz Dance" (written by Eddie Harris and made famous by the second great Miles Davis Quintet) and two Thelonious Monk tunes to free playing on Albert Ayler's "Ghosts." James Carter (alto, tenor, baritone) and Cassius Richmond (alto) fill out the lineup (Bobby LaVell on tenor and Alex Harding on baritone put in appearances), with Cindy Blackman at the drum kit. It's a bluesy, swinging date that features adept solos by Lowe and Carter.

influences:

⏪ Cecil Taylor, John Coltrane, Albert Ayler, Ornette Coleman, Eric Dolphy, Donald Garrett, Sonny Simmons, Bert Wilson, Archie Shepp, Pharoah Sanders, Gene Ammons, King Curtis

⏩ Charles Gayle, Assif Tsahar, Paul Flaherty, Sabir Mateen

Steve Holtje

Lucas

Born Lucas Secon, in Copenhagen, Denmark.

Although the *keep-it-real* set will never admit this Scandinavian-American MC into its ranks, it's refreshing that a rapper like Lucas can make hip-hop his own, twisting it in so many genre-defying ways. Popular inclination seems to lump him with alternarappers, but it's just as well to call him a rap, jazz, and ragtime artist who doesn't care much for boundaries. Perhaps it has something to do with his background: being born in Copenhagen, experimenting with breakdancing and DJing, then getting into rap in his early teens. His conscious immersion in hip-hop culture, if not indigenous to his European roots, is a fact that Lucas celebrates with all the vigor of the old guard of New York, the city to which he moved at the age of 18.

what to buy: *Lucacentric* 🎵🎵🎵 (Big Beat/Atlantic, 1994, prod. Lucas) is a plateful of jazz-funk spontaneity wholly constructed by this rapper, songwriter, and producer. The standout cut, "Lucas with the Lid Off," is an extended metaphor describing, in upbeat bursts of verse, the freedom that comes with tapping a creative subconscious. Drawing aural influences from big-band and dancehall, the tune offers an unprecedented summit of sound. On other musical tangents, Lucas probes dense funk ("CityZen"), while also running off with a contemplative jazz keyboard groove on "The Statusphere."

the rest:

To Rap My World Around You 🎵🎵 (Uptown, 1991)

influences:

⏪ Clifford Brown, Benny Goodman, Digable Planets, M.C. Shan

⏩ Us3

Corey Takahashi

Jon Lucien

Born 1942, in Tortola, British Virgin Islands.

Gifted with a lush baritone voice, Jon Lucien is most at home with the Caribbean and Latin music he heard growing up in the Virgin Islands. Lucien's first instrument was the bass, and he acquired enough skill to start performing in his father's Latin jazz band during his early teens. After being introduced to American jazz (especially the music of Miles Davis and Art Farmer) by a British piano player, he started adding different jazz influences to his repertoire. Lucien came to the States in the early 1970s, working his way around sessions in New York City and playing with musicians like Herbie Hancock. He released a series of albums for different labels but became increasingly dissatisfied with aspects of his personal and professional life. Lucien moved back to the Caribbean (he currently lives in Puerto Rico) in an attempt to escape the problems, returning to New York or Los Angeles only to record music for his albums. On July 17, 1996, he suffered another blow when his daughter, Dalila Lucien, was one of the passengers on TWA Flight 800 that blew up over the coast of Long Island, New York.

what to buy: When Lucien is *on*, he is one of the best midtempo balladeers in the English language. Herbie Hancock called him "the man with the golden throat." Find Lucien the right song, pop some sultry percussion in the background, run the right horn section, and he's awesome, as *Listen Love* 🎵🎵🎵 (Mercury, 1991, prod. Jon Lucien, Jeff Lorber, Edward Reyes) attests. When he's cruising, even as he pours his heart out, Lucien is doing that boring, soulful Caribbean-based New Age swing thing that passes for exotic jazz on Quiet Storm stations. "You Take My Breath Away" is the perfect pop tune, buoyant, jamming, slick.

what to buy next: *Endless Is Love* 🎵🎵🎵 (Shanachie, 1997, prod. Jon Lucien, John Lee, Chuck Loeb) is the first album Lucien did after the death of his daughter, and it's dedicated to her. The songs are good, Lucien's performance is good, the arrangements aren't. There's an automatic bone deduction for use of a drum machine.

the rest:

Mother Nature's Son 🎵🎵🎵 (Mercury, 1993)

influences:

⏪ Miles Davis, Billy Eckstine

⏩ Will Downing

Garaud MacTaggart

Jimmie Lunceford

Born James Melvin Lunceford, June 6, 1902, in Fulton, MO. Died July 12, 1947, in Seaside, OR.

Jimmie Lunceford led a powerhouse swing band in the 1930s and 1940s. He was a highly skilled musician, playing trombone, all of the saxophone family, clarinet, flute, and guitar, but he rarely performed as a soloist on his recordings. The Lunceford Orchestra, in its peak years from about 1934 through 1942, was a brilliant musical unit, a great dance band, and a visual treat, with the members impeccably dressed in different uniforms for each show. The sections performed physical "schtick" with their instruments, trumpets pointing skyward, saxophones swaying, trombones rotating in circles, all the while remaining a high-precision jazz machine executing wildly original charts. The band featured a saxophone section led by the noted alto saxophonist and rehearsal task master Willie Smith and featured many arrangements by Smith, pianist Ed Wilcox, trombonist Ed Durham, trumpeter Sy Oliver, and, later, Billy Moore and Gerald Wilson. The Lunceford Orchestra was one of the first to showcase the high-note trumpet in their arrangements, with Tommy Stevenson and, later, Paul Francis Webster or Snooky Young blasting through the ensembles. James "Trummy" Young gave the band a major trombone soloist and an added vocalist when he joined in the late 1930s. The highly individual drummer Jimmy Crawford, developing a two-beat style at Sy Oliver's insistence, gave the band a distinctive bounce or relaxed beat, which helped to give it identity. Lunceford and his section leaders, with their sense of perfection, along with distinctive arranging, elevated this exciting swing band to a high level that can still be monitored through a rich legacy of recordings.

Lunceford grew up in Denver, where he studied music with Wilberforce J. Whiteman (Paul Whiteman's father) and played alto sax with George Morrison's Orchestra in 1922. He gained a bachelor of music degree at Fisk University, where he met students Willie Smith, Ed Wilcox, and Henry Wells, who all later joined his band. From 1926–29 he taught music at Manassa High School in Memphis, until a band he had formed turned professional. The unit toured and formed residencies in Cleveland, Ohio, and Buffalo, New York, before moving on to New York City in 1933. Lunceford's group had a highly successful six-month stay at the celebrated Cotton Club in Harlem starting in January of 1934. Nightly broadcasts served to enhance the band's reputation; they soon landed a Decca recording contract and began touring extensively, achieving a following and notoriety comparable to that of Ellington and Basie. In 1939 the band switched to Columbia/Vocalion, lost arranger Sy Oliver to Tommy Dorsey, gained trumpeters Gerald Wilson and Snooky Young, and added a 22-year-old arranger, Billy Moore. In 1941 they recorded Wilcox's "Yard Dog Mazurka," which showed up years later in Stan Kenton's band as "Intermission Riff." The Lunceford Orchestra appeared in the film *Blues in the Night* and returned to Decca for a big hit record of the same title. As players like Smith, Wilson, and Young left in the early 1940s, the quality of the band deteriorated, and the once-glorious unit became just another band, lasting until just after Lunceford's death in 1947.

what to buy: *Stomp It Off* 🎵🎵🎵🎵 (Decca, 1992, reissue prod. Orrin Keepnews) offers 21 tracks of auditory proof that 1934–35 was a banner period for the Lunceford organization. There are four interesting nods toward Duke Ellington with "Sophisticated Lady," "Mood Indigo," "Black and Tan Fantasy," and "Solitude" in the program. But the adventurous arrangements show that Willie Smith and Sy Oliver had their own original approaches to the material. An unidentified trio of band members introduce a familiar Lunceford device, the unison vocal, with spirited versions of "Rain," and the delightful "Since My Best Girl Turned Me Down." There are two takes of the popular "Rhythm Is Our Business" with Smith humorously introducing several band members in song. The collection concludes with five tunes from 1935, including Wilcox's easy-going take on "Sleepy Time Gal," and Sy Oliver's swinging vocal on his arrangement of the hoary "Four or Five Times," as the band swings infectiously to the two-beat rhythm that Oliver so often favored. *For Dancers Only* 🎵🎵🎵🎵 (Decca, 1994, reissue prod. Orrin Keepnews) is a continuation of MCA/Decca's chronological Lunceford series that brings back 21 more classic swing sides ranging in date from September 1935 through June 1937. Included are Sy Oliver–arranged gems such as "Swanee River," "My Blue Heaven," "Organ Grinder's Swing," "Linger Awhile," and the title tune. Also included are the Eddie Durham charts on "Avalon," the catchy "Hittin' the Bottle" and "Harlem Shout," Ed Wilcox's swinging approach to "I'll See You in My Dreams," and the clever "I'm Nuts about Screwy Music." This band really swung and these compilations are wonderful introductions to big-band swing and to the Lunceford powerhouse. Swing fans are advised that the entire recorded output of the RCA, Decca, Columbia, Vocalion, and Majestic sides by the Lunceford Orchestra are available on the Jazz Chronological Classics and Masters of Jazz labels, which, while imports, are in wide circulation in the United States.

best of the rest:
Jimmie Lunceford and His Orchestra, 1940 🎵🎵🎵 (Circle, 1940/1994; reissue of *World Transcriptions*)

The Uncollected Jimmie Lunceford & His Harlem Express Live at Jefferson Barracks, Missouri—1944 ♫♫ (Hindsight, 1994)

Jimmie Lunceford and His Orchestra, 1930–1934 ♫♫♫ (Jazz Chronological Classics, 1994)

Jimmie Lunceford and His Orchestra, 1934–1935 ♫♫♫♫ (Jazz Chronological Classics, 1994)

Jimmie Lunceford and His Orchestra, 1935–1937 ♫♫♫♫ (Jazz Chronological Classics, 1994)

Jimmie Lunceford and His Orchestra, 1939 ♫♫♫ (Jazz Chronological Classics, 1994)

Jimmie Lunceford and His Orchestra, 1939–1940 ♫♫♫ (Jazz Chronological Classics, 1994)

Jimmie Lunceford and His Orchestra, 1940–1941 ♫♫♫ (Jazz Chronological Classics, 1994)

Jimmie Lunceford, 1927–1934, Volume 1, No. 12 ♫♫♫ (Masters of Jazz, 1994)

Jimmie Lunceford, 1934, Volume 2, No. 18 ♫♫♫♫ (Masters of Jazz, 1994)

Jimmie Lunceford, 1935–1936, Volume 3, No. 57 ♫♫♫♫ (Masters of Jazz, 1995)

Jimmie Lunceford, 1935–1937, Volume 4, No. 71 ♫♫♫♫ (Masters of Jazz, 1995)

Jimmie Lunceford, 1937–1939, Volume 5, No. 84 ♫♫♫♫ (Masters of Jazz, 1995)

Jimmie Lunceford, The Quintessence, 1934–41 ♫♫♫♫ (Freemeaux & Associates, 1995)

Jimmie Lunceford, 1939, Volume 6, No. 98 ♫♫♫♫ (Masters of Jazz, 1996)

Jimmie Lunceford and His Orchestra, 1941–1945 ♫♫♫ (Jazz Chronological Classics, 1996)

Jimmie Lunceford and His Orchestra, 1937–1939 ♫♫♫♫ (Jazz Chronological Classics, 1997)

influences:

◀◀ Wilberforce J. Whiteman, George Morrison, Don Redman, Fletcher Henderson, Casa Loma Orchestra, Zack Whyte's Band

▶▶ Stan Kenton Orchestra, Sam Donahue Orchestra, Sonny Dunham Orchestra, Tommy Dorsey Orchestra

John T. Bitter

Carmen Lundy

Born November 1, 1954, in Miami, FL.

Carmen Lundy is a gifted jazz singer who writes much of her own material. Though she draws widely from outside the jazz tradition for influences as diverse as country, folk, pop, and soul, her approach is rooted in jazz rhythms and improvisation. Her wide range, including deep resonant chest tones, makes her a highly expressive singer. She is also an accomplished actor and painter. Lundy, sister of bassist Curtis Lundy, began performing professionally while still a teenager. She enrolled at the University of Miami as an opera major, but soon her gospel and blues background drew her toward jazz and she began performing around Miami, and with the school's big band. She moved to New York in the late 1970s, sitting in with the Thad Jones/Mel Lewis Orchestra. She developed a successful stage career, playing the lead in the Duke Ellington review *Sophisticated Ladies* and the role of Billie Holiday in the off-Broadway production *They Were All Gardenias*. Since relocating to Los Angeles in 1991, Lundy has firmly established herself as one of jazz's most promising singers. She has recorded for Blackhawk, Arabesque, Sony/CBS, and JVC, her current label.

what to buy: Though Carmen Lundy performs five well-worn tunes on *Self Portrait* ♫♫♫♫ (JVC, 1995, prod. Akira Taguchi), it's her six original pieces that make this a standout session. Especially impressive are her ballads "Old Friend" and the beautiful "These Things You Are to Me," tunes that might well be picked up by other singers. Accompanied by pianist Cedar Walton, drummer Ralph Penland, bassists John Clayton or Nathan East, and Ernie Watts and Gary Herbig on reeds, Lundy shows she can personalize standards. She delivers a languorous version of "Spring Can Really Hang You Up the Most," a sensuous reading of Jobim's "Triste," and a highly literate version of the Kurt Weill/Ira Gershwin classic "My Ship."

what to buy next: With each release Lundy's voice grows deeper and more resonant, though *Old Devil Moon* ♫♫♫ (JVC, 1997, prod. Akira Taguchi, Carmen Lundy) is a split personality affair. The seven standards, featuring a lithe, responsive rhythm section with Billy Childs (piano), Santi Debriano (bass), and Winston Clifford, are rendered with care by Lundy, especially the Latin-tinged title track, the up-tempo version of "Star Eyes," and "When Your Lover Has Gone," which features some potent tenor work by Frank Foster, who appears on three tracks. But besides her well-crafted ode to impatience, "At the End of My Rope," her four original tunes tend to be over-produced, leaning more toward contemporary pop than straight-ahead jazz. Randy Brecker, Bob Mintzer, Omar Hakin, and Victor Bailey are also featured on a number of tracks. An excellent debut by a singer with tremendous potential, *Good Morning Kiss* ♫♫♫ (Blackhawk, 1986, prod. Carmen Lundy) is a strong jazz-oriented session for which Lundy wrote much of the material herself. Most impressive are her two ballads, the title track and "Quiet Times." Her up-tempo pieces "Time Is Love" and "Perfect Stranger" don't come off quite as well but still demonstrate Lundy's talent for writing strong themes. The album's other highlights include her lilting version of Jobim's "Dindi" with trombonist Steve Turre's gentle accents, and her swinging, eight-minute take on "The Lamp Is Low," which is one of four tracks featuring horn charts by Bobby Watson. The rhythm section features pianist Harry Whitaker, drummer Victor Lewis, and either Curtis Lundy or Ben Brown on bass.

the rest:
Moment to Moment ✍✍✍✍ (Arabesque, 1992)

worth searching for: Bassist Curtis Lundy's first session as a leader, *Just Be Yourself* ✍✍✍✍ (Evidence, 1985, prod. Curtis Lundy, Kenny Washington) features his sister Carmen on two tracks, an undistinguished but sweet ballad, "Funny," and vibraphonist Steve Nelson's boppish tune "Just Be Yourself," which is one of the session's highlights. The other standout tracks are "Jabbo's Revenge" and "Shaw 'Nuff," which feature a trio with Lundy, pianist Hank Jones, and drummer Kenny Washington. Bobby Watson and Nelson are also featured on the session.

influences:
◀◀ Sarah Vaughan, Carmen McRae, Roberta Flack

Andrew Gilbert

Brian Lynch

Born September 12, 1956, in Urbana, IL.

Though many of his peers have received far more attention from the public and press, the fact is that Brian Lynch is one of the most experienced and talented jazz trumpeters of his generation. Growing up in the Milwaukee area, Lynch took advantage of a healthy jazz scene there that found him playing professionally at the age of 16, and gaining valuable knowledge and seasoning through his work with local luminaries Buddy Montgomery and Melvin Rhyne. Following degree studies at the Wisconsin Conservatory, Lynch played briefly with Charles McPherson before heading to New York in 1981. Choice enterprises followed, including a three-year stint with Horace Silver, five years with Toshiko Akiyoshi, and Latin music gigs with Angel Canales and Hector La Voe. Lynch's brassy timbre and fiery approach to improvising make him a natural with both the salsa bands and the hard-bop units on the New York scene. As a result, during the late 1980s it was no surprise to find the trumpeter holding the seat of musical director in pianist Eddie Palmieri's Latin band and in the final edition of the late Art Blakey's Jazz Messengers. Since 1992, Lynch has been a key member of the stimulating Phil Woods Quintet. He continues to record for a variety of labels, including Criss Cross and Sharp

Nine. Able to make a distinctive statement in any musical situation, Brian Lynch is a solid contender for the category of "talent deserving wider recognition."

what to buy: *Back Room Blues* ✍✍✍✍ (Criss Cross Jazz, 1990, prod. Gerry Teekens) was Lynch's second date as a leader and it prominently features his attractive originals. Tenor saxophonist Javon Jackson makes for a robust front-line partner and pianist David Hazeltine begins a fruitful association with the trumpeter that continued in subsequent record dates. *At the Main Event* ✍✍✍✍ (Criss Cross Jazz, 1993, prod. Gerry Teekens) reunites Lynch with mentor and organ player Melvin Rhyne. Also along for the ride are Ralph Moore and guitarist Peter Bernstein. This is groove-centered, tasty stuff that finds everyone in peak form.

what to buy next: *Keep Your Circle Small* ✍✍✍✍ (Sharp Nine, 1995, prod. Marc Edelman) finds Lynch working again with the wonderful pianist David Hazeltine in a quartet setting that really gives him room to stretch as a soloist and composer.

the rest:
Peer Pressure ✍✍✍✍ (Criss Cross, 1987)

influences:
◀◀ Lee Morgan, Woody Shaw

Chris Hovan

Jimmy Lyons

Born December 1, 1933, in Jersey City, NJ. Died May 19, 1986, in New York, NY.

Jimmy Lyons spent most of his career in groups led by pianist Cecil Taylor, where his Charlie Parker–derived sonority provided a direct link to the jazz tradition in Taylor's free-jazz maelstrom. In his teens he was given an alto saxophone by Buster Bailey, was befriended by Elmo Hope, Bud Powell, and Thelonious Monk, and studied with Rudy Rutherford. Lyons began his long association with Taylor in 1960 and appeared on every Cecil Taylor Unit album until his death. From 1978 he performed and recorded as a leader, usually in groups that included bassoonist Karen Borca, drummer Paul Murphy, bassist William Parker, and trumpeter Raphe Malik. He also performed in a duet with drummer Andrew Cyrille. Because Lyons was so closely associated with Taylor, his individual achievements are frequently overlooked. His approach was much more overtly jazz oriented, and his own compositions more songlike. He often constructed his solos from variations and extensions of a few motives, gradually lengthening them into longer lines and often bursting into pure abstract sounds and vocal-sounding cries at the climax of his solo. His sound, and sometimes the shape of his phrases, owed much to Charlie Parker. Tragically, he was just making an impact as a leader in his own right when he died of cancer.

what to buy: Recorded with a trio featuring bassist John Lindberg and drummer Sunny Murray at the Willisau Jazz Festival, *Jump Up/What to Do About* ♫♫♫ (hat ART, 1981, prod. Pia Uehlinger, Werner X. Uehlinger) showcases the fire, daring, and quicksilver intellect of Lyons better than any other he made on his own. His blazing pianoless quintet made music closer to jazz than Taylor's. On *Wee Sneezawee* ♫♫♫ (Black Saint, 1983, prod. Giovanni Bonandrini) there are head solos, head structures, and songlike melodies, but the band still kicks the music away from fixed tempos and tonality for conversational free interplay. Lyons and Cyrille bring out the best in one another. *Something in Return* ♫♫♫ (Black Saint, 1981, prod. Giovanni Bonandrini) is a concentrated, superbly structured, empathetic free-jazz dialogue at a very high level.

what to buy next: *Nuba* ♫♫♫ (Black Saint, 1979, prod. Giovanni Bonandrini) is an intimate and entirely original-sounding trio with singer Jeanne Lee and drummer Cyrille giving beautiful definition and direction to each freely played, atmospheric track. Either of the duets with Cyrille on *Burnt Offerings* ♫♫♫ (Black Saint, 1982, prod. Giovanni Bonandrini) are worth owning. Lyons gives less space to himself on *Give It Up* ♫♫♫ (Black Saint, 1985, prod. Giovanni Bonandrini) than on the earlier quintet date, although his brief ballad feature, "Ballada," is devastating.

worth searching for: Lyons didn't make another album on his own for a decade after *Other Afternoons* ♫♫♫ (BYG, 1969), his stunning debut with Taylor bandmates Cyrille and bassist Alan Silva, joined by guest trumpeter Lester Bowie.

influences:

◀◀ Charlie Parker

▶▶ Rob Brown

Ed Hazell

Johnny Lytle

Born October 13, 1932, in Springfield, OH.

The lightly R&B-influenced recordings of ex-boxer Johnny Lytle have fallen into the category of good, enjoyable, if not earth-shattering, jazz. Though he was a drummer for Ray Charles and later Gene Ammons in the early 1950s, Lytle switched to vibes in the mid-1950s, utilizing a more percussive approach than

some of his contemporaries. He's been a leader since the early 1960s and made several recordings with usually positive results. Though his music is spiced with R&B influences, he has eschewed strictly commercial dates despite obviously having keen pop sensibilities, particularly in the area of composition (his songs have the tendency to make you think you've heard them before even though you haven't). He's spent most of his career on smaller labels and is known as "Fast Hands" for his rapid solos. Though not an innovator, Lytle has consistently been a solid performer and leader for decades.

what's available: *Easy Easy* ♫♫♫ (Muse 1980, 1991/32 Jazz, 1997, prod. Houston Person) combines two Muse recordings, *Fast Hands* from 1980 and *Happy Ground* from 1991, giving a good taste of what Johnny Lytle is about. The fare features nice pop-flavored compositions, good solos, and some great hooks on Lytle's originals. Of the two sessions, *Fast Hands* is better for offering more Lytle compositions. However, *Happy Ground* also has its moments, most notably Lytle's rendition of Freddie Hubbard's "Sunflower." Players include Mickey Tucker (keyboards), David Braham (organ), drummers Idris Muhammed and Greg Bandy, guitarist Melvin Sparks, and others.

worth searching for: With the Muse house band in tow, Lytle leads the cats through standards and his signature originals on *Possum Grease* ♫♫♫ (Muse, 1995, prod. Houston Person). The music on this currently out-of-print album is melodic, but by no means saccharine, with some excellent Houston Person solos in the mix.

influences:

◀◀ Milt Jackson, Lionel Hampton

▶▶ Roy Ayers, Jay Hoggard

Paul MacArthur

Paul Lytton

Born March 8, 1947, in London, England.

A percussionist and instrument maker, Paul Lytton has been one of the figureheads in bringing the amplified world of small sounds and homemade electronic processors to the world of improvised music. Playing in both London and Aachen, Germany, in the late 1960s and early '70s, he began an important duo with saxophonist Evan Parker, a vast influence on later improvisers. This eventually turned into the Evan Parker Trio with the addition of Barry Guy on bass. Lytton also worked in duo with percussionist Paul Lovens, based out of Aachen, and co-founded the fantastic Po-Torch label, which releases free improvised music circling around Lytton, Lovens, and Parker. Lytton is also trained in dentistry; the cover of Derek Bailey's *Guitar Solos 2* shows some picks made by Lytton out of dental plate materials.

what to buy: *Two Octobers* 𝄢𝄢𝄢 (Emanem, 1996) is a fantastic duo with Parker recorded in the early '70s that shows both players' interests in electronics and extending their instruments. Along with Tony Oxley, Lytton was the premiere player of amplified drums, and this is an excellent cross-section of his techniques and ideas.

what to buy next: *The Inclined Stick* 𝄢𝄢𝄢 (Po Torch, 1979), Lytton's only solo disc, follows in the wake of several duo records with master percussionist Paul Lovens, also on Po Torch, and gives a rare insight in Lytton's ideas of space and texture. One of a kind.

the rest:
(With the London Jazz Composer's Orchestra) *Ode* (Incus, 1972)
(With Evan Parker) *Collective Calls (Urban)* (Incus, 1972)
(With Evan Parker) *Live at Unity Theatre* (Incus, 1975)
(With Evan Parker) *Ra 1+2* (Ring, 1976)
(With Paul Lovens) *Was It Me?* (Po Torch, 1977)
(With Evan Parker, Barry Guy, and George Lewis) *Hook, Drift, and Shuffle* (Incus, 1983)
(With Evan Parker and Barry Guy) *Tracks* (Incus, 1983)
(With Evan Parker and Barry Guy) *Atlanta* (Impetus, 1986)
(With the King Ubu Orchestra) *Binaurality* (FMP, 1992)
(With Evan Parker and Barry Guy) *Breaths and Heartbeats* (Rastascan, 1994)
(With Evan Parker and Barry Guy) *50th Anniversary Concert* (Leo, 1994)
(With Evan Parker, Barry Guy, and Marilyn Crispell) *Natives and Aliens* (Leo, 1996)
The Balance of Trade (CIMP, 1996)

influences:
◀◀ Tony Oxley, Hugh Davies

▶▶ Voice Crack, Günter Müller, Adam Bohman

Jim O'Rourke

Harold Mabern

Born March 20, 1936, in Memphis, TN.

Although he has recorded very little as a leader, pianist Harold

Mabern has long been considered by his fellow musicians and in-the-know fans as one of the finest players of his generation. A product of the Memphis scene that also produced the much-revered pianist Phineas Newborn, Mabern is a technically impressive player who makes the most of adventurous harmonic stretches, double-handed unison lines of great intricacy, and a generally daring approach. Following his first important gig in Chicago with the group known as the MJT+3, Mabern headed for New York in 1959 and began to make a name for himself. During the 1960s the impressive list of people he worked and recorded with included Jimmy Forrest, Lionel Hampton, Donald Byrd, Miles Davis, Hank Mobley, J.J. Johnson, Sonny Rollins, Freddie Hubbard, Wes Montgomery, Joe Williams, and Sarah Vaughan. Mabern himself recorded four albums for the Prestige label between 1968 and 1970, and each one is an underappreciated gem of the period. Most recently, Mabern has toured with the Contemporary Piano Ensemble, recorded a duo project with Geoff Keezer in homage to Phineas Newborn, and continues to release his own dates as a leader for the Japanese DIW/Disc Union label.

what to buy: *Wailin'* 𝄢𝄢𝄢𝄢 (Prestige, 1969/1970, prod. Bob Porter) reissues on one CD the albums *Workin' and Wailin'* and *Greasy Kid Stuff*. The latter is particularly rewarding due to the front line that includes trumpeter Lee Morgan and tenor saxophonist Hubert Laws. Mabern's originals are meaty and forward-looking. *The Leading Man* 𝄢𝄢𝄢 (Columbia, 1995, prod. James Williams, Kazunori Sugiyama) is an American compilation of cuts from several dates Mabern recorded for the Japanese DIW/Disc Union label. Most rewarding are the trio tracks with bassist Christian McBride and drummer Jack DeJohnette.

the rest:
Live at Cafe Des Copains 𝄢𝄢𝄢 (Sackville, 1985)
Philadelphia Bound 𝄢𝄢𝄢 (Sackville, 1992)
(With Geoff Keezer) *For Phineas: Two Piano Jazz* 𝄢𝄢𝄢 (Sackville, 1995)

worth searching for: *Straight Street* 𝄢𝄢𝄢 (DIW/Disc Union, 1991, prod. James Williams) is available only on Japanese import but is well worth the price. Working in a trio with Ron Carter and Jack DeJohnette, Mabern contributes some peerless originals, successfully reworks Coltrane's "Crescent" and Stevie Wonder's "Don't You Worry 'Bout a Thing," and is positively astounding on the solo "Apab and Others." *Lookin' at the Bright Side* 𝄢𝄢𝄢 (DIW/Disc Union, 1993, prod. James Williams, Kazunori Sugiyama) is the entire Mabern/McBride/DeJohnette session that was only sampled on the previously mentioned *The Leading Man*. Also available only via Japan, this is Mabern at his most intense and incendiary; listening to this disc is a truly energizing experience.

influences:

⏪ Phineas Newborn, McCoy Tyner

⏩ James Williams, Geoff Keezer, Mulgrew Miller

Chris Hovan

Machito

Born Frank Grillo, February 16, 1915, in Havana, Cuba. Died April 15, 1984, in London, England.

In 1937 Machito arrived in New York City, where he sang and played with Las Estrellas Habaneras, Noro Morales, Xavier Cugat, and Orquesta Siboney. By 1940 he had formed his own band, Machito's Afro-Cubans, and when his brother-in-law, Mario Bauzá, joined the group as musical director, the foundation for one of the greatest Latin bands of all time was laid. Bauzá worked with arrangers like A.K. Salim, John Bartee, and Rene Hernandez to blend Cuban percussion and rhythms with jazz for a sound that revolutionized Latin music. One of Machito's young percussion players from this time, Tito Puente, later took these innovations and polished them still further, but he was probably the only "name" musician to develop from the early 1940s-era bands. Most of the players were originally hired as ensemble players, not spectacular soloists, and the emphasis was on the aggregate, not the individual. The music of Machito's band became a major influence on Stan Kenton and Dizzy Gillespie, while other jazz players like Charlie Parker, Johnny Griffin, Herbie Mann, and Cannonball Adderley either played or recorded with Machito at one point in their careers. During the 1950s Machito's popularity started to slide with the general public, although he continued to make albums on through the early 1980s.

what to buy: *Mucho Macho Machito* 🎵🎵🎵 (Pablo, 1991, prod. various) is a fine collection of Machito's material from the cusp of the 1950s with one of his best bands. The sound has been cleaned up considerably, and songs like "Babarabatiri" and "Asia Minor" cook from beginning to end. Machito is aided by his stalwart trio of arrangers (Bauzá, Salim, and Hernandez) and the addition of jazz players Doc Cheatham, Joe Newman, and Adderley in producing *Kenya* 🎵🎵🎵 (Palladium), some of the finest playing ever released under Machito's name. Their cover of "Tin Tin Deo" is superb, and the underrated Salim's charts for "Oyeme" and "Conversation" are a real treat. The percussion work of Jose Mangual, Candido, and Patato Valdes follows the tradition laid down by Chano Pozo and precedes efforts by Ray

Barretto and Giovanni Hidalgo, among others. This album has been released under other names, including *Latin Soul Plus Jazz* on Tico and, most recently, *Afro Cuban Jazz* on La Mejor Musica. The later album is a mid-price release that changes the sequencing, gets the writing credits wrong, eliminates any liner notes, deletes "Tururato" and adds four tunes from other sessions, including Chico O'Farril's "Mambo Parts 1 & 2."

what to buy next: Other than not having any liner notes or personnel listings, *This Is Machito and His Afro-Cubans* 🎵🎵🎵 (Polydor, 1978, prod. various) is a fine collection of Machito's more jazz-oriented recordings. "Christopher Columbus" is a classic Chu Berry riff that benefits from the Cubop treatment, while mambo cuts like "Sentimental Mambo," "Relax and Mambo," and the fun, if slightly cheesy, "Dragnet Mambo" show why Machito's band was such a hit at dance halls like New York's Palladium.

the rest:

1983 Grammy Award Winner 🎵🎵🎵 (Impulse!, 1983)
Cubop City (1949–50) 🎵🎵🎵 (Tumbao Cuban Classics, 1992)
Tremendo Cuban (1949–52) 🎵🎵🎵 (Tumbao Cuban Classics, 1992)

influences:

⏪ Arsenio Rodriguez

⏩ Dizzy Gillespie, Stan Kenton, Herbie Mann, Tito Puente

Garaud MacTaggart

Mahavishnu Orchestra

Formed 1972.

John McLaughlin, guitar (1972–76); Billy Cobham, drums (1972–74); Jan Hammer, keyboards (1972–74); Jerry Goodman, violin (1972–74); Rick Laird, bass (1972–74); Jean-Luc Ponty, electric violin (1974–75); Michael Narada Walden, percussion (1974–76); Gayle Moran, keyboards, vocals (1974); Ralphe Armstrong, bass (1974–76).

After the release of three solo albums between 1969 and 1971, guitarist John McLaughlin joined forces with Billy Cobham, Jan Hammer, Jerry Goodman, and Rick Laird to form the Mahavishnu Orchestra in 1972. This period in the early 1970s was really the start of an attempt to cross over the genres of jazz and rock music. It was the electrification of jazz or the "fusion" of the two genres. More often than not, the many people who jumped onto this bandwagon seemed to create a watered-down version of both styles and seemed to serve as a turn-off to jazz and rock fans alike. Those who had first experienced this electrification via Miles Davis's explorations were most often repelled by the approach of a new breed of fusion players. Luckily, the players in the Mahavishnu Orchestra took their role as groundbreakers very seriously. Today, their best albums are some of the very few that would make the cut into the jazz history books. The group's debut album, *Inner Mounting Flame*, still remains a classic of the genre. McLaughlin's guitar work takes off where Jimi Hendrix left off. But the decibel level is integrated with a control in the sound that one would more associate with Carlos Santana (with whom Mclaughlin later recorded).

At the beginning of 1974 McLaughlin disbanded the group and later went on to form a new version of the orchestra. In the core group of this new incarnation were McLaughlin, along with Jean-Luc Ponty, Michael Narada Walden, Ralphe Armstrong, and Gayle Moran, plus a few other session players. The 1974 release, *Apocalypse*, an attempt to fuse together not only jazz and rock but also classical elements, features the London Symphony Orchestra under the direction of Michael Tilson-Thomas. Overall, it is intermittently successful at its purpose. By 1975 McLaughlin trimmed the group down to Walden, Ponty, and Armstrong, adding keyboardist Stu Goldberg. Along with a few other studio-session guests, this lineup recorded *Inner Worlds* before McLaughlin finally packed the group in for good in favor of a solo career and other collaborative efforts.

what to buy: *Inner Mounting Flame* ♫♫♫♫♫ (Columbia, 1971, prod. Mahavishnu Orchestra) is a true classic of jazz-rock fusion. The fast-paced, high-decibel music of such compositions as "The Noonward Race" are complemented by the quiet beauty and charm of "A Lotus on Irish Streams."

what to buy next: *Birds of Fire* ♫♫♫♫ (Columbia, 1973, prod. Mahavishnu Orchestra) is another strong effort by the group and the last studio recording by the original line-up. *Visions of the Emerald Beyond* ♫♫♫ (Columbia, 1975, prod. Ken Scott, John McLaughlin) is by the revamped lineup. Producer Ken Scott is perhaps best known for his rock productions, such as Supertramp's *Crime of the Century*.

what to avoid: *Between Nothingness and Eternity* ♫♫ (Columbia, 1974, prod. Mahavishnu Orchestra) is a live recording by the original band. The sound quality is rather murky and the performance is not their best. *Apocalypse* ♫♫♫ (Columbia, 1974, prod. George Martin) is interesting for its incorporation of the London Symphony Orchestra but overall it seems to try to cover too many bases and is only intermittently successful. The final Mahavishnu album, *Inner Worlds* ♫♫ (Columbia, 1975, prod. John McLaughlin, Dennis Mackay), never lives up to the promise of the original releases, with some moments of pleasing music but not enough to make this an album to seek out.

influences:

◀◀ Jimi Hendrix, Carlos Santana, Jeff Beck

▶▶ Reggie Lucas, Frank Marino

Chris Meloche

Kevin Mahogany

Born July 30, 1958, in Kansas City, MO.

Judging from his birthplace, you'd expect singer Kevin Mahogany to be influenced by the Kansas City jazz tradition. And you'd be right. Mahogany has a bluesy KC-influenced vocal style that's a real crowd pleaser. Plus, he's the first truly exciting male vocalist to emerge in a long while. Mahogany began musical studies on piano, clarinet, and saxophones, playing in high school and beyond. When he joined a church choir, he found that singing was his truest passion, although while pursuing music studies at Baker University in Baldwin City, Kansas, he continued to play saxophone and starred in a jazz choir there. He pursued graduate studies at Midwestern State University in Wichita Falls, Texas, then returned to his hometown where he worked mainly with 1960s-styled R&B groups. In the early 1990s, Mahogany fixed his focus on jazz. He appeared on albums by Frank Mantooth and others, and headed for New York with his demo tape in 1992 hoping to land a record deal. Through vibist Gust Tsilis, Mahogany was introduced to Enja. The result was a three-album contract. His first two albums for Enja demonstrated that Mahogany's lush baritone voice is matched by his flawless sense of time as he weaves his way through blues, ballads, and intricate jazz with bold determination.

what to buy: On *Another Time, Another Place* ♫♫♫♫ (Warner Bros., 1997, prod. Matt Pierson), Mahogany kicks off with a scatting version of his original, "Big Rub," a Kansas City swing number, and ends the set with the gospelized and gritty "Parker's Mood/Kansas City." Mahogany comes back strong and hardy with this charming 10-tune collection after his less-than-spectacular Warner debut. Enhancing his vocals are illustrious guests: tenor saxophonist Joe Lovano on three tracks (Mahogany's "Big Rub," Pat Metheny's "Free," Mingus's "Goodbye Porkpie Hat"); singer Randy Travis (dubious collaboration as duet on Mahogany's original blues-swinger, "I Believe She Was Talking About Me"); and his rhythm team Cyrus Chestnut (piano), Dave Stryker (guitar), Ben Wolfe (bass), and Clarence Penn (drums). Mahogany is gutsy and inventive throughout, swings with verve, delivers a gorgeous version of the ballad classic "In the Wee Small Hours of the Morning," bends and shapes his vocals with bluesy bravado, and showcases his considerable art as composer. This solid jazz date (doing what he does best) should bring back his core audience. And it may be his best recording yet. By the time Kevin Mahogany recorded his third Enja album, *You Got What It Takes* 🎵🎵🎵🎵 (Enja, 1995, prod. Matthias Winckelmann), his jazz chops were polished and solid. In a variety of settings that give solo space to his teammates—lyrical pianist James Williams, supportive bassist Michael Formanek, imaginative drummer Victor Lewis, and guest saxophonist Benny Golson—Mahogany displays broad vocal range and builds drama into 13 standards. Mahogany confidently sings a broad selection from gorgeously sweet ballads ("Sophisticated Lady," "My Funny Valentine") to incredibly brisk-paced numbers ("Just in Time," "Yardbird Suite"), to seductive bluesers ("Please Send Me Someone To Love"), and more. Mahogany's delivery is polished. His deep, mature voice puts him in the class of Joe Williams, but Mahogany's no imitator. He's got his own pizzazz that's been simmering since he first began singing at age 12, and his knowledge of the jazz tradition is broad. He gives each song his all, enriching the lyrics by bending notes, sliding up and down the scale with ease, scatting magnificently, and capping some of his lines with unanticipated vocal nuggets. Mahogany totally envelops the listener with his rapture. This is a wonderful album.

what to buy next: Mahogany's second Enja recording, *Songs and Moments* 🎵🎵🎵🎵 (Enja, 1994, prod. Matthias Winckelmann) finds him restructuring 12 standards with a baritone voice deeper than the ocean. Mahogany has his scat form down pat; just listen to him on a fast-paced version of Strayhorn's "Take the A-Train" or Ellington's "Caravan." While some critics are ruthlessly bent toward tearing down his talents and others rave about him as "one of the most exciting jazz singers to come along in many years," fans were thrilled to find Mahogany's deep sexy voice among the crop of fine singers rising to the national scene. Although his immeasurable ability to scat is certainly exciting, Mahogany displays greater confidence on later recordings. But this CD is still a worthwhile listen. Pianist John Hicks, bassist Ray Drummond, drummer Marvin "Smitty" Smith, saxman Arthur Blythe, trombonist Robin Eubanks, trumpeter Michael Mossman, and others add to the attractiveness of this album as do arrangements by Slide Hampton, Freddie Hubbard, and Maria Schneider.

what to avoid: For his Warner label debut *Kevin Mahogany* 🎵🎵 (Warner Bros., 1996, prod. Matt Pierson), the then 38-year-old singer delivers a diluted commercialized mix of blues and R&B, then, almost as an afterthought, adds four jazz tunes at the end of the album. While Mahogany's versatility is evident, and

he's joined by solid jazz players (Kirk Whalum, Rodney Whitaker, Jerome Wiedman, Larry Goldings, and Greg Hutchinson) who would be expected to keep things interesting jazz-wise, that ain't what happens. Confirming their intent, Warner press materials tag the singer as "Warner Bros. Records' newest soul man." Not exactly what jazz purists want to hear.

the rest:
Double Rainbow 🎵🎵🎵🎵 (Enja, 1993)

influences:
◀◀ Jon Hendricks, Bobby McFerrin, Al Jarreau, Grady Tate, Lou Rawls

Nancy Ann Lee

Mike Mainieri

Born July 14, 1938, in New York, NY.

Vibraphonist Mike Mainieri was something of a child prodigy, working his first professional gigs at age four in a trio that toured with Paul Whiteman. By the age of 17, he was playing and arranging for Buddy Rich's sextet. During this period, he also played with legendary artists such as Billie Holiday, Dizzy Gillespie, Coleman Hawkins, and Wes Montgomery. In 1962 he joined the groundbreaking fusion group Jeremy and the Satyrs, led by flutist Jeremy Steig. In the late 1960s he was immersed in the experimental scene as a solo artist and with a conglomeration of musicians collectively known as White Elephant. He went on to form Steps (later, Steps Ahead) in the late 1970s with Michael Brecker, Eddie Gomez, Steve Gadd, and the late Don Grolnick. With various guesting artists and personnel changes, that adventurous group released several albums, including those for the label NYC Records, which Mainieri formed in 1992.

what to buy: Remember the '60s? If it's all rather cloudy, *Mike Mainieri & Friends: White Elephant* 🎵🎵🎵 (NYC, 1996, prod. Mike Mainieri) serves as a charming reminder of some of the adventurous, brilliant, and sometimes rather spacey music played back then. This collection includes tracks created by Mainieri and two dozen or so "friends" on a series of experimental large-group jams that the vibist held from 1962 to 1972. His collaborators include Michael and Randy Brecker, Steve Gadd, and Jon Faddis, who were just kids at the time, but already had the makings of greatness. At the core of this rather eccentric hodgepodge is the 12-minute title track—a dreamy, unceasingly blossoming showcase of youthful musical exuberance. Pass the bong, please. *American Diary* 🎵🎵🎵🎵 (NYC, 1996, prod. Mike Mainieri) is vibist Mainieri's most ambitious work, a quartet date featuring rearrangements of compositions by American classical composers, including Aaron Copland's "Sonata," Samuel Barber's "Overture to the School for Scandal," and Roger Sessions's "Piano Sonata No. 1," as well as Leonard Bernstein's "Somewhere," and Frank Zappa's "King Kong." Zappa? Yes! This pianoless quartet, with Joe Lovano on tenor, Eddie Gomez on bass, and Peter Erskine on drums, utilizes a batch of very eclectic music as a springboard for their peregrinations, and the results mark this as one of the most imaginative jazz recordings of the decade.

best of the rest:
(With Steps Ahead) *Modern Times* 𝄞𝄞𝄞 (Elektra, 1988)
(With Steps Ahead) *Yin Yang* 𝄞𝄞𝄞 (NYC, 1993)
(With Steps Ahead) *Steps Ahead: Live in Tokyo 1986* 𝄞𝄞 (NYC, 1994)
(With Steps Ahead) *Vibe* 𝄞𝄞𝄞 (NYC, 1995)
(With Steps Ahead) *N.Y.C.* 𝄞𝄞𝄞 (Intuition, 1995)

worth searching for: *Blues on the Other Side* 𝄞𝄞𝄞𝄞 (Argo, 1963, prod. Esmond Edwards), Mainieri's first record as a leader, shows remarkable maturity for a 25-year-old, with tasty standards "If I Were a Bell" and "Tenderly" tempered with his own bluesy originals. He swings along with neat, concise musical statements complemented by a delightfully feathery touch and also shows a nice sense of development and rhythmic experimentation on slow ballads. A fine debut.

influences:
◀◀ Milt Jackson, Lionel Hampton, Buddy Rich, Bobby Hutcherson

▶▶ Steve Nelson, Joe Locke, Stephane Harris

see also: *Steps Ahead*

Bret Primack

Adam Makowicz

Born August 18, 1940, in Cesky Tesin, Czechoslovakia.

When Adam Makowicz first came to the United States in 1977, he made a temporary splash as jazz pianist of the hour due to backing from talent-scout extraordinaire John Hammond. Makowicz was possessed of superior technique and was often compared to Art Tatum or Oscar Peterson, whose recordings he first heard on Voice of America radio broadcasts. While Tatum may have provided the initial impetus for the young musician's love of jazz piano, Makowicz was open to many influences. Along with trumpeter Tomasz Stanko, he formed a free-jazz group called the Jazz Darlings back in 1962. Makowicz toured the world with saxophonist Zbigniew Namyslowski throughout

the 1960s and worked with violinist Michal Urbaniak and vocalist Urszula Dudziak before creating yet another group with Stanko in 1975. Since coming to the States, Makowicz has worked with Ben Webster, among others, but he is more often found leading his own group or engaging in solo recitals than in accompanying others.

what to buy: Makowicz seems to have made a close study of American composers Kern, Gershwin, Porter, and Berlin, since much of his concertizing is devoted to material by them. This is good for an album like *The Music of Jerome Kern* 𝄞𝄞𝄞𝄞 (Concord Jazz, 1993, prod. Carl E. Jefferson) because the pianist has lived in these songs, drawing insights from them that might not come through otherwise.

what to buy next: *Adam Makowicz/George Mraz* 𝄞𝄞𝄞 (Concord Jazz, 1994, prod. Carl E. Jefferson, Nick Phillips) is Volume Five in the Maybeck Duo series and a pretty sympathetic outing. Makowicz and Mraz have been playing together off and on for years, and they communicate well. There are the usual showtune covers that pop up in other Makowicz recitals and make for some easy listening but the originals add spice to the mix: "Mito," with its oriental influences, and "Concordance" are perhaps the most interesting, bringing Makowicz's classical training in harmony and theory to bear even though the improvisational aspects can still be heard.

the rest:
(With George Mraz) *Together Wherever We Go* 𝄞𝄞𝄞 (Natasha, 1982)
The Name Is Makowicz 𝄞𝄞𝄞 (Sheffield Lab, 1989)
Plays Irving Berlin 𝄞𝄞𝄞 (VWC, 1992)
Maybeck Recital Series, Volume 24 𝄞𝄞𝄞 (Concord Jazz, 1993)
My Favorite Things: The Music of Richard Rogers 𝄞𝄞𝄞 (Concord Jazz, 1994)

influences:
◀◀ Art Tatum, Oscar Peterson, Erroll Garner

Garaud MacTaggart

Russell Malone

Born November 8, 1963, in Albany, GA.

A self-taught guitarist, Russell Malone has won accolades from Les Paul, Larry Coryell, Jimmy Bruno, and George Benson. His professional experiences include backing pop artists like Regina Belle, Peabo Bryson, and Clarence Carter in addition to work with jazz musicians Jimmy Smith, Harry Connick Jr., Kenny Burrell, Diana Krall, Kenny Barron, Gary Bartz, and Stephen Scott. Malone was also one of the guitarists used in Robert Altman's jazz-based flick, *Kansas City*. His solid sense of swing owes a lot to Benson, Burrell, and Wes Montgomery, which makes him a good choice as a sideman for new traditionalists like Benny Green and Branford Marsalis, who have also employed Malone's skills.

what to buy: With *Black Butterfly* ⚔⚔⚔ (Columbia, 1993, prod. Tracey Freeman), augmented by vibist Steve Nelson on two cuts, Malone and his quartet (pianist Gary Motley, bassist Paul Keller, and drummer Peter Siers) have come up with a pretty decent mainstream jazz album. There are some tributes to guitarists who helped shape Malone's sound—including Wes Montgomery ("Jingles") and Kenny Burrell (the Malone-penned "With Kenny in Mind")—and the title tune is a nice bit of '30s Ellingtonia. The rest of the album is an enjoyable, if workmanlike, performance.

the rest:
Russell Malone ⚔⚔⚔ (Columbia, 1992)

worth searching for: Malone digs down for some deep musical barbeque on Mose Allison's *Gimcracks and Gewgaws* ⚔⚔⚔ (Blue Note, 1998, prod. Ben Sidran). He passes over the jazz licks he usually hangs with for some full-bodied, T-Bone Walker-esque blues guitar on "St. Louis Blues," displaying an aspect of his abilities that a casual listening to his solo albums would never hint at. To let you know that it isn't a one-time thing, he dips back into the blues bag for some serious grease on "The More You Get" before whipping back into more of a straight-ahead jazz mode during his "What Will It Be" solo.

influences:
◀◀ Wes Montgomery, Kenny Burrell, George Benson

Garaud MacTaggart

Junior Mance

Born Julian Clifford Mance Jr., October 10, 1928, in Chicago, IL.

Junior Mance, one of the finest piano players performing today, is easily recognized for his gutsy, blues-infused jazz style. Developing his blues roots while growing up in Chicago, Mance began piano lessons at age eight and credits his piano teacher Dorum Richardson with teaching him everything he needed to know about playing. Earlier influences came from his father, a stride and boogie-woogie pianist, and from listening to his parents' boogie-woogie records by artists such as Albert Ammons, Meade Lux Lewis, and Pete Johnson. Mance's first gig came unexpectedly at age 10, when he sat in as a replacement for a piano player who had taken ill. He ultimately made the deci-

sion to become a professional piano player during his first year at Roosevelt College, signing up for music classes instead of the practical career his family had expected. Mance's illustrious career extends over 40 years and includes stints with some of the most respected musicians in the business. As a member of the Jimmy Dale band in 1947, he met Gene Ammons and joined his band, which fortified his bebop skills and gave him the chance to meet players such as Charlie Parker, Coleman Hawkins, Sonny Stitt, Billy Eckstine, and others. In 1949 Mance got the call to join Lester "Prez" Young, and performed with the saxophonist for a year before departing for army duty. Back home from the service, he accompanied vocalist Dinah Washington for an 18-month stint beginning in 1954, and in 1956 worked with old Army buddies Cannonball and Nat Adderley when the brothers formed their original band. Mance stayed with them until they disbanded in November, 1957. The following year he joined the Dizzy Gillespie quintet before teaming up with Eddie "Lockjaw" Davis and Johnny Griffin two years later. Mance formed his own trio and made his first recording for Verve (the currently out-of-print *Junior*) in 1961. Mance has led his own groups for more than three decades and recorded for a variety of labels, including Capitol, Verve, Riverside, Milestone, and others. As sideman, he has recorded with Gene Ammons, Dinah Washington, Cannonball Adderley, Dexter Gordon, Dizzy Gillespie, and others. A versatile player whose talent has been publicly acclaimed in Canada, Europe, and Japan, Mance retains in his piano style the faint traces of stride piano derived from his childhood influences.

what to buy: Mance's first live recording as a leader in New York City, February 1961 *At the Village Vanguard* ⚔⚔⚔ (OJC, 1996, prod. Orrin Keepnews) offers exceptional examples of Mance's hard-swinging blues and bebop-infused style, and the diversity of his fine piano skills. His rhythmic composition "Looptown" hits you like a gale-force wind in a Chicago winter storm and the lighting-quick tempo is coupled with amazing keyboard articulation. Two other Mance originals, "Letter from Home" and "Smokey Blues" (the tremolo closing is quite impressive), are heart-warming, blues-inspired numbers, brought home by the well-balanced trio consisting of Larry Gales on bass and Ben Riley on drums. Other highlights include "9:20 Special," and "Bingo Domingo," conventional straight-ahead jazz pieces that give further insights into Mance's proficiency. Sackville Records has produced some of the best live sessions of Mance's past and most recent work. An impressive retrospective of this extraordinary pianist's work, *Special* ⚔⚔⚔ (Sackville, 1994, prod. John Norris) compiles studio recordings made at Cherry Beach Sound in 1986 and a live-recorded performance at the famous Café des Copains in Toronto in 1988. Mance's blues roots come through with soulfully relaxed and natural feeling. "I Wish I Knew How It Would Feel to Be Free" is a beautiful piece that carries the down-home essence of an old Negro spiritual, and "If You Could See Me Now" and "In a Sentimental Mood" are well-executed ballads displaying another dimension of Mance's abilities. Just as inspiring, *Jubilation* ⨮⨮⨮⨮ (Sackville, 1994, prod. John Norris) contains a 1994 set live-recorded at the Montreal Bistro in Toronto, Ontario, Canada. The title tune, a rousing number combining blues, boogie-woogie, and tinges of stride, is a timeless vehicle of sheer delight. *Here 'Tis* ⨮⨮⨮⨮⨮, (Sackville, 1992, prod. John Norris) is an excellent tribute to the music of Gillespie, an inspiration and role model for Mance. Performing with the pianist are Bill McBirnie on flute, Reg Schwager on guitar, Kieran Overs on bass, and Norman Marshall Villeneuve on drums. The rich textures created by the addition of flute and guitar nicely augment the session. Mance showcases his superb piano skills on Gillespie standards such as "Con Alma," while "Tour de Force" features Schwager's outstanding guitar work. Mance's solo piano version of Gillespie's Afro-Cuban classic "A Night in Tunisia" totally separates him from his blues roots. This is one of his most pleasing albums.

what to buy next: Influences of stride piano style can occasionally be heard in Mance's playing on *Softly as a Morning Sunrise* ⨮⨮⨮⨮ (Enja, 1994, prod. Horst Weber). But that doesn't mean that Mance doesn't swing, bop, or traverse the blues. Indeed, his keyboard style leans sometimes to a warm cognizance of the Chicago blues as well as bop derivations on this acoustic studio session recorded in July 1994 in Munich. With two superb sidemen—bassist Jimmy Woode and drummer Bob Durham—Mance offers rejuvenating versions of 11 standards and originals by group members. His facile keyboard style, even on ballads, is filled with passion that draws listener attention. *For Dancers Only* ⨮⨮⨮ (Sackville, 1983, prod. John Norris, Bill Smith) is an impressive representation of Mance's duo work with bassist Martin Rivera, an old friend and associate of many years. This CD highlights the influence of Chicago blues on Mance's style, with "Girl of My Dreams," "Run 'Em Around," "Summertime," and the title tune aptly displaying Mance's craft. He doesn't miss on *Junior Mance: At Town Hall, Volume 1* ⨮⨮⨮⨮ (Enja, 1995, prod. Horst Weber), a rousing live-recorded, five-tune performance at Town Hall in New York City on March 30, 1995. The leader is in fine form with bassist Calvin Hill, drummer Alvin Queen, and guest saxophonist Houston Person,

who adds considerable verve to the session on the 10-minute blazing launcher, "Nadja," a Mance original. Person follows Mance's melody lead with a gritty solo on Hoagy Carmichael's "Small Fry," a trudging soul-blues number that shows off Mance's command of the keys. Mance's "Harlem Lullaby" is a beautiful riffy piece, with Person lending his saxy blues-speak to this nighttime vista. Queen and Hill provide substantial support for Mance's exploration. His closer, "Jubilation," which he announces as "the first tune I ever wrote in my life," is a propelling bop spree with everyone in tight-knit unison. Initially, the nearly 16-minute, hard-swinging jouster ("I Cried for You"), with its audience patter, sounds like it was recorded in a club rather than concert hall, but is insignificant in the scope of the whole session. Although it gets off to a rough start, with a three-minute announcement and some sound-production problems on the first track, it's a real foot-tapping pleaser for blues-groove fans. Recorded with the same personnel on the same date and intended as a companion piece, *Junior Mance: At Town Hall, Volume 2* ⨮⨮⨮⨮ (Enja, 1996, prod. Horst Weber) provides an additional five tunes, including 14-plus minutes of the Mance original "Some Other Blues." The kicking opener, Oscar Pettiford's "Blues in the Closet," showcases everyone's skills, but especially highlights Hill's expertise in a fine bass solo. This disc includes chestnuts such as the sweet blues-tainted "My Romance," a lush version of Ellington's "Do Nothin' Till You Hear from Me," and a hip-beat trip to Zawinul's "Mercy, Mercy, Mercy," Both albums are highly recommended.

influences:

◀◀ Charlie Parker, Coleman Hawkins, Lester Young, Albert Ammons, Gene Ammons, Meade "Lux" Lewis, Pete Johnson, Sonny Stitt

Keith Brickhouse and Nancy Ann Lee

Joe Maneri

Born February 9, 1927, in Brooklyn, NY.

Reedman Joe Maneri mixes an encyclopedic knowledge of microtonal music (he's written a respected textbook on the subject) with an acute ear for improvisation. The father of violinist Mat Maneri, he's long been a professor at the New England Conservatory, but didn't have any recordings as a leader released until he was 67 (*Get Ready to Receive Yourself*). Maneri's parents were Sicilian immigrants. He quit school at age 15 to play music professionally, and in the spirit of the true gigging musician took all available work. Of course, that meant lots of wedding jobs (Jewish, Greek, and various Balkan ethnicities) and bar mitzvahs, experiences he absorbed into his musical persona. He was also studying modern classical music, and in the 1940s he got together with a small group of like-minded musicians to experiment with free improvisation and 12-tone music. In 1961 three of Maneri's classical compositions were performed at Carnegie Recital Hall to favorable reviews, and in 1963 Third Stream conceptualist Gunther Schuller hired Maneri to play tenor saxophone on a Third Stream composition by David Reck. Next, Schuller pushed Atlantic Records to sign Maneri, and although the company passed on this opportunity, a Maneri-helmed quartet recorded a demo that finally appeared 35 years later. In 1970 Schuller hired Maneri to teach composition at the New England Conservatory, and Maneri moved to the Boston area and settled into the academic life. He apparently played only rarely in public until Maneri's son Mat and some other area musicians and students prodded Joe into greater activity. In 1995 the English label Leo put out an album, certainly the most startling debut of the year or perhaps the decade, and Maneri finally began to receive the acclaim his truly unique talent merits.

what to buy: The music on *Get Ready to Receive Yourself* ♫♫♫♫ (Leo Lab, 1995, prod. Personasound Productions, Leo Feigin), Maneri's debut album, is as challenging as the most "outside" free jazz, but also generally subdued, which allows better appreciation of his fine gradations of tone quality. All the compositions are group improvisations except for "Body and Soul," which is given a deeply felt reading. Bassist John Lockwood and drummer Randy Peterson provide sensitive accompaniment. Though it's a concert recording (from 1993), *Dahabenzapple* ♫♫♫♫ (Hat Jazz, 1996, prod. Joe Maneri, Mat Maneri, Pia Uehlinger, Werner X. Uehlinger) has no showboating. In fact, it displays a very special intimacy over the course of its three 20-minute-plus improvisations, with Maneri putting so much into each note that a single phrase can carry as much meaning as an entire piece in mainstream jazz. Cecil McBee replaces Lockwood here.

what to buy next: *Let the Horse Go* ♫♫♫♫ (Leo Lab, 1996, prod. Personasound Productions, Leo Feigin) has violinist Mat Maneri, Lockwood, and Peterson, and if anything is even freer and more adventurous than the first Leo CD. The elder Maneri displays a broad range of intonational inflection and microtonal tuning, endowing every note with special feeling. Even the loud moments of full-blast intensity have a lean spareness, with a great deal of space around them, and the predominant quieter moments are reminiscent of the approach of Jimmy Giuffre, if built from different materials and approaches. There

are so many subtle touches that superficial listening just won't do, but deep concentration is always rewarded by this seemingly abstract yet highly emotional music.

what to avoid: *Paniots Nine* ♫♫♫ (Avant, 1998, prod. Joe Maneri) is actually an important document of Maneri's work prior to being "discovered," but it probably shouldn't be approached until after the listener has gained a full appreciation of Maneri's artistry from his 1990s recordings. Seven of the eight tracks on the CD are from the tape Maneri made in 1963 for Atlantic, though the documentation could be clearer—provenance, personnel, and composing credits must be gleaned from Harvey Pekar's well-written liner notes, which lay out the twists and turns of Maneri's history in fine detail (and tantalize with mentions of other private tapes not yet released). The master tapes to the Atlantic demo have been lost, so the sonics are often, well, "archival," and the better-sounding final track, from 1981, seems to end abruptly. However, all this never-before-released material is fascinating, laying bare the Greek and klezmer influences in Maneri's style and showing his quartet melding the eccentric meters into a sort of free-jazz style. The 1981 track has Maneri on clarinet along with a pianist; they play an 11-minute improvisation (called "Jewish Fantasy—At the Wedding" in the liner notes but simply "Jewish Concert" on the track listing) that is predominantly klezmer-inspired but touching on Greek music, jazz, and the blues.

the rest:
(With Joe Morris and Mat Maneri) *Three Men Walking* ♫♫♫♫ (ECM, 1996)
Coming down the Mountain ♫♫♫♫ (Hat Ology, 1998)

worth searching for: *In Full Cry* ♫♫♫♫ (ECM, 1997, prod. Steve Lake) came out in Europe but has not yet appeared in the United States. Hopefully this will soon be rectified. This CD is valuable not only for the expected high quality of the performances, but for what's being performed: mixed in with the original group improvisations are "Tenderly," "Nobody Knows," "Motherless Child," and "Prelude to a Kiss," and hearing the players lovingly break them down and reassemble them is fascinating and moving.

influences:

◀◀ Jimmy Giuffre, Pee Wee Russell

▶▶ Cecil Taylor, Mat Maneri, Assif Tsahar

Steve Holtje

Mat Maneri

Born October 4, 1969, in Brooklyn, NY.

The son of Joe Maneri, violinist Mat Maneri follows in his father's footsteps on a different instrument, using considerable microtonal inflection to color his sound. He also incorporates private study with Miroslav Vitous and Juilliard String Quartet co-founder Robert Koff into his formidable technique and distinctive musical conception. Mat's work in his father's group (see above) and with Matthew Shipp (as heard on the albums *By the Law of Music*, *Flow of X*, and *Critical Mass*) is his most prominent, but his albums as leader or co-leader are gaining him notice in his own right. He has performed in the United States and abroad and worked with such luminaries as Joe Morris, Bob Moses, Bern Nix, Perry Robinson, Cecil McBee, and others.

what to buy: *Fever Bed* 𝄞𝄞𝄞𝄞 (Leo Lab, 1996, prod. Leo Feigin) uses Maneri's regular trio, with bassist Ed Schuller and drummer Randy Peterson. The dynamic levels are quite low, allowing for maximum impact of Maneri's microtonal shadings of pitch. The quietness and the hovering, unemphatic pulse of the music amplify its intensity, drawing the listener into the group's singular free improvisation.

what to buy next: *Acceptance* 𝄞𝄞𝄞 (Hat Ology, 1998, prod. Mat Maneri) stands out from Maneri's other recordings for three reasons: his use of the lower-pitched and darker-toned viola, the larger and more instrumentally colorful group with trombonist Gary Valente and guitarist John Dirac added to the trio (Joe Maneri joins on one track), and deconstructive covers of "My Funny Valentine" and Sonny Rollins's "East Broadway Rundown." The challenge of arranging the more varied textures of a quintet clearly doesn't faze Maneri, who deploys the players across slowly evolving musical landscapes that emphasize subtle timbres and the shapes of the lines. Note that this is a limited edition of 1500 CDs.

the rest:
(With Pandelis Karayorgis) *In Time* 𝄞𝄞𝄞𝄞 (Leo Lab, 1994)
(With Joe Maneri and Joe Morris) *Three Men Walking* 𝄞𝄞𝄞𝄞 (ECM, 1996)

influences:
⏮ Leroy Jenkins, Joe Maneri

Steve Holtje

Albert Mangelsdorff

Born September 5, 1928, in Frankfurt, Germany.

Albert Mangelsdorff is probably the greatest of the free-jazz trombonists who has mastered multiphonics (playing split-tones by simultaneously playing a note and humming through a horn). Mangelsdorff comes from a musical family (his brother Emil is a noted German saxophonist) and he originally studied violin, then guitar. Although jazz was banned in Germany during the war years, Mangelsdorff and his brother attended secret gatherings at the Hot Club in Frankfurt, and in 1940 he decided to pursue jazz. By 1948, at age 20, inspired by the American Armed Forces Radio broadcasts in Europe, he switched to trombone, with Lee Konitz and Lennie Tristano his major inspirations in the 1950s. Mangelsdorff played with Hans Koller and others before leading his own band, broadcasting regularly on Frankfurt radio, and by 1954 winning polls in Germany. In 1958 he visited the United States to perform with the Newport Jazz Festival's international band. The same year, he performed throughout western Europe and in Yugoslavia, leading his own quartets and quintets in concerts and on radio and television. Mangelsdorff recorded the Atlantic album *Animal Dance* with pianist John Lewis in 1962, boosting his international reputation. Early in 1964 he toured Asia for three months, and, not long after, began his development toward free music. Combining the influences of Indian ragas with the more abstract side of improvisation, Mangelsdorff recorded with sitarist Ravi Shankar in 1964 and began to emerge with a notably individualistic style. Worldwide tours followed, including trips to the States for the Newport Festivals in 1965, 1967, and 1969, New Orleans in 1968, Tokyo and Osaka in 1970, and Western and Eastern Europe, further broadening his exposure. From the late 1960s he has been a member of the Globe Unity Orchestra, a large free-music ensemble.

In the early 1970s Mangelsdorff began to develop his multiphonics technique, whereby he played one note and sang another, usually higher, note, sometimes creating chords of up to four notes. This discovery allowed him some creative freedom, and from 1972 he began to perform in unaccompanied trombone concerts, appearing at worldwide festivals, including Monterey, California, in 1975. Mangelsdorff worked with French saxophonist Michel Portal in small combos from 1976–82, and since 1981 he has co-led the French/German Jazz Ensemble with French bassist Jean-François Jenny-Clark. In 1977 he performed and recorded with Barre Phillips, John Surman, and drummer Stu Martin. He toured extensively during the 1980s, working with a variety of groups, including performances and recordings with the United Jazz and Rock Ensemble. Considered to be one of Europe's legendary avant-garde players, Mangelsdorff has been frequently cited in European and American polls, and has won numerous awards for his contributions to the European jazz scene. He is considered a major jazz instrumentalist, an innovator and influential stylist, and a fine composer for small groups and large ensembles. Among Mangelsdorff's many albums, his session with John Lewis and his MPS recordings will be hardest to find.

what to buy: Recorded in Germany in 1983, *Art of the Duo* 𝒥𝒥𝒥𝒥𝒥 (Enja, 1989, prod. Horst Weber) is a duo studio session with Mangelsdorff's inspiration, saxophonist Lee Konitz. On 11 originals the pair creates well-blended, free-jazz dialogue. Mangelsdorff provides structure for Konitz's fashionings, at times emitting deep-toned sounds that simulate a tuba more than a trombone. His dark and eerie harmonic foundations permit Konitz to weave melancholy themes. Noted for his pure intonation and an uncommon art for aqueous, linear playing, Konitz blows cool and noble, fitting neatly into Mangelsdorff's growl effects, ostinatos, and solo profiles. Both instrumentalists stretch and preserve the tradition, displaying creativity throughout. This is an engrossing listen, with both musicians uniquely advancing the form. On *Live in Tokyo* 𝒥𝒥𝒥𝒥 (Enja, 1971/1995, prod. Horst Weber), trombonist Mangelsdorff leads his quartet with Heinz Sauer (tenor saxophone), Günter Lenz (bass), and Ralf Hübner (drums) in their first live-recorded performance (1971) at the jazz club DUG in Shinjuku, Tokyo. This intense free-jazz set captures the musicians as they creatively explore four tunes written by Sauer and Mangelsdorff, with the shortest, "Triple Trip," at 4:05 and the longest, "Mahüsale," at 21:40. Sauer is a real champ on this outing, generating fiery, flowing improvisations. Mangelsdorff keeps his multiphonics to a minimum and sometimes steers the musicians to the inside, but more often this collegial pianoless group engages in free-blowing, harmonically blended sprees that shift tempos, alter dynamics, and showcase each musician's individual ingenuity and virtuosity.

best of the rest:

Three Originals 𝒥𝒥𝒥𝒥 (Verve, 1975–1980/1994)
Triologue Live! 𝒥𝒥𝒥𝒥 (PA/USA, 1976)
Tromboneliness 𝒥𝒥𝒥𝒥 (Sackville, 1976)
Purity 𝒥𝒥𝒥𝒥 (Mood, 1992)

influences:

◀◀ Lee Konitz, Lennie Tristano

▶▶ Ray Anderson

Nancy Ann Lee

Chuck Mangione

Born Charles Frank Mangione, November 29, 1940, in Rochester, NY.

Chuck Mangione brought a sense of New Age aesthetics to melodic jazz. His style is soulful but light, cerebral yet accessible. A masterful technician on trumpet, electric piano, and flugelhorn, his best recordings virtually defined popular jazz in the 1970s and early 1980s. Mangione was inspired to play trumpet by viewing the 1950 film *Young Man with a Horn* (a soapy biography of Bix Beiderbecke with Kirk Douglas in the title role), and drew much encouragement and influence from family friend Dizzy Gillespie. In 1960 Mangione and his older brother, Gap, formed a hard-bop combo called the Jazz Brothers that recorded several well-regarded (but low-selling) LPs for the Jazzland label. After dissolving the band in 1965, Mangione played in the trumpet sections of the Woody Herman and Maynard Ferguson orchestras, before joining Art Blakey and The Jazz Messengers. Mangione credits his stint as the director of their jazz ensemble at the Eastman School of Music (where he earned his bachelor's degree in 1963) for turning his career around. A live recording of the tune "Hill Where the Lord Hides" at his *Friends & Love Concert* led to a deal with Mercury Records. Mangione's career peaked in the mid-1970s at A&M Records when his classic, "Feels So Good," became one of the biggest jazz hits of the decade. Mangione's stylistic change from hard bop to flugelhorn-enhanced melodic jazz was instantly successful with record buyers. He attracted several Grammy nominations with his soundtrack LP for the 1978 film *Children of Sanchez*, which also earned him a Golden Globe Award. In the 1980s, Mangione recorded several LPs for Columbia, but the impact of his sound began to wane, and he decided to take a sabbatical from showbiz. Mangione came back three years later with several high-profile concert events and a self-mocking animated television cameo on *The Simpsons*. The death of Dizzy Gillespie inspired Mangione to return to the trumpet full-time, and he has begun reissuing his back catalog as well as releasing fresh sounds on his own label Feels So Good Records.

what to buy: Mangione's breakthrough hit "Feels So Good," plus several of his most interesting soft jazz tracks from his stay at A&M Records, are on *Greatest Hits* 𝒥𝒥𝒥𝒥 (A&M, 1996, prod. Chuck Mangione). It is a nice introduction to his work, featuring his fine flugelhorn playing on "Children of Sanchez," "Land of Make Believe," and other popular tunes from his earlier albums. This album duplicates his earlier *Best of A&M* recording.

what to buy next: To hear Mangione, his brother Gap, and their early hard-bop style with a quintet, check out *Recuerdo* 𝒥𝒥𝒥𝒥 (OJC, 1991, prod. various).

what to avoid: Mangione's hot streak was clearly over with *Love Notes* 𝒥𝒥 (Columbia, 1982, prod. Chuck Mangione), a meandering, tedious collection.

best of the rest:
Land of Make Believe 𝄞𝄞𝄞𝄞 (Mercury, 1973/1990)
Chase the Clouds Away 𝄞𝄞𝄞 (Rebound Records, 1975/1996)
Feels So Good 𝄞𝄞𝄞 (A&M Records, 1977/1987)
Fun & Games 𝄞𝄞 (Rebound Records, 1980/1994)
Journey to a Rainbow 𝄞𝄞 Columbia, 1983/1990)
Save Tonight for Me 𝄞𝄞 (Columbia, 1986)
Eyes of the Veiled Temptress 𝄞𝄞 (Columbia, 1988)
Hey Baby 𝄞𝄞𝄞 (OJC, 1992)
Compact Jazz 𝄞𝄞 (Verve, 1992)
Greatest Hits 𝄞𝄞 (Intersound, 1993)

worth searching for: Mangione's best live recording to date is *Live at the Village Gate* 𝄞𝄞𝄞 (Feels So Good Records, 1987, prod. Chuck Mangione, Mallory Earl), a two-disc set that features some fine ambience and well-received jams. Also, he won a Grammy for the now out-of-print *Bellavia* 𝄞𝄞𝄞 (A&M, 1975, prod. Chuck Mangione), a superior studio effort.

influences:
◀◀ Dizzy Gillespie, Miles Davis

Ken Burke

The Manhattan Transfer

Formed 1969, in New York, NY.

Tim Hauser (born 1940, in Troy, NY), vocals (1969–present); Laurel Masse (born 1954), vocals (1972–79); Cheryl Bentyne (born in Mt. Vernon, WA), vocals (1979–present); Alan Paul (born 1949, in Newark, NJ), vocals (1972–present); Janis Siegel (born 1952, in Brooklyn, NY), vocals (1972–present).

Over the course of its 25-plus-year career, the Manhattan Transfer has become one of the most popular and acclaimed vocal ensembles in contemporary music. Its repertoire spans jazz, pop, swing, R&B, Brazilian, and doo-wop styles, which the four members perform with ease and high style. The group has earned numerous platinum and gold albums, as well as eight Grammy Awards (group members Janis Siegel and Cheryl Bentyne have also won a Grammy apiece for their arrangements of various tunes). The group also won "Best Vocal Group" honors for 10 years straight—from 1980 to 1990—in the annual *Down Beat* and *Playboy* jazz polls. It won *Playboy's* poll again in 1992.

Taking its name from a 1925 novel by American author John Dos Passos, the Manhattan Transfer was founded in 1969 by Tim Hauser, along with guitarist Gene Pistilli. In 1971 the band released the album *Jukin'*, but the group dissolved the following year, and Hauser took a job driving a cab in New York City. One day his fare was aspiring singer Laurel Masse, and she and

Hauser decided to form a group. At a party, Hauser met Janis Siegel, then a member of a folk group called Laurel Canyon. They then met Alan Paul, who was starring on Broadway in the musical *Grease*. The new group decided to arrange its vocals as if the four voices were the saxophone section of the Count Basie Big Band, and the Manhattan Transfer performed its first concert in June 1973. That line-up recorded four albums, but in 1978 Masse was injured in a car accident and during her recovery she decided not to rejoin the group. Masse was replaced by Cheryl Bentyne, at the time a successful singer in her native Washington. This line-up remains intact.

what to buy: The classic *Vocalese* 𝄞𝄞𝄞𝄞 (Atlantic, 1985, prod. Tim Hauser) is an example of vocal virtuosity. The group set jazz standards to lyrics penned by singer and longtime collaborator Jon Hendricks, using vocals to approximate instrumental solos. The recording sparkles with invention, and standout tracks include "Another Night in Tunisia" with guest appearances by Bobby McFerrin and Hendricks, and "Sing Joy Spring" featuring a solo by Dizzy Gillespie.

what to buy next: *The Manhattan Transfer Anthology: Down in Birdland* 𝄞𝄞𝄞𝄞 (Rhino, 1992, prod. various) is an essential two-CD compilation of the Transfer's best music during its Atlantic years up to 1987. It's an excellent chronicle of the group's development as well as its musical versatility.

what to avoid: *Tonin'* 𝄞𝄞 (Atlantic, 1995, prod. Arif Mardin) is a rather uninspired set of cover songs, most of which were recorded with high-profile guests, including Phil Collins, Bette Midler, Chaka Khan, and Smokey Robinson. There seems to be little connection with either the song or the guest artists; too often, the group is reduced to little more than a background presence and its vocal prowess is never allowed to shine.

best of the rest:
The Manhattan Transfer 𝄞𝄞𝄞𝄞 (Atlantic, 1975)
Coming Out 𝄞𝄞𝄞 (Atlantic, 1976)
The Manhattan Transfer Live 𝄞𝄞𝄞𝄞 (Atlantic, 1978)
Pastiche 𝄞𝄞𝄞 (Atlantic, 1978)
Extensions 𝄞𝄞𝄞𝄞 (Atlantic, 1979)
Mecca for Moderns 𝄞𝄞𝄞𝄞 (Atlantic, 1981)
Bodies and Souls 𝄞𝄞𝄞 (Atlantic, 1983)
Brasil 𝄞𝄞𝄞𝄞 (Atlantic, 1987)
The Offbeat of Avenues 𝄞𝄞𝄞 (Columbia, 1991)
The Christmas Album 𝄞𝄞𝄞 (Columbia, 1992)
Live in Tokyo 𝄞𝄞𝄞 (Rhino, 1996)
Swing 𝄞𝄞𝄞𝄞 (Atlantic, 1997)

worth searching for: On her solo album *At Home* 𝄞𝄞𝄞𝄞 (Atlantic, 1987, prod. Steven Miller), Janis Siegel beautifully show-

The Manhattan Transfer (© Jack Vartoogian)

cases her powerful voice and extraordinary range. She effortlessly runs a stylistic gamut, from a commanding version of Marvin Gaye's "Trouble Man," to the languid ballad "Small Day Tomorrow," to the bluesy "The Million Dollar Secret," to the jazzy and spirited "(If I Had) Rhythm in My Nursery Rhymes."

influences:

◀◀ Count Basie, Fletcher Henderson, Coleman Hawkins, Eddie Jefferson, Lambert, Hendricks & Ross

▶▶ New York Voices

Lucy Tauss

Herbie Mann

Born Herbert J. Solomon, April 16, 1930, in Brooklyn, NY.

Flutist Herbie Mann has incorporated a lot of different music into his jazz improvisations throughout the years. After playing straight-ahead jazz in the 1950s, Mann gradually descended over the next three decades into improvised jazzy-pop, soul-jazz, and world music–influenced music. Although he included top veterans and rising jazz stars in his bands (especially during the 1960s), Mann tended to follow current pop trends, gaining wider audiences but losing many of his core jazz fans. As a youngster, Mann first studied clarinet, and later, after studies at the Manhattan School of Music, became one of the handful of players to make the flute a viable jazz instrument. Mann served in the U.S. Army in Europe, and following his discharge became active as a musician on the West Coast from 1954–57. He began playing, writing, and directing music for television dramas before starting and recording with his own groups. From 1954–58, Mann, doubling on tenor and bass clarinet, often played bebop with players such as Phil Woods, Buddy Collette, Sam Most, Bobby Jasper, and Charlie Rouse. In 1959, in New York, Mann formed his Afro-Jazz Sextet, a group that used several percussionists, including a vibist, along with his flute. He further explored world percussions, making trips to Africa and Brazil during the 1960s, and his band became famous for performances at Newport and appearances at the Village Gate.

In addition to African and Brazilian influences, Mann introduced elements of Arabian, Jewish, and Turkish music into his performances. And, in the late 1960s, he brought in elements from rock on his *Memphis Underground* album, a huge and critical success. By the 1970s Mann had been a producer at Embroyo (a subsidiary of Atlantic Records), and had become one of the most popular jazz flutists, using young sidemen such as Chick Corea and Roy Ayers in his groups. Mann continued to explore the jazz-rock-funk meld in the 1970s, calling his band the Family of Mann. He recorded a reggae album, dabbled in disco, and, after leaving the Atlantic label in 1979, formed his own label, Kokopelli (named after the flute-playing Native American god of harmony, magic, and healing), and began to drift back into jazz. Mann was more popular with fans than critics, and had regularly won *Down Beat* polls from 1957–70 for his music that was always closely related to dance rhythms of the day. He continues to tour and perform at major festivals in the U.S. and Europe, and has recorded exclusively for his Kokopelli label, releasing albums with a world-beat, new age flavor during the late 1980s and 1990s. Many of his recordings from the 1950s–1980s are out-of-print. Throughout his career, regardless of what musical style Mann was exploring, his improvisations on flute have always been confident, joyful, and songlike.

what to buy: With so few of his albums from his Atlantic period in print, *Herbie Mann at the Village Gate* ♫♫♫♫ (Atlantic, 1964/1987, prod. Nesuhi Ertegun) is a treat because it contains his first big hit, "Comin' Home Baby," as well as extended versions of two Gershwin pieces, "Summertime" and "It Ain't Necessarily So." Sidemen include percussionists Ray Mantilla and Chief Bey, bassist Ahmed Abdul-Malik, vibraphonist Hagood Hardy, and drummer Rudy Collins. *Evolution of Mann: The Herbie Mann Anthology* ♫♫♫♫ (Atlantic, 1960–92/Rhino, 1994) compiles in a two-CD set many of his Atlantic hits recorded with an array of musicians, including jazz players such as pianists Chick Corea and Richard Tee, drummers Paul Motian and Steve Gadd, and vibraphonists Dave Pike, Hagood Hardy, and Roy Ayers, in addition to some of the best percussionists. The majority of the selections are drawn from the 1970s, his worst years for jazz, actually. Yet, among the 28 tunes are Mann's classic hits such as "Birdwalk," "Memphis Underground," "Push Push," "Hold On, I'm Comin'," and "Comin' Home Baby." However, the shortcoming of this set is the absence of documentation of Mann's earlier bop-focused years.

what to buy next: *65th Birthday Celebration: Live at the Blue Note–NYC* ♫♫♫♫ (Lightyear, 1997) draws from Mann's week-long engagement to celebrate his 65th birthday in April 1995. On the high-spirited eight tracks he's joined by some of his favorite musicians, many from the Latin-jazz scene such as trumpeter Claudio Roditi, saxophonist Paquito D'Rivera, bassist Eddie Gomez, flutist Dave Valentin, percussionists Milton Cardona, Cyro Baptista, and Café, and a slew of other veterans and young lions. There's enough variety to suit most fans, from Brazilian jazz to funk-jazz, blues, and some straight-ahead tracks. If you want to hear what all the fuss was about in the 1960s, check out *Memphis Underground* ♫♫♫♫ (Atlantic, 1969/1987, prod. Tom Dowd), the huge-selling soul-jazz album that features Mann's sweet and soaring solos with top jazz players such as Roy Ayres (vibraphone) and guitarists Larry Coryell and Sonny Sharrock. Bassist Miroslav Vitous appears on one track. Recorded in Memphis with a local rhythm section (which had played with R&B legends Otis Redding and Sam & Dave), the album blends R&B and country, with jazz improvisations. The grooving title tune enjoyed some well-deserved popularity during its day and the remaining four tunes capture the musicians in high-spirited inventiveness.

best of the rest:

Flute Soufflé ♫♫♫♫ (Prestige/OJC, 1957)
Sultry Serenade ♫♫♫ (Riverside, 1957/OJC, 1997)
Yardbird Suite ♫♫♫♫ (Savoy, 1957/Verve, 1993)
Bird in a Silver Cage ♫♫♫ (Atlantic, 1976)
(With Jasil Brazz) *Caminho De Casa* ♫♫♫ (Chesky, 1992)
Peace Pieces ♫♫♫♫ (Kokopelli, 1995/Lightyear, 1997)
America/Brasil ♫♫♫ (Lightyear, 1997)

influences:

◀◀ Frank Wess, James Moody

▶▶ Joe Farrell, Hubert Laws, Dave Valentin, Eddie Daniels

Nancy Ann Lee

Shelly Manne

Born June 11, 1920, in New York, NY. Died September 26, 1984, in Los Angeles, CA.

A highly musical drummer who could raise the level of any musical situation, Shelly Manne worked and recorded prolifically throughout his career. Bridging the swing and bebop eras, he developed a versatile, responsive style that was rhythmically powerful but also concerned with melodic development. Always open to new sounds, Manne was a dedicated experimentalist, delving into free-form improvising in the early 1950s and recording with Ornette Coleman on one of his first albums. Though Manne was not a particularly influential figure on his instrument, he did create a lasting body of work that stands up today as some of the most consistently rewarding jazz recorded on the West Coast in the 1950s and early 1960s.

Discouraged from learning drums by his tympanist father (who wanted him to play a wind instrument), Manne finally began lessons at age 18 and within a few months was working professionally. By 1939 he was gigging on 52nd Street with bandleaders Bobby Byrne and Joe Marsala (with whom he replaced Dave Tough). Manne spent a few years in the Coast Guard and by 1946, when he began an intermittent relationship with the Stan Kenton band that lasted until 1952, he had recorded with Dizzy Gillespie, Coleman Hawkins, Ben Webster, and Johnny Hodges. Settling in Los Angeles in the early 1950s, Manne quickly became a pillar of Contemporary, recording numerous sessions for the label, including early free-jazz experiments, seminal West Coast jazz sessions, and many swinging, hard-bop oriented albums. His records often featured brilliant arrangers, such as Marty Paich and Bill Holman, and all-star bands, including Art Pepper, Bob Cooper, Curtis Counce, Conte Candoli, Herb Geller, Russ Freeman, and Victor Feldman.

Manne led his own groups from the early 1950s on, usually under the banner Shelley Manne and His Men (or, on ad hoc sessions, Shelly Manne and His Friends). Manne scored a huge jazz hit with his *My Fair Lady* trio album with Andre Previn and Leroy Vinnegar. Extremely busy on the LA studio scene, composing and playing on many film and TV sessions, Manne also ran his popular Shelly's Manne-Hole nightclub from 1960–74. In the mid-1970s, he was a co-founder of the L.A. Four, a chamber jazz group with Bud Shank, Ray Brown, and Laurindo Almeida. He was active musically right up until his unexpected death. Manne recorded for numerous labels, including Impulse!, Verve, Capitol, Atlantic, Concord, Mainstream, Flying Dutchman, Discovery, Interlude, and Savoy.

what to buy: The first volume of the Shelly Manne and His Men series (and his first album for Contemporary), *The West Coast Sound* 𝄞𝄞𝄞𝄞 (Contemporary, 1955/OJC, 1988, prod. Lester Koenig) includes a who's who of West Coast jazz and is a classic of the genre. Covering three septet sessions recorded in 1953 and 1955, the album features excellent tunes and arrangements by Bill Russo, Shorty Rogers, Jimmy Giuffre, and Marty Paich. Art Pepper (alto sax), Bob Cooper (tenor sax), Giuffre (baritone sax), and Bob Enevoldsen (valve trombone) make up the front line of the first session, with Bud Shank replacing Pepper on the second 1953 session. Joe Maini Jr. (alto) and Hol-

man (tenor) join Giuffre and Enevoldsen on the last four tracks. Though this is an arranger's session, this is hard-swinging music with many fine solos. Try and figure out how 1950s West Coast jazz picked up a reputation as bloodless and intellectual listening to the hard-swinging *At the Manne-Hole, Vol. 1* 𝄞𝄞𝄞𝄞 (Contemporary, 1961/OJC, 1992, prod. Lester Koenig). The session features one of Manne's best working quintets, with bebop trumpeter Conte Candoli blowing up a storm, and the fine, Lester Young–influenced tenor saxophonist Richie Kamuca acting as a cool foil with his beautiful sound. Pianist Russ Freeman and bassist Chuck Berghofer complete the powerful, cohesive rhythm section, which drives the band on Dizzy Gillespie's blues "The Champ," and soars through Ellington's rarely played "How Could It Happen to a Dream?" *At the Black Hawk, Vol. 1* 𝄞𝄞𝄞𝄞 (Contemporary, 1959/OJC, 1991, prod. Lester Koenig) was the first of five hard-swinging CDs ultimately released from this live date recorded at the famed San Francisco club. With trumpeter Joe Gordon, tenor saxophonist Richie Kamuca, pianist Victor Feldman, and bassist Monty Budwig, Manne's quintet had no shortage of soloists, and he let them stretch out, with three of the five tunes 12 minutes or longer. The CD includes an alternate take of Frank Rosolino's "Blue Daniel," in addition to "Summertime," "Our Delight," and "Poinciana."

what to buy next: A huge hit when it was released, *My Fair Lady* 𝄞𝄞𝄞𝄞 (Contemporary, 1956/OJC, 1988, prod. Lester Koenig) was a trio date featuring Shelly Manne and His Friends—meaning pianist Andre Previn and bassist Leroy Vinnegar. Manne integrates himself into the trio, so this is really Previn's session, and he sticks fairly close to the melodies from the popular musical. Never a great improvisor, Previn does play with style and imagination, making this a thoroughly enjoyable date. An early edition of Manne's quintet on *More Swinging Sounds* 𝄞𝄞𝄞𝄞 (Contemporary, 1956/OJC, 1993, prod. Lester Koenig) features Stu Williamson (trumpet), Charlie Mariano (alto sax), Russ Freeman (piano), and Leroy Vinnegar (bass) playing Charlie Parker's "Moose the Mooche," Johnny Mandel's jaunty minor key "Tommyhawk," and Bill Holman's fascinating four-part suite "Quartet," a complex 15-minute work that swings from beginning to end. A fine quintet session with longtime collaborators Conte Candoli (trumpet) , Mike Wofford (piano), and Monty Budwig (bass), *Perk Up* 𝄞𝄞𝄞𝄞 (Concord Jazz, 1976/1995, prod. Carl E. Jefferson) also features the great but rarely recorded Memphis alto saxophonist Frank Strozier. Of the album's eight tunes, two are standards, and Strozier, Jimmy Rowles, and Wofford contribute two tunes each to the session. Rowles's gorgeous ballad "Drinkin' and Drivin'" is one of the album's highlights.

what to avoid: Unaccountably, *Mannekind* ♫♫ (Mainstream/MFSL, 1972, prod. Bob Shad) was not only reissued on CD, it was re-released as an expensive hi-fidelity "Original Master Recording," but what's the point of hearing everything if there ain't much to hear? Though Manne rounded up some fine musicians (including Mike Wofford, John Gross, and Gary Barone), there are almost no interesting solos and the band sounds clunky and uninspired. One of the usually dependable Manne's weaker dates.

best of the rest:

"The Three" and "The Two" ♫♫♫♫ (Contemporary, 1954/OJC, 1992)
Swinging Sounds ♫♫♫♫ (Contemporary, 1956/OJC, 1996)
Shelly Manne and His Friends: Bells Are Ringing ♫♫♫♫ (Contemporary, 1956/OJC, 1992)
At the Black Hawk, Vol 2 ♫♫♫♫ (Contemporary, 1959/OJC, 1991)
At the Black Hawk, Vol 3 ♫♫♫♫ (Contemporary, 1959/OJC, 1991)
At the Black Hawk, Vol 4 ♫♫♫♫ (Contemporary, 1959/OJC, 1991)
At the Black Hawk, Vol 5 ♫♫♫♫ (Contemporary, 1959/OJC, 1991)
At the Manne-Hole, Vol. 2 ♫♫♫♫♫ (Contemporary, 1961/OJC, 1992)
2-3-4 ♫♫♫♫ (Impulse!, 1963/1994)

influences:

◀◀ Max Roach, Jo Jones, Dave Tough

Andrew Gilbert

Joseph "Wingy" Manone

Born February 13, 1904, in New Orleans, LA. Died July 9, 1982, in Las Vegas, NV.

Joseph "Wingy" Manone (sometimes spelled "Mannone") was a veritable whirlwind of early jazz. Even though he lost most of his right arm as a youth (severed by a passing street car), Manone was always indefatigable in life. His powerful trumpet playing, sharp dress, quick wit, and weed-smoking hipness provided him with one of the unique personas of jazz. Manone was playing on riverboats professionally by the age of 17. In the early 1920s he traveled extensively and made his first recordings with the Arcadian Serenaders in 1924 in St. Louis. By 1925 he was leading his own band, although he played with other bands off and on, touring the Southwest, Mexico, and California through 1926 (when he returned to the Gulf Coast). In 1927 he went to New York, where he recorded with Red Nichols. Manone then went to Chicago and roomed with Art Hodes. He played a wide variety of venues and was involved in some outstanding recording dates. He briefly went back to New York (where he recorded again) before going on the road.

The 1930s brought Manone his broadest and most lasting fame. His hot road band recorded for Gennett in 1930. Chicago was homebase as Manone played throughout the Midwest until 1934,

when he went back to New York. A stint at the Tap Room, and then the Hickory House on 52nd Street brought him wider exposure via radio and many recording dates (almost 150 titles between 1934 and 1941). Manone also started to appear in some Hollywood films by the late 1940s. He lived in California from 1941 until 1954, where he continued to record and be featured on radio. Manone also continued to travel, and performed in international jazz festivals in his later years, almost right up to his death.

what to buy: For the collector and vintage jazz enthusiast, most of Manone's earliest recordings are available. His first session (recorded in New Orleans) under his own name can be found on *Wingy Manone, 1927–34* ♫♫♫♫ (Classics, 1994, prod. Gilles Petard). "Cat's Head" gives Manone room to display his prowess, while his little seven-piece band provides a glimpse of the hot music still being performed in the Crescent City during the 1920s. His rough-and-ready touring band of 1930 is presented here as well. *Wingy Manone, 1934–35* ♫♫♫♫♫ (Classics, 1995, prod. Gilles Petard) brings us and Manone to New York for some of his best recordings, accompanied by such luminaries as Eddie Miller, Matty Matlock, Gil Bowers, Benny's brother Harry Goodman, Sidney Arodin, Santo Pecora, and others. Performances such as "Swing, Brother, Swing," and "Nickel in the Slot" (which caused record producer Art Satherley to dance about the studio during its recording), may make the listener consider keeping a fire extinguisher handy. Bud Freeman and Jack Teagarden are featured in separate sessions on *Wingy Manone, 1935–36* ♫♫♫♫ (Classics, 1995, prod. Gilles Petard). "Rhythm Is Our Business" with Bud Freeman, and the sober take of "I've Got a Note" with Jack Teagarden are especially fulfilling tracks. *Wingy Manone, 1936* ♫♫♫♫ (Classics, 1995, prod. Gilles Petard) and *Wingy Manone, 1936–37* ♫♫♫♫ (Classics, 1996, prod. Gilles Petard) find Manone switching from Vocalion to Bluebird (RCA Victor), which coincides with his move to the Hickory House. Joe Marsala is the featured clarinetist on most of these titles. Some critics downplay this portion of Manone's career, citing his recordings of pop tunes of the day as banal fodder for the masses. Listen to "West Wind," "Swingin' at the Hickory House," "It Can Happen to You," or the infectious "Floatin' Down to Cotton Town" to dispel that line of thinking. As is the case with any anthology, the listener is inundated with recording after recording by the same group. During any given session, some tunes can be good (and these *are* all good jazz recordings), while one spark can give a particular title the ignition it needs to become a small gem of jazz. That reward of discovery is here in these sessions. The French import label Chronological Classics (commonly referred to as "Classics") will soon finish this Wingy project, one that is certainly worthwhile for those who enjoy small-group swing.

the rest:

The Wingy Manone Collection, Vol. 1: 1927–30 🎵🎵🎵 (Collector's Classics 1994)

The Wingy Manone Collection, Vol. 2: 1934 🎵🎵🎵 (Collector's Classics, 1994)

The Wingy Manone Collection, Vol. 3: 1934–35 🎵🎵🎵🎵 (Collector's Classics, 1994)

The Wingy Manone Collection, Vol. 4: 1935–36 🎵🎵🎵 (Collector's Classics, 1994)

Trumpet Jive 🎵🎵 (Prestige, 1994)

Jim Prohaska

Ray Mantilla

Born June 22, 1934, in New York, NY.

Ray Mantilla is a veteran percussionist who has backed popular artists such as Eartha Kitt, played in numerous bands, and toured and recorded with Herbie Mann, Max Roach, and Al Cohn in the 1960s. From 1963–69 he lived in Puerto Rico, where he led a Latin Band. In 1970 he was a founding member of Max Roach's M'-Boom Re: Percussion band. During the 1970s, Mantilla spent two years with Art Blakey touring Europe and Japan, and recorded in the mid-1970s with Gato Barbieri, Joe Farrell, Richie Cole, Don Pullen, Charles Mingus, Walter Bishop, M'Boom, and Morgana King. In 1979 Mantilla formed his own group, Space Station, a band that performs mostly original music, blending Latin rhythms with bebop in a seamless, impressionistic approach. Mantilla made some recordings with this band for Red Records as well as recording as sideman on numerous recordings.

what to buy: So consistent is the Ray Mantilla Space Station in its approach, the overall success of any of their recordings almost depends on performances by guest artists. In the case of *The Jazz Tribe* 🎵🎵🎵 (Red Records, 1992, prod. Alberto Alberti), it's trumpeter Jack Walrath (and on one tune, tenor saxophonist Steve Grossman). The live-recorded performance at La Spezia Jazz Festival in Italy on December 17, 1990, also includes alto saxist Bobby Watson and the pianist Walter Bishop Jr., bassist Charles Fambrough, and drummer Joe Chambers. Mantilla's percussions keep this illustrious crew working cohesively as they perform eight tunes composed mostly by the various players. You can't really categorize Space Station's complex music. This is not Latin jazz with the usual frontline horns and pulsating rhythmic backing. Mantilla's been there, done that. Although their inventions sometimes lean toward Latin jazz, borrowing from traditional south-of-the-border themes and

rhythms, the leader more often adds textures and colors to straightforward boppers. Their yield is modern-sounding music that's often dreamy, full of dramatic shifts and breaks, and lightly percussive. Contributing significantly to the success of this album, soloists get plenty of space to develop their ideas.

what to buy next: Tenor saxophonist Steve Grossman is the guest with Ray Mantilla Space Station on *Synergy* 🎵🎵🎵🎵 (Red Records, 1994, prod Alberti Veschi, Sergio Veschi), a February 1986 date recorded in an Italian studio. He lends energy to three of the seven eclectic tunes on this session, which is closer to its Latin roots than *The Jazz Tribe*. Mantilla's colleagues on this date include Dick Oatts (saxes/flute), Eddie Martinez (piano), Guillermo Edgehill (bass), and Steve Berrios (drums, percussion). Highlights include over 10 minutes of the Latinate standard "Star Eyes," to which Grossman adds fiery punch.

best of the rest:

Hands of Fire 🎵🎵🎵🎵 (Red, 1984/1993)

Ray Mantilla/Space Station 🎵🎵🎵 (Red, 1988)

Dark Powers 🎵🎵🎵 (Red, 1988/1994)

Nancy Ann Lee

Steve Marcus

Born September 18, 1939, in New York, NY.

Perennially underrated tenor and soprano saxophonist Steve Marcus spent years in the sax sections of the Woody Herman, Buddy Rich, and Stan Kenton big bands, recording infrequently on his own, yet always impressive in whatever the setting. After attending Berklee College of Music, he went on the road with Kenton. Back in New York, he recorded with Gary Burton and the Jazz Composer's Orchestra, worked with Herbie Mann, then returned to road life with Herman. Part of the early fusion movement, Marcus played with Larry Coryell's Eleventh House and formed his own Count's Rock Band. In 1975 he joined Buddy Rich as star soloist and straw boss until the drummer's death in 1987. Today he fronts the Rich reunion band.

what's available: *Smile* 🎵🎵🎵 (Red Baron, 1993, prod. Bob Thiele) is perhaps Marcus's most satisfying recording and sadly the only one in print. He romps passionately with a star rhythm section (pianist John Hicks, bassist Christian McBride, and drummer Marvin "Smitty" Smith) on standards and jazz classics. Though the album was not conceived as an homage, Marcus's takes on Sonny Rollins's "Oleo," Charlie Parker's "Confirmation," Dizzy Gillespie's "Woody 'n' You," and John Coltrane's "Like Sonny," show how the bebop masters shaped his musical point-of-view—swinging, melodic, and full of energy and passion. The evergreen ballad "My One and Only Love," and Charlie Chaplin's "Smile," serve as canvases for his impressionistic soprano. The rhythm section, one of New York's finest, locks up and lends solid support throughout.

influences:

◀◀ John Coltrane, Johnny Griffin, Sonny Rollins

▶▶ Joe Henderson, Javon Jackson, Billy Pierce, Chris Potter

Bret Primack

Rick Margitza

Born October 24, 1961, in Detroit, MI.

An outstanding saxophonist with immense untapped potential, Detroit native Rick Margitza has recorded for Blue Note, SteepleChase, and Challenge as well as gigged with Miles Davis. Margitza started playing the violin at age four. He studied classical piano in elementary school and oboe in junior high school, turning to the alto saxophone after he heard "Bird with Strings." In tenth grade, he switched to tenor, influenced by Michael Brecker and John Coltrane. He attended the Berklee College of Music and the University of Miami but finished his undergraduate work at Loyola University in New Orleans, where he played with Ellis Marsalis. After turning pro, he played and recorded with Maynard Ferguson, Flora Purim, and Airto, then moved to New York in 1988, when he worked with Davis. After signing with Blue Note in 1989, he began a solo career. Margitza has yet to garner the attention he deserves, although his recordings accurately portray his prowess.

what to buy: On *Game of Chance* ♪♪♪♪ (Challenge, 1997, prod. Hein Van de Geyn), Margitza shows he really knows his way around the tenor. But instead of excess double-time and scalar exhibitionism, his improvisations build thoughtfully, an oblique yet vibrant sound burnishing the fire meticulously. His originals are always distinctive, notably "Good Question" and "Jazz Prelude #2," a soprano feature with an early-ECM feel. Margitza is joyous and upbeat as well on "August in Paris," and the Parker-like "Bird Shit," with its tricky bop line and complex harmonies.

what to buy next: On his first release for the Dutch label, *Hands of Time* ♪♪♪♪ (Challenge, 1995, prod. Hein Van de Geyn, Rick Margitza), Margitza's full-bodied tone and melodious approach to improvisation are emboldened by a solid New York rhythm section: pianist Kevin Hayes, bassist George Mraz, and drummer Al Foster. Aside from "Embraceable You," his originals are prominently displayed: "Hip Bop" turns walkin' the bar tenor inside-out, while "Forty-Five Pound Hound" does

the same for the blues. Margitza remains an undiscovered gem. It's hard to go wrong with his rhythm section on *Work It* ♪♪♪♪ (SteepleChase, 1994, prod. Nils Winther), which includes pianist James Williams, bassist George Mraz, and drummer Billy Hart. Perhaps that's why Margitza sounds a little more relaxed than usual. Instead of emphasizing the robustness of his tenor and his compositional prowess, he adopts a more tender and melodic approach to the familiar material here, which includes a haunting treatment of "My Foolish Heart" and a breezy version of "It Could Happen to You." He is very much at home with standards, working the changes and lending his own voice with grace and passion. His last Blue Note date, *This Is New* ♪♪♪♪ (Blue Note, 1992, prod. Matt Pierson), is a standards outing with just two originals. Backed by drummer Jeff "Tain" Watts, bassist Robert Hurst, and pianist Joey Calderazzo, the tenorman plays with the power of a Greek God. Chestnuts such as "On Green Dolphin Street," "Body and Soul," and "Invitation" are re-worked, while the title track and "Just in Time" just plain swing, allowing Margitza to assert his major-league credentials repeatedly. Trumpeter Tim Hagans guests on Margitza's sardonic "Beware of the Door," which, along with his impassioned "Gypsy," document the saxman's potent writing.

worth searching for: Dedicated to "the hope that our children can grow up in a world free of hate," *Hope* ♪♪♪♪ (Blue Note, 1991, prod. Matt Pierson, Rick Margitza) finds Margitza mixing fusion-oriented songs with his own hard-bop/mainstream stylings on this out-of-print CD. The result is imaginative and memorable. Utilizing voices, strings, and brass, and his emotional tenor and soprano, Margitza creates a seamless tapestry that defies categorization. Also check Margitza out on *Color* ♪♪♪♪ (Blue Note, 1989, prod. Matt Pierson, Rick Margitza), a session of originals with a top-notch group that includes Joey Calderazzo (piano), Adam Nussbaum (drums), and Marc Johnson (acoustic bass).

influences:

◀◀ Hank Mobley, Bill Barron, John Coltrane, Michael Brecker

▶▶ Bob Berg, Jerry Bergonzi, George Garzone, Michael Smith

Bret Primack

Kitty Margolis

Born November 7, 1955, in San Mateo, CA.

Rarely does a female jazz vocalist emerge who exhibits the assurance, skill, creativity, and expressiveness to cast her into the same spotlight with the legendary singers Sarah Vaughan,

Ella Fitzgerald, Carmen McRae, or Betty Carter. Kitty Margolis, with her rich contralto, perfect pitch, facile phrasing, strong sense of swing, and ability to reinvent classics, shows great promise. Margolis grew up in San Francisco with the influences of the big-band jazz of Count Basie and Duke Ellington, and singers Ella Fitzgerald and Billie Holiday. She was equally influenced by Bonnie Raitt, and as a seventh grader taught herself to play guitar. Her professional career began in Boston clubs while attending Harvard University. Continuing her education at San Francisco State, she studied jazz with saxophone veteran John Handy, whose playing probably influenced her horn-like lines and swingability. Margolis is a powerful, gifted jazz vocalist who outclasses many of her peers with her sheer inventiveness and musicianship. Critics have described her as "an important new jazz voice," and lauded her for her warmth, exuberant pace, keen pitch, and "the ability to sing a through line, not just fancy riffs." One of the hottest newcomers on the national scene, Margolis has assuredly perfected her wide-ranging craft to include spectacular, fiery scat in the style of the bop-influenced singers. Yet she can just as capably convey hearty note-bending blues moods, sweet Brazilian themes, swingers, and lush ballads. Performing at festivals, concerts, and clubs since she first caught national attention at the 1989 Monterey Jazz Festival, she has been thrilling worldwide audiences. A distinctive vocalist with a style all her own, Margolis has made three critically acclaimed albums for her MAD-KAT label, co-owned with singer Madeline Eastman. For more information, you may visit Margolis's website at http://www.kitty margolis.com/.

what to buy: Margolis gets better with each recording. Start with a recent project, *Straight up with a Twist* ♫♫♫♫ (MAD-KAT, 1997, prod. Alfonso Montuori, Kitty Margolis), an album that lives up to its title. With her strong contralto voice, Margolis is bold in her conversions, injecting unexpected twists of rhythm and melody into warhorse standards such as "Fever," "The Night Has a Thousand Eyes," "All or Nothing at All," "Speak Low," "Wouldn't It Be Loverly," and more. In different settings with her musicians, she employs various approaches, attacking each tune with a mixture of fervent warmth, crisp pitch, timbral diversity, well-informed scat, and adventurous, playful ingenuity. Accompanied by her core band—Spencer Allen (piano, Hammond B-3, synthesizer), Brad Buethe (guitar), Peter Barshay (bass), Scott Morris (drums)—Margolis generates excitement on this well-conceived project. Each tune is saucily reinvented by Margolis, her team, and an array of other spotlighted accompanists and guest soloists, including pianists Paul

Nagle, Kevin Gibbs, and Ruth Davies; trumpeter Roy Hargrove (on three tracks); 73-year-old vocalist Charles Brown (two tracks); and, on one track each, Kenny Brooks (tenor saxophone) and Damien Masterson (harmonica). But while these guests interact admirably with the singer on this explosively hip album, it's Margolis's heady vocals and divine innovations throughout the 13 tunes that make this album the ultimate listen.

what to buy next: On *Evolution* ♫♫♫♫ (MAD-KAT, 1994, prod. Bud Spangler, Kitty Margolis), Margolis fiercely attacks a wide choice of material, from bebop to blues to Brazilian to ballads. Creating punchy horn-like lines, bending notes, smearing or splitting tones, and superbly (yet sparingly) scatting, she leads you through an exciting jazz labyrinth she creates with her Bay-area sidemen. So impressive are her vocals on the 14 tunes that you might initially fail to notice special guest tenor saxman Joe Henderson artistically weaving his lines throughout hers on five tracks. This is an exhilarating album. Her debut recording, *Live at the Jazz Workshop* ♫♫♫♫ (MAD-KAT, 1990, prod. Kitty Margolis, Bud Spangler) was universally praised for her bop-based improvisations, her scatting, and her overall musicianship, backed by pianist All Plank, bassist Scott Reed, and drummer Vince Lateano, at the San Francisco club on June 22, 1988. With her velvety voice that hits low notes with dazzling precision, Margolis reinvents eight ballads and swingers with an innate sense of joyful innovation and a wealth of ideas. Check out her fresh takes on the Miles Davis standard "All Blues" (with lyrics by Oscar Brown Jr.) or her scat artistry on Cole Porter's "I Concentrate on You." This is an impressive debut album, yet she refined her style on subsequent recordings.

influences:

◄◄ Billie Holiday, Ella Fitzgerald, Sarah Vaughan, Hal Stein, John Handy, Sheila Jordan, Al Jarreau, Betty Carter

Nancy Ann Lee

Tania Maria

Born May 9, 1948, in Sao Luis, Maranhao, Brazil.

Tania Maria is a "triple-threat" performer: pianist, vocalist, and composer. She began playing piano at age seven and devoted several years to classical studies; at age 13, however, she developed an interest in jazz and Brazilian pop and has never looked back. After living in Rio and Sao Paulo and weathering a frustrated attempt at a local music career, Maria moved to Paris in 1974. She maintained a full-time residence there until inroads to the U.S. market were opened in 1975. Guitarist and club owner Charlie Byrd brought Tania Maria to Washington,

D.C., to perform, and alerted Concord Records to his amazing find. She has recorded domestically for both Concord and World Pacific/Blue Note and has also released five albums in Europe and four in her native country. Drawing from diverse musical sources, she uses jazz, Caribbean, R&B, funk, pop, and traditional Brazilian styles with equal verve, combining them to great effect. Plenty of Afro-Cuban influence can be heard in Maria's Brazilian jazz. Fiery Montunos abound— she eschews the traditional Brazilian instrumentation, and often the lilting samba and bossa grooves, for burning tumbao-filled marathons featuring congas, bongos, timbales, and funky bass. Nevertheless, if anyone can claim ownership of the bossa nova rhythm, or rend a beautiful Latin-tinged torch song with gut-wrenching affirmation, it is Maria, whose ballad playing and vocalizing are on par with the best. Her highly stylized vocalese includes rhythmic touches of Brazilian Portuguese, pidgen-English, jazz scat, and bluesy melisma; she has been favorably compared to Ella Fitzgerald, Billy Holliday, and Anita O'Day. Maria's crossover experiments delving into pure pop/funk have not been as musically successful or satisfying as her more Latin-oriented ventures, however.

what to buy: *Piquant* 𝄞𝄞𝄞𝄞 (Concord, 1981, prod. Cal Tjader) was a tremendous U.S. debut. Crackling originals like "Yatra-Ta," "Chiclete Com Banana," and "Lemon Cuica" are balanced against classics such as "Triste." Maria puts a special spin on "It's Not for Me to Say." Great selection of tunes, a band that's on fire, and a good recording. *Taurus* 𝄞𝄞𝄞𝄞 (Concord, 1981, prod. Carl E. Jefferson) features the same basic line-up as "Piquant" (with Eddie Duran, guitar; Rob Fisher, bass; Vince Laetano, drums; Willie T. Colon, percussion) plus percussionist Kent Middleton. *Taurus* finds Maria in a more pastoral, bossa/ballad mood and features creative renditions of "Cry Me a River" and John Lennon's "Imagine." This session is not without up-tempo material, however, such as "Que Vengan los Toros" and the burning closer, "Eruption." *Come with Me* 𝄞𝄞𝄞𝄞 (Concord, 1983, prod. Carl E. Jefferson) features bassists Lincoln Goines and John Pena and drummer/percussionists Portinho and Steve Thornton and a mix of up-tempo and medium Latin numbers, funk, and ballads. This one is worth the full retail price for its crowning gem, the slow, simmering, original samba "Nega."

what to buy next: On *The Real Tania Maria: WILD!* 𝄞𝄞𝄞𝄞 (Concord, 1985, prod. Carl E. Jefferson) a great band assists the pianist/singer in presenting incendiary live versions of some of her best material ("Yatra-Ta" and "Sangria" included). *Outrageous* 𝄞𝄞𝄞𝄞 (Concord, 1993, prod. Tania Maria) is another well-

arranged, performed, and presented set of Latin, laid-back, and pop-funk numbers. The hit on this date is "I Can Do It"; what you can't do is get this happy little tune out of your head once you've heard it.

the rest:
Love Explosion 𝄞𝄞𝄞 (Concord, 1984)
Made in New York 𝄞𝄞𝄞 (World Pacific/Blue Note, 1986)
Bela Vista 𝄞𝄞𝄞 (World Pacific/Blue Note, 1990)
The Lady from Brazil 𝄞𝄞𝄞 (World Pacific/Blue Note, 1991)
Forbidden Colors 𝄞𝄞𝄞 (World Pacific/Blue Note, 1991)
The Best of Tania Maria 𝄞𝄞𝄞 (World Pacific/Blue Note, 1993)
Bluesilian 𝄞𝄞𝄞 (TMK, 1996)

influences:
◀◀ Cal Tjader, Flora Purim, Stan Getz
▶▶ Azymuth, Susannah McCorkle, Kevyn Lettau

Gregg Juke

Charlie Mariano
Born November 12, 1923, in Boston, MA.

Primarily known as a Bird-influenced altoist, Mariano is a veteran bebopper with occasional ventures into more modern territory. He was first noticed as a featured soloist with Nat Pierce's band in 1949 and made a reputation for himself around the Boston area. A couple tours with Stan Kenton brought him wider repute, and he formed a critically admired quartet with pianist Toshiko Akiyoshi, whom he married (then later divorced). He played on Charles Mingus's *The Black Saint and the Sinner Lady* in 1963 and later in the decade formed one of the first fusion groups, Osmosis. He traveled in Asia and Europe and incorporated world music and folk music into his style, although at times this has taken him away from his strengths.

what to buy: *Boston All Stars* 𝄞𝄞𝄞 (Prestige, 1952–53, prod. Ira Gitler/OJC, 1990) combines the LPs *The New Sounds from Boston* and *Charlie Mariano Boston All Stars*. Mariano's thin tone and the sometimes pedestrian backing of Mariano's fellow Beantowners will disappoint those who like their bebop bold and brash, but there are nice compositional touches and some good solos, with stars on the two sessions including trumpeters Joe Gordon and Herb Pomeroy and pianist Dick Twardzik (another Kentonite).

what to avoid: *Innuendo* 𝄞 (Lipstick, 1992, prod. Joachim Becker) is dually credited to Mariano and keyboardist Jasper Van't Hof, with drummer Marilyn Mazur filling out the trio. The music is bland fusion with artistic pretensions. With too many smooth synth sounds and an utter lack of aggression, it blends into the background much too easily to be of interest.

the rest:
Live 🎵🎵🎵 (Intuition, 1993)
Adagio 🎵🎵 (Lipstick, 1995)
Seventy 🎵🎵 (Intuition, 1995)

worth searching for: *Toshiko Mariano Quartet* 🎵🎵🎵 (Candid, 1960, prod. Nat Hentoff) is marred somewhat by an out-of-tune piano, but Charlie and wife Toshiko Akiyoshi Mariano are a good team and this is a solid bop/post-bop quartet (with bassist Gene Cherico and drummer Eddie Marshall). The altoist is a more confident and assertive player than on the Prestige sessions, and a more assured composer.

influences:
◄◄ Charlie Parker, Lee Konitz
►► Steve Wilson

Walter Faber

Dodo Marmarosa

Born Michael Marmarosa, December 12, 1925, in Pittsburgh, PA.

Dodo Marmarosa was one of the early bop pioneers, a classically trained pianist who during a very short period became a fixture in the new music scene. His work on several small post-war labels (Atomic, Beltone, Dial, Downbeat, Keynote, Sunset) included support of others and as a leader. Because of his ability to read music, he was in heavy demand by other musicians, including Boyd Raeburn, Lucky Thompson, Slim Gaillard, Wardell Gray, Barney Kessel, and, in sessions that represented his best work, with Charlie Parker on the now-famous Dial sessions. After leaving Pittsburgh at age 16, Marmarosa played with several of the era's best swing bands. While there are recordings that feature his imaginative solos ("The Moose" and "The Great Lie" from Charlie Barnet's *Drop Me off in Harlem* on Decca), much of his big-band work was in rhythm support of the reed and horn sections. In early 1946, after a stint with Boyd Raeburn, Marmarosa and tenor player Lucky Thompson left Raeburn in Los Angeles and formed their own combo, recording several sides on the Downbeat label. Prior to a recording session for Dial, Charlie Parker replaced Joe Albany with Marmarosa after an argument with Albany at a club date. The sessions on Dial are now considered to be classic small-group sides, and it is here that one can discover the precise approach and fast technique of Marmarosa's piano work. In 1947 he was chosen as the most promising jazz pianist by *Esquire* in an assessment that also recognized

Miles Davis, Sonny Stitt, Ray Brown, Milt Jackson, and Sarah Vaughan as tops in their categories. A series of personal tragedies caused Marmarosa to "disappear" from the music scene in the early 1950s and return to Pittsburgh and his family. His mental state continued to deteriorate after a short stay in the army, and his family refused professional help for him. By accident (his car broke down in 1960 on an ill-advised trip to California to see his children) he was stranded in Chicago, where Joe Segal arranged for Marmarosa to record for the Argo label. The actual sessions took place in 1961 and represent his last recordings. Although Marmarosa was active in the Pittsburgh club scene until the late 1960s, his career has essentially been over since 1961, and he lives in Pittsburgh today, existing on a disability pension with other vets, a total recluse.

what to buy: Much of Marmarosa's output is now available on CD, but there are three that represent his best work. Charlie Parker's *The Legendary Dial Sessions, Volume 1* 🎵🎵🎵🎵 (Stash, 1987, prod. Ross Russell) includes the March 1946 recordings of "A Night in Tunisia," "Moose the Mooche," "Ornithology," and "Yardbird." Marmarosa's solos helped define bop piano. *Dodo's Bounce* 🎵🎵🎵 (Fresh Sound, 1991, compilation prod. Jordi Pujol) is a compilation of sessions recorded in Hollywood on the Atomic, Dial, and Downbeat labels with support from Barney Kessel, Lucky Thompson, and others. Marmarosa is featured on all cuts, and his Tatum-like sweeps can be heard on tunes like "Bopmatism" and "Dodo's Dance." *Dodo Marmarosa Pittsburgh 1958* 🎵🎵🎵 (Uptown, 1996, prod. Robert Sunenblick) updates the Marmarosa legacy with previously unreleased sessions in various Pittsburgh locales dating from 1958–62 and includes a 1995 interview in the expansive liner notes. Students of the early bop scene will benefit from the recordings and the notes.

what to buy next: Look for *Up in Dodo's Room* 🎵🎵🎵 (Jazz Classics, 1986, reissue prod. Tony Williams, Will Friedwald), which includes a rehearsal take of "Birdlore" (actually "Ornithology") from the March 1946 Parker/Dial sessions that allows Marmarosa an extended solo. The Chicago recordings are represented by *The Chicago Sessions* 🎵🎵🎵 (Affinity, 1989). These cuts, originally recorded in 1961–62, feature Marmarosa in a trio session and also on sides with the added support of Bill Hardman on trumpet. He deploys unusual chording and rhythmic accompaniments that make this recording excellent.

what to avoid: Pass on the recently released *Dodo Lives* 🎵🎵 (Topaz Jazz, 1997). It's full of material from the big-band days, when Marmarosa was in a supporting role, and/or material covered in other issues of his work.

worth searching for: The adventuresome should seek the LP *West Coast Piano Touch* ♫♫♫ (Vantage, 1952) with Lorraine Geller.

influences:

◀◀ Art Tatum, Erroll Garner, Teddy Wilson

▶▶ Erroll Garner, Mary Lou Williams

Jim Linduff

Branford Marsalis

Born August 26, 1960, in Breaux Bridge, LA.

Twelve years after graduating from younger brother Wynton's band, sax player Branford Marsalis has evolved into that refreshing rarity in jazz: an open-minded neo-traditionalist, an innovative torchbearer equally at home in bop and pop. More outspoken and outrageous than Wynton, Branford has been a fierce critic of the socially unconscious and those who treat jazz as an artform to be preserved rather than nurtured. His touring stints with such rock acts as Sting, Bruce Hornsby, and the Grateful Dead led to vast visibility that reached its zenith in 1992, when he agreed to become the leader of the house band on *The Tonight Show with Jay Leno*. The purist vultures started circling, anxious to catch him pandering to his TV fan club. But Marsalis, working mostly in a loose, aggressive trio format with longtime drummer Jeff "Tain" Watts and bassist Robert Hurst, reacted to his commercial potential by releasing his most difficult, dazzling work; indeed, the swaggering blues of *I Heard You Twice the First Time* (featuring collaborations with Wynton, B.B. King, John Lee Hooker, and the superb cast of Broadway's *The Piano Lesson)* and the gale-force improvisational thrills of the live *Bloomington*—both recorded before he joined *The Tonight Show*—come across as deliciously stubborn declarations of independent thought. Now alternating between full-bore blowing sessions with Watts and bassist Reginald Veal and playful, frenetic hip-hop excursions under his pseudonym, Buckshot LeFonque, Marsalis retains both his relentless commitment to his vision and his biting sense of humor in the face of such societal ills as prejudice and injustice: his 1996 album, the wryly titled *The Dark Keys*, sported watermelon seeds on the cover and a pointed song called "Schott Happens."

what to buy: Recorded live at Indiana University in 1991 but released two years later at the height of his *Tonight Show* stardom, *Bloomington* ♫♫♫♫ (Columbia, 1993, prod. Delfeayo Marsalis) is the chaotic but euphoric sound of an artist at the top of his game. The exhausting, exhilarating performances of

Marsalis, Watts, and Hurst are highlighted by the frantic, 15-minute "Xavier's Lair," a lovely interpretation of "Everything Happens to Me" on which Marsalis slides in the theme from *I Love Lucy,* and a romp through Thelonious Monk's "Friday the 13th" that provokes a young fan to yell out a request for the Grateful Dead's "Dark Star." *The Beautyful Ones Are Not Yet Born* ♫♫♫♫ (Columbia, 1991, prod. Delfeayo Marsalis) is the superb studio catalyst for *Bloomington*, sharing four tracks and the exploratory spirit but adding a fiery duet with saxophonist Courtney Pine on a tribute to Dewey Redman called "Dewey Baby." Of his earlier works, *Renaissance* ♫♫♫ (Columbia, 1987, prod. Delfeayo Marsalis)—featuring pianist Kenny Kirkland and drummer Tony Williams—gives the strongest indication of Marsalis's prowess as player and interpreter by mixing Marsalis and Williams originals with Cole Porter's "Just One of Those Things," J.J. Johnson's "Lament," and Sonny Rollins's "St. Thomas."

what to buy next: A dizzying but delightful excursion into hip-hop, *Buckshot LeFonque* ♫♫♫ (Columbia, 1994, prod. Branford Marsalis, DJ Premier) finds Marsalis teaming with DJ Premier of Gang Starr to create funky collages drawing from such disparate sources as Elton John ("Mona Lisas and Mad Hatters"), Maya Angelou ("I Know Why the Caged Bird Sings"), Albert Collins ("No Pain, No Gain"), and John Coltrane (whose "India" is sampled on "Blackwidow Blues"). Not jazz, but not bad at all.

what to avoid: Perhaps it's the temporary rhythm section (Lewis Nash and Delbert Felix), or maybe it's the unusual recording site (Tokyo), but *Random Abstract* ♫♫♫ (Columbia, 1988, prod. Delfeayo Marsalis) winds up focusing on the first, rather than the second, part of its title, with well-intentioned but wobbly tips of the hat to Ornette Coleman, Wayne Shorter, and John Coltrane.

the rest:

Scenes in the City ♫♫♫ (Columbia, 1983)
Royal Garden Blues ♫♫♫ (Columbia, 1986)
Trio Jeepy ♫♫♫♫ (Columbia, 1989)
Crazy People Music ♫♫♫♫ (Columbia, 1990)
I Heard You Twice the First Time ♫♫♫♫ (Columbia, 1992)
(With Ellis Marsalis) *Loved Ones* ♫♫♫♫ (Columbia, 1996)
The Dark Keys ♫♫♫♫ (Columbia, 1996)
(As Buckshot LeFonque) *Music Evolution* ♫♫♫ (Columbia, 1997)

worth searching for: Marsalis's stunning version of "A Love Supreme" is included on a bonus CD packaged with *Red Hot + Cool: Stolen Moments* ♫♫♫ (GRP, 1994, prod. various). Also check out his tasty backing of galvanizing vocalist Angélique Kidjo on two tracks of *Logozo* ♫♫♫ (Mango/Island Records France, 1991, prod. Joe Galdo).

influences:

◀◀ Wayne Shorter, Sonny Rollins, John Coltrane

▶▶ Joshua Redman

David Okamoto

influences:

◀◀ Ellis Marsalis, Steve Turre, Frank Lacy, Wycliffe Gordon, J.J. Johnson

David Prince

Delfeayo Marsalis

Born June 28, 1965, in New Orleans, LA.

Delfeayo Marsalis, an accomplished trombonist, composer, and arranger, is known mainly for his production work and occasional witty liner-note writing on albums by his more famous older siblings, trumpeter Wynton and saxophonist Branford, and their father pianist Ellis Marsalis. Delfeayo nurtured an interest in engineering and began his career in music as a record producer, studying trombone and studio production at Berklee College of Music. He draws inspiration from precursors like J.J. Johnson, and, prior to making his recording debut as leader in 1992, toured with Ray Charles, Art Blakey's Jazz Messengers, and Abdullah Ibrahim.

what to buy: Evidence presented on two albums as leader indicates that Delfeayo is a talent deserving of wider dissemination. Once you get past the pompous Biblical reference, *Pontius Pilate's Decision* 🎵🎵🎵 (Novus, 1992, prod. Delfeayo Marsalis) is thematically unified, offering burnished tonal canvases that are (a) surprisingly non-doctrinaire and free of programmatic pomposity; (b) not steeped in the bloodless fields of revisionist posturing; (c) capable of being humorous; and, best of all, (d) loose and naturally swinging. As a soloist, Marsalis has a gossamer and tart delivery that bespeaks the best N'awlins tradition without slavishly displaying its "roots." Using a cast of instrumental Young Lions, some of whom work frequently with brother Wynton, he mixes it up in various settings with Jeff "Tain" Watts, Kenny Kirkland, Mark Turner, Marcus Roberts, Wessell Anderson, Reginald Veal, Herlin Riley, and Joshua Redman.

what to buy next: A more recent album, *Musashi* 🎵🎵🎵 (Evidence, 1997, prod. Delfeayo Marsalis), featuring saxophonist Mark Gross, pianist Yuichi Inoue, bassist Shigeo Aramaki, and drummer Masahiko Osaka (plus brother Branford, Papa Ellis, and bass trombonist Bill Reichenbach), is less conceptual, more straight-ahead, and only slightly less successful.

Branford Marsalis (© Jack Vartoogian)

Ellis Marsalis

Born November 14, 1934, in New Orleans, LA.

Even though he's the patriarch of the most powerful dynasty in modern jazz, Ellis Marsalis has performed his most influential work in the classroom rather than the studio. A legendary New Orleans educator who has worked with everyone from sons Wynton, Branford, Delfeayo, and Jason to Harry Connick Jr. and Terence Blanchard, the pianist only started aggressively pursuing a recording career in the last several years; indeed, Wynton has put out more albums over the last decade than his father has during his entire career. Yet such efforts as 1990's *Ellis Marsalis Trio* and 1992's *Heart of Gold* reveal a musician who clearly values graceful simplicity and harmonic warmth over showboating improvisations. His playing is fast and fluent but never reckless, precise but rarely academic. He doesn't pound so much as pounce on the keys, peeking out from under the rhythm section with an understated beauty that draws you in rather than blows you away. Even in his most relaxed moments, covering such standards as "Surrey with the Fringe on Top" or "The Very Thought of You," he avoids lapsing into the supper-club complacency that thwarts many bearers of standards.

what to buy: *Heart of Gold* 🎵🎵🎵 (Columbia, 1992, prod. Delfeayo Marsalis) is a breathtaking collection of swinging originals and elegant standards ranging from "A Nightingale Sang in Berkeley Square" to "Have You Seen Miss Jones," delivered in an intimate acoustic setting. Sidemen include drummer Billy Higgins and bassist Ray Brown.

what to buy next: *Whistle Stop* 🎵🎵🎵 (Columbia, 1994, prod. Delfeayo Marsalis) is a heady, hard-bopping collaboration with Branford that hints at Ellis's romantic side. Instead, most of the disc—especially the five standouts written by the late drummer James Black and originally recorded on a regional '60s album—evokes the ferocious, straight-ahead spirit of an after-hours Bourbon Street jam session.

what to avoid: *Piano in E: Solo Piano* 🎵🎵🎵 (Rounder, 1991, prod. Kalamu Ya Salaam) was recorded in 1986 at New Orleans' Orpheum Theatre and captures Marsalis digging into tunes by Fats Waller, Horace Silver, and Bud Powell. His playing is solid but the solo session lacks the sense of challenge that rhythm sections inspire on his other recordings.

Wynton Marsalis (© Jack Vartoogian)

the rest:

Ellis Marsalis Trio 🎵🎵🎵 (Blue Note, 1990)

A Night at Snug Harbor, New Orleans 🎵🎵 (Evidence, 1995)

(With Branford Marsalis) *Loved Ones* 🎵🎵🎵 (Columbia, 1996)

worth searching for: The generation-crossing *Fathers and Sons* 🎵🎵🎵 (Columbia, 1982) teams Marsalis with then-fledgling talents Wynton and Branford on the first half of this album. The second half features saxophonists Chico and Von Freeman.

influences:

⏪ Dave Brubeck, Hank Jones, Wynton Kelly

⏩ Harry Connick Jr.

David Okamoto

Wynton Marsalis

Born October 18, 1961, in New Orleans, LA.

The majestic powerhouse propelling jazz, as it closes out its first century, is trumpeter Wynton Marsalis. Codifier, arranger, composer, improviser, and head jazz ambassador to the world, Marsalis is an epic figure. Acclaimed in the jazz and classical worlds, he has technical abilities even accomplished trumpeters only dream of. In addition, the cat can swing. Marsalis had enough artistic and commercial success at an early age that (with the help of his intellectual mentor and historic revelation, writer Stanley Crouch, who has written the liner notes to every Wynton Marsalis recording) he was allowed the luxury of conceiving his music in larger scale than the dominant head-solos-head-out construction. The result has been consistently excellent music that achieves and sometimes surpasses the standards set by his predecessors Duke Ellington and Jelly Roll Morton. Marsalis's genius is less that of a revolutionary improviser—though he can flawlessly emulate any style—than of an artist who has internalized most of what has come before him, pushing it beyond excellence. The only jazz streams he hasn't embraced are avant garde and fusion. Like classical composers, Marsalis has addressed his compositions toward large themes and long forms (or long streams of short-but-related pieces) since the mid-1980s. He has received Grammy awards for jazz and classical music and a Pulitzer Prize for 1997's oratorio, *Blood on the Fields.*

what to buy: Marsalis focuses the compositions around a Christian Sunday service on the two-CD set *In This House, on This Day* 🎵🎵🎵🎵 (Columbia, 1994, prod. Steve Epstein). It's a *tour de force,* particularly the second disc, with its "In the sweet embrace of life" motif. For the bebop ideal of extended virtuoso soloing, Marsalis is most naked in the quartet format on *Live at Blues Alley* 🎵🎵🎵🎵 (Columbia, 1988, prod. Steve Epstein, George Butler).

what to buy next: *Wynton Marsalis* 🎵🎵🎵🎵 (Columbia, 1982, prod. Herbie Hancock), a brash debut of the young talent, includes stars Herbie Hancock, Tony Williams, and Ron Carter, with excellent results.

what to avoid: Aside from the opening melody, which displays the technique of Italian opera, *Joe Cool's Blues* 🎵🎵🎵 (Columbia, 1995, prod. Delfeayo Marsalis) is a toss-off for Wynton (paired with his father, Ellis Marsalis).

the rest:
(With Ellis and Branford Marsalis) *Fathers and Sons* 🎵🎵🎵🎵 (Columbia, 1982)
Think of One 🎵🎵🎵🎵 (Columbia, 1983)
Hot House Flowers 🎵🎵🎵🎵 (Columbia, 1984)
Black Codes (From the Underground) 🎵🎵🎵🎵🎵 (Columbia, 1985)
J Mood 🎵🎵🎵🎵 (Columbia, 1985)
The Majesty of the Blues 🎵🎵🎵🎵 (Columbia, 1989)
Crescent City Christmas Card 🎵🎵🎵🎵 (Columbia, 1989)
Tune in Tomorrow 🎵🎵🎵🎵 (Columbia, 1990)
Thick in the South, Soul Gestures in Southern Blue Volume 1 🎵🎵🎵🎵 (Columbia, 1991)
Uptown Ruler, Soul Gestures in Southern Blue Volume 2 🎵🎵🎵🎵 (Columbia, 1991)
Levee Low Moan, Soul Gestures in Southern Blue Volume 3 🎵🎵🎵🎵 (Columbia, 1991)
Blue Interlude 🎵🎵🎵🎵 (Columbia, 1992)
Citi Movement 🎵🎵🎵🎵🎵 (Columbia, 1993)
Blood on the Fields 🎵🎵🎵🎵 (Columbia, 1997)

worth searching for: His multi-volume collection of standards represents Marsalis's deepest exploration of music composed by others. *Marsalis Standard Time: Volume 1* 🎵🎵🎵🎵🎵 (Columbia, 1987, prod. Steve Epstein), *Standard Time, Vol. 2: Intimacy Calling* 🎵🎵🎵🎵 (Columbia, 1990, prod. Steve Epstein), and *Standard Time, Vol. 3: The Resolution of Romance* 🎵🎵🎵🎵 (Columbia, 1990, prod. Delfeayo Marsalis) generally come through with

WYNTON MARSALIS
(WITH JOE HENDERSON)

song "U. M. M. G. (Upper Manhattan Medical Group)"
album Lush Life: The Music of Billy Strayhorn
(Verve, 1991/1992)
instrument Trumpet

Monster Solo

the goods and refute skeptics who thought Marsalis couldn't cut it on standard material.

influences:

◀◀ Duke Ellington, Jelly Roll Morton, Fats Navarro, Clifford Brown, Miles Davis

▶▶ Branford Marsalis, Joshua Redman

Larry Gabriel

Warne Marsh

Born October 26, 1927, in Los Angeles, CA; died December 18, 1987, in Los Angeles, CA.

Tenor saxophonist Warne Marsh (who also played clarinet and flute) is most often remembered for his association with Lennie Tristano. Marsh's ability to spin long, sinuous lines—with occasional liberty-taking on the chords—that bordered on eccentric have caused him to be revered by a number of avante-gardists, notably Anthony Braxton. It should, however, be pointed out that Marsh is primarily a conventional "swinging" saxist with great skills at improvising inventively over standard chord changes. His idiosyncratic style is apparent only in contrast to very conventional tenor players, such as Al Cohn or Zoot Sims.

Marsh's first instrument was the piano. At school he took up the piano-accordion and then switched to alto sax, also playing clarinet. He studied tenor sax with Harry James's star soloist Corky Corcoran, but at the time Tex Benneke was Warne's idol. During the mid-1940s he changed his allegiance to Lester Young and Charlie Parker and remained faithful to them until the end. He was part of the Central Avenue circle of young jazzmen in Los Angeles and had his education enhanced by contact with Dexter Gordon and Wardell Gray. He played with Hoagy Carmichael's group in 1944 and 1945, then went into the army. A short stint in the Buddy Rich band followed. In New York he came in contact with teacher/pianist Lennie Tristano and through him met altoist Lee Konitz, with whom he is often compared, both favoring a highly advanced harmonic conception coupled with a light, refined sax tone. Marsh was an integral part of Tristano's bands (especially his sextet with Konitz) and unlike Konitz stayed faithful to Tristano's precepts pretty much until the end of his career, which came when he collapsed and died on stage during a club gig at Donte's in Los Angeles at the age of 60.

what to buy: Unlike Tristano, Marsh liked working with a strong bassist, and on the 1975 trio date *The Unissued Copenhagen Studio Recordings* ♫♫♫♪ (Storyville, 1997, prod. Arnvid Meyer) he's joined by one of the strongest ever, Niels-Henning Ørsted Pedersen, along with drummer Alan Levitt. Marsh sounds positively unfettered in the absence of a pianist, and anybody who hasn't yet marveled at his improvisatory adeptness should run out and grab this—it's mind-boggling that this session sat on the shelf for so long. This is also a good introduction for newcomers to Marsh's art because by this time his tone wasn't as thin (which can put off some listeners) as 20 years earlier. On a 12-tune collection of familiar standards and two jazz classics, Charlie Parker's "Confirmation" and Miles Davis's "Little Willie Leaps" (there was apparently not much advance preparation for this session, thus no Marsh originals), Marsh absolutely soars. Although his relatively straight rhythmic sense makes his lines flow very smoothly, so that they seem deceptively polite, there are many moments here on the uptempo tunes during which he rips off flurries of notes almost any sax player will envy.

what to buy next: Now available under Lee Konitz's name, the two-CD set *Live at the Half Note* ♫♫♫♫ (Verve, 1994, prod. Lee

Konitz) was recorded in 1959 and initially released on Tristano's label as a Marsh album—with Konitz's solos completely edited out! Konitz was the leader on this gig, however, and it's good to have this date restored to the way it happened. Despite a superstar rhythm section of Bill Evans (piano), Jimmy Garrison (bass), and Paul Motian (drums), in typical Tristano-inspired fashion the focus is very much on the horns, who evince contrasting styles, Marsh warm and flowing, Konitz probing and asymmetrical. The repertoire is a mix of Tristano and Konitz originals, standards such as "It's You or No One," and Charlie Parker's "Scrapple from the Apple." A Marsh album variously titled *Jazz of Two Cities* and *Winds of Marsh* ♫♫♫♫ (Imperial, 1956), which maintains the two-sax frontline format of the Tristano groups—a lineup Marsh favored throughout his career—is currently available on *Intuition* ♫♫♫♫ (Capitol, 1996, prod. Michael Cuscuna), jointly credited to Lennie Tristano and Warne Marsh because it includes Tristano's famous *Crosscurrents* ♫♫♫♫ (Capitol, 1949, prod. Pete Rugolo). The Marsh album, recorded after he'd returned to his hometown, has eight songs plus four mono takes different from the stereo versions, all played by a quintet with Ted Brown (tenor sax), Ronnie Ball (piano), Ben Tucker (bass), and Jeff Morton (drums); Brown provides little contrast with the leader, whose free-flowing inventiveness is not constrained by the tight structures of the mostly original program (there are covers of "Lover Man," "I Never Knew," and the Tchaikovsky piece that was adapted as the pop song "These Are Things I Love"). Though fine, this date is somewhat overshadowed by its historic discmate here. *Crosscurrents* features the Tristano sextet with Marsh and Konitz and shows where Marsh was coming from. It also contains the first recorded free improvisation in jazz history on the tracks "Intuition" and "Digression."

best of the rest:

Star Highs ♫♫♫♪ (Criss Cross, 1982)
A Ballad Album ♫♫♫ (Criss Cross, 1983)
Posthumous ♫♫♫♪ (Interplay, 1990)
(With the Lee Konitz Quintet) *Live at the Montmartre Club vol. 2* ♫♫♫♪ (Storyville, 1993)
Ballad for You ♫♫♫ (Interplay, 1995)
Music for Prancing ♫♫♫♫ (VSOP, 1995)

worth searching for: With Marsh's discography largely out of print, this section has the potential to be the longest in the book. A couple of more recent items may be relatively easy to track down on LP and, unlike so much of the Marsh material now available, was issued as soon as it was made. On *All Music* ♫♫♫ (Nessa, 1976, prod. Chuck Nessa) Marsh shows his fluency in both straight-ahead and avant-garde jazz. "Background Music" seems an ironic title for a piece in the latter style that demands the listener's attention, whereas Marsh's playing during "On Purpose" has an easy, bluesy feel. "Lunarcy," a variation on "How High the Moon," ranges from bop to "out," and then changes to double-time for good measure. The rhythm section of Lou Levy (piano), Jake Hanna (drums), and Fred Atwood (bass) contains some of the premiere Los Angeles players of the mid-1970s; having shared many a bandstand, they mesh seamlessly and support Marsh quite nicely. Partly because of this, and partly because of Warne's creativity and style, the tenor often seems to be free-floating above the rhythm section, but it never sounds lost. *Apogee* 🎵🎵🎵🎵 (Warner Bros., 1978, prod. Walter Becker, Donald Fagen) teams Marsh's fundamentally "cool" style with the more ebullient sound of Pete Christlieb, who seems to bring out some of the more raucous aspects of Marsh's playing. The highlight is "Tenors of the Time," a balls-to-the-wall romp reminiscent of the "cutting contests" of old. Christlieb burns hotly on the first solo, but even following this challenge, Marsh's solo is unhesitating and bursting with fertile ideas. After a brief drum solo with the piano comping behind, the horns play through several choruses as they continue the high-energy pace to the end. Also of particular note is "Magna-Tism," a tune written by Christlieb that is basically an improvisation on "Just Friends." It starts with the two saxes intertwining like double-helix DNA, then settles into the head as Lou Levy (piano), Jim Hughart (bass), and Nick Ceroli (drums) join in. Christlieb takes a lengthy solo, followed by Marsh's in-depth exploration. The two horns then interlock for several choruses, making what can only be described as a joyous noise. An alternately lyrical and angular piano solo ends the tune. Among the other tunes are "I'm Old Fashioned," "Donna Lee," and the first bebop composition by Fagen and Becker (of Steely Dan fame), "Rapunzel," based on the changes of Burt Bacharach's "The Land of Make Believe" (not the tune of the same name by Chuck Mangione).

influences:

◄◄ Lennie Tristano, Lester Young, Charlie Parker

►► Mark Turner, Steve Wilson, Anthony Braxton

Wally Shoup and Debra Pontac

Claire Martin

Born 1967, in London, England.

Though not well known in the United States, singer Claire Martin is quite popular in her native England. Unique and distinc-

tive, the cool-toned, subtle Londoner draws on a variety of influences ranging from Julie London, Chris Connor, and June Christy to rock-era heroines Joni Mitchell and Kate Bush. Quite adventurous in her choice of material, Martin doesn't limit herself to standards—and, in fact, she has demonstrated that the songs of Mitchell, Stevie Wonder, Rupert Holmes, and others can definitely work in a jazz setting. After recording four albums in Britain, Martin ventured to New York in October 1996 to record her first U.S. session.

what to buy: While *The Waiting Game* 🎵🎵🎵🎵 (Honest, 1992, prod. Elliot Meadow) finds Martin tackling Thomas Dolby's "The Key to Your Ferrari" and Joni Mitchell's "Be Cool" with splendid results, *Old Boyfriends* 🎵🎵🎵🎵 (Honest, 1994, prod. Joel E. Siegel) boasts heartfelt interpretations of Rupert Holmes's "Partners in Crime," Tom Waits's "Old Boyfriends," and Artie Shaw's "Moon Ray."

worth searching for: On her excellent British release *Offbeat: Live at Ronnie Scott's Club* 🎵🎵🎵🎵 (Linn, 1995), Martin insightfully finds the jazz potential in Stevie Wonder's "Make Sure You're Sure" and Laura Nyro's "Buy and Sell." Although *Devil May Care* 🎵🎵🎵 (Linn, 1993, prod. Rick Taylor) isn't quite essential, Martin's more devoted followers will enjoy her versions of Buddy Guy's "Save Your Love for Me" and the title song (a Bob Dorough classic). Like *Offbeat*, *Devil May Care* has only been released in the United Kingdom.

influences:

◄◄ Chris Connor, Julie London, June Christy, Joni Mitchell, Kate Bush

Alex Henderson

Mel Martin

Born June 7, 1941, in Sacramento, CA.

Mel Martin is a highly fluent improvisor on a wide array of reed instruments, though he is most often heard on soprano and tenor sax. Working in the advanced mainstream tradition, his style is best described by the name of his repertory band, Bebop and Beyond. Martin started working professionally as a saxophonist as a young teenager, joining the Musician's Union at age 16. He moved to San Francisco in the mid-1960s, participating in the city's burgeoning music scene in jazz, R&B, and pop contexts, recording with Boz Scaggs, Azteca, and Santana. In the mid-1970s, Martin founded the fusion group Listen, which recorded a number of fine albums for Inner City. In 1983, he created Bebop and Beyond, which has recorded albums devoted to the music of Thelonious Monk and Dizzy Gillespie. Martin has led sessions with saxophonists Joe Henderson and Benny Carter and recorded as a sideman in Latin contexts with Mongo Santamaria and Pucho and His Latin Soul Brothers. Very active on the Bay Area jazz scene, Martin has served as musical director for the Keystone All-Stars and assembled big bands for Gillespie, Benny Carter and McCoy Tyner.

what to buy: Far and away Mel Martin's best recording, *Mel Martin Plays Benny Carter* &&&& (Enja, 1996, prod. Mel Martin) features him (on curved soprano, tenor, and flute) with two highly stimulating rhythm sections. On the three tracks recorded live at Yoshi's with the brilliant Roger Kellaway (piano), Jeff Chambers (bass), and Harold Jones (drums), Martin is joined by Carter himself. A highlight is Carter's exotic, dreamy new piece "Zanzibar." Kenny Barron (piano), Rufus Reid (bass), and Victor Lewis (drums) accompany on six tracks, including Carter's best-known tune, "When Lights Are Low," and two Brazilian flavored tunes, "A Kiss from You" and "Summer Serenade." Martin, always a prodigious player, is in highly lyrical form throughout, caressing Carter's melodies with his lush, warm sound.

what to buy next: Not only a fine album, *Bebop and Beyond Play Dizzy Gillespie* (Mesa/Bluemoon, 1994, prod. Mel Martin) &&&& was Gillespie's last studio recording, though his presence is more spiritual than musical. The rhythm section, with pianist George Cables, bassist Jeff Chambers, and either Donald Bailey or Vince Lateano on drums, locks into the grooves, and trumpeter Warren Gale sounds inspired by Diz's presence. Highlights include the medley of "Manteca" and "A Night in Tunisia" and Gillespie's rarely played "Father Time."

the rest:
Listen &&&& (Inner City, 1977)
Growing &&&& (Inner City, 1978)
Other Side Up &&&&& (Catero, 1983)
Bebop and Beyond &&&& (Concord Jazz, 1984)

worth searching for: This out-of-print CD, *Bebop and Beyond Plays Thelonious Monk* &&&& (Mesa/Bluemoon, 1991, prod. Mel Martin) is not just another album of Monk tunes. Martin's arrangements are richly textured and full of imaginative details. With tenor saxophonist Joe Henderson and the remarkable tuba player Howard Johnson, there is no shortage of inspired solos.

influences:
◄◄ John Coltrane, Benny Carter, Sonny Rollins

Andrew Gilbert

Pat Martino
Born Pat Azzara, August 25, 1944, in Philadelphia, PA.

Martino had built himself a reputation as one of the great jazz guitarists when his career was halted by brain aneurysms. After tremendous effort, he eventually managed to rebuild his technique and make an inspiring comeback.

Martino's father, Carmen "Mickey" Azzara, was a club singer who briefly studied guitar with Eddie Lang. He encouraged Pat to take up guitar at age 12. Pat left school in tenth grade to devote himself to music. One of his teachers was Dennis Sandole, who had an older student, John Coltrane, whom Martino met and was influenced by through conversations about music. Martino's technical wizardry won him attention and he soon had work; his first road gig was with organist Charles Earland, a high school friend. Other gigs included soul star Lloyd Price's band, which included a number of "name" jazz musicians. Martino moved to Harlem to soak up the soul-jazz culture and built up a fearsome reputation as a hot soloist. Further sideman gigs in organ groups led by Jack McDuff and Don Patterson followed, and by age 20 Martino was signed by Prestige. By the end of the 1960s he was exploring psychedelic sounds and Eastern/Middle Eastern influences. He spent much of the 1970s recording for Muse, but in 1976 began suffering from severe headaches that were eventually diagnosed as brain aneurysms. Following surgery in 1980, he not only lost all memory of his career (and barely recognized his parents), he was left with no knowledge of how to play guitar. Listening to his old albums and undergoing extensive rehabilitation, including computer therapy, he eventually, amazingly, relearned the instrument and regained his skills.

Martino resumed public appearances in 1987 (the first gig was taped, yielding the Muse album, *The Return*) but dropped out of music again when both of his parents became ill. He finally returned to the studio in 1994, and his career has started to regain its momentum. Martino's presence in the bins has also been increased by the 32 Jazz reissues of his Muse albums; the label promises that by the end of 1998 they will all be in print again.

what to buy: *Heart & Head* &&&&& (32 Jazz, 1998, prod. Joel Dorn) is a low-priced two-CD set consisting of the quartet albums *Consciousness* &&&& (Muse, 1974, prod. Michael Cuscuna) and *Live!* &&&& (Muse, 1972, prod. Don Schlitten). *Consciousness* opens with a smokin' version of Coltrane's "Impressions" and proceeds to cover a lot of ground, including the solo tracks "Passata on Guitar" and Joni Mitchell's "Both Sides

Now." This album is a mature statement of Martino's talents and interests, with the earlier awkwardnesses worked past. He really stretches out on *Live!*, which contains his originals "Special Door" (17:43) and "The Great Stream" (10:28), as well as a cover of the pop hit "Sunny" (10:25). Sometimes lengthy tracks are overly indulgent, but not here, where the band gets in a groove and the solos are hot.

what to buy next: *El Hombre* ♫♫♫♪ (Prestige, 1967/OJC, 1990, prod. Cal Lampley) was Martino's debut as a leader, and he stayed in the soul-jazz-with-organ format he'd been working in with so many greats. Trudy Pitts is the organist, Danny Turner plays flute, and there's traps, congas, and bongos. The thrill is in Martino's idiomatic originals and, much more, in his flights of improvisatory inspiration as he weaves sometimes knotty patterns into swirls of energetic melody. *East!* ♫♫♫♫ (Prestige, 1968/OJC, 1990, prod. Don Schlitten) was the first album on which Martino's stylistic range reached beyond soul-jazz, with the nearly 13-minute title track (penned by bassist Tyrone Brown) an excursion into almost psychedelic realms, modal and drone-based. The other tracks are more straightahead, including Benny Golson's "Park Avenue Petite" and John Coltrane's "Lazy Bird."

what to avoid: Though hardly without merit, *Strings!* ♫♫ (Prestige, 1967/OJC, 1991, prod. Don Schlitten) is fairly formulaic soul-jazz, especially considering the sterling personnel, which include Joe Farrell (tenor sax, flute) and Cedar Walton (piano). Martino would soon become more adventurous, and the later material should take precedence.

the rest:

Baiyina (The Clear Evidence) ♫♫♫ (Prestige, 1968/OJC, 1989)
Desperado ♫♫♫♪ (Prestige, 1970/OJC, 1990)
Footprints ♫♫♫♪ (Muse, 1975/32 Jazz, 1997) a.k.a. *The Visit*
Maker ♫♫♫♪ (Paddlewheel, 1994/Evidence, 1995)
All Sides Now ♫♫♫♪ (Blue Note, 1997)
Cream ♫♫♫♪ (32 Jazz, 1997)

worth searching for: Even after he was an established star, Martino recorded regularly in saxophonist Willis Jackson's organ group. *Willis . . . with Pat* ♫♫♫♫ (32 Jazz, 1998, prod. Willis Jackson, Bob Porter, Don Schlitten; compilation prod. Adam Dorn, Lance Goler) selects highlights from their collaborations on Muse (1974–78) and epitomizes the best aspects of this sort of tenor/organ jazz: soulful, grooving, direct. Jackson's *Bar Wars* ♫♫♫♫ (Muse, 1978/32 Jazz, 1997, prod. Bob Porter, reissue prod. Joel Dorn) is one of the albums picked from for the above compilation. It adds two bonus tracks (alternate takes)

to the original track list and features a superb quintet with Charles Earland (organ), Idris Muhammad (drums), and Buddy Caldwell (congas). Martino, of course, is superbly idiomatic; he never forgot his roots in this music.

influences:

◀◀ Grant Green, Johnny Smith, Wes Montgomery

▶▶ Pat Metheny, Larry Coryell

Steve Holtje

Masada

Formed 1993, in New York, NY. Disbanded in 1997.

John Zorn, alto sax, composer; Dave Douglas, trumpet; Greg Cohen, acoustic bass; Joey Baron, drums. Masada Chamber Ensembles (1994–97) also include: Mark Feldman, violin; Erik Friedlander, cello; Marc Ribot, guitar; Anthony Coleman, piano; David Krakauer, clarinets; John Medeski, organ and piano; Mark Dresser, bass; Kenny Wollesen, drums; Chris Speed, clarinet.

Masada (the place—and symbol) is the fortress in Israel where besieged Jews chose to commit communal suicide rather than submit to captivity. Masada (the group) is the peak of John Zorn's involvement with jazz. Combining Yiddish music (including but not limited to klezmer) with jazz had been done before, but by specifically emphasizing the parallels between Ornette Coleman's early style and the older, modal Eastern/Central European music of Zorn's Jewish ancestors (and by letting the latter dominate rather than treating it as an ingredient to be added for exotic effect), Zorn came up with something new and distinctive.

There are many jazz aspects not specifically traceable to Coleman, of course; that's just a handy comparison. There are moments when Joey Baron's drumming steady four-beat recalls Tony Williams's pulse on Miles Davis's *In a Silent Way*, and some of the freer explorations suggest the Art Ensemble of Chicago. And Douglas's presence is perfect: his work with Balkan scales and rhythms had him on a parallel path in some of his own music.

what to buy: The extreme coherence of the style Zorn has created—not to mention the incredible artistic consistency of the performers—seems to resist the sort of critical parsing that allows for definable gradations of quality. But certainly many fans retain a special fondness for *One/Alef* ♫♫♫♫ (DIW, 1994, prod. John Zorn, Kazunori Sugiyama), where the new amalgam first struck them with its startling rightness: "Jair," the opening track, which alternates klezmer licks and Ornette phrases in a head that's the perfect proclamation of the new style; "Tzofeh" with its ticking insistence; "Ashnah" with its brooding spontaneity, almost-absent pulse, and focus on subtle instrumental textures; the brief "Delin" with what seems like a purely Ornettean head framing a biting bass solo; the cool-strutting "Janohah." Zorn fans looking for his more extreme playing are directed towards *Five/Hei* ✍✍✍✍ (DIW, 1995, prod. John Zorn, Kazunori Sugiyama) for the intense "Hobah," which in the minimal materials of its theme draws not from early Coleman, but instead sounds like a translation to acoustic instruments of one of the harmolodic themes of his Prime Time period—and which then explodes into collectively improvised energy playing straight out of the post-Coltrane school, with Zorn wailing in the altissimo register and Douglas darting sinuously around Zorn's line while Baron thunders underneath.

what to buy next: The leader of the Jews at Masada was named Bar Kokhba. The music on the two-CD set *Bar Kokhba* ✍✍✍✍ (Tzadik, 1996, prod. John Zorn) is performed not by the quartet, but by a number of chamber ensembles, sometimes without drums and with Zorn acting as composer and leader but not playing. "Tannaim," for instance, is a contemplative string trio with Mark Feldman, Erik Friedlander, and Greg Cohen. Practically its opposite, the following tune, "Nefesh," is swinging piano-trio bop—a lament penned by a depressed Horace Silver, perhaps—with John Medeski (sounding rather Monkish in his solo, with touches of early McCoy Tyner in the second half), Mark Dresser, and Kenny Wollesen. This music is more low-key than the quartet, with a corresponding increase in restful beauty during the strings-only numbers and in plaintive soulfulness when the clarinetists wail.

the rest:
Two/Beit ✍✍✍✍ (DIW, 1994)
Three/Gimel ✍✍✍✍ (DIW, 1994)
Four/Dalet ✍✍✍✍ (DIW, 1994)
Six/Nav ✍✍✍✍ (DIW, 1995)
Seven/Zayin ✍✍✍✍ (DIW, 1995)
Eight/Het ✍✍✍✍ (DIW, 1997)
Nine/Tet ✍✍✍✍ (DIW, 1997)
(As the Masada String Trio/Bar Kokhba Sextet) *The Circle Maker* ✍✍✍✍ (Tzadik, 1998)

worth searching for: *Ten* was scheduled for mid-1998. Rumor has it that eventually there will be several live Masada albums and a box set of all the studio recordings, and it looks as if the group will occasionally reunite.

influences:
◀◀ Ornette Coleman, Yiddish music, Don Byron
▶▶ Hasidic New Wave

Steve Holtje

Steve Masakowski
Born September 2, 1954, in New Orleans, LA.

The seven-string guitar has a budding core of young jazz virtuosos making a place for it within the discipline, following the lead of pioneers like Bucky Pizzarelli and George Van Eps. Steve Masakowski, while not as well known nationally as Howard Alden or Jimmy Bruno, certainly has the skills to be considered in the same class. Masakowski was born in the physical cradle of jazz history, educated at Berklee, and returned to New Orleans. He has created his own style with roots in Danny Barker, Joe Pass, Pat Martino, and Jim Hall, adding to the musical ambience of the Big Easy. Masakowski teaches jazz studies at the University of New Orleans and has played and/or recorded with national talent like Emily Remler, Dave Liebman, Mose Allison, Diane Reeves, and Rick Margitza, in addition to such local lights as Ellis Marsalis, Johnny Adams, and Alvin "Red" Tyler. Voted "Best Guitar" in a 1996 *Offbeat* magazine poll, he regularly plays in Astral Project, a New Orleans–based quintet of top-notch session musicians consistently voted best contemporary jazz band in local polls. The band has released two albums to date with Masakowski playing and contributing compositions. As a leader, he has released two albums on his own Prescriptions label, in addition to recording two nationally distributed albums for Blue Note.

what to buy: Sometimes it's what a musician doesn't play that makes him a true virtuoso, looking beyond the physical technique to the heart of the music. Most of the material for *What It Was* ✍✍✍✍ (Blue Note, 1994, prod. David Torkanowsky) comes from the guitarist's pen, but he leaves ample room for other players to vent their skills while not neglecting his own instrumental prowess. "Hector's Lecture" is an interesting Latin excursion featuring the timbales of Hector Gallardo. Rick Margitza's smoldering tenor sax playing on "Budapest" fits the minor-key construction of the piece. "Southern Blue" is a wonderfully off-kilter blues riff with Masakowski slipping around the obvious to make the new.

what to buy next: While not as consistently rewarding as *What It Was*, *Direct AXEcess* ✍✍✍ (Blue Note, 1995, prod. Steve Masakowski, David Torkanowsky) still has its share of rewards. Masakowski brings subtle brilliance to three solo guitar renditions on this album: Thelonious Monk's "Monk's Mood," Hoagy

Carmichael's "New Orleans," and Johnny Mandel's "Emily" (a tribute to guitarist Emily Remler.) The second-line rhythms of "Burgundy," driven by Brian Blade's idiomatic, sympathetic trap playing and Masakowski's partners in Astral Project, David Torkanowsky (piano) and James Singleton (bass), kick up a party.

influences:

◀◀ Danny Barker, Pat Martino, Jim Hall, Joe Pass, Lenny Breau

Garaud MacTaggart

Miya Masaoka

Born January 3, 1958, in Washington, DC.

A master improviser on the 21-string koto, San Francisco Bay Area musician Miya Masaoka employs dozens of personalized techniques (including the use of mallets, bows, and cymbals) to extend the instrument's range beyond that of traditional Japanese music. She's transcribed and performed compositions by Duke Ellington, Thelonious Monk, and Cecil Taylor, and worked with seasoned veterans like Taylor and Pharoah Sanders. Her incisive improvisatory skills can be heard on Ben Goldberg's *Twelve Minor*, Steve Coleman's *Myths, Modes & Means*, and Lisle Ellis's *What We Live Fo(u)r*. While touring in the Netherlands in 1996, a team of technicians at STEIM (the Dutch government-funded Studio voor Elecktro-Instrumentale Muziek) presented her with a custom-built processing unit that can be programmed to improvise along with Masaoka's on-the-spot creations. Despite a growing international reputation, many of the artist's more ambitious projects, like the recent orchestral performance of "What Is the Difference Between Stripping and Playing the Violin?"—a self-described examination of "the commodification of music, the body, ethnicity and eroticism in our market-driven society"—have yet to come out on disc. Masaoka expanded her interest in "hybridized, intercultural, intermedia investigations" when she appeared at the 1997 Monterey Jazz Festival in a trio (with bassist Trevor Dunn and drummer Scott Amendola) augmented by her daughter, DJ Mariko.

what's available: *Compositions-Improvisations* ♫♫♫♫ (Asian Improv, 1994, prod. Miya Masaoka) is Masaoka's brilliant debut, an album startling in its powerful simplicity. It's largely a solo outing with renowned flautist James Newton appearing on "Still/Motion/Ness." Though this recording barely begins to tell the full story, it's a fine introduction to a groundbreaking artist. *Duets* ♫♫♫♫ (Music & Arts, 1997, prod. Fred Maroth) is a live collaboration with George Lewis, featuring two of the music's most compelling improvisers who extend the duet tradition into other universes. Masoka collaborates with Splatter

Trio percussionist Gino Robair and Tom Nunn on *Crepuscular Music* ♫♫♫♫ (Rastascan, 1996, prod. Miya Masaoka, Gino Robair, Tom Nunn). Nunn builds and plays percussive electro-acoustic contraptions called the bug and baboon on this haunting live improvisation which packs enormous intensity into even its most serene passages.

influences:

◀◀ John Coltrane, Cecil Taylor, Butch Morris

Sam Prestianni

Cal Massey

Born January 11, 1928 in Philadelphia, PA. Died October 25, 1972 in Brooklyn, NY.

John Coltrane's recordings of three Cal Massey compositions will keep the obscure trumpeter's name alive. Massey, although a fine (if unassertive) trumpet player, was respected more for his composing and arranging talents. His tunes are often on original chord progressions, with structures sometimes departing from the blues or AABA norms, and rather than just simple unison themes he liked to add countermelodies. His only album as a leader, recorded in 1961 for writer Nat Hentoff's small record label, went unissued (aside from one track on a compilation album) until 1987. He spent much of his subsequent career organizing independent concerts and benefits featuring both avant-garde and mainstream stars who sometimes donated their services out of respect for Massey.

Massey's somewhat impoverished childhood (in a one-parent household) could not obstruct his early interest in music, and in his early teens he was already playing trumpet (in a school band that also included Tommy Turrentine and Ray Brown), soon adding French horn to his skills. By the age of 15 he was already working professionally in area bands. His bosses soon included Jay McShann, Buster Smith, Eddie Vinson, and B.B. King, and in 1951 Charlie Parker recorded Massey's "Fiesta." Massey became friendly with fellow Philadelphians John Coltrane and the Heath brothers, and it was in Massey's band that Coltrane first heard pianist McCoy Tyner. Massey wrote music for Tyner, Freddie Hubbard, Lee Morgan, Jackie McLean, and Archie Shepp, and shortly before his premature death of an apparent heart attack collaborated with Shepp and Stanley Cowell on the musical *Lady Day: A Musical Tragedy,* about Billie Holiday. McCoy Tyner's dedicatory "Folks" is titled after Massey's nickname. Cal's son Zane Massey is a fine saxophonist who has included his father's compositions on both his Delmark albums. In the liner notes to Zane's *Brass Knuckles* it's posited that Cal was blackballed due to his political activism and, as Zane says, "an incident with a very well-known producer at the time."

what to buy: *Blues to Coltrane* 𝄞𝄞𝄞 (Candid, 1987, prod. Nat Hentoff) suffers from poor engineering and a sub-standard piano but is a valuable document. Massey's composing (all five tracks are credited to him) is generally up to the level of his reputation, though "Blues to Coltrane" is just a revamped "Nobody Knows the Trouble I've Seen." Overall, it's an enjoyable bop outing with adventurous post-bop moments—most notably "Father and Son," which also has the most developed arrangement (and another "Nobody Knows the Trouble I've Seen" quote during Massey's carefully nuanced solo). Besides Massey himself on trumpet, the standout solos are by French horn player Julius Watkins. Tenor saxophonist Hugh Brodie is effective if hardly able to stand the inevitable comparison to Coltrane. Pianist Patti Bown wrestles her inadequate instrument to a draw, comping well and occasionally showing interesting ideas in her solos. Holding up the bottom end, though not done any favors in the mix, is bassist Jimmy Garrison.

what to buy next: The Massey material recorded by Coltrane is easily found. The most intricate piece is "The Damned Don't Cry" on *The Complete Africa/Brass Sessions* 𝄞𝄞𝄞𝄞 (Impulse!, 1961, prod. Creed Taylor), the only track on the album not arranged by Eric Dolphy or McCoy Tyner. Its cool timbres and the instrumentation recall Gil Evans. "Bakai" (Arabic for "cry") is on the saxophonist's debut as sole leader, *Coltrane* 𝄞𝄞𝄞𝄞 (Prestige, 1957, prod. Bob Weinstock) and its unusual structure and minor-key chord changes, more complicated than his usual Prestige material, seem to inspire Coltrane. "Nakatini Suite," retitled "Nakatini Serenade," is on *The Believer* 𝄞𝄞𝄞𝄞 (Prestige, 1958, prod. Bob Weinstock) in a Latinized arrangement.

what to avoid: It's unfortunate that Cal's daughter Waheeda, seven years old at the time, sings horribly out of tune on the otherwise lush and lovely "Quiet Dawn" on Archie Shepp's political classic *Attica Blues* 𝄞𝄞 (Impulse!, 1972, prod. Ed Michel). Whatever the political/cultural point may have been, it strongly discourages repeated listening. Massey plays two short flugelhorn solos on the 25-instrument arrangement (complete with strings). His tune "Goodbye to Pops" is the preceding track, though he's not present on it.

worth searching for: Massey's gorgeous ballad "A Baby's Smile" was an outtake from Lee Morgan's *¡Caramba!* 𝄞𝄞𝄞𝄞 (Blue Note, 1968/1996, prod. Francis Wolff, reissue prod.

Michael Cuscuna), but showed up years after the fact as a bonus track on the CD.

influences:

◀◀ Fats Navarro, Freddie Webster, Miles Davis, Gil Evans

▶▶ John Coltrane, Archie Shepp, Zane Massey

Steve Holtje

Zane Massey

Born in 1957, in Philadelphia, PA.

Zane Massey's recordings as a leader are already double his father Cal's album output. Raised in Brooklyn surrounded by great musicians, who often rehearsed at his family's house, Zane was taught not only by his father but also by Frank Foster, Sonny Red, and Jimmy Heath; eventually his father's concerts included young Zane. While still a teenager, his Latin jazz band Young Blood Jazz Men was featured on the ABC-TV black affairs program *Like It Is*. He recorded with Carlos Garnett and later joined Ronald Shannon Jackson's Decoding Society, staying with the group for most of the 1980s and absorbing the harmolodic system. In the meantime he also worked with Sun Ra and Jemeel Moondoc, and in the 1990s he recorded with Roy Campbell and Malachi Thompson for Delmark Records, leading to his albums as a leader. He has also organized the Music under New York big band, which performs in the subway.

what to buy: *Brass Knuckles* 𝄞𝄞𝄞 (Delmark, 1993, prod. Steve Wagner) is a thrilling trio album that reveals Massey's stylistic versatility, from bebop and suggestions of Coleman Hawkins to outside excursions and funk. Throughout, Massey plays with raw excitement, with the bass and drums adequately stoking the rhythmic fires.

what to buy next: The horrible title notwithstanding, *Safe to Imagine* 𝄞𝄞𝄞 (Delmark, 1996, prod. Steve Wagner) offers adventurous playing (if not writing) as Massey occasionally inserts free jazz playing into bebop forms. The quartet format keeps the spotlight securely on the leader, a fortunate development given the merely adequate imaginations of the rhythm trio (pianist Denton Darien sits out three tracks). Could the out-of-tune piano be a tribute to the piano on father Cal's sole album, or is it more likely just shoddy producing?

worth searching for: Of the six Decoding Society albums Massey plays on, *Barbeque Dog* 𝄞𝄞𝄞𝄞 (Antilles, 1983, prod. David Breskin, Ronald Shannon Jackson) best showcases his playing. On his own albums, Massey doesn't play alto sax, but he has three fine alto solos here.

influences:

◀◀ John Coltrane, Sonny Rollins, Coleman Hawkins, Archie Shepp, Cal Massey, Frank Foster, Jimmy Heath, Ronald Shannon Jackson

▶▶ Malachi Thompson, Lee Rozie

Steve Holtje

Material
/Bill Laswell

Formed 1979, in New York, NY.

Bill Laswell, bass, supplemented by whoever he feels like inviting from one session to the next.

Material mastermind Bill Laswell has long mixed genres with unbridled abandon, but within the context of Material itself, jazz has been a constant ingredient, if hardly the only one. Among the busiest producers in music—not so much because he's in demand (though he is: he's produced albums for everyone from Herbie Hancock and Mick Jagger to Motorhead and Iggy Pop) as that he's got such an overflow of ideas he needs to enact—Laswell works on a steady basis for a number of labels, several of them his own to varying degrees (his many ambient and techno projects mostly lie outside the purvue of this book).

Laswell moved to New York in 1978 and within a year had formed Material, initially to back Daevid Allen (Gong). At first it consisted of Laswell (an exceptional bassist), drummer Fred Maher, and synthesizer/keyboardist/tape processor Michael Beinhorn working with a small coterie of fellow avant-gardists or by themselves. The three found work and success as a production team working on modern urban R&B projects, and the breadth of Material's music began increasing. When vast numbers of guest performers were brought in for 1982's *Memory Serves*, the group's future modus operandus was set. An ever-shifting array of performers has kept the group mutating, and Laswell has increased the use of jazz (including Archie Shepp and Wayne Shorter) and world music artists over the years, also adding African and Asian modalities. In 1986 he also co-founded Last Exit, international superstars of the free-improvisation scene. His other jazz-oriented but more ad-hoc groups are SXL (a combination of the Korean percussion quartet Samulnori with a quartet of Laswell, Shankar, Ronald Shannon Kackson, and Alyb Dieng) and Deadline, a one-album stu-

dio project that utilized Steve Turre, Olu Dara, Phillip Wilson, Jonas Hellborg, Manu Dibango, Jaco Pastorius, and others.

what to buy: *Memory Serves* ΔΔΔΔ⍟ (Celluloid/Elektra Musician, 1982, prod. Material, Martin Bisi) was the first Material album to take the guest-star approach to the extreme, and it worked fantastically, with the cream of Downtown NYC's avant/jazz legends (Sonny Sharrock, Billy Bang, Fred Frith, Henry Threadgill, George Lewis, Charles K. Noyes, Olu Dara) concocting music unlike anything ever heard before. But the greatest moment is Laswell's unearthly combination of instrumental virtuosity and timbral imagination on "Silent Land," where he coaxes uncanny harmonics from his bass.

what to buy next: *One Down* ΔΔΔΔ (Celluloid/Elektra, 1982, prod. Material) is Laswell at his funkiest and most commercial (the CD bonus track, "Busting Out," was a dance club hit). The guests range from jazzers to avant types to R&B players, but the most startling performance is "Memories," with 1960s jazz great Archie Shepp playing impassioned solos and Whitney Houston (!), before making her debut album, absolutely soaring on a performance she's never equalled on her own. Since Laswell has devoted so much time recently to ambient music, it's crucial to hear a sampling. *Lost in the Translation* ΔΔΔΔ (Axiom, 1994, prod. Bill Laswell) is credited to Axiom Ambient and labeled "Sound Sculptures by Bill Laswell with contributions from Terre Thaemlitz, The Orb, Tetsu Inoue." Laswell reshapes performances, including Sonny Sharrock, Pharoah Sanders, Nicky Skopelitis, Jah Wobble, Bernie Worrell, Bootsy Collins, Ginger Baker, Liu Sola, and many more, into not the new agey wallpaper much ambient consists of, but rather abstract art music with incredible sensitivity to sonic textures.

what to avoid: Material's *Live from Soundscape* ⍟ (DIW, 1991, prod. Verna Gillis) is rambling, episodic free improvisation with nothing more to offer than isolated moments of instrumental wizardry.

the rest:
Temporary Music ΔΔΔ (Celluloid, 1981)
Red Tracks ΔΔΔ (Red, 1985)
Seven Souls ΔΔ (Virgin, 1989)
The Third Power ΔΔΔ (Axiom, 1991)
Live in Japan ΔΔ⍟ (Restless, 1993)
Hallucination Engine ΔΔ⍟ (Axiom, 1994)

solo outings:
Bill Laswell:
Baselines ΔΔΔΔ (Celluloid/Elektra Musician, 1983)
Hear No Evil ΔΔΔΔ (Venture/Virgin, 1988)

(With Ryuichi Sakamoto and Yosuke Yamashita) *Asian Games* 𝄞𝄞𝄞𝄞
   (Verve, 1994)

SXL:
Live in Japan 𝄞𝄞𝄞 (CBS/Sony Japan, 1987)
Into the Outlands 𝄞𝄞𝄞 (Celluloid/Pipeline, 1988)

Deadline:
Down by Law 𝄞𝄞𝄞 (Celluloid, 1985)

influences:

⏪ John Coltrane, Miles Davis, Sonny Sharrock, Jimi Hendrix, George Clinton

⏩ The Orb, Ben Neill, Mitchell Froom, DJ Spooky, Nona Hendryx, Arthur Baker, Golden Palominos

Steve Holtje

Bill Mays

Born February 5, 1944, in Sacramento, CA.

As a pianist, Bill Mays is a thoroughly trained tradesman. The world needs these kind of people—they are the caretakers of song lore, the nice-sounding players in the ad jingles, the reliable backup musicians and arrangers. Mays moves the music forward under the grand design of an arranger. He was inspired by Earl Hines when he was 16, and by age 18 was playing for Sarah Vaughan (on the recommendation of Jimmy Rowles). With a reputation as a sensitive accompanist, he has worked with singers Al Jarreau, Peggy Lee, Mel Tormé, Frank Sinatra, and Mark Murphy. As a sideman within a group context Mays has played with another impressive list of leaders: Gerry Mulligan, Howard Roberts, Sonny Stitt, Art Pepper, and Bud Shank.

what to buy: On *Bill Mays at Maybeck* 𝄞𝄞𝄞𝄞 (Concord Jazz, 1993, prod. Carl E. Jefferson, Nick Phillips), forced to rely only on himself, Mays shows he is capable of truly interesting playing. The piano intro to "A Nightingale Sang in Berkeley Square" is a clever lead and the rest of the tune is breathtakingly beautiful. Mays's own "Boardwalk Blues" has a wonderfully evocative beginning with a French classical feel, before stretching into a luxurious blues riff, quoting the traditional "Sometimes I Feel like a Motherless Child."

what to buy next: *Bill Mays/Ed Bickert* 𝄞𝄞𝄞 (Concord Jazz, 1994, prod. Carl E. Jefferson, Nick Phillips) proves that pairing these two solid players for the Maybeck Duo date was a no-brainer. Bickert is a fluid guitarist content to lay back in the groove, and Mays does pretty much the same thing on piano. Bickert's soft chording behind Mays's lead on Duke Ellington's "Do Nothing 'till You Hear from Me," and his plush lead over

Mays's feeder rhythm are affably symptomatic of the whole album. Wonderful, responsive playing with fire when needed ("Bick's Bag"), but pleasant rather than soul-shaking.

the rest:
Tha's Delight 𝄞𝄞𝄞 (Trend, 1983)
(With Ray Drummond) *One to One* 𝄞𝄞𝄞 (DMP, 1990)
(With Ray Drummond) *One to One, Volume 2* 𝄞𝄞𝄞 (DMP, 1991)
Kaleidoscope 𝄞𝄞𝄞 (Jazz Alliance, 1992)
An Ellington Affair 𝄞𝄞𝄞 (Concord Jazz, 1993)

influences:

⏪ Earl Hines, Erroll Garner

Garaud MacTaggart

Lyle Mays

Born November 27, 1953, in Wausaukee, WI.

Lyle Mays is probably best known as the keyboardist in the Pat Metheny Group and as Metheny's longtime collaborator, but this tremendously gifted artist is no mere sideman. A composer and solo artist who draws from both jazz and classical traditions, Mays has certainly had a profound impact on the development of the Metheny Group's sound, but he can also place his compositional inventiveness and technical mastery in different contexts.

Growing up in a musical family, Mays was encouraged to perform and create music from an early age, and he further developed his technique during his teens at jazz summer camps. He attended North Texas State University, where he studied composition and arrangement and he earned a Grammy nomination at age 22 for a composition he composed and arranged for the university's big band. After graduating, he toured with saxophonist-clarinetist Woody Herman's Thundering Herd. In 1975, while still a student at North Texas State, Mays met Metheny at the Wichita Jazz Festival in Kansas. Mays was performing with his own group and Metheny was playing in vibraphonist Gary Burton's band. The two discovered a creative kinship, and two years later established the alliance that exists to this day. The two were also part of singer Joni Mitchell's 1979 "Shadows and Light" tour, along with bassist Jaco Pastorius, saxophonist Michael Brecker, and drummer Don Alias. Since 1986 Mays has composed music for several children's recordings for Rabbit Ears Productions, and also composed and performed the score for *Mustang: The Hidden Kingdom,* a 1994 film about a Buddhist enclave narrated by actor Harrison Ford.

what to buy: *Fictionary* 𝄞𝄞𝄞𝄞 (Geffen, 1993, prod. Pat Metheny, Steve Rodby), a live acoustic trio album with drummer Jack De-

Johnette and bassist Marc Johnson, demonstrates Mays's extraordinary improvisational skill and technical finesse, especially on tunes such as the majestic and quirkily titled "Lincoln Reviews His Notes" and the vigorous workout "Hard Eights." DeJohnette and Johnson provide inspired rhythmic support on this elegant recording.

what to buy next: On his solo debut, *Lyle Mays* ♫♫♫ (Geffen, 1986, prod. Lyle Mays, Steven Cantor), Mays paints evocative sonic pictures with his palette of electronic and acoustic sounds. The rich "Highland Aire" features the unmistakable Mays synthesizer voice, while "Mirror of the Heart" has ringing solo piano.

the rest:
Street Dreams ♫♫♫ (Geffen, 1988)

worth searching for: *As Falls Wichita, So Falls Wichita Falls* ♫♫♫ (ECM, 1981, prod. Manfred Eicher), an eclectic trio recording with guitarist Metheny and percussionist-vocalist Nana Vasconcelos, underscores Metheny and Mays's complete accord, whether conjuring the swirling soundscape of the title track or shifting lead voices in the romantic "September Fifteenth (Dedicated to Bill Evans)." *The Road to You* ♫♫♫ (Geffen, 1993, prod. Pat Metheny, Steve Rodby, David Oakes) is a comprehensive document of the Pat Metheny Group's output over the last decade and a half. Mays provides atmospheric synths and a spiky ascending piano solo in "Half Life of Absolution" to heighten the tune's inherent tension, and his powerful soloing helps make "The First Circle" even more dramatic than the original version.

influences:
◀◀ Bill Evans
▶▶ Mitchel Forman

Lucy Tauss

M-Base Collective

1991 in Brooklyn, NY

Cassandra Wilson, vocals; Mark Ledford, vocals; Steve Coleman, alto saxophone; Greg Osby, alto saxophone; Jimmy Cozier, baritone saxophone; Graham Haynes, trumpet; James Weidman, keyboards; Andy Milne, keyboards; David Gilmore, guitar; Kevin Bruce Harris, bass; Reggie Washington, bass; Marvin "Smitty" Smith, drums.

The M-Base style was well established among a floating array of Brooklyn players loosely aligned with Steve Coleman and Greg Osby when this theoretically leaderless project (presum-

ably credited this way for contractual reasons) was laid down for a Japanese label and later picked up for U.S. distribution under a deal with Columbia. It proved to be the first major exposure for a couple of players who would later get contracts as solo artists—Mark Ledford and Andy Milne. Earlier, Kevin Bruce Harris, who'd been with the M-Basers since the beginning, had an interesting if inconsistent album released by a German label helmed by Enja producer Matthias Winckelmann.

what to buy: *Anatomy of a Groove: Current Structural Developments in 21st-Century Creative Black Music* ♫♫♫ (DIW/Columbia, 1992, prod. Steve Coleman) spreads the composing credits around, but the focus is firmly on Coleman, Osby, Smith, and (on the tracks where she participates, mostly contributing wordless vocals) Cassandra Wilson. This is not the most profound music, but the tricky grooves and angular sax lines are always stimulating, and everybody plays well during their moments in the spotlight.

what to avoid: Mark Ledford's *Miles 2 Go* **woof!** (Verve, 1998) pulls out the big-gun guest stars (Pat Metheny, Michael Brecker, Najee, Cyrus Chestnut), but doesn't do much of interest with them. Ledford, besides singing also plays trumpet, keyboard, and guitar, has two main styles. The sappy smooth jazz is merely bland. Much worse are the tracks where he tries to pay tribute to Miles Davis. Anybody want to hear (Ledford's retitled some of these) "So What," "Walkin'," "Blue in Green," "Summertime," "Bye Bye Blackbird," and "Freedom Jazz Dance" with hip-hop/acid jazz beats? I didn't think so.

solo outings:
Kevin Bruce Harris & Militia:
And They Walked amongst the People ♫♫♫ (Tiptoe, 1989)

Andy Milne:
Forward to Get Back ♫♫♫ (D'Note, 1997)

influences:
◀◀ Steve Coleman, Greg Osby
▶▶ Buckshot Lefonque

see also: *Steve Coleman, Graham Haynes, Greg Osby, Marvin "Smitty" Smith, Cassandra Wilson*

Steve Holtje

M'Boom

Formed in 1970, in New York, NY.

Max Roach, drums, marimba, vibraphone, multiple percussion instruments (1970–present); Joe Chambers, marimba, xylophone, bass

marimba, vibraphone (1970–present); Roy Brooks, steel drums, concert tom-toms, tympani, musical saw (1970–present); Omar Clay, xylophone, tympani, bass drum, marimba, bass marimba (1970–present), Warren Smith, tympani, marimba, vibraphone (1970–present); Freddy Waits, gongs, bass drum, concert tom-toms, assorted percussion (1970–present).

M'Boom is quite a unique ensemble in the jazz world, as its members play percussion instruments exclusively. No brass, wind, or string instruments make their way into the compositions, but with the talent involved, M'Boom demonstrates a widely varied percussive palette. Looking at the group's roster, this should come as no surprise, as all the members have made names for themselves in the fields of jazz percussion, composition, and arrangement outside of as well as with M'Boom. Founder Max Roach, in his insistence that rhythm is fundamental to music, created M'Boom as a fluid entity, where sometimes everybody—including road manager Eli Fountain—joins in, while at other times smaller units within the ensemble present their works, as well as works from outside. The name M'Boom is an onomatopoetic echo of a particular percussive sound. Active intermittently, the group has recorded only four albums.

what's available: When *Max Roach—M'Boom* ♪♪♪♪ (Columbia/ Legacy, 1980/1994, prod. Max Roach) was released, it not only found favor among jazzheads but among audiophiles, who found the sound of this release to be pleasing when emitted from high-end audio equipment. But even on a cruddy system, the mix of jazz, ethnic, street-beat, and Caribbean sounds shines. This record contains such M'Boom staples as the insistent chiming of "Onomatopoeia" and the slinky, funky slow-and-low analog proto-hip-hop-dub of "Kujichaglia." Other highlights include a telltale cover of Monk's "Epistrophy" and the never-can-get-enough musical saw work of Roy Brooks on "The Glorious Monster." *Collage* ♪♪♪♪ (Soul Note, 1984/1994) offers diverse compositions from the M'Boomers. Joe Chambers's "Circles" features his excellent vibes and marimba work. The Caribbean flavor comes to the fore towards the end with the steel drum mastery of Roy Brooks on "Jamaican Sun."

worth searching for: Now somewhat scarce but available, *Live at S.O.B.'s—New York* ♪♪♪♪ (Mesa/BlueMoon, 1992, prod. Max Roach) gives a hefty 77-minute serving of both old and new M'Boom charts that features plenty of show-stoppers. Warren Smith skillfully plays the melody to "Blue Monk" on tympani. Roy Brooks, playing musical saw, and Joe Chambers on vibraphone perform a captivating duet on "Body and Soul." Chambers's arrangement of Janet Jackson's "Come Back to Me"

comes off as less preposterous than one might expect for a nice ballad that rubs shoulders with older M'Boom material such as "Circles" and "Gazelle." As usual, this recording demonstrates M'Boom's fluid lineup, with the smaller units being especially impressive. And younger members Steve Berrios and Francisco Mora Jr. integrate both performances and compositions into the mighty M'Boom percussion mix. A 1973-recorded vinyl album and the earliest released M'Boom session, *Re: Percussion* ♪♪♪♪ (Baystate, 1977, prod. Underground, Inc.) features two side-long pieces that contain passages of frantic and intricate percussion patterns, as well as moments of placid, late-night vibes. Unfortunately, this Japan-released date is pretty tough to come by.

influences:

◀◀ Thelonious Monk, Duke Ellington, Chick Webb, Steve Reich

see also: *Max Roach, Joe Chambers, Roy Brooks*

Greg Baise

MC Solaar

Born Claude M'Birali, in France.

Within the global context of hip-hop, MC Solaar is a transcontinental legend. Solaar, along with producer/DJ Jimmy Jay, has been creating smooth, jazzy masterpieces that showcase his liquescent flow since 1990. In fact, it is his uniquely French interpretation of the New York-bred art form that has won him universal praise. The way his words and inflections fit the music provided by Jimmy Jay is uncannily infectious. His rich, mellow baritone is seductive and captivating—whether you understand French or not—and Jimmy Jay's sonic concoctions are tailored to fit Solaar's words like a skin-tight glove. Even though his 1991 French release, *Qui Seme Le Vent Recolte Le Tempo*, achieved multi-platinum status overseas, Solaar didn't actually make an impact stateside until his 1992 duet with Guru on Guru's Jazzmatazz track "Le Bien, Le Mal."

what's available: *Prose Combat* ♪♪♪♪ (Cohiba/Island, 1993, prod. Jimmy Jay) is Solaar's second full-length endeavor, his first to be released in the United States. While rapping solely in his native tongue, Solaar manages to draw on a wide range of lyrical influences (Nietzsche and John Wayne, to name a few) and tackles a variety of subjects and styles, ranging from the effect of American culture on the rest of the world ("Noveau Western") to his French twist on the standard N.Y.C.-styled battle rhyme ("A Dix De Mes Disciples").

worth searching for: MC Solaar's first album is much jazzier and more laid back than *Prose Combat*. Available as a French import, *Qui Seme Le Vent Recolte Le Tempo* ♫♫♫ (Polydor France, 1991, prod. Jimmy Jay) roughly translates to "Who Sows the Wind Receives the Tempo." The title couldn't be more poetically precise, as every track—from the rolling, hypnotic soul-jazz of the title cut to the silky seductiveness of "Victime De La Mode"—is brilliant, proving that Solaar is an MC to be reckoned with. Jimmy Jay released a compilation album, *Jimmy Jay Presente Les Cool Sessions* ♫♫♫ (Virgin France, 1993, prod. Jimmy Jay), which showcases many of France's top MCs, including La Funk Mob, Les Sages Poètes De La Rue, and Lucien, who was immortalized stateside in A Tribe Called Quest's 1990 track "Luck of Lucien."

influences:

◀◀ A Tribe Called Quest, De La Soul, Gang Starr, La Funk Mob, Massive Attack, Tricky

Spence D.

Christian McBride

Born May 21, 1972, in Philadelphia, PA.

Christian McBride quickly shot to first-call acoustic bassist status thanks to dead-on pitch, a profoundly swinging sense of rhythm, solidly supportive tone, and imaginative lines that are more than the usual bop/post-bop walking without overly drawing attention. From playing electric bass in R&B bands (he's proud to say that he owns every single James Brown album), he moved to upright. He moved to New York and studied at Juilliard, finding plenty of session work and playing with any number of jazz greats, including two-and-a-half years in the Freddie Hubbard Quintet (August 1990 through January 1993).

what to buy: *Gettin' to It* ♫♫♫ (Verve, 1995, prod. Richard Seidel, Don Sickler) is a superbly confident first album. McBride is revealed as not only a great bassist but as a pretty good writer too, with a nice amount of variety. He also plays a funky solo version of "Night Train" and performs in a trio with bass elders Milt Hinton and Ray Brown on Neal Hefti's "Splanky." On the other eight tracks he plays with his contemporaries; Cyrus Chestnut (piano) and Lewis Nash (drums) make a good trio with McBride on two tracks, and Roy Hargrove (trumpet), Joshua Redman (tenor sax), and the somewhat older Steve Turre (trombone) join them in various configurations and contribute fervent soloing.

what to buy next: *Number Two Express* ♫♫♫ (Verve, 1996, prod. Richard Seidel, Don Sickler) is nearly as good. Kenny Bar-

ron and Chick Corea (whose "Tones for Joan's Bones" is played) alternate piano duties with elan, the drummer is Jack De-Johnette, and appearances are made by alto saxmen Kenny Garrett and Gary Bartz and vibist Steve Nelson. *Fingerpainting: the music of Herbie Hancock* ♫♫♫ (Verve, 1997), with Nicholas Payton and Mark Whitfield, is more low-key than McBride's albums as sole leader, due to both the instrumentation and the material. Payton on trumpet and Whitfield on guitar work well with McBride, who gets to pay tribute to one of his major compositional influences.

worth searching for: It's a pretty insignificant part of his discography, but anyone wanting all McBride's work as a leader will have to track down the CD single *Double Decker (Deck the Halls with Boughs of Funky Bass)* ♫♫ (Verve, 1994, prod. Richard Seidel, Don Sickler), which technically is McBride's debut as a leader. On the front cover it says "Happy Holidays! a surprise from Verve's newest light," and as that suggests, this was a promo-only Christmas greeting from the label. On it, McBride actually makes something interesting of the material all by himself using just bass and hi-hat.

influences:

◀◀ Ray Brown, Paul Chambers, Wayne Shorter, Herbie Hancock, James Brown

Steve Holtje

Les McCann

Born September 23, 1935, in Lexington, KY.

Keyboardist Les McCann is a soul-jazz pianist and vocalist who won a 1956 U.S. Navy talent contest and gained wider exposure from a subsequent TV appearance on the then-popular *Ed Sullivan Show*. After his discharge from the service, McCann formed a trio in Los Angeles and signed with Pacific Jazz, gaining fans with albums made between 1960–64 such as *Les McCann Plays the Truth* and *The Shout*. His soulful funk piano style was well suited to the 1960s when such groups were at their peak, and after recording for Limelight (1965–67), he signed with Atlantic in 1968 and made (with better-known label-mate, saxophonist Eddie Harris) what is considered his most popular album, *Swiss Movement*. McCann and Harris appeared at the 1968 Montreux Festival together and recorded popular songs such as "Cold Duck Time" and "Compared to What." Two decades later, they were still performing occasional gigs together. McCann's sound is strongly (and enjoyably) gospel-based. He is also a composer of merit, and his songs have been covered by countless jazz musicians, including John Scofield and Regina Carter.

what to buy: Of his albums in print, *Les McCann Anthology: Relationships* ♫♫♫ (Atlantic, 1960/Rhino, 1993, prod. various) provides the most comprehensive overview of McCann's blues-tinged, soulful piano playing and his R&B-styled vocals. The two-CD set, containing 21 tracks, reflects his musical diversity and range from pop-jazz to jazz-funk jams. Only two songs from his work with Eddie Harris appear on this two-CD compilation and other tracks feature his collaborations with organist Richard "Groove" Holmes, the Jazz Crusaders, saxophonists Ben Webster and Stanley Turrentine, and the Gerald Wilson orchestra. The set is not all-inclusive of his Atlantic dates, as it omits McCann's vocal renditions of many tunes and his recordings after 1972. Perhaps another compilation is planned.

what to buy next: *Swiss Movement: Montreux 30th Anniversary Edition* ♫♫♫ (Atlantic, 1970/Rhino, 1996, prod. Nesuhi Ertegun, Joel Dorn) features McCann in his classic six-tune soul-jazz recording with tenor saxophonist Eddie Harris, supported by bassist Leroy Vinnegar and drummer Donald Dean. Included are the classics recorded in the late 1960s at the Montreux Festival, McCann's vocal version of the Gene Harris tune, "Compared to What"; an instrumental rendering of Eddie Harris's "Cold Duck Time"; McCann originals "Kathleen's Theme," "You Got It in Your Soulness," and "Generation Gap"; and, a CD bonus track, Leroy Vinnegar's "Kaftan."

best of the rest:
Much Les ♫♫ (Atlantic, 1969/Rhino, 1993)
On the Soul Side ♫♫♫ (MusicMaster, 1994)
Best of Les McCann Ltd ♫♫♫ (Blue Note, 1996)
Les McCann in New York ♫♫♫ (Blue Note, 1997)

worth searching for: As for his albums with other leaders, among the best picks is *Groove* ♫♫♫♫ (Pacific Jazz, 1961, prod. Richard Bock), a session that features McCann with organist Richard "Groove" Holmes, and tenor saxophonist Ben Webster. Their soulful, robust music includes appealing tunes such as "Seven Come Eleven" and "Deep Purple." Also search the second-hand market for *Les McCann Plays the Truth* ♫♫♫ (Pacific Jazz, 1960) and *The Shout* ♫♫♫ (Pacific Jazz, 1960), recordings that fit into the rock-gospel vein also being plumbed simultaneously by organists Shirley Scott, Jack McDuff, Bobby Timmons, and others. Earthy "soul" muzak with none of the testifying fury that would later come to categorize real soul music. A vinyl album inspired by the 1970s electro-jazz sound, *Layers* ♫♫♫ (Atlantic, 1973, prod. Joel Dorn) showcases the pianist as

instrumentalist and composer. Two suites are included: "Songs from Boston," which contains some fine original expressions that still hold up today (the dreamy electric piano version of his "Sometimes I Cry"), and "Songs from Childhood," which contains six tunes, some of which are built on pretty melodies that depart admirably from McCann's expected soul-jazz leanings. It's been panned by some critics but it's an intriguing listen because it's so different from his larger body of work. McCann experiments with electric piano, ARP synthesizer, clavinet, drums, and tympani. And his cohorts—percussionists Buck Clarke, Ralph MacDonald, and Donald Dean, and bassist Jimmy Rowser—enhance his explorations. It's not one of his best albums, but it displays McCann's writing skills and willingness to experiment. So consider it a find if you run across the LP in used bins.

influences:

◀◀ Bobby Timmons, Carl Perkins

▶▶ Ramsey Lewis, Herbie Hancock

Nancy Ann Lee and Joe S. Harrington

Rob McConnell

Born February 14, 1935, in London, Ontario, Canada.

Although he is an excellent valve trombonist with a gift for melodic, singing solos, Rob McConnell is best known as the band leader and arranger of the Boss Brass, a potent part-time organization featuring many of Canada's best jazz musicians. McConnell began studying music in his teens, learning valve trombone in high school. By the early '60s, inspired by Bob Brookmeyer's smooth, harmonically sophisticated style, McConnell had become one of Canada's premier valve trombonists. From 1965–69 he was featured in Phil Nimmons band, Nimmons 'n' Nine Plus Six. In 1968 McConnell founded the Boss Brass as an all-brass orchestra (and rhythm section) with a repertoire of pop tunes. The group broke up briefly in the late '80s when McConnell moved to L.A. to teach, but reassembled in 1991 and has been together ever since. Over the years the group has featured such superior players as Moe Kaufman and Rick Wilkins (reeds), Ed Bickert and Lorne Lofsky (guitar), Ian McDougall (trombone), and Terry Clarke (drums). As a vehicle for McConnell's swinging and innovative charts, the Boss Brass is about as good an ensemble as a writer could want.

what to buy: Big-band fans won't want to miss *Our 25th Year* ♫♫♫ (Concord Jazz, 1993, prod. Rob McConnell, Phil Sheridan), a driving and oft-times surprising effort by one of the foremost bebop-minded large ensembles in jazz. McConnell's charts are inventive—check out his arrangement of Lionel Hampton's "Flying Home"—and the band plays them with precision and power. And with a host of fine improvisers (trumpeter Guido Basso stands out on "Imagination," for example), this is one of the Boss Brass's more rewarding sessions. After taking a few years off while McConnell moved to L.A. to teach music, the Boss Brass roars back into action with *The Brass Is Back* ✍✍✍ (Concord Jazz, 1991, prod. Phil Sheridan), a potent hard-bop session featuring adventurous compositions and McConnell's inventive charts. Highlights include a bouncy arrangement of Horace Silver's "Strollin'" with a strong solo by guitarist Ed Bickert, Moe Kaufman's fluid alto work on "All the Things You Are," and Guido Basso's charged trumpet playing on Roger Kellaway's "Love of My Life."

what to buy next: McConnell shows off his considerable valve trombone chops with *Three for the Road* ✍✍✍ (Concord Jazz, 1997, prod. Rob McConnell), featuring master guitarist Ed Bickert and bassist Don Thompson. With sketchy arrangements, the focus here is on close listening and spontaneous interplay. Highlights include a gorgeous medley of Henry Mancini tunes, "Two for the Road," "Royal Blue," and "Dreamsville," David Rose's "Our Waltz," and Harold Arlen's "A Sleepin' Bee." One of the best vocal/big band session of the '80s, *Mel Tormé/Rob McConnell and the Boss Brass* ✍✍✍✍ (Concord Jazz, 1986, prod. Carl E. Jefferson) captures both Tormé and the Boss Brass in peak form. Tormé is clearly inspired by McConnell's thoughtful, swinging arrangements and responds with an emotionally charged performance, from the wistful versions of "September Song" and "A House Is Not a Home" to the powerhouse six-part Ellington medley that closes the album.

best of the rest:
The Rob McConnell Jive Five ✍✍✍ (Concord Jazz, 1990)
Brassy and Sassy ✍✍✍ (Concord Jazz, 1992)
Trio Sketches ✍✍✍ (Concord Jazz, 1994)
Overtime ✍✍✍ (Concord Jazz, 1994)
Don't Get around Much Anymore ✍✍✍ (Concord Jazz, 1995)
Play the Jazz Classics ✍✍✍ (Concord Jazz, 1997)

influences:
◀◀ Bob Brookmeyer, Juan Tizol

Andrew Gilbert

Susannah McCorkle

Born January 1, 1946, in Berkeley, CA.

Since the late 1970s, singer Susannah McCorkle has developed into one of the most intelligent and incisive lyric interpreters in jazz. Though she isn't really an improvisor, she is strongly influenced by Billie Holiday and her small, warm voice packs an emotional wallop. A polyglot, she has worked as a translator from Italian, Spanish, French, and German into English, and was inspired to become a jazz singer when she first heard a Billie Holiday record while studying in Paris. Rather than pursue her budding career as a fiction writer, she threw herself into jazz, singing in Rome nightclubs. McCorkle moved to England in 1971 and hooked up with cornetist Dick Sudhalter and pianist Keith Ingham, who worked as her musical director for a number of years. Performing with Bobby Hacket, Ben Webster, and Dexter Gordon helped cement her jazz credentials, and her first New York gig at the Riverboat room in 1975 spread her reputation. She has recorded a series of excellent thematic albums, first for Inner City and PA/USA and later for Concord.

what to buy: The best recording for perusing Susannah McCorkle's vast talent, *From Bessie to Brazil* ✍✍✍✍ (Concord Jazz, 1993, prod. Carl E. Jefferson) covers everything from Paul Simon and Dave Frishberg to two Johnny Mercer/Harold Arlen classics to Jobim's "The Waters of March," which she sings in both Portuguese and her own soulful English translation. Pianist Allen Farnham, her longtime musical director, provides classy, unobtrusive octet charts. Rounding up 14 pre-rock standards that deal with love isn't hard, but with *I'll Take Romance* ✍✍✍✍ (Concord Jazz, 1992, prod. Carl E. Jefferson) McCorkle delivers such a sustained, witty, and heartfelt tribute to the wayward emotion, she makes this album irresistible. McCorkle is accompanied by a swinging four-man rhythm section, led by Allen Farnham (piano) and Basie veteran Frank Wess (tenor sax and flute), who takes a number of highly effective solos. Highlights include her plaintive "My Foolish Heart" and a haunting version of "Spring Is Here." Originally recorded for the Black Lion label while McCorkle was living in England, *The Songs of Johnny Mercer* ✍✍✍✍ (Jazz Alliance, 1977/1996, prod. Chris Ellis) is one of her first albums, and her superb taste, sparkling intelligence, and direct, honest approach to her material is already evident. Accompanied by a small group led by pianist Keith Ingham, McCorkle delves deeply into the Mercer songbook, coming up with such rarely heard treasures as "My New Celebrity Is You," "Harlem Butterfly," and "How Little We Know."

what to buy next: McCorkle's debut on the label she continues to record for, *No More Blues* ✍✍✍✍ (Concord Jazz, 1989, prod. Carl E. Jefferson) is the work of a dedicated student of the American songbook. Looking far beyond the usual, standard suspects, she puts together a winning set with such under-recorded tunes as "P.S. I Love You," Gerry Mulligan's "The Ballad of Pearly Sue," the Gershwin's "Who Cares?," and Dave Frishberg's hilarious "Can't Take You Nowhere." Clarinetist/tenor saxophonist Ken Peplowski directs the top-notch quintet. McCorkle not only sings in beautifully accented Portuguese and Italian on *Sabia* ✍✍✍✍✍ (Concord Jazz, 1990, prod. Carl E. Jefferson), but she also translated most of the lyrics herself. A lovely, sensuous session featuring such appropriate players as Scott Hamilton (tenor sax), Duduka Fonseca (drums), and Cafe (percussion), the album is also the last recording by guitarist Emily Remler before her death. Pianist Lee Musiker wrote the arrangements, which strike a fine balance between Brazilian music and jazz. An album of Irving Berlin tunes, *Let's Face the Music* ✍✍✍✍✍ (Concord Jazz, 1997, prod. Nick Phillips) is a perfect mix of beloved chestnuts ("Heat Wave" "Supper Time" and "Cheek to Cheek") and lesser known tunes ("Love and the Weather," "Better Luck Next Time," and "Waiting at the End of the Road"). The arrangements range from duets, such as a thrilling guitar/vocal version of "How Deep Is the Ocean" with Al Gafa, to trio, quintet, and octet tracks, featuring such fine players as Jerry Dodgion, Greg Gisbert, Conrad Herwig, and Chris Potter. McCorkle brings her usual wit, depth, and humor to the timeless tunes.

the rest:

Over the Rainbow—The Songs of E.Y. "Yip" Harburg ✍✍✍✍ (Jazz Alliance, 1980/1996)

Thanks for the Memories—The Songs of Leo Robin ✍✍✍✍ (PA/USA, 1984)

How Do You Keep the Music Playing ✍✍✍✍ (PA/USA, 1985)

From Broadway to Bebop ✍✍✍✍ (Concord Jazz, 1994)

Easy to Love—The Songs of Cole Porter ✍✍✍✍✍ (Concord Jazz, 1996)

influences:

⏮ Billie Holiday, Peggy Lee

Andrew Gilbert

Jack McDuff

Born Eugene McDuffy, September 26, 1926, in Champaign, IL.

One of the most maligned—yet most thoroughly enjoyed—instruments in the jazz repertoire, the Hammond B-3 gives soul-jazz its soul and jazz-funk its groove. This, of course, means that purists hate it. But, like a barbecue sandwich on a Memphis summer afternoon, the Hammond just is what it is: rich, warm, and undeniably funky. And, whether or not you like the instrument, you can't deny that the undisputed prince of the

Hammond (the king, of course, being Jimmy Smith) has to be Brother Jack McDuff.

McDuff's early work as a bassist in the late '40s soon evolved into self-taught keyboard work with the likes of Willis Jackson. Amazingly, only a few years after he had taught himself the instrument, organist McDuff cut his first sides as a leader for Prestige in 1960. A short string of these dates (including a truly impressive one with Gene Ammons in 1962) soon gave way to widespread success when McDuff revamped his quartet in 1963 with tenor player Red Holloway, drummer Joe Dukes, and a then-little-known guitarist by the name of George Benson. It was this group that was the most successful, both artistically and commercially. However, it didn't last forever and by 1967, the group had splintered, leaving McDuff to settle for pickup bands throughout most of the next 30 years. Powerful though that group may have been, the star of the show was always Brother Jack's soulful way at the keys, a playing style that could effortlessly alternate between lead, harmony, and rhythm while keeping it hot and swingin'. The '70s were filled (as they were for many soul-jazz artists) with pop-fusion records that nonetheless maintained a grittier, funkier feel than their counterparts. A "re-entry" into the game in the late '80s still continues to show McDuff in fine form, though not as greasy.

what to buy: Although it's not quite the fiery soul summit one might expect (due mainly to the fact that collaborator Gene Ammons was still in the throes of addiction and about to go back to jail), *Brother Jack Meets the Boss* ✍✍✍✍ (Prestige/OJC, 1962, prod. Esmond Edwards) is still a cooker. Rooted in bop forms, Ammons and McDuff nonetheless beef it up, turning the session into a bluesy swingfest. *Hot Barbeque/Live!* ✍✍✍✍✍ (Prestige, 1966/Beat Goes Public, 1993, prod. Peter Paul, Lew Futterman) are the perfect two albums to have on one disc. *Hot Barbeque* is, well, hot barbeque, with chomping down on five smokin' originals and even a romp through "Cry Me a River" that's more sexy than sad. *Live!* shows the group in its most comfortable environment as it unremorsefully puts four on the floor and gets down to business. *Down Home Style* ✍✍✍✍ (Blue Note, 1969, prod. Lew Futterman, Larry Rogers), with cover art that will raise your cholesterol just by looking at it, lurches off with McDuff's naughty "The Vibrator" and even takes on a version of the Rascals' "Groovin'." Bluesy, soulful, and unabashedly funky.

what to buy next: For *Honeydripper* ✍✍✍✍ (Prestige/OJC, 1961, prod. Esmond Edwards), McDuff's third session for Prestige as a leader, he found himself in the sterling company of young guitarist Grant Green, as well as drummer Ben Dixon and little-known tenor player Jimmy Forrest (who, for some reason, is given second billing here). Although Brother Jack sticks to the blues (the opening track is appropriately titled "Whap!"), the pressure-cooker this quartet musters up is a joy to behold. *The Heatin' System* 🎵🎵🎵 (Concord, 1995, prod. Allen Farnham), a reasonably successful jaunt for a nearly 70-year-old McDuff, shows he may not be at the height of his powers, but he still has a few bluesy tricks up his sleeves.

the rest:

Tough 'Duff 🎵🎵🎵 (Prestige/OJC, 1960)
Live! 🎵🎵🎵 (Prestige/OJC, 1965)
Color Me Blue 🎵🎵🎵 (Concord, 1992)
Write on, Capt'n 🎵🎵🎵 (Concord, 1993)
(With Joey DeFrancesco) *It's about Time* 🎵🎵🎵 (Concord, 1996)

worth searching for: *Sophisticated Funk* 🎵🎵 (Chess, 1976, prod. Billy Jones) is not a great record—pretty standard, fusion-esque funk fare—but it's worth it for the cover art alone, which depicts a sort of computer-age chastity belt on one of the most naked midsections you'll ever see on an album cover.

influences:

◀◀ Jimmy Smith

▶▶ Lonnie Smith, Joey DeFrancesco

Jason Ferguson

Bobby McFerrin

Born March 11, 1950, in New York, NY.

With its perky jazz-tinged interpretations of Van Morrison's "Moondance," Smokey Robinson's "You Really Got a Hold on Me," and Orleans' "Dance with Me," Bobby McFerrin's self-titled 1982 debut album introduced a talented singer who aspired to be little more than a hipper, happier Al Jarreau. But buried amid the band-accompanied crossover fodder was a two-minute a cappella sprint through Bud Powell's "Hallucinations" that hinted at the vocal gymnastics and improvisatory prowess to come. Once he literally found his voice, McFerrin started performing solo and dazzled crowds with the force and finesse of his singing: Crooning and crowing, scatting and squealing, he hurdled octaves and mimicked everything from muted trumpets to thumping basses with precision and wit. By 1985's *Spontaneous Inventions*, he was dueting with legends like Herbie Hancock and Wayne Shorter and readying himself to redefine vocalese. But he took a pop detour with 1988's irritatingly sunny "Don't Worry Be Happy" and never really found

his way back. McFerrin has spent the past nine years leapfrogging from classical to jazz to world music. His classical collaborations with Yo Yo Ma and the St. Paul Chamber Orchestra and frequent guest conductor appearances—marked by dreadlocks, bare feet, and tuxedo—with symphonies around the country have brought a refreshing respite to the air of pretension that often prevents classical music from reaching young audiences. But McFerrin's unfocused vision makes him more of a happy wanderer than a bold explorer.

what to buy: Recorded live in Germany, *The Voice* 🎵🎵🎵🎵🎵 (Elektra, 1984, prod. Linda Goldstein) presents McFerrin au natural, his voice bobbing and darting like Muhammad Ali in his rope-a-dope prime. The only thing more stunning than the range of material—which includes "Take the 'A' Train," James Brown's "I Feel Good," and Charlie Parker's "Donna Lee"—is the range of his vocalizing, which reaches its jaw-dropping zenith on "T.J.," in which he sounds like he's singing backwards. *Spontaneous Inventions* 🎵🎵🎵🎵 (Blue Note, 1985, prod. Linda Goldstein, Bobby McFerrin) is another live tour de force, mostly solo performances mixed with collaborations with Hancock ("Turtle Shoes"), Shorter ("Walkin'"), Jon Hendricks and the Manhattan Transfer ("Another Night in Tunisia"), and, believe it or not, Robin Williams ("Beverly Hills Blues").

what to buy next: *Bang! Zoom* 🎵🎵🎵 (Blue Note, 1996, prod. Bobby McFerrin, Russell Ferrante), a slick but engaging collaboration with the Yellowjackets, incorporates smooth grooves, African rhythms, and an eerie vocal recreation of Miles Davis's muted trumpet on "Selim."

what to avoid: The dazzling wonder of multitracked vocals drives *Simple Pleasures* 🎵🎵🎵 (EMI, 1988, prod. Linda Goldstein), as McFerrin zeroes in on classics by the Beatles, Cream, the Rascals, and Creedence Clearwater Revival. It's unnecessary not because it's unimpressive, but because it's not jazz.

the rest:

Bobby McFerrin 🎵🎵🎵 (Elektra, 1982)
Medicine Music 🎵🎵🎵 (EMI, 1990)
(With Chick Corea) *Play* 🎵🎵🎵 (Blue Note, 1992)
(With Yo Yo Ma) *Hush* 🎵🎵🎵 (Sony, 1992)
Paper Music 🎵🎵🎵 (Sony, 1995)
The Mozart Sessions 🎵🎵🎵 (Sony, 1996)
Circlesongs 🎵🎵🎵 (Sony, 1997)

worth searching for: OK, this isn't jazz either, but his hilarious, seven-minute condensation of *The Wizard of Oz* on *For Our Children: The Concert* 🎵🎵🎵 (Disney, 1992, prod. George Duke) showcases the breadth of his vocalizing.

influences:

◀◀ Lambert, Hendricks & Ross, Ella Fitzgerald, Al Jarreau

▶▶ Take 6

David Okamoto

Howard McGhee

Born March 6, 1918, in Tulsa, OK. Died July 17, 1987, in New York, NY.

Howard McGhee, or "Maggie" as he was known, was one of the more important bop trumpeters of the 1940s and was instrumental in the formation of the hard-bop trumpet style that would be further developed by Fats Navarro and Clifford Brown. McGhee's career started at the height of the swing era, as he got jobs with Lionel Hampton and Andy Kirk in the early '40s. Also during that time, like so many others, Maggie went through Minton's Playhouse, where he started experimenting with bebop. In 1945 he went with tenor saxophonist Coleman Hawkins to Los Angeles, where the two recorded some important swing-to-bop transitional music under Hawkins's name. While still in California, McGhee recorded with Charlie Parker as part of the Jazz at the Philharmonic tour, and recorded some sides for Dial that were among his most important. After returning to New York, he made some classic recordings with Milt Jackson on Savoy and with Navarro on Blue Note that helped him become one of the most acclaimed trumpeters in jazz by the end of the decade. McGhee would spend most of the '50s veiled in relative obscurity, due in large part to a worsening drug habit. He returned in the early '60s to make some excellent records for Contemporary and Black Lion before falling back into recording inactivity until 1975. From that period on, McGhee made a few nice records on Storyville, although his place in jazz history had been largely forgotten due to his long idle spells.

what to buy: *Howard McGhee & Milt Jackson* ✓✓✓✓✓ (Savoy, 1948/1994, prod. Teddy Reig) is filled with records made at the height of McGhee's period of influence, and they reflect a surprising degree of calm and poise for someone who had so many personal problems at the time. *Maggie's Back in Town* ✓✓✓✓✓ (Contemporary 1961/OJC, 1991, prod. Lester Koenig) was McGhee's first major recording after a long absence, and it is one of his best. Particularly compelling are "Demon Chase" and "Brownie Speaks."

what to buy next: *Sharp Edge* ✓✓✓✓ (Black Lion, 1961/1988, prod. Chris Albertson) is another album made shortly after McGhee's comeback in 1961—and it's another good one. Tenor George Coleman provides a good foil for McGhee, and drummer Jimmy Cobb pushes the two relentlessly.

what to avoid: *The Return of Howard McGhee* ✓✓ (Bethlehem, 1956), McGhee's first comeback, wasn't as successful or as long-lived as the one he would undertake in the early '60s. He sounds unsure and a bit tired.

the rest:
Trumpet at Tempo ✓✓✓✓ (Spotlite, 1946–47/OJC, 1996)
Maggie: The Savoy Sessions ✓✓✓ (Savoy, 1948–52/Denon 1995)
South Pacific Jazz ✓✓✓ (Savoy, 1952)
Cookin' Time ✓✓✓ (Hep, 1967)
Just Be There ✓✓✓ (SteepleChase, 1976)
Jazz Brothers ✓✓✓ (Storyville, 1978)
Live at Emerson's ✓✓✓ (Zim, 1978)
Home Run ✓✓ (Jazzcraft, 1979)
Wise in Time ✓✓✓ (Storyville, 1980)
Young at Heart ✓✓✓ (Storyville, 1980)

worth searching for: The LP *Howard McGhee's All Stars* ✓✓✓✓ (Blue Note, 1950, prod. Alfred Lion) really does feature various line-ups of all stars, including Max Roach and Charlie Parker. But perhaps the most stimulating cuts come from a sextet featuring McGhee with his dazzling protege, Fats Navarro. At times it is difficult to tell the two masters apart, except that McGhee has a thinner tone.

influences:

◀◀ Roy Eldridge, Dizzy Gillespie

▶▶ Fats Navarro, Clifford Brown

Dan Keener

Jimmy McGriff

Born James Harrell McGriff, April 3, 1936, in Philadelphia, PA.

Although Jimmy McGriff grew up in a musical family, with father and mother both pianists and a brother who played drums, music was not his first career. While dabbling with bass, saxophone, drums, vibes, and piano, McGriff served as an MP during the Korean War, and later enrolled at the Pennsylvania Institute of Criminology. While a member of the Philadelphia police force for more than two years, he began moonlighting as a bassist at Pep's Showboat, playing behind blues singers such as Big Maybelle and other 1960s stars. At that point, he decided to concentrate on the organ, which he had first heard in

Bobby McFerrin (© Jack Vartoogian)

church. He studied at Combe College of Music in Philadelphia and at Juilliard in New York. He also took private lessons from jazz-blues masters Jimmy Smith, Richard "Groove" Holmes, Milt Buckner, and classical organist Sonny Gatewood.

McGriff was leading his own blues-based trio in Trenton, New Jersey when a scout for a small record label, Jell, heard the organist's instrumental arrangement of Ray Charles's "I've Got a Woman" and offered him a contract. The single took off, the master was purchased by the Sue label, and in 1962 went to Number Five on *Billboard*'s R&B chart and to Number 20 on the pop chart. More Sue singles followed, including "Bump de Bump" and "All about My Girl," which McGriff reprised on later albums. Throughout his career, he has recorded for many labels, including Solid State, Blue Note, Capitol, United Artists, Groove Merchant, LRC (Lester Recording Catalog), JAM, and, more recently, Telarc and Milestone. McGriff's funky blues sound was successful in the 1960s. He continued to lead small soul-jazz and blues combos in the 1970s, 1980s, and 1990s, including many club dates, concerts, and albums with alto saxophonist Hank Crawford. For most of his career, McGriff played a Hammond B-3, but switched in the 1990s to a modified model known as the Hammond XB-3. He occasionally embarked into electronic fusion, but his synthesizer albums were never as popular as his Hammond work. He has performed throughout the United States and around the world in clubs, concerts, and festivals.

what to buy: *Road Tested* ♫♫♫♫ (Milestone, 1997, prod. Bob Porter) teams McGriff with alto saxophonist Crawford and long-time colleagues guitarist Wayne Boyd and drummer Bernard Purdie. All 10 tracks have a loose, relaxed feel, with McGriff handling the gentle heat of "Summertime." The quartet sears through "Caravan," simmers on "Summertime," and swings on evergreens such as "I Only Have Eyes for You" and "For Sentimental Reasons." *Starting Five* ♫♫♫♫ (Milestone, 1987, prod. Bob Porter) was McGriff's first release for Milestone. He's teamed with two socko saxmen, Rusty Bryant and David "Fathead" Newman, plus guitarists Wayne Boyd and Mel Brown and drummer Bernard Purdie. There may not be a better recorded Hammond version of "Georgia on My Mind" than this one. Then there's the band's funky versions of "Movin' On" and "I'm Getting Sentimental over You." *Greatest Hits* ♫♫♫♫ (Blue Note, 1997, prod. Dean Rudland) is an excellent overview of McGriff's early issues between 1963–70 on various labels, not just Blue Note, but including Sue, Solid State, and Capitol. The organist's most popular B3-burners are here, including "All about My Girl," "The Worm," "Gospel Time," "Kiko," "See See

Rider" and "Fat Cakes." This album is a great retrospective of McGriff's soul-jazz-blues style and his command of the Hammond B-3. Unfortunately, no sidemen are listed for any of the tracks. *The Dream Team* ♫♫♫♫ (Milestone, 1997, prod. Bob Porter) supplies seven exuberant tracks played by favorite McGriff colleagues, including tenor saxophonist Newman, guitarist Brown, and drummer Purdie, with veteran Red Holloway adding his tenor and alto sax sound to the mix. McGriff plays the pine-sap out of his Hammond XB-3, whether stretching out on a countrified ballad like "Ain't It Funny How Time Slips Away," a slow-burning, churchified rendition of "T'Ain't Nobody's Bizness If I Do," or the hard-driving delivery of "Things Ain't What They Used to Be."

what to buy next: *Countdown* ♫♫♫ (Milestone, 1983/1991, prod. Bob Porter) is one of McGriff's forays into a big-band sound, using two saxes and a trombone to supplement his trio. The six pieces effectively deliver the dynamics required for charts such as "Since I Fell for You" and "Shiny Stockings," although true-blue Hammond fans may find the horns somewhat distracting. *Blue to the Bone* ♫♫♫♫ (Milestone, 1988, prod. Bob Porter) features Al Grey's trombone, a rare instrument for the small-organ format, but it works quite well, especially on the two jazz standards, "Don't Get around Much Anymore" and "Secret Love." Saxophonist Bill Easley and guitarist Melvin Sparks supplement McGriff's funky licks, with Bernard Purdie again on drums.

what to avoid: *In a Blue Mood* **woof!** (Headfirst, 1991, prod. Owen R. Husney, Dr. Fink) finds McGriff playing organ and a Kurzweil electric, supplemented by the synthesizer work of Dr. Fink. The electronics dilute the purity of the Hammond on this album and several other issues that resulted in a sound unlike the legendary McGriff. Die-hard fans prefer the 1980s style that he later resumed.

best of the rest:

I've Got a Woman ♫♫♫♫ (Collectables, 1963/1996)
Blues for Mr. Jimmy ♫♫♫♪ (Collectables, 1965/1991)
Right Turn on Blues ♫♫♫♫ (Telarc, 1994)
Blues Groove ♫♫♫♪ (Telarc, 1996)
Tribute to Count Basie ♫♫♫♫ (Lester Recording Catalog/LaserLight, 1996)
Funkiest Little Band in the Land ♫♫♫♪ (LaserLight, 1996)

worth searching for: *The Groover* ♫♫♫♫♫ (JAM, 1982, prod. Esmond Edwards) was this writer's first McGriff LP, and remains a favorite. The six tracks start with Jimmy Forrest's "Night Train," stoked by alto saxophonist Arnold Sterling. A stirring version of Horace Silver's "Song for My Father" features guitarist Billy

Butler, who also enhances the gospel feel of Josef Zawinul's "Mercy, Mercy, Mercy." The final track, "This One's for Ray," is a McGriff tribute to Ray Charles, and features the rare sound of the organist grooving on acoustic piano. If you know someone who has a working LP turntable, dig for this one in the resale-store bins; it'll be well worth the search.

influences:

◀◀ Jimmy Smith, Richard "Groove" Holmes, Milt Buckner, Sonny Gatewood

Patricia Myers

Kalaparusha Maurice McIntyre

Born March 24, 1936, in Clarksville, AR.

As an unsung hero of Chicago's Association for the Advancement of Creative Musicians (AACM), Kalaparusha McIntyre's highly emotive tenor playing—which can switch from outside to inside at the drop of a hat—is often overshadowed by the similarly freewheeling reedwork of compatriot Roscoe Mitchell, on whose *Sound* LP McIntyre made his recorded debut. However, though he has been sorely under-represented on recordings since his 1969 bow, McIntyre's voice is nonetheless a formidable one, and his work with fellow Chicagoans like Muhal Richard Abrams and Kahil El'Zabar is consistently outstanding.

what's available: If there can only be one McIntyre record in print, it might as well be *Forces and Feelings* ♫♫♫♪ (Delmark, 1970, prod. Robert Koester), which is at least as good as his highly acclaimed debut. With the leader issuing forth his trademark flourishes as often as he is relaxing, the seven pieces on the disc (two of which were not on the original release) are much more of an ensemble piece than one would expect, with equal time given to the June Tyson-esque vocalese of Rita Omolokun, the furiously stamping guitar work of Sarnie Garrett, and the frenetic rhythm section of drummer Wesley Tyus and bassist Fred Hopkins. However, the star is still McIntyre, whose playing moves from beautiful melodic accents ("Ananda") to unremorsefully outside screaming ("Fifteen or Sixteen"), with stops at all points in between.

worth searching for: Much in the same vein as *Forces*, *Humility in the Light of the Creator* ♫♫♫♫ (Delmark, 1969), is a more immediately forceful recording without quite as many shades and colors as its follow-up. Still, it's absolutely necessary. *Ram's Run* ♫♫♫♫ (Cadence, 1981), a surprisingly elaborate session (featuring Julius Hemphill, Malachi Thompson, J.R. Mitchell, and no bass player), is a difficult ride with the four AACM stal-

warts pulling out all the theoretical stops. However, nobody ever mistook free jazz for easy listening and *Ram's Run*—especially in comparison to the relatively mediocre work that many of Chicago's best were dishing up at the time—is a little-known gem by a little-known giant.

influences:

◀◀ John Gilmore, Roscoe Mitchell

▶▶ Charles Gayle

Jason Ferguson

Ken McIntyre

Born September 7, 1931, in Boston, MA.

A multi-instrumentalist, as proficient on tenor sax, flute, and bass clarinet as he is on such less-likely instruments as bassoon and oboe, Ken McIntyre has often been overshadowed by the accomplishments of his friend and one-time collaborator Eric Dolphy. However, though he is often regarded as a second-string free player, McIntyre's music—if not his influence—is certainly equal to that of Dolphy. With the exception of a brief stint in the service, he spent his first 28 years in his hometown of Boston, moving to New York only after finishing studies at the Boston Conservatory. Once in the Big Apple, McIntyre got to work making a name for himself and, rather than play numerous sideman gigs, he began making his own records. His two Prestige dates—recorded within a month of one another—showcase a strongly individual reedsman with an acute flair for harmonies and melodic improvisation. Later recordings, most notably his United Artists releases in 1962 and 1963 and his mid- to late '70s work on SteepleChase, were made while McIntyre was splitting his time between teaching and playing. Yet the music suffers none from it, sealing his reputation as a superb, if underappreciated, musician.

what to buy: On the Dolphy collaboration *Looking Ahead* ♫♫♫♫ (Prestige, 1960/OJC, 1994, prod. Esmond Edwards), with an incredibly strong band—Art Taylor (drums), Sam Jones (bass), and Walter Bishop (piano)—to support them, McIntyre and Dolphy go on a Konitz/Marsh-style harmony-fest. Only with these two, the harmonies are more challenging and considerably more improvisatory. Although never too far out (this *was* 1960), the duo's adventurous interplay nonetheless elevates these six tunes (five McIntyre originals and, er, "They All Laughed") far beyond average bebop and the result is an exciting and rewarding record. The highly diverse sessions of *The Complete United Artists Sessions* ♫♫♫♫ (United Artists/Blue

Note, 1962–63/1997, prod. George Wein, Alan Douglas) are taken from two extraordinarily hard-to-find LPs, 1962's *Year of the Iron Sheep* and 1963's *Way Way Out*. In a drastic move away from the blowing sessions of his first three records, McIntyre utilizes not only diverse instrumentations, but also a rather enigmatic compositional style. Not that these records are, as the latter title would imply, "way way out," it's just that with the inclusion of players as diverse as Ahmed Abdul-Malik, Jaki Byard, John Mancebo Lewis, and a 13-piece string section, the pieces here benefit both from McIntyre's formalized music training (he was teaching music in Manhattan public schools) and his wide range of playing capabilities. Although some of *Way Way Out* lapses into monochrome (you can only take so much Schuller-isms before it starts to get dull), it's nonetheless exciting, and, as if to make up for it, the fiery playing on *Year of the Iron Sheep* is spectacular. This double-disc set also tacks on seven unreleased tracks. Essential.

what to buy next: McIntyre's first date as a leader, *Stone Blues* 𝄞𝄞𝄞 (Prestige, 1960/OJC, prod. Esmond Edwards), finds him in not the most illustrious company. The other musicians here—with the exception of Boston drummer Bobby Ward—seemed to have vanished into anonymity after they left the studio, however the mere inclusion of a trombone (played by John Mancebo Lewis) as McIntyre's harmonic foil should clue you in that this isn't your average session. Six McIntyre originals and a soulful version of "I'll Close My Eyes" make up this strong set, which, though certainly not a masterpiece, is a fine showcase for a great player. The excellent set *Hindsight* 𝄞𝄞𝄞𝄞 (SteepleChase, 1974) finds McIntyre the schoolteacher getting down to the real business of playing music after being relatively quiet for a few years. Switching instruments as often as he switches keys, he pulls out all the stops here, bouncing melodic passages off pianist Kenny Drew, who, amazingly enough, seems unfazed by the prospect of accompanying a bassoon. A strong, post-bop set marked by above-average playing by all involved.

the rest:
Open Horizon 𝄞𝄞𝄞 (SteepleChase, 1975)
Chasing the Sun 𝄞𝄞𝄞 (SteepleChase, 1978)

influences:
◀◀ Eric Dolphy, Andrew McGhee, Gigi Gryce
▶▶ Wynton Marsalis, Joshua Redman

Jason Ferguson

Andy McKee

See: Mingus Big Band

Dave McKenna

Born May 30, 1930, in Woonsocket, RI.

Dave McKenna is one of the best swing-oriented pianists to emerge in the 1950s, a hard-driving player who is a master of the solo recital. With his vast knowledge of the Great American Songbook and unflagging rhythmic attack, McKenna is a remarkably consistent recording artist and performer who rarely disappoints. He began playing piano at age seven and taught himself to play jazz by listening to the radio. At 15 had joined the Musicians' Union and some of his first important jobs were with Boots Mussulli (1947), Charlie Ventura (1949), and Woody Herman (1950–51). Drafted in 1951, McKenna served in Korea and rejoined Ventura when he was discharged in 1953. McKenna stayed busy through the 1950s, performing with Buddy Rich and Gene Krupa on a 1956 Jazz at the Philharmonic tour, and playing with Zoot Sims and Al Cohn, Stan Getz, Phil Woods, Ruby Braff, and Bobby Hackett, with whom he worked extensively over the next two decades. He joined the house band at Eddie Condon's in the mid-1960s, performing with Condon, Yank Lawson, Cliff Leeman, and Peanuts Hucko (who opened a club in Denver where McKenna worked frequently in the late 1960s). In 1967, McKenna moved to Cape Cod, where he held down a long-running gig at the Columns Supper Club, where he performed with guest artists such as Joe Venuti, Red Norvo, and Flip Phillips. McKenna made a number of albums through the 1950s and 1960s (for ABC/Paramount, Epic, Bethlehem, and Realm), but starting in the 1970s he became a prolific recording artist, producing a number of fine sessions for small labels such as Halcyon, Shiah, Inner City, Honnydew, and Chiaroscuro. It was through his series of excellent sessions for Concord, starting in 1979, that McKenna began reaching a wider audience. He has recorded in a wide variety of contexts for Concord, both as a leader and a sideman, though his most memorable sessions have been his solo and duo outings.

what to buy: Pianist Dave McKenna is often at his best playing solo and on *A Celebration of Hoagy Carmichael* 𝄞𝄞𝄞𝄞 (Concord Jazz, 1983/1994, prod. Carl E. Jefferson), he pays loving tribute to a great songwriter who produced many fine tunes besides "Stardust," "Lazy River," "The Nearness of You," and of course "Skylark," which are all featured here. McKenna unearths some rarely heard treasures, such as "Moon Country" (which boasts a lyric by Johnny Mercer), "Riverboat Shuffle," and "Lazy Bones." This is mainstream, swing-oriented piano at its best. *You Must Believe in Swing* 𝄞𝄞𝄞𝄞 (Concord Jazz, 1997, prod. Allen Farnham) pairs McKenna with the master bop clarinetist Buddy DeFranco, a stroke of genius on the part of Concord. Not only do these two prodigiously gifted musicians have a ball goading and challenging each other, the duo context leads to unfettered communication in their hard-driving romps where you can really hear every note. The session features DeFranco's bluesy title track and nine standards. Highlights include sweat-inducing romps through "Anthropology" and "The Song Is You," a haunting version of Bronislaw Caper's "Invitation," and a gorgeous reading of "Darn That Dream." McKenna closes the album with a solo version of "Detour Ahead." McKenna's first album for Concord, *No Bass Hit* 🎵🎵🎵🎵 (Concord Jazz, 1979, prod. Carl E. Jefferson) is a trio session with tenor saxophonist Scott Hamilton and drummer Jake Hanna. The material is mostly from the 1930s and 1940s, and the three musicians play with easygoing authority. The music is mostly hard-driving, such as their torrid version of "Drum Boogie" and their revival meeting run through "Get Happy," though the ballad "Long Ago and Far Away" is one of the album's best tracks.

what to buy next: For many of the pianists featured in Concord's Maybeck series, playing a solo recital is a change of pace. For McKenna, the format is second nature, though there's nothing ordinary about the set he turned in on *Live at Maybeck Recital Hall, Vol. 2* 🎵🎵🎵🎵 (Concord Jazz, 1990, prod. Carl E. Jefferson), a particularly memorable session featuring an extended medley of tunes linked by the theme of knowledge (or lack of it). With his beautiful touch, commanding sense of swing, and vast store of tunes, McKenna flows seamlessly from "Teach Me Tonight" with its brief interlude of "School Days," to "An Apple for the Teacher," and transitions into what could be called his "ignorance" medley, with "I Didn't Know About You" flowing into "I Didn't Know What Time It Was" and "I Wish I Knew," etc. His powerful left hand makes a rhythm section superfluous. A rare quartet session for McKenna, *No More Ouzo for Puzo* 🎵🎵🎵🎵 (Concord Jazz, 1989, prod. Carl E. Jefferson) features the excellent young guitarist Gray Sargent and veterans Monty Budwig (bass) and Jimmie Smith (drums). This is a highly rewarding session both for the rich and varied guitar/piano interaction and McKenna's choice of material. Opening with an unusually fast version of "Look for the Silver Lining," a tune that's mostly done as a ballad, the quartet covers such rarely played gems as Jimmy Van Heusen's "Shake Down the Stars," Fats Waller's "Lonesome Me," the Gershwin's "For You, For Me, Forever More" and concludes with a chatty medley of "Talk to Me," "The Talk of the Town," and "Please Don't Talk About Me When I'm Gone." McKenna wrote the funky title track. One of McKenna's best and most imaginative thematic albums, *A Handful of Stars* 🎵🎵🎵🎵 (Concord Jazz, 1993, prod. Carl E. Jefferson) is a solo ses-

sion featuring 15 tunes with the word "star" in the title. The album opens and closes with a fragment of "Estrela, Estrela" giving the album a unified feel. The material ranges from the (overly?) familiar "Stardust" and "Stella by Starlight," which are both given fresh readings, to lesser-known pieces such as "Stardreams" and Carroll Coates's "A Song from the Star," which McKenna introduced on this session. Highlights include "Lost in the Stars" and McKenna's original "Star Kissed."

best of the rest:

Solo Piano 🎵🎵🎵🎵 (Chiaroscuro, 1973/1994)
Dave McKenna Quartet featuring Zoot Sims 🎵🎵🎵🎵 (Chiaroscuro, 1974)
Giant Strides 🎵🎵🎵🎵 (Concord Jazz, 1979/1994)
Left Handed Compliment 🎵🎵🎵🎵 (Concord Jazz, 1980)
Dancing in the Dark 🎵🎵🎵🎵 (Concord Jazz, 1985/1990)
My Friend the Piano 🎵🎵🎵🎵 (Concord Jazz, 1987)
Shadows 'N' Dreams 🎵🎵🎵🎵 (Concord Jazz, 1991)
Concord All-Stars on Cape Cod 🎵🎵🎵🎵 (Concord Jazz, 1992)
Dave McKenna/Gray Sargent: Concord Duo Series, Vol. Two 🎵🎵🎵🎵 (Concord Jazz, 1993)
Dave McKenna/Joe Temperley: Sunbeam and Thundercloud 🎵🎵🎵🎵 (Concord Jazz, 1996)
Easy Street 🎵🎵🎵🎵 (Concord Jazz, 1997)

worth searching for: Though the back of the CD says this music was recorded in 1995, *The Piano Scene of Dave McKenna* 🎵🎵🎵🎵 (Koch Jazz, 1958, prod. Jim Fogelsong) was actually (as the liner notes state) a trio session for Epic from 1958 featuring bassist John Drew and drummer Osie Johnson. McKenna's first trio session shows he had already developed the hard-driving rhythmic authority we've come to expect from him, as well as his sly sense of humor. The CD includes eight unissued alternate takes.

influences:

◀◀ Teddy Wilson, Joe Sullivan, Nat "King" Cole

Andrew Gilbert

McKinney's Cotton Pickers

Formed c. 1926. Disbanded c. 1934.

William McKinney, bandleader and drummer; John Nesbitt, trumpet; Don Redmond, arranger/alto saxophonist/vocalist; Prince Robinson, clarinet; Claude Jones, trombone; Fathead (George) Thomas, vocalist; Dave Wilborn, vocalist.

Originally a quartet out of Paducah, Kentucky, McKinney's Cotton Pickers was one of the great swinging bands of the late 1920s and early 1930s. Formed by former big-band drummer William McKinney around 1923, it originated as the Sinco Septet, then around 1926 evolved into the 10-piece Cotton

Pickers, a show band that performed the funny-hat routines and regularly played the Arcadia Ballroom in Detroit. Nearby at the Greystone Ballroom, the Fletcher Henderson band was performing. McKinney wooed away Henderson's arranger Don Redman and made him musical director. Redman drilled his crew regularly until they mastered his intricate, swinging charts and put together a competitive band of black musicians that matched Henderson's band and the up-and-coming Duke Ellington orchestra. Featuring fine soloists such as trumpeters Sidney DeParis and Joe Smith, and saxophonists Prince Robinson, George Thomas, and Redman, the group quickly earned a reputation on both the jazz and vaudeville circuits before they took up residence at Detroit's Graystone Ballroom. In 1928 they began a series of single recordings, including the RCA Victor hits, "If I Could Be with You One Hour Tonight" and "Baby, Won't You Please Come Home," featuring fine instrumental solos and excellent Redman arrangements. Some all-star sessions included appearances by soloists Coleman Hawkins, Fats Waller, Lonnie Johnson, and others. When Redman departed from the band in 1931 to form his own unit, saxophonist Benny Carter took over as musical director and hired fine players such as Doc Cheatham and Hilton Jefferson to bolster the holdover players. But the band never achieved their former musical heights and made only one more recording before the Depression intervened and the band folded in 1934.

what to buy: The only domestic album available by McKinney's Cotton Pickers, *The Band Don Redmond Built (1928–1930)* (Bluebird, 1990) contains 22 of their best classic Dixieland to swing style recordings after Redmond became the unofficial leader. Includes popular favorites aimed more at a general audience than the fervid collector: "I've Found a New Baby," "Gee Baby, Ain't I Good to You," "I Want a Little Girl," and others, featuring performances from band members such as Benny Carter, Coleman Hawkins, Fats Waller, and others.

the rest:

McKinney's Cotton Pickers—1928–1929 🎵🎵🎵 (Jazz Chronological Classics, 1994)

McKinney's Cotton Pickers—1929–1930 🎵🎵🎵 (Jazz Chronological Classics, 1994)

Nancy Ann Lee

John McLaughlin

Born January 4, 1942 in Yorkshire, England.

After beginning his musical life playing piano and violin, John McLaughlin switched over to the guitar well before entering his

teens. His biggest influences were blues and swing, which eventually led him to gigs playing with such notables as Alexis Korner, Graham Bond, Georgie Fame, and Ginger Baker. After releasing his first solo recording, McLaughlin moved to the United States and soon became a member of Miles Davis's group. He can be heard on Davis's *In a Silent Way*, *Bitches Brew*, *A Tribute to Jack Johnson*, *Live-Evil*, and *Big Fun*.

In 1971 McLaughlin formed the group Mahavishnu Orchestra. Along with Billy Cobham, Jan Hammer, Jerry Goodman, and Rick Laird, McLaughlin managed to shake things up with a brand of jazz-rock fusion unequalled at the time. In fact, their music ranks among the very small number of fusion recordings that still pass the test of time today. Since the disbanding of the Mahavishnu Orchestra, the guitarist has embarked on several musical ventures, such as his recordings with the group Shakti as well as acoustic trio recordings with Al Di Meola and Paco de Lucia.

what to buy: *Extrapolation* 🎵🎵🎵🎵 (Marmalade, 1969/Poly-Gram, 1991, prod. Giorgio Gomelsky) was McLaughlin's first release as a band leader. The quartet with John Surman (sax), Brian Odges (bass), and Tony Oxley (drums) combines the tightness of a rock-centered beat with the more free-form aspects of improvised jazz. A concept that could have easily have fallen apart at the seams works amazingly well for the trio. *My Goals Beyond* 🎵🎵🎵 (Douglas, 1971, prod. John McLaughlin) is an acoustic album featuring musicians Billy Cobham and Jerry Goodman, who would later become a part of the original Mahavishnu Orchestra. The album also includes Dave Liebman and Badal Roy. Serene, animated, and everything in between.

what to buy next: McLaughlin's co-billed collaboration with Carlos Santana, *Love Devotion Surrender* 🎵🎵🎵 (Columbia, 1973, prod. Carlos Santana, John McLaughlin), is full of fiery interplay between two guitarists (shown with their guru, Sri Chinmoy) who make a fine complement to each other, joined by organist Larry Young, plus Cobham, Hammer, and others. The rendition of John Coltrane's "A Love Supreme" is worth the price of admission by itself. *Johnny McLaughlin—Electric Guitarist* 🎵🎵🎵 (Columbia, 1978, prod. John McLaughlin) has a star-studded cast that includes Carlos Santana, Stanley Clarke, Jack Bruce, David Sanborn, Chick Corea, Patrice Rushen, Jack DeJohnette, and ex-Mahavishnus Cobham and Goodman. The result is a mixed bag with more positive than negative elements.

what to avoid: *Adventures in Radioland* 🎵🎵 (Verve, 1986, prod. John McLaughlin) consists of a group of rather lackluster compositions fleshed out with the use of the Synclavier digital synth/sampler. Although the album was issued under the banner of "Mahavishnu," none of the musicians other than McLaughlin ever had anything to do with the original (or subsequent) incarnations of the group. The Bill Evans tribute *Time Remembered* 🎵🎵 (Verve, 1993, prod. John McLaughlin) really doesn't gel in the guitar context.

best of the rest:
Devotion 🎵🎵🎵 (Douglas, 1971)
Where Fortune Smiles 🎵🎵🎵 (Dawn, 1972)
Live at Royal Festival Hall 🎵🎵🎵 (JMT, 1990)
Que Alegria 🎵🎵🎵🎵 (Verve, 1992)
Tokyo Live 🎵🎵🎵 (Verve, 1994)
The Promise 🎵🎵🎵 (Verve, 1996)
The Heart of Things 🎵🎵🎵 (Verve, 1997)

worth searching for: *In a Silent Way* 🎵🎵🎵🎵 (Columbia, 1969, prod. Teo Macero), *Bitches Brew* 🎵🎵🎵🎵 (Columbia, 1970, prod. Teo Macero), and *A Tribute to Jack Johnson* 🎵🎵🎵🎵 (Columbia, 1969, prod. Teo Macero) are fusion at its most rewarding and frequently feature McLaughlin, whose playing Davis always expressed high admiration for.

influences:
⏮ Jimi Hendrix, Wes Montgomery

⏭ Al Di Meola, Vernon Reid

see also: *Mahavishnu Orchestra, Shakti*

Chris Meloche

Jackie McLean

Born John Lenwood McLean Jr., May 17, 1932, in New York, NY.

It would not be an overstatement to declare that Jackie McLean is one of the most important alto saxophonists to emerge from the "School of Hard Bop." When he was 12 years old, McLean's family moved to the thriving cultural neighborhood in the Sugar Hill section of Harlem. His godfather, Norman Cobbs (a saxophonist who played in the church band at Adam Clayton Powell's Abyssiania Baptist Church) presented 14-year old McLean with his first instrument, a soprano saxophone. A year later his parents gave him an alto saxophone. Exposed to Lester Young and Dexter Gordon recordings while working in his stepfather's record store, McLean developed his yen for the harder tenor sound that would influence his later sound and style. He studied with pianist Bud Powell and was inspired by players such as Thelonious Monk and Charlie

---

JACKIE MCLEAN

song "Let's Face the Music and Dance"
album *Swing, Swang, Swingin'*
(Blue Note, 1959/1997)

instrument Alto saxophone

Monster Solo

Parker. By age 19, McLean was making a name for himself; he had already made his recording debut in 1951 with Miles Davis and was developing his style beyond the influences of Charlie Parker. During the 1950s he worked with Charles Mingus, spent three years with drummer Art Blakey's group, and, recording with his own groups, began to develop a reputation as one of the true masters of his instrument. McLean experimented during the 1960s, embracing new developments and introducing adventurous young players such as Charles Tolliver, Tony Williams, Jack DeJohnette, Larry Willis, and (his son) Rene McLean to the scene. At Slug's Saloon in New York's East Village, he began a popular Sunday afternoon jazz series. Since 1971 McLean has been a resident of Hartford, Connecticut. At the Hartt College of the University of Hartford, he developed the jazz degree program and serves as chairman of the African American Music Department. Active in community efforts and founder of the Artists Collective, a non-profit multi-arts cultural center, he has received numerous awards and honors, recorded numerous albums as leader and sideman, and continues to perform worldwide.

McLean's interest in bebop (in general), and Parker (in particular) quickly translated into a forceful and individual instrumental voice of his own. Within five years after his recording with Davis, McLean was signed to Prestige, where he made a string of standards- and blues-based "blowing session" albums before moving over to Alfred Lion's Blue Note label, where he did his most enduring and thrilling work. Later, McLean recorded for the Danish SteepleChase imprint, then dropped out of the scene to concentrate on teaching before resurfacing on tiny Triloka and, later still, Island/Birdology. At present, he is once again back with Blue Note.

what to buy: Midway through the 1980s, at the dawn of the CD era, there weren't more than a handful of albums by McLean in print. Today, you could easily give yourself a hernia trying to carry all of them home, a tribute not only to the power of the marketplace, but also to the consistently high quality of the altoist's work over the more than four decades he's been recording as a leader. Most observers point to *Let Freedom Ring* ✮✮✮✮ (Blue Note, 1962/1988, prod. Alfred Lion) as the watershed outing. Backed by pianist Walter Davis Jr., bassist Herbie Lewis, and drummer Billy Higgins, the album represents McLean's spiritual conversion to Ornette Coleman's "new thing" sound. You can hear the Coleman influence most clearly on the tune "Rene," named after McLean's son. However, the pair of dates that followed would be better still, matching McLean's increasingly "acidic" tone with Grachan Moncur III's impressionistic trombone and (more importantly) his hauntingly complex compositions. *One Step Beyond* ✮✮✮✮✮ (Blue Note, 1963/1995, prod. Alfred Lion) includes Eddie Khan on bass, drummer Tony Williams (making his recording debut), and Bobby Hutcherson's gorgeous and evocative vibraharp. And *Destination Out* ✮✮✮✮✮ (Blue Note, 1963/1995 prod. Alfred Lion) substitutes Larry Ridley and Roy Haynes for Khan and Williams, respectively.

what to buy next: One of the boldest McLean sessions is *New and Old Gospel* ✮✮✮✮ (Blue Note, 1967/1989, prod. Alfred Lion) with the sputtering trumpet of outside avatar Ornette Coleman joining McLean on the frontline backed by a rhythm section of LaMont Johnson, Scott Holt, and Billy Higgins. A less adventurous but equally engaging Blue Note session by McLean is *Jackie's Bag* ✮✮✮✮ (Blue Note, 1959–60/1995, prod. Alfred Lion), a split-session disc that includes some titles with Donald Byrd and Sonny Clark, and others with tenorist Tina Brooks that date from the period of McLean's involvement with the Jack Gelber play, *The Connection. Swing, Swang, Swingin'* ✮✮✮✮ (Blue Note, 1959/1997, prod. Alfred Lion) is an admirable collection of standards with Walter Bishop Jr., Jimmy Garrison, and

Art Taylor, as is *Capuchin Swing* ✮✮✮✮ (Blue Note, 1960, prod. Alfred Lion) on which Jackie is paired with Bishop, Taylor, Blue Mitchell, and Paul Chambers. Among the Prestige titles, both *4, 5 & 6* ✮✮✮✮ (Prestige, 1956/OJC, 1991, prod. Bob Weinstock) and *McLean's Scene* ✮✮✮✮ (Prestige, 1957/OJC, 1992, prod. Bob Weinstock) are particularly lovely, the leader's alto waxing smooth on the albums' standard-heavy tune rosters. From the SteepleChase years comes the lean McLean-Kenny Drew-Alex Riel bassless trio date *Live at Montmartre* ✮✮✮✮ (SteepleChase, 1972/1995, prod. Nils Winther).

what to avoid: McLean's most recent records are his least satisfying. The celebrated tone has grown hard and brittle, at times a parody of his mid-1960s "acid" period, and his solos, while never embarrassing, are nowhere near as interesting as they used to be. Both *The Jackie Mac Attack Live* ✮✮✮ (Birdology, 1993, prod. Jean-Francois Deiber) and *Rhythm of the Earth* ✮✮✮ (Birdology, 1992, prod. Jean-Francois Deiber) fall into this category. *Hat Trick* ✮✮✮ (Blue Note, 1996, prod. Hitoshi Namekata) follows this same pattern, though it does have the advantage of featuring the vibrant piano work of Junko Onishi. Finally, the recently reissued *'Bout Soul* ✮✮✮ (Blue Note, 1967/1997, prod. Francis Wolff) seems a bit formulaic, despite the presence of Woody Shaw and Grachan Moncur III, and the poetry-n-jazz title track is a mistake.

the rest:
Lights Out! ✮✮✮ (Prestige, 1956/OJC, 1990)
Jackie McLean & Co. ✮✮✮✮ (Prestige, 1957/OJC, 1992)
(With John Jenkins) *Alto Madness* ✮✮✮ (Prestige, 1957/OJC)
Strange Blues ✮✮✮ (Prestige, 1957/OJC, 1989)
A Long Drink of the Blues ✮✮✮ (Prestige, 1957/OJC, 1994)
Makin' the Changes ✮✮✮ (New Jazz, 1957/OJC, 1992)
(With Bill Hardman) *Jackie's Pal* ✮✮✮ (Prestige, 1957/OJC)
New Soil ✮✮✮✮ (Blue Note, 1959/1989)
Bluesnik ✮✮✮✮ (Blue Note, 1961/1995)
Tippin' the Scales ✮✮✮✮ (Blue Note 1962/1996)
Dr. Jackle ✮✮✮ (SteepleChase, 1966/1995)
Demon's Dance ✮✮✮✮ (Blue Note, 1967/1997)
A Ghetto Lullaby ✮✮✮✮ (SteepleChase, 1973)
Dynasty ✮✮✮ (Triloka, 1992)
Rites of Passage ✮✮✮ (Triloka, 1992)

worth searching for: It is the material that comprises the less conceptual, more grounded series of albums presently collected on the limited-edition, four-CD set, *Complete Blue Note 1964–66 Jackie McLean Sessions* ✮✮✮✮✮ (Mosaic, 1964–66, prod. Alfred Lion) that marks McLean's high-water point. Available by mail order only, the set contains some truly great music, including 1964's *It's Time* with Charles Tolliver, Herbie Hancock, Cecil McBee, and Roy Haynes; *Action*, also from 1964, with Tolliver, Hutcherson, McBee, and Higgins; the incredibly moving quartet outing, *Right Now* (1965), with Larry Willis, Bob Cranshaw, and Clifford Jarvis that contains the ethereal dedication the then-recently-fallen Dolphy, "Poor Eric"; the dual-trumpet sextet of *Jacknife* (1965) with Tolliver and Morgan, Willis, Ridley, and Jack DeJohnette; the fire-spitting *Consequences*, also from 1965, with Morgan, Harold Mabern, Herbie Lewis, and Billy Higgins, and the so-called *High Frequency* session from 1966 with Willis, Don Moore, and DeJohnette. Eventually, these titles will no doubt find their way on to individual Blue Note discs, but for the time being, the only way to savor this brilliant period of McLean's career is to scoop up the whole shebang at once. And remember, Mosaic's issues are extremely limited, with printings of no more than 7,500 copies of any one title.

influences:

◄◄ Charlie Parker, Dexter Gordon

►► Gary Bartz, Christopher Hollyday, Vincent Herring, Steve Davis

David Prince and Nancy Ann Lee

Rene McLean

Born 1947, in New York, NY.

Although his father is legendary, Rene McLean has established his own voice, playing African, Afro-Latin, and Caribbean music as well as jazz. The recipient of guidance from John Coltrane, private studies with Sonny Rollins, and tutelage from dad Jackie, McLean's first professional gigs were with Tito Puente. But by the early 1970s he was an integral part of the New York jazz scene, working with Sam Rivers, Lionel Hampton, Doug Carn, Tyrone Washington, and the Woody Shaw/Louis Hayes quintet, as well as leading his own groups. With his father, he co-led the Cosmic Brotherhood in the 1970s, and in the late 1980s, teamed with Jackie again. The younger McLean's interest in African studies and culture resulted in many trips to the continent in the 1980s and 1990s, eventually leading to an extended teaching assignment in South Africa, where he currently resides.

what's available: Recorded in South Africa with over 30 local musicians, *In African Eyes* ⵣⵣⵣⵣ (Triloka, 1993, prod. Rene McLean, K.D. Kagel) features the dynamic trumpet of Hugh Masekela as well as McLean's now-mature tenor. This is a true fusion of jazz with the essence of South African township music and its polyrhythmic grooves, not just jazz over an African groove. Percussive, melodic, and energizing, McLean's musical voice adds enthusiasm to the multifaceted music he creates, and he's absolutely joyous on "Soweto Sunrise" and reflective on "Dance Little Mandisa." This is one of the most effective amalgams of jazz and African music ever recorded.

worth searching for: Hard to find, McLean's lively and often impressive debut on *Watch Out!* ⵣⵣⵣⵣ (SteepleChase, 1975/1994, prod. Nils Winther) presages his interest in African music on his "Bilad As Sudan." Grounded in the family tradition, McLean was nearly 30 when he first recorded as a leader and his energy is already enhanced by years of collaboration with seasoned players.

influences:

◄◄ John Coltrane, Sonny Rollins, Jackie McLean

►► Joe Henderson, Javon Jackson, Billy Pierce, Chris Potter

Bret Primack

Jim McNeely

Born May 18, 1949, in Chicago, IL.

In 1975, after graduating from the University of Illinois, McNeely jumped right into the jazz fray, recording or playing with Ted Curson, the Thad Jones-Mel Lewis Jazz Orchestra, Stan Getz, Joe Henderson, Art Farmer, Bobby Watson, Dave Liebman, and Phil Woods. He is not only a talented pianist (Phil Woods has called McNeely "one of the greatest musicians I have ever worked with"), but McNeely has also earned a Grammy nomination as an arranger. He is involved in jazz education, currently teaching at New York University with prior stints at Stanford, Mannes College of Music, the New England Conservatory, and the William Paterson College of New Jersey. McNeely has also served as Associate Musical Director for the Jazz Composers Workshop and an Interest Chairman in Composition and Arranging for the International Association of Jazz Educators. McNeely is the author of *The Art of Comping*, published by Advance Music Publishing.

what to buy: On *At Maybeck, Volume 20* ⵣⵣⵣⵣ (Concord Jazz, 1992, prod. Nick Phillips), McNeely, like Roger Kellaway, has exquisite control of the keyboard and he uses it to serve the music. Even if he lacks the last scintilla of Kellaway's composing skills, the few self-penned songs he performs on this album are worthy samples of his abilities. The eight cover tunes range from familiar jazz starting points like "Body and Soul" and "All the Things You Are," to classic riffs from bebop masters Bud Powell ("Un Poco Loco") and Thelonious Monk ("Bye Ya" and "'Round Midnight"). McNeely's cover of "There Will Never Be

Another You" traipses through all 12 keys without becoming gimmicky.

what to buy next: The trio date *Winds of Change* 🎵🎵🎵 (SteepleChase, 1990, prod. Nils Winther), along with *At Maybeck*, gives a good idea of McNeely's fine piano playing. With a fine blend of originals and covers, the pianist receives sensitive support from bassist Mike Richmond and drummer Kenny Washington. McNeely takes a leisurely stroll through Thad Jones's gorgeous "Quietude" that includes some solid soloing from Richmond over Washington's classy cymbal and brush work. Of the originals, "Brooders Waltz" may be the most thought-provoking, although McNeely's use of a DX-7 II keyboard synthesizer on "Power Gap" walks the line between kitschy and interesting. The trio version of "Bye Ya" on this album is outstanding from Washington's initial spare yet colorful drum solo until the final bar. It compares very well with McNeely's rendition on *At Maybeck*.

the rest:
The Plot Thickens 🎵🎵🎵 (Muse, 1979)
East Coast Blow Out 🎵🎵🎵 (Lipstick, 1991)
The Vanguard Orchestra Plays the Music of Jim McNeely 🎵🎵🎵 (New World, 1997)

influences:
⏪ Wynton Kelly, Art Tatum, Herbie Hancock, McCoy Tyner, Thad Jones, Bob Brookmeyer

⏩ Mike Abene

Garaud MacTaggart

Marian McPartland

Born Marian Turner, March 20, 1920, in Windsor, UK.

Marian McPartland is one of the most beloved figures in jazz, a gifted composer, pioneering educator, creator of the popular National Public Radio broadcast *Piano Jazz* and highly sensitive pianist who has never stopped assimilating new ideas. As a player, she draws on everything from stride, swing, bop and post-bop, though all of her music is marked by her tremendous harmonic knowledge and fey sense of humor. As an interviewer, she has a gift for drawing out musicians and engaging them in probing, straight-forward conversation about their musical ideas.

Born Marian Turner, she studied music at the Guildhall before joining Billy Mayerl's Cavaliers, a four-piano vaudeville act that performed for troops across Europe during World War II. She met cornetist Jimmy McPartland in Belgium and they married before settling in the United States in 1946. They worked to-

gether occasionally in the late 1940s, though her style was considerably more modern than his Chicago Dixieland approach. By 1950, she had her own trio and was working steadily at the New York clubs the Embers and the London House, though it was her long-running gig at the Hickory House (1952–60) with bassist Bill Crow and the brilliant drummer Joe Morello (through 1957) that started her transformation from a good pianist into a jazz institution. She recorded for Savoy, Capitol, and Argo in the 1950s and Time, Sesac, and Dot in the early 1960s. She and Jimmy McPartland divorced in the 1960s, though they remained close friends and remarried weeks before his death in 1991. Like many jazz musicians, she struggled to find steady work through the later 1960s, though eventually she took matters into her own hands and founded her own label, Halcyon (1969–77), on which she released several albums. She recorded three albums for Tony Bennett's Improv label in the mid-1970s and in 1978 signed with Concord where she has recorded many excellent sessions.

Among all her other accomplishments, McPartland is a wonderful writer who contributed many articles and reviews to *Down Beat* in the 1960s and has produced several books, including her priceless collection of profiles and memories of the Hickory House *All In Good Time* (Oxford, 1987). Many of her more interesting *Piano Jazz* broadcasts, which feature her interviews, solo performances and often duets with her guest, have been released by Jazz Alliance.

what to buy: Throughout her career, pianist Marian McPartland has continued to grow and evolve, and in the solo context provided by *Live at Maybeck Recital Hall, Vol. 9* 🎵🎵🎵🎵 (Concord Jazz, 1991, prod. Carl E. Jefferson), her catholic taste, tremendous improvisational skills, and beautiful touch are all in the spotlight. She covers 16 tunes, moving between standards such as "This Time the Dream's on Me," "A Fine Romance," and "It's You or No One," and Ellingtonia, including a stunning version of the complex "Clothed Woman," a swinging romp through "Love You Madly," and Mercer Ellington's "Things Ain't What They Used to Be." Other highlights include a gorgeous version of her gossamer "Twilight World," her bluesy take on Ornette Coleman's "Turn Around," and bittersweet, almost defiant version of Alec Wilder's "I'll Be Around." Internationally recognized as a jazz giant, Benny Carter isn't exactly overlooked, but when McPartland recorded *The Benny Carter Songbook* 🎵🎵🎵🎵 (Concord Jazz, 1990, prod. Carl E. Jefferson) it was the first album dedicated solely to his music (by someone other than himself) in more than two decades. A rich and rewarding quartet session with Carter himself on alto sax, John

Clayton on bass, and Harold Jones on drums, the album features Carter's best-known works, including "When Lights Are Low" with Carter's often neglected bridge, and a trio version of "Key Largo," a Latin-tinged piece from the 1940s made famous by Anita O'Day. McPartland's musical sensibility is perfectly attuned to Carter's, and she renders his tunes with great sensitivity, from the melancholy of "Lovely Woman" to the high-spirited riff tune "Easy Money." McPartland's musical range can be dazzling, as on *In My Life* 𝄞𝄞𝄞𝄞 (Concord Jazz, 1993, prod. Carl E. Jefferson), a trio session with bassist Gary Mazzaroppi and drummer Glenn Davis that ranges from Coltrane to John Lennon, and from Ornette Coleman to Ivan Lins. The album was also the debut of 22-year-old saxophonist Chris Potter (heard on alto and tenor) who plays with startling maturity on Trane's "Red Planet," Coleman's bumpy, red clay tune "Ramblin'," and the standards "Gone with the Wind" and "Close Your Eyes." Other highlights include McPartland's delicate "In the Days of Our Love," Alec Wilder's "Moon and Sand," and "Singin' the Blues," her classy solo tribute to her late husband. This is one of McPartland's most consistently inspired sessions. McPartland used to play Strayhorn's tunes when he came by the Hickory House to catch her trio, and she pays the great composer/arranger a loving tribute with *Plays the Music of Billy Strayhorn* 𝄞𝄞𝄞𝄞 (Concord Jazz, 1987, prod. Carl E. Jefferson), a superior quartet session with Jerry Dodgion (alto sax), Steve LaSpina (bass), and Joey Baron (drums). Dodgion wrote all of the arrangements and his lush alto brings to mind Johnny Hodges (who was featured on so many of these tunes), though McPartland ends the album with a breathtaking solo version of "Daydream," a tune closely associated with the Ellingtonian alto saxophonist. Her trio version of "Lush Life," with its careful attention to the complex melody, would have made composer Strayhorn smile, as would the rollicking opening track, "The Intimacy of the Blues." Other highlights include McPartland's solo version of "Lotus Blossom" and the exotic "Isfahan," with some particularly effective Dodgion alto work.

what to buy next: McPartland has a knack for developing inspired collaborations, and with *Silent Pool* 𝄞𝄞𝄞𝄞 (Concord Jazz, 1991, prod. Nick Phillips) she has found in pianist/arranger Alan Broadbent the perfect person to orchestrate her first session with strings. Built upon a trio with the redoubtable Andy Simpkins (bass) and tasteful Harold Jones (drums), the session is also notable for featuring all McPartland originals. The result is a delicate, moody album with McPartland's lush chords surrounded by sensuous, caressing strings. The music swings, whether it's the jazz waltz "A Delicate Balance" or her concise

tribute "For Dizzy," but it's the various emotional states evoked that make this such affecting music, from the optimistic romanticism of "There'll Be Other Times" to the self-described "Melancholy Mood." Originally released on her own Halcyon label, *Ambiance* 𝄞𝄞𝄞𝄞 (Jazz Alliance, 1970, prod. Marian McPartland) is a loose trio session with many small surprises. Featuring bassist Michael Moore (who wrote four of the 11 tunes) and drummer Jimmy Madson, the album also includes the standards "What Is This Thing Called Love" and "Three Little Words," five tunes by McPartland, including the title track which was inspired by Herbie Hancock, and "Glimpse," where Billy Hart replaces Madson. Moore's unusual "Sounds Like Seven" and McPartland's "Afterglow" are the standout tracks. McPartland pays tribute to one of jazz's great arranger/composers with *Plays the Music of Mary Lou Williams* 𝄞𝄞𝄞𝄞 (Concord Jazz, 1991, prod. Carl E. Jefferson), a trio session featuring her frequent trio mate Bill Douglass (bass) and Omar Clay (drums). Most of the material was originally written for Andy Kirk's Clouds of Joy, the big band in which Williams held down the piano chair. McPartland covers her better known pieces, such as "What's Your Story, Morning Glory?" and "Cloudy," while also unearthing her overlooked themes, including the bluesy tunes "Scratchin' in the Gravel" and "Walkin' and Swingin'," making a strong case for the depth and value of Williams's music. Though cornetist Jimmy and Marian McPartland divorced in the 1960s, they remained close friends and worked together occasionally over the years. For the most part, *A Sentimental Journey* 𝄞𝄞𝄞𝄞 (Jazz Alliance, 1994, prod. Marian McPartland) alternates from track to track between two sextet dates, a 1972 session with Hank Berger (trombone and banjo) and Jack Maheu (clarinet), and a 1973 session with Vic Dickenson (trombone) and Buddy Tate (saxophones). Marian is mostly in a supporting role as Jimmy plays with spirit and mostly solid chops (and does a fine vocal turn on "Basin Street Blues"), though the 1973 session is markedly better, producing some serious fun on "Perdido" and the title track. Most of these tracks were originally released on her Halcyon label.

what to avoid: Though McPartland's *Benny Carter Songbook* CD is one of her better sessions, her broadcast with Carter, *Piano Jazz: McPartland/Carter* 𝄞𝄞𝄞 (Jazz Alliance, 1989, prod. Shari Hutchinson) is one of her least interesting, mainly because he left his alto sax and trumpet at home and plays only piano. She does draw out the normally taciturn Carter, and plays three of his tunes by herself, but their piano duets are non-events.

best of the rest:
Plays the Music of Alec Wilder 𝄞𝄞𝄞𝄞 (Jazz Alliance, 1973)

Concert in Argentina 🎵🎵🎵🎶 (Jazz Alliance, 1974)
Piano Jazz: McPartland/Mary Lou Williams 🎵🎵🎶 (Jazz Alliance, 1978)
Piano Jazz: McPartland/Bill Evans 🎵🎵🎵🎵 (Jazz Alliance, 1978)
Piano Jazz: McPartland/Eubie Blake 🎵🎵🎵🎵 (Jazz Alliance, 1979)
At the Festival 🎵🎵🎵🎶 (Concord Jazz, 1979)
Portrait of Marian McPartland 🎵🎵🎵🎶 (Concord Jazz, 1979)
Piano Jazz: McPartland/Jess Stacy 🎵🎵🎵🎵 (Jazz Alliance, 1981/1995)
Personal Choice 🎵🎵🎵🎶 (Concord Jazz, 1982)
Willow Creek and Other Ballads 🎵🎵🎵🎵 (Concord Jazz, 1985)
Piano Jazz: McPartland/Dizzy Gillespie 🎵🎵🎶 (Jazz Alliance, 1985)
Piano Jazz: McPartland/Milt Hinton 🎵🎵🎵🎵 (Jazz Alliance, 1991)
Piano Jazz: McPartland/Lee Konitz 🎵🎵🎵🎵 (Jazz Alliance, 1991)
Piano Jazz: McPartland/Mercer Ellington 🎵🎵🎶 (Jazz Alliance, 1994)

worth searching for: Recorded live at the 1993 Concord-Fujitsu Jazz Festival, *Silver Anniversary Set* 🎵🎵🎵🎶 (Concord Jazz, 1994, prod. Carl E. Jefferson) is a two-disc set which includes some superior work by McPartland's trio with Bill Douglass (bass) and Omar Clay (drums), including a brilliant version of Ellington's "Prelude to a Kiss." Chris Potter adds his tenor saxophone to the last three tracks, blowing passionately on "I'll Remember April" and "My Foolish Heart," which he concludes with a particularly incisive cadenza. Guitarist Howard Alden's trio and pianist Gene Harris's quartet with tenor saxophonist Scott Hamilton are also featured.

influences:

◀◀ Teddy Wilson, Mary Lou Williams, Duke Ellington, Bill Evans

Andrew Gilbert

Joe McPhee

Born November 3, 1939, in Miami, FL.

A trumpeter since the age of eight, multi-instrumentalist Joe McPhee cites John Coltrane, Ornette Coleman, and Eric Dolphy as the players who led him to the reeds (tenor, alto, and soprano sax, alto clarinet) in the late '60s. He was taken with what he calls their "revolution in sound, breaking with established, popular tradition" and "the risk taking" involved in this type of musicmaking. By the late '70s, McPhee had developed a unique way of building tunes out of improvisational cues, a method he calls "Po Music," after Dr. Edward de Bono's concept of lateral thinking. "Derived from words like possible, positive, poetry and hypothesis," explains McPhee, "Po is a language indicator to show that the process of provocation is being used to move from a fixed set of ideas in an attempt to discover new ones." Simply put, McPhee's Po philosophy is about the process of discovery one goes through when ap-

proaching improvisational problem-solving from a multitude of angles.

McPhee's recorded output has essentially come in three stages. Long out of print, much of his earliest work from 1967–74 was released on Craig Johnson's CjR imprint. In 1974, when Werner Uehlinger first heard the artist while visiting the United States, he was moved to found the eminent Swiss labels, hat HUT and hat ART, specifically to document McPhee's explorations. Those initial albums are no longer available, but a handful of exceptional recordings featuring European improvisers Andre Jaume (reeds) and Raymond Boni (guitar) illustrates McPhee's fruitful collaborations from 1979–90. Over the past few years, McPhee has resurfaced on a number of titles, four of which can be found on the new Cadence offshoot, CIMP (Creative Improvised Music Projects).

what to buy: *Linear B* 🎵🎵🎵🎵 (hat ART, 1990, prod. Pia Uehlinger, Werner X. Uehlinger) is a solid representation of McPhee's mature Po aesthetic. Boni is probably the most startlingly inventive guitarist you've never heard of. The closing track, "Voices," is one of the most moving, non-cliched ballads this side of "Lonely Woman." A largely improvised summit, *Legend Street One* 🎵🎵🎵🎶 (CIMP, 1996, prod. Robert Rusch) features the Joe McPhee Quartet (with fellow tenor saxist Frank Lowe, drummer Charles Moffett, and violinist David Prentice), yielding a structural and conceptual development far broader and more flexible than most through-composed albums. The disc's elastic mood is heightened by its sequencing, which reconfigures the quartet into sub-units of trios, duos, and soloists. Spontaneously recorded with David Prentice after the *Legend Street* sessions, *Inside Out* 🎵🎵🎵🎵 (CIMP, 1996, prod. Robert Rusch) is a set of serene (but not sleepy) duets extending beyond the interplay of soprano sax, alto clarinet, and violin to almost magical "conversations" with the textures, melodies, and rhythms of the birds and bugs in the environment. Dismiss any New Age allusions. Recorded with Survival Unit II, *At WBAI's Free Music Store, 1971* 🎵🎵🎵🎶 (hat ART, 1996, prod. Pia Uehlinger, Werner X. Uehlinger) is a welcome glimpse of McPhee's incipient but already well-developed voice as an improvising band director (on trumpet and tenor sax). Imbued with great beauty, urgency, and political provocation on tunes like "Nation Time" (for activist-poet Amiri Baraka) and "Harriet" (for Underground Railroad conductor Harriet Tubman), the disc reflects McPhee's identification with the spiritual solidarity and anti-establishment fervor of the turbulent late '60s/early '70s. Clifford Thornton on baritone horn and cornet.

what to buy next: *Old Eyes & Mysteries* 🎵🎵🎵🎵 (hat ART, 1992, prod. Pia Uehlinger, Werner X. Uehlinger) is top-form Po music, featuring a septet from 1979 with Jaume and Boni ("Old Eyes") and a trio from 1990 with saxist Urs Leimgruber and drummer Fritz Hauser ("Mysteries"). *Topology* 🎵🎵🎵🎵 (hat ART, 1989, prod. Pia Uehlinger, Werner X. Uehlinger) includes more great Po improvisations from 1981. The singular Irene Schweizer appears on piano, and the revolving lineup performs a distinguished rendition of Mingus's "Pithecanthropus Erectus." On the 1982 quartet recording, *Oleo & A Future Retrospective* 🎵🎵🎵🎵 (hat ART, 1993, prod. Pia Uehlinger, Werner X. Uehlinger), McPhee applies his Po philosophy to Sonny Rollins's "Oleo." The last 35 minutes (four songs) of the disc feature McPhee's core trio with Jaume and Boni. *Legend Street Two* 🎵🎵🎵 (CIMP, 1997, prod. Robert Rusch) offers seven more pieces from the successful *Legend Street* sessions (three duos with Prentice), including a beautiful version of Eric Dolphy's "Something Sweet, Something Tender." More full-throttle than *One*, McPhee goes head to head at times with Prentice, mimicking the timbre of the violin scrape for scrape.

the rest:

(With Rashied Ali, Borah Bergman and Wilber Morris) *The October Revolution* 🎵🎵🎵 (Evidence, 1996)

(With Michael Bisio) *Finger Wigglers* 🎵🎵🎵 (CIMP, 1996)

Common Threads: Live at the Tractor Tavern, Seattle 🎵🎵🎵 (Deep Listening, 1996)

influences:

◀◀ John Coltrane, Albert Ayler, Eric Dolphy

Sam Prestianni

Charles McPherson

Born July 24, 1939, in Joplin, MO.

A passionate, fiery musician whose alto sax style is built on his deep insight into bebop, Charles McPherson is too often pigeonholed as a Charlie Parker disciple. With his searing lyricism and gift for writing memorable melodic lines, he is just reaching the age when his status as a major player should soon be recognized more widely. Raised in Detroit on the same block as pianist Barry Harris and trumpeter Lonnie Hillyer, McPherson started playing alto at age 13. Johnny Hodges was his earliest inspiration, but McPherson heard Parker in 1953 and began exploring bebop. At 17, McPherson was working in the vibrant Detroit scene, and at 20 he moved to New York and soon hooked up with Charles Mingus, with whom he worked intermittently until 1972. One of his most memorable sessions with Mingus was a double-LP recorded at the 1964 Monterey Jazz Festival. He began leading his own bands in 1972, recording a number of fine albums for Xanadu, and in 1978 he settled in San Diego, where he still lives. He played on the *Bird* film soundtrack, recreating some of Parker's famous solos, and was featured on the Jazz at Lincoln Center album *The Fire of the Fundamentals*. He has recorded for Prestige, Mainstream, Discovery, and Arabesque, but considering his stature, has an unfortunately small discography.

what to buy: A superb session with the brilliant trumpeter Tom Harrell, *First Flight Out* 🎵🎵🎵🎵 (Arabesque, 1994, prod. Charles McPherson), was McPherson's first album in years on a label with any distribution. Featuring six McPherson originals as well as tunes by Monk ("Well You Needn't") and Mingus's ("Nostalgia in Times Square," "Goodbye Porkpie Hat," and "Portrait"), the session highlights McPherson's beautiful tone as he and Harrell blend their equally distinctive sounds. The rhythm section is Michael Weiss (piano), Peter Washington (bass), and Victor Lewis (drums). A fine quartet session featuring mostly McPherson originals, *Come Play with Me* 🎵🎵🎵🎵 (Arabesque, 1995, prod. Daniel Chriss, Charles McPherson) also includes Harold Arlen's "Get Happy" taken at a brisk tempo, the perennial ballad "Darn That Dream," and Charlie Parker's "Bloomdido." Mulgrew Miller (piano), Santi Debriano (bass), and Lewis Nash (drums) make up the top-notch young rhythm section. The band sails through "Funhouse," McPherson's reworking of "Limehouse Blues," and his comely ballad "Blues for Camille," written for his young daughter. A high energy session with some of the great second generation boppers, *Bebop Revisited!* 🎵🎵🎵🎵 (Prestige, 1964/OJC, 1992, prod. Don Schlitten) is McPherson's debut as a leader and features the underappreciated trumpeter Carmell Jones, pianist Barry Harris, bassist Nelson Boyd, and drummer Tootie Heath. The playing is consistently inspired and though the album opens with a blazing version of Tadd Dameron's oft-recorded "Hot House," the tunes are hardly overexposed. When was the last time you heard Fats Navarro's "Nostalgia," Charlie Parker's "Si Si," or "Wail" by Bud Powell?

what to buy next: *Con Alma!* 🎵🎵🎵🎵 (Prestige, 1965/OJC, 1995, prod. Don Schlitten) pairs McPherson with fellow Mingus alumnus Clifford Jordan (tenor sax) on a program ranging from Ellington and Monk to Dexter Gordon, Dizzy Gillespie, and Charlie Parker. Monk's rarely played "Eronel" is one of the session's highlights, as is McPherson's slow, torchy blues "I Don't Know." McPherson's old Detroit partner Barry Harris (piano) leads the rhythm section with George Tucker (bass), and Alan

Dawson (drums). Capturing McPherson and trumpeter Lonnie Hillyer's short-lived band in concert, *Live at the Five Spot* 𝄢𝄢𝄢𝄢 (Prestige, 1966/OJC, 1994, prod. Don Schlitten) is a hard-charging bebop session expanded by three tracks on the CD reissue. With Barry Harris (piano) and Ray McKinney (bass) in the rhythm section, the great drummer Billy Higgins is the only non-Detroiter on the album. McPherson wails on his Brazilian flavored version of "Here's That Rainy Day," and uses his trademark bittersweet tone to advantage on "I Can't Get Started."

best of the rest:

Sika Ya Bibi 𝄢𝄢𝄢 (Mainstream, 1972)
New Horizons 𝄢𝄢𝄢𝄢 (Xanadu, 1977)
Free Bop! 𝄢𝄢𝄢𝄢 (Xanadu, 1978)
The Prophet 𝄢𝄢𝄢𝄢 (Discovery, 1983)

worth searching for: A typically blazing set from one of the great bop-influenced alto saxophonists, *Live in Tokyo* 𝄢𝄢𝄢𝄢 (Xanadu, 1976, prod. Don Schlitten) captures McPherson with pianist Barry Harris, bassist Sam Jones, and drummer Leroy Williams. His high octane version of "Bouncin' With Bud" is worth the price of the out-of-print album.

influences:

◀◀ Charlie Parker, Sonny Stitt, Johnny Hodges

Andrew Gilbert

Carmen McRae

Born April 8, 1922 in New York. Died November 10, 1994.

Carmen McRae was a distinctive vocal stylist famous for her ironic, witty interpretations, her smoky voice, and her behind-the-beat phrasing. Although she first learned music as a pianist, her earliest and most enduring influence was vocalist Billie Holiday. McRae's career as a singer began with Benny Carter's orchestra in 1944, and she got jobs with Count Basie and Mercer Ellington later in the 1940s. It was while working as an intermission performer at Minton's that she came under the influence of bebop, and of Sarah Vaughan in particular. McRae's first recordings as a leader were made for Decca in 1954, and she was a hit right away, winning "Best New Singer" in *Down Beat* that year and charting with some hit songs during the next couple of years. McRae would, for the most part, make consistently good records until the early 1990s, gradually accentuating her distinctive vocal traits even more and sounding less like a bopper in the mold of Vaughan.

what to buy: The selections on *Here to Stay* 𝄢𝄢𝄢𝄢 (Decca, 1955–59/GRP, 1992, prod. Milt Gabler, reissue prod. Orrin Keepnews) are among the best McRae cut for Decca in the 1950s, and her Sarah Vaughan influence is very noticeable. Strong, sympathetic backing is provided by guitarist Mundell Lowe, pianist Dick Katz, flautist Herbie Mann, and McRae's husband, Kenny Clarke, on drums on memorable versions of "The Yardbird Suite," "My One and Only Love," and "I Can't Get Started." *Sings "Lover Man" and Other Billie Holiday Favorites* 𝄢𝄢𝄢𝄢 (Columbia, 1962/1997, prod. Teo Macero) preserves material that hadn't been previously available on CD, and thankfully so! McRae is at her boppish best on this collection of holiday standards, including "Yesterdays," "My Man," and "God Bless the Child." The live recording *The Great American Songbook* 𝄢𝄢𝄢𝄢 (Atlantic, 1972/1990, prod. Jack Rael) doesn't really present any more of a "Great American songbook" than most of her other releases, but it stands as McRae's most touching personal statement. The depth and breadth of emotional expression she conveys is remarkable, as is the subtle backing of pianist Jimmy Rowles and guitarist Joe Pass.

what to buy next: Two of the most distinctive female bop vocalists match wits when Betty Carter joins McRae on the delightful *Duets* 𝄢𝄢𝄢𝄢 (Verve, 1996, prod. Richard Seidel). Especially memorable are versions of "Stolen Moments" and "Sophisticated Lady." The two great veterans exchange a little competitiveness and a lot of mutual respect and affection, making this a set worth hearing. McRae made four tribute albums on the Novus label in the 1990s: two for Holiday, one for Thelonious Monk, and *Sarah: Dedicated to You* 𝄢𝄢𝄢𝄢 (Novus, 1991, prod. Larry Clothier), a tribute to Sarah Vaughan. It is interesting that by the time McRae made this album, she was sounding less like "Sassy" than ever before. Nevertheless, this is a fitting and touching tribute, with Shirley Horn accompanying on piano.

what to avoid: *Heat Wave* 𝄢𝄢 (Concord, 1982/1992, prod. Carl Jefferson) is a collaboration with vibraharpist Cal Tjader that doesn't work. Cool Latin pop just isn't McRae's strong suit, nor are tunes by Stevie Wonder or Carlos Santana.

the rest:

Sings Great American Songwriters 𝄢𝄢𝄢𝄢 (Decca, 1955–59/GRP, 1993)
I'll Be Seeing You 𝄢𝄢𝄢𝄢 (Decca, 1955–59/GRP, 1995)
Live: Take Five 𝄢𝄢𝄢 (Columbia Special Products, 1964)

Carmen McRae **(Archive Photos)**

Alive! ♫♫♫♫ (Columbia Legacy, 1965/1994)
Song Time ♫♫♫ (Hindsight, 1970)
It Takes a Lot of Human Feelings ♫♫ (Groove, 1973)
I Am Music ♫♫ (Blue Note, 1975)
Can't Hide Love ♫♫ (Blue Note, 1976/1993)
Live at Ronnie Scott's ♫♫♫ (1978/DRG, 1994)
Live at Bubba's ♫♫♫ (Who's Who in Jazz, 1981/1995)
For Lady Day ♫♫♫♫ (Novus, 1983/1995)
You're Lookin' at Me ♫♫♫♫ (Concord, 1984/1992)
Fine and Mellow: Live at Birdland West ♫♫ (Concord, 1988)
Any Old Time ♫♫♫♫ (Denon, 1990)
Velvet Soul ♫♫♫♫ (Lester Recording Catalog, 1993)
For Lady Day Volume 2 ♫♫♫ (Novus, 1995)

worth searching for: It is surprising that *Carmen Sings Monk* ♫♫♫♫ (Novus, 1990, prod. Larry Clothier), which received so much critical acclaim on its not-so-distant release, should already be out of print, making it annoyingly hard to find. McRae's versions of one Monk classic after another are humorous, profound, and quirky, just like the tunes themselves.

influences:

◀◀ Billie Holiday, Sarah Vaughan

▶▶ Rebecca Paris, Nnenna Freelon

Dan Keener

Jay McShann

Born January 12, 1916, in Muskogee, OK.

One of the last living survivors of the swing era, Jay McShann's musical journey continues unabated; the same "Hootie" McShann who hired the embryonic teenager Charlie Parker as his saxophonist in 1939 fronted the Duke Robillard Band at the 1997 Kansas City Blues and Jazz Fest. McShann, who began playing the piano as a child, had his own band in Kansas City by 1938, and by the early 1940s his enlarged group, fronted by singer Walter Brown, greased by cocky saxman Parker, and catapulted by the huge hit "Confessin' the Blues," could hold its ground against any big band of the period. Led by McShann's powerful piano pumping, his bands always struck a balance between blues and jazz—and they swung like crazy. After he got out of the service and the Basie and Andy Kirk bands went nationwide, McShann recorded in Hollywood with singer Julia Lee before returning to Kansas City, still his base of operations today. Whether playing with big bands or the smaller groups he used in the 1940s (including a nascent R&B combo that included singer Crown Prince Waterford, Numa Lee Davis, and, in his debut recording, Jimmy Witherspoon), McShann remains a

powerful pianist, vocalist, and performer who performs a couple times a month and obviously is not yet content to rest on his considerable laurels.

what to buy: *Hootie's Jumpin' Blues* ♫♫♫♫ (Stony Plain, 1997, prod. Duke Robillard, Holger Peterson) pits the 80-ish pianist with a hard-swinging contemporary group. *The Early Bird Charlie Parker* ♫♫♫♫♫ (MCA, 1982, prod. various) has the studio recordings of the early McShann powerhouse, including "Swingmatism," "Hootie Blues," and "Confessin' the Blues." McShann is the main force behind *Kansas City Blues 1944–49* ♫♫♫♫ (Capitol, 1997, prod. Billy Vera), an exhaustive three-disc look at post–World War II KC line-ups. Besides introducing Witherspoon, he sings up a storm of his own—you wonder why McShann let other singers front the band?—alongside equally noteworthy tracks by Julia Lee and Her Boyfriends, Bus Moten and His Men, Tiny Kennedy, and Walter Brown.

what to buy next: The historical "Wichita transcriptions" and live performances on *Early Bird* ♫♫♫♫ (Stash, 1991, prod. various) capture young gun Charlie Parker at a significant moment in his development and offers more proof that the McShann band could kick anybody's ass off any stage. The much more recent *Swingmatism* ♫♫♫ (Sackville, 1990) offers a tasty choice of updated material, including the gems "Night in Tunisia" and "The Mooche."

the rest:
Goin' to Kansas City ♫♫♫ (New World, 1972/1987)
Hootie's Vine Street Blues ♫♫♫ (Black Lion, 1974/1994)
Solo at Cafe Copains ♫♫♫ (Sackville, 1980)
Air Mail Special ♫♫♫ (Sackville, 1990)
(With John Hicks) *Hootie and Hicks: The Missouri Connection* ♫♫♫ (Reservoir, 1993)
Some Blues ♫♫♫ (Chiaroscuro, 1993)
Piano Playhouse ♫♫♫ (Night Train, 1996)
Just a Lucky So and So ♫♫♫ (Sackville, 1996)
(With Al Casey) *Best of Friends* ♫♫♫ (JSP, 1997)

worth searching for: Jazz giants Herbie Mann, Gerry Mulligan, and John Scofield get down to late-night jazz business on *The Big Apple Bash* ♫♫♫♫ (Atlantic, 1979, prod. Ilhan Mimaroglu), but only on vinyl.

influences:

◀◀ Bennie Moten, Andy Kirk, Harlan Leonard

▶▶ Louis Jordan, Tommy Douglas, Wynonie Harris, Roy Brown, Jimmy Witherspoon, Walter Brown

Leland Rucker

Medeski, Martin & Wood

Formed early 1990s, in New York, NY.

John Medeski, keyboards; Billy Martin, drums, percussion; Chris Wood, bass, harmonica, wood flute.

The songs of Medeski, Martin, and Wood have the improvisatory feel of jazz, but their roots span the music spectrum, making a lot of their material ideal introductory fodder for rockers in transition to jazz. In that way, the trio is quite similar to Charlie Hunter, John Zorn, Marc Ribot, or many of the other new music eclectics. Medeski and Wood originally met in Boston, where they both attended the New England Conservatory of Music prior to moving to New York. Medeski has previously played with the Either/Orchestra and musicians like Dewey Redman and Billy Higgins, in addition to session work with groups as diverse as Blues Traveler and the Klezmatics. Wood's resume includes brief stints with Bob Moses, Randy Weston, and the Either/Orchestra. Martin's experience with New York's new music scene brought him performance credits with Samm Bennett, Ned Rothenberg, and John Lurie although his time with master drummer Bob Moses could be considered his single most important gig from an influence standpoint. In addition to their work together, each member of Medeski, Martin, and Wood is involved in various side projects. Wood is a member of Mark Ribot's Shrek, while Martin performs with John Lurie and (with Medeski) in John Zorn's Masada.

what to buy: *It's a Jungle in Here* ♫♫♫♫ (Gramavision, 1993, prod. Jim Payne) is modern organ trio music for hybrid jazz-rockers with surprisingly effective arrangements from Medeski. While the originals are quite clever, the cover versions of John Coltrane's "Syeeda's Song Flute," King Sunny Ade's "Moti Mo," and a wildly potent medley combining Thelonious Monk's "Bemsha Swing" and Bob Marley's "Lively up Yourself" sample the wide variety of influences forming the band's overall style.

what to buy next: *Friday Afternoon in the Universe* ♫♫♫ (Gramavision, 1994, prod. John Medeski, Billy Martin, Chris Wood, David Baker, Jim Payne) is the stripped-down unit, sans guest stars, that one is most likely to see on the concert tour and, as a result, this album is a lot closer in spirit to what people might hear at one of the group's shows. They whip through a lot of organ trio clichés, but filter those mannerisms through neo-punk jazz attitudes that make the old new again. There's an interesting version of Duke Ellington's "Chinoiserie" to go along with originals like "Last Chance to Dance Trance (Perhaps)" and the quirky "Billy's Tool Box."

Jᴏʜɴ Mᴇᴅᴇsᴋɪ
(ᴡɪᴛʜ Mᴇᴅᴇsᴋɪ, Mᴀʀᴛɪɴ & Wᴏᴏᴅ)

song "Think"
album *Shack-man*
(Gramavision, 1996)
instrument Hammond organ/keyboards

the rest:
Notes from the Underground ♫♫♫ (Accurate, 1992)
Shack-man ♫♫♫ (Gramavision, 1996)

worth searching for: Trumpeter-arranger Ken Schaphorst put together a collection of Harold Arlen tunes *Over the Rainbow* ♫♫♫ (Accurate, 1996, prod. Ken Schaphorst) with Medeski, Martin, and Wood playing four songs.

influences:

⏪ John Coltrane, Larry Young, Miles Davis, Rashied Ali, Bob Moses

⏩ Charlie Hunter, John Zorn, Samm Bennett

Garaud MacTaggart

Brad Mehldau

Born August 23, 1970, in Jacksonville, FL.

An adventurous mainstream pianist, Brad Mehldau fits easily into loose, avant-garde leaning situations, and is a standout player among his generation's rich array of keyboard talent. He started piano lessons at age five and began playing jazz in high school. He moved to New York in the late 1980s and started developing a name for himself through gigs with a number of leading young players, such as Chris Hollyday. He gained widespread exposure during two years with tenor saxophonist Joshua Redman, playing in a hard-driving rhythm section with Christian McBride (bass) and Brian Blade (drums), and appearing on Redman's *MoodSwing* album. Since moving to Los Angeles in 1996, Mehldau has worked intermittently with bassist Charlie Haden in a variety of contexts, and played with Lee Konitz and drummer Joe LaBarbera. He also works around southern California with the group Escape From New York, with saxophonist Ralph Moore, bassist Bob Hurst, and drummer Marvin "Smitty" Smith. His trio, featuring either Larry Grenadier or Darek Oles on bass, and Jorge Rossy on drums, has recorded two excellent albums for Warner Bros. and toured widely in Europe and the U.S.

what to buy: A dazzling sophomore effort by pianist Brad Mehldau, *Vol. 1, The Art of the Trio* ♪♪♪♪ (Warner Bros., 1997, prod. Matt Pierson) features bassist Larry Grenadier and drummer Jorge Rossy playing a set of four standards, four Mehldau originals, and a Beatles tune. The trio's approach is based on the intuitive group sound pioneered by Bill Evans, but they never let the beat fall into the background. Mehldau is most impressive on the standards "I Fall in Love Too Easily," played at a slow, sensuous pace, and "Nobody Else But Me." He also turns Lennon and McCartney's "Blackbird" into an effective, impressionistic jazz opus. His meditative tune "Ron's Place" and delicate ballad "Mignon's Song" indicate Mehldau has a knack for writing melodic fragments for his trio to develop organically into larger themes.

what to buy next: A very impressive debut recording, *Introducing Brad Mehldau* ♪♪♪♪ (Warner Bros., 1995, prod. Matt Pierson) features a trio with Larry Grenadier (bass) and Jorge Rossy (drums) on the first five tracks and Christian McBride (bass) and Brian Blade (drums) on the last four. Mixing standards with four original tunes, Mehldau displays a gift for lyrical phrasing on "It Might as Well Be Spring," while digging into the rapid chord changes of Coltrane's "Countdown" (with the first trio). McBride and Blade, who shared rhythm section duties with Mehldau in Josh Redman's quartet, put a serious groove into the pianist's "London Blues," and stretched out on a 10-minute version of Ellington's "Prelude to a Kiss."

the rest:
Warner Jams, Vol. 1 ♪♪♪♪ (Warner Bros., 1995, prod. Matt Pierson)

worth searching for: Mehldau makes a very strong impression on *Moving In* ♪♪♪♪ (Concord Jazz, 1996, prod. Nick Phillips), a quartet session by the brilliant young saxophonist Chris Potter, heard here mostly on tenor. Mehldau effectively merges into the rhythm section, sharing harmonic ideas with the inventive bassist Larry Grenadier while flowing with the rhythmic textures laid down by powerhouse drummer Billy Hart. Featuring mostly Potter's original tunes, the music provides a wide variety of settings, from grooving blues to a piece influenced by Asian folk music. Mehldau makes the most of the far flung material, responding to each piece on its own terms.

influences:
◀◀ Herbie Hancock, Bill Evans

Andrew Gilbert

Myra Melford
Born January 5, 1957 in Glencoe, IL.

Myra Melford was raised in the Chicago area. Her early piano training included boogie-woogie lessons from Erwin Helfer. She was also influenced by the Association for the Advancement of Creative Musicians and Muhal Richard Abrams and later studied with pianist Art Lande at Washington's Evergreen State College and with the one-of-a-kind Ran Blake. Moving to New York in 1984, she played in bands led by Joseph Jarman, Leroy Jenkins, Henry Threadgill, and Butch Morris, among others. A pair of trio albums on Enemy jump-started her solo career, and two albums for the Swiss label hat ART brought her critical acclaim. Her most recent affiliation is with Gramavision, which issued the eponymous album of her quintet the Same River, Twice, a name reflecting her interest in fluid structure. Her trio albums may have given an incomplete view of her music, because now she's moving further into free jazz territory, though her music retains structural guideposts and premeditated material. She's part of the generation that's less didactic about its stylistic choices, and the way she straddles composition and improvisation in her work reflects that and gets much of its excitement from the friction between the two methods.

what to buy: *The Same River, Twice* ♪♪♪♪ (Gramavision, 1996, prod. Myra Melford, Dave Douglas) builds on the quintet Melford led on *Even the Sounds Shine*, moving towards greater freedom and flexibility. Trumpeter Dave Douglas is an important voice in that process, and his contributions as a player here in his trademark pungent style are supremely assured. Michael Sarin's pointillistic drumming is a big contrast to Melford's other frequent drummer, Reggie Nicholson; Sarin is more prone to drop in funky beats or, conversely, play outside; he dwells more in the moment, an important approach in music this full of sudden contrasts. Rounding out the group, Chris Speed plays tenor sax and clarinet and, instead of a bassist, there's cellist Erik Friedlander; the higher pitch of his instrument makes him more equal with the horns. Much more than in Melford's trio work, this music is about texture and variable pulse, and its exploratory freedoms are excitingly stimulating.

what to buy next: *Alive in the House of Saints* 🎵🎵🎵🎵 (hat ART, 1993, prod. Arnd Richter, Pia Uehlinger, Werner X. Uehlinger) is Melford's best trio album by a fairly wide margin. Perhaps because she'd played with bassist Lindsey Horner and drummer Reggie Nicholson so much more by the time this was made, or maybe just because it's a live recording, the structures are less rigid and the music breathes more and moves more organically. It's still a format where Melford gets deep in a groove and stays there for the length of the piece, and that strategy brings its own rewards and intensities.

what to avoid: Joined as she is by Han Bennink, *Eleven Ghosts* 🎵🎵 (Hat Ology, 1997, prod. Pia Uehlinger, Werner X. Uehlinger) can't help but be interesting, since there are covers of Leroy Carr's "How Long Blues," Scott Joplin's "Maple Leaf Rag," and the traditional tune "Some Relief," not to mention the unusual context—for Melford on record, at least—of playing only with a drummer. But it's the wrong drummer. Though he's very talented and has done fine work in other contexts, Bennink is more disruptive than responsive, and his shtick quickly wears thin. This is one to get after the rest of Melford's albums have been acquired.

the rest:
Jump 🎵🎵🎵 (Enemy, 1990)
Now & Now 🎵🎵🎵🎵 (Enemy, 1991)
Even the Sounds Shine 🎵🎵🎵🎵 (hat ART, 1995)

worth searching for: *The October Revolution* 🎵🎵🎵🎵 (Evidence, 1996, prod. John F. Szwed, Matthews Szwed), a 1994 concert commemorating the Bill Dixon-organized concert series of the same title 30 years before, includes a seven-and-a-half-minute cut by the Myra Melford Trio that stands out as the only released recording of her Trio with a different drummer than Reggie Nicholson: on this occasion Tom Rainey was hitting the skins. It was also her first recording as a leader of someone else's composition: the Butch Morris tune "The Death of Danny Love." The performance is more expansive than her usual trio work, but more defined than her freer quintet music. Two multiple-artists compilations include otherwise unavailable

performances by Melford. *Live at the Knitting Factory, Volume 2* 🎵🎵🎵🎵 (A&M, 1989, prod. Bob Appel) has the superb and fascinating solo performance "Some Kind of Blues," obviously important in the pianist's discography as an example of her unaccompanied work. Less crucial but also of high quality is a live version of "Changes I," a rollicking track by the Same River, Twice group, on *What Is Jazz? 1996* 🎵🎵🎵🎵 (Knitting Factory Works, 1996, prod. Brett Heinz, Mark Perlson), recorded at the eponymous annual festival of the album title.

influences:

◀◀ Muhal Richard Abrams, Ran Blake, Henry Threadgill, Cecil Taylor

▶▶ Matthew Shipp, Chris Chalfant

Steve Holtje

Gil Melle

Born December 31, 1931, in Riverside, CA.

A name familiar only to a very small number of jazz cognoscenti, Gil Melle is probably known only as the person responsible for introducing Blue Note producer Alfred Lion to the illustrious recording engineer Rudy Van Gelder and for composing the theme music to Rod Serling's television series, *Night Gallery.* In all actuality, Melle is a very accomplished baritone saxophonist and composer who made a small number of albums for Blue Note and Prestige in the mid- to late 1950s which have since become highly-prized collector's items. Melle's approach to the baritone horn is quite different than most. His tone is quite dark, with a deep and almost raspy edge to it. As a composer, Melle was writing music in the 1950s that was in advance of the standard fare with its use of modal harmony and 12-tone techniques. With all his talent, Melle was not a popular commodity during his early years, eventually leading to his move to the West coast where he continues to work as a composer for motion pictures and as an advocate of modern electronic music.

what's available: *Primitive Modern/Quadrama* 🎵🎵🎵🎵 (Prestige, 1956/1957, prod. Bob Weinstock) combine two early dates for Prestige on one CD, with Melle working in a quartet with the lamentably underrated guitarist Joe Cinderella. As cerebral as this music is (the liner notes contain lengthy technical explanations), it also displays a great deal of joy and exuberance. *Gil's Guests* 🎵🎵🎵🎵 (Prestige, 1956, prod. Bob Weinstock) finds Melle adding trumpeter Art Farmer, French horn player Julius Watkins, and reedman Hal McKusick to his standard rhythm section for some colorful orchestrations and inspired solos.

worth searching for: *Patterns in Jazz* ♫♫♫♫ (Blue Note, 1956, prod. Alfred Lion) is only available as a Japanese import, but is well worth tracking down. Guitarist Joe Cinderella and trombonist Eddie Bert share the solo honors with Melle's turn on "The Arab Barber Blues," among his finest recorded work.

Chris Hovan

Misha Mengelberg

Born June 5, 1935, in Kiev, the Ukraine, USSR.

Pianist/composer Misha Mengelberg is one of the pre-eminent figures in post-1950s Dutch jazz/improvised music. Although born in the Ukraine, he moved at an early age to the Netherlands, where his father was a conductor. He studied composition at the Royal Conservatory in The Hague but by the early 1960s he was immersed in jazz activity. In 1964 he, along with drummer Han Bennink and bassist Jacques Schols, backed U.S. reedman Eric Dolphy on his last studio session (*Last Date*). In the mid-1970s he formed the I.C.P. 10tet, followed by the I.C.P. Orchestra, a group that still performs works by Mengelberg and its members, as well as those of Duke Ellington, Thelonious Monk, and Herbie Nichols, all major influences on Mengelberg's piano and composition style. Since the early '80s, he has also led small groups and maintained a parallel career as a composer for orchestras and chamber ensembles. Mengelberg's piano style stems from the percussive lineage of such players as Duke Ellington and Thelonious Monk: spare, dissonant, and effective. He will frequently mix his performances with absurdist touches that derive from an early association with the Fluxus movement. (He once recorded a side of an album in duet with his parrot.) Mengelberg's piano work (especially solo) seems to consist of unrelated noodling scribbles that only seem to make sense when the listener draws back and takes in the entire picture. But, despite this, he is a superb and unique accompanist as his quintet and big-band projects attest. He provides soloists with a solid if unpredictable accompaniment that forces them to make unique choices and avoid clichés.

what to buy: *Who's Bridge* ♫♫♫♫ (Avant, 1994, prod. Misha Mengelberg, John Zorn) is probably Mengelberg's most accessible recording. His piano playing is at its most concise and direct with the focus on 11 superb compositions. The expected influences of Monk and Nichols are present—filtered through Mengelberg's unique sensibility. The two CDs of *I.C.P. Orchestra—Bospaadje Konijnenhol I & II* ♫♫♫♫ (I.C.P., 1986–91, prod. Instant Composers Pool) present a stellar (and surprisingly stable) edition of the I.C.P. Orchestra. Best of all is Mengel-

berg's arrangements of six Duke Ellington standards, including a gorgeous, bluer than blue "Mood Indigo." Along with Roswell Rudd's 1982 *Regeneration* (which featured Mengelberg), *Change of Season* ♫♫♫♫ (Soul Note, 1984, prod. Giovanni Bonandrini) helped spearhead the Nichols revival. The all-Nichols program frequently follows Nichols's own arrangements. While Mengelberg's piano is clearly derived (in part) from Nichols with those jabbing, dissonant left hand chords, ultimately it's Mengelberg's unique character that's all over these tunes.

what to buy next: *Impromptus* ♫♫♫ (F.M.P., 1988, prod. Jost Gebers) is a series of 13 tracks that range from the almost miniature to the epic finale that clocks in at 16 minutes. The general tenor is one of tension and edginess and the music is episodic in nature. At times there seems to be no logic to Mengelberg's keyboard rambles. But when one focuses in on his attention to dynamics, his (seemingly) arrhythmic tonal clusters, and bizarre vocalese (it sounds like he's been studying poetry with Cecil Taylor), it begins to make sense. Structurally, *Mix* ♫♫♫♫ (I.C.P., 1994, prod. I.C.P. Geleudsdragers) is almost the polar opposite of *Impromptus*; the two mixes are each nearly 35 minutes in length. The two explorations are full of edgy freneticism that Mengelberg alleviates at the most unexpected moments. Ideas flow by in a fast, almost unrelenting clip. It's difficult but rewarding listening. On *Dutch Masters* ♫♫♫♫ (Soul Note, 1987, prod. Giovanni Bonandrini), the set consists of two Steve Lacy tunes, two by Monk and two by Mengelberg. "Reef" is a buoyant upbeat piece and "Kneebus" is an unusual (especially for Mengelberg) haunting drone-centered work.

worth searching for: Much of Mengelberg's early pre-'80s work, (especially his duets with drummer Bennink) remains unreleased on CD. But *Driekusman Total Loss* ♫♫♫♫ (Vara Jazz, 1964–66) may be the most valuable candidate for reissue. It's the only extant recording of the early Mengelberg quartet with Bennink, Dolphy-esque alto player Piet Nordijk, and bassist Rob Langreis. Here Mengelberg and Bennink sound much more comfortable than they do on Dolphy's *Last Date*, recorded two months later. The final cut is from 1966; Mengelberg's "Remembering Herbie," dedicated to Herbie Nichols, is one of the earliest tributes to this unsung hero.

influences:

◀◀ Thelonious Monk, Lowell Davidson

▶▶ Myra Melford

Robert Iannapollo

Helen Merrill

Born July 21, 1930, in New York, NY.

Not afraid to stretch and take risks, Helen Merrill stands out among singers, with a voice often described as honey-toned and husky. Merrill began her professional career with the Reggie Childs Band when she was 16. She married clarinetist Aaron Sachs in 1947, and had occasion to sit in with musicians, including Charlie Parker, during the early days of bop. She worked with Earl Hines for a few months in 1952, and recorded on the Roost label in 1953. Signing with Mercury to record on the EmArcy label, she recorded with Johnny Richard's Orchestra early in 1954. In December 1954 Merrill recorded the classic sides with Clifford Brown, and in June 1956 the classic sides with Gil Evans. During 1959 she toured England and Europe extensively, remaining in Italy for four years. She returned to the United States in 1967 to work with Dick Katz, recording two albums on the Milestone label. After touring in Japan, she settled in Tokyo in 1967, where she remained for five years, revered by the Japanese people. During that time she recorded 12 albums for the Japanese Victor label. After spending several months in Hong Kong in 1972, Merrill returned to the United States and settled in Chicago, where she formed a 10-piece band with Kenny Soderblom. In 1987 she reunited with Gil Evans for a recording, and has continued to perform, tour, and record.

what to buy: The four-CD set *The Complete Helen Merrill on Mercury* ♫♫♫♫ (EmArcy/Mercury, 1954–58/1994) contains all of Merrill's EmArcy/Mercury sessions. The first CD opens with Merrill's first recordings, done with the Johnny Richards Orchestra in February 1954. She sings "Alone Together," "Glad to Be Unhappy," and "How's the World Treating You?" In addition, this first disc includes the classic sides with trumpeter Clifford Brown, which were recorded on December 22–23, 1954. Brown's sextet included flutist Danny Banks, pianist Jimmy Jones, and guitarist Barry Galbraith. Bassist Milt Hinton and Osie Johnson accompanied Merrill on the December 22 date, and were replaced by bassist Oscar Pettiford and drummer Bobby Donaldson on the 23rd. With arrangements by Quincy Jones, Brown's warm trumpet sound compliments Merrill's voice to perfection. Tunes from these sessions include "Don't Explain," "Born to Be Blue," "You'd Be So Nice to Come Home To," "What's New?," and "Yesterdays." Disc two includes 12 tunes recorded with Hal Mooney as arranger and conductor, and a rhythm section that included pianist Hank Jones, guitarist Barry Galbraith, bassist Milt Hinton, and drummer Sol Gubin, in addition to strings. Recorded on October 21, 22, and 24, 1955, Merrill sings "Just You, Just Me," "Anything Goes,"

"Comes Love," and "End of a Love Affair," demonstrating her abilities as an outstanding song stylist. This disc concludes with four sides recorded on June 26, 1956 with Gil Evans as arranger and conductor. Members of Evans's orchestra included pianist Hank Jones, guitarist Barry Galbraith, bassist Oscar Pettiford, and drummer Joe Morello, among others. The remaining sides with Gil Evans are included on the third CD. Flawlessly arranged and performed, these 12 recordings include some of Merrill's best work, classics such as "By Myself," "Any Place I Hang My Hat Is Home," "He Was Too Good to Me," "I'm a Fool to Want You," and "I'm Just a Lucky So and So." Also included on the third CD is a session recorded February 21, 1957 with the Hal Mooney Orchestra, pianist Marian McPartland, and bassist Milt Hinton. Merrill performs a sultry rendition of "It's a Lazy Afternoon." The fourth CD commences with a session recorded February 27, 1957 with the Hal Mooney Orchestra that also includes McPartland and Hinton. The box set concludes with a session recorded February 21, 1958, with flutist Bobby Jasper, pianist Bill Evans, guitarist George Russell, bassist Oscar Pettiford, and drummer Jo Jones accompanying Merrill. If you are a fan, this is the definitive collection. *Brownie* ♫♫♫♫ (Verve/Gitanes, 1994, prod. Helen Merrill, Jean-Philippe Allard) is a brilliant and respectful tribute to Clifford Brown. Brown's trumpet solos ("Born to Be Blue," "Don't Explain," and "You'd Be So Nice to Come Home To") from the original 1954 sessions were transcribed by Torrie Zito and executed by the trumpet ensemble, which included Lew Soloff, Roy Hargrove, Tom Harrell, and Wallace Roney. The sessions capture the energy of the original sessions, as well as the extraordinary genius of one of the masters. If you can't spring for the four-CD set, check out some of the same material on *Dream of You* ♫♫♫♫ (EmArcy/Mercury, 1954–56/1992, prod. Bob Shad) which includes Merrill's initial classic recording session with Evans, in addition to her work with Johnny Richards. *Collaboration* ♫♫♫♫ (EmArcy, 1988, prod. Kiyoshi Koyama, Helen Merrill) is a more recent session (1987), reuniting Merrill with Evans and living up to the standard set by their original 1956 recordings. Merrill uses a similar approach to the music, and continues to demonstrate the grace and beauty of her voice against the exciting sound of the Gil Evans Orchestra.

what to buy next: *Duets* ♫♫♫ (EmArcy, 1989, prod. Ron Carter) features Merrill and bassist Ron Carter. The bass and voice form a natural acoustic pairing, with the two musicians interacting with grace and ease. *Just Friends* ♫♫♫ (EmArcy, 1989, prod. Kiyoshi Koyama) spotlights Merrill with Stan Getz. The music is both melodic and innovative, and the session includes some unusual choices of material, such as Cleo Laine and Stanley Meyer's "Cavatina" and Joe Raposo's "It's Not Easy Being Green." *Clear out of this World* 🎵🎵🎵 (Verve, 1992, prod. Jean-Philippe Allard) finds Merrill collaborating on a 1991 studio date with Tom Harrell, Wayne Shorter, Roger Kellaway, Red Mitchell, and Terry Clarke on tunes that personally reflect her individual style. One of the best highlights is her interaction with Red Mitchell on "Some of These Days."

Susan K. Berlowitz

Pat Metheny

Born August 2, 1954 in Lee's Summit, MO.

The multi-faceted Pat Metheny gives "contemporary jazz" a good name. One of the biggest jazz stars of the past two decades, he has generally avoided falling into a routine and has gone off on career tangents few other stars would dare explore with their potential fan-alienating characteristics. No contemporary jazz musician (the category has to do with radio-readiness and has recently been called "smooth jazz") has more artistic credibility. Nor does any current guitarist have a more instantly identifiable sound.

Metheny, whose older brother is trumpeter Mike Metheny, played both French horn and (starting at age 13) guitar while growing up near Kansas City. He attended and taught at Berklee School of Music and the University of Miami and joined Gary Burton's band at age 19. He can be heard on the 1974–76 Burton ECM albums *Ring*, *Dreams So Real*, and *Passengers* and on JVC's 1979 *Reunion*). Metheny also began recording for ECM and soon became a star thanks to tuneful compositions that crossed genre boundaries. Since his third album, he has worked frequently with keyboardist Lyle Mays, who is the only permanent member of the Pat Metheny Group besides Metheny himself. Rather than continuously recycle the sound which made him an international attraction, Metheny has continually challenged himself, playing in all sorts of collaborative contexts regardless of whether they seem to fit his style. In the process he has worked with everyone from British avant-gardist Derek Bailey to folk-rock idol Joni Mitchell. He has also proven himself adept in straight-ahead jazz contexts and has consistently championed the work of free-jazz innovator Ornette Coleman, with whom he recorded an excellent album.

what to buy: *Pat Metheny Group* 🎵🎵🎵🎵 (ECM, 1978, prod. Manfred Eicher) was the album that made Metheny a star when its bright, tuneful instrumentals found their way onto some FM radio rock stations. Though some, focusing on the music's

shiny surface, found it shallow, it stands up to repeated listening very well. It certainly didn't sound like anything else being played at that time in any field of music, combining jazz chops and feeling with an attractive, upbeat folksiness—which is not to say that this is folk music, but Metheny's jangling guitarwork speaks in the cadences of the American heartland. This was also where the PMG gelled into its first classic lineup with keyboardist Lyle Mays and the rhythm team which later formed the group Elements, Mark Egan (sounding somewhat like Jaco Pastorius on fretless electric bass at the leader's request) and drummer Dan Gottlieb. *As Falls Wichita, So Falls Wichita Falls* 🎵🎵🎵🎵 (ECM, 1981, prod. Manfred Eicher) is jointly credited to Metheny and Mays, with only percussionist Nana Vasconcelos joining them. The opening title track, all of side one on the original LP, is a 20-minute sonic landscape of considerable imagination and evocative atmosphere. The bell-like piano feature "Ozark," the lovely Bill Evans dedication "September Fifteenth," the pretty (and very folkish) "It's for You," and a gorgeous version of "Amazing Grace" (retitled "Estupenda Graça") perfectly counterbalance the dark moodiness of the first half of the record. Vasconcelos's wordless vocals (the effect would become a cliché on future Metheny albums, though never when Vasconcelos was involved) and his colorful percussion make him invaluable. It's worth noting that Metheny doubles on electric bass quite effectively.

what to buy next: From his first album on, Metheny has played Ornette Coleman tunes. *Rejoicing* 🎵🎵🎵 (ECM, 1984, prod. Manfred Eicher) is a trio album with former Coleman rhythm-section mates Charlie Haden (bass) and Billy Higgins (drums), and though Metheny's guitar tone on this album is a bit too soft to be ideal for the three Coleman classics he programs, it's an ideal format for him to explore this material in. Well, not quite as ideal as actually playing *with* the composer himself, which is what he does on the co-credited *Song X* 🎵🎵🎵🎵 (Geffen, 1986, prod. Pat Metheny). Ornette and his son Denardo (drums) join Metheny, Haden, and Jack DeJohnette (drums) in a scorching program that deals with Coleman's music in his own current style. This is superb free jazz, and though its intensity and the abrasiveness and dissonance of Coleman's harmolodic approach scared off less adventurous Metheny fans, it's one of the high points of his discography.

what to avoid: *We Live Here* 🎵🎵 (Geffen, 1995, prod. Pat Metheny, Steve Rodby, Lyle Mays) leads off with four tracks of lowest-common-denominator smooth jazz, pseudo-hip "street" beats and all. The following title track has more of an edge and a memorable theme, but can't provide enough redemption. The other three tracks are more of a mixed bag, but still below Metheny's usual standard. Not quite so bad but nearly as dispensable is *Still Life (Talking)* ♫♫ (Geffen, 1986, prod. Pat Metheny, Lyle Mays), where the Brazilian touches that used to be a nice change of pace have been formulized. Many tracks are sleep-inducing, and the two best tunes, the excellent "Last Train Home" and the so-so "Third Wind," are heard in livelier versions on the concert album *The Road to You*. Another snorefest is *Secret Story* ♫♫ (Geffen, 1992, prod. Pat Metheny), thanks to overblown arrangements (complete with orchestra) mixed with etiolated world music.

the rest:

Bright Size Life ♫♫♫♫ (ECM, 1976)
Watercolors ♫♫♫ (ECM, 1977)
New Chautauqua ♫♫♫♫ (ECM, 1979)
American Garage ♫♫♫♫ (ECM, 1979)
80/81 ♫♫♫♫ (ECM, 1980)
Offramp ♫♫♫♫ (ECM, 1982)
Travels ♫♫♫♫ (ECM, 1983)
First Circle ♫♫♫♫ (ECM, 1984)
Works ♫♫♫ (ECM, 1985)
Works 2 ♫♫♫ (ECM, 1989)
The Falcon and the Snowman (Soundtrack) ♫♫♫ (EMI, 1985)
Letter from Home ♫♫♫ (Geffen, 1989)
(With Dave Holland and Roy Haynes) *Question and Answer* ♫♫♫♫ (Geffen, 1990)
The Road to You ♫♫♫♫ (Geffen, 1993)
Quartet ♫♫♫ (Geffen, 1996)
Imaginary Day ♫♫♫♫ (Warner Bros., 1997)
(With Derek Bailey, Gregg Bendian, and Paul Wertico) *The Sign of Four* ♫♫♫♫ (Knitting Factory, 1997)

worth searching for: Metheny has regularly varied the settings he's played in, but *Zero Tolerance for Silence* ♫♫♫♫ (Geffen, 1994, prod. Pat Metheny) came as a shock to everyone. It's one of his boldest forays outside the boundaries of contemporary jazz, a solo album that Geffen would only agree to issue as a limited edition (now out of print). Metheny overdubs blasts of free improvisation equally influenced by free jazz (for instance, Sonny Sharrock) and alternative rock (Sonic Youth, Nirvana). The 18-minute "Part 1" is far more intense than his usual style, though some may find it unlistenable, it's not unmusical, built on equal parts repetition and the sonic qualities of an over-amped electric guitar. It's followed by four shorter pieces. "Part 2"'s Ayler-esque melodicism is followed by a bluesy overlaying of riffs; "Part 3" is practically all melody, but full of odd leaps that only slowly slide into tune. "Part 4" minimalistically develops a Blues-Rock riff, skewing it beyond recognition while re-

PAT METHENY
(WITH JOSHUA REDMAN)

song "Whittlin'"
album *Wish*
(Warner Bros., 1993)
instrument Guitar

Monster Solo

calling the structure of Frippertronics; "Part 5" has a touch of acoustic guitar under a fuzzy melody that recalls Captain Beefheart's solo guitar pieces with a middle section in a manic Flamenco style. The overall result is rudely hypnotic. Co-credited to bassist Jaco Pastorius, Metheny, drummer Bruce Ditmas, and pianist Paul Bley, *Jaco* (Improvising Artists, 1976, prod. Paul Bley) was issued by Bley on his label. This 1974 session is strongly influenced by *Bitches Brew*–era electric Miles Davis, alternating lengthy voodoo-chasing excursions and pithy miniatures. Bley's switch to electric piano finds his trademark angularity fitting well with Jaco's throbbing strums, Pat's coiled solos, and Ditmas's shifting pulses. Just 19 years old and still evolving, Metheny sounds like John McLaughlin, but already displays the fluidity he later refined into his more familiar style. Some of Metheny's recent collaborations with other artists are also significant items in his discography. *I Can See Your House from Here* (Blue Note) was made with fellow six-stringer John Scofield, with Steve Swallow on electric and acoustic bass guitar and Bill Stewart on drums. Metheny's customary warm, lyri-

Pat Metheny (© Jack Vartoogian)

cal tone on hollowbody electric and guitar synth (and even acoustic guitar) and his tuneful compositions are equal partners with Scofield's edgy tone and elliptical lines (songwriting credits are split 6-5 in Sco's favor–it's his label, of course). Each accommodates his style to the music of the other, making this a coherent and fascinating project, full of subtle touches. On the bassist's label, the Charlie Haden & Pat Metheny duo album *Beyond the Missouri Sky (Short Stories)* 🎵🎵🎵🎵 (Verve, 1997, prod. Charlie Haden, Pat Metheny) finds Metheny focusing on acoustic guitar. The overall mood is gentle and reflective. Besides fine originals penned separately by Haden and Metheny, there are some very interesting cover choices: pop songwriter Jimmy Webb's "The Moon Is a Harsh Mistress," country legend Roy Acuff's "The Precious Jewel," the traditional tune "He's Gone Away," Johnny Mandel's "The Moon Song," and—most memorably of all of them—two themes by Andrea and Ennio Morricone from the movie *Cinema Paradiso* that perfectly encapsulate the sentimentality (in the best sense) of this collaboration.

influences:

◀◀ Jim Hall, Jimmy Raney, Wes Montgomery, Sonny Sharrock, John McLaughlin, Ornette Coleman

▶▶ John Abercrombie, Bill Frisell, Chieli Minucci

Steve Holtje

Hendrik Meurkens

Born 1957, in Hamburg, Germany.

If any harmonica player has the mettle to match the talents of Toots Thielemans, the acknowledged modern master of the instrument, it's Hendrik Meurkens. Born in Germany to Dutch parents, Meurkens's first instrument was vibraphone, which he mastered in his mid-teens. Hearing Toots Thielemans play, Meurkens was inspired to teach himself to play chromatic harmonica at age 19. In 1977, Meurkens came to the U.S. to pursue jazz studies for three years at Boston's Berklee College of Music. Meurkens became absorbed with native Brazilian music while living in Brazil in the early 1980s, and further developed his skills as musician-composer. Back in Germany during the late 1980s, he composed and arranged music for films and television, and recorded with the Danish Radio Orchestra. Meurkens returned to Brazil in 1989 and recorded his first European-released album there as leader. In 1991, Meurkens was signed by Concord and has made a series of recordings for the label. While the diatonic harmonica is used mostly by blues players, Hendrik Meurkens has smoothly mastered connecting notes on the chromatic harmonica. The instrument lends itself well to the samba-jazz themes on his albums. He fronts his bands as a horn player would, playing so skillfully smooth and fleeting on the instrument that it sounds much like the bandoneon (an Argentinian type of accordion that uses buttons instead of keys).

what to buy: How many different ways can a jazz musician interpret the warhorse tune, "Body and Soul"? On *A View from Manhattan* 🎵🎵🎵🎵 (Concord, 1993, prod. Hendrik Meurkens, Allen Farnham), harmonica player Meurkens does it inventively as a bossa. Capturing a New York jazz sound and mixing it with light Brazilian themes, the German-born Dutchman executes a challenging performance for his third Concord release, mixing it up with sidemen Dick Oatts (saxes, flute), Jay Ashby (trombone), Claudio Roditi (trumpet on his original, "The Monster and The Flower"), Mark Soskin (piano), Harvie Swartz and Leo Traversa (bass), Portinho (drums, percussion), and Carl Allen (drums). After recording sessions around the globe, Meurkens moved to New York in 1992 and this album was recorded there in 1993. The ease with which Meurkens masters a chromatic harmonica is evident in the fluidity of his lines and phrasing. Nice easy rhythms and pleasant solos from his cohorts make *A View from Manhattan* an enjoyable, mostly straight-ahead, listen. Meurkens, a master of the difficult-to-play chromatic harmonica, also plays vibes on *October Colors* 🎵🎵🎵🎵 (Concord, 1995, prod. Hendrik Meurkens), his fifth Concord album. With his cohesive New York–based team, the Sambajazz Quartet, he generates warm, kaleidoscopic excitement with Portinho, one of the best Brazilian drummers in the U.S., and native Brazilians Rogério Botter Maio (electric bass) and Helio Alves (piano). In addition to adroit harmonica technique, Meurkens showcases his talents as composer (five of the 10 tunes are originals), and plays vibraphone equally well on four tracks, including a mellifluous duo with pianist Alves. The title track, "October Colors," is a spirited, romping original that establishes the team's direction and ability to blend jazz with Brazilian beats.

With liberal doses of jazz, Meurkens enhances "Chorinho No. 1," a modernized *chôro* (a musical form developed in Brazil from the late 1800s). Maio's "Tranchan" (translation: "hipness") contains samba characteristics merged with sophisticated chord structures that give it vigor. There are no dull moments on his outing. Meurkens's Sambajazz Quartet creates moods ranging from joyous to dreamy. This is an exceptional listen with great appeal for Brazilian jazz fans.

what to buy next: On *Sambahia* 🎵🎵🎵🎵 (Concord Picante, 1991, prod. Hendrik Meurkens), Meurkens explores a swinging blend of Brazilian jazz and bebop, recorded in 1990 while on tour in Europe with his band, Samba Importado. Meurkens plays harmonica and vibes with equal warmth, intensity, and vitality. His eloquent style on both instruments flows expressively with support from Paquito D'Rivera (alto saxophone, clarinet), Claudio Roditi (trumpet, flugelhorn), Tim Armacost (tenor saxophone), Lito Tabora (piano), Jacaré (bass), Cesar Machado (drums), and Reginaldo Vargas (percussion). The soloists, supported by a great rhythm section, are all extremely talented and versatile and are given ample time to develop their improv ideas. D'Rivera and Roditi are brilliant veteran players who have recorded numerous albums as leaders. Armacost, Vargas, Jacaré, and Tabora are each exquisite in their specialty areas and contribute largely to the success of this session. All but three of the 10 tunes are Meurkens's original compositions. "Two Four Blues" (a samba in 2/4 time) and the title tune are spirited sambas showcasing Meurkens's success with the samba-jazz meld. "A Ilha," originally a bolero, is altered into an easy groove by Jacaré, and features Roditi's mellifluous flugelhorn. D'Rivera is featured in a Parker-like alto solo on Meurkens's arrangement of "Toby's Tune" and then trades fours with Meurkens to demonstrate the latter's notion that similarities of sound exist between alto and harmonica. "Minha Saudade" features Meurkens on a sublime vibraphone solo, with Armacost showing his brilliance on tenor sax. The easy rhythms on this enticing album invite you to sit back, listen, and sip a sangria.

the rest:
Clear of Clouds 🎵🎵🎵🎵 (Concord, 1992)
Slidin' 🎵🎵🎵🎵 (Concord, 1994)
Poema Brasileiro 🎵🎵🎵🎵 (Concord, 1996)

influences:

◀◀ Toots Thielemans, Manfredo Fest, Claudio Roditi

Nancy Ann Lee

Mezz Mezzrow

Born Milton Mezzrow, November 9, 1898, in Chicago, IL. Died August 5, 1972, in Paris, France.

Though never a great jazz musician, Mezz Mezzrow made large contributions to the music by recording a number of classic sessions with soprano saxophone giant Sidney Bechet. Mezzrow's clarinet and tenor sax work was effective on the blues, but he was more important as a cultural figure who defined the perspective and image of the white hipster with his fascinating, opinionated autobiography *Really the Blues*. In many ways he was the prototype for Norman Mailer's "white Negro," though Mezzrow was a loud and self-proclaimed champion of black culture and civil rights. He grew up as part of the Chicago scene with Eddie Condon, Pee Wee Russell, and Bix Beiderbecke, and he remained a passionate partisan of Chicago and New Orleans classic jazz throughout his life. During the late '20s he recorded with Condon, the Jungle Kings, and the Chicago Rhythm Kings, more often on tenor than clarinet. But his reputation among musicians spread more through the high-grade marijuana he sold than his musical prowess. In the mid-'30s he led a number of all-star sessions with integrated bands featuring such swing stars as Benny Carter and Teddy Wilson. Through the support of French jazz critic Hughes Panassie, Mezzrow recorded a brilliant session in 1938 with trumpeter Tommy Ladnier and Bechet that culminated with a classic recording of "Really the Blues." From 1945–47 he led his own record label, King Jazz, which produced some of Bechet's most memorable recordings. Mezzrow moved to France after his triumphant appearance at the 1948 Nice jazz festival. He recorded and toured regularly from 1951–55 with bands featuring Buck Clayton, Jimmy Archey, Gene Sedric, and Lee Collins, and made his last session in 1959. The entire output of Mezzrow's King Jazz label has been reissued on CD.

what to buy: All of Mezz Mezzrow's King Jazz recordings have been reissued in a five-disc set by Storyville, but not in chronological order. *King Jazz Story Volume 2: Really the Blues* (Storyville, 1945–47, prod. Mezz Mezzrow) ✍✍✍✍ features 14 tracks by Mezzrow and Sidney Bechet blowing the blues with a quintet. Bechet dominates the proceedings, playing with ferocious power. Five tracks feature a septet where trumpeter Hot Lips Page gives Bechet some competition, and three solo tracks by pianist Sammy Price round off the album. Though Bechet was far more open-minded about what constituted "real jazz" than Mezzrow, the King Jazz sessions capture the soprano sax master in particularly fine form, despite the material's lack of variety.

what to buy next: Mezzrow wasn't the most imaginative producer, and the music on *King Jazz Story, Volume 1: Out of the Gallion* ✍✍✍ (Storyville, 1945–47, prod. Mezz Mezzrow) reflects his narrow conception of jazz. But with four tracks from a torrid septet session with soprano saxophonist Sidney Bechet and trumpeter Hot Lips Page and 15 tracks of Mezzrow's and Bechet's quintet, there is no shortage of inspired improvisation. High points include "The Sheik of Araby," "Perdido Street Stomp," and an extended version of "The Blues and Freud." Pianist Sammy Price is also featured on three solo tracks.

best of the rest:

King Jazz Story Volume 3: Gone away Blues ✍✍✍ (Storyville, 1945–47)
King Jazz Story Volume 4: Revolutionary Blues ✍✍✍ (Storyville, 1945–47)

influences:

◀◀ Sidney Bechet, Johnny Dodds, Leon Roppolo

Andrew Gilbert

Ron Miles

Born 1963, in Indianapolis, IN.

Trumpeter Ron Miles, who has worked with Bill Frisell since 1994 and was a member of the Ellington Orchestra in the early 1990s, has impeccable educational credentials. At age 10, he started playing trumpet. He studied music at the University of Denver in the early 1970s, then graduated from the Manhattan School of Music in 1986. He returned to DU for his postgraduate degree, then started teaching. In 1992, while in Italy with the show *Sophisticated Ladies,* he attracted the ears of Mercer Ellington and became a member of the Ellington Orchestra. In addition to his work with Frisell, he has played with ex–Cream drummer Ginger Baker's Mile High Polo Club.

what to buy: *My Cruel Heart* ✍✍✍ (Gramavision, 1996, prod. Mark Fuller, Ron Miles), Miles's third recording, brought him to the attention of a wider audience. From grooves that recall mid-1970s Miles Davis to hip-hop rhythms to a modern hard bop to hard blues, the players are all top-notch and adjust to different musical situations with ease.

what to buy next: *Woman's Day* ✍✍✍ (Gramavision, 1997, prod. Hans Wendl) features Frisell prominently and creates a less intense and more reflective Miles as composer. The music is both haunting and surreal. As on the previous recording, the rhythm section of bassist Artie Moore and drummer Rudy Royston shine brightly.

the rest:
Distance for Safety 🎵🎵🎵 (Prolific, 1986)
Witness 🎵🎵🎵 (Capri, 1986)

influences:
◀◀ Bill Frisell, Mercer Ellington, Miles Davis
▶▶ Buckshot LeFonque, Gang Starr

David C. Gross

Bobby Militello

Born March 25, 1950, in Buffalo, NY.

Any alto saxophone player working with Dave Brubeck has the ghost of Paul Desmond to contend with; Bobby Militello copes well with that by playing Desmond's role without slavishly copying the late genius. Left to his own devices, Militello works closer to the '50s funk line of Lou Donaldson on alto and David Newman on tenor. He appeared at the Montreaux Jazz Festival in 1977 as part of the CBS All-Stars and has performed live and recorded with Brubeck, Maynard Ferguson, Bill Holman, Bob Florence, and Ken Navarro, almost typecasting himself as a big-band section player until Brubeck hired him. Since 1983, Militello has continued to work intermittently with Brubeck (including his prominent role in Brubeck's recording of *To Hope: A Celebration—A Mass in the Revised Roman Ritual*), in addition to recording his own material and working a busy freelance schedule from his base in Buffalo, New York, where he also owns a concert venue.

what to buy: *Straight Ahead* 🎵🎵🎵🎵 (Positive Music, 1995, prod. Bobby Militello, Bobby Jones) proves that Militello is a solid player who deserves to be better known than he is. His work with keyboardist Bobby Jones, with whom Militello has made three albums, can be especially rewarding, as this release bears out. Jones is a good pianist but seems most at home on organ, which makes this sextet date a throwback to the '60s organ-group grooves. Trumpeter Jeff Jarvis is a steady presence on the front line with Militello and longtime associate Bob Leatherbarrow keeps the pulse moving from his drum kit. Both Jones and Leatherbarrow contribute material to the session with Jones's "Que Bonito" featuring Militello's fine flute playing and Leatherbarrow's "Flip Flop" providing the tenor player with some rapid fire post-bop moments next to Jones's inventive work on the Hammond B-3.

what to buy next: . . . *heart & soul* 🎵🎵🎵 (Positive Music, 1993, prod. Bobby Militello, Bobby Jones), featuring a stripped-to-the-bone organ trio, is a great deal of retro-fun, with Militello

and Jones alternating leads and drummer Leatherbarrow locking the time in. The exposed setting shows off Militello's skills as a funky, bop inflected reed player. Cover tunes include chestnuts like "Body and Soul," a hopping "Graduation Day," and Horace Silver's "Love Vibrations" (which features an adequate vocal from Militello). All of the musicians on the date contribute songs, with Militello's "Blues for Which Bob" turning into a blowing session and Jones's "Metro Funk" providing the music for an upscale barbecue pit.

the rest:
Easy to Love 🎵🎵🎵 (Positive Music, 1994)

influences:
◀◀ Dave Brubeck, Paul Desmond, Maynard Ferguson
▶▶ Joshua Redman

Garaud MacTaggart

Glenn Miller

Born March 1, 1904, in Clarinda, IA. Reported missing December 15, 1944, on a flight from England to France.

For many people Glenn Miller's name is synonymous with the Big Band/Swing era. While he was never more than a mediocre trombonist, as an arranger he developed perhaps the most distinctive of all the big-band sounds and his band, someone has said, provided the soundtrack for a generation.

Miller grew up poor, in Iowa, Nebraska, and Colorado. There were no musicians in his family and he connected with the trombone only when he found an old one in the basement of a butcher's shop where he was working as an errand boy. The butcher gave him his first lessons. By 1916 he was playing in the Grant City (Missouri) Town Band. After leaving high school he joined a now-unknown band in Laramie, Wyoming, and when it broke up after a year, Miller entered the University of Colorado, where he continued playing and took up arranging. After only two college years he joined the Ben Pollack Orchestra in California, then returned with Pollack to his base in New York and stayed with him until 1928 (Benny Goodman was a fellow band member). In September 1926 Pollack made the first known recordings using Miller's arrangements ("When I First Met Mary" and "'Deed I Do"). As a freelancer in New York he worked as an arranger, played on many studio recordings (including nearly 100 with the Dorsey Brothers Orchestra, for whom he provided at least half the arrangements), was in the pit for several Broadway shows, and on the side studied arranging with Dr. Joseph Schillinger. In 1935 he helped organize

and wrote arrangements for the first American band organized by Ray Noble, and it was during his stint with Noble that he wrote what later became his theme song, "Moonlight Serenade." In 1936 he became an arranger for the famous Glen Gray's Casa Loma Band.

In January of 1937 Miller formed his own band, and in 1938, after a short hiatus, the re-organized band slowly but surely became increasingly popular. At its peak it was one of the highest-paid bands in the nation, with an instantly recognizable sound that sold millions of recordings. The band had a wonderful way with finely arranged ballads, but his biggest hits were instrumental riff tunes such as "Little Brown Jug" (Miller's first swing hit), "In the Mood," "Tuxedo Junction," and "Pennsylvania 6-5000." The Miller arrangements (including many by Jerry Gray, Bill Finegan, and Billy May) were the basic strength of the band, but good soloists were not lacking. Bobby Hackett was the featured trumpet soloist on many of Miller's best-known jazz charts, most famously on "String of Pearls." Tex Beneke handled most of the tenor sax jazz solos (Al Klink, a better soloist, was kept somewhat in the background), and though he was far from being in a class with Hawkins or Webster (or even Klink), Beneke was enormously popular with the band's audiences, probably for his vocals. Miller and the band were featured in two major films, *Sun Valley Serenade* and *Orchestra Wives*.

In mid-1942 Miller volunteered for service in the army, where he put together an all-star service personnel band that first toured the United States on recruiting drives and then, in 1944, was posted to England. On December 15 he was flying ahead of his band to a session in Paris, when his small plane disappeared; a year later he was declared dead. Hollywood honored him with a posthumously released film, *The Glenn Miller Story* in 1953. A Miller "ghost band," currently fronted by Jack O'Brien, is still on the road playing his arrangements, as are other bands around the world; there are recurrent Glenn Miller festivals; music scholarships have been established in his name; and Miller, though gone at age 40, is anything but forgotten.

what to buy: *Glenn Miller: A Memorial* 𝄽𝄽𝄽𝄽 (Bluebird, 1992, prod. Steve Backer) gives an excellent overview of the band's offerings between 1939 and 1942 (and includes one track by the Miller Army Air Force Band), with a good mixture of the band's sweet and swing styles. Almost all of the big hits are here, plus some lesser known but equally engaging arrangements, such as "Song of the Volga Boatmen," "Anvil Chorus," and "Kalamazoo." The ballad style is represented in "Stairway to the Stars," "Sunrise Serenade," "Star Dust," and "Danny Boy." This CD is a re-release of an album from 1969 that sold more than a million copies in its LP format. *The Spirit Is Willing (1939–42)* 𝄽𝄽𝄽𝄽 (Bluebird, 1995, prod. Orrin Keepnews) is a different and welcome take on the Miller band, focusing on "its substantial jazz content," limited to instrumentals, and avoiding the Miller favorites included everywhere else. Some of the early efforts are "King Porter Stomp," "Rug Cutter's Swing" (by Fletcher Henderson's brother Horace), and "Bugle Call Rag, " while the band's later style is reflected in "I Dreamt I Dwelt in Harlem," "Boulder Buff," and "Caribbean Clipper." Billy May's conception of "Take the 'A' Train" as a ballad will surprise you.

what to buy next: For avid fans who want quantity as well as quality, there is *Glenn Miller: The Popular Recordings 1938–1942* 𝄽𝄽𝄽 (Bluebird, 1989), a three-disc set that includes all your favorite Miller recordings and many more treats as well. Miller fans with an historical bent ought to consider *Glenn Miller: The Lost Recordings* 𝄽𝄽𝄽𝄽 (RCA, 1995, prod. Alan Dell), which contains 45 tracks on two discs and contains performances by Miller's Air Force band intended for broadcast to a German audience (to undermine their will to fight). This band maintained and in some ways surpassed the high standards of the civilian band (Miller's civilian band never had the likes of Mel Powell on piano, for example), and the sound quality is excellent (recorded in the famous Abbey Road studios in London).

what to avoid: *In the Digital Mood* 𝄽𝄽 (GRP, 1983, prod. Dave Grusin) presents fairly recent re-recordings of the most popular Miller arrangements by anonymous studio musicians. They are certainly competent, but unless you have a passion for the latest in digital recording technology you're better off with reissues of the original work.

best of the rest:
Pure Gold 𝄽𝄽𝄽𝄽 (Bluebird, 1988)
Classic Glenn Miller: Original Live Recordings 𝄽𝄽𝄽 (Pair, 1989)
The Collector Edition: Glenn Miller 𝄽𝄽𝄽𝄽 (LaserLight, 1991)
Chattanooga Choo Choo: The Number One Hits 𝄽𝄽𝄽𝄽 (Bluebird, 1991)
A Legendary Performer 𝄽𝄽𝄽𝄽 (Bluebird, 1991)
Best of the Big Bands: Evolution of a Band 𝄽𝄽𝄽𝄽 (Columbia/Legacy, 1992)

Glenn Miller **(AP/Wide World Photos)**

Jim Lester

Lucky Millinder

Born Lucius Venable Millinder, August 8, 1900, in Anniston, AL. Died September 28, 1966, in New York, NY.

Lucky Millinder began his career as a tap dancer in Chicago, before becoming a non-playing bandleader. His dancing background and acrobatic showmanship contributed to his vigorous conducting style. After leading an orchestra in France, he assumed the leadership of a major New York swing band, Mills Blue Rhythm Band, in 1934. Originally used by Irving Mills as a substitute group for the Ellington and Calloway bands, the Blue Rhythm Band had already developed its own charging, joyous identity under the direction of Baron Lee. The Blue Rhythm Band broke up in 1938 and Millinder declared bankruptcy. After working with Bill Doggett, Millinder formed a new band under his own name in 1940. The best years for Millinder band came during the early '40s when the band became an incubator for both bop and rhythm and blues. Dizzy Gillespie provided the signs of the bop to come, while the band's blues-based drive pointed to R&B, with such future stars as Sister Rosetta Tharpe and Wynonie Harris as featured vocalists at different stages, pianist/organist Bill Doggett, and tenor saxophonist Sam "The Man" Taylor. Millinder broke up his band in 1952, later working as a liquor salesman and disc jockey.

what to buy: An excellent introduction to the full spectrum of the Millinder band's history is *Back Beats* 🎵🎵🎵🎵 (Pearl, 1996, prod. Tony Watts, Colin Brown). Its 24 tracks range from the classic swing of "Ride, Red, Ride," a 1935 feature for trumpeter Red Allen when Millinder led the Mills Blue Rhythm Band, to the proto-bop of Dizzy Gillespie's solo on "Little John Special." Also included are the band's hits, "I Want a Tall Skinny Papa," sung by Rosetta Tharpe, and "Who Threw the Whiskey in the Well," featuring blues shouter Wynonie Harris.

what to buy next: The various periods of Millinder's career are available in greater detail. For the complete recordings of Millinder's own band in its greatest period, there is *Lucky Millinder 1941–1942* 🎵🎵🎵🎵 (Jazz Chronological Classics, 1993, prod. various). *Ram Bunk Shush* 🎵🎵🎵🎵 (Charly, 1992, prod. various) provides a view of the later band as it moved towards rhythm and blues, with Wynonie Harris, Bill Doggett and Sam "The Man" Taylor prominent.

worth searching for: For swing enthusiasts who want more than the taste provided by the compilation, Millinder's best years with the Mills Blue Rhythm Band are available on *Mills Blue Rhythm Band 1934–1936* 🎵🎵🎵🎵 (Jazz Classics, 1993, prod. various), with tight ensembles and plenty of spots for distin-

guished soloists that include Red Allen, clarinetist Buster Bailey, and trombonist J.C. Higginbotham.

influences:

◀◀ Don Redman, Duke Ellington, Cab Calloway, Count Basie

▶▶ Dizzy Gillespie, Joe Morris

Stuart Broomer

Charles Mingus

Born April 22, 1922, in Nogales, AZ. Died January 5, 1979, in Cuernavaca, MX.

The great bassists working in Mingus's time—Jimmy Blanton, John Kirby, and Oscar Pettiford—all broke ground for bassist Charles Mingus from a performance standpoint. But Mingus's composition skills gave him the edge over his predecessors on the instrument. Even his contemporary, Oscar Pettiford (b. 1922), who wrote classics such as "Tricotism" and "Bohemia After Dark" never made the impact on modern jazz that Mingus did with songs such as "Goodbye Pork-Pie Hat," "Haitian Fight Song," "Jump Monk," and "Better Git It in Your Soul."

Mingus was born into a military family and raised in the Watts district of Los Angeles. In school, he learned to play a variety of instruments including piano, trombone, cello, and bass, finally settling on the latter as his musical weapon of choice in high school. His teachers later included Lloyd Reese for composition, and Red Callender and Herman Rheinshagen (principal bassist of the New York Philharmonic) for technique. Mingus moved to San Francisco and throughout the 1940s and 1950s, he played with jazz legends Louis Armstrong and Barney Bigard. He further enhanced his experience as a sideman with stints in bands led by Lionel Hampton, Red Norvo, Art Tatum, Charlie Parker, and Stan Getz before forming his record label, Debut, in partnership with drummer Max Roach from 1952–1957. By then, he had settled in New York City.

As his activities as composer increased, he formed his Jazz Workshop in 1955, a repertory company and teaching mechanism in which he worked with groups ranging from four to 11 musicians, and shaped performances with verbal cues. He also formed his own publishing company to handle royalties generated from record sales and performances of his works. Throughout the 1950s, Mingus experimented in his Jazz Workshop with extended European-influenced scores, some of which later appeared on a Mercury 1960 release entitled *Pre-Bird* (reissued as *Mingus Revisited*), and on the 1954 release, *Jazzical Moods*. These bands included performers such as future producer Teo Macero, trumpeters Clark Terry, Marcus Belgrave, and Ted Curson; reed players Eric Dolphy, Yusef Lateef, John Handy, Rahsaan Roland Kirk, and Booker Ervin; trombonist Jimmy Knepper; pianist Jaki Byard; and drummer Dannie Richmond, who worked with Mingus for more than 20 years. Many of these musicians played large, continuing roles in the different ensembles Mingus formed throughout the late 1950s and early 1960s, and some of the alumni of the Jazz Workshop sessions continued to perform Mingus's music after his death, becoming the core of the Mingus Dynasty Band (1979–1991) and the Mingus Big Band (1991–present).

The 1950s through the 1960s were probably the most fertile times for Mingus, from both compositional and performance standpoints. Mingus started creating space for fervent gospel shouts and free-jazz elements in his writing, drawing inspiration from socio-political topics, Afro-Latin and Afro-centric themes, and giving a cutting edge vitality to many of his band's performances during this time. Many of his most prominent compositions were created during this time, including "Fables of Faubus," "Goodbye Pork Pie Hat," "Orange Was the Color of Her Dress," and more. The sheer diversity of music that Mingus and his minions recorded during this time is amply documented on albums for the Debut, Candid, Columbia, Impulse!, and RCA labels. Mingus didn't ignore the basic tenets of form learned from his predecessors even as he made room for the future. Instead, he allowed his bandmates to succeed or fail on the merits of their playing within his musical outlines, pushing them with a fierce energy to excel and perform beyond their previous capabilities. These were the days when his sidemen could be fired and rehired or replaced in mid-gig, depending on their leader's wants, needs, and moods. Songs would be started and, if Mingus wasn't pleased with the way they were proceeding, he would stop the band, hectoring them back to the beginning until they made music the way he wanted it. Those who stayed the course for extended periods of time, like Dannie Richmond, Eric Dolphy, Horace Parlan, and Jaki Byard, were challenged to play at their peaks and responded well to their mercurial titan of an employer.

The mid- to late 1960s found Mingus burned out, broke, and temporarily retired from music, but he jumped back into the creative fray in June 1969 and in 1971 was granted a Guggenheim fellowship in composition. That same year, Mingus had his stream-of-consciousness "autobiography," *Beneath the Underdog*, published. Filled with reality and myth, this book was as much about the author's thought processes as it was about the physical details of his life to that point. The tome dropped

CHARLES MINGUS

song "What Love?"
album *Mingus at Antibes*
(Atlantic, 1960/1986)
instrument Bass

names like Fats Navarro, Illinois Jacquet, Duke Ellington, and Count Basie with an easy familiarity even as Mingus peppered his dialogue with the profanity of a gutter philosopher, railing against racism and recounting tales of sexual prowess with equal facility. During the 1970s, he also churned out some fine music with a whole new set of musical collaborators, including trumpeter Jack Walrath, pianist Don Pullen, and saxophonists Ricky Ford and George Adams.

Mingus was diagnosed with amyotrophic lateral sclerosis (Lou Gehrig's disease) in 1977, but he managed to continue composing music with the aid of his wife, Susan, and a friend, Paul Jeffrey, while much of the credit for arranging and orchestrating Mingus's last works belongs to Walrath. Mingus's last recording session in 1978 found him supervising the players from a wheelchair.

Mingus recorded over 100 albums and wrote over 300 scores. After his death in 1979, the National Endowment for the Arts provided grants for a Mingus foundation called Let My Children

Hear Music, which enabled the foundation to catalog all of Mingus's works and present the microfilms to the New York Public Library for research and study purposes. Mingus's masterwork, "Epitaph," a composition of over 500 pages and more than 4,000 measures taking two hours to perform, was discovered during the cataloging process. A Ford Foundation grant helped prepare the score and thirty instrumental parts over five months. The piece was premiered by a 30-piece orchestra conducted by Gunther Schuller at Alice Tully Hall on June 3, 1989, 10 years after Mingus's death.

what to buy: For anyone looking for an introduction to the work of Charles Mingus, *Thirteen Pictures: The Charles Mingus Anthology* ♪♪♪♪ (Rhino, 1993, prod. various) is the place to start. This two-CD set manages to give an abridged version of Mingus's career by hitting some, but definitely not all, of the highlights. Any quibbles longtime fans might have about certain songs being included or not included should be abrogated by the album's success as a primer on the great bassist/composer for the novice listener. It covers material from the Atlantic, Debut, Columbia, Impulse!, and Mercury years with remarkable fairness, even including a performance from the classic album *Money Jungle*, featuring Mingus and drummer Max Roach playing sidemen to Duke Ellington. *Passions of a Man: The Complete Early Atlantic Recordings* ♪♪♪♪ (Atlantic/Rhino, 1997, prod. Nesuhi Ertegun, Ilhan Mimaroglu), a six-CD box set, is an impressive case of the whole being greater than the sum of its parts. It collects material released on six albums and combines them with four previously unreleased alternate takes from the sessions for *The Clown*. Also included is a 1961 interview with Mingus done by Neshui Ertegun that fills up the sixth disc in the set. There are important performances here by Jackie McLean, Booker Ervin, Eric Dolphy, and Rahsaan Roland Kirk to name only a few. Don't confuse this with the impressive three-LP set (now out of print) that was released in 1979 under almost the same title. While that was a wonderful greatest hits set, this CD box set supersedes that by right of its sheer volume. *Mingus Ah Um* ♪♪♪♪ (Columbia, 1960/1990, prod. Teo Macero) is probably the single most accessible album by Mingus, and it includes classic compositions that the bassist would return to many times over the ensuing years. "Goodbye Pork-Pie Hat" (Mingus's tribute to Lester Young) may be his most enduring ballad, having been covered by scads of jazz and pop music artists, but songs like "Fables of Faubus,"

Charles Mingus (© Jack Vartoogian)

"Open Letter to Duke," and "Better Git It in Your Soul" are, in their own ways, just as masterful. The players include saxophonists Booker Ervin, John Handy, Shafi Hadi, trombonists Jimmy Knepper, and Willie Dennis with the impeccable rhythm section of Horace Parlan on piano, Dannie Richmond on drums, and Mingus on bass. *Charles Mingus Presents Charles Mingus* ♪♪♪♪ (Candid, 1961/1988, prod. Nat Hentoff) is the nuclear meltdown of Mingus albums. The leader gave the studio a nightclub ambiance for the session but deleted all the distractions (like cash registers and applause) that often annoyed him in a real life situation. Mingus and the rest of his pianoless quartet (Eric Dolphy on alto saxophone and bass clarinet, trumpeter Ted Curson, and Dannie Richmond on drums) tore into their four-song set with a ferocious energy. The almost telepathic interplay between Dolphy and Curson is worth the price of admission alone on "Folk Forms, No. 1" and Mingus's unique style of song/speech invests the racial politics of "Original Faubus Fables" with a fire lacking in the instrumental version heard on *Mingus Ah Um*.

what to buy next: Mingus's mid-1960s tours of Europe achieved legendary status, especially with the group featured on the two-CD set, *Revenge: The Legendary Paris Concerts* ♪♪♪♪ (Revenge, 1996) (re-mastered by Gene Paul). Along with Mingus, Dolphy, and Richmond, the ensemble featured tenor player Clifford Jordan, pianist Jaki Byard, and trumpeter Johnny Coles. Coles plays on the almost half-hour version of "So Long Eric," but on none of the other tunes because of his sudden, on-stage illness which knocked him out for the rest of the concert and the tour. Byard's neo-ragtime/bop solo on "Parkeriana" packs the history of jazz piano into mere minutes, showing why Mingus really appreciated Byard's versatility. Dolphy is wonderful throughout and Jordan is no slouch either. "Meditations on Integration" features Dolphy's marvelous flute playing and Mingus's skill with an arco bass in some of the composer's most ambitious scoring. Prior to Mingus's unfinished "Epitaph," *The Black Saint and the Sinner Lady* ♪♪♪♪ (Impulse!, 1963/1995, prod. Bob Thiele) contained his greatest long-form work, a "ballet" suite that blended influences from Ellington and Tatum to Debussy and Ravel with a healthy dollop of the composer. Mingus played bass and, on "Mode F-Group and Solo Dance," piano. His cohorts for the session included Charlie Mariano, Jerome Richardson, Jaki Byard, and Don Butterfield, among others (including the ever present Dannie Richmond on drums). *The Complete Debut Recordings* ♪♪♪♪ (OJC, 1990, prod. various) is a phenomenal 12-disc set, mind-boggling in its completeness. From 1951 through 1958, Mingus and drummer Max Roach ran the Debut label as a way of putting their music (and the works of other artists) out on the market. Probably the most notorious release from Debut was *Jazz at Massey Hall*, a live date with Dizzy Gillespie, Bud Powell, Roach, Mingus, and Charlie Parker (cited for contractual reasons on this recording as "Charlie Chan") which documented what was hyped at the time as "the greatest jazz concert ever." If not consistently great, this compilation still documents an important part of Mingus's recorded history and has much to recommend it including strong recordings of "Haitian Fight Song" and "Jump Monk." The personnel in these sessions range from the well known (Miles Davis, Elvin Jones, Mal Waldron, and Wynton Kelly) to lesser lights such as pianist Spaulding Givens, tenor player George Barrow, and drummer Willie Jones.

best of the rest:
Pithecanthropus Erectus ♪♪♪♪ (Atlantic, 1956)
New Tijuana Moods ♪♪♪♪ (RCA Victor, 1957/1996)
Blues and Roots ♪♪♪♪ (Atlantic/Rhino, 1960)
The Clown ♪♪♪♪ (Atlantic, 1961/Rhino, 1989)
Oh Yeah ♪♪♪♪ (Atlantic/Rhino, 1961)
Mingus, Mingus, Mingus, Mingus, Mingus ♪♪♪♪ (Impulse!, 1963/1995)
Mingus Plays Piano ♪♪♪½ (Impulse!, 1963)
Changes One ♪♪♪♪ (Atlantic, 1975/Rhino, 1993)
Mingus at Antibes ♪♪♪♪ (Atlantic, 1976/Rhino, 1994)
Cumbia & Jazz Fusion ♪♪♪♪ (Atlantic, 1978/Rhino, 1994)
Epitaph ♪♪♪♪ (Columbia, 1990)

worth searching for: *Mingus at Monterey* ♪♪♪♪ (Charles Mingus Enterprises, 1966, prod. Charles Mingus) and *Music Written for Monterey, 1965* ♪♪♪½ (Charles Mingus Enterprises, 1966, prod. Charles Mingus) both document music that was and wasn't played at a notorious Monterey, California concert where Mingus claimed the program was too crowded for him to play his compositions the way he wanted. The later release was actually taped a week later at U.C.L.A. and both albums were released through Mingus's mail order company. They were later put out by Fantasy and East Coasting Records, respectively, although both are, for all intents and purposes, unavailable on CD or on vinyl. Now unavailable, *The Complete 1959 CBS Charles Mingus Sessions* ♪♪♪♪♪ (CBS/Mosaic, 1959, prod. Teo Macero) is a limited edition three-CD set that contains all the material used on the *Mingus Ah Um* album plus a wad of rarities, including songs that later found their way onto various out-of-print collections like *Nostalgia in Times Square*. This is one of the classic Mingus ensembles performing absolutely wonderful material. For reading material about Mingus, check out *Mingus: A Critical Biography* by Brian Priestly, published by Da Capo books. It may very well be the definitive printed word on Mingus's life. It includes a massive discography and is filled with the dramatic details of the great bass player's many accomplishments and frustrations.

influences:
◄◄ Duke Ellington, Charlie Parker

►► Malachi Favors, Jack Walrath, Christian McBride, Ricky Ford, Jaco Pastorius

Garaud MacTaggart

Mingus Big Band

Formed 1991, in New York, NY.

Steve Slagle, alto saxophone; Andy McKee, bass; Ryan Kisor, trumpet; Earl Gardner, trumpet; Alex Sipiagan, trumpet; Ronnie Cuber, reeds; Seamus Blake, reeds; John Stubblefield, reeds; Craig Handy, reeds; Ku-Umba Frank Lacy, trombone; Dave Taylor, trombone; Earl McIntyre, trombone; Kenny Drew Jr., piano; Tommy Campbell, drums; Marvin "Smitty" Smith, drums; Adam Cruz, drums.

The 14-piece Mingus Big Band draws from a rotating assemblage of over 100 musicians who make their home at the Time Cafe in New York City, where they perform every Thursday night. Co-musical directors are Steve Slagle and Andy McKee. Charles Mingus left his fellow musicians some 300 compositions to explore when he died in 1979. Since his passing, various ensembles (most notably Mingus Dynasty) have undertaken the task of playing these challenging, often unorthodox, works. The Mingus Big Band is the latest group to meet the challenge. The ensemble grew out of the first complete performance of Mingus's *Epitaph*, an extended work for 31 musicians which premiered in 1989 at Lincoln Center, conducted by Gunther Schuller. Critical acclaim for that concert led to the desire to hear Mingus's work played by larger ensembles and the subsequent cataloging of his scores, which prompted his widow, Sue Mingus, to form the Mingus Big Band in 1991. The ensemble captures the spirit of Mingus's music, a passionate mix of core elements of jazz, swing , blues, and improvisation, as well as love of Duke Ellington, Charlie Parker, gospel music, and judicious use of experimentation. Elements present in the music are lyricism, hard driving hand-clapping joy, turbulence, and anger. By injecting their own musical personalities into the works, Mingus Big Band members remain true to the concept of personal expression that was paramount to the music of bassist-composer Charles Mingus.

what to buy: The Mingus Big Band's best recording, *Live in Time* ♪♪♪♪ (Dreyfus, 1996, prod. Sue Mingus), was live-recorded at the Time Cafe. The strength of the MBB, demonstrated on the two-disc set, is that they aren't interested only in going over old ground with derivative takes on "greatest hits." The band plays energetic, fresh interpretations of well-known Mingus compositions such as "Wednesday Night Prayer Meeting", "Boogie Stop Shuffle" and "E's Flat, Ah's Flat, Too." The ballad "Diane" (also played under the title of "Alice's Wonderland") is a gorgeous song with two melodic strains, either of which could have stood alone. The band captures its lyric quality beautifully. More importantly, the Band explores lesser-known works such as "Number 29," an early 1970s piece Mingus wrote to challenge trumpeters. Arranger Sy Johnson reworked it, spreading the trumpet part to three players—Slagle, trumpeter Randy Brecker, and tenor man John Stubblefield—who carry out most admirably on this version. With the exception of a bootleg recording, Mingus never recorded "The Man Who Never Sleeps," which was arranged as a feature for Brecker. A real highlight is the haunting "Children's Hour of Dreams" from *Epitaph*, a piece without improvisation.

what to buy next: The group's second studio session *Gunslinging Birds* ♫♫♫♫ (Dreyfus, 1995, prod. Sue Mingus) is a well-balanced affair with high-energy romps, including "Gunslinging Bird" and "Jump Monk," and piano pyrotechnics from the prodigious Kenny Drew Jr. Also featured are melodic gems such as the medley of "Noon Night" from *Epitaph* with "Celia." "Reincarnation of a Lovebird" showcases solos by Slagle and Brecker, with Slagle's arrangement truly drawing out the beauty of the piece. *Nostalgia in Times Square* ♫♫♫ (Dreyfus, 1993, prod. Sue Mingus) also contains some fine moments. Craig Handy's tenor brings vitality to the proceedings, especially on "Moanin," "Open Letter to Duke" and a version of "Ecclesiastics" so fervent that even a nonbeliever might be compelled to testify. Seldom-heard Mingus songs are showcased, including "Invisible Lady," "Mingus Fingers" and "Weird Nightmare." Only the title song seems to come off as a bit forced. Maybe it is just one of those pieces that needs actual presence of its composer to make it work.

influences:

◀◀ Charles Mingus, Mingus Dynasty

Dan Polletta

Mingus Dynasty

Formed 1979. Disbanded 1991.

Rotating membership; members on many recordings include: Dannie Richmond, drums; Jimmy Knepper, trombone; Roland Hanna, piano; Don Pullen, piano; George Adams, tenor saxaphone; Craig Handy, tenor saxaphone.

Usually a sextet or septet, Mingus Dynasty, the precursor to the Mingus Big Band, drew on a rotating cast of players. Most albums featured a majority of Mingus veterans. Frequent participants included drummer Dannie Richmond, trombonist (and occasional musical director) Jimmy Knepper, pianists Roland Hanna and Don Pullen, and tenor saxophonists George Adams and Craig Handy. Mingus Dynasty was created by Charles Mingus's widow, Susan Graham Mingus, shortly after the legendary bassist/composer's death in 1979, to keep his music alive. During its decade or so of existence (by the early 1990s it had evolved into the outstanding Mingus Big Band), Mingus Dynasty featured many of the top alumni from the late bassist's bands, touring widely and recording for Elektra, Atlantic, Soul Note, Columbia, and Storyville. Though the group rarely approached the intensity of Mingus-led bands, its concerts sometimes captured the spirit and energy of Mingus performances. Few of Mingus's great compositions had made their way into jazz musician repertoire. Thus, Mingus Dynasty performed an invaluable function in introducing a new generation of players (and fans) to Mingus's breathtakingly rich works.

what to buy: A particularly successful Mingus Dynasty album, *Mingus' Sounds of Love* ♫♫♫♫ (Soul Note, 1988/1994, prod. Giovanni Bonandrini) is a thematic session featuring tunes the bassist wrote for the women in his life. Trombonist Jimmy Knepper's arrangements draw out Mingus's florid romanticism and volatility, and the group he assembled includes such brilliant Mingus veterans as drummer Dannie Richmond, pianist Roland Hanna, and trumpeter Randy Brecker, a Mingus devotee in flutist James Newton, and recent acolytes Craig Handy (tenor sax) and Reggie Johnson (bass). Highlights include the 15-minute version of Mingus's complex "Sue's Changes" and a powerful 12-minute romp through "Ysabel's Table Dance." This was probably Richmond's last recording before his death in early 1988.

what to buy next: An adventurous session covering obscure material or "tunes" that Mingus sang into a tape recorder at the end of his life when he was too weak to write, *The Next Generation* ♫♫♫♫ (Columbia, 1991, prod. Sue Mingus, Delfeayo Marsalis) features a septet that feels like a transition to the Mingus Big Band. Led by trumpeter Jack Walrath, a veteran of Mingus's last great group along with tenor saxophonist George Adams, who dominates much of the album, the session also features a superlative rhythm section with John Hicks (piano), Ray Drummond (bass), and Marvin "Smitty" Smith (drums), and young lions Craig Handy (tenor sax and flute) and Alex Foster (reeds). Highlights include Adams's stunning tenor solo on "Noon Night" from *Epitaph* (Adams was also featured on the posthumous recording of the epic work) and the opening track "Sketch Four," which begins with the tape of Mingus singing the melody as a metronome keeps time.

the rest:

At the Bottom Line 𝄢𝄢𝄢𝄢𝄢 (West Wind, 1979/1995)
Live at Montreux 𝄢𝄢𝄢𝄢 (Atlantic, 1980)
Reincarnation 𝄢𝄢𝄢 (Soul Note, 1982/1994)
Live at the Village Vanguard 𝄢𝄢𝄢 (Storyville, 1984/1994)

worth searching for: Recorded about three months after Mingus's death, *Chair in the Sky* 𝄢𝄢𝄢𝄢𝄢 (Elektra, 1979, prod. Ilhan Mimaroglu) was the first and best Mingus Dynasty album, though it has yet to be reissued on CD. Still, it's not hard to find on vinyl. In addition to the surging "Boogie Stop Shuffle," the avant-trad "My Jelly Roll Soul," and timeless tribute "Goodbye Pork Pie Hat," the group plays three tunes from Mingus's collaboration with Joni Mitchell. Bassist Charlie Haden is the only ringer among such generation-spanning Mingus alumni as Don Pullen (piano), Dannie Richmond (drums), John Handy (alto sax), Joe Farrell (tenor sax), and Jimmy Owens (trumpet and flugelhorn). Farrell is in particularly strong form throughout the album.

Andrew Gilbert

Bob Mintzer

Born January 27, 1953, in New Rochelle, NY.

Bob Mintzer is an acclaimed musician, composer, arranger, author, and educator. Although he's best known for his tenor saxophone playing, he also performs on bass clarinet, soprano saxophone, and the EWI (electronic wind instrument), leading his own big band, and as a member of the popular Yellowjackets. Throughout the '70s and early '80s, Mintzer played with artists such as Tito Puente, Buddy Rich, Art Blakey, Thad Jones/Mel Lewis, Sam Jones, Tom Harrell, Eddie Palmieri, Jaco Pastorius, and David Sanborn. In 1984 he started his own big band, which records for DMP records. Members of the band have included Randy and Michael Brecker, Marvin Stamm, and Peter Erskine. The band has produced 11 albums, four of which were Grammy nominees. In 1990 Mintzer joined the acclaimed contemporary jazz group the Yellowjackets. In recent years he has also performed and recorded with the GRP All-Star Big Band. As an accomplished composer and arranger, Mintzer has published 200 big band arrangements, a saxophone method

book, and several books of etudes and improvisations. Accordingly, he's in great demand as an educator, conducting nearly 20 clinic/workshops a year world-wide, and serving as a saxophone instructor at the Manhattan School of Music.

what to buy: John Coltrane dramatically influenced the way Mintzer plays the saxophone, as well as his writing, so it comes as no surprise that his 1996 big band homage, *Big Band Trane* 𝄢𝄢𝄢𝄢𝄢 (DMP, 1996, prod. Tom Jung, Bob Mintzer), is his finest hour. Of the 10 songs on this CD, three are strongly associated with Coltrane, "My Favorite Things," "Impressions," and "Acknowledgment" from the Coltrane album *A Love Supreme*. The remainder are Mintzer compositions inspired by Coltrane, and they effectively capture the musical piquancy Trane's music embodied. Mintzer is a lucid, cunning writer who crafts tunes with a strong sense of form and melody, as demonstrated on "Prayer for Peace," "Ancestors," and "One People." Stirring soloists include Mintzer and Bob Malach on tenor, Randy Brecker and Marvin Stamm on trumpet, and Phil Markowitz on piano. Rather than copy Coltrane and graft him onto a big band, Mintzer uses Trane as a stepping stone and creates radiant, seasoned music. Trane would have been proud! Mintzer's 18-piece big band is firmly rooted in the tradition of Ellington, Basie's 1950s arrangers, and Gil Evans. Yet, as *Departure* 𝄢𝄢𝄢𝄢𝄢 (DMP, 1993, prod. Tom Jung, Bob Mintzer) so strongly demonstrates, he's on the cutting edge of innovative possibilities as well. This band has a unique character with the sections and ensemble voice combinations presented with a flexibility that makes each instrumentalist's contribution felt on a conscious level. In his solos, Mintzer builds slowly and meticulously and when he unloads, he's a fire-breathing titan. (Note: DMP is an audiophile label and the sound quality on all their recordings is among the best available.) Mintzer joined the Yellowjackets in 1990, and *One Music* 𝄢𝄢𝄢𝄢𝄢 (DMP 1991, prod. Bob Mintzer) was his first small-band project featuring bandmembers Russell Ferrante, Jimmy Haslip, and William Kennedy. Offering a neoteric approach to the standard tenor quartet format, Mintzer creates a neo-bop hybrid on tracks such as "Old Friends" and "The Big Show." Spontaneous and organic, this music may have been recorded in a day or two but it benefits greatly from the fact that it was created by a working group. The 10 straightforward originals that uniquely deploy inventive melodies and complex harmonies could easily lead one to dub this group the Modern Jazz Quartet of the 1990s. Created especially to record *Groovetown* 𝄢𝄢𝄢𝄢𝄢 (Owl, 1996, prod. Bob Mintzer), the New York Jazz Ensemble is a smoking quartet that includes reedman Mintzer, pianist James Williams, bassist Jay Anderson, and drummer Tony Reedus. The quartet was put together as a means of representing New York musicians between ages 30 and 40-something who tend to be overlooked. These four seasoned pros are among the Big Apple's finest and the sum total of their experience as sidemen and leaders makes for a rich and varied musical palate. The bottom line here is intensity, swing, and a sense of urgency, a reflection no doubt of New York itself, especially notable on the animated title track.

what to buy next: On *First Decade* 𝄞𝄞𝄞𝄞 (DMP, 1995, prod. Tom Jung, Bob Mintzer), saxophonist and composer/arranger Mintzer breathes fresh, contemporary life into the big band medium. A 12-song collection from his first seven big band albums on DMP, *First Decade* shows what a man of considerable creative acumen can do with the wealth of resources a big band offers. For this musical feast worthy of a king, Mintzer draws from a regal pool of New York's finest players, outstanding soloists like Michael and Randy Brecker, Peter Erskine, and the late Don Grolnick. Once again he delivers big-band jazz at its finest on *Only in New York* 𝄞𝄞𝄞𝄞 (DMP, 1994, prod. Tom Jung). From start to finish this acoustically precise session, with an all-star line-up that includes Randy Brecker's soulfully intense trumpet and Peter Erskine's effectively energetic percussion, is nothing short of exceptional. *Camouflage* 𝄞𝄞𝄞 (DMP, 1986, prod. Tom Jung, Bob Mintzer) offers more proof that Mintzer is one of the most skillful big band arrangers with burnished ensembles and first rate solos always in evidence. Not his most adventurous effort, the music nevertheless maintains the standard of excellence for which his band is known.

best of the rest:

Spectrum 𝄞𝄞𝄞𝄞 (DMP, 1988)
Urban Contours 𝄞𝄞𝄞𝄞 (DMP, 1989)
Art of the Big Band 𝄞𝄞𝄞 (DMP, 1991)

influences:

⏮ Joe Henderson, Sonny Rollins, Steve Marcus, John Coltrane, Wayne Shorter

⏭ Bob Berg, Bill Evans, Steve Grossman, Dave Liebman, Michael Brecker

Bret Primack

Blue Mitchell

Born Richard Allen Mitchell, March 13, 1930, in Miami, FL. Died May 21, 1979, in Los Angeles, CA.

Richard Allen "Blue" Mitchell was the quintessential hard bop trumpeter, a brilliant musician whose warm, flexible, shining tone made his playing on ballads and blues equally rewarding. Though not an innovator, he helped define the expressive possibilities of late 1950s and 1960s hard bop with his highly personal sound, both through his prolific work as a sideman and his numerous superb sessions as a leader. Mitchell started playing trumpet at 17 and began working around Florida in R&B bands. He made the move to New York in the early 1950s and put in a long stint with Earl Bostic (1953–55). After a brief tour with Sarah Vaughan and Al Hibbler, he moved back to Miami, where Cannonball Adderley heard him playing in 1958 and saw to it that he was brought into the Riverside fold, where he recorded a number of exceptional albums. On the strength of his Riverside debut, Horace Silver hired Mitchell for his quintet, a band that recorded frequently until Silver took a hiatus in 1964. Mitchell and tenor saxophonist Junior Cook took up leadership of the group and continued to record for Blue Note with a series of fine bands including pianists Chick Corea and Harold Mabern, and drummers Roy Brooks, Billy Higgins, and Al Foster (though few of these albums are available on CD). With the crash of the jazz scene in the late 1960s, Mitchell began recording instrumental pop albums and went back to his blues and R&B roots, touring with Ray Charles (1969–71) and John Mayall (1971–73). Settling in Los Angeles, Mitchell worked with Lena Horne and Tony Bennett, and became a key soloist in the big bands of Bill Holman, Bill Berry, and especially Louie Bellson (with whom he was also featured extensively on small group sessions). He co-led a fine quintet with tenor saxophonist Harold Land throughout the late 1970s but the group only made one recording. Mitchell died of cancer at the age of 49.

what to buy: One of the most impressive debut recordings of the era, *Big Six* 𝄞𝄞𝄞𝄞 (Riverside, 1958/OJC, 1991, prod. Orrin Keepnews) features the then-unknown trumpeter Blue Mitchell with trombonist Curtis Fuller and tenor giant Johnny Griffin. Besides introducing Benny Golson's classic tune "Blues March," this session is memorable for the rapport and balance achieved by the three horns. With Wynton Kelly (piano), Wilbur Ware (bass), and Philly Joe Jones (drums), the rhythm section is also first-rate. The first of a number of successful collaborations between Mitchell and tenor saxophonist Benny Golson, *Out of the Blue* 𝄞𝄞𝄞𝄞 (Riverside/OJC, 1958, prod. Orrin Keepnews) is a tasty, unpretentious hard bop session. Opening with Golson's sophisticated "Blues on My Mind," the album originally ended with a down-and-dirty, modern-jazz version of "When The Saints Go Marching In." The CD adds a track that was only available on a compilation. The rhythm section features Wynton Kelly (piano), Art Blakey (drums), and either Paul

Chambers or Sam Jones (bass). A classic hard-bop session, *The Cup Bearers* 🎵🎵🎵🎵 (Riverside, 1962/OJC, 1993, prod. Orrin Keepnews) features Horace Silver's quintet—tenor saxophonist Junior Cook, bassist Gene Taylor and drummer Roy Brooks—with Cedar Walton holding down the piano chair. But this is no ersatz Silver album. Instead, Mitchell brought in a host of excellent tunes by rising young composers, including one each by Walton and Thad Jones and two by trombonist Tom McIntosh. Mitchell really hits his stride on this session, playing with complete authority.

what to buy next: A quality recording all the way around, *Blue Soul* 🎵🎵🎵🎵 (Riverside, 1959/OJC, 1993, prod. Orrin Keepnews) features arrangements by tenor saxophonists Benny Golson and Jimmy Heath. Heath and trombonist Curtis Fuller play on six sextet tracks, while Mitchell plays three tunes with just the rhythm section—pianist Wynton Kelly, bassist Sam Jones, and drummer Philly Joe Jones. Heath, Golson, and Mitchell contribute two strong originals each, but Golson's arrangements make "Polka Dots and Moonbeams" and Horace Silver's "Nica's Dream" two of the more memorable tunes. Jimmy Heath's arrangements for *A Sure Thing* 🎵🎵🎵🎵 (Riverside, 1962/OJC, 1995, prod. Orrin Keepnews) make this a particularly rewarding octet/nonet session featuring trumpeter Clark Terry and baritone saxophonists Pepper Adams (on "West Coast Blues") or Pat Patrick (on Mitchell's "Hip to It"). The charts are tight and focused, forcing Mitchell to solo concisely (as he does brilliantly on "I Can't Get Started") but he also gets a chance to stretch out a bit on a quartet track with Wynton Kelly (piano), Sam Jones (bass), and Tootie Heath (drums). Mitchell's only quartet session for Riverside, *Blue's Moods* 🎵🎵🎵🎵 (Riverside, 1960/OJC, 1994, prod. Orrin Keepnews) showcases his beautiful, luminous trumpet tone on a program that includes bopper such as "Scrapple from the Apple," ballad standards such as "When I Fall in Love," and various funky themes. Wynton Kelly (piano), Sam Jones (bass) and Roy Brooks (drums) provide exemplary accompaniment. When Horace Silver decided to disband in 1964, Mitchell and tenor saxophonist Junior Cook knew they had too good a thing going to simply walk away. *The Thing to Do* 🎵🎵🎵🎵 (Blue Note, 1964/1995, prod. Alfred Lion) was their first post-Silver album, a funky session featuring a promising young pianist named Chick Corea, bassist Gene Taylor and drummer Al Foster.

best of the rest:
Blues on My Mind 🎵🎵🎵🎵 (OJC, 1958/1992)
Smooth as the Wind 🎵🎵🎵🎵 (Riverside, 1961/OJC, 1996)
Step Lightly 🎵🎵🎵🎵 (Blue Note, 1963)

Down with It 🎵🎵🎵🎵 (Blue Note, 1965/Capitol, 1997)
Bring It on Home to Me 🎵🎵🎵🎵 (Blue Note, 1966)
Boss Horn 🎵🎵🎵🎵 (Blue Note, 1966)
Mapenzi 🎵🎵🎵🎵 (Concord Jazz, 1977)

influences:
◄◄ Fats Navarro

Andrew Gilbert

Roscoe Mitchell

Born August 3, 1940, in Chicago, IL.

One of the illustrious musicians to come out of Chicago's Association for the Advancement of Creative Musicians (AACM), multi-instrumentalist Roscoe Mitchell has remained one of the more adventurous innovators blurring the lines between the avant-garde and structured music. He was a charter member of the Art Ensemble of Chicago along with Lester Bowie, Joseph Jarman, and Malachi Favors. Mitchell played clarinet, baritone, and alto in high school and in army bands before leading a hard-bop sextet in Chicago with Joseph Jarman and Henry Threadgill. He also played in a group with Byron Austin, Scotty Holt, and Jack DeJohnette, before joining the experimental band led by Muhal Richard Abrams. Mitchell subsequently formed his own trio, and with his sextet in 1966 recorded *Sound*, the first documentation of the post-Ornette Coleman, second wave of new music. He has performed and recorded with the Art Ensemble of Chicago since the mid-1960s, as well as leading his own groups, particularly his Sound Ensemble, formed in 1980. Mitchell remains active on the free music scene as both a leader and sideman.

what to buy: If you're new to the free music scene, start with *Hey Donald* 🎵🎵🎵🎵 (Delmark, 1995, prod. Robert G. Koester). It's probably one of his most "inside" sessions and you'll gain an appreciation for Mitchell's playing in a quartet setting as he and his teammates glide artfully through 12 songs (mostly originals). Mitchell plays alto, tenor, and soprano saxophones, as well as flute, and gives plenty of space to pianist Jodie Christian, bassist Malachi Favors (both early AACM members), and drummer Albert "Tootie" Heath. Showcasing his wide-ranging chops, Mitchell occasionally leans to the avant garde on this mostly straight-ahead session. When he ventures outside the chord changes, he offers tastefully rendered saxophone improvisations such as "The Band Room," which does, at times, sound like musicians tuning their instruments. Jody Christian contributes the melodic waltz, "Jeremy," a vehicle for Mitchell's lovely flute solo. "Keep On Keeping On," composed by Favors, features his arco (bowed) solos against Mitchell's stretching soprano sax explorations before the whole band creates a spontaneous, cacophonous jolt of avant-garde. Lester Bowie's "Zero" is given a boppish workout with Mitchell on alto sax. One of the prettier tunes is Mitchell's lilting title piece, the longest number at 7:45. Recorded in 1994, the CD is dedicated to Donald Myrick, the late saxophonist and another founding member of the AACM, as well as an original member of Earth, Wind, and Fire. A highly recommended listen from one of the most expressive AACM-influenced musicians. Once duly introduced, you could be ready for Mitchell's sound explorations on his 1966 sextet session, *Sound* 𝄞𝄞𝄞𝄞 (Delmark, 1966/1996, prod. Robert G. Koester), the album that launched his recording career as leader and was the first documentation of AACM music. Mitchell collaborates with Lester Bowie (trumpet, flugelhorn) and Malachi Favors (bass), who would become his partners in the Art Ensemble of Chicago by 1969. Lester Lashley (trombone, cello), Maurice McIntyre (tenor sax), and Alvin Field (drums) round out the crew here. The five-tune CD version differs from the original LP in that an alternate take of "Ornette" is added, and two separate versions of "Sound" are offered rather than the composite on the original vinyl edition. To some ears, their music might seem like doodling or disorganized noise. To fans of the avant-garde, this is a landmark album hinting at how creatively these musicians would collectively forge their myriad soundscapes in successive performances and recordings in the ensuing years. "Sound 1" offers 26-plus minutes of exploration, featuring solo and collective improves from Mitchell, Bowie, and Lashley. One of their most imaginative and playful forays into sound experimentation is "The Little Suite," a colorful inside-out venture that contains nuggets of puckish sound surprises. If you despise squeaks and squawks, stay away. But if you love mind-expanding sounds that take you to another realm, this is an exciting listen and a groundbreaking requisite for your CD collection. If you're curious to see how much music the virtuosic Mitchell can make on an unaccompanied solo session, check out *Sound Songs* 𝄞𝄞𝄞𝄞 (Delmark, 1997, prod. Paul Serrano). Mitchell's linear and timbral discoveries continue as he plays saxophones and flute and an array of instruments on 26 original tunes of this two-CD set. Most selections were studio recorded, except for two live-recorded performances at the University of Wisconsin and at Chicago's Hot House. Half of the tunes are artfully overdubbed, often with layers of unusual percussion (bells, whistles, bicycle horns, toys) and intertwined woodwinds to create textures, add color, and generate excitement. From the serene to the snappy and surly, Mitchell's solo sound experiments are extremely satisfy-

ing for the adventurous listener. On *This Dance Is for Steve McCall* 𝄞𝄞𝄞𝄞 (Black Saint, 1993, prod. Flavio Bonandrini), Mitchell and the Note Factory make their recording debut performing an array of nine tunes composer Mitchell dedicated to his various muses over his 30 years of sound experimentation. He plays saxophones, bamboo flute, and percussion; his side musicians, who have participated in other Mitchell projects, include pianist Matthew Shipp, bassist Jaribu Shahid, bassist-percussionist William Parker, and drummers Tani Tabbal (who also plays hand drums) and Vincent Davis. Recorded after their first two concerts at the New Music Café in New York City, this unusually configured group has a raw, exploratory spirit. There are many highlights and the music is greatly enhanced by the percussionists. Swirling horns create chaos on "The Rodney King Affair," a brief but evocative social-commentary nearly as telling and disturbing as Billie Holiday's "Strange Fruit" was when it was first heard. There are many fine moments on this album, which closes with the dark and eerie title tune, Mitchell's mournful saxophone-led tribute to the late drummer Steve McCall, whose last recording with Mitchell was on the 1986 date, *The Flow of Things*. Ranging from peaceful to piquant, their attractive music makes this a must-have album for Mitchell devotees.

what to buy next: *Roscoe Mitchell and the Sound Ensemble: Live at the Knitting Factory* 𝄞𝄞𝄞𝄞 (Black Saint, 1990, prod. Giovanni Bonandrini) features Mitchell with Hugh Ragin (trumpet, flugelhorn), A. Spencer Barefield (guitar, piano), Jaribu Shahid (bass, congas), and Tani Tabbal (percussion) in a live-recorded performance at New York's Knitting Factory on November 11, 1987. Among the nine selections is a 10-minute variation of the suite-like "Nonaah," a composition with open-ended structure first introduced by Mitchell on the 1973 Art Ensemble of Chicago recording, *Fanfare for the Warriors*. While the titles are intriguing, the music from this version of the Sound Ensemble lacks the intimate cohesiveness of Mitchell's earlier collaborations which included Lester Bowie and Malachi Favors. Yet, the album provides a fresh look at his views on the kinship between composition and improvisation. Recorded in 1983, *Roscoe Mitchell and The Sound and Space Ensembles* 𝄞𝄞𝄞𝄞 (Black Saint, 1983, prod. Giovanni Bonandrini) contains four Mitchell originals and two spontaneously invented Sound Ensemble sprees. Of the arranged pieces, one of the more accessible (though brief) tunes is funkified "You Wastin' My Tyme," featuring Mitchell on lead vocal, and alto and bass saxophones. On the boppish "Linefine Lyon Seven," he leads off with an alto saxophone solo before handing off to trumpeter

Mike Mossman, who delivers it fine and straight up. Tom Buckner, an operatic tenor, adds his splendid voice to the opening and closing peaceful panoramic pieces, but fans of instrumental jazz might find his vocals a distraction.

best of the rest:
(With the Sound Ensemble) *3 X 4 Eye* ✧✧✧ (Black Saint, 1981)
(With Roscoe Mitchell Quartet) *The Flow of Things* ✧✧✧ (Black Saint, 1987/1994)
(With Muhal Richard Abrams) *Duets and Solos* ✧✧✧ (Black Saint, 1993)

see also: *The Art Ensemble of Chicago*

Nancy Ann Lee

Hank Mobley
Born July 7, 1930, in Eastman, GA. Died May 30, 1986, in Philadelphia, PA.

Underrated by critics and underappreciated by the public throughout most of his career, tenor saxophonist Hank Mobley was often capable of inspired work. Most of the definitive hard-bop Blue Note recordings of the late '50s and early '60s include him. His career began with such bebop pioneers as Max Roach, Tadd Dameron, and Dizzy Gillespie. He then became an original Jazz Messenger with Horace Silver and Art Blakey (1954–56). When Silver left the Jazz Messengers, Mobley joined him. While with Silver he began recording under his own name. These recordings reflect his growing assurance and conviction. In 1961 he joined Miles Davis's quintet. The gig should have been his golden ticket, but with Coltrane's departure, Miles's music was in a transition and he faulted Mobley for not being Coltrane or Sonny Rollins. This does a disservice to Mobley's remarkable capabilities. He was an inspired, if fairly traditional, improviser, possessing great rhythmic flexibility and melodic imagination. After his disappointing stay with Davis, he returned to Blue Note. He picked up where he left off, recording straightforward, swinging albums. After touring Europe from 1967–70 Mobley was forced to retire from performing for health reasons. In 1985 he made a non-playing appearance at the Blue Note relaunch concert. Fortunately, some of his best recordings, *Far Away Lands*, *A Slice of the Top*, and *Another Workout*, were finally reissued after languishing in the Blue Note vaults for 20 years. Sadly, Mobley died before receiving the acclaim he deserved.

what to buy: *Soul Station* ✧✧✧✧ (Blue Note, 1960, prod. Alfred Lion) is the definitive Hank Mobley album, swinging from top to bottom and front to back. One of life's great mysteries is why Blue Note didn't release it until 1987. The rhythm section of Wynton Kelly, Paul Chambers, and Art Blakey provides a cohesive and swinging foundation for Mobley's outstanding lyrical solos. "Remember" sets the easy-swinging mood and Mobley's "This I Dig of You" and "Soul Station" have become minor jazz standards. It's not just one of Mobley's best albums—it's one of the best ever.

what to buy next: *Roll Call* ✧✧✧✧ (Blue Note, 1960, prod. Alfred Lion) features the same lineup as Soul Station with the notable addition of Freddie Hubbard, whose solos "Roll Call" and "The Baptist Beat" inject the proceedings with extra fire. *Another Workout* ✧✧✧✧ (Blue Note, 1961, prod. Alfred Lion), like most of Mobley's best, was locked away until Blue Note's mid-'80s resurgence. In the liner notes he credits the influence of Coltrane and Davis with the simplification of his style. Also, his sound is harder and his playing more aggressive. "Gettin and Jettins" even has Mobley exhibiting a strong R&B influence.

what to avoid: *Hard Bop* ✧ (Savoy, 1990) purports to be complete, but is actually only half of *The Jazz Message of Hank Mobley*, which is readily available.

the rest:
The Jazz Message of Hank Mobley, Volume 1 ✧✧✧ (Savoy, 1956)
The Jazz Message of Hank Mobley, Volume 2 ✧✧✧ (Savoy, 1956)
Messages ✧✧✧ (Prestige, 1956)
Tenor Conclave ✧✧✧ (Prestige, 1956)
Hank Mobley and His All-Stars ✧✧✧✧ (Blue Note, 1957)
Peckin' Time ✧✧✧✧ (Blue Note, 1958)
Workout ✧✧✧✧ (Blue Note, 1961/1988)
No Room for Squares ✧✧✧✧ (Blue Note, 1963)
Caddy for Daddy ✧✧✧✧ (Blue Note, 1965)
Dippin' ✧✧✧✧ (Blue Note, 1965)
Turnaround ✧✧✧ (Blue Note, 1965)
Slice of the Top ✧✧✧✧ (Blue Note, 1966)
Far Away Lands ✧✧✧ (Blue Note, 1967)
Hi Voltage ✧✧✧ (Blue Note, 1967)
Blue Note Years: Best of Hank Mobley ✧✧ (Capitol, 1996)

worth searching for: *Thinking of Home* ✧✧✧ (Blue Note, 1970) is a landmark album for Mobley on several counts. It's his last for Blue Note and his last as a leader, but more importantly it's his first foray into extended composition. "Thinking of Home," "Flight," and "Home at Last" make up Mobley's advanced hard-bop suite. Also featured are Woody Shaw and Cedar Walton.

influences:
◄◄ Charlie Parker

►► Joe Henderson, James Spaulding

James Eason

Modern Jazz Quartet

Formed in 1952. Disbanded, 1974. Re-formed, 1981.

John Lewis (born in 1920, in LaGrange, IL), piano; Milt Jackson (born in 1923, in Detroit, MI), vibraharp; Percy Heath, bass; Kenny Clarke, drums (1952–55); Connie Kay (born Conrad Henry Kirnon, April 27, 1927; died 1994), drums/percussion (1955–94); Mickey Roker, drums (early 1990s); Albert "Tootie" Heath, drummer (1995).

Years before this revered chamber-jazz group became the Modern Jazz Quartet and recorded their first album, pianist John Lewis, vibraphonist Milt Jackson, bassist Ray Brown, and drummer Kenny Clarke were working as the rhythm unit in the 1946 version of Dizzy Gillespie's orchestra and they subsequently recorded as the Milt Jackson Quartet in 1951. Percy Health replaced Ray Brown when the group formed and first recorded as the MJQ in 1952. They remained an intact unit even when Clarke left to freelance in New York (before moving to France). In 1955 he was replaced by drummer Connie Kay who would serve the group for the next 20 years. Lewis became the group's musical director, making a long-lasting impact upon the MJQ and expanding their repertoire to include Baroque performances as well as jazz. MJQ arose during the era of cool jazz and became one of the most admired groups, contributing classic tunes such as "Django," "Bag's Groove," and other classics. They recorded for a number of labels since their initial Prestige recording in 1952, and often with guest artists. The group had its final tour before breaking up in 1974 when Jackson quit to pursue other interests. They reunited in 1981 for a tour of Japan, after which Ray Brown became manager and the group's itinerary began to expand. MJQ recorded a 1984 album, and continued to record until Kay's health began to fail in the early 1990s, when Mickey Roker often subbed for him. After Kay's death in 1994, Albert "Tootie" Heath became the MJQ drummer.

Pianist Lewis grew up in Albuquerque, New Mexico. He attended the University of New Mexico, studying music and anthropology and decided to follow music as a career after hearing the Dizzy Gillespie-Charlie Parker group which included vibist Milt Jackson. Lewis eventually became the Gillespie orchestra's pianist-arranger and furthered his development in the Parker-Miles Davis Quintet while he was pursuing advanced studies at the Manhattan School of Music. Lewis's compositions are an important part of the MJQ repertoire. Vibraphonist Milt Jackson was enamored of percussion instruments as a youngster. He studied drums, piano, and vibraharp, ultimately playing in Detroit clubs where Gillespie heard him one night in 1945. Gillespie brought Jackson to New York, paving the way

for Jackson to be recognized as one of the first players to adapt bebop ideas to the vibes. Jackson freelanced extensively after his first stint with Dizzy's band, replaced Terry Gibbs from 1949–50 in Woody Herman's band, and rejoined Gillespie from 1950–52. Jackson plays such a vital role in the group effort, one cannot imagine the MJQ without his soulful, gospel-tinged expressions. After beginning with Jackson's group, Heath's involvement in MJQ deepened over the years from somewhat unobtrusive support with his sturdy resilient sound, to thoughtfully balanced and enlivened solos. He has remained with MJQ since its evolution. By the time he joined MJQ, drummer Kay had worked with Lester Young, Stan Getz, Ben Webster, Charlie Parker, Coleman Hawkins and others. Aside from his reliable timekeeping, his indelible marks on the MJQ were his expert brushwork and his artful use of cymbals, bells, and other percussive aids.

what to buy: You can't go too wrong with any recording by the Modern Jazz Quartet, but for repeated material or brevity of album content, some albums are better than others. For an introduction to the MJQ, start with and branch out from the four-disc, chronological compilation, *MJQ40* ✍✍✍✍ (Atlantic, 1991), containing 53 tunes, all of their biggest hits and more. The boxed set also includes a booklet with extensive notes by Gary Giddins. If that retrospective set is too pricey for starters, another way to acquire a collection of some of the most popular MJQ recordings is on the two-disc set, *Dedicated to Connie* ✍✍✍✍✍ (Atlantic, 1995, prod. Ahmet Ertegun, John Lewis). MJQ elegantly delivers 17 tunes ranging from sweet ballads to swinging bop recorded (in total) at their 1960 concert in Ljubljana, Slovenia. The set kicks off with a four-tune medley of Lewis's European-influenced compositions ("The Little Comedy," "La Cantatrice," "Harlequin," "Fontessa"). Also included are MJQ classics such as "Bag's Groove," "Django," "Vendome," "Skating in Central Park," as well as time-honored tunes such as "'Round Midnight," "It Don't Mean a Thing (If It Ain't Got That Swing)," "How High the Moon," "I Remember Clifford," and other gems. It's a loving tribute to MJQ's late drummer Kay, and a veritable listening feast. A more recently recorded single-disc album, *A 40th Anniversary Celebration* ✍✍✍✍ (Atlantic, 1994, prod. Ahmet Ertegun, Arif Mardin), features one of few MJQ collaborations with other musicians. In studio and live dates in various locations between 1992–93, MJQ mixes it up on 13 mostly swinging selections with vocalist Bobby McFerrin; saxophonists Phil Woods, Illinois Jacquet, Branford Marsalis, Jimmy Heath, and Nino Tempo; trumpeters Harry "Sweets" Edison and Wynton Marsalis; and Freddie

Hubbard (flugelhorn), with Mickey Roker subbing on some tunes for Kay. It's a free-wheeling jazz party, with some fine solos and ensemble work on MJQ favorites. The two-CD set *The Complete Last Concert* 𝄞𝄞𝄞𝄞 (Atlantic, 1974/1989, prod. Ilhan Mimaroglu) was originally released on two LPs as *The Last Concert* and the single LP *More from the Last Concert*. The two-CD reissue was compiled in the original sequence of the November 25, 1974 concert program, and includes two previously unreleased bonus tracks. Lewis, Jackson, Heath, and Kay honor their then two decades together with a total of 22 songs performed before a responsive Lincoln Center audience. It was thought to be MJQ's last concert because Jackson, a pivotal member of the quartet, was leaving the group to pursue his freelance career. Disc one includes dramatic versions of 12 standards ("Summertime," "What's New?," "'Round Midnight," "Confirmation," and others), as well as originals by Lewis and Jackson. Disc two includes 10 tunes, mostly by Lewis, including the ever-present "Django" and Jackson's "Bag's Groove." Among all the MJQ albums out there, the live-recorded Lincoln Center performance is definitely a standout. A 64-minute compilation that draws from five Prestige recordings during the MJQ's two-and-a-half years with the label, *The Artistry of the Modern Jazz Quartet* 𝄞𝄞𝄞𝄞 (Prestige, 1952–55/1986, compilation prod. Ed Michel) presents one way for the uninitiated listener to acquire highlights of the group's first recordings between 1952–55, and their original versions of classics such as "Django," "La Ronde," "Milano," "Ralph's New Blues," and other favorites. If you're not interested in compilations but would rather collect the original albums, the place to begin would be with *Django* 𝄞𝄞𝄞𝄞 (OJC, 1955/1987, prod. Ira Gitler, Bob Weinstock). Recorded in three sessions between June 25, 1953 and January 9, 1955, this CD includes drummer Kenny Clarke's final studio dates with the cohesive MJQ presenting a zestful, eight-tune set that contains original versions of Lewis's "Django," "La Ronde Suite," "Milano," and "Delaunay's Dilemma." Hearing *Concorde* 𝄞𝄞𝄞𝄞 (OJC, 1987, prod. Bob Weinstock), the brief (about 34 minutes) 1955 date that was the first to feature drummer Kay, you might think his playing is rather conservative as he locks in with Heath to accompany Lewis and Jackson. But he helps break the relaxed state with a racing bop version of "I'll Remember April" and the perky title tune finale. High points include the near eight-minute swinging version of "Softly, As in a Morning Sunrise" (where Jackson and Lewis take extended solos), and a romantic Gershwin medley (about the same duration) containing "For You, for Me, Forevermore," "Love Walked In," and "Our Love Is Here to Stay." *Fontessa* 𝄞𝄞𝄞𝄞 (Atlantic, 1956/1989,

prod. Nesuhi Ertegun) is a top-quality session originally engineered by Rudy Van Gelder. Carefully restored on CD-reissue, the album contains seven originals and standards, including Lewis's swinging opener, "Versailles," and the title tune (the centerpiece at 11:12 minutes). A sturdy session, it also features a soulful version of "Angel Eyes," Jackson's cookin' "Bluesology," and pleasing reworkings of "Over the Rainbow" and "Woody 'n' You." *The Modern Jazz Quartet at Music Inn: Volume 2* 𝄞𝄞𝄞 (Mobile Fidelity, 1958/Atlantic Jazz, 1988, prod. Nesuhi Ertegun) covers two 1958 dates in Lenox, Massachusetts, and features tenor saxophonist Sonny Rollins on two tracks (that followed a 1956 session with Jimmy Giuffre at the same site not yet available on CD). This is an unusual session because it contains only two Lewis originals among the six tunes: "Festival Sketch" and "Midsömmer." MJQ launches the set with a romantic, three-ballad medley, next navigates alternating tempos on Charlie Parker's "Yardbird Suite," later reworks "Bags' Groove" (track 5) where Rollins finally joins in, and closes with a swinging version of "A Night in Tunisia," where Rollins sparsely jousts. *For Ellington* 𝄞𝄞𝄞𝄞 (Atlantic, 1988, prod. Nesuhi Ertegun) is an elegant, rhythmically engaging nine-tune homage to composer Duke Ellington, including the CD-bonus track ("Come Sunday"). MJQ gives new life to popular favorites, including their lush interpretation of the ballad "Prelude to a Kiss," tasty toe-tapping versions of "It Don't Mean a Thing" (featuring Kay's cymbals work) and "Rockin' in Rhythm," and more great music that Ellingtonia buffs as well as MJQ fans should find inviting. Reuniting in the studio after a 10-year hiatus to record *Together Again: Echoes (1984)* 𝄞𝄞𝄞𝄞 (Pablo, 1984/1987, prod. Modern Jazz Quartet), Lewis, Jackson, Heath, and Kay prove they have lost none of their edge. The six tunes recorded on March 6, 1984 are among their loveliest on record, especially the lyrical, lightly swinging Jackson original, "Echoes," performed for the first time on this album. Jazz musicians draw from many sources, and Heath's original, "The Watergate Blues," playfully addresses the historical bungled burglary that led many politicos to sing jailhouse blues.

what to buy next: *Topsy: This One's for Basie* 𝄞𝄞𝄞𝄞 (Pablo, 1987, prod. John Lewis) was recorded in 1985, the second album by the reunited MJQ. The tribute actually contains only one tune associated with the Count Basie band, Eddie Durham's swinger, "Topsy II," but all seven tunes are refreshing, swinging readings. Highlights include Jackson's solo performance of "Nature Boy," Lewis's take on the remake of the MJQ standard, "Milano," the collective mastery of shifting time signatures on "Valeria," and Heath's contributions to the perky Lewis original, "D and E," a swinger written with Basie in mind. *Pyramid* 𝄢𝄢𝄢𝄢 (Atlantic, 1960, prod. Nesuhi Ertegun) features Lewis, Jackson, Health, and Kay in six tunes recorded on four separate dates between 1959–60, including fresh versions of their classics "Django," "It Don't Mean a Thing," "Vendome" and others. No quibble with the virtuosic performances, but a drawback of this CD, warranting the lower rating, is its brevity (36:48). Don't expect a stodgy session on *Blues on Bach* 𝄢𝄢𝄢𝄢 (Atlantic, 1974/1987, prod. Nesuhi Ertegun). While the Bach chorale piece, "Jesu Joy of Man's Desiring" is covered wonderfully on the MJQ remake, "Precious Joy," featuring Lewis on harpsichord, much of the rest of the 40-plus minutes of alternating Bach-based fare and blues swings lightly. Although this session doesn't match the vibrancy of some of their other recordings, the four original blues (three by Lewis and one by Jackson) fit neatly into the 1973 session, making this CD featuring Lewis, Jackson, Heath, and Kay an improviser's dream that holds appeal for classical and jazz fans alike. A unique departure for the MJQ, *Place Vendôme* 𝄢𝄢𝄢𝄢 (Philips/Verve, 1989) features the quartet in a 37-minute session with the Swingle Singers, performing seven tunes that meld jazz to classical selections, including the "Air for G String" from the Swingle Singer's best-selling album, *Jazz Sebastian Bach*) and originals by John Lewis. Best is Lewis's lively swinger, "Alexander's Fugue." The two groups blend comfortably to provide a pleasureful listen for fans of the MJQ, light classical music, and vocal jazz.

best of the rest:
Modern Jazz Quartet/Milt Jackson Quartet 𝄢𝄢𝄢𝄢 (Prestige, 1954/1984)
Odds against Tomorrow 𝄢𝄢𝄢𝄢 (Blue Note, 1959/1989)
The Best of the Modern Jazz Quartet 𝄢𝄢𝄢𝄢 (Pablo, 1984–85/1988)
Together Again: Live at the Montreux Jazz Festival '82 𝄢𝄢𝄢𝄢 (Pablo, 1985/1987)

worth searching for: *Paul Desmond and the Modern Jazz Quartet* 𝄢𝄢𝄢𝄢 (Sony/Red Baron, 1971/1993, prod. John Lewis, Ken Glancy, reissue prod. Bob Thiele) is a live-recorded Desmond date captured at New York's Town Hall on Christmas Day, 1971, six years before his death. The seven classics are earmarked by easy rhythms, smooth, sparse lines, and understated phrasing inherent in the MJQs chamber music-like approach to jazz. The one departure is a clever take on the show tune, "Jesus Christ Superstar." Overall, it's a laid-back recording highlighting the supple saxisms of the King of Cool, Paul Desmond.

see also: *Kenny Clarke, Percy Heath, Tootie Heath, Milt Jackson, John Lewis*

Nancy Ann Lee

Charles Moffett

Born September 6, 1929, in Ft. Worth, TX.

With his place in jazz history pretty well sealed by being in Ornette Coleman's explosive 1965–67 trio (that of the Golden Circle dates), as well as appearances with Sonny Rollins, Archie Shepp, and Frank Lowe—not to mention that he fathered bassist Charnett, drummer Cody, and three other musical Moffetts—it's probably not surprising that drummer Charles Moffett didn't venture into leader territory too often. Although he led a trio in 1964 that featured Carla Bley and Pharoah Sanders, Moffett didn't record his first album until 1969. A stint teaching music school followed, along with sporadic playing around the Bay Area. A 1974 collaboration he recorded with his kids has thankfully fallen out of print.

what's available: The opening track on *The Gift* 𝄢𝄢𝄢 (Savoy, 1969, prod. Paul Jeffrey), Moffett's only available outing as a leader, pretty much sums up the *modus operandi*: "Avant Garde Got Soul Too." Featuring his then-seven-year-old drummer son Codaryl (a.k.a. Cody), as well as the slightly older drummer Dennis O'Toole, the elder Moffett is rarely found playing drums on the record. Although he does shine on vibes and the occasional Ornette-like trumpet, most of the groove here is archaically funky, with the disruptions from Codaryl's elementary playing balanced by sympathetic bassman Wilbur Ware's simple bass style.

influences:
◀◀ Elvin Jones

Jason Ferguson

Charnett Moffett

Born June 10, 1967, in New York, NY.

Playing upright bass with Wynton Marsalis's post-bop quintet from 1983–85, teenage Charnett Moffett quickly earned a reputation as a straight-ahead player. So it came as quite a surprise when Moffett (the son of drummer Charles Moffett Sr.) played so much electric bass on his debut album *Net Man* and liberally incorporated R&B and funk elements. Moffett has stressed in interviews that he never considered himself a "jazz purist" and, in fact, his work as a sideman ranges from hard bop gigs with Slide Hampton, Mulgrew Miller, and Monty Alexander to fusion with Stanley Jordan, David Sanborn, and Sonny Sharrock. Unafraid of "outside" playing, he was with Ornette Coleman from 1993–95. Moffett has also recorded some weak "smooth jazz" albums, but his resume has many more pluses than minuses.

what to buy: A departure from the music he'd been playing with Wynton Marsalis, *Net Man* ♫♫♫ (Blue Note, 1986) demonstrated Moffett's proficiency on both the electric and acoustic basses and underscored his passion for fusion as well as straight-ahead post-bop. Ron Carter was still an influence, but his love of fusionists such as Jaco Pastorius and Stanley Clarke was also evident. Fusion is dominant on *Still Life* ♫♫♫ (Evidence, 1996, prod. Charnett Moffett, Hiro Yamashita), an ambitious trio date with keyboardist-pianist Rachel Z and drummer Cindy Blackman. Whether Moffett is being reflective on "Journey" or aggressive on "Ocean Wave," *Still Life* is without a dull moment.

what to avoid: For the most part, *Nettwork* ♫ (Manhattan, 1991, prod. Kenny Kirkland) finds Moffett wasting his talents on sappy, mindless "elevator Muzak" that was obviously recorded strictly for radio airplay. Artistic integrity clearly wasn't a priority on "Angela II," "Spirits," the annoying "Don't Take My Heart Away," and other dreadful cuts that are as embarrassing as they are fluffy.

the rest:
Beauty Within ♫♫♫ (Blue Note, 1990)
Planet Home ♫♫♫ (Evidence, 1996)

influences:

◄◄ Ron Carter, Jaco Pastorius, Stanley Clarke, Jimmy Garrison

Alex Henderson

Grachan Moncur III

Born June 3, 1937, in New York, NY.

Many musicians far less talented than the woefully unknown composer and trombonist Grachan Moncur III have made considerably bigger splashes. Such is the price of honesty and daring. Moncur was born into the tradition. His father, Grachan Moncur II was a bassist with the Savoy Sultans who accompanied great jazz singers such as Billie Holiday and Mildred Bailey. A contemporary of Wayne Shorter's, with whom he played in a Newark school ensemble, Moncur III attended the Manhattan School of Music and Juilliard. The young musician apprenticed with Ray Charles and the Farmer-Golson Jazztet in 1962 before following his muse and becoming the trombonist of choice for a burgeoning 1960s avant-garde movement. His recordings with Sonny Rollins, Jackie McLean, Wayne Shorter, and Lee Morgan were but the first step leading to Moncur's playing with even more "out" musicians such as Archie Shepp, Marion Brown, and Frank Lowe. In addition to his skills on the

trombone, he was also sought out for his writing abilities, contributing effective, interesting material to sessions by Shepp, Beaver Harris, and the Jazz Composers Orchestra plus the bulk of material heard on McLean's classic *Destination Out* album. He also populated his own rare solo recording opportunities (most of which are out of print) with adventurous compositions and fine playing beyond the influences of J.J. Johnson. Even as Moncur was working the new music angle, he never forgot the roots of his art and has played with a variety of more mainstream musicians such as John Patton, Cassandra Wilson, and the Paris Reunion Band.

what's available: After Moncur joined the Art Farmer/Benny Golson Jazztet, he made his most significant musical connection with Jackie McLean, and appeared with McLean's marvelous mid-1960s Blue Note "new thing" groups that included Bobby Hutcherson and Anthony Williams. It was a combination of Moncur's instrumental work and, more importantly, his startlingly fresh and unconventional compositional ideas which prompted Alfred Lion to offer Moncur a shot as a leader. Recorded only months after McLean's *One Step Beyond*, his incredibly nuanced, deeply felt, and highly experimental *Evolution* ♫♫♫♫ (Blue Note, 1963/1996, prod. Alfred Lion) is at least arguably the better album of his two Blue Note recordings and is available as a Japanese pressing. McLean, Hutcherson, Williams, Lee Morgan, and bassist Bob Cranshaw all play with grace, determination and grit, and *Evolution* can easily hold its own among any grouping of putative "best" jazz recordings of the 1960s.

worth searching for: Currently out of print, *Some Other Stuff* ♫♫♫ (Blue Note, 1964, prod. Alfred Lion) finds Moncur leading a quintet featuring young lions who later became giants—Wayne Shorter on tenor sax, Herbie Hancock on piano, Tony Williams on drums, and bassist Cecil McBee. Everyone was playing on the cutting edge of the day and Moncur's writing gives everyone concerned a shot at the adventure. "Gnostic" is a marvelous bit of composition, showcasing the skills Moncur picked up at Juilliard. With his clean trombone playing floating over Hancock's tick-tock pianism, it sounds a lot like the kind of music modern academicians are churning out in the 1990s, but its element of avant-swing invested in the material some 30 years ago by this quintet sets this group apart. Watch for a Japanese pressing of *Some Other Stuff*, but in the meantime, if a search of the used bins yields either of his U.S.-released Blue Note gems, don't scream too loud. You'll also find Moncur contributing to a couple of tracks of Impulse!'s excellent, live, multiple-artist sampler, *The New Wave in Jazz* ♫♫♫♫ (GRP/Impulse!, 1978/1994, prod. Bob Thiele), that also features groups led by John Coltrane, Archie Shepp, and Charles Tolliver. Moncur guested with Joe Henderson, recorded for the import BYG and independent JCOA labels, drifted out of sight, and then resurfaced with a stronger instrumental voice on recordings with tenorist Frank Lowe (*Decision in Paradise*), drummer Beaver Harris and his 360 Degree Music Experience (*Beautiful Africa*), and bassist William Parker (*In Order to Survive*), all found on the Italian-import labels, Black Saint and Soul Note.

influences:

◀◀ J.J. Johnson, Kai Winding, Jimmy Knepper

▶▶ Steve Turre, Ray Anderson, Conrad Herwig

David Prince and Garaud MacTaggart

Thelonious Monk

Born October 10, 1917, in Rocky Mount, NC. Died February 17, 1982, in Weehawken, NJ.

Thelonious Monk was aligned with the bebop movement—he, Charlie Parker, and Dizzy Gillespie are considered the leading innovators of the genre's harmonic advances—yet in many ways (structurally, rhythmically, improvisationally) Monk stood apart from bebop. Ironically, at the same time critics were attacking his highly personal piano style as merely incompetent (mostly because he didn't favor the quicksilver right-hand figures Bud Powell made his fame with), musicians were complaining that Monk's compositions were too hard to learn, full of unexpected yet utterly logical juxtapositions that still sound modern. He insisted that improvisation should be derived from the melody rather than just the changes, another characteristic that set him apart from bebop orthodoxy. It helped that, as is often noted, his frequently witty compositions were more than just a melody over a chord progression. The way Monk stripped away the filigree of bebop, and his seeming disregard of "wrong note" accusations, made him a beacon of integral artistic vision in the face of ignorance and misunderstanding; combined with his deconstruction of everyday jazz structures, it suggests Monk could be called the first jazz post-modernist. And within a decade of his death, his compositions were more popular among jazz performers than ever.

Monk grew up in New York City (near where Lincoln Center is nowadays). By his early teens he was playing professionally as well as accompanying his mother, a singer, in church; he later spent a couple of years touring with an evangelist. Monk also studied at Juilliard, and by the end of the 1930s had regular work, with some of his more famous employers including Lucky

THELONIOUS MONK

song "Bright Mississippi"
album *Monk's Dream*
(Columbia, 1962/1991)
instrument Piano

Millinder (1942), Coleman Hawkins (1943–45), Cootie Williams (1944), who was the first to record Monk's best-known composition, "'Round Midnight," and the Dizzy Gillespie big band. More importantly, he was in the house band at Minton's Playhouse, a Harlem club known as one of the primary New York City breeding grounds of the emerging bebop style. In 1947 he made his first recordings as a leader, 78-rpm discs for Blue Note that remain modernist touchstones to this day.

Monk's career was seriously impeded when he was arrested on drug charges (supposedly the drugs were not his, but he refused to implicate their owner). At that time in New York City, musicians needed a cabaret card from the police to work in clubs, and the drug charge kept him from playing in the city's clubs for six years, forcing Monk to survive on recording sessions and out-of-town gigs. A short and not entirely successful affiliation with Prestige gave way to a long-term attachment with a new label, Riverside, which encouraged his ambitions and was rewarded with the best work of his career. Soon after regaining his cabaret card, Monk had a long run at the Five

Spot Café leading a quartet featuring John Coltrane, and his star once again began rising. He became a big enough attraction that Columbia signed him away from Riverside. Monk began recording for Columbia in 1962, and with major-label money promoting him, his fame spread even further, with tours of Europe and Japan and a *Time* magazine cover story. By the end of the decade, however, diminished health cut into his activities, and his last major tour (with a bebop all-stars band) came in 1971–72. When he died in 1982, he had not officially played in public for six years. His son, T.S. Monk, is a drummer who has had success in both pop and jazz. Among the greats nurtured by Monk were Bud Powell, Sonny Rollins, John Coltrane, and Steve Lacy, and his style was an influence on Randy Weston, Mal Waldron, and other pianists. The most important annual jazz competition for young musicians is named for him. As an innovator, player, composer, and bandleader, Monk will always be counted among the most exclusive elite in the jazz pantheon.

what to buy: *The Complete Riverside Recordings* 𝄞𝄞𝄞𝄞𝄞 (Riverside/Fantasy, 1986, prod. Orrin Keepnews) is a 15-CD set. Is it fair to recommend a box of this size as the first choice? Absolutely, when it's an artist as great as Monk and the box consists of albums as consistently superb and non-redundant as these. Almost all of the original albums are must-owns, and the additional tracks are fascinating for Monk aficionados. And as always with these Fantasy box sets, it's much cheaper than purchasing all or even most of the CDs individually—and no Fantasy box contains more great and timeless music of such variety of context. *Thelonious Monk Plays Duke Ellington* 𝄞𝄞𝄞𝄞𝄞 (Riverside, 1955, prod. Orrin Keepnews) and *The Unique Thelonious Monk* 𝄞𝄞𝄞𝄞 (Riverside, 1956, prod. Orrin Keepnews) are trio albums with Oscar Pettiford on bass; the drummer on the first is Kenny Clarke and on the second is Art Blakey. Producer Orrin Keepnews's idea was to soften the forbidding image that had built up around the public's perception of Monk's music by having the pianist interpret familiar material in his inimitable fashion, and far from sounding like a compromise, the results are both charming and profound, whether on such slight standards as "Liza" and "Tea for Two" or the immortal classics "Honeysuckle Rose," "Mood Indigo," and the rest of the Ellington tunes. The next session, in retrospect, looks like the announcement to the world of Monk's genius (just in case the world hadn't already noticed). *Brilliant Corners* 𝄞𝄞𝄞𝄞 (Riverside, 1956, prod. Orrin Keepnews) adds horns (tenor saxophonist Sonny Rollins throughout; altoist Ernie Henry on three tunes, with trumpeter Clark Terry replacing him on a

fourth), puts Max Roach in the drum seat, and focuses on Monk's unique compositions, especially the tricky and intricate title track. "Ba-lue Bolivar Ba-lues-are" shows that in Monk's hands even a blues takes on unsuspected depth, the pretty "Pannonica" is a classic, and "Bemsha Swing" is an upbeat gem, with Monk's solo piano version of the standard "I Surrender, Dear" delightful filler. With one notable exception, *Thelonious Himself* 𝄞𝄞𝄞𝄞 (Riverside, 1957, prod. Orrin Keepnews) is solo piano performances of standards ("April in Paris," "I Should Care," etc.) and Monk tunes (the stride-inflected "Functional"; the most familiar of all Monk classics, "'Round Midnight," etc.). The box has an abundance of outtakes; both box and album contain, most fascinatingly, 22 minutes of "'Round Midnight" which follows Monk as he works out this new version. And "Monk's Mood" adds tenor saxophonist Coltrane and bassist Wilbur Ware, the first instance of Trane recording with Monk. Just two months later, Monk, Coltrane, Ware, and Blakey were joined by trumpeter Ray Copeland, altoist Gigi Gryce, and tenor legend Coleman Hawkins for *Monk's Music* 𝄞𝄞𝄞𝄞 (Riverside, 1957, prod. Orrin Keepnews), which as the title indicates contains more Monk-penned classics ranging from the gorgeous and delicate "Crepuscule with Nellie" and the quirky "Off Minor," to the familiar "Epistrophy" and "Well, You Needn't," which elicit powerful solos, plus the ballad "Ruby, My Dear" played magisterially by a quartet of Hawkins and the rhythm section. A quartet of Coltrane and the rhythm section (with Shadow Wilson on drums) came next on the three tunes at the heart of *Thelonious Monk with John Coltrane* 𝄞𝄞𝄞𝄞 (Jazzland, 1957, prod. Orrin Keepnews): "Ruby, My Dear," "Nutty," and "Trinkle, Tinkle." These are crucial documents of that historic quartet, though the separate album duplicates Coltrane items from the previous sessions. Sliding baritone sax great Gerry Mulligan into the horn slot produced *Mulligan Meets Monk* 𝄞𝄞𝄞𝄞 (Riverside, 1957, prod. Orrin Keepnews), which works much better than some critics have claimed; Mulligan probes the music from a different perspective than Hawkins and Coltrane and finds different depths, emphasizing contrapuntal aspects of Monk's music that others seemed not to notice. The box also includes an enjoyable session led by Clark Terry at this point. The next Monk-directed sessions yielded this writer's favorite Monk albums of all, *Misterioso* 𝄞𝄞𝄞𝄞 (Riverside, 1958, prod. Orrin Keepnews) and *Thelonious in Action* 𝄞𝄞𝄞𝄞 (Riverside, 1958, prod. Orrin Keepnews), recorded live at the Five Spot Cafe with Johnny Griffin on tenor sax, Ahmed Abdul-Malik on bass, and Roy Haynes on drums (all slightly underrated nowadays, it seems, compared to their genuine stature). Griffin's harmonic mastery and Haynes's motivically based drumming make them perfect complements to the leader's vision, and the generous programs of the separate CDs make these two albums the ideal introduction to Thelonious's oeuvre. From "Rhythm-a-ning" and "Evidence" to "Blue Monk" and "Misterioso," plus such lesser-known gems as "Light Blue" and "Coming on the Hudson," every piece has a purity of focus and avoidance of superfluous gestures rarely equalled in any art form. Another very special project appears on *At Town Hall* 🎵🎵🎵🎵 (Riverside, 1959, prod. Orrin Keepnews), which features Hall Overton's arrangements of Monk tunes for rhythm section and seven horns; bass and drums are Sam Jones and Art Taylor, and the three quartet numbers also recorded that night (but not released at that time) offer the first documentation of Charlie Rouse, who would be Monk's tenor saxophonist of choice for many years to come. The arrangements are totally faithful to the details and spirit of Monk's tunes, and among the horns are baritone saxophonist Pepper Adams, trumpeter Donald Byrd, and altoist Phil Woods. *5 by Monk by 5* 🎵🎵🎵🎵 (Riverside, 1959, prod. Orrin Keepnews) adds trumpeter Thad Jones to the quartet on the immortal "Straight, No Chaser" and "I Mean You," the then-new "Jackie-ing" and "Played Twice" (reminiscent somewhat of the *Brilliant Corners* session for their akimbo trickiness), and the underrated "Ask Me Now." *Thelonious Alone in San Francisco* 🎵🎵🎵🎵 (Riverside, 1959, prod. Orrin Keepnews) captures Monk playing solo and at his most relaxed in a mixture of his tunes and some less-familiar standards. Another San Francisco session the following year, *At the Blackhawk* 🎵🎵🎵🎵 (Riverside, 1960, prod. Orrin Keepnews) is notable for complementing Rouse, Monk, and bassist John Ore with drummer Billy Higgins, trumpeter Joe Gordon, and tenorman Harold Land. *San Francisco Holiday* 🎵🎵🎵🎵 (Riverside, 1960, prod. Orrin Keepnews) as currently constituted in its separate version mixes additional material from this session and others. The Riverside years were concluded, after Monk had moved to Columbia, with the acquisition of two European concert performances by the quartet, *Monk in France* 🎵🎵🎵🎵 (Riverside, 1961) and *Monk in Italy* 🎵🎵🎵🎵 (Riverside, 1961), with Rouse, Ore, and drummer Frankie Dunlop. These are less essential but still quite rewarding listening, though Dunlop isn't quite up to the imaginative standards of Monk's previous drummers.

what to buy next: *The Complete Blue Note Recordings* 🎵🎵🎵🎵 (Blue Note, 1947–52, 1957–58, prod. Alfred Lion/1994, reissue prod. Michael Cuscuna) contains Monk's first major body of work. The earliest work here, the 1947 sessions aren't with stellar musicians, excepting of course drum great Art Blakey, an important collaborator in Monk's uniquely insistent rhyth-

mic innovations; Monk's compositions star instead. In the pre-LP era, everything was recorded for singles issued on 78-rpm discs (thus, all but one of the '47–'52 tracks are under four minutes); the conciseness of necessity is well-suited to Monk's gem-like development of his materials. When vibraphonist Milt Jackson is added in the 1948 and 1951 sessions, the improvising heats up considerably. The 1952 session with another drum great, Max Roach, as well as better horn players (trumpeter Kenny Dorham especially) yielded only six tunes (plus alternates), only one of which Monk continued to play much in future years, but everything is distinctively individualistic. In fact, because such Monk standards as "Thelonious," "Ruby My Dear," "Well You Needn't," "Off Minor," "Introspection," "Monk's Mood," "'Round Midnight," "Evidence," "Misterioso," "I Mean You," "Four in One," "Criss Cross," and "Straight, No Chaser," all of which appear throughout the first three discs' encapsulation of '47–'52, often for the first time, were returned to almost obsessively in his later years, it's the tunes he dropped from his repertoire that keep this collection fresh for dedicated Monk lovers. There are also a pair of Monk tunes ("Misterioso" and "Reflections") from a 1957 Sonny Rollins session that Monk guested on. Jazz fans who for some reason don't want to spring for the entire box can acquire *Genius of Modern Music, Volume 1* 🎵🎵🎵🎵 (Blue Note) and *Genius of Modern Music, Volume 2* 🎵🎵🎵🎵 (Blue Note), which draw on the material on the first three discs of the box set. The final disc contains a recently discovered 1958 Five Spot live gig with a quartet including Coltrane on tenor sax, Ahmed Abdul-Malik on bass, and Roy Haynes on drums. After issuing *Live at the Five Spot: Discovery!* 🎵🎵🎵🎵 (Blue Note, 1993, prod. Michael Cuscuna, T.S. Monk) as a separate CD, the label remastered it for the box set and provided some much-needed pitch correction. Despite the still less-than-pristine recording quality it's of great value, and not just for Coltrane's nascent contributions. Roy Haynes's motivic style made him the drummer most ideally suited to accompany Monk, and Haynes's solos are such masterpieces of thematic development that they're like a drum version of Monk's piano style. And Monk himself is in top form. Monk's Columbia years have gotten a bad rap as a period when he just repeated his old repertoire over and over and was nearly always recorded in the same quartet setting. Eventually these elements became a problem, but he made some fine albums for the company. On his Columbia debut, *Monk's Dream* 🎵🎵🎵🎵 (Columbia, 1962/1991, prod. Teo Macero) it may be true that he'd recorded seven of the eight songs previously, but he sounds absolutely exhilarated, and there's not the slightest sense of routine—though the most exciting track is the new

Thelonious Monk (© Jack Vartoogian)

one, "Bright Mississippi" (a derivative of "Sweet Georgia Brown"). This is the quartet with Charlie Rouse (tenor sax), John Ore (bass), and Frankie Dunlop (drums), and their interaction is positively psychic. The only possible complaint is that the sound's a bit bright and echoey, as if recorded in a tile bathroom, but this was somewhat fashionable at the time and doesn't detract from enjoyment. The two-CD *Big Band and Quartet in Concert* ♫♫♫♫ (Columbia, 1964/1994, prod. Teo Macero, reissue prod. John Snyder) is a sequel to the previous big band album (on Riverside), also arranged by Hall Overton, and fortunately none of the arrangements overlap. There are also solo and quartet numbers. Those looking for unusual Monk repertoire should get *Straight, No Chaser* ♫♫♫♫ (Columbia, 1967/1996, prod. Teo Macero, reissue prod. Orrin Keepnews). It has a nice mix of tunes he'd been playing forever ("Locomotive," the title tune), a standard not noted for being in his repertoire that he nonetheless makes his own ("Between the Devil and the Deep Blue Sea"), and material that was new for him ("Japanese Folk Song," "Green Chimneys"). Monk was ob-

viously still feeling challenged and stimulated, and it shows. And as always, praise is due Rouse, who fit so well with Monk while retaining his own special voice. There's also the bonus inclusion of Monk's solo version of an old hymn, "This Is My Story, This Is My Song," which wasn't issued until after Monk's death. He just plays it straight, with no improvised section, and even flubs his fingering at one point and just stops and replays that chord. But the thick chord voicings make the interpretation special. The other bonus track is the interesting first version of "Green Chimneys." The most recent CD reissue restores editing cuts made to cram the material onto LP when it first came out.

what to avoid: Unlike the two Overton-arranged big band albums, *Monk's Blues* ♫♫ (Columbia, 1969/1993, prod. Teo Macero, reissue prod. John Snyder) sometimes sounds garish and unidiomatic. Oliver Nelson was a fine arranger, but his style clashes with Monk's enough to make the fit uncomfortable. There's still musical enjoyment to be gleaned from this release, but given the vastness of Monk's discography this album should be a low priority. Even less important are the many concert bootlegs of Monk in the 1960s. Given all the quartet recordings he did in the decade, and the availability of high-quality sonic on dates such as *Live at the It Club* and the Mobile Fidelity gold discs listed below, there's not much point in acquiring muddy-sounding versions of the same old songs played by the same old groups, so *Evidence* ♫♫ (Esoldun, 1987); *The Bebop Legends* ♫♫ (Jazz Up/New Sound Planet, 1988), which is half Monk in 1965 and half J.J. Johnson in 1964; *April in Paris* ♫♫ (Bandstand, 1990); and similar barrel-scrapings can be safely ignored by all but the most obsessive completists. Finally, Columbia has recycled its Monk recordings on many compilations, and while there's nothing wrong with that, six out of the 10 tracks on *This Is Jazz 5: Thelonious Monk* **woof!** (Columbia, 1996) are also on *The Composer*, making the new set utterly superfluous while the slightly more generous 11-track collection remains in the catalog.

best of the rest:

Monk ♫♫♫ (Prestige, 1952, 1954/Fantasy Original Jazz Classics, 1982)
Thelonious Monk Trio ♫♫♫♫ (Prestige, 1953–54/Fantasy Original Jazz Classics, 1982)
Thelonious Monk/Sonny Rollins ♫♫♫♫♫ (Prestige, 1953–54/Fantasy Original Jazz Classics, 1982)
In Paris ♫♫♫♫♫ (Vogue, 1954/Vogue/RCA, 1995)
Criss-Cross ♫♫♫♫♫ (Columbia, 1963)
It's Monk's Time ♫♫♫♫ (Columbia, 1964)
Live at the It Club ♫♫♫♫♫ (1964/Columbia, 1982/1998)
Solo Monk ♫♫♫♫ (Columbia, 1965)
Underground ♫♫♫♫ (Columbia, 1968)
The Complete London Collection ♫♫♫♫ (Black Lion, 1971/1996)
Memorial Album ♫♫♫♫♫ (Milestone, 1982)
And the Jazz Giants ♫♫♫♫♫ (Riverside, 1987)
The Composer ♫♫♫♫ (Columbia, 1988)
Standards ♫♫♫♫ (Columbia, 1989)
The Best of Thelonious Monk: The Blue Note Years ♫♫♫♫♫ (Blue Note, 1991)
Live at Monterey Jazz Festival, '63, Volume I ♫♫♫♫ (Storyville, 1994/Mobile Fidelity Sound Lab Ultradisc II, 1997)
Live at Monterey Jazz Festival, '63, Volume II ♫♫♫♫ (Storyville, 1994/Mobile Fidelity Sound Lab Ultradisc II, 1997)

worth searching for: *Art Blakey's Jazz Messengers with Thelonious Monk* ♫♫♫♫♫ (Atlantic, 1957, prod. Nesuhi Ertegun) is much more than Monk filling the piano seat in Blakey's famous quintet. The tenor saxophonist is Johnny Griffin, who the following year would work with Monk extensively, and five of the six tunes are among Monk's most classic compositions. The band is filled out nicely by trumpeter Bill Hardman and bassist Spanky DeBrest. For unknown reasons, Columbia continues to pair two concerts by different bands separated by five years on *Miles & Monk at Newport* ♫♫♫♫ (Columbia, 1994, prod. Teo Macero, reissue prod. Nedra Olds-Neal), which at this point has gone from a single LP to a two-CD set. The Monk half is superb, containing a 1963 concert that included clarinetist Pee Wee Russell (usually associated with Dixieland but quite an open-minded and unique player) sitting in on two lengthy numbers.

influences:

◀◀ Duke Ellington, Fats Waller, Charlie Christian

▶▶ Bud Powell, Mal Waldron, Herbie Nichols, Randy Weston, McCoy Tyner, Cecil Taylor, Ornette Coleman, Eric Dolphy, Steve Lacy, John Coltrane, Barry Harris, Kenny Barron, Marcus Roberts, Sphere, Harry Connick Jr., Steely Dan, Lounge Lizards

Steve Holtje

T.S. Monk

Born December 27, 1949, in New York, NY.

As the son of legendary pianist/composer Thelonious Monk, T.S. Monk (Thelonious Sphere Jr.) has been immersed in jazz since birth, but he didn't decide to devote himself to playing the music until relatively late in his career. A hard-driving drummer, Monk has made his mark as a bandleader, having assembled a superlative sextet that alternates between reviving vintage bop and hard-bop arrangements, and covering original pieces in much the same spirit. Early on, Monk took lessons with Max Roach and Stanley Spector and played on the party circuit before joining his father's band in 1970. He spent two years touring with his father, then worked with him intermittently until Monk Sr. retired in 1975. In the mid-1970s, T.S. played with a fusion band called Natural Essence and from 1974–76 he worked with the Paul Jeffrey Big Band. He formed an R&B group, T.S. Monk, and scored a number of hits. He worked his way back into the jazz scene playing with Clifford Jordan's big band and with Walter Davis Jr. before assembling his own sextet in the late 1980s. Through steady touring and stable personnel the group has turned into one of the premier hard-bop repertory groups in jazz. It has also become an important showcase for young composers working in the advanced hard bop tradition. As chairman of the Thelonious Monk Institute of Jazz for more than a decade, Monk has also made an impact on jazz by sponsoring jazz education programs and an annual contest that has helped advance the careers of players such as Bill Cunliffe, Joshua Redman, Ryan Kisor, and Jacky Terrasson.

what to buy: Monk has maintained his working sextet throughout the 1990s, and *The Charm* 🎵🎵🎵🎵 (Blue Note, 1995, prod. T.S. Monk, Don Sickler) shows how steady work can bind a group together. Though none of the horn players are stars, Don Sickler (trumpet), Bobby Porcelli (alto sax, flute), and Willie Williams (tenor and soprano sax) are a highly potent front line. Veteran pianist Ronnie Mathews and bassist Scott Colley are also top-notch players. The band scores continually here by finding rarely played gems, such as Melba Liston's "Just Waiting," Buddy Montgomery's "Budini," and Walter Davis Jr.'s "Gypsy Folk Tales." *Changing of the Guard* 🎵🎵🎵🎵 (Blue Note, 1993, prod. T.S. Monk, Don Sickler) is the T.S. Monk band's second album and features excellent new jazz tunes such as pianist James Williams's title track, alto saxophonist Bobby Watson's "Appointment in Milano," and pianist Donald Brown's "New York." The session also includes well-known pieces by the senior Monk, "Monk's Dream" and "Crepuscule with Nellie," Kenny Dorham's "Una Mas," and J.J. Johnson's "Kelo" as well as Idrees Sulieman's boppish "Doublemint" and Clifford Jordan's "Middle of the Block" taken at a bruising tempo. Don Sickler (trumpet), Bobby Porcelli (alto sax, flute), Willie Williams (tenor and soprano sax), and Ronnie Mathews (piano) are back from the first album, with bassist Scott Colley the only personnel change.

what to buy next: Trumpeter Don Sickler is as much the star of the T.S. Monk band's debut, *Take One* 🎵🎵🎵🎵 (Blue Note, 1992, prod. T.S. Monk, Don Sickler), as any of the soloists. His transcriptions and arrangements of great bop-oriented tunes make this album a pleasure, from Kenny Dorham's "Monaco" and "Minor's Holiday," to Elmo Hope's "Boa" to Hank Mobley's "Infra-Rae." There's also a healthy dose of senior Monk, with the rarely played "Skippy," and "Think of One," and Max Roach's original arrangement of "'Round Midnight." Except for bassist James Genus, the rest of the band—Sickler, Porcelli, Williams, and Mathews—has remained constant.

the rest:
T.S. Monk on Monk 🎵🎵🎵🎵 (N2K Encoded Music, 1997)

influences:
◀◀ Tony Williams, Max Roach, Art Blakey

Andrew Gilbert

J.R. Monterose

Born Frank Anthony Monterose Jr., January 19, 1927, in Detroit, MI. Died September 16, 1993, in Utica, NY.

A tenor and soprano player of considerable talent, J.R. Monterose performed and recorded frequently in New York through the 1950s in the tradition of Charlie Parker and Lester Young. Monterose came into his own in the mid-1960s after withdrawing to perform at smaller venues in the Midwest and upstate New York. His playing became still more articulate and introspective after returning from Europe, where he lived from 1967–75.

In 1928 Monterose's family moved to Utica, New York. He began playing clarinet in the school band at age 13, and switched to tenor saxophone at 15. He performed with area bands in the late 1940s before moving to New York, where he played with Buddy Rich and Claude Thornhill in the early 1950s. Monterose first recorded with Teddy Charles in 1955, and played with bop groups led by Jon Eardley, Ralph Sharon, and Eddie Bert. He joined Charles Mingus's Jazz Workshop in 1956, but left soon thereafter to join Kenny Dorham's group. He led several recording sessions before moving to Cedar Rapids, Iowa in 1963, where he performed and recorded with Joe Abodeely. Monterose moved to Manchester, England and later Belgium, where he played sporadically and took up the soprano saxophone and classical guitar. He returned to the States in the late 1970s and continued to perform into the 1980s near Albany, New York.

what to buy: In his soprano debut, Monterose is paired with pianist Tommy Flanagan for a mixture of standards and originals on *A Little Pleasure* 🎵🎵🎵🎵 (Uptown, 1981/Reservoir, 1988/1993, prod. Mark Feldman). One can hardly imagine a better framework for Monterose than the equally melodic Flanagan. Their beautiful rendition of "Central Park West" is as gentle as the Coltrane original, without being imitative. The tenor selections are just as delightful, especially Monterose's bouncy original, "Vinnie's Pad." The focus and control Monterose was able to harness during his 14-month club gig at the Tender Trap in Cedar Rapids, Iowa is evident on *In Action* 🎵🎵🎵🎵 (Bainbridge, 1964/1990, prod. Dimitri Sotirarkis, Tony Sotirarkis). He maintains firm phrasing on the boppers "Red Devil" and "Herky Hawkes," and his brief, staccato-like bursts are especially effective on "Waltz for Claire." Monterose is well-miked, but the rest of his ensemble, made up of little-known Midwestern musicians, sounds submerged.

what to avoid: The club setting allows Monterose considerable room for improvisation on *Bebop Loose and Live* 🎵🎵 (Cadence, 1982, prod. Bob Rusch), but the performances might have been better if paired down. In contrast to the taut solos on the releases recommended above, Monterose plays overlong, sprawling solos on the chestnut "What's New" and Kenny Dorham's "Blue Bossa." The contributions from supporting tenor Hugh Brodie are not particularly memorable, and the rhythm section is thrust in the background behind the chatter of club patrons, especially pianist Larry Ham. The album's saving grace is Montrose's tight soprano on "Green Dolphin Street."

influences:

 Coleman Hawkins, Lester Young, Charlie Parker, Sonny Rollins

Jeff Samoray

Buddy Montgomery

Born Charles F. Montgomery, January 30, 1930, in Indianapolis, IN.

The youngest of the Montgomery Brothers, Buddy's associations include work with Lionel Hampton, Joe Turner, and, briefly, Miles Davis. He gained recognition with brothers Wes and Monk in the Montgomery-Johnson Quintet in 1955. Two years later, Buddy and Monk formed the Mastersounds, which occasionally featured Wes. Buddy usually played vibes in this setting. Shortly after disbanding the group in 1960, the three played as the Montgomery Brothers through 1961. During the '60s, Buddy played piano and vibes with a number of groups, but by 1969 focused on piano. During the '70s and '80s, he devoted his time to community and educational projects in Milwaukee, where he was a leading local musician, and later Oakland, California, where he organized the first Oakland Jazz Festival in 1987. Buddy returned to recording in the late '80s with two now-unavailable recordings on the Landmark label. He has since recorded an excellent solo piano album for Concord and has another title due out in 1998.

what's available: *Live at Maybeck Recital Hall, Volume 15* 𝄞𝄞𝄞𝄞 (Concord Jazz, 1992, prod. Carl E. Jefferson), a solo piano date, is another excellent entry in Concord's "Live at Maybeck" series. The material is broad in scope, including standards like "The Man I Love" and less-recorded fare like "This Time I'll Be Sweeter." Montgomery draws from an extensive list of influences and he is a fine interpreter who injects some lounge-style playing without sounding banal.

influences:

 Oscar Peterson, Bud Powell, Art Tatum

▶▶ George Cables

Paul MacArthur

Monk Montgomery

Born William Howard Montgomery, October 10, 1921, in Indianapolis, IN. Died May 20, 1982, in Las Vegas, NV.

While overshadowed as an innovator by his middle brother, the famed guitarist Wes, Monk Montgomery, the oldest of the three

WES **M**ONTGOMERY

song "Blue 'n' Boogie"
album Full House
(Riverside-OJC, 1962/1992)
instrument Guitar

Monster Solo

brothers, is historically one of the most important jazz bassists. Montgomery pioneered electric bass playing in a jazz setting, adopting the instrument in the early 1950s. As late as 1960, he was the only bassist in a major jazz combo to play electric and it is his musical treatment which is credited with influencing other jazz bassists to pick up the instrument. Montgomery played with Lionel Hampton, Art Farmer, and later with his brothers when they formed the Montgomery/Johnson Quintet (1955–56). With brother Buddy (who played piano and vibes), he formed the Mastersounds in 1957 and in 1960 with Wes and Buddy formed the short-lived Montgomery Brothers. After the Montgomery Brothers disbanded, the bassist played with various combos, including stints with Cal Tjader and Red Norvo. Like his brother Buddy, Monk made considerable effort to promote jazz. He helped form the Las Vegas Jazz Society and worked as a jazz disc jockey in Las Vegas.

what's available: Considered one of the best efforts by all three Montgomery Brothers, *Groove Yard* 𝄞𝄞𝄞𝄞 (Riverside, 1961/1994, prod. Orrin Keepnews) gives us the right taste of

Monk, Wes, and Buddy, and shows that even though Wes was the star, Monk and Buddy were also tremendous musicians. Drummer Bobby Thomas joins the brothers on this January 1961 session, and their laid-back approach makes even the most demanding passages seem effortless. The Montgomery Brothers were capable of delivering deceptive West Coast styled jazz that floats out of the speakers so naturally it almost hides the fact that all three were excellent technicians.

influences:

◀◀ Jimmy Blanton, Oscar Pettiford

Paul MacArthur

Wes Montgomery

Born March 6, 1925, in Indianapolis, IN. Died June 15, 1968, in Indianapolis, IN.

One of the most celebrated guitarists in the history of jazz, Wes Montgomery has been a major influence on everyone from George Benson to Lee Ritenour. But he was hardly an overnight sensation. Though he toured with Lionel Hampton from 1948–50, he spent most of the 1950s working day jobs and paying dues on the Indianapolis club circuit. Montgomery, known for a distinctive style that involved extensive use of his thumb, was in his 30s when he starting to enjoy national attention while recording for Riverside and working with producer Orrin Keepnews. Essentially, his albums as a leader can be divided into two categories: his improvisatory hard-bop work for Pacific Jazz (1958–59) and Riverside (1959–63), and his much more commercial pop-jazz and instrumental pop output for Verve and A&M in the mid-to-late 1960s. Though he recorded some straight-ahead jazz for Verve, most of his overproduced Verve recordings predicted the crossover and so-called "smooth jazz" of the 1970s, 1980s, and 1990s. Montgomery had reached the height of his popularity when a heart attack claimed his life at 43.

what to buy: Ranging from his trio sessions with organist Mel Rhyne on *Boss Guitar* ♫♫♫♫ (Riverside, 1963/OJC, 1989, prod. Orrin Keepnews) and *Portrait of Wes* ♫♫♫♫♫ (Riverside, 1963/OJC, 1992, prod. Orrin Keepnews), to his quintet recording with pianist Hank Jones, *So Much Guitar* ♫♫♫♫♫ (Riverside, 1961/OJC, 1987, prod. Orrin Keepnews), Montgomery's work for Riverside was usually superb and you can't go wrong buying any of those sessions. In fact, if you're really a guitar fan, a Wes fan, or have the dough, the recordings of his four years of Riverside are combined in the impressive 12-CD box set, *Wes Montgomery: The Complete Riverside Recordings* ♫♫♫♫♫

(Riverside, 1959–63/OJC, 1993, prod. Orrin Keepnews). The set features 25 of the guitarist's tracks (includes alternate takes) from his small group sessions recorded with some jazz luminaries of the period, and contains a 32-page booklet featuring interviews with Montgomery and various other musicians. (*The Incredible Jazz Guitar of Wes Montgomery* ♫♫♫♫ (Riverside, 1960/OJC, 1987, prod. Orrin Keepnews) is one of the guitarist's classic sessions. Featuring Tommy Flanagan on piano, it introduced such often-recorded originals as "Four on Six" and "West Coast Blues," plus some well-executed standards. This is the album that made Montgomery famous in the jazz realm, and it remains worthy of revisit.

what to buy next: Featuring tenor sax dynamo Johnny Griffin and pianist Wynton Kelly, *Full House* ♫♫♫♫ (Riverside, 1962/OJC, 1992, prod. Orrin Keepnews) is an outstanding live date. Kelly rejoins Montgomery on an equally strong live recording, *Smokin' at the Half Note* ♫♫♫♫, (Verve, 1965/1989), which contains soulful versions of "Four on Six" and Sam Jones's "Unit 7." *Fusion!* ♫♫♫♫ (Riverside, 1963/OJC, 1989, prod. Orrin Keepnews) unites Montgomery with a lush string orchestra, but the arrangements are tasteful (something one cannot say about much of his subsequent work with Creed Taylor), and he still has some room to stretch. *Movin' Along* ♫♫♫♫ (Riverside, 1960/OJC, 1988, prod. Orrin Keepnews), offers a rare chance to hear Montgomery on electric bass guitar.

what to avoid: Avoid it if you come across *Classics, Volume 2* ♫♫ (A&M, 1967–78, prod. Creed Taylor). The 67-minute compilation underscores everything that was wrong with Montgomery's commercial recordings for A&M. Creed Taylor smothers Montgomery's guitar with excessive producing, and the guitarist's improvisatory skills are wasted on note-for-note covers of the pop hits of the day. This album serves primarily as lightweight background music.

best of the rest:

Far Wes ♫♫♫♫ (Pacific Jazz, 1958–59/1990)

The Alternative Wes Montgomery ♫♫♫♫ (Milestone/Fantasy, 1960–63/1990)

Encores, Volume 2: Blue and Boogie ♫♫♫♫ (Milestone/Fantasy, 1962–63/1996)

The Silver Collection ♫♫♫♫ (Verve, 1965–66/1987)

Bumpin' ♫♫♫♫♫ (Verve, 1965/1987/1997)

Wes Montgomery (Archive Photos)

worth searching for: Under the leadership of vibist Milt Jackson, *Bags Meets Wes!* ♫♫♫♫ (Riverside, 1961/OJC, 1992, prod. Orrin Keepnews), is a spirited date that features Montgomery, pianist Wynton Kelly, bassist Sam Jones, and drummer Philly Joe Jones. It contains 10 tunes, including the three alternate takes added to the CD version.

influences:

◀◀ Charlie Christian

▶▶ George Benson, Lee Ritenour

Alex Henderson and Nancy Ann Lee

Tete Montoliu

Born Vincente Montoliu Massana, March 28, 1933, in Barcelona, Spain. Died August 24, 1997, in Barcelona, Spain.

Blind from birth, Tete Montoliu was a skilled pianist who began showing his talent at the age of four and learned to read music in Braille when he was seven. Raised in a musical family by a father who played with the Barcelona Symphony and a mother who loved jazz, Montoliu was exposed to the best of both worlds but, as a youngster, most enjoyed listening to his mother's jazz recordings by Duke Ellington, Fats Waller, and others. He began studies at the conservatory in Barcelona at age 16, continuing until 1953, and played jazz in a Barcelona club at night. He formed his own trio, which Lionel Hampton caught in a local club during one of his visits there and invited him to record with the band in Madrid. Montoliu toured with Hampton in Spain and in Southern France during 1955. During the 1950s–60s, Montoliu played the Cannes Jazz Festival with bassist Doug Watkins and drummer Art Taylor, led a quintet in Barcelona for eight months, performed in Berlin and Copenhagen with his own groups, and accompanied soloists Benny Bailey, Herb Geller, and others. Throughout the years he worked with visiting Americans such as Kenny Dorham, Dexter, Gordon, Ben Webster, Lucky Thompson, and led various groups of his own. He visited New York City in 1967 and performed with various musicians there, but his visits to the U.S. were infrequent. In addition to recording as sideman with a variety of leaders, Montoliu recorded as leader for SteepleChase, Enja, Soul Note, and made one Concord album. Montoliu died of lung cancer at the age of 64 in August, 1997.

what to buy: *A Spanish Treasure* ♫♫♫♫ (Concord, 1991, prod. Carl E. Jefferson) features pianist Tete Montoliu at his lyrical best, performing with bassist Rufus Reid and drummer Akira Tana, on this studio session recorded on June 17, 1991 in Tokyo. The 10-tune session includes standards by Thelonious Monk

("Misterioso"), Tadd Dameron ("Our Delight"), Cole Porter ("All of You"), Miles Davis ("All Blues"), and others which this interactive trio performs with great splash, finesse, and romanticism. It's one of his few CDs available with such illustrious side players and he seems comfortable and inspired. Highly recommended.

what to buy next: A live 1971 date recorded with bassist George Mraz and drummer Joe Nay in Munich, *Body & Soul* ♫♫♫♫♪ (Enja, 1971/1983, prod. Horst Weber) features pianist Montoliu in an energized six-tune set, playing classics such as the title tune, "A Nightingale Sang in Berkeley Square," and "Old Folks," as well as J.J. Johnson's "Lament," and more from their performance at Domicile, a Munich club. Montoliu's performance is energized at this live date, and he demonstrates his flowing, strong right-hand attack, and his percussive approach. *Songs for Love* ♫♫♫♫ (Enja, 1992, prod. Matthias Winckelmann) really plays up Montoliu's romantic side on popular favorites such as "Rainy Day," "Autumn in New York," and two others, as well as four originals. Montoliu is a fiery player whose right hand is frequently very busy, winging over the keys with driving force as he improvises on melody, while his left-hand accompaniment employs mostly sparse chords and walking bass lines. His playing is generally melodic rather than angular, and that goes along with the inspirations he's cited throughout his career.

best of the rest:

(With Niels-Henning Orsted Pedersen, Albert "Tootie" Heath) *Tete!* ♫♫♫♫ (SteepleChase, 1974/1995)
The Music I Like to Play, Vol. 1 ♫♫♫♫ (Soul Note, 1987)
The Music I Like to Play, Vol. 2 ♫♫♫♫ (Soul Note, 1989)
The Music I Like to Play, Vol. 3 ♫♫♫♫ (Soul Note, 1991)
The Music I Like to Play, Vol. 4 ♫♫♫♫ (Soul Note, 1992)

influences:

◀◀ Art Tatum, Bill Evans

Nancy Ann Lee

James Moody

Born March 26, 1925, in Savannah, GA.

Whether he's playing the tenor sax, the alto, soprano, or flute, James Moody does so with the fluidity, deep resonance, and wit that have made him one of the most consistently expressive and enduring figures in modern jazz. Moody joined the seminal bebop big band of Dizzy Gillespie in 1947 and made his mark on a six-bar solo on Gillespie's "Emanon." In 1949 he moved to Europe, where he recorded the masterpiece of improvisation for which he is renowned, "I'm in the Mood for Love." During the 1950s and 1960s, Moody continued to perform in a variety of ensembles, including a three-tenor group with Gene Ammons and Sonny Stitt in 1962. The next year, he rejoined Gillespie and performed in the trumpeter's quintet for the remainder of the decade. In the 1970s Moody moved to Las Vegas, where he began a 10-year stint in the Las Vegas Hilton Orchestra. But after a decade, Moody returned to jazz full time and moved back to New York. He resumed recording in 1985 and received a Grammy nomination for his playing on Manhattan Transfer's *Vocalese* album. He now leads his own group and records for Warner Bros. In 1996 he celebrated his 50th year in the music business.

what to buy: *Return from Overbrook* 𝄞𝄞𝄞𝄞 (Uni/Chess, 1958/1996, prod. Dave Usher) brings together some of Moody's best work from the 1950s. He has always been a reliably exciting improviser and here he plays with his accustomed flair and elegance on chestnuts such as "Parker's Mood," "Body and Soul," and "Easy Living." Bop vocalist Eddie Jefferson, who frequently wrote lyrics to Moody solos, adds his own show-stopping, offbeat wit whenever the opportunity arises. Moody faced many challenges during this period, including financial hardship from a fire that destroyed most of his charts and several instruments as well as fighting a battle with alcohol. His composition, "Last Train from Overbrook" recalls his early days at a mental institution recovering from alcohol addiction. Recorded live at New York's Blue Note during a 70th birthday tribute, *Moody's Party* 𝄞𝄞𝄞𝄞 (Telarc, 1995, prod. Erica Brenner) features Moody's Quartet, with pianist Mulgrew Miller, joined by Grover Washington Jr., Arturo Sandoval, Roy Ayers, and young lion Chris Potter for a set of Moody favorites, including "Parker's Mood," Dizzy's "Groovin' High," and "Pennies from Heaven." Moody hardly seems like he's 70 years old here, and plays with considerable youthful vitality, eliciting a vibrant, glowing sound from his alto, a broader and more plaintive tone from the tenor, and issuing plenty of interesting, modern-minded statements. For *The Blues and Other Colors* 𝄞𝄞𝄞𝄞 (OJC, 1957–1958/1997, prod. Esmond Edwards), the legendary multi-instrumentalist leaves his alto and tenor saxophones at home to present an intriguing two-part program from the mid-1950s. Part one, featuring a sextet, marks his debut on soprano sax, while part two offers an unusual setting of strings, brass, and voice for the Moody flute. In each case, the arrangements are by longtime Moody associate Tom McIntosh, who creates textures that grow adventurous without losing melodic appeal. The most audacious track is "Gone Are the Days," where the chamber group brings Stephen Foster into the Civil Rights '60s; but Moody also wails on soprano in a sanctified version of Ellington's "Main Stem," gives his flute a workout on "Old Folks," and applies his boundless imagination to four of his own originals. On Moody's 1969 album, *Don't Look Away Now!* 𝄞𝄞𝄞𝄞𝄞 (OJC, 1969/1997, prod. Esmond Edwards), a rare document from the period, Moody eschews his usual flute, instead delivering a sax-exclusive recital over an exceptional rhythm section. "When I Fall in Love" and the title track feature his tasty alto. The tongue in cheek "Hey Herb! Where's Alpert?" is vocalist Eddie Jefferson's final appearance on a Moody session. Best of all are two contrasting examples of Moody's tenor at its most expansive, the ballad "Easy Living" and the open-form "Hear Me."

what to buy next: Arranger Gil Goldstein and his assembled trio provide just the right touch of "Moodiness" for the music of Henry Mancini on *Moody Plays Mancini* 𝄞𝄞𝄞𝄞 (Warner Bros., 1997, prod. Matt Pearson, Gil Goldstein). This recording has the romantic feeling of a late-night jazz club and Moody's wonderful improvising on alto, tenor, soprano, and flute, add icing on the cake. With the simple and effective arrangement of "The Pink Panther," a vocal from Moody on the beautiful "Moon River," and a Coltraneish soprano sax treatment of the 3/4-time "Charade," Mancini's music is given a treatment which is modern, yet respects the era in which it was composed. *Young at Heart* 𝄞𝄞𝄞𝄞 (Warner Bros., 1996, prod. Matt Pearson, Gil Goldstein) contains a selection of 10 songs associated with Frank Sinatra, reinterpreted by Moody and arranger Goldstein. At age 71 Moody's sense of swing and phrasing are still impeccable, thanks to his suavely sculpted playing and Goldstein's silken horn and string arrangements. Chestnuts like "Love and Marriage," "Come Fly with Me," and "It Was a Very Good Year" sound both wise and youthful.

influences:

◀◀ Dexter Gordon, Charlie Parker, Dizzy Gillespie, Gene Ammons

▶▶ Booker Ervin, George Coleman, Sonny Rollins, Harold Land

Bret Primack

Jemeel Moondoc

Born August 5, 1951 in Chicago, IL.

Jemeel Moondoc's story is one of perseverance and conviction. He has persisted in his passionate free jazz stylings with little regard for record company indifference, rarely recording as a sideman and ignoring the discouraging words which come his way. In the process, though his recorded efforts have been uneven, he has built a 20-year career and a reputation as a fiery improvisor. However, no matter how unfettered his creativity in the heat of performance, he generally avoids the altissimo clichés of more rigid avant-gardists, and he credits his sound to listening to Lester Young.

Born and raised in Chicago, Moondoc started out on clarinet, later adding flute to his arsenal and playing in an R&B band. Rather than go to college to study architecture on a scholarship, he moved to Boston and played in the James Tatum Blues Band. While in Boston he encountered Ran Blake and, much more the catalyst for his development, first heard Cecil Taylor's music. For the next couple years he followed Taylor from one teaching post to another, playing in Taylor's college rehearsal bands despite not being enrolled at either college. But when the budding alto saxophonist decided to move to New York in 1972, Taylor opined that Moondoc wouldn't be able to make it there.

Moondoc made the move anyway. Unable to get sideman gigs because he had no contacts, he played as a leader on the loft scene. He formed Ensemble Muntu, at the core of which were Moondoc, bassist William Parker, and drummer Rashid Bakr, with members at various times including Arthur Williams (trumpet), Mark Hennen (piano), Roy Campbell (trumpet), Billy Bang (violin), Khan Jamal (vibes), and Ellen Christi (vocals). But in 1980, ironically, Cecil Taylor heard the band and hired away Parker and Bakr.

Moondoc hooked up with the Italian label Soul Note for three mid-1980s albums, which greatly increased his profile. In 1984 formed the Jus Grew Orchestra, which is usually around 15 players strong, and for a while it had a regular Monday night gig. After his final Soul Note release, Moondoc says, the decade-long hiatus from recording that would follow was primarily because he chose to channel his energies into the big band rather than hustle product to record labels. The Jus Grew Orchestra still has no releases to its name; it can't help that the recording budgets of avant-garde jazz imprints tend to be too small to absorb the greater costs of recording such large groups. Meanwhile, there were recordings made with large ensembles led by Butch Morris and Saheb Sarbib. Finally Moondoc reappeared on record as a leader after forming a performing alliance with a pair of veteran Boston improvisors, bassist John Voigt and drummer Laurence Cook. A studio session by the new trio was the first release on the indie Eremite label, featuring Moondoc compositions similar to the bare-bones style of his first and most successful Soul Note album, while a

subsequent appearance at the Amherst, Massachusetts Fire in the Valley Festival was taped for his second Eremite album.

what to buy: *Judy's Bounce* ♫♫♫♫ (Soul Note, 1982, prod. Jemeel Moondoc) finds Moondoc working in the format his playing fits best in, a trio with bass (Fred Hopkins) and drums (Ed Blackwell). The space and freedom it allows him seems to liberate his imagination, or at least not inhibit his improvisations, and he also plays far better on melodically based rather than harmonically based material, reflecting an acknowledged Ornette Coleman (to whom one track is dedicated) influence. With extremely responsive and powerful partners such as Hopkins and Blackwell to spur him on in this live concert, Moondoc— playing with a big sound for an alto saxist—reaches heights of improvisational ecstasy beyond even the nearly as good trio album of 15 years later.

what to buy next: On *Fire in the Valley* ♫♫♫♫ (Eremite, 1997, prod. Michael Ehlers) Moondoc, Voigt, and Cook let it all hang out in an epic 40-minute improvisation that ebbs and flows organically (followed by a minute-and-a-half encore). The rhythm section supports Moondoc with decorative colorations, and Voigt and Cook excel in their own moments in the spotlight.

what to avoid: *Nostalgia in Times Square* **woof!** (Soul Note, 1986, prod. Giovanni Bonandrini) is one of the most unbearable and unrewarding listening experiences ever recorded by a genuinely talented jazz musician, despite an all-star cast of Bern Nix (guitar), Rahn Burton (piano), William Parker (bass), and Dennis Charles (drums). Moondoc, Nix, Burton, and Parker are almost never in tune with each other, which is especially excruciating on this program of the Mingus title tune and three Moondoc originals based on chord changes. Moondoc's fling at playing soprano sax is especially torturous.

the rest:
Konstanze's Delight ♫♫ (Soul Note, 1983)
Tri-P-Let ♫♫♫♫ (Eremite, 1996)

worth searching for: *First Feeding* ♫♫♫ (Muntu, 1977, prod. Piano Magic & Ensemble Muntu) and *Evening of the Blue Men* ♫♫♫♫ (Muntu, 1981) were Moondoc's first recordings. He leads his Ensemble Muntu through sketchily written themes that serve as springboards for fervent free improvisation. Muntu was Moondoc's own company, and these LPs are out-of-print collector's items. *New York Live!* ♫♫♫ (Cadence, 1981) is also only on LP, but remains in print. The later edition of Muntu with trumpeter Roy Campbell plays a 20-minute version of "Salt Peanuts" that avoids the pitfalls of *Nostalgia in Times Square* by using the theme and rhythm but not the changes, playing it free. Campbell's "Thanks to the Creator" is also heard, both tracks coming from a 1980 concert. The flipside is Moondoc's energetic "High Rise" from a 1981 gig, with vocalist Ellen Christi, an acquired taste to say the least, but fitting in better—and singing less—than on *Konstanze's Delight*. Campbell in particular was in good form that night.

influences:

Albert Ayler, Jimmy Lyons, Cecil Taylor, Ornette Coleman, Lester Young

Steve Holtje

Ralph Moore

Born December 24, 1956, in Brixton, England.

A big-toned tenor saxophonist who has fully assimilated John Coltrane's early 1960s sound, Ralph Moore is a top-notch player who constructs cogent, highly nuanced solos. His warm but forceful style has made him one of the busiest tenor players of his generation. When Moore moved to the Oakland, California area in 1972 he had already been playing tenor for a few years. He had attended Boston's Berklee School of Music (1975–78) where he developed strong musical relationships with guitarist Kevin Eubanks and drummer Marvin "Smitty" Smith. Moore moved to New York in late 1980 and put in long stints with Horace Silver (1981–85) and J. J. Johnson. He worked and recorded with veterans such as Ray Brown, Roy Haynes, Dizzy Gillespie, Freddie Hubbard, Kenny Barron, Bobby Hutcherson, Jimmy Knepper, and toured with the Mingus Dynasty band. In the late 1980s, Moore, pianist Renee Rosnes, bassist Larry Grenadier, and drummer Billy Drummond formed the quartet Native Colours, which recorded *One World* for Concord. Since 1995, Moore has been in Los Angeles, where he plays in the *Tonight Show* band and works regularly around Southern California. He has recorded a number of albums for Criss Cross, Landmark, Savoy, and Reservoir.

what to buy: A consistently effective tenor saxophonist, Ralph Moore assembled an excellent quartet for *Who It Is You Are* ♫♫♫♫ (Savoy, 1994, prod. Takao Ogawa), featuring pianist Benny Green, bassist Peter Washington and the great drummer Billy Higgins. Moore displays a rich, muscular tone on "Skylark" and "But Beautiful" and also plays a number of seldom heard gems, such as Idrees Sulieman's "After Your Call" and Lee Morgan's "Delightfully Deggy." Benny Green's funky "Testifyin'" and Moore's Latin romp "Esmeralda" keep things lively.

what to buy next: A serious hard bop session featuring the blazing trumpet of Roy Hargrove and funky piano of Benny Green, *Furthermore* ♫♫♫♫ (Landmark, 1990, prod. Orrin Keepnews) finds Moore keeping some fast company. His tone is still quite Coltranish, but he's incorporating other influences too, especially on relaxed pieces such as Neal Hefti's "Girl Talk." With Peter Washington on bass and either Kenny Washington or Victor Lewis on drums, this band swings fiercely. With Dave Kikoski on piano and veterans Buster Williams on bass and Billy Hart on drums, *623 C Street* ♫♫♫♫ (Criss Cross, 1988/1994, prod. Gerry Teekens) is a high-velocity session that opens with a full throttle version of Bud Powell's "Un Poco Loco" and doesn't slow to a gallop until the closer "Speak Low." Moore plays some strong soprano on Kikoski's "Cecilia," but his tenor work is riveting throughout.

best of the rest:

Round Trip ♫♫♫♫ (Reservoir, 1988/1994)
Rejuvenate! ♫♫♫♫ (Criss Cross, 1989)
Images ♫♫♫♫ (Landmark, 1989)

influences:

John Coltrane, Benny Golson, George Coleman

Andrew Gilbert

Airto Moreira

Born August 5, 1941, in Itaiopolis, Santa Catarina, Brazil.

Airto Moreira is one of the best known percussionists and is largely responsible for introducing Brazilian percussion into American jazz. His blend of avant-garde Brazilian and contemporary free techniques influenced other Brazilian percussionists who arrived in the United States during the late 1960s into the 1970s, and his distinctive use of percussion has now become the standard. Infusing jazz with new rhythms, textures, and tone colors, Moreira has appeared as leader and sideman on numerous recordings, often with his wife, Brazilian jazz vocalist Flora Purim. He has been cited as top percussionist in readers and critics polls of many international magazines.

Moreira grew up in the city of Curitiba and began his musical studies in Brazil from 1948–50 on acoustic guitar and piano. He was performing professionally by his pre-teen years, and formed his own groups after playing in the early 1960s with Sambalanço Trio, the Sambrasa Trio, and Quarteto Novo. A multi-talented instrumentalist who didn't fit into a particular niche, he gravitated toward jazz and progressive interpretations of native Brazilian music styles, traveling extensively in his native country and studying a wide variety of percussion instruments. In 1968 he and Purim moved to the United States, where Moreira spent several months studying with composer-arranger Moacir Santos before becoming involved with the jazz scene. He played with jazz musicians Paul Winter, Wayne Shorter, Cannonball Adderley, and others, dazzling this community with his instrumental prowess on traditional and self-invented instruments. He first gained international notice around 1970 in live performances and recordings with Miles Davis on *Bitches' Brew*, *At Filmore*, and *Live-Evil*. In 1971 he worked with Lee Morgan and played percussion on the seminal eponymous Weather Report album, but didn't join this group because of his commitment to Davis. His role in Davis's group was to use bells, rattles, and shakers to create colors and sounds more than rhythms, and this experience changed Moreira's musical direction. In between gigs with Davis, he recorded two albums as leader: *Natural Feelings* in 1970, and *Seeds on the Ground* in 1970. In 1972 he joined Chick Corea's premier version of Return to Forever, recording on the band's first self-titled fusion LP and leaving the band after recording their 1973 album, *Light as a Feather*. He had relocated to Berkeley, California, in 1973, and also formed and recorded with his own band, Fingers, which lasted for two years. In 1975 he recorded a solo album, *Identity*, which was considered to be one of the decade's best fusion excursions for its dense textures and multiple-tracked, interwoven sounds of myriad instruments. Eventually, Moreira became one of the most in-demand percussionists, working with a variety of jazz artists, including the Crusaders, Freddie Hubbard, Carlos Santana, Herbie Hancock, Gil Evans, Mickey Hart, and Babatunde Olatunji. In the 1980s he was a member of the Al Di Meola Project, and toured with Dizzy Gillespie's United Nation Orchestra. They also led Fourth World, a group that has recorded albums in the 1990s for the import label B&W.

what to buy: Moreira's first album for CTI, and a seminal album that's still fresh-sounding and exciting after all these years, *Free* ♫♫♫♫♫ (CTI, 1972/CBS, 1988, prod. Creed Taylor) features the premier version of Return to Forever with Chick Corea (piano), Stanley Clarke (bass), and Joe Farrell (saxophones/flutes). *Free* was the album that helped spread the word about this incredibly talented Brazilian percussionist. And you'll understand why as you hear Moreira fire up his teammates, including pianists Keith Jarrett and Nelson Ayres, flutist Hubert Laws, guitarist George Benson, bassist Ron Carter, and trombonists Wayne Andre, Garnett Brown, and Joe Wallace. His wife and musical partner, Flora Purim, joins him in vocals on two tracks. The title tune, a Moreira original, is an upbeat percussive spree laced with vocals. A satisfying Moreira album that gives an overview of his broad inter-

ests, *Three-Way Mirror* ♫♫♫♫ (Reference Recordings, 1987, prod. J. Tamblyn Henderson Jr., Airto Moreira) features the percussionist performing eight tunes ranging from native Brazilian numbers, to bebop, to Return to Forever-type fusion. Brazilian vocalist Purim, pianist Kei Akagi, guitarist José Neto, bassist Mark Egan or Randy Tico, and special guest, flutist Joe Farrell (in his last performances) contribute to this fine album. While Moreira and Purim perform at their usual best, Farrell's playing really makes this expertly produced 1985 date a pleasure trip. *The Best of Airto* ♫♫♫♫ (Columbia, 1972–74/1994, prod. Creed Taylor, Billy Cobham, reissue prod. Didier C. Deutsch) draws mostly from the leader's *Free* and *Fingers* albums and contains 10 of Moreira's best tunes recorded between 1972–74 with an array of artists, including Chick Corea or Keith Jarrett (piano), Ron Carter or Stanley Clarke (bass), Eddie Daniels (flute), George Duke (keyboards), and numerous others. Moreira is superb throughout, demonstrating how mightily he adds creative percussive flair to each tune. This is one "best of" album which lives up to its claim, and it's a good introductory album for new fans to discover Airto's talents with Brazilian-jazz beats, and his pyrotechnic penchant for creating exciting tunes that hold up over 20 years later. Plenty of Brazilian melodies, scat-vocals, and swaying modern-edged beats should also satisfy the experienced listener. A serendipitous web-surfing session led to some astounding Airto sessions recorded for the British import label, B&W Music (check for info on the M.E.L.T. 2000 website). If you crave the spontaneity of a jam session among prime innovators, check out *Airto and the Gods of Jazz: Killer Bees* ♫♫♫♫ (B&W Music, 1993, prod. Flora Purim), a unique, modern-sounding album created in California over two weekends in 1989 when percussionist/vocalist Moreira, longing to recreate his NYC loft-session days, assembled a group of all-stars—Hiram Bullock (overdubbed guitars), Stanley Clarke (acoustic/electric bass), Chick Corea (acoustic piano/electronic keyboards), Mark Egan (electric fretless bass), and Gary Meek (tenor/soprano saxophones). Purim makes brief appearances. The album documents one helluva 50-minute jam, with tunes ranging from free-jazz to straight-ahead styles. The title tune grew out of what was initially a beginning soundcheck from Mark Egan. Moreira joins in, playing an Australian bull-roarer, an instrument used by aborigines to banish evil spirits (you've probably witnessed its buzzing in the *Crocodile Dundee* films). Corea and Bullock overdub with some nasty, funk-groove beats. The album contains many fine moments and enough variety to appeal to a wide range of jazz lovers.

what to buy next: Purim and Moreira are co-featured on *The Magicians* ♫♫♫♫ (Concord/Crossover, 1986, prod. Airto Moreira).

A snappy nine-tune session that demonstrates their versatility, it kicks off with a supple version of the Cheatham's "Sweet Baby Blues" before reverting to the couple's familiar Brazilian-jazz blend that draws from their Return to Forever dates. An array of artists are featured, including keyboardists Kei Akagi, George Duke, and Marcos Silva; guitarists Larry Ness, Richard Peixoto, David Zeiher, horn players, and additional drummers and percussionists who add spice to various tunes arranged mostly by Silva. Moreira is responsible for much of the underlying rhythmic excitement. The husband-wife team scores again with *The Sun Is Out* 𝄢𝄢𝄢 (Concord/Crossover, 1987/1989, prod. Airto Moreira, Flora Purim), a recording typical of their work together. Containing a mixture of Purim's vocals supported by her husband's percussion, and a crew that leans to electric guitar/bass-laden, jazz-rock-Brazilian fusion and smooth Brazilian-jazz ballads (mostly written by Moreira and guitarist José Neto), the 10-tune session holds appeal for a couple of jazz camps. Leading his Fourth World band, Moreira also recorded three albums for B&W with various musician assemblages. Since B&W touts itself as "a label without inhibitions, producing music without boundaries," that's exactly what to expect on his Fourth World recordings. He and Flora are constants, and, depending upon where their global travels take them, they meld the region's native rhythms to jazz, often with guitarist Neto as a collaborator. You can't go too far astray with any of these albums. *Fourth World* 𝄢𝄢𝄢𝄢 (B&W Music, 1993, prod. David Garland, Mark St. John) draws inspiration from the Brazilian rainforests. *Fourth World: Live in South Africa, 1993* 𝄢𝄢𝄢𝄢𝄢 (B&W Music/Bootleg.net, 1995) combines Airto and Flora's live-recorded Brazilian-jazz with South African influences, with stimulating results. Recorded during a concert at the Birmhis in Amsterdam, *Encounters of the Fourth World* 𝄢𝄢𝄢𝄢 (B&W Music, 1995, prod. Airto Moreira, Fourth World) continues along the same path, but it's influenced less by Brazilian rhythms and more by jazz-rock fusion. The album features Moreira, Purim, guitarist Neto, bassist/vocalist Gary Brown, keyboardist/flutist Jovino Santos, and special guest, Giovanni Hidalgo (congas/percussion). Each Fourth World album offers an encapsulated, fresh adventure. If you're desirous of a different listen, investigate the sessions Airto recorded in a Johannesburg studio with various South African musicians, including the notable Sipho Gumede, the organizer, whose 1970s band, Sakhile, was a major creative force in South African jazz. The tour (two weeks of recordings and three live concerts with over 50 South African musicians) was sponsored by *Straight No Chaser* magazine and documented on three CDs in the *South Africa: Outernational Meltdown* series. Bolstering a team of superb musicians with his colorful percus-

sions, Moreira is featured most predominantly on *Outernational Meltdown: Free at Last* 𝄢𝄢𝄢𝄢 (B&W Music, 1995, prod. Sipho Sumede), a seven-tune celebration yielding melodically enticing and rhythmically rousing South African jazz from the straight-ahead to the stretched out. It's an ear-expanding journey considerably different from other Airto works, and different, too, from anything you're likely to hear in the United States.

best of the rest:
Seeds on the Ground 𝄢𝄢𝄢 (One Way, 1971/1994)
Struck by Lightning 𝄢𝄢𝄢 (Venture, 1989)
The Other Side of This 𝄢𝄢𝄢 (Rykodisc, 1992)
Operational Meltdown: Jazzin' Universally 𝄢𝄢𝄢𝄢 (B&W Music, 1995)
Operational Meltdown: Healer's Brew 𝄢𝄢𝄢𝄢 (B&W Music, 1995)

influences:

◀◀ João Parahyba, Téo Lima, Robertinho Silva, Oswaldinho da Cuíca, Cyro Baptista, Paulinho da Costa, Guilherme Franco

see also: *Return to Forever, Miles Davis*

Nancy Ann Lee

Joe Morello

Born July 17, 1928, in Springfield, MA.

Joe Morello first played violin as a child, switching to drums as a teenager. He worked with two more of Springfield's finest, Phil Woods and Sal Salvador, in his early years, before moving to New York in 1952. Morello then worked with Johnny Smith, Stan Kenton, and others before joining pianist Marian McPartland's trio. During his three-year stint with McPartland, he recorded with other artists, including Woods, Tal Farlow, Jimmy Raney, Jackie & Roy, and Salvador. He joined the Dave Brubeck Quartet in 1956 and stayed with the group for 11 years. He became known worldwide for his featured solo on Paul Desmond's "Take Five," the first instrumental jazz recording to sell a million copies. It was Morello's uncanny ability to inject a perceived sense of swing into odd meters (5/4, 9/8, and 11/4) that accounted for much of Brubeck's success during his years with the pianist. After Brubeck disbanded the quartet in 1967, Joe did some tours for Ludwig Drums, worked with his own bands around New York, and played in some reunion concerts with Brubeck and McPartland. Although he went blind in 1976, Morello continues to teach about 25 students a week and records for DMP Records. His precise, light-touched, and extremely musical drumming can be heard to good advantage on many Brubeck albums, but *Time Out* is a must.

what's available: On *Going Places* 𝄞𝄞𝄞 (DMP Records, 1993, prod. Joe Morello, Tom Jung), the clean recording achieved by this audiophile label certainly does justice to Joe Morello's delicate, musical drum work. This straight quartet session features Greg Kogan (piano), Ralph Lalama (tenor sax, flute), and Gary Mazzaroppi (bass). It's all pretty much standard fare, except for Morello's drum feature, "Mission Impossible," and his own "Calypso Joe." A very well-performed quartet date with exquisite work from the leader throughout. For *Morello Standard Time* 𝄞𝄞𝄞 (DMP Records, 1994, prod. Tom Jung, Joe Morello), Joe is back with the same quartet as heard on his previous DMP release. This one is just as good, although some may even find it a tad better, possibly due to the choice of material, which includes "Take Five," "Bye Bye Blackbird," "Someday My Prince Will Come," and "Doxy," among the 10 cuts. Again, Joe's drums are clear as a bell.

worth searching for: One of the finest jazz albums of all time, *Time Out* 𝄞𝄞𝄞𝄞 (Columbia, 1959/1997, prod. Teo Macero) highlights best examples of Joe Morello's playing, including his extended drum solo on Paul Desmond's "Take Five," played in 5/4 time. This Brubeck quartet session with Desmond and Eugene Wright (bass) has become a classic album that has been reissued several times (including a version on Columbia's Master Sound Gold CD series). Also included among the seven tunes is the intricate "Blue Rondo a La Turk," played in 9/8 time.

Bill Wahl

Frank Morgan

Born December 23, 1933, in Minneapolis, MN.

Music business myth and a well-coordinated media blitz helped create a storm of late '80s publicity for alto saxophonist Frank Morgan. Here, the publicists argued and the pundits agreed, was the rightful heir to the bebop throne of Charlie Parker, whom Morgan had briefly known when he was first coming up in Los Angeles during the early 1950s. What made the story irresistible was the fact that Morgan, who was a virtual unknown despite his age, was just emerging into the spotlight's bright glare after nearly 30 years spent locked away in the California penal system for a series of offenses associated with his long-standing heroin habit. What the public got in those first heady years of 1986–88 was a virtually nonstop flurry of albums that proved, once and for all, that Morgan could reproduce the general attitude and shape of Bird's riffs, licks, and moods with his eyes closed. He was, in short, a

Young Lion trapped in an older man's body. But as the decade waned, Morgan grew weary of his appointed role as the eternally "new Bird," and so, faced with the challenge of Parker's dazzling speed and nimble harmonic agility, he opted to slow things down to a crawl. Consequently, his next several albums were dominated by syrupy (and, at times, self-pitying and maudlin) balladry. In 1996, however, he began to emerge from this self-imposed emotional straitjacket with an album of uptempo bop standards, and his guest shots with Abbey Lincoln from this same year (on *Who Used to Love*) were economical and particularly coherent.

what to buy: Seen as a whole, Morgan's recorded output is relatively consistent—his "bad" albums aren't that much worse than his best. Still, the more-or-less accepted rule of thumb is, the earlier the Morgan material you purchase, the better off you'll be. In this regard, Morgan's debut as a leader, *Frank Morgan* 𝄞𝄞𝄞 (GNP Crescendo, 1955, prod. Gene Norman), with Wardell Gray, Jack Sheldon, Carl Perkins, Larance Marable, Bobby Timmons, and others, is a reasonably good place to start. Also worth checking out: the "coming out" date with Cedar Walton and Billy Higgins, *Easy Living* 𝄞𝄞𝄞 (Contemporary/OJC, 1986, prod. Richard Bock); the duets with longtime accompanist George Cables on *Double Image* 𝄞𝄞𝄞 (Contemporary, 1986, prod. Richard Bock); and the aforementioned collaboration with Rodney Kendrick's trio, *Bop!* 𝄞𝄞𝄞 (Telarc, 1996, prod. John Snyder). And despite its otherwise hit-and-miss atmosphere, the take of Cables's "Phantom's Progress" on the live date by the so-called Frank Morgan/Bud Shank Quintet, *Quiet Fire* 𝄞𝄞𝄞 (Contemporary, 1987, prod. Richard Bock), offers a glimpse of what Morgan might arrive at were he to drop his "polite" and "happy" pretenses.

what to buy next: The move to Antilles Records in 1989 signaled Morgan's slow-paced decline, but *Mood Indigo* 𝄞𝄞𝄞 (Antilles, 1989, prod. John Snyder), with its vari-sized ensembles and textural diversity, manages to avoid the torpor and the clichés, while his Contemporary Records swansong, *Reflections* 𝄞𝄞𝄞 (Contemporary, 1989, prod. Orrin Keepnews), boasts both Joe Henderson and Bobby Hutcherson among its sidemen. *You Must Believe in Spring* 𝄞𝄞𝄞 (Antilles, 1992, prod. John Snyder) is a series of sax-piano duos with Kenny Barron, Tommy Flanagan, Barry Harris, Roland Hanna, and Hank Jones.

what to avoid: *Love, Lost and Found* 𝄞𝄞 (Telarc, 1995, prod. John Snyder) is the nadir, filled with tepid playing. On the other hand, it does have an interesting bass-alto version of "All the Things You Are," where Morgan inadvertently sounds a bit like

Ornette Coleman. And beware the live-at-the-Vanguard *Bebop Lives!* 🎵🎵 (Contemporary, 1986, prod. Richard Bock), which reeks of over-the-top grandstanding and documents a particularly rancid couple of nights by the late trumpeter/flugelhornist Johnny Coles.

the rest:

Lament 🎵🎵🎵 (Contemporary, 1987)
Major Changes 🎵🎵🎵 (Contemporary, 1987)
Yardbird Suite 🎵🎵🎵 (Contemporary, 1988)
A Lovesome Thing 🎵🎵🎵 (Antilles, 1991)
Listen to the Dawn 🎵🎵🎵 (Antilles, 1994)

influences:

◀◀ Charlie Parker

▶▶ Abraham Burton, Sherman Irbie

David Prince

Lee Morgan

Born July 10, 1938 in Philadelphia, PA. Died February 19, 1972 in New York, NY.

Lee Morgan was only 33 when he was shot dead by a jealous woman in front of a nightclub. One would assume he had a lot more playing to do had he the chance, not to mention his increasing involvement in various political movements. Nonetheless, the incredible amount and quality of music he had created in his brief lifetime has stood the test of time, and Morgan is certain to go down in history as one of the brightest stars the world of jazz trumpet has ever seen.

Something of a prodigy, Morgan had already mastered his instrument by age 15, and it was at this time that he began playing professionally around Philadelphia. By 1956 he had joined Dizzy Gillespie's band, offering up fiery solos that even his boss had to admire. At this time, he began his recording career, both as a leader and as a frequent sideman and soloist on numerous releases, most notably John Coltrane's 1957 masterpiece *Blue Train*. When Gillespie's group disbanded in 1958, Morgan signed up with Art Blakey's Jazz Messengers and played with them for three years. During this period, he was often accused of imitating Clifford Brown, an admitted influence, yet Morgan's bravura brought something extra to his playing, and by the early 1960s he was clearly forging his own style. He bounced around both Philly and New York, recording both on his own and with the Jazz Messengers, including some of that group's finest work (1958's *Moanin'* and 1961's *The Freedom Rider*). After leaving the Messengers in 1961, Morgan's career stalled briefly (mainly due to an all-to-common heroin addiction), but

LEE MORGAN (WITH ART BLAKEY)

song "Moanin'"

album Moanin': Art Blakey and the Jazz Messengers
(Blue Note, 1958/1987)

instrument Trumpet

Monster Solo

by 1964 he had regained his footing and hit it big with his album *The Sidewinder*, featuring the snappy, crossover, smash-hit title track and sympathetic support from tenor saxophonist Joe Henderson. This success inaugurated a remarkable series of consistently impressive records for Blue Note, including another stint with Blakey in 1964–65, and culminating in his popular *Live at the Lighthouse* set in 1970. During the early 1970s Morgan became involved in the Jazz and People's Movement, a group devoted to promoting jazz as a cultural treasure, and he made television appearances protesting the media's booking policies. His senseless death in 1972 sadly robbed the world of a premiere jazzman at the height of his powers.

Morgan's sound virtually defines hard bop. Brash, fast, and acrobatic, he immediately captures the listeners' attention, particularly in his early, Brownie mode. By the late 1960s he had developed an equally powerful introspective side, with incredibly precise use of half-valving techniques, making him one of the most dynamic musicians of his generation. Being a member of the Blue Note stable of artists, Morgan participated in dozens of sessions from some of the finest players of the 1950s and 1960s, from McCoy Tyner to Jimmy Smith, in addition to the 25 albums he recorded as a leader. Frequent collaborators include tenor saxophonist Hank Mobley and drummer Billy Higgins.

what to buy: An absolute classic, *The Sidewinder* 𝄞𝄞𝄞𝄞 (Blue Note, 1964, prod. Alfred Lion) is a set of all-Morgan originals featuring great playing throughout from all parties. Although the tunes are relatively simple, this merely gives the soloists more room to do their thing, especially on "Totem Pole" and the ubiquitous title track. Joined by Hank Mobley, *A-1* 𝄞𝄞𝄞𝄞 (Savoy, 1957, prod. Ozzie Cadena) is early Morgan at his sassiest; his playing is so bold as to occasionally be out of control, but that's part of the fun, and he always pairs well with longtime associate Mobley on tenor.

what to buy next: Morgan's follow-up to *The Sidewinder* (although not released until a few years later), *Search for the New Land* 𝄞𝄞𝄞𝄞 (Blue Note, 1964, prod. Alfred Lion) finds him in a more pensive mood; the selections are beautifully arranged, with the rare (for Morgan) inclusion of guitar, played by the incomparable Grant Green. *The Procrastinator* 𝄞𝄞𝄞𝄞 (Blue Note, 1967, prod. Alfred Lion) features virtually the same band as *Search* (Wayne Shorter, Herbie Hancock, Billy Higgins), but the addition of bassist Ron Carter (fresh from Miles Davis's *Nefertiti* sessions) and vibraphonist Bobby Hutcherson makes the recording an excellent example of latter-day Morgan reaching out to almost avant-garde levels.

what to avoid: *See Autumn* 𝄞 (Picadilly, 1970/1980) comes from a live show broadcast on radio just prior to the superior Lighthouse dates. Essentially a bootleg, this recording isn't so bad for its playing, but iffy sound (the audience is often audible), shoddy presentation (the songs are misidentified), and sketchy song selection reduce its desirability to virtually nil.

the rest:
Introducing Lee Morgan 𝄞𝄞𝄞 (Savoy, 1957)
Lee Morgan Indeed! 𝄞𝄞𝄞 (Blue Note, 1957)
Lee Morgan Volume 2 𝄞𝄞𝄞 (Blue Note, 1957)
(With Wynton Kelly) *Dizzy Atmosphere* 𝄞𝄞𝄞𝄞 (Specialty, 1957)
Lee Morgan Volume 3 𝄞𝄞𝄞𝄞 (Blue Note, 1957)
City Lights 𝄞𝄞𝄞𝄞 (Blue Note, 1957)
The Cooker 𝄞𝄞𝄞𝄞 (Blue Note, 1957)
Candy 𝄞𝄞𝄞𝄞 (Blue Note, 1958)
Here's Lee Morgan 𝄞𝄞𝄞𝄞 (Vee-Jay, 1960)
(With Wayne Shorter, Frank Strozier, and others) *The Young Lions* 𝄞𝄞𝄞𝄞 (Vee-Jay, 1960)
Lee-Way 𝄞𝄞𝄞 (Blue Note, 1960)
(With Thad Jones) *Minor Strain* 𝄞𝄞𝄞 (Roulette, 1961/1990)

Expoobident 𝄞𝄞𝄞 (Vee-Jay, 1961)
Take Twelve 𝄞𝄞𝄞 (Jazzland, 1962)
Rumproller 𝄞𝄞𝄞𝄞 (Blue Note, 1965)
The Gigolo 𝄞𝄞𝄞𝄞 (Blue Note, 1965)
Cornbread 𝄞𝄞𝄞𝄞 (Blue Note, 1965)
Infinity 𝄞𝄞𝄞 (Blue Note, 1965)
Delightfulee 𝄞𝄞𝄞 (Blue Note, 1966)
Charisma 𝄞𝄞𝄞𝄞 (Blue Note, 1966)
The Rajah 𝄞𝄞𝄞 (Blue Note, 1967)
Sonic Boom 𝄞𝄞𝄞𝄞 (Blue Note, 1967)
The Sixth Sense 𝄞𝄞𝄞 (Blue Note, 1968)
Taru 𝄞𝄞𝄞𝄞 (Blue Note, 1968)
Caramba! 𝄞𝄞𝄞 (Blue Note, 1968)
Live at the Lighthouse 𝄞𝄞𝄞𝄞 (Blue Note, 1970)
Lee Morgan 𝄞𝄞𝄞 (Blue Note, 1971)
The Best of Lee Morgan 𝄞𝄞𝄞𝄞 (Blue Note, 1988)

worth searching for: *Tom Cat* 𝄞𝄞𝄞𝄞 (Blue Note/Liberty, 1980, prod. Alfred Lion) sat on the shelves for over a decade. These 1964 sessions feature alto player Jackie McLean, who would appear on a number of Morgan albums, but never better than here; typical of Morgan's mid-1960s, post-*Sidewinder* records, this features a delightfully soulful title cut. Art Blakey and the Jazz Messengers' *Moanin'* 𝄞𝄞𝄞𝄞 (Blue Note, 1958/1987, prod. Alfred Lion) is probably the best example of Morgan's work from his first stint with Blakey's group; the bluesy title cut shows some of the development Morgan had made since first starting out, keeping the explosive bursts of notes in check while exploring the whole range of his horn with sly, swooping effects.

influences:

◀◀ Clifford Brown, Fats Navarro, Dizzy Gillespie

▶▶ Freddie Hubbard, Donald Byrd, Jon Faddis

Eric J. Lawrence

Joe Morris

Born September 13, 1955, in New Haven, CT.

Morris is an avant-garde guitarist who has built an original and energetic personal style on a broad variety of influences, from John MacLaughlin and such horn players as Jimmy Lyons to West African string music and the harmolodic styles of Ornette Coleman and his guitarists Bern Nix and Blood Ulmer. He's as distinctive as any current jazz guitarist, with a very clear plucked tone using practically no sustain and no effects, combining bluesy soul and bebop tidiness with free playing.

Morris moved to Boston in the mid-1970s, found its scene stagnant, and then spent time in Europe. He came back in 1981 and studied with pianist Lowell Davidson, noted for his ESP album. Around that time, Morris cofounded the Boston Improvisors Group and put together a trio with veteran drummer Laurence Cook and young bassist Sebastian Steinberg. They made an album of vigorous outside playing on sometimes complexly organized motifs. Morris released it by starting his own label, Riti (named after a one-stringed African instrument). His 1994 Soul Note album *Symbolic Gesture* was his first record on another label (and the first guitarist-led album in the label's two-decade history) and accelerated the expansion of his U.S. reputation beyond his Boston base. Since then he has been a prolific recording artist, as a leader and with Matthew Shipp, William Parker, Rob Brown, and Joe Maneri.

Besides performing and recording, Morris has lectured on "Transfer of Traditional West African String Music to American Blues Guitar," "Composing for Improvisers," and other topics at Harvard University, New England Conservatory, Berklee College of Music, and elsewhere.

what to buy: The kaleidoscopic, uncategorizable *No Vertigo* 𝄞𝄞𝄞𝄞 (Leo, 1995, prod. Joe Morris, Leo Feigin) is a solo guitar album (one suite is for mandolin) which reveals the anatomy of Morris's music. To say that it suggests Derek Bailey, Cecil Taylor, and Ornette Coleman barely hints at his highly original reworking of such inspirations into a unique style. He can make the most abstract, convoluted lines groove, and when he builds on blues and West African string music, no clichés enter the equation, just appropriate inflections and timbres. *Antennae* 𝄞𝄞𝄞𝄞 (AUM Fidelity, 1997, prod. Joe Morris, Steven Joerg) is a trio record with bassist Nate McBride and drummer Jerome Deupree which sounds like Ornette Coleman on a caffeine rush: fast, twitchy thematic nuggets turned inside out and upside down during intensely focused improvisations. Morris's tune title "Stare into a Lightbulb for Three Years" provides a useful analogy for the music's fixation on returning to those naggingly insistent melodic nodules. On tracks where the pace is relaxed, the blues feeling at the root of the music comes through with striking clarity.

what to buy next: The Joe Morris/Rob Brown Quartet's *Illuminate* 𝄞𝄞𝄞𝄞 (Leo Lab, 1995, prod. Joe Morris, Rob Brown, Leo Feigin) combines the guitarist and alto saxophonist with bassist William Parker and drummer Jackson Krall. On the opening collective improvisation, Morris unleashes machine gun bursts of knotty clusters and twisting lines. Morris's title track is a spare yet often melodic ballad where the guitarist does some rare

(for him) chordal comping under Brown's lush Charlie Parker-esque tone. Brown's 23-minute "Inklings" effectively alternates quiet explorations and feverish outbursts. "Pivotal," another collective improvisation, features Brown playing an Ornette-like lonely melody over spare backing that builds to bustling excitement. Morris's duo album with bassist William Parker, *Invisible Weave* 𝄞𝄞𝄞𝄞 (No More, 1997, prod. Alan Schneider), is completely improvised from start to finish. Morris weaves rapid-fire picking into twisting, hyperactive lines that turn in on themselves in a kinetic style that's exciting but tightly contained, with not a moment of self-aggrandizing flashiness to be heard.

the rest:
(With Rob Brown and Whit Dickey) *Youniverse* 𝄞𝄞𝄞𝄞 (Riti, 1992)
Symbolic Gesture 𝄞𝄞𝄞 (Soul Note, 1994)
Elsewhere 𝄞𝄞𝄞𝄞 (Homestead, 1996)
(With Joe Maneri and Mat Maneri) *Three Men Walking* 𝄞𝄞𝄞𝄞 (ECM, 1996)
You Be Me 𝄞𝄞𝄞 (Soul Note, 1997)
(With Matthew Shipp) *Thesis* 𝄞𝄞𝄞𝄞 (hatOLOGY, 1997)

worth searching for: Morris's early work, covering a decade of pursuing parallel paths on self-released trio albums—gravity-defying, constructions of awesome asymmetricality on the one hand and sweaty, violently askew neo-fusion on the other—can be heard on albums issued on his Riti label (contact ritirec@ici.net). *Wraparound* 𝄞𝄞𝄞 (Riti, 1984, prod. Joe Morris) contains three 1983 live recordings by the Morris/Cook/Steinberg lineup, plus a short solo guitar track. This is restless, probing improvisation using small motivic cells in a free jazz fashion. It is available only on LP at this point. *Human Rites* 𝄞𝄞𝄞 (Riti, 1988) is a two-LP set of 1985–87 dates with two trios. Morris and Steinberg are joined by drummer Thurman Barker on the 1985–86 concert recordings contained on the first LP, while drummer Jerry Deupree is heard on the 1987 studio recordings on the second LP. The track title "Blues & Mathematics: or, all Bird did was tell the truth" gives an idea of the thinking behind this music, which is sometimes more clearly composed than on the first album and more earthily communicative. Not only is Morris superb, playing with emotional directness, Steinberg reveals himself to be a huge acoustic bass talent. On *Sweatshop* 𝄞𝄞𝄞𝄞 (Riti, 1990, prod. Joe Morris) Steinberg plays electric bass in trio with Morris and Deupree. If there were any justice in the world, this half-live, half-studio album would be heard not just by free jazz fans but by fusionheads who would dig its monster grooves and imaginative soloing. *Flip & Spike* 𝄞𝄞𝄞𝄞 (Riti, 1992, prod. Joe Morris, Anne Marcotty

Morris) is by the same group but with Steinberg back on acoustic bass. The music swings hard under Morris's roiling, layered improvisations, which sometimes suggest two or three guitarists interacting.

influences:

◀◀ Bern Nix, James Blood Ulmer, John MacLaughlin, Jimmy Lyons, Cecil Taylor, Lowell Davidson

▶▶ Bruce Eisenbeil

Steve Holtje

Lawrence "Butch" Morris

Born Lawrence Douglas Morris, February 10, 1947, in Long Beach, CA.

Why is one of the finest melodists of his generation so thoroughly obscure? Largely because his melodic gifts coexist with as tenacious a pursuit of the improvisational ideal as is to be found in jazz (a debatable term for much of what Butch Morris does, but the music is all the richer if the inclusionists win the debate). Relatively straight-forward readings of Morris gems like "Spoonin'" and "Fling" are scattered among the records of David Murray and a few other musicians. With Murray's Big Band, Morris is the conductor, cuing improvs within the compositions (including some of his own) with an elaborate gestural language. But when it's Morris's gig, things go further afield, into the realm of a) "conduction" where there is no written, sung, whistled, remembered, or otherwise predetermined music to begin with, only cues to guide what is improvised and how improvisers interact with one another; or into the realm of b) "comprovisation," which overlays cued improvs with written material.

In the early 1970s, Morris played with such West Coast legends as Bobby Bradford, Horace Tapscott, and Charles Moffett. Moffett led a rehearsal band at an Oakland joint called Club 7, and sometimes would put compositions aside and cue the ensemble through group improvisations in a manner Morris had never seen before, slowing them down, or speeding them up, or giving accents for the band to play. Moving to New York in 1976, Morris joined the energy jams on the "loft scene," where the music raged for hours, sometimes leaving Morris concerned that there was no way to preserve, or even to repeat in that very performance, the passing moments of brilliance. Teaching in Rotterdam, he began to build on Moffett's gestural language, progressing toward his first full-blown conduction in 1985. He continues to expand his conductions (they numbered 50 as of early 1995, when he released his opus conduction collection).

Morris also worked on the Robert Altman film, *Kansas City* and is collaborating with Murray, folk-blues singer Taj Mahal, and former Grateful Dead guitarist Bob Weir on a Broadway musical about the life of Negro baseball league star Satchel Paige.

what's available: The comprovisations on *Dust to Dust* 🎵🎵🎵🎵 (New World, 1991, prod. Wayne Horvitz), recorded with percussionist Andrew Cyrille, pianist Myra Melford, and others, may be the best place to begin exploring Morris's music, anchored as it is here with such rolling melodies as "Long Goodbye," and the splintered, staccato Bartok that becomes the basis of "The Bartok Comprovisation." More ambitiously, go for the conduction on the limited-edition 10-CD set *Testament: A Conduction Collection* 🎵🎵🎵🎵 (New World/Countercurrents, 1995, prod. Lawrence D. "Butch" Morris), which chronicles 16 pure conduction sessions recorded between 1988–95 in locations from New York to San Francisco, Japan, and Turkey, mixing up jazz musicians, non-jazz improvisers, and traditional stylists. Though distinctly more powerful when considered as an experiment in progress, the 10 CDs (*Conduction 11, Conduction 15, Conduction 22, Conduction 23, Conduction 25 & 26, Conduction 28 & 31, Conduction 31/35/36, Conduction 38/39/40, Conduction 41, Conduction 50*) are also available individually from New World along with info on ordering the original explanatory booklet for the 10-disc package. What do they sound like? Sometimes like John Cage off Zen and on steroids, as outwardly unrelated ideas layer. Ideas drop out and reappear, build to big band crescendos and maybe cut back to a lone instrumentalist as the first element of the next phase; some conductions last a couple of minutes (although most of the music is in episodes of 20 to about 45 minutes). Morris's broadest strokes recur regularly, as do such core players as trombonist/electronics specialist/live sampler J.A. Deane. But the records can be widely dissimilar, depending on the participants and the chemistry of the performance. Some of these are of particular note. *Conduction 15* is the "jazziest" of the lot, with saxophonist Arthur Blythe as a prominently featured guest. *Conduction 22* may be the most cacophonous, with clashing waves of sound from turntable artist Christian Marclay and electronics from Deane and Günter Müller. *Conduction 25 & 26* includes Morris regulars, jazz-rooted players, and Turkey's traditional Süleyman Erguner Ensemble for the most tintinnabulary (at times) and spell-binding of the collection. *Conduction 50* and *Conduction 28 & 31*, recorded in Tokyo, bring in definite Eastern elements, including Kabuki-esque vocals. Morris refers to *50* as one of his favorites. (For a catalog of nonprofit New World Records, write them at 701 Seventh Avenue, New York, New York 10036.) Another side of Morris the cornetist is well displayed on the trio date *Burning Cloud* 🎵🎵🎵 (FMP, 1996, prod. Jost Gebers). Along with frequent collaborators Deane (trombone, flute, and electronics) and Le Quan Ninh (percussion), it's improv without a safety net or much of a tight rope. On his own records, Morris restricts his playing to seeming prods and punctuation marks. Here, he speaks at length in a language that extends the breathy, voice-like inflections of Don Cherry, Bill Dixon, and Lester Bowie.

worth searching for: Among those works out of print, but worth hunting down is *Homeing* 🎵🎵🎵🎵 (Sound Aspects, 1989, prod. Pedro de Freitas), a comprovisation that returns three times to Morris's haunting "Long Goodbye" melody. *Current Trends in Racism in Modern America* 🎵🎵🎵🎵 (Sound Aspects, 1986, prod. Lawrence D. "Butch" Morris), although not titled as such, was the first conduction, recorded live at the Kitchen in New York City with an 11-piece ensemble including saxophonists Frank Lowe and John Zorn, and Marclay on turntables. More a collage of soloists and less an ensemble work than many later pieces, it remains an unpredictable thrill.

influences:

◀◀ Wayne Shorter, Don Cherry, Bill Dixon, Lester Bowie

▶▶ John Zorn

W. Kim Heron

JELLY ROLL MORTON

song "Seattle Hunch" (take 2)

album Jelly Roll Morton Centennial: His Complete Victor Recordings
(RCA, 1926/1990)

instrument Piano

Monster Solo

Jelly Roll Morton

Born Ferdinand Joseph Lementhe (some sources say La Menthe, Lemott, LaMothe), October 20, 1890, in New Orleans, LA. Died July 10, 1941, in Los Angeles, CA.

Few musicians in the history of jazz were as colorful or gifted as Jelly Roll Morton. A pool hustler, pimp, and notable self-mythologizer, he was also the first great jazz composer and a pianist and vocalist of immense skill. Morton grew up in New Orleans, where he was playing piano in brothels as early as 1902. Around 1904 he became an itinerant musician and traveled the country from New York City to Los Angeles. He worked in a variety of settings, including long stints in minstrel shows, and added regional piano styles to his already impressive command of the ragtime, French quadrilles, light classics, blues, and Caribbean syncopations that he had originally picked up in New Orleans. By the mid-1920s he was living in Chicago, where he recorded with his Red Hot Peppers in 1926–28. These sides are his finest small ensemble recordings, the first recorded examples of real jazz composition-arrangement, and enduring masterpieces of early jazz. Ironically, they were recorded just

as Louis Armstrong was changing the shape of jazz, and Morton's greatest works—with their emphasis on New Orleans collective improvisation and polyphony, as opposed to the virtuoso soloist and the homophony of the emerging big bands, never brought Morton the fame he deserved. In 1928 he moved to New York, and while he made some more impressive recordings there, he was considered out of date, and drifted into an embittered obscurity. He settled in Washington, D.C., where Smithsonian musical folklorist Alan Lomax found him and recorded a remarkable series of solo piano performances and reminiscences at the Library of Congress in 1938. These recordings led to renewed interest in Morton and a handful of new recordings, but in a final cruel irony, he died in 1941 and was again cheated of the recognition he was due.

Morton may not have invented jazz (as he once claimed), but he was certainly among the first to realize its full artistic potential. His arrangements of his compositions, many of them constructed in three distinct sections, unfold in a continuous flux of changing timbre and instrumentation that in no way ob-

scures the music's architectural brilliance and rich design. He could pack a staggering number of devices into a three-minute performance—unison melody lines, stop-time choruses, instrumental breaks, group improvisations—without impeding the sprightly progress of the composition or masking the beauty of his melodies. As a pianist, his ensemble role displayed the same richness as his compositions, and influenced pianists such as Earl "Fatha'" Hines. Morton's youthful wanderings gave him an encyclopedic command of turn-of-the-century popular styles, all of which he played with confidence. An instrumental virtuoso with a keen analytical mind, he synthesized elements of many of these forms into his own style, becoming an indisputable master of jazz performance as well as composition. He sang in a relaxed, earthy tenor that was unpretentious and surprisingly moving.

what to buy: *The Jelly Roll Morton Centennial: His Complete Victor Recordings* ♫♫♫♫ (RCA, 1926/1990, reissue prod. Orrin Keepnews) is a five-CD set containing all the Red Hot Peppers sessions, including dazzling masterpieces like "Grandpa's Spells," "Black Bottom Stomp," and "The Pearls." The later work never equaled these sessions, but there are flashes of brilliance throughout and other New Orleans greats like Henry "Red" Allen, Barney Bigard, and Sidney Bechet appear as sidemen, which alone makes the music worth a listen. The remastering doesn't do justice to the music, but it's essential stuff. All four volumes of Morton's Library of Congress musings are worth owning, but if you have to limit yourself, get *The Pearls: The Library of Congress Recordings, Volume 3* ♫♫♫♫ (Rounder, 1993, prod. Alan Lomax) for its stellar versions of "King Porter Stomp," "The Pearls," and "Bert Williams." For some real insight into how Mr. Morton might have entertained audiences in the seamier establishments he worked, this CD restores the previously censored "Murder Ballad" to its sexually explicit full length. *Winin' Boy Blues: The Library of Congress Recordings, Volume 4* ♫♫♫♫ (Rounder, 1993, prod. Alan Lomax) contains "Creepy Feeling," a superbly paced performance over a slinky tango rhythm (the Spanish tinge that Morton championed) that is perhaps the single best track of these epic recording sessions.

what to buy next: *Kansas City Stomp: The Library of Congress Recordings, Volume 1* ♫♫♫♫ (Rounder, 1993, prod. Alan Lomax) reveals a fascinating and profound portrait of American music on the verge of jazz. Morton plays rags, gospel tunes, blues,

parlor ballads, and light classics, transforming them into jazz before your ears. Immensely exciting music that is both history lesson and art. *Anamule Dance: The Library of Congress Recordings, Volume 2* ♫♫♫♫ (Rounder, 1993, prod. Alan Lomax) offers an ironic, nostalgic version of "Mr. Jelly Lord"; an unflaggingly imaginative "Original Jelly Roll Blues," and another R-rated (and pretty misogynist) blues, "Make Me a Pallet on the Floor."

best of the rest:

Jelly Roll Morton: 1923–24 ♫♫♫♫ (Milestone, 1993)
Last Sessions: The Complete General Recordings ♫♫♫ (Commodore/ GRP, 1997)
Jelly Roll Morton: The Piano Rolls ♫♫♫♫ (Nonesuch, 1997)

worth searching for: *Jelly Roll Morton, Volume 1* ♫♫♫♫ (JSP, 1990, prod. John R.T. Davies) covers the same Red Hot Peppers material as the RCA Centennial collection, but Davies's remastering is infinitely better. If sound quality is really important to you and you don't mind paying the extra money and or hunting for British imports, JSP reissues of Morton's entire Victor catalog are worth it.

influences:

▶▶ Earl "Fatha'" Hines, Charles Mingus, Dick Hyman, James Dapogny

Ed Hazell

Bob Moses

Born January 28, 1948, in New York, NY.

Multi-instrumentalist Bob Moses was playing piano, vibes, and drums (eventually his primary instrument) when he was 10 years old. Within two years he had jammed with Charles Mingus, one of his press agent father's clients. Others included Rahsaan Roland Kirk and Max Roach, and Moses's debut recording came in 1964 on Kirk's *I Talk with the Spirits* (Limelight/Mercury). As a teenage vibraphonist he worked in New York's thriving Latin music scene, and in 1966, at age 18, he co-founded one of the earliest electric jazz-rock groups, Free Spirits (with Jim Pepper and Larry Coryell). Moses and fellow prodigy/childhood friend David Liebman formed the group Open Sky together in the late 1960s and it lasted well into the 1970s on an off-and-on basis in between tours with other artists. The sensitive, swinging drummer has played in a wide variety of jazz contexts with various Gary Burton groups, Jack DeJohnette, Pat Metheny (*Bright Size Life*), Hal Galper, the Brecker Brothers, large groups led by Mike Gibbs and George Gruntz, Steve Kuhn, Emily Remler,

Steve Swallow, and many more. In the early 1980s, his albums *When Elephants Dream of Music* and *Visit with the Great Spirit* brought Moses critical acclaim and a broad audience thanks to colorful, adept arrangements that meld a variety of styles into a seamless, original sound. He has recorded only intermittently since then, partly because he's been expanding his musical palette with trips abroad.

what to buy: Moses had a hit among jazz fans with *When Elephants Dream of Music* ✍✍✍✍ (Gramavision, 1982/1993, prod. Bob Moses, Pat Metheny). The lengthy list of personnel on this album of 13 Moses originals (all but three tunes recorded in NYC studio sessions in April, 1982) draws from a roster of musical innovators in a broad range of adventurous styles from free jazz to fusion and world music, including Bill Frisell (electric guitar), Michael Formanek (acoustic bass), David Friedman (vibes, marimba), Terumasa Hino (cornet), Howard Johnson (electric contrabass, clarinet, tuba), Steve Swallow (electric bass), Nana Vasconcelos (percussion, voice), and numerous others. Moses spurs his ensemble colleagues to generate richly textured instrumental passages, repetitive grooves, and daring solos that range from the ethereal to upbeat, playful, and witty, sometimes enhanced by voices. While Moses creates accessible counterpoint themes to stretch the imagination, he also introduces original tunes to satisfy straight-ahead jazz fans, such as "Embraceable Jew," the dreamy "Black Orchid" (dedicated to Billy Strayhorn), and his big-hearted tribute to Dr. J. But it's on the larger group efforts, edgy pieces with arranged horn segments, that the team performs best and is inspired to stretch out into the most cacophonous fun. This album is the definitive showcase for Moses's tremendous talents and a most engaging listen.

what to buy next: *Devotion* ✍✍✍ (Soul Note, 1996, prod. Bob Moses, Ben Wittman) is partly a reissue of the album *Friends* (Sutra, 1980), though Soul Note wasn't aware of that when Moses sold them these 1979 tapes of his quintet with Terumasa Hino (trumpet), David Liebman (tenor sax), Steve Kuhn (piano), and Steve Swallow (electric bass). In any case, this is a fine album, and one which purist jazz fans may find more approachable than his Gramavision work. His compositions unfold in a highly organic manner, with each section flowing into the next without obvious demarcations. It's as though, having decided that the tonal colors of the instruments and the styles of the players offer contrast enough, Moses wove his music from strands rather than building it from blocks. The subtle free jazz that Jimmy Giuffre conceived in a trio format (to which Swallow was a major contributor) may have pointed towards some of the paths Moses travels down here, though the compositions are

more worked out and a harmonic underpinning is almost always in evidence even if not always the governing feature.

what to avoid: Although *The Story of Moses* ✍ (Gramavision, 1987, prod. Bob Moses) has some typically colorful arrangements and an impressive band (including Pat Metheny, Bill Frisell, David Liebman, and Tiger Okoshi), its melodramatic retelling of the Biblical story—complete with bombastic narration and acting out of the conversations between God and Moses—distracts unbearably from its musical merits.

the rest:
Visit with the Great Spirit ✍✍✍ (Gramavision, 1983)
Time Stood Still ✍✍✍ (Gramavision, 1994)

worth searching for: Perhaps only fellow drummers will be attracted to the German import *Drumming Birds* ✍✍✍ (ITM), Moses's collaboration with downtown NYC percussionist Billy Martin. But this is not a collection of drum duets, rather it's studio-composed music that draws on the wide range of textures and colors these players have available to them thanks to their use of percussion from around the world, as well as drum machines and synthesizers.

influences:

◄◄ Gil Evans, Miles Davis, Charles Mingus, Duke Ellington, Thelonious Monk

►► Pat Metheny, Joe Gallant

Steve Holtje and Nancy Ann Lee

Bennie Moten

Born November 13, 1894, in Kansas City, MO. Died April 2, 1935, in Kansas City, MO.

Bennie Moten led a band that was significant to the history of jazz in that the core of Count Basie's early band evolved out of Bennie Moten's Orchestra, a territory band that enjoyed an esteemed reputation as the best band throughout Kansas, Oklahoma, and Missouri. Moten was a very skilled pianist and his drive as a leader kept him striving to be the best. He first recorded on the OKeh label with a small group in 1923, and again in 1926 with a larger ensemble. Musicians in his band included "Hot Lips" Page, Jimmy Rushing, Count Basie on second piano, Booker Washington, Eddie Durham, Eddie Barefield, Ben Webster, and Walter Page, among others. When the band was on the road, and playing in Kansas City, Moten often let Basie sit in for most of the performance. In 1932 the band recorded their most famous sides for Victor, which included the classic "Moten Swing." When Moten passed away from a bungled tonsillectomy operation in 1935, his brother took over for a short time, and then the band passed into the hands of Count Basie.

what to buy: *Basie Beginnings (1929–1932)* 🎵🎵🎵🎵 (RCA, 1929–32, compilation prod. Orrin Keepnews) captures brilliant and exciting moments from a band that impacted the history of jazz and, with Moten always refining the band, continued to reach new heights. Three sessions are documented on this recording. Six original tunes are included from the first session, which took place October 23–24, 1929 in Chicago for the Victor Record company. Four of the six compositions were collaborations between Moten and Basie. The orchestra included Ed Lewis and Booker Washington on cornet; Thamon Hayes on trombone; Eddie Durham on both trombone and guitar; Harlan Leonard, Jack Washington, and Woody Walder on reeds; Bill "Count" Basie on piano; Buster Moten on accordion; Leroy Berry on banjo; Vernon Page on tuba and Willie McWashington on drums. The band swings hard and cohesively. Also included are nine tunes from the October 27–31, 1930 recording session, which took place in Kansas City. Trumpeter Oran "Hot Lips" Page had, by then, joined the band, along with vocalist Jimmy Rushing, who sings five tunes, including "Won't You Be My Baby," "That Too, Do Blues," "Liza Lee," "When I'm Alone," and "Now That I Need You," as Basie adds vocals to "Somebody Stole My Gal." The last session documented on this CD took place on December 13, 1932, and was recorded in Camden, New Jersey for Victor. Due to Moten's continuous revisions and refinements, the orchestra displays a more sophisticated and smooth swinging sound by 1932. Bassist Walter Page is an important addition to the orchestra, replacing Vernon Page, the tuba player, and Leroy Berry switches from banjo to guitar. Clarinetist and alto saxophonist Eddie Barefield and tenor saxophonist Ben Webster had also joined the Moten organization by then. Seven of the 10 tunes recorded at the 1932 session include the debut of Bennie and Buster Moten's "Moten Swing," as well as "Toby," "The Blue Room," "New Orleans," "Milenberg Joys," and "Lafayette."

the rest:
Bennie Moten 1923–1927 🎵🎵🎵🎵 (Jazz Chronological Classics, 1994)
Bennie Moten 1927–1929 🎵🎵🎵🎵 (Jazz Chronological Classics, 1994)
Bennie Moten 1929–1930 🎵🎵🎵🎵 (Jazz Chronological Classics, 1994)

Susan K. Berlowitz

Paul Motian

Born March 25, 1931, in Philadelphia, PA.

Paul Motian is one of the most interactive drummers in jazz.

Even as his almost wholly textural, free-time method reminds one vaguely of Sunny Murray or Milford Graves, Motian's style is so personal as to be inimitable. His delicately shaded, dynamically varied accompaniment style is always at the service of the music. While he has been a prolific leader, his records are never mere platforms used to display his virtuosity. Rather, they are inevitably vehicles for the realization of a coherent ensemble concept. Sensitive to every sound emitted around him, Motian is a preternaturally reactive player, and as such, a master collaborator. He moved to New York in 1955 and played with a number of musicians, including Gil Evans, Lennie Tristano, Stan Getz, and Thelonious Monk. In 1959 Motian began a relationship with pianist Bill Evans. With Evans, he developed the style for which he has become famous: an elastic, conversational approach that relies less on the maintenance of a steady pulse and more on a communal manner of phrasing. Eventually, in his work with Paul Bley and Keith Jarrett (with whom he did many of his finest recordings), Motian all but gave up on the drummer's traditional time-keeping function in favor of a more purely spontaneous technique of expression. In the 1990s he made a decided turn away from free playing toward a sort of amplified, guitar-driven bebop.

what to buy: Featuring tenorist Joe Lovano (before his major label days) and Bill Frisell (ditto), *Misterioso* 🎵🎵🎵🎵 (Soul Note, 1986, prod. Giovanni Bonandrini) is Motian at his all-encompassing, loose-limbed best. Both Lovano and Frisell appeared on many of Motian's fine 1980s albums; this is the best. Motian's oblique swing and Lovano's dark intensities make a strong pairing.

the rest:
Psalm 🎵🎵🎵🎵 (ECM, 1981)
The Story of Maryam 🎵🎵🎵 (ECM, 1983)
Jack of Clubs 🎵🎵🎵🎵 (Soul Note, 1984)
It Should Have Happened Long Ago 🎵🎵🎵🎵 (ECM, 1984)
One Time Out 🎵🎵🎵 (Soul Note, 1987)
Monk in Motian 🎵🎵🎵 (JMT, 1988)
On Broadway, Volume 1 🎵🎵🎵 (JMT, 1988)
On Broadway, Volume 2 🎵🎵🎵 (JMT, 1989)
On Broadway, Volume 3 🎵🎵🎵🎵 (JMT, 1991)
Motian in Tokyo 🎵🎵🎵🎵 (Soul Note, 1991)
And the Electric Bebop Band 🎵🎵🎵 (JMT, 1992)
Trioism 🎵🎵🎵🎵 (JMT, 1993)

influences:
◀◀ Gil Evans, Thelonious Monk, Max Roach
▶▶ Joe Lovano

Chris Kelsey

Alphonse Mouzon

Born November 21, 1948, in Charleston, SC.

An accomplished drummer by high school, Alphonse Mouzon moved to New York to study music and drama at New York City College and medicine at Manhattan Medical School. He also played in the pit band of the Broadway show *Promises, Promises* while attending New York City College. By 1969 his reputation as a musician had spread to such an extent that a medical career was no longer an option. Mouzon's musical associations read like a Who's Who of modern jazz and pop music. Along with Larry Coryell, he was co-founder of The 11th House, a seminal fusion band of the 1970s. In the early 70s he also played with McCoy Tyner and was a charter member, along with Joe Zawinul and Wayne Shorter, of Weather Report. In the past two decades, he has recorded with Gil Evans, Roy Ayers, George Benson, Herbie Hancock, Dizzy Gillespie, Freddie Hubbard, Les McCann, Stanley Clarke, Ronnie Laws, and Jaco Pastorius. Mouzon also performed with Miles Davis on the 1991 movie soundtrack album *Dingo*. In 1992 he formed Tenacious Records and now records exclusively for the label.

what to buy: Starting his own label has afforded drummer Mouzon the opportunity to extend his sphere of creativity to include producing, composing, arranging, and playing keyboards. He is best when playing live on *As You Wish* ♫♫♫♫ (Tenacious, 1989, prod. Alphonse Mouzon), a 1989 session that features the greatly underrated multi-sax ace Gary Meek. Although the multi-tracked fusion-esque soundscapes that he creates offer the right combination of flurry ear-candy and artsy edges, when he sits down at the drums and really lets loose, as he does on "Give the Drummer Some," watch out. The power and majesty of his percussion is staggering. Admirable solo work throughout by pianist Joachim Becker and bassist Michael Schurmann adds to the proceedings but Meek's tenor and soprano are the real highlight here. Meek, a presence on all but two of the album's 12 tracks, contributes gently snaking soprano lines on cuts like "Thinking of You" and "Obsession," brightening up sometimes heavy-handed background settings. Mouzon successfully covers all the bases on *The Night Is Still Young* ♫♫♫♫ (Tenacious, 1996, prod. Alphonse Mouzon), from melodic soul/funky-smooth jazz to traditional bop in the tradition on this perceptive journey that looks back and forward. A prolific and sometimes adventurous performer, he offers an intriguing look at his dual personality here: the first half of this recording is a straight, swinging set featuring a small group with saxmen Ralph Moore and Eric Marienthal catching the contagious blues groove on "Daddy's Blues," while "Protocol"

finds Mouzon burning up the drum kit as bassist Tony Dumas walks up a storm. Best of all is the joyously brassy, swinging "Waltz for Emma," which Mouzon wrote for his young daughter. The other side of this session in a casual-to-funky contemporary context, with Mouzon playing many synths and other instruments. On musical "travelogues" to Brazil and Africa, he is chops unlimited, playing all the instruments himself.

what to buy next: Drummer Mouzon is a survivor who first came to the attention of jazz listeners with McCoy Tyner's stirring late '60s Quartet, and then as a charter member of Weather Report. He also managed to survive the contrivance of the artificially flavored genre known as contemporary jazz. Somehow, he's taken all his influences and created his own musical amalgam, which always features his driving percussion. Now a composer, percussionist, and pianist, he enlists the musical support of contemporary jazz specialists Lee Ritenour, Russ Freeman, Kirk Whalum, and Brandon Fields on *The Survivor* ♫♫♫ (Tenacious, 1992, prod. Alphonse Mouzon) and the results are colorful, but hardly memorable. This session is just a notch or two above background music. But good background music.

best of the rest:

By All Means ♫♫♫ (Tenacious, 1981/1993)
Back to Jazz ♫♫♫♫ (Tenacious, 1985/1993)
Love Fantasy ♫♫♫ (Tenacious, 1993)
Morning Sun ♫♫♫♫ (Tenacious, 1996)

Bret Primack

Famoudou Don Moye

Born May 23, 1946, in Rochester, NY.

Percussionist Famoudou Don Moye is probably best known for his lengthy association with the free-jazz, ancient-to-modern collaborative, the Art Ensemble of Chicago, formed by members of the AACM (Association for the Advancement of Creative Musicians) which is headquartered in Chicago. Moye studied percussion at Wayne State University in Detroit from 1965–66. In 1968, he traveled to Morocco and Europe with Charles Moore's Detroit Free Jazz band, and worked with Steve Lacy in Rome, North Africa, and Paris. While in Europe, Moye joined the Art Ensemble of Chicago in 1970 when they were in Paris. Replacing Philip Wilson who had left the AEC to tour with the Butterfield Blues Band, Moye fit comfortably with the original members of this avant-garde group—Lester Bowie, Malachi Favors, Joseph Jarman, Roscoe Mitchell—and remains with the AEC today, as well as performing and recording with Lester

Bowie's Brass Fantasy, the Leaders, and the Sun Percussion Summit with Enoch Williamson.

what to buy: If you're curious about the African percussion tradition, give a listen to *Afrikan Song* 🎵🎵🎵🎵 (Southport/AECO. 1996, prod. Famoudou Don Moye), a 15-tune spiritual journey derived from the roots of African singing, theater, and rhythms. Featuring Sun Percussion Summit, a group led by percussionists Famoudou Don Moye and Enoch Williamson, this outing highlights the talents of special guests, percussion masters Mamane Smake and Naby Camara. At times, this group sounds like a chanting, improvised Sun Ra performance. Other times they lean to the modern, delivering an African choral arrangement of the R&B soul ballad, "Just My Imagination," a funk-beat tune, "Big Red Peaches," and a loosely performed spiritual, "By the Rivers of Babylon/Ol' Time Religion." Yet when they focus solely on percussion instrumentals, sometimes lightly supported with echoing wind instruments and an array of African melody instruments, their ancestral music is invigorating. This troupe focuses on creating superb roots harmonies, punctuated with the combined colors and textures of African hand and wind instruments, and storytelling elements. It's an exciting trip for the listener.

what to buy next: *Calypso's Smile* 🎵🎵🎵 (AECO, 1992, prod. Famoudou Don Moye, Joseph Jarman, Isio Saba) features the Joseph Jarman/Famoudou Don Moye Magic Triangle band, with Moye playing traps and an array of percussion instruments. This is a beguiling session with illustrious reedman Joe Jarman and bassist Essiet Okon Essiet, two highly compatible and equally innovative musicians. The trio's seven inside out creations are freely improvised, yet pleasing to the ear. Moye sets the foundations for the African roots-derived songs, adding percussive textures with hand drums, bells, gongs, and other instruments, and painting with bright colors while Jarman creates lovely melodic lines. There's a profound harmonious spirit in their creations which make this an accessible listen.

best of the rest:
Sun Percussion Vol. 1 🎵🎵🎵🎵 (AECO, 1975)
Jam for Your Life 🎵🎵🎵 (AECO, 1991)

worth searching for: If you're hankering to hear more of Moye's creations, it's almost required that you check out his contributions to the Art Ensemble of Chicago. One of the best AEC recordings is the two-disc set *Urban Bushmen* 🎵🎵🎵🎵🎵 (ECM, 1982/1994, prod Manfred Eicher), on which Moye, using his full arsenal of percussion instruments, is featured quite prominently and artistically throughout. It's difficult to imagine

what this group would be without his artistry. If you dig *Urban Bushmen*, you'll also want to hear some other Art Ensemble of Chicago recordings such as *The Third Decade* 🎵🎵🎵🎵 (ECM, 1985/1994, prod. Manfred Eicher), *Full Force* 🎵🎵🎵🎵 (ECM, 1980/ 1994), and *Nice Guys* 🎵🎵🎵🎵 (ECM, 1979/1994). Their eclectic music is highly percussive and freely-improvised, drawing from African-rooted themes and rhythms, and much more.

influences:

◀◀ Ed Blackwell, Max Roach, Art Blakey, Billy Higgins, Andrew Cyrille

▶▶ Kahil El'Zabar, Jamey Haddad

see also: *Art Ensemble of Chicago, Lester Bowie*

Nancy Ann Lee

George Mraz

Born Jiří Mraz, 1944, in Písek, Czech Republic.

George Mraz is a melodious, yet underrated, straight-ahead jazz bassist who has appeared on many jazz albums as sideman and recorded only a few albums as leader. Born in a town 55 miles south of Prague, Mraz began violin studies at age seven, added alto saxophone in high school, and began formal studies on double bass in 1960 when he entered the Prague Conservatory. Though classically trained, Mraz developed an interest in jazz, inspired by the work of Scott LaFaro and Ray Brown. After graduation he spent a year in Munich where he became part of the international jazz scene. In 1968, Mraz came to the U.S. and, on a scholarship, entered Berklee College of Music in Boston. The timing coincided with occupation of Czechoslovakia by the former Soviet Union, and this influenced Mraz's decision to remain in the U.S. He easily found work in the Boston area and it became a busy time for the bassist. Mraz toured with Oscar Peterson (1970–72), worked with Stan Getz (1974–75), and moved to New York, where he became a member of the Thad Jones/Mel Lewis Orchestra (1973–76). He played in a group with Peter Donald and guitarist John Abercrombie, performed with the New York Jazz Quartet founded by Roland Hanna, and with an array of artists including Jimmy Rowles, Zoot Sims, Stan Getz, Pepper Adams, Bill Evans, Jack DeJohnette, John Scofield, and others. Mraz obtained his U.S. citizenship in 1975 (changing his first name to George) and continued to perform, tour, and record with an array of top artists. In 1991, Mraz returned to Prague where he recorded his first album as leader, *Catching Up*, a trio date with Peter Donald and Richie Beirach, released on the Japanese Alfa label. Mraz recorded subsequent albums as leader for the Milestone label, and continues to record as sideman with many jazz artists.

what to buy: After appearing as guest on Mraz's debut album for Milestone, tenor saxophonist Rich Perry became an integral part of Mraz's team with pianist Cyrus Chestnut and drummer Al Foster on the enticing *Bottom Lines* ♫♫♫♪ (Milestone, 1997, prod. Todd Barkan). This is a sprightly bass-focused session riding on adventurous tunes by bassist-composers Jaco Pastorius ("Three Views of a Secret"), Charles Mingus ("Goodbye Porkpie Hat"), Buster Williams ("Christina"), Marcus Miller ("Mr. Pastorius"), Ron Carter ("Little Waltz"), Steve Swallow ("Falling Grace"), and Mraz himself ("Lisa Marie," "Strange Blues"). Mraz is a musician prone to understatement and you have to pay attention to the fundamental subtleties in his sessions. There's lots happening on this session if you listen carefully. Chestnut and Foster are two top innovators and they contribute elegantly to the April, 1997 studio date. Perry is the perfect partner for the harmonious escapades, and one of the highlights on the album is Mraz's unison arco bass playing with Perry's tenorisms on "Mr. Pastorius," which gives a piquant, modish-sounding edge to this tune. Mraz takes more chances on this album and it pays off.

what to buy next: George Mraz has accompanied many artists and can be thought of as one of the stalwart jazz bassists who has performed with the giants. *Jazz* ♫♫♫♪ (Milestone, 1996, prod. Todd Barkan) was his first recording as leader for a U.S. label and his debut on Milestone. Mraz's trio comprises longtime compatriots, pianist Richie Beirach (Larry Willis subs on one track) and drummer Billy Hart. They make a fabulous team. Mraz's classical training in Europe tethers him to the straight-ahead tradition; he neither ventures too far into the avant-garde nor attempts to create swinging, frolicsome interplay. Hart is an alert player who knows when to make a splash and when to yield to the soloists. One of the most sensitive drummers, he creates shading and colors with plenty of cymbals work, alternating with light punches from underneath and with his softly brisk brushwork. Beirach and Mraz share a lyrical bent which relinquishes sweet, elegantly harmonious improvisations. All three musicians create fresh excitement together because they've been collaborating for more than 20 years. Together, this fine team delivers 11 poignantly rich tunes, a few lesser known standards, a couple of Mraz originals, and the pretty, melodic love theme from the film *Cinema Paradiso* (plus a 1:12 reprise). The most noticeably up-tempo tune is Mraz's original, "Pepper," an all-too-brief (1:05) piece that deserves

further exploration. Tenor saxophonist Rich Perry guests with solos on two tracks. Mraz and his trio shine throughout, playing mostly ballads with great artistry, freshness, and flair. The Mraz-Beirach-Hart team also appears on *My Foolish Heart* ♫♫♫♪ (Milestone, 1995, prod. Todd Barkan, Satoshi Hirano), delivering a mixture of 10 standards and originals by Mraz and Beirach. Romantic and only sometimes swinging, this is a sedate session that points up Mraz's songlike bass playing. While this team works well together, Beirach defers to Mraz, and his often dreamy pianisms fail to generate excitement, although on tunes such as Strayhorn's "Passion Flower," his sentimentality fits Mraz's arco (bowed) bass melody lines and exquisite improvisations. Mraz more often takes the melody lead, but on Miles Davis's "Blue in Green" allows the trio to stretch out into freer territory, with Beirach delivering an edgy performance propelled by Hart's explosive drumming.

worth searching for: Mraz is heard best in small groups and the albums with other leaders recommended in this section pair him with the most melodious jazz pianists. Mraz backs pianist Adam Makowicz on *Concord Duo Series, Volume Five* ♫♫♫♪ (Concord, 1994, prod. Carl E. Jefferson). The pianist's lyrical, light keyboard style is influenced by classicism, but he certainly has the capacity to swing hard. With backing from George Mraz, the pianist trades off with ease and fluency. A pleasant, delicate interpretation of 10 standards (including four Makowicz originals). As the Keystone Trio, pianist John Hicks, bassist George Mraz, and drummer Idris Muhammad present nine romantic standards on *Heart Beats* ♫♫♫♪ (Milestone, 1996, prod. Todd Barkan), giving fresh air to familiar songs like "Dancing in the Dark," "It Had to Be You," "Speak Low," and others. Hicks is known for his energy, passion, and melodicism and creates pretty music on this outing. Veterans Mraz and Muhammad are active cohorts, generating plenty of rhythmic spurs and some pleasing solos. A spectacular album. Recorded in New York in September 1991, *Flowers for Lady Day* ♫♫♫♪ (Evidence, 1996, prod. Makoto Kimata, Satoshi Hirano) offers 10 standards associated with singer Billie Holiday, performed by leader Hank Jones (piano), with bassist George Mraz and drummer Roy Haynes. Mraz is lush in his arco playing. Jones, who keeps his conversational expressions mostly in the upper and middle registers, has worked with both players before. Thus his phrasing is familiar to them, which helps secure their tight trio sound. This is a relaxed, pretty (sometimes bubbly) session that includes such gems as "Lover Man," "I'll Never Smile Again," "I'm a Fool to Want You," and more. It's befitting that Jones calls this The Great Jazz Trio. They make great jazz together and, individually, they're legendary romancers of the form. You may also want to check out Mraz's fine work with the New York Jazz Quartet, the best of which is *Surge* 𝄪𝄪𝄪𝄪 (Enja, 1992, prod. Horst Weber), with Roland Hanna (founder/pianist), Frank Wess (flutes, saxophones), and Richard Pratt (drums). It's a lively modern set of five tunes which bring forth the best from each player.

influences:

◀◀ Scott LaFaro, Ray Brown, Ron Carter, Paul Chambers, Doug Watkins

Nancy Ann Lee

Bheki Mseleku

Born 1955, in Durban, South Africa.

Bheki Mseleku is primarily a McCoy Tyner/Keith Jarrett-influenced pianist born in South Africa and living in England. He grew up in South Africa in a poor but musical family and played with local bands, one of which toured in North America in the late 1970s. Mseleku moved to Sweden in 1980 and in his three years there worked with South African expatriate bassist Johnny Dyani and trumpeter Don Cherry; while traveling in Europe he also gigged with other former South Africans, Abdullah Ibrahim, and Chris McGregor. When Mseleku moved to England in 1987 he quickly made an impression with performances at Ronnie Scott's famous London club. After a two-year time out during which he joined a Buddhist community, Mseleku returned to London and music. In late 1991 he put together a band with an American rhythm section (Michael Bowie and Marvin "Smitty" Smith) and local horn players (Steve Williamson, Jean Toussaint, Eddie Parker) that got him a record deal; that group is heard on his debut album, *Celebration*. Verve signed him in 1993 and for his first U.S. release, *Timelessness*, nudged Mseleku closer to the mainstream, attempting to sell him to the American audience with a clutch of mostly famous guest stars: tenormen Joe Henderson, Pharoah Sanders, flutist Kent Jordan, vocalist Abbey Lincoln, drummer Elvin Jones, and pianist Rodney Kendrick. Not surprisingly, the album ended up sounding a bit scattered, though the thinness of Mseleku's compositions was (and remains) more of a problem. The specific South African references in his music set him apart from the familiar influences, however, and he is a tremendously charismatic performer, as best demonstrated on his solo album. Verve continues the guest-star strategy and Mseleku continues to tantalize with his unique talents, which, on record at least, have not yet blossomed to the degree one would expect.

what to buy: *Meditations* 𝄪𝄪𝄪 (Verve, 1994, prod. Russell Herman) contains a solo 1992 concert. If its two lengthy improvisations—32 and 14 minutes—sometimes sound a bit slack, this is nonetheless a compelling album that offers the purest expression of Mseleku's roots. At times his piano playing recalls the tuneful aspects of Keith Jarrett's solo concerts—and he sings along with his playing, too. However, he also sings in a distinctly African style which some may find abrasive and braying but which can grow on open-minded listeners. This truly is a meditative album and should be listened to on that level rather than as an attempt at soloistic virtuosity, though certainly Mseleku is no slouch as a player on either piano or tenor.

what to buy next: There's a cosmic aspect of Mseleku's playing that makes the title of *Star Seeding* 𝄪𝄪𝄪 (Verve, 1995, prod. Bheki Mseleku, Jean-Philippe Allard) appropriate. The multi-instrumentalist, who plays piano, tenor sax, and a little guitar on this album as well as singing on one track, is teamed with the classic Ornette Coleman rhythm section of bassist Charlie Haden and drummer Billy Higgins who offer solid support without hogging the foreground. Mseleku overdubs himself sometimes but never sounds unspontaneous. Though his McCoy Tyner influence is still clear, he's less thunderous than on some previous efforts, and this is definitely his prettiest and most consistent band album so far.

the rest:

Timelessness 𝄪𝄪𝄪 (Verve, 1994)
Beauty of Sunrise 𝄪𝄪𝄪 (Verve, 1997)

worth searching for: The debut album *Celebration* 𝄪𝄪𝄪 (World Circuit, 1992, prod. Russell Herman, Bheki Mseleku, Marvin Smith) made it to the shortlist of England's prestigious Mercury Music Prize. Mseleku's sing-songy themes reference the simplicity of township melodies, but wear thin on repeated hearings; he is much more advanced as a pianist than as a writer. The true hero of *Celebration* is drummer Marvin "Smitty" Smith. Perhaps Mseleku's supreme achievement comes on "Angola," which starts as a chirpily annoying piece of flute pap; he batters it into high gear, with the raw excitement of Smith's propulsion kicking Mseleku into some of his most inspired Tynerisms. The energy continues on the next track, especially when Mseleku, Smith, and soprano saxist Steve Williamson trade fours before the final statement of the theme and then on the extended coda. Those two tunes are the high points; guest appearances include Jean Toussaint (tenor sax) and Courtney Pine (soprano sax).

influences:

◀◀ McCoy Tyner, John Coltrane, Abdullah Ibrahim, Keith Jarrett, Pharoah Sanders

▶▶ Courtney Pine, Steve Williamson

Steve Holtje

Mujician

Formed 1988, in England.

Keith Tippett, piano; Paul Dunmall, reeds; Tony Levin, percussion; Paul Rogers, bass.

The free-improvising British quartet Mujician plays patient, constructive ensemble music that clearly seeks in-depth exploration of each timbral combination made possible by the band's instrumentation. To this end, Paul Dunmall (b. 1953, Welling, England) plays a variety of reed instruments, from the standard saxophones to an E-flat clarinet and a Chinese Shenai. Dunmall and pianist Keith Tippett (b. Bristol, England, 1947) have the most clearly defined histories as improvisers and bring a concomitantly precise and expansive breadth of jazz languages to the musical mix. This is not to downplay the considerable coloristic and non-rhythmic roles played by bassist Paul Rogers (b. Chester, England, 1956) and percussionist Tony Levin (b. Shropshire, England, 1940). Each of this quartet's musicians takes on the others' roles at various times, from Dunmall's rhythmic pocks and blats to the singing quality evinced by Levin on his drum kit.

Mujician's performance history has been largely European, and they have been broadcast on BBC radio, as well as on various other European outlets, including a televised collaboration with Georgian improvisers in Tblisi in the early 1990s. The band has its roots in the late 1960s English avant-garde improvised music scene. Tippett, the most renowned of the quartet, led a variety of aggregates, from small groups to the sprawling Centipede, and recorded with the rock band King Crimson in the early 1970s. Mujician is unique in the British scene for its ability to integrate the abstractions and arrhythmic, amelodic, anti-virtuosic playing of Derek Bailey and the late John Stevens with an extended sense of their own connection with U.S. avant-garde jazz of the 1960s. Where they can begin their often long, completely improvised sets with spacious thought processes that take odd, elongated shapes, they can also spirit through romping, thunderous displays of energy jazz. Dunmall and Tippett take on dynamic force when they are performing at full tilt. Not surprisingly, Dunmall explored spiritual life in a U.S. ashram in the early 1970s, and he exemplifies the link between

all-out expressive performance and a crystallized spiritual vision that has touched John Coltrane, Pharoah Sanders, Albert Ayler, and numerous other free-leaning jazz players.

what to buy: For the extended look at Dunmall's riveting work on the Chinese Shenai, *Birdman* 🎷🎷🎷🎷 (Cuneiform, 1996) is the place to begin listening to Mujician. This lengthy CD also gives you one fully unfurled 30-minute improvisation, as well as a more compact 16-minute piece that shows the storms the quartet can brew in a relatively brief time frame.

what to buy next: The lengthy, uninterrupted follow of *The Journey* 🎷🎷🎷 (Cuneiform, 1992, prod. Derek Drescher) is a fine vantage point on multi-lingual avant-garde jazz. That is, the session allows one to hear the ways an ensemble takes on "group think" through tumultuous roars of energy and dynamic episodes of quietude. *Poem about the Hero* 🎷🎷🎷 (Cuneiform, 1994) is a serial work in five "verses." It's developmental to a point, but if you played it in shuffle mode, the CD would sound as assembled as it does from front to back. It's typically energetic in spots and calmingly spare in parts.

solo outings:

Keith Tippett:
Mujician III 🎷🎷🎷🎷 (FMP, 1987)
The Dartington Concert 🎷🎷🎷🎷 (EG Records, 1992)
Une croix dans l'océan 🎷🎷🎷🎷 (Les Disques Victo, 1996)

Paul Dunmall:
Soliloquy 🎷🎷🎷 (Matchless, 1986)
(With Paul Rogers)*Folks* 🎷🎷🎷🎷(Slam, 1993)
Desire and Liberation 🎷🎷🎷🎷 (Slam, 1997)

influences:

◀◀ John Coltrane Quartet, Pharoah Sanders, Albert Ayler, Art Ensemble of Chicago

▶▶ John Butcher, John Law, Simon Fell, Chris Burn

Andrew Bartlett

Joe Mulholland

Born August 14, 1952, in Battle Creek, MI.

Joe Mulholland grew up in Westfield, New Jersey, started playing piano at age eight, and began studying jazz in high school. He graduated from Williams College with a B.A. in psychology in 1974 and then moved to Boston, studying piano with Harvey Diamond for three years. In 1984 he began attending the New England Conservatory, from which he received a Master's in music in 1986. He has taught at Brown University and Berklee College and composes for film, dance, and theater in addition to his jazz work. Both his albums have been recorded with his sextet, which is built around the rhythm section of himself, bassist Bob Nieske, and drummer Matt Wilson. If Mulholland's albums, especially the earlier one, are hard to find, contact joseph_mulholland@it.berklee.edu or 1-800-871-5261.

what to buy: *Second Sight* ♫♫♫♫ (Jazzheads, 1996, prod. Joe Mulholland) has Gary Valente (trombone), Ken Cervenka (trumpet, flugelhorn), and Michael Moss (alto and soprano saxophone). Though the focus is firmly on Mulholland's post-bop compositions and his rich and varied voicings for the frontline, soloistically the burly yet agile stylings of Valente dominate (no surprise to anyone who's ever heard his brassy tone), which is not to say Cervenka and Moss don't also distinguish themselves. For that matter, Mulholland himself rips off an impressive high-velocity solo on "High Beams." The pieces range from aggressive swingers and jaunty mid-tempo numbers to "Cafe Tables," a 76-bar waltz which is gentle yet slightly fragmented. The moody Piazzolla tango tribute "Astor's Ghost," the only track with a different horn section and drummer, features Nieske bowing a gorgeous melody. Though nothing sounds especially derivative, the spirits of Mingus and the better mid-1960s Blue Note albums frequently peek out from the arrangements. "Scuppy," though still basically tonal, shows Mulholland's more avant-garde side, and throughout the album there's a great concern for tonal colors and ensemble variety; no two tracks sound the same and never is anything simply a drab unison head followed by a string of solos over rhythm.

what to buy next: The horns throughout *Speaking for Myself* ♫♫♫♫ (Bridge, 1990, prod. Joe Mulholland) are Dave Ballou (trumpet, flugelhorn), David Harris (trombone, just as brash-sounding as Valente on the later album), and Allan Chase (saxophones). The CD kicks off with the rollicking "Saturday Night Stomp," soul-jazz of the highest order anchored by Wilson's firm backbeat. All the virtues of the later album are already present here, with just as much variety and care in the arrangements.

influences:
◀◀ Charles Mingus, McCoy Tyner, Miles Davis, Duke Ellington

Steve Holtje

Gerry Mulligan

Born Gerald Joseph Mulligan, April 6, 1927, in Queens, NY. Died January 20, 1996, in Darien, CT.

Modern jazz certainly had its share of icons in the 1950s: Miles Davis, Dave Brubeck, Thelonious Monk, Charles Mingus, Sonny Rollins, and Ella Fitzgerald were all in their prime. Duke Ellington, Count Basie, and (for close to the first half of the decade, anyway) Charlie Parker were still around. Even so, no one was more visible and popular than the lanky baritone saxophonist Gerry Mulligan, whose "pianoless" quartet with Chet Baker caused a sensation when its initial recordings were issued in 1952. Even after his death, Mulligan remains the world's most famous jazz baritone sax player.

Before learning clarinet and various saxophones, Mulligan started out on piano, and became primarily an arranger who wrote for the Johnny Warrington radio band (1944), and bands led by Tommy Tucker and George Paxton in the 1940s. Going to and through New York from 1947–1951 (before settling in California), he worked with drummer Gene Krupa's Orchestra, contributing charts as staff arranger and playing alto with the band. In 1948 he did the same with the Claude Thornhill band. On September 4, 1948, the Miles Davis *Birth of the Cool* group broadcast from the Royal Roost, and by January 1949, Mulligan participated in a series of recording sessions for Capitol which helped introduce the relaxed, anti-frantic, cool-jazz, "West Coast sound" to the jazz world on recordings between 1948–50. Mulligan's other associations during this period included a group of musicians that would shape jazz for the next two decades: Stan Getz, Kai Winding, and those who would become Mulligan's favorite sidemen—Lee Konitz, Jerry Lloyd, Don Ferrara, and Zoot Sims. Again, it was his arrangements for this assemblage of "Five Brothers," that would capture the ears of his fans with their vibrant small-group format.

Early in 1952 Mulligan left New York, spending several months hitchhiking to California where he settled in Los Angeles and had a rocky period with the Kenton band. Still known mostly as an arranger, it was the Los Angeles-based quartet he formed in the early 1950s with trumpeter Chet Baker, bassist "Red" Mitchell, and drummer Chico Hamilton that really focused attention on "Jeru," as Mulligan was also known. That "pianoless" foursome and its immediate successors had a crowd-pleasing, accessible approach to standards, comprising equal parts of Dixieland counterpoint, swing-like pacing, and boppish improvisation that translated into a winning combination. Formed through a series of circumstances that led to the omission of the piano, this quartet would make recordings, under the auspices of producer Richard Bock, that would be hailed by critics as the most innovative in modern progressive jazz. The original Gerry Mulligan Quartet was at its peak of fame in 1954 when a narcotics bust, 90 days in jail, and subsequent legal problems sidelined Mulligan for six months. Over a pay dis-

pute, he and Baker parted and Mulligan headed back to New York City, picking up musicians along the way—bassist Bill Crow, drummer Dave Bailey, and valve trombonist Bob Brookmeyer—all who would remain with him as his group fluxed and changed into various configurations throughout the next decade.

In 1960 Mulligan formed his 13-piece concert band and toured Europe and, in 1964, Japan. After this band folded he freelanced as sideman, working often with pianist Dave Brubeck between 1968 and 1972, and serving as arranger for various groups. In the 1970s Mulligan led the short-lived big band the Age of Steam, headed and toured regularly overseas with a sextet that included vibist Dave Samuels, doubled on soprano for a time, and led a 14-piece band he had assembled. During the 1980s he experimented with a big band that featured electronic instruments, but returned mid-decade to a small-group format, leading a quintet with Scott Hamilton and Grady Tate. During the 1990s he led a "Rebirth of the Cool" band, toured with his quartet, and recorded final sessions for Telarc before his death in 1996.

what to buy: In assessing Mulligan's recorded legacy, it is wise to keep in mind he was a fairly consistent player. His skills never seriously diminished at any time in his career. You could start with his quartet sessions and work your way up to his concert band. One of the best quartet sessions is documented on *At Storyville* 𝄞𝄞𝄞𝄞 (Pacific Jazz, 1957/Blue Note, 1990, prod. Richard Bock), an album that features the baritone saxophonist in live performance at Boston's Storyville Club on December 6, 1956. Out of the 15 tunes on the CD reissue, Mulligan also plays piano (on four tunes), with Bob Brookmeyer (valve trombone, and piano on one tune), Bill Crow (bass), and Dave Bailey (drums). In addition to wittily titled Mulligan originals such as the swing-infected "Bweebida Bwobbida," "Ide's Side," "Bike up the Strand/Utter Chaos," and "Flash," the crew cohesively covers and revives classics such as "Birth of the Blues," "That Old Feeling," "I Can't Get Started," and "Honeysuckle Rose." The CD version adds five previously unissued tracks. Mulligan's Quartet has such a different sound from most of today's groups. *California Concerts, Volume 2* 𝄞𝄞𝄞𝄞 (Pacific Jazz, 1954/Blue Note, 1988, prod. Richard Bock) features Mulligan's quartet with Jon Eardley (trumpet), Red Mitchell (bass), and Chico Hamilton (drums), expanded to an exciting sextet that includes Brook-

meyer (valve trombone, piano) and Zoot Sims (tenor sax) with Larry Bunker taking over the traps set on nine of the 14 selections, some of which are definitive of the Cool era. Mulligan also contributes a few swing originals. *California Concerts, Volume 1* 𝄞𝄞𝄞𝄞 (Pacific Jazz, 1954/Blue Note, 1988, prod. Richard Bock) features the same crew. These are the sessions that initiated the sextet lineup with whom Mulligan would continue to explore during 1955–56 on a series of now out-of-print EmArcy recordings. Each album contains some classic jazz gems, plenty of previously unissued material, and sumptuous interaction among the horns. Both CDs are highly recommended. Mulligan's circa-1959 quartet album with trumpeter/flugelhornist Art Farmer, bassist Bill Crow, and drummer Dave Bailey, *What Is There to Say?* 𝄞𝄞𝄞𝄞 (Columbia, 1959/1994, prod. Gerry Mulligan) may be the best of the bunch, warm, burnished, and gilt-edged. It's also the last of his pianoless quartet albums recorded during the 1950s and contains memorable interpretations of jazz standards such as "Just in Time," "My Funny Valentine" (the latter led by Farmer), and a full-length version of Mulligan's "Utter Chaos" theme song.

what to buy next: For *Re-Birth of the Cool* 𝄞𝄞𝄞𝄞 (GRP, 1992, prod. Gerry Mulligan, John Snyder), Mulligan assembled a team of top musicians, some who had recorded the initial "Birth of the Cool" sessions some 35 years ago, and others who either wanted to play this music or who had exhibited the capacity to do so. Joining Mulligan for this 1992 date are Bill Barber (tuba), Dave Bargeron (trombone), Phil Woods (alto saxophone), Wallace Roney (trumpet), John Clark (French horn), John Lewis (piano), and Ron Vincent (drums). Miles Davis was the trumpeter of choice since he led the original sessions, but his death five months before this session sent Mulligan in search of a trumpeter and Roney, who understands Miles's melodic sense, fit the bill. Mulligan, Barber, and Lewis had played on some of the original "Birth of the Cool" nonet sessions and their presence lends this return visit to the same material (12 tunes) considerable authenticity. Focus is on light tones and tight, intricate arrangements that create smoother, easygoing synthesis between soloist and ensemble. Woods, the chosen replacement for original saxman Lee Konitz who was unavailable, is somewhat restrained but still fluidly eloquent. Overall, this is a nostalgic return visit with many highlights, including Tormé's note-bending, velvety vocals on "Darn That Dream."

Mulligan discovered Brazil rather late in his career and documents his fluid findings with Brazilian vocalist Jane Duboc on *Paraiso: Jazz Brazil* 𝄞𝄞𝄞𝄞 (Telarc, 1993, prod. John Snyder, Gerry Mulligan). Mulligan had heard Duboc while both were on

Gerry Mulligan (© Jack Vartoogian)

tour with their groups in Europe and had said they'd make an album together in the future. Co-writing eight of the album's 11 tunes with Duboc, he is at ease in the genre, masterfully expressing his impressions of the pretty Brazilian rhythms and melodies as he solos and backs Duboc's vocals. Mulligan also revisits Antonio Carlos Jobim's, "Wave," delivering a supple solo on this tune he had recorded in the past. Various percussionists add color and textures to the songs, making this a relaxed and different listen from the baritone saxophonist. *Legacy* 𝄢𝄢𝄢𝄢 (N2K Encoded Jazz, 1996, compilation prod. Ken Poston, Carl Griffin) is an enhanced CD that can be played on any CD player or computer with the appropriate multimedia requirements. The album compiles 10 selections recorded between 1949–96 by Mulligan's quartet, his sextet, nonet, Tentette, and his 13-piece concert band. Included are some of his best solos as well as extraordinary ensemble work from recordings with Chet Baker, Bob Brookmeyer, and others. Besides his virtuosic baritone saxisms, Mulligan was also a spontaneous composer adept at reworking standard chord changes into fanciful fresh improvisations, as showcased on *The Gerry Mulligan Songbook* 𝄢𝄢𝄢𝄢 (Pacific Jazz, 1957/Blue Note, 1996, prod. Richard Bock). Arrangements (mostly by Bill Holman) are for five saxophones featuring Mulligan, Lee Konitz (alto), Allen Eager (alto/tenor), Zoot Sims (alto/tenor), and Al Cohn (baritone/tenor), and the rhythm guitar of Freddie Green (of Count Basie big band fame), bass (Henry Grimes), and drums (Dave Bailey). The saxophonists take plenty of solo room for their clean flowing lines, and offer abundant stylistic variety. Four bonus tracks on the CD reissue are previously unissued tunes recorded the last day of the main session, classics written by Horace Silver ("The Preacher"), Tadd Dameron ("Good Bait"), and Milt Jackson ("Bag's Groove"). Mulligan performed these tunes with Vinnie Burke's string group (guitar, violin, cello, bass, drums). (Note: Don't confuse this CD with another of the same title, but different personnel on the Chiaroscuro label.)

best of the rest:

Mulligan Plays Mulligan 𝄢𝄢𝄢𝄢 (OJC, 1951/1989)

Gerry Mulligan Quartet Featuring Chet Baker Plus Chubby Jackson Big Band 𝄢𝄢𝄢𝄢 (OJC, 1952)

Mulligan Meets Monk 𝄢𝄢𝄢𝄢 (OJC, 1957)

Mulligan Meets the Saxophonists 𝄢𝄢𝄢𝄢 (Verve, 1957, 1959/1987)

(With Scott Hamilton) *Soft Lights and Sweet Music* 𝄢𝄢𝄢 (Concord, 1986)

(With the Gerry Mulligan Orchestra) *Walk on the Water* 𝄢𝄢𝄢 (DRG, 1993),

Verve Jazz Masters, Volume 36 𝄢𝄢𝄢𝄢 (Verve, 1994)

Dream a Little Dream 𝄢𝄢𝄢𝄢 (Telarc, 1994)

Dragonfly 𝄢𝄢𝄢 (Telarc, 1995)

This Is Jazz Number 18 𝄢𝄢𝄢𝄢 (Columbia/Legacy, 1996)

worth searching for: Now out of print, the limited-edition, four-disc set, *The Complete Pacific Jazz Recordings of the Gerry Mulligan Quartet with Chet Baker* 𝄢𝄢𝄢𝄢𝄢 (Pacific Jazz, 1952–57/Blue Note, 1995, prod. Richard Bock), features Mulligan's pianoless quartet recordings with trumpeter Baker. Although this set overlaps with the also-out-of-print Mosaic box set, it includes tracks from Mulligan's work with Baker between 1952–53 and a 1957 reunion date, plus a few earlier titles with pianist Jimmy Rowles as Mulligan was forming his group. A total of 82 consistently pleasureful tracks make this set a welcome addition to any collection. Among the most accessible albums for domestic labels are Mulligan's recordings made for Pacific Jazz during his peak recording years of the '50s and '60s and reissued by Blue Note. You really can't go too far astray with anything Mulligan recorded during this period, but this set will probably only be available through auction services. Also out of print is *The Concert Jazz Band* 𝄢𝄢𝄢𝄢 (Verve, 1960/1991), which features the debut of Mulligan's 13-piece concert band formed in 1959. Highlights include swinging Ellingtonian right on down to a "hit single" reading of Duke's "I'm Gonna Go Fishin'" from the *Anatomy of a Murder* soundtrack.

influences:

◀◀ Lester Young, Harry Carney

▶▶ Ronnie Cuber, Claire Daly

see also: *Miles Davis, Art Farmer, Chet Baker, Dave Brubeck, Bob Brookmeyer*

Nancy Ann Lee and David Prince

Mark Murphy

Born March 14, 1932, in Syracuse, NY.

Mark Murphy is one of the most original and consistently creative male singers in jazz. A daring performer who takes chances on stage, Murphy has turned eclecticism into one of the hallmarks of his style, using his highly personal approach and emphatic sense of swing to interpret a broad range of material, from blues and standards to Brazilian songs and contemporary jazz compositions (for which he sometimes writes a lyric). His scat singing and vocals aren't always as rewarding as his ballad work, but Murphy is a dramatic singer who always brings his particular point of view to his material, interpreting it with his incisive jazz sensibility. He started singing as a teenager in his brother's dance band, and landed his first major gig in 1954 opening for Anita O'Day in San Francisco. Murphy made his first recordings for Milt Gabler on Decca in the mid-1950s, then recorded three forgettable albums for Capitol later in the decade. His two classic albums for Riverside in the early 1960s didn't lead to more work, and he ended up spending a decade in Europe, eventually settling in London, working as an actor in TV and stage productions. He returned to the U.S. in the mid-1970s and began recording a series of fine albums for Muse. A true student of Brazilian music, Murphy recorded a beautiful album of Ivan Lins tunes for Milestone, *Night Mood*. He's also turned his love of Beat-generation writer Jack Kerouac's novels into highly effective jazz/literature projects, such as his Muse album *Bop for Kerouac*. Murphy spends part of each year teaching jazz singing at the University of Graz in Austria and has developed a following on the acid jazz scene in Europe. He has recorded for Audiophile, Milestone, Fontana, Saba, and Muse.

what to buy: Mark Murphy's breakthrough album, *Rah!* 🎵🎵🎵🎵 (Riverside, 1961/OJC, 1994, prod. Orrin Keepnews) is a classic session featuring an all-star jazz big band and charts by Ernie Wilkins. Opening with a heartbreaking version of "Angel Eyes," the album contains the definitive post-Lambert, Hendricks and Ross version of Horace Silver's "Doodlin'," and a roller coaster version of Miles Davis's "Milestones." The tight charts don't allow much room for solos, but with trumpeters Clark Terry and Blue Mitchell, trombonists Jimmy Cleveland and Melba Liston, pianists Bill Evans and Wynton Kelly, and Jimmy Cobb at the drums, Murphy is surrounded by players who know how to swing. *That's How I Love the Blues!* 🎵🎵🎵🎵 (Riverside/OJC, 1962, prod. Orrin Keepnews) is one of the widest ranging explorations of the blues ever put to record. Murphy moves from hip hard bop (Horace Silver's "Senor Blues") to Kansas City blues ("Goin' to Chicago Blues") to show tunes ("Blues in the Night") as if the music was all cut from the same cloth, which of course it is. Al Cohn's charts are as witty and deep as Murphy's singing, making this one of the era's essential vocal albums.

what to buy next: An album only Mark Murphy could pull off, *September Ballads* 🎵🎵🎵🎵 (Milestone, 1988/1992, prod. Larry Dunlap) features tunes by Pat Metheny and Lyle Mays, Chick Corea, Steve Allen, Eliane Elias, Willie Nelson, and Michael Franks. That's more range than most singers cover in a career, and Murphy turns each tune into an effective jazz vehicle. Pianist Larry Dunlap's arrangements make full use of Art Farmer's gorgeous flugelhorn, Larry Coryell's electric guitar, and Oscar Castro-Neves's acoustic guitar. "Time on My Hands" is the only tune that can be called a standard on *I'll Close My Eyes* 🎵🎵🎵🎵

(Muse, 1994, prod. Larry Fallon), but Murphy turns everything he sings into jazz. He even transforms the moldy old Bread tune "If" into a torchy ballad. Trumpeter Claudio Roditi takes a striking solo on the title track.

best of the rest:

Mark Murphy Sings 🎵🎵🎵🎵 (Muse, 1976)
Satisfaction Guaranteed 🎵🎵🎵🎵 (Muse, 1979)
Beauty and the Beast 🎵🎵🎵🎵 (Muse, 1986)
Night Mood 🎵🎵🎵🎵 (Milestone, 1992)
Stolen Moments 🎵🎵🎵🎵 (Muse, 1992)
Song for the Geese 🎵🎵🎵 (RCA/BMG, 1997)

influences:

◀◀ Nat "King" Cole, Peggy Lee, Ella Fitzgerald

▶▶ Kurt Elling

Andrew Gilbert

Turk Murphy

Born Melvin Edward Alton Murphy, December 16, 1915, in Palermo, CA. Died May 30, 1987, in San Francisco, CA.

Turk Murphy was a catalyst in the traditional jazz revival of the 1940s, a jazz trombonist with a robust sound and style, leader of a San Francisco style traditional-jazz band for nearly 40 years, and a gifted and respected composer of rags and jazz tunes. He is revered by hundreds of musicians whose instrumental or band styles were influenced by Murphy. Ten years after his passing, his name remains constant on the lips of his legion of friends and fans.

Murphy grew up in Palermo, a small town nestled in the orange and peach orchards of northern California. Young Murphy heard his grandfather play hoedown fiddle and alto horn, but it was his drummer/trumpet-playing father who introduced him to jazz in the early 1920s. As a lad, Murphy was exposed to Western songs, ragtime, barroom ballads, and brass band marches, and by the time he was 12, he had given up the trumpet for the trombone. Three years later, he was in the musician's union, playing Friday and Saturday night gigs. Somewhere along the line, his football nickname, "The Terrible Turk," was abbreviated and he was simply called "Turk" the rest of his life. From 1933 through 1936 he was a young dance band musician, serving stints in the bands of Will Osborne and Mal Hallett, among others. In 1937 Murphy settled into New Orleans ensemble-style jazz by night and was a garage mechanic in Oakland, California, by day. He began to collect jazz records and sought further lessons in harmony, counterpoint, and composition. The next two years were spent in several traditional jazz bands, while hanging on to his paying day job. He became a charter member of the Lu Watters Yerba Buena Jazz band in 1940 and remained with the popular West Coast revivalist unit until 1949, except for a three-year hiatus as a U.S. Naval Aviation Mechanic First Class. In 1949 Turk Murphy's Jazz Band was formed and Murphy was able to record some of his newer original works such as "Trombone Rag," "Minstrels of Annie Street," "Brother Lowdown," and his haunting closing theme, "Bay City." These tunes are all staples in traditional band books today. Murphy's rough-hewn, good-natured singing was captured along with his trombone on over 40 sides recorded for Good Time Jazz through the spring of 1952. A two-year engagement at the Italian Village in San Francisco ensued and proved to be a turning point in Murphy's career. He subsequently landed a Columbia Records contract and toured extensively throughout the United States and Canada. His arrangement of "Mack the Knife" for Louis Armstrong provided the trumpet player with one of his biggest hits. By 1960 Murphy and his pianist, Pete Clute, had formed a partnership and opened Earthquake McGoon's, a jazz club that became home base for the Murphy band and a mecca for traditional jazz fans. His various bands over the years contained many fine players and he made recordings at home and abroad on over a dozen different labels. On January 10, 1987, shortly before his health failed completely, Murphy was honored at a sold-out jazz concert at Carnegie Hall in New York City. His influence is still felt today in the many traditional jazz groups that embrace the San Francisco style.

what to buy: *Turk Murphy's Jazz Band Favorites* ♪♪♪♪ (Various, 1949–51/Good Time Jazz, 1987, reissue prod. Lester Koenig) offers 21 vintage tracks for fans of West Coast or San Francisco style traditional jazz. Trumpeters Bob Scobey or Don Kinch and reedmen Bob Helm or Bill Napier share solo honors with Murphy's driving trombone. The King Oliver ("New Orleans Stomp"), Louis Armstrong ("Struttin' with Some Barbecue"), and Jelly Roll Morton ("Wolverine Blues") libraries are represented along with several spirituals, rags, barroom ballads, and four of leader Murphy's attractive originals, including his "Trombone Rag," which has evolved into a test piece or challenge for traditional-minded trombonists. Murphy lends his rough and ready vocalizing to several numbers and hits a proper heartfelt mood on "After You've Gone." More of this infectious vintage jazz is on hand in *Turk Murphy's Jazz Band Favorites, Volume 2* ♪♪♪♪ (Various, 1947–52/Good Time Jazz, 1995, prod. Nesuhi Ertegun, Lester Koenig, reissue prod. Ed Michael). Six of the 22 selections were previously unissued, including gems such as the politically incorrect "Red Eye," the hip "Wise Guys," and the tongue-in-cheek "Flamin' Mamie." Completists will want to get

this one. Pianists Wally Rose, Skippy Anderson, and Burt Bales all have fine contributions, as does solid tuba expert, Bob Short (no relation to the famous cabaret singer). Gal singer Claire Austin ends the program in fine fashion with her touching "Oh, Daddy," and performs on an aptly named "Hot Time in the Old Town Tonight." This is undiluted San Francisco-style jazz, still breathing fire after 50 years.

what to buy next: *At the Italian Village 1952–1953* ♪♪♪♪ (Merry Makers, 1952–53/1995, prod. John Gill) was released under the auspices of the San Francisco Traditional Jazz Foundation some 43 years after the taping of the historic 1952 opening concert by clarinetist Bob Helm. Twelve tracks are given over to a full seven-piece ensemble plus Claire Austin on four vocals ("Nobody Knows You When You're Down and Out," "Some of These Days," "Empty Bed Blues," and "Cakewalkin' Babies"). The remaining nine tunes are from a 1953 quintet session with clarinetist Bob Helm and trombonist Murphy, backed by Wally Rose (piano), Dick Lammi (banjo), and Bob Short (tuba). The set lives up to its stated purpose, "helping later generations appreciate some exciting moments in the history of West Coast jazz." *Concert in the Park* ♪♪♪♪ (Merry Makers, 1986, prod. Ted Shafer) is a good example of the last edition of Murphy's San Francisco Jazz Band. Taken live from the 18th Annual Concord Jazz Festival at Todos Santos Plaza in Concord, California, this set shows Murphy stalwarts cornetist Bob Schulz, clarinetist Lynn Zimmer, pianist Ray Skjelbred, tubaist Bill Carroll, and banjo man John Gill in fine support of the trombonist on August 10, 1986, less than a year from playing his final note. This hour of traditional jazz opens with a jaunty "High Society" and closes with the Murphy theme, the haunting "Bay City." Murphy sings the gospel-tinged "This Train" and the Jelly Roll Morton classic, "Sweet Substitute," while Schulz lends his voice to "Sundown Mama," and Gill does "Walkin' the Blues Away."

best of the rest:
Turk Murphy and His San Francisco Jazz Band in Concert, Volume 1 ♪♪♪♪ (GHB, 1972/1994)
Turk Murphy and His San Francisco Jazz Band in Concert, Volume 2 ♪♪♪♪ (GHB, 1972/1994)
(With Turk Murphy's Jazz Band) *San Francisco Jazz* ♪♪♪♪ (Merry Makers, 1985/1993)
(With Turk Murphy's San Francisco Jazz Band) *The Earthquake McGoon Recordings* ♪♪♪♪ (Merry Makers, 1996)

worth searching for: *Lu Watter's Yerba Buena Jazz Band: The Complete Good Time Jazz Recordings* ♪♪♪♪ (Various, 1941, 1942, 1946/Good Time Jazz, 1995, compilation prod. Ralph Kaffel) is a four-CD box set of 98 selections, accompanied by extensive annotation, some of it by the original Watter's trombonist, Turk Murphy. The collection contains the entire Watter's band-recorded output for the Jazz Man and West Coast labels (acquired by Good Time Jazz), plus rare broadcast recordings. Trombonist Murphy and trumpeters Watters and Bob Scobey made up the powerful brass team of this band, which was at the forefront of the New Orleans revival, heavily influencing traditional jazz through the 1940s.

influences:

◀◀ Kid Ory, Lu Watters

▶▶ Original Salty Dogs, South Frisco Jazz Band, West End Jazz Band, Natural Gas Jazz Band, Down Home Jazz Band, Frisco Syncopators, Jim Snyder, Tom Bartlett, Charlie Bornemann, John Gill

John T. Bitter

David Murray

Born February 19, 1955, in Berkeley, CA.

David Murray is one of the most prolific jazzmen of the past two decades, both as a leader and a sideman, and may in fact be the most recorded saxophonist during that time aside from studio musicians. Taught as a child by his mother, a pianist in a Pentecostal church, Murray started on tenor saxophone at age nine and led groups as a teenager. Upon moving to New York City in 1975 he quickly made an impression on the loft scene with his energetic Coltrane/Ayler-derived sound. A founding member of the World Saxophone Quartet, he also played in Jack DeJohnette's Special Edition and the Music Revelation Ensemble.

Murray gradually expanded his style to take in more and more of jazz's history, with specific tributes or dedications to not only Coltrane and Ayler, but also similarly famed tenormen including Ben Webster, Coleman Hawkins, Paul Gonsalves, Lester Young, Sonny Rollins, Charlie Rouse, and Sonny Stitt. Even when tipping his hat to past greats, he maintains his distinctive voice. Obviously versatile, he's equally comfortable caressing a ballad or unleashing bursts of gospel-derived, free-jazz excitement, and his control of his altissimo range is impressive. The most famous bass clarinetist since Eric Dolphy, he led the superb Clarinet Summit quartet with Jimmy Hamilton, John Carter, and Alvin Batiste. Besides the sax and clarinet quartets, he's intermittently led a big band, an octet, separate quartets with pianists John Hicks and Dave Burrell, and all-star groups galore. There has been muttering that in fact he's too prolific for his own good, spewing forth so many albums that they become an

D**AVID** M**URRAY**
(**WITH** W**ORLD** S**AXOPHONE** Q**UARTET**)

song "Come Sunday"
album World Saxophone
Quartet Plays Duke Ellington
(Nonesuch, 1986/1992)

instrument Tenor saxophone

Monster Solo

undifferentiated blur, but that's more a problem of consumer and critical perception than of quality, though he has had his lapses. On the other hand, Murray won the prestigious Jazzpar award in 1991 and has been a frequent poll-topper.

what to buy: The octet is Murray's best format, and *Ming* 𝄞𝄞𝄞𝄞 (Black Saint, 1980, prod. David Murray, Kunle Mwanga) is its undisputed peak, bursting with energy yet thoughtful and unclichéd. "The Fast Life," "The Hill," "Ming," and "Dewey's Circle"—four-fifths of the album—are among Murray's best compositions, and the all-star group with Henry Threadgill (alto sax), Olu Dara (trumpet), Butch Morris (cornet), George Lewis (trombone), Anthony Davis (piano), Wilbur Morris (bass), and Steve McCall (drums) sounds even better than it looks on paper. Murray's arrangements are colorful and give the music a spontaneity and looseness that recall early New Orleans jazz. If there's one thing you can count on in Murray's deep catalog, it's that any quartet album, such as *Morning Song* 𝄞𝄞𝄞𝄞 (Black Saint, 1984), which includes pianist John Hicks, tend to be high-quality, swinging affairs. "Morning Song" is perhaps

Murray's greatest groove tune, building inexorably with each solo chorus as Hicks stokes the burner and drummer Ed Blackwell pounds out the rhythm insistently but imaginatively. This is one of the great tenor sax albums of the past 20 years, with covers of "Body and Soul" and Fats Waller's "Jitterbug Waltz" cementing Murray's relationship with tradition. Two fine trio albums show Murray allowing himself more room to stretch out. *The Hill* 𝄢𝄢𝄢𝄢 (Black Saint, 1988, prod. David Murray) places Duke Ellington's "Take the Coltrane" and Billy Strayhorn's "Chelsea Bridge" amid several Murray classics ("Herbie Miller" has a masterful bass clarinet solo). Post-bop veterans Richard Davis and Joe Chambers are both responsive and prodding. Murray's interaction with the air rhythm section of Fred Hopkins and Steve McCall on *Sweet Lovely* 𝄢𝄢𝄢𝄢 (Black Saint, 1980, prod. Giovanni Bonandrini) is consistently subtle and rewarding. His vast array of timbres and acute control of soft tones are matched by his high-energy blowing and long, limber lines. Highlights are the pretty "Corazon" and an early, roiling incarnation of "Hope/Scope."

what to buy next: The David Murray Big Band is best represented by the 1984 recordings *Live at Sweet Basil, Volume 1* 𝄢𝄢𝄢𝄢 (Black Saint, 1985, prod. David Murray) and *Live at Sweet Basil, Volume 2* 𝄢𝄢𝄢𝄢 (Black Saint, 1986, prod. David Murray). As prolifically as he's recorded, Murray hasn't been heard often enough with this aggregation. Some of the other players include Olu Dara, Baikida Carroll, Craig Harris, Steve Coleman, and Billy Higgins, but the star is definitely Murray, in rowdy, exuberant form amid the grooves of this loosely boisterous 11-man group. His compositions and arrangements offer an updated vision of the big band sound, full of rollicking riffs and wild solos which come equally out of the avant-garde and R&B/JATP traditions. *Special Quartet* 𝄢𝄢𝄢𝄢 (DIW/Columbia, 1991, prod. Bob Thiele) is just that, with pianist McCoy Tyner and drummer Elvin Jones teaming like they did with Coltrane (Fred Hopkins is on bass). Murray knows who he'll be compared to in such company and holds nothing back, providing some of his most full-bodied soloing in years. *Live at the Lower Manhattan Ocean Club, Volumes 1 & 2* 𝄢𝄢𝄢𝄢 (India Navigation, 1978/1989, prod. Bob Cummins) was recorded New Year's Eve 1977 by Murray's early quartet with trumpeter Lester Bowie, Hopkins, and drummer Phillip Wilson. Of the better examples of his early style, this album (which combines two LPs on one CD) best combines availability and cost. In recent years Murray has been getting back to his R&B roots more. *Fo Deuk Revue* 𝄢𝄢𝄢𝄢 (Justin Time, 1997, prod. David Murray, Mamadou Konté, Valérie Malot) combines that quest with the incorporation of

African rhythms and singing, poetry by Amiri Baraka, and rap by Positive Black Soul in a surprisingly successful polyglot. The African drummers are superb, trumpeter Hugh Ragin and trombonist Craig Harris contribute some idiomatic charts, and Murray's clearly fired up and at his most soulful.

what to avoid: *Black and Black* 𝄢 (Red Baron, 1992, prod. Bob Thiele) sounds fairly uninspired. Murray and the other players—Marcus Belgrave, Kirk Lightsey, Santi Debriano, Roy Haynes—never gel, and a pair of limp tunes co-written by Glenn Osser and producer Bob Thiele drag things down even further. This one can be skipped without fear of missing anything worth hearing.

best of the rest:
Flowers for Albert: The Complete Concert 𝄢𝄢𝄢𝄢 (India Navigation, 1976/1997)
Interboogieology 𝄢𝄢𝄢 (Black Saint, 1978)
3D Family 𝄢𝄢𝄢𝄢 (hat HUT, 1978)
Home 𝄢𝄢𝄢𝄢 (Black Saint, 1982)
Murray's Steps 𝄢𝄢𝄢𝄢 (Black Saint, 1983)
Children 𝄢𝄢𝄢𝄢 (Black Saint, 1985)
Recording N.Y.C. 1986 𝄢𝄢𝄢𝄢 (DIW, 1986)
(With Jack DeJohnette) *In Our Style* 𝄢𝄢𝄢 (DIW, 1986)
New Life 𝄢𝄢𝄢𝄢 (Black Saint, 1987)
(With Randy Weston) *The Healers* 𝄢𝄢𝄢𝄢 (Black Saint, 1987)
Lovers 𝄢𝄢𝄢𝄢 (DIW, 1988)
Deep River 𝄢𝄢𝄢𝄢 (DIW, 1989)
I Want to Talk about You 𝄢𝄢𝄢 (Black Saint, 1989)
(With Dave Burrell, Wilber Morris, and Victor Lewis) *Lucky Four* 𝄢𝄢𝄢 (Tutu/Enja, 1989)
Ming's Samba 𝄢𝄢𝄢𝄢 (Portrait/CBS, 1989)
Spirituals 𝄢𝄢𝄢 (DIW, 1990)
Ballads 𝄢𝄢𝄢 (DIW, 1990)
Hope Scope 𝄢𝄢𝄢𝄢 (Black Saint, 1991)
Remembrances 𝄢𝄢𝄢 (DIW, 1991)
Shakill's Warrior 𝄢𝄢𝄢𝄢 (DIW/Columbia, 1991)
David Murray Big Band Conducted by Butch Morris 𝄢𝄢𝄢 (DIW/Columbia, 1991)
A Sanctuary Within 𝄢𝄢𝄢𝄢 (Black Saint, 1992)
MX 𝄢𝄢𝄢 (Red Baron, 1992)
(With Milford Graves) *Real Deal* 𝄢𝄢𝄢𝄢 (DIW, 1992)
Death of a Sideman 𝄢𝄢𝄢𝄢 (DIW, 1992)
Fast Life 𝄢𝄢𝄢𝄢 (DIW/Columbia, 1992/1993)
Body and Soul 𝄢𝄢𝄢 (Black Saint, 1993)
Picasso 𝄢𝄢𝄢𝄢 (DIW, 1993)
Ballads for Bass Clarinet 𝄢𝄢𝄢𝄢 (DIW, 1993)
Tenors 𝄢𝄢𝄢𝄢 (DIW, 1993)
(With Dave Burrell) *Brother to Brother* 𝄢𝄢𝄢 (Gazell, 1993)
Live '93 Acoustic Octfunk 𝄢𝄢𝄢𝄢 (Sound Hills, 1994)
Shakill's II 𝄢𝄢𝄢𝄢 (DIW, 1994)

Saxmen ♫♫♫ (Red Baron, 1994)
The Tip ♫♫♫ (DIW, 1994)
Jug-a-Lug ♫♫♫ (DIW, 1995)
South of the Border ♫♫ (DIW, 1995)
For Aunt Louise ♫♫♫♫ (DIW, 1995)
Quintet with Ray Anderson/Anthony Davis ♫♫♫ (DIW, 1996)
David Murray/James Newton Quintet ♫♫♫♫ (DIW, 1996)
(With Dave Burrell) *Windward Passages* ♫♫♫ (Black Saint, 1997)

worth searching for: *Let the Music Take You* ♫♫♫♫ (Marge, 1978, prod. Gerard Terrones) is a French album with extremely limited distribution in the United States. In quartet with Butch Morris (cornet), Johnny Dyani (bass), and George Brown (drums), Murray improvises ecstatically in his early style, making avant-garde music that's immediately appealing. The title track, not common in his discography, is a real groover. With all the albums Murray's made, there aren't too many unique settings, so *The Jazzpar Prize* ♫♫♫♫ (Enja, 1992, prod. Horst Weber, Arnvid Meyer) with Pierre Dørge's 10-piece New Jungle Orchestra (the name it may be filed under) is worth looking for. Horace Parlan is the highly appropriate pianist, and the (mostly Danish) players acquit themselves well in their usual versatile fashion on the colorful arrangements. There are two Murray tunes, a rousing "Gospel Medley" (vocals by Murray), which unfortunately ends in a fade, two tunes by Dørge (who's a fine guitarist), and a lovely duet with Parlan on Ellington's "In a Sentimental Mood."

influences:

◀◀ John Coltrane, Albert Ayler, Coleman Hawkins, Ben Webster

▶▶ James Carter, Joshua Redman

see also: *Music Revelation Ensemble, World Saxophone Quartet*

Steve Holtje

Sunny Murray

Born James Marcellus Arthur Murray, September 21, 1937, in Idabel, OK.

The man whose percussive style prompted comparisons to "the continuous sound of cracking glass," Sunny Murray is one of the two or three most important drummers to emerge from the avant-garde jazz scene of the early 1960s. He was integral to Cecil Taylor's earthshaking ensembles as well as to the historic trio led by saxophonist Albert Ayler; his liberated concepts of time floated beyond rhythm into a customized dimension of pulse and flow that ideally suited the energies of his bandstand colleagues. After a rough adolescence in Philadelphia, Murray moved to New York in 1956, working with a varied batch of play-

ers: Jackie McLean, Ted Curson, Willie "The Lion" Smith, and Henry "Red" Allen. Once he hooked up with Taylor, with whom he played from 1959 to 1964, there was no looking back. Like many musicians who made their reputations in the heady 1960s, recording for such strident, artist-driven labels as ESP Disk and France's BYG, Murray seems a bit obscure today—yet, as one of the key architects of a musical revolution, he helped put the "free" in free jazz. Long based in France, he continues to perform and record, notably in tandem with earthy, strong-willed tenor players such as David Murray and Charles Gayle.

what to buy: The immediately post-Taylor outing *Sunny Murray* ♫♫♫♫ (ESP, 1966) is highly representative of the period, with a quintet that includes Byard Lancaster (alto sax), Jack Graham (alto sax), Jacques Coursil (trumpet), and another Taylor sideman, bassist Alan Silva. This is not timid music, and it is not for the timid listener: it is a mixture of unrepentent free jazz and ferocious hard-bop-derived playing.

what to buy next: *13 Steps on Glass* ♫♫♫♫ (Enja, 1995, prod. Horst Weber) offers a more recent glimpse into Murray's career. It's a fluid, flexible trio session paced by Philly tenor (and Max Roach mainstay) Odean Pope, who brings a typically edgy lyricism to a set of standards ranging from "Moose the Mooche" to "I Want to Talk about You."

worth searching for: Released by a tiny New York label, *Illuminators* ♫♫♫♫ (Audible Hiss, 1996) is a scorching duo with 1990s free jazz icon Charles Gayle (piano, tenor sax). They had previously worked together for some New York concerts and on Gayle's trio album *Kingdom Come* ♫♫♫♫ (Knitting Factory, 1994), and their rapport is superbly interactive. Murray is often a more spare player than other free jazz drummers, but he really cuts loose in the duo context, and this is a masterful display of the art of free polyrhythms and swinging without a set beat. This also is the most extensive document on record of Gayle's piano playing and will be interesting to his fans for that reason. (Audible Hiss: PO Box 1242, Cooper Station, NY, NY 10276.)

Steve Dollar

Music Revelation Ensemble

Formed 1980, in New York, NY.

James Blood Ulmer, electric guitar; David Murray, tenor saxophone (1980–92); Amin Ali, bass; Ronald Shannon Jackson, drums (1980–88); Cornell Rochester, drums (1989–present).

James Blood Ulmer and Ronald Jackson had played together with Ornette Coleman, and before their solo careers had really taken off, they put together a band with David Murray, whose own career was much talked about but also not where it would be later in the decade. Amin Ali, drum legend Rashied Ali's son, would be a regular collaborator with Ulmer for years to come. This quartet, Ulmer's regular band, was the core group on his breakthrough album *Are You Glad to Be in America?*, recorded in January 1980, and reconvened that June without additional musicians to record a looser album. Ulmer definitely had—and still has—a division in his mind between projects under his own name, which tend to be more rock-oriented and aimed towards the mainstream (or at least his idea of the mainstream), and the Music Revelation Ensemble, which he says is his hardcore harmonic jazz band, focusing on instrumentals rather than songs with vocals.

On the group's first album, recorded for the same German label which had released the World Saxophone Quartet's debut album, this apparently meant a serious free jazz session. The four tracks were between eight and 10 minutes and were very loosely structured. It was definitely Ulmer's band, however, with all four credited to him. But the acclaim for *Are You Glad to Be in America?* led to a contract with Columbia for Ulmer as a solo act, and MRE was put on the back burner. On record the band didn't reappear until 1988, with another Ornette alum, Jamaaladeen Tacuma, in the bass slot. On the third and fourth MRE albums, Ali was back, and Jackson had been permanently replaced by Cornell Rochester. Murray then became unavailable, and since then the trio of Ulmer, Ali, and Rochester has been supplemented (in some cases only for recordings) by a variety of saxophonists: Arthur Blythe, Sam Rivers, Hamiet Bluiett, John Zorn, and Pharoah Sanders, an arrangement which has worked well and seems to stimulate Ulmer's creativity.

what to buy: *In the Name of . . .* 𝄞𝄞𝄞𝄞 (DIW, 1994, prod. James Blood Ulmer, Kazunori Sugiyama) was the first great MRE release after years of good but not always exciting albums. With David Murray having moved to Europe, the sax chair is filled by three alternating veterans: Arthur Blythe (alto sax) and Sam Rivers (soprano and tenor saxes, flute) get three tracks each, with Hamiett Bluiett (baritone sax) on one. The variety—in both timbres and styles—solves a long-standing problem with this group, and Ulmer also wrote some of his best themes.

what to buy next: *Knights of Power* 𝄞𝄞𝄞 (DIW, 1996, prod. James Blood Ulmer, Kazunori Sugiyama) has Blythe and Bluiett splitting sax duties evenly on the eight tracks. Bluiett's fat baritone sax tone gives real heft to the band's sound. The low horn/high horn dichotomy is kept on *Cross Fire* 𝄞𝄞𝄞 (DIW,

1998, prod. James Blood Ulmer, Kazunori Sugiyama), where the guest saxophonists are John Zorn and Pharoah Sanders, opposites in their own ways and yet both well-suited to Ulmer's music. Zorn connects well with its manic intensity, while Sanders fits its spiritual majesty.

the rest:
No wave 𝄞𝄞𝄞 (Moers, 1980)
Music Revelation Ensemble 𝄞𝄞 (DIW, 1988)
Elec. Jazz 𝄞𝄞𝄞 (DIW, 1990)
After Dark 𝄞𝄞𝄞 (DIW, 1991)

influences:
◀◀ Ornette Coleman's Prime Time

▶▶ Ronald Shannon Jackson & the Decoding Society

Steve Holtje

Amina Claudine Myers

Born March 21, 1942, in Blackwell, AR.

Amina Claudine Myers's voice and keyboard artistry has deep roots in the Baptist church of her youth. Her performance history, however, comes mostly from her schooling in European classical techniques (from Philander Smith College in Little Rock, Arkansas) and the nightclubs of the late '60s, where she sang classic jazz riffs while absorbing harmonic influences from records by Ahmad Jamal and Miles Davis. Moving from the South to Chicago for a job teaching in the public schools also brought her into contact with forward-thinking musicians in the Association for the Advancement of Creative Musicians; she also landed gigs with Gene Ammons and Sonny Stitt. Since then, she has worked with a wide variety of musical talent, from singers like Fontella Bass and saxophonist Ricky Ford to guitarist James Blood Ulmer and bassist Bill Laswell—in addition to gigging solo and with her own groups.

what to buy: Uniting Myers's formidable keyboard playing with her strong, bluesy vocals, *Amina Claudine Myers Salutes Bessie Smith* 𝄞𝄞𝄞𝄞 (Leo, 1980, prod. Craig Johnson) is the high-water mark in her solo career. Half the album features four songs associated with the great blues singer Bessie Smith, and there are two longer works written by Myers that pay tribute to the heritage of gutsy female performance, if not specifically to Smith. She is ably abetted by percussionist Jimmy Lovelace and bassist Cecil McBee.

what to buy next: The title tune of *Jumping In the Sugar Bowl* 𝄞𝄞𝄞 (Minor Music, 1984, prod. Stephan Meyner) is pinned on the rapid-fire bass playing of Thomas Palmer, over which Reggie Nicholson's percussion and Myers's piano provide melodic accents tied to the rhythmic chant (based on a childhood game of the same name). Some of Myers's most adventurous keyboard playing is found here, but the rest of the album isn't so much a letdown as it is a welcome change of pace from the relentless opening tune. "Cecil B" is a wonderful tribute to bassist Cecil McBee, while the deliberate "Cameloupe" features Myers, a frequently underrated organist, opting for musical tension over funk and flash.

the rest:

The Circle of Time 𝄞𝄞𝄞𝄞 (Black Saint, 1983)
Country Girl 𝄞𝄞𝄞 (Minor Music, 1986)

worth searching for: Some of Marian McPartland's "Piano Jazz" radio shows are available on compact disc from the Jazz Alliance (a subsidiary of Concord Jazz), including a show aired on August 29, 1991 featuring Myers singing, playing solo piano, and dueting with McPartland. The interview portions of the program are spread between the playing excerpts and shed light on how Myers approaches her material. Their duet on "Mood Indigo" and Myers's vocal on "Call Him/Do You Wanna Be Saved?" are magnificently comfortable. Also, *From the Root to the Source* 𝄞𝄞𝄞 (Soul Note, 1980, prod. Giovanni Bonandrini) features a mighty trio of vocalists (Martha Bass, Fontella Bass, and David Peaston) singing with an impressive trio of instrumentalists including Myers, drummer Phillip Wilson, and bassist Malachi Favors Maghostus.

influences:

◀◀ Nina Simone, Dakota Staton, Ahmad Jamal

▶▶ Cassandra Wilson

Garaud MacTaggart

Najee

Born November 4, 1957.

Najee is one of the most popular and best-selling instrumentalists of the last decade, playing saxophone, flute, and occasional keyboards. However, he suffers from the same problem that Whitney Houston does: inferior material to superior talent. In many quiet storm and smooth jazz formats he is referred to as the black Kenny G. Much of his production is aimed for commercial airplay and mainstream acceptance and sometimes comes off as trite, drowning his brilliance under mediocrity. None of his music is bad, it could just be better. His 1987 debut, *Najee's Theme* established his sound and helped to push contemporary jazz further without pushing the envelope.

what to buy: *Plays Songs from the Key of Life* 𝄞𝄞𝄞𝄞 (Capitol, 1995, prod. George Duke), a tribute to Stevie Wonder's music, is a fully realized work for Najee, who really goes for the gusto. *Tokyo Blue* 𝄞𝄞𝄞𝄞 (Capitol, 1990, prod. Beau Huggins) is the best of his albums. It is smooth, silky, and very hip. The music is played by an array of musicians and is soothing to the ear and non-threatening. Najee's talents are very impressive here and give a glimpse of the level he should always maintain.

what to buy next: *Just an Illusion* 𝄞𝄞𝄞 (Capitol, 1992, prod. Marcus Miller, George Duke, Steven Dubin, Jeff Pescetto, Bryan Loren, Arif Mardin, Fareed, Najee) and *Share My World* 𝄞𝄞𝄞 (Capitol, 1994) both carry on the adult contemporary–smooth jazz sound that provides Najee with a career. Although some of the tracks sound as if they were lifted from those cheesy K-Tel collections, overall they're good efforts.

the rest:

Najee's Theme 𝄞𝄞𝄞 (Capitol, 1987)
Day by Day 𝄞𝄞 (Capitol, 1988)

influences:

◀◀ Grover Washington Jr., George Howard, David Sanborn, Dave Koz

▶▶ James Carter, Alfonzo Blackwell, Christopher Hollyday

Damon Percy

Naked City

Formed in 1989, in New York City. Disbanded in September, 1993.

John Zorn, alto sax; Bill Frisell, lead guitar; Wayne Horvitz, keyboards; Fred Frith, electric bass guitar; Joey Baron, drums; Yamatska Eye, screaming vocals.

Though purists (for whom leader John Zorn has little use) would declare that Naked City isn't jazz, it contains elements of jazz and uses jazz musicians—and Zorn's alto sax abilities and jazz knowledge shouldn't be underrated. Zorn organized his downtown all-star group in 1989, using close friends of his. The group was always extremely eclectic and openminded, drawing on jazz, hardcore thrash, surf, movie themes, funk, and contemporary classical—sometimes several within the same short piece. Zorn was the main composer, but the band's repertoire included covers of movie themes, jazz, and early and modern classical music. There was also the shock value of the occasional screaming vocals by Eye, and cover art depicting violence, domination, torture, death, and sex. In fact, Zorn left the major label Nonesuch when it refused to release *Torture Garden* due to its violent cover art, with the rock indie label Shimmy-Disc issuing it instead. But however much the brutality of the punk/thrash influence may have provoked some listeners, the predominant effect was of superb musicians playing with extreme discipline and without regard to boundaries and categories.

what to buy: Naked City's debut, *Naked City* 🎵🎵🎵🎵 (Nonesuch, 1989, prod. John Zorn, Naked City), is the best starting point for jazz listeners, complete with covers of Johnny Mandel's "I Want to Live" and Ornette Coleman's "Lonely Woman"; movie themes by John Barry, Henry Mancini, Ennio Morricone, and Jerry Goldsmith; and a majestic reading of Georges Delerue's "Contempt" a major highlight. Some of the 19 Zorn originals also suggest soundtrack music, though of an edgy, aggressive sort. The precision with which Zorn, Frisell, et al. wheel through the 26 tracks, all under five minutes and nine less than a minute, is breathtaking.

what to buy next: *Grand Guignol* 🎵🎵🎵🎵 (Avant, 1992, prod. John Zorn) is like two albums on one CD. For nearly 39 minutes it's (mostly contemporary) classical music, from Zorn's darkly moody title track to atmospheric arrangements of pieces by Claude Debussy, Alexander Scriabin, Renaissance composer Roland de Lassus (a.k.a. Orlando di Lasso), Charles Ives (with guest vocal by Bob Dorough), and Messiaen. Following a palate-cleansing break come 33 hardcore/punk/thrash tracks taken from the *Torture Garden* album (all but nine of its tracks), only three lasting longer than a minute. Song titles such as "Jazz Snob Eat Shit," "Piledriver," "Speedfreaks," "Whiplash," and "Thrash Jazz Assassin" convey the flavor of the music, suggesting Hobbes's dictum about life being "nasty, brutish, and short."

the rest:
Heretic 🎵🎵🎵🎵 (Avant, 1993)
Radio 🎵🎵🎵🎵 (Avant, 1993)
Absinthe 🎵🎵🎵🎵🎵 (Avant, 1993)
Black Box 🎵🎵🎵 (Tzadik, 1997)

worth searching for: Eventually we will be gifted with a two-CD set of material recorded live at the old Knitting Factory. It should consist of all the cover tunes Naked City did live, but not as yet released, including jazz (Shirley Scott, John Patton, Dizzy Gillespie, Ornette Coleman), punk (DNA, Live Skull), film com-

posers (Henry Mancini, John Barry, Ennio Morricone), tunes by Funkadelic, and Moroccan Rai music.

influences:

◀◀ Ornette Coleman, DNA, Live Skull, Henry Mancini, John Barry, Napalm Death

▶▶ Bill Frisell, Steve Beresford

Steve Holtje

Ray Nance

Born December 10, 1913, in Chicago, IL. Died January 28, 1976, in New York, NY.

Ray Nance's career was defined by a long association with Duke Ellington, placing him among a great tradition of Ellington trumpeters that includes Cootie Williams, Rex Stewart, Clark Terry, and Cat Anderson. Nance, however, also added other talents to the Duke's repertoire—most notably his violin, but also including some dancing and singing. After coming up with the Earl Hines and Horace Henderson bands in the late 1930s, Nance joined Ellington on a famous night in 1940. That night was November 7, and Ellington's orchestra was giving a concert in Fargo, North Dakota that was captured on tape and immortalized as one of the great jazz concerts in recorded history. Nance's job with the Duke was limited at first to filling the famous "wa-wa" position created by Bubber Miley and the recently departed Cootie Williams, but later expanded to include his other talents. Nance would remain with Ellington, aside from a few breaks, until 1963, shortly after the return of Williams. After that, Nance made a few minor recordings as a leader, but would mostly play in clubs with lesser-known musicians until the end of his career.

what to buy: Among Nance's many contributions to the Ellington catalog are the famous and widely imitated solo on the first version of "Take the 'A' Train," available on the excellent three-CD set, *The Blanton-Webster Band* 🎵🎵🎵🎵🎵 (RCA Bluebird, 1940–42/1986, reissue prod. Bob Porter), and some fine violin playing on the suite *Black, Brown, and Beige* 🎵🎵🎵🎵🎵 (RCA Bluebird, 1944–46)

what to buy next: Credited to Paul Gonsalves and Nance but also featuring Norris Turney on half the album, *Just a-Sittin' and a-Rockin'* 🎵🎵🎵 (Black Lion, 1971/1991, prod. Alan Bates) is a cozy session allowing three fine soloists some limelight outside of their famous employer's band. Among the varying accompanists is pianist Hank Jones. Two more Ellington sessions, including noteworthy work by Nance, should be mentioned.

Duke Ellington Presents . . . 🎵🎵🎵 (Bethlehem, 1956/1994) finds him playing violin and singing on a warm take on "I Can't Get Started" and trumpet solos on "My Funny Valentine" and "Blues," where his two choruses are interestingly shaped at times against the chord progression. And *Duke Ellington Meets Coleman Hawkins* 🎵🎵🎵 (Impulse!, 1962/1995, prod. Bob Thiele), by virtue of being an octet date, also gives the soloists more opportunities to shine, with Nance especially featured on violin on a quintet piece, "The Ricitic," with Hawkins and the rhythm section.

the rest:
Body and Soul 🎵🎵 (Solid State, 1969)

influences:
◀◀ Cootie Williams, Rex Stewart
▶▶ Clark Terry, Harry "Sweets" Edison

Dan Keener

Andy Narell

Born March 18, 1954, in New York City, NY.

Andy Narell was introduced to the steel drums (pans) when his social-worker father started steel orchestras as a way of reducing tensions among street gangs in New York City. Since then Narell has used his formidable technique on this unique instrument to bring it into the jazz fold without neglecting its Caribbean roots. A graduate of the Berklee College of Music, he formed his own label (Hip Pocket) to bring his recordings into the marketplace. He later contracted with Windham Hill, a label known more for new age music than jazz. This broadened his audience base while unfairly trivializing his abilities as an outstanding jazz player among unforgiving jazz "cognoscenti." Narell's link with Windham Hill enabled him to hone his skills as a producer, and he has worked in that capacity with artists like Pete Escovedo, Billy Childs, and Ray Obiedo. On the pop side, he has produced albums for the Bobs and Jimmy Haslip. Narell is also an in-demand session musician, appearing on numerous dates, including releases from Patti LaBelle, Les McCann, and Paquito D'Rivera.

what to buy: Strictly speaking, *The Caribbean Jazz Project* 🎵🎵🎵 (Heads Up, 1995, prod. Caribbean Jazz Project) isn't an Andy Narell album, but a release from the Caribbean Jazz Project, whose three main figures are Narell, vibes player Dave Samuels, and reed man D'Rivera. The blend of Narell and Samuels gives the album a bright, propulsive, open-texture feel without being stereotypically lightweight. D'Rivera's alto

sax and clarinet playing adds an idiomatic Latin flair and tonal bite that counterbalances the percussive pointillism of Narell and Samuels. "Abracadabra," "Three Amigos," and "Paco and Dave" are probably the best tunes to sample from this title.

what to buy next: On *The Hammer* 🎵🎵🎵 (Windham Hill, 1987, prod. Andy Narell), Narell's usual blend of jazz flavoring and Caribbean rhythms is particularly winsome. It provides the matrix for everything else the pan man has done on his own, and tunes like "Jour Ouvert" and the title song are charming.

the rest:
Stickman 🎵🎵🎵 (Windham Hill Jazz, 1981)
Slow Motion 🎵🎵🎵 (Hippocket, 1985)
Light in Your Eyes 🎵🎵🎵🎵 (Windham Hill Jazz, 1989)
Little Secrets 🎵🎵🎵 (Windham Hill Jazz, 1989)
Down the Road 🎵🎵🎵🎵 (Windham Hill Jazz, 1992)
The Long Time Band 🎵🎵🎵 (Windham Hill, 1995)

worth searching for: Narell's skills as a writer for percussion are perhaps best appreciated on other people's albums. The Robert Hohner Percussion Ensemble, on *Different Strokes* 🎵🎵🎵 (DMP, 1991, prod. Robert Hohner, Tom Jung), performs "The Songlines" (from Narell's album *Little Secrets*) using six pan players, bringing out the tune's essential nocturnal delicacy. Narell himself appears on a sampler, *The Bach Variations* 🎵🎵🎵 (Windham Hill, 1994, prod. Dawn Atkinson), playing a solo pan version of Bach's "Jesu, Joy of Man's Desiring."

influences:
◀◀ Ray Holman
▶▶ Pan Ramajay, Jeff Narell

Garaud MacTaggart

Milton Nascimento

Born in 1942, in Rio de Janeiro, Brazil.

Milton Nascimento is one of the most significant figures in Brazilian music, both in terms of performance (as a singer and guitarist) and composition. His vocal abilities are quite phenomenal, gliding from his normal chest voice up to a seamless falsetto. Nascimento's songs have been performed by jazz artists like Sarah Vaughan, Stan Getz, and the Manhattan Transfer. Born in Rio de Janeiro, he was raised in the Brazilian state of Minas Gerais by his adoptive parents. Nascimento played the accordion as a child but had switched to guitar and bass by the time he was a teenager. He also formed an important long-term musical relationship with keyboard player Wagner Tiso when they both played in the same band. Moving to

Belo Horizonte, the capital of Minas Gerais, in 1963, Nascimento played area jazz clubs while attending college. His first big break as a songwriter came in 1966 when a tune he wrote called "Cangmo Do Sal" was performed by the popular Brazilian singer Elis Regina. In 1967 Nascimento was voted best performer at the International Song Festival and one of his songs, "Travessia" ("Bridges"), copped second place in the writing competition. In addition to writing many of his own songs, Nascimento has been closely involved with a cadre of poets and musicians from Minas Gerais called "Clube da Esquina" or "the Corner Club." As a collective, the club released albums under the names of fellow singer/writer L. Borges and Nascimento that were as important and revolutionary in the early '70s as the collaboration between Antonio Carlos Jobim and João Gilberto was in the late '50s. He has also been heavily involved with the New Song movement that swept Latin America in the '60s and '70s, working with major figures within the genre like Pablo Milanes, Silvio Rodriguez, and Mercedes Sosa. In addition, Nascimento is a committed political activist speaking for the indigenous peoples of the Amazon, the environment, and Amnesty International. Jazz musicians started becoming aware of his prodigious talents in the late '60s, when he toured Mexico and the United States in the company of João Gilberto and Art Blakey. Nascimento's first appearance on a U.S. jazz album was on Wayne Shorter's 1974 *Native Dancer*. Shorter returned the favor on Nascimento's 1976 release, *Milton*, which also featured appearances by Herbie Hancock and Raul DeSouza in addition to Brazilian stalwarts Airto Moreira and Toninho Horta. Pianist Barry Harris even wrote a lovely ballad called "Nascimento" that has been performed by Harris and Tommy Flanagan, among others.

what to buy: Jazz aficionados will have to hunt for familiar names like Hubert Laws, Pat Metheny, and Steve Slagle on *Encontros e Despedidas* 𝄞𝄞𝄞𝄞 (Polydor, 1986, prod. Mazola), but they are there. The personnel is geared more towards Nascimento's favorite Brazilian musicians and the result more than justifies his choice. This album leans further into the jazz spectrum then many of his works, and with tunes like "Portal Da Cor" and the title song it could tempt hardcore jazzers to check out the rest of his work. *Minha Historia* 𝄞𝄞𝄞𝄞 (PolyGram Latino, 1994, prod. various) and *The Art of Milton Nascimento* 𝄞𝄞𝄞𝄞 (Verve, 1995, prod. various) are both "best of" compilations, featuring many overlapping tunes. The former has "Travessia," perhaps Nascimento's most famous piece. The latter has 20 songs, compared to 14 for *Minha Historia*. Both retail at about the same price and serve as good introductions.

what to buy next: *Clube da Esquina* 𝄞𝄞𝄞𝄞 (World Pacific, 1972, prod. Milton Miranda) is a classic album, with L. Borges and the rest of Clube Da Esquina. The album blends pop from John Lennon and Paul McCartney with folk song influences from Minas Gerais and elements of bossa nova for a heady mixture that influenced the direction of much '70s Brazilian music. *Nascimento* 𝄞𝄞𝄞𝄞 (Warner Bros., 1997, prod. Russ Titelman, Milton Nascimento) finds Nascimento making a retreat from some of the pop aspects of his later albums. It opens with "Louva-a-Deus (The Praying Mantis)," a percussion fest (a la Oludum) with Nascimento's vocals floating and diving with ease, and "Cuerpo y Alma (Body and Soul)" (not the jazz classic) and "E Agora, Rapaz (And What Now, Man?)" have that indefinable swing native to the best Brazilian music in general and Nascimento's tunesmithing in particular.

best of the rest:

Sentinela 𝄞𝄞𝄞𝄞 (Verve, 1980)
Yauaret J 𝄞𝄞𝄞𝄞 (Columbia, 1988)
Miltons 𝄞𝄞𝄞𝄞 (Columbia, 1989)
Missa Dos Quilombos 𝄞𝄞𝄞𝄞 (Verve, 1992)
Amigo 𝄞𝄞𝄞𝄞 (Warner Bros., 1996)

worth searching for: *Milton* 𝄞𝄞𝄞𝄞 (A&M, 1976), not to be confused with 1989's *Miltons*, is a marvelous album that keeps going in and out of print. Originally released in the United States, it's the first full-length album by Nascimento that received any real distribution. The players include Wayne Shorter and Herbie Hancock, but the songs are the real reason to hunt this album up. "Cravo e Canela" is a classic.

influences:

◄◄ Yma Sumac, João Gilberto, Baden Powell, Heitor Villa-Lobos

►► Novos Baianos

Garaud MacTaggart

Lewis Nash

Born December 30, 1958, in Phoenix, AZ.

Lewis Nash has drummed on so many recorded sessions that you probably already have his work in your collection. Nash says he always banged around on cardboard boxes, pots, and pans, so he took up the drums at age 11, while attending Percy L. Julian Elementary School in Phoenix. He quickly advanced and became a member of Young Sounds of Arizona, a big band made up of all-stars from local high schools. He moved to New York in 1981, when vocalist Betty Carter asked him to work with her. Nash, who plays straight-ahead with a steady but creative hand, has worked with Dizzy Gillespie, Sonny Rollins, Branford Marsalis, Tommy Flanagan, and the Lincoln Center Jazz Orchestra, among others. He remains one of the young lions on the New York scene.

what to buy: *Rhythm Is My Business* 🎵🎵🎵 (Evidence, 1993, prod. Lewis Nash, Naosuke Miyamoto) finds Nash propelling a hummable session. Pianist Mulgrew Miller and vibraphonist Steve Nelson paint the 10 melodies smoothly over Nash's deft rhythms. Tunes include "My Shining Hour" and "Monk's Dream."

worth searching for: Among Nash's best sessions as a sideman are George Adams's *Old Feeling* 🎵🎵🎵 (Blue Note, 1991, prod. Kazunori Sugiyama), Betty Carter's *Look What I Got* 🎵🎵🎵 (Verve, 1988, prod. Betty Carter), Joe Lovano's *Tenor Legacy* 🎵🎵🎵 (Blue Note, 1993, prod. Joe Lovano), and Branford Marsalis's *Random Abstract* 🎵🎵🎵 (Columbia, 1988, prod. Delfeayo Marsalis).

influences:

◀◀ Elvin Jones, Art Blakey, Philly Joe Jones, Max Roach, Roy Haynes, Billy Higgins, Tony Williams, Jimmy Cobb

▶▶ Robert Hurst

Salvatore Caputo

Ted Nash

Born December 28, 1959, in Los Angeles, CA.

As you'd expect with an essentially mainstream tenor saxophonist who grew up in the '60s and '70s, the vision of Ted Nash, son of West Coast session trombonist Dick Nash and namesake of his saxophonist-uncle Ted Nash, encompasses most of the usual stylistic influences. Chief among these is a decidedly '50s-ish John Coltrane, followed by a smattering of Sonny Rollins, a touch of Fletcher Henderson, a smidgen of Wayne Shorter, and, at the outer edges of his attack, an Archie Shepp-like vocal quality.

what's available: Recorded during a 1991 concert, *Out of This World* 🎵🎵🎵 (Mapleshade, 1993, prod. Pierre Sprey) is a sprightly and quite pleasant affair, with Nash's tenor sharing the stage with Frank Kimbrough's piano, Ben Allison's bass, and Tim Horner's drumming. Kimbrough sounds particularly two-fisted on this recording, a factor that no doubt contributes to the overall *joie de vivre* and cooking good spirits of the set.

worth searching for: *Conception* 🎵🎵🎵 (Concord Jazz, 1978) is already deleted from the catalog, so those wanting more Nash on record will have to turn to his sideman shots with Ben Allison,

Marcus Roberts, Mel Lewis, the Kimbrough-led Herbie Nichols Project, and Joe Lovano.

influences:

◀◀ John Coltrane, Sonny Rollins, Fletcher Henderson, Wayne Shorter, Archie Shepp, Dick Nash

▶▶ Joshua Redman

David Prince

Theodore "Fats" Navarro

Born September 24, 1923, in Key West, FL; died July 7, 1950, in New York, NY.

Fats Navarro's career was cut tragically short by his drug addiction and early death, but his legacy remains as one of the greatest trumpeters in jazz history and a founder of the hard-bop trumpet style.

Navarro's early career was spent following in the footsteps of Dizzy Gillespie and Howard McGhee; he joined McGhee in Andy Kirk's trumpet section in 1943, then filled the seat vacated by Gillespie in Billy Eckstine's bop big band in 1945. In 1946, having established himself as a top soloist on a par with Gillespie, Fats left Eckstine in order to record with smaller, less-constraining units. His recordings, first on Savoy as a leader (1946–47), and then on Blue Note (1947–49) with Tadd Dameron, Howard McGhee, and Bud Powell, stand as landmarks in jazz history, setting the stage for many of the developments jazz trumpeting would undergo in the 1950s. Navarro's style was an extension of Gillespie's, with a more distinctive tone and fewer high-note acrobatics. His rapid articulation was a feature absorbed and further refined by Clifford Brown, who acknowledged Navarro as his primary influence in taking the hard-bop style to even greater heights. Unfortunately, Brown, and then Lee Morgan after him, also copied another aspect of Navarro's legacy in dying well before their times, at the peaks of their musical powers. Nevertheless, Fats recorded enough essential music and had enough of an impact on those who followed to be considered among the first rank of jazz trumpeters.

what to buy: The two players mentioned in the title of *Fats Navarro and Tadd Dameron: The Complete Blue Note and Capitol Recordings* 🎵🎵🎵 (Blue Note, 1995, prod. Alfred Lion, Pete Rugolo, reissue prod. Michael Cuscuna) only appear together on 17 of 36 tracks of this two-CD reissue, but this is highly important music nevertheless. Navarro's influential association with Dameron produced such bebop classics as "The Chase," "The Squirrel," "Dameronia," "Lady Bird," and "Sid's Delight." Also featured on this set of recordings from 1947 to 1949 are classic sessions on which Navarro is featured with Bud Powell and with Howard McGhee, and there's even a track where the trumpeter is heard with Benny Goodman's septet on Fats Waller's "Stealin' Apples."

what to buy next: *Memorial* ♫♫♫ (Savoy, 1993, prod. Teddy Reig) preserves some of the best of Navarro's excellent Savoy sides from 1946 and 1947, and finds the great trumpeter duelling with Kenny Dorham and Sonny Stitt, backed by a rhythm section of Bud Powell, Kenny Clarke, and Curley Russell.

what to avoid: There is absolutely nothing wrong with the music on *Fats Navarro with Tadd Dameron* ♫♫♫ (Milestone, 1989, prod. Orrin Keepnews), but listeners would be advised to get the same 1948 material (and more) from the better-sounding and more comprehensive Blue Note set.

the rest:
Nostalgia ♫♫♫ (Savoy, 1947/1958)

worth searching for: There is a much-circulated live recording, bootlegged by a number of less-than-legitimate labels, of a group usually referred to as the Charlie Parker All Stars, which captures his quintet with Navarro, Bud Powell, Curley Russell, and Art Blakey on May 8 and 15, 1950, at Birdland in New York City. The latter date was Navarro's last public appearance and recording, made less than a week before his death from tuberculosis. Fats sounds weary but brilliant in the frontline alongside bebop giant Parker, who can be considered a notable influence on Fats even if he did play alto sax.

influences:
◀◀ Dizzy Gillespie, Howard McGhee, Charlie Parker

▶▶ Clifford Brown, Lee Morgan, Freddie Hubbard, Woody Shaw, Wynton Marsalis

Dan Keener

Buell Neidlinger

Born March 2, 1936, in New York, NY.

Originally trained on the cello, Buell Neidlinger was a prodigy who, at the age of 12, performed with the New York Philharmonic Orchestra. He switched to bass, apprenticing in Dixieland groups and eventually studying with Walter Page and backing such musicians as trumpeter Rex Stewart and tenor saxophonist Ben Webster. In 1955 he became a member of Cecil Taylor's quartet, staying until 1960 and briefly rejoining in 1962, and he also played and recorded with Steve Lacy, Gil Evans, and Freddie Redd. In 1978 he formed the K2B2 label

with saxophonist and frequent collaborator Marty Krystall that has released a steady stream of recordings showcasing Neidlinger in a variety of settings. His group Buellgrass has released two recordings of bluegrass music, taking the compositions of Thelonious Monk and Duke Ellington (as well as originals) as their points of departure. Neidlinger is a stalwart and sturdy bassist who has always added to whatever group situation in which he has played. His playing is characterized by a big sound and a steadfastness that anchors a group with solidity and flexibility. He is a musician with his own vision.

what to buy: *Blue Chopsticks* ♫♫♫♫ (K2B2, 1994, prod. Buell Neidlinger) is a superb tribute to one of Neidlinger's mentors, Herbie Nichols. Neidlinger arranged 11 Nichols compositions for string trio. Don't expect genteel chamber music; these arrangements are delivered with wit and verve and all respects are given to Nichols's timeless and great music. *Rear View Mirror* ♫♫♫♫ (K2B2, 1986, prod. Buell Neidlinger, Marty Krystall) is a sampler of K2B2's earlier, vinyl-only releases, and it covers a wide range of projects. It's a good overview of the label's many and varied releases.

what to buy next: *Big Drum* ♫♫♫♫ (K2B2, 1990, prod. Buell Neidlinger, Marty Krystall) is a live quartet date that contains a little bit of Monk, a little bit of Mingus, a heartfelt composition inspired by the Tiananmen massacre, some blues, and plenty of fine blowing, especially from saxophonist Krystall. Aurora is the trio of saxophonist Krystall, Neidlinger, and Peter Erskine on drums. *Aurora—Aurora* ♫♫♫♫ (Denon, 1988, prod. Jeffrey Weber) is a crackling good record and Neidlinger and Erskine provide a rock solid foundation. Krystall blows a fierce tenor and his allegiance to the tenor tradition from Hawkins and Webster to Coltrane and Ayler is to the fore.

best of the rest:
(With Cecil Taylor) *New York City R&B* ♫♫♫♫ (Candid, 1961)

influences:
◀◀ Thelonious Monk, Herbie Nichols, Cecil Taylor, Wilbur Ware
▶▶ Henry Grimes

Robert Iannapollo

Ben Neill

Ben Neill occupies his own special space between the worlds of electronic music and jazz, and his keen understanding of both genres helps him fashion his own special hybrid. Aside from his synthesizers and samplers, Neill's main instrument is his own specially constructed "mutantrumpet," which has six valves, three bells, and a slide, and in conjunction with computer electronics, enables him to produce an intriguing array of sounds. It's interesting that the name of his unique instrument is the same as that given the highly processed trumpet of Jon Hassell, an ethno-ambient pioneer. (However, Hassell's brass instrument received that name from the exotic, elephantine sounds it produced rather than an unusual physical construction.) Of the myriad electronic composers out there today, Neill stands out as one of the most original, and his jazzy drum and bass solo performance at the 1997 Projekt Festival in Chicago won over a predominately "Goth" crowd, proving his potentially wide appeal. The trumpeter also has taken over as music curator of the Kitchen, a well-known Manhattan art space.

what to buy: On his second album *Tryptical* ♫♫♫ (Antilles, 1996, Ben Neill, Eric Calvi), Neill ventures into dance territory, utilizing trip-hop, polyrhythmic drum and bass, and straight-ahead techno grooves to underlie his spaced-out atmospheres. On different cuts, he teams up with Illbient-style gurus, DJ Olive (from We) and DJ Spooky, who provide turntable effects. The trumpeter brings the melodic inventiveness and free-flowing rhythmic pulse of jazz to an electronic dance arena whose mainstream proponents tend to practice heavy sequencing, repetition, and atonality. The opening cut, "Propeller," also features some driving hand percussion from Don Yallech.

what to buy next: Neill's debut *Green Machine* ♫♫♫ (Astralwerks, 1995, prod. Ben Neill, Mikel Rouse) features some engrossing psychedelic ambient and ambient techno soundscapes. His mutantrumpet plays a strong role on some tracks, while on others he programs gliding ambiences which actively churn forward rather than merely hang in the air. The seven tracks are rather epic but they have much to offer, easily avoiding the wallpaper trappings of generic ambient music.

the rest:
(With David Wojnarowicz) *Itsofomo* (New Tone, 1992)

influences:
◀◀ La Monte Young, Future Sound of London, David Wojnarowicz, Terence McKenna, Rhys Chatham

Bryan Reesman

Oliver Nelson
Born June 4, 1932, in St. Louis, MO. Died October 28, 1975, in Los Angeles, CA.

Nearly everybody dug the late saxophonist, composer, and arranger Oliver Nelson. His tone and attack on both tenor and alto (he also recorded on soprano late in his career) was straightforward and muscular, and his original compositions, clean and uncluttered, were steeped in the swing-into-bop blues tradition. A multi-instrumentalist, composer-arranger Nelson was born into a musical family. His brother played saxophone in a band led by Cootie Williams in the 1940s, and his sister was a singer-pianist. Nelson began his professional career in early 1947, performing with the Jeter-Pillars Orchestra and St. Louis big bands led by Nat Towles and George Hudson. Nelson arranged for and played second alto saxophone in Louis Jordan's big band (1950–51) before playing for two years in a Marine Corps ensemble. He returned to St. Louis where he majored in music composition and theory at Washington University from 1954–57 and pursued further studies at Lincoln University in Jefferson City, Missouri (1958–59). After graduation, he moved to New York, worked briefly with the bands of Erskine Hawkins, Wild Bill Davis, and Louis Bellson, and became the house arranger for the Apollo Theatre. Although he was leading his own groups as early as 1959, he played in and arranged for the Quincy Jones Orchestra from 1960–61, a band that, at the time, included trumpeter Clark Terry, altoist Phil Woods, trombonist Jimmie Cleveland, and other ace players. In addition to playing in the reed sections of the Count Basie and Duke Ellington orchestras, Nelson also worked with small groups and made his recording debut as leader in 1960 with *Meet Oliver Nelson*, an album that won him four stars in a *Down Beat* review at the time. In 1961 Impulse! released Nelson's *Blues and the Abstract Truth*, an album of original music that remains one of the classic albums in jazz, contains one of Nelson's best-known compositions, "Stolen Moments." He moved to Los Angeles in 1967 where he began scoring extensively for television and films. He continued to perform on alto, tenor, and soprano saxophones, and wrote for recording dates during the 1960s and 1970s. Nelson also composed many nonjazz works, which he performed in various settings during his career. He died suddenly on October 28, 1975 of a heart attack.

what to buy: *Blues and the Abstract Truth* ♫♫♫♫ (Impulse!, 1961/1995, prod. Creed Taylor) may be the most transcendent of his recorded works, and to those who ignore Nelson's contributions to the jazz world as arranger/composer, it is viewed as the earmark of his career. In addition to featuring his hearty alto and tenor saxophone performances, the album contains six of Nelson's best compositions, including "Stolen Moments," "Hoe Down," and "Yearnin'," performed with what in retrospect would be considered a "dream team" of sidemen: Eric Dolphy (alto saxophone, flute), Freddie Hubbard (trumpet),

George Barrow (baritone saxophone), Bill Evans (piano), Paul Chambers (bass), and Roy Haynes (drums). This album, which garnered five stars from a *Down Beat* reviewer in 1961, was commended for Nelson's ability to take the music beyond an average blowing session. The album remains one of the all-time best recordings, and is highly recommended for any collection. Also worth investigating for Nelson's talents as arranger/conductor, is his orchestral suite, which merges African rhythms, swing, blues-tinged passages, and a well-arranged brass chorale, as well as his own extraordinary alto and tenor sax improvisations, on *Afro-American Sketches* 🎵🎵🎵🎵 (Prestige, 1961/OJC, 1993, prod. Esmond Edwards). If you're looking for an introduction to this musician, *Oliver Nelson: Verve Jazz Masters 48* 🎵🎵🎵🎵 (Verve, 1962–67/1995, prod. various) is a recommended choice. The album gathers some of his best arrangements, mostly from his 1960s Verve albums, *Full Nelson, Jazzhattan Suite,* and *The Sound of Feeling and the Sound of Oliver Nelson.* This disc contains the first release of Nelson's "Patterns for Orchestra," featuring solos by J.J. Johnson and Grady Tate. It had been planned to include this track on the LP *The Sound of Feeling and the Sound of Oliver Nelson* but the tune "12 Tone Blues" (mistitled as "Patterns for Orchestra") accidentally replaced it. It's one of his best arrangements. Other highlights of this compilation include solos from alto saxophonist Phil Woods ("I Remember Bird," "Penthouse Dawn"), and Nat Adderley, Hank Jones, Patti Bown, Bob Brookmeyer, and others. Nelson himself performs on "You Love but Once." But it isn't his solo that makes this album, it the awesome arrangements that still sound fresh and ebullient today.

what to buy next: Nelson can be heard twice more with Dolphy, both times to good advantage. *Straight Ahead* 🎵🎵🎵🎵 (New Jazz, 1961/OJC, 1990, prod. Esmond Edwards) features slightly more adventurous material performed with pianist Richard Wyands, bassist George Duvivier, and drummer Roy Haynes, while the earlier *Screamin' the Blues* 🎵🎵🎵🎵 (New Jazz, 1960/OJC, 1992, prod. Esmond Edwards) adds trumpeter Richard Williams to the frontline with the same rhythm section. Although it mostly trades off the fame of his earlier album, the sequel *More Blues and the Abstract Truth* 🎵🎵🎵🎵 (Impulse!, 1964/1997, prod. Bob Thiele) contains some fine moments on arrangements of Nelson's original works and features top-notch solos from Phil Woods, Thad Jones, Pepper Adams, Ben Webster, and others.

the rest:
Meet Oliver Nelson 🎵🎵🎵🎵 (OJC, 1959/1993)
(With King Curtis, Jimmy Forrest) *Soul Battle* 🎵🎵🎵🎵 (OJC, 1960/1992)

Taking Care of Business 🎵🎵🎵🎵 (OJC, 1960/1991)
(With Lem Winchester) *Nocturne* 🎵🎵🎵🎵 (OJC, 1960/1992)
(With Joe Newman) *Main Stem* 🎵🎵🎵🎵 (OJC, 1961/1992)
Sound Pieces 🎵🎵🎵🎵 (Impulse!, 1966/1991)
Black, Brown & Beautiful 🎵🎵🎵🎵 (Bluebird, 1970)

influences:

⏪ Johnny Hodges, Sonny Rollins, Charlie Parker, John Coltrane, Wardell Gray, Jimmy Forrest, Thelonious Monk, Gil Evans, George Russell

Nancy Ann Lee and David Prince

New York Composers Orchestra

See: Wayne Horvitz

New York Jazz Quartet

See: Roland Hanna, Frank Wess, George Mraz

Phineas Newborn Jr.

Born December 14, 1931, in Whiteville, TN. Died May 26, 1989, in Memphis, TN.

Technically gifted in every facet of jazz piano playing, Phineas Newborn Jr. never really gained the acceptance and praise due him because of his many absences from the scene, the result of personal and medical problems. Readily considered in the same league with Art Tatum and Bud Powell, Newborn's hardships never detracted from his playing, which was always inspired and animated. His technical mastery was unequaled and he was able to speak in any style while maintaining his own individualistic approach, which combined a soulful blues sensibility with an even-tempered lyricism that was directly accessible. Indeed, his dazzling two-handed octave runs were something of great profundity and they have since been imitated by scores of other pianists.

A product of two musical parents, Newborn began playing around the Memphis area while still in his teens. He moved to New York in 1956 where he worked with Charles Mingus and began recording a number of stimulating albums for the Atlantic, RCA, Roulette, and United Artists labels. With the turn of the decade, Newborn headed to Los Angeles where he met producer Lester Koenig, who supervised a series of quintessential Newborn trio dates for his Contemporary Records label. Unfortunately, Newborn's illnesses took him away from the action on several occasions and for protracted periods of time. Although he would launch limited comebacks during the 1970s and

1980s, Newborn would never really regain his already limited popularity. Worthy of rediscovery, Phineas Newborn deserves a place in jazz history as one of the most brilliant and important jazz pianists of the 20th century.

what to buy: *A World of Piano* 𝄞𝄞𝄞𝄞 (Contemporary, 1961, prod. Lester Koenig) put Newborn in the company of two great rhythm sections—Paul Chambers and Philly Joe Jones for half a set and Sam Jones and Louis Hayes for the other half. By the time this disc plays through, you'll be convinced you have indeed heard a whole world of piano. *Harlem Blues* 𝄞𝄞𝄞𝄞 (Contemporary, 1969, prod. Lester Koenig) was cut with bassist Ray Brown and drummer Elvin Jones. Despite the fact that the three had never played as a group before, the results are tremendous, with Newborn still performing in peak form.

what to buy next: Roy Haynes with Phineas Newborn and Paul Chambers, *We Three* 𝄞𝄞𝄞𝄞 (Prestige/New Jazz, 1958, prod. Esmond Edwards) is a notable set for the empathetic interplay between the trio and for Newborn's soulful and bluesy take on "After Hours," which ranks among the finest renditions of the song on record. *The Great Jazz Piano of Phineas Newborn Jr.* 𝄞𝄞𝄞𝄞 (Contemporary, 1962, prod. Lester Koenig) finds the pianist in his prime, discovering new things to do with an excellent set of jazz standards. Creative, imaginative, and energetic, this set is among Newborn's greatest.

the rest:
The Newborn Touch 𝄞𝄞𝄞 (Contemporary, 1964)
Please Send Me Someone to Love 𝄞𝄞𝄞 (Contemporary, 1969)
Look Out: Phineas Is Back 𝄞𝄞𝄞 (Contemporary, 1976)

worth searching for: *Here Is Phineas: The Piano Artistry of Phineas Newborn Jr.* 𝄞𝄞𝄞𝄞 (Atlantic, 1956, prod. Nesuhi Ertegun) can sometimes be found as an import. This is bebop at its greatest with Oscar Pettiford and Kenny Clarke on board and is the finest example of the pianist's early work.

influences:
◀◀ Art Tatum

▶▶ Harold Mabern, James Williams, Geoff Keezer

Chris Hovan

David "Fathead" Newman

Born February 24, 1933, in Corsicana, TX.

It's hard to find a saxophonist who better exemplifies the "Texas Tenor" ideal. David Newman has that big, full throated, bluesy sound muscular enough to grab your attention yet supple enough that it fits in well in a variety of musical situations. Likewise, he has shown an amazing ability to shine in a staggering variety of situations, whether working as a section man in an R&B band, backing a soul or jazz vocalist, fronting a small jazz group, or even a large orchestra. Even in awkward or overbearing settings Newman's work has been consistently good. Growing up in Dallas, Newman began playing alto saxophone while in the seventh grade. He was influenced early on by the popular Louis Jordan, an influence which is still apparent in his work on both tenor and alto. His nickname "Fathead" was inadvertently bestowed upon him by a music teacher after Newman's failure to navigate an arpeggio on the saxophone. Though Newman, understandably, was not fond of the nickname, it stuck. Falling in with a local scene that included (then unknown) musicians Ornette Coleman and James Clay, Newman was influenced further by Basie associate Buster Smith. He did his first road work with pianist Lloyd Glenn, and went on to play in a variety of R&B groups, including a stint with blues guitarist Lowell Fulson. While with Fulson's band he met Ray Charles, and the pair soon began a musical relationship that lasted nearly a decade. Newman's work with Charles produced many great moments and an immediately recognizable horn-section sound. Newman began recording as a solo artist in 1958 and made a series of moderately successful albums for Atlantic. He left Charles's band—and the music scene at large—in 1963 to settle down with his wife and children, but after a three-year hiatus returned and has remained a visible figure in jazz music circles ever since. Among Newman's studio recordings have been frequent attempts (some of which tried too hard) to appeal more to the masses than to his core audience of jazz listeners. Newman's own contributions to these records are often more respectable than the records themselves. He has also been a great session player, appearing on countless soul, blues, and jazz dates over the years. He's co-led a few excellent releases (30 years apart) alongside fellow Texan James Clay. He's also worked extensively with Herbie Mann, first in Mann's "Family of Mann" during the early 1970s and then recording for Mann's Kokopelli label during the '90s. His longest association has been with saxophonist Hank Crawford, who has joined Newman on scores of recordings over the years.

what to buy: *It's Mister Fathead* 𝄞𝄞𝄞𝄞 (32 Jazz, 1998, reissue prod. Joel Dorn) collects Newman's first four Atlantic LPs, *Fathead—Ray Charles Presents David Newman*, *Straight Ahead*, *Fathead Comes On*, and *House of David* in a wonderful two-CD set. Recorded between 1958 and 1967, they contain Newman's strongest work as a jazz artist. *Fathead* is Newman's steaming

1958 debut in which he led a sextet of musicians from the Ray Charles band (including Hank Crawford on baritone saxophone, trumpeter Marcus Belgrave, and Brother Ray himself on the piano). It includes the minor classic, "Hard Times." *Straight Ahead* and *Fathead Comes On* followed hot on the heels of *Fathead* and are strong, soulful, straight-ahead efforts, with Wynton Kelly and Paul Chambers appearing on the former (a quartet date) and drummer Charlie Persip on hand for both. *House of David* is a mostly successful organ group date from 1967 on which Newman is joined by organist Kossie Gardner and guitarist Ted Dunbar. Another good place to start is the two-disc anthology set *House of David* (Rhino, 1993, prod. Joel Dorn), which borrows its title from the 1967 Atlantic LP. It's a much more balanced overview of Newman's work than *It's Mister Fathead*, collecting examples of his recordings from 1952 up through 1989. A celebration of Newman's versatility, on *House of David* his work as a sideman with Ray Charles is spotlighted on several tracks, as is a taste of his session work with vocalists Aretha Franklin, Dr. John, and Aaron Neville. It's also a decent, if not completely thorough, retrospective of his jazz recordings for Atlantic.

what to buy next: *Lone Star Legend* (32 Jazz, 1997, prod. Joel Dorn) collects two of Newman's early '80s sessions for Muse on one CD. *Resurgence*, recorded in 1980, finds him in the company of Marcus Belgrave, Ted Dunbar, Cedar Walton, Buster Williams, and Louis Hayes for a solid set that marks Newman's return to more serious forms of jazz after a decade of mostly pop-oriented dates. *Still Hard Times* brought old pal Crawford in for a swinging session that echoes the sound of Newman's late '50s recordings, and, of course, the Ray Charles years. On *Mr. Gentle, Mr. Cool* (Kokopelli, 1994, prod. Herbie Mann), Robert Freedman's arrangements provide fresh, if sometimes a bit sedate, setting for Newman's interpretations of 11 Duke Ellington songs. Newman is in top form on tenor, alto, and flute throughout and is particularly effective on ballads like "Prelude to a Kiss." *Fire* (Atlantic, 1989, prod. John Snyder) is a fine live session in which Newman digs into some soul and funk of the Ray Charles/Horace Silver variety. Recorded at the Village Vanguard, Newman gives Stanley Turrentine and Hank Crawford some prime time on stage too.

what to avoid: Unless you're a completist, steer clear of *Back to Basics* (Milestone, 1991, prod. Orrin Keepnews), a reissue of a 1977 session. Some of the overdubbed strings and voices from the original LP release were stripped off the mixes for the '91 reissue, but what's left is still a fairly uninspiring, pop-flavored '70s recording. It's not dreadful, but there are plenty of superior Newman CDs out there.

the rest:
Blue Head (Candid, 1991)
Bigger & Better/The Many Facets of David Newman (Rhino, 1994)
Under a Woodstock Moon (Kokopelli, 1996)

worth searching for: *Heads Up* (Atlantic, 1986, prod. John Snyder) features Newman fronting a quintet that includes vibist Steve Nelson.

influences:

◄◄ Buster Smith, John Hardee, Louis Jordan, Don Wilkerson, Don Byas

►► Wilton Felder, James Clay, Houston Person, Grover Washington Jr.

Dan Bindert

Joe Newman

Born September 7, 1922, in New Orleans, LA. Died July 4, 1992, in New York, NY.

One of the finest trumpeters to emerge during the big band era, Joe Newman's style was all about thrill and exhilaration. He had a broad and brassy tone that cut through any trumpet section and his melodic ideas set him aside from your typical session player. His first important work came in the early 1940s as a member of Lionel Hampton's big band, followed by his initial stint with the Count Basie orchestra from 1943 to 1947. During this period Newman could also be found busy as a sideman with various groups including those of Illinois Jacquet and J.C. Heard. In 1952 he rejoined the Basie band for what would be a fruitful decade. In part of what was known as Basie's "Atomic period," Newman appeared on several of the group's momentous 1950s Roulette sessions. He also would cut a number of commendable records of his own for the RCA and Roulette labels. The next few decades found him working as a session musician, leading his own groups, and serving as educator and jazz advocate. In his role as the latter, he was involved in and eventually became president of a New York-based group known as Jazz Interactions, which promoted jazz education and awareness. Newman's trips overseas included a 1962 Russian tour with Benny Goodman and a 1975 European jaunt with the New York Repertory Orchestra. Active up until his death, he remained a committed jazz musician and statesman of the highest caliber.

what's available: *Jive at Five* (Swingville, 1960/OJC, 1990, prod. Esmond Edwards) pairs Newman with his Basie bandmate Frank Wess and pianist Tommy Flanagan. Underpinned by the solid bass work of Eddie Jones and inspired by the small group swing of Basie, Newman and crew put on tape some of the best and most relaxed jazz of the period. *Good 'n' Groovy* ♫♫♫♪ (Swingville, 1961/OJC, 1994, prod. Esmond Edwards) finds Newman working alongside his other Basie partner, tenor saxophonist Frank Foster. Once again, Flanagan and Jones provide excellent support and the tunes range from swing classics to hard bop delights and even a children's nursery rhyme.

influences:

◀◀ Lionel Hampton, Illinois Jacquet, Count Basie

Chris Hovan

Herbie Nichols

Born January 3, 1919, in New York, NY. Died April 12, 1963, in New York, NY.

Herbie Nichols was a relatively obscure figure even during his lifetime—certainly more jazz fans knew his tune "Lady Sings the Blues" as recorded by Billie Holiday than had heard any of his own records—and only four albums, all trios, were released before his death of leukemia at the age of 44. Somewhat incongruously considering the sophistication of his composing, most of the gigs with which he supported himself were with Dixieland bands or R&B groups. In retrospect, supporters puzzled by the disparity between the quality of Nichols's music and his lack of recognition have tended to point to his apparent distaste for self-promotion. After his premature death, his memory was kept alive by being one of the subjects of A.B. Spellman's 1966 book *Four Lives in the Bebop Business* and by younger musicians on the New York City scene, such as Roswell Rudd, Steve Lacy, and Cecil Taylor, who had worked with him or admired his performances. Although Nichols's music is quite accessible to listeners—he was always concerned with melodic writing—it presented problems to other musicians at the time because structurally it frequently extends normal 32-bar AABA form. In other words, it's not jam session material, instead requiring rehearsal if the musicians aren't going to trip over the unusual phrase lengths. This undoubtedly had something to do with its limited exposure during the composer's lifetime. Musically Nichols frequently gets compared to Thelonious Monk. That's certainly an apt description of his piano playing, though Nichols could be more virtuosic—some of his right-hand runs suggest Art Tatum. To a degree there are also similarities to Monk's harmonic language and sometimes-angular melodies, but Nichols had his own sound and style and could often be

HERBIE NICHOLS

song "The Gig"

album *The Complete Blue Note Recordings*
(Blue Note, 1955–56/1997)

instrument Piano

Monster Solo

much more harmonically complex than Monk. Though there's an introspective hue to Nichols's writing, most of his music also has an appealingly jaunty quality.

what to buy: The invaluable three-CD set *The Complete Blue Note Recordings* ♫♫♫♫ (Blue Note, 1955–56/1997, prod. Alfred Lion, compilation prod. Michael Cuscuna) revamps Mosaic's long-out-of-print five-LP box. There are many memorable tunes here; "The Gig," were it not one of Nichols's most complicated forms, could easily be a jazz standard. The ebullient drummers he worked with at Blue Note—Art Blakey on two sessions and Max Roach on three (the bassists are Al McKibbon and Teddy Kotick)—help bring out the inner joy of his music and provide the interplay with the pianist that he apparently delighted in. This set contains Nichols's three issued Blue Note albums (long unavailable; two were on 10-inch LPs) plus alternate takes and songs unissued at the time. Over the course of 29 originals, one cover (Gershwin's "Mine"), and 48 tracks all told, it becomes clear that Nichols created one of the great unsung legacies of jazz. His self-penned liner notes for his third album are included in the box's booklet; he was a graceful writer who covered music for a Harlem paper.

what to buy next: *Love, Gloom, Cash, Love* ♫♫♫♫ (Bethlehem, 1957, prod. Lee Kraft) has also been issued as *The Bethlehem Session*. Another trio, with George Duvivier on bass and Danny Richmond on drums, it's as valuable and rewarding as the Blue Note material and, sadly, was the last recording of his own music he would make. The title track is a tricky but endearing waltz that ranks among his better-known tunes. Nichols's covers of the standards "Too Close for Comfort" and "All the Way" are interesting for the way in which he can sound distinctive even when the melodies and structures are not his own; he even seems a bit more relaxed and emotive on them.

worth searching for: *I Just Love Jazz Piano* ♫♫♫♫ (Savoy, 1952, prod. Ozzie Cadena) contains the four tracks Nichols recorded for the label, along with unrelated material by three other pianists. Given how little Nichols was able to record, every track is precious. In recent years, his music has increasingly been revived, most notably by two musicians who played with him and by another two several generations younger. Bassist Buell Neidlinger and trombonist Roswell Rudd both played with Nichols in Dixieland bands. Rudd has made two loose trio albums, *The Unheard Herbie Nichols, Volumes 1 and 2* ♫♫♫♫ (CIMP, 1997, prod. Robert D. Rusch). They contain Nichols tunes the pianist himself didn't record (mostly written post-1957), which makes them a project of obvious value even if the arrangements for trombone, electric guitar, and drums take them very far from Nichols's sound world. Rudd also co-led a quintet with soprano saxophonist Steve Lacy, pianist Misha Mengelberg, bassist Kent Carter, and drummer Han Bennink, that split *Regeneration* ♫♫♫♫ (Soul Note, 1983, prod. Giovanni Bonandrini) between Nichols and Monk tunes. He was never able to record his music with horns, so this offers some insight as to the possibilities it contained. With George Lewis and Harjen Gorter filling Rudd's and Carter's slots, *Change of Season* ♫♫♫♫ (Soul Note, 1985, prod. Giovanni Bonandrini) covers only Nichols's tunes, including the composer's own quintet arrangement of the previously unrecorded title tune. These modernists have a fine understanding of the potential of Nichols's compositions, as does Neidlinger, whose *Blue Chopsticks* ♫♫♫♫♫ (K2B2, 1995, prod. Buell Neidlinger) fulfills his promise to the dying Nichols that he'd record his music with horns and strings. Neidlinger (on cello), saxophonist Marty Krystall, and trumpeter Hugh Shick are joined by violin and viola on a quirkily arranged quintet session that's a true delight. Pianist Frank Kimbrough and bassist Ben Allison, who provided the bio and track-by-track

notes on the Blue Note box, have a fine group called the Herbie Nichols Project. *Love Is Proximity* ♫♫♫♫ (Soul Note, 1996, prod. Jazz Composers Collective) offers more orthodox interpretations of the Nichols legacy, in arrangements of varying instrumentation, including saxophonist Ted Nash, trumpeter Ron Horton, and drummer Jeff Ballard. The quintet tracks offer a glimpse of Nichols's expanded vision for his music, and the title track is previously unrecorded.

influences:

◀◀ Thelonious Monk, Art Tatum, Duke Ellington

▶▶ Andrew Hill, Roswell Rudd, Steve Lacy, Misha Mengelberg, Cecil Taylor, Frank Kimbrough, Geri Allen

Steve Holtje

Bern Nix

Born September 21, 1947 in Toledo, OH.

Mostly known for his 1975–87 membership in Ornette Coleman's harmolodic electric group Prime Time, hollowbody electric guitarist Bern Nix has not been recorded nearly as often as his unique sounds merits. Growing up listening to Duane Eddy, the Ventures, Chet Atkins, and blues guitarists, at age 14 Nix's attention was first turned towards jazz by his guitar teachers. He moved into Coleman's famous Prince Street loft in 1975 as the saxophonist put together his first mostly electric group. Nix's role in its democratic approach to group improvisation tended to be spiraling appeggiated figures around which the other players seemed to revolve. Appearances in other projects followed, from ex-Ornette drummer Ronald Shannon Jackson's 1980 debut album and Jemeel Moondoc's *Nostalgia in Times Square* to work with conceptualist Kip Hanrahan, guitarist Elliott Sharp, and post-punk saxophonist/vocalist James Chance's various bands. In the mid-1980s Nix began working more as a leader, forming a trio with bassist William Parker and drummer David Capello, the precursor to Nix's only album as a leader.

what's available: On *Alarms & Excursions* ♫♫♫♫ (New World, 1993, prod. Wayne Horvitz) Nix finally got to present his delicate touch and unpredictable lines as focus rather than contrast, even playing the old standard "Just Friends." Though energetic enough at times, he stresses intricacy and subtlety rather than raucousness (despite the CD title), often playing horn-like lines. Fred Hopkins (acoustic bass) and Newman Baker (drums) offer sympathetic support. This CD proves there's more to harmolodic jazz than the sonic attacks of Ornette Coleman, Blood Ulmer, and Shannon Jackson.

influences:

◀◀ Ornette Coleman, Charlie Christian, Barney Kessel, Freddie King

▶▶ Bill Frisell, Joe Morris

Steve Holtje

Jimmie Noone

Born April 23, 1895, in Cut-Off, LA. Died April 19, 1944, in Los Angeles, CA.

One of the premier New Orleans clarinetists, Jimmie Noone's all too short career ended with his untimely death from a heart attack at age 48. Noone took lessons from Sidney Bechet as a youth. His first paying musical job came as a substitute for Bechet in Freddie Keppard's band. Noone then joined the Young Olympia Band and was a band member from 1914–17, when he left for Chicago and there joined Freddie Keppard's Original Creole Band. When the group disbanded in 1918, Noone went back to New Orleans until summoned back to Chicago by King Joe Oliver to become a member of Oliver's group. He stayed with Oliver until he joined Doc Cooke's large orchestra in 1920 (along with Freddie Keppard). In 1923 he made his first recordings sitting in as a sub with King Oliver's Creole Jazz Band. Noone led his own band at the Apex Club after leaving Doc Cooke in 1928. He briefly teamed with Earl Hines and made some wonderful recordings for Vocalion records during this period. Once the Apex Club closed, Noone played in a number of Chicago clubs and continued to record extensively. He played in and around Chicago until 1942, except for two short stays in New York City, and a long road trip in 1938. By the time World War II broke out, he had headed West and finally settled in California. He had his own band on the Coast, but also played with the bands of Kid Ory and others. Noone recorded and did much radio work right up to the time of his sudden death. For the completist, almost all of Noone's recordings can be found on the Classics label. Having all titles under Noone's name, one will have to sort out the good from the mediocre, but the hot titles are well worth the effort.

what to buy: Noone recorded quite extensively during the late 1920s and early 1930s. However, not all of the material he recorded was what could be considered good jazz. Many titles are pop tunes with pop vocals, with only a hint of Noone's genius in evidence. With that in mind, a good introduction to his playing can be found on *Introduction to Jimmie Noone, 1923–1940* 𝄐𝄐𝄐 (Best/Jazz, 1996, prod. various). This collection includes early titles featuring Noone, as well as the best of the Apex Club titles, plus the high-caliber 1940 Decca recordings. *Apex Blues (1928–30)* 𝄐𝄐𝄐 (MCA, 1994, prod. various) also features the better titles by Noone for Vocalion, where the tunes are jazzy and Noone's punchy clarinet is featured prominently. "Oh Sister Ain't That Hot" and "I Know That You Know" (among other tunes) are excellent.

best of the rest:

Jimmie Noone, 1923–1928 𝄐𝄐𝄐 (Classics, 1994)
Jimmie Noone, 1928–1929 𝄐𝄐𝄐 (Classics, 1994)
Jimmie Noone, 1929–1930 𝄐𝄐𝄐 (Classics, 1994)
Jimmie Noone, 1930–1934 𝄐𝄐𝄐 (Classics, 1994)
Jimmie Noone, 1934–1940 𝄐𝄐𝄐 (Classics, 1994)
The Jimmie Noone Collection 𝄐𝄐𝄐 (Storyville, 1994)
Apex of New Orleans Jazz 𝄐𝄐𝄐 (ASV Living Era, 1997)

influences:

◀◀ Sidney Bechet, Lorenzo Tio Jr.

▶▶ Kenny Davern, Benny Goodman, Frank Powers, Frank Chase

Jim Prohaska

Ken Nordine

Born April 13, 1920, in Des Moines, IA.

Ken Nordine is a true original in a field where we all have some experience: talking. But what distinguishes him from the stereotypical "spoken-word artist" and other jabberers is that he does it with such a genuine sense of improvisation that it can fall under the heading of jazz. At least he thinks so, coining the term "word jazz" to classify his recorded work—which has made him a hilarious, off-the-wall, Grammy nominee, beloved by musical hipsters and commercial producers alike. Nordine grew up in Chicago during the glory days of television and radio. His rich, sonorous voice was well-suited for storytelling and poetry readings, which he would also perform in local clubs with the accompaniment of some of his musician friends during the '50s. Coming to the attention of Dot Records, Nordine was invited to appear on a track from easy-listening bandleader Billy Vaughn titled "The Shifting, Whispering Sands," providing an epic monologue that drove the song to the top of the charts. Throughout the late '50s, Nordine released a series of his own records that featured his surreal stories read over a musical backdrop provided by session musicians like Fred Katz, Richard Marx, Paul Horn, and others. Ad-libbing his way through tracks like "The Sound Museum" and "Faces in the Jazzamatazz," Nordine created a unique mix of witty recitation and jazzy music that was unforgettable, making him an obvious choice to be a pitchman for products ranging from Taster's

Choice coffee to Levi's Jeans. Over the next three decades, Nordine worked consistently, doing several hundred commercials a year, and releasing the occasional record, often on his own cassette-only label. His work continues to be fresh, whimsical, and laced with the soul of bebop bass.

what to buy: The generous collection *The Best of Word Jazz, Volume 1* 𝄢𝄢𝄢 (Rhino, 1990, prod. Tom Mack), the best of Nordine's Dot recordings, demonstrates the aptness of calling this material "Word Jazz."

what to buy next: On *Colors* 𝄢𝄢𝄢 (Philips/Asphodel, 1995, prod. Ken Nordine, Dick Campbell), Nordine offers a series of short monologues about particular colors. They were originally written as radio commercials for a paint company.

influences:

◀◀ Lord Buckley, Lenny Bruce, Jack Kerouac

▶▶ Guru

Eric J. Lawrence

Walter Norris

Born December 27, 1931, in Little Rock, AR.

Prior to the release of his *Live at Maybeck Recital Hall* album in 1990, Norris was a footnote to many U.S. jazz fans as the only pianist to record with Ornette Coleman in the early years of the great saxophonist's career. He actually deserved far better, because he is a fine pianist with great technique and an impressive approach to harmonics. Norris's early, pre-Coleman career found him playing in small groups around the South and in Las Vegas before finally settling in Los Angeles, where he gigged with Stan Getz, Frank Rosolino, and Herb Geller, among others. His post-Coleman employment included stints in New York City with the Thad Jones—Mel Lewis Orchestra and Charles Mingus before finally moving to Germany in 1977, where he ended up teaching improvisation at the Hochschule der Kunste in Berlin.

what to buy: Norris seems to work best in small group settings, and *Hues of Blues* 𝄢𝄢𝄢𝄢 (Concord Jazz, 1995, prod. John Burk), a duet album with master bassist George Mraz, is one of his finest recordings. Their ease together dates back as far as 1974, when they created another wonderful duet album, *Drifting*. While the earlier recording is filled with pleasant moments, this later recording has 20 more years of experience behind it, during which time both players have honed their respective talents even further. John Lewis's "Fontessa" is marvelous, while the title tune is Norris's own superlative, if understated, take on tra-

ditional blues themes. *Live at Maybeck Recital Hall, Volume Four* 𝄢𝄢𝄢𝄢 (Concord Jazz, 1990, prod. Carl E. Jefferson, John Burk) is one of the early gems in the renowned *Maybeck* solo piano series. Norris was visiting the San Francisco area from his expatriate digs in Germany when this particular session was set up and the resulting recording reintroduced him to jazz aficionados. Unlike many of the other *Maybeck* albums, the tunes are almost evenly split between standards like "Body and Soul" and newer material, in this case selections from Norris ("Scrambled" and "Modus Vivendi") or his former students Minako Tanahashi-Tokuyama ("Waltz for Walt") and Joan Johnson Drewes ("It's Always Spring"). Throughout the album, Norris's playing is a marvel of clarity and intriguing harmonic thought.

what to buy next: Tenor sax magician Joe Henderson joins Norris in the delightful quartet date *Sunburst* 𝄢𝄢𝄢 (Concord Jazz, 1991, prod. John Burk). The material covers a wide range of well-chosen standards and some creative new songs. Both the up-tempo title tune and "Rose Petals," an exquisite mid-tempo ballad, were written by Norris and are definite highlights on the album alongside chestnuts like "Stella by Starlight" and Cole Porter's "So in Love." Henderson's playing is fine throughout, but especially noteworthy on John Coltrane's "Naima." *Drifting* 𝄢𝄢𝄢 (Enja, 1974/1978, prod. Matthias Winckelmann) combines two of Norris's earliest recordings as a leader. The first album, *Drifting*, finds the pianist playing with bassist George Mraz while the second album, *Synchronicity*, pairs him with the superlative, if little-known, Hungarian bassist Aladar Pege. The playing on both albums is solid, with wonderful interpretations of "A Child Is Born" and "Spring Can Really Hang You up the Most." It's also a treat to compare the different recordings of "Drifting" and "Spacemaker," seeing how Norris's vision of these works changed over time.

the rest:

Lush Life 𝄢𝄢𝄢 (Concord Jazz, 1991)
Love Every Moment 𝄢𝄢𝄢 (Concord Jazz, 1993)

influences:

◀◀ Art Tatum, Bud Powell, Dinu Lipatti

▶▶ Joan Johnson Drewes, Minako Tanahashi-Tokuyama

Garaud MacTaggart

Kevin Norton

Born January 21, 1956, in Brooklyn, NY.

Kevin Norton's percussion playing mixes vocabularies, even while playing on one particular instrument. His drum-set playing can evoke tonalities that clearly rise from his knowledge of the glockenspiel, marimba, and vibraphone. But his drum playing also influences his playing on those same instruments, lending a sharpness and syncopation to his multi-percussive endeavors. Meanwhile, the glockenspiel and marimba especially provide a rounder, richer set of textures that colors his work and makes Norton a much-sought after and highly regarded drummer. Norton began playing drums at the age of 10 and found an interest in jazz by his teens. He studied music at Hunter College, where he was introduced to bassist Milt Hinton and the Manhattan School of Music. At the latter institution, Norton became well versed in the use of mallets to play percussion instruments, and his mallet expertise has marked nearly all of his professional recordings. He later studied with Barry Altschul, another expert on various percussion instruments. Norton settled into the contemporary downtown New York improvised music scene and began performing with his own groups, Phillip Johnston's groups, and a variety of others. Norton has formed and recorded with Milt Hinton, numerous New Music composers and performers, and many jazz musicians. Saxophonist/composers Anthony Braxton, Phillip Johnston, and David Bindman have both found Norton's playing ideal for extended recordings, as have guitarist James Emery, pianist and band leader Marie McAuliffe, young saxophonist Brandon Evans, improvising vocalist Tyrone Henderson, and Dave Soldier's acclaimed Soldier String Quartet. Norton leads his own trio (George Cartwright, saxophones, Mark Dresser, bass) and a larger group, the Kevin Norton Ensemble.

what to buy: The Kevin Norton Trio debuted with the wildly strong *Integrated Variables* ♫♫♫ (C.I.M.P., 1996, prod. Robert D. Rusch). Norton's dexterity on the whole drum kit showed through, especially on his limber use of the lower-register tom-toms, and saxophonist George Cartwright and bassist Mark Dresser served to highlight Norton's expressive avant-garde stylings and reflect his stirring compositional sense, even when the trio is improvising. His music is decidedly free-leaning and avant-garde, but it also bristles with energy. Furthermore, his percussion work outside the drum kit sparkles and enriches what amounts to a stellar outside jazz session.

what to buy next: Virtually all CDs featuring Norton are worthwhile explorations of the dialogue between free/avant-garde jazz and more mainstream music. His recordings with Anthony Braxton's mid/late 1990s groups are each wondrous, especially *Four Compositions: Quartet, August 19, 1995* ♫♫♫ (Braxton House, 1996, prod. Anthony Braxton). Norton also energizes Phillip Johnston's Big Trouble as they play Johnston's sound-

track for *The Unknown* ♫♫♫ (Avant, 1994, prod. Phillip Johnston). Johnston's uptempo, referentially broad-based music is perfect fodder for Norton's pan-stylism.

influences:

◄◄ Barry Altschul, Max Roach, Ed Blackwell, Milt Hinton, Thurman Barker, Famoudou Don Moye, Bobby Previte

Andrew Bartlett

Red Norvo

Born Kenneth Norville, March 31, 1908, in Beardstown, IL.

Red Norvo, a mallet man extraordinaire, was the first musician to play jazz on the unwieldy xylophone and marimba. He transferred his light touch and deft, swinging style to the vibraharp in the early 1940s about the time he joined Benny Goodman. According to published interviews, Norvo prefers to avoid the term "vibraphone" in favor of the trade name of the Deegan instrument that he plays. He disdained the use of the resonator found on the metal instrument, turning the motor off to avoid any hint of a vibrato. Equally adept at using either two or four mallets, Norvo's distinctive clear, clean, crystalline sound sets him apart from most other vibes players. His concept is one of subtlety, sophistication, and intimacy which has made him a superior kind of chamber-jazz player.

Kenneth (Red Norvo) Norville, at about age 14, worked hard one summer in the railroad years and even sold his beloved pet pony to earn enough money to buy his first instrument. While touring with a marimba band on the vaudeville circuit, Norville acquired his present name when bandleader Paul Ash, who routinely butchered the young redhead's name, introduced him as "Norvo," which was repeated in print by *Variety* magazine. While still in vaudeville, Norvo picked up this habit of gazing out over the keyboard and giving his audience a disarming smile, an essential part of the Norvo persona which has been repeatedly captured in photographs over the years. Hired by Paul Whiteman in the late 1920s, after stints with Victor Young and Ben Bernie, Norvo switched to xylophone, met and married Whiteman vocalist Mildred Bailey, and left in 1933 to embark on a band-leading career in New York. While freelancing and playing one nighters for an otherwise dismal year while waiting for his Local 802 union card, Norvo signed a recording contract with Brunswick which resulted in several memorable jazz xylophone performances. He shared a band with Charlie Barnet, shifting to the piano keyboard when necessary, led a sextet at the Famous Door on 52nd Street late in 1935, and recorded for the then fledgling Decca Company. Highly acclaimed arranger Eddie Sauter was part of this group and, when in 1936, Norvo expanded to a larger band for a Commodore Hotel engagement, Sauter contributed soft, swinging, subdued arrangements which highlighted the leader's beautiful woody xylophone sound against light, moving orchestral ensembles sprinkled with solos by Herbie Haymer and Stew Pletcher. The band went on the road and by 1937, Mildred Bailey joined to add her diminutive voice and big heart to the mix. Soon the pair were touted as "Mr. And Mrs. Swing." Norvo continued to lead big bands and then smaller stylish combos before switching from xylophone to vibes in 1943 just prior to joining the Benny Goodman Quintet in 1944. Norvo led a landmark recording session for Comet in 1945, featuring Dizzy Gillespie and Charlie Parker along with swingsters Teddy Wilson, Slam Stewart, and Flip Phillips.

After 12 years of marriage Norvo and Bailey divorced, but remained friends and sometime collaborators even following Norvo's 1946 marriage to Eve Rogers, a sister of former sideman Shorty Rogers. Norvo went on to become a prominent member of Woody Herman's First Herd and was heavily featured with his former sidemen, Flip Phillips and Shorty Rogers, in a 1946 Woodchopper's album understandably reminiscent of Norvo's early 1940s groups. When Herman disbanded in December 1946, Norvo settled in Santa Monica, California close to the Capitol and Warner recording studios. He did numerable pickup recording dates with such diverse artists as Julia Lee, Benny Carter, Dexter Gordon, The Smart Set, Stan Hasselgard, and his old cohort, Benny Goodman.

In 1950, Norvo introduced an awesome trio that featured memorable interplay between his vibraharp, Tal Farlow's guitar, and Charlie Mingus's bass. Later versions found Jimmy Raney and Red Mitchell taking the guitar and bass chairs, with little or no performance letdown. Norvo led a series of tiros and quintets throughout the 1950s, often appearing in the Las Vegas hotel lounges that boosted Frank Sinatra (a rabid Norvo fan) in the main stage show. Sinatra just liked to listen to Norvo and had the quintet accompany him to Australia for a series of concerts in 1959. Benny Goodman fronted an augmented Norvo quintet for a European tour and a successful four-week stand at Manhattan's Basin Street East to close out the 1950s. Norvo's activities slowed down coincident with a serious ear operation in 1961, and then in the early 1970s, he tried retirement only to reemerge and remain active from the mid-1970s through the mid-1980s. Currently in retirement, Red Norvo is a swing era stalwart who made a successful transition to bop and the modern era.

what to buy: An ideal introduction to vibraharpist Red Norvo is *The Red Norvo Trio with Tal Farlow and Charles Mingus* 🎵🎵🎵🎵

(Savoy, 1950–1951, prod. Dick Bock, Albert Marx/Savoy, 1995, reissue prod. Bob Porter). The 1950 and 1951 trio sessions offer leader Norvo, guitarist Farlow, and bassman Mingus in virtuosic ensemble performances. Each member is at once a soloist, an accompanist, and a rhythm section, as the trio cascades through 20 timeless gems full of appealing solos, rhythmic shifts, and subtle, inventive harmonies. Among other tunes, "Little White Lies," "Cheek to Cheek," and "I'll Remember April" receive outstanding treatment along the way. There are 19 more legendary sides from 1953–1955 on *The Red Norvo Trios* 🎵🎵🎵🎵 (Prestige, 1953–1955/1982 prod. Ralph Kaffel/CD reissue 1995). On these recordings, the inventive bass lines are in the capable hands of Red Mitchell and the fluent, seemingly effortless, guitar work is by Jimmy Raney on all but the last four tracks allotted to the dexterous Tal Farlow. The music here is durable, exciting, and swinging, and epitomizes the best in intimate, chamber-style jazz. For examples of musical communication bordering on telepathic, listen to Cole Porter's "Everything I've Got," (with Raney), or the intricate "Farewell to Arms" (with Farlow), trio jazz of the highest order. A typical Norvo Quintet outing is found on 1957 New Year's eve location recording *The Forward Look* 🎵🎵🎵🎵 (Reference Recordings, 1991, prod. Marcia Martin). Taped around the midpoint in Norvo's lengthy career, the 12 selections are representative of the Norvo repertoire of that time, a half dozen standards such as "Mountain Greenery" and "I'm Beginning to See the Light," and six originals by quintet members or other jazz sources. Norvo's subtle light-textured vibes are aided and abetted by guitarist Jimmy Wyble, reedman Jerry Dodgion, bassist Red Wooten, and drummer John Markham. For a live session played without amplification, these sides are remarkably balanced and devoid of any "clams" or glitches that often plague such efforts. The only misnomer here is the assignment of the title "Saturday Night" to a tune that is obviously "Somebody Else Is Taking My Place." Recommended for small band, swing fans, and for the many Las Vegas lounge visitors of the late 1950s who remember a class jazz act when they hear one.

what to buy next: A collection of 1937–1938 Brunswick/Vocalion sessions, *Red Norvo Featuring Mildred Bailey* 🎵🎵🎵🎵 (Columbia/Legacy, 1993, prod. Michael Brooks) is an appealing entry in the Columbia Best of Big Bands series. Here are Red Norvo, singer Mildred Bailey, along with a little band with a big, big sound, courtesy of innovative arranger Eddie Sauter. The subtle swing of this smooth, dynamic organization is enhanced on these sides by Stew Pletcher's trumpet, Hank D'Amico's clarinet, and the booting tenor sax of Herb Haymer or Jerry Jerome.

Seven vocals are flawlessly handled by singer Mildred Bailey while Norvo and his instrumentalists apply their relaxed, easy swing to 11 tunes, including the acclaimed "Remember" which writer/publisher Neil McCaffrey deemed "three of the most precious minutes from the swing era." Incidentally, pianist Bill Miller, who sparks the rhythm section, is the same Bill Miller who went on to become accompanist to avid Norvo fan, Frank Sinatra. For Norvo completists, Hep Records has started a series of reissues that should result in the entire output of the Norvo Orchestra becoming available on CD. These start with *Jivin' the Jeep* ♪♪♪♪ (Hep, 1993, prod. Alastair Robertson, John R.T. Davies), which displays Norvo's early Brunswick solos and powerful 1934 all-star groups, the 1936 Decca sextets and octets, and several obscure oddities. The generous 26-tune collection represents nine different sessions presented chronologically from April 1933 to March 1936. The first 12 tracks read like a swing who's who, with Jimmy Dorsey, Benny Goodman, Artie Shaw, Jack Jenney, Charlie Barnet, Chu Berry, Teddy Wilson, and Gene Krupa taking their turns as participants. But for many fans, it's the leader's pioneering jazz xylophone solos that steal the show. Norvo's "Dance of the Octopus," an imaginative four-mallet feature, has been called by music authority Gunther Schuller, "the most advanced composition of the early 1930s." Six rare Decca sides, with Norvo hiding under the name Ken Kenny, find the redhead on piano instead of xylophone. The Red Norvo Swing Sextet rounds off this collection with "I Got Rhythm" and "Oh, Lady Be Good," both employing ideal tempos with sparkling solos by Norvo, Herbie Haymer, and Stew Pletcher. *Red Norvo: Volume One, The Legendary V-Disc Masters* ♪♪♪♪ (Vintage Jazz Classics, 1990, prod. various) showcases Norvo's Wartime octet which made some V-discs (radio broadcasts) for the armed forces in 1943. These invaluable sides, restored by Seth Winner, feature Norvo right after he switched to vibraharp, hint at the sound of the Woody Herman Woodchoppers to come, largely due to the presence of future Herman stalwarts Flip Phillips and pianist/arranger Ralph Burns. The octet, dubbed Red Norvo and his Overseas Spotlight Band, has 17 tracks while a lively 1944 Norvo quintet, featuring Aaron Sachs on clarinet and alto sax and Remo Palmieri on guitar, handles the last three titles. These sides are precious for their musical worth, their relative obscurity, and because they serve as prime examples of jazz happenings missed during Petrillo's ill-famed 1942–44 recording ban.

best of the rest:
Rock It for Me ♪♪♪♪ (Hep, 1937–1938)
Wigwammin' ♪♪♪ (Hep, 1939/1996)
Red Norvo Trio ♪♪♪ (OJC,1954)

Red Norvo, Volume Two: The Norvo-Mingus-Farlow Trio ♪♪♪♪ (Vintage Jazz Classics, 1990)
Red Norvo Live at the Blue Gardens ♪♪♪ (MusicMasters, 1992)
Red Norvo Orchestra with Mildred Bailey ♪♪♪♪ (Circle, 1993)
Red Norvo: Fabulous Jam Session ♪♪♪♪ (Spotlite, 1995)
(With Red Norvo, Slam Stewart, Bucky Pizzarelli) *The Rhythm Encounters* ♪♪♪♪ (Jazz Classics, 1996)

worth searching for: *Frank Sinatra with the Red Norvo Quintet Live in Australia, 1959* ♪♪♪♪ (Blue Note, 1997, prod. Will Friedwald) finds "Old Blue Eyes" in the company of Red Norvo in a relaxed, intimate, swinging concert at the West Melbourne Stadium in Australia. Ex-Norvo piano man Bill Miller, then with Sinatra, stretches the band to a sextet for 19 representative tunes from the Sinatra songbook. *Slipped Disc 1945–1946* ♪♪♪♪ (Columbia, 1988, prod. Michael Brooks) features Norvo as a prominent sideman with The Benny Goodman Sextet on 14 of 17 cuts, all with Benny Goodman at the top of his game. Appealing solos abound as Teddy Wilson and Mel Powell split the piano chores with bassman Slam Stewart also getting in some savvy licks. This is exuberant swing! At this writing, *Just a Mood—The Red Norvo Small Bands* ♪♪♪♪ (RCA/Bluebird, 1987, reissue prod. Ed Michel), an essential Norvo collection, is in the cut-out category, but is well worth seeking out for the four exemplary West Coast jazz sessions fronted by the vibes man. Trumpeter Harry Edison, tenor saxophonist Ben Webster, and pianist Jimmy Rowles lend their considerable talents to the four extended "blue" pieces which open the set, with Red Norvo making an infrequent return to xylophone for the 1957 "Just a Mood," a remake of a memorable blues tune done 20 years earlier. A 1954 quintet with Buddy Collette (flute) and Tal Farlow (guitar), sharing the spotlight, showcases four more "blue" tunes, all likeable standards. A 1954 septet tackles four "rose" tunes with trumpeter Shorty Rogers, clarinetist Jimmy Giuffre, and pianist Pete Jolly putting a West Coast stamp on the proceedings.

influences:
▶▶ Peter Appleyard, Gary Burton, Cal Tjader

John T. Bitter

NRG Ensemble
/Hal Russell NRG Ensemble
Formed 1978, in Chicago, IL.

Hal Russell, tenor saxophone, soprano saxophone, trumpet, drums, marimba, zither (1978–92); Mars Williams, tenor saxophone, alto saxophone, soprano saxophone, clarinet, woodflute, didgeridoo, toys (1978–80; 1988–present); Steve Hunt, drums, vibes, marimba,

didgeridoo (1980–present); Brian Sandstrom, bass, trumpet, electric guitar, gong (1980–present); Kent Kessler, bass, bass guitar, didgeridoo, trombone (1985–present); Curt Bley, bass (ca. 1980–1985); Chuck Burdelick, tenor saxophone, alto saxophone, clarinet, flute (1980–ca. 1988); Ken Vandermark, tenor saxophone, bass clarinet, clarinet (1992–present).

One of the great free jazz groups of our time, the NRG Ensemble found its song unsung by public recognition for so long that it's amazing that they persevered long enough to see their popularity soar, an ECM recording contract (!), and the respect and admiration of fans of the cutting edge of jazz. Keep in mind, however, that when Hal Russell founded the Ensemble, he'd already been waiting about 15 years for the right musicians with whom to explore his visionary precepts of composition and free improvisation. Founded in 1978 after Mars Williams became captivated by a performance where Russell tried to perform a duet with his pet dog, NRG remained underground for years. Still, the slow times weren't exactly down times, and even after Williams split for NYC in 1980, the Ensemble practiced constantly in Russell's attic. Soon, NRG was recording dates for Nessa, including a session with the late Ayler alumnus Charles Tyler. Live, not only was NRG calling upon their repertoire of over 400 songs, but they were performing amazing free-jazz song cycles with some borderline ridiculous premises, like their (now unavailable) post-ESP cassette recordings of *The St. Valentine's Day Massacre*, and *Time Is All You've Got*, their avant-garde tribute to Artie Shaw. Projects like these only further showed NRG's commitment to both free jazz and entertainment, a combination that no doubt forms a crux for their appeal. In the late 1980s NRG hooked up with dedicated supporter Steve Lake, Williams returned to the fold, they successfully toured Europe, and they released a couple of CDs on the normally much more placid ECM label. Before Russell died unexpectedly three weeks after quadruple bypass surgery in 1992, he made Williams promise to keep the Ensemble going should he not be around. And that Williams has done. With the addition of young lion Ken Vandermark, the NRG Ensemble now more than ever exists as a hub for the Chicago jazz scene. All of the members keep busy with a plethora of side projects, from rock and acid jazz bands to backing visiting European improvisers. Russell may be gone, but the NRG Ensemble continues to keep his fiery spirit alive.

what to buy: *Hal on Earth* ♫♫♫♫ (Abduction, 1995) began as a cassette-only release in 1989, but was kindly reissued so as to show the jazz world what they were missing out on in the late 1980s. Fire, humor, solid rock tightness, out-of-control freak-outs—it's all here, and each member of the Ensemble con-

tributes compositions multiple instrument prowess to the roster. Especially eardrum shattering is some of Brian Sandstrom's guitar playing, which can sound like an amplified tug-of-war between Sonny Sharrock and Pete Cosey. Although Russell's death left its mark in the hearts of his fans, not too many people were surprised when NRG carried on just as vital as ever with *Calling All Mothers* ♫♫♫♫ (Quinnah, 1994, prod. Steve Lake, Mars Williams). Ken Vandermark throws his kindling into the fire, and the quintet keeps the Russell songbook alive by continuing to perform his songs alongside newer compositions.

what to buy next: Telling the tale from start to finish in over 70 minutes, *The Hal Russell Story* ♫♫♫♫ (ECM, 1992, prod. Steve Lake) is some of the best epic narrative free-jazz that you'll ever find. Unfortunately, it's probably the *only* documentation of their epic narrative free-jazz you'll find since much of their other works in this unique genre are out of print. Tracing his roots in vaudeville and big band up through bop to free jazz, Russell's gruff croak enunciates his life story, finishing almost in time to coincide with the real-time end of the story (Russell died mere weeks after completing this recording). Even with these cold, hard facts, this date favors optimism as opposed to the bittersweet. An added bonus: Russell and company perform a balls-out version of the Fleetwood Mac blues-rocker "Oh Well." *This Is My House* ♫♫♫♫ (Delmark, 1996, prod. Steve Lake, Mars Williams) lacks Russell tunes, but the, ahem, energy level rises over the top for one of the wildest NRG dates in its history.

the rest:
NRG Ensemble ♫♫♫♫ (Nessa, 1981)
(With Charles Tyler) *Generation* ♫♫♫♫ (Nessa, 1982)
Conserving NRG ♫♫♫♫ (Principally Jazz, 1984)
The Finnish/Swiss Tour ♫♫♫♫ (ECM, 1990)

worth searching for: Back in the leaner, pre-ECM days, the NRG Ensemble self-released some extremely limited cassettes, of which only *Hal on Earth* has received widespread reissue. You ought to be saying your prayers every night that some kind soul will reissue such cassette rarities as *Fred*, NRG's free-jazz-cum-vaudeville homage to Mr. Astaire, and *The Sound of Music*, which is *that Sound of Music,* put through an Albert Ayler love-thrashing. The best *Sound of Music* ever? Hopefully, one Thanksgiving you'll be able to decide with your own ears.

influences:
◀◀ Albert Ayler
▶▶ Mars Williams

see also: *Hal Russell, Mars Williams, Charles Tyler*

Greg Baise

Hod O'Brien

Born January 19, 1936, in Chicago, IL.

Hod O'Brien grew up in Connecticut and went to the Manhattan School of Music. The first noteworthy job he had as a pianist was with Oscar Pettiford in 1957, but he also worked with J.R. Monterose, Albert Heath, and Rene Thomas. Eventually, O'Brien returned to school, receiving a degree in psychology and a job with New York University. In the '70s, he opened his own club and gigged with Chet Baker, among others.

what to buy: *Opalessence* 𝄪𝄪𝄪 (Criss Cross, 1985, prod. Gerry Teekens) is a quintet date, with O'Brien acting like a sideman instead of a leader in some cases. Putative sidemen on the gig include trumpeter Tom Harrell (who plays flugelhorn as well), baritone saxophone master Pepper Adams, and a rhythm section of bassist Ray Drummond and drummer Kenny Washington. The playing throughout is fine, sometimes making up for some rather ordinary compositions from O'Brien. Luckily, Harrell and Adams contribute some strong tunes to pick up the slack. Adams's "Joy Road" is the standout selection, and the CD includes the previously unreleased first take of the tune. A cover version of Clifford Brown's "The Blues Walk" gets a fine solo from Adams, the unspoken star of the whole session. There are also some guest vocals by Stephanie Nakasian (on "A Handful of Dust"), who has done some work with Jon Hendricks & Company.

the rest:
Ridin' High 𝄪𝄪 (Reservoir, 1991)

influences:
◀◀ Bud Powell, Red Garland, Wynton Kelly, Erroll Garner

Garaud MacTaggart

Anita O'Day

Born Anita Belle Colton, December 18, 1919, in Chicago, IL.

While she may not have invented the form, Anita O'Day certainly perfected the art of scat-singing. Her crisp enunciation, rhythmic energy, and creative delivery heightened the bebop aspect of big-band jazz. O'Day got her start with the Erskine Tate Orchestra as a marathon dancer and part-time singer. One of her partners was Frankie Laine, whom she constantly quizzed about phrasing, pitch, and song selection. After failing auditions for Benny Goodman and Raymond Scott, O'Day was hired by drummer extraordinaire Gene Krupa for his band in 1941. She and trumpeter Roy Eldridge were key components in making Krupa's band one of the best of that era. O'Day's string of hits ("Let Me Off Uptown," "Alreet," "Bolero at the Savoy") propelled Krupa's outfit to its popular peak just before a drug bust forced him to temporarily fold the band. After a brief stint with Woody Herman, O'Day recorded hits with Stan Kenton's band ("And Her Tears Flowed like Wine," "The Lady in Red"), before returning to Krupa's orchestra. O'Day went solo in 1946, recording with Signature and London, but didn't really find a sympathetic label until she signed with Verve Records in 1952. At Verve, O'Day became a highly respected LP artist, collaborating on great sides with Ralph Burns, Billy May, Jimmy Giuffre, Barney Kessel, Cal Tjader, and Oscar Peterson. Her filmed 1958 appearance at the Newport Jazz Festival, *Jazz on a Summer's Day* (where she scats up a storm on "Tea for Two"), is considered her career high-water mark. O'Day cut top-notch disks and toured worldwide well into the 1960s, until her long-standing addiction to heroin nearly took her life, which she candidly writes about in her 1981 book, *High Times, Hard Times*. Drug-free, she rebounded in the 1970s with a smash appearance at the Berlin Jazz Festival, and took complete charge of her recording career by leasing sides from her own label, Emily Records. O'Day appeared in the 1959 Hollywood film, *The Gene Krupa Story*, and played a small role as a jazz singer in the 1971 film, *Zig-Zag*. In 1997 the National Endowment for the Arts presented O'Day with the American Jazz Masters Award. She has influenced countless singers, including June Christy, Chris Connor, Helen Merrill, but none approached their work with the sense of delightful swing and inventiveness that O'Day had mastered in her mid-career years. Although her voice has deteriorated over the past decade, O'Day has occasionally performed and recorded during the 1990s, but her best work on record occurred in the 1950s.

what to buy: Start with any or all of the following Verve collections, which all capture O'Day in peak form. Compiled from sessions in 1956, *Pick Yourself Up* 𝄪𝄪𝄪𝄪 (Verve, 1956/1991, prod. Norman Granz) finds O'Day displaying solid musicianship as she improvises gleefully through 21 songs. Backed primarily by Buddy Bregman's orchestra and a sextet featuring Paul Smith on piano and Barney Kessel on guitar, she interprets standards such as "Let's Face the Music and Dance," "Stars Fell on Alabama," "Sweet Georgia Brown," "I Won't Dance," "Stompin' at the Savoy," and "Let's Begin." Nine tracks not on the original LP are added to the CD reissue. Bregman, a little-known arranger, has crafted sophisticated, swinging arrangements which high-light fine instrumental solos and excellently crafted section work featuring players such as baritone saxophonist Jimmy Giuffre, trombonist Frank Rosolino, trumpeters Conte and Pete Candoli, and alto saxophonists Herb Geller and Bud Shank, and tenor saxmen Georgie Aud and Bob Cooper. Backed by the Oscar Peterson Quartet, O'Day never sounded better than on *Anita Sings the Most* ♫♫♫♫ (Verve, 1957/1990, prod. Norman Granz), a rather remarkable collaboration featuring inspired versions of "Them There Eyes," "Bewitched, Bothered, and Bewildered," "I've Got the World on a String," "You Turned the Tables on Me," and "They Can't Take That Away from Me." Pianist Peterson's quartet includes guitarist Herb Ellis, bassist Ray Brown, and O'Day's regular drummer, John Poole who contribute some fine solo work. O'Day is in exceptional form throughout. Equally enjoyable, *Verve Jazz Masters 49* ♫♫♫♫ (Verve, 1952–62/1995, prod. Norman Granz, Creed Taylor) compiles 16 tunes from O'Day's years with Verve, offering up such savory collations as "A Nightingale in Berkeley Square," "Angel Eyes," and "I Can't Get Started." Her uptempo version of "Them There Eyes," a classic drafted from her Verve album *Anita Sings the Most*, is performed with Oscar Peterson's quartet and features a lickety-split guitar solo from Herb Ellis. During these years, O'Day was backed by orchestras led by Russ Garcia, Gary McFarland, Billy May, Jimmy Giuffre, Johnny Mandel, and Buddy Bregman, as well as small groups led by pianists Gene Harris, Roy Kral, and Oscar Peterson, and vibraphonist Cal Tjader. And these groups are all documented on this wonderful CD that captures O'Day's honeyed vocals. Compiled from several sessions between 1956 and 1963, *Sings the Winners* ♫♫♫♫♫ (Verve, 1963/1990, prod. Norman Granz) features O'Day performing in both big band and small group settings. She pays tribute to various poll-winning musicians, including homage to Duke Ellington ("Take the 'A' Train"), Oscar Peterson ("Tenderly"), Miles Davis ("Four"), and a zestful scatting tribute to Woody Herman ("Four Brothers"), and to Mary Lou Williams ("What's Your Story Morning Glory?"). This is a classic CD, with seven additional, previously unissued tracks, including "Whisper Not" performed with a trio led by Gene Harris, "Blue Champagne" sung with Bill Holman's big band, "Hershey Bar" backed by the Billy May Orchestra, and "Don't Be That Way" done with a sextet that included trumpeter Harry "Sweets" Edison and pianist Paul Smith. "Peel Me a Grape" is classic O'Day, sung with a quartet which includes vibist Cal Tjader. Most of the tunes on this CD are not repeated on the *Verve Jazzmasters '49* compilation. O'Day's style has impacted the jazz community since her early days with Gene Krupa. These recordings on *I Told Ya I Love Ya, Now Get Out*

♫♫♫♫ (Sony, 1947/Signature, 1991, prod. Bob Thiele) illustrate her energy and innovativeness with both rhythm and melodies. This recording includes the classics, "Hi Ho Trailus Boot Whip," featuring pianist Billy Kyle, and "Malaguena," which features the trombone of Ray Sims, Zoot's older brother. The band is credited in the liner notes by Dan Morgenstern as a top studio crew, however, few of the musicians are named. These recordings are some of her first after leaving the Stan Kenton Band, demonstrating her impeccable phrasing and improvisational skills. Ralph Burns is the pianist on "Ain't Gettin' Any Younger." Other tunes included are "Sometimes I'm Happy," "Ace in the Hole," "Key Largo," and a masterful rendition of "What Is This Thing Called Love."

what to buy next: *Swings Cole Porter* ♫♫♫♫ (Verve, 1954–59/1991, prod. Norman Granz) is another compilation from several sessions with the Billy May Orchestra that finds O'Day paying homage to Cole Porter with interpretations true to her swinging improvisational style. The first 12 tracks, including "Just One of Those Things," "You'd Be So Nice to Come Home To," "All of You," "Get out of Town," and "Night and Day," were recorded on April 2 and 9, 1959, with Billy May and His Orchestra. Band members were not documented at the time of the original recording, and remain unknown today. The CD reissue includes six previously unissued tracks that seem to reflect a more vibrant O'Day than on the original LP release. The extra cuts include "Love for Sale," recorded on January 22, 1952 with a septet led by Ralph Burns, and "Just One of Those Things," recorded in April, 1954 with pianist Arnold Ross, guitarist Barney Kessel, bassist Monty Budwig, and drummer Jackie Mills. On December 8, 1955, O'Day recorded "You're the Top" with the Buddy Bregman Orchestra. Other tunes recorded include "My Heart Belongs to Daddy" recorded with Jimmy Giuffre on April 7, 1959, and "Why Shouldn't I," recorded with Bill Holman on August 17, 1960. The Verve era was O'Day's hot period as a solo act, so you could just as easily be satisfied with *Compact Jazz* ♫♫♫♫ (Verve, 1993, prod. Norman Granz), with tracks recorded between 1952 and 1962 with the Gene Krupa, Buddy Bregman, Billy May, and Marty Paich orchestras. *Mello'day* ♫♫♫ (GNP, 1978/Crescendo, 1992, prod. Leonard Feather) finds the singer backed by Lou Levy, Harvey Newmark, and drummer John Poole. Although her voice isn't quite what it was during her Verve years, the ensemble hits a groove and swings, with some great moments. They perform a touchingly gorgeous rendition of Kurt Weill's "Lost in the Stars."

what to avoid: O'Day was well past her prime when she recorded *At Vine Street Live* ♫♫ (DRG, 1991, prod. Hugh Fordin) and *Rules of the Road* ♪ (Pablo, 1993, prod. Buddy Bregman), in which her voice sounds shot on new versions of her old classics.

best of the rest:

This Is Anita ♫♫♫♫ (Verve, 1955)

I Get a Kick out of You ♫♫♫ (Evidence, 1975/1993)

Live in Person ♫♫♫ (Starline, 1976/1993)

In a Mellow Tone ♫♫♫♫ (DRG, 1989)

Wave: Live at Ronnie Scott's ♫♫ (Castle, 1993)

Meets the Big Bands ♫♫♫♫ (Moon, 1994)

That's That ♫♫♫ (Moon, 1995)

Let Me off Uptown ♫♫♫♫ (Pearl, 1996)

Jazz 'round Midnight ♫♫♫ (Verve, 1997)

Anita O'Day Volume 19 (1941–45) ♫♫♫♫ (L'Art Vocal, 1997)

worth searching for: O'Day's early years swinging with Gene Krupa's big band are chronicled on *Sings with Gene Krupa* ♫♫♫♫ (Tristar, 1994, prod. various), which contains many of their biggest hits from the early '40s. *Drum Boogie* ♫♫♫♫ (Legacy, 1993, compilation prod. Michael Brooks) is another solid collection, with "Drum Boogie," "No Name Jive," "How about That Mess," "Rum Boogie," and more solid cuts with and without O'Day. *Cool Heat* ♫♫♫♫ (Verve, 1959), with O'Day singing the arrangements of Jimmy Giuffre, has not yet been released on CD. Songs on the LP version include "Mack the Knife," "Orphan Annie," and "It Had to Be You," the latter which O'Day interprets from slow tempo which builds to a medium, foot-tapping time, and finishes as if she had entered a race. She also performs "Come Rain or Come Shine" and "The Way You Look Tonight." If you find this LP in the used bins, grab it.

influences:

◀◀ Mildred Bailey, Billie Holiday, Connee Boswell, Frankie Laine

▶▶ June Christy, Chris Connor, Helen O'Connell

Susan K. Berlowitz, Ken Burke, and Nancy Ann Lee

Betty O'Hara

A veteran of the USO circuit and the "all-girl bands," multi-instrumentalist Betty O'Hara played in a Hartford, Connecticut big band and for the Hartford Symphony in the 1950s. She moved to California in 1960, married bass trombonist Barrett O'Hara, and during the 1980s, performed numerous studio sessions for TV and film on trumpet and euphonium. She has toured Japan and Brazil, and performed in the bands of Dizzy Gillespie, Bud Freeman and Tommy Newsom. O'Hara currently plays trombone, cornet and euphonium, arranges, and sings with the West Coast all-female big band, Maiden Voyage. She also co-leads a female jazz quintet, Jazz Birds, and appears frequently as a featured soloist at U.S. festivals.

what's available: Though you won't find her name in jazz encyclopedias, Betty O'Hara's abundant talents, as documented on *Horns Aplenty* ♫♫♫♫ (Magnagraphic Jazz Productions, 1985, prod. Dan Grant/ Delmark, 1995, orig. prod. Robert G. Koester), certainly deserve wider recognition. This is the only recorded sample of her rich-toned instrumental solos and tastefully elegant alto voice currently available. And a fine album it is. O'Hara displays versatile artistry, playing trumpet, and with equal technique and fervor, trombone, euphonium, and flugelhorn. As if her superb playing and singing weren't enough, she also wrote all the instrumental arrangements and contributed an original tune to the mix of 10 swinging standards performed with pianist Johnny Varro, bassist Morty Corb, and drummer/vibraphonist Gene Estes. Time-honored tunes such as Hoagy Carmichael's "Stardust," Duke Ellington's "It Don't Mean a Thing (If It Ain't Got That Swing)," Fat Waller's "Alligator Crawl," and other popular favorites allow O'Hara and friends plenty of stretching room. With minimal overdubbing, O'Hara sometimes creates the sound of a horn-section and devises her own instrumental fill to accompany her vocals. Discovering a player of this caliber on such a well-produced CD is pure joy. O'Hara's a pro. And, witnessing her fronting Maiden Voyage at the 1997 Mary Lou Williams Women in Jazz Festival at the Kennedy Center, I can tell you she's just as rousing in live performance.

Nancy Ann Lee

Old & New Dreams

Formed in 1978.

Don Cherry, trumpet; Dewey Redman, tenor sax; Charlie Haden, bass; Ed Blackwell, drums.

Close to 20 years after Ornette Coleman inaugurated the free-jazz revolution with such albums as *The Shape of Jazz to Come* and *This Is Our Music*, four of his ex-sidemen combined to reinterpret the master's classic repertoire. By the late 1970s, when Old and New Dreams came into being, all its members were prominent leaders in their own right; hence, the band never became a full-time endeavor. Still, on their infrequent concerts and recordings, they transcended nostalgia and produced some memorable work. Old and New Dreams was to Coleman very much as the Herbie Hancock–led VSOP was to Miles Davis: a vehicle for the celebration of an absent legend. Unlike VSOP, however, Old and New Dreams often came close to recapturing the magic of the original.

what to buy: *Old & New Dreams* ♫♫♫♪ (ECM, 1979, prod. Manfred Eicher) is a reminder of how great the original Coleman records were. After Ornette forsook acoustic jazz for his funk (mis)adventures, it was left to his disciples to carry the freebop torch. The music here is so strong, however, that Coleman's actual absence is not particularly felt. It's evident that Cherry, Redman, Haden, and Blackwell had grown a great deal in the period between this and the first Coleman albums; "Lonely Woman," for example, has never sounded better.

what to buy next: *Playing* ♫♫♫ (ECM, 1980, prod. Manfred Eicher) is arguably as fine an album as the first. The band benefits greatly from ECM's sound clarity.

the rest:
One for Blackwell ♫♫♫ (Black Saint, 1987)

influences:
◀◀ Ornette Coleman, Miles Davis
▶▶ Herbie Hancock

Chris Kelsey

King Oliver

Born Joseph Oliver, May 11, 1885, in Abend, LA. Died April 8, 1938, in Savannah, GA.

Cornetist King Oliver was a titanic figure who straddled the world of early New Orleans jazz and its rapid spread through recordings in the 1920s. After trombone lessons as a child, he switched to cornet and was playing in the Melrose Brass Band in 1907, later switching to the prestigious Olympia Brass Band. When Oliver was working in Kid Ory's band in 1917, the trombonist declared him "King" of the New Orleans cornetists, a title that Oliver held without dispute. Veteran bassist Bill Johnson invited Oliver to join him in Chicago in 1919, whereupon Oliver began a residence at the Lincoln Gardens that lasted—with time out for a trip to the West Coast—until 1924. Oliver assumed leadership from Johnson, assembling a band that included Baby Dodds on drums and Johnny Dodds on clarinet. In 1922 he invited the young Louis Armstrong north to join him as second cornetist. This only cemented Oliver's place as the central figure in jazz at the time, a beacon to audiences and especially young musicians. From 1925–27 Oliver led the Dixie Syncopators at the Plantation Cafe, constructing a music that increasingly combined the skills of well-trained "reading" musicians with his more spontaneous, expressive associates from New Orleans, like Johnny Dodds and Kid Ory. A disastrous tour, business mistakes, and failing health combined with changing tastes to undo Oliver's career. When he

moved to New York in 1929, painful dental problems often forced him to cede trumpet solos to Louis Metcalf or Red Allen in his recordings. The later years of Oliver's life were a dismal fall from the celebrity he had known in New Orleans and Chicago. Oliver was one of the major inventors of early jazz, creating a wealth of new sounds through his creative use of mutes and buckets to vary his instrument's sound and introduce imitative vocal effects. In the decade following his first recordings, many of his licks and phrases became the stock-in-trade of young jazz trumpeters. Armstrong, Rex Stewart and Harry James were among those who memorized and performed Oliver's solo choruses from his recording of "Dippermouth Blues."

what to buy: The first choice should be the two-CD *King Oliver's Creole Jazz Band: 1923–1924* ♫♫♫♫ (Retrieval, 1997, prod. various). It's the most complete set of Oliver's greatest work. Though ear witnesses claimed these recordings, made with primitive technology and restricted playing times, did the band little justice, they are unquestionably the first great jazz records, with a combination of sounds and rhythms that had never before been recorded and alive with the glorious ensemble improvisation and emotional power that were the hallmarks of New Orleans music. Among the highlights are two versions of Oliver's great solo feature "Dippermouth Blues" and the dual cornet breaks by Oliver and Armstrong. Oliver's duets with pianist Jelly Roll Morton are also included.

what to buy next: Though his later recordings have been overshadowed by the sheer impact of the Creole Jazz Band, they have distinctive qualities of their own. A good collection is *King Oliver and His Dixie Syncopators, 1926–28* ♫♫♫ (Jazz Chronological Classics, 1994, prod. various), which demonstrates the band's increasing use of arrangement in place of collective improvisation on such tracks as "Deep Henderson." And there are strong performances throughout by Oliver and appearances by Kid Ory on trombone and Johnny Dodds and Omer Simeon on clarinet. *King Oliver 1928–30* ♫♫♫ (Jazz Chronological Classics, 1994, prod. various) has the later New York recordings with surprises that range from the scintillating piano of James P. Johnson to a rendition of Jimmie Rodgers's "Everybody Does It in Hawaii," with country musician Roy Smeck's steel guitar mingling with Oliver's muted horn.

best of the rest:
King Oliver: Volume 2, 1926–31 ♫♫♫ (Topaz, 1995)

worth searching for: To read about the complete life of this essential figure, find the book *King Oliver* by Walter Allen and Brian Rust, revised in 1987 by Laurie Wright, published by Storyville.

influences:

◀◀ Buddy Bolden, Freddie Keppard, Bunk Johnson

▶▶ Louis Armstrong, Bubber Miley, Muggsy Spanier, Red Allen, Doc Cheatham

see also: *Louis Armstrong, Johnny Dodds, Kid Orykl*

Stuart Broomer

One World Ensemble

Formed in 1995, in New York, NY.

Daniel Carter, alto and tenor saxophones, flute, trumpet; Sabir Mateen, tenor saxophone, flute; Yuko Fujiyama, piano; Wilber Morris, bass; Susie Ibarra, percussion.

Bringing together three African American males, all veterans of the New York free-jazz scene, and two younger women of, respectively, Japanese and Filipino heritage, this melting-pot collective plays some of the most well-formed improvisation to be heard nowadays.

what's available: *Breathing Together* ♫♫♫ (Freedom, 1995, prod. Wilber Morris, Samuel Rivers) is the group's only album so far and is a model of collective improvisation. Myriad delicate shadings of tone and timbre abound in this sensually appealing performance. This is free-form jazz that whispers rather than screams, but there's no lack of intensity—you can hear the players listening to each other and developing the music organically. Nor does the music threaten to waft away; "Blues Too" is exactly what its title indicates, a slow-burning blues with a firm beat. It's worth noting that this is among the most crystalline recordings ever granted a free-jazz concert (it captures a gig at the Knitting Factory). The label is not to be confused with the Freedom distributed by Arista back in the 1970s (nor is the owner/producer the saxophonist of the same name). If this CD proves hard to procure, the label can be reached toll-free at 1-888-926-JAZZ.

solo outings:
Wilber Morris:
(With David Murray and Dennis Charles) *Wilber Force* ♫♫♫ (DIW, 1983)

Sabir Mateen:
(With Tom Bruno) *Getting Away with Murder* ♫♫♫ (Eremite, 1997)

influences:

◀◀ Ornette Coleman, Charles Tyler, Marion Brown

Steve Holtje

Junko Onishi

Born April 16, 1967 in Kyoto, Japan.

Japanese pianist Junko Onishi has forged her own style from the fleet and quirky virtuosity of Bud Powell, Bobby Timmons's funky-bluesy hard bop, the off-kilter dissonance of Thelonious Monk, and the thunderous modality of McCoy Tyner. Onishi, who grew up in Tokyo, began playing piano at age four. After graduating from high school in 1986, she moved to Boston to attend Berklee College, where she interacted with Delfeayo Marsalis, Roy Hargrove, and Ryan Kisor (among others) in jam sessions. Her first professional gig came in 1988 when she went on tour to France in Slide Hampton's band. The following year she graduated from Berklee at the top of her class and moved to New York, where she played in the Jesse Davis Quintet, the house band at Augie's. She made a triumphal return to Japan with that group, and in 1990–91 played with small groups led by Gary Thomas, Joe Henderson, and Kenny Garrett. She has also worked with Terence Blanchard, Greg Osby, Mingus Dynasty, and the Mingus Big Band. In 1992 she moved back to Japan and formed the trio heard on her first album, *WOW*, with classmates from her Berklee days. Blue Note began licensing her albums for U.S. release after she began using American rhythm sections, and she also made an album with Jackie McLean in 1996.

what to buy: *Live at the Village Vanguard* ♫♫♫♫ (Somethin' Else/Toshiba-EMI, 1994/Blue Note, 1995, prod. Hitoshi Namekata, Junko Onishi) and *Live at the Village Vanguard II* ♫♫♫♫ (Somethin' Else/Toshiba-EMI, 1994/Blue Note, 1996, prod. Hitoshi Namekata, Junko Onishi) are practically treatises in how to keep the piano trio format sounding current and vital. With an adventurous and wide-ranging program of tunes by Ornette Coleman, Charles Mingus, John Lewis, Gigi Gryce, and Thelonious Monk; the standards "Never Let Me Go," "Tea for Two," "Blue Skies," and "Darn That Dream," the Japanese song "Ringo Oiwake," and an original, these two albums never fall into predictability. Onishi plays with power and invention, and bassist Reginald Veal and drummer Herlin Riley provide empathic, hard-driving accompaniment.

what to buy next: *Piano Quintet Suite* ♫♫♫♫ (Somethin' Else/Toshiba-EMI, 1995/Blue Note, 1996, prod. Hitoshi Namekata, Junko Onishi) finally (not counting the McLean album) puts Onishi in a format with horns, and her writing and arranging for quintet are as fresh and versatile as her trio work. Veteran Marcus Belgrave is a sufficiently adventurous trumpeter that he can follow the leader's leaps from Mingus to

Robert Schumann to Ellington (he even essays a Louis Armstrong-esque vocal on "Take the 'A' Train") as well as the twists of her excellent originals. Alto saxist Eiichi Hayashi sounds like a find, and bassist Rodney Whitaker and drummer Tony Rabeson provide supple underpinning. This album is less driven than her full-bore trio work as Onishi takes advantage of the greater variety of timbres, but it still flexes muscle when appropriate.

what to avoid: "Jackie McLean meets Junko Onishi" says the billing on *Hat Trick* 🎵🎵 (Somethin' Else/Toshiba-EMI, 1996/Blue Note, 1996, prod. Hitoshi Namekata, Jackie McLean), which means you'd probably have to look in McLean's bin to find it. Don't bother. McLean is famous for playing sharp, but that tendency is really out of control here—painfully so. It's especially excruciating on a slow version of "A Cottage for Sale." There's often a feeling that Onishi is subordinating her personality to match what the saxophonist wants to do, as if she's reining in some of her more interesting tendencies for fear of being too modal. How ironic that this is the one Blue Note didn't leave sitting around for a year.

the rest:
Cruisin' 🎵🎵🎵 (Somethin' Else/Toshiba-EMI, 1993/Blue Note, 1994)

worth searching for: The trio album *WOW* 🎵🎵🎵 (Somethin' Else/Toshiba-EMI, 1993, prod. Junko Onishi) is only available in Japan. Is Blue Note afraid the Japanese rhythm section—bassist Tomoyuki Shima and drummer Dairiki Hara—will scare off American record buyers? They shouldn't be; Onishi's mixture of half originals, half excellent choices of jazz tunes (Duke Ellington's "Rockin' in Rhythm," Thelonious Monk's "Brilliant Corners," Ornette Coleman's "Broadway Blues," and that old oddball standard "Nature Boy") more than compensates, and she plays with the same verve and imagination heard on the rest of her trio albums.

influences:
⏪ McCoy Tyner, Bud Powell, Bobby Timmons, Thelonious Monk, Toshiko Akiyoshi

Steve Holtje

Oregon
Formed in 1970, in Los Angeles, CA.

Ralph Towner, guitar, keyboards; Paul Candless, woodwinds; Glen Moore, bass; Collin Walcott (died, 1984), percussion, sitar, tabla; Trilok Gurtu, percussion (1985–mid-90s).

Ralph Towner and Glen Moore first met while at the University of Oregon in 1960, and finding they had common musical ground, they began jamming together. They eventually ventured to Europe and gained valuable playing experience in different circles: Towner studying classical guitar in Vienna and Moore backing expatriate jazzmen like Ben Webster and Dexter Gordon in Copenhagen. They eventually found themselves back in the States in the late '60s, and in 1969 they backed folk singer Tim Hardin at Woodstock. Shortly thereafter they went to Los Angeles to record with Hardin, and met UCLA ethnomusicology grad Collin Walcott, as well as Paul McCandless, who was playing with Paul Winter's Consort. McCandless eventually recruited the three others into Winter's group, and after a short while they realized that they should embark on their own venture, christening themselves Oregon. Their unique sound came to the attention of producer Maynard Solomon, and in 1972 they recorded their debut, *Music of Another Present Era*, for his Vanguard label. They made successful tours of Europe, and regularly recorded for Vanguard, then later Elektra and ECM. On November 8, 1984, their tour bus crashed on a foggy German highway, and Walcott and road manager Jo Harting were both killed. This tragic loss caused the survivors to consider disbanding, but they eventually decided to push forward, and Indian-born Trilok Gurtu was chosen to be Oregon's new percussionist. After Gurtu left, the others have continued as a trio. All of the members have recorded solo material as well. Oregon's disparate influences make for an unclassifiable musical amalgam. Their devotion to improvisation offers a clear connection to jazz, but their frequent use of untraditional rhythmic approaches and non-Western instrumentation creates a culturally diverse sound beyond even the fusion experiments jazzmen like Miles Davis were conducting (Walcott actually played with Davis on his *On the Corner*). They could conceivably be considered a "New Age" group on the basis of their relatively quiet, introspective tone, but their complexity and ability to play as an interacting ensemble bring them well above the level of most performers in that category.

what to buy: A worthy introduction to the group's '70s work, *The Essential Oregon* 🎵🎵🎵 (Vanguard, 1981, prod. Oregon) includes two selections from *Moon and Mind*, their 1979 collection of duets; McCandless's oboe, flute, and clarinet float on top of the songs, with Walcott sprinkling the proceedings with the exotic flavoring of sitar and tabla.

what to buy next: The band's move to a major label does not dilute any of their adventurousness on *Roots in the Sky* 🎵🎵🎵 (Elektra, 1979, prod. Oregon); tracks like "Vessel" and "Ogden Road" are among their most tuneful. Their debut recording,

Music of Another Present Era 🎵🎵🎵 (Vanguard, 1972, prod. Oregon), remains a bold statement; all four members contribute to the songwriting, making for a dynamic collection of sounds from all corners of the musical spectrum.

the rest:

Distant Hills 🎵🎵🎵🎵 (Vanguard, 1973)
Winter Light 🎵🎵🎵🎵 (Vanguard, 1974)
In Concert 🎵🎵🎵 (Vanguard, 1975)
Friends 🎵🎵🎵🎵 (Vanguard, 1977)
Oregon/Elvin Jones Together 🎵🎵🎵 (Vanguard, 1977)
Violin 🎵🎵🎵🎵 (Vanguard, 1977)
Out of the Woods 🎵🎵🎵 (Elektra, 1978)
Moon and Mind 🎵🎵🎵 (Vanguard, 1979)
In Performance 🎵🎵🎵 (Elektra, 1980)
Oregon 🎵🎵🎵 (ECM, 1983)
Crossing 🎵🎵🎵🎵 (ECM, 1985)
Ecotopia 🎵🎵🎵 (ECM, 1987)
45th Parallel 🎵🎵🎵 (Portrait, 1989)
Always, Never, and Forever 🎵🎵🎵 (Intuition, 1992)
Troika 🎵🎵🎵 (Intuition, 1995)
Beyond Words 🎵🎵🎵 (Chesky, 1995)
Northwest Passage 🎵🎵🎵 (Intuition, 1997)

influences:

◀◀ Paul Winter, John Coltrane

▶▶ Turtle Island String Quartet, Roger Eno

Eric J. Lawrence

Original Dixieland Jazz Band

Formed in 1916. Disbanded in 1923. Reunited briefly in 1936.

Nick LaRocco, leader, cornet (1916–36); Eddie Edwards, trombone (1916–36); Alcide "Yellow" Nunez, clarinet (1916); Henry Ragas, piano (1916–19); Johay Stein, drums (1916); Tony Sbarbaro, drums (1917–36); Larry Shields, clarinet (1917–36); Emile Christian, trombone (1919–20); J. Russell Robinson (1919–36).

The Original Dixieland Jazz Band was a white New Orleans quintet who in 1916 went to Chicago, where they performed at the Booster club for a season before going on to New York. In 1917 they opened at Reisenweber's Café in Manhattan, billed as the Original Dixieland Jass Band. Most members of the ODJ band had passed through Papa Jack Laine's Reliance Brass Band and had developed showmanship and wild onstage antics that enhanced their performances. In 1918 this competent New Orleans group released their first recording for the Victor Talking Machine Company, recognized by most historians as the first jazz record. While there existed many other similar groups, others had not recorded. The recording by the ODJ band constituted a revolutionary new sound, a groundbreaking event that popularized Dixieland music at a time when middle-class American families were buying their first home phonograph machines. The two-sided single ("Livery Stable Blues" and "Dixie Jass Band One Step") sold over one million copies in 1917, contributing to the increased demand for Dixieland records, and helping to launch the Jazz age, that wild, exuberant period in history known as the "Roaring Twenties." The ODJ band recorded 20 tracks for Columbia and played their lively syncopated music in London, returning to the United States in 1920. But by 1923 the group had lost much of its popularity and disbanded. They reunited briefly under LaRocca's leadership in 1936 and recorded some Victor sides. Another reunion in 1940, without LaRocca, yielded six Bluebird sides.

what's available: *Original Dixieland Jazz Band: 75th Anniversary* 🎵🎵🎵🎵 (Bluebird, 1917–21/RCA, 1992, prod. various) is a collection of all of the original RCA Victor recordings issued by the band between 1917 and 1921. Included is the song jazz scholars cite as the first jazz recording, "Livery Stable Blues," with its honking, mewling horns imitating barnyard animals. Other lively ensemble pieces include popular favorites such as "Original Dixieland One Step," "Margie," "Jazz Me Blues," "Royal Garden Blues," and "Tiger Rag" that continue to be played by Dixieland and swing-jazz groups today. While there are few extended solos to enhance the tunes, this is a collector's item that should also satisfy newcomers who want to begin their quest into jazz history.

worth searching for: Unless you're a completist, don't spend too much time searching for the compilation, *The Complete Original Dixieland Jazz Band (1917–1936)* 🎵🎵🎵🎵 (RCA, 1995, prod. various), because much of the same material is included on the 75th anniversary recording recommended above. The 24 titles by the ODJ band on the French import CD, *Original Dixieland Jazz Band, Volume 2, First Jazz Recordings* 🎵🎵🎵🎵 (Jazz Archives, 1995, prod. various) duplicates some material from the RCA Victor recordings but also includes some rarities from the band's final sessions, which also makes this a collector's gem.

influences:

◀◀ Buddy Bolden, Jelly Roll Morton, King Oliver

▶▶ Louis Armstrong, Red Allen, Wingy Manone, Bob Crosby, Muggsy Spanier, Mezz Mezzrow, Eddie Condon, Pete Fountain, Yank Lawson

Nancy Ann Lee

The Orphan Newsboys

Formed 1988.

Marty Grosz, guitar, vocals; Peter Ecklund, trumpet, cornet, whistler; Bobby Gordon, clarinet; Greg Cohen, bass; Murray Wall, bass.

Guitarist Marty Grosz is well known for his on-stage wit, using various and often humorous names for the little bands he puts together. One of these, The Orphan Newsboys, an ensemble of tune sleuths and hip revivalists, was not born in the recording studios but was formed at the spur of the moment at Western Pennsylvania's 1988 Conneaut Lake Jazz Party. The band today thrives at festivals, jazz society bashes, club dates, and private parties. The co-leaders of this group of modern-day, strolling minstrels are guitarist Grosz and multi-faceted trumpeter-cornetist-whistler Peter Ecklund. Clarinetist Bobby Gordon and bassist Greg Cohen, are most often the other members. With their fresh outlook and willingness to experiment, The Orphan Newsboys have saved many a festival weekend from the tedium of continual jamming by an endless parade of soloists who just met on-stage.

what to buy: *The Orphan Newsboys Live at the L.A. Classic* ♫♫♫ (Jazzology, 1993, prod. Gus P. Statiras) is a set of 13 evergreens that provides an excellent introduction to this group co-led by Grosz and Ecklund. Live-recorded without frills or enhancements at a concert on Labor Day weekend in 1992, it includes ensemble members Bobby Gordon (clarinet), Greg Cohen (bass), and Hal Smith (drums) in superior small band swing numbers such as the Mercer-Astaire tune, "I'm Building Up to an Awful Letdown," "It's the Talk of the Town," and a lengthy take on "Wabash Blues." *The Orphan Newsboys: Laughing at Life* ♫♫♫♫ (Stomp Off, 1990, prod. Marty Grosz, Doug Pomeroy) is a typical set featuring Ecklund, Grosz, Gordon, and Cohen playing seldom-heard tunes, mostly from the past.

what to buy next: Aptly titled, *The Orphan Newsboys: Rhythm for Sale* ♫♫♫♫ (Jazzology, 1997, prod. Gus P. Statiras) features Ecklund's hot, probing cornet; Marty Grosz's rhythm guitar and Waller-inspired vocals; and Bobby Gordon's wistful Marsala-inspired clarinet. Vinnie Giordano, Murray Wall, and Greg Cohen alternate on bass, and guest reedmen Dan Block, Scott Robinson, and Jack Stuckey pop up on several tracks, as do drummers Hal Smith and Arnie Kinsella. At the core or these performances, The Orphan Newsboys remain both entertaining and musically rewarding as they deliver lively renditions from the band's seemingly inexhaustible book. *The Orphan Newsboys: Extra* ♫♫♫♫ (Jazzology, 1990, prod. Marty Grosz, Peter Ecklund) is another worthy addition to the Orphan Newsboys library. This one has reedman Ken Peplowski and bassist Murray

Wall subbing for Gordon and Cohen, respectively, on several numbers that make for a change of pace. Included are four attractive originals, Grosz's "Krazee Gloo" and "Hudson River Lullaby," and Ecklund's "Lookout!" and "Grey Sky Blues."

see also: *Marty Grosz, Peter Ecklund*

John T. Bitter

Kid Ory

Born Edward Ory, December 25, 1886, in La Place, LA. Died January 23, 1973, in Honolulu, HI.

Kid Ory was the first great trombonist in jazz history, a musician whose experience reached to the music's roots, even to sitting in with the legendary cornet player Buddy Bolden. When Ory formed his own band in 1912, it became one of the most popular in New Orleans, a revolving door through which the best of the city's musicians passed, including Mutt Carey, King Oliver, and Louis Armstrong on cornet and the clarinetists Johnny Dodds, Sidney Bechet, and Jimmie Noone. An early voice in the spread of jazz, Ory was in California by 1919 and led the first black small band to record in the New Orleans style, recording "Ory's Creole Trombone" and "Society Blues" in 1922 as Spike's Seven Pods of Pepper. In 1925 he moved to Chicago where he joined King Oliver's Dixie Syncopators, working with them regularly until 1927. In the same period, he recorded with Jelly Roll Morton and with Louis Armstrong on his Hot Fives and Sevens, the latter including Ory's famous composition "Muskrat Ramble." Ory returned to Los Angeles in 1929, then left the music business in 1933. He spent the swing era first working with his brother on a chicken farm and later taking work as a railroad clerk until resuming performing in 1942. A 1944 radio broadcast with Orson Welles returned him to prominence. While many of his best-known contemporaries had died, including Morton, Oliver, and Johnny Dodds, Ory continued to play the traditional style with great vigor, a powerful and elemental voice whether in counterpoint or solo. With a shifting line-up of skillful and enthusiastic veterans mixing refinement and bluster, Kid Ory's Creole Jazz Band was a jewel of the traditional revival. He continued performing until 1966, when he retired to Hawaii. With the lack of other possibilities in the historical record, Ory can be credited with the assembly, if not the virtual invention, of the fundamental jazz trombone style, the energizing bleats, smears and glissandos that stretch from the birth of the music to the best contemporary players, like Ray Anderson and George Lewis.

what to buy: For an introduction to Ory's pioneering work, *Ory's Creole Trombone: Greatest Recordings 1922–44* ♫♫♫♫ (ASV/

Living Era, 1994, prod. various) is a survey that includes those first recordings of "Ory's Creole Trombone" and "Society Blues;" a sampling of his classic work with Oliver, Armstrong, and Morton; and a brash "High Society" from the Welles radio broadcast. Arguably the best document of his spirited later work is *Kid Ory's Creole Jazz Band (1954)* 🎵🎵🎵🎵 (Good Time Jazz, 1991, prod. Lester Koenig). Ory's rugged trombone is complemented by Alvin Alcorn's clear trumpet leads, Don Ewell's refined piano, and Minor Hall's inventive drumming on repertoire from the traditional warhorse "When the Saints Go Marching In" to "Gettysburg March."

what to buy next: In 1944 Nesuhi Ertegun, later famous as a founder of Atlantic records, started the Crescent label in Los Angeles to record Ory's band. As a result of rather complex negotiations, the results can now be found as either *Kid Ory's Creole Jazz Band 1944–45* 🎵🎵🎵🎵 (Good Time Jazz, 1991) or as *The Legendary Crescent Recordings* 🎵🎵🎵🎵 (GHB, 1995). On either label, it's essential traditional jazz, with the trombonist joined by old associates Mutt Carey on trumpet and Omer Simeon or Darnell Howard on clarinet. The moving "Blues for Jimmie Noone" and the traditional rags, "Maple Leaf Rag." and "1919 Rag," stand out.

best of the rest:

At the Green Room, Volume 1 🎵🎵🎵 (American Music, 1947/1997)
King of the Tailgate Trombone 🎵🎵🎵 (American Music, 1948/ 1995)
Favorites 🎵🎵🎵 (Good Time Jazz, 1956/1987)
Kid Ory's Creole Jazz Band (1956):The Legendary Kid 🎵🎵🎵 (Good Time Jazz, 1990)
This Kid's the Greatest 🎵🎵🎵 (Good Time Jazz, 1992)

influences:

▶▶ George Brunis, Jack Teagarden, Turk Murphy, Roswell Rudd, Ray Anderson

see also: *King Oliver, Louis Armstrong, Jelly Roll Morton*

Stuart Broomer

Greg Osby

Born August 3, 1960, in St. Louis, MO.

Greg Osby started out as an R&B player, and it was only while attending Howard University that he started to gravitate towards jazz. Osby then moved to Boston where he took classes at Berklee in composing and arranging before finally settling in New York City to pursue his career. Early employers included Woody Shaw, Dizzy Gillespie and, most prominently, Jack DeJohnette. Osby is also, for better or worse, lumped in with the M-

Base school of performance, whose most prominent exponent is Steve Coleman. Through his association with Coleman, Osby came into contact with many of the emerging players on the New York jazz scene, including Cassandra Wilson, Geri Allen, and Robin Eubanks. He can also be found playing on albums by Coleman's old boss, bassist Dave Holland, and the fine pianist/composer Andrew Hill. Osby has experimented with blending hip hop and jazz, working with producers Ali Shaheed Muhammed and Street Element to create albums that grafted his acerbic toned alto playing onto rap beats. Of late he has taken the lessons learned from those experiences and his work with M-Base to synthesize his own individual approach to rhythm and harmony even while adapting them to a more mainstream jazz mode.

what to buy: Not since the time Osby worked with giants like Hill and DeJohnette has he taken part in such a coherent jazz album as the no-nonsense *Art Forum* 🎵🎵🎵🎵 (Blue Note, prod. Greg Osby, 1996), filled with original material that hovers near the loft jazz ideal without sacrificing a sense of post-modern romanticism. There is no mucking around with contemporary pop trends (rap), and no excursions into M-Base funk, just plenty of hard-edged playing by a cast of 10 jazz studs ranging from James Williams and Darrell Grant on pianos to Robin Eubanks (trombone) and Jeff Watts (drums).

what to buy next: M-Base cruises in the background of *Further Ado* 🎵🎵🎵🎵 (Blue Note, prod. Greg Osby, 1997), but the thrust of the music is closer to the tradition found in *Art Forum*. While not as strong, *Further Ado*, with its steps away from the jazz/rap hybrid of *Black Book* and *3-D Lifestyles*, seems to confirm the direction Osby will take in future efforts. Blending jazz and rap was a trend in the mid-90s and *Black Book* 🎵🎵🎵 (Blue Note, 1995, prod. Greg Osby) was one of the few hybrids that made the possibilities real instead of creating an inchoate mashing of disparate forms. Pianist Mulgrew Miller has a lot to do with the album's success as a jazz release. Plenty of interesting alto playing from Osby, but if the idea of rap/jazz mutations leaves you queasy, this is probably not the first place to sample his playing.

the rest:
3-D Lifestyles 🎵🎵 (Blue Note, 1993)

worth searching for: Although the group moniker for this project is the M-Base Collective, *Anatomy of a Groove* 🎵🎵🎵🎵 (DIW/Columbia, prod. Steve Coleman, 1992) is basically a Steve Coleman album that features Osby and Coleman running parallel alto riffs up and down the spines of complex grooves. Osby and Cassandra Wilson wrote "Non-Fiction," a lean, slowly shifting piece of neo-space funk that is an album highlight.

influences:

◀◀ Steve Coleman, Von Freeman, Arthur Blythe

▶▶ Gary Thomas

Garaud MacTaggart

Other Dimensions in Music

Formed 1981, in New York, NY.

Roy Campbell, trumpet, flugelhorn, pocket trumpet; Daniel Carter, alto and tenor saxophones, flute, trumpet; William Parker, bass; Rashid Bakr, drums.

The unusually long-lived quartet Other Dimensions in Music is an all-star aggregation of some of New York's most respected free jazz players. Since all the members are busy with their own careers—Campbell and Parker have well-documented work as leaders, Bakr plays with Cecil Taylor, and Carter has a bigger reputation than his small discography would suggest—the group doesn't exist on a regular basis, but when it does come together it's a special occasion, one much-anticipated by devotees of the scene.

what to buy: *Now!* 𝄞𝄞𝄞𝄞 (AUM Fidelity, 1998, prod. Other Dimensions in Music, Steven Joerg) has more variety of structure and style than the group's debut, and the additional eight years of experience, both together and apart, shows in the even tighter cohesion of the members' interaction. The title of "Whispers & Cries of Change" gives a good indication of the breadth of dynamics employed, transcending the reputation New York free musicians have of always playing loudly and with unrelenting intensity. Here, the intensity can be that of a whisper—just as commanding of attention, and giving away its secrets only gradually.

what to buy next: *Other Dimensions in Music* 𝄞𝄞𝄞𝄞 (Silkheart, 1990, prod. Other Dimensions in Music) has four long group improvisations, all over 15 minutes in length. This is some of the most accessible, immediately appealing free jazz to come out of New York, with a great deal of attention paid to varying the instrumental textures and the music's density. The improvisations feel like suites and, whether by arrangement or intuition, sound acutely structured.

influences:

◀◀ New York Contemporary Five

▶▶ One World Ensemble

see also: *Roy Campbell, William Parker*

Steve Holtje

Johnny Otis

Born John Veliotes, on December 28, 1921, in Vallejo, CA.

Drummer, vibraphonist, vocalist, and bandleader Johnny Otis grew up in Berkeley and has been playing jazz and R&B for nearly 60 years. He began playing in Count Otis Matthews's West Oakland House Rockers in the 1930s, and performed in the territory bands of George Morrison and Lloyd Hunter before moving to Los Angeles in 1943 to join Harlan Leonard's Rockets. He also recorded for Philo/Aladdin with Lester Young and Illinois Jacquet. Otis played briefly with Count Basie before forming his own Basie-influenced big band in 1945 with saxophonists Paul Quinichette, Preston Love, and James Van Streeter, and bassist Curtis Counce. The band featured arrangements by Bill Doggett. The Otis Big Band recorded for Excelsior in 1945 with hit single "Harlem Nocturne." The big band broke up in 1946, and Otis started leading smaller R&B combos, sounding often like scaled-down versions of the big bands. At various times, his bands included guitarists Pete Lewis and Jimmy Nolen, and saxophonists Ben Webster, Preston Love, Earle Warren, and James Van Streeter.

Otis was one of the biggest selling artists on the R&B charts in the late 1940s and a major figure in the development of this musical form. He discovered many players who became major artists and stars in their own right, including Little Esther, the Robins, Etta James, Big Mama Thornton, and Jackie Wilson. With the emergence of rock-and-roll, he had a hit record with "Willie and the Hand Jive." He produced numerous recording sessions for a variety of labels including Modern, Savoy, Mercury, Duke/Peacock, and Federal, with artists such as Jimmy Witherspoon, Esther Phillips, Big Mama Thornton, Johnny "Guitar" Watson, and others. During the mid-1960s and 1970s, he continued to champion classic blues and R&B artists and their music. His album *Cold Shot* introduced phenomenal teenage son, Shuggie, on guitar and vocalist Delmar "Mighty Mouth" Evans, and later Otis signed with Epic. Otis produced an afternoon show at the 1970 Monterey Jazz Festival that featured classic R&B performers like Roy Milton, Big Joe Turner, Eddie "Cleanhead" Vinson, Esther Phillips, and others. Otis continues to perform and record, and in 1992 returned to his big band roots with the album, *Spirit of the Black Territory Bands*.

what to buy: *The Original Johnny Otis Show* 𝄞𝄞𝄞𝄞 (Savoy, 1945–1950, prod. Ralph Bass/JVC, 1994, prod. Bob Porter) contains four big band recordings, including two Jimmy Rushing vocals and "Harlem Nocturne," along with hot jump instrumentals with the guitar of Pete Lewis, and vocals by Esther Phillips, Mel Walker, and the Robins. *The Johnny Otis Show Live at Monterey* &&&& (Epic, 1970, prod. Johnny Otis/Legacy, 1993, prod. Lawrence Cohn) captures legendary R&B pioneers Ivory Joe Turner, Esther Phillips, Big Joe Turner, Roy Brown, Eddie "Cleanhead" Vinson, and Roy Milton performing classic songs backed by a terrific band that showcases underrated Clifford Solomon on tenor saxophone.

what to buy next: *The Spirit of the Black Territory Big Bands* &&&& (Arhoolie 1992, prod. Johnny Otis, Tom Morgan) is Otis's homage to the music of the great black big bands, with spirited renditions of songs associated with the bands of Count Basie, Jay McShann, Lionel Hampton, and Duke Ellington, and featuring orchestrations by Otis's son, Shuggie.

the rest:
The New Johnny Otis Show &&&& (Alligator, 1981)
Good Lovin' Blues &&& (Ace (UK) 1990)

worth searching for: *Creepin' with the Cats* &&& (Ace (UK), 1991, prod. Johnny Otis) is a reissue of rare recordings from Otis's Dig/Ultra recordings with a mix of blues, riff-based instrumentals, vocal groups, and rock 'n' roll. *The Johnny Otis Show Live 1970* &&& (Wolf) is the soundtrack of an educational television show Otis produced with Charles Brown, Esther Phillips, Big Joe Turner, Lowell Fulson, Roy Milton, and Cleanhead Vinson to recreate the legendary Barrel House Club. But it is not quite musically up to the level of the Monterey recording. *Johnny Otis Presents the Roots of R&B* &&&& (Laserlight, 1993, prod. Johnny Otis) is a five-volume, budget reissue-series, each with 10 songs taken from 1970s recordings Otis made with artists Charles Brown, Eddie "Cleanhead" Vinson, Louis Jordan, Joe Turner, Richard Berry, Joe Liggins, and others, and with new versions of their most famous songs.

influences:
◀◀ Charles Brown, Nat "King" Cole, Count Basie, Jo Jones, Lionel Hampton

▶▶ Roomful of Blues

Ron Weinstock

Tony Oxley

Born June 15, 1938, in Sheffield, England.

Although known as one of the premier free jazz drummer/percussionsts, Tony Oxley initially made his impact as the house drummer at Ronnie Scott's club in London in the mid-1960s,

backing many visiting U.S. musicians. His early discography finds him behind such unexpected players as pianist Bill Evans and violinist Sugarcane Harris. He was also a drummer on what is arguably guitarist John McLaughlin's best album *Extrapolation.* Oxley was concurrently involved in the early British free jazz experiments (from 1966) and had an early trio with guitarist Derek Bailey and then-bassist (now composer) Gavin Bryars. His first recordings were for CBS and RCA and he used these opportunities to record decidedly modern works using such musicians as Bailey, saxophonist Evan Parker, trumpeter Kenny Wheeler, and trombonist Paul Rutherford. His most high-profile collaboration has been with pianist Cecil Taylor, an association that lasted from 1988 to 1992. Oxley is one of the most intelligent and subtle of Europe's free-jazz percussionists. His fleet, jittery drumming is light (as in airy) and textural yet it pushes the music forward with a powerful momentum. He frequently uses an extended kit and has incorporated electronics into his setup. Great insight into his performing style can be seen in the Cecil Taylor video, *Burning Poles.*

what to buy: The second of Oxley's Celebration Orchestra recordings (the first was the vinyl-only *Tomorrow Is Here* on Dossier), *The Enchanted Messenger* &&&& (Soul Note, 1994, prod. Giovanni Bonandrini) is a massive work divided into 19 sections. The sections are marked out as features for various group combinations and the work is reminiscent of Barry's Guy's early charts for the London Jazz Composer's Orchestra. The masterstroke here is the matching of the vocal artistry of vocalist Phil Minton with that most vocal of trumpeters, Bill Dixon. A powerful and profound big-band recording. A fascinating quartet recording, *Tony Oxley* &&&& (Incus, 1992) matches veterans Oxley and guitarist Derek Bailey with two musicians from the new generation of free improvisers: Pat Thomas on electronics and keyboards and Matt Wand on drum machines and tape switchboard. It's a fruitful collaboration, with Wand's tapes adding some decidedly new sounds to the Incus catalog.

worth searching for: Any of Oxley's three early recordings could stand to be reissued; they have only been heard by a handful of people. *Ichnos* &&&& (RCA, 1971) is an excellent sampling of his early work, one of the finest early recordings of the British free improvisation scene and is a testament to Oxley's group organizing skills as well as his unique drumming.

influences:
◀◀ Art Blakey, Elvin Jones, John Coltrane, Anthony Braxton

▶▶ John Stevens, Jamie Muir

Robert Iannapollo

Makoto Ozone

Born March 25, 1961, in Kobe, Japan.

One of the more important pianists to become famous in the 1980s, Makoto Ozone started playing organ when he was four and began formal piano lessons at 12. He made his professional debut with the Tadao Kitano Arrow Jazz Orchestra in 1976 and attended the Berklee School of Music from 1980 to 1984. He became a fixture in Gary Burton's bands during the '80s and had made 10 solo recordings, though only 1997's *The Trio* is in print. Ozone is a fluid player whose influences range from straight bop to classical and new age.

what's available: *The Trio* 𝄞𝄞𝄞𝄞 (Verve, 1997, prod. Makoto Ozone) is a good, though not exceptional, outing, with 10 compositions written by Ozone. The strongest pieces are the ballads, including "Home," featuring Jon Scofield playing acoustic. The up-tempo pieces, which are in the modern mainstream mode, are also satisfying.

influences:

◀◀ Oscar Peterson, Erroll Garner, Bud Powell, Bill Evans, Chick Corea, Herbie Hancock, Keith Jarrett, Lyle Mays

Paul MacArthur

Oran "Hot Lips" Page

Born January 27, 1908, in Dallas, TX. Died November 5, 1954, New York, NY.

Hot Lips Page was a great swing trumpeter and blues vocalist who early on worked with Ma Rainey, Troy Floyd's band, and others, before joining the legendary Blue Devils from 1928–1931. After the demise of the Blue Devils, Page played in Bennie Moten's Orchestra and was on many of their influential recordings in the early 1930s. It is his trumpet that rides out their trademark tune, "Moten Swing." After Moten's premature death, Page starred among the featured players in Count Basie's band, but went solo just before Basie left Kansas City. Page led a big band which recorded for Victor, and made a number of other recordings with smaller groups. He was featured in Artie Shaw's Orchestra from 1941–42. After that, he mainly freelanced and frequented jam sessions. Page played the Paris Jazz Festival in 1949 along with Sidney Bechet, Miles

Davis, and Charlie Parker. Many of his later recordings were with small jump bands, and bridged the jazz and R&B genres.

what's available: *The Chronological Hot Lips Page, 1938–1940* 𝄞𝄞𝄞𝄞 (Classics, 1991, prod. various) includes small group recordings Page made for Decca and all of the big band sides he recorded for Victor's subsidiary, Bluebird. A septet session in January, 1943 includes Buster Smith on saxophone and clarinet, while a November, 1946 session has Pete Johnson on piano with Page recording "Lafayette" and "South" from the Bennie Moten book. *The Chronological Hot Lips Page, 1940–1944* 𝄞𝄞𝄞𝄞 (Classics), includes small group sessions of blues vocals and hot swing instrumentals for the Bluebird, Commodore, and Savoy labels.

worth searching for: *After Hours in Harlem* 𝄞𝄞𝄞𝄞 (Onyx, 1973, reissue prod. Don Schlitten) is an out-of-print vinyl album of Jerry Newman's 1940–1941 wire recordings from Minton's, valuable for the appearances of stride pianist Donald Lambert and the great Thelonious Monk. Well worth checking out if issued on compact disc, *Basie Beginnings (1929–1932)* 𝄞𝄞𝄞𝄞 (RCA, 1929–32) is a compilation of Bennie Moten big band recordings which includes many of the Moten Band's most famous sides and contains several hot solos from Page.

influences:

◀◀ Louis Armstrong

Ron Weinstock

Jeff Palmer

Born 1951, in Jackson Heights, NY.

A fine organist who has incorporated the influence of Hammond-B3 pioneers Jimmy Smith and Larry Young, Jeff Palmer is a resourceful veteran with a distinctive, hard-driving style. His father was a professional guitarist and Palmer was raised listening to jazz. He started on accordion, but in his early teens began playing an organ his parents had at home. Unlike many organists, Palmer never played the piano. He taught himself the Hammond-B3, which led to steady employment through the 1960s during the height of the instrument's popularity. Palmer has worked with guitarists Grant Green, George Benson, John Scofield, and John Abercrombie, toured with Paul Bley, and recorded sessions for Statiras, Soul Note, Audioquest, and Reservoir.

what to buy: A highly rewarding quartet session with a deep blues feeling, *Shades of the Pine* 𝄞𝄞𝄞𝄞 (Reservoir, 1995, prod. Mark Feldman) surrounds the top flight organist Jeff Palmer with prodigious bandmates in tenor saxophonist Billy Pierce, guitarist John Abercrombie, and drummer Marvin "Smitty" Smith. Palmer wrote all of the nine tunes except for Monk's "Ba-lue Bolivar Ba-lues-are," which turns into an extended workout full of sly, backhanded humor. The group settles into some serious grooves, but avoids soul-jazz cliches throughout due to Smitty's beautifully textured traps work and Pierce's harmonically advanced playing, especially on "Pressure Point" and "Hokus Pokus," where Pierce takes a particularly passionate solo.

what to buy next: An adventurous session by a cooperative quartet, *Abracadabra* &&&& (Soul Note, 1988, prod. Giovanni Bonandrini) features Palmer, Dave Liebman (soprano sax), John Abercrombie (guitar synth), and Adam Nussbaum (drums). The music is loose and atmospheric, and while Palmer wrote much of the material, the tunes are mostly launching pads for improvisational flights. Palmer's organ provides accents and fills, but it's Liebman's passionate soprano work that dominates the well-played, but not particularly memorable session.

the rest:
Laser Wizard &&&& (Statiras, 1986)
Ease On &&&& (Audioquest, 1993)
Island Universe &&&& (Soul Note, 1996)

influences:
◀◀ Larry Young, Jimmy Smith

Andrew Gilbert

Tena Palmer
See: Chelsea Bridge

Eddie Palmieri
Born December 15, 1936, in New York, NY.

Eddie Palmieri started playing the piano when he was eight years old, picking up the rudiments of performance from his older brother Charlie. It was Charlie who introduced Eddie to his first formal teacher in 1949 even though the younger Palmieri was starting to gravitate toward the timbales. This interest in percussion was to remain with him even though he switched back to playing the piano a few years later.

During the mid- and late 1950s Palmieri played for a variety of leaders, the best known of whom were vocalists Vincentico Valdez and Tito Rodriguez. When Palmieri finally went out on his own in 1960, he formed a charanga (along the lines of the ones led by his brother Charlie) called La Perfecta. Jazz ele-

O**RAN** "H**OT** L**IPS**" P**AGE**
(**WITH VARIOUS ARTISTS**)

song "I Got an Uncle in Harlem"
album *Stars of the Apollo*
(Columbia, 1949/1993)
instrument Trumpet and vocals

Monster Solo

ments started creeping into his playing and writing in the mid-1960s just before the band broke up in 1968. Palmieri continued exploring his own personal fusion of Latin music and jazz during the 1970s, with an emphasis on the newer electronic gadgets being brought into the market. His later material shows an increased growth in both arranging and composition (although his electronic experimentation appears less often nowadays) and he, along with Cachao and Tito Puente, can now be considered among the most popular elder statesmen in the world of Latin jazz.

what to buy: *Palmas* &&&& (Elektra/Nonesuch, 1994, prod. Eddie Palmieri) shows the jazz influences in Palmieri's music more than anything he had done up to this time. His association with trumpeter Brian Lynch, trombonist Conrad Herwig, and alto saxophonist Donald Harrison continues past this release, but the formidable front line created by these three talented jazzmen adds an improvisational punch to the awesomely talented Latin rhythm section already on hand. There are no weak tunes among the entire set, making this (despite Palmieri's distinguished catalog of other albums) the one album jazz fans should have. On *Arete* 𝄢𝄢𝄢𝄢 (RMM/Tropijazz, 1995, prod. Eddie Palmieri), listeners should go right to "Definitely In" where Palmieri's slightly skewed arrangement and Tyner-esque piano voicings blend Latin and jazz elements as well as they've ever been done by anyone. "Waltz For My Grandchildren" has a pleasant Monk/Brubeck-goes-Latin feel to it and the rhythm fest at the front end of "Sixes in Motion" is a pulsating delight. The one caveat for this release is based upon Palmieri's vocal groans and moans (à la Keith Jarrett, Oscar Peterson, and Glenn Gould) when he plays piano on the otherwise commendable "Sisters." For some folks, it's an annoyance that might detract from the overall quality of the album.

what to buy next: *Lucumi, Macumba, Voodoo Leyendas* 𝄢𝄢𝄢𝄢 (Sony Discos, 1978/1995, prod. Eddie Palmieri) was a groundbreaking recording for Palmieri in the same way that 1979's *Rican/Struction* was for Ray Barretto, yet it sold poorly. In many ways, this is more a pop album than jazz, but the skillful arrangements incorporating both Brazilian and R&B elements are better than what one would hear on a rock session from the same period. "Colombia Te Canto" and the Santeria-inflected percussion of "Mi Congo Te Llama," as well as the title tune, make this one of Palmieri's more interesting experiments. A solid album throughout, *Vortex* 𝄢𝄢𝄢 (RMM/Tropijazz, 1996, prod. Eddie Palmieri), is marred slightly by a useless, though clever, Latinized arrangement of Beethoven's "Minuet in G" and Palmieri's distracting vocal rumbles and wheezes. Noteworthy tunes include "Iriaida," with it's surprisingly tasteful use of electronic sounds, and "Vanilla Extract," an extended version of Palmieri's earlier hit, "Chocolate Ice Cream."

best of the rest:
Live at Sing Sing , Vol. 1 𝄢𝄢𝄢𝄢 (Tico, 1974/1994)
Champagne 𝄢𝄢𝄢𝄢 (Tico, 1968/1992)
Mozambique 𝄢𝄢𝄢𝄢 (Tico, 1965/1992)
Palo Pa Rumba 𝄢𝄢𝄢𝄢 (Fania, 1984/1992)

worth searching for: Search for two rousing concert albums by the Tropijazz All-Stars that feature long works by Palmieri, "Suite 925-2828" on *Tropijazz All-Stars: Volume One* 𝄢𝄢𝄢𝄢 (Tropijazz, 1996, prod. Ralph Mercado) and "Nobel Cruise" on *Tropijazz All-Stars: Volume Two* 𝄢𝄢𝄢 (Tropijazz, 1997, prod. Ralph Mercado). Other personnel on these albums include Tito Puente, Giovanni Hidalgo, David Valentin, Charlie Sepulveda, J.P. Torres, and David Sanchez.

influences:
◀◀ Tito Puente, Charlie Palmieri, Thelonious Monk, McCoy Tyner, Bud Powell, Benny Golson

▶▶ Michel Camilo, Hilton Ruiz

Garaud MacTaggart

Charlie Parker

Born Charles Christopher Parker, August 29, 1920, in Kansas City, MO. Died March 12, 1955, in New York, NY.

More than any individual apart from Louis Armstrong, virtuoso alto saxophonist Charlie Parker cast his shadow over succeeding generations of jazz musicians. An authoritatively idiomatic Southwest blues shouter who absorbed Lester Young's floating linear phrasing and Art Tatum's harmonic wizardry, Parker stunned his contemporaries on mid-1940s recordings such as "Red Cross," "Now's the Time," and "Ko-Ko" with the brilliance, inventiveness, and innate logic of his solos, executed at unheard-of velocities that bespoke utter mastery of his instrument. Implying his antecedents, but beholden to none, Parker had developed an advanced chromatic and rhythmic language, incorporating sophisticated harmonic/melodic substitutions, absolute command of time and timbre, poetic control of dynamics. The implications of the music he and his contemporaries Dizzy Gillespie, Thelonious Monk, Bud Powell, and Max Roach created in the 1940s and 1950s, inadequately labeled "Bebop," have been only partially absorbed. Parker influenced not only saxophonists but musicians on every instrument. Through his recorded legacy, he continues to astonish us with his freshness and creativity.

what to buy: Since Parker's universally influential, groundbreaking Savoy recordings from 1944–45 and 1947–48 are not issued on CD in a codified manner (see the "Worth Searching For" section), the best place for the uninitiated listener to start a Parker collection is with the beautifully produced, pristinely remastered compilations *Bird's Best Bop* 𝄢𝄢𝄢𝄢, (Verve, 1948–53/1995, prod. Norman Granz) and *Charlie Parker with Strings: The Master Takes* 𝄢𝄢𝄢𝄢 (Verve, 1950–52/1995, prod. Norman Granz). *Best Bop* culls 14 Parker compositions plus two standards performed by small groups on six studio sessions done for Norman Granz. Here are three tracks ("Bloomdido", "Leap Frog", "Relaxing with Lee") from Parker's only recording with Bebop co-founders Dizzy Gillespie and Thelonious Monk. Miles Davis comes back to reconstitute the front line of Parker's 1947–48 working quintet on the mercurial "Au Privave," "She Rote," the definitive "K.C. Blues," and passionate

"Star Eyes" from 1951. His concise statements on "Blues for Alice" and "Swedish Schnapps," accompanied by the unparalleled rhythm section of pianist John Lewis, bassist Ray Brown, and drummer Kenny Clarke, are packed with information. You don't need to hear the lyrics to "The Song Is You" after listening to Parker sing it through his saxophone on a late 1952 session with pianist Hank Jones, bassist Teddy Kotick, and Max Roach. And Parker's astonishing July 1953 solo on his chops-busting original "Confirmation," spurred by Max Roach, sets the standard that all jazz improvisers must aspire to. As for Parker's album with strings, no one ever played with the lyrical fire Parker conjured up on the recordings that comprise this album. His poetic declamations over lush orchestrations on "Just Friends," "Laura," "East of the Sun," "I'm in the Mood for Love," "Easy to Love," "April in Paris," "Repetition," "Rocker," "Autumn in New York," and "Temptation," are classics of their kind. If you have the funds, simply buy the 10-CD box set, *The Complete Charlie Parker on Verve* 𝒜𝒜𝒜𝒜 (Verve, 1946–54/ 1988, prod. Norman Granz, Phil Schaap), compiled with love and the most painstaking discographical exactitude by Parker scholar Phil Schaap. This contains Parker's recordings for Verve in chronological order, including alternate takes and Jazz at the Philharmonic appearances. The sound is superb throughout. Between March 1946 and November 1947, Parker recorded a series of masterpieces for Dial, a small independent label based in Los Angeles. Long unavailable in the States, these works can now be found compiled in the two-CD set, *The Legendary Dial Masters* 𝒜𝒜𝒜𝒜 (Jazz Classics, 1946–47/1994, prod. Ross Russell). Bird's Dial sessions are perhaps the most overtly autobiographical of his recordings, spanning a vast range of emotions and styles, from the anguished depths of the 1946 "Lover Man," the lyric masterpiece "Embraceable You," and the rhythmic abstractions of "Klactoveesedstene." You'll find some of Bird's greatest themes as well, such as "Moose the Mooche," "Yardbird Suite," "Dexterity," "Dewey Square," and "Scrapple from the Apple." The sound quality doesn't match the Verve recordings, but the remasterings are more than adequate. Numerous location and aircheck recordings of Parker performances exist; collecting them can become a delicious obsession. A good place to begin is with the live-recorded *Jazz at Massey Hall* 𝒜𝒜𝒜𝒜 (Debut, 1953/OJC, 1987, prod. Charles Mingus), a document of a 1953 performance at Toronto's Massey Hall, featuring Parker with a quintet of jazz immortals—trumpeter Dizzy Gillespie, pianist Bud Powell, bassist Charles Mingus, and drummer Max Roach. Parker plays with time like a cat with a mouse at the conclusion of his relaxed solo on the reharmonized "Perdido," and you can hear the

CHARLIE PARKER

song "Perdido"
album *Jazz at Massey Hall*
(Debut, 1953/OJC, 1987)
instrument Alto saxophone

Monster Solo

searing intensity of his locutions on "Salt Peanuts," "Wee," and "Night in Tunisia." Gillespie ("my worthy constituent") and Powell matched Parker note for note on this glorious May evening; whoever engineered captured all the instruments with clarity. *Summit Meeting at Birdland* 𝒜𝒜𝒜𝒜 (Tristar, 1950/1997), an aircheck of Parker with trumpet master Fats Navarro, pianist Bud Powell (at his most demonic), and drummer Art Blakey (at his most primal), is this writer's personal Parker desert island pick. Hear "Round Midnight" or "Move" and "Street Beat" to hear jazz played at its highest level. The music on this import CD is the reason why a generation of musicians devoted body and soul to studying Charlie Parker. Fidelity is rather dicey, yet it's still a great listen.

what to buy next: *Bebop and Bird* 𝒜𝒜𝒜𝒜 (Atlantic, 1940–53/ Rhino, 1997) is an intelligently compiled retrospective of Savoy, Dial, and Verve essentials and judiciously selected airchecks. Regarding its merits as an overview, Ornithologists will quibble over this, that, and the next thing—but it's the best available. *Charlie Parker: The Complete Birth of the Bebop* 𝒜𝒜𝒜𝒜 (Stash,

1940–45/1991, prod. Will Friedwald, Norman Saks) contains an unaccompanied "Variations on 'Honeysuckle Rose' and 'Body and Soul'" from 1940, four fully mature 1942 performances with a local Kansas City ensemble, fascinating improvisations by Bird on tenor (his instrument with the unrecorded Earl Hines Orchestra of 1942–43 that incubated Parker, Dizzy Gillespie, and Billy Eckstine) in the most informal situations, an unbearably burning live "Sweet Georgia Brown" from 1945 with Dizzy Gillespie and Don Byas sharing the front line, and three late 1945 airchecks that document the Parker-Gillespie group live from Billy Berg's in Hollywood. You're getting this for the wealth of amazing music, not for the fidelity.

worth searching for: Parker and Gillespie understood each other so well that they sound like one instrument when they play their astonishing unisons on *Dizzy Gillespie: And His Sextets and Orchestra* ♫♫♫♫ (Discovery, 1945–46/1988, prod. Albert Marx) and *Diz 'n' Bird at Carnegie Hall* ♫♫♫♫ (Blue Note, 1947/Roost, 1997, prod. Teddy Reig, Michael Cuscuna). Their sextet recordings on Discovery ("Shaw Nuff" and "Salt Peanuts") are essential; their five quintet collaborations on the Carnegie Hall concert contain some of the most ebullient, virtuosic improvising ever documented. You can't have the full Charles Christopher Parker story without listening to his Savoy recordings. If you don't hear them, you won't know about "Ko-Ko," "Red Cross," "Now's the Time," "Donna Lee," "Parker's Mood," "Ah-Leu-Cha," "Chasin' the Bird," "Constellation," and "Barbados," and you will not know Bird. Savoy issued a series of LPs in the 1950's in chaotic manner, which Denon, the current owner of the great catalog, has incomprehensibly issued in CD packages that replicate the original 30-minute LPs down to the misprints on the back-covers. The sound is good, and any serious listener needs these recordings. Phil Schaap's long-out-of-print, comprehensive, late 1980s remastering, *Bird: The Complete Savoy Recordings* ♫♫♫♫ (Savoy, 1944–48, prod. Buck Ram, Teddy Reig) is the definitive document. Should you ever come upon it, or any of its satellite issues, snap them up. The also-out-of-print mid-1980s compilation *Bird/The Savoy Recordings (Master Takes)* ♫♫♫♫ (Savoy, 1944–48/1985, prod. Bob Porter) is a good substitute, should you find it. Parker's 1941 solos on "Hootie Blues" and "Swingmatism" with the Jay McShann Orchestra, on *The Jay McShann Orchestra: Blues from Kansas City* ♫♫♫♫ (Decca Jazz, 1941–43/GRP, 1992, prod. Dave Dexter, Orrin

Charlie Parker **(Archive Photos)**

Keepnews), first brought his sound to the notice of musicians who hadn't yet heard him live. He didn't record again until 1944. So if locating choice live Parker is a delicious obsession, imagine the ecstasy of hearing early airchecks and transcription recordings that document the period when he was working out his concept.

influences:

◀◀ Louis Armstrong, Lester Young, Buster Smith, Art Tatum, Don Byas, Biddy Fleet

▶▶ John Coltrane, Ornette Coleman, Sonny Stitt, Cannonball Adderley, Jackie McLean, Eric Dolphy, Lou Donaldson, Charles McPherson, Gary Bartz

Ted Panken

Evan Parker

Born April 5, 1944, in Bristol, England.

Among the most important of the European post-free saxophonists, Parker is instantly recognizable, whether playing in groups or solo. He began playing at age 16, spurred by a keen interest in John Coltrane and Paul Desmond. He then moved to London in 1966 and soon met up with John Stevens, Kenny Wheeler, Trevor Watts, and Derek Bailey; they played at the legendary Little Theatre club as the Spontaneous Music Ensemble, which released the classic *Karyobin*. Moving on from SME, Parker began playing in a few regular groups, including duos with Derek Bailey and John Stevens, and with the Music Improvisation Company (featuring Parker, Bailey, Hugh Davies, Jamie Muir, and, later, Christine Jeffries). Parker also co-founded the Incus label with Bailey and percussionist Tony Oxley, which would become possibly the most influential label of improvised music, documenting the incredibly fertile English scene. His duo with percussionist Paul Lytton, beginning in 1969, inspired Parker to experiment with many homemade instruments. Eventually, bassist Barry Guy's arrival cemented Parker's longest and most well-known group, the Evan Parker Trio. Parker's solo playing, which revolutionized the instrument using circular breathing, extreme control of overtones, and multiphonics, created a hybrid of Albert Ayler's new sound world and the long-stream ideas of Terry Riley. In the '90s, Parker has also shown interest in the electronic processing of his instrument's sound and in ensemble playing. As a side interest, Parker has also appeared on records by artists as diverse as the English comics Mortimer and Reeves and reclusive pop genius Scott Walker.

what to buy: *Saxophone Solos* ✍✍✍ (Incus, 1975/Chronoscope, 1994) has a white-hot intensity, and the reissue includes some new tracks.

what to buy next: *50th Birthday Concert* ✍✍✍✔ (Leo, 1994), a two-disc set, is a good way to find out about Parker's two trios, Parker/Paul Lytton/Barry Guy and Parker/Alexander Von Schlippenbach/Paul Lovens. Recorded at a concert honoring Parker's 50th birthday, it features two exemplerary sets from both groups.

what to avoid: The culprit on *Hall of Mirrors* ✍✍ (MM+T, 1990) is Walter Pratti's pedestrian use of electronics to process Parker's free improvising. The uninspired use of delays, harmonizers, and reverbs sound more like a Yamaha demonstration disc than a record of music.

worth searching for: Parker has played on more than 150 albums, including: the Music Improvisation Company's *Music Improvisation Company* ✍✍✍ (ECM, 1970); Derek Bailey and Han Bennink's *Topography of the Lungs* ✍✍✍ (Incus, 1970); Paul Lytton's *Collective Calls* ✍✍✍ (Incus, 1972) and *Live at the Unity Theatre* ✍✍✍ (Incus, 1975); Cecil Taylor and Tristan Honsinger's *The Snake Decides* ✍✍✍ (Incus, 1986); Barry Guy, Eddie Prevost, and Keith Rowe's *Supersession* ✍✍✍ (Matchless, 1990); and Lawrence Casserley's *Solar Wind* ✍✍✍ (Touch, 1997).

influences:

◀◀ Paul Desmond, Albert Ayler, John Coltrane

▶▶ John Zorn, Ned Rothenberg, John Butcher

Jim O'Rourke

Leon Parker

Born 1965, in White Plains, NY.

Leon Parker is the most original and inventive drummer of his generation, a player who has pioneered a new approach to the trap set by radically stripping down his kit to the very basics. Raised in a family of jazz lovers, Parker began playing drums at an early age and by high school was a self-taught percussionist interested in Latin jazz, soul, blues, and funk. He spent time in Barry Harris's Jazz Cultural Theater and with saxophonist Arnie Lawrence before becoming a regular at Augie's from 1987–88, a jam session scene that attracted young players such as Larry Goldings, Peter Bernstein, and Jesse Davis. At Augie's he began experimenting with his stripped-down kit, playing just a cymbal and a snare and eventually just a cymbal. He made his recording debut with bassist Harvie Swartz on *In a Different Light*,

and through Swartz landed a job with Sheila Jordan touring Japan and a gig with Kenny Barron at Bradley's where he played one cymbal. He and his wife Lisa spent most of 1989 in Spain and Portugal, performing on the street. Shortly after returning to New York, Parker began a long-running relationship with Art D'Lugoff's Village Gate, leading a series of trios and groups with musicians such as pianists Bruce Barth, Bill Charlap, and Jacky Terrasson, bassists Ed Howard, Sean Smith, and Ugonna Okegwo, and saxophonists David Sanchez and Joshua Redman. Parker developed a strong musical relationship with tenor saxophonist Dewey Redman, touring Europe with him a number of times. He credits Redman for allowing him the freedom to develop his distinctive rhythmic approach. Parker has played on recordings with Barth and singer Madeleine Peyroux, on Terrasson's two Blue Note CDs and David Sanchez's debut *The Departure*. He has recorded two strong albums of his own.

what to buy: One of the most significant debut albums of the decade, *Above & Below* ✍✍✍✍ (Epicure, 1994, prod. Joel Dorn) opens and closes with percussion solos where Leon Parker uses his body as his instrument. The session covers five originals, two Monk pieces, two standards, and a powerfully swinging version of Juan Tizol's "Caravan," featuring Adam Cruz on percussion and David Sanchez on tenor and soprano saxophones. Parker's explorations of Monk are particularly fascinating, as he turns "Epistrophy" into a complex Afro-Cuban romp with Cruz and tenor saxophonist Mark Turner, and "Bemsha Swing" into a knotty, tempo-shifting joyride with Jacky Terrasson, Ugonna Okegwo, and Cruz.

what to buy next: Parker's second album, *Belief* ✍✍✍✍ (Columbia, 1996, prod. Joel Dorn) is full of highly-rewarding improvised music, though it incorporates a myriad of influences and moves farther away from straight-ahead jazz than his first session. For most of the album he trades the trap set in for various and sundry percussion instruments, and often ends up playing 6/8 time signatures. The album's two highlights, "Belief" and "Ray of Light," feature a pianoless septet with Tom Harrell (trumpet), Steve Wilson (alto sax), and Steve Davis (trombone). Using bells, shakers, dumbek, and wordless vocals, Parker creates a number of striking (and sometimes eerie) aural landscapes, often accompanied by Adam Cruz's percussion work and Natalie Cushman's percussion and vocals.

worth searching for: A thrilling trio session featuring bassist Ugonna Okegwo and drummer Leon Parker, *Reach* ✍✍✍✍ (Blue Note, 1995, prod. Jacky Terrasson) captures Jacky Terrasson reworking three standards and five original tunes. From the playful, dizzying piece "The Rat Race," with its repeated use of *The Twilight Zone* theme, to the lyrical, rhapsodic "Baby Plum," Terrasson writes tunes that seem to develop directly out of his keyboard approach. It's the interaction within the trio that makes this such an enjoyable session, with Okegwo's firm bass work and Parker's beautifully textured drumming creating a highly elastic ensemble sound.

influences:

◀◀ Roy Haynes, Ben Riley

Andrew Gilbert

Maceo Parker

Born February 14, 1943, in Kinston, NC.

With one "Maceo! Blow your horn!" Parker would launch into a jabbing, funky, staccatto sax solo that blew the roof off the mutha and changed soul music forever. His greatest recognition came as the distinctively named sax man in James Brown's band. But after leaving the band and going solo for good in 1990, he shifted into a distinctive brand of soul-jazz. Parker, whose parents both sang (his father also played piano and drums for church services), began his career playing in a band with his brothers. (They performed during intermissions for their uncle's band.) He joined Brown, who led perhaps the most famous funk bands of all time, at age 21.

what to buy: *Roots Revisited* 𝄢𝄢𝄢 (Verve, 1990, prod. Stephan Myner) carries on in the tradition of soul-jazz progenitors like Ray Charles, Hank Crawford, and Stanley Turrentine. "Children's World" shows a distinct James Brown influence, and Sly Stone's "In Time," with guest bassist Bootsy Collins, is Maceo at his best. *Southern Exposure* 𝄢𝄢𝄢 (Jive/Novus, 1993, prod. Stephan Meyner, Maceo Parker) has a roomful of guests, from the New Orleans Rebirth Brass Band to members of the Meters. But the eclectic personnel in no way dilutes the music. The arrangement of "Mercy, Mercy, Mercy" runs at a faster clip than usual, and has a shout chorus that quotes Funkadelic's "Flashlight."

what to buy next: *Mo' Roots* 𝄢𝄢𝄢 (Verve, 1991, prod. Stephan Myner) is from the same mold as *Roots Revisited* and features terrific cover versions of Marvin Gaye's "Let's Get It On" and Horace Silver's "Sister Sadie."

what to avoid: *Life on Planet Groove* 𝄢𝄢 (Verve, 1992, prod. Stephan Myner) is a loose, sprawling live session. Unfortunately, guest saxophonist Candy Dulfer's insipid and blatant David Sanborn imitation detracts from the rest of the album.

EVAN PARKER
(PARKER-GUY-LYTTON
AND MARILYN CRISPELL)

song "Sumach"

album *Natives and Aliens*
(Leo, 1996/1997)

instrument Tenor saxophone

Monster Solo

worth searching for: *Doin' Their Own Thing* 𝄢𝄢𝄢 (House of the Fox, 1970, prod. Maceo Parker) is prototypical early '70s funk. The album is mostly instrumental and crackles with funky soul energy.

influences:

◀◀ Earl Bostic, Louis Jordan, James Brown

▶▶ Prince, David Sanborn, Clarence Clemons, Deee-Lite, Public Enemy, Parliament-Funkadelic

James Eason

William Parker

Born January 10, 1952 in the Bronx, NY.

This veteran bassist has already built a quarter-century career as a ubiquitous presence on the New York free-jazz scene, appearing on records by Charles Gayle, Cecil Taylor, Matthew Shipp, Billy Bang, David S. Ware, Frank Lowe, Bill Dixon, Roscoe Mitchell, Jemeel Moondoc, Rashied Ali's Prima Materia, and many more. As a leader he makes music with a social conscience that nonetheless avoids preachiness; he's also a superbly imagistic poet. The combination of Parker's long experience in jazz and his personal openness have made him a mentor figure on the New York scene.

Parker began playing bass only in his last year of high school, after having played cello. He dates the start of his professional career in 1972, and his dues-paying period encompassed an eclectic range of music, from Maxine Sullivan's group to a Cuban folkloric band in which he was the youngest member. New York's loft scene was important to his development, with such spaces as the Firehouse, Studio Rivbea (where he was one of the house bassists), and Studio We where he played with Andrew Hill, Billy Higgins, and others during a legendary flowering of free jazz. Parker supplemented this on-the-job training with private lessons with bassists Richard Davis, Wilbur Ware, Jimmy Garrison, Milt Hinton, and Art Davis. In 1975 Parker was invited by Don Cherry to play in his group at the Five Spot, the bassist's first gig at a major jazz club. Parker's 1980–91 tenure in various Cecil Taylor groups helped bring him world-wide notice. Since then he's become one of the most-used bassists on the Downtown NY scene and has recorded as a leader. Parker's music builds on some of Taylor's techniques and assumptions but largely reflects Parker's own multi-faceted persona. Its roiling undertow and constant stimulation and ferment seem to have little of the anger associated with free jazz—the force of his playing is better characterized as joyful energy. Beyond Parker's many collaborations and work in other people's groups (notably with David S. Ware and Matthew Shipp), his main focus is on his big band, which he calls the Little Huey Creative Music Orchestra (Little Huey being one of his poetic personas), and the smaller In Order to Survive, which on record has been a quartet and a sextet. These bands often spotlight younger players, with alto saxist Rob Brown, tenorman Assif Tsahar, and drummer Susie Ibarra among those who have begun to be noticed.

what to buy: *Sunrise in the Tone World* 𝄢𝄢𝄢𝄢 (AUM Fidelity, 1997, prod. William Parker, Steven Joerg) is an epic two-CD set which encapsulates Parker's philosophy in musical terms. It aims for—and achieves—a transcendent state which heals the inner being of the listener. This is hardly new-age music, however, and that healing is achieved through ecstatic catharsis. Using graphic scores to structure the performances, Parker provides plenty of room for this group of over 20 players to express themselves individually. Among the familiar names to be heard are Roy Campbell, Steve Swell, Rob Brown, Assif Tsahar,

Gregg Bendian, Cooper Moore, Vinny Golia, and Susie Ibarra. In addition to the moments when specific players are spotlighted, one of the delights of this set is the spontaneous interplay among multiple players and the panoply of instrumental colors deployed by Parker.

what to buy next: *In Order to Survive* 𝄢𝄢𝄢𝄢 (Black Saint, 1995, prod. William Parker) is the first recording of Parker's already classic small group, which here includes alto saxophonist Rob Brown, trombonist Grachan Moncur III, pianist Cooper Moore, trumpeter Lewis Barnes, and drummer Denis Charles (replaced on one of the four tracks by Jackson Krall). The non-hierarchical organization of the music allows the music to ebb and flow as different instruments rise to the surface in an organic, non-egoistic manner and comment on the overall texture while becoming part of it. *Invisible Weave* 𝄢𝄢𝄢 (No More, 1997, prod. Alan Schneider), with Joe Morris, is a dense and intricate guitar-bass recording that was completely improvised from start to finish—free jazz at its most abstract. It is a good representation of Parker's duo work. He can fill the entire sonic canvas himself, especially when he's bowing, while Morris weaves rapid-fire picking into busy, coiling lines. This collaboration yields an introverted album, but digging into its compact sound reveals many bright epiphanies.

the rest:
William Parker:
Testimony 𝄢𝄢𝄢 (Zero In, 1995)

The Little Huey Creative Music Orchestra:
Flowers Grow in My Room 𝄢𝄢𝄢𝄢 (Centering Music, 1994)

In Order to Survive:
Compassion Seizes Bed-Stuy 𝄢𝄢𝄢𝄢 (Homestead, 1996)

influences:
◀◀ Richard Davis, Wilbur Ware, Jimmy Garrison, Art Davis

▶▶ Hill Green, Vattal Cherry, Hal Onserud, Assif Tsahar, Marco Enedi

Steve Holtje

Horace Parlan
Born January 19, 1931, in Pittsburgh, PA.

Parlan overcame the challenge of childhood polio and a partially crippled right hand to develop an idiosyncratic piano style that blended interesting block chords with seemingly scattershot right hand leads. He became one in a series of intriguing pianists for Charles Mingus during the late '50s before joining groups led by Booker Ervin, Eddie "Lockjaw" Davis, Johnny Griffin, and Rahsaan Roland Kirk. Weary of the treatment afforded jazz musicians in America, in 1973 Parlan left for Denmark, where he recorded a batch of albums for Steeple Chase, including two wonderful duet titles with saxophonist Archie Shepp.

what to buy: On *No Blues* 🎜🎜🎜 (SteepleChase, 1976, prod. Nils Winther), alongside awesome bass playing from Niels-Henning Orsted Pedersen and slick drumming by Tony Inzalaco, Parlan produces some fine piano performances. Every tune on this album is a cover version except for Parlan's own "A Theme for Ahmad" (dedicated to Ahmad Jamal); his take on Cedar Walton's "Holy Land" and the Richard Rodgers chestnut "Have You Met Miss Jones?" deserve special notice. For extra measure there is Parlan's classy rendition of "Darn That Dream," which wasn't on the original album release.

what to buy next: On the trio date *Blue Parlan* 🎜🎜🎜♩ (Steeple-Chase, 1979, prod. Nils Winther), Wilbur Little is the bassist and Dannie Richmond, Parlan's former rhythm cohort in the Charles Mingus band, provides the basic pulse on drums. Here's another fine selection of material, including a wonderful take on Mingus's "Goodbye Pork Pie Hat" and a majestically paced "Monk's Mood." Parlan the composer contributes only one original to the mix, a semi-funky theme à la early Herbie Hancock called "Cynthia's Dance."

the rest:
On the Spur of the Moment 🎜🎜🎜 (Blue Note, 1962)
Happy Frame of Mind 🎜🎜🎜♩ (Blue Note, 1963)
Arrival 🎜🎜🎜 (SteepleChase, 1974)
Musically Yours 🎜🎜🎜 (SteepleChase, 1980)
The Maestro 🎜🎜🎜 (SteepleChase, 1980)
Pannonica 🎜🎜♩ (Enja, 1981)
Glad I Found You 🎜🎜🎜 (SteepleChase, 1984)
Like Someone in Love 🎜🎜🎜 (SteepleChase, 1984)
Little Esther 🎜🎜 (Soul Note, 1988)

influences:
⏮ Ahmad Jamal, Bud Powell, Erroll Garner
⏭ Bennie Green, Don Pullen

Garaud MacTaggart

Alan Pasqua

Born June 28, 1952, in NJ.

Alan Pasqua started his professional music career in 1976 as a member of the New Tony Williams Lifetime (at the same time

guitarist Allan Holdsworth joined). At the other end of the musical spectrum, Alan has been a member of the corporate rock groups Giant and Van Stephenson. Through the years he has amassed credits as an in-demand session keyboardist, working extensively with a wide array of musicians that includes Bob Dylan, Eddie Money, Carlos Santana, Rick Springfield, the Temptations, Pat Benatar, Allan Holdsworth, and Ry Cooder. Some of his acclaimed recordings include Ruben Blades's *Nothing but the Truth*, Lee Ritenour's *Alive in L.A.*, Eddie Daniels's *Under the Influence*, Sammy Hagar's *Three Lock Box*, Bryan Duncan's *Mercy*, Whitesnake's *Greatest Hits*, and the soundtracks to *Footloose, Fatal Attraction,* and *The Color Purple.*

Growing up in New Jersey, Pasqua began studing piano at the age of seven. By the time he enrolled at Indiana University, he was already an accomplished classical and jazz pianist. To further his musical proficiency, Pasqua attended the New England Conservatory of Music, studying with Jaki Bayard, Thad Jones, George Russell, and Gunther Schuller. After joining the New Tony Williams Lifetime, the band recorded two albums, *Believe It* and *Million Dollar Legs*, which are considered blueprints in the development of fusion. The stellar list of jazz musicians he has played with since then includes Joe Henderson, Stanley Clarke, Gary Burton, James Moody, Gary Peacock, Eddie Daniels, Peter Erskine, Jack DeJohnette, John Patitucci, Reggie Workman, the Thad Jones & Mel Lewis Jazz Orchestra, Sam Rivers, Sheila Jordan, Joe Williams, Frank Foster, Don Ellis, and Ralph Simon (who produced both of Pasqua's albums as a leader). Pasqua waited until he was 40 to release his debut as a leader, *Milagro*, which exhibits uncommon maturity compositionally as well as musically. He continued the tradition with the release of *Dedications* in 1996; both were recorded for the Postcards label. Listening to these recordings, it is easy to see that Pasqua's earliest musical experiences involved playing in trios. Although both of these recordings are augmented with other players, the spirit of the trio is never abandoned.

what's available: *Milagro* 🎜🎜🎜 (Postcards, 1994, prod. Ralph Simon) is Pasqua's debut as a leader. Pasqua, Jack DeJohnette, Dave Holland, and Michael Brecker—all burning musicians by nature—lay a musical foundation that displays a more subtle strength, building upon compositions that are well-crafted and arranged. The cautious use of other players adds a natural hue to the color and shading. For many critics, this record is stronger than expected. *Dedications* 🎜🎜🎜 (Postcards, 1996, prod. Ralph Simon) is a collection of sensitive, insightful contributions from some very sure-handed musicians. The core trio is Pasqua on piano, Dave Holland on bass, and Paul Motian on drums. Half of the tracks are augmented by Gary Bartz on alto saxophone, Michael Brecker on soprano and tenor saxophone, and Randy Brecker on trumpet. A legendary lineup on some classic-sounding tracks.

influences:

◀◀ Bill Evans, Horace Silver, Hank Jones, McCoy Tyner

Ralph Burnett

Joe Pass

Born Joseph Anthony Jacobi Passalaqua, January 13, 1929, in New Brunswick NJ. Died May 23, 1994, in Los Angeles, CA.

Joe Pass was both the apotheosis of the bop guitar tradition and an innovator who perfected a solo style that turned the guitar into a self-sufficient band. One of the latest blooming jazz giants, Pass began recording the albums that set standards for technical fluency well after he turned 40. Pass became a professional while still in high school, playing in swing bands, including a stint with Tony Pastor. He toured with Charlie Barnet in 1947, but after a tour of duty in the military, drug addiction derailed his career and he didn't return to the scene until the early 1960s. Settling in Los Angeles, Pass began making a name for himself with a series of recordings for Pacific Jazz, including his first classic album, 1963's *For Django*. He spent the next decade playing local gigs, performing with Gerald Wilson, Les McCann, and George Shearing, and touring with Benny Goodman in 1973. That was the year Norman Granz signed him to Pablo, and Pass became a guitar legend with the release of *Virtuoso*, a landmark solo recording that has lost none of its potency over time. During the next two decades, Pass recorded prolifically for Pablo, including sessions with Ella Fitzgerald, Oscar Peterson, Dizzy Gillespie, Milt Jackson, Duke Ellington, and Count Basie, as well as numerous albums of his own, many of which have been reissued on CD. Pass remained active recording and performing right up until his death from cancer, including an extensive tour with "Guitar Summit," a band with Paco Peña, Pepe Romero, and Leo Kottke.

what to buy: The definitive Pass anthology, *Guitar Virtuoso* 🎵🎵🎵🎵 (Pablo, 1997, prod. Norman Granz, Eric Miller) is a four-disc set that covers the fret master's glory years from 1973 to 1992. The first disc contains 17 tracks of Pass's stunning solo guitar work, including four beautiful acoustic pieces from one of his last recordings, *Songs for Ellen*. Disc two covers collaborations with Duke Ellington, Oscar Peterson, Jimmy Rowles, and various small group sessions, while the third disc features live solo and small group performances. The final disc contains

duets with Ella Fitzgerald, John Pisano, Niels Pedersen, and Zoot Sims, and three priceless tracks of Pass (in two rhythm sections) accompanying Sarah Vaughan. There are no treasures from the vault here, and most of the original recordings have been reissued on CD, but *Guitar Virtuoso* is a well-conceived, highly representative selection from Pass's inimitable oeuvre. Like *The Incredible Jazz Guitar of Wes Montgomery*, *Virtuoso* 🎵🎵🎵🎵 (Pablo, 1974/1987, prod. Norman Granz) forever changed what people thought was possible on a guitar. Using conventional technique, Pass supplies his own bass lines and plays rhythmic chords and a melody line simultaneously. He plays mostly standard songs, but there's nothing standard about this jaw-dropping solo album. A must for guitar lovers or fans of jazz guitar. A trio session with bassist Ray Brown and drummer Bobby Durham, *Portraits of Duke Ellington* 🎵🎵🎵🎵 (Pablo, 1974, prod. Norman Granz) is Pass's loving homage to the Duke, a gorgeous album covering nine of the best known tunes from Ellingtonia. There's not a weak track on the album ("In a Mellowtone" and "Solitude" are personal favorites). The second of his five *Virtuoso* sessions, *Virtuoso #2* 🎵🎵🎵🎵 (Pablo, 1977/1987, prod. Norman Granz) finds Pass taking on more contemporary material, including his stunning versions of Coltrane's "Giant Steps," two Chick Corea tunes, and even Marv Albert's "Feelings," which he actually turns into a credible jazz vehicle. His funky romp on Carl Perkins's "Grooveyard" is another highlight.

what to buy next: A relaxed late-night kind of session, *One for My Baby* 🎵🎵🎵🎵 (Pablo, 1989, prod. Eric Miller) pairs Pass's seemingly casual brilliance with the supremely soulful tenor sax of Plas Johnson, the piano and organ of Gerald Wiggins, the rich bass of Andy Simpkins, and the tasteful traps work of Tootie Heath. Besides Pass's two original blues numbers and Milt Jackson's "Bluesology," the tunes are all evergreens, such as "I Remember You," "Poinciana," and "The Song Is You." Pass recorded frequently toward the end of his life, and *Joe Pass & Co.: Joe Pass Quartet Live at Yoshi's* 🎵🎵🎵🎵 (Pablo, 1993, prod. Eric Miller) is one of his best later albums, a swinging live session recorded at Yoshi's Nitespot in Oakland. His working quartet included guitarist John Pisano and drummer Colin Bailey, musicians he had been playing with for three decades, while bassist Monty Budwig (who died only a month after this recording) fits right in with the proceedings. Covering standards, blues, and two Sonny Rollins classics, "Oleo" and "Doxy," Pass plays with his usual relaxed sophistication and casual brilliance. Few guitarists would want to be in a one-on-one situation with Joe Pass, but John Pisano had been playing

with the singular virtuoso for close to 30 years when *Duets*
𝄢𝄢𝄢𝄢 (Pablo, 1996, prod. Eric Miller) was recorded in 1991. A
casual, experimental session, full of stimulating interplay, the
material is mostly extemporaneous riffs suggested by slides
projected on the studio wall, though occasionally they settle
into a tune, such as Horace Silver's "Lonely Woman" or "Alone
Together." *Duets* is a unique addition to Pass's extensive
discography. Another superlative solo outing by Pass, *I Remember Charlie Parker* 𝄢𝄢𝄢𝄢 (Pablo, 1979, prod. Norman
Granz) has an unusual theme. Instead of Bird's tunes, Pass
plays some of the standards that Parker recorded on his two albums with strings. The session contains some of Pass's most
lyrical playing, and his harmonic inventiveness is consistently
inspired. For an object lesson in improvisation, check out his
two completely different takes of "Out of Nowhere" that close
the album.

best of the rest:
Quadrant 𝄢𝄢𝄢𝄢 (Pablo, 1977)
Chops 𝄢𝄢𝄢𝄢 (Pablo, 1978)
Ira, George and Joe 𝄢𝄢𝄢𝄢 (Pablo, 1981/1994)
(With J. J. Johnson) *We'll Be Together Again* 𝄢𝄢𝄢𝄢 (Pablo, 1983)
Blues for Fred 𝄢𝄢𝄢𝄢 (Pablo, 1988)
Appassionato 𝄢𝄢𝄢𝄢 (Pablo, 1990)
Virtuoso Live! 𝄢𝄢𝄢𝄢 (Pablo, 1991)
Songs for Ellen 𝄢𝄢𝄢𝄢 (Pablo, 1992)
Virtuoso #3 𝄢𝄢𝄢𝄢 (Pablo, 1992)
Virtuoso #4 𝄢𝄢𝄢𝄢 (Pablo, 1993)
My Song 𝄢𝄢𝄢𝄢 (Telarc, 1993)
The Best of Joe Pass 𝄢𝄢𝄢𝄢 (Pacific Jazz, 1997)

worth searching for: On paper, pairing Joe Pass with country
music giant Roy Clark seems like a train wreck in the making,
but instead *Roy Clark & Joe Pass Play Hank Williams* 𝄢𝄢𝄢𝄢
(Ranwood, 1995, prod. Ralph Jungheim) comes across like a locomotive roaring through a serene landscape. Remember that
Pass spent the last year of his life touring with the genre-bend-
ing "Guitar Summit." The two guitarists are clearly having a
ball playing Williams's tunes, and on "Honky Tonk Blues" the
supposed divide between country and jazz disappears entirely.
It helps that Pass's quartet, featuring John Pisano (guitar), Jim
Hughart (bass), and Colin Bailey (drums), has three decades of
experience working together.

influences:
◄◄ Charlie Christian, Django Reinhardt
►► Ron Affif, John Pisano, Jack Wilkins

Andrew Gilbert

Jaco Pastorius

Born John Francis Pastorius III, December 1, 1951, Norristown, PA.
Died September 21, 1987, in Fort Lauderdale, FL.

Jaco Pastorius pioneered the electric bass as a solo instrument,
opening doors for generations of players to explore and develop new sounds and techniques. He reached his international career peak during his stint with the premier 1970s fusion band, Weather Report. However, by 1982, when Jaco left
the band, the self-proclaimed "World's Greatest Bass Player"
had begun to deteriorate due to mental illness and to the
abuse of cocaine and alcohol. By 1986, spiritually broken,
physically ailing, penniless, and homeless, Jaco was shunned
by the industry and nearly deserted by his inner circle of
friends who were helpless to save the musician from himself.
By 1987 his increasingly bizarre and self-destructive behavior
(often on stage during performances) culminated in a severe
beating he received after trying to crash an after-hours Fort
Lauderdale bar on September 12, 1987. He was rushed to
Broward County Medical Center, went into a coma, and died on
September 21, 1987.

As a young boy in 1959, Pastorius moved to Fort Lauderdale,
Florida, with his family. He began playing drums in local bands,
and in the summer of 1967 switched to bass guitar, gaining a
reputation as a fine player on gigs as a sideman for visiting R&B
musicians. In the early 1970s he joined Wayne Cochran & the
C. C. Riders and began teaching part-time at the University of
Miami, influencing students Mark Egan and Hiram Bullock. He
then recorded a jazz album with pianist Paul Bley, guitarist Pat
Metheny, and drummer Bruce Ditmas. In 1975 he recorded not
only his eponymous debut solo album, but another Pat
Metheny album (*Bright Size Life*) and two cuts on the Weather
Report album *Black Market* as well. He was then asked to join
Weather Report, and stayed with the group from 1976 to 1982.
During this era—the flowering of jazz/rock fusion—Pastorius
was the greatest electric bassist around, playing with incendiary, lightening-quick speed, immense imagination, and flawless
technical skill. Weather Report's leader, Joe Zawinul, required
his bassist to perform as a soloist rather than serve solely in a
support role. With that freedom, Pastorius generated some of
the most revolutionary solos on his instrument, actually changing the character and rhythmic feel of the Weather Report
sound. But Pastorius was not all funk and no flair. He was able
to execute stunning bass solos on classic bop melodies, such as
the Charlie Parker speedball tune "Donna Lee." Pastorius performed with ease in his fluid, spirited style, exhibiting a plump
tone and using unique smears or vibrato at the end of some

notes. He was also a versatile composer whose original tunes— including "Barbary Coast," "Teen Town," and "Three Views of a Secret"—added to Weather Report's impressive repertoire. His swaggering, bold contributions set the path for a whole new generation of jazz bassists, and a slew of imitators followed in wake; he made the electric bass guitar the preferred instrument in jazz and jazz-rock fusion groups. In 1982 he formed and toured with his Word of Mouth band. His album *Invitation* was released on Warner Bros., and he worked with a sextet that included guitarist Mike Stern, a trio with Hiram Bullock, and toured with Bireli Lagrene. Mental illness and drug abuse halted one of the brightest musical careers in decades.

what to buy: Through uncommon instrumental combinations, *Jaco Pastorius* &&&& (Epic, 1976/1987, prod. Bobby Colomby) presents a flavorful mix of nine tunes that range from funk to love ballads. Pastorius's vast and imaginative musical vision stretches beyond what other bassists were doing at the time, and he sets a new direction for the electric bass. He delivers a tastefully executed version of "Donna Lee" backed only with congas played by Don Alias. He offers a melodic interpretation of his original ballad, "Continuum," with backing from Herbie Hancock and Alex Darqui (both playing Fender Rhodes) and drummer Lenny White. Pastorius also renders a tender solo sitting of his "Portrait of Tracy," a steel-drums backed version of his "Opus Pocus," a Latin romp with Hubert Laws playing piccolo on "(Used to Be a) Cha-Cha," and a beautifully romantic "Forgotten Love," with Herbie Hancock on piano and live strings accompaniment. There's an innocent charm to his playing on this album, making this introduction to bassist-composer Jaco Pastorius a worthy purchase for any CD collection.

what to buy next: Recorded on December 1, 1981, *The Birthday Concert* &&&& (Warner Bros., 1981/1995, prod. Peter Erskine), is a live album featuring Pastorius near the end of his Weather Report stint. Pastorius is in rare form as he celebrates his 30th birthday in front of a bold and brassy big band at Mr. Pip's in Fort Lauderdale, Florida, with friends Michael Brecker (tenor sax), Bob Mintzer (tenor, soprano saxophones, bass clarinet), Don Alias (Congas), and Peter Erskine (drums). The 11 tunes were culled from tapes of two shows and include an intimate version of Pastorius's "Continuum," a fiery version of the jazz classic, "Invitation," and solid performances of other Pastorius originals, "Three Views of a Secret," "Liberty City," "Punk Jazz," and a powerful 10-minute version of "Reza." While this recording contains material previously recorded by Pastorius on his *Invitation* and *Word of Mouth* albums, the presence of Brecker and Mintzer makes this album a tantalizing treat for listeners. Although some

of the guest soloists had performed with Pastorius previously, this night's extraordinary unpublicized (but packed) performance christened Pastorius's Word of Mouth orchestra, which came together on *Word of Mouth* &&&& (Warner Bros., 1981/1988), a diverse, modern session with the band members not acknowledged on the original LP; they are Herbie Hancock, Wayne Shorter, Michael Brecker, Toots Thielemans, Peter Erskine, Jack DeJohnette, Don Alias, Bobby Thomas Jr., Othello Molineaux, Leroy Williams, Dave Bargeron, John Clark, Jim Pugh, Bill Reichenbach, David Taylor, Snooky Young, Howard Johnson (tuba), Tom Scott, James Walker, and George Young. The recording is unique in that it's the culmination of Pastorius's vision, with arrangements written by him. Pastorius's solos are frequently framed in sound vignettes, often with Thielemans in the foreground playing harmonica. The orchestra sometimes sounds like a denser Weather Report, especially in portions of Pastorius's "Liberty City." The album's seven tunes contain a mixture of jazz-rock, oriental themes, percussion-laden avant-garde experiments, and more. It's a listening adventure and knowing what we know about this period of his life, the complex, occasionally raw-sounding music is rather telling. There's enough talent on this debut session to suggest that, had Pastorius lived, the band's full potential might have been truly amazing.

the rest:
Live in New York City, Vol. 1: Punk Jazz &&&& (Big World, 1990)
Live in New York City, Vol. 2: Trio &&&& (Big World, 1991)
Live in New York City, Vol. 3: Promise Land &&&& (Big World, 1991)
Live in New York City, Vol. 4: Trio 2 &&&& (Big World, 1992)
Live in New York City, Vol. 5: &&&& (Big World, 1997)

worth searching for: To learn more about Jaco Pastorius, read the book *Jaco: The Extraordinary and Tragic Life of Jaco Pastorius, "The World's Greatest Bass Player"* by Bill Milkowski (Miller Freeman Books, 1995).

influences:

◀◀ Charlie Parker, Billie Holiday

▶▶ Stanley Clarke, John Patitucci, Jamaaladeen Tacuma, Gerald Veasley

see also: *Weather Report*

Nancy Ann Lee

John Patitucci

Born December 22, 1959 in Brooklyn, NY.

John Patitucci is arguably one of the top acoustic and electric bassists of the 1990s. His speed, clarity, and versatility have brought him wide acclaim and several Grammy nominations. Influenced by the music of the Beatles and Motown artists, Patitucci began playing the bass at age 11. His first musical outlet was playing with his older brother Thomas in a garage band; later, in 1972 when the family moved to northern California, he played with some gospel groups. It was during this period that John began widening his understanding of jazz and was introduced to the music of Miles Davis, Charlie Parker, and John Coltrane. To augment his growing love of jazz, Patitucci entered classical studies at San Francisco State University. He moved to Southern California in 1978 and landed his first professional gig playing with pianist Gap Mangione while studying music at Long Beach State University. After a move to Los Angeles in 1982, John began working with saxophonist Joe Farrell, then wound up playing with Flora Purim and Airto Moriera. As his exposure grew, John was asked to work with such stars as Tom Scott, Robben Ford, Stan Getz, Larry Carlton, Dave Grusin, David Benoit, George Benson, Ernie Watts, Freddie Hubbard, Hubert Laws, Lee Ritenour, and Bob James. In 1985 John accepted his highest-profile job yet when Chick Corea invited him on as an original member of the Elektric and Akoustic bands. Along with the ongoing demands of worldwide tours, John recorded *The Chick Corea Elektric Band*, *Light Years*, *Eye of the Beholder*, *Inside Out*, and *Beneath the Mask* as well as the *Chick Corea Akoustic Band* and *Alive*. John left Corea's band in 1991 to devote more time to personal matters and to focus on his own musical direction. During his tenure with Corea, Patitucci developed his unique 6 string solo voice, which blossomed into a rich solo career including five albums recorded for GRP. His 1993 offering, *Another World*, garnered Patitucci a Grammy nomination for Best Jazz Instrumental Album. He also simultaneously released the critically acclaimed *Heart of the Bass* on Corea's Stretch label and most recently released *One More Angel* for Concord Jazz. Throughout his career, John has consistently won polls for "Best Jazz Bassist" and "Best Acoustic Bassist" from the readers of *Guitar Player, Jazziz,* and other music publications. Although his compositional skills have improved over time, John is regarded most highly for his playing—he performs on acoustic bass with the utmost authority and can make his six-string "sing." Historically, bass players haven't become stars with the regularity that horn and piano players have; nonetheless, Patitucci has secured a place among the great bass innovators of our time.

what to buy: *Heart of the Bass* ♫♫♫♫ (Stretch, 1991, prod. John Patitucci, Chick Corea) showcases Patitucci's orchestral compositions with trumpeter/composer Jeff Beal. Crediting the influ-

ence of renowned orchestrator Claus Ogerman (whom Patitucci joined on his acclaimed work, *Cityscapes*), this recording forges an adventurous path that neatly bridges the jazz and classical idioms. After hearing this concerto, Corea was inspired to compose a set of six new miniatures for bass, piano, and string quartet. Weaving its warm and inviting spell, the bass maintains the lead melodic voice throughout this recording.

what to buy next: *Another World* ♫♫♫♫ (GRP, 1993, prod. John Patitucci) is immersed in the rhythms and spirit of African music. Its hybrid of evocative harmonies and jazz improvisations expands on his previous recordings. It was an introduction to bassist Armand Sabal-Lecco by Michael Brecker that Patitucci credits as a key influence in the creation of this album. The rhythmic foundation is laid by Alex Acuna and Luis Conte, who are joined on seven tracks by Will Kennedy and on three by former bandmate Dave Weckl. Other featured musicians include Jeff Beal, John Beasley, Michael Brecker, Andy Narell, and Steve Tavaglione.

the rest:
John Patitucci ♫♫ (GRP, 1987)
On the Corner ♫♫ (GRP, 1989)
Sketchbook ♫♫♫ (GRP, 1990)
Mistura Fina ♫♫♫ (GRP, 1994)
One More Angel ♫♫♫♫ (Concord Jazz, 1997)

influences:
◄◄ Ron Carter, Eddie Gomez, Dave Holland, Charlie Hayden, Jaco Pastorius, Anthony Jackson

►► Marcus Miller, Will Lee

Ralph Burnett

Don Patterson

Born July 22, 1936, in Columbus, OH. Died February 10, 1988, in Philadelphia, PA.

Patterson started as a pianist but took up the organ in 1959 under the influence of Jimmy Smith. A capable player, he found work with Gene Ammons, Sonny Stitt, and Wes Montgomery, in addition to touring various clubs under his own name, accompanied only by a drummer. Unlike many of his instrumental contemporaries, Patterson virtually shunned the organ's foot pedals, preferring a more pianistic approach that made his solos a little leaner and more austere than those of the competition.

what to buy: *Dem New York Dues* ♫♫♫♫ (Prestige, 1968/1969, prod. Don Schlitten, Bob Porter) combines two albums, 1968's

Opus De Don Patterson and 1969's *Oh Happy Day*. The list of well-known folks playing in support of Patterson is pretty strong, with trumpeters Blue Mitchell and Don Patterson, sax players Junior Cook, George Coleman, and Houston Person, and guitarist Pat Martino. Fine playing is heard in both sessions, but Patterson is only the nominal leader because his musical associates convey far more instrumental personality than he does. The covers of standards like "Stairway to the Stars" and "Perdido" are the most distinguished compositions, but a few originals (notably "Hip Trip" and "Opus De Don") are pretty good, if a tad generic.

what to buy next: The title of *The Genius of the B-3* 🎜🎜🎜 (Muse, 1973, prod. Don Schlitten) is a bit overblown for an organist of solid but not very original talent. This quartet features Eddie Daniels playing saxophones, the underrated Ted Dunbar on guitar, and Freddie Waits handling drums. Songs are well-chosen and everyone plays the kind of riffs one expects to hear in an after hours club, which may explain the classy if commonplace stylings. Not bad, but not great either.

influences:

◀◀ Erroll Garner, Jimmy Smith

▶▶ Larry Goldings

Garaud MacTaggart

John Patton

Born July 12, 1936, in Kansas City, MO.

John Patton started playing piano in 1948 and his first major gig was with R&B singer Lloyd Price (whose big hit was "Lawdy, Miss Clawdy") during the late '50s. While he was performing with Price, Patton started to write tunes for the band, including "Personality," which turned into a minor hit for the singer. By the time Patton left Price, the pianist had discovered the organ and was committed to playing his newfound interest. Saxophonist Lou Donaldson was the first major musician to use Patton's organ playing on a record date—Donaldson's 1962 Blue Note release, *The Natural Soul*. With this recording Patton became part of the talented '60s-era Blue Note stable of house musicians, performing with artists like guitarist Grant Green and vibraphonist Bobby Hutcherson. When organ jazz fell out of favor in the '70s, Patton's subtle, deceptively simple stylings went underground, resurfacing during the early '90s through the efforts of longtime fans like John Zorn.

what to buy: On *Let 'Em Roll* 🎜🎜🎜🎜 (Blue Note, 1965, prod. Alfred Lion), vibist Bobby Hutcherson (who adds a light percus-

sive touch) and guitarist Grant Green provide Patton with the talent needed to push beyond his normal conventions. Most of the tunes are standard blues riffs composed by Patton, but the quartet never lets the playing fall into the ordinary—although their cover of "The Shadow of Your Smile" skirts the edge of lounge act cheese. There is nothing terribly adventuresome about *Boogaloo* 🎜🎜🎜🎜 (Blue Note, 1969, prod. Francis Wolff), but the players slip into a funky groove that defines what acid jazz could be. This is the second album Patton made with flautist and tenor player Harold Alexander, and their obvious aural camaraderie would never be better. Drummer George Edward Brown (about whom little is known) was a talented musician with the ability to bring out the best in other players.

what to buy next: On *Blue Planet Man* 🎜🎜🎜 (Evidence, 1993, prod. Thelma Patton), avant-garde champion and eclectic horn player John Zorn brings his alto to a three-sax lineup on what amounts to Patton's comeback album, after years of neglect by the recording companies. The organist has again written most of the tunes in a comfortable blues mode; his solos are convincing and his funky yet graceful keyboard fills provide sympathetic backdrops for Zorn's impressive array of squeals and honks. However, the undeservedly obscure guitarist Ed Cherry may be the most interesting soloist on the date.

the rest:
Blue John 🎜🎜🎜🎜 (Blue Note, 1964)
Understanding 🎜🎜🎜 (Blue Note, 1969)
Memphis to New York Spirit 🎜🎜🎜 (Blue Note, 1970)

worth searching for: The Japanese import *Minor Swing* 🎜🎜🎜🎜 (DIW, 1995, prod. John Zorn, Kazunori Sugiyama) again matches Zorn and Cherry with Patton. Operating as a quartet (with drummer Kenny Wollesen), Patton and his ensemble distill the music of their 1993 session, creating an overall performance that clearly surpasses the earlier offering. Guitarist Cherry again slashes the edge of avant-garde riffing with his quirky rib-joint comping.

influences:

◀◀ Jimmy Smith, Jack McDuff, Horace Silver, Hampton Hawes, Wynton Kelly

▶▶ John Zorn, Charlie Hunter

Garaud MacTaggart

Mario Pavone

Born 1939 in CT.

Pavone didn't begin playing bass until he was 24, when he was encouraged by his friend guitarist Joe Diorio. Pavone was an industrial engineer who played jazz on the side until the late 1960s when he decided to dedicate himself to music. He played on the New York City loft scene, though his free jazz influences also include the more ensemble-oriented sounds of the AACM, and established himself in groups led by Paul Bley, Bill Dixon, Thomas Chapin, and Anthony Braxton.

what to buy: On *Song for (Septet)* ✃✃✃✗ (New World Countercurrents, 1994, prod. Marty Ehrlich) Pavone's avant-garde experience lends his intricate compositions an angular, unsettling character even though they're mostly tonal. With a solid supporting cast including rising star Peter Madsen (piano), vibist Bill Ware, multi-reedist Marty Ehrlich, and long-time collaborator Thomas Chapin (alto sax, flute), there's a wide variety of tones and textures on this masterful album.

what to buy next: The sextet album, *Dancers Tales* ✃✃✃ (Knitting Factory Works, 1997, prod. Marty Ehrlich) is a bit closer to the mainstream and shows a Mingus influence in the arrangements. Madsen, Ehrlich, and Chapin return, with the pianist in particular being given space for expression—this is not merely an album of heads and horn solos.

the rest:
Toulon Days ✃✃✃ (New World Countercurrents, 1992)

worth searching for: The multiple-artists compilation *What Is Jazz? 1996* ✃✃✃ (Knitting Factory Works, 1996, prod. Brett Heinz, Mark Perlson), recorded live at the eponymous annual festival of the album title, includes a Pavone Sextet track, "Double Diamond," with drummer Mike Sarin fitting well. For a completely different context, there's the Anthony Braxton–Mario Pavone Quintet's *Seven Standards 1996* ✃✃✃ (Knitting Factory Works, 1997, prod. Anthony Braxton, Mario Pavone), with Braxton on piano rather than reeds, plus Dave Douglas (trumpet), Thomas Chapin (alto sax), and Pheeroan Ak Laff (drums). It's a classic bebop format, and they explore tunes by Charlie Parker, Thelonious Monk, and John Coltrane in addition to four standards. As a pianist, Braxton's not up to the high level of the others, but he comps adequately behind their superb solos.

influences:
◄◄ Charlie Haden, Fred Hopkins, Malachi Favors, Henry Grimes, Charles Mingus, John Coltrane

►► Mark Helias

Walter Faber

Cecil Payne

Born December 14, 1922, in Brooklyn, NY.

One of the pioneering bebop baritone saxophonists, Cecil Payne is an agile, light-toned player with a highly melodic approach marked by the influence of both Charlie Parker and Lester Young. He began playing alto sax in high school, studying with 52nd Street veteran Pete Brown, and by the early 1940s was participating on the vital young Brooklyn scene with Max Roach, Duke Jordan, and Randy Weston, with whom Payne later recorded. After serving three years in the Army, Payne returned to Brooklyn in 1946 and was exposed to bebop. He played alto on his recording debut, a 1946 J.J. Johnson date for Savoy that also featured Bud Powell. Later that year he switched to baritone for a gig with Roy Eldridge and landed a job with Dizzy Gillespie's big band, a long stint (1946–49) that established him as one of the most distinctive baritone saxophonists in jazz. In the early 1950s, Payne worked with Tadd Dameron, James Moody, and toured with Illinois Jacquet (1952–54). He performed and recorded with Randy Weston in the mid-1950s, and played on Dameron's excellent *Fountainbleu* album and John Coltrane's *Dakar*. He made a series of recordings with Duke Jordan, including two for Savoy in the mid-1950s, two for Charlie Parker Records in the early 1960s, and one for Spotlight in 1966. He toured with Machito's Afro-Cubans (1963–66), with Lionel Hampton (1964), and took another swing with Woody Herman from 1967–68. Payne dropped out of music briefly but by the end of the decade he was back on the scene, renewing his associations with Weston and Gillespie and working Count Basie (1969–71). He has led his own bands since the 1970s and recorded for Muse, Spotlight, and Delmark.

what to buy: Containing two separate sessions with overlapping personnel, *Stop and Listen to . . . Cecil Payne* ✃✃✃✗ (Fresh Sound, 1961–62/1991, reissue prod. Jordi Pujol) finds baritone sax master Cecil Payne at the peak of his power with an amenable bop-oriented band featuring Clark Terry (trumpet), Duke Jordan (piano), Ron Carter (bass), and Charlie Persip (drums). Warm-toned trombonist Bennie Green rounds out the sextet on the first seven tunes (recorded in March 1962), which include three Payne originals and four pieces by Kenny Drew. The seven quintet tracks (recorded in 1961) include Payne's high-stepping "Communion" and six Charlie Parker tunes. Terry and Payne, two of the most distinctive musicians on their respective instruments, act as inspired foils for each other throughout the album, while Jordan's single note lines are a model of economical bebop. A fine blowing session featuring a host of world class but under-recognized players, *Scotch and*

Nicholas Payton (© Jack Vartoogian)

Milk ⚜⚜⚜⚜ (Delmark, 1997, prod. Robert G. Koester) features the same rhythm section from his first Delmark session—Harold Mabern (piano), John Ore (bass), and Joe Farnsworth (drums). Joining him in the horn section are the two tenors Eric Alexander and Lin Halliday, whose sounds contrast wonderfully, and the tough Detroit trumpeter Marcus Belgrave. Payne gives his bandmates plenty of room to blow and supplied seven of the eight tunes (the standard "If I Should Lose You," a vehicle to showcase Payne's lyricism, is the ringer). Though he has some hard-driving company, Payne displays his dexterity and ferocious bari chops on his up-tempo romp "Et Vous Too, Cecil?," and turns the gently swinging "I'm Goin' In" into a vehicle for his attractive flute work.

what to buy next: Payne's first album as a leader, *Patterns of Jazz* ⚜⚜⚜⚜ (Savoy Jazz, 1956) features two sessions with Payne accompanied by the expert bop rhythm section of Duke Jordan (piano), Tommy Potter (bass), and Art Taylor (drums). Trumpeter Kenny Dorham, already a fully formed jazz giant, plays on

four of the eight tunes. The material includes two standards, including the only ballad (a haunting version of Berlin's "How Deep Is the Ocean"), three Payne originals, and a thrilling run-through of Gillespie's "Groovin' High." The album's two highlights are by Payne's longtime associate Randy Weston, the mysterious, minor key "Chessman's Delight" and the mood shifting "Saucer Eyes," which features a particularly sensitive Dorham solo. Jordan's finely crafted bop lines show why he was one of Bird's favorite pianists.

best of the rest:
Duke Jordan with Cecil Payne and Teddy Edwards ⚜⚜⚜⚜ (Xanadu, 1973/76)
Casbah ⚜⚜⚜ (Stash/Vintage, 1985/1993)
Cerupa ⚜⚜⚜ (Delmark, 1995)

worth searching for: Pianist/composer Randy Weston was still assimilating Monk's influence when he recorded *Jazz à la Bohemia* ⚜⚜⚜⚜ (Riverside/OJC, 1956, prod. Bill Grauer, Orrin Keepnews) at the popular Greenwich Village club Cafe Bohemia. The session features a quartet on six of the eight tracks with Payne, bassist Ahmed Abdul-Malik, and drummer Al Dreares ("You Go to My Head" and "It's Alright With Me" are by the trio). Weston's only original is the mysterious but memorable "Chessman's Delight," a tune recorded by Payne on his debut as a leader a few months before this recording. Payne's highly melodic approach jibes well with Weston's muscular and percussive attack. The two players dig in on an almost 10-minute version of Sid Catlett's "Just a Riff" and the dancing calypso number "Hold 'Em Joe," while Weston turns in a dazzling, expansive version of "You Go to My Head."

influences:

◄◄ Lester Young, Serge Chaloff

►► Nick Brignola, Jack Nimitz

Andrew Gilbert

Nicholas Payton

Born September 26, 1973, in New Orleans, LA.

Young New Orleans trumpeter Payton shares with the young Wynton Marsalis (who encouraged his career) a mellow, Clifford Brown–like tone, an indebtedness to early 1960s Miles Davis's phrasing and melodic conception, and a love for the musical heritage of his hometown. He attracted considerable attention while still in his teens, and after an inconsistent start on record has begun fulfilling that promise.

Both of Payton's parents were musicians; his father, Walter, can be heard on record with the Excelsior Brass Band. From the time he was a toddler, Nicholas was encouraged to make music, and by the age of four he had his first trumpet; at eight he played a Mardi Gras parade with the Young Tuxedo Brass Band, which his father was in. At eleven he was a gigging professional with the All Star Brass Band, which played European festivals as well as the New Orleans streets. He recorded with pianist Marcus Roberts at 17 (on *As Serenity Approaches*) and was touring and recording in Elvin Jones's band while he was still 18. In Jones's much more modern context (he played with him for a couple years) Payton proved he was no mere novelty, acquitting himself as a charismatic and thoroughly schooled trumpeter who had already melded his influences into a distinctive style. The busy Payton has since recorded with Carl Allen, Rodney Whitaker, Black/Note, Jesse Davis, Milt Jackson, Lincoln Center Jazz Orchestra, Renée Rosnes, and Jimmy Smith. He can also be heard and seen in the Robert Altman movie *Kansas City* as part of the all-star band heard throughout the film.

NICHOLAS PAYTON
(WITH DOC CHEATHAM)

song "Epistrophy"

album *Doc Cheatham and Nicholas Payton*
(Verve, 1997)

instrument Trumpet

Monster Solo

what to buy: *Gumbo Nouveau* 𝄞𝄞𝄞𝄞 (Verve, 1996, prod. Nicholas Payton), an album of music by or associated with New Orleans musicians, finds Payton sounding much more at home than on his previous Verve effort. It's hardly the set of clichés the concept might suggest, as the second track demonstrates—likely the slowest and prettiest "When the Saints Go Marching In" ever waxed. He plays "Way Down Yonder in New Orleans" as a langorous ballad, bringing out his most lovingly inflected Miles-like nuances, and applies bebop harmonies to some of the other tunes with unselfconcious ease. There are some rollicking uptempo romps, and his technique is superb this time out. He and pianist Anthony Wonsey interact well, with their duet on Louis Armstrong's "Weather Bird" standing out with its utterly natural flow. On *Doc Cheatham & Nicholas Payton* 𝄞𝄞𝄞𝄞 (Verve, 1997, prod. Andrea du Plessis, Jerry Brock, George Hocutt) Payton lets his inimitable fellow trumpeter, Doc was 91 years old at the time—68 years older than Payton, steal the show on what sadly proved to be Doc's final recording. Payton plays some sensitive obbligatos behind

Cheatham's oh-so-relaxed vocals, and both men play their hearts out, not from competitive urges but from mutual admiration. The surrounding cast of semi-legendary New Orleans-style vets—trombonists Lucien Barbarin and Tom Ebbert, clarinetist Jack Maheu, pianist Butch Thompson, guitarist/banjo player Les Muscutt, bassist Bill Huntington, and drummer Ernie Elly—definitely enhances the project.

what to buy next: *New Orleans Collective* ♫♫♫ (King, 1993/Evidence, 1995, prod. Carl Allen, Vincent Herring) may not be in Payton's bin in stores (look for New Orleans Collective), but it's worth seeking out. He shares the frontline with the alum from Wynton Marsalis's band, Wessell Anderson (alto and sopranino saxes), who writes the majority of the tunes. The band swings, the material is nicely varied, Payton sounds confident, and pianist Peter Martin excels. Bassist Chris Thomas and drummer Brian Blade fill out the quintet.

what to avoid: Payton is too restrained on most of *From This Moment* ♫♫ (Verve, 1995, prod. Delfeayo Marsalis). When he does let go on "It Could Happen to You" his tone is garish and overly brassy and he flubs fast runs. He fares better on the semi-title track, and the ballads are pretty, but that's not enough. One gets the sense that, whether because it was his major label debut or because he wasn't entirely at ease with the rest of the band—Mark Whitfield, guitar; Mulgrew Miller, piano; Reginald Veal, bass; Monte Croft, vibes; Lewis Nash, drums—he never really finds his groove.

the rest:
(With Christian McBride, Mark Whitfield) *Fingerpainting: The Music of Herbie Hancock* ♫♫♫ (Verve, 1997)

worth searching for: A couple Payton guest appearances are rewarding. He plays on the first four tracks of L.A. collective Black/Note's *Nothin' but the Swing* ♫♫♫ (Impulse!, 1996, prod. Mark Anthony Shelby, Willie Jones III), including a cover of Freddie Hubbard's "The Core," and those are among the best tracks on the album. Payton's on five of the 11 cuts on Rodney Whitaker's *Children of the Light* ♫♫♫ (DIW, 1996, prod. Rodney Whitaker, Kazunori Sugiyama), which leads off with a couple of rousing uptempo numbers that let him show off his bebop chops. Later he sounds quite Miles-like on the brooding title track.

influences:
◀◀ Louis Armstrong, Clifford Brown, Miles Davis, Clark Terry, Wynton Marsalis

Steve Holtje

Gary Peacock

Born May 12, 1935, in Burley, ID.

Peacock began studying music seriously when he started playing the drums and piano at age 13. During his late teens he decided to become a professional musician, and after leaving high school he spent six months at the Wesley College of Music in Los Angeles. He was drafted in 1954 and got stationed in Germany where he played in the drum and bugle corps. After his discharge he switched to bass (1956) and toured with Hans Koller, Bud Shank, Bob Cooper, and Gary Crosby. From 1958 to 1961 he gigged and recorded with Barney Kessel, Paul Bley, Ravi Shankar, Don Ellis, and Sonny Simmons. In 1961 his playing moved from hard bop to avant-garde and improvised music. This led him to New York and he played with Archie Shepp, Albert Ayler, Bill Dixon, Don Cherry, and Roswell Rudd. He was a part of the Bill Evans Trio in 1962–63 and toured with Miles Davis from 1964 to 1967. He then dropped out of music to study Eastern philosophy in a quest for a new lifestyle. He went to Japan to study Oriental medicine. Back in the U.S. he enrolled in Washington State University as a microbiology major in 1972. He then joined Paul Bley and Barry Altshul for a tour of Japan in 1976 and began recording as a leader in 1977. Throughout the 1980s and 1990s Peacock has not only recorded as a leader and sideman, he is also an integral part of the Keith Jarrett Trio.

what to buy: Featuring Peacock with Keith Jarrett and Jack DeJohnette, *Tales of Another* ♫♫♫♫ (ECM, 1977, prod. Manfred Eicher) is an introspective weaving of unique musical lines and perspectives. *Shift in the Wind* ♫♫♫♫ (ECM, 1980, prod. Manfred Eicher) is another excellent trio performance with Art Lande on piano and Eliot Zigmund on drums.

the rest:
(With Ralph Towner) *Oracle* ♫♫♫ (ECM, 1994)
(With Bill Frisell) *Just So Happens* ♫♫♫♫ (Postcards 1994)

worth searching for: *December Poems* ♫♫♫♫♫ (ECM, 1979, prod. Manfred Eicher) is a beautiful solo bass recording by the brilliant melodicist.

see also: *Keith Jarrett*

David C. Gross

Duke Pearson

Born August 17, 1932, in Atlanta, GA. Died August 4, 1980, in Atlanta, GA

A man of many talents, Duke Pearson started his career as a modest, yet graceful pianist and would later develop his com-

posing and arranging talents in addition to working as a producer and A&R assistant for the Blue Note label. Like his inspiration, Count Basie, Pearson's style is reflective of an outlook
that calls for simplicity and emotional directness. Nothing Pearson ever played was flashy, yet he communicated in a relaxed
and refined manner that perfectly suited his or his employer's
fancy at any moment. His great skill at crafting catchy melodies
can be gleaned from his two most popular, often-recorded compositions, "Cristo Redentor" and "Jeannine," which are now
considered standards. Pearson's own Blue Note dates, recorded
between 1959 and 1970, are substantial affairs that feature his
writing and particularly strong sidemen. At the end of the 1960s
he would lead a superb big band that was as creative and exciting as the Thad Jones-Mel Lewis Jazz Orchestra but which existed primarily in the studio. It was also during this period that
he would take a great interest in Brazilian music, finding its har-
monically-rich timbre and rhythmic lilt perfectly suited to his
own sensibilities. In later years, Pearson found his activities limited by a bout with multiple sclerosis and by the time of his premature death he had all but dropped out of music.

what to buy: *Wahoo!* 🎵🎵🎵🎵 (Blue Note, 1964, prod. Alfred Lion)
was Pearson's first large group effort for Blue Note. Following
two trio dates cut in 1959, it yielded the fascinating "Bedouin,"
among other fine Pearson originals. Donald Byrd, James Spaulding, and Joe Henderson are all in brilliant form and the results
are impressive. *The Right Touch* 🎵🎵🎵🎵 (Blue Note, 1967, prod.
Francis Wolff) is Pearson's finest date as a leader due in no
small part to his writing, which is colorful, varied, and challenging to all the players involved. The all-star octet includes Freddie
Hubbard, Stanley Turrentine, and James Spaulding.

what to buy next: *Sweet Honey Bee* 🎵🎵🎵🎵 (Blue Note, 1966,
prod. Alfred Lion) has Pearson fronting a sextet with Joe Henderson and Freddie Hubbard. All of the tunes are his and each
one is deserving of some long overdue revival. *I Don't Care
Who Knows It* 🎵🎵🎵 (Blue Note, 1996, prod. Duke Pearson,
Michael Cuscuna) is a compilation of Pearson's second-to-last
dates for Blue Note, all previously unissued and recorded in
1969 and 1970. These are large ensemble sessions that nicely
demonstrate his expertise with Latin and Brazilian influences,
finding Airto and Flora Purim on hand for several choice cuts.

worth searching for: The remainder of Pearson's recordings for
the Blue Note, Atlantic, Prestige, and Polydor labels are unfortunately out-of-print. Both of the following dates featuring
Duke's big band, *Introducing Duke Pearson's Big Band* 🎵🎵🎵🎵
(Blue Note, 1967, prod. Duke Pearson) and *Now Hear This!*

🎵🎵🎵🎵 (Blue Note, 1968, prod. Duke Pearson), have been out-
of-print for some time but are worth looking for if you still own
a turntable. Influential among fellow jazzmen and sought out
by record buffs, they are highly-prized collector's items. *The
Phantom* 🎵🎵🎵🎵 (Blue Note, 1968, prod. Francis Wolff) can be
found via Japan and is Pearson's best effort in the Latin-Brazil-
ian vein. Vibist Bobby Hutcherson and multi-reedman Jerry
Dodgion are deft and animated throughout.

influences:

◀◀ Count Basie, Duke Ellington, Wynton Kelly, John Lewis

Chris Hovan

Ken Peplowski

Born May 23, 1959, in Cleveland OH.

One of the most gifted clarinetists to emerge in the 1990s, Ken
Peplowski is also an excellent tenor saxophonist with a big
breathy sound reminiscent of Ben Webster and Paul Gonsalves.
A highly lyrical player, Peplowski can generate considerable
heat with his light, fluid clarinet work. He is part of a group of
musicians who have expanded on the small group swing tradition, mostly bypassing the harmonic and rhythmic tendencies
of bebop, but Peps draws widely from jazz and classical influences and studies with Sonny Stitt. He began playing clarinet
in the fourth grade and landed his first professional gig with
the Tommy Dorsey ghost band under the direction of Buddy
Morrow (1978–80). He moved to New York in 1980 and began
working in trad and swing settings with Max Kaminsky, Jimmy
McPartland, Ruby Braff, Bob Wilbur, and Joe Bushkin and was
hired by Benny Goodman for what turned out to be his last
band. During the 1980s, Peplowski worked with George Shearing, Hank Jones, Charlie Byrd, and recorded with Mel Tormé,
Peggy Lee and Rosemary Clooney. He began recording a series
of excellent albums for Concord in 1987 and has become a key
member of the label's family, recording with Scott Hamilton,
Howard Alden, Byrd and various saxophone combinations.

what to buy: Ken Peplowski lays claim to the entire jazz tradi-
tion with *Sonny Side* 🎵🎵🎵🎵 (Concord Jazz, 1989, prod. Carl E.
Jefferson), a quintet session with his frequent collaborator
Howard Alden (guitar). Something of a tribute to his mentor
Sonny Stitt, Peps covers such diverse material as Roland Kirk's
"Bright Moments," Monk's "Ugly Beauty," Ellington's "Ring Dem
Bells," and Miles Davis's "Half Nelson," playing alto, tenor, and
clarinet. Though his tone and flowing sax lines make for reward-
ing listening, on clarinet he is among the very best in jazz. Pe-
plowski assembled a brilliant group of veterans for *Mr. Gentle*

and *Mr. Cool* ⚜⚜⚜⚜ (Concord Jazz, 1990, prod. Carl E. Jefferson), including pianist Hank Jones, guitarist Bucky Pizzarelli, and drummer Alan Dawson (Scott Hamilton also sits in on two tracks). The program is mostly standards, but Peps slips in a few ringers, such as Coltrane's gorgeous "Syeeda's Song Flute" and Tadd Dameron's "On a Misty Night." Peps plays beautifully throughout and Jones's elegant solos and Dawson's tasteful drum work make this album one of his best. The third volume in Concord's duo series, *Ken Peplowski/Howard Alden: Concord Duo Series, Vol. 3* ⚜⚜⚜⚜ (Concord Jazz, 1993, prod. Carl E. Jefferson) is immense fun, a thrilling improvisational collaboration with a dose of vaudeville thrown in for good measure. Peps and Alden both have terrific range, covering everything from Jelly Roll Morton's "Why" and Bix Beiderbecke's "In the Dark," to Charlie Parker's "Chasin' the Bird" and Lennie Tristano's "Two Not One." They consistently engage in astonishingly complex interplay, and make it all sound easy (and their asides to the Maybeck Recital Hall audience are often hysterical).

what to buy next: *Steppin' with Peps* ⚜⚜⚜⚜ (Concord Jazz, 1993, prod. Carl E. Jefferson) adds trumpeters Joe Wilder and Randy Sandke, and guitarist Bucky Pizzarelli (on two tunes) to Peplowski's usual quintet instrumentation of guitar (Howard Alden), piano (Ben Aranov), bass (John Goldsby), and drums (Alan Dawson). A loose but focused atmosphere pervades the session, which ranges from Jobim's "Antigua" to Strayhorn's "Johnny Come Lately" and "Lotus Blossom" (featuring a poignant Wilder solo) to Ornette Coleman's "Turnaround," as well as a few standards and originals. A moody album filled with brooding ballads, *It's a Lonesome Old Town* ⚜⚜⚜⚜ (Concord Jazz, 1995, prod. Carl E. Jefferson) is a quintet session with special guests Charlie Byrd, Marian McPartland, and Tom Harrell. Howard Alden (guitar), Allen Farnham (piano), Greg Cohen (bass), and Alan Dawson (drums) make up Peps's world-class band. The focus is on delicate voicings and intricate interplay, as these musicians listen closely to each other. Check out the striking clarinet/trumpet combination on Harrell's "More Than Ever," or the way Cohen's arco bass, Farnham's piano, Alden's guitar, and Peps's clarinet ease into a bossa groove on Jobim's "Zingaro."

best of the rest:
Double Exposure ⚜⚜⚜⚜ (Concord Jazz, 1988/1995)
Illuminations ⚜⚜⚜⚜⚜ (Concord Jazz, 1991)
(With Harry Sweets Edison) *Ken Peplowski Quintet: Live at Ambassador Auditorium* ⚜⚜⚜⚜ (Concord Jazz, 1994)
(With Howard Alden) *Live at Centre Concord: Encore!* ⚜⚜⚜⚜⚜ (Concord Jazz, 1995)

The Other Portrait ⚜⚜⚜⚜ (Concord Concerto, 1996)
A Good Reed ⚜⚜⚜⚜ (Concord Jazz, 1997)

influences:

◀◀ Ben Webster, Lester Young, Paul Gonsalves, Benny Goodman, Tony Scott

Andrew Gilbert

Art Pepper

Born September 1, 1925, in Gardenia, CA. Died June 15, 1982, in Los Angeles, CA.

Art Pepper was one of the greatest alto saxophonists in jazz history and one of the music's most deeply troubled figures. His most significant artistic successes were accompanied by personal setbacks, until the last seven years of his life when he reaffirmed his status as one of jazz's most passionate improvisors on a nightly basis. One of the few alto saxophonists who came of age in the 1940s to forge an approach independent of Charlie Parker, Pepper's warm, passionate, rhythmically forceful style drew on Benny Carter, Lester Young, and elements of Bird. Though his sound changed over the years, including a Coltrane phase in the mid-1960s, Pepper in the end played with a searingly emotional tone that summed up the many travails of his chaotic life. Though Pepper's drug addiction interrupted his career repeatedly, including numerous prison sentences, he recorded prolifically and with amazing consistency. There are virtually no losers among his vast discography. Pepper's brutally honest autobiography *Straight Life,* written with his wife Laurie, is one of the most detailed examinations of a brilliant but tortured psyche in literature.

Pepper started playing clarinet in working-class waterfront bars while tagging along with his longshoreman father. He began playing alto at age 12 and by 17 he was working on Los Angeles' vital Central Avenue scene with Lee Young's band and playing with Dexter Gordon, Charles Mingus, and other major figures. He did short stints with Benny Carter and Stan Kenton before serving in the military (1944–46). Returning to Southern California, he rejoined Kenton as a featured soloist for a long spell (1947–52), the most stable period of his life though it was also when he picked up his heroin habit. He began recording as a leader for Discovery in 1953, furthering his national reputation, but spent much of 1953–55 in prison. He made a series of brilliant recordings for Aladdin in late 1956 and 1957 (reissued on Blue Note) with pianists Carl Perkins, Russ Freeman, and Gerald Wiggins. Also in 1957, he recorded his classic album *Art Pepper Meets the Rhythm Section*, an impromptu quartet session with Miles Davis's band. Throughout the 1950s, Pepper worked extensively as a sideman on numerous West Coast sessions. Pepper finished the decade with a burst of activity, recording a series of definitive albums for Contemporary. He spent much of the 1960s in prison or off the jazz scene, but after a few years in the Synanon program (where he met his wife Laurie) he began a comeback in the early 1970s, culminating with *Living Legend* in 1975 with Hampton Hawes, Charlie Haden, and Shelly Manne. For the next seven years, until his death from a cerebral hemorrhage, Pepper recorded frequently, mostly for Contemporary and Galaxy, and in a variety of contexts from duo sessions with pianist George Cables to a gorgeous album with strings, *Winter Moon*. His slashing attack and cathartic approach on up-tempo numbers was riveting, but the emotionally raw quality of his ballads was even more intense. Many of Pepper's recordings are available and his complete Pacific Jazz, Galaxy, and *Live at the Village Vanguard* sessions have been released in box sets. Numerous live recordings have also been issued since his death.

what to buy: Art Pepper made a number of classic recordings during the 1950s, but *Meets the Rhythm Section* ♫♫♫♫ (Contemporary, 1957/OJC, 1988, prod. Lester Koenig) has to make any short list of his best albums. Miles Davis was in town and Pepper borrowed his rhythm section, the best in jazz, with pianist Red Garland, bassist Paul Chambers, and drummer Philly Joe Jones. Highlights include Pepper's ironically titled "Straight Life," "Birk's Works," and "Star Eyes." The third volume of Blue Note's *Complete Aladdin Recordings: The Art of Pepper* ♫♫♫♫ (Blue Note, 1957/1988, prod. Don Clark) was originally released by Omegatape, an early form of open-reel, stereo pre-recorded tape. Featuring Pepper's working band at the time, with the great pianist Carl Perkins, bassist George Tucker, and drummer Chuck Flores, the session unfolds like a club date. The program consists mainly of standards, though Pepper contributes "Holiday Flight" and "Surf Ride," a tune he recorded numerous times. Pepper's tone is lithe and warm, and he and Perkins take numerous excellent solos. A landmark album pairing Pepper's gorgeous alto with brilliant Marty Paich arrangements, *Art Pepper+Eleven: Modern Jazz Classics* ♫♫♫♫ (Contemporary, 1959/OJC, 1988, prod. Lester Koenig) is an exceptional example of interaction between a featured soloist and a large ensemble. The material consists entirely of bop and cool jazz compositions, and the CD includes alternate takes of "Walkin'" and "Donna Lee." Inspired music from beginning to end, this album is highly recommended. The first of four albums released from Pepper's historic return to New York, *Thursday Night at the Village Vanguard* ♫♫♫♫ (Contemporary,

1977/OJC, 1992, prod. Lester Koenig), was also released by Fantasy as part of a nine-disc set. Accompanied by a stellar rhythm section, with pianist George Cables, bassist George Mraz, and drummer Elvin Jones, this is no-holds-barred music, especially the extended workout on Gordon Jenkins's "Goodbye," and Pepper's "My Friend John." Pepper felt he had something to prove to New York audiences, and he made his point emphatically.

what to buy next: The second volume of Blue Note's *Complete Aladdin Recordings: Modern Art* ♫♫♫♫ (Blue Note, 1957/1988, prod. Don Clark) features pianist Russ Freeman (replaced by Carl Perkins on the last three tunes), bassist Ben Tucker, and drummer Chuck Flores. Pepper's tone hadn't yet taken on the darker edge it would acquire later, and he takes a highly lyrical approach to his original themes, standards, and swing era material. The second to last album Pepper recorded before losing 15 years to heroin addiction and prison, *Smack Up* ♫♫♫♫ (Contemporary, 1960/OJC, 1987, prod. Lester Koenig) features consistently stimulating tunes, such as Harold Land's title track, Benny Carter's "How Can You Lose," and one of the first recordings of an Ornette Coleman tune, "Tears Inside." Pepper's "Las Cuevas De Mario" was written for his dealer, and the CD contains two takes of the previously unknown "Solid Citizens." The fine quintet includes trumpeter Jack Sheldon, pianist Pete Jolly, bassist Jimmy Bond, and the great drummer Frank Butler. An emotionally searing session, *Straight Life* ♫♫♫♫ (Galaxy, 1979/OJC, 1990, prod. Ed Michel) features pianist Tommy Flanagan (his only recording with Pepper), bassist Red Mitchell, and drummer Billy Higgins. Pepper pushes each tune to the limit in extended explorations of "Nature Boy" and "September Song," and turns in a revelatory version of the title track. *Goin' Home* ♫♫♫♫ (Galaxy, 1982/OJC, 1991, prod. Ed Michel) was Pepper's last recording, an intimate, swinging duo session with pianist George Cables, one of his most important collaborators in his last few years. He divides his time between alto and his first horn, clarinet, which he plays with a warm, delicate sound. The ballads, "Lover Man," "You Go to My Head," and "Don't Let the Sun Catch You Cryin'," are particularly emotional.

best of the rest:

The Art Pepper Quartet ♫♫♫♫ (Tampa/OJC, 1956)
The Complete Aladdin, Vol. 1: The Return of Art Pepper ♫♫♫♫♫ (Blue Note, 1957/Capitol, 1988)
The Artistry of Pepper ♫♫♫♫ (Pacific Jazz, 1957/1992)
Gettin' Together! ♫♫♫♫ (Contemporary, 1960/OJC, 1988)
Intensity ♫♫♫♫ (Contemporary, 1960/OJC, 1989)
Living Legend ♫♫♫♫ (Contemporary, 1975/OJC, 1990)
San Francisco Samba ♫♫♫♫ (Contemporary, 1977/1997)
Tokyo Debut ♫♫♫♫ (Galaxy, 1977/OJC, 1995)

Art Pepper: The Complete Village Vanguard Sessions ♫♫♫♫ (Contemporary, 1977/1995)
Landscape ♫♫♫♫ (Galaxy, 1979/OJC, 1991)
Winter Moon ♫♫♫♫ (Galaxy, 1980/OJC, 1991)
Art 'N' Zoot ♫♫♫♫ (Pablo, 1981)
Art Pepper with Duke Jordan in Copenhagen ♫♫♫♫♡ (Galaxy, 1981)
Roadgame ♫♫♫♫ (Galaxy, 1981/OJC, 1993)
Tete-a-Tete ♫♫♫♫ (Galaxy/OJC, 1982)
Art Pepper: The Complete Galaxy Recordings ♫♫♫♫♫ (Galaxy, 1989)

worth searching for: Virtually the only recording of Pepper between 1961–74, *Art Pepper Quartet '64: In San Francisco* ♫♫♫♫ (Fresh Sound, 1964, prod. Jordi Pujol) captures the alto saxophonist at a time when he was strongly influenced by Coltrane (a development that disappointed many of his fans). With pianist Frank Strazzeri, bassist Hersh Hamel, and drummer Bill Goodwin, the music was recorded from a TV appearance and at the Jazz Workshop. The sound quality isn't great, but Pepper plays with considerable intensity, using his new, heavier sound on his originals "The Trip" and "D Section," and revisiting his earlier approach on the standard "Summer Night" and Rollins's "Sonnymoon for Two." The disc also includes a brief interview with Ralph Gleason.

influences:
◀◀ Benny Carter, Lester Young, Charlie Parker

Andrew Gilbert

Ivo Perelman

Born on January 12, 1961, in Sao Paulo, Brazil.

A proficient classical guitarist as a pre-teen, Ivo Perelman played clarinet, trombone, piano, and cello before finding his true voice on the tenor saxophone at the age of 19. He recalls that memorable first encounter with child-like wonder: "It was all melody and air and expression. It felt like an animal, an entity, a living thing. I became one with a living thing." Never one to follow the traditional study methods (he works mostly by ear and without charts, as a "free" improviser), Perelman dropped out of Berklee music school after a semester, traveled abroad, and ended up in Los Angeles in 1986. In L.A. he studied privately to develop his technique and soon began gigging. Three years later, the tiny K2B2 label released his recording debut, *Ivo*, featuring an all-star band, including Airto, Flora Purim, John Patitucci, Peter Erskine, Don Preston, Buell Neidlinger, and Eliane Elias. This album proved to be the first in a one-of-a-kind trilogy of revamped children's tunes with Euro-Brazilian, African, and Tapeba Indian roots. The saxophonist's use of singsong folk ma-

terial as a springboard for improv abstraction echoes the ethos of proto-avant-gardist Albert Ayler. But contrary to myopic critical assessment, Perelman is no clone. "I never even heard Albert Ayler," insists the artist, "until I read that I was supposed to imitate him." The immediacy of Perelman's sound—a variable palette both rich and reedy, rife with muscular attack, soaring melodies, bent phrasing, wily pitch-shifting, blaring split-tones, and ferocious glissandi—has worked to his advantage among the vanguard of New York City's Downtown scene, where he's been active since the early 1990s. Over the past couple of years the saxophonist has recorded with a rare prolificacy, collaborating with such great musicians of the day as Rashied Ali, Marilyn Crispell, Borah Bergman, William Parker, Matthew Shipp, Joe Morris, Dominic Duval, and Gerry Hemingway.

what to buy: *Tapeba Songs* ♫♫♫♫ (Ibeji, 1996, prod. Ivo Perelman) is the final part of the above-mentioned trilogy. Perelman heads an all-Latin ensemble of Jose Eduardo Nazario (percussion), Lelo Nazario (keys), Rodolfo Stroeter (bass), and the incomparable classical guitarist Paulo Bellinati. A young Tapeba girl named Luciana opens "Agua de Manim" with a delightful a capella melody that's picked up and transformed by Perelman's sprawling tenor sax tone. *Strings* ♫♫♫♫ (Leo, 1997, prod. Ivo Perelman) finds Perelman, for the first time on CD, on cello, bringing the gutsy restlessness of his sax playing to this instrument, joined by the brilliant Joe Morris on acoustic guitar. On this unusual improvisation bristling with innovation, Perelman at times drops the four-string and emits vocal outbursts of a primordial fervor. *Strings* is a singular achievement in the history of improvised music. *Children of Ibeji* ♫♫♫♫♡ (Enja, 1992, prod. Ivo Perelman) is number two in the renowned trilogy. Perelman's in heady company with the likes of Don Pullen, Paul Bley, Flora Purim, Andrew Cyrille, Fred Hopkins, and Brandon Ross. The saxophonist is at his most lyrical and inspired interpreting these beautiful folk melodies of his native land.

what to buy next: *En Adir: Traditional Jewish Songs* ♫♫♫♫♡ (Music & Arts, 1997, prod. Ivo Perelman) has the raucous ebullience of a Jewish wedding combined with the exploratory intensity of jazz improvisation. Marilyn Crispell, famous from her Anthony Braxton Quartet tenure, pushes Perelman to soar. Under Gunther Schuller's direction, Perelman interprets fives motifs by Brazil's acclaimed classical composer Heitor Villa-Lobos on *Man of the Forest* ♫♫♫♫♡ (GM, 1994, prod. Gunther Schuller, Ivo Perelman). The impressive ensemble includes Joanne Brackeen, Nana Vasconcelos, Billy Hart, Mark Helias, and a fiery quartet of Latino accompanists. *Blue Monk Variations* ♫♫♫♫ (Cadence Jazz, 1996, prod. Ivo Perelman) offers an impromptu series of solo extrapolations on the Thelonious Monk standard. If you're curious to hear precisely how Perelman dissects and reconstructs melody from multi-tiered vantages, this disc's for you. No matter how far into the cosmos Perelman pushes the tune, the melody retains its character.

the rest:

(With Jose Eduardo Nazario) *Soccer Land* ♫♫♫♪ (Ibeji, 1994)
(With Matthew Shipp and William Parker) *"Came de Terra"* ♫♫♫♪ (Homestead, 1996)
(With Rashied Ali and William Parker) *Sad Life* ♫♫♫♪ (Sad Life, 1996)
(With Rory Stuart) *Revelation* ♫♫♪ (CIMP, 1996)
Slaves of Job ♫♫♫♪ (CIMP, 1996)
Geometry ♫♫♫♪ (Leo, 1997)
(With Marilyn Crispell) *Sound Hierarchy* ♫♫♫♪ (Music & Arts, 1997)

worth searching for: Melodic, accessible, uncompromising, and torrential, *Ivo* ♫♫♫♪ (K2B2, 1989, prod. Marty Krystall) is the monumental debut, and the first part of his trilogy. The top-drawer bandmates are mentioned above.

influences:
◄◄ John Coltrane, Gato Barbieri, Albert Ayler, Brazilian folk songs

Sam Prestianni

Danilo Perez

Born 1966, in Panama City, Panama.

Danilo Perez is one of the most promising young musicians in jazz, a technically dazzling pianist who is part of a vanguard of young Latin American musicians combining Afro-Caribbean influences with bebop and post-bop. A thrilling improvisor who has developed a polyrhythmic group approach, Perez creates and solves musical dilemmas as he solos, working out surprising solutions with his keen rhythmic sensibility. Raised in a musical household, Perez started playing piano at age eight, and studied the Western classical tradition at the National Conservatory in Panama. He didn't really delve into jazz until he came to the United States, ending up in Boston in 1985 to study at Berklee. Before he finished his degree he was working with singer Jon Hendricks, trumpeter Claudio Roditi, and serving as pianist/musical director for Paquito D'Rivera's Havana–New York Music Ensemble. He gained widespread exposure during his four-year stint with Dizzy Gillespie (1989–1992), touring widely with his United Nation Orchestra and the Diamond Jubilee Tribute to Gillespie, which culminated in the live Telarc recording *To Bird with Love*. In addition to his own three excellent albums, Perez has recorded with Arturo Sandoval, Dave Samuels, Richie Zelon, David Sanchez, and Tom Harrell.

what to buy: A brilliant album that seems to flow seamlessly from one tune to the next, *Panamonk* ♫♫♫♪ (Impulse!, 1996, prod. Tommy LiPuma) opens and closes with brief versions of "Monk's Mood." In between, Perez weaves back and forth between four Thelonious Monk classics and "Bright Mississippi," a Monkian take on "Sweet Georgia Brown," four strong original tunes, and "Everything Happens to Me." The band features Avishai Cohen on bass, Terri Lyne Carrington and Jeff "Tain" Watts on drums, and singer Olga Roman on Perez's "September in Rio." His music is full of fire and soul, densely textured and technically demanding. Perez wrote and arranged all the material on *The Journey* ♫♫♫♪ (Novus, 1994, prod. John Snyder), an ambitious work that describes the enslavement of Africans and their experience in the new world through the eventual emergence of a new, free people. Incorporating various African, Cuban, and Caribbean influences, Perez's suites are woven together with rhythmic themes. The core rhythm section of Perez, Ignacio Berroa (drums), and Larry Grenadier is highly effective, as is David Sanchez's tenor and soprano work.

what to buy next: An extremely impressive debut by one of the most exciting young pianists in jazz, *Danilo Perez* ♫♫♫♪ (Novus, 1993, prod. Kathryn King) features an all-star band with Joe Lovano and David Sanchez on tenor and soprano saxophones, Santi Debriano on bass, and Jack DeJohnette on drums. An Afro-Caribbean jazz journey, the album moves between standards such as "Body and Soul" and "Time on My Hands," the bolero "Solo Contigo Basta," and some excellent originals, including "Claudio," Perez's tribute to the Brazilian trumpeter Roditi. And then to mix things up there's Ruben Blades singing on "Skylark," and somehow it works.

influences:
◄◄ Thelonious Monk, Bill Evans, Chick Corea

Andrew Gilbert

Carl Perkins

Born August 16, 1928, in Indianapolis, IN. Died March 17, 1958, in Los Angeles, CA.

One of the great, forgotten hard bop pianists, Carl Perkins was a self-taught musician who developed a spare, funky, rhythmically dynamic style. His use of chords was as harmonically advanced as anyone playing in the mid-1950s. Due to a childhood bout with polio, his left hand was slightly disabled and he played the piano with a distinctive, unorthodox posture, leaning forward with his left arm held parallel to the keyboard. Perkins broke into music in 1948, touring with the R&B bands of Tiny Bradshaw and Big Jay McNeely. He settled in Los Angeles the next year and quickly became one of the busiest pianists on the Los Angeles scene. He worked with Miles Davis in 1950 and became the trumpeter's first-call pianist when he came through town without a band. He recorded with Illinois Jacquet in 1951, then spent two years in the Army. A member of guitarist Oscar Moore's trio intermittently between 1953 and 1955, Perkins also recorded extensively with Art Pepper on some of his best sessions of the mid-1950s. He played in one of the first incarnations of the Max Roach/Clifford Brown Quintet in 1954 and contributed greatly to the success of the classic 1955 album *Dexter Gordon Blows Hot and Cool* and Harold Land's *Harold in the Land of Jazz*, which contains the first recording of Perkins's standard "Grooveyard." He is best known for his recordings with the great hard-bop quintet led by bassist Curtis Counce with Land (tenor sax), Jack Sheldon or Gerald Wilson (trumpet), and Frank Butler (drums). The quintet recorded three excellent albums on Contemporary, including *Carl's Blues*, which was released and dedicated to his memory soon after his death from a heroin overdose. Always the sideman, Perkins recorded only one album under his own name.

what's available: Originally released on the R&B-oriented Dootone label, *Introducing Carl Perkins* 𝄢𝄢𝄢𝄢 (Fresh Sound, 1955) is the legendary pianist's only jazz album as a leader, a trio session featuring his childhood friend from Indianapolis, Leroy Vinnegar (bass), and the ubiquitous Los Angeles drummer Lawrence Marable. With six standards and five Perkins originals, this session is well worth searching out, as Perkins is a perpetually funky player with a very original approach. His ballad work often shines, but it's his highly effective work on his mid-tempo original, "Marblehead," and the up-tempo versions of "Woody 'N' You" and "Just Friends" that leave the lasting impression.

influences:

◀◀ Nat "King" Cole

▶▶ Les McCann, Bobby Timmons, Ramsey Lewis

Andrew Gilbert

Tom Peron
/Bud Spangler Quartet

Formed 1992, in Sacramento, CA.

Tom Peron, trumpet; Bud Spangler, drums; John Wiitala, bass; Jessica Williams, piano (1992–94); Joe Gilman, piano (1995–present).

After years of playing together informally, Peron and Spangler made it official in 1992. Peron was a veteran California-based

trumpeter and Spangler had been a Bay Area radio personality and a member of the Contemporary Jazz Quartet. Their straight-ahead approach is enhanced by Peron's excellent compositions—two on their first recording and four on the second. This is post-bop music in the vein of the CJQ and Miles Davis's acoustic bands of the '60s. Peron is a marvelous, melodic improviser and the group is a tight, sensitive unit.

what's available: Their debut, *Interplay* 𝄢𝄢𝄢 (Monarch, 1994, prod. Tom Peron, Bud Spangler), contains excellent interpretations of standards such as "Oleo" and "We See," but Peron's "Mr. Billou's Groove" and "Trumpeter's Revenge" stand out as substantial and inviting modern bebop. *Dedication* 𝄢𝄢𝄢 (Monarch, 1996, prod. Tom Peron, Bud Spangler) shows a slightly more modern approach, and Peron's compositions are a little more expansive and invite the musicians to stretch out.

influences:

◀◀ Contemporary Jazz Quintet, Miles Davis, Chet Baker, Clifford Brown

Larry Gabriel

Eric Person

Born May 2, 1963, in St. Louis, MO.

Person's father, saxophonist Thomas Person, sparked his son's interest in music (and choice of instruments, which include soprano, sopranino, and alto saxophones, as well as keyboards and slave bells). A product of St. Louis's famed Normandy High School music program, Eric continued his studies at the St. Louis Conservatory of Music. A move to New York paid off with a wide variety of work. There was straight-ahead jazz with Woody Shaw, Jackie McLean, and the big bands of John Hicks and McCoy Tyner, and more adventurous work with several of Chico Hamilton's groups, the Dave Holland Quartet (*Dream of the Elders*), the World Saxophone Quartet (*Moving Right Along*), Franklin Kiermyer (*Kairos*), and a five-album tenure in Ronald Shannon Jackson's Decoding Society. Person has also worked in projects on the fringes of jazz or even outside it: Vernon Reid's Living Colour, guitarist Kelvyn Bell's Kelvynator, and recording work with singer/guitarist Ben Harper on his charting album *The Will to Live*. Person has recorded three albums as a leader with Soul Note and currently has a new working ensemble, Meta-Four. He was seen in cable channel BRAVO's documentary on Blue Note Records.

what to buy: *More Tales to Tell* 𝄢𝄢𝄢 (Soul Note, 1997, prod. Eric Person) moves Person toward the mainstream without compromising his musical principles. Though marred somewhat by overly close and bright recording that can make the album tough on the ears, it reveals Person to be a fine composer and versatile improvisor. The only covers are Miles Davis's "Little Church" and pop star Terence Trent D'Arby's "If You Should Go Before Me," and it speaks well of Person's writing and arranging that they fit in seamlessly.

what to buy next: After his work as a sideman, Person struck out on his own with the fine quartet album *Arrival* &&&& (Soul Note, 1993, prod. Eric Person); Hamilton bandmate Cary DeNigris appears on guitar on two tracks here. The leader's well-structured, organic tunes and thoughtful improvisations shift smoothly through a variety of moods, sometimes suggesting the free-floating modalism of the mid-1960s Miles Davis Quintet.

the rest:
Prophecy &&& (Soul Note, 1994)

worth searching for: Person's work with Chico Hamilton is his most notable in a solidly jazz-oriented context. *My Panamanian Friend* &&&& (Soul Note, 1994, prod. Chico Hamilton) offers the opportunity to hear Person stretch out on seven Eric Dolphy tunes, and he acquits himself well. DeNigris and bassist Kenny Davis fill out the quartet. *Trio!* &&&& (Soul Note, 1993, prod. Chico Hamilton) finds Person, Hamilton, and DeNegris in a more free-wheeling setting, with a third of the pieces composed by Person or co-written with Hamilton.

influences:
◀◀ John Coltrane, Wayne Shorter

Steve Holtje

Houston Person

Born November 10, 1934, in Florence, SC.

Along with Grant Green, Stanley Turrentine, Charles Earland, and Richard "Groove" Holmes, tenor saxophonist Houston Person was at the forefront of the "groove jazz" movement in the late 1960s/early 1970s. A pianist as a child, Person took up tenor sax at age 17 to become one of the more prolific saxophonists on the jazz scene with a style that has served him well both commercially and artistically for over three decades. Person's first major break came when he played with organist Johnny "Hammond" Smith. After he left Smith's group, he began a fruitful solo career, but continued to do extensive work as a sideman, including a long relationship with singer Etta Jones. Since the late 1970s, Person has been the house producer and saxophonist for HighNote (formerly Muse) Records.

As HighNote's session saxophonist of choice, he can always be counted on to deliver tasteful solos with his unique tone. Person's recordings are fun, and though sometimes predictable, generally filled with good playing. While he has strong R&B and blues influences, he is an excellent and underrated straight-ahead player whose funkier jazz dates feature more sophisticated playing than usually heard in such settings.

what to buy: *Goodness!* &&&& (Prestige, 1969, eng. Rudy Van Gelder) is representative of the better groove-based jazz recordings of the late 1960s. The upbeat songs swing, the ballads are interpreted with class, and there's enough R&B to push it over the edge. If you've forgotten just how good this type of jazz could be, throw this on. The Sonny Phillips composition "Jamilah" in particular is one of the best of its kind. A very capable straight-ahead player, Person succeeds in producing a great organless quartet record on *Person-ified* &&&& (HighNote, 1997, prod. Houston Person). Person plays a number of standards with great poise, and what this might lack in adventure it makes up for in beauty and class. Person's interpretations of "I'll Never Stop Loving You," "Stranger on the Shore," and "Gentle Rain" highlight this fine recording. *The Complete Muse Sessions* &&&& (Muse, 1989,1990/32 Jazz, 1997, prod. Houston Person) contains Person's two duet dates with Ron Carter, *Something in Common* and *Now's the Time*. Reissued by 32 Jazz, they are well worth pursuing. Person shines here and Carter is Carter. Interestingly, the sparse setting provides even more evidence that Person is the master of the popular song, as he carries the songs with minimal backing. Both discs are very good, but the second recording, *Now's the Time*, is looser and the interplay is better.

what to buy next: Very representative of Person's bluesy organ dates of late, *The Opening Round* &&&& (Savant, 1997, prod. Houston Person) features Person with Joey DeFrancesco, Person's organist of choice over the past several years, and Rodney Jones, Tracy Wormworth, and Bernard Purdie. The bluesy record combines some jazz standards with some pop hits, including "Let's Stay Together," "What's Goin' On," and "When a Man Loves a Woman." *Lost & Found* &&&& (Muse 1978,1991/ 32 Jazz, 1997, prod. Houston Person) is a reissue of two Person albums, the 1978 *Wildflower* and the previously unreleased *Sweet Slumber* featuring Charles Brown. Not surprisingly, *Sweet Slumber* is a traditional blues record, with Brown's inimitable style the justifiable center of attention. Brown and Person deliver what's expected from their pairing, which makes it worth purchasing. *Wildflower* is typical Person, with Sonny Phillips handling organ chores. Perfectly fine, save for a track or two, but not up to level of *Sweet Slumber*. Houston plays, Etta sings, and guys like Randy Johnston join in a for a blues-filled Christmas that is well above average on *Christmas with Houston Person & Etta Jones* ♫♫♫ (32 Jazz, 1997, prod. Houston Person). *Legends of Acid Jazz* ♫♫♫ (Prestige, 1970–1971/1996, prod. various) is a reissue of two Person albums, *Person to Person!* and *Houston Express*. *Person to Person!* is more rooted in the blues with the classic organ sound, while *Houston Express* puts Person in a larger, more pop-oriented vehicle fronting several brass players. Like most of Person's albums, there are some great tracks, usually a good cover or two, a couple mediocre songs, and an occasional clunker.

influences:

◄◄ Ike Quebec, Stanley Turrentine, Lou Donaldson, Gene Ammons, Illinois Jacquet

►► Grover Washington Jr., Tom Scott, Nat Simpkins

Paul MacArthur

Oscar Peterson

Born August 15, 1925, in Montreal, Quebec, Canada.

Few major jazz musicians have been criticized as scathingly as Oscar Peterson has, which is puzzling considering he's one of the most prodigious pianists in jazz history. Though his early style was derivative of Nat "King" Cole, by the early 1950s he had developed a highly personal style that incorporated elements of Teddy Wilson and Earl Hines and was characterized by flawless technique, vast harmonic knowledge, and the overwhelming power of swing. Frequently faulted for a supposed lack of "soul" (a criticism that doesn't bear scrutiny), Peterson has also been attacked for his ostentatious speed and repetitive phrasing. It's true that his albums suffer from a lack of variety, but he's also one of the most recorded and consistent musicians in jazz history. Peterson gained attention with his tremendous technical skill at a young age, winning an amateur radio contest at 14. He was featured on a weekly radio program in the early 1940s, then developed his touch as an accompanist while working with the Johnny Holms Orchestra in the mid-1940s in Montreal. In the late 1940s, impresario Norman Granz heard Peterson in Canada and presented him at a Carnegie Hall "Jazz at the Philharmonic" concert in 1949. It was the beginning of one of the most prolific artist/producer relationships in jazz history. Granz made Peterson a cornerstone of each new label he founded or was involved with, including Verve, Clef, Norgran, Mercury, and Pablo. While working as Verve's house pianist in the 1950s, Peterson recorded with a Who's Who of jazz royalty, including Billie Holiday, Ella Fitzgerald,

Lester Young, Ben Webster, Coleman Hawkins, and Louis Armstrong. Granz promoted Peterson's career by featuring him on JATP tours in the early 1950s, but Peterson found his musical home with a piano/bass/guitar trio he created (modeled after Nat Cole's) in the mid-1950s. Using tight and intricate arrangements, the Oscar Peterson Trio, featuring Herb Ellis's stinging guitar lines and Ray Brown's powerful, blues-drenched bass work, was one of the most popular and commanding groups in jazz. When Ellis left in 1958, drummer Ed Thigpen came on board, creating another stable and popular trio that lasted until 1965. After a few years in the late 1960s and early 1970s recording for the MPS/BASF label, Peterson rejoined forces with Granz on Pablo, where he recorded frequently with such label stalwarts as Joe Pass, Dizzy Gillespie, Count Basie, Niels-Henning Ørsted Pedersen, Clark Terry, and others. He has continued to tour through the 1980s and 1990s, recording for Telarc, and recovered almost completely from a stroke he suffered in 1993. Many of Peterson's recordings have been reissued on CD, especially his Verve and Pablo sessions. In 1988, lyricist and jazz historian Gene Lees published a fine biography of the pianist, *The Will to Swing*.

what to buy: An excellent two-disc set that documents Peterson with a host of his musical collaborators, *History of an Artist* ♫♫♫♫ (Pablo, 1972–74/1993, prod. Norman Granz) was designed by Granz to recapture various groupings from OP's long career. Besides one solo track (his meditative "Lady of the Lavender Mist") and three duos with Ray Brown, the music features trios with a revolving cast, including guitarists Joe Pass, Irving Ashby, Herb Ellis, and Barney Kessel; bassists Ray Brown, Sam Jones, George Mraz, and Niels Pedersen; and drummers Louis Hayes and Bobby Durham. The level of musicianship is uniformly high, and Peterson is often in astounding form. One of the definitive (and last) recordings by the OP Trio with Herb Ellis and Ray Brown, *At the Concertgebouw* ♫♫♫♫ (Verve, 1957/1994, prod. Norman Granz) was a typically sloppy Granz production (despite the title, the session was recorded at Chicago's Civic Opera House). No matter, the music is simply superb. After playing together for four years, the trio breaths as one. The solos are consistently excellent, but it's the intuitive accompaniment behind the soloists that made this version of the OP Trio so exceptional. Highlights include thrilling versions of Clifford Brown's "Joy Spring" and "Daahoud," a relaxed run through "Bluesology" that should lay to rest the rap about OP being a soulless player, and a medium-tempo take on "I've Got the World on a String" in which OP displays his Nat Cole roots. One of Peterson's most enjoyable sessions, *Oscar Peterson Trio + 1* ♫♫♫♫ (EmArcy, 1964/1984) features his second great trio with bassist Ray Brown and drummer Ed Thigpen, plus special guest Clark Terry on trumpet and flugelhorn. This is also the first time Terry recorded his "mumbles" routine. Terry has one of the most vivacious sounds in jazz, and he is in full flight throughout, even turning the ballads into high-spirited occasions. Peterson and Terry are particularly effective together on the delicate but hard-swinging "Squeaky's Blues" and "Brotherhood of Man," which also features some brilliant traps work by Thigpen. Only the second solo session OP ever recorded, *Tracks* ♫♫♫♫ (MPS, 1971/Verve, 1994, prod. Hans Georg Brunner Schwer) is a tour de force featuring 10 pieces in which Peterson gives his imagination full and unfettered freedom. The results are often breathtaking as he unveils surprise after surprise, changing tempos and keys and breaking into torrid stride passages. He also waxes sensitive on "A Child Is Born" and "Django." But it's his full-throttle versions of "Honeysuckle Rose," "A Little Jazz Exercise," and "Give Me the Simple Life" that leave one's mouth agape.

what to buy next: One of five duo sessions OP recorded with great trumpeters (the others are with Gillespie, Terry, Eldridge, and Faddis), *Oscar Peterson & Harry Edison* ♫♫♫♫ (Pablo, 1975/OJC, 1992, prod. Norman Granz) is a romp in the park on a sunny day, with the two masters treading lightly through seven standards and two bluesy originals. On paper, pairing Sweets Edison's spare, wryly pungent trumpet style with OP's extravagant and effusive piano might seem like a non-starter, but the session is a complete success. A two-disc set that pairs two incomparable masters, *Oscar Peterson et Joe Pass à la Salle Pleyel* ♫♫♫♫ (Pablo, 1975/1997, prod. Norman Granz) opens with seven solo tracks by OP, including a trademark chops-busting run through "Sweet Georgia Brown" and a five-tune Ellington medley, followed by five unaccompanied pieces by Pass. The second disc features a no-holds-barred duo set where OP and Pass play at a preternatural level. Peterson thrived in the trio setting, and *The Trio* ♫♫♫♫ (Pablo, 1973/1991, prod. Norman Granz) was one of the most inspired sessions from his prolific Pablo period. Featuring exceptional support from guitarist Joe Pass and bassist Niels Pedersen, OP turns the piano inside out as he tears though five pieces. Opening with a thrilling version of "Blues Etude," where OP flows through various styles, including stride, boogie woogie, and Nat Cole runs, the set also contains a gorgeous version of Duke Ellington's "Come Sunday." Two masters of swing pair up on *Satch and Josh* ♫♫♫♫ (Pablo, 1975/1988, prod. Norman Granz), a session that unites jazz's greatest minimalist, Count Basie, with Peterson, one of the music's most extravagant embellishers. Accompanied by a peerless rhythm section with guitarist Freddie Green, bassist Ray Brown, and drummer Louie Bellson, Basie (on organ and piano) and OP offer a fascinating series of sketches where their contrasting styles seem to meld effortlessly. Six of the ten tunes are Basie-OP collaborations, though the album's highlights are Basie's classic "Jumpin' at the Woodside" and the standard "These Foolish Things (Remind Me of You)."

what to avoid: Though Peterson and Joe Pass were exceptionally consistent musicians, *Porgy & Bess* ♫♫ (Pablo/OJC, 1976, prod. Norman Granz) is a rare dud in their discographies, mostly due to Peterson's unaccountable decision to use a clavichord, a predecessor to the piano. Pass does his best under the circumstances, sticking exclusively to acoustic guitar, but the circumstances quickly move from novelty to boredom. Gershwin's melodies certainly gain nothing from clavichord treatment, and Peterson never recorded on the instrument again, making this an item of interest only for Peterson fanatics. (This Pablo session should not be confused with OP's fine Verve album, *Plays Porgy and Bess*.)

best of the rest:

The Complete Young Oscar Peterson ♫♫♫♫ (Black and Blue, 1945–49/1994)
Plays the Gershwin Songbooks ♫♫♫♫ (Verve, 1952–59/1996)
The Oscar Peterson Trio at Zardi's ♫♫♫♫ (Pablo, 1955/1994)
Plays Count Basie ♫♫♫♫ (Clef, 1956/Verve, 1993)
Oscar Peterson plays "My Fair Lady" and the Music from "Fiorello!" ♫♫♫♫ (Verve, 1958–60/1994)
Plays Porgy and Bess ♫♫♫♫ (Verve, 1959/1993)
The Jazz Soul of Oscar Peterson/Affinity ♫♫♫♫ (Verve, 1959/1962/1996)
The London House Sessions ♫♫♫♫ (Verve, 1962/1996)
Busting Out with the All Star Big Band ♫♫♫♫ (Verve, 1962/1996)
We Get Requests ♫♫♫♫ (Verve, 1965/1997)
The Good Life ♫♫♫♫ (Pablo, 1973/OJC, 1991)
Oscar Peterson & Clark Terry ♫♫♫♫ (Pablo, 1975/OJC, 1994)
Oscar Peterson & Dizzy Gillespie ♫♫♫♫ (Pablo, 1975/1987)
Oscar Peterson in Russia ♫♫♫♫ (Pablo, 1976/1996)
Montreux '77 ♫♫♫♫ (Pablo, 1977/OJC, 1989)
Nigerian Marketplace ♫♫♫♫ (Pablo, 1982/1988)
Two of the Few ♫♫♫♫ (Pablo, 1983/OJC, 1992)
A Tribute to My Friends ♫♫♫♫ (Pablo, 1984/OJC, 1996)
Oscar Peterson + Harry Edison + Eddie "Cleanhead" Vinson ♫♫♫♫ (Pablo, 1987/1987)
Oscar Peterson Live ♫♫♫♫ (Pablo, 1987)
Saturday Night at the Blue Note ♫♫♫♫ (Telarc, 1991)
Last Call at the Blue Note ♫♫♫♫ (Telarc, 1992)
Encore at the Blue Note ♫♫♫♫ (Telarc, 1993)
Side by Side ♫♫♫ (Telarc, 1994)

The More I See You 🎵🎵🎵🎵 (Telarc, 1995)
Oscar Peterson Meets Roy Hargrove and Ralph Moore 🎵🎵🎵🎵 (Telarc, 1996)
Oscar in Paris 🎵🎵🎵🎵 (Telarc, 1997)

worth searching for: Norman Granz used Peterson frequently as an accompanist, even when his style didn't fit the vocalist, such as OP's many sessions with Billie Holiday. But there's no question that Peterson was the right man for the job on *How Long Has This Been Going On?* 🎵🎵🎵🎵 (Pablo, 1978/1987, prod. Norman Granz), Sarah Vaughan's best Pablo recording. Sassy's voice had attained its full richness, and Peterson matches her incomparable chops without getting in her way. Joe Pass, Ray Brown, and Louie Bellson round out the dream-team rhythm section. Peterson is as effective on Vaughan's slow, sensuous versions of "Midnight Sun" and "Easy Living" as on her romp through "When Your Lover Has Gone," which also features some expert Bellson traps work.

influences:

◀◀ Nat "King" Cole, Teddy Wilson, Earl Hines

▶▶ Monty Alexander, Ross Tompkins, Benny Green, Phineas Newborn Jr.

Andrew Gilbert

Ralph Peterson Jr.

Born May 20, 1962, in Pleasantville, NJ.

Percussionist/composer Ralph Peterson Jr.'s first recording date as a leader began auspiciously with a deliciously syncopated drum stroll from out of the blue that ushered in a sterling version of "Bemsha Swing." Ever since, he has delivered drumming with a chunky Thelonious Monk-ian gait and an Art Blakey-esqe big beat. More recently, he dedicated an entire album to composer/pianist T. S. Monk Sr. The rest varies in quality, to be sure, but regardless, Peterson is one of the most interesting young drummers to come along since the '80s.

what to buy: *Triangular* 🎵🎵🎵🎵 (Blue Note, 1989, prod. Kazunori Sugiyama, Hitoshi Namekata), which remains Peterson's only appearance in a trio setting thus far, is a wickedly clever and terribly accomplished outing, a minor masterpiece of sequencing, pace, and drive. Its octavian eight pieces build in complexity and intensity alike as the record progresses, and Geri Allen's pianistics are

thrilling and exciting throughout. The group is grounded nicely by bassist Essiet Okon Essiet and, in a single instance, Phil Bowler. On the other hand, it is the work of the so-called Fo'Tet, which made its debut with *Ralph Peterson Presents the Fo'Tet* 🎵🎵🎵🎵 (Blue Note, 1991 prod. Kazunori Sugiyama) and was followed at the end of the year with *Ornettology* 🎵🎵🎵🎵 (Blue Note, 1991, prod. Ralph Peterson, Kazunori Sugiyama). Constructed around the impeccable fluidity of clarinetist Don Byron, this earliest incarnation of the Fo'Tet also featured the four-mallet vibraharping of Bryan Carrott (who remains with the band) and the foursquare basswork of Melissa Slocum (who hasn't). Regardless, both albums are excellent. *Presents*, which includes a Byron-penned tribute to Lee Morgan, has the harder, more boppish surfaces. The tribute to Ornette Coleman is, as you'd expect, slightly more conceptual and out, with its quartet core augmented on a pair of tracks by David Murray and Frank Lacy. It concludes with Peterson switching over briefly to the cornet for a reading of "There Is No Greater Love," with a smart, tart melodicism.

what to buy next: By the time the Fo'Tet resurfaced with *The Reclamation Project* 🎵🎵🎵🎵 (Evidence, 1995, prod. John Snyder), Belden Bullock had joined as the band's bassist, and Byron had been replaced by soprano saxophonist Steve Wilson. It's this same lineup that offered *The Fo'Tet Plays Monk* 🎵🎵🎵🎵 (Evidence, 1997, prod. John Snyder). Wilson is a less slippery and inventive conceptualist than Byron, and the resulting reduction in improvisational adventurousness slightly diminishes the overall product. Within the narrower context of this particular edition of the band, however, and despite the Monk album's obviously stunning array of thematic material, *Reclamation* is the stronger effort. Comprised entirely of Peterson originals (some of which are extremely Monkish—"Further Fo" and "Insanity," for example), the record recounts a series of particularly dark hours of the soul.

what to avoid: The Blakey memorial album, *Art* 🎵🎵 (Blue Note, 1994, prod. Ralph Peterson, Kazunori Sugiyama), sure is a letdown. That's partially due to the insidious corporate Demands of the Marketplace that Peterson details in his notes to *The Reclamation Project*; nevertheless, whatever the reason, why bother? Ditto for *Volition* 🎵🎵🎵 (Blue Note, 1990, prod. Kazunori Sugiyama), although it includes yet another interesting performance by Allen. Her solo on "Forth & Back," in fact, really shines.

influences:

◀◀ Art Blakey, Thelonious Monk

▶▶ Don Byron

David Prince

Michel Petrucciani

Born December 28, 1962, in Orange, France.

Petrucciani studied classical piano as a child and first played in concert at 13. After polishing his skills in a family band with his guitarist father (Tony) and bassist brother (Louis), the pianist was soon performing with major jazz figures such as Clark Terry, and by the time he was 19, was recording with Lee Konitz and Charles Lloyd. Soon after, he began recording for Blue Note, achieving considerable popularity in the United States. A pivotal moment in his career occurred when he played at the 1986 Montreux Festival with Jim Hall and Wayne Shorter, a clear sign of the status he had achieved in a very short time. Petrucciani's style combines the subtle harmonic approach of Bill Evans with a forcefully rhythmic attack. Many of his best moments on record have come with former Evans associates such as Hall, Eddie Gomez, and Gary Peacock, with whom he has shown a gift for complex interplay. However, much of his early promise has been dissipated by distracting commercial elements that he regularly adds to his music, like strings, electric piano, and synthesizers. This, along with sometimes rambunctious displays of technique, has limited the interest of his music in recent years.

what to buy: The best of Petrucciani is to be heard on his first American recording, *Pianism* 🎶🎶🎶🎶 (Blue Note, 1987, prod. Mike Berniker), where his lyricism comes to the fore on "Here's That Rainy Day," and his power shows on a roller-coaster ride of "Night and Day." There's subtle interaction on *Power of Three* 🎶🎶🎶🎶 (Blue Note, 1987, prod. David Rubinson), a recording of the 1986 Montreux Festival with Jim Hall on guitar and Wayne Shorter on soprano and tenor. It's testimony to his mastery of a cool, harmonically subtle approach.

what to buy next: Petrucciani's solo encounter with the Ellington repertoire, *Promenade with Duke* 🎶🎶🎶 (Blue Note, 1993, prod. Gilles Avinzac, Michel Petrucciani), is an often lovely excursion, though it concentrates too heavily on the most familiar parts of the landscape, including "Sophisticated Lady," "Satin Doll," and "Caravan." *Michel Plays Petrucciani* 🎶🎶🎶 (Blue Note, 1993, prod. Eric Kressmann, Michel Petrucciani) displays a rather anonymous composing style, but joins Petrucciani with the best rhythm sections of his recording career thus far, with Gary Peacock or Eddie Gomez on bass, and Roy Haynes or Al Foster on drums.

best of the rest:
Marvellous 🎶🎶🎶 (Dreyfus, 1994)
Live 🎶🎶 (Blue Note, 1994)

Au Theatre Des Champs Elysee 🎶🎶🎶 (Dreyfus, 1997)

influences:
◀◀ Bill Evans, Martial Solal, Oscar Peterson

Stuart Broomer

Madeleine Peyroux

Born in Athens, GA.

Madeleine Peyroux may have come out of nowhere with her 1996 debut, *Dreamland*, but her husky voice and sultry phrasing are easily traced to Billie Holiday. Moving to Paris while in her teens, Peyroux joined a group of Latin Quarter buskers called the Lost Wandering Blues & Jazz Band and learned the vintage songs of Holiday, Bessie Smith, and Fats Waller that dominate her repertoire. Yet she is no nostalgia act: echoing Holiday and Smith without mimicking them, she injects a soulful sassiness into her interpretations that sheds some optimistic light on the brooding subject matter. Like Cassandra Wilson, she and co-producer/arranger Greg Cohen update traditional jazz instrumentation by blending guitars, saxophones, and drums with accordions, dobros, marimbas, violins, and harpsichords. The result is a quirky but intimate sound that rings instantly familiar but never predictable.

what's available: *Dreamland* 🎶🎶🎶🎶 (Atlantic, 1996, prod. Yves Beauvais, Greg Cohen) mixes Peyroux's original compositions with classics associated with Holiday ("Getting Some Fun Out of Life"), Fats Waller ("I'm Gonna Sit Right Down and Write Myself a Letter"), Bessie Smith ("Lovesick Blues," "Muddy Water"), Edith Piaf ("La Vie En Rose"), and Patsy Cline ("Walkin' After Midnight"). Adding to the jaw-dropping authenticity of her delivery is the stellar studio band, which includes James Carter, Cyrus Chestnut, Marcus Printup, Leon Parker, and Marc Ribot.

influences:
◀◀ Billie Holiday, Bessie Smith, Ella Fitzgerald

David Okamoto

Phalanx

Formed 1985, in Europe.

James Blood Ulmer, electric guitar; George Adams, tenor saxophone; Amin Ali, bass (1985); Sirone, bass (1987–88); Grant Calvin Weston, drums (1985); Rashied Ali, drums (1987–88).

Phalanx was born when George Adams, a longtime collaborator with Ulmer going back to their days in organ groups, hooked up with the guitarist's touring band, the Black Rock Trio, a meeting documented on a German album with substandard sonics. A more star-studded Phalanx cast—also reflecting Ulmer's history—was assembled for DIW's two New York City albums.

what to buy: There's not much basis for choosing between the DIW albums, so the misleadingly titled *Original Phalanx* 𝄫𝄫𝄫 (DIW, 1987, prod. Kazunori Sugiyama) gets the nod, as much for chronology as anything. The music is a distinctive mix of John Coltrane–inspired free jazz and Ornette Coleman's harmolodics, with Ali's polyrhythmic drumming and Sirone's meaty basslines filling the sound-picture and allowing the others to concentrate on blowing.

what to buy next: *In Touch* 𝄫𝄫𝄫 (DIW, 1988, prod. Kazunori Sugiyama) is another powerful blast of improvisation. As on the earlier DIW album, Ulmer, Adams, and Sirone split the writing credits, but themes are minimal and the emphasis is on spontaneity.

the rest:
Got Something Good for You 𝄫𝄫 (Moers, 1985)

influences:
◀◀ John Coltrane, Ornette Coleman

▶▶ Jean-Paul Bourelly, UYA

Steve Holtje

Flip Phillips

Born Joseph Edward Fillipelli, February 26, 1915, in Brooklyn, NY.

Tenor saxophonist Phillips began his career playing clarinet in a Brooklyn, New York, restaurant band between 1934 and 1939, then with a band led by Frankie Newton in the early 1940s. He switched to tenor sax for a gig with Larry Bennett's band (1942–43). In 1944, his breakthrough gig came when he replaced saxophonist Vido Musso as a featured soloist in Woody Herman's First Herd, and he remained with the big band until the First Herd broke up in 1946. Phillips toured annually with the legendary "Jazz at the Philharmonic" from 1946 to 1957, acquiring a reputation for his venturesome improvisations and for his ability to match his talents against saxophonists such as Charlie Parker and Lester Young. In 1948, Phillips received accolades in both *Down Beat* and *Metronome* polls for best tenor saxophonist. Before retiring to Pompano Beach, Florida in the late 1950s, Phillips co-led a band with Bill Harris that was the core of the ensemble used by Benny Goodman in 1959. He took occasional gigs and emerged occasionally to perform with Benny Goodman's band during his 15-year hiatus. In 1970, he

began recording and traveling again, making annual appearances at the Colorado Jazz Party. By 1975, he had returned to music full time, recording a few sessions and appearing at clubs, festivals, and jazz parties. He toured Europe in 1982 and continued to record and perform with high energy and peak virtuosity throughout the 1980s. Although Phillips can play ballads, stomps, and standards with equal ardor, he is the tenor sax player most often remembered for his squawking sound during a frenetic solo on "Perdido," performed during the JATP tours. Phillips is ranked with those turbulent saxophonists tagged the "honkers and shouters"—Arnett Cobb, Illinois Jacquet, Gene Ammons, King Curtis, and others—whose improvisations often included the screaming, howling, frantic-paced tempos that paved the way for the R&B stylists. His recordings in the 1980s, especially his Concord sessions, demonstrate his full-bodied, burnished sound.

what to buy: Forty years separate tenor saxophonists Flip Phillips and the younger Scott Hamilton. The two came together in the 1987 studio session *A Sound Investment* 𝄫𝄫𝄫𝄫 (Concord, 1987, prod. Carl E. Jefferson) after years of running into each other at jazz parties. Except for Phillips's smear techniques and a few honks, there's almost no audible difference between the then 70-something saxophonist's renderings and those by Scott, under 40 years old at the time. The session performed with John Bunch (piano), Chris Flory (guitar), Phil Flanigan (bass), and Chuck Riggs (drums) includes mostly swinging and bluesy Phillips originals, including "A Sound Investment," "Blues for the Midgets," "With Someone New, " "Great Scott," and "The Claw," along with the Benny Goodman tune "A Smooth One" and others. "With Someone New" is an incredibly lush ballad that gives the saxophonists vent for some warm, smooth solos and harmonic blends. Swing fans will love this tasteful session for the tempos (especially the quickened pace of "Great Scott"), for the single-mindedness of the two saxmen, and for Phillips's original melodies. While you won't find burning blowing on this highly recommended CD, you'll hear some rich-toned, stately tenorisms and swinging jazz at its best.

what to buy next: Playing tenor saxophone and bass clarinet, Flip Phillips joins a crew of Concord swing masters on *Real Swinger* 𝄫𝄫𝄫𝄫 (Concord, 1988, prod. Carl E. Jefferson). The 11-tune mixture contains swing standards and Phillips originals and backs him with one of the most industrious and masterful swing-jazz crews: pianist Dick Hyman, guitarist Howard Alden, rhythm guitarist Wayne Wright, bassist Jack Lesberg, and drummer Charles "Butch" Miles. Highlights include Phillips's deep, woody, bass clarinet solos on the exotic, subtly swinging Slim

Gaillard tune "Vol Vistu Gailey Star," and on the gorgeous combined ballad "It Was a Very Good Year/September Song." Phillips plays tenor sax on the hot racer "Hashimoto's Blues," on Ellington's righteous swinger "Cotton Tail," and finishes the session with a full-bodied solo on the joyous "I Want to Be Happy." Phillips, in top form on both instruments throughout the session, inspires his soul mates to some of their best playing, and everyone shines on this upbeat, lighthearted outing.

best of the rest:
A Melody from the Sky ♫♫♫♫ (Flying Dutchman, 1944–45/Doctor Jazz, 1993)
The Claw: Live at the Floating Jazz Festival (1986) ♫♫♫♫ (Chiaroscuro, 1992)
At the Helm: Live at the 1993 Floating Jazz Festival ♫♫♫♫ (Chiaroscuro, 1994)

influences:
◀◀ Ben Webster
▶▶ Scott Hamilton

Nancy Ann Lee

Pieces of a Dream

Formed 1979, in Philadelphia, PA.

James K. Lloyd, keyboards; Curtis Harmon, drums; Cedric Napoleon, bass, vocals.

Originally discovered by Grover Washington Jr., this talented trio has endured years of moderate success straddling the line between contemporary jazz and R&B, drafting a succession of singers, guitarists, and other instrumentalists to help with the band's layered, funky records. Beginning as a live-oriented unit emphasizing the group's roots in fusion, Pieces moved more toward sequenced sounds along with the rest of the R&B world in the mid-'80s, eventually recording with mostly synthesized drums, keyboards, and bass sounds. Working with Washington and later Guy mastermind Gene Griffin as producers, the group tickled the R&B charts with songs such as "Warm Weather" in 1982 and "Joyride" in 1986.

what to buy: As the group's most propulsive record and the one bearing its funkiest hit, *Joyride* ♫♫♫ (EMI, 1986, prod. Pieces of a Dream) is packed with funky cuts and real playing by flesh-and-blood musicians, something the group would walk away from in later albums.

what to buy next: Including singer Barbara Walker's compelling take on the sultry "Warm Weather," their debut, *Pieces of a Dream* ♫♫♫ (Discovery, 1981, prod. Grover Washington Jr.), al-

lows the band to stretch the boundaries of what musicians could play on a contemporary R&B record. Later, powerhouse vocalists Lance Webb and Norwood turn *'Bout Dat Time* ♫♫♫ (EMI, 1989, prod. James K. Lloyd, Scott A. Cannady, Gene Griffin, Nayan, Randy Bowland, Preston Middleton, Dinky Bingham) into a singing tour de force fueled by totally up-to-date R&B arrangements.

what to avoid: Chock full of predictable grooves and undistinguished playing, *We Are One* **woof!** (Discovery, 1982) presents a strong argument for the sequencing that would later become the band's staple.

the rest:
Makes You Wanna ♫♫♫ (EMI-Manhattan, 1988)
In Flight ♫♫♫ (EMI-Manhattan, 1993)
Goodbye Manhattan ♫♫♫ (Blue Note Records, 1995)
The Best of Pieces of a Dream ♫♫♫ (Blue Note Records, 1996)
Pieces ♫♫♫ (Blue Note, 1997)

worth searching for: Also featuring performances by jazz luminaries such as Washington and Weather Report, *Playboy Jazz Festival* ♫♫♫ (Elektra/Musician) showcases Pieces of a Dream next to some of its biggest influences in a crackling live environment.

influences:
◀◀ Jeff Lorber, George Duke, Grover Washington Jr.
▶▶ D'Angelo, Maxwell

Eric Deggans

Enrico Pieranunzi

Born December 5, 1949, in Rome, Italy.

Pieranunzi is a lyrical post-bop pianist who would be considerably better known to American jazz fans were he based here rather than in his native Italy. However, with his own trio or the Space Jazz Trio he co-leads with bassist Enzo Pietropaoli, he has frequently accompanied American artists as they pass through Italy and has built long-term collaborations with a number of them. The classical structure in his music is no surprise considering he frequently performs with chamber music groups and is a full professor of piano at the Frosinone Conservatory of Music in Rome. Well-versed in both American and European musical traditions, his style is rich with deep inspiration and complex harmony; a strong force of expression pervades every performance by this musician who is also capable of a concrete sweetness. Pieranunzi has a prominent position in the world jazz scene.

what to buy: *Trioscape* (YVP, 1995) shows imagination, rigor, and joy. Highlights are the interesting phrasing of bassist Piero Leveratto and the contrasting drumming styles of Francesco Petreni (refined) and Mauro Beggio (concrete). In trio with drummer André Ceccarelli and bassist Hein Van de Geyn on *Seaward* (Soul Note, 1996, prod. Giovanni Bonandrini), Pieranunzi stands out in his greatness and profundity. *The Night Gone By* (ALFA Jazz, 1996) is the most classic among Pieranunzi trios, with both bassist Marc Johnson and drummer Paul Motian former Bill Evans Trio members (at different times).

what to buy next: Freshness, interplay, and poetry make *Live in Castelnuovo* (Siena Jazz, 1994) one of the best Pieranunzi trio performances with Leveratto and Petreni. *Triologues* (YVP) illustrates the construction and development of Pieranunzi's trio style. *Flux and Change* (Soul Note, 1995, prod. Associazione Culturale Jonica) is an amazing duo album with drummer Paul Motian. They play suites mixing jazz standards, show tunes, originals, and free improvisation, all flowing together organically. Pieranunzi's chiming chords and spiraling melodies are perfectly highlighted by Motian's subtle accents.

what to avoid: *ma l'amore no* (Soul Note, 1997, prod. Flavio Bonandrini) is perhaps an acquired taste for non-Italian listeners, as it features singer Ada Montellanico; much of the singing is in Italian, and the few English efforts sound odd. However, Lee Konitz and Enrico Rava guest on some tracks.

the rest:
Isis (Soul Note, 1981)
New Lands (Timeless, 1984)
What's What (YVP, 1985)
Deep Down (Soul Note, 1986)
(With Chet Baker) *The Heart of the Ballad* (Philology, 1988)
(With Lee Konitz) *Solitudes* (Philology, 1988)
No Man's Land (Soul Note, 1990)
(With Charlie Haden and Billy Higgins) *First Song* (Soul Note, 1990)
The Dream Before Us (IDA, 1990)
Parisian Portraits (IDA, 1990)
(With Phil Woods) *Elsa* (Philology, 1991)
Nausicaa (Quadrivium/Egea, 1993)
Untold Story (IDA, 1993)
Live in Germany (YVP, 1996)

worth searching for: The Charlie Haden–led *Silence* (Soul Note, 1989, prod. Giovanni Bonandrini) is an unforgettable meeting between the great bassist, legendary trumpeter Chet Baker, Pieranunzi, and drummer Billy Higgins. Besides the nearly obligatory "My Funny Valentine," Haden's title track, and bebop standards by Parker, Monk, and Shearing, Pieranunzi's "Echi" is played. Baker's fragile lyricism, Pieranunzi's liquescent chords, Haden's deeply songful tone, and Higgins's precise accents combine in music of subtle beauty. *Bella* (Philology, 1994, prod. Paolo Piangiarelli) is something of an Italian all-star session featuring the smooth and cool sound of Enrico Rava's trumpet over Pieranunzi's Space Jazz Trio with bassist Enzo Pietropaoli and drummer Roberto Gatto.

influences:
◀◀ Lennie Tristano, Bud Powell, McCoy Tyner, Herbie Hancock, Martial Solal, Paul Bley
▶▶ Stefano Battaglia

Giacomo Aula and Steve Holtje

Billie and De De Pierce

Married and began performing together in 1935, in New Orleans, LA.

Billie Pierce (born Wilhelmina Goodson, June 8, 1907, in Marianna, FL. Died September 29, 1974, in New Orleans, LA), piano, vocals; De De Pierce (born Joseph De Lacroix, February 18, 1904, in New Orleans, LA. Died November 23, 1973, in New Orleans, LA), cornet, vocals.

Although he worked primarily as a bricklayer, De De was a self-taught musician who enjoyed popularity playing traditional New Orleans music. During the 1920s he played with many of the famed New Orleans dance bands and was in demand as a member of brass bands for parades. In the 1930s he performed in the riverfront saloons, and in 1935 he married the pianist and singer Billie Pierce. Billie had come to New Orleans in 1929 to replace her older sister, Sadie Goodson, in Buddy Petit's band. She had grown up in a musical family and at age 15 briefly accompanied blues singer Bessie Smith. After they married, Billie and De De usually worked together, mostly in neighborhood dance halls. De De's eyesight began to fail in the 1950s and he temporarily retired, reviving his career in 1965 and making a number of recordings with his wife. He also gained visibility as one of the leaders of the Preservation Hall Jazz Band, which toured the U.S. and Europe.

what's available: *New Orleans: The Living Legends* (Riverside/OJC, 1961/1990, prod. Chris Albertson) includes lively performances by Billie and De De Pierce of blues standards such as "Careless Love" and "Nobody Knows You When You're Down and Out." These classic 1920s tunes have a distinct flavor of New Orleans jazz. On the opener, W. C. Handy's

"St. Louis Blues," pianist Billie solidly supports cornetist De De, who states the melody and agilely improvises around it before Billie takes the lead with her vocals and expressively belts out the blues of a woman ready to travel to St. Louis to get her man back. And so it goes throughout the rest of the album as Billie and De De interpret Clarence Williams's "Gulf Coast Blues," James Cox's "Nobody Knows You When You're Down and Out," and other well-known New Orleans classics. Drummer Albert Jiles joins the husband and wife team for this thoroughly inspired and spontaneous session. This CD is a must-have for classic blues fans and those who favor the traditional New Orleans jazz style.

influences:

◀◀ Buddy Bolden, Louis Armstrong

▶▶ Preservation Hall Jazz Band, Danny and Blue Lu Barker

Susan K. Berlowitz and Nancy Ann Lee

Billy Pierce

Born September 25, 1948, in Hampton, VA.

Billy Pierce is a power saxophonist, one who seems to easily command a plethora of musical languages and weave a touch of each into nearly every solo. Like Harold Land, the tenor saxophonist who chose to remain with his family in Los Angeles rather than endure the incessant touring of the Max Roach–Clifford Brown Quintet of the 1950s, Pierce has chosen to remain more a "local" musician in Boston instead of a New York–based globetrotting post-bop preacher. His teaching job has been a strong priority since he left Art Blakey's Jazz Messengers, with whom he played from 1980 to 1982. He played in and around Boston for a decade before joining Blakey's ace band, which featured the Marsalis brothers, Bobby Watson, and James Williams, among others, during Pierce's short tenure in the group. Just prior to his Blakey stint, and just after it, Pierce recorded with pianist James Williams. Later, he joined Freddie Hubbard's quintet for a short stay before hooking up with drummer Tony Williams's vaunted quintet, where Pierce stayed on for seven years, all the while balancing his Boston life with the demands of Williams's intense ensemble.

Pierce's own recordings began to trickle out in 1985, when Sunnyside released the fine *William the Conqueror*. Shortly thereafter, Sunnyside unloosed *Give and Take* and *Equilateral*, the latter of which garnered accolades for the spare trio setting of pianist Hank Jones, drummer Roy Haynes, and Pierce. In the 1990s, Sunnyside has issued *Rio: Ballads and Bossa*

Novas and *One for Chuck*. Later, Evidence Records reissued a Japanese session, *Epistrophy*, and CIMP released *Froggin' Around*, a limber, throttling trio session co-led by drummer Chris McCann. Especially in the later releases, Pierce shows an unstoppable jubilance and explorative reach that is a constant surprise. The influence of Coltrane is clear on all Pierce's recordings, but he has veered committedly into a freer area for much of his solos and musical logic. Pierce can skid across notes in careening upper-register flights, always dropping back to a hard bop road map that sounds like an Art Blakey session updated for current times. In short, Pierce is a talent who can give off the hoarsest hollers a la Dewey Redman, the most finely wrought fat notes, a la Sonny Rollins, and a good measure of sheer finesse in catapulting scales, a la John Coltrane and Wayne Shorter.

what to buy: Of all the Pierce recordings you're likely to find, *Epistrophy* 𝄢𝄢𝄢 (Evidence, 1995, prod. Big Apple Productions) is the best for pure musicianship. It's a tribute to Thelonious Monk and Sonny Rollins, and Pierce dances Monk's angles and corners as well as he blows torrents of Rollins-esque creativity. That said, the trio of Hank Jones, Roy Haynes, and Pierce sound like a vibrant, lean skeletal mass on *Equilateral* 𝄢𝄢𝄢 (Sunnyside, 1989, prod. James Williams). This is achingly beautiful music, especially Joe Henderson's "Recuerdame," and deserves a spot on any self-respecting jazz fan's shelf.

what to buy next: For unadulterated, powerhouse blowing, *Froggin' Around* 𝄢𝄢𝄢 (CIMP, 1996, prod. Robert D. Rusch) offers Pierce at his fiercest. It's full of long tunes, all built around McCann's spry rhythms and Pierce's penchant for inside/outside musical thinking.

the rest:

Give and Take 𝄢𝄢 (Sunnyside, 1987)
One for Chuck 𝄢𝄢 (Sunnyside, 1991)
Rio 𝄢𝄢 (Sunnyside, 1994)

influences:

◀◀ John Coltrane, Wayne Shorter, Dewey Redman, Sonny Rollins, Art Blakey, David Murray

▶▶ Javon Jackson, James Carter, Mark Shim

Andrew Bartlett

Pigpen

See: Wayne Horvitz

Courtney Pine

Born March 18, 1964, in London, England.

When British saxophonist Courtney Pine's first two albums hit, he sounded and played so much like John Coltrane it was scary. Playing tenor and soprano saxes and bass clarinet, Pine was not content to be just a Coltrane clone. He threw a curve ball with his third U.S. release, *Closer to Home*, which drew from his early experiences in reggae and funk bands, and merged jazz, folk, African-themes, West Indian Ska, and other World music. His 1997 recording, *Underground*, is a hip-hop jazz date, complete with a deejay providing scratches and effects. It appears Pine will be difficult to pin down, but he is no longer just chasing the Trane. A superb technician who's played with some better jazz artists including Art Blakey's Jazz Messengers and Elvin Jones, he is still searching for a distinctive voice.

what to buy: *Modern Day Jazz Stories* ✍✍✍✍ (Antilles/Verve, 1996, prod. Courtney Pine) Pine's foray into acid-jazz stands above the rest of the lot because Pine has an affinity for tradition and can really blow. The assistance of Charnett Moffett, Geri Allen, and guest shots by Eddie Henderson, Cassandra Wilson, and Mark Whitfield don't hurt either. There's also a few Coltrane-inspired, straight-ahead cuts.

what to buy next: In *Within the Realms of Our Dreams* ✍✍✍✍ (Antilles, 1991), the ghost of John Coltrane is channeled through Pine so convincingly it's haunting. Pine's technical display is amazing, albeit extraordinarily derivative. Good support is provided by Charnett Moffett, Jeff "Tain" Watts, and Kenny Kirkland.

the rest:
Closer to Home ✍✍✍ (Antilles/Verve, 1992)

influences:
◀◀ John Coltrane, Albert Ayler, Sonny Rollins, Ornette Coleman, Archie Shepp

Paul MacArthur

John Pizzarelli

Born April 6, 1960, in Paterson, NJ.

During the 1990s, John Pizzarelli has developed into a highly effective rhythm guitarist and a tasteful, albeit limited, small-group swing singer in the tradition of Nat "King" Cole. He studied guitar with his father, the fine jazz guitarist Bucky Pizzarelli, and started making a name for himself when he sat in on a 1980 *Highlights in Jazz* concert with Bucky and Zoot Sims. Fa-

ther and son made a series of records for the Stash label in the 1980s and John picked up a high-profile gig in 1986 with Tony Monte's trio, which made regular radio broadcasts. He made his first album as a leader in 1990, and has continued to develop his charming, though somewhat light-weight, vocal style. His brother, Martin, plays bass in his working trio.

what to buy: John Pizzarelli has turned into an excellent rhythm guitarist and though his vocals will never set the world on fire, he knows what his limits are and works within them. *After Hours* ✍✍✍✍ (Novus, 1995, prod. John Pizzarelli) is his best album so far, a collection of good tunes sung with energy and style. Pizzarelli's trio features his brother Martin on bass and Ray Kennedy on piano, and gets support from special guests Bucky Pizzarelli, trumpeter Randy Sandke, and tenor saxophonist Harry Allen. One of Pizzarelli's most dynamic albums, *Dear Mr. Cole* ✍✍✍✍ (Novus, 1994, prod. Ikuyoshi Hirakawa) features the hard-swinging and dependably funky pianist Benny Green and bassist Christian McBride. Pizzarelli's style borrows so heavily from Nat Cole that a tribute is almost superfluous, but he renders such requisite tunes as "Nature Boy," "Sweet Lorraine," "Honeysuckle Rose," and "Route 66" with sly, occasionally self-deprecating wit and understated style.

what to buy next: Tasteful, swinging arrangements using veteran, session horn players and material selected to fit Pizzarelli's breezy delivery make *All of Me* ✍✍✍✍ (Novus, 1992, prod. John Pizzarelli) an enjoyable experience. Bucky Pizzarelli's guitar adds an extra dose of rhythm, and John's guitar solos don't break up the momentum.

best of the rest:
My Blue Heaven ✍✍✍✍ (Chesky, 1990)
Naturally ✍✍✍✍ (Novus, 1993)
New Standards ✍✍✍✍ (Novus, 1994)
Our Love Is Here to Stay ✍✍✍✍ (Novus, 1997)

influences:
◀◀ Nat "King" Cole

Andrew Gilbert

Dan Plonsey

Born September 1, 1958, in Cleveland, OH.

Dan Plonsey started playing clarinet in the second grade. Three years later he picked up the alto sax. Today, he plays a variety of clarinets and saxophones (including soprano, alto, tenor, and baritone) in addition to more unusual horns like the Laotian mouth organ. Plonsey credits his exposure to Charles Ives,

Iannis Xenakis, Karlheinz Stockhausen, and Mauricio Kagel in his freshman year at Yale as "lifechanging influences." A couple of years later, in 1979, he had an impressionable first encounter with Sun Ra. He took off that summer for the legendary Creative Music Studio in Woodstock, New York, where he studied with Roscoe Mitchell, Anthony Braxton, Leo Smith, and other luminaries of the Association for the Advancement of Creative Musicians and beyond. From 1986 to 1988, the Bay Area composer-improviser attended classes once again with Braxton, while earning an M.A. in music composition from Mills College. As co-founder and curator for two years (from March 1995) of the Beanbender's weekly creative-music series in Berkeley, California, Plonsey fueled the Bay Area improv scene. In an effort to make the venue "an otherworldly presence," he booked both up-and-coming locals and renowned innovators like Parker/Guy/Lytton, John Butcher, Rova Saxophone Quartet, and Nels Cline. As a recording artist, Plonsey is just beginning to come into his own. His ability to fuse the absurd, intellectual, and emotional sides of his personality into both compositions and improvisations gives his music a distinctive voice, which he says arises "from the drama of conflict." A wide-eyed experimentalist, his work ranges from simple melodic frameworks to extraordinary polyphony, at times incorporating elements of over-the-top Dada theater in a bid to make real the unreal.

what to buy: *Ivory Bill* 𝄢𝄢𝄢𝄢 (Music & Arts, 1997, prod. Dan Plonsey, Dan Rathbun) is dedicated to "all animal voices," specifically the ivory-billed woodpecker, whose extinction, says Plonsey, is "against all musical sense." Twenty-two songs, many overdubbed using multiple saxophones (and occasional voice), are organized using an appropriation of Braxton's categorization of saxophone languages. More than a dozen compositional and improvisational strategies are employed, including a kind of bent but soulful phrasing ("microtonal intonational inflections") and the duplication of human and animal voices ("character studies and dramatic interaction").

what to buy next: Featuring monster players Randy McKean, Steve Norton, and Chris Jonas, the Great Circle Saxophone Quartet's *Child King Dictator Fool* 𝄢𝄢𝄢𝄢 (New World, 1997, prod. Great Circle Saxophone Quartet) explores frightening polyphony, especially on Jonas's 13-minute "Snake Tectonics."

the rest:
Dire Images of Beauty 𝄢𝄢𝄢𝄢 (yes.no.lp/retro.P, 1991)

worth searching for: On *Another Curiosity Piece* 𝄢𝄢𝄢𝄢 (Omni Sonic, 1995, prod. John Hinds, Peter Hinds), Plonsey blows

amid the curious extraterrestrial voyages of John (keys, electronics) and Peter (percussion) Hinds of Sun Ra Research fanzine fame. Plonsey's wife, vocalist Mantra Ben-Ya'akova, belts out a few earthquake-size abstractions to further the cosmic ambience.

influences:
◀◀ Sun Ra, Anthony Braxton, Roscoe Mitchell, Albert Ayler

Sam Prestianni

Noel Pointer

Born 1956, in Brooklyn, NY. Died December 19, 1994, in Brooklyn, NY.

A musician who traversed between contemporary jazz and R&B, Noel Pointer started studying violin in the fourth grade. By the time he was 13, he had performed as a guest soloist for the Symphony of the New World Orchestra. Pointer attended the New York High School of Music & Art and attended college at the Manhattan School of Music. During his lifetime, he was a featured soloist for the Chicago Chamber Orchestra and the Detroit Symphony, and became a prominent New York City session musician, accompanying a diverse array of artists, including the Jackson Five, Roberta Flack, Thelonious Monk, Hubert Laws, Miles Davis, and Sammy Davis Jr. Pointer also played in pit orchestras for several Broadway musicals. Though very R&B-influenced, his albums showed much promise in the contemporary jazz setting. Two of his seven solo albums are in print. His debut is notable for some excellent ballads, and a mediocre smooth jazz date from 1993. Pointer died on December 19, 1994, at age 40, of complications resulting from a stroke.

what to buy: Pointer's strong debut, *Phantazia* 𝄢𝄢𝄢 (Blue Note, 1977/1993, prod. Dave Grusin, Larry Rosen), mixes funk pieces with some excellent ballads. The ballads are the strong point, with Pointer's tone reminiscent of Jerry Goodman. Owing much to both the CTI and Dave Grusin's 1970s sound, this outing is somewhat dated, but Pointer's performance of Earl Klugh's "Night Song" is not to be missed.

the rest:
Never Lose Your Heart 𝄢𝄢 (Shanachie, 1993)

influences:
◀◀ Jean-Luc Ponty, Jerry Goodman, Stuff Smith, Stephane Grappelli

▶▶ Sonya Robinson

Paul MacArthur

Ed Polcer

Born February 10, 1937, in Paterson, NJ.

Ed Polcer is a driving cornetist and bandleader entrenched in Eddie Condon–styled jazz. A solid ensemble player with a vast storehouse of tunes at his command, Polcer is also an exciting soloist whose concepts occasionally recall Bobby Hackett, Louis Armstrong, Ruby Braff, and Muggsy Spanier. Polcer's occasional lip trills are close to those of Bunny Berigan, and he is highly adept at filling in behind a vocalist.

Growing up as part of a musical family in Northern New Jersey, where his father and uncle were horn players, Polcer debuted as a xylophone player at age six, and by the early 1950s was occasionally sitting in on cornet at Jimmy Ryan's club on Manhattan's 52nd Street, where he was exposed to the influences of veteran jazz players. Attending Princeton University from 1954–1958, Polcer was active in and eventually led the Nassau Jazz Band, a student Dixieland band. He also gigged with Stan Rubin's Tigertown Five and performed with them in Monaco at the Prince Ranier–Grace Kelly wedding in 1956. After graduation, Polcer played jazz part-time for about 10 years before he left business for full-time music and freelancing in the New York City area. He toured with the Benny Goodman Sextet (1973 and 1975), then helped re-establish Eddie Condon's club, opening as house cornetist and eventually becoming a manager and part owner. All the while, he was evolving into a top-flight, multi-faceted horn player, performing traditional, swing, or semi-modern jazz as required to fit in with club guest stars. Since Condon's closed in 1985 when they lost their lease, Polcer has been a front-runner and organizer on the jazz festival circuit. In recent years, Polcer has also toured with his "Magic of Swing Street" concert show, and performed and recorded with singer Terry Blaine and pianist Mark Shane, as well as remaining an eloquent spokesman for jazz.

what to buy: On *Ed Polcer's All-Stars: Some Sunny Day* 🎜🎜🎜🎜 (Jazzology, 1992, prod. Phil Carroll), leader Polcer upholds the tradition of bands from Nick's and Condon's. With a well-conceived collection of 13 diverse tunes, the band delivers a free-wheeling session with lots of room for solos. Polcer's fiery, driving cornet leads the way, and with clarinetist Allan Vaché, trombonist Bob Havens, pianist Johnny Varro, guitarist Marty Grosz, bassist Jack Lesberg, and drummer Hal Smith, the band puts down relaxed, old-fashioned, swinging, traditional jazz tunes such as "Some Sunny Day," "It All Depends on You," "Spain," the Harold Arlen classic "As Long as I Live," and a bit of ancient jazz history with "Put 'Em Down Blues," "Come Back

Sweet Papa," and "Satanic Blues." The rhythm section adds just the right touch, with ex-Condonites Varro and Lesberg lending experienced hands, along with one of the best rhythm guitarists and chord soloists, Marty Grosz. Hal Smith is the right drummer for this mix of hard-driving and easy-going jazz. *Ed Polcer's All-Stars: Coast to Coast Swingin' Jazz* 🎜🎜🎜🎜 (Jazzology, 1991, prod. Phil Carroll) features the same personnel on a 1990 date. Performing a collection of 13 tunes from the past, they display the same enthusiasm and *joie de vivre* shown on the above date. Bob Haggart replaces Lesberg on bass and some of the tracks take on the flavor of Bob Crosby's Bob Cats. Without attempting to emulate the sound of the old recordings, the band beautifully plays three tunes associated with Bix Beiderbecke ("Louisiana," "Singin' the Blues," "From Monday On"). Whether you call it New York Dixie or updated Traditional, if you like well-constructed solos and swinging ensembles, you'll play this one repeatedly. The choice between these two albums would have to depend on your tune preferences because performances and playing times signify a draw.

what to buy next: *The Magic of Swing Street* 🎜🎜🎜🎜 (BlewZ Manor, 1993, prod. Ed Polcer) features Polcer and his Jazz All-Stars who put on their swing faces for a musical stroll down New York's famous 52nd Street. This fleet sextet features the leader's horn work, Ken Peplowski's clarinet and tenor sax, Tom Artin's trombone, Mark Shane's piano, Frank Tate's bass, and Joe Ascione's drums on a romp through 19 tunes that were played on the legendary street in the 1930s and 1940s. There are musical nods given to Count Basie ("One O'Clock Jump," "Swingin' the Blues"), to John Kirby ("Blue Skies"), to Louis Prima ("Way Down Yonder in New Orleans"), and to the Onyx Club ("The Music Goes 'Round and 'Round"). Jam favorites such as "I Got Rhythm" (featuring breath-taking Peplowski clarinet), "Willow Weep for Me" (highlighting Frank Tate's solid bass solo), and others are included. A rewarding set for the listener. (Available from Jukebox Jazz, P. O. Box 1247, Woodstock, NY 12498). On *A Salute to Eddie Condon* 🎜🎜🎜 (Nagel-Heyer, 1993, prod. Hans Nagel-Heyer) , Polcer leads a troop of touring Americans and two British jazzmen through a 12-tune program of typical Condon fare, recorded live in concert at the Musikhalle in Hamburg, Germany in 1993. Former Condon intermission and band pianist Johnny Varro and bassist Bob Haggart (who was on stage at Town Hall with Eddie Condon in the 1940s) lends an air of authenticity. The familiar Polcer front line, which includes trombonist Bob Havens and clarinetist Allan Vache, is present, along with drummer Butch Miles. Baritone saxophonist Johnny Barnes, and guitarist Jim Douglas out of England's old Alec

Welsh's Condon-styled band, complete the high-powered ensemble. Included is "September in the Rain," the first tune heard when Condon's nightery opened its doors. Solo features abound as Haven's Teagarden-like trombone tackles "I Guess I'll Have to Change My Plan," and Allan Vache's facile clarinet handles "I Used to Love You" in duet with Johnny Varro's sparkling piano. Polcer's lovely muted cornet sound leads the way on the Condon/DeVries tune "Wherever There's Love," with some neat string comping by Douglas and Haggart. Barnes's booming baritone sax sallies forth with "I Believe in Miracles," which also contains a charming vocal by the sax man. The ensemble has a relaxed go at "Wabash Blues," and damn-the-torpedoes charges into "California, Here I Come" and "Hindustan." For completists, seven remaining numbers from this concert are contained on *Jazz Live at the Musikhalle: The First Three Concerts* ♫♫♫♪ (Nagel-Heyer, 1994, prod. Hans Nagel-Heyer).

the rest:
Barbara Lea & Ed Polcer All-Stars at the Atlanta Jazz Party ♫♫♫♪ (Jazzology, 1993)
Jammin' a la Condon ♫♫♫♪ (Jazzology, 1995, prod. George Buck)

worth searching for: *A Night at Eddie Condon's: Ed Polcer and the Condon All-Stars* ♫♫♫♫ (BlewZ Manor, 1992, prod. Ed Polcer) is an out-of-print CD, but cassette versions are available from Jukebox Jazz (P.O. Box 1247, Woodstock, NY 12498). There are some wonderful examples of Ed Polcer, Ken Peplowski, Tom Artin, and Mark Shane on this set made for small band lovers of swing with a traditional touch.

John T. Bitter

Jean-Luc Ponty

Born September 29, 1942, in Avranches, Normandy, France.

The most important jazz violinist of the past two decades, Jean-Luc Ponty has, like many players of his generation, traversed several different paths and musical genres in his career. He usually plays an electric violin and incorporates effects like echo, delay, and distortion to create sounds not normally associated with the instrument. Though predictable at times, Ponty redefined jazz violin and is easily its most popular practitioner.

Classically trained, Ponty was taught to play the violin by his father and the piano by his mother. Focusing on violin at the Paris Conservatory, from which he graduated at age 17, Ponty played with the Concerts Lamoreux Symphony Orchestra in the early 1960s. While at the Conservatory he began playing jazz (as a clarinetist) with some amateur groups. Inspired by the modern jazz of John Coltrane and Miles Davis, he switched to

tenor sax; when he decided to play jazz professionally, he switched back to violin, on which he was most fluent. By the mid-1960s he'd gained notoriety in Europe as a jazz player, and in 1967 he came to the United States where he started working with the George Duke Trio. Duke and Ponty were both associated with Frank Zappa's bands for a time; Ponty worked with the late great composer-guitarist on and off from 1968 to 1975. Ponty formed his first band, the Jean-Luc Ponty Experience, in 1969, but it lasted only two years. After a stint with Elton John, Ponty accepted John McLaughlin's invitation to joining the second Mahavishnu Orchestra in 1974. While he was actually McLaughlin's first choice for the original Mahavishnu Orchestra, immigration problems prevented him from joining and McLaughlin went with Jerry Goodman (who in retrospect was the better musical partner for McLaughlin). Ponty appeared on two Mahavishnu albums, *Apocalypse* and *Visions of the Emerald Beyond*, but left in 1975 because of internal disputes and subsequently pursued his solo career.

The bulk of Ponty's solo work is a hypnotic mixture of jazz/rock, though softer in tone than Mahavishnu, Lifetime, and Return to Forever. At its best, Ponty's late 1970s material was fully developed suites, most notably the excellent *Imaginary Voyage*. It was during this period that Ponty's use of effects increased to the point that his violin was not simply a lead instrument, it created its own harmonies and futuristic sounds that added interesting dimensions to his soundscapes. While Ponty's late 1970s work often had very repetitive backgrounds, his mid-1980s releases, *Individual Choice* and *Open Mind*, used almost Philip Glass–like minimalism. The song "Individual Choice" was used in a short stop-animation film by Louis Schwazberg, which is considered one of the most creative music videos ever produced. Ponty's late 1980s material was less minimal, and in the 1990s he's explored directions in world music and toured with Al Di Meola and Stanley Clarke.

what to buy: Using a whole side of a jazz album for a four-movement suite was still a bold decision in 1976, but the risk paid off on *Imaginary Voyage* ♫♫♫♪ (Atlantic, 1976, prod. Jean-Luc Ponty). The first three movements of the four-part "Imaginary Voyage" suite are highlights of Ponty's career. It begins with an electronic maze that segues into a psychedelic second part. Then there's part III, which has one of the best themes ever recorded and contains some of Ponty's most beautiful playing. If only part IV lived up to the first three parts. The other high spots are the electric square dance "New Country" and the spaced-out "Wandering on the Milky Way." A few weaker tracks keep this from ♫♫♫♫ status, but the great tracks

Jean-Luc Ponty **(Archive Photos)**

are so good they make this a must-have. "New Country" is the only *Imaginary Voyage* track on the two-CD retrospective *Le Voyage: The Jean-Luc Ponty Anthology* ♫♫♫♫ (Rhino/Atlantic, 1996, prod. Jean-Luc Ponty, A.G. Gillis), which covers the Atlantic years (1975–85, plus two tracks from 1993). Thus, it offers buyers hoping to avoid overly duplicative selections a good second choice covering his other Atlantic releases.

what to buy next: The move to minimalism was just beginning on *Mystical Adventures* ♫♫♫♫ (Atlantic, 1981, prod. Jean-Luc Ponty). It's ambitious, well written, and still futuristic. *Tchokola* ♫♫♫♫ (Columbia, 1991, prod. Jean-Luc Ponty) was Ponty's first album to draw extensively from African influnces. It's good to hear him in something different from the typical electronic jazz/rock context, and the new environment was apparently inspiring. Stylistically this may not be everyone's cup of tea, but it's really worth checking out. *Open Mind* ♫♫♫ (Atlantic, 1984, prod. Jean-Luc Ponty) is highly repetitious, but very cool. George Benson's guest apperance is absolutely mesmerising.

what to avoid: Yeah, yeah, yeah, Frank Zappa wrote and arranged *King King* ♫♫ (Pacific Jazz, 1969, prod. Frank Zappa) and George Duke played on it, but this overrated release gets old fast.

best of the rest:
Live at Donte's ♫♫♫ (Blue Note, 1970)
Enigmatic Ocean ♫♫♫♫ (Atlantic, 1977)
Cosmic Messenger ♫♫♫♫ (Atlantic, 1978)
The Gift of Time ♫♫♫ (Columbia, 1987)
Storytelling ♫♫♫ (Columbia, 1989)

worth searching for: The pairing of two jazz violin pioneers produced some wonderful results on *Jean-Luc Ponty/Stephane Grappelli* ♫♫♫♫ (Musidisc France, 1973), though it's nearly impossible to find in the United States. The contrasts between Ponty's electric and Grappelli's acoustic playing yield some unique sounds.

influences:

◀◀ Ray Nance, Stephane Grappelli, Stuff Smith, Svend Asmussen, Miles Davis, John Coltrane

▶▶ Didier Lockwood, John Blake, Michael Urbaniak

Paul MacArthur

Odean Pope

Born October 24, 1938, in Ninety-Six, SC.

Best known for his lengthy stint with drummer Max Roach, Pope's forceful, Coltrane-derived tenor playing and harmonically challenging charts have long been deserving of more recognition. While growing up in Philadelphia, the budding saxophonist was a protege of pianist Ray Bryant, who introduced him to Roach. After touring Europe with the master percussionist, Pope returned home to form Catalyst with his longtime associates, bassist Tyrone Brown and keyboard player Eddie Green. After that group's demise in the mid-'70s, Pope organized the Saxophone Choir, a nine-piece reed corps blended with a rhythm section. Pope continues to record, play, and tour with Roach (whose group he rejoined in 1979), in addition to working with a sax, bass, and drums trio.

what to buy: For his first album with the Saxophone Choir, *The Saxophone Shop* ♪♪♪♪♪ (Soul Note, 1986, prod. Odean Pope), Pope came out firing on all cylinders, turning 12-tone scales into catchy riffs. The title tune (written by Pope) and "Heavenly" (composed by pianist Eddie Green) contain some of the most dynamic playing and writing to be heard within what is basically an avant-garde concept.

what to buy next: *The Ponderer* ♪♪♪♪ (Soul Note, 1991, prod. Odean Pope) shows the Saxophone Choir can sound at times like an enhanced version of the World Saxophone Quartet playing Sun Ra charts. There are three altos (including Byard Lancaster), five tenors (counting the leader), and one baritone to anchor the section with rhythm coming courtesy of pianist Eddie Green, drummer Cornell Rochester, and the bass duo of Gerald Veasley and Tyrone Brown. The bulk of the material was written by Pope or Green, displaying inventive soloists against a well-constructed cushion of reeds. On *Collective Voices* ♪♪♪♪ (CIMP, 1997, prod. Robert D. Rusch) it's good to hear Pope's voice in the exposed format of the piano-less trio. His consistently creative playing is muscular without being overbearing. Bassist Tyrone Brown contributes three songs (including a bottom end showcase called "Bassically Karr," dedicated to the world-renowned classical bassist Gary Karr) while Pope

demonstrates his progressive compositional skills, filling the rest of the album with well-structured tunes that leave plenty of room for fine soloing.

the rest:

Epitome ♪♪♪ (Soul Note, 1994)
Ninety-Six ♪♪♪♪ (Enja, 1996)

influences:

◀◀ John Coltrane, Booker Ervin

▶▶ James Carter, Joshua Redman

Garaud MacTaggart

Art Porter

Born August 3, 1962, in Little Rock, AR. Died November 23, 1996, in Bangkok, Thailand.

Art Porter was one of the more popular smooth jazz saxophonists to emerge in the 1990s. His debut recording in 1992 was a commercial success and was gobbled up by smooth-jazz stations, as were his next three releases. Porter's early music studies were on drums and bass, and, taught by his father, he grew up playing straight-ahead jazz. He began playing saxophone around age 15 and studied at the Berklee College of Music at age 16. He played in nightclubs with his father while still underage (thanks to passage of the Art Porter Bill in Arkansas, which allows underage musicians to perform in clubs and bars as long as a legal guardian is present), and subsequently graduated from Northeastern Illinois University where he earned a degree in music education. Though his solo efforts were smooth-jazz focused, Porter did tour with Jack McDuff, Pharoah Sanders, and the R&B singer Gene Chandler early in his career. His albums are similar to his R&B-influenced contemporaries Kirk Whalum, Najee, and Gerald Albright, though Porter lacked the versatility of his peers, at least on record. In 1996, while in Bangkok, Thailand, Porter drowned during a boating accident.

what to buy: Porter wrote most of the 11 tunes on *Undercover* ♪♪♪ (Verve, 1994, prod. Ronnie Foster, Jeff Lorber, Art Porter), which contains standard smooth-jazz with a few typical throwaway vocal tracks. It does have some nice moments and Jeff Lorber's presence is a plus.

the rest:

Pocket City ♪♪ (Verve, 1992)
Straight to the Point ♪♪ (Verve, 1993)
Lay Your Hands on Me ♪♪ (Verve, 1996)

influences:

⏪ Grover Washington Jr., David Sanborn

Paul MacArthur

Chris Potter

Born January 1, 1971, in Chicago, IL.

One of the most versatile and harmonically insightful young saxophonists in jazz, Chris Potter is a rapidly maturing player who already improvises with a great deal of authority. Heard most frequently on tenor and soprano sax and bass clarinet, Potter also plays alto sax and alto flute. Raised in Columbia, South Carolina, he started playing saxophone at age 11. By his mid-teens he was gigging regularly and at 18 moved to New York to attend the New School (but graduated from the Manhattan School of Music). Taken under the wing of bebop trumpeter Red Rodney, Potter quickly began developing a reputation as one of the most incisive and original young players working in the post-bop tradition. He has quietly racked up more than a score of sideman sessions both with veteran players, including Paul Motian's Electric Bebop Band, the Mingus Big Band, James Moody, Ray Brown, Freddie Hubbard, and Steve Swallow, and with contemporaries such as Ryan Kisor, Joel Spencer, Greg Gisbert, Owen Howard, Steve Million, and Renee Rosnes. His appearance on Marian McPartland's recording, *In My Life*, brought him into the Concord fold, and he has recorded five superb albums for the label and contributed to many sessions by Concord artists, including John Hart and Randy Sandke, and singers Marlena Shaw, Eden Atwood, and Susannah McCorkle. The label has also featured him in ad-hoc saxophone groups and Concord All-Star bands recorded live at the Fujitsu-Concord Jazz Festival.

what to buy: One of the most cutting-edge recordings ever released by Concord, *Unspoken* 𝅘𝅥𝅘𝅥𝅘𝅥𝅘𝅥 (Concord Jazz, 1997, prod. John Burk, Allen Farnham) is a riveting session pairing the brilliant Potter with an all-star band featuring guitarist John Scofield, bassist Dave Holland, and drummer Jack DeJohnette. Sticking almost exclusively to tenor, Potter (who wrote all the material) picks up inspiration from each of the musicians, keying into Sco's liquid blues, Holland's adventurous harmonics, and especially DeJohnette's powerful, multidirectional rhythms. The band steps completely outside on the exhilarating free-form "Time Zone," but most of Potter's tunes are based on intriguing structural or rhythmic motifs, such as the odd recurring rhythmic pattern of "Seven Eleven," or the sly tango at the bottom of "Et Tu, Brute?" Again playing mostly tenor, Chris Pot-

ter explores nine original tunes and the standard "A Kiss to Build a Dream On" on *Moving In* 𝅘𝅥𝅘𝅥𝅘𝅥𝅘𝅥 (Concord Jazz, 1996, prod. Nick Phillips), a quartet session featuring pianist Brad Mehldau, bassist Larry Grenadier, and powerhouse drummer Billy Hart. Potter's tunes range from loose sketches that develop organically and with considerable freedom to more structured pieces. His tenor work on the title track slips into a seemingly simple bluesy groove, while "Pelog" borrows from an Indonesian folk melody. The more you listen to the apparently mild-mannered saxophonist, the more you hear his music is full of the unexpected. The tenth volume in the Concord Duo Series, *Chris Potter/Kenny Werner* 𝅘𝅥𝅘𝅥𝅘𝅥𝅘𝅥 (Concord Jazz, 1996, prod. Carl E. Jefferson), pairs the saxophonist (heard here on tenor and soprano saxophones and bass clarinet) with his long-time collaborator, pianist Kenny Werner. Considering Potter's tango, "The New Left," and Werner's tricky "Boulevard of Broken Time," both players came to the Maybeck Recital Hall concert with challenging material. Werner is a brilliant player with no end of ideas and technique, and he and Potter immediately establish a highly intuitive rapport. Highlights include the obscure old standard "Istanbul, Not Constantinople," Monk's "Epistrophy," and a preternaturally beautiful version of Tom Harrell's "Sail Away."

what to buy next: Potter firmly established himself as one of the most promising young players in jazz with *Concentric Circles* 𝅘𝅥𝅘𝅥𝅘𝅥𝅘𝅥 (Concord Jazz, 1994, prod. Carl E. Jefferson), a quintet session with John Hart (guitar), Kenny Werner (piano), Scott Colley (bass), and Bill Stewart (drums). Potter penned seven of the nine tunes, and effectively uses overdubbing in some places to play his own horn lines. The material ranges between modal themes and more free-jazz directions. Potter plays forcefully, especially on tenor, and Werner improvises considerable daring and passion. *Pure* 𝅘𝅥𝅘𝅥𝅘𝅥𝅘𝅥 (Concord Jazz, 1995, prod. Carl E. Jefferson, John Burk) mixes trio tracks (with bassist Larry Grenadier and drummer Al Foster, a quintet boosted by guitarist John Hart and organist Larry Goldings) with tunes that use extensive overdubbing. The results are quite stimulating, as the leader creates some beautiful voicings on his tune "Bonnie Rose" (bass clarinet, alto flute behind soprano sax) and "Salome's Dance" (saxes with bass clarinet). Potter is especially impressive on Mingus's "Boogie Stop Shuffle" and turns the Lennon-McCartney tune "Fool on the Hill" into an effective jazz mood piece.

worth searching for: One of the best albums of 1997, *Oceans of Time* 𝅘𝅥𝅘𝅥𝅘𝅥𝅘𝅥 (Arabesque, 1997, prod. David Ballou, Billy Hart) is a rare session by the stellar drummer Billy Hart featuring Potter on tenor and soprano sax and bass clarinet, as well as saxophonist John Stubblefield, violinist Mark Feldman, guitarist David Fiuczynski, pianist Dave Kikoski, and bassist Santi Debriano. Encompassing Afro-Caribbean rhythms, backbeats, and polyrhythmic swing, Hart's trap work provides the structure for the septet, and Potter stands out amongst the august company.

influences:

John Coltrane, Dewey Redman, Wayne Shorter

Andrew Gilbert

Bud Powell

Born Earl Rudolph Powell, September 27, 1924, in New York, NY. Died August 1, 1966, in New York, NY.

Personal and other problems marked the tormented life and career of pianist/composer Bud Powell. He was, however, blessed with dazzling and revolutionary technique, and his brilliant, seminal early recordings are as deep in improvisational riches and complexity as any in the history of the music. And yet he also produced some of the most meandering and unfocused performances you'll ever hear. Powell, a much-touted prodigy during his youth in Harlem, starred at the now-famous after-hours jam sessions at Minton's Playhouse in the early 1940s; there he came under Thelonious Monk's tutelage and began imparting his energies to the emerging bop style. During 1942–44, Powell performed in Cootie Williams's band. During a racially-motivated incident in 1945, Powell was severely beaten about the head by Philadelphia police—for the rest of his life he suffered headaches, mental breakdowns, and stays in mental institutions. Despite the chronic health problems inflicted on him, Powell is widely considered the greatest bop pianist, influencing countless later players. He developed a technique in the early 1940s that, at fast and medium tempos, encompassed rapid right-hand melody lines (much like the horns could play) punctuated by random dissonant chords with this left hand. This style soon was adopted by most of the bop pianists of the period. In the late 1940s and early 1950s, Powell performed with his own trio and made occasional appearances in New York clubs with leading boppers such as Charlie Parker, Dizzy Gillespie, Sonny Stitt, J. J. Johnson, and Fats Navarro. Powell was also a composer whose excellent jazz tunes such as "Hallucinations," "Dance of the Infidels," "Tempus Fugit," and "Bouncing with Bud" were recorded by others and have become standards. As Powell's health and musical prowess deteriorated in the 1950s, he curtailed public performances. He moved to Paris in 1959 and led a trio there with Kenny Clarke from 1959 to 1964; he was hospitalized part of the time, however. Following his return to the States in August 1964, Powell made a few concert appearances before abandoning his career. He died in 1966.

what to buy: Seen now, over 30 years after his death, a good percentage of the "poorer" Powell performances have a power and coherence that's lacking in the work of many lesser pianists. Therefore, and despite the variable quality of the material it covers, the four-CD *Bud Powell: The Complete Blue Note and Roost Recordings* ♪♪♪♪ (Blue Note, 1947–53/1994, prod. Alfred Lion, Teddy Reig, Francis Wolff) is an essential document. Beginning with a jaw-dropping series of reconstructions, including "I'll Remember April," "Indiana," and "Somebody Loves Me" from a January 1947 date for Roost (with bassist Curly Russell and drummer Max Roach), and ending with a promenading 1963 reading of "Like Someone in Love" (with Pierre Michelot and Kenny Clarke), the set brings together a number of Powell's indelible recorded moments. The 1949 quintets with Fats Navarro and a teenaged Sonny Rollins are here, as are the three takes of the Latin-flavored masterpiece, "Un Poco Loco" (again with Russell and Roach). Other highlights include a solo rundown of "Parisian Thoroughfare," his broodingly baroque suite "Glass Enclosure" (Powell's musical impressions of stays in mental institutions), and the odd, at times almost barrel-housing, 1957 quartet numbers with Curtis Fuller. Weaker tunes such as the Parker-derived blues "Dry Soul" (with Sam Jones and Philly Joe Jones, from 1958) still reveal the workings of a fertile, complex mind, their often hesitant execution notwithstanding. Five CDs containing takes done for Norman Granz on the Clef and Verve labels, now codified on *The Complete Bud Powell on Verve* ♪♪♪♪ (Verve, 1949–56/1994, prod. Norman Granz, Leroy Lovett), received critical acclaim equal to the Blue Note compilation. Although the set adds up to a treasure trove of impassioned improvisation and crafty invention from Powell's most troubled mid-career period, it is less musically astounding than the Blue Note compilation. The volumes come packaged in one of the handsomest sets imaginable, a miniature replica of those old, classic 78 rpm multi-disc albums, with fabulous artwork and enough annotation and biographical information to keep you reading the whole time the music is playing. Sidemen include Ray Brown, Buddy Rich, George Duvivier, and Art Blakey.

what to buy next: The Powell Trio portion of *Jazz at Massey Hall, Vol. 2* ♪♪♪♪ (Debut/OJC, 1953/1992, prod. Charles Mingus) is another testament to Powell's mastery in the club and concert settings, and the CD reissue includes several bonus tracks. *Bouncing with Bud* 🎵🎵🎵🎵 (Delmark, 1962/1991) is a solid outing that features Powell leading a trio with a 15-year-old Niels-Henning Orsted Pedersen and drummer William Schiopffe. The session of (mostly) racing bop standards, such as "Straight, No Chaser" and "Hot House," was recorded in Copenhagen during Powell's refreshing stay in Europe. His original title tune is included among the seven tunes, as is a pleasant rendering of the ballad "I Remember Clifford." (NOTE: The same material is offered on the pricey, like-titled 24K Gold Disc from Mobile Fidelity; so if sound is your passion, go for the gold.) From Powell's post-1959 Paris period, *A Portrait of Thelonious* 🎵🎵🎵🎵 (Columbia, 1961/Legacy, 1997, prod. Julian Adderley) was produced by Cannonball Adderley and stars "Klook-a-Mop" Clarke and "Lucky" Pierre Michelot; this album captures the essence of the legendary pianist Thelonious Monk in bold technicolor splashes. Included are Monk gems like "Off Minor," "Ruby, My Dear," and "Monk's Mood."

what to avoid: *Bud Plays Bird* 🎵🎵🎵🎵 (Roulette, 1958/Blue Note, 1996, prod. Rudy Traylor) is a 1958 collection with Duvivier on bass and Art Taylor on drums. For anyone other than Powell, this would be considered heavenly—but Bud played these tunes better elsewhere. Another disappointment is the recently reissued Paris meeting with Don Byas, *A Tribute to Cannonball* 🎵🎵🎵 (Columbia, 1961/Legacy, 1997, prod. Julian Adderley). Recorded in Paris, France, in December 1961, only two days before the Monk tribute, this one's pretty much lacking in forward movement.

the rest:
The Amazing Bud Powell, Vol. 1 🎵🎵🎵🎵 (Blue Note, 1949–51/1989)
The Amazing Bud Powell, Vol. 2 🎵🎵🎵🎵 (Blue Note, 1951–53/1989)
Inner Fires 🎵🎵🎵🎵 (Discovery, 1953/1993)
At the Blue Note Café Paris 🎵🎵🎵 (ESP, 1961/1994)
(With Pierre Michelot and Kenny Clarke) *Round about Midnight at the Blue Note* 🎵🎵🎵 (Dreyfus, 1962/1994)
Best of Bud Powell on Verve 🎵🎵🎵🎵 (Verve, 1994)
Jazz Profile 🎵🎵🎵🎵 (Blue Note, 1997)

influences:

◀◀ Earl Hines, Art Tatum, Teddy Wilson

▶▶ Walter Bishop Jr., Hank Jones, Alan Broadbent, George Cables, Wynton Kelly, Thelonious Monk, George Shearing

David Prince and Nancy Ann Lee

B<small>UD</small> P<small>OWELL</small>

song "Cherokee"

album The Complete Bud Powell on Verve
(Verve, 1949/1994)

instrument Piano

Monster Solo

Power Tools
Formed in New York City in 1986.

Bill Frisell, electric guitar; Melvin Gibbs, electric bass; Ronald Shannon Jackson, drums.

With Ronald Shannon Jackson the motivating force, this short-lived downtown NYC supergroup—every player a leader in his own right—made one great album, played concerts intermittently over the next couple of years, and faded away amid the members' many other commitments. Bill Frisell already had a thriving solo career, Jackson was achieving success with his harmolodic group Decoding Society, and Melvin Gibbs was leading two bands (MG and Eye & I) and playing with Vernon Reid. The trio made a strange one-time reappearance at the old Knitting Factory in New York in November 1989; former Miles Davis guitarist Pete Cosey (who had retired from music and was working at the Post Office in Chicago) replaced the unavailable Frisell (Naked City had already formed).

what's available: The atmospheric *Strange Meeting* 🎵🎵🎵🎵 (Antilles, 1987, prod. David Breskin) is arguably the best album

Frisell ever made, and features a number of his best compositions (the title track, "Unscientific Americans," and "When We Go"). It's good to hear Jackson work in a more stripped-down context than his densely instrumented Decoding Society, and Gibbs is the perfect mediator between the more famous members' sounds, solidly defining the music's bottom but infusing his lines with a strong melodic sense.

influences:

⏮ Bill Frisell, Bill Laswell

⏭ Rolf Sturm

Steve Holtje

The Preservation Hall Jazz Band

Formed (informally) in the 1950s, in New Orleans, LA. Officially named in 1961.

Percy Humphrey (born 1903, died 1995), trumpet (1961–95); Willie Humphrey (born 1900, died 1994), clarinet (1961–94); Frank Demond, trombone; Allan Jaffe, tuba (1961–87); Narvin Kimball, banjo; Josiah Frazier, drums; James Miller, piano; and many, many others.

During the 1950s, a New Orleans art dealer, Larry Borenstein, hired veteran jazz musicians to play at his gallery on St. Peter Street. Beginning in 1961 these performances occurred at an unimposing adjacent building at 726 St. Peter Street, which he opened as Preservation Hall. Tuba player Allan Jaffe, now deceased, took over administration and began to book worldwide tours for the band, which has featured a host of the best New Orleans–style players over the years. Representing a wide generational mix, the band includes youngster musicians in their 30s and veterans in their 80s. Despite all of the personnel changes, its sound remains the same—steady, hypnotic, hard-driving century-old music; the usual band formation consists of a front line with clarinet, trombone, and trumpet, and a rhythm section with piano, bass, drums, and banjo. The personnel in the touring groups often differs from the band that regularly performs seven nights a week at the tiny Preservation Hall, where there are usually long waiting lines. Whether touring or at home, PHJB concerts generally end with the recognizable encore of "When the Saints Go Marching In," with the band snaking its way through the audience. PHJB plays the syncopated music created by Louis Armstrong, King Oliver, Jelly Roll Morton, Kid Ory, and others, and the band continues to influence scores of contemporary younger musicians from the Crescent City and elsewhere.

what to buy: *Best of the Preservation Hall Jazz Band* 𝄞𝄞𝄞𝄞 (CBS, 1977–89/1989, prod. various) is a compilation of tracks from various albums featuring the legendary Humphrey brothers. Presenting many of their best performances, it's a good place to start for an introduction to the band. If you're not a fan of "best of" albums, you might want to start with *Preservation Hall Jazz Band, New Orleans, Volume 1* 𝄞𝄞𝄞𝄞 (Columbia, 1977/1992, prod. Irving Steimler), simply because it's the first in a series of delightful albums from the Preservation Hall Jazz Band. This CD contains music that is as close to the band's roots as you're likely hear—other than their earliest recordings backing Sweet Emma Barrett and the husband-wife team of Billie and De De Pierce. Performing on this album are veterans of the New Orleans style Willie Humphrey and Percy Humphrey, brothers who both played in the band nearly up to the times of their deaths. Other band members featured on this CD include Narvin Kimball, Allan Jaffe, Frank Demond, James Miller, and Josiah Frazier. Their music is raw and somewhat unpolished, giving it a certain charm. This disc includes classics such as "Tiger Rag," "Amen," "Over in Gloryland," "Bill Bailey (Won't You Please Come Home)," "His Eye Is on the Sparrow," and more joyful, happy-time music to lift your spirits. If you enjoy this disc, you'll want the whole series that features the Humphrey brothers. *Preservation Hall Jazz Band, New Orleans, Volume II* 𝄞𝄞𝄞𝄞 (Columbia, 1982/1988, prod. Allan Jaffe) features mostly band originals and captures Percy's vocals on PHJB classics such as "Shake It and Break It," "The Bucket's Got a Hole in It," and "Down on the Farm." *Preservation Hall Jazz Band, New Orleans, Volume III* 𝄞𝄞𝄞𝄞 (Columbia, 1983/1987, prod. Allan Jaffe) contains two versions of "Just a Closer Walk with Thee," the dirge-march tempo played at the beginning of legendary New Orleans funeral processions and the joyful style played upon return from the graveyard. A pleasing mix of spirituals and evergreens, including a delightful "Careless Love," which features Percy Humphrey's muted trumpet solo. *Preservation Hall Jazz Band, New Orleans, Volume IV* 𝄞𝄞𝄞𝄞 (Columbia, 1988, prod. Allan Jaffe) finds drummer Josiah Frazier replaced by Frank Parker on this 1986 studio date and the Humphrey brothers at the helm. Allan Jaffe died in 1987 before this album of 10 New Orleans spirituals and standards was released.

what to buy next: For a band that initially no one thought could last, the Preservation Hall Jazz Band is alive and still kickin' on *Preservation Hall Jazz Band Live!* 𝄞𝄞𝄞𝄞 (Sony Masterworks, 1992, prod. Leroy "Sam" Parkins). Over the past 30 years, the PHJB has traveled all over the world, spreading the New Orleans tradition. This is authentic swinging New Orleans roots jazz (razzmatazz!) from the Preservation Hall series, and the first session recorded in the intimacy of the Hall. Featuring a variety of intergenerational musicians, the syncopated, spirited jazz performance is spurred on by a live audience. Trumpeter Percy Humphrey (87 at the time of this recording) and his brother, clarinetist Willie (then 91), appear on six of the 10 tracks, but these live-recorded performances featuring an array of musicians indicate the new generation beginning to step in. Like all their live performances, the various configurations of the PHJB swing with dedication. Highlights include a saucy version of Kid Ory's "Savoy Blues," clarinetist Michael White's solo on the George Lewis classic, "Burgundy Street Blues," and other chestnuts. Jeanette Kimball plays a great rinky-dink piano, especially on "After Hours." The CD ends with their traditional closing number, "When the Saints Go Marching In." *In the Sweet Bye and Bye* ♫♫♫♫ (Sony, 1996, prod. Benjamin Jaffe) features the new generation of players after the deaths of the Humphrey brothers and Allan Jaffe. Michael White replaces clarinetist Willie Humphrey, Wendell Brunious replaces Percy Humphrey, and, for the first time on one of their recordings, the founder's son and Preservation Hall manager, Benjamin Jaffe, performs on acoustic bass and the helicon, a large bass tuba that his father taught him to play. Drummer Josef Lastie Jr. replaced an ailing Frank Parker in 1989. Pianist Ellis Marsalis sits in for Rickie Monie on two spirituals. Frank Demond, 62 years old at the time of this session, and Narvin Kimball are the only remaining members of the band that first recorded for CBS in 1978. Eleven selections include traditional spirituals and popular songs. (Does anyone else remember singing the classic "Do Lord" in grade school in the 1940s?) With vocals by Narvin Kimball and Wendell Brunious, the toe-tappin' session retains its old-time flavor.

influences:

◀◀ Kid Ory, Johnny Dodds, Bix Beiderbecke, Louis Armstrong's Hot Seven, Percy Humphrey and his Crescent City Joymakers, the Dukes of Dixieland

▶▶ Al Hirt, Warren Vache, Ken Peplowski, the Dirty Dozen Brass Band, the Olympia Brass Band, the Rebirth Brass Band, the Alliance Hall Dixieland Band, the World's Greatest Jazz Band, the Heritage Hall Jazz Band

Nancy Ann Lee

The President

See: Wayne Horvitz

Andre Previn

Born Andre Previn, April 6, 1929, in Berlin, Germany.

Previn is a renowned conductor of many prestigious symphony orchestras the world over. He has also won Academy Awards for his work on the musical scores of such motion picture classics as *Porgy and Bess, Gigi, My Fair Lady,* and *Irma la Douce.* Those are fabulous credentials, but many music fans know Previn best as a fine jazz piano cat. Whether he plays sweet and cool on romantic mood pieces, or swings bop-time on standards and show tunes, Previn showcases masterful artistry and the joy of performance.

He studied classical music as a child in Berlin and later in Paris when his family fled the Nazis. His move to Los Angeles in 1938 exposed him to the jazz stylings of Art Tatum, and he was hooked. Previn was always a workhorse, and when he wasn't studying he played piano for radio programs and on film scores, saving jazz for those moments when he needed to blow off some creative steam. Just a teenager when he made his first recordings, Previn initially dug swing music, but after World War II, hard bop began to permeate his style. His trio's playful jazzing up of the score to *My Fair Lady* was a surprise hit, and led to a series of similar reworkings of Broadway themes, standards, and songwriter tributes. He also found time to cut an LP with then-wife Dory Previn (his collaborator on many film songs) and co-write *Coco* for the Broadway stage. While slowly moving away from both jazz and Hollywood, Previn cut his first all-classical LP in 1960, which led to a series of successful romantic mood music discs on Columbia. As always, his playing was fluid and showcased superb technique, but Previn could not deny his ambition to be a full-time conductor of classical music, and he ceased performing in the mid-1960s. After many celebrated years as a conductor, he returned to jazz part time, releasing CDs on various record labels.

what to buy: Previn and his trio (featuring Red Mitchell and Frank Capp) reached a creative apex with *King Size* ♫♫♫♫ (Contemporary, 1960/OJC, 1992, prod. Lester Koenig), transforming six standards into swinging bop. Previn's piano work is especially freewheeling and cool on this fine reissue. For a taste of Previn's "beautiful music" style, *A Touch of Elegance* ♫♫♫♫ (Legacy, 1994, compilation prod. John Snyder, Irving Townsend) is a tribute to the music of Duke Ellington with his tasteful, yet moody, takes on "What's New," "Mack the Knife," "Bye Bye Blackbird," the title track, and many others.

what to buy next: Previn is alone at the piano for *Plays Songs by Jerome Kern* ♫♫♫♫ (Contemporary, 1959/OJC, 1992, prod.

Lester Koenig), with masterful interpretations of "Ol' Man River," "Long Ago and Far Away," and "All the Things You Are." Also, sports buffs who have a hard time getting into jazz ought to check out *Andre Previn/Russ Freeman: Double Play!* ♪♪♪♪ (Contemporary, 1957/OJC, 1992, prod. Lester Koenig), on which Previn gives the bop treatment to such baseball-oriented tunes as "Take Me Out to the Ballgame," "Called on Account of Rain," "Batter Up," and "In the Cellar Blues."

what to avoid: They're cheap and easy to find, but the poor quality of *Some of the Best* ♪♪ (LaserLight, 1996, compilation prod. Rod McKuen) and *More of the Best* ♪ (LaserLight, 1996, compilation prod. Rod McKuen) make them items for indiscriminate bargain-hunters and completists only.

the rest:

Pal Joey ♪♪♪♪ (Contemporary, 1957/OJC, 1991)

Gigi ♪♪♪ (Contemporary, 1958/OJC, 1990)

Plays Songs by Vernon Duke ♪♪♪♪ (Contemporary, 1958/OJC, 1991)

West Side Story ♪♪♪♪ (Contemporary, 1959/OJC, 1990)

Give My Regards to Broadway ♪♪♪ (Columbia Special Products, 1960/1993)

Plays Songs by Harold Arlen ♪♪♪ (Contemporary, 1960/OJC, 1994)

After Hours ♪♪♪ (Telarc, 1989)

The Piano Stylings of Andre Previn (RCA, 1990)

Uptown ♪♪♪♪ (Telarc, 1990)

Plays a Classic American Songbook ♪♪♪ (DRG, 1992)

Andre Previn/Mundell Lowe/Ray Brown: Old Friends ♪♪♪♪ (Telarc, 1992)

What Headphones? ♪♪♪ (Angel, 1993)

The Essence of Andre Previn ♪♪♪♪ (Legacy, 1994)

Andre Previn & His Friends Play "Showboat" ♪♪♪♪ (Deustche Grammophone, 1995)

Ballads—Solo Piano Standards ♪♪♪ (Capitol, 1996)

Jazz at the Musikverein ♪♪♪ (Verve, 1997)

Fats Waller Songbook ♪♪♪ (Simitar, 1997)

worth searching for: Many of Previn's early studio recordings (c. 1945–46) can be found on *Previn at Sunset* ♪♪♪♪ (Black Lion, 1993, reissue prod. Alan Bates); these cuts strongly exhibit the influence of Oscar Peterson. Also, Previn contributes heavily to the success of *Shelly Mann & His Friends* ♪♪♪♪ (OJC, 1996), originally recorded in 1944.

influences:

◀◀ Art Tatum, Oscar Peterson, Pierre Monteaux

▶▶ Roger Williams, Peter Nero, Francis Lai

Ken Burke

Bobby Previte

Born July 16, 1957, in Niagara Falls, NY.

Drummer/composer Bobby Previte studied at Buffalo University and in 1980 moved to New York City where he quickly established himself in the "Downtown" scene, collaborating with cutting-edge innovators such as John Zorn, Wayne Horvitz, Bill Frisell, and Elliott Sharp. An adventurous drummer and an imaginative composer, Previte first recorded his own music in the mid-1980s for the European label Sound Aspects. His own creations are marked by a high-spirited mixture of influences, but they generally maintain a bustling, jazz-based core. Previte has been recognized as an exceptional talent, winning the titles "Composer Deserving of Wider Recognition" (in the 1990 *DownBeat* Critics Poll) and "Hot Jazz Artist of 1991" (from *Rolling Stone*). He has performed his music at major international festivals and toured throughout the United States, Europe, Canada, Australia, and the Far East. In demand as a composer, Previte has written commissioned works for the String Trio of New York, the Philadelphia-based chamber ensemble Relache, and for the Moscow Circus (see his Gramavision album *Music of the Moscow Circus*). The latter piece premiered at the Gershwin Theater in New York City on November 5, 1991. He arranged the Charles Mingus tune "Open Letter to Duke" for Hal Willner's *Weird Nightmare—Meditations on Mingus* recording, and created a new electronic score for the International Puppet Festival, which debuted at the Public Theater in New York City in the fall of 1992. The drummer also continues to regularly tour overseas with his various groups, has recorded during these tours, and conducted numerous workshops, lectures, and master classes in Switzerland, Germany, and Australia, as well as in the United States at the Eastman School of Music in Rochester, New York, and the New School in New York City. Previte continues to work on new projects, including his band the Horse, an 11-piece ensemble that plays jazz of the early 1970s at weekly performances at the Knitting Factory in New York City. The drummer established a new recording label, Depth of Field, which, in September 1997, released *Euclid's Nightmare*, a duo with John Zorn. A new quartet recording from this label was due out in spring 1998. Previte has released over 12 recordings as a leader and appeared on numerous others as a sideman. If you're looking for more info on Previte, see his website (http://members.aol.com/Previte/).

what to buy: *Claude's Late Morning* ♪♪♪♪♪ (Gramavision, 1988/1995, prod. Bobby Previte) features Previte (drums, marimba, keyboards, drum machine, vocals) and some of the finest musicians in the New York City Downtown Scene, such as

Wayne Horvitz (Hammond organ, piano, harmonica), Bill Frisell (electric guitar, banjo), Ray Anderson (tuba, trombone), Joey Baron (drums), and Guy Klucevsek (accordion). Josh Dubin (pedal steel guitar), Carol Emanuel (harp), and Jim Mussen (electronic drums, sampling) also contribute. Previte is a serious composer with a sense of humor that is manifested not only in the titles of these 10 pieces, works that integrate melodies with heavy doses of rhythm, but also in the cohesive musical themes they embody, which range from the ethereal to the clamorous. His wit is evident in the big-beating "Sometimes You Need an Airport," the raucous pulsator "Look Both Ways," the jarring awakener "Claude's Late Morning," and others. The musicians deftly get their ideas across in both arranged and improvised passages. A listening delight. *Music of the Moscow Circus* 🎵🎵🎵🎵 (Gramavision, 1991/1995, prod. Bobby Previte) contains a mixture of moods, avant-garde jazz, Latin-jazz, and extraordinarily imaginative theatrical music designed to be played on a stage. Previte composed and arranged all of the music, some of which evolved from a commission for the Moscow Circus, and plays drums with big, heavy beats on some pieces. The 16 tunes feature Previte (also on keyboards, vocals) in various configurations with New York musicians Jerome Harris (acoustic and electric guitars, vocals), Mark Helias (acoustic and electric bass, vocals), Steve Gaboury (piano, Hammond organ), Carol Emanuel (harp), Mark Feldman (violin), Herb Robertson (trumpet, pocket trumpet, cornet), and Roger Squitero (percussion). Words cannot adequately describe the vividness, creativity, and spirit of the musical feast on this CD. Not only is it ear-expanding, it's music with a heart. You must hear it to appreciate it.

what to buy next: *Weather Clear, Track Fast* 🎵🎵🎵🎵 (Enja, 1991, prod. Bobby Previte) captures Previte leading a hard-driving troupe of prime innovators through seven of his original compositions. Adding more than the usual excitement to Previte's pieces are jazz musicians Don Byron (clarinet, baritone saxophone), Anthony Davis (piano), Anthony Cox (bass), Marty Ehrlich (clarinet, bass clarinet, alto saxophone, flute), Robin Eubanks (trombone), and Graham Haynes (cornet). Steve Gaboury (from Previte's Empty Suits band) sits in for the first tune, "Quinella," a jazz tune he's previously performed live. Many of these players are composers who lead their own groups. With such illustrious company, you can expect the best innovative ensemble music, and that's precisely what these musicians deliver—powerful avant-garde jazz, propelled and racing to the "outside" right from the gate. Previte holds it all together, and these fabulous cats get ample opportunities to strut their solo stuff.

the rest:
Bump the Renaissance 🎵🎵🎵 (Sound Aspects, 1985)
Pushing the Envelope 🎵🎵🎵🎵 (Gramavision, 1987/1995)
Dull Bang, Gushing Sound, Human Shriek 🎵🎵🎵 (Koch Jazz, 1987)
Empty Suits 🎵🎵🎵 (Avant, 1990)
(With Bobby Previte's Empty Suits) *Slay the Suitors* 🎵🎵🎵 (Avant, 1994)
(With Bobby Previte's Weather Clear, Track Fast) *Hue and Cry* 🎵🎵🎵🎵 (Enja, 1994)
(With Bobby Previte's Weather Clear, Track Fast) *Too Close to the Pole* 🎵🎵🎵🎵 (Enja, 1996)
My Man in Sydney 🎵🎵🎵🎵 (Enja, 1997)
Euclid's Nightmare 🎵🎵🎵 (Depth of Field, 1997)
Latin for Travelers 🎵🎵🎵 (Enja, 1997)

influences:
◀◀ Jack DeJohnette, Bob Moses, Ed Blackwell, Paul Motian

Nancy Ann Lee

Sam Price

Born Samuel Blythe Price, October 6, 1908, in Honey Grove, TX. Died April 14, 1992, in New York City, NY.

Sam Price was a marvelous boogie-woogie pianist whose jazz journey included stops in Kansas City, Detroit, and New York during some of the most fecund periods in jazz history (the '30s and '40s). In addition to his music-making skills, Price also had jobs as a public relations man, a record company exec, a photographer, and a nightclub owner, plus less-arts-related occupations as politician and undertaker. Price led groups throughout his life but some of his most important work was done as an accompanist to a wide variety of classic blues singers and jazz giants. His resume included work with Lester Young, Mezz Mezzrow, and Sidney Bechet, plus vocalists Trixie Smith and Sister Rosetta Tharpe. Much of his later career was spent in the company of trumpeter Doc Cheatham.

what to buy: Except for two tunes recorded in 1929 for Brunswick, the collection *1929–1941* 🎵🎵🎵 (Classics, 1993, prod. various) binds together all the titles Price recorded under his own name for Decca during 1940–41. The sessions were done with a free floating, ad hoc group of musicians called the Texas Blusicians. Lester Young is among the players on the April 3, 1941, date (four songs), but he's an ensemble guy, not a soloist.

what to buy next: *Barrelhouse and Blues* 🎵🎵🎵 (Black Lion, 1969, prod. Terry Brown, Alan Bates) is a well-recorded date with a batch of British musicians who have the basics of Price's style down even if they lack the true inspiration necessary to make this spectacular. The mix of originals and cover tunes includes war-horses like "St. James Infirmary" and "Royal Garden Blues," which showcase Price's ability to rise above his surroundings.

the rest:
King of Boogie Woogie 🎵🎵🎵 (Storyville, 1994)

worth searching for: *Rib Joint* 🎵🎵🎵🎵 (Savoy, 1956/1957, prod. Ozzie Cadena), a two-record set, mixes some of Price's best barrelhouse and boogie pianistics with the saxophone of King Curtis and Mickey Baker's guitar for some great party music. Now if it would only come out on CD. . . .

influences:
◀◀ James P. Johnson, Willie Lewis, Hersal Thomas
▶▶ Lloyd Glenn

Garaud MacTaggart

Julian Priester

Born June 29, 1935, in Chicago, IL.

A member of Sun Ra's Arkestra at the beginning (1954–56) and near the end, part of Herbie Hancock's famous sextet (1970–73), one of Max Roach's sidemen (1958–61), and a solo performer in his own right, trombonist Julian Priester has nevertheless been relegated to the sidelines in most jazz histories. It's a most unfortunate occurrence because, along with Grachan Moncur III and Roswell Rudd, he is one of the few players who have kept the poor, misjudged trombone a vital part of the jazz repertoire by continually finding new ways to make it as expressive and melodically integral as an alto sax.

what to buy: *Hints on Light and Shadow* 🎵🎵🎵🎵 (Postcards, 1996, prod. Ralph Simon), a nearly psychedelic summit between Priester and Sam Rivers, finds Priester's trombone providing the only constant, while Rivers switches between flute, piano, tenor, and soprano. Guest Tucker Martine fiddles around on electronics. Largely improvisational, yet anchored by a common structural understanding between the two (a given with great improvisers), *Hints* shows that neither Priester's playing nor his adventurous spirit have dampened with the years.

what to buy next: *Keep Swingin'* 🎵🎵🎵🎵 (Riverside/OJC, 1960, prod. Orrin Keepnews), Priester's debut as a leader, isn't the most distinctive affair, but it's enjoyable nonetheless. The crack rhythm section of Sam Jones on bass and Elvin Jones on drums, Priester's interplay with Jimmy Heath's tenor (excepting the three tracks where Priester goes it alone), and Tommy Flana-

gan's signature piano style combine to create a work that certainly stands on its own.

worth searching for: *Love, Love* 🎵🎵🎵🎵 (ECM, 1974, prod. Julian Priester, Pat Gleeson), an overlooked gem from the early ECM catalog, finds Priester playing bass, tenor, baritone, *and* alto trombones, "post horn," whistle, various percussion instruments, and Arp synths. Accompanied by a generally anonymous supporting cast (except Bill Connors's guitar on the title track), Priester—who had just finished a three-year stint with Herbie Hancock's sextet—takes electro-fusion to an unexpected level. *Love, Love* delivers four outstandingly atmospheric cuts, which, though they seldom get beyond a slow burn, never become background music.

influences:
◀◀ J.J. Johnson
▶▶ Frank Lacy

Jason Ferguson

Prima Materia

Formed 1994, in New York City, NY.

Rashied Ali, drums; Louie Belogenis, tenor sax; Allan Chase, alto and soprano sax; Joe Gallant, bass; William Parker, bass (1994); Greg Murphy, piano (1995–present).

Saxophonist Louie Belogenis contacted former John Coltrane drummer Rashied Ali for this project because he knew what everyone knows in New York City: those gravitating toward "free" jazz must go through Ali as a rite of passage because the drummer has played with all the key figures of the post–Ornette Coleman revolution/evolution. After a few rehearsals with Belogenis and crew, Ali embraced the concept of Prima Materia as an homage to the spirits of Coltrane and other innovators like Albert Ayler. As far as Ali's concerned, nearly all contemporary improvisers have yet to come to terms with Trane and Ayler. Plus, he feels that the general populace has little to no knowledge of these legendary jazz figures. But through Prima Materia, jazz fans will be able to experience at least some of the magic.

what to buy: *Bells* 🎵🎵🎵🎵 (Knitting Factory Works, 1996, prod. Rashied Ali, Louis Belogenis) is the group's most realized work to date. Belogenis, in particular, has by now grown into a formidable interpreter of the material. The melodic framework of Albert Ayler's "Bells" lends itself ideally to heated improvisations from all members of the group.

what to buy next: Whereas the group's debut, *Peace on Earth* ✍✍✍ (Knitting Factory Works, 1994, prod. Louis Belogenis), sounds more like a jam session (albeit a whirlwind one), the Prima Materia concept clicks in full force on Coltrane's extended composition "Meditations" featured on *Meditations* ✍✍✍ (Knitting Factory Works, 1995, prod. Rashied Ali, Louis Belogenis). The inclusion of pianist Greg Murphy adds welcome tonal color to the proceedings. The only drawback is bassist Joe Gallant's short solo during the "Love" section. He's a skilled ensemble player, but his solos sound too rock 'n' roll–derived and thus incongruous among the more abstract improvisation. On the all–John Coltrane debut, *Peace on Earth*, highlights include saxophonist John Zorn as guest blower on "Spiritual" and "Brazilia," and bassist William Parker as the foil to Joe Gallant.

influences:

◀◀ John Coltrane, Albert Ayler

Sam Prestianni

Marcus Printup

Born January 24, 1967, in Conyers, GA.

Though many young trumpet players burst on the scene with significant fanfare during the '90s, for Marcus Printup, a dynamic trumpeter who shows more promise than many of his contemporaries, the attention is deserved. Educated at the University of North Florida in Jacksonville, Printup has won several competitions, including the Thelonious Monk International Trumpet Competition in 1991. His tours include stints with Marcus Roberts, Wynton Marsalis, Carl Allen, and Betty Carter, and he is a member of the Lincoln Center Jazz Orchestra under the direction of Marsalis.

what to buy: Printup's second release, *Unveiled* ✍✍✍ (Blue Note, 1996, prod. Bob Belden, Marcus Printup), which includes mentor Marcus Roberts, shows excellent signs of progress from his debut. His versatility is evident as he echoes the voices of Miles Davis, Clifford Brown, Dizzy Gillespie, Lee Morgan, and Louis Armstrong. Printup is still trying to find his own voice, but the exploration, particularly on Wayne Shorter's "Yes or No" and several originals, is worth hearing.

the rest:

Song for the Beautiful Woman ✍✍✍ (Blue Note, 1995)

influences:

◀◀ Miles Davis, Wynton Marsalis, Freddie Hubbard, Fats

Navarro, Lee Morgan, Clifford Brown, Dizzy Gillespie, Louis Armstrong, Jon Faddis

Paul MacArthur

Professor Longhair

Born Henry Roeland Byrd, December 19, 1918, in Bogalusa, LA. Died January 30, 1980, in New Orleans, LA.

Jelly Roll Morton, in the early part of the 20th century, may have put the "Spanish tinge" into New Orleans' musical vocabulary, but Professor Longhair's rumba-laden rhythms served to define Crescent City piano from the late '40s onward. 'Fess, as he was known to admirers, got his start by watching and listening to the older pianists, and hanging around area clubs to pick up licks from local heroes like Tuts Washington. His first break came when, during a Dave Bartholomew gig, he played piano between Bartholomew's sets, impressing the club owner so much that 'Fess took the star's job right out from under him. The pianist then led a series of groups with names like Professor Longhair and the Four Hairs Combo or Professor Longhair and the Shuffling Hungarians. In 1950 Mercury released a version of "Bald Head" (a previous version of which had been cut for Star Talent as "She Ain't Got No Hair") that made a small dent on the national charts. He later recorded for a series of labels, including Atlantic, Federal, Ebb, and Ron before fading from the public eye during the 1960s. When he was "rediscovered" in 1972, 'Fess was making a living playing cards and sweeping floors in a local record store. That year he re-emerged onto the local and national scene with a spectacular performance at the Louisiana Jazz and Heritage Festival. From then on he made his living touring Europe and the United States, recording albums for Blue Star, Krazy Kat, Alligator, and Atlantic in addition to becoming a star attraction at the New Orleans Mardi Gras.

what to buy: *Fess: The Professor Longhair Anthology* ✍✍✍✍ (Rhino, 1993, prod. various), a fine two-CD set, may be the perfect starting point for someone wishing a well-constructed overview of 'Fess's career from 1950–80. There are plenty of classics to go around, including signature tunes like "She Walks Right In," "Tipitina," and "Mess Around," plus interesting oddities such as "Hadacol Bounce." When 'Fess recorded for Atlantic in 1949 and 1953 he cut some of his finest performances, many of them never released until *New Orleans Piano: Blues Originals, Part 2* ✍✍✍✍ (Rhino, 1973, prod. various). The resulting critical brouhaha was one of the steps that helped bring Longhair back into the limelight. Even though there are other solid collections of his music from the '50s, this may be the definitive single disc album of his early years. The performances on *Crawfish Fiesta* 🎵🎵🎵🎵 (Alligator, 1980, prod. Bruce Iglauer, Andy Kaslow, Allison Kaslow), featuring 'Fess, Dr. John (guitar), and a top-notch group of New Orleans sessioners, are fine, but it is also good to hear some new tunes and interesting variations on some of the pianist's standard fare. Quirky riffs abound on "Willie Fugal's Blues," "Something on Your Mind," and the title song.

what to buy next: Paul McCartney rented the luxury liner *Queen Mary* for a party and hired two New Orleans acts to provide the music: the Meters and Professor Longhair. *Live on the Queen Mary* 🎵🎵🎵🎵 (One Way, 1975, prod. Tom Wilson) documents 'Fess's portion of the evening, and the recording (originally released through Capitol) captured the pianist in fine form. The tunes form the standard set list for him at this time, so there are no real compositional surprises, but the playing and singing on this disc are uniformly wonderful. Pairing 'Fess with guitarist Clarence "Gatemouth" Brown was a wonderful idea and when *Rock 'n' Roll Gumbo* 🎵🎵🎵🎵 (Dancing Cat, 1974, prod. Philippe Rault) originally came out on the French label Barclay, it quickly became a highly sought-after import. Pianist George Winston bought the domestic rights for it, cleaned up the sound, and included material from the session that never made it onto the Barclay release. The result is now available on CD and the opportunity to hear 'Fess on piano and Brown on guitar (or violin on "Jambalaya") is still a wonderful idea. *House Party New Orleans Style: The Lost Sessions, 1971–1972* 🎵🎵🎵🎵 (Rounder, 1987, prod. Quint Davis) came at the beginning of 'Fess's rediscovery and features the pianist in high form alongside guitarist Snooks Eaglin. The music comes from two different sessions, one in New Orleans with 'Fess's usual rhythm section, the other in Memphis with the bassist and drummer from the Meters imported, along with 'Fess and Eaglin, from New Orleans.

what to avoid: 'Fess recorded an interview for Canadian radio that never ended up running due to legal problems. Now it is available as *Fess's Gumbo* 🎵 (Stony Plain, 1996, prod. Keef Whiting), but its worth as a valuable document is lessened by an engineer who forgot to account for Longhair's vocals during the performance part. The playing between the talk segments is fine and it is good to hear 'Fess reminisce about his life, but the singing is so badly recorded/mastered that the vocals are nigh unto inaudible.

the rest:
Big Chief 🎵🎵🎵 (Tomato/Rhino, 1978)
Mardi Gras in New Orleans 🎵🎵🎵 (Nighthawk, 1981)

Rum and Coke 🎵🎵🎵 (Tomato/Rhino, 1982)
Mardi Gras in Baton Rouge 🎵🎵🎵 (Rhino, 1991)
Live in Germany 🎵🎵 (New Rose, 1994)

influences:

◀◀ Tuts Washington, Rocky Sullivan, Archibald, Robert Bertrand

▶▶ Allen Toussaint, Huey Smith, Mac "Dr. John" Rebennack, Fats Domino

Garaud MacTaggart

Arthur Prysock

Born January 2, 1929, in Spartenburg, SC. Died June 14, 1997.

With a baritone voice most FM deejays would kill for, Arthur Prysock became a popular singer in Buddy Johnson's band, scoring a number of big R&B hits between 1944 and 1952. After leaving Johnson, Prysock became a romantic ballad specialist supported by lush arrangements, though he occasionally sang the blues. The romantic approach was a natural fit for Prysock's voice and he enjoyed several hits during the 1950s and 1960s. His recording career slowed down a bit in the 1970s, but singing the Lowenbrau commercials got him back in the national spotlight and he made several appearances on national television shows. Prysock popped back up in the mid-1980s with some good albums on Milestone and continued to tour with his saxophonist brother Red until Red's death in 1993. Prysock would pass away four years later. A good interpreter with an instantly identifiable voice, his awesome low register added to his effectiveness.

what to buy: *Jazz 'Round Midnight* 🎵🎵🎵🎵 (Old Town, 1961–1968/Verve, 1995) is a compilation of Prysock ballads from the 1960s, many about heartbreak (his specialty). The songs are well arranged and Prysock delivers the goods on every cut. The collection of songs represent Prysock at his best, which is pretty damn good. On *Arthur Prysock & Count Basie* 🎵🎵🎵🎵 (Verve/Old Town, 1965/Verve, 1989) Arthur sings and the Count Basie Orchestra plays. The results are as expected and there's nothing wrong with that. *This Is My Beloved* 🎵🎵🎵🎵 (Verve, 1969/1992, prod. Hy Weiss, Pete Spargo) represents a tremendous artistic effort, with Prysock reciting the free-verse poem by Walter Benton about losing a lover to musical accompaniment composed by Mort Garson. Prysock's baritone voice is perfect for such a task and his interpretation has the proper dramatic flair. The music indicates the period this was recorded, but the emotions and reading are timeless. This is what a poetry-set-to-music album should be.

what to buy next: *Compact Jazz* ♫♫♫ (Old Town/Verve, 1963–65/Verve, 1989), a compilation from the early 1960s, is a bit more upbeat and varied than *Jazz 'Round Midnight*. It contains a few tracks available on the *Jazz 'Round Midnight* and the Count Basie album, but enough different good ones to make this worth going after. Of Prysock's mid-1980s recordings for Milestone, *This Guy's in Love with You* ♫♫♫ (Milestone, 1987) is the best. The veteran balladeer still has it in him, belting out the signature bittersweet ballads and a couple upbeat R&B tunes. The on-the-money cover of Brook Benton's hit "Rainy Night in Georgia," and Betty Joplin's counterpoint on three songs, "Everything Must Change" in particular, make this a winner.

the rest:

A Rockin' Good Way ♫♫♫♪ (Milestone, 1985)
Today's Love Songs, Tomorrow's Blues ♫♫♫ (Milestone, 1988)

influences:

◄◄ Joe Turner, Billy Eckstine, Jimmy Rushing, Al Hibbler, Joe Williams

►► Lou Rawls, Barry White, Isaac Hayes, Brook Benton

see also: *Buddy Johnson, Betty Joplin*

Paul MacArthur

Tito Puente

Born Ernest Anthony Puente Jr., April 20, 1923, in New York, NY.

When the rock group Santana recorded "Oye Como Va," a classic Latin hit that Tito Puente had written and recorded, the composer was slightly outraged that such a band would dare sully his music. As soon as the royalty check came (based on massive sales of Santana's first album), Puente discovered the up side of having other people perform his songs. He has prefaced the playing of "Oye Como Va" with that little story many times since then and come to realize that his music has done as much to promote Latin jazz for current audiences as Machito's did for an earlier generation. Puente's musical career began with Latin groups such as the Cuarteto Caney and, after World War II, Xavier Cugat.

In the mid-1940s, after serving in the United States Navy during World War II, Puente came back to New York where Noro Morales and Machito gave the budding percussionist work. By the early 1950s, he had formed his own ensemble, the Piccadilly Boys, and played the Palladium, New York's cultural Mecca for Latin bands. His band meanwhile had mutated into the Tito Puente Orchestra and, with lead vocalist Vincentico

Valdes, proceeded to change the face of Latin music. Puente took the Cuban charanga form (with its flutes and violins) and arranged them in more of a jazz big band context, punching up the brass and reeds for a more powerful sound. He also started using a lot of non-Latin jazz artists like Doc Severinsen within his bands and playing arrangements of jazz standards with a Latin beat. During the 1960s and 1970s Puente recorded albums for GNP, Tico, and Fania with large bands and small groups, continuing the heavy schedule of touring he had developed in the 1950s. By the 1980s Puente's popularity was even stronger than it was in the early 1950s due to a base of fans that included not only the hard-core Latin music lovers, but a fair number of jazz musicians and fans as well.

It was in 1983 that the multi-talented Puente (timbales, drums, marimba, vibraphone, percussion, vocalist, arranger) won the first of his many Grammy Awards, for the album *Tito Puente and His Latin Ensemble on Broadway*. With over 100 albums to his credit, Puente has recorded with most of the major names in Latin music and become a major force in the Latinization of jazz during the last half of the 20th century.

what to buy: The three-CD compilation set, *50 Years of Swing* ♫♫♫♫ (RMM, 1997, prod. various), is a perfect starting place for anyone wanting a well-conceived, albeit abridged, introduction to Tito Puente's music. The 50 songs cover his stints with the major pop labels like MCA and RCA in addition to sampling material from Latin specialty companies Tico and Westside Latino. His big hits "Para Los Rumberos" and "Oye Como Va" are included along with distinguished covers of tunes made famous by Machito ("Tanga" and "Babarabatiri"), renditions of jazz classics like "Lullaby of Broadway" and "Moody's Mood for Love," and distinctly cheesy remakes of pop riffs ("Crystal Blue Persuasion"). The two previously unreleased songs ("Llegue" and "I'm Going to Go Fishing") are adequate performances at best, adding little of real value to the collection, except their hitherto rarity. From the mid-1950s through the early 1960s Puente had one of the hottest bands around, jazz or Latin. The band on *The Best of Dance Mania* ♫♫♫♫ (BMG/International, 1957–1960/1994 prod. Fred Reynolds, Marty Gold) features his second great vocalist (after Vincentico Valdes), Santitos Colon, the remarkable bassist Bobby Rodriguez, and a host of stellar percussionists, including Ray Barretto and Jose Mangual. This CD has 23 cuts, including some previously unreleased outtakes that showcase the care Puente took to craft the perfect performance of a song. His unwillingness to make changes in an arrangement once he had things in place can be heard prior to take #6 of "Estoy Siempre Junto A Ti" where he chides a side-

Tito Puente (l) and Celia Cruz (© Jack Vartoogian)

man for wasting time while the light (signifying that the tape was rolling) was on. *Mambo Beat, Vol. 1* 🎵🎵🎵 (BMG/International, 1956–1957/1994, prod. various) is a well put together collection (compiled by Domingo Echevarria) featuring performances by Puente and his Afro-Cuban Jazz All Star Orchestras in jazz material with a Latin kick. The arrangers include Puente, Marty Holmes, and one of Machito's ace writers, A.K. Salim. The personnel includes jazz musicians Doc Severinsen, Eddie Bert, Gene Quill, and Jimmy Cobb, plus a bevy of Latin percussion kings like Puente (on timbales and vibes), Mongo Santamaria, Willie Bobo, Candido, and Patato Valdes. Standards like "Yesterdays" by Jerome Kern and Oscar Pettiford's "Bohemia After Dark" (renamed "Birdland After Dark") share space with Puente's own wonderful "Night Ritual" and the percussion fest "Ti Mon Bo." On *Live at the Village Gate* 🎵🎵🎵 (RMM, 1992, prod. Alfredo Cruz), Puente heads an all-star group including Mongo Santamaria, Giovanni Hidalgo, Paquito D'Rivera, and Hilton Ruiz through a well-chosen program of jazz favorites and a hip arrangement of his "Oye Como Va." Especially noteworthy are Miles Davis's "Milestones" and Santamaria's "Afro Blue."

what to buy next: With the exception of a big band mini-suite entitled "Night Ritual," *Top Percussion* 🎵🎵🎵 (BMG/International, 1957/1992) is one of the most subversive Latin albums (given the time it first appeared in the marketplace) ever released. Santeria practitioner Puente released this album of polyrhythmic percussion honoring the orishas decades before Milton Cardona's classic *Bembe*. Alongside Mongo Santamaria, Willie Bobo, and a quartet of Cuban vocalists (including the great Mercedita), Puente went for percussion heaven, conducting a textbook example of how exciting and challenging his music can be. Constructed mainly for people with a minimal budget who want to start exploring Puente's voluminous catalog, *El Rey Del Timbal–The Best of Tito Puente and His Orchestra* 🎵🎵🎵 (Rhino, 1997, prod. various) is a good single-disc sampler of Puente's material covering the period from 1949 to 1987. Production is very good but this compilation still does not replace the RMM box set. *Special Delivery* 🎵🎵🎵🎵 (Concord Picante, 1996, prod. John Burk, Tito Puente) is a big band jazz album covering the bebop and post-bop composers that Puente is most comfortable with—Dizzy Gillespie, Thelonious Monk, and Horace Silver. Puente features trumpeter Maynard Ferguson on Gillespie's "Be-Bop" and on the classic tune "On Green Dolphin Street," but his normal complement of players like trumpeters Michael Philip Mossman, Bobby Shew, and Ray Vega are just about as good. Solid playing throughout makes this a good choice for those who want Puente in a "pure" jazz setting. In addition to playing timbales and other assorted percussion instruments, Puente is a gifted vibes player, and *Mambo of the Times* 🎵🎵🎵🎵 (Concord Picante, 1992, prod. John Burk, Allen Farnham, Tito Puente) contains some of his best work in that regard. His playing on Fats Waller's "Jitterbug Waltz" is firmly within the jazz camp even as his supporting cast flits about his melodic statement like Latin fireflies. Puente's vibes work on Billy Strayhorn's beautiful ballad "Passion Flower" is another gem. *The Mambo King* 🎵🎵🎵🎵 (RMM, 1991, prod. Sergio George) is Puente's 100th album, marking a significant milestone in his career. More of a Latin recording than a straight jazz session, the album features Puente joined by major Latin vocal stars like Oscar D'Leon, Celia Cruz, Ismael Miranda, and Tito Nieves. The performance standard is suitably high and the playing is professional yet relaxed. The discography included in the negligible liner notes leads the reader through the honor role of Puente's albums prior to this one.

best of the rest:

Goza Mi Timbal 🎵🎵🎵🎵 (Concord Picante, 1990)
Out of This World 🎵🎵🎵🎵 (Concord Picante, 1991)
In Session 🎵🎵🎵🎵 (RMM, 1994)
Tito's Idea 🎵🎵🎵🎵 (RMM, 1996)

influences:

◀◀ Machito, Mario Bauzá, Dizzy Gillespie, Gene Krupa

▶▶ Guilherme Franco, Cal Tjader, Carlos Santana

Garaud MacTaggart

Don Pullen

Born December 25, 1941, in Roanoke, VA. Died April 22, 1995, in East Orange, NJ.

Don Pullen's early work in local church and R&B groups paved the way for a pianist who was later to be one of the most original and recognizable stylists in jazz. Pullen's style was characterized by a full-bodied, rhythmic, and chordal left hand com-

DON PULLEN

song "Aseeko! (Get Up and Dance)"
album *Don Pullen and the African-Brazilian Connection: Live . . . Again*
(Blue Note, 1993/1995)

instrument Piano

plemented by spiraling right-hand lines that would gradually work themselves up into rushes of cascading notes. He had a percussive style that showed a debt to Monk, but his harmonic conception was less oblique. However, he did not shy away from dissonance. There was also a strong gospel element to his playing that could build certain solo pieces to rousing heights. He moved to New York in 1964, and his first recordings with Giuseppi Logan's group allied him with the free jazz movement. In 1966, in a duo with drummer Milford Graves (a rare format for the time), he recorded the self-produced *Nommo*, which showed him to be an acolyte of Cecil Taylor's pianistics but not yet in possession of his sense of architecture and drama. His re-emergence in 1973 as a member of Mingus's last great quintet heralded a highly individual pianist who brought his gospel, R&B, and avant-garde experience in equal measure to some of Mingus's finest compositions. In 1979 he formed a quartet co-led with tenor saxophonist and fellow Mingus alumnus George Adams. They recorded ten albums through 1987. After that Pullen recorded a number of albums for the Blue Note label, the last four with the African-Brazilian Connection exploring African, Caribbean, and South American rhythms and representing yet another extension of Pullen's fascination with the various idioms of black popular music. Another facet of this was Pullen's return to the organ in 1986 as a member of the band that producer Kip Hanrahan assembled for his Conjure project. He also formed a close association with Canadian saxophonist Jane Bunnett and recorded with her in duet and with her quartet.

what to buy: *Evidence of Things Unseen* &&&& (Black Saint, 1983, prod. Giovanni Bonandrini) is the best solo album to appreciate the full power and beauty of Pullen's piano conception. Everything comes together on the 19-minute "In the Beginning," a piece that marvelously demonstrates Pullen's approach to building up a performance. A complete program. Recorded after the breakup of his 10-year association with the Adams/Pullen quartet, *New Beginnings* &&&& (Blue Note, 1988, prod. Michael Cuscuna) is the sound of Pullen starting anew and obviously loving it. With a program of seven originals ranging from the jaunty bounce of "Jana's Delight" to the swirling power of "Reap the Whirlwind," this is Pullen's piano artistry at full maturity.

what to buy next: A follow up, of sorts, to *New Beginnings*, *Random Thoughts* &&&& (Blue Note, 1990, prod. Michael Cuscuna) uses bassist James Genus and drummer Lewis Nash. The tone is a bit lighter. Genus's walking bass and Nash's snappy brush work propel the title track in a much more literal manner than the Peacock/Williams rhythm section would have. But Pullen's convoluted lines, splashes of dissonance, and powerful keyboard sweeps never trip them up. Pullen was among the few pianists who could match tenor saxophonist George Adams's primal roar, and *Live at the Village Vanguard Vols. 1 & 2* &&&& (Soul Note, 1984, prod. Giovanni Bonandrini) come closest to showing it, from the burning "Necessary Blues (Thank You Very Much Mr. Monk)" to the Pullen classic, the Bo Diddley-esque "Big Alice." *The Sixth Sense* &&&& (Soul Note, 1985, prod. Giovanni Bonandrini) is an unusual quintet date with none of the Pullen standbys, and it's all the stronger for it. Personnel includes Donald Harrison, alto saxophone; Olu Dara, trumpet; Fred Hopkins, bass; and Bobby Battle, drums. The tone is almost light-hearted, the program diverse. Too bad this group wasn't longer lasting.

what to avoid: *Sacred Common Ground* &&& (Blue Note, 1995), Pullen's final album, has the aura of a project not fully realized (although the liner notes state the contrary). It was an attempt

at fusing the music of the African-Brazilian Connection with Native American vocal and rhythm music in collaboration with the Chief Cliff Singers. But the music rarely gels. Pullen's solos are muted, almost as if he were still trying to figure a way into the music.

best of the rest:
(With Sam Rivers) *Capricorn Rising* &&&& (Black Saint, 1975)
(With Jane Bunnett) *New York Duets* &&&& (Music & Arts, 1989)
Kele Mou Bana &&& (Blue Note, 1991)
Ode to Life &&&& (Blue Note, 1992)
Live . . . Again &&&& (Blue Note, 1993)

worth searching for: Recorded with Milford Graves, *Nommo* &&&& (P.G., 1966) catches Pullen at a very early stage in his development, and it sounds like he was in thrall to Cecil Taylor. Pullen has the power, but his ideas don't sound as well thought out. This was originally released in two volumes and hasn't been reissued since. Both volumes would fit nicely on one CD, and a very important part of Pullen's history would be back in circulation.

influences:

◀◀ Thelonious Monk, Cecil Taylor

▶▶ Yosuke Yamashita, D.D. Jackson

Robert Iannapollo

Bernard Purdie

Born June 11, 1939, in Elkton, MD.

Drummer Bernard Purdie began banging on whatever he could find around the house at age six, and bought his first set of drums at age 14. He came to prominence in New York's studio scene shortly after his move there in 1960. He worked and recorded with King Curtis and James Brown, among others, during the 1960s and toured and recorded with Aretha Franklin and Curtis in 1970. In addition to being Franklin's music director, Purdie recorded extensively during the 1970s and was one of the staff drummers for Creed Taylor's CTI Records, mostly being featured on the label's more funk-oriented Kudu subsidiary. During the 1970s, he recorded a solo album for Flying Dutchman (which is long, long out of print) and was heard on albums by a wide variety of artists, including Grover Washington, Louis Armstrong, Dizzy Gillespie, and Gato Barbieri. Since 1980, he has continued to record with numerous artists, including alto saxophonist Hank Crawford. With respect to his work in jazz, Purdie, also known as "Pretty Purdie," is best known for his soulful, precise, uncluttered, and extremely funky style of drumming. Although also proficient in the straight-ahead vein, he was probably the foremost funk/jazz drummer during the 1970s when that style was in its heyday. Whether they know it or not, countless later funk-oriented drummers have assimilated some of Purdie's style.

what's available: After being the drummer for many others for three decades, Purdie came out with *Soul to Jazz,* 𝄞𝄞𝄞𝄞 (ACT Records, 1996, prod. Wolfgang Hirschmann, Siegfried Loch), a refreshingly interesting mix of soul music, funk, and jazz, which should please those who regularly cross those borders. It includes a diverse set of material with such well-known jazz pieces as "The Sidewinder," "Freedom Jazz Dance," "Señor Blues," "The Work Song," and "Moanin'," alongside soul and pop fare like "Superstition," "When a Man Loves a Woman," "Land of 1,000 Dances," and "Gimme Some Lovin'." Purdie is heard with the WDR Big Band, conducted by Gil Goldstein, and guests including Eddie Harris, Michael and Randy Brecker, and vocalist Martin Moss. *Soul to Jazz II* 𝄞𝄞𝄞𝄞 (ACT Records, 1997, prod. Bob Belden) is one of those rare cases where the sequel is better than its predecessor. Volume II finds Pretty Purdie in great form in small group formats. This one is all funk with some gospel, such as the opener "(Sometimes I Feel Like) A Motherless Child," which segues into a funk drum extravaganza, Jack DeJohnette's "New Orleans Strut," which features DeJohnette along with Purdie. I knew this album was a downright winner when they pulled off a creatively funky version of "Theme from Shaft." While Purdie works with the same bassist throughout, some of the other guests who make noteworthy contributions are Stanley Turrentine, Cornell Dupree, Hank Crawford, Vincent Herring, Junior Mance, and Benny Green. The vocals on "Motherless Child" and "Nobody Knows (The Trouble I've Seen)" are also outstanding. Some of the other cuts are "Mister Magic," "Amen," and Turrentine's funky blues "La Place Street." This one's a keeper.

Bill Wahl

Flora Purim

Born March 6, 1942, in Rio de Janeiro, Brazil.

Flora Purim grew up amidst a family of professional musicians and studied piano and guitar. In the mid-1960s she performed in Sao Paulo with her future husband, percussionist Airto Moreira, before moving to America in the late 1960s, where they settled first in New York City and then in Los Angeles. Purim became the featured vocalist in outfits such as Stan Getz's Brazilian-jazz band (1968), Duke Pearson's band (1969–70), and,

later, Return to Forever, the fusion quintet led by Chick Corea with Moreira, Stanley Clarke, and Joe Farrell from 1971–73. Purim's voice is often subtly soft and airy, sometimes scatting around melody lines and soaring above the other instruments and percussion, and she often sings lyrics in Portuguese or English. Although her career was derailed from 1974 to 1975 by a prison term for cocaine possession, she reappeared in 1976 with a semi-successful album on Milestone entitled *Open Up Your Eyes, You Can Fly.* Purim led her own group without Moreira for a while, but resumed working with him in the mid-1980s; they have collaborated regularly since then on a variety of projects worldwide. Check the Internet for informative websites about their ongoing musical activities.

what to buy: Highly influenced by the Fourth World band co-led with Airto, Purim improvises freely on her first album as leader in over five years, *Speed of Light* 𝄞𝄞𝄞𝄞 (B&W, 1995, prod. Airto Moreira, Flora Purim). This UK import represents the percussion-laden, often groove-oriented, yet borderless style in which she is working today. The couple continues their electronic manipulations and overdubbing. However, the results on this album's 12 tunes are excitingly modern-edged and intriguing. In addition to Airto, Purim is joined by a host of musicians, including guitarist José Neto, percussionist Giovanni Hidalgo, drummer Billy Cobham, and others. With this album, it's obviously she has no intention of competing with the many Brazilian jazz vocalists recording today; instead, she is continuing her explorations beyond the traditional, featuring world percussions and often using her voice like an instrument in creations that range from primitive to modern and beyond. If all this electronic experimenting is beyond what your ears can tolerate, check out Purim's vocals on *The Magicians* 𝄞𝄞𝄞 (Concord/Crossover, 1986, prod. Airto Moreira). Imagine this notable Brazilian jazz vocalist convincingly singing the blues-drenched Jeannie Cheatham classic, "Sweet Baby Blues," with backing from George Duke, saxophonist Marry Fettig, and Moreira playing traps. The rest of the album contains a mixture of Brazilian-influenced fusion, typical of the couple's stint with Return to Forever. Pianist Kei Akagi performs with eloquence on a couple of tracks, but his best performance is on his original tune "Jennifer," made contemporary with his keyboard stylings and by Purim's soaring vocals, Airto's percussion, and some fusiony guitar support from David Zeiher. While some of the tracks may sound dated, there's enough versatility here to satisfy most jazz fans.

what to buy next: *Butterfly Dreams* 𝄞𝄞𝄞 (Milestone/OJC, 1973/1988, prod. Orrin Keepnews) ranks among Purim's best early recordings, featuring saxophonist Joe Henderson, pianist George Duke, Moreira, bassist Stanley Clarke, and others. Tunes include a pleasing version of Jobim's "Dindi."

best of the rest:

The Sun Is Out 𝄞𝄞𝄞𝄞 (Concord/Crossover, 1989)
Stories to Tell 𝄞𝄞𝄞 (Milestone/OJC, 1991)
Encounter 𝄞𝄞𝄞 (Milestone/OJC, 1993)

influences:

◀◀ Astrud Gilberto

▶▶ Tania Maria

see also: *Airto Moreira, Return to Forever*

Nancy Ann Lee

Ike Quebec

Born August 17, 1918, in Newark, NJ. Died January 16, 1963, in New York, NY.

Not a household name by any stretch of the imagination, tenor saxophonist Ike Quebec was nonetheless one of the best swing-styled players who came up during the 1940s. Tapping into the husky approach preferred by Coleman Hawkins and Ben Webster, Quebec had a robust and cavernous sound that when combined with an emotional directness made his up-tempo work positively joyous, and his lush ballad performances beautiful enough to bring a tear to the eye. Forward-thinking by nature, Quebec was lucky enough to be part of the developing bebop scene while working in the bands of Kenny Clarke, Benny Carter, and Roy Eldridge. His other activities during the late 1940s and early 1950s included stints with Cab Calloway and Lucky Millinder, recordings for Savoy and Blue Note (his "Blue Harlem" was a jukebox hit of some stature), and a good deal of traveling around the country as a single act. It was also during this period that Quebec worked as a talent scout and A&R man for Blue Note Records. In fact, few are aware that he was responsible for introducing producer Alfred Lion to bebop legends such as Bud Powell and Thelonious Monk. As the 1960s approached, Quebec launched a comeback of sorts with a flurry of recording activity of his own for Blue Note, in addition to several appearances as a sideman on dates by Jimmy Smith, Grant Green, and singer Dodo Greene. Unfortu-

nately, his untimely death cut short any chances of rediscovery by fans and critics until many decades later.

what to buy: *Heavy Soul* 𝄞𝄞𝄞𝄞 (Blue Note, 1961, prod. Alfred Lion) was Quebec's return session for Blue Note and provided ample evidence that he had lost none of his powers. The tenor-bass duo performance of "Nature Boy" is among Quebec's finest recorded moments. *Blue and Sentimental* 𝄞𝄞𝄞𝄞 (Blue Note, 1961/1992, prod. Alfred Lion) is an absolutely resplendent session that finds Quebec fronting an atypical quartet with guitarist Grant Green and the rhythm team of Paul Chambers and Philly Joe Jones. With a brilliant mix of medium cookers and lush ballads, this set is the best place to introduce yourself to Quebec's heartfelt approach.

the rest:

The Art of Ike Quebec 𝄞𝄞𝄞𝄞 (Blue Note, 1961–1962/Capitol, 1992)

worth searching for: Some of Quebec's best work still available appears on his recordings as sideman. *Grant Green: Born to Be Blue* 𝄞𝄞𝄞𝄞 (Blue Note, 1962, prod. Alfred Lion) finds Quebec in the company of guitarist Green, Sonny Clark, Sam Jones, and Louis Hayes. Green and Quebec share most of the solo space and the results are highly rewarding. *Dodo Greene: My Hour of Need* 𝄞𝄞𝄞𝄞 (Blue Note, 1962, prod. Alfred Lion) was arranged by Quebec and features his warm-toned tenor as a perfect foil to Greene's blues-drenched vocals. Two Mosaic sets featuring Quebec as leader, *The Complete '40s Blue Note Recordings of Ike Quebec and John Hardee* 𝄞𝄞𝄞𝄞 (Mosaic, 1944–1946, prod. Alfred Lion) and *The Complete Blue Note 45 Sessions of Ike Quebec* 𝄞𝄞𝄞𝄞 (Mosaic, 1959–1962, prod. Alfred Lion) offer prime examples of Quebec's masterful playing. Once available by mail order, these albums can now only be found by searching used record stores. The former features his early Blue Note sides, while the latter documents some 1960s dates cut originally for release as 45 rpm records.

influences:

◀◀ Coleman Hawkins, Ben Webster, Don Byas

Chris Hovan

Quest

Formed 1981, in New York City.

Dave Liebman, soprano saxophone; Richie Beirach, piano; George Mraz, bass (1981); Ron McClure, bass; Billy Hart, drums.

This collective was an outgrowth of the long-standing collaboration between Liebman and Beirach, and it used the pianist's frequent rhythm section partners. The quartet played everything from gentle jazz tone poems to intense, Coltrane-influenced modal jams and free jazz.

what to buy: Fortunately, the most readily available Quest album is one of its best. Beirach's lush lyricism sets the mood for much of *Natural Selection* ♫♫♫ (Pathfinder, 1988/Evidence, 1994, prod. Quest, David Baker), but the album includes a range of styles. There's even fusion on McClure's catchy "Michiyo," on which he plays a Fender fretless electric bass.

what to buy next: *Midpoint* a.k.a. *Quest III: Live at the Montmartre, Copenhagen, Denmark* ♫♫♫ (Storyville, 1987, prod. Quest) captures a hot concert and emphasizes the group's modal leanings.

the rest:
Quest ♫♫♫ (Palo Alto, 1981)
Of One Mind ♫♫♫♫ (CMP, 1990)

influences:
◀◀ John Coltrane, Wayne Shorter, Herbie Hancock, Lookout Farm

Steve Holtje

Paul Quinichette

Born May 17, 1916, in Denver, CO. Died May 25, 1983, in New York, NY.

Paul Quinichette developed a distinctive approach to the tenor saxophone by using the light-and-breathy sound made popular by Lester Young to deliver a message oriented more from the bebop school than the swing style popularized by Young. Nevertheless, for most of his career he has been referred to as the "Vice Prez" (taking after Young's moniker, "Prez"). During the 1940s, Quinichette toured with several popular big bands of the time, including those led by Jay McShann, Lucky Millinder, Red Allen, and Hot Lips Page. He also gained experience in the popular and R&B genres through his associations with Louis Jordan and Johnny Otis. Much of Quinichette's most memorable work occurred during the 1950s. He did a one-year stint with Count Basie, followed by a gig with Benny Goodman, recordings with Billie Holiday, and a few record dates for the Prestige label, one of which paired him with the innovative John Coltrane. By that decade's end, he left music for a day job, only briefly making a comeback in the 1970s, then retiring again before his death in 1983. Painfully under-recorded, the few documents we do have of Quinichette reveal him to have been a player of notable merit.

what's available: *On the Sunny Side* ♫♫♫♫ (Prestige, 1957, prod. Bob Weinstock) is one of the better examples of the clas-

sic "blowing date." Quinichette is in peak form and he shares the solo honors with John Jenkins, Curtis Fuller, Sonny Red, and Mal Waldron. *Cattin' with Coltrane and Quinichette* ♫♫♫♫♫ (Prestige, 1957, prod. Esmond Edwards) may seem like an unlikely pairing on first impression, but is indeed an animated date that benefits from the contrasts between the two players' approaches.

worth searching for: *Basie Reunions* ♫♫♫♫♫ (Prestige, 1957/1958, prod. Bob Weinstock, Esmond Edwards) is a must-own if you still have a turntable. This 2-LP set brings together sessions that featured Basie alumni such as Buck Clayton, Freddie Greene, Jo Jones, and Walter Page. The results are grand, as is the tradition when explored by those who knew it best.

influences:
◀◀ Lester Young

Chris Hovan

The Quintet of the Hot Club of France
See: Django Reinhardt, Stephane Grappelli

 R

Ma Rainey

Born Gertude Pridgett, April 26, 1886, in Columbus, GA. Died December 22, 1939, in Columbus, GA.

One of the greatest and most influential blues singers of all time, Ma Rainey took the title "Mother of the Blues" early in her career, though nearly a century later it seems a somewhat fanciful claim. Rainey had been performing for some 20 years before she cut her first sides for Paramount in 1923. Her recording career ended a mere five years later in 1928, and when she died of a heart attack in 1939 she was listed by the state of Georgia as a "housekeeper." But over the course of some 100 recordings she fused the sound of rural blues, her experiences in traveling minstrel shows, and black vaudeville theater with a powerfully somber, down-home voice, immortalizing such songs as "See See Rider Blues," "Ma Rainey's Black Bottom," and "Bo-Weavil Blues." That Ma Rainey recorded "classic blues" is also rather dubious. But she was accompanied by an impressive array of early jazz and blues luminaries, including

Louis Armstrong, Fletcher Henderson, Coleman Hawkins, Kid Ory, Buster Baily, "Georgia Tom" Dorsey, Tampa Red, and Blind Blake. Whatever the setting—jug band, jazz band, or simple guitar and piano—it's Ma Rainey's tough, tender, and sometimes tragic singing that comes through on the old 78s. And to the dozens of singers who were influenced by her style—from Bessie Smith to Janis Joplin—Ma Rainey was certainly the prototypical blues mama.

what's available: As with many artists who recorded in the 1920s and 1930s, Rainey's catalog is a confusion of overlapping reissues collected from old 78s and transferred with hit-and-miss results. Of the two most widely available collections, *Ma Rainey's Black Bottom* ♪♪♪♪ (Yazoo, 1990, prod. Nick Perls) has the best sound and cover art—a photo of Ma Rainey with one her stage bands, hand-colored by filmmaker Terry Zwigoff of *Crumb* fame. Rainey is backed by a Fletcher Henderson–led band on "Booze and Blues" (1924), Jimmy Blythe's solo piano on "Don't Fish in My Sea" (1926), and Henderson again with Charlie Green, Buster Baily, and Coleman Hawkins on "Stack O' Lee Blues" (1926). While the sound isn't quite as good, *Ma Rainey* ♪♪♪♪ (Milestone, 1992, prod. Orrin Keepnews) offers an even broader overview of Rainey's shifting array of accompanists. Most exciting for early jazz enthusiasts are three tracks from 1924 featuring Louis Armstrong—"See See Rider Blues," "Jelly Bean Blues," and "Countin' the Blues."

influences:

◄◄ William "Pa" Rainey and the Rabbit Foot Minstrels

►► Bessie Smith, Madeleine Peyroux, Billie Holiday, Etta James, Aretha Franklin, Janis Joplin

Bob Townsend

Jimmy Raney

Born August 20, 1927, in Louisville, KY. Died May 10, 1995, in Louisville, KY.

One of the earliest and most gifted bop-influenced guitarists, Jimmy Raney was a fluid improviser with a subtle, persuasively swinging approach. His soft, quiet sound and gift for melodic statement belied his fiercely swinging attack. Raised in Chicago, he played locally with the Jerry Wald Orchestra before moving to New York and joining Woody Herman for an eight-month stint in 1948. In the next few years he worked with Al Haig, Terry Gibbs, Buddy DeFranco, and Artie Shaw, though it was his classic sessions with Stan Getz (1951–53) that cemented his reputation as a leading modernist. Replacing Tal Farlow, he fit in easily to Red Norvo's advanced swing trio

(1953–54) before recording frequently as a leader in the mid-'50s. From 1954 into the 1960s, however, he worked a supper club gig with pianist Jimmy Lyons, rarely playing jazz outside the studio. He joined forces with Getz again in the early '60s, but soon returned to Louisville and didn't surface again on the jazz scene for nearly a decade. He began playing and recording in New York in 1972 and slowly re-established himself. From the mid-'70s until his death, he toured and recorded regularly, often with his son, guitarist Doug Raney (born August 29, 1956), for a variety of independent labels including Xanadu, PA/USA, SteepleChase, and Criss Cross.

what to buy: Guitarist Jimmy Raney possessed one of the most warm and beautiful guitar sounds in jazz, but he also was capable of swinging with abandon, as he did on the excellent quartet session contained on *Visits Paris Vol. 1* ♪♪♪♪ (Vogue Disques, 1954/BMG, 1996). Accompanied by the great bop pianist Sonny Clark, brilliant bassist Red Mitchell, and drummer Bobby White, Raney displays his harmonic sophistication and gift for lyricism on a program of seven familiar standards. The CD also contains five alternate tracks, including two fascinating and quite different unissued takes of "Stella by Starlight." Other highlights are the two versions of "Body and Soul" and "There'll Never Be Another You." *Two Guitars* ♪♪♪♪ (Prestige, 1957/OJC, 1992, prod. Teddy Charles) pairs Raney with Kenny Burrell, a meeting of two of the most tasteful fret-masters in jazz. Five of the seven tracks feature a septet with Donald Byrd (trumpet), Jackie McLean (alto sax), Mal Waldron (piano), Doug Watkins (bass), and Art Taylor (drums). Each guitarist takes a turn with the rhythm section on a ballad, with Raney offering a gorgeous version of "Out of Nowhere." On the five originals, including three by Waldron and the debut of McLean's classic "Little Melonae," the guitarists generate some heat trading licks, but it's the contrast in their sounds that makes this such a fun session.

what to buy next: *Wisteria* ♪♪♪♪ (Criss Cross, 1986/1991, prod. Gerry Teekens) is a compelling, relaxed trio session featuring the redoubtable Tommy Flanagan (piano) and George Mraz (bass). Full of quiet beauty, the trio turns each tune into a small, finely crafted narrative. High points include the standards "I Could Write a Book," "Out of the Past," and Raney's "Ovals," which features some breathtakingly complex contrapuntal interplay. One of Raney's first albums as a leader, *A* ♪♪♪♪ (Prestige, 1954–55/OJC, 1991, prod. Bob Weinstock), features a quartet session with pianist Hall Overton and a quintet session with trumpeter John Wilson. Raney overdubs a second guitar line on the four quartet tracks, creating an interesting dialogue effect. Though his playing is strong throughout, his bandmates aren't close to his level and the session lacks the energy of his best dates. Still, Raney offers some compelling solos on the ballads "Someone to Watch Over Me," "What's New," and "You Don't Know What Love Is."

best of the rest:
Here's That Raney Day 𝄞𝄞𝄞𝄞 (Black and Blue, 1980)
The Master 𝄞𝄞𝄞 (Criss Cross, 1984/1990)
But Beautiful 𝄞𝄞𝄞𝄞 (Criss Cross, 1990)

worth searching for: A mixed bag pairing an excellent Raney quintet session with a so-so Terry Gibbs session, *Early Stan* 𝄞𝄞𝄞𝄞 (Prestige, 1949–53/OJC, 1991, prod. Bob Weinstock) is a valuable document of Raney's collaboration with tenor giant Stan Getz. Accompanied by Hall Overton (piano), Red Mitchell (bass), and Frank Isola (drums), Raney and Getz share a cool-toned style coupled with a burning rhythmic drive. Their four tracks, including "'Round Midnight" and Raney's intriguing original "Signal," make this a worthwhile purchase for Raney fans. And those classic early '50s recordings with Getz were released in a limited-edition three-disc box set on Mosaic Records, *The Complete Recordings of the Stan Getz Quintet with Jimmy Raney* (Mosaic, 1951–53, prod. various), which is now out of print.

influences:
◀◀ Charlie Christian
▶▶ Jim Hall, Ed Bickert

Andrew Gilbert

Michael Ray

Born in Trenton, NJ.

Trumpeter Michael Ray's background is a curious blend of the earthy and the spacey. Ray's band, the Cosmic Krewe, has a northeastern branch, including a number of players from Vermont, as well as a New Orleans branch. Apart from the logistic possibilities engendered by this arrangement, Ray also manages to keep busy with occasional session work and tours with Sun Ra's Arkestra. The main musical axis about which Ray spins belongs to the late jazz visionary and self-proclaimed space prophet Ra, but he has also played trumpet with Kool & the Gang, a top-selling R&B band during the 1970s and 1980s. Concerts for the Cosmic Krewe are likely to include music written for both sides of Ray's musical personality. Ray has taken some obvious performance riffs from Sun Ra (in addition to appropriating whole portions of Ra's songbook), dressing his band in fanciful, multi-colored costumes that give the concertgoer a visual stimulus to go along with an aural one. He has also included the work of neon art sculptor Jerry Therio in his shows, employing a concept he calls "The Neon-Sound Performances."

what's available: Three of the songs on *Michael Ray & the Cosmic Krewe* 𝄞𝄞𝄞𝄞 (Evidence, 1994, prod. Michael Ray) come from Ray's stint with Sun Ra, while one has its roots in the soulful funk of Kool & the Gang; the rest come from Ray and/or the members of his Cosmic Krewe. The playing is always skillful and the fun level is pretty high, with Ray's trumpet and synthesizer work riding the hard edge of commercial experimentalism. Dave Grippo is an interesting alto player, as evidenced by his work on "Rhythm and Muse," while percussionists Eddie Duran and Gregory Boyd, along with bassist Stacey Starkweather, deserve credit for rock-solid rhythms.

influences:
◀◀ Freddie Hubbard, Miles Davis, Sun Ra
▶▶ Lester Bowie, Graham Haynes

Garaud MacTaggart

The Rebirth Brass Band /The Rebirth Jazz Band

Formed 1983, in New Orleans.

Philip "Tuba Love" Frazier, leader, Sousaphone; Keith "Bass Drum Shorty" Frazier, bass drum, cymbals; Kermit Ruffins, trumpet, vocals (1983–94); Derrick "Khabuky" Shezbie, trumpet (1989–94); Glen Andrews, trumpet, vocals (1992–present); Derek "Dirt" Wiley, trumpet (1989–90); Kenneth "Kenniterry" Terry, trumpet, vocals (1994–present); Reginald Steward, trombone; Keith "Wolf" Anderson, trombone (1983–92); Stafford "Lil' D" Agee, trombone, vocals (1990–present); Tyrus "T" Chapman, trombone (1994–present); John "Prince" Gilbert, tenor saxophone, vocals (1989–present); Roderick Paulin, tenor saxophone (1994); Kenneth Austin, snare drum (1983–89); Ajay "Grab-Grab" Mallery, cymbals, drums (1990–96); Derrick "High Tower" Tabb, snare drum (1996–present); various additional percussionists.

The Rebirth Brass Band was inspired by the Dirty Dozen Brass Band's updating of the New Orleans brass band style, but unlike that group, Rebirth hasn't slipped into overt rock sounds, sticking instead with the traditional parade instrumentation that matches trumpets, trombones, and tuba (well, they do have a tenor sax player) with a small percussion corps (*not* a trap set) playing second-line rhythms. Philip Frazier's Sousaphone is at the root of the group's bold, in-your-face sound, laying down funky (but not funk) basslines and blatting high notes exuberantly. Rebirth adds newer ingredients to the brass band style—Parliament-Funkadelic riffs are quoted, bebop and rock tunes are covered, etc.—but translates them into the New Orleans sound rather than slipping into those other styles. Philip Frazier, whose mother is a gospel singer and organist, put the band together when he was a junior at Joseph S. Clark High School in New Orleans's 6th Ward. The size of the group and its personnel have fluctuated over the years (and even from one gig to the next). Trumpeters Kermit Ruffins and Derrick Shezbie both went on to record solo albums. Rebirth has recorded with Maceo Parker, N'Dea Davenport (ex–Brand New Heavies), G. Love & Special Sauce, Robbie Robertson, and Aaron Neville.

what to buy: If it's precision you want, forget about *Rebirth Kickin' It Live!* ♫♫♫♫ (Rounder, 1991, prod. Ron Levy). But to hear Rebirth on their home turf—the Glass House club in New Orleans, during Mardi Gras in 1990—partying with the rollicking enthusiasm that's the group's trademark is to realize that in this music, spirit counts for far more than accuracy, and chops are defined more by volume than speed. The group's '90s attitude shows in the original "Talk That Shit Now," while its connection to early jazz and the New Orleans tradition shows on covers of "Tin Roof" and "Back o' Town Blues" (done as a medley), "I've Found a New Baby," and "Kidd Jordan's Second Line." There's even a rowdy take on the Hugh Masekela hit "Grazin' in the Grass."

what to buy next: *Rollin'* ♫♫♫ (Rounder, 1994, prod. Keith Keller) contains one of the group's best cover ideas, "Mercy, Mercy, Mercy," which, when they get done with it, sounds like Joe Zawinul rather than Cannonball Adderley wrote it for them—but you'll probably never hear it on the radio because it's in a medley with the band's original "Shake Them Titties." The conceptual coup is "Reggae," which ropes in a bunch of familiar reggae licks in a shotgun wedding between Jamaican and second-line rhythms.

the rest:
Here to Stay ♫♫♫ (Arhoolie, 1986)
Feel Like Funkin' It Up ♫♫♫♫ (Rounder, 1989)
Take It to the Street ♫♫♫♫ (Rounder, 1992)
We Come to Party ♫♫♫ (Gert Town/Shanachie, 1997)

worth searching for: In the band's hometown, the songs "Do Whatcha Wanna" and "I Feel Like Funkin' It Up" were hits on local radio, which may be why *Do Whatcha Wanna* ♫♫♫♫ (Mardi Gras, 1991, prod. Milton Batiste), on a small New Orleans label, includes both of them and "When the Saints Go Marchin' In" as

well. Not only is this album on an indie label, it's credited to Re-Birth Jazz Band, so keep a keen eye out for it. The repertoire surprise this time out is Miles Davis's "All Blues," which works better than you'd think.

solo outings:
Derrick Shezbie:
Spodie's Back ♫♫ (Qwest, 1994)

influences:
◀◀ The Preservation Hall Jazz Band, the Dirty Dozen Brass Band, Louis Armstrong, James Brown

▶▶ The Soul Rebels, the Li'l Rascals

see also: *Kermit Ruffins*

Walter Faber

Dewey Redman

Born May 17, 1931, in Fort Worth, TX.

Avant-gardist Dewey Redman is one of the few saxophonists to come out of the 1960s who wasn't overwhelmed by John Coltrane's influence. He has a distinctive and unique saxophone voice, one that is equally well suited to free jazz or jazz standards. He started on clarinet at age 13 and later played in his high school marching band alongside classmates Ornette Coleman and Charles Moffett. While in high school he switched to alto sax. After college Redman taught in public schools from 1956 to 1959 before moving to California. He settled in San Francisco for seven years and led various groups as well as working with Wes Montgomery and Pharoah Sanders. In 1967, Redman moved to New York and joined Ornette Coleman's band. Coleman had not worked with a second horn since Don Cherry's departure in 1962. In Redman, Coleman found a sympathetic and complementary voice. A second saxophone provided less timbral contrast than Cherry's trumpet, but Redman's loping swing, open lyricism, and broad tone served the group well. The group mainly built on the groundwork previously laid by Coleman. The pair recorded two fine albums for Blue Note with Elvin Jones and Jimmy Garrison. Redman left Coleman in 1974, but his tenure in that band established his reputation as a creative and melodic improviser. He worked with Charlie Haden's Liberation Orchestra, Carla Bley, and Roswell Rudd before joining Keith Jarrett. The recordings made with Jarrett feature Redman at his best. Jarrett's quartet successfully incorporated the free-jazz ideals of Coleman's music without sacrificing its own identity. Redman excelled because of his own strong affinity for melody-based improvisation. *Sur-*

vivor's *Suite* and *Fort Yawuh* stand out as minor masterpieces from this group. Unfortunately, personal conflicts led to the break-up of the band in 1976. Shortly after leaving Jarrett, Redman joined Don Cherry, Charlie Haden, and Ed Blackwell to form Old and New Dreams. In addition to their own compositions, they reinterpreted Ornette Coleman's music in a way that was always challenging and lyrical. Each had first-hand experience that enabled them to avoid the pitfalls that had handcuffed other musicians inspired by free jazz concepts. Their strategy was to combine structure and strong melodic lyricism with group improvisation. They never descended into the directionless atonal squeaking and squawking that torpedoed so many other free-jazz advocates. Everything they played was propelled by the strong, swinging rhythmic pulse of Ed Blackwell. They remained together only briefly but recorded some exceptional albums. Throughout the '80s, Redman appeared on notable recordings with Pat Metheny, Paul Motian, and Charlie Haden's re-formed Liberation Orchestra. His own outings were less consistent, achieving great heights with some, and lacking focus on others. Nonetheless, Dewey Redman is an innovative performer who incorporates blues, bebop, and world music, and even unusual effects, such as singing and speaking into his horn.

what to buy: *Old & New Dreams* 𝄢𝄢𝄢𝄢 (ECM, 1979, prod. Manfred Eicher) features a good mix of Ornette Coleman tunes and originals. It's modern jazz that is fully formed and expertly executed. *Old & New Dreams—A Tribute to Blackwell* 𝄢𝄢𝄢𝄢 (Black Saint, 1990, prod. William Kinnally) is more of the same, and that's good. Captured live, the performances overflow with energy and excitement. *Redman & Blackwell in Willisau* 𝄢𝄢𝄢𝄢 (Black Saint, 1985, prod. Giovanni Bonadrini) is an extension of the excellent duet recordings by Blackwell and Don Cherry ("Mu" and "El Corazon"). The interplay between these two former bandmates is a delight, especially on "Willisee" and "Communication."

what to buy next: *Old & New Dreams—Playing* 𝄢𝄢𝄢𝄢 (ECM, 1981, prod. Manfred Eicher) doesn't have the same energy as the Soul Note live recording, but it showcases the band wonderfully. "Mopti" is an exotic world music excursion that coaxes wonderful solos from Redman and Cherry.

what to avoid: *Coincide* 𝄢𝄢 (Impulse!, 1974, prod. Bob Thiele) features so much sustained dissonance that only the most avant of avant-garde fans will enjoy it.

the rest:
Old & New Dreams 𝄢𝄢𝄢𝄢 (Black Saint, 1976)

Music 𝄢𝄢𝄢𝄢 (Original Jazz, 1978)
Struggle Continues 𝄢𝄢𝄢𝄢 (ECM, 1982)
Living on the Edge 𝄢𝄢𝄢 (Black Saint, 1989)
Choices 𝄢𝄢𝄢 (Enja, 1992)
African Venus 𝄢𝄢𝄢 (Evidence, 1992)
School Work 𝄢𝄢𝄢𝄢 (Mons, 1995)

worth searching for: Unfortunately, most of the recordings on which Redman is the leader are out of print on CD—and most are excellent. Among them, *Tarik* 𝄢𝄢𝄢𝄢 (Affinity, 1969) is an outstanding trio recording. The spare setting pushes Redman to the front.

influences:

◀◀ Charlie Parker, Ornette Coleman

▶▶ Joe Lovano, George Garzone

see also: *Old and New Dreams*

James Eason

Don Redman

Born July 29, 1900, in Piedmont, WV. Died November 30, 1964, in New York, NY.

Although his principal instruments would be clarinet and alto saxophone, Redman was a child prodigy who learned to play most of the band instruments. It was a talent fitting a musician who would become the first major jazz arranger. After graduating at age 20 with a degree in music from Storer College in Harper's Ferry, West Virginia, Redman was soon arranging for Billie Paige's Broadway Syncopators. He settled in New York in 1923 and began arranging for Fletcher Henderson's orchestra. In this period he also recorded as accompanist to many of the classic blues singers of the period—Bessie Smith, Ma Rainey, and Alberta Hunter. A major breakthrough occurred when Louis Armstrong joined the Henderson Orchestra, Armstrong's rhythmic fluency providing the impetus needed for Redman to find ways to make his arrangements swing. Redman left Henderson's band in 1927 to lead the Detroit-based McKinney's Cotton Pickers, building another great proto-swing band in the process. He formed his own group in 1931, using many of the same musicians he had recruited for the Cotton Pickers. In addition to arranging for Henderson, the Cotton Pickers, and his own band, Redman freelanced prolifically, contributing charts to the bands of Paul Whiteman, Count Basie, Ben Pollack, Isham Jones, Jimmy Dorsey, Harry James, and Bing Crosby. He also wrote some durable songs, like "Gee, Baby, Ain't I Good to You," and was an effective vocalist on witty novelty tunes. From 1951 to the late 1950s, Redman worked as arranger/band-

leader for Pearl Bailey. Redman's importance to the rise of big band jazz cannot be exaggerated. With Henderson and McKinney's Cotton Pickers, he was the chief architect of integrating popular orchestral dance music and the elements of jazz, fusing sections with soloists and intertwining written and improvised parts.

what to buy: For an overview of Redman's work, there are two excellent compilations. *Doin' What I Please* ♫♫♫♫ (ASV/Living Era, 1993, prod. Vic Bellerby), with 25 tracks from 1925 to 1938, will provide an excellent introduction to Redman's work, ranging from "Sugarfoot Stomp," featuring Armstrong with the Henderson Orchestra, and takes by McKinney's Cotton Pickers with Fats Waller as guest, to the 1931 "Chant of the Weed," the complex theme song of Redman's own orchestra, and fine arrangements of "I've Got Rhythm" and Ellington's "Sophisticated Lady." Along the way, there are appearances by the greatest musicians of the era, including Coleman Hawkins and Benny Carter. A comparable alternative choice is *Chant of the Weed* ♫♫♫♫ (Pearl, 1996, prod. Tony Watts, Colin Brown), which includes much of the key material.

what to buy next: The alternative is to take the completist approach. For that, the Chronological Jazz Classics series covers all of Redman's work in the thirties under his own name. *Don Redman 1931–1933* ♫♫♫♫ (Jazz Classics, 1994, prod. various) is the most significant of these; it includes terrific instrumental and vocal versions of "Doin' the New Low-down," some of which feature vocals by Cab Calloway and the Mills Brothers.

best of the rest:
Don Redman and His Orchestra 1933–1936 ♫♫♫♫ (Jazz Classics, 1990)
Don Redman and His Orchestra 1936–1939 ♫♫♫♫ (Jazz Classics, 1991)
Don Redman and His Orchestra 1939–1940 ♫♫ (Jazz Classics, 1992)
For Europeans Only ♫♫ (SteepleChase, 1997)

worth searching for: Redman's work with Fletcher Henderson is essential to the rise of the big band era, as well as being often extraordinary and entertaining music. The Armstrong and Henderson connections are best documented on *Fletcher Henderson 1924–1925* ♫♫♫♫ (Jazz Classics, 1994, prod. various). Additional examples of his arrangements for Armstrong can be heard on *Louis Armstrong, Volume IV: Louis Armstrong and Earl Hines* ♫♫♫♫ (Columbia, 1989, prod. Richard M. Jones), which includes a piquant "St. James Infirmary." Redman's earliest recordings with Bessie Smith, from 1923, can be heard on her

Joshua Redman (© Jack Vartoogian)

JOSHUA REDMAN
(WITH ROY HARGROVE)

song "Across the Pond"
album Roy Hargrove
Quintet with the Tenors of Our Time
(Verve, 1994)

instrument Tenor saxophone

Monster Solo

Complete Recordings, Vol. 1 ♫♫♫♫ (Columbia Legacy, 1991, prod. various), but they're of primarily historical interest. He sounds more confident and idiomatic playing alto saxophone on the 1925 "Golden Rule Blues" on *Complete Recordings Vol. 3* (Columbia Legacy, 1992, prod. various).

influences:
◄◄ James Reese Europe, Eubie Blake, King Oliver, Jelly Roll Morton

►► Duke Ellington, Cab Calloway

see also: *Fletcher Henderson, Louis Armstrong, McKinney's Cotton Pickers*

Stuart Broomer

Joshua Redman
Born February 1, 1969, in Berkeley, CA.

Through no fault of his own besides the accident of birth and academic achievement, tenor saxophonist Joshua Redman was the big jazz story of the early and mid-1990s, a gifted but much-hyped musician who provided jazz journalists with a very good story line. The son of the great tenor saxophonist Dewey Redman, Joshua saw little of his father growing up and was raised in Berkeley by his mother, a dancer who exposed him to a wide spectrum of music. Redman participated in the Berkeley High jazz program but he didn't really consider becoming a professional musician until after he graduated summa cum laude from Harvard. After winning the Thelonious Monk Institute's saxophone competition in 1991, he decided to try his hand in the music business instead of attending Yale Law School. He quickly made a strong impression as a mature player with a clear and cogent style, based as much on Gene Ammons as Sonny Rollins. His brief tour with guitarist Pat Metheny, bassist Charlie Haden, and drummer Billy Higgins went a long way in launching his career. Though Redman has been hailed in some quarters as a visionary, he is not an innovative player, though at his best his solos take on a narrative quality, evoking his tenor antecedents while not imitating anyone in particular. Within his first few years on the scene, Redman has recorded with many of the leading musicians in jazz, including drummers Elvin Jones and Paul Motian, tenor saxophonists Joe Lovano and Dewey Redman, trombonist Jimmy Knepper, and pianists John Hicks, Kenny Barron, and Chick Corea.

what to buy: One of the most written about debut albums in recent years, *Joshua Redman* ♫♫♫♫ (Warner Bros., 1993, prod. Matt Pierson) captured the 23-year-old saxophonist playing well beyond his years, with an appealing R&B-ish tone. Pianist Kevin Hays, bassist Christian McBride, and drummer Greg Hutchinson make up the excellent, flexible rhythm section. Redman plays tunes by Monk, Gillespie, James Brown, and the standard "On the Sunny Side of the Street," but it's his own tunes, such as "Wish" and "Sublimation," that best display his emerging sensibility. How many 23-year-old players land a session on their sophomore release with Pat Metheny, Charlie Haden, and Billy Higgins as sidemen? Redman makes the most of his distinguished company on *Wish* ♫♫♫♫ (Warner Bros., 1993, prod. Matt Pierson), an excellent album that ranges from Charlie Parker's "Moose the Mooche" to Ornette Coleman's "Turnaround" to Stevie Wonder's "Make Sure You're Sure." The charged rapport between Metheny and Redman, plus Haden's harmonically-open bass lines, keep Redman on his toes throughout. The album closes with two blistering tracks recorded at the Village Vanguard, including a 12-minute workout on Haden's "Blues for

Pat." Redman moves in a new direction with *Freedom in the Groove* ♫♫♫♫ (Warner Bros., 1996, prod. Matt Pierson), an album featuring his working quintet with guitarist Peter Bernstein joining his old rhythm section—pianist Peter Martin, bassist Chris Thomas, and drummer Brian Blade. Redman's style has come to depend more on riffs and repeated phrases and, with Bernstein's soulful guitar playing both a frontline and rhythm section role, the music is heavily groove-oriented. From the funkified "Can't Dance" to the Middle Eastern–flavored "Hide and Seek," Redman drew from many musical sources in writing all the album's tunes. Though short on melodic interest, the interaction between the musicians keeps the music interesting.

what to buy next: Redman's first album with his working quartet, *MoodSwing* ♫♫♫♫ (Warner Bros., 1994, prod. Matt Pierson) is a highly enjoyable session featuring all his original music. With pianist Brad Mehldau, bassist Christian McBride, and drummer Brian Blade, the rhythm section is first rate and full of fire. With this session it became clear that Redman was solidifying a sound heavily influenced by the great jazz/R&B players from the 1950s, such as Gene Ammons and Red Holloway. A two-disc album recorded live at the Village Vanguard, *Spirit of the Moment* ♫♫♫♫ (Warner Bros., 1995, prod. Matt Pierson) contains some spirited playing, but would have been much stronger if the best tracks were released on one CD. Redman's working band, featuring pianist Peter Martin, bassist Chris Thomas, and drummer Brian Blade, play with a great deal of energy and cohesion, while Redman continues to incorporate more funk and R&B elements into his style. Highlights include the 12-minute versions of Sonny Rollins's "St. Thomas" and Redman's "Herbs and Roots."

worth searching for: One of the more interesting father/son sessions in jazz, *African Venus* ♫♫♫ (Evidence, 1992, prod. Tetsuo Hara) finds then 22-year-old Joshua Redman sitting in on three tracks with his father, Dewey Redman, performing on tenor, alto, musette, and vocals. The contrast in their approaches is fascinating, as Joshua was/is strongly influenced by Coltrane and takes burly, harmonically dense solos on Ellington's "Satin Doll" and his father Dewey's "Venus and Mars." The band features Charles Eubanks (piano), Anthony Cox (bass), Carl Allen (drums), and Danny Sadownick (percussion).

influences:

◄◄ Gene Ammons, Sonny Rollins, Red Holloway, John Coltrane
Andrew Gilbert

Dizzy Reece

Born January 5, 1931, in Kingston, Jamaica.

With a bright, crackling sound, trumpeter Dizzy Reece communicates with an emotionally direct "cry" that has always marked him as an original voice. Unfortunately, he came up during the 1950s and 1960s, a period in jazz history that produced more talented players than the market could sometimes bear. Picking up the trumpet while in his teens, Reece began to make an impact through a stay in England in the late 1950s that found him working with Tubby Hayes and several other top British jazz players. In 1959, the trumpeter moved to New York, recording three albums as a leader for the Blue Note label and one for Prestige. However, Reece's only other notable activity since his initial stateside appearance was a 1968 stint with Dizzy Gillespie and a mid-1980s stay with the Paris Reunion Band. With the reissues boon of the past ten years bringing to light Reece's classic sides, the chance still remains for his name to become better known among the music's fans and collectors.

what's available: *Blues in Trinity* ♫♫♫ (Blue Note, 1958, prod. Alfred Lion, Michael Cuscuna) was cut during Reece's stay in England and features tenor whiz Tubby Hayes and trumpeter Donald Byrd. Dizzy's penchant for minor keys infuses many of the cuts with a wistful melancholy. *Asia Minor* ♫♫♫♫ (Prestige/New Jazz, 1962, prod. Jules Colomby) is Reece's best effort as a leader due not only to his pungent trumpet work but also to his exceptional originals. Cecil Payne, Joe Farrell, Hank Jones, Ron Carter, and Charlie Persip help make this a truly memorable set.

worth searching for: *Star Bright* ♫♫♫♫ (Blue Note, 1959, prod. Alfred Lion) and *Soundin' Off* ♫♫♫ (Blue Note, 1960, prod. Alfred Lion) are two sets that comprise the remainder of Reece's efforts for Blue Note. They are both highly recommended and have become available recently as Japanese imports.

Chris Hovan

Eric Reed

Born June 21, 1970, in Philadelphia, PA.

One of the most rapidly maturing pianists among the multitude of gifted hard bop and post-bop stylists, Eric Reed couples superior technique with endless soul and a probing imagination. Raised in Philadelphia, Reed started playing piano at age two and was steeped in the gospel tradition. He came of age musically in his father's Holiness church. At seven he began studying the Western classical tradition, and moved with his family

to Los Angeles in 1981. In high school he was performing with the Gerald Wilson Orchestra and with John Clayton, and toured with Wynton Marsalis when he was 18, eventually replacing Marcus Roberts in Marsalis's band. Reed has performed with Joe Henderson, Benny Carter, Freddie Hubbard, Joshua Redman, Javon Jackson, Betty Carter, and Charlie Haden, and recorded with saxophonists Wes Anderson, Robert Stewart, and Rickey Woodard, and trumpeters Marcus Printup and Marlon Jordan. Marsalis featured Reed on his albums *Citi Movement*, *In This House, On This Morning*, and *Blood on the Fields*.

what to buy: An ambitious session by a musician of unlimited potential, *Musicale* ♫♫♫♫ (Impulse!, 1996, prod. Tommy LiPuma) contains a wide variety of moods, textures, and instrumentation. Reed covers hard bop with "Black, as in Buhainia," and old-school, New Orleans funk with "Longhair's Rhumba." He revisits his gospel roots with an assist from trombonist Wycliff Gordon on "Baby Sis," and takes a step outside toward 1960s freedom with "Pete and Repete." About half the tunes feature Reed's trio, with bassist Ben Wolfe and drummer Greg Hutchinson, while the other tunes feature a quintet with Wes Anderson (alto sax), Nicholas Payton (trumpet), Ron Carter (bass), and Karriem Riggins (drums).

what to buy next: Reed's sophomore effort is very impressive, highlighting the rapid development of a pianist with tremendous technique and deep soul. *It's Alright to Swing* ♫♫♫♫ (MoJazz, 1993, prod. Delfeayo Marsalis) features eight Reed originals, "You Don't Know What Love Is," and Ellington's "Come Sunday," sung by Carolyn Johnson-White. Reed's trio with Rodney Whitaker (bass) and Greg Hutchinson (drums) plays on half the tracks, with alto saxophonist Wes Anderson joining on five tunes and Wynton Marsalis (billed as E. Dankworth) sitting in on three. Highlights include Reed's deep blue streak on his Coltranish "Undecided" and Anderson's hot alto work on "Third Degree."

the rest:
Soldier's Hymn ♫♫♫ (Candid, 1992)
The Swing and I ♫♫♫♫ (MoJazz, 1995)

influences:
◄◄ Ahmad Jamal, Wynton Kelly, Gerald Wiggins, McCoy Tyr

Andre

Dianne Reeves

Born October 23, 1956, in Detroit, MI.

This versatile singer has refused to b
alternating R&B and jazz albums and

two. She possesses a multi-octave vocal range that's warm, dark, and magesterial on bottom, light and clear on top. She relies equally on R&B, jazz, and gospel phrasing and inflections, and is thus equally effective no matter what the style, mood, or tempo. In concert, her regal presence adds to the authoritative impact of her singing.

Born in Detroit, Reeves moved with her family to Denver when she was two years old. After her high school band competed for and won the opportunity to perform at the annual National Association of Jazz Educators conference, she caught the attention of jazz trumpeter Clark Terry, with whom she performed even while she was attending the University of Colorado. She then moved to Los Angeles in 1976, where she started a long association with jazz pianist Billy Childs (in a cooperative group called Night Flight) and performed with a variety of bands, including the Latin-oriented Caldera, which included not only Eddie del Barrio, later her producer, but also one-time Earth, Wind & Fire keyboardist Larry Dunn. In the early 1980s she toured in groups fronted by Sergio Mendes and Harry Belafonte, and recorded a pair of albums under her own name for the indie label Palo Alto. When Reeves signed to EMI, her producer was her uncle, George Duke. Although her first album was mostly R&B, it included a few tracks tilting toward jazz (Herbie Hancock plays on one, and the two others are jazz standards, "Yesterdays" and "I've Got It Bad and That Ain't Good"), though it was the solidly R&B "Better Days" (also known as "the grandma song") that became a mild hit. Perhaps as a result, her second album stayed away from jazz and aimed for the pop charts (without much success), emphasizing her original material (though a cover of Rickie Lee Jones's "Company" is an effective album closer). The initial pattern was that her EMI albums were R&B and her Blue Note albums were jazz. Then the two styles started to converge. Her 1996 release was not just jazz, but all-star jazz of a very traditional slant. And her 1998 album seemed to chase the success of Cassandra Wilson, with a similar heavy dose of rock and pop covers, more low-key vocals than was Reeves's norm, and sound-alike production; even the album art was similar. If there is often a maddening inconsistency to her albums—always something not quite right about a few tracks—and an unfocused career path, she nonetheless has built up a fairly impressive body of work for a fortysomething jazz singer with eclectic tendencies. If she ever makes a live album, perhaps everything will cohere in the way her volcanic concerts often do.

what to buy: *I Remember* 𝄽𝄽𝄽𝄽 (Blue Note, 1991, prod. Charles !ims, Dianne Reeves, Michael Cuscuna) is uneven—not stylis-

tically but in quality, as it consists of two separate jazz sessions separated in time by two-and-a-half years. The four songs of the 1990 session, with pianist Billy Childs as an extremely sympathetic accompanist on all except a bold "Afro Blue," are strikingly confident. Her heavily gospelized "Love for Sale" may leave purists feeling the song's meaning and mood have been flattened, but it's certainly a thrilling performance vocally; her tender version of Stephen Sondheim's "I Remember Sky" shows that she can be subtle, too. The 1988 material involved a variety of musicians, and the shifting personnel seems to have made her uncomfortable; pianist Mulgrew Miller sounds rather diffident and unrelated.

what to buy next: *Art + Survival* 𝄽𝄽𝄽 (EMI, 1994, prod. Eddie del Barrio, Terri Lyne Carrington) contains Reeves's greatest pop moment, the joyous, gospel-tinged "Come to the River." If some lyrics weren't so one-dimensionally preachy (women's issues, the environment, and a sort of new-age spirituality), this would be an even better album. As it stands, it's by far the best integration on one record of her many styles.

what to avoid: Drawn from her first two albums (plus a guest performance with the group Caldera), *The Palo Alto Sessions 1981–1985* 𝄽 (Blue Note, 1996, prod. various) is strictly for die-hard fans. At the beginning of her recording career, Reeves's voice was too far ahead of her interpretive abilities; too much of her singing consisted of vocal quirks unrelated to the songs at hand. By the second album, her singing had improved markedly, but this compilation selects much more heavily from the first album due to her expressed fondness for the songs themselves.

the rest:
Dianne Reeves 𝄽𝄽𝄽 (EMI, 1987)
Never Too Far 𝄽𝄽 (EMI, 1989)
Quiet After the Storm 𝄽𝄽𝄽 (Blue Note, 1995)
The Grand Encounter 𝄽𝄽𝄽 (Blue Note, 1996)
that day . . . 𝄽𝄽𝄽 (Blue Note, 1998)

worth searching for: The material that was underrepresented on *The Palo Alto Sessions* shows up on *For Every Heart* 𝄽𝄽 (Palo Alto, 1984). Here we see Reeves starting to find her way vocally. This will be of interest to the devoted.

influences:
◀◀ Sarah Vaughan, Carmen McRae, Betty Carter, Chaka Khan
▶▶ Nnenna Freelon

Steve Holtje

Rufus Reid

Born February 10, 1944, in Sacramento, CA.

Bassist Rufus Reid is a major performer and jazz recording artist as well as a full-time educator. The California native received his Associate Arts degree from Olympic College in Bremerton, Washington, in 1969, then furthered his studies as a performance major on the double bass at Northwestern University in Evanston, Illinois, where he earned his Bachelor of Music degree in 1971. Since then, he has become one of Jazz's premiere bassists and a major jazz educator who, since 1979, has served on the faculty of William Paterson University, where he is currently the Director of the Jazz Studies and Performance program. Reid's professional career as a performer began in the late 1960s in Chicago, working with Sonny Stitt, James Moody, Milt Jackson, Curtis Fuller, and Dizzy Gillespie. In the 1970s Reid recorded with Kenny Dorham, Dexter Gordon, Lee Konitz, and Howard McGhee, and toured internationally with the Bobby Hutcherson–Harold Land Quintet, Freddie Hubbard, Nancy Wilson, Eddie Harris, and Dexter Gordon. After moving to the New York City area in 1976, Reid played and recorded with the Thad Jones–Mel Lewis quartet, and began teaching at William Paterson College in Wayne, New Jersey, in 1979. Settling in Teaneck, New Jersey, Reid has continued to perform and record with the best jazz musicians, including Benny Golson, Art Farmer, Bobby Hutcherson, J. J. Johnson, Kenny Burrell, Kenny Barron, Jimmy Heath, and Dave Liebman. Equally well versed in classical music, Reid performed and recorded in 1992 with classical musicians such as Andre Previn, Kathleen Battle, the St. Luke's Chamber Orchestra, and the Wayne Chamber Orchestra. Reid has recorded on over 200 albums as sideman, three under his own leadership—*Perpetual Stroll*, *Seven Minds*, and *Corridor to the Limits* for the Sunnyside label—and, since joining with drummer Akira Tana, has recorded five sessions as TanaReid. The pair continues to conduct master classes and workshops around the world. For his considerable contributions to jazz education, Reid received the prestigious Humanitarian Award from the International Association of Jazz Educators in January 1997.

what to buy: *Seven Minds* 𝄞𝄞𝄞𝄞 (Sunnyside, 1990, prod. Rufus Reid, Francois Zalacain) documents a November 25, 1984 concert performance at William Paterson College with drummer Terri Lyne Carrington and pianist Jim McNeely. Given plenty of solo space on the eight tunes, McNeely plays with fiery energy. Carrington generates deft brushwork and flashy pyrotechnics, depending on the context. This highly interactive mainstream jazz trio is driven from a rhythm-section perspective, featuring unexpected shifts from chorus to chorus, explosive solos from McNeely and Carrington, and Reid's utmost artistic freedom using a variety of techniques that depart from usual bass lines. It's one of Reid's best dates as leader. *Looking Forward* 𝄞𝄞𝄞𝄞 (Evidence, 1995, prod. Akira Tana) is a broadly expressive third TanaReid album containing 10 diverse tunes on which the two distinguished rhythm players lay down splendid polyrhythmic foundations, gently spurring their creative soloists. Guest Tom Harrell doubles warmly on trumpet and flugelhorn on four tunes. Saxophonists Craig Bailey and Mark Turner excel, as does John Stetch on piano. Gifted and flexible, TanaReid players stretch out from straight-ahead to freer jazz styles, as evidenced on "Gold Minor," a modal ballad with a dreamy Japanese motif created by Bailey's flute solos. Elegant flute/horn melodies mark Brubeck's light jubilation, "The Duke." Tana's composition "Skyline" (the longest piece at 8:33) allows time for his tasteful drum solo. This is an engaging album, full of abrupt tempo shifts, expert horn work, and unique tunes composed by Dave Brubeck, Tom Harrell, and Kenny Barron, as well as originals written by band members. On *Yours and Mine* 𝄞𝄞𝄞𝄞 (Concord, 1991, prod. Akira Tana, Rufus Reid), the debut album from TanaReid, the leaders generate a sterling studio session that could only come out of the comfort of their longtime association. Pianist Rob Schneiderman swings with melodic panache, and alto saxophonist Jesse Davis and tenor/soprano saxophonist Ralph Moore add nice touches to make this an A-plus New York studio session (September 1990). Highlights among the 10 tunes (half originals and half standards) include the co-written TanaReid opener, "Some Slinkin'," a racing bop version of "The Song Is You," the TanaReid bass-drums duo on Eddie Harris's "Freedom Jazz Dance," and others. An excellent album.

what to buy next: *Perpetual Stroll* 𝄞𝄞𝄞𝄞 (Theresa, 1981/Sunnyside 1988, prod. Rufus Reid), recorded with the Rufus Reid Trio, is actually the former Dexter Gordon rhythm section featuring Reid, pianist Kirk Lightsey, and drummer Eddie Gladden. On this album, Reid's 28th recording date but his first as leader, the threesome delivers a vibrant six-tune session, interpreting three Reid originals—the tricky title tune; a warm tribute to his wife, "Waltz for Doris"; and the lyrical, pensive centerpiece, "No Place Is the End of the World." The trio also performs the Herbie Hancock gem "One Finger Snap," bass ancestor Oscar Pettiford's "Tricotism," and Lightsey's "Habiba." This is a diverse and engaging debut that highlights the work of these illustrious, though often overlooked, improvisers. On *Blue Motion* 𝄞𝄞𝄞𝄞 (Evidence, 1994, prod. Akira Tana, Rufus Reid) Tana and Reid continue to showcase young musicians, several of whom have been Reid's students. The disc includes strong contributions from saxophonists Craig Bailey and Dan Faulk, along with the reliable piano contributions of veteran Rob Schneiderman. The program contains 10 straight-ahead tunes, mostly originals by group members. While Reid's playing is up to his usual high standards, the empathetic ensemble work on this session also makes it listen-worthy. *Corridor to the Limits* ♫♫♫ (Sunnyside, 1990, prod. Rufus Reid, Francois Zalacain) is a harmonious 10-tune quartet date recorded live during a March 5, 1989 concert at William Paterson College, the site of Reid's teaching post. Performing with Reid are pianist Rob Schneiderman, drummer Victor Lewis, and tenor saxophonist Harold Land, whose warmly-rendered, pensive solos sparkle throughout the concert. Reid's relationship with Land stems from his early 1970s stint with the Bobby Hutcherson–Harold Land group. Land, who flew in from California for the gig, interacts well with this solid, versatile rhythm team. Reid's playing is round-toned and warm, and he's a gracious leader who takes some lengthy engaging solos but doesn't try to hog the spotlight. Everyone collectively and individually makes creative contributions. Adding to the enjoyment of this session is Reid's chosen material, seldom-heard beauties such as Oscar Pettiford's "Swinging 'Till the Girls Come Home," a dreamy reading of Harold Danko's modal piece, "To Start Again," and Reid's contributions on the Thad Jones tune, "Summary." Reid's modern and tricky title tune allows the group to really stretch out at a heated pace, and the closer, Reid's "City Slicker," with its alternating odd meters, swings like a country gate.

the rest:
(With TanaReid) *Passing Thoughts* ♫♫♫♭ (Concord, 1992)
(With Michael Moore) *Doublebass Delights* ♫♫♫♭ (Double-Time, 1996)
(With Tana Reid) *Back to Front* ♫♫♫ (Evidence, 1998)

influences:
◀◀ Oscar Pettiford, Paul Chambers

Nancy Ann Lee

Django Reinhardt

Born Jean Baptiste Reinhardt, January 23, 1910, in Belgium. Died May 16, 1953, in Fontainbleau, France.

The name "Django" has been a mysterious and powerful one in jazz history, and its owner one of the most unique and individualistic of jazz stylists. Reinhardt grew up in a musical Gypsy family, learning to play both violin and guitar proficiently by the time he was 12 years old. In 1928 he was badly injured in a fire,

permanently losing the use of the first two fingers on his fret hand. Inventiveness and talent got him around this disability, as he devised his own fingering method and kept playing. In 1934 Django began a life-long association with violinist Stephane Grappelli, forming the famous Quintet du Hot Club de France and making his first recordings. The Quintet played and recorded throughout Europe in the years leading up to World War II, becoming perhaps the most important group of non-American jazz musicians of the era and creating a distinctive brand of swing using mostly, and often only, stringed instruments. After WWII, Django became popular outside Europe, as he toured the U.S. with Duke Ellington and did some recording. But Django would spend most of the rest of his life in France, where he would continue making great swing music, even experimenting some with electric guitar and be bop. After his early death in 1953, Reinhardt's legend was solidified with the hauntingly famous tribute song "Django," and with the documentary film *Django Reinhardt* by director Paul Paviot. The Django Reinhardt discography available domestically is a confusing mess of overlapping reissues and imports. Completists are urged to stick to the comprehensive Classics reissue series, while more casual listeners should look first at some of the particular releases recommended below.

what to buy: Recorded in 1936–48, *Best of Django Reinhardt* ♫♫♫♫ (Blue Note, 1996, prod. Dan Morgenstern) provides an excellent introduction to the music of the great jazz guitarist, with instructive liner notes by producer Morgenstern. Reinhardt is heard on a mix of early jazz standards like "Limehouse Blues," "You Rascal You," and "Saint Louis Blues" as well as some of his own originals, including "Nuages," "Blues Claire," and "My Serenade." *Peche a la Mouche* ♫♫♫♫♫ (Verve, 1953/1992, prod. Gerard Leveque) features Reinhardt's last recordings. They consist of inventive and distinctive leanings toward bop and electric guitar. This excellent music really makes one wish Django had been around longer to fully explore the territory he ventures into on these recordings.

what to buy next: Reinhardt and Grappelli's group arises fully formed on *First Recordings!* ♫♫♫♫ (Prestige, 1934/OJC, 1997, prod. Don Schlitten). What is most remarkable is how confident and competent they sound, despite the fact that they were staking out totally new territory with their all-string band of European musicians. *Djangology 1949* ♫♫♫♫♭ (RCA, 1949/Bluebird, 1990, prod. Orrin Keepnews) consists of a later reunion of Reinhardt and Grappelli in Italy. The two old friends and compatriots constantly challenge each other and make some stimulating music in the process.

what to avoid: *Gypsy Jazz* 🎵🎵 (Drive Archive, 1994, prod. Don Grierson) is a rather aimless reissue that randomly includes music from several unrelated sessions from late in Django's career (1947–53). The music is fine, but the same stuff can be acquired better ways.

the rest:
1935–1936 🎵🎵🎵 (Classics, 1990)
Djangologie/USA Vols. 1 & 2 🎵🎵🎵 (DRG, 1990)
Django Reinhardt and Stephane Grappelli 🎵🎵🎵 (GNP Crescendo, 1991)
Swing Guitar 🎵🎵🎵 (Jass, 1991)
Django Reinhardt and Friends 🎵🎵🎵 (Pearl, 1992)
1934–1935 🎵🎵🎵 (Classics, 1992)
1937 🎵🎵🎵 (Classics, 1992)
1937: Vol. 2 🎵🎵🎵 (Classics, 1992)
1939–1940 🎵🎵🎵 (Classics, 1992)
1940 🎵🎵🎵 (Classics, 1992)
Compact Jazz: In Brussels 🎵🎵🎵 (Verve, 1992)
Djangology 🎵🎵🎵🎵 (Blue Note, 1993)
1937–1938 🎵🎵🎵 (Classics, 1993)
1938–1939 🎵🎵🎵 (Classics, 1993)
Jazz Masters 38 🎵🎵🎵 (Verve, 1994)
The Indispensable Django Reinhardt 🎵🎵🎵🎵 (RCA, 1994)
Swing de Paris 🎵🎵🎵🎵 (Iris, 1996)
Nuages 🎵🎵🎵 (Arcadia, 1997)

worth searching for: A French import, *Paris 1945* 🎵🎵🎵 (Columbia, 1945, prod. John Hammond) features Reinhardt with an American sextet that includes "Peanuts" Hucko on clarinet and pianist Mel Powell. Highlights include "Homage à Fats Waller" and "Homage à Debussy."

influences:
◄◄ Charlie Christian, Louis Armstrong
►► Charlie Christian, Les Paul

Dan Keener

Emily Remler

Born September 15, 1957, in New York, NY. Died May 4, 1990, in Sydney, Australia.

In his book *Waiting for Dizzy*, Gene Lees accurately described Emily Remler as a "superb musician and on her way to being a great one." The guitarist died before she had a chance to reach that next level. Remler grew up listening to folk and rock music. While attending the Berklee College of Music in the early 1970s, she became familiar with jazz through the recordings of Charlie Christian, Paul Desmond, and, most notably, Wes Montgomery, whose work would prove to be a major influence. After graduation, Remler undertook a second musical education.

She moved to New Orleans, where she immersed herself in that city's eclectic music scene. There, she met guitar legend Herb Ellis, who brought her to the 1978 Concord Jazz Festival, where she was invited to play as part of the "Great Guitars" concert. She returned to New York in 1979 where she worked with singers Nancy Wilson and Astrud Gilberto. In the early 1980s Remler signed with Concord Records. Remler, who battled a long-time heroin addiction, died in 1990.

what to buy: Although Remler is frequently portrayed as a "Wes wannabe" and she would have been first to admit the importance of Montgomery's playing on her own, she accomplished much more than copping his licks as her own voice emerged. Her playing took on a harder edge than Montgomery's and her rhythmic approach certainly wasn't as "in-the-pocket." Remler's own conception is evident on *Catwalk* 🎵🎵🎵🎵 (Concord, 1985, prod. Carl Jefferson), one of two recordings made with trumpeter John D'Earth, bass player Eddie Gomez, and percussionist Bob Moses. This is a post-bop "group" recording in the truest sense of the word with the players interacting through improvisation in a very collective sense (collective doesn't have to mean "free"). Highlights include two Remler originals, the title song, and Moses featured on a West African talking drum on "Mozambique." Remler's single note lines flow, yet aren't silky smooth; they have a bite. D'Earth's trumpet is an excellent complement to Remler's guitar. D'Earth is not interested in playing solos filled with technical bravura. Rather, his sometimes ethereal, sometimes puckish tone fits the mood of the piece. The more straight-ahead Remler is well represented on *East to Wes* 🎵🎵🎵🎵 (Concord, 1988, prod. Carl Jefferson). Backed by the supportive rhythm section of Hank Jones, Buster Williams, and Marvin Smith, Remler demonstrates her capacity to play bop without ever losing her warm sound on originals like "Blues for Herb," Clifford Brown's "Daahoud," and Tadd Dameron's reworking of "What Is This Thing Called Love," which he titled "Hot House." Remler likes a good melody—just listen to her treatment of "Softly as in Morning Sunrise." This warhorse is usually turned into a blowing vehicle but Remler gives the piece a more introspective cast as she takes time to explore its beauty. Another special treat is her acoustic playing on "Snowfall."

what to buy next: Remler's second session, *Take Two* 🎵🎵🎵 (Concord, 1982, prod. Carl Jefferson), is similar to *East to Wes* in its sound. "Pocket Wes" has a stop-and-start theme that is nicely contrasted when it shifts to straight swinging solos by Remler and pianist James Williams. Remler's takes on Dexter Gordon's "For Regulars Only" and her solo version on "Afro

Blue" point out another strength—she never overplays. Like guitarist Jim Hall, she can swing at medium tempo. That understated elegance is also apparent on her debut session as a leader, *Firefly* ♫♫♫ (Concord, 1981, prod. Carl Jefferson), especially on Horace Silver's "Strollin" and Duke's "In a Sentimental Mood." The ghost of Wes emerges as Emily ups the pace on the title tune and Montgomery's "Movin Along," complete with thumb work on the latter.

what to avoid: *This Is Me* ♫ (Justice, 1990, prod. Jeffrey Weber) is Remler's attempt at playing pop instrumentals. When you listen to her play jazz, you'll ask the same question others have about the album: What's the point?

the rest:
Transitions ♫♫♫ (Concord, 1984)
Retrospective, Vol. 1: Standards ♫♫♫♫ (Concord, 1991)
Retrospective, Vol 2: Originals ♫♫♫ (Concord, 1991)

influences:
◀◀ Wes Montgomery, Jim Hall, Herb Ellis, Lenny Breau, Paul Desmond, Joe Pass

Dan Polletta

Return to Forever

Different configurations were established in 1971, 1973, 1977, and 1983.

Chick Corea, keyboards; Stanley Clarke, electric and acoustic bass; Joe Farrell, flutes, sax (1971–72, 1977–78); Airto Moreira, drums, percussion (1971–72); Flora Purim, vocals, percussion (1971–72); Lenny White, drums (1973–77, 1983); Bill Connors, guitar (1973–74); Earl Klugh, guitar (1974); Al Di Meola, guitar (1974–77, 1983); Gary Brown, drums (1977–78); Harold Garrett, horn, trombone (1977–78); Gayle Moran, piano, organ, vocals (1977–78); Jim Pugh, trombone (1977–78); John Thomas, trumpet, flugelhorn (1977–78); James Tinsley, trumpet (1977–78).

The fusion pioneers all had bands with incredibly strong line-ups. Tony Williams had Lifetime. John McLaughlin had the Mahavishnu Orchestra. Chick Corea's showcase band was Return to Forever, and, like Lifetime and Mahavishnu, it hit its peak and burned white hot. Unfortunately, its life as a creative unit was short.

The first Return to Forever featured Corea with Stanley Clarke, Airto Moreira, Flora Purim, and Joe Farrell and played a more subdued style of fusion than the hard-edged styles of Mahavishnu and Lifetime. There was no electric guitar, but there was Clarke's powerful bass and Corea's electric piano explorations while Moreira, Purim, and Farrell provided both jazz and Latin foundations.

Their debut, recorded under Corea's name as *Return to Forever*, is considered one of the important moments in fusion history, with its incredible title track being the stand-out. The group's follow-up, *Light as a Feather*, was more melodic, with some characteristic Corea stylings, and ultimately less radical than the debut. Corea disbanded the first RTF when he decided he wanted to play electric fusion. He re-formed the group in 1973, keeping only Clarke and adding guitarist Bill Connors and drummer Lenny White. If the first RTF was a melodic fusion, an electronic Latin jazz band that drifted off into some interesting explorations, the second version of RTF was a jazz/rock powerhouse owing a tremendous debt to the Mahavishnu Orchestra. Connors's riffs and tone often came straight out of the book of John McLaughlin, and White certainly listened to Billy Cobham. The group even employed trading in the style of Mahavishnu. Though influenced by Mahavishnu, RTF was different in a few important ways. Clarke's style of bass playing, which had classical roots in the first RTF, now was incorporating funk and rock playing. Corea's compositions employed more synthesizer effects, Latin influences, and scripted passages than Mahavishnu, which owed more to John Coltrane and Eastern influences. Connors was replaced by Earl Klugh for one tour in 1974. Klugh was then replaced by Al Di Meola, a 19-year-old guitar wizard who owed much to McLaughlin and Larry Coryell. A more Latin-styled player than Connors, what the youthful star lacked in emotive ability he made up for in technique and ability to play Corea's complex passages. While the band with Di Meola had tons of polish and dance elements to it at times, it lacked the emotive fire of the first Mahavishnu Orchestra, Lifetime, and Coryell's solo work, and some songs sound very dated today. In 1976, RTF released their most commercially successful album, *Romantic Warrior*, which has been unfairly panned in the past. Despite *Romantic Warrior*'s success, Corea would disband this version of RTF shortly after.

Taking Clarke with him once again, Corea formed a third version of RTF in 1977. Recruiting RTF alum Joe Farrell, wife Gayle Moran, and a horn section, this version of RTF was short-lived, much like the version of the Mahavishnu Orchestra that also had a large horn section. In 1983, Corea, Clarke, Di Meola, and White reunited for an RTF tour, but failed to issue a live album. One of the best fusion bands, RTF made an indispensable debut, a few good albums, and a few forgettable ones. Its place as an influential unit is somewhere behind Mahavishnu, Lifetime, and the best of Coryell's solo work, but ahead of Coryell's Eleventh House, Dreams, Passport, and the Brecker Brothers, and probably about on a par with Weather Report. It always had outstanding musicians and generally made good, exciting music.

what to buy: *Return to Forever* 🎵🎵🎵🎵 (ECM, 1972, prod. Manfred Eicher) is a required album in any respectable jazz collection. The 12-minute title track, with Clarke knocking out one of the greatest monster bass riffs ever and Flora Purim screeching, is a haunting delight. The other melodic songs have more of the standard Corea Latin feel, while the opening of "Sometime Ago—La Fiesta" (a 23-minute excursion) starts slowly with the classic electric piano phasing and a beautiful bowed bass solo. It eventually builds into one of Corea's greatest hooks. A must-have, this album misses 🎵🎵🎵🎵🎵 only because of "What Game Shall We Play Today," which is just too lightweight. *Romantic Warrior* 🎵🎵🎵🎵 (Columbia, 1976, prod. Chick Corea) is the fusion equivalent of Mr. Toad's Wild Ride. Filled with hot solos, wild passages, and cool electronic effects, and commercially palatable, this is often despised by critics. Yet, upon further review, it's easy to see why this could be RTF's most successful recording: it's accessible, and the playing—by the Corea/Di Meola/Clarke/White lineup—is outstanding. Although it creates a completely different world than does *Return to Forever*, it's almost as potent.

what to buy next: In essence, *Light as a Feather* 🎵🎵🎵🎵 (Polydor, 1973, prod. Chick Corea) is a lighter version of RTF's first album. Gone is the wild experimentation of the debut title track; what remains is the melodic style from the rest of the album. Overall, that ain't too bad. It's just not revolutionary.

the rest:
Hymn of the Seventh Galaxy 🎵🎵🎵 (Polydor, 1973)
No Mystery 🎵🎵🎵 (Polydor, 1975)
Return to the Seventh Galaxy: The Anthology 🎵🎵🎵🎵 (Verve, 1996)
This Is Jazz #12 🎵🎵🎵 (Columbia, 1996)

influences:
◄◄ Miles Davis, Tony Williams, Lifetime, the Mahavishnu Orchestra

►► Al Di Meola

Paul MacArthur

The Revolutionary Ensemble
Formed 1971. Disbanded 1977.

Leroy Jenkins, violin; Sirone, bass; Frank Clayton, percussion (1971); Jerome Cooper, percussion (1971–77).

Ripe for rediscovery and CD reissues, the idiosyncratic and uncompromising trio the Revolutionary Ensemble recorded relatively little in its six years together. Leroy Jenkins, born in Chicago (March 11, 1932), started playing violin at a young age, then studied with Captain Walter Dyett at Du Sable High School, training ground for many Chicago musicians. An early member of the AACM, he collaborated with his cutting-edge contemporaries in Chicago. He moved briefly to Paris in the company of saxophonist Anthony Braxton, trumpeter Leo Smith, and percussionist Steve McCall (their Creative Construction Company beats even the Revolutionary Ensemble for scarce documentation).

Jenkins founded the Revolutionary Ensemble not long after returning stateside and settling in New York. He has a thin but expressive and personal sound on the violin; ever attentive to timbral nuance, he can be as sweet or raw as he wants. Sirone (born Norris Jones, September 28, 1940, in Atlanta, Georgia), a deeply resourceful and propulsive player with astounding arco (bowed) technique, had been on the New York scene since the mid-1960s. He played with contemporaries such as Dave Burrell and Marion Brown before joining forces and forming a collective with Jenkins. Like Jenkins, Jerome Cooper (born December 14, 1946, in Chicago) studied with Dyett. He'd moved to Europe where he worked with Steve Lacy, the Art Ensemble, Alan Silva, and others before settling in New York and joining the Revolutionary Ensemble (following the departure of drummer Frank Clayton). Cooper is a sometimes minimalist player, which is not to say that he lacks power and imagination. Together the Revolutionary Ensemble put the emphasis on whisper-to-scream group dynamics; on long, open explorations of musical textures; and the AACM trademark of seamless transitions between the composed and improvised. The Jenkins-Sirone rapport is one of the most impressive in the history of the music; Cooper was the rare drummer who could sympathetically bring support and lend structure to what they were doing.

what's available: Only their debut release, *Vietnam 1 & 2* 🎵🎵🎵🎵 (ESP, 1993, prod. the Revolutionary Ensemble), is readily available on CD. From the beginning the Revolutionary Ensemble impressed listeners with its collective sound, with the ability of its members to pull in different directions then find common musical ground.

worth searching for: Grab the vinyl *The People's Republic* 🎵🎵🎵🎵 (A&M, 1976, prod. Ed Michel) or any other black platters you can. The exquisitely recorded *People's Republic* was the RE's only foray into the studio, and it brings out the full body of their sound. The intertwining of bass and violin lines is almost telepathic on Jenkins's ballad "New York," further demonstrating the greatness of the Jenkins-Sirone partnership. In 11 intense minutes, Cooper's "Ponderous Planets" stunningly demonstrates at least three of the group's gambits: textural exploration, extension and elaboration of motifs, and a rocking, propulsive, swinging groove. *Revolutionary Ensemble* ♪♪♪♪ (Inner City, 1978, prod. Matthias Winckelmann, Horst Weber) was recorded in August 1977, shortly before the group's demise, and shows a group nowhere near artistic exhaustion. (It was lack of work, they said, that led to throwing in the towel.) See Jenkins's entry in this book for more information on his solo career. Cooper and Sirone are unrepresented on CD as leaders as of this writing, but look on vinyl for Cooper's *The Unpredictability of Predictability* ♪♪♪♪ (About Time, 1979), a one-musician, live tour-de-force in which Cooper incorporates a West African balafon into his array of percussion instruments. Sirone's *Artistry* ♪♪♪ (Of the Cosmos, 1979, prod. John Silverman), features flutist James Newton, drummer Don Moye, and cellist Muneer Bernard Fennell, but the session lacks the intense interplay of the Revolutionary Ensemble.

influences:

◀◀ The Art Ensemble of Chicago, Max Roach

▶▶ The String Trio of New York

W. Kim Heron

Melvin Rhyne

Born October 12, 1936, in Indianapolis, IN.

While it's an easy task to name any number of Hammond B-3 organ players who have quickly fallen under the spell of innovator Jimmy Smith, it's not as simple to list the few players who've avoided Smith's overpowering influence to develop a sound and manner of their own. Melvin Rhyne is one who managed to carve a niche for himself during the 1960s. His much lighter and less bombastic approach, distinctive use of the organ's stops and settings, and a blue-based style to improvising, mark Rhyne as one of the true original voices on the instrument. Despite his obvious talents, Rhyne's only real claim to fame has been a very prominent stint with Wes Montgomery that found him on the road and in the studio with the guitarist during the early 1960s. Since then, he has resided in the Milwaukee area, where he can be found playing in the local venues and doing some teaching as well. Beginning in 1991, Rhyne began recording for the Criss Cross label, an association that to date has produced three sets as a leader, a few sessions as a sideman, and a renewed interest in his music by both the public and music critics.

what to buy: *Boss Organ* ♪♪♪♪ (Criss Cross Jazz, 1993, prod. Gerry Teekens) is one of the finest organ dates in recent mem-

ory, due to Rhyne's attractive and accessible style. Tenor whiz kid Joshua Redman contributes more than his share of inspired moments too. *Mel's Spell* ♪♪♪♪ (Criss Cross Jazz, 1996, prod. Gerry Teekens) features Rhyne's superb trio with young guitarist Peter Bernstein and drummer Kenny Washington. Intuitive interaction between the players and a superlative set of tunes make this one much more than your average organ trio record.

what to buy next: *The Legend* ♪♪♪ (Criss Cross Jazz, 1991, prod. Gerry Teekens) was Rhyne's return to the recording studio after a lengthy hiatus. While not the event that his later two Criss Cross dates would be, this one will still be rewarding for anyone who appreciates Rhyne's talents.

worth searching for: *Organizing* ♪♪♪♪ (Jazzland, 1960, prod. Orrin Keepnews) was Rhyne's first date as a leader, cut during the period when he was recording for the Riverside/Jazzland labels as part of Wes Montgomery's trio. With Johnny Griffin and Blue Mitchell on board, this long out-of-print album is well worth the search.

Chris Hovan

Marc Ribot

Born May 21, 1954, in Newark, NJ.

This mainstay of the Downtown New York scene, a former member of the Lounge Lizards, is a versatile, inventive guitarist heard frequently and often extensively on albums by Madeleine Peyroux, Medeski, Martin & Wood, Ellery Eskelin, the Klezmatics, John Zorn, David Sanborn, Caetano Veloso, Marisa Monte, Elvis Costello, Tom Waits, Marianne Faithfull, Allen Ginsburg, T-Bone Burnett, and many more. He played in a group called the Real Tones that backed soul singers and other types traveling without a band, people like Wilson Pickett, Solomon Burke (Ribot is on his *Soul Alive!* album), and Chuck Berry. On his own albums, adding many other instruments to his toolbox, Ribot covers an expansive stylistic territory—always in distinctive fashion. Representative of the younger avant-garde that refuses to exclude pop material, he skews familiar tunes and styles into non-Euclidean shapes, and makes avant-garde techniques listener friendly.

what to buy: *Rootless Cosmopolitans* ♪♪♪♪ (Island, 1990, prod. Arthur Moorehead) mixes shockingly deconstructed covers of Sammy Cahn's "I Should Care," Jimi Hendrix's "The Wind Cries Mary," George Harrison's "While My Guitar Gently Weeps," and Duke Ellington's "Mood Indigo" with Ribot originals, positing a fresh amalgam of jazz, rock, and avant-garde.

Exhibiting a wry humor, Ribot's style has nothing to do with fusion in the genre sense, and sometimes produces oddly beautiful abstract structures.

what to buy next: *Shrek* ♫♫♫♫ (Avant, 1994, prod. Marc Anthony Thompson, Marc Ribot) is mostly performed by Ribot's group of that name, which here includes Soul Coughing bassist Sebastian Steinberg. Closing with Albert Ayler's "Bells," this instrumental record is more consistently abstract than *Rootless Cosmopolitans*. On many of Ribot's albums his solo recastings of well-known tunes have been highlights. *Don't Blame Me* ♫♫♫ (DIW, 1995, prod. Gert-Jan Blom, Marc Ribot) has only three originals and includes his takes on jazz standards ("I'm in the Mood for Love," "Don't Blame Me," "Body and Soul," "Dinah," "These Foolish Things," etc.) and Albert Ayler's "Ghosts," Duke Ellington's "Solitude," and Charlie Haden's "Song for Che," making it of obvious interest to jazz fans. The level of concentration required to follow the subtle logic of the terrorism he perpetrates on standards sometimes makes this heavy—but rewarding—listening.

the rest:
The Book of Heads ♫♫♫ (Tzadik, 1995)
Shoe String Symphonettes ♫♫♫♫ (Tzadik, 1997)

worth searching for: Two albums on a small Belgian label are worth hearing. In fact, *Requiem for What's His Name* ♫♫♫♫ (Les Disques du Crepuscule, 1992, prod. Kirk Yano, Marc Ribot) is utterly essential. It's built along the same lines as *Rootless Cosmopolitans* but with slightly greater self-assurance. The irreverent "Yo, I Killed Your God" memorably mocks anti-Semitism and perhaps religion itself, while a cover of Howlin' Wolf's "Commit a Crime" displays a stunning array of stinging blues licks. *Solo Guitar Works of Frantz Casseus* ♫♫♫ (Les Disques du Crepuscule, 1993, prod. Ilana Pelzig Cellum), a tribute to Ribot's Haitian-American guitar teacher, lets him show off impeccable classical guitar technique on lyrical, romantic pieces heavily influenced by the rhythms and harmonies of Haiti. Shrek shows up again on *Subsonic 1* ♫♫♫ (Subsonic/Sub Rosa, 1994, prod. Anthony Coleman), a confusingly split CD that's half Ribot, half solo Fred Frith. Ribot is at his most avant-garde here.

influences:
◀◀ Derek Bailey, Jimi Hendrix, Eugene Chadbourne, Arto Lindsay, Fred Frith, Frantz Casseus, John Zorn, Bill Frisell, Captain Beefheart

▶▶ Brad Schoeppach, David Tronzo, Danny Blume

Steve Holtje

Buddy Rich

Born September 30, 1917, in New York, NY. Died April 2, 1987, in Los Angeles, CA.

One of the most popular drummers in jazz for almost 50 years, Rich was a muscular, flamboyant player with a powerful sense of swing and enormous chops. Unfortunately, despite his great talent, Rich had one of the biggest egos in jazz; a Rich-led band was frequently little more than a vehicle for its leader's rather overstated ensemble style. Still, Rich cooked, plain and simple. Despite his extreme extroversion (or perhaps because of it), his groups were always exciting; they regularly featured top-notch arrangements and such high-caliber soloists as Ernie Watts, Art Pepper, and Phil Wilson.

Rich was born into show business; he played a part in his parents' vaudeville act when he was little more than a year old. He appeared on Broadway as a drummer and tap dancer at age four, and toured the U.S. and Australia from the age of six. At 11, Rich led his first band. From 1937 to 1939 he played with the bands of Joe Marsala, Bunny Berigan, Harry James, Artie Shaw, and Benny Carter. In 1939 he joined Tommy Dorsey's band, with whom he would play (interrupted by a war-time stint in the Marines) until 1945. From that point until 1951, he would lead his own groups and tour variously with Charlie Ventura, Les Brown, and Norman Granz's Jazz at the Philharmonic. Rich spent most of his time between 1953 and 1966 with Harry James, aside from periods with Dorsey (1954–55) and his own group (1957–61). From 1966 to 1974, Rich led his own very successful big band. He spent the late 1970s in New York, playing mostly at his own nightclub, Buddy's Place. He took to the road again in the 1980s, leading another big band of mostly young players. In the 1970s and 1980s, Rich developed a reputation as a lovable, egocentric curmudgeon via frequent appearances on Johnny Carson's *Tonight Show*. According to members of his later groups, that image was only partially earned; Rich's reputed band bus tirades are the stuff of legend.

what to buy: Much of Rich's best work is out of print or hard to find, but the easily acquired *Time Being* ♫♫♫♫ (RCA Bluebird, 1971/1972, prod. Ed Michel) is a fair representation of his excellent early 1970s band, featuring the underrated tenor saxophonist Pat LaBarbera. The Rich bands of this era were prone to occasional covers of undistinguished rock tunes, but when they kick out the stops and swing—as on this record's particularly aggressive "Straight, No Chaser"—they were among the best in the business.

best of the rest:
This One's for Basie ♫♫♫♫ (Verve, 1956)

Swingin' New Band ♪♪♪♪ (Pacific Jazz, 1966)
Big Swing Face ♪♪♪♪ (Pacific Jazz, 1967)
Lionel Hampton Presents Buddy Rich ♪♪♪ (Who's Who, 1977)

influences:

◄◄ Harry James, Gene Krupa, Max Roach

►► Keith Moon, Charlie Watts

Chris Kelsey

Dannie Richmond

Born December 15, 1935, in New York, NY. Died March 16, 1988, in New York, NY.

There are a few sidemen in jazz history who are famous for having brilliantly melded their own personalities with those of a respected leader, allowing the leader's genius to shine through brighter than it might have otherwise. Among these, Billy Strayhorn for his association with Duke Ellington, Charlie Rouse with Thelonious Monk, and Elvin Jones with John Coltrane come to mind; so does Dannie Richmond for his partnership with bassist Charles Mingus. Mingus himself once said, "Dannie Richmond is me with his own sense of will. Instead of hands strumming or bowing, he uses his feet, hands, skin, metal, and wood."

When Richmond joined Mingus in 1956, he was just learning to play the drums, having been a tenor saxophonist in his teens. Nevertheless, he was thrown right into the cauldron with Mingus, and he reacted admirably on Mingus records like *Tijuana Moods* and *East Coasting*. As Richmond's ability as a drummer increased, so did Mingus's confidence in him, and the two became a seamless duo, stretching rhythmic limits and pushing soloists such as Eric Dolphy, Ted Curson, and Booker Ervin to soaring heights on one classic Mingus record after another in the 1960s. Richmond would leave Mingus in 1970 to play and tour with pop acts including Elton John and Joe Cocker, only to rejoin the bassist in 1974. The second stint with Mingus resulted in more great music for the Atlantic label, with a group that included George Adams on tenor, trumpeter Jack Walrath, and pianist Don Pullen. After Mingus's death in 1979, Richmond would continue his legacy, recording with Mingus Dynasty and the Mingus Big Band, as well as with fellow Mingus alumni as a leader and a sideman.

what to buy: The tribute *Ode to Mingus* ♪♪♪♪ (Soul Note, 1979, prod. Giovanni Bonandrini), recorded shortly after the bassist's death in 1979, shows that Richmond had become highly competent as both a drummer and a bandleader. The main attraction is the lengthy title track, but also worth noting are the melodic-sounding multi-tracked drum solo "Olduvai Gorge" and tenor Bill Saxton's work on "Love Bird."

what to buy next: On *Hand to Hand* ♪♪♪♪ (Soul Note, 1980, prod. Giovanni Bonandrini) Richmond and George Adams are joined by fellow Mingus band alumni Jimmy Knepper on trombone and Hugh Lawson on piano for a rousing set of originals. Especially exciting are Lawson's "The Clocker" and Adams's "Yamani's Passion."

what to avoid: The group on *Gentleman's Agreement* ♪♪♪ (Soul Note, 1983, prod. Giovanni Bonandrini) worked together better the first time, on *Hand to Hand*. There's only so much mileage these musicians can expect to get from their old partnerships with Mingus.

the rest:

Plays Charles Mingus ♪♪♪♪ (Timeless, 1980/1997)
The Last Mingus Band A.D. ♪♪♪ (Gatemouth, 1980/Landmark, 1995)
Three or Four Shades of Blues ♪♪♪♪ (Tutu, 1981/1994)

worth searching for: The excellent *In Jazz for the Culture Set* ♪♪♪♪ (Impulse!, 1965, prod. Bob Thiele) was recorded when Richmond was still with Mingus the first time. Pianist Jaki Byard and the harmonica of Toots Thielemans are also featured on this very original sounding set, which ought to be reissued on CD.

influences:

◄◄ Elvin Jones

►► Billy Higgins

Dan Keener

Odd Riisnaes

Born 1953, in Norway.

Riisnaes is a lithe, reedy-toned soprano and tenor saxophonist who covers all of the progressive-mainstream bases, from Ornette Coleman freebop to Miles Davis funk. Riisnaes's style owes much to John Coltrane, though he's cleaner, with more manners. Riisnaes has a firm command of the basic elements of composition and improvisation; his voice is not wildly original, but there's an obvious intelligence and discipline underlying his art. To his credit, Riisnaes relies less on tried and true formulas than many other post-boppers.

what to buy: *Your Ship* ♪♪♪ (Taurus Records, 1995, prod. Odd Riisnaes) shows Riisnaes to be something of an ambitious composer; on this album he writes for combinations ranging

Buddy Rich **(Archive Photos)**

from a soprano sax quartet to a small big band. Stylistically, Risnaes draws from European art and folk traditions, as well as jazz and rock. His sax playing is strong, sure, and melodic. A well-crafted, interesting record.

the rest:
Thoughts ✍✍✍ (Taurus, 1989)
Another Version ✍✍✍✎ (Gemini, 1993)

influences:
⏪ John Coltrane, Jan Garbarek

Chris Kelsey

The Rippingtons
Formed 1986, in Los Angeles, CA.

Russ Freeman, guitars, guitar synthesizers, keyboards, drum programming; Tony Morales, drums (1986–96); Brandon Fields, saxophone (1986–89); Steve Reid, percussion; Jeff Kashiwa, saxophone, EWI (1990–present); Kim Stone, bass; David Anderson, drums (1996–present); Dave Kochanski, keyboards (1996–present).

Dismissed by some serious jazz heads as the epitome of lightweight "fuzak" contemporary jazz, the Rippingtons began mostly as a creation of guitarist/keyboardist/producer Russ Freeman, who used modern sequencing techniques to write, arrange, and perform much of the music on early Rippingtons records himself. Born in Texas and raised in Nashville, Freeman picked up the guitar at age 14 and found himself attracted to jazz greats such as George Benson on one hand and pop artists such as the Beatles on the other. Relocating to attend the University of California at Los Angeles in 1979, the guitarist recorded his first solo album six years later with a group that included percussionist Steve Reid. A year after that, he assembled another record for a Japanese company, this time enlisting such famous friends as Kenny G and David Benoit. Pressed to name his new project while gigging around Los Angeles with a touring band, Freeman called them the Rippingtons because the level of playing was so high ("ripping"). As he assembled more Rippingtons records, Freeman allowed members of the touring band more input into the performance process, eventually recording entire albums as a band in the studio with a live drumkit. In the mid-'90s, Freeman began billing the band as Russ Freeman and the Rippingtons, occasionally assembling solo records and initiating a partnership with old friend Benoit dubbed the Benoit/Freeman Project. The Rippingtons continue to evolve as a band, picking up veteran players with credits including Spyro Gyra, Taj Mahal, and Larry Carlton. Through it all, Freeman has written nearly all of the band's material, championing the sort of commercial sounds condemned by purists but embraced by "smooth-jazz" radio stations nationwide.

what to buy: As the first Rippingtons album featuring a full cast of flesh-and-blood players along with live drums on every cut, *Curves Ahead* ✍✍✍ (GRP, 1991, prod. Russ Freeman) crackles with an energy often missing from previous efforts. It helps that the cast of regulars includes keyboardist Dave Grusin, saxophonist Kirk Whalum, and former Weather Report drummer Omar Hakim, giving a urgent edge to the band's often-easygoing arrangements. *The Best of the Rippingtons* ✍✍✍ (GRP, 1997, prod. Russ Freeman) pulls together the best of the band's cuts from its 11-year career.

what to buy next: Both as an overview of the band's best material and a great showcase for the touring band to cut loose, *Live in L.A.* ✍✍✍ (GRP, 1992, prod. Russ Freeman) presents classic Rippingtons cuts such as "Curves Ahead" and "Tourist in Paradise" in a new light, with particularly fine performances from saxophonist Jeff Kashiwa and ex–Spyro Gyra bassist Kim Stone.

what to avoid: Featuring mostly sequenced arrangements with even the drums programmed, *Tourist in Paradise* ✍✎ (GRP, 1989, prod. Russ Freeman) nearly drowns its generic material in lifeless arrangements, suggesting that the Rippingtons' biggest asset, Freeman's all-encompassing musical vision, may also be their biggest problem.

the rest:
Moonlighting ✍✍ (GRP, 1986)
Kilimanjaro ✍✍✎ (GRP, 1987)
Welcome to the St. James Club ✍✍ (GRP, 1990)
Weekend in Monaco ✍✎ (GRP, 1992)
Sahara ✍✍✍ (GRP, 1994)
(With the Benoit/Freeman Project) *The Benoit/Freeman Project* ✍✍✍
   (GRP, 1994)
Brave New World ✍✍✍ (GRP, 1996)
Black Diamond ✍✍✎ (Windham Hill Jazz, 1997)

worth searching for: Conceived as an all-star team-up featuring the Rippingtons, Benoit, and saxophonist Tom Scott, *Full Swing* ✍✍✍ (Cypress Records, 1988, prod. Russ Freeman) offers another dose of radio-ready commercial jazz from some of the guys who practically invented the genre.

solo outings:
Russ Freeman:
Nocturnal Playground ✍✍✍ (BrainChild Records, 1985)
Holiday ✍✎ (GRP, 1995)

influences:

◄◄ Spyro Gyra, the Crusaders, Bob James

►► Doc Powell, Fourplay

Eric Deggans

Lee Ritenour

Born January 11, 1952, in Hollywood, CA.

Lee Ritenour is well known for his musical versatility, which derives from a childhood spent absorbing the music of jazz guitar legends like Joe Pass, Wes Montgomery, Howard Roberts, and Kenny Burrell, as well as pop and rock stars such as the Byrds, Eric Clapton, Jimi Hendrix, and Jeff Beck. One of L.A.'s top session guitarists through the 1970s, he performed with Steely Dan, Quincy Jones, Herbie Hancock, and Pink Floyd before deciding to establish a solo career in 1976. Since then, his extensive and consistently appealing body of work—which features elements ranging from pop-jazz to funk to straightahead to Brazilian—has made him one of the most popular artists in contemporary jazz. He won a Grammy Award in 1985 for his tune "Early A.M. Attitude," which can be found on *Harlequin*, his duet album with keyboardist Dave Grusin, with whom he has enjoyed a long association. Since 1991 he's also been a member of the highly successful contemporary jazz outfit Fourplay, along with keyboardist Bob James, drummer Harvey Mason, and bassist Nathan East. In 1996 he established his own record label, i.e. Records, along with *Jazziz* magazine publisher Michael Fagien and veteran music industry executive Mark Wexler, which to date has produced two highly successful contemporary jazz albums. Ritenour produced and performed on *A Twist of Jobim*, a star-studded tribute to his friend, the late Antonio Carlos Jobim, and produced *Easy Street* for veteran saxophonist Eric Marienthal.

what to buy: *Harlequin* ♫♫♫♫ (GRP Records, 1985, prod. Dave Grusin, Lee Ritenour) is a duet album with keyboardist Dave Grusin and an example of the kind of musical magic that can be made when two players perform with complete accord. There's a chemistry between players that can't be manufactured. It's either there or it isn't, and it is here, especially on tunes such as the contemporary jazz classic "Early A.M. Attitude" and the playful "Silent Message."

what to buy next: On *Wes Bound* ♫♫♫♫ (GRP Records, 1993, prod. Lee Ritenour) Ritenour tips his hat to one of his most significant influences, Wes Montgomery, but it's not an exercise in emulation. Rather, Ritenour demonstrates his familarity with Montgomery's style as he fits it into a more contemporary

framework. Some of the tunes are covers of Montgomery compositions, such as the swinging "4 on 6"; others are Ritenour's own, such as "Ocean Ave.," which was composed using Montgomery's song structure.

what to avoid: It's strange that two gifted guitarists who share compatible musical backgrounds and influences could come up with an album that displays no sense of musical friendship. With Ritenour and Larry Carlton you're sure to get well-crafted compositions performed with superb technique, but *Larry and Lee* ♫♫ (GRP Records, 1995, prod. Lee Ritenour, Larry Carlton) lacks the kind of back-and-forth that characterizes great duets. The exception is "Remembering J.P.," a tribute to their shared influence, Joe Pass. In general, this is not a collaboration; it's a series of performances, and both players are capable of much more.

the rest:
First Course ♫♫♫♥ (Epic, 1976)
Captain Fingers ♫♫♫♥ (Epic, 1977)
Rio ♫♫♫♫♥ (GRP, 1979)
On the Line ♫♫♫ (Victor Musical Industries, 1983/GRP, 1985)
Earth Run ♫♫♫ (GRP, 1986)
Portrait ♫♫♫ (GRP, 1987)
Festival ♫♫♫♥ (GRP, 1988)
Color Rit ♫♫♥ (GRP, 1989)
Stolen Moments ♫♫♫♫ (GRP, 1990)
Lee Ritenour Collection ♫♫♫♥ (GRP, 1991)
Alive in L.A. ♫♫♫ (GRP, 1997)

worth searching for: *Fourplay* ♫♫♫♫ (Warner Bros., 1991, prod. Lee Ritenour, Bob James, Nathan East, Harvey Mason) is a strong collection of appealing, easily accessible compositions performed by four of the best-respected artists in contemporary jazz. This collection demonstrates the group's comfortable interplay, especially on the leisurely "Midnight Stroll" and the lovely, jazzy "Max-O-Man."

influences:

◄◄ Wes Montgomery, Howard Roberts, Joe Pass

►► Russ Freeman

Lucy Tauss

Ritual Trio

See: Kahil El'Zabar

Sam Rivers

Born September 25, 1930, in El Reno, OK.

Sam Rivers found his decidedly original voice during his musical incubation in Boston, where he attended the Conservatory of Music and hung around after graduation into the mid-1960s, making his breakthrough in his mid-30s as a short-timer with Miles in 1964—he was the saxophonist between George Coleman and Wayne Shorter. Rivers danced along the edge of free jazz with Blue Note's "new thing" crowd in the mid-1960s; he played on recordings by Andrew Hill and Tony Williams, and (as a leader) recorded his own material, as well. He then eschewed the safety net and dove full-bore into improv, often with Dave Holland on bass, Barry Altschul or Thurman Barker on percussion, and Joe Daley on tuba. Typically, Rivers would play tenor, soprano, flute, and piano at various times during a recording session or a performance. He also recorded duets with Holland (*Dave Holland/Sam Rivers, Vol. 1* and *Dave Holland/Sam Rivers, Vol. 2* on Improvising Artists) and alongside Altschul and reedman Anthony Braxton on Holland's incredible *Conference of the Birds*. Concurrently, Rivers wrote (and occasionally performed) fascinating large ensemble works. A force on the New York loft scene with his Studio Rivbea, Rivers's work as a leader seemed to lose focus in the late 1980s as his recordings became less frequent. The late 1990s brought the promise of a Rivers revival from his new base in Florida; and his work on two fairly recent sessions for the Postcards label—*Summit Conference* and *Cerebral Caverns*, led by Reggie Workman—has been stunning. His duet project with Julian Priester for Postcards, *Hints of Light and Shadow*, was interesting if less focused.

what to buy: In the space of three CDs (also available as five LPs), *The Complete Blue Note Recordings of Sam Rivers* ✍✍✍✍ (Mosaic, 1995, prod. Alfred Lion) captures the excitement of Rivers's mid-1960s rapid development beginning with his brisk, confident debut, *Fuschia Swing Song*, in the stirring company of bassist Ron Carter and old Boston hands Jaki Byard (piano) and Tony Williams (drums). It's the record that introduced "Beatrice," the only Rivers composition often played by others, but the title track and several other Rivers pieces here are worth canonical consideration. The package also includes Rivers's three Blue Note follow-up albums and alternate takes. Short of the full Blue Note collection, consider *Dimensions and Extensions* ✍✍✍✍ (Blue Note, 1989, prod. Alfred Lion). As the only Rivers Blue Note otherwise available, it is a 1967 session that, thankfully, is varied enough to suggest the range of Rivers's interests in the last half of the 1960s. "Effusive Melange" features a four-horn line (trumpeter Donald Byrd, alto saxophonist James Spaulding, and trombonist Julian Priester, plus Rivers) that suggests roots in a classic edition of the Jazz Messengers. But there's also a loose, Eastern-sound-

ing tune featuring both Spaulding and Rivers on flute, not to mention a number with just Rivers, drums, and bass (Cecil McBee and Steve Ellington, respectively) pointing to the even more free direction Rivers would take in the 1970s.

what to buy next: *Colours* ✍✍✍✍ (Black Saint, 1983/1994, prod. Giovanni Bonandrini) features Rivers's Winds of Manhattan, an 11-piece reed/woodwinds ensemble sans rhythm section, in a kaleidoscopic range of harmonic colors, but with virtually no soloing.

what to avoid: *Lazuli* ✍✍ (Timeless, 1990, prod. Sam Rivers, Anne de Jong) has the outward trappings of Rivers's better work, but not the spark that brings it alive.

worth searching for: *Streams* ✍✍✍✍ (Impulse!, 1989, prod. Ed Michel), a loose but electric trio date recorded in Montreux with bassist Cecil McBee and drummer Norman Connors, was the first release to herald the free improvising Rivers. *Waves* ✍✍✍✍ (Tomato, 1989, prod. Rivbea Music Company), a kicking quartet session with Holland, Daley, and Barker, was likewise reissued in CD form. On vinyl, go for *Contrasts* ✍✍✍✍ (ECM, 1980, prod. Manfred Eicher), which substitutes trombonist George Lewis for Daley. Also scout around for the five volumes of *Wildflowers: The New York Loft Jazz Sessions* ✍✍✍✍ (Douglas, 1977, prod. Alan Douglas, Michael Cuscuna, Sam Rivers), which chronicle the scene at Rivers's loft over 10 days in 1976; on hand were a handful of veterans from Randy Weston and Marion Brown, as well as newer artists like Henry Threadgill (with the group Air), Oliver Lake, and David S. Ware, whose contributions would come to the fore in the 1980s (or as late as the 1990s, in the case of Ware).

influences:

◀◀ Cecil Taylor, Sonny Rollins, Ben Webster, Ornette Coleman

▶▶ Andrew Hill, Dave Holland, Reggie Workman

W. Kim Heron

Max Roach

Born January 10, 1924, in New Land, NC.

Drummer/percussionist Max Roach has had a 50-year career in Jazz. Along with Kenny Clarke and Art Blakey, Roach is considered a "founding-father" of the bebop style of drumming—he was there at the inception of the genre when Parker, Gillespie, Monk, and others helped push swing towards bop. He was integral in Gillespie's small groups and big band. In the 1950s Roach co-led a quintet with talented trumpeter Clifford Brown, and released a series of classic recordings that featured originals and unique arrangements of standards, including *Brown/Roach Incorporated*, *At Basin Street*, and *Live at the Bee-Hive*. This collaboration was the apex of that era's hard-bop scene, and the quintet could have continued to make tremendous music if not for the tragic and untimely deaths of Brown and Richie Powell (the group's pianist) in a car crash in 1956. Since that time Roach has led his own bands and has worked with nearly every important jazz "modernist" as well. Jazz greats he has performed or recorded with in the last 50 years include Bud Powell, Miles Davis, Thelonious Monk, Herbie Nichols, Kenny Dorham, Clifford Jordan, Eric Dolphy, Anthony Braxton, Oscar Brown Jr., Abbey Lincoln (to whom he was married from 1962 through 1970), Cecil Taylor, and Sonny Rollins. Roach continues to perform and record, as well as teach at the University of Massachusetts–Amherst. His influence on the past half-century of modern jazz is undeniable. Roach's daughter, Maxine Roach, is violist in the Uptown String Quartet, a group that has collaborated with her father on a number of occasions.

what to buy: *Alone Together: The Best of the Mercury Years* 𝄞𝄞𝄞𝄞𝄞 (Verve/PolyGram, 1995, prod. Bob Shad), a double CD compilation of material by Brown and Roach, includes many of the definitive versions of vintage classics culled from the Mercury vaults, plus solo material from both Max and Clifford. "Cherokee," "Joy Spring," "Blues Walk," and "Valse Hot" are all represented, as well as more obscure tracks such as Roach's "Dr. Free-Zee" and "Max's Variations" (with the Boston Percussion Ensemble). *The Max Roach 4 Plays Charlie Parker* 𝄞𝄞𝄞𝄞 (Mercury, 1958/Verve, 1995, prod. Bob Shad) is a nice example of Roach's "piano-less quartet" concept, with superb performances, great recording quality, excellent tune selection (music by or associated with Charlie Parker), and good liner notes. *Max Roach Plus Four* 𝄞𝄞𝄞𝄞 (EmArcy, 1957/Polygram, 1990, prod. Bob Shad) includes material from the original album release, plus tunes from the Roach classic *Jazz in 3/4 Time*. These are some of the first recordings that were made with Roach's new group after Clifford Brown's death. Kenny Dorham's soaring trumpet and Sonny Rollins's impeccable warm tenor are heard throughout. *Deeds, Not Words* 𝄞𝄞𝄞𝄞 (Riverside, 1958/1987, prod. Orrin Keepnews) has an interesting arrangement of "You Stepped Out of a Dream." There are convincing contributions from Ray Draper on tuba, and guest bassist Oscar Pettiford duets with Max on the bonus track "There Will Never Be Another You." Otherwise the bassist is Art Davis, with Booker Little and George Coleman filling out the group. *Percussion Bitter Sweet* 𝄞𝄞𝄞𝄞 (Impulse!, 1961/1993, prod. Max Roach, Michael Cus-

SAM RIVERS

song "Point of Many Returns"

album The Complete Blue Note Sam Rivers Sessions
(Mosaic, 1965/1996)

instrument Soprano saxophone

Monster Solo

cuna) is one of Roach's most famous albums, and shows the political strain that ran strong in much of his work around this time. On a program of superb originals, including the often-covered "Garvey's Ghost," Roach is joined by Eric Dolphy, Booker Little, Julian Priester, Clifford Jordan, Mal Waldron, Art Davis, and Latin percussionists, along with Abbey Lincoln. The arrangements and solos are equally strong on this landmark. At the core of the aptly titled double CD *Historic Concerts* 𝄞𝄞𝄞𝄞 (Soul Note, 1984, prod. Max Roach) are two extraordinary free-improv duets documenting Roach's only collaboration with avant-gardist Cecil Taylor. Taylor's percussive piano style and Roach's melodic drumming are well paired at a high level of inspiration and responsiveness. Added for CD are solo performances from the same 1979 concerts and related interviews. The excellent CD booklet includes not only Lee Jeske's liner notes but also concert reviews by Stanley Crouch, Gary Giddins, and Robert Palmer, adding to the historic flavor.

what to buy next: Somewhat unfairly, Roach's rich and productive period of the late 1970s and 1980s has been overlooked, a

period when he was leading an ace quartet that included trumpeter/flugelhornist Cecil Bridgewater and tenor saxophonist Odean Pope, typically with either Calvin Hill or Tyrone Brown on bass. *Pictures in a Frame* 𝄢𝄢𝄢 (Soul Note, 1979, prod. Giovanni Bonandrini) is one of his best quartet albums. Bridgewater, Pope, Hill, and Roach write stimulating tunes and solo with great verve and depth of feeling. Though mostly a curiosity, the solo final track finds Roach working as pianist and vocalist on a pretty tune of his own devising that's solidly within the standard tradition, yet offers a strong lyric parable. By contrast, *In the Light* 𝄢𝄢𝄢 (Soul Note, 1983, prod. Giovanni Bonandrini) focuses on covers of Thelonious Monk ("Straight No Chaser," "Ruby My Dear"), Tadd Dameron ("If You Could See Me Now," "Good Bait"), and Oscar Pettiford ("Tricotism"), plus two by Roach. Bridgewater and Pope interact well on Roach's modal title track, with Pope using such a wide range on his horn that it sometimes seems he's switching between alto and baritone. The uptempo covers feature Roach's trademark driving swing. *Scott Free* 𝄢𝄢𝄢 (Soul Note, 1985, prod. Giovanni Bonandrini) consists of a 40-minute suite by Bridgewater dedicated to the late bassist Scott LaFaro that offers a winning melange of moods and textures. Bridgewater's fluid solos match the leader's quicksilver drumming, while Pope's robust playing is more aligned with electric bassist Tyrone Brown's solid support, providing built-in contrasts that move the music along. Also worth noting is Roach's more ambitious work with expanded ensembles. On *Max Roach with the New Orchestra of Boston and the So What Brass Quintet* 𝄢𝄢𝄢 (Blue Note, 1996, prod. Max Roach), the percussionist is spotlighted on two separate and distinctly different works. Roach is soloist with the New Orchestra of Boston, which performs Fred Tillis's attractive three-movement suite "Festival Journey," conducted by David Epstein at the University of Massachusetts–Amherst in 1993. The 50-minute composition reflects the American cultural tapestry in rich contemporary classical fare and uniquely focuses on Roach's modern drumming techniques. You won't hear a lot of jazzy licks in this seamless, serious piece, but it does have somewhat of a modern jazz feel and incorporates quotes from gospel hymns as well as several unaccompanied Roach solos. The second tune, "Ghost Dance," is a Roach original. Slightly more than 12 minutes in length, it was recorded two years later with the So What Brass Quintet, which includes Cecil Bridgewater and Frank Gordon (trumpets), Marshall Sealy (French horn),

Steve Turre (trombone), and Robert Stewart (tuba). The piece is based on jazz tonalities and harmonies, with a flavor that smacks of a watered-down Lester Bowie Brass Fantasy. Yet, it's an enticing work that gives each player a chance to solo. And then it ends, leaving you wanting more. Roach is a brilliant craftsman who, throughout both works, brandishes his loose, melodic, polyrhythmic drumming style. Fans of contemporary classical music, drummers, and Max Roach devotees should find this CD an intriguing listen, but it's not his best work. Just different.

what to avoid: *The Max Roach Quartet featuring Hank Mobley* 𝄢 (Debut, 1953/1990) would rate five bones for musical content, with nice performances, tune selection, and arrangements foreshadowing the Dameronian arrangements of the Brown-Roach band. But four bones are subtracted for poor recording quality and/or re-mastering: audible clicks, pops, skips, and dropouts can be heard throughout, as if the mastering was done from an old LP rather than the original master tapes (lost, perhaps?).

best of the rest:

We Insist: Freedom Now Suite 𝄢𝄢𝄢 (Candid, 1958/1992)
Jazz in 3/4 Time 𝄢𝄢𝄢 (EmArcy, 1959)
Drums Unlimited 𝄢𝄢𝄢 (Atlantic, 1960/1988)
Speak, Brother, Speak! 𝄢𝄢𝄢 (Fantasy, 1962/1991)
(With Anthony Braxton) *Birth and Rebirth* 𝄢𝄢𝄢 (Black Saint, 1978)
(With Anthony Braxton) *One in Two—Two in One* 𝄢𝄢𝄢 (hat HUT, 1979)
Live at Vielharmonie 𝄢𝄢𝄢 (Soul Note, 1985)
Easy Winners 𝄢𝄢𝄢 (Soul Note, 1985)
Bright Moments 𝄢𝄢𝄢 (Soul Note, 1987)
Collage 𝄢𝄢𝄢 (PSI, 1988)
(With Dizzy Gillespie) *Max + Dizzy—Paris 1989* 𝄢𝄢𝄢 (A&M, 1990)
Award Winning Drummer 𝄢𝄢𝄢 (Time Jazz, 1990)
To the Max! 𝄢𝄢𝄢 (Bluemoon, 1991)
It's Christmas Again 𝄢𝄢𝄢 (Soul Note, 1994)

worth searching for: Moving in and out of availability, *Max Roach Trio featuring the Legendary Hasaan* 𝄢𝄢𝄢 (Atlantic, 1965/1992, prod. Arif Mardin) is a showcase for the writing and playing of pianist Hasaan Ibn Ali, a Philadelphia legend who sounds like he developed the conception of Thelonious Monk in his own highly personal direction. Tinged with harmonic exoticism and eccentric rhythms, his style deserves to be heard, and you apparently won't find him documented anywhere else. Roach's 1970s material is mostly out of print at this point, but the version of his quartet where Bridgewater's frontline partner was tenor saxophonist Billy Harper was a superb unit. Recorded in 1977 with Reggie Workman on bass, the Japanese LP *Live in Amsterdam* 𝄢𝄢𝄢 (Baystate/RVC, 1984, prod. Max

Max Roach (© Jack Vartoogian)

Roach) consists of sidelong renditions of Roach's "It's Time" and Harper's "Call of the Wild & Peaceful Heart," both attractive themes that stick in the memory. And when the tracks are upwards of 20 minutes each, there's plenty of room for exciting solos. The studio recording *Confirmation* 𝄞𝄞𝄞𝄞 (Fluid, 1978, prod. Alan Wolfson), with Calvin Hill on bass, has a side of classics—Charlie Parker's "Confirmation" and John Coltrane's "Giant Steps"—and a side of three Roach originals. The latter are fine and should disappoint nobody, but hearing Harper and Bridgewater rip into the Bird and Trane items carries a level of visceral excitement that's hard to match.

influences:

◀◀ Chick Webb, Papa Jo Jones, Sid Catlett, O'Neil Spencer, Razz Mitchell, Charlie Parker, Dizzy Gillespie

▶▶ Out of the Blue, Ralph Peterson, Lewis Nash, Marc Edwards

see also: *M'Boom*

Gregg Juke, Steve Holtje, and Nancy Ann Lee

Luckey Roberts

Born Charles Luckeyth, August 7, 1887 (some sources report 1893), in Philadelphia, PA. Died February 5, 1968, in New York, NY.

Roberts deserves to be ranked among the stride piano elite, but his lack of recording activity (only three or four sessions in his career) has left him unknown nowadays except to the cognescenti. This resulted not from hardship or lack of appreciation; rather, for over three decades he pursued the more lucrative path of leading a popular society orchestra. His famous ragtime compositions, written before the stride style developed in New York, were "Pork and Beans" and "Junk Man Rag," while his "Ripples of the Nile" turned into the Glenn Miller hit "Moonlight Cocktail." Roberts was touring the vaudeville circuit by the time he was five years old, though not as a pianist— that had to wait until he was six. (He recalled that he could only play in B-flat at the time, which quickly left the singers straining their vocal cords!) After maturing, he wrote Broadway shows, led his orchestra, and owned the Rendezvous club in Harlem (1942–54), where, of course, he was the house pianist. Later he received hand injuries in a car crash, and suffered a stroke just a few weeks before the Good Time Jazz recording session in 1958—though you'd never know it from his spectacular playing.

what's available: *Luckey & the Lion: Harlem Piano Solos by Luckey Roberts & Willie "The Lion" Smith* 𝄞𝄞𝄞𝄞 (Good Time

Jazz, 1958, prod. Lester Koenig) was originally an LP with Roberts on one side and Smith on the other. Despite his health problems, Roberts displays his flamboyant playing right out of the chute on the rousing "Nothin'" and dazzling right-hand runs on "Spanish Fandango."

worth searching for: *Luckey Roberts & Ralph Sutton* 𝄞𝄞𝄞𝄞 (Solo Art, 1995), with six Roberts tracks recorded in 1946 for Circle, and *Happy Go Lucky* 𝄞𝄞𝄞𝄞 (Period, 1958) are the other jazz sessions he did, though they're nowhere near as easy to find as the Good Time Jazz date above. But *Luckey & the Lion* doesn't include his biggest hits, whereas the 1946 material has "Ripples of the Nile" and "Pork & Beans."

influences:

◀◀ Jesse Pickett, One Leg Willie, Same Gordon, Jack the Bear, Lonnie Hicks, Eubie Blake

▶▶ James P. Johnson, Fats Waller

Steve Holtje

Marcus Roberts

Born August 7, 1963, in Jacksonville, FL.

With his deep gospel and blues roots, Marcus Roberts seemed early in his career to be following the same hard bop path of so many of his peers. But since the early 1990s, Roberts has set out to master pre-bop jazz piano styles. His exploration of stride in particular has deepened his approach to Thelonious Monk and Duke Ellington, and lent his solo recitals a certain drama as he wrestles with the style's two-handed technical demands. Roberts lost his eyesight at the age of five and began playing piano at age eight. He studied music at Florida State University in the early 1980s and was a member of Wynton Marsalis's group from 1985–91. Featured extensively with Marsalis, Roberts's extroverted swing gave the group much of its identity. Winner of the first Thelonious Monk Institute competition, he began recording as a leader in the late 1980s, exploring the music of Jelly Roll Morton, Ellington, Monk, Gershwin, and stride and ragtime with mixed results. He has also toured and recorded in a piano duo with Ellis Marsalis. Roberts is featured on two Jazz at Lincoln Center releases, *The Fire of the Fundamentals* and *They Came to Swing*. Like his former boss Wynton, Roberts has raised hackles with his outspoken criticism of other musicians.

what to buy: Despite the becalming title, *As Serenity Approaches* 𝄞𝄞𝄞𝄞 (Novus, 1992, prod. Delfeayo Marsalis) is a stomping album, a series of solo pieces and duets with pi-

Marcus Roberts (© Jack Vartoogian)

anist Ellis Marsalis, trumpeters Wynton Marsalis, Nicholas Payton, and Scott Barnhart, reed player Todd Williams, and trombonist Ronald Westray. The program mixes standards (including two very different versions of "Cherokee") and vintage jazz tunes from Morton, Ellington, and Waller with Marcus's originals. Roberts's idiosyncratic synthesis of pre-modern techniques with bop-influenced harmonics makes this a fascinating session. Highlights include Roberts's and Wynton Marsalis's interplay on "King Porter Stomp" and Westray's trombone work on "Creole Blues." A highly ambitious solo outing that doesn't always come off, *If I Could Be with You* ♪♪♪ (Novus, 1993, prod. Delfeayo Marsalis) is as interesting for its misses as its hits. Ranging from spirituals and blues to ragtime, stride, swing-era standards, Monk, and Roberts's original tunes, the pianist doesn't have the technique to pull off convincing versions of "Maple Leaf Rag" and "Carolina Shout," though his versions of "Let's Call This" and "Mood Indigo" display considerable taste and insight into the music of Monk and Ellington.

what to buy next: A relaxed trio session featuring bassist Reginald Veal and drummer Herlin Riley, *Gershwin for Lovers* ♪♪♪ (Columbia, 1994, prod. Marcus Roberts) is much less ambitious than many of Roberts's previous albums, which is one of the reasons why it works. The trio, who made up Wynton Marsalis's rhythm section for five years, plays with unhurried precision, creating a wide variety of textures so that the flow of ballads and mid-tempo arrangements never bogs down. The album that became Roberts's manifesto, *Alone with Three Giants* ♪♪♪♪ (Novus, 1991, prod. Delfeayo Marsalis) set his course for the rest of the decade, pitting the solo pianist against the music of Jelly Roll Morton, Duke Ellington, and Thelonious Monk. His technique on Morton's rag "New Orleans Blues" sometimes falters, but he plays Monk (especially "In Walked Bud") with real distinction and his highly percussive version of Ellington's "Black and Tan Fantasy" is the album's highpoint.

best of the rest:
The Truth Is Spoken Here ♪♪♪ (Novus, 1989)

Deep in the Shed 𝄢𝄢𝄢𝄢 (Novus, 1990)
Plays Ellington 𝄢𝄢𝄢𝄢 (Novus, 1995)
Time and Circumstance 𝄢𝄢𝄢 (Columbia, 1996)
Portraits in Blue 𝄢𝄢 (Sony Classical, 1996)
Blues for the New Millennium 𝄢𝄢𝄢 (Columbia, 1997)

worth searching for: On Wynton Marsalis's breakthrough album, *Tune in Tomorrow* 𝄢𝄢𝄢 (Columbia, 1990, prod. Steve Epstein, Delfeayo Marsalis), Roberts shines as he plays with the kind of style and humor often missing in his own performances. Drummer Herlin Riley and Roberts offer a sincere but playfully hip tour through New Orleans shuffles and drags, while Wynton finally exorcizes the ghost of Miles. With two sultry vocals by Shirley Horn, including a drop-dead, beautiful "I Can't Get Started," this is one of the best movie soundtracks of the decade.

influences:

◀◀ Thelonious Monk, Duke Ellington, James P. Johnson, Bud Powell

see also: *Lincoln Center Jazz Orchestra, Wynton Marsalis*

Andrew Gilbert

Clarence "Herb" Robertson

Born February 21, 1951, in Plainfield, NJ.

Herb Robertson may well be one of jazz's most significant trumpeters since the 1950s. His early influences, Al Hirt and Doc Severinson, likely explain Robertson's unmatched penchant for blurting, big, brassy lines and his high-sprited sense of musical bounce. But Robertson's not well known enough outside avant-garde circles for either the several CDs under his own name or the many, many CDs where he appears as a collaborator or sideman to mark a significant commercial success. This is unfortunate in the extreme, for Robertson expertly melds the bright brass of big band trumpeters doing clarion calls with the squiggly explorations of tone and atonalism that came from such pioneers as Bill Dixon in the 1960s and after. But even as a perennial sideman, Robertson consistently makes a solid showing on every session he graces. His mixture of liquid jumps in tone and swirling, energized bends in linear play leave indelible marks everywhere he performs. And his fatness of sound runs parallel to his exquisite compositional sense, whether he's playing a lengthy suite or a robust, free-swinging tune.

Robertson attended Berklee College from 1969 to 1972 and subsequently plied the road with rock and dance bands. But in the 1980s and 1990s, he has been present on dozens of far-reaching sessions. His string of releases on JMT, including *Certified*, a Brass Ensemble session called *Shades of Bud Powell*, the bustling live performance *Xcerpts: Live at Willisau*, Stefan Winter's *The Little Trumpet*, and *Transparency*, appeared to have put Robertson's hard-swinging and playful post-free jazz solidly on the map. But since 1993 Robertson has released only two CDs as a leader, *Falling in Flat Space* and *Sound Implosion*. He's recorded extensively with groups led by alto and baritone saxophonist Tim Berne, saxophonist Andy Laster, bassist Mark Helias, and a roll-call of others, including Michael Moore, Ray Anderson, Lou Grassi, Lindsey Horner, David Sanborn, Phil Haynes, Bobby Previte, Klaus Konig, Paul Lytton, and Gerry Hemingway. Perhaps Robertson's best showings as a side-player come on two CDs from the Joe Fonda/Michael Jefry Stevens Group, where Robertson plays in a seamless weave with pianist Stevens and then bursts out with punchy solos aplenty.

what to buy: Herb Robertson's heated, almost molten trumpet has never sounded freer or more engaging than on *Falling in Flat Space* 𝄢𝄢𝄢 (Cadence Jazz, 1997, prod. Robert D. Rusch). This trio session is as intense as any that loosens a free-playing group from traditional melodic and tonic trappings.

what to buy next: Both of the Joe Fonda/Michael Jefry Stevens CDs, *The Wish* 𝄢𝄢𝄢 (Music and Arts, 1997) and *Parallel Lines* 𝄢𝄢𝄢 (Music and Arts, 1995) are brilliant examples of inside/outside jazz, music that harnesses harmony and melody only to blow past it in cavalcades of skewered energy. Robertson shows again that he can handle the most dexterous tunes and the freest solo materials.

the rest:
Xcerpts: Live at Willisau 𝄢𝄢𝄢 (JMT, 1987)
Shades of Bud Powell 𝄢𝄢𝄢 (JMT, 1988)
Certified 𝄢𝄢𝄢 (JMT, 1991)
Sound Implosion 𝄢𝄢𝄢 (CIMP, 1996)

influences:

◀◀ Bill Dixon, Al Hirt, Doc Severinsen

▶▶ Dave Douglas, Steve Bernstein

Andrew Bartlett and Walter Faber

Betty Roche

Born January 9, 1920, in Wilmington, DE.

A gifted jazz singer with a rich, husky contralto and a distinctive approach to ballads, Betty Roche is best known for her association with Duke Ellington. Strongly influenced by Anita O'Day, Roche was the best jazz singer Ellington hired after the long tenure of Ivie Anderson. Despite singing on one of Ellington's biggest hits, Roche's career never gained momentum and she only made a few recordings. Raised in Atlantic City and New York, Roche broke into music through the amateur competitions at Harlem's Apollo Theatre. She performed and recorded in the early 1940s with the Savoy Sultans and worked briefly with Hot Lips Page and Lester Young. Earl Hines recommended her to Duke Ellington in late 1942, and she made important recordings during each of her two long stints with Ellington (1943–44 and 1952–53). She sang the "Blues" section of Ellington's jazz symphony *Black, Brown and Beige* at its legendary Carnegie Hall debut in 1943 (a performance released by Prestige in 1977 and now available on CD as *The Duke Ellington Carnegie Hall Concerts #1—January 1943*). Roche didn't officially record with Ellington during her first stint because of the 1943 recording ban, and it was Joya Sherrill who ended up making Ellington's *Black, Brown and Beige* album the following year. When Roche finally did record with Ellington in 1952, she scored a monster hit with Billy Strayhorn's theme "Take the 'A' Train," a version that sold eight million copies. After Roche left the band in 1953, the tune became strongly associated with Ray Nance. She recorded a few albums in the next eight years, including two excellent sessions for Prestige, then disappeared from the scene.

what to buy: *Lightly and Politely* ✇✇✇✇✇ (Prestige, 1961/OJC, 1992, prod. Esmond Edwards) was the last recording by the now obscure Betty Roche, which is hard to understand when listening to this recording since she makes a strong impression with her improvisational ease, deft rhythmic phrasing, and direct, emotionally stirring interpretations. Rising above merely competent accompaniment by a quartet led by pianist Jimmy Neeley, Roche takes her time swinging through 10 standards, including three in a row by her former boss Duke Ellington, "Rocks in My Bed," "Just Squeeze Me," and "I Got It Bad . . . ." Other highlights include a lustrous reading of "Someone to Watch Over Me" and sensuous version of "Polka Dots and Moonbeams." This session is highly recommended for fans of jazz singing.

what to buy next: A wonderfully soulful session covering eight top flight standards and Charlie Parker's "Billie's Bounce," *Singin' & Swingin'* ✇✇✇✇ (Prestige, 1960/OJC, 1992, prod. Esmond Edwards) features Bill Jennings on guitar, Wendell Marshall on bass, Jimmy Forrest's blues-drenched tenor saxophone, Ray Haynes's powerful, crisp drumming, and Jack McDuff's tasteful

organ work. Roche is in top form, turning in memorable versions of "Come Rain or Come Shine," "Day by Day," "Until the Real Thing Comes Along," and "Where or When." The only complaint about this session is its 31-minute running time.

the rest:
Take the A Train ✇✇✇✇✇ (Bethlehem, 1956/1977)

worth searching for: Opening with Roche's classic version of Duke Ellington Orchestra's theme song, "Take the 'A' Train," (written, of course, by Billy Strayhorn), *Uptown* ✇✇✇✇✇ (Columbia, 1952–53, prod. George Avakian) is a brilliant album that defies the oft-repeated line that the orchestra was in steep decline in the early 1950s. Sure, the incomparable Johnny Hodges is missed, but Willie Smith's creamy alto gives the band another flavor, and Louie Bellson's dazzling drum work pushed the band to swing harder than it ever had before (Bellson's great composition, "Skin Dee," is also introduced here). Highlights include the clarinet duel between Jimmy Hamilton and Russell Procope on "The Mooche," and a tour de force version of *The Harlem Suite*. Roche's vocal on "'A' Train" was a huge hit, but it's her only contribution to the album.

influences:
◀◀ Anita O'Day, Ivie Anderson

Andrew Gilbert

Claudio Roditi
Born May 28, 1946, in Rio de Janeiro, Brazil.

One of the most exciting trumpeters in jazz, Claudio Roditi has developed a flexible style that encompasses bebop, bossa nova, samba, and Afro-Cuban elements. His deeply felt lyricism, bright, warm sound, and crisp attack make his playing equally effective on ballads and up-tempo material. Raised in the small town of Varghina in the state of Minas Gerais, Roditi started playing trumpet as a youth. At first he listened to Dixieland, but at 13 an uncle introduced him to the music of Chet Baker and Miles Davis. He moved to Rio in 1960 and after a few years broke into the city's burgeoning bossa nova scene. He settled in Boston in 1970, where he studied at Berklee, and played frequently with the great drummer Alan Dawson. He hit New York in 1976 and quickly developed a reputation as a dependably colorful player, recording with Charlie Rouse, Herbie Mann, Michael Franks, and Dom Um Romano. Roditi hooked up with Cuban saxophonist Paquito D'Rivera in 1982, a relationship that has turned into a close musical collaboration encompassing several albums and world tours. He has recorded with a number of singers, including Mark Murphy, Chris Connor, and Michele Hendricks, and was a featured soloist in Dizzy Gillespie's United Nation Orchestra. Roditi has also contributed to a number of Hendrick Meurkens's recent Concord albums, adding considerable texture to the harmonica player's Brazilian sessions. Roditi has recorded for Uptown, Green Street, Milestone, and a series of excellent sessions for Reservoir.

what to buy: Certain concepts just seem right and *Free Wheelin'* &&&& (Reservoir, 1994, prod. Mark Feldman), Claudio Roditi's tribute to the fallen trumpet giant Lee Morgan, is one of them. With nine Morgan tunes, Roditi covers all the bases from the funky hard-bop anthem "The Sidewinder," to the gentle Latin-flavored "Ceora," to the rhythmically complex, modal-feeling "Peyote." Most tunes feature a quintet with Mark Soskin (piano), Buster Williams (bass), Chip White (drums), and the big-toned Argentine tenor saxophonist Andres Boiarsky, though Nick Brignola adds his baritone sax to two tracks and soprano to one. A beautiful marriage of Brazilian music and jazz, *Samba Manhattan Style* &&&& (Reservoir, 1995, prod. Claudio Roditi, Mark Feldman) brings together Roditi's two great loves. He creates a wide variety of moods by rounding out the quintet with a different player on every track, adding saxophonists Greg Abate or Andres Boiarsky, or trombonist Jay Ashby to the rhythm section with Brazilian pianist Helio Alves, bassist John Lee, and drummer Duduka Da Fonseca. Besides the wonderful Brazilian arrangements of Wayne Shorter's "Footprints," Ellington's "In a Sentimental Mood," and Jobim's "Triste" (which features Roditi's vocals), the album features strong original compositions that sustain the album's samba jazz mood.

what to buy next: As the title implies, *Double Standards* &&&& (Reservoir, 1997, prod. Claudio Roditi, Mark Feldman) captures Roditi's dual position as a dedicated student of both jazz and Brazilian music. Covering five Brazilian standards, four jazz tunes, and one original, Roditi utilizes two different bands, though he can't resist mixing genres, as his opening hard bop tune "Reservoir Samba" shows. The session has a relaxed feeling, and highlights include Miles Davis's "So What," and Roditi's gorgeous flugelhorn work on Jobim's "A Felicidade" and "Brigas Nunca Mais." A fine session of Brazilian jazz, *Gemini Man* &&&& (Milestone, 1988, prod. Helen Keane) showcases Roditi's writing, his highly charged trumpet playing, and lush flugelhorn work. Three tunes are probably more than most people want to hear of Roditi's vocals, but with the great pianist Roger Kellaway featured extensively and the expert drumming of Ignacio Berroa and Akira Tana, this is a highly enjoyable album.

best of the rest:
Claudio &&&&&& (Uptown, 1985)
Slow Fire &&&& (Milestone, 1989)
Two of Swords &&&& (Candid, 1990)
Milestones &&&&& (Candid, 1991)
Claudio Roditi — Metropole Orchestra &&& (Mons, 1996)

influences:
◀◀ Dizzy Gillespie, Lee Morgan, Clifford Brown, Art Farmer

Andrew Gilbert

Red Rodney

Born Robert Rodney Chudnick, September 27, 1927, in Philadelphia, PA. Died May 27, 1994, in Boynton Beach, FL.

Red Rodney was the last of the original bebop trumpeters, an august group whose members included Dizzy Gillespie, Fats Navarro, and Miles Davis. Rodney joined Charlie Parker's quintet at the age of 21, and for nearly half a century carried a tradition of musical distinction to listeners worldwide. Although a true bebop innovator in the 1940s and 1950s, Rodney's early contributions to jazz were overshadowed by his chaotic personal life. It was not until his later years that he gained respect as a driving creative force.

He first studied music at Philadelphia's Mastbaum High School, where he was a classmate of Buddy DeFranco and John Coltrane. Rodney became interested in jazz after hearing Dizzy perform. After considerable practice he started sitting in with bands in clubs and, at the Downbeat Club, he met and befriended Gillespie. Impressed by the young trumpeter's musical ability, Gillespie took Rodney to New York and introduced him to Charlie Parker. In 1949 Charlie "Bird" Parker asked Rodney to replace trumpeter Miles Davis, who was leaving to form his own band. Rodney moved to New York City and took his place beside a legend. His experiences with Parker would have a profound and lasting effect on both his music and life. Although 18 months under Bird's wing allowed him to master the intricate harmonies of bebop, he also became addicted to heroin. Accordingly, he faded in and out of the jazz spotlight for nearly a decade after he left Bird. Rodney led dance bands and played in Las Vegas casino orchestras, backing performers such as Elvis Presley, Barbra Streisand, and Sammy Davis Jr. But his love of playing bebop eventually prevailed, and in 1972 he began playing regularly at Donte's jazz club in Los Angeles. He also recorded his first album in 14 years, *Bird Lives!*. After an extended stay in Europe, Rodney returned to the U.S. and formed a group with Ira Sullivan in 1980. They played and recorded together for five years. After parting ways with Sullivan, Rodney formed several new bands featuring up-and-coming jazz musicians whom he had taken under his wing. He also acted as a consultant to actor and director Clint Eastwood during the production of his biographical film on Parker's life, *Bird*. In addition to imparting his first-hand knowledge of Bird and contributing some fiery licks to the soundtrack, he also coached actor Michael Zelnicker on the finer points of being Red Rodney. He made his last public appearance in the summer of 1993 at the Charlie Parker Jazz Festival in New York City. He died on May 27, 1994, of lung cancer. Although the trumpeter endured myriad personal catastrophes during his roller coaster 52-year career, he overcame all odds to record more than 40 albums and to inspire and encourage four decades of jazz trumpeters.

what to buy: At the age of 65, Red Rodney and his incendiary flugelhorn were supercharged by a deep love for the music he played for almost half a century. This collection of bebop standards, *Then and Now* ♫♫♫♫ (Chesky Records, 1992, prod. David Chesky, Bob Belden), is his finest hour. His working band in his final days, which included pianist Gary Dial and saxophonist Chris Potter, was one of his best, and they give "Un Poco Loco," "Confirmation," "Woody 'n You," and eight others a fresh, invigorated face (thanks in part to Bob Belden's arrangements). Rodney focuses exclusively on flugelhorn here but loses none of his intensity. Recorded for the audiophile Chesky label, the acoustics on *Then and Now* offer some of the best sound ever captured on a jazz recording. The CD also includes a fascinating ten minute interview with Rodney in which he discusses jazz past, present, and future.

what to buy next: In and out of jazz in the late 1950s, Red Rodney's occasional sightings proved memorable, and 1957's *Fiery* ♫♫♫♫ (Savoy Jazz, 1957/1993, prod. Ozzie Cadena) was his best from the era. This one is all bebop, played by Rodney and his frequent collaborator, tenor saxophonist and trumpeter Ira Sullivan; also on hand is a rhythm section of Tommy Flanagan on piano, Oscar Pettiford on bass, and either Philly Jo Jones or Elvin Jones on drums. Hard to go wrong with that lineup! Bird favorites "Star Eye" and "Stella by Starlight" are among the highlights, along with Rodney's own "Red Arrow." After nearly five years of collaborating with Ira Sullivan, Red Rodney led his own groups in his final decade. Like Bird and Dizzy had done for him back in the 1940s, he went looking for very promising young musicians and always managed to find them. Consequently, he led one of the best New York–based groups from the mid-1980s to the early 1990s, including a group with reedman Dick Oatts, pianist Gary Dial, bassist Jay Anderson, and drummer Joey Baron. *No Turn on Red* ♫♫♫♪ (Denon,

1986/1989, prod. Gary Dial), arranged and produced by Dial, is a collection of standards like "Greensleeves" and "Young and Foolish" peppered with originals. Here Rodney strays from his bop roots, and the results are most pleasing.

worth searching for: Two Rodney recordings will amply reward efforts to find them. After leaving Bird, Red Rodney paid some heavy personal dues; but he did surface occasionally to remind us of his trumpet prowess. In 1960 he led a quintet for nearly a year at the Red Hill Inn near Philadelphia and recorded *Red Rodney Returns* ♫♫♫♫ (Argo, 1961, prod. Esmond Edwards) for the Chicago-based label. Rodney's trumpet shows no signs of decay here. He plays the trumpet with remarkable proficiency and startling ardor, as does Philly tenor man Billy Root, whose fierce blowing is balanced by confidence and relaxation on the more subdued tracks. "I Remember April," "Red, Hot and Blue," and "Shaw Nuff" are the highlights. After a spell working in Las Vegas backing show business legends like Elvis Presley and Barbra Streisand, Red Rodney returned to his first love, bebop, in 1973 with *Bird Lives!* ♫♫♫♫ (Muse Records, 1973, prod. Joe Fields). Alto saxophonist Charles McPherson (who later lent his sound to the film *Bird*) serves as co-star and he holds up well under the breakneck bebop tempos and stunning ballads. McPherson plays with a fervid lyricism that recalls Parker but doesn't mimic him. A choice rhythm section—pianist Barry Harris, bassist Sam Jones, and drummer Roy Brooks—adds plenty of New York energy as well. Rodney plays with the same fire and passion that has always marked his music. He was a master of the trumpet and of bebop's intricate harmonies, and his warm personality and enthusiasm for the music remain consistent throughout. Word is that 32 Records is putting together a Red Rodney compilation that will bring together the out-of-print Muse sessions—it's supposed to be due out in late 1998 or 1999.

influences:

◀◀ Dizzy Gillespie, Fats Navarro, Miles Davis, Lee Morgan, Woody Shaw

▶▶ Joe Magnarelli, Marcus Printup, Freddie Hubbard, Donald Byrd

Bret Primack

Shorty Rogers

Born Milton Michael Rajonsky, April 14, 1924, in Great Barrington, MA. Died November 7, 1994, in Van Nuys, CA.

Shorty Rogers is remembered primarily for the compositions and arrangements he wrote both for his own groups and the big bands of Woody Herman and Stan Kenton. He also produced some of the most innovative and swinging sounds for small groups playing in the modern West Coast jazz idiom, which he helped define. Rogers excelled as a middle-register trumpet/flugelhorn player. His relative obscurity today is most likely a result of his post-1962 behind-the-scenes career writing musical scores for film and television.

At age five he was a member of his hometown (Lee, Massachusetts) drum and bugle corps. His family moved often, and each time he found a new corps to join, until he was 13. For a Bar Mitzvah gift he received a trumpet and immediately started experimenting with his newly acquired horn. His sister Eve, who later married vibist Red Norvo, introduced him to the music of Benny Goodman, Bunny Berigan, Artie Shaw, and Count Basie; those phonograph records changed his musical life. He graduated from the High School of Music and Art in New York in February 1942 and landed a trumpet job in the Will Bradley Orchestra. Here he met drummer Shelly Manne, who became a friend and close musical associate for the next 42 years. When Bradley disbanded in late 1942, Rajonsky joined Red Norvo's combo, played on famed 52nd Street, and met Norvo's pianist-arranger, Ralph Burns. Drafted into the Army, Rajonsky became a member of the 379th ASF Band and made his first appearance on record, with Cozy Cole, while on leave. Upon his discharge from the service in September 1945, he replaced Conte Candoli in Woody Herman's First Herd. Here he was reunited with Norvo and Burns; this was also the time he started arranging, big-time. When the Herman band broke up at the end of 1946, Rajonsky joined Charlie Barnet, then Butch Stone, and took up residence in Los Angeles where he legally changed his name to Rogers. He went back to Woody Herman for the duration of the boppish Second Herd, where his orchestral writing caught fire, characterized by his punching and blazing brass figures and his ability to make the band swing. When Herman disbanded again, Rogers and Shelly Manne joined Stan Kenton along with Maynard Ferguson, Milt Bernhart, Bud Shank, Art Pepper, and Bob Cooper, all of whom were involved with Rogers's later bands and recordings. Rogers's first record date as leader—October 8, 1951—laid the foundation for what has become known as "West Coast Jazz"; this material was released on Capitol as *Modern Sounds by Shorty Rogers and His Giants*. Rogers had left Kenton, and, tired of life on the road, settled in for almost a year as a member of the Lighthouse All-Stars at Hermosa Beach, California. In 1953 he played occasional gigs with his own band at venues such as the Rendezvous Ballroom at Newport Beach, California, and started an exciting series of dates with his Giants

in the RCA Victor studios. Rogers shifted his brand of West Coast jazz to Atlantic Records in 1955. He returned to RCA Victor the next year and had active roles as an A&R (Artists & Repertoire) man and as an arranger; he also began a series of recordings with various formations of his Giants, groups that ranged in size from a quintet to a nonet to a big band. His last session for RCA took place in April 1961, an ambitious suite entitled *An Invisible Orchard*, which remained unreleased until 1997. During the 1950s Rogers became active writing for the movie studios, and his scoring for films such as *The Wild One* and *The Man with the Golden Arm* are well remembered. After 1962, Shorty Rogers stayed buried in studio soundtrack work, re-emerging twenty years later to briefly revive the Lighthouse All-Stars. Fortunately, for the CD jazz enthusiast, the bulk of Rogers's work for RCA has been reissued and can be found in jazz specialty stores.

what to buy: *The Big Shorty Rogers Express* 🎵🎵🎵🎵 (BMG/RCA, 1994, prod. Jack Lewis) features Rogers and his Giants providing prime examples of classic West Coast modern jazz. Eight tracks from 1953, originally on a 10-inch LP aptly titled *Cool and Crazy*, and four additional tracks from July 1956, are combined in a big band setting to produce an effective, wide-ranging showcase for the 12 attractive Rogers originals. Stan Kenton lent 95 percent of his band for the 1953 date. Art Pepper, Bud Shank, Jimmy Giuffre, and Bob Cooper have some nifty sax solos. Trumpeters on the album constitute a brass who's who, with Conrad Gozzo, Maynard Ferguson, Harry Edison, Conte and Pete Candoli, and leader Rogers all on board. "Blues Express" opens the set with a tight small group theme and then roars into Shorty's solo, followed by Art Pepper's melodic alto. Rogers's longtime band-mate, drummer Shelly Manne, has much to contribute to this innovative session. The closer, "The Sweetheart of Sigmund Freud," is notable for featuring three baritone saxes and a tuba. This IS a cool and crazy album. *Popo* 🎵🎵🎵🎵 (Xanadu, 1978/1994, prod. Bob Andrews, Don Schlitten) features Rogers with Art Pepper recorded at the Lighthouse in late 1951 and preserves a good sampling of Rogers's bebop playing in what is essentially a "blowing" session. Altoist Art Pepper, drummer Shelly Manne, pianist Frank Patchen, and bassist Howard Rumsey also contribute mightily as the quintet roars through the opening Rogers title theme, and dispatches nine additional pop or jazz standards such as "Scrapple from the Apple," "Tin Tin Deo," "Robbins' Nest," and a smoking "Cherokee," offset by ballads like "All the Things You Are" (Pepper's solo) and "What's New?" (Rogers's solo).

what to buy next: Shorty Rogers bowed out of his affiliation with RCA Victor with three 1961 dates and eight tunes conceived by Rogers as a suite entitled *An Invisible Orchard* 🎵🎵🎵🎵 (BMG/RCA, 1997, prod. Dick Pierce). There's a nod toward things celestial here with titles such as "Inner Space," "Saturnian Sunrise," "Light Years," "Like Space," and "Lunar Montunar." A superb rhythm section of pianist Pete Jolly, bassist Red Mitchell, drummer Mel Lewis, and vibist Emil Richards anchors the 18-piece band of ace West Coast jazzmen and studio musicians led by Shorty on flugelhorn. Other primary soloists include Bill Perkins and Harold Land, tenor saxophones; Frank Rosolino, trombone; and Bud Shank and Paul Horn, alto saxophones and flutes. Thanks to RCA Archives for locating the master tapes some 36 years after the last session. The CD should be a must for Shorty Rogers fans and of considerable interest to devotees of West Coast modern jazz. Rogers's return to the jazz scene after years behind studio doors is captured nicely on a live recording, *Bud Shank/Shorty Rogers: California Concert* 🎵🎵🎵🎵 (Contemporary, 1977/OJC, 1997, prod. Richard Bock). Recorded at Orange Coast College, Costa Mesa, California, the May 19, 1985 concert puts the reunited Shank and Rogers in front of an exciting rhythm section (George Cables, piano; Monty Budwig, bass; Sherman Ferguson, drums) in a program of three Rogers originals, three classic jazz pieces, and a wonderful reworking of the old Walter Donaldson tune, "Makin' Whoopee." Rogers displays, both on his horn and in his writing, that he hasn't lost his touch. Listen for his triplet passage on the original "Aurex," and for the unexpected twists and turns of tempo on the lengthy treatment afforded Ellington's "Echoes of Harlem." Both soloists hit a creative ballad mood in "Mia," named for Shorty's daughter. Shank has evolved from a cool to a hot player over the years and he catches fire on Charlie Parker's "Ah-Leu-Cha" and the old Basie classic "It's Sand, Man," written by trumpeter Ed Lewis.

best of the rest:
(With Andre Previn) *Collaboration* 🎵🎵🎵🎵 (RCA, 1955/BMG, 1996)
(With Al Cohn) *East Coast–West Coast Scene* 🎵🎵🎵🎵 (RCA, 1955/BMG, 1996)
Shorty Rogers Plays Richard Rodgers 🎵🎵🎵🎵 (RCA, 1957/BMG, 1996)
(With Shorty Rogers Quintet) *Wherever the Five Winds Blow* 🎵🎵🎵🎵🎵 (RCA, 1957/BMG, 1996)
(With Shorty Rogers and his Giants) *Portrait of Shorty* 🎵🎵🎵🎵 (RCA, 1958/BMG, 1994)
(With Shorty Rogers and his Giants) *"Gigi" in Jazz* 🎵🎵🎵🎵 (RCA, 1958/BMG, 1997)
Manteca/Afro-Cuban Influence 🎵🎵🎵🎵 (RCA, 1958/BMG, 1992)
(With the Shorty Rogers Orchestra) *Chances Are It Swings* 🎵🎵🎵🎵 (RCA, 1959/BMG, 1996)
(With the Shorty Rogers Orchestra featuring the Giants) *The Wizard of Oz* 🎵🎵🎵🎵 (RCA, 1959/BMG, 1996)

SONNY ROLLINS

song "Blue 7"

album *Saxophone Collossus*
(Prestige-OJC, 1956/1987)

instrument Tenor saxophone

Monster Solo

(With the Shorty Rogers Sax Quintet and the Big Band) *The Swingin' Nutcracker* 🎵🎵🎵 (RCA, 1960/BMG, 1996)
(With Bud Shank) *Yesterday, Today and Forever* 🎵🎵🎵🎵 (Concord, 1983)
(With Bud Shank & the Lighthouse All-Stars) *America the Beautiful* 🎵🎵🎵🎵 (Candid, 1991)

worth searching for: *The Complete Atlantic and EMI Jazz Recordings of Shorty Rogers* 🎵🎵🎵🎵 (Mosaic, 1951/1955/1956/1989, compilation prod. Michael Cuscuna, Todd Selbert) has gone out of print, but this four-CD box set of 59 glorious tracks, culled from the Capitol and Atlantic sessions, is a highlight of the recorded legacy of Shorty Rogers and his Giants. Don't walk, run to the cash register if you locate a stray copy of this one.

influences:
◀◀ Bunny Berigan, Harry "Sweets" Edison, Clifford Brown, Miles Davis, Count Basie, Red Norvo, Al Cohn

▶▶ Dave Pell

John T. Bitter

Sonny Rollins

Born Theodore Walter Rollins, September 9, 1930, in New York, NY.

Although it must be a tremendous temptation to the genuinely adventurous artist, radical reinvention isn't for the faint of heart. And if the mighty post-bop tenorist Sonny Rollins never *completely* overhauled his conception or attack, to the extent that you couldn't tell who you were listening to after he came back from one of his celebrated periods of personal examination and woodshedding, still, there aren't that many players who'd even consider making the effort in the first place.

Rollins grew up in a musically rich family, with older siblings who were active in the classical field. Largely self-taught, the younger Rollins was an early bloomer who picked up the demanding intricacies of the bop dialectic with ease and was soon hanging out with the most influential cats around. Parker, Powell, Monk, and Miles were all early supporters. The qualities they heard in the young saxophonist right from the start, and what the critics caught up with a few short years later, were his nimble melodic and harmonic gifts and his sure sense of rhythm and pace. Today it is abundantly clear that Sonny Rollins is among the most commanding individual voices the music has ever had. When the *Village Voice* heralded him as "The Last Jazz Immortal" on the occasion of his 65th birthday, they weren't very far off (the great musical theorist/architect Ornette Coleman is another future resident of jazz's hallowed Mt. Olympus). And although Rollins has written many excellent tunes over the course of his career, it is as an instrumentalist and improvisor that he has made his most musically indelible mark. His robust tone, derived in part from childhood idol Coleman Hawkins, is immediately identifiable, and the complex yet inevitable and utterly logical solo statements he builds have become the benchmarks by which other players are often judged. Above all, Sonny Rollins is the living embodiment of Thelonious Monk's admonition to "play the melody, not the changes."

what to buy: Rollins appeared on record as early as 1949 (in a Bud Powell–led quintet), and by 1951 he'd laid down tracks as a leader. But it wasn't until 1956, after he had voluntarily entered the Federal Penitentiary in Lexington, Kentucky, in order to kick his drug habit, and subsequently joined the Clifford Brown/Max Roach Quintet, that he truly came into his own. The quartet date with Tommy Flanagan, Doug Watkins, and Roach entitled *Saxophone Colossus* ♫♫♫♫ (Prestige, 1956/OJC, 1987, prod. Bob Weinstock) marked the major breakthrough. Bookended with the brilliant calypso-derived line "St. Thomas" and the masterfully constructed "Blue 7," this was the album that prompted

Gunther Schuller to praise Rollins's "thematic" sense of improvisation—what Martin Williams later dubbed "spontaneous orchestration." Following fast on the heels of *Saxophone Colossus* came the inordinately pleasant and highly humorous *Way Out West* ♫♫♫♫ (Contemporary, 1957/OJC, 1988, prod. Lester Koenig), which matched the newly crowned tenor hero with Ray Brown's steady bass and Shelly Manne's exemplary cool-school drumming. This is where Rollins really began to demonstrate his fondness for off-beat pop and Broadway show tunes, and vaudeville material—*Way Out West* includes "Wagon Wheels" and "I'm an Old Cowhand." Also from 1957, and again in the now-familiar sax-bass-drums trio lineup he pioneered, came *A Night at the Village Vanguard, Vol. 2* ♫♫♫♫ (Blue Note, 1957/1988, prod. Alfred Lion) with bassist Wilbur Ware and drummer Elvin Jones. There are now two complete discs from this encounter on the market, and each is worthy of your attention; Volume 2, with the incendiary reading of "Strivers Row," is the stronger individual set. Then, in 1958, Rollins teamed with bassist Oscar Pettiford and (once again) drummer Max Roach to create *The Freedom Suite* ♫♫♫♫ (Riverside, 1958/OJC, 1994, prod. Orrin Keepnews), which was built around a stunning sidelong meditation on integration (and the lack thereof) in American society. The playing is consistently lovely, and the piece's disparate themes reveal themselves as interconnected parts of a whole. In short, an instant classic. Within a year, however, Rollins had disappeared from the scene; he spent the following months practicing on the pedestrian walkway of the Williamsburg Bridge. When he returned, he delivered what is arguably his most finely balanced recording of all time, *The Bridge* ♫♫♫♫ (RCA, 1961/1996, prod. George Avakian). Distinguished by its deft arrangements, mellow overall tone, and the inclusion of guitarist Jim Hall (bassist Bob Cranshaw and drummer Ben Riley round out the group), *The Bridge* is a nearly perfect album, with the spellbinding "John W." at its center, surrounded by a gorgeous "God Bless the Child," a tuneful "Without a Song," and a sprightly "You Do Something to Me." All of Rollins's RCA recordings from 1962–64 are now on a six-CD set, *The Complete Sonny Rollins RCA Victor Recordings* ♫♫♫♫ (RCA, 1962–64/1997, prod. George Avakian). Similarly, the entirety of his output for Prestige is available on a seven-disc set that includes his appearances as a sideman with Monk, J. J. Johnson, and Art Farmer, *Sonny Rollins: The Complete Prestige Recordings* ♫♫♫♫ (Prestige, 1992, prod. Bob Weinstock). Both of these sets earn their high ratings for the sheer weight of gold they contain.

what to buy next: From his earliest solo recordings in 1951 and up through his last extended "retirement" at the end of the

1960s, there really isn't a bad Sonny Rollins album. Indeed, even his less than uniformly pleasing quarter century with Milestone offers ample proof of his continued saxophonic preeminence. That said, there are better places to go than others. *Sonny Rollins Plus Four* ✧✧✧✧ (Prestige, 1956/OJC, 1987, prod. Bob Weinstock) is the historic Brown/Roach Quintet configuration with Richie Powell and George Morrow in a propulsive program that includes Rollins's "Valse Hot" and the cleverly titled "Pent-Up House." Also from 1956, *Tenor Madness* ✧✧✧✧ (Prestige, 1956/OJC, 1994, prod. Bob Weinstock) is centered around the celebrated 13 minute blues face-off between Rollins and John Coltrane that is more a study in complimentary blowing than a "cutting session." Of the three studio albums he made for Blue Note, it is the last of them, *Newk's Time* ✧✧✧✧ (Blue Note, 1957/1990, prod. Alfred Lion), that is most satisfying, with pianist Wynton Kelly, bassist Doug Watkins, and drummer Philly Joe Jones backing the colossal saxophonist on such oddballs as the smarmy Johnny Mathis–associated "Wonderful! Wonderful!" and "Surrey with the Fringe on Top." ("Newk," by the way, is a Rollins nickname that relates back to his physical resemblance to the Brooklyn Dodgers' pitching star of the early 1950s, Don Newcombe.) The other, earlier, Blue Notes are also interesting. *Sonny Rollins* ✧✧✧✧ (Blue Note, 1956/1988, prod. Alfred Lion) is notable for "Decision," the tune that opens the proceedings on a stutter-stepping foot and anticipates later developments in Hard Bop; also notable are the nearly swing-like strains of "Sonnysphere" that close the album on a nostalgic note. *Sonny Rollins, Volume 2* ✧✧✧✧ (Blue Note, 1957/1988, prod. Alfred Lion), on the other hand, boasts J. J. Johnson, Art Blakey, Paul Chambers, and *both* Horace Silver and Thelonious Monk. Another standout from the RCA period is *On the Outside* ✧✧✧✧ (RCA, 1963, prod. George Avakian), a live recording with Don Cherry, Bob Cranshaw, and Billy Higgins that includes a marathon, 25-minute reading of "Oleo" and stands as Rollins's most affecting flirtation with the "new thing." From his brief time with Impulse!, the inadvertently misleading (it sounds like a boxed set) *Sonny Rollins on Impulse!* ✧✧✧✧ (RCA, 1965/1997, prod. Bob Thiele) builds momentum nicely as it proceeds, and culminates in a stupendous reading of "Three Little Words." The sidemen are Ray Bryant, Walter Booker, and Mickey Roker. The double-disc *Silver City* ✧✧✧✧ (Milestone, 1996, prod. Orrin Keepnews, Sonny Rollins) is a well-programmed retrospective of the Milestone years that includes most of the high points. Its appearance more or less obviates the need to pick and choose among the separate releases that marks this most recent epoch in Rollins's career, but you should keep in mind 1972's *Sonny Rollins' Next Album* ✧✧✧✧ (Milestone, 1972/OJC, 1988,

prod. Orrin Keepnews), the record that marked his return with a stirring "Skylark" that is a marvel of concentrated and muscular invention. *Sunny Days, Starry Nights* ✧✧✧✧ (Milestone, 1984/1987, prod. Sonny Rollins) represents another peak, as does *The Solo Album* ✧✧✧✧ (Milestone, 1985/OJC, 1997, prod. Sonny Rollins), which has just been issued for the first time as a CD.

what to avoid: The critics agree, I'm afraid, that 1976's funky-fusion *The Way I Feel* ✧✧ (Milestone, 1976/OJC, 1991, prod. Orrin Keepnews) isn't very good. In fact, the major gripe against Milestone-era Rollins is the inclusion of electric instruments and solidly "commercial" backdrops. Take, for example, a tune such as "Harlem Boys" off *Don't Ask* ✧✧✧ (Milestone, 1979/OJC, 1996, prod. Orrin Keepnews): Rollins's playing is mesmerizing, for sure, but the bump-n-grind background is stultifying. It may be a lot better than listening to David Sanborn with the *Saturday Night Live* band, but as Miles was wont to say, So What?

the rest:
Sonny Rollins with the Modern Jazz Quartet ✧✧✧ (Prestige, 1951, 1953/OJC, 1988)
Moving Out ✧✧✧✧ (Prestige, 1954/OJC, 1987)
Worktime ✧✧✧✧ (Prestige, 1955/OJC, 1989)
Rollins Plays for Bird ✧✧✧ (Prestige, 1956/OJC, 1989)
The Sound of Sonny ✧✧✧✧ (Riverside, 1957/OJC, 1987)
Sonny Rollins and the Contemporary Leaders ✧✧✧✧ (Contemporary, 1958)
St. Thomas in Stockholm ✧✧✧✧ (DIW, 1959)
(With Coleman Hawkins) Sonny Meets Hawk ✧✧✧✧ (RCA, 1963)
Alfie ✧✧✧✧ (Impulse!, 1966/1997)
East Broadway Run Down ✧✧✧✧ (Impulse!, 1967)
Horn Culture ✧✧✧ (Milestone, 1973/OJC, 1993)
The Cutting Edge ✧✧✧ (Milestone, 1974/1990)
Nucleus ✧✧✧ (Milestone, 1975/OJC, 1991)
Don't Stop the Carnival ✧✧✧ (Milestone, 1978/1989)
Easy Living ✧✧✧✧ (Milestone, 1978/OJC, 1996)
Love at First Sight ✧✧✧ (Milestone, 1980/1992)
No Problem ✧✧✧ (Milestone, 1982)
Reel Life ✧✧✧ (Milestone, 1982)
G Man ✧✧✧ (Milestone, 1987)
Dancing in the Dark ✧✧✧ (Milestone, 1988)
Falling in Love with Jazz ✧✧✧ (Milestone, 1989)
Old Flames ✧✧✧ (Milestone, 1993)
Plus 3 ✧✧✧ (Milestone, 1996)

worth searching for: Among the albums that make up *The Complete RCA Victor* set, some are difficult to find as separates. *The Standard Sonny Rollins* ✧✧✧✧ (RCA, 1964, prod. George Avakian) with Herbie Hancock, Jim Hall, David Izenson,

Cranshaw, and Roker is, despite the annoying and abrupt fade-out endings of several of its cuts, a fine record. *Now's the Time* 𝄞𝄞𝄞♩ (RCA, 1964, prod. George Avakian), with Hancock and Thad Jones among the sidemen, traverses bop standards, as does *Sonny Rollins & Co.* 𝄞𝄞𝄞♩ (Bluebird, 1964, prod. George Avakian). *What's New* 𝄞𝄞𝄞♩ (RCA, 1962, prod. George Avakian) included percussionist Machito and was heavy on the calypso/bossa nova tip.

influences:

◀◀ Charlie Parker, Coleman Hawkins, Dexter Gordon

▶▶ Branford Marsalis, James Carter

David Prince

Wallace Roney

Born May 25, 1960, in Philadelphia, PA.

A talented trumpeter, Wallace Roney spent a large part of his artistically impressionable years as a child prodigy in Washington, D.C., where he attended the Duke Ellington School for the Arts and Howard University before briefly enrolling in Boston's Berklee School of Music. His first major gigs were with Abdullah Ibrahim, Chico Freeman, Art Blakey's Jazz Messengers (where he played alongside Wynton Marsalis), and the Tony Williams Quintet. Roney's use of the muted trumpet and his lean style of playing have caused some critics to draw easy (if somewhat misguided) comparisons with Miles Davis. The appearance of a more substantive relationship was furthered when Roney played in the big band that backed up Davis at the 1991 Montreux Jazz Festival, an event at which the master presented the young man with one of his trumpets. Roney also toured with Tony Williams, Herbie Hancock, and Ron Carter in a Davis tribute band.

what to buy: On *Munchin'* 𝄞𝄞𝄞𝄞♩ (Muse, 1995, prod. Don Sickler), Roney leads a talented young quintet including pianist Geri Allen, bassist Christian McBride, drummer Kenny Washington, and, on five cuts, tenor saxophonist Ravi Coltrane. They whip through a well-chosen batch of bop and post-bop standards that hew closely to the musical growth patterns followed by the young Davis. There are tunes from Charlie Parker, Wayne Shorter, Clifford Brown, and Thelonious Monk, plus classy renditions of Davis classics "Solar" and "Smooch." The playing is assured throughout and the soloing honors their predecessors.

Sonny Rollins (© Jack Vartoogian)

The bulk of *Obsession* 𝄞𝄞𝄞♩ (Muse, 1991, prod. Joe Fields) is given over to original post-bop-oriented compositions from band members Roney, drummer Cindy Blackman, and bassist Christian McBride, with the trumpeter's two offerings, "Seven" and the title tune, taking high honors. Tenor and flute man Gary Thomas plays well, if in a less adventurous manner than he does on his own releases. Underrated pianist Donald Brown provides all the right chords and, when given the opportunity to solo (as on Charlie Parker's "Donna Lee"), proves himself worthy of the tradition. The compilation *According to Mr. Roney* 𝄞𝄞𝄞♩ (Muse, 1987–92/32 Jazz, 1998) blends cuts from *Seth Air* and *Intuition* with two tracks from *Verses*, making this double CD release an admirable, if incomplete, document of Roney's earliest years as a leader for Muse Records. The lineups showcase the trumpeter's fine taste in support musicians with older hands Tony Williams, Mulgrew Miller, and Ron Carter helping Roney in the earlier sessions while (then) young lions Jacky Terrasson, Antoine Roney, and Peter Washington give a different generational spin to the later tunes. While the trumpeter has been deemed a Miles Davis clone by some critics, there is enough evidence herein to reveal that Roney was developing his own voice towards the end of his stay with Muse and before he signed with Warner Bros.

what to buy next: The lush arrangements by Gil Goldstein help put the bulk of *Misterios* 𝄞𝄞𝄞♩ (Warner Bros., 1994, prod. Teo Macero, Matt Pierson) within easy analogy distance of Gil Evans's work with Davis. But Gil is no Gil—despite crafting some wonderful backdrops—and neither are the other arrangers featured here, pianist Allen and Roney himself. The song lineup leans heavily toward South America with one tune from Argentinean tango master Astor Piazzolla and compositions from Brazilians Egberto Gismonti and Danilo Caymi. The playing maintains a deceptively easy-going gait with "Michelle," the John Lennon/Paul McCartney piece, the best showcase for the Davis style (if not the substance).

the rest:

Verses 𝄞𝄞𝄞♩ (Muse, 1987)
Intuition 𝄞𝄞𝄞 (Muse, 1988)
The Standard Bearer 𝄞𝄞𝄞♩ (Muse, 1990)
Seth Air 𝄞𝄞𝄞 (Muse, 1992)
Crunchin' 𝄞𝄞𝄞 (Muse, 1993)
The Wallace Roney Quintet 𝄞𝄞𝄞 (Warner Bros., 1996)
Village 𝄞𝄞𝄞♩ (Warner Bros., 1997)

influences:

◀◀ Miles Davis, Clifford Brown, Lee Morgan, Woody Shaw, Booker Little

▶▶ Wynton Marsalis, Roy Hargrove, Ingrid Jensen

Garaud MacTaggart

The Roots

Formed 1987, in Philadelphia, PA.

Black Thought, vocals; Malik B., vocals; Leonard Hubbard, bass; B.R.O.theR. ?uestion/?uestlove, drums; Rahzel the Godfather of Noyze, vocals, percussion; Kamal, keyboards (1995–present).

Gang Starr's DJ Premiere and A Tribe Called Quest's Ali Shaheed gave hip-hop its first notable jazz infusion via their crafty, swinging samples, and Guru's guest-driven Jazzmatazz project followed by introducing the notion of using actual jazz musicians (instead of samples) behind the MC. It was only a matter of time, then, before a group would emerge playing live, jazz-inspired hip-hop without the help of any hired guns. Though Branford Marsalis's Buckshot LeFonque made a fair attempt, the group was far more bop than hip-hop and didn't really register with the rap nation. The Roots leaned just as far the other way, and for that very reason (along with their chops and vision, of course), they were embraced by those rap fans who had been waiting for somebody to stop talking all that jazz and, instead, just play it. By recording their breakthrough *Do You Want More?!!!??!* without the use of samples or even electronic drum machines, the Roots also didn't promise something on wax that they wouldn't be able to deliver live. In fact, their sweaty, relentless performances and impressive musicality earned them a reputation as one of the best, most dynamic live hip-hop acts of the post-Run-D.M.C. era.

what to buy: *Do You Want More?!!!??!* 𝄞𝄞𝄞𝄞 (DGC, 1995, prod. B.R.O.theR. ?uestion, Black Thought, Rahzel, others) has been hailed by some as one of the more progressive recordings in 1990s rap. But that's not quite right. Although the album is certainly different in its approach (a self-contained hip-hop *band* playing without samples?!), the Roots actually look back for inspiration, employing everything from old-soul Fender Rhodes licks and jazz-funk basslines to old-school vocal interplay on such standouts as "Mellow My Man" and "Proceed." Beatboxer extraordinaire Rahzel takes you way back, too, with his vocal percussion work on the "Show'-y ? vs. Rahzel," although it's actually ?uestion himself who proves to be the star of the lyrically positive album with his taut beats and vast vocabulary.

what to buy next: The newly renamed ?uestlove apparently lost his thesaurus before recording the Roots's followup, *Illadelph Halflife* 𝄞𝄞𝄞 (DGC, 1996, prod. ?uestlove, others), as

the album features a narrower range of beats and fills. Samples enter the mix, too, as do guest MCs (Bahamadia, Common, Q-Tip), but the most notable new addition here is the dark tone of the lyrics, which are already bracing for the new millennium. For all the talk about the group's fusing of jazz and hip-hop, the most stunning element of either Roots album actually comes on this record's "Concerto of the Desperado," with Amel Larrieux suddenly in your *aria*.

worth searching for: The Roots call their self-released 1993 debut *Organix* a demo, but the recording is more than just a rough introduction. Although available as a bootleg on the Internet, the album may be reissued in 1998.

influences:

◀◀ Stetsasonic, D.J. Jazzy Jeff & the Fresh Prince, Schoolly D, Sha-Key, Gang Starr/Jazzmatazz, A Tribe Called Quest

▶▶ Erykah Badu, Boogie Monsters, Bahamadia

Josh Freedom du Lac

Michele Rosewoman

Born 1953, in Oakland, CA.

Rosewoman is best known for her quintet, Quintessence, the personnel of which is different on each of its three albums. She is a pianist of lightning reflexes and considerable imagination. Her occasional vocals are never better than adequate, however; but they are significant in that they show her contemporary pop leanings—on her live album, *Spirit*, she sings the Earth, Wind & Fire song of that title. Her style is a mix of post-bop, Latin jazz, some slight African influences, touches of the avant-garde, and—mostly with Quintessence—the akimbo rhythmic accents of the M-Base school.

Rosewoman started playing at age six, and from age 17 studied with pianist Ed Kelly, an Oakland hometown hero who has recorded with Pharoah Sanders. She also had lessons in percussion with Marcus Gordon, in Cuban folkloric music with Orlando "Puntilla" Rios, and in voice with Joyce Bryant. Rosewoman's association with members of the Black Artists Group and the Association for the Advancement of Creative Music prompted her to move to New York in 1978; her New York debut came with Oliver Lake at Carnegie Recital Hall. She has recorded with Billy Bang (the *Rainbow Gladiator* album), Ralph Peterson (*Art*), and Greg Osby (*Greg Osby and Sound Theatre*). Her big band, New Yor-Uba, to which she has devoted considerable time, has not yet been recorded.

what to buy: On *Occasion to Rise* 🎵🎵🎵🎵 (Evidence, 1993, prod. Michele Rosewoman) Rosewoman delivers a fiery trio session, displaying a lively, percussive piano approach that makes for exciting listening. Drummer Ralph Peterson exhibits considerable flair, prodding from under and above, locked with bassist Rufus Reid on this evenly divided session of ten straight-ahead standards and vivid originals. Rosewoman is a powerful player, displaying fertile ideas, uncommon phrasing, and astounding technique. Although she does justice to Ellington's "Prelude to a Kiss" (in solo sitting), Coltrane's "Lazy Bird," Lee Morgan's "Nite Flite," and other standards, Rosewoman's originals are among the most fetching tunes. With her talented teammates she thrashes through "The Sweet Eye of Hurricane Sally," brandishes a highly percussive modern approach on both the title tune and "Eee-Yaa," and finishes the set with "West Africa," a syncopated funk-beat blend that spotlights Peterson.

what to buy next: *Quintessence* 🎵🎵🎵 (Enja, 1989, prod. Matthias Winckelmann) features M-Base initiators Steve Coleman and Greg Osby sharing the frontline on alto sax, with Anthony Cox on bass and Terri Lyne Carrington, perhaps the most sympathetic drummer Rosewoman has worked with. The quirky rhythmic feel of the horns tends to dominate the music, lending the excitement of constant small surprises, and the long-standing collaboration between Coleman and Osby makes them quite effective in tandem. Rosewoman's vigorous playing slips into some avant-garde gestures at times, reminding us of her familiarity with musical contexts that have not been documented on her recordings.

the rest:
The Source 🎵🎵🎵 (Soul Note, 1984)
(With Quintessence) *Harvest* 🎵🎵🎵 (Enja, 1993)
Spirit 🎵🎵🎵 (Blue Note, 1996)

worth searching for: The out-of-print *Contrast High* 🎵🎵🎵 (Enja, 1989, prod. Michele Rosewoman) has a lineup of Quintessence with Greg Osby (alto and soprano sax) and Gary Thomas (tenor sax and flute), bassist Lonnie Plaxico, and drummer Cecil Brooks III. The M-Base rhythms shade into straightforward funk at moments, and Brooks is a much busier drummer than Carrington (or almost any drummer, for that matter); the hyperactivity of the beats can wear thin after a while. But Rosewoman's program of originals contains some striking themes (the Latin waltz "Panambula," for instance, which doesn't include the horns) and nicely voiced arrangements. Her playing is superb throughout.

influences:

◀◀ Herbie Hancock, McCoy Tyner, Thelonious Monk, Chick Corea

▶▶ Geri Allen, Junko Onishi

Steve Holtje and Nancy Ann Lee

Renee Rosnes

Born 1962, in Regina, Saskatchewan, Canada.

A compelling hard-bop pianist, Renee Rosnes was classically trained, starting on the piano at three. She later received formal training in classical performance at the University of Toronto. In the early 1980s she led her own trio in Canada, and occasionally accompanied Dave Liebman and the late Joe Farrell. She moved to New York in 1986 and gained international attention playing with Joe Henderson. Rosnes was signed to Blue Note in 1990, releasing her eponymous debut album and performing with the short-lived group of then promising, young, Blue Note all-stars, Out of the Blue. She also worked with Wayne Shorter, J.J. Johnson, James Moody, Jon Faddis, and Buster Williams. She has also performed and recorded with Native Colours, a quartet led by Billy Drummond.

Rosnes has won several awards, including three Junos (the Canadian equivalent of the Grammy) and been the subject of a CBC (Canadian Broadcasting Company) documentary. Rosnes is also a member of the Jon Faddis–led Carnegie Hall Jazz Band and the Lincoln Center Jazz Orchestra directed by Wynton Marsalis. A respected player, she has released four recordings as a leader, but only the fantastic *Ancestors* is still available in the United States. She's rightfully earned the reputation as excellent player and is becoming an important jazz voice.

what to buy: *Ancestors* 🎵🎵🎵🎵 (Blue Note, 1996, prod. Bob Belden) is an inspired recording rooted in the 1960s bop tradition that shouldn't be missed. Rosnes's playing and compositions are what shine throughout. And part of the credit for this release must go to her sidemen, trumpeter Nicholas Payton, saxophonist Chris Potter, bassist Peter Washington, drummer Al Foster, and percussionist Don Alias, who perform exceptionally well here. If you need convincing that Rosnes is a major player on the jazz scene, this potent date should be more than persuasive.

best of the rest:
As We Are Now 🎵🎵🎵 (Blue Note, 1997)

worth searching for: Rosnes's earliest recordings are currently out of print. *Without Words* 🎵🎵🎵 (Blue Note, 1992, prod. various) highlights Rosnes's trio featuring Buster Williams and Billy Drummond. They cover nine standards with strings accompaniment arranged by Robert Freedman. For the most part *Without Words* avoids the pitfalls of these types of recordings as Freedman is tasteful and owes much to Claus Ogerman. As for Rosnes, her good playing is romantic and sometimes reminiscent of a less technical Oscar Peterson in the same setting. *For the Moment* 𝄞𝄞𝄞 (Blue Note, 1990), a Juno award–winning release, has Joe Henderson providing his sax, and obviously some guidance on seven songs. Rosnes's group tackles standards like "Four in One" and a number of originals. But, it is the standout track "Summer Night" with stellar performances by Henderson and Rosnes that pushes this into the worth seeking category.

influences:

◀◀ Herbie Hancock, Bud Powell, Oscar Peterson, Bill Evans, Wynton Kelly

Paul MacArthur and Nancy Ann Lee

Annie Ross

Born Annabelle Short Lynch, July 25, 1930, in Surrey, England.

Although Annie Ross is best known for her work with the famed vocalese trio, Lambert, Hendricks & Ross, she has achieved numerous accomplishments on her own through the years. As a child, after moving to Los Angeles with her aunt, Ella Logan, Ross appeared professionally as both a singer and an actress. She appeared in Our Gang Follies of 1938, a Little Rascals short film, and in 1942, played Judy Garland's younger sister in the film *Presenting Lily Mars.* When Ross was 16, she attended the American Academy of Dramatic Arts, but because she had problems getting along with her aunt, Ross returned to England, settling in London. In 1952, Ross moved back to the United States and recorded for the first time as a leader. She had written sharp-witted, zany words to "Twisted," the Wardell Gray tune, fitting her words to his saxophone solo. Ross had also written clever lyrics to Art Farmer's composition "Farmer's Market" and Hampton Hawes's "Jackie." The recording that included these tunes created somewhat of a stir in the jazz world. She returned to Europe with Lionel Hampton's Band in 1953 and came back to New York in 1957 to work in a cabaret room called the Upstairs at the Downstairs. In 1958 Ross joined Lambert and Hendricks to form the brilliant vocal trio that would set a standard and continue, even today, to influence jazz vocal groups. While Ross worked as part of the trio, she also recorded three exceptional solo albums that demonstrated her impeccable phrasing, her ability to swing and improvise, and her wide vocal range. In 1962, the trio parted ways, and Ross returned to England, continuing to perform as an actress and singer. During the past few years, Ross has been splitting her time between New York and London, and occasionally performs as a solo act. In 1994 Ross had an acting role as a nightclub singer in the critically acclaimed Robert Altman film *Short Cuts.* She recorded in 1995, and in October 1996 appeared at Birdland in New York City for a week. The following spring she appeared at Carnegie Hall. Although Ross no longer has the range she once had, her diction, phrasing, and delivery are flawless. She continues to swing and perform with style and grace.

what to buy: *Sings a Song of Mulligan* 𝄞𝄞𝄞𝄞 (Pacific/Capitol, 1958, prod. Richard Bock) finds Ross in peak form. She interacts well with the musicians, using her voice as an instrumentalist would. In a style that never stops swinging, Ross displays her versatility, unique phrasing, and amazing range. *A Gasser!* 𝄞𝄞𝄞𝄞 (Pacific Jazz, 1959/Capitol, 1988, prod. Richard Bock) finds Ross improvising at her best with saxophonist Zoot Sims. A brilliant recording.

what to buy next: *Skylark* 𝄞𝄞𝄞 (Pye Recording, 1956/DRG, 1996) compiles recordings from two sessions in 1956, *Annie by Candlelight* and *Nocturne for a Vocalist.* The quartet includes Tony Crombie, Bob Burns, Roy Plummer, and Lennie Rush.

the rest:

Gypsy 𝄞𝄞𝄞 (Pacific, 1959/Capitol, 1995)
Sings a Handful of Songs 𝄞𝄞𝄞 (DCC, 1989/1996)
Music Is Forever 𝄞𝄞𝄞 (DRG, 1996)

influences:

◀◀ Eddie Jefferson, King Pleasure

▶▶ Amy London, Bonnie Sanders

see also: *Lambert, Hendricks & Ross*

Susan K. Berlowitz

Ned Rothenberg

Born September 15, 1956, in Boston, MA.

Virtuoso wind player Ned Rothenberg's playing successfully bridges the worlds of twentieth-century avant-garde composition and jazz-based improvisation via a highly personalized, idiosyncratic approach to reeds and shakuhachi (Japanese end-blown flute). This is not music for the casual listener; with its focus on microscopic detail and extended technique, Rothenberg's music is cerebral in the best sense of the word—challenging, provocative, and ear-expanding—and amply rewards attentive listening.

Rothenberg honed his skills in the late 1970s with Anthony Braxton, appearing on the monumental *Creative Orchestra*. Moving to New York, he became involved with the downtown jazz/new music/no wave crossover scene, notably as a member of the trio Semantics with drummer Samm Bennett and multi-instrumentalist Elliott Sharp. Since then he has worked with a host of collaborators from the fields of jazz, free improvisation, modern classical, and world music, establishing himself as one of the foremost practitioners of his instruments.

Rothenberg's explorations of microtones and the extreme ranges of his instruments are foregrounded in intimate settings, such as his duets with Tuvan overtone singer Sainkho and his New Winds trio with fellow innovators Robert Dick and J.D. Parran. His compositional acumen is showcased in larger ensembles like the all-star nonet Powerlines and the Ned Rothenberg Double Band, the latter of which finds him in unusually funky territory reminiscent of the work of Brooklyn's M-Base players.

what to buy: *Powerlines* 🎵🎵🎵 (New World Countercurrents, 1995, prod. Marty Ehrlich) is the most easily found of Rothenberg's efforts as a leader, and one of his best. Rothenberg's arrangements take full advantage of the broad range of instrumental timbres available from the large ensemble of Rothenberg (alto sax, bass clarinet), Mark Feldman (violin), Ruth Siegler (viola, violin), Erik Friedlander (cello), Mark Dresser (bass), Mike Sarin (drums), Dave Douglas (trumpet), Josh Roseman (trombone), Kenny Berger (baritone sax, bass clarinet), and, on two of the five lengthy tracks, Glen Velez (frame drums). Stylistically, Rothenberg's compositions range from tightly composed contrasts between the opposed sounds of the strings and the horns to loose, rowdy improvising over vamps that build up unstoppably.

what to buy next: You know what you're getting on *The Crux* 🎵🎵🎵 (Leo, 1993, prod. Ned Rothenberg, Marty Ehrlich) by the subtitle: solo wind works 1989–92. Rothenberg plays alto sax on four tracks, bass clarinet on two, and shakuhachi on one. The varied subtleties of his phrasing and inflection combine with his imaginative, often surprising lines to place this album high in the rarified ranks of solo wind recitals.

best of the rest:

(With Paul Dresher) *Opposites Attract* 🎵🎵🎵 (New World Countercurrents, 1991)

(With Steve Lacy, Roy Nathanson, Eric Sleichem) *Antonyms* 🎵🎵🎵 (Sub Rosa, 1994)

(With Sainkho Namchylak) *Amulet* 🎵🎵🎵 (Leo, 1996)

New Winds:

The Cliff 🎵🎵🎵 (SoundAspects, 1989)

Traction 🎵🎵🎵 (Sound Aspects, 1991)

Digging It Harder from Afar 🎵🎵🎵 (Victo, 1994)

Potion 🎵🎵🎵 (Victo, 1998)

worth searching for: The two albums by the Ned Rothenberg Double Band are on a German label and may take some effort to track down, but they are definitely worth the time. *Overlays* 🎵🎵🎵 (Moers Music, 1993, prod. Ned Rothenberg) uses matched trios of alto saxists Rothenberg and Thomas Chapin, electric bassists Jerome Harris (doubling on guitar) and Kermit Driscoll, and drummers Billy Martin (traps) and Adam Rudolph (congas, electric drums). The dark textures and interweaving lines are sometimes lyrical and usually funky. *Real and Imagined Time* 🎵🎵🎵 (Moers Music, 1995, prod. Ned Rothenberg) substitutes Chris Wood for Driscoll and Jim Black (traps) for Rudolph, with Rothenberg and Chapin both doubling on flute (Chapin adds soprano sax as well). The different timbres Rudolph brought are missed a bit, but otherwise this is nearly as good as its predecessor. These CDs can most reliably be obtained through Downtown Music Gallery: dmg@panix.com or (212) 473-0043.

influences:

◀◀ Evan Parker, Anthony Braxton

▶▶ Robert Dick, John Butcher, Wolfgang Fuchs

Dennis Rea and Steve Holtje

Charlie Rouse

Born Charles Rouse, April 6, 1924, in Washington, DC. Died November 30, 1988, in Seattle, WA.

Few sidemen have as close an association with their leader as tenor saxophonist Charlie Rouse had with Thelonious Monk. For more than a decade, Rouse augmented Monk's tricky tunes with a brand of bop that both understated and expanded what the iconoclastic composer was trying to say; and yet he remained his own man, recording frequently before, during, and after his time with Monk and owing only a little stylistically to his longtime employer.

Rouse started out in his early 20s with stints in Billy Eckstine's and Dizzy Gillespie's bands, which gave him a healthy dose of the classic bebop style, which he further explored while working with Tadd Dameron and Fats Navarro. However, a few years later he went in a whole other direction when he was hired to replace his idol, Ben Webster, in Duke Ellington's band in 1949. A missing birth certificate, however, prevented Rouse from acquiring a passport to tour Europe, thus ending his Ellington gig. He easily found other work, though, playing with Count Basie, Clifford Brown, Bennie Green, and Oscar Pettiford. During the late '50s he teamed up with French horn player Julius Watkins to form the group Les Jazz Modes. They were picked up by Atlantic Records in 1957 after a few releases on the small independent Dawn label, but were given such iffy material (songs from the musical *The Most Happy Fella*—ouch!) that interest in the group waned. Thankfully, Rouse's next major project would be long-lasting and an absolute musical classic: serving as second-hand man in Monk's quartet. Rouse took to Monk's music so readily because it allowed him to use both his bop and Ellington experience at the same time, mixing improvisational wit with unusually tuneful melodies. Their collaboration lasted from 1959 to 1970, including many essential recordings for both Riverside and Columbia. Beginning in 1960, Rouse would occasionally make his own records, many of which feature neither Monk compositions nor even Monkish playing; consequently, these recordings clearly demonstrate Rouse's own identifiable style. Yet, it is initially shocking to hear him play with a more traditional pianist. Ultimately, it is Rouse's connection with Monk for which he will be forever remembered, and he was always eager to celebrate the man he played with for so many years. In 1980, along with Kenny Barron, Buster Williams, and former Monk drummer Ben Riley, Rouse formed the group Sphere, initially as a Monk tribute band, although they eventually included originals and other standards in their repertoire, including an album's worth of Charlie Parker tunes. And three of Rouse's final projects exemplify the connection he had with Monk's music: first, a duet with the ultimate Monk cheerleader, Steve Lacy, on "Ask Me Now," included as part of producer Hal Willner's 1984 Monk tribute collection *That's the Way I Feel Now*; second, his participation on Carmen McRae's beautiful 1988 set *Carmen Sings Monk*; and finally, performing as guest of honor at a posthumous Monk birthday celebration (released on CD as *Epistrophy*) just weeks before his own death from lung cancer in 1988.

Rouse played a derivation of hard bop that featured a restraint unusual for most tenor players at the time. Never relying on speed, he soloed with patience and deliberation, careful to never lose sight of the melody. He was fully capable of cooking on the up-tempo tunes, as well as offering up breathy, rich sounds on ballads. All of these traits, along with a rhythmic savviness and overall consistency, made Rouse such a valuable contributor to Monk's quartets.

what to buy: *Thelonious Monk: Criss-Cross* ♫♫♫♫ (Columbia, 1963, prod. Teo Macero), Monk's second album for Columbia, is a good example of what Rouse contributed to Monk's music,

particularly on tracks like "Rhythm-A-Ning," "Hackensack," and the title cut. On *Sphere: Bird Songs* ♫♫♫♫ (Verve, 1988, prod. Joanne Klein, Sphere), Rouse and his '80s group, Sphere, perform exclusively Parker-related compositions, and in this unfamiliar light Rouse shines.

what to buy next: *Takin' Care of Business* ♫♫♫♫ (Jazzland, 1960, prod. Orrin Keepnews) is Rouse's first set as a leader, and he establishes himself as a player in his own right; Blue Mitchell's contributions on trumpet add to the festivities; *Les Jazz Modes* ♫♫♫♫ (Biograph, 1995, prod. Arnold S. Caplin), a two-disc reissue set of the rare Dawn sessions of Rouse's pairing with French Horn player Julius Watkins, transcends the unusualness of the arrangements, except when the irritating soprano starts singing.

the rest:
Unsung Hero ♫♫♫ (Epic, 1960/1961)
Two Is One ♫♫♫ (Strata-East, 1974)
Cinnamon Flower ♫♫ (Casablanca, 1977)
Moment's Notice ♫♫♫ (Storyville, 1978)
The Upper Manhattan Jazz Society ♫♫♫ (Enja, 1981)
(With Sphere) *Four in One* ♫♫♫♫ (Elektra Musician, 1982)
(With Sphere) *Flight Path* ♫♫♫♫ (Elektra Musician, 1983)
Social Call ♫♫♫♫ (Uptown, 1984)
(With Sphere) *Pumpkins Delight* ♫♫♫♫ (Red, 1986)
(With Sphere) *Sphere* ♫♫♫ (Verve, 1987)
(With Sphere) *On Tour* ♫♫♫♫ (Red, 1987)
(With Sphere) *Live at the Umbria Jazz* ♫♫♫♫ (Red, 1988)
Epistrophy ♫♫♫♫ (Landmark, 1989/32 Jazz, 1997)
(With Sphere) *Four for All* ♫♫♫♫ (PolyGram, 1990)

influences:

◀◀ Ben Webster, Wayne Shorter, Thelonious Monk, Charlie Parker

▶▶ Paul Jeffrey

Eric J. Lawrence

Rova Saxophone Quartet /Figure 8

Formed 1977, in San Francisco, CA.

Jon Raskin, saxophone; Larry Ochs, saxophone; Andrew Voight, saxophone (1977–88); Bruce Ackley, saxophone; Steve Adams, saxophone (1988–present).

Arguably the most significant jazz/new-music group in the Bay Area, Rova has been merging conceptual sophistication with passionate vitality for two decades. Since 1978 the band has recorded original compositions, specially commissioned works by other composers like John Carter and Tim Berne, and interpretations of material by experimental-music leaders like Terry Riley and Alvin Curran. Recipients of numerous grants, Rova has performed all over the world, seamlessly integrating closed (composed) and open (improv) forms. Bruce Ackley calls their work a "particularly American hybrid" that encompasses the full jazz tradition (minus overworked bebop), various approaches to the blues, the declaration and power of hard rock, the rhythmic-speech quality of rap, and 20th century classical languages of composers like Xenakis, Stockhausen, and Cage. The group revels in constant metamorphoses of structure, rhythm, timbre, tempo, volume, and spellbinding melody. Although the saxophonists sometimes blow with collision-course intensity, they've been known to temper the uproar with iridescent pianissimo passages. Much to the delight of adventurous music seekers, they also employ a wide range of fascinating techniques to trigger their improvisation, including unpredictable aggregates of rapid-fire polyphony, player-conducted game pieces using cue cards, and numerous other collage methods. At times, the group expands the quartet configuration to an octet (see Figure 8's *Pipe Dreams*) or a larger ensemble (as on *John Coltrane's Ascension* and Larry Ochs's *The Secret Magritte*). They've also recorded with Anthony Braxton (*The Aggregate*), Evan Parker (*The Social Set*), and Henry Kaiser (*Daredevils*). A dozen or so of the band's early vinyl sides are long out of print, but hard-to-find albums like *Invisible Frames*, *This, This, This, This*, or the debut, *Cinema Rovate*, are worth checking out. Rova celebrated its 20th anniversary with a special showcase at the prestigious San Francisco Jazz Festival in 1997.

what to buy: *Saxophone Diplomacy* 🎷🎷🎷🎷 (hat ART, 1991, prod. Eva Soltes, Larry Ochs) is an impressive document of Rova's historic tour of Russia, Latvia, and Romania in 1983. Ochs has said the group's intention was "to become diplomats with a message not being conveyed by the U.S. government" under Reagan's regime. The energy is high and positive. *The Crowd* 🎷🎷🎷🎷 (hat ART, 1992, prod. Pia Uehlinger, Werner X. Uehlinger) is *the* Rova album to get if you want to hear otherworldly beauty and power. A collective composition originally commissioned in 1982 by John Adams for the San Francisco Symphony's New & Unusual Music concert series, *The Crowd* underwent a momentous transformational process before it was recorded in 1985. In the liner notes accompanying *From the Bureau of Both* 🎷🎷🎷🎷 (Black Saint, 1993, prod. Rova Saxophone Quartet), the noted author of *In the Moment* and *Outcats,* Francis Davis, puts this stunning work, and all of Rova's achievements, into clear focus: "Is it jazz? For the sake of jazz,

let's hope so." Terry Riley's *Chanting the Light of Foresight* 🎷🎷🎷🎷 (New Albion, 1994, prod. Rova Saxophone Quartet) is an extraordinary display of determination, skill, and vision. Rova spent almost six years mastering the altered tunings mandated by Riley's score (including what Ochs calls "false fingerings, jaw manipulations, superhuman lungs, and lips of steel") to bring about this major work.

what to buy next: On *Long on Logic* 🎷🎷🎷🎷 (Sound Aspects, 1990, prod. Rova Saxophone Quartet), interpreting compositions by Fred Frith, Henry Kaiser, and the Rova crew, the group brings Frith's wry sense of playfulness to the title track. The tune "Song and Dance" comes across with a unique minstrel-like vibe. *Beat Kennel* 🎷🎷🎷🎷 (Black Saint, 1987, prod. Giovanni Bonandrini), the conclusion of a cycle of overt "jazz"-related investigations (which began with the Steve Lacy homage, *Favorite Street*), is one of Rova's punchiest discs. It includes an Anthony Braxton piece whose title cannot be transcribed on a word processor. *The Works (Volume I)* 🎷🎷🎷🎷 (Black Saint, 1995, prod. Rova Saxophone Quartet) consists of three extended compositions by John Carter, Jack DeJohnette, and Larry Ochs; *The Works (Volume II)* 🎷🎷🎷🎷 (Black Saint, 1997) includes pieces by Tim Berne, Fred Ho, and Jon Raskin. *This Time We Are Both* 🎷🎷🎷🎷 (New Albion, 1991, prod. Rova Saxophone Quartet) documents the group's second venture to Russia and its neighboring countries, recorded in 1989.

the rest:
Rova Plays Lacy—Favorite Street 🎷🎷🎷🎷 (Black Saint, 1984)
(With Anthony Braxton) *The Aggregate* 🎷🎷🎷🎷 (Sound Aspects, 1989)
(With Alvin Curran) *Electric Rags II* 🎷🎷🎷🎷 (New Albion, 1990)
(With Figure 8) *Pipe Dreams* 🎷🎷🎷🎷 (Black Saint, 1994)
John Coltrane's Ascension 🎷🎷🎷🎷 (Black Saint, 1996)
Ptow!! 🎷🎷🎷🎷 (Victo, 1996)

worth searching for: *Invisible Frames* 🎷🎷🎷🎷 (Fore, 1982), *As Was* 🎷🎷🎷🎷 (Metalanguage, 1981, prod. Rova Saxophone Quartet), *This, This, This, This* 🎷🎷🎷🎷 (Moers, 1980, prod. Rova Saxophone Quartet), *The Removal of Secrecy* 🎷🎷🎷🎷 (Metalanguage, 1979, prod. Rova Saxophone Quartet), and *Cinema Rovate* 🎷🎷🎷🎷 (Metalanguage, 1978, prod. Rova Saxophone Quartet) are all hard to find at mainstream record stores. You'll have to dig for them—but it'll be worth it.

solo outings:
Larry Ochs:
The Secret Magritte 🎷🎷🎷🎷 (Black Saint, 1995)

influences:
◀◀ Anthony Braxton, Steve Lacy, Xenakis, Varese

▶▶ Your Neighborhood Saxophone Quartet, Great Circle Saxophone Quartet

Sam Prestianni

Dennis Rowland

Born in Detroit, MI.

Dennis Rowland is a worthy heir to the vocal tradition of Joe Williams and Bill Henderson, a fine blues singer who can also handle standards and ballads with considerable style. His recording career got off to a late start, however, after he spent seven years touring with the Count Basie Orchestra. Surrounded by music as he was growing up, Rowland began singing around Detroit in the mid-'70s. He got his big break in 1977 when Basie hired him; Rowland toured with the band until Basie's death in 1984. But Rowland only appeared on one of Basie's many recordings from this period, contributing two vocals to the 1980 Pablo release *On the Road*. In the mid-'80s, Rowland settled in Phoenix and pursued a career in acting, appearing in a wide range of stage productions. He has released three strong albums for Concord, moving easily between jazz, urban pop, and R&B.

what to buy: A standout among the profusion of tributes released since Miles Davis's death, *Now Dig This!* 𝄞𝄞𝄞𝄞 (Concord Jazz, 1997, prod. Gregg Field) has Rowland covering tunes associated with the late trumpeter, including Oscar Brown Jr.'s version of "All Blues," a mid-tempo version of "I Could Write a Book," and a medley of "The Meaning of the Blues" and J.J. Johnson's "Lament," recreating the seamless feel of the *Miles Ahead* album. With Davis disciples Wallace Roney and Sal Marquez contributing solos and Joe Sample's supple piano work, Rowland's third album on Concord is his best yet.

what to buy next: Rowland's debut, *Rhyme, Rhythm & Reason* 𝄞𝄞𝄞𝄞 (Concord Jazz, 1995, prod. Gregg Field), is the work of an experienced veteran who knows his way around a lyric. His versions of Percy Mayfield's "Please Send Me Someone to Love" and Ida Cox's "Wild Women (Don't Have the Blues)" show his deep blues feeling, while "I'm Afraid the Masquerade Is Over" and "I'm Just a Lucky So and So" (with some expert plunger mute work by Snooky Young) were adapted from Eric Dixon's original Basie charts. Rowland's ballad work on "Your Blase" and "Angel Eyes" is also exemplary.

the rest:
Get Here 𝄞𝄞𝄞 (Concord Jazz, 1996)

worth searching for: Count Basie's *On the Road* 𝄞𝄞𝄞𝄞 (Pablo, 1980, prod. Norman Granz) features Rowland's vocals on two numbers.

influences:
◀◀ Joe Williams, Earl Coleman, Bill Henderson, Count Basie

Andrew Gilbert

Gonzalo Rubalcaba

Born May 27, 1963, in Havana, Cuba.

A graduate of Havana's Institute of Fine Arts, Gonzalo Rubalcaba studied classical piano and played with a wide variety of Cuban musical heroes, including Beny More, the Orquesta Aragon, Irakere, and members of Los Van Van. His talent ensured patronage from such renowned countrymen as Paquito D'Rivera and Chucho Valdes. Rubalcaba formed his own band, Grupo Proyecto, in 1985, then met one of his formidable influences, trumpeter Dizzy Gillespie. Another key figure in bringing Rubalcaba to the awareness of American jazz fans was bassist Charlie Haden, who met the pianist in 1986. Impressed by the young pianist's abilities, Haden arranged for him to perform at jazz festivals in Montreal and Montreux. Because of the lack of normal diplomatic relations between Cuba and the U.S., Rubalcaba was effectively blocked from performing in American jazz venues until 1993, when his American musical allies successfully lobbied the State Department to allow him into the country (technically as a resident of the Dominican Republic). Until then, all of the pianist's recordings were for the Cuban label Egrem. Rubalcaba's music blends a European classical technique with Cuban rhythms like the montuno and the cha-cha without neglecting the post-bop developments of Thelonious Monk, Herbie Hancock, and McCoy Tyner. In addition to his own albums, Rubalcaba has also appeared on releases by Katia Labeque, Ron Carter, Issac Delgado, and Jane Bunnett.

what to buy: The trio date *Diz* 𝄞𝄞𝄞𝄞 (Blue Note, 1994, prod. Gonzalo Rubalcaba) is an homage to trumpeter Dizzy Gillespie, with a playlist of bop-era classics written by Gillespie, Charlie Parker, and others. In addition to the flashing digits of Rubalcaba, there are the formidable talents of his regular drummer, Julio Barreto, and the great bassist Ron Carter. Barreto, in particular, provides a flexible, flashy, driving rhythm that pushes his better-known compatriots to play at their peak. *The Blessing* 𝄞𝄞𝄞𝄞 (Blue Note, 1991, prod. Gonzalo Rubalcaba) features the superb Charlie Haden on bass and Jack DeJohnette on drums; Rubalcaba has a quicksilver technique that nonetheless makes speed subservient to the art. The cover tunes, including the peculiarly effective arrangment of Bill Evans's "Blue in Green," are well chosen, as are the originals.

what to buy next: *Rhapsodia* ♫♫♫ (Blue Note, 1994, prod. Gonzalo Rubalcaba) was nominated for a Grammy award in 1994. It features Rubalcaba's normal quartet in a stunning performance, including wizardly drumming from Julio Barreto and fine trumpet work from Reynaldo Melian. The pianist dives briefly into the fusion bag he was dabbling in with Grupo Proyecto, but the acoustic stuff makes the album strong. The duet album *Flying Colors* ♫♫♫ (Blue Note, 1998, prod. Joe Lovano) has saxophonist Joe Lovano getting top billing on the cover, but Rubalcaba is more than just an accompanist and deserves equal status here. The tone here is more avant-garde oriented than anything either musician has done under his own name, but it is the kind of adventurous playing that always returns to a tonal center somewhere in the tune (even if it is only for a nanosecond). Rubalcaba does his Cecil-Taylor-goes-Latin riffs in "Boss Town" before joining Lovano in an interesting lockstep to the end. The two also engage in some challenging echo play in "Bird Food," and their take on "Hot House" engages in serious exterior decorating on the bones of the melodic structure.

the rest:
Live in Havana ♫♫♫ (Messidor, 1986)
Mi Gran Pasion ♫♫♫♫ (Messidor, 1987)
Giraldilla ♫♫♫ (Messidor, 1989)
Discovery: Live at Montreux ♫♫♫ (Blue Note, 1991)
Images ♫♫♫ (Blue Note, 1992)
Suite 4 y 20 ♫♫♫ (Blue Note, 1993)
Concatenacion ♫♫♫ (Melopea, 1995)
Imagine ♫♫♫ (Blue Note, 1996)
Best of Gonzalo Rubalcaba ♫♫♫ (Milan/Latino, 1997)

worth searching for: Various artists pay homage to the brilliant Brazilian songwriter on *Antonio Carlos Jobim & Friends* ♫♫♫♫ (Verve, 1996, prod. Oscar Castro-Neves, Richard Seidel). Rubalcaba's performance of "Agua De Beber" is outstanding and garnered another Grammy nomination in 1997.

influences:

◄◄ Dizzy Gillespie, Chick Corea, Thelonious Monk, Herbie Hancock, McCoy Tyner, Chucho Valdes

►► D.D. Jackson

Garaud MacTaggart

Vanessa Rubin

Born 1958, in Cleveland, OH.

Like many of the pop/jazz singers who dominated the charts in the late 1940s and early 1950s, Vanessa Rubin is blessed with a beautiful, rich voice and she can swing effectively, but tends to stick close to a song's melody rather than improvise. At times her sound is reminiscent of a young Ernestine Anderson, though without as deep a feeling for the blues. Her first training was in the Western classical tradition and she later started working in jazz settings, singing at Cleveland nightspots with the Blackshaw Brothers organ combo and the Cleveland Jazz All-Stars, featuring Kenny Davis and Ernie Krivda. She moved to New York in 1982 and worked with top-flight pianists such as Kenny Barron, John Hicks, Stanley Cowell, Harold Mabern, and Norman Simmons, and performed with the big bands of Lionel Hampton and Mercer Ellington and Frank Foster's Loud Minority. She has recorded a number of fine albums for Novus.

what to buy: Vanessa Rubin is shown to advantage on *Pastiche* ♫♫♫♫ (Novus, 1993, prod. Vanessa Rubin, Onaje Allan Gumbs), a well-produced session covering standards and jazz compositions such as Wayne Shorter's "Black Nile" and Cedar Walton's "Mosaic." Backed by a flexible rhythm section and a top-notch horn section featuring Steve Turre and trumpeter E.J. Allen, Rubin makes the most of the supportive arrangements, singing with unaffected emotion. Highlights include the bass/vocal duet on "I Only Have Eyes for You" and the swinging, mid-tempo arrangement featuring her subtle interplay with Allen's trumpet on "In a Sentimental Mood." *Soul Eyes* ♫♫♫♫ (Novus, 1992, prod. Onaje Allan Gumbs) is an impressive debut recording by a singer still coming into her own. Backed by a stellar rhythm section featuring Kirk Lightsey (piano), Cecil McBee (bass), and Lewis Nash (drums), and tasteful arrangements by Onaje Allen Gumbs, Rubin interprets a program of standards and jazz tunes. Her soulful, nuanced approach to lyrics serves her well, especially on the Kern/Mercer chestnut "Dearly Beloved," and "Tenderly," a lovely tribute to Sarah Vaughan.

what to buy next: A strange but enjoyable album, *I'm Glad There Is You* ♫♫♫♫ (Novus, 1994, prod. Cecil Bridgewater, Vanessa Rubin) is a tribute to Carmen McRae, though Rubin sounds almost nothing like her and most of the tunes are more strongly associated with Sarah Vaughan. Still, Ruben sings with power and style, scatting effectively on "Yardbird Suite" and introducing a song that should become a standard, "No Strings Attached." A host of guest stars, such as Frank Foster, Kenny

Burrell, Antonio Hart, and Monty Alexander, contribute to the session, but Rubin's voice deservedly holds center stage.

the rest:
Vanessa Rubin Sings ♪♪♪♪ (Novus, 1995)
New Horizons ♪♪♪ (BMG, 1997)

influences:
◀◀ Sarah Vaughan, Nancy Wilson, Ernestine Anderson

Andrew Gilbert

Roswell Rudd

Born November 17, 1935, in Sharon, CT.

Trombonist Rudd began his career in the second half of the 1950s playing in New Orleans/Chicago-style traditional jazz bands. His switch to the avant-garde in the 1960s in some ways was a complete about-face, yet listening to his raucous, overblown tone and spontaneity amid the collective improvisation of free jazz helped perceptive listeners realize the parallels between the two styles. Rudd worked with the underappreciated, nearly legendary pianist Herbie Nichols and then with soprano saxophonist Steve Lacy (another player with a foot in each stylistic camp) and pianist Cecil Taylor (Rudd can be heard on Taylor's *Jumpin' Punkins* and *New York City R&B*). In 1964 Rudd's playing became more radical in the New York Art Quartet, a seminal free jazz group extending the new ideas of ill-fated tenor saxophonist Albert Ayler, with whom Rudd also played. In the second half of the decade Rudd formed an association with tenor saxophonist Archie Shepp (documented on *Mama Too Tight*, *Live in San Francisco*, and more). Other memorable collaborations followed with, among others, Carla Bley, Gato Barbieri, Charlie Haden, and Enrico Rava. He gradually concentrated more on teaching and now lives in upstate New York, only rarely venturing from home for recording sessions and concerts.

what to buy: The Steve Lacy/Roswell Rudd Quartet's *School Days* ♪♪♪♪♪ (hat ART, 1995) contains a 1963 club recording where the soprano saxman and trombonist are joined by fellow incipient modernists Henry Grimes (bass) and Dennis Charles (drums). Pursuing their fascination with Thelonious Monk's compositions in a working band with an all-Monk program, they're very faithful to Monk's heads and structures. They even solo on the changes, though they do indulge their individual tendencies—Rudd raucous and blowzy, Lacy intricate and rapier-like, Grimes exploding notes in pursuit of new timbres. None of the seven tunes—"Bye-Ya," "Brilliant Corners," "Monk's Dream,"

"Monk's Mood," "Ba-Lue Bolivar Ba-Lues-Are," "Skippy," and "Pannonica"—are obvious choices; even three decades later, with Monk's writing deemed sacred canon, only the third and last are much played. The band clearly prefers Monk's subtler creations, which Lacy and Rudd sculpt with carefully shaded performances that mix Monk's angular bebop with modernist tonal colorings and the Dixieland they were schooled in. The frontmen sometimes add spicy counterpoint behind each others' solos, and Charles shows himself to be an excellent bop drummer in the Roy Haynes mode, shadowing their every move. It's especially delightful to hear them trading fours, cooperatively rather than competitively. Lovingly crafted, this is Rudd's most accessible work and a good place to start understanding his style. More crucial to Rudd's personal legacy, though not under his name, are two albums on ESP. Sometimes credited to Albert Ayler, *New York Ear and Eye Control* ♪♪♪♪ (ESP, 1966) is an odd, shambling soundtrack to an art film of the same title. Ayler (tenor sax), Rudd, trumpeter Don Cherry, alto saxophonist John Tchicai, bassist Gary Peacock, and drummer Sunny Murray play some of the freest free jazz ever committed to record, and despite its faults it's often a moving experience. Following in the wake of Ayler's redefinition of free jazz, *New York Art Quartet* ♪♪♪♪ (ESP, 1965) has Rudd, Tchicai, bassist Lewis Worrell, and drummer Milford Graves (plus poet Leroi Jones, later known as Amiri Baraka) offering a somewhat subtler variation on his techniques that is nearly as powerful and offers more variety.

what to buy next: *Regeneration* ♪♪♪♪ (Soul Note, 1983, prod. Giovanni Bonandrini) is credited in unwieldy fashion to Roswell Rudd, Steve Lacy, Misha Mengelberg, Kent Carter, and Han Bennink. Probably the first Herbie Nichols tribute (Rudd played with Nichols in the early 1960s) takes up half this album, while the other half is devoted to Monk tunes. Rudd's broad smears, Lacy's pointed lines, Bennink's nearly parodistic beats, and Mengelberg's versatile comping and startling solos (like a cross between Monk, Bud Powell, and Cecil Taylor) mix humor and affection with serious appreciation. Rudd has also made two loose trio albums, the two volumes of *The Unheard Herbie Nichols* ♪♪♪♪ (CIMP, 1997, prod. Robert D. Rusch). Consisting of Nichols tunes the pianist himself didn't record (mostly written after 1957), the project is of obvious value even if the arrangements for trombone, electric guitar (Greg Millar), and drums (John Bacon Jr.) take them very far from Nichols's sound-world. These albums are closer, however, to Rudd's earthy style.

worth searching for: Rudd is all over the 1981 Monk tribute concert documented on the four-CD set *Interpretations of Monk* ♪♪♪♪ (DIW, 1994, prod. Verna Gillis) (reissued in two parts by Koch in 1997 and 1998). Noted Monkians Rudd, Lacy, and Charlie Rouse appear on all four separate sets led respectively by pianists Muhal Richard Abrams, Anthony Davis, Barry Harris, and Mal Waldron, with Richard Davis on bass and drummers Ed Blackwell and Ben Riley playing two sets each. Though the idioms change from pianist to pianist, all concerned reinterpret Monk's legacy respectfully and challengingly, and Rudd's rowdy playing features prominently. The trombonist's non-tribute work is shamefully underrepresented currently, and some out-of-print LPs need to be sought out for a more complete view. *Everywhere* ♫♫♫ (Impulse!, 1966, prod. Bob Thiele, Roswell Rudd) is not ideally recorded (there are muddy passages) but mixes some relatively swinging tracks (including trombonist Bill Harris's title track) with totally out-there free jazz of the most intense sort on the Rudd originals. Robin Kenyatta (alto sax) and Giuseppi Logan (flute, bass clarinet) distinguish themselves in prominent moments, with Lewis Worrell (bass), Charlie Haden (bass), and Beaver Harris (drums) making an appropriately supportive racket. *Roswell Rudd* ♫♫♫♫ (America) is solidly avant-garde, with Rudd and John Tchicai (alto sax) rollicking through the originals and treating "Pannonica" to a lovely reading. Finn von Eyben (bass) and Louis Moholo (drums) fill out the quartet.

influences:

◀◀ Kid Ory, Thelonious Monk, Herbie Nichols

▶▶ Ray Anderson, Joe Fielder

Steve Holtje

Adam Rudolph

Born September 12, 1955, in Chicago, IL.

Rudolph is a world-music drummer who often works in jazz-related contexts. His most famous jazz associations have been with Yusef Lateef (eight albums), Don Cherry, Herbie Hancock, and Kevin Eubanks, and his most jazz-oriented project as a leader, with his group Moving Pictures, appeared on Soul Note. He specializes in hand drums—congas, djembe, bendir, dumbek, tabla, talking drum, udu—but also plays bamboo flutes, kalimba, didjeridoo, and synthesizers, and multiphonic singing also ranks among his talents. He draws on music literally from around the world (Bali, Cuba, Ghana, Haiti, India, and Morocco), assimilating it with the open-mindedness he absorbed from the AACM artists who were part of his formative musical experiences in his hometown of Chicago. He lived in Ghana in 1977 and later spent time with the Gnawa musicians of Morocco, as has pianist Randy Weston. Another major com-

ROSWELL RUDD
(WITH ARCHIE SHEPP)

song "Syeeda's Song Flute"

album *Four for Trane*
(Impulse!, 1964/1997)

instrument Trombone

Monster Solo

ponent in his style was his study of North Indian tabla drums with Ravi Shankar's tabla player, Pandit Taranath Rao. Rather than playing in imitation of the styles he studies, however, Rudolph synthesizes them into a cross-cultural melting pot that has a jazz/improvising sensibility at its base.

Rudolph's other groups include the percussion quintet Vashti, with Chicago jazz drummer Hamid Drake, Poovalur Srinivasan (South India), Souhael Kaspar (Egypt), and I Nyomen Wenten (Bali), and the Mandingo Griot Society (co-founded with Jali Foday Musa Suso), which blends traditional African music with R&B and jazz. Moving Pictures uses a variable lineup that has included guitarists Wah Wah Watson and Kevin Eubanks, double violinist L. Shankar, harpist Susan Allen, multi-windplayer Ralph Jones III, and many others, and overlaps somewhat with another Rudolph band, Eternal Wind.

what to buy: Recorded with Yusef Lateef, *The World at Peace: Music for 12 Musicians* ♫♫♫♫ (YAL & Meta, 1996, prod. Yusef Lateef, Adam Rudolph) is a two-CD dual release on Lateef's and

Rudolph's labels. It is a major work full of innovative writing that so far is the crowning achievement of Rudolph's career, its high ambition matched by its unfailing achievement. Rudolph and Lateef use unusual compositional processes that include splitting the parts of a given piece between the two composers, who then write independently and put the two halves together after the fact. Lateef was one of the pioneers of the multi-culturalism Rudolph has built his sound around, and this compositional method produces not clashes but rather complementary cogs in meshing wheels. There are more normally composed pieces as well on a CD that brings jazz, blues, and world music together in a gloriously coherent whole. A number of musicians from Moving Pictures are included in the ensemble, with Ralph Jones and trumpeter Charles Moore making especially valuable contributions and Lateef excelling like the venerable master he is.

what to buy next: Credited to Rudolph's Moving Pictures band, *Skyway* &&&& (Soul Note, 1994, prod. Adam Rudolph) includes Jones, Allen, Eubanks, and multi-instrumentalist Jihad Racy on ney and salamiyyah (reed flutes), oud (Arabic lute), kaman (Arabic violin), mijwiz (double clarinet), and rababah (Egyptian fiddle). The sheer variety of timbres, textures, and rhythms is a delight, but there is nothing cut-and-paste about the way it all comes together; the music seems to grow organically, with a pervading feeling of ritual throughout the project.

the rest:

(With Hassan Hakmoun and Don Cherry) *Gift of the Gnawa* &&&& (Flying Fish, 1991)

Adam Rudolph's Moving Pictures &&& (Flying Fish, 1992)

Contemplations &&& (Meta, 1997)

worth searching for: *The Dreamer* &&&& (Meta, 1995, prod. Adam Rudolph) was Rudolph's first release on his Meta label, and uses Moore, guitarist G.E. Stinson, Allen, violinist Jeff Gauthier, Jones, vocalist Kimball Wheeler, narrator Robert Wisdom, and Rudolph's young daughter Hannah on vocals. It's an opera of sorts, and comes as part of a gorgeous package with 12 paintings accompanying texts (inspired by Nietzsche and Schopenhauer) by Nancy Jackson, with each musical piece matched to a painting. Perhaps because the 32-page spiral booklet is nearly the size of two CDs laid top-to-bottom, and thus an awkward size for chain-store bins, it may be easiest to obtain by ordering it directly from Rudolph through his website, www.metarecords.com, where his other Meta releases are available as well. The suite, as one might guess from its title, often has the floating quality of a dream. The music's more composed nature and the texture of Rudolph's synthesizers

and Gauthier's violin combine with Wheeler's classically trained singing to project a more formal feeling than Rudolph's other recordings.

influences:

◀◀ Don Cherry, Yusef Lateef, Fred Anderson, Malawi Nurdurdin, Charles Moore, Pandit Taranath Rao

▶▶ Kevin Eubanks, Hassan Hakmoun

Steve Holtje

Kermit Ruffins

Trumpeter Kermit Ruffins is heavily influenced by Louis Armstrong, both in his trumpet playing and vocals. Like Armstrong, Ruffins got much of his early experience playing on the streets of New Orleans. His mother gave him his first trumpet when he was in eighth grade, and Ruffins's taste for traditional jazz was nurtured from age 15 when he saw his first New Orleans–styled jazz funeral. A series of events led to a 1984 album featuring Ruffins with the ReBirth Brass Band, a romping New Orleans–styled band that he helped to shape in 1983 with Philip and Keith Frazier (tuba and bass drum, respectively) and Keith Anderson (trombone). After a few albums with ReBirth, Ruffins amicably split with the touring band and has been concentrating on his solo career, though he guested on ReBirth's 1994 album. Ruffins has developed into a talented bandleader, writer, singer, and performer. After leaving ReBirth, he formed the Barbecue Swingers, was signed to a solo deal by Justice Records, and has since released three CDs. His Justice contract has been fulfilled and he has opted not to continue with the label.

Ruffins shows a willingness to grow and experiment, which he displays in his live performances in the Crescent City clubs; he is assisted by an array of compatriots on the bandstand, including professionals such as Wessell "Warmdaddy" Anderson, jazz guitarist Mark Whitfield, drummer Herlin Riley, even Wynton Marsalis and University of New Orleans music students. Ruffins also hosts Sunday afternoon jazz jams in his beloved Treme neighborhood, where friends, family, and fans of all ages and backgrounds come to listen. He is also experimenting with the Kermit Ruffins Big Band, a 17- to 20-piece ensemble. Comprised of popular homegrown brass band musicians and up-and-coming modern jazz players, this group performs mostly BBQ Swingers material and other standards. Considering his previous contributions to New Orleans music, one would not expect Ruffins to stagnate. His popularity has increased over his 14 years as a professional musician, and he has appeared as a sideman on albums with the Treme Brass Band, Maceo Parker, and others. Ruffins seems bound to continue pleasing crowds with his upbeat ideas and innovations.

what to buy: Ruffins's debut as leader on Justice Records, *World on a String* 🎵🎵🎵 (Justice, 1992, prod. Randall Hage Jamail) is suggestive of Louis Armstrong, yet the young trumpeter engages listeners with his own unique blowing and singing style on the album's 11 tunes. His trumpet sound is open, brash, and sometimes smoothly muted, and his gravelly vocalizing is mirthful as he revives traditional swing standards such as "Honey Chile," "I've Got the World on a String," "When It's Sleepy Time Down South," and other classics and originals. Pianist Ellis Marsalis (patriarch of that famous musical New Orleans family) heads up a sterling rhythm section with Walter Payton on bass and Shannon Powell on drums. One of the best tracks is Marsalis's duo with Ruffins (on vocals) on the title tune. Guest soloists include Crescent City musicians Doreen Ketchens (clarinet), Lucien Barbarin (trombone), Danny Barker (banjo), and Anthony "Tuba Fats" Lacen (tuba), who come together to perk up the leader's original New Orleans mummer's march, "Kermit's Second Line," and the trad swinger "When My Dreamboat Comes Home." Ruffins can turn on a dime from rousing numbers such as these to sweet, muted or open trumpet solos in a quintet setting (rhythm section and Barbarin) on the ballad "Georgia on My Mind." This is a promising, foot-tapping debut that showcases Ruffins's extensive artistry. His third release as leader, *Hold on Tight* 🎵🎵🎵 (Justice, 1996, prod. Delfeayo Marsalis, Kermit Ruffins), is a 13-tune collection that conveys excitement similar to his inaugural album, and features a solid rhythm team with Victor "Red" Atkins or Walter Lewis on piano, bassist Kevin Morris, and drummer Shannon Powell. This team inspires Ruffins to some of his best playing and singing, especially on the perky version of "Ding Dong the Witch Is Dead" (from the 1939 *Wizard of Oz* film), which also contains a fine solo from ReBirth saxophonist Roderick Paulin. Ruffins's charming original, "Whistlin' Love Birds," receives equal treatment, and everyone shines on the swinger "After You've Gone." With the various ensemble sizes, the guesting New Orleans musicians (including trombonist Corey Henry and veteran pianist-vocalist Walter Lewis), this album is lots of lighthearted fun.

what to buy next: *Big Butter & Egg Man* 🎵🎵🎵 (Justice, 1994, prod. Randall Hage Jamail), Ruffin's second Justice release, features the leader with a totally different team from his debut, but with similar instrumentation. While this outing mostly swings, the rhythm team (Dwight Fitch, piano; Kevin Morris, bass; Jerry Anderson, drums) is not as hardy and cohesive as on *World on a String* or Ruffins's subsequent album, *Hold on*

Tight. Featured musicians included Philip Frazier (tuba) and Corey Henry (trombone). Ruffins sings on six tunes, including the seemingly out of place "Besame Mucho." Best are traditional gems such as Armstrong's "Struttin' with Some Barbecue," containing some of Ruffins's finest trumpet renderings, and the lively New Orleans street beats of "Li'l Liza Jane." Four original tunes underscore Ruffins's burgeoning skills as composer and lyricist, "I'll Drink Ta Dat," "Out of Left Field," "The Undertaker Man," and "Leshianne." This album also establishes that Ruffins has laudable chops for straight-ahead jazz, as he shows in the quintet setting (with saxophonist Roderick Paulin) on his harmonically and rhythmically enticing post-bop original, "Out of Left Field," and the hip, grooving sextet version of Duke Ellington's upbeat "West Indies Jazz Dance," with Ruffins leading Messenger-like front-line horns. While this album has its high points, Ruffins tries to cover a lot of territory and tends to break up the flow and energy and the communal spirit, as well. Yet this album demonstrates the musician's growth, especially as composer and modern improvisor.

best of the rest:

(With ReBirth Brass Band) *Feel Like Funkin' It Up* 🎵🎵🎵 (Rounder, 1989)
(With ReBirth Brass Band) *Kickin' It Live* 🎵🎵🎵 (Rounder, 1991)
(With ReBirth Brass Band) *Take It to the Street* 🎵🎵🎵 (Rounder, 1992)

worth searching for: Check out Kermit Ruffins fronting the ReBirth Brass Band on *Rollin'* 🎵🎵🎵 (Rounder Records, 1994, prod. Keith Keller). Recorded at the end of their 10th year together, this album features the Rebirth Brass Band playing eight raucous, explosive tunes melding jazz, pop, reggae, and traditional New Orleans jazz styles. An outrageously boisterous group with a tuba pumping out underlying dancebeats, ReBirth sometimes sounds like Lester Bowie's Brass Fantasy band and early on introduced Michael Jackson tunes into the repertoire. Yet ReBirth puts its own second-line spin on the brash and brassy tunes, rollin' music that the band originally played in street parades. Everybody is really "on" and Ruffins is prominently featured.

influences:

⏮ Louis Armstrong

see also: *The ReBirth Brass Band*

Nancy Ann Lee

Hilton Ruiz

Born May 29, 1952, in New York, NY.

Hilton Ruiz was something of a child prodigy, appearing on a local New York television show, performing at Carnegie Recital

Hall at the age of eight, and playing in an accordion symphony at nine. He studied classical piano as well as Latin, and received jazz guidance from the late Mary Lou Williams and Cedar Walton. By his early teens, Ruiz was working with a variety of Latin soul bands and, at age 14, recorded with a group called Ray Jay and the East Siders. Before he was 20, Ruiz had worked with Frank Foster, Joe Newman, Cal Massey, Freddie Hubbard, and Joe Henderson—an impressive list for an established player, a truly remarkable list for a relative newcomer. As an adult, Ruiz has also worked and recorded with Rahsann Roland Kirk, Pharoah Sanders, and Charles Mingus. Today, Hilton likes to call himself the original bebop Latin pianist, but he is much more. His own recordings have touched all bases—from straight-ahead funk to Latin soul—in part reflecting a peripatetic lifestyle that has taken him on tours to virtually every part of the world.

what's available: Hilton Ruiz is a pianist/composer with impeccable jazz credentials and, on *Island Eyes* ♫♫♫♫ (Island/RMM Records, 1997, prod. Jack Hooke), he successfully finds room in his music for a vigorous Latin taste without sacrificing its rhythmic and improvisational urgency. With a band that includes some of New York's finest players in both genres, including Tito Puente and Jon Faddis, he gives new life to standards like "Gee Baby Ain't I Good to You," which features John Stubblefield's gutsy tenor and Ruiz on a funky organ, and Sam Jones's "Unit 7," a facile demonstration of bebop with a Hispanic twist. The title track recalls Rollins's "St. Thomas," with Stubblefield's energetic tenor taking no prisoners. Jelly Roll Morton once said that all good jazz had to have a "Latin tinge," a rhythmic twist that added a visceral edge to the straight-ahead jazz groove. On *Hands on Percussion* ♫♫♫♫ (Island/RMM Records, 1995, prod. Jack Hooke) Hilton Ruiz proves Morton right on this 1995 session, where the leader is joined by a group of players who are adept in any genre. Ruiz's "Salute to Eddie," an homage to the great pianist Eddie Palmieri, his "Blues for Cos," dedicated to a certain Mr. Cosby, and his take on "'Round Midnight," feature his cerebral Afro-Caribbean approach, with tasteful percussiveness and melodic invention as hallmarks. Ruiz is an artist of uncommon sensitivity and deep soul, and at the keyboard he cooks, cajoles, and conquers! A collaboration with rising tenor saxman David Sanchez, *Heroes* ♫♫♫♫ (Telarc, 1994, prod. John Snyder) finds Ruiz more laid back, but he loses none of his intensity. Hancock's "Maiden Voyage," Monk's "'Round Midnight," and Parker's "Little Suede Shoes" honor Ruiz's musical heroes. The session is easy-flowing and fun, with Sanchez's tenor providing more than its share of excitement. An ambitious session that finds Ruiz at the helm of a nonet

(three horns and six rhythm), *Manhattan Mambo* ♫♫♫♫ (Telarc, 1992, prod. John Snyder) covers the spectrum of the classic jazz/Latin concord. From mambos à la Perez Prado to Latin versions of Coltrane's "Impressions" and Horace Silver's "Home Cookin'," Ruiz again shows how he can dazzle with his rhythmic and melodic invention. Solos throughout by trumpeter Charlie Sepulveda, trombonist Papo Vazquz, and tenorman David Sanchez enliven the proceedings as well.

worth searching for: Joined by the stellar Buster Williams and Billy Higgins (bass and drums), Hilton Ruiz's debut as leader, *Piano Man* ♫♫♫♫ (SteepleChase, 1995, prod. Nils Winther), demonstrates his profound understanding of the spectrum of Hispanic music and jazz, from samba to clave to bebop, and this is reflected both in his writing and improvisations. Coltrane's "Giant Steps" and "Straight Street" are absolute gems that perfectly illustrate how the fusion of jazz and Latin music can be successful without compromise.

influences:

◄◄ Bud Powell, Art Tatum, Herbie Hancock, Mary Lou Williams, McCoy Tyner, Thelonious Monk

►► Cal Tjader, Charlie Palmieri, Clare Fischer, Eddie Palmieri, Jorge Dalto, Larry Harlow, Michel Camilo, Sonny Bravo

Bret Primack

Jimmy Rushing

Born August 26, 1903, in Oklahoma City, OK. Died June 8, 1972, in New York, NY.

With his clear, strong voice and note-bending style, Jimmy Rushing, known universally as "Mr. Five by Five" for his rotund physique, helped set the standard for blues-inflected Kansas City vocals, but he always preferred jazz to blues. Although he made his living as a pianist in his early years, he concentrated mostly on singing throughout his career. As a teenager, Rushing traveled throughout the Midwest, singing what has become "classic blues" at churches and occasional parties. Rushing first gained notice around 1927 when touring the Southwest and recording with Walter Page's Blue Devils. After a stint with Bennie Moten's band, Rushing became primary vocalist with the Count Basie Orchestra from 1935 to around 1950, singing Basie swing classics such as "Boogie-Woogie" and "Evenin'," and novelty tunes such as "Did You See Jackie Robinson Hit That Ball." When Basie reduced the size of his band around 1950, Rushing eventually struck out on his own leading a band that included Buck Clayton and Dicky Wells. Although he reunited occasionally with the Basie Orchestra (including an appearance at the 1957 Newport Jazz Festival), Rushing freelanced from the 1950s on, recording a series of popular recordings for John Hammond during the 1950s and 1960s, and singing his blues around the country. During the 1960s Rushing was also busy working with bands led by Harry James, Benny Goodman, and Eddie Condon, and recording with Dave Brubeck, Earl Hines, and small groups organized with former Basie sidemen. During the 1950s Rushing appeared in a couple of film documentaries about jazz and had a minor singing and acting role in the 1969 film *The Learning Tree,* about a young African American growing up in Kansas City. Rushing died of leukemia in 1972.

what to buy: Although the most essential Rushing collection would extensively sample the singer's years with the Count Basie Orchestra, *The Essential Jimmy Rushing* ΔΔΔΔ (Vanguard, 1978/1990, prod. John Hammond) is a fine document of Rushing's mid-1950s solo material reissued from a two-LP set (except for two omitted tunes). Rushing recreates a mixture blues and gleeful Kansas City swing standards, including classics such as "Going to Chicago" and "Every Day I Have the Blues," performed with backing from former Basie-ites and swing stars such as tenor saxophonist Buddy Tate, trombonists Lawrence Brown and Vic Dickenson, trumpeter Emmett Barry, drummer Jo Jones, pianist Pete Johnson, guitarist Freddie Greene, and others.

best of the rest:

Gee, Baby, Ain't I Good to You ΔΔΔ (Master Jazz, 1968/New World, 1998)

The You and Me That Used to Be ΔΔΔ (RCA/Bluebird, 1971/1988)

Mister Five by Five ΔΔΔ (Columbia, 1980/Topaz Jazz, 1996)

worth searching for: Rushing is featured on *Count Basie: The Complete Decca Recordings (1937–1939)* ΔΔΔΔ (Decca/GRP-Decca Jazz, 1992, prod. Orrin Keepnews), a three-disc set that magnificently documents the Basie band's first New York recordings from 1937 through 1939. The band's tremendous sense of swing and the soloists' bristling creativity is constantly in evidence; Rushing's work is brilliant, as are the instrumental solos by saxophonists Lester Young and Hershel Evans, trumpeter Buck Clayton, and trombonists Benny Morton and Dickie Wells.

influences:

◀◀ Count Basie, Duke Ellington, Louis Armstrong, Billie Holiday, Bessie Smith

▶▶ Jimmy Witherspoon, Big Joe Turner, Louis Jordan, Dinah Washington

Steve Knopper and Nancy Ann Lee

George Russell

Born June 23, 1923, in Cincinnati, OH.

Composer/pianist George Russell's 1950s theorizing, published in successive editions of *The Lydian Chromatic Concept of Tonal Organization* and hailed as a major contribution to music theory, laid the groundwork for the shift from chord changes to the simpler modal motifs exemplified by Miles Davis's *Kind of Blue* and John Coltrane's *A Love Supreme,* to cite only two high points from a virtual school of jazz writing. But for Russell, rather than a road to outward simplicity, the study of scalar possibilities was a tool for piling on and combining elements for a new kind of complexity, a rather contrary effect in the end. Russell's earliest efforts were recorded by others (his first modal composition remains his most famous: "Cubana Be/Cubana Bop," introduced by Dizzy Gillespie in 1947). His first sessions in the mid-1950s roped in collaborators such as pianist Bill Evans and trumpeter Art Farmer, and early in the 1960s he could call on trumpeter Don Ellis and reedman Eric Dolphy in groups in which Russell took over piano duties himself. ("If I was going to have a group, I had to do something in it," said the newcomer to the keys.) In 1964, he moved to Europe for five years, making his influence felt in Scandinavia, in particular. The arrival of fusion more or less coincided with his exploration of "vertical forms," which layer contrasting motions and textures (think of layers of African percussion). These can be ponderous and fussy at the same time, but at their best can provide a valuable musical experience. The son of a college band instructor, Russell had Fats Waller among the circle of family friends and Jimmy Mundy (an arranger for Benny Goodman) as a neighbor. He first entered jazz as a drummer, but two lengthy sanitarium stays sidetracked him, forcing on him distance and perspective that quite likely aided his quantum reach for a grand musical scheme. His life came full circle in a sense with his own involvement in musical education: since 1969 he has been on the staff of the New England Conservatory. In 1989 he became one of a handful of jazz recipients of the MacArthur Foundation Award, commonly referred to as "the genius grant." In 1995, a London *Times* headline hailed a visit from this "Structuralist of free form."

what to buy: In lieu of an anthology representing the range of Russell's work, make do with the 1977–78 live recordings on *New York Big Band* ΔΔΔΔ (Soul Note, 1977–78/1994, prod. George Russell). Actually the work of two separate first-rate bands, the Swedish Radio Jazz Orchestra, under Russell's direction, renders a surging "Cubana Be/Cubana Bop," with Sabu Martinez supplying the Afro-Cuban kick that Chano Pozo gave the original. The band that Russell led at New York's Village Vanguard handles the rest, delivering such highs as a gospelized take on Russell's 1959 "Big City Blues." Pianist Stanley Cowell, bassist Cameron Brown, and saxophonist Ricky Ford all turn in exemplary solos on various cuts. *New York, N.Y.* ♪♪♪♪ (Decca, 1959/MCA, 1990) is a catchy, late 1950s Russell big band date with pianist Bill Evans and saxophonist John Coltrane turning in more than interesting solos. Jon Hendricks recites a love poem to the Big Apple, putting him in the ranks of the proto-rappers. This recording marked the debut of "Big City Blues," so deservedly revived nearly 20 years later.

what to buy next: Eric Dolphy's fire is one of the elements that nail *Ezz-thetics* ♪♪♪♪ (OJC, 1961/1994, prod. Orrin Keepnews) as the first purchase among Russell's four superior 1960–62 Riverside dates, studio documents of his first working group. Complementing trumpeter Don Ellis and trombonist Dave Baker, alto saxophonist–bass clarinetist Dolphy gave Russell a full horn section of musicians not only at home in his musical world but with abundant chops and ideas to contribute. Too bad this lineup lasted only a single session, the third of the four. But while the next in the series, *The Outer View* ♪♪♪♪ (OJC, 1962/1994, prod. Orrin Keepnews), loses Dolphy and Baker, it boasts an arguably more memorable set of compositions and arrangements, including the suite-like "D.C. Divertimento" (with its touches of Stravinsky) and Russell's unforgettable take on the traditional "You Are My Sunshine." Once heard, the latter's mix of plaintive folk essence (the recording debut for vocalist Sheila Jordan) and modernist flourishes is impossible to forget. A superior Russell fusion date, *Electronic for Souls Loved by Nature—1980* ♪♪♪♪ (Soul Note, 1993, prod. Giovanni Bonandrini) uses a backdrop of electronic and pre-recorded textures for a sextet exploring Russell's vertical forms. Russell is a master at using these massive blocks of sound to build excitement.

what to avoid: The anti-war/anti-imperialist *Listen to the Silence* ♪♪ (Soul Note, 1994, prod. George Russell) is a jazz mass of admirable intent but decidedly uneven effect.

best of the rest:
Stratus Seekers ♪♪♪♪ (OJC, 1962/1989)
Stratusphunk ♪♪♪♪ (OJC, 1962/1995)
The African Game ♪♪♪♪ (Blue Note, 1985/1997)
London Concert, Vols. 1 and 2 ♪♪♪♪ (Stash, 1993)
Vertical Forms VI ♪♪♪♪ (Soul Note, 1994)

worth searching for: *The George Russell Smalltet* ♪♪♪♪ (Bluebird, 1987, prod. Jack Lewis, Fred Reynolds) is a 1956 celebra-

tion of Russell's busy brilliance, his debut as a session leader. Trumpeter Art Farmer and pianist Bill Evans are in excellent form in the combo. *New York, N.Y./Jazz in the Space Age* ♪♪♪♪ (MCA, 1973, prod. Milton Gabler) is a vinyl two-fer that includes the above mentioned *New York, N.Y.* and the 1960 *Space Age* session. Russell said the former summed up his music to date, while the latter mapped his future. Twinned pianists Evans and Paul Bley on two cuts exemplify the forward-looking touches on *Space Age*. Trumpeter Don Cherry is the guest at a 1966 concert, *The George Russell Sextet at Beethoven Hall* ♪♪♪♪ (Saba, 1965, prod. Joachim Berendt), which features Russell's Lydian theory transformations of "Bags' Groove," "Confirmation," and "'Round Midnight." Cherry cooks in particular on "Bags' Groove."

influences:

◄◄ Dizzy Gillespie, Charlie Parker, Charles Mingus, Lester Young, Coleman Hawkins

►► Carla Bley, Steve Swallow, John Coltrane, Bill Evans, Don Ellis, Miles Davis, Jan Garbarek, Palle Mikkelorg, Terje Rypdal

W. Kim Heron

Hal Russell

Born Harold Luttenbacher, August 26, 1926, in Detroit, MI. Died September 5, 1992, in Chicago, IL.

With a career in jazz that went from big band to free jazz, Hal Russell became one of the oldest dogs with some of the newest tricks around. Originally a drummer, Russell started playing professionally during WWII with touring big bands like Woody Herman's, performing a half-dozen sets a day interspersed with all kinds of dance acts, comedians, and movies on vaudeville bills. After the rise of Bird and Diz, Russell became immersed in bop, and he could be found drumming with all of the modern jazz greats at one point or another—he even backed Billie Holiday in a group with Miles Davis. By the early 1960s, after grappling with drug addiction, Russell found employment as a lounge drummer, working with all kinds of variety stars, from Barbra Streisand to Woody Allen. Still, a progressive pulse pounded in Russell's heart, and in the early 1960s Russell drummed with the Joe Daley Quartet. Their foray into free-jazz can be heard on *Newport '63* if you're lucky enough to find it. Daley returned to the world of bop, but Russell kept his free-jazz freak flag flying, becoming more interested in both composing his own tunes and stretching the limits of improvisation. Russell must have had patience by the truckload, because most of his 1970s were spent in Chicago, auditioning members for the NRG Ensemble. Even when the ensemble got off the ground, it was a decade before semblances of success began to arrive. It was worth the wait, however, and his formation of NRG, in hindsight at least, can be seen as quite a significant event in the history of creative music in America. Within a year of the formation of NRG, Russell began to focus on the sax as his axe of choice, rather than drums. Still, he remained versatile and open minded enough to be able to play a variety of instruments, and if a 50-year-old sax novice could do it, you'd better believe that his younger bandmates were expected to serve double-time on various instruments as well. Obviously, a lot of work went into NRG, but even when the Ensemble hit it big, or at least bigger than they had ever been, Russell always found the time not only to participate in a bunch of auxiliary units, but to teach and guide all sorts of younger musicians, from thrashers and rockers to gospel groups. When he died at the age of 66 in 1992, the jazz world lost a vital, unique personality. Fortunately, his acolytes continue to promote his visionary free jazz ideals.

what's available: An amazing solo disc, *Hal's Bells* 𝄞𝄞𝄞𝄞 (ECM, 1993, prod. Steve Lake) isn't a live one-man freak out. Rather, Russell concocted this baby in the studio, overdubbing all of the parts himself, from tenor and soprano saxes to drums and congas. Fifty years in jazz shows off, and his humor is still ever-present, as on the track "Kenny G," wherein a poker-faced Russell pays tribute to the man who brought back the soprano saxophone. The Hal Russell/Joel Futterman Quartet's *Naked Colours* 𝄞𝄞𝄞𝄞 (Silkheart, 1993) gives a rare opportunity to hear Russell in a non-NRG group, and also with a group that features piano (a rarity in the Russell catalog). Russell may have left his Chicago compatriots behind for this date, but he sure didn't leave behind his propensity for going over the top.

worth searching for: Probably the best non-NRG record to demonstrate what Hal Russell was all about is *Destructo Noise Explosion* 𝄞𝄞𝄞𝄞 (ugExplode, 1996), which was Russell's only public performance with the Flying Luttenbachers. Recorded at Northwestern University's WNUR studios on June 2, 1992, Russell shares the free jazz limelight with drummer Weasel Walter and saxophonist Chad Organ in a ramshackle ruckus where two 20-year-olds and a senior citizen create one of the great unknown free-jazz forty-five minutes of the 1990s. Originals by Walter and Russell get equal time, while Ayler tunes and music from *The Edge of Night* get bum-rushed with a punk-jazz fervor. Though Russell left the Luttenbachers on less-than-friendly terms, Walter continued the aggressive, humorous, and flip

free-jazz with several other Flying Luttenbachers lineups. Nowadays the Flying Luttenbachers carry on with Walter, an electric guitarist, and an electric bassist, and they are heavily influenced by New York No Wave and Scandinavian death metal(!). Too bad Russell isn't still around to join in the fracas—he'd surely continue to serve as an inspiration to players a third his age.

influences:

◀◀ Gene Krupa, Albert Ayler

▶▶ NRG Ensemble, Mars Williams, Ken Vandermark, Weasel Walter

see also: *NRG Ensemble*

Greg Baise

Pee Wee Russell

Born Charles Ellsworth Russell, March 27, 1906, in St. Louis, MO. Died February 15, 1969, in Alexandria, VA.

Relatively few recordings were released under clarinetist Pee Wee Russell's name in his lifetime, but his career was long and particularly fruitful. He played with early jazz legend Bix Beiderbecke in the 1920s and appeared with Thelonious Monk at the 1963 Newport Festival. In between he was associated with Red Nichols, Red Allen, Eddie Condon, and Louis Prima. Near the end of his life, he began recording for Impulse! in an easy-going, Gerry Mulligan–like group whose book included material by Monk, John Coltrane, and Ornette Coleman. Russell's idiomatic tone and often unconventional choice of notes were his dual trademarks. In the lower register, he would growl and slur, layering warm quavering tremolos onto held notes. At the upper end of the clarinet (he occasionally blew tenor sax, as well) he conveyed a light, woody, and gossamer sound with breathy undertones. During his lifetime there were those who contended that he couldn't really play his horn at all. In this respect, he was not so different from Ornette Coleman. Today, that unfortunate trend is reversing, and he is experiencing a welcome upswing in popularity among collectors and historians.

what to buy: Of the available Russell-led dates, the 1961 session with Coleman Hawkins, Bobby Brookmeyer, Jo Jones, Milt Hinton, pianist Nat Pierce, and trumpeter Emmett Berry, *Jazz Reunion* 𝄞𝄞𝄞𝄞 (Candid, 1961, prod. Nat Hentoff), is especially attractive. Russell was, by all accounts, a shy and self-deprecating man, and this trait translates to his approach within this group's context. He refuses to put himself into the spotlight, preferring to let the other frontliners have the first solo say. But

Russell's statements are uniformly wonderful, if a bit understated, including "Mariooch," with the other horns sitting out. The compilation *Pee Wee Russell: Jazz Original* &&&& (Commodore, 1938/1944, prod. Milt Gabler) includes sessions under the leadership of guitarist Condon and cornetists Mugsy Spanier and Wild Bill Davison, as well as eight sides credited to Russell's "Hot Four" (pianist Jess Stacy, bassist Sid Weiss, and drummer George Wettling) and four by the "Three Deuces" (Russell, pianist Joe Sullivan, and Zutty Singleton). The CD includes the Deuces' 1941 version of the insistently up-tempo "Jig Walk," the performance Russell called his personal favorite; the sinewy, snaky "Deuces Wild"; and several attractive slow-paced blues (most notably "D. A. Blues").

what to buy next: *Portrait of Pee Wee* &&&& (Esoteric, 1958/DCC, 1991, prod. William Fox) presents the dixieland-revivalist side of Russell. The group includes Ruby Braff, Bud Freeman, Vic Dickenson, Nat Pierce (again), bassist Charles Potter, and drummer Karl Kiffe in a program of standards and a couple of Russell originals.

worth searching for: The albums Russell made for Impulse! with trombonist Marshall Brown, bassist Russell George, and drummer Ronnie Bedford have never been reissued, though this will likely be remedied as GRP's Impulse! campaign continues. The 1965 date, *Ask Me Now!* &&&& (Impulse!, 1965), is quite marvelous. Although he only had three years left to him at this point, Russell's work is exemplary.

influences:

◄◄ Omer Simeon

►► Kenny Davern, Don Byron

David Prince

Terje Rypdal

Born August 23, 1947, in Oslo, Norway.

Terje Rypdal is a powerful electric guitarist with a strong interest in tonal color. He used to play in some of Norway's top rock bands, but the first time many non-Scandinavians ever heard of him was when he was rumored to be Miles Davis's guitarist for the *Bitches Brew* sessions before the great trumpeter signed John McLaughlin instead. There are some superficial similarities in styles between McLaughlin and Rypdal, but the former leans more towards the quick pick while Rypdal invests his playing with great washes of sound and long, drawn-out chord sequences. Albums from the early '70s like *What Comes After* and *Whenever I Seem to Be Far Away* show why Davis consid-

ered the Norwegian guitarist; Rypdal's later releases, however, pull him further away from Davis's direction at the time. For the past few decades, Rypdal has worked with many prominent European jazz artists, including Jan Garbarek, John Surman, and Barre Phillips, helping define the aesthetic for Manfred Eicher's ECM label. His wide-open, intense performances and recordings are logical extensions of both Rypdal's and Eicher's fascination with 20th-century classical composers like Ligeti, Part, and Penderecki. It also explains Rypdal's continued interest in writing works like the violin concerto he titled "Undisonus" (for which he won 1984's Composition of the Year award from the Society of Norwegian Composers).

what to buy: Combined with some of Rypdal's most fiery guitar performances, Palle Mikkelborg's trumpet playing has a lot to do with the success of *Skywards* &&&&✓ (ECM, 1997, prod. Manfred Eicher). His soft-focused brass playing provides a tonal contrast to the electronics and string backdrop heard through most of the recording, even as Rypdal stacks unusual power chords like an air-traffic controller. This is one of the most consistently rewarding albums in Rypdal's oeuvre—even if it does sound like the jazz title Pink Floyd never released. Rypdal uses the rhythm section of his rock group (bassist Bjorn Kjellemyr and drummer Audun Kleive) on *If Mountains Could Sing* &&&& (ECM, 1995, prod. Manfred Eicher), but the result is a surprisingly tight yet flexible jazz-inflected release. The guitarist uses a string trio (violin, viola, and cello) for contrast, and there are moments that acquire a chamber-music semblance. But when the power trio kicks in, as it does in "Private Eye," the energy level is jacked up appropriately.

what to buy next: *Works* &&&& (ECM, 1994, prod. Manfred Eicher), collected from seven different albums recorded before 1982, gives a good picture of Rypdal's broad, soaring tone and long, stinging lines. Improvisation comes more from the classical or rock traditions even though Rypdal has been considered more of a jazz musician outside the confines of his native Norway. Rypdal uses a group called the Chasers for more rock-oriented instrumental performances, and *The Singles Collection* &&&&✓ (ECM, 1989, prod. Manfred Eicher)—posing with tongue in cheek as a greatest-hits compilation—is the band's only release with anything other than novelty value. "Sprott" is the kind of killer riff Jeff Beck would do if he wasn't so wrapped up in technical onanism.

the rest:

Odyssey &&&✓ (ECM, 1975)

Waves &&& (ECM, 1978)

(With Miroslav Vitous and Jack DeJohnette) *Terje Rypdal, Miroslav Vitous & Jack DeJohnette* 🎵🎵🎵 (ECM, 1979)
Descendre 🎵🎵🎵 (ECM, 1980)
(With the Chasers) *Chaser* 🎵🎵 (ECM, 1985)
(With the Chasers) *Blue* 🎵🎵 (ECM, 1987)
(With David Darling) *Eos* 🎵🎵🎵 (ECM, 1988)
Undisonus 🎵🎵🎵 (ECM, 1990)
Q.E.D. 🎵🎵🎵 (ECM, 1993)

influences:

◀◀ Jimi Hendrix, Gustav Mahler, Gyorgy Ligeti

▶▶ Glenn Branca

Garaud MacTaggart

Sade

Born Helen Folsade Adu, January 16, 1959, in Lagos, Nigeria.

Reared as the daughter of an African father and English mother, Sade made a minor name for herself as a clothes designer during the 1980s before turning heads in London as lead singer for the jazz-funk band Pride. Joined by keyboardist Andrew Hale, bassist Paul Denman, and guitarist/saxophonist Stuart Matthewman, Sade organized her own self-named band in 1984, eventually forging a mix of cool-school jazz and smoldering funk that brought the group to worldwide attention. Though critics have often focused on Sade herself—a coffee-colored beauty with a fashion model's face and jazzy, delicate vocal chops—the publicity-shy singer has always insisted that Sade be viewed as a band. And while some have found the group's laid-back instrumental mix a bit boring, its signature sound has garnered a wide and loyal fan base.

what to buy: It's not until her second album, *Promise* 🎵🎵🎵🎵 (Portrait, 1986, prod. Robin Millar, Sade), that Sade begins to live up to the promise of her own jazz/pop/soul sound. Veering from the percolating hit "The Sweetest Taboo" to the jazzy minor-chord lament "Mr. Wrong" and the semi-funky, lounge-tinged workout "Never as Good as the First Time," the singer's detached cool mixes with her crack backing band to bring some truly inspired moments. Coming back after a four-year layoff, Sade added '90s-style reggae touches for her best effort yet, *Love Deluxe* 🎵🎵🎵🎵 (Epic, 1992, prod. Sade), a heady mix of tunes fueled by the burning, sensual grooves "No Ordinary Love" and "Cherish the Day."

what to buy next: *The Best of Sade* 🎵🎵🎵🎵 (Epic, 1994, prod. various) is a smart collection of the key tracks from her four albums.

what to avoid: Though Sade's debut, *Diamond Life* 🎵🎵🎵 (Portrait, 1985, prod. Robin Millar), made a splash by introducing the world to her jazz-influenced ice-queen persona, the songs here are a little too restrained—excepting the hit single "Smooth Operator."

the rest:
Stronger Than Pride 🎵🎵🎵 (Epic, 1988)

worth searching for: The promotional only *Interview Deluxe* (Epic, 1992) brings a bit of insight from the interview-shy Sade.

influences:

◀◀ Nina Simone, Billie Holiday, Marvin Gaye

▶▶ Des'ree, Me'Shell Ndegeocello

Eric Deggans

Dino Saluzzi

Born Timoteo Saluzzi, May 20, 1935, in Campo Santa, Argentina.

Dino Saluzzi has a deep and abiding interest in the folk-music traditions of his native country, acquiring them through his membership in a clan of musicians. He learned the bandoneon (an accordion-like instrument) from his father and, despite an academic background in avant-garde classical music acquired through later studies, Saluzzi has always used folk elements as the basis for his compositions. In that regard he is a lot like fellow countryman Astor Piazzolla, whose interest in the tango spurred him to experiment with the form. Saluzzi uses the same elements in combination with milongas, camdombe rhythms, and music from the Andean Indian tradition to make a whole new hybrid. Saluzzi has entered the world-music market in the company of jazz performers like Charlie Haden, Edward Vesala, and George Gruntz, adding piquant, folk-rooted improvisations and colors to their music. Despite this, he is best known in South America for his membership in an experimental ensemble called Musica Creativa.

what to buy: *Cite de la Musique* 🎵🎵🎵🎵 (ECM, 1997, prod. Manfred Eicher) provides an introduction to Saluzzi's jazzier side. Along with bassist Marc Johnson and his son/guitarist, Jose M. Saluzzi, the senior Saluzzi's wizardly bandoneon playing has reached the synthesis of jazz and Argentine tango that was only hinted at in earlier recordings. Despite some quick pattering percussion on songs like "El Rio y el Abuelo" the overall impression is still sensuous and reflective rather than raucous. For *Mojotoro* ♫♫♫ (ECM, 1992, prod. Manfred Eicher), Saluzzi hired three other talented Saluzzis and a trio of outsiders. The blend of two bandoneons by Dino and Celso with reed work by Felix (Saluzzis, all) swings in the same lush yet ascetic fashion as many ECM albums. He has some of the same stylistic conceits as Piazzola and Gato Barbieri, but the collective combination of Argentine passion and classical training doesn't take away from anyone's individuality.

what to buy next: With *Rios* ♫♫♫ (Intuition, 1995, prod. Lee Townsend), Saluzzi is first among equals in a trio with bassist Anthony Cox and vibes/marimba player David Friedman. The interplay between bandoneon and marimba is especially pleasing to the ear, but the music owes more to the vibrant folk roots of Argentina than it does to the traditional jazz bastions of New Orleans, Chicago, or New York. On *Andina* ♫♫♫ (ECM, 1988, prod. Manfred Eicher), Saluzzi makes his bandoneon jump and mourn through intense, folk-based melodies, much as Piazzolla, Strayhorn, and Kodaly did for their respective cultures.

the rest:
Kultrum ♫♫♫ (ECM, 1983)
Once Upon a Time—Far Away in the South ♫♫♫ (ECM, 1986)

influences:
◀◀ Astor Piazzolla
▶▶ Celso Saluzzi

Garaud MacTaggart

Joe Sample

Born February 1, 1939, in Houston, TX.

Pianist Joe Sample is best known for playing fusion and electric pop-jazz, but his roots are acoustic hard bop. In the late 1950s he co-founded the Jazz Crusaders with trombonist Wayne Henderson, tenor saxophonist Wilton Felder, and drummer Stix Hooper. This hard bop/post-bop powerhouse was greatly influenced by Art Blakey's Jazz Messengers, but what made the band unconventional was its lack of a trumpeter and the interaction of Henderson's trombone and Felder's tenor. Their sound changed considerably in the early 1970s, when they dropped "Jazz" from their name and abandoned bop in favor of a more commercial but equally appealing jazz/funk/soul style. It wasn't until later in the decade that Sample began to seriously pursue a career outside of the Crusaders. Though he'd recorded

the little known bop date *Fancy Dance* in 1969, it was 1978's *Rainbow Seeker* that made Sample a hit on his own and popularized him in the "crossover" market.

what to buy: Undeniably his greatest accomplishment, *Carmel* ♫♫♫♫ (MCA, 1978, prod. Joe Sample, Stix Hooper, Wilton Felder) boasts such melodic, introspective gems as "A Rainy Day in Monterrey" and the title song and proved that commercial appeal and artistic integrity aren't mutually exclusive. Meanwhile, *Collection* ♫♫♫ (GRP, 1978/1985, prod. various) focuses on his work for MCA in the late 1970s and early to mid-1980s and paints a generally impressive picture of Sample as both a composer and a soloist. A few weak cuts are included, but classics like "Sunrise" and "Fly with the Wings of Love" show how rewarding and charismatic he can be.

what to buy next: After recording so much gently introspective work on his own, Sample returned to a grittier, more Crusaders-ish jazz-funk style on *Did You Feel That?* ♫♫♫ (Warner Bros., 1994, prod. Stewart Levine). From Lee Morgan's "The Sidewinder" to earthy, down-home originals like "Viva De Funk" and "Just Chillin'," this CD was a most welcome surprise.

the rest:
Fancy Dance (Gazell, 1969)
Rainbow Seeker (MCA, 1978)
Voices in the Rain (MCA, 1980)
Spellbound (Warner Bros., 1989)
Invitation (Warner Bros., 1983)

Alex Henderson

David Sanborn

Born July 30, 1945, in Tampa, FL.

David Sanborn may be the world's most widely recorded and imitated R&B saxophonist. He made his reputation as an impressive soloist with numerous rock bands, and he has created what has become the definitive commercial alto sax sound. As a child Sanborn overcame a major obstacle. He suffered polio, was put in an iron lung, and subsequently took up a wind instrument as physical therapy. After studying music at Northwestern and Iowa universities in time for the "Summer of Love," Sanborn moved to the West Coast and got his first major gig with the Paul Butterfield Blues Band. He stayed with Butterfield from 1967 to 1971 (the band performed at Woodstock),

David Sanborn (© Jack Vartoogian)

then toured with Stevie Wonder in 1972–73. After playing with Gil Evans's band in 1973, Sanborn took several rock-oriented jobs. He played with the Brecker Brothers in 1975, and was a featured soloist for David Bowie, James Taylor, the Eagles, the Rolling Stones, and Aretha Franklin. Sanborn has led his own groups and taken several high profile gigs since the early '80s. He hosted a radio show for NPR, a TV show for NBC, contributed solos to numerous commercials and TV themes, and sat in regularly on *Late Night with David Letterman*. His TV show was famously eclectic: Sonny Rollins, Leonard Cohen, Miles Davis, Aaron Neville, Slim Gaillard, Hank Ballard, and Sun Ra were among the guests. Diverse lineups and unusual musical pairings were its strengths. And its downfall. Too hip for TV, the show was canceled after two seasons. Sanborn is an exciting and emotive performer who is influenced as much by Maceo Parker as Charlie Parker. Ironically, he is so popular and imitated that his own early recordings often sound trite and generic. The one weakness of his solo work is that it exhibits a sameness from one album to the next. There isn't much difference between *As We Speak*, *Backstreet*, and *Straight from the Heart*. This is testimony to Sanborn's consistent musicianship as well as the limits of his brand of fusion. He has never put out a bad album, but with a few exceptions, he hasn't put out a truly inspired one. However, his recent work has demonstrated a jazzier, more experimental influence.

what to buy: Until *Another Hand* ♪♪♪♪ (Elektra, 1991, prod. Hal Willner), Sanborn rarely took chances on his albums. This is the most ambitious album of his career. With Charlie Haden, Joey Baron, and Bill Frisell, the music draws more from New York's downtown jazz scene than the recording-studio fusion normally associated with Sanborn. He ventures away from the comfortable "fuzak" of his previous albums. Lou Reed's "Jesus" glows, and shows the depth of Sanborn's expressiveness. *Upfront* ♪♪♪♪ (Elektra, 1992, prod. Marcus Miller), a return to Sanborn's standard funk fare, retains plenty of edge from *Another Hand*. His version of Ornette Coleman's "Ramblin'" is proof of that. The music on the album evokes the best of the soul/jazz records of the '60s. "Bang Bang" is the quintessential party tune.

what to buy next: *Heart to Heart* ♪♪♪♪ (Warner Bros., 1978, prod. John Simon) switches easily from typical Sanborn fusion to densely orchestrated Gil Evans tunes like "Short Visit." *As We Speak* ♪♪♪♪ (Warner Bros., 1981, prod. Marcus Miller) rounds up all the usual suspects and features Sanborn on soprano.

what to avoid: If his work with Gil Evans is the right way to feature Sanborn with a larger orchestra, *Concerto* **woof!** (Warner Bros., 1990, prod. Tommy Lipuma) is the wrong way. Musical wallpaper.

the rest:
Taking Off ♪♪♪♪ (Warner Bros., 1975)
Sanborn ♪♪♪ (Warner Bros., 1976)
Love Songs ♪♪♪ (Warner Bros., 1976)
Hideaway ♪♪♪♪ (Warner Bros., 1979)
Voyeur ♪♪♪♪ (Warner Bros., 1980)
As We Speak ♪♪♪ (Warner Bros., 1981)
Backstreet ♪♪♪ (Warner Bros., 1982)
Straight to the Heart ♪♪♪ (Warner Bros., 1984)
Change of Heart ♪♪♪ (Warner Bros., 1987)
Close Up ♪♪♪ (Reprise, 1988)
Hearsay ♪♪♪ (Elektra, 1994)
Best of David Sanborn ♪♪♪♪ (Warner Bros., 1994)
Pearls ♪♪♪♪ (Elektra, 1995)
Songs from the Night Before ♪♪♪ (Elektra, 1996)

worth searching for: Gil Evans's *Svengali* ♪♪♪♪ (Atlantic Act, 1972) forces Sanborn away from his pet phrases and familiar licks. Sanborn's bright, cutting tone works well over the close harmonies of Evans's arrangements.

influences:

◀◀ Ray Charles, Stevie Wonder, Hank Crawford, Jackie McLean

▶▶ Warren Hill, Najee, Dave Koz, Jay Beckenstein

James Eason

David Sanchez

Born 1968, in Guaynabo, Puerto Rico.

One of the leading young musicians forging a fertile synthesis of Afro-Caribbean music and jazz, David Sanchez is a powerful tenor saxophonist with the potential to become a major voice on the instrument. With his lightning-quick reflexes, finely-honed sense of rhythm, and sophisticated post-bop harmonic vocabulary, Sanchez combines the strengths of two musical traditions in an approach more flexible than much Latin jazz. Sanchez started playing congas at age eight and picked up the tenor sax four years later. He graduated from a performing arts high school and moved to New York in 1988, determined to become a professional musician. While enrolled at Rutgers University he studied with Kenny Barron, John Purcell, and Ted Dunbar, and began to establish a strong reputation in New York's Latin-jazz circles. In 1990, Paquito D'Rivera and Claudio Roditi brought him to the attention of Dizzy Gillespie, who hired him for his United Nation Orchestra and various small group performances. He has recorded with many of the leading figures in both Latin and straight-ahead jazz, including, respectively, Charlie Sepulveda, Danilo Perez, Hilton Ruiz, and Roy Hargrove; and Leon Parker, Kenny Drew Jr., Rachel Z, Ryan Kisor, and Slide Hampton's Jazz Masters.

what to buy: Sanchez moves seamlessly between Latin and straight-ahead vehicles on *Sketches of Dreams* ����� (Columbia, 1995, prod. John Snyder), an excellent session highlighting his facility in both genres and his forceful synthesis of the two. He and Roy Hargrove make a fiery frontline on the first two tunes and Sanchez's title track. Danilo Perez and Dave Kikoski split piano duties and share solo responsibilities with Sanchez and the Latin percussion, which is particularly effective on the high-voltage version of Jackie McLean's "Little Melonae." Sanchez shows off his lyrical side, with shades of Stanley Turrentine, on "Falling in Love with Love" and "It's Easy to Remember." Playing all his own tunes except for a tasty, concise version of Monk's "Four in One," Sanchez continues his mutual exploration of the Afro-Caribbean rhythms and jazz in the highly charged *Street Scenes* ����� (Columbia, 1997, prod. Billy Banks, Charles Fishman, David Sanchez). Alto saxophonist Kenny Garrett sits in on two tunes, burning with Sanchez on the album's closer "The Elements," but it's pianist Danilo Perez who shares center stage and points the way toward a profound synthesis of Latin influences and jazz. Sanchez's forceful tenor work surges with energy, especially on his two versions of the title track, but he also knows when more is less, as on "The Soul of El Barrio," backed just by bass and congas. And considering his sensuous soprano work on the moody ballad "Carmina," Sanchez is also developing his chops on the smaller horn.

what to buy next: A debut worthy of Dizzy Gillespie's last protégé, *The Departure* ����� (Columbia, 1994, prod. Bobby Watson) features five of his original tunes, a slashing tribute to Diz on "Woody 'N' You," a melodic hard bop work out on Jimmy Heath's "CJ," and some fine ballad work on Alec Wilder's "I'll Be Around." Featuring Danilo Perez (piano), either Peter Washington or Andy Gonzalez (bass), and Leon Parker (drums), the highly dynamic rhythm section, occasionally augmented by percussionist Milton Cardona, creates finely textured settings for Sanchez's hard-edged tenor work, moving seamlessly between the Latin and jazz grooves. Trumpeter Tom Harrell joins Sanchez on three tunes, blending his luminous tone with Sanchez's tenor and evoking a Miles Davis mood on Sanchez's "Santander."

worth searching for: Almost a manifesto by the new wave of young Latin-jazz musicians, *Algo Nuestro* ����� (Antilles, 1993,

prod. Charlie Sepulveda) is a smokin' session by trumpeter Charlie Sepulveda with Sanchez on tenor and soprano, pianist Edward Simon, bassist Andy Gonzalez, drummer Adam Cruz, Latin percussionist Richie Flores, and special guests. Sanchez contributes two excellent tunes, the almost avant garde "Mal Social," and the haunting, soulful "Nina's Mood." Highly recommended.

influences:

◄◄ Sonny Rollins, Stanley Turrentine, Michael Brecker

Andrew Gilbert

Poncho Sanchez

Born October 30, 1951, in Laredo, TX.

Along with his former boss Cal Tjader, Poncho (Ildefonso) Sanchez is one of the two great non-Caribbean Latin-jazz bandleaders. A virtuoso conguero, Sanchez leads one of the most consistent and versatile (not to mention employed) Latin bands in jazz. Growing up in Norwalk, California in a large Mexican-American family (he was the youngest of 11 kids), Sanchez taught himself flute, guitar, and percussion before learning the congas at age 18. Though it took him a while to break into the close-knit Latin percussion circles, he soon began working with local Southern California bands. Hired by Tjader in 1975, he played a central role in the popular group until Tjader's death in 1982. Sanchez formed his own band the same year and recorded two albums for Discovery, then signed on with Concord Picante. His band has become one of the label's staples, recording a series of consistently well-crafted albums, often featuring special guests. Part of the band's strength is its stability — the Banda brothers (Tony on bass and Ramon on timbales) have been with Sanchez since the beginning. With his large book of Latin and modern jazz charts, Sanchez fits easily into any musical context, working regularly at clubs, festivals and concerts.

what to buy: As the title says, *Para Todos* ����� (Concord Picante, 1994, prod. Carl E. Jefferson, John Burk) has something for everyone, including a very funky dose of tenor saxophonist Eddie Harris, who fits right in with Sanchez's typically well-played Latin jazz. Sanchez puts an Afro-Cuban twist on modern jazz tunes by Gerry Mulligan, Harold Land, J.J. Johnson, and Art Farmer, and spurs Harris to some very satisfying low-down tenor work on his great theme "Cold Duck Time." Sanchez's formula of tight, swinging arrangements, strong improvisors, and a mixed program of jazz and Latin themes reaches a perfect balance on *Papa Gato* ����� (Concord Picante, 1987, prod. Carl

E. Jefferson), one of his better sessions. Saxophonist Justo Almario, trumpeter Sal Cracchiolo, and trombonist Art Velasco all take advantage of their solo space, and the band is in excellent form on Horace Silver's "Senor Blues," Gillespie's "Manteca," and "Tania," a lovely tune by the band's pianist Charlie Otwell. A meeting of two Latin jazz giants, *Chile Con Soul* 𝄫𝄫𝄫𝄫 (Concord Picante, 1990, prod. Frank Marrone, Allen Farnham) features one of the best versions of Sanchez's band with the great timbales player Tito Puente sitting in on two tracks, including one of the most emphatic versions of "Lover, Come Back to Me" ever recorded. Other highlights include pianist Charlie Otwell's title track, Eddie Palmieri's "Con Migo," and Cal Tjader's "Soul Burst."

what to buy next: An excellent Latin jazz session by one of the best bands in the business, *Fuerte!* 𝄫𝄫𝄫𝄫 (Concord Picante, 1994, prod. Chris Lang) features spirited solos by trumpeter Sal Cracchiolo, trombonist Art Velasco, and tenor saxophonist Kenny Goldberg, who also contributes two strong tunes. Sanchez keeps things interesting by varying the mood with a bolero and the West African-derived "Alafia" by pianist Charlie Otwell, as well as a smoking Latin version of Clifford Brown's "Daahoud" to close the album. In some sense every album Sanchez has made is a tribute to Cal Tjader, but for *Soul Sauce* 𝄫𝄫𝄫𝄫 (Concord Picante, 1995, prod. Carl E. Jefferson, John Burk) he recreates the great bandleader's sound by bringing vibraphonist Ruben Estrada into the band. Sanchez picked out a host of tunes associated with Tjader, including Clare Fischer's "Morning" and Mongo Santamaria's "Tu Crees Que." Sanchez's love and respect for his former boss comes through on every track. A must for Latin percussion fans, *Conga Blue* 𝄫𝄫𝄫𝄫 (Concord Picante, 1996, prod. John Burk, Nick Phillips) features the great conguero Mongo Santamaria sitting in on five tracks, including a brief but blazing version of Herbie Hancock's "Watermelon Man." The band is in fine form, with many solo opportunities for trombonist Alex Henderson, saxophonist Scott Martin, and trumpeter Stan Martin.

best of the rest:

Sonando 𝄫𝄫𝄫𝄫 (Concord Picante, 1983)
El Conguero 𝄫𝄫𝄫𝄫 (Concord Picante, 1987)
Bien Sabroso 𝄫𝄫𝄫𝄫 (Concord Picante, 1988)
La Familia 𝄫𝄫𝄫𝄫 (Concord Picante, 1988)
Cambios 𝄫𝄫𝄫𝄫 (Concord Picante, 1991)
El Mejor 𝄫𝄫𝄫𝄫 (Concord Picante, 1992)
A Night With Poncho Sanchez Live: Bailar 𝄫𝄫𝄫𝄫 (Concord Picante, 1993)
Baila Mi Gente-Salsa 𝄫𝄫𝄫𝄫 (Concord Picante, 1996)
Freedom Sound 𝄫𝄫𝄫𝄫 (Concord Picante, 1997)

influences:

◀◀ Mongo Santamaria, Cal Tjader, Tito Puente

Andrew Gilbert

Pharoah Sanders

Born Ferrell Sanders, October 14, 1940, in Little Rock, AR.

Saxophonist Pharoah Sanders moved to Oakland in 1959, worked for awhile with R&B and avant-garde musicians in San Francisco, then moved to New York City in 1962 where he played with Rashied Ali, Don Cherry, Sun Ra, John Gilmore, and other avant-garde artists before recording his first solo album for ESP, *Pharoah's First Album*. The recording led to Sanders being invited to join forces with John Coltrane's group from 1965 to 1967. He appeared on most of Coltrane's last albums, bringing a ferocious voice to the recordings. Sanders left the band shortly before Coltrane's death and continued recording as a solo artist with the rather disappointing *Tauhid*. It wasn't until the release of *Karma* in 1969 that he seemed to find a voice of his own. This album was augmented by the vocal stylings of Leon Thomas and contained what would become Sanders's signature tune, "The Creator Has a Master Plan." His recorded output from 1970 to 1980 did little to further his direction. Recording ballads and standards didn't seem to please his audience and did not appear to win him any new fans. It wasn't until 1994 when things started to happen to again bring Sanders back to the center of attention in the jazz world. He guested as tenor saxophonist on drummer Franklin Kiermyer's 1994 Evidence album *Solomon's Daughter*, and issued a quartet recording as leader, *Crescent with Love*. The former placed him in a group of musicians that seemed to bring the fire back into his playing. The latter was a double disc of works either written by or often performed by John Coltrane. Although it was largely made up of ballads, this recording seemed to contain the spark that was missing in other efforts of this nature. Perhaps it was just the timing of the release, but it seemed to mark a comeback for Sanders's career and garnered much critical praise. His 1995 album, *Message from Home*, was produced by the prolific Bill Laswell. While some fans did not appreciate the world-fusion style of the approach, this album also gained a lot of attention.

what to buy: If there is one Sanders recording that would rank as a classic, *Karma* 𝄫𝄫𝄫𝄫 (Impulse!, 1969/1995, prod. Bob Thiele) would be it. On this album the band includes Lonnie Liston Smith (piano), and Reggie Workman or Ron Carter (bass), along with the vocalizations of Leon Thomas. "The Creator Has a Master Plan" originally spanned nearly both sides of the original LP, and was finally edited into a continuous flow with the 20-bit remastered version of the CD release. *Tauhid* 🎧🎧🎧 (Impulse!, 1966/1993, prod. Bob Thiele), Sanders's debut on the label, includes a notable performance by the late guitarist Sunny Sharrock.

what to buy next: *Crescent with Love* 🎧🎧🎧 (Evidence, 1994, prod. Big Apple Productions, Tetsuo Hara), a tribute to John Coltrane, includes "Naima," "Crescent," and "After the Rain," as well as standards such as "Misty" and "Body and Soul." This collection of ballads showed Sanders's indebtedness to the quieter side of Coltrane. *Message from Home* 🎧🎧🎧 (Verve, 1996, prod. Bill Laswell) offers a shot of world-fusion music on the funky side under the watchful eye of Bill Laswell. One more direction for Sanders.

what to avoid: *Africa* 🎧🎧 (Timeless, 1988/1993, prod. Wim Wigt) and *Moon Child* 🎧🎧 (Timeless, 1993, prod. Wim Wigt) contain sadly dull and lifeless collections of music (with rare exceptions).

best of the rest:
Pharoah's First Album 🎧🎧🎧 (ESP, 1964/1994)
Jewels of Thought 🎧🎧 (Impulse!, 1969)
Deaf Dumb Blind 🎧🎧 (Impulse!, 1970)
Thembi 🎧🎧 (Impulse!, 1971)
Black Unity 🎧🎧🎧 (Impulse!, 1971/1997)
Live at the East 🎧🎧🎧 (Impulse!, 1971)
Village of the Pharoahs 🎧🎧 (Impulse!, 1973)
Elevation 🎧🎧 (Impulse!, 1973)
Love in Us All 🎧🎧🎧 (Impulse!, 1973)
Love Will Find a Way 🎧 (Arista, 1977)
Beyond a Dream 🎧🎧 (Arista, 1978)
Journey to the One 🎧🎧🎧 (Evidence, 1980)
Rejoice 🎧🎧🎧 (Evidence, 1981)
Heart Is a Melody 🎧🎧🎧 (Evidence, 1982/1993)
Shukuru 🎧🎧 (Evidence, 1985/1992)
Welcome to Love 🎧🎧🎧 (Evidence, 1993)
Naima 🎧🎧🎧 (Evidence, 1995)

influences:
⏮ John Coltrane, Albert Ayler, Eric Dolphy
⏭ David S. Ware, Charles Gayle, Rob Brown

Chris Meloche

Randy Sandke

Born May 23, 1949, in Chicago, IL.

Way back at University High (whose alumni also include trombonists Ray Anderson and George Lewis) in Chicago's Hyde Park, folks knew trumpeter Randy Sandke was ticketed for a major musical career. The fast track to the big time turned into a long march when Sandke's chops were wrecked—with a ruptured larynx—playing too-loud jazz-rock with Michael Brecker at the University of Indiana. Sandke put down the trumpet for 10 years, moved to New York, took up guitar, and worked musical and other jobs through the '70s. A roommate, Michael Gribbroek, convinced him to pick up the horn again and Sandke was soon making up for lost time. Gigs with New York bands in the "traditional" vein, Sandke's first and abiding musical love, led to work with Bob Wilber and then Benny Goodman, whom he played with until Goodman died in 1986. In the following decade Sandke has emerged in his own right as a fluid, highly skilled player and a creative modern-traditionalist voice. On recordings, most tracks stay within the four to six-minute range—strategically programmed for airplay, perhaps, but not artistically limited, as Sandke's experience with swing-era veterans enables him to make significant statements with no wasted time. On up-tempo cuts, his work conjures a spirit of celebration reminiscent of Clifford Brown.

what to buy: Four CDs on Concord, recorded between 1993 and 1996, represent Sandke's state of the art to date. All are versatile and well-conceived, making innovative statements on material ranging from pre-swing vintage through hard-bop. *The Chase* 🎧🎧🎧🎧 (Concord, 1995) features Ray Anderson's surrealist trombone, and don't miss what these cats do with not-often-recorded tunes "Ill Wind" and "The Folks Who Live on the Hill." Other performers are saxophonists Chris Potter, Scott Robinson, and Michael Brecker, with rhythm section Ted Rosenthal (piano), John Goldsby (bass), and Marvin "Smitty" Smith (drums).

what to buy next: Also notable are *Calling All Cats* 🎧🎧🎧🎧 (Concord, 1996), *Get Happy* 🎧🎧🎧🎧 (Concord, 1994), and *I Hear Music* 🎧🎧🎧🎧 (Concord, 1993). The latter two include Ken Peplowski (tenor saxophone, clarinet), Ray Kennedy (piano), John Goldsby (bass), and Terry Clarke (drums), with trombonist Robert Trowers added on *Get Happy*. Nice work here on one of Thelonious Monk's hard tunes, "Humph," and Charles Mingus's "Boogie Stop Shuffle." *Calling All Cats* is the most adventurous, including Sandke (on piano) playing his Bix Beiderbecke tribute, "In a Metatone," his arrangement of a work by medieval composer Machaut, and a moving "Blues A'Poppin'" by Cootie Williams. This pianoless (except Sandke's own track) recording includes Howard Alden's guitar and saxophonists Scott Robinson, Chuck Wilson, and Gary Keller; Joel Helleny (trombone); Michael Moore (bass), and Dennis Mackrel (drums).

worth searching for: In the more strictly "traditional" vein, Sandke leads the live tribute recording *We Love You Louis! The New York Allstars Play the Music of Louis Armstrong* ♫♫♫ (Nagel-Heyer). With Kenny Davern on clarinet joining Sandke on a five-piece front line with trombonist Helleny, David Ostwald on tuba, and second trumpet player Byron Stripling, this is a historically sensitive work. Unfortunately, while some cuts (notably "Savoy Blues") work beautifully, an overly conservative rhythm section keeps most of the work from rising to its full potential. Randy Sandke's earliest recording as a leader, first issued as the LP *New York Stories*, now appears on *The Sandke Brothers* ♫♫♫♫ (Stash, 1985). An ambitious first project, all seven cuts with Randy are his own compositions; the rest of the CD belongs to Randy's older brother and first mentor, Jordan Sandke. Randy plays with familiar partners Michael Brecker (tenor saxophone), Joel Helleny (trombone), and John Goldsby (bass), along with Jim McNeeley (piano) and Kenny Washington (drums).

influences:

◀◀ Louis Armstrong, Bix Beiderbecke, Bunny Berigan, Clifford Brown, Buck Clayton, Harry James, Jordan Sandke

David Finkel

Arturo Sandoval

Born November 6, 1949, in Artemisa, Havana, Cuba.

Afro-Cuban jazz, called Cubop when it arose in the 1940s with the late Dizzy Gillespie as its prime innovator, is alive today partly through Gillespie's protégé, multi-talented Cuban trumpeter Arturo Sandoval. Sandoval believes that no matter whether you call it Latin jazz or Afro-Cuban jazz, it's the same combination of jazz harmonies and lines with the Afro-Cuban rhythms. Gillespie, a legendary trumpeter and bandleader, met his Afro-Cuban jazz mentor, Mario Bauzá, in 1937. Then at the forefront of developing bebop, Gillespie felt jazz needed some outside influences. So, with the help of Cuban trumpeter Bauzá and Chano Pozo, a conga player, Gillespie merged Afro-Cuban polyrhythms with bebop harmonies. Sandoval continues to do the same thing with his Latin Train band (formed in the mid-1990s) and his other groups. He creates compositions that infuse jazz with Afro-Cuban rhythms instead of merely adding Latin percussion to a jazz tune.

Sandoval began playing music at age 13 in a village band where he learned the rudiments of theory and percussion. He selected the trumpet after playing many instruments, and in 1964 began three years of classical trumpet studies at the Cuban National School of the Arts. By age 16 he'd earned a place in an all-star national band and had his first exposure to jazz recordings by Dizzy Gillespie, who would become his idol and mentor. After a stint in the military (during which he continued to play with the Orquesta Cubana de Música Moderna), Sandoval co-founded Irakere, a Grammy-winning group that melded traditional Cuban music, jazz, classical, and rock into an explosive mixture. This band quickly became a sensation worldwide, and their appearance at the 1978 Newport Jazz Festival in New York introduced them to American audiences and resulted in a recording contract with Columbia. Sandoval left Irakere in 1981, formed his own international touring band, and captured honors as Cuba's best instrumentalist in 1982, 1983, and 1984. He also performed as a classical trumpeter with the BBC Symphony in London and with the Leningrad Symphony in the former Soviet Union.

Sandoval was thrilled to finally meet his mentor in 1977 when Dizzy Gillespie was in Cuba to perform. Though Sandoval couldn't speak a word of English, he chauffeured Gillespie into the black neighborhoods to hear musicians play guaguanco and rumba in the streets. Gillespie was surprised when his "driver" performed that evening with Irakere. Impressed with the young musician, Gillespie took him under his wing. Sandoval recorded and toured internationally with Gillespie's United Nation Orchestra and appeared on the 1992 recording, *Live at Festival Hall*. In fact, it was while touring with this Grammy Award-winning orchestra in Rome in July 1990 that Sandoval requested political asylum. With help from Gillespie and then Vice-President Dan Quayle, Sandoval resettled with his family in Miami, where he now teaches full-time at Florida International University. Sandoval continues to tour extensively, performing jazz, of course, but also classical music with symphony orchestras. He has lectured in the U.S. and overseas and has written and performed on several film soundtracks, including *The Perez Family*, *The Mambo Kings*, and *Havana*.

what to buy: After Sandoval established his wide-ranging talents on a few GRP albums, he hit big with the album his fans had been waiting for: *Arturo Sandoval & the Latin Train* ♫♫♫♫ (GRP, 1996, prod. Arturo Sandoval), an album of 11 Afro-Cuban jazz classics featuring one of Sandoval's hottest bands. Their Cuban grooves and Sandoval's soaring solos could shake dust from club rafters and coax fans to dance in the aisles. Augmented by vocalists and a host of percussionists, the Latin Train band simmers with the expert musicianship of musical director Kenny Anderson (saxophones), Otmaro Ruiz (piano), David Enos (bass), Aaron Serfaty (drums), and Manuel "Equi"

Castrillo (percussion). Sandoval's clean, crisp tone and polished technique are astounding. You'll be reminded of Dizzy, especially when Sandoval hits those shrieking high notes. The high-energy tunes are balanced by beautiful Latin ballads such as "Waheera," sweetened with "strings" briefly before the tempo shifts. The band embraces danceable grooves that include mambo, danzon, son montuno, guajira, guaracha, songo, and chachacha. If you can't discern one style from another, just let your head and feet feel the beats. *I Remember Clifford* 🎵🎵🎵🎵 (GRP, 1992, prod. Papito, Carl Griffin, Rudy Perez, Arturo Sandoval) is Sandoval's second album as leader after emigrating from Cuba to the United States in 1990—and it could easily be retitled "I Remember Bebop." On this tribute to trumpeter Clifford Brown, Sandoval demonstrates his mastery of the post-bop tradition with racing lines and controlled playing (with little high-register screeching). He is superbly backed by a rhythm section that includes Kenny Washington (drums), Kenny Kirkland (piano), and Charnett Moffett (bass). Guesting on some tracks are tenor saxists Ernie Watts, David Sanchez, and Ed Calle. Keyboardist Felix Gomez plays on the title tune. Through sparing use of electronic manipulation, Sandoval creates a trumpet "choir" on five tracks. The leader's playing is technically proficient and enjoyable throughout, but Sandoval's solo on the title ballad best demonstrates his capacity for compassionate, warm-toned playing, and that sentimental track alone makes this CD a worthy buy. Add his tantalizing treatments of standards such as "Daahoud," "Joy Spring," "Cherokee," "I Get a Kick Out of You," and you can't go wrong with this album. Sandoval returned to straight-ahead jazz with *Swingin'* 🎵🎵🎵🎵 (GRP, 1996, prod. Arturo Sandoval), an album showcasing his talents as composer (he wrote seven of the 11 tunes). He performs superbly on both trumpet and flugelhorn in this small-group setting, and is backed by a rhythm team that includes Joey Calderazzo (piano), John Patitucci (acoustic bass), and Greg Hutchinson (drums). A variety of guest soloists make significant contributions, including Eddie Daniels (clarinet), Ed Calle (tenor sax), Dana Deboe (trombone), Michael Brecker (tenor sax), Mike Stern (guitar), and Clark Terry (trumpet, flugelhorn). If straight-ahead jazz is your bag, this is the Sandoval album you'll want to own.

what to buy next: *Danzón* 🎵🎵🎵🎵 (GRP, 1994, prod. Arturo Sandoval, Richard Eddy) is full of exciting rhythms, soaring solos, and plentiful surprises (for one, Bill Cosby sings). A fun-filled celebration of Afro-Cuban music in the style of the legends, late and living, this 11-tune album shows the full range of Sandoval's talents as player of trumpet, flugelhorn, piano, timbales, and percussion, as well as singer and composer/arranger. In addition to playing some high-note trumpet, Sandoval sings scat vocals on a hot version of "Groovin' High." A vast powerhouse of talented guest artists maintain the matchless vitality of this album. Joining Sandoval on various tracks are vocalist Gloria Estefan, pianist Danilo Perez, guitarist Rene Luis Toledo, flutist Dave Valentin, percussionist Giovanni Hidalgo, and saxophonist Ed Calle. Highlights are many on this must-own disc of danceable rhythms. *Dream Come True* 🎵🎵🎵🎵 (GRP, 1993, prod. Michel Legrand, Arturo Sandoval) finds Sandoval performing ten bop-to-ballad standards with pianist Michel Legrand, who also conducts a full studio orchestra on a few tracks. Sandoval maintains superb command of his instruments, playing open and muted trumpet and flugelhorn. His passionate performances are beautifully accompanied by his colleagues Peter Erskine (drums), Brian Bromberg (bass), Ernie Watts (tenor sax), and trombonist Bill Watrous (whose lengthy solo on "Dahomey Dance" is a delight). An array of other musicians comprise the studio orchestra, enhancing the trumpeter's solos on "Little Sunflower," "To Diz with Love," "How Do You Keep the Music Playing," and the Sandoval original, "Vida Real." While the orchestra-backed numbers are beautiful, the small-group tracks are equally enjoyable; these include the Sandoval-Legrand duet that pays homage to Dizzy Gillespie; the lush, sentimental ballad reading of "Con Alma"; and Sandoval's Afro-Cuban original, "Blue," a boppish treat performed with Legrand, Bromberg, Erskine, Watrous, and Watts. For an introduction to Sandoval's extraordinary high-register trumpet playing, check out *The Best of Arturo Sandoval* 🎵🎵🎵🎵 (Milan Latino, 1997, prod. various), a compilation of Sandoval's Bernstein to bop to Latin-fusion performances, along with some originals. You may have to adjust the treble-bass controls on your audio setup, but you'll appreciate the trumpeter's open and muted virtuosity on the diverse mixture of tunes. Best are Sandoval's modernized, 15 minute version of his mentor's classic, "A Night in Tunisia," and his catchy original, "Blues en Dos Partes." While this is not one of Sandoval's best albums, it's worthy of a listen and you might get lucky and find this disc in the used bins. Don't expect *Tumbaito* 🎵🎵🎵🎵 (Messidor, 1986/1991, prod. Detlef Englehard, Götz A. Wörner) to be fused with Latin jazz. It's contemporary, funky, and sometimes straight-ahead after the opener, "A Night in Tunisia." The session includes Sandoval's former all-star group: Hilario Duran (piano), Jorge Chicoy (guitar), Jorge Reyes (bass), Bernardo Garcia (drums), and Reinaldo Valera (percussion), and showcases the leader's ability to forge links with bebop, blues, funk, Cuban rhythms, and classical elements. It also shows off Sandoval's ability to "screech and shout." (You might have to close your windows for "Tunisia Blues.") "Nuestro Blues," which begins with a vigorous piano head and seems promising, also includes too many loud layers of music—too much to sort out. Five selections are originals; the best are "Los Elefantes," a lovely lush ballad with Sandoval playing an even, full-toned flugelhorn; and "Relax" (by then you might need to!), which features some fine piano work from Duran. The title tune features Sandoval playing a lovely muted trumpet head with underlying Latin rhythms, and an increasing contemporary funk bass line that evolves into high-volume pyrotechnics again.

the rest:

The Classical Album 𝄞𝄞𝄞𝄞𝄞 (RCA Victor/Red Seal, 1994)
En Concerto 𝄞𝄞𝄞𝄞 (Habacan, 1992)
Flight to Freedom 𝄞𝄞𝄞 (GRP, 1991)

worth searching for: A date that reunites Sandoval with leader Paquito D'Rivera, *Reunion* 𝄞𝄞𝄞𝄞𝄞 (Messidor, 1991, prod. Götz A. Wörner, Uwe Feltens) features the former members of the groundbreaking Orquesta Cubana de Música Moderna and the innovative Irakere. With side players fluent in Afro-Cuban rhythms, bassist David Finck, guitarist Fareed Haque, percussionist Giovani Hidalgo, pianist Danilo Perez, and drummer Mark Walker, Sandoval sizzles in solos, especially when he slows things down for his rendition of "Body & Soul" with Perez and Finck. The trumpeter teams notably with D'Rivera for a racing version of Dizzy Gillespie's Cubop number, "Tanga," as well as D'Rivera's title tune written specially for the session. He trades the spotlight with D'Rivera's sax on a fluid version of the Chucho Valdés bolero, "Claudia." A totally engaging album from start to finish.

influences:

◀◀ Dizzy Gillespie, Clifford Brown

Nancy Ann Lee

Mongo Santamaria

Born Ramon Santamaria, April 7, 1922, in Jesus Maria, Havana, Cuba.

Born in a poor district of Havana known for its Afro-Cuban culture, Mongo Santamaria originally studied the violin but switched to drums before dropping out of school to become a professional musician. As a young man he traveled to the U.S. via Mexico, arriving in New York City with fellow congo player Armando Peraza in 1949. Billed as the Black Cuban Diamonds, they were performing during a time when Latin music was changing course and spawning an array of mambo groups from big bands to small combos. Perez Prado led probably the biggest crossover band to reach non-Latin audiences, and master conguero Mongo Santamaria worked with Prado's band before joining Tito Puente for six years. Santamaria recorded with Dizzy Gillespie in 1954, then relocated to the West Coast where he joined San Francisco–based vibist Cal Tjader (somewhat of a pacesetter himself in Latin jazz) from 1958 to 1961. While on the West Coast, Santamaria began recording his own albums with a straight-Latin *charanaga* band, debuting with *Mambo* and *Yambu*. His popular tune, "Afro Blue," from his earliest albums eventually became a jazz standard recorded by countless musicians. But his biggest hit would be the Herbie Hancock tune "Watermelon Man," which the pianist brought to a New York nightclub one night in 1962 where Santamaria's band was performing to an audience of about three people. Hancock began to demonstrate his new tune, the musicians gradually joined in, and the tune became part of Santamaria's repertoire. Producer Orrin Keepnews heard it, and had it recorded as a single by the Battle label in 1962. It became a huge hit, topping pop charts in 1963. It remains Santamaria's theme song and the tune that most fans remember him by. Throughout the 1960s Santamaria led his own groups containing both jazz and Latin players, including Brazilian Joao Donato on piano. Santamaria became tremendously popular running long-lasting bands that combine traditional *charanga* with jazz brass sections, wind instruments, and piano solos. His bands in the early 1960s included pianist Chick Corea and flutist Hubert Laws, as well as Brazilian and Cuban musicians. Santamaria formed a New York–based group in 1961, and, between 1965 and 1970, made a series of recordings for Atlantic and Columbia that combined R&B and soul tunes with Latin rhythms and jazz, a hot danceable combination that brought him greater fame. Santamaria continued to mix musical genres in the 1960s and 1970s, and has since returned to his Afro-Cuban roots, recording for Vaya, Pablo, Concord Picante, Chesky, Milestone, and other labels.

what to buy: If you're a fan of Latin rhythms or just want to hear the albums that started Santamaria's career, check out *Afro-Roots* 𝄞𝄞𝄞𝄞 (Prestige, 1958/1989, prod. various), which combines 12 tunes from Santamaria's 1959 session for Fantasy (originally released as *Mongo*), and the nine selections recorded in 1958 (originally released as *Yambu*). Just as the title implies, these 21 percussion-laden tunes cut to the quick, with Santamaria featuring native rhythms based on chants and rituals that date back to their Cuban origins. One track features the playing of vibist Cal Tjader and pianist Vince Guaraldi, hinting at his more jazz-oriented albums to come. Timbalero Willie Bobo appears on this album, creating (at the time of this recording) some of the most exciting Afro-Cuban rhythmic exchanges fans had ever heard. If you're more interested in hearing overt jazz influences, pick up *Skins* 𝄞𝄞𝄞𝄞 (Milestone, 1962/1976/1990, prod. Orrin Keepnews), which features 10 tunes by a 1964 version of Santamaria's band first documented on the Riverside recording *Mongo Explodes!* and nine tunes recorded by the 1962 version of "the Mongo Santamaria Afro-Latin Group" (originally issued as *Go, Mongo!*). The 1964 band included jazz players such as Hubert Laws (piccolo, flute, tenor sax) and guesting soloists Nat Adderley (cornet) and Jimmy Cobb (drums), in addition to Santamaria's regular lineup. Capers and Sheller were writing some great tunes by then, and this album has numerous highlights and catchy beats that tried to recapture the success of "Watermelon Man." (They come close with the instrumental track, "Corn Bread Guajira.") The band performing the tunes for the first Riverside date in 1962 was originally thrown together by Santamaria and his manager (because Santamaria at the moment of signing had no band), and includes a young Armando Corea at the piano (before he became known by his nickname "Chick"), and Chicago musicians Paul Serrano (trumpet), Pat Patrick (flutes, saxophones), and others. Obviously, this CD offers historical value as well as some good music. Following a series of Fantasy albums that featured authentic Afro-Cuban rhythms, Santamaria's octet was booked in 1962 into the Black Hawk Cafe, a San Francisco club where they recorded most of the music you hear on *At the Blackhawk* 𝄞𝄞𝄞𝄞 (Fantasy, 1962/1994). His pianist/trombonist Joao Donato is obviously well-versed in Latin music and jazz, and flutist Rolando Lozano (who plays unadorned wood flute) sounds like any accomplished jazz musician. Along with Santamaria's supportive and solo work on hand drums, there are plenty of great moments contributed by the musicians (including baritone saxophonist Pat Patrick on one tune) performing the 14 tunes written mostly by group members. The jazz standards, "Tenderly," "All the Things You Are," "Body and Soul," and "Close Your Eyes" are given Latinate treatment, and the authentic Afro-Cuban numbers are equally exciting. The music compiled on this CD was originally released on *Mighty Mongo* and *Viva Mongo*. Riding on the success of his 1963 hit single of Herbie Hancock's "Watermelon Man" (and Santamaria's album of the same name), Santamaria appeared at the Village Gate in New York City with his band on September 2, 1963 and made the live-recorded *Mongo at the Village Gate* 𝄞𝄞𝄞𝄞 (Riverside, 1963/OJC, 1990, prod. Orrin Keepnews). By now the up-front horns feature Marty Sheller (trumpet), Bobby Capers and Pat Patrick (flutes, saxes), with a rhythm section that includes Santamaria, Rodgers Grant

(piano), Victor Venegas (bass), and Frank Hernandez (drums), plus two other Latin percussionists. Along with originals by Santamaria (including the bonus track "Para Ti"), there are tunes by band members and others. Highlights are many, but especially notable are Sheller's trumpet solos. Santamaria performs a skin-against-skins solo on "My Sound" that's a knockout. His mastery as a conguero was long established, but this recording documents his continuing growth and the rigor of his new music that would pave the way for today's bands, such as Jerry Gonzalez and the Fort Apache Band.

what to buy next: On *Sabroso!* 𝄞𝄞𝄞𝄞 (Fantasy, 1959/1993), Santamaria leads a band based on classic Latin *charanga* format of flute and violin (with Latin percussion) and *pachanga,* the rage among New York's Latin teenagers around 1961. The 13 tunes capture the band in a performance recorded in San Francisco in the early 1960s. No jazz musicians collaborate on this recording, but the danceable rhythms and format on this CD are attractive. *Our Man in Havana* 𝄞𝄞𝄞𝄞 (Fantasy, 1959/1993), which compiles recordings made in Havana in the 1960s with Willie Bobo and other percussionists, vocalists, and instrumentalists from Cuba, is equally enticing, and you can hear how this music had begun to influence the development of Latin-jazz. With *Mongo Returns* 𝄞𝄞𝄞𝄞 (Milestone, 1995, prod. Todd Barkan), the then 73-year old percussionist comes home to the label that issued his 1963 top-ten hit, a cover version of Herbie Hancock's "Watermelon Man." Santamaria maintains a palatable, diverse mix of nine modernized Afro-Cuban jazz tunes laced with smatterings from his 1970s fusion days. The session features a tight, melodic horn section and solo fabrications from Eddie Allen (trumpet and flugelhorn), Robert DeBellis (alto and baritone saxes, flute), and Roger Byam (tenor and soprano saxophones, flute). Mongo is on the spot, illustrious and supportive as conguero and leader. Musical conductor Marty Sheller contributes three modern-edged tunes. Highlights include a seductive version of Ary Barroso's "Bahia" that features Allen's pretty muted-trumpet solos and a Latinized interpretation of Marvin Gaye's "When Did You Stop Loving Me, When Did I Stop Loving You." Allen also proves his prowess as composer with two funky originals—"Ol' School Groove" and "Slyck 'n' Slyde." Most of the 12 musicians comprise Santamaria's regular working group for the past decade (guest pianist Hilton Ruiz and bassist John Benitz, excluded). Pianist Oscar Hernandez, an array of percussionists (Louis Bauzo, Greg Askew, Steve Berrios), and the horn team generate spacious, fresh Latin-jazz grooves that are enriched by fine solos. The pretty melodies and easy rhythms will charm you. *Brazilian Sunset* 𝄞𝄞𝄞𝄞 (Candid, 1992, prod. Alan Bates, Mark Morganelli) features percussionist Santamaria with an array of prime musicians conversant in Afro-Cuban jazz for a 1992 live-recorded performance at Birdland, New York City. Perhaps because the gig was captured before an appreciative audience, the 12 tunes really kick, spurred by the leader's colorful percussions. Santamaria remains in the forefront on the 12 tunes (seven originals), laying down great rhythms for his soloists—musical director Eddie Allen (trumpet, flugelhorn), Jimmy Crozier (alto and baritone saxes, flute), Craig Rivers (tenor sax, flute), with support from the fine rhythm players Ricardo Gonzalez (piano), Guillermo Edgehill (bass), Johnny Almendra (drums, timbales), and Eddie Rodriguez (percussion). The version of Marty Sheller's "Gumbo Man" maintains distinctive 1970s funk flair tinged with shifting Latin rhythms. Mongo's original, "Sofrito," features an excellent baritone sax solo (taken either by Rivers or Crozier, liner notes vary). Another take on Santamaria's most memorable 1963 hit, "Watermelon Man," adds to the festive atmosphere.

best of the rest:

Arriba! 🎵🎵🎵🎵 (Fantasy, 1959/1996)
Mongo Introduces La Lupe 🎵🎵🎵🎵 (Riverside, 1963/Milestone, 1993)
Afro Blue 🎵🎵🎵🎵 (Concord Picante, 1987/1997)
Mambo Mongo 🎵🎵🎵 (Chesky Records, 1993)
Mongo's Greatest Hits 🎵🎵🎵🎵 (Fantasy, 1995)

influences:

◀◀ Luciano "Chano" Pozo y Gonzales, Willie Bobo

▶▶ Carlos Santana, Jerry Gonzalez

Nancy Ann Lee

Gray Sargent

Guitarist Sargent works the Boston-to-Providence corridor with considerable success, building a local reputation that hasn't yet spread much beyond those boundaries. When he has gigged in other areas it is often as a sideman for pianist Dave McKenna or as part of a Concord Jazz package tour. Sargent, whose clean, concise playing is deserving of wider recognition, has also played and recorded with neo-swing artists like Ruby Braff and Scott Hamilton.

what's available: *The Gray Sargent Trio* 🎵🎵🎵 (Concord Jazz, 1993, prod. Carl E. Jefferson, John Burk) is Sargent's only solo album, with his longtime associates bassist Marshall Wood and drummer Ray Mosca. Their occasional employer, pianist Dave McKenna, sits in on five of the 11 tunes. The playing is well phrased throughout but it is almost too tasteful with no fire-in-

the-belly performances (with the possible exception of cuts featuring McKenna) to juice up easy lopes through "A Nightingale Sang in Berkeley Square" and "Love Is a Many Splendored Thing."

influences:

◀◀ Dave McKenna, Stanley Clarke, Charlie Christian

Garaud MacTaggart

Stefan Scaggiari

Born in Evansville, IN.

Stefan Scaggiari graduated from the Eastman School of Music in 1968 and promptly joined the Marine Band, where he spent much of his time playing political functions in Washington, D.C. After leaving the military, Scaggiari stayed on in the capital city, making his living as a cocktail pianist in restaurants and leading jam sessions in area clubs. It was at one of these gigs, during the mid-'80s, that he made an impression on Susan Stamberg of National Public Radio, who invited him to play on her show, *Weekend Edition*. Scaggiari became the house pianist for the program, playing the show's theme song week after week for three years. He later picked up a gig as musical director at an Annapolis jazz club, the King of France Tavern, where he began an association with jazz chanteuse Carol Sloane; this job led to a recording contract with Concord Jazz Records. Scaggiari is a talented accompanist for singers and visiting jazz dignitaries, but he's only adequate as leader of his own trio. His ability to feed discreet yet distinct melodic lines for vocalists like Ethel Ennis and Carol Sloane or instrumentalists like Phil Woods and Herb Ellis makes him a valued commodity on nightclub bandstands.

what to buy: *Stefan Out* 🎵🎵🎵 (Concord Jazz, 1995, prod. Nick Phillips), his third album for Concord Jazz, finds Scaggiari still playing tasteful piano—but there are a few semi-adventurous, fiery cover tunes. He does a handful of classics by the Gershwins, Cole Porter, and Harold Arlen, but Scaggiari also includes sparkling performances of Cedar Walton's "Bolivia" and Chick Corea's "Windows" to go with two well-thought-out originals, "Felix" and "When You're Around."

what to buy next: On *That's Ska-jar-e* 🎵🎵🎵 (Concord Jazz, 1992, prod. Carl E. Jefferson, John Burk), his medley of Eddie Harris's "Freedom Jazz Dance" and the Gershwins' "I Got Rhythm" starts the album off on good footing. But the rest finds Scaggiari falling back into the nightclub pianist role with which he is so familiar. They're good tunes played well, but that's it, no special insights.

the rest:

Stefanitely ♪♪♥ (Concord Jazz, 1993)

worth searching for: Scaggiari's best role (for the present) is as an accompanist, and to hear him at his peak with singer Carol Sloane can be a real pleasure. Listen to his sensitive backdrop for Sloane on her album *Heart's Desire* (Concord Jazz, 1992, prod. Carl E. Jefferson, John Burk).

influences:

◀◀ Ellis Larkins, Gerry Wiggins

▶▶ Bill Mays

Garaud MacTaggart

Maria Schneider

Born November 27, 1960, in Windom, MN.

Maybe Maria Schneider will be the one to help jazz craft a more accurate definition of "big band." More than evoking the "good old days" when big bands delivered unthreatening pop instrumentals unsullied by "radicals" such as Parker, Monk and Gillespie, Schneider's large ensemble extends another less-acknowledged tradition, that of the jazz orchestra performing serious original works which swing, rather than empty exercises in nostalgia.

Schneider received proper training to undertake the task, earning her undergraduate degree in theory and composition at the University of Minnesota and her master's at Eastman School of Music. She studied privately with Rayburn Wright and Bob Brookmeyer, two musicians whose knowledge of writing and arranging for large ensembles is unsurpassed. In the mid-1980s, Brookmeyer introduced her to jazz orchestra leader/drummer Mel Lewis, who encouraged Schneider to form her own band as the best outlet for her writing. Before undertaking that big step, Schneider seized the opportunity in 1985 to work with her musical idol, Gil Evans. She remained with Evans until he died in the spring of 1988. The following year, Schneider and her then husband, trombonist John Fedchock, formed a big band. (The two later went their separate ways personally and professionally.) Since 1993, Schneider's Orchestra has been the Monday night band at Visione's in New York City.

what's available: Schneider has two recordings on Enja which showcase her talents as bandleader, composer, and arranger, *Evanescence* ♪♪♪♪ (Enja , 1994, prod. Maria Schneider) and

Coming Out ♪♪♪♪ (Enja, 1996, prod. Maria Schneider). Both albums reflect pre-fusion Gil Evans influences, but are not slavish imitations of his work. Schneider crafts pieces which take advantage of the dynamics a large ensemble can produce. Schneider's arrangements are not just up-tempo, brassy flag-wavers. Her orchestra can play quietly. Coupled with her fresh exploration of large-group tone colors, Schneider's pieces have an engaging capacity to build and release tension in a subtle fashion. Her works unfold slowly, with themes evolving at an unhurried pace. In these days of "give-it-to-me-now," Schneider's approach can be refreshing. But, at times, some songs lose their steam because they go on too long. Similar to the best of Evans's work, soloists are integrated into the arrangements so they never sound strung together but rather rise above and retreat into the ensemble. The highlight of Schneider's 1994 album is the title composition. Through her well-crafted arrangement, the piece builds in intensity and gives way to Rich Perry's tenor solo and Tim Hagans's muted trumpet over humming brass. Schneider's more pastoral-sounding 1996 album places a greater emphasis on writing for ensemble, and features as a centerpiece an impressionistic three-part suite, "Scenes from Childhood," commissioned for the 1995 Monterey Jazz Festival. A minor caveat for these sessions and Schneider's work in general—if you are a jazz fan who likes an overt or even indirect dose of the blues in your music, you won't find much in Schneider's work. But she certainly has a fresh take on what has mostly been a tired subject.

influences:

◀◀ Gil Evans, Bob Brookmeyer, Mel Lewis, Duke Ellington, Gerry Mulligan Concert Jazz Band

Dan Polletta

Rob Schneiderman

Born June 21, 1957, in Boston, MA.

Rob Schneiderman is a gifted pianist, arranger and composer with a strong reputation as a dynamic accompanist and a developing one as a leader of his own sessions. Versed in the bop and post-bop tradition, Schneiderman plays with a beautiful touch and a deceptively relaxed-sounding, on-the-beat feel. He is a lyrical player who relishes a finely crafted melody, and his own solos reflect his strong sense of structure. Growing up in San Diego, Schneiderman started playing piano under the guidance of his mother, a piano teacher. He began playing jazz as a teenager with guitarist Peter Sprague and started working locally at high school parties and a small local nightclub. By the late 1970s, Schneiderman was working regularly with fellow San Diegan, alto saxophonist Charles McPherson, and began working with such top-flight players as Eddie Harris and Sonny Stitt when they came through town. He moved to New York in the early 1980s, landing regular work with Harris, Chet Baker, Art Farmer, James Moody, and Clifford Jordan, among others. He has recorded with J.J. Johnson and TanaReid, the band led by drummer Akira Tana and bassist Rufus Reid. Since the mid-1990s, Schneiderman has lived in the San Francisco Bay Area, where he is pursuing a doctorate in mathematics and continues to play occasional local gigs. He has made a series of excellent albums for Reservoir.

what to buy: A session marked by sensitive group interplay and thoughtful, inspired solos, *Dark Blue* 𝄞𝄞𝄞𝄞 (Reservoir, 1994, prod. Mark Feldman) is an exemplary album on every level. The rhythm section—Schneiderman, bassist Peter Washington and drummer Lewis Nash—plays with tasteful zest, while tenor saxophonist Ralph Moore and trumpeter Brian Lynch both sound confident and inspired throughout. Schneiderman penned five of the album's nine tunes, including the title track, a clever minor blues, and the Miles-ishly modal "Smoke Screen." Lynch contributed the moody, impressionistic "Silent Conversation" and takes a gorgeous solo on the Ray Noble standard "The Touch of Your Lips." A stellar quartet session featuring the formidable rhythm section team of Akira Tana (drums) and Rufus Reid (bass), *New Outlook* 𝄞𝄞𝄞𝄞 (Reservoir, 1988, prod. Mark Feldman) highlights the versatile trombone work of Slide Hampton, who manages to sound like a different player on each tune. Schneiderman composed four of the eight tunes, though he writes with such an ear for melody it's hard to tell his work from the standards. His playing is a relaxed counterpoint to Hampton's hard-charging style, though Schneiderman also plays with considerable, if understated energy.

what to buy next: *Smooth Sailing* 𝄞𝄞𝄞 (Reservoir, 1990, prod. Mark Feldman) features the kind of trio a leader would kill for, players who listen closely and contribute constantly to shape the flow of the music, especially behind someone else's solo. Schneiderman recruited his boss in the TanaReid group, bassist Rufus Reid, and the redoubtable drummer Billy Higgins for this thoroughly enjoyable date. The material includes Schneiderman's attractive originals and standards such as "It Never Entered My Mind" and "You Stepped Out of a Dream," which ends with a long, exhilarating series of drum/piano trade-offs. A light, dancing trio session with a fresh, first-take feel to it, *Keepin' in the Groove* 𝄞𝄞𝄞𝄞 (Reservoir, 1996, prod. Mark Feldman) pairs Schneiderman with his former bosses,

bassist Rufus Reid, and drummer Akira Tana, on a program of classic and lesser-known jazz tunes. Highlights include the funky version of Bud Powell's title track, the lovely, loping version of Eddie Harris's "Deacceleration," and an irresistibly gentle version of Wayne Shorter's "This Is for Albert."

influences:

◀◀ Red Garland, Bill Evans, Bud Powell, Herbie Hancock

Andrew Gilbert

Diane Schuur

Born 1953, in Seattle, WA.

A self-professed disciple of Dinah Washington, Diane Schuur has spent the past decade veering from Brazilian to adult-contemporary pop to blues in hopes of escaping the daunting "next Ella" pigeonhole that set her up for unfair and unrealistic expectations. Blinded after birth in a hospital accident, Schuur got her big break in 1979 when she was invited to sing with Dizzy Gillespie at the Monterey Jazz Festival. She became one of the first acts signed to Dave Grusin and Larry Rosen's GRP label in 1984 after they spotted her singing with Stan Getz on a PBS-televised White House concert. Her Grammy-winning 1987 collaboration with the Count Basie Orchestra showcased the roof-raising power of her voice and endeared her to the burgeoning audience of new jazz listeners enticed by the sonic clout of the then-fledgling compact disc. But conquering the contemporary jazz market so early in her career left Schuur searching for material to challenge her formidable vocal skills. GRP has steered her toward numerous conceptual jazz-vocal projects, but perhaps she'd be better suited to rekindling the gospel and R&B roots she celebrated on 1988's underrated *Talkin' 'Bout You*.

what to buy: The live *Diane Schuur and the Count Basie Orchestra* 𝄞𝄞𝄞 (GRP, 1987, prod. Morgan Ames, Jeffrey Weber) captures Schuur in a sassy, scat-laden big-band summit on such standards as "I Loves You Porgy," her signature rendition of "Travelin' Light," and a thrilling horn-driven romp through Aretha Franklin's "Climbing Higher Mountains." On the other end of the vocal spectrum, *In Tribute* 𝄞𝄞𝄞 (GRP, 1992, prod. Andre Fischer), an homage to jazz heroines such as Ella Fitzgerald, Sarah Vaughan, Billie Holiday, and Dinah Washington, marks her transition from bluesy belter to soulful stylist. Her versions of "Guess I'll Hang My Tears Out to Dry" and "God Bless the Child" are marked by hushed authority rather than pyrotechnic gymnastics.

what to buy next: On *Talkin' 'Bout You* 𝄞𝄞𝄞 (GRP, 1988, prod. Steven Miller), Schuur taps into her gospel and R&B roots on a

Diane Schuur (© Jack Vartoogian)

repertoire-stretching set with three Ray Charles covers and Helen Humes's "Hard Drivin' Mama II."

what to avoid: Her anemic debut album, *Deedles* ♪ (GRP, 1984, prod. Dave Grusin, Larry Rosen), is dragged down by tepid versions of Billy Joel's "New York State of Mind" and Jackson Browne's "Rock Me on the Water," not to mention the annoying omnipresence of the dated Yamaha DX-7 keyboard.

the rest:
Schuur Thing ♪♪♪ (GRP, 1985)
Timeless ♪♪♪♪ (GRP, 1986)
Pure Schuur ♪♪♪ (GRP, 1991)
Love Songs ♪♪♪ (GRP, 1993)
(With B.B. King) *Heart to Heart* ♪♪♪ (GRP, 1994)
Love Walked In ♪♪♪ (GRP, 1996)
Blues for Schuur ♪♪♪ (GRP, 1997)

worth searching for: Schuur sings a lovely version of "The Christmas Song" on the first volume of *A GRP Christmas Collection* ♪♪♪ (GRP, 1988, prod. Michael Abene).

influences:
◀◀ Dinah Washington, Ella Fitzgerald, Sarah Vaughan
▶▶ Dianne Reeves, Anita Baker

David Okamoto

Irene Schweizer

Born 1941.

A member of the European avant-garde, pianist Irene Schweizer is one of the best and most versatile pianists around. After barging headfirst into the all-male bastions of both the London and Berlin free-music scenes, Schweizer made her mark early as a soloist (on FMP) and with various groups, including Barry Guy's London Jazz Composers Orchestra. Later collaborations—including an amazing series of piano/drum duet records—as well as a consistent stream of quality solo work and sessions as a leader have earned her great respect. Although her work is consistently challenging (and occasionally violent), its underlying humor and adventurousness make her music exciting, enjoyable, and approachable.

what to buy: On *Piano Solo, Vols. 1 & 2* 𝄞𝄞𝄞𝄞𝄞 (Intakt, 1990, prod. Rosemarie A. Meier), Schweizer's piano shines in a variety of musical contexts. These two solo records, recorded over three days, show her at the height of her powers, careening between improvisations, blues, and even an Irving Berlin tune. A more recent solo album, *Many and One Direction* 𝄞𝄞𝄞𝄞 (Intakt, 1996), is nearly as good. With *Irene Schweizer & Han Bennink* 𝄞𝄞𝄞𝄞 (Intakt, 1995, prod. Rosemarie A. Meier, Patrick Landolt), which is the best of Schweizer's several piano/drum duet records, she finds a more than able accomplice in Dutch looney tune Han Bennink. Although piano/drum duets aren't all that rare, they can be disconcerting if you're not accustomed to the style; yet the interplay between Schweizer's dense, harmonic passages and Bennink's propulsively free rhythms results in a dynamic improvisational duo. Although Schweizer has worked with bassist JoNlle LJandre and vocalist Maggie Nicols on several occasions, *Splitting Image* 𝄞𝄞𝄞𝄞 (Intakt, 1994/1997, prod. Rosemarie A. Meier) is by far their best work together. Schweizer's glisteningly frenetic piano work finds marvelous accompaniment from LJandre's solid alternations between violent banging and fully expressive arco playing. And Nicols's multi-octave singing, with lyrics about ice cream and love, makes the album strangely powerful and truly rewarding.

the rest:

Irene Schweizer & Louis Moholo 𝄞𝄞𝄞𝄞 (Intakt, 1986)
Irene Schweizer & Gunter Sommer 𝄞𝄞𝄞𝄞 (Intakt, 1987)
Irene Schweizer & Andrew Cyrille 𝄞𝄞𝄞 (Intakt, 1988)
Irene Schweizer & Pierre Favre 𝄞𝄞𝄞𝄞 (Intakt, 1990)

worth searching for: *The Storming of the Winter Palace* (Intakt, 1988) is a fine collaboration between Schweizer, Nicols, LJandre, drummer Gunter Sommer, and trombonist George Lewis. For some reason it's currently unavailable. It's well worth getting if you find it, though: given the incredibly swinging outness of this adventure, it's great to hear Lewis and Nicols duke it out on a couple of numbers.

Jason Ferguson

John Scofield

Born December 26, 1951, in Dayton, OH.

John Scofield has become one of jazz's leading guitarists by constantly challenging himself. Raised in Wilton, Connecticut,

young Scofield absorbed a variety of sounds and styles, everything from the Beatles to John Coltrane. After attending the Berklee College of Music, where he studied with Mick Goodrick and Gary Burton, he joined Gerry Mulligan in 1974. In the following years larger audiences heard Scofield in the fusionesque George Duke/Billy Cobham Band. As the guitarist performed as a sideman with prestigious bandleaders, he simultaneously launched his solo career in Europe. Scofield enjoyed immediate success in a variety of musical configurations, the most popular being a trio with Steve Swallow and Adam Nussbaum. Scofield's association with Miles Davis (1982–85) boosted his reputation enough to allow him to break away from sideman work and concentrate fully on his own endeavors. The John Scofield Quartet, the latest chapter in the continuing development of his solo career, is a marked departure from the electric funk of his earlier groups. Scofield's recent collaborators have included saxman Joe Lovano and organist Larry Goldings. He also recorded an album with the late saxophonist Eddie Harris.

what to buy: *Quiet* 𝄞𝄞𝄞𝄞𝄞 (Verve, 1997, prod. John Scofield, Steve Swallow) is a rare acoustic guitar session for John Scofield, utilizing a horn section along with his working quartet and special guest Wayne Shorter. Scofield wrote the tunes and did the arrangements with the help of long-time collaborator, bassist Steve Swallow. A recent addition to his creative arsenal, the nylon-stringed acoustic guitar well-serves his concise improvisations, in which he displays the same concern for finely-etched melody that characterizes his memorable compositions. In a clean, understated style, he exploits the affinity intimate-sounding nylon strings have for romantic melodies. And, taking a page from the arranging book of his hero, Gil Evans, he creates moody, Spanish-tinged chamber-jazz settings for his compositions. Shorter's playing is memorable as well, especially on the gorgeous ballad "Away with Words." John Scofield was thinking about soul jazz when he recorded *Hand Jive* 𝄞𝄞𝄞𝄞𝄞 (Blue Note, 1994, prod. Lee Townsend), a 1993 date featuring his Quartet and special guest Eddie Harris. It was Harris and Les McCann who created a significant pre-fusion groove back in the 1960s with their appealing version of the tune "Compared to What," and Scofield succeeds in capturing that dynamic immediately on his "I'll Take Les" and the other nine tunes, as well. There's an earthiness, lots of structural adventurousness, and a down-home interplay between Harris and Scofield that add up to big fun on *Hand Jive*. *Groove Elation!* 𝄞𝄞𝄞𝄞𝄞 (Blue Note, 1995, prod. Lee Townsend) oozes and drips with the retro hybrid of funk, spirituals, blues, and soul jazz that infuses these catchy tunes and inspires some first rate soloists. This album marks the first time Scofield augmented his group with horns, and it's a significant creative highpoint in his distinctive career. Scofield wrote the charts himself, and they land all their punches in the right places, accenting and commenting on his ingeniously angled melodies. His solos sail along on his lilting, strutting melodicism and his rich subtext of pop music referents. The real masterpiece is "Peculiar," which perfectly distills the essence of the funk-jazz cocktail that Scofield has served up for the last five years; at the same time it suggests a new level of complexity in his writing. *What We Do* ♪♪♪♪ (Blue Note, 1993, prod. John Scofield) is Scofield's third recording with tenor saxophonist Joe Lovano, and it's a more straight-ahead trip than their earlier funk-oriented sessions. There are a variety of moods and settings here that bring out the best in these players: the appropriately titled "Call 911," focusing on Lovano's urgent tenor; "Camp Out," which walks the fine line between freedom and normality; and "Little Walk," where Lovano and Scofield play as one. *What We Do* is a most welcome addition to Scofield's considerable discography. *Pick Hits Live* ♪♪♪♪♪ (Gramavision, 1994, prod. John Scofield) was recorded live in Tokyo in 1987, when Scofield's guitar was at its most explosive. The influence of Miles Davis is very evident here; paying his dues with Miles put him in much greater control of the guitar. He's nothing short of audacious. Aside from a beautiful solo-guitar piece, "Georgia on My Mind," the album is dominated by Dennis Chambers's jazz P-Funk groove. *Out Like a Light* ♪♪♪♪ (Enja, 1981, prod. John Scofield) is from a 1981 trio date, recorded live in Munich, that also produced the CD *Shinola*. The group is absolutely locked in synch on five extended tracks, with Scofield's guitar, Steve Swallow's bass, and Adam Nussbaum's drums working as one. Swallow's playing is so strong that it puts a more tasteful face on the guitar trio format. This was done before Scofield joined Miles, and he was still getting his sound and approach together; but this working group does indeed have its act together (and check out the beautiful solo guitar rendition of "Melinda").

what to buy next: Joined by bassist Darryl Jones, drummer Omar Hakim, and keyboardist Don Grolnick, Scofield strikes a funky techno-groove on *Still Warm* ♪♪♪♪ (Gramavision, 1989, prod. Steve Swallow). Jones and Hakim are beatmasters supreme, and combined with Grolnick's fascinating keyboard textures and Scofield's sharp, hotly articulated guitar, this is state of the art fusion. *Rough House* ♪♪♪ (Enja, 1994, prod. John Scofield) is an early Scofield date, made before Scofield joined Miles and after the guitarist worked with Charles Mingus

and Gary Burton, so the music is an informed amalgam of free-flowing bop and an intelligent sort of bluesy rock. The session features Hal Galper on piano, Stafford James on bass, and Adam Nussbaum on drums. Galper and Scofield are great together on uptempo romps like "Triple Play," with Nussbaum burning as well. *Shinola* ♪♪♪ (Enja, 1993, prod. John Scofield) is taken from the same live 1991 trio date in Munich that produced *Out Like a Light*. There's a loose, exploratory feel on these rambling trio tracks. *Live* ♪♪♪ (Enja, 1977, prod. John Scofield), Scofield's first date as a leader, features Richie Beirach on piano, George Mraz on bass, and Joe LaBarbera on drums. An inspired debut mixing styles and settings, the album includes the standard "Softly As in a Morning Sunrise" and the adventurous "Air Pakistan." There's plenty of action packed jazz funk on *Loud Jazz* ♪♪♪ (Gramavision, 1989, prod. Steve Swallow), an energetic, animated 1987 session that includes George Duke and guitarist Hiram Bullock.

influences:

◀◀ B.B. King, Otis Rush, George Benson, Pat Martino, Jim Hall

▶▶ Pat Metheny, Mike Stern, Kevin Eubanks, John Abercrombie, Ted Dunbar, Steve Khan

Bret Primack

Jimmy Scott

Born July 17, 1925, in Cleveland, OH.

With his androgynous appearance and near-soprano voice—the result of a hormonal imbalance—Jimmy Scott is often mistaken for a jazz chanteuse. The confusion might have thrown audiences back in the late '40s, when Scott was singing with Lionel Hampton's band, but it has helped turn him into a hip enigma in the '90s as he has become the toast of New York's club circuit. Scott's solo career never matched the heights of his talent: he scored a handful of R&B hits in the '50s as Little Jimmy Scott but got snared in a relentless tangle of record company politics. Scott went into early retirement in the mid-'60s, partly to care for his ailing father, but re-emerged in the '80s with a flurry of career-rejuvenating appearances: Bill Cosby used his rendition of "Evening in Paradise" in his sitcom; Lou Reed drafted him to sing backing vocals on *Magic and Loss*; Alec Baldwin and Kim Basinger asked him to warble "All of Me" at their wedding; and David Lynch hired him to croon "Sycamore Trees" in the final episode of *Twin Peaks*. Signed to Sire/Warner Bros. in 1992 after he was discovered singing at Doc Pomus's funeral, Scott continues make fine albums, even though his voice nowadays isn't as strong as his convictions.

what to buy: *Dream* ♪♪♪♪ (Sire/Warner Bros., 1994, prod. Mitchell Froom) is a startlingly beautiful, achingly intimate showcase for Scott's delicate phrasing and laid-back supper-club panache. Backing him on such nightclub staples as "Don't Take Your Love from Me," "It Shouldn't Happen to a Dream," and "I'm Through with Love" are Ron Carter, Milt Jackson, Junior Mance, and Red Holloway. *Heaven* ♪♪♪ (Warner Bros., 1996, prod. Craig Street), his haunting collaboration with pianist Jacky Terrasson, mixes soul-baring spirituals with reverent covers of Bob Dylan's "When He Returns," Talking Heads' title track, and country artist Julie Miller's "All My Tears."

the rest:
All the Way ♪♪♪ (Sire/Warner Bros., 1992)
Lost and Found ♪♪♪ (Rhino/Atlantic, 1993)
All Over Again ♪♪♪ (Savoy Jazz, 1995)

worth searching for: The soundtrack *Twin Peaks: Fire Walk with Me* ♪♪ (Warner Bros., 1992, prod. David Lynch, Angelo Badalamenti) features a reprise of Scott's rendition of "Sycamore Trees."

influences:

◀◀ Sarah Vaughan, Charles Brown

▶▶ Julee Cruise, Simply Red, Lou Reed, Jai

David Okamoto

Shirley Scott

Born March 14, 1934, in Philadelphia, PA.

Though she's best known for her organ playing—especially with saxophonist Stanley Turrentine in the 1960s—Shirley Scott's first love is piano, which she studied from age six. She also took up trumpet successfully and won a scholarship. Her family was musical and her early experiences were at her father's club playing in her brother's band. With the popularity of the Hammond B-3 organ, Scott, then 19, began working a club date where the owner provided an organ and she quickly learned how to play. Sometime around 1953, Eddie "Lockjaw" Davis came to Philadelphia for a gig and needed a replacement for his organist who had quit. Scott filled in and shortly after that recorded her first album. Since then, she has recorded about 50 albums as leader and performed and recorded with Eddie "Lockjaw" Davis's group (1955–60) and with Stanley Turrentine (1960–71). (They married in 1961, divorced in 1971.) She also recorded with Jimmy Forrest (1978), Dexter Gordon (1982), Joe Newman, and Al Grey. Scott has recorded for the Prestige, Impulse!, Atlantic, Chess/Cadet, Strata-East, Muse, and Candid

labels. Her Hammond B-3 playing on her early albums has a percussive, biting approach that exploits the instrument's full range. Her straight-ahead, bebop piano artistry is particularly notable on her more recent piano trio recordings for Candid. In the early 1990s, Scott began teaching jazz and piano at her alma mater, Cheyney University. In 1992, Scott showed up as musical director and pianist for Bill Cosby's Philadelphia-produced television show, *You Bet Your Life*. She continues to perform and tour internationally, playing both piano and organ.

what to buy: Her first album in some time, *Blues Everywhere* ♪♪♪♪ (Candid, 1992, prod. Mark Morganelli) features Shirley Scott leading a piano trio recorded live at Birdland in New York City in November 1991 with bassist Arthur Harper and drummer Mickey Roker. Scott shows a powerful keyboard style (likely influenced by her organ technique), a strong two-handed approach that sports her thick block chords on the blues numbers. On boppers, her single-line right-hand runs are kept interesting by interspersing chords to create a light swing feel. Roker and Harper are comfortable helping her create deeper grooves, and they take some fine solos throughout the set. Among the seven tunes, Scott includes two originals: the hard-swinging "Blues Everywhere," and her powerful, nearly nine-minute contrapuntal piece "Oasis," which delightfully switches rhythms and features fine solos from her team mates. She also serves up lovely versions of warhorse standards like a waltzing "Autumn Leaves," a boppish, uptempo "Embraceable You," and a delicately reflective version of "'Round Midnight." This is a most memorable piano trio album that captures Scott and her cohorts in peak form. For a sampling of Scott's fabulous organ work of the 1960s, one of the CD reissues readily available, *Soul Shoutin'* ♪♪♪♪ (Prestige, 1963/1994, prod. Ozzie Cadena), combines two previous Prestige albums recorded in 1963, six tunes from *The Soul Is Willing* and the five tunes from *Shirley Scott & Stanley Turrentine/Soul Shoutin'*. She and tenor saxophonist Stanley Turrentine enjoy the rhythm backing of Major Holley and Earl May sharing bass duties, and the righteous rhythm master Grasella Oliphant on drums. The 11 tunes include four memorable originals from Turrentine ("The Soul Is Willing," "I Feel All Right," "Deep Down Soul," and the title tune). They also play other soulful numbers ("Secret Love," "Gravy Waltz," "In the Still of the Night") that compare favorably to the boppish and swinging fare that Jimmy Smith was creating during the same era. It's definitely jazz, but with a bluesy edge that gives it utmost appeal. Scott shines on her solos throughout, playing with loads of soul and authoritative technique. Turrentine is also in superior shape, generating wonderful soul-jazz tenorisms. This album is highly recommended.

what to buy next: From the piano trio session recorded live at Birdland in New York City in November 1991 (see above), though released three years later, *Skylark* 𝄢𝄢𝄢 (Candid, 1995, prod. Mark Morganelli, Alan Bates) features Shirley Scott playing with bassist Arthur Harper and drummer Mickey Roker. The seven tunes include a lovely 11-minute version of "Alone Together," a pretty bossa nova reading of Horace Silver's "Peace," and more with her comfortably tight trio. A pleasing listen all the way through, especially when she digs into bluesy grooves as she does on her head-nodding original, "McGee and Me." *A Walkin' Thing* 𝄢𝄢𝄢 (Candid, 1996, prod. Alan Bates) captures a 1992 studio session Scott made with bassist Arthur Harper, drummer Aaron Walker, Terell Stafford (trumpet), and Tim Warfield (tenor saxophone). If you expect to hear that stinging sound of the old-fashioned Hammond B-3, you'll be disappointed. Although Scott's chops are fine, the organ sounds muted. Plus, on the tunes where the horn players revel, she can barely be heard. Yet there are highlights among the eight tunes that make this a worthy listen. On the 10-minute title gem by Benny Carter, Scott takes one of her best solos and creates deep-groove, walking bass lines that provide launching pads for the eager young soloists. Another jewel is Scott's take on the classic soul standard, "When a Man Loves a Woman," done as a seductive, gospel-tinged unaccompanied solo. Warfield and Stafford have worked together in the past, and their front-line horns, as well as their individual soloing, are excellent on this outing.

best of the rest:
Blue Flames 𝄢𝄢𝄢 (Prestige, 1964/OJC, 1994)
Queen of the Organ 𝄢𝄢𝄢 (Impulse!, 1964/1993)

Nancy Ann Lee

Stephen Scott

Born March 13, 1970, in New York, NY.

Stephen Scott is a dazzling pianist and arranger who was already playing with Betty Carter at the age of 18 (she called him a "genius" and he appears on her 1987 recording *Look What I Got*). Leaving Carter, Scott recorded two albums with the Harper Brothers, was a pivotal member of Roy Hargrove's highly-praised first quintet, appeared on Joe Henderson's Grammy-winning *Lush Life*, performed on albums by Bobby Watson, Sonny Rollins, and Justin Robinson, and has recorded five solo albums in a leadership capacity. Scott's solo debut for

Verve in 1991, *Something to Consider*, won tremendous critical acclaim, but it was recently deleted from the PolyGram catalog. His subsequent recordings have been better, showing his continued progress. A creative musician, Scott has passed the "player with potential" phase to become a pianist, composer, and arranger to be reckoned with. He is one of the best of the "young lions."

what to buy: With a lineup that includes Branford Marsalis, Ron Blake, Jesse Davis, Kenny Garrett and Russell Malone, Scott's latest recording, *The Beautiful Thing* 𝄢𝄢𝄢 (Verve, 1997, prod. Stephen Scott, Richard Seidel), is his most adventurous. His approach is often modern, with fusion tones on "Afterthoughts and Reflections," and an acoustic smooth jazz feel on the title track. But it is also rich in tradition, with a faithful version of "This Little Light of Mine," a Tyneresque rendition of "I Love Lucy" (the theme from the TV show), and a fantastic reading of Kenny Dorham's "La Mesha." Though broad in scope, *The Beautiful Thing* is a cohesive statement confirming not only that Stephen Scott has arrived, but he is here to stay. Scott's second release, *Aminah's Dream* 𝄢𝄢𝄢 (Verve, 1993, prod. Brian Bacchus, Stephen Scott), is a burner that shows significant growth from his debut. Inspired by bassist Ron Carter and drummer Elvin Jones, Scott is in fine form. His ideas show more focus and his compositions are better developed on this fantastic follow-up that avoids the sophomore jinx.

what to buy next: The Roy Hargrove/Christian McBride/Stephen Scott Trio performs on *Parker's Mood* 𝄢𝄢𝄢 (Verve, 1995, prod. Richard Seidel, Don Sickler). The three core members of the original Roy Hargrove Quintet pay tribute to Charlie Parker by playing 16 songs from his songbook with excellent results. The players stretch beyond straight bebop, adding vocabulary from other traditions to make this something more than three young cats playing Bird.

the rest:
Renaissance 𝄢𝄢𝄢 (Verve, 1995)

influences:
◄◄ Herbie Hancock, Bud Powell, Wynton Kelly, Ahmad Jamal, McCoy Tyner

Paul MacArthur

Tony Scott

Born Anthony Sciacca, June 17, 1921 in Morristown, NJ.

Scott would be far better known if he were less of a nomad. After establishing himself as one of the few great bebop clarinetists, he left the U.S. in 1959, upset by the deaths of a number of musician friends and by the lack of respect for his instrument (he also plays alto and baritone saxophones, piano, guitar, and marimba). Following a period of travels throughout Asia, he returned to the U.S. in 1965, but moved to Italy in the following decade and has since spent time in Africa and the Middle East. He has also wandered musically, recording new age, electronic, and ambient music. But Scott's warm, dark clarinet tone (strongly influenced by tenor saxophonist Ben Webster) and melodic sense remain distinctive.

Scott attended Julliard from 1940 to 1942 and studied composition privately with Stefan Wolpe. He worked as a sideman with many of the greats of the swing era in his apprentice years, including a short stint in the Ellington band. Scott's recorded debut as a leader came in 1946 on three tracks for the Gotham label (run by the Sam Goody record store) leading a septet including Dizzy Gillespie (under the alias B. Bopstein), Webster, and Trummy Young, with Sarah Vaughan on vocals. He wrote arrangements for and accompanied Billie Holiday; he was also Harry Belafonte's music director for a while. Scott's emotive style and refined technique made him a poll-topping clarinetist in the 1950s, and it's unfortunate that so little of his work prior to his departure is currently available. While he was in Japan in 1964 he recorded music designed for meditation, anticipating in some ways the new age trend of coming decades. He says he has turned down jazz work that he felt would take him away from his true musical interests; fortunately he has recorded some uncompromised but definitely jazz albums for the Philology label in Italy.

what to buy: *Sung Heroes* ♪♪♪♪ (Sunnyside, 1989, prod. Tony Scott) contains 1959 material that has also appeared under the title *Dedications*. Most of the album is with Bill Evans, Scott La-Faro, and Paul Motian; on one track the leader plays piano. Except for one wailing blues, the mood is somber, as many of the dedicatees were recently dead. There's not the slightest hint of maudlin sappiness, however; some tracks approach abstractness, although the majority are quite melodic.

what to buy next: *African Bird: Come Back! Mother Africa* ♪♪♪♪ (Soul Note, 1984, prod. Tony Scott) gives a taste of Scott's integration of world music into his style without going as far from jazz as *Music for Zen Meditation*, undoubtedly because the main influence here is African. There is a lot of African percussion on these tracks, and the kalimba (thumb piano) and marimba are prevalent as well. The album is dedicated "To the Spirit of Charlie Parker," and Scott's clarinet playing remains

clearly bop-derived, though by this point there are many other ingredients.

best of the rest:
Music for Zen Meditation ♪♪♪ (Verve, 1964/1998)
The Clarinet Album ♪♪♪♪ (Philology, 1993)

worth searching for: On *Homage to Billie Holiday—Body and Soul* ♪♪♪♪ (Philology, 1995, prod. Paolo Piangiarelli), which he recorded with Franco D'Andrea, Scott remembers his friend with intimate clarinet/piano duos on songs associated with her. Scott's solo take on "God Bless the Child" is especially moving, as are his liner notes, a personal account of Billie's last concert and troubled last days. Philology is a small Italian label, but at the moment its distribution in the U.S. is fairly extensive.

influences:

◀◀ Charlie Parker, Ben Webster

▶▶ Buddy DeFranco, Jimmy Giuffre, Perry Robinson, Don Byron

Walter Faber

Gil Scott-Heron

Born April 1, 1949 in Chicago, IL.

Starting as an angry, somewhat one-dimensional and unsympathetic poet, Gil Scott-Heron broadened his outlook and empathy to become an astute and articulate observer of socio-political issues, always retaining enough of his anger with injustice to give his work an edge. Early on he incorporated music into his art, and eventually became an effective singer in a mildly jazzy R&B context. Scott-Heron debuted with an album of poems accompanied by percussion, 15 short tracks that packed a big wallop and, as much as they were of their time, remain relevant (which says as much about the United States as it does about the poet). On his next record he added more music to his sound but continued to rap. Whether or not listeners shared the sentiments of such hard-hitting tracks as "Whitey on the Moon" (which criticized spending money on the space program while there was poverty in the inner city) or the famous "The Revolution Will Not Be Televised" (the mature Scott-Heron would not be guilty of the cheap shot at "hairy-armed women's liberationists"), it was clear he had a way with words and a distaste for the hypocrisy and BS of politicians, regardless of their race. After three albums on Flying Dutchman (owned by John Coltrane producer Bob Thiele), he made one classic album on Strata-East and then became the first artist signed by Arista. All the while he was adding more and more music to his records, and his Arista albums were typically pop-oriented R&B and funk, abetted by his long collaboration with flutist/keyboardist Brian Jackson (who sometimes took the lead vocals and often shared billing on the albums). They even made an anti-drinking ditty, "The Bottle," appealing enough that it was a dance hit in 1974. His 10-year Arista period overlapped considerably with the Reagan Era, inspiring two of his best political songs, "'B' Movie" and "Re-Ron," and found him taking an increasingly universal outlook as reflected in the classic "(What's the Word) Johannesburg," which he performed as one of *Saturday Night Live*'s first musical guests. But his #30-charting 1975 Arista debut was his only album to reach the Top 50, and urban hits such as the anti-drug "Angel Dust" never broke out into the mainstream, though his popularity was broad-based enough that he was more than a cult artist. After parting ways with Arista, Scott-Heron was not picked up by another label. The early '90s, surprisingly, found him combatting substance abuse. Apparently winning the battle, he made a comeback with one album for TVT and received props from the more thoughtful present-day rappers for his influence and example.

what to buy: *The Revolution Will Not Be Televised* 🎵🎵🎵🎵 (RCA, 1988, prod. Bob Thiele) is audacious and revolutionary (in several senses of the word). This newer version (an LP compilation with the same title had less material) adds bits from his first two albums on Flying Dutchman to the entire *Pieces of a Man* 🎵🎵🎵🎵 (Flying Dutchman, 1973, prod. Bob Thiele).

what to buy next: *The Best of Gil Scott-Heron* 🎵🎵🎵🎵 (Arista, 1984, prod. various) is the only Arista album still in print, a scandalous situation made even worse by the fact that it still skimpily consists of the same nine tracks as when it came out on LP. It has the best-known Arista tracks—"Winter in America," "The Bottle," "Johannesburg," "Angel Dust," "'B' Movie," "Re-Ron," etc. and is the only option for those not willing to search used LP bins.

what to avoid: It's not hard to avoid *1980* 🎵 (Arista, 1980, prod. Gil Scott-Heron, Brian Jackson, Malcolm Cecil), since it's out of print, but the combination of overly disco-ized production and running out of material and ideas after putting out albums at a furious pace make this Scott-Heron's limpest album. After the thoughtful, articulate anti-nuke plant "We Almost Lost Detroit" on *Bridges*, "Shut 'Um Down" was mere sloganeering, showing as much imagination as the album title.

the rest:
Small Talk at 125th and Lenox 🎵🎵🎵 (Flying Dutchman, 1972)

Free Will 🎵🎵🎵🎵 (Flying Dutchman, 1972)
Winter in America 🎵🎵🎵🎵 (Strata/East, 1974)
The First Minute of a New Day 🎵🎵🎵 (Arista, 1975)
It's Your World 🎵🎵🎵🎵 (Arista, 1976)
Bridges 🎵🎵🎵🎵 (Arista, 1977)
Secrets 🎵🎵🎵🎵 (Arista, 1978)
The Mind of Gil Scott-Heron 🎵🎵🎵🎵 (Arista, 1978)
Real Eyes 🎵🎵🎵🎵 (Arista, 1980)
Reflections 🎵🎵🎵🎵 (Arista, 1981)
Moving Target 🎵🎵🎵🎵 (Arista, 1982)
Minister of Information: Live 🎵🎵🎵 (Castle Communications, 1994)
Spirits 🎵🎵🎵 (TVT, 1994)

worth searching for: *From South Africa to South Carolina* 🎵🎵🎵🎵🎵 (Arista, 1975, prod. Gil Scott-Heron, Brian Jackson, the Midnight Band) is not only one of the greatest political albums of the '70s, it's also got some of the best grooves, funky but often infused with elliptical African rhythm patterns. Not only does it connect the racism in "Johannesburg" and "South Carolina (Barnwell)," it also showcases a gentle, personalized optimism on "Beginnings (First Minute of a New Day)" and "A Lovely Day." The only flaw is Jackson's strained, out-of-tune singing on some tracks.

influences:

◀◀ Langston Hughes, Amiri Baraka, Last Poets

▶▶ Sekou Sundiata, Public Enemy, KRS-One, Spearhead, Dana Bryant

Steve Holtje

Mitch Seidman

Born November 27, 1953, in Long Branch, NJ.

Stylistically situated somewhere between the art-bop of Lennie Tristano and Jimmy Giuffre's Third-Stream sensibilities is where you'll find the mellow, understated guitarist Mitch Seidman.

what's available: Seidman's debut, *Fretware* 🎵🎵🎵🎵 (Brownstone Recordings, 1994, prod. Harvie Swartz, Mitch Seidman), is the more boppish of his two albums to date. It boasts a particularly fine supporting cast of Harvie Swartz (of Sheila Jordan fame) on bass, Alan Dawson on drums, and, on several tracks, either Charlie Kohlhase (on alto or baritone saxophone) or Leonard Hochman (tenor sax or bass clarinet). The material is easygoing and attractive, with Lee Konitz's "It's You" and Kohlhase's "Dyani" being the standouts. On the former, Kohlhase's alto waxes particularly Lee-like, while on the latter, Swartz's bass comes on like Richard Davis in full "Music Matador" flight. *Ants in a Trance* 🎵🎵🎵🎵 (Brownstone, prod. Mitch Seidman, Harvie

Swartz) changes the instrumental lineup to a string-heavy guitar, bass (Swartz, again), and viola (Ella Lou Weiler), augmented by Hochman on bass clarinet. Dark and pithy, the musical emphasis here is decidedly Third Stream, with the chamber-like appeal of Chico Hamilton's mid-'50s quintets, especially on the opening cover of Thelonious Monk's "Bye-Ya" and Seidman's brooding title tune. Versions of Dave Brubeck's "In Your Own Sweet Way," Giuffre's "Frog Legs," and Zoller's "Homage to O.P." (Oscar Pettiford) are also here.

influences:

Jimmy Raney, Tal Farlow, Attila Zoller, Jim Hall, Miles Davis, Sonny Rollins, Bill Evans

David Prince

Pete Selvaggio

Born December 15, 1941, in Cleveland, OH.

Growing up in Cleveland, Pete Selvaggio began playing accordion at age nine and quickly learned the instrument to surprise his father, who was away on a trip to Italy. Selvaggio's teacher, Joe Trolli, had written many polkas played by the Frankie Yankovic band in Cleveland, and under Trolli's instruction, the young Selvaggio excelled on the instrument. Selvaggio eventually played everything from Italian folk tunes to polkas, and European classical music, inspired by his mother who was a trained violinist. He studied at the Cleveland Institute of Music, and at the age of 16, Selvaggio was featured during the Summer Pops programs of the Cleveland Orchestra. Hearing the 1950s pop-jazz trio recordings of Chicago accordionist Art Van Damme inspired Selvaggio to explore jazz. Throughout high school, Selvaggio played accordion in a jazz ensemble that included trombonist Jiggs Whigham. Word of Selvaggio's talent got around. He joined the popular accordion-organ-guitar trio, The Three Suns, for three years, and at age 23 relocated to New York where he freelanced in between tours with Guy Lombardo's Royal Canadians, an eight-year association during which Selvaggio played accordion, piano (the latter learned during a hiatus from the band), and sang. Selvaggio returned to Cleveland where his all-around musicianship has enlivened the scene for over two decades. In 1992, Selvaggio lent Old World charm to Cleveland saxophonist Ernie Krivda's album, *Ernie Krivda Jazz* on Cadence Records. Krivda figured prominently in Selvaggio eventually getting his self-produced session on the Koch Jazz label. (The session was originally a limited cassette release under another title.) Selvaggio also regularly plays piano and sings with the revived 1950s vocal quartet, The Four Lads, and has occasionally performed with The Cleveland Orchestra. But it's his accordion mastery that's his real gift. Look for another release sometime in 1998.

what's available: Pete Selvaggio's debut album as leader, *Galleria* 𝄞𝄞𝄞𝄞 (Koch Jazz, 1996, prod. Ernie Krivda), features the accordionist charmingly reinventing eight diverse standards with long-time Cleveland collaborators, a well-matched crew that includes guitarist Bob Fraser, bassist Bill Plavan (who died in 1997), and drummer Val Kent. Selvaggio is a soulful, expressive player, a keen improviser who draws from musical fare of today and the past four decades. His version of Cole Porter's "Dream Dancing," given samba seasoning, is elegant. The team does eight minutes of sweet justice to Fats Waller's "Jitterbug Waltz," warmly reinvents the 1950s classic "Stranger in Paradise" (based on Borodin themes), and beautifully remakes Charlie Haden's "First Song." Selvaggio's solos are masterful and impassioned throughout, but it is his warmly lyrical version of "Ballad of the Sad Young Man" that should bring tears to your eyes. Whether playing uncomplicated single-lines or adding drama with chorded passages, or tampering with tempos, Selvaggio is a hit. Tenor saxophonist Ernie Krivda guests on his original title tune, a rapidly flowing number that puts each player in the spotlight, and on the seductive "Wild Is the Wind." A magnificent debut from an accordion virtuoso and definitely a musician to track.

influences:

Dick Contino, Art Van Damme, Eddie Monteiro

see also: *Ernie Krivda*

Nancy Ann Lee

Charlie Sepulveda

Born in New York, NY.

A fiery, fat-toned trumpeter, Charlie Sepulveda is one of the leading young musicians developing a hard-driving synthesis of post-bop jazz and Afro-Caribbean rhythms. Sepulveda was born in the Bronx, but moved with his family to Caguas, Puerto Rico when he was a child. He began learning trumpet at age 12 and was soon playing at a local Pentecostal church. A friend introduced him to the music of Clifford Brown and Lee Morgan, sparking his passion for jazz and horn-laden pop music groups such as Earth, Wind & Fire and Chicago. By age 15, Sepulveda was playing professionally with some of Puerto Rico's leading bands, from the avant garde Le Masacre to established stars such as Willie Rosario, Cortijo, and Bobby Valentin, and the groups Salsa Fever and Batacumbele. Sepulveda joined Eddie Palmieri's band and moved to New York in the late 1980s. He has recorded with Palmieri, Hilton Ruiz, Steve Turre, and Tito Puente, and toured with Dizzy Gillespie's United Nation Orchestra, performing alongside Dizzy and Wynton Marsalis on the concert recording *To Diz with Love*.

what to buy: Trumpeter Charlie Sepulveda's second session for Antilles, *Algo Nuestro* 𝄞𝄞𝄞𝄞 (Antilles, 1993, prod. Charlie Sepulveda), is a blazing session that brings together many of the leading young Latin musicians forging an irresistible synthesis of Afro-Caribbean rhythms and advanced jazz harmonies and improvisation. Sepulveda's sextet features David Sanchez (tenor and soprano sax), Ed Simon (piano), Andy Gonzalez (bass), Adam Cruz (drums), and Richie Flores (percussion). The trumpeter tips his hat to his former bandleader with a flag waving version of Eddie Palmieri's "Puerto Rico." Sepulveda introduces three of his own tunes, including the powerfully swinging opening track "El Gringo," and the title track, which translates as "Our Thing." Other highlights include Sanchez's "Mal Social," which inspires some of Sepulveda's most compelling trumpet work, and pianist Donald Brown's "Episode from a Village Dance."

what to buy next: Something of a disappointment, *Watermelon Man* 𝄞𝄞𝄞 (RMM, 1996, prod. Charlie Sepulveda) is an enjoyable commercial effort that backs off from Sepulveda's earlier, more challenging sessions. Herbie Hancock's title track is fatally overproduced, though there are also moments of great power and purity, such as the duet between Sepulveda and pianist Dario Eskanaci on the trumpeter's tune "Julia." Another highlight is Luis Demetrio's "Apoyate En Mi Alma," featuring a playful vibes solo by Tito Puente. Sepulveda's band, The Turnaround, includes tenor saxophonist Eric Leed, keyboardist Renato Neto, pianist Eskenaci, bassist John Benitez, drummer Johnny Almendra, and percussionist Anthony Carrillo.

the rest:
New Arrival 𝄞𝄞𝄞𝄞 (Antilles, 1991)

worth searching for: The extraordinary pianist Hilton Ruiz pays homage to various musical giants on *Heroes* 𝄞𝄞𝄞𝄞 (Telarc, 1994, prod. John Snyder), a sometimes overwhelming session featuring a dream team of Latin percussionists—Steve Berrios, Ignacio Berroa, Giovanni Hidalgo, Tito Puente and Carlos "Patato" Vales. The horn section ain't too shabby either, with David Sanchez, Steve Turre, and Sepulveda, whose duet with Ruiz on Dizzy Gillespie's "Con Alma" is one of the session's highlights.

influences:
◀◀ Dizzy Gillespie, Clifford Brown

Andrew Gilbert

Doc Severinsen

Born Carl H. Severinsen, July 7, 1927, in Arlington, OR.

One of the most visible trumpet players of the last 40 years, Carl H. "Doc" Severinsen is a consummate professional who can execute a wide variety of musical genres with equal skill. Whether a bandleader, guest star, or hired hand, Severinsen has never allowed his legendary sartorial style or immense fame to intrude upon the character of his music.

The son of an Oregon dentist, he was nicknamed "little doc," and began playing trumpet at the age of seven. As a teenager, Severinsen won the Music Educator's National Contest, and was good enough to tour with the Ted Fiorito Orchestra. After World War II, he played trumpet and flugelhorn with bands led by Charlie Barnet, Tommy Dorsey, and Benny Goodman, before joining NBC as a staff musician in 1949. When he wasn't playing on the big network variety shows of the 1950s and early 1960s (the *Steve Allen* show among them), Severinsen recorded solid jazz with the likes of Stan Getz, Tito Puente, Gene Krupa, Milt Jackson, and softer, more commercial sounds with Dinah Washington and Ray Conniff. When Johnny Carson took over *The Tonight Show* from Jack Paar in 1963, Severinsen was the assistant bandleader behind Skitch Henderson. Carson discovered he had better comedic chemistry with the affable trumpet player than the dour Henderson, and by 1967 made Severinsen the band leader of his nightly program. Always a colorful dresser, Severinsen began wearing increasingly wild outfits to accommodate the jokes in Carson's monologues, and crystallized his TV persona as the goofy hipster. TV fame led to a series of well-received jazz and pop LPs on the Command, RCA, Epic, and ABC labels, as well as being voted the Top Brass Player in over a dozen Playboy music polls. When Carson left *The Tonight Show* in 1992, so did Severinsen, who has since led successful tours with his TV band and been named the Principal Pops Conductor for the Phoenix Symphony, The Minnesota Orchestra, The Milwaukee Symphony, and Buffalo Philharmonic Orchestra. Though Doc Severinsen is past 70 years old, he still has a pretty good lip.

what to buy: Severinsen's best recording with his fabled *Tonight Show* Band is *Once More . . . With Feeling!* 𝄞𝄞𝄞𝄞 (Amherst, 1991, prod. Jeff Tyzik). In addition to the band's fine regular soloists, 14 popular jazz standards, and refreshing, colorful charts (written mostly by top arrangers Bill Holman and Tommy Newsom), this CD features guest appearances by Wynton Marsalis and Tony Bennett on one tune each. Includes classic gems such as "St. Louis Blues," "I Can't Get Started" (featuring Bennett, "Avalon" (with Marsalis), "What Is This Thing Called Love," and "Body and Soul."

what to buy next: Almost as good are *Doc Severinsen & the Tonight Show Orchestra* ♪♪♪ (Amherst, 1990, prod. Jeff Tyzik) and *Tonight Show Band, Vol. 2* ♪♪♪ (Amherst, 1990, prod, Jeff Tyzik), where the group alternates between playing big-band standards and fusion workouts in their inimitable, polished style.

what to avoid: There's too much Cincinnati Pops and not enough Severinsen on *Erich Kunzel/Cincinnati Pops* ♪♪ (Telarc, 1991, prod. Robert Woods, Elaine Martone).

best of the rest:

Facets ♪♪ (Amherst, 1988)
Doc Severinsen & Xebron ♪♪ (Passport Records, 1989)
Ja-Da ♪♪ (MCA, 1992)
Lullabies and Goodnight ♪♪ (Critique, 1992)
Good Medicine ♪♪ (RCA Bluebird, 1992)
Doc Severinsen & Friends ♪♪ (MCA Special Products, 1992)
Two Sides of Doc Severinsen ♪♪♪ (The Right Stuff, 1993)
Merry Christmas from Doc Severinsen & the Tonight Show Orchestra ♪♪♪♪ (Amherst, 1992, prod. Jeff Tyzik)

worth searching for: The out-of-print *Tonight Show Band, Vol.1* ♪♪♪♪ (Amherst, 1986, prod. Jeff Tyzik) won a Grammy for Best Jazz Instrumental–Big Band, for Doc and the boys in 1987. Also, Severinsen has guested as soloist on several sessions with conductor Erich Kunzel and the Cincinnati Pops Orchestra. If you're a real completist, you'll definitely want *Big Band Hit Parade* ♪♪♪♪ (Telarc, 1988, prod. Robert Woods), *Erich Kunzel/ Cincinnati Pops Orchestra: Fiesta* ♪♪ (Telarc, 1990, prod. Robert Woods), *Unforgettably Doc* ♪♪♪ (Telarc, 1992, prod. Robert Woods, Elaine Martone), and *Christmas With the Pops* ♪♪♪♪ (Telarc, 1993, prod. Robert Woods).

influences:

◄◄ Harry James, Ray Anthony

►► Herb Alpert, Chuck Mangione

Ken Burke

Shakti

Formed in 1975. Disbanded in 1977.

John McLaughlin, acoustic guitar, vocals; L. Shankar, violin, viola, vocals; Zakir Hussain, tabla, timbales, bongos, congas, dholak drums, naal, triangle, vocals; T.H. (Vikku) Vinayakram, ghatam, mridangam, kanjeera, moorsing, vocals; R. Raghavan, mridangam, (1975).

When John McLaughlin recorded his first album with Shakti in 1975, it came out of left field, confounding fans and critics alike. Shakti, which means "creative intelligence, beauty, and power" played a form of fusion, but instead of merging jazz and rock, it combined traditional North and South Indian ragas and rhythmic patterns with Western jazz, blues, and rock influences, and improvisation. Like McLaughlin's two previous Mahavishnu Orchestras, the tempos were fast, the meters intricate, the percussion intense, and the solos often played at blinding speed. Unlike Mahavishnu, Shakti's instrumentation and sound was more Indian than Western (McLaughlin was the only Western musician), the music was entirely acoustic, and it never achieved major mainstream popularity.

Between 1975 and 1977, Shakti made three recordings for Columbia: *Shakti*, *Handful of Beauty*, and *Natural Elements*. Each album featured over-the-top performances and complex rhythms and percussion solos. McLaughlin played a custom-made acoustic guitar (it's design was based on the Indian Vina and included sympathetic strings—also called drone strings—and a scalloped fretboard). L. Shankar effortlessly traversed between Indian and Western styles (it's easy to spot Jerry Goodman's influence in Shankar's playing). At its peak, Shakti successfully blended several disparate musical genres with technical virtuosity. Unfortunately, its Indian sound was a difficult sell for Columbia Records, who never properly marketed the group, and after their third release the group disbanded. McLaughlin has pursued several different musical directions since Shakti's breakup, though he and Zakir Hussain did reunite in 1995 for one track on McLaughlin's excellent release *The Promise,* and he toured with Hussain, T.H. (Vikku) Vinayakram, and Hariprasad Chaurasia in 1997.

what's available: All three of Shakti's albums have been released on CD, but none are currently available domestically. *The Best of Shakti* ♪♪♪♪ (Columbia Records, 1975–1977, prod. John McLaughlin/Moment Records, 1994, prod. Zakir Hussain) is a compilation released on Moment Records (a subsidiary of Sony headed by Zakir Hussain). The album includes selections from all three albums and shows that, at their best, Shakti could be an intense powerhouse as "Joy" and "Mind Ecology" demonstrate, and play beautiful pieces like "Two Sisters" with emotion. Though a compelling argument could be made for the inclusion of "Lotus Feet" or one or two other songs, music on this collection explains why Carlos Santana once said Shakti was, "the most intense music that I've felt since John Coltrane was alive."

influences:
⏪ Ravi Shankar, Mahavishnu Orchestra

see also: *John McLaughlin, Mahavishnu Orchestra*

Paul MacArthur

Mark Shane

Born April 18, 1946, in Perth Amboy, NJ.

Mark Shane brings his classic jazz piano style, full of buoyant swing and lyrical improvisation, to personal appearances and recording dates, whether under his own banner, or as musical director for singer Terry Blaine, or as sideman with Ed Polcer, Bob Wilber, Marty Grosz, Randy Sandke, Sam Pilafian, Peter Ecklund, or the Empire Brass.

Shane's early jazz influences came from recordings of jazz giants Teddy Wilson, Earl Hines, Fats Waller, Louis Armstrong, Coleman Hawkins, Lester Young, and Benny Goodman. He grew up listening to his aunt, a piano player whom he claims had a "big, fat, left-hand sound." Shane studied classical piano early on and later took harmony lessons from a local pro. He subsequently gigged around the Catskills, and by the time he moved from New Jersey to Philadelphia, he had acquired a degree in biology. He worked in the University of Philadelphia veterinary school for two years, playing at night and on weekends, before moving to Boston where he encountered "some hard bumps and funky gigs" along with gaining experience, learning new tunes, and playing six nights a week. Shane moved to New York City where jobs got better. In the late 1970s, he worked in the house band with bassist Red Balaban and cornetist Ed Polcer at the third Eddie Condon's jazz club. Shane began a lengthy association with reedman Bob Wilber at the Hyatt Regency in New Orleans in 1979, a quartet which included bassist Milt Hinton and drummer Bobby Rosengarden. Shane recorded and toured with Wilber in the Smithsonian Jazz Repertory Ensemble well into the 1980s. He appeared on the soundtrack of the 1984 film *The Cotton Club,* and went on to film work on *Brighton Beach Memoirs, Biloxi Blues,* and the popular 1988 film, *Working Girl.* Shane also appeared with the Lester Lanin and Peter Duchin society orchestras during this period and played many balls, cotillions, openings, fund-raisers and prestigious private parties, including Presidential Inaugural Balls in Washington. While featured with Peter Duchin (1984–1988), Shane began playing piano for singer Terry Blaine during band intermissions, an association which led to a three-and-a-half-year duo engagement at New York's Café Society, and a 1992 recording (issued under Shane's name) with some friends from Condon's. Many from that same bunch recorded on Blaine's well-known 1994 CD, *Whose Honey Are You.* For about the past decade, Shane has toured throughout the United States and Europe, often with singer Blaine, but also with various jazz instrumentalists.

what's available: A collection of 15 swing-oriented tunes, *Blue Room* ♪♪♪♪ (Kamadisc, 1992, prod. Doug Wood) offers a well-balanced mix of band numbers and strictly rhythm-section pieces. It could well have been dedicated to the late Teddy Wilson, as the framework suggests Wilson's delightful sessions recorded between 1935 and 1945. Blaine sings "Did I Remember?" and "Eeny Meeny Miney Mo," both associated with Billie Holiday when she was working with pianist Wilson. Shane also sings himself, rather charmingly, on several Waller-tinged numbers. Ed Polcer (cornet), Spanky Davis (trumpet), Tom Artin (trombone), and Ken Peplowski (tenor sax and clarinet) all lend their superlative support to Shane who plays as if 52nd Street was still going full-tilt. Guitarist Frank Vignola, alternating bassists Bill Crow and Earl May, and drummer Danny D'Imperio provide solid rhythm backgrounds. Shane has built a following among piano devotees, and listening to his quicksilver versions of "Shine" and "Blue Room" demonstrates why. Recommended for swing-piano fans and 52nd Street nostalgia buffs. A set of 16 Swing-era tunes, *On Treasure Island* ♪♪♪♪ (Jukebox Jazz, 1996, prod. Tom Desisto), showcases Shane's solo jazz piano on six numbers and brings his smooth, Teddy Wilson-esque keyboard mannerisms into focus on three duo, three trio, two quartet, and two full-band numbers as well. Cornetist Ed Polcer joins Shane for a groovy, loping "Tiger Rag," and turns on the warmth with his muted ballad feature, "I Don't Know Whether I'm Coming or Going." Trombonist Tom Artin joins with Shane and Imperio for a go at Fats Waller's catchy riff tune, "Yacht Club Swing," and then jaunts out with the trio on the venerable, "Some of These Days." Dan Block makes the most of his clarinet feature with the trio on "Get Rhythm in Your Feet." Blaine sings a foot-tapping "One, Two, Button Your Show," a poignant "On the Sentimental Side," and then joins the full ensemble for a rousing "Shakin' the Blues Away," a fitting closer to this lively collection. Shane's rhythm mates throughout these sides are the steady Frank Tate on string bass and the tasteful drummer, Joe Ascione. Shane's CDs are available in many record stores, and also can be purchased by mail from Jukebox Jazz, P. O. Box 1247, Woodstock, NY 12498.

worth searching for: Mark Shane performs as sideman on some selections of *Travelin' Light with Sam Pilafian & Friends* ♪♪♪♪ (Telarc, 1991, prod. Elaine Martone), an album featuring 13 quartet performances by the extraordinary tuba player Sam

Pilafian (of Empire Brass), with guitarist Frank Vignola and rhythm guitarist Jimmy George. Because of the capabilities of the participants, what was essentially a jam session on standards turns into a chamber-jazz group of the highest order. Shane fans will dig "Avalon, " "If I Only Had a Brain," and "I Found a New Baby," among others. Shane's playing is well-featured on this most unusual date. If the thought of a tuba soloist doesn't scare you off, the album is well-worth hearing.

influences:

◀◀ Teddy Wilson, Fats Waller, James P. Johnson, Earl Hines, Art Tatum

see also: *Terry Blaine*

John T. Bitter

Bud Shank

Born May 27, 1926, in OH.

Bud Shank reinvented himself as a hard bopper in the 1980s, but for decades he was one of the alto sax's finest representatives of "cool jazz"—a softer, more subtle approach to bebop. Originally from Ohio, Shank moved to Los Angeles in the 1940s and became a fixture in West Coast jazz circles. Shank, who was known for a light style comparable to Lee Konitz, played with Charlie Barnet in the late 1940s and Stan Kenton in 1950–51 and soon became a member of the Lighthouse All-Stars. This '50s band was so named because Shank, trumpeter Shorty Rogers, tenor saxman Bob Cooper, and other members played together regularly at the Lighthouse, a legendary jazz club in the Hermosa Beach suburb. During the '50s, Shank (who also played the flute) teamed up with Brazilian guitarist Laurindo Almeida for the groundbreaking *Brazilliance* sessions. The 1960s found Shank doing his share of film scores and soundtracks without giving up jazz, and in the 1970s he formed the L.A.4 with Almeida, Ray Brown, and Chuck Flores. Shank gave listeners some major surprises in the 1980s when he gave up the flute for good, toughened his alto considerably, and went for a more aggressive hard bop approach. In the early '90s, he co-led a Lighthouse All-Stars Reunion with Rogers.

what to buy: Recorded in 1953 and 1958, the superb Shank/Almeida collaborations reissued on *Brazilliance, Vol. 1* ♫♫♫♫ (Capitol, 1991, prod. Richard Bock) and *Brazilliance, Vol. 2* ♫♫♫♫ (Capitol, 1991, prod. Richard Bock) boast a landmark fusion of cool jazz and Brazilian music that predicted the bossa nova explosion of the early 1960s. While the *Brazilliance* sessions favor softness and restraint, Shank offered a tougher ap-

proach to Brazilian jazz on *Tomorrow's Rainbow* ♫♫♫♫ (Contemporary, 1989, prod. Bud Shank, David Keller). Keyboardist Marcos Silva, guitarist Richard Piexoto, and other Brazilian players clearly bring out the best in Shank, who is at his most soulful on treasures ranging from the rueful "The Colors of Despair" to the optimistic "The Railroad." Shank plays the flute exclusively on *Crystal Comments* ♫♫♫♫ (Concord, 1980, prod. Bud Shank), an intimate trio date featuring Bill Mays primarily on electric piano and Alan Broadbent mostly on acoustic piano. Given how much warmth he brings to the flute on "I'll Take Romance" and "On Green Dolphin Street," one can't help but wish Shank hadn't given it up entirely several years later.

what to buy next: Recorded in January 1956, when Shank was only 29, *Live at the Haig* ♫♫♫♫ (Bainbridge, 1956) illustrates the richness of "cool jazz" and features the lyrical pianist Claude Williamson. Reborn as a hard bopper, Shank spares no passion on *I Told You So!* ♫♫♫♫ (Candid, 1993, prod. Alan Bates, Mark Morganelli), recorded live at New York's Birdland. The session unites him with pianist Kenny Barron, bassist Lonnie Plaxico, and drummer Victor Lewis. On "Limehouse Blues" and George Cables's "I Told You So!" Shank is much more Phil Woods–ish than he was in his youth, and leaves no doubt that he was enjoying the change immensely.

best of the rest:

Sunshine Express ♫♫♫ (Concord, 1976)
That Old Feeling ♫♫♫♫ (Contemporary, 1986)
Live at Jazz Alley ♫♫♫♫ (Contemporary, 1986)
(With the Roumanis String Quartet) *Drifting Timelessly* ♫♫♫♫ (Capri, 1991)

worth searching for: Led by Shank and Shorty Rogers, and featuring Conte Candoli and Bob Cooper, the Lighthouse All-Stars were reunited with exciting results on *America the Beautiful* ♫♫♫♫ (Candid, 1991, prod. Bud Shank, Shorty Rogers, David Keller). From Bud Powell's "Un Poco Loco" to Rogers's "Lotus Bud," the group goes for a harder sound than it was known for in the 1950s.

influences:

◀◀ Lee Konitz

▶▶ Laurindo Almeida, João Gilberto

Alex Henderson

Sonny Sharrock

Born August 27, 1940, Ossining, NY. Died May 26, 1994, Ossining, NY.

The late Sonny Sharrock, avant-garde jazz guitarist extraordinaire, first gained attention playing free jazz with Pharoah Sanders in the late '60s, and closed his recording career with music for the *Space Ghost* cartoon show. In between came gigs with Miles Davis and Herbie Mann. Ear-splitting atonal solos made him a six-string legend, but he never lost touch with his jazz and blues roots. His rare 1970s albums are out of print, but the mid-'80s brought a heralded comeback under the aegis of producer Bill Laswell. At the time of his death of a heart attack, he had just been signed by RCA.

Sharrock didn't start playing guitar until he was 20 years old; he preferred saxophone, but asthma prevented him from playing horn. Even as a guitarist he conceived of music as a horn player, which helps explain the ease with which he fit into the free jazz scene of New York in the mid-1960s, when no other guitarists of significance did. His torrid work on Pharoah Sanders's *Tauhid* suggests a mix of Coltrane and Sanders translated to strings. Other recordings in this period included Marzette Watts's *Marzette Watts* and Byard Lancaster's *It's Not Up to Us*. Sharrock's lengthiest sideman gig came, somewhat surprisingly, with jazz flutist Herbie Mann. Though Mann's idiom was mainstream jazz-pop, he carried Sharrock in his band from 1967 through 1973 in the face of much criticism—since Sharrock didn't tame down his fiery soloing in this context. Fans would walk out of concerts when Sharrock's big solo came, and Mann, who has sometimes been characterized as a musical lightweight chasing pop trends, deserves considerable credit for continuing to feature the younger guitarist. Sharrock recorded regularly with Mann—*Live at the Whisky A Go Go*, *Memphis Two-Step*, *Memphis Underground* (a crossover hit which also included Larry Coryell), *Concerto Grosso in D Blues*, *Windows Opened*, *Stone Flute*, and more—and most of these albums contain at least one priceless, lengthy blast of Sharrock skronk.

In this period, Sharrock also recorded with Roy Ayers (*Stoned Soul Picnic*), Don Cherry (*Eternal Rhythm*), Wayne Shorter (*Super Nova*), Steve Marcus Quartet (*Green Line*), and even Miles Davis, though his presence on *A Tribute to Jack Johnson* remained uncredited for years. Produced by Mann, he debuted as a leader in 1969 with *Black Woman*, which included his wife Linda on vocals; this and two other long-out-of-print releases in the 1970s firmly established in the mind of the record industry that he was not a commercial proposition, though nowadays collectors salivate at the mere mention of their titles. After 1975's *Paradise* there was a six-year gap in his discography until he hooked up with producer/bassist Bill Laswell's group Material on *New York Improvisations 1981*. Laswell included Sharrock in various projects, most memorably the free-jazz su-

pergroup Last Exit; he recorded the guitarist on whichever label Laswell was working for (or running) at the time, most notably Enemy (note that though the Enemy releases can be somewhat difficult to find, they are not—despite what some will say—currently unavailable). When Sharrock put together a permanent band in the late 1980s, it sometimes leaned more toward rock than jazz, moving away from the free-form playing that had made him famous. His power remained generally undiminished, however.

what to buy: *Into Another Light* ♫♫♫♫ (Enemy, 1996, prod. Bill Laswell) is producer Bill Laswell's well-chosen selection of 1986–91 tracks. Though it contains no previously unreleased material and is barely 50 minutes, it does cut across record label boundaries to present a complete cross-section of the music Sharrock released under his own name in that time: lush solo electric guitarscapes, driving band efforts, a collaboration with Sanders and Elvin Jones, and a duet with fellow guitarist Nicky Skopelitis. Sharrock's ballsy, fusion-like themes are memorable, and his coruscating performances are sometimes mind-blowing. It's a useful introduction to the second half of Sharrock's career. For jazz listeners, *Ask the Ages* ♫♫♫♫♫ (Axiom, 1991, prod. Bill Laswell, Sonny Sharrock) will be the most attractive album overall. Sharrock is reunited with Sanders, who plays with all his old power, while polyrhythm juggernaut Elvin Jones's drumming gooses the proceedings relentlessly. Charnett Moffett is adequate on bass. This is ecstatic music that, while sophisticated in its own ways, hits listeners on a gut level.

what to buy next: *Guitar* ♫♫♫♫ (Enemy, 1986, prod. Sonny Sharrock, Bill Laswell) introduced the uncategorizable Sharrock to a new and broader audience ready to digest his unique amalgam of jazz, avant-garde, blues, rock, and world music stylings. These solo electric guitar pieces pile skirling, bright melodies atop darkly shimmering backdrops—it's full of majestic beauty. *Seize the Rainbow* ♫♫♫♫ (Enemy, 1987, prod. Sonny Sharrock, Bill Laswell) captures Sharrock's band before he added keyboards and tamed his guitar attack. The ferocious double-drum rhythm section of Pheeroan AkLaff and Abe Speller with monster electric bassist Melvin Gibbs rips through the aggressive themes with muscular glee, with a few more trance-like but no less powerful tracks for variety.

what to avoid: *Highlife* ♫♫ (Enemy, 1990, prod. Sonny Sharrock) dilutes Sharrock's vision to such an extent that even Pharoah's "Venus/Upper Egypt" (from *Tauhid*) and Trane's "Giant Steps" sound bland. Dave Snider's cheesy electric keyboards make some of the tracks sound uncomfortably like TV show themes, though in a different context the melodies of a few would be majestic. Sharrock's tone is still great, but playing as "inside" as he does here, with this kind of production, tilts the style uncomfortably close to mediocre fusion.

the rest:

Dance with Me, Montana 🎵🎵🎵 (Marge, 1982)

Live in New York 🎵🎵🎵 (Enemy, 1989)

Faith Moves 🎵🎵🎵🎵 (CMP, 1991)

worth searching for: Pharoah Sanders's *Tauhid* 🎵🎵🎵🎵 (Impulse!, 1967, prod. Bob Thiele) is the earliest recording of Sharrock's guitar playing and shows him in the kind of full-bore free jazz blowing context that produced his unique approach. Sharrock's long-out-of-print early albums are uneven but worthwhile. *Black Woman* 🎵🎵🎵🎵 (Vortex, 1969, prod. Herbie Mann) is an odd grab-bag, very much of its time, which often uses chant-like material (including the Auvergne lullaby "Bailero," somewhat misidentified as French), sounding like a cross between Pharoah Sanders's *Karma* and slowed-down gospel, as the launch pad for freer excursions. The first appearance of Sharrock's "Blind Willie" is played solo on acoustic guitar, emphasizing its drone underpinning and relationship with country blues, a la Blind Willie Johnson. Dave Burrell plays piano on much of the album, Milford Graves is the drummer, and this remains, sadly, a record more talked-about than heard. *monkey-pockie-boo* 🎵🎵🎵🎵 (BYG, 1970) is the most far-out of all, with Linda's vocals at their most extreme (recalling Patty Waters and Yoko Ono) and the music basically a free-form rave-up. Co-credited to Linda, *Paradise* 🎵🎵🎵 (Atco, 1975, prod. Ilhan Mimaroglu) sounds like Sharrock's big pop move, but it's so weird, Linda's vocals are so avant-garde, and Sonny's guitar playing so imaginative, that the rock/funk beats and electric keyboards couldn't tip this over into "sellout." Significant for containing Sharrock's last recording, *Space Ghost* 🎵🎵 (Cartoon Network, 1994, prod. Keith Crofford) was a limited edition promo EP put out to publicize the cartoon of the same title, for which Sharrock, on November 19, 1993, recorded the theme song. He apparently is not heard on all the tracks here, and may only be on the theme itself—a distinction glossed over by the liner notes.

influences:

◄◄ Blind Willie Johnson, John Coltrane, Albert Ayler

►► Marc Ribot, Bill Frisell, Caspar Brötzmann, Pete Cosey, Thurston Moore, William Hooker

Steve Holtje

Artie Shaw

Born Arthur Jacob Arshawsky, May 23, 1910, in New York, NY.

Mainly self-taught, Artie Shaw was playing alto saxophone in a dance band in his early teens, and by his mid-teens switched to the clarinet and worked as music director/arranger with Austin Wylie's band in Cleveland, Ohio. With Irving Aaronson's band, Shaw traveled in 1929 to New York where he sat in at late-night jam sessions, including those organized by an early mentor, pianist Willie "The Lion" Smith. When he was 19, Shaw discovered the scores of Igor Stravinsky and Claude Debussy, a factor that would influence much of his future music making, as evidenced by Shaw's first experiments with string sections in the context of his first professional band. Shaw perfected his playing and became a highly sought-after session musician, especially on alto saxophone and clarinet. He attended Columbia University (to study literature) in the first of his periodic "retirements" from the music business. Shaw re-entered the musical fray in 1934, rejoining the session scene he worked in prior to his collegiate experience, and working with many top-notch musicians of the day including Wingy Manone, Red Norvo, the Dorsey Brothers, and Bunny Berrigan.

Shaw finally became a bandleader in his own right in 1936 (with a recording contract for Brunswick Records) after debuting a piece he wrote for octet ("Interlude in B Flat"), which included four string players. This short-lived band experimented with a few interesting recordings before Shaw had to break up the group in early 1937 due to lack of bookings. His next band was formed with an eye toward the more conventional big band market. It was during this time that Shaw recorded his first massive hit, "Begin the Beguine." From then until 1942, when Shaw joined the navy, he led one of the most popular bands of the Big Band/Swing era, employing sterling musicians such as Billie Holiday, Georgie Auld, Buddy Rich, and Johnny Guarnieri. Hits recorded by the band included "Frenesi," "Indian Love Call," "Back Bay Shuffle," and the band's theme, "Nightmare." This period saw the rise of a fan-generated conflict between aficionados of Shaw and the other major clarinet player of the day, Benny Goodman. Neither of the musicians were involved in the hostilities, but their fans debated the merits of their heroes in the press, in concert, and in conversation. Shaw also managed to include a string section in his bands during this time, harkening back to his first efforts of 1936. Another feature of his groups then was the Gramercy Five, a band within the band that allowed Shaw the opportunity for more sonic experimentation, especially with Guarnieri playing harpsichord instead of the piano used in the big band context. Shaw also

Artie Shaw **(AP/Wide World Photos)**

had at least two abortive periods of "retirement" during this period before jumping back into the band business. During his Navy years, Shaw was put in charge of an all-star band which entertained World War II troops fighting in the Pacific. After leaving the Navy, he formed another series of bands before entering his longest "retirement" in the mid-1950s to devote himself to literary pursuits.

In addition to his short stories written in the mid-1950s and 1960s, Shaw wrote his autobiography, *The Trouble With Cinderella,* in 1952, and a trio of short stories in the 1960s, *I Love You, I Hate You, Drop Dead!,* in addition to operating Artixo Productions, a film distribution and production company.

what to buy: Despite the favorable reputation of the Gramercy Five sessions, *The Last Recordings, Vol. 1: Rare & Unreleased* ♫♫♫♫ (Music Masters, 1992, prod. Artie Shaw), a two-CD set of tunes from 1954, could very well contain Shaw's finest music within a small group format. His restless brand of perfectionism has Shaw breaking out of the mold for the last time, since these

are among his final recordings. Performances are strong throughout with a fine mix of originals by Shaw and a well-chosen batch of standards. The rhythm section of pianist Hank Jones, bassist Tommy Potter, and Irv Kluger is a high-class constant along with Shaw on clarinet. Vibes player Joe Roland and guitarist Tal Farlow play on the New York dates while Joe Puma plays guitar on the Hollywood sessions. *Begin the Beguine* ♫♫♫♫ (RCA/Bluebird, 1938–41/1988, prod. various) is probably the best single volume to start with if someone just wants a taste of Shaw's major hits. It is filled with 20 of Shaw's most popular chart-toppers, including "Frenesi," "Star Dust," and "Back Bay Shuffle." All of the material covered comes from the classic 1938–1941 period when singers Billie Holiday, Helen Forrest, and Tony Pastor were with the band. The band within a band on *The Complete Gramercy Five Sessions* ♫♫♫♫ (RCA./Bluebird, 1989, prod. various) allows Shaw, with a select handful of musicians, to step out of the bigger group format and play music that swings harder and more progressively than his larger ensemble. Included are eight tunes from the 1940 version of the Five and seven from the 1945 edition. The harpsichord of 1940 gives way to the piano of 1945, but that provides the only minor quibble about which version of the Gramercy Five is better. Of interest to fans are two takes on Shaw's "Mysterioso," in addition to classics such as "Special Delivery Stomp" and "Scuttlebutt." The recordings on *The Indispensable Artie Shaw: 1944–45* ✍✍✍ (RCA, 1944–45/1986/1995, reissue prod. Jean-Paul Guiter) date from when Shaw had come back to the States after his tour of the South Pacific theater of operations. His new band featured a large brass/reed section, and the rhythm quartet of piano, guitar, bass, and drums. While they cover a lot of Gershwin tunes in addition to a sprinkling of other standards and Shaw originals, their charts were written by notables such as Eddie Sauter, Dave Rose, and Ray Conniff. Although this particular band didn't have quite the commercial success of his earlier outfits, Shaw managed to come up with a jazz classic ("Little Jazz") that featured trumpeter Roy Eldridge. There are also a handful of tunes from Shaw's last formal Gramercy Five ensemble, a lineup that included Eldridge, Dodo Marmarosa, and Barney Kessel.

what to buy next: Shaw stepped out from his career as a session musician to lead his first band in 1936. The import CD *In the Beginning—1936* ✍✍✍ (Hep, 1994, prod. A. Robertson, J.R.T. Davies) documents the June–December period of that year when Shaw led his innovative "string quartet" group, which included the usual complement of rhythm and brass/reed instruments in addition to a small string section. It was an experiment that garnered critical acclaim but modest commercial success. There are elements of "schmaltz" to be found here, but Shaw's clarinet playing is superb throughout, and the performances swing far more than the stuff that was being done by his contemporaries Glen Gray or Lawrence Welk (especially on material like "It Ain't Right" and "Copenhagen"). *More Last Recordings: The Final Sessions* ✍✍✍ (MusicMasters, 1993, prod. Artie Shaw) contains additional tunes from the 1954 small-group sessions that MusicMasters dipped into for their superb *The Last Recordings, Vol. 1: Rare & Unreleased* release. This two-CD set contains some interesting takes on standards long associated with Shaw. His clarinet playing is supple and adventurous throughout, and this infects his performances of "Frenesi," "Stardust," and "Back Bay Shuffle" with an almost bebop flair. Pianist Hank Jones and guitarist Tal Farlow deserve particular mention for the way they urge the music from the past into the (then) present.

best of the rest:

Frenesi ✍✍✍ (RCA, 1992)

Personal Best ✍✍✍ (RCA, 1992)
Artie Shaw: 1936 ✍✍✍ (Classics,1996)
Artie Shaw: Greatest Hits ✍✍✍ (RCA, 1996)

influences:

◀◀ Willie "The Lion" Smith, Claude Debussy, Igor Stravinsky, Jimmy Dorsey, Barney Bigard

▶▶ Bob Wilber, Dick Johnson

Garaud MacTaggart

Marlena Shaw

Born Marlena Burgess, 1944, in New Rochelle, NY.

Singer Marlena Shaw has known for most of her life how to win over an audience. She made her first appearance at Harlem's famed Apollo Theatre at age 10. By age 20 she was entertaining lounge audiences at swanky resort hotels—an experience that was an important factor in her development as a stylist. Possessing a voice that can handle pop, jazz, and R&B equally well, her greatest talent may be the engaging manner she brings to a variety of music. Unfortunately, Shaw has frequently recorded in surroundings that were too slick, too trendy, or too middle-of-the-road. One of her early releases on Cadet provided her with a hit, a vocal version of "Mercy, Mercy, Mercy" that struck a chord with pop and R&B singles-buyers in 1967. Her work also made an impression on Count Basie, who hired her that year. Shaw sang with the Basie band until 1972. Recording for Blue Note in the early '70s and Columbia later in the decade, Shaw's recordings became increasingly layered with thicker and thicker coatings of commercial gloss, eventually approaching generic disco. Still, Shaw's gift for improvisational storytelling resulted in some truly memorable songs, including "Shaw Biz/Suddenly It's How I Like to Feel/Shaw Biz (Reprise)" and a great version of the Goffin/King song "Go Away Little Boy," which became a modest R&B hit in 1977. Shaw recorded a pair of solid releases for Verve in the late '80s, and she now seems to be gaining more of the respect she has long deserved; she appeared as a guest on releases by Joe Williams and Jimmy Smith and recorded two solid Concord CDs with a higher-than-ever jazz-to-pop quotient.

what to buy: *It Is Love* ✍✍✍ (Verve, 1987, prod. Ron Berinstein), recorded before a live audience in the intimate Vine Street club in Hollywood, displays Shaw's talents in the best possible light. And the tasteful backing trio (featuring pianist Buddy Montgomery) proves flexible enough to handle Shaw's versatility with ease. She's is in fine voice here, singing a wide range of material, including a funky version of "Unforgettable," a down-home "Rockin' Chair Blues," and a loungey but inspired medley pairing "Nobody Knows You When You're Down and Out" and "That's Life." Best of all is the charming 10-minute version of "Go Away Little Boy," a song that always works better live than on studio recordings.

what to buy next: Her two '90s Concord discs, *Elemental Soul* 𝄞𝄞𝄞 (Concord, 1997, prod. John Burk) and *Dangerous* 𝄞𝄞𝄞 (Concord, 1996, prod. John Burk), mix standards with lesser-known jazz songs, plus a few Shaw originals. Fans of her '70s material will want *The Best of Marlena Shaw* 𝄞𝄞𝄞 (Blue Note, 1997, prod. various), which includes the memorable "You, Me & Ethel."

the rest:
Love Is in Flight 𝄞𝄞 (Verve, 1988)
Who Is This Bitch Anyway? 𝄞𝄞 (Blue Note, 1993)

worth searching for: Most of her late '70s recordings for Columbia are both heavily disco-flavored and unavailable on CD. But *Sweet Beginnings* 𝄞𝄞 (Columbia, 1977, prod. Bert de-Coteaux) is worth getting if you find it (and still have a turntable); it's got her hit version of "Go Away Little Boy."

influences:

◀◀ Nancy Wilson, Gloria Lynne, Esther Phillips, Dakota Staton, Lou Rawls

▶▶ Angela Bofill, Phyllis Hyman, Anita Baker, Natalie Cole

Dan Bindert

Woody Shaw

Born December 24, 1944, in Laurinburg, NC. Died May 10, 1989, in New York, NY.

One of the great trumpeters of the 1970s and 1980s, Woody Shaw bridged the gap between hard bop and the so-called avant garde by respecting tradition while playing with controlled freedom. In the early 1960s, at the invitation of Eric Dolphy, Shaw traveled to Europe to work with the saxophonist, who died shortly after Shaw arrived. Shaw stayed in Paris and played with Kenny Clarke and Bud Powell. In 1965, after returning to New York, he replaced Carmel Jones as the trumpeter in Horace Silver's Quintet; after recording with Silver, he became a regular on Blue Note Records. During the late 1960s, Shaw played with Jackie McLean, Hank Mobley, Donald Byrd, McCoy Tyner, and Art Blakey. In 1973 Shaw began leading his own groups, though he had extended stints in the Junior Cook/Louis Hayes Quintet and with Dexter Gordon. Shaw recorded for Muse, Red Records, and Timeless, as well as three

brilliant and critically acclaimed releases for Columbia. His group proved to be quite popular, but, perhaps because of certain personal problems, this success never parlayed into true jazz stardom. Failing eyesight curtailed his career, and his death resulted from injuries incurred when he was hit by a subway in New York City at the age of 45.

what to buy: *Dark Journey* 𝄞𝄞𝄞𝄞 (Muse, 1965–87/32 Jazz, 1997, prod. Joel Dorn) is a 15-track compilation of Woody Shaw's best work for the Muse label, recorded between 1965 and 1987. The pianists alone are worth the price of admission: Herbie Hancock, Muhal Richard Abrams, Cedar Walton, Kenny Barron, Kirk Lightsey, Larry Young, and Onaje Allen Gumbs. Of course, Shaw's trumpet playing throughout is brilliant, thanks to his open approach to music and improvisation. Songs like "The Moontrane," "Tetragon," and "Cassandranite" show off Shaw's ability to create whole compositions rather than simply graft new melodies on standard changes. The care and intelligence that he invested in his music is celebrated on *Moontrane* 𝄞𝄞𝄞𝄞 (32 Jazz, 1997, prod. Joel Dorn), a 1974 date that features the stellar trumpeter with a septet. *Moontrane* was his first use of a three-horn front line, and the success of the sound led him to utilize the configuration in his working group and subsequent recordings. Shaw's trumpet, like the compositions, is unforgettable on this album. The title track was written when he was only 18-years old; it debuted on Larry Young's 1965 Blue Note classic, *Unity*, which featured Shaw, Joe Henderson, and Elvin Jones. Also, the work of trombonist Steve Turre, 26 at the time of the recording, is not to be missed. Woody Shaw spent considerable time in Europe in his final years, and *In My Own Sweet Way* 𝄞𝄞𝄞𝄞 (In + Out, 1989, prod. Frank Kleinschmidt) documents two concerts from 1987 that feature the trumpeter and a European rhythm section. Shaw is in top form, as are Fred Henke on piano, Neil Swainson on bass, and Alex Deutsch on drums (their names may be unfamiliar but their music is not). An exhilarating version of Shaw's "Joshua C." that runs nearly 14 minutes is clearly the highlight, along with Shaw's moving tribute to friend Larry Young, "The Organ Grinder." *Last of the Line* 𝄞𝄞𝄞𝄞 (32 Jazz, 1997, prod. Joel Dorn), a two-CD set from Joel Dorn's new 32 Jazz label, brings together two classic Woody Shaw sessions, *Cassandranite*, recorded in 1965, and *Love Dance*, done 11 years later. The 1965 group includes Joe Henderson and Herbie Hancock, and the five tracks represent the state-of-the-art in jazz for the mid-60s. At the time, Henderson and Shaw had been working together in Horace Silver's group, and the music clearly benefits from their knowledge of and familiarity with each other. The five tracks on *Love Dance* include a variety of moods, settings, and textures, as well as Shaw's stunning compositions and brilliant trumpet.

what to buy next: Shaw's working groups were a potent musical force, and in the early 1980s the frontline included his trumpet and Steve Turre's trombone, giving them a sound unlike any other working group of the era. *Lotus Flower* 𝄞𝄞𝄞𝄞 (Enja, 1982/1995, prod. Horst Weber) includes sterling solo work from all involved, notably by a then-rookie Mulgrew Miller on piano. The album also features two of Shaw's finest tunes, "Song of Songs" and "Lotus Flower." Like many other musicians, Shaw fled New York in the late 1960s for the West Coast. His ambitious 1972 session, *Song of Songs* 𝄞𝄞𝄞𝄞 (OJC, 1972/1997, prod. Lester Koenig), was recorded in Los Angeles with pianist George Cables for the Contemporary label. As always, Shaw's pungent trumpet shines, his harmonically distinctive style a unique spin-off of Freddie Hubbard. Nineteen-year-old drummer Woody "Sonship" Theus, who later played with Charles Lloyd, performs with maturity far beyond his years, driving the music with intensity that recalls the best of Elvin Jones or Tony Williams. *Bemsha Swing* 𝄞𝄞𝄞 (Blue Note, 1997, prod. Michael Cuscuna) is a 1986 jam session–like date heavy on Monk tunes recorded live at Detroit's Baker's Keyboard Lounge and features Shaw with three of the Motor City's finest players, a young Geri Allen on piano, Robert Hurst on bass, and veteran Roy Brooks (of Horace Silver fame) on drums. Everyone is in excellent form here, especially Allen, and although this was one of Shaw's later sessions, his personal problems obviously had little effect on his creativity.

influences:

◀◀ Dizzy Gillespie, Clifford Brown, Fats Navarro, Freddie Hubbard, Lee Morgan

▶▶ Tim Hagens, Joe Magnarelli, Nicholas Payton, Roy Hargrove

Bret Primack

George Shearing

Born August 13, 1919, in London, England.

George Shearing is a classically trained pianist and a natural jazz improviser whose 1949 quintet was one of the first small jazz groups to gain widespread popularity. The historic original version of the George Shearing Quintet included piano, vibraphone, guitar, bass, and drums, and featured plenty of interplay between piano and vibes. Since his earliest recordings, Shearing has demonstrated his "locked-hands" technique—a block chord style that developed from Milt Buckner's earlier model and from the chordal playing of the Glenn Miller saxophone section. Shearing's quintet lasted until 1978, and some of the talent to pass through the group included Cal Tjader, Gary Burton, Toots Thielemans, Joe Pass, Israel Crosby, and Vernel Fournier.

Blind since birth, Shearing began playing piano at age three when he would pick out tunes he heard on the radio. He received limited musical training at the Linden Lodge School for the Blind in London, which he attended from age 12 to 16. He more readily absorbed what he heard on recordings by Fats Waller, Teddy Wilson, Art Tatum, and other pianists, teaching himself how to play boogie-woogie and blues on the piano. He made his first recording in 1936. He came to America in 1947, and, with help from Leonard Feather, he settled in New York where he joined the thriving bebop scene. Before forming his quintet, Shearing replaced Erroll Garner in the Oscar Pettiford Trio and led a quartet with Buddy DeFranco (1948). In the late 1950s, Shearing began performing classical concerts with symphony orchestras, in which he sometimes included arrangements featuring his quintet. From the late 1970s he has performed mostly as a soloist or in duos. Among the bassists Shearing has worked with are Brian Torff, Don Thompson, and Neil Swainson. Following his move to the Telarc label in the 1990s, Shearing began a series of recordings in trio settings, as well as other projects. Shearing's best-known composition, "Lullaby of Birdland," was written in 1952 as the theme for the legendary jazz club and its radio broadcasts.

what to buy: If you're just getting acquainted with George Shearing, his small group recordings are recommended, particularly his lively duets, which clearly demonstrate his polished style. Two of the best available albums recorded by Shearing are his duets with the highly expressive bassist Brian Torff. *Blues Alley Jazz* 𝄞𝄞𝄞𝄞 (Concord, 1980/1989, prod. Carl E. Jefferson), recorded in October 1979, documents a nine-tune set at the famed Washington D.C. jazz club. Virtuosic performances of Billy Taylor's "One for the Woofer" and other lesser-known pieces (including a delightful Torff original, "High and Inside") showcase skillful exchanges that are often full of wit, elegant lyricism, and swinging vitality. Torff shows great flexibility, generating spirited solos, gentle arco (bowed) work, and lightning-quick pizzicato stylings, matching Shearing's wit (he is this writer's favorite Shearing bassist). Recorded the following year at the Concord Jazz Festival in August 1980, *On a Clear Day* 𝄞𝄞𝄞𝄞 (Concord, 1980/1993, prod. Carl E. Jefferson) gets a slightly higher rating for the material, which includes a Shear-

George Shearing (l) and Jean "Toots" Thielemans **(Archive Photos)**

ing-Torff version of the leader's "Lullaby of Birdland" as well as classics such as "Love for Sale," "Have You Met Miss Jones?," "Happy Days Are Here Again," and two brilliant compositions by Torff. Both albums include one tune featuring Shearing's vocals. These albums are among his earliest recordings with the Concord label. Torff appeared on one more Concord recording with Shearing, *An Evening with George Shearing & Mel Tormé*, before he was replaced by bassist Don Thompson. For a live-recorded festival performance, *Dexterity* 🎵🎵🎵🎵 (Concord, 1988, prod. Carl E. Jefferson) is one of the best. An acoustically perfect, pleasurable listen recorded at the 1987 Fujitsu-Concord Jazz Festival in Japan, this 11-tune set includes duos with bassist Neil Swainson, Shearing solos, and two tunes with singer Ernestine Anderson backed simply by Shearing and Swainson (the hip swinger "As Long As I Live" and a classy version of the soul standard "Please Send Me Someone to Love"). While much of the set swings sedately, Shearing and Swainson also deliver a top-drawer, lyrical version of Michel Legrand's ballad "You Must Believe in Spring." An Ellington medley is

icing on the cake, with Shearing segueing from the bouncy "Take the 'A' Train" into a poignant version of "In a Sentimental Mood," and through three other Duke tunes. He closes the set with yet another version of his biggest pop hit since 1952, "Lullaby of Birdland." It's an attractive album that demonstrates the full power of Shearing's piano artistry. Shearing switched to the Telarc label with *I Hear a Rhapsody* 🎵🎵🎵🎵 (Telarc, 1992, prod. John Snyder), a live-recorded performance with bassist Neil Swainson and drummer Grady Tate at the Blue Note in New York City, in February 1992. This tasty trio album is one of his best, not only for the 11-tune mix, but for Shearing's exceptional rapport with Swainson and Tate—especially on swinging versions of "The End of a Love Affair" and "The Masquerade Is Over," and their boppish takes on "Birdfeathers" and "Wail." This album is highly recommended, as is their follow-up 11-tune album from the same live-recorded engagement, *Walkin'* 🎵🎵🎵🎵 (Telarc, 1995, prod. John Snyder). The slightly higher rating is a purely subjective recommendation based on the slightly more popular material.

what to buy next: On *Breakin' Out* ♫♫♫ (Concord, 1987, prod. Carl E. Jefferson), Shearing joins with veteran bassist Ray Brown and drummer Marvin "Smitty" Smith for a set containing 10 (often swinging and blues-tinged) standards and his original "Break Out Blues." This was Shearing's first recording with bassist Ray Brown and it's a choice New York studio session recorded in May 1987. After this session, Shearing and Brown did some classical concerts together. Smith adds extra panache to this outing with his splashy drumming, especially notable on the graceful trio take on Ellington's "Day Dream." (But Smith is not as understated and tasteful as drummer Grady Tate in Shearing's subsequent trio sessions recorded for Telarc.) A pleasing session of duets with guitarist Jim Hall, *First Edition* ♫♫♫ (Concord, 1982, prod. Carl E. Jefferson) offers an array of eight relaxed selections (two by Hall, one from Shearing) in a quasi–chamber-jazz setting. Some spirited interaction occurs on Hall's "Careful," a 16-bar blues based on a double-diminished scale that gives it a Middle-Eastern flavor, first recorded on a 1959 Jimmy Giuffre date. Shearing and Hall prove to be well-suited collaborators. A lively two-piano set with Hank Jones, *The Spirit of 176* ♫♫♫ (Concord, 1989, prod. Carl E. Jefferson) contains 14 tunes ranging from classic boppers to lush ballads. By the way, the number "176" in the title refers to the number of keys on two 88-key pianos. Highlights are many, particularly since these two players exhibit similarly relaxed and melodious styles as well as capabilities for Monkish bop expressions ("I Mean You" and "Ask Me Now"). An exceptional showcase for Shearing's tremendous talent, *Grand Piano* ♫♫♫ (Concord, 1985/1987, prod. Carl E. Jefferson) features an entire solo piano session with Shearing performing 10 romantic standards, including captivating, lyrical versions of the Rodgers-Hart standard, "It Never Entered My Mind," Kurt Weill's "Mack the Knife," Vernon Duke's "Taking a Change on Love," and Cole Porter's "Easy to Love." Alone worth the price of the album is Shearing's classically-tinged version of Antonio Carlos Jobim's classic "How Insensitive," performed as an exquisite ballad rather than with the usual Brazilian rhythms. Shearing's refined technique is readily apparent as he creates moods ranging from sensitive and melancholy to joyously upbeat and swinging. *Grand Piano* is a splendid listen that draws from the entire jazz piano tradition. In October 1986 Shearing recorded a follow-up album, *More Grand Piano* ♫♫♫ (Concord, 1987, prod. Carl E. Jefferson), which features his solo piano performances of 11 classics. Most enjoyable are his seductive readings of the ballad "You Don't Know What Love Is," his swing-tempo take on "East of the Sun," and a lush, lyrical reading (showcasing his locked-hands chordal technique) of the warhorse "I Can't Get Started." Some of these standards date back to his quintet days.

what to avoid: Shearing's playing is mostly overshadowed by the horn players among the six accompanying musicians on *In Dixieland* ♫♫♫ (Concord, 1989, prod. Carl E. Jefferson), and except for a couple of solo sittings and melody heads, you don't hear much from the pianist. However, if you like Dixieland (particularly from the Concord family of musicians) and don't miss hearing Shearing's piano, the album is okay.

best of the rest:

(With Carmen McRae) *Two for the Road* ♫♫♫ (Concord, 1980)
(With Marian McPartland) *Alone Together* ♫♫♫ (Concord, 1981)
An Evening with George Shearing and Mel Tormé ♫♫♫ (Concord, 1982)
(With Don Thompson) *Live at the Café Carlyle* ♫♫♫ (Concord, 1984)
(With Mel Tormé) *An Elegant Evening* ♫♫♫ (Concord, 1986)
Compact Jazz ♫♫♫ (Verve, 1987)
(With Mel Tormé) *A Vintage Year* ♫♫♫ (Concord, 1989)
(With the Robert Farnon Orchestra) *How Beautiful Is Night* ♫♫♫ (Telarc, 1993)
(With the New George Shearing Quintet) *That Shearing Sound* ♫♫♫ (Telarc, 1994)
(With Neil Swainson, Louis Stewart) *Paper Moon: The Music of Nat King Cole* ♫♫♫ (Telarc, 1996)
Favorite Things ♫♫♫ (Telarc, 1997)

worth searching for: Fans born before World War II should find *Mel & George "Do" World War II* ♫♫♫ (Concord, 1991, prod. Carl E. Jefferson) a nostalgic collection of 13 tunes (19 if you include tunes encapsulated in two medleys) featuring Mel Tormé. Shearing's trio with bassist Neil Swainson and drummer Donny Osborne plays three solo numbers before they are joined by "The Velvet Fog." Their performance was recorded live at Paul Masson Mountain Winery, in Saratoga, California, in two sets on September 2 and 3, 1990. (It was obviously an outdoor concert and you can hear the crickets loudly chirping!) The album contains plenty of popular American songbook favorites by composers Sammy Cahn, Harold Arlen, Johnny Mercer, Irving Berlin, Duke Ellington, and others. Tormé is in fine form throughout.

influences:

◀◀ Fats Waller, Teddy Wilson, Art Tatum, Erroll Garner, Bud Powell, Hank Jones

Nancy Ann Lee

Archie Shepp

Born May 24, 1937, in Ft. Lauderdale, FL.

Shepp's saxophone career began in R&B bands around Philadelphia, then expanded with the '60s avant-garde, and, most recently, changed direction again as he explores jazz roots as an elder statesman. The rough blues elements of his playing lent originality to his voice in the '60s, and added excitement (and sometimes sloppiness) to his later, more traditional jazz performances. After graduating from Goddard College with a degree in dramatic literature, Shepp moved to New York City, where his first important gig was in 1960 with Cecil Taylor. He moved to another series of crucial, reputation-sealing stints working as a co-leader (with John Tchicai and Don Cherry) of the New York Contemporary Five and various groups with trumpeter Bill Dixon. In 1964 Shepp began showing up in concert and on record with John Coltrane. Shepp also maintains a commitment to the dramatic arts, having written plays and poems (most of them concerned with racial inequality, art, and Afrocentric political issues); his theatrical works include the plays *The Communist* and *Junebug Graduates Tonight,* plus *Lady Day: A Musical Tragedy* (written with trumpeter Cal Massey). The saxophonist has also held a variety of academic positions, teaching at the University of Buffalo and at the University of Massachusetts at Amherst, among others.

what to buy: *Goin' Home* ✍✍✍✍ (SteepleChase, 1977, prod. Nils Winther), a duet album with pianist Horace Parlan, is without a doubt the most beautiful and sensitive release Shepp has ever taken part in. *Goin' Home* contains his arrangements of classic gospel songs plus a previously unissued rendition of Duke Ellington's "Come Sunday." Shepp was to return to this format with Parlan a few more times after this, but only *Trouble in Mind,* an album of blues tunes, even comes close to this soulful recital. As producer, Coltrane gave the tribute album *Four for Trane* ✍✍✍✍ (Impulse!, 1965, prod. John Coltrane) a certain credibility. Coltrane had already been deemed a god by many avant-garde musicians, and with this album Shepp's burgeoning talent received the imprimatur of the master. As expected, Coltrane tunes (including "Naima") dominate the playlist, but Shepp gets his compositional licks in with the powerful "Rufus (Swung His Face to the Wind . . .)."

what to buy next: *Trouble in Mind* ✍✍✍✍ (SteepleChase, 1980, prod. Nils Winther), the companion album to *Goin' Home,* is a wonderfully programmed and played set of slow to mid-tempo blues riffs. Parlan's playing sets the tone for Shepp's surprisingly tender ballad performances. "Make Me a Pallet on the Floor" and the Earl Hines classic, "Blues in Third," are particularly effective. The sidemen for the Charlie Parker tribute, *Lady Bird* ✍✍✍✍ (Denon, 1979, prod. Yoshio Ozawa), push Shepp to perform these bop classics at his best. He peaks during the conventional "Relaxin' at Camarillo," although he later works in

some of his patented R&B-cum-avant-garde blaring honks on "Now's the Time." Pianist Jaki Byard is especially effective in his solo spots while bassist Cecil McBee and drummer Roy Haynes keep the pulse cruising. *Fire Music* ✍✍✍ (Impulse!, 1965, prod. Bob Thiele) is a record whose importance within Shepp's catalog outstrips much of its initial artistic value. The blend of political polemic, ferocious soloing, and borderline kitsch was symptomatic of the times, and the initial reaction from progressive audiences was more laudatory than it perhaps deserved. Despite these hindsight drawbacks, the playing is more rewarding than a lot of the era's cutting-edge music, and some of the players on this session (Ted Curson, Marion Brown, David Izenzon, and Joe Chambers, for instance) went on to make substantial contributions to the art.

best of the rest:
Live in San Francisco ✍✍✍ (Impulse!, 1966)
Mama Too Tight ✍✍✍ (Impulse!, 1966)
Steam ✍✍✍ (Enja, 1977)
On Green Dolphin Street ✍✍✍ (Denon, 1978)
Tray of Silver ✍✍✍ (Denon, 1979)
(With Max Roach) *The Long March* ✍✍✍ (hat ART, 1979)

worth searching for: *The Way Ahead* (Impulse!, 1968, prod. Bob Thiele), sadly out of print, features a powerful, cutting-edge sextet and four tunes that reveal two sides of Shepp—as a burgeoning new-music stud and as a tradition-loving pseudo-historian. Each song is written by a group member (except Duke Ellington's "Sophisticated Lady"), with the truest avant-roots performance Shepp ever gave relegated to Walter Davis's "Damn If I Know (The Stroller)," where the sax screams and blurts hardcore blues through a futuristic filter.

influences:
◀◀ Ben Webster, Coleman Hawkins, Charlie Parker, John Coltrane, Sonny Rollins, Ornette Coleman

Garaud MacTaggart

John Sheridan

Born John Fredric Sheridan, January 20, 1946, in Columbus, OH.

John Sheridan began private piano studies in September 1953. Around this time he realized that he wanted a career in music; he claims his life was changed forever in 1954 (when he was eight) when his father brought home a recording of the 1938 Benny Goodman Carnegie Hall concert. During his childhood he was also taken with the piano playing of Jess Stacy and Teddy Wilson, who remain two of his primary influences. Continuing his piano studies, Sheridan also started studying clarinet in the summer of 1956, and was active in band and orchestra programs throughout his school years. He also began working professionally at local dances, concerts, state and county fairs, and appeared on the TV show *Ruth Lyon's Fifty-Fifty Club,* which originated in Cincinnati, Ohio. Sheridan received a Bachelor of Music degree from Capitol University in June 1968. That summer he enlisted in the U.S. Navy, spending time at Little Creek, Virginia at the U.S. Navy School of Music. He eventually took an assignment with the U. S. Navy Band in Washington, D.C. where he began arranging music. After military service, Sheridan relocated to Texas where he enrolled at North Texas State University, earning his Master of Music degree in May 1977. While in the Dallas–Fort Worth area, he played and arranged for the Mal Fitch Orchestra (1972–74), was rehearsal pianist and orchestrator for the Casa Mañana Summer Musicals (1974–78), and worked with Tommy Loy's Upper Dallas Jazz Band (1973–79). He also worked with the Joyce Wilson Quartet, the Jack Wyatt Quartet, Johnnie "Scat" Davis's Band, and led his own quartet. It was with Loy that Sheridan met trumpeter Jim Cullum Jr. and accepted an offer in 1979 to join the Jim Cullum Jazz Band in San Antonio, Texas, where Sheridan remains at present.

Serving as principal arranger and pianist for the Cullum Band, Sheridan has written over 1,000 arrangements for the ensemble, many of which have been heard on *Riverwalk Live at the Landing,* the Public Radio International weekly broadcast series that stars the Cullum band and guests. As an arranger, Sheridan was responsible for the Cullum band albums, *Porgy and Bess,* *'Tis the Season to Be Jammin',* and much of the material heard in *Hooray for Hoagy, Super Satch, Shootin' the Agate,* as well as most of the jazz content found in the CD series, *Riverwalk Live at the Landing.* Outside of the Cullum band, Sheridan has continued a professional relationship begun in 1988 with Dick Hyman, with whom he frequently performs in a two-piano format. He has also performed in the same context with Ralph Sutton, Eddie Higgins, Derek Smith, and Johnny Varro. He has arranged extensively for singer Banu Gibson, contributing to her symphonic repertoire and writing many charts for her band, including those featured on her 1955 Christmas CD, *'Zat You, Santa Claus?* As his busy schedule permits, he makes occasional appearances as pianist on the jazz party circuit and has performed at the Central Illinois Jazz Festival, the Pensacola Jazz Festival, and several Conneaut Lake jazz parties, where he fits into jazz groups of any size or style. With several recording projects of his own behind him and more in the planning stages, Sheridan is a bright star on the jazz horizon.

what to buy: John Sheridan and his Dream Band is featured on *Something Tells Me* 𝄡𝄡𝄡𝄡 (Arbors, 1997, prod. John Sheridan), an album that displays the leader's formidable keyboard and arranging skills. A swinging octet setting honors the songwriting talents of Harry Warren, Richard Whiting, and Johnny Mercer. Seventeen songs are right out of the swing era, and instrumentals sound fresh and inspired. The versatile bunch of musicians were specially chosen by Sheridan (hence the "Dream Band" handle). Randy Reinhart and Dan Barrett both double on trumpet or cornet and trombone. Brian Ogilvie and Ron Hockett each play clarinet or alto/tenor sax. With such diversity of horns at his command, Sheridan makes the most of the multi-layered musical textures available to him, and breathes new life into overlooked songs such as "Can't Teach My Old Heart New Tricks," "About a Quarter to Nine," "Silhouetted in the Moonlight," and the great old "Have You Got Any Castles, Baby?" Each front-line member is an agile, inventive soloist, and many solo gems enhance the set. The solid rhythm support is left to veteran bassist Bob Haggart, guitarist Reuben Ristrom, and drummer Jeff Hamilton. Sheridan's piano has many satisfying moments, but the leader is content to share the solo spotlight with his talented band members. The charts range from the sketchy road map variety with loose jamming ("Japanese Sandman") to tight, complex reminders of the fine John Kirby style ("I'd Love to Take Orders from You"). Bob Haggart uncorks his special brand of whistling for a loping, easy ramble on "Ride, Tenderfoot, Ride" (worth the price of the CD). This one should appeal to swing fans, mainstream jazz buffs, moviegoers, and tune sleuths. John Sheridan and his Buddies Four star on *Butterscotch* 𝄡𝄡𝄡𝄡 (Triangle Jazz Ltd., 1992, prod. Tom Rippey, Dick Rippey), a laid-back, relaxed quintet outing with plenty of room for Sheridan's fleet, two-handed piano artistry and his featured solos on "Oh, Baby" and "Sunday." Joining Sheridan from the ranks of the Jim Cullum Jazz Band are bassist Don Mopsick and guitarist Howard Elkins. Trumpeter Randy Reinhart and Texas tenorman Alfredo "Fred" Salas make up an abbreviated front line and participate on most tracks. Among the 14 tunes, homage is paid to Fats Waller with "I'd Rather Call You Baby" and "Up Jumped You with Love," to Joe Sullivan with "My Little Pride and Joy," and to Bunny Berigan with "More Than You Know," which is constructed on the changes of "I Can't Get Started." The title tune is an ode to Sheridan's favorite ice cream topping, but there's nothing syrupy about this attractive original featuring Sheridan's piano.

what to buy next: Dan Barrett and John Sheridan are two world-class musicians who share a penchant for exploring lovely, obscure melodies. Co-starring on *Two Sleepy People* 🎵🎵🎵🎵 (Arbors, 1996, prod. Rachel Domber, Mat Domber), they dig into gems such as "Why Do I Lie to Myself About You?," "I Like the Likes of You," "Who Loves You?," "Remember Me," and eight others. The title tune begins and ends the session with Barrett opening on cornet and closing the set on trombone. There are some generous helpings of Sheridan's splendid piano stylings that display his remarkable touch. The versatile Barrett employs a variety of open and muted trombone sounds, switching occasionally to cornet to vary the textures and tonal colors. The CD is a superb introduction to both of these swinging musicians who are keeping pace with today while glancing back at a glorious musical past. John Sheridan collaborates on *My Very Good Friend* 🎵🎵🎵 (Bear Fruit Productions, 1997, prod. David J. Gibson) with former U.S. Navy bandmate, tuba player Marty Erickson. The two old friends got together in San Antonio, Texas, for a loosely organized duet session and laid down 15 swinging tracks that almost defy description. Imagine encountering Charlie Parker's "Yardbird Suite" and "My Little Suede Shoes," or Carl Perkins's "Grooveyard" in a tuba-piano context! Erickson plays a Willson 3400 E-flat tuba which he helped design. He was a Navy Band member for 25 years before he retired to a career as a tuba clinician soloist. This reunion with his ex-Navy buddy works out fine for open-minded fans who can appreciate the intimacy of this unusual duo recording. Other tunes on the album include "You Took Advantage of Me," "I Let a Song Go Out of My Heart," "My One and Only Love," and "Tea for Two"; this CD is available from Bear Productions, 11814 Chapel Bells Way, Clarksville, MD 21029-1172, (410)531-4990.

worth searching for: Banu Gibson's *Livin' in a Great Big Way* 🎵🎵🎵🎵 (Swing Out, 1991, prod. Banu Gibson) is a superior vocal album blessed with artful piano accompaniment split between two keyboard wizards, John Sheridan and David Boeddinghaus. Each pianist tackles eight tunes backing Gibson. *'Zat You, Santa Claus* 🎵🎵🎵🎵 (Swing Out, 1995, prod. Banu Gibson) is a swinging Christmas CD by Banu Gibson and the New Orleans Hot Jazz group for which John Sheridan did all the arrangements. Included are three attractive Sheridan originals: "Christmas Will Be a Little Lonely This Year," "Christmas on the Bayou," and "Santa, Swing Me a Christmas Tune"; the latter two were co-written with Gibson. The 14-tune holiday collection offers obscure gems such as "Christmas Night in Harlem," "Christmas in New Orleans," and "At the Christmas Ball." Full of hot, bright sounds by the band and vocal stylings from a great gal, this is an enjoyable alternative to the frequently overdone holiday musical fare.

influences:

◀◀ Teddy Wilson, Jess Stacy, Dave Bowman, Bill Evans, Earl Hines, Dick Hyman, Dave McKenna, Oscar Peterson, Gene Schroeder, Ralph Sutton, Benny Carter, Bob Haggart, Fletcher Henderson, Matty Matlock, Billy May, Jimmy Mundy, Eddie Sauter, Conrad Salinger, Don Walker

see also: *Banu Gibson*

John T. Bitter

Matthew Shipp

Born December 7, 1960, in Wilmington, DE.

Arguably the most important pianist of his generation, Shipp has become an important figure on the New York avant-jazz scene. His playing is more pan-harmonic than atonal and rarely sounds like such avowed influences as Andrew Hill and Bill Evans, more often suggesting harmonically adventurous 20th-century classical composers, especially Scriabin. His lines rumble and swirl in a thoughtful, organic way, punctuated by massive chiming chords.

Shipp began playing piano at age five; he credits hearing Ahmad Jamal's music with first inspiring him to seriously explore jazz. An important early influence was noted educator Robert "Boysie" Lowery, who had been Clifford Brown's teacher (Brown's and Shipp's mothers had been friends). After attending the University of Delaware, he studied with Dennis Sandole (teacher of John Coltrane, James Moody, Art Farmer, etc.) and Ran Blake. Moving to New York in 1985, Shipp resisted going the usual route of itinerant sideman, working instead as a leader and in the bands of musicians—Roscoe Mitchell, David S. Ware, schoolmate Rob Brown, drummer Marc Edwards, guitarist Joe Morris—who view him as more of an equal collaborator. For a while in the mid-'80s he led a loose group of shifting membership aptly called Convection, which included at various times William Parker, Abdul Wadud, Akua Dixon Turre, Steve McCall, and Dennis Charles. Shipp's relationship with Ware has been especially fruitful, and listeners seeking the full picture of Shipp's development are advised to pick up the Ware Quartet albums, which feature the Shipp Trio, as well as the pianist's work as a leader. Shipp feels he works best with other players he can spontaneously bounce ideas off of, and his discography is full of duo and trio recordings, with bassist William Parker his most regular cohort.

what to buy: Credited to the Matthew Shipp "String" Trio, *By the Law of Music* 🎵🎵🎵🎵 (hat ART, 1997, prod. Art Lange, Pia, Werner X. Uehlinger) matches Shipp with violinist Mat Maneri and bassist William Parker for a 12-movement suite that, in parts, is the furthest he's strayed from jazz. The styles include suggestions of serial technique and texture, piano passages suggesting Bach inventions refracted through the prism of free jazz, a progression-based, jazzy-bluesy hoedown reminiscent of Herbie Nichols, and free-improv energy music built from Coltranesque successions of sound blocks. The overall texture is varied by interspersing solo and duo sections, and throughout the performances project intelligence, passion, and intensity in equal proportions. The closing coda is a raucous yet noble cover of Duke Ellington's "Solitude" in which Shipp's insistent chords are balanced by Maneri's sweetly melodic frosting. The sound quality is superbly clear on what will eventually be seen as one of the supreme albums of its decade. The solo piano album *Symbol Systems* 𝄞𝄞𝄞𝄞 (No More, 1995, prod. Alan Schneider) was intended to be a duo, but the other player didn't show up. It certainly sounds assured. With no other players, *Symbol Systems* clearly displays how unique his gestural language is, though its angularity can recall Mal Waldron (especially on "Frame") when Shipp's spiky energy subsides briefly. The influence of Scriabin is evident as well, lending his lines a sense of majesy. The quartet album *The Flow of X* 𝄞𝄞𝄞𝄞 (2.13.61, 1997, prod. Matthew Shipp) sounds like an all-out blowing session. Violinist Mat Maneri, who's more to the forefront than Shipp himself, has a tone that sometimes suggests Stephane Grappelli; otherwise he's not particularly beholden to any jazz violin paradigms, playing either like an improvising classical violinist or a horn player. The most interesting track is the least free, "Flow of Silence," on which drummer Whit Dickey swings more than ever before, at least on record.

what to buy next: On the duo album *Zo* 𝄞𝄞𝄞𝄞 (Rise, 1993/213CD, 1994) there's a primal power in Shipp's playing that reaches toward ultimate emotional expression. The easiest way to approach his music may be the radical recasting of "Summertime," which trembles with the suppressed violence of oppression and the edginess that heat and humidity bring on. His massive chords state the melody over and over as bassist William Parker squiggles frenetically against it or bows mournfully, with occasional excursions away from the melody into freer expressions of the moods it suggests. The other three tracks are more far-out but equally potent and often subtle. Consisting of three tracks totalling 41 minutes, the very "outside" *Critical Mass* 𝄞𝄞𝄞𝄞 (213CD, 1995) is built equally of rooted massiveness and soaring lightness, with violinist Mat Maneri's addition to Shipp's usual trio with Parker and Dickey placing even more of an emphasis than usual on quick-minded inter-

play. There is great strength in this challenging music, especially apparent in Shipp's tolling chords at the beginning of "Virgin Complex" and in Parker's throbbing acoustic bass throughout; but the strength here is built from tensile flexibility, not rigidity.

what to avoid: The Shipp/Roscoe Mitchell duo album *2-Z* 𝄞𝄞 (2.13.61, 1996) finds the AACM saxophone legend playing with claustrophobia-inducing density, laying out conceptual slabs of sound that lack interest on other levels. Shipp, tailoring his playing to Mitchell's, ends up sounding less inspired than usual.

the rest:
Circular Temple 𝄞𝄞𝄞𝄞 (Quinton, 1990/Infinite Zero, 1994)
Points 𝄞𝄞𝄞𝄞 (Silkheart, 1991)
Prism 𝄞𝄞𝄞𝄞 (Brinkman, 1996)
Before the World 𝄞𝄞𝄞𝄞 (FMP, 1997)
(With Joe Morris) *Thesis* 𝄞𝄞𝄞𝄞 (hatOLOGY, 1997)
The Multiplication Table 𝄞𝄞𝄞𝄞 (hatOLOGY, 1998)

worth searching for: Still in print but never available except on LP, *Sonic Explorations* 𝄞𝄞𝄞 (Cadence Jazz, 1988, prod. Matthew Shipp, Rob Brown, Bob Rusch) was Shipp's debut on record. If not as assured or as broad-based stylistically as his later work, it's nonetheless well worth hearing, and aside from the six-section title suite there are interesting takes on "Oleo" and "Blue in Green." The multiple-artists live compilation *What Is Jazz? 1996* 𝄞𝄞𝄞𝄞 (Knitting Factory Works, 1996, prod. Brett Heinz, Mark Perlson) was recorded at the annual festival of the album title and includes a powerful solo Shipp track not available elsewhere. Many David S. Ware Quartet albums with Shipp are important in chronicling Shipp's development; especially noteworthy moments include the title track on *flight of i* 𝄞𝄞𝄞𝄞 (DIW/Columbia, 1992, prod. Kazunori Sugiyama), where the leader displays impressive circular breathing technique over some of Shipp's most Scriabinesque chording, and the two monolithic renditions of "Autumn Leaves" on *Third Ear Recitation* 𝄞𝄞𝄞𝄞 (DIW, 1993, prod. Kazunori Sugiyama). Rob Brown's *Blink of an Eye* 𝄞𝄞𝄞𝄞 (No More Records, 1997, prod. Alan Schneider) is a duo with Shipp that consists of three live free improvisations; although the first two are each in the half-hour range, they are masterfully sustained thanks to keen responsiveness. Brown and Shipp alternate contrasting styles and matching figures, with the congruity of their wild flurries aligned via underlying musical logic. The volume and density of their intertwining figures may fluctuate, but intensity and imagination never flag.

influences:
◄◄ Cecil Taylor, Andrew Hill, Bill Evans, Thelonious Monk, Alexander Scriabin, J.S. Bach

▶▶ Myra Melford

Steve Holtje

Bobby Short (tuba)

Born August 26, 1911. Died April 4, 1976, in Shellville, CA.

During the last revival of Dixieland jazz in San Francisco, which began in the late 1940s, you could hear bands such as the Yerba Buena Jazz Band, the Turk Murphy Jazz Band, Bob Scobey's Dixielanders, Monty Ballou's Castle Jazz Band, and other traditional bands that were rebelling against the evolution of swing jazz. Bobby Short was a tuba player who found work during this revival period, playing with Jack Teagarden and performing and recording with Monty Ballou's Castle Jazz Band, which had started in Portland, Oregon in 1955. Short played traditional jazz with Turk Murphy in San Francisco during the early 1950s and occasionally doubled on cornet and trumpet. After a stint with Bob Scobey (1956–58), Short rejoined Murphy's group from 1958–61. Short continued to record with the Castle Jazz Band and with bands led by Clancy Hayes and Lu Watters.

worth searching for: Discover examples of Bob Short's tuba artistry on the Dixieland jazz recordings of the Bob Frisco Scobey Band available from the Fantasy catalog. *Direct from San Francisco* ♫♫♫ (Good Time Jazz, 1992) contains Dixieland classics such as "Jazz Me Blues," "A Closer Walk with Thee," "Ja-Da," and other tunes performed with trumpeter/leader Bob Scobey, trombonist Jack Buck, clarinetist Bill Napier, and banjoist/vocalist Clancy Hayes. Also available on the Good Time Jazz label, *Famous Castle Jazz Band* ♫♫♫♫ (Good Time Jazz, 1992) finds Short with the band led by Marty Ballou performing lively, time-treasured tunes such as "Sweet Georgia Brown," "Royal Garden Blues," "Careless Love," "Tiger Rag," "Kansas City Stomp," and others. This is one of the best of the discs representative of this revival period of San Francisco–based Dixieland jazz. Another recording featuring Short's playing with the Bob Scobey band featuring banjo/vocalist Clancy Hayes is *Raid the Juke Box* ♫♫♫ (Good Time Jazz, 1994). The band plays favorites from the juke box era, including "Love Letters in the Sand," "All Shook Up," "So Rare," "Blueberry Hill," and "Bye Bye Love."

Nancy Ann Lee

Bobby Short (vocalist)

Born September 15, 1926, in Danville, IL.

Bobby Short is a cabaret singer who respects and understands the lyric content of the songs in his vast repertoire. He's in a class by himself: he's an impeccable dresser, his smile is stunning, and his husky baritone voice is frequently tinged with a touch of laryngitis that in no way detracts from its appeal. His piano playing shows influences of Nat Cole and Art Tatum, two of his long-time friends. Short's diction, delivery, personality, and all-around savoir faire allow him the ability to connect and communicate with his audiences in ways unlike many other performers.

Bobby Short left Danville at age 11, with his family's blessing, to perform in vaudeville as a child singer-pianist in Chicago, 125 miles north of his home. Later he spent a year in New York City where he got booked at various clubs, including Harlem's famous Apollo Theatre. Early in 1938 Short returned to Danville and remained there for four years while he finished high school. Then he was off to the Capitol Lounge in Chicago. In 1943 he went to Omaha, Nebraska, where he met Nat Cole; then he toured to Milwaukee where he befriended Art Tatum. The next 20 years were spent performing in clubs on both coasts, occasionally in Florida or the Midwest. In 1954 Short acquired the savvy Phil Moore as his manager and sometime music director. Short sold a tape to Atlantic Records, which subsequently landed him a recording contract. Surviving the mid-1960s club doldrums, Short replaced George Feyer at the Café Carlyle in New York City's Carlyle Hotel in 1968; he was recommended for the gig by the Ertegun's at Atlantic Records. From '68 to the present day, Bobby Short has been presenting his stylized versions of lyrics from the Great American Songbook for four to eight months a year at this intimate Madison Avenue spot. As long as Short is performing, the works of composers Cole Porter, Rodgers and Hart, Jerome Kern, Vernon Duke, and George and Ira Gershwin are in good hands. Short's legions of fans and those who are about to discover this one-of-a-kind singer can kick back and enjoy the large part of his recorded output that remains available on CD.

what to buy: *50 by Bobby Short* ♫♫♫♫ (Atlantic, 1950s–80/1986, prod. various) offers a look back on Bobby Short's recorded output on Atlantic from the 1950s to the 1980s. This two-CD compilation contains 50 tracks of sophistication, swing, and tasteful treatment of both evergreens and obscurities such as "Manhattan," "From This Moment On," "I've Got Five Dollars," "Sand in My Shoes," "I Love You, Samantha," "It's Bad for Me," "Changes," "Bojangles of Harlem," and "Our Love Is Here to Stay." *Late Night at the Café Carlyle* ♫♫♫♫ (Telarc, 1992, prod. John Snyder) features 17 standards and lesser known songs recorded by the Bobby

Short Trio from June 20–22, 1991 at his comfortable home base. His swinging companions, bassist Beverly Peer and drummer Robert Scott, admirably support the singer-pianist as they ease and swing through chestnuts such as "Night and Day," "Drop Me Off in Harlem," "Body and Soul," "Street of Dreams," "Every Time We Say Goodbye," and nine other tunes. The freshness and charm obvious to the audience attending these live performances transfers nicely to the compact disc. For similar material in an 11-piece band setting, pick up *Celebrating 30 Years at the Café Carlyle* ♫♫♫♫ (Telarc, 1997, prod, John Snyder). This collection reprises 14 of the songs associated with Short during his stay at the Madison Avenue nitery, all done up in new arrangements with strong instrumental support from outstanding bassist Frank Tate, drummer Klaus Suonsaari, and eight instrumentalists, including saxophone genius Scott Robinson and reedman Loren Schoenberg.

what to buy next: *Swing That Music* ♫♫♫ (Telarc, 1993, prod. John Snyder) features Short with the Howard Alden–Dan Barrett Quintet. Short plays the role of the hot sophisticate, singing 13 songs arranged by Barrett with the quintet providing a swinging backdrop. Barrett's trombone, Howard Alden's guitar, and Chuck Wilson's alto sax, clarinet, and flute all sparkle in the vocal accompaniments, ensemble settings, and solo spots that fall between the singer's choruses. Bassist Frank Tate, drummer Jackie Williams, and pianist Short make a formidable rhythm team. The 1936 standard "Gone with the Wind" receives definitive handling and the rarely heard Sam Coslow/Tom Satterfield "Restless" is especially effective. Several of the other tunes are off the beaten path—"Take Love Easy," "Killin' Myself," "Ghost of Yesterday," "Sleep, Baby, Don't Cry"—and are treated kindly by the crew. For a generous taste of Bobby Short's piano playing and a sampling of his thoughts on music, try a delightful hour of *Marian McPartland's Piano Jazz with Guest Bobby Short* ♫♫♫♫ (Jazz Alliance, 1994, prod. Shari Hutchinson). A November 10, 1986 broadcast for McPartland's National Public Radio *Piano Jazz* series, the recording documents nine musical tracks interspersed with conversation as host McPartland and guest Short go one-on-one, managing four piano duets, three Short solos, two McPartland solos, and two vocals by Short.

best of the rest:
Bobby Short is K-Ra-Zy for Gershwin ♫♫♫♫ (Atlantic, 1959/1990)
The Mad Twenties ♫♫♫♫ (Atlantic, 1959/1994)
Bobby, Noel & Cole ♫♫♫♫ (Atlantic, 1971, 1972/1989)
Celebrates Rodgers and Hart ♫♫♫♫♫ (Atlantic, 1975/1994)
Guess Who's in Town ♫♫♫♫ (Atlantic, 1987)
Songs of New York ♫♫♫♫ (Telarc, 1995)

influences:
◄◄ Mabel Mercer, Hildegarde, Nat King Cole, Art Tatum

John T. Bitter

Wayne Shorter

Born August 25, 1933, in Newark, NJ.

Wayne Shorter has made a profound impact on jazz as an improviser, composer, and conceptualizer. Throughout his career he has broken rules and stretched boundaries. His compositions extend form and harmony yet retain an impeccable sense of structure and melodic development. His solos are full of unexpected melodic leaps and rhythmic twists that, once heard in full, become perfectly logical. Shorter's strength is in exploring bold new concepts while remaining connected to traditional tenets.

Born and raised in Newark, New Jersey, Shorter had easy access to New York's abundant jazz scene in the 1940s and 1950s. He would often cut classes to go see various big bands. Attending the Newark High School of Music and Art, he started on clarinet at the age of 16 but switched to tenor saxophone. He improved so rapidly that he was soon sitting in with Sonny Stitt. Shorter developed a reputation as an advanced and adventurous tenor player. Known as "the kid from Newark," he shared a bandstand with jazz luminaries such as Max Roach, Horace Silver, Jackie McLean, Kenny Clarke, and Oscar Pettiford. He even attracted the attention of John Coltrane who would occasionally discuss music and practice with him. Shorter graduated from New York University with a music degree before serving in the U.S. Army from 1956 to 1958. He maintained his good standing in the jazz community despite being away for three years. After the Army, Shorter joined Maynard Ferguson's band, where he first met Joe Zawinul. He left Ferguson in 1959 when he heard Art Blakey was looking for a tenor player for the Jazz Messengers. From 1959 to 1964, as musical director for the Jazz Messengers, Shorter matured as a soloist and composer. His playing and compositions added a great deal of variety and diversity to the hard-bop setting. From Blakey he also learned important lessons about musical storytelling and quickly grabbing the audience's attention. In 1960, on Coltrane's recommendation, Miles Davis asked Shorter to join his band. But because of his obligation to Blakey, Shorter declined and remained with the Jazz Messengers.

Prior to joining Blakey, Shorter recorded three albums for Vee Jay: *Introducing Wayne Shorter*, *Second Genesis*, and *Wayning Moments*, subsequently reissued on a now-out-of-print CD with additional cuts not on the original release. They are conventional hard-bop excursions with a trumpet and tenor front line. Each album is a mix of standards and originals. Shorter's playing exposes his indebtedness to melody players like Lester Young and Sonny Rollins. He seems to approach each solo as an opportunity to compose a new melody, and the track "Devil's Island" on *Wayning Moments* is a brief but notable illustration of this skill.

When he finally signed up with Miles in 1964, Shorter brought a sense of musical exploration to the band that had been missing since Coltrane's departure in 1960. With Shorter, Herbie Hancock, Tony Williams, and Ron Carter, Miles had a formidable collection of composers as well as instrumentalists. Shorter was particularly prolific, contributing tunes such as "E.S.P.," "Pinocchio," "Nefertiti," and "Footprints." Strangely, his playing took on two distinct styles: in the studio he played elliptical, sparse, and probing solos; in live performances (such as on *The Complete Live at the Plugged Nickel Sessions*) his playing is marked by an increased complexity, density, and fervor. But overall, the abstract and impressionistic aspects of his playing deepened. During this period Shorter also led several excellent, often brilliant, sessions for Blue Note. These recordings effectively merged avant-garde concepts with a hard-bop sensibility, reflecting the influences of Blakey and Davis. Less rhythmically daring than Miles's band, Shorter's outings are underlined with a fairly conventional swing. But the music tested formal, melodic and harmonic boundaries and rules. Away from the pressure cooker of a high profile gig, Shorter's albums breathe and unfold organically. Shorter's compositions and solos departed from standard conventions, trading in unpredictable harmonies, sparse melodies, and unusual or extended forms. *Speak Like a Child*, *Etcetera*, and *JuJu* are excellent representations of his tremendous, often subtle abilities. And with "Speak Like a Child," "Yes or No," "JuJu," and "Deluge," Shorter contributed unique, distinctive tunes that have since entered the standard jazz repertoire. Toward the end of his tenure with Davis, Shorter began performing on soprano saxophone as much as tenor. Unlike others, he has carved a unique identity on soprano completely distinct from his tenor sound. He has conquered the intonation and timbral difficulties that plague other tenor players. With a tone that is singing and melancholy, Shorter has helped set the standard of excellence on the instrument and become one of its most accomplished practitioners.

By 1970, Shorter formed Weather Report with Joe Zawinul. The band pursued the kind of expansive, electronic jazz introduced by Miles Davis on *Nefertiti* and *In a Silent Way*. At first the music was open and free flowing, later becoming more arranged and structured. By the mid-1970s Zawinul's influence began to dominate Weather Report. Shorter was under-utilized—often featured only in the statement of a melody or on incidental background figures. He was more prominent as a guest soloist on records by Steely Dan and Joni Mitchell. At any rate, his 15 years with Weather Report were his longest stay with any group, and albums such as *Night Passage*, *Black Market*, and *Sweetnighter* feature some outstanding Shorter contributions. After defining the jazz fusion canon and contributing many remarkable recordings, Weather Report disbanded in 1986.

During the 1970s Shorter also recorded once under his own name. The album *Native Dancer* combines Brazilian music with jazz in ways unlike previous bossa nova excursions. The music stays truer to Brazil rhythmically and incorporates the more intricate harmonies of late 1960s Miles and early 1970s Weather Report. However, it was as much Milton Nascimento's album as Shorter's. Only three of the nine tunes are Shorter's, and his solo space is limited. Nevertheless, the collaboration is quite successful and the album is exceptional. At the same time, Shorter toured as part of V.S.O.P., a band that reunited him with ex-Miles sidemen Herbie Hancock, Ron Carter and Tony Williams and featured Freddie Hubbard in the trumpet chair. The music consisted primarily of reinterpretations of their work with Miles. The first release by the group was a refreshing contrast to their individual electronic outings. Shorter's solos on "Dolores" and "Byrdlike" show that playing in Weather Report had not compromised his ability to play in a more conventional jazz setting. *Tempest in the Colosseum* and *Live under the Sky*, both recorded in Japan, find the band a little more relaxed and comfortable with each other.

After the Weather Report era, Shorter continued pursuing jazz fusion but he was not relegated to a supporting role. His first release, *Atlantis*, is ambitious and complex. Compositions such as "The Three Marias" and "Endangered Species" are minor masterpieces of sophisticated orchestration and motivic development that also leave room for Shorter's improvisations. The albums *Phantom Navigator* and *Joy Ryder* were less ambitious and a bit disappointing in comparison. After *Joy Ryder*, Wayne took some time off from his solo career. He toured with Carlos Santana in 1988, and with the Miles Davis Tribute Band in 1992. The Tribute Band, similar to V.S.O.P. except with Wallace Roney on trumpet, is slightly more predictable and less energetic than its V.S.O.P. predecessor. After his brief sabbatical, Shorter returned in 1995 to the studio with the album *High Life*. The

album received equal amounts of acclaim and criticism when it was released. The merits of the music are not revealed easily or immediately. The album features a great deal of subtle, sophisticated interplay and counterpoint that requires added attention from the listener. More recently, Shorter recorded an album of duets with longtime bandmate Herbie Hancock. Given the abilities of the two participants, *1+1* is a deep and tremendously rewarding collaboration.

Shorter is often labeled a Coltrane disciple. While he has the capacity to play dense, multi-note solos similar to Coltrane's "sheets of sound," Shorter never pursued the harmonic patterns or formula (see "Giant Steps" and "Countdown") of Coltrane. In addition, his lyrical, open, declarative melodies, heightened by great rhythmic diversity and complexity, point to a strong Lester Young and Sonny Rollins influence. But Shorter transcends such simple comparisons. He is a unique and singular musician, one who has clearly staked out his own territory and continues to grow and develop. Shorter's legacy as a composer ranks him second only to Monk or Ellington. His continued excellence as an improviser marks him as one of the most important instrumentalists of his generation.

what to buy: *JuJu* ♫♫♫♫ (Blue Note, 1964/1996 , prod. Alfred Lion) is a subtle and pensive album. It represents the first step in Shorter's development as a sophisticated composer and improviser. His first quartet recording for Blue Note finds him working with two members of Coltrane's rhythm section (McCoy Tyner and Elvin Jones). Their presence gives the proceedings freedom, space, and drive. All six Shorter originals from the session have become classics. *Speak No Evil* ♫♫♫♫♫ (Blue Note, 1964/1988, prod. Alfred Lion) is yet another important album filled with classic compositions. Freddie Hubbard brings a necessary fire and passion to the recording. The only possible complaint is the number of inferior imitators created by the enormous impact of this album. *Et Cetera* ♫♫♫♫ (Blue Note, 1965/1995, prod. Alfred Lion) is an all-time best. Shorter's solos flow naturally and subtly from the compositions. The overall tone is dark and haunting. The compositions are not as long-lived as others of Shorter's, but they are minimalist gems. It is incomprehensible that Blue Note left this one unreleased for more than 10 years. *Adam's Apple* ♫♫♫♫ (Blue Note, 1966/1988, prod. Alfred Lion) is full of classic Shorter compositions and outstanding solos. "Adam's Apple," "El Gau-

cho," and "502 Blues" have become jazz standards. It's particularly interesting to hear Shorter's version of "Footprints" as he originally wrote it.

what to buy next: *Night Dreamer* ♫♫♫♫ (Blue Note, 1964/1987, prod. Alfred Lion) was Shorter's first album for Blue Note, and it set the tone for most of what would follow. Elvin Jones, McCoy Tyner, and Reggie Workman provide strong support throughout. The album has been unfairly overshadowed by subsequent Shorter releases. "Charcoal Blues" is a quirky, almost Monk-like blues that shows off Shorter's ability to take chances without losing sight of the original melody. *Soothsayer* ♫♫♫♫ (Blue Note, 1965/1990, prod. Alfred Lion) features a good mix of up-tempo Blakey-ish cookers like "Angola" with more distinct Shorter compositions such as "Lady Day." And having three horns allows Shorter to flex his arranging muscles. Interestingly, the recording features possibly the first recording of Tony Williams with McCoy Tyner. *All Seeing Eye* ♫♫♫♫ (Blue Note, 1966/1994, prod. Alfred Lion) is a programmatic journey into cosmological and religious territory. The album is inspired by nothing less than the creation of the universe to its destruction at the hands of the Devil. The five-horn frontline is wonderfully exotic and provocative. *Schizophrenia* ♫♫♫♫ (Blue Note, 1967/1995, prod. Francis Wolff) is a more conventional hard bop session for Shorter. The sextet configuration is reminiscent of the Jazz Messengers, but the addition of James Spaulding on flute expands the timbral range. "Tom Thumb" is a jazz bossa in the mold of Horace Silver's "Song for My Father." "Schizophrenia" starts mysteriously and develops into a straight-ahead cooker. *Super Nova* ♫♫♫♫♫ (Blue Note, 1969/1988, prod. Alfred Lion) showcases Shorter on soprano more prominently than ever before. The music ranges from sweet and melancholy to daring and avant garde. Shorter's version of Jobim's poignant "Dindi" is outstanding.

best of the rest:

Introducing Wayne Shorter ♫♫♫ (Vee-Jay, 1959)
Second Genesis ♫♫♫ (Vee-Jay, 1960/Le Jazz, 1994)
Wayning Moments Plus ♫♫♫♫ (Vee-Jay, 1962)
Moto Grosso Feio ♫♫♫ (Blue Note, 1970)
Native Dancer ♫♫♫♫♫ (Columbia, 1974/1990)
Atlantis ♫♫♫♫ (Columbia, 1985/1995)
Phantom Navigator ♫♫♫ (Columbia, 1987)
Joy Ryder ♫♫ (Columbia, 1988)
High Life ♫♫♫♫ (Verve, 1995)
1+1 ♫♫♫♫♫ (Verve, 1997)

worth searching for: *Odyssey of Iska* ♫♫♫ (Blue Note, 1970/1996) is an interesting companion to *Moto Grosso Feio*.

Wayne Shorter **(Archive Photos)**

Recorded on the same day with the same personnel (with the notable exception of Chick Corea and Jack DeJohnette switching instruments), the music is extremely ethereal and open.

influences:

◀◀ Lester Young, Charlie Parker, John Coltrane, Sonny Rollins

▶▶ Branford Marsalis, Gary Thomas, Bill Evans (sax), Rick Margitza, Sam Newsome

see also: *Weather Report, Art Blakey, Miles Davis*

James Eason

Alan Silva

Born January 22, 1939, in Bermuda.

Silva was raised in New York City, where he studied piano and violin as a child, later taking trumpet lessons from Donald Byrd. In the early 1960s, Silva turned his full attention to the string bass and the burgeoning avant-garde scene. After appearing with pianist Burton Greene at the October Revolution concerts in 1964, Silva worked with the leading figures of the movement, including Cecil Taylor, Albert Ayler, the Jazz Composers Orchestra, and Bill Dixon. In the late 1960s and 1970s, he led a group called the Celestial Communication Orchestra. A longtime resident of Paris, Silva has been an important contributor to European free improvisation, playing with, among others, the large collective Globe Unity Orchestra. Silva created an original style on the bass, bowing high harmonics to create the illusion of much higher-pitched string instruments. With it, he builds dense accompaniments and solos that seem suspended between a string section and electronic music.

what's available: There is only one CD currently available on which Silva is the leader: a reissue of his first date as leader, *Alan Silva* 𝅘𝅥𝅘𝅥𝅘𝅥𝅘𝅥 (ESP, 1968/1994, prod. Bernard Stollman). It includes vibraphonist Karl Berger, pianist Dave Burrell, and drummer Barry Altschul in two long and dense group improvisations that emphasize layered percussion and keyboards.

worth searching for: Silva's outstanding recording with Albert Ayler is *Live in Greenwich Village* 𝅘𝅥𝅘𝅥𝅘𝅥𝅘𝅥 (Impulse!, 1967, prod. Bob Thiele), with Silva joining cellist Joel Freedman in providing an almost orchestral carpet of sound for the leader's tenor on "For John Coltrane." On Cecil Taylor's *Unit Structures* 𝅘𝅥𝅘𝅥𝅘𝅥𝅘𝅥 (Blue Note, 1966, prod. Alfred Lion), Silva's bowed bass is paired with Henry Grimes's pizzicato. Silva adds some startlingly fresh tone colors, while Grimes provides the propulsion, resulting in one of the most effective uses of two basses ever recorded. From there it's on to vinyl, both old and fairly recent. Released as a two LP set and still available in that form, *Das Lied* 𝅘𝅥𝅘𝅥𝅘𝅥𝅘𝅥 (Po Torch, 1991, prod. Paul Lovens) is a 1981 quartet performance with pianist Alexander Von Schlippenbach, saxophonist Evan Parker, and percussionist Paul Lovens. It's an exceptional performance of free improvised music, brawling and serene by turn, as is the out-of-print LP by the same quartet, *Anticlockwise* 𝅘𝅥𝅘𝅥𝅘𝅥 (FMP, 1981, prod. Jost Gebers).

influences:

◀◀ Paul Chambers, Scott LaFaro, Art Davis, Gary Peacock

▶▶ Peter Kowald, Barry Guy, William Parker

see also: *Albert Ayler, Cecil Taylor, Bill Dixon*

Stuart Broomer

Horace Silver

Born September 2, 1928, in Norwalk, CT.

Silver is an enormously influential instrumentalist, composer, and bandleader who is one of the primary architects of hard bop. He first rose to prominence as a member of saxophonist Stan Getz's quartet in 1950–51. A 1952 recording date with Lou Donaldson led to Silver's 28-year association with the Blue Note label, for which he made his most important recordings. In 1953 he joined drummer Art Blakey to co-lead the Jazz Messengers. The cooperative quintet made several memorable albums, including two with a young Clifford Brown, *Live at Birdland* in 1954 and *Live at Cafe Bohemia*, with Kenny Dorham and Hank Mobley, in 1955. In 1954 Silver recorded with Miles Davis. In 1956 he left the Jazz Messengers and formed his own quintet. While leading his own band in the mid- to late 1950s, he also recorded as a sideman with Mobley, Dorham, Sonny Rollins, Lee Morgan, J.J. Johnson, and others associated with Blue Note's hard bop sound. Aside from a short period of retirement in the late 1970s and early 1980s, Silver has continued to lead bands in the mold of his original quintet. Over the years, his groups have included such notable saxophonists as Joe Henderson, Mobley, Clifford Jordan, Michael Brecker, Junior Cook, and Benny Golson; and trumpeters such as Dorham, Donald Byrd, Art Farmer, Blue Mitchell, Randy Brecker, Tom Harrell, and Woody Shaw. Silver has occasionally added a third horn or augmented the quintet with extra brass, strings, percussion, or a choir, but his basic formula has remained unchanged for over 40 years.

Silver's impact on jazz is three-fold. His instrumental style laid the groundwork for many of hard bop's innovations. It grew out of the influence of Bud Powell, especially in the way the left-hand rhythm supports right-hand lines. However, Silver pared down Powell's effusiveness, tightening it to short, boldly etched melodies varied and extended in the right hand and accompanied by insistent, regularly spaced chording in the left to build enormous tension and swing. The rhythmic drive and powerful melodic simplicity of the blues, R&B, and gospel are also an important component of Silver's playing, as are Latin rhythms. In addition, as a bandleader he established the instrumentation of the standard small jazz combo from the 1950s forward: tenor saxophone, trumpet, piano, bass, and drums. Finally, Silver is a superb jazz composer. His melodies have an elegance and economy comparable to Thelonious Monk's, but his use of gospel and blues gives them a much more direct emotional appeal that often masks their sophistication. He arranges these tunes for his quintet with signature voicings that help establish his music as some of the most distinctive, as well as consistently upbeat and popular, in jazz.

what to buy: Joe Henderson was a front-line voice to equal the leader's, which helps lift *Song for My Father* ♫♫♫♫ (Blue Note, 1964, prod. Alfred Lion) a cut above even Silver's high standards. The title track is, of course, a classic, but don't overlook the rest of the album. *Tokyo Blues* ♫♫♫♫ (Blue Note, 1962, prod. Alfred Lion) is the peak performance by Silver's classic quintet with Junior Cook and Blue Mitchell. Silver's solo on "Sayonara Blues" is an absolute masterpiece of sustained tension, melodic development, and sanctified soul. It's guaranteed to set toes tapping. For half of *Cape Verdean Blues* ♫♫♫♫ (Blue Note, 1965, prod. Alfred Lion), J.J. Johnson joins Henderson and Woody Shaw to form one of Silver's strongest horn sections. The results are predictably burning. The title track is a Latin-tinged followup to "Song for My Father," but the uptempo "Nutville" and the medium "The African Queen" are the highlights.

what to buy next: *Jody Grind* ♫♫♫♫ (Blue Note, 1966, prod. Alfred Lion) is a finger-popper from beginning to end, with the title track being one of Silver's many grooving masterpieces. "Grease Piece" features one of Silver's most down-and-dirty, percussive solos on record. On *Further Explorations by the Horace Silver Quintet* ♫♫♫♫ (Blue Note, 1958, prod. Alfred Lion), an edition of the quintet that features Art Farmer and Clifford Jordan turns in a consistently driving and inventive set. This is an overlooked gem in the Silver discography. *Horace Silver and the Jazz Messengers* ♫♫♫♫ (Blue Note, 1954, prod. Alfred Lion) has the original band with Dorham and Mobley, who throw themselves into Silver's music with youthful enthusiasm. The

H ORACE S ILVER

song "Doin' the Thing"

album *Doin' the Thing: The Horace Silver Quintet at the Village Gate*
(Blue Note, 1961/1988)

instrument Piano

Monster Solo

gospel touches in "The Preacher" and blues groove of "Doodlin'" point the way to Silver's classic period in the 1960s.

what to avoid: *The United States of Mind, Phase 3-All* ♫ (Blue Note, 1972, prod. Alfred Lion) reminds that it's a good rule of thumb to beware of any Silver album with lyrics. With all due respect to the sincerity of Silver's spiritual beliefs and their positive intent, his lyrics can be downright embarrassing, even when sung by a vocalist as good as Andy Bey. *It's Got to Be Funky* ♫♫ (Columbia, 1993, prod. Horace Silver) is a disappointing, overproduced release with a brass section that's only partially saved by merely acceptable soloing from Silver and saxophonist Eddie Harris. There are also four vocals, including the silly "Dufus Rufus" and "The Hillbilly Bebopper."

best of the rest:

The Horace Silver Trio ♫♫♫♫ (Blue Note, 1953)
Blowin' the Blues Away ♫♫♫♫ (Blue Note, 1959)
Horace-Scope ♫♫♫♫ (Blue Note, 1960)
Re-Entry ♫♫♫♫ (RAM, 1994)
Pencil Packin' Papa ♫♫♫ (Columbia, 1994)

The Hardbop Grandpop 🎵🎵🎵 (Impulse!, 1996)
A Prescription for the Blues 🎵🎵🎵 (Impulse!, 1997)

worth searching for: *Doin' the Thing* 🎵🎵🎵🎵 (Blue Note, 1961, prod. Alfred Lion) is a scorching live album by the Mitchell-Cook quintet with Silver in a particularly aggressive mood, goading the band forward.

influences:

◀◀ Thelonious Monk, Bud Powell

▶▶ Ramsey Lewis, Les McCann, Bobby Timmons

Ed Hazell

Sonny Simmons

Born August 4, 1933, in Sicily Island, LA.

An underrated player, Simmons has synthesized all the major post-war developments in saxophone playing into his own instantly recognizable style. In his improvising one hears echoes of Charlie Parker, Ornette Coleman, and John Coltrane: Simmons combines Coleman's vocal qualities, Parker's variety of phrasing and aggressiveness, and the advanced harmonic ideas and spiritualism of Coltrane and Dolphy. His erratic career has worked against his receiving the acknowledgment he desires.

Simmons first played tenor saxophone in the R&B bands of Lowell Fulson, Earl Bostic, and Charles Brown, but gave it up to concentrate on jazz after hearing Charlie Parker on the "Jazz at the Philharmonic" tour in Oakland in 1950. In 1962 he recorded with Prince Lasha on *The Cry!* and then moved to New York, where he recorded with Eric Dolphy on *Iron Man* (1963) and with Elvin Jones on *Illumination* (1963), and made his first albums as a leader with bands featuring his wife, trumpeter Barbara Donald. He also played with Sonny Rollins, Don Cherry, John Coltrane, and other New York avant-gardists. In the late 1960s Simmons moved back to the West Coast, where he has lived since. From 1967 to 1969 he was a member of the Firebirds, a quintet with Prince Lasha, Charles Moffett, Buster Williams, and Bobby Hutcherson. After making his currently out-of-print double album *Burning Spirits* (1971), Simmons didn't make a significant recording for 23 years. Simmons returned to active playing in 1994 with *Ancient Ritual*, one of the jazz world's most inspired comebacks.

what to buy: A magnificent comeback, *Ancient Ritual* 🎵🎵🎵🎵 (Qwest, 1994, prod. Craig Morton) features Simmons's son Zarak on drums and Charnett Moffett on bass in a trio program of blistering medium-tempo originals during which Simmons

never falters. Simmons plays with blues-drenched authority and rigorous freedom on *Staying on the Watch* 🎵🎵🎵🎵 (ESP, 1966, prod. Bernard Stollman), the better of his two early ESP disks. This album also features trumpeter Donald and a young John Hicks on piano. *Transcendence* 🎵🎵🎵🎵 (CIMP, 1996, prod. Bob Rusch) is another fire-breathing trio session, with simpatico youngster Michael Marcus and longtime collaborator Charles Moffett. Simmons engages in memorable duo exchanges with each and plays a lovely unaccompanied solo.

what to buy next: On *American Jungle* 🎵🎵🎵 (Qwest, 1997, prod. Craig Morton), Simmons again makes a case for his stature as an alto player, accompanied by a standard rhythm section featuring Travis Shook on piano, Reggie Workman on bass, and Cindy Blackman on drums. He even finds something new to say on the well-worn "My Favorite Things." Not as sharply focused as his other ESP date, *Music from the Spheres* 🎵🎵🎵 (ESP, 1966, prod. Bernard Stollman) again features trumpeter Donald as well as the impressive, if little-known, tenor saxophonist Bert Wilson. Simmons sticks to tenor saxophone throughout *Judgment Day* 🎵🎵🎵 (CIMP, 1996, prod. Bob Rusch), where he's joined by Marcus, Moffett, and bassist Steve Neil. On tenor, Simmons loses some of the more lyrical vocal qualities of his alto playing, but he plays with commitment and fire throughout, and his feature on "The Call for Old Sirus" is impressive.

what to avoid: *Backwoods Suite* 🎵🎵 (West Wind, 1982, prod. Ulli Blobel) is a disappointing and confused set that's well below par for Simmons, despite the presence of drummer Billy Higgins.

the rest:

Rumasuma 🎵🎵🎵 (Contemporary, 1969)

worth searching for: Perhaps Simmons's masterpiece, *Manhattan Egos* 🎵🎵🎵🎵 (Arhoolie, 1969, prod. Sonny Simmons, Chris Strachwitz), a quartet date with Donald, includes the stunning "Coltrane in Paradise."

influences:

◀◀ Charlie Parker, Ornette Coleman, Eric Dolphy, John Coltrane

▶▶ Gary Bartz

Ed Hazell

Nina Simone

Born February 21, 1933, in Tyron, NC.

Nina Simone is a true original—a vocalist whose repertoire has ranged from jazz, blues, and gospel to Broadway and Tin Pan

Alley tunes, and beyond those "accepted" styles to folk, pop, and rock. Her individuality and willingness to take musical risks have won her scores of devotees over the years, but also cost her some recognition among those who say she is not a jazz singer.

Simone grew up with dreams of becoming a concert pianist. She got far enough along this road to have been studying piano at the prestigious Julliard school in the 1950s. But Simone felt that, as a black woman, there were too many obstacles keeping her from attaining that goal, and she started taking more seriously the jobs she had been getting as a pianist/vocalist in Atlantic City. In the late 1950s Simone began recording on the Bethlehem label, and in 1959 her famous version of Gershwin's "I Loves You (Porgy)" gave her a top-20 hit. Simone's recordings of the early 1960s for the tiny Colpix label have stood as her most enduring, especially among jazz fans. For the rest of the 1960s and the early 1970s, her records would become more popularly flavored, but every bit as eclectic. For most of the next two decades, Simone would be away from recording in the U.S., settling temporarily in various places in Europe and Africa. In the early 1990s, Simone underwent a minor resurgence, with a new album for Asylum and an autobiography entitled *I Put a Spell on You.*

what to buy: The two-CD set *Anthology: The Colpix Years* 🎵🎵🎵🎵🎵 (Rhino 1996, prod. David Nathan, James Austin, Gary Peterson) combines the best tracks from Simone's most stimulating period (1959 to 1966). Her eclecticism is in full force, and so is her incredible soulfulness. Songs range from jazz standards ("Willow Weep for Me," "Fine and Mellow," "Solitude") and blues and gospel to many of Simone's own political protest anthems.

what to buy next: Some of the songs on *At the Village Gate* 🎵🎵🎵🎵 (Colpix, 1961/Roulette, 1991, prod. Cal Lampley, Michael Cuscuna) are also on the Rhino anthology, but the performance is worth hearing in its entirety. Simone's voice goes effortlessly from plaintive on Cole Porter's "Just in Time" and Rodgers and Hart's "Too Good to Me" to mellow on the folk song "House of the Rising Sun" to angry on "Brown Baby" and bitterly ironic on "Children Go Where I Send You." Simone also shows off her piano chops on "Bye Bye Blackbird." Covering the years 1964 through 1967, *Don't Let Me Be Misunderstood* 🎵🎵🎵🎵 (Mercury, 1988, prod. various) is one of the many compilations drawing from Simone's recordings on Mercury and Philips. The selection presents an eclectic selection of mostly ballads, including the title track, "Ne Me Quitte Pas," "Don't Explain," and "Wild Is the Wind." This is a good introduction to Simone's mid-1960s sound.

what to avoid: *Baltimore* 🎵 (CTI, 1978/Legacy, 1995, prod. Creed Taylor) marked a comeback of sorts for Simone, who hadn't recorded for six years—but it's a real stinker. Simone apparently had no say whatsoever in the choice of tunes, and one can't imagine she wanted the reggae-tinged backing either. Songs include such diversely awful hits as Randy Newman's title track and Hall & Oates's "Rich Girl".

the rest:
Best of the Colpix Years 🎵🎵🎵🎵 (Colpix, 1959–63/Roulette, 1992)
At Newport 🎵🎵🎵 (Colpix, 1961)
Broadway, Blues, Ballads 🎵🎵🎵 (Verve, 1964/1993)
In Concert/I Put a Spell on You 🎵🎵🎵 (Philips, 1964–65/Verve, 1990)
Pastel Blues/Let It All Out 🎵🎵🎵 (Mercury, 1965/1990)
Wild Is the Wind/High Priestess of Soul 🎵🎵🎵 (Philips 1966–67/Verve, 1990)
Saga of the Good Life and Hard Times 🎵🎵🎵 (RCA, 1967–68/1997)
Sings the Blues 🎵🎵🎵🎵 (Novus, 1967/1991)
The Essential Nina Simone 🎵🎵 (RCA, 1972/1993)
Essential, Vol. 2 🎵🎵 (RCA, 1972/1994)
Songs of the Poets 🎵🎵🎵 (Edsel, 1976/1993)
Live at Ronnie Scott's 🎵🎵🎵 (DRG, 1984/1994)
A Single Woman 🎵🎵🎵🎵 (Asylum, 1993)
After Hours 🎵🎵🎵 (Verve, 1995)
Ultimate Nina Simone 🎵🎵🎵🎵 (Verve, 1997)

worth searching for: *Nina at Town Hall* 🎵🎵🎵🎵 (Colpix, 1960, prod. Bob Blake, Jack Gold) was one of Simone's first for Colpix, and it includes memorable renditions of "Black Is the Color of My True Love's Hair," "The Other Woman," and "Cotton Eyed Joe."

influences:
◀◀ Billie Holiday, Carmen McRae
▶▶ Dianne Reeves, Harry Belafonte

Dan Keener

Zoot Sims

Born John Haley Sims, October 29, 1925, in Ingelwood, CA. Died March 23, 1985, in New York, NY.

Zoot Sims was one of the most distinctive of the many cool-toned tenor saxophonists who based their styles on Lester Young, though later in his career his sound reflected a deep appreciation of Ben Webster. With his beautiful, sleek tone and superb sense of swing, Sims could generate great momentum from the first note of a tune. Raised in a vaudeville family, Sims learned the show business trade as a youth, playing clarinet and drums and then tenor sax at age 13. He began touring with dance bands at age 15, joining Benny Goodman's big band in

1943, a relationship that continued intermittently through the 1970s, including international tours in 1950, 1958, 1962, 1972 and 1976. He recorded for the first time in 1944 with pianist Joe Bushkin, and towards the end of the war moved out to California where he played with Big Sid Catlett. After serving in the army he spent 1946–47 with Goodman and from 1947 to 1949 played with Woody Herman, where he was part of the legendary Four Brothers sax section with Stan Getz, Jimmy Giuffre, and Herbie Steward. In the early 1950s, Sims played briefly with Stan Kenton and made his first recording as a leader on Prestige. In the mid-1950s he toured with Gerry Mulligan's bands and formed a lasting musical partnership with fellow tenor man Al Cohn. Late in his career he mastered the soprano saxophone, recording an entire album with the horn on Pablo, playing with a gentle, highly mellifluous approach. From the mid-1950s through his death from cancer Sims recorded prolifically, including sessions with Joe Pass, Count Basie, Harry "Sweets" Edison, and a series of spirited tenor battles with Cohn and lyrical collaborations with pianist Jimmy Rowles. Sims was a very consistent player who rarely turned in a poor performance. Many of his recordings are available.

what to buy: A hard swinging session reissued by Evidence, *Either Way* 🎵🎵🎵🎵 (Evidence, 1961/1992, prod. Fred Miles) features the working band led by Sims and Cohn, with Mose Allison on piano, Bill Crow on bass, and Gus Johnson on drums. The like-minded (and sounding) saxophonists spur each other on, though the session is as notable for the three tracks by the excellent but completely forgotten Philadelphia singer, Cecil "Kid Haffey" Collier, who belts "Sweet Lorraine," "I Like It Like That," and "Nagasaki" in a style reminiscent of Jimmy Rushing. Sims and Cohn do a fine job playing complimentary fills behind Collier and picking up his bluesy swagger in their solos. Recorded at San Francisco's famed Keystone Korner in 1983, *On the Korner* 🎵🎵🎵🎵 (Pablo, 1994, prod. Todd Barkan) captures Sims playing with the lithe, stripped-to-essentials style of his late career. Accompanied by a highly responsive rhythm section composed of pianist Frank Collett, bassist Monty Budwig, and drummer Shelly Manne, Sims plays authoritative versions of "Dream Dancing," "If You Could See Me Now," and "I'll Remember April." His soprano work on Ellington's "Tonight I Shall Sleep" and "Pennies from Heaven" is exquisite and sounds unlike that of anyone else. *Passion Flower* 🎵🎵🎵🎵 (Pablo, 1980/OJC, 1997, prod. Norman Granz) is a gem of an album, a rare Zoot Sims big band session featuring Benny Carter arrangements of eight Ellington compositions and Billy Strayhorn's title track. Sims's tone had begun to take on shades of Ben Webster

late in his career, and his sound here is streamlined and gloriously lush. The choice of tunes gives Sims a wide range of moods, from the high stepping "I Let a Song Go out of My Heart" to the wistful "Your Love Has Faded" to the plaintive "I Got It Bad." The all-star band, led by Jimmy Rowles's sparkling piano, plays Carter's charts with vigor and precision.

what to buy next: Johnny Mandel's songs make a perfect vehicle for Sims's burnished tenor on *Quietly There* 🎵🎵🎵🎵 (Pablo, 1984/OJC, 1993, prod. Norman Granz), an album recorded almost exactly a year before Sims death. With the exceptional but underrated pianist Mike Wofford, bassist Chick Berghofer, drummer Nick Ceroli, and Victor Feldman on percussion, Sims covers both Mandel's standards ("Emily" and "A Time for Love") and his less frequently played jazz pieces ("Low Life" and "Zoot"). Sims never needed a rhythm section to swing and on *Blues for Two* 🎵🎵🎵🎵 (Pablo, 1982/OJC, 1991, prod. Norman Granz) he and guitarist Joe Pass, who was an orchestra all by himself, play a daring set of duets. Together they made an inspired pair, playing with a confident but relaxed feel. Sims sails through the standards "Dindi," "Pennies from Heaven," "Black and Blue," and "Remember," caressing each melody while Pass accompanies and takes a number of fine solos. The two players collaborated on the title track and "Takeoff." Bill Holman, one of modern jazz's great arrangers, wrote the charts and conducted the ten-piece band on *Hawthorne Nights* 🎵🎵🎵🎵 (Pablo, 1976/OJC, 1995, prod. Norman Granz), a finely tailored suite of eight tunes for Sims's lyrical tenor. Trombonist Frank Rosolino and trumpeters Snooky Young and Oscar Brashear also take some excellent solos, but it's the way Holman has written to Sims's lithe melodic approach that makes this such a rewarding album. The tunes include two Holman originals, Ellington's "Mainstem," and "I Got It Bad," and the standards "More Than You Know" and "Only a Rose."

best of the rest:

Zoot Sims in Paris 🎵🎵🎵🎵 (Vogue, 1950–53/BMG, 1995)
Quartets 🎵🎵🎵🎵 (Prestige, 1951/OJC, 1987)
Morning Fun 🎵🎵🎵🎵 (Black Lion, 1956/1990)
And the Gershwin Brothers 🎵🎵🎵🎵 (Pablo, 1975/OJC, 1990)
Zoot Plays Soprano 🎵🎵🎵🎵 (Pablo, 1976/OJC, 1996)
(With Jimmy Rowles) *If I'm Lucky* 🎵🎵🎵🎵 (Pablo, 1977/OJC, 1992)
(With Harry "Sweets" Edison) *Just Friends* 🎵🎵🎵🎵 (Pablo, 1978/OJC, 1991)
For Lady Day 🎵🎵🎵🎵 (Pablo, 1978/1991)
(With Jimmy Rowles) *Warm Tenor* 🎵🎵🎵🎵 (Pablo, 1978/OJC, 1996)

worth searching for: An impromptu feeling, hard-swinging session, *Somebody Loves Me* 🎵🎵🎵🎵 (LRC, 1989) pairs Sims on tenor and soprano with guitarist Bucky Pizzarelli, bassist Milt Hinton, and drummer Buddy Rich. With no liner notes or recording credits on the CD, one could guess the first 10 tracks (mostly standards) are from the late '70s. The last four tunes, featuring Sims on tenor with Lionel Hampton, Teddy Wilson, George Duvivier, and Buddy Rich, could be from the early '70s, but whenever they were recorded, the music is highly enjoyable, especially the nine-minute jam on Hampton's "Ham Hock Blues."

influences:

◀◀ Lester Young, Ben Webster

▶▶ Ken Peplowski, Rickey Woodard

Andrew Gilbert

Frank Sinatra

Born December 12, 1915, in Hoboken, NJ. Died May 14, 1998, in Los Angeles, CA.

Although he's the consummate pop singer (possibly the only one to put out hit records in five different decades), Frank Sinatra without jazz is unimaginable. The seductive slow boil of his crooning days and the muscular swing-pop hybrid he perfected in the 1950s owe much to an innate understanding of jazz mechanics. He took the notes the songs demanded as mere guidelines to a more complete performance that was both dramatic and musical. A perfectionist, Sinatra demanded multiple runthroughs of songs so that arrangements would shine. Nonetheless, each Sinatra performance was a practiced improvisation that would vary according to the dynamics of the moment.

An only child who was doted on by his Italian immigrant parents, the teen-aged Sinatra began singing professionally against their wishes. But he stubbornly clung to his ambitions, and his mother, resigned to the fact, found him a breakthrough gig at the Rustic Cabin in Englewood, New Jersey, in the late 1930s. By 1939 he had signed on with Harry James's orchestra, and then moved on to Tommy Dorsey's big band. Sinatra's voice jumped out of the speakers on "I'll Never Smile Again," the first vocal he recorded with Dorsey. By the time they played New York's Paramount Theater in 1942, Sinatra's affect on the crowd was electric, and the bobbysoxers screamed and swooned in their seats. Dorsey was miffed that his singer was getting a better reaction than the band. Sinatra soon left to start a solo career that contributed mightily to a change of focus in the music business, from big bands to individual singers.

Sinatra's youthful style was sweet. He sang ballads with a deceptively breathless voice, a near-whisper, holding notes with the slightest of quavers, sounding sincere and more vulnerable and sensuous than any mainstream pop singer before him. (He admits Billie Holiday's singing was a major influence on him.) When his career as a crooner went bust toward the end of the 1940s, he methodically reinvented himself as a mature singer (and movie actor). At age 37 he signed with Capitol Records and began to refocus his image as a swinging, rambunctious bon vivant, who sometimes got very low in the wee, small hours of the morning—and developed a confident, huskier sound to match. Despite the swagger of his approach, Sinatra maintained an interesting humility in concert, dutifully giving credit to the songwriters and arrangers who gave him the material that was his springboard.

In the 1960s he continued to do swinging material, but also ventured into folk-influenced contemporary pop and even soft rock. He "retired" in 1971 only to come back in 1973 and continued releasing records up until 1985. Although his voice was deteriorating (his upper register became raw and his pitch sometimes wavered), his interpretive skills diminished only slightly. He remained a major draw on the concert circuit until his retirement in 1995. His hiatus from recording after his 1985 album, *L.A. Is My Lady*, until his 1993 album, *Duets*, seems to acknowledge that "the Voice" didn't sound good enough for the studio anymore. The *Duets* approach, in which all the duets were reportedly recorded separately, suggests that Sinatra needed studio tweaking to make coherent recordings. You can hear technology clamp down the sound as Sinatra loses his breath at the end of phrases. However, these records were big events that extended Sinatra's hit-making punch into the 1990s.

what to buy: *The Capitol Years* ♫♫♫♫ (Capitol, 1990, prod. Ron Furmanek) offers a succinct overview of Sinatra's classic period in three CDs. His best work during this time was in collaboration with Nelson Riddle, whose arrangements on such tunes as "I've Got the World on a String" nailed the optimistic, prime-of-life feeling Sinatra brought to his singing. (Sinatra was also successful working with Gordon Jenkins, whose arrangements had a more stately, reflective feeling, and Billy May, whose arrangements swung more forcefully than Riddle's.) If the price tag for the four-CD set is too high, *Best of the Capitol Years* ♫♫♫♫ (Capitol, 1992, compilation prod. Wayne Watkins) and *Frank Sinatra: The Capitol Collectors Series* ♫♫♫♫ (Capitol, 1989, compilation prod. Ron Furmanek) offer excellent single-CD overviews. Capitol released 23 Sinatra albums from 1953 to 1961, and 16 of them were conceived by the singer as cohesive units (ushering in the era of the concept album); they were later collected in a box called *Concepts* ♫♫♫♫ (Capitol, 1992, prod. Voyle Gilmore, David Cavanaugh). If you prefer to buy them separately, all 16 are must-buys, although in CD form some questionable bonus tracks have been added (fortunately they're added after the original program, which makes it easy to play back the original, coherent LP sequence). *The Complete Capitol Singles Collection* ♫♫♫♫ (Capitol, 1996, compilation prod. Brad Benedict) is a four-CD set that lives up to its title with A-sides and B-sides, many of which had not been available on CD before. *The Columbia Years (1943–1952): The Complete Recordings* ♫♫♫♫ (Columbia, 1993, compilation prod. Didier C. Deutsch) collects on 12 CDs the Sinatra sides that defined a new role for pop singers. They were revolutionary then and enjoyable now; a four-disc distillation called *The Best of the Columbia Years: 1943–1952* ♫♫♫♫ (Columbia, 1995, compilation prod. Didier C. Deutsch) was released in 1995 for the budget-conscious.

what to buy next: *The Song Is You* ♫♫♫♫ (RCA, 1993, prod. Paul Williams) is the definitive collection of Sinatra's work with Tommy Dorsey, on five CDs. (RCA distilled the box down to one CD in 1994's *I'll Be Seeing You* ♫♫♫♫ (RCA, 1994, prod. Paul Williams).) *The Reprise Collection* ♫♫♫♫ (Reprise, 1990, compilation prod. Mo Ostin, Joe McEwen, James Isaacs) isn't as satisfying as the collections of earlier work, yet it presents a picture of adventurous maturity. Sinatra was a chart-buster in his early Columbia years and after his comeback at Capitol, but he cooled down some after he started his own label, Reprise, in 1961. Pop-radio tastes had changed, after all. He wasn't exactly passed by, though, as such chart successes as "Strangers in the Night," "My Way," and "Theme from *New York, New York*" attest. However, Sinatra turned a lower pop-radio profile into an opportunity to make albums that took some interesting chances, including jazzy collaborations with Count Basie, Duke Ellington, and Antonio Carlos Jobim. In its four CDs, *The Reprise Collection* is a bit overlong, yet it covers a much longer period than the Capitol collection—from a 1960 recording of "Let's Fall in Love" all the way to a 1986 recording of "Mack the Knife." It also yields some previously unreleased gems, including the much-speculated-upon "Zing! Went the Strings of My Heart," recorded in 1960. In 1991, the condensed, single-CD *Sinatra Reprise: The Very Good Years* ♫♫♫♫ (Reprise, 1991) was reissued. The label went the other way in 1995, releasing *The Complete Reprise Studio Recordings* ♫♫♫♫ (Warner Bros., 1995) on 20 discs. Yikes! Essential for completists, but even at a discount the price tag is out there.

what to avoid: *Duets* ♫ (Capitol, 1993, prod. Phil Ramone) and *Duets II* ♫ (Capitol, 1994, prod. Phil Ramone) may have revived

Sinatra's recording career, but consist of mostly meaningless (and chemistry-less) re-recordings. This is said with infinite sadness. For the first time in his career, Sinatra had to depend on others to carry him. For two-thirds of the over-ambitious *Trilogy* ♫♫ (Reprise, 1980/1988, prod. Sonny Burke), Sinatra summed up where he was in the late 1970s. The gorgeous Nelson Riddle arrangement of George Harrison's "Something" and the swaggering "Theme from *New York, New York*" became virtual signature tunes of the early autumn of Sinatra's career. Conceived as a three-LP look at the past, the present, and the future, Sinatra could have skipped the future part. The LP-long Gordon Jenkins suite pondering the future was goofy at best, ponderous at worst, and dwelled more on Sinatra the celebrity than Sinatra the musician. A boiled-down, single album from these sessions could have been dynamite.

best of the rest:

Songs for Swingin' Lovers! ♫♫♫♫ (Capitol, 1956/1997)
A Swingin' Affair! ♫♫♫♫ (Capitol, 1957/1991)
Come Fly with Me ♫♫♫♫ (Capitol, 1957/1987)
(Frank Sinatra Sings for) Only the Lonely ♫♫♫♫ (Capitol, 1958/1997)
Come Dance with Me! ♫♫♫♫ (Capitol, 1958/1996)
No One Cares ♫♫♫♫ (Capitol, 1959/1991)
Frank Sinatra with the Red Norvo Quartet: Live in Australia 1959 ♫♫♫♫ (Capitol, 1959/1997)
Nice 'N' Easy ♫♫♫♫ (Capitol, 1960/1991)
Sinatra's Swingin' Session!!! ♫♫♫♫ (Capitol, 1960/1987)
Sinatra/Basie ♫♫♫♫ (Reprise, 1963/1988)
September of My Years ♫♫♫♫ (Reprise, 1965/1988)
Francis Albert Sinatra and Antonio Carlos Jobim ♫♫♫♫ (Reprise, 1967/1988)
Francis A. Sinatra & Edward K. Ellington ♫♫♫♫ (Reprise, 1968/1988)
Sinatra and Sextet: Live in Paris ♫♫♫♫ (Reprise, 1994)
V-Discs Columbia Years: 1943–45 ♫♫♫♫ (Columbia, 1994)
Portrait of Sinatra ♫♫♫♫ (Columbia, 1997)

worth searching for: There are a wealth of radio, TV, and concert performances available on small labels that aren't often easy to find at your local CD store. The place to start is with such 1940s material as *The Unheard Frank Sinatra, Vols. 1–4* ♫♫♫♫ (Vintage Jazz Classics, 1990) and then such 1950s material as *Perfectly Frank* ♫♫♫♫ (BCD, 1990). (The holy grail for Sinatra searchers, including this one, is *From the Vaults*—only 750 copies were said to have been pressed.)

influences:

◄◄ Billie Holiday, Bing Crosby

►► Tony Bennett, Harry Connick Jr., Kurt Elling

Salvatore Caputo

Steve Slagle

See: Mingus Big Band

Carol Sloane

Born 1937, in Providence, RI.

One of the finest singers in jazz, Carol Sloane has a gorgeous, rich voice strongly reminiscent of Ella Fitzgerald but she has a more incisive approach to lyrics. Rooted in bop, Sloane is a singer's singer who can find new insights in standards, swing with complete authority, and make contemporary material sound like it was written for a jazz singer. Over the years her voice has aged beautifully, gaining texture, while her approach to lyrics has become more emotionally direct and inviting. Sloane started singing professionally as a young teen and at 18 toured Germany with a musical comedy troupe. She spent two years in the late 1950s with the Les and Larry Elgart Orchestra and started making a name for herself when she subbed for Annie Ross in the Lambert, Hendricks & Ross vocal group. Jon Hendricks made sure she was booked at the 1961 Newport festival, where her *a cappella* version of "Little Girl Blue" caused something of a sensation. She recorded a couple of albums for Columbia in the early 1960s but mostly dropped off the jazz scene for the rest of the decade and didn't make it back to a recording studio until 1977 (though a live album of a 1964 gig with Ben Webster, *Carol and Ben*, was released by Honeydew). Since the early 1980s, she has finally come into her own and her late-blooming career has been documented with a series of excellent albums on Progressive, Eastwind, Contemporary, and especially Concord.

what to buy: A long-lost session recorded shortly after Carol Sloane's 1961 triumph at Newport, *Out of the Blue* 𝄞𝄞𝄞𝄞 (Koch, 1962, prod. Mike Berniker), was reissued in 1996 by Koch. Sloane is still very much under the sway of Ella Fitzgerald, but she has her own approach to phrasing. Bill Finegan's arrangements frame her voice wonderfully and Jim Hall, Barry Galbraith, Clark Terry, and Bob Brookmeyer (who also contributed two arrangements) all take strong solos. Highlights include "Little Girl Blue," "My Ship," and "My Silent Love," which features trumpeters Terry and Nick Travis playing beautiful little figures behind her vocals. Though Sloane still brings Ella to mind, on *When I Look in Your Eyes* 𝄞𝄞𝄞𝄞 (Concord Jazz, 1991, prod. John Burk) her debt to Carmen McRae is also apparent. Accompanied by pianist Bill Charlap, bassist Steve Gilmore, drummer Ron Vincent, and guitarist Howard Alden, Sloane is in top form on this ultimately classy session featuring mostly standards and a few discoveries. The sense of momentum she generates on "Old Devil Moon" defies gravity, while her languorous version of "Midnight Sun" makes time stop. Her light-as-air version of "Isn't This a Lovely Day" and melancholy rendering of "Something Cool" are also highlights. *Love You Madly* 𝄞𝄞𝄞𝄞 (Contemporary, 1989, prod. Helen Keane) marked Sloane's return to her proper place among the jazz elite. Backed by an all-star band with Art Farmer and Clifford Jordan, Kenny Barron, Rufus Reid, and Akira Tana, she selects an equally appropriate group of tunes. From Louis Armstrong's "Someday You'll Be Sorry" and Ellington's "Love You Madly" to the standards "That Old Devil Called Love" and "My Foolish Heart," Sloane puts her personal stamp on these standards, which are all attractively arranged by Richard Rodney Bennett. Her exquisite duets with guitarist Kenny Burrell on "I Wish I'd Met You," and "For All We Know" are also highlights.

what to buy next: A heartfelt tribute from one master to another, *The Songs Carmen Sang* 𝄞𝄞𝄞𝄞 (Concord Jazz, 1995, prod. Allen Farnham, Carol Sloane) is Sloane's love letter to Carmen McRae. Sloane has long been inspired by McRae's phrasing and literate approach to lyrics, so she doesn't have to change anything to evoke the late singer. Phil Woods sits in on alto and clarinet on half the tunes, playing in and around Sloane with such swing and precision they sound like old partners. The excellent rhythm section features Bill Charlap (piano), Michael Moore (bass), and Ron Vincent (drums). No living jazz singer handles lyrics with the intelligence and style of Sloane, and on *The Real Thing* 𝄞𝄞𝄞𝄞 (Contemporary, 1990, prod. Helen Keane) she brings her inimitable approach to 13 tunes of varying vintage. Her duet with Grady Tate on the medley of "Makin' Whoopee" and "The Glory of Love" is a hoot and, in an example of brilliant programming, she follows it with the definitive version of Billy Strayhorn's achingly lonely "Something to Live For." Her reading of "Too Late Now" is also for the ages. With Phil Woods on alto and clarinet, Mike Renzi on piano and keyboards, Rufus Reid on bass, and Tate on drums, Sloane has all the support she needs.

best of the rest:

Sophisticated Lady 𝄞𝄞𝄞𝄞 (Audiophile, 1985)
Heart's Desire 𝄞𝄞𝄞𝄞 (Concord Jazz, 1992)
Sweet and Slow 𝄞𝄞𝄞𝄞 (Concord Jazz, 1993)
The Songs Sinatra Sang 𝄞𝄞𝄞𝄞 (Concord Jazz, 1996)

influences:

◄◄ Ella Fitzgerald, Carmen McRae

Andrew Gilbert

Bessie Smith

Born April 15, 1894, in Chattanooga, TN. Died September 26, 1937, in Clarksdale, MS.

Bessie Smith is without question the greatest of all classic blues and jazz performers. She began her career as a vaudeville dancer while still in her teens, but her potential as a singer sparked Ma Rainey's interest early on. She established herself while touring with Rainey's Rabbit Foot Minstrels, and by 1923 she moved to New York, where she lived in Harlem. She soon signed with Columbia and issued "Downhearted Blues" and "Gulf Coast Blues"; performed with pianist Fletcher Henderson, the record sold 780,000 copies in less than six months. Subsequent recordings with Henderson's small group bolstered Smith's reputation and garnered her tours as a bona fide star on the TOBA (Theater Owners Booking Association) circuit. By 1925, and for the next three years, she starred in her own touring summer tent show, *Harlem Frolics*. Her new show in 1928, *Mississippi Days,* was equally successful. By this period, Smith had recorded with giants such as James P. Johnson, Fletcher Henderson, and Louis Armstrong. However, in the late 1920s, the TOBA circuit was hurt by the Depression, the advent of talking films, and other factors, and Smith's popularity began to wane. In 1933 she made her last classic recordings for John Hammond, featuring jazz musicians Jack Teagarden, Coleman Hawkins, and Benny Goodman. She appeared in stage shows and toured with Broadway troupes. Smith died tragically in an automobile accident in 1937, just as she was beginning to make in-roads with a new, decidedly more contemporary, swing-oriented style.

Smith's voice has withstood the test of time. "Jailhouse Blues" is an early example of her mastery of slides, "drop-offs," and other melismatic embellishments, fully realized on later recordings such as "Careless Love" and "Whip It to a Jelly." Her judicious use of guttural inflections on tunes like "Cemetery Blues" and "Dirty No-Gooder's Blues" further illustrates her artistry. Through careful employment of these and other vocal devices, Smith convincingly conveyed many moods on recordings. She fully deserved the title "Empress of the Blues."

what to buy: *The Complete Recordings, Vol. 2* ♪♪♪♪♪ (Columbia/Legacy, 1991, prod. Lawrence Cohn) contains sides recorded between April 1924 and November 1925, in a well-suited, small-group setting. (Louis Armstrong is one of the most notable accompanists.) In contrast to earlier recordings, Smith's vocal delivery is markedly more authoritative at this juncture in her career, as evidenced by the plaintive numbers "Reckless Blues" and "Careless Love Blues." The highlight is "St. Louis Blues," a masterpiece of controlled tension. *The Complete Recordings, Vol. 3* ♪♪♪♪ (Columbia/Legacy, 1992, prod. Lawrence Cohn) contains more recordings from Smith's artistic zenith (late November 1925 to mid-February 1928). Highlights include the magnificent "Back Water Blues," "After You've Gone," "Muddy Water," "Trombone Cholly," "Lock and Key," and "A Good Man Is Hard to Find." For those wanting but one representative set.

what to buy next: *The Complete Recordings, Vol. 1* ♪♪♪♪ (Columbia/Legacy, 1991, prod. Lawrence Cohn) contains Smith's first 38 recordings, among them the magnificent debut, "Down Hearted Blues," the blues-inflected pop tune "Baby Won't You Please Come Home," and her mesmerizing rendition of "T'ain't Nobody's Bizness If I Do." Most sides feature her with sparse and rather pedestrian piano accompaniment. *The Complete Recordings, Vol. 4* ♪♪♪♪ (Columbia/Legacy, 1993, prod. Lawrence Cohn) showcases Smith's late 1920s and early 1930s recordings. As the Depression hit America, vaudeville was on the decline and fewer people were listening to the blues. Sadly, by July of 1930, Smith could do no better than bottom billing at Harlem's Apollo Theater. Understandably, her voice had begun to show signs of wear by the time of these sessions, yet recordings like "Empty Bed Blues" and "Nobody Knows You When You're Down and Out" are nevertheless powerful. *The Complete Recordings, Vol. 5: The Final Chapter* ♪♪♪ (Columbia/Legacy, 1996, prod. Lawrence Cohn) contains the rest of Smith's 1931 recordings and a 1933 session for OKeh, along with alternate takes, the *St. Louis Blues* soundtrack, and a 72-minute interview with Smith's niece, Rudy Smith. The 1933 session is especially fine and hints at the new musical directions Smith was exploring at the time of her death. The rest of this set will find more favor with collectors and serious fans.

best of the rest:

Bessie Smith 1925–33 ♪♪♪♪ (Nimbus, 1987)
The Collection ♪♪♪♪ (Columbia, 1989)
Empress of the Blues ♪♪♪ (Charly, 1992)
Bessie Smith 1923 ♪♪♪ (Classics, 1994)
Bessie Smith 1923–24 ♪♪♪ (Classics, 1994)

influences:

◀◀ Ma Rainey

▶▶ Mahalia Jackson, Odetta, Jimmy Rushing, Ella Fitzgerald, Billie Holiday

D. Thomas Moon and Nancy Ann Lee

Cecilia Smith

Born in Cincinnati, OH.

The vibraphone was introduced in the U.S. as a "steel marimba" in 1916 and, while male musicians such as Milt Jackson, Lionel Hampton, Gary Burton, and Bobby Hutcherson have contributed to making it a jazz instrument, few females have earned a spot in jazz history as vibraphone players. Cecilia Smith is the exception. Raised in Cleveland, Ohio, Smith is a U.S. master of the four-mallet technique and the first woman vibraphonist to record as a leader. After earning her degree in music at Berklee College of Music in Boston, Smith released, in 1993, the first of four albums for the small independent Brownstone label. Currently living in Brooklyn, New York, Smith continues to perform in concert settings, clubs, festivals, arts and educational institutions, and other venues in New York and throughout the country. Smith has collaborated with many jazz notables, including Milt Hinton, Mulgrew Miller, Billy Pierce, Ralph Moore, Cecil Bridgewater, and others. She serves as a music therapist and educator for several NYC non-profit institutions, has taught at Berklee and Cornell University, and is an accomplished composer who performed her commissioned score for a 1995 feature-length film, *Naked Acts.*

what to buy: The second release from the Cecilia Smith Quartet, *CSQ, Volume II* 𝄞𝄞𝄞𝄞 (Brownstone, 1995, prod. Jack Wertheimer), proves not only that performer, composer, and leader Smith is an expert on the bars, but she's a capable leader who maintains lightly swinging, tight grooves with pianist Frank Wilkins and drummer Ron Savage—two fine players from the Boston area who return on this outing from her previous recording. Bassist Steve Kirby adds verve with his plucky pizzicato and smooth bowed technique. Guest saxophonist Billy Pierce generates excitement on three tracks. Smith's musicianship is impressive. She displays a responsive, fluid approach on 12 original compositions and freshly arranged standards. An artful interpreter, Smith masters the instrument with unique phrasing and time. She injects cool freshness into classics such as "Every Time We Say Goodbye," "Old Devil Moon," and "Darn That Dream." Her pallette is broad; she brings colors from many musical influences into her playing, including the 1970s Midwest funk she heard growing up. Smith exhibits a distinctive, lyrical warmth that sets her apart from other vibists.

what to buy next: As she did on her preceding album, *High Standards*, Smith tries to please too many people on *Leave No Stone Unturned* 𝄞𝄞𝄞 (Brownstone, 1997, prod. Cecilia Smith),

her most recent recording as leader. In addition to her regular sidekicks, Frank Wilkins (piano), Steve Kirby or Lonnie Plaxico (bass), and Ron Savage (drums), she spotlights an array of guests of varying talent. Obviously best is veteran Gary Bartz, who plays soprano sax on the opener ("Sand Box," a solid bop number by Wilkins) and alto sax on Tadd Dameron's "Our Delight" (arranged by Cecil Bridgewater). Trumpeter Cecil Bridgewater guests on two tracks, as does soprano/alto saxophonist Greg Osby. Cellist Eileen Fulson makes a cameo appearance, vocalist Armstead Christian appears on two tracks, and guitarist Freddie Bryant on two tracks. While Smith attempts to keep her albums interesting, so many stylists from different bags confuse the listener. However, there are some high points on this 10-tune set that includes five Smith originals.

the rest:
The Takeoff 𝄞𝄞𝄞 (Brownstone, 1993)
High Standards 𝄞𝄞𝄞 (Brownstone, 1996)

influences:
◄◄ Milt Jackson, Gary Burton, Bobby Hutcherson

Nancy Ann Lee

Hal Smith

Born July 30, 1953, in Indianapolis, IN.

Hal Smith is one of the most versatile and musically knowledgeable drummers working within the traditional and swing jazz idioms. His adaptability and familiarity with jazz drumming history allows him to fit into whatever style of band he is working with at the moment. His influences are many and wide-ranging, and include Dave Tough, Sidney Catlett, Zutty Singleton, Fred Higuera, and Chick Webb, among numerous others. Although chiefly self-taught, Smith studied in 1983 with another of his favorites, Jake Hann. Smith has led a nomadic career with residencies in La Jolla, Los Angeles, Portland, San Francisco, San Antonio, Cincinnati, St. Paul, Chicago, and New Orleans. In demand for record dates, Smith, at this writing, has made over 125 LP and CD appearances with countless bands.

Hal Smith took up the drums in 1963 after being inspired by the Firehouse Five Plus Two, playing at Disneyland. He attended California State University, graduating in 1976 with a B.A. in journalism, which has served him well as a prolific writer of liner notes for Stomp Off, GHB, Triangle Jazz, and Jazzology recordings. A career in music beckoned while he was still in college and he became the regular drummer for the South Frisco Jazz Band (1970–1973). By 1978, he had become a full-time musician. Smith played with the Golden State Jazz Band and Terry

Waldo's Gutbucket Syncopators in the late 1970s. In the early 1980s, Smith became a charter member of Chicago Rhythm, was briefly with Jim Cullum's Jazz Band and then hooked up with trumpeter Chris Tyle and vocalist-guitarist Rebecca Kilgore in the swing-oriented band Wholly Cats. From late 1983 to 1986, he was a member of the Butch Thompson Trio on the popular public radio series *Prairie Home Companion,* while doubling with the Hall Brothers Jazz Band. In the late 1980s, he led the Hal Smith Trio, the Hal Smith Rhythmakers, and the Down Home Jazz Band, reviving a band he had off and on between 1971 and 1977 that played on the West Coast, Lu Watters–San Francisco style. During 1988 and 1989, Smith toured with the popular group Banu Gibson and Her New Orleans Jazz. He also subbed for drummer Wayne Jones with the Original Salty Dogs, the Sons of Bix, and James Dapogny's Chicago Jazz Band. In the 1990s, Smith has increasingly led his own groups, including two traditionally styled groups, Down Home Jazz Band and the New Orleans Wanderers, and a band echoing the old Bob Scobey Frisco Band, the Frisco Syncopators, which he co-leads with Chris Tyle. He toured Germany with his California Swing Cats, featuring Rebecca Kilgore, who is also featured along with clarinetist Bobby Gordon in Smith's little swing band, the Roadrunners. Smith is active on the jazz festival scene at home and abroad, remains a member of the Butch Thompson Trio, frequently guests with the Orphan Newsboys, and plays with the Silver Leaf Jazz Band and with Tim Laughlin's New Orleans All-Stars. Smith is a jazz chameleon, changing styles at will, and blending in with his intelligent drumming.

what to buy: Since Hal Smith's CDs can vary stylistically, the order of preference in obtaining them would relate to their style content for most jazz enthusiasts. Hal Smith's Roadrunners should be required listening for swing addicts in need of a musical fix, and his *Rhythm, Romance and Roadrunners!* ♫♫♫♫ (Triangle Jazz, 1996, prod. Dick Rippey, Tom Rippey) features Bobby Gordon's lyrical clarinet or Rebecca Kilgore's gentle, lilting voice out in front. Playing old-fashioned swing, this stellar quintet digs into 20 gems. The leader's drums are ever tasteful and fit comfortably into the swing groove. Piano man Ray Skjelbred, with his keen understanding of the Jess Stacy–Joe Sullivan approach, is on hand with the kind of classic jazz piano solos that are all too rare today. Bassist Mike Duffy anchors the rhythm section, and Kilgore (also a guitarist) plays solid rhythm guitar. Tunes are varied and were chosen and played with loving care. The resulting music is timeless. A second session of 20 tunes was recorded by the same team, *Hal Smith's Roadrunners, Vol. 2* ♫♫♫♫ (Triangle Jazz, 1997, prod. Tom Rippey, Dick

Rippey). *Down Home Jazz Band: Dawn Club Joys* ♫♫♫♫ (Stomp Off, 1992, prod. Hal Smith) is Volume 5 (the first on CD) of the eight-volume series that pays homage to the West Coast Traditional–San Francisco style of Lu Watters, Turk Murphy, and Bob Scobey. Leader Hal Smith emulates Watters's drummer Bill Dart on this disc, which is enhanced by the presence of clarinetist Bob Helm, a charter member of the Lu Watters Yerba Buena Jazz Band. Cornetists Chris Tyle and Bob Schulz, trombonist Tom Bartlett, pianist Ray Skjelbred, banjo player Jack Meilahn, and tuba player Mike Bezin flesh out the ensemble. San Francisco–style traditionalists will revel in the 20 authentic-sounding tracks laid down by these dedicated revivalists. If this is your bag, there are three more volumes on CD, and chances are you'll also enjoy the Frisco Syncopators who play in the traditional cum-swing style of the Bob Scobey Frisco Jazz Band.

what to buy next: Initially organized for a March 1995 tour of Germany, the quintet Hal Smith leads on *Hal Smith's California Swing Cats: Swing, Brother, Swing* ♫♫♫♫ (Jazzology, 1995, prod. Hal Smith) recorded 15 foot-tapping, feel-good tunes destined to leave listeners in a downright buoyant mood. Clarinetist Tim Laughlin garners plenty of solo pace with sprightly, up-tempo solos on the swingers, and contrasting, elegant, warm-and-woodsy tones on the ballads. Rebecca Kilgore's outstanding eight vocals are worth the price of the set, especially her renditions of "Thou Swell," "You," and "I Can't Believe That You're in Love with Me." Chris Dawson lends his Teddy Wilson–style piano to the proceedings, while Marty Eggers keeps the beat going with his huge-toned bass. Kilgore fills in beautifully with her rhythm guitar, and leader Smith comes through with sensitive rhythm support, forsaking solos space until the closing tribute to Chick Webb on Gershwin's "Liza." This kind of combo is all too rare now. Luckily, the band was able to return the next year to put down 16 more tracks on *California Swing Cats: Stealin' Apples* ♫♫♫♫ (Jazzology, 1997, prod. Hal Smith), featuring new member Tom Roberts on piano, and nine more delectable Kilgore vocals. A reunion of sorts occurred at the 1988 San Diego Traditional Jazz Festival as Smith and six of his former band mates put together a fine Condon-style band documented on *Hal Smith's Rhythmakers: California, Here I Come* ♫♫♫♫ (Jazzology, 1989, prod. George H. Buck). The free-wheeling ensembles, hot solos, and good-natured vocals are highlighted in this fine batch of 15 old pop tunes, warhorses, and standards, performed by Chris Tyle (cornet), Bobby Gordon (clarinet), Jack Meilahn (guitar), Mike Duffy (bass), and drummer Smith. An enlivened session with appeal for fans of Chicago-styled traditional jazz.

the rest:

The Hal Smith–Chris Tyle Frisco Syncopators: Milneburg Joys ♫♫♫ (GHB, 1989)

The Frisco Syncopators: San Francisco Bound ♫♫♫ (Stomp Off, 1991)

The Frisco Syncopators: Firehouse Stomp ♫♫♫ (Stomp Off, 1992)

Down Home Five Strut Miss Lizzie ♫♫♫ (Stomp Off, 1994)

Down Home Jazz Band: Back to Bodega ♫♫♫ (Stomp Off, 1994)

Down Home Jazz Band: Paddle Wheelin' Along ♫♫♫ (Stomp Off, 1995)

Frisco Syncopators: Come Rest Your Ears ♫♫♫ (Yerba Buena, 1995)

Hal Smith & Creole Sunshine Jazz Band: Bourbon Street Memories ♫♫♫ (GHB, 1996)

worth searching for: Smith also appears on a session under Tyle's leadership, *Chris Tyle's New Orleans Rover Boys: A Tribute to Benny Strickler* (Stomp Off, 1991, prod. Bob Erdos). A traditional romp in the classic San Francisco style of Lu Watters, this is a tribute to the late Stricker, who took a band into the Dawn Club in 1942 when the draft for World War II had decimated the Watters band. This CD is a personal favorite of drummer Smith, who takes a sideman's role here on a mix of West Coast traditional, old favorites, warhorses, and Western swing.

influences:

◀◀ Sid Catlett, Dave Tough, Baby Dodds, Chick Webb, Gene Krupa, Ben Pollack, Ray Bauduc, Kaiser Marshall, Vic Berton, Zutty Singleton, Nick Fatool, Bill Dart, Tony Sbarbaro, Fred Higuera, Smokey Stover, Wayne Jones, Jake Hanna, Lloyd Byasee, Minor Hall, Ormond Downes, George Wettling

John T. Bitter

Jabbo Smith

Born Cladys Smith, December 24, 1908, in Pembroke, GA. Died January 16, 1991.

Jabbo Smith has earned cult status among many jazz enthusiasts for his pioneering trumpet playing in the 1920s and 1930s—he has been frequently compared to Louis Armstrong. Much of Smith's childhood was spent at the Jenkins Orphanage in Charleston, South Carolina, where jazz was taught to many budding young musicians. By the age of 16 he had mastered the trumpet and trombone and was already playing professionally; he headed to New York to play with Harlem pianist Charlie Johnson, with whom he later made his first recordings. Before he was 20 Smith had become one of New York's most popular trumpeters, working with James P. Johnson, Fats Waller, and, most notably, Duke Ellington, performing a memorable trumpet solo on "Black and Tan Fantasy." In 1929 Smith formed his own band, the Ryhthm Aces, which featured a unique collection of instruments: clarinet, tuba, piano, Ikey Robinson's banjo, and, of course, Smith's trumpet (along with his irresistible vocals). His recordings during this period were reminiscent of Armstrong's "Hot Five" sound, particularly the ferocious "Jazz Battle," "Take Me to the River," and "Sau-Sha Stomp." This is perhaps Smith's most popular (and finest) work. All original compositions, they reveal a completely original style in phrasing, sound, and rhythm. By the time swing came to dominate jazz in the late 1930s, Smith's career was dwindling, plagued by bad choices and erratic behavior. His contemporaries compared him to Armstrong, Dizzy Gillespie, and Roy Eldridge, but general critical consensus has so far failed to admit him to the pantheon of jazz trumpet players.

what's available: Thankfully, all of Smith's finest work has been preserved on *The Complete 1929/1938 Sessions* ♫♫♫♫ (Jazz Archives, 1993), an indispensable two-CD set featuring four dozen tracks. The CD covers Smith's recordings from 1929 to 1938, including his work with Waller, Charlie Johnson, James P. Johnson, and Ellington, and his 1929 studio dates with his Rhythm Aces. The CD finishes with Smith's last recordings under his name, the 1938 sessions with Jabbo Smith and His Orchestra, featuring one of his loveliest songs, the sublime "Rhythm in Spain."

worth searching for: For the complete Jabbo Smith, outtakes and all, check out his recordings with some of his contemporaries. *Duke Ellington 1927–1928* ♫♫♫ (Classics 542) features Smith's work with Ellington, including "Black and Tan Fantasy." *The Complete Charlie Johnson Sessions* ♫♫♫♫ (Hot 'n' Sweet) offers a complete roundup of the great jazz pianist's work, including his recordings with Smith. One of Fats Waller's buddies on the album *Fats and His Buddies* ♫♫♫ (RCA Bluebird, 1992, prod. Orrin Keepnews) is Jabbo, heard on a 1928 Louisiana Sugar Babes session with Garvin Bushell, James P. Johnson, and Waller (on pipe organ). Smith's cornet playing can be found on a 1926 session by little-known cornetist Thomas Morris, collected on *When a 'Gator Hollers* ♫♫♫ (Frog). Legendary Harlem pianist Willie "The Lion" Smith also worked with Jabbo. Their collaboration is featured on *Willie "The Lion" Smith and His Cubs* ♫♫♫♫ (Timeless, 1993). Pianist and jugman Clarence Williams made some raucous recordings with Smith, available on *Clarence Williams 1926–27* ♫♫♫ (Classics 718).

influences:

◀◀ Louis Armstrong

▶▶ Hot Lips Page, Doc Cheatham, Roy Eldridge, Dizzy Gillespie

James Bradley

Jimmy Smith

Born James Oscar Smith, December 8, 1925, in Norristown, PA.

Before Jimmy Smith, the organ traditionally had been relegated to movie theaters, sports stadiums, churches, and roller rinks. But Smith's soulful blend of blues, bebop, and swing revolutionized the instrument in the 1950s and 1960s. With his foot-pedal bass lines, percussive left-hand chording, and funky right-hand solos, he sounded like a big band. Smith studied the piano as a child and by the age of nine was performing on the radio. After serving in the Navy during WWII, he attended the Hamilton School of Music in 1948 and the Ornstein School of Music from 1949 to 1950. Tired of out-of-tune pianos on the job and inspired by previous organists such as Bill Doggett and Wild Bill Davis, Smith began to play the Hammond in 1951. He formed a trio in 1955 that briefly featured John Coltrane. He practiced for years in a Philadelphia warehouse on a rented organ and played extensively in the area before getting the opportunity to play in New York. A successful stint at New York's Cafe Bohemia led to gig at Birdland and then to an appearance at the 1957 Newport Jazz Festival, bringing Smith to the attention of fans and other musicians. Around this same time, Freddie Hubbard brought a tape of Jimmy Smith to Ira Gitler, who took it to Bob Weinstock at Prestige. Weinstock passed on signing Smith, but Alfred Lion at Blue Note snapped him up the next week. Smith recorded several excellent dates at Blue Note with superb support from sidemen such as Ike Quebec, Jackie McLean, Kenny Burrell, and Stanley Turrentine. In 1963 Smith was lured away to Verve records, where his popularity continued to grow with jazz (and blues) fans after he recorded mid-'60s international hit singles like "A Walk on the Wild Side" and "Got My Mojo Working." Many of the Verve sessions featured big bands arranged by Oliver Nelson or Lalo Schifrin. However, much of Smith's late 1960s output was weighed down by attempts at crossover success. He was including too many cheesy rock covers that diminished his reputation and didn't highlight his strengths. Although his recorded output during the 1970s was inconsistent, Smith continued to tour. But by the mid-1970s his earthy, funky style of jazz had fallen out of favor. He decided to stop touring and moved to California and opened a nightclub. Smith resumed touring in the early 1980s and signed again with Blue Note, recording music more suited to him. In his concert performances well into the 1990s, Smith demonstrated the musical magic (and bawdiness) that allowed him to hold enthusiastic audiences in the palm of his hand. It is difficult to fully appreciate the impact Jimmy Smith had when he first surfaced on the scene. He was the first to develop a modern, clean organ sound that combined bebop and blues.

His walking bass lines were sophisticated and modern, executed by the swiftest feet since Fred Astaire. His punchy chords and fiery solo lines brought the bebop sensibilities of Bud Powell to the organ. Jimmy Smith exploded on the jazz scene, revolutionized the Hammond B-3, and set the standard for subsequent organ groups. And he's still going at it.

what to buy: *The Sermon* ♐♐♐♐ (Blue Note, 1957/1987, prod. Alfred Lion) is Smith's first recording for Blue Note and features the 20-minute version (from the LP) of the tune that would become Smith's bluesy anthem on future recordings and concert performances. Smith is one of few organists who works well with horns behind him, and this session features trumpeter Lee Morgan, trombonist Curtis Fuller, alto saxist Lou Donaldson, the very underrated tenorist Tina Brooks, as well as guitarist Kenny Burrell or Eddie McFadden, and drummer Art Blakey or Donald Bailey, who all contribute marvelously. Containing mostly standards, the album is a well-structured jam session. With such a strong band playing familiar material there's no way you can go wrong. It's a swinging, straight-ahead, typical Blue Note date. *Back at the Chicken Shack* ♐♐♐♐♐ (Blue Note, 1960/1987, prod. Alfred Lion) has the "grease" that one expects from Jimmy Smith. Recorded the same day as *Midnight Special*, this is soul-jazz with deep, funky grooves. Saxophonist Stanley Turrentine is given plenty of opportunity to shine, along with guitarist Kenny Burrell and drummer Donald Bailey. Highlights include the title tune and a catchy version of "On the Sunny Side of the Street" that was not released on the original version of the album. The album is quintessential Jimmy Smith, and so is *Midnight Special* ♐♐♐♐ (Blue Note, 1960/1989, prod. Alfred Lion), from the same studio session. Featuring tunes such as "One O'Clock Jump," "Jumpin' the Blues," and the title tune, it's in the same soulful mode as *Back at the Chicken Shack*. You can't go wrong with either album—both are highly recommended. For fans who still prefer their organ-jazz served up with a sprinkling of blues seasoning, check out *Got My Mojo Working/Hoochie Coochie Man* ♐♐♐♐ (Verve, 1966/1997, prod. Creed Taylor). This CD combines two LPs recorded in 1965 and 1966, respectively; at the time, they set both jazz and blues fans on their ears. (Smith won the 1965 *Down Beat* Readers Poll for his instrument.) Smith works the hell out of his Hammond B-3 on *Got My Mojo Working*, singing raw vocals of the title tune, and growling through "High Heel Sneakers." He also lays down classic, kicking B-3 jazz versions of "Johnny Come Lately," "C-Jam Blues," and "Hobson's Hop," with backing horns artfully arranged by Oliver Nelson. Two dates are documented on *Got My Mojo Working*: the December 16, 1965 session included guitarist Kenny Burrell, bassists Ron Carter or Ben Tucker, and drummer Grady Tate; the next day, Burrell and Tate returned, with George Duviver on bass, plus a horn section that includes Jerome Richardson (baritone sax), Phil Woods (alto sax), Romeo Penque (tenor sax, flute), and Ernie Royal (trumpet). *Hoochie Coochie Man* includes a larger crew, an orchestra that features luminaries such as Joe Newman, Melba Liston, Phil Woods, Jerry Dodgion, Willie Ruff, and others. Burrell and Tate are back for this June 14, 1966 session, with Richard Davis on bass, and Oliver Nelson again serving as arranger-conductor. This date included Nelson's "Blues and the Abstract Truth," Smith's cover of the John Lee Hooker tune "Boom Boom," and other B-3 groovers.

what to buy next: No matter which decade you pick, Smith's sure to have some dazzling albums. After an absence of 23 years, Smith returned to Verve for one of his best jazz-focused sessions, *Damn!* ♫♫♫♪ (Verve, 1995, prod. Richard Seidel, Don Sickler). This session was drummer Arthur Taylor's last recording, and captures Smith performing nine classics he's done before, but this time he's joined, in various configurations, by trumpeters Roy Hargrove and Nicholas Payton; saxophonists Abraham Burton, Ron Blake, Mark Turner, and Tim Warfield; guitarist Mark Whitfield; and a deep-grooving rhythm section with bassist Christian McBride and veteran drummers Bernard Purdie or Arthur Taylor. Everyone gets to stretch out on tunes by Horace Silver ("Sister Sadie"), Dizzy Gillespie ("Woody 'N' You"), Herbie Hancock ("Watermelon Man"), Charlie Parker ("Scrapple from the Apple"), James Brown ("Papa's Got a Brand New Bag"), and others. With all the fiery, hot-paced solos and Smith's vitalized playing, there's never a dull moment on this must-own album. Recorded in Hollywood on January 12–14, 1993, *Sum Serious Blues* ♫♫♫ (Milestone, 1993, prod. Johnny Pate) shows that Jimmy Smith is as entertaining today as he was 30 years ago. Smith leads off with the blues-groover title tune, then yields to Phil Upchurch who gets to show off his soulful guitar style, with Andy Simpkins on bass and Michael Baker on drums. Reminiscent of Smith's albums orchestrated by Oliver Nelson in the 1960s, this CD features a classy and brassy horn section with Buddy Collette (alto saxophone), Ernie Fields Jr. (baritone sax), Herman Riley (tenor sax), Maurice Spears (bass trombone), and Oscar Brashear (trumpet). The menu is a fine feast of straight-ahead, swinging jazz and toe-tappin' blues tunes constructed on Pate's arrangements that leave wide open spaces for Smith's improvisations and horn solos. Smith's gravelly voice earnestly embraces the soul-ballad, "Hurry Change, If You're Comin'," and he works his vo-

JIMMY SMITH

song "Back at the Chicken Shack"
album *Back at the Chicken Shack*
(Blue Note, 1960/1987)
instrument Hammond organ

Monster Solo

cals in front of the subdued horn section, then finishes with a fine organ solo. Vocalist Marlena Shaw fits right in with the crew, singing on "You've Changed" and "(I'd Rather) Drink Muddy Water." An eight-minute workout of Smith's classic "The Sermon" will take you right to church with its gospel-tinged, bluesy truths, and you'll gain further appreciation for the tight interaction between Smith and Upchurch. And that's before Smith's deep-grooved original, "Open for Business," which features a splashy Upchurch solo, a gritty bari burst from Fields, and Smith's growling organ-grinding. An early 1960s date, *Prayer Meetin'* ♫♫♫♪ (Blue Note, 1963/1988, prod. Alfred Lion) is only slightly weaker than *Midnight Special* or *Chicken Shack*, recorded around the same time. The personnel is pretty much the same, with Smith mixing it up with saxophonist Stanley Turrentine, Donald Bailey, and guitarist Quentin Warren. Most of the music was recorded on February 8, 1963, except for two tunes from a 1960 session that add bassist Sam Jones. The performances lack the same energy and pop of the earlier recordings, but still manage to cover all the expectations from a Jimmy Smith record. This was Smith's last album for the label until 1986, when he recorded *Go for Watcha Know*. The two-disc set *Walk on the Wild Side: The Best of the Verve Years* ♪♪♪♪ (Verve, 1995) is the best way to explore Smith's post–Blue Note career without having to wade through countless groovy rock and pop covers. Musicians include guitarists George Benson, Kenny Burrell, and Wes Montgomery, as well as saxophonist-arranger Oliver Nelson.

best of the rest:

Home Cookin' ♪♪♪♪ (Blue Note, 1958/1996)
Crazy Baby! ♪♪♪♪ (Blue Note, 1960/1989)
Open House/Plain Talk ♪♪♪♪ (Blue Note, 1960/1992)
Bashin' The Unpredictable Jimmy Smith ♪♪♪♪ (Verve, 1962/1995)
I'm Movin' On ♪♪♪♪ (Blue Note, 1963/1995)
The Cat ♪♪♪♪ (Verve, 1964)
Christmas Cookin' ♪♪♪ (Verve, 1964/1992)
Organ Grinder Swing ♪♪♪ (Verve, 1965)
Cat Strikes Again ♪♪♪ (LaserLight, 1980/1992)
All the Way Live ♪♪♪♪ (Milestone, 1981)
Off the Top ♪♪♪ (Elektra, 1982)
Go for Watcha' Know ♪♪♪♪ (Blue Note, 1986/1996)
Prime Time ♪♪♪ (Milestone, 1989)
Fourmost ♪♪♪ (Milestone, 1991)
Master ♪♪♪♪ (Blue Note, 1994)

worth searching for: *Groovin' at Small's Paradise, Vol. 1* ♪♪♪♪ (Blue Note, 1957) finds Smith uptown serving up soulful music with both hands and both feet. The energy abounds on this live session. It showed up briefly as a Japanese pressing but deserves to be released domestically. Also hard to find, *Dynamic Duo* ♪♪♪♪ (Verve, 1966, prod. Creed Taylor) features Smith with Wes Montgomery, with whom he had a lot in common. Both were extremely popular and influential musicians and skilled improvisors of sophisticated and soulful jazz. While they both often covered material that was beneath them, they are in excellent form on this date—a complementary duo with each one inspiring and inciting the other to new heights.

influences:

◄◄ Wild Bill Davis, Milt Buckner, Bud Powell, Horace Silver

►► Shirley Scott, Jimmy McGriff, Larry Young, Joey DeFrancesco

James Eason and Nancy Ann Lee

Leo Smith

Born December 18, 1941, in Leland, MS.

This trumpeter's soloing and writing synthesizes African, Asian, blues, and jazz influences into a unique and entirely contemporary sound. In his brass playing, jazz allusions trample historical dividing lines, with brilliant Louis Armstrong high notes and Cootie Williams growls finding unexpected homes next to Don Cherry smears and Lester Bowie blatts. Smith also plucks the African mbira and the Chinese koto as a Delta bluesman would, and he tempers the blue rawness of his singing with a reggae lilt. In recent years, a sing-song lyricism has invaded his otherwise rigorous abstractions (the influence of his Rastafarianism?), but he remains a master colorist with an entirely idiosyncratic sense of form.

Smith joined the Association for the Advancement of Creative Musicians in 1967 and appeared on Anthony Braxton's *Three Compositions of New Jazz* the same year. In 1969, he moved to Paris and joined the Creative Construction Company, which included Braxton, violinist Leroy Jenkins, and sometime drummer Steve McCall; the group recorded a historic New York City concert in 1970. Smith then moved to Connecticut, where he founded his own record label, Kabell, which operated until 1986. On Kabell, he issued a pioneering solo album in 1971, and several albums by his changing ensemble, New Delta Ahkri, whose members included vibraphonist Bobby Naughton, saxophonist Henry Threadgill, and bassist Wes Brown. In the '70s he was also a founding member of the Creative Musicians Improvising Forum (CMIF), a Connecticut-based musicians' cooperative patterned after the AACM, which sponsored concerts through the state. Smith recorded three Incus albums with Derek Bailey's Company in 1977 and two albums for FMP in 1979 and 1981 with a free-improvisation trio of German bassist Peter Kowald and drummer Gunter Sommer. In 1979 he co-led a big band with Roscoe Mitchell, touring Europe and recording two albums for the Moers label. By the mid-'80s Smith had openly embraced Rastafarianism and took the name Wadada. His new band, Sphinx, performed a jazz-rock-reggae fusion, although it never recorded. In 1993, he was awarded the Dizzy Gillespie Chair at the California Institute of Arts.

what to buy: *Go in Numbers* ♪♪♪♪ (Black Saint, 1980, prod. Leo Smith) is the best and most representative example of Smith's group conception available (until his Nessa LP *Spirit Catcher* or the Kabell albums are reissued). It's a somber, although never dull, exploration of tone color and spacious rhythm. *Procession of the Great Ancestry* ♪♪♪♪ (Chief, 1983, prod. Chuck Nessa) contains rapturous evocations of jazz trumpeters Miles Davis, Booker Little, Roy Eldridge, and Dizzy Gillespie played with stately calm by Smith mainstay Bobby Naughton, bassist Joe Fonda, and Chicago percussionist Kahil el Zabar, one of Smith's most sympathetic drummers. After a decade without a new group album, Smith came back with the extraordinary *Tao-Njia* 𝄐𝄐𝄐𝄐 (Tzadik, 1993, prod. Wadada Leo Smith). This album is marked by an even deeper, more confident, and imaginative use of African American, classical, and world music influences.

what to buy next: On *Kulture Jazz* 𝄐𝄐𝄐 (ECM, 1992, prod. Steve Lake), his third solo album, Smith's avant-griot evocations of his artistic, spiritual, and blood ancestors test the ability of African American music to assimilate other traditions, generate new forms, and absorb new sounds.

worth searching for: *Reflectativity* 𝄐𝄐𝄐𝄐 (Kabell, 1975, prod. Leo Smith), a 1974 concert recording with bassist Wes Brown and pianist Anthony Davis, is one of the overlooked masterpieces of the 1970s. The group plays Smith's elusive music with great seriousness and sympathy.

influences:
◀◀ Don Cherry, Miles Davis

Ed Hazell

Lonnie Smith

Born 1943, in Buffalo, NY.

Organist Lonnie Smith's first instrument was a trumpet. As a kid he was interested in early R&B, and he formed a vocal group known as the Supremes while still in high school. He finally started playing the organ (without taking the usual first step for budding organists, the piano) under the influence of Bill Doggett and Jimmy Smith. After leaving Buffalo for New York City, Smith found himself working with guitarists George Benson and Grant Green before joining saxophonist Lou Donaldson on the sessions that resulted in the hit album *Alligator Boogaloo*. Since then, Smith has released a slew of albums for Blue Note and several other prominent jazz labels, in addition to session work for Lou Donaldson, Red Holloway, Eric Gale, Jimmy Ponder, and the Essence All-Stars. Smith has become one of the top organists in the country with a style that relies less on speed than in forming the ultimate funky groove.

what to buy: *Live at Club Mozambique* 𝄐𝄐𝄐 (Blue Note, 1995, prod. Francis Wolff), recorded live on May 21, 1970 in Detroit, is the kind of greasy funk that's at the heart of what modern aficionados now call "acid jazz." There is solid playing from Smith throughout, with Ronnie Cuber on baritone and Dave Hubbard on tenor flying over drummer Joe Dukes (formerly with Jack McDuff) and some local percussion players. Guitarist George Benson joins his former employee as guest artist for some fine playing, especially on the album's closer, "Seven Steps to

Heaven." It's hard to believe this album actually sat in the vaults for 25 years before being released. Adventurous playing is not something normally associated with Lonnie Smith, but the trio tunes he cut for Venus Records, *Afro Blue* 𝄐𝄐𝄐 (Venus/MusicMasters, 1997), with guitarist John Abercrombie and drummer Marvin "Smitty" Smith, are fairly brave outings for the master of the comfortable groove. This tribute to John Coltrane brings the organist into modal territory that the late Larry Young used to explore, and, while not as technically gifted as Young, Smith more than holds his own. Abercrombie isn't forced to carry as much of the load on this release as he is on the two Jimi Hendrix tributes, *Foxy Lady* and *Purple Haze*, but his playing challenges the organist into one of his most cerebral, yet moving, performances.

what to buy next: *Move Your Hand* 𝄐𝄐𝄐 (Blue Note, 1969, prod. Francis Wolff), a live set recorded at Club Harlem in Atlantic City, New Jersey, was a pretty big hit for Smith. His only sideman of note from a more modern perspective is Smith's longtime associate, baritone sax player Ronnie Cuber. The remaining players do a fine job, though, keeping the groove in firm control despite the incongruous cover of Donovan's "Sunshine Superman." "Dancin' in an Easy Groove" was recorded at the same time as the rest of the album but never released before. As for *Purple Haze* 𝄐𝄐𝄐 (Venus/MusicMasters, 1995, prod. Todd Barkan), Jimi Hendrix is one of the few rock player/composers to have found acceptance within certain parts of the jazz community, with the Gil Evans arrangement of "Little Wing" coming to mind quickest. That an organist would dare to attempt these tunes would be sheer effrontery if Hendrix hadn't used the instrument as color on so many of his albums, or if there weren't a great guitarist like John Abercrombie on the date. The arrangements draw the songs past the 13-minute mark for three out of four songs, and the playing fills the space well; but this is an album aimed more at Hendrix/Abercrombie fans—with Smith's role reduced to an important sideman instead of a session leader.

the rest:
Drives 𝄐𝄐𝄐 (Blue Note, 1970)
Foxy Lady 𝄐𝄐𝄐 (Venus/MusicMasters, 1996)

worth searching for: Some of Smith's best playing has been as a quasi-sideman in semi-superstar groups like those found on *Chartbusters!* 𝄐𝄐𝄐 (NYC, 1995, prod. Todd Barkan, Milan Simich). There are a batch of 1960s-era post-bop standards on that release with Smith and drummer Lenny White figuring in on every one. Other sidemen include guitarists David Fiuczynski, John Scofield, and Hiram Bullock, with Craig Handy doing all the tenor sax work.

influences:

◀◀ Bill Doggett, Jimmy Smith

▶▶ Ronnie Foster, Leon Spencer, Bobby Watley

Garaud MacTaggart

Lonnie Liston Smith

Born December 28, 1940, in Richmond, VA.

Lonnie Liston Smith has often been confused with organist Lonnie Smith, but they most definitely aren't the same. While the organist has focused on soul-jazz and hard bop, Lonnie Liston Smith is a McCoy Tyner–influenced electric keyboardist and acoustic pianist who started out playing straight-ahead jazz but became best known for his fusion recordings. In the 1960s and early 1970s, Smith's work as a sideman for Gato Barbieri, Rahsaan Roland Kirk, Pharoah Sanders, and others showed how expressive and spiritual he could be in an acoustic post-bop setting, but he went electric during an association with Miles Davis and continued to embrace fusion when he founded his own group, the Cosmic Echoes, in the mid-1970s. After recording his share of strong fusion dates in the mid-to-late 1970s, Smith wasn't heard from as often in the 1980s. The early '90s found him offering weak NAC-type releases that left a lot to be desired creatively.

what to buy: Smith expressed a very deep spirituality on his debut album, *Astral Traveling* ✍✍✍✍ (Flying Dutchman, 1973, prod. Bob Thiele), and the equally superb *Expansions* ✍✍✍✍ (Flying Dutchman, 1975, prod. Bob Thiele), both of which offer an inspired blend of jazz, soul, and funk. As much as *Expansions* and *Visions of a New World* ✍✍✍✍ (RCA, 1975, prod. Bob Thiele) appealed to R&B audiences, the influence of John Coltrane, McCoy Tyner, and Pharoah Sanders was still there. Smith's producer, Bob Thiele, had in fact worked with Coltrane. In 1986 Smith made a surprising return to acoustic post-bop with his fine trio date, *Make Someone Happy* ✍✍✍✍ (Doctor Jazz, 1986, prod. Bob Thiele).

what to buy next: Though not quite as strong as *Expansions*, *Reflections of a Golden Dream* ✍✍✍ (RCA, 1976) and *Renaissance* ✍✍✍ (RCA, 1976) show how imaginative Smith can be. For all its commercial appeal, the sleek *Loveland* ✍✍✍ (Columbia, 1978) is quite enjoyable and could be called "mood music with a difference."

what to avoid: Though *Love Goddess* ✍✍ (Startrak, 1991) contains a few nice straight-ahead numbers—including Miles Davis's "Blue in Green" and Kenny Dorham's "Blue Bossa"—it

is dominated by homogenized "elevator Muzak" obviously made with rigid radio formats in mind. Even weaker is the highly commercial *Magic Lady* ✍ (Startrak, 1991), which contains a noteworthy remake of Smith's enchanting "Quiet Moments," but, on the whole, is soulless and quite forgettable.

influences:

◀◀ McCoy Tyner, John Coltrane, Pharoah Sanders, Charles Lloyd

Alex Henderson

Louis Smith

Born Edward Louis Smith, May 20, 1931, in Memphis, TN.

Rather than devoting himself to the full-time profession of jazz musician, this trumpeter has made two careers for himself, teaching and playing. He has taught instrumental music in high schools and colleges from Atlanta to Memphis to his current hometown, Ann Arbor, Michigan. He has also recorded on instruction tapes and CDs for Caris Music Services alongside musicians like Jimmy Knepper, Bobby Watson, Billy Hart, and John Abercrombie. As a leader, Smith has signed an impressive number of world-class jazz masters to act as his sidemen. His first date included Cannonball Adderley, recording under his alias "Buckshot LaFunke," and Smith has also led sessions with Charlie Rouse, George Coleman, Roland Hanna, Billy Hart, Junior Cook, and Kenny Washington. After graduating from high school, Smith won a music scholarship to Tennessee State University, later transferring to the University of Michigan for his post-graduate work. After a tour of duty in the Army, Smith taught school in Atlanta. He recorded his first album, *Here Comes Louis Smith*, in 1957 for Transition, a Boston-based label that went out of business. Blue Note picked up the masters and signed the young trumpeter to a contract. By 1958, Smith found himself playing on sessions for Kenny Burrell, joining the Horace Silver Quintet for a few months of touring and recording his second release, *Smithville*.

what to buy: *Just Friends* ✍✍✍ (SteepleChase, 1978, prod. Nils Winther) had been Smith's first recording date in 20 years and came about through the efforts of producer Nils Winther. Though Smith is the leader, saxophonist George Coleman and pianist Harold really stand out. The four Smith-penned tunes allow plenty of room for the players to stretch out, with Coleman especially effective on the opener, "Blues for Jimmy."

what to buy next: With youth comes speed, and *Here Comes Louis Smith* ✍✍✍ (Blue Note, 1957, prod. Tom Wilson) is a fast-paced bebop date with fine playing from Smith in his Clifford Brown mode, but the real story comes from the playing of Cannonball Adderley, with pianists Duke Jordan and Tommy Flanagan. Smith wrote four of the six tunes, and his "Brill's Blues" deserves to be played more often. The unison passages in "Val's Blues" are a little ragged, but Adderley saves the day with a rare combination of aplomb and fire, while Smith's soloing hints at the player he could have been if he had devoted less time to academic pursuits. *Ballads for Lulu* 𝄢𝄢𝄢 (SteepleChase, 1990, prod. Nils Winther), an album of chestnuts like "Laura" by Johnny Mercer and "Time After Time" by Sammy Cahn, show off Smith's steady balladry to good effect. Pianist Jim McNeely is impressive as well. The one caveat is that, at 70 minutes, the CD is too long.

the rest:
Prancin' 𝄢𝄢𝄢 (SteepleChase, 1979)
Strike Up the Band 𝄢𝄢𝄢 (SteepleChase, 1991)
Silvering 𝄢𝄢𝄢 (SteepleChase, 1993)
I Waited for You 𝄢𝄢𝄢 (SteepleChase, 1996)

influences:
◀◀ Clifford Brown
▶▶ Joe Magnarelli, Phil Ranelin

Garaud MacTaggart

Marvin "Smitty" Smith

Born June 24, 1961, in Waukegan, IL.

The drummer for the *Tonight Show* Band led by Kevin Eubanks, Marvin "Smitty" Smith is a talented and flexible drummer who has been a popular player for over a decade. He joined the Jon Hendricks band at 20, and has since played with such divergent artists as Sonny Rollins, David Murray, Sting, Dave Holland, the Frank Foster/Frank Wess Big Band, and Bobby Watson. As a leader, his playing owes much to Art Blakey, but he is also excellent in the fusion and funk settings (his vocals on the *Tonight Show* are always a treat). He also has a tremendous sense of humor, which has highlighted some of his live performances.

what to buy: Smitty is in fine form on *The Road Less Traveled* 𝄢𝄢𝄢 (Concord Jazz, 1989, prod. Allen Farnham), and his compositions are more adventurous than on his debut. The octet setting allows for some unique arrangements, and the playing, particularly from pianist James Williams and trumpeter Wallace Roney, is very good.

the rest:
Keeper of the Drums 𝄢𝄢𝄢 (Concord Jazz, 1987)

influences:
◀◀ Kenny Clarke, Jack DeJohnette, Art Blakey, Max Roach, Philly Joe Jones, Tony Williams

Paul MacArthur

Stuff Smith

Born Hezekiah Leroy Gordon Smith, August 14, 1909, in Portsmouth, OH. Died September 25, 1967, in Munich, Germany.

Violinist Stuff Smith was mostly self-taught and developed a style that was highly syncopated, hoarse-toned, and raucous, contrasting vastly with the European-gypsy influences of his peers. He was an extraordinary fiddler whose performances lit up Manhattan's 52nd street in 1936. Smith studied early with his father and performed in the family band. By age 15, Smith was working as a professional musician. From 1926 to 1928 he performed with Alphonso Trent, then briefly with Jelly Roll Morton. Smith lived in Buffalo for several years, then moved to New York in 1936, where, playing amplified violin, he led a quintet at the Onyx Club with trumpeter Jonah Jones, drummer Cozy Cole, and others. After Fats Waller died, Smith led Waller's band in 1943. Norman Granz recorded several exceptional 1950s Verve sessions with Smith. The violinist toured extensively during the 1960s and settled in Copenhagen in 1965.

what to buy: While much of Smith's discography is either on import labels or out-of-print albums with domestic labels, it's meaningful to honor the roots of jazz and long-gone stellar stylists like violinist Stuff Smith. Guitarist Herb Ellis, a prime statesman of swing 12 years Smith's junior, claims that Stuff's trio was the first professional jazz group he ever sat in with. They come together again on the appropriately titled *Together!* 𝄢𝄢𝄢𝄢 (Epic, 1963/Koch Classics, 1995, prod. John Hammond), a reissue of their spunky 1963 Hollywood studio session produced by John Hammond. The tight, steadily swinging, nine-tune session features Smith and Ellis with Bob Enevoldsen (tenor sax, valve trombone), and solid rhythm players Lou Levy (piano), Shelly Manne (drums), and Al McKibbon (bass). Ellis interacts pleasingly with Stuff and injects some hard-swinging, mellifluous solos, but it's definitely Stuff's stuff and Enevoldsen's valve trombone solos that steal the scene. The spectacular disc includes three previously unreleased takes and original photos and liner notes by Leonard Feather. "Stuff" is really happening! *Violins No End* 𝄢𝄢𝄢𝄢 (Pablo, 1957/OJC, 1996, prod. Norman Granz) finds Stuff Smith playing four duets with

Stephane Grappelli (the leader) recorded in a Paris studio session in May 1957 with Oscar Peterson (piano), Herb Ellis (guitar), Ray Brown (bass), and Jo Jones (drums). The remaining three selections feature Smith in a 1957 concert at Salle Pleyel, Paris, with the same rhythm team. Smith's playing has a rawer, bluesy edge to it, while Grappelli's playing is more fluid and romantic. Smith often plays chordal harmonies, and he swings hot and hard on the seven minutes of "Desert Sands," one of the album highlights. Smith also delivers a waltz-to-swing version of "How High the Moon" and shows supreme mastery of his instrument on the ballad "Moonlight in Vermont."

best of the rest:

Stuff Smith, 1936–1939 𝄐𝄐𝄐𝄐 (Jazz Chronological Classics, 1996)

Stuff Smith: Live at the Montmartre 𝄐𝄐𝄐𝄐 (Storyville, 1965/1994)

Nancy Ann Lee

Willie "The Lion" Smith

Born November 25, 1897, in Goshen, NY. Died April 18, 1975, in New York, NY.

Willie the Lion ranks high among the greats of stride piano, that virtuosic New York style that demanded a left hand of steel. If James P. Johnson was the technical giant and Fats Waller the nonpareil entertainer, Smith was the suave sophisticate (the three often traveled New York's "rent party" circuit together). His ornate style can be heard further down the jazz road in Art Tatum's baroque profusions, and Duke Ellington wrote "Portrait of the Lion" in tribute to Smith.

With his rather incredible complete monicker being William Henry Joseph Bonaparte Bertholoff Smith, Willie the Lion grew up in Brooklyn and earned his nickname fighting in France in World War I. There seems to be no photographic evidence that Smith was ever less than impeccably turned out in the finest suits, or even that he ever appeared in public without a fat cigar clenched in his teeth. His music reflects that sense of style; there's never anything unkempt about it. He was a musician his entire life, toured the world, wrote a magnificently self-aggrandizing autobiography, and was a dyed-in-the-wool New Yorker until the day he died.

what to buy: *The Chronological Willie "The Lion" Smith 1938–1940* 𝄐𝄐𝄐𝄐 (Classics, 1993) gets the nod over the other items in Classics' series for the abundance of superb solo piano—the 14 tracks recorded for Commodore on January 10, 1939, are quite arguably the most durable part of the Lion's legacy (and the more memorable solo items on the other vol-

umes, only one or two each in any case, are heard here in different versions). Not surprisingly, "Finger Buster" is an uptempo showpiece, but it's urbane numbers such as "Morning Air" and "Echoes of Spring" that are more typical of the fancy style Smith was known for. The eccentric accent pattern of "Rippling Waters" is quite tricky in its syncopations. There are four tracks of the less interesting material with a band (although the instrumentals "Rushin'" and "Noodlin'" are fine, the two numbers with vocals barely feature Smith) and four tracks with Smith and vocalist Big Joe Turner, where Smith sounds fine if a bit overpowered by the mismatch with the blues shouter. There's also the curiosity "Three Keyboards," where Smith plays celeste while Joe Bushkin and Jess Stacy share piano duty, and "The Lion and the Lamb," a two-piano duet with Smith and Bushkin. But it's the piano tracks, which are positively spine-tingling, that will bring listeners back over and over.

what to buy next: *Echoes of Spring* 𝄐𝄐𝄐 (Milan, 1992) was recorded live in Paris in 1965. Playing solo in his late 60s, Smith shows that his technique, if a shade below the precision of his earlier days, is still up to the demands of such uptempo romps as "Here Comes the Band." He reprises some of his most famous originals as well as a few charming vocal numbers. Of special interest are two deconstructions of "Tea for Two," a Chopin Polonaise, James P. Johnson's demanding "Carolina Shout," and a seven-minute, 45-second medley of four Johnson numbers, including "Charleston." There's also an eight-minute, 40-second medley of items by other famous pianists, from Eubie Blake, Luckey Roberts, and Fats Waller to Duke Ellington, Vernon Duke, and others.

the rest:

Luckey & the Lion: Harlem Piano Solos by Luckey Roberts & Willie "The Lion" Smith 𝄐𝄐𝄐𝄐 (Good Time Jazz, 1958)

Pork and Beans 𝄐𝄐𝄐 (Black Lion, 1966)

The Chronological Willie "The Lion" Smith 1925–1937 𝄐𝄐𝄐 (Classics, 1992)

The Chronological Willie "The Lion" Smith 1937–1938 𝄐𝄐𝄐 (Classics, 1992)

worth searching for: On blues singer Leadbelly's *Where Did You Sleep Last Night* 𝄐𝄐𝄐𝄐 (Smithsonian Folkways, 1996, prod. Moses Asch), Smith can be heard accompanying on "4, 5, and 9" (a.k.a. "Hollywood and Vine"), recorded in 1946. Smith is not featured but can be heard playing boogie-woogie behind the vocal and the loose jams in the breaks.

influences:

◄◄ Scott Joplin, Eubie Blake, James P. Johnson

►► Fats Waller, Duke Ellington, Art Tatum

Steve Holtje

Paul Smoker

Born May 8, 1941, in Muncie, IN.

Paul Smoker is a trumpeter so steeped in the tradition of his instrument that he regularly includes classics like Bix Beiderbecke's "Davenport Blues" and Louis Armstrong's "Cornet Chop Suey" in his sets. Yet, he also performs in groups of free improvisation with players like Derek Bailey, Peter Brotzmann, and George Lewis. It's this all-encompassing view of jazz that gives his music its strength. Smoker grew up in Davenport, Iowa, and began playing in clubs in Chicago as a teenager. He graduated with a doctorate in music from the University of Iowa in 1974 and taught at Coe College until 1990. He began making a name for himself and his trio (with bassist Ron Rohovit and drummer Phil Haynes) in the early 1980s. Their first recording was a self-produced effort, *QB* (1984), with a guest appearance by Anthony Braxton, and it received great acclaim. The trio toured Europe, which led to three albums recorded for the German Sound Aspects label. In 1987, Smoker and Haynes formed Joint Venture with saxophonist Ellery Eskelin and bassist Drew Gress. They released three albums for the German Enja label. Eskelin left the group in 1996, and his position has been filled by several reed players, most frequently clarinetist Don Byron. Smoker has been involved in several side projects, including a brass ensemble and compositions for big band that have yet to be recorded. He has also performed and recorded with Anthony Braxton (most notably in his Charlie Parker Project), percussionist Gregg Bendian, and Phil Haynes's Four Horns and a What group.

Smoker's trumpet playing is powerful and he uses the complete range of his horn. He can perform acrobatic feats on his instruments, yet he is also a player of great sensitivity, especially on ballads. His earliest influences included Clifford Brown, Maynard Ferguson, and Doc Severinsen (who was a teacher). He also cites John Coltrane as a major influence and cites Anthony Braxton's first solo saxophone album, *For Alto*, as an important turning point.

what to buy: *Alone* ✍✍✍ (Sound Aspects, 1986, prod. Paul Smoker, Phil Haynes) is one of the trio's best-organized records. It begins with a "Prelude" for bass and drums that her-

alds a suite (of sorts), the centerpiece of which is Phil Haynes's title track, a piece that develops slowly and organically. The second half of the set is a tribute to past influences: Smoker's hyperfast "Mingus Among Us," Juan Tizol's "Caravan," and Armstrong's "Cornet Chop Suey." The program is rounded out by a trio, "Postlude," which ties it all together. An apex for the trio. Everything that's good about this group is found on *Genuine Fables* ✍✍✍ (hat ART, 1988, prod. Paul Smoker): their personal, hard-driving brand of freebop on Haynes's "Total Eclipse," their textural and tonal exploration (with a rare use of electronics on the trumpet) on Smoker's epic-length "Tetra," a nod to his instrument's tradition on a growling "St. Louis Blues," a nod to the modern tradition on Mingus's "Fables of Faubus," and two unexpected standards, "Laura" and "Hello Young Lovers." Smoker and reed player Golia met as the front line for Gregg Bendian's *Countparts*. The duo formed this quartet with bassist Ken Filiano from Golia's band and drummer Phil Haynes from Smoker's group on *Halloween '96* ✍✍✍ (C.I.M.P., 1996, prod. Robert D. Rusch). Golia is on baritone throughout and the combination with Smoker is effective. Both players use the entire range of their instruments, and their contrast and interplay serves the material well. Smoker revises his "Ynori/Lobmag" (originally recorded by Joint Venture) for group exploration rather than solo sequences. His other original, "Nailenrac," adopts the development strategy of his trio with a long organic exposition building to an amazing climax.

what to buy next: *Joint Venture-Ways* ✍✍✍ (Enja, 1989, prod. Joint Venture, David Baker) is an improved record over the group's first. There are no standards and all band members contribute compositions except for Eskelin. Opening with Haynes's "Roberta's Changes," the band breathes fire on this prime example of freebop. Smoker contributes two compositions: "Gambol/Irony" consists of a group line that evolves into a solo spot for each member; "Caverns" starts with a slow prelude before kicking into uptempo for a loopy main theme that provides wide-open space for solos. *Joint Venture* ✍✍✍ (Enja, 1987, prod. Joint Venture), the first effort of the quartet of Smoker and Haynes with saxophonist Ellery Eskelin and bassist Drew Gress, is a well-thought-out effort with a mix of standards and originals. They start with a "Lush Life" that's both close to the original (in Eskelin's saxophone) yet abstracted by commentary by the rest of the group. "Chorale and Descendance" is an exploration of the various avenues of contemporary jazz. Recorded at the same sessions as *Alone*, the material on *Come Rain or Come Shine* ✍✍✍ (Sound Aspects, 1986, prod. Paul Smoker, Phil Haynes) hardly sounds like outtakes. It has a lively version of the Art Ensemble of Chicago's "Old Time Southside Dance" and a wry interpretation of the title track. But this album has less of a whole feeling than its predecessor.

influences:

◄◄ Clifford Brown, Maynard Ferguson, Doc Severinsen, John Coltrane

Robert Iannapollo

Gary Smulyan

Born 1955.

Smulyan is a talented baritone sax player, as evidenced by his prime placement in the 1990 *JazzTimes* Critics' Poll of Emerging Talent and the 1993 *Down Beat* Critics' Poll. He has played in a wide assortment of ensembles, including stints with Woody Herman's Thundering Herd, the Mel Lewis Jazz Orchestra, the Phillip Morris Super Band, the Joe Henderson Big Band, and the Carnegie Hall Jazz Band. As a session player, Smulyan has recorded with jazz artists like Barbara Lea, Mike LeDonne, and Kevin Mahogany, and worked with pop singer Diana Ross.

what to buy: Pepper Adams was one of the great baritone saxophone players of all time, but his writing never received much attention (compared to his contemporary, Gerry Mulligan), so Smulyan's *Homage* ♪♪♪♪ (Criss Cross, 1983, prod. Gerry Teekens) was a welcome idea. All eight tunes come from Adams's pen, receiving sympathetic, swinging performances from Smulyan, pianist Tommy Flanagan, bassist Ray Drummond, and drummer Kenny Washington.

what to buy next: *The Lure of Beauty* ♪♪♪♪ (Criss Cross, 1991, prod. Gerry Teekens) shows Smulyan has a firm grasp of hard bop trademarks in his writing to go along with his technical expertise. He also has former Charles Mingus trombone kingpin Jimmy Knepper to help instill life into the session. The end result is a well-chosen mix of covers ("Boos's Blues" by Quincy Jones is a good album opener) and originals (especially the ballad, "Moonlight on the Nile") played by talented musicians. While not essential, it's still a pretty good listen.

the rest:

Saxophone Mosaic ♪♪♪ (Criss Cross, 1994)

influences:

◄◄ Pepper Adams, Harry Carney

►► Ronnie Cuber. Nick Brignola

Garaud MacTaggart

Jim Snidero

Born on May 29, 1958, in Washington, DC.

Although the number of jazz musicians today who are making the alto saxophone their instrument of choice is a small one, Jim Snidero surely can be counted among those few who have developed a individualistic voice while further developing the innovations suggested by Charlie Parker and Jackie McLean. A graduate of the jazz studies program at the University of North Texas, Snidero hit the New York scene in 1981 and began touring with organist Jack McDuff. Two years later, he took the lead alto chair in the Toshiko Akiyoshi big band, a position he still holds today. Along the way, Snidero worked with a number of important artists, including Frank Sinatra and Eddie Palmieri. While not as well known as he should be, Snidero has maintained an active recording, teaching, and touring schedule. He's recorded as a leader for various overseas labels, most notably Red Records and Criss Cross Jazz, the latter also being a forum for many of his sideman appearances. Snidero makes no apologies for an approach that is within the tradition and focused heavily on his tart and fluid tone. Indeed, his sound has become more individualistic through the years and his heated improvisations never fail to electrify and reward the attentive listener.

what to buy: *Vertigo* ♪♪♪♪ (Criss Cross Jazz, 1996, prod. Gerry Teekens) benefits from the great blend that Snidero shares with tenor ace Walt Weiskopf. There are several Snidero originals and the mood is spirited and bucolic. This is probably among the alto's finest efforts as a leader. *Blue Afternoon* ♪♪♪♪ (Criss Cross Jazz, 1993, prod. Gerry Teekens) features Snidero with front line partner Brian Lynch on trumpet. With Benny Green, Peter Washington, and Marvin "Smitty" Smith on hand, the focus is on spirited hard bop with positive results.

what to buy next: *Mixed Bag* ♪♪♪ (Criss Cross Jazz, 1988, prod. Gerry Teekens) was Snidero's first effort for Criss Cross; an intriguing affair due to the rhythm section, which includes pianist Benny Green and drummer Jeff "Tain" Watts. Snidero's full and robust alto is in fine form on a few originals and some well-selected standards.

the rest:

While You Were Here ♪♪♪♪ (Red, 1994)
Jim Snidero Live ♪♪♪♪ (Red, 1994)
San Juan ♪♪♪♪ (Red, 1997)

worth searching for: *Storm Rising* ♪♪♪♪ (Ken Music, 1990, prod. Jim Snidero, Ken Fujiwara) is a gorgeous quartet session that was available for a short time on the now-defunct Ken

Music label. Worth looking for, this one catches a fine band on a day when everyone was obviously in top shape.

influences:

◄◄ Cannonball Adderley, Jackie McLean, Charlie Parker

Chris Hovan

Soft Machine

Formed 1966, in Canterbury, England.

Daevid Allen, guitar, vocals (1966–67); Robert Wyatt, drums, vocals (1966–71); Kevin Ayers, bass, vocals (1966–68); Mike Ratledge, keyboards (1966–76); Larry Nolan, guitar (1966); Andy Summers, guitar (1968); Hugh Hopper, bass (1967–73); Elton Dean, sax (1969–72); Phil Howard, drums (1971–72); John Marshall, drums (1972–81); Karl Jenkins, sax, piano (1972–79); Alan Holdsworth, guitar (1973–75, 1980–81); John Ethridge, guitar (1975–81); Alan Wakeman, sax (1976); Steve Cooke, bass (1976–79); Rick Sanders, violin (1976–79); Lyn Dobson, sax, flute (1969); Mick Evans, trombone (1969); Mark Charig, cornet (1969).

Soft Machine formed in 1966 out of the seminal Canterbury group Wilde Flowers. The earliest lineup included Robert Wyatt and Kevin Ayers (both from Wilde Flowers) along with Daevid Allen and Mike Ratledge. Guitarist Larry Nolan was also in the band in its earliest days. He was later replaced for a short period in 1968 by Andy Summers (later, of the Police) before a stint with Eric Burdon and the Animals. In their initial period, the group earned a reputation as one of the prominent British psychedelic bands by playing at London venues like UFO and the Roundhouse (with the likes of Pink Floyd and Tomorrow). Their brand of psychedelia lent itself to long improvisational jams.

By the time of their debut album, *Soft Machine*, the group had trimmed down to the trio of Wyatt, Ayers, and Ratledge. For their second album, *Volume 2*, they were still a trio, but bassist Hugh Hopper replaced Ayers. Various shifts in personnel occurred on subsequent albums. Their *Third* album, containing jazz elements, added Elton Dean, and *Fourth* featured the same lineup. In the interim, Wyatt was replaced by Phil Howard on drums. But before Howard had a chance to enter the studio with the group, John Marshall entered the picture and, with him as drummer, the band released the predictably entitled *Fifth* album. After two lackluster albums, *Six* was a step in a more positive direction, showcasing the current lineup in both the studio and live performances. By this time Dean had left the group and been replaced by Karl Jenkins on saxophone and piano. After their *Seven* album, featuring Marshal, Ratledge,

Jenkins, and new bassist Roy Babbington, the band switched affiliations to the Harvest label. During this period, they issued two more studio albums and a live LP before calling it quits in 1979. The band later re-formed to record a final studio album released in 1981 before putting the group to rest once and for all.

what to buy: *Third* 𝄞𝄞𝄞 (Columbia, 1970/1991, prod. Soft Machine) was perhaps the band's shining moment. This was their first release that would really get them classified in the jazz genre. While the whole band is at peak form, the newly added Elton Dean has some stellar moments on saxophone. The original LP contained only one track per side and showed off the long jazz-oriented jams for which the band had become famous.

what to buy next: *Six* 𝄞𝄞𝄞 (CBS, 1973/One Way Records, 1996, prod. Soft Machine) shows both the studio and live concert sides of the band. This was the first album to include the sax and piano work of Karl Jenkins.

what to avoid: Stay away from *Land of Cockayne* 𝄞 (Harvest, 1981/One Way Records, 1996, prod. Mike Thorne); it probably would have been better for the group to have stayed in mothballs than to reunite and issue this bland collection of tunes. *Fourth* 𝄞𝄞 (CBS, 1971/1995, prod. Soft Machine) and *Fifth* 𝄞𝄞 (CBS, 1972, prod. Soft Machine) were, respectively, Wyatt's last and Marshall's first recording with the group. Neither album is much to write home about.

best of the rest:

Soft Machine 𝄞𝄞𝄞 (Probe, 1968/One Way Records, 1993)
Volume 2 𝄞𝄞𝄞 (Probe, 1969)
Six 𝄞𝄞𝄞 (CBS, 1973/One Way Records, 1993)
Seven 𝄞𝄞 (CBS, 1973/One Way Records, 1996)
Bundles 𝄞𝄞𝄞 (Harvest, 1975)
Softs 𝄞𝄞 (Harvest, 1976/See For Miles, 1995)
At the Beginning (Charley, 1977)
Alive and Well—Recorded in Paris 𝄞𝄞𝄞 (Harvest, 1978/See For Miles, 1995)

worth searching for: *Triple Echo* 𝄞𝄞𝄞𝄞 (Harvest, 1977, prod. various) is a triple LP that consists of two albums of material from other LPs as well as both sides of their debut single. The third album features BBC radio sessions produced for the program Top Gear. These sessions also document the short period in 1969 when the band was a seven-piece outfit.

influences:

◄◄ Wilde Flowers

►► Gong, Caravan, Matching Mole, 801, Quiet Sun

Chris Meloche

Martial Solal

Born August 23, 1927, in Algiers, North Africa.

In some ways, Martial Solal is France's answer to Oscar Peterson. He's a tremendous technician influenced by Art Tatum, and like Peterson, has been lambasted by critics for using too many notes. Unlike Peterson, he does not have a plethora of in-print material available in the U.S. He is not as deeply rooted in jazz tradition as Peterson, but is a more adventurous composer. Classically trained, Solal worked in Algiers before moving to Paris in 1950. He became internationally known for his appearances at night clubs and jazz festivals in the United States during the 1960s and has played with some jazz legends, including Django Reinhardt, Don Byas, Lucky Thompson, Kenny Clarke, Sidney Bichet, Lee Konitz, and Stephane Grappelli. Solal has also been active in the French movie industry, scoring over 30 films.

what to buy: Solal performs several standards solo on *Bluesine* ♫♫♫♫ (Soul Note, 1983, prod. Giovanni Bonandrini). The interpretations are very good and filled with Solal's typically difficult and dense passages. *Bluesine* is a well thought out and intelligent recording with some enjoyable fiery moments.

the rest:
Duo in Paris ♫♫♫ (Dreyfus, 1975)
Martial Solal Big Band ♫♫♫♪ (Dreyfus, 1984)

influences:
◀◀ Fats Waller, Oscar Peterson, Art Tatum, Bud Powell

Paul MacArthur

Muggsy Spanier

Born Francis Joseph Spanier, November 9, 1906, in Chicago, IL. Died February 12, 1967, in Sausalito, CA.

Muggsy Spanier played coronet in a predictable, melody-based style from the time he began his professional career in 1921 with Elmer Schoebel's band. Spanier first recorded in 1924, performed with Chicago dance bands until 1929, and became absorbed in the school of white musicians developing the Chicago swing style, such as clarinetist Frank Teschemacher, pianist Jess Stacy, tenor saxman Bud Freeman, and guitarist/banjo player Eddie Condon. Spanier became one of the finest players in Chicago and was present on many famous recording sessions, including those by the Chicago Rhythm Kings with Red McKenzie. But the Depression hit and Spanier and scores of other musicians were looking for work. Spanier joined Ted Lewis's novelty orchestra as a prime soloist (along with bandmates Jimmy Dorsey, George Brunis, Benny Goodman, and others who passed through the band), played the Kit Cat Club in London with the orchestra (1930), and performed in two films with this band in 1929 and 1935. After he replaced Harry James in Ben Pollack's orchestra at the end of 1936, Spanier, playing a gig in New Orleans, became ill (some sources say it was too much alcohol; others claim he had surgery for a serious illness) and was hospitalized at the Touro Infirmary in New Orleans. Upon his recovery, he headed for Chicago where he opened with his eight-piece Ragtime Band (considered his best band by historians) at the Sherman Hotel's Old Town Room on April 29, 1939. The group recorded 16 performances for RCA's Bluebird label that were later dubbed "the Great 16" because they virtually defined the New Orleans revival movement and made the band popular in the United States and Europe. In spite of performances in Chicago and New York, the demand for big bands was increasing, and the small group disbanded for lack of work after 18 months. Spanier briefly rejoined Lewis, led a recording group in 1940 with Sidney Bechet (the Big Four), and played in Bob Crosby's Bob Cats band (1940–41). Leaving Crosby, he formed a successful big band of his own between 1941 and 1943, and subsequently played in small New Orleans–style groups (often as leader) and with Earl Hines during the 1950s. He toured Europe in 1960, played the Newport Festival in 1964 (though not in good health) and a few other gigs before his death in 1967.

what to buy: *The Ragtime Band Sessions* ♫♫♫♫ (Bluebird, 1939/1995, reissue prod. Orrin Keepnews) contains lovingly restored, rare reissues of "the Great 16," the New Orleans–styled tunes that made his Ragtime Band popular. This CD contains the original 16 classic sides, plus alternate takes, bringing the total to 24. Sound quality is perfect as Spanier delivers his brawny big-tone solos and melody leads that inspired his sidemen and lifted the swinging band off the ground. With recordings to consider, Spanier had tinkered with personnel, and after Bob Casey was switched from guitar to bass, the band swung hard (you'll hear booming pulse on these tunes). The clarinet of Rod Cless was also critical to the band sound and his solos are exquisite. Included among the 16 classics are "Big Butter and Egg Man" (two takes), "I Wish I Could Shimmy Like My Sister Kate," "Dippermouth Blues," "Livery Stable Blues (Barnyard Blues)," "Dinah," and other delightful romps.

what to buy next: *Muggshot* ♫♫♫♫ (ASV, 1924–1942/1993) contains chronologically organized samples of Spanier's playing with a variety of bands, including some live-recorded sides of his orchestra in New York in 1939. Classics such as "I've

Found a New Baby," recorded in 1928 by the Chicago Rhythm Kings, feature Spanier and players such as Frank Teschemacher, Mezz Mezzrow, Eddie Condon, Gene Krupa, and other luminaries of the Chicago swing style. Among the bands highlighting Spanier are the Bucktown Five (a 1924 side with Volley DeFaut on clarinet), Ray Miller and His Orchestra (1929), Mound City Blues Blowers (1931), Bechet-Spanier Big Four (1939), and Bob Crosby and His Bob Cats (1942). Classic tunes performed by these groups include "Royal Garden Blues," "The Darktown Strutters' Ball," "Relaxin' at the Touro" (an original by Spanier and Buskin), and "Hesitatin' Blues." Spanier is not always featured as prominently on these recordings as he is on the album recommended above, but the 24 tunes, all original takes, are interesting for their historical merit.

best of the rest:

Muggsy Spanier 1939–1942 🎵🎵🎵 (Jazz Chronological Classics, 1939–42/1994)

Muggsy Spanier 1944 🎵🎵🎵 (Jazz Chronological Classics, 1944/1997)

influences:

◀◀ Joe "King" Oliver, Louis Armstrong

Nancy Ann Lee

Spanish Fly
/Sex Mob

Formed in New York, NY.

Spanish Fly: Steven Bernstein, trumpet, slide trumpet, cornet, flugelhorn, vocals; David Tronzo, electric slide guitar, prepared guitar; Marcus Rojas, tuba, tuba percussion, tuba singing. Sex Mob: Steven Bernstein, slide trumpet; Briggan Krauss, alto sax; Tony Scherr, acoustic bass; Kenny Wollesen, drums.

Spanish Fly is a unique collective trio on the downtown N.Y.C. scene that mixes loose arrangements and free improvisation and is dedicated to the proposition that humor and avant-garde jazz are not musically exclusive (Rahsaan Roland Kirk and Lester Bowie are the attitudinal forefathers of this music). All three members have impressive resumés. Bernstein is music director of the Lounge Lizards and worked with head Lizard John Lurie on the soundtrack of *Get Shorty*. He also wrote arrangements for the band in Robert Altman's *Kansas City* and was musical director of the group when it later toured. His session credits range from hip-hop/acid jazz trio Digable Planets to jazz/klezmer clarinetist Don Byron (*Bug Music*), Carla Bley's Very Big Band, and two Medeski, Martin & Wood albums. Rojas has been a member of Howard Johnson's Gravity, Philip John

ston's Big Trouble, Henry Threadgill's Very Very Circus, and the Jazz Passengers. Tronzo (who tends to go by just his last name) is a fellow occasional Jazz Passenger and Big Trouble–maker and has recorded with David Sanborn (*Another Hand*) and Leni Stern (*Secrets*). Drummer Ben Perowsky often joins the group, which flits from funk to New Orleans parade music to klezmer to free improv in an appealing amalgam of styles that somehow manages not to fly apart from centrifugal force.

Bernstein also leads Sex Mob, a quartet of players with equally impressive C.V.s that tends to feature even more guest appearances. The tendency to groove long and hard makes this group a bit more stylistically coherent, and the many cover tunes drawn from across the whole history of pop and jazz are rearranged in Frankensteinian style with infectious affection.

what to buy: Spanish Fly's *Rags to Britches* 🎵🎵🎵 (Knitting Factory, 1993, prod. Hal Willner) ignores genre boundaries to incorporate funky off-kilter grooves, dirges, Hendrix and Ellington tunes, and plenty of outside spice. Their delicate yet oddly resilient contraptions contain many unusual sonic effects, not just from the juxtaposition of the three superbly balanced instrumental sounds but also from such techniques as Rojas singing through his instrument and banging on it, and some very metallic effects from Tronzo—though there's nothing pretentious or impenetrable about these methods. Ben Perowsky contributes drums and percussion on three of the 13 numbers.

what to buy next: Spanish Fly's *Fly by Night* 🎵🎵🎵 (Accurate, 1996) combines music written for a ballet with an old limited-edition EP (*Insert Tongue Here*); Perowsky is a regular presence. Some tracks are as abstract as these guys get—make no mistake, the frequent humor subtracts nothing from their deep musicality. Tronzo Trio's *Roots* 🎵🎵🎵 (Knitting Factory Works, 1994, prod. Tronzo, Jimi Zhivago) busts slide guitar out of the confines of blues into indefinable realms. On this instrumental album, mostly with electric bassist Stomu Takeishi and drummer Jeff Hirshfield, Tronzo (who also plays the similar dobro) covers Irma Thomas, Thelonious Monk, Duke Ellington, and Eddie Harris for funky context, but it's his originals that break new ground. Underpinned by bass and drums, he twists together blues, jazz, and the avant-garde interest in pure sound to produce a knotty yet accessible style all his own.

worth searching for: Sex Mob's *Din of Inequity* is scheduled for release as this is written. Then again, it's been scheduled for over a year—guys this in-demand have trouble getting together in the studio. Who knows if the title will even be the same when it's finally issued? But based on the group's live shows, where they've turned "The Macarena" into a spooky good time, and the promo single *Sign of the Times* ♫♫♫♫ (Knitting Factory Works, 1998), which deconstructs the Prince hit of the same title and the Paul McCartney Bond movie theme "Live and Let Die," the full-length CD will be a wild ride where some of the songs played will wake up in the hospital asking, "What hit me?"

influences:

◀◀ Art Ensemble of Chicago, Lounge Lizards, Kamikaze Ground Crew, Lester Bowie's Brass Fantasy

▶▶ Babkas

Steve Holtje

Glenn Spearman

Born February 14, 1947, in New York, NY.

After being introduced to the "free" music of late-period John Coltrane and the energy players of the mid-1960s, by 1969 tenor saxophonist Glenn Spearman had begun playing in San Francisco and Los Angeles with Charles Tyler, Donald Garrett, and Butch and Wilbur Morris. Then someone turned him on to Frank Wright. He traveled to Paris to hook up with Wright, and the elder saxist kind of took him on as a protégé. Spearman stayed on in Europe, living in Rotterdam for four years. In 1977, he met Cecil Taylor through Wright, and inspired by Taylor, moved to New York by 1978. There he worked with Taylor's trumpeter Raphe Malik, and in 1981 returned to the Bay Area and began a lifelong partnership with drummer Donald Robinson.

After Spearman released a powerful set of duets with Robinson, *Night after Night*, he worked with Taylor on a number of projects, and in the subsequent years collaborated with players like William Parker, Bill Dixon, and Paul Murphy. In 1990, he founded the Double Trio with Robinson, bassist Ben Lindgren, pianist Chris Brown, percussionist William Winant, and Rova saxophonist Larry Ochs. In 1994, Lisle Ellis replaced Lindgren on the upright. In late 1995, Spearman teamed up with Marco Eneidi to co-lead a 21-piece Creative Music Orchestra, roughly derived from Cecil Taylor's large-scale efforts.

Spearman once told this writer, "I'm never gonna stop playing this way," referring to how he often dives into screaming improvisation after the first few bars. One can hear this resolve at work on any of his recordings, and on the most recent two with his acclaimed Double Trio, *Smokehouse* and *The Fields*, his execution is startlingly acute.

what to buy: *The Fields* ♫♫♫♫ (Black Saint, 1996 , prod. Don Paul, Larry Ochs) is one of the most fiery jazz records of the decade. Compositions by both Spearman and Ochs fuel mighty improvisations from the entire ensemble. The addition of Ellis, an amazingly intuitive player, provides a much more attuned harmonic foundation for the solo flights of Spearman and Ochs. On *Smokehouse* ♫♫♫♫ (Black Saint, 1994, prod. Larry Ochs), The Double Trio's energetic concept fully comes together for the first time on disc. A couple of live tracks typify the group's explosive concert performances.

the rest:

(With Double Trio) *Mystery Project* ♫♫♫♪ (Black Saint, 1994)
(With Paul Murphy, William Parker as Trio Hurricane) *Suite of Winds* ♫♫♫♪ (Black Saint, 1994)
(With Marco Eneidi) *Creative Music Orchestra* ♫♫♫♪ (Music & Arts, 1997)

worth searching for: *Night after Night* ♫♫♫♫ (Musa–Physics, 1981, prod. Glenn Spearman) offers impressive duets with drummer Donald Robinson for which Spearman has been called John Coltrane to Robinson's Rashied Ali. Still available in a vinyl-only format, the saxophonist augments his tenor playing with a rare appearance on bass clarinet.

influences:

◀◀ John Coltrane, Frank Wright, Cecil Taylor

Sam Prestianni

Sphere

Formed 1979, in New York, NY. Disbanded 1988.

Charlie Rouse (died 1988), tenor saxophone; Kenny Barron, piano; Buster Williams, bassist; Ben Riley, drums.

With the exception of pianist Kenny Barron, all of Sphere's members had an association with Thelonious Monk, most notably Charlie Rouse, whose idiosyncratic tenor playing was a major factor in Monk's band from 1959 until 1970. The group's debut album, in 1982, was successful enough to ensure the continuance of Sphere as a side project to the members' other gigs. What started out as a living memorial to Monk's music later grew to include other material from the heyday of bebop and originals by group members. With Rouse's death in 1988, the group ceased performing.

what to buy: *Sphere on Tour* ♫♫♫♫ (Red, 1985, prod. Giovanni Bonandrini) is a well-played document of Sphere in concert, with plenty of musicianship to go around. Even if it lacks the last bit of energy and inspiration that many of the group's earlier releases displayed, *Sphere on Tour* is still a solid album with a particularly charming version of "Well You Needn't."

what to buy next: *Pumpkins Delight* ♫♫♫ (Red, 1986, prod. Alberto Alberti, Sergio Veschi, Umbria Jazz Festival staff) is another good concert by the band, recorded this time at the Umbria Jazz Festival. The band had evolved past its roots in the Monk canon to include material written by the members. Buster Williams's "Christina" is a fine ballad deserving of more performances but, while the rest of the songs all have their points, the date never gets beyond solid to inspirational.

worth searching for: Sphere's best recordings are all out of print. The band's first album, *Four in One* ♫♫♫♫ (Elektra/Musician, 1982), is a marvelous collection of Monk tunes including the title piece and a nifty version of "Eronel." *Bird Songs* ♫♫♫♫ (Verve, 1988) features material either composed by or closely associated with Charlie Parker and also served as a valedictory salute to tenor man Rouse, who died just prior to the album's release.

influences:

◄◄ Thelonious Monk, Charlie Parker

Garaud MacTaggart

Spirit of Life Ensemble
Formed 1975.

Founder/leader Daoud-David Williams, percussion; Clifford Adams, trombone, vocals; Mamdouh Bahri, guitar; Tony Branker, trumpet; Everald Brown, congas; Greg Bufford, drums; Beldon Bullock, bass; Winston Byrd, trumpet; Bryan Carrott, vibraphone; Richard Clements, piano; Michael Cochran, piano; Ted Curson, trumpet; Carlos D. De-Saixas, trombone, percussion; Carlos Francis, trumpet; Mark Gross, alto/tenor saxophones, flute; Onaje Allen Gumbs, piano; Cleve Guyton, alto sax, flute; Darryl M. Hall, bass; Winard Harper, drums; Talib Kibwe, alto/soprano saxophones, musical director; Marcus McLaurine, bass; Jann Parker, vocals; Patrick Rickman, trumpet; James Stewart, tenor sax.

The Spirit of Life Ensemble, founded in 1975 by leader/percussionist Daoud-David Williams, is now a collective of about 40 musicians, about half of whom perform on a fairly regular basis and include outstanding players such as saxophonist Talib Kibwe (who serves as music director), and other talented musicians mentioned above. Williams apprenticed in groups led by Charles Tyler, Pharoah Sanders, Ted Curson, Phillip Harper, Ryo Kawasaki, Onage Allen Gumbs, Victor Jones, Malachi Thompson, and other leaders. His band grew out of an arts coalition in

Jersey City, the Ascension Workshop, and their modern, dynamically exciting creations draw from a wide spectrum of jazz and world music. Since mid-1995, they have performed regularly at the Sweet Basil Jazz Club in New York's Greenwich Village, every Monday night as the house big band, usually with a 10- to 18-member group. The band has its own label, Rise Up Productions, for which they recorded their first album in 1984, and they have recorded four more albums, three of which are available on CD. Although the band tours internationally, they maintain their ties to the Jersey City community in outreach programs and appearances in area schools and colleges.

what to buy: Recorded during live performances at the 5 Spot in New York City on May 12–13, 1995, *Live! At the 5 Spot* ♫♫♫♫♫ (Rise Up Productions, 1996, prod. Talib Kibwe, James Stewart, Mamdouh Bahri, Kenny Mead) demonstrates just how explosive this band can be with all their colorful and catchy rhythms. There are no weak tracks among the nine tunes. Fresh takes on standards such as "Caravan," "Nature Boy," "Moanin'," and other rhythmically challenging charts keep things moving along swiftly. This band creates abundant excitement with their spirited traditional mix of Afro-Cuban rhythms spiked with bebop and modern jazz elements, well-written arrangements performed with cohesion and liveliness, and all the hardy blowing from the soloists. This is a most tantalizing listen that matches bands such as Dizzy Gillespie's and others that have mastered similar musical blends.

what to buy next: A versatile album, though less fiery than *Live! At the 5 Spot*, *Live at Pori Jazz* ♫♫♫♫ (Rise Up Productions, 1997, prod. Ted Curson) features a Spirit of Life 16-member ensemble performing a mixture of eight standards and originals by band members. Recorded at the 1996 Pori Jazz Festival in Finland, their exhilarating musical tapestry weaves Afro-Cuban and Latin rhythms with various elements of jazz, with soloists frequently injecting their improvisations with playful "quotes" from familiar tunes. There's a bundle of talent in this band, and the musicians work their way deftly through the straight-up jazz version of "On a Clear Day" (featuring the talented vocalist Jann Parker). They show just as much finesse on reedman Stewart's Mingus-inspired number, "Sneak Out," and perform with exceptional flair as a unit on the nearly 10-minute "L'Odysee Africane," composed by Talib Kibwe. With Jann Parker and her phenomenal vocal range, expert sense of time, and relaxed phrasing, you have one helluva listen.

the rest:

Inspirations ♫♫♫ (Zazou/Rise Up Productions, 1992)

influences:

◀◀ Dizzy Gillespie, Paquito D'Rivera

Nancy Ann Lee

Victoria Spivey

Born October 15, 1906, in Houston, TX. Died October 3, 1976, in New York, NY.

You can hear Victoria Spivey winking along to her powerful, deceptively agile piano-pounding as she sings songs like "Let's Ride Tonight," "I Got Men All over This Town," and "I'm a Red Hot Mama." Borrowing innuendo from Bessie Smith and a ragtime piano style from Scott Joplin himself, Spivey was a popular Texas performer in the late 1920s, and a pal of well-known guitarist Lonnie Johnson, with whom she recorded several duets. In her early career years, her playing also crossed over into jazz and she recorded using jazz sidemen such as Louis Armstrong and Red Allen. After appearing in the 1929 film *Hallelujah,* the singer-songwriter spent most of the 1930s in vaudeville where she fronted Lloyd Hunter's orchestra on tour. In the 1940s she toured with the Olsen and Johnson musical revue *Hellzapoppin',* which toured following release of the 1941 Universal film. She continued to perform for a while after moving to Harlem, but retired in 1952 to take care of her family. In the early 1960s, she reunited with Johnson, appeared with Turk Murphy's band, recorded a few albums, and became a reasonably popular personality in guest radio and club appearances.

what to buy: *Woman Blues!* ✔✔✔✔ (Bluesville/Original Blues Classics, 1961, prod. Kenneth Goldstein, Len Kunstadt) is her reunion album with Lonnie Johnson, and it's really fun. Spivey seems delighted to be recording, her piano dances eloquently with Johnson's smooth guitar, and despite the presence of the festive "Christmas without Santa Claus," the songs are subtly (and not-so-subtly, as in the blatantly man-trapping "I Got Men All over This Town") sexy.

what to buy next: *And Her Blues, Vol. 2* ✔✔✔ (Spivey, 1972), recorded on Spivey's own label, is a tour of her jazz material from 1961 to 1972; it's not as energetic as *Woman Blues!* but still a nice document of a great singer and pianist.

the rest:
Complete Recorded Works—Vol. 1 (1926–27) ✔✔✔ (Document, 1995)
Complete Recorded Works—Vol. 2 (1927–29) ✔✔✔ (Document, 1995)
Complete Recorded Works—Vol. 3 (1929–36) ✔✔✔ (Document, 1995)
Complete Recorded Works—Vol. 4 (1936–37) ✔✔✔ (Document, 1995)

worth searching for: Spivey's first two "comeback" albums, *Idle Hours* ✔✔✔ (Bluesville, 1961), with Johnson, and *Songs We Taught Your Mother* ✔✔✔✔ (Bluesville, 1961), with fellow blueswomen Alberta Hunter and Lucille Hagamin and a big jazz band, are tough to find but important documents of her career progression.

influences:

◀◀ Bessie Smith, Scott Joplin, Art Tatum, Lonnie Johnson

▶▶ Katie Webster, Saffire—The Uppity Blues Women, Koko Taylor, Ray Charles, Sippie Wallace, Hadda Brooks, Alberta Hunter

Steve Knopper and Nancy Ann Lee

Splatter Trio

Formed 1987, in San Francisco, CA.

Gino Robair, percussion, electronics; Myles Boisen, doubleneck electric guitar/bass, casio; Dave Barrett, multiple saxophones, saxcello, ocarina, DX-7.

Splatter Trio sounds like no other creative-music ensemble. Slaves to no genre and butchers of most (as the band name suggests), the threesome tends to smash riffs, beats, and atmospheres and spray the fragments into constantly morphing sound shapes. Whether interpreting original compositions or improvising freely, when in peak performance, Splatter's scattered collisions give the music an extraordinary edge. Each member of the band employs a variety of extended techniques to stretch the improvisational possibilities: Dave Barrett sometimes blows multiple horns at once; Myles Boisen often applies metallic files and other devices to his custom doubleneck; and Gino Robair makes his cymbals sing with a bow and uses a gang of noise-makers (from marbles to dog toys to small motors) to expand his percussive range. In the past year, the group began investigating musical forms previously out of reach by performing live to its own improvisations, pumped through a club's sound system from a pair of preprogrammed CD players. Beyond their collective efforts as a trio (and individual collaborations with artists like the Rova Saxophone Quartet, Anthony Braxton, and Club Foot Orchestra), Robair ran the Dark Circle Lounge creative-music series at San Francisco's Hotel Utah for three years and heads Rastascan Records, while Boisen runs the Guerrilla Euphonics recording studio. (At present, the trio is on hiatus for a couple of years—though it did appear at the Knitting Factory's 1997 New York Jazz Festival—while Barrett sojourns in Mexico.)

what to buy: Combining the exploratory energy of punk kids on their first four-track with the musical savvy of world-class improvisers, for *Hi-Fi Junk Note* ✍✍✍✍ (Rastascan, 1995, prod. the Splatter Trio) the Splatter Trio exploded genres and let Boisen reconstruct the debris with deft computer editing. He whittled 12 Digital Audio Tapes of multi-jointed improvisations into 56 minutes that recall the machine madness of Survival Research Laboratories and the hyper-real intensity of a Peter Greenaway film. Open meter and timbral nuance supersede the usual fare of notes, chords, and classic time signatures. Post-modern fragments from all over the musical map are warped into a cohesive dynamic of haunting electronics, avant-garde blowing, and off-kilter rhythms. *Jump or Die—Splatter Trio & Debris Play Braxton* ✍✍✍✍✍ (Music & Arts, 1994, prod. Gino Robair, Steve Norton), a historic recording, is the only known instance of a band interpreting compositions from Anthony Braxton's complex oeuvre using only the composer's scores and the musicians' instincts. Splatter Trio, Boston quintet Debris, and Randy McKean, Tom Plsek, and Gregg Bendian work as a remarkable collective, shifting the personnel to fit the pieces, some of which are superimposed with both acoustic and electronic instrumentation.

what to buy next: *The Splatter Trio* ✍✍✍✍ (Rastascan, 1989, prod. the Splatter Trio), the band's striking debut, documents its earliest scored pieces, which pack all the excitement and unpredictability of the improvisations into a concise, tight (but flexible) song-based format. *Anagrams* ✍✍✍✍ (Rastascan, 1992, prod. the Splatter Trio) is a heady recording of mostly improvised pieces (with a sprinkling of pre-written songs, including the delirious "Tango Big Boy" and antic "Splatter vs. the Titans"). Ralph Carney, Steve Clarke, and Fred Lonberg-Holm guest as a trumpet trio on "Matching Tye."

the rest:
Fistful of Dewey ✍✍ (Racer, 1992)

solo outings:
Myles Boisen:
Guitarspeak ✍✍✍✍ (Rastascan, 1994)

Gino Robair:
(With Anthony Braxton) *Duets, 1987* ✍✍✍✍ (Rastascan, 1987)
Other Destinations ✍✍✍✍ (Rastascan, 1989)
(With Oluyemi Thomas) *Unity in Multiplicity* ✍✍✍ (Rastascan, 1996)
(With Miya Masaoka & Tom Nunn) *Crepuscular Music* ✍✍✍✍ (Rastascan, 1996)
Singular Pleasures ✍✍✍ (Rastascan, 1997)

influences:
◀◀ Ornette Coleman, Anthony Braxton

▶▶ The Bay Area creative-music community

Sam Prestianni

Spyro Gyra
Formed 1975.

Jay Beckenstein, saxophones (1975–present); Jeremy Wall, keyboards (1975–78); Tom Schuman, keyboards (1978–present); Rick Strauss, guitars (1977–78); Fred Rapillo, guitars (1978); Chet Catallo, guitars (1978–84); Julio Fernandez, guitars (1984–89 and 1991–present); Jay Azzolina, guitars (1989–90); Tom Walsh, drums (1975–77); Duffy Fornes, drums (1977); Ted Reinhardt, drums (1977–78); Eli Konikoff, drums (1978–84); Richie Morales, drums (1984–90); Tony Cintron, drums (1990); Joel Rosenblatt, drums (1991–present); Jim Kurzdorfer, bass (1975–80); David Wofford, bass (1980–83); Kim Stone, bass (1983–86); Roberto Vally, bass (1987); Oscar Cartaya, bass (1988–91); Scott Ambush, bass (1992–present); Dave Samuels, vibes, marimba (1983–93); Emile Umbopha Latimer, percussion (1976–77); Gerardo Velez, percussion (1978–85); Manolo Badrena, percussion (1986–87); Marc Quinones, percussion (1989–90).

There are two Spyro Gyras. One is a fantastic live contemporary-jazz band that plays a good collection of songs, takes risks, and shows off considerable jazz chops. The other is a record-making machine, and the most commercially successful jazz band of the past 20 years. It produces tight albums and is often lambasted by critics for its commercialism (something an early '80s *Down Beat* interview with Beckenstein did little to negate). Spyro Gyra (a misspelling of spirogyra, a scientific term for pond scum algae) was formed c. 1974 by saxophonist Jay Beckenstein and keyboardist Jeremy Wall. In 1978, the band's eponymous debut album was well received and a commercial success, but the subsequent album, *Morning Dance*, started Spyro Gyra's climb to a steady, top-selling jazz act.

The band's frequent cast changes have led to some interesting turns over the years. The mid-'80s stuff is more fusion, less R&B than the earlier work, and the mid- to late '90s material is more commercial and less adventurous. Spyro Gyra will best be remembered as a band that broke commercial barriers with catchy melodies and pleasant arrangements at a time when fusion was losing the attention of the masses and its first generation of players.

what to buy: *Access All Areas* ✍✍✍ (Amherst, 1984, prod. Jay Beckenstein, Richard Calandra) is a collection of peak live performances with the band playing some of the better songs from its first seven years. Unfortunately, the CD reissue omits "Old

San Juan" from the original LP release. *Morning Dance* 𝄞𝄞𝄞𝄞 (Amherst, 1979, prod. Jay Beckenstein, Richard Calandra), one of the best-selling jazz albums of all time, includes the pop-classic title track and the great "Starburst." While many of the compositions and instrumentation do not stand up well over time, the soloing is good. *Catching the Sun* 𝄞𝄞𝄞𝄞 (MCA, 1980, prod. Jay Beckenstein, Richard Calandra), Spyro Gyra's third outing, continued its refinement. On *Breakout* 𝄞𝄞𝄞𝄞 (Amherst, 1986, prod. Jay Beckenstein, Richard Calandra), the title track and "Bob Goes to the Store" (an even better live tune) are some of the standouts.

what to buy next: The debut, *Spyro Gyra* 𝄞𝄞𝄞 (Amherst, 1978, prod. Jay Beckenstein, Richard Calandra), created the map for the group's next 20 years. Some songs are banal, some dated, but the ones that survive, like "Cascade" and "Leticia," have better soloing—and a sense of tension and release missing from much of the band's output since the early '90s. *Alternating Currents* 𝄞𝄞𝄞 (Amherst, 1985, prod. Jay Beckenstein, Richard Calandra) includes "Shakedown," one of Spyro Gyra's best songs. *Rites of Summer* 𝄞𝄞𝄞𝄞 (GRP, 1988, prod. Jay Beckenstein) breaks free of the typical Spyro Gyra mold with a more modern sound and a Yellowjackets-influenced tone. *Three Wishes* 𝄞𝄞𝄞𝄞 (GRP, 1992, prod. Jay Beckenstein), one of Spyro Gyra's better '90s albums, contains more interesting compositions and arrangements than usual for the group, with more emphasis on melodic playing.

what to avoid: You'd be safe to fast forward past the banal *Fast Forward* 𝄞𝄞 (GRP, 1990). *Dreams beyond Control* 𝄞 (GRP, 1993, prod. Jay Beckenstein) is even more commercial than normal, with some awful vocals. It's geared toward commerce and little else.

the rest:
Carnival 𝄞𝄞𝄞 (Amherst, 1980)
Freetime 𝄞𝄞𝄞 (Amherst, 1981)
Incognito 𝄞𝄞𝄞 (Amherst, 1982)
City Kids 𝄞𝄞𝄞 (Amherst, 1983)
Stories without Words 𝄞𝄞𝄞 (Amherst, 1987)
Point of View 𝄞𝄞𝄞 (GRP, 1989)
Love & Other Obsessions 𝄞𝄞 (GRP, 1995)
Heart of the Night 𝄞𝄞 (GRP, 1996)
20/20 𝄞𝄞 (GRP, 1997)

influences:
◀◀ Weather Report, Crusaders
▶▶ Yellowjackets, Wishful Thinking, C'est What

Paul MacArthur

Mary Stallings

Born in San Francisco, CA.

Long one of the most gifted, swinging vocalists in jazz, Mary Stallings spent decades as a local San Francisco legend before reestablishing her national profile in the mid-1990s. Like Carol Sloane with Ella Fitzgerald, Stallings immediately calls to mind Dinah Washington with her bluesy phrasing and penchant for holding long notes at the beginning and end of phrases. But Stallings's voice is a little softer than Washington's and she finds her own insights in lyrics. Stallings knew she wanted to be a singer at a young age, and as a child sang formally in churches and concert settings throughout California. Encouraged by her uncle, saxophonist Orlando Stallings, she listened closely to the great jazz singers. By age 14, Stallings was appearing in Bay Area night clubs and was soon performing with such luminaries as Ben Webster, Cal Tjader, Red Mitchell, Teddy Edwards, and the Montgomery Brothers (Wes, Buddy, and Monk). Before graduating from high school she joined R&B pioneer Louis Jordan's Tympani Five. While singing at San Francisco's Blackhawk nightclub she caught the attention of Dizzy Gillespie, who asked her to join him on several West Coast gigs, culminating in an acclaimed appearance at the 1965 Monterey Jazz Festival. She spent a year in the late 1960s performing in Nevada with Billy Eckstine, and toured with the Count Basie Orchestra from 1969–72. She spent most of the 1970s and 1980s in semi-retirement, though she did a South American tour with Gillespie and worked occasional club dates with pianist Ed Kelly and saxophonist Pharoah Sanders. Since 1994, she has recorded three excellent albums for Concord.

what to buy: One of the best vocal albums of the decade, *Spectrum* 𝄞𝄞𝄞𝄞 (Concord Jazz, 1996, prod. John Burk) features Mary Stallings with a group of tried and true professionals who know what accompanying a singer is all about. Pianist Gerald Wiggins leads the rhythm section with Ron Eschete (guitar), Andy Simpkins (bass), and Paul Humphrey (drums). Trumpeter Harry "Sweets" Edison contributes to six tunes—check out his sly commentary on "No Love, No Nothin'" and perfectly modulated solo on "Day Dream"—and tenor saxophonist Rickey Woodard plays on four tunes. Alan Broadbent provides lovely woodwind charts on "Just as Though You Were Here" and "I Thought About You." Stallings sings with precision and finely calibrated emotional nuance throughout, capturing perfectly the pathos of "Solitude" and the wistfulness of "Some Other Time." A relaxed, highly swinging session highlighted by the combustible chemistry between Stallings and pianist Monty Alexander, *Manhattan Moods* 𝄞𝄞𝄞𝄞 (Concord Jazz, 1997, prod.

Allen Farnham) covers a variety of moods, from the sensuously slow, torchy rendering of the bop anthem "How High the Moon," to the Basie-ish groove of "Sweet and Lovely," to the playfully swinging version of "Surrey with the Fringe on Top." Bassist Ben Wolfe and drummer Clyde Lucas round out the rhythm section, while Hendrik Meurkens adds some gorgeous harmonica work on two tracks and plays vibes on "He Was Too Good to Me." Dick Oatts plays flute on "How High the Moon" and "He Was" and soprano sax on Carroll Coates's "I Have a Feeling." Though often thought of as a Dinah Washington disciple, Stallings's close listening to Billie Holiday shows up on "Ghost of a Chance" and "You Go to My Head."

what to buy next: Stallings's first album for a significant label in 33 years (!), *I Waited for You* ⅃⅃⅃⅃ (Concord Jazz, 1994, prod. Carl E. Jefferson) is a feel-good session with pianist Gene Harris's quartet, featuring Ron Eschete (guitar), Luther Hughes (bass), and Paul Humphrey (drums). Though the presence of horns is sometimes missed, Stallings and Harris share a deep affinity for the blues, and the pianist takes a break from his usual build-to-a-crescendo style to play some highly lyrical passages. Highlights include the two Benny Carter tunes, "Blues in My Heart" and the bossa nova chart of "Only Trust Your Heart," and the wonderfully swinging opener "Where or When."

worth searching for: Though it hasn't been reissued on CD, *Cal Tjader Plays, Mary Stallings Sings* ⅃⅃⅃ (Fantasy/OJC, 1961) is available on LP and cassette and it's an enjoyable session with Stallings singing a host of standards. She and Tjader's band don't have a great rapport but the music is well played and swinging, and she sings with a strong blues feeling.

influences:

◀◀ Dinah Washington, Billie Holiday, Carmen McRae

Andrew Gilbert

Marvin Stamm

Born May 23, 1939, in Memphis, TN.

Trumpeter Marvin Stamm's first big break in jazz came after graduation from North Texas State University, where he was discovered by Stan Kenton. He became Kenton's trumpet soloist for two years, and later toured worldwide with Woody Herman.

Settling in New York in late 1966, Stamm quickly established himself as a busy jazz and studio trumpeter. A member of the Thad Jones/Mel Lewis Jazz Orchestra and the Duke Pearson Big Band, he also recorded with Bill Evans, Quincy Jones, Oliver Nelson, Charles Mingus, Freddie Hubbard, Stanley Turrentine, Frank Foster, and George Benson, among many others. In 1982, eschewing the lucrative studio scene, he focused on playing jazz, and since that time has worked with John Lewis's American Jazz Orchestra, the Bob Mintzer Big Band, the George Gruntz Concert Jazz Band, Louis Bellson's big band and quintet, and, at times, with the big bands of composers Maria Schneider and Rich Shemaria. Active in jazz education, Stamm visits universities and high schools across the U.S. and abroad as a performer, clinician, and mentor. Stamm also continues to lead his own groups.

what's available: Stamm's second MusicMasters session, *Mystery Man* ⅃⅃⅃⅃ (MusicMasters, 1992, prod. Jack Cortner), is a well-conceived and -produced set that features one standard and nine diverse originals by Kenny Wheeler, Lar Jansson, and tenor saxophonist Bob Mintzer. Moving from duo, to quartet, to quintet, to sextet, soloists Stamm and Mintzer and pianist Bill Charlap are soft and tender on "Old Ballad" and "My Funny Valentine" and fluidly ablaze on the 12/8 blues "Giuseppe" and Mintzer's "Re-Re." Throughout, drummer Terry Clarke drives the machine with refined precision, swinging mightily. Stamm's trumpet chops are displayed in abundance as well, but with taste and substance instead of grandstanding. Spirited playing abounds on Marvin Stamm's first recording in the nine years since he returned to full-time jazz playing, *Bop Boy* ⅃⅃⅃⅃ (MusicMasters, 1990, prod. Jack Cortner). Stamm and producer Jack Cortner programmed the set with an eye toward varying tempos and moods, and the material, combined with a high level of musicianship from Stamm and his collaborators (tenor men Bob Mintzer and Bob Malach, pianist Phil Markowitz, bassist Mike Richmond, and drummer Terry Clarke), make *Bop Boy* a real winner. From note one on Mintzer's burning "Reunion" to Kurt Weill's lovely ballad, "My Ship," a duo with Stamm and Markowitz, the emphasis here is on first-rate musicianship and top-notch soloing. *Live at the Yardbird—The Marvin Stamm/Bob Stroup Quintet* ⅃⅃⅃⅃ (Wilson & Stroup Music Group, 1996, prod. Bob Stroup) is a live album, recorded in Edmonton, Alberta. It features Marvin Stamm in a quintet setting with the late Bob Stroup, formerly of Woody Herman's band. The sound of the trumpet/trombone frontline and the usually spirited soloists take this one a notch or two above the usual blowing session. Standards "My Ideal," "Alone," and Miles Davis's "All Blue" are featured here, along with several intriguing originals by Ted Nash and Thad Jones. Trombonist Stroup certainly knew his away around the horn at any tempo, as heard on his original, "The Weenies Are Winning."

influences:

◀◀ Sam Noto, Clifford Brown, Harry James

▶▶ Lew Soloff, Randy Brecker, Sal Marquez, Tom Harrell

Bret Primack

Dakota Staton

Born June 3, 1932, in Pittsburgh, PA.

A dynamic singer whose star rose quickly in the middle 1950s, Dakota Staton has never attained the notoriety deserving of her talent. She studied at the Filion School of Music in Pittsburgh and sang professionally with her sisters as well as singing with her brother's orchestra. Moving to New York, Dakota took part in a jam session at the Baby Grand club, in Harlem, in 1954. She caused a stir and landed a record contract with Capitol in 1955. With the popularity of her first recording, *The Late, Late Show*, Dakota was voted most promising newcomer by *Down Beat*'s readers. In 1958, she recorded with George Shearing. Moving to Europe in 1965, Dakota performed and spent time in England and Germany. She returned to New York in 1970, and has continued to perform and record on into the 1990s. Sometime between the 1950s and the 1990s, she took the name Aliyah Rabia. No matter what names she uses, the gifted singer's power, stage presence, and natural swingability instantly grab audiences.

what to buy: On the classic recording *The Late, Late Show* ♫♫♫♫ (Capitol, 1957/Collectables, 1991), Staton is showcased at her best, delivering 12 tunes in the sentimental style of 1950s singers. Accompanied by a studio orchestra led by Van Alexander and highlighting pianist Hank Jones and trumpet soloist Jonah Jones, the 1957 studio session captures Staton as she flawlessly and passionately interprets each tune. Though she may remind some folks of Teresa Brewer and other singers of that era, Staton's sound is bigger and her style is all her own as she swings and draws the listener into her world. Tunes include a swinging rendition of "Broadway," a seductive reading of "Summertime," and a great rendition of "A Foggy Day," on which she briefly scats (accompanied by an unidentified trombonist and vibraphonist). Alexander's lovely arrangements are crafted to set off Staton's strong, insightful vocals.

what to buy next: With Manny Albam's brilliant arrangements, Dakota, with a strong voice, fronts the all-star big band with great facility on *Dakota Staton with the Manny Albam Big Band* ♫♫♫♫ (LRC, 1990, prod. Sonny Lester). Highlights include gritty, bluesy versions of "Country Man," "Cry Me a River," and "Confessin' the Blues," among others.

worth searching for: Dakota's deep, husky voice has stood the test of time but many of her albums are unavailable. *Dakota*

Staton ♫♫♫♫ (Muse, 1990, prod. Houston Person) is a great recording that includes her often-used pianist Bross Townsend in addition to tenor saxophonist Houston Person. Search the used bins for that Muse session and also for *Darling Please Save Your Love for Me* ♫♫♫ (Muse, 1991, prod. Houston Person), which finds Staton still in fine form, singing with great emotion and depth. If you come across the Capitol LP version of Staton's 1958 session with George Shearing, *In the Night* (Capitol, 1958), snatch it up. It's not been released on CD.

influences:

◀◀ Billie Holiday, Etta James, Jo Stafford, Nancy Wilson

▶▶ Rosemary Clooney, Blossom Dearie, Cleo Laine

Susan K. Berlowitz

Jeremy Steig

Born September 23, 1943, in New York, NY.

Coming of age in rock and roll's infancy, Jeremy Steig understood that music as well as he did jazz, and that set the tone for a career that has continually crossed boundaries. Steig, the son of artist William Steig, started playing flute when he was 11. By the mid-'60s Steig had added playing with singer-songwriters such as Tim Hardin and Richie Havens to his bag of jazz gigs. Eventually he evolved an interest in electronics as well, and he was on the cutting edge of fusion music through the '70s. Today he alternates between a mature, reflective sound and a funkier groove. A virtuoso who also plays piccolo and bass flute, Steig has played with the likes of Joe Henderson, Eddie Palmieri, Yoko Ono, and Tommy Bolin. He has worked often with bass player Eddie Gomez, having a fine affinity for Gomez's evocative, creamy style.

what's available: *Jigsaw* ♫♫♫ (Triloka, 1992, prod. Walter Becker, Mitchell Markus, K.D. Kagel, Paul A. Sloman) is the album still in print that best displays Steig's range as a leader and composer. The players include Lee Ann Ledgerwood on piano, John Beasley on synthesizer, and the guitar of George Wadenius. *Something Else* ♫♫♫ (LaserLight, 1996, prod. Sonny Lester) is a funky outing with a single producer and amounts to a collaboration with keyboard player Jan Hammer. *Outlaws* ♫♫♫ (Enja, 1976, prod. Jeremy Steig, Eddie Gomez) is a more reflective album, the first recorded duo collaboration with Eddie Gomez.

worth searching for: The out-of-print *Music for Flute & Double Bass* ♫♫♫♫ (CMP, 1978, prod. Eddie Gomez, Jeremy Steig) is an even better collaboration between Gomez and Steig. One of the best sessions under Steig's leadership, also now out of print, was *Rain Forest* 🎵🎵🎵🎵 (CMP, 1981, prod. Jeremy Steig), a forward-looking session with Karl Ratzer on electric guitar, Mike Nock on synthesizer and electric piano, Gomez on bass, and Jack DeJohnette on drums, aided and abetted by the Latin percussion of Ray Barretto and Nana Vasconcelos. The Lee Ann Ledgerwood–led session called *You Wish* 🎵🎵🎵🎵 (Triloka, 1991, prod. Walter Becker) is also worth getting. Steig is featured on four tracks to very good effect. Drummer Danny Gottlieb's *Brooklyn Blues* 🎵🎵🎵🎵 (Big World, 1990, prod. Danny Gottlieb) is a virtually straight-ahead session and Steig shines.

influences:

◀◀ Miles Davis, John Coltrane, Bill Evans

▶▶ Hubert Laws, James Newton

Salvatore Caputo

Steps Ahead

Formed 1979.

Michael Brecker, tenor sax (1979–86); Mike Mainieri, vibes (1979–present); Don Grolnick, piano (1979–83); Eliane Elias, piano (1983–84); Warren Bernhardt, piano (1984–86); Eddie Gomez, bass (1979–86); Victor Bailey, bass (1986); Daryl Jones, bass (1986); Tony Levin, bass (1989); Steve Gadd, drums (1979–82); Peter Erskine, drums (1982–86); Steve Smith, drums (1986–92).

Formed originally by vibist Mike Mainieri as an all-star group to tour Japan, Steps Ahead became the most prominent fusion group of the 1980s. Originally called Steps, the core personnel consisted of Mainieri, Michael Brecker, and Eddie Gomez. Each was an experienced session musician capable of fitting into a variety of settings. Because of the diverse backgrounds of the members, the band was able to attract a wide variety of fans. At a time when jazz was struggling more than usual to find a mass audience, Steps Ahead generated a lot of interest. Certain neoconservative contingencies notwithstanding, the band played a vital role in the resurgence of jazz in the early '80s, playing festivals and successful world tours. This was not a collection of soloists content to engage in blowing sessions. This was a group of seasoned vets joining together to make music—its members listened, reacted to, and supported each other. Their sophisticated balance was reminiscent of the Modern Jazz Quartet, though they deftly combined synthesizers and electronic effects with acoustic bass and vibes. With the departure of Brecker, Gomez, and Erskine in 1986 and 1987, the focus shifted to Mainieri and a shifting cast of part-time musicians.

what to buy: *Modern Times* 🎵🎵🎵🎵 (Elektra, 1984, prod. Steps Ahead) highlights the trademark Steps Ahead sound, with terrific interplay among the members, a good mix of jazz and funk, and terrific solos. "Safari" features Mainieri's electric vibes, sequencers, and synthesizers to good effect. "Radioactive" charges ahead with various synthesizer effects, and Brecker's solo is surprisingly motivic.

what to buy next: *Magnetic* 🎵🎵🎵🎵 (Elektra, 1986, prod. Steps Ahead) is the last to include Michael Brecker. He goes out in style, however, with an excellent EWI (Electronic Wind Instrument) version of "In a Sentimental Mood."

what to avoid: *NYC* 🎵🎵 (Intuition, 1989, prod. Mike Mainieri) is the first without Michael Brecker, Eddie Gomez, or Peter Erskine, and the music suffers for it. It's not entirely bad, just inferior in comparison to their previous work.

the rest:
Step by Step 🎵🎵🎵 (Denon, 1980)
Smokin' in the Pit 🎵🎵🎵🎵 (Denon, 1982)
Paradox 🎵🎵🎵 (Denon, 1982)
Yin-Yang 🎵🎵 (NYC, 1992)
Vibe 🎵🎵 (NYC, 1994)
Live in Tokyo 1986 🎵🎵 (NYC, 1995)

worth searching for: *Steps Ahead* 🎵🎵🎵🎵 (Elektra, 1983, prod. Steps Ahead) is similar to *Modern Times* but with Eliane Elias in the piano chair. The U.S. debut demonstrates the subtle combination of acoustic bass and vibes in a semi-fusion setting. Brecker's solos, particularly on "Pools" and "Northern Cross," served as a textbook for a generation of tenor players.

influences:

◀◀ Weather Report, the Brecker Brothers

▶▶ Spyro Gyra, Yellowjackets, Fattburger

James Eason

Mike Stern

Born January 10, 1953, in Boston, MA.

An artist of extraordinary versatility, Mike Stern possesses one of the most distinctive guitar voices in contemporary jazz: an intense, ferocious jazz-rock-blues-inflected roar. At the same time, he can switch gears completely and turn in a performance of delicately lyrical eloquence. Stern first picked up the guitar at age 12; he didn't decide to pursue a career in music until his late teens, when he enrolled in Boston's Berklee College of Music in 1971, studying under such masters as Pat Metheny and Mick Goodrick. In 1976 Stern joined Blood, Sweat, and Tears and met bass master Jaco Pastorius, who became a close friend. Following his two-year stint in Blood, Sweat, and Tears, Stern joined drummer Billy Cobham's fusion band. One night, while the group was performing at New York's Bottom Line club, Miles Davis saw the guitarist and offered him a spot in his band. Stern remained with Davis from 1981 until 1983 (and briefly in 1985), appearing on the albums *The Man with the Horn*, *We Want Miles*, and *Star People*. After leaving Davis's band, Stern played in Pastorius's Word of Mouth ensemble and later in an electrified version of the band Steps Ahead. Stern made his debut as a solo artist in 1986 and has since released eight albums, two of which, *Is What It Is* and *Between the Lines*, earned Grammy nominations. He also performs as a sideman in various groups; in 1986 he joined saxophonist Michael Brecker's quintet, and he appears on the Brecker Brothers' Grammy-nominated 1992 reunion album *Return of the Brecker Brothers*. He has also toured with saxophonist Joe Henderson and recorded with guitarists Jim Hall and Pat Martino.

what to buy: Stern is best known for his contemporary approach, but *Standards (and Other Songs)* ✍✍✍✍ (Atlantic, 1992, prod. Gil Goldstein) demonstrates his facility with straightahead styles. This is a tasteful, gracefully executed collection of standards and Stern originals. Standout tracks include a lovely, spare version of Horace Silver's "Peace" and the captivating original "Lost Time."

what to buy next: *Odds or Evens* ✍✍✍✍ (Atlantic, 1991, prod. Jim Beard) is an example of Stern's effortless versatility and impressive technique. The compositions are inventive and varied, and Beard has effectively set Stern's powerful playing against equally solid rhythms. Standout tunes include the title track, in which an explosive Stern is matched by equally forceful saxophonist Bob Berg; "Seven Thirty," which finds Stern wrapping his guitar sinuously around a loose rhythm; and "Common Ground," a smooth tune that intensifies into a ringing power ballad.

what to avoid: *Time in Place* ✍✍ (Atlantic, 1988, prod. Steve Khan) is not a bad recording, but Stern isn't enough in evidence, preferring to let saxophonists Michael Brecker and Bob Berg drive the album. When he does solo, Stern turns in some solid performances, particularly on "After All" and his pensively eloquent lead on "Before You Go."

the rest:
Upside Downside ✍✍✍✍ (Atlantic, 1986)
Jigsaw ✍✍✍✍ (Atlantic, 1989)
Is What It Is ✍✍✍✍ (Atlantic, 1994)
Between the Lines ✍✍✍ (Atlantic, 1996)
Give and Take ✍✍✍✍ (Atlantic, 1997)

influences:

◀◀ Miles Davis, B.B. King, Jimi Hendrix, Jim Hall, Wes Montgomery

Lucy Tauss

Stetsasonic /Daddy-O /Prince Paul /Gravediggaz

Formed 1981, in Brooklyn, NY.

Daddy-O (born Glenn Bolton), vocals; Delite (born Martin Wright), vocals; Fruitkwan (born Bobby Simmons), vocals, drums; Wise (born Leonard Roman), beatbox; DBC (born Marvin Nemley), keyboards, turntables, drums; Prince Paul (born Paul Houston), turntables, samplers.

If to some hip-hop represented the promise of postmodern method, the ultimate egalitarian fusion of all sounds and genres, then it needed someone to make the commercial leap. So it was up to such innovators as Stetsasonic, billed as the "original hip-hop band," to become the musical recombinant that could demonstrate the range of forms available to the next generation of sampler-dependent producers and post-hip-hop instrumentalists. It's no surprise that it would be Stet that would summarize hip-hop's musical strategy in the manifesto entitled "Talking All That Jazz." Main Stet alum Prince Paul would go on to apply his lessons directly with "sons" De La Soul, setting the stage for hip-hop's sonic and artistic entropy.

what to buy: When Stet decided to throw out coherence and flow with its interests, the group came up with the endlessly enjoyable *In Full Gear* ✍✍✍✍ (Tommy Boy, 1988, prod. Stetsasonic), a map for many of the vectors hip-hop and pop music generally would take in the next decade. There's a look back to the Last Poets and the Watts Prophets on Daddy-O's "Freedom or Death." The revisionist Sly & the Family Stone on "It's in My Song" points to Rage Against the Machine. There's a concession to the James Brown sampling craze on "DBC Let the Music Play," a venture into dancehall on "The Odad," and a reverent take on "Miami Bass." And "Talking All That Jazz" anticipates both Us3 and Gang Starr, while Prince Paul's "Music for the Stetfully Insane" prefigures MoWax and the instrumental hip-hop craze.

what to buy next: A crew merging live drumming with drum machines, turntables, old-school-influenced MCs, and a human beatbox could go in many directions, and the debut, *On Fire* 𝄞𝄞𝄞 (Tommy Boy, 1986, prod. Stetsasonic), finds the band feeling out its possibilities at a transitional period in hip-hop. Much of the album sounds like A&R by the numbers—a metal-rap fusion track here, a Def Jam–styled track there, a Roxanne-type track and a bunch of park-jam rhymes over drum machines. The exuberance of the rhyme trio energizes the basic 808 thump of "4 Ever My Beat" and "My Rhyme." "Go Stetsa 1" is the real gem, with Nawthar Muhammed's powerful drum rolls and memorable verses from the entire crew. *Blood, Sweat & No Tears* 𝄞𝄞𝄞 (Tommy Boy, 1991, prod. Stetsasonic) doesn't reach nearly as far as its predecesor, *In Full Gear*, but maintains a steady, relaxing groove. Daddy-O and Delite keep their rhymes positive and direct while Prince Paul's off-kilter humor provides the counterpoint.

the rest:
Daddy-O:
You Can Be a Daddy but Never Be Daddy-O 𝄞𝄞𝄞 (Island, 1993)

The Gravediggaz:
6 Feet Deep 𝄞𝄞𝄞 (Gee Street, 1994)
The Pick, the Sickle, and the Shovel 𝄞𝄞𝄞𝄞 (Gee Street, 1997)
Six Feet Deep 𝄞𝄞𝄞 (Gee Street, 1997)

Prince Paul:
Psychoanalysis 𝄞𝄞𝄞 (WordSound, 1996)

influences:
◀◀ Run-D.M.C., Public Enemy
▶▶ De La Soul, MoWax, Dr. Octagon, the Roots

Jeff "DJ Zen" Chang

John Stevens
/Spontaneous Music Ensemble

Born June 10, 1940, in Brentford, England. Died September 13, 1994.

A major figure in the history of free improvisation in England, drummer Stevens co-led the hugely influential Spontaneous Music Ensemble. With his voracious musical curiousity he also made significant contributions to jazz-rock and jazz-world fusions, and to free jazz. Stevens co-founded the Spontaneous Music Ensemble in 1965 with saxophonist Trevor Watts and trombonist Paul Rutherford. The SME attracted a veritable who's who of English free improvisation—Evan Parker, Derek Bailey, Barry Guy, Dave Holland, and Kenny Wheeler were all regular participants in prominent club sessions. The group, with rotating members, sometimes expanded to a big band called the Spontaneous Music Orchestra. From the late '70s

until Stevens's death, the ensemble performed less regularly and most often included violinist Nigel Coombes and guitarist Roger Smith, and in its final three years, saxophonist John Butcher. The SME's music was generally quiet and highly detailed; Stevens played a pared-down drum kit with small cymbals to achieve subdued volumes and varied tonal colors. Fixed tempos, melodies, and a traditional rhythm section-plus-soloists approach were discarded in favor of explorations of rhythmic cells, timbre, and collective development. Stevens was exceptionally busy with projects outside the SME, even recording with John Lennon and Yoko Ono. He led a jazz-rock fusion band, Away, which included guitarist Alan Holdsworth; the John Stevens Dance Orchestra; a big band called Freebop; a jazz-world music ensemble called Folkus; and various quartets and quintets that played in a number of modern idioms. With Away, he played long, flowing jazz-rock patterns and drove the band. In Folkus, he employed folk-derived rhythms in various time signatures. In big bands and freebop settings he was also a driving, sometimes overbearing, drummer with a highly interactive style.

what to buy: *Karyobin* 𝄞𝄞𝄞𝄞 (Chronoscope, 1968, prod. Eddie Kramer), an early SME recording, features Kenny Wheeler, Evan Parker, Derek Bailey, Dave Holland, and Stevens in a series of brilliantly concentrated, brightly colored, dry-textured improvisations that sounded like nothing else. It's delicate, abstract music that's still a challenge after 30 years. *Face to Face* 𝄞𝄞𝄞𝄞 (Emanem, 1973, prod. Martin Davidson), a performance by a version of SME featuring just Trevor Watts and Stevens, is as close as two people get to playing as one. They are totally absorbed in the process of music-making, taking a series of small, bird-like gestures and elaborating on them in wonderfully unexpected ways. *A New Distance* 𝄞𝄞𝄞 (Acta, 1994), a late edition of SME with John Butcher and Roger Smith recorded just months before Stevens's death, finds him still searching for new instrumental sounds and novel improvisational shapes and structures.

what to buy next: On *Quintessence 1 (1973–4)* 𝄞𝄞𝄞 (Emanem, 1997, prod. Martin Davidson), Stevens, Parker, Watts, Bailey, and bassist Kent Carter turn in an SME performance that's classic in every way, with 40 minutes of tightly focused, daring improvisation that never loses direction for a minute. The CD reissue includes additional material by a Stevens-Watts-Carter trio from another date. *Quintessence 2 (1973–4)* 𝄞𝄞𝄞 (Emanem, 1997, prod. Martin Davidson) contains the second, equally brilliant set from the 1974 concert, plus Stevens-Watts duets. *John Stevens Works: Big Band and Quintet* 𝄞𝄞𝄞 (Konnex, 1993, prod. John Stevens, Manfred Schiek), a reissue of two sessions recorded under Stevens's name, includes a rousing big-band tribute to Albert Ayler and a hard-swinging free jazz quintet session with marked Ornette Coleman overtones. *John Stevens Works: Re-Touch and Quartet* ♫♫♫ (Konnex, 1993, prod. John Stevens, Manfred Schiek), the only available example of Stevens's fusion work, is a meandering jazz-rock improvisation with Holdsworth, Jeff Young, and Barry Guy that succeeds only intermittently. Made during the same big band session listed above, the quartet collectively improvises on a short Stevens composition that they recorded several other times.

best of the rest:

Spontaneous Music Ensemble: Summer 1967 ♫♫♫ (Emanem, 1997)
Spontaneous Music Ensemble: Hot and Cold Heroes, 1980 & 1991 ♫♫♫ (Emanem, 1997)

worth searching for: The hard-to-find *So What Do You Think?* ♫♫♫ (Tangent, 1971, prod. Mike Steyn) is another early date that ranks with the SME's best.

influences:

◀◀ Sunny Murray, Phil Seamans, Ornette Coleman

Ed Hazell

Bill Stewart

Born October 18, 1966, in Des Moines, IA.

Stewart is a New York City–based drummer whose kaleidoscopic, pointillistic playing combines Tony Williams's pulse with Gerry Hemingway's akimbo accents. He moved to New York from Minneapolis in the late 1980s and soon found a wealth of opportunities as a sideman—playing with everyone from John Scofield, Jim Hall, Marc Copland, Larry Goldings, and John Scofield to James Brown and Maceo Parker.

what to buy: Though *Snide Remarks* ♫♫♫ (Blue Note, 1995, prod. Bob Belden, Bill Stewart) is firmly within the jazz camp, there are twentieth-century classical influences in the harmonies and scales. Stewart's uptempo tunes are quirky and serpentine, embodying his rhythmic sense melodically, while his slow tunes are more impressionistic tone poems than ballads. He has a hushed sense of wonder and mystery on tracks such as "Soul Harbor" and "Space Acres." Pianist Bill Carrothers, who, like all the musicians here, has worked with Stewart before (dating back to when they both lived in Minneapolis), spins out post-bebop lines on the fast numbers and his trademark pastel harmonies (Richie Beirach is the closest comparison) on the rest. Although Carrothers complements

Stewart's conception perfectly, it's the horns—trumpeter Eddie Henderson and tenor saxist Joe Lovano—who take the meatiest solos (the bassist is Larry Grenadier). Lovano revels in the chance to stretch out, with well-constructed improvisations that have just enough looseness to be inviting. Whether fiery or contemplative, all of Henderson's solos are fluid and scintillating. And though this is a drummer's album, Stewart shows off not with extended solos, but rather with masterful pacing and accents within the fabric of the music.

what to buy next: Stewart's writing is even better on *Telepathy* ♫♫♫ (Blue Note, 1997, prod. Bob Belden, Bill Stewart), which continues in the same vein as its predecessor. Using the same rhythm team, *Telepathy* has Steve Wilson (alto and soprano saxes) and Seamus Blake (tenor sax) in the horn slots. The haunting "These Are They" starts the album on an uneasily contemplative note, a bold programming move. A couple of tunes later, "Happy Chickens" perks things up considerably with its funky hard-bop riffs and rhythms, and Thelonious Monk's "Rhythm-a-ning" gets a superb rethinking. The focus on this album is much more on Carrothers, who distinguishes himself throughout.

the rest:

Think Before You Think ♫♫♫ (Jazz City, 1990/Evidence, 1998)

influences:

◀◀ Philly Joe Jones, Elvin Jones, Tony Williams, Gerry Hemingway, Thelonious Monk, Horace Silver, Maurice Ravel, Andrew Hill

Steve Holtje

Rex Stewart

Born February 22, 1907, in Philadelphia, PA. Died September 7, 1967, in Los Angeles, CA.

Rex Stewart was one of the great trumpeters of the 1930s, a hard-blowing player who made up for his technical limitations with a huge bag of half-valve effects that allowed him to approximate human speech with his horn. His ability to play highly expressive, squeezed and bent notes and use them with great musical flair made him a key element in Duke Ellington's orchestras of the 1930s and 1940s. Stewart's family moved to Washington, D.C. in 1914 and he got his start playing on riverboats plying the Potomac. His idol was Louis Armstrong, but early on he realized he didn't have the technique to imitate Satchmo, so he began developing his energetic approach. He played with Elmer Snowden in 1925 and replaced Armstrong in the Fletcher Henderson Orchestra in 1926, but quit because he felt he wasn't ready for the gig and joined (Fletcher's brother) Horace Henderson's band at Wilberforce College. He rejoined Henderson's band in 1928 and stayed for five years as a featured soloist in what was still the country's leading jazz orchestra. Stewart joined Ellington in 1934 and stayed through the orchestra's greatest years, leaving in 1945. Ellington quickly incorporated Stewart's unique "talking" style into the band's palette, and featured his cornet work in many tunes. He toured extensively with Jazz at the Philharmonic between 1947–51, partly dropped out of jazz in the middle of the decade, then led a Fletcher Henderson reunion band from 1957–58. He was a regular at Eddie Condon's club from 1958–59, and then settled on the West Coast. Working as a disc jockey and as a critic he began writing for *Down Beat*. His profiles have been collected in *Jazz Masters of the '30s*, one of the first and still best books on jazz written by a jazz musician. Named after one of his biggest hits with Ellington, his wonderful, self-deprecating autobiography, *Boy Meets Horn,* was published posthumously.

what to buy: Made up of three small-group Ellington sidemen sessions originally recorded for HRS, *Rex Stewart and the Ellingtonians* ♫♫♫♫ (Riverside/OJC, 1990, prod. various) features four tracks with Stewart, Lawrence Brown, Barney Bigard, Billy Kyle, Brick Fleagle, Wellman Braud, and Dave Tough, and four tracks with a quartet featuring Kyle, John Levy, and Cozy Cole. The 1940 septet session has a light, Dixieland feel to it, while the 1946 quartet tracks, all written by Stewart, give him plenty of space to expound with his unique, highly expressive trumpet style. The last two tracks (from 1946) feature pianist Jimmy Jones's Big Eight and don't include Stewart. A two-disc collection of Ellington side projects recorded between 1934–38, *Duke Ellington: Small Groups, Vol. 1* ♫♫♫♫ (Columbia/Legacy, 1991, prod. Helen Oakley) features Stewart on about 12 of the 45 tracks, including four excellent tunes (three by Stewart) with Duke at the piano, recorded on a July 7, 1937 session by Stewart and His 52nd Street Stompers. Other sessions feature Ellington's other trumpet star, Cootie Williams, Barney Bigard, and Johnny Hodges. This is seminal small group swing.

best of the rest:
The Big Reunion ♫♫♫♫ (Fresh Sound, 1957)
Porgy and Bess Revisited ♫♫♫♫ (Warner Bros., 1958)

worth searching for: *Trumpet Jive!* ♫♫♫♫ (Prestige, 1992, prod. Esmond Edwards) was the name of an album Stewart recorded in 1944–45 with the fine trad trumpeter Wingy Manone. The last 14 tunes are from *The Happy Jazz of Rex Stewart*, an album made up of a 1945 swing session with trombonist/vibraphonist Tyree Glenn and alto saxophonist Earl Bostic, and a 1960 trad session on which he sings three tunes. Stewart is in fine form, though he's a little too generous in giving his bandmates solo space.

influences:
◄◄ Louis Armstrong, Jabbo Smith

Andrew Gilbert

Robert Stewart
Born August 17, 1969, in Oakland, CA.

Robert Stewart is a bluesy tenor saxophonist who fits easily into R&B, bebop, and post-bop contexts. A natural swinger with a big sound reminiscent of Gene Ammons and Dexter Gordon, he was raised in Oakland and started playing tenor in high school. One of his first influences was late 1960s' Pharoah Sanders, but some of his first professional gigs were with blues bands and organ combos, and he continues to work on the West Coast blues circuit. Stewart spent about seven months in the Los Angeles hard-bop combo Black Note in 1992, and has worked with Max Roach, Billy Higgins, Benny Golson, McCoy Tyner, and Eddie Harris, and toured with drummer Winard Harper. He was also featured on Wynton Marsalis's *Blood on the Fields* album and tour, and has worked on a variety of the trumpeter's projects.

what's available: A down-and-dirty organ combo date, *In the Gutta* ♫♫♫♫ (Qwest, 1996, prod. Robert Stewart, Craig Morton) is a hard-blowing blues session featuring Larry Bradford on Hammond B3 organ, Ralph Byrd on guitar, and Ranzel Merritt on drums. Stewart does a fair job as a blues shouter on two original tracks and shows off his lyrical side with an extended version of "Misty." On Bill Doggett's "Honky Tonk," Booker T. Jones's "Green Onions," and his original "West Virginia Red," Stewart plays with the kind of spirited swagger that made R&B such popular jukebox fair in the 1950s.

worth searching for: Stewart was in a Coltrane phase when he recorded *Judgement* ♫♫♫♫ (World Stage Records, 1994, prod. Dennis Sullivan, D.J. Riley), an impressive debut session featuring pianist Eric Reed, bassist Mark Shelby, and the great drummer Billy Higgins. Stewart is in a relaxed mood and plays with considerable self-assurance throughout, letting his beautiful sound pour out of his horn. He strolls his way through two standards, "Invitation" and "As Time Goes By," and six straight-ahead originals, including the very Tranish "Serene" and the lovely, mid-tempo title track.

influences:

 Gene Ammons, John Coltrane, Dexter Gordon, Eddie Harris

Andrew Gilbert

Sonny Stitt

Born February 2, 1924, in Boston, MA. Died July 22, 1982, in Washington, DC.

Sonny (Edward) Stitt is often pegged as Charlie Parker's most avid disciple, but he had reached many of the same harmonic and rhythmic insights in the early 1940s independent of Bird. A blazing alto saxophonist with an archetypical bebop sound, Stitt was also a highly charged tenor player, though his approach was strongly influenced by Lester Young. He was capable of breathtaking ballad work on either horn. He landed his first major gig as an alto saxophonist with Tiny Bradshaw in the early 1940s and hooked up briefly with Billy Eckstine's seminal bop big band, playing alongside Gene Ammons and Dexter Gordon. Soon after he moved to New York he worked with Dizzy Gillespie (1945–46) and recorded with Kenny Clarke. Drug problems kept him off the scene for a number of years and when he returned he was playing tenor as a way to distinguish himself from Parker. He co-led one of the first great tenor duel bands with Ammons (1950–52) and began leading his own combos. After Parker's death in 1955 he began playing alto again, touring with Jazz at the Philharmonic and Dizzy Gillespie in the late 1950s, and with Miles Davis in 1960–61. He toured with the Giants of Jazz in 1971–72, a band featuring Gillespie, Monk, Kai Winding, Al McKibbon, and Art Blakey. Though Stitt was a very prolific and consistent musician, rarely turning in a poor performance in his 100 or so albums as a leader, he was often at his best when jousting with other saxophonists or in similar competitive situations.

what to buy: Collecting three classic bebop sessions, *Sonny Stitt/Bud Powell/J. J. Johnson* ◊◊◊◊ (Prestige, 1949–50/OJC, 1989, prod. Bob Weinstock) features two quartet dates with Stitt on tenor and Bud Powell (piano), Curly Russell (bass) and Max Roach blazing through "All God's Chillun Got Rhythm," "I Want to Be Happy," and "Fine and Dandy." The quintet date features Stitt with J. J. Johnson (trombone), John Lewis (piano), Nelson Boyd (bass), and Roach on eight tracks, including three Johnson tunes and Lewis's "Afternoon in Paris." Stitt's first recordings on tenor find him combining elements of Lester Young and Dexter Gordon with his own harmonic vocabulary in a highly satisfying synthesis. Powell is in excellent form throughout, playing with astounding rhythmic dexterity and harmonic inventiveness. Stitt became

one of the preeminent bebop tenor players in the early 1950s, and *Prestige First Sessions, Vol. 2* ◊◊◊◊ (Prestige, 1950–51/1992, prod. Bob Weinstock) documents him with a variety of rhythm sections and sextets (he also plays alto on two tracks). Though there are four vocal tracks by the deservedly obscure Teddy Williams and Larry Townsend, Stitt is the featured soloist throughout and he plays with tremendous poise and energy, including a number of first-rate ballad performances. He is backed by pianists such as Duke Jordan, Kenny Drew, and Junior Mance while Art Blakey and Wesley Landers do most of the drum work. One of Stitt's best albums from the 1960s, *Soul People* ◊◊◊◊ (Prestige, 1964/1993, prod. Ozzie Cadena) pairs him with the great tenorman Booker Ervin, a supremely soulful player with a highly distinctive sound who inspires Stitt to some prodigious blowing. With Don Patterson on organ and Billy James on drums, all five tracks with Stitt and Ervin come in at about nine minutes or more, giving them plenty of room to stretch out. The CD also includes Stitt on Miles Davis's "Tune Up" with guitarist Grant Green replacing Ervin, and Patterson playing "There Will Never Be Another You" with a trio. Sonny Stitt never sounded better than on the 1972 Muse album *Tune-Up*, which features a "bopophilic" rhythm section with Barry Harris (piano), Sam Jones (bass), and Alan Dawson (drums). The nine-minute workout on "I Got Rhythm" is what jazz is all about. This album has been combined with another formerly out-of-print Muse album, *Congestion*, and reissued as *Endgame Brilliance* ◊◊◊◊ (32 Jazz, 1997, prod. Don Schlitten).

what to buy next: *Kaleidoscope* ◊◊◊◊ (Prestige, 1950–52/1992, prod. Bob Weinstock) is the companion album to *Prestige First Sessions, Vol. 2*, a collection of dates featuring Stitt with a three-trumpet octet, a sextet backing a forgettable singer, and three different rhythm sections. Stitt switches between alto and tenor (and on two tracks baritone), playing with tremendous energy and authority on each horn. His versions of "Imagination" and "Cherokee" with Junior Mance, Gene Wright, and Art Blakey are two of the highlights. A quartet session recorded in Japan less than two years before Stitt died of cancer, *The Good Life* ◊◊◊◊ (Evidence, 1994, prod. Takao Ishizuka) features pianist Hank Jones, bassist George Duvivier, and drummer Grady Tate on a program of standards and Stitt's brief opening number, "Deuce's Wild." A relaxed, focused session with only two tunes coming in longer than five minutes, Stitt plays some majestic ballads, including "Polka Dots and Moonbeams" and a succinct "Autumn Leaves." Though Tate's voice is attractive on "My Funny Valentine" and "Body and Soul," one vocal track would have been sufficient.

what to avoid: This anthology of Stitt's Prestige recordings is hardly what its title suggests. On half of the organ-combo dates on *Soul Classics* 𝄞𝄞 (Prestige, 1962–1972/1988, prod. various) Stitt plays the electric Veritone saxophone, making his beautiful sound largely unrecognizable. The novelty wears off very quickly.

best of the rest:

At the Hi-Hat 𝄞𝄞𝄞𝄞 (Roulette/Capitol, 1954/1993)
Sonny Stitt Sits in with the Oscar Peterson Trio 𝄞𝄞𝄞𝄞 (Verve, 1957–1959/1991)
Stitt Meets Brother Jack 𝄞𝄞𝄞𝄞 (Prestige/OJC, 1962/1992)
Night Letter 𝄞𝄞𝄞𝄞 (Prestige, 1963/1969, prod. Ozzie Cadena, Bob Porter)
The Last Sessions, Vols. 1 & 2 𝄞𝄞𝄞𝄞 (Muse, 1982)

influences:

◄◄ Charlie Parker, Lester Young, Dexter Gordon, Gene Ammons

►► Lou Donaldson, Ken Peplowski

Andrew Gilbert

Straight Ahead

Formed around 1984, in Detroit, MI.

Eileen Orr, keyboards, vocals; Marion Hayden, bass, vocals; Gaylelynn McKinney, drums, vocals; Regina Carter, violin, vocals; Cynthia Dewberry, flute, vocals.

Straight Ahead, a Detroit-based quintet, began its collective life under the tutelage of vocalist Miche Braden, who was looking for a first-rate, swinging, no-jive straight-ahead—and all-female—resident jazz backup band. The group's wide musical repertoire isn't distinctively "feminist," but its very existence and longevity make a powerful statement about women's ascendance in jazz. After backing the singer for several years in clubs, the combination stayed together when Braden left Detroit to pursue a successful show business career. Having learned a lot about vocal technique in the process, the group added collective vocalizing to its arsenal as well as adding a lead singer. It has become Detroit's most popular working jazz small group for festival and club dates, regrettably too few and far between for a full-time living. From Straight Ahead's inception, the core of the group has been Eileen Orr, Marion Hayden, and Gaylelynn McKinney. Orr is experienced and works regularly in jazz, blues, and Latin/Caribbean piano; Hayden is the busiest gigging bassist in town; and McKinney, the group's youngest member and a product of Detroit's musical McKinney family, is a sharp and clean drummer with full control of dynam-

ics and polyrhythms. The core trio ensures a solid and richly textured foundation underneath whatever eclectic direction the music goes. Other personnel have rotated through, the most forceful being bebop-and-beyond violinist Regina Carter, who came home to Detroit after living in Germany and became a mainstay of Straight Ahead before moving to New York (where she has joined the String Trio of New York and recorded with Mark Helias). Both Carter and Cynthia Dewberry, who was lead vocalist and flutist during most of the 1990s, appear on the Straight Ahead recordings to date.

A caveat: Straight Ahead's recorded output, while reasonably representative of the group's wide-ranging repertoire and technical facility, hasn't yet come close to the energy of its live performances. For example, the nearly four-minute version of McKinney's "7 Minutes 2-4" on the inaugural *Look Straight Ahead* recording only hints at the drum solo she performs in concert on this high-octane 7/4 theme. Nor do the recordings fully convey the group's powerful virtuosity in the "pure" bebop realm. "Hallucinations" (by Bud Powell) on *Look Straight Ahead* is a nice snapshot, at least. Atlantic Records seems oriented more toward the "smooth" sound trying to penetrate the fusion market. This impression is reinforced by the presence, on about half the tracks, of a background synthesizer (this is a drawback only if you share this reviewer's jaundiced view that synthesizers equal brain death). The electronics are hardly necessary considering what Orr can do pianistically and what the whole group can do vocally.

what to buy: *Straight Ahead's Greatest Hits* 𝄞𝄞𝄞 (Atlantic, 1996, prod. various), compiled from their three Atlantic releases (see below), pretty well features the ensemble's recorded range as it's evolved since the early 1990s.

what to buy next: Depending on stylistic choice, you might try the most recent Straight Ahead recording, *Dance of the Forest Rain* 𝄞𝄞𝄞 (Atlantic, 1995, prod. Bob Belden). It's the most ambitiously produced set, adding the colorful guitar work of Fareed Haque, Brazilian percussionist Guilherme Franco, and, on various tracks, Detroit-born saxophonists Kenny Garrett and Norma Jean Bell, as well as other backgrounders. Garrett's alto illuminates McKinney's four-part "Suite Arthur." Listen to the band's venture into jazz-rap on "Step into the Projects." Well-crafted and contemporary.

worth searching for: Currently out-of-print, their first and best album, *Look Straight Ahead* 𝄞𝄞𝄞 (Atlantic, 1992, prod. Lenny White), includes among the 10 diverse tunes what is probably the group's most enduringly popular collective vocal, "You

Touch Me," composed by Carter and Orr (with additional words credited to Maureen Daily); the tune also appears in a better-mixed version on their *Straight Ahead's Greatest Hits*. Also hard to find, their second album, *Body and Soul* ΔΔΔ (Atlantic, 1993, prod. Lenny White), features a mixture of 10 originals and standards performed by Cynthia Dewberry and Regina Carter, plus the core trio of Orr, Hayden-Banfield, and McKinney. Labeled as tunes "in the tradition," the crew gives excellent mainstream readings to jazz standards such as "Hot House," "Body and Soul," and "No Moe." Labeled as tunes "in transition" are Carmen Lundy's "Never Let You Go" and Ralph Towner's "Icarus." The album also features originals by group members.

David Finkel

Billy Strayhorn

Born November 29, 1915, in Dayton, OH. Died May 31, 1967, in New York, NY.

One of jazz's greatest composer/arrangers, Billy Strayhorn played an essential role in the Duke Ellington Orchestra from the time he was hired as a lyricist in 1939 until his death from cancer in 1967. Though Strayhorn's particular contributions were often overlooked during his life, he has gained much wider recognition in the past decade. A sensitive, swinging pianist whose style was marked by great harmonic sophistication and a beautiful touch, Strayhorn could also perfectly imitate Ellington's more percussive, expansive approach. His body of tunes, including the Ellington orchestra's theme song "Take the 'A' Train" (which Ellington always introduced by giving him credit), is one of the most beautiful and finely crafted *oeuvres* in American music.

Raised in Pittsburgh, Strayhorn began writing songs and musical reviews while still in high school. He was already a preter-naturally gifted songwriter before joining the Ellington sphere, composing such stunning art songs as "Lush Life" and "Something to Live For." He began collaborating with Ellington in 1939, at first supplying lyrics but quickly assuming the role of Ellington's cherished collaborator, writing arrangements for the orchestra and such classic instrumentals as "Chelsea Bridge," "Rain Check," and "Johnny Come Lately." After the mid-1940s, Ellington and Strayhorn began sharing credit for many of their collaborations, which led to the widespread misconception that their music was indistinguishable. In truth, when working on their own, Strayhorn and Ellington had profoundly different compositional styles. The depth of their musical pairing is probably unprecedented, with Strayhorn involved in every aspect of the band's creative life, from leading small group ses-

sions with Ben Webster, Cootie Williams, Barney Bigard, and Johnny Hodges, to co-composing and arranging hundreds of tunes and extended works such as *The Deep South Suite, A Drum Is a Woman, Such Sweet Thunder,* and *The Perfume Suite.* Outside of the Ellington organization, Strayhorn recorded only a few sessions of his own during his life, most of which are now available on CD. His death inspired Ellington to record one of the orchestra's last great albums, *And His Mother Called Him Bill.* David Hadju's 1996 biography of Strayhorn, *Lush Life,* played an important role in disentangling Strayhorn's accomplishments from Ellington's, and shed light on Strayhorn's genius and the way he navigated through life as a semi-public figure and a quietly, though openly, gay man.

what's available: This revelatory set of unreleased material, *Lush Life* ΔΔΔΔ (Red Baron, 1964–65/Sony, 1992, prod. Duke Ellington, Mercer Ellington), is absolutely essential for those interested in Billy Strayhorn or lovers of Ellingtonia. Most of the 20 tracks were recorded in 1965 and feature Strayhorn at the piano with an exemplary quintet including Clark Terry (trumpet and flugelhorn), Bob Wilbur (clarinet), Wendell Marshall (bass), and Dave Bailey (drums), with Ellington sharing piano duties on "Smada" and "Just A-Settin' and A-Rockin'." Willie Ruff's French horn joins the quintet on five tracks, adding considerable warmth to the arrangements. Terry is in supremely high spirits throughout, bringing tremendous emotional vibrancy to such well-known Strayhorn tunes as "Raincheck," "Chelsea Bridge," and an extended version of "Passion Flower." Strayhorn accompanies the serviceable singer Ozzie Bailey on four tunes, and plays three tunes by himself, among the only solo piano pieces he ever recorded. Perhaps the most memorable track is the album's first, with Strayhorn accompanying his own vocals on "Lush Life." Of the very few albums Strayhorn recorded during his life, *The Peaceful Side* ΔΔΔ (Capitol, 1961/1996, prod. Alan Douglas) was the most intimate and personal. Reworking 10 tunes previously recorded by the Ellington orchestra, Strayhorn pairs down each tune to its essence. Recorded in Paris, the session features Strayhorn's piano backed by bassist Michel Goudret on five tracks, the Paris String Quartet on two (including a gentle ballad version of "Take the 'A' Train"), and by the Paris Blue Notes vocal group on three tracks. Highlights include the duo versions of "Passion Flower" and "Something to Live For," and the breathtaking string arrangement on "A Flower Is a Lovesome Thing." A completely obscure album when it was released, it was reissued in 1996.

worth searching for: Strayhorn was a magnificent composer, with few recordings as leader to his credit. More often, his works were recorded by numerous others. To hear his wonderful music performed, seek out the following recordings. One of Ellington and Strayhorn's last collaborations, *The Far East Suite—Special Mix* 𝄢𝄢𝄢𝄢 (Bluebird, 1966/RCA, 1995, prod. Brad McCuen) is also one of Duke's best extended works of the 1960s, a highly lyrical nine-piece evocation of their long 1963 State Department–sponsored tour of Asia. The CD reissue adds four alternate takes, including Strayhorn's haunting ballad "Isfahan," featuring Johnny Hodges, and the clever "Bluebird of Dheli," which features Jimmy Hamilton. Strayhorn and Ellington never appropriate other musical traditions, rather they brilliantly utilize their vast orchestral jazz vocabulary in recreating their travels. An essential album for Ellington and Strayhorn fans. One of the finest Billy Strayhorn tributes ever recorded, Art Farmer's *Something to Live For* 𝄢𝄢𝄢𝄢 (Contemporary, 1987, prod. Helen Keane) is a brilliant quintet session with Clifford Jordan (tenor sax), James Williams (piano), Rufus Reid (bass), and Marvin "Smitty" Smith (drums). Farmer's achingly poignant flugelhorn sound and deep harmonic insight make him particularly well-suited to explore Strayhorn's music, while Jordan and Williams both bring their passionate lyricism and hard-swinging romanticism to the seven Strayhorn classics, including "Isfahan," "Johnny Come Lately," and "Raincheck." The album that finally brought tenor saxophonist Joe Henderson the audience and recognition his playing had so long warranted, *Lush Life: The Music of Billy Strayhorn* 𝄢𝄢𝄢𝄢 (Verve, 1992, prod. Richard Seidel, Don Sickler) features trumpeter Wynton Marsalis, pianist Stephen Scott, bassist Christian McBride, and drummer Greg Hutchinson. The session alternates instrumentation on each track, and includes one solo piece (a tour de force version of "Lush Life" that concludes the album), a duo with each member of the rhythm section, two trios, one quartet and three pieces with the full quintet. Henderson's soft-edged, deeply mysterious sound meshes perfectly with Strayhorn's tunes, and he cuts right to the emotional heart of Strayhorn's music, opening the album with a gorgeous tenor/bass duet on "Isfahan." Other highlights include the duets with Scott and Hutchinson on "Lotus Blossom" and "Take the 'A' Train," respectively, and the darkly playful version of "U.M.M.G." featuring the quintet and some pointed trumpet work by Marsalis. Pianist Marian McPartland used to play Strayhorn's tunes when he came by the Hickory House to catch her trio, and she pays the great composer/arranger a loving tribute with *Plays the Music of Billy Strayhorn* 𝄢𝄢𝄢𝄢 (Concord Jazz, 1987, prod. Carl E. Jefferson), a superior quartet session with Jerry Dodgion (alto sax), Steve LaSpina (bass), and Joey Baron (drums). Dodgion wrote all the arrangements and his lush alto brings to mind

Johnny Hodges (who was featured on so many of these tunes), though McPartland ends the album with a breathtaking solo version of "Daydream," a tune closely associated with the Ellingtonian alto saxophonist. Her trio version of "Lush Life," with its careful attention to the complex melody, would have made Strayhorn smile, as would the rollicking opening track, "The Intimacy of the Blues." Other highlights include McPartland's solo version of "Lotus Blossom" and the exotic "Isfahan," with some particularly effective Dodgion alto work. Drawing widely from the Verve archives, the label assembled *Lush Life: The Billy Strayhorn Songbook* 𝄢𝄢𝄢𝄢 (Verve, 1996, prod. various), an anthology of 15 Strayhorn tunes performed by various jazz artists, released in conjunction with David Hadju's Strayhorn biography of the same name. The music ranges from Cecil Taylor's angular rendering of "Johnny Come Lately" to Stan Getz's haunting live version of "Blood Count." Though there are some unaccountable choices made (why include Billy Eckstine singing Ellington's "Satin Doll" or Ella Fitzgerald's blithe version of the wrenching "Something to Live For"?), there are three tunes that taken alone are worth the CD's price. Strayhorn's string arrangement for Ben Webster's version of "Chelsea Bridge" is a classic, and his piano work on Johnny Hodges's version of "Three and Six," featuring Webster, Ray Nance, Lawrence Brown, and Roy Eldridge, displays a mature style quite distinct from Ellington's. The album ends with a thrilling, star-studded nine-minute Norman Granz jam session on "Take the 'A' Train," with Eldridge, Benny Carter, Don Byas, and Coleman Hawkins. Ellington wrote his heart-wrenching tribute to his alter ego (included in the CD liner notes) the day Strayhorn died, and it's as eloquent and moving as the music on *And His Mother Called Him Bill* 𝄢𝄢𝄢𝄢 (Bluebird, 1967/1987, prod. Brad McCuen), which was recorded three months after Strayhorn's death. The album covers a wide range of Strayhorn's tunes, from his early masterpieces "Daydream" and "Rain Check," to his late works "U.M.M.G." and "Blood Count," which features one of the most emotionally-charged solos Johnny Hodges ever recorded, an angry outpouring at Strayhorn's loss. The Ellington orchestra still contained many of its most individual voices, and Cootie Williams, Clark Terry, Jimmy Hamilton, Paul Gonsalves, and Harry Carney all make their love for Strayhorn clear. The original album ended with Ellington's devastating solo version of "Lotus Blossom," recorded while the orchestra was packing up its instruments, though the CD reissue defuses the gesture by changing the order of the tracks.

influences:
◀◀ Duke Ellington

▶▶ Melba Liston, Gil Evans

Andrew Gilbert

The String Trio of New York

Formed October 1977, in New York, NY.

James Emery, guitar; John Lindberg, bass; Billy Bang, violin (1979–87); Charles Burnham, violin (1988–92); Regina Carter, violin (1993–present).

Don't be fooled by the String Trio of New York's misleading moniker: far from being parlor fare for the blue-haired set, this is gutsy, improvised music stripped down to its acoustic essence. Core members and Braxton alumnae James Emery and John Lindberg—joined sequentially over the years by Billy Bang, Charles Burnham, and Regina Carter—have quietly labored in the shadows for nearly two decades, building an impressive body of uncompromising (and commercially unrewarding) work that is remarkable in its purity and consistency. Despite its somewhat austere instrumentation, the trio patrols a wide dynamic range and can build up a formidable head of steam when the occasion calls for it. The group is equally comfortable inside and outside of time and changes, and frequently ventures into free territory. Lindberg's playing is simultaneously vocal and propulsive, while Emery unleashes exhilarating torrents of brittle notes on his classical and soprano guitars. Billy Bang is arguably the most mature, exciting, and adventurous of the three violinists, and any of the titles featuring him come highly recommended. His successor, Charles Burnham (known for his work in James Blood Ulmer's Odyssey trio), brought a folkish element to the trio's music with his warm tone and rootsy melodic sense, contrasting the classical leanings of current violinist Regina Carter, a fixture in New Age schlockmeister Yanni's group but also a solo jazz artist who can really tear it up live, though her albums as a leader haven't shown that side of her.

what to buy: *Area Code 212* ♪♪♪♪ (Black Saint, 1981, prod. Giovanni Bonandrini) mixes jazz, blues, avant-garde, and a bit of flamenco feeling from Emery on a generally appealing and accessible program that splits the compositional duties evenly among its six tunes. There's plenty of variety: Emery's moody "Coho," Bang's uptempo "Bang's Bounce," with its unison theme statement sounding like an Albert Ayler head, Lindberg's catchy "Twixt C and D," etc. This was the group's second album, but the first where all the elements cohered.

what to buy next: With Carter playing in a more straight-ahead style than on her commercial solo albums, *Blues . . . ?* ♪♪♪♪

(Black Saint, 1995) is a swinging acoustic delight from start to finish. A rambunctious Bird medley and a burning take on Lee Morgan's "Speedball" are highlights on a record redefining its title subject. There are also covers of Miles Davis's "Freddie the Freeloader" and Duke Ellington's "I'm Afraid," with the rest of the material band originals. The John Lindberg Ensemble's *Bounce* ♪♪♪♪ (Black Saint, 1997, prod. Flavio Bonandrini) is the bassist's most satisfying record outside the String Trio, neither too composed nor too loose. He's joined by trumpeter Dave Douglas, saxophonist Larry Ochs (co-leader of the Rova Sax Quartet), and drummer Ed Thigpen. They probe new areas of improvisation, with the groundbreaking ideas of Douglas and Ochs melded with Lindberg's original compositions.

the rest:
(With Billy Bang) *First String* ♪♪♪♫ (Black Saint, 1979)
(With Billy Bang) *Common Goal* ♪♪♪ (Black Saint, 1982)
(With Billy Bang) *Rebirth of a Feeling* ♪♪♪♪ (Black Saint, 1984)
(With Billy Bang) *Natural Balance* ♪♪♪ (Black Saint, 1987)
(With Regina Carter) *Intermobility* ♪♪♪ (Arabesque 1993)
(With Regina Carter) *Octagon* ♪♪♪ (Black Saint, 1994)

worth searching for: The two albums on Stash with Charles Burnham are hard to find in the wake of the label's demise, but are worth the extra effort. They both offer an abundance of tunes covering the spectrum of jazz classics—a new development at the time, and to a degree unmatched since, though Burnham also shows himself to be a capable composer. With just one original each by the members, *Ascendant* ♪♪♪ (Stash, 1990, prod. Fred Brightman) boasts Charlie Parker's "Ah-Leu-Cha," Chick Corea's "Straight Up and Down," Jimmy Garrison's "Ascendant," Ellington's "Heaven," John Lewis's "Skating in Central Park," Mingus's "Nostalgia in Times Square," and Monk's "Nutty." The great surprises on the album are Jimi Hendrix's "Manic Depression" and "Little Wing," and Erik Satie's "Gymnopedie No. 1"; they make one wonder if the group had noted the success of the genre-mixing albums of the Kronos and Turtle Island String Quartets. *Time Never Lies* ♪♪♪♪ (Stash, 1991, prod. Fred Brightman) continues in a similar vein, but the covers this time are all solidly "in the tradition": "Ramblin'" (Ornette Coleman), "St. Louis Blues" (W.C. Handy), "Celia" (Bud Powell), "Peggy's Blue Skylight" (Mingus), "Honeysuckle Rose" (Waller), and "After the Rain" (Coltrane). Also, there are two originals each by the members, which overall makes for a more comfortable mix for jazz fans.

solo outings:
James Emery:
Turbulence ♪♪♫ (Knitting Factory Works, 1991)

John Lindberg:

Dimension 5 𝄢𝄢𝄢 (Black Saint, 1982)

Give and Take 𝄢𝄢𝄢 (Black Saint, 1983)

Trilogy of Works for Eleven Instrumentalists 𝄢𝄢𝄢 (Black Saint, 1985)

(With Albert Mangelsdorff, Eric Watson) *Dodging Bullets* 𝄢𝄢𝄢 (Black Saint, 1992)

(With Albert Mangelsdorff, Eric Watson, Ed Thigpen) *Quartet Afterstorm* 𝄢𝄢𝄢 (Black Saint, 1994)

Resurrection of a Dormant Soul 𝄢𝄢𝄢 (Black Saint, 1996)

(With Eric Watson) *Soundpost: Works for Piano and Double Bass* 𝄢𝄢𝄢 (Music & Arts, 1996)

influences:

◀◀ Stephane Grappelli, Django Reinhardt, the Fourth Way, Shakti, Oregon

▶▶ Eyvind Kang, Mark Feldman, Jason Hwang, Ralph Towner

see also: *Billy Bang*

Dennis Rea and Steve Holtje

Frank Strozier

Born June 13, 1937, in Memphis, TN.

Overshadowed by contemporaries such as James Spaulding and Jackie McLean, alto saxophonist Frank Strozier has never really received the attention and acclaim his talent deserves. The early years of his career were spent in Chicago, where he worked with Booker Little, George Coleman, and Harold Mabern. By the end of the 1950s he moved to New York and was a vital member of the group MJT+3, which included Mabern, bassist Bob Cranshaw, and drummer Walter Perkins. That group and Strozier himself led several record dates for the Vee-Jay label that have since become valuable collector's items. Further New York gigs included short stints with Miles Davis and Roy Haynes. Later, Strozier settled on the West Coast where he worked with Don Ellis, Chet Baker, and Shelly Manne. Since the 1970s, Strozier has kept a very low profile, playing infrequently and recording a few albums for various small independent record labels. With a biting and intense tone and a style that is fiery and spirited, Strozier has always been a valuable musician. Unfortunately, none of his vintage recordings are available on CD, making his continued obscurity all the more frustrating.

what's available: *Remember Me* 𝄢𝄢𝄢 (SteepleChase, 1976, prod. Nils Winther) was cut upon Strozier's return to New York in the mid-1970s. Although not as incendiary as some of his earlier sides, this set is still a good example of the altoist in fine form.

worth searching for: *Fantastic Frank Strozier—Plus* 𝄢𝄢𝄢𝄢 (Vee-Jay, 1960, prod. Sid McCoy) was briefly available on CD but then quickly disappeared when the company went bankrupt. This historic meeting with trumpeter Booker Little is one of Strozier's finest efforts and the reissue features several bonus cuts. *March of the Siamese Children* 𝄢𝄢𝄢𝄢 (Jazzland, 1962, prod. Orrin Keepnews) is another hard-to-find piece that ranks among the finest records produced for the Jazzland label. Both Strozier and pianist Harold Mabern are at their creative bests.

influences:

◀◀ Charlie Parker

Chris Hovan

Strunz & Farah

Formed in 1979, in Los Angeles, CA.

Jorge Strunz, guitar; Ardeshir Farah, guitar; Luis Conte, percussion (guest musician since 1980); Guillermo Guzman, electric bass (1990–93); Juanito "Long John" Oliva, Afro-Cuban percussion, cajon (1990–94); Luis Perez Ixoneztli, pre-Columbian winds and percussion, vocals (1990–93); Paul Tchounga, drums (1990–present); Eliseo Borreo, electric bass, vocals (1993–present); Cassio Duarte, percussion (1994–present).

While they often get pegged as Flamenco or New Age, this fiery, world beat combo falls into neither category. Led by the acoustic guitar pyrotechnics of Jorge Strunz and Ardeshir Farah, the six-piece band assimilates Afro-Latin, Arabic, and Spanish influences into a melting pot that transcends easy categorization. The group's sound has progressed and matured since its inception, moving from the raw power of *Mosaico*, to the nocturnal moods of *Misterio*, to the fascinating world fusion sounds of *Primal Magic*. Each album offers its own trademark, whether it's the progressive structures of *Guitarras* or the primal world beat of *Americas*. What keeps their music fresh is that Strunz & Farah have played in other formats. Strunz recorded four albums with the 1970s Latin/jazz fusion group Caldera, and Farah played pop music with Iranian musicians in the late 1970s. Although many world music groups do not tend to sell in large numbers, the duo has done very well over the years. *Primal Magic* and *Americas* are both close to Gold, with the latter being nominated for a Grammy for Best World Music album in 1992.

what to buy: Their live album, *Live* 𝄢𝄢𝄢 (Selva, 1997, prod. Strunz & Farah, Kathlyn Powell), nicely captures the duo's inspiring energy. Songs from their last three recordings are played in the set, and the musicians really get to display their chops, from the powerful rhythm section to the extended solos of the guitarists themselves, who sound like they could race across the frets all night long. *Primal Magic* 𝄢𝄢𝄢 (Mesa/Blue Moon, 1990, prod. Strunz & Farah) started a newer trend among young Flamenco/Spanish guitar wannabes. While Flamenco stylings certainly play a part in the music, the exotic pre-Columbian winds of Luis Perez and the band's Afro-Latin rhythm section flesh out an exotic, sophisticated sound that is both mystical and uplifting, yielding an inspired recording. *Americas* 𝄢𝄢𝄢 (Mesa/Blue Moon, 1992, prod. Strunz & Farah) followed this path as well and is also quite noteworthy. Finally, *Mosaico* 𝄢𝄢𝄢 (Mesa/Blue Moon, 1982) features some truly blistering guitar work that will not fail to move you. There is no such thing as a bad Strunz & Farah record. But fans of their 1990s material will probably find *Misterio* 𝄢𝄢𝄢 (AudioQuest, 1991) very mellow. It consists of Strunz & Farah and guitarist Ciro Hurtado (on three tracks) without a rhythm section. *Misterio* still stands on its own and offers romantic guitar musings perfect for late-night listening.

best of the rest:
Frontera 𝄢𝄢𝄢𝄢 (Milestone, 1984)
Guitarras 𝄢𝄢𝄢𝄢 (Milestone, 1985)
Heat of the Sun 𝄢𝄢𝄢 (Selva, 1995)

Bryan Reesman

Dave Stryker

Born 1957.

Although Stryker's guitar playing has a rough-hewn blues tinge, it finds its best moments in tandem with either the funky organ gospel preached by his first major mentor, Jack McDuff, or the hard-edged, soulful jazz saxophone of his later employer, Stanley Turrentine. While his playing definitely has roots in the soul jazz scene, Stryker has the ability to go outside standard blues riffs and into jazz modes at a moment's notice. He left his home in Omaha, Nebraska, for the competitive scene of New York City in 1980, carving out a nice-sized niche for himself in the process. In addition to working with Turrentine and McDuff, the guitarist has also played gigs alongside Kevin Mahogany, Dizzy Gillespie, Freddie Hubbard, Steve Slagle, and Lonnie Smith. Stryker has received performance grants from the National Endowment for the Arts in 1981, 1988, and 1990, in addition to producing album-length tributes to Grant Green and Billy Rogers, two important influences on his playing.

what to buy: *Nomad* 𝄢𝄢𝄢𝄢 (Steeple Chase, 1995, prod. Nils Winther) proves that putting Stryker in front of Bill Warfield's big band was a wonderful idea. Instead of coming up with another organ trio date or small group gig, this album allows Stryker to showcase his essential versatility in a format not usually known for its kindness to guitar soloists. Some of the personnel included on this album show up on previous releases by the guitarist (including Steve Slagle and Bob Parsons), which may explain the exacting yet comfortable groove many of these tunes display.

what to buy next: *Blue to the Bone* 𝄢𝄢𝄢 (Steeple Chase, 1996, prod. Nils Winther) sets Stryker in the midst of a talented wind/reed quartet and a solid rhythm trio for a series of original, blues-based tunes. It's a perfect bit of typecasting. Stryker wrote most of the material and arranged it in collaboration with Bob Parsons. Songs like the low-down organ group groove of "Bayou Blues" and "Tchoupitoulas St.," with its second-line pulse, are good fits for Stryker's talents.

the rest:
Guitar on Top 𝄢𝄢𝄢 (Ken, 1992)
Full Moon 𝄢𝄢𝄢 (Steeple Chase, 1994)
Strike Zone 𝄢𝄢𝄢 (Steeple Chase, 1994)
Blue Degrees 𝄢𝄢𝄢 (Steeple Chase, 1995)
Stardust 𝄢𝄢𝄢 (Steeple Chase, 1995)
The Greeting 𝄢𝄢𝄢 (Steeple Chase, 1996)

worth searching for: Stanley Turrentine's *T Time* 𝄢𝄢𝄢 (Music Masters, 1995, prod. Alan Abrahams) features a pleasant little groove written by Stryker called "Side Steppin'" with a solo from the guitarist/composer. Stryker works the post-midnight funk groove with a swing often lacking in the throwaway songs this genre seems to generate. He is also listed (with Kenny Drew Jr.) as co-arranger of Ivan Lins's beautiful Brazilian ballad, "The Island."

influences:
◄◄ Aaron "T-Bone" Walker, Grant Green, Billy Rogers, Matt Murphy
►► John Scofield

Garaud MacTaggart

John Stubblefield

Born February 4, 1945, in Little Rock, AR.

Not the most famous saxophonist to come out of Little Rock, but miles better than Bill Clinton, Stubblefield looked like a rising star in the 1980s but never saw his career take off the way that those of some contemporaries did. It wasn't from lack of talent or distinctiveness, and his available recordings (not enough of his catalog, alas) are all solidly enjoyable.

During his college years, Stubblefield was already going on the road with well-known R&B bands (the Drifters, Solomon Burke, Jackie Wilson, etc.). He isn't often thought of as an AACM musician, but he joined after moving to Chicago following his graduation. He studied with AACM founder Muhal Richard Abrams and ex–Miles Davis tenorman George Coleman, which suggests broader interests than his available work as a leader shows (then again, he can be heard on Delmark albums by Joseph Jarman and Kalaparusha Maurice McIntyre). Moving to New York in 1971, he provided another informative dichotomy, playing with pianist Mary Lou Williams, who has been famous since the original big-band era; the Collective Black Artists big band; and a number of other large groups, from the Thad Jones/Mel Lewis band to Tito Puente's orchestra. He appeared on record with Miles Davis, McCoy Tyner, Dollar Brand (Abdullah Ibrahim), Lester Bowie, and more, plus pop gigs with Marvin Gaye and Diana Ross. He even co-wrote a jingle for Revlon. For a while in the 1980s he taught at Rutgers University. More recently he has been a member of the repertory group Mingus Big Band.

what to buy: Aside from its swinging title track, *Countin' on the Blues* 𝄢𝄢𝄢 (Enja, 1987, prod. Matthias Winckelmann) isn't the genre exercise its title implies. The opening track, Mulgrew Miller's attractive "Remembrance," is the blues refracted through the prism of early 1960s John Coltrane. Some tracks aren't strictly related to the blues, and hints of Wayne Shorter's 1960s Blue Note period crop up in other pieces. Baritone saxophonist Hamiet Bluiett shares the frontline with the leader, and the contrast is stimulating. Miller sounds quite at home (especially when taking the McCoy Tyner role); Charnett Moffett (bass) shines in several features and Victor Lewis (drums) prods the rhythm acutely. Strict jazz purists may blanche at the short closing track, a fusiony number with a touch of synth and Moffett's percolating electric bass, but it's done tastefully.

what to buy next: More solidly bebop-oriented than some future offerings would be, *Confessin'* 𝄢𝄢𝄢 (Soul Note, 1985, prod. Giovanni Bonandrini) gets the nod for the way Cecil Bridgewater fills out the frontline on trumpet and flugelhorn. In this context, Stubblefield's blues "More Fun" sounds a bit like a tribute to the Cannonball Adderley Quintet with Nat Adderley, though his curling soprano sax lines keep it from becoming a parody. Mulgrew Miller is a more satisfying pianist here than he would become in the next decade, and Rufus Reid (bass) and Eddie Gladden (drums) fill out the rhythm section nicely. With the nine-minute album-closing title track, Stubblefield finally mines the rich vein of modalism and produces his most appealing sound. *Morning Song* 𝄢𝄢𝄢 (Enja, 1993, prod. Harry

Whitaker) is slightly marred by a few early cuts on which the leader's tendency to play sharp gets painfully close to Jackie McLean-like extremeness; otherwise it's a fine quartet effort with pianist George Cables, bassist Clint Houston, and Victor Lewis. His "A Night in Lisbon" is the sort of modal setting in which Stubblefield excels but doesn't play in often enough, while Mickey Tucker's "Slick Stud & Sweet Thang" is a surprisingly greasy bit of soul-jazz that brings out Stubblefield's gospel roots in satisfying fashion.

worth searching for: *Bushman Song* 𝄢𝄢𝄢𝄢 (Enja, 1986, prod. Matthias Winckelmann) is out of print; perhaps the label now blushes at its commercial tint. Listeners not allergic to Stubblefield's occasional overdubbing of himself, or to Geri Allen's electric piano and Yamaha DX-7, or Charnett Moffett's electric bass—factors on only three of the seven tracks—will find an appealingly tuneful collection of Stubblefield compositions. Some of the songs have plenty of depth to them (though "Calypso Rose" is as lightweight as he gets). Plus there's Victor Lewis's funky but complex backbeats and Mino Cinélu's colorful percussion (plus a vocal on the one track he wrote). The ten-minute-plus "East Side—West Side" in particular offers that gotta-have-it modality that marks Stubblefield's best work, with a superb extended tenor solo. It's amusing, too, to read Stanley Crouch's liner notes: you can feel him gritting his teeth as he tries to squeeze out enough backhanded approval of some of the sounds on this record to collect his check.

influences:

◀◀ Wayne Shorter, John Coltrane, Billy Harper, Don Byas

▶▶ Joshua Redman

Steve Holtje

Rolf Sturm

Born June 18, 1962, in Lewisburg, PA.

Sturm attended the Baldwin-Wallace Conservatory, the Berklee College of Music, and Bucknell University. He got his BFA in Jazz Guitar from Ithaca College, and he has studied privately with Jim Hall, John Abercrombie, Bill Frisell, and Joe Pass. Whether playing acoustic or electric guitar, he has a fast, clean technique that he unfurls in knotty lines sometimes reminiscent of Pat Martino, or more effects-treated lines a la Bill Frisell. Sturm has been heard in many contexts: John Zorn's Cobra, the Walter Thompson Orchestra, Joe Gallant's Illuminati, groups led by Jimmy Knepper, Marty Fogel, Frank London, and Ellen Christi, the tango band New York–Buenos Aires Connection, the rock group ATB (All Terrain Band), and even backing the Mills Brothers and country singer Eddy Arnold. He also composes modern classical music and has performed and recorded in that field.

what's available: The Sturm Brothers' *Back Home* 🎵🎵🎵 (Water Street, 1997) contains duos (with bassist Hans Sturm) and trios (with percussionist Glen Velez) covering a wide range of styles and moods, from straight-ahead and contemporary jazz to blues to a mournful tango. Hans (a fine acoustic player) is an equal partner, and the brothers split the composing credits (five tracks each). They are adept at giving each piece a distinctive feel, yet the album coheres nicely. This independent release is distributed by North Country/Cadence.

influences:

◀◀ Jim Hall, John Abercrombie, Bill Frisell, Joe Pass, Pat Martino

Steve Holtje

Ira Sullivan

Born Ira Brevard Sullivan Jr., May 1, 1931, in Washington, DC.

Ira Sullivan is a multi-instrumentalist who grew up in a musical family and, at a young age, began to learn trumpet and saxophone from his parents. He concentrated on tenor saxophone during his high school years, but it was really on trumpet that he began to make a name for himself in Chicago during the 1950s. Early in the decade Sullivan was a member of the house band at the famous Bee Hive club, where he worked with Charlie Parker, Roy Eldridge, Sonny Stitt, Lester Young, Howard McGhee, and Wardell Gray. He played with Art Blakey in New York for a brief period (1956), but never spent much time on the road. At some point Sullivan also took up and perfected flute playing, altering his bebop chops into a freer style. In early 1962 Sullivan and his quartet made a live-recorded tribute album to Charlie Parker, *Bird Lives!*, and then, surprising his fans and colleagues in the early 1960s, Sullivan settled with his family in Florida, where he been steadily working on the local scene. His appearances outside of Florida have been rare, as have his recordings as leader. In 1980, Sullivan formed a quintet with his friend Red Rodney and made some recordings with the trumpeter. Sullivan also recorded on sessions for the Delmark label led by Chicago-based players Lin Halliday and Jim Cooper. Sullivan shows a willingness to experiment, and his albums are usually fresh and exciting, though many of his earliest dates are out-of-print.

what to buy: *Blue Stroll* 🎵🎵🎵 (Delmark, 1997, prod. Robert G. Koester) captures a 1959 session that comes off more as a jam

than an organized studio date, but it's valuable because leader Sullivan pairs with tenor saxophonist Johnny Griffin on the front line, along with Chicago musicians Jodie Christian (piano), Vic Sproles (bass), and Wilbur Campbell (drums). Sullivan plays mostly trumpet, but adds some baritone sax, peck horn, and alto sax on the six straight-ahead tunes (which include an alternate take of "Wilbur's Tune"). The best track is the nearly 20-minute blowout on the bluesy bopper "Bluzinbee" (one of the best single tunes on record), with Sullivan taking the first solo, a burly baritone venture, followed by Griffin's alto solo, Sullivan on trumpet, Griffin on tenor, Sullivan on peck horn, Griffin on baritone, Sullivan on alto sax, and, finally, a drum solo from Campbell. The then-young musicians showed plenty of promise on this session made 40 years ago. This CD is a great listen.

the rest:
Nicky's Tune 🎵🎵🎵 (Delmark, 1994)

worth searching for: Ira Sullivan teams up with leader/guitarist Joe Diorio on a more recent session, *The Breeze and I* 🎵🎵🎵 (RAM Records, 1994, prod. Raimondo Meli Lupi), an airy, melodious album that highlights Diorio's romantic influences upon Sullivan, who plays flute, alto flute, soprano and alto saxophones, and percussion, with expertise, passion, and sweet harmoniousness on the 10 tunes. It's a serene album featuring lush and lovely standards such as "I Wish You Love," "Beautiful Love," "Day by Day," and other plums. Missing, though, is Sullivan's trademark tune, "Amazing Grace," with which he closes all his live performances. Yet the real grace here is heard in Sullivan's and Diorio's warm-toned interactions.

influences:

◀◀ Charlie Parker, Clark Terry, Harry "Sweets" Edison, Lester Young, Coleman Hawkins, Sonny Rollins

▶▶ Joshua Redman, Tom Harrell, Brad Goode

Nancy Ann Lee

Joe Sullivan

Born Dennis Patrick Terence Joseph O'Sullivan, November 6, 1906, in Chicago, IL. Died October 13, 1971, in San Francisco, CA.

One of the most powerful and exciting pianists in all of jazz, Joe Sullivan found himself growing up in Chicago at absolutely the best time and place to learn and create jazz. Classically trained as a youth, Sullivan was already leading his own small group by age 17. He toured in vaudeville, and by the mid-1920s had settled into regular band and radio work throughout Chicago. Along with a number of other Chicago musicians, Sullivan migrated to

New York City by the late 1920s, as regular work became scarce in Chicago because of the increasingly national nature of radio work and the expanding recording industry that was based in the East. Sullivan moved to California by the mid-1930s as a member of George Stoll's Orchestra. He was a regular accompanist to Bing Crosby and made a number of records and films with him. Bing recommended Sullivan to his younger brother Bob Crosby, and Sullivan joined the Crosby organization in 1936. His tenure was cut short by a bout with tuberculosis, which hospitalized him at a sanatorium in California for almost the entire year of 1937. Once recovered, he again played with Bing Crosby before re-joining the Bob Crosby outfit back in New York for a short period in 1939. He left Crosby to form his own fine band at Cafe Society. Some other brief gigs ensued, then he went back out to the West Coast during the war. After the war Sullivan returned to New York to perform with Eddie Condon's gang, then once again returned to California where he played a long residence at the Hangover Club in San Francisco. Sullivan was active in jazz festivals and various club dates during the 1960s until ill health and copious drinking forced him out of music almost entirely.

what's available: All of Joe Sullivan's earliest recordings under his own name can be found on *Joe Sullivan, 1933–1941* 𝄞𝄞𝄞𝄞 (Classics, 1995, prod. Gilles Petard). This includes his four solos recorded by John Hammond for Columbia in 1933 and his equally interesting four solos for Decca in 1935. Either version of "Little Rock Getaway" (the only title recorded for both labels) is impressive as a showpiece for Sullivan's Chicago-style barrelhouse piano. The Decca version has a longer and quite different intro than the one on Columbia, and it's taken at a faster pace. However, the differences only highlight Sullivan's prowess and do not signify either version being better than the other. "Gin Mill Blues" from the Columbia session displays Joe's talent for the blues. His rolling, low-octave bass midway through the solo evokes images of couples slow dancing and tightly embraced in a wooden-floored barrelhouse somewhere. "Minor Mood" for Decca is a minor masterpiece in jazz piano. Sullivan brings together Chicago-style treble (a la Earl Hines) with Harlem stride bass to provide a truly wonderful offering. His Cafe Society band was one of the earliest working mixed bands caught on record. It was a wonderful small band (including Ed Hall on clarinet and Benny Morton on trombone) that did not last long. Some nice recordings here, including perhaps one of the prettiest ballads recorded during the swing era: "I've Got a Crush on You" with vocal by Helen Ward.

worth searching for: Much of Joe Sullivan's work, either as a sideman or under his own name, is still un-reissued. His solo

efforts for the Sunset label in 1944 and 1945 are quite good and deserve to be available again. His solo and quartet recordings for Disc records in 1945 made it to LP, but not to CD. Sullivan's wonderful *New Solos from an Old Master* 𝄞𝄞𝄞𝄞 (Riverside, 1951) also has not yet been reissued on CD. Sullivan recorded some real hot sessions with Red Nichols in 1930 with such titles as "China Boy" and "Shim-Me-Sha-Wabble." Other sessions worth searching for include the McKenzie-Condon Chicagoans titles from 1927 and the Chicago Rhythm King session from 1928. Joe's recordings with both Benny Goodman and Joe Venuti in 1933 are exemplary. Due to their overall superior musical quality, these particular recordings should be mandatory for any serious jazz student and aficionado.

Jim Prohaska

Maxine Sullivan

Born Marietta Williams, May 13, 1911, in Homestead, PA. Died April 7, 1987, in New York, NY.

With her small, clear voice and precise, unhurried phrasing, Maxine Sullivan (born Marietta Williams) was a songwriter's singer, a consistently swinging, unadorned song stylist who improvised around the edges of a tune while staying close to the melody. Her emotionally direct delivery and classy stage presence allowed her the rare ability to interpret songs as if they were written for her, which in some cases they were. (Her own debut recording introduced "Gone With the Wind," and she also was the first to sing "Darn That Dream.") Sullivan got her start singing in Pittsburgh nightspots, eventually landing work on radio broadcasts. She moved to New York in the mid-1930s and was hired to sing during intermissions at the Onyx Club, where she was heard by bandleader Claude Thornhill. He recruited her to sing two of his arrangements of the Scottish songs "Annie Laurie" and "Loch Lomond," and the latter became a huge hit that launched her solo career. Sullivan married bassist and combo leader John Kirby and starred for two years on the CBS radio show *Flow Gently Sweet Rhythm,* the only national broadcast of the time featuring African American artists. She played the Cotton Club with Louis Armstrong and toured with Benny Goodman in 1941. She scored a number of hits with other folk novelty numbers in the late 1930s and early 1940s, but Sullivan left show business for much of the war, the first of her many retirements. She began working again occasionally in the late 1950s, and in the mid-1960s opened a long engagement at the Washington, D.C. club Blues Alley, launching her comeback in earnest. From 1969 on she was working regularly, singing at Dick Gibson's jazz parties with the World's Greatest

Jazz Band, and recording with Earl Hines, Bob Wilbur, Bobby Hackett, and Dick Hyman. She recorded with increasing frequency toward the end of her life, making arguably her best jazz recordings in her seventies.

what to buy: One of only three albums Maxine Sullivan recorded in the 1950s, *A Tribute to Andy Razaf* ✍✍✍✍ (DCC, 1956/1991, prod. Leonard Feather) was the first album devoted to one of popular music's great lyricists. Accompanied by a superb small group featuring trumpeter Charlie Shavers, clarinetist Buster Bailey, saxophonist Jerome Richardson, and a rhythm section led by the redoubtable pianist Dick Hyman, Sullivan sings straight-forward versions of Razaf's collaborations with Fats Waller, Eubie Blake, and others. Her cool, restrained but sassy vocal style fits Razaf's clever lyrics perfectly, especially on "Keepin' Out of Mischief Now," "Honeysuckle Rose," "Ain't Misbehavin'," and the wistful "Memories of You." A highly recommended album. *Uptown* ✍✍✍✍ (Concord Jazz, 1985, prod. Takao Ishizuka) pairs Sullivan with tenor saxophonist Scott Hamilton's neo-swing quintet, featuring John Bunch (piano), Phil Flanagan (bass), Chris Flory (guitar), and Chuck Riggs (drums). With her controlled, swinging phrasing and clear-eyed, unsentimental approach to lyrics, Sullivan sings 10 vintage swing-era tunes without a hint of nostalgia. Highlights include "I Thought About You," "I Got a Right to Sing the Blues," and two Howard Dietz–Arthur Swartz standards, "Something to Remember You By" and "By Myself." Hamilton's warm-toned tenor work compliments Sullivan's small, supple voice effectively throughout the session.

what to buy next: By limiting the program to tunes Harold Arlen and Ted Koehler wrote for Cotton Club reviews, *The Great Songs from the Cotton Club by Harold Arlen and Ted Koehler* ✍✍✍✍ (Stash/MFSL, 1984, prod. Ken Bloom, Bill Rudman, Keith Ingham) had to include a few second-rate tunes. But accompanied by pianist Keith Ingham's quintet, Sullivan makes the most of the selections (all written between 1931–34), singing with impeccable taste and unfailing swing. Highlights include "As Long As I Live," "Ill Wind," "Stormy Weather" and "I've Got the World on a String." (Note: The Great Songs album will be reissued in 1998 on Harbinger Records.) Recorded live in Tokyo less than a year before her death, *Swingin' Sweet* ✍✍✍✍ (Concord Jazz, 1986, prod. Takao Ishizuka) features Sullivan with tenor saxophonist Scott Hamilton's quintet (the same personnel as *Uptown*). Singing 14 swing-era tunes, including the rarely performed "A Hundred Years from Today" and "Cheatin' on Me," she was never in better jazz form. A highly enjoyable album.

best of the rest:

The Biggest Little Band in the Land ✍✍✍✍ (Circle, 1940–41)
Spring Isn't Everything ✍✍✍ (Audiophile, 1989/1994)
Maxine Sullivan Sings the Music of Burton Lane ✍✍✍✍ (Stash/MFSL, 1985,1991/Harbinger, 1998)

worth searching for: Completed just months before her death, *Together: Maxine Sullivan Sings the Music of Jule Styne* ✍✍✍✍ (Atlantic, 1987, prod. Ken Bloom, Bill Rudman, Keith Ingham) captures Sullivan in her best jazz form, her voice a little raspy with age but her sense of swing and impeccable phrasing intact. Singing 16 songs from the pen of Jule Styne, from 1926's "Sunday" to 1983's "Killing Time," Sullivan gives definitive readings of Styne standards such as "Bye Bye Baby," "Things We Did Last Summer," and "Just in Time." Trumpeter Glenn Zottola, trombonist George Masso, and reed player Phil Bodner make the most of their solo space in pianist Keith Ingham's artful arrangements. (Note: This album will be available in 1998 on Harbinger Records.)

influences:

◀◀ Ethel Waters, Mildred Bailey

▶▶ Susannah McCorkle

Andrew Gilbert

Sun Ra

Born Herman Blount, May 14, 1914, in Birmingham, AL. Died May 30, 1993, in Birmingham, AL.

During the 1950s, when such revolutionary figures as Ornette Coleman and Cecil Taylor began carving out niches for their singular sounds, Herman Blount, a little-known pianist, changed his name to Sun Ra, claimed to be from Saturn, and set about rearranging the entire concept of big band jazz. Ra's early years playing around Chicago, solo and with the Fletcher Henderson band, were undistinguished. Even after assembling his Arkestra, their music—increasingly based on African-style polyrhythms, radical harmonics, and Ra's unorthodox compositions—seldom found large audiences until the late 1960s when the psychedelic youth culture connected with the music, colorful costumes, and Ra's mystic philosophy. More than 100 musicians graced the Arkestra over the years, including Craig Harris, Julian Priester, Billy Bang, and Vincent Chauncey, but a core that included reed players John Gilmore, Marshall Allen, and Laurdine "Pat" Patrick, bassist Ronald Boykins, and vocalist June Tyson stayed with the group for decades. For a period in the 1960s and 1970s, the band lived together communally in Philadelphia, and Ra's most consistent label work was for his own Saturn Records. Sources show that there are more than

500 Sun Ra albums. Ra's work breaks roughly into three periods: big band/hard bop exotica during the 1950s; outer and outer free jazz during the 1960s; and swing from the mid-1970s until his death. Ra's longtime saxophonists (John Coltrane acknowledged Gilmore as an influence) were a key element of his sound as he pushed the music further into mystical abstractions without forgetting that it was the beat that made peoples' asses shake. While the music seemed advanced, the Arkestra's stage presence, complete with singers and dancers that sometimes cavorted in the audience, was straight out of vaudeville.

what to buy: The free jazz landmark *The Magic City* 𝄞𝄞𝄞𝄞𝄞 (Saturn, 1965/Evidence, 1993, prod. Infinity Inc., Alton Abraham, reissue prod. Jerry Gordon) is a high point for Ra—and for anyone else. Its mysterious ebbs and flows slowly build to musical tidal waves with eerie synthesizer work, agitated piano, and exultant saxophone solos.

what to buy next: *Mayan Temples* 𝄞𝄞𝄞𝄞 (Black Saint, 1990, prod. Giovanni Bonandrini) was one of Ra's final studio albums and offers a fine summation of his late period, mixing up standards ("Alone Together"), big band exotica, and one long, exploratory piece. Included is a wonderful reading of "El Is the Sound of Joy," which prefigured Coltrane's "Giant Steps."

best of the rest:

Supersonic Jazz 𝄞𝄞𝄞𝄞 (Saturn, 1956/Evidence, 1991)

Sun Song 𝄞𝄞𝄞𝄞 (Delmark, 1957/1990)

Sound of Joy 𝄞𝄞𝄞 (Delmark, 1957)

Jazz in Silhouette 𝄞𝄞𝄞𝄞 (Saturn, 1958/Evidence, 1991)

Sun Ra Visits Planet Earth/Interstellar Low Ways 𝄞𝄞𝄞𝄞 (Saturn, 1958, 1960/Evidence, 1992)

Angels and Demons at Play/The Nubians of Plutonia 𝄞𝄞𝄞𝄞 (Saturn, 1959, 1960/Evidence, 1993)

Sound Sun Pleasure 𝄞𝄞𝄞 (Saturn, 1960, 1973/Evidence, 1991)

We Travel the Spaceways/Bad and Beautiful 𝄞𝄞𝄞𝄞 (Saturn, 1960, 1961/Evidence, 1992)

Fate in a Pleasant Mood/When Sun Comes Out 𝄞𝄞𝄞𝄞 (Saturn, 1961, 1963/Evidence, 1993)

Cosmic Tones for Mental Therapy/Art Forms of Dimensions Tomorrow 𝄞𝄞𝄞 (Saturn, 1962, 1963/Evidence, 1992)

Other Planes of There 𝄞𝄞𝄞𝄞 (Saturn, 1964/Evidence, 1992)

The Heliocentric Worlds of Sun Ra, Vol. 1 𝄞𝄞𝄞𝄞 (ESP, 1965)

Monorails and Satellites 𝄞𝄞𝄞 (Saturn, 1966/Evidence, 1991)

Pictures of Infinity 𝄞𝄞𝄞 (Black Lion, 1968)

Holiday for Soul Dance 𝄞𝄞𝄞 (Saturn, 1969/Evidence, 1991)

Atlantis 𝄞𝄞𝄞 (Saturn, 1969/Evidence, 1993)

Solar Myth Approach 𝄞𝄞𝄞𝄞 (Affinity, 1970)

My Brother the Wind II 𝄞𝄞𝄞 (Saturn, 1970/Evidence, 1992)

Space Is the Place 𝄞𝄞𝄞𝄞 (Blue Thumb, 1972/Impulse!, 1998)

Unity 𝄞𝄞𝄞𝄞 (Horo, 1977)

JOHN GILMORE (WITH SUN RA)

song "The Shadow World"

album *The Magic City*
(Evidence, 1965/1993)

instrument Tenor saxophone

Solo Piano 𝄞𝄞𝄞 (Improvising Artists, Inc., 1977)

St. Louis Blues 𝄞𝄞𝄞 (Improvising Artists, 1978)

Visions 𝄞𝄞𝄞 (SteepleChase, 1978)

Sunrise in Different Dimensions 𝄞𝄞𝄞𝄞 (hat HUT, 1981)

Strange Celestial Road 𝄞𝄞𝄞 (Rounder, 1985)

Reflections in Blue 𝄞𝄞𝄞 (Black Saint, 1987)

Live at Pitt-Inn 𝄞𝄞𝄞𝄞 (DIW, 1988)

Hours After 𝄞𝄞𝄞 (Black Saint, 1989)

Out There a Minute 𝄞𝄞𝄞 (Enigma, 1990)

Somewhere Else 𝄞𝄞𝄞 (Rounder, 1993)

Soundtrack to Space Is the Place 𝄞𝄞𝄞𝄞 (Evidence, 1993)

Live at the Hackney Empire (Leo, 1994)

Live from Soundscape 𝄞𝄞𝄞 (DIW, 1994)

The Singles 𝄞𝄞𝄞 (Evidence, 1996)

worth searching for: There are literally hundreds of Sun Ra LPs that are either out of print or were distributed by Saturn only at Arkestra concerts. Here's a trio of noteworthy gems. On a German label, *It's After the End of the World* 𝄞𝄞𝄞𝄞 (MPS, 1972, prod. Joachim Berendt) captures the Arkestra at two 1970 festival concerts in Germany during a particularly strong and fertile

Sun Ra (© Jack Vartoogian)

period. Ra is playing an especially wide variety of keyboards and the band stretches out on three of the five tracks. *Pathways to Unknown Worlds* ♪♪♪♪ (Saturn, 1973/Impulse!, 1975, prod. Alton Abraham) is a bit easier to find because it's one of the Saturn albums Impulse! licensed in the 1970s (when it was owned by ABC). It's a screaming, totally out-there session with Marshall Allen going off on some long, scorching solos—just about as close as Sun Ra ever got to the energy stream of free jazz. The double LP *Live at Montreux* ♪♪♪♪ (Inner City, 1976, prod. Sun Ra) documents one of the larger versions of the Arkestra, 20 pieces, and drummer Clifford Jarvis really drives the group. Sun Ra's lengthy solo piano intro to the side-long "Take the 'A' Train" is a must-hear, as is Marshall Allen's impassioned second solo on "Of the Other Tomorrow."

solo outings:
John Gilmore:
(With Cliff Jordan) *Blowing in from Chicago* (Blue Note, 1957/1994)
(With Paul Bley, Paul Motian, Gary Peacock) *Turning Point* (1968/Improvising Artist, Inc., 1975)

influences:
◀◀ Fletcher Henderson, Duke Ellington

▶▶ Art Ensemble of Chicago, John Coltrane, Michael Ray and the Cosmic Krewe, Medeski, Martin & Wood, Parliament-Funkadelic

Larry Gabriel and Steve Holtje

Supersax
Formed 1972, in Los Angeles, CA.

Med Flory, clarinet; Buddy Clark, trombone; Bill Perkins; Warne Marsh; Jay Migliori; Conte Candoli; Jake Hanna; Carl Fontana; Jack Nimitz; Lanny Morgan; Lou Levy; Frank De La Rosa.

Supersax bases its entire style and sound on the classic performances of the late great Charlie Parker. A nine-member band, their five-piece sax section impressively replicates Parker's solos in unison. The result is a powerful wall of sound that is as uplifting for the listener as it is technically innovative. Clarinetist Med Flory had begun transcribing Parker's solos with an eye toward forming this type of band during the mid-1960s. It wasn't until 1972 that he and trombonist Buddy Clark were able to pull together musicians accomplished enough to execute the group's concept. Clark left the group after its third LP, but Flory kept various line-ups going, cutting LPs for Capitol, Verve, MPS, and Columbia into the late '80s. On Columbia, Supersax often sweetened its sound with help from the L.A. Voices and string sections, a move that irritated purists, but their underlying instrumental tone stayed in the hard-bop groove all the way. Supersax regrouped for a final LP after Clint Eastwood's 1989 film *Bird* rekindled interest in the music of Parker. Tribute groups don't come any better than this.

what to buy: Most of the Supersax catalog is out-of-print. Fortunately, their Grammy-winning debut and best overall LP, *Supersax Plays Bird* ♫♫♫♫ (Capitol, 1972/Blue Note, 1991, prod. John Palladino), is still available. Featuring their original line-up, the group brings fresh harmonic life to 10 classic slices of Charlie Parker, including "Ko Ko," "Parker's Mood," "Just Friends," and "Lady Be Good." Wild stuff for all you bop fans.

what to buy next: A later line-up of Supersax reemerged to cut *Stone Bird* ♫♫♫ (Columbia, 1989, prod. Ed Yelin), which contains some re-recordings of their earlier material, but still cooks on such numbers as "Salt Peanuts," "K.C. Blues," and "Scrapple from the Apple."

worth searching for: Supersax's live concert LP, *Chasin' the Bird* ♫♫♫ (Verve, 1977), has a stronger improvisational feel than many of their studio albums, and its extended solos make this a must-have item for fans. Supersax makes a guest appearance on Joe Williams's *In Good Company* ♫♫♫ (Verve, 1989), which is still in print and features contributions from Marlena Shaw, Shirley Horn, and Henry Johnson.

influences:

◀◀ Charlie Parker, Joe Maini, Count Basie Saxophone Quartet, Gerry Mulligan, Woody Herman, Stan Kenton

▶▶ L.A. Voices, Twenty-Ninth Street Saxophone Quartet, New York Saxophone Quartet

Ken Burke

John Surman

Born August 30, 1944, in Tavistock, Devon, England.

American listeners first heard Surman on guitarist John McLaughlin's 1969 album *Extrapolation*, the same year Surman started working as a leader after spending most of the decade with British bandleader Mike Westbrook. Considered one of the best English avant-garde saxophonists, perhaps second only to Evan Parker, Surman (who also plays bass clarinet, synthesizer, and piano) has had a long relationship with ECM and has recorded a number of demanding solo albums.

what to buy: *Adventure Playground* ♫♫♫♫ (ECM, 1992, prod. Manfred Eicher) is a superb collaboration between Surman and the trio of Paul Bley (piano), Gary Peacock (bass), and Tony Oxley (drums). The group often leaves a great deal of space, both between the members and in their own playing, which combines with their unpredictability to produce an element of quiet suspense throughout the album. Surman wrote four of the tracks, Bley two, Peacock and Oxley one each, and Carla Bley the final track on a recording where every sound seems absolutely right yet utterly spontaneous.

what to buy next: *Stranger Than Fiction* ♫♫♫♫ (ECM, 1994, prod. Manfred Eicher) is only the second album recorded by Surman's regular quartet with pianist John Taylor, bassist Chris Laurence, and drummer John Marshall. When the group's low-key intensity sometimes builds slowly but inexorably, the contrast of these fuller sections is ecstasy-producing while remaining abstractly songful. Even in the quartet's quietest moments, however, they probe the depths of the music. Lyricism has rarely been so profound.

best of the rest:

Upon Reflection ♫♫♫ (ECM, 1979)
(With Jack DeJohnette) *The Amazing Adventures of Simon Simon* ♫♫♫♫ (ECM, 1981)
Such Winters of Memory ♫♫♫ (ECM, 1983)
Withholding Pattern ♫♫♫ (ECM, 1985)
Private City ♫♫ (ECM, 1988)
Road to St. Ives ♫♫♫ (ECM, 1990)
(With John Warren) *The Brass Project* ♫♫♫ (ECM, 1993)
(With Karin Krog, Terje Rypdal, Vigleik Storaas) *Nordic Quartet* ♫♫♫♫ (ECM, 1995)

worth searching for: The trio consisting of electric guitarist John Abercrombie, bassist Marc Johnson, and drummer Peter Erskine is joined by Surman (who contributes one piece) on *November* ♫♫♫♫ (ECM, 1993, prod. Manfred Eicher). It's an album of atmosphere more than of songs or instrumental flash, and Surman tilts the mood to the *noir* side with his two low-register horns (baritone sax and bass clarinet). The predominant pleasure lies in hearing the musicians listening and responding to each other on this successful communal record. For a sample of early Surman, the easiest-to-find source is John

McLaughlin's *Extrapolation* 🎵🎵🎵 (Polydor, 1969, prod. Giorgio Gomelsky). With Surman, bassist Brian Odges, and Oxley, the guitarist made one of the most exciting and stimulating debut albums ever. Surman plays in a burlier, more aggressive style than can be heard on his later ECM albums.

influences:

◀◀ Jimmy Giuffre, Wayne Shorter

▶▶ Jan Garbarek

Walter Faber

Ralph Sutton

Born November 4, 1922, in Hamburg, MO.

Ralph Earl Sutton considers himself a traditional swing pianist. His playing is often in the Harlem stride tradition, featuring a powerful left hand like his predecessors, Fats Waller, James P. Johnson, and Willie "The Lion" Smith. His right hand spins melodies, dashing, plunging, and hovering all over the keyboard. For over 50 years, Sutton has been dispensing his brand of joyous swing, mellow and memorable melodic improvisation laced with unbridled humor, and consistently remains one step ahead of the best of his competition. Drawing from an ever-broadening base of jazz tunes, vintage pop tunes, and standards, he rarely plays a tune twice the same way.

The son of a country-style fiddler, Sutton grew up near St. Louis and had six years of classical piano training beginning at an early age. He performed with his father's group at local dances and joined Jack Teagarden's band at age 19 after the famous trombonist-leader heard him play at a prom at the Missouri State Teacher's College in Kirksville. After Army service interrupted his career, Sutton performed staff radio work in St. Louis. He became active on the New York jazz scene, appearing in 1947 on the weekly radio show *This Is Jazz*, before working as the intermission pianist at Eddie Condon's club (1948–1956). Tired of New York living, Sutton moved to San Francisco in 1956, worked with Bob Scobey, played intermission piano at the Easy Street club, and gigged around town until he settled in Aspen, Colorado in 1964. Always an individualist, Sutton didn't mind working during the skiing season in the Rocky Mountains where his wife had a supper club. In 1968, Sutton was a founding member of the World's Greatest Jazz Band, which was born out of a series of Colorado jazz parties. Sutton played, toured, and recorded regularly with that group until 1974. Since then he has performed at jazz festivals, concerts, and occasional club dates around the globe, and has recorded extensively at

home and abroad. There remains a genuine sense of joy about Ralph Sutton's playing, which surely must provide therapeutic value to mainstream jazz lovers.

what to buy: Sutton's turn at the Maybeck Recital Hall, *Ralph Sutton at Maybeck* 🎵🎵🎵 (Concord, 1993, prod. Carl E. Jefferson) is Volume 30 in this remarkable piano recordings series produced in Berkeley, California. The August 1993 date finds Sutton in a retrospective mood performing 12 tunes which have been closely identified with him over the years. Four Fats Waller songs ("Honeysuckle Rose," "Clothes-Line Ballet," "Ain't Misbehavin'," and the tongue-in-cheek "Viper's Drag") and two Beiderbecke pieces ("In a Mist" and "In the Dark") are dispatched with loving care, as is "Echo of Spring," the elegant Willie "The Lion" Smith composition which is high among Sutton's favorites. "Love Lies," an obscurity that Sutton embraced in his Teagarden days, is performed along with the almost-forgotten Irving Berlin tune, "Russian Lullaby." This collection is a fitting introduction to this swinging piano veteran's work. A nifty New York quartet session from August 1983, *Partners in Crime* 🎵🎵🎵 (Sackville, 1983, prod. Mark Hewitt) finds pianist Sutton and veteran bassist Milt Hinton in the company of two visiting Australians, trumpeter Bob Barnard and his brother, drummer Len Barnard. Bob's trumpet eases into a comfortable groove, somewhere between Bobby Hackett and Louis Armstrong in concept, and he holds his own with Sutton whose performance on the 10 selections is inspired. A later CD recorded in Sydney, Australia in May 1991, *Ralph Sutton: Easy Street* 🎵🎵🎵 (Sackville, 1991, prod. Jim McLeod) reunites the Barnards and Sutton in 13 trio and duo performances.

what to buy next: Reminiscent of the mid-1980s "Stridemonster" duo dates by Hyman and the late Dick Wellstood, *Dick Hyman–Ralph Sutton* 🎵🎵🎵 (Concord, 1994, prod. Carl E. Jefferson) is an exciting meeting between two legendary jazz pianists. There are romping and stomping duo choruses on "Dinah" and "I Found a New Baby," which understandably brought rousing ovations from the crowd at the Maybeck Recital Hall where this performance was recorded in November 1993. Among the 12 joyous tracks are a thoughtful duet version of "Emaline," and a rollicking "The World Is Waiting for the Sunrise." Each artist gets a solo turn, Sutton on "Everything Happens to Me," and Hyman on "Ol' Man River." In a day when good sound is the norm, sound production here is warm and outstanding, as are the performances. *Ralph Sutton Quintet with Ruby Braff* 🎵🎵🎵 (Storyville, 1996, prod. William A. MacPherson, George C. Tyler) features four veteran jazzmen in a relaxed club date session from three decades ago. Ruby Braff (cornet), Milt Hinton (bass), the late Mousie Alexander (drums), and leader Ralph Sutton on piano put their special jazz stamp on 12 standard tunes. Only one of the tunes, "On the Sunny Side of the Street," was previously issued on an obscure Blue Angel LP. The set shows a melodic Sutton who stays within the swing idiom on numbers such as "Gone With the Wind," "Exactly Like You," and the lovely "Memories of You." Braff, with his passionate style full of subtle surprises, is very effective in this setting. His lyrical variations bring a freshness to songs that were already old when this was recorded years ago. Even "Wang Wang Blues," "Shine," and "Limehouse Blues" sound new. A great set for those who would like to hear what a younger Sutton and Braff sounded like back in the 1960s.

best of the rest:

Ralph Sutton Quartet 🎵🎵🎵🎵 (Storyville, 1977/Storyville 1995)

Last of the Whorehouse Piano Players: The Original Sessions 🎵🎵🎵🎵 (Chazz Jazz, 1980/Chiaroscuro, 1992)

Ralph Sutton: At Café Des Copains 🎵🎵🎵🎵 (Sackville, 1983)

Ralph Sutton and Jay McShann: Last of the Whorehouse Piano Players 🎵🎵🎵🎵 (Chiaroscuro, 1989)

Eye Opener 🎵🎵🎵🎵 (J&M, 1990/Solo Art, 1997)

More At Café Copains 🎵🎵🎵🎶 (Sackville, 1988)

Luckey Roberts–Ralph Sutton: The Circle Recordings 🎵🎵🎵🎶 (Solo Art, compilation 1995)

Alligator Crawl 🎵🎵🎵🎵 (Solo Art)

Sunday Session 🎵🎵🎵🎶 (Sackville, 1996)

Ralph Sutton Trio: Live at Sunnie's, Vol. 1 🎵🎵🎵🎵 (Storyville, 1997)

influences:

◀◀ Fats Waller, James P. Johnson, Willie "The Lion" Smith, Art Tatum

John T. Bitter

Steve Swallow

Born October 4, 1940, in New York, NY.

Steve Swallow spent his childhood in Fair Lawn, New Jersey, where he began playing acoustic bass at age 14 after studying piano and trumpet. He attended Yale University where he studied composition with Donald Martino, and during leisure hours played swing jazz with many notables, including Pee Wee Russell, Buck Clayton, and Vic Dickenson. Swallow left Yale in 1960 and moved to New York City, where he began to play with Paul Bley, the Jimmy Giuffre Trio, and a sextet led by George Russell that included Eric Dolphy and Thad Jones. During these years he also performed with João Gilberto, Sheila Jordan, and bands led by Benny Goodman, Marian McPartland, Chico Hamilton, Al Cohn/Zoot Sims, Clark Terry, and Bob Brookmeyer/Chick

Corea. From late 1956 through 1967, Swallow toured with the Stan Getz Quartet, which then included Gary Burton, whose group Swallow joined in 1968 and with whom he has continued to work for three decades, appearing on more than 20 of Burton's recordings. Swallow began writing music when he joined the Art Farmer Quartet in 1964, and many of his songs have been recorded by notable jazz artists such as Bill Evans, Chick Corea, Stan Getz, Gary Burton, Phil Woods, and others.

After switching from acoustic to electric bass in 1970, Swallow moved to Bolinas, California, where he wrote the music for an ECM duet album with Burton, *Hotel Hello*. Returning to the East Coast in 1974, Swallow taught at the Berklee College of Music for two years. Awarded a National Endowment for the Arts grant in 1976, he set the poetry of Robert Creeley to music, yielding another ECM album, *Home*. During this decade he also performed with such diverse soloists as Dizzy Gillespie, Michael Brecker, Bob Moses, Steve Lacy, Michael Mantler, and others. In 1978 Swallow joined the Carla Bley band, and he continues to perform and record with Bley extensively in myriad settings. Since 1980 Swallow has often performed with, recorded with, and produced albums for guitarist John Scofield. Swallow has also produced several albums with Carla Bley, including the 1985 session *Night-Glo*, which was written to feature him; his 1987 album *Carla* features original compositions written to feature her pianisms. During the 1980s he also performed and recorded with Andy Sheppard, Paul Motian, Joe Lovano, Ernie Watts, Paul Bley, Henri Texier, and others. His duo concerts with Carla Bley since 1988 have been performed throughout Europe, the United States, South America, and Japan, and they have released two duet albums, *Duets* (1988) and *Go Together* (1993) as well as other recordings together. Throughout the 1990s Swallow has performed often, recorded albums with John Scofield and Pat Metheny (*I Can See Your House from Here*), toured internationally, and recorded albums with Carla Bley and a variety of other jazz artists.

what to buy: Playing his five-string bass, Swallow mixes it up with a lively septet on *Steve Swallow* 🎵🎵🎵🎵 (ECM, 1994, prod. Steve Swallow, Carla Bley), a New York City studio session recorded in 1991 with Steve Kuhn (piano), Carla Bley (organ), Karen Mantler (synthesizer, harmonica), Hiram Bullock (guitar), Robby Ameen (drums), and Don Alias (percussion). Guest soloists Gary Burton (vibes) and John Scofield (guitar) greatly enhance the session, which highlights nine modern numbers ranging from Brazilian jazz to jazz-funk, composed and arranged by Swallow. The energetic music sounds as hip and fresh today as when it was made, and the musicians and soloists perform superbly throughout. This album is highly recommended.

what to buy next: For music fans just learning about jazz, it's suggested that you start with simply-layered music and move on to more complex and textured sounds as your ears get acclimated. To further understand the role of the bass in jazz, these duo recordings between pianist Carla Bley and bassist Steve Swallow are recommended. *Duets* 𝄞𝄞𝄞𝄞 (ECM, 1988, prod. Carla Bley, Steve Swallow) features the pair performing nine duets. Original compositions by both musicians yield opportunities to create unusual piano-bass explorations that range from the straight-ahead, Monkish, and lightly swinging ("Baby Baby," "Romantic Notions #3"), to accessible uptempo sprees with Swallow creating walking basslines ("Walking Batteriewoman"), to ballads with lovely folk-influenced melodies ("Útviklingssang"), to gentle Latinate numbers ("Ladies in Mercedes," "Remember," and the nearly nine-minute suite-like "Reactionary Tango—Parts 1/2/3"), and more. This is a resplendent duet album, particularly for late-night listening. Recorded in 1992, another duet session, *Go Together* 𝄞𝄞𝄞𝄞 (ECM, 1993, prod. Carla Bley, Steve Swallow) finds the bassist in sprightly form as he switches between melody lines and a supportive role to Bley's pianisms on the opener "Sing Me Softly of the Blues." As with their earlier album, there is a splendid suite-like piece, "Masquerade in 3 Parts," this time by Swallow. Again, their original improvised music is delightfully listener friendly without smacking too much of the European classical tradition. Plus, the liner booklet contains wittily captioned snapshots reminding you of those dime-store photo machines and hinting at the warm, attractive quality of their music together.

best of the rest:
Home 𝄞𝄞𝄞 (ECM, 1979/1994)
Carla 𝄞𝄞𝄞 (ECM, 1986–87/1994)
Real Book 𝄞𝄞𝄞 (ECM, 1994)
Deconstructed 𝄞𝄞𝄞 (ECM, 1997)

worth searching for: Check the Carla Bley section in your local record store for one of Swallow's best albums, capturing live-recorded trio performances with Bley and British tenor/soprano saxophonist Andy Sheppard during their 1994 tour of France, Italy, Austria, Germany, Turkey, and England. *Songs with Legs* 𝄞𝄞𝄞𝄞 (Watt Works, 1996, prod. Carla Bley, Steve Swallow) is one of their most exciting ventures, yielding exceptional collaborations built on six original "inside-out" compositions and arrangements by Bley. This trio's musical output walks and talks, with Bley's diverse music serving as fuel for their actions. Everyone plays exceptionally well, yielding a most enjoyable listen, especially on tunes such as the gospelized, nearly eight-minute sermon, "The Lord Is Listenin' to Ya, Hallelujah!," featuring a raw-toned tenor sax solo from Sheppard. Other highlights include the perky walker, "Chicken," and a novel, 10-minute interpretation of Thelonious Monk's "Misterioso." Swallow's presence is felt throughout. One of Swallow's dates with the John Scofield Trio, *Out Like a Light* 𝄞𝄞𝄞𝄞 (Enja, 1981, prod. John Scofield) documents a 1981 live-recorded date in Munich that also produced the CD *Shinola*. Five extended tracks (mostly Scofield originals) feature Scofield's guitar, Swallow's acoustic bass, and Adam Nussbaum's drums working as a tight unit. Swallow's strong playing lays tasteful foundations for this guitar trio format, and he often takes moments in the spotlight playing guitar-like melodies in inspired solos. Despite the fact that the group was formed the same year this performance was recorded, there's an easy give-and-take among these musicians as they work their way through mainstream to jazz-rock fusion styles.

see also: *John Scofield, Carla Bley*

Nancy Ann Lee

The Sweet Baby Blues Band
See: Jeannie & Jimmy Cheatham and the Sweet Baby Blues Band

Steve Swell
Born December 6, 1954, in Newark, NJ.

Trombonist Steve Swell was born and raised in New Jersey, where he studied at Jersey City State College before moving into professional musical life in New York City in the first part of the 1970s. Swell played countless gigs prior to 1983, when he toured with Lionel Hampton's band for nearly a year. He then moved on to brief stints with Buddy Rich and pianist Jaki Byard's Apollo Stompers, with whom Swell first recorded in late 1984. He then traveled headlong into New York's avant-garde jazz scene, first with composer Makanda Ken McIntyre and then with Jemeel Moondoc, William Parker, Zane Massey, Roy Campbell, Herb Robertson, Joey Baron, Tim Berne, Phillip Johnston, Perry Robinson, Lou Grassi, and others. Swell currently leads or co-leads several groups: the New York–based quartet ZigZag, a Russian-based free improvisational quintet, a trio with saxophonist Will Connell and drummer Lou Grassi, a large ensemble, the Out and About Quartet with fellow trombonist Roswell Rudd, and a duo with bassist Ken Filiano. Swell has picked up the lead in the world of improvising trombone. He's got the vivacious energy and wit of Roswell Rudd, with whom he studied in the mid-1970s. Swell also has a fast-moving imagination that liberally doses all his solos and compositions with sly hints of pre-bebop jazz, touches of marching brass swagger, and far-reaching explorations of what his horn can achieve outside the realms of standard tonality, execution, and structure. Most of all, Swell injects his music with a considerable degree of whole-hearted joy and a clear sense that he is having fun while playing. In the late 1990s, as he reaches into his forties, perhaps Swell has arrived at a point where he can exercise his considerable creativity while maintaining a secure and stable career as a first-call improviser, composer, and bandleader. His recordings with Phillip Johnston's Big Trouble are now matched by powerful showings with saxophonist Michael Marcus, drummer Tom Schmidt, and vocalist Mary LaRose.

what to buy: *Out and About* 𝄢𝄢𝄢𝄢 (CIMP, 1996, prod. Robert D. Rusch) introduced the Steve Swell Quartet with Roswell Rudd. With his former student in the lead, Rudd blustered and fat-toned his way to a point of sheer excellence on Swell's imaginitive compositions. The music is fairly avant-garde, but it is also highly accessible and even riotously fun.

what to buy next: Another Steve Swell Quartet, this time with saxophonist Mark Whitecage, presents *Moons of Jupiter* 𝄢𝄢𝄢 (CIMP, 1997, prod. Robert D. Rusch), a powerhouse showing for Whitecage and Swell. The buttery energy created by twin trombonists Rudd and Swell is not present here, as Whitecage has a far more precise instrument and execution. In this precision is a quicker, tighter ensemble sound, and the fun the quartet has proves that Swell runs like a champion in all settings. With soprano saxophonist Chris Kelsey, Swell made an inventive duo CD, *Observations* 𝄢𝄢𝄢 (CIMP, 1996, prod. Robert D. Rusch). Although Swell is clearly leaps beyond the merely adequate playing of Kelsey, the pair have a fine avant-garde improvisational chemistry that serves to throw great attention to the trombone's clearly flawless delivery.

worth searching for: Phillip Johnson's Big Trouble presents one of the best silent film scores of the 1990s with *The Unknown* 𝄢𝄢𝄢 (Avant, 1993, prod. Phillip Johnston), and one of the prime reasons the music works so smashingly is Steve Swell. His trombone solos are so limber, so engaging, and so chock full of high-kicking wit, that Johnston's score could not be in better hands when Swell is in the nominal lead taking his several solos.

influences:

◀◀ Roswell Rudd

▶▶ Craig Harris, Frank Lacey

Andrew Bartlett

Gabor Szabo

Born March 8, 1936, in Budapest, Hungary. Died February 26, 1982, in Budapest, Hungary.

Hungarian guitarist Gabor Szabo brought some of his homeland's Gypsy mysticism with him when he fled the Communists in 1956. He ended up in California, studied at the Berklee College of Music, and wound up participating in the early '60s West Coast jazz scene as a member of Chico Hamilton's group. He distinguished himself with a nimble touch and a distinctive style, creating an almost Indian-sounding drone with the lower strings (he does play sitar on some records), and *Down Beat* recognized him by naming him "best new guitarist" in 1964. In 1965 Szabo played in groups led by Gary McFarland and fellow Hamilton graduate Charles Lloyd before starting his own career as a leader. He recorded a series of albums for Impulse!, most notably the live set *The Sorcerer*, featuring the steady back-up of second guitarist Jimmy Stewart. Rock elements began creeping into his work, resulting in a predilection for syrupy dross that would plague Szabo for the rest of his career. He continued to record and tour, including frequent trips back to Hungary to support the local jazz scene there. It was during a 1982 visit that Szabo became ill and died, robbing the world of an unusual talent.

what to buy: Szabo's unique style comes into focus on *The Sorcerer* 𝄢𝄢𝄢𝄢 (Impulse!, 1967, prod. Bob Thiele), a live date from the Jazz Workshop in Boston; trippy originals mix traditional jazz riffs with hypnotic, Gypsy-influenced lines, not to mention the unexpectedly appropriate covers of Sonny Bono's "The Beat Goes On" and the bossa-nova classic, "O Barquinho."

what to buy next: Probably Szabo's purest jazz record, *Spellbinder* 𝄢𝄢𝄢 (Impulse!, 1966, prod. Bob Thiele) features former employer Chico Hamilton on drums, Ron Carter on bass, and Latin percussion from Willie Bobo. Included is the Szabo original "Gypsy Queen," later made into a huge hit by Santana.

what to avoid: The beginning of the end for Szabo's true jazz career came on *Gabor Szabo 1969* 𝄢𝄢 (Skye, 1969, prod. Norman Schwartz); playing covers of Joni Mitchell and Beatles tunes was a bad idea.

best of the rest:

Gypsy '66 𝄢𝄢𝄢 (Impulse!, 1966)
Jazz Raga 𝄢𝄢 (Impulse!, 1966)
The Best of Gabor Szabo 𝄢𝄢𝄢𝄢 (Impulse!, 1968)
Bacchanal 𝄢𝄢𝄢𝄢 (DCC, 1968)
The Szabo Equation: Jazz, Mysticism, Exotica 𝄢𝄢𝄢𝄢 (Jazz Heritage, 1968/1992)

(With Bobby Womack) *High Contrast* ♫♫♫ (Blue Thumb, 1970)
Mizrab ♫♫♫ (CTI, 1972)

influences:

◄◄ Tal Farlow, Charlie Byrd

►► Al Di Meola

Eric J. Lawrence

Lew Tabackin

Born Lewis Barry Tabackin, March 26, 1940, in Philadelphia, PA.

Lew Tabackin, a gifted saxophonist whose technique and tone show influences of Ben Webster, Lester Young, and Sonny Rollins, is equally accomplished as a flute player, often drawing from Asian classical music. Tabackin majored in flute studies at the Philadelphia Conservatory of Music (1958–62). After a stint in the Army, he played with Tal Farlow and Don Friedman before moving to New York in 1965. There he began working with Maynard Ferguson, Clark Terry, the Thad Jones–Mel Lewis Orchestra, Joe Henderson, Donald Byrd, Elvin Jones, the *Tonight Show* band, and others. He led his own trio during 1968–69 and toured overseas where he conducted jazz workshops and appeared as soloist with the Danish Radio Orchestra. Tabackin married Toshiko Akiyoshi and toured Japan with her in 1970 and 1971. In 1972 they moved to Los Angeles and ran a workshop band which evolved into the critically acclaimed Toshiko Akiyoshi Orchestra, featuring Akiyoshi's arrangements and Tabackin's artistry as soloist. The couple returned to New York in 1983. Since then Tabackin has collaborated with numerous small groups and recorded a few albums as leader.

what to buy: *I'll Be Seeing You* ♫♫♫♫ (Concord, 1997, prod. Carl E. Jefferson) features the leader powerfully conveying his musical message with a straight-ahead saxophone style that rivals that of Sonny Rollins. With stellar team support from pianist Benny Green, bassist Peter Washington, and drummer Lewis Nash, Tabackin generates an exceptional nine-tune studio session (recorded in New York in April 1992) with many highlights. The leader is capable of a wide range of expressions, from his kinetic, full-toned tenor readings of appealing boppers such as "I Surrender, Dear," "I'll Be Seeing You," and "In Walked Bud," to his breathy tenorisms on the Monk ballad "Ruby My Dear," to

his graceful, Asian-influenced flute playing on Coltrane's "Wise One" and the Latin-influenced "Chic Lady" (a composition by his wife, Toshiko Akiyoshi). Highly recommended.

what to buy next: On *Tenority* ♫♫♫♫ (Concord Records, 1996, prod. Allen Farnham), Tabackin's fourth Concord album, the distinguished jazz flutist and tenor saxophonist known for his smooth, supple, and sweetly articulate playing exalts standards such as "Autumn Nocturne," "Sentimental Journey," "You Stepped out of a Dream," and other popular favorites. The New York studio session focuses on the veteran jazzman's deep-toned tenor expressions, supported by bassist Peter Washington, drummer Mark Taylor, and lyrical pianist Don Friedman. These musicians, plus guesting trumpeter Randy Brecker, mix it up in various trio and quartet settings. For the first time on his Concord recordings, the leader adroitly stretches from straight-ahead to the outer edge on three pianoless quartet versions of jazz standards performed with Brecker, Washington, and Taylor, making this one of Tabackin's most varied and adventurous albums.

the rest:

(With Hank Jones, Dave Holland, Victor Lewis) *Desert Lady* ♫♫♫♫♫ (Concord, 1990)

(With Benny Green, Peter Washington, Lewis Nash) *What a Little Moonlight Can Do* ♫♫♫♫♫ (Concord, 1994)

Nancy Ann Lee

Jamaaladeen Tacuma

Born Rudy McDaniel, June 11, 1956, in Hempstead, NY.

Tacuma (McDaniel before he converted to Islam) sang doo-wop as a teenager in Philadelphia and started to play the bass at age 13, gigging in R&B bands and making his professional debut in organist Charles Earland's band while still a teenager. When Tacuma was 19, guitarist Reggie Lucas introduced him to Ornette Coleman and he was included in Ornette's groundbreaking Prime Time band from its inception, appearing on the seminal Prime Time albums *Dancing in Your Head*, *Of Human Feelings*, and *Body Meta*. Tacuma's virtuosic and highly melodic style on his trademark Steinberger (headless) bass was a good fit in Coleman's democratically organized Harmolodic music, and has also made him a popular session player with everyone from Jeff Beck, Joe Cocker, Stevie Wonder, Todd Rundgren, and Nile Rodgers to James Blood Ulmer, Olu Dara, Vernon Reid, Julius Hemphill, and David Murray. The bassist even had a pop music fling of his own in the first half of the 1980s, leading the quintet Cosmetic, which released one album and a few rare singles.

what to buy: *House of Bass: The Best of Jamaaladeen Tacuma* 🎵🎵🎵🎵 (Gramavision/Rykodisc, 1994, prod. Jamaaladeen Tacuma, Jonathan F.P. Rose) offers a cross section of Tacuma's first five jazz albums on Gramavision. Tacuma explores the outer boundaries of fusion, mingling Coleman's harmonies, classical dabblings, and a variety of world music styles (especially Middle Eastern modalities) with heavy funk. Tacuma's sinuous basslines are adorned by such high-powered guests as saxmen Julius Hemphill, David Murray, and Byard Lancaster, cornetist Olu Dara, guitarists Vernon Reid and Ronnie Drayton, and drummer Bill Bruford. *Showstopper* 🎵🎵🎵🎵 (Gramavision, 1983, prod. Jamaaladeen Tacuma) was Tacuma's debut. Not content with any one style, he features progressive R&B, fusion, world music, the Ebony String Quartet, and opera singer Wilhemina Fernandez of the cult French film classic *Diva*. The first half of the album is relatively focused, with four cuts by his avant-funk quintet Jamaal.

what to buy next: Dedicated to multi-talented actor and African American icon Paul Robeson, *Renaissance Man* 🎵🎵🎵🎵 (Gramavision, 1984, prod. Jamaaladeen Tacuma) swings from out-funk to cerebral composition and is also half-Jamaal. A cover of Ornette Coleman's "Dancing in Your Head" features the composer on alto sax. *Music World* 🎵🎵🎵🎵 (Gramavision, 1986, prod. Jamaaladeen Tacuma) was made during a world tour, with tracks recorded in France, Turkey, Japan, and the U.S. capturing the moods and styles of the aforementioned countries using such musicians as Andy and Jerry Gonzalez (bass and congas), Jean Claude Asselin (electric mandolin), Yavuz Ozizik (keyboards), Abdur Rahim (sax), and Kazumi Watanabe (electric guitar).

the rest:
(With Cosmetic) *So Tranquilizin'* 🎵🎵 (Gramavision, 1984)
Jukebox 🎵🎵🎵 (Gramavision, 1987)
Boss of the Bass 🎵🎵🎵 (Gramavision, 1991)
Sound Symphony 🎵🎵🎵 (Moers, 1992)
The Night of Chamber Music 🎵🎵🎵 (Moers, 1993)
Dreamscape 🎵🎵🎵 (DIW, 1996)

worth searching for: *Gemini* 🎵🎵🎵🎵 (ITM Pacific, 1987, prod. Jamaaladeen Tacuma, Wolfgang Puschnig) is an interesting duet recording with Wolfgang Puschnig on alto sax, hojak, programming, and vocals.

influences:

◀◀ James Jamerson, Buddy Miles, Michael Henderson
▶▶ Albert MacDowell, Chris Walker

David C. Gross and Steve Holtje

Aki Takase

Born January 26, 1948, in Osaka, Japan.

Pianist Aki Takase received her earliest piano training from her mother, a piano teacher, who gave her daughter classical lessons from the age of three. Takase also played acoustic bass in an all-woman band in high school, and after graduation studied piano at Tohogakuen University of Tokyo. Inspired by recordings of Charles Mingus, Ornette Coleman, and John Coltrane, she began learning on her own how to improvise. Takase got her first professional gigs in 1971 and by age 25 was leading her own groups. She recorded with saxophonist Dave Liebman in the early 1980s, and appeared with her trio at the Berlin festival. Takase has worked with artists such as Cecil McBee, Sheila Jordan, and Bob Moses, and a solo piano concert at the East-West Festival in Nuremberg brought her critical acclaim. She played regularly in a duo with Maria Joao from 1988–1994, and maintained a busy touring schedule. During the mid-1990s, she toured with Rashed Ali and Reggie Workman (a trio which yielded the recording *Clapping Music*), formed a septet, and recorded with the Toki String Quartet, as well as working as a solo performer. While Takase focuses on jazz improvisation, she draws from the broadest palette to include elements from the Japanese musical tradition as well as from European Classical music. Takase also plays the koto, a traditional Japanese 17-string, zither-like instrument, but it is her unmatched, multifarious piano performances and her skills as composer-arranger that rank her as a top innovator among her contemporaries.

what to buy: Aki Takase is joined by bassist Reggie Workman and drummer Sunny Murray on the live-recorded *Clapping Music* 🎵🎵🎵🎵 (Enja, 1995, prod. Barbara Ruger, Horst Weber), a nine-tune session that includes originals by Takase, Charles Mingus, Thelonious Monk, and other composers. During the 1960s (a period in American jazz which seems to have greatly influenced Takase), Workman was John Coltrane's bassist and Murray collaborated with Albert Ayler and Cecil Taylor. Brought together originally by producer Weber, the three innovators worked together in 1993, and their affinity for ear-expanding, seamless performances together is evident on this illustrious set, especially on their nine-and-a-half minute interpretation of Mingus's "Boogie Stop Shuffle." On such classics as "Do You Know What It Means to Miss New Orleans" and Coltrane's "Reflections" and "Oska-T," Takase demonstrates that she is entrenched in the entire jazz tradition, able to impart impressionistic pianisms which draw from the earliest jazz styles to the present. Buy any one of her albums and you'll be richly rewarded. By her ninth album, *Oriental Express* ♪♪♪♪♫ (Enja, 1996, prod. Barbara Ruger), there's no question about Aki Takase's penchant for composing fresh material and leading sizzling modern sessions. For this fittingly titled album, Takase wrote arrangements for the five tunes (includes her three originals) and leads her six sidemen in a rollicking, inside-out session that provides ample space for her sidekicks to solo with surprising bluesy suppleness and to conduct avant-garde marauds. Exceptionally fine solo (and ensemble) work from trombonist Hiroshi Itaya, tenor/baritone saxophonist Hiroaki Katayama, alto/soprano saxist Eiithi Hayashi, and trumpeter Issei Igarashi (who would baffle blindfolded test-takers with their New York avant-garde sound) engages listeners with the nearly 25-minute homage to Charles Mingus's "So Long Eric/Duke's Choice/Goodbye Pork Pie Hat." Equally mesmerizing are Takase's works ("In and Out," "Open The Door," and the title tune) and "Point," a piece by (her husband) pianist Alex V. Schlippenbach. Her rhythm mates, bassist Nobuyoski Ino and drummer Shota Koyama, display their artistry and knowledge of the American jazz tradition. Takase is virtuosic; her playing is full of rich ideas and surprising musical twists which draw from the entire jazz tradition..

what to buy next: Takase's willingness for experimentation yields an exciting album with the Toki String Quartet and an equally adventurous bassist Nobuyoshi Ino on *Close Up of Japan* ♪♪♪♪♫ (Enja, 1993, prod. Horst Weber), an eight-tune album of standards and Takase originals that merge American free jazz, European chamber music, and Japanese influences. Takase's own broadly-based performances (using approaches from deeply romantic to percussive and cutting edge) provide extraordinary stimulation, especially her avant-garde, churning piece "Presto V.H" and her romantic title ballad. Ino can make his bass sound like a growling bear or a deep-toned sweet instrument. Surprises abound as Takase and Ino interact passionately on a daringly bold and beautiful version of Charlie Haden's "Song for Che." Takase's virtuosic piano artistry (as well as her skills as arranger) are amply displayed on the 11-minute poignant treatment of Astor Piazzolla's "Winter in Buenos Aires." An exceptional album that should appeal to fans of new music. A solo piano studio session of 13 standards and originals, *Shima Shoka* ♪♪♪♪ (Enja, 1990, prod. Horst Weber) features Takase demonstrating her strong two-handed approach and an ability to spontaneously compose using a variety of piano techniques (including tweaking the piano strings). Takase is a self-determined player who carves her own path through her ebullient originals and classics such as

Coltrane's "Giant Steps," Mingus's "Goodbye Pork Pie Hat," and Rollins's "Valse Hot." She definitely has an idea-rich style all her own, which she capably exhibits on this provocative outing. On *Perdido* ♪♪♪♪ (Enja, 1982, prod. Horst Weber), Takase is documented in a masterful live-recorded performance at the East-West Festival in Nuremberg, Germany, on June 19, 1982. Playing both piano and koto (sometimes in the same tune), Takase delivers one of her highly acclaimed, career-making performances (and you'll hear why). Though she draws from her European classical training as well as avant-garde players such as Don Pullen, Cecil Taylor, and the like, Takase is truly a one-of-a-kind artist, capable of some of the freshest improvisations imaginable. And this early album only hints at what was yet to come.

the rest:
(With Maria Joao) *Looking for Love* ♪♪♪ (Enja, 1993)
(With David Murray) *Blue Monk* ♪♪♪♪ (Enja, 1994)

influences:

◀◀ Bill Evans, Bud Powell, Herbie Hancock, Charles Mingus, John Coltrane, Ornette Coleman, Gary Peacock, Charlie Haden, Maurice Ravel, Claude Debussy, Erik Satie, Bela Bartok

Nancy Ann Lee

Tom Talbert

Born August 4, 1924, in Crystal Bay, MN.

A particularly fine arranger/composer, Tom Talbert is obscure even by the standards of jazz's most overlooked craft, probably due to his infrequent and hard-to-find recordings. First exposed to jazz through listening to the radio, he began studying arranging and piano in high school. He moved to California in the mid-1940s, leading an experimental orchestra that at times featured such advanced musicians as pianists Dodo Marmarosa and Claude Williamson, and saxophonists Hal McKusick, Lucky Thompson, and Art Pepper. The band worked and recorded intermittently through 1949, sessions that have been reissued on Sea Breeze. When Stan Kenton formed his Innovations band in 1950, a number of Talbert's players joined and Talbert wrote arrangements for Kenton. He toured with Anita O'Day in 1947, and in 1950 moved to New York where he picked up freelance work writing for the big bands of Buddy Rich, Claude Thornhill, Boyd Raeburn, Machito, and Tony Pastor, and combos led by Oscar Pettiford, Marian McPartland, Kai Winding, and Charlie Ventura. In the mid-1950s, Talbert recorded a session with singer Patty McGovern and his classic *Bix Duke Fats* album, which has been reissued by Sea Breeze. He spent much of the 1960s and early 1970s in the Midwest, working with a large ensemble. He moved to Los Angeles in the mid-1970s, began writing for TV, and assembled a septet, later expanded into a big band, to play his charts. He has recorded a number of fine albums for Sea Breeze.

what to buy: Though it was hailed as a masterpiece when it was first released on Atlantic, *Bix Duke Fats* ♫♫♫♫ (Modern Concepts, 1956/Sea Breeze, 1994, prod. Tom Talbert) is a long lost gem that was reissued on CD. Talbert uses different instrumentation for each of the composers, covering four tunes by Waller, three by Beiderbecke, two by Ellington, and one original. The sessions feature top-flight jazzmen such as pianist George Wallington, trumpeter Joe Wilder, trombonists Jimmy Cleveland and Eddie Bert, and alto saxophonist Herb Geller, though the star is Talbert's inventive, finely textured arrangements. The pianoless octet he uses for Beiderbecke's "In a Mist," "Candlelights," and "In the Dark" includes bassoon and French horn, and his arrangements effectively highlight the impressionist influences in Bix's music. Geller's lush alto is featured throughout the Ellington pieces, most memorably on a rhythmically tame but harmonically tasty version of "Ko-Ko." Wilder's beautiful, warm trumpet and Cleveland and Bert's expert trombone work are featured on the Waller tracks, where Talbert manages to translate some of Fats's irrepressible spirit into his arrangements.

what to buy next: Talbert knows to look for gold in a gold mine, and he hits pay dirt again and again on *Duke's Domain* ♫♫♫♫ (Sea Breeze, 1994, prod. Tom Talbert), a brilliant big band session exploring the music of Ellington and Strayhorn. Talbert contributes his own homages to each of the great composers, and splits the rest of the album between them, covering five Strayhorn pieces, including a fascinating version of the obscure "After All," and three pieces and a medley by Ellington. His voicings are often strikingly beautiful, and there are many deft touches throughout, such as the French horn introduction to "Chelsea Bridge." Featured musicians include trumpeters Bob Summers and Steve Huffsteter, trombonist Andy Martin, pianists Tom Garvin and Tom Ranier, and saxophonist Gary Foster.

best of the rest:
Tom Talbert Jazz Orchestra 1946–1949 ♫♫♫♫♫ (Sea Breeze, 1995)
Louisiana Suite ♫♫♫♫ (Sea Breeze, 1977/1994)
Things As They Are ♫♫♫ (Sea Breeze, 1987/1994)
The Warm Cafe ♫♫♫♫ (Modern Concepts/Sea Breeze, 1993)

influences:
◀◀ Duke Ellington, Gil Evans

Andrew Gilbert

TanaReid
See: Rufus Reid

Horace Tapscott
Born April 6, 1934, in Houston, TX.

True genius is an often-overlooked and unwanted commodity in today's instantly disposable, "product"-oriented atmosphere that celebrates mindless replication and entertainment-as-diversion far more than thought-provoking originality. A pianist, composer, and community activist, Horace Tapscott is, despite his virtually unknown status, a towering musical genius who only makes about one record each decade, if you discount the series of albums for the minuscule Nimbus label that have documented most of his moves over the past 20 years. But like Randy Weston, Andrew Hill, Mal Waldron and others of this ilk, he deserves to be revered and treasured. After moving to Los Angeles with his family when he was 11, Horace Tapscott started out as a trombonist, landing a gig with Gerald Wilson's big band by the early 1950s. While serving in the air force he made the switch to piano. He later toured briefly with Lionel Hampton, but soon decided to act locally rather than globally, and formed his famed Pan-Afrikan People's Arkestra in 1961. The Arkestra, based in a neighborhood church and dedicated to developing the talents of youth in the South Central Los Angeles community, presents free concerts and workshops. Tapscott still occasionally ventures out of the 'hood to play club and concert gigs, however, in a wide variety of settings including solo piano, piano-drum and piano-bass duos, trio, and quintet. His music, which is mainly modally concerned, is commanding—when he leans into a piano, you take notice, and hear the joy and the sorrow, the ancient to the future, the now and the ever after.

what to buy: In the past couple of years, things have been looking up. New York's Arabesque label has taken an interest in Tapscott, and have thus far issued a pair of excellent albums. *Thoughts of Dar-Es Salaam* ♫♫♫♫ (Arabesque, 1997, prod. Ray Drummond, Daniel Chriss) is a stunning set that teams Tapscott's booting keyboard with Drummond's steady bass work and Jabali Billy Hart's powerful, yet nuanced, drumming. *Thoughts* includes a breakneck treatment of Sonny Rollins's "Oleo" and a ringing "Now's the Time" alongside seven Tapscott compositions, including the Weston-like strains of "As a

Child" (note how the cover shot alludes to Weston's own *With These Hands*) and the happy "Social Call." *Aiee! The Phantom* 𝄢𝄢𝄢 (Arabesque, 1996, prod. Daniel Chriss, Adam Abeshouse) is nearly as good, with Reggie Workman, Andrew Cyrille, and the Detroit-based trumpeter Marcus Belgrave. What keeps it from ascending to the heights of *Dar-Es Salaam* is the appearance of the youthful and unformed alto playing of Abraham Burton on a few of the record's tracks. Still, given the paucity of available Tapscott material, this one will do quite nicely.

what to buy next: Of the Nimbus albums, you'd be well-advised to check out *Flight 17* 𝄢𝄢𝄢 (Nimbus, 1978, prod. Tom Albach), an expansive recital by the Pan-Afrikan People's Arkestra. The lengthy title cut, which begins with Tapscott delving into the piano's soundboard to create an otherworldly prelude that is soon joined by a quavering string obligato over which the rest of the ark bray and whine, is a magnificent sustained workout. At the other end of the manpower rainbow sits the so-called *Tapscott Sessions, Vol. 8* 𝄢𝄢𝄢 (Nimbus, 1991, prod. Tom Albach), the latest in an ongoing series of solo piano recordings that includes lengthy, filigreed versions of Monk ("Crepuscule with Nellie"), Waldron ("Fire Waltz"), and Weston ("Little Niles"), as well as his own "As a Child."

worth searching for: In 1989, hat ART's Werner X. Uehlinger taped a couple of nights at a Los Angeles venue, the Catalina Bar & Grill, and released the results as *The Dark Tree, Volumes 1 & 2* 𝄢𝄢𝄢𝄢 (hat ART, prod. Werner Uehlinger, G. G. Schmid). John Carter's clarinet is a perfect foil of the leader's piano, and the Cecil McBee–Andrew Cyrille rhythm section can't be beat. These titles have recently been deleted, but they are well worth searching out. So is Tapscott's first date as a leader, *The Giant Is Awakened* 𝄢𝄢𝄢𝄢 (Flying Dutchman, 1969, prod. Bob Thiele), which also marked the recording debut of altoist Arthur Blythe. The dual-basses of David Bryant and Walter Savage Jr., and the drumming of longtime associate Everett Brown Jr., round things out. Most of the remaining Nimbus issues have yet to make it onto compact disc, but they include *The Call* 𝄢𝄢𝄢 (Nimbus, 1978, prod. Tom Albach) and *Live at the I.U.C.C.* 𝄢𝄢𝄢 (Nimbus, 1981, prod. Tom Albach), both of which are by the Arkestra; *At the Crossroads* 𝄢𝄢𝄢 (Nimbus, 1980, prod. Tom Albach), a keyboard-drum duo with Everett Brown Jr.; *Dial B for Barbra* 𝄢𝄢𝄢 (Nimbus, 1981, prod. Tom Albach), which is a sextet date; and the two volumes of *Live at Lobero, Vol. 1* 𝄢𝄢𝄢 (Nimbus, 1982, prod. Tom Albach) and *Live at Lobero, Vol. 2* 𝄢𝄢𝄢 (Nimbus, 1982, prod. Tom Albach), featuring a trio with Roberto Miranda on bass and Sonship on percussion.

David Prince

Vladimir Tarasov

Born 1947, in Archangelsk, USSR.

As drummer for the Ganelin Trio, Tarasov has more than staked his claim as one of the most important Eastern European percussionists around. However, the marvelous series of records (all titled, or subtitled, *Atto*—"act" in Italian) he's cut as a leader since 1985 has sealed his reputation as a fantastic percussionist and a forward-thinking, highly intellectual composer/improviser.

what to buy: *Atto III: Drumtheatre* 𝄢𝄢𝄢𝄢 (Sonore, 1988/1994, prod. Peter Motovilov), the third of Tarasov's solo endeavors, is undoubtedly his best. With Tarasov alone responsible for the many percussion sounds on this disc, this nearly 40-minute drum piece (laced with overdubs of extremely odd and often funny sounds) is a vibrant masterpiece, showcasing Tarasov's mastery of the craft, as well as his inescapable political awareness.

what to buy next: On *Atto V* 𝄢𝄢𝄢 (Sonore, 1991/93, prod. Peter Motovilov), Tarasov, as one of the only players who can get away with 30- and 40-minute drum solos that don't bring the listener to the brink of suicide, plays consistently delightful solo "attos." This fifth edition finds the drummer in a relatively straightforward situation, with the samples and effects rarely overshadowing his playing (as they do on *Monotypes*, for instance). With Tarasov drumming and conducting the 15-piece Baltic Art Orchestra, the mammoth *Live at Jazz Baltica* 𝄢𝄢𝄢 (Sonore, 1994/1996, prod. Peter Motovilov) is surprisingly rewarding. Although it's difficult to tell the depth of compositional detail that went into it, the interplay of startlingly fresh improvisation and clearly thought-out context makes this disc the best of Tarasov's large band excursions.

the rest:

Atto I: Something Has Happened against the Marine Background 𝄢𝄢𝄢 (Sonore, 1985/1995)
Atto II: Monotypes 𝄢𝄢 (Sonore, 1986/1995)
Atto IV 𝄢𝄢𝄢𝄢 (Sonore, 1989/1994)
Atto VI 𝄢𝄢𝄢 (Sonore, 1991/1993)
Atto VII: Water Music 𝄢𝄢𝄢 (Sonore, 1992/1994)
Atto VIII: Sonore 𝄢𝄢𝄢 (Sonore, 1993)
(With Ilya Kabakov) *Olga, Something Is Burning* 𝄢𝄢𝄢 (Sonore, 1993)
(With the Lithuanian Art Orchestra) *Waltz Atto* 𝄢𝄢𝄢 (Sonore, 1993)
(With the Thundering Dragon Percussion Group) *Chinese Project* 𝄢𝄢𝄢 (Sonore, 1994)
(With Vladimir Miller and Vitas Pilbavicicus) *Frontiers* 𝄢𝄢𝄢 (Leo Lab, 1995)

worth searching for: The one-off date *Red & Blue* (Historical Performance, 1988, prod. Peppo Spagnoli) teams Tarasov up with his Ganelin partner Vladimir Chekasin, as well as the only Italian free jazz legend, altoist Mario Schiano. Although Schiano has collaborated with a wide range of musicians, this combination—thanks to the thick Lithuanian accents of Tarasov and Chekasin—is fresh and sympathetic.

Jason Ferguson

Buddy Tate

Born February 22, 1913, in Sherman, TX.

One of the few remaining swing-era players, tenor saxophonist Buddy Tate first made a name for himself as a member of the Count Basie band during the 1930s. His husky, warm, and burnished sound was true to form with the other heavyweights of the time, such as Ben Webster, Coleman Hawkins and Herschel Evans. However, Tate's delightful swagger and exuberance, not to mention his distinctive clarinet playing, helped him to stand apart from his contemporaries. Throughout the 1930s, 1940s, and 1950s, Tate was an in-demand player and he worked with a variety of popular big bands, including those led by Nat Towles, Lucky Millinder, Hot Lips Page, Jimmy Rushing, and Andy Kirk. Over the following few decades, Tate led his own band in a lengthy stay at Harlem's Celebrity Club, in addition to recording a fine series of albums for the Prestige label. During the 1970s, the saxophonist kept busy as a touring artist in Europe and through his work with Benny Goodman, Jay McShann, and Paul Quinichette. Tate has lately been heard from on rare occasions, yet he continues to play and record sporadically. His recent stint with Lionel Hampton proved that he is still a committed player with something meaningful and distinctive to say.

what to buy: Both of the following quintet dates are important because they feature Tate in the company of swing-era trumpeter Buck Clayton: *Buck & Buddy* ♫♫♫♫ (Prestige Swingville/ OJC, 1960, prod. Esmond Edwards) and *Buck & Buddy Blow the Blues* ♫♫♫♫ (Prestige Swingville/OJC, 1961, prod. Esmond Edwards). The material is familiar and the performances are sublime and inspired. Of particular interest are the few cuts that feature Tate's seldom-recorded clarinet work.

what to buy next: *Groovin' with Tate* ♫♫♫♫ (Prestige/ Swingville, 1959–1961, prod. Esmond Edwards) combines on one CD the original albums *Tate's Date* and *Groovin' with Tate*. While the latter is a pleasant quartet outing, the former is an exciting large group date that features many of Tate's col-

leagues from the Harlem nightspot, Celebrity Club. The empathy they obviously share make this a joyous romp that never fails to reward.

the rest:
Buddy Tate and His Buddies ♫♫♫ (Chiaroscuro, 1973)
The Ballad Artistry of Buddy Tate ♫♫♫♫ (Sackville, 1981)
Just Jazz ♫♫♫♫ (Reservoir, 1984)

worth searching for: *Tate-a-Tate* ♫♫♫♫ (Prestige/Swingville, 1960, prod. Esmond Edwards) is only currently available on vinyl, but is worth looking for if you still own a turntable. With Clark Terry and Tommy Flanagan on board, Tate goes for broke and the results are invigorating.

influences:
◀◀ Herschel Evans, Coleman Hawkins, Ben Webster

Chris Hovan

Grady Tate

Born January 14, 1932, in Durham, NC.

Few musicians gain notoriety on more than one axe, but Grady Tate has received acclaim both as a solid jazz drummer and melodic baritone singer. As a youth Tate played drums and sang at church and social functions until his voice changed. At that point he abandoned singing, focusing solely on drums through his teen years. While a member of the U.S. Air Force Band he started singing again, fronting a 21-piece unit, but after he left the service his drumming sidetracked his singing career. In 1959 he backed "Wild" Bill Davis, and a couple of years later he was playing for Quincy Jones. An excellent drummer, Tate has worked for some of the best jazz players and popular singers, including Duke Ellington, Count Basie, Stan Getz, Jimmy Smith, Benny Goodman, Wes Montgomery, Ray Charles, Tony Bennett, Lena Horne, Della Reese, and Sarah Vaughan. Tate relaunched his singing career in 1968 and has made a number of recordings usually as a singer. As a drummer, Tate is a well-respected player. As a singer, he is a good performer most obviously influenced by Joe Williams.

what to buy: With a solid quartet behind him, on *TNT* ♫♫♫♫ (Milestone, 1991, prod. Bob Porter) Tate sings 10 standards with the warmth and enthusiasm necessary to make this a winner. Less pop-influenced than many of his albums, he actually comes across better in this setting, suggesting he should pursue more straight-ahead singing dates in the future. A very pleasant affair.

Art Tatum **(Archive Photos)**

what to buy next: *Body & Soul* ♪♪♪ (Milestone, 1993) is a vocal very typical of a pop/jazz recording from the late 1980s/early 1990s. Tate's voice is in fine form. Nice, but not much more.

influences:

◀◀ Max Roach, Philly Joe Jones, Joe Williams, Billy Eckstine

Paul MacArthur

Art Tatum

Born October 13, 1909, in Toledo, OH. Died November 5, 1956, in Los Angeles, CA.

Ask any jazz keyboardists prior to 1960 to name their favorite piano player, and they almost invariably say Art Tatum. For sheer technical mastery, Tatum had no peer at the time (and perhaps only Cecil Taylor has rivaled him since), but his harmonic and linear invention, lush tone, and relaxed swing also helped make him the pianist's pianist.

Tatum was born blind in one eye and with only partial sight in the other. Although he could read sheet music with glasses or by using the Braille method, he learned to play primarily by ear off of piano rolls, radio, records, and from other musicians in the Toledo area. In 1932 he came to New York as the accompanist for singer Adelaide Hall. Tatum was a prodigy and, even at this early juncture, he essentially had all the elements of his style in place; his four earliest recorded piano solos can be heard on the album *Piano Starts Here*. In the 1930s, his reputation was primarily as an unaccompanied soloist, but he could be an adept small combo player, as shown by a 1941 session backing blues singer Joe Turner and an all-star session with Coleman Hawkins recorded for Commodore Records in 1943. In early 1944 he established a trio patterned after Nat "King" Cole's which featured Slam Stewart on bass and either Tiny Grimes or Everett Barksdale on guitar. Beginning in 1953, Tatum began an association with producer Norman Granz that resulted in the recordings on which his reputation largely rests today—a monumental 121 unaccompanied solos and a series of small group sessions with Benny Carter, Buddy DeFranco, and Ben Webster, among others. He remained an active performer up until his death from uremia in 1956. Although Tatum performed regularly in concert halls, clubs, and on radio primarily in Hollywood, New York, and Chicago, he remained more of a critical and musicians' favorite than a popular star.

Tatum synthesized jazz piano styles of his day into a grand and florid style that also incorporated advanced harmonies, radical leaps in logic, and unusual phrase lengths. He exerted a strong, direct influence on pianists of the bop generation and indirectly on all pianists afterwards. Tatum's left hand figures demonstrate his admiration for Fats Waller and other Harlem stride pianists, while his intricate right-hand lines and his habit of abandoning the beat show the influence of Earl Hines. In his solo performances he often favored rubato introductions before launching into variations and reharmonizations of the tune. Tatum rarely if ever remained in tempo for an entire performance, breaking up stride passages with blindingly fast, ornate lines that seemingly disregard the tempo, only to land squarely in place when they end. He never entirely abandoned a melody for long, often disguising it in fantastically reharmonized form or in intricate variations. His constant referral to the melody led to charges that he was not a genuine improviser. These charges were compounded by his habit of playing many of his recorded solos note for note or with minor variations in concert, and occasional over-reliance on favorite phrases and devices. But after-hours tapes and other live recordings show that Tatum continued to grow and take risks as an improviser throughout his entire career. In groups, Tatum's dense, busy style, confounding harmonies, and rhythmic sophistication could paralyze lesser horn players, but those who found a way to cope with his outpourings were clearly inspired. Despite his extreme sophistication, Tatum was a relaxed and often unpretentious and entertaining player who delighted himself and his audiences with his remarkable abilities.

what to buy: *The Complete Pablo Solo Masterpieces* ♪♪♪♪♪ (Pablo, 1991, prod. Norman Granz) is the Sistine Chapel of solo jazz piano. There has never been a single achievement by another pianist to equal this overwhelming display of piano technique and improvisatory imagination, recorded in a mere four studio sessions from December 1953 through January 1955. The seven CDs in the box are also available individually, but Tatum is so consistently brilliant throughout these sessions that there is virtually no reason to recommend one over another. If you can't afford the box, choose a CD that contains tunes you like and listen in awe to what Tatum does with them. Each session on *The Complete Pablo Group Masterpieces*

Art Tatum

song "I Wish I Were Twins"
album *The Standard Sessions*
(Music and Arts, 1935/1995)
instrument Piano

Monster Solo

♪♪♪♪♪ (Pablo, 1991, prod. Norman Granz) has a different character, depending on the other featured soloist, but these group recordings are almost the equal of Tatum's solo recordings for Granz. Again the entire box is worth owning, but more distinctions are possible. The meeting with the imperturbable, soulfully mellow Ben Webster is probably the crowning glory of the group dates. Benny Carter's aristocratic elegance and intelligence also mesh beautifully with Tatum's. Clarinetist Buddy DeFranco also finds lots of common ground with Tatum. The piano trio date is a tightly synchronized group showcase for Tatum. The sessions with Lionel Hampton and Roy Eldridge bring out the lighter, cheerier side of Tatum's playing. Only the sextet with Harry Edison, Hampton, and Barney Kessel fails to live up to the exulted standards set by the others.

what to buy next: *20th Century Piano Genius* ♪♪♪♪ (Verve, 1996, prod. Richard Seidel) refutes those who say Tatum was a formulaic player, as this informal session at the home of a Hollywood friend finds Tatum in a consistently inventive mood. Technically mind-boggling, as usual, but also lighthearted at times.

The Complete Capitol Sessions, Volumes 1 & 2 🎵🎵🎵 (Capitol, 1949) contains more sterling solo performances, including masterful versions of "Willow Weep for Me" and "Aunt Hagar's Blues." The trio with Stewart and Barksdale constrains Tatum harmonically and rhythmically, and on a couple tracks it sounds like he's merely going through the motions.

best of the rest:

Piano Starts Here 🎵🎵🎵🎵 (Columbia, 1933, 1949)
The Standard Transcriptions 🎵🎵🎵🎵 (Music & Arts, 1935–43)
Classic Early Solos (1934–37) 🎵🎵🎵🎵 (Decca, 1991)

worth searching for: *God Is in the House* 🎵🎵🎵🎵 (Onyx, 1972, prod. Don Schlitten) presents a remarkable portrait of the genius relaxing after hours that ranges from tossed-off duets with a club owner playing whisk brooms on a chair to a truly memorable encounter with the unjustly neglected trumpeter Frankie Newton.

influences:

◀◀ Earl Hines, Fats Waller

▶▶ Oscar Peterson, Tommy Flanagan, Hank Jones, Adam Makowicz, Bud Powell, Lennie Tristano

Ed Hazell

Art Taylor

Born April 6, 1929, in New York, NY. Died February 6, 1995, in New York, NY.

As one of the house drummers for both the Prestige and Blue Note labels, Art Taylor can be found on countless numbers of archetypal record dates from the 1950s and 1960s. His popularity with both his employers and fellow musicians is not hard to understand. Taylor's style was about providing the best support for the soloist while maintaining his own polyrhythmic voice. His crisp snare drum patterns and tasteful drum fills and solos fit perfectly with the extroverted hard bop that was coming out of New York at the time. Taylor's first appearance of note was with Howard McGhee in 1948, and he followed that up with short stints with Coleman Hawkins, Donald Byrd, and pianists Bud Powell and George Wallington. An extensive period of recording activity following that found him working with John Coltrane (he's the drummer on the legendary *Giant Steps* album), Mal Waldron, Miles Davis, Thelonious Monk, Budd Johnson, and Red Garland, just to name a few. Beginning in 1963, Taylor would spend the next 20 or so years living in France and Belgium where he played with such fellow expatriates as Dexter Gordon and Johnny Griffin. It is also during this

period that he would compile his frank and revealing book of interviews with jazz musicians collected in *Notes and Tones*. In the early 1990s, Taylor returned to an active role as a leader with the re-formation of his group known as Taylor's Wailers. The band was important not only for the two impressive recordings they made, but for the valuable exposure given to such up-and-comers as tenor saxophonist Willie Williams, pianists Marc Cary and Jacky Terrasson, and alto saxophonist Abraham Burton. Sadly, Taylor's premature death cut short what could have been a viable unit for launching young jazz talents.

what to buy: *A.T.'s Delight* 🎵🎵🎵🎵 (Blue Note, 1960/1996, prod. Alfred Lion) is a brilliantly arranged session that pairs trumpeter Dave Burns and saxophonist Stanley Turrentine on the front line with Wynton Kelly and Paul Chambers in the rhythm section. Adding to the excitement are the spirited exchanges between Taylor and conga drummer Potato Valdez on a few cuts and the appearance of two stellar Kenny Dorham compositions. *Mr. A. T.* 🎵🎵🎵🎵 (Enja, 1991, prod. Matthias Winckelmann) was Taylor's return to the Rudy Van Gelder studios (where he was so busy recording during the 1950s that he left one drum set there all the time) and to recording activity with his Wailers. Walter Bolden's choice compositions and a fiery band with Willie Williams, Abraham Burton, and Marc Cary all help make this Taylor's greatest record of his career.

what to buy next: *Taylor's Tenors* 🎵🎵🎵 (New Jazz, 1959/OJC, 1994, prod. Esmond Edwards) is essentially a blowing session, but what a fine one it is! Charlie Rouse and Frank Foster make a killer tenor pair, and pianist Walter Davis is no slouch either. An inspired selection of material includes Monk's "Straight, No Chaser" and "Rhythm-a-Ning." *Wailin' at the Vanguard* 🎵🎵🎵🎵 (Verve, 1992, prod. Brian Bacchus) is a live and charged set caught at the famous Village jazz spot and features some vital playing from Willie Williams, Abraham Burton, and pianist Jacky Terrasson. Unfortunately, this would be the swan song for Taylor's Wailers.

the rest:

Taylor's Wailers 🎵🎵🎵 (New Jazz, 1957/OJC, 1992)

influences:

▶▶ Kenny Washington, Lewis Nash, Billy Drummond

Chris Hovan

Billy Taylor

Born July 24, 1921, in Greenville, NC.

Most of the world knows Dr. Billy Taylor as a TV personality from his appearances on *CBS Sunday Morning,* but insiders are aware of his dedication to the idiom as an educator and spokesperson, as well as an archetypal trio pianist who was employed in Ben Webster's group within three days after arriving in New York City after graduation from Virginia State College in 1942. Taylor jumped into the thriving 52nd Street scene, working with an array of stylists including Billie Holiday, Ella Fitzgerald, Coleman Hawkins, Eddie South, Stuff Smith, Cozy Cole, Roy Eldridge, and numerous others. Taken under the wing of Art Tatum, Teddy Wilson, and Joe Jones, Taylor gigged with a variety of stylists including a stint with Machito's Afro-Cuban band, touring Europe with the Don Redman orchestra, and replacing Erroll Garner in the Slam Stewart Trio. A busy musician during those days, Taylor performed in New York, Boston, and Washington, D.C., and was house pianist at Birdland in New York City from 1949–1951, where he backed Charlie Parker, Lee Konitz, Gerry Mulligan, Miles Davis, Roy Eldridge, Dizzy Gillespie, and a host of other jazz luminaries. The Birdland stint became his learning ground and prepared him for a year-long engagement in 1951 at Club Le Downbeat, where his trio included bassist Charles Mingus and drummer Charlie Smith. Earl May replaced Mingus when the legendary bassist left to form his own group. Taylor's trio was joined by the legendary Cuban drummer, Candido, in the early 1950s.

Taylor made recordings with a variety of jazz artists for Roost, Prestige, Riverside, ABC Paramount, Impulse!, Mercury, Capitol, and other labels during the 1950s, and started his own publishing company (Duane Music Inc.). He also began to write about jazz and present lectures and clinics to music teachers, and to focus on expanding jazz audiences through the use of radio and television exposure. He was musical director of the first jazz series produced by the National Educational Television network, where his band included trumpeter Doc Severinsen, reedman Tony Scott, trombonist Jimmy Cleveland, guitarist Mundell Lowe, Earl May or Eddie Safranski on bass, and Ed Thigpen or Osie Johnson on drums. Taylor continued his educational activities and cofounded New York's Jazzmobile programs. For three years in the early 1970s, Taylor served as musical director of the televised *David Frost Show,* then returned to radio where he helped build the biggest jazz radio audience in New York for WLIB. Taylor began work on his doctorate during his stint with Frost, earning his degree in several years. Although his time was devoted to arts advocacy, during the 1970s Taylor managed to write some commissioned works for large jazz ensembles, and continued to perform with his trio. He hosted the National Public Radio broadcast, *Jazz Alive,* which was followed by a series

which traced the history of jazz, *TaylorMade Piano.* He toured extensively, performing in concert halls, community centers, and with symphony orchestras around the world.

In the middle of this bustling period of activity he was offered the job of arts correspondent for *CBS Sunday Morning,* a task that continued into the 1990s and for which he has profiled more than 150 jazz artists. Taylor also hosted his own jazz piano show on the Bravo cable TV channel, composed additional works during the 1980s–1990s, and continued a busy lecture schedule as well as serving since 1994 as artistic advisor for an ongoing jazz concert series at the John F. Kennedy Center for the Performing Arts. He has won numerous awards, including two Peabodys, an Emmy, the NEA's Jazz Masters Fellowship, and others. In recent years Taylor has recorded for Concord, GRP, Arcadia, and his Taylor-Made label. He has written over 300 original compositions, and published the book *Jazz Piano: A Jazz History.* His current working trio is with bassist Chip Jackson and drummer Steve Johns.

what to buy: *Billy Taylor Trio* ♪♪♪♪ (Prestige, 1952–1953/1995) is a pleasant album that documents the early years of the pianist's trio when he was one of the busiest musicians in New York. His first trio dates were recorded in the mid-1940s when he was newly arrived in New York and still under Art Tatum's influences. However, the 20 tunes on this disc were made nearly a decade later with bassist Earl May and drummer Charlie Smith, and show that Taylor had come into his own, using a chordally-rich technique (especially on ballads) and his lightening-quick, single-line runs on up-tempo swingers. If you believe that the world's most prominent jazz educator can't play, check out his reflective performances of mostly standards. While there's not a weak tune in the bunch, highlights include an amazingly speedy version of "Lover" which converts to waltz tempo at the end, a swinging reading of "They Can't Take That Away from Me," a Monk-tinged reading of the swinger "Give Me the Simple Life," a tidy, tasteful, toe-tapping "Let's Get Away from It All," and delicate, rich interpretations of "Little Girl Blue" and "Tenderly," among other jazz standards. This CD reissue combines his two LPs, *Billy Taylor Trio, Vol. 1* and *Billy Taylor Trio, Vol. 2* and is a must-own for anyone interested in Taylor; it's the gem of a classic piano jazz trio recording made during this period. Turn the calendar ahead four decades, and you have the wonderfully enlivened session *It's a Matter of Pride* ♪♪♪♪ (GRP, 1994, prod. Michael Abene, Billy Taylor), featuring a cross-generational, Taylor-led team with two of the best younger jazz lions, bassist Christian McBride and drummer Marvin "Smitty" Smith. They artfully perform 10 Taylor originals written between the 1940s and 1970s, highlighting guest soloists Stanley Turrentine (tenor saxophone on three tracks), Grady Tate (vocals on two numbers), and Ray Mantilla (congas on the Latinate "Picture This" and "I'm a Lover"). Taylor is at his eloquent best throughout the swinging and bopping session, proving that despite his role as a jazz spokesperson in recent years, he still has spectacular magic in those fingers. A rare recording in any arena, *My Fair Lady Loves Jazz* ♪♪♪♪ (Impulse!, 1965/1994, prod. Creed Taylor) finds Taylor gliding and swinging through Quincy Jones's jazz arrangements from the score of the popular Broadway show and subsequent film *My Fair Lady.* If you dug the tunes the Lerner–Loewe team introduced to the world, you'll love this February 1957 session that features Taylor with bassist Earl May, drummer Ed Thigpen, and baritone saxophonist Gerry Mulligan (on four tracks) enhancing classics such as "The Rain in Spain," "I've Grown Accustomed to Her Face," and other popular favorites given jazz bounce and verve. Among other soloists featured in the medium-size ensemble are Charles Fowlkes (baritone sax), Jimmy Cleveland (trombone), and Ernie Royal (trumpet). You'll be glad you sprung for this album when you hear their bossa version of "The Rain in Spain." Taylor is superb at the helm throughout. After hearing this session you'll wonder why arranger Jones went so far astray into the pop field when he has the talent for writing such riveting jazz arrangements.

what to buy next: *Homage* ♪♪♪♪ (GRP, 1995, prod. Michael Abene, Billy Taylor) features Taylor with the Turtle Island String Quartet on Taylor's commissioned three-movement title suite (a tribute to violinists Eddie South and Stuff Smith, bassist Slam Stewart, cellist/bassist Oscar Pettiford, and others). Taylor has appeared as sideman on recordings with TISQ in the past, and their work together is engaging, lively, and swinging. Yet on this Grammy-nominated disc Taylor excels on the 10 remaining original tunes performed with his trio featuring bassist Chip Jackson and drummer Steve Johns (with percussionist Jim Saporito augmenting five tunes). Among the album's many highlights are the gently swaying "Kim's Song," the near–avant-garde "Hope and Hostility" (which prominently features Jackson), Taylor's solo piano version of the Waller-influenced ragtime tune "Uncle Bob," and a deeply entrenched blues, "Two Shades of Blue." Taylor's jazz rapping on the catchy tune "On This Lean, Mean Street" belies his age. Trio tunes are pert, animated, melodically pleasing and tap into Taylor's vast stylistic artistry. This is one of his best recent trio albums. With the same trio, Taylor recorded *Music Keeps Us Young* ♪♪♪♪ (Arkadia, 1997, prod. Bob Karcy, Billy Taylor), an

album of five standards and six originals that launched Bob Karcy's Arkadia label. There's a magic happening with this straight-ahead trio, no doubt due equally to the material and the tight companionship (after three years of working together) between Taylor and his younger sidekicks. Jackson, from Rockville Center, New York, has performed with a host of top-name jazz players, including Elvin Jones, Gary Burton, Horace Silver, Betty Carter, Stan Getz, and others. Johns is from Boston and has backed Gary Bartz, Nat Adderley, George Russell, and others. The trio generates fresh readings of classics such as "Lover Come Back to Me," "Up Jumped Spring," "Naima," "Body and Soul" (the longest tune at 10:38), and an impassioned reading of Taylor's bluesy, "I Wish I Knew How It Would Be to Feel Free," which served as the anthem of the civil rights movement in the 1960s and was used in the film *Ghosts of Mississippi.* For the ear-pleasing mixture of ballads, swing tunes, and blues, this album is highly recommended. On his own Taylor-Made label, *You Tempt Me* ♪♪♪♪ (Taylor-Made, 1989, prod. Billy Taylor, Jim Anderson) is an equally impressive trio set with lyrical bassist Victor Gaskin and tasteful drummer Curtis Boyd, recorded on June 24, 1985. The album's focus is Taylor's six-part jazz suite *Make a Joyful Noise,* inspired by the 100th Psalm and originally commissioned by Robert Shaw for the Atlanta Symphony. Taylor conveys his spirituality on the deeply-felt and reverent "Let Us Make a Joyful Noise/Spiritual," with Gaskin's lovely bowed solo and Boyd's soft brushwork greatly enriching the 11-minute piece. Other highlights from this suite include Boyd's talents on the traps on the enlivened rhythms of "Rejoice," the peacefully melodic "Prayer," the lilting hallelujah chorus "Celebrate," and the finale, "Walking in the Light," a seven-minute spree that amply highlights Gaskin and the enthusiastic exchange between Taylor and Boyd. The joyful Taylor title tune, with its catchy rhythms, is a listening delight, as is the swinger "Tom, Vaguely." Taylor also artfully engineers a respectful, delicate piano-bass duo reading of Ellington's "Take the 'A' Train," the only standard amidst the eight tunes. This is a must-own album that displays some of Taylor's most delicate and celebratory improvisations. Still listed in print at the time of this writing, *Dr. T* ♪♪♪♪ (GRP, 1993, prod. Dave Grusin, Larry Rosen) is an illustrious collection of 10 standards and originals which opens with a hard-swinging alteration of the usual ballad, "I'll Remember April," featuring Taylor with his excellent, regular rhythm team, Victor Gaskin (bass) and Bobby Thomas (drums). Baritone saxophonist Gerry Mulligan lends his romantic cool composure to "'Round Midnight," his sterling sense of swing on his original "Line for Lyons," and a memorably lush version of the Taylor original, "Just the Thought of You." Taylor hadn't recorded with Mulligan since the 1950s, but with his trio backs Mulligan with elegant ease throughout, making this a choice addition for any collection.

best of the rest:
The Billy Taylor Trio with Candido ♫♫♫♪ (Prestige, 1954/OJC, 1991)
With Four Flutes ♫♫♫♪ (Riverside, 1959/OJC, 1994)
Solo ♫♫♫♪ (Taylor-Made, 1988)
White Nights & Jazz in Leningrad ♫♫♫♪ (Taylor-Made, 1988/1993)

worth searching for: While Taylor has more vibrant sessions in print, completists will want to search for the CD *Among Friends* ♫♫♫♪ (Harrison Digital Publications, 1992), which features the Billy Taylor Trio, with Victor Gaskin (bass) and Bob Thomas (drums), enhanced by the inventions of tenor/soprano saxophonist Fred Tillis. Recorded at the University of Massachusetts in 1991, these old friends deliver a 10-tune session that includes one original each from Taylor ("A Bientot") and Tillis ("The Holidays"), with the rest of their inventions focused on gems by Charlie Parker ("Confirmation"), Benny Carter ("When the Lights Are Low"), Antonio Carlos Jobim ("How Insensitive"), Ellington ("It Don't Mean a Thing"), and others.

influences:
◄◄ Teddy Wilson, Art Tatum, Erroll Garner

►► Cyrus Chestnut, Ahmad Jamal

Nancy Ann Lee

CECIL TAYLOR

song "With (Exit)" (master take)
album Conquistador
(Blue Note, 1966/1989)

instrument Piano

Monster Solo

Cecil Taylor

Born Cecil Percival Taylor, March 15, 1930, in Long Island City, NY.

Cutting a definitive path through the complex thicket of post-bop jazz, contemporary classical music, and experimental noise-mongering that has made the latter half the 20th century so darned interesting, Cecil Taylor has deployed his art as equal parts mystic evocation, avant-garde battle cry, architectonic razzle-dazzle, and aesthetic tough-man contest. The process, which really got going after the classically trained composer left the New England Conservatory of Music in the mid-1950s, continues into Taylor's fifth decade of public performance. He is one of the handful of demigods in the vanguard wing of jazz—or creative improvised music, as some prefer. He's a touchstone for three generations of like-minded musicians, the single degree of separation between such disparate (but eagerly exploratory) collaborators as Gil Evans and Thurston Moore (of noisy art-rock outfit Sonic Youth). Now pitched somewhere between grand diva and free-jazz grandpappy, Taylor founded an entire school of hyper-dynamic pi-

anism that lifts off from the varied examples of Bud Powell, Thelonious Monk, and Duke Ellington to create a fierce, captivating and ultimately elegant soundscape of shifting textural layers and resounding accents; approach the keyboard, he once said, as if it were "88 tuned drums"—or 96, given his preference for German-made Bosendorfers. A radical figure whose place in jazz is somewhat akin to John Cage's in classical music, Taylor incorporates dance and poetry into his performances, flirting with shamanistic, stream-of-consciousness utterances and impromptu movement that finds him shaking his graying dreadlocks while he prances in gym sweats. Taylor suffered for his art in the 1960s, his dues-paying days as a dishwasher duly noted by writer A.B. Spellman in his celebrated book *Four Lives in the Bebop Business*. Decades on, Taylor was the recipient of a MacArthur Foundation "genius grant." A 1988 festival in Berlin, commemorated by an astounding 11-CD box set on the German label FMP, cemented his Olympian status in performances with a flock of European improvisers.

what to buy: Taylor has recorded prolifically, yet much of his catalog slips in and out of print or exists on pricey or obscure European labels. But a great entry point is *Nefertiti: The Beautiful One Has Come* 🎵🎵🎵🎵 (Revenant, 1997), a domestic indie reissue of a classic 1962 concert with drummer Sunny Murray and alto saxophonist Jimmy Lyons—two of Taylor's most important partners. The two CDs boast some previously unreleased material. Recorded at the Cafe Monmartre in Paris, the music finds Taylor with one foot in tradition and the other in the future, essentially birthing his signature style. Think of Picasso and Braque inventing Cubism, and imagine what *that* might have sounded like, and you can get an idea of why this record is so important. From here, it's probably a matter of what *kind* of Cecil you prefer.

what to buy next: *Unit Structures* 🎵🎵🎵🎵 (Blue Note, 1966, prod. Alfred Lion) marks a breakthrough, establishing a group identity for Taylor's concepts, which as the title implies function in an almost molecular fashion. Lyons returns, with Andrew Cyrille on drums, two bassists (Alan Silva and Henry Grimes), Eddie Gale Stevens Jr. on trumpet, and Ken McIntyre on various reeds. It's a challenging record, as dense and complex as any of the period's towering highwire acts, yet rich in beauty and intellectual bravado. It's a distressing comment on mainstream jazz's backward-mindedness that nothing like this happens on major labels today. A decade later, *One Too Many Salty Swift and Not Goodbye* 🎵🎵🎵🎵 (hatART, 1991) finds a 1978 Taylor unit blowing the roof off a Stuttgart concert hall. The volatile ensemble—Lyons, as ever, with trumpeter Raphe Malik, violinist Ramsey Ameen, bassist Sirone, and drummer Ronald Shannon Jackson—matches and even exceeds the leader's gift for surging electrical flow, everyone staking out and defining their individual space amid roiling give-and-take. Lyons and Malik make especially sympathetic foils for each other, setting a sharp tone with a heraldic opening duet.

best of the rest:

Jazz Advance 🎵🎵🎵 (Blue Note, 1956)

Looking Ahead! 🎵🎵🎵🎵 (OJC, 1958)

The World of Cecil Taylor 🎵🎵🎵🎵 (Candid, 1960)

Conquistador! 🎵🎵🎵🎵 (Blue Note, 1966)

Silent Tongues 🎵🎵🎵🎵 (Freedom, 1975)

Dark Unto Themselves 🎵🎵🎵🎵 (1976/Enja, 1990)

Cecil Taylor Unit 🎵🎵🎵🎵 (New World, 1978)

3 Phasis 🎵🎵🎵🎵 (New World, 1978)

It Is in the Brewing Luminous 🎵🎵🎵🎵 (hat ART, 1980)

(With Max Roach) *Historic Concerts* 🎵🎵🎵🎵 (Soul Note, 1984)

Olu Iwa 🎵🎵🎵🎵 (1986/Soul Note, 1994)

For Olim 🎵🎵🎵🎵 (Soul Note, 1987)

Alms/Tiergarten (Spree) 🎵🎵🎵🎵 (FMP, 1988)

The Hearth 🎵🎵🎵🎵 (FMP, 1988)

Always a Pleasure 🎵🎵🎵 (FMP, 1996)

worth searching for: Taylor's latter-day prime is heard on *Looking (Berlin Version)* 🎵🎵🎵🎵 (FMP, 1990, prod. Jost Gebers), featuring the extraordinary Feel Trio (drummer Tony Oxley, bassist William Parker). The 72-minute set veers between the pianist's bracing tempos—ideas and idioms zip by as if on fast-forward—and a mellowing sense of incantatory gesture. The former is fed by Parker's dizzying, bowed harmonics, the latter enhanced by Oxley's uniquely omniversal bank of percussive tools. FMP is a German label that has provided considerable documentation of Taylor over the past decade; its releases can be obtained through the Cadence mail-order catalog if not found in your local store.

influences:

◀◀ Bud Powell, Thelonious Monk, Duke Ellington

▶▶ Marilyn Crispell, Matthew Shipp

Steve Dollar

John Tchicai

Born April 28, 1936, in Copenhagen, Denmark.

Tchicai has one of the most instantly recognizable sounds in jazz, a light, dry, vocal keen with a carefully controlled vibrato. His solos are deliberately constructed themes and variations played with a relaxed swing but developed with surprising leaps and twists.

After meeting Archie Shepp and Bill Dixon at the Helsinki Jazz Festival in 1962, he moved to New York City in 1963, where he enjoyed the most productive three years of his career. With Shepp and trumpeter Don Cherry he was coleader of the New York Contemporary Five, a band whose impact was larger than its short life in 1963 and 1964. With Roswell Rudd he cofounded another short-lived band, the New York Art Quartet, whose polyphonic free improvisations were among the most radical of its day. In addition, Tchicai appeared as a sideman on several landmark recordings of the New York avant-garde, including John Coltrane's *Ascension,* Archie Shepp's *Four for Trane,* and Albert Ayler's *New York Eye and Ear Control.* Tchicai returned to his native Denmark in 1966, where he founded the Cadentia Nova Danica big band (1967–73) and worked with the Strange Brothers in the later part of the decade. In the 1980s Tchicai toured and recorded with several prominent groups and artists, including the New Jungle Orchestra, the Cecil Taylor Orchestra of Two Continents, and tenor saxophonist Charles Gayle, then switched his main instrument from alto to tenor saxophone. In the early 1990s he moved to California, where he performed around San Francisco and taught at the University of California at Davis.

what to buy: *The New York Art Quartet and Imamu Amiri Baraka* 🎵🎵🎵🎵 (ESP, 1964, prod. Bernard Stollman) is a benchmark recording of the 1960s New York avant-garde, as remarkable for the intensity of its group interaction as for individual solos. Tchicai and trombonist Roswell Rudd are unlikely but perfectly matched foils, and the polyrhythmic outpourings of drummer Milford Graves are awe-inspiring. *Grandpa's Spells* 🎵🎵🎵🎵 (Storyville, 1993, prod. Arnvid Meyer, Peter Danstrup) ranges confidently from the Jelly Roll Morton title track to free improvisation. With touches of mordant humor and spiky playing from Dutch pianist Misha Mengelberg, it's one of Tchicai's best recent recorded performances. *Timo's Message* 🎵🎵🎵🎵 (Black Saint, 1984, prod. Giovanni Bonandrini) is an excellent showcase for Tchicai the soloist. He digs into the grooves by the quartet's two bassists, and his improvisations at times burst into ecstatic warbling; clearly, he's enjoying himself.

what to buy next: A duet with Polish bassist Vitold Rek, *Satisfaction* 🎵🎵🎵 (Enja, 1991, prod. Christiane Schulte-Strathaus, Vitold Rek) has an easygoing rapport with some marvelous soprano sax improvising and poetry recitals. On *Love Is Touching* 🎵🎵🎵 (X-Talk, 1995, prod. John Tchicai), the backup band, a California group called the Archetypes, isn't nearly at Tchicai's level, but it plays with enthusiasm and Tchicai is in good form.

what to avoid: *Merlin Vibrations* 🎵🎵 (Planisphare, 1983, prod. John Tchicai) is a classic "You had to be there" album: probably fun for the musicians to play and enjoyable for the audience, but doesn't translate well to recording.

worth searching for: Far too much Tchicai is out of print, including *Afrodisiaca* 🎵🎵🎵🎵 (MPS, 1969, prod. Joachim Berendt), a splendid recording by a 30-piece edition of Cadentia Nova Danica that blends African grooves with free jazz fire.

Ed Hazell

Jack Teagarden

Born Jack Weldon Leo Teagarden, August 29, 1905, in Vernon, TX. Died January 15, 1964, in New Orleans, LA.

Trombonist-vocalist Jack Teagarden is one of the true giants of jazz. His unique tone and braggadocio style of playing make him identifiable with just one measure of music—even

the playing of one note sometimes can be enough to give Teagarden away. Born to a musical family, Teagarden was playing trombone by the age of 10. His dad was an amateur trumpet player; his mother played piano, as did his sister, Norma; brother Charlie played trumpet; and brother Clois played drums. By age 15, Teagarden was playing with various bands, and he toured the Southwest and Mexico extensively through the mid-1920s. By then, he had become almost legendary to those who had heard him, and his fame preceded his trip to New York in 1927. His first recordings (with the Roger Wolfe Kahn and Ben Pollack Orchestras) show a trombonist whose skill was almost unmatched by any other jazz trombonist, black or white. Teagarden became fast friends with the other titans who were shaping the jazz world of the time: Benny Goodman, Coleman Hawkins, Louis Armstrong, Bix Beiderbecke, Fats Waller, and Red Allen, among others. A number of recording sessions (many of which seem more like organized jam sessions) were issued from this period. Teagarden's voice was just as good as his trombone playing, making his presence on a record date a most treasured event.

Teagarden played with Ben Pollack's band on and off for a good part of the late 1920s and early 1930s. He played briefly with Red Nichols at the Hotel New Yorker and on some excellent recordings for Brunswick during this period. He formed his own band briefly during 1933 and played at the Vienna Gardens, located in the 1933 Chicago World's Fair grounds (and also recorded four titles for Columbia). The Depression caused Teagarden to seek steady income, which he found with Paul Whiteman's Orchestra. Teagarden stayed on for five years and then left Pops in 1938 to form his own big band. The business end of the music profession was ultimately too much for Teagarden and he disbanded his group near the end of World War II. The war years may have been Teagarden's best artistic period. His 1943 and 1944 sessions with the Capitol Jazzmen on Capitol, George Wettling on Keynote, and Louis Armstrong on V-Disc are breathtaking. After the war and his dissolution of his band, he joined Louis Armstrong's All-Stars, playing with Louis until 1951. Upon leaving Louis, Teagarden formed his own small group. He toured right up to his death in 1964.

what to buy: Teagarden's Victor recordings covered a wide variety of settings and spanned much of his career. These are chronicled in the two-CD set, *The Indispensable Jack Teagarden, 1928–1957* 🎵🎵🎵 (RCA, 1995, prod. various) and start with his first recorded solo as a sub (for Miff Mole!) with Roger Wolfe Kahn's Orchestra on "She's a Great, Great Girl," and end with the wonderful Bud Freeman's Chicagoans titles. Equally diverse but more focused on his earlier output are two CDs: *I Gotta Right to Sing the Blues* 𝄞𝄞𝄞𝄞 (ASV Living Era, 1992, prod. various) and *The Best of Big T* 𝄞𝄞𝄞𝄞 (Topaz, 1995, prod. various), each of which cover pretty much the same ground. The best of Teagarden's work with Paul Whiteman, Frankie Trumbauer (see the Trumbauer entry for Teagarden's complete output under Tram's leadership), Wingy Manone, Ben Pollack, and others are featured here. Off and on, from 1930 until 1934, Teagarden led bands under his own name. *A Hundred Years from Today* 𝄞𝄞𝄞𝄞 (Conifer, 1994) chronicles the best of these titles, while *Jack Teagarden, 1930–1934* 𝄞𝄞𝄞𝄞 (Jazz Chronological Classics, 1994, prod. Gilles Petard) does its usual job of completeness in acceptable sound. Teagarden's first leadership date for ARC (American Record Company) produces standard Depression fare, until Teagarden comes and saves the day on "You're Simply Delish." The recording dates get better, especially the 1931 Columbia session with Fats Waller. The ride-out on "Chances Are" is so exquisite that it elevates this recording almost to desert island status. Teagarden's Brunswick sessions from 1933 and 1934 provide excellent examples of Teagarden's singing prowess and are showcases for his trombone. In fact, for the first Brunswick date, Teagarden was featured on the original 78rpm recordings as a vocal star and not the orchestra leader. For examples of Teagarden's later work, the best reissues currently available can possibly be found on the wonderful limited edition set, *The Complete Capitol Fifties Jack Teagarden Sessions* 𝄞𝄞𝄞𝄞 (Mosaic, 1995, prod. Charlie Lourie, Michael Cuscuna). This tasteful set has outstanding sound and content, superlative vocals and trombone solos by Teagarden, and wonderful improvisational as well as arranged venues to showcase the irrepressible talent of Big T.

what to buy next: The balance of the Jazz Chronological Classics series *Jack Teagarden, 1934–1939* 𝄞𝄞𝄞 (Jazz Chronological Classics, 1994); *Jack Teagarden, 1939–1940* 𝄞𝄞 (Jazz Chronological Classics, 1994); *Jack Teagarden, 1940–1941* 𝄞𝄞 (Jazz Chronological Classics, 1995); and *Jack Teagarden, 1941–1943* 𝄞𝄞𝄞 (Jazz Chronological Classics, 1996) feature Teagarden's big band. Many instrumental titles are quite good, and Teagarden shines on both vocal and solo outings. The sweet titles and ballads really slow the band down, and will no doubt do the same for the listener. Teagarden's wartime band was also quite good. He recorded for Standard Transcriptions, the best of which can be found on *Masters of Jazz, Vol. 10—Jack Teagarden, 1941–1944* 𝄞𝄞𝄞𝄞 (Storyville, 1941–1944/1994). Also worth pursuing are the excellent HRS titles from 1940, which can be found on *Jack Teagarden–Pee Wee Russell* 𝄞𝄞𝄞 (Origins of Jazz, 1990).

the rest:
Jack Teagarden Live in Chicago, 1960–1961 𝄞𝄞 (Jazzland, 1993)
Jack Teagarden and His All Stars 𝄞𝄞 (Jazzology, 1993)
Club Hangover Broadcasts 𝄞𝄞𝄞 (Arbors Jazz, 1996)

see also: *Frank Trumbauer, Wingy Manone*

Jim Prohaska

Richard Teitelbaum
Born 1939.

Originally more of a classical pianist, Richard Teitelbaum actually spent his early musical years combining biofeedback research with contemporary composition in the radical electronic composition group Musica Elettronica Viva, which also counted Frederick Rzewski as a member. However, a meeting in 1969 with Anthony Braxton opened Teitelbaum's ears more to possibilities of improvisation and, though most of his work retains a slightly academic/classical flair, he may be the premier free jazz electronicist.

what to buy: On *Concerto Grosso* 𝄞𝄞𝄞 (hat ART, 1985, prod. Pia Uehlinger, Werner X. Uehlinger), Teitelbaum has George Lewis and Anthony Braxton improvise with computers to go along with the human performance. It's an unbalancing interaction that, on one hand, puts Lewis and Braxton on their toes, but on the other hand sounds contrived and technologically challenged.

what to avoid: *Sea Between* (Victo, 1987) 𝄞, a duet between Teitelbaum and violinist Carlos Zingaro from the 1987 edition of Victoriaville's "Festival de Musique Actuelle," is about as sterile as a "free jazz" recording can be. Teitelbaum, fully enamored by digitalia (all his keyboards here are resolutely digital, with the expected thin, antiseptic sound), encouraged Zingaro to do the same and the one instrument that might inject some human levity into the proceedings winds up MIDI-controlled. It probably seemed like a good idea at the time.

worth searching for: A phenomenal collaboration with Braxton, *Time Zones* 𝄞𝄞𝄞𝄞 (Freedom/Arista, 1977, prod. Richard Teitelbaum, Michael Cuscuna) is, unfortunately, long out-of-print, but it's a rather easy LP find. To hear Braxton improvise and interact with Teitelbaum's array of Moogs is not to be missed. However, to hear Braxton get down on the contrabass clarinet . . . needless to say, it's a rather odd moment.

Jason Ferguson

Jacky Terrasson

Born November 27, 1965, in Berlin, Germany.

One of the most dynamic and exciting young pianists in jazz, Jacky Terrasson has developed a style that involves sudden shifts in tempo and dynamics, and a radical deconstruction of standard melodies. While drawing on Red Garland, Wynton Kelly, and Keith Jarrett, his trio style features an idiosyncratic mix of lyricism and sometimes jarring twists and turns. Raised in Paris, he studied the European classical tradition between the ages of five and 12, when he discovered jazz and began taking lessons with American expatriate Jeff Gardner. He attended Berklee (1985–86) but left after a year for a regular gig in Chicago. After a year of army service back in France, he settled in Paris and worked in clubs backing singers, including a six-month stint with Dee Dee Bridgewater. He made the move to New York in 1990 and eventually landed a gig with drummer Art Taylor (1991–92), recording with his Taylor's Wailers band on *Wailin' at the Vanguard*. Through his work on tenor saxophonist Javon Jackson's first Blue Note album, Terrasson hooked up with singer Betty Carter and spent eight months in her group. At the same time, he won the 1993 Thelonious Monk Institute's piano competition. His working band of the mid-1990s, featuring bassist Ugonna Okegwo and drummer Leon Parker, created something of a sensation with its highly charged rhythmic approach. In 1997, Terrasson toured with Cassandra Wilson after writing the arrangements and leading his trio on a jointly credited Blue Note release with the singer, *Rendezvous*, a torchy though low-energy exploration of standards. Terrasson has also recorded a number of sessions with trumpeter Wallace Roney, saxophonists Javon Jackson, Antoine Roney, and Ravi Coltrane, and singer Jimmy Scott.

what to buy: A thrilling trio session featuring bassist Ugonna Okegwo and drummer Leon Parker, *Reach ♫♫♫♫* (Blue Note, 1995, prod. Jacky Terrasson) captures Terrasson reworking three standards and five original tunes. From the playful, dizzying piece "The Rat Race," with its repeated use of *The Twilight Zone* theme, to the lyrical, rhapsodic "Baby Plum," Terrasson writes tunes that seem to develop directly out of his keyboard approach. It's the interaction within the trio that makes this such an enjoyable session, with Okegwo's firm bass work and Parker's beautifully textured drumming creating a highly elastic ensemble sound.

what to buy next: *Jacky Terrasson ♫♫♫♫* (Blue Note, 1995, prod. Jacky Terrasson) is the pianist's U.S. debut (he recorded an album in 1993 with Okegwo and Parker for the Japanese label Venus), a fascinating session where you can hear him working out his approach with the trio. He moves between totally revamping standards such as "I Love Paris" and "My Funny Valentine" to paying loving attention to the melodies of the two Jule Styne/Sammy Cahn classics, "I Fall in Love Too Easily" and "Time After Time." Though his playing sometimes comes off as coldly intellectual, his exceptional technique and surfeit of ideas make this a rewarding album.

worth searching for: Originally released on the Japanese Alfa label, *Sax Storm ♫♫♫♫* (Evidence, 1993, prod. Satoshi Hirano, Todd Barkan) is a hard-blowing session by the quintet Grand Central, a band led by saxophonists Antoine Roney and Ravi Coltrane. Terrasson, bassist Santi DeBriano, and drummer Cindy Blackman make up the formidable rhythm section. Though it's mostly a blowing session for the two horns (who really spur each other on during the classic tenor battle tune "Blues Up and Down"), Terrasson takes a number of strong solos, especially on Roney's "The Awakening," where he references *The Twilight Zone* theme, and the standard "All the Things You Are."

influences:

◀◀ Ahmad Jamal, Red Garland, Wynton Kelly, Keith Jarrett

Andrew Gilbert

Clark Terry

Born December 20, 1920, in St. Louis, MO.

If there's one single musician performing today whose longevity in the music business qualifies him as an Ambassador of Jazz Music, it's Clark Terry. In an amazing career spanning over 50 years to date, Terry continues to delight audiences by communicating a passion and love for his music in worldwide concert performances. Widely known for his good humor on stage, he enjoys a career full of travel, and as a frequent visitor and one-time resident of Berne, Switzerland, has a hotel suite dedicated to him at The Inner Enge Hotel, decorated with personal artifacts collected throughout his life. One of his most cherished items, a letter from his idol, the maestro himself, Louis Armstrong, warmly dispenses advice to an impressive young trumpet player, "Keep playing that trumpet boy, because you can blow your ass off!" And blowing trumpet and flugelhorn is exactly what Terry has accomplished in a fascinating yet sometimes difficult career fraught with the perils of the day, which started as a young man of 13 growing up in St. Louis, Missouri.

Terry grew up in a family of 10 children and at age nine moved in with his oldest sister and her husband, a tuba player with

Dewey Jackson's band, the Musical Ambassadors. As a youngster watching the band practice, Terry met trumpet player Louis Caldwell, who assigned him the duty of watching his horn during breaks. Returning from break one day, Caldwell caught Terry trying to blow his trumpet and told him he was going to grow up to be a trumpet player. Soon after, he became a member of the local drum and bugle corps and has been playing music ever since. Leaving high school during his senior year to help support his family, he got his first gig as a professional through his brother-in-law, playing with a band named Dollar Bill and His Small Change. From this start, he went on to work with bands such as the Reuben and Cherry Carnival Show, Ida Cox and Her Dark Town Scandal, and Fate Marable's Riverboat Band.

Entering the Navy in 1942, Terry performed with the Navy band and, upon discharge in 1945, joined Lionel Hampton's band for close to a year before returning to St. Louis to work with George Hudson at the Club Plantation. Between the years of 1947 and 1948 Terry traveled to California to join Charlie Barnett's big band, and became a member of Basie's Big Band shortly before the band broke up due to financial difficulties. He remained with Basie as a member of his octet until 1951, and it was during this time period that Terry convinced Basie to hire Ernie Wilkins, who wrote some of the band's biggest hits. In 1951 Terry joined the Ellington band and remained with the band until 1959. From late 1959 to 1960, Terry toured Europe as a member of Harold Arlen's *The Free and Easy Show* and as a member of the Quincy Jones Orchestra, returning to become a regular member of the NBC Orchestra and *The Tonight Show* Band. Terry continued to record on several recording dates and for a short period in the 1970s led his own band, Clark's Big Bad Band.

During an illustrious career, Terry has performed and recorded with legendary figures such as Lester Young, Milt Hinton, Quincy Jones, Ben Webster, Oscar Peterson, Ray Brown, Jerry Mulligan, and many more great musicians. Terry's pioneering work using half-valve techniques and distinct use of muted effects helped to influence the young Miles Davis, who also hailed from St. Louis. Terry is a staunch supporter of jazz education and continues to devote time to young musicians, teaching improvisational techniques beyond the books and manuals. He has received four honorary doctorate degrees and has had two music schools named after him. He maintains a busy career today, performing for audiences worldwide, and has come to be admired for his infectious style of humor fused with his impressive skills on trumpet and flugelhorn, as well as his familiar style of singing and scatting.

what to buy: Terry has been a member of both the Basie and Ellington bands. He has not always received his due as an individual stylist, yet he is responsible for some of the most innovative jazz recordings to come out of the era. Some of his best work can be found on his first recording as leader, *Clark Terry* &&&&& (EmArcy, 1955/Verve, 1997, prod. Bob Shad). A CD in the Verve Elite Edition series of limited edition historical recordings, it also contains bonus tracks from the Leonard Feather–produced MGM LP, *Cats vs. Chicks*. The album features an all-star lineup of illustrious musicians such as Jimmy Cleveland, Cecil Payne, Horace Silver, Oscar Pettiford, Wendell Marshall, Art Blakey, and select arrangements by Quincy Jones. The tracks from *Cats vs. Chicks* features sidemen Urbie Green, Lucky Thompson, Horace Silver, Tal Farlow, Oscar Pettiford, and Kenny Clark. Percy Heath, Terry Pollard, Norma Carson, and Mary Osborne appear on select tracks throughout the CD. Accompanied by these excellent musicians, Terry showcases his multifaceted talents. Many fine tracks (such as "Double Play"), demonstrate Terry's exceptional, smooth trumpet assisted by the consistent drive of Silver's piano and Pettiford on bass. "Co-op" swings at a nice bop tempo and features the horns of Cleveland and Payne tightly interacting with Terry. Other noteworthy tunes are "The Countess," "Chuckles," "Mamblues," and "Cat Meets Chick." For an insightful adventure into more of Clark Terry's work, *The Happy Horns of Clark Terry* &&&&& (Impulse!, 1964/1994, prod. Bob Thiele) is a gem of a recording, featuring some of the most outstanding musicians in the business, such as Phil Woods on alto sax and clarinet, Ben Webster on tenor sax, Roger Kellaway on piano, Milt Hinton on bass, and Walter Perkins on drums. Instead of listening to one particular number, put on the CD and enjoy the ride. Tunes like "Return to Swahili," "Ellington Rides Again," and "Impulsive" capture Terry's ingenious talent on trumpet and flugelhorn. His presentation and flawless execution turn out an enriched sound, yet not so brazen as to overshadow his illustrious sidemen. "Do Nothin' 'Til You Hear from Me," a tender ballad with an incredible opening chorus set by Webster's glorious sound, prepares the stage for Terry's invigorating flugelhorn solo, which is sharp and full of bite and brings new intimacy to this wonderful Ellington standard. One of Terry's most exciting later recordings is *Portraits* &&&&& (Chesky Records, 1988, prod. Norman Chesky), which compiles tunes dedicated to legendary trumpeters by a man whose own trumpet has thrilled his audiences for over 50 years. This is an excellent recording not only for the musicians it honors but for the lifetime of experience Terry brings with him to this date. The depth of commitment combined with his infectious good humor still carries over into his music like a radiant beacon on a dark night. Joined by Don Friedman on piano, Victor Gaskin on bass, and Lewis Nash on drums, this release offers an affectionate account of Terry musically reminiscing about old friends. Check out Terry's original, "Finger Filibuster," which opens with his trademark scatting. "Ciribirbin," a tribute to Harry James, is a Latin-inspired tune containing lovely piano work by Friedman, the consistent drive of drummer Lewis Nash, and Terry's dashing trumpet enhanced by muted effects. The delightfully poignant ballet on "I Can't Get Started" hails Bunny Berigan with Terry lending warm, lyrical charm on flugelhorn. *In Orbit* ✍✍✍ (Riverside, 1958/OJC, 1987, prod. Orrin Keepnews) is an extraordinary release featuring Terry on flugelhorn (possibly the first time this instrument is used as the lead horn in a jazz date) combined with the auspicious presence of Thelonious Monk, one of the major figures of modern jazz. Assistance by Sam Jones (bass) and Philly Joe Jones (drums) makes this recording one of Terry's finest accomplishments. Five swift Terry originals exhibit his skilled proficiency on flugelhorn and are enhanced by Monk's influence. Highlights include "In Orbit," a swinging tribute to Terry's flugelhorn creativity. "Let's Cool One," written by Monk, lends itself to Monk's trademark piano style and showcases Jones's drumming, and Terry's memorable original, "Argentia," gives vent to the rich tones of his flugelhorn, Monk's impressive phrasing, and Jones's sweeping bass solo.

what to buy next: Some of the most extensive work recorded by Clark Terry for the respected Riverside label in the 1950s can be found on OJC. *Serenade to a Bus Seat* ✍✍✍ (Riverside, 1957/OJC, 1993, prod. Orrin Keepnews) is a swinging bebop affair. Terry's debut recording on the Riverside label consists of five Terry originals plus two standards performed with an incredible entourage of sidemen, including Paul Chambers (bass), Philly Joe Jones (drums), Johnny Griffin (tenor sax), and Wynton Kelly (piano), who also appear on the Riverside label for the first time with this recording. Key tunes such as the title number, "Serenade to a Bus Seat" (written in memory of those long journeys while a member of the big bands), jumps right from the opening. Griffin's sax is hot, and all Quintet members equally share the limelight spurred by the brilliant, searing rhythm combination of Jones and Chambers. Terry's playing is flawless as he moves into the standard "Stardust" with clear resonant texture, and he's followed by Griffin's equally impressive solo. The tunes "Boardwalk," "Boomerang," and "Digits," exceptionally fine numbers written by Terry, are rich, well-balanced yet swinging tunes showcasing his individualized sound and accompaniment from his amazing array of talented side-

men. This CD is a must for the serious music listener. *Duke with a Difference* ✍✍✍ (Riverside, 1957/OJC, 1990, prod. Orrin Keepnews) is a rather unique dedication to his boss at the time, Duke Ellington. Taking traditional Ellington tunes and departing from the disciplined, orchestrated arrangements to create a non-Ellington treatment of the music, allows Terry freedom of expression. The cuts employ tenorman Paul Gonsalves and altoist Johnny Hodges, players who were at some point important members of the Ellington band. The CD offers a warm lighthearted treatment of Duke's music led by Terry, especially numbers like "Cotton Tail," a swinging sensation which allows Terry and members of his quintet a chance to strut their individual talents. "Just Squeeze Me, (But Don't Tease Me)," one of Duke's show piece tunes opens harmoniously, features Terry using half-valve techniques during his solo, and blends the delightful work of altoist Hodges and tenorist Gonsalves combined with the trombones in the ensemble, making this a well-rounded interpretation. The hauntingly beautiful voice of Marian Bruce is featured on the all-time favorite, "In a Sentimental Mood," with backing from Billy Strayhorn on piano, Tyree Glenn on vibes, Jimmy Woode on bass, and Sam Woodyard on drums, and assistance from trombonists Quentin Jackson and Britt Woodman, to make this one of Terry's most thorough works. Terry's fourth Riverside CD, *Top and Bottom Brass* ✍✍✍ (Riverside, 1959/OJC, 1993, prod. Orrin Keepnews), offers a beautifully arranged display of harmonic unison between Terry's trumpet or flugelhorn and the superb playing by tubaist Don Butterfield. The rhythm sections features Jimmy Jones on piano, Sam Jones on bass, and Arthur Taylor on drums. The luxurious sound of brass combined with this rhythm section startles the imagination on tunes such as the warm, affectionate version of "My Heart Belongs to Daddy," a quick-tempoed "Top and Bottom Brass," and flowing harmonic horns on the pleasant "Mardi Gras Waltz." *Memories of Duke* ✍✍✍ (OJC, 1980/1990, prod. Norman Granz) is a masterpiece of a recording bringing together some of Terry's longtime friends for a session dedicated to Duke Ellington. Guitarist Joe Pass, bassist Ray Brown, pianist Jack Wilson, and drummer Frank Severino join Terry on an array of Duke's trademark tunes, including a fast-moving version of "Sophisticated Lady" which features Terry's enlightened, muted lead trumpet and Pass's moving and well-articulated solo, and pleasing readings of other Ellington gems such as "Cotton Tail," "Come Sunday," "Passion Flower," and "Echoes of Harlem." *Yes, The Blues* ✍✍✍ (OJC, 1981/1995, prod. Norman Granz) contains a collection of tunes teaming him up with his old partner, alto saxman Eddie "Cleanhead"

Vinson, who achieved fame as a blues player but is just as comfortable playing jazz. Coming together for the first time since 1947, (when Terry was a member of his 16-piece band) they deliver seven tunes. The opening number, "Diddlin'," features Terry playing a solo on his mouthpiece. Art Hillary's down-home bluesy feeling on organ coupled with Terry's trumpet solo make this a sassy remembrance of the blues. Other highlights include Terry's growling trumpet and muted solos on the rousing "Railroad Porter Blues" (enhanced by Vinson's vocals and help from "Harmonica George" Smith and Hillary on organ), and "Swingin' the Blues," a beboppish, up-tempo take featuring Hillary on piano. *Live at the Village Gate* ♫♫♫ (Chesky Records, 1990, prod. David Chesky) and *The Second Set* ♫♫♫ (Chesky Records, 1990, prod. David Chesky, Steve Kaiser) are the triumphant result of Terry's November 19 and 20, 1980 live recording dates in New York City at The Village Gate, three weeks before his 70th birthday. *The Second Set* as the name suggests, was recorded on the second evening of this club engagement and released five years after the actual recording date in honor of Terry's 75th birthday. Both releases contain all original compositions written and arranged by Terry and are excellent recordings capturing his natural showmanship. *Live at the Village Gate* and *The Second Set* team Terry up with pianist Don Friedman, bassist Marcus McLauren, and drummer Kenny Washington, as well as the accomplished tenor and soprano saxophones of Jimmy Heath. Paquito D'Rivera joins this fine crew for a guest appearance on *Live at the Village Gate* and the tune "Silly Samba," a change of pace from the rest of the evening's performance, is a swinging samba characteristic of D'Rivera's bravado and Terry's mastery on flugelhorn. Heath and Terry are highlighted throughout, but the rhythm section deserves special mention. Highlights include "Simple Waltz," "Opus Ocean," and "Ode to a Flugelhorn," exceptionally fine tunes full of intensity brought by Terry to his live performances. An obscure recording, *Live in Chicago—Vol. 1* ♫♫♫, (Monad Records, 1976/1995, prod. Alonzo King, Buddy Scott) is worthy of mention because it features Terry in a live performance at Ratso's in Chicago with his longtime partner Ernie Wilkins on alto and tenor sax, Marty Harris on piano, Victor Sproles on bass, and Ed Saple on drums. The sound quality is good for a 1976 live recording, and the spontaneous interaction of the musicians comes through with sincerity not often captured in live recordings. Tunes such as "Secret Love," "Celito Lindo," and "On the Trail," are well-executed and alive with the vibrancy of Terry's multifaceted playing, but also exhibit the acclaimed playing of Ernie Wilkins, known for his incredible writing and arrangements.

worth searching for: Other inspiring releases featuring Terry include four recordings made with his longtime associate, trombonist Bob Brookmeyer. One of their recording dates *The Power of Positive Swinging* ♫♫♫, (Mainstream Records, 1965/1993, prod. Bob Shad) is an exciting, totally unpretentious collaboration containing a relaxed cohesion of swinging tunes backed by the capable efforts of Roger Kellaway on piano, Bill Crow on bass, and Dave Bailey on drums. Terry is featured on "Battle Hymn of the Republic," an innovative interpretation featuring his fluid use of the high register blended with his mute treatments along with Brookmeyer's solid trombone making one intriguing number. "Ode to a Flugelhorn" jumps off to a fast moving pace with exchanges between Terry and Brookmeyer and an exquisite flugelhorn solo from Terry. Another masterful collaboration finds Clark Terry teamed up with a bevy of musicians who without doubt are considered members of the who's who of jazz. *The Alternate Blues* ♫♫♫ (OJC, 1980/1992, prod. Norman Granz) finds Terry fitting in nicely with Dizzy Gillespie, Freddie Hubbard, Oscar Peterson, Ray Brown, Joe Pass, and Bobby Durham. The album conveys a casual, informal atmosphere, as if these legendary musicians had nothing better to do than get together for a little impromptu recording session. If one were to use this album as a barometer, it should give a hint of the magnitude of Terry's exceptional talent. The "Alternate Takes" (one through four) are a combination of repeat takes because of an error in rhythm section accompaniment. Both Gillespie and Hubbard electing to play eight-bar blues, forgot Terry elected to play twelve-bar blues, and didn't switch into twelve-bars until the final take when they finally got it down. Making this an incredibly fresh-sounding and inspired display of each trumpet player's individual talents, this CD was made in the spirit of a "cutting" session, a contest jam to determine who had the right stuff. With what could be considered one of the greatest rhythm sections, the trumpeters are inspired to work responsively and competitively. "Wrap up Your Troubles in Dreams" is an amazing piece presenting everyone's combined and individual talents with arresting solos from Terry, Gillespie, and Hubbard. Pianist Peterson works in perfect unison, with his amazing lightning fingering movement supported with Pass's well-positioned riffs, Brown's incredible fills, and Durham's succinct driving.

influences:

◀◀ Louis Armstrong, Roy Eldridge, Bunny Berigan, Louis Caldwell, Doc Cheatham

▶▶ Miles Davis, Terence Blanchard, Nicholas Payton

Keith Brickhouse

Sister Rosetta Tharpe

Born Rosetta Nubin, March 20, 1921, in Cotton Plant, AK. Died October 9, 1973, in Philadelphia, PA.

In his book *Invisible Republic: Bob Dylan's Basement Tapes*, rock critic Greil Marcus conjures an image from 1966 of Dylan sitting in the dressing room of London's Royal Albert Hall, picking out the notes to Sister Rosetta Tharpe's "Strange Things Happening Everyday." It's moments before one of the folkie faithful was to shout: "Judas!" And Dylan was to scream back: "You're a liar!" In the decade between 1938 and 1948, Sister Rosetta Tharpe was the queen of gospel song. Like Dylan, Tharpe was an artist whose raw talent, musical curiosity, and flamboyance could not be contained. The voice of his generation, Dylan "went electric." Gospel's first national star, Sister Rosetta dyed her hair red, donned mink, and played electric guitar with a vengeance that not only blurred the lines between jazz, gospel, blues, and country, but between the sacred and profane.

The precocious daughter of an old-time gospel shouter, Katie Bell Nubin (Mother Bell), Tharpe grew up playing Holiness conventions, migrating from Arkansas to Chicago. After signing with Decca in 1938, she recorded such gospel hits as "Rock Me," "That's All," and her signature song, "This Train," as well as risque numbers such as "I Want a Tall Skinny Papa." She also performed as a vocalist (and sometimes guitarist) in the Cotton Club Revue with Cab Calloway and his orchestra. And by the time she died in 1973, she had played with an incredible array of musicians, including Count Basie, Lucky Millinder, Benny Goodman, Louis Jordan, Sam Price, Roy Acuff, Red Foley, and Muddy Waters. "There's something about the gospel blues that's so deep the world can't stand it," Tharpe once said. And it's only recently that the depth of her influence on that hybrid form, and its echo in so much of American music, has been fully understood and appreciated.

what's available: *Complete Recorded Works, Vol. 1 (1938–1941)* 𝄞𝄞𝄞𝄞 (Document, 1995, prod. Johnny Parth) collects Sister Rosetta's first recordings, most done two months prior to her appearance in the historic "Spirituals to Swing" concert at Carnegie Hall on December 23, 1938. Opening with a series of solo guitar and vocal tracks, it's evident that Tharpe's playing owes much to Big Bill Broonzy. *Vol. 1* also includes tracks from several 1941 sessions with Lucky Millinder and his Orchestra—notably a breezy big band take on the blues standard "Trouble in Mind" and "Rock Daniel," a boogie-woogie spiritual that features the kind of brilliantly innovative guitar solo that would become her stock in trade, reaching its zenith on a rocking

electric version of "That's All." *Complete Recorded Works, Vol. 2 (1942–1944)* 𝄞𝄞𝄞 (Document, 1995, prod. Johnny Parth) continues Tharpe's move toward a secular sound in a major way with "I Want a Tall Skinny Papa." It also includes an incendiary version of "This Train," recorded live with Louis Jordan and His Tympany Five, and the song many consider her most influential, "Strange Things Happening Every Day," recorded with the Sam Price Trio. All 53 tracks on *Vol. 1* and *Vol. 2* are transfers from original (mostly 78 RPM) recordings, and the sound isn't always first-rate. But these chronological compilations really are complete.

influences:

⏮ Thomas A. Dorsey

⏭ Jerry Lee Lewis, Bob Dylan

Bob Townsend

Toots Thielemans
/Jean Thielemans

Born Jean Baptiste Thielemans, April 29, 1922, in Brussels, Belgium.

Toots Thielemans is largely responsible for introducing the chromatic harmonica as a jazz instrument. Inspired after hearing the pop harmonica sounds of Larry Adler in the movies, Thielemans started playing the harmonica at age 17 while in college. But after he contracted a lung infection, he taught himself to play guitar by listening to Django Reinhardt recordings, and was soon playing in clubs all over Brussels. He did take up harmonica again and after World War II, Thielemans performed in American GI clubs in Europe. Thielemans emigrated to the U.S. in 1948, shared the bill with saxophonist Charlie Parker at the Paris International Jazz Festival in May 1949, and toured with the Benny Goodman Sextet in 1950. From 1953 to 1959, he played guitar (and some harmonica) with the George Shearing Quintet. Thielemans subsequently formed his own group, but he continued to freelance with other leaders and do studio work. His whistling while he played guitar caught the ear of arranger-producer Quincy Jones and he used Thielemans on a number of successful recordings. During the 1960s, Thielemans began regular tours of Europe where he recorded his most popular composition, "Bluesette," in 1962, which featured him on guitar and whistling. This worldwide hit made him an in-demand player in the U.S. and he has continued playing harmonica and whistling on various studio dates, for film soundtracks such as the *Midnight Cowboy* theme song, for TV themes, and on pop and jazz recordings. Thielemans is a bop-oriented player, but he's able to play a variety of jazz styles, which are evident on his many recordings as leader and sideman since the 1960s. In 1981, Thielemans had a major stroke, but he has mostly recovered and continues to play. He began incorporating Brazilian rhythms in his music and gathered Brazil's best musicians to perform on his "Brasil Project" albums in the early 1990s.

what to buy: Thielemans plays harmonica and guitar on *Man Bites Harmonica* ♫♫♫♫ (Riverside/OJC, 1958). Despite the curious album title, this is one of the leader's best early dates, a cool jazz session of eight tunes featuring Thielemans with baritone saxophonist Pepper Adams, pianist Kenny Drew, bassist Wilbur Ware, and drummer Art Taylor. His lyrical improvisations, especially on harmonica, are flawlessly performed, especially on love ballads such as "Don't Blame Me." Adams's rich-toned bari is the perfect foil for the high register sound of the harmonica, especially when they unite for the melody lead to Louis Armstrong's saucy tune, "Strutting with Some Barbecue." And when Thielemans takes up the guitar, his sound, fluency, and sense of swing are reminiscent of Joe Pass, notably so on the bopping Ray Bryant number, "18th Century Ballroom." Along with Thielemans's fine performances, the unusual instrumentation and tasty jazz servings make this a listening feast. Thielemans's first recording as leader after a 12-year hiatus, *Only Trust Your Heart* ♫♫♫♫ (Concord, 1988, prod. Fred Hersch) finds the leader starring solely on harmonica, supported by Fred Hersch on piano, Harvie Schwartz on bass (subbed by Marc Johnson on two tracks), and Joey Baron on drums. The trio is tight and light, with Baron creating plenty of splashy and expansive polyrhythms to spur Thielemans's mellow-toned solos and keep the 12 romantic swingers, boppers, ballads, and bossas moving forward. Hersch's artistry is extremely supportive to the harmonica player and every bit as captivating as he supports Thielemans's mellifluous solos. The leader sways with the Brazilian-jazz classic "Estate," generates soprano sax-like bop lines on Wayne Shorter's "Speak No Evil," sweeps through the Latinate title tune, and navigates hornlike lines on the tricky Thelonious Monk tune, "Little Rootie Tootie." *Only Trust Your Heart* is a first-rate listen.

what to buy next: *Brasil Project* ♫♫♫♫ (Private Music, 1992, prod. Miles Goodman, Oscar Castro-Neves) is recommended for fans who can't get enough Brazilian jazz and primarily for the nine-and-a-half minute lilting Brazilian-jazz version of Thielemans's "Bluesette," which includes wonderful vocals from Ivan Lins, Djavan, Joao Bosco, Caetano Veloso, Milton Nascimento and Dori Caymmi (in duet), and Thielemans's gui-

tar and whistling. No session dates are listed for the 13 tunes recorded in studios in Los Angeles, New York, and Rio De Janeiro, but just about everybody who is anybody in Brazilian jazz is present, including Eliane Elias (piano), Oscar Castro-Neves (keyboards), Ricardo Silveira (electric guitar), to name a few. And, scattered throughout the various musician configurations with Thielemans (who plays harmonica on all tracks), are jazz musicians Marc Johnson (bass), Mark Isham (trumpet), Dave Grusin (piano), and Lee Ritenour (acoustic guitar). *Brasil Project II* ♫♫♫♫ (Private Music, 1993, prod. Miles Goodman, Oscar Castro-Neves) provides more good listening from all of these musicians with Thielemans at the helm improvising on harmonica through the 13 tunes. In addition to most of the same musicians who appeared on the previous album, bassist Brian Bromberg adds distinctive flair to this session. Thielemans leads the session *Do Not Leave Me* ♫♫♫♫ (Stash/Vintage Jazz, 1989, prod. Emmanuel Chamboredon, Toots Thielemans) with Fred Hersch and Joey Baron, with Marc Johnson on bass. The album offers 48 minutes of lush jazz recorded live at Palais de Beaux Arts, in Brussels, on June 19, 1986. The Jacques Brel title tune, translated to French, "Ne Me Quitte Pas," is a global classic, and Thielemans's pleading interpretation, performed as a soulful duo with Hersch, is passionate and stirring. Other tunes include Miles Davis's "Blue N' Green" and "All Blues," Hoagy Carmichael's "Stardust," the warhorse "Autumn Leaves," a modernized version of Ivan Lins's "Velas," and a short version of the Thielemans theme song, "Bluesette."

best of the rest:

Toots Thielemans: The Silver Collection ♫♫♫♫ (Polydor, 1985)
Footprints ♫♫♫♫ (Verve, 1991)
For My Lady ♫♫♫♫ (EmArcy, 1991)
East Coast West Coast ♫♫♫♫ (Private Music, 1992)
Verve Jazz Masters 59 ♫♫♫♫ (Verve, 1996)

worth searching for: If you are broad-minded or seeking a different listen, search for Thielemans's performance on two tracks of *The French Collection—Jazz Impressions* ♫♫♫♫ (EMI, 1989, prod. Mike Berniker, Ettore Stratta). On this 11-tune album that combines jazz and the works of classical composers Debussy, Ravel, Fauré, and Satie, Thielemans does a beautiful job. He interprets Fauré's "Sicilienne, Op 78" in a quartet setting led by pianist Fred Hersch (musical director and arranger), phrasing with a jazz mentality and swinging lightly over Hersch's bubbling accompaniment; they are swept along by drummer Joey Baron's brushwork. Thielemans performs equally well on Poulenc's "Cantiena from Flute Sonata," a dramatically haunting, European-sounding melody, upon which the harmonica player improvises mostly in the upper range, like a soprano voice. The recording also features bassist Steve Laspina and guest soloists James Newton (flute), Kevin Eubanks (guitar), and Eddie Daniels (clarinet). This is one of the best albums of its type.

influences:

◄◄ Larry Adler, John Coltrane, Django Reinhardt, Joe Pass, Antonio Carlos Jobim

►► Hendrik Meurkens, Kenny Burrell

Nancy Ann Lee

Gary Thomas

Born June 10, 1961, in Baltimore, MD.

An aggressive saxophone solist with a disinctive sound, Gary Thomas is unafraid to experiment. He is comfortable with funk, standards, M-Base, and rap. He first came to prominence playing with Miles Davis in the late '80s. He injected his unique style into Davis's fusion, refusing to regurgitate generic licks. He later became an integral part of Jack DeJohnette's Special Edition. He and altoist Greg Osby stretched harmonic conventions and experimented with electronic effects. He also contributed some excellent flute work while with DeJohnette. As a sideman and on his own projects, Gary Thomas is at the forefront of younger players challenging the status quo of the neoconservative contingency.

what to buy: *By Any Means Necessary* ✗✗✗✗ (JMT, 1989, prod. Stefan Winter) typifies Thomas's music. Serpentine melodies over odd-metered funk are deftly handled. A superior version of "You're under Arrest," more exotic and compelling than Davis's original, highlights the disc. Anthony Cox's funky upright bass gives the music added warmth and resonance.

what to buy next: *Code Violations* ✗✗✗✗ (Enja, 1988, prod Matthias Winckelmann) is extremely funky in an unpredictable and uncliched way. Thomas doubles on flute with excellent results. It's only his second session as a leader, but Thomas's musical concepts are fully formed.

what to avoid: *Kold Kage* ✗✗ (JMT, 1991, prod. Gary Thomas) is disappointing compared to previous outings. The overly dense setting seems to prevent the music from locking in as solidly as it should. The attempts at incorporating rap deserve an "A" for effort, but come across stiff and forced.

the rest:

Seventh Quadrant ✗✗✗✗ (Enja, 1987)

While the Gate Is Open ✗✗✗✗ (JMT, 1989)
Till We Have Faces ✗✗✗ (JMT, 1992)
Exile's Gate ✗✗✗ (JMT, 1993)
Overkill ✗✗✗✗ (JMT, 1996)

worth searching for: On Jack DeJohnette's *Irresistible Forces* ✗✗✗✗ (MCA, 1987, prod. Jack DeJohnette), Thomas combines with alto saxist Greg Osby to inject their M-Base influences into DeJohnette's music. The two saxmen turn up the heat on Osby's "Osthetic."

influences:

◄◄ Dexter Gordon, Wayne Shorter

►► Kenny Brooks, Sam Newsome

James Eason

Luther Thomas

Born June 23, 1950, in St. Louis, MO.

Thomas developed on the St. Louis scene and was a member of that city's Black Artists Group (BAG), similar to Chicago's AACM. He moved to New York in the 1970s, as did several other BAG members, and played in a wide variety of contexts, including the various groups of alto saxophonist/"no wave" punk-funk bandleader James Chance.

what to buy: *BAGin' It* ✗✗✗✗ (CIMP, 1996, prod. Robert D. Rusch) uses Thomas's all-star quartet with trumpeter Ted Daniel, bassist Wilber Morris, and drummer Denis Charles, which has worked together off and on since 1984. The idiom is partially arranged free jazz—what Thomas, with a nod to Butch Morris, calls "semi-conduction." Charles's intricate polyrhythms and ability to lay down a deep groove that's not a steady beat are keys to the success of this music, which is often quite sparsely constructed.

what to buy next: The blowing session *Saxcrobatic Fanatic* ✗✗✗✗ (CIMP, 1997, prod. Robert D. Rusch) matches Thomas with two colleagues from his BAG days, electric guitarist Kelvyn Bell and drummer Ronnie Burrage. From the start Thomas is clearly "on" and bursting with ideas, and this is much more of a showcase for his free-flowing improvisatory wizardry than his other albums.

what to avoid: *Yo' Momma* ✗ (Moers, 1981, prod. Burkhard Hennen, Luther Thomas, Axel Markens), billed as a Luther Thomas & Dizzazz recording, is a mix of off-kilter funk-rock and really bad rap. The only thing worse than Thomas's crude rapping is his even cruder (in several senses) lyric writing. There's some wild blowing, and the grooves are interesting, but there's no getting around the horrible stuff in the foreground.

the rest:

(With Joseph Bowie–Luther Thomas/Saint Louis Creative Ensemble) *Can't Figure Out (Whatcha Doin' to Me)* ♫♫♫ (Moers, 1979)

worth searching for: Thomas's group with Daniel, Morris, and Charles is joined by keyboardist Charles Eubanks on *Don't Tell* ♫♫ (Creative Consciousness, 1994). The CD is too short (31:25), and Eubanks's tinkly synthesizers emphasize the low-budget production values, but Thomas is sufficiently under-recorded that this is nonetheless worth hearing. Thomas's tart compositions are tonal with unexpected jumps in the progressions, and the solos, though never very outside, feel unfettered; Daniel in particular sounds good.

influences:

◄◄ Ornette Coleman, Oliver Lake

Steve Holtje

Butch Thompson

Born Richard Enos Thompson, November 28, 1943, in Marine-on-St. Croix, MN.

Butch Thompson's mass-market reputation rests on his key role in Garrison Keillor's popular public radio program, *A Prairie Home Companion,* for which he provided background music, solos, and witty repartee during a 12-year period beginning in 1974. Thompson's interest in traditional jazz grew out of his experiences playing clarinet in the Hall Brother's Jazz Band, a Minneapolis-St. Paul–area band that occasionally backed up touring early jazz giants like George Lewis, Kid Thomas, and Eubie Blake. He has since become one of the foremost scholars of Jelly Roll Morton's music and played piano in the off-Broadway show *Jelly Roll,* which won an Obie Award in 1995. Like many of his idols, Thompson has recorded music for player pianos, but unlike them, he uses modern technological conveniences such as floppy disks and CDs to do so. Thompson's discs for Music Systems Research (a modern player piano manufacturer) include ragtime and Christmas programs.

what to buy: Other people have played Scott Joplin's material and had a great deal of success doing so, but never before have these tunes been played with the lilt and swing that Thompson gives them on *Thompson Plays Joplin* ♫♫♫♫ (Daring, 1998, prod. Mason Daring). This is truly a revelatory recording, with Thompson treating these songs like they are

old friends and not just academic delights to be waded through. On *The 88's: Good Old New York* ♫♫♫♫ (Daring, 1989, prod. Mason Daring, Adam Maffei), Thompson takes a musical tour of New York jazz roots, including material from the pens of Eubie Blake, Jelly Roll Morton, Willie "the Lion" Smith, Thomas "Fats" Waller, a James P. Johnson.

what to buy next: *Butch and Doc* ♫♫♫♫ (Daring, 1994, prod. Mason Daring, Andrea du Plessis), an album of classic tunes by Duke Ellington, Billy Strayhorn, and others, includes trumpeter/vocalist Doc Cheatham and beguiles the listener into hearing the music more than the craft. Cheatham's chops may be a little shaky at times but he still blows amazingly well for a nonagenarian and his vocals add an endearing sweetness to the mix. "Rosetta" is a subtle marvel, while the piano playing on "If Dreams Come True" stands with the best stuff he has ever done.

the rest:

Jelly Roll Morton Piano Solos ♫♫♫♫ (Biograph, 1968)
The 88's: New Orleans Joys ♫♫♫♫ (Daring, 1989)
The 88's: Chicago Breakdown ♫♫♫♫ (Daring, 1989)
The 88's: Minnesota Wonder ♫♫♫ (Daring, 1992)
The Butch Thompson Trio Plays Favorites ♫♫♫ (Solo Art, 1992)
Yulestride ♫♫♫ (Daring, 1994)
Lincoln Avenue Blues ♫♫♫♫ (Daring, 1995)
Lincoln Avenue Express ♫♫♫♫ (Daring, 1997)

influences:

◄◄ Jelly Roll Morton, Fats Waller

►► Judy Carmichael, Ralph Sutton, James Dapogny

Garaud MacTaggart

Lucky Thompson

Born June 16, 1924, in Columbia, SC.

Although not always acknowledged as such, saxophonist Lucky Thompson was one of the first modern innovators in regard to his approach to the soprano saxophone. With a warm sound marked by minimal vibrato, and a more technically-advanced sense of melodic development, Thompson was the link between swing-era legend Sidney Bechet and contemporary players Steve Lacy and John Coltrane. In addition, his mature tenor saxophone work was also distinctive for his strong sense of swing combined with the vocabulary of be-bop. During the 1940s, Thompson first made a name for himself while working in the big bands of Billy Eckstine, Don Redman, and Lionel Hampton. Later, he became a part of the be-bop revolution fostered by Dizzy Gillespie and Charlie Parker, both of whom he recorded with. Miles Davis's legendary 1954 *Walkin'* session would benefit from Thompson's fine playing. During the next few decades, although remaining somewhat underappreciated, the saxophonist stayed busy working in Stan Kenton's band, teaching at Dartmouth, living for two extended stays in France, and recording a few sessions of considerable merit. One of the great mysteries of jazz, Thompson dropped out sometime in the mid-1970s and little has been heard from him since.

what to buy: *Tricotism* ♫♫♫♫ (ABC Paramount, 1956/Impulse!, prod. Creed Taylor) is one of Thompson's early masterpieces. Trio tracks and a quartet/quintet session find the saxophonist in the company of Hank Jones, Jimmy Cleveland, and Oscar Pettiford, among others. *Lucky Strikes* ♫♫♫♫ (Prestige/OJC, 1964, prod. Don Schlitten) was one of three pristine dates Thompson cut for Prestige, this one easily the gem of the trio. A strong cast (Hank Jones, Richard Davis, and Connie Kay) and exceptional originals such as "Prey-Loot" and "Mid-Nite Oil" make for some distinctive and rewarding music.

what to buy next: *Happy Days* ♫♫♫ (Prestige, 1963/1965, prod. Don Schlitten) contains two Prestige dates, one a moody ballad collection of Jerome Kern standards and the other a selection of such well-known items as "People" and "Happy Days Are Here Again." Thompson's soprano and tenor work is all warmth and grace!

the rest:
Lucky Thompson and Gigi Gryce in Paris ♫♫♫ (Vogue/GRP, 1956)
Lord, Lord, Am I Ever Gonna Know ♫♫♫ (Candid, 1961)

influences:
◄◄ Don Byas
►► Eric Alexander, Tad Shull

Chris Hovan

Malachi Thompson
Born August 21, 1949, in Chicago, IL.

A veteran of Chicago's Association for the Advancement of Creative Musicians (AACM), trumpeter Malachi Thompson is an iconoclastic, enterprising musician. He leads several ensembles, including his regular Freebop Band (documented on his first Delmark album in 1989) and his Africa Brass big band (formed in 1991). He has recorded six albums as leader for the Delmark label, and has recorded as sideman for a variety of labels. A devoted historian, Thompson is involved in spearheading the revival of the Sutherland Hotel on Chicago's South side.

Thompson received his first trumpet at age 11, began classical studies with a musician in his church band, and took weekly lessons at a music instrument company. His interest in jazz was sparked when his mother (an avid music fan who shared her jazz record collection with her son) took him to see Count Basie perform. Thompson began to learn the language of jazz by combining what he heard on recordings with what he learned through his associations with musicians. An Art Blakey record featuring trumpeter Bill Hardman inspired Thompson to play bebop. In the meantime, Thompson was developing his classical chops, and by seventh grade, beat out the competition for lead trumpet in the concert band.

During the 1960s, Chicago's music scene was flourishing with active players such as John Stubblefield, Eddie Harris, Gene Ammons, and others. After a dispute with his parents over his playing club gigs, Thompson moved out into his own apartment. Throughout his teens, Thompson had been gigging a few nights a week and, by his high school graduation in 1967, was performing with R&B bands, big bands, and was backing touring R&B artists. He began to tour, playing "bread-and-butter" R&B gigs with a variety of musicians.

Thompson performed his first jazz gig with the AACM, fulfilling a requirement that young musicians produce a concert of original music. He began playing with the AACM big band, learning the principles and the AACM philosophy of integrity and experimentation. As he shifted from playing stock charts to challenging, experimental music by Henry Threadgill and Muhal Richard Abrams, Thompson was enthralled and encouraged. He recorded his debut album, *The Seventh Son*, in 1972. Before he left Chicago for New York in 1974, Thompson had met saxophonist Carter Jefferson, with whom he would eventually form a quintet and begin a 20-year association that lasted until Jefferson's death on December 9, 1993. The last time Thompson saw Jefferson, they recorded a tribute tune Thompson wrote, "CJ's Blues," which appears on Thompson's *47th Street* album.

At the coaxing of Jefferson, Thompson moved in 1974 to New York City, where he had been playing gigs on tour since he was 18. Thompson remained in New York for nine years, freelancing most of the time, playing with small groups led by Jackie McLean and Joe Henderson, and with the Sam Rivers big band. From 1975 to 1980, Thompson and Norman Spiller co-led Brass Proud, the forerunner of Lester Bowie's Brass Fantasy and a band featuring seven trumpets and a rhythm section. Olu Dara, Tommy Terrentine, Victor Lewis, and others were in the band and they worked around New York and along the East Coast. Thompson was also still leading his Freebop band. It was back during New York City's "loft" days, and Thompson absorbed all that he could until he burned out and moved to Washington D.C. after his marriage ended in divorce. While D.C. was a hotbed of activity, Thompson remained a road musician, working mostly with the short-lived New York Hot Trumpet Repertory Company, featuring trumpeters Lester Bowie, Olu Dara, Wynton Marsalis, and Stanton Davis.

Thompson left D.C. and lived in Vienna, Austria, for a few years. He had been working frequently in Europe with the Freebop band, and after moving there, he participated in special projects with David Murray, Oliver Lake, Stan Davis, and Philip Wilson, and performed in large ensembles and with all-star big bands. He was doing well until 1989 when he was diagnosed with a rare form of lymphoma. He returned to Chicago for treatment and spiritual renewal, and today is cancer-free.

Thompson is a member of the Sutherland Community Arts Initiative, a community-based organization that seeks to restore music to the Sutherland Hotel and Ballroom located at 47th and Drexel (Thompson's old neighborhood) on Chicago's South side. It was there during the 1960s that jazz artists such as Dizzy Gillespie, Miles Davis, John Coltrane, Nancy Wilson, Gene Ammons, Sonny Stitt, James Moody, and others performed.

Thompson teaches music through the Urban Gateways arts education program. In 1995, Thompson was recognized for his lifelong achievements as a recipient of the Arts Midwest Jazz Master Award. He was selected as 1996 *Chicago Tribune* Chicagoan of the Year, and was a 1997 Chicago Endowments for the Arts honoree for his support of the arts and his community involvement through arts residencies. On September 18, 1997, Thompson's stage production, *The Sutherland,* opened at the Victory Gardens Theater. Highly autobiographical, it is a musical about a young musician who grows up in the shadow of the Sutherland Hotel, leaves the U.S. to go on a European tour, and returns to discover that the tight-knit neighborhood he knew has deteriorated. Some of the music is performed on Thompson's 1997 Delmark CD, *47th Street.*

what to buy: Representing Thompson's most ambitious and polished recorded project to date, *47th Street* ✍✍✍✍ (Delmark, 1997, prod. Robert G. Koester, Steve Wagner) is his 10-selection tribute to a vibrant period of black Chicago history when 47th Street on Chicago's South side was a thriving center of economic vitality and cultural activity. Containing Thompson's originals, rearranged standards, and some selections from his stage production, *The Sutherland,* the album draws from the entire jazz tradition. With two separate rhythm teams, the fare

alternately swings traditionally, stretches harmonically into free-blowing turf, and combines fine mainstream jazz section work with extraordinary solos from Thompson, tenor saxophonist Billy Harper, alto/soprano saxophonist Joe Ford, and the late tenor saxman Carter Jefferson. Instrumental settings vary and some tunes feature vocals, the most notable being Dee Alexander's rendering of the title theme. Among album highlights are "CJ's Blues," a pleasing, low-key trio number featuring Thompson (on muted trumpet) with Jefferson and bassist John Whitfield; the 13-minute free-jazz centerpiece, "Some Freebop for Monk"; and Thompson's fine solos on his rhythmically and melodically engaging "African Sun Dance," performed with Ford, Jefferson, and the rhythm team of Kirk Brown (piano), bassist Whitfield, drummer Nasar Abadey, and percussionist Dr. Cuz. For the listener, *47th Street* is a full-scale jazz experience, an ear-expanding album highlighting Thompson's trumpet mastery and many other peak moments. On *Buddy Bolden's Rag* ✍✍✍✍ (Delmark, 1995, prod. Robert G. Koester, Steve Wagner) Thompson continues his work to establish new traditions in jazz, keeping one foot squarely in jazz brass history and the other staunchly placed on the cutting edge. Thompson's Africa Brass band (four trumpets, four trombones, plus bass, percussion, and drums) and featured guest trumpeter, Lester Bowie, take the listener on a nine-tune spree, leaping from various styles and eras. If you enjoy AACM-school jazz that combines the present with the ancient, lyrical themes with freestyle playing and catchy rhythms, you'll dig this entertaining album.

what to buy next: *New Standards* ✍✍✍✍ (Delmark, 1994, prod. Robert G. Koester) features various musicians who had performed in Thompson's Freebop band up to the time of this recording. Longtime colleague, the late tenor man Carter Jefferson, is prominently featured, along with Joe Ford (alto/soprano saxophones), Sonny Seals (saxophone), and Steve Berry (trombone). Other musicians include Ron Bridgewater (tenor sax), Nasar Abadey or Avreeayl Ra (drums), John Whitfield (bass), and Kirk Brown (piano). Thompson strives to establish jazz tunes he feels should become "new standards," including Wayne Shorter's "Pinocchio," the time-shifting arrangement of Victor Feldman's "Joshua" (from the Miles Davis songbook), and Thompson's humorous arrangement of Harold Arlen's "If I Only Had a Brain," from the *Wizard of Oz.* He also contributes two originals, "Dyhia Malika" and his four-piece medley "Chicago Soundscapes." There's enough variety to please a broad spectrum of jazz fans on Thompson's critically acclaimed album *Lift Every Voice* ✍✍✍✍ (Delmark, 1993, prod. Robert G. Koester), recorded with his Africa Brass band and his Freebop Band after his trip to Africa and Egypt the preceding year. The journey broadened Thompson's perspective and the eight selections contain styles from straight-ahead jazz to African-beat themes. Included are innovative takes on traditional songs such as "Old Man River" and "Nobody Knows the Trouble I've Seen," John Coltrane's "Transition," and Thompson's four originals.

the rest:
Spirit 𝄞𝄞𝄞 (Delmark, 1989)
The Jaz Life 𝄞𝄞𝄞 (Delmark, 1992)

influences:
◀◀ Booker Little, Miles Davis, Woody Shaw

Nancy Ann Lee

Claude Thornhill

Born August 10, 1909, in Terre Haute, IN. Died July 1, 1965 in New York, NY.

If there truly was a Birth of the Cool, Claude Thornhill was its father. After study at the Cincinnati Conservatory and the Curtis Institute, Thornhill spent the 1930s working and recording with several big names in jazz, including Benny Goodman (1934–35), Bud Freeman (1935), and Billie Holiday (1938). Thornhill, through his arranging skills, was largely responsible for Maxine Sullivan's 1938 hit with "Loch Lomond" (the pair once being referred to as the Beardless Svengali and the Sepia Trilby). Thornhill crossed paths with Gil Evans in the California band of Skinnay Ennis. After forming his own band in 1940, Thornhill reached back to this association, bringing Evans in as arranger in 1941.

The Thornhill band of 1941–1948 was one of the most innovative of the big bands (Thelonious Monk once referred to Thornhill's band as one of his favorites). In addition to Thornhill's taste for compositions inspired by such European classical composers as Ravel and Debussy, Evans provided the band with groundbreaking charts of bop tunes by Charlie Parker ("Anthropology," "Yardbird Suite"), Miles Davis ("Donna Lee"), and Sir Charles Thompson ("Robbins Nest"). In addition to the material, Thornhill and Evans began to experiment with the very composition of the band, adding several instruments foreign to jazz bands (i.e. french horns, tuba, and flute), as well as having as many as seven reed players, all able to double on clarinet. These developments (with Evans's departure from the band in 1948) led directly to Davis's legendary Birth of the Cool sessions. No fewer than seven Thornhill alumni (Evans, Gerry

Mulligan, Lee Konitz, trumpeter/composer John Carisi, tuba player Bill Barber, and french horn players Junior Collins and Sandy Seigelstein) were involved in the sessions as either players, arrangers, composers, or sometimes all three.

Through the 1950s, Thornhill recorded sporadically, doing an album of Mulligan arrangements in 1953 among others. Sadly, all of Thornhill's later work under his own name is currently out of print in the U.S.

what to buy: All of the highlights of Thornhill's 1940s band can be found on the single-disc collection *Claude Thornhill—Best of the Big Bands* 𝄞𝄞𝄞𝄞 (CBS, 1990, reissue prod. Michael Brooks). His bebop arrangements are here as well as his biggest hit (and signature tune), "Snowfall." Also included is an Evans arrangement of a segment of the "Nutcracker Suite" not covered in Ellington's treatment.

what to buy next: *Gerry Mulligan Tentet & Quartet* 𝄞𝄞𝄞 (GNP/Crescendo, 1996, prod. Gene Norman) features Thornhill's arranging talents.

worth searching for: The out-of-print LP *Two Sides of Claude Thornhill* (Kapp) helps fill in some of the gaping holes in the Thornhill discography.

influences:
◀◀ Paul Whiteman, Duke Ellington

▶▶ Miles Davis's "Birth of the Cool" band, Gil Evans Orchestra, Gerry Mulligan Concert Jazz Band

Larry Grogan

Henry Threadgill

Born February 15, 1944, in Chicago, IL.

Saxophinist-flutist-clarinetist Henry Threadgill is a major composer, bandleader, and improviser. He was involved with the Association for the Advancement of Creative Musicians from the start, introduced via Muhal Richard Abrams's Experimental Band. Yet even during this early period, Threadgill's interests lay far beyond the strictly defined parameters of so-called jazz. In the '60s, in addition to working with bop and avant-garde groups, the artist also performed with gospel, blues, polka, Latin, and marching bands, and more recently expanded his range to include works for Indonesian and modern dance, film, theater, and symphonic productions. Citing genre-defining explorers like Duke Ellington and Charlie Parker, Threadgill is convinced that "the DNA of jazz is a conglomerate of everything." This inclusive attitude, and his commitment to growth through

change, places him among the ranks of contemporary world-influenced composer-improvisers like Anthony Braxton, Ornette Coleman, and Cecil Taylor.

Threadgill first came to prominence as a composer with Air, an extraordinary trio (originally with Fred Hopkins and Steve McCall) that set the standard for small-group improvisation in the '70s and '80s. By the late '70s, he began experimenting with compositions for larger ensembles. *X-75, Volume 1* features a nonet with four bass players and Amina Claudine Myers on vocals. A short time later, he founded his Sextett, which was actually a seven-piece group with rotating members, including Pheeroan Aklaff, Diedre Murray, and Frank Lacy. The Sextett laid the groundwork for Very Very Circus, an oddly configured septet featuring Gene Lake, Brandon Ross (currently Cassandra Wilson's guitarist), and Marcus Rojas (Spanish Fly's tuba player). After releasing Very Very Circus' *Too Much Sugar for a Dime*, co-produced by Bill Laswell, Threadgill moved on, much to the dismay of some fans and critics who don't jibe with his recent developments. From *Song Out of My Trees* forward, the artist began scoring pieces for smaller chamber groups and incorporating overt influences from his sojourns in Trinidad, Venezuela, and India (where he now makes his home). Further, Threadgill started to drop entirely out of the proceedings as a player and focus the spotlight on his compositions—another move which bothered longtime supporters of his spirited improvisations. In 1996, he made his latest radical shift by introducing his otherworldly Make a Move quintet with Ross, Tony Cedras (accordion, harmonium), Stomu Takeishi (electric fretless bass), and J.T. Lewis (drums).

what to buy: *Too Much Sugar for a Dime* 🎵🎵🎵🎵 (Axiom, 1993, prod. Bill Laswell, Henry Threadgill) is the very best demonstration of Very Very Circus' odd and beautiful power grooves. Think of ornately adorned, stomping elephants on an extraterrestrial voyage. Unusual arrangements of guitars sweeping like pianos and tubas fuel intricate melodic movement among all the voices. And Threadgill's resonant saxophone buoys the spirit of the compositions with unflagging energy. With *Song out of My Trees* 🎵🎵🎵🎵 (Black Saint, 1994, prod. Giovanni Bonandrini), though Threadgill bows out on two of the five tunes, the world-class players more than do justice to his compositions. This is the great "chamber group" recording, with a rotating ensemble cast, including (among others) Myra Melford

(piano), Brandon Ross (alto guitar), James Emery (soprano guitar), Tony Cedras (accordion), and Amina Claudine Myers (harpsichord, organ). "Over the River Club," with three guitars, bass, and piano, is one of Threadgill's finest investigations of stratified harmonic movement. *Easily Slip into Another World* 🎵🎵🎵🎵 (RCA/Novus, 1988, prod. Ed Michel) is the most energized of the Sextett's improvisational recordings. The album opens with Olu Dara's "I Can't Wait Till I Get Home." *Spirit of Nuff . . . Nuff* 🎵🎵🎵🎵 (Black Saint, 1991, prod. David Stone, Henry Threadgill), almost Ellingtonian in its breadth and beauty, contains more prime Very Very Circus interpretations of new Threadgill compositions.

what to buy next: *You Know the Number* 🎵🎵🎵🎵 (RCA/Novus, 1987, prod. Ed Michel) is the most buoyant of the Sextett recordings, with no vocal asides. It contains perhaps the heaviest personnel (same as on *Easily Slip*): Rasul Siddik (trumpet), Frank Lacy (trombone), Diedre Murray (cello), Fred Hopkins (bass), Pheeroan Aklaff (drums), Reggie Nicholson (drums). *Where's Your Cup?* 🎵🎵🎵🎵 (Columbia, 1997, prod. Bill Laswell, Henry Threadgill) prevalently uses Cedras's harmonium to give the music a strange feel—part eerie, part transcendent. Fretless bassist Takeishi—a twentysomething former Slayer aficionado—adds an extra dose of odd intensity to Threadgill's moving compositions. Although *Carry the Day* 🎵🎵🎵🎵 (Columbia, 1995, prod. Bill Laswell, Henry Threadgill) has been dismissed by quite a few non-believers (which makes it an easy score in the used CD bins), the augmented Very Very Circus—with an Asian-cum-Latino ensemble of instrumentalists (pipa, accordion, violin), percussionists and singers—creates a pan-ethnic streetfair atmosphere that makes for tangible myriad alternative realities. *Makin' a Move* 🎵🎵🎵🎵 (Columbia, 1995, prod. Bill Laswell, Henry Threadgill) provides more Very Very Circus "Plus" investigations. Highlights include the non-VVC contributions like "Noisy Flowers" (for Myra Melford and a six-string quartet), "Refined Poverty" (for Threadgill, on alto, and a cello trio), and "The Mockingbird Sin" (for guitar quartet and cello trio).

the rest:
X-75, Volume 1 🎵🎵🎵 (Arista/Novus, 1979)
(With the Sextett) *When Was That?* 🎵🎵🎵🎵 (About Time, 1982)
(With the Sextett) *Just the Facts and Pass the Bucket* 🎵🎵🎵🎵 (About Time, 1983)
(With the Sextett) *Subject to Change* 🎵🎵🎵🎵 (About Time, 1985)
(With the Sextett) *Rag, Bush and All* 🎵🎵🎵🎵 (RCA/Novus, 1989)
(With the Very Very Circus) *Live at Concepts* 🎵🎵🎵 (Taylor Made, 1991)

Henry Threadgill (© Nancy Ann Lee)

influences:
⏪ Duke Ellington, Muhal Richard Abrams
⏩ Spanish Fly, Dave Douglas

Sam Prestianni

Bobby Timmons

Born December 19, 1935, in Philadelphia, PA. Died March 1, 1974, in New York, NY.

Pianist Bobby Timmons will forever be remembered for the soul-jazz classics that he penned in the sixties, such as "Moanin'," "This Here," and "Dat Dere." The fact remains that he started out as a technically-gifted bebop pianist with a light touch and a highly rhythmic approach who just happened to find the popular funk style a natural outgrowth of his own artistic development. Throughout the 1950s, Timmons worked with such notables as Chet Baker, Kenny Dorham, Sonny Stitt, and Maynard Ferguson. By the beginning of the next decade he became a vital member of two of the most popular jazz groups of the period—Art Blakey's Jazz Messengers and the Cannonball Adderley Quintet. In fact, one could get a good idea of his superb piano work by merely consulting any number of albums recorded by Blakey or Adderley with Timmons at the piano. At the same time, he was leading his own trios and recording extensively for Riverside Records and later for the Prestige label. By the end of the 1960s, the soul-piano boom that Timmons had largely founded was being taken over by such names as Ramsey Lewis and Les McCann, meaning that Timmons's career eventually saw a decline that ended with his untimely death in 1974 at the age of 38. Worthy of rediscovery, Timmons's recorded output is indeed large. Further investigation will show him to have had more talent than even his popular stature would suggest.

what to buy: *This Here is Bobby Timmons* ♪♪♪♪ (Riverside/OJC, 1960, prod. Orrin Keepnews) makes for an impressive debut and one of the pianist's best efforts, with Sam Jones and Jimmy Cobb making for a true "super trio." *Workin' Out* ♪♪♪♪ (Prestige, 1964/1966, prod. Ozzie Cadena, Cal Lampley) pairs on one CD the original albums *Workin' Out* and *Soul Man*. While the former is an exceptional date that pairs Timmons with vibist Johnny Lytle, it's the latter set that is a genuine classic. Ron Carter, Wayne Shorter, and Jimmy Cobb make up a truly exciting cast and such originals as Carter's "Little Waltz" and Shorter's "Tom Thumb" are not to be missed.

what to buy next: *In Person* ♪♪♪♪ (Riverside/OJC, 1961, prod. Orrin Keepnews) finds Timmons in the company of bassist Ron Carter and drummer Tootie Heath for a live set that finds everyone inspired and in top form. *Sweet and Soulful Sounds* ♪♪♪♪ (Riverside/OJC, 1962, prod Orrin Keepnews) is probably one of the best of Timmon's studio dates from the period. An excellent choice of material and the work of bassist Sam Jones and drummer Roy McCurdy make this more than just your average piano trio album.

the rest:
Soul Time ♪♪♪♪ (Riverside/OJC, 1960)
Easy Does It ♪♪♪♪ (Riverside/OJC, 1961)
Born to Be Blue ♪♪♪♪ (Riverside/OJC, 1963)

influences:
⏪ Bud Powell
⏩ Ramsey Lewis, Benny Green

Chris Hovan

The Billy Tipton Memorial Saxophone Quartet

Formed 1988, in Seattle, WA.

Amy Denio, alto saxophone (1988–96); Marjorie de Muynck, soprano, alto, tenor saxophones (1988–95); Babs Helle, baritone saxophone (1988–91); Stacy Loebs, alto, tenor saxophones (1988–91); Barbara Marino, baritone, alto saxophones (1991–present); Jessica Lurie, alto, tenor saxophones (1992–present); Maya Johnson, tenor, soprano saxophones (1995–96); Annelise Zamula, tenor, soprano, alto saxophones (1996–present); Sue Orfield, soprano and tenor saxophones (1997–present); Pam Barger, drums (1993–present).

This quartet named themselves after the late Dorothy Lucille Tipton who adopted a male identity to get by in the jazz world of the Pacific northwest. She kept her secret intact for more than 50 years—amazingly, even from three wives, or so the story goes—until dying from a bleeding ulcer in 1991.

In their 10 years of existence personnel has slowly shifted with none of the founding members on board any longer and with the addition of a full-time drummer. However, their general approach has remained unchanged. They possess a keen sense of history and a broad, rich compositional base (primarily from Amy Denio and Jessica Lurie), but what sets them apart from the more commonly articulated presentations of saxophone quartets are their forays into the musics of elsewhere and other times. Bulgarian, Klezmer, and other Eastern European folk styles coexist naturally and proudly with more contemporary Western strains. So naturally, in fact, that it seems like a bunch of dancing cousins have come to visit.

what's available: Don't be misled by the cover of *Saxhouse* ♫♫♫ (Knitting Factory Works, 1993, prod. BTMSQ). It's a snapshot moment of all four sax-bearing women caught mid-wail atop a bus on a big city street. This is not, thankfully, a presentation of performance—guerilla saxophone screech 'n' skronk. The album clearly delineates their agenda, with reeds taking on a range of folk and dance music not normally associated with the instrument. They succeed in making it all sound like they were made for each other. *Box* ♫♫♫ (New World Records, 1996, prod. BTMSQ) continues the story, finessing the recording process itself, while Lurie jumps to the fore with her writing this time out.

worth searching for: *Make It Funky God* ♫♫♫ (Horn Hut, 1994, prod. BTMSQ) is an extended-play CD released on their own label. Sold at their performances and via mail order, it's a fine companion to their pair of full-length outings.

solo outings:

Amy Denio:

Birthing Chair Blues ♫♫♫ (Knitting Factory Works, 1991)

Tongues ♫♫♫ (FOT Records, 1993)

influences:

◀◀ World Saxophone Quartet, Henry Cow

David Greenberger

Wayman Tisdale

Born June 6, 1964, in Tulsa, OK.

When he was in fifth grade, NBA power forward Wayman Tisdale began playing bass in his father's church. Inspired by the lead-bass style of Stanley Clarke and the funky grooves of Marcus Miller and the Gap Band's Robert Wilson, Tisdale kept playing pop-jazz through high school, college, the Olympics (he was a basketball gold medalist in 1984), and in the NBA off-seasons. He signed with Motown's MoJazz subsidiary when a friend of his took the completed tapes of *Power Forward* to some label executives for an anonymous listening session. The executives were interested and very surprised to find out the session leader was Tisdale.

what to buy: Tisdale hooked up with a cast of pop-jazz characters, including his inspiration, Marcus Miller, for the surprisingly accomplished, creamy pop-jazz of *Power Forward* ♫♫♫ (MoJazz, 1995, prod. Wayman Tisdale, various). Tisdale's grooves pulse with the light funk that's perfect background for the jacuzzi.

what to buy next: In typical sophomore effort style, *In the Zone* ♫♫ (MoJazz, 1996, prod. Wayman Tisdale, various) slips from the mark Tisdale set in his debut. It's pleasant enough in the background, but has a hard time taking the foreground.

influences:

◀◀ Stanley Clarke, Marcus Miller

Salvatore Caputo

Cal Tjader

Born Callen Radcliffe Tjader Jr., July 16, 1925, in St. Louis, MO. Died May 5, 1982, in Manila, Philippines.

Diehard Latin-music fans decry his cool jazz tendencies and hard-core jazzers lament his Latin daliances, but Tjader's dedication to the music helped to popularize and promote Latin jazz to the average jazz fan. He was an important conduit between the two styles, and his contributions served as a prelude to the Latin-rock fusion of Santana.

Tjader got started in show business at an early age. At age 4 he joined his parents' vaudeville act. At age 7 he was dancing with Bill "Bojangles" Robinson in the movie *The White of the Dark Cloud of Joy.* A few years later, the family moved to northern California and Cal's interests turned to the drums. After a three-year hitch as a Navy medic during World War II, Tjader returned to California and continued to study music at San Francisco State. In 1948, he joined Dave Brubeck's octet as the drummer. He then joined the George Shearing Quintet in 1953, giving him important national exposure and igniting his interest in Latin music. He formed his own group, which included Armando Peraza (from Shearing's group), Willy Bobo, and Mongo Santamaria. His timing was excellent: the country was caught in a mambo craze, and Tjader's music was a perfect fit. In 1965, he had a hit with a reworked version of Dizzy Gillespie's "Guachi Guaro," renamed "Soul Sauce." The following year he toured with Eddie Palmieri and recorded the outstanding *El Sonido Nuevo,* a groundbreaking mix of the hot salsa of Palmieri and cool jazz of Tjader. This was a marked departure from previous Latin-jazz ventures like those by Stan Getz, who mixed cool jazz with cool samba to make bossa nova. Tjader stayed on the West Coast and continued to perform and record throughout the '70s and '80s with a wide range of musicians, including Clare Fischer, Herbie Hancock (under the psuedonym Dawili Gonga), and Pancho Sanchez. He died suddenly while on tour in Manila.

what to buy: *Monterey Concerts* ♫♫♫♫ (Fantasy, 1959) collects volumes one and two of *Concert by the Sea* on one CD. The band featured Willie Bobo and Mongo Santamaria and sets the standard for the genre. It's a nice mix of jazz standards and Latin originals like "Afro Blue." *Soul Sauce* ♫♫♫♫ (Verve, 1965, prod. Creed Taylor) has the hit "Guachi Guaro" and includes Donald Byrd, Kenny Burrell, and Willie Bobo.

what to buy next: *El Sonido Nuevo* 𝄞𝄞𝄞 (Verve, 1966, prod. Creed Taylor) captures the groundbreaking blend of cool jazz and hot salsa. The album is more subdued than *Soul Sauce*, but still sparkles on numbers like "Ritmo Uni" and "Unidos."

what to avoid: *Cal Tjader Plays/Mary Stallings Sings* 𝄞 (Fantasy, 1961) has too much Mary, not enough Cal.

the rest:
Good Vibes 𝄞𝄞 (Concord Jazz, 1951)
Mambo with Tjader 𝄞𝄞 (Fantasy, 1954)
Tjader Plays Mambo 𝄞𝄞 (Fantasy, 1954)
Black Orchid 𝄞𝄞𝄞 (Fantasy, 1956/1993)
Latin Kick 𝄞𝄞𝄞 (Fantasy, 1956)
Los Ritmos Calientes 𝄞𝄞𝄞 (Fantasy, 1957/1992)
Latin Concert 𝄞𝄞𝄞 (Fantasy, 1958)
Jazz at the Blackhawk 𝄞𝄞𝄞 (Fantasy, 1959)
Latino! 𝄞𝄞𝄞 (Fantasy, 1960)
Sona Libre (Verve, 1963)
Cal Tjader's Greatest Hits 𝄞𝄞𝄞𝄞 (Fantasy, 1965)
The Best of Cal Tjader 𝄞𝄞𝄞𝄞 (Verve, 1968)
Plugs In 𝄞𝄞𝄞 (DCC Jazz, 1969)
Primo 𝄞𝄞𝄞 (Fantasy, 1970/OJC, 1992)
Descarga 𝄞𝄞𝄞 (Fantasy, 1971)
Tambu 𝄞𝄞𝄞 (Fantasy, 1973)
Amazonas 𝄞𝄞𝄞 (Fantasy, 1975)
Here and There 𝄞𝄞𝄞 (Fantasy, 1976)
Huracan 𝄞𝄞 (Laserlight, 1978)
La Onda Va Bien 𝄞𝄞𝄞 (Concord Picante, 1979)
Gozame! Pero Ya 𝄞𝄞𝄞 (Concord Picante, 1980)
Fuego Vivo 𝄞𝄞𝄞 (Concord Picante, 1981)
Shining Sea 𝄞𝄞𝄞 (Concord Picante, 1981)
Heat Wave 𝄞𝄞𝄞 (Concord Picante, 1982)
Sentimental Moods 𝄞𝄞𝄞 (Fantasy, 1996)

worth searching for: *Stan Getz/Cal Tjader Sextet* 𝄞𝄞𝄞𝄞 (Fantasy, 1958/OJC, 1990) is a terrific collaboration between the two men who would become the standard-bearers for Latin jazz fusion. Vince Guaraldi, Billy Higgins, Eddie Duran, and Scott LaFaro round out the proceedings expertly. It was originally a Tjader album, but with the saxophonist's fame now greater, it's listed under Getz's name.

influences:
◄◄ Milt Jackson, George Shearing
►► Vince Guaraldi, Mark Levine

James Eason

T.J. Kirk

Formed 1993, in San Francisco, CA.

Charlie Hunter, eight-string guitar, bass; Will Bernard, guitar; John Schott, guitar; Scott Amendola, drums.

The quirkiest offspring of the longtime marriage between jazz and funk, T.J. Kirk is a Bay Area quartet dedicated to playing the music of Thelonious Monk, James Brown, and Rahsaan Roland Kirk—usually at the same time. Fronted by former Disposable Heroes of Hiphoprisy guitarist Charlie Hunter, T.J. Kirk was born as James T. Kirk (Paramount Pictures eventually denied the group permission to use the *Star Trek* moniker) and its repertoire was designed to provide band members with artillery to silence noisy, inattentive crowds. But once-a-week gigs and growing audiences soon blossomed into one of the coolest, and most literal, examples of fusion to come along since Return to Forever. No word yet on whether the group will pursue its ongoing threat to splinter into Charles Nelson Riley, which would combine the music of Charles Mingus, Prince Rogers Nelson (a.k.a. the artist formerly known as Prince), and former Monk drummer Ben Riley.

what to buy: Relentlessly funky grooves and driving, dueling guitars turn *T.J. Kirk* 𝄞𝄞𝄞 (Warner Bros., 1995, prod. Lee Townsend) into an outrageous tour de force. It's a pity that publishing company concerns forced the musicians to break down their funny hybrid titles like "Cold Sweaty Panic" (Brown's "Cold Sweat" with Kirk's "Rip, Rig and Panic"), "I Got to Move Bud" (Brown's "I Got to Move" and Monk's "In Walked Bud"), and "Shufflegate" (Monk's "Shuffle Boil" and Brown's "You Can Have Watergate") into straightforward, medley-like track listings.

the rest:
If Four Was One 𝄞𝄞𝄞 (Warner Bros., 1996)

influences:
◄◄ Weather Report, Return to Forever

David Okamoto

Charles Tolliver

Born March 6, 1942, in Jacksonville, FL.

One of the most important artistic relationships this clarinetist was to develop started in 1969 when he formed a quartet called Music, Inc. with pianist Stanley Cowell. They later (1971) started a record label called Strata-East to distribute their own recordings as well as works by other artists, including poet-singer Gil Scott-Heron. Raised in New York City, Tolliver got a cornet from his grandmother when he was 8 and proceeded to learn the instrument on his own. After graduating from high school, he attended Howard University in Washington, D.C., where he studied pharmacy. Before he could complete his degree requirements, Tolliver moved back to New York City, where his first important gig was with alto saxophonist Jackie McLean. The first album Tolliver appeared on was McLean's *It's Time*. Tolliver also was the 1968 *Down Beat* Critics Poll winner on trumpet. Tolliver was fairly active about releasing his own albums through the 1980s but has since concentrated on studio and concert work.

what to buy: Recorded with Music, Inc. while on tour in Europe, *The Ringer* ♪♪♪♪ (Freedom/Black Lion, 1970, prod. Alan Bates, Chris Whent) could be the finest studio recording by the trumpeter. All of the tunes were written by him, and Tolliver's playing walks an accessible, swinging, post-bop line. Pianist Stanley Cowell is a solid alternate soloist. On *Impact* ♪♪♪♪ (Strata-East, 1975, prod. Charles Tolliver, Alan Bates), Tolliver leads a big band with a top notch batch of soloists through one of his most exciting albums. The revamped versions of the title tune and "Plight" from *The Ringer* are wonderful.

what to buy next: *Grand Max* ♪♪♪ (Black Lion, 1972, prod. Charles Tolliver, Alan Bates), recorded live at the Loosdrecht Jazz Festival in the Netherlands, features a fine quartet of musicians working with Tolliver. The title tune refers to Tolliver's former employer Max Roach.

the rest:
Live at Historic Slugs, Volumes 1 & 2 ♪♪♪♪ (Strata-East, 1970)
Music Inc. & Big Band ♪♪♪♪ (Strata East, 1972)
Impact ♪♪♪ (Enja, 1972)
Live in Tokyo ♪♪♪ (Strata-East, 1974)
Compassion ♪♪♪ (Strata-East, 1978)
Live in Berlin, Volume 1 ♪♪♪♪ (Strata-East, 1988)
Live in Berlin, Volume 2 ♪♪♪ (Strata-East, 1988)

influences:

◀◀ Clifford Brown, Freddie Hubbard

▶▶ Marlon Jordan, Roy Hargrove, Tim Hagans

Garaud MacTaggart

Mel Tormé

Born Melvin Howard Tormé, September 13, 1925, in Chicago, IL.

Mel Tormé is a gifted multitalented show business personality who in the course of his 75-plus years has been a respected jazz singer, an actor, composer, arranger, pianist, drummer, author, child radio performer, and raconteur. His hobbies are numerous and his collections imposing. Among other things, he is an aficionado of World War I aircraft and of American movies. Tormé has been a professional singer for over 60 years and his voice, prior to a debilitating stroke in August 1996, has always contained a youthful zest. In his earlier days, his high husky voice led him to be dubbed "The Velvet Fog," but after the 1950s, he sang more from his diaphragm, dispensing with what he calls "head tones." His voice has a wide range and he goes from low to high register with apparent ease. Tormé has superb control and flexibility, and as he grew older he developed a more heightened sense of swing.

Mel Tormé started in show business at age four as a Monday night feature act with the Coon-Saunders Orchestra at the Black Hawk in Chicago. At age six, he was on stage in a children's review run by bandleader Paul Ash. In 1933, he was "Jimmy the Newsboy" on the radio soap opera *Song of the City,* and for the next several years (until his voice changed) he could be heard on the radio acting in shows such as *Little Orphan Annie* and *Jack Armstrong, The All-American Boy,* among others. At age 15, he published his song "Lament to Love," which was recorded by Harry James. And in August 1942, just before turning 17, he joined the Chico Marx Orchestra as singer and vocal arranger, and eventually replaced George Wettling as the band's drummer. Tormé appeared in his first film, *Higher and Higher,* with Frank Sinatra. In 1944, he took over a vocal group, which he named the Mel-Tones, and started recording for Decca and Musicraft. In 1946, he cowrote the holiday evergreen, "The Christmas Song," with his partner Robert Wells. Tormé appeared in several more films, including the MGM musical *Good News,* and still managed to tour and do club dates around the country. Over the years, recording dates with Capitol, Columbia, Atlantic, Bethlehem, and Verve ensued and Tormé continued to refine his vocal skills while involved in television, authoring books, arranging music, and making personal appearances at home and abroad. His activities and source materials suffered a bit in the 1960s when rock music started to prevail, but Tormé fell back on the classic ballads and swing songs from the "Great American Songbook," and starting in 1982 he released a series of well-produced, straightforward albums from Concord Jazz. The Concord albums were often done in the company of fellow jazz performers such as pianists George Shearing and John Colianni, saxophonists Frank Wess and Ken Peplowski, bassists John Leitham, Bob Maize, and Neil Swainson, and drummer Donny Osborne, with orchestration

led and arranged by Rob McConnell and Marty Paich. Thanks to exposure on the hit TV series *Night Court,* Tormé remained visible playing himself in some broad comedy sketches. Even with this renewed activity Tormé somehow found time to publish six books, all very readable. Throughout the 1980s and early 1990s, Tormé brought his brand of ballad, scat, and jazz singing on theater tours, jazz festivals, and concert visits throughout the world, usually with a troupe of jazz players, until his unfortunate stroke in August, 1996. Thanks to his many available CDs, his voice has not been silenced.

what to buy: *The Mel Tormé Collection, 1944–1985* ♫♫♫♫ (Rhino, 1996, compilation prod. Dave Kapp) compiles the singer's recordings from Decca, Coral, Musicraft, Capitol, Sony/Columbia, PolyGram/Verve, and other labels on a four-CD, 92-track retrospective of Mel Tormé's recording career up to his latter-day recordings for Concord. A box set with a 62-page illustrated booklet with an essay by Will Friedwald and additional annotation by Tormé, this highly recommended collection is a great way to become acquainted with the renowned vocalist or to replace any scratchy Tormé 78s or LPs you might own. *Mel Tormé Swings Shubert Alley* ♫♫♫♫ (Verve, 1959/ 1989) finds the singer at the top of his game performing vocal magic on a dozen first-rate Broadway show tunes. The Marty Paich Orchestra, with 11 handpicked West Coast sidemen, complements Tormé and deserves equal billing on one of the finest jazz vocal albums to reach compact disc. Alto saxophonist Art Pepper, tenor saxophonist Bill Perkins, and trombonist Frank Rosolino make the most of their brief solo spots and blend in well with the flexible, swinging, assured delivery and dynamic range of the Tormé pipes. The solid rhythm section of pianist Paich, bassist Joe Mondragon, and drummer Mel Lewis is augmented by Red Callendar's tuba, which effectively provides a full bottom sound in the ensembles. "Just in Time," "All I Need Is the Girl," "Hello Young Lovers," "The Surrey with the Fringe on Top," "Too Darn Hot," and remaining tunes have never had such great treatment. This is vintage Tormé and a perfect example of the musical whole being equal to the sum of its parts.

what to buy next: *Velvet and Brass* ♫♫♫♫ (Concord Jazz, 1995, prod. John Burk) features the singer in a perfect fit with Rob McConnell and the Boss Brass band. Thirteen tracks, arranged and conducted by Rob McConnell, contain a satisfying mix of jazz ballads, Latin rhythms, and straight-ahead swingers conveying a variety of styles and tempos punctuated with lots of burnished brass. The lovely opener, Jerome Kern's "Nobody Else but Me," and the closing take on the Paul Madeira–Jimmy Dorsey tune "I'm Glad There Is You" are reason enough to seek out this album. Another rewarding blend of consummate musicianship, good taste, and solid source material occurs with *Mel Tormé Sings Fred Astaire* ♫♫♫♫ (Bethlehem, 1957/1994). This November 1956 Hollywood session finds singer Tormé in one of his earlier collaborations with the Marty Paich Dek-Tette, singing 12 evergreens by composers George and Ira Gershwin, Irving Berlin, Jerome Kern, and Johnny Mercer on this tribute to one of Tormé's idols, Fred Astaire. This edition of the Dek-Tette features Herb Geller (alto saxophone), Jack Montrose (tenor sax), and the trumpets of Pete Candoli and Don Fagerquist, all of whom demonstrated the validity of the West Coast jazz approach. Tormé glides comfortably through the Astaire songbook with "A Foggy Day," "A Fine Romance," "Cheek to Cheek," and an up-tempo "The Way You Look Tonight," among the winning performances.

the rest:
(With the Mel-Tones) *A Foggy Day* ♫♫♫ (Musicraft/Discovery, 1945–47/1989)
(With the Mel-Tones) *There's No One but You* ♫♫♫ (Musicraft/Discover, 1945–47/1989)
Spotlight on Mel Tormé ♫♫♫♫ (Capitol, 1949–51/1994)
Easy to Remember ♫♫♫♫ (Hindsight, 1953–1963/1994)
Mel Tormé in Hollywood ♫♫♫♫ (Coral/Decca, 1954/1992)
It's a Blue World ♫♫♫♫ (Bethlehem, 1955/1994)
Tormé ♫♫♫♫ (Verve, 1958/1898)
(With the Mel-Tones) *Back in Town* ♫♫♫♫♫ (Verve, 1959/1991)
Right Now ♫ (Sony/Columbia, 1960)
Ellington/Basie Songbook ♫♫♫♫♫ (Verve, 1960/1991)
Swingin' on the Moon ♫♫♫♫ (Verve, 1960)
Songs of New York ♫♫♫♫ (Atlantic, 1964/1987)
That's All ♫♫♫ (Columbia, 1965/1997)
Live at Maisonette ♫♫♫♫♫ (Atlantic, 1975)
Encore at Marty's, New York ♫♫♫♫♫ (DCC, 1982)
An Evening with George Shearing and Mel Tormé ♫♫♫♫♫ (Concord, 1982)
(With George Shearing) *An Elegant Evening* ♫♫♫♫♫ (Concord, 1986)
(With George Shearing) *An Evening at Charlies* ♫♫♫♫♫ (Concord, 1986)
Mel Tormé–Rob McConnell and the Boss Brass ♫♫♫♫♫ (Concord, 1986)
Compact Jazz ♫♫♫♫ compilation (Verve, 1987)
(With George Shearing) *Top Drawer* ♫♫♫♫♫ (Concord, 1988)
(With George Shearing) *A Vintage Year* ♫♫♫♫♫ (Concord, 1988)
(With the Marty Paich Dek-Tette) *Reunion* ♫♫♫♫♫ (Concord, 1988)
(With the Marty Paich Dek-Tette) *In Concert in Tokyo* ♫♫♫♫♫ (Concord, 1989)

Mel Tormé and Peggy Lee **(Archive Photos)**

Night at the Concord Pavilion 🎵🎵🎵🎵 (Concord, 1990)

Smooth as Velvet 🎵🎵🎵🎵 (Pickwick/Laserlight, 1991)

(With George Shearing) *Mel and George Do World War II* 🎵🎵🎵🎵 (Concord, 1991)

Fujitsu-Concord Jazz Festival 🎵🎵🎵🎵 (Concord, 1991)

(With Cleo Laine) *Nothing without You* 🎵🎵🎵 (Concord, 1992)

Christmas Songs 🎵🎵🎵 (Telarc, 1992)

Sing, Sing, Sing 🎵🎵🎵🎵 (Concord, 1993)

The Great American Songbook: Live at Michael's Pub 🎵🎵🎵🎵 (Telarc, 1993)

16 Most Requested Songs 🎵🎵🎵 (Columbia, 1993)

A Tribute to Bing Crosby 🎵🎵🎵 (Concord, 1994)

Jazz 'Round Midnight 🎵🎵🎵🎵 compilation (Verve, 1994)

A&E: An Evening with Mel Tormé Live from the Disney Institute 🎵🎵🎵🎵 (Concord, 1996)

My Night to Dream 🎵🎵🎵🎵 (Concord, 1997)

influences:

◀◀ Jackie Cain, Roy Kral, Frank Sinatra, Ella Fitzgerald, Louis Armstrong, Bing Crosby, Fred Astaire, Nat "King" Cole, Woody Herman

▶▶ Harry Connick Jr., Mandy Patinkin, Johnny Hartman

John T. Bitter

Ralph Towner

Born March 1, 1940, in Chehalis, WA.

Along with Keith Jarrett, and Jan Garbarek, Ralph Towner, both as a solo artist and with his band Oregon, has defined the chamber jazz sound of the ECM label for over two decades. Though best known as an accomplished and influential guitarist, Towner actually didn't pick up the instrument until his early twenties. As a child he studied trumpet and also taught himself piano. He studied composition at the University of Oregon and after graduation took up guitar, taking lessons in Vienna under Karl Scheit. Towner played in small jazz groups in the mid-1960s and ended the decade as a member of the Paul Winter Consort. The Consort's seminal album *Icarus*, which contains three Towner compositions, including the classic title track, is not only Winter's best, but set the benchmark for New Age music, one rarely approached by today's practitioners. When the Paul Winter Consort disbanded in 1970, Towner formed Oregon with Consort bandmates Glen Moore, Colin Walcott, and Paul McCandless. The group merged classical, folk, Indian, jazz, and other "world" influences to play a genre that would eventually be called chamber jazz by some and New Age by others. Regardless of the term, the quartet has played an exciting form of mostly acoustic music that has earned justifiable critical and audience praise.

Towner's solo career has included appearances on Weather Report's *I Sing the Body Electric*, duets with Gary Burton and John Abercrombie, and several solo albums on ECM. His guitar playing is deeply rooted in the classical style, but he draws from bebop, free jazz, Indian, and other influences. Though he also plays piano, French horn, and synthesizer on some of his albums, it is his guitar playing that justifiably garners most of the attention. He is an excellent player who has influenced many players in the classical, folk, and new age genres, though few play with his brilliance.

what to buy: *Diary* 🎵🎵🎵🎵 (ECM, 1974/1994, prod. Manfred Eicher) is generally regarded as his best solo recording (at least until he recorded *Ana*). Towner plays guitar, piano, and gong, in some cases all three through overdubbing (showing he can accompany himself quite nicely). "Icarus" is the high point of the affair, with its piano lead and captivating rhythm guitar. Though *Diary* influenced the New Age movement, the New Age players only grasped the mood and some of its prettier points. They failed to grasp Towner's intensity, use of dissonance, or creativity. A splendid effort. *Solstice* 🎵🎵🎵🎵 (ECM, 1975/1994, prod. Manfred Eicher) is more energetic, jazzier, and bluesier than most of Towner's recordings, partially a response to drummer Jon Christensen's straight-ahead playing. Eberhard Weber and Jan Garbarek round out the quartet and are in good form, as is Towner who plays with unusual intensity. Compositionally, this is one of Towner's better efforts, with "Nimbus" possessing an excellent hook and some awesome playing by Weber. *Matchbook* 🎵🎵🎵🎵 (ECM, 1975, prod. Manfred Eicher) offers a classic duet with Gary Burton that, while reflective of ECM's mid-1970s chamber jazz movement, stands up very well over 20 years later. Though rather tranquil, *Matchbook's* high points, "Icarus" and "Goodbye Pork Pie Hat," are seductive. *Ana* 🎵🎵🎵🎵 (ECM, 1997, prod. Manfred Eicher) makes the ultimate solo guitar statement as a lesson in composition, playing, and creativity. Towner incorporates classical, folk, jazz, pop, and avant-garde influences in an absorbing and never disjointed fashion. This masterful solo recording is 48 minutes of bliss. A must have for any acoustic guitar student or fan.

what to buy next: Containing mostly original material recorded in Europe, *Solo Concert* 🎵🎵🎵🎵 (ECM, 1980/1994, prod. Manfred Eicher) includes the compositions "Train of Thought" and "Zoetrope," which are the best, and Towner's cool rendition of "Nardis." *Slide Show* 🎵🎵🎵🎵 (ECM, 1986, prod. Manfred Eicher) is the second duet with Gary Burton showing that lightning does strike twice. Less serene than *Matchbook*, *Slide Show*'s peak moments are many and the frisky playing is enjoyable. While Towner has obviously influenced Pat Metheny, his arrangements on *Open Letter* &&&& (ECM, 1994, prod. Manfred Eicher) show Metheny has also influenced him. Less cerebral and more fun than some of Towner's work, the playing is no less excellent. His use of synthesizer for color is effective and Peter Erskine adds some good, if uneventful, touches. The only Towner recording that has some obvious traces of John McLaughlin is *City of Eyes* &&& (ECM, 1989/1994, prod. Manfred Eicher).

the rest:

Trios/Solos &&& (ECM, 1973)
Souls and Shadows &&& (ECM, 1977)
Old Friends, New Friends &&& (ECM, 1979/1994)
Blue Sun &&& (ECM, 1983/1994)
Lost and Found &&& (ECM, 1996)

influences:

◀◀ John Fahey, Charlie Byrd, Julian Bream, John Williams, Carlos Montoya, Andres Segovia

▶▶ Michael Hedges, William Ackerman, Tuck Andress, Pat Metheny

Paul MacArthur

Trance Mission

Formed 1992, in San Francisco, CA.

Beth Custer, B-flat, alto, and bass clarinets, trumpet, percussion, voice; Stephen Kent, didgeridoos, cello, percussion, voice; John Loose, percussion (1992–97); Eda Maxym, vocals, samples (1997–present); Kenneth Newby, Indonesian winds, percussion, atmospheric treatments (samples); Peter Reason, drums, percussion, samples (1997–present).

Trance Mission had a successful start to its career. Its 1993 debut was the second release for the San Francisco–based City of Tribes label and sold over 10,000 copies with little mainstream promotion. This was proof that the band's eclectic blend of world music and jazz sounds would find an audience craving such aural adventures. One element that has always stood out is the clarinet playing of Custer, unusual not only for its placement within the tribal milieu, but also in terms of her melodic, jazz-inflected approach. As the Bay area ensemble has developed, so has its sound. The raw, jazzy tones conjured up by its early music have given way to dreamier Fourth World imagery as ambient electronics have

seeped into the later works. Simultaneously, the layers of percussion have increased, with the music focusing less on clarinet and didgeridoo as the leading instruments. While the world fusion and jazz influences remain at the heart of the sound, the band's increased use of both electronics and the studio to produce enhanced atmospheric works has helped progress its sound, which appeals to both world and ambient fans alike. The members of Trance Mission are involved in many other projects released through the City of Tribes label. In fact, COT artists frequently collaborate, which has lead to some dynamic recordings with Trance Mission players.

what to buy: *Head Light* &&&& (City of Tribes, 1996, prod. Simon Tassano) sees Trance Mission moving into more ethno-ambient territory, although many strong rhythmic elements easily keep much of it from being pigeonholed in that genre. It's the quartet's best effort to date. Producer Tassano certainly has influenced the band's sound with his spatial enhancements, and this time out, he actually stripped away some of the layers of tracks the band recorded to give the album an equally dense and spacious feel, creating a clear mix. One of the most memorable pieces is the title track, which features Custer's processed alto clarinet mirroring an electric guitar as it cuts across the ambiences and primal drumming. And "Worksong" spotlights the multitracked, otherworldly vocals of Maxym, who also sings for the Beasts of Paradise.

what to buy next: Trance Mission's sophomore effort, *Meanwhile…* &&& (City of Tribes, 1994, prod. Simon Tassano), is more psychedelic and intense than their debut and shows the band progressing into less structured, more improvisatory territory. The clarinet playing becomes more Middle Eastern sounding, and Newby begins to become more of a presence in the group's sonic tapestry. Loose provides some kit playing on half the tracks as well. A couple of the songs have some odd poetry recitations over them, but these hardly detract from the driving beat of such works as "Go Play Outside!" *Trance Mission* &&& (City of Tribes, 1993, prod. Oliver DiCicco) began the group's fusion odysseys and features some up-tempo cuts, including "Folk Song," which literally sounds like a jazz club gone tribal. Custer's clarinet playing is a dominant force on the album, her higher-pitched wind sounds rising above the music but complemented by the lower tones of Kent's growling didgeridoo. A solid beginning for the group.

influences:

◀◀ Miles Davis, John Coltrane, Jon Hassell, Brian Eno, the Beatles

Bryan Reesman

Tribal Tech

Formed 1985, in Los Angeles, CA.

Scott Henderson, electric guitar; Gary Willis, electric bass; Pat Coil, keyboards (1985–87); David Goldblatt, keyboards (1988–90); Scott Kinsey, keyboards (1992–present); Steve Houghton, drums (1985–88); Joey Heredia, drums (1990); Kirk Covington, drums (1992–present).

One of the hottest fusion groups of the 1990s, Tribal Tech's tough-edged music is far from the saccharine, radio-conscious music of so many current fusion groups. Built around Scott Henderson's screaming guitar licks and Gary Willis's often Jaco-esque basslines, the quartet's a mix of Weather Report's layered approach and Return to Forever's aggressiveness, but bluesier than either.

Henderson studied with guitarist Joe Diorio at Los Angeles' Guitar Institute of Technology, then played with Jean-Luc Ponty, the first version of the Chick Corea Elektric Band, and Zawinul Syndicate. Willis became known in the bands of Wayne Shorter and Allan Holdsworth. Their collaboration, Tribal Tech, adds a keyboardist and a drummer (saxophonist Bob Sheppard also played in some of the earliest incarnations).

what to buy: *Reality Check* 🎵🎵🎵🎵 (Bluemoon, 1995, prod. Scott Henderson, Gary Willis) is the group's most recent release at this writing, though another album is supposedly in the works. After a soft, lyrical "Stella by Starlight" comes the brash, flashy "Stella by Infra-Red High Particle Neutron Beam," and Scott Henderson's crunching guitar heroics on the latter set the tone for the remainder of the CD, though not everything's that intense. There are some funky grooves, and Scott Kinsey's keyboards sometimes reference mid-period Weather Report. For all the unbridled energy and flashy virtuosity, there's remarkably little self-indulgence, and occasional lyricism.

what to buy next: The 76-minute-plus *Primal Tracks* 🎵🎵🎵 (Bluemoon, 1994, prod. Scott Henderson, Gary Willis) compiles selections from Tribal Tech's early *Dr. Hee*, *Nomad*, and *Tribal Tech* albums, all originally on Relativity. The overall quality is quite high and this offers a nice cross section of TT styles. The virtuosic Henderson solo album *Dog Party* 🎵🎵🎵 (Mesa, 1994, prod. Scott Henderson) finds him jamming hot blues outside the Tribal Tech context (there are even horns and harmonica). It's convincing and fun, complete with a few good-humored vocals.

the rest:
Spears 🎵🎵🎵 (Passport, 1985/Relativity, 1990)
Illicit 🎵🎵🎵🎵 (Bluemoon, 1992)
Face First 🎵🎵🎵🎵 (Bluemoon, 1993)

solo outings:
Scott Henderson:
Tore Down House 🎵🎵🎵 (Mesa, 1997)

influences:
◀◀ Tony Williams Lifetime, John McLaughlin, Return to Forever, Weather Report, John Scofield

▶▶ Frank Gambale, Pat Coil

Steve Holtje

A Tribe Called Quest

Formed 1988, in Queens, NY.

Q-Tip (born Jonathan Davis), vocals; Phife (born Malik Taylor), vocals; Jarobi, vocals (1988–91); Ali Shaheed Muhammad, DJ.

Celebrated for its easy funkiness and positive vibe, A Tribe Called Quest has set trends for nearly a decade. Along with DJ Premier, Ali Shaheed Muhammad is most responsible for moving hip-hop production away from Afrika Bambaataa's breakbeat canon and towards 1960s and 1970s jazz fusion. Q-Tip's ability to naturalize rhythm rhyming as part of the total musical flow makes him one of the best rappers ever to grace a mic. And Phife's earthy humor grounds the group and prevents Tribe from becoming highbrow.

what to buy: The group's first three records are all highly recommended. *People's Instinctive Travels and the Paths of Rhythm* 🎵🎵🎵🎵 (Jive, 1990, prod. A Tribe Called Quest) is set up as a personal journey into a realized Afrocentric aesthetic, moving from birth through discovery and loss—and, finally, to comfort and pride. While the unseen hand of the Jungle Brothers is there, Q-Tip dominates the record. Yet the humor leavens the morality plays. *The Low End Theory* 🎵🎵🎵🎵 (Jive, 1991, prod. A Tribe Called Quest) has been praised for creating the so-called hip-hop-jazz sound, but that minimizes the album's considerable achievement. *The Low End Theory* not only presents the group at the height of its confidence and creative powers, it also attempts to place hip-hop within the black cultural continuum as a whole. On "Excursions," Q-Tip and Ali map the path from be-bop to the Last Poets and then into the 1990s. On the very next track, "Buggin Out," the trio applies its low end theory (we're talking low end in the sense of class, ass, and bass) and Phife emerges as a rhyme animal. On "Jazz," Phife epitomizes the group's—and all of hip-hop's—great leap forward when he declares: "The low end theory's here, so it's time to wreck shop!" An absolute classic. *Midnight Marauders* 🎵🎵🎵🎵 (Jive, 1993, prod. A Tribe Called Quest) has a different, if no less ambitious, goal: it seeks to redefine black pop on singles like "Oh My God," "Award Tour," and "Electric Relaxation." Ali's sound is expansive, subtle, and hook-filled, and Q-Tip and Phife have never been more direct in approach.

what to buy next: After the first three Tribe records, *Beats, Rhymes and Life* ✍✍✍ (Jive, 1996, prod. A Tribe Called Quest) sounds like a big letdown, as if the group has discovered limits it can't overcome. Q-Tip admits as much on "Keep It Moving," saying: "Hip-hop/A way of life/It doesn't tell you how to raise a child or treat a wife." "1nce Again" even sounds like a step backward, reprising *The Low End Theory*'s "Check the Rhime" and "Verses from the Abstract" in a refinement of a formula that's strictly for the radio.

worth searching for: *Revised Quest for the Seasoned Traveller* ✍✍✍ (Jive UK, 1992, prod. various) is an interesting import, featuring mostly uptempo British remixes from the first two albums.

influences:

◀◀ Jungle Brothers, Biz Markie, Public Enemy, De La Soul, K-Rob

▶▶ Main Source, Hieroglyphics, Dream Warriors, Brand Nubian, Da Bush Babees, Us3

Jeff "DJ Zen" Chang

LENNIE TRISTANO

song "Requiem"
album Lennie Tristano/
The New Tristano
(Atlantic, 1956/1962/Rhino, 1994)
instrument Piano

Monster Solo

Lennie Tristano

Born March 19, 1919, in Chicago, IL; died November 18, 1978, in New York, NY.

While his recording career lasted barely 20 years, pianist Lennie Tristano had a profound impact on the sound of jazz, although he remains a controversial figure. Supporters argue that his theories turned improvisation into a science, relying on precision, intelligence, and virtuosity to bring jazz to the level of classical music. Others find him so calculating as to have removed the warmth in the music, overemphasizing technique at the expense of feeling. In any case, Tristano opened up a whole new level of playing, whether it be with his experiments in overdubbing or in his forays into what would later be called "free jazz," insuring his legacy to be, as the cliche goes, a musician ahead of his time.

Born during a measles epidemic, Tristano was afflicted with a condition that left him completely blind by age 11. But he began studying music at an early age, first learning piano from his opera singer mother, then studying woodwinds and music theory at a school for the blind. He eventually graduated with a de-

gree in music from the American Conservatory in Chicago in 1943, all the while establishing himself as a player of note in the local clubs. He also began teaching privately, and by 1945 counted future notables and collaborators Lee Konitz and Billy Bauer among his students. A relocation to New York a year later further upped Tristano's profile, as he performed with Charlie Parker and Dizzy Gillespie and was named *Metronome* magazine's Musician of the Year in 1948. He continued teaching, now including Warne Marsh as a pupil, and together with Marsh, Konitz, and Bauer formed a sextet in 1949. This unit recorded *Crosscurrents*, a short but ground-breaking set of tunes that influenced both the "cool" and "free" jazz camps with its willful austerity; while the record didn't sell well, it certainly caused a lot of talk in the jazz community. By 1951, Tristano had enough students to open his own school, the first jazz school of its kind, and hired Konitz, Marsh, and other former students as instructors. However, as many of these talented staff members would eventually leave to further their own playing careers, Tristano was forced to close the school and return to private teaching in 1956. For the next decade, he focused almost exclusively on teaching, performing the rare club date and recording even less, and by 1968 he had retired from the music scene. But interest in Tristano has remained constant, with a French television documentary airing in 1973 and with the regular stream of private recordings made commercially available since his death in 1978; these appear mostly on the small independent label, Jazz Records, which he founded and is now run by his daughter, drummer Carol Tristano (production input is provided by Lennie's former students Connie Crothers and Lenny Popkin).

Tristano's style owes much to the popular bop techniques of his day, yet his ideas took him much further. He believed in avoiding "emotional coloration" in his playing, resulting in flat, measured notes that focused on melodic explorations. He used time signature changes, block-chording, dissonance, and even multi-tracking to create complex, ultra-cool performances that often require repeat listenings to fully appreciate. Tristano surrounded himself with like-minded musicians such as Konitz and Marsh, whose devotion to the pianist bordered on the cultish. Together they would practice until everyone's timing was perfectly in sync with one another, often using Bach fugues as rehearsal exercises, and the result was a group that played like a well-oiled machine, capable of imaginative flights of improvisation, but in complete awareness of the other players. The rhythm section would often get the short end of Tristano's stick, as he sought only a regular, consistent beat, devoid of inflection, to provide a backdrop for the soloists; flashy drummers need not apply. While his recordings remain obscure to the general listener, his exacting standards as a teacher continue to influence each new generation of jazz players.

what to buy: Over the course of the seven short tracks on *Crosscurrents* ♫♫♫♫ (Capitol, 1949, prod. Pete Rugolo) Tristano and acolytes Lee Konitz on alto sax, Warne Marsh on tenor sax, Billy Bauer on guitar, and a competent but faceless rhythm section (just the way Tristano liked it) offer up their thorny variations on bop, with tracks such as "Wow" and "Crosscurrent" serving as textbook examples of Tristano's methods. However, the real eye-openers are "Intuition" and "Digression," which present a couple of minutes of proto-free playing that is unhampered by an imposed structure, yet tied together by the musicians' complete understanding of their instruments and of each other. Although not available on its own, this set of recordings appears on a number of collections, most notably *Intuition* ♫♫♫♫ (Capitol, 1996), jointly credited to Lennie Tristano and Warne Marsh because it includes a 1956 Marsh album (originally on Imperial) variously titled *Jazz of Two Cities* and *Winds of Marsh*.

what to buy next: *Lennie Tristano/The New Tristano* ♫♫♫♫ (Atlantic, 1956/1962/Rhino, 1994, prod. Lennie Tristano) contains two later-period Atlantic albums reissued on one CD. Unaccompanied piano solos, some multi-tracked experiments, and a live set with his 1955 quartet reveal a truly original thinker at work.

the rest:
The Complete Lennie Tristano on Keynote ♫♫♫♫ (Mercury, 1946–47/1987)
Descent into the Maelstrom ♫♫♫ (Inner City, 1952–66)
The Lennie Tristano Quartet ♫♫♫♫ (Atlantic, 1955/1981)
New York Improvisations ♫♫♫ (Elektra Musician, 1983)
Continuity ♫♫♫ (Jazz Records, 1985)
Complete Atlantic Recordings of Lennie Tristano, Lee Konitz & Warne Marsh ♫♫♫♫ (Mosaic, 1997)

worth searching for: The posthumous releases of Tristano material on Jazz Records contain valuable documentation of his groups beyond what came out on commercial recordings, though at the cost of inferior sonics. *Wow* ♫♫♫ (Jazz Records, 1991, prod. Lenny Popkin) was recorded live by Billy Bauer around 1950 and captures a sextet with Tristano, Bauer, Konitz, Marsh, and unidentified bass and drums. The wire recording offers distant, one-dimensional sound with speed fluctuations, but we get to hear Bauer, Konitz, and Marsh play Bach's Fugue in D Minor, BWV 899, as well as Tristano, Bauer, and Konitz originals. *Live in Toronto 1952* ♫♫♫ (Jazz Records, 1982/1989, prod. Russell Rockman, Connie Crothers) has much clearer (if hardly perfect) sound for a quintet performance with Tristano, Konitz, Marsh, drummer Al Levitt, and bassist Peter Ind. Such Tristano classics as "Lennie's Pennies" and "317 East 32nd" get lengthier workouts than on commercial recordings, with the saxophonists spinning out gorgeous, flowing lines that float serenely above the rhythm section. Jazz Records can be contacted at P.O. Box 30273, NY, NY 10011-0103.

influences:

◀◀ Roy Eldridge, Art Tatum, Bud Powell

▶▶ Lee Konitz, Warne Marsh, Bill Evans, Connie Crothers, Charles Mingus, Phil Woods, Carol Tristano, Lennie Popkin, Richard Tabnik, Mark Diorio, Mark Turner

Eric J. Lawrence

Frankie Trumbauer

Born May 30, 1901, in Carbondale, IL. Died June 11, 1956, in Kansas City, MO.

Frank Trumbauer was a very gifted musician who was proficient on a wide variety of instruments, even at an early age. He settled on the C-Melody sax as his instrument of choice when he turned professional in 1918. After a stint in the service, he played with a number of Chicago bands until landing a job with Jean Goldkette's organization. Trumbauer headed one of Goldkette's many units, leading a band at the Arcadia Ballroom in St. Louis. It was here that Bix Beiderbecke joined the band. Eventually, Bix and Trumbauer (nicknamed "Tram") joined Goldkette's main unit and started recording together. During this period, Tram organized a pickup group from the Goldkette outfit and recorded for OKeh. Some of these recordings (all featuring Bix) have become some of the high watermarks of jazz ("Riverboat Shuffle," "Singin' the Blues," "I'm Comin' Virginia," and others).

With the disbanding of the Goldkette band, Beiderbecke, Trumbauer, and a few other alumni joined Paul Whiteman's Orchestra. Whiteman featured Beiderbecke and Trumbauer in public and on record, as the two musicians' rapport would get played out in their famous chase choruses. This culminated on the tune "Borneo" for OKeh, where the clever interplay between the two becomes virtually intuitive. Beiderbecke and Trumbauer try to play what each thinks the other's next chorus will be. At the end, Trumbauer takes his last four-bar break, which is a perfect foil for Beiderbecke. In Beiderbecke's response, one can almost hear his smile come through his tone as he takes the ride out. This was a wonderful time for both musicians. Trumbauer stayed with Whiteman until 1932. He fronted his own band for about a year, then rejoined Whiteman about the same time as Jack Teagarden did in 1933. He and Teagarden, along with Teagarden's brother Charlie, formed a small novelty group ("The Three 'T's'") within the band. As in earlier days, Trumbauer fronted a small studio group while with Whiteman. He recorded for Brunswick with Jack Teagarden as one of the featured soloists with the group. When Trumbauer left Whiteman in 1937, he ended up on the West Coast. He then formed his own big band, but started getting more involved with aviation (a personal passion). During World War II, he was a test pilot. After the War, he briefly returned to music, but left it for good in 1947.

what's available: Although there are a number of CD reissues of Frankie Trumbauer recordings, most will be listed under Bix Beiderbecke's name (please refer to the Bix Beiderbecke entry). However, a recent set of CDs on the Old Masters (TOM) label have been released that highlight Tram's career sans Beiderbecke. The first CD, *Tram! Volume 1* ♫♫♫♫ (The Old Masters 107, 1997, prod. various), features Trumbauer on his earliest recordings, which include the Benson Orchestra, Paul Whiteman, the Mound City Blue Blowers, the legendary Bee Palmer

tests, and his earliest OKeh's without Beiderbecke. *Tram! Volume 2* ♫♫♫♫ (The Old Masters 108, 1997), continues with the non-Beiderbecke OKehs, and includes some real gems. Although some collectors equate post-Bix to mean no musical interest with regard to Tram's career, these sessions produce some sparkling recordings. Titles such as "I Like That" (better known as "Loved One") and "Love Ain't Nothin' but the Blues" suffer little as a result of no Bix. "Happy Feet" and "Deep Harlem" are other examples of both fine arranging and some nice solo work by Trumbauer and others. The final CD, *Tram! Volume 3* ♫♫♫♫ (The Old Masters 109, 1997), is Trumbauer's band on Brunswick. These include all of the titles with Jack Teagarden in this pullout unit from the Paul Whiteman Orchestra. These are all very satisfying recordings.

see also: *Bix Beiderbecke*

Jim Prohaska

Assif Tsahar

Born June 11, 1969, in Tel Aviv, Israel.

Just starting to make a name for himself, this Brooklyn resident owes an obvious debt to Coltrane (who doesn't?) but has incorporated other influences, including Charles Gayle's energy and a few melodic figurations, Sonny Rollins's intuitive improvisational structures, and Archie Shepp's varied textural palette. He also has a lyrical streak that makes him a formidable and affecting ballad player, a less-than-common trait among free jazz saxophonists. Tsahar moved to New York in 1990 and got a diploma from Mannes, where he studied classical theory, and a Bachelor's degree in music from the New School. Before recording as a leader, Tsahar had been heard with William Parker's Little Huey Creative Music Orchestra on the albums *Flowers Grow in My Room* and *Sunrise in the Tone World*.

It's worth noting that Tsahar's wife and frequent collaborator on drums, Susie Ibarra, is also a rising star who has played with Parker as well as in the David S. Ware Quartet and briefly with John Zorn's Masada. She has studied with Milford Graves and other free jazz drummers and combines that with her percussion group (Gamalan, Kulintang) work for a highly individual sound.

what to buy: A trio album with Parker and Ibarra, *Shekhina* ♫♫♫♫ (Eremite, 1997, prod. Michael Ehlers) is Tsahar's first release as a leader, and he springs forth with a potent, fully formed style that marks him as an important new voice on his instrument. It's always a revelation to find avant-gardists worth

Tuck & Patti (© Jack Vartoogian)

hearing even in their quiet moments, when excitement and momentum can't carry them, as on the tender "Hidden Heart," where Parker contributes a moving arco section at the end that Tsahar interacts well with while Ibarra's sensitive cymbal work adorns the melodies. Ibarra's imaginative use of non-trapset percussion spices the textures nicely, and she and Parker continually nudge the music forward. If you can't find the CD, contact the label directly at eremite@javanet.com.

what to buy next: *Ein Sof* 𝄢𝄢𝄢𝄢 (Silkheart, 1998, prod. Assif Tsahar) continues in the same vein as its predecessor, using the same trio, and is just as excellent. The group distinguishes itself equally in quiet moments and full throttle moments, and just as important, there's a genuine dynamic continuum in between the extremes as the pieces ebb and flow organically, building climaxes in an unforced way. The leader is extremely impressive, always with something to say, never seeming to merely mark time until the next idea comes along, and the group interplay is at a high level of responsiveness.

influences:
◀◀ John Coltrane, Charles Gayle, Sonny Rollins

Steve Holtje

Tuck & Patti

Tuck Andress, guitar (born October 25, 1952, in Tulsa, OK); Patti Cathcart, vocals (born October 4, 1950, in San Francisco, CA).

Husband-wife duo Tuck Andress and Patti Cathcart have been making beautiful music together for more than a decade, blending the thick, soulful licks of his Gibson L-5 electric guitar with her husky, gospel-trained singing to create an unapologetically hopeful celebration of both divine and romantic love. In the early 1980s, they became a fixture at the Fairmont Hotel's Venetian Room in San Francisco, where they mixed Ella Fitzgerald and Joe Pass tunes with covers of Steely Dan's "Peg" and the theme from *Grease*. Signed to new age kingpin Windham Hill's jazz subsidiary in 1987, they quickly established an intimate, spellbinding sound by recording live with-out overdubs in their Menlo Park, California, home studio. Their repertoire still leans heavily on originals, standards, and contemporary covers ranging from Jimi Hendrix to Cyndi Lau-per. But since graduating to Epic Records in 1995, Tuck & Patti have started experimenting with percussion, processing tech-niques, and the occasional saxophone. Yet, the heart of their sound remains the nuances—the audible breaths, the squeaks of fingers on guitar strings, the purposeful silences—that speak volumes.

what to buy: *Dream* ♪♪♪♪ (Windham Hill Jazz, 1991, prod. Patti Cathcart) is Tuck & Patti's musical manifesto, a passionate plea for racial unity, world peace, and true love. "We can change this world, but first you're gonna have to dream," Cathcart sings. The cover choices are typically eclectic—"One Hand, One Heart" from *West Side Story,* Jimmy Cliff's "Sitting in Limbo," Horace Silver's "Togetherness," Stevie Wonder's "I Wish"—but their vision has crystallized.

what to buy next: *Love Warriors* ♪♪♪ (Windham Hill Jazz, 1989, prod. Patti Cathcart) is equally hopeful but a little more playful than *Dream,* thanks to a swinging romp through the Beatles' "Honey Pie," Hendrix's "Castles Made of Sand/Little Wing," and their own "Hold Out, Hold Up and Hold On."

what to avoid: The contract-fulfilling *The Best of Tuck & Patti* ♪♪♪ (Windham Hill Jazz, 1994) draws highlights from their three Windham Hill albums, but loses the thematic thread that neatly ties their messages together.

the rest:
Tears of Joy ♪♪♪ (Windham Hill Jazz, 1988)
Learning How to Fly ♪♪♪♪ (Epic, 1995)

worth searching for: The lovely holiday ballad "Christmas Wish" can be found on the compilation *Winter, Fire & Snow: Songs for the Holiday Season* ♪♪♪ (Atlantic, 1995, prod. vari-ous).

solo outings:
Tuck Andress:
Reckless Precision ♪♪♪♪ (Windham Hill Jazz, 1990)
Hymns, Carols and Songs about Snow ♪♪♪ (Windham Hill Jazz, 1991)

influences:
◀◀ Wes Montgomery, Sarah Vaughan, Ella Fitzgerald
▶▶ Dianne Reeves

David Okamoto

Mickey Tucker

Born April 28, 1941, in Durham, SC.

One of many to suffer from a lack of name recognition and criti-cal acclaim, pianist Mickey Tucker is a supremely talented mainstream player who also happens to be an accomplished composer and organ player. Tucker's highly-developed har-monic sense and crystal-clear tone put him on par with just about any other pianist of his generation. Since taking up the piano while in his teens, he has worked as a school teacher, an arranger for the R&B group Little Anthony and the Imperials, and appeared with a lengthy list of jazz artists, including Roland Kirk, Willis Jackson, Art Blakey, Eric Kloss, and Sonny Fortune. During the 1970s, Tucker toured Africa and Europe with Art Blakey's Jazz Messengers and recorded several times for the Xanadu and Muse labels (sadly, all of these are cur-rently unavailable). The next decade found him working with the newly-revived Farmer/Golson Jazztet before taking up resi-dence in Australia. Not as often recorded as he should be, Tucker has lately been leading sessions for SteepleChase Records that rank among the finest work of his career.

what to buy: *Blues in Five Dimensions* ♪♪♪♪ (SteepleChase, 1989, prod. Nils Winther) features some down and dirty perfor-mances from Tucker and a stellar quartet that includes guitarist Ted Dunbar. This one really does explore the blues in all its di-mensions! *Hang in There* ♪♪♪♪ (SteepleChase, 1991, prod. Nils Winther) finds Tucker leading a sextet of talented youngsters, including Javon Jackson, Greg Gisbert, Donald Harrison, and Marvin "Smitty" Smith. There is much incendiary playing from all involved, but especially from Tucker, who seems to be spurred on at every moment by Smith's propulsive drumming.

the rest:
Sweet Lotus Lips ♪♪♪♪ (Denon, 1993)

influences:
◀◀ Hampton Hawes, Art Tatum, Phineas Newborn Jr.

Chris Hovan

Big Joe Turner

Born May 18, 1911, in Kansas City, MO. Died November 24, 1985, in In-glewood, CA.

Big Joe Turner was a bartender in prohibition-era Kansas City when he first began shouting the blues. His work with pianist Pete Johnson in the 1930s and 1940s helped popularize boogie woogie and laid the groundwork for the R&B revolution of the 1950s. Turner's first records, "Roll 'Em Pete," and "Cherry Red," were made for Vocalion in 1939. Through the 1940s he recorded swing, jazz, and some pretty raw blues, shouting about the joys of sex, sin, and boogie with some of the hottest players of that period (Johnson, Meade Lux Lewis, and Freddie Slack, to name a few). In 1951, he signed with Atlantic and was suddenly at the forefront of a hot new trend called R&B. Atlantic's musicians played a little sweeter, and their engineering was a helluva lot better, but Turner's approach hadn't changed a bit. At his commercial peak, Turner appeared in two motion pictures, *Rhythm and Blues Revue* (1955) and *Shake Rattle and Rock* (1956). When rock 'n' roll became the province of white teenagers, Turner's days as a hitmaker came to an end, though he made many superb recordings for Atlantic until 1959. Turner churned out records for Savoy, RCA/Bluebird, Bluesway, and Blues Time, among others, but didn't find another long-term deal until he signed with Norman Granz's Pablo Records in the 1970s. Though he recorded many well-regarded jazz LPs with Dizzy Gillespie, Milt Jackson, Roy Eldridge, and Eddie "Cleanhead" Vinson, Joe Turner never really stopped rocking. Even when old age, obesity, and diabetes forced him to sit while singing, he would pound out the beat with his cane and sing with impressive power until the day he died.

what to buy: Turner's vocals are hot and juicy on *Have No Fear, Big Joe Turner Is Here* 𝄞𝄞𝄞𝄞 (Savoy Jazz, 1984/1995, compilation prod. Bob Porter; original producer Herb Abramson), a superb 26 track collection of tunes cut for the National label (c. 1945–47) with Pete Johnson, Albert Ammons, Wild Bill Moore, and Red Saunders. The killer "My Gal's a Jockey," "Sally Zu-Zazz," and "I'm Still in the Dark" are included. Also, check out *Tell Me Pretty Baby* 𝄞𝄞𝄞𝄞 (Arhoolie, 1992, prod. Jack Lauderdale), which features more of Turner's great sides with Pete Johnson and his orchestra (c. 1947–49) and includes the ribald "Around the Clock Blues (parts 1 & 2)" and nearly two dozen slabs of wild, swinging boogie. If you want to indulge yourself further, get *Big, Bad and Blue: The Big Joe Turner Anthology* 𝄞𝄞𝄞𝄞 (Rhino, 1994, prod. James Austin), a 61-song, three-disc set comprising Turner's best sides for several labels from the 1930s through the 1950s. An instant history lesson and lots of cool boogie as well.

what to buy next: Those who dig the big beat of early rock 'n' roll are well-advised to consider purchasing *Rhythm & Blues Years* 𝄞𝄞𝄞𝄞 (Rhino, 1986, reissue prod. Bob Porter) or *Greatest Hits* 𝄞𝄞𝄞𝄞𝄞 (Rhino, 1987, reissue prod. Bob Porter), which feature the best from his Atlantic Records era. *The Boss of the Blues* 𝄞𝄞𝄞𝄞 (Rhino, 1981, prod. Nesuhi Ertegun) is a 10-track reproduction of Turner's 1956 Atlantic LP that still cooks today.

Despite an ugly cover, *Shake, Rattle, & Roll* 𝄞𝄞𝄞𝄞 (Tomato, 1994, prod. various) is a really good budget compilation with many strong Atlantic sides and great notes by Pete Welding. To hear Turner on stage in his rockin' prime, there is *Big Joe Rides Again* 𝄞𝄞𝄞𝄞 (Rhino, 1987, prod. Nesuhi Ertegun), containing 10 songs from his 1959 Carnegie Hall appearance. *Blues Train* 𝄞𝄞𝄞𝄞 (Muse, 1995, prod. Doc Pomus, Bob Porter) is a reissue of Turner's 1983 LP with Roomful of Blues, and *Jumpin' with Joe: The Complete Aladdin & Imperial Recordings* 𝄞𝄞𝄞 (ERG, 1996) has a couple of hot duets with Turner rival Wynonie Harris.

what to avoid: Turner rerecorded his big hits several times, some of which pop up on *The Best of Joe Turner* 𝄞𝄞𝄞 (Pablo, 1987, prod. Norman Granz), which is mostly material from the 1970s, not his all-time classics. And beware *Stormy Monday* 𝄞𝄞 (Pablo, 1991, prod. Norman Granz), a reissue of one of Turner's lesser LPs from 1976.

the rest:
The Midnight Special 𝄞𝄞𝄞 (Pablo, 1987)
Bosses of the Blues 𝄞𝄞𝄞 (RCA Bluebird, 1989)
Flip, Flop, and Fly 𝄞𝄞𝄞 (Pablo, 1989)
I've Been to Kansas City, Vol. 1 𝄞𝄞𝄞𝄞 (MCA Special Products, 1990)
Singing the Blues 𝄞𝄞𝄞 (Mobile Fidelity, 1990)
The Trumpet Kings Meet Joe Turner 𝄞𝄞𝄞𝄞 (OJC, 1990)
Everyday I Have the Blues 𝄞𝄞𝄞 (OJC, 1991)
Kansas City Here I Come 𝄞𝄞𝄞𝄞 (OJC, 1992)
Let's Boogie: The Freedom Story 1959–64 𝄞𝄞𝄞 (Collectables, 1992)
Texas Style 𝄞𝄞𝄞 (Evidence, 1992)
Every Day in the Week 𝄞𝄞𝄞 (Decca Jazz, 1993)
Life Ain't Easy 𝄞𝄞𝄞 (OJC, 1994)
In the Evening 𝄞𝄞𝄞 (OJC, 1995)
Things That I Used to Do 𝄞𝄞𝄞 (OJC, 1995)
Honey Hush 𝄞𝄞𝄞 (Jewel, 1996)
Patcha, Patcha All Night Long 𝄞𝄞𝄞 (OJC, 1996)
Shouting the Blues 𝄞𝄞𝄞 (Eclipse, 1996)
Joe Turner's Blues 𝄞𝄞𝄞 (Topaz Jazz, 1998)

worth searching for: For those who dig the great boogie and jazz pianists: Big Joe is backed by Pete Johnson, Freddie Slack, Willie "The Lion" Smith, and Art Tatum on *The Complete 1940–44* 𝄞𝄞𝄞𝄞 (Official, 1991), which features 25 tracks from his Decca days. *Early Big Joe 1940–44* 𝄞𝄞𝄞𝄞 (MCA Special Products, 1980) is easier to track down, but has only 14 cuts.

influences:
◀◀ Pete Johnson, Jimmy Rushing

▶▶ Wynonie Harris, Roy Brown, Bill Haley, B.B. King

Ken Burke

Norris Turney

Born September 8, 1921, in Wilmington, OH.

A multi-reed player who specializes on alto sax, Norris Turney showed interest in music at a young age and he and his siblings were encouraged by his parents. He was also influenced by his grandmother's singing of church music, by his cousin's blues recordings, and by combos that played at his aunt's weekend rent parties. Turney started piano lessons early on, and after difficulties coordinating his left hand and right hand playing, asked his parents for a saxophone. His father surprised him with an old C-Melody saxophone when he was about 13 years old and he began taking lessons. A year later, his father presented him with an alto saxophone, and Turney soon organized a high school band that played locally and for school dances. Turney's first professional job at age 18 was at a Cincinnati strip joint, The Cat and Fiddle. Turney remained in Cincinnati for about three years until a territory band led by Bill Tye came down from Columbus, and Turney joined Tye for a year, after which he worked in Toledo, Youngstown, Akron, and other cities until 1950, sometimes leading his own band. Turney returned to Cincinnati where he worked with A.B. Townsend's band at the Cotton Club for nearly two years. He left with saxophonist Weasel Parker for St. Louis where he joined the Jeter-Pillars Orchestra for two years. Next, Turney joined Tiny Bradshaw's touring jump-band in Chicago, remaining with the band for a year before going to New York and joining Billy Eckstine's band in 1944. After a year and a half with Eckstine, Turney returned to Cincinnati and played with various Ohio bands, occasionally working with Youngstown native, pianist Ace Carter, before moving on to Massachusetts and eventually New York in 1950. Toughing it out for a year, Turney left New York City to join Elmer Snowden's band in Philadelphia from 1951 to 1952. For the next few years, Turney freelanced, and performed with the bands of Charlie Gaines and Bullmoose Jackson. In 1957, he returned to Ohio, met his wife Marilee, and they settled permanently in New York in 1960 after which Turney continued to work with many bands, most notably with Ray Charles in 1957. In 1969, then age 48, Turney joined Duke Ellington, playing occasional trombone parts, then replacing the ailing saxophonist Johnny Hodges. After his four-year stint with Ellington, Turney played Broadway shows for a decade before rejoining the jazz scene as a freelancer. By the mid-1980s, Turney was in demand again, touring internationally and teaching. Until some 1990s albums, Turney never really did much recording, except for earlier dates with Snooky Young and Roy Eldridge. Turney joined the Lincoln Center Jazz Orchestra in 1988. In 1994, he received the prestigious Arts Midwest Jazz Master Award, recorded a highly acclaimed album in 1995 for Mapleshade, and, in 1997, began touring northern Europe with Claude "Fiddler" Williams and Red Richards (the latter died on March 12, 1998). After 30 years in New York City, Turney resettled in Kettering, Ohio, where he now resides.

what's available: Turney finally gets his due with his only album as leader, *Big Sweet 'n' Blue* ♪♪♪♪ (Mapleshade, 1996, prod. Larry Willis, Pierre Sprey, Dave Barber), recorded on April 5–6, 1993, with an intergenerational band that is basically Nat Adderley's rhythm section: pianist Larry Willis (b. 1942), bassist Walter Booker (b. 1933), and drummer Jimmy Cobb (b.1929). Each of these veteran musicians has backed notable jazz luminaries on numerous sessions and they provide exquisite, understated accompaniment as Turney displays bluesy verve on his originals "Blues for Edward," "Blues in B," and the dreamy "Checkered Hat." He delivers heartfelt, torchy versions of the ballads "Here's That Rainy Day" and "Street of Dreams," and is reverential with ardent Ellingtonian expressions, creating a lilting version of "In a Mellow Tone," a seductive rendering of Strayhorn's "Blood Count," and a graceful reading of "Come Sunday." Turney couldn't have found more empathetic team mates. This is a wonderful album that finds Turney, 72 years old at the time of this recording, in rarest, relaxed form. Although the fare is mostly a collection of luxuriant ballads, Turney coaxes so much heat from his horn it's awe-inspiring. After hearing this album, you'll understand why Ellington wrote songs to feature this alto saxophonist.

influences:
◀◀ Benny Carter, Willie Smith, Johnny Hodges

Nancy Ann Lee

Steve Turre

Born September 12, 1948, in Omaha, NB.

Steve Turre has developed into a fine trombonist and is also known for his artistry playing an array of various sized seashells from around the world. Turre is also an excellent composer-arranger who leads his own groups, including his shell choir. In addition, since 1984 he's been a regular member of the band on the weekly television show *Saturday Night Live*. Turre grew up amidst a musical family in the San Francisco Bay area of California, listening to recorded music of his Mexican-American heritage as well as blues and jazz. After a brief attempt at playing violin, Turre settled on playing trombone at age 10. He began his professional career playing for dances and parties while still in junior high school. After high school graduation,

Turre went on to study music at Sacramento State University, and played on weekends with the Frisco-based salsa band led by brothers Pete and Coke Escovado, an experience that would launch his career-long involvement with this musical style.

Turre recorded with the Latin-rock group Santana in 1970, and from 1968 played sporadically with Roland Kirk. In 1972, Turre was hired to tour with the Ray Charles band. The following year, he joined Art Blakey's Jazz Messengers and toured Europe with the Thad Jones–Mel Lewis Orchestra. During the 1970s, he worked with an array of jazz musicians, including Chico Hamilton, Woody Shaw, and Rahsaan Roland Kirk. Turre was a member of and wrote arrangements for trombonist Slide Hampton's World of Trombones, and also worked as composer-arranger for Max Roach, as well as leading his own quartet and performing (or touring) with bands led by Cedar Walton, Hugh Masekela, Eddie Palmieri, Pharoah Sanders, Archie Shepp, and others. He's also performed with Manny Oquendo's Libre where he recognized the spiritual connection between the shells and hand drums, and by 1970, he eventually embraced that concept with the development of his shell choir. By 1979, in another stint with Kirk's band, Turre's virtuosic chops on seashells were featured up front. During a tour of Mexico with Woody Shaw, Turre experienced an epiphany when he learned from relatives that his ancestors had played seashells. He began to develop his shell choir concept in earnest, melding his shell choir sound with Afro-Cuban rhythms, bebop, and swing. He presented his first shell choir concert at Verna Gillis's Soundscape loft in New York City. During the 1980s, Turre worked with McCoy Tyner, Poncho Sanchez, Hillton Ruiz, and Tito Puente, and beginning in 1987, showcased his talents before wide-ranging audiences as a member of Dizzy Gillespie's United Nation Orchestra. Turre teaches privately and performs clinics, master classes, and workshops at colleges and universities. In addition to performing with his shell choir, a group that features four trombonists who double on shells, he has also performed and recorded regularly with Lester Bowie's Brass Fantasy, and occasionally joins the Leaders and the Timeless All-Stars. Turre has made several recordings as leader for Stash, Antilles, and Verve.

what to buy: From the first notes of the leader's shell-playing on *Steve Turre* ♫♫♫♫♫ (Verve, 1997, prod. Billy Banks), you know you're going to hear an exceptional jazz album. Turre leads off with an excellent bossa nova arrangement of Ellington's "In a Sentimental Mood," which contains vocals by the husky-voiced Cassandra Wilson, Turre's sublime trombone solo, and strings accompaniment from Akua Dixon's (Turre's

wife) Quartette Indigo. All that in the first tune is a huge clue to the musical feast offered within the remaining five tunes, featuring guesting soloists Jon Faddis (trumpet), Randy Brecker (trumpet/flugelhorn), J.J. Johnson (trombone), and others. Track two features Turre playing a shell solo with a 13-piece brass ensemble on his appealing "The Emperor," highlighting unique instrumental sounds and catchy Afro-Cuban rhythms. Of the six tunes on the album, all but two are imaginative Turre originals. Appearing with Turre on most tunes is his trombone/shells crew featuring Robin Eubanks, Jimmy Bosch, and Douglas Purviance. The rest of the all-star musicians participating (looks like a who's who of adventurous jazzmakers in New York City) varies from track to track, with heavy emphasis on rhythm, thanks to Milton Cardona, Porthino, Manny Oquendo, Victor Lewis, and other rhythm masters, and the presence of the melodic bassist Andy Gonzalez (of Fort Apache Band fame). Enjoyable from first note to last, this album is a spiritual journey as well for the listener and provides the best overview of Turre's awesome talents as performer, leader, and composer-arranger. By the time *Sanctified Shells* ♫♫♫♫♫ (Antilles, 1993, prod. Billy Banks) hit the market, many jazz fans were aware of Turre's shell playing from his appearances with groups led by others, particularly Dizzy Gillespie's United Nation Orchestra. But, since Turre had not documented his concept on recordings, few people were aware of his playing with this core group of trombonists—Robin Eubanks, Reynaldo Jorge, Clifton Anderson—who double on shells. Yielding to his ancestral muse, Turre presents 10 tantalizing original tunes featuring either himself or his shell choir, three of them cowritten with Kimati Dinizulu. Andy Gonzalez adds his lyrical bass to most selections, and numerous top-name drummers/percussionists add flair to this serendipitous session. One of the catchiest numbers is Turre's "Gumbo," which features the shell choir with bassist Gonzalez, drummer Herlin Riley, and Milton Cardona on hand drums. Add brass, a bit of Afro-Cuban rhythm, and you have "Macho (Para Machito)," which proves Turre absorbed the lessons from his stint with salsa bands. While his eponymous album reviewed above shows a better developed approach to his broad musical spectrum, *Sanctified Shells* hints at what was to come and is a must-own album once you become beguiled by Turre's creativity.

what to buy next: Of equal interest, *Rhythm Within* ♫♫♫♫♫ (Antilles, 1995, prod. Billy Banks) was released between the aforementioned albums, and again features the core shell choir (this time with Robin Eubanks, Jamal Haynes, and Frank Lacy). Turre contributes all the arrangements and five compositions among the nine tunes. Guest soloists include pianist Herbie Hancock, trumpeter Jon Faddis, and tenor saxophonist Pharoah Sanders, who each appear on selected tracks. One of the best tunes is the subdued, soulful reading of Buddy Johnson's seductive pop hit, "Since I Fell for You," featuring a plunger bone solo from Turre, an open bone solo from 75-year-old Brent Woodman, shell solos from Turre, and backing from the shell choir, bassist Andy Gonzalez, drummer Victor Lewis, and shakeres players Milton Cardona and Jimmy Delgado. The fare also includes the Miles Davis classic "All Blues," and muted bone solos from Turre and Jamal Haynes on the straight-ahead chestnut "Body and Soul." Ranging from free to funky, from bop-oriented to soulfully bluesy, to African-tinged themes and groove-beats, all of Turre's musical influences are brought to the fore, including tinges of the AACM (Association for the Advancement of Creative Musicians) derived from his collaborations with Lester Bowie's Brass Fantasy. Not as fiery as *Steve Turre* but a tad more jazzy than *Rhythm Within*, this album is enjoyable for the selected material, for Turre's playing and arrangements, and for the guest appearances. Extensive liner notes from Turre explain his rationale in creating each uncommon tune. Once you're into Turre's music, you'll want to own this one, too. *Right There* 🎵🎵🎵🎵 (Antilles, 1991, prod. John Snyder) is probably the most straight-ahead session Turre has recorded to date. Most of the eight standards and originals are performed by Turre (trombone, shells) with a rhythm section that includes pianist Benny Green, bassist Buster Williams, and drummer Billy Higgins, enhanced with John Blake on violin and Akua Dixon Turre on cello. That's the predominant setting. Add to that group two guest soloists, trumpeter Wynton Marsalis and saxophonist Benny Golson, who contribute to Turre's originals "Woody & Bu" and "Unfinished Rooms." On the piece "Descarga de Turre," Turre mixes it up with a totally Latin-influenced crew, including flutist Dave Valentin, bassist Andy Gonzalez, pianist Willie Rodriguez, and percussionists. Everyone shines. Yet, although this is an enjoyable session, it's not as unique-sounding as Turre's subsequent sessions. However, the album does point up Turre's ability to compose in any musical milieu and to intelligently interpret Ellingtonia, as evidenced on his elegant muted trombone solo on "Echoes of Harlem."

influences:

◀◀ Curtis Fuller, Julian Brewster, J.J. Johnson, Woody Shaw, Rahsaan Roland Kirk, Slide Hampton, Art Blakey, McCoy Tyner, Dizzy Gillespie, Manny Oquendo

▶▶ Robin Eubanks, Craig Harris, Jimmy Bosch, Jamal Haynes

Nancy Ann Lee

Stanley Turrentine

Born April 5, 1934, in Pittsburgh, PA.

Possessed of one of the biggest, baddest tenor sax sounds on the planet, Turrentine is a soul-jazz monster. His sense of swing is powerful and unique. His manner of phrasing is alternately lissome and blunt; his expression, tough and tender. There's a paradoxical vulnerability to Turrentine's rough-hewn style, which lies at the core of his appeal. Though he made his name in funky organ trios led by Jimmy Smith and Shirley Scott (who was Turrentine's wife for a time), his swing-oriented tenor is at home in virtually any straight-ahead context.

In the early 1950s, Turrentine toured with the R&B bands of Earl Bostic, Ray Charles, and Lowell Fulson. In 1959–60 Turrentine gigged and made his first recordings with Max Roach's band. His first dates as leader came with Blue Note in 1959. At the same time he played and recorded with Smith. Turrentine recorded a series of popular, funk-based albums for Blue Note in the 1960s. In the 1970s, his albums became increasingly commercial and overproduced, though Turrentine's playing remained at a very high level. Turrentine has, throughout the last several years, returned to his soul and straight-ahead jazz roots—to his great benefit as an artist.

what to buy: *Sugar* 🎵🎵🎵🎵 (CTI/CBS Associated, 1970, prod. Creed Taylor) is not just one of the best things ever put out by the label, it's excellent by any standard. Consistently funky and swinging, with a pre-fusion George Benson on guitar and Freddie Hubbard on trumpet, this record places Turrentine in the best possible context: at the helm of small combo, playing straight-ahead with great feeling and minimum fuss. The title track became a jazz standard.

what to buy next: *The Best of Stanley Turrentine: The Blue Note Years* 🎵🎵🎵🎵 (Blue Note, 1960/1984, prod. various) is a compendium of Turrentine's best work for the label, featuring a Who's Who of 1960s jazz-funksters.

what to avoid: *The Best of Mr. T* 🎵🎵 (Fantasy, 1975/1978, prod. various) is a most misleading title. Turrentine's Fantasy years were considerably less than fantastic—fusion in its least interesting, most saccharine form.

best of the rest:

Stan "The Man" 🎵🎵🎵 (Bainbridge, 1959)
Up at Minton's 🎵🎵🎵🎵 (Blue Note, 1961)
(With Shirley Scott) *Let it Go* 🎵🎵🎵🎵 (GRP/Impulse!, 1964/1966)
Don't Mess with Mr. T 🎵🎵🎵🎵 (CTI/CBS Associated, 1973)

Stanley Turrentine (© Jack Vartoogian)

Pieces of Dreams 𝄢𝄢𝄢 (OJC, 1974)
Z.T.'s Blues 𝄢𝄢𝄢 (Blue Note, 1985)
Wonderland 𝄢𝄢𝄢 (Blue Note, 1986)
More Than a Mood 𝄢𝄢𝄢 (Music Masters, 1992)
If I Could 𝄢𝄢𝄢 (Music Masters, 1993)

influences:

◄◄ Coleman Hawkins

Chris Kelsey

Turtle Island String Quartet

Formed 1985, in the Bay Area, San Francisco, CA.

Darol Anger, violin (1985–present); Mark Summer, cello (1985–present); David Balakrishnan, violin (1985–93); Tracy Silverman, violin (1993–present); Irene Sazer, viola (1985–90); Katrina Wreede, viola (1990–93); Danny Seidenberg, viola (1993–present).

Once described by Darol Anger as a bunch of frustrated guitarists who somehow ended up with these "little boxes," the

Turtle Island String Quartet is not the first string quartet to venture outside the classical realm with commercial success, but, with the exception of the Kronos Quartet, it is the most important. Silverman, Summer, and Seidenberg all have solid classical credentials, while Anger, a founding member of the David Grisman Quintet, is considered one of the fathers of the "new acoustic" style. The Quartet has generally been successful taking the string quartet outside of the classical dimension, incorporating jazz, bluegrass, rock, blues, folk, Latin, and other genres in their playing. Their repertoire includes compositions by Jimi Hendrix, Tower of Power, Miles Davis, Pat Metheny, Ralph Towner, Dizzy Gillespie, and Horace Silver, but unlike the Kronos Quartet, whose selections are equally eclectic, they rarely sound like a classical quartet trying to play jazz. Instead, beginning with its second record, *Metropolis*, the Quartet has sounded like a jazz quartet. Summer's tremendous bass foundation allows the rest of the quartet to go in unsafe directions that could rarely be called classical. The Quartet is merely good on record, as opposed to live, where it is absolutely captivating.

what to buy: On *On the Town* ♫♫♫ (Windham Hill, 1991, prod. Darol Anger, David Balakrishnan), the TISQ perform 12 standards, with more traditional arrangements and soloing than usual. The addition of the Billy Taylor Trio on three songs adds a welcome dimension to the string-quartet sound, which may be difficult for jazz fans to digest in large doses. This is by far the most accessible and mainstream date in the TISQ catalog. It also swings.

the rest:
Turtle Island String Quartet ♫♫♫ (Windham Hill, 1988)
Metropolis ♫♫♫ (Windham Hill, 1989)
Who Do We Think We Are? ♫♫♫♫ (Windham Hill, 1994)

worth searching for: *Skylife* ♫♫♫ (Windham Hill, 1990), a deleted title, contains four excellent tracks—Chick Corea's "Señor Mouse," Summer's "Ensenada," Balakrishnan's "Tremors," and Robert Johnson's "Crossroads"—that represent some of TISQ's best playing. Eric Clapton is rumored to have told Summer that TISQ's version of "Crossroads" was better than Cream's.

influences:

◀◀ Kronos Quartet, Stuff Smith, David Grisman, Stephane Grappelli, John Blake, Jerry Goodman

▶▶ Uptown String Quartet, String Trio of New York

Paul MacArthur

29th Street Saxophone Quartet

Formed 1982, in New York, NY.

Jim Hartog, baritone saxophone; Ed Jackson, alto saxophone; Rich Rothenberg, tenor saxophone; Bobby Watson, alto saxophone.

Hartog and Jackson met at the New England Conservatory in 1977, and after both had moved to New York, they decided to form a sax quartet. Rothenberg was drafted in 1982 when he played a big band date with them, and with a tour booked for their incipient quartet, another permanent alto player had to be found. When Hartog bumped into Watson at a Christmas party at a saxophone repair shop, they had their man—and their best known player. The group was named for the street Hartog lived on when the group rehearsed at his apartment.

Like the World Saxophone Quartet before them, initially the 29th Streeters focused on collective improvisation, but they soon moved in a more traditional and arranged direction, and of the many sax quartets around nowadays, they are perhaps the closest to big band writing, and definitely the most

straight-ahead. Two albums for the Italian label New Note were licensed by Antilles for issue in the U.S. the same year the latter released the group's major label debut, though at this point that seems to have turned out to be a one-shot deal. The group's most recent release was recorded in 1993 for another Italian label, Red, which has considerably broader U.S. distribution than New Note.

what to buy: The quartet's most recent album, *Milano New York Bridge* ♫♫♫♫ (Red, 1994, prod. 29th Street Saxophone Quartet, Sergio Veschi), is a tightly arranged album containing Billy Strayhorn's "Chelsea Bridge," Herbie Hancock's "Maiden Voyage," Thelonious Monk's "Bye Ya" and "Reflections," Charles Mingus's "Ibis," Sonny Rollins's "Pent Up House," Duke Ellington's "Take the Coltrane," and the standards "Somewhere," "Love for Sale," and "How About You," plus three originals for variety. The rich voicings and relaxed grooves are practically reason enough in themselves to listen, and all four saxophonists shine in solo spotlights.

what to buy next: *Your Move* ♫♫♫ (Antilles, 1992, prod. Brian Bacchus) is a highly tuneful program, all band originals with the exception of pianist Rodney Kendrick's blues "Jimmy Kay." Between lush riffing that recalls the Ellington sax section, traditional structures, and the many catchy melodies, it's easy to imagine putting words to many tracks and perhaps coming up with a few attractive pop hits in the process. The predominant mood is mellow, but with enough variety of texture to keep individual tracks from blurring together.

the rest:
Watch Your Step ♫♫♫ (New Note, 1985/Antilles, 1992)
The Real Deal ♫♫♫ (New Note, 1987/Antilles, 1992)
Live ♫♫♫♫ (Red, 1988)
Underground ♫♫♫ (Antilles, 1991)

worth searching for: Ed Jackson's *Wake Up Call* ♫♫♫♫ (New World CounterCurrents, 1994), his debut as a leader, uses an octet including Rothenberg and past collaborator Tom Varner (French horn), who contributes two typically episodic tunes. An eclectic player and composer, Jackson frequently shifts gears rhythmically and stylistically, but maintains an internal logic. The opening dissection of Monk's "Played Twice" provides an appealing blueprint of his arranging methods.

influences:

◀◀ World Saxophone Quartet, Duke Ellington, Charles Mingus

Steve Holtje

Charles Tyler

Born July 20, 1941, in Cadiz, KY. Died June 27, 1992, in Toulon, France.

Tyler, another under-recorded 1960s avant-gardist, died at the age of 50 after an on-again, off-again career from which little remains in print. His highly vocal tone shows a strong Ayler influence, and he had a penchant for unusually instrumented groups, which helps his albums stand out from the free jazz pack.

Tyler's mother was half Indian, and he was born on an Indian reservation, although he grew up in Cleveland (at 14 he met the Ayler brothers, who also lived there). He started playing when he was six years old, first on clarinet and then on alto sax, and picked up baritone later on, playing the big horn while in an Army band. He moved to New York City in 1965 and soon was recording with Albert Ayler (on the ESP classics *Bells* and *Spirits Rejoice*). A year later he recorded his first album as a leader and played in the Turn of the Century Orchestra, a free jazz all-stars aggregation. But after recording his sophomore album in 1967, he left New York and studied under David Baker (who played cello on Tyler's second album) at Indiana University. He transferred to the University of California. One source says he also lived in Denver for a while and played with a rock band, then moved to Los Angeles, teaching to support his family.

Tyler returned to New York in late 1973 and participated in the then-thriving loft scene. He also started his own record label, Ak-Ba, which put out two of his albums (good luck trying to find them!). In the 1980s he was a member of violinist Billy Bang's groups and also recorded with vibist Khan Jamal (*Dark Warrior* on SteepleChase) and with Hal Russell's NRG Ensemble. He spent much of the decade living in Europe (Copenhagen and Paris), playing in settings ranging from bebop and African music with French groups, to Sun Ra when the Arkestra was touring in Europe.

what to buy: *Charles Tyler Ensemble* ♫♫♫♫ (ESP, 1966) remains a free jazz classic over 30 years after it marked Tyler's debut as a leader. Though the sound is somewhat dim (drummer Ronald Shannon Jackson sounds especially distant), Tyler is right up front and sounds magnificent, moving from contemplative quiet moments to energetic effulgence. The most unusual touch is having Charles Moffett play chimes (not throughout the album). Fellow Aylerites Henry Grimes (bass) and Joel Friedman (cello) fill out the group.

what to buy next: *Eastern Man Alone* ♫♫♫ (ESP, 1967) is a string-heavy session with Tyler on alto, a cellist (David Baker), and two bassists (Brent McKesson, Kent Brinkley). The initial

reaction may be that Tyler doesn't play enough on his own session, but once that's put aside there is some fine collective soloing by the strings, which, because there are no drums to clutter the sound picture, can be heard better than on most ESP discs. And when Tyler is playing, the contrast between his vocal tone (sometimes he sounds more like a tenor than an alto, actually) and the bowed strings is special.

the rest:
Saga of the Outlaws ♫♫♫ (Nessa, 1978)
Autumn in Paris ♫♫♫ (Silkheart, 1988)

worth searching for: *Live at Green Space* ♫♫♫ (Anima, 1982, prod. John Mingione) is a duo between Billy Bang (violin, mbira) and Tyler. It's a bit diffuse at times, but at its peak this is swinging, penetrating improvisation. Bang's *Rainbow Gladiator* ♫♫♫♫ (Soul Note, 1981, prod. Giovanni Bonandrini) is an exuberant, swinging quintet session with Tyler on both alto and baritone saxes, plus Michele Rosewoman (piano), Wilbur Morris (bass), and Dennis Charles (drums). The material is played with raw excitement and generous humor, and of items in print at the moment, this contains Tyler's best 1980s playing.

influences:

◀◀ Albert Ayler, Ornette Coleman

▶▶ Charles Gayle, Assif Tsahar

Steve Holtje

McCoy Tyner

Born December 11, 1938, in Philadelphia, PA.

Among the most distinctive and influential pianists in jazz, Tyner is also a superb composer and arranger whose deep discography as a leader can stand alongside anyone's. Tyner has sometimes unjustly been noted more for his enormously well-known work with the classic John Coltrane Quartet from 1960 to 1965, where he constructed a dense modal style that stands as a pianistic prototype. But the epitome of Tyner's mature sound is found on his mid-1970s albums for Milestone, where he had a sympathetic producer in Orrin Keepnews, who was never short on ideas and encouraged his artists' own conceptual ambitions. Of special note is that this maturation took place in a period when many jazz artists succumbed to commercial pressures in various ways, whether by switching to electric instruments, incorporating rock into their styles, or simplifying their music. With the exception of taking a few R&B sideman gigs in the late 1960s (with Jimmy Witherspoon and Ike & Tina Turner) and allowing a few questionable guest appearances on his later albums for Columbia, Tyner resisted all such compromises. Furthermore, he has continued to evolve over the years and has maintained a consistency of artistic excellence nearly unmatched by any of his peers.

Tyner, whose mother was a pianist, grew up in the fertile music community of Philadelphia, where Bud and Richie Powell were neighbors. It was in Philly that Tyner first met and worked with John Coltrane. The pianist spent a half a year working with Art Farmer and Benny Golson's Jazztet, then moved to New York and joined Coltrane's group. Perhaps no other pianist of the time could have come up with a style assertive and hefty enough to stand alongside the tremendous forces of Coltrane's tireless sax improvisations and Elvin Jones's polyrhythmic drumming. Tyner was an integral part of such milestone Coltrane albums as *My Favorite Things*, *Coltrane Plays the Blues*, *Olé*, *Africa/Brass*, *Crescent*, *A Love Supreme*, *Ascension*, and *Meditations*. At the same time, he was gradually building a career as a leader, at first on Impulse!, the same label as Coltrane. He left Coltrane's group in 1965, disturbed by the fact that, with the addition of Rashied Ali and Pharoah Sanders, his playing was often drowned out in concert by the two-drum barrage of Jones and Ali.

Soon after leaving Coltrane, Tyner switched his label affiliation to Blue Note, making a number of fine albums which, alas, have been ill-served by its current reissue policy. Fortunately he's much better represented in Milestone's catalog, and it was his Milestone work (from 1972 through 1980) that made it eminently clear that he was a creative force in his own right beyond the reputation he had built working with Coltrane. In 1981 Tyner switched to Columbia, which didn't really know what to do with him; there then followed a long period in which he recorded for a variety of labels in the U.S. and abroad, with his return to the revived Blue Note label producing some especially fine albums. Another revived label, Impulse!, signed him in 1995. A devout Muslim all his adult life, he carries himself with dignity and grace—always reflected in his spiritually charged music—and continues to make music that rises to the high personal standard he has established.

what to buy: A pair of live albums with underrecorded tenor and soprano saxophonist Azar Lawrence are the most brilliant of the many sparkling gems found in Tyner's 1970s Milestone catalog. *Atlantis* ♪♪♪♪♪ (Milestone, 1974, prod. Orrin Keepnews) and *Enlightenment* ♪♪♪♪♪ (Milestone, 1973, prod. Orrin Keepnews) recapture the vastness and overflowing creative spirit of the classic Coltrane Quartet, but with Tyner's own spe-

McCoy Tyner

song "Sahara"
album Sahara
(Milestone, 1972/OJC, 1991)
instrument Piano

cial flavor dominating. The solo piano of "In a Sentimental Mood" on *Atlantis* offers a nostalgic but entirely relevant nod from one master to another, and is also something of a sonic breather after the epic title track (rhythmically stoked by drummer Wilby Fletcher's powerful polyrhythms). The highlights of *Enlightenment* are the contrasting moods of the three-movement title suite and the 25-minute blues workout "Walk Spirit, Talk Spirit." Tyner has always excelled in trio settings, and two of the most exciting came on one album, *Supertrios* ♪♪♪♪♪ (Milestone, 1977, prod. Orrin Keepnews), where he combines with Ron Carter and Tony Williams (who steps his playing up several notches to match Tyner's energy) on six tracks and Eddie Gomez and Jack DeJohnette on the other half of the CD (originally a two-LP set). Tyner's romantic side is much more apparent here than in his larger ensemble settings. The McCoy Tyner Big Band doesn't come together very often, and when it does it's an event to celebrate. *Uptown/Downtown* ♪♪♪♪♪ (Milestone, 1988, prod. McCoy Tyner, Eric Miller) simply overflows with joy, from the hearty embrace of "Love Surrounds Us" to the romping fun of "Blues for Basie." Among the soloists stepping out from the 15-piece band to good effect are Joe Ford, Junior Cook, Ricky Ford, Steve Turre, and (on every track, and rightly so) Tyner himself.

what to buy next: Tyner's early work as a leader is of more than mere historical interest. The most successful of his Impulse! trio albums is *Nights of Ballads and Blues* 𝄞𝄞𝄞 (Impulse!, 1963, prod. Bob Thiele) with Steve Davis (bass) and Lex Humphries (drums). Monk and Ellington covers, standards, and the original "Groove Waltz" show the pianist in a very different light (and consciously so) than his contemporaneous work with Coltrane. The first album Tyner made after breaking with Impulse!, *The Real McCoy* 𝄞𝄞𝄞𝄞 (Blue Note, 1967, prod. Alfred Lion), features a swinging powerhouse quartet with Joe Henderson, Ron Carter, and Elvin Jones. Noteworthy tracks are the exuberant "Passion Dance" and the lovely ballad "Search for Peace." Henderson, who shines throughout with thoughtful, full-bodied solos, is one of the few tenors of the time whose strong individuality could make moot the inevitable Coltrane comparisons. The only flaw lies in the disappointing fade-out ending of "Passion Dance." How good an arranger is Tyner? So good that even that most dreaded of jazz concepts, the "with strings" album, ends up being a tour de force in his hands. On *Fly with the Wind* 𝄞𝄞𝄞𝄞 (Milestone, 1976, prod. Orrin Keepnews) Tyner wisely wrote the charts himself rather than going the usual route of hiring an outside arranger to add generic, simple charts as "sweetener." Tyner deploys the strings not as a single mass of complementary sound but as independent sections, and the memorable title track is a classic. Hubert Laws also adds to the album's success with some nice flute solos. The two-CD trio album *Live at Sweet Basil* 𝄞𝄞𝄞𝄞 (King, 1989/Evidence, 1995, prod. Horst Liepolt) serves the dual purpose of spotlighting Tyner's long association with Avery Sharpe (bass) and Aaron Scott (drums) and of exhibiting the somewhat pared-down playing style the pianist moved towards in the late 1980s, reincorporating bebop in ways he hadn't shown in years. The program is also an excellent mix of Monk and Coltrane favorites, standards, and a couple of Tyner originals. As the years have gone by, Tyner has gradually been captured more often in solo settings, but *Soliloquy* 𝄞𝄞𝄞𝄞 (Blue Note, 1992, prod. Michael Cuscuna) edges out its competitors thanks to superb sound and a program of tunes he's visited less frequently, including interesting takes on "Willow Weep for Me" and Bud Powell's "Bouncin' with Bud." If any proof is needed that Tyner the writer continues to excel, *Infinity* 𝄞𝄞𝄞𝄞 (Impulse!, 1995, prod. Michael Cuscuna) has several wonderful recent originals, with "Happy Days" (celebrating a trip to Senegal) in particular likely to become a Tyner standard.

Tenor saxophonist Michael Brecker joins the trio and acquits himself well, even on the direct challenge of an interesting arrangement of Coltrane's "Impressions."

what to avoid: Tyner's consistency is such that none of his in-print albums is less than good. There are a couple out-of-print efforts fans might see in used-LP bins, however, which may not be worth the expense. *Inner Voices* 𝄞𝄞 (Milestone, 1977, prod. Orrin Keepnews) might seem potentially interesting because of the presence of Earl Klugh and Ron Carter, but four of its five tracks are dragged down by wordless vocals treated like a lead melody instrument. It might have worked better if not for the voices having a very artificial, inhuman tone and being deployed as an inflexible block. Only "Uptown," voiceless but with a nice horn arrangement and a trumpet solo by Jon Faddis, wears well on repeated listening. *Looking Out* 𝄞𝄞 (Columbia, 1982, prod. McCoy Tyner) has its attractions (the wonderful composition "Love Surrounds Us Everywhere") and curiosities (electric guitarist Carlos Santana, vocalist Phyllis Hyman), but the dated faux-CTI production, worsened by Jerry Hey's hack string arrangements on two tracks, keeps this album very low on the Tyner rankings. And for that matter, Santana adds little beyond a few jarring solos, and Hyman's unsubtle pop-jazz singing actually distracts from the music.

best of the rest:

Inception 𝄞𝄞𝄞 (Impulse!, 1962)
Plays Ellington 𝄞𝄞𝄞 (Impulse!, 1964)
Today and Tomorrow 𝄞𝄞𝄞𝄞 (Impulse!, 1966/1991)
Extensions 𝄞𝄞𝄞𝄞 (Blue Note, 1970/1996)
Sahara 𝄞𝄞𝄞𝄞 (Milestone, 1972/OJC, 1991)
Echoes of a Friend 𝄞𝄞𝄞𝄞 (Milestone, 1972)
Song for My Lady 𝄞𝄞𝄞 (Milestone, 1973)
Song of the New World 𝄞𝄞𝄞𝄞 (Milestone, 1973)
Trident 𝄞𝄞𝄞𝄞 (Milestone, 1975)
Together 𝄞𝄞𝄞𝄞 (Milestone, 1979)
4x4 𝄞𝄞𝄞𝄞 (Milestone, 1980)
Horizon 𝄞𝄞𝄞 (Milestone, 1980)
Dimensions 𝄞𝄞𝄞 (Elektra, 1984)
(With Jackie McLean) *It's about Time* 𝄞𝄞𝄞 (Blue Note, 1985)
Revelations 𝄞𝄞𝄞𝄞 (Blue Note, 1989)
Things Ain't What They Used to Be 𝄞𝄞𝄞𝄞 (Blue Note, 1990)
Remembering John 𝄞𝄞𝄞𝄞 (Enja, 1991)
New York Reunion 𝄞𝄞𝄞𝄞 (Chesky, 1991)
44th Street Suite 𝄞𝄞𝄞𝄞 (Red Baron, 1991)
(With McCoy Tyner Big Band) *The Turning Point* 𝄞𝄞𝄞𝄞 (Verve, 1992)

McCoy Tyner (© Jack Vartoogian)

(With McCoy Tyner Big Band) *Journey* 𝄞𝄞𝄞 (Birdology, 1993)
(With Bobby Hutcherson) *Manhattan Moods* 𝄞𝄞𝄞 (Blue Note, 1994)
Prelude and Sonata 𝄞𝄞 (Milestone, 1995)
The Best of McCoy Tyner: The Blue Note Years 𝄞𝄞𝄞 (Blue Note, 1996)

worth searching for: It's not surprising with an artist as prolific as Tyner that some gems have not yet appeared on CD or have drifted into unavailability. The superb *Focal Point* 𝄞𝄞𝄞𝄞 (Milestone, 1975, prod. Orrin Keepnews) is one of Tyner's very best albums. His horn arrangements masterfully contrast instrumental timbres, and the front line—Gary Bartz (sopranino, soprano, and alto saxes, clarinet), Joe Ford (flutes, soprano and alto saxes), and Ron Bridgewater (soprano and tenor saxes)—are consistently inspired. Charles Fambrough (bass), Eric Kamau Gravatt (drums), and Guilherme Franco (congas, percussion, tabla) play with an intensity to match Tyner's own. And most of all, this has some of Tyner's most memorable themes, notably "Mes Trois Fils," "Indo-Serenade," and (with Tyner on the title instrument) "Mode for Dulcimer." The concert album *The Greeting* 𝄞𝄞𝄞 (Milestone, 1978, prod. Orrin Keepnews) is noteworthy for a sextet version of "Fly with the Wind" and for excellent playing by George Adams (tenor and soprano saxes, flute) and Joe Ford (flute, alto sax). Charles Fambrough is on bass, with Sonship on drums and orchestra bells and Guilherme Franco on percussion and berimbau. Recorded at a Japanese festival gig, *Passion Dance* 𝄞𝄞𝄞𝄞 (Milestone, 1979, prod. Ed Michel) is another Milestone album vastly deserving reissue. A monumental performance of Coltrane's "Moment's Notice" with guests Ron Carter and Tony Williams kicks things off. Carter and Williams also join Tyner on "Song of the New World." The album's other three pieces are piano solos, and on the thrilling title track Tyner deploys his bass notes, massive chords, fleet modal lines, and trademark trills in such a fashion that it seems the work of an entire band rather than just one instrument. Recorded in 1980 with a 13- to 15-piece band, with arrangements by Tyner, Jimmy Heath, Slide Hampton, and Frank Foster, *13th House* 𝄞𝄞𝄞𝄞 (Milestone, 1982, prod. Orrin Keepnews) appeared after Tyner had left Milestone for Columbia. The Foster and Heath arrangements are of their own compositions, which can stand alongside the leader's own for rich instrumental tones, polyphonic splendor, and irresistible tunefulness. *La Leuenda de la Hora* 𝄞𝄞𝄞𝄞 (Columbia, 1981, prod. McCoy Tyner) inaugurated Tyner's Columbia period successfully and stands out due to the strong Afro-Cuban flavor of four of its five tracks (with the other being his blues "Walk Spirit, Talk Spirit"). It's another magnificent feat of arranging, complete with a small string section and an animated front line of

Hubert Laws, Bobby Hutcherson, Paquito D'Rivera, Chico Freeman, and Marcus Belgrave.

influences:

◀◀ Thelonious Monk, John Coltrane, Bud Powell, Art Tatum, Igor Stravinsky, Claude Debussy, Duke Ellington

▶▶ Chick Corea, Joanne Brackeen, Hilton Ruiz, Francesca Tanksley, Marilyn Crispell, Myra Melford, Yosuke Yamashita, Mulgrew Miller

Steve Holtje

James Blood Ulmer

Born February 2, 1942, in St. Matthews, SC.

Ulmer rose to fame with Ornette Coleman in the 1970s, followed by a series of critically acclaimed albums as a leader. A strong blues element was always in his style, mixed with quirky phrasing and note choices that led Coleman to say Ulmer was playing harmolodically before they even met in 1972. Ulmer's scintillating array of guitar tones and his jagged, unpredictable lines simultaneously stand out from yet complement seemingly any style, and in his own music he has mixed together harmolodics, rock, and the blues. He also sings, and his mush-mouthed vocals have a certain Jimi Hendrix/bluesman charm.

Ulmer grew up listening to gospel, country, and his father's big band records. The family had a gospel vocal group which Ulmer was drafted into early on. He began playing guitar at age four, and years later admired Wes Montgomery. After coming of age in Pittsburgh and Ohio, he spent five years in Detroit, mostly playing with organist Hank Marr at the Blue Bird club. After Ulmer moved to New York, he recorded with organists Larry Young (*Lawrence of Newark*) and Big John Patton (*Accent on the Blues*, *Memphis to New York Spirit*), as well as with tenor saxophonist Joe Henderson (*Multiple*), and even played in Art Blakey's Jazz Messengers briefly and with ex-Coltrane drummer Rashied Ali's free jazz group—a much more adventurous context than the others mentioned. Later Ulmer recorded with alto saxophonist Arthur Blythe (*Lenox Avenue Breakdown*). In 1972 drummer Billy Higgins introduced Ulmer to Coleman, and the guitarist played with Coleman for much of the next three years, though the group—with Dewey Redman, Charlie Haden or Sirone, and Higgins or Ed Blackwell—never released any work including Ulmer. In this period, to get a bigger sound, Ulmer started using his bottom string as a drone, tuning the entire instrument to the same note (which he calls "harmolodic tuning").

It was in 1978 with Ornette—and initially released on the Coleman-run record label Artists House—that Ulmer made his first released album as a leader, *Tales of Captain Black*, billed as simply James Blood. (Most listeners will find that the album suffers from the awkward drumming of Ornette's son Denardo, though diehard harmolodicists disagree.) A year earlier there was a free jazz quartet recording with tenor saxophonist George Adams, bassist Cecil McBee, and drummer Doug Hammond that offers an interesting contrast to the more structured harmolodic music he was perfecting in the same period. Ulmer's artist breakthrough came on 1980's epochal *Are You Glad to Be in America?*, recorded for a British independent label, followed by a three-album stint on Columbia from 1981 to 1983. Since then, the majority of Ulmer's releases have come on Japanese and German labels (picked up to varying degrees for U.S. distribution), with the exceptions being Bill Laswell–produced projects.

In the 1980s, Ulmer also formed the group Music Revelation Ensemble, for his most hardcore harmolodic outings. Initially it was a quartet with tenor saxophonist David Murray, ex-Coleman drummer Ronald Shannon Jackson, and electric bassist Amin Ali (Rashied Ali's son), though only Ali remains in the group to the present day and the size has expanded. (Ulmer can also be heard on Murray's *Children*). The band Phalanx reunited Ulmer with Rashied Ali and included tenor saxophonist George Adams and bassist Sirone.

Ulmer continues to be a presence on the New York City scene and in foreign record store bins. He made an album of Ornette Coleman tunes in 1996 and at this writing (March 1998) has released just his second recording made for a U.S.-based label in the last decade.

what to buy: *Are You Glad to Be in America?* 𝄞𝄞𝄞𝄞𝄞 (Rough Trade, 1980, prod. James Blood Ulmer/DIW, 1995, prod. James Blood Ulmer, Kazunori Sugiyama) is a harmolodic bombshell, spraying sonic shrapnel in every direction. Ulmer only sings on two of the 10 tracks, focusing instead on giving himself and the horns (David Murray, Oliver Lake, and Olu Dara) fast, intricate heads and plenty of solo space. Part of the album's sound is defined by the two-drummer team of Ronald Shannon Jackson and Calvin Weston, who generally avoid using their cymbals

and concentrate instead on sharp snare accents and rumbling tom-tom patterns that sound like a cross between a marching band and African drumming, with bassist Amin Ali locking into their beats. And throughout, Ulmer's guitar lines bubble and buzz in barely restrained whiplashes of bent notes and scrabbling strums with the occasional wah-wah-heavy riffing thrown in for good measure.

what to buy next: How did an album as wild and free as *Odyssey* 𝄞𝄞𝄞𝄞 (Columbia, 1983/Columbia Legacy, 1996, prod. James Blood Ulmer) not only come out on a major label, but get reissued? Ulmer took the blend of blues and avant-garde jazz guitar he'd perfected playing with Ornette Coleman and put it in a stripped-down context. He devised a new tuning so he could play basslines and rhythm riffs or lead lines simultaneously, then put together a trio with electric violinist Charles Burnham and drummer Warren Benbow—plus his thick, mumbled vocals, of course. The result sounds like nobody else, and like an ideal version of jazz-funk for a less commercial world. Grab it quick before it goes out of print again. Nearly as exciting is the reunion of this trio, credited to Odyssey the Band and logically titled *Reunion* 𝄞𝄞𝄞𝄞 (Knitting Factory, 1998, prod. James Blood Ulmer).

what to avoid: Despite the album's title and the band name (The James Blood Ulmer Blues Experience), on *Blues Allnight* 𝄞𝄞 (In+Out, 1990/Rounder) all the song structures are verse-chorus or verse-bridge-chorus, plus solos—not a 12-bar blues is heard (nor is this a jazz album). The chugging "She Ain't So Cold" sounds like a country song written by the Ramones; "I Don't Know Why" has a gospelish feel mixed with metallic guitar squiggles and fuzztone power chords. There are tracks where Winnie Leyh's unimaginative synthesizer chords intrude, and throughout, longtime Ulmer bassist Amin Ali and drummer Grant Calvin Weston play only basic rhythms. Ulmer never sounds challenged.

the rest:
Tales of Captain Black 𝄞𝄞𝄞 (Artists House, 1978/DIW, 1996)
Revealing 𝄞𝄞𝄞 (In+Out, 1990)
Black and Blues 𝄞𝄞 (DIW, 1991)
Harmolodic Guitar with Strings 𝄞𝄞𝄞𝄞 (DIW, 1993)
Blues Preacher 𝄞𝄞𝄞 (DIW/Columbia, 1994)
Live at the Bayerischer Hof 𝄞𝄞𝄞 (In + Out, 1995/Rounder, 1996)
Music Speaks Louder Than Words: James Blood Ulmer Plays the Music of Ornette Coleman 𝄞𝄞𝄞𝄞 (DIW, 1996/Koch Jazz, 1997)

worth searching for: A lot of Ulmer's catalog is out-of-print, whether because of defunct companies or major label indifference. *Free Lancing* 𝄞𝄞𝄞𝄞 (Columbia, 1981, prod. James Blood

Ulmer) vied for commercial success, slightly, and thus emphasizes rock and funk more than Ulmer's very best recordings, but his vision isn't compromised. There are three basic groups here: the *Are You Glad to Be in America?* band minus Jackson; a trio of Ulmer, Ali, and Weston; and that trio plus second guitarist Ronnie Drayton and a trio of female backup singers. The follow-up, *Black Rock* 🎵🎵🎵 (Columbia, 1982, prod. James Blood Ulmer) errs slightly in giving Irene Datcher and Amin Ali lead vocals, but is otherwise another taut offering (by Ulmer's standards) featuring fine guitar playing. *America—Do You Remember the Love?* 🎵🎵🎵 (Blue Note, 1987, prod. Bill Laswell, James Blood Ulmer) doesn't fulfill the promise suggested by its all-star lineup of Ulmer, bassist Bill Laswell, drummer Jackson, and Nicky Skopelitis (12-string guitar and banjo). The players seem subdued, and Ulmer's new songs are uneven. But it has its high points—the way "After Dark" throbbingly builds up the mock-ominous contrasts of "Black Sheep"—and the droning sound is hypnotically attractive. *Part Time* 🎵🎵🎵 (Rough Trade, 1984) captures the *Odyssey* trio live at the Montreux Jazz Festival in 1983, though four of the seven tracks are songs from the original album. It's still fine music, if a bit more shambling. The trio is joined by Ali on *Live at the Caravan of Dreams* 🎵🎵🎵 (Caravan of Dreams, 1986, prod. Kathelin Hoffman), but Ali is superfluous and ends up clogging the sound. Not out-of-print but perhaps hard to find because of its billing is *South Delta Space Age* 🎵🎵🎵 (Antilles/Verve, 1995, prod. Bill Laswell, James Blood Ulmer). In spite of being billed as by Third Rail, an all-star group of Ulmer, Bill Laswell (bass), Ziggy Modeliste (drums), Bernie Worrell (organ, clarinet), and Amina Claudine Myers (organ, electric piano, vocals), all the music is written or cowritten by Ulmer, who also plays guitar and sings lead vocals. If not particularly ambitious, it's an enjoyable, soulful funk-blues amalgam; a second effort is forthcoming.

influences:
◀◀ Wes Montgomery, Ornette Coleman
▶▶ Jean-Paul Bourelly

see also: *Music Revelation Ensemble, Phalanx*

Steve Holtje

Us3
Formed 1991, in London, England.

Geoff Wilkinson, producer; KCB, rapper (1995–present); Shabaam Sahdeeq, rapper (1995–present); Mel Simpson, keyboards (1991–94).

Heretics or heroes? Us3, which deftly weaves samples from vin-tage jazz recordings with hypnotic raps and hip-hop grooves, has been described as both, depending whether you're talking to jazz purists or young dance music fans. In 1992, the band released a single called "And the Band Played Boogie" that lifted riffs from Blue Note recordings. Rather than sue, Blue Note signed producing partners Geoff Wilkinson and Mel Simpson and gave the band carte blanche with the label's extensive catalog. The resulting album, 1993's *Hand on the Torch*, was propelled by the irresistible "Cantaloop (Flip Fantasia)." The song, a major MTV-driven dance floor hit, layered live trumpets, hip-hop rhythms, rapper Rahsaan, emcee Pee Wee Marquette's introduction from Art Blakey's 1954 *A Night in Birdland, Vol. 1*, and the piano hook from Herbie Hancock's "Cantaloupe Island." The success of that album has been credited with re-igniting commercial interest in Blue Note's reissues. Following Simpson's defection, Wilkinson teamed with East Coast rappers KCB and Shabaam Sahdeeq for 1997's *Broadway & 52nd*.

what to buy: The dazzling *Hand on the Torch* 🎵🎵🎵 (Blue Note, 1993, prod. Mel Simpson, Geoff Wilkinson) is the joyful sound of two kids turned loose in a playground—namely, the Blue Note vaults, where they sample everything from Art Blakey dialogue to snippets of Horace Silver's "Song for My Father," Bobby Hutcherson's "Goin' Down South," and Donald Byrd's "Steppin' into Tomorrow," creating a seamless, relentlessly funky whole.

the rest:
Broadway & 52nd 🎵🎵🎵 (Blue Note, 1997)

influences:
◀◀ Gil Scott-Heron, Gang Starr, Digable Planets
▶▶ Buckshot LeFonque

David Okamoto

Jai Uttal
Born Doug Uttal, in New York, NY.

This talented vocalist/multi-instrumentalist studied classical piano as a child before also learning to play banjo, harmonica, and electric guitar. His diverse musical abilities were reflected in his learning a wide range of styles and absorbing everything from Jimi Hendrix to John Coltrane to modern classical music. By age 19, he became entranced by the music of world famous Indian musician Ali Akbar Khan and was compelled to move to California to study voice and the 25-string sarod under Khan's guidance. Uttal was later able to apply his Indian classical training to the other forms of music he played during the 1970s and 1980s, including reggae, punk, Motown, and blues. During the 1970s (after changing his name to Jai), he made many pilgrimages to India while also studying music in California under various tutors. One of those Indian treks was incredibly influential—he lived and played amongst Bengalese street musicians named the Bauls, communicating with them entirely through music, and the lessons learned there would permanently alter his musical course.

Uttal has been categorized both as a world and jazz musician, but his music blends those elements with pop and fusion to form a signature sound that is full of warmth and romanticism. The musician originally began his recording career with his 1990 debut *Footprints*, an album that found him taking his inspirational journeys to India (particularly his time spent with the Bauls) and applying it to his Western heritage. In other words, the improvisatory nature of certain Indian styles were appropriated into more structured forums such as pop and electronic music. The composer/musician formed the Pagan Love Orchestra (which includes multi-instrumentalist Peter Apfelbaum and keyboardist Kit Walker) to interpret his early works live, but he began to see the greater possibilities of working with a live band, hence their appearance on all of his albums after *Footprints*.

As his work has progressed, Uttal has moved away from works that center more on him and work in a group setting (including occasional songwriting collaborations), one which includes guitar, trombone, violin, bass, and percussion. The electronic influences of his debut soon were stripped away and replaced by more pop-based sounds, which later lead to fusion and even a few reggae influences. Uttal's main instrument is the dotar, which sonically resembles a sitar but possesses a crisper sound with less twang. It dominates his first two albums, but as his music has matured, he has let the sounds of the Pagan Love Orchestra become stronger and more independent. No matter what album you listen to, though, the sound of Uttal and his orchestra is very distinct. Uttal has also performed on albums by the Hieroglyphics Ensemble, Tulku, the Peter Apfelbaum Sextet, and Gabrielle Roth & the Mirrors, and has produced two albums for Ali Akbar Khan.

what to buy: While his latter two releases are more orchestrated and quite sonically rich, his debut has more of an immediate, and lasting, visceral impact. *Footprints* 𝄞𝄞𝄞𝄞 (Triloka, 1990, prod. Jai Uttal) is more of a solo project and features a larger amount of electronic music–based pieces. The intense trance sounds of "Madzoub (God Intoxicated)" and "Bus Has Come" are engrossing, as is the Tangerine Dream–like se-

quencer freefall of "Snowview." Trumpter Don Cherry and vocalist Lakshmi Shankar lend their talents to some of the tracks. Jai Uttal and the Pagan Love Orchestra's latest, *Shiva Station* 𝄞𝄞𝄞𝄞 (Triloka, 1997, prod. Jai Uttal), was mixed by Bill Laswell, and it features songs with lyrics and chants in Sanskrit, Hindi, Bengali, and English. It shows the group getting tighter and more cohesive, with the album possessing a more lush and orchestrated feel than previous works (see below). While not as groundbreaking as the other releases, it is a warm, passionate affair. Some of it rocks, and a couple tunes get jazzy. And Uttal's romantic lyrics are more personal and less conventional this time out.

what to buy next: Uttal's second outing, *Monkey* 𝄞𝄞𝄞 (Triloka, 1992, prod. Jai Uttal), is the first disc with the Pagan Love Orchestra and features some well-done pop ballads given intriguing Eastern twists. Uttal's impassioned singing elevates them above standard world pop fare. There are also plenty of catchy world instrumentals featuring Uttal's dotar playing at their center, and while the sound here is sparser than subsequent works, it's engaging. *Beggars and Saints* 𝄞𝄞𝄞 (Triloka, 1995, prod. Jai Uttal) is another good release, albeit one that will grow on you more with each listen. The Pagan Love Orchestra is given more of a chance to shine, integrating Indian instruments with Western rock and brass instrumentation. The album leans more towards a fusion and less of a pop sound than before, and subliminal ambient touches weave into different spots.

Bryan Reesman

Warren Vache Jr.

Born February 21, 1951, in Rahway, NJ.

Along with tenor saxophonist Scott Hamilton, cornetist Warren Vache pioneered the mid-'70s revival of small group swing. His lustrous warm tone, complete control of his horn (cornet, flugelhorn), and sometimes daring improvisational runs make him a consistently rewarding player. Raised in a highly musical family—his father is noted jazz historian and bassist Warren Vache, Sr., and his brother is trad clarinetist Alan Vache—he studied early on with Pee Wee Erwin and made a name for himself among swing-era veterans working with Benny Goodman,

Bob Wilbur, and Vic Dickenson. He began leading his own sessions in the mid-1970s, often recording with Hamilton and accompanying singer Rosemary Clooney on some of her finest Concord albums. He furthered his reputation on the mainstream jazz scene through numerous appearances at jazz parties. Vache has recorded a number of his own fine albums for Concord and Muse. He has also worked as an actor, most notably in the film *The Gig*, a wonderfully unpretentious ode to amateur jazz musicians.

what to buy: A supremely elegant trio session with pianist John Bunch and bassist Phil Flanigan, *Midtown Jazz* 🎵🎵🎵 (Concord Jazz, 1983/1992, prod. Carl E. Jefferson) captures cornetist Warren Vache at his most lyrical. The set consists mostly of ballads, ranging from standards such as "I'm Old Fashioned," "I'll Remember April," and "Out of Nowhere," to contemporary tunes such as Johnny Mandel's beautiful "A Time for Love" and Henry Mancini's "Two for the Road." Vache also covers two modern jazz classics, playing an ingeniously un-boppish version of Bud Powell's "Tempus Fugit" and a fascinating version of Thelonious Monk's "Rhythm-A-Ning," based on an arrangement by Clark Terry and Bob Brookmeyer. A drummer is not missed as the trio swings with confidence and Vache plays some astounding high runs at the lowest volume possible. A highly successful session featuring Vache with the top-flight rhythm section of Richard Wyands (piano), Michael Moore (bass), and Billy Hart (drums), *Horn of Plenty* 🎵🎵🎵🎵 (Muse, 1994, prod. Don Sickler) ranges widely across the jazz trumpet landscape, evoking Buddy Bolden, Louis Armstrong, Bix Beiderbecke, Buck Clayton, Clifford Brown, and Miles Davis. Tenor saxophonist Houston Person and trombonist Joel Helleny fill out the sextet on Sonny Stitt's classic "The Eternal Triangle," a wonderfully playful version of Armstrong's "Struttin' with Some Barbecue," and a sensuous run through Davis's "All Blues," featuring Vache's muted cornet. The album's highlights include a sensitive duet between Vache and the underrated guitarist Joe Puma on his tune "Bix Fix," and a chance-taking duo version of "Buddy Bolden's Blues" pairing Vache with Moore's sturdy bass. Wyands plays with grace and admirable flexibility throughout the session and Hart's drum work is typically tasteful and alert.

what to buy next: Small group 1980s swing at its best, *Easy Going* 🎵🎵🎵 (Concord Jazz, 1987/1997, prod. Carl E. Jefferson) features Vache on cornet and flugelhorn, Howard Alden on guitar, Dan Barrett on trombone, John Harkins on piano, Jack Lesberg on bass, and Chuck Riggs on drums. As the title suggests, the group inhabits its material with easygoing authority, playing inventively within the neo-swing context. Vache mostly

steers clear of the predictable and well-trod, hewing to such relatively obscure tunes as "It's Been So Long," "Little Girl," and "Mandy Make Up Your Mind." Vache is particularly ardent on Ellington's "Warm Valley" and deeply evocative on Carroll Coates's "London by Night." He even sings a lyric written by his father on Bobby Hackett's "Michelle." Featuring a versatile septet, *Talk to Me Baby* 🎵🎵🎵 (Muse, 1996, prod. Don Sickler) brings together Vache with saxophonist Bill Easley, trombonist Joel Helleny, guitarist Howard Alden, pianist Richard Wyands, bassist Michael Moore, and drummer Alvin Queen. Helleny is especially effective on "Polka Dots and Moonbeams," while Easley's lyrical tenor work on "You'll Never Know" perfectly meshes with Vache's mellow cornet. Vache fans will be particularly interested in the four tracks with just Alden and Moore, where the trio attains a light-as-air, free-floating sensibility with Vache's horn gliding from note to note. Vache is especially effective on the two trio tracks, "The Eels Nephew" by Bud Freeman and Billy Strayhorn's "Isfahan."

best of the rest:

Scott Hamilton and Warren Vache 🎵🎵🎵 (Concord Jazz, 1978)
Polished Brass 🎵🎵🎵🎵 (Concord Jazz, 1979)
Iridescence 🎵🎵🎵🎵 (Concord Jazz, 1981)
Warm Evenings 🎵🎵🎵 (Concord Jazz, 1989)

influences:

◀◀ Bobby Hackett, Ruby Braff

Andrew Gilbert

Bebo Valdes

Born October 9, 1918, in Quivican, Cuba.

Bebo Valdes is the father of renowned Cuban pianist Chucho Valdes, but he deserves to be considered on his own merits. Certainly by the time he left Quivican for Havana in 1936, the senior Valdes had already acquired an impressive keyboard technique, enabling him to find a series of jobs in many local bands. In addition to his work as musical director at Havana's famous Tropican Night Club, Valdes can also be considered one of the primary forces in the Cuban jam session (known as a *descarga*) alongside bassist Cachao (Israel Lopez). He also appeared on many radio and television concerts during the late '50s with his group, Sabor de Cuba. The pianist left Cuba in 1960 for Mexico, where Valdes became associated for a short time with a record label as a musical director and pianist. He then lived in Spain, taking part in a tour by the reconstructed Lecuona Cuban Boys before moving to Stockholm, Sweden.

what to buy: *Bebo Rides Again* ♫♫♫♫ (Messidor, 1995, prod. Paquito D'Rivera), the first album Bebo Valdes recorded in 35 years, finds the pianist/arranger in fine form. Amid an impressive array of Latin talent, the master pianist finds room for a solo spot ("Oleaje"), on which he trips lightly through a lovely fantasia with impeccable elan.

what to buy next: The 20 songs on the collection *Mayajigua* ♫♫♫♫ (Caney, 1995, prod. various) were recorded in Havana in 1957 and 1960, documenting one of the best Cuban ensembles of the day, Bebo Valdes y Su Orquesta Sabor de Cuba. There is a nice array of rhythms displayed in the program, from montunos, mambos, and boleros to rumbas, guarachas, and danzones. The big band's playing and arranging are all quite good, with special emphasis given to a tremendous trumpet section featuring Alejandro "El Negro" Vivar and "Chocolate" Armenteros on the classic "El Manisero," to name one highlight.

the rest:
Descarga Caliente ♫♫♫♫ (Caney, 1995)

influences:
◀◀ Rene Hernandez, Arsenio Rodriguez, Ernesto Lecuona

▶▶ Chucho Valdes, Gonzalo Rubalcaba

Garaud MacTaggart

Chucho Valdes

Born Jesus Valdes, October 9, 1941, in Quivican, Cuba.

Chucho Valdes has been one of the major forces on the Cuban jazz scene since the late '60s, when he formed Orquesta Cubana de Musica Moderna with trumpeter Arturo Sandoval and reed player Paquito D'Rivera. From there the trio helped Irakere get off the ground in 1973. Son of Cuban music legend Bebo Valdes, Chucho is a formidable pianist in his own right and a composer of some repute. As a jazz piano player, he owes much to Art Tatum and McCoy Tyner, but leavens that with roots sunk deep in the rhythms of his homeland.

what to buy: *Cuba Jazz* ♫♫♫♫ (TropiJazz, 1996, prod. Ralph Mercado, Eddie Rodriguez), one of the strongest Latin-jazz albums of the '90s, is listed as "Paquito D'Rivera presents Cuba Jazz featuring Bebo and Chucho Valdes," but it is Chucho's album more than anyone else's. His piano playing and arranging touches are all over the album and his duet with the senior Valdes (on "Peanut Vendor") is marvelous.

what to buy next: Listening to Valdes's performances on *Lucumi: Piano Solo* ♫♫♫♫ (Messidor, 1988, prod. Gotz A. Worner)

makes one realize where Cuban players like Gonzalo Rubalcaba and Hilario Diaz got their roots. He wrote all the material, and his playing is superb, with supple ballads like "Jica" acting as wonderful counterweights to dance-inflected tunes like "Mambo Influenciado" and "Osun." Valdes has created a solo piano album for Latin jazz fans that may serve as a touchstone for future generations.

the rest:
Solo Piano ♫♫♫♫ (World Pacific, 1993)
Pianissimo ♫♫♫ (Molito, 1994)
Chucho Valdes Live ♫♫♫ (RMM, 1998)

worth searching for: Valdes composed and arranged all the material on Irakere's *Live at Ronnie Scott's* ♫♫♫♫ (World Pacific, 1993, prod. Pete King, Chris Lewis), which offers a good sense of Valdes's perspective in his long-standing ensemble. Of particular note is his playing on "Cuando Canta El Corazon," the greatest workout is the nearly 13-minute "Flute Notes."

influences:
◀◀ Bebo Valdes, Art Tatum, Horace Silver, McCoy Tyner, Ernesto Lecuona

▶▶ Gonzalo Rubalcaba, Hilario Diaz

Garaud MacTaggart

Ken Vandermark

Born September 22, 1964, in Warwick, RI.

Over the past few years, Vandermark has exploded onto the Chicago jazz scene. He fronts or co-fronts a number of mind-blowing bands, including Caffeine, Steam, Steelwool Trio, and various combos bearing his surname. He's amassed an impressive discography, releasing no less than seven albums in one year. An integral force in Chicago's creative-music community, Vandermark collaborates with all the local heavyweights. He grew up in the Boston area, picking up trumpet in fourth grade and switching to tenor saxophone in 11th grade. In 1989, he relocated to the more dynamic Chicago environment, landing a temporary slot in Hal Russell's famous NRG Ensemble and quickly proving with gigantic lungs and amazing stamina for overblowing free jazz. When Russell died in 1992, Vandermark joined NRG full-time, as frontline composer and co-tenor saxophonist. NRG producer and devotee Steve Lake says Vandermark infused "this exhilaratingly intense band (with) a further shot of adrenaline."

what to buy: The Vandermark 5's *Single Piece Flow* ♫♫♫♫♫ (Atavistic, 1997, prod. Ken Vandermark) is perhaps the best place to start for jazz fans wary of the saxophonist's sometimes overpowering, loud-and-free blowouts. Not to say there's any lack of energy or freedom here. But this is clearly Vandermark's most swinging album. It's tight yet varied in approach, with eight compositions dedicated to a different individual, from Jackie Chan to Johnny Hodges, and each inspiring an appropriately distinctive mood. On *Fred Anderson/DKV Trio* 𝄞𝄞𝄞𝄞 (Okkadisk, 1997, prod. Ken Vandermark, Bruno Johnson), Chicago improvisational fixture Fred Anderson, a tenor saxophonist, leads this dynamic set featuring Vandermark's latest combo. Anderson's compositions and thoughtful improvisations coax Vandermark to tap a more sensitive side not often heard when he's on his own. The juxtaposition of Anderson's deep warmth and Vandermark's anxious invention creates white-hot jams. Steam's *Real Time* 𝄞𝄞𝄞𝄞 (Eighth Day Music, 1997, prod. Steam) marks Vandermark's coming of age. Bouncing his improvisation off pianist Jim Baker's harmonic accompaniment, Vandermark plays in a voice all his own, barking and howling with gleeful abandon, but still driving home sweet melody. The NRG Ensemble's *Calling All Mothers* 𝄞𝄞𝄞𝄞 (Quinnah, 1994, prod. Steve Lake, Mars Williams) is a monster. Tunes like "Punch and Judy" and "Chasin' My Tail" underscore the group's devotion to the energy jazz aesthetic. Beyond the manic eruptions, the album succeeds because of the intensely focused songwriting.

what to buy next: The Steelwool Trio's *International Front* 𝄞𝄞𝄞𝄞 (Okkadisk, 1995, prod. Ken Vandermark) is one of Vandermark's heaviest projects. Despite the allusions to extreme abrasiveness ("Steelwool"), the intensity is rarely less than palatable. For the Baker-Hunt-Vandermark trio's *Caffeine* 𝄞𝄞𝄞 (Okkadisk, 1994, prod. Jim Baker), Vandermark tears through extended, incendiary free-blowing that lives up to the group's Caffeine moniker. Often overwhelmingly intense, the music still seduces listeners. The Vandermark Quartet's *Solid Action* 𝄞𝄞𝄞 (Platypus, 1994, prod. Mason Taylor) is unique for its instrumentation (bass, drums, sax, clarinets, violin, guitar, cornet) and hard-rock-level energy. Some of the noisy tunes come on steady-grooving with slamming backbeats, wailing guitar jams, and savage riffs.

the rest:
STANDARDS: Four Improvising Trios (Chicago) with Ken Vandermark 𝄞𝄞𝄞 (Quinnah, 1995)
Utility Hitter 𝄞𝄞𝄞 (Quinnah, 1996)
Hoofbeats of the Snorting Swine 𝄞𝄞𝄞 (Eighth Day Music, 1996)
This Is My House 𝄞𝄞𝄞 (Delmark, 1996)
Blow Horn 𝄞𝄞𝄞 (OKKA disk, 1997)
Baraka 𝄞𝄞𝄞 (OKKA disk, 1997)
a meeting in chicago 𝄞𝄞𝄞 (Eighth Day Music, 1997)

worth searching for: The DKV Trio's *Live at Lunar Cabaret* 𝄞𝄞𝄞𝄞 (OKKA, 1997, prod. Bruno Johnson), a superb live set from Vandermark's trio, starts off almost inaudibly, eventually building to monumental proportions. Imaginative mood swings from an incredibly empathetic unit. Only 600 copies were issued.

influences:
◀◀ Albert Ayler, Eric Dolphy, Ornette Coleman, Cecil Taylor

Sam Prestianni

Tom Varner

Born June 17, 1957, in Morristown, NJ.

Tom Varner is the leading jazz French horn player of his generation and a creative small-group arranger capable of transcending jazz's boundaries without losing its root feeling. He took private lessons from French horn great Julius Watkins and studied with Ran Blake, George Russell, and Jaki Byard at the New England Conservatory, influencing his music's eclectic character and stylistic crossbreeding—the serialism of Berg and Webern meets Thelonious Monk's angular bop structures, Ornette Coleman's pantonal melodicism, and funky 12-bar blues.

Varner formed a group with saxophonist Ed Jackson while in Boston, and they have continued working together regularly since Varner moved to New York City in 1979. As a sideman, he's played and/or recorded with a litany of big names including Steve Lacy, Dave Liebman, George Gruntz, John Zorn, Bobby Watson, LaMonte Young, and Miles Davis with Quincy Jones at Montreux in 1991, appearing on over 30 albums.

what to buy: *Martian Heartache* 𝄞𝄞𝄞𝄞 (Soul Note, 1997, prod. Tom Varner) zips through styles the way some guys go through chords—it almost seems as if there's a new one every bar or two. "Keep It Up" alternates cool chords from horns-minus-rhythm-section, a funky groove suggestive of James Brown, up-tempo post-bop, and short unaccompanied solos, all these styles progressively becoming more and more intertwined over the track's 7:45 length. There are a few pretty tracks, too, including the album closer, "Lady Gay," an old country song featuring guest vocalist Dominique Eade. But it's the whiplash effects that make the album exciting, and Varner's turn-on-a-dime arrangements are masterful.

what to buy next: On *The Mystery of Compassion* 𝄞𝄞𝄞𝄞 (Soul Note, 1993, prod. Bobby Previte) Varner's ingenious charts are played by an occasionally augmented quintet of Ed Jackson (alto sax) and Rich Rothenberg (tenor sax)—half the 29th

Street Saxophone Quartet—Mike Richmond (bass), and Tom Rainey (drums). Varner explores the full range of instrumental textures in distinctive fashion on a personal milestone.

the rest:

Tom Varner Quartet 𝄢𝄢𝄢 (Soul Note, 1981)

Motion/Stillness 𝄢𝄢𝄢 (Soul Note, 1983/1995)

Long Night Big Day 𝄢𝄢𝄢𝄢 (New World CounterCurrents, 1991)

worth searching for: *Jazz French Horn* 𝄢𝄢𝄢 (New Note, 1986, prod. Tom Varner, Jim Hartog) lets Varner display his chops in a straight-ahead quintet with Jim Snidero (alto sax), Kenny Barron (piano), Mike Richmond (bass), and Victor Lewis (drums). Jazz classics by Charlie Parker ("Quasimodo"), Bud Powell ("So Sorry Please"), and Duke Ellington ("Come Sunday"), standards (Kurt Weill's "Lost in the Stars," Cole Porter's "I Love You"), Varner tunes based on familiar changes ("Blues for Z," the flag-waver "What Is This Thing Called First Strike Capability"), and the moody original ballad "April Remembrances" are all chordal and mostly bebop, and the way Varner flies through the changes of the "What Is This Thing Called Love" derivative at top speed is miraculous for a French horn player. *Covert Action* 𝄢𝄢𝄢 (New Note, 1988, prod. Tom Varner, Jim Hartog) also has a few familiar tracks ("Happy Trails," "They Say It's Wonderful," and Monk's "Let's Call This") but is more stripped down—just Varner, Richmond, and drummer Bobby Previte—and the originals don't always reference bebop.

influences:

◀◀ Julius Watkins, Ornette Coleman, John Zorn

▶▶ Vincent Chauncey, Ed Jackson

Steve Holtje

Nana Vasconcelos

Born August 2, 1944, in Recife, Brazil.

Along with Airto Moreira, Brazilian percussionist Nana Vasconcelos is one of the most important purveyors of the colorful and polyrhythmic music style that is a cultural treasure of his native country. What makes him especially valuable is his ability to adapt his multi-cultural approach to a variety of musical genres. After making an early debut with his father's band while still in his teens, Vasconcelos worked for a time with the celebrated Milton Nascimento before coming to the U.S. in the 1970s as a member of Gato Barbieri's band. Later that decade, the percussionist teamed with fellow Brazilian Egberto Gismonti before helping to form the group Codona, which combined a variety of "world music" styles and featured trumpeter

Don Cherry and the late Collin Walcott. Throughout this period, Vasconcelos recorded for the ECM label with the various aforementioned ensembles, including a memorable early 1980s stay with the Pat Metheny Group. The foundation of Vasconcelos's multi-layered sound, which often includes vocals, guitar, and hand percussion, is the berimbao. This native instrument includes a hollow gourd and attached bowed-shape piece of wood that stretches a wire strand, its resonance closely resembling that of a slack guitar string. As a proponent of the rich musical legacy that Brazil has to offer, Vasconcelos remains one of the country's most valuable exports.

what to buy: *Saudades* 𝄢𝄢𝄢𝄢 (ECM, 1979, prod. Manfred Eicher) is a great place to experience Vasconcelos's talent as it is a virtual tour-de-force for his resplendent approach. *Duas Vozes* 𝄢𝄢𝄢𝄢 (ECM, 1984, prod. Manfred Eicher) is a date co-led with Egberto Gismonti that finds the pair exploring a variety of traditional songs and spontaneous duets with fascinating results.

what to buy next: *Storytelling* 𝄢𝄢𝄢 (EMI, 1995, prod. Nana Vasconcelos) features Vasconcelos utilizing a more contemporary approach. The overall effect is still one of multi-layered textures, yet electronics have a more prominent role.

the rest:

Lester 𝄢𝄢𝄢 (Soul Note, 1985)

worth searching for: Highlighting the unique rapport shared by two major talents, *Egberto Gismonti: Danca Das Cabecas* 𝄢𝄢𝄢𝄢 (ECM, 1976, prod. Manfred Eicher) features several lengthy pieces for percussion and Gismonti's guitar. *Pat Metheny/Lyle Mays: As Falls Wichita, So Falls Wichita Falls* 𝄢𝄢𝄢𝄢 (ECM, 1980, prod. Manfred Eicher) is one of the three sets that Vasconcelos recorded with Metheny and it's the best of the bunch due to the expansive title track, which benefits greatly from Vasconcelos's uncanny percussion work. *Codona 3* 𝄢𝄢𝄢 (ECM, 1983, prod. Manfred Eicher) summarizes the chamber music approach of this atypical group that owed much of its vitality and rhythmic variety to Vasconcelos.

Chris Hovan

Sarah Vaughan

Born March 27, 1924, in Newark, NJ. Died April 3, 1990, in Los Angeles, CA.

Possessed of one of the most glorious voices in popular music, Sarah Vaughan was jazz's greatest diva. A virtuoso with complete control of pitch, timbre, and dynamics, Vaughan used her rich contralto voice like a horn, embellishing melodies with the kind of imaginative leaps and compositional structure of the most profound instrumental improvisors. She could transform even the weakest material into effective jazz vehicles with her effortless swing and sophisticated bebop-derived harmonic sensibility. Though she didn't scat often, she was among the very best when she did. Her improvisational approach changed over the years, and in the late 1950s and 1960s her sound became, at times, almost operatically ornate, though this tendency decreased later in her career. Vaughan's voice grew deeper and richer as she aged but she lost virtually none of her control, lending her late recordings a depth and texture unlike anything in jazz or popular music. From her first recordings with Billy Eckstine's bebop orchestra in the mid-1940s through the end of her career, Vaughan compiled a discography that is among the most significant and influential in jazz. Though she became a pop star and recorded many pop dates of limited interest to jazz fans, she usually performed with a jazz trio, and continued to make jazz albums throughout her career.

Vaughan started singing in Newark's Mt. Zion Baptist Church as a child. She studied piano and at age 12 began playing organ in church, too. She won her first amateur night at Harlem's legendary Apollo Theatre in 1942 and the next year she was heard by singer Billy Eckstine, who recruited her as a backup singer and pianist for Earl Hines's band. When Eckstine left Hines to form his own band, bringing along a host of bebop pioneers, Vaughan came too, and she made her first recordings with the orchestra in late 1944. She recorded a classic version of "Lover Man" with Dizzy Gillespie and Charlie Parker in 1945 and, after a brief stint with bassist John Kirby's swing-oriented combo from 1945 to 1946, she struck out on her own. She gained widespread exposure touring with Jazz at the Philharmonic in 1948 and became a pop star after she signed with Columbia in 1949, scoring numerous hits with romantic pop ballads and show tunes. Her only pure jazz date during her five years with the label was a classic 1950 session with Miles Davis and Budd Johnson. Between 1954 and 1963 her contract with Mercury provided a much more satisfying arrangement, producing many pop albums but also her masterpieces on Mercury's jazz label EmArcy with Clifford Brown, Count Basie, Ernie Wilkins, and especially her trio with Roy Haynes. Though she signed a similar arrangement with Roulette (1960–63), leading to some excellent recordings with arrangements by Benny Carter and Gerald Wilson, her jazz releases dwindled in the mid-1960s, and after a fine Mercury session with Thad Jones and Manny Albam in early 1967, she didn't return to a recording studio until 1971.

Vaughan spent the last decade of her career recording for Mainstream and Pablo, where she ended her career with a series of remarkable albums paired with Oscar Peterson, Roland Hanna, and the Count Basie Orchestra, and exploring Brazilian songs and the music of Duke Ellington. Though she continued performing up until about six months before her death from lung cancer, Vaughan didn't record another straight-ahead jazz album after 1982.

what to buy: One of the definitive early Sarah Vaughan albums, *Swingin' Easy* ♪♪♪♪ (EmArcy, 1954/1957/Verve, 1992, prod. Bob Shad) only contains 36 minutes of music, but she is dazzling throughout. The classic "Shulie a Bop," with the introduction of her trio worked into the tune, has been much imitated. Eight of the tracks were recorded in 1954 with pianist John Malachi, bassist Joe Benjamin, and drummer Roy Haynes, while the other tunes are from 1957, with Haynes, pianist Jimmy Jones, and bassist Richard Davis. The only meeting between the two jazz legends, *Sarah Vaughan with Clifford Brown* ♪♪♪♪ (EmArcy, 1954/Verve, 1990, prod. Bob Shad) is an essential album for any jazz collection. Ernie Wilkins's arrangements for the sextet featuring Brown (trumpet), Paul Quinchette (tenor sax), Herbie Mann, (flute) and Sassy's working trio with Jimmy Jones (piano), Joe Benjamin (bass), and Roy Haynes (drums), frame her voice perfectly. Her versions of "September Song," "Jim," and "Lullaby of Birdland" have never been surpassed. The CD reissue of *Sarah Vaughan at Mister Kelly's* ♪♪♪♪ (EmArcy, 1957/Verve, 1991, prod. Bob Shad) contains more than twice the music of the original album! Recorded live at the Chicago nightspot, Vaughan sounds wonderfully relaxed despite the microphones, proceeding with aplomb after flubbing the lyric to "How High the Moon." Her trio was among the best, with pianist Jimmy Jones, bassist Richard Davis, and especially drummer Roy Haynes, who spent six years with Vaughan and had the taste and reflexes to keep up with her. Arguably the best of Vaughan's Pablo recordings, *How Long Has This Been Going On?* ♪♪♪♪ (Pablo, 1978/1987, prod. Norman Granz) features Sassy in beautiful voice with Oscar Peterson, Joe Pass, Ray Brown, and Louie Bellson, all of whom are the most musical of accompanists. The session is loose and relaxed, allowing Vaughan to stretch out while singing 10 well-worn standards. Her slow, sensuous versions of "Midnight Sun" and "Easy Living," triumphant take of "I've Got the World on a String," and romp through "When Your Lover Has Gone" are definitive jazz statements.

Sarah Vaughan **(AP/Wide World Photos)**

what to buy next: With under 34 minutes of music, *In the Land of Hi-Fi* 𝄞𝄞𝄞𝄞 (EmArcy, 1955/Verve, 1989, prod. Bob Shad) leaves you wanting more of Vaughan's gorgeous, swinging voice. Soaring through a dozen standards with superb arrangements by Ernie Wilkins, Vaughan offers astonishing versions of "Cherokee" and "How High the Moon," showing why both tunes became bop anthems. Fortunately, Wilkins's arrangements allow some space for solos by the top flight band, including a number of spots for Cannonball Adderley's fiery alto work. One of the best albums of jazz vocal duets ever recorded, *Sarah Vaughan and Billy Eckstine: The Irving Berlin Songbook* 𝄞𝄞𝄞𝄞𝄞 (EmArcy, 1957, prod. Bob Shad) captures the two old friends singing 11 Berlin classics. Among the many highlights are the two numbers Irving Berlin wrote for Rogers and Astaire, "Isn't This a Lovely Day" and "Cheek to Cheek." Hal Mooney's orchestrations aren't distinguished but the band does include Harry "Sweets" Edison, and Sassy and Mister B exhibit energy so exuberant, even the pedestrian charts can't slow them down. A delicate, haunting addition to Vaughan's large discography, *After Hours* 𝄞𝄞𝄞𝄞 (Roulette, 1961/1997, prod. Teddy Reig) is a unique session finally reissued on CD, featuring her vocals backed by just the exquisite guitar work of Mundell Lowe and limber bass of George Duvivier. Only the most confident singer would attempt an entire album with such minimal accompaniment, and Sassy turns the session into a classic with unforgettable versions of "My Favorite Things," "Ill Wind," and "In a Sentimental Mood." Vaughan's last straight-ahead session, *Crazy and Mixed Up* 𝄞𝄞𝄞𝄞 (Pablo, 1982/1987, prod. Sarah Vaughan) features guitarist Joe Pass, pianist Roland Hanna, bassist Andy Simpkins, and drummer Harold Jones. Singing standards such as "Autumn Leaves" and "You Are Too Beautiful," Vaughan makes the well-worn tunes sound fresh with her amazingly rich and still supple voice. She also covers two tunes by Brazilian songwriter Ivan Lins, "Love Dance" and "The Island," and Hanna's attractive ballad "Seasons."

what to avoid: An unlikely project to say the least, *The Mystery of Man* 𝄞𝄞 (Kokopelli, 1984) finds Vaughan in West Germany singing poetry written by Pope John Paul II as translated by Gene Lees with an orchestra conducted by Lalo Shifrin. Seriously. It's a long story, but suffice it to say the music is ponderous and only the presence of two of Lees's own tunes prevents this from being a shaggy, shedding dog.

best of the rest:

Sarah Vaughan 𝄞𝄞𝄞𝄞 (Laserlight, 1945)
The Divine Sarah Vaughan 𝄞𝄞𝄞𝄞 (Columbia, 1949–53)

The George Gershwin Songbooks, Vol. 1 𝄞𝄞𝄞𝄞 (EmArcy, 1955/Verve, 1990)
The George Gershwin Songbooks, Vol. 2 𝄞𝄞𝄞𝄞 (EmArcy, 1955/Verve, 1990)
Sings Broadway: Great Songs from Hit Shows 𝄞𝄞𝄞 (Verve/Mercury, 1956/1995)
Misty 𝄞𝄞𝄞 (Mercury, 1958, 1963/Verve, 1990)
Count Basie & Sarah Vaughan 𝄞𝄞𝄞𝄞 (Roulette, 1961)
You're Mine You 𝄞𝄞𝄞𝄞 (Fresh Sound/Roulette, 1962)
The Benny Carter Sessions 𝄞𝄞𝄞𝄞𝄞 (Roulette, 1962–63/1994)
Sings Soulfully 𝄞𝄞𝄞𝄞 (Roulette, 1963/1993)
Sassy Swings the Tivoli 𝄞𝄞𝄞𝄞𝄞 (EmArcy, 1963/1988)
Sassy Swings Again 𝄞𝄞𝄞𝄞𝄞 (Mercury, 1967/1989)
Send in the Clowns 𝄞𝄞𝄞 (Columbia Legacy/Mainstream, 1974/1995)
I Love Brazil! 𝄞𝄞𝄞𝄞𝄞 (Pablo, 1977/1994)
Copacabana 𝄞𝄞𝄞𝄞 (Pablo, 1979/1988)
Duke Ellington Songbooks, Vol. 1 𝄞𝄞𝄞𝄞𝄞 (Pablo, 1979/1987)
Duke Ellington Songbooks, Vol. 2 𝄞𝄞𝄞𝄞𝄞 (Pablo, 1979/1987)
Send in the Clowns 𝄞𝄞𝄞𝄞 (Pablo, 1981)
Gershwin Live! 𝄞𝄞𝄞 (CBS, 1982/1987)

worth searching for: Released posthumously, *Soft and Sassy* 𝄞𝄞𝄞𝄞 (Hindsight, 1961/1994, prod. Pete Kline) captures Vaughan singing standards and show tunes such as "Poor Butterfly," "Tenderly," and "Serenata," but instead of being encumbered by a studio orchestra, she's swinging free and easy with Roland Hanna (piano), Richard Davis (bass), and Percy Brice (drums). Sassy polishes off most of the tunes in two or three minutes during this wonderfully relaxed session.

influences:

◄◄ Ella Fitzgerald

►► Nnenna Freelon, Vanessa Rubin, Carmen Lundy

Andrew Gilbert

Joe Venuti

Born Giuseppi Venuti, September 6, 1903, in Philadelphia, PA. Died August 14, 1978, in Seattle, WA.

The undisputed father of jazz violin, Joe Venuti employed a searing tone and flawless bow technique to create some of the most inventive and energetic solos of the swing era. Venuti and his partner, guitarist Eddie Lang, played with Bert Estlow's and Red Nichols's respective bands before they hit the big time with Jean Goldkette's orchestra in 1924. Goldkette seemed to be the unofficial farm system for Paul Whiteman's orchestra. Many of Goldkette's discoveries (including the Dorsey Brothers) were lured away by Whiteman, the self-proclaimed "King of Jazz," with promises of bigger pay and solo turns in the spotlight. So it was with Venuti and Lang, who joined Whiteman in 1929. Whether working solo or in their own combo, the Blue Four, Venuti and Lang were tremendously popular session musicians who cut sides with just about every major swing band of their era. After Lang's death in 1933 (during a botched tonsillectomy), Venuti made several attempts at leading his own bands well into the 1940s; none were successful. A popular featured performer on Bing Crosby's radio show, Venuti also made appearances in such films as *Garden of the Moon, Sing, Helen, Sing,* and *Syncopation.* Though he never really stopped working, the ravages of alcoholism put Venuti's career in a tailspin by the early 1960s. Acclaimed appearances at the Newport Jazz Festival and England's Jazz Expo rekindled public interest and led to a series of well-received recordings with Earl Hines, George Barnes, Zoot Sims, and many others. While bravely fighting cancer during the 1970s, Venuti continued taking gigs and recording, playing with impressive verve and skill until his death.

what to buy: You can sample Venuti's groundbreaking, early period with Eddie Lang on *Stringin' the Blues* 𝅘𝅥𝅘𝅥𝅘𝅥 (Topaz Jazz, 1995, prod. various), which features guest appearances by the Dorsey Brothers, King Oliver, and Bing Crosby during the late 1920s and early '30s. *Fiddlesticks* 𝅘𝅥𝅘𝅥𝅘𝅥 (Happy Days, 1994) combines recordings with Venuti and Lang's group, Blue Four, with exciting sessions with Charlie and Jack Teagarden during the early to late '30s. Or you could opt for *Violin Jazz 1927–34* 𝅘𝅥𝅘𝅥𝅘𝅥 (Yazoo, 1991) , a nice sampler of both periods.

what to buy next: A particularly delightful later outing, *Joe Venuti and Zoot Sims* 𝅘𝅥𝅘𝅥𝅘𝅥 (Chiaroscuro, 1994, prod. Hank O'Neal) features Venuti and sax legend Sims on some solid small group swing. Smartly reworked standards such as "I Got Rhythm," "I'll See You in My Dreams," and "I Surrender Dear" showcase the soloists at their best.

the rest:
(With George Barnes) *Gems* 𝅘𝅥𝅘𝅥 (Concord Jazz, 1975/1994)
(With Eldon Shamblin, Curely Chalker, Jethro Burns) *'S Wonderful: 4 Giants of Swing* 𝅘𝅥𝅘𝅥𝅘𝅥 (Flying Fish, 1976/1992)
(With Dave McKenna) *Alone at the Palace* 𝅘𝅥𝅘𝅥𝅘𝅥) (Chiaroscuro, 1977/1992)
(With Stephane Grappelli) *Best of the Jazz Violins* 𝅘𝅥𝅘𝅥 (Lester Recording Catalog, 1989)
Sliding By 𝅘𝅥𝅘𝅥 (Gazell, 1991)
Pretty Trix 𝅘𝅥𝅘𝅥 (IAJRC, 1992)
Joe Venuti in Chicago, 1978 𝅘𝅥𝅘𝅥 (Flying Fish, 1993)
Essential Joe Venuti 𝅘𝅥𝅘𝅥 (Vanguard Classics, 1995)
15 Jazz Classics 𝅘𝅥𝅘𝅥𝅘𝅥 (Omega, 1995)

SARAH VAUGHAN
(WITH VARIOUS ARTISTS)

song "Ain't Misbehavin'"
album *Stars of the Apollo*
(Columbia, 1950/1993)
instrument Vocals

Monster Solo

worth searching for: Venuti's work with Eddie Lang never sounded better than on *Great Original Performances 1926–33* 𝅘𝅥𝅘𝅥𝅘𝅥 (Mobile Fidelity, 1992), a now out-of-print digitally remastered compilation of superior quality.

influences:

◀◀ Paul Whiteman, Eddie Lang

▶▶ Stephane Grappelli, Django Reinhardt, Stuff Smith

Ken Burke

Harold Vick

Born April 3, 1936, in Rocky Mount, NC. Died November 13, 1987, in New York, NY.

Harold Vick is one of the tenor saxophonists who became known to jazz listeners through organ groups during the '60s soul-jazz era. His brawny but smooth tenor sound was important to quite a few tenor/organ recordings during that decade. Vick began playing semi-professionally while a student at

Howard University in Washington, D.C., in the late '50s. After backing touring acts of the day at the famed Howard Theatre, Vick joined Red Prysock's band, and later played with R&B stars like Ruth Brown and Lloyd Price. His first real success came with groups led by Jack McDuff in the early '60s. He recorded his only release for Blue Note in 1963 and waxed two (now scarce) releases later in the decade for RCA/Victor. Vick recorded one album each for Strata-East and Muse during the '70s and also played with Jimmy McGriff, Shirley Scott, and Jack DeJohnette's group Compost. Later work as a sideman included a stint with Abbey Lincoln.

what's available: *Steppin' Out* ♫♫♫ (Blue Note, 1996, prod. Alfred Lion) contains some strong blowing from Vick, who also wrote five of the six tunes—mostly bluesy and uncomplicated, but above the average soul-jazz fare.

worth searching for: *Don't Look Back* ♫♫♫ (Strata-East, 1974/Universal Sounds, 1997, prod. Harold Vick), reissued on vinyl, was an ambitious break from Vick's organ-group past, proving his range was wider than his '60s work would indicate. He composed and arranged all six tracks, and is featured on a variety of reeds, including bass clarinet, alto flute, and soprano sax, though he's still most impressive on tenor. *Commitment* ♫♫♫ (Muse, 1978) is not as adventurous as *Don't Look Back*, but it's an enjoyably straightforward tenor-plus-rhythm outing.

influences:

◄◄ Gene Ammons, Red Prysock, George Coleman

►► Houston Person, Don Braden, Eric Alexander

Dan Bindert

Frank Vignola

Born December 30, 1965, in Islip, Long Island, NY.

Frank Vignola started playing guitar when he was five and banjo at 12. He grew up listening to the recordings of Django Reinhardt, Charlie Christian, George Barnes, and Wes Montgomery. At family parties, when relatives and friends brought guitars, banjos, mandolins, and accordions for jam sessions, he listened and soon joined in. The youth won a Canadian banjo championship at the age of 14, and later played with the New York Banjo Ensemble. He graduated with honors from the Cultural Arts Center of Long Island. At 20, Vignola formed a five-piece band called the Hot Club. The group's three guitars, violin, and acoustic bass emulated the 1930s sound of the famed Reinhardt–Stephane Grappelli Quintette du Hot Club of France. The band had a 20-week booking at

Michael's Pub in New York, and a featured spot at the 1988 Newport Jazz Festival.

"Versatile" should be Vignola's middle name, since he honed a variety of jazz styles as a leader and sideman in both posh clubs and local hangouts in New York, New Jersey, and Boston. Equally adept at acoustic guitar, electric guitar, and banjo, he worked gigs with Leon Redbone, Ringo Starr, Milt Hinton, and Billy Mitchell, and has played and/or recorded with Les Paul, Woody Allen, Jon Hendricks, Frank Wess, and Ken Peplowski. He also performed on Johnny Carson's *Tonight Show,* and on PBS with ragtime pianist Max Morath. In 1991, Vignola and tuba player Sam Pilafian started touring and recorded four albums as the duo Travelin' Light. The pair played major jazz venues in the United States and Europe and both joined the music faculty of Arizona State University, where Vignola established a jazz-guitar program before moving back East. During the summer of 1997, his more contemporary quartet, Unit Four, performed in Sweden, Switzerland, and at Lincoln Center in New York. Vignola's trademark is solid rhythm, but he also delivers the dazzling runs of Django Reinhardt and Charlie Christian. He is known for a combination of blazing right-hand strumming, blues-tinged single-note choruses, and chordal improvisations.

what to buy: Since the early 1990s, Vignola has led a trio with bassist John Goldsby and drummer Joseph Ascione, adding guests for recording sessions. *Appel Direct* ♫♫♫♫ (Concord, 1993, prod. Carl Jefferson, John Burk) has Junior Mance on piano, Billy Mitchell on tenor sax, and Sam Pilafian on tuba. Vignola's dual strengths as a rhythm player and exciting riff-taker come through strongly on all 12 tracks, especially on "Appel Direct," a Grappelli-Reinhardt original that features Mance's classy work. The musical fare ranges from bop to blues, swing to funk, Fats Waller ("Jitterbug Waltz") to Cole Porter ("Love for Sale"), and from Duke Pearson's "Jeannine" to Rodgers and Hammerstein's "It Might As Well Be Spring," and Vignola proves he is master of all genres. Goldsby complements with rich resonance and stirring bowed work and Ascione ably underscores with sticks and brushes. The most surprising track is "Ready 'n Able," featuring Mitchell's tenor, Vignola's banjo, and Pilafian's tuba, and it somehow works without becoming a novelty tune. *Let It Happen* ♫♫♫♫ (Concord, 1994, prod. Carl Jefferson) starts with the basic Vignola-Goldsby-Ascione trio plus guests—David Grisman adds mandolin on five tracks, soprano/alto saxophonist Arnie Lawrence is on two, and clarinetist Ken Peplowski is on one track. Again, lots of variety, with lots of Latin flavor, from "Tico Tico" to Jobim's lesser-known

"Ligia" and the oldie "Spanish Eyes." Grisman's energy and fleetness match Vignola's throughout, but Ascione's bongos often are a bit pervasive. Of the 12 tracks, Reinhardt's obscure "Fleche d'Or" gets funky with Peplowski's clarinet taking the Grappelli violin riffs. Horace Silver's "Ah So" is super-fueled and Vignola's treatment of Glenn Miller's "String of Pearls" is creatively arranged. The album represents a move toward Vignola's future sound.

what to buy next: *Look Right, Jog Left* 𝅘𝅥𝅮𝅘𝅥𝅮𝅘𝅥𝅮𝅘𝅥𝅮 (Concord, 1996, prod. Glen Barros, John Burk) is the initial issue of Unit Four, Vignola's trio plus keyboardist Allen Farnham. This is a more contemporary Vignola, playing both electric and acoustic, as Goldsby adeptly alternates basses. Aided by Farnham's synth work and Ascione's drive, the quartet burns through 12 tracks. The 10 originals range from lyrical and Latin to hard-rocking and bluesy. Farnham's synthesized B-3 sound on "The Antidote" is commanding, while Ascione's drum groove propels "Jonathan's Wine." The album is a departure from Vignola's first two sessions as a leader, and it lets his versatility shine through even more. Brief solo-guitar interludes, each cleverly titled "Vignolette," give a refreshing change of pace.

what to avoid: *Getting It Together* **woof!** (Summit Records, 1995, prod. Sam Pilafian, Frank Vignola) is a beginning jazz improvisation course, complete with instructional booklet. Vignola and Pilafian play 14 tracks of tuba-guitar/banjo grooves to which a student adds his or her instrument for practice.

the rest:
(With Travelin' Light) *Travelin' Light* 𝅘𝅥𝅮𝅘𝅥𝅮𝅘𝅥𝅮 (Telarc, 1991)
(With Travelin' Light) *Makin' Whoopee* 𝅘𝅥𝅮𝅘𝅥𝅮𝅘𝅥𝅮 (Telarc, 1993)
(With Travelin' Light) *Christmas with Travelin' Light* 𝅘𝅥𝅮𝅘𝅥𝅮𝅘𝅥𝅮 (Telarc, 1993)
Cookin' with Frank and Sam 𝅘𝅥𝅮𝅘𝅥𝅮𝅘𝅥𝅮 (Concord, 1995)

worth searching for: *The Concord Jazz Guitar Collective* 𝅘𝅥𝅮𝅘𝅥𝅮𝅘𝅥𝅮𝅘𝅥𝅮 (Concord, 1995) showcases the three-guitar coalition of Vignola, Howard Alden, and Jimmy Bruno, backed by bassist Jim Hughart and drummer Colin Bailey. Vignola plays electric on "Perdido," "Four Brothers" and "Ornithology." He takes up the acoustic for "Seven Come Eleven," "Body and Soul," "Donna Lee," and Reinhardt's lovely "Song d'Automne." Alden plays electric; Bruno both acoustic and electric.

influences:

◀◀ Django Reinhardt, Charlie Christian, Wes Montgomery, George Barnes, Joe Pass, Herb Ellis, Bucky Pizzarelli

Patricia Myers

Leroy Vinnegar
Born July 13, 1928, in Indianapolis, IN.

One of the most active and dependably swinging bassists on the West Coast in the 1950s and 1960s, Leroy Vinnegar perfected a highly propulsive walking bass style that was both rhythmically effective and harmonically sophisticated. Though he didn't solo often, his huge sound and penchant for plucking an open string to accent his lines make his work easy to recognize. A high school friend of pianist Carl Perkins, Vinnegar made his reputation in the early 1950s playing in the house rhythm section of Chicago's Beehive club, accompanying traveling musicians such as Charlie Parker, Sonny Stitt, Lester Young, Howard McGhee, and Johnny Griffin. He moved to Los Angeles in 1954 as Art Tatum's substitute bassist and soon became the city's first-call bassman. He recorded with most of L.A.'s leading musicians, including tenor saxophonists Stan Getz, Teddy Edwards, and Harold Land, trumpeter Shorty Rogers, guitarist Barney Kessel, and pianists Andre Previn and Les McCann, with whom he recorded, respectively, the hit albums *My Fair Lady* and *Swiss Movement*. He also recorded important sessions with Sonny Rollins, Kenny Dorham, and Phineas Newborn Jr. Television, movie, and studio work preoccupied him for much of the 1960s, though he continued to play jazz. Health problems sidelined him in the 1980s and he moved to Portland, where he has become an important part of the Pacific Northwest jazz scene.

what to buy: A fine session with the overly cute idea of collecting tunes with a pedestrian theme, *Leroy Walks!* 𝅘𝅥𝅮𝅘𝅥𝅮𝅘𝅥𝅮𝅘𝅥𝅮 (Contemporary, 1957/OJC, 1990, prod. Lester Koenig), features Victor Feldman (vibes), Gerald Wilson (trumpet), Teddy Edwards (tenor sax), Tony Bazley (drums), and Vinnegar's childhood friend pianist Carl Perkins (who died less than a year after this album). Vinnegar plays with his usual drive but sticks mostly to rhythm section duty, letting his bandmates take most of the solos. The result is well-played hard bop, though not an especially inspired session.

what to buy next: Notable mostly as the recording debut of trumpeter Freddie Hill, *Leroy Walks Again!* 𝅘𝅥𝅮𝅘𝅥𝅮𝅘𝅥𝅮 (Contemporary, 1962–63/OJC, 1990, prod. Lester Koenig) is another solid session featuring a host of top Los Angeles players, including Teddy Edwards (tenor sax), Roy Ayers (vibes), and Mike Melvoin (piano). Vinnegar's tribute to his late friend pianist Carl Perkins, the waltz "For Carl," is one of the session's highlights, along with Edwards's straight-ahead blues, "Wheelin' and Dealin'."

the rest:
Walkin' the Basses 🎵🎵🎵 (Contemporary, 1993)

worth searching for: A hugely popular album and a landmark of jazz funk, *Swiss Movement* 🎵🎵🎵🎵 (Rhino, 1969/Atlantic, 1996, prod. Nesuhi Ertegun, Joel Dorn) captures tenor saxophonist Eddie Harris in an impromptu concert appearance at Montreux with pianist Les McCann's band, featuring expatriate trumpeter Benny Bailey, Vinnegar, and drummer Donald Dean. Vinnegar played more inventively on other sessions, but he's rarely sounded as funky. The CD reissue includes Vinnegar's "Kaftan," a wonderful mid-tempo, gospel-flavored piece with a particularly thoughtful Harris solo.

influences:

◀◀ Jimmy Blanton, Oscar Pettiford, Tommy Potter

▶▶ Paul Chambers, Scott LaFaro

Andrew Gilbert

Eddie "Cleanhead" Vinson

Born December 18, 1917, in Houston, TX. Died July 2, 1988, in Los Angeles, CA.

"Cleanhead" Vinson's voice cracked as badly as that of a 12-year-old boy with his first chin hairs, but adoring female fans had no complaints about the man's macho swagger. Though Eddie Vinson was a bop-styled alto saxophonist first, he was also an earthy, ribald blues singer in the tradition of blues shouters such as Big Joe Turner. Called "Cleanhead" after he became bald as a result of an accident with a lye hair straightener, Vinson took off in the late 1930s with Chester Boone's big band, blowing tenor sax with fellow Texans Illinois Jacquet and Arnett Cobb, and stayed with the band from 1935 to 1941, during which time it changed leaders to Milt Larkin (1936), and Floyd Ray (1940). He detoured to play behind Big Bill Broonzy for a year, then found his home as a saxophonist and vocalist with Cootie Williams after moving to New York. It was with Williams that Vinson hit with his monster blues squeal, "Cherry Red Blues," which he would record repeatedly over his 50-year career. Going it alone, Vinson led big bands in the mid-1940s and a septet in 1948 that included John Coltrane, Red Garland, and Johnny Coles. Vinson continued to prove his mettle with the top sax aces of his day, blowing with everyone from Cannonball Adderley to Ben Webster, and performing with Count Basie, Johnny Otis, Arnett Cobb, and Buddy Tate during the 1970s and 1980s. From the 1940s, Vinson churned out three dozen sides for Mercury as well as recordings for Bethlehem, Riverside, Delmark, and other labels. Vinson joined fellow blues shouter Joe Turner in churning out sessions for the Pablo label in the 1960s and 1970s, then toured regularly with Etta James until his death by a heart attack in 1988.

what to buy: *Blues, Boogie and Bop: The 1940s Mercury Sessions* 🎵🎵🎵🎵🎵 (Verve, 1995, prod. Richard Seidel, Kazu Yanagida), a prohibitively-expensive, limited-edition, seven-box set, contains nearly three dozen Vinson sides from the late 1940s. Packaged in a plastic copy of a postwar-era radio, it contains exhaustive notes and superbly-reproduced jazz and blues winners by Witherspoon, Albert Ammons, Professor Longhair, Jay McShann, and Helen Humes. *Battle of the Blues, Vol. 3* 🎵🎵🎵🎵 (King, 1988, prod. Syd Nathan), a reproduction of the 1950s-vintage King album, splits 16 cuts evenly between Vinson and fellow lungsman Jimmy Witherspoon. Vinson goes over the top on "Person to Person" and "Ashes on My Pillow" and hauls out a Cherry Red soundalike on "Somebody Done Stole My Cherry Red." Witherspoon's no-nonsense, Kansas City shouting is a fine compliment to Cleanhead's Texas twisters.

what to buy next: There are only five Vinson tracks on *Cootie Williams and His Orchestra 1941–44* 🎵🎵🎵🎵 (Classics, 1995), but they include his historic 1944 version of "Cherry Red." The rest are up-tempo, big band instrumentals with some of bop pianist Bud Powell's earliest performances.

the rest:
Kidney Stew Is Fine 🎵🎵🎵🎵 (Delmark, 1969)
I Want a Little Girl 🎵🎵🎵 (Pablo/OJC, 1981/1995)
Blues in the Night Vol. 1: The Early Show 🎵🎵🎵 (Fantasy, 1992)
Cherry Red 🎵🎵🎵 (One Way, 1995)
Cleanhead's Back in Town 🎵🎵🎵 (Bethlehem, 1996)

influences:

◀◀ Louis Jordan

▶▶ Cannonball Adderley

see also: *Johnny Coles, Johnny Otis, Cootie Williams*

Steve Braun and Nancy Ann Lee

The Visitors

Formed 1968. Disbanded 1976.

Earl Grubbs, soprano sax, tenor sax; Carl Grubbs, alto sax.

Graduates of the Mastbaum school, one of the finest jazz education programs in the country, the Visitors were just the Grubbs brothers, Earl (1942–89) and Carl (born 1944) and whichever musicians they plucked out of the fertile Philadelphia gene pool at the time. Cousins of Naima Coltrane (John's first wife, and yes, they would cover her tribute song), the brothers were often taught by Trane himself while they were still in their teens; they were practicing the "Giant Steps" progression before the LP came out. The Grubbs recorded four spiritually-searching LPs in the early 1970s, often covering Coltrane tunes or interpolating his riffs into original pieces, and coming to very much represent the profound and totalizing effect that Coltrane had on acoustic jazz for about 15 years into the late 1970s. The two would modulate or fugue together, soprano and alto sounding like a single Coltrane on tenor, and their recordings are archetypal examples of the far-outing of the Philadelphia sound, exploring Eastern-ish harmonies against modal structures and extraneous percussion—the peaceful fire so popular at the time. Yes, perhaps bong hits were involved, but art is art, dude. As the 1970s descended, responsibility (or whatever) called and the Grubbs moved onto other things. Earl played with Odean Pope's big band and Carl played funk with a group called Airwaves. Carl later moved to Baltimore where he still occasionally plays out and teaches. He has a solo record that he sells out of his house.

what to buy: A young pre-fusion Stanley Clarke is all over *In My Youth* 𝄞𝄞𝄞𝄞 (Muse, 1972, prod. Skip Drinkwater, Dennis Wilen) and adds a bass feel similar to the one he provided for LP recordings with Pharoah Sanders. The album is one of few from the Grubbs brothers available on CD, and includes an alternate take of the title track, Sid Simmons on piano, and their version of "Giant Steps."

the rest:
Rebirth 𝄞𝄞𝄞𝄞 (Muse, 1974)
Motherland 𝄞𝄞𝄞𝄞 (Muse, 1976)

worth searching for: A beautiful feel inhabits all of the Visitors LPs, but the Grubbs brothers preferred their first one, *Neptune* 𝄞𝄞𝄞𝄞 (Muse, 1971, prod. Skip Drinkwater) featuring shifting personnel, with pianist John Hicks on bass (!), pianists Rahn Burton, Grubbs's cohort Sid Simmons, and a cast of co-Philadelphians. If you like Norman Connor's early work, or anyone within spitting distance of late Atlantic/early Impulse! Coltrane, this should tickle your fancy. Reissued on LP in the 1980s, so it's not to hard to track down.

influences:

◄◄ John Coltrane

►► Courtney Pine

D. Strauss

Roseanna Vitro

Born February 28, 1954, in Hot Springs, AR.

A talented and soulful jazz singer with an impressive range, Roseanna Vitro deserves to be much better known. Vitro lived in Texarkana, Arkansas, and later moved to Houston, where she sang blues and rock during the early to mid-1970s before becoming jazz-oriented and singing with Arnette Cobb. Vitro moved to New York in 1980 and soon found herself working with Lionel Hampton. Vitro's debut album, *Listen Here*, was released on Texas Rose in 1984, and, as leader, she went on to record for Skyline, Chase, Concord, and Telarc.

what to buy: Joined by talents such as tenor player George Coleman and pianist Fred Hersch, Vitro is especially inspired on the impressive *Softly* 𝄞𝄞𝄞𝄞 (Concord, 1993, prod. Paul Wickliffe, Roseanna Vitro). The title is either misleading or ironic because a very passionate and soaring Vitro doesn't hesitate to let loose on versions of "Softly, As in a Morning Sunrise," "Falling in Love with Love," and "I'm Through with Love." And she's equally uninhibited on *Passion Dance* 𝄞𝄞𝄞𝄞 (Telarc, 1996, prod. Paul Wickliffe), which contains some emotional alto sax solos by Gary Bartz, and finds Vitro excelling on jazz standards such as Benny Golson's "Whisper Not" and Eddie Harris's "Freedom Jazz Dance."

what to buy next: Vitro salutes one of her idols with thrilling results on *Catchin' Some Rays: The Music of Ray Charles* 𝄞𝄞𝄞𝄞 (Telarc, 1997, prod. Paul Wickliffe). Vitro's versions of "One Mint Julep," "Lonely Avenue," and other songs associated with Charles have as much to do with jazz as they do with R&B, and she never allows her love of the soul man to obscure her own identity.

the rest:
Listen Here 𝄞𝄞𝄞𝄞 (Texas Rose, 1984)
A Quiet Place 𝄞𝄞𝄞𝄞 (Skyline, 1987)

worth searching for: Though not quite as strong as *Softly* or *Passion Dance*, *Reaching for the Moon* 𝄞𝄞𝄞𝄞 (Chase, 1993, prod. Paul Wickliffe) is an enjoyable and heartfelt date that offers noteworthy interpretations of "Yesterdays," "In a Sentimental Mood," and Brazilian composer Ivan Lins's "The Island." Saxmen George Coleman and Joe Lovano have some nice spots.

influences:

◄◄ Sarah Vaughan, Carmen McRae, Ella Fitzgerald

Alex Henderson

Freddy Waits

See: M'Boom

Mal Waldron

Born August 16, 1926, in New York, NY.

Pianist Mal Waldron is without question one of the most unique jazz pianists in the history of the music. Like Thelonious Monk and Herbie Nichols, Waldron has developed a sound and approach that is uniquely his own and devoid of clichés and identifiable influences. He possesses a dark and brooding sound combined with a pointed and angular attack. Waldron often relies on minor keys, and his use of space and repetition creates a tension-and-release that is often overwhelming. Initially a classical player, Waldron became more and more interested in jazz while studying at Queens College and he made his first recordings with Ike Quebec, Della Reese, and Charles Mingus. During the 1950s, he worked and recorded with his own groups, in addition to serving as house pianist for Prestige Records. For two years prior to Billie Holiday's death, Waldron worked as her accompanist. He also played an integral part in the short-lived Eric Dolphy/Booker Little Quintet. The mid-1960s then marked the end of the first period of Waldron's career. He suffered a nervous breakdown at the time, which took away his ability to play the piano. Over the next few years he had to relearn and redevelop his technique, which he did largely by listening to his own older recordings. By the end of the decade Waldron had moved to Europe where he worked with Steve Lacy, Archie Shepp, and recorded often for a variety of labels, including ECM, Enja, Muse, hat ART, and Soul Note. Now into his seventies, Mal Waldron continues to record on a regular basis and is a popular attraction on the European and Japanese circuits. As it should be with an artist of his stature, the majority of his historically important albums are currently in print, making it possible for one to trace the evolution and rise to prominence of this exceptional pianist.

what to buy: *Mal 4* 🎵🎵🎵🎵 (Prestige-New Jazz/OJC, 1958, prod. Bob Weinstock) is the best place to hear Waldron in an early trio setting. His dark lyricism comes through brilliantly on a choice set of originals and standards. *The Quest* 🎵🎵🎵🎵 (New Jazz/OJC, 1961, prod. Esmond Edwards) is Waldron's all-time masterpiece, due in no small part to a wonderful set of origi-

nals and the appearances of Booker Ervin and Eric Dolphy. This is a classic not to be missed!

what to buy next: *Free at Last* 🎵🎵🎵🎵 (ECM, 1969, prod. Manfred Eicher) was the first album done for ECM and the first recording for Waldron upon his arrival in Europe. This is another of his classic trio dates and one that is timeless in its originality and beauty. *The Git-Go-Live at the Village Vanguard* 🎵🎵🎵🎵 (Soul Note, 1986, prod. Giovanni Bonandrini) is one of Waldron's better recent efforts. Working in a quintet format and stretching out on lengthy performances, there is more fire and drive here than in some of Waldron's studio dates of the same period.

the rest:
Mal 1 🎵🎵🎵 (Prestige/OJC, 1956)
Mal 2 🎵🎵🎵🎵 (Prestige/OJC, 1957)
Left Alone 🎵🎵🎵🎵 (Bethlehem, 1957)
Mal 3: Sounds 🎵🎵🎵🎵 (Prestige-New Jazz/OJC, 1958)
Impressions 🎵🎵🎵🎵 (Prestige-New Jazz/OJC, 1959)
Black Glory 🎵🎵🎵🎵🎵 (Enja, 1971)
Hard Talk 🎵🎵🎵🎵 (Enja, 1974)
Sempre Amore 🎵🎵🎵🎵 (Soul Note, 1986)
Left Alone '86 🎵🎵🎵🎵🎵 (Evidence, 1986)
The Seagulls of Kristiansund: Live at the Village Vanguard 🎵🎵🎵🎵 (Soul Note, 1986)
Our Colline's a Treasure 🎵🎵🎵 (Soul Note, 1987)
Crowd Scene 🎵🎵🎵🎵 (Soul Note, 1989)
Where Are You? 🎵🎵🎵 (Soul Note, 1989)
(With Jeanne Lee) *After Hours* 🎵🎵🎵 (Owl, 1994)
My Dear Family 🎵🎵🎵🎵 (Evidence, 1994)

Chris Hovan

Dan Wall

Born in Atlanta, GA.

Dan Wall comes from three generations of professional pianists and began his own career at age 14. Wall established his reputation as a jazz pianist in Atlanta during the 1970s before heading to New York. During the 1980s he worked New York City clubs and recorded with Steve Grossman, Eddie Gomez, Jeremy Steig, Joe Chambers, and accompanied singers such as Dakota Staton and Sheila Jordan. Long before he began playing the Hammond B-3 in a co-op trio with John Abercrombie in 1992, Wall had mastered the monster instrument. But Abercrombie's trio with drummer Adam Nussbaum was a progressive group that ventured far beyond the expected bluesy grooves of a B-3 group. Besides recording with Abercrombie and others, Wall has recorded (on piano) with tenor saxophonist Ernie Krivda, and in 1995 released his first album as leader, playing the organ. He has toured extensively and appeared in radio and television broadcasts throughout Europe, Canada, Japan, and the U.S. He currently resides in a suburb of Cleveland, Ohio.

what's available: Hammond B-3 organist Dan Wall leads a trio with guitarist Karl Ratzer and drummer Adam Nussbaum on *Off the Wall* 𝄢𝄢𝄢𝄢 (Enja, 1997, prod. Matthias Winckelmann). Guest soloists include Ingrid Jensen (trumpet, flugelhorn) and Lester LaRue (guitar). Though Wall is certainly capable of deep blues grooves, and teases the listener with such riffs on this nine-tune session, this is not that kind of organ trio. Wall, who wrote seven of the tunes, takes more risks with harmony, building on a modern framework that stretches the organ trio format even beyond the expected fusion sound. Wall is not a flashy guy prone to loud, hard-edged improvisations. Rather, he is a tasteful, melody-focused player who is just as likely to stay inside the changes as he does on "Carol's Bridge," a tune cowritten with his wife, singer Carol Veto. Jensen's attractive muted trumpet solo highlights "Waltz for John" and Wall's playing is equally inspired. Since Wall contributed plenty of original tunes during his stint with the John Abercrombie Trio and uses the same drummer, this session sounds a lot like that cooperative (especially their album *Speak of the Devil*). The main differences are the central focus on his innovative, often driving and enlivened B-3 executions, and his creative compositions which give him opportunities for all-embracing jazz expressions.

see also: *John Abercrombie, Ernie Krivda*

Nancy Ann Lee

Bennie Wallace
Born November 18, 1946, in Chattanooga, TN.

Imagine Eric Dolphy and Sonny Rollins (c. 1964) "walking the bar" in some old honky-tonk, playing Thelonious Monk tunes, and you'd have some idea of what Bennie Wallace sounds like. His honking, heavily arpeggiated style can sometimes suggest the saxophone's circus roots, but he provides enough humor, emotion, and intensity to remain a safe distance from the abyss.

Wallace started on clarinet at age 12 but switched to tenor a few years later. As a teenager he played with local country bands and R&B groups. In 1971, shortly after graduating from the University of Tennessee as a clarinet major, he moved to New York City. Through the early '80s, he toured extensively throughout Europe with the George Gruntz and NDR big bands.

He has recorded for various record labels, including Blue Note. He also achieved success with film scores like *White Men Can't Jump.*

what to buy: Like Sonny Rollins, Wallace's playing is strongest in a trio setting unencumbered by a pianist's comping. And the stronger the trio, the better. Dave Holland and Elvin Jones provide the right support on *Big Jim's Tango* 𝄢𝄢𝄢𝄢 (Enja, 1982, prod. Horst Weber) so Wallace really soars, particularly on "My Heart Belongs to Daddy" and "Big Jim Does the Tango for You."

what to buy next: *The Free Will* 𝄢𝄢𝄢 (Enja, 1980, prod. Matthias Winckelmann) finds Wallace expertly complemented by Tommy Flanagan, Dannie Richmond, and Eddie Gomez. "Back Door Beauty" is a pretty jazz waltz that is transformed by Flanagan's solo. On *Plays Monk* 𝄢𝄢𝄢 (Enja, 1981, prod. Matthias Winckelmann) Wallace emulates Monk so his solos come out distinctly idiosyncratic. His debt to Sonny Rollins is particularly evident on "'Round Midnight."

what to avoid: *Mystic Bridge* 𝄢𝄢 (Enja, 1982, prod. Horst Weber) is less focused and more lackluster than other recordings. Chick Corea's playing seems at odds with Wallace's.

the rest:
Fourteen Bar Blues 𝄢𝄢𝄢 (Enja, 1978)
Sweeping through the City 𝄢𝄢𝄢𝄢 (Enja, 1984)
Brilliant Corners 𝄢𝄢𝄢𝄢 (Denon, 1986)
Art of the Saxophone 𝄢𝄢𝄢𝄢 (Denon, 1987)
Bordertown 𝄢𝄢𝄢 (Blue Note, 1987)
Old Songs 𝄢𝄢𝄢𝄢 (JVC, 1993)
Talk of the Town 𝄢𝄢𝄢 (Enja, 1993)

worth searching for: *Twilight Time* 𝄢𝄢𝄢𝄢 (Blue Note, 1985) is a rollicking and diverse outing, featuring Stevie Ray Vaughan, Dr. John, and John Scofield. The songs range from "Is It True What They Say about Dixie?" and "Tennessee Waltz" to the New Orleans–centric "Saint Expedito" and "All Night Dance." Wallace's extended cadenza on the title track makes the disc worth the price.

influences:
◀◀ Sonny Rollins, Eric Dolphy

James Eason

Fats Waller
Born Thomas Wright Waller, May 21, 1904, in New York, NY. Died December 15, 1943, in Kansas City, MO.

Fats Waller, one of the great showmen of jazz, a terrific organist, an underrated solist, and an important figure who worked with Bessie Smith, Sidney Bechet, and Fletcher Henderson, first became famous in the '20s with enduring hits such as "Honeysuckle Rose" and "Ain't Misbehavin'."

Waller, whose father was a street-corner preacher with his own trucking business, began his career playing organ during his father's services. His first paying job came when he was 15 years old as he became the house organist at the Lincoln Theatre. In the early 1920s, he became a protege of the great Harlem stride pianist James P. Johnson, and through him he cut player piano rolls and lined up his first recording date. He also started accompanying a number of classic blues singers (including Bessie Smith and Alberta Hunter) and writing songs.

By the end of the '20s, Waller was becoming a force in New York City jazz. He did regular radio broadcasts and had already recorded with stars like Fletcher Henderson, Clarence Williams, and Sidney Bechet, and his songs were garnering both commercial and critical acclaim. With Andy Razaf, grandson of the former Madagascarian consul to the United States, he created such classics as "Honeysuckle Rose," "Ain't Misbehavin'," and "My Fate Is in Your Hands." With his recording career also in full swing, Waller made substantial contributions to dates led by Ted Lewis and Jack Teagarden. By the mid-'30s, Waller had created one of the finest small jazz groups of the time with the sextet Fats Waller and his Rhythm, and though he recorded a lot of material mandated by his record company—much of it trite, hackneyed themes—he still imbued it with wit and humor. (Gems included "Christopher Columbus," "Until the Real Thing Comes Along," and "Cabin in the Sky.") He also appeared in a variety of short films (including *Stormy Weather,* with Lena Horne) and radio shows, toured Europe, and played the organ in Paris' Notre Dame Cathedral. On a return train trip from Hollywood to New York City, after working a solo piano gig at the Zanzibar Room, he died of pneumonia.

what to buy: *Turn on the Heat—Piano Solos* 𝒜𝒜𝒜𝒜 (RCA/Bluebird, 1991, prod. various), which includes multiple takes from 1929 RCA sessions, is a must-have for anyone with more than a passing interest in great piano playing. It includes more than half the record dates from 1927 through 1934, the period when Waller's reputation as a pianist was beginning to pick up steam nationally. Classics like "Handful of Keys," "Ain't Misbehavin'," and "Smashing Thirds" are the highlights, but it is also instructive to hear the differences in two run-throughs of "Carolina Shout," the showpiece written by his mentor, James P. Johnson. *Greatest Hits* 𝒜𝒜𝒜𝒜 (RCA Victor, 1996, prod. various) has been around in various forms since the dawn of the LP era, but the CD remastering has improved it tremendously. It's a good sam-

pler for the neophyte, containing 14 big Waller hits, but the label could have included far more material. *Breakin' the Ice . . . The Early Years, Part 1 (1934–1935)* 𝒜𝒜𝒜𝒜 (RCA/Bluebird, 1995, prod. various) and *I'm Gonna Sit Right Down . . . The Early Years, Part 2 (1935–1936)* 𝒜𝒜𝒜𝒜 (RCA/Bluebird, 1995, prod. various) have better overall sound than the corresponding releases for Classics, although the latter contains better discography information. Songs like "A Porter's Love Song to a Chambermaid" and "Honeysuckle Rose" were deserved hits, but the solos on "Then I'll Be Tired of You" (from trumpeter Herman Autrey and altoist Mezz Mezzrow) and the bouncy instrumental "Serenade for a Wealthy Widow" are underrecognized classics. "I Got Rhythm," "Dinah," and the title song from the second album are higlights of *Part 2.*

what to buy next: The standard Fats Waller hits like "Ain't Misbehavin'" and "Honeysuckle Rose" aren't on *Fats and His Buddies* 𝒜𝒜𝒜𝒜 (RCA/Bluebird, 1992, reissue prod. Orrin Keepnews), but it's still the perfect single-disc complement for a greatest hits set. On material from 1927 through 1929, Waller plays in three different group configurations, revealing his skills at the pipe organ. The Louisiana Sugar Babes' material with James P. Johnson on piano and Waller on organ is particularly delightful, though it doesn't quite capture the two men's greatness. *Fats Waller and His Rhythm, The Middle Years: Part I* 𝒜𝒜𝒜𝒜 (RCA/Bluebird, 1992, prod. various) and *A Good Man Is Hard to Find, The Middle Years: Part II* 𝒜𝒜𝒜𝒜 (RCA/Bluebird, 1995, prod. various) represent 1936 to 1940, during which Waller reveled in vocal shtick. He still played prodigious piano, but seemed to realize that pop tastes preferred bouncy melodies, cleversounding lyrics, and outrageous mugging rather than straightforward instrumental genius. But these performances aren't trite, especially when compared to much of the stuff his contemporaries were unleashing in faux Waller style. Especially affecting are his takes on "Yacht Club Swing," "Hold Tight," and the alternate takes of "I'll Dance at Your Wedding," where maudlin sentimentality, fortunately, loses to the pianist's formidable wit and skill. *The Jugglin' Jive of Fats Waller and his Orchestra* 𝒜𝒜𝒜𝒜 (Sandy Hook, 1985), a document of 1938 radio broadcasts from New York City, reveal Waller's live performance genius. The disc is filled with shameless mugging, double entendre asides, and plenty of classic Waller cuts, including "Honeysuckle Rose" and "Ain't Misbehavin'," with little gems like "Pent up in a Penthouse" and "Hallelujah."

what to avoid: There are a couple Waller titles on the market that unwary buyers could pick up in a careless moment and regret later. *Low Down Papa* 𝒜𝒜𝒜 (Biograph, 1990, prod. Arnold S.

Caplin) is actually quite interesting, taking player piano rolls that Waller "cut" for the QRS and Play-A-Roll companies, putting them on a modern player piano, and then recording the result in digital sound. *Fats at the Organ* **woof!** (ASV, 1992) is another matter, however, because it takes piano rolls and transcribes them for organ. While Waller did play the organ, the approach he used was different than the one he used for piano, making these mechanical transcriptions more than one step away from the real thing.

best of the rest:

Last Years: Fats Waller and His Rhythm, 1940–1943 ♫♫♫ (RCA, 1989)
1936 ♫♫♫ (Classics, 1995)
1936–1937 ♫♫♫ (Classics, 1995)
1937 ♫♫♫ (Classics, 1995)
1929–1934 ♫♫♫ (Classics, 1996)
1934–1935 ♫♫♫ (Classics, 1996)
1935 ♫♫♫ (Classics, 1996)
1935, Vol. 2 ♫♫♫ (Classics, 1996)
1935–1936 ♫♫♫ (Classics, 1996)
1937, Vol. 2 ♫♫♫ (Classics, 1996)
1937–1938 ♫♫♫ (Classics, 1996)
1939 ♫♫♫ (Classics, 1998)

worth searching for: Maurice Waller wrote a biography of his famous father with Anthony Calabrese, *Fats Waller* (Macmillan/Schirmer Books, 1977), which reads well, if a tad starchy. The senior Waller was also one of the first major jazz artists ever bootlegged, pre-dating all those European concert recordings that keep showing up on the market—organ solos from the RCA vaults emerged when some enterprising soul compiled them and released two 10-inch vinyl albums on the Jolly Roger label.

influences:

◀◀ Luckey Roberts, James P. Johnson, Willie "the Lion" Smith

▶▶ Art Tatum, Teddy Wilson, Count Basie

Garaud MacTaggart

George Wallington

Born Giancinto Figlia, October 27, 1924, in Palermo, Sicily, Italy. Died February 15, 1993, in New York, NY.

Although the names of Bud Powell and Thelonious Monk are more commonly mentioned when considering the early bebop piano stylists, George Wallington played a significant part in the development of the new music. A native of Italy, Wallington was the son of an opera singer and he immigrated to the United States with his family just prior to his first birthday. His earliest work of considerable merit was as part of the Dizzy Gillespie group, the first bebop combo to play on New York's famed 52nd Street. Through the mid-1950s, Wallington worked with an impressive number of jazz luminaries, including Charlie Parker, Red Rodney, Zoot Sims, Gerry Mulligan, Serge Chaloff, Kai Winding, and Terry Gibbs. He would also form and lead his own quintet that featured up-and-comers of the time trumpeter Donald Byrd and altoist Phil Woods, making several consummate albums for the Prestige label prior to the end of the decade. Any one of these recordings will reveal the great fluidity and technical expertise that marked Wallington's archetypal playing. A cerebral musician in some ways, he nonetheless played with a great deal of swing and joyful exuberance. A sad loss for jazz fans, Wallington left the music scene in 1960 to labor in his family's business, only briefly returning in the mid-1980s to record three albums. His death in 1993 cut short any chances of further musical activity and possible rediscovery by a new generation of jazz listeners and followers.

what to buy: *Jazz for the Carriage Trade* ♫♫♫♫ (Prestige, 1956/OJC,1991, prod. Bob Weinstock) is a hard-bop delight that prominently features Donald Byrd and Phil Woods. A tasty program that includes Tadd Dameron's "Our Delight" provides solid inspiration for all the soloists, particularly Wallington. *The New York Scene* ♫♫♫♫ (New Jazz, 1957/OJC, 1992, prod. Bob Weinstock) benefits from the solid front line of Byrd and Woods and from several of their original tunes. In addition, drummer Nick Stabulas proves to be a propulsive and valuable player who has been sadly forgotten.

what to buy next: *Jazz at Hotchkiss* ♫♫♫♫ (Savoy, 1957/Savoy Jazz, 1995, prod. Ozzie Cadena) would be Wallington's last recording before his retirement from music. The incendiary bop mood is again in full force with Wallington's ballad original, "Before Dawn," a standout.

the rest:

The George Wallington Trios ♫♫♫ (Prestige, 1949–51/OJC, 1991)
Live at the Cafe Bohemia ♫♫♫ (Prestige, 1955/OJC, 1992)
Pleasure of a Jazz Inspiration ♫♫♫ (VSOP, 1985/1995)

Chris Hovan

Winston Walls

Born 1939, in Ironton, OH.

Based out of Charleston, West Virginia, keyboardist Winston Walls is a club circuit legend deserving of a wider audience. His technique, harmonic concept, and stage presence is a collection of qualities that lesser, more popular organists would love to have, but Walls seems destined to wander the back roads of fame, a textbook example of potential hampered by the vagaries of fate. Walls is the son of blues pianist Harry Van Walls, and he began playing piano in church as a youth, although he first tasted the life of a professional musician by playing drums for organist Bill Doggett. This led to Walls's first gigs as an organist, as he stopped playing drums and started adapting his piano technique to the organ. As an organist, Walls hit the road as a sideman for R&B acts like Dionne Warwick, Al Green, and the Ike and Tina Turner Revue while his jazz gigs found him playing alongside Lou Donaldson and Sonny Stitt. With a growing family to support, Walls also took on a series of colorful jobs, as a stand-up comic and a professional wrestler. At one time Walls and Jack McDuff were both looking for a guitarist to join their bands and the competition for a young guitarist named George Benson was fairly hot and heavy, with McDuff finally getting the nod from the future jazz giant. Since that time Walls has continued working with a series of regional players, but not until recording his only album (so far) did he get a chance to work again with a musician of national stature. Ironically it was with his old rival and friend, Jack McDuff.

what's available: *Boss of the B-3* 𝄢𝄢𝄢𝄢 (Schoolkids, 1993, prod. Stephen Bergman, Michael Lipton), a live recording, documents a vanishing jazz music rite: the organ battle. Part of the album features Walls and McDuff wailing on each other with fierce delight, telling tales and escalating the groove to a blazing fire before rolling low-down, soulful chords along the bass pedals. McDuff's tone is the lighter, more percussive one, while Walls's sound is massive, all-encompassing in technique, volume, and showmanship. Walls's rendition of "How Great Thou Art" is a virtuoso performance with a range of tonal color and chordal nuance that places him comfortably among the giants on his instrument.

influences:

◀◀ Bill Doggett, Richard "Groove" Holmes, Jimmy McGriff, Jack McDuff

▶▶ Bobby Watley

Garaud MacTaggart

Jack Walrath

Born May 5, 1946, in Stuart, FL.

The last in a distinguished line of trumpeters to work for Charles Mingus, Jack Walrath also served as chief arranger for the great bassist/composer during Mingus's last few years. Before that, he had worked in various R&B bands (including a year spent with Ray Charles) and a fistful of Latin ensembles in addition to playing in jazz groups. After Mingus's death, Walrath started his own band, the Masters of Suspense, in addition to playing with the Mingus Dynasty, among others. Walrath's playing is not, strictly speaking, from the Miles Davis or Clifford Brown schools of performance—it sounds more like the exuberant, wide-open style of Louis Armstrong crossed with the twisted humor of Lester Bowie.

what to buy: The title of *Out of the Tradition* 𝄢𝄢𝄢𝄢 (Muse, 1992, prod. Don Sickler), a 1990 Masters of Suspense session, is a bit tongue-in-cheek, as most of the playlist contains classics from Duke Ellington, Harold Arlen, Mingus, and others, plus a twisted version of the Bach cantata "Wachet Auf!" that the trumpeter calls "Wake up and Wash It Off!" There is also a wonderful rendition of "Brother Can You Spare a Dime" with a superb bass solo. *Hipgnosis* 𝄢𝄢𝄢𝄢 (TCB, 1995, prod. Peter Burli), recorded while the Masters of Suspense were on their first European tour, showcases Walrath's genial refusal of the status quo. This time, with the exception of Mingus's "Eclipse," all the tunes were composed by the trumpeter. In addition to Walrath's usual sterling performance, guitarist David Fiuczynski serves as another demented soulmate to the leader's already idiosyncratic vision of humor and art.

what to buy next: *Serious Hang* 𝄢𝄢𝄢𝄢 (Muse, 1994, prod. Don Sickler, Jack Walrath), with another Masters of Suspense edition, approximates the sound of funky organ groups from the '60s doing a futuristic workout. Along for the ride this time are guitarist Fiuczynski and Walrath's former Mingus compatriot, Don Pullen, playing organ. The trumpeter/leader covers a lot of ground, arranging a Bulgarian folk tune ("Izlyal E Delyo Haidoutin"), a James Brown classic ("Get on the Good Foot"), and the almost obligatory Mingus composition ("Better Get Hit in Your Soul"), in addition to a couple tunes from Pullen and himself. Half the material on *Portraits in Ivory and Brass* 𝄢𝄢𝄢𝄢 (Mapleshade, 1994, prod. Larry Willis, Jack Walrath, Pierre Sprey) consists of duets between Walrath and pianist Larry Willis. While this album reveals that Walrath is not a pretty player, it does show that his instrumental intellect and compositional skills make him an effective player. Especially interesting is his tune "Monk's Feet," an uncanny simulacre of Thelonious Monk's style that avoids aping it slavishly.

the rest:

In Montana 𝄢𝄢𝄢 (Jazz Alliance, 1980)
Wholly Trinity 𝄢𝄢𝄢𝄢 (Muse, 1986)
Gut Feelings 𝄢𝄢𝄢 (Muse, 1991)
Hi Jinx 𝄢𝄢𝄢 (Stash, 1993)

In Europe 🎵🎵🎵 (SteepleChase, 1995)
Journey Man 🎵🎵🎵🎵 (Evidence, 1996)

influences:

◀◀ Charles Mingus, Thelonious Monk, Louis Armstrong

▶▶ Lester Bowie

Garaud MacTaggart

Cedar Walton

Born January 17, 1934, in Dallas, TX.

Pianist Cedar Walton is one of modern jazz's great accompanists, a supremely elegant bop-based stylist who is known for his indefatigable swing and well-constructed solos. He is also a fine composer who has penned a number of standards, including "Bolivia," "Holy Land," "Ugetsu," and "Mode for Joe." Walton's first influence was his mother, a piano teacher who started instructing him at a young age. He studied music at the University of Denver in the early 1950s and moved to New York in 1955, but was soon drafted into the Army; he played with Eddie Harris, Don Ellis, and Leo Wright while stationed in Germany. Returning from the Army, he quickly broke into the New York scene, debuting on trumpeter Kenny Dorham's forgettable session of vocals *This Is the Moment*, and landing a steady gig with J.J. Johnson from 1958 to 1960. Walton participated in John Coltrane's classic 1959 *Giant Steps* album (including many out takes that surfaced on Rhino's Coltrane box set *The Heavyweight Champion*) and replaced McCoy Tyner in Art Farmer and Benny Golson's Jazztet (1960–61) when Tyner joined Trane's quartet. Walton really made his mark during his three-year stint with Art Blakey (1961–64), contributing a number of tunes and arrangements to the book of what was arguably the greatest incarnation of the Jazz Messengers, featuring Freddie Hubbard, Wayne Shorter, and Curtis Fuller. After a couple of years as Abbey Lincoln's accompanist (1965–66), Walton became the house pianist for Prestige, forming a rhythm section partnership with drummer Billy Higgins that ranks as one of the great collaborations in modern jazz (a relationship that continues today). Walton also played on many excellent Blue Note and Riverside sessions in the mid-1960s with trumpeter Lee Morgan and tenor saxophonists Hank Mobley, Jimmy Heath, Clifford Jordan, and Joe Henderson. Walton formed a group with Mobley in the early 1970s, rejoined Blakey in 1973 for a tour of Japan, and formed a trio and then quartet with Higgins in the mid-1970s that eventually recorded under the name Eastern Rebellion, featuring a succession of bassists and saxophonists including Clifford Jordan, George Coleman, Bob Berg, Ralph Moore, and Vincent Herring. In the late 1960s and 1970s, Walton recorded a number of albums using keyboards and experimenting with electronics, but since the 1980s he has worked almost exclusively in acoustic contexts. Walton has recorded extensively for Muse, SteepleChase, Red, Criss Cross, and Timeless (both as a leader and with the Timeless All-Stars), though many of these albums have not been reissued yet on CD. Walton continues to be one of the busiest accompanists in jazz, recording with both veteran players and up-and-coming musicians.

what to buy: Walton plays mostly his own tunes on *Cedar!* 🎵🎵🎵🎵 (Prestige, 1967/OJC, 1993, prod. Don Schlitten), a strong, hard-blowing session that features a number of trio pieces with Leroy Vinnegar (bass) and Billy Higgins (drums), and quartet and quintet tracks with the underrated tenor saxophonist Junior Cook and trumpeter Kenny Dorham, who takes a beautiful solo on Walton's "Turquoise Twice." Walton's mid-tempo reworking of Ellington's "Come Sunday," featuring the quintet, is another highlight. Everything comes together on *Eastern Rebellion* 🎵🎵🎵🎵 (Impulse!, 1975, prod. Cedar Walton), a majestic quartet session featuring tenor saxophonist George Coleman, bassist Sam Jones, and drummer Billy Higgins. Coleman has never sounded better than on the 10-minute version of Walton's standard "Bolivia," powered by Jones's propulsive bass work. Walton waxes lush and lyrical on Coltrane's "Naima" and Coleman stretches out on Walton's "Mode for Joe." A highly recommended album. Recorded live at Yoshi's Nitespot in Oakland in 1989, *Ironclad* 🎵🎵🎵🎵 (Monarch, 1995, prod. Bud Spangler) is a typically swinging trio date featuring bassist David Williams and drummer Billy Higgins. Among Walton's many fine trio sessions, this one stands out for his four original compositions, including the multifaceted 14-minute title track and the Latin-tinged "Fiesta Español." Check out Higgins's subtle march pattern on Walton's "N.P.S." The trio also turns in gorgeous nine-minute versions of "My Old Flame" and "Over the Rainbow." Acoustic straight-ahead jazz wasn't thriving when Walton, tenor saxophonist Clifford Jordan, bassist Sam Jones, and drummer Louis Hayes recorded the 1974 Muse releases *A Night at Boomer's, Vol. 1* and *A Night at Boomer's, Vol. 2*, but these two albums gave the lie to the "jazz is dead" line. These albums have been combined and reissued on a single CD as *Naima* 🎵🎵🎵🎵 (32 Jazz, 1997, prod. Don Schlitten). The first volume is a hard-charging session highlighted by Walton's "Holy Land" and Sonny Rollins's "St. Thomas." The second volume focuses more on lush standards, such as Coltrane's "Naima," "Stella by Starlight," and an almost 12-minute tour de force, "Blue Monk." Exceptional music.

what to buy next: Walton's first album exclusively featuring his own tunes and arrangements, *Composer* 🎵🎵🎵🎵 (Astor Place, 1996, prod. Don Sickler) is the work of a master craftsman using only the best materials. Bassist Christian McBride and drummer Victor Lewis share rhythm section duties, while Roy Hargrove (trumpet), Vincent Herring (alto sax), and Ralph Moore (tenor and soprano sax) fill out the sextet, giving Walton a potent, hard-bop oriented band. Walton's playing is typically swinging and incisive throughout, but it's the imaginative ways he uses the band to develop his melodic themes that make this an important addition to his discography. The 25th volume in the Maybeck Recital Hall Series, *Cedar Walton at Maybeck Recital Hall, Vol. 25* 🎵🎵🎵🎵 (Concord Jazz, 1993, prod. Carl E. Jefferson) captures him in an expansive and serious mood. A solo sitting, there's no real new ground here, just gorgeous playing by a musician who has come to represent the very best of bebop-based piano work. Unfortunately, he only covers two originals, a blues he wrote for the occasion and "Bremond's Blues." Otherwise he finds gold in well-worn standards such as "Stella by Starlight," "Darn That Dream," and his first recorded version of "Sweet Lorraine." The first Eastern Rebellion album in about a decade, *Mosaic* 🎵🎵🎵🎵 (MusicMasters, 1992, prod. John Snyder) features a new version of the quartet with tenor saxophonist Ralph Moore and bassist David Williams joining the inimitable partnership of Walton and drummer Billy Higgins. Each player contributes at least one tune to the session, including a thrilling, breakneck version of Walton's title track. Other highlights include Freddie Hubbard's "Sunflower," Moore's lyrical work on "My One and Only Love," and Sam Jones's "Bittersweet," a tune from the first Eastern Rebellion album.

what to avoid: Two trio tracks, "I Should Care" and Clare Fischer's "Pensativa" with bassist Reggie Workman and drummer Tootie Heath, keep *Soul Cycle* 🎵🎵 (Prestige, 1969/OJC, 1995, prod. Don Schlitten) from being a dog, 'cause the rest of the session features Walton on a personality-erasing electric piano, attempting to score hits with, at the worst, a lame version of Stevie Wonder's "My Cherie Amour." Even the presence of saxophonist James Moody doesn't redeem this one.

best of the rest:
Spectrum 🎵🎵🎵 (Prestige, 1968–69/1994)
Breakthrough! 🎵🎵🎵🎵 (Cobblestone/Muse, 1977)
Eastern Rebellion 2 🎵🎵🎵 (Timeless, 1979)
The Maestro 🎵🎵🎵🎵 (Muse, 1981)
Bluesville Time 🎵🎵🎵🎵 (Criss Cross, 1985/1994)
Cedar Walton Plays 🎵🎵🎵 (Delos, 1987)
First Set 🎵🎵🎵🎵 (SteepleChase, 1987/1994)
Second Set 🎵🎵🎵🎵 (SteepleChase, 1988/1994)
As Long As There's Music 🎵🎵🎵🎵 (Muse, 1990)
St. Thomas 🎵🎵🎵🎵 (Evidence, 1991)
My Funny Valentine 🎵🎵🎵 (Evidence, 1991)
Among Friends 🎵🎵🎵🎵 (Evidence, 1992)
Manhattan Afternoon 🎵🎵🎵🎵 (Criss Cross, 1993)
Simple Pleasure 🎵🎵🎵🎵 (MusicMasters, 1993)
Cedar's Blues 🎵🎵🎵🎵 (Red, 1995)
The Art Blakey Legacy 🎵🎵🎵🎵 (Evidence, 1997)

influences:

◀◀ Bud Powell, Kenny Drew, Red Garland

▶▶ Mulgrew Miller, George Cables

Andrew Gilbert

David S. Ware

Born November 7, 1949, in Plainfield, NJ.

David Ware is a tenor saxophonist of power and imagination. Although Ware is identified with free jazz, Sonny Rollins was a mentor, and in his own way Ware draws on the breadth of jazz history. He has a broad, meaty tone in all ranges of his horn, even in the altissimo register. In 1990 he began recording with a quartet including pianist Matthew Shipp and bassist William Parker, and with changes in the drum chair, that has been Ware's group ever since and has become one of the most cohesive units on the scene. Ware made his first album as a leader in 1988 for the Swedish label Silkheart, and in 1990 he recorded his first two quartet albums for the same company. At that time the drummer was Marc Edwards, with whom Ware had played in the Cecil Taylor Unit. Whit Dickey later held the drum chair, and lately has been replaced by Susie Ibarra.

Ware started playing around age 11, taking up alto and baritone sax and bass in school while practicing tenor sax outside school. He moved to Boston in 1967, going to college, studying with Charlie Mariano and Joe Viola, and performing with Michael Brecker, Herb Pomeroy's big band, and Bob Neloms. He moved to New York City in 1973 and in 1974 played with Cecil Taylor for the first time. He was a regular member of Taylor's band for a year and a half in 1976–77, as documented on *Dark to Themselves*. His time with Taylor has had a continuing influence on Ware's music. He realized later that, young and bursting with energy, he hadn't been fully exploiting the potential of Taylor's compositions—he had been improvising above them rather than from within them, using the materials they contained. This realization helped make him a more melodic player and writer, which is not to say his intense free jazz outlook was compromised, just deepened. It was in the 1970s that

Ware, who had met Sonny Rollins while still in his mid-teens, began practicing regularly with the tenor statesman. After leaving Taylor's group, Ware joined drummer Andrew Cyrille's Maono and can be heard with Cyrille on *Metamusician's Stomp* on Black Saint, *Special People* on Soul Note, and more. In the same period he also played in the groups of two other drummers, Milford Graves and Beaver Harris, and performed as a leader on the loft scene.

Dutch filmmaker Coco Schrijber made a 25-minute documentary about Ware, *In Motion,* which was released in Europe. It mixes concert footage of Ware's powerful quartet with an interview taped as he drove his cab around Manhattan (his rent-paying gig since 1981) at nighttime.

what to buy: *flight of i* 𝄞𝄞𝄞𝄞 (DIW/Sony, 1992, prod. Kazunori Sugiyama) is the best of the early albums with Marc Edwards on drums. It's perhaps the most accessible of Ware's albums, and not only because it contains two familiar standards, "There Will Never Be Another You" and "Yesterdays." The opening track, "Aquarian Sound," is a modal groover with an easy-to-follow structure. On the stunning title track, Ware's sustained circular-breathing solo flies with hair-raising intensity above bell-like chords that vividly show Shipp's relation to Scriabi-nesque harmony. This is free jazz, yes, but not in the sense of free improvisation; even at its most "outside" *flight of i* shows careful planning, and the quartet's method of building its music from Ware-penned patterns is at its clearest. *Third Ear Recitation* 𝄞𝄞𝄞𝄞 (DIW, 1993, prod. Kazunori Sugiyama) is framed by two versions of the standard "Autumn Leaves," with Shipp's big piano chords playing it straight—cocktail piano on steroids—as Ware goes outside the chord changes in passionate blowing and drummer Whit Dickey plays three rhythms at once. On Ware's originals (the bulk of the album), Shipp alternates between skitters across the keyboard and solemn chords built on fourths over which Ware improvises like a man obsessed with transcendence.

what to buy next: After a period of somewhat insular complexity on the Homestead albums, *Wisdom of Uncertainty* 𝄞𝄞𝄞𝄞 (AUM Fidelity, 1997, prod. David S. Ware) returned the quartet to a less dense expression of its ideas. Ware's burly tone is capable of surprising agility, and when he's got the space to move around in, the diversity of his influences comes through more audibly. On her second album with the group, drummer Susie Ibarra's pointillistic (and emergingly muscular) playing provides a springboard for all with her multiplicity of rhythmic subdivisions. The group as a whole packs a gigantic impact, but

DAVID S. WARE

song "Utopic"
album *Wisdom of Uncertainty*
(AUM Fidelity, 1997)
instrument Tenor saxophone

there are also moments of pensive beauty, as on the tinkling introduction of "Sunbows Rainsets Blue." *DAO* 𝄞𝄞𝄞𝄞 (Homestead, 1996, prod. David S. Ware) was Ware's best Homestead disc, an abstract concept album that loosely builds off Taoist tenets to liberate expression and creativity. Constructing music spontaneously and organically from motivic cells, the quartet amplifies strong emotional expression through varied near-repetition that intensifies hypnotically.

the rest:
Passage to Music 𝄞𝄞𝄞 (Silkheart, 1988)
Great Bliss, vol. 1 𝄞𝄞𝄞 (Silkheart, 1990)
Great Bliss, vol. 2 𝄞𝄞𝄞 (Silkheart, 1990)
Earthquation 𝄞𝄞𝄞𝄞 (DIW, 1994)
Cryptology 𝄞𝄞𝄞 (Homestead, 1995)
Godspelized 𝄞𝄞𝄞𝄞 (DIW, 1996)

worth searching for: The multiple-artist compilation *What Is Jazz? 1996* 𝄞𝄞𝄞𝄞 (Knitting Factory Works, 1996, prod. Brett Heinz, Mark Perlson), recorded at the eponymous annual festival, includes the otherwise unavailable "In This Love," a hurricane-force gust of free improv.

influences:

◀◀ Frank Wright, John Coltrane, Albert Ayler, Gene Ammons

▶▶ Charles Gayle, Assif Tsahar, Glenn Spearman

Steve Holtje

Wilbur Ware

Born Bernard Ware, September 8, 1923, in Chicago, IL. Died September 9, 1979, in Philadelphia, PA.

Although he recorded only one album as a leader, Wilbur Ware made his mark as the house bassist for Riverside Records, participating on some of the label's finest recordings. Ware developed his playing around the rhythm, with a heavy, percussive style. Yet he was flexible enough to be in demand from a wide variety of players, including Lee Morgan, Zoot Sims, Sonny Rollins, and Grant Green. He began his music career teaching himself banjo, but after his father gave him a bass, Ware knew he had found his instrument. He started doing gigs around town and in New York, eventually playing with Stuff Smith, Roy Eldridge, Sonny Stitt, Joe Williams, and Eddie "Cleanhead" Vinson, among others. In the mid-'50s, Ware hooked up with Thelonious Monk and recorded regularly with his group, including a 1957 date at the Five Spot with John Coltrane. He worked prolifically until an illness forced him into semi-retirement in 1963, but continued to work sporadically with groups including Clifford Jordan, Blue Mitchell, Archie Shepp, and Sun Ra until his death.

what to buy: *Sonny Rollins: A Night at the Village Vanguard, Vols. 1 & 2* ♪♪♪♪ (Blue Note, 1958, prod. Alfred Lion) is a classic, as evidenced on the adventurous playing on "Softly As in a Morning Sunrise."

what to buy next: *The Chicago Sound* ♪♪♪♪ (Riverside, 1958, prod. Orrin Keepnews), Ware's only album as a leader, is exceptional, although the saxophonists (both fellow Chicagoans) get most of the highlights. Ware is his usual role-playing self—steady and inventive, but satisfied to remain relatively in the background.

influences:

◀◀ Jimmy Blanton, Walter Page

▶▶ Ray Brown, Richard Davis

Eric J. Lawrence

Dinah Washington

Born Ruth Lee Jones, August 29, 1924, in Tuscaloosa, AL. Died December 14, 1963, in Detroit, MI.

Honored with a postage stamp by the U.S. Postal Service in 1993, 30 years after her death, Dinah Washington's popularity as a blues, gospel, jazz, and pop singer has continued to swell as we move into the new millennium. Buoyed by the success of "Soft Winds" and "Blue Gardenia" in the film *The Bridges of Madison County,* Mercury has continued to release new compilations of her work and reissue older releases, allowing new generations to discover her artistry as a vocalist and performer. Born in Alabama, Washington moved to Chicago at age three. She played piano at church, won a talent contest for singing "I Can't Face the Music" at age 15, and had joined Lionel Hampton's band as a singer by 18. However, Decca, the label Hampton was signed with, was not interested in Washington, so she began recording with Hampton backing her up on some of her early sides with songs penned by jazz critic Leonard Feather, who had been impressed by her debut at the Apollo. These were bluesy songs that led to more associations with great players such as Milt Jackson and Charles Mingus in 1945. Known to be volatile, Washington finally left Hampton's band in 1946, the same year she was signed with the newly formed Mercury Records, an association that would last 15 years.

As Washington's career progressed, she drifted further away from the blues, although she did pen and record "Long John Blues," a tantalizing double entendre about a dentist, in 1947. Her singing became more jazz influenced throughout the remainder of the 1940s, and she eventually became a leading stylist who was able to become a successful crossover artist in the 1950s. Washington's vocals on love songs touched audiences, and her personal life was as tumultuous as the emotions she sang, as she married nine different times. Eventually, she began incorporating more popular standards by the likes of Irving Berlin, Cole Porter, and the Gershwins, finally scoring a pop song hit with "What a Diff'rence a Day Makes," but she sang the lyrics as "makes" leading to some collections using the wrong title for the song. From this point on, Washington used lush orchestras to back her up, and she sang mostly slow ballads, trying to repeat the formula. One way that she continued to follow that popular vein was by teaming up with Brook Benton for duets such as "Baby, You've Got What It Takes." She signed with Roulette in 1961, but her music was not as compelling. However, she did make *Back to the Blues* in 1962, and demonstrated what she still could do vocally on blues songs. Dead at 39 from an overdose of alcohol and diet pills, Washington's catalog continues to grow, and her influence on blues, jazz, and pop music is steady as ever.

what to buy: The import *Dinah Washington—The Complete Volume 1* 𝄞𝄞𝄞𝄞 (Official, 1988) is definitive for the early blues sides that Washington cut between 1943 and 1945. It opens with "Evil Gal Blues," penned by Leonard Feather specifically for her, as well as three other cuts he wrote, including "Salty Papa Blues," which opens with some muted trumpet while Washington's voice sounds seductive and tough at the same time, a trick she uses on Charles Mingus's "Pacific Coast Blues," too. These 17 tracks alone would be enough to secure Washington's place in the blues. The two discs of *First Issue: The Dinah Washington Story (The Original Recordings)* 𝄞𝄞𝄞𝄞 (Mercury, 1993, prod. Michael Lang, Richard Seidel) offer a great overview of Washington's career on Mercury, and also include two of the early sides from Keynote. Disc one is the better, and it includes Washington compositions such as "Postman Blues," which sounds like a personal letter to an old lover, and "Record Ban Blues," which captured the woes of artists like Washington for the upcoming record ban of 1947. Disc two has its highlights: "Blue Gardenia," "Lover, Come Back to Me," and a cover of Bessie Smith's "Back Water Blues." *The Complete Dinah Washington on Mercury, Vol. 1 (1946–49)* 𝄞𝄞𝄞𝄞 (Mercury, 1987, prod. Kiyoshi Koyama) is the first of seven boxed sets that Mercury did in the late 1980s covering the nearly 500 sides she recorded for the label. The set contains some tasty selections spread across the three discs, including alternate takes and previously unavailable material. While a bit much, it does capture that peak early period when Washington first got signed by Mercury.

what to buy next: *What a Diff'rence a Day Makes* 𝄞𝄞𝄞𝄞 (Mobile Fidelity Sound Lab, 1997) is the way to really hear Washington's vocals; her voice is as close, intimate, and crisp as being in the front row—the best of her pop music releases. Her ease at making us feel the nostalgia in "I Remember You," or her conviction that she has "locked her heart" in "I'm Thru with Love," are only the appetizers for the velvety and dreamy "What a Diff'rence a Day Makes." While most critics write off her late 1950s and early 1960s releases, *Back to the Blues* 𝄞𝄞𝄞𝄞 (Roulette, 1997, prod. Henry Glover) captures that moment when Washington made an effort to return to her roots, and while it might not quite get there, she handles the material in such a way that it recalls her best singing on those early records. Recorded only a year before her death, Washington, who co-wrote six of the tracks, sings with a conviction about relationships that rings quite true for the road she had traveled.

She closes the album with "Me and My Gin," and there's an ominous sense that she's long been living the song.

what to avoid: *Dinah '63* 𝄞𝄞 (Roulette, 1963/1990, prod. Henry Glover) is a return to the pop material that Washington was mining over those last years, but this set is especially pallid. She covers such tunes as "I Left My Heart in San Francisco" and "Bill," but they are pedestrian compared to her earlier work in popular tunes.

the rest:
The Bessie Smith Songbook 𝄞𝄞𝄞𝄞 (EmArcy, 1986)
Compact Jazz 𝄞𝄞𝄞𝄞 (Mercury, 1986)
The Complete Dinah Washington on Mercury, Vol. 2 (1950–52) 𝄞𝄞𝄞𝄞 (Mercury, 1987)
The Complete Dinah Washington on Mercury, Vol. 3 (1952–54) 𝄞𝄞𝄞𝄞 (Mercury, 1988)
The Complete Dinah Washington on Mercury, Vol. 4 (1954–56) 𝄞𝄞𝄞𝄞 (Mercury, 1988)
The Complete Dinah Washington on Mercury, Vol. 5 (1956–58) 𝄞𝄞𝄞𝄞 (Mercury, 1989)
Verve Jazz Masters 19 𝄞𝄞𝄞𝄞 (Verve, 1994)
Blue Gardenia 𝄞𝄞𝄞𝄞 (EmArcy, 1995)

influences:
◄◄ Bessie Smith

►► Etta James, Natalie Cole, Rachelle Ferrell

John Koetzner

Grover Washington Jr.

Born December 12, 1943, in Buffalo, NY.

Perhaps no artist is more frustrating to jazz purists than Grover Washington Jr. They want to dismiss him as a pop saxophonist, but they know they can't because he's an excellent improviser, a good writer, a smooth performer, and he can play straight-ahead with the best. But what really irks them is, with the possible exception of David Sanborn, no other sax player has inspired so many banal imitators. At least Washington can play—well.

The multi-reedman's success has had some interesting twists. Though he'd built up a solid reputation as a session player for Charles Earland and John Hammond, and became one of the house musicians for CTI, his first solo recording, *Inner City Blues*, was the result of Crawford missing a scheduled recording date. The album was a hit and Washington's next few recordings, like many of the CTI albums of the period, merged traditional jazz and soul. They were also popular and put Washington in more demand as a session player. In the late '70s, Washington jumped to Motown, where his sound became smoother and more refined. But it was *Winelight*, his second release on Elektra, that put him over the top. The smooth, R&B-laced jazz record yielded the Top Two smash "Just the Two of Us," which featured Bill Withers on vocals, went gold, and took home two Grammys (the irony here is Withers was signed to Columbia, yet this turned out to be the soul singer's biggest hit). After a few more pop-jazz albums, which were good but had the typical throwaway vocal tracks, Washington co-led a straight-ahead date with Kenny Burrell on 1984's *Togethering* and recorded his first straight-ahead date as a solo leader in 1988 with *Then and Now*, which solidified his reputation as a serious player.

Washington continues to be the top sax player in adult-contemporary jazz, keeping on top of new trends and applying them when they fit his style with good and bad results. He is also an excellent marketer and showman who keeps live audiences mesmerized. His albums have spawned many imitators, but those imitators usually only focus on his tone or his grooves, and not on his playing, which is rooted in the tradition of John Coltrane, Sonny Rollins, Stanley Turrentine, and Cannonball Adderley. Despite the occasional rut, Washington is likely to be on top for a long time and hopefully will return to recording his superb traditional albums.

what to buy: *Winelight* 𝄞𝄞𝄞𝄞 (Elektra, 1980, prod. Grover Washington Jr., Ralph MacDonald), the quintessential smooth-jazz recording, has serious hooks and serious playing. Washington plays sexy and hot, and no sax player sounds better blowing over a groove. The must-have album, still fresh after 15 years, is the type of soul-jazz that inspired some to take up the sax and others to dim the lights. On *Then and Now* 𝄞𝄞𝄞𝄞 (Columbia, 1988, prod. Grover Washington Jr.), surrounding himself with Ron Carter, Tommy Flannagan, Herbie Hancock, and Marvin Smitty Smith, Washington proved he could lead a great straight-ahead date. On *All My Tomorrows* 𝄞𝄞𝄞𝄞𝄞 (Columbia, 1994, prod. Todd Barkan, Grover Washington Jr.), Washington plays euphoric straight-ahead ballads with a number of excellent sidemen, including Eddie Henderson, Robin Eubanks, Hank Jones, and Freddy Cole.

what to buy next: *Inner City Blues* 𝄞𝄞𝄞 (Kudu, 1972/Motown, 1995), the auspicious debut, contains two Marvin Gaye songs, a Bill Withers song, some standards, arrangements by Bob James, strings, electric piano, and the CTI house band, and Washington shows he's not afraid to stretch out. *Come Morning* 𝄞𝄞𝄞 (Elektra, 1981), the follow-up to *Winelight*, didn't do the impossible by equaling it, but it is pleasant listening.

what to avoid: *Strawberry Moon* 𝄞𝄞 (Columbia, 1987) is one of the very few times Washington sounds as wimpy as his imitators.

the rest:
Mr. Magic 𝄞𝄞𝄞 (Kudu, 1975/Motown, 1995)
Paradise 𝄞𝄞𝄞 (Elektra, 1979)
The Best Is Yet to Come 𝄞𝄞𝄞 (Elektra, 1982)
Inside Moves 𝄞𝄞 (Elektra, 1984)
Anthology of Grover Washington Jr. 𝄞𝄞𝄞 (Elektra, 1985)
Time out of Mind 𝄞𝄞 (Columbia, 1989)
Next Exit 𝄞𝄞 (Columbia, 1992)
Soulful Strut 𝄞𝄞𝄞 (Columbia, 1996)

worth searching for: The balance of gritty (like his Kudu/CTI recordings) to polished (like his Motown dates) is just right on *Reed Seed* 𝄞𝄞𝄞𝄞 (Motown, 1978), as Washington sometimes blasts through with vigor, and sometimes seduces. His closing statements on Billy Joel's "Just the Way You Are" stay with you the rest of the night. *Skylarkin'* 𝄞𝄞𝄞𝄞 (Motown, 1980), more than any other recording, foreshadows *Winelight*. The playing is more erratic, but in some cases it's even smoother. Because Motown obviously doesn't know what to do with its jazz catalog, it should license it to a company that would give this and Washington's other Motown material proper attention. A collaboration with Kenny Burrell, *Togethering* 𝄞𝄞𝄞𝄞 (Blue Note, 1985) has what you'd call a lineup: Washington, Burrell, Ron Carter, Jack DeJohnette, and Ralph MacDonald. Any questions about Washington's ability to play "serious" jazz were put to rest with this fantastic release. The only pity is Washington and Burrell haven't made a follow-up—and the fact that this is out-of-print.

influences:

◀◀ Cannonball Adderley, John Coltrane, Stanley Turrentine, Eddie Harris, Sonny Rollins, Dexter Gordon, Gene Ammons

Paul MacArthur

Rob Wasserman

A talented though peripheral bassist on the jazz scene, Rob Wasserman plays a unique blend of jazz, bluegrass, folk, and rock. An excellent technician, Wasserman attended the San Francisco Conservatory of Music, and after a brief stint with the New Wave band Oingo Boingo he became a member of David Grisman's group in the late 1970s. Though he's played with a number of jazz figures, including Stephane Grappelli, he's garnered more acclaim in the bluegrass, folk, and rock circles for his associations with Grisman, the Grateful Dead, and Bob Weir's group Ratdog.

what to buy: *Solo* ✍✍✍ (Rounder, 1982, prod. David Grisman) contains 13 original solo bass performances, a challenging 30 minutes for both the listener and the player. There are some good melodies and Wasserman employs some interesting tricks, but, while this is an excellent playing clinic, it is lacking in strong compositions.

what to buy next: The other two available Wasserman albums are farther from jazz in varying degrees. *Duets* ✍✍✍ (MCA Jazz, 1988, prod. Rob Wasserman, Clare Wasserman) is, as advertised in its title, duets, sometimes with jazz musicians (Bobby McFerrin, Stephane Grappelli) but more often with pop singers (Aaron Neville, Jennifer Warnes, Ruben Blades, Rickie Lee Jones, Dan Hicks, Lou Reed). But jazz fans will find some of the material familiar, as "Autumn Leaves," "One for My Baby," "Stardust," "Angel Eyes," and "Over the Rainbow" figure in the program. *Bob Weir/Rob Wasserman: Live* ✍✍✍ (Grateful Dead Records, 1997, prod. John Cutler, Howard Danchik) pairs the bassist with Grateful Dead guitarist Bob Weir, who sings on all of the tracks. Not a jazz album at all, it still is a good folk-based, acoustic album that will appeal to fans of the Dead, Ratdog, and David Grisman.

worth searching for: Now out-of-print, *Trios* ✍✍✍ (GRP, 1994, prod. Rob Wasserman, John Cutler) is an eclectic recording of Wasserman in different trio settings, two of which are historic: the first appearance of Brian and Carnie Wilson together on record (a very good pop song), and the last recording made by Willie Dixon (some fun blues). Also joining in the festivities are Branford Marsalis/Bruce Hornsby, Edie Brickell/Jerry Garcia, and Neil Young/Bob Weir. By and large this really isn't a jazz record, but it's recommended because the different settings highlight Wasserman's versatility and there are some exceptional performances.

influences:

◀◀ Jimmy Blanton, Scott LaFaro, Charlie Haden, Dave Holland

Paul MacArthur

Benny Waters

Born January 23, 1902, in Brighton, MD.

Saxophonist Benny Waters has lived through all the major jazz eras and the entire history of jazz recording. He was playing jazz as it was being invented, and in late 1997 and into early 1998, Waters was still active, touring Europe for 10 weeks, per-

forming with the Max Weinberg Seven on the *Conan O'Brien Show,* celebrating the October release of his album *Live at 95* with a week-long engagement at Sweet Basil in New York City, and appearing at the 25th Annual International Association of Jazz Educators conference in New York City in January, 1998.

Waters grew up in a musical family, with three brothers and three sisters. By age five he was playing piano, and by age seven was giving piano recitals. His oldest brother, also a prodigy, introduced Waters to the E-flat clarinet. His mother died when Waters was eight and he went to live in Haverford, Pennsylvania, to be raised by his aunt and uncle, Mamie and Fred Garner. There, he began his professional career while still in high school playing hot syncopated music in the dance band of Charlie Miller (1918–21). Waters learned to play saxophones while with this pre-jazz band. Around age 18, Waters entered the Boston Conservatory of Music where he studied piano and theory. While at the Conservatory, Waters simultaneously taught private clarinet instruction, training Harry Carney years before the saxophonist joined the Duke Ellington Orchestra. While in Boston, Waters (playing piano) also worked with Johnny Hodges, who was then playing soprano sax. By this time, Waters was playing all the saxophones and his gigging (often out-of-town) was overshadowing his studies. In 1924, Waters went to New York to play a show at Harlem's Lafayette Theatre, and while there heard Louis Armstrong with Fletcher Henderson's Orchestra. Inspired, Waters left Boston and school and, based in Philadelphia, sought full-time work as a dance band musician.

The turning point in his career came in the summer of 1926 when Waters was invited to join the band of pianist Charlie Johnson in Atlanta. He remained with the band from the time it traveled to New York, became the house band (until 1932) at Small's Paradise in Harlem, until it folded around 1933. During the next two decades, he worked with a number of groups, including six months with Fletcher Henderson in 1935 and stints with Hot Lips Page, Claude Hopkins, and Jimmie Lunceford, recording with the latter two bands. Waters led his own band for four years in the 1940s and joined drummer Roy Milton's R&B band before hooking up with Jimmy Archey's Dixieland band for a month-long European tour. He easily found work in Europe, decided to expatriate, quit drinking, and eventually settled in Paris where he worked steadily from 1952 to 1992. He led a little group for about a decade in a Pigalle neighborhood club where Johnny Griffin, Dexter Gordon, Thelonious Monk, Bud Powell, and Sonny Criss would often sit in. Then, at age 67, Waters started a solo career, touring all over Europe. In 1979, he began his annual trips back to the USA. He recorded in 1987 for the first time as leader, an album for Muse titled *From Paradise (Small's) to Shangri-la*. Waters returned to the United States for cataract surgery, an operation which failed and left him blind. Undeterred, Waters resumed his career in New York City, practicing every day and receiving rave reviews for his performances on alto and tenor saxophones, clarinet, and for his baritone vocals. When you hear his recordings, you'll be gladdened (that he was still around for the sessions) and saddened (that we were deprived of 40 years of his contributions).

what to buy: Benny Waters was 85-years old when *From Paradise (Small's) to Shangri-la* 𝄡𝄡𝄡𝄡 (Muse, 1989, prod. Phil Schaap) was recorded in 1987 and, hearing his flawless robust-toned saxophone playing (alto and tenor), his smooth clarinet renderings, and his fine baritone voice, you'd never guess his age. Teamed with Don Coates (piano), Earl May (bass), and Ronnie Cole (drums), Waters delivers nine tunes with wonderful swinging vitality, often switching within one tune to play both alto and tenor, and putting his horns down momentarily to deliver, with crisp perfection, vocal versions of the novelty tunes, "Hit That Jive Jack" and "Romance without Finance." Originally released on LP, the CD reissue adds the bonus track, "'S' Wonderful." Whether singing or blowing his fluid saxisms, Waters never falters for one second. His spirited playing, supported by a skillful rhythm team, remains excellent all the way through this strong set. Waters climbed on the bandstand at the historically named new Birdland on Manhattan's West 44th Street on January 23, 1997 to record *Benny Waters Birdland Birthday: Live at 95* 𝄡𝄡𝄡𝄡 (Enja, 1997, prod. Matthias Winckelmann). The well-planned, nine-tune set performed with Mike LeDonne (Hammond b-3 organ, piano), Howard Alden and Steve Blailock (guitar), Earl May (bass), and Ed Locke (drums) highlights some fine blowing by the 95-year old. As evidenced on the first track, an up-tempo boppish version of "Exactly Like Me," Waters maintains (if not leads) the hard-swinging pace and hits the finishing upper register notes with crisp precision. When he slows the pace for his drawling original, "Blues Amore," his alto saxophone tone ranges from full-bodied blowing to soft subtleness injected with raspy seductive notes, with LeDonne embellishing the mood on the B-3, and Alden soloing with finesse. Waters sings and scats on the swinging version of "Everybody Loves My Baby," then picks up his alto to backing by the bouncy piano chops of LeDonne and punching rhythms from May and Locke. Just listen to his melody head on his original, "Callin' the Cats," a jump-swing number that should have you up and dancing. Throughout this live-recorded date, Wa-

ters, at 95, is a more imaginative and engaging improviser (at any tempo) than many players in their thirties. If you buy one of these albums, you'll want both.

what to buy next: Waters is at comfortable ease with his contemporaries (ranging in age from middle 60s to early 90s) on *Statesmen of Jazz* 𝄡𝄡𝄡𝄡 (American Federation of Jazz Societies, 1995, prod. Arbors Records), a December 20, 1994 session that prominently features him with Clark Terry (flugelhorn, trumpet), Joe Wilder (flugelhorn), Al Grey (trombone), Buddy Tate (tenor saxophone), Milt Hinton (bass), Claude Williams (violin), Jane Jarvis (piano), and David "Panama" Francis (drums). Waters gets some fine spotlighted moments on the album of 10 classics (some contributed by band members). This is no jam, but a well-planned studio session offering some of the hottest soloing and best ensemble work on record.

Nancy Ann Lee

Ethel Waters

Born October 31, 1896, in Chester, PA. Died September 1, 1977, in Chatsworth, CA.

After working in vaudeville in Baltimore and Philadelphia, singer Ethel Waters moved to New York in 1919, toured with Fletcher Henderson's Black Swan Troubadours during the 1920s, and made her first recordings for Black Swan, "Down Home Blues" and "Oh Daddy." Waters could sing the blues like Bessie Smith, yet was an adept jazz vocalist with a sterling sense of swing and was one of the first true jazz singers to record. An early star on the vaudeville and TOBA (Theater Owners Booking Association) circuits before drifting into upscale jazz and pop, she used her polished singing approach for show tunes, taking starring roles in revues such as "Africana" and "Paris Bound." Waters was the first black singer to work with a white band when she was with Benny Goodman and the Dorsey Brothers in 1929. She appeared at the Cotton Club in 1933, where she first became associated with the song "Stormy Weather," and she followed that stint with important roles in musicals and an appearance at Carnegie Hall in 1938. She was also a dramatic actress appearing in plays and Hollywood films, including *Cabin in the Sky,* the 1943 movie in which she sang "Happiness Is Just a Thing Called Joe." In 1948–49, Waters toured with Fletcher Henderson as her accompanist and in 1957 had her own Broadway show, "An Evening with Ethel Waters." An accomplished author, she wrote two autobiographies, including 1951's best-selling *His Eye Is on the Sparrow* and 1972's *To Me It's Wonderful*. Illness forced her to retire from show business, but she sang spirituals for evangelist Billy Graham in the 1960s and 1970s.

what to buy: Nearly everything in Waters's discography is on import labels. Completists will want to investigate the six volumes in the imported Jazz Chronological Classics series, because they document Waters's fascinating progression from "Down Home Blues" to "Sweet Georgia Brown" to "Someday Sweetheart" to "Porgy." The best volume for the average jazz fan is *1931–1934* 𝄢𝄢𝄢𝄢 (Classics, 1997, prod. Gilles Petard). Containing 23 tracks, two of which feaeture Waters singing with the Duke Ellington Orchestra—"I Can't Give You Anything but Love" and "Porgy"—this volume probably has the most appeal, as it also includes the original version of "Stormy Weather" as well as jazz gems such as "Don't Blame Me," "Harlem on My Mind," and other favorites that were popular well into successive decades.

what to buy next: Of the earlier Classics volumes, best are *1925–1926* 𝄢𝄢𝄢𝄢 (Classics, 1997, prod. Gilles Petard), which features Smith singing 23 playful blues and jazz classics, some with backing from Fletcher Henderson on piano, and *1926–1929* 𝄢𝄢𝄢𝄢 (Classics, 1994, prod. Gilles Petard), which finds James P. Johnson in the piano chair. Other volumes include sides with Jack Teagarden, Fletcher Henderson, Benny Goodman, and the Dorsey brothers, and versions of "Dinah" and "Stormy Weather."

influences:

◀◀ Bessie Smith, Ma Rainey, Victoria Spivey

▶▶ Billie Holiday, Mildred Bailey, Aretha Franklin, Dinah Washington, Mahalia Jackson

Steve Knopper and Nancy Ann Lee

Patty Waters

Ah, the mysterious Patty Waters. A singer by trade but not by talent, the two dates she cut for ESP in the mid-'6os are unparalleled in bizarreness; even the caliber of the musicians accompanying her—Burton Greene, Ran Blake, Giuseppi Logan—is ultimately overshadowed by her emotional, untrained wailings.

what's available: It's difficult to decide which is better, *Patty Waters Sings* 𝄢𝄢𝄢 (ESP, 1965) or *College Tour* 𝄢𝄢𝄢 (ESP, 1966), for while her debut has a rambling 13-minute *something* called "Black Is the Color of My True Love's Hair," the utterly surreal aspect of Waters & Co. plowing through "Wild Is the Wind" and "It Never Entered My Mind" ultimately takes the cake.

Jason Ferguson

Bill Watrous

Born June 8 1939, in Middletown, CT.

Trombonist Bill Watrous is one of the best, yet largely unheralded, trombonists working today. His earliest introduction to music came from his father, who was a trombonist, and Watrous played in traditional jazz bands as a teenager. During his Navy days, he played in a jazz band and studied with Herbie Nichols. Throughout the 1960s and into the 1970s, trombonist Watrous paid his dues blowing in big bands of Kai Winding, Quincy Jones, Johnny Richards, Woody Herman, and others, and later led and recorded two Columbia albums with his Manhattan Wildlife Refuge (1973–76) in New York before resettling in Southern California in 1976. He played in Los Angeles studio bands for the Merv Griffin and Dick Cavett television shows. These days, Watrous works often with composer Pat Williams and has appeared on his albums. Watrous did only about two years of studio work after moving to California. He has concentrated on his performance career and performs occasionally with his big band as well as other local gigs. He also plays European jazz festivals, and is a jazz educator who conducts numerous workshops and clinics around the country. He's recorded for Famous Door, Soundwings, GNP, and other labels, most of which are out-of-print. Watrous is also a vocalist and in mid-1997 was considering recording a Chet Baker tribute on which he planned to include his vocals.

what to buy: On *Space Available* 𝄢𝄢𝄢𝄢 (Double-Time Records, 1997, prod. Bill Watrous, Hank Cicalo), Watrous's first big band album as leader since 1973, the trombonist uses top-name West Coast players, most of whom have been with him since 1978. Recorded like a live album, the studio session was completed in two days without rehearsal. He has said this 17-musician band is more foreward-looking, sounding more like a New York band (such as the Thad Jones–Mel Lewis unit with whom Watrous recorded) than a West Coast group. Hard-swinging, winning arrangements by Tom Kubis, Gordon Goodwin, Frank Perowsky, and Ken Kaplan allow generous space for Watrous and featured soloists—trumpeters Steve Huffsteter, Bill Liston, and Bob Summers, and saxophonists Gene Burkurt and Sal Lozano. Pianist Shelly Berg, bassist Trey Henry and drummer Randy Drake comprise the sterling rhythm section (and Watrous's working quartet). This is a highly recommended album.

best of the rest:

Bone-Ified ♪♪♪♪ (GNP, 1992)

worth searching for: Though you'll probably have to really search for this album, Watrous can also be heard on the recording *The Brass Connection* ♪♪♪♪ (Innovation Records, prod. Doug Hamilton, Phil Sheridan). Anyone who digs the sounds of straight-ahead, Basie-tradition swing, and brass ensemble playing would find this session recorded in Toronto a pleasant listen. Augmenting the 10-musician ensemble are guest soloists such as Watrous, Jiggs Whigham, Carl Fontana, and Ian McDougall. Watrous shines in the spotlight on McDougall's "Night after Night after Night," mastering the intricately switching tempos and emitting a gorgeously warm and luxurious tone; and on the Bill Holman arrangement of the classic ballad "When Your Lover Has Gone," Watrous's soulful melody head and improvisations display his trombone mastery.

influences:

◄◄ Carl Fontana, J.J. Johnson, Urbie Green

►► John Fedchock, Conrad Herwig

Nancy Ann Lee

Bobby Watson

Born August 23, 1953, in Lawrence, KS.

In 1977, quite a few eyebrows were raised when drummer Art Blakey, the nurturer of many jazz greats, started touting the country kid in overalls with the alto saxophone as his latest great discovery. Eyebrows remained up in amazement as Bobby Watson let loose with a Parkeresque run of notes. Watson's sweet, full tone evokes both memories of Johnny Hodges and the blues-tinged beauty of the church music Watson played as a child. Since those early days as a Jazz Messenger, Watson has, for the most part, fulfilled Blakey's expectations.

Watson studied music at the University of Miami. After graduation, when the opportunity arose for an education with Art Blakey, Watson grabbed it and spent five years as a Jazz Messenger, eventually becoming the band's musical director. Watson did the same thing Benny Golson did for Blakey in the late 1950s, he helped kick-start a group that had become stagnant. He also brought to the group his energetic playing and something else Blakey needed, a songwriter to fit the Messenger groove. The best example of Watson's contribution to the Messengers is displayed on *Album of the Year*, featuring the best of Blakey's later bands, including a precocious trumpeter named Wynton Marsalis. After leaving Blakey in 1981, Watson formed

the first edition of his long-running band, Horizon. Watson demonstrated his diversity working as a sideman in George Coleman's hard-bop octet, Sam Rivers's experimental Winds of Manhattan ensemble, and drummer Panama Francis's Savoy Sultans. Watson was having a hard time finding a label to record his band, so he and bassist Curtis Lundy formed their own label, New Note, in 1983. A few years later, Watson helped found the 29th Street Saxophone Quartet. He signed with Blue Note in the late 1980s and a few years later switched to Columbia where he recorded both small group sessions and an album with the big band he formed in early 1990s.

what to buy: While several of Watson's finer sessions have fallen out of print, good dates to explore exist. Watson has a bit of a populist streak, which some critics have unfairly dismissed as being facile. The alto player has a good dose of old school appreciation for creating solos that capture attention, sometimes with burning intensity or sweet lyricism, occasionally with humor. Like Horace Silver, Watson isn't afraid of writing slick, finger-popping, catchy melodies as vehicles for improvisations. One of Watson's strongest albums is *Love Remains* ♪♪♪♪ (Red, 1988, prod. Bobby Watson), a quartet recording with pianist John Hicks, bassist Curtis Lundy, and drummer Marvin Smith. The album has its requisite cookers like "The Mystery of Ebop" and "Sho Thang." The title composition is one of Watson's most beautiful pieces ever, demonstrating the depth of emotion he can create when he puts his mind to it . The same band made an album under Hicks's name, *Naima's Love Song* ♪♪♪♪ (DIW, 1988, prod. Shigenobu Mori, John Hicks, Bobby Watson), which is worth grabbing.

what to buy next: Evidence has begun to reissue some of Watson's earlier works as a leader. All the dates recorded in 1983 are rendered with a *joie de vivre* usually lacking in jazz, a spirit reflected in his tunes and his tone, it can be alternately sweet and light, or biting and a bit angry. *Beatitudes* ♪♪♪ (Evidence, 1997, prod. Bobby Watson, Curtis Lundy) and *Jewel* ♪♪♪ (Evidence, 1993, prod. Bobby Watson) feature many of the same songs, played by a quartet on the former and a sextet on the latter. The Watson original, "To See Her Face," which appears on both albums, contains elements frequently present in Watson's tunes, a theme launched in a straight, swinging groove linked to a Latin bridge. Lundy's ballad "Orange Blossom " also appears on both albums. Watson learned well from Blakey. He doesn't play everything in his first chorus, but instead builds his solos to satisfying resolution. If you like a fuller sound, opt for *Jewel. Beatitudes* merits a tail wag for its gospel-influenced title tune and the Watson swingers "On the One" and "E.T.A."

Gumbo 🎵🎵🎵 (Evidence, 1994, prod. Bobby Watson, Curtis Lundy) introduces trumpeter Melton Mustafa and baritone saxophonist Hamiet Bluiett (who plays only the title tune). Highlights include a popping version of Sam Jones's "Unit Seven" and a most engaging Watson waltz, "Wheel within a Wheel." The melody is like many Watson originals, simple yet memorable. There are several hummable songs on *Present Tense* 🎵🎵🎵 (Columbia, 1992, prod. Bobby Watson, Don Kolesky), including another version of "Love Remains." The album takes advantage of the underrated composing and playing talents of longtime Watson collaborator, drummer Victor Lewis.

what to avoid: Unfortunately for his fans, Bobby crosses over on *Urban Renewal* 🎵🎵 (Kokopelli, 1995, prod. Tim Patterson). A comparison of this album to *Love Remains* or to the hard-to-find *Post-Motown Bop* places the superficial *Urban Renewal* in its proper place.

the rest:
Advance 🎵🎵🎵 (Enja, 1985)
Appointment in Milano 🎵🎵🎵 (Red, 1988)
Round Trip 🎵🎵🎵 (Red, 1988)
Solo Saxophone Album 🎵🎵🎵 (Red, 1993)
Tailor Made 🎵🎵🎵 (Columbia, 1993)
Midwest Shuffle 🎵🎵 (Columbia, 1994)

worth searching for: That Watson's music is a truer reflection of the term "contemporary jazz" than wimpy pop instrumentals is nowhere better demonstrated than on *Post-Motown Bop* 🎵🎵🎵🎵 (Blue Note, 1991, prod. Bobby Watson, Matt Pierson). While rooted in the Jazz Messenger tradition, the album captures writing and rhythms that reflect the sounds of today in a way that doesn't pander. Pianist Ed Simon, bassist Carroll Dashiell, and Lewis create a good groove without sacrificing the fluidity and creativity that is lacking in most "contemporary jazz." With a nine-piece band, Watson demonstrates his appreciation of Johnny Hodges on *The Year of the Rabbit* 🎵🎵🎵 (New Note, 1989, prod. Bobby Watson, Jim Hartog), a concert recording of a fun-loving, free-wheeling tribute to the alto giant.

influences:
◀◀ Charlie Parker, Johnny Hodges, Art Blakey

Dan Polletta

Charlie Watts
Born June 2, 1941, in Islington, London, England.

Though his fame has come from being the drummer for the Rolling Stones (and with good reason), Charlie Watts played jazz before joining the legendary rock band and often played with jazz groups between Rolling Stones' tours. In the 1990s, Watts started recording jazz albums with his quintet, though only one of their four recordings is still available domestically. Watts's music is mainstream, owing much to the bebop tradition, and it is good jazz. Much like his work with the Rolling Stones, his jazz drumming is not of the bombastic, pyrotechnic style, but that of the timekeeper who is at times creative. In such a roll, he is both credible and enjoyable.

what to buy: On *Long Ago & Far Away* 🎵🎵🎵 (Virgin Records, 1996), Watts's Quintet, along with the London Metropolitan Orchestra, serves as a backdrop for vocalist Bernard Fowler, who sings 14 standards with generally good, sometimes stunning results. The arrangements by alto saxophonist Peter King are carefully crafted and the playing, particularly from the Quintet, is solid. *Long Ago & Far Away* is smooth and very appealing, if not challenging. Like earlier Linda Rondstadt treatments of jazz standards (and this is better) it's the type of music your friends will undoubtedly ask you about if you throw it on, even if it's a little syrupy. Includes classics such as "I've Got a Crush on You," "More Than You Know," "I Should Care," "What's New," and "In a Sentimental Mood."

the rest:
A Tribute to Charlie Parker: With Strings 🎵🎵🎵 (Continuum, 1992)
Warm & Tender 🎵🎵🎵 (Continuum, 1993)

influences:
◀◀ Philly Joe Jones, Louis Bellson, Jo Jones

Paul MacArthur

Ernie Watts
Born October 23, 1945, in Norfolk, VA.

Ernie Watts's career as a saxophonist has established him as a resourceful musician with widespread talents and strength to play in a diversity of backgrounds. Up to the 1990s, it was as sideman or guest soloist that he gained critical attention. Following attendance at Berklee College of Music, Watts's first significant employment included a 1966 to 1968 stint with the Buddy Rich band, after which Watts moved to Los Angeles, where he landed a most favorable spot in 1972 as a regular performer in NBC's *Tonight Show* band. He worked with Gerald Wilson and Oliver Nelson and recorded with Bobby Bryant and Jean-Luc Ponty in the 1960s. During the 1970s he played with notables such as Lee Ritenour, Stanley Clarke, and his idol,

Cannonball Adderley. In 1982, Watts received a Grammy Award for his performance on the soundtrack to the film *Chariots of Fire*. Watts's own output in the early 1980s did not reach the heights of making any original, pure statements one would expect from a musician with such a broad musical background. What seems to have changed his course is his affiliation with Charlie Haden's Quartet West in the mid-1980s. The series of recordings made with this group convey Watts's rich lyrical sense and his integrity and warmth. In the 1990s, Watts began to make recordings that were compositionally strong and marked by his gift of improvisational playing. While some of the recordings Watts made in the 1990s attempt to blend various approaches to R&B, World music, pop music, and vocals, and are challenging in their accessibility, the straight-ahead jazz recordings with his own quartet best display Watts's gifts as a performer.

what to buy: While the JVC recordings exhibit Watts's talents as leader and soloist, because they vary in settings and players there is a lack of consistency. What works best for Watts is when he surrounds himself in a smaller group (preferably, a quartet) with musicians whose playing inspires each other. *Unity* 🎵🎵🎵🎵 (JVC, 1995, prod. Akira Taguchi) is Watts's finest recording, featuring an unusual two-bass quartet. Showcasing his ability to all-out swing in fine solos that shimmer, shine, glow, and let go, the music is distinguished by a robust group of stellar musicians whose chemistry is clear and abundant. The album contains 11 standards and originals (four) by Watts, and one each from drummer Jack DeJohnette and electric bassist Steve Swallow. Pianist Geri Allen and acoustic bassist Eddie Gomez round out the harmonious team as they distribute up-tempo tunes and ballads that are crisp and alive. *Reaching Up* 🎵🎵🎵🎵 (JVC, 1994, prod. Akira Taguchi, Ernie Watts) works in much the same way as *Unity*. With music that swings hard, Watts's fine lyrical and energetic playing is fueled by a quartet with Mulgrew Miller (piano), Charles Fambrough (bass), and Jack DeJohnette (drums). Trumpeter Arturo Sandoval plays on two tunes and adds more spark to the music's fire. Containing 10 standards and originals, the recording is a strong workout in modern jazz tempos that emphasize muscle, in contrast to the flexibility of Watts's 1996 release. Watts's debut on JVC, *The Ernie Watts Quartet* 🎵🎵🎵🎵 (JVC, 1987/1992, prod. Akira Taguchi), features him playing alto, soprano, and tenor saxophones. His playing is vigorous, subtle, and sensual. With a quartet that includes Pat Coil on piano, Joel DiBartolo on bass, and Bob Leatherbarrow on drums, Watts is allowed to soar, twist, and maneuver his lyrical way through composi-

tions. All tunes are done with elegance and soul and served up rich and cooking, yet there is often a relaxed pop feeling to some of the tunes. Included are renditions of "My One and Only Love," "Skylark," and "Body and Soul."

what to buy next: *The Long Road Home* 🎵🎵🎵 (JVC, 1996, prod. Akira Taguchi) shows Watts pursuing a bluesy direction with compositions played less to exhibit Watts's talents and more to create a smoky, raw atmosphere that is grounded in passionate, soulful twists of jazz grooves. In addition to two tracks that feature the vocals of Carmen Lundy, the album highlights the group of top-notch musicians, including Kenny Barron on acoustic piano, Reggie Workman on acoustic bass, and, on three tracks, guitarist Mark Whitfield. Though mainly a ballad-oriented album, two Charles Mingus tunes are included, as well as originals by the leader. While Watts plays with smooth elegance, and the band provides excellent accompaniment, the listener is left wanting a bit more sweat.

what to avoid: *Project Activation Earth* 🎵🎵 (Amherst, 1989, prod. Leonard Silver, Jeff Tyzik) and *Afoxe* 🎵🎵 (CTI, 1993, prod. Creed Taylor) use larger ensembles of players and approaches ranging from fusion (*Project Activation Earth*) to an odd mixture of everything from soul to New Age to world music (*Afoxe*). These attempts at large production fail to sustain accessible levels of direction. While the playing by Watts and company on both recordings reflects their talents, there is a loss of intimacy and personal punch.

worth searching for: As a regular member of Charlie Haden's Quartet West, Watts's strong and rich lyrical style merged nicely with the film noir sound Haden explored on a series of recordings on the Verve label. The best recording of the series, *Now Is the Hour* 🎵🎵🎵🎵 (Verve, 1996, prod. Charlie Haden, Ruth Cameron) shows Watts playing in a confident, muscular pre-bop style that, like the rest of the music, is both dark and romantic; subtle, but consistently inspiring.

Gregory Kiewiet

Weather Report

Formed 1970, in New York, NY. Disbanded 1985.

Josef Zawinul, keyboards; Wayne Shorter, saxophones; Miroslav Vitous, bass (1970–73); Alphonse Mouzon, drums (1970), Airto Moreira, percussion (1970); Eric Gravatt, drums (1971–72); Dom Um Romao, percussion (1971–73); Ishmael Wilburn, drums (1972); Andrew N. White III, bass, French horn (1973); Herschel Dwellingham, drums (1973); Muruga, percussion (1973); Alphonso Johnson, bass (1973–75); Alyrio Lima, drums (1974); Ndugu (Leon) Chancler, percus-

Weather Report **(Archive Photos)**

sion (1974); Chester Thompson, drums (1975); Jaco Pastorius, bass (1976–79); Alex Acuna, percussion (1976); Manolo Badrena, percussion (1976); Peter Erskine, drums (1978–81); Victor Bailey, bass (1982–85); Jose Rossy, percussion (1982–85); Omar Hakim, drums (1982–85)

Led by Zawinul and Shorter—both part of Miles Davis's landmark jazz-rock experiments during the late 1960s, Weather Report was a visionary band that managed to infuse its high-voltage jazz with rock 'n' roll excitement and world-music exoticism. Unlike many fusion experiments that fizzled, Weather Report's sound was compelling and seemed to sweep the listener along, prompting Zawinul to dub it "parade music." The unique sound and accessibility quickly earned a following beyond normal jazz aficionados. Zawinul, classically trained on the piano in his native Austria, created a vibrant, full-bodied sound using layers of cutting-edge synthesizers while the rhythm section built deep, complex foundations. Shorter, with his bebop jazz background, soared above and through the mix with sharp, angular saxophone lines. When Pastorius added his compositional skill and darting jazz-funk flourishes on fretless bass, Weather Report experienced its greatest commercial success, earning a gold record with 1977's *Heavy Weather* and the hit, "Birdland." Zawinul and Shorter announced in the spring of 1996 that they planned to re-form Weather Report later in the year.

what to buy: *Heavy Weather* ♪♪♪♪ (Columbia, 1977/1997, prod. Josef Zawinul, Jaco Pastorius, Wayne Shorter) is a compelling blend of ebullience ("Birdland," "Teen Town") and beauty ("A Remark You Made," "Harlequin"). The energy level nears meltdown status on *Mysterious Traveler* ♪♪♪♪ (Columbia, 1974/1987, prod. Josef Zawinul), with its adventurous title track and the mesmerizing "Nubian Sundance."

what to buy next: *Black Market* ♪♪♪♪ (Columbia, 1976/1987, prod. Josef Zawinul, Jaco Pastorius) bristles with Latin and African rhythms and exotic melodies. The triumvirate of Zawinul-Shorter-Pastorius hits its compositional peak on *Mr. Gone* ♪♪♪♪ (Columbia, 1978/1991, prod. Josef Zawinul, Jaco Pastorius), creating high drama with instrumental music.

what to avoid: It took a few albums for Weather Report to find its form amid all those influences, so the first two discs, *Weather Report* ♪♪ (Columbia, 1971/1992, prod. Josef Zawinul, Wayne Shorter) and *I Sing the Body Electric* ♪♪ (Columbia, 1972/1990, prod. Josef Zawinul, Wayne Shorter) offer too few glimpses into the magic ahead.

the rest:

Sweetnighter ♪♪♪ (Columbia, 1973/1996)
Tale Spinnin' ♪♪ (Columbia, 1975/1994)
8:30 ♪♪ (Columbia, 1979/1994)
Night Passage ♪♪♪ (Columbia, 1980/1987)
Procession ♪♪ (Columbia, 1983)
Domino Theory ♪♪♪♪ (Columbia, 1984)
Sportin' Life ♪♪♪ (Columbia, 1985)
This Is This ♪♪♪♪ (Columbia, 1987)
This Is Jazz 10: Weather Report ♪♪♪♪ (Columbia, 1996)

worth searching for: Though Weather Report's best albums are unified pieces, a couple best-of collections allow for sampling of different periods in the group's evolution. Both Japan's *Star Box* ♪♪♪ (Sony, 1993, prod. various) and Britain's *Weather Report: The Collection* ♪♪♪ (Castle, 1990, prod. various) offer key tracks and good introductions to the group.

influences:

◀◀ Miles Davis, Charlie Parker, Dizzy Gillespie, John Coltrane

▶▶ Herbie Hancock, Chick Corea, Steps Ahead

see also: *Miles Davis*

David Yonke

Chick Webb

Born William Webb, February 10, 1909, in Baltimore, MD. Died June 16, 1939, in Baltimore, MD.

Drummer-bandleader Chick Webb had a short-lived career, but his contributions to jazz drumming influenced players such as Gene Krupa and many other contemporaries. A childhood accident left Webb with a deformed spine, but he nevertheless began playing drums in a local band by age 11. Webb went to New York City in 1924 and freelanced until he formed his own band two years later. Early members of his band included Johnny Hodges, Bobby Stark, and later, Benny Carter and Jimmy Harrison. Webb played on a platform amidst his band and, though unable to read music, cued members with his drumming. Despite his size, he was a propulsive player whose speed and rhythmic skills were even more dazzling in live performances than on his recordings. His band worked Harlem clubs and recorded one session for Brunswick in 1931, and con-

tinued to struggle for wider notice. At the urging of Benny Carter and other associates, in 1934 Webb hired the 17-year old singer Ella Fitzgerald (who had been appearing at amateur contests at the Apollo Theatre). After Webb began to regularly feature her on recordings, the band enjoyed its broadest popularity from June 1935 until February 1939. Although Ella Fitzgerald's name became bigger than the Webb orchestra (which had been primarily a dance band specializing in the fox trot and boogie-woogie–influenced swing), they achieved popularity with frequent engagements broadcast from the Savoy Ballroom and a lengthy series of recordings for Decca. Although Webb's failing health was in steady decline, he managed to record eight studio sides for Decca on April 21, 1939, plus continue live radio broadcasts through May, 4, 1939, before he died of spinal tuberculosis. Following his death, Ella Fitzgerald led the band for two years until July of 1941.

what to buy: *An Introduction to Chick Webb, 1929–1939* ♪♪♪♪♪ (Best of Jazz, 1994, reissue prod. Gilles Petard) almost equally splits the 22 tunes between sides recorded with and without Fitzgerald. This compilation was made by a panel of experts (Preston Love, Kurt Mohr, Duncan Schiedt, Johnny Simmen, Jerry Valburn) rather than one individual (something almost unheard of in the business of jazz). On this wonderful compilation, Webb's drumming drives orchestras led by Louis Armstrong, Mezz Mezzrow, as well as his own orchestras. Besides Webb's first issued recording ("Dog Bottom"), there's even a rare track ("My Honey's Loving Arms") with Webb driving the Gotham Stompers, a small combo of Ellington soloists, featuring vocalist Ivie Anderson. There really isn't a dull track, but you'll probably best enjoy those tracks that feature Webb propelling his Orchestra though fast-paced swing numbers (recorded in 1937) such as "Sweet Sue, Just You" and "Harlem Congo." The latter features his drum solo and shifting tempos. Ella Fitzgerald sings her popular classics, "A-Tisket, A-Tasket" (recorded in 1938) and "Undecided" (recorded in 1939), as well as others. Listen to the entire album and you'll marvel at what a versatile rhythm master Webb was, no matter whether he was driving his orchestra or a small ensemble, or backing a singer or an instrumental soloist.

what to buy next: *Standing Tall* ♪♪♪♪ (Almac Records/Drive Archive, 1996) isn't a definitive, career-spanning album by Chick Webb and his Orchestra, although it does provide some fine examples of his playing and leadership in live-recorded radio broadcasts from February 10, 1939 and (mostly) May 4, 1939 (six weeks before his death). The band's personnel included many notable names, although players such as Benny Carter and

Louis Jordan had left the band by these recordings. There are plenty of highlights among the 12 tunes, including fine solos from trumpeter Taft Jordan, trombonist Sandy Williams, and top-notch ensemble work. Tunes include a surprising take on the John Phillip Sousa march, "Stars and Stripes Forever," and a tempo-shifting version of "My Wild Irish Rose," featuring Webb's hard-driving artistry and combustive solo breaks. Ella Fitzgerald sings popular classics such as "If I Didn't Care," the novelty tune "Chew, Chew, Chew (Your Bubble Gum)," and others. This album would be of interest to completists, but also provides an excellent example of one of the most popular swing bands of that period—even without Ella Fitzgerald.

best of the rest:
Spinnin' the Web ♫♫♫♫ (Decca, 1929–1939/1994)
Chick Webb, 1929–1936 ♫♫♫♫♫ (Jazz Chronological Classics, 1994)
Chick Webb, 1935–1938 ♫♫♫♫ (Jazz Chronological Classics, 1994)

worth searching for: *Ella Fitzgerald: The Early Years, Part 2* ♫♫♫♫ (Decca Jazz, 1993, prod. various) is a two-CD set that contains 42 tunes featuring the vocalist. Noticeably best, disc one features 1939 sessions (February 17, April 21, and March 2), near the end of Ella's stint with the Chick Webb Orchestra, only months before Webb's death in June. Amazingly, his energy drives his swinging band through delightful hits such as "Unde-cided," "'Tain't What You Do," "My Heart Belongs to Daddy," "Chew, Chew, Chew (Your Bubble Gum)," and other classics featuring generous choruses from the Webb Orchestra. After his death, the orchestra was kept intact, but following the departure of a number of original members, lost a lot of spirit. Later-recorded dates (June 29, August 18, October 12, 1939, and various 1940 and 1941 dates) on disc two, though technically top-notch, lacked the impact of Webb's presence. The set also includes Fitzgerald performances with her Savoy Eight band, an ensemble of Webb Orchestra members, featuring Webb on drums. Lovingly restored, the selections feature the famous singer performing many tunes she first made classics.

influences:
▶▶ Sid Catlett, Bill Beason, Jesse Price, Gene Krupa

see also: *Ella Fitzgerald*

Nancy Ann Lee

Eberhard Weber

Born on January 22, 1940, in Stuttgart, Germany.

Bassist Eberhard Weber has been hailed for his unique voice, melding jazz with a European contemporary classical style, and since the inception of the five-string, electro-acoustic bass, Weber has been one of the leading proponents of the instrument. Weber learned cello at age six from his father (a music teacher), and began playing bass at 16, performing in the school orchestra and for parties and dances. He met Wolfgang Dauner in the late 1960s and they worked together for the next eight years in the group Et Cetera. Weber also worked with Dave Pike in the 1970s, and formed his own group, Colours, in 1974. Weber has collaborated regularly with Jan Garbarek and Gary Burton, and has written film scores and performed and recorded solo with looping devices making his one bass sound like a full orchestra. Weber records as a leader mostly for the ECM label and, while some of those recordings are hard to find in the U.S., check out the ECM website for more details on obtaining Weber's CDs by mail order.

what to buy: If you must label music, then many of the post-1960s works recorded by Weber lean more toward a sophisticated, enlightened New Age and World Fusion rather than the avant-garde, hard-core post-bop, swing, or straight-ahead jazz styles. But Weber's already been there, done (at least some of) that. In America, some of his work of the 1970s and 1980s might fall into the realm of Classical "New Music" being made by 20th-century composers, except that Weber's highly improvisatory work contains many jazz elements, some jazz-rock fusion, and other influences. An adept composer with a vision, Weber proves on his second solo recording, *Pendulum* ♫♫♫♫ (ECM, 1994, prod. Eberhard Weber), that one man with a bass (multiple overdubs and an electric echo unit) can sound like an orchestra. Weber creates astonishing depth and texture, a sound tapestry mastered with only one instrument. As he has in the past when working with other musicians, he builds on his melodic originals to create an array of moods that most listeners should find fairly friendly. *Silent Feet* ♫♫♫♫ (ECM, 1978, prod. Manfred Eicher) finds Weber with his touring group, Colours, with Rainer Bruninghaus (piano, synthesizer), Charlie Mariano (soprano saxophone, flutes), and introduces drummer John Marshall, who works well with the crew, often punching up from underneath and adding percussive flair to Weber's three originals to make the nearly 43-minute session an exceptional listen. Mariano is a wonderfully aggressive improviser, a Weber frequent collaborator (at least in the late 1970s) who works tightly with the bassist and pianist on this outing, and helps create the desired climates, colors, and textures for each piece. You'll marvel at the role of the bass in this session and how Weber's improvs and comping inspires the other musicians.

what to buy next: Not one of his best sessions, but one that could become addictive with repeated listening, *Later That*

Evening 𝄞𝄞𝄞 (ECM 1982, prod. Manfred Eicher) finds bassist Weber in a 1982 studio session with Paul McCandless (soprano sax, oboe, English horn, bass clarinet), Bill Frisell (guitar), Lyle Mays (piano), and Michael DiPasqua (drums, percussion). Each of the four Weber compositions is unique, colorful, and dynamic, ranging in duration from the eerily floating six-and-a-half minute title tune punctuated with Weber's deep-toned electric bass improvisations, to the churning, shifting tempos and panoramic excitement of the full group on the 16-plus-minute, "Death in the Carwash."

best of the rest:

The Colours of Chloe 𝄞𝄞𝄞𝄞 (ECM, 1973/1994)
Yellow Fields 𝄞𝄞𝄞𝄞 (ECM, 1974)
The Following Morning 𝄞𝄞𝄞𝄞 (ECM, 1976)
Fluid Rustle 𝄞𝄞𝄞 (ECM 1979/1994)
Works 𝄞𝄞𝄞 (ECM, 1985/1994)

influences:

◀◀ Steve Reich, Pat Metheny, Ralph Towner, Lucky Thompson

▶▶ Bill Connors, Jaco Pastorius

Nancy Ann Lee

Ben Webster

Born Benjamin Francis Love Webster, March 27, 1909, in Kansas City, MO. Died September 20, 1973, in Amsterdam, Netherlands.

One of the "Big Three" tenor saxophone players of the '30s and '40s (along with Coleman Hawkins and Lester Young), Ben Webster carved a unique niche for himself. His full-bodied tone, warm vibrato, and bluesy melodies straddled the middle ground between Hawkins's harmonic explorations and Young's lyrical journeys.

After violin lessons as a child, Wesbter learned to play piano (his neighbor, boogie-woogie virtuoso Pete Johnson, taught him to play the blues). He performed in a few southwestern bands, but worked primarily as a soloist. While performing as an accompanist for silent movies at a theatre in Amarillo, Texas, Webster met Budd Johnson, who showed him some saxophone basics. A visiting Willis Handy Young hired Webster to play in his Young Family Band (along with saxophonist/son Lester), and the elder Young taught Webster proper saxophone technique and how to read music. It was with Benny Moten's orchestra that Webster acheived some acclaim, as a featured performer on landmark recordings like "Lafayette" and "Moten Swing." Still showing a strong Hawkins influence, Webster's playing was described as "unrestrained growling through chord changes."

During the rest of the '30s, Webster played in the bands of Andy Kirk, Fletcher Henderson (replacing Lester Young, who had, in turn, replaced Coleman Hawkins), Benny Carter, Willie Bryant, Cab Calloway, and Teddy Wilson. In 1940 (after brief visits in 1935 and 1936), he joined Duke Ellington's orchestra, along with Billy Strayhorn and Jimmy Blanton, and the trio sparked the Ellington band to new heights. As a result, Webster became Ellington's first major tenor soloist, and was featured prominently on many famous recordings, including "Cotton Tail," "Chelsea Bridge" and "All Too Soon." It was with Ellington that Webster began to fully realize his saxophone style and musical identity. Although he returned to Ellington's band briefly in 1948, Webster spent the bulk of the '40s performing and recording frequently as both a leader and a sideman. His own small groups performed regularly at the many clubs on New York's 52nd Street. By the '50s, Webster moved to the West Coast to be near his ailing mother, and he recorded with Art Tatum, Coleman Hawkins, and Billie Holiday. After his mother's death, he moved back to New York, and, on a tour with Jazz at the Philharmonic, visited Europe for the first time in 1965. Propelled partly by changing trends in jazz and partly by a lack of work, Webster relocated and settled in Copenhagen and Amsterdam. From 1965 until his death in 1973, he continued to record and tour for his devoted European fans.

what to buy: *Ben Webster Meets Oscar Peterson* 𝄞𝄞𝄞 (Verve, 1959, prod. Norman Granz) provides the one-two punch of an experienced rhythm section in support of a masterful tenor player. The entire session is overflowing with relaxed confidence from all parties. Webster's take on "In the Wee, Small Hours of the Morning" is sublime and, in many ways, surpasses Sinatra's version. *Soulville* 𝄞𝄞𝄞 (Verve, 1957, prod. Norman Granz) finds Webster supported once again by Oscar Peterson, Ray Brown, Stan Levey, and Herb Ellis on guitar. "Late Date" is a wonderful example of Webster's blues playing—deeply rooted in the Kansas City tradition, he growls and groans and puts the listener in the middle of a late-night jam session. On "Makin' Whoopee," he's at his sensuous best, shading each phrase with timbral subtleties and shadings. The final three tracks are the only studio recordings of Webster's piano playing. He wasn't quite as adept on the piano as on the tenor, but it is still fascinating to hear. *Meets Gerry Mulligan* 𝄞𝄞𝄞 (Verve, 1959, prod. Norman Granz) opens with the haunting melody of "Chelsea Bridge," one of Webster's signature tunes with Ellington, and moves on to straight-ahead Mulligan originals with Webster getting the lion's share of solo space. Recorded during Webster's stay in California, the two had been playing together for some time before they entered the studio and their rapport is evident. The disc contains five extra tracks left off the original LP, three of which are Webster compositions.

what to buy next: *Ben & Sweets* ♫♫♫ (Columbia, 1962, prod. Mike Berniker) finds two masters in top form, as Edison's impishly witty playing serves as an excellent foil to Webster's more gruff and sumptuous playing. The session has the relaxed feel of old friends getting together to blow on familiar tunes. *Soulmates* ♫♫♫ (OJC, 1963) and *Travelin Light* ♫♫♫♫ (Milestone, 1957 Orrin Keepnews), both influenced by Lester Young and Johnny Hodges, feature a young Joe Zawinul, years before Weather Report. Webster's version of "Travelin Light" is notable in its poignancy and sensitivity.

what to avoid: Buck Clayton and Ben Webster rarely play together on *Ben & Buck* ♫♫ (Storyville, 1967). The numbers, recorded live in Belgium, are features for one or the other, and when they do play together it is at a tempo too fast for Webster's style.

the rest:
Complete Ben Webster on EmArcy ♫♫♫ (EmArcy, 1953)
King of the Tenors ♫♫♫♫ (Verve, 1953)
Sophisticated Lady ♫♫♫♫ (Verve, 1954)
Ballads ♫♫♫ (Verve, 1954)
Music for Loving: Ben Webster with Strings ♫♫♫ (Verve, 1955)
The Soul of Ben Webster ♫♫♫ (Verve, 1957)
Tenor Giants ♫♫♫ (Verve, 1957)
Ben Webster and Associates ♫♫♫ (Verve, 1959)
At the Renaissance ♫♫♫ (OJC, 1960)
Live at Pio's ♫♫♫♫ (Enja, 1963)
Live! ♫♫♫♫ (Storyville, 1963)
See You at the Fair ♫♫♫ (Impulse!, 1964)
Gone with the Wind ♫♫ (Black Lion, 1965)
There Is No Greater Love ♫♫ (Black Lion, 1965)
The Jeep Is Jumping ♫♫♫♫ (Black Lion, 1965)
Swingin' in London ♫♫♫♫ (Black Lion, 1965)
Black Lion Presents Ben Webster ♫♫♫♫ (Black Lion, 1965)
Stormy Weather ♫♫♫♫ (Black Lion, 1965)
Meets Bill Coleman ♫♫ (Black Lion, 1967)
Plays Ballads ♫♫ (Storyville, 1967)
Big Ben Time ♫♫♫ (EmArcy, 1967)
Ben Meets Don Byas ♫♫ (Verve, 1968)
For the Guv'nor (Tribute to Duke Ellington) ♫♫♫ (Charly, 1969)
At Work in Europe ♫♫ (Prestige, 1969)
My Man: Live at the Montmartre 1973 ♫♫♫ (SteepleChase, 1973)
Atmosphere for Lovers and Thieves ♫♫♫♫ (Black Lion, 1974)

worth searching for: *The Sound of Jazz* ♫♫♫♫♫ (Columbia/Sony, 1958, prod. George Avakian, Irving Townsend), the soundtrack to the landmark 1958 TV broadcast, is a phenomal document of

BEN WEBSTER (WITH THE DUKE ELLINGTON ORCHESTRA)

song "Cotton Tail"
album *Cotton Tail*
(RCA Bluebird, 1940/1997)
instrument Tenor saxophone

a true jazz summit meeting. In addition to Ben Webster, the personnel includes jazz luminaries like Lester Young, Coleman Hawkins, Billie Holiday, Red Allen, and Gerry Mulligan. The pinnacle moment is the group's stellar performance of "Fine and Mellow," on which Billie Holiday sings the first chorus followed by solos from Webster, Young, and, a few choruses later, Hawkins. The only minor complaint is the recording is of the dress rehearsal, and not the actual broadcast, and features Mal Waldron's "Nervous" instead of Thelonious Monk's performance of "Blue Monk." *Giants of the Tenor Sax: Ben Webster/Don Byas* ♫♫♫♫ (Commodore, 1944, prod. Milt Gabler) is vintage Ben Webster, shortly after he left Ellington, performing with Sid Catlett. The disc also contains the excellent Don Byas/Slam Stewart duets from Town Hall in 1945.

influences:
◀◀ Coleman Hawkins, Johnny Hodges, Benny Carter

▶▶ Scott Hamilton, Branford Marsalis, Archie Shepp, Bennie Wallace

James Eason

Dave Weckl

Born 1960, in St. Louis, MO.

An aggressive drummer known for almost superhuman agility and precision, Weckl pioneered a contemporary approach to jazz drums—triggering sound samples, sequences, and effects from behind the drum kit. Raised in a house filled with music, thanks to his piano-playing dad, Weckl was drawn to the drums via his boyhood hero, Buddy Rich. Eventually he studied jazz at the University of Bridgeport, Connecticut, making a name with the jazz-fusion band Nitesprite before moving to New York. He won a seat in fusion auteur Michel Camilo's band, and word of Weckl's prodigious talent soon spread through the city's jazz scene, helped by early boosters such as former Weather Report drummer Peter Erskine. Drafted by jazz piano legend Chick Corea after playing sessions for everyone from Madonna to George Benson, Weckl brought a machine-like precision to Corea's cutting-edge Elektric Band, which melded state-of-the-art synthesizer and sequencer technology with jazz complexity. Following seven years of work with that outfit, Weckl went solo in 1993, assembling a series of records filled with adventurous keyboard and percussive work until he lost his recording deal a few years later.

what to buy: As a showcase for his prodigious drumming talent and the facility of his keyboard-playing partner Jay Oliver, *Heads Up* ♫♫♫ (GRP, 1992, prod. Dave Weckl, Jay Oliver) is an excellent platform—melding interesting tunes with guest turns by Elektric Band cohorts Eric Marienthal, John Patitucci, and Randy Brecker.

what to avoid: The biggest criticism to dog Weckl's playing since he revolutionized jazz drumming in the '80s is his feel—which favors a multitude of notes and an impersonal precision that doesn't sit well with funk or more laid-back grooves. This is most evident on his solo debut, *Master Plan* **woof!** (GRP, 1990, prod. Dave Weckl, Jay Oliver), on which the fast chops leave little room for emotion or expression.

the rest:
Light Years ♫♫♫♪ (GRP, 1987)
Eye of the Beholder ♫♫♪ (GRP, 1988)
(With the Akoustic Band) *Chick Corea Akoustic Band* ♫♫♫♪ (GRP, 1989)
(With the Elektric Band) *The Chick Corea Elektric Band* ♫♫♫♪ (GRP, 1989)
Inside Out ♫♫♫ (GRP, 1990)
Beneath the Mask ♫♫♫ (GRP, 1991)
Akoustic Band Alive ♫♫♫ (GRP, 1991)
Hard Wired ♫♫♫ (GRP, 1994)

worth searching for: It's supposed to be an instructional tape for drummers, but Weckl's *Contemporary Drummer + One* ♫♫♫ (DCI Music Video, Inc., 1987) also offers some pretty interesting tunes, framed by blazing drum licks from the master. As an added bonus, he includes music so you can follow along.

influences:
◀◀ Billy Cobham, Buddy Rich, Steve Gadd
▶▶ Carter Beauford, Dennis Chambers, Jeff Greenblatt

Eric Deggans

George Wein

Born October 3, 1925, in Boston, MA.

Jazz impresario George Wein is as legendary as his festivals, the spark plug of New York–based Festivals Productions, Inc., which produces some 1,000 music events annually. In addition to his work as a producer, Wein is an accomplished pianist whose group, dubbed the Newport Jazz Festival All-Stars, has toured the U.S., Europe, and Japan for many years.

George Theodore Wein started studying classical piano at the age of eight, but by the time he was 15, jazz became his passion. After college, he got a job playing piano for $90 a week at a Chinese restaurant and also began booking a local Jazz club. The gigs were successful so he leased a room at Boston's Copley Square Hotel and called it Storyville. It soon became Boston's leading Jazz venue. In July 1954, he created the world's first all-jazz festival in Newport, Rhode Island, but after the 1971 riot, he moved the three-day event to New York. Since moving to the Big Apple, Wein has booked practically every living Jazz musician of note to play at the Newport Jazz Festival–New York, the Kool Jazz Festival, and the JVC Festival, often presenting them in cleverly conceived thematic configurations. Although he remains busy as a producer, he tours occasionally with a hand-picked group he calls the Newport Jazz Festival All-Stars.

what to buy: On *Newport Jazz Festival All-Stars: Bern Concert '89* ♫♫♫♫ (Concord Records, 1990, prod. Carl E. Jefferson), George Wein takes a page from the book of Norman Granz and his Jazz at the Philharmonic recordings, putting together an all-star band that includes such diverse saxmen as Ricky Ford, Scott Hamilton, and Norris Turney, as well as cornetist Warren Vache, and George Wein himself on piano. But instead of the JATP patented duels, this is a straight-ahead, hard-edged, and friendly session, where everyone gets plenty of solo space and uses it to good advantage

what to avoid: *Swing That Music* **woof!** (Columbia Records, 1993, prod. George Wein), an all-star date organized around Wein's piano is perhaps one of the most boring Jazz records ever made. If this is any indication of Wein's keyboard chops, there's a message here: George Wein, keep your day job!

worth searching for: In a group that includes the legendary Pee Wee Russell on clarinet, brash cornetist Ruby Braff, and tenorman Bud Freeman, George Wein pretty much stays in the background on *George Wein & the Newport All-Stars* 🎵🎵🎵🎵 (Impulse!, 1962, prod. Bob Thiele) and lets these veterans swing comfortably. Earl Hines's inspiration is obvious through Wein's brief solos and he displays a fine feeling for the blues as well. To his credit, Wein lays down a solid beat and is adept at comping for other soloists and also good at making up head arrangements on tunes like "Crazy Rhythm," "The Bend's Blues," and "JaDa," which proves to be a real rouser. But even though Wein's name is at the top of the bill, it's the wizened veterans that really shine here.

influences:

◀◀ Earl Hines

▶▶ Dave McKenna, Dick Wellstood

Bret Primack

Dick Wellstood

Born November 25, 1927, in Greenwich, CT. Died September 24, 1987, in Palo Alto, CA.

The late Dick Wellstood is remembered by many as an accomplished stride pianist, but that is akin to seeing the proverbial tip of the iceberg. Wellstood evolved initially from a two-fisted, Joe Sullivan–like approach to the keyboard, into a mature piano stylist in the Harlem stride tradition of Thomas "Fats" Waller, James P. Johnson, and Willie "The Lion" Smith, with added Ellington overtones and subtle elements of Thelonious Monk and other modernists. For the uninitiated, Wellstood's complex harmonies may be an acquired taste. But to the discerning listener, Wellstood's technique and thorough examination of the entire range of the piano and his unhackneyed handling of his varied sources of material is still a revelation. He remains, a decade after his untimely death, a complete piano player with a highly personal style.

Widowed when Wellstood was three years old, his mother functioned as a church organist and also gave piano lessons. While attending public schools in various parts of New England, Wellstood found that playing boogie-woogie piano after lunch at school drew attention. In the summer of 1944, at age 16, he heard James P. Johnson and Willie "The Lion" Smith at the Pied Piper in New York, and they made lasting impressions on the budding jazzman. From 1946 to 1950, Wellstood played with his chum, Bob Wilber, and made his recording debut in 1947 as a member of Wilber's Wildcats. In 1949, he recorded with Sidney Bechet. Wellstood played with veteran trombonist Jimmy Archey, starting in 1950, and toured Europe with that band in 1952. About that time, he received private music lessons in the Boston and New York areas. Always a brilliant scholar, Wellstood studied law in 1953 while playing intermittently with trumpeter Roy Eldridge and with trombonist Conrad Janis's Tailgate Five. Soon qualified as a lawyer, he did not practice law until the mid-1980s. Wellstood played intermissions at the first Condon's in 1956, was house pianist at the Metropole (1959–61), then played Nick's (1961–63). He played with luminaries such as Red Allen, Ben Webster, Coleman Hawkins, and Wild Bill Davison. The pianist joined the Gene Krupa Quartet for three years, touring South America (1965) and Israel (1966), and then moved into a band job in New Jersey, continuing a long association with clarinetist Kenny Davern.

Always open to diversity, Wellstood appeared on Bob Dylan's first album, and also recorded with folk singer Odetta. As band work diminished in the early 1970s, he played with Paul Hoffman's society orchestra, while concentrating on developing a career as a solo pianist. He became a full-time soloist in 1974, but continued doing occasional band dates and record dates with friends Marty Grosz, Kenny Davern, Vince Giordano, Andy Stein, and Dan Barrett. He recorded many albums that attest to his keyboard prowess, including everything from ragtime to bop in his repertoire. In the mid-1980s, Wellstood and guitarist Marty Grosz, along with cornetist Dick Sudhalter and reedman Joe Muranyi, formed a wonderful little band that specialized in performing neglected songs and original tunes in interesting and sometimes unusual ways. First dubbed as the Bourgeois Scum, they became known and later recorded as the Classic Jazz Quartet. When Wellstood, the heart and soul of the group, died of a heart attack in 1987, the band dissolved and became an unforgettable musical memory for those who had heard it.

what to buy: *Dick Wellstood: Live at the Sticky Wicket* 🎵🎵🎵🎵 (Arbors, 1997, prod. Diane McClumpha Wellstood) offers a joyous surprise for the avid jazz piano collector who discovers this entire evening's performances by the one and only "Stridemonster," Dick Wellstood. Captured at the Sticky Wicket Pub in Hopkinton, Massachusetts, on a chilly November night in 1986, this two-CD set of 41 tunes commemorates Wellstood on the tenth anniversary of his death. The warm, relaxed atmosphere of these previously unissued tunes is enhanced by Wellstood's banter with his appreciative audience. From the opening romp through Shearing's "Lullaby of Birdland," through the rousing closer, Friml's "March of the Musketeers," the listener is privy to Wellstood's imaginative excursions into a repertoire that includes the works of Joplin, Waller, Johnson, Coltrane, Parker, the Gershwins, Rodgers, and Morton. This one is a must for Wellstood's legions of fans or for anyone interested in checking out the work of a truly original jazz master. A set of 17 worthy gems, *Dick Wellstood and His All-Star Orchestra* 𝄫𝄫𝄫𝄫 (Chiaroscuro, 1973, prod. Hank O'Neal/Chazz Jazz, 1981, prod. Charlie Baron/Chiaroscuro reissue compilation, 1992) takes eight tracks from a 1973 Chiaroscuro duet date of Wellstood and reedman Kenny Davern, and adds all nine cuts from the Chazz Jazz Blue Three sessions that took place at Hanratty's in New York City in 1981. Wellstood and Davern are old hands at intuitive improvisation and spontaneous interplay. There is also plenty of musical jousting and subtle jesting by the clarinetist-soprano saxist and the keyboard wizard, with Bobby Rosegarden's clean and crisp drumming added for the trio numbers. Tunes derive from the Armstrong, Condon, and Morton songbooks, but also include "Blue Monk," an upbeat "Oh, Peter!," and "Fast As a Bastard," an up-tempo reworking, taken at an almost impossibly fast clip, of Ellington's "Jubilee Stomp." This one is a must for swing-minded traditionalists and fans of these major talents.

what to buy next: An invaluable addition to the National Public Radio series, *Marian McPartland's Piano Jazz with Guest Dick Wellstood* 𝄫𝄫𝄫 (Jazz Alliance, 1994, prod. Dick Phipps), captures an hour of jazz piano music and interesting conversation from June 27, 1981, providing further insight into the Wellstood persona. Twelve tunes are woven in and about McPartland's interview with Wellstood, including three delightful piano duets on "Lulu's Back in Town," "'Deed I Do," and "Fine and Dandy." The inventive mind and the extraordinary touch of the late Dick Wellstood are on full display on *This Is the One . . . Dig!* 𝄫𝄫𝄫 (Audiophile, 1977, prod. George H. Buck/Solo Art, 1994, prod. Dick Burwen, Dick Wellstood), a set of 16 pieces from an October 12, 1975 studio date in Lexington, Massachusetts. "Sir Richard Wellstride," as admirers often called him, strides and strolls through tunes ranging from the James P. Johnson classics "Mule Walk" and "Snowy Morning Blues," to a harmonically rich version of John Coltrane's "Giant Steps," with some Cole Porter, Fats Waller, Richard Rodgers, and Niccolo Paganini tossed into the rewarding mix—a bonanza for classic jazz piano buffs.

best of the rest:

Dick Wellstood Alone 𝄫𝄫𝄫 (Jazzology, 1971/Solo Art, 1997)

Bob Wilber–Dick Wellstood: Duet 𝄫𝄫𝄫𝄫 (Parkwood, 1984/Progressive, 1995)

Dick Wellstood: Ragtime Piano Favorites 𝄫𝄫𝄫 (Special Music, 1987)

Never in a Million Years 𝄫𝄫𝄫𝄫 (Challenge, 1995)

worth searching for: A two-CD set, *The Classic Jazz Quartet* 𝄫𝄫𝄫𝄫 (Jazzology compilation, 1995, prod. Donald Kurtz, Richard Sudhalter), the 31-tune collection captures the entire recorded output of this classy little band of swinging traditionalists. Cornetist Dick Sudhalter and reedman Joe Muranyi form the front line for the unbeatable rhythm team of guitarist Marty Grosz and anchor-man, pianist Dick Wellstood. There is plenty of solo space all-around, a brace of vocals by Marty and the Band, and some clever arrangements by each of the participants. All of the 1984 Jazzology LP sides and the 1985 Vineyard date for Stomp-Off are included, along with nine previously unreleased cuts from a March 1986 private party session in North Salem, New York. This was a thinking-man's band, offering attractive originals and obscure standards, much lively jazz, a mix of subtle and not-so-subtle humor, and downright good-natured fun.

John T. Bitter

Kenny Werner

Born 1951, in Brooklyn, NY.

When leading his own groups or in solo recital, classically trained pianist Kenny Werner's improvisations venture into long-form mystical experiences, even as he grounds his flights of fancy in a solid, post-bop tradition. A graduate of Boston's Berklee School of Music, Werner has developed an impressive resume, performing and recording with Charles Mingus, Dizzy Gillespie, Lee Konitz, and Archie Shepp, among others. He has also taught at New York City's New School and in a number of master classes, clinics, and seminars.

what to buy: Werner, bassist Ratzo Harris, and drummer Tom Rainey have been playing as a unit since the '80s, so they can create a sense of familiarity verging on telepathy. *Live at Visiones* 𝄫𝄫𝄫 (Concord Jazz, 1995, prod. Allen Farnham) reveals their approach to classic material, because all the songs were either pop chestnuts like "Stella by Starlight" and "There Will Never Be Another You" or newer jazz standards by Miles Davis, Wayne Shorter, and John Coltrane. Werner is especially impressive on Chick Corea's "Windows."

what to buy next: On *Kenny Werner at Maybeck* ♫♫♫ (Concord Jazz, 1994, prod. Nick Phillips), Werner covers "Someday My Prince Will Come" and opens the program with an almost 13-minute improvisation titled "Roberta Moon," which illustrates his tendency to take a phrase into linear hyperspace, running with the moment and away from the original melody.

the rest:

Uncovered Heart ♫♫♫ (Sunnyside, 1990)
Introducing the Trio ♫♫♫ (Sunnyside, 1990)
Press Enter ♫♫♫♪ (Sunnyside, 1992)
Meditations ♫♫♫ (SteepleChase, 1993)
Copenhagen Calypso ♫♫♫ (SteepleChase, 1994)

influences:

◀◀ Bill Evans, Bud Powell, Al Haig

▶▶ Chick Corea, Keith Jarrett

Garaud MacTaggart

Paul Wertico

Born January 5, 1953, in Chicago, IL.

Paul Wertico started playing drums at the age of 12 and became a professional by the age of 15. Self-taught on the drum set, he developed his unique musical concept by listening not only to jazz and rock, but to a variety of musical styles from all over the world. He then applied elements of these styles to his drumming in a melodic as well as rhythmic fashion. Wertico's playing has been compared to that of "an Impressionist painter," while he has also been described as "an inspired madman" and "a restless innovator."

In 1983, Wertico became a member of the world renowned Pat Metheny Group. Wertico's versatility has enabled him to appear in a wide variety of musical settings besides Metheny's popular group, including acid jazz with folk/soul singer Terry Collier; playing big-band charts with writer/arranger Nelson Riddle; an award winning blues-rock album with singer/guitarist Ellen McIlwaine (in a trio with bassist Jack Bruce); backing up singer Rosemary Clooney; adult contemporary fusion-jazz with the group Special EFX; as well as backing up touring acts like the Drifters, Little Anthony, the Coasters, the Shirrelles, Mary Wells, even Phyllis Diller and Joan Rivers.

what's available: Exotic textures, polyrhythms, and robust ideas mark *the Yin and the Yout* ♫♫♫♫ (Intuition Records, 1993, prod. Howie Morrell), the debut solo recording of Pat Metheny band drummer Paul Wertico. A folksy and down-home album, it contains an amalgam of styles ranging from traditional Peruvian music to free jazz, yet it never loses sight of the sensibility that unifies them. Wertico succeeds in creating a fresh-sounding and unpretentiously experimental set of ideas, swerving freely from world music, as on the album's seductive opening cut, "Peruvian Folk Song," to percussion/synthesizer tone paintings. In honor of Maestro Roach, Wertico plays an electronic drum solo entitled "The Max Factor," full of taste and textures. The all-star cast includes Dave Liebman on soprano saxophone, Bob Mintzer on tenor saxophone, former Flecktone Howard Levy on pennywhistle and Jew's harp, and Dave Holland on acoustic bass.

influences:

◀◀ Buddy Rich, Shelly Manne, Louis Bellson

▶▶ Dave Weckl, Greg Bissonette

Bret Primack

Fred Wesley

Born 1944, in Mobile, AL.

Famed for his time with both James Brown (starting in 1968) and Parliament-Funkadelic and its various offshoots, trombonist Fred Wesley has consistently been the most jazz-oriented of the many horn players (such as saxophonists Maceo Parker and Pee Wee Ellis) in those and similar contexts—but then, he also played in the Count Basie big band. Since Wesley was often the James Brown band's musical director (Brown said he preferred Wesley's arranging to Ellis's, and that Wesley had a better sense of rhythm), it was logical that he would be the leader of the JBs when they recorded as a separate act. Later, in the period when P-Funk mastermind/ringleader George Clinton was recording his sprawling organization under as many names (and for as many different labels) as possible, the horn section of Wesley, Parker, and trumpeters Rick Gardner and Richard "Kush" Griffith was christened the Horny Horns, with Wesley the leader. In the years since all those bands' heydays, Wesley has worked off and on with Brown and Clinton, and more frequently with Parker and Ellis as the JB Horns, also appearing on Parker's albums (and Parker on Wesley's). Starting in 1990, Wesley's albums have focused on jazz, with his funk impulses being mostly channeled into his non-leader work. As a jazz trombonist he favors an extremely rich and darkly mellifluous tone, which sets him apart from most current peers, though he requires distinctive contexts to make it into a compelling sonic package.

what to buy: *New Friends* ♫♫♫♫ (Antilles/Island, 1990, prod. Stephan Meyner, Fred Wesley) is a tour-de-force that puts Wesley solidly in the jazz tradition but connects it with R&B at the same time through a series of inspired covers: Duke Ellington's "Rockin' in Rhythm," Clyde McPhatter & the Drifters' lascivious "Honey Love," Thelonious Monk's "Bright Mississippi" and "Blue Monk," the Dells' "Love We Had Stays on My Mind" (with a great vocal on Wesley's version by Carmen Lundy), Quincy Jones's "Plenty, Plenty Soul," Dizzy Gillespie's "Birks Works," and Elmo Hope's "Eyes So Beautiful." Equally impressive is Wesley's remake of his Horny Horns tune "Peace Fugue," rewritten for four trombones, and his jazzy "For the Elders" allows everyone to stretch out. "D-Cup and Up" is the only outright funk number, but it's as deeply grooving as anything he's ever done. The other players are young, respected jazz musicians who know how to get down, making this album a varied joy from start to finish.

what to buy next: The first two albums billed as by Fred Wesley and the Horny Horns, *A Blow for Me, a Toot for You* 🎵🎵🎵 (Atlantic, 1977, prod. George Clinton, William "Bootsy" Collins) and *Say Blow by Blow Backwards* 🎵🎵🎵 (Atlantic, 1979/AEM, 1994, prod. George Clinton, William "Bootsy" Collins, Fred Wesley), sometimes sound like they were thrown together without much care, with flubbed notes and half-assed vocals, and a number of tunes recycled from P-Funk albums. But for all that there are still great moments, and whatever happens, it's funky. And surprisingly, the two new remixes per CD work well. *The Final Blow* 🎵🎵🎵🎵 (AEM, 1994, prod. George Clinton) seems to be from the same period as the two albums that actually got issued, but is tighter, more musically interesting and inventive, and doesn't suffer from the lackadaisical mass vocals of the other efforts—five of the seven tracks are instrumentals, with only minimal lead vocals on the other two—and "Bells" might be the best thing they ever did.

what to avoid: The JB Horns' *Pee Wee, Fred & Maceo* 🎵 (Gramavision, 1990, prod. Jim Payne) is pedestrian hackwork, by-the-numbers funk that's not even very funky and all blurs together indistinguishably. *To Someone* 🎵🎵 (Hi Note/Rough Trade, 1990) is Wesley's most hardcore jazz album, but his tone is a bit blowzy, which after a while becomes irritating on a quartet date where he's the only horn. Even worse, bassist Ken Walker's lines are turgid and unimaginative.

the rest:
(With Fred Wesley & the JBs) *Damn Right I Am Somebody* 🎵🎵🎵 (People/Polydor, 1974)
(With Fred Wesley & the New JBs) *Breakin' Bread* 🎵🎵🎵 (People/Polydor, 1974)
Comme Ci Comme Ca 🎵🎵🎵 (Antilles/Island, 1991)
Swing and Be Funky 🎵🎵🎵 (Minor Music, 1992)

worth searching for: Fred Wesley & the JBs' *Doing It to Death* 🎵🎵🎵 (People/Polydor, 1973, prod. James Brown) features the #1 R&B title hit. If the rest feels a bit like filler, it's damn funky filler, and one wonders why this LP (and for that matter the other J.B.'s stuff) has been out-of-print for so long (though the 10-minute title track is available on various James Brown anthologies). The four-group collection *Jim Payne's New York Funk! Vol. 1* 🎵🎵🎵 (Gramavision, 1993, prod. Jim Payne) includes three tracks by a Wesley-led quintet including Kenny Garrett (alto sax) recorded specifically for this anthology (among the other bands is a Pee Wee Ellis group with Clyde Stubblefield on drums). The import-only *Amalgamation* 🎵🎵🎵🎵 (Minor Music, 1994, prod. Stephan Meyner, Fred Wesley) is so funky that even a cover of Wham's "Careless Whisper" grooves, though the highlight is the tightly percolating "Herbal Turkey Breast."

influences:

◄◄ James Brown, Parliament-Funkadelic, J.J. Johnson

►► Tower of Power, Brand New Heavies, Heavy Metal Horns

Steve Holtje

Frank Wess

Born January 4, 1922, Kansas City, MO.

Reedman Frank Wess began developing his considerable chops in dance, theater, and club bands until 1941. During World War II, he served in the Army Band as assistant bandleader and clarinet soloist (1941–45) and led a 17-piece swing band that accompanied Josephine Baker, performing for the Allied Troops in Africa. When the War ended, he toured with the the Billy Eckstine Orchestra (1946–47) and with bands led by Eddie Heywood (1947), Lucky Millinder (1948), and Bullmoose Jackson (1948–49). He studied the flute, then joined the Count Basie Orchestra as one of the principal composer-arrangers from 1953 to 1964, playing tenor, some alto, but was best known as the player who popularized the flute in jazz. In 1964, Wess left the Basie band to freelance in New York, where he performed at concerts and clubs, taught and conducted workshops and clinics, did some composing and arranging, and played for Broadway shows, television, and studio work. He wrote and performed with Clark Terry's occasional big band from 1969, and was a founding member of the New York Jazz Quartet in 1974. He worked with Philly Joe Jones's Dameronia band (1981–85), and co-led a quintet with former Basie bandmate, saxophonist Frank Foster from 1984 to 1986. Wess was coleader of the Frank Wess–Harry Edison Orchestra (documented on a Concord recording, *Dear Mr. Basie*). In addition to recording numerous sessions as sideman and leader, Wess added several movie soundtracks to his list of accomplishments. Wess has a warm, relaxed, fluid, and always swinging saxophone style, but is probably known best for his flute playing.

what to buy: Wess has an extraordinary knack for making a tune sound terrific, no matter which instrument he picks up. He plays tenor saxophone, alto saxophone, flute, and bass flute on *Tryin' to Make My Blues Turn Green* ₰₰₰₰ (Concord, 1994, prod. Carl E. Jefferson), an album recorded with pianist Richard Wyands, bassist Lynn Seaton, drummer Gregory Hutchinson, trumpeters Cecil Bridgewater and Greg Gisbert, trombonist Steve Turre, and reedman Scott Robinson. The talented, small, tightly-unified team sometimes sounds like a big band as they forge their way through 12 tunes (five Wess originals) with horns locked in unison and the kicking rhythm section spurring them along. When these cats swing, they swing hard; when they lean to lush and lovely, their playing is full of tenderness and warmth. In addition to writing most of the spectacular arrangements, Wess plays bass flute on one of the most beautiful ballads ever, Kenny Burrell's "Listen to the Dawn," to which Turre adds gorgeous color with his conch shells artistry. This is a great straight-ahead session and a recording that represents the magic that is supposed to happen when musicians come together in the studio. Some of Wess's best work can be found on recordings with the New York Jazz Quartet, a cooperative group founded by Roland Hanna in the 1970s. One of the best of these sessions, *Surge* ₰₰₰₰ (Enja, 1992, prod. Horst Weber), features Wess (who replaced Hubert Laws in 1974) playing flute and saxophones with pianist Roland Hanna, bassist George Mraz, and drummer Richard Pratt. Wess contributes two originals to the modern six-tune studio set (recorded on February 19, 1977)—the romping title tune on which he plays flute and soprano sax and the Far East–influenced ballad "Placitude," a vehicle for his bass and soprano flute renderings. Although Wess is widely known for creating Basie-like swing, his performances with the empathetic personnel in this version of the New York Jazz Quartet prove that the reedman is a consummate musician who can create a broad range of straight-ahead stylings. Just listen to his modern saxisms on Hanna's up-tempo funkified "Big Bad Henry." You won't find any standards here; the diverse six pieces are written by quartet members and provide tasteful and sophisticated jazz that showcases the best talents of these musicians. A second New York Jazz Quartet date, *Oasis* ₰₰₰₰ (Enja, 1981, prod. Matthias Winckelmann), recorded on February 13, 1981, replaces drummer Richard Platt with Ben Riley. Wess is still a

champ, delivering a rich tenor sax solo on his original "Don't Come, Don't Call," which opens the set. Wess contributes a 13-minute, diverse three-movement suite, "The Patient Prince," which ranges from classically-tinged jazz to hard-driving bop, and features Wess, playing both flute and tenor sax, and captures each of the other musicians in spotlighted moments. Hanna dominates the session, contributing bluesy grounders, "Funk House" (performed as a duo with bassist Mraz), "Cram It Damn It" (a funk tune that gives Wess space for bluesy flute licks), the straight-up, waltzing "It's Just a Social Gathering" (which gives everyone a solo shot), and the dreamy title ballad. *Surge* is the more vibrant of the two albums, but there's some really lovely and lyrical jazz on *Oasis*. Buy both albums to get a complete picture of the all-embracing expressions of Wess and his cohorts. The hard-swinging, precise rhythms of the 16-member Frank Wess Orchestra heard on *Entre Nous* ₰₰₰₰₰ (Concord, 1991, prod. Carl E. Jefferson) were recorded live at the 1990 Fujitsu-Concord Jazz Festival in Japan. The first number sets the tone for the whole album, with the band generating a hot Basie-grooved Wess original, "Order in the Court." The rhythm team—pianist Tee Carson, bassist Eddie Jones, and drummer Dennis Mackrel—drives this band like a steamin' locomotive through the remaining nine tunes, a mixture of lushly orchestrated ballads and blues-grooved swingers. Don't be upset that Wess solos only on three tunes (his imprint is otherwise all over this album), including an elegant flute solo on his gorgeous original ballad, "Entre Nous," which he also arranged. Wess has put together a stellar band of excellent soloists, and highlights include Art Baron's muted trombone solos on "Blues in the 2%" and "Pit Pat Blues," Joe Newman's trumpet and vocals on "St. James Infirmary," and Tee Carson's piano solos on several numbers. Wess is a consummate musician, a well-rounded reedman, a composer who writes the stuff of standards (why isn't everyone playing his tunes?), and an accomplished arranger. While Wess doesn't play much on this CD, it showcases all his best talents.

what to buy next: *Dear Mr. Basie* ₰₰₰₰ (Concord, 1990, prod. Carl E. Jefferson) finds the Frank Wess–Harry Edison Orchestra in live-recorded performance at the 1989 Fujitsu-Concord Jazz Festival in Japan. What's unique (and blessed) about this big band date is the incredible lineup that includes (mostly) the senior statesmen of jazz, 15 of them former Basie-ites: Snooky Young, Joe Newman, Al Aaron, Ray Brown (trumpets); Al Grey, Grover Mitchell, Benny Powell, Michael Grey (trombones); Marshal Royal, Curtis Peagler, Billy Mitchell, Bill Ramsey (saxophones); Ronnell Bright, piano; Eddie Jones, bass; Gregg Field, drums. Solos from these Basie-band stalwarts provide many highlights. Wess's flute solo on "The Very Thought of You" is lush and lovely. Up-tempo Basie band classics such as "Jumpin' at the Woodside" and "One O'Clock Jump," the wonderful Wess originals "Blue on Blue" and "All Riled Up," as well as two Neal Hefti standards ("Whirly Bird" and "Li'l Darlin'"), and other classics, make this tribute to Basie a lovable listen. Fans of the Hammond B-3 organ will dig this CD from Town Crier Recordings, *Going Wess* 𝄞𝄞𝄞𝄞 (Town Crier, 1993, prod. Claudia Marx), featuring Frank Wess (tenor sax/flute) with Bobby Forrester (Hammond B-3 organ) and Clarence "Tootsie" Bean (drums). The organ/saxophone combination has worked for jazz musicians such as Shirley Scott/Stanley Turrentine, and it fares equally well for the swingin' Wess and the facile Forrester, an organist who has collaborated with Stanley Turrentine, George Coleman, and other horn players. Wess adds extra flair with his flute improvs and Forrester is at ease at the B-3, as he and drummer Bean (a working unit since 1978) help leader Wess keep the session of 10 standards classy and lightly groovin'. Nice album with many highlights. Reedmen and former Basie-ites Frank Wess and Frank Foster teamed in the studio in 1984 to make *Frankly Speaking* 𝄞𝄞𝄞𝄞 (Concord, 1985, prod. Bennett Rubin), a battle of the tenors (on three tunes) as well as a showcase for their other instrumental and composing-arranging endeavors. Backed by a rhythm dream team—Kenny Barron, piano; Rufus Reid, bass; Marvin "Smitty" Smith, drums—both Franks glide through the eight-tune set with experienced team and solo work. One of their best collaborations is featured on the 1930s hit, "When Did You Leave Heaven?," where Wess blends his flute with Foster's tenor sax before they break out into solos on Barron's gospel-blues chords and the wide-gaited rhythm. Also enjoyable is the Neal Hefti tune "Two Franks," a jumpin' spree with the two tenorists going at it in the way of a 1940s "cutting" contest, blowing fast and hard and blending their melody lines. In this case, it's a draw.

influences:

◀◀ Lester Young, Coleman Hawkins

▶▶ Holly Hofmann, Lew Tabackin, Hubert Laws, Ken Peplowski

Nancy Ann Lee

Randy Weston

Born April 6, 1926, in Brooklyn, NY.

Randy Weston has been a pioneer in emphasizing the African roots of jazz and the connections between the two styles, something he was doing even before he lived in Africa for six years. In addition, he is a superb pianist and composer whose jazz waltz "Hi-Fly" has become a standard. Weston is greatly respected by his fellow musicians and by hard-core jazz fans, but has not received the mainstream acclaim a creator of his accomplishments would seem to merit, which has resulted in too much of his catalog lapsing from availability.

Weston grew up in Brooklyn, where his father had a West Indian restaurant frequented by jazz musicians. Weston has frequently commented on the sense of community he felt growing up in that environment, and many of his sidemen, such as Cecil Payne, were childhood friends. It was Randy's father who first taught him about African history and who encouraged his piano studies. He started his professional career later than many, at age 23, and then not in a jazz context but rather as accompanist to blues singer Bull Moose Jackson. Subsequent jobs were with Eddie "Cleanhead" Vinson, trumpeter Kenny Dorham, and drummer Art Blakey, and Weston became friends with Thelonious Monk and studied informally with him. In 1954 Weston became the first modern musician to record for the fledgling Riverside label, and it was his albums for that company that first gained him a nationwide reputation. "Hi-Fly," "Little Niles," and a number of other jazz waltzes became popular vehicles with other musicians, establishing him as an important writer.

In 1960 Weston recorded an influential album for Roulette, the five-movement suite *Uhuru Afrika*. It used large-group arrangements by trombonist Melba Liston, who had previously arranged for Weston's quintet; they have continued to work together, off and on, ever since. *Uhuru Afrika* had an all-star cast that prominently featured the percussion of Babatunde Olatunji, Candido, and Armando Peraza, plus drummers Max Roach, Charlie Persip, and G.T. Hogan along with 13 all-star horn players. It was the strongest expression yet of Weston's interest in Africa. By this time he was regularly featuring drummer Big Black in his groups, emphasizing the African element even outside of such special projects. The following year he visited Nigeria, returning in 1963. A similar album was recorded that year, *Highlife*, which has been combined with *Uhuru Afrika* on a limited edition CD. He also spent a year touring New York City elementary schools with his sextet with a History of Jazz program, giving 40 concerts in that time that traced the history of the music from Africa through the Caribbean, the black church, New Orleans jazz, etc. The program was sponsored by Pepsi-Cola and the players worked for union scale.

Weston toured North Africa in the beginning of 1967, sponsored by the U.S. State Department, and decided to settle there. He spent most of his time until 1973 in Africa, opening his African Rhythms Club in Tangier. In that period he had no records released, a drought broken by an atypical 1972 album on CTI, *Blue Moses*, which found him pressured into playing electric piano, which he continued to do on a few tracks on his follow-up record, the much better *Tanjah*, where he once again worked with Melba Liston. He then lived in France and Africa again, though this time around he continued to release records while based abroad. He returned to the United States in the early 1990s and began a fruitful association with Verve that has yielded his most mature statements. He has continued to work in Morocco on occasion, and he made an album with some of the Gnawa musicians whose style has had the strongest influence on his style, as heard in the magnificent "Blue Moses" and "The Healers." His small group African Rhythms, which works as a sextet or septet, has been his touring group for much of the decade.

what to buy: The bold, questing two-CD set *The Spirits of Our Ancestors* (Antilles, 1992, prod. Randy Weston, Brian Bacchus, Jean-Philippe Allard) explores jazz's Africanicity, with Weston's angular piano style set jewel-like amidst Melba Liston's arrangements for an almost-big band. Guests Pharoah Sanders on tenor sax and gaita (a high-pitched African horn) and trumpet legend Dizzy Gillespie show how expansive the parameters of Weston's vision are, but everything's grounded in loping rhythms that swing no matter how far-out the playing gets. It contains a number of classic Weston tunes, from "Blue Moses," "The Healers," and "African Cookbook" to "African Village Bedford-Stuyvesant" (heard in two versions), "African Sunrise," and "A Prayer for Us All"—10 tracks in all, and though there's a one-CD selection available, the entire original album is a must-own. *Portraits of Thelonious Monk: Well You Needn't* (Verve, 1990, prod. Jean-Philippe Allard) and *Self Portraits: The Last Day* (Verve, 1990, prod. Jean-Philippe Allard), along with *Portraits of Duke Ellington: Caravan* (see below), make up a trilogy recorded in three days in Paris with Jamil Nasser (bass), Idris Muhammad (drums), and Eric Asante (percussion). Hearing Weston take on seven Monk themes not as an imitator but rather as a mature artist who has fully absorbed the Monkian oeuvre into his own is both an immensely satisfying listen and a closing of the circle. *Self Portraits*, as the title suggests, finds Weston playing his own music, mixing new material with well-known classics ("Berkshire Blues," "Night in Medina"), which sound definitive in this context.

what to buy next: For a taste of Weston's early work, it's hard to beat *With These Hands* (Riverside, 1956, prod. Orrin Keepnews, Bill Grauer). His quartet with Cecil Payne (baritone sax), Ahmed Abdul-Malik (bass), and Wilbert Hogan (drums) runs through a standards-based program that also includes two originals, with "Little Niles" making its first appearance. This is Weston at his most mainstream, in the style that first brought him acclaim. *Monterey '66* (Verve, 1994, prod. Randy Weston) captures a titanic concert that sat unreleased in Weston's private collection until almost two decades later. A band with Ray Copéland (trumpet, flugelhorn), Booker Ervin (tenor sax), Payne, Bill Wood (bass), Lenny McBrowne (drums), and Big Black (congas) stretches out on the Weston classics "Afro Black," "Little Niles," "Berkshire Blues," and the monumental "African Cookbook," among others. Cook it does, with hypnotic intensity. It was soon afterward that Weston broke up this group and had his recording hiatus. The solo piano recital *Marrakech in the Cool of the Evening* (Verve, 1994, prod. Randy Weston, Jean-Philippe Allard), recorded in the ballroom of a Moroccan hotel, has a wonderful intimacy. To an extent, Weston's in a reminiscing mood, playing Nat "King" Cole's "In the Cool of the Evening," a Dizzy Gillespie medley, Fats Waller's "Jitterbug

RANDY WESTON

song "A Night in Mbari"

album *Saga*

(Verve, 1995)

instrument Piano

Waltz," and Billy Strayhorn's "Lotus Blossom." On the other ten tracks, Weston surveys some of his less frequently played originals, making this album a fine adjunct to *Self Portraits*.

what to avoid: "String Arrangements by Melba Liston," says the banner headline on the cover of *Earth Birth* 🎵🎵 (Verve, 1997, prod. Jean-Philippe Allard). As good an arranger as Liston has been in band contexts, this is a disappointment. One problem seems to be that in Weston's mind "strings" equals mellow (not to mention waltz—the first four tracks are in 3/4, with another later on pushing the percentage above half the album). The energy and density of his piano style is largely missing here, appearing mostly in his famed "Little Niles," and drummer Billy Higgins and bassist Christian McBride are also too polite. Most fatally, the string arrangements feature too much corny unison writing and are thus redolent of sappy 1950s productions intended as classy background or makeout music. You can easily find better versions of "Pam's Waltz," "Hi-Fly," "Berkshire Blues," etc.

best of the rest:
Get Happy 🎵🎵🎵 (Riverside, 1955)
Jazz a la Bohemia 🎵🎵🎵 (Riverside, 1956)
How High the Moon 🎵🎵🎵 (Biograph, 1956)
Uhura Africa/Highlife 🎵🎵🎵🎵 (Roulette, 1961/64, /Capitol, 1990)
Berkshire Blues 🎵🎵🎵🎵 (1965/Black Lion, 1978)
Blue Moses 🎵🎵🎵 (CTI, 1972)
Tanjah 🎵🎵🎵🎵 (Polydor, 1973/Verve, 1995)
Carnival: Live at Montreux '74 🎵🎵🎵🎵 (Freedom, 1975)
Blues to Africa 🎵🎵🎵🎵 (Freedom, 1975)
(With David Murray) *The Healers* 🎵🎵🎵 (Black Saint, 1987)
(With Vishnu Wood) *Perspective* 🎵🎵🎵 (Denon, 1989)
Volcano Blues 🎵🎵🎵🎵 (Antilles, 1993)
Splendid Master Gnawa Musicians of Morocco & Randy Weston 🎵🎵🎵 (Antilles, 1994)
(With African Rhythms) *Saga* 🎵🎵🎵🎵 (Verve, 1995)

worth searching for: It's hugely disappointing that the first volume of the Portraits trilogy, *Portraits of Duke Ellington: Caravan* 🎵🎵🎵🎵 (Verve, 1990, prod. Jean-Philippe Allard), is being allowed to go out-of-print. Whether on "Caravan" and "C Jam Blues" or lesser-known Ellingtonia, these tracks shed light on a Weston influence less remarked on than Monk's. The parallels between the Ellington band's sound and the orchestral fullness and far-reaching nature of Weston's playing become clear. The out-of-print *Trio and Solo* 🎵🎵🎵 (Riverside, 1955–56, prod. Orrin Keepnews, Bill Grauer) doesn't contain Weston's first Riverside session, but the six tracks from January 1955 (five with bassist Sam Gill and drummer Art Blakey) are the next-earliest, and—according to producer Keepnews's liner notes on the four-CD box set *The Riverside Records Story* 🎵🎵🎵🎵 (Riverside/Fantasy, 1997, prod. Orrin Keepnews)—they were the first Keepnews was happy with. One of the trio numbers can be heard on that collection. A subsequent LP eventually included four solo piano tracks from September 1956 that were not released at the time, and these examples of Weston's early solo style (mostly ballads) along with Blakey's presence on the trio numbers make this album worthy of reissue. It is also greatly to be hoped for that Weston's three late 1950s albums for United Artists will reappear. *Little Niles* 🎵🎵🎵 (United Artists, 1958) and *Destry Rides Again* 🎵🎵🎵 (United Artists, 1959), both with a sextet featuring tenor great Johnny Griffin, and especially *Live at the Five Spot* 🎵🎵🎵🎵 (United Artists, 1959), with a quintet whose frontline consists of Coleman Hawkins and Kenny Dorham, found Weston's style maturing rapidly and contain much great playing.

influences:
⏪ Thelonious Monk, Art Tatum, Duke Ellington
⏩ Rodney Kendrick

Steve Holtje

Kirk Whalum
Born 1958, in Memphis, TN.

Although tenor saxophonist Kirk Whalum's roots lie in gospel and Southern soul, he has become one of the most popular jazz/pop artists of the last decade. Critics have categorized him as strictly a jazz musician, but have chided him for leaning more on pop stylings and less on his innate jazz sensibilities. True, Whalum has found great success and mainstream exposure through his pop and R&B recordings and collaborations, but he has never compromised his influences. Whalum grew up in Memphis influenced by church music and playing horn in his father's church choir. As a teenager, Whalum earned a music scholarship to Texas Southern University in Houston. It was here that he formed his own band and by 1979 was opening for such artists as Bob James, who invited Whalum to play on his Columbia album, *12*. Whalum soon earned a deal with Columbia Records. Since then he's toured with an array of contemporary pop and jazz artists, including the group Take 6, Marcus Miller, George Benson, Luther Vandross, Larry Carlton, and singers Nancy Wilson and Michael Franks. Whalum's 1985 debut, *Floppy Disk,* hinted at the smooth silky sound that would become the hallmark of many 1980s instrumentalists, including George Howard, James Carter, and Najee. A steady stream of successful records helped to cement Whalum's standing in the industry.

However, his most important contribution to music came in 1992. Whalum's sax solo on Whitney Houston's "I Will Always Love You," from the mega-platinum soundtrack album *The Bodyguard,* boosted his visibility and appeal. He has toured with Whitney Houston during the past several years, a stint that has included performances in South Africa and a White House reception for Nelson Mandela. Whalum continues to be an in-demand session player in addition to recording his own albums as leader. He is currently based in Los Angles.

what to buy: *Cache* 𝄞𝄞𝄞 (Columbia, 1992) is the best representation and most complete effort in Whalum's catalog so far. His playing is superb and the musical selections are more jazz-tinged than on his other works. The quiet storm favorite "Love Is a Losing Game," featuring vocals by Jevetta Steele, is a pleaser, as are stellar renditions of "Over the Rainbow" and the Babyface composition, "Love Saw It." Most artists don't hint at a particular style or niche until their third or fourth release. Whalum's first release, *Floppy Disk* 𝄞𝄞𝄞 (Columbia, 1985, prod. various), establishes his artistry. With the help of mentor Bob James, Whalum delivers a solid set of smooth grooves and scintillating riffs.

what to buy next: With *In this Life* 𝄞𝄞𝄞 (Columbia, 1995), his fifth album as leader, Whalum takes us on a more musically diversified, spiritually enriched journey. On this collection, he reaches for his gospel influences and love of country music. Mostly ballads are featured, with "I Turn to You" and the title track taking center stage. *The Promise* 𝄞𝄞𝄞 (Columbia, 1989) is another collection of solid tunes delivered by Whalum in his sincere, straightforward style.

the rest:
And You Know That 𝄞𝄞𝄞 (Columbia, 1988)
Colors 𝄞𝄞𝄞 (Columbia, 1997)

influences:
◀◀ Bob James, Grover Washington Jr., Dave Koz, David Sanborn, Kenny G, Jonathan Butler

Damon Percy

Kenny Wheeler

Born January 14, 1930, in Toronto, Canada.

As he approaches age 70, Kenny Wheeler can count himself as one of the few truly original voices in the area of contemporary jazz. His introspective trumpet work is marked by a rich and burnished tone, and his immediately recognizable composi-

tions are rare in their originality and lyricism. A native of Canada, Wheeler first picked up the trumpet in his teens. Following studies at the Toronto Conservatory, he moved to England in the early 1950s, where he worked with Johnny Dankworth's band over a six-year period. During the next decade, Wheeler became deeply influenced by Europe's burgeoning avant garde scene. In addition to recording his rare 1968 debut recording, *Windmill Tilter,* he logged valuable experience with Tony Oxley, Michael Gibbs, Anthony Braxton, the Globe Unity Orchestra, and the Spontaneous Music Ensemble. By the mid-1970s, Wheeler was an active recording artist for the ECM label where he developed a small, but substantial catalog. He also became a distinctive member of bassist Dave Holland's group between 1983 and 1987, contributing some of his finest recorded work to the Holland sessions *Jumpin' In*, *Seeds of Time*, and *The Razor's Edge*. Self-effacing and content to labor in the shadows of obscurity, Wheeler continues to be one of jazz music's most valuable composers and trumpeters.

what to buy: *Gnu High* 𝄞𝄞𝄞𝄞 (ECM, 1975, prod. Manfred Eicher) finds Wheeler leading a quartet with pianist Keith Jarrett taking on a prominent role. The music is richly melodic and varied and one would be hard pressed to find a better set of music to come from a decade that produced few artifacts of lasting value. *Music for Large and Small Ensembles* 𝄞𝄞𝄞𝄞𝄞 (ECM, 1990, prod. Manfred Eicher) is one of only two existing recordings to display Wheeler's talent for writing in a big band setting. One of the two discs in this set is taken up by the lengthy "Sweet Time Suite," a virtual tour-de-force for displaying Wheeler's exceptional writing and trumpet work. This is a highly memorable collection that provides required listening.

what to buy next: *Deer Wan* 𝄞𝄞𝄞𝄞𝄞 (ECM, 1977, prod. Manfred Eicher) features fellow ECM heavies John Abercrombie, Dave Holland, Jack DeJohnette, and Jan Garbarek, and the results are uniformly high. *The Widow in the Window* 𝄞𝄞𝄞𝄞𝄞 (ECM, 1990, prod. Manfred Eicher) is a quintet date with pianist John Taylor and guitarist John Abercrombie. You'll find inspired solo work from all and a collection of Wheeler's finest compositions.

the rest:
Double, Double You 𝄞𝄞𝄞𝄞𝄞 (ECM, 1983)
Welcome 𝄞𝄞𝄞𝄞 (Soul Note, 1986)
Flutter By, Butterfly 𝄞𝄞𝄞𝄞 (Soul Note, 1987)
Paul Bley and Kenny Wheeler 𝄞𝄞𝄞𝄞 (Justin Time, 1996)
Angel Song 𝄞𝄞𝄞𝄞 (ECM, 1997)

worth searching for: *Kayak* 𝄞𝄞𝄞𝄞 (Ah Um, 1992, prod. Nick Purnell) was cut and produced in England, Wheeler's home for over four decades. Available as an import, this disc features a large ensemble and includes such British stars as Chris Pyne, Dave Horler, and John Taylor. The program of Wheeler originals is typical of his high standards of originality.

influences:
▶▶ Tom Harrell

Chris Hovan

Rodney Whitaker
Born February 22, 1968, in Detroit, MI.

Bassist Rodney Whitaker began musical studies on violin at age eight, mastering the instrument within five years. He reluctantly switched to bass at age 13, but gained enthusiasm for his new instrument after hearing a Paul Chambers recording. Whitaker progressed through the Detroit public school system, receiving solid instruction from educators Ed Quick and Jerome Stasson, and while still in high school was recommended to saxophonist Donald Washington, leader of the ensemble Bird/Trane/Sco/Now! Whitaker remained with the group throughout high school, mastering the bebop style. He participated in workshops led by Marcus Belgrave, performed European classical music with the Detroit Civic Orchestra, studied privately with Detroit Symphony musicians, and began to write. His accomplishments attracted attention from established Detroit musicians, and drummer Leonard King hired 15-year old Whitaker to work in his group. Whitaker also worked with drummer Francisco Mora, saxophonist Chris Pitts, pianist/composer Kenn Cox, and saxophonist Donald Walden's group. Word spread to New York and Whitaker replaced bassist Bob Hurst in the Terence Blanchard–Donald Harrison Quintet for a year, leaving with Blanchard who struck out on his own. Whitaker spent two years with Blanchard, then joined Roy Hargrove's band for nearly four years. Whitaker recorded his debut album, *Children of the Light*, in September 1995. He's also worked with Kenny Garrett, and performed and toured with the Lincoln Center Jazz Orchestra. Whitaker shows talent equal to another prominent young bassist, Christian McBride, and is definitely a talent to watch.

what's available: *Children of the Light* 🎵🎵🎵 (Koch Jazz, 1996, prod. Rodney Whitaker, Kazunori Sugiyama), originally issued in Japan on DIW, features Whitaker surrounded by an excellent team that includes trumpeters Nicholas Payton or Wallace Roney, pianists Geri Allen or Cyrus Chestnut, drummers Kariem Riggins or Greg Hutchinson, and guesting hometown soloists, tenor saxophonist James Carter and flutist Cassius Richmond.

Whitaker leads this edgy, restless session with considerable artistry. The 11 selections include Whitaker's rearranged standards and exhilarating originals and display his mastery of his instrument. Check out his original compositions: "Woman Child," a soulful, African-beat piece that gives dominant voice to his free-ranging bass expressions and the dark harmonies of "(Queen) Roz," written to favor contributions from Payton, Carter, Allen, and Riggins.

worth searching for: You'll find more of the same stimulating straight-ahead jazz and some lovely ballads on Roy Hargrove's quintet session, *Of Kindred Souls* 🎵🎵🎵🎵 (Novus, 1993, prod. Larry Clothier, Roy Hargrove). Whitaker lays down solid, deep-toned foundations for solos by Hargrove (trumpet/flugelhorn) and Ron Blake (tenor/soprano sax), and locks in consistently with drummer Greg Hutchinson and their other rhythm mate, pianist Marc Cary. An excellent session featuring standards such as "Everything I Have Is Yours," "My Shining Hour," and some Whitaker originals, "Mothered," "Childhood," and "Love's Lament," as well as fresh material from other members of the group. Whitaker backs leader Terence Blanchard on *Terence Blanchard* 🎵🎵🎵🎵 (Columbia, 1991, prod. Delfeayo Marsalis), another session featuring a youthful crew—pianist Bruce Barth, drummers Jeff Watts or Troy Davis, and guest soloists Branford Marsalis or Sam Newsome on tenor sax. The musicians give fresh voice to a pleasing mixture of standards and Blanchard originals, exhibiting mastery of the intricate harmonies and interacting with intelligence and maturity. Whitaker's playing is prominently best on a time-switching, swinging version of the warhorse, "I'm Getting Sentimental Over You," and on the grand finale, a quartet version of "Amazing Grace."

influences:
◀◀ Paul Chambers, Pops Foster, Jimmy Blanton, Oscar Pettiford

Nancy Ann Lee

Mark Whitecage
Born June 4, 1937, in Litchfield, CT.

Highly respected on the New York free jazz circuit, Hoboken, New Jersey–based multi-instrumentalist Mark Whitecage has been underrecorded as a leader and has not achieved the public attention his talents deserve, though his fellow musicians appreciate his alert artistry and frequently draw on his talents. Since arriving on the scene in the late 1960s, Whitecage has recorded with Gunter Hampel (five albums), Saheb Sarbib (five albums), Mario Pavone (two), Jeanne Lee (two), Steve Swell (one), and others; he has also performed with Anthony Braxton and Perry Robinson. He was one of the motivating forces behind the Improvisors Collective, a cooperative concert-organizing group based at Context Studios and which eventually spawned the Vision Festival—at the first Visionfest, Whitecage's performance was one of the highlights.

what to buy: *Caged No More* ♪♪♪♪ (CIMP, 1996, prod. Robert D. Rusch) adds cellist Tomas Ulrich to Whitecage's regular trio with bassist Dominic Duval and drummer Jay Rosen. It's entirely spontaneous improvisation, the context in which New York City listeners are perhaps most accustomed to hearing Whitecage. Spotlighting the quartet's superb interactivity, this is free jazz of unusual spareness and subtlety (which is not to say the musicians don't sometimes work up quite a head of steam) in which the music flowers with unforced naturalness.

what to buy next: *Free for Once* (CIMP, 1996, prod. Robert D. Rusch) features Duval and Rosen. Some tracks are more premeditated than anything on the above CD. A couple of the faster tunes suggest hard-swinging post-bop, while darker and moodier tracks recall Ornette Coleman's haunted tone and elastic lines. The sax-bass-drums format allows Whitecage to move freely from inside to outside on a flexible, stimulating session. Though structure always remains a strong factor, often the trio explodes into all-out free blowing, though in the midst of one such foray Whitecage quotes "Billy Boy" and at an earlier point a tango even breaks out!

worth searching for: *Mark Whitecage & Liquid Time* ♪♪♪♪ (Acoustics, 1991, prod. Otfried Müller) is on Whitecage's own label and is a must-hear for legendary drummer Peter LeMaitre, whose premature death four months after this session robbed the New York scene of one of its most sensitive and open drummers. Also on the date are pianist Michael Jefry Stevens and bassist Joe Fonda, both regular collaborators of Whitecage's, and trumpeter Dave Douglas. The musical idiom is not free jazz, but complex post-bop of the most adventurous sort, though not without a certain tunefulness. Douglas's carefully shaded trumpet tones complement the leader's equally varied sax style. Stevens is the leader of the duo CD *Short Stories* ♪♪♪♪ (Red Toucan, 1997, prod. Michael Jefry Stevens) and wrote all the material, which is chord-based and often quite lyrical. Not available at press time, but scheduled for release are Whitecage's *4+3=5* (CIMP, 1998) with Joseph Scianni and *Consensual Tension* (CIMP, 1998).

influences:

◀◀ Ornette Coleman, Air, Joe Chambers

▶▶ Rob Brown

Steve Holtje

Paul Whiteman

Born March 28, 1880, in Denver, CO. Died December 26, 1967, in Doylestown, PA.

While Paul Whiteman was important in the history of jazz, it was more for the band members he hired than for the music he played. Even though he toured as "The King of Jazz," Whiteman preferred blending symphonic and pop musics with just a hint of jazz to give it flavor. This was just the approach needed to bring "respectability" to jazz among the upper crust. To be fair, Whiteman hired the best possible musicians (many of them excellent jazz practitioners) and paid them better than anyone else in the business. The role call of major figures that passed through his band is impressive, including Bix Beiderbecke, Jimmy and Tommy Dorsey, Joe Venuti, Jack Teagarden, Bunny Berrigan, and Eddie Lang. If you count the singers he hired, names like Bing Crosby, Mildred Bailey, and Johnny Mercer pop out at you. Whiteman first came to public notice in the early 1920s, when he and his band recorded a song called "Whispering" that sold phenomenally well for its time. He commissioned George Gershwin to write "Rhapsody in Blue" and premiered the piece (with the composer playing the piano) in 1924's famous "An Experiment in Modern Music" concert in New York's Aeolian Hall. (Ferde Grofe, who had arranged both "Whispering" and the version of "Rhapsody in Blue" heard in Aeolian Hall later became famous with orchestral pieces like "The Grand Canyon Suite" and "The Mississippi River Suite.") The success of this concert led Whiteman to feature symphonic arrangements of other American composers including Victor Herbert, William Grant Still, and Duke Ellington. The 1930s were ushered in with Whiteman starring in an Academy Award—winning film (for "Best Interior Decoration") called *The King of Jazz*. Busby Berkeley engaged in his usual flamboyant scene-shifting for this picture, and Bing Crosby made his first celluloid appearance as part of Whiteman's male vocal group, the Rhythm Boys. By the end of the decade Whiteman and his orchestra found it harder to get jobs as the big band era was starting to swing closer to its demise. During the '40s he appeared in a few more movies (including 1947's *The Fabulous Dorseys*) but a larger portion of his time was spent as a musical director for the American Broadcasting Company and hosting his own television show. He had by then given up his band, although he still made guest appearances fronting other orchestras.

what to buy: *Paul Whiteman and His Orchestra* ✍✍✍ (Pearl, 1990, prod. various) covers the period from 1921 to 1934 and has most of the big Whiteman hits, including "Whispering" and its hit parade follow-up, "Japanese Sandman." Standards like "Nola," "Deep Purple," and "Liebestraum" fill up the set, but interesting jazz moments peek through in the band's versions of "St. Louis Blues" and "Wabash Blues."

what to buy next: While *The King of Jazz* ✍✍✍ (ASV/Living Era, 1996, prod. various) covers roughly the same time period, there is more of an emphasis on jazz inflection here. As in the other set, Beiderbecke, Teagarden, and Venuti are present, as are singers Crosby and Bailey, but it also offers Whiteman's early recording of "Rhapsody in Blue" for Gershwin fans.

worth searching for: The out-of-print *The Complete Capitol Recordings of Paul Whiteman and His Orchestra* ✍✍✍ (Capitol, 1995) is still worth hunting up for anyone interested in the back end of Whiteman's career. Johnny Mercer, a former singer with Whiteman's band, was one of the three cofounders of Capitol, and he coaxed his old boss into recording for the label during the '40s. The resultant material wasn't as popular with the audiences of the time, wrapped up as they were in swing and bebop bands of the day, but Whiteman managed to wax a few charmers anyhow. Included is Billie Holiday vocalizing on "Traveling Light" under the alias of "Lady Day."

influences:
▶▶ Lawrence Welk

Garaud MacTaggart

Mark Whitfield

Born October 6, 1966, in Lindenhurst, NY.

A 1987 Berklee School of Music graduate, guitarist Mark Whitfield released his first album, the blues-oriented *The Marksman*, about the time that every jazz player under 25 was getting a record contract. Whitfield began his musical studies at an early age, playing bass until his family relocated to Seattle where he landed a spot as guitarist in the school band. Mostly self-taught, Whitfield's exceptional abilities became apparent in a high school jazz competition sponsored by Berklee where he subsequently enrolled with a full scholarship. After graduation, he relocated to New York. Like many of his contemporaries, he showed promise, and has lived up to that promise. Stylistically Whitfield's a hard-bop stylist, though he has flirted with pop-jazz on occasion. His guitar influences include George Benson (who encouraged Whitfield to pursue working with organist Jack McDuff), Wes Montgomery, Kenny Burrell, and Grant Green. Whitfield has established himself as one of the top jazz guitarists of his generation.

what to buy: With accompaniment by a 21 piece orchestra on all but three cuts, *Forever Love* ✍✍✍ (Verve, 1997, prod. Richard Seidel, Mark Whitfield) is everything a jazz album with strings should be—seductive, compelling, romantic, provocative, dramatic, and refined. Though it's an album of ballads, the perfectly-sequenced songs cover much territory and Whitfield's playing, particularly on "Nature Boy" and "Forever," is hypnotic. The inclusion of three solo acoustic guitar pieces and vocalist Diana Krall on two songs adds the right balance to the affair. This is a truly rewarding artistic statement.

what to buy next: With an all-star veteran team—pianist Kenny Barron, bassist Ron Carter, and drummer Jack DeJohnette—for support, Whitfield does some serious playing on his sophomore effort, *Patrice* ✍✍✍ (Warner Bros., 1991, prod. Mark Whitfield, Ricky Schultz). He stretches out and the compositions are more challenging than on his debut. A Grant Green influence is strong on many cuts, but Whitfield also plays some nice acoustic pieces. After the George Benson styled pop-jazz *Mark Whitfield*, the guitarist came back with *True Blue* ✍✍✍ (Verve, 1994, prod. Richard Seidel, Don Sickler), a straight-ahead date with blues, standards, and bop. This is a good rebound with some solid playing and "Save Your Love for Me" is a keeper. A theme album dedicated to New York City, *7th Avenue Stroll* ✍✍✍ (Verve, 1995, prod. Richard Seidel, Don Sickler) offers standards written about the city such as "Sunday in New York" and "Harlem Nocturne." The session is filled with convivial playing from expert sidemen (pianists Tommy Flanagan and Stephen Scott, bassists Dave Holland and Christian McBride, and drummer Al Foster) and Whitfield's characteristic discipline shows throughout. With solid results, three of the hottest (and best) Generation X jazz players—Whitfield, bassist Christian McBride, and trumpeter Nicholas Payton—cover 14 Herbie Hancock compositions on *Fingerpainting: The Music of Herbie Hancock* ✍✍✍ (Verve, 1997, prod. Richard Seidel, Don Sickler). The material includes Hancock's funk classics, his straight-ahead standards, and some of his movie music. The trio's interpretations show great affinity for the material and the only drawback is the sparse setting as there are some moments that just demand a larger ensemble.

the rest:
The Marksman ✍✍✍ (Warner Bros., 1990)
Mark Whitfield ✍✍✍ (Warner Bros., 1993)

influences:

◀◀ Wes Montgomery, Charlie Christian, George Benson, Joe Pass, Grant Green, Kenny Burrell

Paul MacArthur

Weslia Whitfield

Born September 15, 1947, in Santa Maria, CA.

One of the most incisive and intelligent interpreters of lyrics working in the jazz/cabaret tradition, Weslia Whitfield is a singer who swings effectively on up-tempo numbers and brings a lustrous sensuality to ballads. She only improvises around the edges of a melody, but her strong, clear voice and direct, emotionally unadorned approach transforms even well-worn standards into highly personal material. Few singers can match the richness of her repertoire, which is full of obscure gems and standards reunited with their rarely heard verses. Trained in opera, Whitfield began singing in night clubs in the early 1970s, exploring the Great American Songbook. She slowly developed a devoted following around the San Francisco Bay Area and by the late 1980s had established herself as one of the premier jazz-influenced cabaret performers, a singer most comfortable working with jazz musicians. She performs almost exclusively with pianist/arranger Mike Greensill, a highly sensitive accompanist who is also her husband. Whitfield has recorded a number of excellent albums and sang "When Lights Are Low" with Benny Carter on his MusicMasters *Songbook* album.

what to buy: Singer Weslia Whitfield's best album yet, *Teach Me Tonight* ♫♫♫♪ (HighNote, 1997, prod. Orrin Keepnews) is an intimate session featuring pianist Mike Greensill (Whitfield's husband), bassist Michael Moore, drummer Joe LaBarbera, and reed master Noel Jewkes. With five tunes by the great Sammy Cahn, the album could have been marketed as a tribute, as Whitfield turns the title track into an irresistible plea and slows the usually mid-tempo "I've Heard That Song Before" to a ballad and restores the rarely heard verse. She also captures the exact balance of desperation and hope in "All My Tomorrows," which features some particularly moving tenor work by Jewkes. Other highlights include Whitfield's gorgeous duet with Moore on "Just in Time" and her storyteller's take on the Gershwin's "It Ain't Necessarily So." Greensill's tasteful, understated arrangements stay out of Whitfield's way while providing just the right level of support. *Seeker of Wisdom and Truth* ♫♫♫♪ (Cabaret, 1994, prod. Orrin Keepnews) is a superior collection of songs, performed with impeccable taste. Whitfield, accompanied by pianist

Mike Greensill, bassist John Goldsby and drummer Tim Horner, brings her probing, emotionally direct style to standards such as "My Favorite Things," "The Gypsy in My Soul," and "The Very Thought of You." With "I Believe in You," from *How to Succeed in Business . . .* and a medley from the Fred Astaire movie *Royal Wedding,* she translates stage and movie tunes into swinging vehicles that stand on their own. Her beautiful version of Billy Eckstine's ballad "I Want to Talk about You" and the obscure Cole Porter number "Come to the Supermarket" are among the album's highlights.

what to buy next: Whitfield has established herself as a singer with an uncanny skill for cutting through the layers of sentiment and nostalgia accumulated by standards to find the emotional essence of a lyric and melody. With *Beautiful Love* ♫♫♫♪ (Cabaret, 1993, prod. Orrin Keepnews) she displays a gift for breathing life into tunes rarely heard outside the shows for which they were written, such as Rodgers and Hammerstein's "Wonderful Guy," Lerner and Lowe's "Show Me," and a raucous version of Frank Loesser's "Sit Down, You're Rockin' the Boat." Whether bringing her unbridled sensuality to the torchy standards "Don't Go to Strangers" and "Beautiful Love," or waxing faux naive with "Let There Be Love" and "I Just Found Out about Love," Whitfield finds the perfect emotional tone for each tune she sings. Pianist Mike Greensill's arrangements are so right and unobtrusive it's easy to miss just how well-crafted they are. Bassist Dean Riley and drummer Tom Duckworth round out the trio. Accompanied by pianist Mike Greensill and bassist Dean Riley, Whitfield mostly sticks to tunes less taken on *Lucky to Be Me* ♫♫♫♪ (Landmark, 1990, prod. Orrin Keepnews), a session that features some of the more obscure works by such well-known composers as Rodgers and Hart ("This Funny World"/"He Was Too Good to Me"), Cole Porter ("Do I Love You?"), Irving Berlin ("Be Careful, It's My Heart"), and Duke Ellington (represented by the wonderful "Don't You Know I Care?"). Whitfield's precise phrasing makes even unknown tunes, such as the Tommy Wolf/Victor Feldman ballad "A Face Like Yours," sound like a standard. She is especially delightful when she turns her attention to three chestnuts by Howard Dietz and Arthur Schwartz, including the tongue-in-cheek "Rhode Island Is Famous for You" and the rueful but spirited "By Myself."

the rest:
Just for a Thrill ♫♫♫♪ (Myoho, 1986)
Until the Real Thing Comes Along ♫♫♫♪ (Myoho, 1988)
Nobody Else but Me ♫♫♫♪ (Myoho, 1989)
Live in San Francisco ♫♫♫♪ (Landmark, 1991)

influences:

◀◀ Sylvia Sims, Margaret Whiting

Andrew Gilbert

Gerald Wiggins

Born May 12, 1922, in New York, NY.

An elegant and highly versatile pianist best known for his taste-ful, swinging work accompanying many fine singers, Gerald Wiggins has played blues, swing, bop, and hard-bop over the course of his long career. Wiggins came of age when Teddy Wilson and Nat "King" Cole were the dominant piano influences, and Wig worshiped at the altar of Art Tatum. He had the technique and harmonic insight to adjust to the changes wrought by bebop, though like Hank Jones he has always maintained a strong connection to the older styles through his attention to melody and occasional use of stride and boogie woogie. Wiggins landed his first job on the road with comedian Stepin Fetchit in the early 1940s. He broke into the big bands with Les Hite when Dizzy Gillespie was in the trumpet section, then made a tour of the South with Louis Armstrong's orchestra in 1943. He worked with Benny Carter's orchestra before being drafted and spending two years stationed in Seattle (1944–46). After the service, he moved to San Francisco where he was recruited by Chico Hamilton to accompany Lena Horne. He settled in Los Angeles in the early 1950s and made a career of accompanying vocalists such as Dinah Washington, Kay Starr, Ernie Andrews, Nat "King" Cole, Joe Williams, Ella Mae Morse, Eartha Kitt, Helen Humes, and Jimmy Witherspoon. Active on L.A.'s vital Central Avenue scene in the early 1950s, he recorded with many top West Coast players, such as Art Pepper, Teddy Edwards, and Zoot Sims. He worked in the studios as a music director and vocal coach in the 1960s (one of his students was Marilyn Monroe) while continuing to play Los Angeles area club dates. Over the years, Wiggins has recorded for many independent labels, including Muse, Trend, Palo Alto, Hemisphere, Specialty, Challenge, and Black & Blue, though most of these recordings are extremely hard to find. He has been featured on a number of Concord sessions as a leader and as a sideman on a number of Scott Hamilton albums, including *Radio City*, Clark Terry and Red Holloway's *Locksmith Blues*, Mary Stallings's excellent *Spectrum*, and on the Frank Capp Juggernaut albums recorded after Nat Pierce's death in 1992. He was also on Joe Pass's Pablo album *One for My Baby*.

what to buy: The eighth volume in Concord's solo piano series, *Live at Maybeck Recital Hall, Vol. 8* 𝄞𝄞𝄞𝄞 (Concord Jazz, 1991,

prod. Carl E. Jefferson) is one of the program's gems, a wide-ranging tour through the best of the American Songbook played by a master with a sly sense of humor and a beautiful touch. His ideas roll out with such a relaxed and graceful feel, it's easy to get caught up in flow and miss his sophisticated and witty improvisation. "I Should Care," "Don't Blame Me," and the opening "Yesterdays" are some of the highlights on this first-rate album. Simply put, *Soulidarity* 𝄞𝄞𝄞𝄞 (Concord Jazz, 1996, prod. John Burk) is feel-good music that captures Wiggins with his longtime collaborator bassist Andy Simpkins and drummer Paul Humphrey in a trio with a simpatico, unpretentiously swinging approach. Wig works his way through a host of great songs from Irving Berlin's first hit, 1912's "Alexander's Ragtime Band," to Thad Jones's classic from the 1960s, "A Child Is Born." His two originals, "Strip City" from a Marilyn Monroe film and "Surprise Blues," add some spice to the proceedings.

what to buy next: A fine trio session featuring Joe Comfort (bass) and Jackie Mills (drums), *Relax and Enjoy It* 𝄞𝄞𝄞𝄞 (Contemporary/OJC, 1961, prod. Lester Koenig) captures Wig's working group playing a typical set of attractive standards such as "One for My Baby" and "My Heart Stood Still," as well as an unusual arrangement of the folk tune "Frankie and Johnny." Wig shows off his gorgeous touch on the Ellington medley of "Just Squeeze Me" and "Satin Doll."

best of the rest:

Music from Around the World in 80 Days 𝄞𝄞𝄞 (Specialty, 1956/OJC, 1991)

Gerald Wiggins Trio 𝄞𝄞𝄞𝄞 (VSOP, 1956/1997)

worth searching for: Originally released on Motif Records, *Reminiscin' with Wig* 𝄞𝄞𝄞𝄞 (Fresh Sound, 1957) is a trio session featuring bassist Eugene Wright and drummer Bill Douglass. Wig is in a mischievous mood, inserting quotes and finishing tunes with stomping final choruses. Besides Jerome Kern's "They Didn't Believe Me," the tunes are all rarely covered pieces such as "In My Merry Oldsmobile" and "That Old Gang of Mine."

influences:

◀◀ Art Tatum, Nat "King" Cole

▶▶ Benny Green, Eric Reed

Andrew Gilbert

Bob Wilber

Born Robert Sage Wilber, March 15, 1928, in New York, NY.

Bob Wilber is a pre-bop reeds player and composer-arranger who studied with Sidney Bechet in 1946–47, performed in a band in high school that included Dick Wellstood, and as a teenager sat in at Jimmy Ryan's club in New York City. Following World War II, Wilber led the revival of traditional jazz on the East Coast with his band the Wildcats, led bands at the Savoy and Storyville Club in Boston, and subbed for Bechet at the Nice Festival in 1948. After Army service (1952–54), Wilber became a member of the cooperative group the Six, which created a blend of modern and traditional jazz. In the late 1950s, he worked with Bobby Hackett, Jack Teagarden, and Eddie Condon, and toured with Benny Goodman in 1958 and 1959. Wilber was a founding member of the World's Greatest Jazz Band in 1969 and, with Kenny Davern, co-led the group Soprano Summit from 1974 to 1978. This group was reunited in 1990 and is still active as the Summit Reunion. Wilber is dedicated to the preservation of the jazz tradition, and in the late 1970s served as director of the Smithsonian Jazz Repertory Ensemble. He formed his own record company, Bodeswell, and from 1980 to 1983 led the Bechet Legacy, became director of jazz studies at Wilkes College in 1982, and wrote the soundtrack score for the 1984 film *The Cotton Club,* for which he won a Grammy Award. In 1987, Wilber published his autobiography, *Music Was Not Enough* (Macmillan). The next year, Wilber led a Carnegie hall tribute concert celebrating the 50th anniversary of the famous Benny Goodman concert. For his lifelong contributions to the jazz idiom, Wilber was elected a member of the Senior Statesmen of Jazz, along with many musicians who are in their eighties and nineties. In 1997, Wilber was co-billed with clarinetist Michael White in a Lincoln Center Jazz Orchestra tribute to Sidney Bechet. Wilber, who has homes in Arizona and the Cotswolds in England, continues to perform on clarinet and saxophones in the swing and Dixieland styles, and to record, compose, arrange, lecture, and write articles.

what to buy: *Reunion at Arbors* 𝄢𝄢𝄢𝄢 (Arbors, 1998, prod. Bob Wilber, Kenny Davern) features Bob Wilber and Kenny Davern merging their special chemistries on a pleasing set of nine studio-recorded classics, including sterling versions of warhorses such as "Sentimental Journey," "The Sheik of Araby," "Who's Sorry Now," and other hot-to-medium swing marvels and ballads. The musical relationship of the leaders dates back to Dick Gibson's Colorado Jazz Party in 1974, when the pair delivered an impromptu saxophone duet on "The Mooche." It was so well received that the principals formed and co-led the group Soprano Summit from 1974 to 1978, with a rhythm section that usually included guitarist Marty Grosz, bassists Milt Hinton or George Duvivier, and Bobby Rosengarden on drums. Since they reunited in the mid-1980s, they've been creating that old magic

under the name of Summit Reunion and have recorded a number of albums during the 1990s. This album is different for its inclusion of pianist Dave Frishberg, the singer/songwriter known for classics such as "My Attorney Bernie," "Peel Me a Grape," and others, and who has worked with both of the leaders in other bands. Drummer Ed Metz Jr., bassist Bob Haggart, and guitarist Bucky Pizzarelli simmer under solos by Wilber and Davern and keep the rhythmic pulses strong and steady throughout. A lushly orchestrated session of swingers and ballads recorded in England on October 10, 1994, *Bean: Bob Wilber's Tribute to Coleman Hawkins* 𝄢𝄢𝄢𝄢 (Arbors, 1995, prod. Harvey Bard, Rachel Domber, Mat Domber) features tenor saxophonists Harry Allen, Antti Sarpila (Wilber's student from Finland), and Tommy Whittle on the front line with Wilber. The group first collaborated when they performed a 1993 concert in England titled "The Swing Makers." Backed by Mick Pyne (piano) (who died on May 25, 1995 before the album was released), Dave Cliff (guitar), Dave Green (bass), and Clark Tracey (drums), the tenor saxophonists perform choruses as a tight unit and generate some excellent improvised solos. Their recreations of what Hawkins sounded like in a sax section make this 17-tune session a delightfully crafted tribute to the highly influential Coleman Hawkins, whose rich-toned, fluid saxisms inspired not only Wilber and his cohorts, but countless others worldwide. Although Wilber defers lots of spotlight space to his teammates, this tribute to one of his major inspirations bears his imprint throughout.

what to buy next: A laid-back session of classics and Wilber originals, *Horns A-Plenty* 𝄢𝄢𝄢 (Arbors, 1994) features the leader playing clarinet, curved and straight soprano saxophones, and tenor and alto saxes with sparkling support from pianist Johnny Varro, bassist Phil Flanigan, and drummer Ed Metz Jr. A pleasant session of medium-tempo swingers, popular favorites such as "Make Believe," "Smoke Gets in Your Eyes," "This Can't Be Love," and other delights. Soothing and smooth, *Horns A-Plenty* ranks among Wilber's best recordings. Although he has been writing for and leading big bands for years, Wilber had never recorded with a big band until *Bufadora Blow-Up* 𝄢𝄢𝄢 (Arbors, 1997, prod. Bob Wilber). The album features the Bob Wilber Big Band in a live performance at the 1996 March of Jazz presented by Arbors Records, and highlights the leader's composing-arranging skills for a big band. Among the 16 tunes are swing classics such as "It's Been So Long," "Goodnight My Love," "I'm Checking Out, Goom Bye" (featuring vocals by Wilber's wife, Joanne "Pug" Horton), "Jumpin' at the Woodside," and more. In addition to Wilber (alto, soprano saxophones, clarinet), lead soloists include Jerry Jerome (trumpet), Dick Hyman (piano), Dan Barrett (trombone), and others. The varied swing tempos, fine material, expert leadership, and excellent soloists make this intimate performance (with Wilber announcing) pure listening pleasure.

best of the rest:
(With Soprano Summit) *In Concert* ✷✷✷✷ (Concord, 1976/1992)
Ode to Bechet ✷✷✷✷ (Jazzology, 1982/1996)
Summit Reunion ✷✷✷✷ (Chiaroscuro, 1990)
Live at Concord '77 ✷✷✷✷ (Concord, 1991)
Soprano Summit ✷✷✷✷ (Chiaroscuro, 1994)
Bob Wilber & Bechet Legacy ✷✷✷✷ (Challenge, 1995)
Nostalgia ✷✷✷ (Arbors, 1996)

worth searching for: You may also want to check out the video version of *Bufadora Blow-Up* from Arbors, which features the musicians playing all of the tunes that are on the CD, plus interesting interviews with Wilber and his wife, singer Joanne "Pug" Horton, revealing facts about their lives and careers, including video tours of their homes in England and Arizona.

influences:
◀◀ Sidney Bechet, Benny Goodman, Artie Shaw, Coleman Hawkins, Johnny Hodges, Charlie Parker, Benny Carter, Frank Wess, Kenny Davern, Ralph Sutton, Dick Wellstood, Buddy DeFranco

▶▶ Ken Peplowski, Scott Hamilton, Chuck Hedges

see also: *Dan Barrett, Kenny Davern, Marty Grosz, Keith Ingham, Eddie Condon*

Nancy Ann Lee

Barney Wilen

Born Bernard Jean Wilen, March 4, 1937, in Nice, France. Died May 27, 1996, in Nice, France.

This saxophonist first came to international reknown in the mid-'50s, making concert appearances with Kenny Clarke, Benny Golson, and Bud Powell. He also recorded soundtrack albums with Miles Davis and Art Blakey's Jazz Messengers. Son of an American father and a French mother, Wilen spent his early years in the U.S., before moving to France in 1947. He became a formidable young talent, performing with American expatriate jazz musicians and other touring players. After building his formidable reputation, he moved to Africa in 1968, living there until 1973 when he returned to Nice. During this time, Wilen studied different musical cultures and modes of playing, experimenting with free jazz and Indian classical performances.

Upon his return to France, Wilen partook of further musical trends, investigating fusion jazz and Afro-centric rhythms before finally reverting back to his bop beginnings.

what to buy: *French Ballads* ✷✷✷✷ (IDA, 1987, prod. Philippe Vincent), a disc of French ballads, is heavy on material by Michel Legrand, but there are also a couple tunes from Django Reinhardt, Edith Piaf's signature piece ("La Vie En Rose"), and Frank Sinatra's signature, "My Way." Wilen is a wonderful ballad player and he has a gorgeous tone on tenor and baritone.

what to buy next: On *New York Romance* ✷✷✷ (Venus/Sunnyside, 1994, prod. Todd Barkan), Wilen is backed up by a solid East Coast ensemble (pianist Kenny Barron, bassist Ira Coleman, and drummer Lewis Nash) and they do a good job of covering the program on this disc. In addition to standards by Cole Porter, Kurt Weill, and Burton Lane, they also run through some '60s jazz classics by Duke Jordan ("No Problem") and Lou Donaldson ("Blues Walk").

best of the rest:
Wild Dogs of the Ruwenzori ✷✷✷ (IDA, 1989)
Movie Themes from France ✷✷✷ (Timeless, 1990)
Sanctuary ✷✷✷ (IDA, 1991)

worth searching for: Wilen's soundtrack work with Art Blakey, *Les Liàisons Dangereuses* (Fontana, 1960), and Miles Davis, *L'ascenseur Pour L'echafaud* (Fontana, 1957), are available again after years of catalog neglect.

influences:
◀◀ Sonny Rollins, Ben Webster, Lester Young

▶▶ Jean-Louis Chautemps, Hubert Fol, Georges Grenu

Garaud MacTaggart

Jack Wilkins

Born June 3, 1944, in New York, NY.

Jack Wilkins has become one of the busiest mainstream guitar players on the New York jazz scene. Known for an approach that incorporates a pianist's touch with classical guitar technique, he has recorded with Michael Brecker, Phil Woods, Stan Getz, and Dizzy Gillespie.

what to buy: A two-CD set that consolidates material from the LPs *The Jack Wilkins Quartet* and *You Can't Live Without It*, *Merge* ✷✷✷✷ (Chiaroscuro, 1977, prod. Hank O'Neal) offers a bracing shot of Wilkins, backed by talents such as Michael Brecker, Eddie Gomez, and Jack DeJohnette.

what to buy next: Featuring a host of unknown New York session guys, *Alien Army* 🎵🎵🎵 (Music Masters, 1992, prod. Leroy Parkins) serves up tasty guitar licks in a comfortable setting.

what to avoid: Compared to his other efforts, *Mexico* 🎵🎵 (CTI, 1992, prod. Creed Taylor) is a little pedestrian—but still a competent effort by one of mainstream jazz' hottest guitarists.

the rest:
Windows 🎵🎵🎵 (Mainstream, 1973)
Call Him Reckless 🎵🎵🎵 (Music Masters, 1989)

worth searching for: Wilkins's work on Project G-7's *A Tribute to Wes Montgomery* 🎵🎵🎵 (Evidence, 1992, prod. Akira Tana) places him alongside better-known guitarists Kenny Burrell and Kevin Eubanks.

influences:
◀◀ Wes Montgomery, Kenny Burrell, Joe Pass

▶▶ Mark Whitfield, Norman Brown

Eric Deggans

"Buster" Williams

Born Charles Williams, April 17, 1942, in Camden, NJ.

An excellent but often-overlooked bassist, Buster Williams gained prominence in the 1960s playing for Gene Ammons, Sonny Stitt, Dakota Staton, Betty Carter, Sarah Vaughan, Nancy Wilson, and Miles Davis. He sat in the Jazz Crusaders' revolving bass chair from 1967 to 1969, then became a member of Herbie Hancock's underrated but groundbreaking groups from 1969 to 1972. After leaving Hancock, he played with Dexter Gordon and Mary Lou Williams before joining the legendary Ron Carter Quartet. Williams has been primarily a sideman, playing with a wide array of artists, most notably Kenny Barron, with whom he was a member of the Thelonious Monk tribute group Sphere. Though an inventive and respected player, he tends to be taken for granted in the jazz community, which is a shame, because few bassists possess his talent.

what to buy: *Tokudo* 🎵🎵🎵 (Denon, 1989) is a trio date with Kenny Barron and Ben Riley, with all three men in excellent form. Williams's playing is crisp and well-conceived.

what to buy next: *Two as One* 🎵🎵🎵 (Red) is a duo album with Barron.

influences:
◀◀ Oscar Pettiford, Paul Chambers, Ray Brown, Jimmy Blanton

Paul MacArthur

Charles "Cootie" Williams

Born July 10, 1911, in Mobile, AL. Died September 15, 1985, in New York, NY.

Cootie Williams was one of the most famous, and most important, among the great tradition of Ellington trumpeters. He got his start with the Young Family Band (which included tenor saxophonist Lester) when he was but 14 years old. Williams went to New York in 1928 and played with Chick Webb and Fletcher Henderson before replacing Bubber Miley in the famous plunger position in Duke Ellington's band in 1929. Cootie was a major component of Duke's orchestra as it swung to the forefront of the big band era in the 1930s, and he was routinely featured in tunes such as "Echoes of Harlem" and, of course, "Concerto for Cootie." In 1940 Williams left Ellington to join the immensely popular Benny Goodman, where he was featured for about a year. After leaving Goodman, Williams led a semi-successful big band of his own through the 1940s, which at times included up-and-coming musicians like Bud Powell and Charlie Parker. In the 1950s, Cootie had drifted into relative obscurity, only to return to a rejuvenated Ellington group in 1962 as a featured soloist. He stayed with the Ellington band even past Duke's death, until Williams's own retirement around 1978.

what to buy: All of the CDs currently available consisting of Williams's output from the '40s overlap to some degree, making choosing between them something of a toss-up. The material on *Echoes of Harlem* 🎵🎵🎵🎵 (Pearl, 1996), however, is excellent. Williams is, of course, the main star, but also check out young alto Charlie Parker, singer Eddie "Cleanhead" Vinson, tenor Eddie "Lockjaw" Davis, and pianist Bud Powell in his very first recordings. Also contained on this import is the very first recording of Thelonious Monk's classic composition "'Round Midnight," which few people know was cowritten by Williams.

what to buy next: Fans of classical music will know how RCA prided itself, and rightfully so, on it's "Living Stereo" records of the late 1950s and early '60s. *Cootie Williams in Hi-Fi* 🎵🎵🎵🎵 (RCA 1958, prod. Fred Reynolds/1995, prod. Rolf Enoch) is a rare example of when they carried over the hi-fi technology into the jazz realm, with very nice results. Cootie's bravado is in full force in front of a mostly anonymous, but solid, big band on tried and true standards like "Caravan" and "Concerto for Cootie."

what to avoid: There's not much in Williams's small discography that is truly worth avoiding, and most of the music on *Cookin' with Cootie* 🎵🎵 (Drive Archive 1996, prod. Don Grierson), recorded in 1945, is just fine. But this reissue falls short of some of the others that cover much of the same material, in that it leaves out many of the more notable performances from the era, like "Honeysuckle Rose" and "Echoes of Harlem." Also, sound quality is rather poor.

the rest:

Typhoon 𝄢𝄢𝄢 (Swingtime, 1950)
The Big Challenge 𝄢𝄢𝄢 (Jazztone, 1957)
The Solid Trumpet of Cootie Williams 𝄢𝄢𝄢 (Moodsville, 1962)
1941–1944 𝄢𝄢𝄢 (Classics, 1995)

worth searching for: Recorded with Rex Stewart, *Cootie and Rex* 𝄢𝄢𝄢𝄢 (Jazztone, 1957) is perhaps the two greatest of all Ellingtonian trumpeters paying tribute to and dueling with each other. What is most remarkable about hearing the two together is how both are able to make the trumpet sound amazingly like the human voice, but in different ways: Cootie with a plunger and Stewart with valve tricks and the like.

influences:

⏮ Bubber Miley, Louis Armstrong

⏭ Ray Nance, Clark Terry, Wynton Marsalis

Dan Keener

Clarence Williams

Born October 8, 1893, in Plaquemine Delta, LA. Died November 6, 1965, in New York, NY.

Clarence Williams is perhaps one of the most influential yet most underrecognized giants of early jazz. Williams was not an outstanding hot jazz piano player (although some of his solos are quite good), but he was prolific in his recording output, and exceedingly influential in arranging many, many fine recording sessions during the 1920s. Moreover, his compositions comprise some of the most recognized and popular jazz titles of the Golden Age of Jazz. He spent most of his early years in New Orleans, although he did some touring with minstrel and vaudeville groups. Along with Armand J. Piron, he toured with W.C. Handy's Orchestra, and then formed a music publishing company with Piron. The partnership dissolved, precipitating Williams's move to Chicago where he opened a number of music shops before moving to New York in 1920. Williams's association with the major record labels of the day (Victor, OKeh, and Columbia) allowed his New York publishing business to flourish. He directed many recording sessions plus served as an accompanist on a great number of blues recordings. He also was an arranger, leader, and A&R (Artists & Repertoire) man for the OKeh and Columbia Race series of records. Williams led a number of different bands that appeared in clubs around New York. His recording connections allowed him to both record and broadcast quite regularly. His wife, Eva Taylor, also appeared with him. By the mid-1930s, he concentrated more on the publishing business, and less on recording. He sold his publishing business during the war, and retired to running an antique/second hand store until his death.

The dilemma with Clarence Williams is what to buy. He led groups from the early 1920s through the mid-1930s. All recordings are jazz, yet some are truly classic performances while others are merely quaint examples of Black pop music of the period. The listener's decisions can be driven by who is on a particular track (e.g., Louis Armstrong, Sidney Bechet, King Oliver, James P. Johnson, Ed Allen, Cecil Scott, etc.) or the size of the group (small groups such as the Washboard Four/Five groups and the Blue Five versus the larger "Jazz Kings" and Orchestra titles).

what to buy: For completeness, the Jazz Chronological Classics, commonly referred to as "Classics," series is the most comprehensive Clarence Williams set ever issued. The sound can be uneven, but this may well be the only way the average jazz fan will be able to own most of Williams's jazz output. The series includes: *Clarence Williams, 1921–1924* 𝄢𝄢𝄢𝄢 (Jazz Chronological Classics, 1994, prod. Gilles Petard), *Clarence Williams, 1924–1926* 𝄢𝄢𝄢𝄢 (Jazz Chronological Classics, 1994, prod. Gilles Petard), *Clarence Williams, 1926–1927* 𝄢𝄢𝄢𝄢 (Jazz Chronological Classics, 1994, prod. Gilles Petard), *Clarence Williams, 1927* 𝄢𝄢𝄢𝄢 (Jazz Chronological Classics, 1994, prod. Gilles Petard), *Clarence Williams, 1927–1928* 𝄢𝄢𝄢𝄢 (Jazz Chronological Classics, 1994, prod. Gilles Petard), *Clarence Williams, 1928–1929* 𝄢𝄢𝄢𝄢 (Jazz Chronological Classics, 1994, prod. Gilles Petard), *Clarence Williams, 1929* 𝄢𝄢𝄢𝄢 (Jazz Chronological Classics, 1995, prod. Gilles Petard), *Clarence Williams, 1929–1930* 𝄢𝄢𝄢𝄢 (Jazz Chronological Classics, 1995, prod. Gilles Petard), *Clarence Williams, 1930–1931* 𝄢𝄢𝄢𝄢 (Jazz Chronological Classics, 1995, prod. Gilles Petard), *Clarence Williams, 1933* 𝄢𝄢𝄢𝄢 (Jazz Chronological Classics, 1995, prod. Gilles Petard), *Clarence Williams, 1933–1934* 𝄢𝄢𝄢𝄢 (Jazz Chronological Classics, 1996, prod. Gilles Petard), *Clarence Williams, 1934* 𝄢𝄢𝄢𝄢 (Jazz Chronological Classics, 1996, prod. Gilles Petard), and *Clarence Williams, 1934–1937* 𝄢𝄢𝄢𝄢 (Jazz Chronological Classics, 1997, prod. Gilles Petard). The highlights of Clarence Williams's output on Jazz Chronological Classics may be helpful in focusing on what may be of interest. The earliest titles include many Sidney Bechet solos, most of which are exhilarating. "Kansas City Man Blues" (July 1923) and "New Orleans Hop Scop Blues" (October 1923) are two standout favorites.

When Louis Armstrong arrives in New York (becoming a member of Fletcher Henderson's band), he joins up with his New Orleans pals on a number of recording sessions led by Williams, and sparks really fly. Bechet and Armstrong really hit it off on "Everybody Loves My Baby" (November 1923) and the fiery "Cakewalkin Babies from Home" (January 1925), among others. By the end of 1925, Louis left New York and did not record with Williams again. The Clarence Williams dates that follow Armstrong's departure are somewhat uneven, but not dull by any standard. Both recording dates that feature the tune "Candy Lips" (the Jazz Kings of January 25, 1927, and the Washboard Four of January 29, 1927) are exceptional studies in small group jazz. The Jazz Kings version is a clarinet duet with rhythm accompaniment, while the Washboard Four side drops one clarinet and replaces it with the wonderful horn of Ed Allen. A number of nice larger band titles follow, including a date that features Coleman Hawkins at a point of transition, heralding things to come. He offers a powerhouse solo on "Dreamin' the Hours Away" (January 1928). King Oliver is next to join the recording festivities. Oliver is featured in duet with Ed Allen (and a lovely pairing it is!) on the Washboard Five session of May 23, 1928. The Orchestra date with "Mountain City Blues" (June 1928) is another fine outing for Oliver and well-deserved kudos go to Williams as the arranger for the date. A much larger band is featured on the QRS recording session ("Long, Deep, and Wide," "Speakeasy," etc.) (August 1928). Most of the 1929 sessions are split between the Jazz Kings and Washboard Band groups. "You Don't Understand" and "Oh Baby, What Makes Me Love You So" from November, 1929 include James P. Johnson on some very tasty piano. Most of the titles recorded in 1930 are of the highest caliber. All material is well-recorded, and the various bands fronted by Williams include some of the cream of New York's black jazz musicians of the period. The material recorded from 1934 on sometimes loses its sparkle. Some tracks seem "old-fashioned" by the standards of other music recorded at the same time. Other tracks such as "The Stuff's Here and It's Mellow," or "Tell the Truth" and "Sashay, Oh Boy" (these latter two may not even be a Williams group!) are quite good, as is the entire RCA/Bluebird session from 1937. Some of the latter recordings notwithstanding, Clarence Williams's music is essential to any vintage jazz collection and the whole series should be considered. For a more eclectic review of Clarence Williams's music, *Clarence Williams and the Jazz Kings, Vol. 1* ๕๕๕๕ (Frog, 1997, prod. various) and *Clarence Williams and the Jazz Kings, Vol. 2* ๕๕๕๕ (Frog, 1997, prod. various) are available. These CDs focus on the instrumental groups as well as the accompaniments to such blues

singers as Lucille Hegamin, Ethel Waters, Lizzie Miles, Bertha Idaho, and others.

what to buy next: Robert Parker's Digital Stereo products are well known and well regarded. *Clarence Williams, 1927–1934* ๕๕๕ (Robert Parker, 1994) is no exception, but only highlights Williams's career. This also may be a good introduction to Clarence Williams for the novice listener. Two series have started but not completed their Clarence Williams reissue projects, and only time will tell whether they will be completed or not. These include: *Clarence Williams, Vol. 1* ๕๕๕ (Collectors Classics, 1994, prod. various) and *Clarence Williams, Vol. 2* ๕๕๕๕ (Collectors Classics, 1994, prod. various), plus *Clarence Williams, Complete Sessions, Vol. 1, 1923* ๕๕๕ (EPM/Hot 'N Sweet, 1996, prod. various), *Clarence Williams, Complete Sessions, Vol. 2, 1923–1925* ๕๕๕ (EPM/Hot 'N Sweet, 1996, prod. various), *Clarence Williams, Complete Sessions, Vol. 3, 1925–1926* ๕๕๕ (EPM/Hot 'N Sweet, 1996, prod. various), and *Clarence Williams, Complete Sessions, Vol. 4, 1926–1927* ๕๕๕๕ (EPM/Hot 'N Sweet 1996, prod. various). The sound on all of these is quite good and not as uneven as the Classics sometimes tend to be. However, the Classics series is complete, and these are not. For hardcore Clarence Williams fans, *Clarence Williams & the Blues Singers, Vol. 1, 1923–1928* ๕๕ (Document, 1995, prod. various) and *Clarence Williams & the Blues Singers, Vol. 2, 1927–1932* ๕๕ (Document, 1995, prod. various) feature Clarence as accompanist to a variety of cabaret-style, black, mostly female singers of varying quality. Williams's work is generally bland on these. Thus, these CDs may be best-suited for the jazz historian and collector.

Jim Prohaska

Claude Williams

Born February 22, 1908, in Muskogee, OK.

By the time Claude Williams moved to Kansas City in 1928, the city was a hot bed for swing, and since Williams played most string instruments he was able to find work. His favored instrument has been violin, on which, from his earliest performing days, he could produce horn-like jazz improvisations inspired by Charlie Parker and Lester Young. His first recordings were made for the Brunswick label in 1928, playing guitar and violin with the Twelve Clouds of Joy (a band led first by Terrence Holder, then by Andy Kirk) with pianist Mary Lou Williams arranging and composing. The band made their New York debut at the Roseland Ballroom and at Harlem's Savoy. Upon returning to Kansas City, the band became part of the thriving scene where musicians at 50 clubs near 18th and Vine battled it out in jams and cutting contests. After working awhile in Kansas City, Claude Williams headed for Chicago where he was playing guitar with Eddie Cole's band (brother of Nat "King" Cole). When assembling his first band in 1936, Count Basie found Williams and hired him and put him in a prominent role (playing rhythm guitar) that garnered him brief national fame before he was replaced by Freddie Green. In the 1940s, Claude freelanced with various bands in the Midwest, and by the 1950s was using amplification on his fiddle. He worked in Los Angeles with Roy Milton's Blues Band (1951–52), and in 1953 moved back to Kansas City to lead his own combo on fiddle and guitar. Saxophonist Eddie "Cleanhead" Vinson was a member of that group. Williams led his own groups and freelanced around Kansas City throughout the 1960s, toured Europe in the 1970s, and worked and recorded with pianist Jay McShann into the 1980s. His last album to feature his guitar work was his 1980 album *Fiddler's Dream*. Since then, he has focused exclusively on violin. Williams continued his freelance work and recorded a couple of albums during the 1980s and 1990s and began touring Europe in 1997. Williams has won numerous awards, including his 1989 induction into the Oklahoma Jazz Hall of Fame. He celebrated his 89th birthday teaching students at the Smithsonian National Museum of American History, and continued an active schedule with overseas tours, club appearances, an ocean cruise, and other engagements.

what to buy: *SwingTime in New York* 𝄞𝄞𝄞𝄞 (Progressive, 1995, prod. Russ Dantzler) documents a September 5, 1994, studio gig with then 86-year-old Williams in peak form, swingin', fiddlin', and romancin' his way through a spectacular set of 14 classics (11 done in one take each) with superb support from veterans Sir Roland Hanna (piano), excellent swing drummer Joe Ascione, Earl May (bass), and music director Bill Easley (tenor sax, flute, clarinet). Williams's lush bowings on the ballad "Laura" (with fine rhythm team backing that includes Ascione's whispery brushwork and Easley's lovely flute solo) is one of many highlights; there are plenty more. Williams's occasional vocals add to the delight of this outing (especially his revisit to one of his first-learned songs, "You've Got to See Your Mama Ev'ry Night or You Can't See Mama at All"). Plus, he nods to one of his inspirators with a novel boppin' take on "Lester Leaps In." There's heartfelt rapport among these musicians (all but Hanna have previously worked with Williams) to fortify the leader's fiddlin' fashionings on this well-rounded set.

what to buy next: *King of Kansas City* 𝄞𝄞𝄞𝄞 (Progressive, 1997, prod. Claude Williams, Russ Dantzler) hits hearty grooves right

from the start, bolstered by a sideteam that includes the Claude Williams Swing String Trio—Williams, guitarist Rob Fleeman, bassist Bob Bowman—with drummer Todd Strait, and guests, saxophonist Kim Park and vocalists Karrin Allyson and Lisa Henry. Williams performs 13 standards, singing on "St. Louis Blues" and "Gee Baby, Ain't I Good to You?" The diverse session isn't as much Kansas City swing–styled as you'd wish for, but Williams gets some especially hot fiddle licks in on Arnett Cobb's jump-tune "Smooth Sailing." It's amazing that, age 89 at the time of this recording, Williams still has energy for an all-day session in the studio. *Live at J's, Vol. 1* 𝄞𝄞𝄞𝄞 (Arhoolie, 1993, prod. Russ Dantzler, Chris Strachwitz) features the fiddler mixing it up on 12 tunes live-recorded during two Spring 1989 performances at "J's," a New York venue. Williams's fiddle sings and swings on classics such as "(Going To) Kansas City," "Our Love Is Here to Stay," "After You've Gone," "Cherokee," and other standards, as well as two delightful originals, an amazing lightening-quick hoedown on "The Fiddler" and Williams's vocals and waltzing tempo on his ballad "You're My Desire." Guitarist James Chirillo, pianist Ron Mathews, drummers Akira Tana or Grady Tate, and bassist Al McKibbon add sparking energy to the toe-tappin' tunes. *Live at J's, Vol. 2* (Arhoolie, 1993, prod. Russ Dantzler, Chris Strachwitz), from the same live dates with the same personnel, contains 11 more tunes, standards to which Williams (81-years old at this gig) adds his spirited fiddling flair. Williams draws from his past with warhorses such as the pretty Victor Young song "100 Years from Today," Ellington's "Take the 'A' Train" and "Don't Get around Much Anymore," as well as contributing his "Fiddler's Dream" and "That Certain Some-One." Williams's fluency, polished technique, and blissfully swinging personalized style (somewhere between the warm romanticism of Stephane Grappelli and bluesy verve of Stuff Smith) will make you wonder why he doesn't have more recordings as leader to his credit.

worth searching for: Williams is at comfortable ease with his contemporaries (ranging in age from middle sixties to early nineties) on *Statesmen of Jazz* 𝄞𝄞𝄞𝄞 (American Federation of Jazz Societies, 1995, prod. Arbors Records), a session recorded on December 20, 1994 that prominently features him with Clark Terry (flugelhorn, trumpet), Joe Wilder (flugelhorn), Al Grey (trombone), Benny Waters (alto saxophone), Buddy Tate (tenor saxophone), Milt Hinton (bass), Jane Jarvis (piano), and David "Panama" Francis (drums). These musicians have been collaborating or crossing paths for decades and represent much of the good jazz that has been heard in various venues and on recordings for many decades. With an accumulated 500 years of experience among the nine musicians, they've racked up credits with legends such as King Oliver, Louis Armstrong, Duke Ellington, Count Basie, Andy Kirk, Cab Calloway, Roy Eldridge, Lester Young, and countless other jazz luminaries. Thus what you hear on this album of 10 classics (some contributed by band members) is performed with informed gentility. This is no jam, but a well-planned studio session offering some of the hottest soloing and best ensemble work on record. It is a must-own album, a slice of authentic jazz history that finds everyone at their elegant best.

influences:

◀◀ A.J. Piron, Joe Venuti, Eddie South, Stephane Grappelli, Stuff Smith

▶▶ Ray Nance, John Frigo, Vassar Clements, Matt Glaser, Randy Sabien, Tom Morley

Nancy Ann Lee

Daoud-David Williams

See: Spirit of Life Ensemble

"Fiddler" Williams

See Claude Williams

James Williams

Born March 8, 1951, in Memphis, TN.

A champion of the modern mainstream piano style first introduced by Art Tatum and later developed by Phineas Newborn Jr., James Williams has proven to be one of the finest contemporary players of his generation, in addition to being a valued supporter of young talent and a record producer in his own right. Williams was initially influenced by 1960s soul and the gospel music of the African American church. He spent time working and studying in his native Memphis before heading to Boston in 1972 for a five-year stint as an instructor at the Berklee College of Music. During this period he worked with a number of name artists including Woody Shaw, Joe Henderson, and Clark Terry. His stay with Art Blakey's Jazz Messengers (1977–81) brought Williams his first taste of public and critical acclaim. During the 1980s and 1990s, Williams worked extensively as a sideman with players such as Bobby Hutcherson and Tom Harrell. He has fronted some impressive groups of his own and recorded a number of valuable albums in addition to producing the work of other artists (e.g., Harold Mabern, Donald Brown, Billy Pierce) for such labels as Concord, Sunnyside, EmArcy, and DIW/Disc Union. An admitted student and pur-

veyor of the music of Phineas Newborn Jr., Williams also leads the Contemporary Piano Ensemble, a group that includes his peers Harold Mabern, Geoff Keezer, and Mulgrew Miller, and is dedicated to fostering the legacy of Newborn and others of his ilk. Williams's own style is marked by a prodigious technique, a fluent two-handed attack, and a rich harmonic knowledge that makes his music always sound fresh and engaging.

what to buy: *Alter Ego* ♫♫♫♫ (Sunnyside, 1984, prod. James Williams, Francois Zalacain) is one of the best showcases for Williams's writing. A fine cast that includes guitarist Kevin Eubanks and Billy Pierce also helps elevate this outing to a higher plane than your average mainstream fare. *Talkin' Trash* ♫♫♫♫ (DIW/Columbia, 1993, prod. James Williams, Kazunori Sugiyama) finds Williams in the company of the legendary Clark Terry, saxophonist Billy Pierce, vibist Steve Nelson, bassist Christian McBride, and drummer Tony Reedus. Everyone was obviously inspired by Terry's presence and the trumpeter's humorous vocal numbers are a highlight amidst a session that is absolutely flawless.

what to buy next: *Progress Report* ♫♫♫♫ (Sunnyside, 1985, prod. James Williams, Francois Zalacain) features Eubanks and Pierce, like the aforementioned *Alter Ego*, and once again finds the material fostering animated performances. *Meets the Saxophone Masters* ♫♫♫♫ (DIW/Disc Union, 1991, prod. James Williams, Kazunori Sugiyama) pits Williams and his trio against tenor legends George Coleman, Joe Henderson, and Billy Pierce for a blowing date of considerable worth.

the rest:

Up to the Minute Blues ♫♫♫♫ (DIW/Disc Union, 1994)
At Maybeck Recital Hall ♫♫♫♫ (Concord, 1996)
Truth, Justice, and Blues ♫♫♫ (Evidence, 1996)

influences:

◀◀ Art Tatum, Hampton Hawes, Phineas Newborn Jr.

▶▶ Geoff Keezer

Chris Hovan

Jessica Williams

Born March 18, 1948, in Baltimore, MD.

When it comes to playing a sterling game of musical free association, pianist Jessica Williams is about as good as they get. Her best inventions are built around endlessly intertwining, seamless streams of references to all sorts of things. Bits of popular song, quips from the classics (both African American and European), punning allusions, engaging non sequiturs—

these devices and more routinely find their way into the mix. She'll do "A Night in Tunisia," for instance, as if it'd been written by Monk, from its opening chording and rhythm that recall "Epistrophy," all the way down to the splashing dissonant accents and a couple of quotes from "Mysterioso." Only much, much later does it turn Gillespian, briefly, echoing the call from "Salt Peanuts." In the midst of a "Mack the Knife" that features stabbing, staccato effects via hand-dampened strings, she suddenly blurts out an ingenuous "I love him" as an aside; a snippet of the theme from *Mary Hartman, Mary Hartman* will crop up in any number of comedic situations. Clarity of line, fine technical command, and an almost encyclopedic knowledge of the various eras and styles that comprise jazz history are also features of Williams's seemingly limitless bag of tricks. After studying formal theory at Baltimore's Peabody Conservatory for a while, her rebellious nature converted her to jazz and improvisation. Gigging up and down the East Coast once she'd graduted from the public school system, taking whatever nightclub work she could find, it was an offer to join Philly Joe Jones's mid-1970s band that proved to be the big break. Later, she took up residence at San Francisco's Keystone Korner, where she assumed the role of "house pianist," which seasoned her by exposure to an endless succession of touring pros. Until her most recent release, *Jessica's Blues*, trio and solo were the only ways she was represented on record as a leader, with a nearly non-existent sideperson discography.

So why isn't Jessica Williams better known? That's a good question, of course, though it doesn't offer up many easy answers. For starters, let's just say she is, by all accounts, a very private person. Her lifestyle can safely be labeled as radical by mainstream American standards, judged by the openly pro-gay stance of her 1993 release on Hep (don't forget that prior to the recent declarations of sexual independence by Fred Hersch, Gary Burton, and Andy Bey, the subject was rarely discussed openly). Despite such irrelevant extra-musical considerations, the fact remains that her music is extremely accessible. Suffice it to say, then, that her decision to remain aloof from major music business centers and customs—she's currently somewhere in the rural Pacific Northwest, self-producing cassettes of experimental electronic music and doing the occasional indie album date—combined with a steadfast refusal to compromise artistic vision, have all played a part in her obscurity.

what to buy: Things, however, have been looking up ever since she signed with recently resurgent Candid Records in 1995, distributed by the exemplary jazz division at Koch International. Of the pair of uniformly excellent albums she has thus far done for the label, *Higher Standards* 𝄞𝄞𝄞𝄞 (Candid, 1997, prod. Jessica Williams, Alan Bates) is the more impressive, an assured outing in a trio setting that finds bassist Dave Captein and drummer Mel Brown offering outstanding support throughout a program of . . . well . . . standards. This is, in fact, the disc that has both the stunning version of "A Night in Tunisia" and the "Mack the Knife" mentioned above, plus a striking "Get Out of Town" that opens to Williams working keys and soundboard, simultaneously, which sets up an especially attractive melodic/rhythmic atmosphere. *Gratitude* 𝄞𝄞𝄞𝄞 (Candid, 1996, prod. Jessica Williams, Alan Bates) is a solo recital that brings a number of her own compositions into the picture. Among these, the dedication to bassist Leroy Vinnegar entitled "The Sheikh" is particularly strong, with more healthy doses of Williams's arresting, harp-like soundboard work. Deeper into the album she combines fragments of "Just You, Just Me" with portions of "Evidence" to create the slyly Monkian round "Justice," and there are plenty of nods to John Coltrane woven into the album's scheme and fabric. The sound of both Candid discs is, by the way, superb. And another fine solo recital, this time live, can be found on the Jessica Williams volume of the ongoing series *At Maybeck Hall Volume 21* 𝄞𝄞𝄞𝄞 (Concord, 1992, prod. Nick Phillips), another disc that offers pristine sound as well as convincing musicianship.

what to buy next: The bulk of the remainder of the Jessica Williams catalog is found on the small Canadian imprint Jazz Focus. *Inventions* 𝄞𝄞𝄞𝄞 (Jazz Focus, 1995, prod. Jessica Williams, Philip Barker) is a trio with frequent collaborators Jeff Johnson on bass and Dick Berk on drums (plus a solitary cover/solo performance, "Tea for Two"). Dedications to fellow-88ers "Toshiko" (Akiyoshi) and Duke (Ellington, "Nightwatch") and 'Trane, again, plus a crisp "Clean Blue Lou," a description of a Philip K. Dick character who's achieved Buddhahood in this lifetime. Alone again in 1994 for *Arrival* 𝄞𝄞𝄞𝄞 (Jazz Focus, prod. Jessica Williams, Philip Baker) or caught in the act at Atwaters in Portland, Oregon, to create a relaxed, grooveful group of *Encounters* 𝄞𝄞𝄞𝄞 (Jazz Focus, 1995, prod. Jessica Williams, Philip Baker) with the above-mentioned Vinnegar and the wonderful Mel Brown on drums, Williams is nothing if not polished and consistent. . . . *And Then, There's This* 𝄞𝄞𝄞𝄞 (Timeless, 1990, prod. Tim Merritt), done with John Witala on bass and Kenny Wolleson on drums, is rife with allusions. "Nichols' Bag" acknowledges Williams's deep debt to Herbie Nichols, hence its double-entendre title; the "House That Rouse Built" dovetails with Monk's "Bemsha Swing" and "I Mean You." Most instructive in drawing stylistic parallels, though, may be the marvelously spun "Newk's Fluke," an *homage a* Sonny Rollins that goes to the very source of her use of quotes from widespread sources as a form of narrative shorthand.

the rest:
The Next Step ♫♫♫ (Hep Jazz, 1993)
Momentum ♫♫♫ (Jazz Focus, 1996)
Jessica's Blues ♫♫♫ (Jazz Focus, 1997)

worth searching for: Charlie Rouse's *Epistrophy* ♫♫♫ (Landmark, 1992/32 Jazz, 1997, prod. Orrin Keepnews, reissue prod. Joel Dorn) is taken from a 1988 concert that paid tribute to Thelonious Monk (and was the tenor saxophonist's final recording). It includes Williams sitting in on "Blue Monk." She refigures the theme slightly but is perfectly suited to the spirit of the piece.

influences:

◀◀ Meade Lux Lewis, Dodo Marmarosa, Hampton Hawes, Thelonious Monk, Sonny Rollins, John Coltrane, Herbie Nichols

▶▶ Rodney Kendrick, Geri Allen, Gonzalo Rubalcaba

David Prince

Joe Williams

Born Joseph Goreed Williams, December 12, 1918, in Cordele, GA.

Joe Williams is the last of the great big band singers, a powerful baritone with the rare ability to offer definitive versions of blues, standards, and ballads. A warm performer with a confidently swinging style, Williams brought an urbane sophistication to a role pioneered in the Count Basie band by Jimmy Rushing. Raised in Chicago, Williams began singing in nightclubs while still a teenager. He worked with Jimmy Noone in the late '30s and performed with Coleman Hawkins and Lionel Hampton in the early '40s. A tour with Andy Kirk and his Clouds of Joy in 1946–47 led to Williams's first recording, but he continued to struggle. In the late '40s he had brief stints with the Albert Ammons/Pete Johnson band and the Red Saunders band back in Chicago. In 1950 he worked with trumpeter Hot Lips Page and the septet Count Basie founded after breaking up his big band. Williams scored a minor hit with King Kolax in 1951 with "Everyday I Have the Blues," which would become one of his signature songs, but he scuffled for another few years before hooking up with Basie again in 1954. During his seven-year tenure with the revitalized Basie band, Williams became an international star and was one of the key elements behind Basie's resurgence. Williams worked with trumpeter Harry "Sweets" Edison's small group from 1961 to

1962 and has toured with his own rhythm section ever since. Over the years Williams occasionally reunited with Basie and also recorded memorable sessions with the Thad Jones–Mel Lewis Orchestra, the Capp/Pierce Juggernaut, Cannonball Adderley, and George Shearing. As of this writing, Williams continues to perform and record with the energy and chops of a man half his age.

what to buy: The first and still definitive Williams/Basie album, *Count Basie Swings, Joe Williams Sings* ♫♫♫♫ (Verve, 1955/1993, prod. Norman Granz), is a powerhouse session with tight, driving arrangements. Many of the tunes, "Every Day I Have the Blues," "The Comeback," "In the Evening," and "Alright, Okay, You Win," are still in Williams's repertoire. An essential purchase for big band and jazz vocal fans. A classic session pairing two jazz institutions at the peak of their powers, *Joe Williams and the Thad Jones/Mel Lewis Orchestra* ♫♫♫♫ (Blue Note, 1966/1994, prod. Alfred Lion) features Jones's complex but streamlined arrangements. Williams responds with tour de force versions of "Smack Dab in the Middle" and "It Don't Mean a Thing . . ." where he scats up a storm. Also memorable is his hilarious version of "Evil Man Blues." Recorded live at Hollywood's Vine Street Bar and Grill, *Ballad and Blues Master* ♫♫♫♫ (Verve, 1992, prod. Eulis Cathey) captures the great singer in a relaxed, swinging mood. With his longtime accompanist, pianist Norman Simmons, leading a crack rhythm section featuring the soulful guitarist Henry Johnson, Williams displays his remarkable versatility, crooning ballads such as "Everyday (I'll Fall in Love)" and "A Hundred Years from Today," then tearing into the raunchy blues of "Who She Do" and a three-song medley that ends the album.

what to buy next: For his second album with Basie, *The Greatest!!* ♫♫♫ (Verve, 1957, prod. Buddy Bregman), Williams wanted to show he wasn't just a bluesman. He proves himself to be a top-shelf jazz singer capable of transforming pop tunes and ballads into swinging vehicles. There's hardly a weak track among the 12 tunes, but standouts include Ellington's "I'm Beginning to See the Light," the Gershwins's "Our Love Is Here to Stay" and "'S Wonderful," and the Mercer/Arlen gem "Come Rain or Come Shine." Taken from the same performances from which *Ballad and Blues Master* was drawn, *Every Night: Live at Vine St.* ♫♫♫ (Verve, 1987, prod. Miriam Cutler, David Kreisberg, Ron Berinstein) features Williams at his best with his excellent working rhythm section. Highlights include his much-copied arrangement linking "Every Day I Have the Blues" with Miles Davis's "All Blues," a raucous version of "Roll 'Em Pete," and a beautifully rendered "Too Marvelous for Words." A di-

Joe Williams (© Jack Vartoogian)

verse selection of material makes *In Good Company* 🎵🎵🎵🎵 (Verve, 1989, prod. Miriam Cutler, Ron Berinstein) one of Williams's more representative albums. Accompanied by his erstwhile rhythm section piloted by pianist Norman Simmons, Williams sings two duets with Marlena Shaw, including a classic version of "Is You Is or Is You Ain't My Baby." Though his two duets with Shirley Horn, backed by her trio, are a little disappointing, the two tunes with Supersax ("Just Friends" and "Embraceable You") work well.

best of the rest:

Every Day: Best of the Verve Years 🎵🎵🎵🎵 (Verve, 1954–89/1993)

At Newport '63/Jump for Joy 🎵🎵🎵🎵 (Collectables, 1963/BMG, 1997)

Joe Williams Live 🎵🎵🎵🎵 (Fantasy, 1974/OJC, 1990)

Prez Conference: Prez and Joe 🎵🎵🎵🎵 (GNP, 1979/Crescendo, 1986)

Live at Orchestra Hall, Detroit 🎵🎵🎵🎵 (Telarc, 1993)

Here's to Life 🎵🎵🎵 (Telarc, 1994)

Feel the Spirit 🎵🎵🎵 (Telarc, 1995)

influences:

⏪ Jimmy Rushing, Billy Eckstine

⏩ Kevin Mahogany

Andrew Gilbert

Mars Williams

Well-grounded in both the avant-jazz and the rock worlds, Mars Williams can produce a pedigree as mind-boggling as some of the note-salvos fired with such agility from the bells of his saxes. Everyone knows that he's the current spokesperson for the NRG Ensemble, and that he founded said group with Hal Russell in 1978. You might know that he also gigged full-time with the Waitresses (of the MTV hit "I Know What Boys Like") and later became a member of the Psychedelic Furs. But how about that sax on Billy Idol's *Rebel Yell*, or those reeds on *The Power Station*? That's our man Mars as well, and in short, the man is capable of playing in quite a diverse range of idioms.

Luckily for all of the free jazz fans out there, Williams returned to Chicago and the NRG Ensemble in 1988, one of several factors that seemingly pushed NRG over the edge and into the limelight. Jazz has always been near the center of Williams's heart, and after leaving Chicago in 1980, he studied with Roscoe Mitchell in Madison before leaving for New York. Even while gigging in rock bands in NYC, Williams found the time to occasionally operate on the periphery of the Zorn/Laswell downtown scene. But that's nothing compared to how busy Williams is now. Besides such full-time endeavors as the NRG Ensemble and Liquid Soul, Williams can be found in more than a handful of other projects in the Chicago area. His group Witches and Devils keeps the music of Albert Ayler alive with the help of Ken Vandermark and the dynamic avant-garde cellist Fred Lomberg-Holm, and with a group called Slam, Williams perpetrates some thrash-jazz mania. His Crown Royals exercise some retro-lounge-swing moves while trying not to be confused with the Royal Crown Revue. And he has a duo or two with Vandermark: Cinghiale, which plays originals, and the Sun Ra Project, which does the public the service of presenting previously unreleased Sun Ra songs. Next time you're in Chicago, odds are that you'll see him.

what's available: The public's loudest shouts for Williams probably get generated for his crossover mersh group Liquid Soul. Their eponymous release, *Liquid Soul* ♫♫♫ (Ark 21, 1996, prod. Mars Williams), blends brass and beats, funk and acid jazz, hip-hop and hard bop. This large group (including turntablist Jesse De La Pena) mixes covers of classics like "Equinox" and "Freddie the Freeloader" with cybermodern tunes like "Afro Loop" and "Java Junkie." If this slick effort leaves you longing for some of Williams's roots, you might be better off with *Hoofbeats of the Snorting Swine* ♫♫♫♫ (Eighth Day Music, 1996, prod. Mars Williams, Ken Vandermark) by Cinghiale, which is his duo with NRG-mate Ken Vandermark. Here, the NRG frontline loudly explores free improv and post-Ayler tunesmithery with a blown battery of reed instruments, a far cry from the slick-a-phonics of Liquid Soul.

worth searching for: Probably not dissimilar to how NRG must have started out, *Eftsoons* ♫♫♫♫ (Nessa, 1981) is a loud and crazy duo LP for Williams and Hal Russell, featuring some bells-together scrape-action and plenty of over-the-top blowing.

influences:
◀◀ Albert Ayler, Hal Russell

see also: *NRG Ensemble*

Greg Baise

Mary Lou Williams

Born Mary Scruggs, May 8, 1910, in Atlanta, GA. Died May 28, 1981, in Durham, NC.

Pianist Mary Lou Williams was a highly regarded instrumentalist, primarily a swing stylist and gifted composer who contributed to the success of many notable jazz orchestras during the big band era. But more important, she is the only major jazz artist who lived and *adapted her playing style* throughout the development of all of the jazz eras: spirituals, ragtime, the blues, Kansas City swing, boogie woogie, bop or modern, and avant-garde. Williams grew up in Pittsburgh and performed from age six to 16 at parties and in vaudeville using the name Mary Lou Burley (her stepfather's surname). In 1925, she joined a group led by baritone saxophonist John Williams, whom she married in 1927, and afterwards performed as Mary Lou Williams. They headed for Memphis, John's home, and then to Oklahoma City, and when Andy Kirk took over Terrence Holder's band (with John Williams as member), Mary Lou began to do some arranging for the band in 1928. By 1930, she had became the chief composer and arranger in Andy Kirk's band, supplying five or six arrangements a week, and the fame of this Kansas City–based band was largely due to her distinctive arrangements and original compositions, and her piano playing. During the same period, she was also writing and arranging for bands led by Benny Goodman, Earl Hines, and Tommy Dorsey. In 1942, Williams and her husband were divorced, and she left Kirk's band to return to Pittsburgh. She formed her own band that included the young drummer Art Blakey, and shortly after married trumpeter Harold "Shorty" Baker. In 1943, they moved to New York, where Williams was eventually drawn into the bop scene, contributing scores to Dizzy Gillespie's big band. Young bop players such as pianists Thelonious Monk and Budd Powell, and arranger Tadd Dameron congregated at her apartment during the 1940s. Williams joined Duke Ellington's Band where she served as staff arranger for six months, writing about 15 pieces, including "Trumpet No End" in 1946. That same year, three movements of her *Zodiac Suite* were performed at Town Hall by the New York Philharmonic Orchestra at Carnegie Hall.

But she was feeling frustrated; the more she experimented, the greater the gulf between demands of entertaining and her need to grow as a musician. In 1952, she escaped to Europe where she performed with trios and quartets in England and France for two years. In 1954, Williams returned to New York and, disillusioned about the business, retired from music.

She converted to Catholicism about this time, and established a charitable foundation, a ministry to assist musicians wrestling with alcoholism, drug addiction, and illness. Coaxed back into the music business by fellow musicians and her spiritual advisors, she began playing publicly again in 1957, joining Dizzy Gillespie at the Newport Jazz Festival and taking jobs in New York's premier jazz clubs. She started and ran her own record label from 1955 to 1963 and during the 1960s began to compose sacred works for orchestra, including "Mary Lou's Mass" (which was later choreographed by Alvin Ailey), and "The Lord's Prayer." During the 1970s, with Father Peter O'Brien as her personal manager, Williams had a lengthy engagement at the Cookery in New York (documented on the 1975 album *At the Cookery*) and she continued to explore the art form, even participating in a daring two-piano concert with Cecil Taylor in 1977 (documented on the album *Embraced*). Williams also began devoting her time to educational activities and in 1977, joined the faculty of Duke University, where she taught the history of jazz, wrote arrangements, and gave private instruction until she was incapacitated in 1980. She died of cancer in 1981. After her death, a major tribute to Mary Lou Williams was held at Town Hall in New York City, with pianists Barbara Carroll, Hazel Scott, and Rose Murphy, and a big band conducted by trombonist-arranger Melba Liston performing Williams's compositions and arrangements from the 1930s to the 1970s.

what to buy: You could buy any CDs recorded by Mary Lou Williams, but one that is a good introduction to her role in jazz history is the documentation of her radio appearance with Marian McPartland. It must have been a thrill for Marian McPartland to host her major influence and her friend (since 1949) on *Piano Jazz: McPartland/Williams* ♫♫♫ (The Jazz Alliance, 1978/1995, prod. Dick Phipps). McPartland once told this writer that upon her arrival in the USA from England in 1946, one of the first things she did was to befriend her idol, Mary Lou Williams. Those familiar with McPartland's *Piano Jazz* broadcast series for National Public Radio know that she intersperses piano performances by guests with conversation about the artist's career. Williams claimed she was then the only living jazz musician who adapted her style throughout the various eras from boogie woogie to bop, and beyond, and talks about her stints with artists from Fats Waller to Cecil Taylor. Williams (backed by bassist Ronnie Boykins) plays her original tunes, including a soft blues ("Baby Man"), the blues ballad that was a hit for the Lunceford band ("What's Your Story, Morning Glory?"), a swing piece by Ellington ("The Jeep Is

Jumpin'"), a modal piece ("Medi No. 2"), a lovely rendition of the standard "I Can't Get Started," and other illuminating works that display Williams's flexibility and command of the keyboard. A must-own album for fans of piano jazz, Mary Lou Williams, and jazz historians. Critics disagree in their assessments of *Embraced* ♫♫♫ (Pablo, 1978/OJC, 1995, prod. Mary Lou Williams, Cecil Taylor), which finds Mary Lou Williams performing with avant-garde pianist Cecil Taylor in what could possibly be the most exciting two-piano concert in jazz history. First, you have to be open to hearing avant-garde jazz, then perhaps even slightly be admiring of Cecil Taylor's work, a pianist who's been known to alienate audiences everywhere with audacious, lengthy, percussive solo piano performances. Then, too, it would be helpful to understand that Mary Lou Williams was always on the cutting edge of new traditions, constantly seeking new sounds. She had explored the avante-garde scene during the 1960s, taking boogie woogie chords and turning them on their edge harmonically to create something different. Although she is generally classified in jazz textbooks and other tomes as a Kansas City swing player, she was constantly evolving and her intelligence and skills took her far beyond her roots. She even influenced Thelonious Monk. Knowing all this, you might be ready for the 10 selections (mostly written by Williams) which (in titles at least) range from a spiritual, to ragtime, to Kansas City swing, to bop, and beyond. While Taylor dominates the concert, Williams could equally play with strength and voracity beyond the edge. There is so much energy in this live-recorded performance, you'll feel the heat. While such concerts are unusual in Williams's discography, and *Embraced* is a distinct departure from Williams's recorded works, it does remain an ear-bending experience for the adventurous listener.

best of the rest:

Mary Lou Williams: 1927–1940 ♫♫♫♫ (Jazz Chronological Classics, 1927–40/1994)

The Zodiac Suite ♫♫♫ (Smithsonian, 1945/Folkways, 1995)

Zoning ♫♫♫ (Smithsonian, 1974/Folkways, 1995)

Live at the Cookery ♫♫♫ (Chiaroscuro, 1975/1994)

Solo Recital/Montreux Jazz Festival 1978 ♫♫♫♫ (Pablo, 1978/OJC, 1998)

influences:

◀◀ Fats Waller, Earl Hines, Count Basie

▶▶ Marian McPartland, Bud Powell, Thelonious Monk, Tadd Dameron, JoAnne Brackeen, Geri Allen, Hilton Ruiz

Nancy Ann Lee

Tony Williams

Born December 12, 1945, in Chicago, IL. Died February 23, 1997, in New York, NY.

Tony Williams could have been remembered for simply being the child-prodigy drummer who, at age 17, helped propel Miles Davis's influential mid-'60s group. However, far more than that, Williams was a major force behind Blue Note's highly rewarding, experimental mindset in the '60s, as well as the prime mover behind jazz-rock fusion.

Discovered by Sam Rivers as a 13-year old, Williams soon found himself regularly gigging with the free thinking instrumentalist and others in the Boston area. Before long, Williams had moved to New York to become part of the jazz play *The Connection,* and his career took off, with session work on many influential Blue Note albums (Eric Dolphy's *Out to Lunch,* for one) and, thanks to an introduction to Miles Davis from Jackie McLean, he landed the coveted drum chair in Davis's band in 1963. He stayed there for six years, but also recorded two crucially exploratory solo albums—*Lifetime* and *Spring*—both of which helped propel the "new school" from a nebulous concept to a concerted effort. At the very point Davis was deciding to head off into the land of electricity, Williams had his own ideas and, in 1969, formed Lifetime with organist Larry Young and guitarist John McLaughlin. The first three records the group recorded—though universally panned throughout the jazz community—were sophisticated and raw, and among the first (and best) "fusion" to make considerable impact on a rock audience. Their fourth album didn't turn out so well, however, and in 1972 Williams disbanded Lifetime, only to unveil a newer, slicker (and, eventually, more successful) version three years later. Featuring prog-rock guitar whiz kid Allan Holdsworth, this Lifetime was more jazz-funk than jazz-rock and, in comparison to the previous group, fairly thin. That group, too, broke up, and it wasn't until 1985 that Williams rediscovered his bearings, releasing the first in a series of straight-ahead bop records with a group of enthusiastic young players. In 1992, he disbanded that group and returned his focus to pop-fusion. He died at 51 of heart problems.

what to buy: The masterwork *Spring* 🎵🎵🎵🎵 (Blue Note, 1965, prod. Alfred Lion) isn't quite as exploratory as *Lifetime,* but its solid quintet (Wayne Shorter, Sam Rivers, Herbie Hancock, Gary Peacock, and Williams) stretches post-bop forms to a near-breaking point, with Williams and Rivers playing so closely together it's scary. *The Tony Williams Lifetime Anthology* 🎵🎵🎵🎵 (Verve, 1969–72/PolyGram Chronicles, 1997, prod. various), spookily released two days after Williams's unex-

pected death, is a fitting eulogy. It corrals most of the best bits from his early '70s records (as well as a few middling cuts from 1972's disappointing *The Old Bum's Rush*), presenting a solid picture of how heavy and free jazz-rock fusion could be. Larry Young's organ work is among his best, crunchy but not overtly funky; McLaughlin's guitar is turned up to 11; ex-Cream bassist Jack Bruce's vocals are expectedly melodramatic; and Williams's drumming provides much of the improvisational thrust. The glow-in-the-dark packaging is a little cheesy, but the music inside is an essential addition to any rock or jazz music library. *Tokyo Live!* 🎵🎵🎵🎵 (Blue Note, 1995, prod. Tony Williams) is surprisingly strong, especially considering the rather uneventful output of Williams's previous two decades. Getting down to some seriously swinging bop business with a crew of up-and-comers—Wallace Roney, Bill Pierce, Mulgrew Miller, Ira Coleman—Williams careens gracefully through two CD's worth of strong tunes (the only clinker here is a misguided take on the Beatles' "Blackbird").

what to buy next: About 60 percent of *Emergency!* 🎵🎵🎵🎵 (Polydor, 1969, prod. Monte Kay, Jack Lewis) can be found on the aforementioned *Anthology,* but this single-disc collection is essential on its own. The first of the Lifetime records, this features just a trio—Williams, Young, and McLaughlin—and all eight selections here are phenomenally electric. With *Tony Williams Lifetime—The Collection* 🎵🎵🎵 (Columbia, 1975–76), in crass pursuit of a little more cabbage, Williams dramatically revamped Lifetime into a much slicker, more song-oriented beast. This CD collects its two Columbia records and, though obviously not as good as the Polydor era (Alan Holdsworth is in the band), the disc has its moments, most of which come from Williams's drumming. *Best Of* 🎵🎵🎵 (Blue Note, 1985–91/1996, compilation prod. Michael Cuscuna) is the only studio recording you need of Williams's work from 1985 to 1991. Pretty slick hard bop and not really pop-oriented, this would be excellent work from a newcomer, but it's rather disappointing from the exploratory Williams.

what to avoid: *Wilderness* (ARK 21, 1996, prod. Tony Williams), a rather dull, fusion-esque set, finds Williams in the thoroughly modern company of Michael Brecker, Stanley Clarke, and Herbie Hancock. Williams's playing is typically strong, but the material (most surprisingly written by Williams) is nearly flaccid. It's pure background music and a disappointing last record.

the rest:
Foreign Intrigue 🎵🎵🎵 (Blue Note, 1985)
Civilization 🎵🎵🎵 (Blue Note, 1986)
Angel Street 🎵🎵🎵 (Blue Note, 1988)

Native Heart 𝒥𝒥𝒥 (Blue Note, 1989)
The Story of Neptune 𝒥𝒥𝒥𝒥 (Blue Note, 1991)

worth searching for: For some reason, Williams's Blue Note debut, *Lifetime* 𝒥𝒥𝒥𝒥𝒥 (Blue Note, 1964/1987, prod. Alfred Lion), fell out of print after its initial reissue in 1987, which is most unfortunate. With the drummer in the estimable company of Rivers, Hancock, and Peacock, as well as Bobby Hutcherson, Richard Davis, and Ron Carter, it's hardly surprising this is among the best examples of the mid-'60s Blue Note new school. Occasional blasts of melodic genius flash within bristling improvisatory passages, creating a dark, disorienting album that rests as much on Williams's exciting, unpredictable drumming as it does on the ever-interesting tenor work of Rivers. *Joy of Flying* 𝒥𝒥 (Columbia, 1978) is actually quite a bad fuzak record, but well worth the bargain bin price, if only for the utterly incongruous (and out-there) duet with Cecil Taylor that closes it out.

influences:

◀◀ Philly Joe Jones, Max Roach

▶▶ Jack DeJohnette

Jason Ferguson

Steve Williamson

Born 1964, in London, England.

One of several black British jazz players to emerge in the late 1980s, alto/soprano saxophonist Steve Williamson is a solid technician whose style merges post-bop with funk and avant-garde. He took up sax at 16 and along with intensely studying Charlie Parker and John Coltrane, played in reggae bands. He also became interested in the sounds of George Clinton and his bands Parliament and Funkadelic, and has been sorting out the influences of the jazz and funk genres ever since. Williamson has worked with Art Blakey, Wynton Marsalis, Gil Scott-Heron, Cassandra Wilson, and Abbey Lincoln, and shows much promise, but where he'll end up is still hard to tell.

what's available: *Journey to the Truth* 𝒥𝒥 (Verve, 1994, prod. Steve Williamson) makes it to this section by default, as it is the only Steve Williamson album in print. A cross between funk, avant-garde, and rap, it is nothing special. The problem is none of the genres are played very well, and as a cohesive unit it just doesn't gel. Williamson is a capable player, but this does not represent his abilities well.

worth searching for: *A Waltz for Grace* 𝒥𝒥𝒥 (Verve, 1990), Williamson's debut release, now unavailable, while not a spec-

tacular recording, had its moments. He flirted with funk and the avant-garde, and had some success marrying the two. But the high points were the ballads, where, despite his love of playing on the edge, proved to be his strongest area.

influences:

◀◀ Charlie Parker, John Coltrane, Steve Coleman, Rahsaan Roland Kirk, Ornette Coleman

Paul MacArthur

Willie & Lobo

Formed 1991, in Puerto Vallarta, Mexico.

Willie Royal, violin; Wolfgang Fink, acoustic guitars.

Willie Royal and Wolfgang "Lobo" Fink first met in 1983, but timing wasn't right for their collaboration. By the time they met again in 1991 in the house band at a club in Puerto Vallarta, wandering Willie had been playing his fiery violin stylings in about 30 bands, and Bavarian guitarist Lobo had perfected his strong, clean, Flamenco guitar licks with gypsies in the caves of Grenada, Spain, before moving to Mexico. After the pair became musical soulmates (and avid surfing buddies), they released their first Mesa/BlueMoon album in 1993, capturing fans and hitting *Billboard* charts for 33 weeks with their eclectic, engagingly fresh sound that combines gypsy music, Cajun, Tex-Mex, Middle-Eastern, tango, and jazz improvisations. They've released five recordings for Mesa/BlueMoon, and their music has also been immortalized in a novel by author Robert Waller, *Puerto Vallerta Squeeze*. Willie & Lobo released a collective album of the same name in 1996. They tour extens ively as a duo, but when they record for Mesa/BlueMoon it's generally with an array of sidemen.

what to buy: Willie & Lobo, together for about three years prior to their debut recording, *Gypsy Boogaloo* 𝒥𝒥𝒥𝒥 (Mesa/Blue-Moon, 1993, prod. Rick Braun, George Nauful), demonstrate instrumental mastery and impassioned improvisational skills on the 11 (mostly original) tunes ranging from romantic tone poems to exploding crescendos. Their invigorating meld of global music inspires magnificent interaction and virtuosic solos. Willie (violin) and Lobo (guitar) are accompanied by Efrain Toro (percussion), Cliff Hugo (acoustic bass and electric bass), Rick Braun (keyboard, synthesizer, and trumpet) and George Nauful (12-string guitar). Every track is engaging and inspired. Their second album, *Fandango Nights* 𝒥𝒥𝒥𝒥 (Mesa/BlueMoon, 1994, prod. George Nauful, Rick Braun), features the pair performing another array of 13 lively, dramatic originals augmented by guest soloists and a great percussion team. Guitarist Jeff Golub, cellist Suzie Katayama, soprano saxist Steve Kujala, and keyboardist-producer Braun are spotlighted guests. Finest moments include a march-tempo Virginia reel ("Royal Reel") written by Willie and dedicated to his father (an Air Force Colonel), and a sweet, melodic song, "Pablo," titled after Willie's five year old son. Lobo wrote many of the tunes on the album and his Flamenco mastery stands out. Willie plays his newly-acquired, 150 year old violin which he had converted to five strings (to combine the normal violin sound with the deeper tone of a viola) and uses a special pick-up that enhances his sound, making the difference in his instrument sound noticeably improved from their first album. *Between the Waters* 𝄢𝄢𝄢𝄢 (Mesa/BlueMoon, 1995, prod. Dominic Camardella, George Nauful) finds the pair playing 13 engagingly diverse originals, with musicians Brad Dutz, George Nauful, Rick Braun (flugelhorn on one tune), Cliff Hugo (bass), Gary Meek (soprano sax), and others. Close your eyes, listen, and imagine sun-drenched sand dunes, blue ocean waters, and warm, south-of-the-border breezes. The synergistic musical capers of these free-wheeling vagabonds may force you to head for Puerto Vallarta. The "gypsy-surfer dudes" do it again with their fifth album, *Caliente* 𝄢𝄢𝄢𝄢 (Mesa/BlueMoon, 1997, prod. Rick Braun, George Nauful). Another spirited and fresh adventure, this CD features 11 tracks with guest appearances by trumpeter Braun (on "Puerto Vallarta Squeeze," a new version of the title tune from their previous CD) and guitarist Marc Antoine ("Napali"). Percussionists contribute generously to the listening pleasures. Attractive counterpoint rhythms throb like heartbeats under Royal's lush melody lines on contemplative tunes such as "Desert Sun" and "Arena Caliente," and on the exhilarating "Noche De Tangier" repeated bass guitar riffs and swirling percussions intertwine with Willie's gypsy violin fashionings. Their well-paced selections, fine arrangements, ear-pleasing harmonies, and enlivened rhythms make *Caliente* pure listening delight from start to finish. You can't miss with any one of the above albums. If Willie & Lobo win you over, you'll want all of their albums.

what to buy next: *Puerto Vallarta Squeeze* 𝄢𝄢𝄢 (Mesa/BlueMoon, 1996, George Nauful, Rick Braun, Domenic Camardella) combines selections from earlier Willie & Lobo albums and capitalizes on Waller's novel. Not much new here, except the title tune. But if you're looking for an introduction to Willie & Lobo music, this is a good place to start as it contains many of their best tunes.

Nancy Ann Lee

Larry Willis

Born December 20, 1942, in New York, NY.

A valued sideman, Larry Willis is a sophisticated interpreter with a broad background and inventive style. While attending the Manhattan School of Music, he started playing with Jackie McLean and made his recording debut on McLean's 1965 album *Right Now*. Since then, he has been in demand, having played on more than 250 albums and performed with musicians as diverse as Miles Davis, Hugh Masekela, Herb Alpert, Nat and Cannonball Adderley, Carla Bley, and Stan Getz. From 1972 to 1977 he was the keyboardist for Blood, Sweat, & Tears, an erratic period in the band's history with some tremendous high points (their rendition of "Maiden Voyage" on *New Blood*), and some artistic failures (their disco work on *Mirror Image*). Willis's playing with the group, however, was always solid, and he left BS&T before it became nothing more than a backing band for David Clayton-Thomas. During the past 20 years, Willis has led some great dates, playing fusion, funk, and straight-ahead with excellent interpretative ability. He is music director of Mapleshade Productions, and though he has only a few domestic albums in print, he appears as sideman on many of Mapleshade's recordings.

what's available: On the spectacular *Solo Spirit* 𝄢𝄢𝄢𝄢 (Mapleshade, 1993, prod. Pierre M. Sprey), Willis interprets nine spirituals in a solo setting, where he allows each song to develop without rushing a single note. The 14-minute version of "Motherless Child" is one of the finest moments on record. *Portraits in Ivory and Brass* 𝄢𝄢𝄢𝄢 (Mapleshade, 1992, prod. Larry Willis, Jack Walrath, Pierre M. Sprey), co-led by trumpeter Jack Walrath and occasionally featuring bassist Steve Novosel, is an almost sparse affair, with no drums and Mapleshade's wooden studios. Not surprisingly, this setting lends itself exceptionally well to ballads.

worth searching for: *Inner Crisis* 𝄢𝄢𝄢𝄢 (Groove Merchant, 1973), cut while Willis was a member of Blood, Sweat, & Tears, contains six great Willis compositions, ranging from fusion to funk to straight-ahead. "Journey's End" and the title track are among the best compositions of that era.

influences:

◄◄ Oscar Peterson, Bud Powell, Horace Silver, John Lewis, Wynton Kelly, Ramsey Lewis, Hank Jones

Paul MacArthur

Cassandra Wilson (© Jack Vartoogian)

Cassandra Wilson

Born December 5, 1955, in Jackson, MS.

The Mississippi-raised Wilson came to New York in 1982, already a professional singer. Besides working with the already established Dave Holland and New Air, she collaborated with the musicians gathered around alto saxophonist Steve Coleman who were inventing a style they called M-Base. At the beginning of her recording career she was also identified with this style due to her appearances on several Coleman-led albums and her use of that pool of musicians on her first two albums. She started moving away from that dense, funky sound on her third album, *Blue Skies*, a standards collection. Though it was not an entirely successful move—whatever the claims of her hardcore fans, Wilson is too willfully mannered in her singing on jazz material—it did bring her to the attention of the jazz mainstream.

Wilson reverted to electric bands featuring original material plus a few standards reworked in eccentric ways. Though her career lost sales momentum, her reputation as a promising singer continued to grow, leading Blue Note to sign her. Pairing her with producer Craig Street provided the fresh start she needed, and her reworked style and focus—sparse instrumentation, laid-back vocals, and greater variety of cover material—helped her cross over to the more sophisticated segment of the pop audience. She is now one of the most popular and commercially successful young jazz singers on the scene, and her style and choice of material has become a much-copied template for other singers looking to expand beyond the standards audience.

what to buy: *Blue Light 'Til Dawn* 𝄞𝄞𝄞𝄞 (Blue Note, 1993, prod. Craig Street) was Wilson's commercial breakthrough. In a departure from her previous work, she stripped her music to its barest essence: rhythm, blues, and her supple, languid phrasing. A number of songs, including a pair of Robert Johnson covers ("Come on in My Kitchen" and "Hellhound on My Trail"), are built on Brandon Ross's spare steel-string guitar lines. Others feature equally skeletal instrumentation. A take on Joni

Mitchell's "Black Crow" with just Don Byron's clarinet and six percussionists, and the standard "You Don't Know What Love Is," with only Ross and violinist Charlie Burnham, are a few examples. Even numbers with lusher arrangements (her self-penned title track and Van Morrison's "Tupelo Honey") are sweet but sinewy, and the album's quiet intimacy captured the fancy of many listeners. *Point of View* &&&& (JMT, 1986, prod. Steve Coleman, Stefan F. Winter) was Wilson's first album and remains a high point of her catalog, offering a telling contrast with her Blue Note material. The band consists of alto saxophonist Steve Coleman, bassist Lonnie Plaxico (heard on acoustic and electric instruments), drummer Mark Johnson, bluesy guitarist Jean-Paul Bourelly, and trombonist Grachan Moncur III. The first three musicians especially were associated with the M-Base style, and Wilson works within its sharp angles and cutting rhythms on a program mostly consisting of band originals. The high point is guitarist Jean-Paul Bourelly's ultra-funky "I Thought You Knew," Wilson's pretty ballad "I Am Waiting," and a reverential version of Miles Davis's "Blue in Green" with her original lyrics added. The overall feeling of energy makes the slow tunes stand out.

what to buy next: On Wilson's second album, *Days Aweigh* &&&& (JMT, 1987, prod. Stefan F. Winter), Coleman, Bourelly, and Johnson return, joined by pianist/synthesizer player Rod Williams and either acoustic bassist Kenny Davis or electric bassist Kevin Bruce Harris, with cornetist Olu Dara on the tune he wrote and trumpeter Graham Haynes on six of the other eight tracks. An up-tempo cross between bebop and M-Base on Cole Porter's "Let's Face the Music and Dance" is exciting, but the highlight is Wilson's gorgeous and slightly oddball ballad "Subatomic Blues," on which she alternates between a floating head voice and her lower and heftier contralto. *New Moon Daughter* &&&& (Blue Note, 1995, prod. Craig Street), the follow-up to *Blue Light 'Til Dawn*, finds Wilson again mixing her jazz into unusual contexts, with only two jazz-associated covers, "Strange Fruit" (Billie Holiday) and "Skylark" (Hoagy Carmichael). There's rock ("Love Is Blindness" by U2), pop ("Last Train to Clarksville" by the Monkees), blues (Son House's "Death Letter"), and country (Hank Williams Sr.'s "I'm So Lonesome I Could Cry" and Neil Young's "Harvest Moon"), plus five originals. The mood is quiet and brooding (and usually acoustic guitar–based) except on the gently undulating cover of the Monkees' "Last Train to Clarksville," which Wilson manages to make sound mature.

what to avoid: *Rendezvous* && (Blue Note, 1997, prod. Bob Belden) with Jacky Terrasson takes Wilson's style on her previous two albums to extremes. Rather than creating intimacy, Wilson's use of the same languid, laid-back vocal approach on every song merely sounds blasé (and makes such classics as "It Might As Well Be Spring" sound one-dimensional). Terrasson's efforts to spice up the proceedings end up sounding out of place, although his playing is good. *After the Beginning Again* && (Polydor K.K., 1992/JMT, 1994, prod. Cassandra Wilson) is the least important of Wilson's JMT albums and only finally appeared in the U.S. in the wake of her Blue Note success. It's especially marred by James Weisman's unctuous piano stylings. Wilson's own songs work better (in a mellow, funky fusion vein) than the covers. "'Round Midnight" sounds archly mannered, though "Baubles, Bangles and Beads" would be okay with a less-cute pianist.

the rest:
Blue Skies &&& (JMT, 1988)
Jump World &&& (JMT, 1990)
She Who Weeps &&& (JMT, 1991)
Live &&& (JMT, 1991)
Dance to the Drums Again &&& (DIW/Columbia, 1992)

worth searching for: Trombonist Steve Turre's *Steve Turre* &&&& (Verve, 1997, prod. Billy Banks) features Wilson as guest vocalist on a samba-ized cover of Duke Ellington's magnificent "In a Sentimental Mood." Wilson is heard in a completely different context on New Air's *Air Show No. 1* &&& (Black Saint, 1986, prod. Giovanni Bonandrini) in a group led by then-husband Henry Threadgill. The weirdly haunting "Don't Drink That Corner My Life Is in the Bush," "Apricots on Their Wings" (which she redid on her second album), and especially her scatting on "Side Step" feature her vocals at their artiest. Wilson was an integral part of the M-Base group Steve Coleman and Five Elements. *World Expansion (By the M-Base Neophyte)* &&&& (JMT, 1987, prod. Steve Coleman) remains the high point of the M-Basers, with Wilson and superdiva D.K. Dyson splitting the vocal chores backed by Geri Allen (piano), Kelvyn Bell (guitar), Harris and Johnson, the leader, trombonist Robin Eubanks, and Haynes. Wilson sings lead on three tracks and is truly a part of the ensemble, stretching and bending her notes like an instrument. With Dyson gone from *Sine Die* &&& (Pangaea/I.R.S., 1988, prod. Steve Coleman), Wilson is featured even more.

influences:
◀◀ Billie Holiday, Peggy Lee, Nina Simone
▶▶ Dianne Reeves, Diana Krall

see also: *M-Base Collective*

Steve Holtje

Gerald Wilson

Born September 4, 1918, in Shelby, MS.

Though Gerald Wilson was an accomplished trumpeter, his most significant accomplishments came through his work as an arranger and bandleader. Though he learned his craft during the swing era, he easily made the transition into modern jazz, producing some of the most advanced big band charts of the mid and late '40s. Raised in Memphis as a youth, he began studying music seriously in high school after his family moved to Detroit. He landed a job in Jimmie Lunceford's trumpet section, replacing Sy Oliver, and during his four-year tenure (1939–42), he developed his skills as an arranger and composer. He moved to Los Angeles in 1942 and worked in the big bands of Les Hite and Benny Carter and spent the mid-'40s playing in Willie Smith's Navy band with Ernie Royal and Clark Terry. When he returned to Los Angeles he began to assemble a band for singer Herb Jeffries, but after Jeffries balked, Wilson turned the group into one of the first large ensembles to incorporate the new language of bebop, with such top-flight players as trumpeters Snooky Young and Teddy Buckner, trombonist Melba Liston and pianist Jimmy Bunn. From 1944 to 1946, Wilson's band worked on L.A.'s thriving Central Avenue and toured nationally, but he decided to disband in order to pursue further musical education. His reputation as an arranger was firmly established in the late '40s when Duke Ellington, Dizzy Gillespie, and Count Basie all recorded his charts. He formed another band in 1952, working in San Francisco and making an aborted tour with Billie Holiday. He contributed some strong trumpet work to bassist Leroy Vinnegar's *Leroy Walks!* and on a couple of Curtis Counce quintet recordings on Contemporary in the mid '50s, but spent much of the decade writing arrangements for jazz/pop sessions with singers such as Ella Fitzgerald, Julie London, Al Hibbler, Sarah Vaughan, Nancy Wilson, and Johnny Hartman.

He formed his best known band in the early '60s, an all-star ensemble with tenor saxophonists Teddy Wilson and Harold Land and guitarist Joe Pass. The group didn't tour but made some excellent albums for World Pacific. In the '70s, Wilson wrote scores for TV and film, started his own radio show and began a second career as a jazz educator at UCLA. His big band has been a mainstay on the L.A. scene from the '60s, a group that often mixes veterans such as Oscar Brashear, Thurman Green, and Snooky Young with up-and-coming young players. Unfortunately, few of Wilson's recordings for Excelsior, Trend, Discovery, and World Pacific are available on CD.

what to buy: Composer/arranger/bandleader Gerald Wilson's first recording of the '90s, *State Street Sweet* ♫♫♫♫ (MAMA Foundation, 1995, prod. Gerald Wilson, Douglas Evans) is a creative, high-powered session featuring his excellent charts and strong soloists. The disc is split between strong new material, such as "Lakeshore Drive" and the title track, and some of the strongest tunes written for his great '60s band, such as "Carlos," "The Feather," and "The Serpent." A number of longtime Wilson associates, including Plas Johnson and Snooky Young, join in, but the album is also a showcase for such young talents as saxophonist Randall Willis, from the B Sharp Quartet, pianist Brian O'Rourke, and Gerald's son, guitarist Anthony Wilson (who won the 1996 Thelonious Monk competition for composers).

what to buy next: It might seem strange that Southern California, a region where jazz history has often been neglected, has pioneered the commercial recording of jazz oral histories, but then, there are so many great stories to tell. *Suite Moments* ♫♫♫♫ (MAMA Foundation, 1996, prod. Harvey Robert Kubernik, Douglas Evans) is a two-disc set (produced by the same folks who recorded Buddy Collette's audiobiography) of Wilson telling the story of his career, from his days with Jimmie Lunceford, his relationships with Ellington and Basie, and various other jazz luminaries, to his experiences as a bandleader. There are no major scoops here, but Wilson is a sharp raconteur, and his wry, bemused take on the music biz comes through clearly.

worth searching for: A strong hard bop session led by the superb bassist Leroy Vinnegar, *Leroy Walks!* ♫♫♫♫ (Contemporary, 1957/OJC, 1984, prod. Lester Koenig) features Wilson on trumpet with Victor Feldman (vibes), Teddy Edwards (tenor sax), Tony Bazley (drums), and the highly original pianist Carl Perkins. Edwards and Feldman are the main soloists, but Wilson contributes some strong ensemble work with his muted horn and supple solo on "Walkin'."

influences:

◀◀ Duke Ellington, Tadd Dameron

▶▶ Stan Kenton, John Clayton, Melba Liston

Andrew Gilbert

Nancy Wilson

Born February 20, 1937, in Chillicothe, OH.

By the mid-1960s, Nancy Wilson's distinctive sound had shifted from jazz to pop and R&B, although she would continue to shift gears between styles throughout her career. Like many singers,

Nancy Wilson (© Jack Vartoogian)

Wilson developed at an early age, singing in choirs and dance bands as a teenager in Columbus, Ohio. In 1956 she joined Rusty Bryant's Carolyn Club Band and made her first recordings for Dot Records. Her next collaboration was with Cannonball Adderley in 1959. Still hooked on straight-ahead jazz, Wilson recorded her first hit with Adderley, "Save Your Love for Me," in 1962. From there she picked up a more pop-oriented style and a new momentum, putting 33 albums on the charts between 1962 and 1977. Some of the hit songs from that period include "Peace of Mind," "Don't Come Running Back to Me," "Face It Girl, It's Over," and "Now I'm a Woman." Wilson's "How Glad I Am" won a Grammy for Best R&B Song in 1964. In 1983 she won a song festival award in Tokyo and recorded five albums for Japanese labels over the next few years. During that time she also made one pop record in the U.S., *The Two of Us*, with Ramsey Lewis. Wilson let the stops out on her pop sensibilities when she made *With My Lover Beside Me* with Barry Manilow, who performed on and produced the album. Her latest album, *If I Had My Way*, proves that, regardless of style, this singer is

still going strong. In addition to her heavy touring schedule, in recent years Wilson has hosted a popular documentary series for National Public Radio that highlights people, places, and events in jazz.

what to buy: *Ballads, Blues, and Big Bands: The Best of Nancy Wilson* ♫♫♫ (Capitol, 1996/1996, prod. various) is a three-disc set of Wilson's recordings between 1959 and 1969. Sixty songs include many of her best jazz performances with orchestras led by Billy May, Oliver Nelson, Gerald Wilson, and smaller groups led by George Shearing and Cannonball Adderley. Wilson sings popular jazz songs composed by Duke Ellington, Billy Strayhorn, Hoagy Carmichael, Bill Evans, Rodgers and Hart, the Gershwins, Johnny Burke, and numerous other top writers. If you want to hear Wilson doing her roots music, this is the album.

what to buy next: If you don't want to lay out the cash for the three-CD set, check out *Best of Nancy Wilson: The Jazz and Blues Sessions* ♫♫♫ (Blue Note, 1996, prod. various), which highlights the singer performing orchestral arrangements by

Billy May, Oliver Nelson, and Gerald Wilson, as well as smaller groups led by Cannonball Adderley and George Shearing. Among the 17-tune collection, she sings jazz standards such as "Green Dolphin Street," "Stormy Monday," "You Don't Know Me," and Antonio Carlos Jobim's Brazilian-jazz gem, "Wave." *Nancy Wilson/Cannonball Adderley* ����� (Capitol, 1961/1993) features saxophonist Adderley and the hit "Save Your Love for Me."

the rest:

Yesterday's Love Songs, Today's Blues ��� (Blue Note, 1963/1991)
Welcome to My Love �� (Blue Note, 1967/1994)
Lush Life ��� (Capitol 1967/1995)
But Beautiful ���� (Capitol, 1969/1990)
Keep You Satisfied ��� (Columbia, 1986/1989)
Forbidden Lover ���� (Columbia, 1987)
Nancy Now! ��� (Columbia, 1988)
Lady with a Song ���� (Columbia, 1990)
I Wish You Love ��� (CEMA Special Products, 1992/1994)
Love, Nancy ��� (Columbia, 1994)
Spotlight on Nancy Wilson ��� (Capitol, 1995)
If I Had My Way ���� (Columbia, 1997)

worth searching for: *The Two of Us* ���� (Columbia, 1984), her enjoyable collaboration with Ramsey Lewis that marked her last appearance on *Billboard*'s pop album chart.

influences:

◀◀ Little Jimmy Scott, Nat King Cole, Billy Eckstine, LaVern Baker, Dinah Washington, Ruth Brown

▶▶ Patti LaBelle, Anita Baker, Phyllis Hyman

Norene Cashen

Steve Wilson

Born February 9, 1961, in Hampton, VA.

Since arriving in New York City in 1987 to replace Kenny Garrett in the popular cooperative group O.T.B. (Out of the Blue, a group dedicated to the classic Blue Note sound), alto/soprano saxophonist Steve Wilson has been one of the city's busiest and most respected musicians. He blends tart soulfulness and harmonic erudition, plays bebop with Charlie Parker–like lucidity and rhythmic sinuousness, and renders a ballad like he was preaching the lyric. The Tidewater area native began playing at the age of 12, and by the middle years of high school was playing with contemporaries Billy Drummond and James Genus in various garage bands together or with other groups, funk bands, horn bands, and jam sessions.

After a year on the road with R&B singer Stephanie Mills, Wilson entered the strong jazz program at Virginia Commonwealth University; he performed and lived around the Richmond, Virginia, area until 1987. He's worked and recorded with Ralph Peterson, Buster Williams, Mulgrew Miller, Donald Brown, Renee Rosnes, Michelle Rosewoman, Johnny King, Don Braden, Bruce Barth, Leon Parker, the Carnegie Hall Jazz Orchestra, and the Smithsonian Jazz Masterworks Orchestra, to name a few. As of this writing he's performing with Chick Corea's new Origin sextet.

what to buy: Wilson's status as sideman par excellence has tended to obscure the fact that he's one of the most original voices on the scene. Take the delightful *Four for Time* ���� (Criss Cross, 1996, prod. Gerry Teekens), with an empathetic quartet featuring pianist Bruce Barth, bassist Larry Grenadier, and drummer Leon Parker, featuring Wilson on alto all the way. The group had worked together a full week before the recording; chance-taking prevails throughout. The freely expressed music, loose and open-ended, is serendipitous, with the musicians exhibiting great sensitivity, wit, and adventurous spirit. Their elastic sense of swing is only part of the wide spectrum of collective inside-out improvisations. Wilson's previous album, *Step Lively* ���� (Criss Cross, 1993, prod. Gerry Teekens), features his playing with Freddie Bryant (guitar), Cyrus Chestnut (piano), Dennis Irwin (bass), Greg Hutchinson (drums), and Daniel Sadownick (percussion), in a simmering in-the-pocket date that counterpoints Latin and Soul tropes with post-bop explorations that's every bit as fresh and satisfying.

what to buy next: *Blues for Marcus* ��� (Criss Cross, 1993, prod. Gerry Teekens), with Steve Nelson (vibes), Bruce Barth (piano), James Genus (bass), and Lewis Nash (drums), seems a bit less focused and compositionally distinctive than the two that succeeded it. The musicianship is top-shelf, and there are many brilliant moments, including inspired interpretations of Ornette Coleman's "Jayne," Roland Kirk's "The Haunted Melody," and Joe Chambers's "Patterns," and the driving original title track.

the rest:

New York Summit ���� (Criss Cross, 1994)

influences:

◀◀ Eddie Harris, Rahsaan Roland Kirk, Cannonball Adderley, Charlie Parker

Ted Panken

Teddy Wilson

Born Theodore Shaw Wilson, November 24, 1912, in Austin, TX. Died July 31, 1986, in New Britain, CT.

Teddy Wilson grew up in Tuskegee, Alabama, where his parents worked for the university. After a brief spell at Talladega College, he moved to Chicago, eventually finding work with Jimmie Noone, Speed Webb, and Louis Armstrong, among others. Wilson also started touring the after hours clubs in the company of one of his idols, Art Tatum, playing piano duets and making a name for himself. One night in 1933, while subbing on a gig for Earl Hines, Wilson was heard by record producer John Hammond who convinced Benny Carter that the young pianist would be the perfect fit for his band. With this endorsement (and cash sent by Carter to cover his cost of transportation), Wilson moved to New York City. Playing with Carter and various other musicians (including recording sessions under his own name with high caliber players like Billie Holiday, Ben Webster, and Johnny Hodges) further honed Wilson's skills. This attracted the attention of Benny Goodman, then at the height of his powers as a bandleader. By 1936 Wilson had broken the color barrier by becoming the first black member of a prominent white jazz group when he joined Goodman's trio. From then until 1939, when he finally left Goodman's employ, Wilson found himself participating in some of his boss' finest small group recordings. His association with Goodman also had given him the name recognition with the masses that would tempt him into leading his own big band. This short-lived ensemble drew upon Wilson's contacts to pack the group with stars like Ben Webster, Doc Cheatham, J.C. Heard, and Al Casey. Despite the musical firepower of the band, Wilson and his group were never able to make the kind of commercial dent in the marketplace that would guarantee the band's survival as a unit. From 1940 on, Wilson would end up touring and recording with small groups or as a solo artist. He also worked staff jobs in various New York radio and television studios in addition to teaching at the Juilliard School and joining Goodman for occasional reunion tours.

what to buy: *1937* 𝅘𝅥𝅘𝅥𝅘𝅥𝅘𝅥 (Classics, 1991, prod. various) may be the best available set to display what Teddy Wilson's wonderful 1930s-era bands sounded like. Certainly the recording lineups are impressive, with Billie Holiday, Ellingtonians Harry Carney and Johnny Hodges and Basie-ites Lester Young, Walter Page, and Freddie Green—just a sampling of the all-stars gathered here. Classic jazz interpretations of "Mean to Me" and "I'll Get By" are only a few of the tunes to emerge from the sessions included here. *With Billie in Mind* 𝅘𝅥𝅘𝅥𝅘𝅥𝅘𝅥 (Chiaroscuro, 1972,

TEDDY WILSON
(WITH THE BENNY GOODMAN TRIO)

song "Body and Soul"
album *Original Benny Goodman Trio and Quartet Sessions, Volume 1: After You've Gone*
(Bluebird, 1935/1987)
instrument Piano

Monster Solo

prod. Hank O'Neal) features solo piano renditions of tunes associated with the great Billie Holiday—a fine tribute to Wilson's former band singer. Especially effective are versions of "What a Little Moonlight Can Do," "Body and Soul," and "Miss Brown to You," but Wilson makes all the songs swing with grace and a wistful, emotional undercurrent. The inclusion of six previously unavailable cuts is an added bonus.

what to buy next: More fine performances with Billie Holiday and appearances by stars like Benny Goodman, Ben Webster, and Johnny Hodges make *1934–35* 𝅘𝅥𝅘𝅥𝅘𝅥 (Classics, 1990, prod. various) another highlight in Classics' journey through Wilson's bands of the 1930s and '40s. It is also interesting to compare the Holiday versions of "What a Little Moonlight Can Do" and "Miss Brown to You" with the solo renditions on Wilson's tribute album (mentioned above). There is also a fine version of "Rosetta" that does justice to one of Wilson's pianistic idols, Earl Hines. *Cole Porter Standards* 𝅘𝅥𝅘𝅥𝅘𝅥 (Black Lion, 1978, prod. Alan Bates), a solo piano release, features stunningly beautiful interpretations of 20th-century masterpieces and a classy improvisation ("Too Darn Blue") inspired by its surroundings. The swing is palpable on tunes like "Just One of Those Things" and "I Get a Kick out of You," but it also infuses ballad material such as "Why Shouldn't I" and "Easy to Love." Surely this should be considered one of the finest Cole Porter tribute albums available.

best of the rest:

(With Lester Young) *Pres & Teddy* ♪♪♪♪ (Verve, 1957)
Runnin' Wild ♪♪♪ (Black Lion, 1974)
Revisits the Goodman Years ♪♪♪♪ (Storyville, 1980)
1935–36 ♪♪♪♪ (Classics, 1991)
1936–37 ♪♪♪♪ (Classics, 1991)
1938 ♪♪♪♪ (Classics, 1991)
1939 ♪♪♪♪ (Classics, 1991)
How High the Moon ♪♪♪♪ (Tradition, 1997)

worth searching for: The double album set, *Concert in Argentina* ♪♪♪♪ (Halcyon, 1975, prod. Alejandro Szterenfeld), is the result of a 1974 concert in Buenos Aires, Argentina, featuring Marian McPartland, Ellis Larkins, Earl Hines, and Teddy Wilson. Each pianist gets a whole side to themselves, and Wilson uses his to play standards by Gershwin, Waller, and well-articulated versions of "Body and Soul," "Flying Home," and Hines's "Rosetta." While the Wilson sides alone are fine, when combined with performances by three other outstanding pianists, the whole set moves into the "Why isn't this on CD?" category.

influences:

◀◀ Earl Hines, Art Tatum, Willie "the Lion" Smith

▶▶ Marcus Roberts, Marian McPartland

Garaud MacTaggart

Lem Winchester

Born March 19, 1928, in Philadelphia, PA. Died January 13, 1961, in Indianapolis, IN.

Although one can only speculate, had Lem Winchester not been killed during a freak gun accident, it is possible that he could have emerged as one of the more consequential vibraphonists of his generation. A police officer by day, Winchester played several instruments before ultimately deciding on the vibes, largely due to the influence of Milt Jackson. Over the course of the 1958 Newport Jazz Festival, Winchester's soulful sound caught the ears of several record producers, and in no time he was recording on his own for the Prestige label and working with heavy hitters such as Ramsey Lewis, Benny Golson, Tommy Flanagan, Oliver Nelson, and Etta Jones. Although the vibraphone is one of the trickier instruments on which to ac-

quire a personalized sound, Winchester's style was quickly developing just prior to his death. His attack was fast and full-bodied, with just a hint of vibrato. He was able to tackle quick-fire bebop lines and to deliver the blues with original flavor and intent. Despite a modest catalog of recordings, Winchester remains a revered player in the minds of those most enamored with the jazz of the 1950s and 1960s.

what to buy: *Winchester Special* ♪♪♪♪ (Prestige/New Jazz, 1959, prod. Esmond Edwards) was the vibist's first date as a leader. It features Benny Golson and Tommy Flanagan on a well-chosen set that includes the Winchester originals "Down Fuzz" and "The Dude." *Lem's Beat* ♪♪♪♪ (Prestige/New Jazz, 1960, prod. Esmond Edwards) finds Winchester in a sextet featuring saxophonists Curtis Peagler and Oliver Nelson. Nelson also provides the arrangements. From start to finish, this set finds everyone in peak form.

what to buy next: *Another Opus* ♪♪♪♪ (Prestige/New Jazz, 1960, prod. Esmond Edwards) is a bit lighter than Winchester's other recordings, but very melodic and rewarding, nonetheless. Pianist Hank Jones and the flute of Frank Wess are added bonuses.

worth searching for: *Lem Winchester and the Ramsey Lewis Trio* ♪♪♪♪ (Argo, 1958, prod. Esmond Edwards) is a hard record to come by, but well worth looking for in light of the early glimpse it gives us of Winchester's talents.

influences:

◀◀ Milt Jackson, Lionel Hampton

Chris Hovan

Kai Winding

Born Kai Chresten Winding, May 18, 1922, in Aarhus, Denmark. Died May, 6, 1983, in Yonkers, NY.

Kai Winding was most notable as a bop trombonist who brought a distinctive sound to the trombone section of the Stan Kenton big band. Winding arrived with his family in the U.S. in 1934 and began playing trombone in 1937 while attending Stuyvesant High School. He played in a burlesque house band during a summer season, joined the Shorty Allen band in 1940, and worked with Sonny Dunham, Alvino Rey, and others in 1941. Winding joined the Coast Guard in 1942 and played in a service band. During this period he made his recording debut with Roy Stevens on the Manor label. From October of 1945 to January 1946, Winding performed with the Benny Goodman Orchestra, but made no recorded solos. The trombonist toured with Stan

Kenton (1946–47), worked with small combos led by Charlie Ventura (1947–48), Tadd Dameron (1948–49), and contributed brief solos to the first of Miles Davis's nonet sessions that resulted in *Birth of the Cool* (1949). Winding led a small band with singer Buddy Stewart for awhile in 1948, and in 1949 headed groups in New York City clubs, made TV appearances, worked as a studio musician (recording jingles and music for industrial films), and performed on pop and jazz jobs until the fall of 1954 when he teamed up with fellow trombonist J. J. Johnson to form a quintet. After this group broke up, Winding formed a septet in 1956 that featured four trombones and a rhythm section. This group made many appearances on college campuses between 1958 and 1960, and during this time Winding also toured Europe with J. J. Johnson (1958) and appeared at the 1959 Playboy Jazz Festival as well as other festivals. In 1962 Winding became musical director at the New York City Playboy Club. The following year he began experimenting with unusual instrumentations, sometimes enhanced with electric instruments behind a 12-piece brass ensemble, and recorded successful non-jazz albums such as *More* (1963) and *Mondo Cane #2* (1964) aimed at the commercial market. Winding co-led the second version of the World's Greatest Jazz Band with Eddie Condon at the Roosevelt Grill in 1969 before moving to California where he joined the staff band on the Merv Griffin TV show in the early 1970s. Winding reformed his four trombone group for the Concord Jazz Fest and other engagements, and toured internationally with the Giants of Jazz in 1971 and 1972 and with Lee Konitz. With Curtis Fuller, Winding led the group Giant Bones (1979–80). Winding's style ranges from the exuberant, rough, and biting tone of his days with Kenton, to the restrained solos with Davis, to a delicate sound evident on his recordings with J. J. Johnson.

what to buy: Strings enhance the trombone musings created by Kai Winding, J. J. Johnson, and Bennie Green on the OJC limited edition CD *With Strings* ♪♪♪♪ (Prestige, 1952, 1954/OJC, 1989), adding sweetened appeal to classics such as "Stardust," "There's a Small Hotel," "Embraceable You," "Bag's Groove," and other classics. (Note: This CD is listed in the Muze system under J. J. Johnson.) The same threesome recorded *Trombone by Three* ♪♪♪ (Prestige/OJC, 1992), a collection of standards and originals performed with Sonny Rollins, Kenny Dorham, Gerry Mulligan, John Lewis, Max Roach, Roy Haynes, Art Blakey, and others. ♪

what to buy next: *Nuf Said* ♪♪♪ (Bethlehem/Charly, 1994) features Kai Winding with J. J. Johnson performing 17 tunes (including alternate takes) with pianist Dick Katz and drummer Al Harewood. Although the two trombonists display similar styles and novice ears will have trouble determining who's playing, this album is enjoyable for the material and their interactions on various takes of popular classics such as "Lover," "Thou Swell," "It's All Right with Me," and more.

best of the rest:
In Cleveland 1957 ♪♪♪ (Status, 1994)

influences:

◀◀ J. C. Higginbotham, Vic Dickenson, Dicky Wells, J. J. Johnson, Herbie Harper

▶▶ Al Grey, Jimmy Cleveland, Frank Rosolino, Slide Hampton, Curtis Fuller, Bill Watrous, Jiggs Whigham, Steve Turre, Conrad Herwig, Paul Ferguson

Nancy Ann Lee

Jimmy Witherspoon

Born August 8, 1923, in Gurdon, TX. Died September 18, 1997, in Los Angeles, CA.

Vocalist Jimmy Witherspoon was an artist who was at home in both the jazz and blues fields, not unlike his contemporaries Jimmy Rushing, Big Joe Turner, and Joe Williams. Brought up in the African American church, Witherspoon was first influenced by gospel music and began singing while in the Navy. In the mid-1940s, before becoming a solo artist, he spent some time with the legendary Jay McShann. His 1959 appearance at the Monterey Jazz Festival led to a great deal of critical and popular acclaim, and during the next decade he led a wonderful series of albums for the Prestige label and toured extensively throughout Europe. A bout with throat cancer in the early 1980s kept him from the scene for a time, but he recovered and returned to performing for a time. Witherspoon remained such a popular attraction for his entire career due to his great way with a lyric. Each word was clear and concise, and he loved to stretch and bend notes for the maximum effect. A true original, Witherspoon was one of the best blues and jazz vocalists around.

what to buy: *Goin' to Kansas City Blues* ♪♪♪♪ (RCA, 1957, prod. George Avakian) reunited Witherspoon with Jay McShann's group (the vocalist first worked with the band leader in 1945). Great tunes, a fine group of soloists that includes Kenny Burrell, Al Sears, and J.C. Higginbotham, and Witherspoon's top-notch vocal work make this one a classic. *Blues Around the Clock* ♪♪♪♪ (Prestige/OJC, 1963, prod. Ozzie Cadena) is the best of Witherspoon's Prestige dates and a concise example of his way with the blues. In addition, he gets great backing from an organ combo led by Paul Griffin.

what to buy next: *Some of My Best Friends Are the Blues* 𝄞𝄞𝄞 (Prestige/OJC, 1964, prod. Lew Futterman) features Witherspoon belting some soulful ballads in front of a big band led by arranger and tenorist Benny Golson. *Blues for Easy Livers* 𝄞𝄞𝄞𝄞 (Prestige/OJC, 1966, prod. Peter Paul) is a small group date that includes such name jazz players as Pepper Adams, Bill Watrous, Roger Kellaway, Richard Davis, and Mel Lewis. Certainly not among Witherspoon's more well-known sides, this one is due for rediscovery as is it one of his better efforts of the '60s.

the rest:
Jimmy Witherspoon and Jay McShann 𝄞𝄞𝄞𝄞 (Black Lion, 1947–1949)
The Spoon Concerts 𝄞𝄞𝄞 (Fantasy, 1959)
Baby, Baby, Baby 𝄞𝄞𝄞 (Prestige, 1963)
Evenin' Blues 𝄞𝄞𝄞 (Prestige, 1963)
Rockin' L.A. 𝄞𝄞𝄞 (Fantasy, 1988)

Chris Hovan

Francis Wong
Born April 13, 1957, in San Francisco, CA.

Francis Wong has been widely recognized as a leader of the West Coast's burgeoning Asian American jazz community since his recording debut in 1984 on Jon Jang's radical album *Are You Chinese or Charlie Chan?* Starting on violin at the age of 10, Wong moved on to the sax by the end of junior high. In 1987, he began investigating numerous indigenous instruments of Asia, like the shinobue, yokobue, and erhu. Although the tenor saxophone is his primary axe, Wong's also an expressive composer-improviser on flute, clarinet, and violin.

Wong founded the Great Wall Quartet (with Jang, Mark Izu, E.W. Wainwright Jr., and Hafez Modirzadeh) in 1990 to perform jazz tunes, original works, pieces by contemporary Asian American composers, and Chinese classical and folk material. After releasing the group's inaugural effort in 1993, Wong has appeared as a leader or co-leader on six other albums. He has also collaborated on a number of Jon Jang and Glenn Horiuchi recordings, and performed live with such luminaries as James Newton, George Lewis, and Cecil Taylor. In addition to his work as a composer-performer, Wong heads Asian Improv Arts in San Francisco, an organization that sponsors showcases for Asian American musicians and artists, including the annual Asian American Jazz Festival and Asian Improv Records. Wong is also a four-time grant recipient from the California Arts Council Artist in Residency program, and is on the faculty at San Francisco State University and the New College of California. He is

currently working on a large ensemble concept with vocalist/writer Genny Lim.

what to buy: The eight-part title track comprises the bulk of this second recording by the Francis Wong Quartet, *Pilgrimage* 𝄞𝄞𝄞𝄞 (Music & Arts, 1997, prod. Francis Wong), which features Wong's Ming ensemble—pianist Glenn Horiuchi, percussionist Elliot Humberto Kavee, and special guest percussionist Royal Hartigan. The piece, which the artist says "is a loosely composed suite that deals with some of my ideas about transformation and rites of passage," paints a composite portrait of Wong's improvisational frameworks. The dynamics range from barely audible moments on indigenous instruments to booming drums and saxophone. It is thoroughly original and engaging throughout. The Ming trio's torrential debut, *Ming* 𝄞𝄞𝄞𝄞𝄞 (Asian Improv Records, 1995, prod. Francis Wong, Julie Hatta), like *Pilgrimage*, features what is commonly referred to as jazz as only one of many ingredients of the music. Horiuchi's free piano playing on a variation of the classic Chinese theme "Autumn Moon Reflected on the Peaceful Lake" rivals the best of that "genre." The introduction of the three-part piece "Persistence of Vision," on shamisen, flute, and cello (Kavee can play percussion and cello simultaneously), is quiet, beautiful, and hypnotic. "An Urgency in Our Insurgency" speaks to the lifeline of the so-called avant-garde. Wong's recording debut as a leader with a crack band, *Great Wall* 𝄞𝄞𝄞𝄞 (Asian Improv, 1993, prod. Francis Wong), is marked by a striking John Coltrane influence that bolsters the saxophonist's sound, particularly soaring on "Conversations," a dual tenor workout with Modirzadeh. Traditional Asian melodies like "Autumn Moon Reflected on the Peaceful Lake," "Alishan (Song of Ali Mountain)," and the title track flourish in this format of the jazz quartet.

what to buy next: *Devotee* 𝄞𝄞𝄞𝄞 (Asian Improv, 1997, prod. Francis Wong, Julie Hatta) is an important album with Genny Lim and Francis Wong's Ming trio examining the foundations of ethnicity and what race means in contemporary America. The Ming ensemble supports Lim's theatrical storytelling-singing with Kavee on drums and cello, Horiuchi on shamisen and piano, and Wong on sax, violin, erhu, flute, and clarinet.

the rest:
(With Tatsu Aoki) *Chicago Time Code* 𝄞𝄞𝄞 (Asian Improv, 1995)
(With Kavee) *Duets I* 𝄞𝄞𝄞𝄞 (Asian Improv, 1996)
(With Tatsu Aoki, Dave Pavkovic Trio) *Urban Reception* 𝄞𝄞𝄞𝄞 (Southport, 1996)

influences:
◀◀ John Coltrane, Sonny Rollins, Albert Ayler

▶▶ Vijay Iyer

Sam Prestianni

Anthony Wonsey

Born September 21, 1971, in Chicago, IL.

A rapidly maturing pianist with a light, fluid touch and an ear for melody, Anthony Wonsey is a student of the lyrical bop tradition by way of Tommy Flanagan and Cedar Walton (through Mulgrew Miller). He began playing piano at age six and received early instruction from his mother, a classical pianist, and Zilner Randolph, who was Louis Armstrong's musical director for much of the 1930s. He attended Berklee on a full scholarship and since the mid-1990s has distinguished himself on the New York scene as one of the leading pianists of his generation. He has recorded with trumpeters Nicholas Payton and Eddie Allen, drummer Carl Allen, and saxophonist Phil Woods; toured with alto saxophonists Kenny Garrett and Chris Holliday, singer Nnenna Freelon, and drummer Elvin Jones; and gigged with saxophonists Vincent Herring, Mark Turner, Antonio Hart, and Donald Harrison, and trumpeter Roy Hargrove. Wonsey has recorded two albums on Evidence.

what to buy: An excellent trio session featuring bassist Christian McBride and drummer Carl Allen, *Another Perspective* ✍✍✍ (Evidence, 1997, prod. Satoshi Hirano) is an impressive sophomore effort that finds pianist Anthony Wonsey deep in Bud Powell territory. Covering four Powell tunes, including the rarely played "Duid Deed," taken at a torrid tempo, and the altered minor blues "Blue Pearl," which features a highly effective arrangement that uses vamps to transition between sections, Wonsey plays with marked maturity and probing intelligence. Other highlights include a graceful version of Hank Jones's "We're All Together" and his lyrical original "Song for Constance." As a trio, the three players make a highly cohesive unit, balancing power with emotional nuance.

what to buy next: A very impressive debut recording, *Anthonyology* ✍✍✍ (Evidence, 1996, prod. Satoshi Hirano) features Wonsey's trio with bassist Christian McBride and drummer Carl Allen playing a varied collection of 10 tunes. He contributes three of his own pieces, including the high-stepping Bud Powellish "Hey Jimmy," and the disturbing, verging-on-atonal "Faces of a Clown." Most impressive is his work on the rarely-played Wynton Kelly gem "Temperance" and George Shearing's "Conception." Though his personality doesn't always come through on standards, he never settles for the obvious, for in-

stance linking "It Might as Well Be Spring" and "Sweet Lorraine" in a medley to close the album.

worth searching for: A highly-charged quintet session led by trumpeter Eddie (a.k.a. E.J.) Allen, *R 'n' B* ✍✍✍ (Enja, 1995, prod. Matthias Winckelmann) features alto saxophonist Donald Harrison, Wonsey, bassist Christian McBride, and powerhouse drummer Marvin "Smitty" Smith. Consisting entirely of Allen's originals, the music involves constantly shifting rhythms, from Afro-Caribbean beats to soul shuffles and outright swing. Wonsey fits right into the proceedings, always in step and ready to slip in an idea or two.

influences:

◀◀ Hank Jones, Tommy Flanagan, Mulgrew Miller

Andrew Gilbert

Rickey Woodard

Born August 5, 1950, in Nashville, TN.

A big-toned tenor saxophonist with deep blues roots, Rickey Woodard is a hard swinging player who can launch a tune with fierce momentum from the first note. His tenor style draws from both swing era and mainstream, modern jazz players such as Don Byas, Wardell Grey, and Gene Ammons, and his ballad approach displays traces of Dexter Gordon's lyric consciousness. His alto tone is less distinctive and he's de-emphasized the horn in recent years. Raised in Nashville, Woodard didn't have much choice but to go into music, joining his five brothers and sisters in the family's R&B band. As part of the children's musical education, Woodard's father made them listen to Duke Ellington, Count Basie, Lucky Thompson, and Ray Charles. Woodard joined Charles in 1980 and spent about eight years on the road with his band. He settled in Los Angeles in 1988 and has become a pillar of the Southern California jazz scene, featured in the Clayton–Hamilton Jazz Orchestra, Jeannie and Jimmy Cheatham's Sweet Baby Blues Band, and the Frank Capp Juggernaut. Woodard toured with Horace Silver in the mid-1990s and Silver showcased his tenor work on his 1994 Columbia album *Pencil Packin' Papa*. Woodard has performed with Benny Carter and Harry "Sweets" Edison, and works around Southern California with his own combo and a popular three tenor group with revolving personnel including Plas Johnson, Harold Land, Charles Owens, Pete Christlieb, and Herman Riley.

what to buy: With a powerhouse rhythm section and two lyrical but hard-blowing horns, *The Silver Strut* ✍✍✍ (Concord Jazz, 1996, prod. Nick Phillips) is an excellent, unpretentious hard bop session. Woodard hired his sometime-bosses John Clayton (bass) and Jeff Hamilton (drums) to anchor the rhythm section along with the great pianist Cedar Walton, and paired his bluesy tenor with the brilliant but underappreciated trumpeter Oscar Brashear on a program of originals, hard bop anthems (Hank Mobley's "Take Your Pick" and Walton's "Firm Roots"), and standards (a Latin-ized "Lover Man" and "Stardust"). The deeply soulful Woodard excels in impromptu blowing sessions, and on *The Tokyo Express* ☆☆☆☆ (Candid, 1992, prod. Mark Morganelli) he plays a program of standards with an ad hoc rhythm section covering three distinct jazz eras. Veteran drummer Joe Chambers is an under-recorded master with a distinctive way of driving a group, pianist James Williams matches Woodard in the soul department, and the young Christian McBride plays with remarkable maturity. The stomping 11-minute title track alone makes this session a winner, though Joe Henderson's "Recorda-Me" kicks things off with a bang.

what to buy next: Woodard plays alto on his opening tune, "Icicle," as well as on "Tadd's Delight," but sticks mostly to his warmer-toned tenor on *Yazoo* ☆☆☆☆ (Concord Jazz, 1994, prod. John Burk), a fine hard bop session with Ray Brown (trumpet), Cedar Walton (piano), Jeff Littleton (bass), and Ralph Penland (drums). Though only a few of the tunes are blues, Woodard infuses everything he plays with a down-home feeling, swaggering through Dexter Gordon's "Fried Bananas" and a sultry "September in the Rain." Walton's classic "Holy Land" and Woodard's Horace Silver-ish "Turbulence" are session highlights.

the rest:
California Cooking! ☆☆☆☆ (Candid, 1991)
The Frank Capp Trio Presents Rickey Woodard ☆☆☆☆ (Concord Jazz, 1991)
Quality Time ☆☆☆☆ (Concord Jazz, 1995)
The Tenor Trio ☆☆☆☆☆ (JMI, 1997)

worth searching for: Woodard is in a lyrical mood on *Night Mist* ☆☆☆☆ (Fresh Sound, 1992, prod. Rickey Woodard), a loose, relaxed session with pianist Eric Reed, bassist Tony Dumas, and the polished drummer Roy McCurdy. Woodard plays some highly effective hard bop on Nat Adderley's "Teaneck" and Charlie Parker's "Billie's Bounce," but his beautiful sound is really shown to advantage on the ballad "Good Morning Heartache" and the mid-tempo version of "Secret Love."

influences:
◀◀ Dexter Gordon, Gene Ammons, David "Fathead" Newman

Andrew Gilbert

Phil Woods
Born Phillip Wells Woods, November 2, 1931, in Springfield, MA.

Along with his peers, Cannonball Adderley and Jackie McLean, Phil Woods is a premier alto saxophonist in jazz. Entrenched in the bebop tradition since the late 1940s, he's a masterful expressionist admired by fans and colleagues alike for his consistent fluency, bold locutions, and fresh-sounding inventions. Woods's distinctive style, rife with his idiomatic expressions, is instantly recognizable.

Woods began saxophone lessons when he was 12, studying with Harvey LaRose in Springfield, and before graduating from high school, traveled to New York to study theory with pianist Lennie Tristano. After graduation from high school, Woods headed for new York City in 1948 and spent one summer at Manhattan School of Music, then transferred to Juilliard as a clarinet major. At night, he was hitting the 52nd Street scene where he began making a name for himself at bop jam sessions. Woods briefly apprenticed with the big band of Charlie Barnet in 1954 and with Jimmy Raney in 1955; he then worked with George Wallington and participated in State Department–sponsored tours to the Middle East with Dizzy Gillespie in 1956. Woods became one of New York's busiest sidemen, leading his own combos in the late 1950s, and recording his first of many albums as leader (especially his group co-led with fellow altoist, known as "Phil and Quill"). He played in the Buddy Rich band (1958–59) and, as a founding member of the Quincy Jones band, toured Europe in 1959 and 1960, and with the Benny Orchestra toured the Soviet Union in 1962. In the early 1960s, Woods starred in a nonet led by Thelonious Monk. After 11 years of doing studio work, and as rock took over the USA, Woods moved to Europe in 1968 where he spent four years (until 1972) leading his avant-garde leaning European Rhythm Machine with pianist George Gruntz, bassist Henri Texier, and drummer Daniel Humair.

After returning to the States in 1973, Woods settled briefly in Los Angeles where he formed a short-lived electronic quartet before moving to the Delaware Gap region in eastern Pennsylvania, where an enclave of musicians included his future quintet members. In 1973, Woods conceived his acoustic quintet, forming his first version the following year with pianist Mike Melillo, bassist Steve Gilmore, guitarist Harry Leahy, and drummer Bill Goodwin, a successful group that, after a few personnel changes, still tours today. The group recorded first in 1975, producing *The New Phil Woods Album*, and played together sporadically for two years before getting more work. Leahy joined the group and they recorded *Live from the Showboat*, an album that broke through under the name of the Phil Woods Six (with the addition of Brazilian percussionist Alyrio Lima).

On the success of this album, the band won the 1977 Grammy for Best Jazz Performance by a small group. (Six months later, RCA dropped the album from its catalog and two albums later, dropped the group!) Leahy left in 1978 and the group worked as a quartet before Tom Harrell (1983–89) joined to make it a quintet. Subsequent changes have included pianists Hal Galper (1980–90), Jim McNeely (1990–95), and Bill Charlap; Harrell was succeeded by Hal Crook (1989–92) and Brian Lynch. Gilmore and Goodwin have been with the group since its start, and have helped develop fresh repertoire for this adventurous tight-knit quintet. The band has over 300 songs in its book, developed over the past 20-plus years. With consistent high quality, Woods has continued performing and recording from the time of his first album as leader in 1954. In addition to his favored alto saxophone, he has occasionally doubled on clarinet. Although Woods has not recorded for a major American label since 1978, you can find his albums recorded from the 1950s to the present on a variety of labels, including Prestige, Savoy, RCA, Mode, Epic, Candid, Impulse!, MGM, Verve, Enja, Chesty Red, Antilles, Concord, Philology (an Italian label devoted to Woods's music), and others.

what to buy: Among the earliest documents of Phil Woods's alto saxophone playing are two sessions compiled on *Early Quintets* 𝄞𝄞𝄞𝄞 (Prestige, 1954/OJC, 1995, prod. various) when Woods was a 22-year old bursting with mature, fluid, bop energy. The four-track session that impressed Bob Weinstock enough to sign Woods to a contract with Prestige stems from a 1954 session (originally recorded on 10-inch LP) featuring the alto saxophonist with leader Jimmy Raney (guitar), John Wilson (trumpet), Bill Crow (bass), and Joe Morello (drums). The second session, a 1959 Dick Hyman Quintet date, was previously unissued before the original 12-inch LP of this Prestige disc was released. Woods's adoration of Charlie Parker is evident, but the eight selections also demonstrate that at a young age he had already developed his distinctive sound, combining Parker's influence with his own attack and innate sense of swing and momentum. Recorded on November 25, 1955, *Woodlore* 𝄞𝄞𝄞 (Prestige, 1955/OJC, 1989, prod. Bob Weinstock) marks the first date with Woods as the only horn, originally documented on his first 12-inch LP. With his supportive rhythm team—John Williams (piano), Teddy Kotick (bass), Nick Stabulas (drums)—Woods demonstrates the alto saxophone style that, whether playing careening bop or warm satiny ballads, would change little in future decades. The saxman's sumptuous performance on the Neal Hefti romancer, "Falling in

Love All Over Again," demonstrates his talents for picking and performing great material, and "Woodlore" and "Strollin' with Pam" highlight his early skills as composer. Sticking close to his Parker-like bop roots, Woods excels as leader on *Pairing Off* 𝄞𝄞𝄞𝄞 (Prestige, 1956/OJC, 1991), a swinging septet session of top-ranked players recorded on June 15, 1956. Altoists Woods and Gene Quill share the front line in different pairings with Kenny Dorham and Donald Byrd (trumpets), supported by a superb rhythm team of Tommy Flanagan (piano), Doug Watkins (bass), and Philly Joe Jones (drums). Woods composed three of the four tunes. His 14-minute opener, "The Stanley Stomper," swings with classy flair and "Pairing Off," a fast-paced 12-minute spree on which all soloists mix it up, make this an exhilarating date. Another early date, *The Young Bloods* 𝄞𝄞𝄞𝄞 (Prestige/OJC, 1956) features 25-year old Woods and trumpeter Donald Byrd (about a month before his 24th birthday), both rising stars, on the front line with rhythm backing from pianist Al Haig (who had backed Charlie Parker and Dizzy Gillespie), bassist Teddy Kotick, and drummer Charlie Persip. The six tunes (mostly by Woods) skillfully harvest the bop tradition. If you don't care what Woods sounded like when he was in his twenties and want to hear his more recent recordings, you have many choices, from dates with his quintet, to Woods and his quintet fronting a jazz orchestra, to a duet session with pianist Jim McNeely, to Woods playing clarinet on a Brazilian-jazz session, and an array of other notable dates. A two-CD set featuring the Phil Woods Quartet, *European Tour Live* 𝄞𝄞𝄞𝄞 (Red Records, 1995, prod. Alberto Alberti, Sergio Veschi) features Woods's quartet with pianist Mike Melillo, a live-recorded performance in Perugia, Italy, on November 12, 1980, the year before he would be replaced by Hal Galper. With his rhythm team that also includes Steve Gilmore (bass) and Bill Goodwin (drums), Woods generates some of his finest alto sax solos on these two discs. The nine-tune assortment on the two discs features standards and Woods originals, ranging from bop to ballads, which the quartet performs with breathtaking prowess. *Bop Stew* 𝄞𝄞𝄞𝄞 (Concord, 1988, prod. Carl E. Jefferson) captures a live-recorded performance at the 1987 Fujitsu-Concord Jazz Festival by the Phil Wood Quintet, one of seven Festival dates. Although Woods always strives for high quality, the added impetus of the perceptive and enthusiastic Japanese audience at Kan-i Hoken Hall in Tokyo probably contributes to the success of this critically-acclaimed performance, a sparkling collection of boppers, blowouts, and ballads featuring Woods's regular lineup with Galper, Gilmore, Goodwin, and Harrell. Galper's title tune is the piece de resistance, along with a nine-minute-plus version of "Poor Butterfly" (featuring

Woods on clarinet), and three Woods's originals. Recorded with the same personnel, *Bouquet* 𝄞𝄞𝄞𝄞 (Concord, 1989, prod. Carl E. Jefferson) is drawn from another performance at the 1987 Fujitsu-Concord Jazz Festival. With the exception of "Willow Weep for Me," the crew covers lesser-known gems and originals by band members arranged at various tempos from bop to ballads. Everyone is in rare form on both dates, but trumpeter Harrell's contributions (original tunes and solos) add significantly to the attractiveness of these companion CDs. A divine date recorded in June 1990 after trombone player Hal Crooks joined the Quintet, *All Bird's Children* 𝄞𝄞𝄞𝄞 (Concord, 1991, prod. Carl E. Jefferson) contains an accessible mix of nine tunes arranged by Woods (Hal Galper's "Gotham Serenade," Woods's originals "My Man Benny" and "Ole Dude," Benny Carter's "Just a Mood") and Crooks ("Ixtlan," "From This Moment On," "With a Song in My Heart"). Woods and Crook blend warmly on the front line and everyone plays their passionate, innovative best. This is the farewell recording date for pianist Hal Galper, and his exceptional heartfelt lyricism is felt throughout. Woods and pianist Jim McNeely perform a series of 10 duets on *Flowers for Hodges* 𝄞𝄞𝄞𝄞 (Concord, 1991, prod. Carl E. Jefferson), which proves how well-suited to Woods's style pianist McNeely was during his tenure with the quintet (1990–95). McNeely is an underrated player whose melodic, idea-rich inventions really work with Woods's soaring and supple saxisms on this June, 1991 session. The fare contains their originals as well as Ellingtonia attributable to the great Johnny Hodges, who was Woods's earliest inspiration. The empathetic duets offer sincere homage and yield a few charming surprises, especially on the Woods original, "Hodges." *Flowers for Hodges* is highly recommended. The live-recorded Phil Woods Quintet date documented on *Full House* 𝄞𝄞𝄞𝄞 (Milestone, 1992) features (for the first time) Woods with trombonist Hal Crook and pianist Jim McNeely, with rhythm regulars Steve Gilmore (bass) and Bill Goodwin (drums). McNeely adds energy to the band, as well as contributing agreeable original tunes. During his tenure with the band (1989–92), Crook's presence changes the band's sound slightly, giving it a cooler-toned edge. With excellent soloing and support, both he and McNeely bring much to the date. Recorded at Catalina's Bar and Grill in Hollywood, California, on September 12, 1991, the album features six tunes (none by Woods) written by McNeely, Crook, and lesser-knowns such as Johnny Mandel's "Here's to Alvy," Al Cohn's "Pensive," and Enrico Pieranunzi's waltz "Hindsight" (featuring Woods on clar-

inet). For the tight energy, warmer tones, and melodious inventiveness (especially McNeely), this version of the quintet is one of this writer's favorites. If you desire to compare the first 20 years of Woods's various configurations of his quartet/quintet, the limited edition five-disc Mosaic set, *The Phil Woods Quartet/Quintet: 20th Anniversary Set* (Mosaic, 1976–1992/1995, prod. Bill Goodwin) compiles (previously unreleased) dates from the group's earliest performances (June 1, 1976) to the version of the band captured on August 3, 1992, with trumpeter Brian Lynch and pianist Jim McNeely. The venues range from live concerts in Japan and Finland, to club dates at Catalina's Bar and Grill in Hollywood and Ronnie Scott's in London, to three separate studio sessions. This set provides one way to trace the evolution of the Phil Woods quintet. But it's not the final chapter.

what to buy next: Though Woods apprenticed in the 1950s with an array of big bands, he's only occasionally led, arranged and composed, *and recorded* with a big band such as that heard on *Celebration!* 𝄞𝄞𝄞𝄞 (Concord, 1997, prod. Bill Goodwin). The nine-tune studio session of originals and standards features the Festival Orchestra, notable for its association with the Celebration of the Arts Festival founded by Woods and Rick Chamberlain in 1978 and held annually in Eastern Pennsylvania. The session (recorded January 21, 22, 1997) features a 16-musician band that incorporates Woods's regular working quintet, highlighted in combo spots and wonderful solos from Woods, Brian Lynch (trumpet), Bill Charlap (piano), Hal Crook (trombone), Bill Goodwin (drums), and Steve Gilmore (bass). *My Man Benny, My Man Phil* 𝄞𝄞𝄞𝄞 (MusicMasters, 1990) features Woods collaborating tightly with then 82-year-old Benny Carter (alto sax, trumpet) on a relaxed 10-tune session of mostly originals by the two principals. Supported by Chris Neville on piano, George Mraz (bass), and Kenny Washington (drums), the two saxophonists perform with cool-headed energy and panache. This is a mutually respectful meeting of two giants in the jazz world and, though they've performed together regularly at Dick Gibson's annual jazz party, they've only recorded once together before this (*Further Definitions*, a 1961 sax ensemble album that included Woods, Carter, Coleman Hawkins and Charlie Rouse). This is a rare recording that belongs in any collection. On *Phil Woods Quintet Plays the Music of Jim McNeely* 𝄞𝄞𝄞𝄞 (TCB, Switzerland, 1996, prod. Bill Goodwin) alto saxophonist Woods leads a sparkling, hard-driving, cohesive team through seven bebop (and beyond) compositions from pianist Jim McNeely on this February, 1995 session recorded at Red Rock Stu-

Phil Woods (© Jack Vartoogian)

dios in Saylorsburg, Pennsylvania. Woods, trumpeter Brian Lynch, pianist McNeely, bassist Steve Gilmore, and drummer Bill Goodwin perform McNeely's works written especially for the Quintet (with one exception). Lynch's amazing solos are generated in the same vein as Woods's—angular, hastened, and crisp. Woods's bright alto sound, combined with tightly-arranged horn parts, gives this group a distinctive sound. Woods describes McNeely's compositions as "difficult (but) fun to play," yet this team makes the demanding music seem effortless and stimulating. A great listen and an excellent showcase for McNeely as composer-performer. *Heaven* 𝄞𝄞𝄞𝄞 (Blackhawk, 1985/Evidence, 1996, prod. Bill Goodwin) captures a December 1984 session featuring the Phil Woods Quintet with new member Tom Harrell. They reinvent six tunes, including Ellington's "Heaven" and "Azure," Brubeck's "The Duke," and more. With rhythm cohorts Hal Galper (piano), Gilmore (bass), and Goodwin (drums), Woods plays alto sax, and doubles on clarinet on this lyrical, straight-ahead session. The group had already been working together for five years when Harrell (who contributes the bebop rusher "Occurrence") joined them on this album originally released in 1985 on Blackhawk. The crew artfully interprets Sam Rivers's "222" and the chestnut "I'm Getting Sentimental Over You." Thematically, the focus of this session is on lightly swinging, blues-based Ellingtonia, yet it retains a bebop flavor. *Heaven* is a divine listen with Woods and crew at their inventive best. Multi-instrumentalist Phil Woods believes "if there's any future for jazz it's going to draw from a tighter fusion between the music of South America, the islands, and that whole scene." With this in mind, Woods took a year to create one of his most beautiful albums to date. *Astor and Elis* 𝄞𝄞𝄞𝄞 (Chesky, 1996) features Woods playing mostly clarinet and a little alto sax on this dual tribute to the late nuevo tango–jazz master Astor Piazzolla, and to Elis Regina, a virtuosic female singer who blended jazz with her sweet native Brazilian stylings before she died tragically in 1982 at age 36. Woods magnificently displays both his classically trained side (remnants of student days at Juilliard) and his masterful jazz chops. His fine musician team features cellist Eric Friedlander whose playing on all but three tracks contributes significantly to the album's radiance, Phil Markowitz (synthesizer), David Finck (bass), Duduka Da Fonseca (drums/percussion), and Bill Charlap (piano). They expertly capture the South-of-the-border moods and pure jazz passion on 11 tunes by Piazzolla, Dizzy Gillespie ("the father of it all" whose bebop inspired South Americans), and Milton Nascimento, and Woods. *Astor and Elis* was one of this writer's top picks for best album of 1996. While it's not his usual bebop, it's

still a gorgeous CD that should appeal to fans who admire Phil's adventurousness and subtle South American rhythms. *Mile High Jazz: Live in Denver* 𝄞𝄞𝄞𝄞 (Concord, 1996, prod. Bill Goodwin) finds Woods with his regular working quintet—bassist Steve Gilmore and drummer Bill Goodwin (his henchmen since 1974), pianist Bill Charlap (since 1995), and trumpeter Brian Lynch (since 1992). Woods excels on this April, 1996 live-recorded straight-ahead session at Vartan's Jazz Room in Denver. Six tunes are split evenly between group originals and lesser-known standards. From Charlap's gate-opener, "Blues for K.B.," a fast-paced bopper that prominently features each soloist and tight, two-horn interactions, a kicking set ensues. Woods allows time for each tune to unfold (only one is under 10 minutes), thus nothing seems chopped, hastened, or predictable. Woods's original, "Song for Sass," a gently swaying, mid-tempo Latinized number gives vent to the kind of soloing that has earned the saxman herds of fans. This is no ordinary session. A variety of vamps and interludes enhance the robust arrangements, yielding one of Woods's most harmonically intriguing and vibrant recorded sessions.

best of the rest:

Pot Pie 𝄞𝄞𝄞 (Prestige, 1955/OJC, 1996)
(With Phil Woods Quartet and Gene Quill) *Phil & Quill with Prestige* 𝄞𝄞𝄞𝄞 (Prestige, 1957/OJC, 1996)
Four Altos 𝄞𝄞𝄞 (Prestige/OJC, 1957)
(With Red Garland) *Sugan* 𝄞𝄞𝄞𝄞 (Prestige, 1957/OJC, 1994)
Bird Feathers 𝄞𝄞𝄞 (Prestige/OJC, 1957)
(With Phil Woods's Little Big Band) *Evolution* 𝄞𝄞𝄞𝄞𝄞 (Concord, 1988)
(With the Big Bang Orchestra) *Embraceable You* 𝄞𝄞𝄞 (Philology, 1989)
(With Tommy Flanagan, George Mraz, Kenny Washington) *Here's to My Lady* 𝄞𝄞𝄞𝄞 (Chesky, 1989)
(With Phil Woods's Little Big Band) *Real Life* 𝄞𝄞𝄞𝄞 (Chesky, 1990)
(With Phil Woods Quintet plus Hal Crook) *Flash* 𝄞𝄞𝄞𝄞 (Concord, 1990)
(With the Catania City Brass Orkestra) *Phil on Etna* 𝄞𝄞𝄞𝄞 (Philology, 1990)
(With Enrico Pieranunzi) *Elsa* 𝄞𝄞𝄞 (Philology, 1991)
Alto Summit 𝄞𝄞𝄞 (Milestone, 1996)

influences:

◀◀ Johnny Hodges, Benny Carter, Charlie Parker, Cannonball Adderley, Jackie McLean, Oliver Nelson

▶▶ Joe Lovano, Greg Abate, Antonio Hart, John Handy

Nancy Ann Lee

Reggie Workman

Born June 26, 1937, Philadelphia, PA.

A powerful and expressive bassist, Reggie Workman accrued

credits during the 1960s ranging from Art Blakey and the Jazz Messengers (*Free for All*), to John Coltrane (he often replaced Jimmy Garrison with Coltrane groups, including some selections on *Live at the Village Vanguard*), to the Blue Notes' "new thing" crowd (Wayne Shorter's *Adam's Apple*), and later avant-garde players such as David Murray (*Morning Song*). Yet, Workman has been woefully underrecorded as a leader. A tuba, piano, and euphonium player before turning to the bass at around 18, Workman played first in R&B groups and, in 1958, earned his first notable jazz association working with Gigi Gryce. He has also been active in music education, teaching at a number of Eastern colleges and universities.

what to buy: *Summit Conference* ♫♫♫♫ (Postcards, 1994, prod. Ralph Simon) reunites Workman with some of his 1960 Blue Note contemporaries (saxophonist Sam Rivers, pianist Andrew Hill, and trombonist Julian Priester) and turns the "new thing" of three decades ago into a kind of revved up classicism. It's no preparation, however, for *Cerebral Caverns* ♫♫♫♫ (Postcards, 1995, prod. Ralph Simon), a moody masterpiece of a recording, featuring Rivers and Priester, plus pianist Geri Allen, percussionist-sampler-electronics manipulator Gerry Hemingway, harpist Elizabeth Panzer, percussionist Al Foster, and tabla player Tapan Modak. No configuration of musicians is repeated in the eight cuts, and the cuts themselves play on the mix-and-match possibilities, as when Modak and Priester duet at length before being joined by nearly the full crew on "Ballad Exploration." Elsewhere, Allen is pushed to some of her most aggressive playing on record—and some of her most lyrical. Yet for all the range, this never sounds disjointed.

what to buy next: Try *Images* ♫♫♫ (Music and Arts, 1990, prod. Reggie Workman). From the lineup, including clarinetist Don Byron, vocalist Jeanne Lee, and pianist Marilyn Crispell, this should have been a sensational live date, but something seems to have been lost in the translation from the stage, a problem even more apparent on *Altered Spaces* ♫♫♫ (Leo, 1993, prod. Reggie Workman, Leo Feigin) with much the same group and the added distraction of mediocre sound.

W. Kim Heron

World Saxophone Quartet

Formed 1976, in New York, NY.

Julius Hemphill, alto, tenor, and soprano saxophones, flute (1977–89); David Murray, tenor sax, bass clarinet; Oliver Lake, alto, tenor, and soprano saxophones, flute, poetry; Hamiet Bluiett, baritone saxophone,

alto clarinet, contra-alto clarinet, flute, alto flute; Arthur Blythe, alto saxophone (1990–92, 1994–95); James Spaulding, alto saxophone (1993); Eric Person, alto and soprano saxophones (1993); John Purcell, saxello, English horn, flute, alto flute (1996–present).

The World Saxophone Quartet, one of the first permanent sax quartets to record regularly without a rhythm section, grew out of a 1974 four-sax project led by Anthony Braxton that included Oliver Lake, Hamiett Bluiett, and Julius Hemphill. The latter three reconvened for a festival performance in 1976 and added rising star David Murray. At first the members' backgrounds in free jazz made the quartet primarily a vehicle for improvisation, but all four had broader interests than that, and they moved towards an integration of improvisation with compositions and arrangements, which was probably necessary for the group if it hoped to continue along its rhythm section-less path. The model for this lay, paradoxically, in the big bands of the 1930s and 1940s, and the WSQ's arrangements often have the spontaneous looseness allied with precision (another paradox, it would seem, until one has heard them perform) of the Count Basie band playing head arrangements. Rhythmic precision proved to be the instrument that allowed the group to not only play without a rhythm section, but make listeners forget that it didn't use one. And with baritone sax player Bluiett's fat tone and solid ostinati anchoring the quartet, the strong R&B and gospel feel that all the members (especially Hemphill, who was long the quartet's dominant arranger) liked to use had a solid groove foundation.

After debuting on a German label with slight U.S. distribution, the WSQ moved to the Italian label Black Saint, which at the time was distributed by PolyGram in the States. It's from this period that the group's classic albums date. After switching to Elektra/Musician, the group began recording theme albums of other people's music—*Plays Duke Ellington* and *Rhythm & Blues*, the latter consisting of soul and R&B classics—which broadened its appeal but weakened its focus. In addition, Hemphill's health began failing. Arthur Blythe filled in for him off and on in concert situations, and finally replaced him, although Hemphill did not leave the group voluntarily and the break was not amicable. Blythe's recorded debut came on *Metamorphosis*, which is of greater significance in the addition of African drummers and, on three tracks, electric bassist Melvin Gibbs. Some fans saw these moves as a diminution of the group's identity, a sign that the quartet was grasping for ideas in the post-Hemphill era.

The contentious James Spaulding lasted for all of two tracks during a 1993 recording session and was replaced by Eric Person for the bulk of the album, *Moving Right Along*. The following year's *Breath of Life* found Blythe stepping in again, temporarily, but once again the radical change was the use of Fontella Bass (vocals), Donald Smith (piano), Amina Claudine Myers (organ), Fred Hopkins (bass), and drummers Gene Lake and Ronnie Burrage. More recently John Purcell has stepped into the gap and has been given much of the say in the group's direction, and both of the quartet's albums on its current label, Justin Time, use additional players.

what to buy: The band's fourth album remains its most appealing and coherent statement. *Revue* 𝄢𝄢𝄢𝄢 (Black Saint, 1982, prod. World Saxophone Quartet) is full of Ellingtonian scoring alternated with gutbucket riffing and patches of free improvisation. One of the most exciting tactics is for three of the horns to riff behind a soloist in flight. Conversely, sometimes Bluiett nails down the tune with his huge baritone sound on a repeating figure while the other three horns improvise intertwining lines above him. At times, individual players speak their piece unaccompanied, and the textures are varied even more by Hemphill and Lake playing flutes. This is a kaleidoscopic triumph. The previous album, *W.S.Q.* 𝄢𝄢𝄢𝄢 (Black Saint, 1981), took Hemphill's ensemble arranging to then-new heights, though he still left plenty of room for individual members to make soloistic statements. The players' background in free music shows in the broad range of timbres they deploy, which beyond even the differences in their horns allows them to contrast their parts effectively.

what to buy next: The sophomore effort *Steppin'* 𝄢𝄢𝄢𝄢 (Black Saint) was the first album on which the freeform music of the group's origin gave way to arranging genius. Hemphill's compositions, destined to be the heart of the WSQ, come to the fore, and Hamiet Bluiett's strong baritone sax grooves hold it all together no matter how frenzied the solos become. The lush voicings and adrenalized improvisations of the original quartet are heard in concert in December 1985 on *Live at the Brooklyn Academy of Music* 𝄢𝄢𝄢𝄢 (Black Saint, 1986, prod. World Saxophone Quartet). Hemphill's compositional mastery provides three of the five tracks, but an epic version of Murray's swinging "Great Peace" is the highlight.

what to avoid: *Four Now* 𝄢𝄢 (Justin Time, 1996, prod. John Purcell, World Saxophone Quartet) displays a group that's run out of new musical ideas, with the prolific Hemphill long gone and Murray, Lake, and Bluiett—John Purcell being the latest fourth member—seemingly hoarding their better tunes for solo albums. They've even run out of new gimmicks (the quartet's

again joined by African drummers), so this venerable group goes through the motions on underdeveloped arrangements, occasionally saved by energetic solos.

the rest:
Live in Zurich 𝄢𝄢𝄢 (Black Saint, 1984)
Plays Duke Ellington 𝄢𝄢𝄢𝄢 (Elektra/Musician, 1986)
Dances and Ballads 𝄢𝄢𝄢 (Elektra/Musician, 1987)
Rhythm & Blues 𝄢𝄢𝄢𝄢 (Elektra/Musician, 1989)
Metamorphosis 𝄢𝄢𝄢 (Elektra/Musician, 1990)
Breath of Life 𝄢𝄢𝄢 (Elektra/Nonesuch, 1994)
Moving Right Along 𝄢𝄢𝄢𝄢 (Black Saint, 1994)
Takin' It 2 the Next Level 𝄢𝄢 (Justin Time, 1997)

worth searching for: *Point of No Return* 𝄢𝄢𝄢𝄢 (Moers, 1977) was the quartet's debut on album and remains its most "outside" statement. Recorded for a German label, its availability in the U.S. is sporadic at best. Though not as carefully arranged as the subsequent albums and with less variety of instrumental color, it remains exciting improvisationally for listeners with a taste for the adventurous.

influences:
◀◀ Duke Ellington, Charles Mingus

▶▶ 29th Street Saxophone Quartet, Your Neighborhood Saxophone Quartet

Steve Holtje

Frank Wright
Born July 9, 1935, in Grenada, MS. Died May 17, 1990, in Germany.

A vanguard avant-gardist, the Reverend Frank Wright (who was, in fact, ordained) never received the respect he deserved for his immensely expressive and passionate tenor saxophone work, although he lead a popular band (by free jazz standards) in Europe through the early 1970s. Part of the reason for this was his expatriatism (he emigrated to France in 1969), and part was the small faction of R&B and gospel-influenced free players he commited himself to. (Wright started out as an R&B bassist before a fateful 1963 meeting with Albert Ayler, home in Cleveland on his poverty sabbatical from Cecil Taylor's band). His sax could preach your head off and, in his last few years, increasingly took on church trappings. Unlike Sonny Stitt, Wright was sadly underrecorded, although he did play with many of the era's leading lights, including John Coltrane, Sunny Murray, and Cecil Taylor, whose big band he often bolstered well into the 1980s. He can be heard to great effect on the sublime *Winged Serpent (Sliding Quadrants)* and *Olu Iwa*.

what to buy: *Your Prayer* 𝄞𝄞𝄞 (ESP-Disk, 1967, prod. Frank Wright) is a time capsule of the 1960s avant-garde, featuring a caterwauling five-man lineup. *One for John* 𝄞𝄞𝄞 (BYG, 1970, prod. Jean Georgakarakos, Jean-Luc Young) produced one of free jazz's classic quartets (Noah Howard, alto sax; Bobby Few, piano; Alan Silva, bass; Muhammad Ali, drums).

what to buy next: *Kevin, My Dear Son* 𝄞𝄞𝄞 (Sun, 1978, prod. Sebastien Bernard) includes vocalese pioneer Eddie Jefferson, who comes off as a rougher-voiced Leon Thomas, and drummer Philly Joe Jones, who evidently learned a few things from his collaborations with Archie Shepp and Anthony Braxton. Playing is relatively more modal, but cacophonous and sloppy in the best possible manner. Bobby Few's "Cowboys and Indians" includes plenty of war-whooping. The Sonny Rollins–influenced *Frank Wright Trio* 𝄞𝄞𝄞 (ESP-Disk, 1965, prod. Frank Wright) has Henry Grimes on bass and Tony Price on drums. *Stove Man, Love Is the Word* 𝄞𝄞𝄞 (Sandra, 1979) is a fiery live sextet date.

the rest:
Frank Wright–Noah Howard 𝄞𝄞𝄞 (Catfish)
Uhuru Na Umoja 𝄞𝄞𝄞 (America)
Last Polka in Nancy 𝄞𝄞𝄞 (Center of the World, 1974)
Solos, Duets Vol. 1 𝄞𝄞𝄞 (Sun, 1976)
Solos, Duets Vol. 2 𝄞𝄞𝄞 (Sun, 1976)
Shouting the Blues 𝄞𝄞𝄞 (Sun, 1978)

influences:

 Albert Ayler, John Coltrane

▶▶ Charles Gayle, David S. Ware

D. Strauss

 Y

Yosuke Yamashita

Born February 26, 1942, in Tokyo, Japan.

Yamashita began attracting attention in 1969 with a bassless trio that stayed together until 1983. Due to his early free jazz leanings, he was called "the Japanese Cecil Taylor," but there's more to his style than that sort of high-energy playing, and lately he more resembles Don Pullen, who like Yamashita is a hard-to-categorize pianist who combines the music of several cultures and moves smoothly from chord structures to rapturously adventurous solos favoring eccentric right-hand runs.

However, Yamashita's individuality is such that no comparison takes in all his facets. Yamashita is best known in the United States for a series of albums on Antilles and Verve with Cecil McBee on bass and Pheeroan AkLaff on drums, what Yamashita calls his New York Trio. The group covers a lot of musical ground, from jazz standards to free improvisation and much in between, including modality, complex rhythms, and arrangements of Japanese folk tunes.

Though his mother was a piano teacher, Yamashita started out on the piano without using music, playing familiar melodies while adding chords underneath. He later learned to read music during three or four years of violin lessons. His parents' jazz records introduced him to the music, and his brother played the drums in swing and Chicago-style jazz groups with his college friends, who practiced in the family home. Yamashita was invited to play with them and recalls that the first tune he played was "On the Sunny Side of the Street." His enjoyment of improvisation melded with this jazz experience to put him on a new path. He began studying theory and chords, and went to music college to study composition at the same time.

He soon became attracted to free improvisation, which is the context in which he came into the public eye, but over the years he combined his inside and outside playing in a structured, disciplined approach that retained the fire of free jazz even as his personal style evolved to a less willfully wild approach—in effect, he says, he plays free on the chord progressions.

what to buy: Yamashita had to carefully choose his American collaborators in his "New York Trio" for flexibility and imagination—enough power to stand alongside Yamashita's sonic fireballs, yet enough restraint and attention to match his moments of delicacy. McBee brings to the task a full, rounded tone that can either anchor the sound or stand out in counterpoint, while AkLaff has the power and hard-driving swing of Elvin Jones or Art Blakey and the intricacy and polyrhythmic command of Max Roach. The trio's *Sakura* 𝄞𝄞𝄞𝄞 (Antilles, 1991, prod. Roppei Iwagami) was its third but was Yamashita's first worldwide release with them and is particularly interesting because it consists of interpretations of Japanese traditional and folk songs. There is a sonic relationship between Japanese scales and blues scales, which are both strongly pentatonic even when they include more notes. As might be expected, *Sakura* represents Yamashita's music at its earthiest and in some ways its most melodic.

what to buy next: On *Kurdish Dance* 𝄞𝄞𝄞 (Polydor KK Japan, 1992, prod. Yosuke Yamashita/Antilles/Verve, 1993) the pianist has two solo numbers and is backed on the other six tracks by McBee and AkLaff. Tenor saxophonist Joe Lovano joins in on four tracks; "4th Street Up" is the furthest out Yamashita had then played on his Verve releases. This is highly structural music full of energy and imagination. After he had composed the title track, which has an 8/9 time signature, he was told it sounded like a Kurdish folk rhythm, hence the name. On *Dazzling Days* 𝄢𝄢𝄢 (Verve, 1994, prod. Yosuke Yamashita) he again uses McBee and AkLaff and, on three of the CD's eight tracks, Lovano, who takes more liberties in this context than on his own Blue Note albums. Yamashita's piano style is so striking, with his thick bebop harmonies erupting into dazzling dissonant runs and atonal flurries, that his finely crafted compositions can be overshadowed at first. They run the gamut from virtuosic post-bop to warm ballads to hypnotic modal themes to odd-metered, world music-inflected grooves—all structurally resilient and offering improvisatory opportunities galore.

what to avoid: Heard as an experimental pop album, *Asian Games* 𝄢𝄢(Verve Forecast, 1993, prod. Bill Laswell) with Bill Laswell and Ryuichi Sakamoto was interesting at the time it came out, but the rhythms are dated and banal, and Yamashita ends up functioning as a sound effect (if a particularly agile and imaginative one) amid the droning beats and electronics.

the rest:
A Tribute to Mal Waldron 𝄢𝄢𝄢𝄢 (recorded 1980/Enja, 1988)
It Don't Mean a Thing 𝄢𝄢𝄢𝄢 (DIW, 1985)

worth searching for: Enja was an important supporter of Yamashita and was the label that introduced him to the West, but all but one of his albums for the label have lapsed from print. Perhaps the one most deserving resurrection is *Banslikana* 𝄢𝄢𝄢𝄢 (Enja, 1976, prod. Horst Weber, Matthias Winckelmann), a solo piano album mixing six Yamashita originals (including the memorable title track) with covers of "A Night in Tunisia" and "Autumn Leaves." Yamashita's imagination roams freely, and a listen to this album makes his Cecil Taylor influence clear. *Ways of Time* 𝄢𝄢𝄢𝄢 (Verve, 1994, prod. Yosuke Yamashita) and *Spider* 𝄢𝄢𝄢𝄢 (Verve, 1995, prod. Yosuke Yamashita), both recorded with the New York Trio, went unreleased in the U.S. until Verve finally brought them in, sort of, stickered as "Special Import/Limited Edition" (so act quickly). Yamashita's playing is more exciting on *Spider*, but Tim Berne's presence spices up three tracks on *Ways of Time*, including one where Joe Lovano also plays. In addition, Lovano is on two other tracks that don't include Berne. The two-horn track has some spicy interplay and nicely woven lines, while the final track, with Berne on baritone sax, finds him and Yamashita feeding off each others' energy in outside forays that make it the album's highlight.

influences:
◄◄ Cecil Taylor, Don Pullen, Mal Waldron
►► Marilyn Crispell, Myra Melford

Steve Holtje

The Yellowjackets

Formed in 1981.

Russell Ferrante, keyboards (1981–present); Jimmy Haslip, bass (1981–present); Robben Ford, guitar (1981–83); Marc Russo, alto saxophone (1983–90); William Kennedy, drums (1986–present); Bob Mintzer, saxophones, EWI, bass clarinet (1991–present).

Seventeen years after their self-titled debut album, the Yellowjackets continue to please their core fans and gain new admirers with their special "rhythm and jazz" blend that sets them apart from other major jazz fusion groups. The Yellowjackets originally formed as a backup unit for guitarist Robben Ford and made their debut in 1981 with a light, cohesive R&B sound. Although personnel have changed over the years, founding members Ferrante and Haslip remain with the band. Ford left the group in 1983 for a solo career and was replaced by alto saxophonist Marc Russo who remained with the band until 1990, pushing the group into new and stronger jazz directions. Replacing Russo in 1991, tenor saxophonist Bob Mintzer has added even more jazz credibility to the group with his arsenal of instruments that includes soprano sax, bass clarinet, and EWI (electric wind instrument). William Kennedy joined the band in 1986, bringing influences of African, Brazilian, and world music rhythms to the Yellowjackets sound. All of the members have broad musical tastes that enhance the band's unique mixture of acoustic and electric jazz, classical music, and funk in live concerts and on recordings. The Yellowjackets have racked up around 15 albums, the most recent of which is *Blue Hats*. Previous albums have featured special guest producer Jan Erik Kongshaug (*The Spin*, 1989, and *Greenhouse*, 1991) and artists Alex Acuna (percussionist) and Vince Mendoza (arranger) on *Greenhouse*, and Bobby McFerrin (vocalist on *Dreamland*, 1995). The band received Grammy Awards in 1986 (for Best R&B Instrumental Recording for "And You Know That" from the *Shades* album) and 1988 (Best Jazz Fusion Performance for the *Politics* album). In 1995 the Yellowjackets received their ninth Grammy nomination for *Dreamland*, their first Warner Bros. release since returning to the label after a ten-year absence. In addition to touring internationally, the Yel-

The Yellowjackets **(AP/Wide World Photos)**

lowjackets have scored and performed music for Hollywood films and participated in diverse projects, including a performance of Ferrante's arrangement of "Behold the Lamb of God" from Handel's *Messiah* (1992). With all the individual and combined talents of these musicians, the Yellowjackets strive to create music that is fresh, modern, and beyond categorization.

what to buy: One thing about this band is they compose *all* of their own wonderful music; rarely do they record standards. If you haven't heard the Yellowjackets for awhile (or never), you might want to check out their 1997 disc, *Blue Hats* ♫♫♫♫ (Warner Bros., 1997, prod. the Yellowjackets), a loose, highly improvised session with lots of solos, no guests, and no overdubs, probably one of their most pensive, melodic, and wholehearted jazz-focused efforts. While the Yellowjackets are a musical family that play as a tight unit, it's the chameleon-like Mintzer who bumps this nine-tune session (dedicated to keyboardist Don Grolnick) to a higher plateau, playing with equal passion, proficiency, fluidity, and rich tone, both tenor and so-

prano saxophones, the EWI, and bass clarinet. His gorgeous bass clarinet solo on the breezy "Statue of Liberty," one of the best straight-ahead acoustic numbers on the album, is alone worth the album price. Whether you're an old or new Yellowjackets fan, or prefer fusion or straight-ahead jazz, you'll find *Blue Hats* an ear-pleasing listen. Upbeat and punchy, *Run for Your Life* ♫♫♫♫ (GRP, 1994, prod. the Yellowjackets) highlights the talents of all, including bassist Jimmy Haslip with his Jaco Pastorius-like licks on the opener "Jacket Town," an exciting tune with Mintzer and Ford on the front-line. The nine tunes on this session (dedicated to Richard Tee) lean to the R&B side, with guests Robben Ford (guitar), Steve Croes (synclavier), and Judd Miller (synthesizer programming) making significant contributions. "Runferyerlife" is a racing bop spree that Mintzer masters in Parker-like style, with Ferrante and the rest of the rhythm section keeping up the barreling pace. Ferrante is the focus on a lot of the tunes (as well as Mintzer), and as with all of the Yellowjackets' albums, there's more than one musical flavor represented on this exuberant outing to satisfy well-rounded listening tastes.

what to buy next: Not as blue-hued as *Blue Hats* but containing more of an upbeat jazz-funk-fusion blend on the 10 tunes, *Dreamland* 𝄢𝄢𝄢 (Warner Bros., 1995, prod. the Yellowjackets) finds the band joined by trumpeter Chuck Findley, percussionist Luis Conte, and a guest appearance by vocalist Bobby McFerrin on the ethereal samba, "Summer Song." Catchy funk-tinged rhythms, Findley's muted trumpet, and Mintzer's bass clarinet improvs make "Blacktop" and "Turn in Time" zesty, toe tappin' treats. Though electric keyboards are his main bag, Ferrante also plays acoustic piano, and it's a dazzling venture when he does. These musicians have learned how to please their fans. Each tune is distinctive and their musical blend contains a little bit of funk, some fusion, and some solely mainstream jazz such as the upbeat "A Walk in the Park." *Dreamland* is a smooth listen with many fine solos.

best of the rest:

Yellowjackets 𝄢𝄢𝄢 (Warner Bros., 1981/1988)
Samuri Samba 𝄢𝄢𝄢𝄢 (Warner Bros., 1984/1988)
Mirage a Trois 𝄢𝄢𝄢𝄢 (Warner Bros., 1985/1989)
Four Corners 𝄢𝄢𝄢𝄢𝄢 (GRP, 1987/1997)
Live Wires 𝄢𝄢𝄢 (GRP, 1991)
Like a River 𝄢𝄢𝄢𝄢𝄢 (GRP, 1992)
Collection 𝄢𝄢𝄢 (GRP, 1995)

influences:

◀◀ The Crusaders, Spyro Gyra, Pieces of a Dream, Steps Ahead

▶▶ Special EFX, Fattburger

Nancy Ann Lee

John Young

Born 1922, in Chicago, IL.

Pianist John Young never earned fame much beyond his Chicago base, but he enjoyed a five-decade career as an in-demand jazz pianist. Young attended DuSable High School, studying with legendary music educator Captain Walter Henri Dyett. His early influences were piano giant Earl "Fatha" Hines, Art Tatum, and horn players Charlie Parker and Lester Young. Young joined Andy Kirk's swinging big band in 1942, playing the circuit between Chicago, Cleveland, and Detroit for the next five years. He eventually gave up the rigors of the road to remain in Chicago. He joined Jay Burkhart's big band in 1948, and also played in the Dick Davis quartet, replacing Herman Blount, who would later change his name to Sun Ra. During the 1950s,

Young focused on trio work in the Chicago area, playing South side venues such as the Cadillac Lounge, Kitty Kat Club, and Roberts Show Lounge, and accompanying visiting artists such as Joe Williams, Nancy Wilson, and Carmen McRae. He also led his trio behind guests such as Ben Webster, Coleman Hawkins, Dexter Gordon, and others, and recorded an album with Gene Ammons and Zoot Sims. From the early 1970s, Young worked with Chicago tenor saxophonist Von Freeman and others, and his playing covered a wide span of styles, from swing to bebop, and beyond to the boundaries of free jazz. As leader, he recorded on the Delmark, Argo/Chess, and Major labels, and also recorded as sideman with Andy Kirk, Frank Foster, Al Grey, Von Freeman, and others for a variety of labels.

what's available: The only album in print for John Young as a leader is his Delmark CD, *Serenata* 𝄢𝄢𝄢 (Delmark, 1992, prod. Robert G. Koester), a well-mastered reissue of September 25 and 26, 1959 sessions with bassist Victor Sproles and drummer Phil Thomas. A brief, but pleasurable session of 11 tunes (including three alternate takes) displaying the talents that made Young one of Chicago's jazz mainstays, the tight trio recording covers varying tempos and styles delivered with verve and imagination. Young's prowess at the piano is admirably demonstrated and you can't help wondering why his fluent, lyrical straight-ahead jazz statements didn't bring him greater recognition. Alternate takes of three selections are included bringing the time to just over 41 minutes, with two versions each of "Circus," "Baby Doll," and "I Don't Wanna Be Kissed." Best are his "Cubana Chant" with its melody head quoting from familiar Afro-Cuban riffs before evolving into a hard-swinging spree, the first take of the blues drag "Baby Doll," and his mambo version of the title tune.

influences:

◀◀ Earl "Fatha" Hines, Art Tatum

Nancy Ann Lee

Larry Young
/Khalid Yasin Abdul Aziz

Born October 7, 1940, in Newark, NJ. Died March 30, 1978, in New York, NY.

Young started out on piano and began playing in various R&B groups around Elizabeth, New Jersey. In the late '50s, he switched his focus to organ, picking up one-nighters with passing stars like Lou Donaldson and B.B. King. When he was 20, Young recorded his first album, *Testifying*, with a soulful technique that marked him a player to watch. In the mid-'60s, he moved to Blue Note Records, where he showed a style of remarkable clarity and a sophisticated grasp of harmony (Young was listening heavily to John Coltrane's concepts at this time) on sessions with Grant Green, Joe Henderson, Lee Morgan, and Donald Byrd. He began working with Miles Davis, John McLaughlin, and Jimi Hendrix, and performed in drummer Tony Williams's groundbreaking fusion jazz group, Lifetime. Young (known today by his Islamic name, Khalid Yasin Abdul Aziz) then continued session work and released an occasional solo album. He died after complications from a stomach problem.

what to buy: *The Complete Blue Note Recordings of Larry Young* 🎵🎵🎵🎵 (Mosaic, 1993, prod. Alfred Lion, Francis Wolff), a limited edition set, contains all the material Blue Note released with Young as a leader or with accompanying guitarist Grant Green during the mid- to late '60s. It's a key acquisition for jazz organ aficionados. *The Art of Larry Young* 🎵🎵🎵🎵 (Blue Note, 1992, prod. Alfred Lion, Francis Wolff), given the cost and availability of the Mosaic set, may be the next best bet, with a fine sampling drawn from Young's various Blue Note releases. Especially valuable is a performance of Victor Feldman's "Seven Steps to Heaven" and the organ/drums duet "Visions." *Unity* 🎵🎵🎵🎵 (Blue Note, 1965, prod. Alfred Lion) is the finest of Young's Blue Note albums, and it features the organist with drummer Elvin Jones, tenor saxophonist Joe Henderson, and trumpeter Woody Shaw. *Unity* features three compositional debuts from Shaw including "The Moontrane" and "Zoltan," plus an awesome duet from Young and Jones on "Monk's Dream" (this also appears on *The Art of Larry Young*).

what to buy next: The first of Young's influential Blue Note titles, *Into Something* 🎵🎵🎵 (Blue Note, 1964, prod. Alfred Lion) was a quartet date with Young, drummer Elvin Jones, tenor saxophonist Sam Rivers, and guitarist Grant Green. The two versions of "Ritha" (one with Rivers and one without) are almost worth the price of admission by themselves. *Groove Street* 🎵🎵🎵 (OJC, 1962, prod. Esmond Edwards) is the last Young album released by Prestige, a quartet date that introduces the organist's composition "Talkin' 'Bout J.C."

the rest:
Testifying 🎵🎵🎵 (OJC, 1960)
Young Blues 🎵🎵🎵 (OJC, 1960)

influences:
◀◀ Jimmy McGriff, John Coltrane

▶▶ Winston Walls, Barbara Dennerlein

Garaud MacTaggart

LESTER YOUNG

song "D.B. Blues"
album *The Complete Aladdin Recordings*
(Blue Note, 1945/1995)
instrument Tenor saxophone

Lester Young

Born August 27, 1909, in Woodville, MS. Died March 15, 1959, in New York, NY.

"Prez"—short for "President," the nickname Billie Holiday gave him—was an original hipster and part of the foundation of modern tenor saxophone jazz improvisation. With a high yet warm tone and an engaging improvisational style, Young was one of the two pillars of tenor jazz during his day and a seminal influence on the development of bebop. Jazz enthusiasts of the late 1930s were either in the Prez camp (he was a laid-back, rhythmic improviser who seldom strayed far from the melody) or in the Coleman Hawkins camp (an aggressive, complex improviser). After early years that included playing hot music in a family band and a few other stops, Young became a major attraction with Count Basie during the 1930s. His subsequent career included classic work on stints with others (he was Holiday's favorite accompanist) and an uneven but substantive solo career. His was the style that formed the bridge between swing and bebop, and even helped inspire the post-bop cool

school. His idiosyncratic speech mannerisms in large part became the basis for hip language and he provided nicknames for
many, such as "Lady Day" and "Sweets" Edison. Without the
Prez influence, jazz tenor would sound very different.

what to buy: Prez is more known for specific solos rather than
any particular album. *Prized Pres* 🎵🎵🎵🎵 (Official, 1936–57) compiles some of his best work in a number of different settings, including some backbone-shivering collaborations with Holiday.

what to buy next: Young seemed to shine when there were
great musicians to push him and *Lester Young with the Oscar
Peterson Trio* 🎵🎵🎵🎵 (Verve, 1997, prod. Norman Granz) provides some post-Basie punch, including a couple of great takes
of "I Can't Get Started."

best of the rest:
Lester Young 1936–1944 🎵🎵🎵🎵 (Jazz Portraits)
Lady Day and Prez 🎵🎵🎵🎵 (Giants of Jazz)
Classics in Swing 🎵🎵🎵🎵 (Commodore, 1938–44)
Complete Aladdin Recordings 🎵🎵🎵🎵 (Blue Note, 1945/1995)
Carnegie Blues 🎵🎵🎵🎵 (PolyGram, 1946)
Lester Swings 🎵🎵🎵🎵 (PolyGram, 1951)
The President Plays 🎵🎵🎵🎵 (Verve, 1952)
Pres and Sweets 🎵🎵🎵🎵 (Verve, 1955)
Pres and Teddy 🎵🎵🎵🎵 (Verve, 1956)
Jazz Giants '56 🎵🎵🎵🎵 (PolyGram, 1956)
Laughin' to Keep from Cryin' 🎵🎵🎵 (Verve, 1958)
Lester Young and Piano Giants 🎵🎵🎵🎵 (Pablo)
Newly Discovered Performances 🎵🎵🎵 (ESP, 1975)
Complete Lester Young 🎵🎵🎵🎵 (Mercury)
Lester Young Story, Vols. 1–3 🎵🎵🎵🎵 (Columbia, 1977)
Master Takes 🎵🎵🎵🎵 (Savoy/Arista, 1980)
Jazz Masters 30 🎵🎵🎵🎵 (Verve/PolyGram, 1994)

worth searching for: Some of Young's best solos were driven
by the Basie band and *Lester Young Memorial Album* 🎵🎵🎵🎵
(Fontana, 1936–40) captures those early golden years. The
classic "Lester Leaps In" alone is well worth the price.

influences:

◀◀ Frank Trumbauer, Jimmy Dorsey, Louis Armstrong, Count
Basie

▶▶ Charlie Parker, Dexter Gordon, Gerry Mulligan

Larry Gabriel

Snooky Young

Born Eugene Edward Young, February 3, 1919, in Dayton, OH.

"Snooky" Young, once called "the most dependable trumpet
player in the business" by Buck Clayton and Count Basie, is rec-

ognized as one of the best lead trumpet players to have come
through the Basie organization. Young began performing at an
early age with his family's band, the Black and White Revue,
traveling on the vaudeville circuit during the late 1930s. A true
disciple of the late Louis Armstrong, Young first saw Armstrong
while standing outside the Palace Ballroom in Dayton, and
though too young to enter the Ballroom, Armstrong made an indelible impression (as with many young trumpeters of the era)
and became Young's lifelong idol. Young went on to join the Jimmie Lunceford Orchestra in 1939 at the age of 19, and stayed
with the band for three years. During the course of his illustrious career, Young has performed with renowned big bands led
by Chic Carter, Les Hite, Benny Carter, Gerald Wilson, Lionel
Hampton, Lee and Lester Young, and Charles Mingus. Young
was an original member of the Thad Jones–Mel Lewis Band, and
a member of the NBC Orchestra under the direction of Doc Severinsen on the *Tonight Show* hosted by Johnny Carson. In addition to his session work, Young is also credited with several film
soundtracks, including *Blues in the Night,* but is mainly remembered for his various stints as section leader while a member of
the Count Basie Band.

Young first joined Basie in 1942, sitting in for Buck Clayton who
was out for a month because of his tonsils. Going on to perform
with Les Hite and Benny Carter, Young returned to play with
Basie in 1943, afterwards working with Gerald Wilson's Big
Band and Lionel Hampton before once again returning to the
Basie Band from 1945 to 1947. At this point, Young quit the
road and returned home to Dayton where he formed his own
band and worked locally and throughout the Midwest for the
next 10 years. During this time, he is known to have opened up
the Flame Show Bar in Detroit and is documented as accompanying singer Billie Holiday in her performance at Club Valley. In
1957, he returned to play with Basie including a European tour,
and stayed with Basie until 1962 before joining the NBC Orchestra. Young has recorded on approximately 45 records. His
work as a section leader can be found on recordings with
bands of Jimmie Lunceford (1939–42), Lionel Hampton (1942),
Count Basie (1943, 1957–62), Thad Jones and Mel Lewis, and
most recently, with Frank Capp's Juggernaut band in 1995.

what's available: Recognized as an outstanding musician and
an excellent soloist, he is considered by his peers to be a powerhouse in any trumpet section. Unfortunately, as is the case with
many lead players of the Big Band era, although recording with
many of the most influential bands of the century, Young has
few recordings as leader to his credit. Having only made three
recordings as a leader, the only CD currently in print is *Snooky*

and *Marshal's Album* 🎵🎵🎵 (Concord Jazz, 1978/1989 prod. Carl E. Jefferson). Trumpeter Snooky Young and saxophonist Marshal Royal come together on this exceptional recording showcasing their talents with sidemen Louie Bellson (drums), Ray Brown (bass), Freddie Green (guitar), and Ross Tompkins (piano). A special guest appearance by vocalist Scat Man Crothers makes this album a delight to listen to and a plus for any record collection. The album includes a fine version of "Cherry" that features a beautiful exchange between the two soloists. "Mean Dog Blues," originally written by Scat Man Crothers for Snooky Young, is a true blues number performed in the spirit of the genre by Young. The medley "You've Changed/I'm Confessin'/ Come Sunday" melds melodic interpretations of Louis Armstrong's tune "Confessin'" with a heartfelt version of Duke Ellington's classic from *Black, Brown, and Beige Suite* and features Young in a masterful solo performance.

influences:

◀◀ Louis Armstrong, Roy Eldridge, Harry "Sweets" Edison

Keith Brickhouse

Rachel Z

Born Rachel Nicolazzo, c. 1963, in New York, NY.

Dubbed "Rachel Z" by Steps Ahead bandmate Mike Mainieri, the contemporary keyboardist was classically trained in voice from age two and studied piano from age seven. Rachel Z graduated from the New England Conservatory in 1984 with a "Distinction in Performance" and has studied with pianists John Hicks, JoAnne Brackeen, and Richie Beirach. She has toured with Al Di Meola, Najee, Bobby Watson, Wayne Shorter, and Lenny White, been a member of Steps Ahead and the Arsenio Hall Show Band, and was an integral part of Wayne Shorter's 1995 release, *High Life*. A versatile keyboardist, Z is at home in both the contemporary and hard bop settings and shows signs of growth in each. A joint venture agreement announced in December 1997 between her label, NYC Records, and the GRP Recording Company to promote and market NYC artists should give her career a boost.

what to buy: Though Rachel Z's first album was split evenly between mainstream and contemporary cuts, it was somewhat de-

rivative. Although *Room of One's Own* 🎵🎵🎵 (NYC Records, 1996) is more traditional, it is also more exploratory and rewarding for the listener. Titled after the 1929 published feminist essay by Virginia Woolf (which asserts that a woman must have money and a room of her own if she is to create), the album includes original tunes dedicated to famous women. The jazz-fusion influences of Herbie Hancock, Miles Davis, and the Yellowjackets are still easily spotted here, but Rachel Z does take risks, often with good payoffs. Sideplayers include bassist Tracey Wormworth, drummers Cindy Blackman and Terri Lyne Carrington, tenor/soprano saxophonist George Garzone, and violinist Regina Carter.

the rest:

Trust the Universe 🎵🎵🎵 (Columbia, 1993)

influences:

◀◀ Herbie Hancock, Wynton Kelly, Bill Evans, Chick Corea, McCoy Tyner, John Hicks, JoAnne Brackeen, Richie Beirach

Paul MacArthur and Nancy Ann Lee

Bobby Zankel

Born December 21, 1949, in Brooklyn, NY.

A long-time resident of Philadelphia, saxophonist Bobby Zankel is a darling of Bob Rusch's Cadence Jazz/CIMP labels. A well-rounded innovative musician who stretches into the avantgarde, Zankel first gained notice during the 1970s as a member of Cecil Taylor's Unit Core Ensemble and as part of the Melvin Rhyne–George Brown Trio. Establishing his career in Philadelphia by 1975, Zankel collaborated with an array of musicians that included Hank Mobley, Lester Bowie, the Dells, Jymmie Merritt, and Edgar Batemen. Zankel moved to New York for a period in the mid-1970s where he joined the jazz loft scene with players such as Sam Rivers, Sunny Murray, Ray Anderson, and others. Since the 1980s, Zankel's talents as soloist, composer, and arranger have garnered him commissions and grants for his works for theater, dance, and other performing arts. Zankel cites as inspirators Charles Mingus, Ornette Coleman, Charles Rouse, Cecil Taylor, and other legendary explorers, which present clues to where he's coming from. Considering the broad-based talent he displays on his four albums, one wonders why Zankel isn't more widely known.

what to buy: Aside from his skills as performer and leader, Bobby Zankel's first album for Cadence, *Seeking Spirit* 🎵🎵🎵🎵 (Cadence, 1992, prod. Bob Rusch) highlights his skills as composer and arranger with two separate groups recorded nearly a year apart in 1991 and 1992. Ten original tunes kick off with a fairly straight-ahead "Heritage" performed with an eight-musician ensemble (including Zankel), and gradually evolve into freely-improvised, high-energy efforts such as "Evolution," performed with pianist Uri Caine, bassist Tyrone Brown, and drummer David Gibson. The modern-sounding larger group features established players such as Odean Pope (tenor sax) and Johnny Coles (trumpet), along with other fine players. Zankel's well-conceived, textured (sometimes cacophonous) arrangements for the larger group sport tight unified horns and complex, snappy rhythms. As a soloist, Zankel displays raw power and idea-rich fluency, and his quartet numbers add to the diversity and creativity of this enticing listen. Zankel leads a driving horn-fronted septet on *Emerging from the Earth* ♫♫♫♫ (Cadence, 1995, prod. Robert D. Rusch), his second album for the label. His deftly-arranged eight originals work together as a suite, laying foundations that propel dissonant, churning power and intensity. Stan Slotter (trumpet, flute) tightly shares horn duties with Zankel. Violinist John Blake solos brilliantly and twists supporting lines around the horns. Uri Caine (piano), Tyrone Brown (bass), Ralph Peterson Jr. (drums), and Ron Howerton (percussion) push the soloists with pulsating, shifting rhythms and create astounding interplay.

what to buy next: Zankel's most recent outing for the audiophile label CIMP (Creative Improvised Music Projects) finds him leading a softer-edged, melodic, but nonetheless vibrant quintet on *Prayer and Action* ♫♫♫♫ (CIMP, 1997, prod. Robert D. Rusch). His interactions with trumpeter John Swana are supported by solid underpinnings from vibraphonist Bryan Carrott, bassist Tyrone Brown, and drummer Ralph Peterson Jr. Ranging from airy pieces to a groove-oriented finale, the six Zankel originals rendered by this pianoless quintet display energy and intelligence similar to Zankel's earlier albums. Zankel's trio on *Human Feeling* ♫♫♫ (CIMP, 1996, prod. Robert D. Rusch) features pianist Marilyn Crispell (one of the best among avant-garde innovators) and drummer Newman Baker. Zankel coaxes some wide-ranging sounds from his alto sax on this five-tune session of freely-improvised originals (Crispell contributes one tune). Most of Zankel's harmonically advanced music on this 1995 trio date comes from his works for dance and ballet. This is no ordinary session and while Zankel interacts creatively with Crispell and Baker, the recording lacks the ear-pleasing colors, textures, and cohesiveness predominant in his other works.

influences:

◄◄ Sam Rivers, Ornette Coleman, John Gilmore, Thelonious Monk, Charles Mingus, Cecil Taylor

Nancy Ann Lee

Frank Zappa

Born December 21, 1940, in Baltimore, MD. Died December 4, 1993, in Los Angeles, CA.

Frank Zappa—guitarist, composer, arranger, lyricist, librettist, satirist, and scatologist—comes to jazz through the back door. Although his music doesn't often swing (except in some parody situations), it features a high order of rhythmic and harmonic sophistication and makes daunting technical demands of performers. Zappa's interest in avant-garde music, stemming from his love of 20th-century composer Edgar Varese, put him in tune with the experimental mood of many late '60s jazz performers, who were taking their music in similarly far-out directions. Zappa often was packaged on concert bills with jazz performers, including a tour with Duke Ellington and a near-legendary show with Roland Kirk (pre-Rahsaan) sitting in. As much as Miles Davis's *Bitches Brew* and *In a Silent Way*, Zappa's *Hot Rats* helped sow the seeds of the highly commercial jazz-fusion wave of the mid-'70s—an ironic outcome given Zappa's reputation for being on the fringe. Incredibly prolific, Zappa released more than 50 albums in his lifetime containing, with very few exceptions, nothing but Zappa compositions, and nearly as much unreleased material sits in his family's archives. The feat was all the more remarkable since he composed, arranged, performed, and produced much of it in the spaces between tour stops.

what to buy: Zappa's most pleasing and focused work is *Hot Rats* ♫♫♫♫ (Bizarre/Reprise, 1969/Rykodisc, 1995), on which the clear, sharp melodies of "Peaches En Regalia" and "Little Umbrellas" coupled with a straighter-than-usual rhythmic drive, sweet harmonic textures, and dynamic arrangements make it easy on the ears without sacrificing musical meat. Two relatively open-ended jam pieces—"Willie the Pimp" and "Gumbo Variations"—display Zappa's considerable guitar chops. *Uncle Meat* ♫♫♫♫ (Bizarre/Reprise, 1969/Rykodisc, 1995) represents the height of Zappa's ambitions, including the avant-jazz rock of "King Kong," the off-center doo-wop of "The Air," and the post-Stravinsky flavor of "Uncle Meat" and "Dog Breath." However musically anarchic and eclectic, *We're Only in It for the Money* ♫♫♫♫ (Verve, 1968/Rykodisc, 1995) and *Lumpy Gravy* ♫♫♫♫ (Verve, 1968/Rykodisc, 1995) can be viewed as one long piece. *Money* proves a bit dated because of topical satire—for instance, the impact of the *Sergeant Pepper's Lonely Hearts Club Band* cover spoof is blunted and so is the use of "Hey Joe" as the basis for "Flower Punk"—but the music holds up and its scope is much broader than anything rock offered until that time. Zappa recorded most of *Jazz from Hell* ♫♫♫♫ (Rykodisc, 1986) alone on the Synclavier, offering some of his edgiest work of the '80s with such tunes as "Night School" and the title cut. Zappa's "classical" arrangements of "Dog Breath Variations" and "Uncle Meat" are the higlights of *The Yellow Shark* 𝄢𝄢𝄢𝄢 (Barking Pumpkin, 1993). In addition, Ensemble Modern, working under Zappa's direction, turns in the best orchestral reading in his catalog. *Civilization Phaze III* 𝄢𝄢𝄢𝄢 (Barking Pumpkin, 1994) is the album Zappa was working on as cancer consumed him. A continuation of the *Money* and *Lumpy Gravy* "life inside a piano" scenario, *Civilization* is a moody piece that addresses death sardonically (how else?). It doesn't have the novel charm of the earlier installments, but with Zappa playing Synclavier for the bulk of the album, the music comes across as a passionate epitaph by this avowedly non-passionate sonic scientist.

what to buy next: The other initial Mothers of Invention albums—*Freak Out* 𝄢𝄢𝄢𝄢 (Verve, 1966/Rykodisc, 1995), *Absolutely Free* 𝄢𝄢𝄢𝄢 (Verve, 1967/Rykodisc, 1995), and *Cruising with Ruben and the Jets* 𝄢𝄢𝄢𝄢 (Verve, 1968/Rykodisc, 1995)—are all a hoot, a breath of irreverent air just when rock music started to take itself seriously. Oddly enough, Zappa took himself very seriously in a humorous way. *Burnt Weeny Sandwich* 𝄢𝄢𝄢𝄢 (Bizarre/Reprise, 1969/Rykodisc, 1995) is a seamless melange of Mothers instrumentals from the road and studio bracketed by two doo-wop covers. *Lather* 𝄢𝄢𝄢𝄢 (Rykodisc, 1996) was originally intended to be a four-LP release in 1977 but a business dispute thwarted that plan. (Much of the music was released in separate, extremely cheesy packaging in *Zappa in New York*, *Studio Tan*, *Sleep Dirt*, and *Orchestral Favorites*.) *Lather* sums up where Zappa was after a little more than a decade in show business. *Over-Nite Sensation* 𝄢𝄢𝄢𝄢 (DiscReet, 1973/Rykodisc, 1995) and *Apostrophe* 𝄢𝄢𝄢𝄢 (DiscReet, 1974/Rykodisc, 1995) represent another album tandem that finds Zappa reinvigorated as the "frontman" for a new group of Mothers. *Shut Up 'n Play Yer Guitar* 𝄢𝄢𝄢𝄢 (Barking Pumpkin, 1981/Rykodisc, 1986) lives up to its title by offering solos from live performances that stand up like written-out compositions.

what to avoid: The *!@#$% of the Mothers* 𝄢 (Verve, 1970) and *The Mothers of Invention: Golden Archive Series* 𝄢𝄢 (MGM, 1970) are retrospectives that incompetently chop up Zappa's music from the Verve years. *Just Another Band from L.A.* 𝄢𝄢 (Bizarre/Reprise, 1972; Rykodisc, 1995) represents about the lowest point in Zappa's catalog. The music just sits there. So does the humor.

the rest:
Weasels Ripped My Flesh 𝄢𝄢𝄢 (Bizarre/Reprise, 1970/Rykodisc, 1995)
Chunga's Revenge 𝄢𝄢𝄢 (Bizarre/Reprise, 1970/Rykodisc, 1995)

Fillmore East, June 1971 𝄢𝄢𝄢 (Bizarre/Reprise, 1971/Rykodisc, 1995)
Waka/Jawaka 𝄢𝄢𝄢 (Bizarre/Reprise, 1972/Rykodisc, 1995)
The Grand Wazoo 𝄢𝄢𝄢𝄢 (Bizarre/Reprise, 1972/Rykodisc, 1995)
Roxy & Elsewhere 𝄢𝄢𝄢𝄢 (DiscReet, 1974/Rykodisc, 1995)
One Size Fits All (DiscReet, 1975/Rykodisc, 1995)
(With Captain Beefheart) *Bongo Fury* 𝄢𝄢𝄢 (DiscReet, 1975/Rykodisc, 1995)
Zoot Allures 𝄢𝄢𝄢 (Warner Bros., 1976/Rykodisc, 1995)
Zappa in New York 𝄢𝄢𝄢 (DiscReet, 1978/Rykodisc, 1995)
Studio Tan 𝄢𝄢𝄢 (DiscReet, 1978/Rykodisc, 1995)
Sleep Dirt 𝄢𝄢 (DiscReet, 1979/Rykodisc, 1995)
Orchestral Favorites 𝄢𝄢 (DiscReet, 1979/Rykodisc, 1995)
Sheik Yerbouti 𝄢𝄢𝄢 (Zappa, 1979/Rykodisc, 1995)
Joe's Garage: Act 1 𝄢𝄢𝄢 (Zappa, 1979/Rykodisc, 1995)
Joe's Garage: Acts 2 & 3 𝄢𝄢 (Zappa, 1979/Rykodisc, 1995)
Tinsel Town Rebellion 𝄢𝄢𝄢 (Barking Pumpkin, 1981/Rykodisc, 1995)
You Are What You Is 𝄢𝄢𝄢 (Barking Pumpkin, 1981/Rykodisc, 1995)
Ship Arriving Too Late to Save a Drowning Witch 𝄢𝄢𝄢 (Barking Pumpkin, 1982/Rykodisc, 1995)
Man from Utopia 𝄢𝄢 (Barking Pumpkin, 1982/Rykodisc, 1995)
Baby Snakes 𝄢𝄢 (Barking Pumpkin, 1983/Rykodisc, 1995)
Zappa, Vol. 1 𝄢𝄢𝄢 (Barking Pumpkin, 1983)
Boulez Conducts Zappa: The Perfect Stranger 𝄢𝄢𝄢 (Angel/EMI, 1984/Rykodisc, 1995)
Them or Us 𝄢𝄢 (Barking Pumpkin, 1984/Rykodisc, 1995)
Thing-Fish 𝄢𝄢 (Barking Pumpkin, 1984/Rykodisc, 1995)
Francesco Zappa, 1984 𝄢𝄢 (Barking Pumpkin, 1984/Rykodisc, 1995)
Old Masters Box 1 𝄢𝄢𝄢𝄢 (Barking Pumpkin, 1985)
Old Masters Box 2 𝄢𝄢𝄢 (Barking Pumpkin, 1986)
Old Masters Box 3 𝄢𝄢𝄢 (Barking Pumpkin, 1986)
Frank Zappa Meets the Mothers of Prevention 𝄢𝄢𝄢 (Rykodisc, 1985)
Does Humor Belong in Music? 𝄢𝄢 (Rykodisc, 1986)
Zappa, Vol. 2 𝄢𝄢𝄢 (Rykodisc, 1986)
Guitar 𝄢𝄢𝄢𝄢 (Rykodisc, 1988)
You Can't Do That on Stage Anymore, Vol. 1 𝄢𝄢𝄢 (Rykodisc, 1988)
You Can't Do That on Stage Anymore, Vol. 2 𝄢𝄢𝄢𝄢 (Rykodisc, 1988)
Broadway the Hard Way 𝄢𝄢𝄢 (Rykodisc, 1988)
You Can't Do That on Stage Anymore, Vol. 3 𝄢𝄢𝄢 (Rykodisc, 1989)
The Best Band You've Never Heard in Your Life 𝄢𝄢𝄢 (Rykodisc, 1991)
Make a Jazz Noise Here 𝄢𝄢𝄢 (Rykodisc, 1991)
You Can't Do That on Stage Anymore, Vol. 4 𝄢𝄢𝄢 (Rykodisc, 1991)
Beat the Boots!! 𝄢𝄢𝄢 (Foo-Ee, 1991)
You Can't Do That on Stage Anymore, Vol. 5 𝄢𝄢𝄢 (Rykodisc, 1992)
Beat the Boots 2! 𝄢𝄢 (Foo-ee, 1992)
You Can't Do That on Stage Anymore, Vol. 6 𝄢𝄢𝄢 (Rykodisc, 1992)
Playground Psychotics 𝄢𝄢 (Rykodisc, 1992)
Ahead of Their Time 𝄢𝄢𝄢𝄢 (Rykodisc, 1993)
Zappa, Vols. 1 & 2 𝄢𝄢𝄢𝄢 (Rykodisc, 1995)
Strictly Commercial: The Best of Frank Zappa 𝄢𝄢𝄢𝄢 (Rykodisc, 1995)
The Lost Episodes 𝄢𝄢𝄢 (Rykodisc, 1996)

Frank Zappa Plays Frank Zappa: A Memorial Tribute 🎵🎵🎵 (Barking Pumpkin, 1996)
Have I Offended Someone? 🎵🎵🎵 (Rykodisc, 1997)
Strictly Genteel 🎵🎵🎵 (Rykodisc, 1997)

worth searching for: Zappa produced a number of albums for other artists and *King Kong* (World Pacific, 1969/Blue Note, 1993), a Jean-Luc Ponty session, was the best. Ponty's first fusion effort gave Zappa an opportunity to work out full-blown arrangements that were not dependent on multiple overdubs but on a strong cast of players. "Twenty Small Cigars" and "King Kong" are stand-out tracks. *Mothermania* 🎵🎵🎵 (Verve, 1969) is essentially a greatest non-hits album, compiled under Zappa's direction, from the Verve years that includes a few interesting and rare alternate takes. Although *200 Motels* 🎵🎵🎵 (United Artists, 1971) doesn't hang together too well, we get to hear Zappa throwing everything against the wall. Most interesting are the a cappella choral selections such as "A Nun Suit Painted on Some Old Boxes," which are unlike anything he did before or after. *Zappa's Universe* 🎵🎵🎵 (Verve, 1993) features Zappa followers like Mike Kenneally doing an enjoyable live musical production of Zappa's work, although Zappa wasn't involved in the performance or production.

influences:

◀◀ Edgar Varese, Duke Ellington, Johnny "Guitar" Watson, Spike Jones

▶▶ Steve Vai, Rudy Schwartz Project, Dweezil Zappa, Meridian Arts Ensemble

Salvatore Caputo

Joe Zawinul

Born July 7, 1932, in Vienna, Austria.

Just as Ellington had his orchestra, Zawinul has his synthesizers. Only recently has technology advanced enough to make it easy for others to coax the kind of sounds out of a synth that Zawinul has been getting for decades. He has the unique ability to humanize and "de-synthesize" electronic instruments. Additionally, he is an accomplished composer, daring improviser, and an early pioneer of jazz-rock fusion.

Zawinul started on accordion at age six, then studied classical piano and composition at the Vienna Conservatory. Foreshadowing his approach to synthesizers, Zawinul preferred the accordion because he could more easily manipulate the timbre. He would take pieces of felt and cover the sound holes in different ways, thus making his first forays into music synthesis. Hearing George Shearing and Errol Garner inspired him to play jazz. He worked with Austrian saxophonist Hans Koller in 1952 and began to gig with his own trio in Germany and France. In 1958, Zawinul won a scholarship to Berklee College of Music. He left after only one week to go with Maynard Ferguson's band. He then worked briefly with Slide Hampton and served as Dinah Washington's accompanist from 1959 to 1961. After a one-month gig with Harry "Sweets" Edison, Zawinul joined Cannonball Adderley. These gigs were conventional and mainstream, and took Zawinul away somewhat from his timbral experimentations. However, they did allow him the opportunity to more fully absorb the jazz language.

During his nine-year stay with Cannonball, he evolved from a mainstream, hard-bop pianist to a soul/jazz pianist to a jazz/rock pioneer. With Adderley, Zawinul was able to further develop his compositional skills, writing "Walk Tall," "Country Preacher," and the hit "Mercy, Mercy, Mercy." When he wrote "Mercy, Mercy, Mercy" the electric piano was found mostly in pop groups and cheap cocktail lounges, but Zawinul heard the inherent funkiness in the instrument and the success of the song helped steer the band into the electronic era. This affinity for unusual sounds also brought him to the attention of Miles Davis. He wrote "In a Silent Way," "Pharoah's Dance," and "Double Image" for Davis. These compositions helped establish the electric piano as a viable jazz instrument and not merely a cheap substitute for a grand piano.

Zawinul left Adderley to form Weather Report with Shorter in 1971. Weather Report allowed him to pursue more sophisticated synthesized timbres. He graduated from the electric piano to more sophisticated and expressive synthesizers and developed reed-like and string-like timbres that enhanced, reinforced, and strengthened Wayne Shorter's saxophone. The group's first albums were primarily improvised, later becoming more structured. He also incorporated unique keyboard configurations and techniques. Zawinul would program his keyboard in the opposite direction (i.e. ascending to descending, and vice versa) or he'd program random events so that the same note struck twice wouldn't yield the same pitch. Zawinul once again provided a popular hit with "Birdland." After more than a decade of success Weather Report broke up in 1985.

Zawinul went on to explore new musical territory on his own. He immediately formed Weather Update, which, because of legal issues regarding the name similarities, quickly became Zawinul Syndicate. His music became more synthesizer-heavy and groove-oriented without becoming ponderous or heavy-handed. Ethnic, jazz, and electric music were artfully combined. Zawinul's method of composing became more expansive. He would compose by recording hours and hours of improvisations, then transcribing them for band. Because of recent acoustic dogma, Zawinul's importance has been marginalized. Undaunted, he continues to grow and explore as a composer and improviser. His music continues to inspire and uplift. The pendulum will swing back, and he'll be appreciated for his tremendous contribution to jazz and fusion.

what to buy: *My People* 𝄌𝄌𝄌 (Escapade, 1996, prod. Joe Zawinul) is a rich and varied album. Zawinul deftly combines jazz and world music. Despite the wide range of the music on the album, underpinning everything is a tremendously strong groove. The disc exemplifies what Zawinul is about: danceable, wide-ranging, evocative music. *Zawinul* 𝄌𝄌𝄌 (Atlantic, 1991) features remakes of "In a Silent Way" and "Double Image," both from Miles Davis's early electric jazz experiments. Guest appearances from Herbie Hancock and Wayne Shorter give the album additional Miles Davis credibility. The disc serves as an unofficial sequel to Davis's *In a Silent Way* or *Nefertiti*.

what to buy next: *Lost Tribes* 𝄌𝄌𝄌 (Columbia, 1992, prod. Joe Zawinul) is a transitional album that picks up where *Dialects* left off and points to where Zawinul was headed with *My People*. Zawinul's trademark angular rhythms and surprising melodies abound. *Rise & Fall of the Third Stream/Money in the Pocket* 𝄌𝄌𝄌𝄌 (Rhino, 1996, prod. Joel Dorn) shows two different sides of Zawinul. The first half of the disc features the Third Stream compositions of saxophonist William Fischer and carefully balances classical, avant-garde, and mainstream jazz. It's occasionally diffuse and meandering, but Zawinul seems to make the most of it. The second half is a terrific, straight-ahead set of primarily Zawinul compositions rooted in the kind of funky hard bop popularized by Cannonball. Pepper Adams and Joe Henderson provide many of the highlights.

the rest:
Immigrants 𝄌𝄌𝄌 (Columbia, 1988)
Black Water 𝄌𝄌𝄌 (Columbia, 1989)
Beginning 𝄌𝄌𝄌 (Fresh Sound, 1990)
Stories of the Danube 𝄌𝄌𝄌 (PolyGram, 1996)

worth searching for: *Dialects* 𝄌𝄌𝄌𝄌 (Columbia, 1986, prod. Joe Zawinul) is Zawinul's outstanding post–Weather Report solo debut. "The Harvest" is a wild and wonderful combination of sounds and world rhythms, and Bobby McFerrin's pseudo-African scatting propels "Waiting for the Rain."

influences:
◀◀ Bud Powell, Art Tatum, George Shearing, Erroll Garner

see also: *Weather Report*

James Eason

Denny Zeitlin

Born April 10, 1938, in Chicago, IL.

Pianist Denny Zeitlin's open-sounding chording will remind listeners of Bill Evans, with whom Zeitlin is most often compared. Yet Zeitlin was also influenced by the early avant-garde pianists, as well as free jazz improvisors like Ornette Coleman, whose compositions Zeitlin likes to cover. For this reason, his music tends to be freer and more complex than Evans's, but is just as warm and expressive. Zeitlin began recording in the early 1960s while still studying medicine at Johns Hopkins University. Often teamed with bassist Charlie Haden, he made a series of well-regarded albums for Columbia that await CD reissue. Over the next two decades he devoted more time to psychiatry practice but continued to perform occasional gigs on the West Coast. In the 1970s, Zeitlin dabbled with electronic keyboards and worked on the soundtrack to the film *Invasion of the Body Snatchers*. Since the 1980s, he has returned to the acoustic piano, continuing to perform and record with some regularity. Less adventurous listeners should feel confident in exploring Zeitlin's recordings; in contrast to other avant-garde pianists of his generation, Zeitlin's music is warmly romantic and will appeal to mainstream jazz fans.

what to buy: As with so many other pianists, Maybeck Recital Hall brought out the best in Zeitlin. His concert CD *Live at Maybeck, Volume 27* 𝄌𝄌𝄌 (Concord, 1993, prod. Carl E. Jefferson) features some of his strongest arrangements—almost orchestral in their conception—and most compelling performances. Underrated as a composer, Zeitlin features some appealing originals in this recital.

what to buy next: Zeitlin worked with Charlie Haden many times early in his career but the only available document of their partnership is a later session of duets, *Time Remembers One Time Once* 𝄌𝄌𝄌 (ECM, 1983/1994, prod. Manfred Eicher). More recently, Zeitlin teamed up with Dave Friesen on *Concord Duo Series, Volume Eight* 𝄌𝄌𝄌 (Concord, 1995, prod. Nick Phillips). The richer-sounding Haden is a much better partner, and their rapport, cultivated over years of collaboration, is really something special. However, both CDs show this underrecorded pianist in excellent form and are well worth acquiring.

what to avoid: Although undeniably gifted and imaginative, Zeitlin occasionally allows a little blandness to seep into his playing. Though currently out-of-print, his album *Homecoming* ♫♫ (Living Music, 1986, prod. Paul Winter, Denny Zeitlin) was meant to showcase the gentle side of his music, yet is somewhat lacking in personality. The compositions (all by Zeitlin) cannot compare to his contributions to the Maybeck recital. With its placid atmosphere, this recording will remind some listeners of the New Age piano style; one could argue that Zeitlin was an influence on that genre.

worth searching for: In the late 1980s, Zeitlin recorded for the New Age label Windham Hill. *Trio* ♫♫♫ (Windham Hill, 1988, prod. Denny Zeitlin) and *In the Moment* ♫♫♫♫ (Windham Hill, 1989, prod. Denny Zeitlin) are currently out-of-print but should be easy enough to find in a used CD store. Listeners disappointed by the meandering *Homecoming* need not worry. Unlike most Windham Hill releases, these albums are straight jazz, featuring some of Zeitlin's strongest statements as an improvisor.

influences:
◄◄ Bill Evans, Paul Bley, Ornette Coleman

Will Bickart

Zony Mash
See: Wayne Horvitz

John Zorn
Born September 2, 1953, in New York, NY.

The multiplicity of musics that John Zorn is involved with ranges from avant-garde cut-ups to Japanese bar bands, from chamber music to hard-core punk rock, from film music to klezmer. And, yes, jazz, with the boundaries (not that Zorn is ever a man to concern himself with the lines between styles) between jazz and some of his other improvised endeavors rather blurred. His quartet Masada, for instance, combines jazz and Yiddish music. He frequently uses jazz musicians in his groundbreaking "game pieces" (the most famous being *Cobra*) in which a prompter uses pre-arranged signals to cue one, some, or all of the players to do specific things, perhaps for only a second or two. He has also recorded on the albums of a wide variety of jazz musicians, including Frank Lowe, Thomas Chapin, Butch Morris, Marc Ribot, Medeski, Martin and Wood, Big John Patton, and others. A visionary entrepreneur, he has founded several labels dedicated to cutting edge music, the most significant for jazz fans being avant and Tzadik.

what to buy: Billed as the Sonny Clark Memorial Quartet, which is as much pianist Wayne Horvitz's band as Zorn's, *Voodoo* ♫♫♫♫ (Black Saint, 1986) is the place for timid mainstream jazz fans to assure themselves that, yes, he has impeccable bebop chops on alto sax. As its title indicates, it's a tribute to the underrecognized Blue Note pianist/composer almost forgotten after his premature death at age 31 in 1963, and the tunes are glorious. All concerned (Ray Drummond's on bass, and longtime Zorn and Horvitz collaborator Bobby Previte's on drums) pay tribute to a legendary pianist. Zorn takes off into the stratosphere enough that hard-core Zorn fans will also enjoy this. *Spy vs. Spy* ♫♫♫♫ (Elektra/Musician, 1989, prod. John Zorn), which consists entirely of tunes written by Ornette Coleman, is also a tribute album to a jazz great, but with a difference. A quintet of Zorn, fellow altoist Tim Berne, drummers Joey Baron and Michael Vatcher, and bassist Mark Dresser blast through much of the album at a furious pace (many tracks last just a minute or two), playing tunes from across the many stages of Coleman's career with the intensity of the energy school of free jazz married to the hectic fury of hard-core punk. For contrast after the initial shock, the second half of the album slows down, though the tension hardly lets up. With the perception of Coleman moving from avant-garde provocateur to jazz icon, this album re-radicalizes his vision.

what to buy next: The treatment of classic jazz material by Zorn's trio with trombonist George Lewis and electric guitarist Bill Frisell falls somewhere between the above extremes on *News for Lulu* ♫♫♫♫ (hat ART, 1988, prod. Pia Uehlinger, Werner X. Uehlinger) and *More News for Lulu* ♫♫♫♫ (hat ART, 1992, prod. Pia Uehlinger, Werner X. Uehlinger). The repertoire is classic bebop/post-bop tunes written by Clark, Kenny Dorham, Hank Mobley, and Freddie Redd, with the addition of one tune each by Misha Mengelberg and Big John Patton on the second album. While the material isn't redefined anywhere near as radically as the Ornette Coleman classics were, their context is definitely altered and updated, revealing new facets of the material. For Zorn in his most free-form improvising context—but within an aesthetic not unfamiliar to open-minded jazz fans—it's hard to beat his trio with guitarist Derek Bailey and George Lewis as heard on *Yankees* ♫♫♫♫ (Celluloid/OAO, 1983). The on-the-fly structures and evocative timbres contain a world of stimulating sounds and ideas.

best of the rest:
The Classic Guide to Strategy ♫♫♫ (Lumina Records, 1983, 1986/ Tzadik, 1996)
Cobra ♫♫♫♪ (hat HUT, 1987/1991)

Kristallnacht ♫♫♫♫ (Tzadik, 1995)

(With Derek Bailey, William Parker) *Harras* ♫♫♫♫♪ (Avant, 1995)

worth searching for: The two-LP *That's the Way I Feel Now: A Tribute to Thelonious Monk* ♫♫♫ (A&M, 1984, prod. Hal Willner) includes Zorn (game calls, alto sax, clarinets), Arto Lindsay (guitar, vocal), Wayne Horvitz (piano, organ, celeste, electronics), and M.E. Miller (drums, timpani) interpreting the pianist's "Shuffle Boil." But you'll have to rummage through the used LP bins, because the one-CD version unfortunately omits this track. (Were the game calls too far-out for A&M?) On the two-CD set *The Colossal Saxophone Sessions* ♫♫♫ (King, 1993/Evidence, 1995, prod. Joe Chambers), a dozen saxophonists ranging from legends to up-and-comers are mixed and matched on 20 tracks. Zorn can be heard on compositions by Wayne Shorter and Archie Shepp, and on "Promptus," jointly written by Zorn and multi-instrumentalist/producer Joe Chambers (whose intricate 1960s Blue Note albums have a cult following). Playing alongside Lee Konitz, Frank Morgan, David Murray,

Donald Harrison, and Shepp, Zorn fits right in and more than holds his own. To hear Zorn at greater length, check out organist John Patton's *Minor Swing* ♫♫♫♫ (DIW, 1995, prod. John Zorn, Kazunori Sugiyama) where Zorn is the only horn in a quartet that also includes guitarist Ed Cherry and drummer Kenny Wollesen. This is swinging, deeply bluesy soul-jazz played at a higher level of creativity than is normally associated with that genre. Zorn is also heard on Patton's *Blue Planet Man* ♫♫♫ (King, 1993/Evidence, 1995, prod. Thelma Patton), but is one of three saxes and is thus heard less often on a session which, in any case, lacks the intense focus of the later recording.

influences:

◄◄ John Cage, Karlheinz Stockhausen, Anthony Braxton, Sonny Clark, Ornette Coleman, Napalm Death

►► UYA, Django Bates, Universal Congress of . . .

see also: *Masada, Naked City*

Steve Holtje

musicHound *Jazz*

Resources and Other Information

Compilation Albums

Books, Magazines, and Newsletters

Web Sites

Record Labels

Radio Stations

Music Festivals

If you're looking for some good jazz
music by a variety of performers,
these compilation albums would be a
good place to start. (We've broken
the list down by type of music to
make your life a little easier.)

Acid Jazz & Hip-Hop

Best of Acid Jazz, Vol. 2 🎵🎵🎵 (Acid Jazz,
1997)

The Birth of the Third Stream 🎵🎵🎵🎵 (Columbia Legacy, 1996)

Blue Break Beats, Vol. 1 🎵🎵🎵 (Blue Note,
1992)

Blue Break Beats, Vol. 2 🎵🎵🎵 (Blue Note,
1992)

Blue Break Beats, Vol. 3 🎵🎵 (Blue Note,
1997)

Legends of Acid Jazz: Hammond Heroes
🎵🎵🎵🎵 (Prestige/Fantasy, 1998)

*Move to Groove: The Best of 1970s Jazz-
Funk* 🎵🎵🎵 (Verve, 1995)

Rare Grooves 🎵🎵🎵🎵 (Blue Note, 1996)

*Straight No Chaser: The Most Popular,
Most Sampled Songs from the Vaults
of Blue Note* 🎵🎵🎵🎵🎵 (Blue Note,
1994)

Stolen Moments: Red Hot + Cool 🎵🎵🎵🎵
(Impulse!/GRP, 1994)

UP&down Club Sessions, Vol. 1 🎵🎵🎵
(Prawn Song/Mammoth, 1995)

UP&down Club Sessions, Vol. 2 🎵🎵
(Prawn Song/Mammoth, 1995)

Afro-Cuban, Brazilian, & Latin Jazz

Afro Cuban Jazz 1947 🎵🎵🎵🎵 (Giants of
Jazz, 1995)

Afro Cubano Chant 🎵🎵🎵🎵 (Hip Bop
Essence/Silva Screen, 1995)

Antonio Carlos Jobim Songbook 🎵🎵🎵🎵🎵
(Concord, 1997)

The Best of Latin Jazz: Compact Jazz 🎵🎵🎵
(Verve, 1993)

Jazz 'Round Midnight: Bossa Nova 🎵🎵🎵🎵
(Verve, 1994)

Nova Bossa Nova: Jazz Influence 🎵🎵🎵🎵🎵
(Arkadia Jazz, 1997)

The Original Mambo Kings...Afro-Cubop
🎵🎵🎵🎵🎵 (Verve, 1993)

Red Hot & Rio 🎵🎵🎵🎵 (Antilles, 1996)

Talkin' Verve with a Twist 🎵🎵🎵 (Verve,
1997)

TropiJazz All-Stars 🎵🎵🎵🎵 (TropiJazz/RMM,
1996)

TropiJazz All-Stars: Live!, Vol. 2 🎵🎵🎵🎵
(TropiJazz/RMM, 1997)

A Twist of Jobim 🎵🎵🎵 (Verve, 1997)

United Rhythms of Messidor 🎵🎵🎵🎵 (Messidor, 1994)

*Wave: The Antonio Carlos Jobim Song-
book* 🎵🎵🎵🎵 (Verve, 1996)

Avant-Garde & On the Edge

Jazz Underground: Live at Smalls 🎵🎵🎵🎵
(Impulse!, 1998)

Knitting Factory Tours Europe 1991
🎵🎵🎵🎵🎵 (Knitting Factory, 1991)

Live at the Knitting Factory, Vol. 1 🎵🎵🎵🎵🎵
(A&M, 1989)

Live at the Knitting Factory, Vol. 2 🎵🎵🎵🎵
(A&M, 1989)

Live at the Knitting Factory, Vol. 3 🎵🎵🎵🎵🎵
(A&M, 1989)

Live at the Knitting Factory, Vol. 4 🎵🎵🎵🎵
(A&M, 1990)

Live at the Knitting Factory, Vol. 5 🎵🎵🎵🎵
(A&M, 1991)

What Is Jazz? Festival 1996 🎵🎵🎵🎵🎵 (Knitting Factory, 1996)

Best Of & Label Samplers

The Best of Impulse!, Vol. 2 🎵🎵🎵🎵
(MCA/Impulse!, 1988)

Best of Jazz 'Round Midnight 🎵🎵🎵 (Verve,
1996)

Bethlehem Sampler 🎵🎵🎵 (Charly, 1997)

Blue Box: Best of Blue Note 🎵🎵🎵🎵🎵 (EMI,
1997)

*Blues, Boogie and Bop: The Best of the
1940s Mercury Sessions* 🎵🎵🎵🎵
(Verve, 1995)

*The Concord Jazz Collector's Series Sam-
pler* 🎵🎵🎵🎵 (Concord, 1993)

Critics' Pick Sampler, Vol. 1 🎵🎵🎵🎵🎵 (Black
Saint/Soul Note, 1997)

Critics' Pick Sampler, Vol. 2 🎵🎵🎵🎵🎵 (Black
Saint/Soul Note, 1997)

The Debut Records Story 🎵🎵🎵🎵
(Debut/Fantasy, 1997)

Delmark 40th Anniversary: Jazz 🎵🎵🎵🎵
(Delmark, 1993)

Disques Vogue in Paris: Highlights 🎵🎵🎵🎵
(RCA Victor, 1995)

Drop Acid and Listen to This 🎵🎵🎵🎵 (Knitting Factory Works, 1997)

Hit Jazz 🎵🎵🎵🎵🎵 (32 Jazz, 1997)

Introducing the Verve Jazz Masters 🎵🎵🎵🎵 (Verve, 1994)

Jazz Central Station: Global Poll Winners, Vol. 1 🎵🎵🎵🎵 (N2K, 1996)

Jazz Collection, Vol. 2 🎵🎵🎵 (MusicMasters, 1991)

Jazz Showcase 🎵🎵🎵🎵 (Telarc, 1994)

A Little Magic in a Noisy World 🎵🎵🎵🎵 (ACT Music, 1996)

MCA Presents a Sampler of Decca Jazz (1927–1949) 🎵🎵🎵🎵 (Decca/MCA, 1990)

Original Jazz Classics: The Prestige Sampler 🎵🎵🎵🎵 (OJC, 1988)

Prestige All-Stars: Roots 🎵🎵🎵🎵 (Prestige/OJC, 1957/1996)

Red Hot on Impulse! 🎵🎵🎵🎵🎵 (Impulse!/GRP, 1994)

Resist New Groove 3: Constructions in Subjazz and Pulse 🎵🎵 (Resist, 1997)

The Riverside Records Story 🎵🎵🎵🎵🎵 (Debut/Fantasy, 1997)

The Songlines Anthology 🎵🎵🎵🎵 (Songlines, 1996)

This Is Jazz 21 🎵🎵🎵🎵 (Columbia, 1996)

The UP Compilation, Vol. 2 🎵🎵🎵 (Unity/Page Records, 1998)

Verve Jazz Masters 60: The Collection 🎵🎵🎵 (Verve, 1996)

Verve's Grammy Winners 🎵🎵🎵 (Verve, 1994)

The Verve Story, 1944-1984 🎵🎵🎵🎵 (Verve, 1994)

Warner Jams, Vol. 1 🎵🎵🎵🎵 (Warner Bros., 1995)

What a Wonderful World 🎵🎵🎵 (Red Baron/Sony, 1995)

Blue Jazz

Blues for Tomorrow 🎵🎵🎵🎵 (Riverside/OJC, 1994)

Earthy 🎵🎵🎵 (Prestige/OJC, 1991)

New Blue Horns 🎵🎵🎵🎵 (Riverside/OJC, 1995)

The Prestige Blues-Swingers: Outskirts of Town 🎵🎵🎵🎵 (Prestige/OJC, 1992)

Cinema Sounds (Soundtrack Albums)

The Bridges of Madison County 🎵🎵🎵🎵 (Malpaso/Warner Bros., 1995)

Fallen Angels 🎵🎵🎵🎵🎵 (Verve, 1993)

Get Shorty 🎵🎵🎵🎵 (Antilles, 1995)

Jazz Goes to the Movies 🎵🎵🎵 (Timeless, 1994)

Kansas City 🎵🎵🎵🎵 (Verve, 1995)

L.A. Confidential 🎵🎵🎵 (Restless, 1997)

Malcolm X 🎵🎵🎵 (Qwest/Reprise, 1992)

Crooners and Warblers

Bethlehem Vocal Sampler, Vol. 1 🎵🎵🎵 (Bethlehem, 1987/1996)

Billie, Ella, Lena, Sarah! 🎵🎵🎵🎵 (Columbia/Legacy, 1980/1994)

East Coast Jive 🎵🎵🎵 (Apollo/Delmark, 1994)

The Essential Jazz Singers 🎵🎵🎵🎵 (Verve, 1996)

The Great Jazz Vocalists Sing Ellington and Strayhorn 🎵🎵🎵🎵 (Blue Note, 1997)

Jazz Singers 🎵🎵🎵 (Prestige, 1994)

The Jazz Voice 🎵🎵🎵 (Knitting Factory Works, 1997)

Pennies from Heaven: Capitol's Gentlemen of Song, Vol. 2 🎵🎵🎵🎵 (Capitol, 1995)

Songs That Made the Phone Light Up 🎵🎵🎵 (32 Jazz, 1997)

Vocal Sampling: Una Forma Mas 🎵🎵🎵🎵 (Sire, 1995)

West Coast Jive 🎵🎵🎵 (Apollo/Delmark, 1992)

Dixieland and New Orleans Beats

Best of Bourbon Street 🎵🎵🎵🎵 (ProArte/ProJazz, 1989)

Compact Jazz: Best of Dixieland 🎵🎵🎵 (Verve, 1989)

The Mercury Records Jazz Story 🎵🎵🎵🎵 (Verve, 1995)

New Orleans Jazz Giants: 1936–1940 🎵🎵🎵🎵 (JSP, 1994)

We Dig Dixieland Jazz 🎵🎵🎵🎵 (Savoy, 1993)

Deck the Halls

Christmas in New Orleans: R&B, Jazz & Gospel 🎵🎵🎵 (Mardi Gras Records, 1992)

A Concord Jazz Christmas 🎵🎵🎵🎵 (Concord, 1994)

A Concord Jazz Christmas 2 🎵🎵🎵🎵 (Concord, 1996)

Jazz Christmas: Hot Jazz for a Cool Night 🎵🎵🎵 (BMG/MusicMasters, 1992)

Jazz Christmas Party 🎵🎵🎵🎵 (Warner Bros., 1997)

Jazz for Joy (A Verve Christmas Album) 🎵🎵🎵 (Verve, 1997)

Jazz to the World 🎵🎵 (Blue Note, 1995)

Justin Time for Christmas 🎵🎵🎵🎵 (Justin Time, 1995)

An NPR Jazz Christmas with Marian McPartland and Friends 🎵🎵🎵🎵 (NPR Classics, 1997)

Santa's Bag: An All-Star Jazz Christmas 🎵🎵🎵🎵🎵 (Telarc, 1994)

A Traditional Jazz Christmas 🎵🎵🎵🎵 (GRP, 1997)

Drums and Beats

Anthology of Jazz Drumming, Vol. 1 🎵🎵🎵 (Masters of Jazz, 1997)

Anthology of Jazz Drumming, Vol. 2 🎵🎵🎵 (Masters of Jazz, 1997)

Early Jazz & The Roaring Twenties

From Ragtime to Jazz 🎵🎵🎵🎵 (Timeless, 1997)

From Ragtime to Jazz: Vol. 2, 1916–1922 🎵🎵🎵🎵 (Timeless, 1997)

The Jazz Age: New York in the Twenties 🎵🎵🎵🎵 (Bluebird/RCA, 1991)

Jazz Ltd., Vol. 1 🎵🎵🎵🎵🎵 (Delmark, 1994)

Jazz the World Forgot: Jazz Classics of the 1920s, Vol. 1 🎵🎵🎵🎵 (Yazoo, 1996)

Jazz the World Forgot: Jazz Classics of the 1920s, Vol. 2 🎵🎵🎵🎵 (Yazoo, 1996)

New Orleans in the '20s 🎵🎵🎵🎵 (Timeless, 1993)

Roaring Twenties 🎵🎵🎵🎵 (ProArte/ProJazz, 1991)

Specialty Legends of Boogie Woogie 🎵🎵🎵 (Specialty, 1992)

Stride Piano Summit 🎵🎵🎵🎵 (Milestone, 1991)

Education and History

The Instrumental History of Jazz 🎵🎵🎵🎵🎵 (N2K, 1997)

History of Jazz 🎵🎵🎵🎵 (BMG/MusicMasters, 1998)

RCA Beginner's Guide to Jazz 🎵🎵🎵🎵🎵 (Bluebird/RCA, 1996)

Geographic Jazz

Chicago Hot Bands, 1924–1928 🎵🎵🎵🎵 (Timeless, 1997)

Jazz from Atlanta: 1923–29 🎵🎵🎵🎵 (Timeless, 1997)

Jazz in California 🦴🦴🦴 (Timeless, 1997)
Jazz in St. Louis 🦴🦴🦴 (Timeless, 1997)
Jazz in Texas 🦴🦴🦴 (Timeless, 1997)
Jazz Men—Detroit 🦴🦴🦴🦴 (Savoy, 1993)
New York Stories 🦴🦴🦴🦴 (Blue Note, 1992)
Obscure and Neglected Chicagoans 🦴🦴🦴🦴 (IAJRC, 1994)
West Coast Jazz Summit 🦴🦴🦴🦴 (MONS, 1996)

Guitars Galore

Come Together: Guitar Tribute to the Beatles, Vol. 2 🦴🦴 (NYC, 1995)
The Concord Jazz Guitar Collection, Volumes 1 and 2 🦴🦴🦴 (Concord, 1981)
The Concord Jazz Guitar Collection, Volume 3 🦴🦴🦴🦴 (Concord, 1992)
Jazz Guitar Classics 🦴🦴🦴🦴 (OJC, 1990)
Pioneers of Jazz Guitar 🦴🦴🦴 (Yazoo, 1992)

The Great American Songbook Composers

All the Things You Are: The Jerome Kern Songbook 🦴🦴🦴 (Verve, 1996)
Anything Goes: The Cole Porter Songbook . . . 🦴🦴🦴 (Verve, 1992)
The Billy Strayhorn Songbook 🦴🦴🦴 (Concord, 1997)
Blue Skies: The Irving Berlin Songbook 🦴🦴 (Verve, 1996)
Blues in the Night: The Johnny Mercer Songbook 🦴🦴🦴 (Verve, 1997)
Cheek to Cheek: The Irving Berlin Songbook 🦴🦴🦴 (Verve, 1997)
Cole Porter in Concert: Just One of Those Live Things 🦴🦴🦴🦴 (Verve, 1994)
The Complete Cole Porter Songbooks 🦴🦴🦴🦴 (Verve, 1993)
The Complete Gershwin Songbooks 🦴🦴🦴🦴 (Verve, 1995)
The Complete Jerome Kern Songbooks 🦴🦴🦴🦴 (Verve, 1997)
The Complete Rodgers & Hart Songbooks 🦴🦴🦴🦴 (Verve, 1996)
Fine Romance: Jerome Kern Songbook 🦴🦴🦴🦴 (Verve, 1994)
The Hoagy Carmichael Songbook 🦴🦴🦴🦴🦴 (BMG/RCA, 1990)
How Deep Is the Ocean: The Irving Berlin Songbook 🦴🦴 (Verve, 1997)
I Get A Kick Out of You: Cole Porter Songbook, Vol. 2 🦴🦴🦴🦴 (Verve, 1991)
Isn't It Romantic?: The Rodgers & Hart Songbook 🦴🦴🦴🦴 (Verve, 1996)

Jazz 'Round Midnight: Gershwin 🦴🦴🦴🦴 (Verve, 1998)
Lush Life: The Billy Strayhorn Songbook 🦴🦴🦴🦴 (Verve, 1996)
My Funny Valentine: The Rodgers & Hart Songbook 🦴🦴🦴 (Verve, 1995)
S' Marvelous: The Gershwin Songbook 🦴🦴🦴 (Verve, 1994)
S' Paradise: The Gershwin Songbook 🦴🦴🦴🦴 (Verve, 1995)
S' Wonderful: Concord Jazz Salutes Ira Gershwin 🦴🦴🦴🦴 (Concord, 1996)
S' Wonderful: The Gershwin Songbook 🦴🦴🦴🦴 (Verve, 1992)
S' Wonderful: The Jazz Giants Play George Gershwin 🦴🦴🦴🦴 (Prestige/Fantasy, 1997)
Soft Lights and Sweet Music: The Jazz Giants Play Irving Berlin 🦴🦴🦴🦴 (Prestige/Fantasy, 1997)
Stardust: The Jazz Giants Play Hoagy Carmichael 🦴🦴🦴🦴🦴 (Prestige/Fantasy, 1997)
That Old Black Magic: The Harold Arlen Songbook 🦴🦴 (Verve, 1997)
We'll Have Manhattan: The Rodgers & Hart Songbook 🦴🦴🦴 (Verve, 1993)
We'll Meet Again: The Love Songs of World War II 🦴🦴🦴🦴🦴 (MCA/Smithsonian, 1993)
Yesterdays: The Jerome Kern Songbook 🦴🦴🦴🦴 (Verve, 1997)

Ivory Ticklers

B-3in': Organ Jazz 🦴🦴🦴🦴 (32 Jazz, 1997)
Modern Jazz Piano Album 🦴🦴🦴🦴 (Savoy, 1995)
Piano Players & Significant Others 🦴🦴🦴🦴 (BMG/MusicMasters, 1990)

Jammin'

All-Star Jam Sessions 🦴🦴🦴🦴🦴 (Moon Jazz, 1995)
Fabulous Pescara Jam 🦴🦴🦴 (Philology, 1997)
Jazz Loft Sessions 🦴🦴🦴🦴 (Douglas, 1997)
Jelly Roll Morton's Jams 🦴🦴🦴 (Verve, 1993)
The Pablo All-Stars Jam: Montreux '77 🦴🦴🦴🦴 (Pablo Live/OJC, 1977/1989)

Jazz in Concert

Carnegie Hall Salutes the Jazz Masters: Verve 50th Anniversary 🦴🦴🦴🦴 (Verve, 1994)

Eastwood after Hours: Live at Carnegie Hall 🦴🦴🦴🦴🦴 (Malpaso/Warner Bros., 1997)
From Spiritual to Swing: Carnegie Hall Concerts, 1938–1939 🦴🦴🦴🦴🦴 (Vanguard, 1987)
Giants of Jazz—In Berlin '71 🦴🦴🦴🦴 (Verve, 1988)
Jazz at the Philharmonic: At the Montreux Jazz Festival, 1975 🦴🦴🦴🦴 (Pablo/OJC, 1975)
Jazz at the Philharmonic: Frankfurt, 1952 🦴🦴🦴🦴 (Pablo, 1952/1997)
Jazz at the Philharmonic: Hartford, 1953 🦴🦴🦴🦴 (Pablo, 1953)
Jazz at the Philharmonic in Tokyo: Live at the Nichigeki Theatre, 1953 🦴🦴🦴🦴🦴 (Pablo, 1953/1990)
Jazz at the Philharmonic: Jazz at the Santa Monica Civic, '72 🦴🦴🦴🦴 (Pablo, 1972)
Jazz at the Philharmonic: London, 1969 🦴🦴🦴🦴 (Pablo, 1969)
Jazz at the Philharmonic, 1983 🦴🦴🦴🦴 (Pablo/OJC, 1983)
Jazz at the Philharmonic: Return to Happiness, Tokyo, 1983 🦴🦴🦴🦴 (Pablo, 1983)
Jazz at the Philharmonic: The First Concert 🦴🦴🦴🦴🦴 (Verve, 1994)
JVC Jazz Festival Live! A Night of Chesky Jazz 🦴🦴🦴🦴 (Chesky, 1992)
The New Wave in Jazz 🦴🦴🦴🦴🦴 (Impulse!, 1968/1978, Impulse!/GRP, 1994)
The October Revolution 🦴🦴🦴🦴🦴 (Evidence, 1996)
Once by Company 🦴🦴🦴🦴 (Incus, 1989)

Lounge & Dance

Oscillatin' Rhythm 🦴🦴 (Capitol, 1997)
Uptown Saturday Night 🦴🦴🦴🦴 (PolyGram, 1997)

Saxophone Surplus

The Colossal Saxophone Sessions 🦴🦴🦴🦴🦴 (King, 1993/Evidence, 1995)
Romantic Sax for Lovers 🦴🦴 (Verve, 1987)
Tenor Conclave 🦴🦴🦴🦴 (OJC, 1990)

Smooth Sounds: Fusion and Contemporary Jazz

Basstorius—Bass Talk, Vol. 3 🦴🦴🦴 (Hot Wire, 1994)
Fuse One 🦴🦴🦴🦴 (BMG/MusicMasters, 1980–81/1995)

1997 Panasonic Jazz Festival 🎵🎵🎵 (International Music Factory, 1997)

Smooth Elements: Smooth Jazz Plays Earth, Wind & Fire 🎵🎵🎵 (Shanachie, 1997)

Swing & Big Band

Big Band Collection 🎵🎵🎵🎵 (Special, 1993)

Big Bands in Hi-Fi, Vol. 2: In the Mood 🎵🎵🎵🎵 (Capitol, 1995)

Gentle Duke: The Ellington Soloists Play Duke 🎵🎵🎵🎵 (Prestige/Fantasy, 1997)

Giants of Small-Band Swing, Vol. 1 🎵🎵🎵🎵 (Riverside/OJC, 1990)

Giants of Small-Band Swing, Vol. 2 🎵🎵🎵🎵 (Riverside/OJC, 1990)

Great Swing Bands 🎵🎵🎵 (Hindsight, 1995)

Harlem Big Bands 🎵🎵🎵🎵 (Timeless, 1994)

100 Greatest Jazz & Swing Hits 🎵🎵🎵 (Affinity, 1994)

Swing—Not Spring 🎵🎵🎵🎵 (Savoy, 1993)

Tributes

For the Love of Monk 🎵🎵🎵🎵 (32 Jazz, 1997)

Hub Art: A Celebration of the Music of Freddie Hubbard 🎵🎵🎵🎵 (Hip Bop Essence/Silva Screen, 1995)

Interpretations of Monk, Vol. 1: Afternoon Concert 🎵🎵🎵🎵 (DIW, 1994/Koch Jazz, 1997)

Interpretations of Monk, Vol. 2: Evening Concert 🎵🎵🎵🎵 (DIW, 1994/Koch Jazz, 1998)

Jazz Celebration: A Tribute to Carl Jefferson 🎵🎵🎵🎵 (Concord, 1996)

Opus De Funk: The Jazz Giants Play Horace Silver 🎵🎵🎵🎵 (Prestige/Fantasy, 1997)

Tribute to Lee Morgan 🎵🎵🎵🎵 (NYC, 1995)

Wavelength Infinity: A Sun Ra Tribute 🎵🎵🎵🎵 (Rastascan, 1995)

Weird Nightmare: Meditations on Mingus 🎵🎵🎵 (Columbia, 1992)

Can't get enough information about jazz music? Here are some books, magazines, and newsletters you can check out for further information. Happy reading!

Books

BIOGRAPHIES

American Musicians II: Seventy-Two Portraits in Jazz
Whitney Balliett (Oxford University Press, 1996)

Around about Midnight: A Portrait of Miles Davis
Eric Nisenson (Da Capo Press, 1996)

As Though I Had Wings: The Lost Memoir
Chet Baker (St. Martins Press, 1997)

Ascension: John Coltrane and His Quest
Eric Nisenson (St. Martins Press, 1993)

Bass Line: The Stories and Photographs of Milt Hinton
Milt Hinton and David G. Berger (Temple University Press, 1991)

Benny Goodman and the Swing Era
James Lincoln Collier (Oxford University Press, 1989)

Benny Goodman, Listen to His Legacy (Studies in Jazz, No. 6)
D. Russell Connor (Scarecrow Press, 1988)

Benny Goodman: Wrappin' It Up (Studies in Jazz, No. 23)
D. Russell Connor (Scarecrow Press, 1996)

Beyond Category: The Life and Genius of Duke Ellington
John Edward Hasse (Da Capo Press, 1995)

Billie Holiday
Stuart Nicholson (Northeastern University Press, 1995)

Billie's Blues: The Billie Holiday Story, 1933–1959
John Chilton and Buck Clayton (Da Capo Press, 1989)

Bird: The Legend of Charlie Parker
Robert George Reisner (Da Capo Press, 1988)

Bird Lives! The High Life and Hard Times of Charlie (Yardbird) Parker
Ross Russell (Da Capo Press, 1996)

Bird's Diary: The Life of Charlie Parker, 1945–1955
Ken Vail (Harvill Press, 1996)

Blue Flame: Woody Herman's Life in Music
Robert C. Kriebel (Purdue University Press, 1995)

Celebrating the Duke: And Louis, Bessie, Billie, Bird, Carmen, Miles, Dizzy, and Other Heroes
Ralph J. Gleason (Da Capo Press, 1995)

Charlie Christian
Peter Broadbent (Hal Leonard Publishing Corp., 1997)

Charlie Parker (Black Americans of Achievement)
Ron Frankl (Chelsea House, 1992)

Charlie Parker: His Music and Life (Michigan American Music Series)
Carl Woideck (University of Michigan Press, 1996)

Charlie Parker Played Be Bop
Chris Raschka (Orchard Books, 1992)

Chasin' the Trane: The Music and Mystique of John Coltrane
J.C. Thomas (Da Capo Press, 1988)

Cleo
Cleo Laine (Simon & Schuster, 1997)

Coltrane: A Biography
Cuthbert Ormond Simpkins (Black Classic Press, 1988)

Count Basie (Black Americans of Achievement)
Bud Kliment and Nathan Irvin Huggins, eds. (Chelsea House, 1992)

Crazeology: The Autobiography of a Chicago Jazzman (Music in American Life Series)
Bud Freeman (University of Illinois Press, 1989)

Crazy Fingers: Claude Hopkins Life in Jazz
Claude Hopkins and Warren W. Vache (Smithsonian Institute Press, 1992)

Dance of the Infidels: A Portrait of Bud Powell
Francis Paudras (Da Capo Press, 1998)

Dancing to a Black Man's Tune: A Life of Scott Joplin (Missouri Biography Series)
Susan Curtis (University of Missouri Press, 1994)

Dexter Gordon: A Musical Biography
Stan Britt (Da Capo Press, 1989)

Dizzy Gillespie (Black Americans of Achievement)
Tony Gentry (Chelsea House, 1994)

Django Reinhardt
Charles Delaunay (Da Capo Press, 1988)

Duke Ellington (Black Americans of Achievement)
Ron Frankl (Chelsea House, 1988)

Duke Ellington (Impact Biography)
Eva Stwertka and Eve Stwertka (Franklin Watts, Inc., 1994)

Duke Ellington: Jazz Composer
Ken Rattenbury (Yale University Press, 1993)

Duke Ellington: The Piano Prince and His Orchestra
Andrea Davis Pinkney (Disney Press, 1998)

Ella Fitzgerald: A Biography of the First Lady of Jazz
Stuart Nicholson (Scribner, 1994)

Ellington: The Early Years (Music in American Life Series)
Mark Tucker (University of Illinois Press, 1991)

Fats Waller
Maurice Waller (Macmillan General Reference, 1997)

First Lady of Song: Ella Fitzgerald for the Record
Geoffrey Mark Fidelman (Birch Lane Press, 1994)

Forces in Motion: The Music and Thoughts of Anthony Braxton
Graham Lock and Nick White (Da Capo Press, 1989)

From Satchmo to Miles
Leonard Feather (Da Capo Press, 1988)

Glenn Miller and His Orchestra
George Thomas Simon (Da Capo Press, 1988)

Good Morning Blues: The Autobiography of Count Basie
Albert Murray (Da Capo Press, 1995)

Great African Americans in Jazz (Outstanding African Americans Series)
Carlotta Hacker (Crabtree Pub., 1997)

The Great Jazz Pianists: Speaking of Their Lives and Music
Len Lyons and Veryl Oakland (Da Capo Press, 1989)

High Times, Hard Times
Anita O'Day (Limelight Editions, 1989)

I Guess I'll Get the Papers and Go Home: The Life of Doc Cheatham
Doc Cheatham (Cassell Academic, 1998)

It's About Time: The Dave Brubeck Story
Fred Hall (University of Arkansas Press, 1996)

Jack Teagarden: The Story of a Jazz Maverick
Jay D. Smith, et al (Da Capo Press, 1988)

Jaco: The Extraordinary and the Tragic Life of Jaco Pastorius, "The World's Greatest Bass Player"
by Bill Milkowski (Miller Freeman Books, 1995)

Jazz Greats (20th-Century Composers)
David Perry (Phaidon/Chronicle Books, 1996)

Jazz People
Dan Morgenstern (Da Capo Press, 1993)

Quincy Jones (I Have a Dream)
Stuart A. Kallen (Abdo & Daughters, 1996)

John Coltrane
Bill Cole (Da Capo Press, 1993)

John Coltrane and the Jazz Revolution of the 1960s
Frank Kofsky (Pathfinder Press, 1998)

Keith Jarrett: The Man and His Music
Ian Carr (Da Capo Press, 1992)

King of Ragtime: Scott Joplin and His Era
Edward A. Berlin (Oxford University Press, 1994)

Leader of the Band: The Life of Woody Herman
Gene Lees and Graham Lees (Oxford University Press, 1995)

A Life in Ragtime: A Biography of James Reese Europe
R. Reid Badger (Oxford University Press, 1995)

Louis Armstrong: A Cultural Legacy
Marc H. Miller, ed., et al (University of Washington Press, 1994)

Louis Armstrong: An Extravagant Life
Laurence Bergreen (Broadway Books, 1997)

Louis Armstrong Odyssey: From Jane Alley to America's Jazz Ambassador
Dempsey J. Travis (Urban Research Press, 1997)

Lush Life: A Biography of Billy Strayhorn
David Hajdu (Farrar Straus & Giroux, 1996)

Madame Jazz: Contemporary Women Instrumentalists
Leslie Gourse (Oxford University Press, 1995)

Marshal Royal: Jazz Survivor (Bayou Press)
Marshal Royal and Claire P. Gordon (Cassell Academic, 1997)

Miles: The Autobiography
Miles Davis and Quincy Troupe (Touchstone Books, 1990)

Miles Davis: The Early Years
Bill Cole (Da Capo Press, 1994)

The Miles Davis Companion: Four Decades of Commentary
Gary Carner, ed. (Schirmer Books, 1996)

Miles' Diary: The Life of Miles Davis 1947-1961
Ken Vail (Harvill Press, 1997)

Mingus: A Critical Biography
Brian Priestley (Da Capo Press, 1988)

Mingus/Mingus: Two Memoirs
Janet Coleman and Al Young (Critical Arts Book Co., 1989)

Monk
Laurent De Wilde (Shooting Star Press, 1997)

Music Is My Mistress
Duke Ellington (Da Capo Press, 1988)

Outcats: Jazz Composers, Instrumentalists, and Singers
Francis Davis (Oxford University Press, 1990)

Pee Wee Russell: The Life of a Jazzman
Robert Hilbert (Oxford University Press, 1993)

Pres: The Story of Lester Young
Luc Delannoy (University of Arkansas Press, 1993)

Sassy: The Life of Sarah Vaughan
Leslie Gourse (Da Capo Press, 1994)

Satchmo
Gary Giddins (Da Capo Press, 1998)

Satin Dolls: The Women of Jazz (Musicbooks)
Andrew G. Hager (Michael Friedman/Fairfax Publishing, 1997)

Sidney Bechet: The Wizard of Jazz
John Chilton (Da Capo Press, 1996)

The Song Stars: The Ladies Who Sang with the Bands and Beyond
Richard Grudens (Celebrity Profiles Inc., 1997)

Space Is the Place: The Lives and Times of Sun Ra
John F. Szwed (Pantheon Books, 1997)

Spirit Catcher: The Life and Art of John Coltrane
John Fraim (Greathouse, 1996)

Stan Getz: A Life in Jazz
Donald L. Maggin (William Morrow & Co., 1996)

Straight, No Chaser: The Life and Genius of Thelonious Monk
Leslie Gourse (Schirmer Books, 1997)

Suits Me: The Double Life of Billy Tipton
Diane Wood Middlebrook (Houghton Mifflin, 1998)

Swing, Swing, Swing: The Life & Times of Benny Goodman
Ross Firestone (W.W. Norton & Co., 1994)

Talking Jazz: An Oral History
Ben Sidran (Da Capo Press, 1995)

Thelonious Monk: His Life and Music
Thomas Fitterling (Berkeley Hills Books, 1997)

Three Kilos of Coffee: An Autobiography
Manu Dibango (University of Chicago Press, 1994)

Too Marvelous for Words: The Life and Genius of Art Tatum
James Lester (Oxford University Press, 1995)

Wes Montgomery
Adrian Ingram (Hal Leonard Publishing Corp., 1993)

Wishing on the Moon: The Life and Times of Billie Holiday
Donald Clarke (Penguin USA, 1995)

The Woodchopper's Ball: The Autobiography of Woody Herman
Woody Herman and Stuart Troup (Limelight Editions, 1994)

Woody Herman: Chronicles of the Herds
William D. Clancy and Audree Coke Kenton (MacMillan Publishing Co., 1995)

The World of Count Basie
Stanley Dance (Da Capo Press, 1985)

The World of Duke Ellington
Stanley Dance (Da Capo Press, 1981)

GENERAL INTEREST

The Art of Jazz : Ragtime to Bebop
Martin T. Williams (Da Capo Press, 1988)

Bebop: The Music and Its Players
Thomas Owens (Oxford University Press, 1996)

Bebop and Nothingness: Jazz and Pop at the End of the Century
Francis Davis (Schirmer Books, 1996)

The Best Damn Trumpet Player: Memories of the Big Band Era and Beyond
Richard Grudens and Frankie Laine (Celebrity Profiles Inc., 1996)

The Big Band Almanac
Leo Walker (Da Capo Press, 1989)

The Big Bands
George Thomas Simon (Schirmer Books, 1981)

The Birth of Bebop: A Social and Musical History
Scott Deveaux (University of California Press, 1997)

Black Music
Leroi Jones and Imamu Amiri Baraka (Da Capo Press, 1998)

Blue: The Murder of Jazz
Eric Nisenson (St. Martins Press, 1997)

Blues Up and Down: Jazz in Our Time
Tom Piazza (St. Martins Press, 1997)

But Beautiful: A Book about Jazz
Geoff Dyer (North Point Press, 1996)

Central Avenue Sounds: Jazz in Los Angeles
Chlora Bryant (Editor), et al (University of California Press, 1998)

A Century of Jazz: From Blues to Bop, Swing to Hiphop—A Hundred Years of Music, Musicians, Singers and Styles
Roy Carr (Da Capo Press, 1997)

Chicago Jazz: A Cultural History, 1904-1930
William Howland Kenney (Oxford University Press, 1994)

The Chronicle of Jazz
Mervyn Cooke (Abbeville Press, Inc., 1998)

The Color of Jazz: Race and Representation in Postwar American Culture
Jon Panish (University Press of Mississippi, 1997)

The Creation of Jazz: Music, Race, and Culture in Urban America (Music in American Life)
Burton W. Peretti (University of Illinois Press, 1992)

Dancing in Your Head: Jazz, Blues, Rock, and Beyond
Gene Santoro (Oxford University Press, 1994)

Different Drummers: Jazz in the Culture of Nazi Germany
Michael H. Kater (Oxford University Press, 1992)

Down Beat: 60 Years of Jazz
Frank Alkyer and John McDonough, eds. (Hal Leonard Publishing Corp., 1995)

Drummin' Men: The Heartbeat of Jazz: The Swing Years
Burt Korall (Schirmer Books, 1990)

Early Jazz: Its Roots and Musical Development
Gunther Schuller (Oxford University Press, 1986)

Free Jazz (The Roots of Jazz)
Ekkehard Jost (Da Capo Press, 1994)

The Freedom Principle: Jazz after 1958
John Litweiler (Da Capo Press, 1990)

From Birdland to Broadway: Scenes from a Jazz Life
Bill Crow (Oxford University Press, 1993)

From Jazz to Swing: African-American Jazz Musicians and Their Music, 1890-1935 (Jazz History, Culture, and Criticism Series)
Thomas J. Hennessey (Wayne State University Press, 1994)

Frontiers of Jazz
Ralph De Toledano, ed. (Pelican Pub. Co., 1994)

Goin' to Kansas City (Music in American Life)
Nathan W. Pearson, Jr. (University of Illinois Press, 1988)

Hard Bop: Jazz and Black Music 1955-1965
David H. Rosenthal (Oxford University Press, 1993)

The History of Jazz
Ted Gioia (Oxford University Press, 1997)

Hot Jazz and Jazz Dance
Roger Pryor Dodge (Oxford University Press, 1996)

In the Moment: Jazz in the 1980s
Francis Davis (Da Capo Press, 1996)

Inside Jazz
Leonard G. Feather (Da Capo Press, 1988)

Introduction to Jazz History
Donald D. Megill and Richard S. Demory (Prentice Hall, 1996)

Jackson Street After Hours: The Roots of Jazz in Seattle
Paul De Barros (Sasquatch Books, 1993)

Jammin' at the Margins : Jazz and the American Cinema
Krin Gabbard (University of Chicago Press, 1996)

Jazz: A Century of Change
Lewis Porter, ed. (Schirmer Books, 1997)

Jazz Styles: History & Analysis
Mark C. Gridley (Prentice Hall, 1996)

Jazz
Michael Burnett (Oxford University Press, 1986)

Jazz
Paul O. Tanner, et al (McGraw Hill, 1998)

Jazz: A History of the New York Scene
Samuel R. Charters and Leonard Kunstadt (Da Capo Press, 1988)

Jazz Age: Popular Music of the 1920s
Arnold Shaw (Oxford University Press, 1987)

Jazz: America's Classical Music
Grover Sales and Graham Lees (Da Capo Press, 1992)

Jazz: An Introduction
Edward Lee (Parkwest Publications, 1997)

Jazz Anecdotes
Bill Crow (Oxford University Press, 1991)

The Jazz Exiles: American Musicians Abroad
Bill Moody (University of Nevada Press, 1993)

Jazz from the Beginning
Garvin Bushell, et al (University of Michigan Press, 1991)

Jazz in American Culture (American Ways Series)
Burton W. Peretti (Ivan R Dee, 1997)

Jazz in Its Time
Martin Williams (Oxford University Press, 1991)

Jazz is
Nat Hentoff (Proscenium Pub., 1984)

The Jazz Life
Nat Hentoff (Da Capo Press, 1988)

Jazz Lives
Graham Lees and John Reeves (McClelland & Stewart, 1992)

Jazz Masters of the '20s
Richard Hadlock (Da Capo Press, 1988)

Jazz Masters of the Fifties
Joe Goldberg (Da Capo Press, 1988)

Jazz Masters of the Thirties (MacMillan Jazz Masters Series)
Rex William Stewart (Da Capo Press, 1988)

Jazz Matters: Reflections on the Music and Some of Its Makers
Doug Ramsey and Gene Lees (University of Arkansas Press, 1989)

Jazz on Record: A History
Brian Priestly (Billboard Publications, 1991)

The Jazz Revolution: Twenties, America, and the Meaning of Jazz
Kathy J. Ogren (Oxford University Press, 1992)

The Jazz Scene: An Informal History from New Orleans to 1990
W. Royal Stokes (Oxford University Press, 1991)

Jazz Singing: America's Great Voices from Bessie Smith to Bebop and Beyond
Will Friedwald (Da Capo Press, 1996)

Jazz Spoken Here: Conversations with Twenty-Two Musicians
Wayne Enstice and Paul Rubin (Da Capo Press, 1994)

Jazz: The American Theme Song
James Lincoln Collier (Oxford University Press, 1993)

Jazz: The 1980s Resurgence
Stuart Nicholson (Da Capo Press, 1995)

The Jazz Tradition
Martin Williams (Oxford University Press, 1993)

The Joy of Jazz: Swing Era, 1935-1947
Tom Scanlan (Fulcrum Pub., 1996)

Keep Cool: The Black Activists Who Built the Age of Jazz
Ted Vincent (Pluto Press, 1995)

The Melody Lingers on: Scenes from the Golden Years of West Coast Jazz
Jo Brooks Fox and Jules L. Fox (Daniel & Daniel Pub., 1996)

New Musical Figurations: Anthony Braxton's Cultural Critique
Ronald M. Radano (University of Chicago Press, 1993)

Ornate With Smoke
Sterling Plumpp (Third World Press, 1998)

The Passion for Jazz
Leonard G. Feather (Da Capo, 1990)

Rags and Ragtime: A Musical History
David A. Jasen and Trebor Jay Tichenor (Dover Publications, 1989)

Red and Hot: The Fate of Jazz in the Soviet Union 1917-1991
S. Frederick Starr (Limelight Editions, 1994)

Riding on a Blue Note: Jazz and American Pop
Gary Giddins (Oxford University Press, 1981)

Singers and the Song II
Gene Lees (Oxford University Press, 1998)

Sitting in: Selected Writings on Jazz, Blues, and Related Topics
Hayden Carruth (University of Iowa Press, 1993)

Stir It Up: Musical Mixes from Roots to Jazz
Gene Santoro (Oxford University Press, 1997)

Stomping the Blues
Albert Murray (Da Capo Press, 1989)

Stormy Weather: The Music and Lives of a Century of Jazzwomen
Linda Dahl (Limelight Editions, 1989)

Story of Jazz
Marshall W. Stearns (Oxford University Press, 1985)

Swing Changes: Big-Band Jazz in New Deal America
David W. Stowe (Harvard University Press, 1994)

Swing Out: Great Negro Dance Bands
Gene Fernett (Da Capo Press, 1993)

Swing to Bop: An Oral History of the Transition in Jazz in the 1940s
Ira Gitler (Oxford University Press, 1987)

Swingin' the Dream: Big Band Jazz and the Rebirth of American Culture
Lewis A. Erenberg (University of Chicago Press, 1998)

Texan Jazz
Dave Oliphant (University of Texas Press, 1996)

Unzipped Souls: A Jazz Journey Through the Soviet Union
William Minor (Temple University Press, 1995)

Up from the Cradle of Jazz: New Orleans Music Since World War II
Jason Berry, et al (Da Capo Press, 1992)

Waiting for Dizzy
Gene Lees and Graham Lees (Oxford University Press, 1991)

We Called It Music: A Generation of Jazz
Eddie Condon, et al (Da Capo Press, 1992)

What Jazz Is: An Insider's Guide to Understanding and Listening to Jazz
Jonny King (Walker & Co., 1997)

What to Listen for in Jazz
Barry Kernfeld (Yale University Press, 1997)

The Wonderful Era of the Great Dance Bands
Leo Walker (Da Capo Press, 1990)

The World of Jazz
Rodney Dale (Book Sales, 1996)

Magazines and Newsletters

Billboard
1515 Broadway
New York, NY 10036
(212) 764-7300

Cadence
Cadence Building
Redwood, NY 13679

CMJ New Music Monthly
11 Middleneck Rd., Ste. 400
Great Neck, NY 11021
(516) 466-6000

Coda
PO Box 1002
Station "O"
Toronto, Ontario M4A 2N4

Canada
(250) 335-2911

Down Beat
102 N. Haven Rd.
Elmhurst, IL 60126
(800) 535-7496

Gene Lees Jazzletter
PO Box 240
Ojai, CA 93024-0240
E-mail: jazzlet@ix.netcom.com

ICE
PO Box 3043
Santa Monica, CA 90408
(800) 647-4ICE

Jazziz
3620 NW 43 St.
Gainesville, FL 32606
(352) 375-3705

Jazz Now
PO Box 19266
Oakland, CA 94519-0266
(800) 840-0465
E-mail: jazzinfo@jazznow.com

The Jazz Report
14 London St.
Toronto, Ontario M6G 1M9
Canada

JazzTimes
8737 Colesville Rd., 5th Floor
Silver Spring, MD 20910
(301) 588-4114

Marge Hofacre's Jazz News
PO Box 16826
San Diego, CA 92176
(619) 283-9583

Mississippi Rag
PO Box 19068
Minneapolis, MN 55419
(619) 861-2446

Musician
1515 Broadway
New York, NY 10036
(212) 536-5208

Rolling Stone
1290 Avenue of the Americas, 2nd Floor
New York, NY 10104
(212) 484-1616

Strictly Jazz
PO Box 492008
College Park, GA

Jazz music has a tremendous presence in cyberspace. Point your Web browser to these pages for more information on your favorite artists, E-zines, jazz venues, and more.

Artists

Geri Allen
http://kzsu.stanford.edu/~cathya/
geriallen.html

Mose Allison
http://www.bluenote.com/allison.html
http://www.mcs.net/~modika/mose.
html

Herb Alpert
http://www.geffen.com/almo/
herbalpert/
http://www.rudyscorner.com/

Louis Armstrong
http://www.foppejohnson.com/
armstrong/

Chet Baker
http://home.ica.net/~blooms/
bakerhome.html
http://hotel.prosa.dk/~jes/chet.htm
http://www.book.uci.edu/Jazz/
CDLists/ChetBaker_CDL.html

Beeblebrox
http://copper.ucs.indiana.edu/
~mherzig/beeblebrox.html

Bix Beiderbecke
http://www.riverwalk.org/bix.htm

Tony Bennett
http://www.music.sony.com/Music/
ArtistInfo/TonyBennett/

George Benson
http://www.mca.com/grp/grp/artists/
benson.rel.html
http://www.mcarecords.com/amp15/
f.benson.html

Tim Berne/Screwgun Records
http://home.sprynet.com/sprynet/
ssmith36/mainpage.htm

Terence Blanchard
http://www.music.sony.com/Music/
ArtistInfo/TerenceBlanchard.html

Jane Ira Bloom
http://www.tuna.net/janeirabloom/
home.html

Lester Bowie
http://www.trb.ayuda.com/~dnote/
lester.html

Dave Brubeck
http://www.schirmer.com/composers/
brubeck_bio.html

Gary Burton
http://www.ecmrecords.com/ecm/
artists/440.html

Doc Cheatham
http://www.npr.org/programs/
jazzprofiles/cheatham.html

Stanley Clarke
http://hem.passagen.se/nils30/

Billy Cobham
http://www.mca.com/grp/grp/artists/
cobham.rel.html

Nat "King" Cole
http://www.tip.net.au/~bnoble/
natkcole/nat_cole.htm

Ornette Coleman
http://www.harmolodic.com/
http://www.eyeneer.com/Jazz/Ornett
e/index.html

John Coltrane
http://www.trailerpark.com/flamingo/
trane/
http://www.rio.com/~ryans/influence/
coltrane/
http://www.acns.nwu.edu/jazz/artists/
coltrane.john/
http://sd.znet.com/~bydesign/
coltrane.john/
http://www.siba.fi/~eonttone/trane.
html

Harry Connick Jr.
http://www.hconnickjr.com/
http://www.connick.com/connick.html
http://weber.u.washington.edu/~no1
husky/harry/connick.html

Chick Corea
http://www.aent.com/concord/bios/
corea.html

Bing Crosby
http://www.kcmetro.cc.mo.us/
pennvalley/biology/lewis/crosby/
bing.htm
http://www.geocities.com/Bourbon
Street/3754/bing.html

http://www.tir.com/~rtw/bing.htm

Miles Davis
http://www.music.sony.com/Music/
ArtistInfo/MilesDavis/
http://users.cybercity.dk/~ccc6517/
http://www.nettally.com/dbird/miles
m.htm
http://www.wam.umd.edu/~losinp/
music/md-list.html

Jack DeJohnette
http://www.pk.edu.pl/~pmj/
dejohnette/

Al Di Meola
http://www.eskimo.com/~bpentium/
dimeola/

Bill Dixon
http://www.sover.net/~wrdixon/

Eric Dolphy
http://epoch.cs.berkeley.edu:8000/
personal/jmh/music/dolphy.html
http://farcry.neurobio.pitt.edu/Eric.
html

Tommy Dorsey
http://www.teleport.com/~rfrederi/
wtommy01.htm
http://spaceformusic.com/
tommydorsey.html

Madeline Eastman
http://www.madelineeastman.com/

Duke Ellington
http://duke.fuse.net/
http://www.dnsmith.com/ellington/
http://www.ilinks.net/~holmesr/
duke.htm

Kevin Eubanks
http://www.mca.com/grp/grp/artists/
eubanks.rel.html

Bill Evans
http://members.aol.com/UserRRR00/
BETrio.html

Maynard Ferguson
http://www.xs4all.nl/~maynard/
http://www.netins.net/showcase/
maynard/
http://www.geocities.com/Times
Square/Castle/2685/maynard.html

Ella Fitzgerald
http://www.enviromedia.com/ella/
http://www.public.iastate.edu/
~vwindsor/Ella.html
http://www.seas.columbia.edu/~tts6/
ella.html

Bela Fleck
http://www.flecktones.com/
http://www.epix.net/~jpowlus/

Fourplay
http://www.fourplayjazz.com

Michael Franks
http://www.michaelfranks.com

Stan Getz
http://www.book.uci.edu/Jazz/
CDLists/StanGetz_CDL.html

Dizzy Gillespie
http://www.mca.com/grp/grp/artists/
gillespie.rel.html

Benny Goodman
http://www.flash.net/~rdreagan/
index.shtml
http://qlink.queensu.ca/~3pje2/
bg.html

Stephane Grappelli
http://www.digitalrain.net/bowed/
grapelli.htm

Dave Grusin
http://www.mca.com/grp/grp/artists/
grusin_dave.rel.html
http://www.geocities.com/Hollywood/
Academy/1201/

Herbie Hancock
http://www.mercuryrecords.com/
mercury/artists/hancock_herbie/
hancock_herbie.html
http://www.netspace.org/~was/
music_11/hjh.html

Billie Holiday
http://users.bart.nl/~ecduzit/billy/
index.html

Shirley Horn
http://www.verveinteractive.com/
horn.html

Freddie Hubbard
http://www.columbia.edu/~jes79/
freddisc.html

Ahmad Jamal
http://www2.cybernex.net/~ajamal/
http://www.npr.org/programs/
jazzprofiles/jamal.html

D.D. Jackson
http://www.ddjackson.com

Bob James
http://www.ubl.com/ubl/cards/007/
6/94.html
http://www.bobjames.com

Al Jarreau
http://www.fortunecity.com/lavender/
fullmonty/33/index.html

Antonio Carlos Jobim
http://nortemag.com/tom/

Etta Jones
http://home.earthlink.net/
~americanlg/ettaj.htm

Scott Joplin
http://www.scottjoplin.org/
http://www.ddc.com/~decoy/sjop.htm

Stan Kenton
http://hiwaay.net/~crispen/kenton/
http://www.geocities.com/Bourbon
Street/5046/

Rebecca Kilgore
http://www.teleport.com/~rkilgore/
index.html/

Rahsaan Roland Kirk
http://falcon.cc.ukans.edu/~sgalic/
roland.htm

Gene Krupa
http://www.geocities.com/Bourbon
Street/Delta/3898/
http://www.concentric.net/~thompjr/
gene_krupa/index.shtml

Steve Lacy
http://wwwusers.imaginet.fr/
~senators/

Ramsey Lewis
http://jazzusa.com/ramsey/bio.htm

Dave Liebman
http://www.upbeat.com/lieb

Jeff Lorber
http://www.lorber.com/jeff.html

Manhattan Transfer
http://www.west.net/~jrpprod/tmt/
tmt.html
http://www.singers.com/manhattan
transfer.html

Branford Marsalis
http://www.music.sony.com/Music/
ArtistInfo/BranfordMarsalis/news.
html

Wynton Marsalis
http://www.ubl.com/artists/012491.
html
http://www.jazzworld.com/Artist_
Info/wyntonmarsalis/

Kitty Margolis
http://www.kittymargolis.com

Pat Martino
http://www.patmartino.com

Bobby McFerrin
http://www.bobbymcferrin.com/
home.html

Pat Metheny
http://www.patmethenygroup.com/

Glenn Miller
http://www.heartland.net/local/
pages/glenn-miller/member.htm

Charles Mingus
http://www.mingusmingusmingus.
com/

Thelonious Monk
http://www.achilles.net/~howardm/
tsmonk.html

Wes Montgomery
http://glolink.com/WES/

Airto Moreira & Flora Purim
http://www.asahi-net.or.jp/
~uh6k-ogr/af/welcome.html

Gerry Mulligan
http://bookweb.cwis.uci.edu:8042/
Jazz/Mulligan2253.html
http://www.geocities.com/Bourbon
Street/Delta/1724/

Charlie Parker
http://www.wam.umd.edu/~losinp/
music/bird.html
http://www.cmgww.com/music/
parker/parker.html

Courtney Pine
http://www.ejn.it/mus/pine.htm

Jean-Luc Ponty
http://www.ponty.com/

Bobby Previte
http://members.aol.com/Previte

Tito Puente
http://www.nando.net/prof/caribe/
PuenteTito.html

Rebirth Brass Band
http://www.ikoiko.com/rebirth

Rufus Reid
http://www.ejn.it/index.htm

Buddy Rich
http://biged.simplenet.com/buddy/

Max Roach
http://www.jazzworld.com/Artist_
Info/maxroach/maxin2.html

Marcus Roberts
http://cyboard.com/jchrissco/bios/
MR_bio.html

Sonny Rollins
http://www.duke.edu/~bab7/rollins.
html

Adam Rudolph/Meta Records
http://www.metarecords.com

Joe Sample
http://prarecords.com/artists/sample/

David Sanborn
http://gull.me.es.osaka-u.ac.jp/
~yasuo/inst/david

Diane Schuur
http://www.dianeschuurfanclub.com/

John Scofield
http://www.c-and-c.si/sco/

Gil Scott-Heron
http://pubweb.acns.nwu.edu/
~jas923/heron.html

Artie Shaw
http://www.artieshaw.com/

Sun Ra
http://www.fusebox.com/~jimr/
http://www.holeworld.com/stellar.
html
http://www.eyeneer.com/Jazz/Sunra/

Toots Thielemans
http://houbi.simplenet.com/belpop/
groups/toots.htm

Henry Threadgill
http://www.ejn.it/mus/threadgi.htm

McCoy Tyner
http://nuinfo.nwu.edu/jazz/artists/
tyner.mccoy/

Sarah Vaughan
http://www.geocities.com/Vienna/
8244/

Weather Report
http://members.harborcom.net/
~jmayer/jordu/weather.htm
http://www.sainet.or.jp/~head/wr.
html

Cassandra Wilson
http://www.geocities.com/Bourbon
Street/4587/

Phil Woods
http://cyboard.com/jchrissco/bios/
PW_bio.html
http://www.upbeat.com/philwoods/
index.htm

Yellowjackets
http://www.yellowjackets.com/

E-Zines

Billboard Online
http://www.billboard.com/

Guitar Player Online
http://www.guitarplayer.com/

Guitar World Online
http://www.guitarworld.com/

ICE Magazine
http://www.webcom.com/~ice/

Jazz Friends Review
http://tri-millenia.net/jfr/welcome.
htm

Jazz Now Magazine
http://www.dnai.com/~jazzinfo/

JazzZine
http://members.aol.com/jazzzine/
index.html

Kansas City Jam/Jazz Ambassador Magazine
http://www.kansascity.com/kcjazz/

OffBeat Magazine
http://www.neosoft.com/~offbeat/
home.html

Trombone Journal
http://www.trombone.org/

Wired
http://www.wired.com

General Information and Fun Sites

All About Jazz
http://www.allaboutjazz.com/

Apollo Theatre
http://www.apolloshowtime.com

Centerstage, Chicago Jazz Artists
http://www.centerstage.net/chicago/
music/whoswho/directory.html

European Improvised Music
http:www.shef.ac.uk/misc/rec/ps/
efi/RS

Great Day in Harlem
http://www.beatthief.com/greatday/greatday.html

Instrument Jokes
http://www.mit.edu/people/jcb/jokes

Internet Bass Links
http://www.odyssee.net/~addison/bass1

The Jazz Composers Collective
http://www.jazzcollective.com/

The Jazz Corner
http://www.jazzcorner.com/

Jazz Violin
http://www.dappu.calarts.edu/~chung/jazzviolin.html

Jenny's Jazz Archive of Jazz Improvisation
http://www.ohio.net/~osvaths/old_tips.html

Red Hot and Cool Jazz
http://members.aol.com/Jlackritz/jazz/index.htm

Toronto Jazz (DuMaurier)
http://www.tojazz.com/

WNUR People of Jazz Index
http://www.new.edu/WNUR/jazz/artists/

Jazz Clubs (Venues), USA

Catalina's, Hollywood, CA
http://jazznet.com/CATALINA/

Dimitriou's Jazz Alley, Seattle, WA
http://www.jazz-alley.com

The Jazz Bakery, Los Angeles, CA
http://jazznet.com/JAZZBAKERY/

Jazz Clubs in New York City
http://www.mediabridge.com/nyc/entertainment/jazz.html

Jazz Clubs Worldwide
http://www.jazz-clubs-worldwide.com

The Knitting Factory, New York, NY
http://www.knittingfactory.com/

Kuumbwa Jazz Center, Santa Cruz, CA
http://www.jazznet.com/~lmcohen/KUUMBWA

Sculler's Jazz Club, Boston, MA
http://www.scullersjazz.com

Sweet Basil, New York, NY
http://www.sweetbasil.com

Yoshi's, West Oakland, CA
http://www.yoshis.com/

Organizations and Agencies

A Cappella Web Directory
http://www.casa.org/web_directory.html

American Federation of Jazz Societies
http://www.worldmall.com/wmcc/afjs/

American Federation of Musicians
http://www.afm.org

Central PA Friends of Jazz
http://www.pajazz.org

Earshot Jazz Home Page
http://www.accessone.com/earshot

International Saxophone Home Page
http://www.saxophone.org

International Society of Bassists
http://www.jmu.edu/bassists/links.html

Jazz at Lincoln Center
http://www.jazzatlincolncenter.org/

Jazz Institute of Chicago
http://www.jazzinstituteofchicago.org/

Jazz Journalists Association
http://www.jazzhouse.org/

MAMA Foundation
http://www.mamajazz.org

National Endowment for the Arts
http://www.arts.endow.gov

The Northeast Ohio Jazz Society Home Page
http://www.worldnetoh.com/~nojs/

San Francisco Traditional Jazz Foundation
http://www.sftradjazz.org/

Radio

Gavin Online Magazine
http://www.gavin.com

KLON Radio
http://www.csulb.edu/~klon/klon2/klon.html

NPR Radio
http://www.npr.org/

WBGO 88.3 FM
http://www.wbgo.org/

WNUR-FM
http://www.acns.nwu.edu/jazz/

Various
http://www.radio.audionet.com

Research and History

The Clarinet in Jazz Since 1945
http://www.eclipse.net/~fitzgera/matt/clar1945.html

Concordia University Archives
http://www.archives3.concordia.ca/jazz.html

Historic New Orleans Collection
http:www.hnoc.org

The Institute of Jazz Studies, Rutgers University
http://www.rci.rutgers.edu/~schwart/jazz.htm

The International Lyrics Server
http://www.lyrics.ch

Internet Resources for Music Scholars
http://www.rism.harvard.edu/MusicLibrary/InternetResources.html

Jazz Central Station
http://jazzcentralstation.com/

Musicians' Intellectual Law & Resources Links
http://www.aracnet.com/~schornj/index.html

Red Hot Jazz Archives
http://www.technoir.net/jazz/c.html

CD Sales Sites

CDnow
http://www.cdnow.com/

CD Universe
http://www.cduniverse.com

CD World
http://cdworld.com

The Intelligent Network
http://www.tunes.com/

Jazz Record Mart
http://www.idsonline.com/delmark/jrm.history.com

Music Boulevard
http://www.musicblvd.com/

1-800-Every CD
http://www.everycd.com

Record Labels

Antilles
http://www.antillesnet.com/

Arabesque Jazz Recordings
http://www.arabesqrec.com

Arbors Records
http://www.arborsjazz.com/

Arkadia Records
http://www.arkadiarecords.com/

Ark21
http://www.ark21.com

Atlantic Records
http://www.atlantic-records.com/

Biograph Records
http://www.biograph.com

Black Saint
http://www.blacksaint.com

Blue Note Records
http://www.bluenote.com/

Chesky Records
http://www.chesky.com/music

CIMP
http://www.cadencebuilding.com

Concord Records
http://www.aent.com/concord/

Consolidated Artists Productions
http://www.jazzbeat.com

Delmark Records
http://www.idsonline.com/delmark/
delmark.home.htm

DMP Records
http://www.dmprecords.com

Doubletime Records
http://www.doubletimejazz.com/

ECM Records
http://www.ecmrecords.com/

Enja Records
http://www.enjarecords.com/

Fantasy Records
http://www.fantasyjazz.com/

GRP Records
http://www.mca.com/grp

Harmolodic Records
http://www.harmolodic.com/

Heads Up Records
http://www.jazzbytes.com/headsup.
html

Heart Music
http://www.heartmusic.com/

IGMOD Records
http://www.igmod@igmod.com/

In + Out Records
http://harp.rounder.com/rounder/
profiles/iout.html

Jazzheads Records
http://www.jazzheads.com

Jazzology Records
http://www.jazzology.com

Justice Records
http://www.justicerecords.com/

Justin Time Records
http://www.justin-time.com/

K-Jazz Productions
http://www.k-jazz.com/

The Knitting Factory Records
http://www.knittingfactory.com/

Koch International
http://kochint.com/

Kokopelli Records
http://www.koko.com/

Lipstick & Jazzline Records
http://www.move.de/amm/

Lost Chart Records
http://www.total.net/~lostchar/
lcenglish.html

Meltdown Records
http://www.meltdownrecords.com/

Mobile Fidelity Sound Lab
http://www.mofi.com/

Nagel-Heyer Records
http://www.nagelheyer.de/

PolyGram Online
http://www.polygram.com/polygram/

RCA Victor
http://www.rcavictor.com/

Reprise Records
http://www.repriserec.com

Rhino Records
http://www.rhino.com

Riverwalk Live at the Landing
http://www.riverwalk.org/

Rounder Records
http://www.rounder.com/

Shanachie Records
http://www.shanachie.com

Silkheart Records
http://www.silkheart.se/

Smithsonian Folkways Recordings
http://www.si.edu/folkways/start.
html

Sony Music Online
http://www.music.sony.com/music/
index2.html

Southport Records
http://www.chicagosound.com

Sunnyside Records
http://www.sunnysidezone.com/

Telarc International
http://www.dmn.com/telarc/

Tower Records
http://www.towerrecords.com/

Triloka Records
http://www.triloka.com/

Turnip Seed Records
http://www.turnipseed.com/

Verve Interactive
http://www.verveinteractive.com/

Warner Bros.
http://www.wbn.com/

Windham Hill
http://www.windham.com/

The following record labels are just some of the labels that have important jazz catalogs. You may want to contact them if you have questions regarding specific releases.

Accurate
PO Box 390115
Cambridge, MA 02139
(617) 277-6262
Fax: (617) 277-1924

Alpha Phonics
PO Box 1112
Midtown Station
New York, NY 10018
(718) 738-6082
Fax: (718) 845-5822

Altenburgh
PO Box 154
Mosinee, WI 54455
(715) 693-2230

Antilles
825 Eighth Ave., 26th Floor
New York, NY 10019
(212) 333-8000

Arabesque Recordings
32 W. 39th St., 11th Floor
New York, NY 10018
(212) 730-5000
Fax: (212) 730-8316
E-mail: arabesqrec@aol.com

Arbors Records
1700 McMullen-Booth Rd. #C-3
Clearwater, FL 33759

(813) 726-7494
Fax: (813) 724-1745
E-mail: mrd@gate.net

Ark 21
14724 Ventura Blvd., Penthouse
Sherman Oaks, CA 91403
(818) 461-1700
Fax: (818) 461-1745
E-mail: publicity@ark21.com

Arkadia Records
34 E. 23rd St.
New York, NY 10010
(212) 533-0007
Fax: (212) 979-0266
E-mail: arkadiany@aol.com

Atlantic Records
1290 Avenue of the Americas
New York, NY 10104
(212) 707-2000
E-mail: web@atlantic-records.com

AUM Fidelity
PO Box 170147
Brooklyn, NY 11217
(718) 369-0913/81
Fax: (718) 369-0981

Biograph Records
35 Medford St., Ste. 203
Somerville, MA 02143
(617) 426-7500
Fax: (617) 426-5222
E-mail: cd@biograph.com

Black Saint
PO Box 4292
Great Neck, NY 11023
(516) 482-7325

Fax: (516) 829-7190
E-mail: sphere@blacksaint.com

Blue Jackel Entertainment
322 Hicksville Rd.
Bethpage, NY 11714
(516) 932-1608

Blue Note Records
304 Park Avenue South, 3rd Floor
New York, NY 10010
(212) 253-3000
Fax: (212) 253-3099

Cannonball Records
1660 Lake Dr. West
Chanhassen, MN 55317
(612) 361-6302

Chesky Records
355 W. 52nd St., 6th Floor
New York, NY 10019-6239
(212) 586-7799
Fax: (212) 262-0814
E-mail: chesky@pipeline.com

Chiaroscuro Records
830 Broadway
New York, NY 10003
(212) 473-0479

CIMP
Cadence Building
Redwood, NY 13679
(315) 287-2852
Fax: (315) 287-2860
E-mail: cimp@cadencebuilding.com

Concord Records
2450-A Stanwell Dr.
Concord, CA 94520
(510) 682-6770

Fax: (510) 682-3508
E-mail: concordrecords@aent.com

Consolidated Artists Productions
290 Riverside Dr., Ste. 11-D
New York, NY 10025
(212) 222-5159
Fax: (212) 864-3449
E-mail: bebopyo@aol.com

DA
PO Box 3
Little Silver, NJ 07739

Delmark Records
4121 N. Rockwell
Chicago, IL 60618
(773) 539-5001
Fax: (773) 539-5004
E-mail: delmark@midwest.idsonline.com

DMP Records
PO Box 15835 Park Sq. Stn.
Stamford, CT 06901
(203) 327-3800
E-mail: dmp_comments@dmn.com

Doubletime Records
PO Box 1244
New Albany, IN 47151-1244
(800) 293-8528
Fax: (812) 923-1971
E-mail: dtjazz@thepoint.net

ECM Records
E-mail: ecm-info@ecmrecords.com

Enja Records
PO Box 190333
Munich, Germany D-80603
Fax: +49 (0) 89 167 8810
E-mail: info@enjarecords.com

Eremite
PO Box 812
Northampton, MA 01061
(413) 584-9592
E-mail: eremite@javanet.com

Evidence Music
1100 E. Hector St., #392
Conshohocken, PA 19428
(610) 832-0844

Fantasy Records
2600 Tenth St.
Berkeley, CA 94710
(510) 549-2500
Fax: (510) 486-2015
E-mail: info@fantasyjazz.com

Flying Note
PO Box 1027

Canal Station
New York, NY 10013-1027
(914) 496-3105
Fax: (914) 496-0438

FMP/Free Music Production
PO Box 100 227, D-10562
Berlin, Germany

Gazell
PO Box 527
Mansfield Center, CT 06250
(203) 429-1062

GRP Records
555 W. 57th St., 10th Floor
New York, NY 10019
(212) 424-1000
Fax: (212) 424-1007

Harmolodic Records
E-mail: info@harmolodic.com

hat ART
4106 Therwil
Switzerland
Fax: 011-4161-721-6655

Heads Up International
4204 Russell Rd., Ste. K
Mukiteo, WA 98275
(206) 349-1200
Fax: (206) 349-1166
E-mail: dave@headsup.com

Heart Music
PO Box 160326
Austin, TX 78716-0326
(512) 795-2375
Fax: (512) 795-9573
E-mail: info@heartmusic.com

High Note Records
106 W. 71st St.
New York, NY 10023
(212) 873-2020

Igmod Records
855 Village Center Dr., Ste. 317
Saint Paul, MN 55127
(612) 787-0577
Fax: (612)644-9142
E-mail: igmod@aol.com

Improvising Artists, Inc.
PO Box 4292
Great Neck, NY 11023

India Navigation
PO Box 818
Blairstown, NJ 07825
(516) 725-9206
Fax: (516) 725-9211

Jazzheads Records
PO Box 523
Planetarium Station
New York, NY 10024-0523

Jazzology Records
1206 Decatur St.
New Orleans, LA 70116
(504) 525-1776
Fax: (504) 523-2629
E-mail: fred.hatfield@sstar.com

Jen-Bay
109 West Blvd.
East Rockaway, NY 11518
(516) 599-6589
E-mail: jenbayjazz@compuserve.com

Justice Records
3215 W. Alabama
Houston, TX 77098
(713) 520-6669
Fax: (713) 525-4444
E-mail: justice@justicerecords.com

Justin Time Records
5455 rue Paré, Ste. 101
Montreal, Quebec, Canada H4P 1P7
(514) 738-9533
Fax: (514) 738-9533

K-Jazz Productions
Dennis Sheppard
c/o K-Jazz Productions
330 E. 38th Street #8L
New York, NY 10016
(212) 986-7023
Fax: (212) 986-7024
E-mail: dennis@k-jazz.com

Knitting Factory
74 Leonard St.
New York, NY 10013
(212) 219-3006
Fax: (212) 219-3401

Koch International
2 Tri Harbor Ct.
Port Washington, NY 11050-4617
(516) 484-1000
Fax: (516) 484-4746
E-mail: koch@kochint.com

Leo
The Cottage, 6
Anerley Hill, London SE19 2AA
England
E-mail: leorec@atlas.co.uk

Lost Chart Records
5505 St. Laurent Blvd. #4202
Montreal, Quebec, Canada H2T 1S6

(514) 276-4760
E-mail: lostchar@total.net

MAMA Foundation
555 E. Easy St.
Simi Valley, CA 93065

Mesa/Bluemoon
209 E. Alameda Ave., Ste. 101
Burbank, CA 91502
(818) 841-8585

META
2024 Glencoe Ave.
Venice, CA 90291
(310) 397-1316
Fax: (310) 397-7116

Mobile Fidelity Sound Lab
105 Morris St.
Sebastopol, CA 95472
(707) 829-0134
Fax: (707) 829-3746
E-mail: mofi@mofi.com

MoJazz
825 Eighth Ave., 29th Floor
New York, NY 10019-1736
(212) 445-3353

Nagel-Heyer Records
Rugenbarg 85
Hamburg, Germany 22549
+49 40 801784
Fax: +49 40 801784
E-mail: nhrjazz@aol.com

Natasha Imports
PO Box 427
Margaretville, NY 12455

New Albion
584 Castro St., #515
San Francisco, CA 49114
(415) 621-5757
Fax: (415) 621-4711

New World
701 Seventh Ave.
New York, NY 10036
(212) 302-0460
Fax: (212) 944-1922

No More
PO Box 334
Woodmere, NY 11598
E-mail: nomore@bway.net

NYC
(800) 266-4NYC
Fax: (212) 633-9773
E-mail: nyc@jazzonln.com

PolyGram
825 Eighth Ave., 26th Floor
New York, NY 10019
(212) 333-8000
Fax: (212) 333-8402

Postcards
225 Lafayette St.
New York, NY 10012

Ram
PO Box 4292
Great Neck, NY 11023

RCA Victor
1540 Broadway, 36th Floor
New York, NY 10036
(212) 930-4000
E-mail: rcavictor@digitopia.com

Red
PO Box 4292
Great Neck, NY 11023

Reprise Records
3300 Warner Blvd.
Burbank, CA 91505-4694
(818) 846-9090
Fax: (818) 846-8474
E-mail: toreprise@aol.com

Rhino Records
10635 Santa Monica Blvd., 2nd Floor
Los Angeles, CA 90025-4900
(310) 474-4778
Fax: (310) 441-6575
E-mail: drrhino@rhino.com

Riti
E-mail: ritirec@ici.net

Riverwalk Live at the Landing
Pacifc Vista Productions
101 H St., Ste. D
Petaluma, CA 94952
(800) 41-RIVER
Fax: (707)-765-0132
E-mail: mophandl@txdirect.net

Rounder Records
One Camp St.
Cambridge, MA 02140
(617) 354-0700
Fax: (617) 491-1970
E-mail: info@rounder.com

Screwgun
104 St. Marks Ave.
Brooklyn, NY 11217

Silkheart Records
Dalagatan 33
S-113 23 Stockholm, Sweden

+46-8-33 56 83
Fax: +46-8-34 99 18
E-mail: info@silkheart.se

Sirocco Jazz
PO Box 136
Altrincham WA15 9FE
England

Shanachie Records
13 Laight St., 6th Floor
New York, NY 10013
(212) 334-0284
Fax: (212) 334-5207
E-mail: shanach@idt.net

Smithsonian Folkways Recordings
955 L'Enfant Plaza, Ste. 2600, MRC 914
Washington, DC 20560
(202) 287-3251
Fax: (202) 287-3699
E-mail: folkways@aol.com

Songlines
1003-2323 W. 2nd Ave., Apt. 1003
Vancouver, British Columbia V6K 1J4
Canada
(604) 737-1632
E-mail: tfeif@songlines.com

Sony Music
550 Madison Ave.
New York, NY 10022-3211
(212) 833-8000
Fax: (212) 833-7120
E-mail: sonymusiconline@sonymusic.com

Soul Note
PO Box 4292
Great Neck, NY 11023

Southport Records
3501 N. Southport
Chicago, IL 60657
(773) 281-8510
Fax: (773) 472-4330
E-mail: sparrow@chicagosound.com

Sunnyside Communications
348 W. 38th St., #12B
New York, NY 10018
(212) 564-4606
E-mail: sunnyside@ibm.net

Telarc International
23307 Commerce Park Rd.
Cleveland, OH 44122
(216) 464-2313
Fax: (216) 464-4108
E-mail: comments@telarc.com

32 Jazz
250 W. 57th St.

New York, NY 10107

Triloka Records
306 Catron St.
Santa Fe, NM 87501
(505) 820-2833

Turnip Seed Records
E-mail: turnip@turnipseed.com

2.13.61
PO Box 691
Prince St. Station
New York, NY 10012

Verve Records
825 Eighth Ave., 26th Floor

New York, NY 10019
(212) 333-8000
Fax: (212) 333-8194
E-mail: vervemail@us.polygram.com

Victo
C.P. 460
Victoriaville, Quebec G6P 6T3
Canada
(819) 752-7912
Fax: (819) 758-4370

Warner Bros.
3300 Warner Blvd.
Burbank, CA 91505-4694
(818) 846-9090

Fax: (818) 846-8474
E-mail: wbrpinc@wbr.com

Water Street Music
PO Box 224
Fairview, NJ 07022

Windham Hill
8750 Wilshire Blvd.
Beverly Hills, CA 90211-2713
(310) 358-4800
Fax: (310) 358-4805
E-mail: consumers@windham.com

The following are some of the U.S. radio stations that feature a jazz format. Please be advised that radio station formats often change like the weather. Your best bet would be to check the local radio listings in the cities below. (Radio station listings courtesy of BIA Publishing.)

Alaska

Anchorage
KNIK (105.3 FM)

Arizona

Phoenix
KYOT (95.5 FM)

Tucson
KUAT (1550 AM)

Arkansas

Little Rock
KYFX (99.5 FM)

Marked Tree
KJBR (93.7 FM)

California

Bakersfield
KSMJ (96.5 FM)

Carmel
KRML (1410 AM)

Carmel
KXDC (101.7 FM)

Copperopolis
KRVR (105.5 FM)

Davis
KQBR (104.3 FM)

Fair Oaks
KSSJ (94.7 FM)

Fowler
KEZL (96.7 FM)

Goleta
KMGQ (106.3 FM)

Independence
KDAY (92.5 FM)

Indio
KJJZ (102.3 FM)

Los Angeles
KTWV (94.7 FM)

San Diego
KIFM (98.1 FM)

San Francisco
KKSF (103.7 FM)

Sebastopol
KJZY (93.7 FM)

Shingle Springs
KRRE (101.9 FM)

Visalia
KSLK (96.1 FM)

Colorado

Denver
KHIH (95.7 FM)

Security
KSKX (105.5 FM)

Connecticut

Pawcatuck
WKCD (107.7 FM)

Florida

Key West
WCNK (98.7 FM)

Lakeland
WSJT (94.1 FM)

Marco
WGUF (98.9 FM)

Miami Beach
WLVE (93.9 FM)

Midway
WJZT (100.7 FM)

Miramar Beach
WSBZ (106.3 FM)

San Carlos Park
WDRR (98.5 FM)

St. Augustine
WFSJ (97.9 FM)

Vero Beach
WGYL (93.7 FM)

Winter Park
WLOQ (103.1 FM)

Georgia

La Grange
WJZF (104.1 FM)

Statesboro
WPTB (850 AM)

Hawaii

Hilo
KNWB (97.1 FM)

Pearl City
KUCD (101.9 FM)

Idaho

Boise
KBSU (730 AM)

Illinois

Chicago
WNUA (95.5 FM)

Farmington
WJPL (96.5 FM)

Harvey
WBEE (1570 AM)

Indiana

Louisville
WSJW (103.9 FM)

Kansas

Haysville
KWSJ (105.3 FM)

Kentucky

Newport
WNOP (740 AM)

Russellville
WJZC (101.1 FM)

Massachussetts

Boston
WSJZ (96.9 FM)

Plymouth
WPLM (99.1 FM, 1390 AM)

Michigan

Detroit
WVMV (98.7 FM)

Glen Arbor
WJZJ (95.5 FM)

Mackinaw City
WLJZ (94.5 FM)

Mio
WAVC (93.9 FM)

Pentwater
WEWM (94.1 FM)

Minnesota

St. Louis Park
KMJZ (104.1 FM)

Mississippi

Meridian
WNBN (1290 AM)

West Point
WKBB (100.9 FM)

Missouri

Liberty
KCIY (106.5 FM)

St. Charles
KIRL (1460 AM)

New Mexico

Albuquerque
KEZF (101.3 FM)

New York

Albany
WHRL (103.1 FM)

Auburn
WHCD (106.9 FM)

New York
WQCD (101.9 FM)

North Carolina

Harrisburg
WCCJ (92.7 FM)

Ohio

Cincinnati
WNOP (740 AM)

Elyria
WNWV (107.3 FM)

Fairfield
WVAE (94.9 FM)

Greenville
WLSN (106.5 FM)

Lancaster
WJZA (103.5 FM)

Richwood
WZJZ (104.3 FM)

Oklahoma

Broken Arrow
KOAS (92.1 FM)

Edmond
KTNT (97.9 FM)

Oregon

Lake Oswego
KKJZ (106.7 FM)

Pennsylvania

Philadelphia
WJJZ (106.1 FM)

Pittsburgh
WJJJ (104.7 FM)

South Carolina

Charleston
WJZK (96.9 FM)

Florence
WYNN (540 AM)

Loris
WVCO (94.9 FM)

Texas

Ft. Worth
KOAI (107.5 FM)

Killeen
KAJZ (93.3 FM)

Terrell Hills
KCJZ (106.7 FM)

Waco
KBCT (94.5 FM)

Utah

Ogden
KBZN (97.9 FM)

Virginia

Norfolk
WJCD (105.3 FM)

Woodbridge
WJZW (105.9 FM)

Washington

Seattle
KWJZ (98.9 FM)

West Virginia

Romney
WJJB (100.1 FM)

Wisconsin

Brillion
WEZR (107.5 FM)

Milwaukee
WJZI (93.3 FM)

If you want to see some jazz music performed live, we suggest you check out some of these North American music festivals.

UNITED STATES

Alabama

Alexander City
Alexander City Jazz Festival
2 days in mid-June
Contact: (205) 329-8084

Florence and Shoals region
W.C. Handy Music Festival
7 days in August
Various venues in Florence and nearby towns
Contact: (205) 766-7642

Alaska

Juneau
Juneau Jazz and Classics Festival
Two weekends in May
Contact: (907) 463-3378

Arizona

Sedona
Sedona Jazz on the Rocks
3-day weekend in September

Contact: (800) 638-4253 or (520) 282-1985

California

Blue Jay
Blue Jay Jazz Fest
Various weekly concerts in July, August
Contact: (909) 337-0705

Concord
Fujitsu Concord Jazz Festival
3 days in July
Concord Pavilion
Contact: (510) 671-3100
Fax: (510) 676-7262

Idyllwild
Idyllwild Jazz in the Pines
Last weekend in August
Campus of the Idyllwild School of Music and the Arts
Contact: (909) 659-5404

Irvine
West Coast Jazz Party
Labor Day weekend
Irvine Marriott at John Wayne County Airport
Contact: Jazzline: (714) 724-3602; Irvine Marriott Hotel: (714) 553-0100

Long Beach
Long Beach Jazz Festival
Weekend in August
Lagoon
Contact: (562) 436-7794

Los Angeles
UCLA Jazz & Reggae Festival
2 days, Memorial Day weekend
UCLA Campus
Contact: (310) 825-9912

Los Angeles
Playboy Jazz Festival
Weekend in June
Hollywood Bowl
Contact: Hotline: (310) 449-4070
Fax: (310) 246-4077

Los Angeles
Hollywood Bowl
Various single dates in July, August, September
Hollywood Bowl
Contact: (213) 850-2000

Mammoth Lakes
Jazz Jubilee
4 days in July
Contact: (760) 934-2478

Oakville
Robert Mondavi Winery Summer Festival
Various dates in July, August
Contact: (888) 769-5299

Redlands
Redlands Bowl Summer Music Festival
Various dates in July, August
Redlands Bowl
Contact: (909) 793-7316

Rohnert Park
Sonoma County Dixiejazz Festival
Weekend in August
Contact: (707) 539-3494

Sacramento
Sacramento Jazz Jubilee
Weekend in May
Contact: (916) 372-527

San Francisco
Stern Grove Festival
Various dates, June through August
Sigmund Stern Grove, 19th Ave. at Sloan Blvd.
Contact: (415) 252-6252

San Francisco
Jazz & All That Art on Fillmore
2 days, Fourth of July weekend
Contact: (415) 346-9162

San Jose
San Jose Jazz Festival
Weekend in early August
Contact: (408) 288-7577

San Mateo
Jazz on the Hill
Weekend in mid-June
College of San Mateo
Contact: (650) 574-6694

Vallejo
Shoreline Jazz, Art and Wine Festival
Weekend in late August

Vallejo waterfront
Contact: (707) 643-3653

Colorado

Boulder
Mile High Jazz Camp
6 days in July
University of Colorado at
    Boulder
Contact: (303) 492-6352
Fax: (303) 492-5619

Breckenridge
Genuine Jazz in July
Weekend in July
Breckenridge, floating stage
    at base of Peak 9
Contact: (970) 453-6018

Grand Junction
Northwest Art & Jazz Festival
Weekend in mid-June
Contact: (970) 245-2926

Snowmass Village
Janus Jazz Aspen at Snowmass
*Various dates, June through
    September*
Contact: (970) 920-4996

Telluride
Telluride Jazz Celebration
*Various dates, July through
    August*
Contact: (888) 827-8081
(970) 728-7009
Fax: (970) 728-5834
E-mail: Paul_machado@info-
    zone.org
Website: http://infozone.
    telluride.co.us:80/
    TellJazz.html

Vail
Vail Jazz Party
Labor Day weekend
Marriott's Mountain Resort
    Hotel
Contact: (888) 824-5526
(970) 476-6266
Fax: (970) 476-6556
E-mail: vjf@vail jazz.org

Winter Park
Winter Park Jazz & American
    Music Festival
Weekend in mid-July

Amphitheater at Winter Park
    Resort
Contact: (800) 903-PARK

Connecticut

Goshen
The Litchfield Jazz Festival
Weekend in August
Goshen Fairgrounds
Contact: (860) 567-4162
E-mail: lpai@ct1.nai.net
Website: http://www.
    litchfieldct.com/clt/lpa

Hartford
Greater Hartford Festival of
    Jazz
4 days in late July
Bushnell Park Performance
    Pavilion
Contact: (860) 722-6231
Fax: (860) 688-4677

Moodus
The Great Connecticut Tradi-
    tional Jazz Festival
Weekend in August
Sunrise Resort
Contact: (800) 468-3838
E-mail: hotevent@snet.net

Delaware

Rehoboth Beach
Rehoboth Beach Jazz Festival
4 days in mid-October
Contact: (503) 232-3000
Fax: (503) 232-2336

Wilmington
Clifford Brown Jazz Festival
5 days in June
Rodney Square
Contact: (888) 328-5887

District of Columbia

Washington, D.C.
Kennedy Center Mary Lou
    Williams Women in Jazz
    Festival
3 days in May
Contact: (800) 444-1324
(202) 467-4600

Website: http://kennedy-
    center.org

Washington, D.C.
Jazz & Arts Fest
*Various dates, June through
    August*
Contact: (202) 783-0360
E-mail: districtcurators@
    jazzarts.org
Website: http://www.jazzarts.
    org

Washington, D.C.
Thelonious Monk International
    Jazz Competition and Gala
2 days in late September
Baird Auditorium
Contact: (202) 364-7272
Fax: (202) 364-0176

Florida

Clearwater
Clearwater Jazz Holiday
4 days in October
Coachman Park
Contact: (813) 461-5200
Fax: (813) 724-6547

Hollywood
Hollywood Jazz Festival
Weekend in late November
Young Circle Park
Contact: (954) 921-3404
Fax: (954) 921-3572

Jacksonville
WJCT's Jacksonville Jazz Festi-
    val
7 days in the fall
Metropolitan Park
Contact: (904) 358-6336
Fax: (904) 354-6846

Miami
Florida International University
    Jazz Festival
3 days in April
Florida International University
Contact: (305) 348-3442
Fax: (305) 348-4073
E-mail: dunscomb@fiu.edu

Sarasota
Sarasota Jazz Festival
7 days in late March
Contact: (941) 366-1552
Fax: (941) 366-1553

E-mail: SaraJazzCl@aol.com

Georgia

Atlanta
Atlanta Jazz Festival
8 days in May
Contact: (404) 817-6815
Fax: (404) 817-6827
E-mail: cultural affairs@
    mindspring.com

Atlanta
JVC Jazz Festival—Atlanta
July
Contact: Atlanta Symphony
    Orchestra
(404) 733-4886
Fax: (404) 733-4999

Atlanta
Montreux Atlanta Music Festi-
    val
*8 days surrounding Labor Day
    weekend*
Piedmont Park
Contact: Atlanta Bureau of
    Cultural Affairs
(404) 817-6815
Fax: (404) 817-6827
E-mail: culturalaffair@
    mindspring.com

Idaho

Caldwell
Jazz at the Winery
*Weekend performances
    throughout June, July*
Contact: (800) 743-9549

Illinois

Chicago
Marshall Vente Jazz Festival
Late January
Jazz Showcase
Contact: (630) 968-3339
Fax: (630) 968-5940

Chicago
Chicago Jazz Festival
Labor Day weekend
Petrillo Music Shell, Grant
    Park
Contact: (312) 744-3370

Website: http://www.ci.chi.il.
us/WM/Special Events/

Highland Park
Jazz at Ravinia
4 days in June
Ravinia Park
Contact: (800) 433-8819
Website: http://www.ravinia.
org

Rock Island and Moline
Quad-Cities Jazz Festival
Weekend in May
Contact: (309) 762-0736
Fax: (309) 762-5123

Indiana

Elkhart
Elkhart Jazz Festival
Weekend in late June
Contact: (800) 597-7627

Iowa

Clarinda
Glenn Miller Birthplace Society
4 days in mid-June
Contact: (712) 542-2461

Davenport
Bix Beiderbecke Memorial
Jazz Festival
4 days in late July
Various venues, including Le
Claire Park, banks of the
Mississippi River
Contact: (319) 324-7170

Kansas

Topeka
Topeka Jazz Festival
Weekend in May
Topeka Performing Arts Center
Contact: (785) 267-1315

Wichita
Wichita Jazz Festival
8 days in mid-April
Contact: (316) 684-1100
(316) 722-6051
Fax: (316) 722-1959

Louisiana

New Orleans
New Orleans Jazz & Heritage
Festival
10 days in April, May
Contact: (504) 522-4786
Fax: (504) 522-5456
Website: http://www.nojazz
fest.com

Maine

Brunswick
Maine Festival
4 days in early August
Thomas Point Beach
Contact (202) 772-9012
Fax: (207) 772-3995
E-mail: mainearts@maineart.
org

Rockland
North Atlantic Blues Festival
2 days in mid-June
Public landing at Rockland
Contact: (207) 596-6055
E-mail: bluesman@midcoast.
com

Maryland

Annapolis
Annapolis Jazzfest
Weekend in June
St. John's College Campus
Contact: (410) 647-8718
Fax: (410) 647-0998

Columbia
Baltimore/Washington Jazzfest
Weekend in May
Contact: (410) 730-7105
Fax: (410) 715-3047
E-mail: AfricanArtMuseum@
erols.com

Columbia
Capital Jazz Fest
First weekend in June
Merriweather Post Pavilion
Contact: (301) 218-0404
(888) 378-FEST
Website: http://www
capitaljazz.com

**Columbia & Lake
Kittamagundi**
Columbia Festival of the Arts
10 days in June
Contact: (410) 715-3044
(410) 715-3043
E-mail: colfest@erols.com

Takoma Park
Takoma Park Jazzfest
A Saturday in May
Jecquie Park
Contact: (301) 589-4433

Massachusetts

Boston
Boston Globe Jazz & Blues
Festival
8 days in June
Contact: (617) 929-2649
Fax: (617) 929-2606
E-mail: M_caci@globe.com

Boston
Boston Harborfest
6 days in early July
Contact: (617) 227-1528
Fax: (617) 227-1886
E-mail: festival@boston
harbor.com

Lenox
Tanglewood
Labor Day weekend
Contact: (800) 274-8499

Michigan

Ann Arbor
Ann Arbor Summer Festival
Various dates, June & July
Power Center for the Perform-
ing Arts
Contact: (734) 647-2278

Detroit
Montreux Detroit Jazz Festival
Labor Day weekend
Contact: (313) 963-7622
Fax: (313) 963-2462
Website: http://www.
montreuxdetroitjazz.com

Mackinac Island
Grand Hotel Labor Day Jazz
Weekend
Labor Day weekend

Contact: (517) 349-4600
Fax: (517) 349-5504

Missouri

Kansas City
Kansas City Blues & Jazz Festi-
val
Weekend in July
Penn Valley Park
Contact: (800) 530-5266
Fax: (816) 531-2583
E-mail: kcbnj@qni.com
Website: http://www.kc
bluesjazz.org

Sedalia
Scott Joplin Ragtime Festival
5 days in June
Contact: (660) 926-2271
Fax: (660) 826-5054
E-mail: ragtimer@scottjoplin.
org

New Jersey

Cape May
Cape May Jazz Festival
Weekend; dates vary
Contact: (609) 884-7200
Fax: (609) 884-7277

East Hanover
International Jazz Day
One day in May
Contact: (201) 887-3167

Madison
Atlantic Mutual's Jersey Jazz-
Fest
Weekend in late June
Fairleigh Dickinson University
Contact: (800) 303-6557

New York

Long Island
Long Island Jazz Festival
*Weekend in late July/early Au-
gust*
Planting Fields Arboretum,
Oyster Bay
Contact: (516) 922-0061
Fax: (516) 922-0770
E-mail: artsfriend@aol.com

New York
JVC Jazz Festival New York
13 days in June
Contact: (212) 501-1390

New York
Texaco New York Jazz Festival
15 days in June
The Knitting Factory Club and
other locations
Contact: (212) 219-3006
Fax: (212) 219-3401
E-mail: sonya@knitting_
factory.com
Website: http://www.
nyjazzfest.com

New York
52nd Street Jazz Festival
1 day in July
52nd Street from Lexington to
Seventh Avenue
Contact: (212) 809-4900
(212) 799-7418

New York
Washington Square Music
Festival
1 day in July
Washington Square Park
Contact: (212) 431-1088
Fax: (212) 226-6788
E-mail: fgassoc@aol.com

New York
Panasonic Village Jazz Festival
10 days in mid-August
Greenwich Village
Contact: (212) 989-5149
Fax: (212) 691-0039
E-mail: jb@intlmusic.com

New York
Charlie Parker Jazz Festival
Last Sunday in August
Tompkins Square Park, Char-
lie Parker Place
Contact: (973) 377-1729

Saratoga
Freihofer's Jazz Festival—
Saratoga
Weekend in late June
Contact: (518) 587-3330

Syracuse
Syracuse Jazz Fest
Weekend in early June
Clinton Square

Contact: (315) 437-5627
Website: http://www.
syracusejazzfest.com/

North Carolina

Asheville
Wonderful Winery Jazz Week-
end
*Various summer weekends
and a September weekend*
The Winery in Asheville
Contact: (800) 543-2961

Raleigh
Artsplosure Spring Jazz & Art
Festival
4 days in mid-May
Contact: (919) 832-8699

Ohio

Cleveland
Tri-C JazzFest
10 days in April
Cuyahoga Community College
and other sites
Contact: (216) 987-4400
Fax: (216) 987-4422

Columbus
Capital University Jazz Week
Festival
*6 days in late March/early
April*
Capital University Conserva-
tory of Music
Contact: (614) 236-6285
Fax: (614) 236-6935

Strongsville
Earlyjas Fall Festival
3 days in mid-September
Holiday Inn
Contact: (330) 644-5957
Fax: (330) 896-4811

Oklahoma

Guthrie
Jazz Banjo Festival
Weekend in May
Contact: (405) 260-0529

Tulsa
Juneteenth on Greenwood
Heritage Festival

3 days in mid-June
Oklahoma Jazz Hall of Fame
Contact: (918) 596-1001
Fax: (918) 596-1005

Oregon

Gresham
Mt. Hood Festival of Jazz
*Weekend in late July/early Au-
gust*
Contact: (503) 231-0161

Pennsylvania

Chadd's Ford
Labor Day Weekend Jazz Festi-
val
Labor Day weekend
Contact: (610) 388-6221

Delaware Water Gap
Delaware Water Gap Celebration of the Arts (COTA)
3 days in September
Contact: (717) 424-2210

Erie
Erie Art Museum Blues & Jazz
Festival
Weekend in August
Frontier Park
Contact: (814) 459-5477
Fax: (814) 452-1744
E-mail: erieartm@erie.net

Harrisburg
Central PA Mellon Jazz Festival
Weekend in mid-June
Contact: (800) 807-1010
(717) 540-1010
Fax: (717) 540-7735
E-mail: pajazz@epix.net

Penn's Landing
Jam on the River
Weekend in May
Great Plaza at Penn's Landing
Contact: (215) 636-3300
Fax: (215) 636-3327

Philadelphia
Peco Energy Jazz Festival
Weekend in mid-February
Contact: (215) 636-3300
Fax: (215) 636-3327

Philadelphia
University of the Arts Festival
7 days in April
University of the Arts
Contact: (215) 875-2206
Fax: (215) 545-8056

Pittsburgh
Mellon Jazz Festival
10 days in mid-June
Contact: (610) 667-3559
E-mail: info.fest@fpiny.com

Whitehall
Lehigh Valley Blues & Jazz
Festival
Weekend in July
Lehigh Valley
Contact: (610) 261-2888

Rhode Island

Newport
JVC Jazz Festival at Newport
Weekend in August
Fort Adams State Park and the
Newport Casino
Contact: (401) 847-3700

Newport
Newport Jazz Festival at Sea
*6-day cruise following the
Newport Jazz Festival*
Aboard the Queen Elizabeth 2
Contact: (800) 433-0493

South Carolina

Charleston
Spoleto Festival U.S.A.
*17 days, usually beginning the
first week in June*
Contact: (803) 722-2764
Fax: (803) 723-6383
Website: http://www.
charleston.net/spoleto

Tennessee

Franklin
Franklin Jazz Festival
*Weekend in late July/early Au-
gust*
Town Square, downtown
Franklin
Contact: (615) 791-5025
(615) 790-5541

Kingsport
Triangle Jazz Party
Weekend in May
Contact: (423) 246-3644

Nashville
Tennessee Jazz and Blues Society Concert Series
Thursday outdoor series, from May through August
Contact: (615) 889-2941

Nashville
National Guitar Summer Workshop
5 days in July
Contact: (800) 234-6479
Fax: (860) 567-0374
E-mail: NGSW@aol.com

Vermont

Burlington
Discover Jazz Festival
6 days in June
Contact: (802) 863-7992

Virginia

Hampton
Hampton Jazz Festival
Weekend in June
Mill Point Park, downtown Hampton
Contact: (757) 838-4203

Newport News
Virginia Waterfront International Arts Festival
Weekend in May
Christopher Newport University
Contact: (757) 664-6492
Fax: (757) 664-6838

Norfolk
Town Point Jazz and Blues Festival
Weekend in May
Town Point Park
Contact: (757) 441-2345
Fax: (757) 441-5198
E-mail: festevent@series 2000.com

Orkney Springs
Shenandoah Valley Music Festival Jazz Weekend

Weekend in August
Contact: (540) 459-3396
E-mail: svmf@shentel.net

CANADA

Alberta

Calgary
Calgary International Jazz Festival
13 days beginning in mid-June
Contact: (403) 233-2628

Edmonton
International Jazz Festival
11 days in late June/early July
Contact: (403) 432-7166

British Columbia

Vancouver
Du Maurier International Jazz Festival
10 days in mid-June
Contact: (604) 682-0706

Nova Scotia

Halifax
Du Maurier Atlantic Jazz Festival
9 days in mid-July
Contact: (800) 567-5277

Ontario

Toronto
Du Maurier Downtown Jazz
10 days in June
Contact: (416) 973-3000

Toronto
JVC Jazz Festival Toronto
4 days in late August
Contact: (416) 973-4600

Quebec

Montreal
Festival International de Jazz de Montreal
12 days beginning in early July
Contact: (888) 515-0515
Website: http://www. montrealjazzfest.com

musicHound Jazz

Indexes

Five-Bone Album Index

Band Member Index

Producer Index

Roots Index

Category Index

The following albums achieved the highest rating possible—5 bones—from our discriminating MusicHound *Jazz writers. You can't miss with any of these recordings. (Note: Albums are listed under the name of the entry (or entries) in which they appear and are not necessarily albums by that individual artist or group. The album could be a compilation album, a film soundtrack, an album on which the artist or group appears as a guest, etc. Consult the artist or group's entry for specific information.)*

Ahmed Abdul-Malik
Misterioso (Riverside, 1958)
Thelonious in Action (Riverside, 1958)

Muhal Richard Abrams
Blu Blu Blu (Black Saint, 1991)
Familytalk (Black Saint, 1993)
The Hearinga Suite (Black Saint, 1989)
Levels and Degrees of Light (Delmark, 1967)
Think All, Focus One (Black Saint, 1995)

George Adams
America (Blue Note, 1989)
Changes One (Atlantic/Rhino, 1975)
Live at Montmarte (Timeless, 1986)
Live at Village Vanguard, Vol. 1 & Vol. 2 (Soul Note, 1985)

Johnny Adams
Walking on a Tightrope: The Songs of Percy Mayfield (Rounder, 1989)

Julian "Cannonball" Adderley
Alabama Concerto (Riverside, 1958)
Black Messiah (Capitol, 1970)
Cannonball Adderley Quintet in San Francisco (Riverside, 1959)
Mercy, Mercy, Mercy! (Capitol, 1966)
Somethin' Else (Blue Note, 1958)

Nat Adderley
Dizzy's Business (Milestone, 1993)
That's Right! (Riverside, 1960)

Air
Air Show No. 1 (Black Saint, 1986)
Live Air (Black Saint, 1977)
New Air Live at Montreux International Jazz Festival (Black Saint, 1983)

Toshiko Akiyoshi
Carnegie Hall Concert (Columbia, 1992)
Tales of a Courtesan (RCA, 1976)

Howard Alden
Your Story—The Music of Bill Evans (Concord Jazz, 1994)

Monty Alexander
Echoes of Jilly's (Concord Jazz, 1997)

Geri Allen
Twenty One (Blue Note, 1994)

Henry "Red" Allen
World on a String (RCA/Bluebird, 1957/1991)

Mose Allison
Allison Wonderland: The Mose Allison Anthology (Atlantic, 1994)
Greatest Hits (OJC, 1988)

Alloy Orchestra
New Music for Silent Films (Accurate Records, 1994)

Laurindo Almeida
Brazilliance, Vol. 1 (World Pacific, 1953)

Ray Anderson
Don't Mow Your Lawn (Enja, 1996)
Heads and Tales (Enja, 1996)
It Just So Happens (Enja, 1987/1992)
Slideride (hat ART, 1994)

Louis Armstrong
Hot Fives and Hot Sevens, Vol. 2 (Columbia, 1988)
Hot Fives and Hot Sevens, Vol. 3 (Columbia, 1989)
Hot Fives, Vol. 1 (Columbia, 1988)
Louis Armstrong Plays W.C. Handy (Columbia, 1954/1997)

Art Ensemble of Chicago
Fanfare for the Warriors (Atlantic, 1974)
Kabalaba (AECO, 1978)
People in Sorrow (Nessa, 1969)
Song For (Delmark, 1991)
Sound (Delmark, 1996)
Spiritual (Black Lion, 1997)
This Dance Is for Steve McCall (Black Saint, 1993)
Urban Bushmen (ECM, 1982/1994)
Works (ECM, 1994)

Albert Ayler
In Greenwich Village (Impulse!, 1967)
Spiritual Unity (ESP-Disk, 1964)

Derek Bailey
Aida (Dexter's Cigar, 1976/1997)

Chet Baker
The Best of the Gerry Mulligan Quartet with Chet Baker (Pacific Jazz, 1991)
Complete Pacific Jazz Live Recordings (Mosaic, 1954)
Complete Pacific Jazz Studio Recordings of the Chet Baker Quartet with Russ Freeman (Mosaic, 1953–56)
Quartet: Russ Freeman and Chet Baker (Pacific Jazz, 1956)

Ginger Baker
Going Back Home (Atlantic, 1994)

Billy Bang
Rainbow Gladiator (Soul Note, 1981)

Carlos Barbosa-Lima
Music of the Brazilian Masters (Concord Picante, 1989)

Danny Barker
Save the Bones (Orleans, 1991)

Charlie Barnet
Complete Charlie Barnet, Vols. 1–6 (Bluebird, 1935–42)

Sweet Emma Barrett
Sweet Emma—New Orleans: The Living Legends (Riverside, 1961)

Count Basie
April in Paris (Verve, 1956)
Basie (Roulette, 1957/1994)
Basie in London (Verve, 1957/1988)
Basie, Lambert, Hendricks, Ross (Europa/Giganti Jazz)
Beaver Junction (VJC, 1991)
The Complete Decca Recordings (Decca)
The Complete Roulette Live Recordings of Count Basie and His Orchestra (Roulette, 1959–62)
The Complete Roulette Studio Recordings of Count Basie and His Orchestra (Roulette, late 1950s–early 1960s)
The Count at the Chatterbox (Jazz Archive, 1974)
Count Basie and the Kansas City Seven (Impulse!, 1962/1996)
Count Basie at Newport (Verve, 1957/1989)

Count Basie Swings, Joe Williams Sings (Verve, 1955/1993)
Sing Along with Basie (Roulette, 1959/1991)

Alvin Batiste
Clarinet Summit, Vol. 2 (India Navigation, 1985)
In Concert at the Public Theater (India Navigation, 1983)
Musique d'Afrique Nouvelle Orleans (India Navigation, 1984)
Southern Bells (Black Saint, 1987)

Mario Bauzá
My Time Is Now (Messidor, 1993)
Tanga (Messidor, 1992)

Sidney Bechet
Best of Sidney Bechet on Blue Note (Blue Note, 1939–53/1994)
Really the Blues (Living Era, 1993)
Volume 2: 1923–1932 (Masters of Jazz, 1992)

Bix Beiderbecke
Bix Beiderbecke and the Wolverines (Timeless, 1993)
Bix Beiderbecke, Vol. 1: Singin' the Blues (1927) (Columbia, 1990)
Bix Beiderbecke, Vol. 2: At the Jazz Band Ball (1927–28) (Columbia, 1991)
The Complete New Orleans Rhythm Kings, Vol. 2 (1923) /The Complete Wolverines (1924) (King Jazz, 1923–24/1992)
Masters of Jazz Series: The Complete Bix Beiderbecke (Media 7, 1997)

Richie Beirach
Antarctica (Pathfinder, 1985/Evidence, 1994)
Kahuna, Keeper of Secrets (Trio, 1978)
Sunday Songs (Blue Note, 1992)

Bob Belden
PrinceJazz (Somethin' Else/Toshiba-EMI, 1994)

Marcus Belgrave
Working Together (Detroit Jazz Musicians Co-op Productions, 1992)

Louie Bellson
Duke Ellington: Black, Brown & Beige (MusicMasters, 1992)
Duke's Big Four (Pablo, 1974)

Gregg Bendian
Bang! (Truemedia Jazzworks, 1994)
Counterparts (CIMP, 1996)

Tony Bennett
Forty Years: The Artistry of Tony Bennett (Columbia, 1991/1997)
I Left My Heart in San Francisco (Columbia, 1962/1988)
The Tony Bennett/Bill Evans Album (Fantasy/OJC, 1975)
Tony Bennett: Jazz (Columbia, 1987)

Han Bennink
I.C.P. Orchestra Performs Nichols and Monk (I.C.P., 1984–86)
Peter Brotzman Octet Machine Gun (F.M.P, 1968)

Bob Berg
Another Standard (Stretch, 1997)
Enter the Spirit (Stretch, 1997)
Games (Jazz Door, 1992)
New Birth (Xanadu, 1978)
Steppin'—Live in Europe (Red, 1994)

Borah Bergman
The October Revolution (Evidence, 1996)
Reflections on Ornette Coleman and the Stone House (Soul Note, 1995)

Bunny Berigan
Bunny Berigan and His Boys 1935–36 (Classics, 1993)
Mound City Blues Blowers (Timeless, 1994)
Portrait of Bunny Berigan (ASV Living Era, 1992)
Swingin' High (Topaz, 1993)

Dick Berk
One by One (Reservoir, 1996)

Peter Bernstein
Freedom in the Groove (Warner Bros., 1996)
More Urban Tones (Criss Cross Jazz, 1996)

Steve Berrios
And Then Some! (Milestone, 1996)
First World (Milestone, 1995)
Mongo Returns (Milestone, 1995)

Chu Berry
Cab Calloway 1939–40 (Classics)
Cab Calloway 1940 (Classics)
The Calloway Years: 1937–41 (Merrit)
Chu Berry Story 1936–39 (Jazz Archives)
Giants of the Tenor Sax (Commodore, 1938–1941)

Barney Bigard
Duke Ellington: Small Groups, Vol. 1 (Columbia, 1934–38)
Louis Armstrong Plays W.C. Handy (Columbia, 1954/1986)

Eliane Elias
Eliane Elias Plays Jobim (Blue Note, 1990)
The Three Americas (Blue Note, 1997)

Duke Ellington
And His Mother Called Him Bill (Bluebird, 1967/1988)
The Blanton-Webster Band (RCA, 1940–42/1987)
Carnegie Hall Concerts, January 1943 (Prestige, 1943/1991)
Early Ellington: The Complete Brunswick and Vocalion Recordings, 1926–31 (Decca, 1926–31/1994)
Ellington at Newport (Columbia, 1956/1987)
The Great Paris Concert (Atlantic, 1963/1989)
Money Jungle (United Artists, 1962/Blue Note, 1989)
Uptown (Columbia, 1952/1987)

Don Ellis
Electric Bath (GNP/Crescendo, 1996)
New Ideas (OJC, 1963)

Herb Ellis
Roll Call (Justice, 1991)
Together! (Epic, 1963/Koch Classics, 1995)

Kahil El'Zabar
Big Cliff (Delmark, 1995)
The Continuum (Delmark, 1998)
Jitterbug Junction (CIMP, 1997)

Bobby Enriquez
Live! In Tokyo (GNP/Crescendo, 1983)
The Prodigious Piano of Bobby Enriquez (GNP/Crescendo, 1991)

Peter Erskine
From Kenton to Now (Fuzzy Music, 1995)
Peter Erskine (Contemporary/OJC, 1982)

Booker Ervin
The Freedom Book (Prestige, 1964/OJC, 1995)
The Space Book (Prestige, 1964/OJC, 1996)

Ellery Eskelin
Figure of Speech (Soul Note, 1993)
Green Bermudas (Eremite, 1996)

Robin Eubanks
World Expansion (By the M-Base Neophyte) (JMT, 1987)

Bill Evans
Cross-Currents (Fantasy, 1978)

Everybody Digs Bill Evans (Riverside, 1959)
Explorations (Riverside, 1961)
Highlights from Turn Out the Stars (Warner Bros., 1996)
Interplay (Riverside, 1963)
Marian McPartland's Piano Jazz with Guest Bill Evans (Jazz Alliance, 1978)
Moonbeams (Riverside, 1962)
New Jazz Conceptions (Riverside, 1957)
Paris Concert, Edition One (Elektra, 1980)
Portrait in Jazz (Riverside, 1960)
Sunday at the Village Vanguard (Riverside, 1961)
Waltz for Debby (Riverside, 1962)

Gil Evans
The Individualism of Gil Evans (Verve, 1964/1988)
Live at Sweet Basil (King, 1984/Evidence, 1992)
Live at Sweet Basil, Volume II (King, 1984/Evidence, 1992)
Out of the Cool (Impulse!, 1961/1996)

Douglas Ewart
The Bamboo Forest (Arawak, 1990)

Charles Fambrough
The Proper Angle (CTI, 1991)

Art Farmer
Blame It on My Youth (Contemporary, 1988)
Farmer's Market (Prestige/OJC, 1956)
Meet the Jazztet (Chess/MCA, 1960)
Portrait of Art Farmer (Contemporary/OJC, 1958)
Something to Live For: The Music of Billy Strayhorn (Contemporary, 1987)

Joe Farrell
Outback (CTI, 1971)
Sonic Text (Fantasy/OJC, 1990)

Ella Fitzgerald
The Best of Ella Fitzgerald & Louis Armstrong on Verve (Verve, 1997)
Compact Jazz: Ella & Duke (Verve, 1957–66/1993)
The Complete Ella Fitzgerald & Louis Armstrong on Verve (Verve, 1997)
The Concert Years (Pablo, 1994)
Ella Abraca Jobim (Pablo, 1980–81/1991)
Ella in London (Pablo, 1974/1987)
Ella: The Legendary Decca Recordings (Decca Jazz, 1995)
First Lady of Song (Verve, 1949–66/1994)

The Jerome Kern Songbook (Verve, 1963/1987)
Love Songs: Best of the Verve Songbooks (Verve, 1996)
Newport Jazz Festival: Live at Carnegie Hall (Columbia, 1973/Legacy, 1995)
75th Birthday Celebration (Decca, 1938–55/GRP, 1993)
Sings the George and Ira Gershwin Songbook (Verve, 1959/1987)
Sings the Rodgers & Hart Songbook, Volumes I & II (Verve, 1956/1997)

Bob Florence
With All the Bells and Whistles (MAMA Foundation, 1995)

Jimmy Forrest
Most Much (Prestige, 1961)
Soul Battle (Prestige, 1960)

Sonny Fortune
From Now On (Blue Note, 1996)

Frank Foster
Frankly Speaking (Concord, 1984)
Two for the Blues (Pablo, 1983/OJC, 1993)

Gary Foster
Concord Duo Series, Volume Four (Concord, 1995)

Bud Freeman
Bud Freeman 1939–1940 (Jazz Chronological Classics, 1995)

Russ Freeman
At the Manne Hole, Volume I (Contemporary, 1959/OJC, 1992)
At the Manne Hole, Volume II (Contemporary, 1962/OJC, 1992)
Chet Baker: Boston 1954 (Pacific Jazz, 1954/1997)
Russ & Chet (Contemporary, 1955)
The Three and the Two (Contemporary, 1954/OJC, 1994)
West Coast Live (Pacific Jazz, 1954/Blue Note, 1998)

Freestyle Fellowship
Inner City Griots (Island, 1993)
To Whom It May Concern (Sun, 1991)

Johnny Frigo
Debut of a Legend (Chesky, 1994)
Live from Studio in New York City (Chesky, 1989)
Roll Call (Justice, 1991)

David Frishberg
Can't Take You Nowhere (Fantasy, 1986)
Classics (Concord, 1983/1991)
Getting Some Fun out of Life (Concord, 1977)
Live at Vine Street (OJC, 1984/1994)

Curtis Fuller
The Complete Blue Note/United Artists Curtis Fuller Sessions (Mosaic Records, 1996)
The Curtis Fuller Jazztet with Benny Golson (Savoy, 1959)

Charles Gabriel
Live at the Kerrytown Concert House (Gabriel Historical Society, 1995)

Steve Gadd
Burning for Buddy—Vols. I and II (Atlantic, 1996 and 1997)

Slim (Bulee) Gaillard
Slim Gaillard: Laughing in Rhythm (Verve, 1994)

Ganelin Trio
Concerto Grosso (Sonore, 1980/1995)
Poco-a-Poco (Leo, 1978/1988)

Erroll Garner
Concert by the Sea (Columbia, 1956/1987)
Erroll Garner Collection 1: Easy to Love (EmArcy/Verve, 1988)
The Erroll Garner Collection 2: Dancing on the Ceiling (EmArcy/Verve, 1989)

Giorgio Gaslini
Ayler's Wings (Soul Note, 1991)

Stan Getz
The Girl from Ipanema: The Bossa Nova Years (Verve, 1964/1989)
Jazz Samba (Verve, 1963)
People Time (Verve, 1992)

Terry Gibbs
Air Mail Special (Contemporary, 1990)
Dream Band (Contemporary, 1959/1986)
Kings of Swing (Contemporary, 1992)
Memories of You (Contemporary, 1992)
Terry Gibbs Dream Band, Volume 4: Main Stem (Contemporary 1961/1991)
Terry Gibbs Dream Band, Volume 5: The Big Cat (Contemporary, 1961/1991)

Banu Gibson
Battle of the Bands: San Antonio vs. New Orleans (Pacific Vista, 1994)

Livin' in a Great Big Way (Swing Out CD, 1994)

João Gilberto
Getz/Gilberto (Verve, 1964)
The Legendary João Gilberto (World Pacific, 1990)

Dizzy Gillespie
Diz and Roy (Verve, 1954/1994)
Dizzy Gillespie: His Sextets and Orchestra (Musicraft, 1945–46/1988)
Dizzy Gillespie: The Complete RCA-Victor Recordings (RCA, 1946–49/1995)
Dizzy's Diamonds: The Best of the Verve Years (Verve, 1954–64/1992)

Jimmy Giuffre
1961 (ECM, 1961)

Ben Goldberg
Here by Now (Music and Arts, 1997)
Junk Genius (Knitting Factory Works, 1996)
Masks & Faces (Nine Winds, 1991/Tzadik, 1996)
Twelve Minor (Avant, 1997)

Vinny Golia
Against the Grain (Nine Winds, 1993)
The Art of Negotiation (CIMP, 1996)
Commemoration (Nine Winds, 1994)
The Gift of Fury (Nine Winds, 1981)
haunting the spirits inside them . . . (Music & Arts, 1995)
Portland, 1996 (Nine Winds, 1996)
Triangulation (Nine Winds, 1996)
Worldwide & Portable (Nine Winds, 1990)

Benny Golson
Benny Golson's New York Scene (Contemporary/OJC, 1957)
Live (Dreyfus, 1991)
Meet the Jazztet (Chess/MCA, 1960)
The Modern Touch (Riverside/OJC, 1957)

Jerry Gonzalez & the Fort Apache Band
Crossroads (Milestone, 1994)

Benny Goodman
Air Play (Signature, 1989)
Benny Goodman Carnegie Hall Jazz Concert (Columbia, 1987)
Benny Goodman: Complete Capitol Small Group Recordings (Mosaic, 1993)
Jam (Swing House, 1983)
On the Air, 1937–1938 (Columbia, 1993)
Session (Swing House, 1981)
Treasure Chest Series (MGM, c. 1959)

Dexter Gordon
The Complete Blue Note Sixties Sessions (Blue Note, 1996)
Our Man in Paris (Blue Note, 1963/1988)

Dusko Goykovich
After Hours (Enja, 1995)
Balkan Connection (Enja, 1996)
Bebop City (Enja, 1995)
Soul Connection (Enja, 1994)

Wardell Gray
The Chase! (Dial, 1947)
Wardell Gray Memorial Album, Volume 2 (Prestige, 1950/1952/OJC, 1992)

Grant Green
The Best of Grant Green, Volume I (Blue Note, 1993)
The Complete Blue Note Recordings of Larry Young (Mosaic, 1993)
Green Street (Blue Note, 1961)

Phillip Greenlief
Phillip Greenlief/Trevor Dunn (Evander Music, 1996)

Al Grey
Me 'n' Jack (Pullen Music, 1996)

Johnny Griffin
A Blowing Session (Blue Note, 1957/1988)
The Congregation (Blue Note, 1957/1994)

Henry Grimes
Albert Ayler in Greenwich Village (Impulse!, 1967)
Conquistador (Blue Note, 1967)
Unit Structures (Blue Note, 1966)
Where Is Brooklyn? (Blue Note, 1966)
Witches and Demons (Arista Freedom, 1975)

Don Grolnick
The Complete Blue Note Recordings (Blue Note, 1997)

Steve Grossman
Time to Smile (Dreyfus Jazz, 1994)

Dave Grusin
The Gershwin Collection (GRP, 1991)

Gigi Gryce
The Rat Race Blues (Prestige/New Jazz, 1960)

Vince Guaraldi
A Flower Is a Lovesome Thing (Fantasy, 1957/1994)

Charlie Haden
Beyond the Missouri Sky (Verve, 1997)
Charlie Haden, the Montréal Tapes with Gonzalo Rubalcaba and Paul Motian (Verve, 1998)
Dream Keeper (Blue Note, 1991)
Haunted Heart (Gitanes/Verve, 1992)
Night and the City (Verve, 1998)
Now Is the Hour (Gitanes, 1996)

Al Haig
Shaw 'Nuff (Musicraft, 1945–46)

Jim Hall
The Bridge (Victor Jazz, 1962/1996)
The Complete Landmark Sessions (32 Jazz, 1997)
Dedications & Inspirations (Telarc, 1994)
Jazz Guitar (Pacific, 1957/Capitol)
Live at Village West (Concord, 1984)
Something Special (MusicMasters, 1993)

Lin Halliday
East of the Sun (Delmark, 1992)

Chico Hamilton
Man from Two Worlds (Impulse!, 1962/1963)

Scott Hamilton
At Last (Concord Jazz, 1989)
Major League (Concord Jazz, 1986)
Radio City (Concord Jazz, 1990)
Scott Hamilton with Strings (Concord Jazz, 1993)
Soft Lights and Sweet Music (Concord Jazz, 1986)

Lionel Hampton
After You've Gone: The Original Benny Goodman Trio and Quartet Sessions, Volume 1 (Bluebird, 1935–37/1987)
Hamp and Getz (Verve, 1955)
His Best Records with the Jazz Masters, Volume 2 (Black and Blue, 1938–39)
Lionel Hampton and His Orchestra (1937–38) (Classics, 1937–38)
Lionel Hampton and His Orchestra (1938–39) (Classics, 1938–39)
Midnight Sun (Decca, 1946–47/1993)

Slide Hampton
Slide Hampton and the JazzMasters—Dedicated to Diz (Telarc, 1993)

Herbie Hancock
Empyrean Isles (Blue Note, 1964/1987)
Maiden Voyage (Blue Note, 1965/1987)

Mwandishi: The Complete Warner Bros. Recordings (Warner Bros., 1970–72/1994)
My Point of View (Blue Note, 1963/1996)

John Handy
Karuna Supreme (MPS, 1980)
Live at the Monterey Jazz Festival (Koch Jazz, 1996)

W.C. Handy
Louis Armstrong Plays W.C. Handy (Columbia, 1954/1997)

Sir Roland Hanna
Perugia (Freedom, 1975)

Billy Harper
In Europe (Soul Note, 1979)
Live on Tour in the Far East, Volume 1 (SteepleChase, 1992)
Live on Tour in the Far East, Volume 2 (SteepleChase, 1993)
Live on Tour in the Far East, Volume 3 (SteepleChase, 1995)

Tom Harrell
Form (Contemporary, 1990)
Moon Alley (Criss Cross, 1986)
Passages (Chesky, 1993)
Upswing (Chesky, 1993)
Visions (Contemporary, 1991)

Eddie Harris
Artist's Choice: The Eddie Harris Anthology (Rhino, 1994)

Billy Hart
Quartets: Live at the Village Vanguard (Blue Note, 1994)

Johnny Hartman
All of Me (Bethlehem Jazz, 1956/1993)
John Coltrane & Johnny Hartman (Impulse!, 1963)

Hampton Hawes
All Night Session, Vol. 1 (Contemporary/OJC, 1958)
All Night Session, Vol. 2 (Contemporary, 1958/OJC, 1991)
All Night Session, Vol. 3 (Contemporary, 1958/OJC, 1991)
Everybody Likes Hampton Hawes: Trio, Vol 3 (Contemporary, 1956/OJC, 1990)
For Real! (Contemporary/OJC, 1958)
Four! (Contemporary/OJC, 1958)
The Green Leaves of Summer (Contemporary/OJC, 1964)

Hampton Hawes Trio, Volume One (Contemporary/OJC, 1955)
Live at the Jazz Showcase in Chicago (Enja, 1973/1996)
The Seance (Contemporary/OJC, 1969)
This Is Hampton Hawes, The Trio: Vol. 2 (Contemporary/OJC, 1956)

Roy Haynes
Cracklin' (New Jazz, 1963/OJC, 1994)
Out of the Afternoon (Impulse!, 1962/1996)
Te Vou! (Dreyfus, 1994)

Jimmy Heath
On the Trail (Riverside, 1964/OJC, 1994)

Percy Heath
Django (Prestige, 1953–55)
Walkin' (Prestige, 1954)

Mark Helias
Loopin' the Cool (Enja, 1996)

Jonas Hellborg
The Silent Life (Day Eight, 1991)
Temporal Analogues of Paradise (Day Eight, 1996)

Julius Hemphill
Dogon A.D. (Mbari, 1972/Freedom, 1977)

Bill Henderson
Bill Henderson with the Oscar Peterson Trio (Verve, 1963/1989)
His Complete Vee-Jay Recordings, Vol. 1 (Vee-Jay, 1959–60/1993)
His Complete Vee-Jay Recordings, Vol. 2 (Vee-Jay, 1960–61/1993)

Eddie Henderson
Dark Shadows (Milestone, 1996)
Mwandishi: The Complete Warner Bros. Recordings (Warner Archives, 1994)

Fletcher Henderson
Fletcher Henderson, 1924, Vol. 3 (Classics)
Fletcher Henderson: 1924–1925 (Classics)
Fletcher Henderson: 1932–1934 (Classics)
A Study in Frustration (Columbia, 1923–1938/1994)

Joe Henderson
Milestone Years (Milestone, 1994)
Mode for Joe (Blue Note, 1966)

Woody Herman
The First Herd (Le Jazz, 1996)
The 1940s—The Small Groups: New Directions (Columbia, 1988)
The Thundering Herds, 1945–1947 (Columbia, 1988)

Woody Herman, The V-Disc Years, Vols. 1 & 2, 1944–46 (Hep, 1994)

John Hicks
East Side Blues (DIW/Disc Union, 1988)

Andrew Hill
The Complete Blue Note Andrew Hill Sessions (1963–66) (Mosaic)
Point of Departure (Blue Note, 1964)

Earl "Fatha" Hines
Earl Hines Plays Duke Ellington (New World Records, 1988)
Earl Hines Plays Duke Ellington, Vol. Two (New World Records, 1997)
Tour de Force (Black Lion, 1973)
Tour de Force Encore (Black Lion, 1973)

Milt Hinton
Piano Jazz: McPartland/Milt Hinton (Concord/Jazz Alliance, 1991)

Art Hodes
The Complete Art Hodes Blue Note Sessions (Mosaic, 1990)
Pagin' Mr. Jelly (Candid, 1989)

Johnny Hodges
Caravan (Prestige, 1992)
Complete Johnny Hodges Sessions: 1951–55 (Mosaic, 1989)
Duke Ellington Small Groups, Volume 1 (Columbia/Legacy, 1991)
The Duke's Men: Small Groups, Volume 2 (Columbia/Legacy, 1993)
Everybody Knows Johnny Hodges (Impulse!, 1964)
Hodge Podge (Legacy/Epic, 1995)
Johnny Hodges at Sportpalast, Berlin (Pablo, 1993)
Passion Flower: 1940–46 (Bluebird, 1995)
A Smooth One (Verve, 1979)
Triple Play (Bluebird, 1967)

Billie Holiday
The Complete Decca Recordings (GRP, 1991)

Bill Holman
Brilliant Corners (JVC, 1997)
A View from the Side (JVC, 1995)

Richard "Groove" Holmes
Blue Groove (Prestige, 1966–1967)
Soul Message (Prestige, 1965)

Adam Holzman
The Big Picture (Lipstick, 1996)

Shirley Horn
Close Enough for Love (Verve, 1989)
You Won't Forget Me (Verve, 1991)

Wayne Horvitz
Miss Ann (Tim/Kerr, 1995)

Freddie Hubbard
Breaking Point (Blue Note, 1964)
Hub-Tones (Blue Note, 1962)

Helen Humes
Helen (Muse, 1981)
Helen Humes and the Muse All-Stars (Muse, 1980)
Songs I Like to Sing! (Contemporary/OJC, 1960)
Swingin' with Humes (Contemporary/OJC, 1961)
'Tain't Nobody's Biz-ness If I Do (Contemporary/OJC, 1959)

Dick Hyman
Moog: The Electric Eclectics of Dick Hyman (Varese Sarabande, 1969/1997)

Abdullah Ibrahim
Duke Ellington Presents the Dollar Brand Trio (Reprise, 1963)
Tintinyana (Kaz, 1988)

Chuck Israels
Kronos Quartet: The Complete Landmark Sessions (Landmark, 1985–1986/32 Jazz, 1997)

Javon Jackson
Me and Mr. Jones (Criss Cross Jazz, 1992)

Milt Jackson
Bags and Trane (Atlantic, 1959/1988)
Bags Meets Wes! (Riverside, 1961/OJC, 1987)
The Big 3 (Pablo, 1975/OJC, 1994)
For Someone I Love (Riverside, 1963/OJC, 1990)
Genius of Modern Music, Vol. 2 (Blue Note, 1951–52)
Night Mist (Pablo, 1977/OJC, 1994)

Ronald Shannon Jackson
Eye on You (About Time, 1980)
Mandance (Antilles/Island, 1982)

Willis "Gator Tail" Jackson
Bar Wars (32 Jazz, 1977)
Willis Jackson with Pat Martino (Prestige, 1964)

Ahmad Jamal
Ahmad's Blues (Chess, 1959/GRP, 1994)
At the Pershing/But Not for Me (Chess, 1958/MCA, 1990)
Big Byrd: The Essence Part 2 (Verve, 1996)
Chicago Revisited: Live at Joe Segal's Jazz Showcase (Telarc, 1993)

Harry James
The Chronological Harry James Orchestra, 1937–1939 (Jazz Classics, 1996)
The Harry James Years, Vol. 1 (Bluebird/RCA, 1993)
Wrappin' It Up: The Harry James Years, Vol. 2 (Bluebird/RCA, 1995)

Jon Jang
Tiananmen! (Soul Note, 1993)

Joseph Jarman
Fanfare for the Warriors (Atlantic, 1973)
Naked (DIW, 1986)

Keith Jarrett
At the Blue Note (ECM, 1995)
Keith Jarrett at the Blue Note: The Complete Recordings (ECM, 1995)
Bye Bye Blackbird: A Musical Tribute to Miles Davis (ECM, 1993)
Facing You (ECM, 1972/1994)
The Impulse! Years, 1973–1974 (Impulse!, 1977/1997)
The Köln Concert (ECM, 1975/1994)
Mysteries: The Impulse! Years, 1975–76 (Impulse!, 1975–76/1996)
Nude Ants (ECM, 1979/1980/1994)
Solo Concerts: Bremen/Lausanne (ECM, 1973)

The Jazz Passengers
Broken Night Red Light (Crespuscle, 1987)
Deranged and Decomposed (Crespuscle, 1988)
Implement Yourself (New World, 1990)
Jazz Passengers in Love (High Street, 1994)
Live at the Knitting Factory (Knitting Factory, 1991)
Plain Old Joe (Knitting Factory, 1993)

Eddie Jefferson
The Jazz Singer (Evidence, 1959–65/1993)

Antonio Carlos Jobim
Man from Ipanema (Verve, 1995)

Budd Johnson
Let's Swing (Swingville, 1960/OJC, 1993)

Buddy Johnson
Buddy and Ella Johnson 1953–1964 (Bear Family, 1992)
Walk 'Em: The Decca Sessions (Decca, 1941–1952/Ace/UK, 1996)

J.J. Johnson
The Great Kai and Jay (Impulse!, 1961)

James P. (Price) Johnson
Snowy Morning Blues (Decca Jazz, 1991)

Pete Johnson
The Boss of the Blues (Atlantic, 1956)

Elvin Jones
Illumination! (Impulse!, 1963)
Live at the Lighthouse, Vols. 1 & 2 (Blue Note, 1972)
Youngblood (Enja, 1992)

Etta Jones
Don't Go to Strangers (Prestige, 1960)

Hank Jones
Somethin' Else (Blue Note, 1958/1986)

Sam Jones
The Chant (Riverside, 1961/OJC, 1994)
Down Home (Riverside, 1962/1995)

Thad Jones
The Complete Blue Note/UA/Roulette Recordings of Thad Jones (Mosaic, 1956–1959)
The Complete Solid State Recordings of the Thad Jones/Mel Lewis Orchestra (Mosaic, 1966–1970)
Fabulous Thad Jones (Debut, 1955)
Mean What You Say (Milestone, 1966)

Clifford Jordan
Blowing in from Chicago (Blue Note, 1957)

Louis Jordan
Five Guys Named Moe: Original Decca Recordings, Volume 2 (Decca, 1949–1952/1992)
Let the Good Times Roll: The Complete Decca Recordings, 1938–54 (Bear Family, 1994)

Sheila Jordan
Portrait of Sheila (Blue Note, 1962/1989)

Bruce Katz
Grateful Heart: Blues and Ballads (Bullseye, 1996)

Geoff Keezer
Here and Now (Blue Note, 1990)

World Music (DIW/Disc Union, 1992)

Stan Kenton
City of Glass (Capitol, 1947–53/1995)

Freddie Keppard
The Complete Freddie Keppard, 1923–27 (King Jazz, 1996)

Talib Kibwe
The Spirits of our Ancestors (Antilles, 1992)

Andy Kirk
Andy Kirk, 1929–31 (Classics, 1994)

Rahsaan Roland Kirk
Does Your House Have Lions: The Rahsaan Roland Kirk Anthology (Rhino, 1993)
Rahsaan—The Complete Mercury Recordings (Mercury, 1961–65/PolyGram, 1990)
The Vibration Continues (Atlantic, 1968–74)

Lee Konitz
Zounds (Soul Note, 1991)

Peter Kowald
Die Jungen: Random Generators (Free Music Production, 1979)
Open Secrets (Free Music Production, 1988)
Paintings (Free Music Production, 1981)

Ernie Krivda
Ernie Krivda Jazz (Cadence, 1992)
Perdido (Koch, 1998)

Kronos Quartet
The Complete Landmark Sessions (Landmark, 1985–1986/32 Jazz, 1997)

Steve Kuhn
Looking Back (Concord, 1991)
Years Later (Concord, 1993)

Steve Lacy
Futurities (hat ART, 1984)
Prospectus (hat ART, 1983)
Vespers (Soul Note, 1993)
The Way (hat ART, 1979)

Scott LaFaro
Beauty Is a Rare Thing: The Complete Atlantic Recordings of Ornette Coleman (Atlantic/Rhino, 1993)
Bill Evans Trio: Sunday at the Village Vanguard (OJC, 1961/1987)
Free Jazz (Atlantic, 1961/1987)

Lambert, Hendricks & Ross
Everybody's Boppin' (Columbia, 1959–61/1989)
The Hottest New Group in Jazz (Columbia, 1960/1996)
Sing a Song of Basie (Impulse!, 1957/GRP, 1992)
The Swingers! (Pacific Jazz, 1959/Blue Note, 1995)
Twisted: The Best of Lambert, Hendricks, and Ross (Rhino, 1992)

Harold Land
The Fox (Contemporary, 1959/OJC, 1988)
Harold in the Land of Jazz (Contemporary, 1958 /1988)
A Lazy Afternoon (Postcards, 1995)
Mapenzi (Concord Jazz, 1977/1990)
San Francisco (Blue Note, 1970/Capitol, 1995)
Total Eclipse (Blue Note, 1967/Capitol, 1996)
West Coast Blues! (Jazzland, 1960/OJC, 1996)

Last Exit
The Noise of Trouble: Live in Tokyo (Enemy, 1987)

Last Poets
Be Bop or Be Dead (Axiom, 1993)
The Blue Guerrilla (Collectables, 1990)
Hustler's Convention (Celluloid, 1984)
Last Poets (Celluloid, 1984)

Yusef Lateef
The African-American Epic Suite (ACT/Blue Jackel, 1994)
The World at Peace: Music for 12 Musicians (YAL & Meta, 1996)

Hubert Laws
In the Beginning (CTI, 1974/Sony Legacy, 1997)

Peggy Lee
Black Coffee & Other Delights: The Decca Anthology (Decca/MCA, 1952–56/1994)
Capitol Collector's Series, Volume 1, The Early Years (Capitol, 1945–50/1997)

Michel Legrand
Legrand Jazz (Columbia, 1960/Philips, 1989)

Peter Leitch
Colours and Dimensions (Reservoir, 1996)
Duality (Reservoir, 1995)
Exhilaration (Reservoir, 1993)

Mean What You Say (Concord Jazz, 1990)
Up Front (Reservoir, 1997)

John Leitham
Lefty Leaps In (USA Music Group, 1996)

Lou Levy
Clap Hands, Here Comes Charlie! (Verve, 1961/1989)

Mel Lewis
Definitive Thad Jones, Volume 1 (Music-Masters, 1989)
Live at the Village Vanguard (DCC, 1980/1991)
Lost Art (MusicMasters, 1990)
Mel Lewis (VSOP, 1957/1995)

Ramsey Lewis
The In Crowd (Argo, 1965/Chess, 1990)

Dave Liebman
Classic Ballads (Candid, 1991)
Homage to Coltrane (Owl/Blue Note, 1987)
Miles Away (Owl/Blue Note, 1995)
New Vista (Arkadia Jazz, 1997)
Return of the Tenor (Doubletime, 1996)
Songs for My Daughter (Soul Note, 1995)
A Tribute to John Coltrane (Columbia/Blue Note, 1987)
Voyage (Evidence, 1996)
West Side Story Today (Owl/Blue Note, 1990)

Abbey Lincoln
Straight Ahead (Candid, 1961/1988)
You Gotta Pay the Band (Verve, 1991)

Melba Liston
Earth Birth (Verve, 1997)
The Spirits of Our Ancestors (Antilles, 1992)
Tanjah (Verve, 1973/Polydor, 1995)
Uhuru Afrika/Highlife (Roulette, 1960)
Volcano Blues (Antilles, 1993)

Charles Lloyd
Charles Lloyd in the Soviet Union (Atlantic, 1967)
Forest Flower (Atlantic, 1967/Rhino, 1995)

Mike Longo
Dawn of a New Day (CAP, 1997)

Harold Mabern
Lookin' at the Bright Side (DIW/Disc Union, 1993)
Wailin' (Prestige, 1969/1970)

Kevin Mahogany
Another Time, Another Place (Warner Bros., 1997)

Mike Maineri
American Diary (NYC, 1996)
Blues on the Other Side (Argo, 1963)

Joe Maneri
Dahabenzapple (Hat Jazz, 1996)
Get Ready to Receive Yourself (Leo Lab, 1995)
In Full Cry (ECM, 1997)
Let the Horse Go (Leo Lab, 1996)

Albert Mangelsdorff
Art of the Duo (Enja, 1989)
Live in Tokyo (Enja, 1971/1995)

The Manhattan Transfer
The Manhattan Transfer Anthology: Down in Birdland (Rhino, 1992)
Vocalese (Atlantic, 1985)

Shelly Manne
At the Manne-Hole, Vol. 1 (Contemporary, 1961/OJC, 1992)
At the Manne-Hole, Vol. 2 (Contemporary, 1961/OJC, 1992)
"The Three" and "The Two" (Contemporary, 1954/OJC, 1992)
The West Coast Sound (Contemporary, 1955/OJC, 1988)

Joseph "Wingy" Manone
The Wingy Manone Collection, Vol. 3: 1934–35 (Collector's Classics, 1994)
Wingy Manone, 1934–35 (Classics, 1995)

Ray Mantilla
The Jazz Tribe (Red Records, 1992)

Rick Margitza
Game of Chance (Challenge, 1997)
Hands of Time (Challenge, 1995)
Hope (Blue Note, 1991)
This Is New (Blue Note, 1992)
Work It (SteepleChase, 1994)

Kitty Margolis
Straight up with a Twist (MAD-KAT, 1997)

Tania Maria
Piquant (Concord, 1981)
Taurus (Concord, 1981)

Dodo Marmarosa
The Legendary Dial Sessions, Volume 1 (Stash, 1987)

Wynton Marsalis
Black Codes (From the Underground) (Columbia, 1985)
Citi Movement (Columbia, 1993)
In This House, On This Day (Columbia, 1994)
Marsalis Standard Time: Volume 1 (Columbia, 1987)
Wynton Marsalis (Columbia, 1982)

Warne Marsh
Crosscurrents (Capitol, 1949)
Intuition (Capitol, 1996)

Claire Martin
Offbeat: Live at Ronnie Scott's Club (Linn, 1995)
Old Boyfriends (Honest, 1994)
The Waiting Game (Honest, 1992)

Mel Martin
Bebop and Beyond Plays Thelonious Monk (Mesa/Bluemoon, 1991)
Mel Martin Plays Benny Carter (Enja, 1996)

Masada
Bar Kokhba (Tzadik, 1996)
Eight/Het (DIW, 1997)
Five/Hei (DIW, 1995)
Nine/Tet (DIW, 1997)
One/Alef (DIW, 1994)
Seven/Zayin (DIW, 1995)
Six/Vav (DIW, 1995)
Three/Gimel (DIW, 1994)
Two/Beit (DIW, 1994)

Cal Massey
The Complete Africa/Brass Sessions (Impulse!, 1961)

MC Solaar
Qui Seme Le Vent Recolte Le Tempo (Polydor France, 1991)

Les McCann
Les McCann Anthology: Relationships (Atlantic, 1960/Rhino, 1993)

Susannah McCorkle
Easy to Love — The Songs of Cole Porter (Concord Jazz, 1996)
From Bessie to Brazil (Concord Jazz, 1993)
I'll Take Romance (Concord Jazz, 1992)
Let's Face the Music (Concord Jazz, 1997)
No More Blues (Concord Jazz, 1989)
Over the Rainbow — The Songs of E.Y. "Yip" Harburg (Jazz Alliance, 1980/1996)

The Songs of Johnny Mercer (Jazz Alliance, 1977/1996)
Thanks for the Memories—The Songs of Leo Robin (PA/USA, 1984)

Jack McDuff
Hot Barbeque/Live! (Prestige, 1966/Beat Goes Public, 1993)

Jimmy McGriff
The Dream Team (Milestone, 1997)
Road Tested (Milestone, 1997)
Starting Five (Milestone, 1987)

Ken McIntyre
Looking Ahead (Prestige, 1960/OJC, 1994)

Dave McKenna
A Celebration of Hoagy Carmichael (Concord Jazz, 1983/1994)
Dancing in the Dark (Concord Jazz, 1985/1990)
A Handful of Stars (Concord Jazz, 1993)
Live at Maybeck Recital Hall, Vol. 2 (Concord Jazz, 1990)
You Must Believe in Swing (Concord Jazz, 1997)

McKinney's Cotton Pickers
McKinney's Cotton Pickers—1928–1929 (Jazz Chronological Classics, 1994)
McKinney's Cotton Pickers—1929–1930 (Jazz Chronological Classics, 1994)

John McLaughlin
Bitches Brew (Columbia, 1970)
In a Silent Way (Columbia, 1969)

Jackie McLean
Complete Blue Note 1964–66 Jackie McLean Sessions (Mosaic, 1964–66)

Rene McLean
In African Eyes (Triloka, 1993)

Marian McPartland
The Benny Carter Songbook (Concord Jazz, 1990)
In My Life (Concord Jazz, 1993)
Live at Maybeck Recital Hall, Vol. 9 (Concord Jazz, 1991)
Piano Jazz: McPartland/Bill Evans (Jazz Alliance, 1978)
Piano Jazz: McPartland/Eubie Blake (Jazz Alliance, 1979)
Piano Jazz: McPartland/Jess Stacy (Jazz Alliance, 1981/1995)
Piano Jazz: McPartland/Lee Konitz (Jazz Alliance, 1991)

Piano Jazz: McPartland/Milt Hinton (Jazz Alliance, 1991)
Plays the Music of Billy Strayhorn (Concord Jazz, 1987)
Willow Creek and Other Ballads (Concord Jazz, 1985)

Joe McPhee
Inside Out (CIMP, 1996)
Linear B (hat ART, 1990)
Old Eyes & Mysteries (hat ART, 1992)
Oleo & A Future Retrospective (hat ART, 1993)
Topology (hat ART, 1989)

Charles McPherson
Bebop Revisited! (Prestige, 1964/OJC, 1992)
Con Alma! (Prestige, 1965/OJC, 1995)
First Flight Out (Arabesque, 1994)
Free Bop! (Xanadu, 1978)
Live in Tokyo (Xanadu, 1976)

Carmen McRae
The Great American Songbook (Atlantic, 1972/1990)

Jay McShann
The Early Bird Charlie Parker (MCA, 1982)

Brad Mehldau
Moving In (Concord Jazz, 1996)

Gil Melle
Patterns in Jazz (Blue Note, 1956)
Primitive Modern/Quadrama (Prestige, 1956/1957)

Helen Merrill
Brownie (Verve/Gitanes, 1994)
Collaboration (EmArcy, 1988)
The Complete Helen Merrill on Mercury (EmArcy, 1954–58/Mercury, 1994)
Dream of You (EmArcy, 1954–56/Mercury, 1992)

Glenn Miller
Glenn Miller: A Memorial (Bluebird, 1992)
Glenn Miller: The Lost Recordings (RCA, 1995)
The Spirit Is Willing (1939–42) (Bluebird, 1995)

Charles Mingus
Charles Mingus Presents Charles Mingus (Candid, 1961/1988)
The Complete 1959 CBS Charles Mingus Sessions (CBS/Mosaic, 1959)
Mingus Ah Um (Columbia, 1960/1990)

Thirteen Pictures: The Charles Mingus Anthology (Rhino, 1993)

Mingus Dynasty
Chair in the Sky (Elektra, 1979)

Bob Mintzer
Big Band Trane (DMP, 1996)
Departure (DMP, 1993)
First Decade (DMP, 1995)
Groovetown (Owl, 1996)
One Music (DMP 1991)
Only in New York (DMP, 1994)

Blue Mitchell
Big Six (Riverside, 1958/OJC, 1991)
Blue Soul (Riverside, 1959/OJC, 1993)
Blues on My Mind (OJC, 1958/1992)
The Cup Bearers (Riverside, 1962/OJC, 1993)
Down with It (Blue Note, 1965/Capitol, 1997)
Mapenzi (Concord Jazz, 1977)
Out of the Blue (Riverside/OJC, 1958)
A Sure Thing (Riverside, 1962/OJC, 1995)
The Thing to Do (Blue Note, 1964/1995)

Roscoe Mitchell
Hey Donald (Delmark, 1995)
Sound (Delmark, 1966/1996)
Sound Songs (Delmark, 1997)
This Dance Is for Steve McCall (Black Saint, 1993)

Hank Mobley
Soul Station (Blue Note, 1960)

Modern Jazz Quartet
The Complete Last Concert (Atlantic, 1974/1989)
Dedicated to Connie (Atlantic, 1995)
Django (OJC, 1955/1987)
Fontessa (Atlantic, 1956/1989)
For Ellington (Atlantic, 1988)

Grachan Moncur III
Evolution (Blue Note, 1963/1996)

Thelonious Monk
And the Jazz Giants (Riverside, 1987)
Art Blakey's Jazz Messengers with Thelonious Monk (Atlantic, 1957)
At Town Hall (Riverside, 1959)
The Best of Thelonious Monk: The Blue Note Years (Blue Note, 1991)
Big Band and Quartet in Concert (Columbia, 1964/1994)
Brilliant Corners (Riverside, 1956)
The Complete Blue Note Recordings (Blue Note, 1947–52, 1957–58)

COLLECTABLES RECORDS INC.
P.O. BOX 35
NARBERTH, PA 19072

THANK YOU for purchasing this compact disc. We hope that you enjoy it. If you would like to receive our **FREE** compact disc catalog or our **FREE** 7" vinyl singles catalog, please call us at:

TOLL FREE NUMBER

1-800-336-4627

Or fill out this card and mail it back to us:

Name: _____

Address: _____

City: _____ State: _____ Zip: _____

☐ PLEASE SEND ME A FREE COMPACT DISC CATALOG.
☐ PLEASE SEND ME A FREE 7" VINYL SINGLES CATALOG.

Compact Disc Title Purchased: _____

Where Item Was Purchased: _____

Comments & Suggestions: _____

COLLECTABLES RECORDS INC. P.O. BOX 35 NARBERTH, PA 19072
☎ (800) 336-4627 ☎ (610) 649-7565 FAX: (610) 649-0315

The Complete Riverside Recordings (Riverside/Fantasy, 1986)
5 by Monk by 5 (Riverside, 1959)
Genius of Modern Music, Volume 1 (Blue Note)
Genius of Modern Music, Volume 2 (Blue Note)
Live at the Five Spot: Discovery! (Blue Note, 1993)
Memorial Album (Milestone, 1982)
Miles & Monk at Newport (Columbia, 1994)
Misterioso (Riverside, 1958)
Monk's Dream (Columbia, 1963)
Monk's Music (Riverside, 1957)
Thelonious Alone in San Francisco (Riverside, 1959)
Thelonious Himself (Riverside, 1957)
Thelonious in Action (Riverside, 1958)
Thelonious Monk Plays Duke Ellington (Riverside, 1955)
The Unique Thelonious Monk (Riverside, 1956)

T.S. Monk
The Charm (Blue Note, 1995)

Monk Montgomery
Groove Yard (Riverside, 1961/1994)

Wes Montgomery
Bags Meets Wes! (Riverside, 1961/OJC, 1992)
Boss Guitar (Riverside, 1963/OJC, 1989)
Full House (Riverside, 1962/OJC, 1987)
The Incredible Jazz Guitar of Wes Montgomery (Riverside, 1960/OJC, 1987)
Portrait of Wes (Riverside, 1963/OJC, 1992)
So Much Guitar (Riverside, 1961/OJC, 1987)
Wes Montgomery: The Complete Riverside Recordings (Riverside, 1959–63/OJC, 1993)

Tete Montoliu
A Spanish Treasure (Concord, 1991)

James Moody
The Blues and Other Colors (OJC, 1957–1958/1997)
Don't Look Away Now! (OJC, 1969/1997)
Moody's Party (Telarc, 1995)
Return from Overbrook (Uni/Chess, 1958/1996)

Ralph Moore
Furthermore (Landmark, 1990)
Rejuvenate! (Criss Cross, 1989)

Airto Moreira
Encounters of the Fourth World (B&W Music, 1995)
Free (CTI, 1972/CBS, 1988)
Outernational Meltdown: Free at Last (B&W Music, 1995)

Joe Morello
Time Out (Columbia, 1959/1997)

Lee Morgan
Moanin' (Blue Note, 1958)
The Sidewinder (Blue Note, 1964)

Joe Morris
Flip & Spike (Riti, 1992)

Lawrence "Butch" Morris
Dust to Dust (New World, 1991)
Homeing (Sound Aspects, 1989)
Testament: A Conduction Collection (New World/Countercurrents, 1995)

Jelly Roll Morton
Anamule Dance: The Library of Congress Recordings, Volume 2 (Rounder, 1993)
The Jelly Roll Morton Centennial: His Complete Victor Recordings (RCA, 1990)
Jelly Roll Morton, Volume 1 (JSP, 1990)
Kansas City Stomp: The Library of Congress Recordings, Volume 1 (Rounder, 1993)
The Pearls: The Library of Congress Recordings, Volume 3 (Rounder, 1993)
Winin' Boy Blues: The Library of Congress Recordings, Volume 4 (Rounder, 1993)

Bob Moses
When Elephants Dream of Music (Gramavision, 1982/1993)

Bennie Moten
Basie Beginnings (1929–1932) (RCA, 1929–32)

George Mraz
Surge (Enja, 1992)

Gerry Mulligan
At Storyville (Pacific Jazz, 1957/Blue Note, 1990)
California Concerts, Volume 1 (Pacific Jazz, 1954/Blue Note, 1988)
California Concerts, Volume 2 (Pacific Jazz, 1954/Blue Note, 1988)
The Complete Pacific Jazz Recordings of the Gerry Mulligan Quartet with Chet Baker (Pacific Jazz, 1952–57/Blue Note, 1995)

What Is There to Say? (Columbia, 1959/1994)

Mark Murphy
Beauty and the Beast (Muse, 1986)
Mark Murphy Sings (Muse, 1976)
Rah! (Riverside, 1961/OJC, 1994)
Satisfaction Guaranteed (Muse, 1979)
That's How I Love the Blues! (Riverside/OJC, 1962)

David Murray
Ming (Black Saint, 1980)
Morning Song (Black Saint, 1984)

Naked City
Absinthe (Avant, 1993)
Grand Guignol (Avant, 1992)
Heretic (Avant, 1993)
Naked City (Nonesuch, 1989)

Ray Nance
The Blanton-Webster Band (RCA Bluebird, 1940–42/1986)

Theodore "Fats" Navarro
Fats Navarro and Tadd Dameron: The Complete Blue Note and Capitol Recordings (Blue Note, 1995)

Oliver Nelson
Afro-American Sketches (Prestige, 1961/OJC, 1993)
Blues and the Abstract Truth (Impulse!, 1961/1995)

Phineas Newborn Jr.
The Great Jazz Piano of Phineas Newborn Jr. (Contemporary, 1962)
Here Is Phineas: The Piano Artistry of Phineas Newborn Jr. (Atlantic, 1956)
A World of Piano (Contemporary, 1961)

Herbie Nichols
The Complete Blue Note Recordings (Blue Note, 1955–56/1997)
Love, Gloom, Cash, Love (Bethlehem, 1957)

Red Norvo
Just a Mood—The Red Norvo Small Bands (RCA/Bluebird, 1987)
The Red Norvo Trio with Tal Farlow and Charles Mingus (Savoy, 1950–1951)

NRG Ensemble
Hal on Earth (Abduction, 1995)

Anita O'Day
I Told Ya I Love Ya, Now Get Out (Sony, 1947/Signature, 1991)

Pick Yourself Up (Verve, 1956/1991)
Sings the Winners (Verve, 1963/1990)

King Oliver
King Oliver's Creole Jazz Band: 1923–1924 (Retrieval, 1997)

Original Dixieland Jazz Band
The Complete Original Dixieland Jazz Band (1917–1936) (RCA, 1995)
Original Dixieland Jazz Band: 75th Anniversary (Bluebird, 1917–21/RCA, 1992)

Kid Ory
Kid Ory's Creole Jazz Band (1954) (Good Time Jazz, 1991)
Ory's Creole Trombone: Greatest Recordings 1922–44 (ASV/Living Era, 1994)

Johnny Otis
The Johnny Otis Show Live at Monterey (Epic, 1970)

Oran "Hot Lips" Page
Basie Beginnings (1929–1932) (RCA, 1929–32)

Eddie Palmieri
Palmas (Elektra/Nonesuch, 1994)

Charlie Parker
Bird: The Complete Savoy Recordings (Savoy, 1944–48)
Bird/The Savoy Recordings (Master Takes) (Savoy, 1944–48/1985)
Charlie Parker with Strings: The Master Takes (Verve, 1950–52/1995)
The Complete Charlie Parker on Verve (Verve, 1946–54/1988)
Dizzy Gillespie: And His Sextets and Orchestra (Discovery, 1945–46/1988)
The Legendary Dial Masters (Jazz Classics, 1946–47/1994)
Summit Meeting at Birdland (Tristar, 1950/1997)

Leon Parker
Reach (Blue Note, 1995)

William Parker
Sunrise in the Tone World (AUM Fidelity, 1997)

Joe Pass
Chops (Pablo, 1978)
Duets (Pablo, 1996)
Guitar Virtuoso (Pablo, 1997)
I Remember Charlie Parker (Pablo, 1979)
Ira, George and Joe (Pablo, 1981/1994)

Joe Pass & Co.: Joe Pass Quartet Live at Yoshi's (Pablo, 1993)
Portraits of Duke Ellington (Pablo, 1974)
Roy Clark & Joe Pass Play Hank Williams (Ranwood, 1995)
Virtuoso (Pablo, 1974/1987)
Virtuoso Live! (Pablo, 1991)
Virtuoso #2 (Pablo, 1977/1987)
Virtuoso #3 (Pablo, 1992)
Virtuoso #4 (Pablo, 1993)
We'll Be Together Again (Pablo, 1983)

Jaco Pastorius
The Birthday Concert (Warner Bros., 1981/1995)
Jaco Pastorius (Epic, 1976/1987)

Gary Peacock
December Poems (ECM, 1979)

Duke Pearson
Now Hear This! (Blue Note, 1968)
The Phantom (Blue Note, 1968)
The Right Touch (Blue Note, 1967)

Ken Peplowski
Illuminations (Concord Jazz, 1991)
It's a Lonesome Old Town (Concord Jazz, 1995)
Ken Peplowski/Howard Alden: Concord Duo Series, Vol. 3 (Concord Jazz, 1993)
Live at Centre Concord: Encore! (Concord Jazz, 1995)
Mr. Gentle and Mr. Cool (Concord Jazz, 1990)
The Other Portrait (Concord Concerto, 1996)
Sonny Side (Concord Jazz, 1989)
Steppin' with Peps (Concord Jazz, 1993)

Art Pepper
The Art of Pepper (Blue Note, 1957/1988)
Art Pepper: The Complete Galaxy Recordings (Galaxy, 1989)
Art Pepper: The Complete Village Vanguard Sessions (Contemporary, 1977/1995)
Art Pepper+Eleven: Modern Jazz Classics (Contemporary, 1959/OJC, 1988)
The Artistry of Pepper (Pacific Jazz, 1957/1992)
The Complete Aladdin, Vol. 1: The Return of Art Pepper (Blue Note, 1957/Capitol, 1988)
Gettin' Together! (Contemporary, 1960/OJC, 1988)
Goin' Home (Galaxy, 1982/OJC, 1991)
Intensity (Contemporary, 1960/OJC, 1989)

Landscape (Galaxy, 1979/OJC, 1991)
Living Legend (Contemporary, 1975/OJC, 1990)
Meets the Rhythm Section (Contemporary, 1957/OJC, 1988)
Modern Art (Blue Note, 1957/1988)
Roadgame (Galaxy, 1981/OJC, 1993)
Smack Up (Contemporary, 1960/OJC, 1987)
Straight Life (Galaxy, 1979/OJC, 1990)
Tete-a-Tete (Galaxy/OJC, 1982)
Thursday Night at the Village Vanguard (Contemporary, 1977/OJC, 1992)
Tokyo Debut (Galaxy, 1977/OJC, 1995)
Winter Moon (Galaxy, 1980/OJC, 1991)

Ivo Perelman
Strings (Leo, 1997)
Tapeba Songs (Ibeji, 1996)

Danilo Perez
The Journey (Novus, 1994)
Panamonk (Impulse!, 1996)

Carl Perkins
Introducing Carl Perkins (Fresh Sound, 1955)

Oscar Peterson
At the Concertgebouw (Verve, 1957/1994)
History of an Artist (Pablo, 1972–74/1993)
How Long Has This Been Going On? (Pablo, 1978/1987)
Oscar Peterson & Clark Terry (Pablo, 1975/OJC, 1994)
Oscar Peterson & Harry Edison (Pablo, 1975/OJC, 1992)
Oscar Peterson et Joe Pass a la Salle Pleyel (Pablo, 1975/1997)
The Oscar Peterson Trio at Zardi's (Pablo, 1955/1994)
Oscar Peterson Trio + 1 (EmArcy, 1964/1984)
Plays Count Basie (Clef, 1956/Verve, 1993)
Plays the Gershwin Songbooks (Verve, 1952–59/1996)
Tracks (MPS, 1971/Verve, 1994)
The Trio (Pablo, 1973/1991)

Ralph Peterson Jr.
Triangular (Blue Note, 1989)

Flip Phillips
Real Swinger (Concord, 1988)
A Sound Investment (Concord, 1987)

Enrico Pieranunzi
Live in Castelnuovo (Siena Jazz, 1994)
Trioscape (YVP, 1995)

The George Russell Smalltet (Bluebird, 1987)
New York, N.Y. (Decca, 1959/MCA, 1990)
New York, N.Y./Jazz in the Space Age (MCA, 1973)
The Outer View (OJC, 1962/1994)

Joe Sample
Carmel (MCA, 1978)

David Sanchez
Street Scenes (Columbia, 1997)

Poncho Sanchez
Chile Con Soul (Concord Picante, 1990)
Conga Blue (Concord Picante, 1996)

Pharoah Sanders
Karma (Impulse!, 1969/1995)

Arturo Sandoval
Arturo Sandoval & the Latin Train (GRP, 1996)
The Classical Album (RCA Victor/Red Seal, 1994)
I Remember Clifford (GRP, 1992)
Reunion (Messidor, 1991)

Mongo Santamaria
AfroRoots (Prestige, 1958/1989)
Mongo's Greatest Hits (Fantasy, 1995)
Skins (Milestone, 1962/1976/1990)

Rob Schneiderman
Dark Blue (Reservoir, 1994)
Keepin' in the Groove (Reservoir, 1996)
New Outlook (Reservoir, 1988)

John Scofield
Groove Elation! (Blue Note, 1995)
Hand Jive (Blue Note, 1994)
Out Like a Light (Enja, 1981)
Quiet (Verve, 1997)
What We Do (Blue Note, 1993)

Shirley Scott
Blues Everywhere (Candid, 1992)
Soul Shoutin' (Prestige, 1963/1994)

Pete Selvaggio
Galleria (Koch Jazz, 1996)

Charlie Sepulveda
Heros (Telarc, 1994)

Shakti
The Best of Shakti (Columbia Records, 1975–1977)

Bud Shank
Brazilliance, Vol. 1 (Capitol, 1991)

Brazilliance, Vol. 2 (Capitol, 1991)
Tomorrow's Rainbow (Contemporary, 1989)

Sonny Sharrock
Ask the Ages (Axiom, 1991)
Guitar (Enemy, 1986)

Artie Shaw
The Last Recordings, Vol. 1: Rare & Unreleased (Music Masters, 1992)

Woody Shaw
Dark Journey (Muse, 1965–87/32 Jazz, 1997)
In My Own Sweet Way (In + Out, 1989)
Last of the Line (32 Jazz, 1997)
Moontrane (32 Jazz, 1997)

George Shearing
On a Clear Day (Concord, 1980/1993)

Archie Shepp
Goin' Home (SteepleChase, 1977)

John Sheridan
Livin' in a Great Big Way (Swing Out, 1991)
Something Tells Me (Arbors, 1997)

Matthew Shipp
Blink of an Eye (No More Records, 1997)
By the Law of Music (hat ART, 1997)
flight of i (DIW/Columbia, 1992)
Third Ear Recitation (DIW, 1993)

Bobby Short (vocalist)
50 by Bobby Short (Atlantic, 1950s–80/1986)
Late Night at the Café Carlyle (Telarc, 1992)

Wayne Shorter
Adam's Apple (Blue Note, 1966/1988)
Et Cetera (Blue Note, 1965/1995)
JuJu (Blue Note, 1964/1996)
Speak No Evil (Blue Note, 1964/1988)

Alan Silva
Unit Structures (Blue Note, 1966)

Horace Silver
Song for My Father (Blue Note, 1964)
Tokyo Blues (Blue Note, 1962)

Nina Simone
Anthology: The Colpix Years (Rhino 1996)

Zoot Sims
And the Gershwin Brothers (Pablo, 1975/OJC, 1990)
Blues for Two (Pablo, 1982/OJC, 1991)

For Lady Day (Pablo, 1978/1991)
Hawthorne Nights (Pablo, 1976/OJC, 1995)
Just Friends (Pablo, 1978/OJC, 1991)
Morning Fun (Black Lion, 1956/1990)
On the Korner (Pablo, 1994)
Passion Flower (Pablo, 1980/OJC, 1997)
Zoot Plays Soprano (Pablo, 1976/OJC, 1996)

Frank Sinatra
Best of the Capitol Years (Capitol, 1992)
The Capitol Years (Capitol, 1990)
The Columbia Years (1943–1952): The Complete Recordings (Columbia, 1993)
The Complete Capitol Singles Collection (Capitol, 1996)
Concepts (Capitol, 1992)
Frank Sinatra: The Capitol Collectors Series (Capitol, 1989)

Carol Sloane
Love You Madly (Contemporary, 1989)
Out of the Blue (Koch, 1962)
The Real Thing (Contemporary, 1990)
The Songs Carmen Sang (Concord Jazz, 1995)
The Songs Sinatra Sang (Concord Jazz, 1996)
When I Look in Your Eyes (Concord Jazz, 1991)

Bessie Smith
The Complete Recordings, Vol. 2 (Columbia/Legacy, 1991)
The Complete Recordings, Vol. 3 (Columbia/Legacy, 1992)

Jabbo Smith
The Complete Charlie Johnson Sessions (Hot 'n' Sweet)
The Complete 1929/1938 Sessions (Jazz Archives, 1993)

Jimmy Smith
Back at the Chicken Shack (Blue Note, 1960/1987)

Leo Smith
Reflectativity (Kabell, 1975)
Tao-Njia (Tzadik, 1993)

Lonnie Liston Smith
Astral Traveling (Flying Dutchman, 1973)
Expansions (Flying Dutchman, 1975)
Make Someone Happy (Doctor Jazz, 1986)
Visions of a New World (RCA, 1975)

Stuff Smith
Together! (Epic, 1963/Koch Classics, 1995)

Jim Snidero
Vertigo (Criss Cross Jazz, 1996)

Soft Machine
Triple Echo (Harvest, 1977)

Muggsy Spanier
The Ragtime Band Sessions (Bluebird, 1939/1995)

Glenn Spearman
The Fields (Black Saint, 1996)

Spirit of Life Ensemble
Live! At the 5 Spot (Rise Up Productions, 1996)

Splatter Trio
Duets, 1987 (Rastascan, 1987)
Guitarspeak (Rastascan, 1994)
Hi-Fi Junk Note (Rastascan, 1995)
Jump or Die—Splatter Trio & Debris Play Braxton (Music & Arts, 1994)
Other Destinations (Rastascan, 1989)

Mary Stallings
Spectrum (Concord Jazz, 1996)

Marvin Stamm
Bop Boy (MusicMasters, 1990)
Mystery Man (MusicMasters, 1992)

Dakota Staton
Dakota Staton (Muse, 1990)
The Late, Late Show (Capitol, 1957/Collectables, 1991)

John Stevens
Karyobin (Chronoscope, 1968)

Rex Stewart
Duke Ellington: Small Groups, Vol. 1 (Columbia/Legacy, 1991)

Sonny Stitt
Endgame Brilliance (32 Jazz, 1997)
Kaleidoscope (Prestige, 1950–52/1992)
The Last Sessions, Vols. 1 & 2 (Muse, 1982)
Sonny Stitt/Bud Powell/J. J. Johnson (Prestige, 1949–50/OJC, 1989)
Soul People (Prestige, 1964/1993)

Billy Strayhorn
. . . And His Mother Called Him Bill (Bluebird, 1967/1987)
The Far East Suite—Special Mix (Bluebird, 1966/RCA, 1995)

Lush Life (Red Baron, 1964–65/Sony, 1992)
Lush Life: The Billy Strayhorn Songbook (Verve, 1996)
Lush Life: The Music of Billy Strayhorn (Verve, 1992)
Plays the Music of Billy Strayhorn (Concord Jazz, 1987)
Something to Live For (Contemporary, 1987)

Frank Strozier
Fantastic Frank Strozier Plus (Vee-Jay, 1960)
March of the Siamese Children (Jazzland, 1962)

Joe Sullivan
Joe Sullivan, 1933–1941 (Classics, 1995)

Maxine Sullivan
Together: Maxine Sullivan Sings the Music of Jule Styne (Atlantic, 1987)
A Tribute to Andy Razaf (DCC, 1956/1991)

Sun Ra
Live at Montreux (Inner City, 1976)
Live at Pitt-Inn (DIW, 1988)
The Magic City (Saturn, 1965/Evidence, 1993)
Mayan Temples (Black Saint, 1990)
Other Planes of There (Saturn, 1964/Evidence, 1992)
Pathways to Unknown Worlds (Saturn, 1973/Impulse!, 1975)
Sun Song (Delmark, 1957/1990)
Sunrise in Different Dimensions (hat HUT, 1981)

John Surman
Adventure Playground (ECM, 1992)
Extrapolation (Polydor, 1969)

Steve Swallow
Songs with Legs (Watt Works, 1996)
Steve Swallow (ECM, 1994)

Lew Tabackin
I'll Be Seeing You (Concord, 1997)

Aki Takase
Clapping Music (Enja, 1995)

Tom Talbert
Bix Duke Fats (Modern Concepts, 1956/Sea Breeze, 1994)
Duke's Domain (Sea Breeze, 1994)

Horace Tapscott
Thoughts of Dar-Es Salaam (Arabesque, 1997)

Vladimir Tarasov
Atto III: Drumtheatre (Sonore, 1988/1994)

Buddy Tate
Buck and Buddy (Prestige Swingville/OJC, 1960)
Buck and Buddy Blow the Blues (Prestige Swingville/OJC, 1961)
Tate-a-Tate (Prestige/Swingville, 1960)

Art Tatum
The Complete Pablo Group Masterpieces (Pablo, 1991)
The Complete Pablo Solo Masterpieces (Pablo, 1991)

Art Taylor
Mr. A. T. (Enja, 1991)

Billy Taylor
Billy Taylor Trio (Prestige, 1952–1953/1995)
It's a Matter of Pride (GRP, 1994)
My Fair Lady Loves Jazz (Impulse!, 1965/1994)
Solo (Taylor-Made, 1988)
You Tempt Me (Taylor-Made, 1989)

Cecil Taylor
Alms/Tiergarten (Spree) (FMP, 1988)
Looking (Berlin Version) (FMP, 1990)
Nefertiti: The Beautiful One Has Come (Revenant, 1997)

John Tchicai
Afrodisiaca (MPS, 1969)
The New York Art Quartet and Imamu Amiri Baraka (ESP, 1964)

Richard Teitelbaum
Time Zones (Freedom/Arista, 1977)

Jacky Terrasson
Reach (Blue Note, 1995)

Lucky Thompson
Lucky Strikes (Prestige/OJC, 1964)
Tricotism (ABC Paramount, 1956/Impulse!)

Malachi Thompson
47th Street (Delmark, 1997)

Henry Threadgill
Carry the Day (Columbia, 1995)
Easily Slip into Another World (RCA/Novus, 1988)
Makin' a Move (Columbia, 1995)
Rag, Bush and All (RCA/Novus, 1989)
Song out of My Trees (Black Saint, 1994)
Spirit of Nuff . . . Nuff (Black Saint, 1991)

Frank Wess
Entre Nous (Concord, 1991)
Surge (Enja, 1992)
Tryin' to Make My Blues Turn Green (Concord, 1994)

Randy Weston
Portraits of Thelonious Monk: Well You Needn't (Verve, 1990)
The Spirits of Our Ancestors (Antilles, 1992)

Kenny Wheeler
Deer Wan (ECM, 1977)
Gnu High (ECM, 1975)
Music for Large and Small Ensembles (ECM, 1990)
The Widow in the Window (ECM, 1990)

Mark Whitfield
Forever Love (Verve, 1997)

Gerald Wiggins
Live at Maybeck Recital Hall, Vol. 8 (Concord Jazz, 1991)

Bob Wilber
Reunion at Arbors (Arbors, 1998)
Soprano Summit (Chiaroscuro, 1994)

Claude Williams
SwingTime in New York (Progressive, 1995)

James Williams
Alter Ego (Sunnyside, 1984)
Progress Report (Sunnyside, 1985)
Talkin' Trash (DIW/Columbia, 1993)

Jessica Williams
Higher Standards (Candid, 1997)

Joe Williams
Count Basie Swings, Joe Williams Sings (Verve, 1955/1993)
Every Day: Best of the Verve Years (Verve, 1954–89/1993)
Joe Williams and the Thad Jones/Mel Lewis Orchestra (Blue Note, 1966/1994)

Tony Williams
Lifetime (Blue Note, 1964/1987)
Spring (Blue Note, 1965)
The Tony Williams Lifetime Anthology (Verve, 1969–72/PolyGram Chronicles, 1997)

Larry Willis
Solo Spirit (Mapleshade, 1993)

Cassandra Wilson
World Expansion (By the M-Base Neophyte) (JMT, 1987)

Lem Winchester
Winchester Special (Prestige/New Jazz, 1959)

Jimmy Witherspoon
Goin' to Kansas City Blues (RCA, 1957)

Francis Wong
Ming (Asian Improv Records, 1995)
Pilgrimage (Music & Arts, 1997)

Rickey Woodard
The Tenor Trio (JMI, 1997)

Phil Woods
All Bird's Children (Concord, 1991)
Bop Stew (Concord, 1988)
Bouquet (Concord, 1989)
European Tour Live (Red Records, 1995)
Evolution (Concord, 1988)

Flowers for Hodges (Concord, 1991)
Pairing Off (Prestige, 1956/OJC, 1991)

Reggie Workman
Cerebral Caverns (Postcards, 1995)

World Saxophone Quartet
Revue (Black Saint, 1982)

Larry Young
The Art of Larry Young (Blue Note, 1992)
The Complete Blue Note Recordings of Larry Young (Mosaic, 1993)
Unity (Blue Note, 1965)

Lester Young
Carnegie Blues (PolyGram, 1946)
Complete Lester Young (Mercury)
Jazz Giants '56 (PolyGram, 1956)
Lady Day and Prez (Giants of Jazz)
Lester Young and Piano Giants (Pablo)
Lester Young Memorial Album (Fontana, 1936–40)
Lester Young Story, Vols. 1–3 (Columbia, 1977)
Pres and Teddy (Verve, 1956)
Prized Pres (Official, 1936–57)

Frank Zappa
Uncle Meat (Bizarre/Reprise, 1969/Rykodisc, 1995)
We're Only in It for the Money (Verve, 1968/Rykodisc, 1995)

John Zorn
Kristallnacht (Tzadik, 1995)
More News for Lulu (hat ART, 1992)
News for Lulu (hat ART, 1988)
Spy Vs. Spy (Elektra/Musician, 1989)
Yankees (Celluloid/OAO, 1983)

Can't remember what band a certain musician or vocalist is in? Wondering if a person has been in more than one band? The Band Member Index will guide you to the appropriate entry (or entries).

Abercrombie, John *See* Gateway

Abramovich, Uri *See* Ganelin Trio/Vyacheslav Ganelin

Aceyalone *See* Freestyle Fellowship

Ackley, Bruce *See* Rova Saxophone Quartet/Figure 8

Acuna, Alex *See* Weather Report

Adams, Clifford *See* Spirit of Life Ensemble

Adams, George *See* Mingus Dynasty; Phalanx

Adams, Steve *See* Rova Saxophone Quartet/Figure 8

Afifi, Osama *See* B Sharp Jazz Quartet

Agee, Stafford "Lil' D" *See* The Rebirth Brass Band/The Rebirth Jazz Band

Ahmed, Omar *See* Jackie McLean/Abdul Kareem/Omar Ahmed

AkLaff, Pheeroan *See* Air/New Air

Alexander, Aaron *See* Babkas

Ali, Amin *See* Music Revelation Ensemble; Phalanx

Ali, Rashied *See* Phalanx; Prima Materia

Allen, Daevid *See* Soft Machine

Allen, Eddie *See* Nancie Banks Orchestra

Altschul, Barry *See* Circle

Ambush, Scott *See* Spyro Gyra

Amendola, Scott *See* T.J. Kirk

Amis, Dave *See* Dedication Orchestra

Anderson, David *See* The Rippingtons

Anderson, Keith *See* Dirty Dozen Brass Band; The Rebirth Brass Band/The Rebirth Jazz Band

Andress, Tuck *See* Tuck & Patti

Andrews, Glen *See* The Rebirth Brass Band/The Rebirth Jazz Band

Andrews, Revert *See* Dirty Dozen Brass Band

Anger, Darol *See* Turtle Island String Quartet

Armstrong, Ralphe *See* Mahavishnu Orchestra

Austin, Kenneth *See* The Rebirth Brass Band/The Rebirth Jazz Band

Ayers, Kevin *See* Soft Machine

Aziz, Khalid Yasin Abdul *See* Larry Young/Khalid Yasin Abdul Aziz

Azzolina, Jay *See* Spyro Gyra

B.R.O.theR. ?uestion?uestlove *See* The Roots

Badrena, Manolo *See* Spyro Gyra; Weather Report

Bahri, Mamdouh *See* Spirit of Life Ensemble

Bailey, Victor *See* Steps Ahead; Weather Report

Bakr, Rashid *See* Other Dimensions in Music

Balakrishnan, David *See* Turtle Island String Quartet

Ballou, Dave *See* Either/Orchestra

Bang, Billy *See* The String Trio of New York

Bankhead, Harrison *See* Eight Bold Souls/Ed Wilkerson Jr.

Banks, Nancie *See* Nancie Banks Orchestra

Barber, Billy *See* Flim & the BB's

Barbuto, Steve *See* Avenue Blue/Jeff Golub

Bargero, Dave *See* Blood, Sweat & Tears

Barnes, Allan *See* The Blackbyrds

Baron, Art *See* Lincoln Center Jazz Orchestra

Baron, Joey *See* Joey Baron/Baron Down; Masada; Naked City

Barrero, Tony *See* Nancie Banks Orchestra

Barrett, Dave *See* Splatter Trio

Barron, Kenny *See* Sphere

Batiste, Lionel Paul Jr. *See* Dirty Dozen Brass Band

Bavan, Yolande *See* Lambert, Hendricks & Ross/Lambert, Hendricks & Bavan

Beckenstein, Jay *See* Spyro Gyra

Beckett, Harry *See* Dedication Orchestra

Beirach, Richie *See* Quest

Belgrave, Marcus *See* Lincoln Center Jazz Orchestra

Belogenis, Louie *See* Prima Materia

Bennink, Han *See* Clusone 3

Bentyne, Cheryl *See* The Manhattan Transfer

Berg, Bill *See* Flim & the BB's

Berger, David *See* Lincoln Center Jazz Orchestra

Bernard, Will *See* T.J. Kirk

Bernhardt, Warren *See* Steps Ahead

Bernstein, Steven *See* Lounge Lizards; Spanish Fly/Sex Mob

Berrios, Steve *See* Jerry Gonzalez & the Fort Apache Band

Bienenfeld, Lolly *See* Diva

Biggins, Jim *See* Avenue Blue/Jeff Golub

Black Thought *See* The Roots

Blackwell, Ed *See* Old & New Dreams

Blake, Michael *See* Lounge Lizards

Blake, Seamus *See* Mingus Big Band

Bley, Curt *See* NRG Ensemble/Hal Russell NRG Ensemble

Bloedow, Oren *See* Lounge Lizards

Bluiett, Hamiet *See* World Saxophone Quartet

Blume, Danny *See* Lounge Lizards

Blythe, Arthur *See* The Leaders; World Saxophone Quartet

Boisen, Myles *See* Splatter Trio

Borreo, Eliseo *See* Strunz & Farah

Bowden, Mwata *See* Eight Bold Souls/Ed Wilkerson Jr.

Bowie, Lester *See* Art Ensemble of Chicago; The Leaders

Bowne, Dougie *See* Lounge Lizards

Brand, Dollar *See* Abdullah Ibrahim/Dollar Brand

Branker, Tony *See* Spirit of Life Ensemble

Braxton, Anthony *See* Circle

Brecker, Michael *See* Steps Ahead

Brecker, Randy *See* Blood, Sweat & Tears

Briscoe, Chris *See* Dedication Orchestra

Brooks, Roy *See* M'Boom

Brötzmann, Peter *See* Globe Unity Orchestra; Last Exit

Brown, Everald *See* Spirit of Life Ensemble

Brown, Gary *See* Return to Forever

Brown, Les *See* Les Brown/Les Brown & His Band of Renown

Bryant, Clora *See* Jeannie & Jimmy Cheatham & the Sweet Baby Blues Band

Bufford, Greg *See* Spirit of Life Ensemble

Bullock, Beldon *See* Spirit of Life Ensemble

Burdelick, Chuck *See* NRG Ensemble/Hal Russell NRG Ensemble

Burnham, Charles *See* The String Trio of New York

Butterfly *See* Digable Planets

Byrd, Winston *See* Nancie Banks Orchestra; Spirit of Life Ensemble

Callender, Red *See* Jeannie & Jimmy Cheatham & the Sweet Baby Blues Band

Campbell, Roy *See* Other Dimensions in Music

Campbell, Tommy *See* Mingus Big Band

Candless, Paul *See* Oregon

Candoli, Conte *See* Supersax

Capitol Q *See* Dream Warriors

Carlson, John *See* Either/Orchestra

Carlton, Larry *See* Crusaders/Jazz Crusaders; Fourplay

Carmichael, Greg *See* Acoustic Alchemy

Carrott, Bryan *See* Lounge Lizards; Spirit of Life Ensemble

Carson, Reggie *See* B Sharp Jazz Quartet

Cartaya, Oscar *See* Spyro Gyra

Carter, Daniel *See* One World Ensemble; Other Dimensions in Music

Carter, Regina *See* Straight Ahead; The String Trio of New York

Castellanos, Gilbert *See* Black/Note

Catallo, Chet *See* Spyro Gyra

Cathcart, Patti *See* Tuck & Patti

Chambers, Joe *See* M'Boom

Chancler, Ndugu (Leon) *See* Weather Report

Chapman, Tyrus "T" *See* The Rebirth Brass Band/The Rebirth Jazz Band

Charig, Mark *See* Soft Machine

Chase, Allan *See* Prima Materia

Cheatham, Jeannie *See* Jeannie & Jimmy Cheatham & the Sweet Baby Blues Band

Cheatham, Jimmy *See* Jeannie & Jimmy Cheatham & the Sweet Baby Blues Band

Chekasin, Vladimir *See* Ganelin Trio/Vyacheslav Ganelin

Cherry, Don *See* Old & New Dreams

Christian, Emile *See* Original Dixieland Jazz Band

Cifelli, Barbara *See* The Jim Cifelli New York Nonet

Cifelli, Jim *See* The Jim Cifelli New York Nonet

Cintron, Tony *See* Spyro Gyra

Clark, Buddy *See* Supersax

Clark, Tom *See* BeebleBrox

Clarke, Kenny *See* Modern Jazz Quartet

Clarke, Stanley *See* Return to Forever

Clay, Gordon *See* Groove Collective

Clay, Omar *See* M'Boom

Clayton, Frank *See* The Revolutionary Ensemble

Clayton-Thomas, David *See* Blood, Sweat & Tears

Clements, Richard *See* Spirit of Life Ensemble

Cobham, Billy *See* Mahavishnu Orchestra

Cochran, Michael *See* Spirit of Life Ensemble

Cohen, Greg *See* Masada; The Orphan Newsboys

Coil, Pat *See* Tribal Tech

Coleman, Anthony *See* Masada

Coleman, Steve *See* M-Base Collective

Collins, Phil *See* Brand X

Colomby, Bobby *See* Blood, Sweat & Tears

Connors, Bill *See* Return to Forever

Conte, Luis *See* Strunz & Farah

Cooke, Steve *See* Soft Machine

Hunter, Charlie *See* T.J. Kirk

Hussain, Zakir *See* Shakti

Hyman, Jerry *See* Blood, Sweat & Tears

Ibarra, Susie *See* One World Ensemble

Immel, Dan *See* BeebleBrox

Ixoneztli, Luis Perez *See* Strunz & Farah

J-Sublimi *See* Freestyle Fellowship

Jackson, Ed *See* 29th Street Saxophone Quartet

Jackson, Isaiah *See* Eight Bold Souls/Ed Wilkerson Jr.

Jackson, Milt *See* Modern Jazz Quartet

Jackson, Ronald Shannon *See* Music Revelation Ensemble; Power Tools

Jacobs, Perk *See* The Blackbyrds

Jaffe, Allan *See* The Preservation Hall Jazz Band

James, Bob *See* Fourplay

James, Simon *See* Acoustic Alchemy

Jarman, Joseph *See* Art Ensemble of Chicago

Jarobi *See* A Tribe Called Quest

Jeanrenaud, Joan *See* Kronos Quartet

Jeffers, Jack *See* Nancie Banks Orchestra

Jenkins, Karl *See* Soft Machine

Jenkins, Leroy *See* The Revolutionary Ensemble

Jewell, Russell *See* Either/Orchestra

Johnson, Aaron *See* Nancie Banks Orchestra

Johnson, Alphonso *See* Weather Report

Johnson, Jimmy *See* Flim & the BB's

Johnson, Maya *See* The Billy Tipton Memorial Saxophone Quartet

Johnson, Richard *See* Nancie Banks Orchestra

Johnson, Vinnie *See* Nancie Banks Orchestra

Jones, Brad *See* The Jazz Passengers

Jones, Claude *See* McKinney's Cotton Pickers

Jones, Daryl *See* Steps Ahead

Jones, Percy *See* Brand X

Jones, Willie III *See* Black/Note

Joseph, Charles *See* Dirty Dozen Brass Band

Joseph, Kirk *See* Dirty Dozen Brass Band

Kamal *See* The Roots

Kareem, Abdul *See* Jackie McLean/Abdul Kareem/Omar Ahmed

Kashiwa, Jeff *See* The Rippingtons

Katsimpalis, Tom *See* Biota

Katz, Steve *See* Blood, Sweat & Tears

Kay, Connie *See* Modern Jazz Quartet

KCB *See* Us3

Kent, Stephen *See* Trance Mission

Kessler, Kent *See* NRG Ensemble/Hal Russell NRG Ensemble

Kibwe, Talib *See* Spirit of Life Ensemble

Kiely, Danny *See* BeebleBrox

Kienle, Peter *See* BeebleBrox

Killgo, Keith *See* The Blackbyrds

Kimball, Narvin *See* The Preservation Hall Jazz Band

King Lou *See* Dream Warriors

Kinsey, Scott *See* Tribal Tech

Kisor, Ryan *See* Mingus Big Band

Klugh, Earl *See* Return to Forever

Knepper, Jimmy *See* Mingus Dynasty

Knight, Joe *See* Nancie Banks Orchestra

Knox, Richard *See* Dirty Dozen Brass Band

Kochanski, Dave *See* The Rippingtons

Kohlhase, Charlie *See* Either/Orchestra

Konikoff, Eli *See* Spyro Gyra

Kooper, Al *See* Blood, Sweat & Tears

Kowald, Peter *See* Globe Unity Orchestra

Krakauer, David *See* Masada

Krauss, Briggan *See* Babkas; Spanish Fly/Sex Mob

Kuramoto, Dan *See* Hiroshima

Kuramoto, June *See* Hiroshima

Kurzdorfer, Jim *See* Spyro Gyra

LaCroix, Jerry *See* Blood, Sweat & Tears

Lacy, Ku-Umba Frank *See* Mingus Big Band

Ladybug/Mecca *See* Digable Planets

Laird, Rick *See* Mahavishnu Orchestra

Lake, Oliver *See* World Saxophone Quartet

Lambert, Dave *See* Lambert, Hendricks & Ross/Lambert, Hendricks & Bavan

LaRocco, Nick *See* Original Dixieland Jazz Band

Laronga, Barbara *See* Diva

Laswell, Bill *See* Material/Bill Laswell

Latimer, Emile Umbopha *See* Spyro Gyra

Ledford, Mark *See* M-Base Collective

Lee, Rodney *See* B Sharp Jazz Quartet

Leff, Jeff *See* Phillip Johnston/Big Trouble

Levin, Tony *See* Mujician; Steps Ahead

Levine, Jeff *See* Avenue Blue/Jeff Golub

Levy, Howard *See* Béla Fleck & the Flecktones

Levy, Lou *See* Supersax

Lewis, John *See* Modern Jazz Quartet

Lewis, Roger *See* Dirty Dozen Brass Band

Liebman, Dave *See* Quest

Lightsey, Kirk *See* The Leaders

Lima, Alyrio *See* Weather Report

Lindberg, John *See* The String Trio of New York

Lindsay, Arto *See* Lounge Lizards

Lipsius, Fred *See* Blood, Sweat & Tears

Lloyd, James K. *See* Pieces of a Dream

Loebs, Stacy *See* The Billy Tipton Memorial Saxophone Quartet

Long, Barbara *See* Hiroshima

Loose, John *See* Trance Mission

Lumley, Robin *See* Brand X

Lurie, Evan *See* Lounge Lizards

Lurie, Jessica *See* The Billy Tipton Memorial Saxophone Quartet

Lurie, John *See* Lounge Lizards

Lyons, Cliff *See* The Jim Cifelli New York Nonet

Mahone, James *See* Black/Note

Mainieri, Mike *See* Steps Ahead

Malik B. *See* The Roots

Mallery, Ajay "Grab-Grab" *See* The Rebirth Brass Band/The Rebirth Jazz Band

Malone, Tom *See* Blood, Sweat & Tears

Maricle, Sherrie *See* Diva

Marini, Lou Jr. *See* Blood, Sweat & Tears

Shezbie, Derrick "Khabuky" *See* The Rebirth Brass Band/The Rebirth Jazz Band

Shields, Larry *See* Original Dixieland Jazz Band

Shorter, Wayne *See* Weather Report

Shur, Itaal *See* Groove Collective

Siegel, Janis *See* The Manhattan Transfer

Silverman, Tracy *See* Turtle Island String Quartet

Simpson, Mel *See* Us3

Sipiagan, Alex *See* Mingus Big Band

Siraisi, Genji *See* Groove Collective

Sirone *See* Phalanx; The Revolutionary Ensemble

Slagle, Steve *See* Mingus Big Band

Smith, Marvin "Smitty" *See* M-Base Collective; Mingus Big Band

Smith, Nolan *See* Jeannie & Jimmy Cheatham & the Sweet Baby Blues Band

Smith, Steve *See* Steps Ahead

Soloff, Lew *See* Blood, Sweat & Tears; Lincoln Center Jazz Orchestra

Somer, Erwin *See* Free Music Quintet

Spangler, Bud *See* Tom Peron/Bud Spangler Quartet

Spaulding, James *See* World Saxophone Quartet

Speed, Chris *See* Masada

Squitero, Roger *See* Avenue Blue/Jeff Golub

Stein, Johay *See* Original Dixieland Jazz Band

Steward, Reginald *See* The Rebirth Brass Band/The Rebirth Jazz Band

Stewart, James *See* Spirit of Life Ensemble

Stone, Kim *See* The Rippingtons; Spyro Gyra

Strauss, Rick *See* Spyro Gyra

Strunz, Jorge *See* Strunz & Farah

Stubblefield, John *See* Jerry Gonzalez & the Fort Apache Band; Mingus Big Band

Sugarman, Neal *See* Nancie Banks Orchestra

Summer, Mark *See* Turtle Island String Quartet

Summers, Andy *See* Soft Machine

Swanson, Edwin *See* Nancie Banks Orchestra

Swell, Steve *See* Joey Baron/Baron Down; Phillip Johnston/Big Trouble

Tabb, Derrick "High Tower" *See* The Rebirth Brass Band/The Rebirth Jazz Band

Tarasov, Vladimir *See* Ganelin Trio/Vyacheslav Ganelin

Taylor, Chris *See* Either/Orchestra

Taylor, Dave *See* Mingus Big Band

Taylor, Louis *See* Jeannie & Jimmy Cheatham & the Sweet Baby Blues Band

Tchounga, Paul *See* Strunz & Farah

Temperley, Joe *See* Lincoln Center Jazz Orchestra

Terry, Kenneth "Kenniterry" *See* The Rebirth Brass Band/The Rebirth Jazz Band

Theberge, Chris *See* Groove Collective

Thielemans, Jean *See* Toots Thielemans/Jean Thielemans

Thomas, Fathead (George) *See* McKinney's Cotton Pickers

Thomas, John *See* Return to Forever

Thomas, Rob *See* The Jazz Passengers

Thompson, Chester *See* Weather Report

Threadgill, Henry *See* Air/New Air

Tinsley, James *See* Return to Forever

Tippett, Keith *See* Dedication Orchestra; Mujician

Toney, Kevin *See* The Blackbyrds

Towner, Ralph *See* Oregon

Towns, Efrem *See* Dirty Dozen Brass Band

Tronzo, David *See* Lounge Lizards; Spanish Fly/Sex Mob

Turner, John *See* Either/Orchestra

Turney, Norris *See* Lincoln Center Jazz Orchestra

Ulmer, James Blood *See* Music Revelation Ensemble; Phalanx

Vally, Roberto *See* Spyro Gyra

van der Locht, Peter *See* Free Music Quintet

Vandermark, Ken *See* NRG Ensemble/Hal Russell NRG Ensemble

Veal, Reginald *See* Lincoln Center Jazz Orchestra

Velez, Gerardo *See* Spyro Gyra

Vicek, Dana *See* Lounge Lizards

Vinayakram, T.H. (Vikku) *See* Shakti

Vitous, Miroslav *See* Weather Report

Voight, Andrew *See* Rova Saxophone Quartet/Figure 8

Von Essen, Oliver *See* Nancie Banks Orchestra

von Schlippenbach, Alexander *See* Globe Unity Orchestra

Vonnegut, Dan *See* BeebleBrox

Wadenius, George *See* Blood, Sweat & Tears

Waits, Freddy *See* M'Boom

Wakeman, Alan *See* Soft Machine

Walcott, Collin *See* Oregon

Walden, Michael Narada *See* Mahavishnu Orchestra

Wall, Jeremy *See* Spyro Gyra

Wall, Murray *See* The Orphan Newsboys

Walsh, Tom *See* Spyro Gyra

Ware, Bill *See* Groove Collective; The Jazz Passengers

Warleigh, Ray *See* Dedication Orchestra

Washington, Kenny *See* Lincoln Center Jazz Orchestra

Washington, Reggie *See* M-Base Collective

Watson, Bobby *See* 29th Street Saxophone Quartet

Webb, Nick *See* Acoustic Alchemy

Weber, Raymond *See* Dirty Dozen Brass Band

Weidman, James *See* M-Base Collective

Weiss, Jerry *See* Blood, Sweat & Tears

Weisz, Deborah *See* Diva

Wess, Frank *See* Lincoln Center Jazz Orchestra

Weston, Grant Calvin *See* Lounge Lizards; Phalanx

Wheeler, Kenny *See* Dedication Orchestra

BAND MEMBER INDEX

The Producer Index lists
the albums in MusicHound
Jazz that have a producer
noted for them. Under
each producer's name is
the name of the artist or
group in whose entry the
album can be found, fol-
lowed by the album title. If
an album is produced by
more than one individ-
ual/group, the album
name will be listed sepa-
rately under the names of
each of the producers.
(Note: The entry in which
the album can be found is
not necessarily that of the
artist or group whose
album it is. The album
could be a compilation
album, a film soundtrack,
an album on which the
artist or group appears as
a guest, etc. Consult the
artist or group's entry for
specific information.)

Greg Abate
Greg Abate, *Dr. Jekyll & Mr.
Hyde*

Ahmed Abdullah
Ahmed Abdullah, *Liquid Magic*

Michael Abene
Eddie Daniels, *Under the In-
fluence*
Mercer Ellington, *Digital Duke*
Diane Schuur, *A GRP Christ-
mas Collection*
Billy Taylor, *Homage*
Billy Taylor, *It's a Matter of
Pride*

Adam Abeshouse
Horace Tapscott, *Aiee! The
Phantom*

Alton Abraham
Sun Ra, *The Magic City*
Sun Ra, *Pathways to Un-
known Worlds*

Alan Abrahams
Dave Stryker, *T Time*

Muhal Richard Abrams
Muhal Richard Abrams, *Blu
Blu Blu*
Muhal Richard Abrams, *The
Hearinga Suite*
Muhal Richard Abrams, *Think
All, Focus One*

Herb Abramson
Ruth Brown, *Rockin' in
Rhythm—The Best of
Ruth Brown*
St. Elmo Hope, *The Final Ses-
sions*
Eddie Jefferson, *The Jazz
Singer*

Aceyalone
Freestyle Fellowship, *All Balls
Don't Bounce*

Pepper Adams
Pepper (Park) Adams, . . .
Plays Charlie Mingus

Julian "Cannonball" Adderley
Julian "Cannonball" Adderley,
Black Messiah
Don Byas, *A Tribute to Can-
nonball*
James Clay, *The Sound of the
Wide Open Spaces*
Dexter Gordon, *Resurgence*
Budd Johnson, *Budd Johnson
& the Four Brass Giants*
Sam Jones, *Down Home*
Clifford Jordan, *Spellbound*
Bud Powell, *A Portrait of The-
lonious*
Bud Powell, *A Tribute to Can-
nonball*

Nat Adderley
Nat Adderley, *Blue Autumn*

Jamey D. Aebersold
Jerry Bergonzi, *Just Within*

Air
Air/New Air, *Air Mail*
Air/New Air, *Air Song*

Toshiko Akiyoshi
Toshiko Akiyoshi, *Remember-
ing Bud: Cleopatra's
Dream*

Toshiko Akiyoshi, *Tanuki's
Night Out*

Tom Albach
Horace Tapscott, *At the Cross-
roads*
Horace Tapscott, *The Call*
Horace Tapscott, *Dial B for
Barbra*
Horace Tapscott, *Flight 17*
Horace Tapscott, *Live at
Lobero, Vol. 1*
Horace Tapscott, *Live at
Lobero, Vol. 2*
Horace Tapscott, *Live at the
I.U.C.C.*
Horace Tapscott, *Tapscott
Sessions, Vol. 8*

Alberto Alberti
Zusaan Kali Fasteau, *After Na-
ture*
Zusaan Kali Fasteau, *Manzara*
Joe Henderson, *An Evening
with Joe Henderson*
Ray Mantilla, *The Jazz Tribe*
Sphere, *Pumpkins Delight*
Phil Woods, *European Tour
Live*

Chris Albertson
Sweet Emma Barrett, *Sweet
Emma—New Orleans: The
Living Legends*
Meade "Lux" Lewis, *The Blues
Piano Artistry of Meade
Lux Lewis*
Howard McGhee, *Sharp Edge*

Spyro Gyra, *Spyro Gyra*
Spyro Gyra, *Three Wishes*

Joachim Becker
Charlie Mariano, *Innuendo*

Walter Becker
Pete Christlieb, *Apogee*
Dave Kikoski, *Persistent Dreams*
Warne Marsh, *Apogee*
Jeremy Steig, *Jigsaw*
Jeremy Steig, *You Wish*

Richie Beirach
Richie Beirach, *Antarctica*
Richie Beirach, *Self-Portraits*
Richie Beirach, *Sunday Songs*
Richie Beirach, *Trust*

Bob Belden
Bob Belden, *PrinceJazz*
Bob Belden, *Shades of Blue*
Bob Belden, *When Doves Cry: The Music of Prince*
Richie Cole, *Kush: The Music of Dizzy Gillespie*
Miles Davis, *Miles Davis & Gil Evans: The Complete Columbia Studio Recordings*
Peter Delano, *Bite of the Apple*
Marcus Printup, *Unveiled*
Bernard Purdie, *Soul to Jazz II*
Red Rodney, *Then and Now*
Renee Rosnes, *Ancestors*
Bill Stewart, *Snide Remarks*
Bill Stewart, *Telepathy*
Straight Ahead, *Dance of the Forest Rain*
Cassandra Wilson, *Rendezvous*

Vic Bellerby
Sidney Bechet, *Really the Blues*
Don Redman, *Doin' What I Please*

Louie Bellson
Louie Bellson, *Live at Joe Segal's Jazz Showcase*

Louis Belogenis
Prima Materia, *Bells*
Prima Materia, *Meditations*
Prima Materia, *Peace on Earth*

Gregg Bendian
Derek Bailey, *The Sign of 4*

Gregg Bendian, *Bang!*
Gregg Bendian, *Banter*
Gregg Bendian, *Counterparts*
Gregg Bendian, *Gregg Bendian's Interzone*
Gregg Bendian, *The Sign of 4*
Alex Cline, *Gregg Bendian's Interzone*

Brad Benedict
Frank Sinatra, *The Complete Capitol Singles Collection*

Sathima Bea Benjamin
Abdullah Ibrahim/Dollar Brand, *Ekaya (Home)*

Danny Bennett
Tony Bennett, *Astoria: Portrait of the Artist*

Dave Bennett
Art Hodes, *Pagin' Mr. Jelly*

Don Bennett
Don Bennett, *Solar: The Don Bennett Trio*

Robert Bennett
Cecilia Coleman, *Cecilia Coleman: Home*

Han Bennink
Clusone 3, *I Am an Indian*

David Benoit
David Benoit, *American Landscape*
David Benoit, *Christmastime*
David Benoit, *Urban Daydreams*
David Benoit, *Waiting for Spring*

George Benson
George Benson, *Big Boss Band*

Joachim Berendt
George Russell, *The George Russell Sextet at Beethoven Hall*
Sun Ra, *It's After the End of the World*
John Tchicai, *Afrodisiaca*

Steve Beresford
Steve Beresford, *Signals for Tea*
Dedication Orchestra, *Ixesha*

Dedication Orchestra, *Spirits Rejoice*

Bob Berg
Bob Berg, *Another Standard*
Bob Berg, *Backroads*
Bob Berg, *Cycles*
Bob Berg, *Enter the Spirit*
Bob Berg, *In the Shadows*

Thilo Berg
Jeff Hamilton, *Dynavibes*
Jeff Hamilton, *Jeff Hamilton Trio: Live!*
Allan Harris, *Here Comes Allan Harris*
Allan Harris, *It's a Wonderful World*

Ed Berger
Benny Carter, *Harlem Renaissance*

Borah Bergman
Borah Bergman, *Reflections on Ornette Coleman and the Stone House*

Stephen Bergman
Winston Walls, *Boss of the B-3*

Jerry Bergonzi
Jerry Bergonzi, *Lineage*
Jerry Bergonzi, *Standard Gonz*
Jerry Bergonzi, *Tilt*

Ron Berinstein
Shirley Horn, *I Thought About You*
Marlena Shaw, *It Is Love*
Joe Williams, *Every Night: Live at Vine St.*
Joe Williams, *In Good Company*

Sebastien Bernard
Frank Wright, *Kevin, My Dear Son*

Tim Berne
Babkas, *Fratelli*
Tim Berne, *. . . theoretically*
Mark Dresser, *Force Green*

Mike Berniker
Count Basie, *The Essential Count Basie, Vol. 1*
Count Basie, *The Essential Count Basie, Vol. 2*

Count Basie, *The Essential Count Basie, Vol. 3*
Johnny Coles, *The Warm Sound*
Cleo Laine, *A Beautiful Thing*
Michel Petrucciani, *Pianism*
Carol Sloane, *Out of the Blue*
Toots Thielemans/Jean Thielemans, *The French Collection—Jazz Impressions*
Ben Webster, *Ben & Sweets*

Steve Berrios
Steve Berrios, *And Then Some!*
Steve Berrios, *First World*

Sandro Berti-Ceroni
Steve Grossman, *In New York*
Steve Grossman, *Time to Smile*

Don Better
Holly Hofmann, *Just Duet*
Holly Hofmann, *Tales of Hofmann*

Big Apple Productions
Billy Pierce, *Epistrophy*
Pharoah Sanders, *Crescent with Love*

Scott Billington
Johnny Adams, *Good Morning Heartache*
Johnny Adams, *The Verdict*
Johnny Adams, *Walking on a Tightrope: The Songs of Percy Mayfield*
James Booker, *Resurrection of the Bayou Maharajah*
James Booker, *Spiders on the Keys*
Ruth Brown, *R+B = Ruth Brown*
Dirty Dozen Brass Band, *Jelly*
Dirty Dozen Brass Band, *Voodoo*

Dinky Bingham
Pieces of a Dream, *'Bout Dat Time*

Walter Bishop Jr.
Walter Bishop Jr., *Bish Bash*

Martin Bisi
Material/Bill Laswell, *Memory Serves*

Wild Bill Davison, *Wild Bill Davison with the Alex Welsh Band*
Peter Ecklund, *Ecklund At Elkhart*
Bud Freeman, *California Session*
Bud Freeman, *Superbud*
Milt Hinton, *Back to Bass-ics*
George Lewis (clarinet), *New Orleans Funeral and Parade*
Ed Polcer, *Jammin' a la Condon*
Hal Smith, *Hal Smith's Rhythmakers: California, Here I Come*
Dick Wellstood, *This Is the One . . . Dig!*

Thomas Buckner
Borah Bergman, *First Meeting*

Peter Bunetta
Kenny G, *Silhouette*

John Burk
Howard Alden, *Take Your Pick*
Karrin Allyson, *Fujitsu–Concord 27th Jazz Festival*
Louie Bellson, *Their Time Was the Greatest!*
Bob Berg, *Another Standard*
Kenny Burrell, *Lotus Blossom*
Allen Farnham, *Play-cation*
Jimmy Heath, *As We Were Saying . . .*
Walter Norris, *Hues of Blues*
Walter Norris, *Live at Maybeck Recital Hall, Vol. 4*
Walter Norris, *Sunburst*
Chris Potter, *Pure*
Chris Potter, *Unspoken*
Tito Puente, *Mambo of the Times*
Tito Puente, *Special Delivery*
Poncho Sanchez, *Conga Blue*
Poncho Sanchez, *Para Todos*
Poncho Sanchez, *Soul Sauce*
Gray Sargent, *The Gray Sargent Trio*
Stefan Scaggiari, *That's Ska-jar-e*
Marlena Shaw, *Dangerous*
Marlena Shaw, *Elemental Soul*
Carol Sloane, *When I Look in Your Eyes*
Mary Stallings, *Spectrum*

Mel Tormé, *Velvet and Brass*
Frank Vignola, *Appel Direct*
Frank Vignola, *Look Right, Jog Left*
Gerald Wiggins, *Soulidarity*
Rickey Woodard, *Yazoo*

Sonny Burke
Frank Sinatra, *Trilogy*

Peter Burli
Jack Walrath, *Hipgnosis*

Terry Burns
Laura Caviani, *Dreamlife*

Thomas C. Burns
Al Grey, *Fab*

Tom Burns
Bob Cooper, *Pete Christlieb–Bob Cooper: Live*

Ronnie Burrage
D.D. Jackson, *Bang On!*

Kenny Burrell
Kenny Burrell, *Ellington Is Forever, Volume I*
Kenny Burrell, *Ellington Is Forever, Volume II*
Kenny Burrell, *Then Along Came Kenny*

Gary Burton
Gary Burton, *Astor Piazzolla Reunion*
Gary Burton, *Departure*
Gary Burton, *Face to Face*
Eddie Daniels, *Benny Rides Again*

Dick Burwen
Dick Wellstood, *This Is the One . . . Dig!*

Lee Bush
Ernie Krivda, *The Art of the Ballad*
Ernie Krivda, *Golden Moments*
Ernie Krivda, *Perdido*

Dr. George Butler
Toshiko Akiyoshi, *Carnegie Hall Concert*
Terence Blanchard, *Terence Blanchard*
Nnenna Freelon, *Nnenna Freelon*

Bobby Hutcherson, *Live at Montreux*
Elvin Jones, *Live at the Lighthouse, Vols. 1 & 2*
Wynton Marsalis, *Live at Blues Alley*

Jonathan Butler
Jonathan Butler, *Head to Head*

Donald Byrd
The Blackbyrds, *Action/Better Days*
The Blackbyrds, *The Blackbyrds/Flying Start*
The Blackbyrds, *City Life/Unfinished Business*
Donald Byrd, *And 125th Street, N.Y.C.*

Don Byron
Don Byron, *Bug Music*
Don Byron, *No Vibe Zone*

George Cables
George Cables, *By George: George Cables Plays the Music of George Gershwin*

Ozzie Cadena
Julian "Cannonball" Adderley, *Spontaneous Combustion*
Dorothy Ashby, *The Jazz Harpist*
Mildred Bailey, *Me and the Blues*
Charlie Byrd, *Midnight Guitar*
Kenny Clarke, *Bohemia after Dark*
Ted Curson, *Fire down Below*
Curtis Fuller, *Blues-Ette*
Curtis Fuller, *The Curtis Fuller Jazztet with Benny Golson*
Curtis Fuller, *New Trombone*
Wilbur Harden, *Mainstream 1958—The East Coast Jazz Scene*
Wilbur Harden, *Tanganyika Strut*
Roy Haynes, *Cracklin'*
Red Holloway, *The Burner*
Red Holloway, *Live!*
Willis "Gator Tail" Jackson, *Gentle Gator*
Willis "Gator Tail" Jackson, *Willis Jackson with Pat Martino*
Hank Jones, *Quartet/Quintet*
Lee Morgan, *A-1*

Herbie Nichols, *I Just Love Jazz Piano*
Sam Price, *Rib Joint*
Red Rodney, *Fiery*
Shirley Scott, *Soul Shoutin'*
Sonny Stitt, *Night Letter*
Sonny Stitt, *Soul People*
Bobby Timmons, *Workin' Out*
George Wallington, *Jazz at Hotchkiss*
Jimmy Witherspoon, *Blues around the Clock*

Uri Caine
Uri Caine, *Sphere Music*

Richard Calandra
Spyro Gyra, *Access All Areas*
Spyro Gyra, *Alternating Currents*
Spyro Gyra, *Breakout*
Spyro Gyra, *Catching the Sun*
Spyro Gyra, *Morning Dance*
Spyro Gyra, *Spyro Gyra*

Jorge Calandrelli
Eddie Daniels, *Breakthrough*

Joey Calderazzo
Joey Calderazzo, *The Traveler*

Dominic Camardella
Ottmar Liebert/Luna Negra, *Solo para Ti*
Willie & Lobo, *Between the Waters*

Ruth Cameron
Charlie Haden, *Charlie Haden, the Montréal Tapes with Gonzalo Rubalcaba and Paul Motian*
Charlie Haden, *Night and the City*
Charlie Haden, *Now Is the Hour*
Ernie Watts, *Now Is the Hour*

Dick Campbell
Ken Nordine, *Colors*

Gigi Campi
Ernest Harold "Benny" Bailey, *Fire, Heat and Guts*

Scott A. Cannady
Pieces of a Dream, *'Bout Dat Time*

Steven Cantor
Lyle Mays, *Lyle Mays*

Roberto Capasso
Bix Beiderbecke, *The Complete New Orleans Rhythm Kings, Vol. 2 (1923) /The Complete Wolverines (1924)*
Freddie Keppard, *The Complete Freddie Keppard, 1923–27*

Arnold S. Caplin
Eubie Blake, *The Greatest Ragtime of the Century*
Eubie Blake, *Memories of You*
Scott Joplin, *Elite Syncopations, Classic Ragtime from Rare Piano Rolls*
Scott Joplin, *The Entertainer, Classic Ragtime from Rare Piano Rolls*
Scott Joplin, *King of the Ragtime Writers*
Charlie Rouse, *Les Jazz Modes*
Fats Waller, *Low Down Papa*

Michael Caplin
Dave Kikoski, *Dave Kikoski*

Andrew Caploe
Phillip Johnston/Big Trouble, *Flood at the Ant Farm*
Phillip Johnston/Big Trouble, *The Unknown*

Frank Capp
Frank Capp, *The Frank Capp Juggernaut: In a Hefti Bag*
Frank Capp, *Frank Capp Juggernaut: Play It Again, Sam*
Frank Capp, *Frank Capp Quartet Featuring Rickey Woodard: Quality Time*
Frank Capp, *Juggernaut Strikes Again!*

Alyson L. Careaga
Charles Gayle, *Everything*

Caribbean Jazz Project
Paquito D'Rivera, *The Caribbean Jazz Project*
Andy Narell, *The Caribbean Jazz Project*

Larry Carlton
Larry Carlton, *Discovery*

Larry Carlton, *Last Night*
Lee Ritenour, *Larry and Lee*

Judy Carmichael
Judy Carmichael, *Judy Carmichael . . . and Basie Called Her Stride*

Hope Carr
Don Byron, *No Vibe Zone*

Terri Lyne Carrington
Dianne Reeves, *Art + Survival*

Bakida Carroll
Bakida Carroll, *Door of the Cage*
Bakida Carroll, *Shadows and Reflections*

Phil Carroll
Ed Polcer, *Ed Polcer's All-Stars: Coast to Coast Swingin' Jazz*
Ed Polcer, *Ed Polcer's All-Stars: Some Sunny Day*

Benny Carter
Benny Carter, *The Best of Benny Carter*
Benny Carter, *Live and Well in Japan*

Betty Carter
Betty Carter, *The Audience with Betty Carter*
Betty Carter, *The Betty Carter Album*
Betty Carter, *Droppin' Things*
Betty Carter, *Look What I Got*
Lewis Nash, *Look What I Got*

Joe Carter
Art Farmer, *Art Farmer, Lee Konitz with the Joe Carter Quartet & Trio*

John Carter
Bobby Bradford, *Dauwhe*
John Carter, *Dauwhe*

Regina Carter
Regina Carter, *Something for Grace*

Ron Carter
Ron Carter, *The Bass and I*
Ron Carter, *Etudes*
Ron Carter, *Jazz, My Romance*
Christopher Hollyday, *Reverence*

Helen Merrill, *Duets*

Oscar Castro-Neves
Joe Henderson, *Double Rainbow*
Toots Thielemans/Jean Thielemans, *Brasil Project*
Toots Thielemans/Jean Thielemans, *Brasil Project II*

Patti Cathcart
Tuck & Patti, *Dream*
Tuck & Patti, *Love Warriors*

Eulis Cathey
Gary Bartz, *Blues Chronicles: Tales of Life*
Antonio Hart, *For Cannonball & Woody*
Joe Williams, *Ballad and Blues Master*

Dave Caughren
Earl "Fatha" Hines, *Piano Solos*

David Cavanaugh
Benny Goodman, *Hello Benny*
Benny Goodman, *Made in Japan*
Frank Sinatra, *Concepts*

Laura Caviani
Laura Caviani, *Dreamlife*

Malcolm Cecil
Ginger Baker, *Falling off the Roof*
Gil Scott-Heron, *1980*

Ilana Pelzig Cellum
Marc Ribot, *Solo Guitar Works of Frantz Casseus*

Yves Chamberland
Stephane Grappelli, *Flamingo*
Steve Grossman, *In New York*

Joe Chambers
John Zorn, *The Colossal Saxophone Sessions*

Emmanuel Chamboredon
Toots Thielemans/Jean Thielemans, *Do Not Leave Me*

Channel Classics Studio
Willem Breuker, *De Onderste Steen*

Thomas Chapin
Thomas Chapin, *Insomnia*
Thomas Chapin, *Sky Piece*
Thomas Chapin, *You Don't Know Me*

Denis Charles
Joel Forrester, *No . . . Really!*

Teddy Charles
Pepper (Park) Adams, *. . . Plays Charlie Mingus*
Teddy Charles, *Collaboration West*
Teddy Charles, *Wardell Gray Memorial, Vol. 2*
Booker Ervin, *The Book Cooks*
Wardell Gray, *Wardell Gray Memorial Album, Volume 1*
Booker Little, *Booker Little and Friend*
Jimmy Raney, *Two Guitars*

Sam Charters
Dave Burrell, *Brother to Brother*
Dave Burrell, *Daybreak*

Allan Chase
Allan Chase, *Dark Clouds with Silver Linings*

Jay Chattaway
Maynard Ferguson, *Conquistador*

Don Cherry
Don Cherry, *MultiKulti*
Don Cherry, *Relativity Suite*

David Chesky
Ana Caram, *Maracanã*
Ana Caram, *The Other Side of Jobim*
Ana Caram, *Rio after Dark*
Eddie Daniels, *Real Time*
Paquito D'Rivera, *Havana Café*
Paquito D'Rivera, *Portraits of Cuba*
Paquito D'Rivera, *Tico! Tico!*
Johnny Frigo, *Debut of a Legend*
Johnny Frigo, *Live from Studio in New York City*
Fred Hersch, *The Fred Hersch Trio Plays . . .*
Peggy Lee, *Moments like This*
Red Rodney, *Then and Now*

John Coltrane, *The New Wave in Jazz*
Eddie Condon, *The Complete CBS Recordings of Eddie Condon and His All-Stars*
Chick Corea, *Now He Sings, Now He Sobs*
Tadd Dameron, *The Complete Blue Note and Capitol Recordings of Fats Navarro and Tadd Dameron*
Miles Davis, *The Complete Live at the Plugged Nickel 1965*
Miles Davis, *Highlights from the Plugged Nickel*
Buddy DeFranco, *The Complete Verve Recordings of Buddy DeFranco Quartet/Quintet with Sonny Clark*
Eric Dolphy, *The Complete 1961 Village Vanguard Recordings*
Kevin Eubanks, *Live at Bradley's*
Gil Evans, *The Individualism of Gil Evans*
Gil Evans, *Out of the Cool*
George Freeman, *Birth Sign*
Curtis Fuller, *The Complete Blue Note/United Artists Curtis Fuller Sessions*
Dizzy Gillespie, *Diz 'n' Bird at Carnegie Hall*
Benny Goodman, *Benny Goodman: Complete Capitol Small Group Recordings*
Dexter Gordon, *The Complete Blue Note Sixties Sessions*
Benny Green, *Kaleidoscope*
Benny Green, *That's Right!*
Sir Roland Hanna, *Perugia*
Billy Hart, *Quartets: Live at the Village Vanguard*
Julius Hemphill, *Reflections*
Joe Henderson, *State of the Tenor*
Woody Herman, *Keeper of the Flame: Complete Capitol Recordings of the Four Brothers Band*
Art Hodes, *The Complete Art Hodes Blue Note Sessions*

Bobby Hutcherson, *Manhattan Moods*
Joseph Jarman, *Fanfare for the Warriors*
Thad Jones, *The Complete Blue Note/UA/Roulette Recordings of Thad Jones*
Thad Jones, *The Complete Solid State Recordings of the Thad Jones/Mel Lewis Orchestra*
Charles Lloyd, *A Night in Copenhagen*
Joe Lovano, *Quartets*
Warne Marsh, *Intuition*
Pat Martino, *Consciousness*
Cal Massey, *!Caramba!*
Thelonious Monk, *The Complete Blue Note Recordings*
Thelonious Monk, *Live at the Five Spot: Discovery!*
Theodore "Fats" Navarro, *The Complete Fats Navarro and Tadd Dameron on Blue Note and Capitol*
Herbie Nichols, *The Complete Blue Note Recordings*
Charlie Parker, *Diz 'n' Bird at Carnegie Hall*
Duke Pearson, *I Don't Care Who Knows It*
Don Pullen, *New Beginnings*
Don Pullen, *Random Thoughts*
Dizzy Reece, *Blues in Trinity*
Dianne Reeves, *I Remember*
Sam Rivers, *Wildflowers: The New York Loft Jazz Sessions*
Max Roach, *Percussion Bitter Sweet*
Shorty Rogers, *The Complete Atlantic and EMI Jazz Recordings of Shorty Rogers*
Woody Shaw, *Bemsha Swing*
Nina Simone, *At the Village Gate*
Jack Teagarden, *The Complete Capitol Fifties Jack Teagarden Sessions*
Richard Teitelbaum, *Time Zones*
McCoy Tyner, *Infinity*
McCoy Tyner, *Soliloquy*

Randy Weston, *Uhura Africa/Highlife*
Tony Williams, *Best Of*

John Cutler
Rob Wasserman, *Bob Weir/Rob Wasserman: Live*
Rob Wasserman, *Trios*

Miriam Cutler
Shirley Horn, *I Thought About You*
Joe Williams, *Every Night: Live at Vine St.*
Joe Williams, *In Good Company*

Gene Czerwinski
Stan Kenton, *Stan Kenton 50th Anniversary Celebration: The Best of Back to Balboa*

Paquito D'Rivera
Paquito D'Rivera, *Bebo Rides Again*
Paquito D'Rivera, *Havana Café*
Paquito D'Rivera, *A Night in Englewood*
Paquito D'Rivera, *Paquito D'Rivera Presents: Forty Years of Cuban Jam Session*
Paquito D'Rivera, *Tico! Tico!*
Bebo Valdes, *Bebo Rides Again*

Claire Daly
Joel Forrester, *No . . . Really!*

Foppe Damste
Marion Brown, *Porto Nova*

Helen Oakley Dance
Barney Bigard, *Duke Ellington: Small Groups, Vol. 1*

Stanley Dance
Paul Gonsalves, *Mexican Bandit Meets Pittsburgh Pirate*
Earl "Fatha" Hines, *Tour de Force*
Earl "Fatha" Hines, *Tour de Force Encore*

Howard Danchik
Rob Wasserman, *Bob Weir/Rob Wasserman: Live*

Eddie Daniels
Eddie Daniels, *Beautiful Love*
Eddie Daniels, *Benny Rides Again*
Eddie Daniels, *Breakthrough*
Eddie Daniels, *Under the Influence*

John Dankworth
Cleo Laine, *A Beautiful Thing*
Cleo Laine, *Blue & Sentimental*

Peter Danstrup
John Tchicai, *Grandpa's Spells*

Russ Dantzler
Claude Williams, *King of Kansas City*
Claude Williams, *Live at J's, Vol. 1*
Claude Williams, *SwingTime in New York*

James Dapogny
James Dapogny, *Hot Club Stomp*
James Dapogny, *Laughing at Life*
James Dapogny, *On the Road*
James Dapogny, *Original Jelly Roll Blues*

Mason Daring
Butch Thompson, *Butch and Doc*
Butch Thompson, *The 88's: Good Old New York*
Butch Thompson, *Thompson Plays Joplin*

Dave G
Clever Jeff, *Jazz Hop Soul*

Kenny Davern
Kenny Davern, *Breezin' Along*
Kenny Davern, *Kenny Davern and the Rhythm Men*
Kenny Davern, *Stretchin' Out*
Bob Wilber, *Reunion at Arbors*

Martin Davidson
John Carter, *Tandem 1 & 2*

Bobby Gordon, *Don't Let It End*
Bobby Gordon, *The Music of Pee Wee Russell*
Al Grey, *Matzoh and Grits*
Bob Haggart, *Bob Haggart's Swing Three: Hag Leaps In*
Rebecca Kilgore, *I Saw Stars*
John Sheridan, *Two Sleepy People*
Bob Wilber, *Bean: Bob Wilber's Tribute to Coleman Hawkins*

Rachel Domber
Dan Barrett, *Jubilesta!*
Dan Barrett, *Two Sleepy People*
Ruby Braff, *Being with You*
Ruby Braff, *Calling Berlin, Volume 1*
Ruby Braff, *Calling Berlin, Volume 2*
John Bunch, *John Bunch Solo*
John Bunch, *Struttin'*
David Frishberg, *Double Play*
Bobby Gordon, *Bobby Gordon Plays Bing*
Bobby Gordon, *Don't Let It End*
Bobby Gordon, *The Music of Pee Wee Russell*
Al Grey, *Matzoh and Grits*
Bob Haggart, *Bob Haggart's Swing Three: Hag Leaps In*
Rebecca Kilgore, *I Saw Stars*
John Sheridan, *Two Sleepy People*
Bob Wilber, *Bean: Bob Wilber's Tribute to Coleman Hawkins*

Frank Donovan
Jimmy Dorsey, *Perfidia*

Michael Dorf
Charles Gayle, *Avant Knitting*

Adam Dorn
The Jazz Passengers, *Individually Twisted*

Joel Dorn
Don Braden, *Organic*
Gary Burton, *Alone at Last*
John Coltrane, *The Heavyweight Champion: The Complete Atlantic Recordings*
Hank Crawford, *Mr. Blues Plays Lady Soul*
Eddie Harris, *Electrifying Eddie Harris/Plug Me In*
Billie Holiday, *The Complete Commodore Recordings*
The Jazz Passengers, *Individually Twisted*
Rahsaan Roland Kirk, *The Case of the 3-Sided Dream in Audio Color*
Rahsaan Roland Kirk, *Does Your House Have Lions: The Rahsaan Roland Kirk Anthology*
Rahsaan Roland Kirk, *The Inflated Tear*
Yusef Lateef, *The Complete Yusef Lateef*
Yusef Lateef, *The Doctor Is in . . . and Out*
Yusef Lateef, *Hush 'n' Thunder*
Yusef Lateef, *The Man with the Big Front Yard*
Yusef Lateef, *Yusef Lateef's Detroit*
Hubert Laws, *The Laws of Jazz/Flute By-Laws*
Pat Martino, *Bar Wars*
Pat Martino, *Heart & Head*
Les McCann, *Layers*
Les McCann, *Swiss Movement: Montreux 30th Anniversary Edition*
David "Fathead" Newman, *House of David*
David "Fathead" Newman, *It's Mister Fathead*
David "Fathead" Newman, *Lone Star Legend*
Leon Parker, *Above & Below*
Leon Parker, *Belief*
Woody Shaw, *Dark Journey*
Woody Shaw, *Last of the Line*
Woody Shaw, *Moontrane*
Leroy Vinnegar, *Swiss Movement*
Jessica Williams, *Epistrophy*
Joe Zawinul, *Rise & Fall of the Third Stream/Money in the Pocket*

Bob Dorough
Bob Dorough, *Schoolhouse Rock!*

Frank Dorritie
Al Cohn, *Standards of Excellence*
Barney Kessel, *Solo*

Alan Douglas
Dave Burrell, *High One High Two*
Chick Corea, *Turkish Women at the Bath*
Kenny Dorham, *Matador/Inta Something*
Duke Ellington, *Money Jungle*
King Pleasure, *Moody's Mood for Love*
Ken McIntyre, *The Complete United Artists Sessions*
Sam Rivers, *Wildflowers: The New York Loft Jazz Sessions*
Billy Strayhorn, *The Peaceful Side*

Dave Douglas
Dave Douglas/Tiny Bell Trio/New & Used, *Five*
Dave Douglas/Tiny Bell Trio/New & Used, *Live in Europe*
Dave Douglas/Tiny Bell Trio/New & Used, *Serpentine*
Myra Melford, *The Same River, Twice*

Tom Dowd
John Lewis, *The Wonderful World of Jazz*
Herbie Mann, *Memphis Underground*

Will Downing
Will Downing, *Love's the Place to Be*

Hamid Drake
Peter Brotzmann, *Dried Rat Dog*

Dream Warriors
Dream Warriors, *And Now the Legacy Begins*
Dream Warriors, *Subliminal Simulation*

Dreams
Michael Brecker, *Dreams*

Derek Drescher
Mujician, *The Journey*

Mark Dresser
Mark Dresser, *The Cabinet of Dr. Caligari*
Mark Dresser, *Force Green*
Mark Dresser, *Invocation*

Francis Dreyfus
Benny Golson, *Domingo*
Stephane Grappelli, *Flamingo*

Frank Driggs
Lloyd "Tiny" Grimes, *I Miss You So*
Fletcher Henderson, *A Study in Frustration*
Earl "Fatha" Hines, *Live at the Village Vanguard*
Johnny Hodges, *Hodge Podge*

Skip Drinkwater
The Visitors, *In My Youth*
The Visitors, *Neptune*

Ray Drummond
Ray Drummond, *Continuum*
Ray Drummond, *The Essence*
Ray Drummond, *Excursion*
Ray Drummond, *Vignettes*
Horace Tapscott, *Thoughts of Dar-Es Salaam*

Andrea du Plessis
Doc Cheatham, *Doc Cheatham & Nicholas Payton*
Butch Thompson, *Butch and Doc*

Steven Dubin
Najee, *Just an Illusion*

Marty Duda
Bill Doggett, *The Right Choice*

George Duke
The Blackbyrds, *Action/Better Days*
Angela Bofill, *Tell Me Tomorrow*
Randy Brecker, *Detente*
George Duke, *The Clarke/Duke Project*
George Duke, *Muir Woods Suite*
Rachelle Ferrell, *Rachelle Ferrell*
Everette Harp, *Everette Harp*
Hiroshima, *Go*
George Howard, *Attitude Adjustment*

Don Grusin
David Benoit, *Urban Day-
dreams*

Vince Guaraldi
Vince Guaraldi, *A Charlie
Brown Christmas*
Vince Guaraldi, *A Flower Is a
Lovesome Thing*

Jean-Paul Guiter
Sidney Bechet, *The Complete,
Vol. 1 & 2*
Sidney Bechet, *The Complete,
Vol. 3 & 4*
Sidney Bechet, *The Complete,
Vol. 5 & 6*
Artie Shaw, *The Indispensable
Artie Shaw: 1944–45*

Onaje Allan Gumbs
Stanley Jordan, *Bolero*
Vanessa Rubin, *Pastiche*
Vanessa Rubin, *Soul Eyes*

Tom Guralnick
Tom Guralnick, *Broken Dances
for Muted Pieces*
Tom Guralnick, *Pitchin'*

Guru
Gang Starr, *Daily Operation*
Gang Starr, *Guru's Jazzmatazz:
Vol. I*
Gang Starr, *Hard to Earn*
Gang Starr, *No More Mr. Nice
Guy*

O. Gust
Pepper (Park) Adams, *En-
counter!*

Mladen Gutesha
Ernest Harold "Benny" Bailey,
Islands

John Guth
The Jim Cifelli New York
Nonet, *Bullet Train*

Tommy Gwaltney
Buck Clayton, *Goin' to Kansas
City*

Gary Haase
Lionel Hampton, *For the Love
of Music*

Charlie Haden
Charlie Haden, *Beyond the
Missouri Sky*

Charlie Haden, *Charlie Haden,
the Montréal Tapes with
Gonzalo Rubalcaba and
Paul Motian*
Charlie Haden, *Haunted Heart*
Charlie Haden, *Night and the
City*
Charlie Haden, *Now Is the
Hour*
Hank Jones, *Steal Away*
Pat Metheny, *Beyond the Mis-
souri Sky (Short Stories)*
Ernie Watts, *Now Is the Hour*

John Haeny
John Klemmer, *Fresh Feathers*

Roy Halee
Blood, Sweat & Tears, *Blood,
Sweat & Tears 3*

Doug Hall
Elements, *Whirlwind*

Chico Hamilton
Eric Person, *My Panamanian
Friend*
Eric Person, *Trio!*

Doug Hamilton
Bill Watrous, *The Brass Connection*

Jeff Hamilton
Monty Alexander, *Reunion in
Europe*

John Hammond
Ray (Raphael) Bryant, *Con
Alma*
Charlie Christian, *The Genius
of the Electric Guitar*
Miles Davis, *Sketches of
Spain*
Herb Ellis, *Together!*
Ella Fitzgerald, *Newport Jazz
Festival: Live at Carnegie
Hall*
John Handy, *Live at the Mon-
terey Jazz Festival*
John Handy, *New View*
John Handy, *Second John
Handy Album*
Billie Holiday, *The Quintes-
sential Billie Holiday*
Ahmad Jamal, *Poinciana*
Jo Jones, *The Essential Jo
Jones*
Django Reinhardt, *Paris 1945*

Jimmy Rushing, *The Essential
Jimmy Rushing*
Stuff Smith, *Together!*

John Hammond Jr.
Don Ellis, *Electric Bath*

Gunter Hampel
Gunter Hampel, *Celestial
Glory*
Gunter Hampel, *Dialog*
Gunter Hampel, *The 8th of
July, 1969*
Gunter Hampel, *Fresh Heat,
Live at Sweet Basil, New
York*
Gunter Hampel, *Jubilation*

Herbie Hancock
Herbie Hancock, *Dis Is da
Drum*
Herbie Hancock, *Future Shock*
Herbie Hancock, *Headhunters*
Herbie Hancock, *Monster*
Herbie Hancock, *Mwandishi:
The Complete Warner
Bros. Recordings*
Herbie Hancock, *The New
Standard*
Wynton Marsalis, *Wynton
Marsalis*

Bernie Hanighen
Billie Holiday, *The Quintessential Billie Holiday*

Kip Hanrahan
Kip Hanrahan, *All Roads Are
Made of the Flesh*
Kip Hanrahan, *Conjure: Music
for the Texts of Ishmael
Reed*
Kip Hanrahan, *Desire Devel-
ops an Edge*

Fareed Haque
Fareed Haque, *Deja Vu*
Fareed Haque, *Opaque*

Tetsuo Hara
Carl Allen, *The Dark Side of
Dewey*
Andrew Cyrille, *Ode to the Liv-
ing Tree*
Joshua Redman, *African Venus*
Pharoah Sanders, *Crescent
with Love*

Satoshi Harano
Jerry Gonzalez & the Fort
Apache Band, *Moliendo
Café*

Paul Hardcastle
Paul Hardcastle, *Cover to
Cover*

J.W. Hardy
Bobby Bradford, *Seeking*
Bobby Bradford, *West Coast
Hot*

Roy Hargrove
Roy Hargrove, *Approaching
Standards*
Roy Hargrove, *Habana*
Roy Hargrove, *Of Kindred
Souls*
Roy Hargrove, *With the Tenors
of Our Time*
Rodney Whitaker, *Of Kindred
Souls*

Joe Harley
Kei Akagi, *Mirror Puzzle*
Joey Calderazzo, *Secrets*
Bruce Katz, *Crescent Crawl*
Bruce Katz, *Mississippi Moan*
Bruce Katz, *Transformation*

Billy Harper
Billy Harper, *Capra Black*
Billy Harper, *Somalia*

Craig Harris
Craig Harris, *F-Stops*

Billy Hart
Billy Hart, *Oceans of Time*
Chris Potter, *Oceans of Time*

Jim Hartog
Tom Varner, *Covert Action*
Tom Varner, *Jazz French Horn*
Bobby Watson, *The Year of
the Rabbit*

Jeff Haskell
Buddy DeFranco, *Whirligig*

Larry Hathaway
Ray (Raphael) Bryant, *Ray's
Tribute to His Jazz Piano
Friends*

Julie Hatta
Francis Wong, *Devotee*
Francis Wong, *Ming*

Tim Hauser
The Manhattan Transfer, *Vocalese*

Graham Haynes
Graham Haynes, *Nocturne Parisian*
Graham Haynes, *Transition*

Phil Haynes
Paul Smoker, *Alone*
Paul Smoker, *Come Rain or Come Shine*

Roy Haynes
Roy Haynes, *Te Vou!*

Robert E. Heal
Peter Appleyard, *Barbados Cool*

Jimmy Heath
Antonio Hart, *Don't You Know I Care*

Norman Hedman
Bill Henderson, *Live in Concert with the Count Basie Band*

Wally Heider
Jimmy Dorsey, *1939–1940*
Sammy Kaye, *Sammy Kaye & His Orchestra: 22 Original Big Band Recordings 1941–44*

Brett Heinz
Thomas Chapin, *What Is Jazz? 1996*
Myra Melford, *What Is Jazz? 1996*
Mario Pavone, *What Is Jazz? 1996*
Matthew Shipp, *What Is Jazz? 1996*
David S. Ware, *What Is Jazz? 1996*

Mark Helias
Ray Anderson, *Don't Mow Your Lawn*
Ray Anderson, *What Because*
Ray Anderson, *Wishbone*
Mark Helias, *The Current Set*
Mark Helias, *Loopin' the Cool*

Jonas Hellborg
Jonas Hellborg, *Ars Moriende*
Jonas Hellborg, *The Bassic Thing*

Jonas Hellborg, *Elegant Punk*
Jonas Hellborg, *Jonas Hellborg Group*
Jonas Hellborg, *Temporal Analogues of Paradise*
Jonas Hellborg, *The Word*

Gerry Hemingway
Marilyn Crispell, *Marilyn Crispell & Gerry Hemingway Duo*

Julius Hemphill
Julius Hemphill, *Dogon A.D.*
Julius Hemphill, *Fat Man and the Hard Blues*
Julius Hemphill, *Five Chord Stud*
Julius Hemphill, *Reflections*

Big Daddy Henderson
Hiroshima, *Hiroshima*

J. Tamblyn Henderson Jr.
Airto Moreira, *Three-Way Mirror*

Scott Henderson
Tribal Tech, *Dog Party*
Tribal Tech, *Primal Tracks*
Tribal Tech, *Reality Check*

Wayne Henderson
Ronnie Laws, *Fever*
Ronnie Laws, *Friends and Strangers*
Ronnie Laws, *Pressure Sensitive*

Burkhard Hennen
Luther Thomas, *Yo' Momma*

Mike Hennessey
Ernest Harold "Benny" Bailey, *For Heaven's Sake*
Stephane Grappelli, *Shades of Django*
Kirk Lightsey, *Saying Something*

Nat Hentoff
Ernest Harold "Benny" Bailey, *Big Brass*
Jaki Byard, *Blues for Smoke*
Ted Curson, *Charles Mingus Presents Charles Mingus*
Don Ellis, *Out of Nowhere*
Art Farmer, *Portrait of Art Farmer*
Don Friedman, *Out Front*

Benny Golson, *Benny Golson's New York Scene*
Abbey Lincoln, *Straight Ahead*
Booker Little, *Out Front*
Charlie Mariano, *Toshiko Mariano Quartet*
Cal Massey, *Blues to Coltrane*
Charles Mingus, *Charles Mingus Presents Charles Mingus*
Pee Wee Russell, *Jazz Reunion*

David Hentschel
Brand X, *Manifest Destiny*

Cynthia B. Herbst
Julius Hemphill, *Fat Man and the Hard Blues*
Julius Hemphill, *Five Chord Stud*
Fred Hersch, *Memento Bittersweet*

Karl Hereim
Ellery Eskelin, *Jazz Trash*

Russell Herman
Bheki Mseleku, *Celebration*
Bheki Mseleku, *Meditations*

Amy Herot
Dave Brubeck, *Time Signatures: A Career Retrospective*

Nano Herrera
Steve Grossman, *Con Amigos*

Vincent Herring
Nicholas Payton, *New Orleans Collective*

Fred Hersch
Fred Hersch, *The Fred Hersch Trio Plays . . .*
Fred Hersch, *Heart Songs*
Fred Hersch, *Passion Flower: Fred Hersch Plays Billy Strayhorn*
Toots Thielemans/Jean Thielemans, *Only Trust Your Heart*

Monika Herzig
BeebleBrox, *Quantumn Tweezers*
BeebleBrox, *Raw Material*

Mark Hewitt
Ralph Sutton, *Partners in Crime*

John Hicks
John Hicks, *East Side Blues*
John Hicks, *Naima's Love Song*
Bobby Watson, *Naima's Love Song*

Billy Higgins
Billy Higgins, *Mr. Billy Higgins*

David A. Himmelstein
Earl "Fatha" Hines, *Grand Reunion*

John Hinds
Dan Plonsey, *Another Curiosity Piece*

Peter Hinds
Dan Plonsey, *Another Curiosity Piece*

Ikuyoshi Hirakawa
Larry Goldings, *Caminhos Cruzados*
John Pizzarelli, *Dear Mr. Cole*

Satoshi Hirano
Nat Adderley, *Mercy, Mercy, Mercy*
Richie Beirach, *My Foolish Heart*
Cindy Blackman, *Sax Storm*
Tommy Flanagan, *Sea Changes*
George Mraz, *Flowers for Lady Day*
George Mraz, *My Foolish Heart*
Jacky Terrasson, *Sax Storm*
Anthony Wonsey, *Another Perspective*
Anthony Wonsey, *Anthonyology*

Wolfgang Hirschmann
Bob Brookmeyer, *Electricity*
Bernard Purdie, *Soul to Jazz*

Richard James Hite
W.C. Handy, *W.C. Handy's Memphis Blues Band*

Laurence Hobgood
Kurt Elling, *Close Your Eyes*
Kurt Elling, *The Messenger*

1
3
2
8

carl e. jefferson

PRODUCER INDEX

PRODUCER INDEX

Ralph MacDonald
Grover Washington Jr., *Wine-light*

Teo Macero
Geri Allen, *Eyes . . . In the Back of Your Head*
Geri Allen, *Misterios*
Geri Allen, *Twenty One*
Louie Bellson, *Duke Ellington: Black, Brown & Beige*
Dave Brubeck, *Time Out*
Charlie Byrd, *The Touch of Gold*
Miles Davis, *Agharta*
Miles Davis, *Bitches Brew*
Miles Davis, *The Complete Live at the Plugged Nickel 1965*
Miles Davis, *Get up with It*
Miles Davis, *Highlights from the Plugged Nickel*
Miles Davis, *In a Silent Way*
Miles Davis, *Kind of Blue*
Miles Davis, *The Man with the Horn*
Miles Davis, *Miles & Monk at Newport*
Miles Davis, *Miles Smiles*
Miles Davis, *Milestones*
Miles Davis, *On the Corner*
Miles Davis, *Pangaea*
Miles Davis, *Sketches of Spain*
Miles Davis, *A Tribute to Jack Johnson*
Duke Ellington, *First Time! The Count Meets the Duke*
Maynard Ferguson, *Chameleon*
Ella Fitzgerald, *Newport Jazz Festival: Live at Carnegie Hall*
Chico Hamilton, *Drumfusion*
Woody Herman, *Woody's Winners*
J.J. Johnson, *J.J. Inc.*
J.J. Johnson, *The Trombone Master*
Lambert, Hendricks & Ross/Lambert, Hendricks & Bavan, *Everybody's Boppin'*
Ramsey Lewis, *Sun Goddess*
Lounge Lizards, *Live from the Drunken Boat*

Lounge Lizards, *The Lounge Lizards*
John McLaughlin, *Bitches Brew*
John McLaughlin, *In a Silent Way*
John McLaughlin, *A Tribute to Jack Johnson*
Carmen McRae, *Sings "Lover Man" and Other Billie Holiday Favorites*
Charles Mingus, *The Complete 1959 CBS Charles Mingus Sessions*
Charles Mingus, *Mingus Ah Um*
Thelonious Monk, *Big Band and Quartet in Concert*
Thelonious Monk, *Miles & Monk at Newport*
Thelonious Monk, *Monk's Blues*
Thelonious Monk, *Monk's Dream*
Thelonious Monk, *Straight, No Chaser*
Joe Morello, *Time Out*
Wallace Roney, *Misterios*
Charlie Rouse, *Thelonious Monk: Criss-Cross*

Tom Mack
Ken Nordine, *The Best of Word Jazz, Volume 1*

Dennis MacKay
Brand X, *Unorthodox Behaviour*
Al Di Meola, *Scenario*
Mahavishnu Orchestra, *Inner Worlds*

William A. MacPherson
Ralph Sutton, *Ralph Sutton Quintet with Ruby Braff*

Adam Maffei
Butch Thompson, *The 88's: Good Old New York*

Mahavishnu Orchestra
Mahavishnu Orchestra, *Between Nothingness and Eternity*
Mahavishnu Orchestra, *Birds of Fire*
Mahavishnu Orchestra, *Inner Mounting Flame*

Mike Mainieri
George Garzone, *Alone*
George Garzone, *Four's and Two's*
Mike Maineri, *American Diary*
Mike Maineri, *Mike Mainieri & Friends: White Elephant*
Steps Ahead, *NYC*

Kousaku Makita
Jack DeJohnette, *Zebra*

Valérie Malot
David Murray, *Fo Deuk Revue*

Joe Maneri
Joe Maneri, *Dahabenzapple*
Joe Maneri, *Paniots Nine*

Mat Maneri
Joe Maneri, *Dahabenzapple*
Mat Maneri, *Acceptance*

Chuck Mangione
Chuck Mangione, *Bellavia*
Chuck Mangione, *Greatest Hits*
Chuck Mangione, *Live at the Village Gate*
Chuck Mangione, *Love Notes*

Herbie Mann
David "Fathead" Newman, *Mr. Gentle, Mr. Cool*
Sonny Sharrock, *Black Woman*

Michael Mantler
Carla Bley, *Escalator over the Hill*

Arif Mardin
Roy Ayers, *Impressions of the Middle East*
Betty Carter, *'Round Midnight*
Regina Carter, *Something for Grace*
Eddie Harris, *Electrifying Eddie Harris/Plug Me In*
Eddie Harris, *The In Sound/Mean Greens*
Freddie Hubbard, *Backlash*
The Manhattan Transfer, *Tonin'*
Modern Jazz Quartet, *A 40th Anniversary Celebration*
Najee, *Just an Illusion*
Max Roach, *Max Roach Trio featuring the Legendary Hasaan*

Rick Margitza
Rick Margitza, *Hands of Time*
Rick Margitza, *Hope*

Kitty Margolis
Kitty Margolis, *Evolution*
Kitty Margolis, *Live at the Jazz Workshop*
Kitty Margolis, *Straight up with a Twist*

Tania Maria
Tania Maria, *Outrageous*

Sherrie Maricle
Diva, *Leave It to Diva*

Axel Markens
Luther Thomas, *Yo' Momma*

Mitchell Markus
Jeremy Steig, *Jigsaw*

Clair Marlo
Pat Coil, *Just Ahead*

Fred Maroth
Miya Masaoka, *Duets*

Timothy Marquand
Beaver Harris, *From Ragtime to No Time*

Frank Marrone
Poncho Sanchez, *Chile Con Soul*

Branford Marsalis
Branford Marsalis, *Buckshot LeFonque*

Delfeayo Marsalis
Kenny Kirkland, *Kenny Kirkland*
Branford Marsalis, *The Beautyful Ones Are Not Yet Born*
Branford Marsalis, *Bloomington*
Branford Marsalis, *Random Abstract*
Branford Marsalis, *Renaissance*
Delfeayo Marsalis, *Musashi*
Delfeayo Marsalis, *Pontius Pilate's Decision*
Ellis Marsalis, *Heart of Gold*
Ellis Marsalis, *Whistle Stop*
Wynton Marsalis, *Joe Cool's Blues*

Wynton Marsalis, *The Resolution of Romance*
Mingus Dynasty, *The Next Generation*
Lewis Nash, *Random Abstract*
Nicholas Payton, *From This Moment*
Eric Reed, *It's Alright to Swing*
Marcus Roberts, *Alone with Three Giants*
Marcus Roberts, *As Serenity Approaches*
Marcus Roberts, *If I Could Be with You*
Marcus Roberts, *Tune in Tomorrow*
Kermit Ruffins, *Hold on Tight*
Rodney Whitaker, *Terence Blanchard*

Billy Martin
Medeski, Martin & Wood, *Friday Afternoon in the Universe*

Christine Martin
Holly Cole, *Jazz to the World*

George Martin
Mahavishnu Orchestra, *Apocalypse*

Marcia Martin
Red Norvo, *The Forward Look*

Mel Martin
Mel Martin, *Bebop and Beyond Plays Thelonious Monk*
Mel Martin, *Mel Martin Plays Benny Carter*

Elaine Martone
Doc Severinsen, *Erich Kunzel/Cincinnati Pops*
Doc Severinsen, *Unforgettably Doc*
Mark Shane, *Travelin' Light with Sam Pilafian & Friends*

Albert Marx
Dick Berk, *More Birds, Less Feathers*
Alan Broadbent, *Better Days*
Eric Dolphy, *Gongs East!*
Dizzy Gillespie, *Dizzy Gillespie: His Sextets and Orchestra*

Al Haig, *Shaw 'Nuff*
Red Norvo, *The Red Norvo Trio with Tal Farlow and Charles Mingus*
Charlie Parker, *Dizzy Gillespie: And His Sextets and Orchestra*

Claudia Marx
Frank Wess, *Going Wess*

Steve Masakowski
Steve Masakowski, *Direct AX-Ecess*

Miya Masaoka
Miya Masaoka, *Compositions-Improvisations*
Miya Masaoka, *Crepuscular Music*

Harvey Mason
Lee Ritenour, *Fourplay*

George Massenberg
Flim & the BB's, *New Pants*

Material
Material/Bill Laswell, *Memory Serves*
Material/Bill Laswell, *One Down*

Lyle Mays
Pat Coil, *Schemes and Dreams*
Lyle Mays, *Lyle Mays*
Pat Metheny, *Still Life (Talking)*
Pat Metheny, *We Live Here*

Mazola
Milton Nascimento, *Encontros e Despedidas*

Robin McBride
Charles Earland, *The Great Pyramid*

Rob McConnell
Rob McConnell, *Our 25th Year*
Rob McConnell, *Three for the Road*

Sid McCoy
Bill Henderson, *His Complete Vee-Jay Recordings, Vol. 1*
Bill Henderson, *His Complete Vee-Jay Recordings, Vol. 2*
Frank Strozier, *Fantastic Frank Strozier—Plus*

Brad McCuen
Duke Ellington, *And His Mother Called Him Bill*
Lionel Hampton, *Reunion at Newport 1967*
J.J. Johnson, *Say When*
Billy Strayhorn, *And His Mother Called Him Bill*
Billy Strayhorn, *The Far East Suite—Special Mix*

Joe McEwen
Joe Beck, *Circle in the Round*
Tony Bennett, *Tony Bennett: Jazz*
Frank Sinatra, *The Reprise Collection*

Bobby McFerrin
Bobby McFerrin, *Bang! Zoom*
Bobby McFerrin, *Spontaneous Inventions*

Andy McKaie
Bing Crosby, *Bing Crosby: His Legendary Years 1931–1957*
Bing Crosby, *Bing's Gold Records*
Billie Holiday, *The Complete Decca Recordings*

Rod McKuen
Andre Previn, *More of the Best*
Andre Previn, *Some of the Best*

John McLaughlin
Al Di Meola, *Friday Night in San Francisco*
Al Di Meola, *The Guitar Trio*
Al Di Meola, *Passion, Grace & Fire*
Mahavishnu Orchestra, *Inner Worlds*
Mahavishnu Orchestra, *Visions of the Emerald Beyond*
John McLaughlin, *Adventures in Radioland*
John McLaughlin, *Johnny McLaughlin—Electric Guitarist*
John McLaughlin, *Love Devotion Surrender*
John McLaughlin, *My Goals Beyond*
John McLaughlin, *Time Remembered*

Shakti, *The Best of Shakti*

Jackie McLean
Junko Onishi, *Hat Trick*

Rene McLean
Rene McLean, *In African Eyes*

Jim McLeod
Ralph Sutton, *Ralph Sutton: Easy Street*

Ron McMaster
João Gilberto, *The Legendary João Gilberto*

Chip McNeill
Maynard Ferguson, *Live from London*

Marian McPartland
Marian McPartland, *Ambiance*
Marian McPartland, *A Sentimental Journey*

Charles McPherson
Charles McPherson, *Come Play with Me*
Charles McPherson, *First Flight Out*

Kenny Mead
Spirit of Life Ensemble, *Live! At the 5 Spot*

Elliot Meadow
Claire Martin, *The Waiting Game*

John Medeski
Medeski, Martin & Wood, *Friday Afternoon in the Universe*

Rosemarie A. Meier
Irene Schweizer, *Irene Schweizer & Han Bennink*
Irene Schweizer, *Piano Solo, Vols. 1 & 2*
Irene Schweizer, *Splitting Image*

Myra Melford
Myra Melford, *The Same River, Twice*

Misha Mengelberg
Misha Mengelberg, *Who's Bridge*

Marc Shaiman
Harry Connick Jr., *When Harry Met Sally*

Bud Shank
Bud Shank, *America the Beautiful*
Bud Shank, *Crystal Comments*
Bud Shank, *Tomorrow's Rainbow*

Nat Shapiro
Michel Legrand, *After the Rain*

Sonny Sharrock
Sonny Sharrock, *Ask the Ages*
Sonny Sharrock, *Guitar*
Sonny Sharrock, *Highlife*
Sonny Sharrock, *Seize the Rainbow*

Artie Shaw
Artie Shaw, *The Last Recordings, Vol. 1: Rare & Unreleased*
Artie Shaw, *More Last Recordings: The Final Sessions*

Mark Shelby
Teodross Avery, *Nothin' But the Swing*
Black/Note, *Nothin' But the Swing*
Nicholas Payton, *Nothin' but the Swing*

Don Shelton
Bob Florence, *Funupmanship*
Bob Florence, *With All the Bell and Whistles*

Archie Shepp
Marion Brown, *Three for Shepp*
Bill Dixon, *Archie Shepp–Bill Dixon Quartet*

Bob Sheppard
Bill Cunliffe, *A Rare Connection*

John Sheridan
John Sheridan, *Something Tells Me*

Phil Sheridan
Ed Bickert, *This Is New*
Rob McConnell, *The Brass Is Back*
Rob McConnell, *Our 25th Year*

Bill Watrous, *The Brass Connection*

Judith Sherman
Robin Holcomb, *Little Three*

Shelley M. Shier
Dorothy Donegan, *Live at the 1990 Floating Jazz Festival*

Matthew Shipp
Matthew Shipp, *The Flow of X*
Matthew Shipp, *Sonic Explorations*

Steve Sholes
Al Hirt, *Our Man In New Orleans*
Al Hirt, *The Sound of Christmas*

Wayne Shorter
Weather Report, *Heavy Weather*
Weather Report, *I Sing the Body Electric*
Weather Report, *Weather Report*

Don Sickler
Geri Allen, *Crunchin'*
Cindy Blackman, *Telepathy*
Donald Brown, *Car Tunes*
Donald Brown, *Cause and Effect*
Donald Brown, *People Music*
Donald Brown, *Send One Your Love*
Donald Brown, *Sources of Inspiration*
Ricky Ford, *Shorter Ideas*
Ricky Ford, *Tenor Madness Too!*
Joe Henderson, *Lush Life: The Music of Billy Strayhorn*
Christian McBride, *Double Decker (Deck the Halls with Boughs of Funky Bass)*
Christian McBride, *Gettin' to It*
Christian McBride, *Number Two Express*
T.S. Monk, *Changing of the Guard*
T.S. Monk, *The Charm*
T.S. Monk, *Take One*
Wallace Roney, *Munchin'*
Stephen Scott, *Parker's Mood*
Jimmy Smith, *Damn!*
Billy Strayhorn, *Lush Life*

Warren Vache Jr., *Horn of Plenty*
Warren Vache Jr., *Talk to Me Baby*
Jack Walrath, *Out of the Tradition*
Jack Walrath, *Serious Hang*
Cedar Walton, *Composer*
Mark Whitfield, *Fingerpainting: The Music of Herbie Hancock*

Tony Sidotti
Holly Hofmann, *Duo Personality*

Ben Sidran
Mose Allison, *Ever Since the World Ended*
Mose Allison, *Gimcracks and Gewgaws*
Russell Malone, *Gimcracks and Gewgaws*

Fred Siebert
Hank Jones, *Master Class*

Glenn Siegel
Ed Blackwell, *Walls-Bridges*

Joel E. Siegel
Shirley Horn, *Softly*
Claire Martin, *Old Boyfriends*

Greg Silberman
Ran Blake, *The Short Life of Barbara Monk*

Horace Silver
Horace Silver, *It's Got to Be Funky*

Leonard Silver
Ernie Watts, *Project Activation Earth*

Jim Silverman
Craig Harris, *Tributes*

John Silverman
The Revolutionary Ensemble, *Artistry*

Milan Simich
Lonnie Smith, *Chartbusters!*

Sonny Simmons
Sonny Simmons, *Manhattan Egos*

John Simon
Blood, Sweat & Tears, *Child Is Father to the Man*
Gil Evans, *Priestess*
Gil Evans, *Where Flamingos Fly*
Charles Lloyd, *Of Course, of Course*
David Sanborn, *Heart to Heart*

Ralph Simon
Harold Land, *A Lazy Afternoon*
Alan Pasqua, *Dedications*
Alan Pasqua, *Milagro*
Julian Priester, *Hints on Light and Shadow*
Reggie Workman, *Cerebral Caverns*
Reggie Workman, *Summit Conference*

Lew Simpkins
Gene "Jug" Ammons, *Red Top*

Mel Simpson
Us3, *Hand on the Torch*

Israel Sinfonietta
Lionel Hampton, *For the Love of Music*

Genji Siraisi
Groove Collective, *We the People*

Ib Skovgaard
Geri Allen, *Some Aspects of Water*
Kenny Drew, *The Squirrel*

Slickaphonics
Ray Anderson, *Modern Life*

Carol Sloane
Carol Sloane, *The Songs Carmen Sang*

Paul A. Sloman
Jeremy Steig, *Jigsaw*

Bill Smith
Wild Bill Davison, *Jazz Giants*
George Lewis (trombone), *The George Lewis Solo Trombone Album*

Cecilia Smith
Cecilia Smith, *Leave No Stone Unturned*

1
3
5
2

steam

Buddy DeFranco, *Like Some-
one in Love*
Marty Grosz, *Songs I Learned
at My Mother's Knee and
Other Low Joints*
The Orphan Newsboys, *The
Orphan Newsboys Live at
the L.A. Classic*
The Orphan Newsboys, *The
Orphan Newsboys:
Rhythm for Sale*

Steam
Ken Vandermark, *Real Time*

Jeremy Steig
Jeremy Steig, *Music for Flute
& Double Bass*
Jeremy Steig, *Outlaws*
Jeremy Steig, *Rain Forest*

Irving Steimler
The Preservation Hall Jazz
Band, *Preservation Hall
Jazz Band, New Orleans,
Volume 1*

Steps Ahead
Steps Ahead, *Magnetic*
Steps Ahead, *Modern Times*
Steps Ahead, *Steps Ahead*

Chip Stern
Ginger Baker, *Going Back
Home*

Jim Stern
Azar Lawrence, *Bridge into
the New Age*

Mike Stern
Bob Berg, *In The Shadows*

Stetsasonic
Stetsasonic/Daddy-O/Prince
Paul/Gravediggaz, *Blood,
Sweat & No Tears*
Stetsasonic/Daddy-O/Prince
Paul/Gravediggaz, *In Full
Gear*
Stetsasonic/Daddy-O/Prince
Paul/Gravediggaz, *On Fire*

John Stevens
John Stevens/Spontaneous
Music Ensemble, *John
Stevens Works: Big Band
and Quintet*
John Stevens/Spontaneous
Music Ensemble, *John*

Stevens Works: Re-Touch
and Quartet*

Michael Jefry Stevens
Mark Whitecage, *Short Stories*

Bill Stewart
Bill Stewart, *Snide Remarks*
Bill Stewart, *Telepathy*

James Stewart
Spirit of Life Ensemble, *Live!
At the 5 Spot*

Robert Stewart
Robert Stewart, *In the Gutta*

Mike Steyn
John Stevens/Spontaneous
Music Ensemble, *So What
Do You Think?*

Kevin Stoller
Khani Cole, *Piece of My Heart*

Mike Stoller
Ruth Brown, *Rockin' in
Rhythm—The Best of
Ruth Brown*

Bernard Stollman
Paul Bley, *Closer*
Alan Silva, *Alan Silva*
Sonny Simmons, *Music from
the Spheres*
Sonny Simmons, *Staying on
the Watch*
John Tchicai, *The New York Art
Quartet and Imamu Amiri
Baraka*

David Stone
Henry Threadgill, *Spirit of Nuff
. . . Nuff*

Thomas Stöwsand
Globe Unity Orchestra, *Improvisations*

Chris Strachwitz
Pete Johnson, *Tell Me Pretty
Baby*
Sonny Simmons, *Manhattan
Egos*
Claude Williams, *Live at J's,
Vol. 1*

Ettore Stratta
Tony Bennett, *Astoria: Portrait
of the Artist*
Eddie Daniels, *Breakthrough*

Ramsey Lewis, *A Classic Encounter*
Toots Thielemans/Jean Thielemans, *The French Collec-
tion—Jazz Impressions*

Craig Street
Don Byron, *Blue Light 'til
Dawn*
Holly Cole, *Temptation*
Fareed Haque, *For One Who
Knows*
Javon Jackson, *A Look Within*
Jimmy Scott, *Heaven*
Cassandra Wilson, *Blue Light
'Til Dawn*
Cassandra Wilson, *New Moon
Daughter*

Bob Stroup
Marvin Stamm, *Live at the
Yardbird—The Marvin
Stamm/Bob Stroup Quintet*

Strunz & Farah
Strunz & Farah, *Americas*
Strunz & Farah, *Live*
Strunz & Farah, *Primal Magic*

Carl Sturken
Dave Koz, *Dave Koz*
Dave Koz, *Lucky Man*

Dick Sudhalter
Kenny Davern, *Never in a Mil-
lion Years*
Dick Wellstood, *The Classic
Jazz Quartet*

Kazunori Sugiyama
George Adams, *Old Feeling*
Geri Allen, *Maroons*
Jean-Paul Bourelly, *Fade to Ca-
cophony*
Jean-Paul Bourelly, *Freestyle*
Jean-Paul Bourelly, *Saints &
Sinners*
James Carter, *JC on the Set*
James Carter, *Jurassic Classics*
Dave Douglas/Tiny Bell Trio/
New & Used, *Sanctuary*
Milford Graves, *The Real Deal*
Robert Hurst III, *One for
Namesake*
Robert Hurst III, *Robert Hurst
Presents: Robert Hurst*
Ronald Shannon Jackson,
What Spirit Say

Harold Mabern, *The Leading
Man*
Harold Mabern, *Lookin' at the
Bright Side*
Masada, *Five/Hei*
Masada, *One/Alef*
Music Revelation Ensemble,
Cross Fire
Music Revelation Ensemble,
In the Name of . . .
Music Revelation Ensemble,
Knights of Power
Lewis Nash, *Old Feeling*
John Patton, *Minor Swing*
Nicholas Payton, *Children of
the Light*
Ralph Peterson Jr., *Art*
Ralph Peterson Jr., *Ornettol-
ogy*
Ralph Peterson Jr., *Ralph Pe-
terson Presents the Fo'Tet*
Ralph Peterson Jr., *Triangular*
Ralph Peterson Jr., *Volition*
Phalanx, *In Touch*
Phalanx, *Original Phalanx*
Matthew Shipp, *flight of i*
Matthew Shipp, *Third Ear
Recitation*
James Blood Ulmer, *Are You
Glad to Be in America?*
James Blood Ulmer, *Music
Speaks Louder Than
Words: James Blood
Ulmer Plays the Music of
Ornette Coleman*
James Blood Ulmer, *Tales of
Captain Black*
David S. Ware, *flight of i*
David S. Ware, *Third Ear
Recitation*
Rodney Whitaker, *Children of
the Light*
James Williams, *Meets the
Saxophone Masters*
James Williams, *Talkin' Trash*
John Zorn, *Minor Swing*

Dennis Sullivan
Black/Note, *43rd & Degnan*
Robert Stewart, *Judgement*

Sipho Sumede
Airto Moreira, *Outernational
Meltdown: Free at Last*

Bill Summers
Herbie Hancock, *Dis Is da Drum*

*Rhythm Kings, Vol. 2
(1923) /The Complete
Wolverines (1924)*
Freddie Keppard, *The Complete Freddie Keppard,
1923–27*

Charles Tolliver
Charles Tolliver, *Grand Max*
Charles Tolliver, *Impact*

David Torkanowsky
Steve Masakowski, *Direct AX-
Ecess*
Steve Masakowski, *What It
Was*

Irving Townsend
Rosemary Clooney, *Blue Rose*
Miles Davis, *Sketches of
Spain*
Chico Hamilton, *The Chico
Hamilton Special*
Chico Hamilton, *Drumfusion*
Lambert, Hendricks &
Ross/Lambert, Hendricks
& Bavan, *Everybody's
Boppin'*
Andre Previn, *A Touch of Ele-
gance*

Lee Townsend
Joey Baron/Baron Down,
Down Home
Marty Ehrlich, *Emergency
Peace*
Jerry Granelli, *Another Place*
Jerry Granelli, *News from the
Street*
Charlie Hunter, *Bing, Bing,
Bing!*
Charlie Hunter, *Ready . . .
Set . . . Shango!*
Charlie Hunter, *The Return of
the Candyman*
Marc Johnson, *Right Brain Pa-
trol*
Marc Johnson, *The Sound of
Summer Running*
Hank Jones, *The Oracle*
Dino Saluzzi, *Rios*
John Scofield, *Groove Elation!*
John Scofield, *Hand Jive*
T.J. Kirk, *T.J. Kirk*

Ed Trabanco
John Bunch, *The Best Thing
for You*

Jack Tracy
Art Farmer, *Blues on Down*
Terry Gibbs, *Terry Gibbs
Dream Band, Volume 5:
The Big Cat*
Woody Herman, *Verve Jazz
Masters 54: Woody Her-
man*

Rudy Traylor
Johnny Hartman, *And I
Thought about You*
Bud Powell, *Bud Plays Bird*

A Tribe Called Quest
A Tribe Called Quest, *Beats,
Rhymes and Life*
A Tribe Called Quest, *The Low
End Theory*
A Tribe Called Quest, *Midnight
Marauders*
A Tribe Called Quest, *People's
Instinctive Travels and the
Paths of Rhythm*

Glenn Trilley
Chelsea Bridge, *Blues in
Sharp Sea*

Lennie Tristano
Lennie Tristano, *Lennie Tris-
tano/The New Tristano*

Tronzo
Spanish Fly/Sex Mob, *Roots*

Assif Tsahar
Assif Tsahar, *Ein Sof*

Don Turnipseed
JoAnne Brackeen, *Power Talk*

**29th Street Saxophone
Quartet**
29th Street Saxophone Quartet, *Milano New York
Bridge*

George C. Tyler
Ralph Sutton, *Ralph Sutton
Quintet with Ruby Braff*

McCoy Tyner
McCoy Tyner, *La Leuenda de la
Hora*
McCoy Tyner, *Looking Out*
McCoy Tyner, *Uptown/Down-
town*

Jeff Tyzik
Doc Severinsen, *Doc Severin-
sen & the Tonight Show
Orchestra*
Doc Severinsen, *Merry Christ-
mas from Doc Severinsen
& the Tonight Show Or-
chestra*
Doc Severinsen, *Once More . . .
With Feeling!*
Doc Severinsen, *Tonight Show
Band, Vol.1*
Ernie Watts, *Project Activation
Earth*

Pia Uehlinger
Ran Blake, *That Certain Feel-
ing*
Anthony Braxton, *Charlie
Parker Project 1993*
Anthony Braxton, *Willisau
(Quartet) 1991*
Dave Burrell, *Windward Pas-
sages*
John Carter, *Seeking*
Pierre Favre, *Arrivederci La
Choutarse*
Don Friedman, *Thingen*
Jimmy Giuffre, *Emphasis,
Stuttgart 1961*
Steve Lacy, *Futurities*
Steve Lacy, *Remains*
Steve Lacy, *School Days*
Steve Lacy, *The Way*
Jimmy Lyons, *Jump Up/What
to Do About*
Joe Maneri, *Dahabenzapple*
Joe McPhee, *At WBAI's Free
Music Store, 1971*
Joe McPhee, *Linear B*
Joe McPhee, *Old Eyes & Mys-
teries*
Joe McPhee, *Oleo & A Future
Retrospective*
Joe McPhee, *Topology*
Myra Melford, *Alive in the
House of Saints*
Myra Melford, *Eleven Ghosts*
Rova Saxophone Quartet/Fig-
ure 8, *The Crowd*
Richard Teitelbaum, *Concerto
Grosso*
John Zorn, *More News for Lulu*
John Zorn, *News for Lulu*

Werner X. Uehlinger
Ran Blake, *That Certain Feeling*

Anthony Braxton, *Charlie
Parker Project 1993*
Anthony Braxton, *Willisau
(Quartet) 1991*
Dave Burrell, *Windward Pas-
sages*
John Carter, *Seeking*
Pierre Favre, *Arrivederci La
Choutarse*
Don Friedman, *Thingen*
Jimmy Giuffre, *Emphasis,
Stuttgart 1961*
Steve Lacy, *Futurities*
Steve Lacy, *Remains*
Steve Lacy, *School Days*
Steve Lacy, *The Way*
Jimmy Lyons, *Jump Up/What
to Do About*
Joe Maneri, *Dahabenzapple*
Joe McPhee, *At WBAI's Free
Music Store, 1971*
Joe McPhee, *Linear B*
Joe McPhee, *Old Eyes & Mys-
teries*
Joe McPhee, *Oleo & A Future
Retrospective*
Joe McPhee, *Topology*
Myra Melford, *Alive in the
House of Saints*
Myra Melford, *Eleven Ghosts*
Rova Saxophone Quartet/Fig-
ure 8, *The Crowd*
Matthew Shipp, *By the Law of
Music*
Horace Tapscott, *The Dark
Tree, Volumes 1 & 2*
Richard Teitelbaum, *Concerto
Grosso*
John Zorn, *More News for Lulu*
John Zorn, *News for Lulu*

Lars Goran Ulander
Jerry Bergonzi, *Emergence!*

James Blood Ulmer
Music Revelation Ensemble,
Cross Fire
Music Revelation Ensemble,
In the Name of . . .
Music Revelation Ensemble,
Knights of Power
James Blood Ulmer, *America—
Do You Remember the
Love?*
James Blood Ulmer, *Are You
Glad to Be in America?*
James Blood Ulmer, *Black
Rock*

Which artists or groups have had the most influence on the acts included in MusicHound Jazz? The Roots Index will help you find out. Under each artist or group's name—not necessarily a jazz act—are listed the acts found in MusicHound Jazz that were influenced by that artist or group. By the way, John Coltrane is the influence champ: he appears in the ◀◀ section of a whopping 113 artists or groups.

John Abercrombie
Nels Cline
David Fiuczynski
Bill Frisell
Rolf Sturm

Muhal Richard Abrams
Air
A. Spencer Barefield
Eight Bold Souls
Myra Melford
Henry Threadgill

Pepper Adams
Hamiet Bluiett
Nick Brignola
Ronnie Cuber
Gary Smulyan

Julian "Cannonball" Adderley
Arthur Blythe
Jesse Davis
George Duke
Bill Easley
Sonny Fortune
Kenny Garrett
John Handy
Antonio Hart
Sam Jones
Jim Snidero
Grover Washington Jr.
Steve Wilson
Phil Woods

King Sunny Ade
Peter Apfelbaum

Larry Adler
Toots Thielemans

Air
Mark Whitecage

Toshiko Akiyoshi
Junko Onishi

Rashied Ali
Marc Edwards
Franklin Kiermyer
Medeski, Martin & Wood

Geri Allen
Bruce Katz

Napoleon "Snags" Allen
Lloyd "Tiny" Grimes

Red Allen
William "Bill" Johnson Coleman
Peter Ecklund

Herb Alpert
Rick Braun
Mac Gollehon

Barry Altschul
Kevin Norton

Albert Ammons
Vince Guaraldi
Junior Mance

Gene Ammons
James Carter
Ellery Eskelin
Von Freeman
Red Holloway
Joseph Jarman
Frank Lowe
Junior Mance
James Moody
Houston Person
Joshua Redman
Robert Stewart
Sonny Stitt
Harold Vick
David S. Ware
Grover Washington Jr.
Rickey Woodard

Ernestine Anderson
Denise Jannah
Vanessa Rubin

Fred Anderson
Muhal Richard Abrams

Adam Rudolph

Ivie Anderson
Betty Roche

Ernie Andrews
Bill Henderson

Ray Anthony
Doc Severinsen

Ron Anthony
Ron Affif

Peter Apfelbaum's Heiroglyphics Ensemble
Lounge Lizards

Don Apiazo
Mario Bauzá

Archibald
Professor Longhair

Louis Armstrong
Ahmed Abdullah
Henry "Red" Allen
Chris Barber
Bix Beiderbecke
Marcus Belgrave
Tony Bennett
Roland Bernard "Bunny" Berigan
Lester Bowie
Cab Calloway
Doc Cheatham
Buck Clayton
Nat "King" Cole
William "Bill" Johnson Coleman

Chris Kelsey
Steve Lacy
Mezz Mezzrow
Jimmie Noone
Bob Wilber

Jeff Beck
Avenue Blue
Al Di Meola
Frank Gambale
Mahavishnu Orchestra

Fred Beckett
J.J. Johnson

Captain Beefheart
Marc Ribot

Bix Beiderbecke
Chet Baker
Roland Bernard "Bunny" Berigan
Ruby Braff
Doc Cheatham
Jim Cullum
Wild Bill Davison
Peter Ecklund
The Preservation Hall Jazz Band
Randy Sandke

Richie Beirach
Django Bates
Rachel Z

Louie Bellson
Mel Lewis
Charlie Watts
Paul Wertico

Tony Bennett
Harry Connick Jr.
Allan Harris
Johnny Hartman

George Benson
Ron Affif
Lenny Breau
Zachary Breaux
Jonathan Butler
Mark Elf
Kevin Eubanks
Fourplay
Paul Jackson Jr.
Henry Johnson
Randy Johnston
Ronny Jordan
Stanley Jordan
Russell Malone
John Scofield

Mark Whitfield

Jerry Bergonzi
Don Braden

Bunny Berigan
Ruby Braff
Shorty Rogers
Randy Sandke
Clark Terry

Irving Berlin
Clusone 3

Leonard Bernstein
Michel Legrand

Chu Berry
George Adams
Gene "Jug" Ammons
Yusef Lateef

Vic Berton
Hal Smith

Jimmy Bertrand
Lionel Hampton

Robert Bertrand
Professor Longhair

Barney Bigard
Bill Easley
Woody Herman
Artie Shaw

Walter Bishop Jr.
Benny Green

Black Sabbath
The Grassy Knoll

Ed Blackwell
Billy Higgins
Famoudou Don Moye
Kevin Norton
Bobby Previte

Eubie Blake
Duke Ellington
James P. (Price) Johnson
Don Redman
Luckey Roberts
Willie "The Lion" Smith

John Blake
Turtle Island String Quartet

Ran Blake
Myra Melford

Art Blakey
Carl Allen
Dick Berk
Steve Berrios
Cindy Blackman
JoAnne Brackeen
Norman Connors
Billy Hart
Tootie Heath
Billy Higgins
Elvin Jones
T.S. Monk
Famoudou Don Moye
Lewis Nash
Tony Oxley
Ralph Peterson Jr.
Billy Pierce
Marvin "Smitty" Smith
Steve Turre
Bobby Watson

Jimmy Blanton
Ray Brown
Ron Carter
Paul Chambers
Richard Davis
Eddie Gomez
Milt Hinton
Sam Jones
Monk Montgomery
Leroy Vinnegar
Wilbur Ware
Rob Wasserman
Rodney Whitaker
"Buster" Williams

Carla Bley
Dave Douglas
Kip Hanrahan
Phillip Johnston

Paul Bley
Richie Beirach
Lowell Davidson
Don Friedman
Keith Jarrett
Enrico Pieranunzi
Denny Zeitlin

Blood, Sweat & Tears
Randy Brecker

Blues Project
Blood, Sweat & Tears

Hamiet Bluiett
James Carter

Arthur Blythe
Greg Osby

Willie Bobo
Steve Berrios
Mongo Santamaria

Buddy Bolden
King Oliver
Original Dixieland Jazz Band
Billie and De De Pierce

Boogie Woogie Red
Mr. B

James Booker
Harry Connick Jr.

Dexter Bordon
Jim Hall

Victor Borge
Dorothy Donegan

Earl Bostic
Arthur Blythe
Thomas Chapin
Maceo Parker

Connee Boswell
Ella Fitzgerald
Anita O'Day

Lester Bowie
James Carter
Dave Douglas
Lawrence "Butch" Morris

Lester Bowie's Brass Fantasy
Spanish Fly

Dave Bowman
John Sheridan

JoAnne Brackeen
Rachel Z

Kirt Bradford
Arthur Blythe

Ruby Braff
Rebecca Coupe Franks
Warren Vache Jr.

Dollar Brand
Lounge Lizards

Anthony Braxton
Gregg Bendian
Marion Brown
Don Byron
Mark Dresser

Mark Helias
Tony Oxley
Dan Plonsey
Ned Rothenberg
Rova Saxophone Quartet
Splatter Trio
John Zorn

Julian Bream
Bill Connors
Ralph Towner

Lenny Breau
Earl Klugh
Steve Masakowski
Emily Remler

Michael Brecker
Rick Margitza
David Sanchez

The Brecker Brothers
Steps Ahead

Julian Brewster
Steve Turre

Bob Brookmeyer
Curtis Fuller
Rob McConnell
Jim McNeely
Maria Schneider

The Brotherhood of Breath
Dedication Orchestra

Charles Brown
Ray Charles
Johnny Otis
Jimmy Scott

Clifford Brown
Marcus Belgrave
Terence Blanchard
Rick Braun
Tom Browne
Donald Byrd
Don Cherry
Ted Curson
Wilbur Harden
Tom Harrell
Eddie Harris
Eddie Henderson
Freddie Hubbard
Howard Johnson
Booker Little
Lucas
Wynton Marsalis
Lee Morgan
Nicholas Payton

Tom Peron/Bud Spangler
  Quartet
Marcus Printup
Claudio Roditi
Shorty Rogers
Wallace Roney
Randy Sandke
Arturo Sandoval
Charlie Sepulveda
Woody Shaw
Louis Smith
Paul Smoker
Marvin Stamm
Charles Tolliver

H. Rapp Brown
Last Poets

James Brown
Fela Anikulapo-Kuti
Miles Davis
The Jazz Passengers
Christian McBride
Maceo Parker
The Rebirth Brass Band
Fred Wesley

Lawrence Brown
Glenn Ferris
Bill Harris

Marion Brown
Noah Howard
One World Ensemble

Ray Brown
Ron Carter
Paul Chambers
Stanley Clarke
Mark Dresser
Bruce Gertz
Percy Heath
Sam Jones
John Leitham
Christian McBride
George Mraz
"Buster" Williams

Ruth Brown
Nancy Wilson

Dave Brubeck
Vince Guaraldi
Keith Jarrett
Ellis Marsalis
Bobby Militello

Jack Bruce
Mark Egan

Lenny Bruce
Ken Nordine

John Bruno Sr.
Jimmy Bruno

Ray Bryant
Mr. B
Stanley Cowell

Rusty Bryant
Red Holloway

Elwood Buchanan
Miles Davis

Roy Buchanan
Stanley Jordan

Lord Buckley
Ken Nordine

Milt Buckner
Bill Doggett
Jimmy McGriff
Jimmy Smith

Teddy Bunn
Lloyd "Tiny" Grimes

Kenny Burrell
A. Spencer Barefield
Ed Bickert
Ron Eschete
Kevin Eubanks
Eric Gale
Henry Johnson
Randy Johnston
Peter Leitch
Russell Malone
Mark Whitfield
Jack Wilkins

Gary Burton
Cecilia Smith

Jonathan Butler
Kirk Whalum

Jaki Byard
Harold Danko
D.D. Jackson

Don Byas
James Carter
Teddy Edwards
Frank Foster
Benny Golson
Paul Gonsalves
Jim Hall
Yusef Lateef

David "Fathead" Newman
Charlie Parker
Ike Quebec
John Stubblefield
Lucky Thompson

Lloyd Byasee
Hal Smith

Charlie Byrd
Gabor Szabo
Ralph Towner

Don Byron
Masada

John Cage
Peter Kowald
John Zorn

Jackie Cain
Mel Tormé

Louis Caldwell
Clark Terry

Blanche Calloway
Cab Calloway

Cab Calloway
Mario Bauzá
Billy "Mr. B" Eckstine
Lucky Millinder

Elizete Cardozo
João Gilberto

Hoagy Carmichael
Harry Connick Jr.

Stokely Carmichael
Last Poets

Harry Carney
Pepper (Park) Adams
Hamiet Bluiett
Don Byron
Serge Chaloff
Howard Johnson
Gerry Mulligan
Gary Smulyan

Benny Carter
Stan Getz
Lee Konitz
Lincoln Center Jazz Orchestra
Mel Martin
Art Pepper
John Sheridan
Norris Turney
Ben Webster

Bill Doggett
Louis Jordan
Lonnie Smith
Winston Walls

Eric Dolphy
Art Ensemble of Chicago
Anthony Braxton
Don Byron
Richard Davis
Marty Ehrlich
Vinny Golia
Joseph Jarman
The Jazz Passengers
Rahsaan Roland Kirk
Oliver Lake
Frank Lowe
Ken McIntyre
Joe McPhee
Pharoah Sanders
Sonny Simmons
Ken Vandermark
Bennie Wallace

Lou Donaldson
Houston Person

The Doors
Adam Holzman

Kenny Dorham
Nat Adderley
Chet Baker
Lester Bowie
Bobby Bradford
Mark Egan
Art Farmer
Tom Harrell

Bob Dorough
Steve Beresford
Michael Franks

Jimmy Dorsey
Les Brown
Tommy Dorsey
Benny Goodman
Artie Shaw
Lester Young

Tommy Dorsey
Benny Goodman
Sister Rosetta Tharpe

Ormond Downes
Hal Smith

Dream Warriors
Clever Jeff
Digable Planets

Kenny Drew
Cedar Walton

Paquito D'Rivera
Jerry Gonzalez & the Fort
    Apache Band
Spirit of Life Ensemble

Lawrence Duhe
Sidney Bechet

George Duke
Alex Bugnon
Pieces of a Dream

The Dukes of Dixieland
Dirty Dozen Brass Band
The Preservation Hall Jazz
    Band

Ted Dunbar
Vic Juris

Johnny Dyani
Dedication Orchestra

Walter Dyett
Ronnie Boykins

Billy Eckstine
Ernie Andrews
Freddy Cole
Johnny Hartman
Herb Jeffries
Jon Lucien
Arthur Prysock
Grady Tate
Joe Williams
Nancy Wilson

Harry "Sweets" Edison
James Carter
Shorty Rogers
Ira Sullivan
Snooky Young

Either\Orchestra
Ben Allison

Roy Eldridge
Ernest Harold "Benny" Bailey
Clifford Brown
Terry Gibbs
Dizzy Gillespie
Al Hirt
Howard McGhee
Clark Terry
Lennie Tristano
Snooky Young

Duke Ellington
Toshiko Akiyoshi
Chris Anderson
Art Ensemble of Chicago
Charlie Barnet
Bob Belden
Blood, Sweat & Tears
Claude Bolling
Willem Breuker
Cab Calloway
The Jim Cifelli New York Nonet
Nat "King" Cole
Harry Connick Jr.
Andrew Cyrille
Tadd Dameron
Anthony Davis
Richard Davis
Either/Orchestra
Mercer Ellington
Gil Evans
Tommy Flanagan
Joel Forrester
Vinny Golia
Woody Herman
Fred Ho
Abdullah Ibrahim
Jon Jang
Duke Jordan
Kronos Quartet
Lincoln Center Jazz Orchestra
Melba Liston
Wynton Marsalis
M'Boom
Marian McPartland
Lucky Millinder
Charles Mingus
Thelonious Monk
Bob Moses
Joe Mulholland
Herbie Nichols
Duke Pearson
Marcus Roberts
Jimmy Rushing
Maria Schneider
Billy Strayhorn
Sun Ra
Tom Talbert
Cecil Taylor
Claude Thornhill
Henry Threadgill
29th Street Saxophone Quar-
    tet
McCoy Tyner
Randy Weston
Gerald Wilson
World Saxophone Quartet
Frank Zappa

Mercer Ellington
Ron Miles

Don Ellis
Either/Orchestra
John Klemmer

Herb Ellis
Emily Remler
Frank Vignola

Brian Eno
Trance Mission

Eric B. & Rakim
Gang Starr

Booker Ervin
Odean Pope

Kevin Eubanks
Ronny Jordan

Eureka Brass Band
Dirty Dozen Brass Band

Eureka Jazz Band
Eric Dolphy

James Reese Europe
Fletcher Henderson
Don Redman

Bill Evans
Kei Akagi
Richie Beirach
Ran Blake
Lenny Breau
Alan Broadbent
Gary Burton
John Campbell
Bill Charlap
Cecilia Coleman
Marc Copland
Chick Corea
Bill Cunliffe
Harold Danko
Kenny Drew Jr.
Don Friedman
Don Grolnick
Herbie Hancock
Fred Hersch
Bob James
Keith Jarrett
Joachim Kuhn
Steve Kuhn
Art Lande
Andy LaVerne
Lyle Mays
Marian McPartland

Mingus Dynasty
Mingus Big Band

Blue Mitchell
Tom Harrell

Joni Mitchell
Robin Holcomb
Claire Martin

Razz Mitchell
Max Roach

Red Mitchell
Chuck Israels

Roscoe Mitchell
Muhal Richard Abrams
A. Spencer Barefield
Ari Brown
Rob Brown
Joseph Jarman
Kalaparusha Maurice McIntyre
Dan Plonsey

Hank Mobley
Junior Cook
Rick Margitza

Zigaboo Modaliste
Billy Hart

Miff Mole
Tommy Dorsey

Grachan Moncur III
Craig Harris
The Jazz Passengers

Thelonious Monk
Muhal Richard Abrams
Joe Albany
Mose Allison
Art Ensemble of Chicago
A. Spencer Barefield
Ran Blake
Carla Bley
Paul Bley
Arthur Blythe
Joe Bonner
Donald Brown
Gary Burton
George Cables
Don Cherry
Ornette Coleman
John Coltrane
Lowell Davidson
Anthony Davis
Miles Davis

Walter Davis Jr.
Eric Dolphy
Dorothy Donegan
Kenny Drew Jr.
Joel Forrester
Erroll Garner
Giorgio Gaslini
Charles Gayle
Dizzy Gillespie
Ben Goldberg
Darrell Grant
Benny Green
Barry Harris
Fred Hersch
St. Elmo Hope
Abdullah Ibrahim
Keith Jarrett
Rodney Kendrick
Kronos Quartet
Abbey Lincoln
Lincoln Center Jazz Orchestra
Lounge Lizards
M'Boom
Misha Mengelberg
Bob Moses
Paul Motian
Buell Neidlinger
Oliver Nelson
Herbie Nichols
Junko Onishi
Eddie Palmieri
Danilo Perez
Ralph Peterson Jr.
Don Pullen
Marcus Roberts
Michele Rosewoman
Charlie Rouse
Gonzalo Rubalcaba
Roswell Rudd
Hilton Ruiz
Matthew Shipp
Horace Silver
Sphere
Bill Stewart
Cecil Taylor
McCoy Tyner
Jack Walrath
Randy Weston
Jessica Williams
Bobby Zankel

Pierre Monteaux
Andre Previn

Eddie Monteiro
Pete Selvaggio

Little Brother Montgomery
Mr. B
Danny Barker

Wes Montgomery
Ron Affif
Avenue Blue
Joe Beck
George Benson
Peter Bernstein
Jean-Paul Bourelly
Zachary Breaux
Larry Carlton
Larry Coryell
Ted Dunbar
Mark Elf
Herb Ellis
Lisle Ellis
Ron Eschete
Tal Farlow
Bill Frisell
Eric Gale
Henry Johnson
Randy Johnston
Hubert Laws
Peter Leitch
Russell Malone
Pat Martino
John McLaughlin
Pat Metheny
Emily Remler
Lee Ritenour
Mike Stern
Tuck & Patti
James Blood Ulmer
Frank Vignola
Mark Whitfield
Jack Wilkins

Carlos Montoya
Ralph Towner

James Moody
Holly Hofmann
Eddie Jefferson
King Pleasure
Herbie Mann

Keith Moon
Bill Bruford

Charles Moore
Adam Rudolph

Oscar Moore
George Freeman
Lloyd "Tiny" Grimes

Joe Morello
Jerry Granelli

Lee Morgan
Joshua Breakstone
Tom Browne
Russell Gunn
Brian Lynch
Marcus Printup
Claudio Roditi
Red Rodney
Wallace Roney
Woody Shaw

Ennio Morricone
Alloy Orchestra

Butch Morris
Miya Masaoka

George Morrison
Jimmie Lunceford

Ferdinand "Jelly Roll" Morton
James Booker
James Dapogny
Dick Hyman
Rahsaan Roland Kirk
Lincoln Center Jazz Orchestra
Wynton Marsalis
Original Dixieland Jazz Band
Don Redman
Butch Thompson

Sal Mosca
Connie Crothers

Bob Moses
Medeski, Martin & Wood
Bobby Previte

Bennie Moten
Count Basie
Erskine Hawkins
Lincoln Center Jazz Orchestra
Jay McShann

Paul Motian
Babkas
Peter Erskine
Bobby Previte

Tony Mottola
Jimmy Bruno

Famoudou Don Moye
Alex Cline
Kevin Norton

Ali Shaheed Muhammad
DJ Krush

ROOTS INDEX

The Category Index represents an array of categories put together to suggest some of the many groupings under which jazz music and jazz artists can be classified. The Hound welcomes your additions to the existing categories in this index and also invites you to send in your own funny, sarcastic, prolific, poignant, or exciting ideas for brand new categories.

Afro-Cuban, Brazilian, & Latin Jazz
Cachao
Ana Caram
Paquito D'Rivera
Dizzy Gillespie
Jerry Gonzalez & the Fort
    Apache Band
Machito
Airto Moreira
Eddie Palmieri
Tito Puente
Flora Purim
Claudio Roditi

Avant-Garde, Modal, and Free Jazz
AACM (Association for the Advancement of Creative Musicians)
Muhal Richard Abrams

Art Ensemble of Chicago
Albert Ayler
Billy Bang
Tim Berne
Ran Blake
Paul Bley
Arthur Blythe
Anthony Braxton
Don Byron
Betty Carter
John Carter
Don Cherry
Ornette Coleman
John Coltrane
Chick Corea
Marilyn Crispell
Eric Dolphy
Marty Ehrlich
Bill Evans
Malachi Favors
Charlie Haden
Herbie Hancock
Julius Hemphill
Dave Holland
Joseph Jarman
Keith Jarrett
Leroy Jenkins
Elvin Jones
Steve Lacy
Oliver Lake
Cecil McBee
Myra Melford
Pat Metheny
Charles Mingus
Roscoe Mitchell
Airto Moreira
Butch Morris
David Murray
Evan Parker

Jaco Pastorius
Gary Peacock
Don Pullen
Dewey Redman
Pharoah Sanders
Sonny Sharrock
Wayne Shorter
Sonny Simmons
Sun Ra
Jamaaladeen Tacuma
Cecil Taylor
Henry Threadgill
James "Blood" Ulmer
Reggie Workman
Joe Zawinul

Banjo Bosses
Danny Barker
Béla Fleck

Bebop
Gene Ammons
Ray Brown
Red Callender
Kenny Clarke
Al Cohn
Sonny Criss
Tadd Dameron
Miles Davis
Kenny Dorham
Gil Evans
Tal Farlow
Stan Getz
Dizzy Gillespie
Dexter Gordon
Roy Haynes
Woody Herman
Ahmad Jamal
Hank Jones
John Lewis

Dodo Marmosa
Thelonious Monk
James Moody
Gerry Mulligan
Charlie Parker
Oscar Peterson
Flip Phillips
Bud Powell
Max Roach
George Shearing
Zoot Sims
Sonny Stitt
Billy Taylor
Lucky Thompson

Big Bands
Count Basie
Cal Calloway
Capp-Pierce Juggernaut Band
Benny Carter
Diva
Jimmy Dorsey
Tommy Dorsey
Billy Eckstine
Duke Ellington
Maynard Ferguson's Big Bop
    Nouveau
Globe Unity Orchestra
Charlie Haden's Liberation
    Music Orchestra
Woody Herman Herds
Illinois Jacquet
Harry James
Thad Jones–Mel Lewis Orchestra
Stan Kenton
Machito
Glen Miller
Mingus Big Band

Red Norvo
Maria Schneider Orchestra
Artie Shaw
Sun Ra Arkestra
Gerald Wilson

Colors
Henry "Red" Allen
Afro Blue Band
Avenue Blue
Black Note
Blackbyrds
Ari Brown
Charles Brown
Clifford Brown
Donald Brown
Jeri Brown
Les Brown
Marion Brown
Ray Brown
Rob Brown
Ruth Brown
Tom Browne
Red Callender
Red Garland
Benny Green
Dodo Green
Grant Green
Wardell Gray
Al Grey
Red Holloway
Blue Mitchell
Red Norvo
Red Rodney
Yellowjackets

**Composers, Arrangers, &
Songwriters**
Cannonball Adderley
Nat Adderley
Mose Allison
Eubie Blake
Carla Bley
Lester Bowie
Dave Brubeck
Ornette Coleman
John Coltrane
Chick Corea
Tadd Dameron
Bob Dorough
Duke Ellington
Bill Evans
Gil Evans
Dave Frishberg
Dizzy Gillespie
Benny Golson
Slide Hampton
Herbie Hancock
Fletcher Henderson

Bill Holman
Antonio Carlos Jobim
J.J. Johnson
James P. Johnson
Quincy Jones
Scott Joplin
Charles Mingus
Thelonious Monk
Butch Morris
Jelly Roll Morton
Bob Moses
Oliver Nelson
Charlie Parker
Bobby Previte
Tito Puente
Sonny Rollins
Maria Schneider
Wayne Shorter
Horace Silver
Billy Strayhorn
McCoy Tyner

Cool Jazz & West Coast Style
Chet Baker
Bob Brookmeyer
Dave Brubeck
Bob Cooper
Miles Davis
Paul Desmond
Gil Evans
Jimmy Giuffre
Vince Guaraldi
Jim Hall
Chico Hamilton
Bill Holman
Barney Kessel
Lee Konitz
Shelly Manne
Gerry Mulligan
Art Pepper
Andre Previn
Shorty Rogers
Bud Shank
Zoot Sims
Lennie Tristano
Leroy Vinnegar

Crooners & Divas
Mose Allison
Karrin Allyson
Ernestine Anderson
Eden Atwood
Mildred Bailey
Danny Barker
Tony Bennett
Terry Blaine
Dee Dee Bridgewater
Charles Brown
Jeri Brown

Ruth Brown
Cab Calloway
Ana Caram
Ray Charles
June Christy
Rosemary Clooney
Freddy Cole
Nat "King" Cole
Ida Cox
Bing Crosby
Connie Crothers
Bob Dorough
Dominique Eade
Madeline Eastman
Billy Eckstine
Kurt Elling
Rachelle Ferrell
Ella Fitzgerald
Banu Gibson
Allan Harris
Johnny Hartman
Bill Henderson
Al Hibbler
Alberta Hunter
Denise Jannah
Al Jarreau
Eddie Jefferson
Betty Joplin
Louis Jordan
Sheila Jordan
Rebecca Kilgore
Cleo Laine
Lambert, Hendricks & Ross
Peggy Lee
Abbey Lincoln
Carmen Lundy
Kevin Mahogany
Manhattan Transfer
Kitty Margolis
Bobby McFerrin
Carmen McRae
Helen Merrill
Mark Murphy
Anita O'Day
John Pizzarelli
Flora Purim
Diane Reeves
Betty Roche
Annie Ross
Vanessa Rubin
Jimmy Rushing
Diane Schuur
Jimmy Scott
Frank Sinatra
Carol Sloane
Bessie Smith
Dakota Staton
Maxine Sullivan
Mel Tormé

Big Joe Turner
Sarah Vaughan
Rosanna Vitro
Dinah Washington
Ethel Waters
Joe Williams
Cassandra Wilson
Nancy Wilson
Jimmy Witherspoon

Dixieland Revival
Judy Carmichael
Eddie Condon
James Dapogny
Art Hodes
Dick Hyman
Dave McKenna
Joe Sullivan
Ralph Sutton
Jack Teagarden
Dick Wellstood

Early Jazz
Albert Ammons
Lil Hardin Armstrong
Louis Armstrong
Paul Barbarin
Sidney Bechet
Bix Biederbecke
Barney Bigard
Buddy Bolden
Eddie Condon
Wild Bill Davidson
Baby Dodds
Johnny Dodds
Tommy Dorsey
Bud Freeman
Benny Goodman
W. C. Handy
Earl Hines
James P. Johnson
Gene Krupa
Nick LaRocca
George Lewis
Mead Lux Lewis
Wingy Manone
Mezz Mezzrow
Glenn Miller
Miff Mole
Jelly Roll Morton
Joe "Tricky Sam" Nanton
Red Nichols
Jimmy Noone
Joe "King" Oliver
Kid Ory
Don Redman
Willie "The Lion" Smith
Muggsy Spanier
Frank Teschemacher

Claude Thornhill
Frankie Trumbauer
Joe Venuti
Fats Waller
Jimmy Yancey

Flute Fanciers
Jane Bunnett
Eric Dolphy
Holly Hofmann
Hubert Laws
Herbie Mann
Ira Sullivan
Frank Wess

Fusion
George Benson
Blood, Sweat & Tears
Michael Brecker
Randy Brecker
Donald Byrd
Stanley Clarke
Billy Cobham
Chick Corea
Larry Coryell
The Crusaders
Miles Davis
Al Di Meola
George Duke
Mark Egan
Peter Erskine
Kenny G
Steve Gadd
Frank Gambale
Herbie Hancock
Eddie Harris
Bob James
Steve Khan
John Klemmer
Hubert Laws
Ronnie Laws
David Liebman
Jeff Lorber
John McLaughlin
Pat Metheny
Alphonse Mouzon
Najee
Jaco Pastorius
John Patitucci
David Sanborn
John Scofield
Spyro Gyra
Mike Stern
Jamaaladeen Tacuma
Tribal Tech
Weather Report
Dave Weckl
Tony Williams
Yellowjackets

Joe Zawinul

Groovy Groups
Toshiko Akiyoshi Big Band
Art Ensemble of Chicago
Nanci Banks Orchestra
Blood, Sweat & Tears
Lester Bowie's Brass Fantasy
Jeannie & Jimmy Cheatham
      and the Sweet Baby Blues
      Band
Chelsea Bridge
Clusone 3
Jim Cullum Jazz Band
Dirty Dozen Brass Band
Eight Bold Souls
Jerry Gonzalez & the Fort
      Apache Band
The Jazz Passengers
Spike Jones City Slickers
Lambert, Hendricks & Ross
Last Poets
Lincoln Center Jazz Orchestra
Manhattan Transfer
M-Base Collective
M'Boom
McKinney's Cotton Pickers
Medeski, Martin & Wood
Old and New Dreams
Original Dixieland Jazz Band
Orphan Newsboys
Pieces of a Dream
Preservation Hall Jazz Band
Rebirth Brass Band
Return to Forever
Rippingtons
(Kahil El'Zabar's) Ritual Trio
Spirit of Life Ensemble
Straight Ahead
Billy Tipton Memorial Saxo-
      phone Quartet
Us3
The Visitors
Weather Report
World Saxophone Quartet
Yellowjackets

Hard Bop
Pepper Adams
Cannonball Adderley
Nat Adderley
Benny Bailey
Kenny Barron
Bob Berg
Art Blakey
Randy Brecker
Tina Brooks
Clifford Brown
Kenny Burrell

Ron Carter
Paul Chambers
Billy Cobham
John Coltrane
Miles Davis
Kenny Dorham
Kenny Drew
Booker Ervin
Art Farmer
Tommy Flanagan
Curtis Fuller
John Gilmore
Benny Golson
Gigi Gryce
Tom Harrell
Barry Harris
Louis Hayes
Jimmy Heath
Percy Heath
Joe Henderson
Elvin Jones
Hank Jones
Philly Joe Jones
Sam Jones
Thad Jones
Wynton Kelly
Harold Land
Yusef Lateef
Ramsey Lewis
Junior Mance
Jack McDuff
Jimmy McGriff
Jackie McLean
Charles McPherson
Billy Mitchell
Blue Mitchell
Hank Mobley
J. R. Monterose
Wes Montgomery
Lee Morgan
Oliver Nelson
Sonny Rollins
Shirley Scott
Woody Shaw
Horace Silver
Jimmy Smith
Stanley Turrentine
McCoy Tyner
Wilbur Ware
Phil Woods
Reggie Workman

Hip Harmonica
Hendrik Meurkens
Toots Thielemans

Keepin' Up with the Joneses
Elvin Jones
Etta Jones

Hank Jones
Jo Jones
Oliver Jones
Philly Joe Jones
Quincy Jones
Sam Jones
Spike Jones
Thad Jones

Mainstream & Modern
Carl Allen
Bob Berg
Terence Blanchard
Ray Brown
Benny Carter
Ricky Ford
Larry Goldings
Benny Green
Jake Hanna
Roy Hargrove
Tom Harrell
Milt Hinton
Johnny Hodges
Jo Jones
Marlon Jordan
Geoff Keezer
Joe Lovano
Brian Lynch
Wynton Marsalis
Joshua Redman
Marvin "Smitty" Smith

The Mighty Smiths
Bessie Smith
Cecilia Smith
Hal Smith
Jabbo Smith
Jimmy Smith
Lonnie Liston Smith
Dr. Lonnie Smith
Louis Smith
Marvin "Smitty" Smith
Stuff Smith
Willie "The Lion" Smith

Organists
Milt Buckner
Wild Bill Davis
Joey DeFrancesco
Barbara Dennerlein
Bill Doggett
Larry Goldings
Richard "Groove" Holmes
Jack McDuff
Jimmy McGriff
Amina Claudine Myers
Jeff Palmer
Don Pullen
Melvin Rhyne
Shirley Scott